BARRON'S

HOW TO PREPARE FOR THE

GED

HIGH SCHOOL
EQUIVALENCY EXAM

13TH EDITION

30247
90030

Murray Rockowitz, Ph.D.
Former Chairman, Board of Examiners,
New York City Board of Education
Former Principal,
John Philip Sousa Junior High School,
New York City
Former Chairman, English Department,
Charles Evans Hughes High School,
New York City

Samuel C. Brownstein
Former Chairman, Biology Department,
Wingate High School, Brooklyn, New York

Max Peters
Former Chairman, Mathematics Department,
Wingate High School, Brooklyn, New York

Ira K. Wolf, Ph.D.
Teacher of Mathematics,
Benjamin N. Cardozo High School,
Bayside, New York

Johanna M. Bolton
Instructor, Adult High School Program,
Daytona Beach Community College,
Daytona Beach, Florida

Robert Feinstein
GED Instructor for Adult Educational Services,
Northport-East Northport School District,
Northport, New York

Sally Ramsey
Former GED Instructor,
Southeastern Illinois College,
Harrisburg, Illinois

Louis Gotlib
Science Teacher,
Wissahickon Senior High School,
Ambler, Pennsylvania

Kelly A. Battles
Language Arts Teacher,
St. Augustine, Florida

BARRON'S

All inquiries should be addressed to:
Barron's Educational Series, Inc.
250 Wireless Boulevard
Hauppauge, New York 11788
http://www.barronseduc.com

Library of Congress Catalog No. 2003058340

International Standard Book No. (without CD-ROM) 0-7641-2603-2
International Standard Book No. (with CD-ROM) 0-7641-7711-7

Library of Congress Cataloging-in-Publication Data

How to prepare for the GED high school equivalency exam /
Murray Rockowitz ... [et al.].— 13th ed.
       p.   cm.
   At head of title: Barron's.
    ISBN 0-7641-2603-2 (alk. paper)—ISBN 0-7641-7711-7 (book with CD)
   1. General educational development tests—Study guides.   2. High school equivalency examinations—Study guides.   I. Title: Barron's how to prepare for the GED high school equivalency exam.   II. Title: GED.   III. Rockowitz, Murray.   IV. Barron's Educational Series, Inc.

LB3060.33.G45R63   2004
373.126′2—dc22   2003058340

PRINTED IN THE UNITED STATES OF AMERICA
9 8 7 6 5 4 3 2

CONTENTS

Chapter 20 • Fractions and Measurement 492

Chapter 21 • Decimals and Percents 509

Chapter 22 • Data Analysis 526

Chapter 23 • Algebra...534

PREFACE

This edition includes the most recent changes in the content and format of the tests of General Educational Development (GED) required to qualify for a High School Equivalency Diploma. The authors, all specialists in various areas of the high school curriculum, have developed practice exercises and tests that reflect these changes and provide extensive preparation for the GED Examination.

TO THE READER

"Until recently, all we asked of job applicants was that they be able to sign their names and find their way to the time clock. Now they've got to have a high school diploma." These words of an electronics manufacturer are a warning to the student and jobseeker of today.

IF   you want an interesting job—one that does not lead to a dead end;

IF   you want to be accepted into a good company's apprenticeship program;

IF   you want to advance on the job from a one-operation task to the technician or troubleshooting level;

IF   you want to continue your studies at a technical school;

IF   you want to get a technical or junior professional Civil Service position;

IF   you want to be accepted in a specialized assignment in the Armed Forces;

you must have a high school diploma.

If you have not yet completed high school, this book will help you earn that precious diploma by passing a High School Equivalency Examination. All fifty states, the District of Columbia, many U.S. territories, and most Canadian provinces have programs that enable you to do this.

To help you,

we have carefully analyzed the latest GED tests, and, on the basis of that analysis, have prepared materials that provide:

- explanations of key ideas,
- concise summaries of each topic,
- thorough drill exercises,
- realistic practice tests.

All you need add is the determination to use these materials according to the schedule we have suggested. If you do, you will gain the confidence and knowledge you need to pass the High School Equivalency Examination and earn your high school diploma.

TO THE INSTRUCTOR

If you are using this book in a class preparing for the High School Equivalency Examination, please note that:

- all necessary background materials have been included;
- after every principle, appropriate illustrations may be found;
- after each topic and subtopic, there are ample drill exercises;
- sample reading selections have been thoroughly analyzed;
- answers for all exercises have been included and, in most cases, explanations for the correct answer are given.

You will **not** have to go to any other sources for additional materials. We have included more than enough practice and drill for any student in your class who seeks the High School Equivalency Diploma.

INTRODUCTION TO THE GED EXAMINATION

CHAPTER 1: Preparing for the GED Examination

Everything you need to know about the GED Examination process, along with hints and strategies for studying and test taking. Also, an overview of the new GED exam.

CHAPTER 2: A Diagnostic Examination

A Diagnostic Examination that will tell you how strong or weak you are in each of the five test areas. This information will allow you to apply your study efforts to the areas where you need them most.

Preparing for the GED Examination

The Importance of the GED Examination

The General Educational Development or GED Examination offers anyone who has not completed his or her high school diploma a way to earn a High School Equivalency Certificate. This is the equivalent of a high school diploma, and it is necessary for those who want to continue their education in college or another career-oriented program. Having a high school diploma today is also very important if you want a good job.

EDUCATION PAYS
Median annual earnings of workers aged 25 to 64, in 2000 dollars.

BACHELOR DEGREE OR MORE
SOME COLLEGE
HIGH SCHOOL GRADUATE
HIGH SCHOOL DROPOUT

MEN

$50,000 / 40 / 30 / 20 / 10 / 0
'76 '80 '85 '90 '95 '00

WOMEN

$50,000 / 40 / 30 / 20 / 10 / 0
'76 '80 '85 '90 '95 '00

Source: Labor Department

Study these graphs briefly. Note that the black line indicates the average annual earnings of high school graduates aged 25 to 64. The bottom gray line represents the average annual earnings of high school dropouts of similar age. Compare the two lines for 2000. You see that high school graduates earned much more than high school dropouts. Men earned nearly $10,000 a year more; women earned over $5,000 a year more. Over the span of years from age 25 to age 64, a male high school graduate earns about $400,000 more than a high school dropout; the woman graduate earns over $200,000 more. *It pays to have a high school diploma.*

This book has been written to help you prepare to take the GED Examination. It contains reviews of the subject material, practice exercises, and even practice tests, all of which will familiarize you with the content and format of the actual examination. Over two million people have already used this book to help them pass the GED Examination. You can too!

The Five GED Test Areas

The GED Examination is divided into five tests:

1. Language Arts, Writing
2. Social Studies
3. Science
4. Language Arts, Reading
5. Mathematics

The five tests are designed to measure the knowledge and skills that a student should have acquired after four years in high school. One important thing about the tests is that, even though the questions may involve a specific area of study such as science, you don't have to memorize specific facts, details, dates, or even exact definitions. Much of this information is given to you in the test itself. You have to be able to read and understand the material that is presented and then to answer questions about it.

With the exception of the essay part of the Writing Skills test, all of the questions in the GED Examination are multiple-choice. You will be given a brief statement, short passage, map, table, or diagram, and then you will have to answer one or more multiple-choice questions about this material. This book will help you learn how to analyze and use information presented in these various ways.

TIMETABLE OF A
HIGH SCHOOL EQUIVALENCY EXAMINATION
TOTAL: 7 HOURS, 25 MINUTES

	Section	Time Allowed	Number of Test Items	Description
Test 1	The Language Arts, Writing Test Part I	75 minutes	50	Sentence Structure (30%) Usage (30%) Mechanics (25%) Organization (15%)
	Part II	45 minutes		Essay on a given topic
Test 2	The Social Studies Test	70 minutes	50	History (40%) Geography (15%) Civics and Government (25%) Economics (20%)
Test 3	The Science Test	80 minutes	50	Biology (50%) Earth Science Chemistry } 50% Physics
Test 4	The Language Arts, Reading Test	65 minutes	40	Literary Text (poetry, drama, prose before 1920, prose 1920–1960, prose after 1960) (75%) Nonfiction Text (nonfiction prose, critical reviews, business documents) (25%)
Test 5	The Mathematics Test Part I (with a calculator)	45 minutes	25	Numbers and Operations (25%) Geometry (25%) Measurement and Data Analysis (25%) Algebra (25%)
	Part II (without a calculator)	45 minutes	25	(same as above)

Commonly Asked Questions About the GED Tests

1. *Who can take the GED tests?* Adults who meet the eligibility requirements established by their state, territorial, or provincial departments of education can take the GED tests.

2. *Where are the GED tests given?* The American Council on Education (ACE) maintains an informative Web site (*http://www.acenet.edu/calec/ged*) that lists testing centers in all 50 states and several territories outside the United States, along with other valuable GED-related material. For testing centers and administrative contacts nearest your home, you can also try calling or visiting your local high school.

3. *What score is required to earn a High School Equivalency Diploma?* The standard score requirements vary for each state, territory, or province. You will find that in some states a candidate must earn a minimum score of 410 on each of the five test areas or a minimum average score of 450 for the five tests. The majority of states require a minimum average score of 450 and no individual test score below 350 or 410.

4. *What types of questions are on the GED tests?* Part II of the Writing Skills test requires a written essay. For the other test questions, you will be given information in the form of a written passage, graph, diagram, map, or table, and asked to answer one or more multiple-choice questions based on the information presented. Five answer choices are given for each question.

5. *How can experience outside the classroom help me pass the GED tests?* Many people worry about the difficulty of taking the GED Examination, especially if they've been out of school for a long time. What you should realize is that learning continues after you leave school. You read newspapers and follow political events; you travel and talk to many different people; you listen to the radio, watch television, and go to the movies. All of these experiences are forms of learning and add to your educational background.

6. *Why are maturity and motivation strong assets?* More mature students have experiences that will help them visualize or understand situations that may be involved in a problem on the GED Examination. Also, older students understand the need for good study habits and have the self-discipline to work regularly in this book. With the mature decision to study for the GED tests, half the battle is over. Many educators know that motivation, the desire to learn, is the first step toward success.

7. *When are you ready to take the GED Examination?* After reviewing and doing the practice exercises, take the practice tests in Unit VIII, and score your results. If your scores are in the category Good or Excellent, you are probably ready to walk into the examination room with confidence. If, however, you did not attain such scores, do not apply for the GED Examination until you have studied further. Concentrate on the areas in which you are weak. This chapter includes a thirty-session study schedule (see pages 8–9).

Organizing Your Plan of Study

SOME STUDY HINTS

Educators agree that, for learning to be efficient, certain steps must be followed. As a mature person, you will probably appreciate the value of carefully following these ten tips for successful study.

1. **Physical conditions.** Find a quiet place. Tolerate no distraction—noise or music. Do not work in an overheated room.

2. **Timing.** You will learn faster and remember longer if you study in several short sessions rather than in one long session. Do not attempt to study for an entire weekend. Fatigue will set in after a few hours. It is wiser to spend some time each day rather than to "cram" your work into one or two days.

3. **Schedule for study.** A study schedule must be workable, realistic, practical, and, above all, suited to you and your other obligations. Decide which days and hours you can spare for study. Make a schedule, and stick to it.

4. **Using odd moments.** Put spare time and wasted moments to work. Riding on the bus or train may be a good time to mem-

orize troublesome spelling words and to study rules of grammar or definitions of unfamiliar terms.

5. **Efficiency.** Most people find that learning occurs faster in the early part of the day. Perhaps you can work into your schedule some time for study before your day's work begins or on weekend mornings. Certainly you should not schedule study in the later hours of the evening.

6. **Review periods.** On certain days, plan to review. Take stock of yourself in these study periods. This review will serve at least two purposes. It will definitely reinforce the learning, and the gratification of knowing that you have acquired new material will stimulate you to learn more.

7. **Writing while you learn.** Wherever possible, write what you are studying. Spelling can best be learned by writing. Get into the habit of writing down key ideas of the passages you read. This writing will focus attention on your learning, will help you avoid distractions that may cause your mind to wander, and will provide an opportunity to check up on yourself. Also, educators believe that the more senses employed while studying, the more effective the learning will be.

8. **Reading.** The best way to improve reading comprehension is by practicing reading. You will find that a great part of the test involves the interpretation of reading material. Read your newspaper very carefully. Make it a habit to read the editorials. If possible, engage a member of your family or a friend in frequent discussions of the ideas presented in your newspaper. Of course, this book has specific reading exercises on the various phases of the test. But remember: there is no substitute for general reading.

9. **The dictionary.** The most important single book, in addition to this one, that can help you prepare for the High School Equivalency Examination is the dictionary. It is important to have one nearby as you study. A suggested inexpensive dictionary is the pocket-size paperback edition of *Webster's New World Dictionary of the American Language.*

10. **S Q 3R.** A popular way to remember the five important steps needed to study effectively is the S Q 3R method.

    • S stands for *survey.* You examine the material to be learned to get a general idea of the content.

    • Q stands for *question.* You turn the topic, the title of the section you are studying, into a question or questions. For example, if the title of the section is "Drawing Conclusions," you turn it into a challenging question: "How do I draw conclusions from what I read?"

    • The first of the three R's stands for *read.* You use the reading skills that are taught in this book, such as locating the main idea, finding details, reading critically, detecting propaganda, determining cause and effect, and comparing and contrasting ideas.

    • The second R stands for *recite.* You close the book and speak aloud from memory. Include especially the main ideas you have located and any name, word, or fact you find difficult to remember.

    • The third R stands for *review,* which literally means to "view" or see again. You look over your notes, the lines you have highlighted, or the outline you have made. Do this again until you are sure you have mastered the material, for example, spelling words that trouble you or a rule of punctuation you find hard to remember.

This is a summary of the S Q 3R method of study:

S urvey
Q uestion
R ead
R ecite
R eview

BEFORE THE TEST DATE

1. **Use this book wisely.** It can help you achieve your goal—the High School Equivalency Diploma. After you take the Diagnostic Test, you will discover your specific weaknesses and can concentrate your review on these areas. Study the examination strategies, and apply them when you do the exercises and take the practice tests.

2. **Practice reading and writing.** Besides using the material in this book, spend more time reading. Read the local newspaper and some magazines. Also practice writing. Write letters to friends and relatives. Instead of using the telephone, use your pen.

3. **Don't rush to take the tests.** Don't be in too big a hurry to apply for the GED Examination. First be sure that you are prepared by taking the exercises and tests in this book. Even though most states will let you retake the tests after a waiting period, a notice that you failed the first time is unpleasant and may even discourage you from trying again. Instead of rushing into the examination and trusting to good fortune for a passing grade, it's better to wait until you know that you're ready. Also, don't procrastinate and cram all your study into the last few days. This rarely works. It's much better to set a realistic study schedule that gives you enough time to prepare.

4. **Know what to expect.** By the time you finish the preparation material in this book, you will be familiar with all the kinds of questions you will encounter on the GED tests. The exercises and practice test questions in this book are very similar to the actual test questions. Knowing what to expect will relieve some of your anxiety about taking the exam.

5. **Be relaxed.** It's a good idea to relax the evening before you take the GED Examination. A good night's sleep will help you to think logically; you'll be well rested and alert. Also, do not eat a heavy meal, which will make you feel dull and sleepy, before you take the test.

Tactics and Strategies in the Examination Room

1. **Allow plenty of time to get to the test site.** Taking a test is pressure enough. You don't need the extra tension that comes from worrying about whether you will get there on time.

2. **Read all directions and questions carefully.** Answer the question given, not one you expected. Look for key words, such as *except*, *exactly*, and *not*. Carefully examine tables, graphs, and diagrams so you don't miss important information.

3. **Don't expect trick questions.** A straightforward presentation is used in all test sections.

4. **When you have difficulty finding an answer, eliminate choices that are definitely wrong.** Then consider the remaining choices.

5. **Don't let one or two challenging questions upset you.** Some questions are definitely harder than others. Remember you do not have to get 100 percent on this examination. No one does.

6. **Don't get bogged down on any one question.** If a question is taking too much time, circle it and make a guess. Then, if you have time at the end of the examination, go back and review the circled questions.

7. **Change answers only if you have a good reason for doing so.** Don't change your answer on a hunch or a whim. Most often the first judgment that you make is correct.

8. **Check answer order frequently.** Make sure you are putting your answers in the right spaces.

9. **Use your time wisely.** After taking the practice tests in this book, you will be familiar with the proper pace needed to complete each test.

10. **Be careful not to make stray pencil marks on the answer sheet.** These may interfere with the rating of your performance. If you wish to change an answer, be sure to erase your first mark completely. The rating machine will automatically mark an answer wrong if more than one choice is made. Also, do not fold or crease the answer sheet.

11. **Answer all questions, even if you have to guess.** Your score will be determined by the number of correct answers; no points are deducted for wrong answers. For this reason it is better to guess at an answer than to not respond at all. Of course, wherever possible, eliminate as many wrong answers as you can before guessing. Every answer you eliminate improves your chance of guessing correctly.

12. **Remain as calm as possible.** If you consider yourself a person who "goes to pieces" on tests, cheer up! Psychologists claim that more than 90 percent of us think we don't perform well on tests *of any kind.* Nobody likes tests. But more than 80 percent of the people who have taken the High School Equivalency tests in the New York area, for example, have passed them. They must be doing something right. And so can you—with the right attitude and careful preparation.

A Suggested Study Schedule

The task of reading this book and learning the material may seem impossible—after all, it's a big book! If, however, you divide everything up into thirty lessons, the job suddenly becomes much easier. The teachers who prepared this material for you have done just that—they have arranged everything into small lesson "bites." Another benefit is that, if you follow their plan, you will not have the problem of jumping from one subject to another and being worried that you may be missing something important.

If you find that you cannot manage the time necessary for the thirty-lesson plan outlined below, you can easily divide the work into sixty sessions. In any case, if you follow this plan and check off each task as it is accomplished, when you are finished, you will be prepared to walk into the GED Examination with confidence.

1. Read Chapter 1 to familiarize yourself with the GED Examination. Analyze the Examination Timetable. Examine the general study hints, tactics, and strategies in this chapter. Plan a schedule for study. Refer to the table of contents of this book to become acquainted with your "self-tutor."

2. In Chapter 2, take the Language Arts, Writing test and the Social Studies test (Diagnostic Examination). Study the analyses of correct answers. Make a note of your weaknesses.

3. In Chapter 2, take the Science test and the Language Arts, Reading test (Diagnostic Examination). Study the analyses of correct answers. Make a note of your weaknesses.

4. In Chapter 2, take the Mathematics test (Diagnostic Examination). Analyze your errors, and note the topics on which you committed the most errors.

5. In Chapters 3 and 4, study the sections on sentence structure and usage. Do the practice exercises. Check the answers and the answer analyses.

6. In Chapters 5, 6, and 7, study the sections on mechanics, organization, and additional writing skills. Do the practice exercises. Check the answers and the answer analyses.

7. In Chapter 8, study and do all practice exercises on the sample paragraphs. Check the answers and the answer analyses.

8. Study and do all practice exercises in Chapter 9. Write several essays using suggested topics.

9. Now it is time to take the Language Arts, Writing test, Parts I and II (Practice Examination One) in Unit VIII. Check your answers. Analyze your errors. Study the analyses of the correct answers.

10. In Chapter 10, study the analyzed passages on the basics in social studies.

11. In Chapter 10, study the basics for interpreting tables, graphs, and maps. Do the practice exercises.

12. Study the "Glossary of Social Studies Terms" in Chapter 11. In Chapter 12, do the concept questions as well as the reading passage questions, and analyze your errors.

13. Now it is time to take the Social Studies test (Practice Examination One) in Unit VIII. Check your answers. Analyze your errors.

14. In Chapters 13 and 14, read about the Science test. Study the sample questions. Check your areas of weakness. Study the "Glossary of Scientific Terms." Check any terms that are unfamiliar.

15. In Chapter 15, do the practice exercises in biology. Refer to the glossary in Chapter 14 for troublesome terms.

16. In Chapter 15, do the practice exercises in earth science. Refer to the glossary in Chapter 14 for troublesome terms.

17. In Chapter 15, do the practice exercises in chemistry and physics. Refer to the glossary in Chapter 14 for troublesome terms.

18. Now it is time to take the Science test (Practice Examination One) in Unit VIII. Check your answers. Analyze your errors. Study the analyses of correct answers.

19. In Chapter 16, study the material on reading skills and skills in interpreting literature. Study the material on nonfiction text.

20. In Chapter 17, do the practice exercises on literature and nonfiction text.

21. Now it is time to take the Language Arts, Reading test (Practice Examination One) in Unit VIII. Check your answers. Analyze your errors. Study the analyses of correct answers.

22. In Chapter 19, study the material on basic operations.

23. In Chapters 20–21, review the sections on fractions, decimals, and percents. Do the practice exercises. Check your answers.

24. In Chapters 22–24, review the sections on geometry, data analysis, and algebra. Do the exercises. Check your answers.

25. Read the test-taking strategies in Chapter 25. Take the practice mathematics test in Chapter 26. Check your answers.

26. Now it is time to take the Mathematics test (Practice Examination One) in Unit VIII. Check your answers. Analyze your errors.

27. You are now ready to take Practice Examination Two in Unit VIII. Take the Language Arts, Writing test, Parts I and II. Check your answers. Analyze your errors. Study the analyses of correct answers.

28. Take the Social Studies test (Practice Examination Two). Check your answers. Analyze your errors. Study the analyses of correct answers.

29. Take the Science test and the Language Arts, Reading test (Practice Examination Two). Check your answers. Analyze your errors. Study the analyses of correct answers.

30. Take the Mathematics test (Practice Examination Two). Check your answers. Analyze your errors. Study the analyses of correct answers.

A WORD ABOUT TIME

Don't try to learn everything or take every practice test in one session. Work at your own speed and in your own way. A book can't be completely flexible—but we urge you to be flexible. Use this book to suit your individual needs. If you need review in math but feel pretty confident about English, concentrate on math. If you want to try the exams first and skip a study section, do so. Remember that High School Equivalency Examinations are given frequently. Remember also that in most states you can take one test at a time—or two, or three, or all five. Remember especially that, if you fail one test, you can take another...and another. However, you will probably take all five tests and pass them all the first time you try. That is what this book aims to help you do.

THE NEW GED EXAMINATION

Standardized tests change from time to time. The GED Examination, as you may already know, changed in 2002. Although much of the new exam tests the same concepts in the same way as past GED Exams, the new exam also differs from its predecessors in some significant respects. As you prepare for your GED Exam, you must familiarize yourself with these differences.

The purpose of the following overview is to outline these changes as they affect each part of the exam: Writing Skills, Parts I and II; Social Studies; Science; Literature and the Arts; and Mathematics. This overview describes in detail the changes to each part of the exam, and points you to relevant items in the book that will be especially helpful to you in your preparation to deal with these changes. It also provides some examples of new question types. As you work your way through this book, therefore, you should consult this test overview regularly.

If you revisit this overview regularly in conjunction with the rest of the book, you will be well prepared for the GED Exam. Good luck on test day!

LANGUAGE ARTS, WRITING, TEST 1, PART I

As in the past, **Language Arts, Writing Test 1**, Part I tests your knowledge of the content of written English—sentence structure, the ability to recognize correct and incorrect sentences—sentence fragments and run-on sentences; correct usage, agreement, case of pronouns, verb forms; mechanics of capitalization and punctuation. Passages 12–20 sentences long are still used. Now paragraphs are lettered, and titles are given to instructional and informational documents. Within each passage there are errors you have to find and correct, or recognize as correct; sentences you are asked to combine; and alternative ways to write sentences, all of these in a multiple-choice format. In some you are given the sentence to be corrected and five possible answers. In some questions, one possible answer is, "no correction is necessary." Three types of errors are retained from the old test: errors in sentence structure, errors in usage, and errors in mechanics: punctuation and capitalization. The three types of items are the same as in the old test: correction of errors in a sentence or a number of sentences; revision of a stem with an underlined part that may be correct or incorrect; construction shift, the rewriting of a stem that is correct but that you will be asked to write in a different way. Also, there are 5 fewer questions in this test, making the total 50 instead of 55.

WHAT IS NEW IN THE GED?

1. Sentence structure is now weighted 30%, usage 30%, and mechanics 25%. Tested will be homonyms (words with the same sound as another word or words but with a different spelling and meaning, such as *to, two, too*); possessives (form of a noun or pronoun that shows ownership, such as *boy's hat, ladies' hats*), and contractions (shortened form of a word or words by omission of a letter, such as *do not, don't; they are, they're*). Fewer uses of the comma will be tested, emphasizing only those that prevent confusion in meaning, as in "Let's eat Frank before we go to work." "Let's eat, Frank, before we go to work."

Homonyms

Turn to page 164. The final paragraph on the page lists 40 frequently used groups of homonyms, most of them groups of two, fewer of three. Check the meaning of each homonym and use each in a sentence so you don't confuse them. An example is: "*There* are many exact words." "They used *their* words carefully."

Possessives and Contractions

Turn to page 158, under Apostrophe. Study the examples.

The three most troublesome contractions are *it's, you're,* and *they're. It's* is a contraction of *it is* (the second "i" is omitted). *Its,* without the apostrophe, is a possessive. "The dog wagged *its* tail." Here nothing is omitted; it is not a contraction. *You're* is a contraction of *you are. Your* is a possessive. "You wore *your* coat." The

same is true for *they're,* contracted from *they are. Their* is a possessive.

Here are 25 of the most frequently used contractions:
aren't, can't, couldn't, doesn't, don't, hadn't, hasn't, haven't, he'd, he's, I'd, isn't, I've, let's, mustn't, shouldn't, there's, wasn't, we'd, weren't, we've, won't, wouldn't, you'll, you've

For each, indicate the two words of which it is a contraction, for example *aren't—are not.* Be careful where you put the apostrophe. *Doesn't* is correct; *does'nt* is not.

Commas

Failure to use commas can often result in confusion. Here are some examples: "While we were eating the bird started singing." "If you want to shoot the sergeant will show you how." Commas can also change the meaning of a sentence. Compare "Please let me have some honey." with "Please let me have some, honey." Always try to determine if a comma is needed to clarify the meaning.

2. The new GED has a change in the weight of the three question types. Correction questions are now weighted at 45%, down from 50%. You are asked to correct errors in organization, sentence structure, usage, and mechanics in one sentence, a number of sentences, or a complete paragraph. Construction shift items have been raised to 20%. These test only mechanics and sentence structure. You are asked to rewrite a stem using an alternate structure (another way to write the sentence). Revision questions test skills in sentence structure, usage, and mechanics by having part of the stem underlined and having you choose from five possible corrections. These remain weighted at 25%.

To prepare for correction and revision questions, review pages 115–131 for sentence structure; pages 132–151 for usage; 152–167 for mechanics. Then study the following questions and the answer analyses on the pages indicated.

Sentence structure

Page 34, question 3; page 38, question 25. Answer analyses are on page 97. Page

594, question 1; page 596, question 12; page 599, question 25. Answer analyses are on page 664. Page 681, question 17; pages 682–683, questions 25 and 28; page 686, question 43. Answer analyses are on page 745.

Usage

Page 34, question 1; page 37, question 19. Answer analyses are on page 97. Page 599, question 27; page 600, question 28; page 604, question 47. Answers and analyses are on pages 660–661. Page 678, question 3; page 684, question 31. Answers and analyses are on page 745.

Construction shift—Rewriting sentences

Page 40, question 30; page 43, question 49; analysis on pages 97–98; page 594, question 3; page 596, question 13; page 603, question 45; analysis on pages 660–661; page 681, question 18; page 684, question 34; page 685, question 36; page 686, question 44; page 688, question 50; analysis on pages 745–746.

Construction shift—Combining sentences

Page 41, question 38; analysis on page 98; page 595, question 8; page 596, question 11; page 598, question 19; page 604, question 50; analysis on pages 660–661; page 680, question 13; page 681, question 19; page 683, question 27; page 684, question 35; analysis on page 745.

3. Sentence structure, usage, and mechanics are now worth 85%. A new content area, organization, is now weighted at 15%, an important change. This involves moving sentences in a paragraph to improve logic and clarity; removing irrelevant sentences; identifying, moving, inserting topic sentences (a statement of the main idea or unifying thought); and joining or dividing paragraphs to improve clarity.

4. The content of the passages that are the basis for the questions in the Language Arts, Writing Test, Part I has been broadened to include, in addition to informational passages, "how to" (practical subjects) and business documents. The following are among the passages you will find that embody this change:

- Page 193, How to Save
- Page 196, How to Be a Better Consumer
- Page 198, How to Control Household Pests
- Page 200, How to Make a Household Inventory
- Page 594, How to Make Food Safe
- Page 598, How to Prevent Drug Abuse
- Page 600, How to Prevent Home Accidents
- Page 680, How to Purchase Camping Equipment
- Page 685, How to Buy Auto Insurance
- Page 687, How to Find Help in a New Community You Move To

LANGUAGE ARTS, WRITING, TEST 1, PART II

In this part, as in the old test, you are asked to write an expository essay in 45 minutes. The length of the essay is now 250 words rather than the 200 words as in the old test. In the essay you are asked to explain, describe, or interpret a particular idea, situation, or experience by using your own personal life and information, as in the current test. See page 217 for a sample expository essay. Study page 225, The Expository Outline, and follow through on pages 219–221, Setting Up an Expository Essay. There are additional sample essays on pages 220–221 and 229.

The essay directions will be thorough and specific:

- You must write on the assigned topic ONLY.
- You will have 45 minutes to write on your assigned essay topic.

The essay required in the new GED test is now given a score from 1–4 (with 4 being the highest) based on the following:

- Response to prompt
- Organization
- Development and details
- Conventions of edited English
- Word choice

The scoring guide is as follows:

4. Effective
3. Adequate
2. Marginal
1. Ineffective (A score of 1 will require that you retake the entire Language Arts, Writing Test 1.)

1. Do not leave any blank pages.
2. Write legibly *in ink* so that the evaluators will be able to read your writing.
3. Write on the assigned topic. If you write on a topic other than the one assigned, you will not receive a score for the Writing Skills Test.
4. Write your essay on the lined pages of the separate answer sheet booklet.

Part II is a test to determine how well you can use written language to explain your ideas. In preparing your essay, take the following steps:

1. Read the DIRECTIONS and the TOPIC carefully.
2. Plan your essay before you write. Use the scratch paper to make any notes. These notes will be collected but not scored.
3. Before you turn in your essay, reread what you have written and make any changes that will improve your essay.
4. Your essay should be long enough to develop the topic adequately and should be approximately 250 words.

The assigned topic will be clearly indicated. Here are some sample topics to practice on.

1. If you could choose to spend a day with a particular person, whom would you choose? In your essay, indicate the reasons you would choose that person.
2. If you had a choice of a travel destination, indicate the place and the reasons why you chose it.
3. All of us have beliefs we hold dear. Choose one such belief and indicate the reasons why you chose it.
4. We all have favorite memories. Choose the memory you most cherish and give the reasons why it is dear to you.
5. "A friend in need is a friend indeed," goes the saying. Choose an experience you had helping a friend or being helped by a friend. Indicate why the experience is memorable.

Finally, review page 229, Allot Your Time (the essay is now 250 words), and Revising the Essay on the same page, concentrating on items 1, 2, 3, 5, and 6 on the checklist.

SOCIAL STUDIES, TEST 2

The following will indicate the four main changes or new emphases, and guide you in your preparation by showing how the materials in this book can be of the greatest use.

1. The test will emphasize history and government including civics; 40% will be history with United States history 25% and world history 15%.
2. More questions will be based on maps, tables, cartoons, and photographs—the graphic and visual.
3. Each test will include part of at least one *historical* document, for example, the United States Constitution, and at least one *practical* document chosen from sources dealing with your life as a citizen and a consumer. Both global (international) and United States (national) settings will be included.
4. Questions requiring analysis of prose and graphic materials will be emphasized.

The multiple-choice questions will be based on both *prose* (texts, speeches, newspapers, news magazines, and documents) and *visuals* (maps, graphs, tables, political cartoons, and photographs). Both single-question items and sets of questions based on the selections will be included.

Four types of thinking will be tested as in previous versions of the examination:

1. Questions requiring comprehension—understanding of information and ideas and the meaning they may imply (20%).
2. Questions requiring application—ability to use the information and ideas you understand in new situations (20%).
3. Questions involving analysis—ability to go beyond mere comprehension and application to recognize cause and effect, to determine the writer's point of view, assumptions, and errors, and to distinguish fact from opinion (40%).

4. Questions involving evaluation—determine how the facts presented lead to the conclusions reached, their accuracy, and how they are influenced by the author's point of view or bias (20%).

EMPHASIS ON HISTORY AND GOVERNMENT

Begin with the American History outline on pages 299–302, noting the eight major sections. Look up any words you do not know in the glossary beginning on page 308. Some examples are: Puritan, colony, abolitionist, Reconstruction, immigration, isolationism, New Deal, and Cold War.

First read the history selection on page 247, answer the questions, and study the answer analyses. For further reading go to History—Social Studies practice on pages 326–329, and, after reading the five selections, answer questions 26–40. The correct answers with explanations are on pages 335–336.

Review the World History outline on pages 306–308. The Diagnostic Test and the two practice examinations contain many question sets (groups of questions) and single questions on U.S. and world history; the Diagnostic Test, sets 15–16 and 29–31, and questions 20 and 38. Practice Exam One, set 15–17, question 20; set 31–33, and questions 7, 39, and 40; Practice Exam Two, set 17–19, questions 13 and 41.

For government, begin with the Civics and Government outline on page 306, noting the key areas—meaning of democracy, the political system, the party system, elections, the three branches of government and their functions, and state and local governments. Again look up the meanings of words you don't know on pages 311–314, particularly amendment, cabinet, checks and balances, civil rights, Congress, constitution, executive, federal, judicial, legislature, republic, Supreme Court, and vote. Go to page 245 for the reading dealing with political conventions in Civics and Government, answer the questions, and study the answer analyses. Further readings are on pages 321–323 with answers and analyses on pages 334–335. Other questions on the three tests are: Diagnostic—set 1–3; questions 25, 34; set 41–43, question 44; and set 48–49; Practice

Exam One—set 4–6, question 8; sets 21–22, 34–35; Practice Exam Two—sets 1–3, 4–6, question 21; set 24–26, and questions 30 and 40.

While history and government (political science) questions are 65% of the test, be sure to study economics and geography in the same way that you did for history and government.

GRAPHIC AND VISUAL

More questions will be based on the graphic and the visual: maps, tables, graphs, cartoons, and photographs. Here's how to study for each of these:

- For *tables*, study pages 253–255, following the steps indicated for reading tables. Note the title, locate facts, find relationships between facts, and draw conclusions from them. Other tables and graphs are on page 264 with questions and answers on pages 271 and 272; Diagnostic Test—set 26–28; Practice Exam One—questions 18 and 50; sets 23–25, 49–50; Practice Exam Two—questions 43 and 47—a total of 8 tables.

- For *graphs*, study pages 255–258 for examples, questions, answers, and answer analyses of the three main types of graphs: (1) the pie or circle graph, (2) the bar graph, and (3) the line graph. All three types are fully explained.

  In the section Additional Practice with Tables, Graphs, and Maps, page 262, questions 5–11 and 31–33 deal with pie graphs, questions 12–15, 16–18, 19–20, 34–35, 36–37 deal with bar graphs. In the Diagnostic Test, sets 7–8, 21–22, question 23; sets 26–28, 39–40 deal with bar graphs; question 34 contains a pie graph. In Practice Exam One, set 10–11 has a line graph. In Practice Exam Two sets 10–12, 22–23 have pie graphs, set 33–34 a bar graph; questions 37–39 contain both bar and pie graphs.

- For *maps*, a detailed treatment is on pages 258–261 covering the aids that help you read maps: title, legend, latitude and longitude, scale of miles, grids to locate places, and measurement of distances between them. Additional practice is on page 262 (pollution), page 267 (refugees), and page 332 (the Middle East).

- Another means of visual presentation, *political cartoons*, is on pages 272–276 including a discussion of their value and the steps in interpreting them. Practice is provided by five political cartoons dealing with topics such as political campaign financing, television coverage of elections, human rights in China, the electoral college, and the minimum wage. More cartoons are found in the three tests: Diagnostic Test—questions 44 and 50; Practice Exam One—question 9 and sets 21–22 and 34–35; Practice Exam Two—set 7–8, questions 13, 21, and 32.
- A new feature of the Social Studies test is the interpretation of photographs. The saying goes: "A picture is worth a thousand words." A photograph can be a powerful political weapon; examples are a photo of a Vietcong solider shot point-blank in the head, a terrified Jewish boy, hands behind his head, with Nazi soldiers pointing guns at him. On pages 280–282 are five photographs that make political statements: Photograph 1 depicts a presidential campaign rally. Theodore Roosevelt is speaking to attentive listeners before a backdrop of a welcome sign, an eagle, symbol of the United States, and the bull moose, symbol of his political party. Photograph 3 protests the use of child labor; note the small young boys working the huge machine. Photograph 5 points up an all-black segregated classroom, students and teacher. Look for more photographs in your daily newspaper.

HISTORICAL DOCUMENTS

Each test will feature at least one *historical* document. Turn to pages 277–280 for typical important historical documents, such as the first two paragraphs of the Declaration of Independence, an excerpt from the Monroe Doctrine, an amendment from the Bill of Rights in the United States Constitution; the Preamble to the Universal Declaration of Human Rights adopted by the United Nations in 1948. Study these and the analyses of the answers to the questions. Eight additional documents and speeches can be found in the three tests: Diagnostic Test—set 15–16, Lincoln's Gettysburg Address; question 20, the Monroe and Truman Doctrines compared; set 29–31, President Lyndon B.

Johnson's speech. Practice Exam One—set 4–6, an important Supreme Court decision; set 19–20, the Great Society message of President Lyndon B. Johnson. Practice Exam Two—set 1–3, from the writings of Alexander Hamilton; set 24–26, from Jefferson's Inaugural Address, question 30 from a decision of Supreme Court Justice Oliver Wendell Holmes.

PRACTICAL DOCUMENTS

Each test will feature a *practical* document. Turn to pages 282–288 for typical practical documents, such as an Internal Revenue Service publication dealing with a job search, a proposition to be voted on in an election, a technology company's annual report, an internal corporate bulletin dealing with safety, and the original 2000 census form. All of these require close reading because they are government and business documents. The questions and answers will help you interpret these documents. For further practice, see the Diagnostic Test set 4–6 dealing with product warranties for consumers; set 26–28 with Federal Reserve information; Practice Exam One—set 49–50 dealing with a public opinion poll; Practice Exam Two—set 10–12 with data from the Congressional Budget Office; set 37–39 with data on the national debt from the Office of Management and Budget; question 47 based on a tax table.

ANALYSIS OF PRINTED TEXTS

Questions stressing analysis of printed texts will be more numerous. To prepare for these, turn first to page 277. (The new test now has 40% of the questions requiring analysis instead of the 30% indicated.) Study carefully the answer and the analysis of the question dealing with democracy. Continue on pages 278–288.

Another feature of the new test is the inclusion of a set of questions that combine several of the social studies areas. An example of this is set 15–17 on page 610 in which history, government, and economics are involved. While analysis is stressed, ample practice is provided for comprehension (understanding of the text); see page 289, application (using comprehension in a new setting); pages 290–291, 294–295, and evaluation (judging accuracy and the author's interpretation), pages 292–293.

If you use this study guide properly, you will be well prepared for the new GED Social Studies test.

SCIENCE, TEST 3

There have been some changes made to the GED Science test. You will find that this book provides you with an excellent preparation for the test and the material in this study guide is highly relevant to the new test.

The test is still a multiple-choice format with five choices per question. The scoring for the test is the same as in previous years. All of the test-taking hints that this book provides are valuable. For example, if the correct answer to a question is not immediately obvious, it is a good strategy to try to eliminate incorrect choices to narrow down the choices.

There is no need for you to memorize any equations. There are very few calculations on the GED science section and those that do exist involve some basic calculations such as addition, subtraction, or multiplication. In the event that a formula is needed, it will be provided to you.

Probably the biggest difference between the old test and the new one is that there are fewer lengthy passages followed by several questions and more brief passages followed by a single question. This is to allow each question to focus on a specific topic or concept. You will also find that the new test tries to make use of more practical examples. For instance, instead of a question that describes the motion of a pendulum, you might find a question, or series of questions, that deals with a swing. The concept is the same, but you are using a common object to illustrate it.

There has been a slight redistribution of the topic contents as well: a greater emphasis on life sciences and environmental topics on the new version of the GED. On the new version of the test, more questions will deal with the life sciences—mainly biology—or environmental science—including ecology. There are questions from all areas of the physical sciences as well, including chemistry, physics, and earth and space science.

The test does not seek to see how much vocabulary you have memorized or how much science you may recall from school. Instead, the emphasis is on applying basic concepts and thinking things through. In this respect, the test remains unchanged.

The new version of the GED uses the National Science Education Standards as a guideline. Below you will find a short summary of the standards and some of the examples of each.

CONTENT STANDARD A: SCIENCE AS INQUIRY

- Abilities needed to perform scientific inquiry
- Understanding the nature of scientific inquiry

This section refers to the ability to understand a well-planned experiment, including the use of control (or comparison) groups. This version of your Barron's GED study guide already has many questions regarding this topic; see, for example, the passage containing questions 72 and 73 in the biology practice section.

CONTENT STANDARD B: PHYSICAL SCIENCE

- The structure of atoms
- The properties and structure of matter
- Chemical reactions
- Motion and forces
- Conservation of energy and the concept of entropy
- Interactions of energy and matter

This standard deals mainly with the physical sciences such as chemistry and physics.

The science practice sections on chemistry and physics cover these topics, and there are many more questions in the practice exams.

CONTENT STANDARD C: LIFE SCIENCE

- The cell
- The molecular basis of heredity
- Evolution of life
- The interdependence of organisms
- Matter, energy, and organization in living systems
- Behavior

The science practice section on biology covers these topics. Keep in mind that not every biology question fits exactly into each of the topics above. The new standards are general guidelines that can be used to help organize information for you.

CONTENT STANDARD D: EARTH AND SPACE SCIENCE

- Energy in the earth
- Geochemical cycles (rock and mineral cycles)
- Origin and evolution of the earth and the moon
- Origin and evolution of the universe

This topic area also includes meteorology and the water cycle.

CONTENT STANDARD E: SCIENCE AND TECHNOLOGY

- Technological design
- General understanding about science and technology

This section deals with the applications of science. For example, the earth science practice passage dealing with different forms of energy and their uses fits into this category; see earth science practice, questions 1–3. In addition, there are questions in the physics and chemistry sections that also deal with applications of science; see physics practice questions 18–20.

CONTENT STANDARD F: SCIENCE IN PERSONAL AND SOCIAL PERSPECTIVES

- Personal and community health
- Population growth
- Natural resources
- Environmental quality
- Natural and human-induced hazards
- Local, national, and global challenges in science and technology

Many of the questions dealing with this content standard are those that stress some real-world applications. Questions dealing with water or air quality would be good examples of topics covered under this content standard.

CONTENT STANDARD G: HISTORY AND NATURE OF SCIENCE

- Science as a human endeavor
- Nature of scientific knowledge
- Historical perspectives

This content standard deals with the manner in which scientific knowledge is gained (through experimentation) and some historical perspectives on the acquisition of this knowledge. Keep in mind that you will not be expected to have memorized any names of scientists or dates regarding discoveries. Instead, you are more likely to see a passage dealing with the history of a concept, such as models or the structure of the atom, and then to see a few questions dealing with that passage. Remember that all of the information you will need to answer the questions will be contained in the passage.

As you study for the GED, it may help to see into which content standard questions or groups of questions fit. Keep in mind that not every question or passage will fit neatly into a single category, but you should find that paying close attention to the study material, the questions, and answers with explanations will allow you to be successful on the science section of the GED.

LANGUAGE ARTS, READING, TEST 4

This test keeps a number of features of the old GED Examination, but the title has been changed to **Language Arts: Reading**.

1. Selections of 300 to 400 words will be drawn from respected writers of prose fiction and nonfiction, poetry, and drama. The texts will have been written from pre-1920 to after 1960 to date, both classical and modern.
2. The subject matter and authors will continue to reflect many different cultural backgrounds. Diversity will be emphasized as in the past.
3. Each selection will continue to be introduced by a purpose question to help you, the reader, focus on the meaning and intent of the passage. It will be of the "why" and the "how" variety.

4. The questions will be in the same multiple-choice format.
5. The test will include prose, poetry, and drama with four to eight questions designed to test your reading comprehension on several levels of difficulty: to understand, to apply your understanding, to analyze specific parts of a passage, and to synthesize the parts of the passage into a whole.
6. As is now the case, 75% of the questions will be literary texts divided among prose, poetry, and drama with at least one selection from each. Various passages from classical and modern writing will continue to be represented; 25% will be nonfiction prose.

WHAT'S NEW?

1. In *content* and *context* there is greater emphasis on diversity of the selections. Various ethnic groups are included. To help you prepare for these kinds of texts, a number of authors of different backgrounds are represented in the current edition.
   - *African-Americans* included are the dramatist Lorraine Hansberry—*A Raisin in the Sun* selection on page 76, novelist and essayist Alice Walker, author of *The Color Purple*—her memoir of her mother on page 445, Maya Angelou's prose selection on page 73 and a poem on page 443, and Naomi Long Madgett's poem "I've Come This Far to Freedom" on page 444.
   - *Hispanics* are represented by two Nobel Prize winners for Literature—Pablo Neruda, a Chilean author, with his selection on page 436, and Spanish author Juan Ramon Jimenez, with a selection from *Platero and I* on page 446.
   - *Jewish* authors included are Nobel laureate Isaac Bashevis Singer who wrote in Yiddish—a selection from his short story "Short Friday" appears on page 634, Mary Antin who came to America from Poland and wrote in Yiddish and English in *The Promised Land* about opportunity in the United States—selection on page 637, and Emma Lazarus whose poem on the Statue of Liberty is analyzed on pages 426–429.

   - A selection by a *Native American* from the memoir of Chief Red Fox is on page 77.
   - A selection from the best-selling *The Joy Luck Club* by Asian American author Amy Tan is on page 437.
2. Women writers included are the five above-mentioned African-Americans, as well as Mary Antin, Amy Tan, Emma Lazarus, short story writer Sarah Orne Jewett, poet Sara Teasdale, and Katherine B. Day, a dramatist (*Life with Father*).
3. Various regions of the United States and Canada produced Washington Irving (New York), Sarah Orne Jewett (Maine), Henry Thoreau (Massachusetts), William Allen White (Kansas), Mark Twain (Missouri), and Farley Mowat (Canada).
4. Another change in the literary texts comprising 75% of the test is a broader range of time periods in which the texts were written, and the time periods are more specifically defined into three, more classical passages written pre-1920, passages written between 1920 and 1960, and more modern passages written after 1960. Here again the current edition will be of great help. Selections written prior to 1920 are drawn from "Rip Van Winkle" by Irving, page 447; *Walden* ("Why did the author go to the woods?") by Thoreau, pages 447–448; "What Is a Camp of War-wounded Like?" by Walt Whitman, page 422; "What Are Feuds?" by Mark Twain, pages 449–450; "Ozymandias" by Percy Shelley, page 417; and selections by Lazarus, page 426; Jewett, pages 448–449, and Mary Antin, page 637. Selections written between 1920 and 1960 include those from *A Raisin in the Sun*, page 76, *Life with Father*, page 418, *Death of a Salesman*, pages 429–430, *Our Town*, page 717, poems by Auden, page 451, and Teasdale, page 720, from *Platero and I*, page 446, and "Short Friday," page 634. Since 1960 we have here selections from the works of Neruda, page 436, Tan, page 437, Walker, page 445, and Angelou, pages 73 and 443. There will be one selection from each of these periods.

   In addition there is an 8- to 25-line poem and one drama selection. Eleven poems with questions and analyzed answers are included in the current edition of the GED. They are found on pages

74, 75, 417, 421, 443, 444, 450, 451, 718–719, and 720. It is most important that you study the six skills in Reading Poetry on pages 425–426.

For the drama selection you can prepare by studying the seven selections with questions and analyzed answers on pages 76, 418–419, 429–430, 452, 453–454, 636–637, and 717. Here, too, it is most important that you study Reading Drama on page 429 and the seven skills listed in the Summary of Interpretation of Drama Reading on page 431.

5. Nonfiction questions are based on three selections chosen from nonfiction prose. They deal with a variety of subjects.
   - Read the following and study the analyses of the answers to the questions: a humorous essay by Andy Rooney on differing personality types, pages 442–443, the reading habits of kids, pages 456–457, Hollywood, page 455, the offensive behavior of people, pages 716 and 722–723, the immigrant experience, page 633, and an appreciation of an American woman author, page 724.
   - There are autobiographical accounts of a Chilean poet, page 436, a Canadian, page 441, a black woman, page 443, a Jewish immigrant, page 637, and a Spanish author, page 446. There will be one such selection on the GED.
   - At least one selection will deal with reviews of art and the performing arts. Read an appreciation of the paintings of the versatile Renaissance man, Leonardo da Vinci, pages 457–458. The most comprehensive selection and treatment of a performing art is on pages 431–432, which deals with puppetry on children's TV and Jim Henson's Muppets. Study the questions and answer analyses on pages 432–433.

6. A completely new feature is a business-related document such as a company bulletin or an annual report. One such selection will be on the test. You will find a selection from an actual corporate report on page 284. It states the scope of the company's operations and its efforts to improve profits. An actual company bulletin is reproduced on page 285. It seeks to cut down on the greatest cause of accidents by company drivers: backing of vehicles. Study these and the analyzed answers on page 285.

The format of the questions has not changed.

READING SKILLS

The emphasis on reading skills has shifted to higher and more difficult levels. Comprehension and application questions are now only 35% of the test—20% comprehension and 15% application. Analysis questions (reference to specific parts of a passage) are allocated 30–35%, and synthesis questions (drawing on the passage as a whole) are similarly allocated 30–35%.

Comprehension

Comprehension tests a basic understanding of the meaning and purpose of the writing. It tests your ability to restate information in other words (paraphrase), summarize the main idea, and explain the thought conveyed by the text. Read the discussions on pages 413–414 and on pages 415–416. Questions that focus on the *main idea* are: page 72, question 5; page 74, question 16 ("which phrase best expresses the idea"); page 423, question 1; page 426, question 1; page 444, question 36; page 450, question 71; page 451, question 76; page 634, question 15; page 637, question 31 ("the best title for this selection"); page 718, question 15 ("which word best expresses the main idea"), and page 720, question 21 ("the main idea of the poem").

For *details*, read page 417. Some questions on details are: page 73, question 13 (reference of a pronoun), page 443, question 33 (situations), page 458, question 120 (studies), page 716, question 2 (examples of unattractive behavior).

Application questions

Application questions test your ability to use information and ideas from the passage in a different situation. A good example is question 25 on page 720 where you are asked to apply the meaning of the term "barter" to the text of the poem. Others include page 437, question 5 ("legends"), page 438, question 10 ("hard times"), page 440, question 16 ("symbol"), page 444, question 42 ("destination"), page 445, question 48 ("evidence"), and page 450, question 74 (the "church incident"). Study the answer analyses to questions on these passages.

Analysis questions

Analysis questions ask you to break down the information in the text to its parts and make several references to specific parts of a passage. You will have to draw conclusions, understand consequences (cause and effect), or arrive at other ideas suggested or implied by the passage. Read pages 418–420 on making inferences. In addition, you may be asked to identify such qualities as tone and mood (see page 418) or arrive at what is suggested from language sometimes used in an unusual way. These questions will give you practice in analysis. *Cause and effect*: page 78, question 34 (effect of love of nature). *Drawing conclusions and deductions and making inferences*: page 79, question 36; page 437 question 2; page 437, question 6; page 442, question 28; page 443, questions 34, 35; page 447, question 56; page 634, question 12; page 636, question 21 ("make an assumption"); page 637, questions 26, 27; page 717, question 7; page 718, question 12 (conclusion regarding theme). *Projecting outcomes*: page 77, question 27 ("the family will"), page 77, question 28 ("the head of the house will be"); page 635, questions 19, 20 ("will probably"); and page 637, question 30 ("will"). Study these with the analyzed answers.

Synthesis questions

Synthesis questions, the most difficult kind, require putting parts together to make a whole from different parts of a text or from two texts. You will have to make connections between the parts, determine how the text is organized, the overall tone or purpose of the text, or bring to the passage outside knowledge to integrate with it. This will become clear from these examples: page 74, question 19 (point of view); page 75, question 25 (impact); page 430, question 2 (construct a prior event); page 430, question 6 (situation); page 444, question 41 (kind of poem); page 724, question 40 (effect of whole). *Mood or attitude*: page 77, question 31; page 448, question 64 (tone); page 450, question 75 (attitude); page 451, question 80 (source of power); page 455, question 101 (attitude); page 632, question 1 (how mood is expressed); page 723, question 31 (writer's attitude); *Organization*: page 75, question 24.

A major change is the inclusion of expanded synthesis questions, combining information from two parts within a passage. A good example is on page 78, a comparison of two plays, *Romeo and Juliet* by Shakespeare and *West Side Story*. Question 37 asks you to find in the text a comparison of the language of the two plays; question 38 centers on the common weaknesses of the plays; questions 39 and 40 focus on the similarities and differences between the couples in the plays. In answering each of the questions you have to connect parts within the text, comments on *Romeo and Juliet* and *West Side Story*, and make a synthesis to answer the question. Remember to study the answer analyses on pages 105–106.

Study the above materials that are already in this edition of the GED book and you will be well prepared for the new GED.

MATHEMATICS, TEST 5

The new Mathematics section of the GED Exam will be somewhat different from old exams. Here's a summary of the important changes:

1. ***Fewer questions.*** The number of questions will be reduced from 56 to 50 and will be split into Parts I and II, each of the parts having 25 questions.
2. ***Use of a calculator.*** For Part I, you will be given a Casio fx-260SOLAR calculator at the testing site, which you have the option of using to help solve all questions in this part only.
3. ***Use of an answer grid.*** For 10 of the 50 questions on the test, you will not be offered multiple choice but must come up with answers on your own. You will then be required to "bubble in" these answers on an answer grid.

The good news is that the new test doesn't appear to be any more difficult than the old one. The concepts tested and the level of complexity of the questions are virtually the same as those included in past exams, and are covered thoroughly in this book. With the added privilege of being able to use a calculator for Part I, you will almost certainly find the new test easier.

USING THE CASIO FX-260SOLAR CALCULATOR

Before taking Part I, you will be issued a Casio fx-260SOLAR calculator and then given a few minutes to practice using it. You don't have to use the calculator, but it is strongly recommended that you do so. It can really help you to avoid computational errors that lead to incorrect answers and can dramatically reduce the time it takes to solve certain problems, giving you more time to spend on the tougher questions. After Part I is over, you must return the calculator and complete Part II without it.

If you have had some past experience using a calculator, it will help you in operating the Casio fx-260, which works like virtually all hand-held calculators. If you have never used a calculator, however, it is a good idea to purchase or borrow one to practice on prior to taking the GED. The most effective way to practice is to use the fx-260, which is available in retail stores for about $10 or can be ordered from the GED Fulfillment Center by calling (301) 604-9073.

As you take the practice exams in this book, use the calculator to help solve only about half the questions. Because you will still be required to do your own calculations for many of the questions, it's important to keep your computational skills strong and avoid overdependence on the calculator.

On page 20 is a basic diagram of the Casio fx-SOLAR calculator that will be issued to you. Please note that the calculator has a lot more function keys than you will need to use on the test.

Here are some basic rules to keep in mind when using a calculator:

- Press the keys firmly, checking the display window to make sure you have entered numbers accurately.
- Press AC (or similar key) after completing each problem to completely clear it. Pressing C will erase just the last number entered.
- Numbers and the decimal point will appear on the display window, but operations signs (like + or × or ÷) will not.

Example One (Basic Operations)

28.3 ft.

52 ft.

How many square feet of carpet are required to cover the entire office floor in the diagram above?

PRESS   *28.3*,   then ×,   then *52*,   then =

Answer: 1471.6 sq. ft.

Example Two (Working with Parentheses)

Find: 12(117 ÷ 13) − 68

PRESS   *12* × [(⋯ *117* ÷ *13* ⋯)] − *68* =

Answer: 40

Note: The fx-260 has parentheses keys, but some other calculators don't.

Example Three (Working with Fractions)

Broadway	**3/4 mile**
Alice Avenue	**2 1/2 miles**
Stockton Street	**4 miles**

According to the highway exit sign above, how much further past Broadway is Alice Avenue?

PRESS   *2* a b/c *1* a b/c *2* − a b/c *3* a b/c *4* =

Answer: 1 3/4 miles

Note: Not all calculators are able to compute fractions.

Example Four (Working with Signed Numbers)

What is the value of the following expression?

–3(–6 + 8) – (–12)

PRESS *3* +/– × [(··· *6* +/– + *8* ···)] – *12* +/– =

Answer: 6

Note: Some calculators allow you to enter negative numbers using the – key.

Example Five (Working with Exponents)

A container that holds crushed gravel is in the shape of a cube, with each side measuring 17 feet. What is the volume: of the container?

PRESS *17* X^y *3* =

Answer: 4,913 cu. ft.

Example Six (Working with Square Roots)

The square root of 138 is between what two whole numbers?

PRESS *138* SHIFT X^2

Answer: between 11 and 12

FINDING AN ANSWER AND USING AN ANSWER GRID

On 10 questions out of the 50 on the test, multiple-choice answers will not be provided. You must come up with an answer yourself and then record it on a grid (see illustration).

Example One (Recording Whole Numbers)

m∠*CBD* = 132°

What is the measure in degrees of ∠*ACB*?
(Using what you've learned about triangles and supplemetary angles in Chapter 24, you calculate the correct answer to be 42°.)

Answer: 42°

You can fill in the answer grid for this response in four different ways; all are correct (see illustration below). Make sure to write the answer in the top horizontal row of boxes and then "bubble in" the corresponding numbers below. Don't worry about including the degrees sign (°); it's unnecessary.

Example Two (Recording Numbers with Decimals)

Sharon and her coworkers want to purchase a portable CD player as a going-away present for their boss. The player costs $86.99. Sharon collects $47.35 from her coworkers and contributes $20 herself. How much more does she need to make the purchase?

Answer: $19.64

Here, there is only one way to complete the grid. Note that the decimal point *must* be recorded and takes up an entire column. Recording the $ sign is unnecessary.

Example Three (Recording Fractions)

A plumber measures a piece of pipe to be 1 5/8 inches. How much does he need to trim from the pipe to make it fit a connection that is 1 3/8 inches long?

Answer: 2/8 or **1/4**

The grid can be completed in the following ways, all of which are correct.

Example Four (Recording Points on a Coordinates Plane Grid)

Two lines intersect at a point with coordinates of (5, –3). Show the location of the intersecting point on the grid below.

Answer: see grid

Note: The coordinate plane grid illustrated is just like the rectangular coordinate grid in Chapter 23. However, the *x* and *y* axes are not labeled, so it's essential that you memorize which is which. There will most probably be only two questions out of the 50 requiring you to fill in this type of grid.

PRACTICE STRATEGIES FOR QUESTIONS WITHOUT MULTIPLE CHOICE

Learning to fill in the answer grid is rather easy. The challenging part of the new test is feeling confident about the answers you calculate without actually seeing them confirmed with a multiple choice. Much of the practice in the instructional chapters requires you to come up with answers on your own, so that kind of practice should help instill confidence in your work. It's also suggested strongly in Chapter 25 that, except when using the method of "Plugging In," you should always calculate an answer first and then compare it to the multiple-choice offerings.

A Diagnostic Examination

The direction sheets, mathematics formulas,* and question formats of this examination are constructed like the actual test you will take. The examination consists of five parts.

Tests		Questions	Time Allowance
Test 1:	The Language Arts, Writing Test, Part I	50	1 hour, 15 minutes
	The Language Arts, Writing Test, Part II	Essay	45 minutes
Test 2:	The Social Studies Test	50	1 hour, 10 minutes
Test 3:	The Science Test	66	1 hour, 35 minutes
Test 4:	The Language Arts, Reading Test	40	1 hour, 5 minutes
Test 5:	The Mathematics Test, Part I	25	45 minutes
	The Mathematics Test, Part II	25	45 minutes
	Total:		7 hours, 20 minutes

For this examination, we have included an answer sheet and a self-appraisal chart. Mark yourself on each test, checking your answers against the answer key. Read the answer explanations to be sure you understand the correct answer choices. After you have calculated the scores for all five tests, refer to the self-appraisal materials to determine your subject area strengths and weaknesses as well as your total GED score.

The main purpose of the test is to help you discover your strengths and your weaknesses. IMPORTANT: You should spend more time studying those chapters that deal with the tests in which you are weakest. In that way, you will improve your score when you take the two practice examinations at the end of this book.

SIMULATE TEST CONDITIONS

To make conditions similar to those on the actual examination, do not take more time than that allowed for each test.

---

*Directions and mathematics formulas are reprinted by permission of the GED Testing Service of the American Council on Education.

Answer Sheet for the Diagnostic Examination

TEST 1: THE LANGUAGE ARTS, WRITING TEST

1. ① ② ③ ④ ⑤
2. ① ② ③ ④ ⑤
3. ① ② ③ ④ ⑤
4. ① ② ③ ④ ⑤
5. ① ② ③ ④ ⑤
6. ① ② ③ ④ ⑤
7. ① ② ③ ④ ⑤
8. ① ② ③ ④ ⑤
9. ① ② ③ ④ ⑤
10. ① ② ③ ④ ⑤
11. ① ② ③ ④ ⑤
12. ① ② ③ ④ ⑤
13. ① ② ③ ④ ⑤
14. ① ② ③ ④ ⑤
15. ① ② ③ ④ ⑤
16. ① ② ③ ④ ⑤
17. ① ② ③ ④ ⑤
18. ① ② ③ ④ ⑤
19. ① ② ③ ④ ⑤

20. ① ② ③ ④ ⑤
21. ① ② ③ ④ ⑤
22. ① ② ③ ④ ⑤
23. ① ② ③ ④ ⑤
24. ① ② ③ ④ ⑤
25. ① ② ③ ④ ⑤
26. ① ② ③ ④ ⑤
27. ① ② ③ ④ ⑤
28. ① ② ③ ④ ⑤
29. ① ② ③ ④ ⑤
30. ① ② ③ ④ ⑤
31. ① ② ③ ④ ⑤
32. ① ② ③ ④ ⑤
33. ① ② ③ ④ ⑤
34. ① ② ③ ④ ⑤
35. ① ② ③ ④ ⑤
36. ① ② ③ ④ ⑤
37. ① ② ③ ④ ⑤
38. ① ② ③ ④ ⑤

39. ① ② ③ ④ ⑤
40. ① ② ③ ④ ⑤
41. ① ② ③ ④ ⑤
42. ① ② ③ ④ ⑤
43. ① ② ③ ④ ⑤
44. ① ② ③ ④ ⑤
45. ① ② ③ ④ ⑤
46. ① ② ③ ④ ⑤
47. ① ② ③ ④ ⑤
48. ① ② ③ ④ ⑤
49. ① ② ③ ④ ⑤
50. ① ② ③ ④ ⑤

TEST 2: THE SOCIAL STUDIES TEST

1. ① ② ③ ④ ⑤
2. ① ② ③ ④ ⑤
3. ① ② ③ ④ ⑤
4. ① ② ③ ④ ⑤
5. ① ② ③ ④ ⑤
6. ① ② ③ ④ ⑤
7. ① ② ③ ④ ⑤
8. ① ② ③ ④ ⑤
9. ① ② ③ ④ ⑤
10. ① ② ③ ④ ⑤
11. ① ② ③ ④ ⑤
12. ① ② ③ ④ ⑤
13. ① ② ③ ④ ⑤
14. ① ② ③ ④ ⑤
15. ① ② ③ ④ ⑤
16. ① ② ③ ④ ⑤
17. ① ② ③ ④ ⑤
18. ① ② ③ ④ ⑤
19. ① ② ③ ④ ⑤
20. ① ② ③ ④ ⑤
21. ① ② ③ ④ ⑤
22. ① ② ③ ④ ⑤

23. ① ② ③ ④ ⑤
24. ① ② ③ ④ ⑤
25. ① ② ③ ④ ⑤
26. ① ② ③ ④ ⑤
27. ① ② ③ ④ ⑤
28. ① ② ③ ④ ⑤
29. ① ② ③ ④ ⑤
30. ① ② ③ ④ ⑤
31. ① ② ③ ④ ⑤
32. ① ② ③ ④ ⑤
33. ① ② ③ ④ ⑤
34. ① ② ③ ④ ⑤
35. ① ② ③ ④ ⑤
36. ① ② ③ ④ ⑤
37. ① ② ③ ④ ⑤
38. ① ② ③ ④ ⑤
39. ① ② ③ ④ ⑤
40. ① ② ③ ④ ⑤
41. ① ② ③ ④ ⑤
42. ① ② ③ ④ ⑤
43. ① ② ③ ④ ⑤
44. ① ② ③ ④ ⑤

45. ① ② ③ ④ ⑤
46. ① ② ③ ④ ⑤
47. ① ② ③ ④ ⑤
48. ① ② ③ ④ ⑤
49. ① ② ③ ④ ⑤
50. ① ② ③ ④ ⑤

TEST 3: THE SCIENCE TEST

1. ① ② ③ ④ ⑤
2. ① ② ③ ④ ⑤
3. ① ② ③ ④ ⑤
4. ① ② ③ ④ ⑤
5. ① ② ③ ④ ⑤
6. ① ② ③ ④ ⑤
7. ① ② ③ ④ ⑤
8. ① ② ③ ④ ⑤
9. ① ② ③ ④ ⑤
10. ① ② ③ ④ ⑤
11. ① ② ③ ④ ⑤
12. ① ② ③ ④ ⑤
13. ① ② ③ ④ ⑤
14. ① ② ③ ④ ⑤
15. ① ② ③ ④ ⑤
16. ① ② ③ ④ ⑤
17. ① ② ③ ④ ⑤
18. ① ② ③ ④ ⑤
19. ① ② ③ ④ ⑤
20. ① ② ③ ④ ⑤
21. ① ② ③ ④ ⑤
22. ① ② ③ ④ ⑤

23. ① ② ③ ④ ⑤
24. ① ② ③ ④ ⑤
25. ① ② ③ ④ ⑤
26. ① ② ③ ④ ⑤
27. ① ② ③ ④ ⑤
28. ① ② ③ ④ ⑤
29. ① ② ③ ④ ⑤
30. ① ② ③ ④ ⑤
31. ① ② ③ ④ ⑤
32. ① ② ③ ④ ⑤
33. ① ② ③ ④ ⑤
34. ① ② ③ ④ ⑤
35. ① ② ③ ④ ⑤
36. ① ② ③ ④ ⑤
37. ① ② ③ ④ ⑤
38. ① ② ③ ④ ⑤
39. ① ② ③ ④ ⑤
40. ① ② ③ ④ ⑤
41. ① ② ③ ④ ⑤
42. ① ② ③ ④ ⑤
43. ① ② ③ ④ ⑤
44. ① ② ③ ④ ⑤

45. ① ② ③ ④ ⑤
46. ① ② ③ ④ ⑤
47. ① ② ③ ④ ⑤
48. ① ② ③ ④ ⑤
49. ① ② ③ ④ ⑤
50. ① ② ③ ④ ⑤
51. ① ② ③ ④ ⑤
52. ① ② ③ ④ ⑤
53. ① ② ③ ④ ⑤
54. ① ② ③ ④ ⑤
55. ① ② ③ ④ ⑤
56. ① ② ③ ④ ⑤
57. ① ② ③ ④ ⑤
58. ① ② ③ ④ ⑤
59. ① ② ③ ④ ⑤
60. ① ② ③ ④ ⑤
61. ① ② ③ ④ ⑤
62. ① ② ③ ④ ⑤
63. ① ② ③ ④ ⑤
64. ① ② ③ ④ ⑤
65. ① ② ③ ④ ⑤
66. ① ② ③ ④ ⑤

TEST 4: THE LANGUAGE ARTS, READING TEST

1. ① ② ③ ④ ⑤
2. ① ② ③ ④ ⑤
3. ① ② ③ ④ ⑤
4. ① ② ③ ④ ⑤
5. ① ② ③ ④ ⑤
6. ① ② ③ ④ ⑤
7. ① ② ③ ④ ⑤
8. ① ② ③ ④ ⑤
9. ① ② ③ ④ ⑤
10. ① ② ③ ④ ⑤
11. ① ② ③ ④ ⑤
12. ① ② ③ ④ ⑤
13. ① ② ③ ④ ⑤
14. ① ② ③ ④ ⑤
15. ① ② ③ ④ ⑤

16. ① ② ③ ④ ⑤
17. ① ② ③ ④ ⑤
18. ① ② ③ ④ ⑤
19. ① ② ③ ④ ⑤
20. ① ② ③ ④ ⑤
21. ① ② ③ ④ ⑤
22. ① ② ③ ④ ⑤
23. ① ② ③ ④ ⑤
24. ① ② ③ ④ ⑤
25. ① ② ③ ④ ⑤
26. ① ② ③ ④ ⑤
27. ① ② ③ ④ ⑤
28. ① ② ③ ④ ⑤
29. ① ② ③ ④ ⑤
30. ① ② ③ ④ ⑤

31. ① ② ③ ④ ⑤
32. ① ② ③ ④ ⑤
33. ① ② ③ ④ ⑤
34. ① ② ③ ④ ⑤
35. ① ② ③ ④ ⑤
36. ① ② ③ ④ ⑤
37. ① ② ③ ④ ⑤
38. ① ② ③ ④ ⑤
39. ① ② ③ ④ ⑤
40. ① ② ③ ④ ⑤

TEST 5: THE MATHEMATICS TEST, PART I

1. ① ② ③ ④ ⑤

2. ① ② ③ ④ ⑤

3.

```
      / / /
    . . . .
    0 0 0 0 0
    1 1 1 1 1
    2 2 2 2 2
    3 3 3 3 3
    4 4 4 4 4
    5 5 5 5 5
    6 6 6 6 6
    7 7 7 7 7
    8 8 8 8 8
    9 9 9 9 9
```

4. ① ② ③ ④ ⑤

5. ① ② ③ ④ ⑤

6.

```
      / / /
    . . . .
    0 0 0 0 0
    1 1 1 1 1
    2 2 2 2 2
    3 3 3 3 3
    4 4 4 4 4
    5 5 5 5 5
    6 6 6 6 6
    7 7 7 7 7
    8 8 8 8 8
    9 9 9 9 9
```

7. ① ② ③ ④ ⑤

8. ① ② ③ ④ ⑤

9. ① ② ③ ④ ⑤

10. ① ② ③ ④ ⑤

11. ① ② ③ ④ ⑤

12. ① ② ③ ④ ⑤

13. ① ② ③ ④ ⑤

14.

```
      / / /
    . . . .
    0 0 0 0 0
    1 1 1 1 1
    2 2 2 2 2
    3 3 3 3 3
    4 4 4 4 4
    5 5 5 5 5
    6 6 6 6 6
    7 7 7 7 7
    8 8 8 8 8
    9 9 9 9 9
```

15. ① ② ③ ④ ⑤

16. ① ② ③ ④ ⑤

17. ① ② ③ ④ ⑤

18. ① ② ③ ④ ⑤

19.

```
      / / /
    . . . . .
    0 0 0 0 0
    1 1 1 1 1
    2 2 2 2 2
    3 3 3 3 3
    4 4 4 4 4
    5 5 5 5 5
    6 6 6 6 6
    7 7 7 7 7
    8 8 8 8 8
    9 9 9 9 9
```

20. ① ② ③ ④ ⑤

21. ① ② ③ ④ ⑤

22.

```
      / / /
    . . . .
    0 0 0 0 0
    1 1 1 1 1
    2 2 2 2 2
    3 3 3 3 3
    4 4 4 4 4
    5 5 5 5 5
    6 6 6 6 6
    7 7 7 7 7
    8 8 8 8 8
    9 9 9 9 9
```

23. ① ② ③ ④ ⑤

24. ① ② ③ ④ ⑤

25.

```
      / / /
    . . . .
    0 0 0 0 0
    1 1 1 1 1
    2 2 2 2 2
    3 3 3 3 3
    4 4 4 4 4
    5 5 5 5 5
    6 6 6 6 6
    7 7 7 7 7
    8 8 8 8 8
    9 9 9 9 9
```

TEST 5: THE MATHEMATICS TEST, PART II

26. ① ② ③ ④ ⑤

27.

28. ① ② ③ ④ ⑤
29. ① ② ③ ④ ⑤
30. ① ② ③ ④ ⑤
31. ① ② ③ ④ ⑤
32. ① ② ③ ④ ⑤
33. ① ② ③ ④ ⑤
34. ① ② ③ ④ ⑤
35. ① ② ③ ④ ⑤

36. ① ② ③ ④ ⑤
37. ① ② ③ ④ ⑤
38. ① ② ③ ④ ⑤
39. ① ② ③ ④ ⑤
40. ① ② ③ ④ ⑤
41. ① ② ③ ④ ⑤
42. ① ② ③ ④ ⑤
43. ① ② ③ ④ ⑤
44. ① ② ③ ④ ⑤
45. ① ② ③ ④ ⑤
46. ① ② ③ ④ ⑤

47.

48. ① ② ③ ④ ⑤

49. ① ② ③ ④ ⑤

50.

DIAGNOSTIC EXAMINATION

TEST 1: LANGUAGE ARTS, WRITING, PART I

Directions

The Language Arts, Writing test is intended to measure your ability to use clear and effective English. It is a test of English as it should be written, not as it might be spoken. This test includes both multiple-choice questions and an essay. These directions apply only to the multiple-choice section; a separate set of directions is given for the essay.

The multiple-choice section consists of paragraphs with numbered sentences. Some of the sentences contain errors in sentence structure, usage, or mechanics (spelling, punctuation, and capitalization). After reading the numbered sentences, answer the multiple-choice questions that follow. Some questions refer to sentences that are correct as written. The best answer for these questions is the one that leaves the sentence as originally written. The best answer for some questions is the one that produces a sentence that is consistent with the verb tense and point of view used throughout the paragraph.

You should spend no more than 75 minutes on the multiple-choice questions and 45 minutes on your essay. Work carefully, but do not spend too much time on any one question. You may begin working on the essay part of this test as soon as you complete the multiple-choice section.

To record your answers, mark the numbered space on the answer sheet beside the number that corresponds to the question in the test.

FOR EXAMPLE:

Sentence 1: **We were all honored to meet governor Phillips.**

What correction should be made to this sentence?

(1) insert a comma after <u>honored</u>   ① ② ● ④ ⑤
(2) change the spelling of <u>honored</u> to <u>honered</u>
(3) change <u>governor</u> to <u>Governor</u>
(4) replace <u>were</u> with <u>was</u>
(5) no correction is necessary

In this example, the word "governor" should be capitalized; therefore, answer space 3 would be marked on the answer sheet.

GO ON TO THE NEXT PAGE

TEST 1: LANGUAGE ARTS, WRITING, PART I

<u>Questions 1–9</u> refer to the following paragraph.

(1) A combination of attributes make vegetable gardening a national hobby with both young and old. (2) For an ever-increasing number of individuals seed catalogs and the thoughts of spring gardening provide a happy escape from the winter doldrums. (3) Vegetable gardeners unanimously agree that many home-grown vegetables picked at their peak of maturity have quality. seldom found in vegetables purchased from commercial markets. (4) From Spring to late Fall, a well-planned and maintained garden can provide a supply of fresh vegetables, thus increasing the nutritional value of the family diet. (5) Freezers make it possible to preserve some of the surplus vegetables to be enjoyed at a later date other vegetables can be stored for a few months in a cool area. (6) Not to be overlooked is the finger-tip convenience of having vegetables in the backyard; this in itself justifies home gardening for many individuals. (7) In addition, vegetable gardening provides excercise and recreation for both urban and suburban families. (8) Although your initial dollar investment for gardening may be nominal, one cannot escape the fact that gardening requires manual labor and time. (9) Neglecting jobs that should be performed on a regular basis may result in failure and a negative feeling toward gardening.

1. Sentence 1: **A combination of attributes make vegetable gardening a national hobby with both young and old.**

   What correction should be made to this sentence?

   (1) insert a comma after <u>attributes</u>
   (2) change <u>make</u> to <u>makes</u>
   (3) capitalize vegetable gardening
   (4) reverse <u>with</u> and <u>both</u>
   (5) no correction is necessary

2. Sentence 2: **For an ever-increasing number of individuals seed catalogs and the thoughts of spring gardening provide a happy escape from the winter doldrums.**

   What correction should be made to this sentence?

   (1) remove the hyphen from <u>ever-increasing</u>
   (2) change <u>number</u> to <u>amount</u>
   (3) insert a comma after <u>individuals</u>
   (4) insert a comma after <u>catalogs</u>
   (5) no correction is necessary

3. Sentence 3: **Vegetable gardeners unanimously agree that many home-grown vegetables picked at their peak of maturity have <u>quality. seldom</u> found in vegetables purchased from commercial markets.**

   Which of the following is the best way to write the underlined portion of this sentence? If you think the original is the best way, choose option (1).

   (1) quality. seldom
   (2) quality. Seldom
   (3) quality seldom
   (4) quality; seldom
   (5) quality, seldom

4. Sentence 4: **From Spring to late Fall, a well-planned and maintained garden can provide a supply of fresh vegetables, thus increasing the nutritional value of the family diet.**

   What correction should be made to this sentence?

   (1) remove capitals from <u>Spring</u> and <u>Fall</u>
   (2) remove the hyphen from <u>well-planned</u>
   (3) remove the comma after <u>vegetables</u>
   (4) change <u>thus</u> to <u>however</u>
   (5) no correction is necessary

GO ON TO THE NEXT PAGE

TEST 1: LANGUAGE ARTS, WRITING, PART I

5. A new paragraph can

(1) be started after sentence 3
(2) be started after sentence 4
(3) be started after sentence 6
(4) be started after sentence 7
(5) not be started

6. Sentence 6: **Not to be overlooked is the finger-tip convenience of having vegetables in the backyard; this in itself justifies home gardening for many individuals.**

What correction should be made to this sentence?

(1) insert a comma after <u>overlooked</u>
(2) change the spelling of <u>vegetables</u> to <u>vegtables</u>
(3) replace the semicolon after <u>backyard</u> with a comma
(4) change the spelling of <u>gardening</u> to <u>gardning</u>
(5) no correction is necessary

7. The topic sentence of this paragraph is

(1) sentence 1
(2) sentence 2
(3) sentence 3
(4) sentence 8
(5) sentence 9

8. Sentence 8: **Although your initial dollar investment for gardening may be nominal, one cannot escape the fact that gardening requires manual labor and time.**

What correction should be made to this sentence?

(1) change <u>Although</u> to <u>Because</u>
(2) remove the comma after <u>nominal</u>
(3) change <u>one</u> to <u>you</u>
(4) change <u>requires</u> to <u>require</u>
(5) no correction is necessary

9. Sentence 9: **Neglecting jobs that should be performed on a regular basis may result in failure and a negative feeling toward gardening.**

What correction should be made to this sentence?

(1) insert a comma after <u>jobs</u>
(2) insert a comma after <u>basis</u>
(3) change <u>may result</u> to <u>results</u>
(4) change <u>and</u> to <u>despite</u>
(5) no correction is necessary

Questions 10–19 refer to the following paragraph.

(1) In coming years, families will need to learn to turn to there computers for assistance. (2) With the increasing amounts of information a family is required to process, the home computer will become a necessity for both decision making and family record storage and retrieval.   (3) A home communications revolution is predicted with the arrival of the home computer. It will serve as a source and processor of information. (4) A virtually infinite amount of information from many sources will be at the instantaneous disposal of the family for more efficient decision making. (5) The computer will plan meals, turn lights on at appropriate times keep track of family members' schedules, calculate budget information, and oversee credit, spending, and bank accounts. (6) Just as home equipment frees the homemaker from the labor of housekeeping, the computer release's family members from some repetitious managerial duties. (7) The home terminal may serve as a home education center for children's homework and part of the lifelong learning program of parents and elderly family members. (8) The change that will have the most immediate effect on family decision making will be increased discretionary time. (9) For economic reasons, many families will decide to use their "free" time to hold a second job. (10) With the increasing interest in personal development, a segment of the time might be allotted by some to develop

GO ON TO THE NEXT PAGE

TEST 1: LANGUAGE ARTS, WRITING, PART I

alternative interests through lifelong educational programs that will facilitate career changes, to increase skills for effective citizenship, and learning new skills to enhance their family living.

10. Sentence 1: **In coming years, families will need to learn to turn to there computers for assistance.**

    What correction should be made to this sentence?

    (1) remove the comma after <u>years</u>
    (2) change <u>will need</u> to <u>need</u>
    (3) change the spelling of <u>assistance</u> to <u>assistence</u>
    (4) change the spelling of <u>there</u> to <u>their</u>
    (5) no correction is necessary

11. Sentence 2: **With the increasing amounts of information a family is required to process, the home computer will become a necessity for both decision making and family record storage and retrieval.**

    What correction should be made to this sentence?

    (1) change <u>With the</u> to <u>Despite</u>
    (2) change <u>is</u> to <u>are</u>
    (3) remove the comma after <u>process</u>
    (4) change the spelling of <u>necessity</u> to <u>neccesity</u>
    (5) no correction is necessary

12. Sentence 3: **A home communications revolution is predicted with the arrival of the home <u>computer. It</u> will serve as a source and processor of information.**

    Which of the following is the best way to write the underlined portion of the sentence? If you think the original is the best way, choose option (1).

    (1) computer. It
    (2) computer, It
    (3) computer, it
    (4) computer it
    (5) computer; It

13. Sentence 4: **A virtually infinite amount of information from many sources will be at the instantaneous disposal of the family for more efficient decision making.**

    What correction should be made to this sentence?

    (1) insert a comma after <u>information</u>
    (2) insert a comma after <u>sources</u>
    (3) insert a comma after <u>family</u>
    (4) change the spelling of <u>efficient</u> to <u>eficient</u>
    (5) no correction is necessary

14. Sentence 5: **The computer will plan meals, turn lights on at appropriate times keep track of family members' schedules, calculate budget information, and oversee credit, spending, and bank accounts.**

    What correction should be made to this sentence?

    (1) remove comma after <u>meals</u>
    (2) insert comma after <u>times</u>
    (3) change <u>members'</u> to <u>member's</u>
    (4) change the spelling of <u>schedules</u> to <u>skedules</u>
    (5) no correction is necessary

15. Sentence 6: **Just as home equipment frees the homemaker from the labor of housekeeping, the computer release's family members from some repetitious managerial duties.**

    What correction should be made to this sentence?

    (1) change <u>Just as</u> to <u>Although</u>
    (2) change the spelling of <u>equipment</u> to <u>equiptment</u>
    (3) remove the comma after <u>housekeeping</u>
    (4) change <u>release's</u> to <u>releases</u>
    (5) no correction is necessary

GO ON TO THE NEXT PAGE

TEST 1: LANGUAGE ARTS, WRITING, PART I

16. Sentence 7: **The home terminal may serve as a home education center for children's homework and part of the lifelong learning program of parents and elderly family members.**

    If you rewrote sentence 7 beginning with

    Children's homework and part of the lifelong learning program of parents and elderly family members

    the next words should be

    (1) are served
    (2) may serve
    (3) may be served
    (4) serve
    (5) will serve

17. Sentence 8: **The change that will have the most immediate effect on family decision making will be increased discretionary time.**

    What correction should be made to this sentence?

    (1) change will have to having
    (2) change the spelling of effect to affect
    (3) change family to family's
    (4) change will be to is
    (5) no correction is necessary

18. Sentence 9 should be

    (1) left as it is
    (2) placed last
    (3) placed after sentence 2
    (4) placed after sentence 6
    (5) omitted

19. Sentence 10: **With the increasing interest in personal development, a segment of the time might be allotted by some to develop alternative interests through lifelong educational programs that will facilitate career changes, to increase skills for effective citizenship, and learning new skills to enhance their family living.**

    What correction should be made to this sentence?

    (1) change the spelling of development to developement
    (2) change the spelling of through to thorough
    (3) remove the comma after changes
    (4) change learning to to learn
    (5) no correction is necessary

Questions 20–28 refer to the following paragraphs.

(1) To lessen the threat of faulty car repair work or repair frauds, they're a number of constructive steps you can take. (2) While these measures can't offer full protection, it is wise insurance against dented pocketbooks and expanded time schedules.

(3) First, never wait until a small problem becomes a big and costly one. (4) Always takes your car in for a check at the first sign of trouble.

(5) But before you take the car in, make a list of all problems and "symptoms" so you are prepared to describe the trouble as accurately and specifically as possible.

(6) Don't just ask to have the car put in "working order," (7) that kind of general statement can lead directly to unnecessary work.

(8) On your initial visit, make certain you get a copy of the work authorization that you sign or a general estimate of the total cost of the repairs. (9) Don't leave until you do.

(10) Ask the repair garage to telephone you when the exact work to be done has been determinned. (11) When you receive the call, say you now want to return to the station to obtain another work order itemizing the cost of each repair to be made.

GO ON TO THE NEXT PAGE

TEST 1: LANGUAGE ARTS, WRITING, PART I

20. Sentence 1: **To lessen the threat of faulty car repair work or repair frauds, they're a number of constructive steps you can take.**

    What correction should be made to this sentence?

    (1) change <u>lessen</u> to <u>lesson</u>
    (2) remove the comma after <u>frauds</u>
    (3) change the spelling of <u>they're</u> to <u>there are</u>
    (4) change <u>can</u> to <u>might</u>
    (5) no correction is necessary

21. Sentence 2: **While these measures can't offer full protection, it is wise insurance against dented pocketbooks and expanded time schedules.**

    What correction should be made to this sentence?

    (1) change <u>While</u> to <u>Nevertheless</u>
    (2) change <u>it is</u> to <u>they are</u>
    (3) change <u>insurance</u> to <u>insurence</u>
    (4) insert a hyphen in <u>pocketbooks</u>
    (5) no correction is necessary

22. Sentence 3: **First, never wait until a small problem becomes a big and costly one.**

    What correction should be made to this sentence?

    (1) change <u>first</u> to <u>firstly</u>
    (2) remove the comma after <u>first</u>
    (3) change the spelling of <u>until</u> to <u>untill</u>
    (4) change <u>becomes</u> to <u>will become</u>
    (5) no correction is necessary

23. Sentence 4: **Always takes your car in for a check at the first sign of trouble.**

    What correction should be made to this sentence?

    (1) change <u>takes</u> to <u>take</u>
    (2) change <u>always</u> to <u>allways</u>
    (3) change <u>your</u> to <u>your'e</u>
    (4) insert a comma after <u>check</u>
    (5) no correction is necessary

24. Sentence 5: **But before you take the car in, make a list of all problems and "symptoms" so you are prepared to describe the trouble as accurately and specifically as possible.**

    What correction should be made to this sentence?

    (1) change <u>take</u> to <u>will take</u>
    (2) remove the comma after <u>in</u>
    (3) change <u>are</u> to <u>will be</u>
    (4) change the spelling of <u>specifically</u> to <u>specificaly</u>
    (5) no correction is necessary

25. Sentences 6 and 7: **Don't just ask to have the car put in "working <u>order," that</u> kind of general statement can lead directly to unnecessary work.**

    Which of the following is the best way to write the underlined portion of this sentence? If you think the original is the best way, choose option (1).

    (1) order," that
    (2) order" that
    (3) order": that
    (4) order". that
    (5) order." That

GO ON TO THE NEXT PAGE

TEST 1: LANGUAGE ARTS, WRITING, PART I

26. Sentence 8: **On your initial visit, make certain you get a copy of the work authorization that you sign or a general estimate of the total cost of the repairs.**

    What correction should be made to this sentence?

    (1) change the spelling of <u>initial</u> to <u>initail</u>
    (2) remove the comma after <u>visit</u>
    (3) insert a comma after <u>sign</u>
    (4) change the spelling of <u>estimate</u> to <u>estemate</u>
    (5) no correction is necessary

27. Sentence 10: **Ask the repair garage to telephone you when the exact work to be done has been determinned.**

    What correction should be made to this sentence?

    (1) insert a comma after <u>you</u>
    (2) insert a comma after <u>work</u>
    (3) insert a comma after <u>garage</u>
    (4) change the spelling of <u>determinned</u> to <u>determined</u>
    (5) no correction is necessary

28. Sentence 11 should be

    (1) left as it is
    (2) placed first
    (3) placed after sentence 5
    (4) placed before sentence 9
    (5) omitted

<u>Questions 29–37</u> refer to the following paragraphs.

(1) Total dollars available, family tastes storage and preparation facilities, end use, and item cost all affect a buying decision. (2) Unit pricing can help by taking the guesswork out of the price factor and simplifying cost comparisons.

(3) Unit price is just what its name implies— the price per unit. (4) To be more specific, unit pricing gives you the cost per ounce or per pound or per 100 or per square foot. (5) This price per unit enables you to ready find the best buy, dollarwise, among several items in different-size packages with different total prices.

(6) Thousands of retail food chain stores now have unit pricing programs. (7) Such programs are required by local laws in several areas, but generally the programs are voluntary.

(8) Stores that offer unit pricing generally use a shelf tag system—a label on the shelf edge below the item gives the name of the item, the size, the total price, and the unit price.

(9) When unit pricing was first introduced the shelf tag system posed some problems because keeping the tags on the shelves in the right location can be difficult. (10) But as unit pricing has gained acceptance, some of these mechanical problems has been overcome, and the label information has become more usable from the shoppers' standpoint.

29. Sentence 1: **Total dollars available, family tastes storage and preparation facilities, end use, and item cost all affect a buying decision.**

    What correction should be made to this sentence?

    (1) insert a comma after <u>tastes</u>
    (2) change <u>all</u> to <u>each</u>
    (3) change <u>affect</u> to <u>effect</u>
    (4) change the spelling of <u>buying</u> to <u>bying</u>
    (5) no correction is necessary

GO ON TO THE NEXT PAGE

TEST 1: LANGUAGE ARTS, WRITING, PART I

30. Sentence 1: **Total dollars available, family tastes storage and preparation facilities, end use, and item cost all affects a buying decision.**

    What correction should be made to this sentence?

    (1) change <u>family</u> to <u>family's</u>
    (2) change <u>affects</u> to <u>affect</u>
    (3) change the spelling of <u>decision</u> to <u>desicion</u>
    (4) insert a comma after <u>storage</u>
    (5) no correction is necessary

31. Sentence 2: **Unit pricing can help by taking the guesswork out of the price factor and simplifying cost comparisons.**

    What correction should be made to this sentence?

    (1) change <u>can</u> to <u>could</u>
    (2) change <u>by taking</u> to <u>to take</u>
    (3) insert a hyphen in <u>guesswork</u>
    (4) insert a comma after <u>factor</u>
    (5) no correction is necessary

32. Sentences 3 and 4: **Unit price is just what its name implies—the price per unit. To be more specific, unit pricing gives you the cost per ounce or per pound or per 100 or per square foot.**

    Which of the following is the best way to write the underlined portion of these sentences? If you think the original is the best way, choose option (1).

    (1) . To be more specific
    (2) , To be more specific
    (3) ; To be more specific
    (4) : To be more specific
    (5) —To be more specific

33. Sentence 5: **This price per unit enables you to ready find the best buy, dollarwise, among several items in different-size packages with different total prices.**

    What correction should be made to this sentence?

    (1) remove the commas before and after <u>dollarwise</u>
    (2) change <u>ready</u> to <u>readily</u>
    (3) change <u>among</u> to <u>between</u>
    (4) change <u>size</u> to <u>sized</u>
    (5) no correction is necessary

34. Sentences 6 and 7: **Thousands of retail food chain stores now have unit pricing programs. Such programs are required by local laws in several areas, but generally the programs are voluntary.**

    The most effective combination of sentences 6 and 7 would include which of the following groups of words?

    (1) and such programs
    (2) although such programs
    (3) whereas such programs
    (4) programs that are
    (5) programs some being

35. Sentence 8: **Stores that offer unit pricing generally use a shelf tag <u>system—a label</u> on the shelf edge below the item gives the name of the item, the size, the total price, and the unit price.**

    Which of the following is the best way to write the underlined portion of this sentence? If you think the original is the best way, choose option (1).

    (1) system—a label
    (2) system. a label
    (3) system; a label
    (4) system: a label
    (5) system, a label

GO ON TO THE NEXT PAGE

TEST 1: LANGUAGE ARTS, WRITING, PART I

36. Sentence 9: **When unit pricing was first introduced the shelf tag system posed some problems because keeping the tags on the shelves in the right location can be difficult.**

    What correction should be made to this sentence?

    (1) change was to had been
    (2) insert a comma after introduced
    (3) change there to their
    (4) insert commas before and after in the right location
    (5) no correction is necessary

37. Sentence 10: **But as unit pricing has gained acceptance, some of these mechanical problems has been overcome, and the label information has become more usable from the shoppers' standpoint.**

    What correction should be made to this sentence?

    (1) change the spelling of acceptance to acceptence
    (2) remove the comma after acceptance
    (3) change the spelling of usable to useable
    (4) change has been overcome to have been overcome
    (5) no correction is necessary

Questions 38–47 refer to the following paragraphs.

(1) You are going to move. (2) That statement will ring true for most Americans. (3) You will be the exception if you maintain your present residence for the rest of your life. (4) About one in five persons moves each year, put another way, the average person moves once every 5 years.

(5) Again dealing in averages most moves of household goods are completed without difficulty, although some are not. (6) The moving experience can be uneventful, but it should be recognized that many of the factors involved can lead to frustrations, uncertainties, and expected course of action that suddenly must be changed.

(7) Most moves envolve fulfilment of a positive development. (8) A promotion has come through, (9) or perhaps an opportunity to move to a better climate. (10) Maybe there's a long-sought chance to be closer to the home folks or the grandchildren.

(11) On the other side of the coin, a familiar neighborhood is being left behind. (12) The personal effort that must be put into a move can leave family members exhausted just at the time when they need to be at their sharpest.

38. Sentences 1 and 2: **You are going to move. That statement will ring true for most Americans.**

    The most effective combination of sentences 1 and 2 would include which of the following groups of words.

    (1) would be a statement that will ring
    (2) is a statement that will ring
    (3) might be a statement that will ring
    (4) being a statement that will ring
    (5) will be a statement that will ring

39. Sentence 3: **You will be the exception if you maintain your present residence for the rest of your life.**

    What correction should be made to this sentence?

    (1) change will be to are
    (2) change the spelling of exception to exeption
    (3) insert a comma after exception
    (4) change your to you're
    (5) no correction is necessary

40. Sentence 4: **About one in five persons moves each year, put another way, the average person moves once every 5 years.**

    Which of the following is the best way to write the underlined portion of this sentence? If you think the original is the best way, choose option (1).

    (1) year, put
    (2) year, although put
    (3) year, and put
    (4) year, because put
    (5) year, or put

GO ON TO THE NEXT PAGE

TEST 1: LANGUAGE ARTS, WRITING, PART I

41. Sentence 5: **Again dealing in averages most moves of household goods are completed without difficulty, although some are not.**

    What correction should be made to this sentence?

    (1) insert a comma after <u>averages</u>
    (2) insert a hyphen in <u>household</u>
    (3) change the spelling of <u>difficulty</u> to <u>dificulty</u>
    (4) remove the comma after <u>difficulty</u>
    (5) no correction is necessary

42. Sentence 6: **The moving experience can be uneventful, but it should be recognized that many of the factors involved can lead to frustrations, uncertainties, and expected course of action that suddenly must be changed.**

    What correction should be made to this sentence?

    (1) change the spelling of <u>experience</u> to <u>experiance</u>
    (2) remove the comma after <u>uneventful</u>
    (3) change <u>but</u> to <u>and</u>
    (4) change <u>course</u> to <u>courses</u>
    (5) no correction is necessary

43. Sentence 7: **Most moves envolve fulfilment of a positive development.**

    What correction should be made to this sentence?

    (1) change <u>most moves</u> to <u>most every move</u>
    (2) change <u>envole</u> to <u>could envolve</u>
    (3) change <u>envolve</u> to <u>involve</u>
    (4) change the spelling of <u>development</u> to <u>developement</u>
    (5) no correction is necessary

44. Sentences 8 and 9: **A promotion has come <u>through, or</u> perhaps an opportunity to move to a better climate.**

    Which of the following is the best way to write the underlined portion of these sentences? If you think the original is the best way, choose option (1).

    (1) through, or
    (2) through. or
    (3) through : or
    (4) through ; or
    (5) through—or

45. Sentence 10: **Maybe there's a long-sought chance to be closer to the home folks or the grandchildren.**

    What correction should be made to this sentence?

    (1) change <u>there's</u> to <u>they're is</u>
    (2) remove the hyphen from <u>long-sought</u>
    (3) add an apostrophe to <u>folks</u>
    (4) change the spelling of <u>grandchildren</u> to <u>grandchildern</u>
    (5) no correction is necessary

46. The topic sentence of this paragraph is

    (1) sentence 1
    (2) sentence 4
    (3) sentence 6
    (4) sentence 9
    (5) sentence 11

GO ON TO THE NEXT PAGE

TEST 1: LANGUAGE ARTS, WRITING, PART I

47. Sentence 12: **The personal effort that must be put into a move can leave family members exhausted just at the time when they need to be at their sharpest.**

    What correction should be made to this sentence?

    (1) insert commas around that <u>must be put into a move</u>
    (2) change <u>can</u> to <u>could</u>
    (3) change the spelling of <u>exhausted</u> to <u>exausted</u>
    (4) insert a comma after <u>time</u>
    (5) no correction is necessary

<u>Questions 48–50</u> refer to the following paragraphs.

   (1) In fishing, the first step for the angler is to upgrade his equipment so that the availible range of lures, line weights, distances, etc., is substantially increased. (2) Usually a spinning reel and rod are selected as the next phase in advancement.
   (3) The spinning reel consist's of a stationery spool carrying a length of monofilament line, a bail, or pickup device to direct the line onto the reel; and a crank that rotates the pickup device, restoring the line to the spool.
   (4) In operation, the lure, attached to the monofilament line and dangling several inches beyond the rod tip, is cast by swinging the rod from a position slightly behind the shoulder through a forward arc to a position in front at approximately eye level.
   (5) Proper timing of the finger pressure on the line as it leaves the reel, combined with the rod acceleration, control the distance the lure will travel.
   (6) Lures as light as a sixteenth of an ounce with two-pound test monofilament line will provide enjoyable sport with any of the panfish, heavier lures and lines will more than adequately subdue far larger fish.
   (7) Lures are available in a near infinite range of weights, sizes, shapes, and colors and include such items as spoons, spinners, jogs, plugs, and bugs as well as natural baits.
   (8) With adequate spinning gear, anyone is prepared to pursue the fascinating and challenging game fish. (9) This category includes the world-famous and aristocratic salmon, the trout, the chars, the grayling, the basses, and the pike family.

48. Sentence 2 should be

    (1) left as it is
    (2) placed last
    (3) placed after sentence 5
    (4) placed before sentence 8
    (5) omitted

49. Sentence 2: **Usually a spinning reel and rod are selected as the next phase in advancement.**

    If you rewrote sentence 2 beginning with

    <u>The next phase in advancement</u>

    the next words would be

    (1) are selected a spinning
    (2) are selecting a spinning
    (3) selects a spinning
    (4) is the selection of a spinning
    (5) will be selecting a

50. Sentence 3: **The spinning reel consist's of a stationery spool carrying a length of monofilament line, a bail, or pickup device to direct the line onto the reel; and a crank that rotates the pick up device, restoring the line to the spool.**

    What correction should be made to this sentence?

    (1) change <u>consist's</u> to <u>consists</u>
    (2) change the spelling of <u>length</u> to <u>lenth</u>
    (3) remove the comma after <u>line</u>
    (4) insert a comma after <u>device</u>
    (5) no correction is necessary

GO ON TO THE NEXT PAGE

TEST 1: LANGUAGE ARTS, WRITING, PART II

This part of the Writing Skills test is intended to determine how well you write. You are asked to write an essay that explains something, presents an opinion on an issue, or concentrates on retelling a personal experience.

PROMPT

As a child we have many experiences ranging from funny to unfortunate. In the Mark Twain story, *Tom Sawyer*, we find young Tom in many unforgettable situations from being lost in a cave to returning in time for his own funeral. Each of us has a personal story from childhood that seems to be told over and over at family reunions, birthdays, or around friends. Perhaps your personal experience happened on a fishing trip, at school, or on a campout.

DISCUSSION QUESTION

Think of a personal childhood experience that seems to be told over and over again. It may be funny, sad, exciting, or just something out of the ordinary. What personal experience comes to mind?

Directions

Write an essay of about 250 words in which you recount this personal event. Give supporting details in your essay. You have 45 minutes to write on this topic.

CHECK YOURSELF

- Read carefully the prompt, discussion question, and directions.
- Decide if the prompt is expository, persuasive, or narrative.
- Plan your essay before you begin.
- Use scratch paper to prepare a simple outline.
- Write your essay on the lined pages of a separate answer sheet.
- Read carefully what you have written and make needed changes.
- Check for focus, elaboration, organization, conventions, and integration.

END OF EXAMINATION

TEST 2: SOCIAL STUDIES

Directions

The Social Studies test consists of multiple-choice questions intended to measure general social studies concepts. Most questions are based on short readings that often include a graph, chart, or figure. Study the information given and then answer the question(s) following it. Refer to the information as often as necessary in answering the questions.

You should spend no more than 70 minutes answering the questions. Work carefully, but do not spend too much time on any one question. Be sure you answer every question. You will not be penalized for incorrect answers.

To record your answers, mark the numbered space on the answer sheet beside the number that corresponds to the question in the test.

FOR EXAMPLE:

Early colonists of North America looked for settlement sites that had adequate water supplies and were accessible by ship. For this reason, many early towns were built near

(1) mountains
(2) prairies
(3) rivers
(4) glaciers
(5) plateaus

① ② ● ④ ⑤

The correct answer is "rivers"; therefore, answer space 3 would be marked on the answer sheet.

GO ON TO THE NEXT PAGE

TEST 2: SOCIAL STUDIES

Questions 1–3 are based on the following passage.

The governor is empowered to veto single items of the budget bill, appending to each a message, and to return the same to the legislature if it is still in session. Such items can be enacted over his veto. This authority, not possessed by the president of the United States, lays a heavy responsibility on the governor for the integrity of the budget in all its parts.

All bills passed within the last ten days of a legislative session fall under what is called the "30-day" rule. None can become a law unless within 30 days (Sundays included) it has been signed by the governor.

The veto power is not used sparingly. More than one out of four bills falls to the deadly stroke of the executive pen.

1. The passage indicates that the governor

    (1) vetoes about one fourth of the bills
    (2) vetoes about three fourths of the bills
    (3) vetoes all bills during the legislative session
    (4) vetoes no bills during the legislative session
    (5) uses the veto power very sparingly

2. The "30-day" rule applies to

    (1) the time limit for exercising the veto
    (2) the pocket veto
    (3) the amount of time in which to appeal the governor's action
    (4) bills passed within the last ten days of a legislative session
    (5) the limitation on passing a law over the governor's veto

3. The governor's veto power is greater than that of the president in that the governor has the ability to

    (1) take as much time as he wishes before signing a bill
    (2) veto a bill in less than 10 days
    (3) ignore all bills during the last month of the legislature
    (4) veto single items of the budget bill
    (5) override the two-thirds vote of the legislature

Questions 4–6 are based on the following passage.

The consumer's first line of defense is information. Before you buy any product—especially before you make a major purchase of any kind—get all the information you can about the manufacturer's guarantee or warranty provisions.

Remember, a guarantee is a statement by the manufacturer or vendor that he stands behind his product or service. Guarantees and warranties usually have limitations or conditions, so get all promises in writing.

Before you buy any product or service covered by a guarantee or warranty, make sure you resolve these questions:

—What, exactly, is covered?

—Whom should you call when you need repairs under the warranty?

—Must repairs be made at the factory or by an "authorized service representative" to keep the warranty in effect?

—Who pays for parts, for labor, for shipping charges?

—How long does the warranty last?

—If pro rata reimbursement is provided, what is the basis for it?

—If the warranty provides for reimbursement, is it in cash or credit toward a replacement?

Keep the warranty and sales receipt for future reference.

4. The advice given to the consumer in this passage deals chiefly with

    (1) business ethics
    (2) unconditional guarantees
    (3) product safety
    (4) unwarranted promises
    (5) pre-purchase information

5. Guarantees and warranties, the passage implies, should be

    (1) conditional
    (2) in writing
    (3) made by the salesman
    (4) cancelable
    (5) dependent on the use of the product

GO ON TO THE NEXT PAGE

TEST 2: SOCIAL STUDIES

6. Warranties usually include all of the following EXCEPT

   (1) what is covered
   (2) who does the repairs
   (3) where the repairs are made
   (4) who pays for expenses incurred in doing the repairs
   (5) return of monies paid

Questions 7 and 8 are based on the following chart.

MEDIAN AGE IN THE UNITED STATES

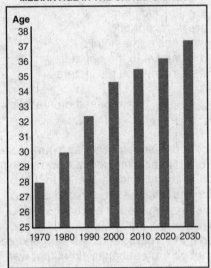

7. Which situation will be most likely to occur after the period shown in the graph?

   (1) Advertisers will increase their emphasis on youth.
   (2) The size of the average family will increase.
   (3) School districts will build more elementary schools.
   (4) The cost of the Social Security program will rise.
   (5) Population will begin to decline.

8. Which factor would most likely reverse the direction of the trend indicated by the graph?

   (1) development of a cure for cancer
   (2) a large increase in the birth rate
   (3) a prolonged period of economic depression
   (4) an increase in infant mortality
   (5) pollution control

9. Government policies designed to foster economic growth by encouraging greater consumption would probably meet with the greatest opposition from which group?

   (1) labor leaders
   (2) business executives
   (3) military leaders
   (4) environmentalists
   (5) individual entrepreneurs

Questions 10 and 11 are based on the following cartoon.

10. What is the main idea of the cartoon?

   (1) The world lacks sufficient energy resources to survive much longer.
   (2) Concerns of environmentalists have had little impact on the actions of industrialists.
   (3) The struggle between energy and the environment cannot be resolved.
   (4) The need to produce energy comes into conflict with the need to preserve the environment.
   (5) A stalemate has been arrived at between industrialists and environmentalists.

GO ON TO THE NEXT PAGE

TEST 2: SOCIAL STUDIES

11. In dealing with the situation referred to in the cartoon during the late 1970s, the United States federal government generally followed a policy that

    (1) gave priority to energy demands over environmental concerns
    (2) sided with environmentalists against corporations
    (3) sought new energy sources outside the United States
    (4) attempted to divert national attention to other issues
    (5) dealt evenhandedly with industrialists and environmentalists

12. The presidents of the United States from the time of World War II to the present have been most influential in the area of

    (1) civil rights
    (2) urban affairs
    (3) foreign affairs
    (4) states rights
    (5) human rights

Questions 13 and 14 are based on the following passage.

Not all place names on maps refer to visible locations. When a name refers to a specific place, it can be easy to get a mental picture of it. When you see a name such as Arctic Circle, Antarctic Circle, Tropic of Cancer, or Tropic of Capricorn, you do not get a mental picture in the same way. These imaginary markers on the Earth's surface usually appear on maps as dotted blue lines. When you travel across one of them, you cannot detect it with the human eye or feel it against your skin.

The Tropics of Cancer and Capricorn are named after constellations of stars. Historians believe that ancient Roman geographers were the first to refer to these two imaginary lines as Cancer and Capricorn.

The Tropic of Cancer runs parallel to the equator at latitude 23°27'N. It marks the northernmost point at which the sun appears directly overhead at noon. The name refers to the constellation Cancer (the Crab), which first becomes visible in the Northern Hemisphere on June 20, 21, or 22, near the summer solstice.

The Tropic of Capricorn runs parallel to the equator at about latitude 23°27'S. It designates the southernmost point at which the sun appears directly overhead at noon. The name refers to the constellation Capricorn (the Goat), which first becomes visible in the Southern Hemisphere on December 21 or 22, near the winter solstice.

13. The Arctic and Antarctic Circles are

    (1) mental pictures
    (2) imaginary markers
    (3) dotted blue lines
    (4) visible locations
    (5) easily detected

14. The Tropic of Cancer and the Tropic of Capricorn are similar in that they

    (1) are specific places
    (2) are of recent origin
    (3) mark the same points
    (4) run parallel to the equator
    (5) were named by navigators

Questions 15 and 16 are based on the following passage.

Fourscore and seven years ago our fathers brought forth on this continent a new nation, conceived in liberty, and dedicated to the proposition that all men are created equal.

Now we are engaged in a great civil war, testing whether that nation, or any nation so conceived and so dedicated, can long endure. We are met on a great battlefield of that war. We have come to dedicate a portion of that field as a final resting-place for those who here gave their lives that that nation might live. It is altogether fitting and proper that we should do this.

But, in a larger sense, we cannot dedicate—we cannot consecrate—we cannot hallow—this ground. The brave men, living and dead, who struggled here, have consecrated it far above our poor power to add or detract.

—Abraham Lincoln

15. In the first paragraph, the speaker refers to

    (1) the Declaration of Independence
    (2) the Articles of Confederation
    (3) the United States Constitution
    (4) the Northwest Ordinance
    (5) the Monroe Doctrine

16. The purpose of the speech was to

    (1) commemorate a battle
    (2) remember the founding of our nation
    (3) dedicate a cemetery
    (4) deplore civil war
    (5) seek political support in an election

GO ON TO THE NEXT PAGE

TEST 2: SOCIAL STUDIES

Questions 17–19 are based on the following chart, which lists some characteristics of Nations *A* and *B*.

Factors of Production	*Nation A*
Land (natural resources)	Relative scarcity
Labor	Relative abundance
Capital	Relative abundance
Business management	Relative abundance

Factors of Production	*Nation B*
Land (natural resources)	Relative abundance
Labor	Relative abundance
Capital	Relative scarcity
Business management	Relative scarcity

17. Which economic decision would most probably be in the best interests of Nation *A*?

    (1) permitting an unfavorable balance of payments
    (2) seeking foreign markets
    (3) attracting investments from foreign nations
    (4) encouraging immigration
    (5) increasing imports

18. During the early 19th century, which nation most nearly resembled Nation *A*?

    (1) the United States
    (2) Great Britain
    (3) Russia
    (4) Turkey
    (5) China

19. If Nation *B* wishes to industrialize, how can it best encourage its own citizens to invest their capital in domestic industries?

    (1) by permitting an unfavorable balance of payments and seeking colonies
    (2) by permitting an unfavorable balance of payments and encouraging immigration
    (3) by attracting investments from foreign nations and encouraging immigration
    (4) by instituting high protective tariffs and giving tax concessions to business
    (5) by lowering taxes on imports

20. "Our policy in regard to Europe . . . is not to interfere in the internal concerns of any of its powers"—President Monroe, 1823

    "It must be the policy of the United States to support free peoples who are resisting attempted subjugation by armed minorities or by outside pressures."—President Truman, 1947

    The most valid conclusion to be drawn from these statements is that

    (1) President Truman followed President Monroe's theory of foreign relations
    (2) during the 19th and 20th centuries, the United States was not interested in international affairs
    (3) during the 19th century, events in Europe did not affect the United States
    (4) President Truman changed the policy of President Monroe
    (5) conditions were different in 1947 from those in 1823

Questions 21 and 22 are based on the following graphs.

Of all women with children under 6 and living with their husbands, how many work?

60	18.6%
65	29.3%
70	30.3%
75	36.7%
80	45.1%
85	53.4%
90	58.9%
96	62.7%

Of all working women with children under 6 and living with their husbands, how many work...

	FULL TIME	PART TIME
60	69.6%	30.4%
65	68.8%	31.2%
70	64.9%	35.1%
75	64.9%	35.1%
80	64.9%	35.1%
85	65.7%	34.3%
90	64.2%	35.8%
96	62.8%	37.2%

Source: Bureau of Labor Statistics

Of all woman who work, how many have children under 6 years old?

60	12.8%
65	14.1%
70	14.4%
75	15.3%
80	14.6%
85	16.1%
90	16.7%
96	16.8%

GO ON TO THE NEXT PAGE

TEST 2: SOCIAL STUDIES

21. The period with the greatest increase in the percentage of working women having children under 6 and living with their husbands was

    (1) '60–'65
    (2) '70–'75
    (3) '80–'85
    (4) '85–'90
    (5) '90–'96

22. The percentage of women working part time remained steadiest between

    (1) '60 and '70
    (2) '70 and '80
    (3) '75 and '85
    (4) '80 and '90
    (5) '90 and '96

Question 23 is based on the following graph.

Weather and Climate

Source: *Current Events*, 1990 (adapted)

23. Which area, as illustrated in the graph, would be warmest and driest?

    (1) A
    (2) B
    (3) C
    (4) D
    (5) E

Question 24 is based on the following diagram.

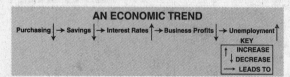

AN ECONOMIC TREND

Purchasing ↓ → Savings ↓ → Interest Rates ↑ → Business Profits ↓ → Unemployment ↑

KEY
↑ INCREASE
↓ DECREASE
→ LEADS TO

24. Which is occurring in the economy illustrated above?

    (1) increase in real income
    (2) devaluation of currency
    (3) growth
    (4) recession
    (5) recovery

25. "All forms of life developed from earlier forms. In every case the fittest survived and the weak died out. It is the same for people and nations."

    This passage expresses a view most often found in

    (1) fundamentalism
    (2) social Darwinism
    (3) liberalism
    (4) utopian socialism
    (5) egalitarianism

Questions 26–28 are based on the following graph.

A Snapshot of Family Finances

Percentage of families in each income group. In 1998 dollars.

	1989	1992	1995	1998
Family income *median, before-tax*	32,800	$30,400	$32,700	**$33,400**
Family net worth *median*	59,700	56,800	60,900	**71,600**
Percentage of all families with stock holdings *direct or indirect*	31.6%	36.7%	40.4%	**48.8%**
Median value of holdings *for families with holdings*	$10,800	$12,000	$15,400	**$25,000**
Debt as a percentage of total family assets	12.4%	14.6%	14.7%	**14.4%**
Families with debt payments that are 40 percent or more of income	10.1%	10.9%	10.5%	**12.7%**

Source: *Federal Reserve*

26. The largest percent of families was in the income group of

    (1) less than $10,000
    (2) $10,000 to $25,000
    (3) $25,000 to $50,000
    (4) $50,000 to $100,000
    (5) $100,000 and over

27. The largest increase in income between 1989 to 1998 was in the group

    (1) less than $10,000
    (2) $10,000 to $25,000
    (3) $25,000 to 50,000
    (4) $50,000 to $100,000
    (5) $100,000 and over

GO ON TO THE NEXT PAGE

TEST 2: SOCIAL STUDIES

28. According to the table, the following rose every year from 1989 to 1998:

    (1) family income
    (2) family net worth
    (3) families with stock holdings
    (4) family debt
    (5) debt payments 40% or more of income

Questions 29–31 are based on the following passage.

We must pursue a course designed not merely to reduce the number of delinquents. We must increase the chances for young people to lead productive lives.

For these delinquent and potentially delinquent youth, we must offer a New Start. We must insure that the special resources and skills essential for their treatment and rehabilitation are available. Because many of these young men and women live in broken families, burdened with financial and psychological problems, a successful rehabilitation program must include family counseling, vocational guidance, education and health services. It must strengthen the family and the schools. It must offer courts an alternative to placing young delinquents in penal institutions.

—Lyndon B. Johnson

29. The emphasis in this speech is on

    (1) diagnosis and research
    (2) prevention and rehabilitation
    (3) rehabilitation and research
    (4) treatment and diagnosis
    (5) research and diagnosis

30. The main purpose of this speech is to

    (1) provide federal financial aid
    (2) give advice to broken families
    (3) support research and experimentation
    (4) praise "halfway houses"
    (5) advocate legislation to combat juvenile delinquency

31. The passage implies that

    (1) delinquents cannot lead productive lives
    (2) detention of delinquents is unnecessary
    (3) delinquency is caused by family problems
    (4) the federal government must assume responsibility for preventing juvenile delinquency
    (5) courts must place young delinquents in the proper penal institutions

Questions 32 and 33 are based on the following photograph.

32. The purpose of this photograph is to show

    (1) how dangerous it is to transport merchandise without a cover
    (2) how vulnerable merchandise is when in the open
    (3) different ways of transporting milk
    (4) how milk jugs were transported by train
    (5) the first covered wagon to transport milk

33. The photograph was probably taken

    (1) during the 1940s
    (2) during the 1950s
    (3) during the 1960s
    (4) during the 1970s
    (5) during the 1980s

GO ON TO THE NEXT PAGE

TEST 2: SOCIAL STUDIES

Question 34 is based on the following graph.

1992 Presidential Election Results

Popular Vote   Electoral Vote

34. Which generalization is supported by the information provided by the graph?

    (1) The electoral vote often fails to reflect the popular vote.
    (2) The House of Representatives settles presidential elections in which third-party candiates participate.
    (3) The electoral college system weakens the two-party system.
    (4) Electoral college members often vote against their party's candidates.
    (5) Electoral votes result in closer elections.

Questions 35–37 are based on the following graph.

Average Amount of Time Each Day Spent Doing Each Activity (*hours:minutes*)

	Children 2 to 7	Children 8 to 18
Watching TV	1:59	3:16
Listening to CDs or tapes	0:21	1:05
Reading	0:45	0:44
Listening to the radio	0:24	0:48
Using the computer	0:07	0:31
Playing video games	0:08	0:27
Using the Internet	0:01	0:13

Percentage of Children Who Use a Computer Each Day

All children	42%
2–7 years old	26
8–18 years old	51
White	45
Black	39
Hispanic origin	28
Low income	29
Middle Income	40
High income	50

35. The survey mentions all of the following media EXCEPT

    (1) TV
    (2) reading
    (3) radio
    (4) Internet
    (5) movies

36. The most likely computer user according to the graph would be

    (1) an 8- to 18-year-old white
    (2) a low-income 2- to 7-year-old
    (3) a middle-income Hispanic
    (4) a high-income 2- to 7-year-old
    (5) a 2- to 7-year-old black

37. The dominant medium for children from 2 to 18 is

    (1) TV
    (2) reading
    (3) radio
    (4) computer
    (5) Internet

38. A primary source is an eyewitness account of an event or events in a specific time period. Which would be an example of a primary source of information about life in the 18th-century American colonies?

    (1) a diary of a colonial shopkeeper
    (2) a painting of the colonial period by a 20th century artist
    (3) a novel about the American Revolutionary War
    (4) a reproduction of furniture used during the colonial period
    (5) a social history of the period

GO ON TO THE NEXT PAGE

TEST 2: SOCIAL STUDIES

<u>Questions 39 and 40</u> are based on the following graph.

Median Weekly Earnings of Full-Time Female Workers, 25 and Over, by Educational Attainment *(In 1998 dollars)*

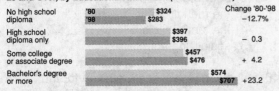

	'80		Change '80-'98
No high school diploma	$324	$283 ('98)	−12.7%
High school diploma only	$397	$396	− 0.3
Some college or associate degree	$457	$476	+ 4.2
Bachelor's degree or more	$574	$707	+23.2

Women's Median Earnings by Race and Educational Attainment, 1998

Sources: *Bureau of Labor Statistics, RFA Dismal Sciences*

39. Between 1980 and 1998, weekly earnings fell the most for women with

    (1) no high school diploma
    (2) a high school diploma
    (3) some college study
    (4) an associate degree
    (5) a bachelor's degree

40. By background, women's earnings for whites and Hispanics exceeded that of blacks who had

    (1) no high school diploma
    (2) a high school diploma
    (3) an associate degree
    (4) a bachelor's degree
    (5) more than a bachelor's degree

<u>Questions 41–43</u> are based on the statements made by Speakers *A*, *B*, *C*, *D*, and *E*.

<u>Speaker *A*:</u> Government could not function very well without them. The flow of information they provide to Congress and the federal agencies is vital to the functioning of our democratic system.

<u>Speaker *B*:</u> Yes, but the secrecy under which they generally operate makes me suspicious that they are influencing lawmakers in improper ways.

<u>Speaker *C*:</u> Don't forget that they not only try to influence Washington opinion but also attempt to shape public opinion across the nation in order to create a favorable climate for their views.

<u>Speaker *D*:</u> That's true. Any politician who ignores 40,000 letters does so at great risk. We have to pay attention to them whether we accept their views or not.

<u>Speaker *E*:</u> I agree with Speaker *C*. Public opinion is essential to the functioning of our American way of life.

41. Which group are the speakers most likely discussing?

    (1) lawyers
    (2) reporters
    (3) government workers
    (4) media analysts
    (5) lobbyists

42. Which speaker is most concerned about the impact of the methods used by this group upon democratic government?

    (1) *A*
    (2) *B*
    (3) *C*
    (4) *D*
    (5) *E*

43. Which speaker implies that lawmakers frequently must deal with a great many issues about which they know very little?

    (1) *A*
    (2) *B*
    (3) *C*
    (4) *D*
    (5) *E*

GO ON TO THE NEXT PAGE

TEST 2: SOCIAL STUDIES

Question 44 is based on the following cartoon.

"AND A HAPPY ELECTION YEAR TO YOU, TOO"

44. Which statement best summarizes the main point of the above cartoon?

(1) The citizen's vote is a powerful means of influencing legislators seeking reelection.
(2) Citizens are dependent upon the legislative branch of government for protection.
(3) Federal and state legislators usually agree on major campaign issues.
(4) The public generally does not favor consumer protection legislation.
(5) Voters are easily fooled by politicians seeking votes.

Questions 45–47 are based on the following passage.

The people and groups that provide the stimulation and contact necessary for social development—the socializing agents—usually fall into two classes: (1) those people with authority over the individual, such as parents and teachers, and (2) those in positions of equality with him or her—age peers, such as playmates or a circle of friends. Since the family is the socializing agent during the critical first years of life, it naturally has had great influence. But because of the increased specialization of the functions of the family, the rapidity of social change that tends to divide the generations, and the high degree of mobility and social fluidity, the peer group is of growing importance in modern urban life.

45. Parents, teachers, and age peers share the role of

(1) people with authority over the individual
(2) peer group members
(3) the friendly circle
(4) the family circle
(5) socializing agents

46. All of these reasons are given for the increased role of peers in an individual's social development EXCEPT

(1) social mobility
(2) social fluidity
(3) generation gap
(4) growing number of peers
(5) specialization of family functions

47. The family, in modern urban life, is

(1) exerting influence
(2) growing in importance
(3) being replaced by the peer group
(4) filling a broadening role
(5) influential only in the early years of life

Questions 48 and 49 refer to the following statements made by Speakers *A*, *B*, and *C*.

Speaker *A*: Increased contact among nations and peoples is characteristic of our times. A single decision by OPEC or a multinational corporation can send ripples of change throughout our global society.

Speaker *B*: If we are to survive, all passengers on our Spaceship Earth must participate in efforts to solve the issues that threaten humankind—poverty, resource depletion, pollution, violence, and war.

GO ON TO THE NEXT PAGE

TEST 2: SOCIAL STUDIES

Speaker *C:* We must understand that no single culture's view of the world is universally shared. Other people have different value systems and ways of thinking and acting. They will not see the world as we do.

48. Which concept is discussed by both Speakers *A* and *B*?

(1) self-determination
(2) nationalism
(3) conservation
(4) interdependence
(5) protectionism

49. Speaker *C* indicates a desire to reduce

(1) ethnocentrism
(2) globalism
(3) social mobility
(4) religious tolerance
(5) interdependence

Question 50 is based on the following cartoon.

"Witnesses for the Prosecution"

50. The cartoon is concerned primarily with determining responsibility for which situation?

(1) use of poison gas during World War I
(2) slave labor camps in the Soviet Union during the Stalin era
(3) the Holocaust in Europe during the 1930s and 1940s
(4) apartheid practices in South Africa
(5) the blitzkrieg of World War II

END OF EXAMINATION

TEST 3: SCIENCE

Directions

The Science test consists of multiple-choice questions intended to measure the general concepts in science. The questions are based on short readings that often include a graph, chart, or figure. Study the information given and then answer the question(s) following it. Refer to the information as often as necessary in answering the questions.

You will have 95 minutes to answer the questions. Work carefully, but do not spend too much time on any one question. Be sure you answer every question. You will not be penalized for incorrect answers.

To record your answers, mark the numbered space on the answer sheet beside the number that corresponds to the question in the test.

FOR EXAMPLE:

Which of the following is the smallest unit?

    (1) solution   ① ② ● ④ ⑤
    (2) molecule
    (3) atom
    (4) compound
    (5) mixture

The correct answer is "atom"; therefore, space 3 would be marked on the answer sheet.

Note: *The science sections of the two practice tests at the end of this book, like the science section on the actual GED exam, consist of 50 questions. This section has 66 questions in order to diagnose better your strengths and weaknesses in science.*

GO ON TO THE NEXT PAGE

TEST 3: SCIENCE

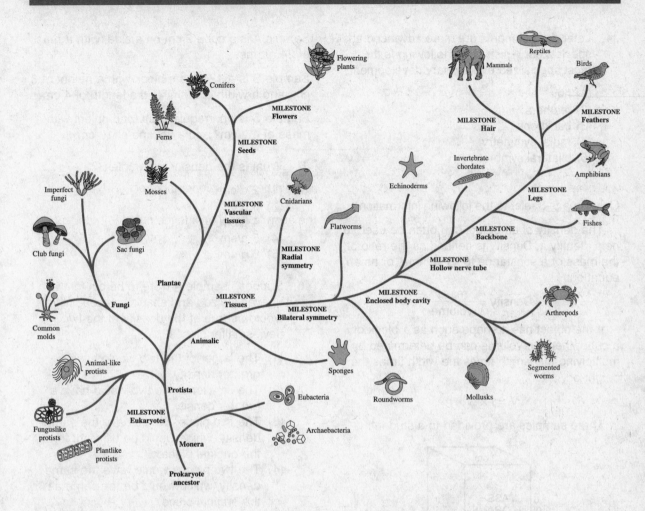

Questions 1–4 refer to the figure above.

The figure above shows the evolutionary relationships between the major classes of organisms. Branch points show common ancestors, and each branch represents a new class of organisms.

1. Which milestone came latest in evolution?

   (1) tissues
   (2) bilateral symmetry
   (3) feathers
   (4) flowers
   (5) backbone

2. Which of the following shows the correct order of emergence, from earliest to latest?

   (1) mosses, ferns, conifers
   (2) conifers, mosses, ferns
   (3) ferns, mosses, conifers
   (4) ferns, conifers, mosses
   (5) conifers, ferns, mosses

3. If groups that shared common ancestors are more likely to be closely related, which groups are most closely related evolutionarily?

   (1) echinoderms and mollusks
   (2) birds and reptiles
   (3) round worms and segmented worms
   (4) protists and molds
   (5) echinoderms and fishes

GO ON TO THE NEXT PAGE

TEST 3: SCIENCE

4. Later developments are more advanced and specialized. Which of the following is the most specialized evolutionary development?

    (1) hair
    (2) feathers
    (3) backbone
    (4) radial symmetry
    (5) bilateral symmetry

Questions 5–8 refer to the following information.

The density of an object can often be used to help identify it. Density is defined as the ratio of the mass of a substance to its volume, or as an equation:

$$\text{Density} = \frac{\text{mass}}{\text{volume}}$$

If the object has a shape such as a block or a cube, then the volume can be determined by multiplying the length times the width times the height or

$$V = l \times w \times h$$

Three samples are provided to a student:

A

B

C

Sample A is a cube 2 cm on a side, with a mass of 24 grams.

Sample B is a 120 gram block with a height of 3 cm, and a width of 2 cm, and a length of 4 cm.

Sample C is an irregularly shaped object with a mass of 4 g/cm^3 and a volume of 10 cm.

5. What is the density of sample B?

    (1) 2 g/cm^3
    (2) 3 g/cm^3
    (3) 4 g/cm^3
    (4) 5 g/cm^3
    (5) 6 g/cm^3

6. Suppose sample A were to be cut into two unevenly sized and shaped pieces. What would be true of the density of the two new, smaller pieces?

    (1) The larger of the two would have a greater density.
    (2) The smaller of the two would have a greater density.
    (3) The two pieces would have the same density, which would be different from the original piece.
    (4) The two pieces would have the same density, which would be the same as the original piece.
    (5) There is not enough information to tell.

7. When a balloon is heated its volume doubles. What happens to its density?

    (1) The density doubles.
    (2) The density quadruples.
    (3) The density stays the same.
    (4) The density is cut in half.
    (5) There is not enough information to tell.

8. What is the mass of sample C?

    (1) 20 g
    (2) 30 g
    (3) 40 g
    (4) 60 g
    (5) 80 g

GO ON TO THE NEXT PAGE

TEST 3: SCIENCE

9. An island may form when material expelled by an undersea volcano gradually builds up and rises above the surface of the water. This has happened in numerous places in the Pacific Ocean. Over time, however, another island may begin to form some distance from the first. It is possible that chains of islands, such as the Hawaiian Islands, were formed in this way. One reason for this may be that

    (1) the volcano moves along the bottom of the ocean
    (2) the plates of earth and rock that cover the interior of planet Earth are slowly moving, taking the islands with them
    (3) when the first island was finished, some leftover lava started another island
    (4) volcanoes erupted in places where islands were going to be formed
    (5) volcanic eruptions have had nothing to do with the formation of islands

10. The figure above shows a sonar wave being sent out from a ship, hitting the bottom of the ocean and bouncing back to the ship. By knowing the speed of the sound wave and the time the wave travels, the depth to the bottom of the ocean can be determined. The sonar wave travels at 1,000 meters per second. If it takes 4 seconds for the wave to travel to the bottom of the ocean and return, how deep is the ocean at that location?

    (1) 500 meters
    (2) 1,000 meters
    (3) 2,000 meters
    (4) 4,000 meters
    (5) 8,000 meters

Questions 11–13 refer to the following passage.

Most of us have played with magnets from the time we were very young. Magnets may be man-made or occur naturally. The earliest of magnets come from the ancient Greeks, who used a mineral known as magnetite, which they noticed could repel or attract certain metals. Interestingly, if a magnet is broken in half, each piece will then have its own north and south poles.

In general, all magnets, no matter what their shape, have both a north and south pole. Like poles attract each other; unlike poles repel each other. A compass works because it uses a freely rotating magnet that be attracted or repelled by the naturally magnetic poles of the earth.

One of most common applications of magnets is in creating an electromagnet, which is caused when an electric current moves through a magnetic material, such as an iron nail.

11. What type of magnet can be controlled by adjusting the flow of electric current, such as might be used in a scrap yard to pick up, and then drop large pieces of metal?

    (1) magnetite
    (2) an electromagnet
    (3) a naturally occurring magnet
    (4) a bar magnet
    (5) a magnet with two north poles

12. Which end of a compass will face north?

    (1) the north pole
    (2) the south pole
    (3) either end, depending on whether it is above or below the equator
    (4) it depends what the magnet is made of
    (5) it depends what metals are around the compass

13. Alnico magnets are used in industry because they have a great deal of strength for their size. What must be true of an alnico magnet?

    (1) It must have an electric current going through it.
    (2) It must be attracted to all metals.
    (3) It must be a naturally occurring magnet.
    (4) It must have both a north and a south pole.
    (5) None of the above must be true.

GO ON TO THE NEXT PAGE

TEST 3: SCIENCE

Questions 14–16 refer to the following article.

The two most common types of engines are the gasoline internal combustion engine and the diesel engine. Each has its own advantages and disadvantages in specific situations. In the gasoline internal combustion engine used in most automobiles and lawn mowers, a mixture of gasoline and air is mixed together and ignited by a spark from a spark plug. The air provides the necessary oxygen that allows combustion to take place.

The diesel engine works by mixing the fuel and air under very high pressures, which heats the mixture to a very high temperature, causing it to ignite. The high pressures used require a very strong construction for the walls of the cylinders and engine. Diesel engines can be more difficult to get started, but once going, they are inexpensive to run, as the fuel they require costs less than gasoline.

14. Which of the following is true of the internal combustion engine but not the diesel engine?

    (1) It requires both fuel and air.
    (2) It is less expensive to operate.
    (3) It requires a spark plug.
    (4) It operates by compressing the air and fuel mixture to ignite it.
    (5) It needs less air.

15. Why are diesel engines used for trucks that travel long distances?

    (1) Gasoline is not available everywhere.
    (2) Diesel fuel is less expensive than gasoline.
    (3) Internal combustion engines pollute.
    (4) Spark plugs are unreliable.
    (5) The engines have stronger walls.

16. Which type of engine would a race car use and why?

    (1) internal combustion because it is cheaper to operate
    (2) internal combustion because it weighs less
    (3) internal combustion because it uses less fuel
    (4) diesel because it does not require a spark plug
    (5) diesel because the engine is stronger

Questions 17–19 refer to the following article.

All nations agree that cooperative efforts are needed in research to study and predict earthquakes. In July 1956 the first World Conference on Earthquake Engineering was held in Tokyo. Its purpose was to share information about the prediction of earthquakes and methods of constructing buildings and bridges that can withstand the shocks.

What causes earthquakes? The crust of the Earth is a broken mosaic of pieces, bounded by deep cracks called faults. When forces deep inside the Earth move these pieces, tremendous shock waves start from the faults. Shock waves in the crust, from whatever source, can be detected by seismographs all over the world. If the earthquake occurs beneath the ocean, it produces an enormous wave, called a tsunami, that can do much damage when it arrives at a shore.

17. What is the most frequent cause of major earthquakes?

    (1) movements within the Earth
    (2) folding
    (3) landslides
    (4) submarine currents
    (5) tsunamis

18. How can earthquake destruction be minimized?

    (1) more frequent use of seismographs
    (2) better construction of buildings
    (3) quicker methods of evacuation
    (4) early detection and warning
    (5) better control of tsunamis

19. Nuclear explosions can be detected by seismographs because they

    (1) cause tsunamis
    (2) occur on geologic faults
    (3) cause earthquakes
    (4) produce shock waves in the crust
    (5) compress the rock

GO ON TO THE NEXT PAGE

TEST 3: SCIENCE

Atom	# protons	# neutrons	# electrons	Atomic mass (amu)	Most common ionic charge	Common compound with Cl
Sodium	11	12	11	23	+1	NaCl
Potassium	19	20	Y	39	+1	W
Calcium	20	20	20	40	+2	$CaCl_2$
Magnesium	12	X	12	24	+2	$MgCl_2$
Aluminum	13	14	13	27	+3	Z

Questions 20–23 refer to the table above.

The table above shows the composition of some common atoms, their most common charges when they form ions, and some common compounds of their ions. Neutral atoms have equal numbers of protons and electrons. Protons and neutrons each have a mass of 1 atomic mass unit (amu), whereas the mass of an electron is generally ignored as it is so small.

20. What is the value of Y, the number of electrons in a potassium atom?

    (1) 19
    (2) 20
    (3) 23
    (4) 34
    (5) 35

21. What is the value of X, the number of neutrons in a magnesium atom?

    (1) 6
    (2) 12
    (3) 24
    (4) 36
    (5) 48

22. What would be the formula for potassium chloride, represented by W in the table above?

    (1) KCl
    (2) K_2Cl
    (3) KCl_2
    (4) K_2Cl_2
    (5) Cl_2K

23. What is the formula of aluminum chloride, represented in the table by Z?

    (1) AlCl
    (2) $AlCl_2$
    (3) $AlCl_3$
    (4) Al_2Cl
    (5) Al_3Cl

Questions 24–29 refer to the following article.

Photosynthesis is a complex process involving many steps. Water in the soil is absorbed by the roots of a plant, rises through tubules called xylem, and moves through the stems and into the leaves. Carbon dioxide, diffused from the air through the stomata and into the leaf, comes into contact with the water and dissolves. The solution of carbon dioxide in water then diffuses through the cell walls and into the cells. Organelles within the cell, called chloroplasts, contain chlorophyll, a green pigment that captures light energy from the sun and transforms it into chemical energy. This chemical energy acts to convert the carbon dioxide and water into other compounds. These compounds become more and more complex until finally a sugar is produced. Oxygen is given off as a by-product of the photosynthetic process.

24. Which plant structure is directly involved in the making of sugar?

    (1) stoma
    (2) xylem
    (3) cell wall
    (4) plasma membrane
    (5) chloroplast

GO ON TO THE NEXT PAGE

TEST 3: SCIENCE

25. To carry on photosynthesis, the water of the soil must be transported to the leaf. Which structure conducts soil water to the leaf?

    (1) chlorophyll
    (2) stoma
    (3) xylem
    (4) phloem
    (5) chloroplasts

26. What is/are the main product(s) of photosynthesis?

    (1) chlorophyll only
    (2) sugars and water
    (3) water and oxygen
    (4) oxygen only
    (5) oxygen and sugars

27. Sugar is composed of carbon, hydrogen, and oxygen. In the process of photosynthesis, what is the source of these chemical elements?

    (1) carbon dioxide alone
    (2) water alone
    (3) either the carbon dioxide or the water
    (4) both the carbon dioxide and the water
    (5) neither the carbon dioxide nor the water

28. What is the function of chlorophyll in photosynthesis?

    (1) serves as a source of carbohydrate
    (2) produces carbon dioxide
    (3) changes light energy to chemical energy
    (4) supplies chemical energy
    (5) provides the green color

29. Carbon dioxide enters a plant by way of the

    (1) roots
    (2) xylem
    (3) plasma membrane
    (4) stomata
    (5) intercellular spaces

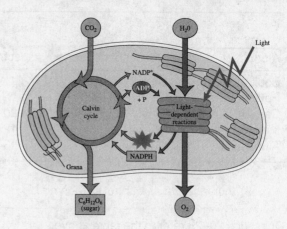

30. The figure above shows a schematic of photosynthesis. Which of the following must be present for plants to produce sugars?

    I. light
    II. carbon dioxide
    III. water

    (1) I only
    (2) II only
    (3) I and II only
    (4) II and III only
    (5) I, II, and III

GO ON TO THE NEXT PAGE

TEST 3: SCIENCE

31. Green plants, in sunlight, absorb carbon dioxide to produce glucose, releasing oxygen in the process. Which of the following would be most likely to increase the rate at which this process goes on?

    (1) Increase the amount of oxygen in the air.
    (2) Add glucose to the soil.
    (3) Move the plants into the shade.
    (4) Reduce the amount of carbon dioxide in the air.
    (5) Increase the amount of carbon dioxide in the air.

Questions 32–34 refer to the following article.

In the process of evolution, some individuals in a population of organisms possess physical traits that allow them to have an advantage in survival over other members of their species. These changes may help them better attract mates, find food, hide from predators, or defend themselves. The individuals with a survival advantage will be more likely to pass their genes on to future generations, thus allowing the species to evolve over time.

A bird's bill usually defines the type of food that the bird eats. Some hunting birds have sharp hooked bills. Other birds have slender bills to extract nectar from flowers. The interesting bill of the South American toucan is huge and brightly colored and can be as long as half the length of the the bird's body. This bill is useful in picking fruit.

32. What is the probable reason that African hornbills closely resemble the South American toucan, even though the two species are unrelated?

    (1) The resemblance is purely a coincidence.
    (2) There has been an interchange of genetic material between the two species of birds.
    (3) The two species of birds have evolved from a common ancestor.
    (4) Both species of birds are fruit eaters in tropical rain forests.
    (5) The toucans have migrated from Africa.

33. When the Industrial Revolution introduced great smoke-belching factories into England, a certain species of moth found itself threatened. These white moths lived on the bark of light-colored trees, where they were virtually invisible to predators. When smog from the factories turned everything in the area black with soot, the trunks of the trees were not immune. As time passed, the population of this moth dropped dramatically. The chief reason for the decline may have been that

    (1) because the white moths were now visible against the sooty bark, they were easier for birds to catch
    (2) the soot was poisonous to the moths
    (3) the soot killed off the moth's primary source of food
    (4) the soot destroyed the moth's eggs
    (5) the moths had to find other trees because the old ones were now too dark

34. Snakes are solitary creatures. With a few exceptions, they crawl off to live alone after they hatch. Occasionally a female snake will lay a trail of a special scent called a pheromone. The reason for laying this trail is that the only life process a snake cannot carry on alone is

    (1) respiration
    (2) hibernation
    (3) reproduction
    (4) regulation
    (5) locomotion

GO ON TO THE NEXT PAGE

TEST 3: SCIENCE

35. Potassium is receiving special attention as an important nutritional requirement. Potassium ions help conduct an electric charge that is important in the transmission of nerve impulses and muscle contraction. Foods such as bananas and dried apricots are rich in potassium. These foods are recommended for persons who lose potassium because their medication causes the loss of body water. Why might the heart malfunction because of loss of potassium?

    (1) The heart needs banana and apricot
    (2) The heart absorbs much potassium
    (3) High blood pressure can be treated
    (4) Low blood pressure can be treated
    (5) Contraction of heart muscles requires potassium

36. Oxides of carbon, sulfur, and nitrogen, which occur in the stack gases of coal-burning plants, react with atmospheric water to form acids. The pollution caused by stack gases may be responsible for all the following forms of environmental damage EXCEPT

    (1) physical deformity of developing fish
    (2) corrosion of buildings
    (3) death of many forest trees
    (4) damage to human lungs
    (5) sewage contamination of water supplies

37. The laws that control recombination of genes seem to be much the same for all sexually reproducing organisms. These laws are studied by statistical analysis of large numbers of offspring for several generations. Which of the following organisms would be most useful in experiments to study the laws of recombination of genes?

    (1) bacteria
    (2) human beings
    (3) mice
    (4) dogs
    (5) oak trees

38. The early atmosphere of the Earth had no oxygen. It was first produced when bacteria developed the green pigment that made photosynthesis possible. In which of the following groups is the sequence in which organisms appeared on Earth presented correctly?

    (1) animals, green bacteria, nongreen bacteria
    (2) green bacteria, animals, nongreen bacteria
    (3) animals, nongreen bacteria, green bacteria
    (4) nongreen bacteria, green bacteria, animals
    (5) nongreen bacteria, animals, green bacteria

39. The graph below shows the changes in the populations of wolves and moose in a northern forest for a period of 6 years. What is the most reasonable explanation of the facts shown?

WOLF AND MOOSE POPULATIONS 1970–1980

    (1) Moose produce more offspring when there are few wolves.
    (2) When there are many moose, there are more recreational hunters.
    (3) Wolves produce more offspring when there are many moose.
    (4) Both wolf and moose populations vary according to the weather conditions.
    (5) Wolf populations have no relationship to the availability of moose.

GO ON TO THE NEXT PAGE

TEST 3: SCIENCE

Question 40 is based on the following diagram.

SOIL
ROCK LAYER *A*
ROCK LAYER *B*
ROCK LAYER *C*
ROCK LAYER *D*

40. When sediments are deposited in the ocean, new layers form on top of preexisting layers. The sediments may eventually turn into fossil bearing rocks. What might a geologist conclude about fossils found in the rock layers shown in the diagram above?

    (1) All the fossils are of the same age.
    (2) The relative ages of the fossils cannot be determined.
    (3) The fossils in rock layer *D* are older than those in layer *A*.
    (4) The fossils in rock layer *B* are older than those in layer *C*.
    (5) The fossils in rock layer *A* are older than those in layer *B*.

41. The AIDS virus is transmitted from an infected person by direct introduction of his or her blood or other body fluids into the body of another person. An individual can contract AIDS by any of the following means EXCEPT

    (1) breathing the air expelled by a person with the disease
    (2) sexual intercourse with an infected person
    (3) using a hypodermic needle that had been used by someone with the disease
    (4) receiving a blood transfusion from an infected person
    (5) passage of the virus from a pregnant woman into the fetus she is carrying

42. Some corn plants may have genes that make them immune to the poisonous effects of herbicides. These genes can arise spontaneously by mutation, and will then be passed on to future generations. What might a plant breeder do to develop a line of corn that would not be killed by herbicides?

    (1) Apply herbicides to cause mutations.
    (2) Prevent mutations by careful control of environmental conditions.
    (3) Find immune plants by applying herbicides and breeding the survivors.
    (4) Withhold all fertilizers and breed the plants that survive.
    (5) Withhold all herbicides and breed whichever plants mutate.

43. Since World War II, new varieties of rice have been developed that produce two or three times as much grain when they are grown with heavy doses of chemical fertilizers. A farmer should decide NOT to use these varieties if

    (1) he or she is accustomed to growing more familiar varieties of rice
    (2) he or she is cultivating only a small plot
    (3) his or her farm is in an unusually wet climate
    (4) there is no way he or she can obtain the seed of the new varieties
    (5) the fertilizer needed costs more than the value of the extra grain

44. Why do you feel cool when you get out of the surf on a dry day?

    (1) Evaporating water removes heat from the body.
    (2) Evaporation produces heat.
    (3) Condensation cools the body.
    (4) The air is cooler than the surf water.
    (5) Sea breezes make you feel cooler.

GO ON TO THE NEXT PAGE

TEST 3: SCIENCE

Questions 45–49 refer to the following article.

Today some plants are cloned to produce millions of offspring from a small piece of the original plant. Plant cloning is possible because each plant cell contains a complete blueprint, in the form of chromosomes, for reproducing itself. After a piece of the plant is placed in a growth medium, special plant growth hormones, called auxins and cytokinin, are added to stimulate the production of new plants. The new plants are genetically identical to the original plant and to each other.

The equipment and processes used in cloning are more expensive than those used for other forms of vegetative propagation. The advantage of cloning is that large numbers of plants are produced in a short period of time. For example, a million plants of a new variety can be cloned in about six months. This process is very useful for developing strains of disease resistant crops or plants that not only can survive in a difficult climate but also will produce a large harvest.

45. For which reason is cloning used to reproduce plants?

(1) Plants with a large degree of genetic variability are produced.
(2) Plants are produced more cheaply than by other vegetative methods.
(3) Plants are produced by the sexual process, resulting in seeds.
(4) A large number of plants are produced in a short period of time.
(5) Plants with large degrees of variation are produced.

46. It is possible to clone plants that are identical to their parent plants because

(1) scientists have developed blueprints to make so many different plants
(2) every plant cell is the same
(3) chromosomes carry identical genetic blueprints from the parent plant
(4) hormones are used to induce plants to reproduce
(5) plants are easy to grow under the correct conditions

47. Which statement describes the hormones auxin and cytokinin?

(1) They are forms of vegetative propagation.
(2) They can develop into a zygote.
(3) They stimulate the production of new plants.
(4) They inhibit the production of new plants.
(5) They are forms of asexual reproduction.

48. How is cloning defined?

(1) a form of sexual reproduction
(2) a form of vegetative propagation
(3) an inorganic hormone
(4) an inorganic component of the growing medium
(5) an auxin

49. An important difference between plants produced by cloning and plants grown from seed is that

(1) cloned plants are healthier
(2) cloned plants are identical to the parent plant
(3) plants grown from seed are identical to the parent plant
(4) plants grown from seed are better adapted to the conditions in which the plants are grown
(5) cloned plants do not need as much care

50. If particles are to be considered water-soluble, they must dissolve in water. In this case, the resulting solution will be clear. Sometimes, however, some of the substance will settle out of the solution, leaving a precipitate on the bottom of the container.

Why do we find the instruction "Shake well before using" on the labels of some medicines?

(1) The liquid is a solution.
(2) The mixture is not a solution.
(3) The particles are the size of molecules.
(4) The particles are not visible.
(5) Light goes through the solution.

GO ON TO THE NEXT PAGE

TEST 3: SCIENCE

Questions 51–53 refer to the following table.

The table below shows some common acids and bases and some of their common properties. (Note: tasting chemicals is never recommended.)

Substance	pH	Taste	Litmus color
Lemon juice	2	Sour	Red
Vinegar	3	Sour	Red
Water	7 (neutral pH)	None	No change
Soapy water	9	Bitter	Blue
Ammonia	10	Bitter	Blue

51. Sour milk would most likely have which of the following pH values?

    (1) 11
    (2) 10
    (3) 8
    (4) 7
    (5) 4

52. An unknown solution has a pH of 10. Which of the following properties would it likely have?

    (1) tastes sour and turns litmus blue
    (2) tastes sour and turns litmus red
    (3) tastes bitter and turns litmus blue
    (4) tastes bitter and turns litmus red
    (5) tastes sour and leaves litmus unchanged

53. Many cleaners use either acids or bases to help dissolve dirt and grease. Ammonia is a common base often used in cleaning glass and vinegar is also often used as a cleaning solution. Suppose someone mixed an ammonia solution and a vinegar solution to make a cleaning solution. How would this new mixture most likely work?

    (1) There is not enough information to tell.
    (2) It would work even better since it is made from two good cleaners.
    (3) The ammonia would work, but the vinegar would not.
    (4) The solution would be neutral and would most likely not be an effective cleaner.
    (5) The vinegar would work, but the ammonia would not.

54. Which of the following general rules is the best explanation of the way an ice cube cools a drink?

    (1) Cold moves to objects of higher temperature.
    (2) Heat moves to objects of higher density.
    (3) Heat moves to objects of lower density.
    (4) Cold moves to objects of lower temperature.
    (5) Heat moves to objects of lower temperature.

Questions 55 to 58 are based on the following passage and diagram.

When air rises, it expands, and this change makes it cool down. Conversely, when air sinks, it is compressed and becomes warmer. As air cools down, its relative humidity rises; when the relative humidity reaches 100%, moisture condenses out of the air.

The diagram shows the prevailing wind directions and air temperatures at different elevations on both sides of a mountain.

55. What is the approximate air temperature at the top of the mountain?

    (1) 12°C
    (2) 10°C
    (3) 0°C
    (4) 7°C
    (5) 4°C

GO ON TO THE NEXT PAGE

TEST 3: SCIENCE

56. On which side of the mountain and at what elevation is the relative humidity probably 100%?

    (1) on the windward side at 0.5 km
    (2) on the windward side at 2.5 km
    (3) on the leeward side at 1.0 km
    (4) on the leeward side at 2.5 km
    (5) on the leeward side at 1.5 km

57. How does the temperature of the air change as the air rises on the windward side of the mountain between sea level and 0.5 kilometer?

    (1) The air is warming because of compression of the air.
    (2) The air is warming because of expansion of the air.
    (3) The air is cooling because of compression of the air.
    (4) The air is cooling because of expansion of the air.
    (5) The air is warmed and cooled because of expansion of the air.

58. Which feature is probably located at the base of the mountain on the leeward side (location *X*)?

    (1) a dry, desertlike region
    (2) a jungle
    (3) a glacier
    (4) a large lake
    (5) a river

59. Human activities produce or add all these pollutants EXCEPT

    (1) sound
    (2) pollen
    (3) radiation
    (4) smoke
    (5) carbon oxides

Questions 60 and 61 are based on the following passage and diagram.

The block marked *A* is being pulled uphill at constant speed by the falling weight. Since the speed is constant, the force pulling the block uphill must be equal in magnitude to the force holding it back. This opposing force is called friction.

60. How would the situation change if a larger weight were used?

    (1) Nothing would be different.
    (2) Both the block and the weight would accelerate instead of going at a constant speed.
    (3) Both the block and the weight would be going at a higher constant speed.
    (4) The weight would accelerate, but the block would still travel at constant speed.
    (5) Both the block and the weight would slow down.

61. While you are probably most familiar with animals that have an internal skeleton, called an endoskeleton, certain organisms have their skeletons on the outside of their bodies. This exoskeleton is an excellent means of support and protection, but as the animal grows, its skeleton does not. Because of this, the exoskeleton has to be shed or molted now and then.

    Animals with an exoskeleton are called invertebrates. Of the animals listed below, which one is *not* an invertebrate?

    (1) lobster
    (2) turtle
    (3) snail
    (4) horseshoe crab
    (5) spider

GO ON TO THE NEXT PAGE

TEST 3: SCIENCE

Bottle	Male flies in bottle	Female flies in bottle	Flypaper present?	Food	Light
One	10 wingless, 10 winged	10 wingless, 10 winged	Yes	Yes	Yes
Two	10 wingless, 10 winged	10 wingless, 10 winged	No	Yes	yes

Questions 62–66 refer to the following information.

The following experiment was carried out to se if there were situations in which a wingless fly might have an advantage over the normal, winged fly. The experimental set-up is described by the table above.

62. Which of the following is the independent variable in the experiment?

  (1) the presence of food in the bottles
  (2) the amount of light provided to the flies
  (3) the presence of flypaper in the bottles
  (4) the sex of the flies
  (5) the experiment has a control

63. In which bottle would it be predicted that the wingless flies might have an advantage?

  (1) bottle 1
  (2) bottle 2
  (3) both bottles
  (4) neither bottle
  (5) it depends on the type of food provided

64. What would be an appropriate variable to measure at the end of the experiment?

  (1) the weight of the flies
  (2) the number of flies alive
  (3) the amount of food the flies had consumed
  (4) the response of the flies to light and darkness
  (5) the differences in survival between male and female flies

65. In nature, wingless flies sometimes arise spontaneously. This is called

  (1) a law of nature
  (2) a mutation
  (3) a gene
  (4) an allele
  (5) a spontaneous generation

66. What general principle of nature would be explained by finding that most of the flies with wings died on the flypaper?

  (1) Flypaper is an effective means of control of insects.
  (2) Fruit flies exist in nature in many different forms.
  (3) Evolution favors the forms with the best survival values.
  (4) The survival value of a trait depends on the environment in which the organism lives.
  (5) Processes in natural ecosystems cannot be simulated in the laboratory.

END OF EXAMINATION

TEST 4: LANGUAGE ARTS, READING

Directions

The Language Arts, Reading test consists of excerpts from pre-1920, 1920–1960, and post-1960 literature, articles about literature or the arts, and at least one business document. Each excerpt is followed by multiple-choice questions about the reading material.

Read each excerpt first and then answer the questions following it. Refer to the reading material as often as necessary in answering the questions.

Each excerpt is preceded by a "purpose question." The purpose question gives a reason for reading the material. Use these purpose questions to help focus your reading. You are not required to answer these purpose questions. They are given only to help you concentrate on the ideas presented in the reading materials.

You should spend no more than 65 minutes answering the questions. Work carefully, but do not spend too much time on any one question. Be sure you answer every question. You will not be penalized for incorrect answers.

To record your answers, mark the numbered space on the answer sheet beside the number that corresponds to the question in the test.

FOR EXAMPLE:

It was Susan's dream machine. The metallic blue paint gleamed, and the sporty wheels were highly polished. Under the hood, the engine was no less carefully cleaned. Inside, flashy lights illuminated the instruments on the dashboard, and the seats were covered in rich leather upholstery.

The subject ("It") of this excerpt is most likely

(1) an airplane   ① ② ● ④ ⑤
(2) a stereo system
(3) an automobile
(4) a boat
(5) a motorcycle

The correct answer is "an automobile"; therefore, answer space 3 would be marked on the answer sheet.

GO ON TO THE NEXT PAGE

TEST 4: LANGUAGE ARTS, READING

Questions 1–5 refer to the following business document.

HOW MUST EMPLOYEES' WORK ENVIRONMENT BE FLEXIBLE?

Window Solutions for Networks Employee Handbook

Telecommuting

(1) The Company is committed to creating a flexible work environment that balances the needs of our customers, employees, and the Company. (2) Therefore, the Company tries
(5) to be creative in its approach to work styles and location. (3) Telecommuting arrangements may be made on an "as needed basis" or set up on a regular schedule. (4) In either case, it is preferred that
(10) employees spend time working in the office whenever possible. (5) This allows employees to be accessible to customers and creates a sense of consistency and cooperation among work groups. (6) When
(15) employees desire to work at home, the Company asks that they do so in a manner that is in keeping with a workstyle of accessibility, communication, and productivity. (7) All telecommuting arrangements are subject
(20) to approval by the employee's manager. (8) In general, the following principles should be used in telecommuting.
• (9) Employees should make arrangements with their manager at least 1 week before
(25) telecommuting.
• (10) Employees should check in with the office on a regular basis.
• (11) Employees should inform their manager of their whereabouts so they may
(30) be reached easily.
• (12) Working at home means working for the Company, not taking time off to do projects not related to the Company.
• (13) Employees should not routinely work
(35) at home on days before or following vacations or holidays.
• (14) Under regular circumstances, telecommuting should not be used more than 1 day a week or more than 3 days a
(40) month.

1. What is the meaning of "telecommuting"?
   (1) working primarily on the phone
   (2) working from home
   (3) working at the office
   (4) working on a computer
   (5) answering phones for the Company

2. According to the document, which one of the following is a principle used in telecommuting (lines 19–40)?
   (1) telecommuting should be done at least 4 days a month
   (2) working from home on days before or following vacations or holidays is acceptable
   (3) check in with the office at least once every hour
   (4) employees should give their manager information of their whereabouts
   (5) taking a vacation is the same as working at home

3. Which of the following would be an example of "a manner that is in keeping with a workstyle of accessiblity, communciation, and productivity" (lines 16–18)?
   (1) employee routinely checks in with his manager
   (2) employee communicates via cell phone
   (3) employee calls customers from the office
   (4) employee informs manager of his whereabouts only once
   (5) employee produces less work while telecommuting

4. If the Company wanted to dismiss an employee for improper telecommuting, which of the following would be a valid reason?
   (1) employee regularly used telecommuting more than 3 days each month
   (2) employee checked in with the office
   (3) employer didn't give time off to the employee
   (4) employer failed to inform employee of telecommuting policy
   (5) Company has a no-fault policy

GO ON TO THE NEXT PAGE

TEST 4: LANGUAGE ARTS, READING

5. What is the main purpose of the Company's telecommuting policy?

   (1) to reduce the employees' workload
   (2) to create a more flexible and balanced work environment for today's employees
   (3) to give more vacation time
   (4) to allow for direct communication between customer and employee
   (5) to save the Company money

Questions 6–10 refer to the following excerpt from a work of prose fiction.

WHAT CAN A BEREAVED FATHER DO?

Iona sees a hall porter with some sacking, and decides to talk to him.

"Friend, what sort of time is it?" he asks.

"Past nine. What are you standing here for? Move on."

Iona moves on a few steps, doubles up, and abandons himself to his grief. He gives a tug at the reins; he can bear it no longer. "The stables," he thinks, and the little horse, as if it understood, starts off at a trot.

One of the cabdrivers around the stove half gets up, grunts sleepily, and stretches toward a bucket of water.

"Do you want a drink?" Iona asks him.

"Don't I want a drink!"

"That's so? Your good health! But listen, mate—you know, my son is dead...Did you hear? This week, in the hospital...It's a long story."

Iona looks to see what effect his words have, but sees none—the young man is fast asleep again. Just as much as the young one wants to drink, the old man wants to talk. Is it nothing to tell?

"I'll go and look after my horse," thinks Iona; "there's always time to sleep. No fear of that!"

When he is alone, he dares not think of his son; he can speak about him to anyone, but to think of him, and picture him to himself, is unbearably painful.

"That's how it is, my old horse. There's no more Kuzma Ionitch. Now let's say, you had a foal, you were this foal's mother, and suddenly, let's say, that foal went out and left you to live after him. It would be sad, wouldn't it?"

The little horse munches, listens, and breathes over its master's hand...

Iona's feelings are too much for him, and he tells the little horse the whole story.

6. In this story it is ironic that

   (1) the cabdriver wants a drink
   (2) the hall porter tells Iona to move on
   (3) Iona tells his story to his horse
   (4) Iona has run out of food for his horse
   (5) the horse had a foal

7. Iona goes to take care of his horse. He does so most probably to

   (1) have something to do
   (2) protest the high cost of feed
   (3) show his great love for his horse
   (4) prove that he does not resent the cabdriver's action
   (5) remove his feelings of guilt

8. The setting for this story is probably a 19th-century

   (1) American city
   (2) eastern European city
   (3) northern European farm
   (4) American small town
   (5) English city

9. The author's purpose in using the present tense is most probably to

   (1) make the story seem modern
   (2) increase the length of the story
   (3) heighten the reader's sense of immediacy
   (4) write the story as consciously as possible
   (5) reinforce the first-person point of view

10. Iona's situation is brought home to the reader when he

    (1) asks the hall porter for the time
    (2) asks the cabdriver for a drink
    (3) talks to himself
    (4) fights off sleep
    (5) compares himself to a foal's mother

GO ON TO THE NEXT PAGE

TEST 4: LANGUAGE ARTS, READING

Questions 11–15 refer to the following excerpt from a work of prose nonfiction.

HOW DID A MOTHER AND A SON REACT TO A TRAGEDY?

After living nearly two years in Cairo, I had brought my son Guy to enter the University of Ghana in Accra. Guy was seventeen and quick. I was thirty-three and
(5) determined. We were Black Americans in West Africa, where for the first time in our lives the color of our skin was accepted as correct and normal. The future was plump with promise. For two days Guy and I
(10) laughed. On the third day, Guy, on a pleasure outing, was injured in an automobile accident. One arm and one leg were fractured and his neck was broken.

July and August stretched out like fat men
(15) yawning after a sumptuous dinner. They had every right to gloat, for they had eaten me up. Gobbled me down. Consumed my spirit, not in a wild rush, but slowly, with the obscene patience of certain victors. I
(20) became a shadow walking in the white hot streets, and a dark spectre in the hospital.

Trying utterly, I could not match Guy's stoicism. He lay calm, in a prison of plaster from which only his face and one leg and
(25) arm were visible. His assurances that he would heal and be better than new drove me into a faithless silence.

Admittedly, Guy lived with the knowledge that an unexpected sneeze could force the
(30) fractured vertebrae against his spinal cord, and he would be paralyzed or die immediately, but he had only an infatuation with life. He hadn't lived long enough to fall in love with this brutally delicious experience.
(35) He could lightly waft away to another place, if there really was another place, where his youthful innocence would assure him wings, a harp, and an absence of nostalgic yearning. My wretchedness reminded me
(40) that, on the other hand, I would be rudderless. We had been each other's home and center for seventeen years. He could die if he wanted to and go off to wherever dead folks go, but I, I would be left without a
(45) home.

—Maya Angelou

11. The narrator notes that there are differences between herself and Guy in both age and

   (1) education
   (2) temperament
   (3) intelligence
   (4) agility
   (5) devotion

12. Which literary device is used in line 14?

   (1) understatement
   (2) hyperbole
   (3) simile
   (4) onomatopoeia
   (5) metaphor

13. The word *they*, as used in line 15, is intended to mean the

   (1) certain victors
   (2) days of July and August
   (3) fat men
   (4) narrator's thoughts
   (5) West Africans

14. The narrator portrays the delicate nature of her son's life with the words

   (1) "seventeen and quick"
   (2) "dark spectre"
   (3) "hadn't lived long"
   (4) "lightly waft away"
   (5) "infatuation with life"

15. What does the imagery in lines 19 and 21 convey about the narrator's situation?

   (1) Her sudden helplessness seemed unreal.
   (2) Her physical health had deteriorated.
   (3) She was a Black American walking freely in a once white-only area.
   (4) She was undefeated by the adversity of life.
   (5) She was uncertain about her future.

GO ON TO THE NEXT PAGE

TEST 4: LANGUAGE ARTS, READING

Questions 16–20 are based on the following poem.

WHAT IS IT LIKE WHEN ELECTRIC POLES REPLACE TREES?

On their sides, resembling fallen timbers
    without rough
Barks—a hundred feet apart—lie power
    poles.
Just yesterday, this road was edged
    With eucalyptus; in aisles
Between rows of trees, seats for the aged.
Now tree odors hover in the air, residues of
    life.
The poles are erected. The frigid,
    Passionless verticals
        Strive
To fill the socket-shaped holes
Left by trees. Identical, cement-wedged
Below, parasitically fastened to live wires
    above,
Tree imposters, never to be budged
    From a telegraphic owl's
Knowitallness, they stand—rigid!
Sad children, wishing to climb, scan the
    miles
And miles of uninterrupted electric forests for
    leaves.

16. Which phrase best expresses the ideas of this poem?

    (1) the new trees
    (2) the promising verticals
    (3) improving the landscape
    (4) on climbing trees
    (5) tree odors

17. The poet seems to resent the power poles'

    (1) rough barks
    (2) new odors
    (3) lifelessness
    (4) expensiveness
    (5) electric charge

18. In this poem, the children are sad because

    (1) the poles are too slippery to climb
    (2) the poles are too rigid to climb
    (3) they have been forbidden to climb the poles
    (4) the poles have replaced the trees
    (5) they have grown to love the owls

19. The poet's point of view is expressed by the use of such phrases as

    (1) fallen timbers
    (2) power poles
    (3) passionless verticals
    (4) socket-shaped holes
    (5) live wires

20. An example of a poetic figure of speech is found in the words

    (1) tree odors
    (2) cement-wedged
    (3) tree imposters
    (4) sad children
    (5) scan the miles

GO ON TO THE NEXT PAGE

TEST 4: LANGUAGE ARTS, READING

Questions 21 to 25 refer to the following poem.

WHAT IS THE REACTION OF A TEACHER TO HIS STUDENT'S DEATH?

I remember the neckcurls, limp and damp
    as tendrils;
And her quick look, a sidelong pickerel
    smile;
(5) And how, once startled into talk, the light
    syllables leaped for her,
And she balanced in the delight of her
    thought,
A wren, happy, tail into the wind,
(10) Her song trembling the twigs and small
    branches.
The shade sang with her;
The leaves, their whispers turned to kissing;
And the mold sang in the bleached valleys
(15)   under the rose.

Oh, when she was sad, she cast herself
    down into such a pure depth,
Even a father could not find her:
Scraping her cheek against straw;
(20) Stirring the clearest water.

My sparrow, you are not here,
Waiting like a fern, making a spiny shadow.
The sides of wet stones cannot console me,
Nor the moss, wound with the last light.

(25) If only I could nudge you from this sleep,
My maimed darling, my skittery pigeon.
Over this damp grave I speak the words of
    my love:
I, with no rights in this matter,
(30) Neither father nor lover.
       —Theodore Roethke, "Elegy for Jane"

21. The poet wrote this poem mainly to

    (1) describe Jane
    (2) criticize Jane
    (3) mourn Jane
    (4) remember Jane
    (5) forget Jane

22. The poet's feeling for Jane, as indicated in the poem, is one of

    (1) awe
    (2) reverence
    (3) regret
    (4) nostalgia
    (5) love

23. To what does the poet repeatedly compare Jane?

    (1) a flower
    (2) a shooting star
    (3) a bird
    (4) a small pet
    (5) a lovely song

24. The change that takes place in the poem starting on line 21 is that the poet

    (1) becomes resigned
    (2) recollects further details
    (3) compares himself to a father
    (4) talks directly to the dead student
    (5) becomes more angry at his loss

25. The poem is powerful in its impact on the reader because the poet feels he

    (1) is like a father to Jane
    (2) is like a lover to Jane
    (3) is like a teacher to Jane
    (4) has no right to write the poem
    (5) is responsible for her tragedy

GO ON TO THE NEXT PAGE

TEST 4: LANGUAGE ARTS, READING

Questions 26–30 refer to the following excerpt from a play.

HOW DOES THE FAMILY RESPOND TO LINDNER'S OFFER?

WALTER: I mean—I have worked as a chauffeur most of my life—and my wife here, she does domestic work in people's
(5) kitchens. So does my mother, I mean—we are plain people . . .

LINDNER: Yes, Mr. Younger—

WALTER: [*Really like a small boy, looking down at his shoes and then up
(10) at the man*] And—uh—well, my father, well, he was a laborer most of his life.

LINDNER: [*Absolutely confused*] Uh, yes—

WALTER: [*Looking down at his toes once
(15) again*] My father almost beat a man to death once because this man called him a bad name or something, you know what I mean?

(20) LINDNER: No, I'm afraid I don't.

WALTER: [*Finally straightening up*] Well, what I means is that we come from people who had a lot of pride. I mean—we are very
(25) proud people. And that's my sister over there and she's going to be a doctor—and we are very proud—

LINDNER: Well—I am sure that is very
(30) nice, but—

WALTER: [*Starting to cry and facing the man eye to eye*] What I am telling you is that we called you over here to tell you that we are
(35) very proud and that this is—this is my son, who makes the sixth generation of our family in this country, and that we have all thought about your offer and we
(40) have decided to move into our house because my father—my father—he earned it. [MAMA *has her eyes closed and is rocking back and forth as though she
(45) were in church, with her head*

nodding the amen yes] We don't want to make no trouble for nobody or fight no causes— but we will try to be good
(50) neighbors. That's all we got to say. [*He looks the man absolutely in the eyes*] We don't want your money. [*He turns and walks away from the man*]

(55) LINDNER: [*Looking around at all of them*] I take it then that you have decided to occupy.

BENEATHA: That's what the man said.

LINDNER: [*To* MAMA *in her reverie*] Then I
(60) would like to appeal to you, Mrs. Younger. You are older and wiser and understand things better I am sure...

MAMA: [*Rising*] I am afraid you don't
(65) understand. My son said we was going to move and there ain't nothing left for me to say. [*Shaking her head with double meaning*] You know how these
(70) young folks is nowadays, mister. Can't do a thing with 'em. Good-bye.

LINDNER: [*Folding up his materials*] Well— if you are that final about it...
(75) There is nothing left for me to say. [*He finishes. He is almost ignored by the family who are concentrating on* WALTER LEE. *At the door* LINDNER *halts and looks
(80) around*] I sure hope you people know what you're doing. [*He shakes his head and exits*]

—Lorraine Hansberry, *A Raisin in the Sun*

26. The story Walter tells about his father almost beating a man to death for calling him a name is

   (1) an anecdote
   (2) a lie
   (3) a warning
   (4) a dream
   (5) an allusion

GO ON TO THE NEXT PAGE

TEST 4: LANGUAGE ARTS, READING

27. From this point on, the family will

    (1) stay in the ghetto
    (2) try for a new life
    (3) sell their house
    (4) retreat to the South
    (5) fight for causes

28. After this incident, the head of the house will be

    (1) Travis
    (2) Mama
    (3) Walter
    (4) Ruth
    (5) Beneatha

29. Mr. Lindner

    (1) understands the Youngers
    (2) despises the Youngers
    (3) is sympathetic to the Youngers
    (4) is tolerant of the Youngers
    (5) disagrees with the Youngers

30. The word that best describes Walter's family is

    (1) plain
    (2) vicious
    (3) proud
    (4) trouble-making
    (5) uncooperative

Questions 31–35 refer to the following passage.

HOW DOES AN INDIAN CHIEF REMEMBER HIS CHILDHOOD?

I have acted in the movies and in Wild West shows, and served as an interpreter between the Indian and the White man. I have met presidents and kings, writers, scientists, and artists. I have had much joy and received many honors, but I have never forgotten my wild, free childhood when I lived in a tepee and heard the calling of the coyotes under the stars . . . when the night winds, the sun, and everything else in our primitive world reflected the wisdom and benevolence of the Great Spirit. I remember seeing my mother bending over an open fire toasting buffalo meat, and my father returning at night with an antelope on his shoulder. I remember playing with the other children on the banks of a clean river, and I shall never forget when my grandfather taught me how to make a bow and arrow from hard wood and flint, and a fishhook from the rib of a field mouse. I am not sentimental but memories haunt me as I review scenes from those days before I was old enough to understand that all Indian things would pass away.

The average American child of today would enjoy the privileges I had out there on the unspoiled prairie one hundred years ago. I was usually awake in time to see the sun rise. If the weather was warm, I went down to the river that flowed near our village and dipped water out of it with my hands for a drink, then plunged into it. The river came down out of the hills, ferrying leaves, blossoms, and driftwood. Fish could be seen in the pools formed near the rapids over which it rippled. Birds nested and flew among the banks, and occasionally I would see a coon or a fox in the brush. Hawks circled overhead, searching the ground for mice or other small animals for their breakfast, or to feed the young in their nests. There were never enough hours in a day to exhaust the pleasure of observing every living creature—from the orb spider spinning his magic and all but invisible web to the bald eagles on their bulky nests atop the tallest trees, teaching fledglings how to eject safely.

—Memoirs of Chief Red Fox

31. The mood of the selection is one of

    (1) nostalgia
    (2) bitterness
    (3) resignation
    (4) envy
    (5) anticipation

GO ON TO THE NEXT PAGE

TEST 4: LANGUAGE ARTS, READING

32. One of the most important of the chief's memories is that of

    (1) Wild West shows
    (2) many honors
    (3) meeting presidents and kings
    (4) family members
    (5) coyotes

33. The writer's primitive world was characterized by

    (1) evidence of the Great Spirit
    (2) fishhooks
    (3) bow and arrow
    (4) the call of the coyotes
    (5) night winds

34. The writer's love of nature led him to

    (1) observe it closely
    (2) benefit from its warmth
    (3) collect specimens
    (4) search for small animals
    (5) sleep late

35. Nature a hundred years ago was preferable to nature today because it was more

    (1) varied
    (2) wild
    (3) magical
    (4) friendly
    (5) unspoiled

Questions 36–40 refer to the following commentary on the plays *Romeo and Juliet* and *West Side Story*.

HOW DO *ROMEO AND JULIET* AND *WEST SIDE STORY* COMPARE?

What glorious verse falls from the lips of Shakespeare's boys and girls! True, there is a rollicking jazzy vigor in such songs of *West Side Story* as the one of Officer Krupke, but it
(5) pales alongside the pyrotechnical display of Mercurio's Queen Mab speech. There is tenderness in "Maria," but how relatively tongue-tied is the twentieth-century hero alongside the boy who cried, "He jests at scars
(10) that never felt a wound." "Hold my hand and we're halfway there," say Maria and Tony to each other, and the understatement touches us. But "Gallop apace, you fiery-footed steeds" and the lines that follow glow with a glory that
(15) never diminishes. The comparisons of language could be multiplied, and always, of course, Shakespeare is bound to win.

Without its great poetry *Romeo and Juliet* would not be a major tragedy. Possibly it is
(20) not, in any case; for as has frequently been remarked, Shakespeare's hero and heroine are a little too slender to carry the full weight of tragic grandeur. Their plight is more pathetic than tragic. If this is true of them, it
(25) is equally true of Tony and Maria: for them, too, pathos rather than tragedy. But there is tragedy implicit in the environmental situation of the contemporary couple, and this must not be overlooked or underestimated.
(30) Essentially, however, what we see is that all four young people strive to consummate the happiness at the threshold on which they stand and which they have tasted so briefly. All four are deprived of the opportunity to do
(35) so, the Renaissance couple by the caprice of fate, today's youngsters by the prejudice and hatred engendered around them. All four are courageous and lovable. All four arouse our compassion, even though they may not
(40) shake us with Aristotelian fear.

Poets and playwrights will continue to write of youthful lovers whom fate drives into and out of each other's lives. The spectacle will always trouble and move us.

GO ON TO THE NEXT PAGE

TEST 4: LANGUAGE ARTS, READING

36. The author of the selection implies that

    (1) the songs of *West Side Story* lack strength
    (2) the language of *West Side Story* leaves us cold
    (3) the language of *Romeo and Juliet* lacks the vigor of that of *West Side Story*
    (4) the poetry of *Romeo and Juliet* will prevail
    (5) the speech of *West Side Story* can compete with the verse of *Romeo and Juliet*

37. In comparing the language of *Romeo and Juliet* with that of *West Side Story* the author

    (1) takes no position
    (2) likes each equally
    (3) favors that of *Romeo and Juliet*
    (4) favors that of *West Side Story*
    (5) downplays the differences

38. Both plays share a common weakness. That weakness is

    (1) the stature of their heroes and heroines
    (2) the absence of deep emotion
    (3) their dramatic construction
    (4) the lack of substance of their themes
    (5) the lack of linguistic power

39. The couples in the two plays share all of the following EXCEPT

    (1) a pathetic situation
    (2) lack of opportunity to achieve happiness
    (3) courage
    (4) inability to instill fear in the reader
    (5) inability to arouse pity in the reader

40. The couples in the two plays differ in the nature of

    (1) their plight
    (2) their ultimate fate
    (3) the cause of their tragic situation
    (4) their attractiveness
    (5) their love for one another

END OF EXAMINATION

TEST 5: MATHEMATICS

Directions

The Mathematics test consists of multiple-choice and alternate format questions intended to measure general mathematics skills and problem-solving ability. The questions are based on short readings that often include a graph, chart, or diagram.

You should spend no more than 45 minutes answering the questions. Work carefully, but do not spend too much time on any one question. Be sure you answer every question. You will not be penalized for incorrect answers.

Formulas you may need are given on page 81. Only some of the questions will require you to use a formula. Not all the formulas given will be needed.

Some questions contain more information than you will need to solve the problem. Other questions do not give enough information to solve the problem. If the question does not give enough information to solve the problem, the correct answer is "Not enough information is given."

You may use a calculator on Part I.

To record your answers, mark the numbered space on the answer sheet beside the number that corresponds to the question in the test.

FOR EXAMPLE:

If a grocery bill totaling $15.75 is paid with a $20.00 bill, how much change should be returned?

(1) $5.26
(2) $4.75
(3) $4.25   ① ② ● ④ ⑤
(4) $3.75
(5) $3.25

The correct answer is "$4.25"; therefore, answer space 3 would be marked on the answer sheet.

GO ON TO THE NEXT PAGE

TEST 5: MATHEMATICS

FORMULAS

Description	Formula
AREA (*A*) of a:	
square	$A = s^2$; where s = side
rectangle	$A = lw$; where l = length, w = width
parallelogram	$A = bh$; where b = base, h = height
triangle	$A = \frac{1}{2} bh$; where b = base, h = height
trapezoid	$A = \frac{1}{2}(b_1 + b_2) \, h$; where b = base, h = height
circle	$A = \pi r^2$; where π = 3.14, r = radius
PERIMETER (*P*) of a:	
square	$P = 4s$; where s = side
rectangle	$P = 2l + 2w$; where l = length, w = width
triangle	$P = a + b + c$; where a, b, and c are the sides
circumference (*C*) of a circle	$C = \pi d$; where π = 3.14, d = diameter
VOLUME (*V*) of a:	
cube	$V = s^3$; where s = side
rectangular container	$V = lwh$; where l = length, w = width, h = height
cylinder	$V = \pi r^2 h$; where π = 3.14, r = radius, h = height
square pyramid	$V = \frac{1}{3}(\text{base edge})^2 h$
cone	$V = \frac{1}{3} \pi r^2 h$
Pythagorean theorem	$c^2 = a^2 + b^2$; where c = hypotenuse, a and b are legs, of a right triangle
distance (*d*) between two points in a plane	$d = \sqrt{(x_2 - x_1)^2 + (y_2 - y_1)^2}$; where (x_1,y_1) and (x_2,y_2) are two points in a plane
slope of a line (*m*)	$m = \dfrac{y_2 - y_1}{x_2 - x_1}$; where (x_1,y_1) and (x_2,y_2) are two points in a plane
MEASURES OF CENTRAL TENDENCY	mean = $\dfrac{x_1 + x_2 + \ldots + x_n}{n}$; where the x's are the values for which a mean is desired, and n = number of values in the series
	median = the point in an ordered set of numbers at which half of the numbers are above and half of the numbers are below this value
simple interest (*i*)	$i = prt$; where p = principal, r = rate, t = time
distance (*d*) as function of rate and time	$d = rt$; where r = rate, t = time
total cost (*c*)	$c = nr$; where n = number of units, r = cost per unit

GO ON TO THE NEXT PAGE

TEST 5: MATHEMATICS, PART I

Directions: You will have 45 minutes to complete this section. You may use a calculator.

1. On 5 successive days a deliveryman listed his mileage as follows: 135, 162, 98, 117, 216. If his truck averages 14 miles for each gallon of gas used, how many gallons of gas did he use during these 5 days?

   (1) 42
   (2) 52
   (3) 115
   (4) 147
   (5) 153

2. Parking meters in Springfield read: "12 minutes for 5¢. Maximum deposit 50¢." What is the maximum time, in hours, that a driver may be legally parked at one of these meters?

   (1) 1
   (2) 1.2
   (3) 12
   (4) 2
   (5) Not enough information is given.

Question 3 is based on the following figure.

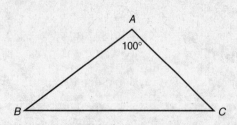

3. If $AB = AC$ and m $\angle A = 100°$, what is the measure of $\angle B$ in degrees?
   Mark your answer in the circles on the grid on the answer sheet.

4. The ABC Department Store had a special sale on shirts. One group sold at $15 per shirt, and another group sold at $18 per shirt. If 432 shirts were sold at $15 each and 368 shirts were sold at $18 each, the number of dollars taken in at the shirt sale may be represented as

   (1) $800(15 + 18)$
   (2) $(15)(368) + (18)(432)$
   (3) $(15)(800) + (18)(800)$
   (4) $33(432 + 68)$
   (5) $(15)(432) + (368)(18)$

5. A hockey team won X games, lost Y games, and tied Z games. What fractional part of the games played were won?

   (1) $\dfrac{X}{X + Y + Z}$

   (2) $\dfrac{X}{XYZ}$

   (3) $\dfrac{X}{XY}$

   (4) $\dfrac{X}{X + Y}$

   (5) $\dfrac{X}{X - Y - Z}$

6. One-half the students at Madison High School walk to school. One-fourth of the rest go to school by bicycle. What part of the school population travels by some other means?
   Mark your answer in the circles on the grid on the answer sheet.

GO ON TO THE NEXT PAGE

TEST 5: MATHEMATICS, PART I

7. Which of the following graphs shows the solution set for the inequality $2x > 4$?

(1)

(2)

(3)

(4)

(5)

8. An aquarium is in the form of a rectangular solid. The aquarium is 3 feet long, 1 foot 8 inches wide, and 1 foot 6 inches high. What is the volume, in cubic feet, of the aquarium?

   (1) 6.16
   (2) 6.4
   (3) 7.5
   (4) 7.875
   (5) 8.64

9. A flagpole casts a shadow 16 feet long. At the same time, a pole 9 feet high casts a shadow 6 feet long. What is the height, in feet, of the flagpole?

   (1) 18
   (2) 19
   (3) 20
   (4) 24
   (5) Not enough information is given.

10. The enrollment of a college is distributed as follows:

    360 freshmen
    300 sophomores
    280 juniors
    260 seniors

    The freshman class makes up what percent of the total enrollment?

    (1) 18%
    (2) 20%
    (3) 25%
    (4) 30%
    (5) Not enough information is given.

11. A purse contains 6 nickels, 5 dimes, and 8 quarters. If one coin is drawn at random from the purse, what is the probability that the coin drawn is a dime?

    (1) $\frac{5}{19}$
    (2) $\frac{5}{14}$
    (3) $\frac{5}{8}$
    (4) $\frac{5}{6}$
    (5) $\frac{19}{5}$

12. The leaders in the Peninsula Golf Tournament finished with scores of 272, 284, 287, 274, 275, 283, 278, 276, and 281. What is the median of these scores?

    (1) 273
    (2) 274
    (3) 276
    (4) 278
    (5) 280

13. The cost of a dozen ballpoint pens and 8 pencils is $4.60. If the cost of the pens is 3 for $0.97, what is the cost, in cents, of 1 pencil?

    (1) 6
    (2) 8
    (3) 8.5
    (4) 9
    (5) 9.5

14. The scale on a map is 1 inch = 150 miles. The cities of Benton and Dover are $3\frac{1}{2}$ inches apart on this map. What is the actual distance, in miles, between Benton and Dover?

    Mark your answer in the circles on the grid on the answer sheet.

GO ON TO THE NEXT PAGE

TEST 5: MATHEMATICS, PART I

Question 15 is based on the following figure.

15. What is the perimeter of the figure?

    (1) $8a + 5b$

    (2) $9a + 7b$

    (3) $7a + 5b$

    (4) $6a + 6b$

    (5) $8a + 6b$

Question 16 is based on the following chart.

SPEAKER SALE	
1/3 off listed prices	
40 Watts	$159.99
60 Watts	$183.99
80 Watts	$219.99
All Installations	$150

16. Kirsten wants to purchase a pair of car speakers. The list above indicates prices for each pair, not including the 1/3 discount. If she buys the 40-watt speakers at the discounted price and has them installed, what will her total bill be, including 8% sales tax?

    (1) over $400

    (2) between $225 and $250

    (3) between $250 and $260

    (4) between $260 and $270

    (5) between $270 and $280

17. The Men's Shop advertised a spring sale, including the following sale items.

    ties: 3 for $23
    shirts: 3 for $43
    slacks: $32.75 per pair
    jackets: $58.45 each

    What is the price of 6 ties, 3 shirts, 2 pairs of slacks, and 1 jacket?

    (1) $157.20

    (2) $180.20

    (3) $189.95

    (4) $202.95

    (5) $212.95

18. In which of the following lists are the numbers written in order from greatest to smallest?

    (1) $0.80, 19\%, 0.080, \frac{1}{2}, \frac{3}{5}$

    (2) $0.80, \frac{1}{2}, 0.080, \frac{3}{5}, 19\%$

    (3) $0.80, \frac{3}{5}, \frac{1}{2}, 19\%, 0.080$

    (4) $\frac{1}{2}, 0.80, \frac{3}{5}, 19\%, 0.080$

    (5) $\frac{3}{5}, \frac{1}{2}, 19\%, 0.080, 0.80$

19. If an airplane completes its flight of 1,364 miles in 5 hours and 30 minutes, what is its average speed, in miles per hour? Mark your answer in the circles on the grid on the answer sheet.

20. The distance between two heavenly bodies is 85,000,000,000 miles. This number, written in scientific notation, is

    (1) 8.5×10^{-10}

    (2) 8.5×10^{10}

    (3) 85×10^{9}

    (4) 0.85×10^{-9}

    (5) 850×10^{7}

GO ON TO THE NEXT PAGE

TEST 5: MATHEMATICS, PART I

21. What is the value of $3ab - x^2y$ if $a = 4$, $b = 5$, $y = 3$, and $x = 2$?

    (1) 18

    (2) 24

    (3) 48

    (4) 54

    (5) 72

Question 22 is based on the following graph.

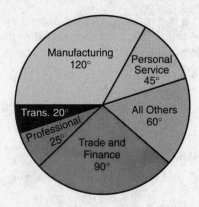

This circle graph shows how 180,000 wage earners in a certain city earned their livings during a given period.

22. The number of persons engaged in transportation in the city during this period was?

    Mark your answer in the circles on the grid on the answer sheet.

23. A hiker walks 12 miles due north. Then he turns and walks 16 miles due east. At this point, how many miles is the hiker from his starting point?

    (1) 12

    (2) 16

    (3) 18

    (4) 20

    (5) Not enough information is given.

Question 24 is based on the following figure.

24. If $\overline{BF}$ bisects $\angle ABC$, $\overline{CD}$ bisects $\angle ACB$, m$\angle ABC = 68°$, and m$\angle ACB = 72°$, then m$\angle BEC =$

    (1) 90°

    (2) 98°

    (3) 100°

    (4) 110°

    (5) 120°

25. The dimensions of the hallway below are 6.5 ft. and 7.2 ft. If the area is to be covered with carpet at $2.10 per square foot, how much would carpeting for the hallway cost?

Mark your answer in the circles on the grid on the answer sheet.

GO ON TO THE NEXT PAGE

TEST 5: MATHEMATICS, PART II

Directions: You will have 45 minutes to complete questions 26–50. You may NOT use a calculator; otherwise, directions are the same as in Part I. You MAY refer to the *Formulas* sheet.

26. John weighed 192 pounds. His doctor put him on a diet, which enabled him to lose at least 4 pounds per month. What was John's exact weight after 6 months on the diet?

    (1) 160 lb.
    (2) 165 lb.
    (3) 167 lb.
    (4) 168 lb.
    (5) Not enough information is given.

27. Mr. Ames bought a bond for $10,000. The bond yields interest at $8\frac{1}{2}$ % annually. If the interest is paid every 6 months, how much is each interest payment in dollars?
    Mark your answer in the circles on the grid on the answer sheet.

28. Given the equation $x^2 - x - 12 = 0$, which of the following give(s) a complete solution of the equation?

    (1) 4 only
    (2) −4 only
    (3) 3 and 4
    (4) −3 and 4
    (5) −4 and 3

29. The ratio of men to women at a professional meeting was 9:2. If there were 12 women at the meeting. Which equation could be used to find the number of men at the meeting?

    (1) $\frac{12}{x} = \frac{9}{2}$
    (2) $24x = 180$
    (3) $\frac{9}{2} = \frac{x}{12}$
    (4) $7x = 24 + 9$
    (5) Not enough information is given.

30. What is the slope of the line that passes through point A (2,1) and point B (4,7)?

    (1) $\frac{1}{3}$
    (2) $\frac{2}{3}$
    (3) $\frac{3}{2}$
    (4) 2
    (5) 3

31. In a basketball game Bill scored three times as many points as Jim. Together they scored 56 points. How many points did Bill score?

    (1) 14
    (2) 28
    (3) 42
    (4) 48
    (5) Not enough information is given.

Question 32 is based on the following graph.

32. The graph shows the lengths of some famous rivers correct to the nearest hundred miles.

    Which one of the following statements is correct?

    (1) The Thames is more than one-half as long as the Seine.
    (2) The Dnieper is 1,200 miles long.
    (3) The Euphrates is about 250 miles longer than the Rio Grande.
    (4) The Rio Grande is about 1,000 miles longer than the Seine.
    (5) The Thames is about 100 miles long.

GO ON TO THE NEXT PAGE

TEST 5: MATHEMATICS, PART II

Question 33 is based on the following graph.

RECEIPTS AND EXPENDITURES

33. The graph shows receipts and expenses for the years indicated. The receipts are designated by shaded bars and the expenses by striped bars. The year in which receipts exceeded expenses by $100,000 was

    (1) 1984
    (2) 1985
    (3) 1986
    (4) 1987
    (5) 1988

34. If 1 pencil costs y cents, then 6 pencils will cost, in cents,

    (1) $6y$

    (2) $\dfrac{y}{6}$

    (3) $\dfrac{6}{y}$

    (4) $y + 6$

    (5) $\dfrac{y}{2}$

35. Mr. Martin earns $12 per hour. One week Mr. Martin worked 42 hours; the following week he worked 37 hours. Which of the following indicates the number of dollars Mr. Martin earned for the 2 weeks?

    (1) $12 \times 2 + 37$
    (2) $12 \times 42 + 42 \times 37$
    (3) $12 \times 37 + 42$
    (4) $12 + 42 \times 37$
    (5) $12(42 + 37)$

36. Kwan's recipe for lemonade requires 8 ounces of lemon juice for every quart of water used. To prepare for a large party, he uses 4 gallons of water. How much lemon juice is needed?

    (1) 108 ounces
    (2) 5 quarts
    (3) 96 ounces
    (4) 1 gallon
    (5) $2\frac{1}{2}$ quarts

Question 37 is based on the following figure.

37. In the figure $\overrightarrow{AB} \parallel \overrightarrow{CD}$, $\overrightarrow{CE}$ bisects $\angle BCD$, and $m\angle ABC = 112°$. Find $m\angle ECD$.

    (1) 45°
    (2) 50°
    (3) 56°
    (4) 60°
    (5) Not enough information is given.

GO ON TO THE NEXT PAGE

TEST 5: MATHEMATICS, PART II

38. Mrs. Garvin buys a bolt of cloth 22 feet 4 inches in length. She cuts the bolt into four equal pieces to make drapes. What is the length of each piece?

    (1) 5 ft.

    (2) 5 ft. 7 in.

    (3) 5 ft. 9 in.

    (4) 6 ft. 7 in.

    (5) Not enough information is given.

<u>Questions 39 and 40</u> are based on the following graph.

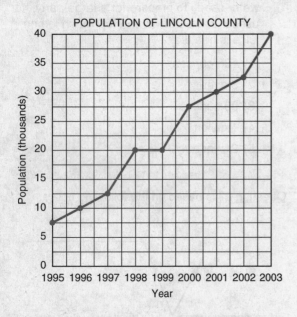

POPULATION OF LINCOLN COUNTY

The graph shows the growth in population in Lincoln County between the years 1995 and 2003.

39. What was the population of Lincoln County in the year 2000?

    (1) 20,000

    (2) 25,000

    (3) 26,000

    (4) 27,500

    (5) 30,000

40. The amount of population growth in Lincoln County between 1995 and 1996 was the same as which of the following?

    (1) 1996–1997 as well as 1997–1998

    (2) 1996–1997 as well as 2000–2001

    (3) 2000–2001 as well as 2002–2003

    (4) 1997–1998 as well as 1998–1999

    (5) 1998–1999 as well as 2000–2002

41. A box is in the form of a rectangular solid with a square base of side x units in length and a height of 8 units. The volume of the box is 392 cubic units. Which of the following equations may be used to find the value of x?

    (1) $x^2 = 392$

    (2) $8x = 392$

    (3) $8x^3 = 392$

    (4) $8x^2 = 392$

    (5) $8 + x^2 = 392$

42. There were three candidates at a school board election. Mrs. Clay received twice as many votes as Mr. Dunn, and Mr. Arnold received 66 votes more than Mr. Dunn. How many votes did Mrs. Clay receive?

    (1) 209

    (2) 275

    (3) 320

    (4) 402

    (5) Not enough information is given.

GO ON TO THE NEXT PAGE

TEST 5: MATHEMATICS, PART II

Question 43 is based on the following figure.

43. If $AB = AC$, $\overline{AD} \perp \overline{BC}$, and m∠$B$ = 68°, what is the value of x?

   (1) 12°
   (2) 22°
   (3) 32°
   (4) 44°
   (5) 68°

Question 44 is based on the following information.

In the figure below line $\overrightarrow{PQ}$ is parallel to line $\overrightarrow{RS}$.

44. What is the value of x?

   (1) 15
   (2) 20
   (3) 25
   (4) 30
   (5) 35

45. The square root of 30 is between which of the following pairs of numbers?

   (1) 3 and 4
   (2) 4 and 5
   (3) 5 and 6
   (4) 6 and 7
   (5) 15 and 16

Question 46 is based on the following figure.

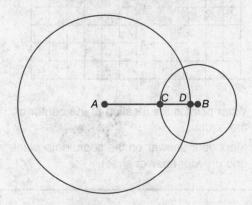

46. The radius of circle A measures 20 inches, and the radius of circle B measures 8 inches. If CD = 6 inches, find AB, in inches.

   (1) 22
   (2) 24
   (3) 25
   (4) 28
   (5) Not enough information is given.

GO ON TO THE NEXT PAGE

TEST 5: MATHEMATICS, PART II

47. The graph of a square is shown on the grid below.

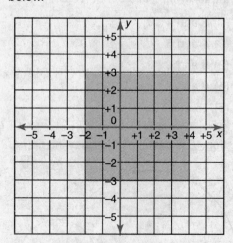

What point is the location of the center of the square?

Mark your answer on the coordinate plane grid on your answer sheet.

48. A woman buys *n* pounds of sugar at *c* cents a pound. She gives the clerk a $1.00 bill. The change she receives, in cents, is

   (1) $nc - 100$
   (2) $n + c - 100$
   (3) $100 - (n + c)$
   (4) $100 - nc$
   (5) Not enough information is given.

49. If $x = 10$, each of the following is true **EXCEPT**

   (1) $3x + 1 > 12$
   (2) $2x - 3 < 25$
   (3) $x^2 + 1 > x^2 - 1$
   (4) $4x - 1 = 39$
   (5) $2x - 7 < 7 - 2x$

Question 50 is based on the following figure.

50. Mr. Denby planned to build a house on the plot of ground shown. What is the area, in square feet, of this plot of ground?

   Mark your answer in the circles on the grid on the answer sheet.

END OF EXAMINATION

Answer Keys, Summaries of Results, and Self-Appraisal Charts

TEST 1: LANGUAGE ARTS, WRITING, PART I/PAGE 33

I. CHECK YOUR ANSWERS, using the following answer key:

1. **2**	11. **5**	20. **3**	29. **1**	38. **2**	47. **5**
2. **3**	12. **1**	21. **2**	30. **2**	39. **5**	48. **1**
3. **3**	13. **5**	22. **5**	31. **5**	40. **5**	49. **4**
4. **1**	14. **2**	23. **1**	32. **1**	41. **1**	50. **1**
5. **5**	15. **2**	24. **3**	33. **2**	42. **4**	
6. **5**	16. **3**	25. **5**	34. **4**	43. **3**	
7. **1**	17. **5**	26. **5**	35. **3**	44. **1**	
8. **3**	18. **1**	27. **4**	36. **2**	45. **5**	
9. **5**	19. **4**	28. **1**	37. **4**	46. **2**	
10. **4**					

II. SCORE YOURSELF:

Number correct:

Excellent _____
45–50

Good _____
39–44

Fair _____
33–38

III. EVALUATE YOUR SCORE: Did you get at least 35 correct answers? If not, you need more practice for the Language Arts, Writing, Part I test. In any event, you can improve your performance to Excellent or Good by analyzing your errors.

IV. ANALYZE YOUR ERRORS: To determine your areas of weakness, list the number of correct answers you had under each of the following categories (which correspond to the content areas of the Language Arts, Writing, Part I test), and compare your score with the average scores specified in the right-hand column. Review the answer analysis section beginning on page 97 for each of the questions you got wrong, and give yourself more practice in your weak areas with the appropriate material in Unit II before attempting Practice Examination One.

Content Areas	Items	Your Score	Average Score
Sentence Structure	3, 12, 16, 25, 29, 32, 34, 38, 40, 44, 49		7
Usage	1, 8, 19, 20–21, 23–24, 30, 33, 37, 42		7
Mechanics			
Possessives/contractions/ homonyms	10, 15, 43, 50		3
Punctuation	2, 14, 26, 35, 36, 41		3
Capitalization	4		1
Organization	5, 7, 18, 28, 46, 48		4
No correction	6, 9, 11, 13, 17, 22, 27, 31, 39, 45, 47		7

Total _____

TEST 2: SOCIAL STUDIES/PAGE 45

I. CHECK YOUR ANSWERS, using the following answer key:

1. **1**	11. **1**	21. **1**	31. **3**	41. **5**
2. **4**	12. **3**	22. **2**	32. **4**	42. **2**
3. **4**	13. **2**	23. **5**	33. **1**	43. **1**
4. **5**	14. **4**	24. **4**	34. **1**	44. **1**
5. **2**	15. **1**	25. **2**	35. **5**	45. **5**
6. **5**	16. **3**	26. **3**	36. **1**	46. **4**
7. **4**	17. **2**	27. **4**	37. **1**	47. **1**
8. **2**	18. **2**	28. **3**	38. **1**	48. **4**
9. **4**	19. **4**	29. **2**	39. **1**	49. **1**
10. **4**	20. **4**	30. **5**	40. **3**	50. **3**

II. SCORE YOURSELF:

Number correct:

Excellent _____
45–50

Good _____
40–44

Fair _____
35–39

III. EVALUATE YOUR SCORE: Did you get at least 35 correct answers? If not, you need more practice for the Social Studies test. In any event, you can improve your performance to Excellent or Good by analyzing your errors.

II. ANALYZE YOUR ERRORS: To determine your specific weaknesses, list the number of correct answers you had under each of the following categories (which correspond to the content areas of the Social Studies test), and compare your score with the average scores specified in the right-hand column. Review the answer analysis section beginning on page 99 for each of the questions you got wrong, and give yourself more practice in your weak area with the appropriate material in Unit IV (including the "Glossary of Social Studies Terms") before attempting Practice Examination One.

Content Areas	Items	Your Score	Average Score
Political Science	1–3, 12, 29–31, 34, 41–43, 44, 48–49		8
Economics	4–6, 9, 17–19, 21–22, 24 26–28, 35–37, 39–40		10
History	15–16, 20, 25, 32–33, 38, 50		5
Geography	7–8, 10–11, 13–14, 23, 45–47		7

Total _____

TEST 3: SCIENCE/PAGE 56

I. CHECK YOUR ANSWERS, using the following answer key:

1. **3**	12. **2**	23. **3**	34. **3**	45. **4**	56. **2**
2. **1**	13. **4**	24. **5**	35. **5**	46. **3**	57. **4**
3. **2**	14. **2**	25. **3**	36. **5**	47. **3**	58. **1**
4. **4**	15. **2**	26. **5**	37. **3**	48. **2**	59. **2**
5. **4**	16. **2**	27. **4**	38. **4**	49. **2**	60. **2**
6. **4**	17. **1**	28. **3**	39. **3**	50. **2**	61. **2**
7. **4**	18. **2**	29. **4**	40. **3**	51. **5**	62. **3**
8. **3**	19. **4**	30. **5**	41. **1**	52. **3**	63. **1**
9. **2**	20. **1**	31. **5**	42. **3**	53. **4**	64. **2**
10. **3**	21. **2**	32. **4**	43. **5**	54. **5**	65. **2**
11. **2**	22. **1**	33. **1**	44. **1**	55. **5**	66. **4**

II. SCORE YOURSELF:

Number correct:

Excellent _____
60–66

Good _____
49–59

Fair _____
40–48

III. EVALUATE YOUR SCORE: Did you get at least 40 correct answers? If not, you need more practice for the Science test. In any event, you can improve your performance to Excellent or Good by analyzing your errors.

IV. ANALYZE YOUR ERRORS: To determine your specific weaknesses, encircle the number of each question that you got wrong. This will reveal the specific science area that needs emphasis in planning your study program. After studying the answer analysis section beginning on page 102 for each of the questions you got wrong, list the terms that you feel need further explanation and study them in the "Glossary of Scientific Terms." Then give yourself more practice in your weak areas with the appropriate material in Unit V before attempting Practice Examination One.

Content Areas	Items	Your Score	Average Score
Biology	1–4, 24–39, 41–43, 45–49, 59, 61–66		24
Earth Science	9–13, 17–19, 40, 44, 55–58		7
Chemistry	20–23, 44, 50–52		6
Physics	5–8, 14–16, 53–54, 60		7

Total _____

TEST 4: LANGUAGE ARTS, READING/PAGE 70

I. CHECK YOUR ANSWERS, using the following answer key:

1. **2**	9. **3**	17. **3**	25. **4**	32. **4**	39. **4**
2. **4**	10. **5**	18. **4**	26. **3**	33. **1**	40. **3**
3. **1**	11. **2**	19. **3**	27. **2**	34. **1**	
4. **1**	12. **3**	20. **3**	28. **3**	35. **5**	
5. **2**	13. **2**	21. **3**	29. **5**	36. **4**	
6. **3**	14. **4**	22. **5**	30. **3**	37. **3**	
7. **1**	15. **1**	23. **3**	31. **1**	38. **1**	
8. **2**	16. **1**	24. **4**			

II. SCORE YOURSELF:

Number correct:

Excellent _____
36–40

Good _____
32–35

Fair _____
28–31

III. EVALUATE YOUR SCORE: Did you get at least 28 correct answers? If not, you need more practice for the test on Language Arts, Reading. In any event, you can improve your performance to Excellent or Good by analyzing your errors.

IV. ANALYZE YOUR ERRORS: To determine your specific weaknesses, first list the number of correct answers you had under each of the following categories and compare your score with the average scores specified in the right-hand column. After studying the answer analysis section beginning on page 105 for each of the questions you got wrong, study the material in the section *Basic Reading Skills* and the section *Reading Prose, Poetry, and Drama* in Unit VI as well as the "Glossary of Literary Terms" to strengthen your weak areas before attempting Practice Examination One.

Reading Skills	Items	Your Score	Average Score
Locating the Main Idea	5, 16, 21		3
Finding Details	2, 12, 17–18, 23–24, 32–33, 38–40		11
Inferring Meaning	1, 13–15, 19–20, 22, 34–35		6
Making Inferences	3, 4, 7, 10, 25, 36–37		5
Determining Tone and Mood	6, 9, 26–27, 31		4
Inferring Character	11, 28–30		3
Inferring Setting	8		1

Total _____

Now, to see how your scores in the content area of Language Arts, Reading test compare with the average scores in the right-hand column, list your score for each of the following:

Literary Forms	Items	Your Score	Average Score
Prose Fiction	6–15		7
Prose Nonfiction	1–5, 31–40		17
Poetry	16–25		7
Drama	26–30		3

Total _____

TEST 5: MATHEMATICS/PAGE 80

I. CHECK YOUR ANSWERS, using the following answer key:

1. **2**	11. **1**	21. **3**	31. **3**	41. **4**
2. **4**	12. **4**	22. **10,000**	32. **4**	42. **5**
3. **40**	13. **4**	23. **4**	33. **5**	43. **2**
4. **5**	14. **525**	24. **4**	34. **1**	44. **3**
5. **1**	15. **2**	25. **98.28**	35. **5**	45. **3**
6. **3/8, or .375**	16. **5**	26. **5**	36. **4**	46. **1**
7. **5**	17. **5**	27. **425**	37. **3**	47. **(1,0)**
8. **3**	18. **3**	28. **4**	38. **2**	48. **4**
9. **4**	19. **248**	29. **3**	39. **4**	49. **5**
10. **4**	20. **2**	30. **5**	40. **2**	50. **10,400**

II. SCORE YOURSELF:

Number correct:

Excellent _____
40–50

Good _____
32–49

Fair _____
28–31

III. EVALUATE YOUR SCORE: Did you get at least 28 correct answers? If not, you need more practice for the Mathematics test. In any event, you can improve your performance to Excellent or Good by analyzing your errors.

IV. ANALYZE YOUR ERRORS: To determine your specific weakness, list the number of correct answers you had under each of the following skill areas, and compare your score with the average scores specified in the right-hand column. After studying the answer analysis section beginning on page 106 for each of the questions you got wrong, give yourself more practice in your weak areas with the appropriate material in Unit VII before attempting Practice Examination One.

Content Areas	Items	Your Score	Average Score
Numbers and Basic Operations	1, 2, 4, 12, 19, 26, 35, 45		5
Fractions and Measurements	6, 11, 36, 38		2
Decimals and Percents	10, 13, 18, 20, 27, 29		3
Data Analysis	14, 16, 17, 22, 32, 33, 39, 40		4
Algebra	5, 7, 8, 15, 21, 28, 31, 34, 41, 42, 48, 49		7
Geometry	3, 9, 23, 24, 25, 30, 37, 43, 44, 46, 47, 50		7

Total _____

YOUR TOTAL GED SCORE

The Language Arts, Writing Test   _____

The Social Studies Test   _____

The Science Test   _____

The Language Arts, Reading Test   _____

The Mathematics Test   _____

Total _____

Answer Analysis

TEST 1: LANGUAGE ARTS, WRITING, PART I/PAGE 33

1. **2** There is an error in usage. The subject of the sentence is *combination*, which is singular. A singular verb, *makes*, is required for agreement.

2. **3** The error is in punctuation. A comma is needed to set off an introductory phrase.

3. **3** There is a sentence fragment beginning with *seldom*. This is corrected by removing the period and joining the fragment to the rest of the sentence.

4. **1** There is an error in capitalization. Seasons are *not* capitalized.

5. **5** This paragraph has one main idea and cannot be divided in two.

6. **5** No correction is necessary.

7. **1** The first sentence makes a general statement about the attributes of vegetable gardening. The other sentences in the paragraph support this main idea.

8. **3** The usage error is in the shift in person in two pronouns that refer to the same person. The second-person pronoun *your* in the introductory clause requires a continuation of the second person, *you*, in the main clause.

9. **5** No change is necessary.

10. **4** The correct homonym is *their*, meaning belonging to them. The computers belong to them (families).

11. **5** No correction is necessary.

12. **1** The original is correct. Two sentences are needed.

13. **5** No correction is necessary.

14. **2** A comma is required to set off items in a series.

15. **2** There is no need for an apostrophe in *releases*. The verb must agree with its subject, and in this sentence, both should be singular.

16. **3** The meaning of the sentence requires *may be served*.

17. **5** No correction is necessary.

18. **1** Sentence 9 should be left as it is because it elaborates on *discretionary time* in the previous sentence.

19. **4** There is an error in usage. Parallel structure requires the use of infinitives: *to develop, to increase, to learn* (rather than *learning*).

20. **3** The sentence requires the use of *there are* rather than *they are (they're)*. *They are a number of...steps* doesn't make sense.

21. **2** The pronoun *they* agrees with plural noun *measures*.

22. **5** No correction is necessary.

23. **1** The subject of the sentence is you (understood). Therefore, the verb to agree with a singular subject is *take*.

24. **3** The future tense should be used for an action taking place in the future, that is, when you take the car in.

25. **5** Two sentences are necessary to correct the run-on sentence. To accomplish this, a period after *order* and a capitalized *That* are needed.

26. **5** No correction is necessary.

27. **4** The correct spelling is *determined*.

28. **1** Sentence 11 should be left as it is because it is the logical last course of action for the passage.

29. **1** A comma is needed to set off items in a series.

30. **2** The plural subject *all* requires the verb *affect*.

31. **5** No correction is necessary.

32. **1** The original way is the best among the choices offered.

33. **2** *Readily* is an adverb that modifies the verb *to find*.

34. **4** The relative pronoun *that* avoids the unnecessary use of the words *such programs*.
35. **3** A semicolon is used to separate independent clauses in a sentence.
36. **2** A comma is used after an introductory clause.
37. **4** The plural subject, *some*, requires the verb *have been overcome*.
38. **2** Making "You are going to move" the subject of the verb *is* eliminates the need for "That statement" and effectively combines the two sentences.
39. **5** No correction is necessary
40. **5** *Or* is correct because "another way" to state the fact is given.
41. **1** A comma is used after an introductory phrase.
42. **4** There is more than one course of action; therefore, *courses* is the correct choice.

43. **3** The proper word for this sentence is *involve*.
44. **1** The original is correct because *or* connects two independent clauses (*has come through* is understood after *an opportunity to move to a better climate*).
45. **5** No correction is necessary.
46. **2** The main idea of this passage is that *the average person moves once every 5 years*.
47. **5** No correction is necessary.
48. **1** The first sentence tells the first step of fishing; therefore, it must be left as the first sentence of the first paragraph in order to keep the chronologic order of steps.
49. **4** Rewriting the sentence with *The next phase* as the subject requires a singular verb, *is*, in the present tense.
50. **1** A verb that agrees with a singular subject does not require an apostrophe.

TEST 1: LANGUAGE ARTS, WRITING, PART II/PAGE 44

SAMPLE ESSAY

> I remember the day that I fell of the back of my brother's bicycle. The memory is still so vivid in my mind. I will always remember it.
>
> It was a beautiful spring day in 1967 when my older brother and I decided to go bike riding on the same bike. My brother's bicycle was an old Easy Rider with a saddle seat and a fender that went over the back tire. The fender was my "seat." As I straddled the back tire on the fender and we began our journey up a large hill I remember telling him, "I'm slipping off the fender!" "Just hold on," was his reply. I tried but my little seven-year old hands just couldn't do the trick. I slid right onto the asphalt roadway. My hands and knees took the brunt of the force and as I got up I looked down to see two very badly skinned knees. Crying, my brother helped me hobble back to the house where my mother was none too sympathetic with the sight of my terribly skinned knees. In fact, she was upset with me too because I was to wear a short dress the next night for my Bible School Program. She had warned me not to ride on the back of the bike. I suppose I should have listened.
>
> What a day that was in 1967. It still seems like yesterday when I sat straddled on that old bicycle just before slipping off. I'll never forget it.

TEST 2: SOCIAL STUDIES/PAGE 45

1. **1** The last paragraph of the passage states clearly that the governor's veto power is not used sparingly, and that more than one out of four bills fails to receive approval.

2. **4** The second paragraph of the selection deals with the "30 day" rule. The first sentence of this paragraph states that all bills passed within the last ten days of the legislative session are covered by this rule.

3. **4** The first sentence of the first paragraph states that the governor has the power to veto single items of the budget bill. This is an authority not possessed by the president of the United States.

4. **5** Nearly all of the selection deals with a plan of action for use before the consumer buys. See the second sentence and also the first words of the third paragraph.

5. **2** The consumer is advised to get all promises in writing.

6. **5** It is specifically mentioned that pro rata (or partial) return of moneys and credit toward a replacement may be part of a warranty.

7. **4** By 2030, increasing numbers of Americans will reach the age that makes them eligible for Social Security benefits.

8. **2** A large increase in the birth rate would cause the average age to become lower since the many babies added to the population would counteract the older Americans.

9. **4** Persons concerned with the natural environment fear that an emphasis on greater production and consumption will mean further pollution of the air (by factory smokestacks and apartment house incinerators) and of rivers, lakes, and streams (by industrial wastes and sewage disposal); and increased problems of solid waste disposal and rising noise levels.

10. **4** There is no movement toward a solution to the energy problem as long as the two cyclists representing energy and environment keep pedaling in different directions.

11. **1** A fivefold increase in the price of imported crude oil from 1973 to 1980 severely affected the U.S. economy and forced a search for alternative domestic sources of energy, despite possible immediate negative effects on the environment.

12. **3** This is directly related to the big change from isolationism to internationalism in U.S. foreign policy. From 1920 to 1940 we had no political or military ties to non-American countries, and we never joined the League of Nations. Since World War II, which ended in 1945, the United States has pursued policies of collective security. President F. D. Roosevelt called for the United Nations, of which we are a charter member. President Truman committed U.S. aid to Europe through the Marshall Plan, the Truman Doctrine, and NATO. Subsequent presidents have continued economic aid to Asia and Africa, military assistance to Middle East and Asian nations, and commitments to Korea and Vietnam. President Kennedy started the Peace Corps, and President Nixon tried to negotiate peace in Vietnam and in Israel. Each of the other choices involves areas in which the Congress, the Supreme Court, and the states have been more influential than the president.

13. **2** The passage states that the Arctic and the Antarctic are "imaginary markers on the Earth's surface."

14. **4** It is stated that both the Tropic of Cancer and the Tropic of Capricorn run parallel to the equator.

15. **1** The Gettysburg Address was delivered in 1863. Fourscore and seven years

earlier—that is, 87 years earlier—the Declaration of Independence had been signed. It declared the liberty of the thirteen colonies and stated that all men are created equal.

16. **3** The speech was delivered at the Gettsyburg cemetery. In the second paragraph, Lincoln states that this is the purpose of the occasion.

17. **2** Lacking land for agriculture, Nation *A* will use its abundant labor, capital, and management skills to develop industry. The resulting products can be sold to domestic and foreign markets.

18. **2** In the 1800s, Great Britain led the world in manufactures and resembled Nation *A* in factors of production.

19. **4** Nation *B*, with its natural resources and labor, must encourage new industries by protectionist tariffs and by tax concessions to attract capital investment.

20. **4** The purpose of the Truman Doctrine, as opposed to President Monroe's policy of noninterference, was to support the governments of Greece and Turkey against direct and indirect Communist aggression. In 1947 Greece was in especially weakened condition following Nazi occupation during World War II, and was under attack by Communist guerrilla bands.

21. **1** From '60 to '65, the increase was 29.3% minus 18.6%, or 10.7%, greater than for any other interval.

22. **2** Between '70 and '80, the percentage of women working part time remained unchanged at 35.1%.

23. **5** Area E is farthest from a large body of water and moisture from the ocean by the prevailing winds would fall as rain before reaching Area E.

24. **4** A recession takes place in the economy when purchasing, saving, and business profits go down. The result is an increase in unemployment and a period of reduced economic activity—a recession.

25. **2** Social Darwinism became popular in the second half of the 19th century. It applied Darwin's theory of natural selection to people and nations, attempting thereby to justify the widening gap between the rich and the poor in the United States.

26. **3** The income group, $25,000 to $49,999, is at or close to 30%, more than any of the others.

27. **4** The largest increase was in the $50,000 to $99,999 group, from 20% to 25%.

28. **3** The number of families with stock holdings increased in each of the years indicated.

29. **2** The purpose of this speech by President Lyndon Johnson was to help troubled young people lead productive lives. In dealing with delinquent and potentially delinquent youth, he was concerned first about preventing them from getting into trouble; then, if they did, in helping them to become useful citizens. These ideas are stated in the first two paragraphs.

30. **5** President Johnson states that he recommends the Juvenile Delinquency Prevention Act of 1967.

31. **3** Family counseling is recommended because so many delinquents "live in broken families, burdened with . . . problems."

32. **4** The photograph depicts an early transportation method of milk by train.

33. **1** The photograph was taken when trains were still the most common form of transportation of goods, which was during the 1940s.

34. **1** Comparing the two graphs reveals that the electoral vote is much different from the popular vote.

35. **5** The movies are not mentioned as a media type.

36. **1** The 8- to 18-year-olds has the highest percentage, 51%, and whites at 45% have a higher computer use than Blacks and Hispanics.

37. **1** As an activity, watching TV is well ahead of the other six mentioned.

38. **1** A primary source is an eyewitness account of an event, such as a description in a diary, or an artifact constructed in a specific time period.

39. **1** With a drop of 12.7%, the weekly earnings fell the most for women with no high school diploma.

40. **3** The graph indicates that median earnings for whites and Hispanics exceeded those for Blacks with an associate degree.

41. **5** Lobbyists are representatives of special-interest groups who attempt to influence congressmen by providing information, preparing bills, and testifying at hearings.

42. **2** (*B*) Lobbyists sometimes use undesirable ways of influencing legislation by giving gifts and campaign contributions. The laws they sponsor may not benefit the general public.

43. **1** (*A*) Thousands of bills in many areas are introduced during each session of Congress. These must be handled by standing committees who try to bring expertise to each subject.

44. **1** Out of concern for their own reelection, legislators (the Boy Scouts in the cartoon) introduce consumer protection bills during an election year.

45. **5** Parents, teachers, and age peers are mentioned in the two classes of socializing agents.

46. **4** In the last sentence, all of the reasons are mentioned except the *number* of peers. The group is mentioned as being of increasing importance.

47. **1** The passage, in the second sentence, refers to the great influence of the family.

48. **4** Speaker *A* is talking about a world made smaller by modern technology. Speaker *B* agrees and adds that the problems of any area now become the problems of all humankind. Both feel that, as the world becomes one community, interdependence is a factor in world survival.

49. **1** Ethnocentrism is the view that one's own culture is superior to all others. Speaker *C* is calling for the appreciation of other people's value systems and ways of life.

50. **3** The extermination of over six million people, nearly all Jews, by the Nazi regime in Germany is called the Holocaust.

TEST 3: SCIENCE/PAGE 56

1. **3** Feathers are a late branch on this tree and thus came latest in evolution. Notice that tissues came much earlier in the branching process.

2. **1** The branch coming straight up from plantae shows that mosses came before ferns, which came before conifers.

3. **2** Birds and reptiles are late branches on the animal branch of the phylogenetic tree. Notice that they are also right next to each other.

4. **4** The latest of these evolutionary developments is feathers, which appear at the end of the animal branch of the tree.

5. **4** The volume of the block is 3 cm × 2 cm × 4 cm or 24 cm^3. The mass is given as 120 grams. Using the density formula provided, 120g/24cm^3 = 5 g/cm^3, Choice 4.

6. **4** Cutting an object into smaller pieces does not change its identity, and does not change its density. It is true that the volume of the new piece would be smaller, but the mass would be smaller as well. Notice that Choice 3 looks similar to Choice 4, but that the second part of the response is different. Make sure you read all of the choices completely before you select your answer.

7. **4** A balloon that is heated does not undergo any change in mass. You are told that the volume doubles. Thus, when doing a density calculation, you would be dividing the same mass by twice the volume. Dividing by twice as big a number gives half the answer. For example, a 100 gram balloon with a volume of 50 cm^3 would have a density of 2 g/cm^3. If the volume doubles to 100 cm^3, the new density would be 1 g/cm^3 (half of the original).

8. **3** If density is mass divided by volume, then mass is density times volume, so 4g/cm^3 times 10 cm^3 = 40g.

9. **2** According to the theory of continental drift and plate tectonics, the surface of the Earth is moving. The undersea volcanic vent, however, opens deep into the center of the Earth and is stable. One theory about the formation of the Hawaiian Islands suggests that a section of the Earth moves over the volcanic vent, which spews forth enough material to form an island; then, as a new section of Earth moves over the vent, another island is formed.

10. **3** The total time for the sound wave to go from the boat to the bottom and back is 4 seconds. It took 2 seconds to go down and 2 seconds to return. Therefore, 2 seconds × 1,000 meters/second = 2,000 meters.

11. **2** Only an electromagnet has the ability to be turned on or off. Notice that Choice 5 is an impossibility, so that you could disregard this answer at once.

12. **2** Since opposite poles of a magnet attract, the north pole of the earth should attract the south pole of a compass needle. It does not matter where on earth you are, this is always true.

13. **4** The passage clearly states that all magnets have a north and a south pole, so that must be true of the magnet referred to in the question, regardless of the type of magnet it is.

14. **2** The passage states that the diesel engine is less expensive to operate. Choice 1 is true of both engines. The amount of air used is not mentioned at all in the passage (Choice 5)

15. **2** On long trips, cost of fuel would be a major consideration so the less expensive diesel fuel would be an advantage.

16. **2** Internal combustion engines weigh less and a race car is concerned with speed and little else. Cost is not a factor, nor is availability of spark plugs.

17. **1** Earthquakes are the result of the movement of rock masses below the Earth's surface, resulting in breaking rock layers and displacement (fault) of segments of the layer at the breaking point. The folding of rock layers results from the action of lesser forces acting over a longer period of time. The forces produced by landslides are too small to create an earthquake.

18. **2** The 1989 earthquake in San Francisco killed many people because older buildings and roadways were not built to withstand such a severe shock. The more modern buildings survived.

19. **4** It is shock waves in the crust that a seismograph detects, whether they are produced by earthquakes or by nuclear explosions.

20. **1** Because atoms are electrically neutral, the number of protons (positive charges) must equal the number of electrons (negative charges). Thus, there must be 19 electrons in a potassium atom.

21. **2** The mass number is the number of protons and neutrons added togeher. Because the mass number is 24 and the number of protons is 12, there must be 24 – 12 = 12 neutrons in a magnesium atom.

22. **1** Potassium and sodium both form ions of charge +1. Because sodium combines with chloride to make the compound NaCl, potassium, with the same ionic charge, likely forms the compound KCl.

23. **3** Aluminum forms an ion of charge +3. Ions with charge +1 combine in 1-to-1 ratios with chloride, those that form a +2 ion combine in a 1-to-2 ratio, so aluminum should combine in a 1-to-3 ratio. Note that you do not have to know how to write chemical formulas to follow the patterns in the data provided to you.

24. **5** Many parts of the plant are involved, but it is in the chloroplasts that the actual chemical process takes place.

25. **3** Water from the soil is conducted through the xylem.

26. **5** Chemical energy is needed to split water into H^+ (combined in the glucose) and O_2.

27. **4** Hydrogen and carbon dioxide are successively built up into sugars.

28. **3** Chlorophyll in the chloroplasts of the cells transforms the energy of light into chemical energy.

29. **4** The stomata are openings through which carbon dioxide enters the leaf.

30. **5** Note that the figure shows you that light, water, and carbon dioxide all go into the plant system to produce sugars. Thus all three are required, and choice 5 is the correct answer.

31. **5** Since carbon dioxide is used in photosynthesis, increasing the supply would speed up the process.

32. **4** The birds have come to resemble each other because they have evolved to adapt to the same lifestyle. Choices 2, 3, and 5 contradict the statement that the birds are unrelated.

33. **1** According to the information, the white moths were invisible to predators against the light-colored bark. When the trees were darkened by soot, however, the moths were very easy to see.

34. **3** The only life process that a snake cannot perform alone is reproduction.

35. **5** Since the heart is a muscle with nerves that conduct impulses, potassium is an important nutrient. Many prescription drugs that heart patients take have a tendency to remove excess water. Dissolved potassium is thus lost.

36. **5** Stack gases combine with atmospheric water to produce acid rain, which can damage embryos, buildings, trees, and lungs.

37. **3** Mice have many offspring, with a short time between generations. Choice 1 is wrong because bacteria do not reproduce sexually. Choices 2 and 4 are wrong because dogs and humans, while of great practical interest, are not as prolific as mice. Oak trees are extremely prolific, but they have to grow for many years before they produce acorns.

38. **4** The passage implies that green bacteria evolved from nongreen forms, which must have been on earth first. Animal life requires oxygen, so it must have come after the green bacteria changed the atmosphere.

39. **3** The wolf population peaked a year after the peak of the moose population, so many wolves must have been born when the moose population was at its highest.

40. **3** The fossils in rock layer *D* are older than those in layer *A*. Fossils are found in sedimentary rocks. Sedimentary rocks are formed as layer upon layer of material is deposited. The oldest sediment layer *D* was laid down first and appears at the bottom. The youngest layer is at the top.

41. **1** Breathing air is not a form of direct transmission of body fluids. In sexual intercourse, each person has intimate contact with the body fluids of the other, so Choice 2 is wrong. Choices 3, 4 and 5 all involve transmission of blood from person to person.

42. **3** The breeder's problem is to locate the immune plants, which will be those that survive when herbicides are applied.

43. **5** Choice 1 is wrong; a farmer might follow this practice, but it is not what he *should* do. Choice 4 is wrong because you are asked the basis on which he should decide. There is no reason to suspect that Choices 2 and 3 are relevant.

44. **1** When evaporation occurs, heat is required to change a liquid (here, water) to a gas. Evaporation is a cooling process.

45. **4** Cloning is used to produce a large number of plants in a short period of time. According to the passage, one million plants can be cloned in about 6 months.

46. **3** According to the passage, each cell contains chromosomes, a complete blueprint for reproducing itself.

47. **3** The hormones auxin and cytokinin stimulate the production of new plants. Hormones are substances that regulate the growth and reproduction of organisms.

48. **2** Cloning is defined as a form of vegetative propagation. Vegetative propagation is a form of asexual reproduction; that is, only one parent is required.

49. **2** Sexual reproduction processes mix the heredities of the two parents, and produce offspring different from both. In cloning and other vegetative methods, there is no change in the genotype.

50. **2** The medicine is a suspension, not a solution. All incorrect choices are characteristic of solutions.

51. **5** Sour milk is acidic and must have a pH value of less than 7. Only choice 5 is an acidic pH.

52. **3** A substance with a pH of 10 is a base. Bases taste bitter and turn litmus blue. Note that both conditions must be met.

53. **4** Many cleaners work because they are either acidic or basic. Mixing an acid and a base usually leads to a neutral solution, which would negate any of the cleaning effects from acidic or basic solutions. It is rare for a science question to not give you enough information to solve a problem.

54. **5** Heat is a form of energy that moves spontaneously from regions of higher temperatures to lower. Cold is not a thing; the word here is used as an adjective.

55. **5** On the west side of the mountain, the temperature is dropping 3°C for each 0.5 km. At 2.5 km the temperature is 7°C. At the top it is 3° less, or 4°C. The same results would be obtained by using data from the east side of the mountain, where the temperature is dropping 5°C for each 0.5 km.

56. **2** When precipitation occurs, the relative humidity is 100%. In the diagram, precipitation is occurring on the windward side of the mountain at an elevation of 2.5 km.

57. **4** As the air rises, it expands. When it expands, it cools. You may have noticed that the air rushing out of a tire feels cool. This is because the air is expanding.

58. **1** As the air descends on the leeward side of the mountain, it becomes warmer. As a result, there will rarely be precipitation there. The lack of precipitation will produce an arid region. The deserts in the southwestern part of the United States are located on the leeward sides of mountain ranges.

59. **2** Some plants release pollen to the atmosphere. Human activity does not greatly affect the amount of pollen in the atmosphere. Substances are usually considered pollutants when they are added to the environment by human activity. Any portion of the environment can become polluted, including the atmosphere, the hydrosphere, or the lithosphere. The environment is said to be polluted when more of some substance is added than would normally be present. If, for example, large amounts of waste are dumped into a river, the water becomes polluted. Fish and other living organisms in the river may die if the pollution level becomes too great.

60. **2** The block and the weight are tied together, so they must always have the same speed. If the force moving the block becomes larger than the friction, the block must accelerate.

61. **2** Although a turtle has a hard outer shell similar to an exoskeleton, it also has an internal skeleton and is classified as a vertebrate.

62. **3** The independent variable in an experiment is the factor or variable directly manipulated by the experimenter, in this case the presence of the flypaper.

63. **1** Bottle 1 has flypaper in it, which although not a "natural" thing, in this case could create a situation where not flying was an advantage.

64. **2** The most obvious variable to be measured to see if there was a genuine advantage to wingless or winged flies is the number of flies that have survived. Choice 2 is the best answer.

65. **2** Mutations are changes in the genes in an organisms. Although they are the result of gene changes (or different alleles appearing), the actual change is known as a mutation.

66. **4** In most circumstances in nature, it must be expected that wings are useful. This experiment sets up an artificial environment in which the survival values are reversed. Some such environment might well exist in nature.

TEST 4: LANGUAGE ARTS, READING/PAGE 70

1. **2** The document describes a flexible form of working from home, telecommuting.

2. **4** The third principle listed says that "employees should inform their manager of their whereabouts so they may be reached easily."

3. **1** An employee who "routinely checks in with his manager" shows that he is communicating well.

4. **1** The last principle states that telecommuting should not be used more than 3 days in a month.

5. **2** The policy's first statement says, "The Company is committed to creating a flexible work environment. . . ."

6. **3** Only an animal is awake to listen to Iona.

7. **1** Iona feels he must do something since he can always sleep later.

8. **2** The name of Iona's son, Kuzma Ionitch, is a clue to an eastern European setting.

9. **3** The present tense gives a feeling that the events described are happening now.

10. **5** Iona asks the horse to put herself in the position of a foal's mother who loses her foal.

11. **2** Guy is "quick," and the narrator is "determined." There is a contrast also, in their reactions to the accident and the possibility of death.

12. **3** A simile is a direct comparison that uses the word *like* or *as*.

13. **2** The pronoun *they* refers to the subjects of the preceding sentence, July and August.

14. **4** If the narrator's son were to die, he would "lightly waft" or float away.

15. **1** The narrator became a shadow and a spectre, a ghost, both of which are intangible or unreal.

16. **1** The power poles are replacing the eucalyptus and thus are, in a sense, new trees.

17. **3** The poet calls the power poles "frigid" and "passionless."

18. **4** The children realize they cannot climb the "new trees" and miss the old ones.

19. **3** The poet considers the electric poles incapable of feeling ("passionless verticals") since they are not like trees, which are members of the Plant Kingdom and draw life from the earth.
20. **3** "Tree imposters" is a metaphor in which the poles are compared to false-pretending people.
21. **3** Line 25 states that the poet cannot be consoled. He wishes he could wake Jane from "this sleep"—death.
22. **5** In line 28, he speaks of "my love."
23. **3** Jane is referred to as "a wren," "my sparrow," and "my skittery pigeon."
24. **4** The poet goes from "she" to "her" to "you."
25. **4** In line 29, he indicates he has "no rights in this matter."
26. **3** Walter indirectly indicates that Lindner can expect the same treatment if Lindner insults him.
27. **2** It can be inferred that a better home will be part of a new life.
28. **3** Mama says, "My son said we was going to move," so Walter will be the head of the house.
29. **5** As he leaves, Lindner shakes his head in disagreement.
30. **3** Walter says, "We are very proud people."
31. **1** The author repeats "I remember" and says he has "never forgotten" and "shall never forget."
32. **4** The chief remembers his mother cooking, his father returning from hunting, his grandfather teaching him.
33. **1** The writer says his world reflected the wisdom and benevolence of the Great Spirit.
34. **1** The author writes, "There were never enough hours in a day to exhaust the pleasure of observing every living creature."
35. **5** The author describes the privileges he had on the "unspoiled prairie one hundred years ago."
36. **4** The author says that, in comparisons of language, Shakespeare is bound to win.
37. **3** The author says, among other unfavorable comparisons, that the songs of *West Side Story* pale next to the speech of Mercutio.
38. **1** The passage states that Romeo and Juliet "are a little too slender" to carry the play and this is "equally true of Tony and Maria."
39. **4** The passage observes that the heroes and heroines do "not shake us with...fear."
40. **3** Romeo and Juliet suffer from "the caprice of fate," while Tony and Maria suffer from prejudice and hatred.

TEST 5: MATHEMATICS/PAGE 80

1. **2** First find the total mileage.

$$135 + 162 + 98 + 117 + 216 = 728 \text{ mi.}$$

Divide the total mileage (728) by the number of miles covered for each gallon of gas used (14) to find the number of gallons of gas needed.

$$728 \div 14 = 52 \text{ gal.}$$

2. **4** Since 5¢ will pay for 12 min. $0.50 will pay for $10 \times 12 = 120$ min. 120 min. = 2 hr.

3. **40** If $AB = AC$, then $\angle ABC$ is an isosceles triangle and base angles B and C have equal measures: $m\angle B = m\angle C$.
Let $x = m\angle B = m\angle C$.

The sum of the measures of the angles of a triangle is 180°, so

$$\begin{aligned} x + x + 100 &= 180 \\ 2x + 100 &= 180 \\ 2x &= 180 - 100 = 80 \\ x &= 40 \end{aligned}$$

4. **5** Since 432 shirts were sold at $15 each, the number of dollars taken in was 15×432.

Since 368 shirts were sold at $18 each, the number of dollars taken in was 18×368.

The total amount taken in was $15 \times 432 + 18 \times 368$, which may be written as

$$(15)(432) + (368)(18).$$

5. 1 The total number of games played was $X + Y + Z$.

The number of games won was X.

The fractional part of the games won was $\dfrac{X}{X + Y + Z}$

6. 3/8 or .375

$\dfrac{1}{2}$ of the pupils walk to school.

$\dfrac{1}{4}$ of the other $\dfrac{1}{2} = \dfrac{1}{4} \times \dfrac{1}{2} = \dfrac{1}{8}$ use bicycles.

$$\dfrac{1}{2} + \dfrac{1}{8} = \dfrac{4}{8} + \dfrac{1}{8} = \dfrac{5}{8}$$

of the pupils either walk or use bicycles.

Therefore, $1 - \dfrac{5}{8} = \dfrac{3}{8}$ use other means.

7. 5 Since $2x > 4$, then

$$x > \dfrac{4}{2} = 2.$$

The only choice that is greater than 2 is 3.

8. 3 Since the aquarium is in the shape of a rectangular solid, its volume is given by the formula $V = lwh$. To find the volume in cubic feet, express each of l, w, and h in feet.

Length, l, is 3 ft.

Width, $w = 1$ ft. 8 in. $= 1\dfrac{2}{3}$ ft. $= \dfrac{5}{3}$ ft.

Height, h, is 1 ft. 6 in. $= 1\dfrac{1}{2}$ ft. $= \dfrac{3}{2}$ ft.

$$V = 3 \times \dfrac{5}{3} \times \dfrac{3}{3} = \dfrac{15}{2} = 7.5 \text{ cu. ft.}$$

9. 4 Let $x =$ height of flagpole. The two poles and their shadows can be represented by two triangles.

Since the triangles are similar, the lengths of corresponding sides are in proportion.

Set up the proportion:

$$\dfrac{h \text{ (flagpole)}}{h \text{ (pole)}} = \dfrac{l \text{ (flagpole shadow)}}{l \text{ (pole shadow)}}$$

$$\dfrac{x}{9} = \dfrac{16}{6}$$

$$6x = 9 \times 16 = 144$$

$$x = \dfrac{144}{6} = 24$$

10. 4 The total enrollment is

$360 + 300 + 280 + 260 = 1{,}200$

The part of the total enrollment that represents the freshmen is

$$\dfrac{360}{1{,}200} = \dfrac{36}{120} = \dfrac{3}{10} = 30\%.$$

11. 1 The purse contains $6 + 5 + 8 = 19$ coins, 5 of which are dimes. Therefore, the probability of drawing a dime is $\dfrac{5}{19}$.

12. 4 When an odd number of scores are arranged in increasing order, the median is the middle number. In this case, there are 9 numbers, so the median is the fifth number.

$$272, 274, 275, 276, 278, 281, 283, 284, 287$$
$$\downarrow$$
$$\text{median}$$

13. 4 The pens cost 3 for \$0.97.

Cost of 1 dozen pens $= 4(\$0.97)$
$= \$3.88$.

Cost of 8 pencils $=$
$\$4.60 - 3.88 = \$0.72$.

Cost of 1 pencil $= \$0.72 \div 8$
$= 9$ cents.

14. 525 Since 1 in. on the map represents 150 mi., 3 in. represents

$3(150) = 450$ mi., and $\dfrac{1}{2}$ in.

represents $\dfrac{1}{2}(150) = 75$ mi.

Then $3\dfrac{1}{2}$ in. represents

$450 + 75 = 525$ mi.

15. **2** To find the perimeter of the figure, find the sum of the lengths of the four sides:

$$2a + b + a + 3b + 3a + b + 3a + 2b$$
$$= 9a + 7b.$$

16. **5** $\$159.99 \times \dfrac{2}{3} =$

$106.66 (40-watt speakers after discount)

$$
\begin{array}{r}
\$106.66 \\
+\$150 \text{ (installation)} \\
\hline
\$256.66 \\
\times \quad 1.08 \text{ (sales tax)} \\
\hline
\end{array}
$$

$277.19, which falls between $270 and $280

17. **5** Since 3 ties sold for $23,
6 ties cost 2($23) = $46.
3 shirts cost $43.
Since slacks sold for $32.75 per pair,
2 pairs of slacks cost
2($32.75) = $65.50.
1 jacket cost for $58.45.
$46 + $43 + $65.50 + $58.45
= $212.95

18. **3** Write all the numbers as decimals, so that it is easier to arrange the numbers in order of size.
19% = 0.19,
$\dfrac{1}{2} = 0.50$, and $\dfrac{3}{5} = 60$.

The correct order from greatest to smallest is
0.80, 0.60, 0.50, 0.19, 0.080
or 0.80, $\dfrac{3}{5}$, $\dfrac{1}{2}$, 19%, 0.080
The correct choice is (3).

19. **248** To find the average speed, in miles per hour, divide the distance, in miles, by the time, in hours. Since 5 hr. and 30

min. is $5\dfrac{1}{2}$, or 5.5 hr., divide 1,364 by 5.5: 1364 ÷ 5.5 = 248.

20. **2** To write a number in scientific notation, write it as the product of a number between 1 and 10 and a power of 10. In this case, the number between 1 and 10 is 8.5. In going from 8.5 to 85,000,000,000, you move the decimal point 10 places to the right. Therefore 85,000,000,000 = 8.5×10^{10}.

21. **3** $3ab - x^2y = 3(4)(5) - (2)(2)(3)$
   $= 60 \quad - 12 = 48$

22. **10,000** The sum of the measures of the angles around the center of the circle is 360°. The fraction that represents the part of the total number of workers engaged in transportation is $\dfrac{20}{360} = \dfrac{1}{18}$.
$\dfrac{1}{18}$ of 180,000 = $\dfrac{180,000}{18}$ = 10,000

23. **4** In the right triangle use the Pythagorean theorem.

$$x^2 = (12)^2 + (16)^2$$
$$= 144 + 256 = 400$$
$$x = \sqrt{400} = 20$$

24. **4** Since m∠ABC = 68° and $\overline{BF}$ bisects ∠ABC, then m∠EBC = $\dfrac{1}{2}$ (68) = 34°.
Since m∠ACB = 72° and $\overline{CD}$ bisects ∠ACB, then m∠ECB = $\dfrac{1}{2}$ (72) = 36°.

Since the sum of the measure of the angles of a triangle is 180°,

m∠EBC + m∠ECB + m∠BEC = 180°
34 + 36 + m∠BEC = 180°
70 + m∠BEC = 180°
m∠BEC = 180 – 70 = 110°

25. **98.28**

$$6.5$$
$$\underline{\times\ 7.2}$$
$$46.8 \text{ sq. ft. (area of hallway)}$$
$$\underline{\times\ 2.10} \text{ (price of carpet/sq. ft.)}$$

$98.28 (total price of the carpet)

26. **5** You know that John Davis lost *at least* 4 lb. each month. But he may have lost much more. Not enough information is given to determine his exact weight after the 6-month period.

27. **425** The annual interest on $10,000 at $8\frac{1}{2}\%$ is $10,000 × 0.085 = $850.

Thus, every 6 months Mr. Ames receives $\frac{1}{2}$ of $850 = $425.

28. **4** Factor the left-hand side of $x^2 - x - 12 = 0$:

$(x - 4)(x + 3) = 0$,
$x - 4 = 0$ **or** $x + 3 = 0$
$x = 4$ **or** $x = -3$

29. **3** Using the first ratio of 9:2, set up a second with the information given, then convert to an equation using fractions.

$$\frac{9 \text{ (men)}}{2 \text{ (women)}} = \frac{x \text{ (unknown \# of men)}}{12 \text{ (known \# of women)}}$$

30. **5** Slope of $\overrightarrow{AB}$

$$= \frac{\text{change in } y\text{-coordinates}}{\text{change in } x\text{-coordinates}}$$

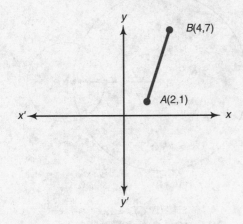

Slope of $\overrightarrow{AB} = \dfrac{7 - 1}{4 - 2} = \dfrac{6}{2} = 3$

31. **3** Let x = number of points scored by Jim, and
$3x$ = number of points scored by Bill.

$$x + 3x = 56$$
$$4x = 56$$
$$x = 56 \div 4 = 14$$
$$3x = 3(14) = 42$$

32. **4** Note that each subdivision line on the vertical axis represents 200 mi. The Rio Grande is about 1,500 mi. long, and the Seine is about 500 mi. long. Therefore, the Rio Grande is about 1,000 mi. longer than the Seine.

33. **5** In 1988, the receipts were $600,000 and the expenses were $500,000. In 1988, receipts exceeded expenses by $100,000.

34. **1** Six pencils will cost 6 times as much as 1 pencil. Since y is the cost of 1 pencil, the cost of 6 pencils is 6 times $y = 6y$.

35. **5** In 2 weeks Mr. Martin worked a total of (42 + 37) hr. and earned $12 for each hour. Therefore, the total number of dollars he earned was 12(42 + 37).

36. **4** There are four quarts in a gallon. Kwan has multiplied the usual recipe by 16 (1 qt. × 16 = 4 gal.) for the party.
Thus, multiply the lemon concentrate by 16.
$16 \times 8 =$ 128 oz. then divide by 32 (oz./qt.)
4 qt. = 1 gal.

37. **3** Since pairs of alternate interior angles of parallel lines have equal measures, m∠BCD = m∠ABC. Thus m∠BCD = 112°.

$$m\angle ECD = \frac{1}{2}\, m\angle BCD$$
$$= \frac{1}{2}(112°) = 56°$$

38. **2** 22 ft. 4 in. = 22(12) + 4 = 268 in.

    268 ÷ 4 = 67 in. per piece
    $\frac{67}{12} = 5\frac{7}{12}$
    Each piece is 5 ft. 7 in. in length.

39. **4** According to the graph, the population in 2000 was midway between 25,000 and 30,000.

    25,000 + 30,000 = 55,000
    55,000 ÷ 2 = 27,500

40. **2** Lincoln County's population increased by 2,500 (or one vertical line up on the graph) between 1995 and 1996. This is true of both 1996–1997 and 2000–2001. The other choices can be eliminated because either one or both years did not show the 2,500-person increase.

41. **4** Use the formula $V = lwh$ to represent the volume of the rectangular solid.

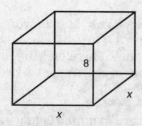

    $V = x \cdot x \cdot 8 = 8x^2$
    $8x^2 = 392$

42. **5** Since the total number of votes cast is not given, an equation to solve the problem cannot be set up.

43. **2** If $AB = AC$, $m\angle C = m\angle B = 68°$. Since $\overline{AD} \perp \overline{BC}$, $m\angle ADC = 90°$.

    Since the sum of the measures of the angles of a triangle is 180°:
    68 + 90 + m∠x = 180
    158 + m∠x = 180
    m∠x = 180 − 158 = 22°

44. **3** Since PQ is parallel to RS, alternate interior angles are equal: $2x = x + 25$. Subtracting x from each side yields $x = 25$.

45. **3** Since $5^2 = 25$ and $6^2 = 36$, $\sqrt{30}$ is between 5 and 6.

46. **1** AD = radius of large circle = 20 in. BC = radius of small circle = 8 in.

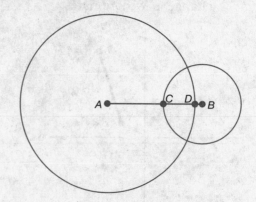

    $CD = 6$
    $DB = BC − CD = 8 − 6 = 2$
    $AB = AD + DB = 20 + 2 = 22$ in.

47. **(1,0)** The square measures 6 units ×
6 units. Its center coordinates are
(1,0). Your grid should be marked
accordingly.

48. **4** To find the cost of n lb. of sugar at c
cents per pound, multiply n by c to
obtain nc.

To find the change received subtract
nc cents from 100 cents. The result is
$100 - nc$.

49. **5** Check each inequality or equation in
turn.
(1) $3(10) + 1 > 12$, $30 + 1 > 12$. True
(2) $2(10) - 3 < 25$, $20 - 3 < 25$. True
(3) $10^2 + 1 > 10^2 - 1$.
$100 + 1 > 100 - 1$. True
(4) $4(10) - 1 = 39$, $40 - 1 = 39$. True
(5) $2(10) - 7 > 7 - 2(10)$,
$20 - 7 < 7 - 20$. Not true
The correct choice is (5).

50. **10,400** Divide the given figure into two
rectangles by drawing a dotted line.

Width of rectangle A =
$100 - 20 = 80$
Length of rectangle A = 120
Area of rectangle A =
$(80)(120) = 9,600$ sq. ft.
Area of rectangle B =
$40 \times 20 = 800$ sq. ft.
Area of figure = $9,600 + 800 =$
$10,400$ sq. ft.

CHAPTER 3:   Sentence Structure

We identify run-on sentences and sentence fragments. Parallel structure, misplaced modifiers, and writing correct sentences are thoroughly covered.

CHAPTER 4:   Usage

Key areas of usage are limited to agreement, case of nouns and pronouns, and errors in verb form and tense. A glossary defines usage terms and provides examples of each.

CHAPTER 5:   Mechanics

Fifteen basic rules of capitalization are listed. Basic rules are presented for each of the *nine* punctuation marks. Basic spelling rules are presented, specifically homonyms, possessives, and contractions.

CHAPTER 6:   Organization

You will learn how to use transitions, how to appropriately divide text, how to identify topic sentences, unity, and coherence in different types of text.

CHAPTER 7:   Additional Writing Skills

You will learn the differences between 30 pairs of words frequently confused or misused. A Basic 650-Word Vocabulary is presented. Kinds of wordiness are demonstrated.

CHAPTER 8:   Practice with Sample Test Paragraphs

We have provided sample paragraphs and questions based on them, similar to those on the GED. These contain, with explanations, examples of the sentence correction, sentence revision, and construction shift items on the GED and will thus give you experience with the kind of materials you will face on the examination.

Sentence Structure

A sentence is the basic means of communicating an idea.

A sentence may be defined as a group of words having a subject and a predicate (see Glossary of Usage, pages 148–151) and expressing a complete thought. Each sentence should be separated from the one that follows it by some form of end punctuation such as a period, a question mark, or an exclamation point.

Run-On Sentences

In one important group of errors, you may fail to separate two or more sentences by using the proper punctuation. Instead, you may either use no punctuation at all or incorrectly use a comma. The general term for this group of errors is the *run-on sentence* or, if a comma is incorrectly used, the *comma splice.*

Here are frequently made errors and the ways in which they may be corrected.

Type 1

The run-on sentence can result from an incorrectly used or omitted conjunction (connecting word) or adverb.

EXAMPLE

WRONG:
Joe was elected class president *x* he is very popular.

CORRECT:
Joe was elected class president *because* he is very popular.

"Joe was elected class president" and "he is very popular" are both independent sentences. The two sentences have been run together because there is no end punctuation between them. This error can be corrected by simply placing a period between the two sentences. A better way to correct this error, however, is to look for a relationship between the two sentences. The first sentence, "Joe was elected class president," is a result of the second, "he is very popular." It is, therefore, possible to join the two sentences using the conjunction *because.* Joe was elected president *because* he is very popular.

EXAMPLES

WRONG:
Joe is very popular *x* therefore he was elected class president.

Joe is very popular *x* thus he was elected class president.

CORRECT:
Joe is very popular and, as a result, he was elected class president.

Joe is very popular. Therefore, he was elected class president.

Joe is very popular; therefore, he was elected class president.

To correct this, you must substitute a conjunction, such as, *and* for the adverbs *therefore* and *so* or break the run-on sentence at the point marked *x* with either a period or a semicolon.

PRACTICE

Some of these sentences have errors; others are correct. Rewrite correctly the sentences that contain errors. Write "correct" for those that have no errors.

1. Hector studied very hard, so he passed the test.
2. Maria was very beautiful therefore she was chosen queen of the prom.
3. Avital has lots of friends she is very good-natured.

ANSWERS

1. Correct.
2. Maria was very beautiful. Therefore, she was chosen queen of the prom.
3. Avital is very good-natured and, as a result, she has lots of friends.

Type 2

EXAMPLES

WRONG:
Joe worked hard *x* he was bound to succeed.

CORRECT:
Joe worked *so* hard *that* he was bound to succeed.

WRONG:
Joe worked hard *x* consequently he was bound to succeed.

CORRECT:
Joe worked hard. *Consequently,* he was bound to succeed.

CORRECT:
Since Joe worked hard, he was bound to succeed.

PRACTICE

1. Since the employer required a high school diploma, I had to pass the GED test.
2. Helena was a good shopper she saved lots of money.

ANSWERS

1. Correct.
2. Helena was a good shopper. Consequently, she saved lots of money.

Type 3

EXAMPLES

WRONG:
Joe disliked English *x* he got a good mark anyhow.

CORRECT:
Joe disliked English, *but* he got a good mark anyhow.

WRONG:
Joe disliked English *x* nevertheless he got a good mark.

CORRECT:
Joe disliked English. *Nevertheless,* he got a good mark.

Although Joe disliked English, he got a good mark.

WRONG:
Joe disliked English *x* however he got a good mark.

CORRECT:
Joe disliked English. *However,* he got a good mark.

PRACTICE

1. The politician did not do much campaigning nevertheless he was elected.
2. Although the team rallied, it lost the game.

ANSWERS

1. The politician did not do much campaigning. Nevertheless, he was elected.
2. Correct

Type 4

EXAMPLES

WRONG:
Joe is excellent in mathematics *x* he is also good in English.

CORRECT:
Joe is excellent in mathematics, *and* he is also good in English.

WRONG:
Joe is excellent in mathematics *x* furthermore he is good in English.

CORRECT:
Joe is excellent in mathematics. *Furthermore,* he is good in English.

WRONG:
Joe is excellent in mathematics *x* besides he is good in English.

CORRECT:
Joe is excellent in mathematics. He is *also* good in English.

Joe is excellent in mathematics. *Besides*, he is good in English.

PRACTICE

1. Fernando is an excellent violinist he is a fine violist as well.
2. The telecast raised much money for muscular dystrophy research, furthermore it was very entertaining.

ANSWERS

1. Fernando is an excellent violinist; he is a fine violist as well.
   or
   Fernando is an excellent violinist. Besides, he is a fine violist.
2. The telecast raised much money for muscular dystrophy research. Furthermore, it was very entertaining.

Type 5
EXAMPLE

WRONG:
Joe is always imitating the coach, he respects him greatly.

CORRECT:
Joe is always imitating the coach *whom* he respects greatly.

In the above example, *coach* is the word (noun) described and *whom he respects greatly* is the descriptive clause.

PRACTICE

1. The class elected Juan president of the class they liked him best of all the candidates.
2. Anna was the best student the class admired her.

ANSWERS

1. The class elected Juan, whom they liked best of all the candidates, president of the class.
2. Anna, whom the class admired, was the best student.

Type 6
EXAMPLE

WRONG:
Did Joe win x he was the best candidate.

CORRECT:
Did Joe win? He was the best candidate.

"Did Joe win?" is an interrogative sentence that asks a question. "He was the best candidate" is a declarative sentence that makes a statement. Often students combine, in error, the question and the answer given to it.

PRACTICE

1. Is Conchita home? I have to speak to her.
2. Did you go to see the play it was very entertaining.

ANSWERS

1. Correct.
2. Did you go to see the play? It was very entertaining.

Type 7

This run-on sentence error involves the punctuation of quotations. Therefore, refer to "Basic Rules of Punctuation" beginning on page 155.

EXAMPLE

WRONG:
"Joe won," he said, "I thought he was the best runner."

CORRECT:
"Joe won," he said. "I thought he was the best runner."

"Joe won." He said, "I thought he was the best runner."

PRACTICE

1. "Come in," said the hostess, "I'm happy to see you."
2. "Study hard," advised the teacher. "You'll pass the test."

ANSWERS

1. "Come in," said the hostess. "I'm happy to see you."
2. Correct.

Sentence Fragments

In another important group of errors, you may fail to complete the sentence. (You will remember that a sentence is defined as a group of words having a subject and a predicate and expressing a complete thought.) In the kind of error called a *sentence fragment*, either the subject is left out, so that a predicate is left standing by itself (e.g., "Wish you were here.") or a part of the predicate is broken off from the sentence and made to stand by itself (e.g., "Walking down the street.").

Type 1

EXAMPLE

WRONG:
> Am having a wonderful time. Wish you were here.

CORRECT:
> *I* am having a wonderful time. *I* wish you were here.

In each case, without the subject it is impossible to know *who* is doing the action indicated in the predicate.

PRACTICE

1. Miss you. Will be home tomorrow.
2. Great idea. Wish you luck.

ANSWERS

1. We miss you. We'll be home tomorrow.
   or
   I miss you. I'll be home tomorrow.
   or
   They miss you. They'll be home tomorrow.
2. That's a great idea. I (We) wish you luck.

Type 2

EXAMPLE

WRONG:
> Joe studied hard. Passed all his tests and was graduated.

CORRECT:
> Joe studied hard, passed all his tests, and was graduated.

Note that *studied hard*, *passed all his tests*, and *was graduated* are all parts of the predicate, and they all tell us something about Joe.

PRACTICE

1. Don collected baseball cards. Played the piano and excelled in sports.
2. Donna went to school. Worked as a baby-sitter.

ANSWERS

1. Don collected baseball cards, played the piano, and excelled in sports.
2. While Donna went to school, she worked as a baby-sitter.

Type 3

EXAMPLES

WRONG:
> Joe got a good mark in English. Although he doesn't like the subject.
> [Adverbial clause]

CORRECT:
> Joe got a good mark in English, although he doesn't like the subject.

WRONG:
> Joe has an English teacher. Whom he likes very much. [Adjective clause]

CORRECT:
> Joe has an English teacher whom he likes very much.

PRACTICE

1. Fern is popular. Because she is considerate.
2. I enjoy being with Jill. Who is very amusing.

ANSWERS

1. Fern is popular, because she is considerate.
2. I enjoy being with Jill, who is very amusing.

Type 4

EXAMPLES

WRONG:
Joe got up early. To go to school.

CORRECT:
Joe got up early to go to school.

WRONG:
Joe worked hard. Studying his lessons.

CORRECT:
Joe worked hard studying his lessons.

WRONG:
Walking down the street. Joe thought about his job.

CORRECT:
Walking down the street, Joe thought about his job.

EXAMPLES

> **IMPORTANT NOTE:**
>
> A clause and a phrase can be detached in error either at the *beginning* or at the *end* of the sentence.

WRONG:
Joe went to the movies. With his friend.

CORRECT:
Joe went to the movies with his friend.

WRONG:
Joe enjoyed himself. At the movies.

CORRECT:
Joe enjoyed himself at the movies.

PRACTICE

1. Looking around the room. Cynthia saw her friend.
2. Frances practiced daily, doing her exercises on the piano.
3. I was too tired. To go to the supermarket.

ANSWERS

1. Looking around the room, Cynthia saw her friend.
2. Correct.
3. I was too tired to go to the supermarket.

Type 5

EXAMPLE

WRONG:
Joe enjoys all sports. Baseball, football and swimming.

CORRECT:
Joe enjoys all sports: baseball, football, and swimming.

Sports is the object; baseball, football, and swimming are nouns in apposition equivalent in meaning. Note that the colon is used to introduce listings. See the section "Basic Rules of Punctuation" beginning on page 139.

EXAMPLE

WRONG:
Joe admires the captain of the team. Ron Jones.

CORRECT:
Joe admires the captain of the team, Ron Jones.

PRACTICE

1. Miguel collects antiques. Stamps and coins.
2. Dick met his fiancee's mother, Mrs. Ellis.

ANSWERS

1. Miguel collects antiques, stamps, and coins.
2. Correct.

Type 6

EXAMPLE

WRONG:
Joe has excelled in his studies. Also in sports and extracurricular activities.

CORRECT:
Joe has excelled in his studies, in sports, and in extracurricular activities.

PRACTICE

1. Noel spent his spare time at the movies. Also at the pool and at the gym.
2. Sheila helped at home, in school, and at church.

ANSWERS

1. Noel spent his spare time at the movies, the pool, and the gym.
2. Correct.

PRACTICE WITH RUN-ON SENTENCES AND SENTENCE FRAGMENTS

Beneath each sentence you will find five ways of writing the underlined part. Choose the answer that makes the best sentence. Answer 1 is always the same as the underlined part and is sometimes the right answer. This is the sentence revision type of multiple-choice item.

1. Yolanda had a passion for <u>fruits; melons,</u> pineapples, grapefruits, and pears.

    (1) fruits; melons,
    (2) fruits. melons,
    (3) fruits, melons,
    (4) fruits: melons,
    (5) fruits. Melons,

2. "Take your umbrella," suggested the boy's <u>mother. "It</u> might rain."

    (1) mother. "It
    (2) mother," it
    (3) mother,". It
    (4) mother: "It
    (5) mother:" it

3. "Why he didn't come home on <u>time." stated</u> the parent, "is beyond me."

    (1) time." stated
    (2) time? "stated
    (3) time"? stated
    (4) time, "Stated
    (5) time," stated

4. The teacher told her <u>student to bring his</u> books to class every day.

    (1) student to bring his
    (2) student that he should bring his
    (3) student he should bring his
    (4) student: bring your
    (5) student—bring your

5. Arnold studied <u>hard he</u> wanted to make the honor roll.

    (1) hard he
    (2) hard because he
    (3) hard: He
    (4) hard, he
    (5) hard. since he

6. Have you been to the <u>museum it</u> has an excellent exhibition.

    (1) museum it
    (2) museum, it
    (3) museum? it
    (4) museum? It
    (5) museum which

7. "The Red Sox won the pennant," <u>said the sportscaster, "I</u> thought they were the best team."

    (1) pennant," said the sportscaster, "I
    (2) pennant." said the sportscaster, "I
    (3) pennant", said the sportscaster, "I
    (4) pennant," said the sportscaster. "I
    (5) pennant." said the sportscaster. "I

8. The student replied <u>that he is</u> living here for the last three years.

    (1) that he is
    (2) that "He is
    (3) that, "He is
    (4) that he was
    (5) that he has been

9. <u>I should agree to the proposal if I were</u> in your situation.

    (1) I should agree to the proposal if I were
    (2) I would agree to the proposal if I would be
    (3) I would agree to the proposal if I was
    (4) I would agree to the proposal, if I was
    (5) I would agree to the proposal; if I were

10. The employer refused the worker the <u>raise besides,</u> he threatened to fire him.

    (1) raise besides,
    (2) raise, besides,
    (3) raise: besides.
    (4) raise. besides
    (5) raise. Besides,

11. Studying hard. Miss you. Write.

    (1) Studying hard. Miss you. Write.
    (2) I am studying hard. Miss you. Write.
    (3) I am studying hard. I miss you.
        Write.
    (4) Studying hard; miss you; write.
    (5) Studying hard: miss you. Write.

12. To succeed in school: Juan attended
    regularly, did his homework, and studied
    hard.

    (1) school: Juan
    (2) school. Juan
    (3) school, Juan
    (4) school—Juan
    (5) school Juan

13. Why didn't you come I waited for hours
    for your arrival.

    (1) come I
    (2) come, I
    (3) come; I
    (4) come: I
    (5) come? I

14. Joanne didn't like to study she passed
    the examination anyhow.

    (1) study she
    (2) study and she
    (3) study, and she
    (4) study: but she
    (5) study, but she

15. They objected to me staying.
    Nevertheless, I remained at the
    gathering.

    (1) me staying. Nevertheless, I
    (2) me staying, nevertheless I
    (3) my staying, nevertheless, I
    (4) my staying. Nevertheless I
    (5) my staying. Nevertheless, I

16. Can't be at your wedding send all our
    love.

    (1) Can't be at your wedding send
    (2) Can't be at your wedding; send
    (3) Can't be at your wedding; we send
    (4) Can't be at your wedding, we send
    (5) We can't be at your wedding, but we
        send

17. Although Vincent and Giuseppe,
    buddies during the Vietnam War, hadn't
    met for over five years.

    (1) Giuseppe, buddies during the
        Vietnam War, hadn't met
    (2) Giuseppe buddies during the
        Vietnam War hadn't met
    (3) Giuseppe, buddies during the
        Vietnam War, didn't meet
    (4) Giuseppe were buddies during the
        Vietnam War yet hadn't met
    (5) Giuseppe were buddies during the
        Vietnam War, they hadn't met

18. Will you come to my party I'd be happy
    to have you there.

    (1) party I'd
    (2) party. I'd
    (3) party; I'd
    (4) party: I'd
    (5) party? I'd

19. "This is most unusual," said Jorge," the
    mail has never come late before."

    (1) Jorge, "the
    (2) Jorge, "The
    (3) Jorge. "The
    (4) Jorge; "The
    (5) Jorge: "The

ANSWER KEY

1. **4**	5. **2**	9. **1**	13. **5**	17. **5**
2. **1**	6. **4**	10. **5**	14. **5**	18. **5**
3. **5**	7. **4**	11. **3**	15. **5**	19. **3**
4. **1**	8. **5**	12. **3**	16. **5**	

WHAT'S YOUR SCORE?

_____ right,	_____ wrong
Excellent	18–19
Good	15–17
Fair	12–14

If you scored lower, study the kinds of run-
on sentences and sentence fragments illustrated in this section.

ANSWER ANALYSIS

1.4 See Type 5 under "Sentence Fragments." The nouns in apposition with *fruits* should be preceded by a colon. See Rule 1 under "The Colon."

2.1 No error.

3.5 See "The Comma," as it refers to the divided quotation where commas are used to set off the speaker.

4.1 No error.

5.2 See Type 1 under "Run-on Sentences." A cause for Arnold's studying hard is needed to bring the two sentences together.

6.4 See Type 6 under "Run-on Sentences." Two sentences of different kinds are improperly run together.

7.4 See Type 7 under "Run-on Sentences." The two sentences are improperly run together because there is a divided quotation.

8.5 The present perfect tense is required since the student has been living here up to the present time.

9.1 Correct as is.

10.5 See Type 4 under "Run-on Sentences." In this run-on sentence, an additional idea is incorrectly connected to the first idea.

11.3 See Type 1 under "Sentence Fragments." The subjects of the first two sentences are improperly left out. In *Write,* the subject *you* is understood.

12.3 See Type 4 under "Sentence Fragments." The Important Note mentions that a phrase may, in error, be detached at the beginning of the sentence. Here, it is "To succeed in school." The colon detaches the phrase; the comma connects it to the sentence.

13.5 Two sentences of different kinds are incorrectly run together.

14.5 See Type 3 under "Run-on Sentences." A conflicting idea is incorrectly connected to the idea it apparently contradicts.

15.5 See Problem 3 under "Some Special Problems" of "Case of Nouns and Pronouns."

16.5 See Type 1 under "Sentence Fragments." The subject of the sentence is improperly left out. In addition, see Type 3 under "Run-on Sentences." A conflicting idea is incorrectly connected to the idea it apparently contradicts.

17.5 See Type 4 under "Sentence Fragments" (particularly **Important Note**). This is an example of a detached clause at the beginning of the sentence.

18.5 See Type 6 under "Run-on Sentences." Two sentences of different kinds are incorrectly run together. "Will you come to my party?" is an interrogative sentence; "I'd be happy to have you there" is a declarative sentence.

19.3 See Type 7 under "Run-on Sentences." Two different sentences are run together improperly because there is a divided quotation.

Parallel Structure

A major error in structure is failure to keep parts of the sentence that perform the *same purpose* in the *same form.* This is called an error in parallel structure.

Here is an example of such an error.

Type 1

EXAMPLE

WRONG:

Joe likes *swimming, fishing,* and, if he has the time, *to take* a long walk.

The sentence tells us three things Joe likes. They are related to us by words that are the objects of the verb *likes,* and they serve the same purpose. But are their forms alike? Let us line them up vertically.

Joe likes swimming
             fishing
             to take a long walk

No, they are not. *Swimming* and *fishing* are verbs used, in the *-ing* form, as nouns. *To take,* however, is an infinitive. Words having the same function should have the same form. Then, the sentence has parallel structure. The sentence should read:

Joe likes swimming
              fishing
              taking a long walk

CORRECT:

Joe likes *swimming, fishing,* and, if he has the time, *taking a long walk.*

PRACTICE

1. Irene enjoys baking, cooking, and to prepare meals.
2. Julie excels at embroidering, crocheting, and hooking rugs.

ANSWERS

1. Irene enjoys baking, cooking, and preparing meals.
2. Correct.

Type 2

Here is another example of lack of parallel structure.

EXAMPLE

WRONG:

Jane and Jim took part *in* baseball games, *in* swimming *contests,* and *in learning* about golf.

The sentence tells us three things in which Jane and Jim took part. All three are objects of the preposition *in.* They serve the same purpose, yet the form of one of them is different.

Jane and Jim took part
      in baseball *games*
      in swimming *contests*
      in *learning* about golf

Two are nouns; the third is a verb used, in the *-ing* form, as a noun. To maintain parallel structure, the third must also be a noun.

Jane and Jim took part
      in baseball *games*
      in swimming *contests*
      in *golf lessons*

Lessons is a noun. The structure of the items in the sentence is now parallel.

CORRECT:

Jane and Jim took part *in* baseball *games, in* swimming *contests,* and *in* golf *lessons.*

PRACTICE

1. Ben took courses in computers, in mathematics, and in learning about fine arts.
2. Jesse couldn't decide on a career in education, in business, or becoming a doctor.

ANSWERS

1. Ben took courses in computers, in mathematics, and in fine arts.
2. Jesse couldn't decide on a career in education, in business, or in medicine.

Type 3

Here is another type of error in parallel structure.

EXAMPLE

WRONG:

The backers failed to realize *the success of the show* or *how long it would run.*

Two things were realized: both are objects of the infinitive *to realize.* Yet one is a noun, *success;* the other a noun clause, *how long it would run.* Since both fill the same purpose in the sentence, they should have the same form. Either both should be nouns or both should be noun clauses. You may correct this sentence in either of two ways to achieve parallel structure.

CORRECT:

The backers failed to realize the *success* of the show or the *length* of its run. [Two nouns]

The backers failed to realize *how successful the show would be* or *how long it would run.* [Two noun clauses]

PRACTICE

1. Jane needed financial support and being encouraged.
2. Arnold was not aware of his strength or how good-looking he was.
3. The movie was entertaining and it instructed us as well.

ANSWERS

1. Jane needed financial support and encouragement.
2. Arnold was not aware of how strong or how good-looking he was.
3. The movie was entertaining and instructive.

Type 4

Here is another type of error in parallel structure.

Note: Certain pairs of words in English connect parts of a sentence that are equal in importance—*parallel elements.* You are familiar with a number of them:

> both...and
> either...or
> neither...nor
> not only...but also
> whether...or

Remember to use these *immediately before* the parallel element each accompanies.

A few examples will make this point clear.

EXAMPLES

WRONG:

Chiquita was *both* asked to work the switchboard *and* to address envelopes.

Note that only one of the words, *and*, precedes an infinitive, *to address*. Both should precede the infinitives, *to work* and *to address*.

Chiquita was asked　*both* to work
　　　　　　　　　and to address

CORRECT:

Chiquita was asked *both* to work the switchboard *and* to address envelopes.

Here is another example.

WRONG:

The basketball star *not only* was popular *but also* modest.

The basketball star was
　　　　　　　　not only popular
　　　　　　　　but also modest

CORRECT:

The basketball star was *not only* popular *but also* modest.

PRACTICE

1. Carmen was interested neither in sports nor in books.
2. He was not only smart but also handsome.

ANSWERS

1. Correct.
2. Correct.

If you want to remember the idea behind parallel structure, here are two examples— one simple, one profound.

> Something *old*
> Something *new*
> Something *borrowed*
> Something *blue*

Note that *Something* is followed by four different adjectives.

Finally, here is a splendid example from Abraham Lincoln's Second Inaugural Address. (The parallel elements are underlined.) "With <u>malice</u> toward <u>none</u>, with <u>charity</u> for <u>all</u>, with <u>firmness</u> in the <u>right</u> as God gives us to see the right, let us finish the work we are in, <u>to bind</u> up the nation's wounds, <u>to care</u> for him who shall have borne the battle and for his widow and his orphan, <u>to do</u> all which may achieve and cherish a just and a lasting peace among ourselves and with all nations."

PRACTICE WITH PARALLEL STRUCTURE

Beneath each sentence you will find five ways of writing the underlined part. Choose the answer that makes the best sentence. Answer 1 is always the same as the underlined part and is sometimes the right answer. These are included in the sentence correction type of multiple-choice item.

1. <u>To strive for perfection, to serve one's fellow man, to help</u> the needy are ideals all should try to follow.

   (1) To strive for perfection, to serve one's fellow man, to help

(2) To strive for perfection, serving one's fellow man, helping

(3) Striving for perfection, serving one's fellow man, and to help

(4) Striving for perfection, to serve one's fellow man, helping

(5) To strive for perfection. To serve one's fellow man. To help

2. Jones, the president of the union and <u>who is also a member of the community group</u>, will be in charge of the negotiations.

(1) who is also a member of the community group,

(2) since he is a member of the community group

(3) a member of the community group

(4) also being a member of the community group

(5) , in addition, who is a member of the community group

3. Marie is good-looking, <u>with intelligence, and has youth.</u>

(1) with intelligence, and has youth

(2) intelligent, and has youth

(3) intelligent, and is youthful

(4) , with intelligence, and youthful

(5) intelligent, and youthful

4. The instructor told the student <u>to hold the club lightly, keeping his eye on the ball and drawing the club back quickly, but too much force should not be used</u> on the downward stroke.

(1) to hold the club lightly, keeping his eye on the ball and drawing the club back quickly, but too much force should not be used

(2) to hold the club lightly, keep his eye on the ball, and drawing the club back quickly, and too much force should not be used

(3) to hold the club lightly, keep his eye on the ball, draw the club back quickly and not use too much force

(4) to hold the club lightly, keep his eye on the ball, draw the club back quickly and too much force should not be used

(5) he should hold the club lightly, keeping his eye on the ball, drawing the club back quickly, and not using too much force

5. He is rude, gruff, <u>and doesn't think of the feelings of others or of showing consideration to</u> others.

(1) and doesn't think of the feelings of others or of showing consideration to

(2) and doesn't think of or show consideration to

(3) thoughtless, and inconsiderate of

(4) thoughtless of others and of showing consideration to

(5) thoughtless of others' feelings, and lacking in consideration to

ANSWER KEY

1. **1**   2. **3**   3. **5**   4. **3**   5. **3**

WHAT'S YOUR SCORE?

_____ right,	_____ wrong
Excellent	5
Good	4
Fair	3

If you scored lower, review this section and study the examples of correct parallel structure.

ANSWER ANALYSIS

1. **1** No error.
2. **3** The nouns in apposition must be parallel to one another. "Jones, the *president*...and a *member*...."
3. **5** This is a case of parallel structure involving three adjectives.
4. **3** Four infinitives in parallel form are much clearer than the mixture of an infinitive (*to hold*), two participles (*keeping* and *drawing*), and a clause (*too much force should not be used*).
5. **3** Parallel structure requires the use of four adjectives (*rude, gruff, thoughtless*, and *inconsiderate*) instead of two adjectives (*rude, gruff*) and two phrases (*of the feelings..., of showing...*) following the unnecessary verb *doesn't think*.

Misplaced Modifiers

A modifier is a word or a group of words that help describe another word or group of words by giving a more exact meaning. The modifier may be an adjective (a *big* house) or an adverb (walk *slowly*), an adjective clause (the man *who came to dinner*) or an adjective phrase (Jeanie *with the light brown hair*), an adverbial clause (he arrived *when the clock struck twelve*) or an adverbial phrase (he arrived *on time*). Very often, confusion in meaning takes place when a modifier is used incorrectly.

A modifier that is misplaced in a sentence may cause confusion in meaning.

Type 1

EXAMPLE

WRONG:

Fred cut himself while shaving *badly*.

The word *badly* is a misplaced modifier. It is an adverb that modifies the meaning of the verb *cut* and, therefore, should be placed where there is no doubt about what it modifies. (It certainly isn't intended to modify *shaving*.)

CORRECT:

Fred cut himself *badly* while shaving.

The meaning is completely changed by the placement of the modifier. Now the sentence means what the writer intended to say.

Type 2

EXAMPLE

WRONG:

The fire was put out before any damage was done *by the firefighters*.

The phrase *by the firefighters* is a misplaced modifier. It modifies the verb *put out* and, therefore, should be placed near the verb it modifies. The writer certainly did not mean to say that the firefighters did any damage, yet this is the message conveyed. Once again, the misplaced modifier completely confuses the meaning.

CORRECT:

The fire was put out *by the firefighters* before any damage was done.

Type 3

EXAMPLE

WRONG:

What do you think of Bill Clinton *as a foreign diplomat*?

The adjective phrase *as a foreign diplomat* is obviously not intended to modify Bill Clinton, who cannot possibly be one. It should be placed near the word it modifies, *you*.

CORRECT:

As a foreign diplomat, what do you think of Bill Clinton?

What do you, *as a foreign diplomat*, think of Bill Clinton?

> By now, you may have figured out the rule that will save you from misplacing modifiers. *Always place the modifier, be it a word or a group of words, as near as possible to the word it modifies* so that the reader will not be in any doubt about the meaning of the sentence.

Here's a humorous example of a misplaced modifier to help you remember the rule.

WRONG:

They were *almost* married for five years.

To save the couple from gossip, you must place the modifier, *almost*, near the word it modifies, *five*.

CORRECT:

They were married for *almost* five years.

PRACTICE

1. Julia almost won all the prizes that were awarded.
2. The girl was dancing with her boyfriend in the red dress.
3. What do you think of Shakespeare as an English teacher?

ANSWERS

1. Julia won almost all the prizes that were awarded.
2. The girl in the red dress was dancing with her boyfriend.
3. As an English teacher, what do you think of Shakespeare?

DANGLING MODIFIERS

In the preceding examples, the modifier was misplaced. It should have been placed clearly and unmistakably near the word or words it modified. At least, though, there was a word in the sentence with which the modifier belonged. In the case of the *dangling modifier,* the problem is that there is no word or words to which the modifier clearly refers.

Here are some examples.

EXAMPLE 1

WRONG:

Standing on the corner, *the car* passed me by.

It is important to note that merely turning the incorrect sentence around will not keep the modifier from dangling.

WRONG:

The car passed me by, *standing* on the corner.

The sentence has to be rewritten to read:

CORRECT:

While I was *standing* on the corner, the car passed me by.

Standing is now part of the verb and is no longer dangling.

EXAMPLE 2

WRONG:

Speeding down the track at ninety miles an hour, *the stalled car* was demolished by the train.

The stalled car obviously can't be speeding. The dangling modifier, *speeding,* can refer only to the train. This is an easy one to correct.

CORRECT:

Speeding down the track at ninety miles an hour, *the train* demolished the stalled car.

EXAMPLE 3

WRONG:

At ten, my parents took me on a trip to California.

The phrase *at ten* is dangling since it does not have a noun it clearly modifies. Who was ten? Surely not the parents. The phrase has to be converted into a clause to correct the error.

CORRECT:

When I was ten, my parents took me on a trip to California.

> ### HOW CAN DANGLING MODIFIERS BE AVOIDED?
>
> *Dangling modifiers can be avoided by following an introductory phrase immediately with the word it modifies.*

Note the following examples.

EXAMPLE 4

WRONG:

To get good grades, *lessons* must be prepared carefully.

CORRECT:

To get good grades, *you* must prepare your lessons carefully.

EXAMPLE 5

WRONG:

After graduating from school, my father got me a good job.

CORRECT:

After I was graduated from school, my father got me a good job.

EXAMPLE 6

WRONG:

Watching the baseball game, the frank-furters tasted delicious.

CORRECT:

Watching the baseball game, I ate delicious frankfurters.

EXAMPLE 7

WRONG:

His leg was injured *while playing* tennis.

CORRECT:

He injured his leg *while playing* tennis.

EXAMPLE 8 (A humorous one)

WRONG:

Walking around in the zoo, my eye was caught by the gorilla.

Did you ever see an eye walking?

CORRECT:

As *I* was *walking around in the zoo*, the gorilla caught my eye.

PRACTICE

1. Sightseeing in Washington, D.C., the White House was my first stop.
2. Struggling in the water, the lifeguard saw me.
3. To earn an equivalency diploma, the GED test must be passed.

ANSWERS

1. When I was sightseeing in Washington, D.C., the White House was my first stop.
2. The lifeguard saw me while I was struggling in the water.
3. To earn an equivalency diploma, you must pass the GED test.

Now we come to the case of the modifier that can modify, not one, but two words or phrases.

Here's an example.

EXAMPLE 1

WRONG:

Does a man live here with a wife and a child *named Johnny?*

Who is named Johnny, the man or the child? The sentence is unclear as it stands. If the man is named Johnny, then this is how the question should have been written.

CORRECT:

Does a man *named Johnny* live here with a wife and a child?

If, however the child is named Johnny, the sentence has to be changed to put *Johnny* near the word *child*, thus making them equivalent.

CORRECT:

Does a man live here with a wife and a child, *Johnny?*

Here are some other two-way modifiers.

EXAMPLE 2

WRONG:

Plans for withdrawing troops *gradually* were drawn up by the government.

There are two possible meanings here: that the troops will be withdrawn gradually *or* that the plans were drawn up gradually. The writer probably meant:

CORRECT:

Plans for the gradual withdrawal of troops were drawn up by the government.

EXAMPLE 3

WRONG:

Because we studied hard *for a week* we were ready for the examination.

Did we study hard for a week, or were we ready for the examination for a week? It is not clear from the sentence what the writer intended. A comma, put in the right place, will help get rid of the two-way modifier.

CORRECT:

Because we studied hard for a week, we were ready for the examination.

PRACTICE

1. Because we had no classes for a week we were on vacation.
2. After I passed the GED test with the help of the teacher I got a job.
3. Hopes for recovering from the operation quickly were dashed by the doctor.

ANSWERS

1. Because we had no classes, for a week we were on vacation.
   or
   Because we had no classes for a week, we were on vacation.

2. After I passed the GED test, with the help of the teacher I got a job.
   or
   After I passed the GED test with the help of the teacher, I got a job.
3. Hopes for recovering quickly from the operation were dashed by the doctor.
   or
   Hopes for recovering from the operation were quickly dashed by the doctor.

PRACTICE WITH MODIFIERS

Beneath each sentence you will find five ways of writing the underlined part. Choose the answer that makes the best sentence. Answer 1 is always the same as the underlined part and is sometimes the right answer.

1. <u>Turning</u> the corner, my eye caught sight of the house where I used to live.

   (1) Turning
   (2) After turning
   (3) Having turned
   (4) When turning
   (5) When I turned

2. The <u>horse, ridden by the experienced jockey with the broken leg, had</u> to be destroyed.

   (1) horse, ridden by the experienced jockey with the broken leg, had
   (2) horse ridden by the experienced jockey with the broken leg had
   (3) horse with the broken leg ridden by the experienced jockey had
   (4) horse with the broken leg ridden by the experienced jockey, had
   (5) horse with the broken leg, ridden by the experienced jockey, had

3. The interviewee was <u>asked, "What is your opinion of Elizabeth Taylor as a movie critic?"</u>

   (1) asked, "What is your opinion of Elizabeth Taylor as a movie critic?"
   (2) asked his opinion of Elizabeth Taylor as a movie critic.
   (3) asked "What his opinion was of Elizabeth Taylor as a movie critic?"
   (4) asked, "As a movie critic, what is your opinion of Elizabeth Taylor?"
   (5) asked as a movie critic "What is your opinion of Elizabeth Taylor?"

4. <u>Wagging its tail, the dog food was quickly consumed by the happy puppy.</u>

   (1) Wagging its tail, the dog food was quickly consumed by the happy puppy.
   (2) Wagging it's tail, the dog food was quickly consumed by the happy puppy.
   (3) The happy puppy quickly consumed the dog food wagging its tail.
   (4) Wagging its tail, the happy puppy quickly consumed the dog food.
   (5) The dog food was quickly consumed by the happy puppy wagging it's tail.

5. <u>At the age of ten, my parents took me</u> to Disneyland.

   (1) At the age of ten, my parents took me
   (2) At the age of ten my parents took me
   (3) My parents took me at the age of ten
   (4) My parents took me aged ten
   (5) At the age of ten, I was taken by my parents

6. The secretary located the picture of the senator looking through the files.

   (1) The secretary located the picture of the senator looking through the files.
   (2) The secretary located the senator's picture looking through the files.
   (3) Looking through the files, the senator's picture was located by the secretary.
   (4) Looking through the files, the secretary located the picture of the senator.
   (5) Looking through the files the picture of the senator was located by the secretary.

7. The Smiths were almost married ten years before they had their first child.

   (1) were almost married
   (2) were married almost
   (3) almost were married
   (4) had been almost married
   (5) had been married almost

8. We finally agreed on a price for the picture of the ship that hung in the balcony.

   (1) picture of the ship that hung
   (2) picture of the ship that was hung
   (3) picture of the ship that hanged
   (4) ship's picture that hung
   (5) ship's picture that hanged

9. Our guest let us know that he would be arriving next week in his last letter.

   (1) that he would be arriving next week in his last letter
   (2) that he was arriving next week in his last letter
   (3) that he will arrive next week in his last letter
   (4) in his last letter that he would be arriving next week
   (5) in his last letter that he was arriving next week

10. My mother lives in the house on the hill that she just bought.

    (1) house on the hill that she just bought
    (2) house on the hill she just bought
    (3) house she just bought on the hill
    (4) house on the hill which she just bought
    (5) house, she just bought, on the hill

ANSWER KEY

1.	**5**	3.	**4**	5.	**5**	7.	**5**	9.	**4**
2.	**5**	4.	**4**	6.	**4**	8.	**4**	10.	**3**

WHAT'S YOUR SCORE?

_____ right,   _____ wrong

Excellent	9–10
Good	8
Fair	7

If you scored lower, review the corrected examples in this section

ANSWER ANALYSIS

1. **5** The way the sentence reads with the dangling modifier, the *eye* is *turning the corner.*
2. **5** *With the broken leg* is a misplaced modifier. Also see Rule 8 under "The Comma." In this sentence, commas are required to set off *ridden...jockey.*
3. **4** Again there is a misplaced modifier. *Movie critic* should be placed near the word it modifies—*interviewee.*
4. **4** The dangling modifier gives the impression that the *dog food was wagging its tail.* The possessive pronoun *its* does not have an apostrophe.
5. **5** The dangling modifier, *At the age of ten,* erroneously modifies *parents.*
6. **4** The dangling modifier *looking through the files* gives the mistaken impression that *the picture* was doing the looking.
7. **5** The modifier, *almost,* is misplaced. It should be near *ten years,* which it modifies. Also see "Misplaced Modifiers." The past perfect tense, *had been married,* is needed because the years of marriage in the past *preceded* the birth of the child, also in the past.
8. **4** The modifier, *that hung in the balcony,* should be near the noun, *picture,* which it modifies. See "Misplaced Modifiers." The past tense of *hang* (an object) is *hung.*
9. **4** The misplaced modifier, *in his last letter,* gives the mistaken impression

that the guest would be arriving *in* the letter. The phrase should be near *know*, which it modifies.

10. **3** *She just bought* modifies *house* and should be placed next to it.

Writing Correct Sentences

1. Poorly written sentences result when necessary words are omitted.

EXAMPLE

WRONG:

Deborah is as bright *x* if not brighter than her sister.

If the words *if not brighter than* are temporarily removed from the sentence, the sentence reads "Deborah is as bright... *x* her sister," clearly a sentence that makes no sense. If *as* is added at the point indicated, however, the sentence makes sense.

CORRECT:

Deborah is as bright as, if not brighter than, her sister.

OR BETTER STILL

Deborah is as bright as her sister, if not brighter.

2. Poorly written sentences result when you needlessly shift the construction of your sentences or your point of view. This happens in a number of ways.

EXAMPLE

WRONG:

Jim was a loyal friend, but self-discipline was lacking in him.

In this sentence, the subject of the, main clause is Jim. For some reason, the writer chose to shift to another subject, self discipline, although it was not necessary to do so.

CORRECT:

Jim was a loyal friend, but he lacked self-discipline.

EXAMPLE

WRONG:

We traveled in Israel, where archeological sites interested us.

CORRECT:

We traveled in Israel, where we were interested in archeological sites.

3. The verb may be shifted unnecessarily from the active to the passive voice or from one tense to another.

EXAMPLE

WRONG:

Alice enjoyed the movies, and television was also enjoyed by her.

Wherever possible, the active verb, *enjoyed*, should be used in preference to the passive, *was enjoyed*, because it expresses an idea more effectively. Having correctly started with an active verb, it is simply illogical to shift to the passive voice. In the first sentence, Alice *enjoyed* movies actively, but then television was *enjoyed* (the passive verb).

CORRECT:

Alice enjoyed movies and also television.

4. The number and person of the pronoun may be shifted unnecessarily.

EXAMPLE

WRONG:

If one wishes to succeed, they should work hard.

In this sentence, there is a shift in number from the singular pronoun *one* to the plural pronoun *they*. The number of the pronoun should be kept consistent.

CORRECT:

If *one* wishes to succeed, *one* should work hard.

OR

If *they* wish to succeed, *they* should work hard.

Usage

4

Agreement

SUBJECT AND VERB

A common error is failure to provide agreement between subject and verb. The basic rule is:

THE VERB MUST AGREE WITH ITS SUBJECT IN *NUMBER* AND IN *PERSON*.

Number

1. If the subject is *singular* (there is only one person or thing spoken about), the verb must be *singular*.
2. If the subject is *plural* (there is more than one person or thing spoken about), the verb must be *plural*.

Person

The verb must agree with the subject in *person*.

EXAMPLE

Singular	
I study	–First Person
You study	–Second Person
He	
She } studies	–Third Person
It	
Plural	
We study	–First Person
You study	–Second Person
They study	–Third Person

(See the "Glossary of Usage" (page 148) for a complete definition of *person*.)

There are two difficulties to overcome.

1. **What is the subject?**

   Ask yourself, "What is spoken about?" Ordinarily, you should have no trouble. Sometimes, however, the *subject and the verb are separated* by a number of intervening words.

   EXAMPLE

   Joe, despite the fact that he was a newcomer, *was* elected president.
   [*Joe* is still the subject—singular.]

   The intervening words may contain a plural.

   EXAMPLE

   Joe, together with all his friends, *was* welcomed warmly.
   [*Joe* is still the subject—singular.]

2. **Is the subject singular or plural?**

   EXAMPLE

   A *box* of chocolates *is* on the table.
   [*Box*, the subject, is singular.]

   Most of the time, *pronouns* will be involved in this type of error. Some pronouns that can cause confusion are:

Singular Pronouns		**Singular or Plural Pronouns**
anybody	neither	any
anyone	nobody	all
each	no one	more
either	one	most
everybody	somebody	none
everyone	someone	some

However, *compound subjects* may also be involved. When a subject has more than one part and the parts are connected by *and* or by a word or groups of words similar in meaning to *and,* it is considered a *compound subject* and is plural.

EXAMPLES

Joe *and* his friend *are* here.

To study hard, to play hard, to enjoy life are desirable aims.

Her outstanding contribution to school athletics, her service as class officer, and her excellent scholastic record qualify her for the position of president.

EXCEPTION

A compound subject that consists of two singular subjects connected by *either...or,* or *neither...nor* is considered a singular subject.

EXAMPLE

Neither Joe nor his friend *is* here.

NOTE:

Agreement is always with the number of the part of the subject nearest the verb.

EXAMPLE

Neither Joe nor I *am* voting for Frank.

Sometimes the subject comes after the verb. It is still the subject and may be singular or plural.

EXAMPLE

Pasted in the upper right-hand corner of the envelope were two ten-cent stamps.

[*Stamps* is the subject, even though it is the last word in the sentence. The verb is plural because the subject, *stamps,* is plural.]

SOME SPECIAL PROBLEMS

1. Agreement of subject and certain irregular verbs

The addition of the negative contraction *n't,* should not result in an error you would not make if the *n't* were omitted.

EXAMPLE

WRONG:
It don't matter.

CORRECT:
It doesn't matter.

You would never say, "It do matter." You would say, "It does matter."

Sometimes the reversal of subject and verb in a question causes an error that would not be made in a declarative sentence.

EXAMPLE

WRONG:
Was you there?

CORRECT:
Were you there?

2. Use of singular or plural after *there* at the opening of a sentence

The use of *is* or *are* depends on the *noun or pronoun that follows* the verb.

EXAMPLE

WRONG:
There's many ways to show you care.

CORRECT:
There are many ways to show you care.

3. Subjects that are plural in form but singular in meaning

The mere fact that a noun ends in *s* doesn't make it plural.

NOUNS WITH SINGULAR MEANINGS

economics	mumps
mathematics	news
measles	physics

---

4. Subjects that are singular in form but plural in meaning

Despite what you might think, these subjects take a *singular* verb when the group involved is thought of as a single unit.

NOUNS WITH PLURAL MEANINGS

army	group
class	orchestra
club	team
crowd	

EXAMPLE

The crowd *was* dispersed by the police.

PRACTICE

1. Economics is my most difficult subject.
2. The group of students are gathering at the office.
3. Neither Jules nor I are coming to the meeting.
4. There's a great many problems to be solved.
5. The teacher, together with her students, are going to the theater.

ANSWERS

1. Correct.
2. The group of students is gathering at the office.
3. Neither Jules nor I am coming to the meeting.
4. There are a great many problems to be solved.
5. The teacher, together with her students, is going to the theater.

PRONOUN AND ANTECEDENT

Another common error is failure to provide agreement between a pronoun and the noun it is replacing, its *antecedent*. The basic rule is:

A PRONOUN MUST AGREE WITH ITS ANTECEDENT IN *NUMBER, GENDER, AND PERSON.*

Number

If the antecedent is singular, the pronoun replacing it is singular.

EXAMPLE

Joe does *his* homework.
[The pronoun *his* takes the place of Joe. *Joe* is singular (one person); therefore, the pronoun is singular]

Gender

If the antecedent is masculine, the pronoun replacing it is masculine. If the antecedent is feminine, the pronoun replacing it is feminine.

EXAMPLE

Susan does *her* homework.

Person

Note above that both *Joe* and *Susan* are in the third person. Therefore, the pronouns replacing each must be in the third person—*his, her.*

How do you find the antecedent? Sometimes it is not easy to determine what noun the pronoun is replacing. The *antecedent may be separated from the pronoun* that takes its place by a number of words or by a phrase.

EXAMPLES

Joe is a *boy* who does *his* work.
[*boy*—antecedent; *his*—pronoun]

One of the boys who walked to school was late to *his* class.
[*one*—antecedent; *his*—pronoun]

The same procedure should be used to *determine the number of the pronoun when it replaces a compound subject.*

EXAMPLE

Joe and his *friend* brought *their* books.

When *either...or* or *neither...nor* connects singular subjects, the pronoun is singular.

EXAMPLE

Neither Joe *nor* his friend brought *his* book.

However, a pronoun that refers to a singular and a plural antecedent connected by *or* or *nor* agrees in number with the closer antecedent.

EXAMPLE

Either Kathy *or* the boys should explain *their* reasons.

SOME SPECIAL PROBLEMS

1. Pronouns that appear to be plural but are, in fact, singular

Some pronouns appear to refer to more than one person, but they never refer to more than one person *at a time*. Others may be either singular or plural.

Singular Pronouns		Singular or Plural Pronouns
anybody	neither	any
anyone	nobody	all
each	no one	more
either	one	most
everybody	somebody	none
everyone	someone	some

The following sentence may sound a little strange to you, but it is correct.

EXAMPLE

Every student must do *his* homework every day.

2. Pronouns that refer to nouns that appear to be plural but are singular in form

These pronouns require a verb in the singular.

EXAMPLE

The team continued *its* winning streak.

3. Pronouns with indefinite antecedents

The antecedent must be clear or the sentence rephrased.

EXAMPLE

WRONG:
Frank told Joe to take *his* books to school.
[To whom does *his* refer—to Frank or to Joe? The sentence must be rewritten to clear up this confusion.]

CORRECT:
Frank told Joe to take Frank's books to school for him.

OR BETTER

Frank said to Joe: "Take my books to school for me."

PRACTICE

1. Will everyone who has the right answer raise their hands?
2. Every participant must do his best.
3. The mother told her daughter to take her laundry to the laundromat.
4. One of my friends who went to school with me lost his mother.
5. Either the workers or the foreman are expected to attend.

ANSWERS

1. Will everyone who has the right answer raise his hand?
2. Correct.
3. The mother told her daughter, "Take my laundry to the laundromat."
4. Correct.
5. Either the workers or the foreman is expected to attend.

PRACTICE IN AGREEMENT

In each sentence, five parts are underlined and numbered. Where there is an error in agreement, choose the number of the underlined part that contains the error. If there is no error, choose answer 5. No sentence contains more than one error. These are included in the sentence correction type of multiple-choice item.

1. Luis, accompanied by <u>his</u> friend <u>are</u>
             (1)   (2)
waiting to see whether you and <u>I</u> <u>are</u>
                    (3)(4)
joining them. <u>No error</u>
            (5)

2. <u>There</u>, Mr. Chairman, <u>is</u> all the
  (1)   (2)
reports that the committee prepared
in <u>its</u> work as well as the notes <u>that</u>
   (3)   (4)
were taken. <u>No error</u>
           (5)

3. <u>There's</u> several ways for the city to
   (1)

   solve <u>its</u> fiscal problems, but <u>one</u> of
   (2)   (3)

   them is not to lose <u>its</u> integrity.
   (4)

   <u>No error</u>
   (5)

4. News from abroad <u>is</u> that each country
   (1)

   is supporting <u>its</u> own policies despite
   (2)

   the fact that <u>ours</u> <u>are</u> superior to
   (3)   (4)

   theirs. <u>No error</u>
   (5)

5. Let everyone who <u>agrees</u> raise <u>his</u>
   (1)   (2)

   hand so that neither George nor I <u>am</u>
   (3)

   in doubt about what the majority opinion

   <u>is.</u> <u>No error</u>
   (4)   (5)

6. Margaret asked Rosa to take <u>her</u>
   (1)

   clothes to the cleaners and to make

   certain that <u>none</u> of <u>them</u> <u>were</u> in need
   (2)   (3)   (4)

   of repair. <u>No error</u>
   (5)

7. Watching <u>our</u> game <u>were</u> Fred and his
   (1)   (2)

   father and his mother, together with

   <u>their</u> other children and <u>their</u> neighbors.
   (3)   (4)

   <u>No error</u>
   (5)

8. <u>Each</u> American must ask <u>himself</u>:
   (1)   (2)

   "<u>Don't</u> it matter if we pollute <u>our</u>
   (3)   (4)

   environment?" <u>No error</u>
   (5)

9. "Neither <u>I</u> nor <u>they</u> <u>are</u> attending
   (1)   (2) (3)

   the game," we said to <u>its</u> promoter.
   (4)

   <u>No error</u>
   (5)

10. <u>Everyone</u> gave <u>her</u> opinion that a blue
    (1)   (2)

    and white suit <u>was</u> the best choice for
    (3)

    Liz to wear although there <u>were</u>
    (4)

    exceptions. <u>No error</u>
    (5)

Answer Key

1. **2**	3. **1**	5. **5**	7. **5**	9. **5**
2. **2**	4. **5**	6. **1**	8. **3**	10. **5**

WHAT'S YOUR SCORE?

_____right,   _____wrong

Excellent	9–10
Good	8
Fair	7

If you scored lower, restudy this section, concentrating on the rules and examples.

Answer Analysis

1. **2** Luis, the subject of the sentence, is singular, so the verb should be singular: *is* instead of *are*.
2. **2** The subject of the sentence, *reports*, follows the verb. Since the subject is plural, the verb should be plural: *are*, not *is*.
3. **1** The subject is *ways*, which follows the verb. The verb must be plural to agree with the plural subject. *There's* should be *There are*.
4. **5** No error.
5. **5** No error.
6. **1** The antecedent of *her* is not clear. Is it Margaret or Rosa? Depending on the answer, *her* should be changed to *Margaret's* or *Rosa's*.
7. **5** No error.
8. **3** The correct form of the third person singular of the verb *do* is *does*. *Doesn't it...is* correct.
9. **5** No error.
10. **5** No error.

Case of Nouns and Pronouns

NOUNS

In English, the form of a noun rarely changes because of its case (its relation to other words in the sentence). Only in the *possessive case* do the forms of most nouns change.

Nominative Case

EXAMPLE

Frank hit Joe.
[*Frank* is the subject.]

Objective Case

EXAMPLES

Joe hit *Frank*.
[*Frank* is the object.]

Ellen ate the *salad*.
[*Salad* is the object.]

Possessive Case

EXAMPLE

Cesar's friend went away.
[A noun requires an apostrophe to indicate possession.]

PRONOUNS

Nearly all pronouns have different forms in the nominative, objective, and possessive cases. Only the pronoun forms *you* and *it* do NOT change when the case changes from *nominative* to *objective* or vice versa.

Nominative Case (for subjects)	Possessive Case	Objective Case (for objects)
I	my, mine	me
you	your, yours	you
he	his	him
she	her, hers	her
it	its	it
we	our, ours	us
they	their, theirs	them
who	whose	whom
whoever	–	whomever

BASIC RULES FOR THE CASE OF PRONOUNS

Nominative

1. The subject of a verb (a noun or a pronoun) is in the nominative case. This is true whether the subject is singular or compound.

   EXAMPLE

   WRONG: Me and Frank are good friends.
   CORRECT: Frank and *I* are good friends.

2. A predicate pronoun, whether singular or plural, is in the nominative case.

   EXAMPLES

   They thought that the visitor was *he*.

   Frank and Joe knocked on the door. "It is *they*," Sue said.

3. Pronouns in apposition with nouns in the nominative case are also in the nominative case.

   EXAMPLE

   The two *contestants*, *she* and *I*, were tied for first place.

Objective

4. The object of a verb (a noun or pronoun) is in the objective case. This is true whether the object is singular or compound.

   EXAMPLE

   They applauded *him* and *her*.

   Did they face Frank and *us* in the contest?

5. The object of a proposition is in the objective case. This is true whether the object is singular or compound.

   EXAMPLES

   Everyone but *her* did the homework.

   Between *you* and *me*, Sue is my best friend.

6. Pronouns in apposition with nouns in the objective case are also in the objective case.

   EXAMPLES

   They gave the prizes to the *winners, her and me*.

   For *us amateurs*, it is fun to watch professionals perform.

7. The subject of an infinitive is in the objective case; the same is true for the object of an infinitive.

   EXAMPLES

   We asked *him* to go.

   We wanted him to ask *them* to come along.

Possessive

8. Pronouns in the possessive case, unlike nouns in the possessive case, *never* have an apostrophe.

   EXAMPLES

   The dog wagged *its* tail.

   We have met the enemy and they are *ours*.

   She has *hers;* they have *theirs*.

SOME SPECIAL PROBLEMS

1. The case of pronouns coming after a comparison involving *than* or *as*

EXAMPLE

Joe received more votes than *I*.

The problem of deciding the case, and therefore the form, of the pronoun is complicated by the fact that the verb following *I* is understood.

Joe received more votes than I (did).

This is, therefore, a special instance of Rule 1: The subject of a verb is in the nominative case. This rule is true even if the verb is understood.

2. The case of the relative pronoun *who* or *whom*

Determine whether the relative pronoun is the subject or the object in its clause, and don't be fooled by words that come between the subject and the verb.

EXAMPLES

Who do you think *was elected* president? [*Who* is the subject of *was elected* and is therefore in the nominative case.]

Whom did you invite to the party? [*Whom* is the object of *did invite* and is therefore in the objective case.]

The same rule applies to *whoever* and *whomever*.

EXAMPLES

Give the book to *whoever asks* for it. [*Whoever* is the subject of *asks* and is in the nominative case.]

He impressed *whomever he approached*. [*Whomever* is the object of *approached* and is in the objective case.]

3. The case of pronouns (or nouns) coming before verbs ending in *-ing* and used as nouns

EXAMPLE

I do not object to *his* going with me.

Going is a verb form ending in *-ing* and used as a noun—object of the preposition *to*.

The possessive case, *his*, must be used. This is a fine point, but it often appears on tests.

Here are several more examples:

EXAMPLES

Fatigue was the cause of *Frank's* falling asleep at the wheel.

My going to school daily helped my work.

The television program interfered with *Sue's* and *Joe's* doing their homework.

4. The case of shift in pronoun reference

Unnecessary shift in pronoun reference is another common error. This involves pronouns that refer to the same person in the same sentence.

EXAMPLE

WRONG:
If *one* has a good sense of humor, *you* will probably be popular.

CORRECT:
If *one* has a good sense of humor, *one* will probably be popular.

If *you* have a good sense of humor, *you* will probably be popular.

Remember to be consistent in your use of pronouns. Do not shift from a pronoun in one person (*one* is in the third person) to another pronoun in another person (*you* is in the second person) unless the two pronouns refer to different people.

PRACTICE

1. Dolores was prettier than her.
2. Juana didn't like us asking her all those questions.
3. Who can you trust with your money these days?
4. Whoever thought of this idea is a genius.
5. Who do you feel deserves the prize?
6. When one works hard, he feels he deserves a raise.

ANSWERS

1. Dolores was prettier than she.
2. Juana didn't like our asking her all those questions.

3. Whom can you trust with your money these days?
4. Correct.
5. Correct.
6. When one works hard, one feels one deserves a raise.

PRACTICE WITH NOUNS AND PRONOUNS

In each sentence, five parts are under-lined and numbered. Where there is an error in case, choose the number of the underlined part that contains the error. If there is no error, choose answer 5. No sentence contains more than one error.

1. If I were she, I would not
   (1)   (2)
   exchange hers for mine. No error
                (3)   (4)   (5)

2. Whom, do you think, should be asked
   (1)
   to send his regrets to them and me?
             (3)   (4)   (5)
   No error
   (5)

3. It is they whom we invited, not him
       (1)   (2)   (3)
   and her. No error
       (4)   (5)

4. She and I decided to give ours to
   (1)   (2)   (3)
   whoever we pleased. No error
   (4)   (5)

5. They and I gave the prize to the
   (1)   (2)
   winners, him and her. No error
             (3)   (4)   (5)

6. The winners, he and she, were
                 (1)   (2)
   welcomed to the society by us and
                               (3)
   them. No error
   (4)   (5)

7. Did Joe and him meet John and her
                (1)   (2)

in the finals when they eliminated
their opponents and ours? No error
(3)   (4)   (5)

8. Between you and I, it's their problem,
           (1)   (2) (3)
   not ours. No error
       (4)   (5)

9. Whose going to get more votes than I,
   (1)
   he or she? No error
   (3)   (4)   (5)

10. For us newcomers, his going upset
        (1)   (2)
    us, me particularly. No error
    (3) (4)   (5)

ANSWER KEY

1. **5**	3. **5**	5. **5**	7. **1**	9. **1**
2. **1**	4. **4**	6. **5**	8. **2**	10. **5**

WHAT'S YOUR SCORE?

_____right,	_____wrong
Excellent	9–10
Good	8
Fair	7

If you scored lower, restudy this section, concentrating on the rules and examples.

ANSWER ANALYSIS

1. **5** No error.
2. **1** The relative pronoun that begins the sentence is the subject of *should be asked* and should therefore be in the nominative case, *who.*
3. **5** No error.
4. **4** This word is the object of the preposition *to*, so it should be in the objective case. *Whomever* is correct.
5. **5** No error.
6. **5** No error.
7. **1** This word is part of the subject and should be in the nominative case. *He* is correct.

8. **2** *Me* is correct since the objective case is required for the object of the preposition *between.*
9. **1** A subject and verb are required, not a possessive pronoun. *Who's* (or *who is*) is correct.
10. **5** No error.

Verbs

The *verb*, the part of the sentence that indicates the action carried out by the subject, *also indicates* when the action was carried out. It does so by its tense.

TENSE

The most widely used tenses are the

present,
past, and
future.

An additional tense is the present perfect, which is less frequently used, and sometimes causes difficulty.

This tense requires the use of a helping verb (*have*) and the past participle of the verb.

Verb: *to live*	
Present tense:	live
Past tense:	lived
Future tense:	shall live
Present perfect tense:	has, have lived

Examples of the use of tense:
Note the way in which the rest of each sentence is affected.

Present tense: I *live* in New York *now.*
Past tense: I *lived* in New York *last year.*
Future tense: I *shall live* in New York *next year.*
Present perfect tense: I *have lived* in New York for *five years.*

VERB FORMS

The principal parts of *to live, to see, to do,* and *to lie* are:

Verb	Past	Past Participle
live	lived	lived
see	saw	seen
do	did	done
lie	lay	lain

Many of the difficulties you have with verbs involve the *irregular verbs.* These change form in either the past or the past participle or in both. The most frequent error is the use of the wrong part of the verb, most often the past participle for the simple past.

EXAMPLES

WRONG:
I seen him do it.

CORRECT:
I *saw* him do it.

WRONG:
I done it.

CORRECT:
I *did* it.

Note: The present perfect tense is formed with *has* or *have* plus the past participle.

EXAMPLE

I *have seen* enough; I am glad to leave.

Study the following lists of most frequently confused verbs.

FREQUENTLY USED IRREGULAR VERBS

Verb	Past Tense	Present Perfect Tense
be	I was	I have been
beat	I beat	I have beaten
become	I became	I have become
begin	I began	I have begun
bite	I bit	I have bitten
blow	I blew	I have blown
break	I broke	I have broken
bring	I brought	I have brought
buy	I bought	I have bought
catch	I caught	I have caught
choose	I chose	I have chosen
come	I came	I have come
dig	I dug	I have dug
do	I did	I have done
draw	I drew	I have drawn
drink	I drank	I have drunk
eat	I ate	I have eaten
fall	I fell	I have fallen
fly	I flew	I have flown
freeze	I froze	I have frozen
get	I got	I have got *or* gotten
give	I gave	I have given
go	I went	I have gone
grow	I grew	I have grown
have	I had	I have had
know	I knew	I have known
lay	I laid (place)	I have laid
lead	I led	I have led
lie	I lay (recline)	I have lain
lose	I lost	I have lost
make	I made	I have made
ride	I rode	I have ridden
ring	I rang	I have rung
rise	I rose	I have risen
run	I ran	I have run
say	I said	I have said
see	I saw	I have seen
shake	I shook	I have shaken
sink	I sank	I have sunk
speak	I spoke	I have spoken
swim	I swam	I have swum
swing	I swung	I have swung
take	I took	I have taken
teach	I taught	I have taught
tear	I tore	I have torn
think	I thought	I have thought
throw	I threw	I have thrown
win	I won	I have won
write	I wrote	I have written

50 OTHER IRREGULAR VERBS

Verb	Past Tense	Present Perfect Tense
arise	I arose	I have arisen
awake	I awaked *or* awoke	I have awaked *or* awoke
bear	I bore	I have borne *or* born
bend	I bent	I have bent
bind	I bound	I have bound
build	I built	I have built
creep	I crept	I have crept
deal	I dealt	I have dealt
dive	I dived, dove	I have dived
drive	I drove	I have driven
drown	I drowned	I have drowned
feed	I fed	I have fed
feel	I felt	I have felt
fight	I fought	I have fought
find	I found	I have found
flee	I fled	I have fled
forget	I forgot	I have forgotten
forgive	I forgave	I have forgiven
hang (an object)	I hung	I have hung
hang (a person)	I hanged	I have hanged
hide	I hid	I have hidden
hold	I held	I have held
kneel	I knelt	I have knelt
leave	I left	I have left
lend	I lent	I have lent
meet	I met	I have met
mistake	I mistook	I have mistaken
pay	I paid	I have paid
prove	I proved	I have proved *or* proven
seek	I sought	I have sought
sell	I sold	I have sold
send	I sent	I have sent
sew	I sewed	I have sewed *or* sewn
shine	I shone	I have shone
shrink	I shrank	I have shrunk
sing	I sang	I have sung
slay	I slew	I have slain
slide	I slid	I have slid
sleep	I slept	I have slept
spend	I spent	I have spent
spring	I sprang	I have sprung
steal	I stole	I have stolen
strike	I struck	I have struck
swear	I swore	I have sworn
sweep	I swept	I have swept
swing	I swung	I have swung
wake	I waked *or* awoke	I have waked *or* woken
wear	I wore	I have worn
weep	I wept	I have wept
wind	I wound	I have wound

PRACTICE

1. They begun to improve after much practice.
2. Aaron brung the book I needed to school.
3. My friends had drunk all the lemonade at the party.
4. The valise that had lain out in the rain was soaked.
5. The batter swang the bat at the wild pitch.
6. The hostess had laid out the cookies beautifully on the table.
7. The oarsman almost drownded when the winds blew up.
8. The choir sung all the songs on the program.
9. The sun shined all day.
10. The guest awoked before I did.

ANSWERS

1. They began to improve after much practice.
2. Aaron brought the book I needed to school.
3. Correct.
4. Correct.
5. The batter swung the bat at the wild pitch.
6. Correct.
7. The oarsman almost drowned when the winds blew up.
8. The choir sang all the songs on the program.
9. The sun shone all day.
10. The guest awoke before I did.

A SPECIAL PROBLEM

The irregular verbs you have just studied present difficulties when used in simple sentences. Even more difficult are complex sentences (see the "Glossary of Usage" on page 148). In these sentences, you have to figure out the time (or tense) relationship between the verbs in the two clauses.

What is the proper sequence of tenses for verbs in the main and dependent clauses of a complex sentence?

This can vary, but some common sequences follow.

VERB SEQUENCES	
Main Clause	**Dependent Clause**
Present tense: I *gain* weight	**Present tense:** when I *eat* too much.
Present tense: I *believe*	**Past tense:** that he *studied* for the examination.
Past tense: The audience *applauded*	**Past tense:** when the soloist *finished*.
Future tense: I *shall leave*	**Present tense:** when he *comes*.

PRACTICE

PRACTICE

After Patrick attended high school for four years, he earned a diploma.

ANSWER

Correct.

PRACTICE WITH VERBS

In each sentence, five parts are underlined and numbered. Choose the number of the underlined part that contains the error. If there is no error, choose answer 5. No sentence contains more than one error.

1. He was <u>suppose</u> to <u>lay</u> the book on
         (1)   (2)
   the table after he <u>brought</u> it home
                (3)
   from the man from whom he had
   <u>taken</u> it. <u>No error</u>
   (4)   (5)

2. After the pitcher <u>threw</u> a fast ball,
             (1)
   the batter <u>swung</u> the bat and
         (2)
   <u>hit</u> the ball to left field, where it was
   (3)
   <u>caught.</u> <u>No error</u>
   (4)   (5)

3. The child <u>awoke</u> when the parent
         (1)
   <u>brung</u> the gift he had <u>chosen</u> and
   (2)   (3)
   <u>gotten</u> into the bedroom. <u>No error</u>
   (4)   (5)

4. After he <u>drunk</u> his milk, the athlete
         (1)
   <u>dived</u> into the pool and <u>swam</u> ten
   (2)   (3)
   laps more than he <u>said</u> he would.
             (4)
   <u>No error</u>
   (5)

5. I <u>lay</u> in bed dreaming of the places I
    (1)
   had <u>seen,</u> the friends I had not
       (2)
   <u>forgotten</u>, and the new friends I had
      (3)
   <u>met</u>. <u>No error</u>
   (4)   (5)

6. When I <u>wrote</u> her that I wanted it
        (1)
   <u>done,</u> Rita <u>hung</u> the picture that had
   (2)   (3)
   <u>lain</u> on the floor. <u>No error</u>
   (4)   (5)

7. The entertainer <u>sung</u> the song I had
           (1)
   <u>sung</u> when you <u>saw</u> me, and I was
    (1)   (2)
   <u>shaken</u> by the coincidence. <u>No error</u>
    (4)   (5)

8. He would have <u>drownded,</u> had I not
            (1)
   <u>bent</u> the board which pinned him
   (2)
   down and then <u>broken</u> it with the
            (3)
   tool I had <u>found.</u> <u>No error</u>
         (4)   (5)

9. I <u>arose;</u> I <u>sprang</u> after the mugger; I
    (1)   (2)
   <u>struck</u> him; I <u>threw</u> him to the ground.
    (3)   (4)
   <u>No error</u>
   (5)

10. The suspect admitted: "I <u>done</u> it. I
               (1)
    <u>crept</u> into the apartment. I <u>fought</u>
    (2)   (3)
    with the man. I <u>tore</u> his clothes."
            (4)
    <u>No error</u>
    (5)

ANSWER KEY

1. **1**	3. **2**	5. **5**	7. **1**	9. **5**
2. **5**	4. **1**	6. **5**	8. **1**	10. **1**

Answer Analysis

1.1 The past participle of *suppose* is *supposed*.

2.5 No error.

3.2 The past tense of *bring* is *brought*.

4.1 The past tense of *drink* is *drank*.

5.5 No error.

6.5 No error.

7.1 The past tense of *sing* is *sang*.

8.1 The past participle of *drown* is *drowned*.

9.5 No error.

10.1 The past tense of *do* is *did*.

Adjectives and Adverbs

An **adjective** is used to describe a noun or pronoun.

EXAMPLE

He wore a *dark* hat.

An **adverb** is used to modify a verb, an adjective, or another adverb.

EXAMPLE

He played *very poorly.*
[*Poorly* modifies *played; very* modifies *poorly.*]

There are times, however, when adjectives and adverbs may be confused. This confusion can be caused by

Use of a verb that describes a condition, not an action

If the verb is not used as an action verb, or if the verb describes a condition, then an *adjective rather than an adverb* must follow it. Why? The reason is that the adjective really modifies the subject and not the verb.

VERBS THAT DESCRIBE A CONDITION

look	be
feel	am
taste	is
seem	are
become	was
smell	were
grow	has been
sound	had been

EXAMPLES

He looks *sick.*
[*Sick* describes *he.*]

I feel *good.*
[*Good* describes *I.*]

The fruit tastes *sweet.*
[*Sweet* describes *fruit.*]

Adjectives or adverbs that have the same form

ADJECTIVES AND ADVERBS WITH THE SAME FORM

fast	long
slow	ill
deep	sharp

EXAMPLES

He worked very *fast.*

He cut *deep* into the skin.

SOME SPECIAL PROBLEMS

1. Adjectives that indicate the degree to which they describe nouns

Degree is indicated in one of two ways:

- the adverb *more* or *most* is placed before the adjective;

- The suffix *-er* or *-est* is added to the adjective.

EXAMPLES

He was *more quiet* than she.

He was *quieter* than she.

He was the *most friendly* person there.

He was the *friendliest* person there.

What is the problem? It is that you must use the *more* or *-er* form when two and only two persons or things are involved. Similarly, you must use the *most* or *-est* form when three or more persons or things are involved. Never use *both* in the same sentence.

EXAMPLES

He was the *shyer* of the two.

He was the *most shy* among the three of them.

NOTE:

Some irregular adjectives do not follow these rules. The most frequently used are:

	Comparative (Comparison between two people or things)	Superlative (Comparison among more than two people or things)
bad	worse	worst
far	farther	farthest
good	better	best
many, much	more	most

---

2. Incorrect use of a negative adverb and a negative adjective in the same sentence

EXAMPLE

WRONG:
He does*n't* do *no* work.
[A negative adverb—*n't [not]* and a negative adjective—*no*]

CORRECT:
He doesn't do *any* work.

PRACTICE

1. The orchestra sounded superb.
2. Alfredo waited long for his reward.
3. Enrique was the noisiest student in the class.
4. Of the three children, the youngest was the worst.

ANSWERS

1. Correct.
2. Correct.
3. Correct.
4. Correct.

PRACTICE WITH ADJECTIVES AND ADVERBS

In each sentence, five parts are underlined and numbered. Choose the number of the underlined part that contains the error. If there is no error, choose answer space 5. No sentence contains more than one error.

1. Hardly <u>hadn't</u> he <u>quietly</u> and <u>painfully</u>
        (1)   (2)   (3)
built the sand castle than it was
<u>swiftly</u> torn down. <u>No error</u>
   (4)   (5)

2. Although I feel <u>good</u>, I look <u>sick</u>
                   (1)   (2)
because I ate <u>sparingly</u> and
                  (3)
<u>improperly. No error</u>
   (4)   (5)

3. <u>Gladly</u> I'll say that he <u>surely</u> hit the
   (1)   (2)
ball <u>real</u> <u>well</u>. <u>No error</u>
     (3)   (4)   (5)

4. Anita was the <u>most</u> <u>intelligent</u> girl
          (1)   (2)

   although she didn't dress <u>well</u> or act
                          (3)

   <u>properly.</u> <u>No error</u>
    (4)   (5)

5. The lunch, which was <u>lovingly</u> and
                  (1)

   <u>carefully</u> prepared, tastes <u>deliciously</u>
    (2)   (3)

   and is <u>healthful.</u> <u>No error</u>
       (4)   (5)

6. He worked <u>fast</u>; I worked <u>slow</u>. He
      (1)   (2)

   rested <u>frequently</u>; I worked <u>continuously</u>.
        (3)   (4)

   <u>No error</u>
    (5)

7. It doesn't seem <u>right</u> that some
         (1)

   flowers that look <u>ugly</u> smell <u>sweet</u>
           (2)   (3)

   while others that look pretty smell
   <u>bad</u>. <u>No error</u>
   (4)   (5)

8. Doesn't Chico succeed just as <u>good</u>
               (1)

   as Carlos though he isn't as
   <u>hard-working</u>, <u>serious</u>, and
    (2)   (3)

   <u>conscientious</u>? <u>No error</u>
    (4)   (5)

9. The <u>worse</u> of the two storms ended
     (1)

   as <u>quickly</u> and <u>suddenly</u> as it had
     (2)   (3)

   begun, leaving us <u>ill</u> with fear.
            (4)

   <u>No error</u>
    (5)

10. He spoke <u>deliberately</u> and chose
        (1)

   his words <u>carefully</u>, with the result
        (2)

   that his speech cut <u>deep</u> and he was
          (3)

   the <u>more</u> effective of the two speakers.
    (4)

   <u>No error</u>
    (5)

ANSWER KEY

| 1. 1 | 3. 3 | 5. 3 | 7. 5 | 9. 5 |
| 2. 5 | 4. 5 | 6. 5 | 8. 1 | 10. 5 |

WHAT'S YOUR SCORE?

    _____right,   _____wrong
Excellent   9–10
Good   8
Fair   7

If you scored lower, restudy this section, concentrating on the rules and examples.

ANSWER ANALYSIS

1. **1** To avoid a double negative, the correct word is *had*.
2. **5** No error.
3. **3** The word modifies the adverb *well*, so it should be an adverb—*really*.
4. **5** No error.
5. **3** The verb *tastes* requires a predicate adjective. *Delicious* is correct.
6. **5** No error.
7. **5** No error.
8. **1** This word modifies the verb *Does(n't) succeed*, so an adverb, *well*, is required.
9. **5** No error.
10. **5** No error.

Glossary of Usage

ACTIVE VERB Verb whose subject is the doer of the action that the verb is indicating. (The batter *hit* the ball.)

ADJECTIVE Part of speech that helps describe a noun or pronoun by giving it a more exact meaning. (*big* house; *many* friends; *this* pencil)

ADVERB Part of speech that helps describe a verb, an adjective, or another adverb by giving it a more exact meaning. (walks *slowly*; *very* pretty)

AGREEMENT This refers to parts of a sentence that are alike in gender, number, and person such as a subject and its verb and a pronoun and its antecedent. (*I study. He studies. The dog* wagged *its* tail.)

ANTECEDENT Noun that is replaced with a pronoun. (*EVERYONE* will please remove *his* hat. *WALKING* is *what* I like to do most.)

ANTONYM Word that is opposite in meaning to another word. (happy, sad)

APPOSITION Condition describing two nouns, next to each other in a sentence, that are equivalent in meaning. (my brother, Joe; Mrs. Brown, the secretary)

AUXILIARY VERB Verb that helps another word show voice or tense. (I *would have* forgotten. She *had* left.)

CASE Form of a noun or pronoun that shows its relation to the other words in a sentence.
Nominative case of pronouns has the forms *I, you, he, she, we, they, who,* and is used as the subject of a verb or as a predicate noun. (*They* go. It is *we.*)
Possessive case shows possession. In nouns, it is formed with the apostrophe: (Frank's). Possessive pronouns include *mine, yours, his, hers, its, ours, theirs, whose.* (*Note:* There is no apostrophe in any possessive pronoun.)
Objective case of pronouns has the forms *me, you, him, her, us, them, whom,* and is used as the object of a verb, object of a preposition, subject or object of an infinitive. (They hit *him.* They gave it to *him.* I want *him* to go. I want to hit *him.*)

CLAUSE Group of words in a sentence that contains a subject and a predicate.
Independent clauses can stand alone. (He played well.)
Dependent clauses (adverb, adjective, or noun clauses) cannot stand alone. (He played well *although he was hurt.* The book *that I read* was very interesting. *That he recovered* was a miracle.)

COMPARISON Change of form in adjectives and adverbs to show increase in amount or quality. (strong, strong*er*, strong*est*; good, bett*er*, be*st*)
Comparative refers to a greater degree in quality or quantity of one item or person with respect to another. (smart*er* of the two)
Superlative refers to a greater degree in the quality or quantity of one item or person with respect to two or more others. (larg*est* of the three)

COMPLEX SENTENCE Sentence that has one independent clause and at least one dependent clause. (We are happy *that you came.*)

COMPOUND-COMPLEX SENTENCE Sentence that has two independent clauses and at least one dependent clause. (*Joe sang* and *Joan played the song that she had been studying.*)

COMPOUND PREDICATE Two or more predicates usually joined by *and* or *or.* (He *goes to school by day* and *works at night.*)

COMPOUND SENTENCE Sentence that has two independent clauses. (*Joe sang* and *Joan played the piano.*)

COMPOUND SUBJECT Two or more subjects that take the same verb. (*Frank* and *I* will come.)

CONJUNCTION Part of speech that connects words, phrases, or clauses. (bread *and* butter; "to be *or* not to be"; She came *when* I left.)

CONSONANT Letter other than *a, e, i, o, u* (which are considered vowels) or *y* (which is considered a semivowel).

DASH Punctuation mark that shows a pause or break in a sentence. (He may not come—but why should I worry?)

DIRECT OBJECT Noun or pronoun that receives the action of the verb. (Jon struck *him.* Give *it* to Gerry.)

DIRECT QUOTATION Use of the exact words of the speaker. (The teacher said, "Do your homework.")

FIRST PERSON Pronoun and verb forms that refer to the person or persons speaking. (*I, we; my, our; me, us; am, are*)

FUTURE TENSE Time of verb that shows a happening yet to take place. (He *will retire* next year.)

GENDER Classification of nouns and pronouns into three groups: masculine, feminine, and neuter. A *masculine* pronoun is *he;* a *feminine* pronoun is *she;* a pronoun in the *neuter* gender is *it.*

GLOSSARY Listing of difficult or unusual words occurring in a book with their definitions. It is usually found in the back of the book. This glossary is at the end of the chapter to which it relates.

HOMONYM Word with the same sound as another word or words but with a different spelling and meaning. (to, too, two; pear, pair)

HYPHEN Mark (-) used to form a compound adjective (two-faced), to join certain prefixes to words (ex-president) or to separate words into syllables (En-glish).

IDIOM Group of words that, taken together, differs in meaning from the individual words used separately. (once upon a time)

INDIRECT OBJECT Word that shows, without any preposition, to whom or for whom the action in the sentence is taking place. (He gave *me* a pen.)

INDIRECT QUOTATION Quotation that does not use the exact words of the speaker. (The candidate said [that] he would accept the nomination.)

INFINITIVE Verb form that is usually indicated by *to* before the verb. Sometimes *to* is understood. (I want *to go*. He made me *laugh.)*

INTERJECTION Independent word that expresses strong feeling. (ah! oh! alas!)

INTERROGATIVE SENTENCE Sentence that asks a question. (Did he leave?)

INTRANSITIVE VERB Verb that has no object. (He *stands.* I *sit.)*

MODIFIER Word or group of words that help describe another word or group of words by giving a more exact meaning. See ADJECTIVE, ADVERB.

NOMINATIVE CASE Form of the noun or pronound that is the subject or predicate noun in a sentence. *(She* is *president.)*

NOUN Part of speech that is the name of a person, place, or thing. (George Washington; New York; toy)

NUMBER Change in the form of a noun, pronoun, adjective, or verb to show whether there is one *(singular)* or more than one *(plural)* (man, men; he, they; this, these; is, are)

OBJECT Noun or pronoun that names the person or thing acted upon by the verb. (She brought the *book.* I admire *her.)*

OBJECTIVE CASE Form of the noun or pronoun that shows it is the person or thing that receives the action. (I hit *him.)*

OBJECT OF A PREPOSITION Noun or pronoun that follows a preposition that controls it. (with *me*; between *you* and *me*; among *him* and *them)*

PARALLELISM (PARALLEL STRUCTURE) Two parts of a sentence that are given the same form, and therefore have the same

importance, in the sentence. (He eats *both* meat *and* vegetables. *Not only* the relatives were invited *but also* the friends. Beth enjoys *jogging, skating,* and skiing.)

PARTICIPLE Form of a verb that is used both as an adjective and as part of a verb. (the *sleeping* child; am *going*; have *gone)*
present participle (going)
past participle (gone)

PART OF SPEECH One of eight categories into which words in a sentence are assigned: *noun, pronoun, verb, adjective, adverb, preposition, conjunction, interjection.*

PASSIVE Form of verb that is used when the subject of the sentence receives the action. (The watch *was given* to Joe. The man *was laid* to rest.)

PAST TENSE Time of verb that shows that an action has been completed. (He *went.* We *did go.)*

PERSON Form of pronoun or verb that tells whether the person (or persons) speaking is doing the action *(first person)*; a person being spoken to is doing the action *(second person);* or the person spoken about is doing the action *(third person).* (*We* left for home. *You* stayed here. *They* arrived late.)

PHRASE Group of words without a subject and predicate, usually introduced by a preposition, that has a use in a sentence like that of a noun, adjective, or adverb. (*In the park* is where I like to sit. Jeannie *with the light brown hair.* He ran *to first base.)*

PLURAL Form of noun, pronoun, adjective, or verb that indicates that more than one person, place, or thing is being spoken about in the sentence. (boys; they; these; are)

POSSESSIVE Form of noun or pronoun that shows ownership. *(girl's* pencil; *ladies'* hats; *its* paw)

PREDICATE Part of the sentence that tells something about the subject (what the subject does, what is done to the subject, or what is true about the subject). (The boy *went home quickly.* This milk *tastes sour.)*

PREFIX Addition (usually a single syllable) to the beginning of a word that adds to or changes the meaning of the word. (*impossible; ex*-president; *re*view; *pre*fix)

PREPOSITION Part of speech that shows the relationship between a noun or pronoun that is its object, and some other word in the sentence. (Mary went *to* the library.)

PRESENT PERFECT TENSE   Time of verb that shows an action that started in the past and is continuing or has just been completed in the present. It requires the use of an auxiliary verb in the present tense and the past participle. (He *has been* our friend for years.)

PRESENT TENSE   Time of verb that shows an action that is going on now. There are three forms of this tense—he *says*, he *is saying*, he *does say*.

PRONOUN   Part of speech that is used in place of a noun. (John came. *He* was welcome.) The four main kinds of pronouns are:
demonstrative (this, that, these, those);
personal (I, you, he, she, it, we, they);
possessive (mine, yours, his, hers, ours, theirs);
relative (that, what, who, which).

PROPER NOUN   Noun that refers to an individual person, place, or thing. (George Washington; New York City; City Hall)

ROOT   Basic part of a word, without prefixes or suffixes, that gives the main meaning of the word. (*cred*—believe; with prefix *in* and suffix *ible*—in *cred* ible— unbelievable)

RUN-ON (or COMMA SPLICE) SENTENCE   Two sentences that are made into one by mistake. They are separated either by a comma or by no punctuation at all. (Wrong: Kay is class president, she is my friend. Correct: Kay is class president. She is my friend.)

SENTENCE   Group of words containing a subject and a predicate and expressing an independently complete thought. (*He came early*.) Three chief kinds of sentences are:
declarative (makes a statement);
interrogative (asks a question);
imperative (gives a command).

SENTENCE FRAGMENT   Group of words that may contain a subject and a predicate but that fails to express a complete thought and is, by error, punctuated as if it did. (Wrong: Hoping to hear from you. Correct: I am hoping to hear from you.)

SINGULAR   Form of noun, pronoun, adjective, or verb that refers to one person, place, or thing in a sentence. (boy; he; this; is)

SUBJECT   Part of the sentence that does the action or is spoken about. (*He* hit the ball. *The watch* was given to the man.)

SUFFIX   Addition to the ending of a word that adds to or changes its meaning. (hand*ful*; quick*ly*; act*or*)

SYLLABLE   Smallest group of sounds, consisting of a vowel sound, and one or more consonant sounds that are pronounced as a unit. (con-so-nant)

SYNONYM   Word that is very similar in meaning to another word. (happy—glad)

TENSE   Time of an action, indicated by the verb as *present, past, future, present perfect*. These are the most widely used tenses in English.

USAGE   Actual use of language by the people at large. *Good usage* is the actual use of language by educated persons and other persons in positions of importance.

VERB   Part of speech that indicates the action carried out by the subject or that tells something about the subject. (He *hit* the ball. She *was* in the garden.)

VOWELS   Letters representing the sounds *a, e, i, o, u.* The letter *y* is considered a semivowel, as in *slowly*.

Mechanics

Mechanics deals with capitalization, punctuation, and spelling (especially homonyms, possessives, and contractions).

Capitalization. Fifteen basic rules are provided with applications for each.

Punctuation. Basic rules and examples are given for each of the major punctuation marks: period, question mark, exclamation point, comma, semicolon, colon, apostrophe, parentheses and quotation marks.

Spelling. A total of 650 words has been included in three lists for you to study. Study the basic rules for homonyms, possessives, and contractions.

CAPITALIZATION

BASIC RULES OF CAPITALIZATION

1. Capitalize the first word of a sentence.

   EXAMPLE

   We went to the theater.

2. Capitalize the first word of a direct quotation.

   EXAMPLE

   He said, "Don't give up."

3. Capitalize the first word of a line of poetry.

   EXAMPLE

   "Poems are made by fools like me..."

4. Capitalize proper nouns (names of specific persons, places, or things).

   EXAMPLES

   Winston Churchill; Mr. James Jones; New York City; Main Streeet; City Hall
   Note: Capitalize names of family members when used in place of their actual name.

   CORRECT
   I need you, Mom.
   Grandma went to the store today.

5. Capitalize proper adjectives (adjectives formed from proper nouns).

   EXAMPLES

   American; Shakespearean

6. Capitalize names of specific organizations or institutions.

   EXAMPLES

   Sousa Junior High School; Columbia University; American Red Cross; Federal Bureau of Investigation

7. Capitalize days of the week, months of the year, and holidays. (*Note:* Do *not* capitalize seasons, e.g., winter.)

   EXAMPLES

   Sunday; June; Thanksgiving

8. Capitalize languages. (*Note:* These are the *only* school subjects that are capitalized.)

   EXAMPLES

   French; Hebrew
   I study English, Spanish, biology, mathematics, and social studies.

9. Capitalize races and religions.

   EXAMPLES

   Hindu; Christian

10. Capitalize references to the Deity and to the titles of holy books.

    EXAMPLES

    the Almighty; the Old Testament; the Koran

11. Capitalize titles of people when they are followed by a name, being careful to capitalize both the title and the name. (*Note:* If a specific person is meant, the name may, at times, be omitted.)

    EXAMPLES

    President Lincoln; Dr. Schweitzer; Her Majesty the Queen

12. Capitalize titles of works of literature, art, and music.

    EXAMPLES

    War and Peace (note that articles, short prepositions, and conjunctions such as *and* are not capitalized in titles); *American Gothic;* Beethoven's Fifth Symphony

13. The pronoun *I* is capitalized at all times.

    EXAMPLES

    I walked one mile south to the school.

14. Sections of the country are capitalized, but directions are not.

    EXAMPLES

    I lived in the South for five years.
    We traveled south.

15. Capitalize specific places and addresses, but do not capitalize the second half of a hyphenated number.

EXAMPLE

Times Square; 25 Main Street; 65 West Thirty-third Street.

PRACTICE

1. Junior belongs to the Boy scouts.
2. My favorite subject in school is English.
3. New York City is about 250 miles south of Boston.
4. The bible is a holy book to millions.
5. Salt Lake city is in Utah.
6. My cousin shouted, "be careful!"
7. Donna's cat was named sandy.
8. My home is located near broadway.
9. Most inhabitants of Israel are jewish.
10. Labor day occurs in September.

ANSWERS

1. Junior belongs to the Boy Scouts.
2. Correct.
3. Correct.
4. The Bible is a holy book to millions.
5. Salt Lake City is in Utah.
6. My cousin shouted, "Be careful!"
7. Donna's cat was named Sandy.
8. My home is located near Broadway.
9. Most inhabitants of Israel are Jewish.
10. Labor Day occurs in September.

PRACTICE WITH CAPITALIZATION

The following sentences contain problems in capitalization. If there is an error, select the one underlined part that must be changed to make the sentence correct. If there is no error, choose answer 5. No sentence contains more than one error. These are included in the sentence correction type of multiple-choice item.

1. Peter Winkle of West Virginia, the last
                        (1)
   doubtful republican name to be called
                (2)
   on May 16, was, like Ross, a "nobody."
      (3)   (4)
   No error
   (5)

2. Most of our compound words
   beginning with Indian can be traced
                    (1)
   to the white man's contact with these
   original Americans; thus we have
              (2)
   Indian summer, Indian file and Indian
   (3)   (4)
   giver. No error
          (5)

3. Her sons have used books in the way
   her father, the Hon. John F.
                    (1)   (2)
   Fitzgerald, mayor of Boston, used
                (3)
   Thanksgiving turkeys as elaborate
   (4)
   calling cards. No error
                   (5)

4. As the 800-foot-long tanker *Houston*
                                  (1)
   passed beneath the Verrazano Bridge,
                        (2)   (3)
   the captain ordered its speed
       (4)
   reduced. No error
            (5)

5. The English teacher assigned the
       (1)
   Poe story "Murders in The Rue
   (2)   (3)   (4)
   Morgue." No error
            (5)

6. He lived on Twenty-First Street, at
                (1)   (2)   (3)
   the corner of Broadway. No error
                 (4)   (5)

7. The Frick Museum is located East of
       (1)   (2)   (3)
   Central Park. No error
           (4)   (5)

8. He failed <u>C</u>hemistry and <u>F</u>rench but
           (1)   (2)
   passed <u>E</u>nglish and <u>S</u>panish. <u>No error</u>
          (3)   (4)   (5)

9. I attended <u>D</u>awson <u>S</u>chool and
              (1)   (2)
   <u>S</u>outhern <u>U</u>niversity. <u>No error</u>
   (3)   (4)   (5)

10. <u>M</u>r. and <u>M</u>rs. Jones and <u>F</u>amily invite
    (1)   (2)   (3)   (4)
    you to a party at their home.
    <u>No error</u>
    (5)

Answer Key

1.	**2**	3.	**5**	5.	**4**	7.	**3**	9.	**5**
2.	**5**	4.	**5**	6.	**2**	8.	**1**	10.	**4**

WHAT'S YOUR SCORE?

_____right,	_____wrong
Excellent	9–10
Good	8
Fair	7

If you scored lower, restudy this section, concentrating on the rules and examples.

Answer Analysis

1. **2** See Rule 6. Capitalize names of specific organizations.
2. **5** No error.
3. **5** No error.
4. **5** No error.
5. **4** Unimportant words in the title of a literary work are not capitalized.
6. **2** In an address, the second part of a hyphenated number is not capitalized.
7. **3** Directions are not capitalized.
8. **1** Only languages, among school subjects, are capitalized.
9. **5** No error.
10. **4** This word refers to a general group and, therefore, is not capitalized.

PUNCTUATION

BASIC RULES OF PUNCTUATION

The Period
The period is used after
- a sentence that makes a statement;

  EXAMPLE

  He arrived on time.

- a sentence that gives a command;

  EXAMPLE

  Sit up straight.

- some abbreviations and contractions.

  EXAMPLES

  Mr., A.M., etc.

The Question Mark
The question mark is used after a sentence that asks a question.

EXAMPLE

Did you like the game?

The Exclamation Point
The exclamation point is used after a sentence that emphasizes a command or that conveys strong feeling.

EXAMPLES

Stop writing immediately!

What a pleasant surprise!

The Comma
The comma is used

- to separate a word or words that indicate the person to whom a remark is addressed, known as direct address;

  EXAMPLE

  John, please come here.

- to separate a word or words that add information about the noun, known as appositives;

  EXAMPLE

  Nancy, my secretary and receptionist, is very efficient.

- to set off expressions or phrases that are inserted in the sentence and that interrupt the normal word order;

  EXAMPLE

  Notre Dame, in my opinion, will win the championship.

- after introductory phrases and clauses, particularly when they are long (more than three words) or when the meaning may be temporarily confused if the comma is omitted;

  EXAMPLE

  When the dog jumped up, Darryl's parents became frightened.

- to separate independent clauses of a compound sentence joined by a conjunction such as *and, but, for, nor, or, so,* or *yet,* unless the sentences are short;

  EXAMPLE

  Joe decided to attend the game, but I remained at home.

  but (if the sentences are short)

  Joe returned but I remained.

- to separate items in a series;

  EXAMPLE

  The box contained books, toys, games, and tools.

- before the text of a quotation; in a divided quotation, commas are used to set off the speaker;

EXAMPLES

The teacher said, "Return to your seats."
"Return to your seats," said the teacher, "so we may continue the lesson."

- to set off clauses and phrases that are not essential to the meaning of the sentence;

EXAMPLE

Jan, who was seated beside me, left early.
[Note that the clause "who was seated beside me" is not essential to the sentence, which, without it, would read, "Jan left early."]

    but

The students who studied hard passed the test.
[The clause "who studied hard" is essential since only the students who studied hard passed. Without this clause the meaning intended by the writer—that students who did not study hard failed—would not be clear to the reader.]

- after the salutation in a friendly letter;

EXAMPLE

Dear Dad,

- after the complimentary close in all letters;

EXAMPLE

Sincerely,

- between the day of the month and the year when writing a date;

EXAMPLE

May 23, 2003

- between the city and the state when writing an address.

EXAMPLE

St. Augustine, FL 32086

Note: **Do NOT use commas . . .**
- between a subject and its verb when the verb immediately follows the subject;

EXAMPLE

The boys on the team celebrated their victory.

- to separate parts of a compound predicate or a compound subject.

EXAMPLES

They enjoyed a good dinner and saw a play.

Sally and Jose make great teammates.

The Apostrophe

The apostrophe is used
- in a contraction to show that letters have been omitted;

EXAMPLE

Don't stop pretending to have a good time.

- to show possession;

EXAMPLE

My brother's dog has been through obedience training.

- to show plural of single letters.

EXAMPLE

Susan made straight A's in geography class.

Quotation Marks

Quotation marks are used
- around titles of songs or poems;

EXAMPLE

My favorite song is "Imagine" by John Lennon.

- around titles of chapters;

EXAMPLE

I particularly enjoyed Chapter 3, "Your Pet as a Companion."

  - around titles of articles.

EXAMPLE

In today's paper, there was an article entitled "Hurricane looms in Gulf waters."

Parentheses

Parentheses are used to enclose any words that explain or add to an idea or ideas contained in a sentence. Parentheses are always used in pairs (that is, one opens and the other closes the included word or words).

EXAMPLE

Frank Jones (author of *Ideas That Work*) has written many best sellers.

The Semicolon

The semicolon is used . . .
- to separate independent clauses in a sentence; either a semicolon or a comma may be used when the clauses are short;

EXAMPLE

I came; I saw; I conquered. (or I came, I saw, I conquered.)

- to separate items in a series when these items contain commas.

EXAMPLE

The guests included William H. Rehnquist, Chief Justice of the United States; Colin Powell, Secretary of State; and Edward Kennedy, Senator.

The Colon

The colon is used . . .

- to introduce a series or a list of items;

  EXAMPLE

  These items were included on the shopping list: fruit, vegetables, meat, fish, and ice cream.

- before a restatement, an illustration, or an explanation of the main idea of the sentence;

  EXAMPLE

  I have but one rule of conduct: Do unto others as you would be done by.

- after the salutation of a business letter.

  EXAMPLE

  Dear Sir:

PRACTICE

1. Invite Constance my sister to the dance.
2. What nonsense!
3. Eli, if you ask me, is the smartest of them all.
4. After Ruth rested at home she felt better.
5. The childrens' clothing department was well stocked.
6. Your country expects only one thing from you citizens; do your duty.
7. Present at the meeting were General Smith, Army Chief of Staff: Admiral Jones, Chief of Naval Operations: and General Gray, Commanding General of the Marine Corps.
8. Maria indicated that she wouldnt come.
9. My parents warned me, "Dont be late."

ANSWERS

1. Invite Constance, my sister, to the dance.
2. Correct.
3. Correct.
4. After Ruth rested at home, she felt better.
5. The children's clothing department was well stocked.
6. Your country expects only one thing from you citizens: Do your duty.
7. Present at the meeting were General Smith, Army Chief of Staff; Admiral Jones, Chief of Naval Operations; and General Gray, Commanding General of the Marine Corps.
8. Maria indicated that she wouldn't come.
9. My parents warned me, "Don't be late."

PRACTICE WITH PUNCTUATION

The following sentences contain problems in punctuation. Choose the number of the underlined part that must be changed to make the sentence correct. <u>No sentence contains more than one error.</u> If there is no error, choose answer 5. These are included in the sentence correction type of multiple-choice item.

1. Consider, for example, the widespread
        (1)   (2)
   notion that a clean environment can
   be obtained by reducing our
   dependence on "technology". No error
        (3)   (4)   (5)

2. However, we often get careless; we
       (1)   (2)
   say, "It's close enough, or "Who cares
                  (3)
   anyway." No error
      (4)   (5)

3. Gasoline and whisky have much in
   common: they're both blended, both
      (1) (2)   (3)
   distilled—and both have something of
      (4)
   a kick. No error
        (5)

4. The object therefore, is to clean up
          (1)   (2)
   the air: the higher the vapor
      (3)
   pressure, the more likely it is that
      (3)
   gasoline will evaporate. No error
                (5)

5. At 6 PM tomorrow, however, they will
      (1)   (2)   (3)
   be fed into a 12-inch diameter
   pipeline, each entering at a different
      (4)
   point. No error
      (5)

6. Mr. James Smith, President
        (1)
   The Line Company_
            (2)
   16 Fifth Street_
            (3)
   Lansing, Arizona 47962
   Dear Mr. Smith,
            (4)
   <u>No error</u>
      (5)

7. 1413 Sixth Street_
               (1)
   Columbus_Florida_
         (2)   (3)
   March 5, 1984
         (4)
   <u>No error</u>
      (5)

8. "Are you coming?" he asked.
                (1)
   "Yes."
      (2)
   "When?"
         (3)
   "Now."
         (4)
   <u>No error</u>
      (5)

9. "You take care of your problems,"
                          (1)
   said those to whom we addressed our
   questions, "and we'll take care of
         (2)(3)
   ours". <u>No error</u>
      (4)   (5)

WHAT'S YOUR SCORE?

_____right,	_____wrong
Excellent	9–10
Good	8
Fair	7

If you scored lower, restudy this section, concentrating on the rules and examples.

ANSWER ANALYSIS

1. **4** At the end of a sentence, the period should be placed between the quotation marks and the word (*technology.*").
2. **4** The question mark is used after a sentence that asks a question.
3. **5** No error.
4. **1** See rule 3 under "The Comma." The comma is used to set off expressions or phrases that are inserted in the sentence and that interrupt the normal word order.
5. **1** See rule 3 under "The Period." The period is used after most abbreviations.
6. **4** A colon is required after the salutation of a business letter.
7. **2** In an address, a comma is used between the city and the state.
8. **5** No error.
9. **4** The period should be enclosed within the quotation marks.

Spelling

Spelling mistakes on the new GED test consist of homonyms, contractions, and possessives. First, review the basic rules of spelling. Then, move on to the list of homonyms and the practice exercises. Finally, study the rules for contractions and the rules for forming possessives. Complete all practice exercises, and you will be well prepared for this section of the test.

BASIC RULES OF SPELLING

1. Plurals of most nouns are formed by adding *s* to the singular.

   EXAMPLE

   house, hous*es*

2. When the noun ends in *s, x, ch,* or *sh,* the plural generally is formed by adding *es.*

   EXAMPLES

   gas, gas*es*
   box, box*es*
   witch, witch*es*
   dish, dish*es*

3. a. The plural of a noun ending in *y* preceded by a consonant is formed by changing *y* to *i* and adding *es.*

   EXAMPLE

   lady, lad*ies*

   b. The plural of a noun ending in *y* preceded by a vowel does not change *y* to *i* EXCEPT for words ending in *quy.*

   EXAMPLES

   toy, toy*s*
   but
   soliloquy, soliloqu*ies*

4. a. A word that ends in *y* preceded by a consonant usually changes *y* to *i* before a suffix unless the suffix begins with *i.*

   EXAMPLE

   beauty, beaut*iful*

   b. A word that ends in *y* preceded by a vowel usually keeps the *y* when a suffix is added.

   EXAMPLE

   coy, coy*er*

5. a. A word that ends in silent *e* generally keeps the *e* when a suffix beginning with a consonant is added.

   EXAMPLE

   care, care*ful*

   b. A word that ends in silent *e* generally drops the *e* when a suffix beginning with a vowel is added.

EXAMPLES

believe, believ*able*
move, mov*ing*

6. **Exceptions to Rule 5.**
Words ending in *ce* and *ge* keep the letter *e* before *able* and *ous*.

EXAMPLES

notice, notic*eable*
change, chang*eable*
courage, courag*eous*

7. A one-syllable word that ends in one consonant following a short vowel generally doubles the consonant before a suffix that begins with a vowel.

EXAMPLES

big, big*gest*
thin, thin*ner*

8. A word of more than one syllable that ends in one consonant following one short vowel generally doubles the final consonant before a suffix beginning with a vowel *if* the accent is on the last syllable.

EXAMPLES

omít, omit $\boxed{t}$*ed*
        regrét, regret $\boxed{t}$*ing*
           allót, allot $\boxed{t}$*ed*

9. The letter "i" is generally used before "e" except after "c."

EXAMPLES

bel*ie*ve, rec*ei*ve

There are many exceptions, as:

    either
    neither
    neighborhood
    weigh
    leisure

10. An apostrophe is used to show that a letter has been omitted in a contraction.

EXAMPLES

it is, it's
they are, they're

11. An abbreviation is always followed by a period.

EXAMPLE

etc.

12. Nouns of Latin origin ending
    —in *us* become *i* in the plural,

    EXAMPLE

    rad*ius*, rad*ii*

    —in *a* become *ae* in the plural,

    EXAMPLE

    formul*a*, formul*ae*

    —in *um* become *a* in the plural,

    EXAMPLE

    medi*um*, medi*a*

    —in *is* become *es* in the plural.

    EXAMPLE

    ax*is*, ax*es*

13. The suffix *ful* is spelled with a single *l*.

    EXAMPLES

    help*ful*
    tablespoon*ful*

    (*Note:* The word *full* itself is the only exception.)

MOST FREQUENTLY CONFUSED HOMONYMS

A common error is the confusion of two words having the <u>same pronunciation</u> but <u>different spellings and meanings</u>. These are called *homonyms.* In this humorous sentence—"A doctor must have lots of patients (patience)"—there is no way of our knowing which word the speaker means if the sentence is spoken. Therefore, we don't know how to spell the word. The words *patients* and *patience* are homonyms.

Forty-four groups of homonyms follow. Be certain to check the meaning of each word in each group so that you can figure out the spelling from the meaning of the word as it is used in a sentence.

air; heir	meat; meet
all together; altogether	pail; pale
ate; eight	pair; pear
aunt; ant	patience; patients
blew; blue	peace; piece
bough; bow	principal; principle
brake; break	read; red
buy; by	right; write
cent; scent; sent	road; rode
coarse; course	sew; so; sow
for; four	stationary; stationery
forth; fourth	steal; steel
grate; great	straight; strait
groan; grown	some; sum
hear; here	son; sun
him; hymn	their; there; they're
hole; whole	threw; through
hour; our	to; too; two
knew; new	way; weigh
know; no	witch; which
lead; led	wood; would
mail; male	your; you're

CONTRACTIONS AND POSSESSIVES

Knowing where and when to use the apostrophe is an important skill. Use the following guidelines to help you.

RULES FOR CONTRACTIONS

1. When forming a contraction, always place the apostrophe in the spot of the missing letter(s).

   EXAMPLE

   cannot = can't; is not = isn't;
   they are = they're; should not = shouldn't

2. There are some irregularly formed contractions.

   EXAMPLES

   will not = won't

RULES FOR POSSESSIVES

1. When forming possessives, write "'*s*" after the word that is possessing.

   EXAMPLES

   Sally's book (the book belongs to Sally)

   children's books (the books belong to the children)

   author's viewpoint (the viewpoint belongs to the author)

2. When forming possessive plural nouns, just place an apostrophe after the "s."

   EXAMPLES

   authors' viewpoints (the viewpoints belong to more than one author)

   books' pages (the pages belong to more than one book)

PRACTICE WITH SPELLING

For each sentence, choose the correct homonym, contraction, or possessive noun/pronoun to fill in the blank.

1. Prince William is the _____ to the English throne.

   (1) air
   (2) heir

2. Our school's _____ communicates well with his students.

   (1) principal
   (2) principle

3. If there is one thing I _____, it's that many countries fear the United States military.

   (1) know
   (2) no

4. Of _____ I want to take a vacation!

   (1) course
   (2) coarse

5. We set _____ on our great adventure to the Florida Keys.

   (1) fourth
   (2) forth

6. My cousin has _____ many pets.

   (1) to
   (2) too
   (3) two

7. In church, the choir sang a beautiful _____.

   (1) him
   (2) hymn

8. The short stop _____ the ball just in time to make the third out.

   (1) through
   (2) threw

9. When my family members are finally _____, we have a great time.

   (1) all together
   (2) altogether

10. I _____ wait to tell my best friend that I got a job!

    (1) ca'nt
    (2) can't

11. The economy _____ improve when people are afraid to buy stocks.

    (1) wo'nt
    (2) won't

12. My dog likes the smell of _____.

    (1) daisies'
    (2) daisies

13. Susan wants to be an illustrator for _____ books.

    (1) children's
    (2) childrens'

14. _____ cousin works for the CIA.

    (1) Sallys'
    (2) Sally's

15. My _____ Judy is a stay-at-home mom.

    (1) aunt
    (2) ant

16. A letter carrier delivers _____.

    (1) mail
    (2) male

17. Pencil _____ can be poisonous if swallowed by young children.

    (1) led
    (2) lead

18. I learned to _____ clothes from my mother.

    (1) sew
    (2) so
    (3) sow

19. The gym has a set of _____ bikes that I like to ride.

    (1) stationary
    (2) stationery

20. The _____ group decided to do volunteer work together as a service project.

    (1) hole
    (2) whole

21. It _____ my fault that the vase was broken by the puppy; I told you to place it on a higher shelf.

    (1) wasn't
    (2) was'nt

22. The doctor sees about one hundred _____ a day.

    (1) patients
    (2) patience

23. If you are over _____, you should try diet and exercise.

    (1) wait
    (2) weight

24. When _____ homework becomes too much to complete, it is time to start budgeting your time.

    (1) your
    (2) you're

25. _____ are many types of American Indian tribes that still live in the United States.

    (1) There
    (2) Their
    (3) They're

26. The soccer team _____ three tournaments in a row!

    (1) one
    (2) won

27. A spider actually eats _____ own web when he's finished with it.

    (1) his
    (2) it's

28. When _____ work to be done, I'd rather take a nap!

    (1) theirs
    (2) there's

29. The boys thought the bowling alley was all _____ for the evening.

    (1) theirs
    (2) there's

30. When _____ finished debating an issue, the senators return to their offices in the capitol building.

    (1) there
    (2) their
    (3) they're

Organization

BASIC RULES OF ORGANIZATION: UNITY AND COHERENCE

On the GED exam, questions referring to organization in writing make up 15% of the exam. Organization means that the writing has both unity and coherence. Unity and coherence make your writing clear and easy to comprehend.

UNITY

Unity: To bring individual thoughts and ideas together in an organized manner.

- In a sentence, it is important to write only *one thought* at a time.

- In a paragraph, it is important to organize several supporting sentences that relate to only *one idea.*

- In an essay, it is important to organize several paragraphs of ideas that support only *one thesis.*

TOPIC SENTENCES

The unifying idea in a paragraph is demonstrated through the use of a topic sentence. A topic sentence may occur in one of four places in a paragraph:

1. at the beginning, stating the unifying idea of the paragraph
2. at the middle, building up to a point, then expanding on an idea
3. at the end, presenting a well-developed argument followed by a convincing conclusion
4. nowhere; sometimes the topic sentence may not be stated, but implied

PRACTICE

1. **Where is the topic sentence in the following paragraph?**

She has shown me the awesome tranquilty of nature. She gives me the bigger half of the cookie when there's only one left. She doesn't buy me fancy clothes, or take me to expensive restaurants. Instead, she tells me about the rose garden she planted a few years back and the quilt she just started. She always seems to know the answer to my "Why?" questions. She is my mother, my best friend and confidant.

ANSWER

1. At the end: "She is my mother, my best friend and confidant."

COHERENCE

Coherence: To bring several related ideas together around a central theme and in an organized manner.

- Use transitions in paragraphs from sentence to sentence and in essays from paragraph to paragraph.

Pasta is easy to make. To make enough pasta for four people, **first** put two cups of water and a teaspoon of salt in a large pot. Bring the salted water to a boil over high heat. **Then** add 16 ounces of pasta. **When** the water returns to a boil, lower the heat to medium high and slightly stir the pasta to keep pieces from sticking together. Let the pasta cook for 8 to 10 minutes, and **then** remove the pot from the heat. **Immediately** pour the pasta into a colander to remove the water. **Finally**, run cool water over the pasta to keep it from becoming sticky. **Now** you may serve it with your favorite sauce.

- Use parallelism (phrases and clauses that have the same grammatical structure).

EXAMPLE

Rabbits can become as tame and domesticated as cats **if they are** handled gently on a daily basis and **if they are** taught to use a litter box.

- Use an organizational pattern: chronological order, spatial order, order of importance, specific to general or general to specific, and problem/solution.

EXAMPLE (of chronological order)

Travelers must be aware of the restrictions for carry-on items today. When **first** arriving at the airport, travelers must check any luggage that will not fit in the overhead bins. Any ordinary objects with a sharp point that could be used as a weapon, such as nail files, needles, and knives, must be checked at this stage in the traveling. **Secondly**, travelers must be prepared to be searched at the passenger screening station. Here, federal security officers direct travelers through metal detectors and assist them in placing all carry-on items through the x-ray machines. At this point, if any contraband items are spotted, they are confiscated. **Finally**, the traveler may be randomly searched again just before boarding the plane.

COMMON TRANSITIONS

Without transitions, your writing will not flow smoothly. Transitions are words and phrases that connect one idea to the next, one sentence to the next, or one paragraph to the next.

Transitions are important because they are the "glue" that holds your ideas together. But be careful not to overuse transitions in your writing; too many transitions can cause as much confusion as too few.

Therefore, you don't necessarily need a transition between every idea or every sentence, but it is a good idea to use a transition between each paragraph. Transitions usually come near the beginning of a paragraph. However, you should use a transition wherever it works best.

NINE TYPES OF TRANSITIONS

1. *Transitions that* **add**: additionally, again, along with, also, and, another, as well, besides, equally important, finally, for example, for instance, further, furthermore, in addition, likewise, moreover, next, together with, too.
2. *Transitions that* **signal time**: about, after, afterward, as soon as, at, at the same time, before, during, earlier, finally, first, immediately, in the meantime, later, last, meanwhile, next, next week, next time, next year, now, prior to, second next, soon, then, third, till, today, tomorrow, until, when, yesterday.
3. *Transitions that* **indicate place**: above, across, against, along, alongside, amid, among, around, away from, back of, behind, below, beneath, beside, between, beyond, by, down, here, in front of, in the center of, in the middle of, inside, into, near, off, on top of, outside, over, there, throughout, to the left, to the right, under, up.
4. *Transitions that* **emphasize**: again, another key point, first thing to remember, for this reason, frequently, important to realize, indeed, in fact, in short, in summary, key point, most important information, on the negative side, on the positive side, surprisingly, to emphasize, to point out, to repeat, with this in mind.
5. *Transitions that* **illustrate**: for example, for instance, in other words, put another way, seems clear from this, simply stated, stated differently, that is, to clarify, to illustrate the point.
6. *Transitions that* **show cause and effect**: as a result, for this reason, then, therefore.
7. *Transitions that* **compare**: accordingly, also, as, by comparison, comparable to, in conjunction with this, in the same manner, in the same way, just as, like, likewise, similarly, sometimes.
8. *Transitions that* **contrast**: although, as opposed to, but, conversely, counter to, even so, even though, however, in spite of this, in the meantime, nevertheless, on the contrary, on the other hand, otherwise, sometimes, still, yet.
9. *Transitions that* **summarize**: accordingly, all in all, as a result, consequently, due to, in closing, in conclusion, in short, in sum-

mary, in the last analysis, finally, lastly, logical conclusion is, therefore, thus, to conclude.

PRACTICE

Circle the best transition to complete the sentence.

1. I looked <u>across/behind</u> the basketball court to find my opponent about to shoot a three-pointer.
2. <u>When/Before</u> I woke up from my nap, I found the dog had eaten my cake!
3. I learned how to read quicker; <u>as a result/for example</u> I have been making better grades.
4. The store owner locked up each night; <u>however/accordingly</u>, the thief was still able to break in and steal more than a thousand dollars worth of merchandise.
5. My sister has <u>yet/therefore</u> to discover what she wants to do with her life.

ANSWERS

1. across
2. When
3. as a result
4. however
5. yet

PARALLEL STRUCTURE

Parallelism in a coherent paragraph occurs when phrases and clauses have the same grammatical structure. Parallel structure provides clarity in the writing. On the other hand, faulty parallelism disrupts the balance of grammatical structure. Parallelism appears in the following: outlines, lists, compound structures, comparisons, and contrasted elements. Study the two basic guidelines for parallel structure:

1. It is important to balance

   - nouns with nouns; adjectives with adjectives, etc.

EXAMPLE

The History of Sports
    I. Famous **Players**
        A. Deceased
        B. Living
    II. Great **Coaches**
    III. Championship **Teams**

   - phrases with phrases

EXAMPLE

To wonder about the planet is **to question** the entire universe.

   - clauses with clauses

EXAMPLE

I wanted to know **that I was safe** and **that everyone else was safe**, too.

2. To make your writing parallel, repeat

   - a preposition
   - an article
   - the "to" of the infinitive
   - the introductory word of a phrase or clause

PRACTICE

Rewrite each sentence, correcting the faulty parallelism.

1. She learned to pay attention and take notes.
2. My brother and sister love to play volleyball.
3. The dog chased the cat behind the table and a wall!

ANSWERS

1. She learned to pay attention and to take notes.
2. My brother and my sister love to play volleyball.
3. The dog chased the cat behind the table and up a wall!

PARAGRAPH ORGANIZATION

There are four main ways to organize a paragraph:

1. Start with a topic sentence, then add supporting sentences.
2. Start with detailed sentences that support one idea and end with a topic sentence.
3. Start with a statement of the topic, then restrict the idea and illustrate it.
4. Start with a question or statement of problem, then answer and explain a solution.

PRACTICE

1. **What type of organization does this paragraph illustrate?**

What I have most wanted to do throughout the past ten years is to make political writing into an art. My starting point is always a feeling of partisanship, a sense of injustice. When I sit down to write a book, I do not say to myself, "I am going to produce a work of art." I write it because there is some lie that I want to expose, some fact to which I want to draw attention, and my initial concern is to get a hearing. But I could not do the work of writing a book, or even a long magazine article, if it were not also an aesthetic experience. Anyone who cares to examine my work will see that even when it is downright propaganda it contains much that a full-time politician would consider irrelevant. I am not able, and I do not want, completely to abandon the world view that I acquired in childhood. So long as I remain alive and well I shall continue to feel strongly about prose style, to love the surface of the earth, and to take a pleasure in solid objects and scraps of useless information. It is no use trying to suppress that side of myself. The job is to reconcile my ingrained likes and dislikes with the essentially public, non-individual activities that this age forces on all of us.

—George Orwell, "Why I Write"

2. **What type of organization does this paragraph illustrate?**

Dealing with the [lime]stone itself involves a whole new set of machines. Great mobile engines called channelers, powered by electricity, chug on rails from one side of the bed to the other, chiseling ten-foot-deep slots. Hammering and puffing along, they look and sound and smell like small locomotives. By shifting rails, the quarries eventually slice the bed into a grid of blocks. The first of these to be removed is called the key-block, and it always provokes a higher than usual proportion of curses. There is no way to get to the base of this first block to cut it loose, so it must be wedged, hacked, splintered and worried at, until something like a clean hole has been excavated. Men can then climb down and, by drilling holes and driving wedges, split the neighboring block free at its base, undoing in an hour a three-hundred-million-year-old cement job.

—Scott Russell Sanders
from "Digging Limestone"

3. **What type of organization does this paragraph illustrate?**

In October 1347 a Genoese fleet made its way into the Messina harbor in northeast Sicily. Its crew had "sickness clinging to their very bones." All were dead or dying, afflicted with a disease from the Orient. The Messinese harbor masters tried to quarantine the fleet, but it was too late. It was not men but rats and fleas that brought the sickness, and they scurried ashore as the first ropes were tied to the docks. Within days, the pestilence spread throughout Messina and its rural environs and, within six months, half the region's population died or fled. This scene, repeated thousands of times in ports and fishing villages across Eurasia and North Africa, heralded the coming of the great natural disaster in European history—the Black Death.

—Robert S. Gottfried, *The Black Death*

4. **What type of organization does this paragraph illustrate?**

American humor rested less on inherent wit or sharp observation of human filings than on rough drolleries full of exaggeration and strange usage for its own sake. The speech became noisy and profuse. It imitated sounds of sucking and smacking and cracking and slicing and chipping and sawing and thumping and poking and digging and clapping and exclaiming and hushing. It stuck in extra syllables for elegance and comic surprise. It liked to repeat in the same word the sound of dental consonants that gave a jerky, droll effect. It made comedy out of mouth-widening vowel sounds and speech-yodels whose effect depended upon a swallowed l—the gobble of the North American turkey. It was at times almost an abstract sound. Its character stripped of known words and their meaning, and left only with sound, might still suggest the meaning intended, along with the hard, simple, and at times lyrically beautiful life from which it came.

—*Sons of Democracy*

ANSWERS

1. Starts with topic sentence, then adds supporting sentences.
2. Starts with statement of problem, then explains a solution.
3. Starts with detailed sentences and ends with topic sentence.
4. Starts with a statement of the topic, then restricts and illustrates it.

TEXT DIVISION

In a piece of writing, it is important to organize all of the paragraphs around a central theme and to separate the paragraphs appropriately from each other.

The most logical time to make a paragraph break (or beginning of a new paragraph) is when there is a shift in

- time or place
- a sequence from one point to the next
- emphasis for the sake of clarity
- dialogue from one speaker to another
- focus from one idea to the next

BASIC GUIDELINES FOR UNITY AND COHERENCE

To achieve and identify unity and coherence in writing, there are a few basic guidelines to follow. Ask yourself the following questions to identify whether or not the piece of writing has unity and coherence:

1. Is there a topic sentence that states only one main idea?
2. Are enough details (elaboration) given to clearly explain the main idea?
3. Is there unity? (Does every sentence refer to the main idea?)
4. Are the ideas arranged in a logical order?
5. Are the ideas connected with transitions?

Practice Paragraphs and Questions on Organization

<u>Questions 1–3</u> refer to the following passage.

What is the purpose of chess?

(1) People know little about this fascinating game. (2) A common saying among those who know this game best is that the winner of the game is the one who makes the next-to-the-last mistake. (3) Even among grandmasters, the secret of success is not superior strategy but the failure to make tactical errors. (4) The purpose of the game is the opponent's skillful exploitation of a mistake made at any point in the game. (5) It is rare, nonetheless, that a game lasts for 100 moves. (6) The average number of moves is usually somewhere around 45, and the shortest game can consist of only 2 moves.

1. The topic sentence of this paragraph is

    (1) sentence 1
    (2) sentence 2
    (3) sentence 3
    (4) sentence 4
    (5) sentence 5

2. Sentence 1 should be

    (1) left as it is
    (2) placed last
    (3) placed after sentence 3
    (4) placed after sentence 6
    (5) omitted

3. A new paragraph can

    (1) be started after sentence 2
    (2) be started after sentence 3
    (3) be started after sentence 4
    (4) be started after sentence 5
    (5) not be started

<u>Questions 4–6</u> refer to the following passage.

How did the Soviet Union fall?

(A)

(1) Although the peasants occasionally rioted and rebelled, they continued to believe the old myths about how much their tsar loved them. (2) So their uprisings were usually directed against the nobility and local gov-

ernment officials, and were poorly organized and easy to suppress. (3) Russia's factory workers prior to the twentieth century were too few and unorganized to sustain a coherent movement. (4) Russia's revolutionary movement did not emerge from the peasants or workers, the two most oppressed groups in Russia. (5) Instead, it was Russia's small, educated classes, those exposed to foreign ideas, that beginning in the 1820s produced its revolutionaries. (6) At first they were nobles—the only people in Russia at the time with a Western-type education. (7) In 1825 a group of noble army officers tried to overthrow the tsar. Their effort failed, and harsh punishment followed.

(B)

(8) Beginning in the 1840s and especially after 1860, as education spread, most revolutionaries came from the middle and lower classes. (9) The crucial point about these people is what they wanted for Russia. (10) Most of them did not want a society with a constitutional, democratic government and a free-enterprise economic system similar to what they saw in Western Europe or the United States. (11) Instead, Russian revolutionaries were socialists who believed a country's economy should be in the hands of the people as a whole and that every person should receive an equal share of that economy's wealth. (12) Some Russian socialists hoped the economy would be controlled at the local level, while others believed it should be run by a powerful, centralized state. (13) All of them, however, opposed the free-enterprise, capitalist system because they felt it caused inequality and forced most people to live in poverty. (14) They also distrusted constitutional democracy as it existed in the West, mainly because they felt that political institutions in capitalist societies were manipulated and controlled by the rich at the expense of the poor.

—"The Rise and Fall of the Soviet Union" by Michael Kort

4. The topic sentence of paragraph (A) is

   (1) sentence 1
   (2) sentence 2
   (3) sentence 3
   (4) sentence 4
   (5) sentence 5

5. Sentence 4 should be

   (1) left as it is
   (2) placed first
   (3) placed after sentence 1
   (4) placed after sentence 8
   (5) omitted

6. A new paragraph can

   (1) be started after sentence 2
   (2) be started after sentence 3
   (3) be started after sentence 4
   (4) be started after sentence 5
   (5) not be started

Questions 7–9 refer to the following passage.

What would happen if animals were allowed their freedom?

(1) Among watchdogs in Seattle, Berkeley was known generally as one of the best. (2) Not the smartest, but steady. (3) A pious German shepherd (Black Forest origins, probably), with big shoulders, black gums, and weighing more than some men, he sat guard inside the glass door of Tilford's Pet Shoppe, watching the pedestrians scurry along First Avenue, wondering at the derelicts who slept ever so often inside the foyer at night, and sometimes he nodded when things were quiet in the cages behind him, lulled by the bubbling of the fishtanks, dreaming of an especially fine meal he'd once had, or the little female poodle, a real flirt, owned by the aerobic dance teacher (who was no saint herself) a few doors down the street; but Berkeley was, for all his woolgathering, never asleep at the switch. (4) He took his work seriously. (5) Moreover, he knew exactly where he was at every moment, what he was doing, and why he was doing it, which was more than can be said for most people, like Mr. Tiflord, a real gumboil, whose ways were mysterious to Berkeley. (6) Sometimes he treated the animals cruelly, or taunted them; he saw them not as pets but profit. (7) Nevertheless, no vandals, or thieves had ever brought trouble through the doors or windows of Tilford's Pet Shoppe, and Berkeley, confident of his power but never flaunting it, faithful to his master though he didn't deserve it, was certain that none ever would.

—"Menagerie, A Child's Fable" by Charles Johnson

7. The topic sentence of this paragraph is

   (1) sentence 1
   (2) sentence 2
   (3) sentence 3
   (4) sentence 4
   (5) sentence 5

8. Sentence 1 should be

   (1) left as it is
   (2) placed first
   (3) placed after sentence 4
   (4) placed after sentence 8
   (5) omitted

9. A new paragraph can

   (1) be started after sentence 2
   (2) be started after sentence 3
   (3) be started after sentence 4
   (4) be started after sentence 5
   (5) not be started

ANSWER KEY

1. **2**   3. **3**   5. **2**   7. **1**   9. **5**
2. **5**   4. **4**   6. **3**   8. **1**

ANSWER ANALYSES

1. **2** The main idea of the paragraph is the role of errors in the playing of chess.
2. **5** The sentence is irrelevant to the topic.
3. **3** The paragraph shifts from its main idea to a subordinate one after sentence 4—the length of games.
4. **4** The main idea of paragraph (A) is to make the point that Russia's revolution did not come from the peasants or workers; the rest of the paragraph proves that statement.
5. **2** Because sentence 4 is the main idea, it would read clearly if it were placed first.
6. **3** A new topic, the educated Russians who tried to overthrow the tsar, is mentioned in sentence 5 and the following sentences support it; therefore, it should be the beginning of a new paragraph.
7. **1** The entire passage describes who Berkeley is, and sentence 1 introduces the reader to Berkeley.
8. **1** Because it is important to know who Berkeley is, sentence 1 must remain the first sentence, for coherence.
9. **5** A new paragraph cannot be started because the entire passage is just introducing the reader to Berkeley.

WHAT'S YOUR SCORE?

_____ right,   _____ wrong
Excellent   9
Good   8
Fair   7

If you scored lower, review the corrected examples in this section.

Additional Writing Skills

Correct Use of Words

Here are thirty pairs of words that are frequently confused and misused. Study the distinctions between the words in each pair. An example of the correct use of each member of the pair is given.

ACCEPT, EXCEPT

The verb **accept** means "to receive something" or "to agree to something." **Except** is most frequently used as a preposition meaning "leaving out." The use of *except* as a verb meaning "to leave out" is rare.

EXAMPLES

He was chosen to *accept* the gift.

Everyone came *except* him.

AGGRAVATE, IRRITATE

The verb **aggravate** means "to make worse." The verb **irritate** means "to annoy." In general, a person is *irritated*; a situation or a condition is *aggravated*.

EXAMPLES

Constant rubbing tended to *aggravate* the already painful wound.

The behavior of the child *irritated* all the guests.

ALREADY, ALL READY

Already is an adverb of time meaning "previously." **All ready** means exactly what the two words indicate—all prepared.

EXAMPLES

When I arrived, he had *already* left.

When I arrived, I found them *all ready* for the meeting.

ALTOGETHER, ALL TOGETHER

Altogether is an adverb of degree meaning "completely." **All together** means exactly what the two words indicate—all the persons in a group.

EXAMPLES

He was *altogether* unprepared for the assignment.

We found the team *all together* in the locker room.

AMONG, BETWEEN

Among is used when more than two persons or things are involved. **Between** is used when only two persons or things are involved. (You needn't be concerned with the rare exceptions to these rules.)

EXAMPLES

Frank, Joe, and Ed shared the expenses *among* them.

Jane and Joan shared the expenses *between* them.

AMOUNT, NUMBER

Amount is used for things or ideas that cannot be counted, and is usually followed by a singular noun—*money, talent, courage*. **Number** is used for persons or things that can be counted.

EXAMPLES

Sue carried a large *amount* of cash.

The *number* of accidents this year is greater than we thought.

I needed a large *amount* of money.

I needed a large *number* of dollars to pay my bills.

In the third example, the word *money* is thought of as a single unit. In the fourth, the word *dollars* is thought of as individual items that can be counted.

AROUND, ABOUT

Around is correctly used to indicate direction in a circle around an object. **About** should be used when number or size is indicated.

EXAMPLES

They walked *around* the house.

There were *about* 50,000 fans in the stadium.

The rug was *about* nine feet wide.

AS, LIKE

Only **as** can introduce a clause. **Like** cannot serve as a conjunction to introduce a clause; it is most frequently used as a preposition meaning "similar to."

EXAMPLE

WRONG:

This cereal tastes good *like* a cereal should.

CORRECT:

This cereal tastes good *as* a cereal should.

CORRECT:

He wanted everyone to be *like* him.

BEAT, BET

Beat means "to defeat." **Bet** means "to wager," or "to gamble something of value," on the result of a game.

EXAMPLES

Frank *beat* Jack in straight sets in their tennis match.

I *bet* five dollars that Joan would outrun Jane.

BESIDE, BESIDES

Beside means "at the side of." **Besides** means "in addition."

EXAMPLES

He came over to sit *beside* me.

There were nine others present *besides* Joe.

BORROW, LEND

Borrow means that the borrower is on the taking end of the transaction. **Lend** means that the lender is on the giving end of the transaction.

EXAMPLES

Please let me *borrow* ten dollars from you.

I'll be glad to *lend* the ten dollars to you.

BOTH, EACH

Both refers to two objects or persons taken together. **Each** refers to one or more objects or persons taken individually.

EXAMPLES

Both my pens cost ten dollars.

(Note: Don't use *both* in the above example if you mean that the cost of the two pens was twenty dollars. *Both* means the pair of pens.)

Each of my pens cost five dollars.

BRING, TAKE

Bring is used when the movement in the sentence is toward the speaker or the writer. **Take** is used when the movement in the sentence is away from the speaker or the writer.

EXAMPLES

Bring the pencils to me, please.

Take these books to the principal's office.

CAN, MAY

Can is used to indicate the ability to do something. **May** is used when permission is sought to do something, most frequently in the form of a question.

EXAMPLES

I *can* tie a slip knot.

May I have the car tonight?

FEWER, LESS

The correct use of these words follows the same rules as those indicated for **amount** and **number**. **Fewer** is used for persons or things that can be counted. **Less** is used for things or ideas that cannot be counted. (Note that *less* is usually followed by a singular noun, *fewer* by a plural noun.)

EXAMPLES

The number of accidents this year is *fewer* than we thought.

We enjoyed *less* freedom this year than last.

HANGED, HUNG

Hanged refers to a specific kind of execution that has taken place. **Hung** refers to something that has been suspended from an object.

EXAMPLES

The murderer was *hanged*.

The picture was *hung* on the hook attached to the wall.

IMPLY, INFER

Imply is used to indicate that the speaker or the writer is making a hint or suggestion. **Infer** is used to indicate that the hint or suggestion made by the speaker was taken by the audience, which drew a conclusion from it.

EXAMPLES

I mean to *imply* that he didn't get the job done.

I *infer* from your remarks that he was lazy.

IN, INTO

In is used to indicate that something is already in a place. **Into** is used to indicate that someone or something is moving from the outside to the inside of a place.

EXAMPLES

The dog is *in* the living room.

The dog dashed *into* the living room from the kitchen.

LATEST, LAST

Latest means "the most recent in a series." **Last** means "final."

EXAMPLES

The popular candidate was seen talking with his *latest* rival.

He appeared on television for the *last* time before his retirement.

LEARN, TEACH

Learn is used to indicate that knowledge or behavior is being acquired. **Teach** is used to indicate that knowledge or behavior is being provided.

EXAMPLES

He tried to *learn* how to hang-glide.

I tried to *teach* him how to hang-glide.

MYSELF, ME

Myself may be used properly in one of two ways. It can be used for emphasis, or it can be used as the object of an action verb with *I* as the subject. (*Never* use *myself* when *I* or *me* is correct.)

EXAMPLES

I *myself* will attend to this matter.

I hit *myself* in the hand.

WRONG:
He gave the awards to Frank and myself.

CORRECT:
He gave the awards to Frank and me.

WRONG:
Frank and myself will get the awards.

CORRECT:
Frank and I will get the awards.

POUR, SPILL

Pour means "to cause a liquid to flow deliberately." **Spill** means "to cause a liquid to flow accidentally or unintentionally."

EXAMPLES

The hostess *poured* coffee for her guests.

The hostess was embarrassed when she *spilled* the coffee on her guest's dress.

PRECEDE, PROCEED

Precede means "to come or go before" something or someone. **Proceed** means "to go on," particularly after an interruption.

EXAMPLES

Jimmy Carter *preceded* Ronald Reagan as president of the United States.

The speaker *proceeded*, after he was interrupted by a heckler.

PRINCIPAL, PRINCIPLE

Principal may be used in two ways. It can denote the head of a school, or it can be used as an adjective meaning "the main" or "the most important." **Principle** is used to indicate a law or a rule of conduct.

EXAMPLES

The *principal* addressed the teachers and the parents.

He was the *principal* speaker at the graduation exercises.

We are dedicated to the *principle* that all men are created equal.

QUITE, QUIET

The adverb **quite** means "completely" or "very." The adjective **quiet** means "still" or "calm."

EXAMPLES

He was *quite* angry when he lost the game.

After his fit of temper, he became *quiet*.

RAISE, RISE

Raise means "to lift" or "to bring up" something or someone. **Rise** means "to get up" or "to go up"; it does *not* take an object.

EXAMPLES

The guard *raised* his rifle when he heard a sound.

He *rises* in the morning when the sun rises.

ROB, STEAL

One is said to **rob** a *person* or an *institution* such as a bank by taking property or valuables from it. One is said to **steal** *an object* such as personal property or valuables from someone or some institution.

EXAMPLE

The criminal was caught in the act of trying to *rob* the bank.

The criminal tried to *steal* the man's wallet.

SET, SIT

Set means "to put something in a certain place." **Sit** means "to be seated."

EXAMPLES

The delivery boy *set* the packages on the kitchen floor.

Please *sit* in this chair.

STAND, STAY

You **stand** when you are on your feet. (The past tense is *stood*.) You **stay** when you remain in a given place. (The past tense is *stayed*.)

EXAMPLES

He *stood* all the way home in the bus.

He *stayed* at the stadium until the game was over.

STATIONARY, STATIONERY

Stationary means "not moving" or "still." **Stationery** refers to writing paper, envelopes, and other office supplies.

EXAMPLES

The *stationary* animal provided an excellent target for the hunter.

The student bought his notebooks at the *stationery* store.

FREQUENT ERRORS IN WORD USE

1. **DON'T USE** the expression *could of,* *should of,* or *would of.* Instead, use the correct expression (with *have*) for which any of these spoken distortions is an incorrect substitute.

   WRONG:

   He could of been the winner if he had tried.

   CORRECT:

   He *could have* been the winner if he had tried.

2. **DON'T USE** the expression *different than.* Instead, use *different from.*

   WRONG:

   Playing baseball is different than playing softball.

   CORRECT:

   Playing baseball is *different from* playing softball.

3. **DON'T USE** incorrect prepositions.

   WRONG:

   May I borrow a dollar off you?

   CORRECT:

   May I borrow a dollar *from* you?

   WRONG:

   Come over our house for a party.

   CORRECT:

   Come *to* our house for a party.

4. **DON'T USE** *don't* in the third person singular. Use *doesn't,* which is the contraction of *does not.*

   WRONG:

   He don't belong here.

   CORRECT:

   He *doesn't* belong here.

5. **DON'T USE** *who's* when you mean *whose.* *Whose* should be used to show possession. *Who's* is a contraction of *who is.*

   WRONG:

   I know who's book this is.

   CORRECT:

   I know *whose* book this is.

PRACTICE WITH CONFUSED AND MISUSED WORDS

In each sentence, five parts are underlined and numbered. Choose the number of the underlined part that contains the error. If there are no errors, choose number 5. This kind of error is included in the sentence correction type of multiple-choice item.

1. The <u>number</u> of persons present this
      (1)
   time <u>was</u> much different <u>than</u> the
      (2)   (3)
   number <u>that</u> came last time.
        (4)
   <u>No error</u>
    (5)

2. <u>Fewer</u> visitors were allowed <u>in</u> our
    (1)   (2)
   hospital <u>than</u> <u>yours</u>.   <u>No error</u>
        (3)   (4)   (5)

3. We were <u>already</u> to leave <u>as</u> we had
         (1)   (2)
   been instructed had it not been for
   <u>him</u> and <u>her</u>. <u>No error</u>
    (3)   (4)   (5)

4. <u>Bring</u> this book to <u>whoever</u> you
    (1)   (2)
   think is most deserving <u>besides</u> <u>me</u>.
                   (3)   (4)
   <u>No error</u>
    (5)

5. Geraldo and <u>I</u> asked Conchita and
           (1)
   <u>him</u> whether <u>they'd</u> <u>except</u> the gift.
    (2)   (3)   (4)
   <u>No error</u>
    (5)

6. Anyone <u>may</u> ask a question about
        (1)
   any problem bothering <u>him</u> because
                 (2)
   it's the <u>kind of</u> situation which is
        (3)
   most <u>aggravating</u>. <u>No error</u>
      (4)   (5)

7. <u>Enclosed</u> <u>are</u> checks that
      (1)   (2)

   cover all the expenses <u>except</u> <u>hers</u>.
                  (3)   (4)

   <u>No error</u>
    (5)

8. Give the book to <u>whoever</u> asks for
                  (1)

   it despite the large <u>number</u> of
                 (2)

   requests and say it is a gift from
   <u>him</u> and <u>myself</u>. <u>No error</u>
    (3)   (4)   (5)

9. He considered it <u>altogether</u> <u>likely</u>
                 (1)   (2)

   that <u>less</u> accidents would occur
      (3)

   this year than last <u>since</u> the speed
                (4)

   limit was changed. <u>No error</u>
              (5)

10. Hector felt that, <u>among</u> the three of
              (1)

    us who ran for office, the <u>number</u>
                   (2)

    of votes <u>should have proven</u> that
            (3)

    the winners were Enrique and
    <u>myself</u>. <u>No error</u>
     (4)   (5)

ANSWER KEY

| 1. **3** | 3. **1** | 5. **4** | 7. **5** | 9 **3** |
| 2. **2** | 4. **1** | 6. **4** | 8. **4** | 10. **4** |

WHAT'S YOUR SCORE?

_____ right,   _____ wrong

Excellent	9–10
Good	7–8
Fair	6

If you scored lower, restudy this section, concentrating on the differences between the pairs of words and the ten errors in word use to avoid.

ANSWER ANALYSIS

1. **3** Use *different from* rather than *different than*.
2. **2** *Into* must be used to indicate that the visitors are moving from the outside to the inside of the hospital.
3. **1** *All ready* must be used in the meaning of *all* prepared.
4. **1** *Take* should be used when the movement in the sentence is away from the speaker or writer.
5. **4** *Accept* is used to mean "to receive something."
6. **4** The verb *irritate* should be used since the required meaning is "annoying."
7. **5** No error.
8. **4** Since neither emphasis nor an object of an action verb is required, *me* should be used.
9. **3** *Fewer* should be used since the accidents can be counted.
10. **4** Since neither emphasis nor an object of an action verb is needed in this sentence, *I* should be used.

Wordiness: The Problem of Too Many Words

Wordiness, the use of more words than is necessary, is a frequent weakness of many speakers and writers. It is particularly undesirable when it confuses the reader.

Some sentences contain words or phrases that are unnecessary.

EXAMPLE

My friend *he* is a baseball fan.

In this sentence, both the noun *friend* and the pronoun *he* are unnecessary when referring to the same person. A pronoun takes the place of a noun. The sentence should read:

"My friend is a baseball fan."

OR

"He is a baseball fan."

EXAMPLE

This *here* pen writes better than that *there* one.

Both *here* and *there* are not needed. *This* means nearer than another person or thing referred to as *that*.

EXAMPLE

Take your feet off *of* the table.

Off means "so as to be no longer on." The word *of* in the sentence is superfluous.

EXAMPLE

Whatever he does, he does *it* well.

The pronoun *it* isn't needed. In fact, the pronoun replaces nothing in the sentence and what *it* refers to isn't clear.

Some sentences contain words that are repetitive since they restate parts of the meaning of other words in the sentence.

EXAMPLE

I have a friend *of mine* who helps me with my housework.

In this sentence, *mine* means "belonging to me," and the idea is already contained in the words *I have*. Therefore, *of mine* should be eliminated from the sentence.

EXAMPLE

I have to be at work at 9 A.M. *in the morning*.

In this sentence, A.M. means "ante meridiem" or "before noon." It conveys the idea of *morning*. Therefore, the phrase *in the morning* isn't needed.

EXAMPLE

Congress has decided to refer the matter *back* to committee.

The word *refer*, contains a prefix (*re-*) which means "back." Therefore, the word *back* is unnecessary. A similar incorrect expression is "return back."

Some sentences contain words that unnecessarily repeat other words in the sentence.

EXAMPLE

We left after *the conclusion of* the concert.

After means "later than," so the words *the conclusion of* are unnecessary.

EXAMPLE

Helen Keller wrote an autobiography *of her life*.

An *autobiography* is the story of one's life; *of her life* should be omitted.

EXAMPLE

In my opinion, *I think* the criminal should be pardoned.

In this sentence, *think* means to "hold an opinion," so either *in my opinion* or *I think* can safely be dispensed with.

PRACTICE

1. That there book belongs to me.
2. Despite the rain, the umpires decided to continue on with the game.
3. Please refer back to page 12 in the book.
4. My parents they are completely devoted to me.
5. I usually go to bed at 11:00 P.M. at night.
6. When I was eighteen years old, I was graduated from high school.

ANSWERS

1. That book belongs to me.
2. Despite the rain, the umpires decided to continue the game.
3. Please refer to page 12 in the book.
4. My parents are completely devoted to me.
5. I usually go to bed at 11:00 P.M.
6. When I was eighteen, I was graduated from high school.

PRACTICE WITH WORDINESS

Beneath each sentence you will find five ways of writing the underlined part. Choose the answer that makes the best sentence. Answer 1 is always the same as the underlined part and is sometimes the right answer.

1. After the conclusion of the game, my friend, he decided to return back home.

   (1) After the conclusion of the game, my friend, he decided to return back
   (2) After the conclusion of the game, my friend decided to return back
   (3) After the conclusion of the game, my friend decided to return

(4) After the game, my friend decided to return back

(5) After the game, my friend decided to return

2. At this <u>point in time, type up five copies of this here</u> contract.

(1) point in time, type up five copies of this here
(2) point in time, type five copies of this here
(3) time, type five copies of this
(4) time, type five copies of this here
(5) time, type up five copies of this

3. Because we cooperated <u>together, we divided up the work on the report that was assigned.</u>

(1) together, we divided up the work on the report that was assigned
(2) together, we divided the work on the report that was assigned
(3) , we divided up the work on the report that was assigned
(4) , we divided the work on the assigned report
(5) , we divided up the work on the assigned report

4. Mr. Steele, <u>who was president of the company, repeated again what he had said while we were having</u> dinner.

(1) who was president of the company, repeated again what he had said while we were having
(2) who was president of the company, repeated what he had said while we were having
(3) president of the company, repeated what he had said while we were having
(4) president of the company, repeated again what he had said during
(5) president of the company, repeated what he had said during

5. At 8:00 P.M. <u>in the evening, he continued on his walk, which was enjoyable.</u>

(1) in the evening, he continued on his walk, which was enjoyable
(2) he continued on his walk, which was enjoyable
(3) he continued on his enjoyable walk
(4) in the evening, he continued his enjoyable walk
(5) he continued his enjoyable walk

6. <u>A large crowd of people waited outside of</u> the building.

(1) A large crowd of people waited outside of
(2) A crowd waited outside
(3) A crowd waited outside of
(4) There was a large crowd of people who waited outside of
(5) There was a large crowd who waited outside of

7. The senator <u>rose up to say that, in his opinion, he thought the bill should be referred back to</u> committee.

(1) rose up to say that, in his opinion, he thought the bill should be referred back to
(2) rose up to say that he thought the bill should be referred back
(3) rose up to say that he thought the bill should be referred
(4) rose up to say that, in his opinion, the bill should be referred
(5) rose to say that he thought the bill should be referred

8. My wife wanted <u>that I should return to school when I was thirty years of age</u>.

(1) that I should return to school when I was thirty years of age
(2) that I should return back to school when I was thirty years of age
(3) me to return back to school when I was thirty years of age
(4) me to return to school when I was thirty years of age
(5) me to return to school when I was thirty

ANSWER KEY

1. **5**	3. **4**	5. **5**	7. **5**
2. **3**	4. **5**	6. **2**	8. **5**

WHAT'S YOUR SCORE?

_____ right,   _____ wrong

Excellent	7–8
Good	6
Fair	5

If you scored lower, review the four kinds of wordiness illustrated in this section.

ANSWER ANALYSIS

1. **5** *The conclusion of*, *he*, and *back* are all included in the meanings of other words in the sentence.

2. **3** *Point in*, *up*, and *here* are all included in the meanings of other words in the sentence.

3. **4** *Together* and *up* are included in the meanings of other words in the sentence. The adjective *assigned* is preferable stylistically to the adjective clause *that was assigned*.

4. **5** *Again* is unnecessary. The appositive, *president*, is preferable to the adjective clause *who was president*. The preposition *during* is preferable to the adverb clause *while we were having*.

5. **5** *In the evening* and *on* are included in the meanings of other words in the sentence. The adjective *enjoyable* is preferable to the adjective clause *which was enjoyable*.

6. **2** The words *large* and *of* are unnecessary. *That* is preferable to *who* when it refers to a neuter noun such as *crowd*.

7. **5** The words *up*, *in his opinion*, and *back* are unnecessary.

8. **5** The words *years of age* are unnecessary. The expression *that I should* is clumsy and can easily be replaced by the words *me to*.

A Basic 650-Word Vocabulary

Here is a list of 650 basic words to help you build your vocabulary. For each word, a definition is provided. You should use these lists together with a good dictionary such as *Webster's New World Dictionary of the American Language*.

200 USEFUL NOUNS

ACCESS (means of) approach or admittance (to records)

ACCORD agreement

AFFLUENCE abundance; wealth (age of _____)

AGENDA list of things to be done or discussed (at a meeting)

ALIAS assumed name (Fred Henry, _____ John Doe)

ANIMOSITY great hatred (toward strangers)

ANTHOLOGY collection of writings or other creative work such as songs

ATLAS book of maps

AUDACITY boldness

AVARICE greed for wealth

AWE feeling of respect and wonder (in _____ of someone's power)

BIGOTRY unwillingness to allow others to have different opinions and beliefs from one's own

BLEMISH defect (on one's record)

BONDAGE slavery

BOON benefit (a _____ to business)

BRAWL noisy fight

BREVITY shortness

BULWARK strong protection (a _____ against corruption)

CALIBER quality (a person of high _____)

CAMOUFLAGE disguise, usually in war, by changing the appearance of persons or material

CASTE social class or distinction

CATASTROPHE sudden disaster (an earthquake)

CHRONICLE historical record

CLAMOR uproar

CONDOLENCE expression of sympathy (extended _____ to a bereaved)

CONNOISSEUR expert judge (of paintings, food)

CONSENSUS general agreement

CONTEXT words or ideas just before or after a given word or idea (meaning of a word in a given _____)

CRITERION standard of judgment (good or poor by this _____)

CRUX the essential point (the _____ of the matter)

DATA known facts (_____ were found through research)

DEBUT first appearance before an audience (actor, pianist)

DELUGE great flood (rain or, in a special sense, mail)

DEPOT warehouse

DESTINY predetermined fate (it was his _____ to)

DIAGNOSIS determination of the nature of a disease or a situation

DILEMMA situation requiring a choice between two unpleasant courses of action (he was in a _____)

DIN loud, continuing noise

DISCORD disagreement

DISCREPANCY inconsistency (in accounts, in testimony)

DISSENT difference of opinion (from a decision)

DROUGHT long spell of dry weather

ELITE choice part or element (of society)

ENVIRONMENT surrounding influences or conditions

EPOCH period of time associated with an important person or event (the _____ of spaceflight)

ERA period of time marked by an important person or event (the Napoleonic _____)

ESSENCE basic nature (of the matter)

ETIQUETTE rules of social behavior that are generally accepted

EXCERPT passage from a book or a document

EXODUS departure, usually of large numbers

FALLACY mistaken idea; reasoning that contains an error

FANTASY imagination (he indulged in _____)

FEUD continued deadly hatred (between two families)

FIASCO complete, humiliating failure

FIEND inhumanly cruel person

FINALE last part or performance

FLAIR natural talent (for sports)

FLAW defect

FOCUS central point (of attention)

FOE enemy

FORMAT physical appearance or arrangement (of a book)

FORTITUDE steady courage (when in trouble)

FORUM a gathering for the discussion of public issues

FOYER entrance hall (to a building or dwelling)

FRAUD deliberate deception

FRICTION rubbing of the surface of one thing against the surface of another

FUNCTION purpose served by a person, object, or organization

GHETTO section of a city where members of a particular group (formerly religious, now usually racial) live

GIST essential content (of a speech or an article)

GLUTTON one who overeats or indulges in anything else to excess

GRIEVANCE complaint made against someone responsible for a situation believed to be unjust

HAVOC great damage and destruction (wreak _____ on)

HAZARD danger

HERITAGE inheritance either of real wealth or of a tradition

HOAX deliberate attempt to trick someone, done either with serious intent or as a joke

HORDE crowd

HORIZON limit (of knowledge, experience, or ambition)

HUE shade of color

HYSTERIA wild emotional outburst

IDIOM expression peculiar to a language that, as a whole, has a different meaning from the words that comprise it (hit the road)

ILLUSION idea or impression different from reality

IMAGE likeness or reflected impression of a person or object

INCENTIVE spur or motive to do something (profit _____)

INCUMBENT present holder of an office

INFLUX flowing in (of money into banks, tourists into a country)

INFRACTION violation of a rule or a law

INITIATIVE desire or ability to take the first step in carrying out some action (often a new plan or idea)

INNOVATION introduction of a new idea or method

INTEGRITY moral and intellectual honesty and uprightness

INTERIM meantime (in the _____)

INTERLUDE period of time between two events (_____ between the acts of a play)

INTRIGUE secret plot

INTUITION knowledge derived through instinct rather than thought

ITINERARY route followed on a trip, actual or planned

JEOPARDY risk of harm (put into _____)

KEYNOTE main theme (He sounded the _____ of the convention)

LARCENY theft (The jury couldn't decide whether the crime was grand or petty _____)

LAYPERSON one who is not a member of a particular profession (from the point of view of a _____)

LEGACY material or spiritual inheritance (from a parent)

LEGEND story passed on from generation to generation and often considered to be true

LORE body of traditional knowledge (nature _____)

MALADY disease (incurable _____)

MANEUVER skillful move (a clever _____)

MARATHON contest requiring endurance

MEDIA means of communication (_____ of radio and television)

MEMENTO object that serves as a reminder (a _____ of the war)

METROPOLIS main city of a state or region (or any large city)

MORALE state of mind as it affects possible future action (The troops had good _____)

MULTITUDE a large number

MYTH a story that is a traditional explanation of some occurrence, usually in nature (the _____ of Atlas holding up the heavens)

NICHE suitable and desirable place (He found his _____ in the business organization)

NOMAD wanderer

NOSTALGIA desire to return to past experiences or associations

ODYSSEY long journey

OMEN something that is believed to predict a future event (an evil _____)

OPTIMUM best possible quantity or quality (He participated to the _____)

OVATION enthusiastic reception usually accompanied by generous applause (He received a tumultuous _____)

OVERSIGHT failure to include something through carelessness (His name was omitted because of an _____)

PAGEANT public spectacle in the form of a stage performance or a parade (a historical _____)

PANORAMA clear view of a very broad area

PARADOX statement of a truth that appears to contradict itself (a 20-year-old who had only five birthdays because he was born on February 29)

PASTIME way of spending leisure time (He took up golf as a _____)

PAUPER very poor person

PEER an equal in age, social standing, ability, or other feature

PHENOMENON event that can be scientifically explained, such as the tides

PITFALL trap

PITTANCE very small sum of money (He survived on a _____)

PLATEAU area of level land located at a height

PLIGHT condition, usually unfavorable (the sorry _____ of the refugees)

POISE calm and controlled manner of behavior (He showed _____ in difficult situations)

PREDICAMENT unpleasant situation from which it is difficult to free oneself (He found himself in a _____)

PREFACE introductory statement to a book or speech

PRELUDE something that is preliminary to a more important act or work

PREMISE statement from which a conclusion is logically drawn (Granted the _____ that..., we may conclude...)

PREMIUM amount added to the usual payment or charge (He paid a _____ for the seats)

PRESTIGE respect achieved through rank, achievement, or reputation

PRETEXT reason given as a cover-up for the true purpose of an action (He gave as a _____ for stealing the ring, his sentimental attachment to it)

PRIORITY something that ranks before others in importance (He gave _____ to his studies)

PROCESS step-by-step system for accomplishing some purpose (the _____ of legislation)

PROSPECT outlook for the future (the _____ of peace)

PROXIMITY nearness

PSEUDONYM assumed name, usually by an author (Mark Twain, _____ of Samuel Clemens)

PUN play on words depending on two different meanings or sounds of the same word (Whether life is worth living depends on the *liver*)

QUANDARY uncertainty over a choice between two courses of action (He was in a _____ between the careers of law or medicine)

QUERY question

QUEST search (_____ for knowledge)

RARITY something not commonly found (A talent like his is a _____)

REFUGE place to which one can go for protection (He found _____ in the church)

REMNANT remaining part (_____ of the troops)

REMORSE deep feeling of guilt for some bad act (He felt _____ at having insulted his friend)

RENDEZVOUS a meeting or a place for meeting

REPLICA an exact copy (_____ of a painting)

REPRIMAND severe criticism in the form of a scolding (He received a _____ from his superior)

RESIDUE remainder

RESOURCES assets, either material or spiritual, that are available for use

RESPITE temporary break that brings relief (_____ from work)

RÉSUMÉ summary

REVERENCE feeling of great respect (_____ for life)

ROBOT one who acts mechanically or like a mechanical man

ROSTER list of names (_____ of guests)

SABOTAGE deliberate damage to vital services of production and supply, usually to those of an enemy in wartime

SAGA long tale, usually of heroic deeds

SALUTATION greeting, written or spoken (The _____ of a letter may be "Dear Sir")

SARCASM use of cutting remarks

SATIRE attack upon evil or foolish behavior by showing it to be ridiculous

SCAPEGOAT person who is blamed for the bad deeds of others

SCENT distinctive smell

SCOPE entire area of action or thought (the _____ of the plan)

SEGMENT part or section of a whole (_____ of a population)

SEQUEL something that follows from what happened or was written before (_____ to a novel)

SILHOUETTE outline drawing in black

SITE location of an object or an action (original _____ of a building)

SLANDER untruth spoken or spread about a person that damages his or her reputation

SLOGAN motto that is associated with an action or a cause (Pike's Peak or bust!)

SLOPE slant (_____ of a line)

SNARE trap

SOLACE comfort (She found _____ in work)

SPONSOR person or organization that endorses and supports an individual, an activity, or a cause

SPUR something that moves one to act (a _____ to sacrifice)

STAMINA ability to fight off physical difficulties such as fatigue and cold

STATURE height reached physically or morally (a man of great _____)

STATUS standing, social or professional

STIMULUS any encouragement to act

STRATEGY skillful planning and execution (the _____ in a battle)

STRIFE conflict (_____ between labor and management)

SUMMIT the highest point (the _____ of his career)

SUPPLEMENT amount added to complete something (_____ to a budget)

SURVEY broad study of a topic (a _____ of employment)

SUSPENSE tenseness brought about by uncertainty as to what will happen

SYMBOL something that is used to represent something else (Uncle Sam is a _____ of the United States)

SYMPTOM indication of something (_____ of disease)

SYNOPSIS brief summary

TACT ability to say and do the appropriate thing

TALLY record of a score or an account (the _____ of the receipts)

TECHNIQUE method or skill in doing work (the _____ of an artist)

TEMPERAMENT natural disposition, often to act in a contrary manner (He displayed a changeable _____)

TEMPO pace of activity (The _____ of life is increasing)

TENSION mental or emotional strain (She was under great _____)

THEME topic of a written work or a talk

THRESHOLD starting point (the _____ of a career)

TINT shade of color

TOKEN sign that stands for some object or feeling (a _____ of esteem)

TONIC something that is a source of energy or vigor

TRADITION body of customs and beliefs received by one generation from another

TRAIT distinguishing feature (_____ of character)

TRANSITION movement from one situation to another (_____ from dictatorship to democracy)

TRIBUTE display of respect or gratitude (He paid a _____ to his parents)

TURMOIL disturbance (great _____ at the meeting)

TUTOR private teacher

ULTIMATUM final ("Take it or leave it") offer

UNREST restless dissatisfaction

UPHEAVAL sudden overthrow, often violent

UTENSIL useful implement (a kitchen _____)

UTOPIA ideal place or society

VALOR courage

VENTURE undertaking that involves risk

VICINITY neighborhood

VICTOR winner

VIGOR vitality

VIM energy

VOW solemn pledge

WAGER bet

WHIM sudden notion or desire

WOE great sorrow (He brought _____ to his friends)

WRATH intense anger (He poured his _____ on his enemies)

ZEAL eager desire

ZEST keen enthusiasm (_____ for competition)

200 USEFUL VERBS

ABSOLVE free from guilt (for a crime)

ACCEDE agree to (a request)

ACCELERATE speed up

ADJOURN put off to a later time (a meeting)

ADVOCATE act in support of (revolution)

ALLEGE claim

ALLOT assign (a share)

ALLUDE refer to (a book)

ALTER change

ASSENT agree

ATONE make up for (a sin)

AUGMENT add to

AVERT prevent

BAN forbid

BAR exclude

CEDE give up (territory)

CHASTISE punish

CITE mention in order to prove something

COERCE force

COLLABORATE work with someone

COMMEND praise

CONCUR agree

CURTAIL cut short or reduce

DEDUCE draw a conclusion from given facts

DEEM consider

DEFER postpone

DELETE remove or erase (a word)

DEPLORE regret

DEPRIVE keep someone from having or getting something

DESPISE scorn

DETAIN delay temporarily

DETECT uncover something that is not obvious

DETEST hate

DETRACT take away from

DEVOUR eat greedily

DIGRESS depart from the subject under consideration

DILUTE weaken by adding something less strong (a mixture)

DISINTEGRATE fall apart

DISPEL drive away

DISPERSE scatter

DISRUPT break up

DISTORT present incorrectly (facts)

DIVERGE go in different directions

DIVULGE reveal

EJECT throw out

ENCOUNTER meet

ENDEAVOR try

ENHANCE increase the quality or value of

ENSUE follow as a result

ERR make a mistake

ERUPT break out

EVADE avoid or escape from someone or something

EXCEED surpass

EXTOL praise highly

FALTER stumble

FAMISH starve

FEIGN pretend

FLOURISH thrive

FOIL prevent

FORSAKE abandon

FRUSTRATE prevent someone from achieving a goal

GAUGE estimate

HARASS disturb constantly

HEAVE lift and throw

HEED pay attention to (advice)

HINDER keep back

HURL throw with force

IGNITE set fire to
IMMERSE plunge into a liquid
IMPAIR damage
IMPLY suggest
INCITE arouse
INFER come to a conclusion based on something known
INSTIGATE spur to action
INTERROGATE question
INTIMIDATE frighten by making threats
IRK annoy

JEER poke fun at (by sarcastic remarks)

LAMENT feel sorrow for
LAUNCH set in motion
LOP cut off
LURE tempt
LURK remain hidden, usually for an evil purpose

MAGNIFY enlarge
MAIM cripple
MIMIC imitate
MOCK ridicule
MOLEST annoy

NARRATE tell (a story)
NAVIGATE steer (a ship)
NEGATE deny

ORIENT adjust oneself or someone else to a situation or place
OUST expel

PEND remain undecided
PERFECT complete
PERPLEX puzzle
PERTAIN have reference to
PERTURB upset greatly
PERUSE read carefully
PRECLUDE prevent something from happening
PRESCRIBE order (for use or as a course of action)
PRESUME take for granted
PREVAIL win out over
PROBE investigate thoroughly
PROCURE obtain
PROSPER be successful
PROTRUDE project
PROVOKE arouse to action out of irritation
PRY look closely into

QUELL subdue

REBATE give back, usually part of an amount paid
REBUKE reprimand
RECEDE move backward

RECONCILE bring together by settling differences
RECTIFY correct
RECUR happen again
REFRAIN keep from
REIMBURSE pay back
REITERATE repeat
REJECT refuse to take
RELINQUISH give up
REMINISCE recall past happenings
REMUNERATE pay for work or other service done
RENOUNCE give up (a claim)
RENOVATE restore (a house)
REPENT regret (a sin)
REPOSE rest
REPROACH blame
REPULSE drive back (an attack)
RESTRAIN hold back
RETAIN keep
RETALIATE return in kind (a blow for a blow)
RETARD delay
RETRIEVE get back
REVERE have deep respect for

SCAN look at closely; look over quickly
SCOFF mock
SCORN treat with contempt
SCOUR clean thoroughly; move about widely in a search
SCOWL look angry
SEEP ooze
SEETHE boil
SEVER divide
SHED throw off (clothing)
SHIRK seek to avoid (duty or work)
SHUN avoid
SHUNT turn aside
SIFT sort out through careful examination (evidence)
SIGNIFY mean
SINGE burn slightly
SKIM read over quickly
SMITE hit hard
SNARL tangle
SOAR fly high in the air
SPURN reject scornfully
STARTLE surprise
STIFLE suppress (feelings)
STREW scatter
STRIVE try hard
STUN daze
SUBSIDE lessen in activity
SUCCUMB yield to
SUFFICE be enough
SURGE increase suddenly
SURMOUNT overcome (an obstacle)
SUSTAIN support
SWAY move back and forth

TAMPER meddle with
TARNISH discolor
TAUNT reproach mockingly
THAW melt
THRASH defeat thoroughly
THRIVE prosper
THROB beat insistently
THRUST push forcefully and suddenly
THWART prevent someone from achieving a goal
TINGE color slightly
TORMENT afflict with pain
TRANSFORM change the appearance of
TRANSMIT send along
TRUDGE walk slowly and wearily

UNDERGO experience
UNDO return to condition that existed before something was done
USURP seize power illegally
UTILIZE make use of
UTTER speak

VACATE make empty
VANQUISH conquer
VARY change
VEND sell
VERIFY prove the truth of
VEX annoy
VIBRATE move back and forth
VIOLATE break (a law)
VOUCH guarantee

WAIVE give up (a right or privilege)
WANE decrease in strength
WAVER sway back and forth
WHET sharpen
WIELD put to use (power or a tool such as a club)
WITHSTAND hold out against (pressure)
WREST pull violently

YEARN long for
YIELD give up

250 USEFUL ADJECTIVES

ADAMANT unyielding
ADEPT skilled
ADROIT skillful
AESTHETIC having to do with beauty
AGILE nimble
AMBIDEXTROUS equally skilled with both hands
AMENABLE disposed to follow (advice)
AMIABLE friendly
APT suitable

ARDENT passionate
ARROGANT over proud
ARTICULATE able to express oneself cleary (an _____ person)
ASTUTE shrewd
AUTHENTIC genuine

BARREN unfruitful
BIZARRE strange
BLAND gentle; soothing
BLATANT overloud
BOISTEROUS rambunctious
BRUSQUE rudely brief

CALLOUS unfeeling
CANDID honest
CASUAL offhand
CHIC stylish
CHRONIC continuing over a long period of time
CIVIC municipal
CIVIL courteous
COLOSSAL huge
COMPATIBLE capable of getting along together
CONCISE brief but complete
CRAFTY sly
CREDIBLE believable
CUMBERSOME bulky
CURT rudely brief

DEMURE modest; reserved
DEROGATORY belittling
DESOLATE lonely
DESTITUTE poverty-stricken
DETERGENT cleansing
DEVIOUS indirect
DEVOID completely free of (feeling)
DEVOUT very religious
DIMINUTIVE tiny
DIRE dreadful
DISCREET careful
DISINTERESTED impartial
DISMAL gloomy
DISTRAUGHT driven to distraction
DIVERSE varied
DOMESTIC having to do with the home
DOMINANT ruling
DORMANT sleeping
DRASTIC extreme (changes)
DREARY gloomy
DUBIOUS doubtful
DURABLE lasting
DYNAMIC energetic

EARNEST intensely serious
EBONY black
ECCENTRIC peculiar (behavior)
EDIBLE fit to be eaten
EERIE weird

ELEGANT tastefully fine
ELOQUENT powerfully fluent in writing or speech
ELUSIVE hard to get hold of
EMINENT distinguished (author)
EPIC heroic in size
ERRATIC not regular
ETERNAL everlasting
ETHNIC having to do with race
EXORBITANT unreasonable (price)
EXOTIC foreign
EXPLICIT clearly indicated
EXTEMPORANEOUS spoken or accomplished with little preparation
EXTENSIVE broad

FANATIC extremely enthusiastic
FEASIBLE possible to carry out (a _____ plan)
FEEBLE weak
FERTILE productive
FERVENT warmly felt
FESTIVE in the spirit of a holiday (celebration)
FICKLE changeable
FLAGRANT noticeably bad (violation)
FLEET swift
FLIMSY not strong (platform)
FLUENT smooth (speech)
FORMIDABLE fear-inspiring because of size or strength (enemy)
FRAGILE easily broken
FRAIL delicate
FRANK outspoken
FRATERNAL brotherly
FRIGID extremely cold
FRUGAL thrifty
FUTILE useless

GALA festive
GALLANT courteously brave (conduct)
GENIAL kindly
GIGANTIC huge
GLUM gloomy
GORY bloody
GRAPHIC vividly realistic
GRATIS free
GRIM sternly forbidding (future)
GROSS glaringly bad (injustice)
GRUESOME horrifying

HAPHAZARD chance
HARSH disagreeably rough
HEARTY friendly (welcome)
HECTIC feverish
HEINOUS outrageous (crime)
HIDEOUS extremely ugly
HILARIOUS very merry, mirthful
HOMOGENEOUS of like kind (group)

HORRENDOUS horrible
HOSTILE unfriendly (unwelcome)
HUMANE merciful
HUMBLE modest
HUMID damp

IMMACULATE spotlessly clean
IMMENSE very large
IMMINENT about to happen (storm)
IMPARTIAL unbiased
IMPERATIVE necessary
IMPERTINENT rude
IMPROMPTU without any preparation (remarks)
IMPUDENT rudely bold
INCESSANT uninterrupted
INCLEMENT rough (weather)
INCOHERENT not clearly connected
INDELIBLE unable to be erased
INDIFFERENT showing no interest
INDIGENT poor
INDIGNANT very angry
INDISPENSABLE absolutely necessary
INDUSTRIOUS hard-working
INEPT ineffective
INFAMOUS having a bad reputation
INFINITE endless
INFLEXIBLE unbending
INGENIOUS clever
INNATE inborn
INNOCUOUS harmless
INSOLENT boldly rude
INTENSIVE thorough (study)
INTERMITTENT starting and stopping (rain)
INTOLERANT unwilling or unable to respect others or their beliefs
INTRICATE complicated
INVINCIBLE unable to be conquered
IRATE angry
IRRATIONAL unreasonable

JOVIAL good-humored
JUBILANT joyous

LABORIOUS demanding a lot of work
LATENT hidden (talent)
LAVISH extremely generous (praise)
LAX loose (discipline)
LEGIBLE easily read (print)
LEGITIMATE lawful (claim)
LETHAL fatal
LOATH reluctant
LOFTY very high
LUCID clear
LUCRATIVE profitable (business)

MAJESTIC grand (building)
MALICIOUS spiteful
MALIGNANT harmful

MAMMOTH gigantic
MANUAL done by the hands (labor)
MARINE of the sea (life)
MARTIAL warlike
MASSIVE bulky and heavy
MEAGER scanty
MENIAL lowly (task)
METICULOUS extremely careful
MILITANT aggressive
MOBILE movable (home)
MUTUAL reciprocal (admiration)

NAIVE innocently simple
NAUSEOUS disgusting
NEGLIGENT neglectful
NEUROTIC describing the behavior of a person suffering from an emotional disorder
NIMBLE moving quickly and easily
NONCHALANT casual and unexcited
NOTABLE important (person)
NOTORIOUS well-known in an unfavorable way (criminal)
NULL having no effect

OBESE very fat
OBJECTIVE free from prejudice (analysis)
OBNOXIOUS extremely unpleasant (behavior)
OBSOLETE out-of-date (machine)
OBSTINATE stubborn
OMINOUS threatening (clouds)
OPPORTUNE timely
ORTHODOX usually approved (religious beliefs)
OUTRIGHT complete

PARAMOUNT chief (importance)
PASSIVE not active (participation)
PATHETIC pitiful
PERILOUS dangerous
PERTINENT relevant
PETTY relatively unimportant
PIOUS devoutly religious
PLACID calm (waters)
PLAUSIBLE apparently true (argument)
POIGNANT keenly painful to the emotions
POMPOUS self-important (person)
PORTABLE capable of being carried (radio)
POSTHUMOUS taking place after a person's death (award)
POTENT powerful (drug)
POTENTIAL possible (greatness)
PRECARIOUS risky
PRECISE exact
PREDOMINANT prevailing
PREPOSTEROUS ridiculous
PREVALENT widespread
PRIMARY fundamental (reason)
PRIME first in importance or quality

PRIMITIVE crude (tools)
PRIOR previous (appointment)
PRODIGIOUS extraordinary in size or amount (effort)
PROFICIENT skilled
PROSAIC ordinary
PRUDENT discreet (advice)
PUNY small in size or slight in strength (effort)
PUTRID rotten

QUAINT pleasantly odd (custom)

RAMPANT spreading unchecked (violence)
RANCID having the bad taste or smell of stale food (butter)
RANDOM decided by chance (choice)
RASH reckless
RAUCOUS harsh (sound)
REFLEX referring to an involuntary response (action)
REGAL royal
RELENTLESS persistent (chase)
RELEVANT pertinent
REMOTE far distant (time or place)
REPULSIVE disgusting
REPUTABLE respectable (doctor)
RESIGNED submitting passively to (one's fate)
RESOLUTE firmly determined
RETICENT speaking little (child)
RIGID stiff
ROBUST strong and healthy
ROWDY rough and disorderly (mob)
RUGGED rough
RUTHLESS pitiless (dictator)

SAGE wise (advice)
SALUTARY healthful (climate)
SANE mentally sound
SCANTY meager
SCHOLASTIC having to do with school and education (record)
SCRUPULOUS careful and honest (accounting)
SEDATE dignified
SERENE calm
SHEER very thin (stockings); utter (nonsense)
SHREWD clever in one's dealings (businessperson)
SIMULTANEOUS happening at the same time (events)
SINGULAR remarkable; strange (behavior)
SINISTER threatening evil
SKEPTICAL showing doubt (attitude)
SLENDER small in size or amount (contribution)
SLUGGISH slow-moving
SNUG comfortable

SOBER serious
SOLEMN grave (occasion)
SOLITARY lone
SOMBER dark and gloomy (outlook)
SOPHISTICATED wise in the ways of the world
SPARSE thinly scattered
SPIRITUAL referring to the spirit or soul
SPONTANEOUS happening as a result of natural impulse (reaction)
SPORADIC happening at irregular times (shooting)
SPRY nimble
STALWART robust
STARK bleak (outlook)
STATELY dignified
STATIC stationary
STATIONARY not moving
STEADFAST firm
STERN severe (look)
STOUT fat; firm (resistance)
STRAIGHTFORWARD honest (answer)
STRENUOUS demanding great energy (exercise)
STURDY strongly built
SUAVE smoothly polite (manner)
SUBLIME inspiring admiration because of noble quality (music)
SUBSIDIARY less important (rank)
SUBSTANTIAL having considerable numbers or size
SUBTLE suggested delicately (hint)
SULLEN resentful
SUMPTUOUS costly (meal)
SUNDRY various
SUPERB of a high degree of excellence
SUPERFICIAL not going beyond the obvious (examination)
SUPERFLUOUS beyond what is needed
SUPERLATIVE superior to all others (performance)
SUSCEPTIBLE easily affected by

TANGIBLE capable of being touched; actual (results)
TARDY late (student)
TART having a sharp taste (food)
TAUT tightly stretched (rope)
TEDIOUS long and tiresome (study)
TENACIOUS holding fast (grip)
TENTATIVE temporary for a period of trial (agreement)
TEPID lukewarm (water)
TERMINAL concluding
TERSE brief but expressive (comment)
TIDY neat (appearance)

TIMELY happening at a desirable time (arrival)
TIMID shy
TIRESOME tiring
TITANIC having enormous size or strength
TORRID intensely hot
TRANQUIL calm (waters)
TRANSIENT passing away after a brief time
TRIFLING having little importance
TRITE ordinary (remark)
TRIVIAL insignificant
TURBULENT agitated

ULTIMATE final (conclusion)
UNANIMOUS in complete agreement (decision)
UNASSUMING modest
UNCANNY unnatural (accuracy)
UNDAUNTED not discouraged
UNDERHAND sly
UNIQUE being the only one of its kind (specimen)
UNRULY disorderly (crowd)
UNWIELDY clumsy to use, usually because of size (implement)
UPRIGHT honest (citizen)
UTMOST most extreme (in distance, height or size)

VAIN futile (attempt); conceited (person)
VALIANT brave
VALID (legally) sound (argument)
VAST very large in extent or size (distances)
VEHEMENT violent in feeling (protest)
VERBATIM word for word (report)
VERSATILE able to perform many tasks well (athlete)
VIGILANT watchful (sentry)
VILE highly disgusting (conduct)
VISIBLE able to be seen (object)
VITAL essential (contribution)
VIVACIOUS lively
VIVID bright (color)
VULNERABLE open to attack (position)

WARY cautious
WEARY tired
WEE very small
WEIGHTY important (decision)
WHOLESOME causing a feeling of well-being (entertainment)
WILY cunning (magician)
WITTY amusingly clever (remark)
WORDY using too many words (reply)
WORTHY deserving (choice)
WRETCHED miserable

Practice with Sample Test Paragraphs

This chapter presents a fully analyzed sample GED test paragraph and three additional paragraphs, with answers, for practice.

PRACTICE TEST PARAGRAPH 1

The following items are based on a paragraph that contains numbered sentences. Some of the sentences may contain errors in sentence structure, usage, or mechanics. <u>A few sentences, however, may be correct as written.</u> Read the paragraph and then answer the items based on it. For each item, choose the answer that would result in the most effective writing of the sentence or sentences. The best answer must be consistent with the meaning and tone of the rest of the paragraph.

(1) Savings has been referred to as the tool for accomplishing future goals. (2) After a family has decided on a savings plan the decision on how to invest wisely must be made. (3) Life insurance is a way to provide immediate financial protection for the loss of income through the death of the breadwinner. (4) Once children are expected, the need arises for life insurance. (5) Life insurance is purchased to cover the cost of the funeral, to pay the expenses of the last illness, and to provide income for the survivors. (6) When planning for this type of financial protection, be sure to consider all resources the survivors will have to use (earning ability as well as financial) the amount of income that will meet necessities, and finally the cost of such a program. (7) Concentrate insurance dollars on the breadwinner, and buy the type of insurance that will give the most protection for the cost. (8) A savings account is the second leg of the stool for a savings program. (9) It is here where a family keeps the money that it may need immediately or plans to use within the near future. (10) After the family will protect itself with insurance for the survivors and with a savings account, it is then ready to invest in other possible channels. (11) At this point a family needs to consider these channels in line with its distant goals and with the economy.

1. Sentence 1. **Savings has been referred to as the tool for accomplishing future goals.**

   What correction should be made to this sentence?

   (1) change <u>has</u> to <u>have</u>
   (2) change the spelling of <u>referred</u> to <u>refered</u>
   (3) insert a comma after <u>to</u>
   (4) change the spelling of <u>accomplishing</u> to <u>acomplishing</u>
   (5) no correction is necessary

2. Sentence 2. **After a family has decided on a savings plan the decision on how to invest wisely must be made.**

   What correction should be made to this sentence?

   (1) change <u>has</u> to <u>have</u>
   (2) insert an apostrophe after <u>savings</u>
   (3) insert a comma after <u>plan</u>
   (4) change the spelling of <u>decision</u> to <u>descision</u>
   (5) change <u>how to invest</u> to <u>how to have invested</u>

3. Sentence 3. **Life insurance is a way to provide immediate financial <u>protection for the</u> loss of income through the death of the breadwinner.**

   Which of the following is the best way to write the underlined portion of this sentence? If you think the original is the best way, choose option (1).

   (1) protection for the
   (2) protection. For
   (3) protection, for
   (4) protection; for
   (5) protection—for

4. Sentences 4 and 5. **Once children are expected, the need arises for life insurance. Life insurance is purchased to cover the cost of the funeral, to pay the expenses of the last illness, and to provide income for the survivors.**

   The most effective combination of these sentences would include which of the following groups of words?

   (1) insurance, life insurance is
   (2) insurance that is purchased
   (3) insurance, in fact life insurance
   (4) insurance, that is to say life insurance
   (5) insurance life insurance is then purchased

5. Sentence 6. **When planning for this type of financial protection, be sure to consider all resources the survivors will have to use (earning ability as well as financial) the amount of income that will meet necessities, and finally the cost of such a program.**

   What correction should be made to this sentence?

   (1) change <u>when planning</u> to <u>having planned</u>
   (2) insert a comma after the second parenthesis
   (3) substitute quotation marks for the parentheses
   (4) change the spelling of <u>necessities</u> to <u>neccessities</u>
   (5) remove the comma after <u>necessities</u>

6. Sentence 7. **Concentrate insurance dollars on the breadwinner, and buy the type of insurance that will give the most protection for the cost.**

   What correction should be made to this sentence?

   (1) capitalize <u>breadwinner</u>
   (2) insert a hyphen between <u>bread</u> and <u>winner</u>
   (3) change <u>will give</u> to <u>gives</u>
   (4) remove <u>the</u> before <u>most protection</u>
   (5) no correction is necessary

7. Sentences 8 and 9. **A savings account is the second leg of the stool for a savings program. It is here where a family keeps the money that it may need immediately or plans to use within the near future.**

   The most effective combination of these sentences would include which of the following groups of words?

   (1) program where a family
   (2) program for which a family
   (3) program here where a family
   (4) program in which a family
   (5) program to which a family

8. Sentence 10. **After the family will protect itself with insurance for the survivors and with a savings account, it is then ready to invest in other possible channels.**

What correction should be made to this sentence?

(1) change <u>will protect</u> to <u>protects</u>
(2) insert a comma before <u>and</u>
(3) remove the comma after <u>account</u>
(4) change <u>then</u> to <u>therefore</u>
(5) no correction is necessary

9. The topic sentence of this paragraph is

(1) sentence 1
(2) sentence 2
(3) sentence 5
(4) sentence 8
(5) sentence 11

ANSWER KEY

1. **1**	3. **1**	5. **2**	7. **1**	9. **2**
2. **3**	4. **2**	6. **5**	8. **1**	

ANSWER ANALYSIS

1. **1** (1) is correct because savings is considered a plural noun; therefore, it requires a verb that agrees. (2) is not correct because *referred* is correctly spelled. (3) is wrong because no comma is needed here. (4) is wrong because *accomplishing* is correctly spelled. (5) is wrong because a correction is necessary.

2. **3** (1) is not correct because *family* may be considered a collective noun in the singular. (2) is wrong because no apostrophe is necessary since the idea of possession is not involved. (3) is correct because a comma *is* necessary after an introductory clause. See rule 4. (4) is incorrect because *decision* is spelled correctly. (5) is wrong because *to invest* is the correct tense since the investment has not yet taken place.

3. **1** This is so because the original is the best way. In (2), a period would result in a sentence fragment. In (3), (4), and (5), no punctuation is necessary after *protection.*

4. **2** In (1) the change would result in a run-on sentence. (2) is correct because *that is purchased* is an adjective clause describing *insurance.* In (3), (4), and (5), all the corrections would result in run-on sentences.

5. **2** In (1), the present tense is correct and should not be changed. In (2), a comma should be inserted in a series according to rule 6, so this is correct. (3) is wrong because no one is being quoted. (4) is incorrect because *necessities* is the correct spelling. In (5), the comma is needed to punctuate a series.

6. **5** This is so because no correction is necessary. (1) is incorrect because breadwinner is not a proper noun (see rule 4) and should not be capitalized. (2) is wrong because breadwinner is a single word that does not need a hyphen. In (3), *will give* is the correct tense because the future tense is required and, therefore, there should be no change. In (4), *the* is necessary because a definite article is needed. Therefore (5) is the correct answer.

7. **1** This is a tricky question because it calls for the *most effective combination.* (1) is the most effective combination because the adjective clause immediately follows the noun, *program,* that it describes. (2), (4), (5) are awkward and not as effective. (3) is incorrect because an adjective clause is required.

8. **1** The family protects itself in the *present* so the present tense, not the future tense, is needed. In (2), no comma is needed where only two items are involved: insurance and savings. In (3), the comma after *account* is necessary after an introductory clause. (4) is wrong because *then* is correct since it means "at that time." (5) is incorrect because there is an error in the sentence.

9. **2** (1) is wrong because it mentions only the relationship between savings and future goals. (2) is correct because the entire paragraph describes how to wisely invest in a savings plan. (3) is wrong because it mentions one way to invest in a savings plan. (4) is wrong because it mentions only a savings account. (5) is wrong because it tells what a family needs to consider before deciding on a savings plan.

Three Additional Sample Test Paragraphs with Answer Analyses

Refer to page 193 for directions in answering the questions based on these paragraphs.

Important: Do not answer any question until you have read and analyzed all the possible choices. You will have to draw on your knowledge of sentence structure, usage, and mechanics, all of which may be involved in a single question.

PRACTICE TEST PARAGRAPH 2

(1) To improve consumer choice use good buying strategies and tactics to carry out the basic plan. (2) Price's and quality can vary greatly in buying food, auto insurance, or dandruff treatments. (3) A watermelon is a better buy at certain times of the year because of transportation costs. (4) Air conditioning may be a good buy at other times. (5) A used car may be adequate for many purposes. (6) A turnip is nutritious. (7) The choice available makes your personal consumer decision process complex, but the potential savings and improvements is huge compared to poor results from not shopping harder. (8) A great deal of regret can be avoided by obtaining reliable information in consumer education courses consumer magazines, and numerous books and pamphlets. (9) Unfair and deceptive practices of a few businesses would largely disappear, if consumers practiced self-defense. (10) Such defense means being well informed. (11) Consumers can assist in improving product safety, help to maintain reasonable prices, and raising the quality of goods not only by buying wisely, but by addressing themselves to economic and consumer problems. (12) Theres a mutual responsibility among consumers to seek and to improve the ways in which producers make and sell their products and services.

1. Sentence 1. **To improve consumer choice use good buying strategies and tactics to carry out the basic plan.**

   What correction should be made to this sentence?

   (1) insert a comma after <u>choice</u>
   (2) change <u>strategies</u> to <u>stratagies</u>
   (3) insert a comma after <u>strategies</u>
   (4) change <u>to</u> to <u>and</u>
   (5) no correction is necessary

2. Sentence 2. **Price's and quality can vary greatly in buying food, auto insurance, or dandruff treatments.**

   What correction should be made to this sentence?

   (1) remove the comma after <u>quality</u>
   (2) remove the apostrophe from <u>Price's</u>
   (3) change <u>can</u> to <u>could</u>
   (4) remove the comma after <u>food</u>
   (5) no correction is necessary

3. Sentences 3 and 4. **A watermelon is a better buy at certain times of the year because of transportation costs. Air conditioning may be a good buy at other times.**

   The most effective combination of sentences 3 and 4 would include which of the following words?

   (1) costs, although air
   (2) costs, and air
   (3) costs, but air
   (4) costs, however air
   (5) costs, whereas air

4. Sentence 7. **The choice available makes your personal consumer decision process complex, but the potential savings and improvements is huge compared to poor results from not shopping harder.**

   What correction should be made to this sentence?

   (1) change the spelling of <u>available</u> to <u>availible</u>
   (2) remove the comma after <u>complex</u>
   (3) change <u>but</u> to <u>and</u>
   (4) change <u>is</u> to <u>are</u>
   (5) no correction is necessary

5. Sentence 8. **A great deal of regret can be avoided by obtaining reliable information in consumer education courses consumer magazines, and numerous books and pamphlets.**

   What correction should be made to this sentence?

   (1) change <u>can</u> to <u>could</u>
   (2) change <u>by obtaining</u> to <u>if you obtained</u>
   (3) insert a comma after <u>courses</u>
   (4) remove the comma after <u>magazines</u>
   (5) no correction is necessary

6. Sentence 9. **Unfair and deceptive practices of a few businesses would largely disappear, if consumers practiced self-defense.**

   What correction should be made to this sentence?

   (1) change the spelling of <u>businesses</u> to <u>busineses</u>
   (2) change <u>would</u> to <u>should</u>
   (3) remove the comma after <u>disappear</u>
   (4) change the spelling of <u>disappear</u> to <u>disapear</u>
   (5) no correction is necessary

7. Sentences 9 and 10. **Unfair and deceptive practices of a few businesses would largely disappear, if consumers practiced <u>self-defense. Such</u> defense means being well-informed.**

Which of the following is the best way to write the underlined portion of this sentence? If you think the original is the best way, choose option (1).

(1) self-defense. Such
(2) self-defense such
(3) self-defense, such
(4) self-defense; such
(5) self-defense, nevertheless such

8. Sentence 11. **Consumers can assist in improving product safety, help to maintain reasonable prices, and raising the quality of goods not only by buying wisely, but by addressing themselves to economic and consumer problems.**

   What correction should be made to this sentence?

   (1) remove the comma after <u>safety</u>
   (2) change <u>help</u> to <u>helping</u>
   (3) change <u>but</u> to <u>and</u>
   (4) change the spelling of <u>addressing</u> to <u>adressing</u>
   (5) no correction is necessary

9. Sentence 12. **Theres a mutual responsibility among consumers to seek and to improve the ways in which producers make and sell their products and services.**

   What correction should be made to this sentence?

   (1) change the spelling of <u>Theres</u> to <u>There's</u>
   (2) change <u>among</u> to <u>between</u>
   (3) change <u>to seek</u> to <u>and seek</u>
   (4) change <u>and</u> to <u>or</u>
   (5) no correction is necessary

ANSWER KEY

1. 1	3. 2	5. 3	7. 1	9. 1
2. 2	4. 4	6. 5	8. 2	

ANSWER ANALYSIS

1. **1** There is an error in punctuation. A comma is used after an introductory phrase.

2. **2** There is an error in spelling. *Prices* does not possess anything; therefore, it does not require an apostrophe.

3. **2** A conjunction is required because the two independent clauses are equally important.

4. **4** There is an error in usage. A plural subject, *savings and improvement*, requires a plural verb, *are*.

5. **3** There is an error in punctuation. A comma is required to separate items in a series.

6. **5** No correction is necessary.

7. **1** The original is correct. All other choices result in run-on sentences.

8. **2** There is an error in usage. The use of the participle *helping* is required to parallel the participles *improving* and *raising*.

9. **1** There is an error in spelling. *There's* is a contraction of *there is*, the subject and verb needed to make this sentence.

PRACTICE TEST PARAGRAPH 3

(1) Household insects seem to have an incredible ability to escape extinction. (2) Cockroaches for example which have been on earth millions of years longer than human beings, can subsist on any kind of food. (3) They thrive in all parts of the world, some species prefer a human home to other habitats. (4) Once they enter it they use countless instinctive tricks to keep from being killed or evicted. (5) You can control household pests. (6) Do systematic house cleaning. (7) The best way to rid your home of practically all insect pests is by a combination of good housekeeping practices and proper use of the right insecticide. (8) It is easier to prevent pests from infesting your home than it is to get rid of them after they are established. (9) Household insects seek available food in places where they can hide and breathe. (10) If one eliminates these attractions from your home, the insects will look elsewhere for them. (11) Keep storage cabinets, kitchen drawers, and washtubs clean. (12) Frequent scrubbings with hot water and soap will do the job.

1. Sentence 2. **Cockroaches for example which have been on earth millions of years longer than human beings, can subsist on any kind of food.**

   What correction should be made to this sentence?

   (1) insert commas before and after <u>for example</u>
   (2) change <u>which</u> to <u>who</u>
   (3) remove the comma after <u>human beings</u>
   (4) change <u>can subsist</u> to <u>have subsisted</u>
   (5) no correction is necessary

2. Sentence 3. **They thrive in all parts of the <u>world, some species</u> prefer a human home to other habitats.**

   Which of the following is the best way to write the underlined portion of this sentence? If you think the original is the best way, choose option (1).

   (1) world, some species
   (2) world. Some species
   (3) world some species
   (4) world but some species
   (5) world because some species

3. Sentence 4. **Once they enter it they use countless instinctive tricks to keep from being killed or evicted.**

   What correction should be made to this sentence?

   (1) change <u>it</u> to <u>man's home</u>
   (2) insert a comma after <u>it</u>
   (3) change <u>being killed</u> to <u>having been killed</u>
   (4) change <u>or</u> to <u>and</u>
   (5) no correction is necessary

4. Sentences 5 and 6. **You can control household pests. Do systematic house cleaning.**

   The most effective combination of sentences 5 and 6 would include which of the following groups of words?

   (1) pests and do
   (2) pests if they try to do
   (3) pests while doing
   (4) pests by doing
   (5) pests having done

5. Sentence 7. **The best way to rid your home of practically all insect pests is by a combination of good housekeeping practices and proper use of the right insecticide.**

If you rewrote sentence 7 beginning with

A combination of good housekeeping practices and proper use of the right insecticide is

the next word(s) would be

(1) indeed
(2) therefore
(3) furthermore
(4) for example
(5) however

6. Sentence 8. **It is easier to prevent pests from infesting your home than it is to get rid of <u>them after</u> they are established.**

Which of the following is the best way to write the underlined portion of this sentence? If you think the original is the best way, choose option (1).

(1) them after
(2) them. After
(3) them, after
(4) them; after
(5) them, and after

7. A new paragraph should be started after

(1) sentence 2
(2) sentence 4
(3) sentence 8
(4) sentence 10
(5) sentence 11

8. Sentence 10. **If one eliminates these attractions from your home, the insects will look elsewhere for them.**

What correction should be made to this sentence?

(1) change <u>your</u> to <u>one's</u>
(2) remove the comma after <u>home</u>
(3) change <u>will</u> to <u>would</u>
(4) change <u>elsewhere</u> to <u>somewhere else</u>
(5) no correction is necessary

9. Sentences 11 and 12. **Keep storage cabinets, kitchen drawers, and wash-tubs clean. Frequent scrubbings with hot water and soap will do the job.**

The most effective combination of sentences 11 and 12 would include which of the following groups of words?

(1) and frequent scrubbings
(2) by frequent scrubbings
(3) because frequent scrubbings
(4) since frequent scrubbings
(5) as a matter of fact frequent scrubbings

Answer Key

1. **1**	3. **2**	5. **5**	7. **2**	9. **2**
2. **2**	4. **4**	6. **1**	8. **1**	

Answer Analysis

1. **1** There is an error in punctuation. Commas are used to set off clauses that are inserted into a sentence.
2. **2** There is an error in sentence structure. As written, this is a run-on sentence. A period is needed to divide the two sentences, and the second sentence must start with a capital letter.
3. **2** There is an error in punctuation. A comma is needed to set off the introductory clause.
4. **4** The sentences are best combined by changing the second sentence into an adverbial phrase modifying the verb *control.*
5. **5** *However* is used when the idea in a sentence differs from the idea in the preceding sentence. In this case, the preceding sentence mentioned one method of control. This sentence refers to a combination of methods.
6. **1** The original is correct, since *after they are established* is an adverbial clause modifying *get rid of.*

200 Language Arts, Writing, Test 1, Part I

7. **2** The first four sentences describe how insects seem to thrive. The last eight sentences all elaborate on how you can control household insects.

8. **1** There is an error in the use of the pronouns—a needless shift from the third person *one* to the second person *your.* If you use more than one pronoun to refer to the same person, you must be consistent. The words *If one eliminates* must be followed by *from one's home.*

9. **2** The best combination is *by frequent scrubbings,* which modifies the verb *keep* and makes the words *will do the job* unnecessary.

PRACTICE TEST PARAGRAPH 4

(1) Among your important records are a thorough household inventory. (2) Before this can be of much value, in case of fire or burglary, youll need to supply some details. (3) Be sure to list the item date bought, purchase price, model number if it applies, brand name, dealer's name. (4) And general description (color, size, style, electric or gas, etc.) (5) Don't forget to include a realistic lump sum in your list for clothes and jewelry if you don't itemize these. (6) This information serves a triple purpose. (7) It helps you to determine the value of your possessions so you can have adequate insurance protection. (8) It helps you if it becomes necessary for you to make an insurance claim. (9) Some families take pictures of they're rooms to help identify possessions. (10) One copy of the household inventory should be put in your safe deposit box; you may wish to give a copy to your insurance company.

1. Sentence 1. **Among your important records are a thorough household inventory.**

   What correction should be made to this sentence?

   (1) change <u>your</u> to <u>you're</u>
   (2) change <u>are</u> to <u>is</u>
   (3) change <u>thorough</u> to <u>through</u>
   (4) change the spelling of <u>inventory</u> to <u>inventary</u>
   (5) no change is necessary

2. Sentence 2. **Before this can be of much value, in case of fire or burglary, youll need to supply some details.**

   What correction should be made to this sentence?

   (1) remove the comma after <u>value</u>
   (2) remove the comma after <u>burglary</u>
   (3) change youll to you'll
   (4) change <u>to supply</u> to <u>to have supplied</u>
   (5) no correction is necessary

3. Sentence 3. **Be sure to list the item date bought, purchase price, model number if it applies, brand name, dealer's name.**

   What correction should be made to this sentence?

   (1) insert a comma after <u>item</u>
   (2) capitalize <u>date bought</u>
   (3) remove the comma after <u>applies</u>
   (4) change <u>dealer's</u> to <u>dealers</u>
   (5) no correction is necessary

4. Sentences 3 and 4. **Be sure to list the item date bought, purchase price, model number if it applies, brand name, dealer's <u>name. And</u> general description (color, size, style, electric or gas, etc.)**

   Which is the best way to write the underlined portion of this sentence? If you think the original is the best way, choose option (1).

   (1) name. And
   (2) name. and
   (3) name and
   (4) name, and
   (5) name, And

5. Sentence 5. **Don't forget to include a realistic lump sum in your list for clothes and jewelry if you don't itemize these.**

   What correction should be made to this sentence?

   (1) change <u>Don't</u> to <u>Dont</u>
   (2) change the spelling of <u>realistic</u> to <u>reelistic</u>
   (3) insert a comma after <u>sum</u>
   (4) change the spelling of <u>clothes</u> to <u>cloths</u>
   (5) no correction is necessary

6. Sentences 6 and 7. **This information serves a triple <u>purpose. It</u> helps you to determine the value of your possessions so you can have adequate insurance protection.**

Which of the following is the best way to write the underlined portion of this sentence? If you think the original is the best way, choose option (1).

(1) purpose. It
(2) purpose it
(3) purpose It
(4) purpose, so it
(5) purpose although it

7. Sentence 8. **It helps you if it becomes necessary for you to make an insurance claim.**

What correction should be made to this sentence?

(1) insert a comma after <u>you</u>
(2) change <u>you</u> to <u>one</u>
(3) change <u>becomes</u> to <u>will become</u>
(4) change the spelling of <u>necessary</u> to <u>neccessary</u>
(5) no correction is necessary

8. Sentence 9. **Some families take pictures of they're rooms to help identify possessions.**

What correction should be made to this sentence?

(1) change the spelling of <u>they're</u> to <u>their</u>
(2) insert a comma after <u>rooms</u>
(3) change to <u>help</u> to <u>which helps</u>
(4) change the spelling of <u>possessions</u> to <u>posessions</u>
(5) no correction is necessary

9. Sentence 10. **One copy of the household inventory should be put in your safe deposit box; you may wish to give a copy to your insurance company.**

What correction should be made to this sentence?

(1) change <u>should be</u> to <u>is to be</u>
(2) change the semicolon after <u>box</u> to a colon
(3) change <u>may</u> to <u>might</u>
(4) capitalize insurance company
(5) no correction is necessary

ANSWER KEY

1. **2**	3. **1**	5. **5**	7. **5**	9. **5**
2. **3**	4. **4**	6. **1**	8. **1**	

ANSWER ANALYSIS

1. **2** There is an error in usage. The subject of the sentence is *inventory*, which is singular. The verb, therefore, must also be singular, *is*, since subject and verb must agree in number.
2. **3** The error is in spelling. The proper contraction of *you will* is *you'll* with the apostrophe indicating that letters are omitted.
3. **1** There is a punctuation error. Commas are needed to set off items in a series.
4. **4** Inclusion of the phrase *and general description* in the previous sentence removes the sentence fragment. A comma is necessary because the phrase is one of a series of phrases.
5. **5** No correction is necessary.
6. **1** The original is correct. Two separate sentences are required.
7. **5** No correction is necessary
8. **1** The error is in spelling. *Their* is a possessive pronoun meaning "belonging to them."
9. **5** No correction is necessary.

WHAT'S YOUR SCORE?

Total your score on the four practice test paragraphs (the analyzed paragraph and the three additional sample test paragraphs).

_____ right,	_____ wrong
Excellent	32–36
Good	27–31
Fair	22–26

CHAPTER 9: The Essay

The purpose of the GED Essay test is to test your ability to write. It does this by requiring you to write an essay of about 250 words in which you explain something, present an opinion on an issue, or retell a personal experience. The purpose of the test is not to show how much you know about a particular subject, but how well you can relate your ideas. In this chapter, through examples and practice, you will learn essential skills from sentence structure to completed essays that will help improve your ability to create structured and focused essays.

The Essay

What Is an Essay?

Before you can begin your essay it is necessary that you understand what it is you are writing. An essay is a short theme based on a main idea and details. On the GED test you will be given a *prompt* to write about. You will write sentences that are complete, varied, and correct. You will build them into focused paragraphs that are combined into your final essay.

The *Language Arts, Writing, Part II* section will show you how to write an essay by going through ten segments beginning with the sentence and moving to paragraphs and then the essay. Sentence structures, punctuation, and grammatical elements may be reviewed in full in the *Language Arts, Writing, Part I*.

The Sentence

What is a sentence?

A sentence is a group of words that make a complete thought. In this complete thought there is a subject that tells what the sentence is about and a predicate that tells what the subject does. Sentences express the thoughts and ideas of people through speaking or writing. To make sure that a thought or idea is completely understood, the sentence must be spoken or written clearly and correctly.

EXAMPLES

CORRECT SENTENCES:

Judy will take the five o'clock train home from work.
Please call for a reservation.
Wow, that was a great baseball game!
What is for supper?

These sentences are all grammatically correct. They are complete, begin with capital letters, and end with correct punctuation marks.

INCORRECT SENTENCES:

Gets up early in the morning.
The long black train.
Jan and Mark and Terry and Lee.
The busy intersection is a dangerous place for children they may get hurt!

The first three sentences in the incorrect examples above are sentence fragments. This means they are lacking a subject or a predicate. The last sentence is a run-on sentence.

Gets up early in the morning is lacking a subject. Who or what gets up early in the morning? We can correct this sentence by adding the subject "cat" to the sentence. *The cat gets up early in the morning.*

The long black train is lacking a predicate. What does it do? This sentence can be corrected by adding the predicate "is loaded with freight." *The long black train is loaded with freight.*

Jan and Mark and Terry and Lee is a sentence fragment; it is written poorly and does not contain a predicate. When there is a multiple subject or series of words, they should be connected with commas such as *Jan, Mark, Terry, and Lee will ride the bus to town.*

The busy intersection is a dangerous place for children they may get hurt may sound like a correct sentence, but actually it is two sentences together. This is called a run-on sentence. It should be made into two complete sentences. *The busy intersection is a dangerous place for children. They may get hurt.* Notice that each new sentence has a subject and a predicate.

TYPES OF SENTENCES

There are four basic types of sentences. They are declarative, interrogative, exclamatory, and imperative.

Declarative sentences make a statement. They are a "telling" sentence. This type of sentence states an idea and ends with a period.

EXAMPLES

The sky is blue.
The roses have thorns.
Sandie and Larry are going shopping in the mall.
Flowers need plenty of water to survive the heat of summer.

Interrogative sentences ask a question. An interrogative sentence ends with a question mark

EXAMPLES

What are you wearing to the dance?
Does the baby need changing?
Did you forget to buy the milk?
Did Christy pick up the mail?

Exclamatory sentences state strong emotion. An exclamatory sentence ends with an exclamation point.

EXAMPLES

Watch out for that car!
The weather report is saying there is a tornado warning!
That bee is after me!
The damage to the park is unbelievable!

Imperative sentences make a request or command. They are sometimes confused with the interrogative sentences, but imperative sentences do not ask a question. With a request or command, the person to whom the statement is directed does not need to give an answer. These sentences end with a period.

EXAMPLES

Please pick up Jordan from football practice.
Don't smoke around the baby.
Wash the dishes when you are finished with the meal.
Please return the movie to the video store.

PRACTICE—TYPES OF SENTENCES

Decide what each type of sentence is and write the correct letter beside the statement.

A. declarative   B. interrogative
C. exclamatory   D. imperative

1. _____The young boy sat by the lake watching his reflection.
2. _____Where are you going on Saturday?
3. _____Charlie was admiring his new car.
4. _____Please turn the stereo down.
5. _____I just won a stuffed gorilla at the fair!
6. _____There are days when I think time passes very slowly.
7. _____The parade is starting!
8. _____Meet me at the pizza parlor.
9. _____When are you driving Diego to the game?
10. _____There is a wonderful new program on television tonight.

ANSWER KEY

1. **A**	3. **A**	5. **C**	7. **C**	9. **B**
2. **B**	4. **D**	6. **A**	8. **D**	10. **A**

PRACTICE—SENTENCE COMPONENTS

In order for a sentence to be written correctly it must have several components such as correct capitalization, punctuation, subjects, and predicates. These components help the reader to correctly determine the intended meaning of the statement.

THE BASIC RULES FOR CAPITALIZATION ARE AS FOLLOWS:

- Always capitalize the first word in a sentence.
- Always capitalize important words in a title.
- Always capitalize proper nouns (specific names of people, places, or things).
- Always capitalize the word *I*.

EXAMPLES

This glass jar would make a lovely vase.
Have you ever seen *The Wizard of Oz*?
The Statue of Liberty is located in New York Harbor.
Marci and I are attending the University of Kentucky in the fall.

USE OF PUNCTUATION

Punctuation is important in a sentence to allow the reader to fully understand the meaning of a sentence. A sentence followed by a question mark clearly shows that a question was being asked. An exclamation point at the end of a sentence shows that a sentence is being said with strong emotion, and a period at the end of a sentence tells the reader that a statement is being said. That statement may be telling a fact, opinion, or making a request or command. There are other punctuation marks that may be included in a sentence such as commas, quotation marks, colons, apostrophes, parentheses, and semicolons. These different types of punctuation may be reviewed in *Language Arts, Writing, Part I*.

PRACTICE—ENDING PUNCTUATION

Place the correct punctuation mark at the end of each sentence.

1. I wonder what the weather will be like today
2. Tell me about when you were a child
3. What is the best way to get to New York from Denver
4. Help me wrap this package
5. That is really amazing
6. The museum had over ten thousand visitors in the last month
7. What a wonderful time we had
8. Where is my new watch
9. The keys to the car are on the kitchen table
10. This book is one of the best I have ever read

ANSWERS

1. period
2. period
3. question mark
4. period
5. exclamation mark
6. period
7. exclamation mark
8. question mark
9. period
10. exclamation mark

SUBJECT AND PREDICATES

Every sentence must have a *subject* and a *predicate*. A subject tells who or what the sentence is about. The subject in a sentence can be a noun or pronoun, or it could be simply an understood subject. A noun is a person, place, or thing. A pronoun is a word that takes the place of a noun. An understood subject would be one that is not stated, but understood by the reader such as in an imperative sentence.

EXAMPLES

Grandmother's blue dish/fell to the floor with a crash.
The old quilt/was tattered.
I/gathered the walnuts from the ground
Turn the radio down.

The above subjects and predicates are separated by a slash mark. In the first example *Grandmother's blue dish* is the subject and *fell to the floor with a crash* is the predicate. In the second example, *The old quilt* is the subject and *was tattered* is the predicate. In the third example, *I* is the subject and *gathered the walnuts from the ground* is the predicate. The last example has an understood subject. This is an imperative sentence that makes a command. The understood subject would be the person to whom the sentence is referred.

SUBJECTS

A subject may be simple or complete. A simple subject means the key word that the sentence is about. A complete subject includes the simple subject and all the words that go with it.

EXAMPLES

The limb of the tree scratched the clear window.
The small black fox caught a mouse from the field.

The limb of the tree would be the complete subject, while *limb* would be the simple subject. In the second example, *The small black fox* would be the complete subject and *fox* would be the simple subject.

Subjects in a sentence may also be compound. This means there are two or more subjects that share the same verb.

EXAMPLES

Rodney and Carolee are planning a picnic lunch at the park.
Chicago and St. Louis have similar weather.
Amanda, Paul, and Tom worked overtime at the factory.

The compound subject in the first sentence would be *Rodney* and *Carolee*; the second sentence would be *Chicago* and *St. Louis*. The compound subjects in the third sentence would be *Amanda, Paul,* and *Tom.*

PRACTICE—SUBJECTS

Circle the complete subjects in the following sentences. Underline the simple subjects. If the subject is understood, write *understood* at the end of the sentence.

1. The picture frame sits neatly on the office desk.
2. Follow the light with your eyes.
3. The small yellow car made an illegal turn.
4. He watches scary movies in the dark.
5. Brenda's new jeans have a slight tear in the knee.
6. The green light has turned red.
7. The mall is very crowded with shoppers.
8. Watch the weather report tonight.
9. I heard a bird chirping from a distant tree.
10. Art is a fun hobby.

ANSWERS

1. (The picture frame) sits neatly on the office desk.
2. Follow the light with your eyes. (Understood)
3. (The small yellow car) made an illegal turn.
4. (He) watches scary movies in the dark.
5. (Brenda's new jeans) have a slight tear in the knee.
6. (The green light) has turned red.
7. (The mall) is very crowded with shoppers.
8. Watch the weather report tonight. (Understood)
9. (I) heard a bird chirping from a distant tree.
10. (Art) is a fun hobby.

PREDICATES

The predicate in a sentence tells what the subject *does*. It has a verb form. The verb form may be an action verb or linking verb. Just like the subject, there may be a simple predicate and a complete predicate. A simple predicate would be the one word that tells what the subject does, while a complete predicate would be all the words that go with the verb.

EXAMPLES

The busy school bus picked up the children for school.
Our main course for dinner is beef stew.

In the first sentence the simple predicate would be *picked* and the complete predicate would be *picked up the children for school.* In the second sentence the simple predicate would be *is* and the complete predicate would be *is beef stew.* The first sentence shows an action verb as the predicate while the second sentence shows a linking verb as the predicate. You may review the difference between these two types of verbs in the *Writing Skills, Part I.*

Sentences may also contain *compound predicates.* This means there are two or more verbs in the predicate that share the same subject.

EXAMPLES

The bird chirped and fluttered around the cage.
Stadium fans clapped, yelled, and stomped as the team entered.

The compound predicate in the first example would be *chirped* and *fluttered,* and in the second example *clapped, yelled,* and *stomped.*

Sentences may also have a *compound subject* and a *compound predicate.*

EXAMPLES

The carpenter and plumber looked over the plans and wrote a report.
The teacher, principal, and students played games and rode rides at the school carnival.

Carpenter and *plumber* are the subjects in the first sentence. *Looked* and *wrote* make up the compound predicate. In the second example, *teacher, principal,* and *students* are the subjects and *played* and *rode* are the predicates.

PRACTICE—SUBJECT AND PREDICATE

Part A
Put a check mark next to sentences that contain both the subject and the predicate.

1. _____ There is a large black snake crawling across the road.
2. _____ Where are you going for lunch?
3. _____ June stapled her project papers together.
4. _____ Leaves in the afternoon.
5. _____ Watch out for the car!
6. _____ The local radio station plays country music.
7. _____ The tiny brown mouse.
8. _____ Sandwiches for the party.
9. _____ The twins were wearing identical outfits.
10. _____ The car was making.

Part B
Write the letter that corresponds with the underlined part of the sentence.

A. simple subject   D. complete predicate
B. simple predicate   E. compound subject
C. complete subject   F. compound predicate

1. _____ The <u>motor</u> on the car was running hot.
2. _____ A replacement window <u>was ordered for the house</u>.
3. _____ <u>Dogs and horses</u> are useful animals on a ranch.
4. _____ I <u>attended</u> the Thanksgiving Day Parade.
5. _____ The motorcycles <u>skidded and raced</u> past the crowd.
6. _____ <u>A blaring fire alarm</u> was alarming patients in the hospital.
7. _____ December <u>is</u> a very cold month in the northern states.
8. _____ Several <u>thorns</u> are protruding from the base of the rosebush.
9. _____ The small child <u>picked up the blue crayon from the floor</u>.
10. _____ <u>All available volunteers</u> are helping with the disaster.

ANSWERS

Part A
Sentences 1, 2, 3, 5, 6, and 9 should be checked.

Part B

1. **A**	3. **E**	5. **F**	7. **B**	9. **D**
2. **D**	4. **B**	6. **C**	8. **A**	10. **C**

EFFECTIVE SENTENCE STRUCTURE

TYPES OF SENTENCE STRUCTURES

It is important when writing an essay to make sure that each sentence written is clear and has correct structure. There are different types of sentences that can be part of an essay. These different types of sentences give the essay variety, depth, and a greater sense of interest for the reader. Try some of these types of sentences when you begin your essay.

A *simple sentence* is usually made of an independent clause. An independent clause simply means the sentence contains a subject and a predicate. An independent clause can stand alone.

EXAMPLE

> The fisherman caught a ten-pound catfish.

The fisherman would be the subject; *caught a ten-pound catfish* would be the predicate.

A *compound sentence* contains two independent clauses and they are usually combined with a conjunction such as and, or, but, or so.

EXAMPLE

> The fisherman caught a ten-pound catfish, but it managed to get away.

This sentence has two complete sentences combined with the word *but*. The first independent clause is *The fisherman caught a ten-pound catfish*, and the second is *it managed to get away*. In the first independent clause *The fisherman* is the subject, and *caught a ten-pound catfish* is the predicate. In the second independent clause *it* is the subject and *managed to get away* is the predicate.

A *complex sentence* is made up of one independent clause and one or more dependent clauses (also called a *subordinating clause*). There are several types of subordinating clauses such as appositives, adjectives, adverbs, nouns, and prepositionals. A dependent clause cannot stand alone as a sentence.

EXAMPLE

Aunt Fay, *my mother's sister*, is a very creative artist.

The italicized part of the sentence is a subordinating phrase called an *appositive*, which tells more about the subject *Aunt Fay*. Make sure that you separate the appositive by commas.

SUBJECT/VERB AGREEMENT

When you write a sentence, make sure that the subject and the verb agree. In other words, make sure to use the correct verb form with the subject. (Review *Writing Skills, Part I* for complete listing.)

INCORRECT USAGE OF SUBJECT/VERB AGREEMENT

The mums, in the garden, is beautiful in the fall.
I is going to the festival at the park.
Sue and Jackie brung fresh baked pie for the bake sale.
They gives each year to their favorite charity.

CORRECT USAGE OF SUBJECT/VERB AGREEMENT

The mums, in the garden, are beautiful in the fall.
I am going to the festival at the park.
Sue and Jackie brought fresh baked pie for the bake sale.
They give each year to their favorite charity.

Different styles of sentences and ideas develop the essay into a more enjoyable reading experience. Try using some of these ideas in your writing.

COMPARING AND CONTRASTING IDEAS

Comparing and *contrasting* means the way ideas are alike and different. If you are writing a narrative essay about the time you rode a mule into the Grand Canyon, you may want to include some comparing and contrasting.

EXAMPLE

I began the long journey down into the canyon on the back of a mule. The mule was a more sure-footed animal than the horse. I was glad to know that since the path was so narrow.

In this passage there is a contrasting idea of how the mule is unlike the horse. The mule is sure footed and the horse is not.

You may also want to include some sentences that compare. Suppose you were writing a persuasive essay about why farmers should or should not add growth hormones to cattle feed.

EXAMPLE

The hamburger used in many fast-food restaurants is from cattle that have been fed growth hormones. The hamburger that I use at home is from a cow we raised and later butchered. It was not given any type of growth hormone. It seems to me that the hamburger meat from both types of cattle has the same flavor.

This paragraph compares the taste hamburger from the two types of cattle.

A VENN DIAGRAM

To make it easier to develop comparing and contrasting ideas you may want to draw a Venn diagram. This will help you outline your ideas. A Venn diagram is a simple diagram made up of two intertwining circles. Each outer loop represents how the two ideas are different. The center loop represents how the ideas are alike.

EXAMPLE

If you wanted to compare and contrast the mule and the horse, this is how the Venn diagram would look.

Mule	**Similar**	**Horse**
sure footed	looks similar	may slip on rock
very strong	can be ridden	used for pleasure
used for working	used on farms	shorter hears
long-eared		is able to reproduce
braying voice		longer tails
offspring of		fast moving
horse and donkey		

PRACTICE—VENN DIAGRAM

Make a Venn diagram on a separate piece of paper. Choose from the following ideas.

> computers and typewriters
> daycare and stay-at-home moms
> college degree and high school degree
> video rental and movie theaters
> e-mail and postal letters

ANSWERS

(Answers will vary.)
Computer: Has many programs, has more equipment, has more capabilities than a typewriter, has a monitor for viewing work.
Typewriter: Used only as a word procesor, uses ribbon for printing.
Same: Both use electricity, both have a keyboard, both are word processors.

CAUSE AND EFFECT

Another way to make your essay more interesting is by including a cause-and-effect relationship of ideas. A cause is what happens first in the relationship of ideas; the effect is secondary.

EXAMPLES

> The fierce storm blew the large straw hat from my head. It promptly landed in a large mud puddle.
> A careless match was thrown from the window of a passing car. It landed in a stack of dry leaves which quickly began to burn.
> Over Thanksgiving I ate more than my usual amount. At Christmas the dress I wanted to wear was too small.

In the first example the cause would be the *fierce storm* and the effect would be *the hat landed in a large mud puddle.* Keep in mind that the fierce storm would have to happen before the hat could land in a large mud puddle. This makes the fierce storm the cause. The second example shows *the match* as the cause and *the leaves burning* as the effect. The cause in the last example is *I ate too much at Thanksgiving* and the effect would be *the dress was too small.*

PRACTICE—CAUSE AND EFFECT

Put a check mark next to the sentences that have a cause-and-effect relationship.

1. _____ Greg played his guitar and Jane sang.
2. _____ Monica's hair began to get wet as she walked in the rain.
3. _____ The police officer gave Mike a ticket when he discovered his license had expired.
4. _____ The cereal became soggy soon after it was poured into the milk.
5. _____ Someone had torn a page from the magazine.
6. _____ The milk began to soak into the carpet soon after the baby dropped the bottle from her crib.
7. _____ The paper shredded when the printer jammed.
8. _____ The full moon rose over the lake.
9. _____ Keisha switched on the light just as the bulb blew out.
10. _____ The snow was covering most of the mid-western states.

ANSWERS

Sentences 1, 2, 3, 4, 6, 7, and 9 all contain cause-and-effect relationships.

TIME ORDER

Time order words give the reader a sense of *when* things happen and the *correct order.* These types of words may include, first, second, third, next, later, afterwards, soon, and finally. If you were writing a personal narrative about how to make your favorite cake, you would need to add time order words to help with the correct order. This makes the sequence of events more clearly understood.

EXAMPLE

> Before I start baking I always check to make sure I have the proper ingredients. First, I read through the recipe carefully. Then I gather together all the ingredients that I will need. I place them on the counter within easy reach. After I have the ingredients, I begin mixing them in the proper order.

This paragraph shows the use of time order words. It makes the sentences of the paragraph relate to one another by moving from one step to the next in the correct order.

PRACTICE—TIME ORDER WORDS

On a separate sheet of paper practice using time order words in paragraphs. Below are some ideas for paragraphs.

My morning routine
How to play tennis
Buying a new car
Learning a new dance
Making a scrapbook
Planting a garden
Baking bread
Preparing for an interview
Assembling a product
Home fire dril

ANSWERS

(Answers will vary.)

EXAMPLE

Planting a garden takes a lot of planning. First, there is finding a perfect place in your yard to place it. Second, you need to buy all the supplies to use such as shovels and seeds. Next, you will have to plant the garden according to the planting instructions. Finally, if you maintain it well, you will have a beautiful garden full of fresh vegetables or flowers.

WORDS IN CONVERSATION

Another way to vary sentences used in an essay is to include conversation. Written conversation is called *dialogue*. The correct way to write dialogue is to put it within quotation marks. However, remember that only the spoken part of the dialogue is put into quotation marks and not who said it. Also remember that the first word in a quotation is capitalized unless it is a continuation.

EXAMPLES

"Where did you go on vacation?" asked Emma.
"We went to the Smokey Mountains in Tennessee," replied Bill.

Emma asked, "Have you ever been there before?"
"No," replied Bill, "last year we went to the Everglades."

You can vary your sentence structure by putting the names of the person speaking at the beginning, middle, or end of your sentences. Notice that if you place the person who is speaking in the middle of the sentence, you will have two sets of quotation marks. You would not capitalize the first word in the continuation of that quotation. If a question is asked in dialogue, make sure you put the question mark at the end of the question being asked and not at the end of the sentence unless the quotation ends there. For example, look at the first and third examples.

A statement such as *Juan said he missed his train* is not dialogue. This is a statement written in the third person and does not contain the person's exact words. This is called an *indirect quotation*. It does not have quotation marks around it.

EXAMPLES

Wendy said that she would leave next Monday.
John said that Minnie is feeling much better today.
The barking dog told its owner that someone was nearby.
Jeremy nodded in reply.

Make sure that periods, question marks, and exclamation points are inside the quotation marks. Make sure that the names of people that are speaking are not inside the quotation marks.

PRACTICE—QUOTATIONS

Put a check mark next to the correctly written dialogue.

1. _____ "Jimmy said that his new job started on Monday."
2. _____ "Mommy, can I have another cookie?" asked Jenny.
3. _____ "Wow," said Margaret, "you did a great job!"
4. _____ "Did you know, asked Sammy, That I collect stamps?"
5. _____ "Yes," said Francine, "I knew that!"

6. _____ "While you were gone I cleaned the house," she said.

7. _____ He hurriedly answered, "I'll be right there!"

8. _____ Jack said he would like to go to the movies with us.

9. _____ "When did Jonathan call," asked Danielle?

10. _____ "This morning," mother answered with a smile.

ANSWERS

Sentences 2, 3, 5, 6, 7, 8, and 10 are all correct sentences.

RUN-ON SENTENCES

What makes writing sentences hard is the way we speak. We don't always speak in correct sentences and many times we run our sentences together. Therefore, when we write sentences, we often want to write the way we speak.

Run-on sentences occur when you have more than one sentence combined with only one punctuation mark at the end. This makes for an unusually long incorrect sentence that will take away from your essay.

When you write your essay, try to avoid this mistake by checking each sentence for a subject and predicate. If you have more than one subject or predicate in a sentence you may have a run-on sentence. You should always proofread your work.

EXAMPLES

INCORRECT:

William and Beverly walked from the grocery store to the park they watched the children play on the swings.
It was beginning to get cold outside the furnace in the house seemed to keep running on and on.
The traffic accident on Ninth Street was the result of someone falling asleep at the wheel he should have been more careful.

CORRECT:

William and Beverly walked from the grocery store to the park. They watched the children play on the swings.
It was beginning to get cold outside. The furnace in the house seemed to keep running on and on.
The traffic accident on Ninth Street was the result of someone falling asleep at the wheel. He should have been more careful.

PRACTICE—SENTENCE WRITING

Practice writing some sentences of your own and give them to someone to read over. The more you write, the better your writing style.

What Is a Paragraph?

A paragraph is a group of related sentences. It is made up of a main idea (topic sentence) and detail sentences. The main idea focuses on what the paragraph will be about while the detail sentences add support to the topic. The first line in a paragraph must be indented (moved over). Make sure to watch the margins on both sides of the paper and do not write more than a few letters over the right margin. In a paragraph remember not to move to the left-hand margin every time you begin a new sentence, but begin the next sentence promptly after the last.

EXAMPLES

INCORRECT PARAGRAPH SETUP:

Computers have greatly affected our lives. Students use the computer to research classroom projects.
Some people use computers to shop for clothes or even food.
Still others use the computer to keep in touch with family and friends.

CORRECT PARAGRAPH SETUP:

Computers have greatly affected our lives. Students use the computer to research classroom projects. Some people use computers to shop for clothes or even food. Still others use the computer to keep in touch with family and friends.

MAIN IDEAS AND DETAILS

A paragraph needs a main idea. The main idea is usually the first sentence in a paragraph, but it doesn't necessarily have to be. When you write your main idea, make sure that the sentence is a broad statement. This will make it easier for you to write detail sentences.

EXAMPLES

There are several differences between satellite television and cable.
Eating from the four basic food groups will help you stay healthy.
My family is very special to me.
Having a fire safety plan is important.

All of the above examples are broad enough to allow the writer to create numerous detail sentences. Let's use the first example and write some details for it.

There are several differences between satellite television and cable. First, cable usually has fewer channels to choose from while satellite television gives you a greater variety. Second, with satellite television you may be able to rent the equipment or you may purchase it. With cable there is no equipment to purchase. Finally, the price is a factor. Depending on the programs you desire, the satellite system may end up costing you more money.

Notice in the above example that the main idea is the first sentence. All of the sentences in the paragraph relate to it. Each detail sentence has something to do with the differences between satellite television and cable. Notice the use also of time order words and the correct setup of the paragraph. Time order words are not necessary in every paragraph, but can be helpful in setting it up.

Let's use the second main idea example and write a paragraph for it.

Eating from the different food groups will help you stay healthy. Your body needs nutrients supplied by each of the four basic food groups. The meat group supplies the needed proteins to keep your energy level high. The dairy group gives you calcium for strong teeth and bones. The vegetable and fruit group provides many vitamins such as A and C. The bread group gives you carbohydrates, which provide you with energy. Missing out on any one of these groups may cause you to become sick.

Try writing detail sentences for the other two examples. Remember to write details that follow the main idea.

PRACTICE—EDITING DETAIL SENTENCES

Read the following two paragraphs and delete the detail sentences that do not follow the main idea.

My family and I went to the apple orchard last fall. The trees seemed to be loaded down with the sweet juicy fruit. There were many apples that had fallen to the ground. These apples were bruised. There was a large owl sitting in the top of a tree. We picked three bushels of apples before it was time to leave. What a great day at the orchard!

My last camping trip was an experience I would rather forget. It seemed we had been walking for hours before the group leader decided she had found the perfect spot for the night. We had just begun to unpack our gear when I looked down to find a large black snake making its way toward me. I tried to move out of its path but it seemed to follow me. The snake was from a nonpoisonous species. I tripped over a stone and fell back just as the group leader scooted the snake in a different direction with a large stick. I don't think I slept at all that night thinking about that snake.

ANSWERS

Paragraph 1: Remove sentence, "There was a large owl sitting in the top of a tree." *Paragraph 2:* Remove sentence, "The snake was from a nonpoisonous species."

COMBINING PARAGRAPHS

Once you understand the basics of writing a paragraph you are ready to combine several paragraphs together. When we combine paragraphs together in a theme or essay, we still have to keep the paragraphs focused on the topic. Each paragraph does not have to follow the same topic sentence, but each must be related to the overall main idea of the essay.

PRACTICE—MAIN IDEA IN PARAGRAPHS

Read through the following example of an essay. Underline the main idea in each paragraph as you read. Notice that each main idea relates to the main topic of recycling. Each paragraph in the essay discusses different aspects of why recycling is important.

EXAMPLE

Topic for essay: Recycling Is Important to the Future of America.

Recycling is an important factor for the future of America. It helps to keep pollution down, keeps our landfills from filling up, and helps save some natural resources.

Recycling helps keep the pollution levels down in our society. Newspapers that were once burned can now be returned for recycling. Aluminum cans are less likely to be thrown on the sides of the road because they can be turned in for money. Old tires that were once discarded have been recycled by being chopped up and made into playground coverings. It seems that there are many innovative ways to convert old trash into useful materials.

By recycling materials we can prevent many tons of garbage from being emptied into public landfills. It takes years for many of the items dumped into landfills to decay. Some items take hundreds of years to decay. This slow decay prevents the reuse of landfills, which in turn causes more land to be used.

The earth has only a limited supply of natural resources, and when they are gone there will be no more. By recycling materials made from natural resources we can prevent or slow down the use of these important natural resources.

In summary, recycling is an important factor for the future of America. It helps to keep pollution down, keeps our landfills from filling up, and helps save some natural resources. It would be nice if everyone in America would participate in this practice.

PRACTICE—PARAGRAPHS WITH MAIN IDEAS AND DETAILS

Choose from the following topics and write a paragraph with a main idea and three to five detail sentences.

My favorite pet
Learning to drive
A rewarding experience
A special person
A nerve-racking experience
Violence on television
My favorite job
A scary encounter

ANSWERS

EXAMPLE

My favorite pet is my dog, Charlie. She is a cute Cocker Spaniel puppy. I have taught her many tricks during the few weeks since she came to live with me. She is very lovable. Each day when I come home from work she greets me at the door. I just love her!

(Other answers will vary.)

PRACTICE

What would be the main idea for each group of sentences below? Write a main idea for each group of sentences and then rewrite each group in paragraph form. Add or delete words as necessary.

Group A
Family and friends are gathered together.
The turkey is roasting in the oven.
The children are watching the parade on television.
Main idea _____

Group B
Jayna walks through the rows of books.
She fills out the card in her book.
It is very quiet inside the room.
Main idea _____

Group C
Joel's knee looks badly injured.
The doctor examines the wound.
Stitches are required for the cut.
Main idea _____

Group D
The copy machine was making a funny noise.
The secretaries tried to correct the problem.
A red light was blinking on the control panel.
Main idea _____

ANSWERS

(Sentence will vary.)

EXAMPLE

Group A—It is Thanksgiving Day at the Harris home.

Group B—Jayna visits the local library.

Group C—Joel gets hurt at the football game.

Group D—The office copy machine is broken again!

Types of Essays

What are the different types of essays?

Basically there are three different types of essays. They are persuasive, expository, and narrative. Depending on the topic that will be given to you on your GED test, you will be able to pick out what type of essay you need to write and set it up with ease. Expository and persuasive essays are set up in five paragraphs while narratives can be set up in three or four. In this section we will go through the three different types of essays and what makes each unique. In the next few segments we will go through setting up the essays and actually begin writing.

Remember, you are not graded on how much you know about the subject but how well you can relate your ideas on paper.

THE PERSUASIVE ESSAY

This type of essay requires you to take a stand on an issue and develop an argument explaining why you have made this particular choice. You will need to use personal experiences in your explanations or information that you know. This essay is set up in five paragraphs.

EXAMPLE

PROMPT

Many states have enacted laws throughout the years to help people stay safe. One such law that has been passed in many states is the seat belt law.

DISCUSSION QUESTION

Do you feel that states have the right to tell people they must wear a seat belt in an automobile?

SAMPLE PERSUASIVE ESSAY

Seat belt laws have been enacted in many states. I feel that they are very important for the safety of all Americans. This law saves countless lives each year, makes sure our children are safe, and gives me a sense of security when I get behind the wheel of a car. I believe that seat belt laws are very important and should be enforced in every state.

There are many people alive today because of the enforced seat belt laws. This law makes sure that people who ordinarily don't wear seat belts in automobiles are restrained in case of an accident. I know personally that the seat belt laws work because I, who was once a non-seat belt wearer, was in an accident. I only wore the seat belt because of this law. I was lucky. It saved my life when my car rolled over one night on a rain-slick road. Instead of being thrown out of the car and possibly killed or injured, I was safe.

Children are also safer because of this law. It is required by law that all children be restrained in a car safety seat or seat belt. This keeps the child safe in case of an accident. It also gives the adult driving the comfort of knowing the child is not moving around the automobile where he or she could be injured by opening a door and falling out.

When I get behind the wheel of a car and snap on my seat belt, I feel comfortable knowing that I have a better survival rate should I be in an accident. I want to make sure that I am here to enjoy life for a long time, and by wearing a seat belt in the car I know that I am increasing my odds of surviving an accident.

Seat belt laws are important to me and should be to everyone! They help save lives, keep our children safe, and give me security in the automobile. I would recommend that every state have seat belt laws.

THE EXPOSITORY ESSAY

This essay requires you to explain, describe, or interpret a particular situation, experience, or idea by again using personal experiences or information. This essay is set up in five paragraphs.

EXAMPLE

PROMPT

There have been many great books written through the years. Think of three books that you have read that have affected your life in some way. It may have affected you in a small way or a profound way.

DISCUSSION QUESTION

What are three books that you have read that have affected you in some way?

SAMPLE EXPOSITORY ESSAY

Books have always been a big part of my life. I have read many books through the years but three of my favorite books are, *The King, the Mouse, and the Cheese*, *Little Women*, and *Silas Marner*. I have read these many times and each time I do, they add joy to my life.

The King, the Mouse, and the Cheese was the first book I remember reading.

When I was in second grade we were required to do a book report. This book was my choice. I remember my mother reading the book with me and helping me decide what I would say about the book. On the day of the report I stood at the front of the room and quickly reported on the story. The class loved it and everyone wanted to check the book out of the library. This book gave me the joy of reading and made me want to continue.

When I was a teenager, *Little Women* quickly became a favorite of mine. It was a story of four sisters and how they grew from girls into young women. This story discussed friendship, love, and war. It gave me a sense of family and an appreciation for my own.

The last book on my favorite list is, *Silas Marner*. This is a story written by George Eliot. It is about a man who loved gold and came to realize that a little girl was more important that all the gold in the world. It gave me a wonderful message that there are more important things than material possessions.

Books can be a wonderful asset to anyone's life. These marvelous stories can bring fulfillment, appreciation, and values.

THE NARRATIVE ESSAY

This type of essay requires you to recount a personal experience by using sequencing skills, details, or descriptions. It is basically recounting a "story" of what has happened to you. This essay is set up in three or four paragraphs.

EXAMPLE

PROMPT

Everyone seems to have a memorable event that took place in his or her life. Think of an event that seems to stand out in your memory.

DISCUSSION QUESTION

What made this event different from all of the others? Was it a time of great happiness or sadness? Was it funny?

SAMPLE NARRATIVE ESSAY

The event that is most memorable to me was a Mother's Day in 1978. This was the day that my brother and I decided to take our mom out for a wonderful day at the museum and dinner. What started out as good intentions ended up costing us more than we anticipated.

The day started out fine as we left our home in my brother's big old black car and traveled two hours into the city to the museum. As soon as we arrived at the museum we noticed that the day was already getting warm. We went quickly inside the air-conditioned museum and spent several hours wandering around looking at the entire collection of paintings, statues, and even automobiles. After we looked at everything in the museum, we decided we were getting hungry and were eager to go to eat dinner. We left the building and found the car. As my brother turned the key all we heard was a terrible grinding noise that told us we weren't going anywhere. Stuck! My brother went inside and called a tow truck to take the car in for repairs. My mother gave my brother money to fix the car and then she and I waited at the museum for his return. This was a time before cell phones were being used and we had no idea how long it was going to take. In the meantime, it was getting hotter and we were getting hungrier. We went back into the museum and looked around for several more hours until closing time. We then had no choice but to go outside and sit in the stifling heat. We were miserable! Finally, the familiar big old black car came into view and we gladly jumped in. The first place we went was to eat.

What started out as a nice trip ended up being a day of misery. Mother's Day, 1978, will be one I will never forget. I'm sure my mother and brother feel the same way.

Setting Up an Essay

When you take your GED Language Arts, Writing, Part II test, you will be given a prompt and/or a discussion question. You will write your essay on this question.

The prompt on the Language Arts, Writing, Part II test will be a subject that will be familiar to you. You will not be graded on how much you know about the material but how well you can relate your ideas.

In this segment we will go through the three types of essays (expository, persuasive, and narrative) from beginning to end. There will be explanations for each paragraph included in the essay along with the essay in its entirety. You will be able to see and understand the process of a three-, four-, or five-paragraph essay.

What must be included in an essay?

An essay must have a clear *focus* that states the *main idea*. *Details* are needed to support that focus. The essay must be set up in a format that makes sense and allows the essay to be read easily and understood by the reader.

Essays have three main parts:

1. The first is an *introduction*. This is the main idea of the essay. The introduction is the first paragraph of the essay. Without an introduction the essay would have no focus and would be hard to understand.
2. The second part of the essay is the *body*. The body is the "meat" of the essay. This is where the supporting details are added. The body of the essays we will write will have one, two, or three paragraphs.
3. The last part of an essay is the *conclusion*. This is the final paragraph of the essay. Not only is it important to have a focus and supporting details but it is equally important to make sure you summarize your essay by tying all the ideas together at the end.

SETTING UP AN EXPOSITORY ESSAY

EXPOSITORY PROMPT

Throughout the year there are many holidays that people in the United States celebrate. Some are religious holidays such as Christmas and Easter, while other holidays celebrate the lives of famous Americans such as George Washington and Abraham Lincoln.

DISCUSSION QUESTION

Think of some holidays that are important to you. Why are these holidays important to you?

HOW TO SET UP AN EXPOSITORY ESSAY

Focus: What is the main idea that the essay will be about?

Think—is it about Christmas, Easter, George Washington, and Abraham Lincoln or is it about you? This essay is about you and particular holidays that you relate to your personal life.

First Step: Decide on *three* specific ideas to explain, describe, or interpret in your essay.

Think: What are three holidays that you enjoy? Let's say that you enjoy Veteran's Day, Independence Day, and Christmas. These three holidays will become your second, third, and fourth paragraph in your five-paragraph essay once a main idea and details are established. The first paragraph in your essay will be an introduction and the last a summarization.

Main Idea: What is the main idea of the essay going to be? Look again at the prompt and see what the discussion question is asking: "Why are these holidays important to you?" You cannot use this statement as your main idea for the essay, but you can reword it to make it into a main idea: "Holidays are important to me." Now you have your main idea.

First Paragraph: The first paragraph begins with the main idea of the essay and includes the three ideas you want to discuss.

Think: What was the main idea of the essay? What were the three ideas you wanted to explain?

EXAMPLE

Holidays are important to me. There are many holidays I enjoy, but the three I enjoy most are Veteran's Day, Independence Day, and Christmas.

This paragraph now includes your main idea of the essay and the three ideas (holidays, in this case) that will be discussed. You may note that this paragraph is made up of only two sentences, yet it relays perfectly the main idea of the essay and the three ideas you are going to discuss. You may however add an extra sentence to help express the main idea.

EXAMPLE

Holidays are important to me. There are many holidays I enjoy, but the three I enjoy most are Veteran's Day, Independence Day, and Christmas. These holidays all have a special meaning to my family and me.

Second Paragraph: You are now ready to set up your second paragraph. In this paragraph you will take your first idea (Veteran's Day) and create a topic sentence (main idea) for the paragraph and then create detail sentences that support the idea.

Think: What would be a good main idea for your second paragraph if the idea you are writing about is Veteran's Day? Mentally take notes of details about why Veteran's Day is important to you. Is it because you have veterans in your family? Is it because you have lost loved ones in a war? Is it because you get a day off from work to be with your family? Whatever the reason, think of a main idea for this paragraph. When you write your main idea for the paragraph make sure it is broad enough to cover several sentences of discussion; for example, "Veteran's Day is an honorable holiday." This is a broad statement that allows you to add on sentences that *explain* why it is important to you. If your main idea was "Veteran's Day is important to me because my father was in the Vietnam War," your detail sentences would be limited to a discussion of your father in the Vietnam War.

EXAMPLE

Veteran's Day is an honorable holiday. It is a day when I think about the men and women serving our country in the military. Veteran's Day is a day on which I think about the men and women who gave their life for me so that I may have freedom. On this day I take my children to the Veteran's Day services so that they will learn to appreciate and respect the veterans of the past and present in our country.

Third Paragraph: The third paragraph relates to the second idea (holiday) from your introductory paragraph. In this case it is Independence Day. The third paragraph is set up in the same way as the second.

Think: Create a main idea or topic sentence. Mentally think of detail sentences that you want to include. Again, try to think of a broad main idea. It will be easier to think of details to go along with it.

EXAMPLE

Independence Day is a great summer holiday. On Independence Day my family gathers together for our annual family reunion. The kids have a great time lighting sparklers and playing traditional games outdoors. We top off the end of the day by watching the great display of fireworks.

This paragraph has a broad main idea and all details are focused on it. It also includes personal supporting details.

Fourth Paragraph: The fourth paragraph uses your final or third idea (holiday) from your introductory paragraph. This idea is Christmas. Again, this paragraph is set up just as paragraphs two and three.

Think: Create a main idea for your third idea (holiday). This would be about Christmas. What could you write that would be broad enough to include supporting details? If you wrote, "I receive many gifts for Christmas," your detail sentences would be limited to only those gifts you received. If you wrote, "Of all the holidays, Christmas is my favorite," you would have a much broader approach to adding on details.

EXAMPLE

Of all the holidays, Christmas is my favorite. Christmas is a time of joy and generosity in my family. It is a

time when all of my family gathers together in front of the fireplace to sing Christmas carols. I love to watch the little children in my family open their gifts on Christmas morning. It seems to be almost magical.

Fifth Paragraph: This is the last paragraph and its purpose is to summarize the entire essay. As with the other four paragraphs, this paragraph also needs a main idea. This paragraph may also need special phrases to show closure such as: "In summary," "In conclusion," "In short," etc.

Think: Create a main idea that would summarize the entire essay. This paragraph does not need as many detail sentences as the other paragraphs but one or two would help support the summarization. What was the entire essay about? What do you need to include in your summarization of the entire essay? Make sure to put in the three ideas you have been explaining.

EXAMPLE

In summary, there are many holidays that are important to my family and me. Three of these holidays are Veteran's Day, Independence Day, and Christmas.

The word count for the entire essay is 256 words. You can clearly see that each paragraph is focused, contains main ideas and details, has structure, and yet is simple. Take a look at what the entire essay would look like written together. Notice how it flows easily from one paragraph to the next.

Holidays are important to me. There are many holidays I enjoy, but the three I enjoy most are Veteran's Day, Independence Day, and Christmas. These holidays all have a special meaning to my family and me.

Veteran's Day is an honorable holiday. It is a day when I think about the men and women serving our country in the military. Veteran's Day is a day on which I think about the men and women who gave their life for me so that I may have freedom. On this day I take my children to the Veteran's Day services so that they will learn to appreciate and respect the veterans of the past and present in our country.

Independence Day is a great summer holiday. On Independence Day my family gathers together for our annual family reunion. The kids have a great time lighting sparklers and playing traditional games outdoors. We top off the end of the day by watching the great display of fireworks.

Of all the holidays, Christmas is my favorite. Christmas is a time of joy and generosity in my family. It is a time when all of my family gathers together in front of the fireplace to sing Christmas carols. I love to watch the little children in my family open their gifts on Christmas morning. It seems to be almost magical.

In summary, there are many holidays that are important to my family and me. Three of these holidays are Veteran's Day, Independence Day, and Christmas.

SETTING UP A PERSUASIVE ESSAY

PERSUASIVE PROMPT

At any given evening, with most any family relaxing at home, there will be the familiar ringing of the telephone. Usually its neighbors, friends, or family, but every so often it is a telemarketer trying to get us to purchase numerous items ranging from new tires, credit cards, or siding, to insurance. Sometimes we decide to purchase these items, and sometimes we become annoyed at their constant calling.

DISCUSSION QUESTION

How do you feel about telemarketers calling your home? Do you feel they are a vital part of our economy by providing a service to people or do you feel they are interrupting your personal time with your family?

HOW TO SET UP A PERSUASIVE ESSAY

Focus: What is the main idea of the essay going to be about? It is about telemarketers calling your home. The main question is, how do you feel about this? You are required to take a stand on this issue. Do you feel that these calls are important or are they an invasion of your privacy?

First Step: Decide what your stand is on the issue. Next, think of *three* specific reasons why you feel the way you do.

Think: What are the three reasons that you do or do not like telemarketers calling your home. Let's say your stand is that you do not like them calling your home. Here are your three possible reasons:

1. The first reason you do not like them calling is because you do not want to spend your time at home being pressured by salespeople.
2. Your second reason may be that you do not trust people selling items over the phone.
3. Your third reason may be that you don't need or want the product that is being offered.

Main Idea: Take a look at the essay prompt and question. What is the main idea of the essay going to be? Remember to make your first statement or main idea broad enough that you will be able to write a lot about it. You will begin your first paragraph with the main idea of the essay and include your three reasons. Remember, in a persuasive essay you are required to take a stand so this essay is written in the first person, "I." Your main idea may be stated something like this: "There are many reasons why I don't like telemarketers calling my home."

First Paragraph: The first paragraph is the introduction. It will begin with your main idea and have one or two more sentences that support the main idea. Remember to include in your introduction your three reasons why you feel the way you do. This will be the focus of the body of the essay.

Think: What was your main idea? What were your three reasons?

EXAMPLE

There are many reasons why I don't like telemarketers calling my home. Three of these reasons are that they interrupt my family time, I don't trust giving out financial information to them over the phone, and I don't always need or want the products they offer.

This paragraph now includes your main idea of the essay and three reasons why you don't like telemarketers calling your home. Notice that the paragraph is made up of only two sentences. You may want to add a third sentence to help support the main idea.

EXAMPLE

> There are many reasons why I don't like telemarketers calling my home. Three of these reasons are that they interrupt my family time, I don't trust giving out financial information over the phone, and I don't always need or want the products they offer. I know telemarketers have a job to do, but I just don't like the interruptions they cause.

Second Paragraph: You are now ready for your second paragraph. This is the body of the essay. In this paragraph you will take the first reason from your introduction and create a main idea. Then you will create supporting details for the main idea.

Think: What would be the main idea for your second paragraph? Your first reason in your introduction states: "They interrupt my family time." You will need to use these words to create your main idea. You may write, "When telemarketers call my home I feel that they interrupt my family time." Now you need to think of at least three more sentences that would support how you feel about this particular reason.

EXAMPLE

> When telemarketers call my home I feel that they interrupt my family time. It seems that every time my family and I sit down to dinner, the phone rings. Instead of spending time with my children I end up listening to several minutes of chatter. I hate to be rude and hang up the phone, but I admit that is what I sometimes have to do to get back to my family.

Third Paragraph: The third paragraph relates to your second reason in your introduction. The second reason you don't like telemarketers calling is, "I don't feel comfortable giving out financial information over the phone." The third paragraph is still the body of the essay and it is set up just as the second paragraph with a main idea and details.

Think: Create a main idea using your second reason. It may be, "I don't feel comfortable giving out financial information over the phone to a telemarketer." After you have your main idea, you would need to think of about three sentences that support the main idea of your third paragraph.

EXAMPLE

> I don't feel comfortable giving out financial information over the phone. I don't know the person on the other end and it could be someone dishonest. I realize that not all telemarketers are dishonest. It's just that it makes me nervous to give out credit card information when anyone could be listening.

Fourth Paragraph: This paragraph is set up like the second and third paragraphs and is also part of the body of the essay. The main idea of the fourth paragraph relates to your third reason in your introduction. Your third reason was, "I don't always need or want the products they are selling."

Think: What would be a good main idea using your last reason? Think of about three sentences that will support your main idea for the fourth paragraph. Your last main idea may be, "Telemarketers don't usually offer any products that I would be interested in purchasing."

EXAMPLE

> Telemarketers don't usually offer any products that I would be interested in purchasing. It seems that most telemarketers who call my home try to send me information on acquiring credit cards. Some try to sell expensive encyclopedias or even light bulbs. One telemarketer even offered to sell me siding for my brick home!

Fifth Paragraph: This the last paragraph in your five-paragraph persuasive essay. It is also called the conclusion. It is important that you summarize your entire essay and draw a conclusion in this paragraph.

Think: Create a main idea that would summarize the entire essay. What was the essay about? What was your stand on the issue? Make sure that you put in the three reasons you explained in your conclusion.

EXAMPLE

I don't like telemarketers calling my home. There are many reasons for this. Some of these reasons are that they interrupt my family time, I don't feel comfortable giving out financial information over the phone, and I don't usually need or want any of the products they are selling.

You have now completed your persuasive essay. Let's take a look at how the entire essay would look when it is put together. The word count for this essay is 280 words. It doesn't take very many sentences to make up the 250 words you need to write in your essay. The persuasive essay we just wrote has only three or four sentences in each paragraph.

There are many reasons why I don't like telemarketers calling my home. Three of these reasons are that they interrupt my family time, I don't trust giving out financial information over the phone, and I don't always need or want the products they offer. I know telemarketers have a job to do, but I just don't like the interruptions they cause.

When telemarketers call my home I feel that they interrupt my family time. It seems that every time my family and I sit down to dinner, the phone rings. Instead of spending time with my children I end up listening to several minutes of chatter. I hate to be rude and hang up the phone, but I admit that is what I sometimes have to do to get back to my family.

I don't feel comfortable giving out financial information over the phone. I don't know the person on the other end and it could be someone dishonest. I realize that not all telemarketers are dishonest. It's just that it makes me nervous to give out credit card information when anyone could be listening.

Telemarketers don't usually offer any products that I would be interested in purchasing. It seems that most telemarketers who call my home try to send me information on acquiring credit cards. Some try to sell expensive encyclopedias or even light bulbs. One telemarketer even offered to sell me siding for my brick home!

In summary, I don't like telemarketers calling my home. There are many reasons for this. Some of these reasons are that they interrupt my family time, I don't feel comfortable giving out financial information over the phone, and I don't usually need or want any of the products they are selling.

SETTING UP A NARRATIVE ESSAY

The narrative essay is set up differently than the expository or persuasive essays. It can have three, four, or even five paragraphs. It is usually easier to set it up in three or four. In the following example we will set it up into three paragraphs. It still has the same three basic parts: the introduction, body, and conclusion. In the narrative essay each paragraph will represent one of the basic parts. Remember that the narrative essay is written in the first person and discusses a personal issue.

NARRATIVE PROMPT

Do you remember when you got your first real job? It may have been one when you were still in high school. Maybe it was at the service station across town or being a waiter or waitress. How did you feel about this job? Try to recall how you felt about your first job.

DISCUSSION QUESTIONS

Think about your first job. How did you feel about it? How did you get this job? What made it so special?

HOW TO SET UP A NARRATIVE ESSAY

Focus: What is the main idea of your essay going to be about? It is about your first job and why it was important to you.

First Step: Decide what you want your main idea sentence to say.

Think: Your first sentence or main idea needs to state what type of job you are going to discuss in your essay.

Main Idea: Suppose that your first job was as a waitress or waiter in a restaurant. Your first sentence may be, "I will never forget my first job as a waitress in a small-town café."

First Paragraph: In your first paragraph you will need to include your main idea sentence and at least one or two other sentences to help support the main idea. Remember that the first paragraph is the focus for the entire essay.

EXAMPLE

> I will never forget my first job as a waitress in a small-town café. I was only sixteen years old and felt so excited. This was the beginning of my independence.

This simple paragraph focuses on the first job and its importance to the writer.

Second Paragraph: The second paragraph in the narrative essay is the body of the essay. Since the essay is written in the first person and tells about an experience of the writer, it is important to put in time order the words that show sequencing of details. Begin the body of the essay with the first event you want to share. Then continue in order. Put in thoughts and feelings as you write your sentences.

EXAMPLE

> The summer after I turned sixteen my mother thought it was time for me to find a summer job. She had heard that there was an opening for a waitress in a small local café. I wasn't too happy about giving up my life of leisure for the summer, but I decided to give it a try. The pay for the job was a dollar an hour, which I thought was a lot of money. I started my job on the first day washing dishes. I washed and washed. After a few days, I was promoted to pouring coffee at the snack bar. I thought this was great compared to the dishwashing and even managed to make a tip now and then. Later on, I was given the job of waiting on the customers. It wasn't as easy as it looked and I made my share of mistakes. Finally, by the end of the summer I had made a little money, but what was most important was the experience I gained.

Make sure that your detail sentences refer to the main idea of the essay. Keep your sentences in sequence. Notice that the writer above uses time order words such as *after a*

few days, *later on*, and *finally*. This allows the reader to understand exactly what order the actions in the paragraph are taking place.

Third Paragraph: The final paragraph in the narrative essay is the conclusion. This paragraph sums up the entire essay.

EXAMPLE

> My first job was a great experience for me. It helped me to gain my first taste of independence while also gaining some great experience.

The word count for the entire narrative essay is 227 words. Let's take a look at how it would read when put together.

> I will never forget my first job as a waitress in a small-town café. I was only sixteen years old and felt so excited. This was the beginning of my independence.
>
> The summer after I turned sixteen my mother thought it was time for me to find a summer job. She had heard that there was an opening for a waitress in a small local café. I wasn't too happy about giving up my life of leisure for the summer, but I decided to give it a try. The pay for the job was a dollar an hour, which I thought was a lot of money. I started my job on the first day washing dishes. I washed and washed. After a few days, I was promoted to pouring coffee at the snack bar. I thought this was great compared to the dishwashing and even managed to make a tip now and then. Later on, I was given the job of waiting on the customers. It wasn't as easy as it looked and I made my share of mistakes. Finally, by the end of the summer I had made a little money, but what was most important was the experience I gained.
>
> My first job was a great experience for me. It helped me to gain my first taste of independence while also gaining some great experience.

Creating Quick Outlines for Essays

Creating a quick outline before you write your essay will save you some time in writing. It will help to keep your essay in focus. Below we will go through three outlines for the previous essays. When you create an outline, you will need to jot down your ideas on scrap paper and not include this in your actual essay, but only use it as a reference.

THE EXPOSITORY OUTLINE

The expository essay was written in a five-paragraph form. Therefore, you will need to number your outline into five sections and write your main idea for each paragraph beside each number. Remember when writing your outline that your first paragraph is the introduction and contains your three main points. Paragraphs two, three, and four will be about the three main points. Typically, outlines are written in Roman numerals.

EXAMPLE

I. Holidays are important to me.

II. Veteran's Day is an honorable holiday.

III. Independence Day is a great summer holiday.

IV. Of all the holidays, Christmas is my favorite.

V. In summary, there are many holidays that are important to my family and me.

Once you have your five main paragraph outlines, you can insert your detail sentence ideas under each main idea.

IMPORTANT HOLIDAYS TO ME

I. Holidays are important to me.
   A. Holidays I enjoy are Veteran's Day, Independence Day and Christmas
   B. Holidays have special meaning

II. Veteran's Day is an honorable holiday.
   A. Men and women in the service
   B. Take children to services

III. Independence Day is a great summer holiday.
   A. Family reunion
   B. Kids play games
   C. Watch fireworks

IV. Of all the holidays, Christmas is my favorite.
   A. Generosity
   B. Family gathers together
   C. Opening gifts

V. In summary, there are many holidays that are important to my family and me.
   A. Veteran's Day, Independence Day, and Christmas

Do not spend a great deal of time jotting down your outline. The outline is meant to save you time. Your detail sentences do not necessarily have to be written out completely in your outline. They can be fragments that you can add on to when you write your complete essay. From the above outline you can use the ideas to create your sentences for your five-paragraph essay. Compare the above outline of "Important Holidays to Me" to the complete essay.

THE PERSUASIVE OUTLINE

The persuasive essay was also written in five-paragraph form. To begin the persuasive outline number your five paragraphs with Roman numerals and write a main idea for each paragraph. The first sentence in your outline is going to state your stand on the issue you will be writing about. This is the focus of the essay. The next three sentences in your outline will be about your three points explaining why you made this stand. Your final sentence is the main idea for your conclusion.

EXAMPLE

I. I don't like telemarketers calling my home.

II. Telemarketers interrupt my family time.

III. I don't like giving out financial information.

IV. I don't like the products from tele-
    marketers.

V. There are many reasons I don't like
   telemarketers calling.

After writing your main ideas for each paragraph, continue with adding your details to
each paragraph. For each detail sentence
assign a letter of A, B, C, etc.

**WHY I DON'T LIKE
TELEMARKETERS
CALLING MY HOME**

I. I don't like telemarketers calling my
   home.
   A. Interrupt family time, financial
      information, and don't need or
      want products

II. Telemarketers interrupt family time.
    A. Phone rings during family time
    B. Hanging up on callers

III. I don't feel comfortable giving out
     financial information.
     A. I don't know person calling
     B. Credit card information

IV. Telemarketers don't offer products I
    need or want.
    A. Offer products such as credit
       cards
    B. Offer products such as encyclo-
       pedias or light bulbs

V. I don't like telemarketers calling my
   home.
   A. Interrupt family time, financial
      information, and products

Compare the above outline with the persuasive essay on telemarketers. Notice again
that some sentences are written as fragments. This is for the purpose of jotting the
outline ideas down quickly. You can add
more words when you write the actual essay.

THE NARRATIVE OUTLINE

The narrative outline is written in a three-
paragraph form. Number your three main
idea sentences with Roman numerals and
then write the main idea for each paragraph.
Remember, in a narrative essay the first
paragraph is the introduction, the second is
the body, and the third is the conclusion.

EXAMPLE

I. I will never forget my first job as a
   waitress.

II. My mother thought it was time for
    me to get a job.

III. My first job was a great experience.

After you have decided what you want your
main ideas to be in your narrative essay,
continue with detail sentences for each paragraph.

MY FIRST JOB

I. I will never forget my first job as a
   waitress.
   A. Felt excited
   B. New experience

II. My mother thought it was time for
    me to get a job.
    A. Heard about an opening
    B. Gave up summer vacation
    C. Was paid a dollar an hour
    D. Washed dishes
    E. Promoted to pouring coffee
    F. Waited on customers
    G. Made some mistakes
    H. Made money and gained experi-
       ence

III. My first job was a great experience.
     A. Helped me gain independence
        and experience

Notice in the narrative essay outline that
most details are added to the second section,
which is the body of the essay. Make sure
that when you add your details they are in
order of occurrence. Compare the outline to
the actual narrative essay.

Writing the Essay

Before you begin to write your own essay let's take a look at some words and phrases that you may include in your essay to make it more complete and also words that you may want to limit.

VERBS

Make sure to use the correct verb tense in your sentence.

create	appreciate
influence	require
experience	dashed
commit	develop
decide	compare
provide	manage
consider	educate
recommend	expand
introduce	convince
convey	apply
supply	question
support	inform
restrict	increase
retain	focus
achieve	

ADJECTIVES

Use these words before a noun to create a more interesting sentence.

useful	young
tactful	uncertain
lovely	safe
elaborate	common
elegant	modern
merry	marvelous
keen	knowledgeable
fresh	steady
historical	vital
weary	powerful
generous	persistent
informative	cautious
beneficial	outspoken
simple	careful

ADVERBS

Use these words to modify a verb, adjective, or another adverb.

slowly	somewhat
reassuringly	apparently
perfectly	never
carefully	really
yesterday	surely
very	easily
twice	fast
quietly	near
forever	awfully
sometimes	strangely
more	suddenly

TIME AND SPACE ORDER WORDS AND PHRASES

Use these words in your narrative essay to show sequence or in your expository or persuasive essays to help explain ideas.

first	subsequently
second	then again
third	further
next	after
later	above
after that	beyond
soon after	nearby
afterwards	far off
previously	in front
last	to the right
then	to the left

WORDS AND PHRASES THAT SHOW CONTRASTING THOUGHTS

although	yet
but	however
nevertheless	rather
on the other hand	still
on the contrary	

WORDS AND PHRASES THAT HELP ILLUSTRATE AND EXPLAIN AN IDEA

for example	for this reason
for instance	truly
to illustrate	to emphasize
thus	again
in other words	to repeat
that is to say	in fact
as has been said	

CONNECTING WORDS

Be careful that you do not overuse these words and create run-on sentences.

and	nor
or	for
but	

WORDS THAT SUMMARIZE

These words may be used at the conclusion of your essay.

in conclusion	in brief
in summary	all in all
to sum up	as a result
in short	therefore
in sum	finally

WORDS THAT ADD INFORMATION

again	in addition to
in addition	another
for instance	also
next	for example
also	for instance
as well as	in other words
finally	that is

WORDS TO LIMIT IN YOUR ESSAY

because	but
and	maybe
so	stuff
then	things (Be specific!)

ESSAY PRACTICE

Below is a prompt for a practice essay. On a separate sheet of paper write a quick outline and then begin your essay. Remember that the outline is for your own benefit and is not to be turned in with the essay. Time yourself as you write.

PROMPT

American people have become more health conscious in the past few years. More people seem to be exercising regularly and watching what they eat.

DISCUSSION QUESTION

What are some ways that you can help yourself to become healthier or maintain your own good health?

Write an essay of about 250 words in which you explain or present your reasons for this topic. You have 45 minutes to write on this topic.

SAMPLE ANSWER

After you finish writing your essay compare it to the sample essay below. You may have come up with similar ideas. Everyone will not choose the same three points to write about in their essay. As long as you can provide clear, focused main ideas and details to back them up, you should be on the road to success!

Since the above prompt was an expository theme, you should have written five paragraphs. Look now at the sample outline.

SAMPLE OUTLINE

I. There are many ways in which I stay healthy.
   A. eat right
   B. exercise daily
   C. try not to worry

II. I always try to eat the right types of food each day.
   A. eat from the four main food groups
   B. drink plenty of water

III. Before I begin each day I make sure I exercise at least ten minutes.
  A. start out with stretching exercises
  B. work up to more strenuous exercise

IV. Worry has a big effect on my health.
  A. simple things don't bother me
  B. relaxing

V. There are many ways to stay healthy but I choose to eat right, exercise, and not worry.

SAMPLE ESSAY FROM OUTLINE

MAINTAINING GOOD HEALTH

There are many ways in which I can stay healthy. I try to eat right, exercise daily, and try not to worry. If I do all of these things I feel better emotionally and physically.

I always try to eat the right types of food every day. Eating from the four basic food groups always helps. By doing this I make sure I get all the vitamins and minerals that I need each day. I also drink plenty of water instead of soft drinks with added sweeteners. I feel that this is better for me.

Before I begin each day I make sure I exercise at least ten minutes. I begin with stretching exercises. Later, I work up to more strenuous exercises that really get my heart rate up.

Worry has a big effect on my health. I try not to let things worry me as before. I don't let simple things bother me. I usually take a few minutes each day to relax.

There are many ways to stay healthy, but I choose to eat right, exercise, and not worry. With the combination of these three things, how can I go wrong?

In the above sample the word count is 195 words. Once you have your outline written, the paragraph doesn't take that long to write. Just remember to jot down phrases in your outline and don't worry about trying to come up with the "perfect" outline. No one will see it but you!

ALLOT YOUR TIME

Remember that you have a maximum time of 45 minutes. Use the following guidelines.

1. Read the instructions completely and make sure you understand what you are going to write about—three to five minutes.
2. Make your outline—five to ten minutes. (If you have a good outline to follow your essay will flow much easier and take less time!)
3. Writing the 250-word essay—twenty to twenty-five minutes.
4. Revising and editing your essay—five minutes.

Keep these times in mind as you go in to write your essay. They will be most helpful.

REVISING THE ESSAY

This segment will give you some ideas on how to revise your essay once you have it written. Remember to always reread your essay once you have completed it. If you have allotted your time, you should have five to ten minutes to complete this very important part of essay writing.

Below is a set of guidelines to follow when revising your essay.

CHECK YOURSELF

1. Check for the main idea in the first paragraph of all three types of essays.
2. Check for your *three* points in your first paragraph of a persuasive or expository essay.
3. Check to make sure in the persuasive and expository essays that the second, third, and fourth paragraphs include a topic sentence related to the three points in your first paragraph.
4. Check to make sure in your narrative essay that you include sequencing and time order words.
5. Do your detail sentences in each paragraph stick to the topic? Keep the focus of the essay.
6. Check for run-on sentences, correct punctuation, capitalization, subject/verb agreement, and spelling.

7. Check for summarization at the end of the essay. Do you have a clear ending for your essay?
8. Do you have a clear and focused introduction, body, and conclusion?
9. Do you have about 250 words in your essay?

EDITING EXERCISE FOR THE ESSAY

Below is an essay with major mistakes. Jot down in the margins the problems that you see with the essay, then check any that you found with the rewritten essay.

BEING A GOOD CITIZEN

Everyone has ideas on how to be a good citizen. I believe that people need to be aware of current events and help other people.

In order to be a good citizen a person should be aware of the current events. If a person is informed good about what is taking place in the world then that person can in turn act on that information. Such as voting. Voting is something every person should do some people don't like to vote. It is a person's right and responsibility to vote in an election and make sure that we have responsible people running our government. Our government today is in need of strong leaders.

I believe everyone should help other people. I have a friend that volunteers their services at the nursing home. There are several nursing homes near here. Volunteering at your child's school is also a wonderful way to help other people this helps the child with class work or even homework.

I think being a good citizen is a great idea!

---

focus. The last paragraph was made up of only one sentence. You should never have a one-sentence paragraph in your essay. Introductory words in a sentence should be separated with a comma such as, "In order to be a good citizen, a person should....". Changing the word "good" to "well" and placing it before the verb in the sentence "If a person is informed good about what is taking place in the world...." makes better sense. Good is an adjective and is used to describe a noun; well is an adverb that tells more about the verb.

REVISION OF "BEING A GOOD CITIZEN"

Everyone has ideas on how to be a good citizen. I believe that people need to be aware of current events, help other people, and keep in touch with public officials.

In order to be a good citizen, I feel that a person should be aware of the current events. If a person is well informed about what is taking place in the world, that person in turn can act on that information.

A good citizen should help other people. There are many ways to help others. A few of these ways would be to volunteer in nursing homes or school.

Citizens should keep in touch with public officials. Everyone should know their local, state, and federal elected public officials that represent them. These people provide valuable input to governmental issues.

Being a good citizen is important. I believe that to be a good citizen a person should be aware of current events, help other people and keep in touch with public officials.

In the revision of "Being a Good Citizen," you can see that major reconstruction of the format was needed. In the first paragraph of the original essay there were only two points expressed when there should have been three. There were several run-on sentences and details that didn't pertain to the topic. The paragraphs began to ramble without a

EDITING EXERCISE FOR THE ESSAY

On the following page is an essay with a few mistakes. See if you can find them in about five to ten minutes.

THE NEGATIVE IMPACT OF TELEVISION ON CHILDREN

Today it seems that children spend entirely too much time in front of the television. I feel that television has a negative effect on children because it takes up much of their free time it provides a child with much publicized violence and a child doesn't get much exercise while sitting in front of a television for hours on end.

When a child has free time I believe that child should be using it for more constructive things like studying or socializing with friends instead of sitting in front of a television watching it hour after hour and not really learning anything it seems they are just being intertained.

There is entirely too much violence on television. If a child watches television unsupervised they may be watching violent programs that the parents aren't aware of. These types of actions that they see on television may seem acceptable to the child and later the child may become involved in unacceptable behavior and the parents wouldn't want that to happen.

Sitting in front of the television daily also keeps the child from doing any physical activities. A child needs to be actively involved in types of physical stimulation that will burn off calories and keep a child's muscles strong.

I believe that television provides a negative impact on children. When children watch too much television it takes up a lot of their free time, it provides a child with visions of violence, and takes away time that a child could be exercising or playing.

In the revision of "The Negative Impact of Television on Children," there were only a few mistakes that you should have found in your ten-minute revision. First, there are some punctuation errors. There should be two commas in the series of the first paragraph. There should also be a comma after the introductory word group, "When a child has free time, I believe...." The second paragraph is made up of one very long incorrect sentence. It should be broken down into smaller sentences. Some words may be omitted because they are unnecessary and take away from the essay. There is also a spelling mistake in the second paragraph—*intertained* should be spelled *entertained*. The third paragraph has problems with an extremely long sentence. The word "and" should not be used in it. The sentence should be broken down into smaller sentences.

REVISION OF "THE NEGATIVE IMPACT OF TELEVISION ON CHILDREN"

Today it seems that children spend entirely too much time in front of the television. I feel that television has a negative effect on children because it takes up much of their free time, it provides a child with much publicized violence, and a child doesn't get much exercise while sitting in front of a television for hours on end.

When children have free time, I believe they should be using it for more constructive things like studying or socializing with friends. I believe they would learn more by doing this than watching television hour after hour. It seems they are just being entertained.

There is entirely too much violence on television. If children watch television unsupervised, they could be watching violent programs that the parents are not aware of. The type of violent actions children see may become acceptable to them. They may later try some of these violent actions.

Sitting in front of the television daily also keeps children from doing any physical activities. Children need to be actively involved in types of physical stimulation that will burn off calories and keep their muscles strong.

I believe that television provides a negative impact on children. When children watch too much television it takes up a lot of their free time, it provides them with visions of violence, and takes away time that they could be exercising or playing.

ESSAY PRACTICE

It is now time to put everything together that you have read and create your own essay.

PROMPT

Most people go though life one day at a time accomplishing things along the way. Some people accomplish great education or wealth; others accomplish skills at writing, music, or nurturing. Sometimes, simple accomplishments mean more than great ones. Try to think of what your greatest accomplishments are in life.

DISCUSSION QUESTION

What are your greatest accomplishments?

Write an essay of about 250 words in which you discuss this topic. Give supporting details and examples for every point you make. You have 45 minutes to write on this topic.

CHECK YOURSELF

1. Read carefully the prompt, discussion question, and directions.
2. Decide if the prompt is expository, persuasive, or narrative.
3. Plan your essay before you begin.
4. Use scrap paper to prepare a simple outline.
5. Write your essay on the lined pages of a separate sheet of paper.
6. Read carefully what you have written and make needed changes.
7. Check for focus, elaboration, organization, conventions, and integration.

PRACTICE PROMPTS FOR ESSAYS

This segment will provide you with practice prompts for essays. Remember, the more you practice, the better you will become at writing essays.

EXPOSITORY PROMPTS

Collections
In the News
Fun Games to Play
Favorite Television Programs
My Friends
My Spare Time
Funny Sights
Dangerous Experiences
Favorite Songs
Running a Household
Sticking to a Budget
Automobile Safety
Weather Hazards
Celebrations
Auction Purchases
Favorite Animals
Amusement Parks
World Problems
Women in Politics
What I Hope to Gain by Getting My GED

NARRATIVE PROMPTS

My Greatest Adventure
Relatives Visit
The Family Vacation
My Greatest Lesson
Never Again!
My Favorite Hobby
A Joyful Experience
My Experience in the Army
My Greatest Luck
A Sad Day
Moving Day
My First Home
My Experience with Technology
Something I Haven't Told
My Last Day of Work
The Greatest Game I've Ever Seen!
My Most Challenging Day
My Most Nervous Day
A Childhood Experience
A Proud Day in My Life

PERSUASIVE

Is the death sentence constitutional?

Do talk shows go too far?

Should the Ten Commandments be posted in schools?

Should the number of immigrants be restricted in the United States?

Should all work places have mandatory drug testing?

Should high school students be required to pass a test to graduate?

Do you think the United States should use only metric measurements?

Should the government provide homes for all of the homeless?

Do you believe in life on other planets?

Should the rich pay more taxes?

Should there be video cameras on streets that record people for the Internet?

Should there be seat belts on school buses?

Should the government allow advertisements to be placed on school buses?

Should gambling be allowed in every state?

Should E-Commerce have to pay taxes?

Do we still need a Selective Service?

Are planes really safe?

Should there be a time limit for people on welfare?

Should there be a "cut-off" age for people running for president?

Should there be more censorship on television?

PRACTICE ESSAY

(Answers will vary.)

You could have written the practice essay as expository or narrative. If you wrote it as expository you should have followed these guidelines: You should have five paragraphs in your essay. The first is the introduction with the second, third, and fourth being the body. The fifth paragraph would be your summary of the essay. You could have written this essay in two different ways: One, you could have thought of three specific accomplishments that you have had in your life and written about them including main ideas and details. The second way would be for you to have thought of one main accomplishment in your life and given three specific reasons why this was such a great accomplishment for you. You would have used the three specific reasons as your main ideas for the body of the essay.

If you wrote the essay as narrative you should have written the essay in this way: First there should be a three or four paragraph set up. Narrative paragraphs are written in the first person with a sequence of events taking place. You should have listed in your first paragraph your main idea, stating what your greatest accomplishment was. The second and third paragraphs would be a logical sequence of events, explanations, and support telling about your greatest accomplishment. You last paragraph would be the summarization of the essay.

RUBRIC

This segment will give you some insight on how your essay will be scored.

When you write your essay and submit it to be scored, it will be read by two trained readers. These two readers will base the score they give you on an "overall effectiveness" of the essay. Essays will be assigned a score of 1 to 4, with one being the lowest and four the highest. They will be looking at areas such as:

- **Focus:** The clarity of your ideas to the topic of the essay.
- **Elaboration:** How well you explain and support your ideas or opinions.
- **Organization:** The logical flow and structure of the essay.
- **Conventions:** The standard use of written English.
- **Integration:** The overall effectiveness of the essay.

The readers will not count each mistake that is made and make a deduction of points, but will instead look at the overall effectiveness of the essay for scoring. You may make several small mistakes with grammar or punctuation and still end up with a 4 on the score as long as the essay is well focused, supported, and organized.

On the next page is the official GED Essay Scoring Guide. This will give you a good idea of how your essay will be graded.

GED ESSAY SCORING GUIDE

The GED Testing Service has defined the four levels of GED Essays:

4 – Effective

3 – Adequate

2 – Marginal

1 – Ineffective (It is important to note that a score of 1 will require you to retake the entire Language Arts, Writing, Test 1.)

Papers will show *some or all* of the following characteristics.

Upper-half papers make clear a definite purpose, pursued with varying degrees of effectiveness. They also have a structure that shows evidence of some deliberate planning.

Level 4 writing is *competent.*

Papers scored as a 4 are clearly organized with effective support for each of the writer's major points. The writing offers substantive ideas. The surface features are consistently under control, despite an occasional lapse in usage.

Level 3 writing is *sufficient.*

Papers scored as a 3 usually show some evidence of planning or development. Support, though sufficient, tends to be less extensive or convincing than that found in a paper scored as a 4. The writer generally observes the conventions of accepted English usage. Some errors are present, but they are not severe enough to interfere significantly with the writer's main purpose.

Level 2 writing is *acceptable.*

Papers scored as a 2 are characterized by a marked lack of development or inadequate support for ideas. The level of thought apparent in the writing is frequently unsophisticated or superficial, often marked by a listing of unsupported generalizations. Instead of suggesting a clear purpose, these papers often present conflicting purposes. Errors in accepted English usage may seriously interfere with the overall effectiveness of these papers.

Level 1 writing is *insufficient.*

Papers scored as a 1 leave the impression that the writer has not only *not* accomplished a purpose, but has not made any purpose apparent. The dominant feature of these papers is the lack of control. The writer stumbles both in conveying a clear plan for the paper and in expressing ideas according to the conventions of accepted English usage.

Level 0 writing is *not able to be scored.*

The zero score is reserved for papers which are blank, illegible, or written on a topic other than the one assigned.

Now, keeping this scoring guide in mind, study the following treatments of the unfavorable effects on health of smoking.

Paper 1

The major effects of smoking include a shortened life span. Each year nearly half a million Americans die prematurely as a result of smoking. Smoking is responsible for 30 percent of all cancer deaths in the United States, including those from lung cancer.

Smoking weakens the heart's ability to function, leading to heart attacks and strokes. In addition, tens of thousands die from chronic lung disease linked to smoking.

Women who smoke during pregnancy are ten times more likely to have miscarriages. Also, the babies of smoking mothers tend to have lower birth weights.

Finally, there is the risk of death or severe illness for those who are exposed to second-hand smoke: lung cancer, emphysema, bronchitis, pneumonia, or heart disease.

Paper 2

Smoking has many unfavorable effects. It affects the health of the smoker in many ways. It results in shortness of breath. It causes tobacco stains.

Smoking becomes a habit that is hard to break smokers become addicted to cigarettes because of the nicotine.

Smoking is also very expensive three packs a day cost about $50 a week which could buy alot of food and necesities.

If you have a family, they are affected by second-hand smoke. Children learn to smoke by imitating there parents.

That's why you shouldn't smoke.

Paper 3

Smoking has bad affects. Millions of americans smoke they spend a great deal of money on cigarettes.

Smoking is bad for you. It destroys your health and causes Cancer. You may think its grown up to smoke but it really isnt.

Smoking also hurts the ones around you. Who inhale your smoke. Women who are pregnant might hurt they're babies.

Smokers pollute the air. And make it hard for others around them to breath.

This is why you should think twice before you light up.

Paper 1 has excellent organization of materials relating to the subject. Paragraphing is logical. Specific facts are presented, and everything relates directly to the topic. There are no errors in sentence structure, punctuation, or capitalization.

Paper 2 has elements of organization. Each of the first four paragraphs makes a single argument.

This paper has two main weaknesses. First, the arguments are not backed up by any relevant facts. One of the effects mentioned (tobacco stains) is unimportant, while important effects on health are omitted. In addition, there are a number of errors. Paragraph two has a run-on sentence, as has paragraph three. *A lot* is misspelled as *alot*,

and *necessities* as *necesities*; also, there should be a comma after *week*. In paragraph four, an incorrect pronoun refers to family— *they* instead of *it*, and *there* should be replaced by *their*. Although this paper has good organization, the errors would reduce the rating to a 3.

Paper 3, is poorly organized. Irrelevant material is included (money spent, grown-up feeling). Statements are repeated and not documented (causes cancer). Also, there are many errors in accepted English usage. There are sentence errors—a run-on sentence in the first paragraph, and sentence fragments in the third and fourth paragraphs. There are several spelling errors; *affects* should be *effects*; *its* should be *it's*; *isnt* should be *isn't*; *they're* should be *their*; *breath* should be *breathe*. *Americans*, not *americans*, and *cancer*, not *Cancer*, are correct. Sentences are very short, even childish.

There is no doubt that Paper 1 will receive a 4, but Paper 3 will receive a 1.

SOCIAL STUDIES
TEST 2

CHAPTER 10: Reading and Interpreting Social Studies Materials

The basic skills in reading social studies materials are thoroughly treated. A special section deals with basics in interpreting tables, graphs, and maps, and two additional sections that deal with interpreting political cartoons and historical photographs.

CHAPTER 11: Handling Social Studies Skills Questions

The four basic kinds of skills questions are analyzed with examples of each. Twenty questions offer practice in dealing with questions testing comprehension, application, analysis, and evaluation. An outline of study for all the social studies is included. The Glossary of Social Studies Terms is a mini-dictionary with clear and simple definitions.

CHAPTER 12: Social Studies Practice

The 64 questions based on passages, tables, cartoons, photographs, and maps provide ample practice in reading and interpreting social studies materials.

Reading and Interpreting Social Studies Materials

How to Read Civics and Government, History, Economics, and Geography

Reading in the social studies requires a number of skills that are common to all reading materials. When you read in any subject, you want to identify the *main ideas* of the writer. So, too, in social studies you need to get at the key thoughts being expressed.

LOCATING THE MAIN IDEA

If you read too slowly, you may miss the main point because you have gotten too involved in details. It is important, therefore, that you first read the selection through to the end rather quickly *before* you turn to the questions.

Where do you look for the main idea? Most often you will find it in the topic sentence, usually the first sentence in the passage. Sometimes, however, the writer will withhold the main idea until the last sentence, building up to it throughout the entire selection. At other times, the writer will include both a main idea and an important secondary (or subordinate) idea.

To train yourself in **locating the main idea**, ask yourself the same questions that will be asked of you on the examination.

1. What is the main idea of the passage?
2. What is the best title for the passage?
3. If I were choosing a suitable headline for the article in a newspaper, what headline would I choose?
4. What is the *topic sentence* of this paragraph or paragraphs; *that is, the sentence that includes the ideas contained in all the other sentences?*

FINDING DETAILS

After you have determined the main idea, the next step is to *locate the facts supporting the main idea or details* that flow from the main idea. If, for example, the main idea of a passage is that democracy is the best form of government, the author will undoubtedly provide facts or reasons to support this statement or include facts that show the superiority of democracy to other forms of government. If the main idea is a general conclusion that many persons with physical disabilities have overcome them and become famous, details would probably include such examples as Helen Keller and Franklin D. Roosevelt.

How do you locate a detail? You go back to the selection a second or third time to dig it out of the passage. It most frequently will come in the middle or toward the end of the selection. Sometimes clues in the passage steer you to the detail or fact in question. Clues for locating details may read:

An example is...

One reason is...

An argument in support of (or against)...is...

A reason for...is...

To train yourself in **locating details**, ask yourself these questions:

1. What examples are given to illustrate the main point?
2. What reasons are offered to support the author's position?
3. What arguments for or against a proposal does the author present?
4. When, where, how did something happen?
5. What did someone do?
6. Why did he or she do it?

To find the proper detail, it will be necessary for you to *learn how to skim,* that is, to read rapidly to locate the piece of information you are seeking. You can do this only if you know specifically what you need to find in a given selection and limit your reading to finding only that fact.

DETERMINING ORGANIZATION

Note the manner in which the writer organizes his or her material. This will help you to follow the author's thoughts effectively. The writer may organize his or her material chronologically, that is, in the order in which a series of events happened. Alternatively, the writer may organize the material logically by presenting the arguments *for* a position in one paragraph and the arguments *against* in another. Or the writer may present his or her ideas in the order of their importance,

with the most important ideas first. This, in fact, is the way a newspaper article is written—"from the top down"—in case the reader doesn't have time to finish it all.

If you can determine the organization of a passage, you can zero in on the relationship between the main parts of a passage.

CLUES TO FINDING THE RELATIONSHIP BETWEEN THE MAIN PARTS OF A PASSAGE

Sequence of ideas is indicated by such words as:

first	next	finally
second	further	

Additional ideas are indicated by such words as:

and	furthermore	likewise
besides	also	in addition

Opposing or contrasting ideas are indicated by such words as:

on the other hand	but	yet
however	still	although

DRAWING CONCLUSIONS

Another step involves *drawing conclusions from the material presented.* Conclusions are often indicated by such words as:

thus	accordingly	consequently
therefore	so	as a result

Sometimes, however, the author does not draw the conclusion, but leaves it to you, the reader, to do so. You infer the conclusion from the materials presented; you draw the inference as a result of details you have noted and the relationships you have determined (time sequence, logical order, cause-and-effect, among others). Thus, if an author indicates that a given president vetoed many bills, you might infer that the president and the Congress differed in their thinking about legislation, perhaps because the Congress was controlled by a political party different from that of the president.

To train yourself to **make inferences** properly in order to draw a conclusion, ask yourself these questions:

1. What do I think will happen next? (inference or prediction as to the outcome)
2. Putting these arguments together, what conclusion can I reach?
3. If one result was caused by something, will a similar effect take place in another situation where the same cause is operating?
4. What is the writer suggesting, rather than saying outright?

READING CRITICALLY

In addition to drawing conclusions and making inferences, it is essential in social sciences that you react to what you have read. Often you must judge the material you are reading, not merely understand it. Historians, political scientists, economists, sociologists, and anthropologists often present one side of the story, their side, but there is almost always another side. In other words, they may "slant" the material to suit their bias by including only facts and arguments favorable to their own view and omitting everything else. It is essential for you to *read critically.* Do *not* accept everything that is written just because it appears in print.

You must develop the habit of challenging the author by raising questions, judging the completeness and truth of the information presented, and distinguishing fact from opinion.

A *statement of fact* is one that can be proved true by consulting a reliable source of information such as an encyclopedia, an almanac, or an official government document. Here is an example.

EXAMPLE

The federal government spends billions of dollars each year helping states with aid to needy persons: needy through unemployment, disability, or family problems.

This statement can be verified by consulting the official federal budget.

A *statement of opinion or belief* is one that expresses the feelings, thoughts, or beliefs of a person or persons, and that cannot be proved to be true by reference to any reliable source at the present time.

EXAMPLE

It is believed that by the year 2004, population will have outstripped food production and starvation will be widespread.

This is a prediction in the form of a statement or belief attributed to an unidentified source ("It is believed...") that cannot be proved until the year 2004. It is possible that others may have their own beliefs. In any case, the statement is definitely not a fact.

Note that certain words are clues to statements of opinion.

WORDS THAT ARE CLUES TO STATEMENTS OF OPINION

claim	probably
believe	possibly
think	might
consider	should (have)
will be	could (have)
likely	ought

WORDS THAT PROBABLY REFLECT OPINION RATHER THAN FACT

better	undesirable
worse	necessary
desirable	unnecessary

REMEMBER: Always apply the test, "Can this statement be proved by reference to a reliable source?"

It is important to distinguish fact from opinion in the printed word when writers unconsciously allow their opinions or biases to enter into their writing. It is even more important to do so when a writer slants his or her material deliberately.

You can **read critically** if you ask your-self the following questions:

1. Why is the author writing this selection?
2. What is the author trying to get me, the reader, to believe?
3. Is the author presenting a balanced or one-sided view of the situation?
4. Is the author omitting essential information?
5. Is the author appealing to my mind or to my emotions and prejudices?
6. Does the author have some hidden reason for writing what he or she writes?
7. Is the author accurate? Or does he or she deal in half-truths?
8. Does the author use words with specific agreed-upon meanings, or does he or she use words that are "loaded" because they have special meanings?

DETECTING PROPAGANDA AND PROPAGANDA TECHNIQUES

When writers deliberately spread ideas or opinions to benefit themselves or institutions to which they belong or to damage opponents or opposing institutions, they are engaging in propaganda. A propagandist tries to influence your thinking or behavior and to turn your opinions and actions in a certain direction. He or she uses words that appeal to your emotions—your fears, your loves, your hates—rather than to your reason, to your ability to think clearly, in order, ultimately, to make you do things in a way you never ordinarily would do.

Seven common techniques in propaganda are:

1. *Name-calling.* The writer tries to influence you by attaching a bad name to an individual, group, nation, race, policy, practice, or belief.

   EXAMPLE

   It would be wise to pay no attention to that loony liberal (or retarded reactionary, depending upon the writer's point of view).

   Certain names are loaded with emo-

tional overtones: Fascist, Red, Nazi, Commie. You must note carefully in what way and for what purpose these terms are used. Name-calling is a common propaganda technique.

2. *Glittering generalities.* The writer attaches "good" names to people and policies, in the hope that you will accept them without really looking into the facts.

   EXAMPLE

   The writer appeals to our emotions by using such "good" terms as *forward-looking, peace-loving, straight-shooting,* and *idealistic.*

   We all love progress, peace, honesty, and idealism so we tend to accept rather than challenge. Always ask the questions "why" and "how" when "good" terms are applied to people and policies.

3. *Transfer.* The writer tries to use the approval and prestige of something or some institution we respect to get us to accept something else in which he or she is interested.

   EXAMPLE

   Most Americans are law-abiding and respect their police officers. One who writes on behalf of an athletic league supported by the local police will try to get you to transfer your approval of the police to the athletic league he or she is sponsoring.

   Always examine the person or institution receiving the transfer on its own merits rather than on the merits of the original institution you love and respect.

4. *Testimonial.* Advertisements on television and radio make wide use of testimonials. A top athlete endorses a breakfast cereal. A beautiful actress recommends a cosmetic cream. An ex-senator testifies to the value of a credit card. A testimonial is a recommendation made by someone on behalf of a person, a product, or an institution.

   But is the athlete an expert on nutrition? Is the actress an expert on skin care? Is the politician an expert on personal money management? REMEMBER: these people are being paid to make these testimonials. You must ask yourself whether the person making the testimonial is expert enough to do so before you believe what you read or hear.

More subtle is newspaper reporting that is based on *indirect* testimonials.

EXAMPLES

Official circles report...; It was learned from a senior government official...; A reliable source stated...

Always ask *which* circles, *which* official, *which* source. Be careful of any information that comes from a high *unidentified* source.

5. *Card-stacking.* The writer attempts to get you to see only one side of a particular issue. To do so, he or she will use half-truths and omit the other side of the argument. Examples occur frequently in "authorized" biographies that present a person's life in glowing terms, including all the good qualities while omitting or toning down the poor ones. When reading about an issue, always note whether both sides have been discussed or whether the cards have been stacked by the writer on one side of the issue only.

6. *Bandwagon.* The writer tries to make you go along with the crowd. Since most people like to follow the trend, they will respond favorably to such statements as "Nine out of ten Americans prefer..." or "...sells more... than all other companies put together." In politics, the bandwagon technique is often seen in action in national political conventions. "Join the swing to...."

The bandwagon-approach writer does not want you to think clearly for yourself. You should always ask *why* you should join the others, and not do so because your emotions have gotten the better of you.

REMEMBER:

A critical reader

- does not believe everything he or she reads simply because it is in print;
- accepts as true only statements that can be proved or that are made by reliable authorities;
- separates fact from opinion, recognizes emotional language and bias, and is aware of slanting by omission.

DETERMINING CAUSE AND EFFECT

A reading skill frequently used in social studies involves determining the relationship between events. Events rarely occur in isolation. They are generally the result of other events that happened earlier.

EXAMPLE

The Japanese bombed Pearl Harbor on December 7, 1941. The United States then declared war on Japan.

The bombing of Pearl Harbor was the cause; the declaration of war was the result or effect of the bombing. Always try, when reading of an event, to determine its cause or causes. *Here is a question involving cause and effect:*

QUESTION

1. President Franklin D. Roosevelt's New Deal policy led to numerous government agencies, created in an effort to combat the effects of the Great Depression. One major result of this policy was to

   (1) weaken the power of the chief executive
   (2) strengthen the policy of laissez-faire
   (3) increase the power of the federal government
   (4) expand the importance of states' rights
   (5) lessen the need for judicial review

ANSWER AND ANALYSIS

The question asks for a result of President Franklin D. Roosevelt's New Deal policy. The opposite results occurred from those listed as Choices 1, 4, and 5; that is, the New Deal strengthened the power of the chief executive; weakened the importance of states' rights, and increased the need for judicial review. Choice 2, the policy of laissez-faire, provides for little or no interference by government in the affairs of business, clearly an incorrect response. Only Choice 3 is correct because the New Deal program called for executive action to advance economic recovery and social welfare.

COMPARING AND CONTRASTING IDEAS AND ORGANIZATIONS

Another frequently needed skill in social studies reading involves the ability to compare and contrast institutions and events. You may be asked to compare American democracy with French democracy, contrast democracy with communism, compare the platforms of the Republicans and Democrats, or contrast the role of women in the eighteenth century with their role in the twentieth.

QUESTION

1. The careers of Theodore Roosevelt and Franklin D. Roosevelt were similar because each man

   (1) was an outstanding military leader before becoming president
   (2) led the cause for international peace, but involved the United States in a war
   (3) succeeded to the presidency upon the death of the preceding president
   (4) believed in a strong presidency and acted accordingly
   (5) represented the same political party

ANSWER AND ANALYSIS

You are asked to compare the careers of two American presidents. Franklin D. Roosevelt was not an outstanding military leader before becoming president. Theodore Roosevelt did not involve the United States in a war. Franklin D. Roosevelt did not succeed to the presidency

upon the death of the preceding president. Theodore Roosevelt was a Republican; Franklin D. Roosevelt, a Democrat. Thus Choices 1, 2, 3, and 5 are incorrect. Choice 4 is correct because both Roosevelts were strong presidents: Theodore Roosevelt was a trust buster, had a Square Deal policy, and pursued an expansionist foreign policy; Franklin D. Roosevelt carried out New Deal policies and a Good Neighbor policy with Latin America, and he led the nation for most of World War II.

LEARNING SOCIAL STUDIES VOCABULARY AND DERIVING MEANING FROM CONTEXT

In social studies as in science, vocabulary is of critical importance. Words found in social studies may

- represent complicated ideas, such as *nationalism, referendum, mercantilism;*
- imply a whole set of ideas, such as *feudalism, militarism, bimetallism;*
- have meanings specific to the social studies although they have other meanings as well, such as *Axis, act, shop;*
- come from foreign languages, such as *apartheid, junta, laissez-faire;*
- have meanings that go beyond the usual ones, such as *dove, plank, scab.*

Try to derive the correct meaning from the *context*—the words with which the term appears in a sentence.

You can **check your understanding of the meaning of the vocabulary** in a given selection by asking yourself:

1. What is the key word in the sentence (paragraph, selection)?
2. What is the meaning of the word in *this* sentence (context)?
3. What is the exact meaning (denotation) of the word in this selection?
4. What is the extended meaning (connotation) of the word in this selection? (What does it *suggest* as well as say?)
5. What is the effect of a given word on me?
6. What is the special meaning of this word in social studies?

Practice with Social Studies Readings

A representative selection in each of the social studies follows, together with questions based on it. Read each of the selections and try to answer the questions *without* referring to the answer analyses that follow. Then check your answers by carefully reading the analyses. Each of the sets of questions following the selections contains a question that

- is aimed at testing whether you can *locate the main idea* ("The best title for the selection is...");
- is designed to test your ability to *locate details* ("One difference between _____ and _____ is...");
- requires you to show your *knowledge of social studies vocabulary* ("All of the following words used in economics are correctly paired with their meanings EXCEPT...");
- forces you to *make a conclusion or predict an outcome* ("We can conclude that..." "It is most likely that...").

In addition, there are questions designed to test your ability to

- *find reasons* that the author uses to support an argument;
- *follow the organization* of a selection;
- *identify the position taken by the author* (or any bias he or she may have).

CIVICS AND GOVERNMENT, WITH ANSWERS AND ANSWER ANALYSIS

There are the following four key committees at a political convention.

➤ The *Credentials Committee*. This group decides who is an official delegate entitled to vote.

➤ The permanent *Organization Committee*, which picks the convention's officers, including the chairperson. This official decides who can speak at the convention and who cannot.

➤ The *Rules Committee*, which makes the rules by which the convention and the party organization are run.

➤ The *Resolutions and Platform Committee*, which writes the party platform. Usually, a

convention lasts about four days. Typically, a temporary convention chairperson opens the convention with a *keynote address*, which is meant to set the tone of the convention—and quite frequently does. The real business of the day, however, goes on behind the podium, where the Credentials Committee settles disputes over *delegate credentials*.

On the second day the *party platform* is read, debated, and usually voted upon. A *permanent chairperson* is installed, and the convention is asked to approve the reports of its major committees.

On the third day actual *nominations* for presidential candidates are taken. States are called alphabetically at the Republican Convention, by lottery at the Democratic. Each state may nominate one candidate, second a nomination already made, yield (surrender the floor to another state), or pass. After each nomination there is usually a loud demonstration for the nominee.

Balloting begins only after nominations have been closed. A *simple majority*—one more than half the votes—is all that is needed to win. Every Republican presidential candidate since 1948 and every Democratic one since 1952 has won on the first ballot. If no one wins a simple majority on the first ballot, the vote is taken again until a candidate is picked.

By the fourth day a *presidential nominee* has usually emerged. He, in turn, addresses party leaders and tells them whom he prefers for *vice president*. Usually he gets his way.

Finally, the two candidates make their *acceptance speeches*, go through a few ceremonial events, and the *convention ends*.

1. The main idea of the above selection is

   (1) choosing a president and vice president
   (2) four key committees
   (3) how Republican and Democratic conventions differ
   (4) conventions: American political dramas
   (5) how conventions are organized and run

2. The vice-presidential candidate is chosen by the

   (1) party leaders
   (2) roll-call vote
   (3) Rules Committee
   (4) permanent convention chairman
   (5) presidential nominee

3. In the next convention, it is most likely that the party candidates will be nominated by

   (1) simple majority on the second ballot
   (2) plurality on the second ballot
   (3) two-thirds vote on the first ballot
   (4) simple majority on the first ballot
   (5) plurality on the first ballot

4. The INCORRECTLY paired group below is

   (1) Organization Committee—convention chairperson
   (2) permanent chairperson—keynote address
   (3) nominees—acceptance speeches
   (4) states—nominations
   (5) simple majority—choice of nominee

5. One difference between Republican and Democratic conventions is the way in which

   (1) committees are organized
   (2) convention chairpersons are chosen
   (3) nominations for presidential candidates are made
   (4) balloting takes place
   (5) party platforms are decided

6. The writer of this selection has organized the passage

   (1) logically
   (2) psychologically
   (3) chronologically
   (4) argumentatively
   (5) critically

NOTE:
The words in the questions that are defined in the "Glossary of Social Studies Terms" (page 308) are *ballot, convention, majority, nominate, party, platform* and *plurality.*

ANSWER KEY

1. **5** 2. **5** 3. **4** 4. **2** 5. **3** 6. **3**

ANSWER ANALYSIS

1. **5** Question 1 calls for the main idea of the selection. The possible answers generally fall into several categories. *One of the choices* will be incorrect or irrelevant; that is, it will have nothing to do with the question. *Other choices* will focus on details and not on the main idea. *Still another choice* will be too general, too vague. *The correct answer* will be broad in scope yet specific enough to indicate the main idea or purpose of the article. Choice 5 is correct because it indicates the main idea of the article, which is to explain how conventions are organized by committees and how they are run to accomplish their purposes, namely, nominating a presidential and a vice-presidential candidate and adopting a party platform. Choice 1, choosing a president and vice president, is incorrect since the convention merely nominates. It chooses the presidential and vice presidential candidates who may become president and vice president if elected. Choices 2 and 3 deal with details—the committee structure and the one point of difference between the Republican and the Democratic conventions. Choice 4 is too broad; conventions may be American political dramas but that is *not* the main idea or purpose of this selection.

2. **5** This question requires you to locate a detail, albeit an important detail, in the passage. Skimming (reading rapidly) through the passage, you will note the term *vice president* for the first time in the next to last paragraph. It is there you will find the correct answer—Choice 5. The presidential nominee tells the party leaders whom he prefers for vice president.

contemporary American institutions. What is the principle? That government fills a need for a community that the community itself cannot fill or fill well. Choice 1 is incorrect since education is a function the states have traditionally performed. Choice 2 is incorrect since the U.S. Chamber of Commerce is a private organization, not a federal agency. Choice 3 is incorrect since the National Guard is under state jurisdiction in peacetime. Choice 4 is incorrect because Public Service Commissions are generally state agencies. By the process of elimination, Choice 5 is correct. The Federal Aviation Administration regulates air commerce, including a national system of airports and air traffic control, an interstate function that a state ("community") cannot efficiently perform.

5. **4** This question calls for recall of a detail mentioned in the passage. Although the founders of our republic "strongly believed in private enterprise," they "chose to make the post office a government monopoly." This is an example of how flexible they were. The correct answer is 4. The other choices are irrelevant.

6. **1** Involved here are four statements that are false according to the passage and one that is true. Each statement has to be considered in light of what is said in the passage, and four must be discarded. Choices 3, 4, and 5 contradict what is said: government has actually broadened its role; Americans have always been willing to accommodate to change; our creed of democracy is not fixed. Choice 2 is not answerable solely on the evidence given in the passage, since we are not told the size of the shares of profit that capital and labor receive. Only Choice 1 is true: our political parties wish to retain "the existing political and economic order." They differ, however, on the rate of speed at which to change it.

7. **3** This question requires an inference on your part. "From what I have read," you must ask yourself, "what is the author's view of the issue he discusses?" The issue is change and the author obviously applauds it. Choice 3—favorable—is the correct answer. Why? The reason is found in the first two sentences. All the rest of the passage merely gives examples of change. The author cites the fact that the United States is "next to the oldest continuous government in the world." He is proud of that and he attributes that fact, in the next sentence, to our willingness to accommodate ourselves to change. Therefore, change must be good if it enables our government to survive.

Thus far, we have thoroughly analyzed the answers to two passages in political science and history. We have *located the main ideas* of each selection. We have dealt with the problem of *identifying* various kinds of *details*. In each selection, your *knowledge of social studies vocabulary* was tested. Finally, you were required to *draw inferences and predict outcomes*. The remaining four selections will give you further practice in these reading skills. We will analyze only those questions that introduce new reading techniques or that present special problems. Be certain to check your answers against the correct answers that follow the questions. If you made an error, do not hesitate to go back to the selection and read it through once more.

ECONOMICS, WITH ANSWERS AND ANSWER ANALYSIS

Could the United States fall into the depths of another Great Depression?

Economists can't say for sure. Most feel, however, that past depressions have taught us how to avoid economic disaster.

We've learned, for example, of the need for:

• *Government regulation of the stock market.* The Securities Act of 1933 made stock dealings less of a shell game by bringing them out into the open. The Securities Exchange Act of 1934 set up the Securities and Exchange Commission (S.E.C.), which acts as a sort of official consumer watchdog group. One of its jobs is to warn the investing public against the sort of crazy speculating that preceded the 1929 crash.

- *A permanent Council of Economic Advisers to take the economy's pulse for the government.* The Employment Act of 1946 created the Council of Economic Advisers. Its recommendations in 1949, 1958, 1969, and 1985 observers feel, helped keep the recessions of these years from becoming depressions.
- *A Federal Deposit Insurance Corporation (F.D.I.C.) to promise government backing of bank deposits.* The F.D.I.C. insures certain bank deposits. Such insurance has so far prevented the type of bank runs— panic withdrawals—that forced thousands of banks to close their doors in the early 1930s.
- *A federal relief system for jobless people.* State and local governments struggled to provide relief for the poor in the early years of the Great Depression. For the most part, they failed. They, too, ran out of money.

The New Deal introduced Social Security, a government pension plan. Government insurance followed for workers who are laid off or can't work because of injuries. Veterans' benefits and public assistance (welfare) are two other forms of government help in which Washington became involved during the 1930s.

These *transfer funds*, as they are called, don't merely help the recipients. In the long run, they help the whole economy by giving people buying power. This buying power helps keep up the demand for bonds. Thus, it helps keep factories open and factory workers employed.

For these and other reasons, many economists believe that we are now in better control of the U.S. economy, which is one of the strongest in the world.

NOTE:

The words *crash, depression, inflation, panic, speculation, welfare,* and *unemployment* are all in the Economics section of the "Glossary of Social Studies Terms."

---

1. The selection emphasizes
   - (1) the effects of the Great Depression
   - (2) the contributions of the New Deal
   - (3) the strength of the U.S. economy
   - (4) ways to avoid economic disaster
   - (5) the role of people's buying power

2. All of the following are associated with the New Deal EXCEPT
   - (1) Social Security
   - (2) Council of Economic Advisers
   - (3) veterans' benefits
   - (4) welfare
   - (5) unemployment insurance

3. All of the following were characteristics of the Great Depression that economists sought to correct EXCEPT
   - (1) stock market speculation
   - (2) bank failures
   - (3) unemployment
   - (4) soaring inflation
   - (5) poverty

4. The federal government stepped in where state and local governments failed in
   - (1) regulating the stock market
   - (2) backing bank deposits
   - (3) providing relief for the jobless
   - (4) providing veterans' benefits
   - (5) introducing Social Security

5. Which of the following statements is NOT true?
   - (1) The United States avoided depressions in each decade following the Great Depression.
   - (2) Bank panics have been avoided since the Great Depression.
   - (3) The Securities and Exchange Commission alerts investors to the kind of stock market activity that preceded the Great Depression.
   - (4) Transfer funds help the unemployed.
   - (5) We have learned how to prevent another Great Depression.

6. We can conclude from the author's presentation that he sees another Great Depression as

(1) inevitable
(2) likely
(3) unlikely
(4) impossible
(5) predictable

ANSWER KEY

1. **4** 2. **2** 3. **4** 4. **3** 5. **5** 6. **3**

ANSWER ANALYSIS

Let us look at questions 5 and 6.

5. **5** Question 5 gives you five statements, one of which is false. You have to check each statement against the passage. Choice 1 is true since the passage states that the recommendations of the Council of Economic Advisers helped avoid depressions in 1949, 1958, 1969 and 1985. Choice 2 is true since the passage states the Federal Deposit Insurance Corporation "has so far prevented" bank runs. Choice 3 is also true since the Securities and Exchange Commission has, as one of its responsibilities, warned the public against speculation. Choice 4 is true because unemployment insurance is included in transfer funds. Choice 5 is *not* true since economists are not certain we can avoid another Great Depression, although most of them may feel that way.

6. **3** Question 6 asks you to make an inference, one of the most difficult reading skills. The author concludes the article on an optimistic note—"economists believe that we are now in better control" of our economy, which is "one of the strongest in the world." Therefore, we are safe in inferring or drawing the conclusion that the author sees another Great Depression as unlikely, Choice 3.

GEOGRAPHY, WITH ANSWERS AND ANSWER ANALYSIS

Geography may be subdivided into several areas of study.

Physical Geography   In the study of physical (natural) geography, stress is laid upon the natural elements of man's environment. These include topography, soils, earth materials, earth-sun relationships, surface and underground water, weather and climate, and native plant and animal life. Physical geography must also include the impact of man on his physical environment as well as those influences omnipresent in nature.

Cultural Geography   In cultural geography emphasis is placed upon the study of observable features resulting from man's occupation of the earth. These features include population distribution and settlement, cities, buildings, roads, airfields, factories, railroads, farm and field patterns, communication facilities, and many other examples of man's work. Cultural geography is one of the very significant fields of geographic inquiry.

Economic Geography   In economic geography, the relationship between man's efforts to gain a living and the earth's surface on which they are conducted are correlated. In order to study how man makes a living, the distribution of materials, production, institutions, and human traits and customs are analyzed.

Regional Geography   In regional geography the basic concern is with the salient characteristics of areas. Emphasis is placed upon patterns and elements of the natural environment and their relationships to human activities. By using the regional technique in studying geographic phenomena, what otherwise might be a bewildering array of facts is brought into focus as an organized, cohesive pattern.

Systematic Geography   It is also feasible to study the geography of a small area or the entire surface of the earth in systematic fashion. Settlement, climates, soils, landforms, minerals, water, or crops, among others, may be observed, described, analyzed, and explained. Research in systematic geography has proved to be very valuable.

1. This passage describes geography's

   (1) growth
   (2) scope
   (3) importance
   (4) role in the social sciences
   (5) principles

2. The difference among the five areas of geography described is one of

   (1) method
   (2) importance
   (3) emphasis
   (4) recency
   (5) objectivity

3. A student interested in the influence of a geographical feature of a region on available jobs would study

   (1) physical geography
   (2) cultural geography
   (3) economic geography
   (4) regional geography
   (5) systematic geography

4. A meteorologist would likely be most interested in

   (1) physical geography
   (2) cultural geography
   (3) economic geography
   (4) regional geography
   (5) systematic geography

5. An urban sociologist would probably study

   (1) physical geography
   (2) cultural geography
   (3) economic geography
   (4) regional geography
   (5) systematic geography

6. A person studying the problems of the Middle East will use the approach found in

   (1) physical geography
   (2) cultural geography
   (3) economic geography
   (4) regional geography
   (5) systematic geography

7. A conservationist studying the effects of such human activities as strip mining and land erosion would turn to

   (1) physical geography
   (2) cultural geography
   (3) economic geography
   (4) regional geography
   (5) systematic geography

8. That aspect of geography that seeks to study in a planned and orderly way the geography of a small area is

   (1) physical geography
   (2) cultural geography
   (3) economic geography
   (4) regional geography
   (5) systematic geography

ANSWER KEY

1. **2**   2. **3**   3. **3**   4. **1**   5. **2**   6. **4**
7. **1**   8. **5**

ANSWER ANALYSIS

Four of the questions—3, 6, 7, and 8—deal with definitions. Two call for knowledge of terms in addition to those defined in the passage.

2. **3** Question 2 is a little tricky, but, if you read closely, you will notice that the author uses the words *stress* and *emphasis* in his definitions of the various areas of geography.

Questions 4 and 5 are, in effect, two-step questions. First, you must define the term in the question. Then, you must recall the definition of the area of geography to which it relates.

4. **1** In question 4, you must know that a meteorologist is concerned with weather. Only then can you identify physical geography as his or her primary interest.

5. **2** In this question, you must know that an urban sociologist studies cities, an area of interest to the cultural geographer.

Practice with Interpreting Tables, Graphs, Maps

Since study of the social sciences involves the gathering and interpretation of facts, you will frequently encounter various methods for presenting the facts you need. Most often, these facts will be presented in the form of tables or charts, graphs, or maps. Let us deal with each of these methods in turn.

TABLES

The ability to read tables is an important skill because tables are the most common means of presenting data in the social studies.

What is a table? It is an arrangement of figures, usually in one or more columns, which is intended to show some relationship between the figures. In political science, a table may show the growth of the number of eligible voters in national elections. In economics, a table may show the annual incomes of various groups within the population of a country. A table may also show the relationship between two factors, for example, between the amounts of education of various groups as related to their annual incomes.

First note the title of the table: Sizes, Populations, and Densities of the World's Largest Nations and Regions.

Now, look at the headings of the columns in the table. Six headings are given: Country, Size, Population 1968, Population 1990, People per Square Mile 1968, People per Square Mile 1990.

Next, locate the columns to which each heading is related. In the first column, the different countries or areas of the world are listed. The next column gives their sizes in square miles. The next two columns list population figures for 1968 and 1990, and the last two give the numbers of people per square mile for the same two dates.

Just how do you read a table? First you read the title of the table to determine just what figures are being presented. The title is usually at the top of the column or columns of figures. Let us use the following table as a typical illustration.

Having identified the title, the column headings, and the columns to which they relate, you are now in a position to *locate facts.*

SIZES, POPULATIONS, AND DENSITIES OF THE WORLD'S LARGEST NATIONS AND REGIONS

1	2	3	4	5	6
		Population (U.N. Estimate)		People per Square Mile	
Country	Size (sq. mi.)	1968	1990	1968	1990
USSR*	8,600,000	238,000,000	290,122,000	28	33.5
Canada	3,850,000	21,000,000	26,620,000	5	7.5
China	3,700,000	730,000,000	1,133,000,000	197	306.7
United States	3,600,000	200,000,000	251,394,000	57	68.3
Brazil	3,300,000	88,000,000	150,368,000	27	45.8
India	1,200,000	534,000,000	853,373,000	437	698.0
Other Areas					
Japan	143,000	101,000,000	123,692,000	706	848.0
Southeast Asia	1,692,000	270,000,000	447,000,000	159	262.9
Middle East	3,784,000	261,000,000	306,400,000	69	81.0
Africa— south of the Sahara	8,600,000	254,000,000	500,000,000	30	62.2

Note the great increase of population in the 22 years that separate the two sets of figures. Scientists estimate that the earth's present population will double in the next 50 years sooner.

*Note that "USSR" refers to the all the former republics of the former Soviet Union.

QUESTIONS

1. What is the size of the United States?
2. What was the population of India in 1968? What is the U.N. estimate of the population of India in 1990?
3. What was the number of people per square mile in Japan in 1990?
4. What country's population grew to over 1 billion between 1968 and 1990?

ANSWERS

1. **3,600,000 square miles**
2. **534,000,000   853,373,000**
3. **848.0**
4. **China**

ANSWER ANALYSIS

1. The second column from the left lists sizes. Put your finger at the top of that column, and move it down until you locate the figure on a line with United States—3,600,000.
2. Locate the column for population in 1968. Put your finger at the top of the column, and move it down to the figure on a line with India—534,000,000. Do the same for 1990.
3. Locate the column for people per square mile in 1990. Find the number on a line with Japan—848.0.
4. To answer this question, you have to locate two populations, one in 1968 and one in 1990. You also must locate a figure that is over 1 billion. Scan both columns of population figures. Only one is over 1 billion, that of China in 1990. In the column to the immediate left for 1968, the figure for China's population is 730,000,000, so that figure grew to 1,133,000 in 1990.

Now you are ready to *find relationships between facts.* This type of question requires you to locate one figure and then relate it to at least one other figure.

QUESTIONS

1. What is the basic trend of the world's population?
2. What is the basic trend in the number of people per square mile?
3. From 1968 to 1990, what country or area had the smallest increase in population?

4. In what country or area did the number of people per square mile double?

ANSWERS AND ANALYSIS

1. Compare column 4 (pop. 1990) with column 3 (pop. 1968). In every instance, the population in 1990 is greater. The conclusion can be reached that population is increasing all over the world.
2. Compare column 6 (people per square mile—1990) with column 5 (people per square mile—1968). The conclusion can be reached that the number of people per square mile is increasing all over the world.
3. Subtracting the figures in column 3 (pop. 1968) from those in column 4 (pop. 1990), it is apparent that Canada had the smallest increase, 5,620,000, in population.
4. Comparing the figures in columns 5 and 6 for people per square mile in 1968 and 1990, it is clear that in Africa—south of the Sahara the number of people per square mile more than doubled, from 30 to 62.2.

Now you can proceed to the most difficult skill of all—*inferring conclusions from the facts presented.* Sometimes you can draw a conclusion from the table alone. Other times, you must add facts from your general knowledge.

QUESTIONS

1. What conclusion can you draw from Japan's population figures?
2. What conclusion can you draw about the population in Africa—south of the Sahara?
3. What major problem may exist for Canada's population?
4. What common problems may China, India, and Japan experience?

ANSWERS AND ANALYSIS

1. Japan has the most crowded population in the world, with attendant problems of housing, health, and transportation among others.
2. The half-billion population of Africa—south of the Sahara is spread over 8,600,000 square miles. This fact will result in problems of distribution of goods and services to the countries of the area.

3. A similar problem exits for Canada, with the added possibility that adequate manpower may not be available.

4. The high population density in each country suggests potential difficulty in providing food, shelter, and other essential services to the inhabitants.

SUMMARY OF HOW TO READ A TABLE

1. Note the title.
2. Look at the column headings.
3. Locate the column to which the other columns are related.
4. Locate facts.
5. Find relationships between facts.
6. Infer conclusions from the facts presented.

GRAPHS

THE CIRCLE (PIE) GRAPH

Tables, as you have just seen, are composed of columns of figures selected to show the relationship between facts that the social studies writer considers important. Very often, the author will present these same facts in another way so that you can visualize them more readily and draw conclusions more easily. The writer does this by means of a graph.

Let us look at the following set of facts arranged in a table. They concern the principal religions of the world in the year 1991.

PRINCIPAL RELIGIONS OF THE WORLD, 1991

Buddhist	6%
Christian	33%
Hindu	13%
Islam	18%
No religion	21%
Other	1%
Para-religions	8%

Looking at these facts in table form, you find it hard to draw any ready conclusions. But when you see them in the form of a circle (pie) graph, you are able to immediately visualize the relationships that exist between them.

PRINCIPAL RELIGIONS OF THE WORLD, 1991

LEGEND
- Christian
- Islam
- Hindu
- Buddhist
- Other*
- Para-religions**
- No religion

* Includes Sikh, Jains, Bahai, Shinto, Taoist, and Jewish
** Includes Chinese folk religionists, New-religionists, and tribal religionists

Now use this graph to answer the following questions.

QUESTIONS

1. Which religion has the most followers?
2. Which of the individually named religions has the fewest followers?
3. Which two religions account for more than half of the world's population?
4. Which proportion of the world's people do not practice a religion?

ANSWERS

1. **Christian**
2. **Buddhist**
3. **Islam and Christianity**
4. **21%**

ANSWER ANALYSIS

The answers almost leap up at you from the circle graph. The Christian religion has by far the largest slice of the circle; all of the religions combined under "Other" are hardly visible. By visually combining the various slices of the pie, you can see that the Christian and Islamic religions account for just over half of the total pie. By referring to the legend and then back to the pie, you can see that a large slice of the pie represents people who practice no religion. Just by inspection, you can estimate the number at around one-fifth or 20% of the total. The actual figure (21%) is provided.

The circle graph can also help you to compare visually two sets of facts. Here are a circle graph and a graph of another type (the bar graph).

SHARE OF TOTAL ENERGY, 1995

Note the title—Share of Total Energy, 1995

Note the unit used—percent of 100

Note the date—1995

Note the major categories—petroleum, natural gas, renewable energy, coal, nuclear electric

Study both graphs carefully and answer the following questions.

QUESTIONS

1. What are the most important sources of energy?
2. To reduce our dependence on oil imports, the use of which sources would have to be increased?
3. What percent of total energy does conventional hydroelectric power contribute?

ANSWERS AND ANALYSIS

1. Three sources—petroleum, natural gas, and coal—amount to 70% of total energy.
2. The percents of the other sources—natural gas, coal, renewable energy, and nuclear electric—would have to be increased from their current total of 62%.

3. The circle graph tells you that renewable energy contributes 8% of the total energy consumed. Now look at the bar graph. Conventional hydroelectric power contributes half of renewal energy, or 4% of total energy.

THE LINE GRAPH

This common type of graph shows relationships between facts by plotting points on a coordinate plane (two lines are involved) and connecting them with straight lines.

As an example, let us construct a line graph based on the following data about world population growth between 1650 and 2000 (estimated).

Year	World Population in Millions
1650	550
1750	725
1850	1175
1900	1600
1950	2490
1993	5554
2000 (est.)	6500

To construct the graph, draw a horizontal line and, perpendicular to it, a vertical line. Let:

- the horizontal line (technically known as the *abscissa*) represent the period of years from 1650 to 2000 (est.);
- the vertical line (technically known as the *ordinate*) represent world population.

To plot the line graph, start with the first line of data—year 1650, world population 550 million. Go up the ordinate 550, and place a dot there. Then find the next date, 1750, on the abscissa and go up the ordinate and place a dot opposite 725. Next find the date 1850 on the horizontal line and go up to a point opposite 1175. Place a dot there. Continue to do the same thing for each year on the table. Then draw a straight line from dot to dot to complete the graph.

What can you tell or visualize from this line graph?

World population (millions)

Year

QUESTIONS

1. What is the trend of the world population?
2. What was the world population in 1900?
3. In what 50-year period was the increase the greatest?
4. In the period covered by the graph, approximately how many times did the population grow?

ANSWERS

1. **The trend is sharply upward.**
2. **1600 million.**
3. **1950–2000 (est.).**
4. **About 12 times, from 550 million to 6500 million.**

ANSWER ANALYSIS

1. The plotted line always trends upward, with the slant becoming steeper in recent decades to indicate accelerating population growth.
2. First find the year 1900 on the abscissa. Then move your finger straight up to the point in line with the ordinate indicating the population. The number is 1600 million.
3. The growth is greatest where the line is steepest—between 1950 and 2000 (est.).
4. The population grew from 550 million to 6500 million, or about 12 times.

THE BAR GRAPH

A bar graph is very much like the line graph we just studied. There is the same visual presentation of one set of facts in relation to another set. There is the same horizontal line (*abscissa*) representing one set of facts. The same vertical line (*ordinate*) represents the other set.

For a bar graph, however, you do not put a dot at the point that represents one fact in relation to another, nor do you connect those points by lines. Instead, you make bars of equal width and of heights that indicate the relationship. Thus you could change the line graph you just studied to a bar graph by making a bar for each point identified.

The bar graph below is entitled "Aging Societies." It gives the percentages of population 65 and over for five countries at four different times, two past and two projected. It also indicates by small pie graphs the percentages of health spending in 1993, in each country, for people 65 and over as a share of total health care spending.

AGING SOCIETIES

Source: Organization of Economic Cooperation and Development

Use these graphs to answer the following practice questions.

QUESTIONS

1. In what country will the government have to spend the most in the year 2020 for health care for the aging?

   (1) Japan
   (2) Germany
   (3) France
   (4) Britain
   (5) United States

2. Which country will have the greatest population under 65 in 2020?

   (1) Japan
   (2) Germany
   (3) France
   (4) Britain
   (5) United States

3. Which countries have the most similar aging characteristics?

   (1) Japan and Germany
   (2) Germany and France
   (3) France and Britain
   (4) Britain and the United States
   (5) Japan and the United States

4. Which country will have the least stable growth of population over 65 for the rest of this century?

   (1) Japan
   (2) Germany
   (3) France
   (4) Britain
   (5) United States

5. What country was the least responsive to the health-care needs of its aging population in 1993?

   (1) Japan
   (2) Germany
   (3) France
   (4) Britain
   (5) United States

ANSWER KEY

1. **1**   2. **5**   3. **3**   4. **1**   5. **2**

ANSWER ANALYSIS

1. **1** In 2020, 25% of the population of Japan will be 65 or older, at least 4% more than any other country in the graph.

2. **5** In 2020, the United States will be the only country with an over-65 population below 20%.

3. **3** For France and Britain, percents are nearly identical for 1995, 2000, and 2010. The two countries will have the identical percent of population 65 or older in 2020, and in 1995 differed by less than 1% in percent of health care spending for the elderly as a share of total health-care spending.

4. **1** Japan will have an increase in population over 65. The other countries will remain at the same level.

5. **2** The pie graphs show that Germany spent least, approximately 9 to 10% less than France and Britain, for similar numbers of elderly.

MAPS

A map is a visual representation of all or part of the surface of the earth. A map may or may not include a number of aids to help you visualize the surface it is depicting. It will always include a *title*. If the map uses symbols, it will always include a *legend* (or key) to give the meaning of those symbols. It may also include:

- latitude and longitude to indicate direction and help you to find a specific location;
- a scale of miles to indicate what distance on the map equals a specific distance in miles on land;

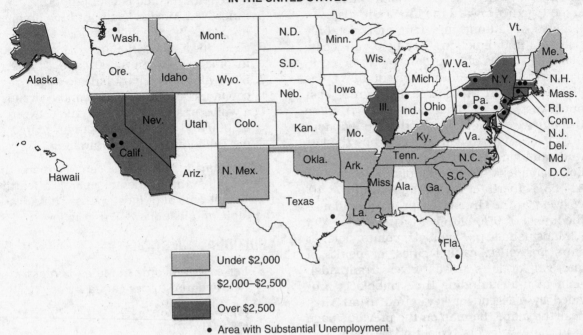

**PER CAPITA INCOME AND UNEMPLOYMENT
IN THE UNITED STATES**

Under $2,000

$2,000–$2,500

Over $2,500

• Area with Substantial Unemployment

• a grid, or square, usually identified by a set of letters on one axis (vertical or horizontal) and a set of numbers on the other, so that a place can be found in, for example, a grid identified as F 3 or H 7;

Important aids that you must learn to use in order to read a map are its *title* and its *legend* (or key). Since ancient times, maps have played a unique role in presenting information about the world, and maps are extremely useful in locating places and distances in any part of the world.

In the 1500s Gerardus Mercator, a Dutch mapmaker, coined the word *atlas* to describe a collection of maps. The atlas is unique because only it, with its maps, actually shows *where* things are located in the world. Only on a map can the countries, cities, roads, rivers, and lakes covering a vast area be seen all at once in their relative locations. Routes between places can be traced, trips planned, boundaries of neighboring countries examined, distances between places measured, and the paths of rivers and the sizes of lakes visualized.

Places can be found by looking up the place name in the index at the back of the atlas. There is usually a letter-number key next to the name of the place, **A3**, for example. This will help you find the place on a grid or square on the map. The letters are usually located to the left or right of the map, the numbers to the top or bottom of the map.

Sometimes, if the place is big enough, you can find it on the map visually.

Distances between places can be figured by using the scale of miles, usually on the bottom of the page.

Place a ruler over the scale to find how many miles a given ruling is, then place the ruler between two places on the map to find the length. For example, if a distance on the scale is 20 miles to one inch and the distance on the map is $1\frac{1}{2}$ inches, the distance is $1\frac{1}{2}$ times 20, or 30 miles between the two points on the map. Determining directions can be done by using a series of lines drawn across the map—the lines of latitude and longitude. Lines of latitude are drawn east and west, from left to right. Lines of longitude are drawn north and south, from top to bottom.

The lines of latitude appear as curved lines; the lines of longitude are straight lines that come together toward the top of the map.

Lines of latitude and longitude not only help you find direction, they help you locate places. Parallels of latitude are numbered in degrees north and south of the equator. Lines of longitude are numbered in degrees east and west of an imaginary line running through Greenwich, England, near London. Any place on earth can be located by the latitude and longitude lines running through it. For example, Chicago, Illinois, is located at 41° 53' N (north of the equator), and 87° 40' W (west of the Greenwich prime meridian—the line of 0° 0' longitude).

Maps usually use symbols, points, dots, or stars (for cities, capital cities, or points of interest), or lines (roads, rivers, railroads). Help in understanding the symbols is provided by a legend or key found in an atlas near the map. The map on the previous page is in many respects typical of the maps you will encounter. The following questions will sharpen your skills in map reading.

QUESTIONS

1. What is the *title* of the map?
2. What three indications make up the *legend*?
3. What does ● mean?
4. What is the average per capita income of the population of the state of New York?
5. What is the average per capita income of the population of the state of New Mexico?
6. What is the average per capita income of the population of the state of Iowa?
7. Which state has a larger per capita income, Alaska or Hawaii?

ANSWERS AND ANALYSIS

1. The title of the map is "Per Capita Income and Unemployment in the United States." See the heading above the map.
2. The dark blue areas indicate per capita income over $2,500; the white areas indicate per capita income between $2,000 and $2,500; the light blue areas indicate per capita income under $2,000.
3. The ● indicates an area with substantial unemployment.

4. Since New York is a dark blue area, its per capita income is over $2,500.
5. Since New Mexico is a light blue area, its per capita income is under $2,000.
6. Since Iowa is a white area, its per capita income is between $2,000 and $2,500.
7. Since Alaska is a dark blue area (per capita income over $2,500) and Hawaii is a white area (per capita income between $2,000 and $2,500), Alaska has a larger per capita income than Hawaii.

This map introduces a complication, the idea of substantial unemployment, a feature that is not typical of most maps. That idea is the topic of questions 3–7 that follow.

ADDITIONAL QUESTIONS

1. Per capita income in Maine is most nearly equal to per capita income in

   (1) Washington
   (2) Idaho
   (3) Utah
   (4) Nevada
   (5) Missouri

2. Which generalization is best supported by the map?

   (1) All New England states have per capita incomes of over $2,000.
   (2) All states along the Atlantic seaboard have a high per capita income.
   (3) All southern states have incomes below $2,000.
   (4) All states along the Pacific coast have per capita incomes of $2,000 or over.
   (5) Most states have per capita incomes over $2,500.

3. According to the map, in which state is unemployment a major problem?

   (1) Pennsylvania
   (2) Florida
   (3) Alabama
   (4) Texas
   (5) Washington

4. Which state has both a per capita income of between $2,000 and $2,500, and an area with substantial unemployment?

   (1) Kansas
   (2) Ohio
   (3) Kentucky
   (4) Mississippi
   (5) California

5. Which state has a high per capita income and substantial unemployment?

   (1) Florida
   (2) Louisiana
   (3) Minnesota
   (4) California
   (5) Nevada

6. Unemployment is less of a problem in Indiana than in

   (1) Massachusetts
   (2) Tennessee
   (3) Mississippi
   (4) Louisiana
   (5) Arizona

7. Which conclusion concerning the state of Tennessee is supported by the map?

   (1) It is larger than Montana and richer than Mississippi.
   (2) It has more unemployment than Georgia and was richer than Kentucky.
   (3) It is as rich as Arkansas and poorer than Nevada.
   (4) It had less unemployment than Oklahoma and more unemployment than Georgia.
   (5) It is smaller than Minnesota and richer than Illinois.

ANSWER KEY

1. **2**   2. **4**   3. **1**   4. **2**   5. **4**   6. **1**
7. **3**

ANSWER ANALYSIS

1. **2** The answer is Choice 2 since both states are light blue areas, with per capita incomes under $2,000.

2. **4** Choice 4 is correct. California had a per capita income of over $2,500; Washington and Oregon had incomes between $2,000 and $2,500; all have incomes of $2,000 or over per capita. Choice 1 is incorrect since Maine has an income of less than $2,000. Choice 2 is wrong since three states—North Carolina, South Carolina, and Georgia—have incomes lower than $2,000. Choice 3 is incorrect since Texas, Florida, and Virginia have incomes above $2,000. Choice 5 is incorrect; only 10 states have per capita incomes over $2,500.

3. **1** On the map, Pennsylvania has six dotted areas with substantial unemployment; Florida, Washington, and Texas have one each and Alabama has none. Choice 1 is correct.

4. **2** You have to find a white area with a dot. Only Ohio, Choice 2, fits these criteria.

5. **4** You have to find a dark blue area with several dots. Only California, Choice 4, fits this description.

6. **1** You need to locate a state with more than one dot since Indiana has one such dot. The correct answer is Choice 1, Massachusetts, which has two dots.

7. **3** The map compares Tennessee with other states with regard to per capita income *and* unemployment. Choice 1 is wrong since Montana is larger. Choice 2 is wrong since Tennessee is not richer than Kentucky but the same. Choice 4 is wrong since Tennessee has more unemployment than both Oklahoma and Georgia. Choice 5 is incorrect since Tennessee is poorer than Illinois. Choice 3 is correct; both Tennessee and Arkansas have per capita incomes of less than $2,000, while Nevada has a per capita income of over $2,500.

Now it is time for further practice. The following practice exercises will give you ample preparation in reading tables, graphs, and maps for the GED Examination.

ADDITIONAL PRACTICE WITH TABLES, GRAPHS, AND MAPS

Read each of the following questions carefully. Select the best answer.

Questions 1–4 are based on the following map.

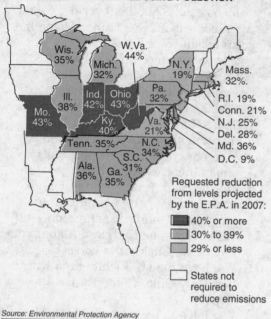

NEW GOALS FOR REDUCING POLLUTION

Requested reduction from levels projected by the E.P.A. in 2007:

- ■ 40% or more
- ▓ 30% to 39%
- ▒ 29% or less

- □ States not required to reduce emissions

Source: Environmental Protection Agency

1. According to the map, the state that probably will have the most pollution is

   (1) Missouri
   (2) Indiana
   (3) Ohio
   (4) Kentucky
   (5) West Virginia

2. The states that have exactly similar goals in the reduction of pollution are

   (1) Michigan, Pennsylvania, Massachusetts
   (2) Missouri, Indiana, Ohio
   (3) Alabama, Georgia, South Carolina
   (4) Virginia, Connecticut, Maryland
   (5) New York, Rhode Island, New Jersey

3. The area with the lowest requested reduction in pollution is

   (1) Virginia
   (2) District of Columbia
   (3) Rhode Island
   (4) New York
   (5) Connecticut

4. Pollution appears to be lowest in the region of

   (1) the Midwest
   (2) the Great Lakes
   (3) the Southeast
   (4) the Middle Atlantic States
   (5) the Deep South

Questions 5–11 are based on the following graphs.

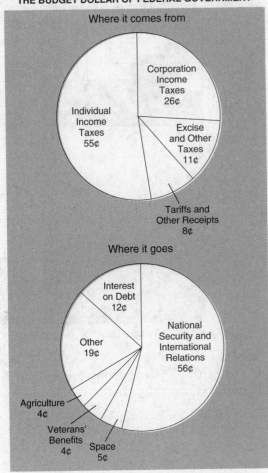

THE BUDGET DOLLAR OF FEDERAL GOVERNMENT

Where it comes from

Corporation Income Taxes 26¢

Individual Income Taxes 55¢

Excise and Other Taxes 11¢

Tariffs and Other Receipts 8¢

Where it goes

Interest on Debt 12¢

Other 19¢

National Security and International Relations 56¢

Agriculture 4¢

Veterans' Benefits 4¢

Space 5¢

5. Forty-five percent of the national income is derived from

(1) individual income taxes, excise taxes, and tariffs
(2) corporation income taxes, excise taxes, and tariffs
(3) individual income taxes, corporation income taxes, and excise taxes
(4) individual income taxes, corporation income taxes, and tariffs
(5) individual income taxes and excise taxes

6. The largest amount of the national income is expended on

(1) health and welfare
(2) national security and international relations
(3) space
(4) interest on debt
(5) veterans' benefits

7. The two areas on which equal amounts of the national income are expended are

(1) agriculture and veterans' benefits
(2) space and agriculture
(3) health and welfare and interest on debt
(4) veterans' benefits and space
(5) space and all others

8. The amount of income received from the collection of excise and other taxes approximately equals the amount expended for

(1) interest on debt
(2) health and welfare
(3) space
(4) agriculture
(5) veterans' benefits

9. What is the biggest source of income for the federal government?

(1) tariffs
(2) excise taxes
(3) corporation taxes
(4) individual income taxes
(5) other receipts

10. The combined expenditure for agriculture and veterans' benefits equals that for the income category entitled

(1) excise and other taxes
(2) health and welfare
(3) interest on debt
(4) tariffs and other receipts
(5) national security

11. The income from individual income taxes most nearly equals the expenditure for

(1) national security and international relations
(2) health and welfare
(3) space
(4) veterans' benefits
(5) all others

Questions 12–15 are based on the following graphs.

12. According to the graphs, the population census takes place

   (1) every 10 years
   (2) every 20 years
   (3) every 30 years
   (4) every 50 years
   (5) irregularly

13. The 1990 census reveals that the largest age group is that between

   (1) 5 and 15
   (2) 15 and 25
   (3) 25 and 35
   (4) 35 and 45
   (5) 45 and 55

14. The birth to 5-year group is larger in each census than the

   (1) 5 to 15
   (2) 35 to 45
   (3) 45 to 55
   (4) 65 to 75
   (5) over 75

15. The group that will have grown the most in percentage between 1950 and 2010 is the

   (1) 5 to 15
   (2) 15 to 25
   (3) 25 to 35
   (4) 35 to 45
   (5) over 75

COASTAL LANDS AT RISK

If sea levels rose by 20 inches by the year 2100, as scientists expect, coastal areas would be at risk. Here are some examples of shoreline losses, in square miles.

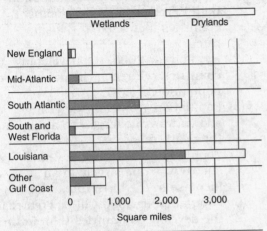

The New York Times

WHERE THE POPULATION GROWS FASTEST
Total world population in billions

*Projected

Source: The Washington Post, July 1990 (adapted)

16. According to the graph, if sea levels rose 20 inches by the year 2100, the coastal lands that would be most affected are in

    (1) the South Atlantic
    (2) the Mid-Atlantic
    (3) Louisiana
    (4) Other Gulf Coast
    (5) Florida

17. The coastal drylands that would be most affected are in the

    (1) Mid-Atlantic
    (2) South Atlantic
    (3) South and West Florida
    (4) Other Gulf Coast
    (5) New England

18. Which statement is true, according to the graph?

    (1) The northeast United States would be more affected than the Gulf Coast.
    (2) The East Coast would be more affected than the Gulf Coast.
    (3) The Gulf Coast would be the hardest hit.
    (4) Generally the wetlands would be affected more than the drylands.
    (5) The shoreline is greater on the Atlantic than on the Gulf.

19. Which statement is best supported by the data in the graph?

    (1) The rate of world population growth has begun to decrease.
    (2) The world's population tripled between 1970 and 1989.
    (3) Most of the world's population lives in economically developing countries.
    (4) The population of economically developed countries consumes most of the world's resources.
    (5) The world is nearing zero population growth.

20. Which factor best accounts for the difference in the growth rate between developing and developed countries as shown in the graph?

    (1) increased family planning in developed countries
    (2) increasing pollution in developed countries
    (3) the breakdown of extended families in developing countries
    (4) the rise of single-parent families throughout the world
    (5) the greater likelihood of wars in developing countries

21. The greatest difference in population growth between developing and developed countries took place (or will take place) in the year

    (1) 1980
    (2) 1989
    (3) 2000
    (4) 2010
    (5) 2020

Questions 22–24 are based on the following graphs.

DEVELOPED COUNTRIES

DEVELOPING COUNTRIES

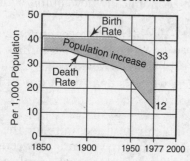

RATE OF POPULATION INCREASE = BIRTH RATE – DEATH RATE
Source: United Nations Population Division

22. Which statement is best supported by the information in the graphs?

    (1) In the years shown, population in both developed and developing countries increased at the same rate.
    (2) By the year 2000, the developing countries will reach the point of zero population growth.
    (3) Population growth in the years shown was due largely to a drop in the death rate.
    (4) Population growth in the years shown was due largely to an increase in the birth rate.
    (5) Population in 2000 will be greater in the developed countries than in the developing countries.

23. According to the graphs, in the developed countries

    (1) the birth rate surpassed the death rate for the years shown
    (2) the death rate surpassed the birth rate for the years shown
    (3) the population is growing at an increased rate
    (4) the birth rate is increasing
    (5) the death rate is increasing

24. According to the graphs, a comparison of developed and developing countries shows that

    (1) the birth rate and the death rate have always been greater in the developing countries
    (2) only the birth rate has been greater in the developing countries
    (3) only the death rate has been greater in the developing countries
    (4) birth and death rates have been similar in both
    (5) population increases have been similar in both

Questions 25–30 are based on the following illustration.

THE MILLIONS UPROOTED: WHERE THE REFUGEES HUDDLE

Bosnia and Herzegovina
Over 2 million

Turkey
500,000 to 2 million

Iraq
1 million

Iran
Over 2.5 million

Azerbaijan
500,000

Afghanistan
1.2 million

Middle East
Over 3 million

Pakistan
1.2 million

Algeria
195,000

Nepal
110,000

Mexico
32,000

Guinea
420,000

Sudan
400,000;
4 million
internally
displaced

Thailand
115,000

Colombia
900,000

Myanmar
1 million

Sierra Leone and Liberia
Over 800,000

Sri Lanka
1 million

Ivory Coast
300,000

Ethiopia
340,000

India
Over 250,000

Angola
1.2 million

Uganda
265,000

Congo
330,000

Burundi
1 million

Foreign refugees
Internally displaced refugees
Both

Source: United Nations Commissioner for Refugees

The New York Times

25. According to the map, the country with the largest number of foreign refugees is

(1) Algeria
(2) Congo
(3) Azerbaijan
(4) Uganda
(5) Iran

26. The country with the largest number of internally displaced refugees is

(1) Sudan
(2) Angola
(3) Afghanistan
(4) Pakistan
(5) Myanmar

27. The European country with the largest number of refugees is

(1) Turkey
(2) France
(3) Italy
(4) Bosnia
(5) Greece

28. The number of countries that have over 1 million refugees is

(1) 3
(2) 5
(3) 6
(4) 8
(5) 10

29. The continent with the fewest number of refugees is

(1) North America
(2) South America
(3) Europe
(4) Africa
(5) Asia

30. The country for which the number of refugees is least precise is

(1) Colombia
(2) Algeria
(3) Turkey
(4) Nepal
(5) Thailand

Questions 31–33 are based on the following graph.

SOURCES OF UNITED STATES ENERGY

Total Oil = 40.6%

Figures represent estimated percentage of sources for U.S. energy consumption in 1986.

Source: U.S. Department of Energy

Questions 34–35 are based on the following graph.

HEALTH CARE IN THE UNITED STATES

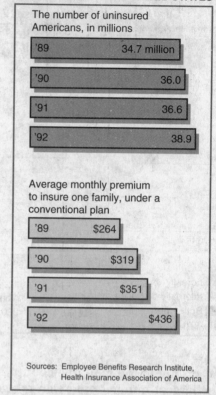

Sources: Employee Benefits Research Institute, Health Insurance Association of America

31. According to the graph,

    (1) oil contributes more to U.S. energy than coal and natural gas
    (2) OPEC (Arab) oil is the smallest contributor to U.S. energy
    (3) OPEC oil exceeds non-OPEC oil as a source of U.S. energy
    (4) natural gas is the largest single source of U.S. energy
    (6) hydro energy and nuclear energy exceed foreign oil as sources of U.S. energy

32. According to the graph, the largest single source of U.S. energy is

    (1) coal
    (2) natural gas
    (3) domestic oil
    (4) nuclear and hydro
    (5) OPEC and non-OPEC foreign oil

33. It can be inferred from the graph that foreign sources account for what percentage of U.S. energy?

    (1) 27.3%
    (2) 26.4%
    (3) 22.3%
    (4) 13.3%
    (5) 10.2%

34. According to the graph, the most valid conclusion that can be drawn is that

    (1) health care is not available for most Americans
    (2) the number of Americans not insured for health has reached a peak
    (3) the premiums for conventional plans for health care cannot be afforded by most Americans
    (4) health care is becoming less available and more costly to American families
    (5) the rate of increases in health care costs is declining

35. The average monthly premium to insure one family

    (1) had its greatest increase from 1989 to 1990
    (2) had its greatest increase from 1990 to 1991
    (3) had its greatest increase from 1991 to 1992
    (4) saw a decrease in the rate of increases
    (5) increased at a rate of 50% in the four-year period 1989–1992

Questions 36–37 are based on the following graph.

PERCENTAGES OF WORKERS WITH YEAR-ROUND FULL-TIME JOBS

Census Bureau

36. According to the graph, during the period shown:

    (1) the number of men working full time increased dramatically.
    (2) the number of women working full time increased dramatically.
    (3) the number of men working full time fell slightly.
    (4) the total number of men and women working full time leveled off.
    (5) the total number of men and women working full time decreased.

37. From the figures given in the graph, there probably was a recession in the years

    (1) 1967–1973
    (2) 1974–1978
    (3) 1979–1985
    (4) 1985–1990
    (5) 1991–1996

Questions 38–40 are based on the following chart.

ECONOMIC AND SOCIAL PROFILES OF SELECTED COUNTRIES—EAST ASIA

	Populations (Millions est.)		Per Capita Income	GNP (billions of dollars)	Literacy Rate (%)		Doubling Population Time (Years)
	1976	1990	1989	1989	1976	1992	
Japan	113	124	23,730	2,920	99	100	exceeds 100
Korea (South)	36	43.2	4,400	186.5	88.5	96	70
Korea (North)	16	21.8	1,240	28	NA	95	38
China (Peoples Republic)	852	1,150	360	393	40	73	48
Taiwan (Republic of China)	16.3	20.5	7,480	150	86	94	61

Source: *Encyclopedia Britannica Book of the Year 1992*

38. Which of the following is true according to the chart?

    (1) Taiwan leads China in both per capita income and literacy rate.
    (2) Taiwan is the least populated country.
    (3) North Korea is wealthier than South Korea.
    (4) South Korea leads China in GNP.
    (5) The population of North Korea showed the least growth between 1976 and 1990.

39. The country with the greatest increase in population and literacy rate is

    (1) Japan
    (2) North Korea
    (3) South Korea
    (4) China
    (5) Taiwan

40. Individuals are benefiting most from the GNP in

    (1) Japan
    (2) North Korea
    (3) South Korea
    (4) China
    (5) Taiwan

WHAT'S YOUR SCORE?

_____right, _____wrong

Excellent	36–40
Good	32–35
Fair	28–31

If you scored lower, you may need more review. Reread the section, "Practice with Interpreting Tables, Graphs, Maps" (page 253), and try again.

ANSWER ANALYSIS

1. **5** West Virginia has a proposed level of 44%, the highest percentage indicated.
2. **1** All three states have levels of 32%.
3. **2** The District of Columbia, at 9%, has by far the lowest projected level of pollution.
4. **4** The Middle Atlantic states, with the exception of Maryland have projected levels of pollution of less than 30%.
5. **2** These three sources provide 26%, 11%, and 8%, respectively, for a total of 45%.
6. **2** National security and international relations represent 56% of the national expenditure.
7. **1** Four percent is expended on each.
8. **1** Excise and other taxes bring in 11%, 12% is spent on interest on debt.
9. **4** Fifty-five percent of federal income comes from individual income taxes.
10. **4** These add up to 8%, the amount received from tariffs and other receipts.
11. **1** Income from individual income taxes is 55%; expenditure for national security and international relations is 56%.
12. **2** The titles of the bar graphs are the 1950 census, 1970 census, 1990 census, and 2010 census; here is a 20-year gap between them.
13. **3** Over 40 million persons are between 25 and 35.
14. **5** In each census, there are more in the birth to 5-year group than the over-75 group.
15. **2** The 15 to 25 age group will grow from 21% to 46%, more than any other age group.
16. **3** Louisiana would lose about 3600 square miles, at least 1000 square miles more than anywhere else.
17. **2** The loss to South Atlantic drylands would constitute about 900 square miles, hundreds of square miles more than the Mid-Atlantic and South and West Florida.
18. **3** The Gulf Coast and Louisiana would lose about 4300 square miles, the total of all the other areas combined.
19. **3** The graph shows that most of the world's population lives in economically developing nations. In 1989, 4.03 billion, of a total world population of 5.23 billion, or 80% of the total, lived in developing nations.
20. **1** Inspection of the figures shows that the growth rate is higher in developing than in developed nations; people in developing nations have less access to family-planning assistance.
21. **5** In 2020, the gap as shown in the graph is 6.94 minus 1.35 or 5.59 billions, greater than for any other year.
22. **3** While the graph for developed countries shows a steady balance between declining birth and death rates, the graph for developing countries shows a relative population increase that grows from about 1875 to the present because the death rate drops more and more compared with the birth rate.
23. **1** The birth rate line is consistently above the death rate line.
24. **1** The birth rate and the death rate lines for the developing countries have always been higher than those for the developed countries.
25. **5** Iran has over 2.5 million foreign refugees. The other choices all have fewer than half a million.
26. **1** Sudan has 4 million internally displaced persons.
27. **4** Bosnia has over 2 million internally displaced refugees.
28. **5** The following countries have over 1 million refugees—Angola, Iraq, Burundi, Sudan, Sri Lanka, Iran, Afghanistan, Pakistan, Myanmar, and Bosnia.
29. **1** Only Mexico in North America has refugees, and they total 32,000.
30. **3** Turkey's refugee population is indicated as having a range between 500,000 to 2 million.
31. **2** OPEC (Arab) oil, contrary to popular belief, is the smallest contributor to United States energy, 2.3%.
32. **3** Domestic oil counts for 27.3% of United States energy.
33. **4** 13.3% is the total of OPEC and non-OPEC contributions.
34. **4** Health care is becoming less available because fewer and fewer people have insurance and each year it gets more costly for a family.

35. **3** The increase was $85 a month per family—$351 to $436.
36. **2** The percentage of women working full time in 1976 was 40%. In 1996, it was 55%, an increase of 15% in 20 years. The percentage of men in the same period of time grew half as much, from 62% to 70%.
37. **2** The percentage of both men and women working dropped visibly in the years 1974–1978, to 62% and 40%, respectively, from consistently higher levels prior to that period, probably because fewer jobs were available.
38. **1** Inspection of the chart shows that per capita income in Taiwan is 7480, many times that in China, 360. Taiwan had literacy rates of 86 in 1976 and 94 in 1992, much higher than those of China for the same dates.
39. **4** The population of China grew from 852 to 1150 and the literacy rate grew from 40% to 73%; these increases were greater than than those of any other country listed.
40. **1** Japan has a per capita income far greater than that of any other country in the chart. The same is true for its gross national product.

Basics in Interpreting Political Cartoons

Political cartoons, as a distinct art form, first became important in the second half of the nineteenth century. Two cartoonists, in particular, achieved great fame during that period.

Thomas Nast, of *Harper's Weekly*, attacked Tammany Hall in 1869, when Boss Tweed and his Ring were in control of New York City. His most famous cartoon, "The Tammany Tiger Loose—'What are you going to do about it?'" led to the voting out of Ring officials and Tweed's conviction and jailing for grand larceny. This cartoon is on page 273.

Joseph Keppler, who founded *Puck*, the first humorous weekly in the United States, used color to powerful effect in his cartoons. A famous cartoon, "Bosses of the Senate," attacked the financial interests represented in the U.S. Senate. This cartoon is on page 273.

1. Most cartoons deal with a single important issue, usually an election campaign issue, questions of peace or war, or corruption in government.
2. The cartoonist frequently uses an exaggerated likeness, or caricature, of some well-known person or institution, for example, Uncle Sam, as the main focus of attention. Or he or she may use or create a familiar symbol to represent an important idea; a dove for peace, a tiger for Tammany Hall.
3. Reading is kept to a minimum so that the appeal is largely visual. A few words at most are used to drive home an idea, so the visual appeal of the political cartoon is universal. Boss Tweed pointed out that, even if his followers could not read, they could "look at the d___n pictures." Thus the cartoonist presents an issue in simplified form, stripped of all relatively unimportant details, in a way that his readers can understand.
4. The cartoonist graphically presents his or her own point of view or that of a newspaper or magazine. The cartoonist is usually openly anticorruption or anti-war, and portrays the object of his or her criticism in the ugliest manner possible.

Because of the visually appealing use of a caricature and/or a symbol focusing critically on a single important issue, the political cartoon is a powerful means of shaping public opinion. Its appeal to the emotions is difficult to equal, and its influence continues to the present day.

How, then, do you interpret a political cartoon when you encounter it on the High School Equivalency Examination?

Here are a few suggestions, using the Nast and Keppler cartoons.

Step 1. *Identify the caricatures or symbols used in the cartoon.* For historical cartoons, you may need some social studies background. In contemporary cartoons, the caricatures and symbols are easier to identify.

In the Nast cartoon, Boss Tweed, sitting in the gallery under the standard reading TAMMANY SPOILS, is a symbol of political power. The tiger represents Tammany Hall, the corrupt political club, and the woman in the tiger's claws is the dead Republic surrounded by the breakdown of law and the destroyed democratic freedom of the ballot.

Step 2. *Identify the issue being exposed or criticized by the cartoonist.* In the case of Nast, it is the undermining of the democratic process by a corrupt political boss and his cronies. In the Keppler cartoon, it is the taking over of the U.S. Senate by monopolies and trusts.

Step 3. *Determine the point of view being expressed by the cartoonist.* In the Nast cartoon, the snarl on the face of the tiger and the exaggerated size of Boss Tweed show how vicious the cartoonist considers the political boss, his organization (the Tweed Ring), and Tammany Hall to be. In the Keppler cartoon, the bloated stomachs of the trusts and their ugly facial expressions convey the cartoonist's disgust.

Now turn to a third cartoon, study it, and try to answer the questions based on it.

QUESTIONS

1. What issue is the subject of this cartoon?
2. What do the elephant and the donkey represent?
3. What is each trying to do?
4. What point of view is the cartoonist expressing?

ANSWERS AND ANALYSIS

1. The issue is campaign-funding abuse, as indicated on the cookie jar.
2. The elephant is the traditional symbol of the Republican party; the donkey, of the Democratic party.
3. Each has a hand in the cookie jar and is trying to extract money for the campaign.
4. The cartoonist finds both parties at fault even though he portrays the equally guilty Republicans expressing disapproval of the Democrats.

Practice with Interpreting Political Cartoons

1. The main purpose of Mike Thompson's cartoon is to

   (1) portray the conflict between Republicans and Democrats
   (2) show the superiority of the Republicans over the Democrats
   (3) show the superiority of the Democrats over the Republicans
   (4) show that Republicans and Democrats are both at fault in campaign fund-raising
   (5) show that Democrats do not feel guilty about their campaign fund-raising

2. The cartoonist achieves his purpose by

   (1) exaggerating the conduct of both parties
   (2) arousing our sympathy for both parties
   (3) portraying the humor of the conduct of both parties
   (4) favoring Republicans over Democrats
   (5) showing the irony of the Republicans' conduct

4. What is the main idea of the cartoon?

   (1) Labor camps remain China's primary method of punishing political prisoners.
   (2) The Chinese consider the United States an ungrateful trading partner.
   (3) Economic development in China has been achieved by ignoring human rights issues.
   (4) The Chinese believe that human rights are unimportant to the United States.
   (5) The United States should benefit from the cheap prices of Chinese products.

3. What is the main idea of the cartoon?

   (1) Families that watch television are the most informed about politics.
   (2) The speeches of candidates often fail to attract the voters' attention.
   (3) More voters should watch cable television.
   (4) Television networks are not acting in politically responsible ways.
   (5) Families approve of television coverage of political campaigns.

ANSWER ANALYSIS

1. **4** Choice 4 is correct because the cartoonist indicates that both parties have their hands in the cookie jar and are guilty of campaign fund-raising abuses. Neither party is superior to the other, nor does either feel guilty.

2. **5** The irony arises from the fact that each party has a hand in the jar, yet the Republican elephant is faulting the Democratic donkey for an abuse of which both are equally guilty.

3. **2** Although the viewers approve of free air time for presidential candidates, they ignore the candidates and view other programs.

4. **3** Labor camps in China violate the human rights of the Chinese who are not free to leave, work long hours under extremely poor conditions, and receive little wages.

5. **3** Since the popular vote is sometimes not reflected in the electoral college vote, the value of the vote of the American citizenry is diminished.

6. **4** Though there is some benefit in the increase of the minimum wage, the gap between the wage and the cost of living is still very large so the benefit is merely a token benefit.

5. What is the main idea of the cartoon?

   (1) The electoral college has more value now than it did in the past.
   (2) Only Congress should have the power to elect a president.
   (3) The electoral college decreases the value of a citizen's vote.
   (4) Free elections in the United States have almost disappeared.
   (5) The electorate chooses the electoral college.

6. The point of view expressed in this cartoon is that the 1997 increase in the minimum wage would

   (1) significantly reduce the gap between the rich and the poor
   (2) encourage the poor to appreciate the concern of politicians
   (3) help workers climb the ladder of success
   (4) be unlikely to provide any major benefit to the poor
   (5) lower taxes for workers

Practice with Interpreting Historical Documents

Interpreting historical documents means reading them carefully and deciding what is the main purpose behind the document. Sometimes you are simply asked from what the document text was taken. Pay close attention to any vocabulary words that may be mentioned in the text; these may be included in the questions to follow. Many questions ask "which of the following EXCEPT." In cases like these, eliminate the choices that ARE examples of the statement. Then choose the one best answer that is NOT an example.

DOCUMENT 1

THE DECLARATION OF INDEPENDENCE

When in the Course human events it becomes necessary for one people to dissolve the political bonds which have connected them with another, and to assume among the powers of the earth, the separate and equal station to which the Laws of Nature and of Nature's God entitle them, a decent respect to the opinions of mankind requires that they should declare the causes which impel them to the separation.

We hold these truths to be self-evident, that all men are created equal, that they are endowed by their Creator with certain unalienable Rights, that among these are Life, Liberty and the pursuit of Happiness. That to secure these rights, Governments are instituted among Men, deriving their just powers from the consent of the governed. That whenever any Form of Government becomes destructive of these ends, it is the Right of the People to alter or to abolish it, and to institute new Government, laying its foundation on such principles and organizing it's powers in such form, as to them shall seem most likely to effect their Safety and Happiness.

QUESTIONS

1. The main purpose of the Declaration of Independence is to

   (1) justify separation from another government
   (2) obey laws of nature
   (3) earn a decent respect for others' opinions
   (4) influence the course of human events
   (5) join the powers of the earth

2. All of the following rights are included EXCEPT

   (1) life
   (2) liberty
   (3) pursuit of happiness
   (4) equal opportunity
   (5) safety

3. The Declaration states that governments derive their powers from

   (1) the powers of the earth
   (2) the Laws of Nature
   (3) the Laws of Nature's God
   (4) the opinions of mankind
   (5) the governed

ANSWER KEY

1. **1**   2. **4**   3. **5**

ANSWER ANALYSIS

1. **1** The Declaration states that "a decent respect to the opinions of mankind requires that (a people) should declare the causes which impel them to the separation."
2. **4** All the rights are mentioned except equal opportunity, although that might be interpreted as being included in the pursuit of happiness.
3. **5** It is stated that governments derive "their just powers from the consent of the governed."

DOCUMENT 2

UNITED STATES CONSTITUTION
Amendment VI

In all criminal prosecutions, the accused shall enjoy the right to a speedy and public trial, by an impartial jury of the State and district wherein the crime shall have been committed, which district shall have been previously ascertained by law, and to be informed of the nature and cause of the accusation; to be confronted with the witnesses against him; to have compulsory process for obtaining witnesses in his favor, and to have the Assistance of Counsel for his defense.

QUESTIONS

1. The above passage is

    (1) part of the Declaration of Independence
    (2) part of the Bill of Rights of the Constitution
    (3) part of the Articles of Confederation
    (4) part of the Preamble to the Constitution
    (5) a requirement of the Supreme Court

2. The amendment requires that an accused should have all of the following EXCEPT

    (1) counsel for the defense
    (2) a jury from the state where the crime took place
    (3) witnesses in his favor
    (4) reasons for the trial
    (5) a confidential trial

3. The amendment enumerates the

    (1) civil rights of accused criminals
    (2) responsibilities of the federal government
    (3) duties of the witnesses
    (4) duties of the defense counsel
    (5) duties of the courts

ANSWER KEY

1. **2**   2. **5**   3. **1**

ANSWER ANALYSIS

1. **2** The passage is Amendment VI of the United States Constitution and part of the Bill of Rights.

2. **5** The first four choices are rights of the accused criminal. The last, Choice 5, is prohibited. A speedy and public trial must take place.

3. **1** The amendment gives the civil rights of the accused criminal: a speedy and public trial; an impartial jury, a knowledge of the reasons for his accusation, the right to confront witnesses against him, the right to have witnesses for him, the right to a defense counsel.

DOCUMENT 3

"In the discussions to which this interest has given rise, and in the arrangements by which they may terminate, the occasion has been deemed proper for asserting as a principle in which rights and interests of the United States are involved, that the American continents, by the free and independent condition which they have assumed and maintain, are henceforth not to be considered as subjects for future colonization by any European power. . . . We owe it, therefore, to candor and to the amicable relations existing between the United States and those powers to declare that we should consider any attempt on their part to extend their system to any portion of this hemisphere as dangerous to our peace and safety. With the existing colonies or dependencies of any European power we have not interfered and shall not interfere. But with the governments who have declared their independence and maintain it, and whose independence we have, on great consideration and on just principles, acknowledged, we could not view any interposition for the purpose of oppressing them or controlling in any other manner their destiny by any European power in any other light than as the manifestation of an unfriendly disposition toward the United States."

QUESTIONS

1. The statement that "the American continents . . . are henceforth not to be considered as subjects for future colonization by any European power" is known as

   (1) the Declaration of Independence
   (2) Washington's Message to Congress
   (3) the Articles of Confederation
   (4) the Monroe Doctrine
   (5) the Truman Doctrine

2. The United States would

   (1) retaliate if colonized
   (2) interfere with existing European colonies
   (3) ignore the actions of European powers
   (4) view colonization as an unfriendly act
   (5) break off relations with the interfering European power

3. The passage states that this statement of policy is based on

   (1) the freedom and independence the United States has maintained
   (2) the friendly relations between it and European powers
   (3) its success as a colony
   (4) its right to interfere with European powers
   (5) its control of its destiny

ANSWER KEY

1. **4**   2. **4**   3. **1**

ANSWER ANALYSIS

1. **4** The statement is known as the Monroe Doctrine announced to Congress by President James Monroe on December 2, 1823.
2. **4** The message mentions "an unfriendly disposition" as a consequence.
3. **1** The justification for the doctrine is maintaining the "free and independent condition of the United States."

DOCUMENT 4

UNIVERSAL DECLARATION OF HUMAN RIGHTS
Preamble

Whereas recognition of the inherent dignity and of the equal and inalienable rights of all members of the human family is the foundation of freedom, justice and peace in the world,

Whereas disregard and contempt for human rights have resulted in barbarous acts which have outraged the conscience of mankind, and the advent of a world in which human beings shall enjoy freedom of speech and belief and freedom from fear and want has been proclaimed as the highest aspiration of the common people,

Whereas it is essential, if man is not to be compelled to have recourse, as a last resort, to rebellion against tyranny and oppression, that human rights should be protected by the rule of law,

Whereas the people of the United Nations have in the Charter reaffirmed their faith in fundamental human rights, in the dignity and worth of the human person and in the equal rights of men and women and have determined to promote social progress and better standards of life in larger freedom,

Now, Therefore, The General Assembly proclaims...

This Universal Declaration of Human Rights...

QUESTIONS

1. The Preamble states that the rule of law can

   (1) prevent barbarous acts
   (2) prevent contempt for human rights
   (3) outrage the world's conscience
   (4) disregard human rights
   (5) prevent rebellion against tyranny

2. The purposes of the Universal Declaration are to do all of the following EXCEPT

   (1) protect human rights
   (2) promote freedom of speech
   (3) achieve freedom from fear
   (4) prevent war
   (5) promote social progress

3. The Declaration has as its justification all of the following EXCEPT

    (1) equal rights of men and women
    (2) observance of fundamental freedoms
    (3) justice in the world
    (4) rebellion against tyranny
    (5) dignity and worth of all peoples

ANSWER KEY

1. **5**   2. **4**   3. **4**

ANSWER ANALYSIS

1. **5** It states that the protection of the rule of law will make unnecessary recourse to rebellion against tyranny.
2. **4** War is not mentioned in the Preamble.
3. **4** Rebellion against tyranny is mentioned only as a last resort.

Practice with Interpreting Photographs

Interpreting historical photographs means studying them carefully and deciding what is the main purpose behind the photograph. Sometimes you are simply asked from what location the photograph was taken. Pay close attention to every person and item in the photograph. Other questions ask you to identify the photo. Most important, you may be asked the purpose behind the photograph (why it was taken or why it is famous). Take time to analyze the photograph. Identify key political figures, if any, location, and important subjects in the photograph. All of these are important clues to the meaning behind the photograph.

PHOTOGRAPH 1

QUESTION

1. This photograph was taken

    (1) in a courtroom
    (2) at an open air debate
    (3) at a political campaign rally
    (4) a sports event
    (5) a celebration

ANSWER ANALYSIS

1. **3** The photograph was taken of President Theodore Roosevelt at a political rally.

PHOTOGRAPH 2

QUESTION

2. This is a photograph of

   (1) a business meeting
   (2) a presidential meeting
   (3) a questioning of a witness
   (4) a public trial
   (5) a political confrontation

ANSWER ANALYSIS

2. **2** President Harry Truman, who succeeded Franklin D. Roosevelt, meets with government officials.

PHOTOGRAPH 3

QUESTION

3. The purpose of this photograph is to depict

   (1) the illegal use of child labor
   (2) factory conditions
   (3) a strict foreman
   (4) ill-clothed children
   (5) oyster shucking

ANSWER ANALYSIS

3. **1** Young children were illegally used in a sweatshop to make clothing.

PHOTOGRAPH 4

QUESTION

4. The purpose of this photograph is to show

   (1) obedient children
   (2) the pledge of allegiance
   (3) objection to saluting the flag
   (4) an American classroom
   (5) equality of the sexes

4. **2** All of the children are pledging allegiance to the country.

PHOTOGRAPH 5

QUESTION

5. The purpose of this photograph is to picture

(1) a mathematics class
(2) a disobedient student
(3) an inadequate classroom
(4) a segregated classroom
(5) neglected children

ANSWER ANALYSIS

5. **4** The photograph depicts a classroom in which Black children are segregated. All the people in the picture are Black—pupils and teacher.

Practice with Interpreting Practical Documents

Interpreting practical documents means reading a business or government document. Read the entire document carefully, noting lists or words that are bolded. Key points are usually listed and numbered or bulleted. Many of the questions accompanying these documents are to test whether or not you can read and interpret the document. Sometimes the purpose of the document is questioned; the answer to this can often be found in the headline or bolded words.

INTERNAL REVENUE SERVICE PUBLICATION 529

Job Search Expenses

You can deduct certain expenses in looking for a new job in your present occupation, even if you do not get a new job. You cannot deduct these expenses if:

(1) You are looking for a job in a new occupation, or
(2) There was a substantial break between the ending of your last job and your looking for a new one.

You cannot deduct your expenses if you are seeking employment for the first time.

Employment and outplacement agency fees. You can deduct employment and outplacement agency fees you pay in looking for a new job in your present occupation.

Résumé. You can deduct amounts you spend for typing, printing, and mailing copies of a résumé to prospective employers if you are looking for a new job in your present occupation.

Travel and transportation expenses. If you travel to an area and, while there, you look for a new job in your present occupation, you may be able to deduct travel expenses to and from the area. You can deduct the travel expenses if the trip is primarily to look for a new job.

QUESTIONS

1. You can deduct expenses if you are a mechanic

   (1) looking for a new job as a computer programmer
   (2) returning to work after many years
   (3) looking for your first job
   (4) looking for a job in another garage
   (5) going back to school

2. Expenses that can be deducted include all of the following EXCEPT

   (1) cost of distributing your résumé
   (2) travel time primarily for personal activity
   (3) travel looking for a new job in a new area as a mechanic
   (4) travel looking for a new job as a mechanic in your present area
   (5) certain travel and transportation expenses

3. The main purpose of this regulation is to

   (1) get more tax money from job seekers
   (2) ease the burden of job seekers
   (3) catch violators of Internal Revenue Service regulations
   (4) list allowable deductions
   (5) list expenses that are not deductible

ANSWER KEY

1. **4**   2. **2**   3. **2**

ANSWER ANALYSIS

1. **4** It is specifically stated that you can deduct expenses if you are looking for a job in your present occupation. The mechanic, in this case, will still be a mechanic in another garage.
2. **2** The expenses for a trip on personal business cannot be deducted.
3. **2** The instructions of the Internal Revenue Service help job seekers by allowing them to deduct legitimate expenses.

VOTE ON A COUNTY PROPOSITION TO APPROVE AN AMENDMENT TO A LAW

Shall "Local Law" adopted by the County amending the laws of the County Commissioner of Public Works with respect to the local Community College be approved?

BACKGROUND: This local law is subject to a vote because it would change the powers of the Commissioner of Public Works as laid out in the County Charter. All construction projects at the College are now undertaken by the County through its Department of Public Works (DPW). Currently, all College projects are supervised by DPW, which sometimes also performs the work with County workers but often contracts it out. If the law is approved, DPW would no longer have control over public works on the Community College campus; instead, the College would supervise improvement projects directly with its own personnel. The College would no longer pay DPW to supervise improvement projects.

QUESTIONS

1. At present, construction projects at the College are directly performed by

   (1) the County
   (2) the Commissioner of Public Works
   (3) the Department of Public Works
   (4) the Community College
   (5) the contracted personnel

2. The local law, which must be approved by the voters, would give control of improvement projects to

   (1) the Commissioner of Public Works
   (2) the Department of Public Works
   (3) the Community College
   (4) the County Charter
   (5) the County workers

3. The proposed change would affect all of the following EXCEPT

   (1) the Commissioner of Public Works
   (2) the Department of Public Works
   (3) the role of the Community College
   (4) the supervision of the Community College
   (5) local law

ANSWER KEY

1. **3**   2. **3**   3. **4**

ANSWER ANALYSIS

1. **3** Construction projects are now undertaken by the County through its Department of Public Works.
2. **3** The College would supervise improvement projects directly.
3. **4** Supervision *of* the Community College is not mentioned in the passage. Supervision *by* the College is.

ANNUAL REPORT—CORPORATION X

The Company designs, manufactures and markets personal computers and related personal computing and communicating solutions for sale primarily to education, creative, consumer, and business customers. Substantially all of the Company's net sales to date have been derived from the sale of personal computers. The Company manages its business primarily on a geographic basis. The Company's geographic operating segments include the Americas, Europe, Japan, and Asia Pacific. Each geographic segment provides similar hardware and software products and similar services. During 1998, the Company continued and essentially completed a restructuring plan commenced in 1996 aimed at reducing its cost structure, improving its competitiveness, and restoring sustainable profitability. The Company's restructuring actions included the termination of employees, closure of facilities, and cancellation of contracts.

The Company's personal computers are characterized by their ease of use, innovative industrial designs and applications base, and built-in networking, graphics and multimedia capabilities. The Company offers a wide range of personal computing products, including personal computers, related peripherals, software, and networking and connectivity products.

QUESTIONS

1. The annual report of the corporation includes all of the following EXCEPT its

   (1) products
   (2) geographic operating segments
   (3) restructuring actions
   (4) marketing
   (5) cost of products

2. The company's main source of income comes from

   (1) personal computers
   (2) peripherals
   (3) software applications
   (4) networking products
   (5) connectivity products

3. The company's income has come from all of the following EXCEPT

   (1) schools
   (2) corporations
   (3) individual consumers
   (4) investments
   (5) creative customers

ANSWER KEY

1. **5**   2. **1**   3. **4**

ANSWER ANALYSIS

1. **5** The first four choices are mentioned in the report. Cost of products is mentioned nowhere.
2. **1** The report mentions that substantially all the net sales have been from the sales of personal computers.
3. **4** Investments are not mentioned as a source of income. Schools, businesses, and customers—individual and creative—are.

SAFETY BULLETIN OF CORPORATION X
SUBJECT: BACKING OF VEHICLES

It has been estimated that the average driver has his vehicle in reverse less than 1% of the time, but backing produces a substantially greater percentage of vehicle accidents. This is understandable because a driver often has restricted vision while backing.

Backing can be avoided by using a few simple rules:

—Plan your route and make immediate decisions on parking which will keep backing to a minimum.

—Always back into a parking space. This allows full visibility when pulling out.

If backing cannot be avoided:

Walk behind your vehicle before you enter it.

Align the mirrors for maximum view.

Check clearances and know your vehicle.

Turn your head while backing. Don't rely on mirrors alone.

Back slowly and be ready to stop at any moment.

Sound the horn if there is a possibility that someone might walk behind your vehicle.

Avoid blind-side backing. Backing to the right is dangerous because you are backing blind.

QUESTIONS

1. Proper backing is important because

   (1) it cannot be avoided
   (2) the driver has to do it constantly
   (3) the driver has full visibility
   (4) it is the cause of many avoidable accidents
   (5) the driver makes immediate decisions

2. Backing accidents occur because the driver

   (1) has limited visibility
   (2) backs into a parking space
   (3) backs in slowly
   (4) sounds his horn
   (5) is ready to stop

3. All of the following are possible causes of backing accidents EXCEPT

   (1) inadequate clearance
   (2) reliance solely on mirrors
   (3) blind-side backing
   (4) aligned mirrors
   (5) inadequate visibility

4. The purpose of the bulletin is to remind drivers to

   (1) plan
   (2) always avoid backing
   (3) rely on mirrors
   (4) prevent backing accidents
   (5) walk behind the vehicle

ANSWER KEY

1. **4**   2. **1**   3. **4**   4. **4**

ANSWER ANALYSIS

1. **4** Backing produces a greater percentage of accidents for the time needed for it—1%.
2. **1** The bulletin states that the driver has restricted view while backing.
3. **4** Drivers are reminded to align mirrors to prevent backing accidents. All the other choices are causes.
4. **4** The bulletin is intended to prevent backing accidents by cautioning drivers to avoid backing where possible and to observe safe backing procedures.

United States Census 2000

U.S. Department of Commerce • Bureau of the Census

This is the official form for all the people at this address. It is quick and easy, and your answers are protected by law. Complete the Census and help your community get what it needs — today and in the future!

Start Here

Please use a black or blue pen.

1. How many people were living or staying in this house, apartment, or mobile home on April 1, 2000?

Number of people

INCLUDE in this number:
- foster children, roomers, or housemates
- people staying here on April 1, 2000 who have no other permanent place to stay
- people living here most of the time while working, even if they have another place to live

DO NOT INCLUDE in this number:
- college students living away while attending college
- people in a correctional facility, nursing home, or mental hospital on April 1, 2000
- Armed Forces personnel living somewhere else
- people who live or stay at another place most of the time

2. Is this house, apartment, or mobile home — *Mark* ☒ *ONE box.*

☐ Owned by you or someone in this household with a mortgage or loan?
☐ Owned by you or someone in this household free and clear (without a mortgage or loan)?
☐ Rented for cash rent?
☐ Occupied without payment of cash rent?

3. Please answer the following questions for each person living in this house, apartment, or mobile home. Start with the name of one of the people living here who owns, is buying, or rents this house, apartment, or mobile home. If there is no such person, start with any adult living or staying here. We will refer to this person as Person 1.

What is this person's name? *Print name below.*

Last Name

First Name   MI

OMB No. 0607-0856: Approval Expires 12/31/2000

Form **D-1**

4. What is Person 1's telephone number? *We may call this person if we don't understand an answer.*

Area Code + Number

5. What is Person 1's sex? *Mark* ☒ *ONE box.*
☐ Male   ☐ Female

6. What is Person 1's age and what is Person 1's date of birth?
Age on April 1, 2000

Print numbers in boxes.
Month   Day   Year of birth

→ **NOTE: Please answer BOTH Questions 7 and 8.**

7. Is Person 1 Spanish/Hispanic/Latino? *Mark* ☒ *the "No" box if* **not** *Spanish/Hispanic/Latino.*
☐ **No,** not Spanish/Hispanic/Latino   ☐ Yes, Puerto Rican
☐ Yes, Mexican, Mexican Am., Chicano   ☐ Yes, Cuban
☐ Yes, other Spanish/Hispanic/Latino — *Print group.* ↙

8. What is Person 1's race? *Mark* ☒ *one or more races* to indicate what this person considers himself/herself to be.
☐ White
☐ Black, African Am., or Negro
☐ American Indian or Alaska Native — *Print name of enrolled or principal tribe.* ↗

☐ Asian Indian   ☐ Japanese   ☐ Native Hawaiian
☐ Chinese   ☐ Korean   ☐ Guamanian or Chamorro
☐ Filipino   ☐ Vietnamese   ☐ Samoan
☐ Other Asian — *Print race.* ↙   ☐ Other Pacific Islander — *Print race.* ↙

☐ Some other race — *Print race.* ↙

→ **If more people live here, continue with Person 2.**

Person 2

Your answers are important!
Every person in the Census counts.

1. What is Person 2's name? *Print name below.*
Last Name

First Name   MI

2. How is this person related to Person 1? *Mark* ☒ *ONE box.*

☐ Husband/wife
☐ Natural-born son/daughter
☐ Adopted son/daughter
☐ Stepson/stepdaughter
☐ Brother/sister
☐ Father/mother
☐ Grandchild
☐ Parent-in-law
☐ Son-in-law/daughter-in-law
☐ Other relative — *Print exact relationship.* →

If NOT RELATED to Person 1:

☐ Roomer, boarder
☐ Housemate, roommate
☐ Unmarried partner
☐ Foster child
☐ Other nonrelative

3. What is this person's sex? *Mark* ☒ *ONE box.*

☐ Male   ☐ Female

4. What is this person's age and what is this person's date of birth? *Print numbers in boxes.*

Age on April 1, 2000   Month   Day   Year of birth

→ **NOTE: Please answer BOTH Questions 5 and 6.**

5. Is this person Spanish/Hispanic/Latino? *Mark* ☒ *the* **"No"** *box if* **not** *Spanish/Hispanic/Latino.*

☐ **No,** not Spanish/Hispanic/Latino   ☐ Yes, Puerto Rican
☐ Yes, Mexican, Mexican Am., Chicano   ☐ Yes, Cuban
☐ Yes, other Spanish/Hispanic/Latino — *Print group.* ↗

6. What is this person's race? *Mark* ☒ *one or more races* to indicate what this person considers himself/herself to be.

☐ White
☐ Black, African Am., or Negro
☐ American Indian or Alaska Native — *Print name of enrolled or principal tribe.* ↗

☐ Asian Indian   ☐ Japanese   ☐ Native Hawaiian
☐ Chinese   ☐ Korean   ☐ Guamanian or Chamorro
☐ Filipino   ☐ Vietnamese   ☐ Samoan
☐ Other Asian — *Print race.* ↗   ☐ Other Pacific Islander — *Print race.* ↗

☐ Some other race — *Print race.* ↗

→ **If more people live here, continue with Person 3.**

Person 3

Census information helps your community get financial assistance for roads, hospitals, schools, and more.

1. What is Person 3's name? *Print name below.*
Last Name

First Name   MI

2. How is this person related to Person 1? *Mark* ☒ *ONE box.*

☐ Husband/wife
☐ Natural-born son/daughter
☐ Adopted son/daughter
☐ Stepson/stepdaughter
☐ Brother/sister
☐ Father/mother
☐ Grandchild
☐ Parent-in-law
☐ Son-in-law/daughter-in-law
☐ Other relative — *Print exact relationship.* →

If NOT RELATED to Person 1:

☐ Roomer, boarder
☐ Housemate, roommate
☐ Unmarried partner
☐ Foster child
☐ Other nonrelative

3. What is this person's sex? *Mark* ☒ *ONE box.*

☐ Male   ☐ Female

4. What is this person's age and what is this person's date of birth? *Print numbers in boxes.*

Age on April 1, 2000   Month   Day   Year of birth

→ **NOTE: Please answer BOTH Questions 5 and 6.**

5. Is this person Spanish/Hispanic/Latino? *Mark* ☒ *the* **"No"** *box if* **not** *Spanish/Hispanic/Latino.*

☐ **No,** not Spanish/Hispanic/Latino   ☐ Yes, Puerto Rican
☐ Yes, Mexican, Mexican Am., Chicano   ☐ Yes, Cuban
☐ Yes, other Spanish/Hispanic/Latino — *Print group.* ↗

6. What is this person's race? *Mark* ☒ *one or more races* to indicate what this person considers himself/herself to be.

☐ White
☐ Black, African Am., or Negro
☐ American Indian or Alaska Native — *Print name of enrolled or principal tribe.* ↗

☐ Asian Indian   ☐ Japanese   ☐ Native Hawaiian
☐ Chinese   ☐ Korean   ☐ Guamanian or Chamorro
☐ Filipino   ☐ Vietnamese   ☐ Samoan
☐ Other Asian — *Print race.* ↗   ☐ Other Pacific Islander — *Print race.* ↗

☐ Some other race — *Print race.* ↗

→ **If more people live here, continue with Person 4.**

QUESTIONS

1. Which of these would be included in answering the census form?

   (1) an inmate in a federal prison
   (2) a person living in Evanston, Illinois, and attending Northwestern University
   (3) a pilot at an Air Force base in Alaska
   (4) a person living in the apartment
   (5) a traveling salesman away most of the year

2. All of the following are asked about EXCEPT

   (1) age
   (2) employment
   (3) telephone number
   (4) race
   (5) date of birth

3. All of the following are mentioned as Spanish/Hispanic/Latino EXCEPT

   (1) Dominican
   (2) Puerto Rican
   (3) Mexican
   (4) Chicano
   (5) Cuban

1. **4**   2. **2**   3. **1**

ANSWER ANALYSIS

1. **4** The form asks for the people living or staying in the apartment. All the others are not to be included.
2. **2** No mention is made of employment. All the other choices are specifically mentioned.
3. **1** Dominicans are not mentioned although they might be included in other Spanish/Hispanic/Latino groupings.

Handling Social Studies Skills Questions

The Social Studies test no longer tests your ability to recall information such as dates, isolated facts, or events. It now emphasizes higher level skills. It does so by testing your ability to understand the written word or graphics, to analyze and apply the given information and ideas, and to evaluate the accuracy of the information and the conclusions based on it.

Comprehension Items

Twenty percent of the test, or about 10 items, require you to understand the meaning and purpose of written material, passages or quotations, and information contained in maps, graphs, tables, and political cartoons. These items test your ability to restate information, summarize ideas, and identify incorrectly stated ideas. The question will usually include a quotation and be followed by the words "This most nearly means" or "The best explanation of this statement is" or "The author believes or suggests."

EXAMPLE

A CODE

Never DO, BE, or SUFFER anything in soul or body, less or more, but what tends to the glory of God.

Resolved, never to lose one moment of time; but improve it the most profitable way I possibly can.

Resolved, to think much, on all occasions, of my own dying, and of the common circumstances which attend death.

Resolved, to maintain the strictest temperance in eating and drinking.

QUESTION

1. The author of the code believes that people should be mainly concerned with

   (1) monetary issues
   (2) luxuries
   (3) patriotism
   (4) spiritual matters
   (5) politics

ANSWER AND ANALYSIS

The passage reflects the ideas of Puritanism, a code that stresses spiritual concerns.

You can answer this question correctly if you read the passage carefully and decide what is being emphasized. Then, look for the answer that identifies that emphasis. In this question, the emphasis is on living for the glory of God, concern for one's manner of dying, and discipline in such material concerns as eating and drinking. The spiritual is stressed. Indeed, you can answer the question even if you do not know it is the Puritan Code that is being quoted. The correct choice is 4.

Application Items

Thirty percent of the test, or about 15 items, require you to use information and ideas in a situation other than that indicated to you in the question. Applying information and ideas is a high-level skill because you must not only understand the general content, but also be able to transfer it to the context of a particular situation. In other words, you must go from the general information you are given to a specific case.

EXAMPLE

The principle of judicial review provides for the judiciary to determine the constitutionality of both state and federal laws.

QUESTION

1. Which action best illustrates the principle of judicial review?

   (1) Congress enacts civil rights legislation.
   (2) The Senate approves appointment of federal judges.
   (3) An act of Congress is struck down by the Supreme Court.
   (4) The states refuse to cooperate with the federal authorities in crime control.
   (5) Congress overrides a presidential veto.

ANSWER AND ANALYSIS

The principle of judicial review means the power of the U.S. Supreme Court to rule on the constitutionality of acts of Congress, state legislatures, executive officers, and lower courts. The only choice that involves a court action is Choice 3, a specific application of this principle to an act of Congress. You must apply the principle of judicial or court reexamination to an act of Congress.

The purpose of another form of question or item on the High School Equivalency Examination Social Studies test is to test your ability to apply given information that defines ideas in historical documents, divisions of subject matter in the social studies, systems of government, economics, psychology, and groups of basic concepts in the five areas of the social studies. You will have to

1. understand information that is presented in defined categories, usually five in number;
2. relate a situation, action, or event to those categories;
3. arrive at an application of the information in the categories to the given situation, action, or event.

An illustration will make this clear. In this example, the information presented in defined categories is the central idea of each of five articles of the Bill of Rights, the first ten amendments to the Constitution.

EXAMPLE

The first ten amendments to the Constitution make up the Bill of Rights ratified by Congress in 1791. Parts of five of the amendments read as follows:

(A) Article 1—Congress shall make no law...abridging the freedom of speech or of the press.
(B) Article 2—The right of the people to keep and bear arms shall not be infringed.
(C) Article 5—No person...shall be compelled in any criminal case to be a witness against himself, nor be deprived of life, liberty, or property, without due process of law.
(D) Article 7—The right to trial by jury shall be preserved.
(E) Article 8—Excessive bail shall not be required...nor cruel and unusual punishments inflicted.

The questions that follow deal with three ways in which the given information can be used by three individuals in three different situations.

QUESTIONS

Indicate the amendment (article) most likely to be cited in support of his or her position by

1. an opponent of capital punishment

   (1) Article 1
   (2) Article 2
   (3) Article 5
   (4) Article 7
   (5) Article 8

2. a member of the National Rifle Association

(1) Article 1
(2) Article 2
(3) Article 5
(4) Article 7
(5) Article 8

3. a person accused of a criminal act who is testifying at his or her trial

(1) Article 1
(2) Article 2
(3) Article 5
(4) Article 7
(5) Article 8

ANSWERS AND ANALYSIS

You must apply the categorized information to each situation.

The correct answer to question 1 is Choice 5. An opponent of capital punishment will cite Article 8's prohibition against cruel and unusual punishment.

The correct answer to question 2 is Choice 2. A member of the National Rifle Association will cite Article 2, "The right of the people to keep and bear arms shall not be infringed."

The correct answer to question 3 is Choice 3. The person on trial might "take the Fifth," citing the provision of Article 5 that "no person...shall be compelled in any criminal case to be a witness against himself."

Try another item set in this format.

EXAMPLE

Psychology is the science of behavior and of human thought processes. There are a number of closely interrelated branches of human psychology.

(A) Social psychology investigates the effect of the group on the behavior of the individual.
(B) Applied psychology puts to practical use the discoveries and theories of psychology as in industrial psychology.
(C) Clinical psychology diagnoses and treats mental disorders and mental illnesses.
(D) Comparative psychology deals with different behavioral organizations of animals including human beings.
(E) Physiological psychology attempts to understand the effects of body functions on human behavior.

QUESTIONS

Each of the following describes a proposed study. Indicate which branch of psychology is most clearly involved.

1. A company wants to study the effects of music piped into a factory where workers are on an assembly line.

(1) Social psychology
(2) Applied psychology
(3) Clinical psychology
(4) Comparative psychology
(5) Physiological psychology

2. A drug rehabilitation center wants to study the role of peer pressure on a teenager in a drug prevention program.

(1) Social psychology
(2) Applied psychology
(3) Clinical psychology
(4) Comparative psychology
(5) Physiological psychology

3. A grant is available for a study of schizophrenia, a disorder characterized by hallucinations and delusions.

(1) Social psychology
(2) Applied psychology
(3) Clinical psychology
(4) Comparative psychology
(5) Physiological psychology

ANSWERS AND ANALYSIS

The correct answer to question 1 is Choice 2. Applied psychology puts the findings of industrial psychologists to practical use, in this case for people who work on an assembly line.

The correct answer to question 2 is Choice 1. Social psychologists are concerned with the effects of groups, in this case teenagers, who put pressure on their peers to use drugs.

The correct answer to question 3 is Choice 3. Clinical psychologists would apply for the grant because of their interest in schizophrenia, a mental disorder.

Analysis Items

Thirty percent of the test, or about 15 items, require you to break down information into its parts to determine their interrelationships. These items involve the ability to identify cause-and-effect relationships, separate fact from opinion, separate conclusions from supporting statements, and show that you can recognize assumptions on which conclusions are based.

QUESTION

Democracy may be defined as government by the people directly or through representatives chosen in free elections. Which quotation from the Declaration of Independence best describes the fundamental principle of democracy in the United States?

(1) "imposing taxes on us without our consent"
(2) "governments long established should not be changed for light and transient causes"
(3) "depriving us, in many cases, of the benefits of trial by jury"
(4) "deriving their just powers from the consent of the governed"
(5) "quartering large bodies of armed troops among us"

ANSWER AND ANALYSIS

Not only must you understand the meaning of each possible answer, but you must analyze it to determine which is a *fundamental* principle of government in the United States. First you must understand; then you must analyze.

You have to go through all of the following steps:

Choice 1: imposing taxes without consent—meaning taxation without representation
Choice 2: governments long established should not be changed for light causes—meaning change in government must be for good reason
Choice 3: benefits of trial by jury—meaning the right to trial by jury
Choice 4: deriving powers from consent of the governed—meaning the government gets its power from those it governs, the people
Choice 5: quartering armed troops—meaning compulsion to keep soldiers in homes

Now the test of a *fundamental* principle of government in the United States must be applied to each.

Choice 1 is not fundamental; it is a grievance.
Choice 2 refers not to the government of the United States, but to changing governments in general.
Choice 3, trial by jury, is an important right, but it is not as fundamental as Choice 4, which states that the U.S. government is a democracy in which the people rule through their elected representatives. This is an absolutely fundamental principle.
Choice 4 is the only correct interpretation that can be made.
Choice 5 refers to unauthorized quartering of soldiers—important, but not fundamental.

Evaluation Items

Twenty percent of the test, or about 10 items, are the most difficult. You must make judgments about the soundness or accuracy of information. These questions test your ability to determine whether facts are adequately documented or proved, whether they are appropriately used to support conclusions, and whether they are used correctly or incorrectly in the presentation of opinions or arguments.

QUESTION

Which statement is an opinion rather than a fact?

(1) France was involved in the Vietnam conflict before the United States entered it.
(2) There are tensions between mainland China and Taiwan.
(3) Peace will be achieved by regional agreements throughout the world.
(4) Great Britain has become a full member of the European Common Market.
(5) The United States is a member of the North Atlantic Treaty Organization.

ANSWER AND ANALYSIS

Five statements are presented. Four are facts that can be proved or verified by evidence—that France was involved in Vietnam; that mainland China and Taiwan have tensions; that Great Britain is a member of the

European Common Market; that the United States is a member of the North Atlantic Treaty Organization. Choice 3, peace will be achieved by regional agreements throughout the world, is an opinion or a hypothesis—not a fact—and it remains to be proved.

Practice with Social Studies Skills Questions

COMPREHENSION

1. During the last 150 years, immigrants were attracted to the United States because manpower needs increased. This occurred when the United States was experiencing periods of

   (1) economic expansion
   (2) economic depression
   (3) war
   (4) political change
   (5) stability

2. "The privilege to be involved and to conduct a business in any manner that one pleases is not guaranteed by the Constitution. The right to engage in certain businesses may be subject to various conditions. Laws regulating businesses have been found to be valid. We find no justification to reject the state law under question."

   Which is best illustrated by the passage?

   (1) residual powers
   (2) legislative consent
   (3) judicial review
   (4) executive order
   (5) executive privilege

3. Which is a basic assumption of the graduated income tax?

   (1) The ability to pay increases as wealth increases.
   (2) Each wage earner should contribute to the government the same percentage of his or her income.
   (3) The middle class should bear the burden of financing the government.

   (4) Citizens should pay the costs of government services in proportion to their use of such services.
   (5) Taxes on the wealthy should not be too great.

4. "In a sense the people of the Third World were forced to help pay for the Industrial Revolution in the West."

   Which statement most clearly supports this viewpoint?

   (1) The colonizing powers encouraged industries in their colonies.
   (2) Western nations depended upon raw materials from their colonies.
   (3) Financial centers of the world blocked investments in these new nations.
   (4) The Third World is now experiencing an Industrial Revolution.
   (5) The Third World supplied most of the manpower needed by the West.

5. "Public opinion is of major significance in social control."

   The author of this statement most probably means that

   (1) the influence of public opinion on government leaders is very limited
   (2) problem solving is simplified when public opinion is not known
   (3) public opinion may be predicted accurately, especially in the time of national crisis
   (4) government officials must pay attention to public opinion in the formulation of policies
   (5) polls provide little help to lawmakers

ANALYSIS

THE BUSINESS CYCLE

6. If economic indicators place the economy at a point on the cycle between 1 and 2, then the Council of Economic Advisers would most likely suggest which action to the president?

   (1) planned deficit spending
   (2) increasing income tax rates
   (3) lowering interest rates
   (4) increasing government expenditures
   (5) encouraging higher wages

7. "The showpieces are, with rare exceptions, the industries dominated by a handful of large firms. The foreign visitor, brought to the United States...visits the same firms as do the attorneys of the Department of Justice in their search for monopolies."

   The best explanation of this seemingly contradictory behavior is that

   (1) only the largest corporations will allow foreign visitors to inspect their factories
   (2) both State and Justice Department officials oppose the development of monopolies
   (3) the developing countries of the world are interested only in large corporations
   (4) the largest corporations often pioneer in research and production methods
   (5) small firms do not welcome foreign investment

8. "Why, by interweaving our destiny with that of any part of Europe, entangle our peace and prosperity in the toils of European ambition, rivalship, interest, humor, or caprice?"

   Which action by the United States best reflects the philosophy expressed in this quotation?

   (1) passage of legislation restricting immigration
   (2) rejection of the Treaty of Versailles
   (3) enactment of the Lend-Lease Act
   (4) approval of the United Nations Charter
   (5) membership in the North Atlantic Treaty Organization

9. "If a nation expects to be ignorant and free, in a state of civilization, it expects what never was and never will be."

   Which idea is most strongly supported by this statement?

   (1) the government's right to tax
   (2) universal suffrage
   (3) a strong central government
   (4) compulsory education
   (5) abolition of slavery

10. "Ours is a country where people...can attain to the most elevated positions or acquire a large amount of wealth...according to their talents, prudence, and personal exertions."

    This quotation most clearly supports the idea that

    (1) upward social mobility and the work ethic are closely related
    (2) economic collectivism is part of American life
    (3) regulated capitalism reflects private initiative
    (4) the United States has a centrally controlled economic system
    (5) the U.S. economic system favors the wealthy

APPLICATION

11. Which is the most valid statement concerning the problem of balancing human wants with limited resources?

    (1) It exists only in societies with a free enterprise economy.
    (2) It has been solved in nations with strong governmental controls over economic activity.
    (3) It has become less of a problem with the advancements in technology.
    (4) It exists in all societies, no matter what the economic system.
    (5) It will be solved by the year 2000.

Handling Social Studies Skills Questions 295

12. A "strict constructionist," one who would permit the federal government to exercise only those powers specifically granted by the U.S. Constitution, would favor which of the following actions?

   (1) the institution of programs for social reform
   (2) annexation of territory by the United States
   (3) bypassing constitutional restraints
   (4) limiting the power of the federal government
   (5) increasing the power of the states

A basic principle of the U.S. Constitution is the division of governmental power in the executive, the legislative, and the judicial branches. Legislative powers are vested in Congress; judicial powers, in the Supreme Court and federal court system; executive powers, in the president and his governmental machinery. Thus, a system of checks and balances exists among the three branches of government.

Each of the following is an example of the system of checks and balances in operation. Identify the one branch that is checking the other by choosing the appropriate response.

13. Congress overrides a presidential veto.

   (1) the executive checks the legislative
   (2) the executive balances the judicial
   (3) the judicial balances the legislative
   (4) the legislative checks the executive
   (5) the legislative checks the judicial

14. The Senate refuses to confirm a presidential nominee for an ambassadorship.

   (1) the executive checks the legislative
   (2) the executive balances the judicial
   (3) the judicial balances the legislative
   (4) the legislative checks the executive
   (5) the legislative checks the judicial

15. The president nominates a Supreme Court justice.

   (1) the executive checks the legislative
   (2) the executive balances the judicial
   (3) the judicial balances the legislative
   (4) the legislative checks the executive
   (5) the legislative checks the judicial

EVALUATION

16. Which statement would be most *difficult* to prove?

   (1) Japan's emperors have reigned but have seldom ruled.
   (2) The workers of the United States are better workers than those of Japan.
   (3) In the post-World War II period, the United States was the source of much cultural borrowing by the Japanese.
   (4) Japanese technology in the 1970s was more advanced than it was in the 1940s.
   (5) The cost of living in Japan has been rising ever since World War II.

17. Which statement would be most *difficult* to prove?

   (1) Popular ideas of third parties in the United States tend to be adopted by the major political parties.
   (2) The Articles of Confederation rendered more authority to the state government than to the federal government.
   (3) The Sherman Antitrust Act was used to reduce the effectiveness of labor unions.
   (4) World War II was necessary in order to end the Great Depression.
   (5) The right to vote has been extended in the twentieth century.

18. Which information about country *X* would be most useful to the head of a government establishing a foreign policy toward country *X*?

   (1) an analysis of the national resources and goals of country *X*
   (2) a file containing the major public statements made by the leaders of country *X* concerning their nation's foreign policies
   (3) an analysis by religious leaders of the major religious groups and beliefs of the people of country *X*
   (4) a newspaper report summarizing the treaties and international agreements of country *X*
   (5) knowledge of the party to which leaders of country *X* belong

19. Which statement expresses an opinion rather than a fact?

    (1) The United States did not join the League of Nations.
    (2) At one time, the United States was on the gold standard.
    (3) President Franklin D. Roosevelt made unnecessary concessions to the Russians at Yalta.
    (4) The Oregon Dispute was settled by extending the 49th parallel to the Pacific Ocean.
    (5) The United States is a member of NATO.

20. "The privilege to be involved and to conduct a business in any manner that one pleases is not guaranteed by the Constitution. The right to engage in certain businesses may be subject to various conditions. Laws regulating businesses have been found to be valid. We find no justification to reject the state law under question."

    Which concept would most likely be REJECTED by the author of this passage?

    (1) laissez-faire
    (2) welfare
    (3) competition
    (4) profit motive
    (5) antitrust legislation

ANSWER KEY

1. **1**	5. **4**	9. **4**	12. **4**	15. **2**	18. **1**
2. **3**	6. **2**	10. **1**	13. **4**	16. **2**	19. **3**
3. **1**	7. **4**	11. **4**	14. **4**	17. **4**	20. **1**
4. **2**	8. **2**				

WHAT'S YOUR SCORE?

_____right,	_____wrong
Excellent	19–20
Good	15–18
Fair	13–14

If your score was low, the explanation of the correct answers below will help. Analyze your errors. Reread the appropriate sections in this chapter. There are more skills questions in the two full-length practice examinations at the end of this book.

ANSWER ANALYSIS

1. **1** Immigrants have been attracted when there were opportunities for farming on cheap, fertile land; and for jobs in factories and mines and in building transportation lines. Immigration has fallen off during wars, when it was dangerous and difficult to travel, and during depressions, when jobs were not available.

2. **3** Judicial review is the power of the Supreme Court to determine the constitutionality of laws of Congress and the states, and the acts of government executives. The hypothetical decision in the passage is the result of the Supreme Court's being willing to hear a case on appeal from a lower court because a constitutional issue was involved.

3. **1** The graduated income tax raises the *rate* of taxation as one's income increases. For example, a family of four earning $55,000 pays a federal income tax at a higher rate than a similar family having a taxable income of $25,000.

4. **2** From about 1870 on, the growth of European industrialization led to increased demand for African copper, precious woods, diamonds, gold and (later) uranium; and the development of rubber and cocoa plantations by U.S. firms and Western European nations. In Asia, areas such as Malaya and Indonesia furnished rubber, tin, and petroleum to the West.

5. **4** Social controls are composed of two parts. There are, first, the laws against what society defines as criminal actions, such as malicious destruction of property or the sale of narcotics. Those laws are enforced by police and courts to the extent of their ability and efficiency. Then there are the informal controls, based upon the human desire for the good opinion of others, that society exerts upon its members. Teenage fads illustrate the control exerted by group conformity. Public opinion in general is a powerful factor in social control. Political leaders know that they cannot stray too far from public opinion without risking loss of control, for example, with

respect to imposing a state sales tax where none exists.

6. **2** A major economic aim of government is to smooth out the extremes of the business cycle in order to avoid "boom and bust." During the period of economic expansion and prosperity indicated in the question, a rise in income tax rates would reduce disposable income, slowing the rate of inflation that can shorten the period of expansion. Another reason for higher tax rates under these conditions is to create a budget surplus to repay part of the national debt.

7. **4** Foreign businesspersons and engineers are interested in both the techniques of large-scale production and the research and development programs that can be afforded only by such large and wealthy firms as Xerox, IBM, Intel, and DuPont. This research is responsible for patents that create monopolies over techniques and products—e.g., xerography, nylon fibers—that may attract the attention of the antitrust division of the Department of Justice.

8. **2** The Treaty of Versailles provided for a League of Nations, but the view expressed in the quotation prevailed. The United States never joined the League of Nations.

9. **4** This statement of Thomas Jefferson strongly supports compulsory education. To implement it, Jefferson designed a system of public education from elementary school through secondary school and then the university.

10. **1** Upward social mobility or movement refers to the potential ability of anyone in America to move up in socioeconomic status. If one has talent, plans carefully ("prudence"), works hard ("personal exertions"), one can advance in American society.

11. **4** The central problem of *all* economic systems is how best to use limited resources to meet unlimited human needs and desires.

12. **4** A *strict construction* would permit the federal government to exercise only the powers specifically delegated in the Constitution, restricting the use of the elastic clause. A *broad construction* would favor more flexibility in the interpretation of the elastic clause, thus leading to more power for the federal government.

13. **4** Legislative powers are vested in Congress, but the president must sign bills enacted by Congress before they become law. The presidential veto is a check of the executive on the legislature. However, Congress may override a president's veto by a two-thirds vote in each house, in which case, as in this item, the legislative branch checks the executive branch.

14. **4** The Constitution provides that a majority vote of the Senate is needed to confirm appointment of ambassadors. In this instance, the legislative branch is exercising a check on the executive.

15. **2** The Constitution grants the president (executive) the power to appoint "judges of the Supreme Court" with the advice and consent of the Senate. The executive branch is given this power over the judicial branch; the Supreme Court cannot choose its own judges.

16. **2** The term *better* involves many factors, and it would be difficult to reach an agreement about *what* was to be measured, let alone *how* to measure the many factors.

17. **4** Each of the other choices can be substantiated by objective, factual evidence, such as examples of minor-party ideas that major parties have adopted, a restrictive list of the powers the Constitution gives to the national government, and examples of the use of the Sherman Act against labor unions. In the twentieth century women and 18-year-olds have been given the vote. The above facts are generally accepted and agreed upon. That is not true for the controversial statement linking the Great Depression and World War II.

18. **1** One nation should understand the purposes and resources of another in order to carry on intelligent dealings with it. An analysis of those items is particularly valuable.

19. **3** We may define a fact as a statement that can be proved or verified and about which most people agree. An opinion is a personal conclusion that may be based on factual information,

one's own biases and background, and even wishful thinking. An opinion is not verifiable, and people tend to disagree about opinions; for example, which team will win next year's World Series or Superbowl game, who is the world's greatest musician, whether a particular presidential action was wise or foolish.

20. **1** The paragraph approves of state laws that regulate business in the public interest. Laissez-faire is an economic policy that provides for little or no interference by government in the affairs of business, so the author of this passage would most likely reject it.

Outline of Study for the Social Studies Test

Although the Social Studies test does not ask you to recall specific facts, reading passages are based on the topics that are covered in the high school curriculum. The more you know about these topics, therefore, the easier it will be for you to understand the reading passages.

Use the following outline of topics that may appear on the Social Studies test to guide you in your review.

ECONOMICS

I. The meaning of economics
II. How businesses behave
   A. How business is organized
   B. Economic markets
   C. Capitalism
   D. Supply and demand
   E. How prices are determined
   F. Competition and monopoly
III. Production
   A. Role of production
   B. Deciding what and how to produce and distribute
   C. Production of goods and services
   D. Uses and rewards of factors of production
IV. The individual as a consumer
   A. Consumer problems and responsibilities
      1. The American standard of living: wages, working conditions, food, shelter, clothing, health care, educational and recreational activities
      2. Factors influencing price and quality of goods: supply and demand (Note: Simple illustrations; e.g., snowstorm in citrus fruit belt, drought, strikes)
      3. Business organizations as they affect the consumer, independent stores, chain stores, cooperatives
      4. Consumer information services: private and government aids
      5. Consumer protection
         a. Credit associations: origin, functions
         b. Protective legislation: Bureau of Standards, price controls, Food and Drug Administration, grading and labeling
      6. Installment buying: advantages and disadvantages
      7. Advertising: values, government curbs
      8. Inflation; deflation; effects on the consumer
   B. Responsibilities of consumers
      1. Saving; budgeting
      2. Economical buying and use of materials and possessions
V. The individual as a worker
   A. Choice of a vocation
      1. Occupational trends
      2. Qualifications and preparation
      3. Employment opportunities
      4. City, state, national, and private employment services
   B. Rights and responsibilities as a worker
      1. Bargaining individually and collectively
      2. Producing efficiently; conserving wisely; consuming intelligently
   C. Problems of capital and labor
      1. Labor's struggle for economic freedom
         a. Against evils of industrialism; against monopoly
         b. Development of trade unionism
      2. Rights and responsibilities of labor and management
      3. Recent trends toward labor-management cooperation
      4. Problems of increasing central-

ization: large corporations, large labor unions, government controls, and services

  D. Labor and the economy
    1. Labor market—union and nonunion labor
    2. Distribution of income—profit and wages
    3. Collective bargaining, strikes, picketing
    4. Productivity
  E. Government employees
    1. Types of service
    2. Means of securing positions: merit system, history of Civil Service
    3. Economic status and problems

VI. Economics and financial institutions
  A. Money and monetary policy
  B. Banking and interest
  C. Financial institutions other than banks

VII. Government's role in the economy
  A. Taxes and other sources of revenue
  B. Government expenditures

VIII. How the overall economy behaves
  A. Measuring the economy
  B. How the economy grows
  C. Problems of growth
  D. Economic fluctuations—business cycles
  E. Inflation and deflation
  F. Policies for stabilization of the economy
  G. Formulating modern economic policy

IX. United States and the world economy
  A. International trade
  B. Foreign exchange and the balance of payments

X. Other economic systems
  A. Comparative economics
  B. Communism and socialism
  C. Economics of underdeveloped nations

XI. Contemporary problems of the American economy
  A. Social economic problems—poverty in plenty
  B. Economic security
  C. Economy problems of agriculture
  D. Problems of urbanization

XII. Molders of economic thought (Adam Smith, John Maynard Keynes, John Stuart Mill, Karl Marx, Thomas Malthus, et al.)

AMERICAN HISTORY

I. Beginnings of America
  A. Old World backgrounds
  B. The new lands
    1. The explorers: their motives, achievements, utilization of natural gateways to America
    2. Geographic factors and their effects on life in new lands
    3. Leaders: Spanish, Portuguese, Dutch, French, English
  C. Colonization and growth of settlements
    1. Reasons for leaving Europe
    2. Diversity of cultural origin; effects on patterns of life in New World
    3. Effects of economic and geographic influences: on agricultural development, growth of commerce and industry, transportation and communication, social and cultural life
    4. Growth of ideals of religious freedom: the Puritans, Roger Williams, the Quakers and William Penn, the Baltimores and Maryland
    5. Characteristic examples of self-government: Virginia, Massachusetts, New York, Pennsylvania, Rhode Island
    6. Conflicting ideals and systems: political, industrial, economic, social
  D. French and Indian War, 1754–1763: causes, effects, significance
  E. Democracy in colonial times
    1. European influences
    2. Contributions of immigrants toward shaping American ideal
    3. Influence of geographic factors
    4. Leaders of early democratic ideals: Patrick Henry, James Otis, Samuel Adams, John Adams, Benjamin Franklin
    5. Zenger case: freedom of the press
  F. Establishing the new nation: growth of democracy
    1. The American Revolution: causes, leaders, events, results
    2. The Declaration of Independence: Thomas Jefferson
    3. The Articles of Confederation, 1781–1789; weaknesses

4. The Constitution
   a. The Constitutional Convention: main compromises, struggle for adoption
   b. Contributions: James Madison, George Washington, Alexander Hamilton
   c. Adoption; provision for amendment
   d. Study of the Constitution: federal nature of our government; division of powers between federal government and states; separation of powers: executive, legislative, judicial
   e. Bill of Rights: origin, adoption, significance

II. The expansion of the United States
   A. Original extent of thirteen states and territories
   B. Northwest Ordinance, 1787: foundation of our expansion and colonial policy; its effects on later history
   C. Growth of continental United States of America (Louisiana Purchase, Florida Purchase, annexation of Texas, acquisition of Oregon Territory, Mexican Cession)
   D. The frontier
      1. Meaning: description of frontier life, geographic influences
      2. Influence of frontier on American life
      3. Leaders: Daniel Boone, Brigham Young, Kit Carson
   E. Acquisition of territory beyond continental United States (Alaska, Pacific Islands, Hawaii, Guam, Philippines, Caribbean area, Puerto Rico, Panama Canal Zone, Virgin Islands): how acquired, present status

III. Development of democratic way of life
   A. Roots of American democracy in colonial and early American periods
      1. European sources; colonial experience; influence on making of Constitution; Bill of Rights
      2. Problems confronting new nation: organization of federal government, interpretation of Constitution

3. Federalists vs. Anti-Federalists; beginning of political parties
4. Leaders: Washington, Hamilton, John Adams, Jefferson, Madison
   B. Jeffersonian Democracy (Jefferson's ideas on democracy; agrarian versus commercial influences; War of 1812; effects on American life; Era of Good Feeling, 1816–1823)
   C. Jacksonian Democracy (meaning; evidences in economic, social, and political life; extension of suffrage; humanitarian reforms— care of sick, criminals, needy; early cooperative movement)

IV. National unity versus sectionalism
   A. Factors that promoted nationalism (Monroe Doctrine; Supreme Court decisions; development of an American culture)
   B. Factors that promoted sectionalism (differences in ways of earning a living; industrialism of the North; plantation-holding system of the South; acquisition and settlement of new territory)
   C. Major issues of sectionalism (Tariff; the Bank; internal improvement; admission of new states; slavery)
   D. Slavery (origin; influence of geographic factors on slavery as an institution; effect of inventions [Eli Whitney's cotton gin]; Missouri Compromise; Abolitionists— Garrison, Stowe; growing tension between North and South)
   E. Civil War (election of Abraham Lincoln, 1860; highlights of the war; leaders and events; Emancipation Proclamation; results of war)
   F. Reconstruction Period
      1. Problems: the plight of freed slaves; readmission of the seceded states; the rebuilding of the South; contribution of reconstructed states to South; high taxes and corruption; "carpetbaggers," "scalawags," the Ku Klux Klan
      2. Significance of constitutional amendments: XIII, XIV, XV
      3. Effects of Reconstruction

V. The industrial era
   A. Geographic background
      1. The physiographic regions of the

United States: Atlantic Coastal Plain, Appalachian Highlands, Great Central Plain, Cordilleran Highlands
2. Geographic study of each region: differences in location, climate, topography, natural resources; man's utilization and control of natural environment; effects on life of people, types of industries, products; interdependence of peoples of different regions
3. Geographic reasons for location and growth of big cities: New York, Philadelphia, Boston, Chicago, Denver, Seattle, New Orleans, San Francisco, Detroit, Pittsburgh

B. The Industrial Revolution
1. Meaning
2. Causes: inventions, wealth of raw materials, abundant labor supply, ready markets, capital
3. Inventions
   a. European: textile machinery, steam engine
   b. American: cotton gin, steamboat, sewing machine, telegraph, farming machines, newer processes for steel manufacture, later inventions
4. Effects on social, industrial, and political life
5. Significance in our lives today

C. Development of our business economy
1. America's riches: abundant natural resources; energetic, inventive people
2. Domestic and international trade
   a. Bases of trade: needs of people, climatic variations, unequal distribution of natural resources
   b. Exports; imports; tariffs
3. Development of industries (geographic basis)
   a. Agriculture: chief agricultural regions of the United States, life and problems of the farmer, chief products

   b. Transportation and communication: significance in our industrial development
   c. Commerce
   d. Mining: coal, iron, oil, copper
   e. Manufacturing industries: steel, oil, textiles, automobiles, machinery, motion pictures, radio and television
   f. The factory system: effects on worker, methods of work, and population movements
   g. Growth of cities

D. Recent trends
1. Regional developments: Tennessee Valley Authority, Boulder Dam, Grand Coulee, Bonneville, Missouri Valley
2. Conservation: need for; work of Theodore Roosevelt, Franklin Roosevelt, Gifford Pinchot, Rachel Carson and others
3. Social legislation: Social Security Act; care of aged, dependent, unemployed
4. Increase of government controls
5. Contemporary contacts of the family with the federal and the state government: taxes, draft, education

VI. Our American heritage
A. Our democratic institutions and ideals
1. Division of power between the central government and the states
2. Bill of Rights and Civil Liberties; Four Freedoms
3. Development of Women's Rights movement; leaders
4. Extension of democracy to social and economic life; free tax-supported educational system; legislative restrictions against discrimination in employment

B. Development of an American culture
1. Influence of American literature
2. Influence of science
3. Growth of art, architecture, and music

C. Education for democracy
1. Organs of information and opinion: schools and colleges, news-

papers, periodicals, radio, movies, pressure groups
2. Propaganda: its meaning and recognition

D. Our people
1. Story of immigration; "Americanizing" the immigrant
2. Contribution of various peoples to our culture
3. Problems of groups of diverse racial, religious, and national origins
4. Intercultural understandings and appreciations

E. Democracy vs. totalitarianism

VII. Growth of America as a world power
A. Our foreign policy
1. Washington's Farewell Address—isolation and neutrality
2. Jefferson's "no entangling alliance"
3. The Monroe Doctrine: origin, provisions, importance
4. Westward Expansion: Louisiana and Florida purchases; Mexican War; Oregon Treaty
5. Overseas Expansion: Spanish-American War
6. America's relations with the Far East and Japan: opening of Japan; Open-Door Policy, 1899
7. Relations of United States with Latin America; life and culture of people; leaders of several Latin American countries; Pan-Americanism; Good Neighbor Policy; present relations
8. The Panama Canal: acquisition; construction; importance

B. The United States and World War I
1. Origin and causes of World War I
2. Entry of the United States into the war
3. Peace problems
4. League of Nations; Woodrow Wilson

C. The United States and World War II
1. Origin and causes of World War II
2. Reason for U.S. participation
3. Outcomes of World War II

D. Post World War II
1. Emergence of new nations
2. The Cold War
3. The Truman Doctrine

4. The Marshall Plan
5. Regional organizations: OAS, NATO, CENTO, OAU; Benelux, EU, Colombo Plan, GATT
6. The Korean War
7. The Civil Rights and Feminist movements
8. The spread of nuclear weapons and efforts to contain them
9. Space exploration
10. The Vietnam War
11. The Third World

VIII. The United States as a member of the United Nations
A. Historical background of peace movements
B. Events leading to formation of the United Nations
C. Organization
D. Main current problems
E. Role of United States in world affairs

GEOGRAPHY

I. The individual in his or her relationships to the earth
A. The earth as the home of man
1. The earth as a globe: principal features, size, shape, relation to other heavenly bodies, revolution and rotation, inclination of the axis, great circles, the equator and the measurement of latitude, the prime meridian and the measurement of longitude, relative sizes and positions of land masses and water areas, the atmosphere, effects on human living
2. Representations of the earth
a. Maps; globes
b. Types and uses of map projections; relation of map to globe
3. Climate
a. Climatic controls: latitude, altitude, topography, distance from the sea, prevailing winds, ocean currents (study of major climatic regions of world: tropical rain forest, tropical savanna, tropical desert, maritime, humid continental, continental steppe, con-

tinental desert, Mediterranean subtropical, humid subtropical, taiga, tundra, polar ice cap)

b. Effects on human living: on energy and temperament, on natural resources, on occupations and industries, on population movements

4. Topography

a. Chief topographical features of earth: plains; plateaus; mountains; valleys; continents; bodies of water—oceans, lakes, seas, rivers

b. Relation to human living: transportation and communication; population movements

5. Natural resources: their utilization, conservation, effect on human living

6. People: cause and effect of population distribution and movements, present trends

7. The air age: relation of shape of earth to development effects of air age on human living

II. The individual in his or her relationships to the life and culture of peoples of different lands

A. Latin America, our southern neighbor

1. Reasons for our interest

2. Geographic influences: relative location, comparative area, range in latitude, climatic range, topography (mountains—Andes; volcanoes; plateaus—Brazilian highlands, Altiplano; plains—pampas; rivers—Amazon, Orinoco)

3. Natural regions and countries

4. People

a. Composition and distribution of the population, sharp regional differences, effects of racial diversity, economic and social groups; education and culture; role of the church—population trends (fast growth) and movements; contributions to world culture—foods, vocabulary

b. Utilization of resources for development of industry; mode of life in agricultural, grazing, mining, and limited industrial areas; one-crop countries; big landowners, inadequate food supply; urban centers

5. Transportation and communication problems (poor topography, lack of roads and railroads)

6. Trade relations: characteristic products, imports, exports (only raw materials), world markets, port cities

7. Significance of region in the world community

B. Canada—our northern neighbor

1. Reasons for our interest; common bonds

2. Natural regions and provinces

3. Geographic influences: relative location (latitudinal factor), comparative area, climatic range, topography, natural resources, effects on life of people

4. People; size and distribution of population; causes and effects of two national cultures; utilization of resources of land and adjacent waters for development of industries; mode of life in different regions; interdependence of regions; newer trends in industrialization; population movements; urban centers

5. Transportation and communication handicaps; effects of air age

6. Trade: characteristic products; imports, exports (agriculture, wheat, automobiles, forest products, fish, furs, minerals); trade relations with United States, Great Britain, other countries; ports

7. Place in British Commonwealth; in world community

C. Northern and western Europe

1. Reasons for our interest

2. Regions and countries included (23 nations in northwest Europe, southern Europe, middle (central) Europe, Scandinavia)

3. Geographic influences; strategic location; comparative area;

climatic factors; bodies of water; nature of coastline; variety and location of resources; effects on life of people

4. People: 300 million, composition, distribution (urbanization); low population growth; diversity of skills; multilingual—60 languages, ethnic minority problems; similarities and contrasts in education and culture; life and work in various regions; maximum use of resources of environment (land and sea) for development of industry and agriculture; locations of agricultural areas and industrial centers; contributions of various national groups to world culture; cultural centers

5. Trade: characteristic products, farming, food surpluses; major industrial products, imports, exports, trade centers; role of European Union (EU), role of European Free Trade Association (EFTA), world markets, port cities

6. Transportation and communication facilities; effects of air age

7. Current problems: colonial policies, regional problems, American relations with European countries, trade barriers, postwar problems.

8. Significance of region in world community

D. Mediterranean region and Near East, including southwest Asia
1. Reasons for our interest
2. Natural regions and countries
3. Strategic points: Suez Canal, Dardanelles, Bosporus, Gibraltar
4. Mediterranean climate (desert areas of little rainfall); topography—great mountain systems (Alps), major rivers, northern European plains; natural resources—two-thirds of world's oil reserves, effects on life of people
5. People: 400 million, distribution of population (small density); diverse cultural backgrounds;

methods of utilizing resources for limited agricultural and limited industrial development; mode of life in different regions; population trends and movements; urban centers

6. Transportation and communication

7. Trade: characteristic products; imports, exports (oil), importance of trade route through Suez Canal; trade centers and ports; world markets

E. Eastern Europe
1. Reasons for our interest
2. Natural regions and countries in the area: Poland, Czech Republic, former Yugoslavia, Balkan nations, Russia and CIS
3. Geographic influences; comparative area and extent; climatic range; topography—mountains (Carpathians, Urals), rivers (Volga); natural resources—coal, effects on life of people
4. People: size and distribution of population; diversity of nationalities and cultures; utilization of resources: mode of life in agricultural (Ukraine), forest, and mining areas; industry (in Czech Republic) and in the growing manufacturing centers; effects of government land policies; program of expansion
5. Trade: limited foreign trade; emphasis on internal trade; effects of lack of good ports; characteristic products—coal, oil, agriculture; imports and exports
6. Significance of region in world community

F. The Far East
1. Reasons for our interest
2. Natural and climatic regions; countries—China, Japan, India, southeast Asia, south Asia, the two Koreas, Taiwan, the Philippines, Indonesia
3. Geographic influences: relative location; comparative area and extent (one-third of the earth's surface); types of climate: tundra, taiga, grasslands of steppes, monsoons (southeast

Asia), tropical rainforests (Indonesia), humid subtropical (south China), humid continental (north China), desert (Gobi); topography—mountains (Himalayas), plateaus (Mongolia), desert (Gobi), active volcanoes, rivers—Yangtze, Yellow, Indus, Ganges, Mekong, deltas; natural resources—coal, oil, iron ore, tungsten; effects on lives of people

4. People: 60% of total world population; unequal distribution (one-third in urban centers); social classes (India), racial and cultural diversity: Mongoloid, Caucasoid, Negroid; high birth rate

5. Mode of life: adverse climatic conditions; utilization of natural resources; types and methods of agriculture—need for intensive soil cultivation, prevalence of subsistence crops; home industries; factors limiting industrial expansion; trends toward industrialization

6. Transportation and communication problems in greater part of region; topographic handicaps

7. Trade: characteristic products— two-thirds agricultural (wheat, rice, spices), imports, exports (tea, silk), world markets reached mostly by air

G. Australia and New Zealand
1. Reasons for our interest
2. Natural regions: western plateau, Red Heart, Great Barrier Reef
3. Geographic influences: remoteness; comparative area—3 million square miles; mild climate; low population destiny; natural resources (iron ore, gold)
4. People: 17 million, including 200,000 aborigines; population concentrated in coastal cities; effects of remoteness on life and culture; mode of life in different regions (cities, outback); high level of industrialization; agricultural regions; urban centers; effects of progressive government
5. Transportation and communication: importance of internal

travel by air because of vast distances
6. Trade: 25% of world's wool (sheep-raising in New Zealand), meat (beef, lamb), wheat as principal exports; imports; trade centers, ports, trade relations with United Kingdom and United States
7. Problems of immigration and multiculturalism
8. Place in British Commonwealth; in world community

H. Africa
1. Natural regions and countries
2. Geographic influences: 10% of world area, 5000 miles from north to south, 4600 miles from east to west; second largest continent; climatic range— tropical rainforest, grasslands, desert (Sahara), the Rift Valley, rivers (Nile, Zambezi), effects on life of people
3. People: size, distribution (70% Black); native and European cultures; effects of exploitation by European powers; mode of life in mining, grazing, agricultural regions; handicaps limiting development of resources; special case of South Africa
4. Transportation and communication problems; no railroads; lack of capital
5. Trade: exports—tropical crops, minerals; imports—machinery, manufactured goods; problem of smooth coastline and few natural harbors; lack of skilled labor
6. Potential for future development

III. World Trade
A. Bases of world trade (Needs of people; climatic variations; unequal distribution of natural resources)
B. Importance of trade in our economic, political, and cultural life
C. Man's role in world trade
1. Making of goods: raw materials; capital; labor; transportation; inventions and improved processes that make possible better utilization of natural and human resources
2. Marketing of goods: transporta-

tion; land, water, and sky routes; influence of government policies on the flow of goods; effect of trade on group living

3. Utilization of goods and services; production, consumption, law of supply and demand; surpluses and shortages; effects of prosperity or depression in one region on other regions

4. Importance of communication and its effect on trade; major agencies of communication; effects of airplane and of computers and other new inventions

D. Relation of world trade to world peace

IV. Toward a better world

A. The development of better understanding among peoples; reasons why understanding is essential; factors that tend to foster understanding; factors that tend to foster disunity and conflict; suggested methods of dealing with such problems

B. Implications of atomic age: peacetime development; atomic energy and war; need for international control of atomic energy

C. International organization: past efforts to bind people of the world together; creation of the United Nations; functioning of the United Nations; future hopes for world unity

CIVICS AND GOVERNMENT

I. Nature of political systems
A. Government and society—importance and basic role of government
B. Types of modern governments
C. Meaning of democracy

II. American political system
A. Foundations of American government; modern political and economic systems; heritage
B. Declaration of Independence and U.S. Constitution
C. American federalism

III. American political process
A. Political party system
B. Right to vote and voter behavior
C. Nominations and elections

D. Public opinion and pressure groups (lobbyists)

IV. National executive branch
A. Office and powers of the president
B. Functions
C. Vice president
D. President's cabinet

V. National legislative branch
A. Nature, structure, and powers of Congress
B. Functions
C. Roles of Congress

VI. National judiciary branch
A. American system of justice—importance of law and the legal system
B. Federal court system and role of Supreme Court
C. Judicial process and administration of law
D. Civil liberties and civil rights
E. Goal of equal justice for all

VII. State governments
A. Nature and functions of state governments
B. State executive, legislative, and judiciary branches
C. Financing state and local governments

VIII. Local governments
A. Importance
B. Governing the communities—cities, towns, counties
C. Financing

IX. Government and the general welfare
A. Federal revenues and expenditures
B. Money and banking policies
C. Our government and business—capitalism
D. Labor and Social Security
E. Agriculture and conservation

X. The United States in today's world
A. American foreign policy
B. U.S. and international organizations
C. Population explosion; technological revolution; meeting social responsibilities—health, education, welfare, crime, and other social issues

WORLD HISTORY

I. The Dawn of Civilization (c. 3000–1500 B.C.)
A. Mesopotamia
1. Sumeria
2. Babylonia

3. Assyria
4. Chaldea
B. Egypt
   1. Role of Pharaohs
   2. Religion
   3. Sciences

II. The Spread of Civilization (c. 1500–500 B.C.)
A. Hittites
   1. Iron
B. Phoenicians
   1. Trade
C. Hebrews
   1. Jewish monotheism
   2. The Old Testament
   3. The Ten Commandments
D. Lydians
   1. Coins
E. Ancient Persians
   1. Zoroasterianism

III. Aegean Civilization (c. 1200 B.C.)
A. Crete
B. Troy

IV. Ancient Greece (Hellenic)
A. Homeric Age (1000 B.C.)
B. Greek Gods
C. City States (900 B.C.)
   1. Spartan military
   2. Athenian democracy
      a. Pericles (461 B.C.) "Golden Age"
      b. Architecture
      c. Philosophy
D. Persian Wars
E. Peloponnesian Wars
F. Hellenistic Period
   1. Macedonian conquests
   2. Alexander the Great (334 B.C.)

V. Ancient Rome
A. Etruscan
B. Roman republic (509 B.C.)
   1. Rome conquers Italy
   2. Rome conquers world
   3. The Caesars (49 B.C.)
C. Roman contributions
   1. Latin language
   2. Religion
   3. Engineering (roads)
D. Decline and Fall (300–476 A.D.)
   1. Barbarian invasions

VI. Asia
A. India (563 B.C.)
   1. Buddha
B. Chinese Empire (770–256 B.C.)
   1. Confucius
   2. Taoism

VII. Rise of Christianity (c. 30–529 A.D.)
A. Christ as Messiah
B. The New Testament
C. Spread by Peter and Paul
D. Papacy created
E. Monasticism

VIII. Byzantine Civilization
A. Constantine (312 A.D.)
B. Justinian (527 A.D.)
C. Byzantine Empire (610–1453 A.D.)

IX. Islam
A. Mohammed (570 A.D.)
   1. Allah
   2. Mecca
B. Moslem conquests
C. Contributions
   1. Mathematics and science
   2. Medicine

X. Medieval Society
A. Feudalism (800–1250)
   1. The Manor
      a. Lord
      b. Knighthood
   2. Chivalry
B. Church
   1. The Popes
   2. The Hierarchy
   3. Clergy (Monks)
   4. Crushing of heresy
C. The Crusades (1096)
   1. Commerce—Guilds
D. Medieval governments
   1. France—Charlemagne
   2. England—Alfred the Great, William the Conqueror
   3. The Magna Carta (1215)
E. Culture
   1. Romance languages
   2. Gothic architecture

XI. China
A. Genghis Khan (1162)
B. Kublai Khan (1218)

XII. Africa
A. Kingdom of Songhay

XIII. Renaissance (1350–1600)
A. Printing (1450)
B. Art
   1. Painting
      a. DaVinci, Michelangelo, Rembrandt
C. Literature
   1. Dante—*Divine Comedy*
   2. Cervantes—*Don Quixote*
   3. Chaucer—*Canterbury Tales*
   4. Shakespeare—Plays
D. Ruling families
   1. Medici

2. Borgia
E. Cities
   1. Venice
   2. Florence
XIV. Reformation
  A. Martin Luther (1519)
  B. Protestantism
    1. John Calvin
  C. Anglicanism
    1. Henry VIII (1509)
    2. Elizabeth I (1558)
  D. Catholic Counter-Reformation
    1. The Inquisition
    2. The Jesuits
  E. Religious Wars
XV. Scientific Revolution (1500–1700)
  A. Astronomy—Copernicus
  B. Physics—Galileo
  C. Mathematics—Newton
XVI. European Expansion
  A. Exploration
    1. Portuguese—Prince Henry, Vasco da Gama
    2. Spanish—Columbus, Magellan
  B. The Americas
    1. Mayans (900–1200)
    2. Aztecs (1360)
    3. Incas (1493)
    4. Conquistadors—Cortez, deSoto, La Salle, Pizarro
XVII. Absolute Monarchy
  A. Spain—Ferdinand and Isabella (1479)
  B. France—Louis XIV (1661)
  C. Prussia—Frederick the Great (1740)
  D. Russia—Peter the Great (1682); Catherine the Great (1762); Romanov (1613–1917)
XVIII. Western Civilization
  A. French Revolution (1789–1799)
  B. Napoleon (1799–1815)
  C. The Industrial Revolution
    1. Railroads (1820)
    2. Steel (1856)
  D. The Rise of Nationalism
    1. France—Bourbons
    2. Prussians
    3. Hapsburgs
    4. Kingdom of Italy (1861)
    5. German Empire—Bismarck (1871)
    6. Austria-Hungary (1867)
XIX. Europe (1914–1945)
  A. World War I (1914–1918)
    1. Defeat of Germany
  B. Rise of Communism

    1. Lenin, Stalin
  C. Rise of Nazism
    1. Hitler
    2. The Holocaust
  D. Rise of Fascism
    1. Mussolini
  E. World War II (1939–1945)
    1. Defeat of Germany and Japan
    2. Use of atomic bomb
XX. 1945–Present
  A. Cold War
    1. Marshall Plan, Berlin Wall
  B. NATO vs. Warsaw Pact
  C. Downfall of Soviet Union
  D. People's Republic of China (1949) Mao
  E. Korean War (1950–1953)
  F. Vietnam War (1964–1973)
  G. Cuban Revolution
    1. Castro
  H. Middle East
    1. Emergence of Israel (1948)
    2. Persian Gulf War (1990–1991)
  I. Achievements in Space
  J. European Community

Glossary of Social Studies Terms

In social studies, as in science, vocabulary is of critical importance. The following selected subject-area vocabulary lists consist of words from the five social sciences—history (see below), civics and government (page 311), economics (page 314), and geography (page 318). The definitions have been simplified, and in the simplification some aspects of the definition have been omitted. If a definition is not clear, be certain to consult a dictionary. In any event, be sure to review the section "Learning Social Studies Vocabulary and Deriving Meaning from Context" in Chapter 10 (page 244).

Don't forget: The glossary defines a number of terms that are likely to be used on the test. Be sure to consult the glossary when you encounter unfamiliar terms in the questions in the next chapter.

HISTORY

ABOLITIONIST one who favored abolishing slavery in the United States prior to the Civil War

AGGRESSION attack by one country on another without any provocation

ANNEXATION addition of territory to an already existing country or state

APARTHEID policy of racial segregation and discrimination against blacks and other non-Europeans practiced by the Republic of South Africa until 1990

APPEASEMENT policy of giving into the demands of an enemy power in an effort to maintain peace

ARMISTICE temporary stopping of war by agreement of both sides before a peace treaty is signed

ARYAN term wrongly used by the Nazis to refer to a person of German or northern European descent

AXIS in World War II, the countries—Nazi Germany, Fascist Italy, and Japan—that fought against the United States and its allies

BLACKLIST list of people or organizations to be avoided in trade or denied employment because of government policy or suspected disloyalty

BLOCKADE action taken to cut off trade and communication with an enemy

BOONDOGGLE spending of public money to create unnecessary jobs

BOURGEOISIE the middle class

BOYCOTT refusal to deal with a country or an organization for political or economic reasons

CHARTER in colonial times, a grant from the English ruler to a person or corporation giving certain rights and privileges of settlement

CIVIL WAR American war between the northern and southern states (1861–1865)

COLD WAR diplomatic and economic conflict between nations short of actual warfare

COLONY settlement in a distant land that remains under control of the country from which its settlers came

COMPROMISE agreement in which each side gives up some things it wanted

CONSERVATION policies and practices that aim at preservation of natural resources such as forests and wildlife

COUP D'ETAT sudden overthrow of a government by force

DECREE order of a government or a church

DESEGREGATION removal of separation of races in public places such as schools

DISARMAMENT reduction in arms and armed forces as a result of agreement between nations

DISCRIMINATION prejudice in the treatment of one group, as compared with another, in such matters as jobs, housing, and admission to schools

DOCTRINE principle or belief or a set of principles or beliefs

DOVE one who espouses the cause of peace and/or pursues a conciliatory policy in foreign affairs

EDICT official proclamation or decree

EMANCIPATION setting free of a slave or anyone else in bondage

EMBARGO official order preventing ships from entering or leaving the ports of a country for the purpose of commerce

EMIGRATION movement of a person or persons from one country to settle in another

EMPIRE group of states, colonies, or territories joined together under the rule of a dominant power

EVOLUTION theory that plants and animals develop from earlier life forms by the passing down, from one generation to the next, of variations that help them to survive

FAIR DEAL continuation and development of the principles of the New Deal by the Truman administration

FEMINISM movement to win for women, rights equal to those of men in political, social, and economic areas

FEUDALISM medieval (9th to 15th centuries) social and economic organization of society in Europe

GENOCIDE systematic killing off of an entire national, racial, or cultural group

HAWK one who advocates an aggressive and warlike approach to foreign policy

HERESY a religious belief opposed to doctrine established by the church

IMMIGRATION movement of a person into a new country to settle there

IMPERIALISM policy of a nation to extend its power by establishing colonies and controlling territories, raw materials, and world markets

INDUSTRIAL REVOLUTION social and economic changes brought about by the development of large-scale industrial production

INTEGRATION incorporation of different racial or ethnic groups into free and equal association in a society or an organization

ISOLATIONISM policy of a country that is based on unwillingness to take part in international affairs

MANDATE authority given by the League of Nations to one nation to administer a territory or geographic region

MANIFESTO public declaration by a government of intention to act or of action taken

MEDIEVAL referring to the period in Europe between the 9th and 15th centuries

MILITARISM belief that the military should dominate the government and that military efficiency is the ideal of the state

MONARCHY government in which supreme power rests with a king, queen, or emperor and where such power may be absolute or limited

MONOTHEISM doctrine that there is only one God

NATIONALISM doctrine that the interests and security of one's own country are more important than those of other nations or international groups

NAZISM system in Germany (1933–1945) that controlled all activities of the people, fostered belief in the supremacy of a Fuhrer (Leader), and promoted the German people as a master race and the establishment of Germany as the dominant world power

NEW DEAL principles and policies of liberal democrats as advocated under the leadership of President Franklin Roosevelt

NONAGGRESSION referring to an agreement between two nations not to attack one another

OPINIONS, ATTITUDES AND BELIEFS a person's preferences or positions on public matters based on thought or emotion: opinions are short-term, attitudes are more lasting, beliefs deal with the more basic values of life

PACIFISM belief that conflicts between nations should be settled by peaceful means rather than by war

PACT agreement or treaty between nations

PAN-AMERICANISM belief in political, economic, social, and cultural cooperation and understanding between the nations of North, Central, and South America

PARLIAMENT the legislative body of Great Britain, consisting of the House of Lords and the House of Commons

PARTITION division of a geographic area into two or more countries or into areas annexed to already existing countries

PLEBISCITE direct vote of all eligible voters on an important political issue

PREJUDICE hostile attitude without foundation in fact or knowledge toward an ethnic group or any member of it

PROHIBITION in the United States, the period between 1920 and 1933 when the manufacture and sale of alcoholic drinks was forbidden by federal law

PROPAGANDA systematic spread of ideas or doctrines with a view to convincing others of their truth, using repetition and, in some cases, distortion

PROTECTORATE weaker state protected and in some instances controlled by a stronger state

PROVISIONAL referring to a government that functions temporarily until a permanent government is established

PURITAN Protestant in 16th and 17th century England and America who sought greater reform in the Church of England

QUOTA greatest number of persons who may be admitted, as to the United States or to an institution such as a college

RACE one of three primary divisions of humans—Caucasian, Negro, and Mongoloid—differing in physical characteristics

RATIFICATION granting of formal approval, as to a constitution or a treaty

REACTIONARY extreme conservative, one who opposes progress or liberalism

RECIPROCAL applying by mutual agreement to both parties or countries concerned, as in trade

RECONSTRUCTION period after the Civil War (1865–1877) during which the Confederate states were controlled by the federal government and recognized prior to readmission to the Union

RENAISSANCE period (14th through 16th centuries) of revival in learning and the arts in Europe

REPARATION payment by a defeated nation for damages done to persons and property of the victorious country in a war

SANCTIONS measures taken by a group of nations to force another to stop a violation of international law that it is considered to have made

SATELLITE a small state that is dependent on a larger, more powerful state and must, as a result, maintain similar policies

SECTIONALISM placing of the interests of a section of a country ahead of those of the nation

SEDITION acts that tend to foment rebellion against the existing government

SEGREGATION policy or practice of compelling racial and ethnic groups to live apart from each other

SELF-DETERMINATION right of a people to determine its own form of government independently

SHARECROPPER farmer who does not own land but works it for a share of the crop

SOVEREIGNTY supreme and independent political authority of a state

STATUS QUO the existing political, social, and economic order

STEREOTYPE fixed belief regarding a person, group, or idea that is held by a number of people and allows no individuality or critical judgment

SUFFRAGETTE woman who works actively for the right of women to vote

TOLERATION freedom to hold religious beliefs different from those in authority

TRUSTEESHIP authority from the United Nations to a country to administer a territory or region

VALUES social principles, goals, or standards held or accepted by an individual, class or society

WHIG member of a political party that supported limitation of presidential power and opposed the Democrats in the United States (1836–1856); also a person who supported the American Revolution

ZIONIST supporter of the movement to establish a Jewish national state in Palestine; now, a supporter of the State of Israel

CIVICS AND GOVERNMENT

ACT document made into law by a legislative body

ADMINISTRATION term of office of the executive branch of government

AGENCY bureau that administers a governmental function

ALIEN one who owes allegiance to a government or country other than the country in which he resides

ALLEGIANCE duty of a citizen to his or her government

ALLIANCE formal agreement between nations to achieve a common purpose

AMENDMENT change or revision made in a constitution or a law

AMNESTY general pardon to a group of persons, freeing them from punishment for offenses against a government or society

ANARCHY complete absence of government and law with resulting disorder

APPELLATE court that can receive appeals and reverse the decisions of lower courts

APPORTIONMENT allotment of representatives to a group in proportion to their members

APPROPRIATION money made available by formal act of a legislative body for a specific public purpose

AT-LARGE official chosen by all the voters of a particular election district

AUTONOMY self-government

BALLOT (1) the paper on which a vote is recorded (2) the right to vote

BICAMERAL legislature made up of two houses, such as a Senate and an Assembly or a Senate and a House of Representatives

BILL preliminary form of a law proposed to a legislative body

BIPARTISAN representing or composed of members of two parties

BLOC combination of legislators or nations that acts as a unit with a common interest or purpose

BOSS politician who controls a political machine and has influence over legislation and appointments to office

BUREAUCRACY government that functions through departments that follow given rules and have varying degrees of authority in the organization

CABINET group of advisers to the head of a country who usually administer governmental departments

CAMPAIGN program of activities designed to elect a candidate to political office

CAUCUS closed meeting of party members to decide policy or to select candidates for office

CENSURE reprimand voted by a governmental body of one of its members or of the government or its cabinet

CENTER in politics, a party or group that follows policies between the left (which advocates change) and the right (which opposes it)

CHECKS AND BALANCES system of government that provides for each branch (executive, legislative, and judicial) to have some control over the others

CIVIL LIBERTIES rights to think, speak, and act without interference that are guaranteed to the individual by law and custom

CIVIL RIGHTS rights that are guaranteed to the individual by the Constitution and by acts of Congress; e.g., right to vote

CIVIL SERVICE those in the employ of government who got their positions through open competitive examination on the basis of merit

COALITION temporary alliance of countries or parties for action to achieve some purpose

COMMISSION government agency with administrative, judicial, or legislative powers

COMMITTEE group chosen by a legislative body to consider a particular law or topic

CONFERENCE meeting of committees from two branches of a legislature to settle differences in a bill they have enacted

CONFIRMATION approval by a legislative body of an act or appointment by an executive

CONGRESS the legislature of the United States, consisting of the Senate and the House of Representatives

CONSERVATIVE person or party that tends to oppose change in government and its institutions

CONSTITUTION system of fundamental laws and principles, written or unwritten, by which a people is governed

CONVENTION gathering of members or delegates of a political group for a specific purpose, such as choosing a candidate for office

DELEGATE (1) representative to a convention (2) person empowered to act on behalf of those who choose him or her

DEMOCRACY government by the people directly or through representatives chosen in free elections

DICTATORSHIP state ruled by one who has absolute power and authority

ELECTION choosing by vote among candidates for public office

EXECUTIVE the branch of government charged with administering the laws of a nation

FASCISM a system of government characterized by power in the hands of a dictator, suppression of opposition parties, and aggressive nationalism (Italy, 1922–1945)

FEDERAL referring to a system of government in which a constitution divides powers between the central government and such political subdivisions as states

FILIBUSTER tactics, such as nonstop oratory, used by a minority in a legislative body to delay action on a bill

FOREIGN POLICY course of action adopted by a country in its dealings with other nations

FREEDOM civil or political liberty

GOVERNMENT established system of political administration by which a country or its subdivisions is ruled

HEARING session of a legislative committee in which evidence bearing on possible legislation is obtained from witnesses

IMPEACH to bring charges against a public official for wrongdoing prior to possible trial and removal from office if a conviction is obtained; **IMPEACHMENT** the act of bringing such charges

INAUGURATION formal induction into office of a public official

INDICTMENT formal accusation of someone with the commission of a crime, usually after investigation by a grand jury of charges made by a prosecutor

INITIATIVE right of a citizen to bring up a matter for legislation, usually by means of a petition signed by a designated number of voters

INJUNCTION court order preventing a person or group from taking an action that might be in violation of the law

JUDICIAL referring to the courts and their functions or to the judges who administer these functions

JURISDICTION authority of a government or court to interpret and apply the law

LAW bill that has been approved by a legislative body and signed by the chief executive

LEFT members of a legislative body who take more radical and liberal political positions than the other members

LEGISLATION laws made by a legislative body, such as a Senate

LEGISLATURE group of persons having the responsibility and authority to make laws for a nation or a political subdivision of it

LIBERAL individual or political party whose beliefs stress protection of political and civil liberties, progressive reform, and the right of an individual to govern him- or herself

LOBBY to attempt to influence legislators to support bills that favor some special group or interest

MACHINE political organization under the leadership of a boss and his lieutenants that controls party policy and job patronage

MAJORITY (1) number of votes for a candidate that is greater than the votes for all the other candidates put together (2) party in a legislative body that commands the largest number of votes

MINORITY political group that is smaller than the controlling group in a government or legislature and does not have the necessary votes to gain control

MUNICIPAL referring to local government such as that of a city, town, or village

MUNICIPALITY city or town that has the power to govern itself

NATURALIZE to give the rights of citizenship to a noncitizen or alien

NEUTRALITY policy of a government that avoids taking sides directly or indirectly in disputes between other nations

NOMINATE to name a candidate for election to public office

ORDINANCE law enacted by local governmental authority

OVERRIDE action taken by a legislative body to enact a law that has been disapproved (vetoed) by the chief executive of a political unit such as a nation or state

PARDON official release from (continued) legal punishment for an offense

PARTISAN position or vote that follows party policy ("the party line")

PARTY organization of persons who work to elect their candidates to political office to further the governmental philosophy and causes in which they believe

PATRONAGE power of a political organization or its representative to give jobs

PETITION request for specific legal or judicial action that is initiated and signed by an interested individual or group of individuals

PLANK one of the items in a party program or platform

PLATFORM statement of the policies and principles of a political party or its candidate for office

PLURALITY number of votes by which the winning candidate in an election defeats his or her nearest opponent

POLL (1) vote as recorded by a voter (2) count of votes cast (3) questioning of a group of people chosen at random on their views on political and other matters

PRECINCT subdivision of a town or city that serves as an election unit

PRESSURE GROUP group of people who seek to change government law or policy through the use of lobbies, propaganda, and media

PRIMARY vote by members of a political party to choose candidates for political office or for some other political purpose

PROGRESSIVE person or party that stands for moderate political and social change or reform

PUBLIC OPINION views of a people, generally as they influence social and political action

QUORUM minimum number of a legislative body that must be present before the body can legally conduct business

RADICAL person or party that stands for extreme political and social change

RATIFY give formal approval to a document such as a treaty or constitution

RECALL right of or action taken by vote of the people or by petition to remove a public official from office

REFERENDUM practice of submitting to direct popular vote a proposed law or an act that has been passed by a legislative body

REFORM political movement designed to correct abuses in government by changes in the law

REGIME form or manner of government or rule

REGISTRATION signing up of a person in his or her election district to enable that person to vote

REGULATE to control or bring under the control of government or a government agency

REPRESENTATIVE member of a legislative body chosen to act on behalf of those who elected him or her to represent them

REPUBLIC government in which power remains with all the citizens, who are entitled to vote and who elect representatives who act for them and are responsible to them

RESOLUTION formal statement of opinion or intention voted by a legislative or other group

REVIEW reexamination by higher judicial authority of the proceedings or decision of a lower court

REVOLUTION complete overthrow, usually by force, of an established government or political system

RIGHT (1) members of a legislative body who hold more conservative views than the other members (2) that which belongs to an individual by law or tradition, such as the right to free speech

SELF-GOVERNMENT government of a people by its own members or their representatives instead of by some outside power

SENIORITY consideration given to length of service in a legislative body in making assignments to important positions or to membership in committees of that body

SOCIAL SECURITY federal system of old age, unemployment, and disability insurance for employed and dependent persons

SOVEREIGNTY supreme and independent power or authority in government

SPEAKER public official who presides over a law-making body such as the House of Representatives or an assembly

STATE any of the political units that constitute the federal government

STATUTE law passed by a legislative body

SUBPOENA written order to a person to appear in court or before a legislative body to give evidence

SUBVERSIVE referring to an act or a person that would tend to overthrow the existing government

SUFFRAGE right to vote in political elections or on political matters

SUMMONS written order to appear in court, addressed to a person who may be involved in or have knowledge of a crime

SUPREME COURT highest federal court whose decisions are final and take precedence over those of all other courts

TENURE (1) length of time a person holds office (2) an individual's right to hold office until retirement or death

TESTIFY to present evidence in a court under oath

TICKET list of candidates nominated for election by a political party

TOTALITARIAN kind of government in which one political party is in power to the exclusion of all others

TREASON betrayal of one's country by actively helping its enemies in their attempt to overthrow it or defeat it in war

TREATY formal agreement, entered into by two or more nations, dealing with commerce or policies

URBAN having to do with a town or city

VETO act or power of a chief executive to turn down a bill passed by a legislative body by actually rejecting it or refusing to sign it

VOTE to cast a ballot or take any other necessary action to express one's choice in an election of a candidate for office or of any proposal for legislative change

ECONOMICS

ARBITRATION attempt to settle, or settlement of, a dispute by submitting it to a third party designated to decide it after hearing evidence presented by both sides

ASSET property and resources of all kinds of a person or a corporation

AUTOMATION production and distribution of goods automatically by mechanical and electronic, rather than human, means

BALANCE OF PAYMENTS relationship between a nation's outflow of money (imports, foreign aid) and inflow of money (exports, gifts)

BALANCE SHEET financial statement balancing the assets, liabilities and net worth of an individual or a business

BANKING practice of receiving, keeping, lending, or issuing money and making easier the exchange of funds

BANKRUPTCY financial condition in which a person or business is found legally unable to pay creditors

BARTER system of trading in which one good is exchanged for another without the use of money

BUDGET statement of an individual, business, or government in which expected incomes are allocated as expenses in designated necessary areas

BUSINESS buying and selling of commodities and services for a profit

CAPITALISM economic system based on private ownership of the means of production with freedom of private enterprise to earn a profit under free market (competitive) conditions

CARTEL combination of businesses to establish a national or international monopoly by limiting competition

CASTE social class or group formed on the basis of birth or wealth, existing under strict rules within a social system, with little or no movement into or out

CENSUS official count of the population of a country (required every ten years in the United States by the Constitution)

CERTIFICATE document that shows that a person owns stock and is entitled to the benefits and liabilities of a stockholder

COLLECTIVE BARGAINING negotiation between management and labor regarding wages, hours, working conditions, and other benefits

COMMERCE large-scale buying and selling of goods involving transportation of the goods between cities or countries

COMMODITY any good that is bought or sold in a commercial transaction

COMMUNISM economic system based on ownership of all property by the state and, in Marx's view, on equal distribution of economic goods through revolutionary means

COMPENSATION payment given as recompense for an injury or loss, as to a worker who has been hurt on the job

COMPETITION in a free enterprise system, the attempts by rival businesses to get customers for the goods they manufacture or distribute

CONSUMER one who uses goods or services out of need

CONSUMER PRICE INDEX single number that compares consumer prices in one year with prices paid by consumers in previous years

CONTRACT agreement between two or more people or companies to do something, set forth in writing or orally, and enforceable by law

CORPORATION group of individuals who possess shares and have the privileges and obligations of a single person, with limited liability

COST amount of money, labor, and other expenses involved in producing or obtaining goods or services

CRAFT (members of) trade requiring special skills, such as printing

CRASH sudden decline in market values of shares in a business

CREDIT money, based on a person's economic standing, that he or she is allowed to borrow and repay at a later date

CREDITOR person or institution to whom money is owed

CURRENCY money, such as coin or bank notes, that is in circulation in a country

CUSTOMS duty or tax levied by a government on imported and exported goods

CYCLE in business, a sequence of events that occurs and recurs in a given order and involves boom, downturn, depression or recession, and recovery

DEBT obligation of an individual or corporation to pay something to a creditor

DEFICIT amount by which a corporation's or a government's debts are greater than its credits or assets

DEFLATION fall in prices brought about by a decrease in spending

DEMAND desire and ability to pay for goods and services usually within a given price range at a given time

DEPLETION using up of natural resources such as oil and timber

DEPOSIT money put into a bank or given in partial payment for something purchased

DEPRECIATION decrease in value of business property or equipment through "wear and tear"

DEPRESSION period of low business activity, wide unemployment, and falling prices

DEVALUATION lowering of the exchange value of one currency with respect to another by decreasing the amount of gold backing it

DISCOUNT amount deducted from the original price of something sold

DISCRIMINATION unfavorable treatment of persons based on negative prejudgments made without regard to fact

DISTRIBUTION process of making goods and services available to consumers, as well as the promotion of the buying and selling of these goods and services

ECONOMICS science that deals with the production, distribution, and consumption of goods and services

ECONOMIC SYSTEM manner in which a nation's resources are used, and goods and services are produced and distributed

ECONOMY structure and functioning of a nation's economic system

ENTREPRENEUR person who enters into business and risks his or her skills, time, and money in the hope of earning a profit

EQUILIBRIUM market price at which supply equals demand

EXCISE tax on the production, sale or use of certain commodities within a country

EXPORT goods sold by one country to another

EXTENDED FAMILY family that includes other relatives (grandparents, uncles and aunts, cousins, in-laws) beyond the immediate nuclear family (parents and children)

FISCAL having to do with taxes, public revenues, or public debt

FOREIGN EXCHANGE currency that can be used to pay international debts

FRINGE benefit given by an employer that, although not paid directly as wages, involves a cost to the employer

GOODS merchandise

GROSS NATIONAL PRODUCT (GNP) total value of a nation's annual output of goods and services

IMPORT goods brought into by one country from another

INCOME money received by a person or business organization for work or services performed or from investment or property

INDUSTRY businesses as a group that are engaged in manufacturing

INFLATION rise in prices caused by an increase in the amount of money in circulation or by an increase in the amount of spending resulting from greater demand than supply

INPUT amount of money and/or manpower invested in a project or process

INSTALLMENT system of credit in which goods purchased are paid for over a period of time by partial payments

INTEREST (1) charge for money borrowed, usually expressed as a percentage of the money lent (2) money paid to a depositor for money left in a bank for a stated period

INVESTMENT money put into a business or property in the hope of receiving income or earning a profit

LABOR economic group of wage-earning workers

LEVY tax imposed or collected by a government or other authority

LIABILITY debt owed by a business, a corporation, or an individual

LOCKOUT prevention by an employer of his or her workers from working during a dispute

LOSS amount by which the cost of an article sold is greater than the selling price

MANAGEMENT those who direct the affairs of a business or industry

MARGIN difference between the cost and the selling price of a product

MARKET buying and selling of goods or property

MEDIATION entry of a third party into a dispute between management and labor, with the intention of settling it fairly

MERGER combination of two or more businesses or corporations in which one of them eventually controls the other(s)

MONETARY having to do with the money of a country

MONEY coin or paper stamped by government authority, used as a medium of exchange and measure of value

MONOPOLY exclusive control of a product or service in a market so that prices for the product or service can be fixed and competition eliminated

NOTE written promise to pay a debt, such as a promissory note

OBSOLESCENCE process by which the plant and equipment of a business become outdated and can no longer be used efficiently to produce the goods needed

OUTPUT work done or amount produced by a person, machine, or assembly line in a given period

OVERHEAD costs involved in running a business, such as those for rent and electricity

PANIC period in which fear of economic collapse results in frenzied attempts to convert property, goods, and securities into cash

PARTNERSHIP form of business organization in which two or more people put money or property into a business and share the profits or losses

POVERTY extreme lack of the things necessary to sustain life, such as food, shelter, and clothing

PRICE amount of money or its equivalent for which anything is bought, sold, or offered for sale

PRODUCTION creation of economic value by making goods and services available to meet the needs of consumers

PRODUCTIVITY degree of ability to produce goods and services of economic value

PROFIT amount by which the selling price of an article sold is greater than the cost

PROPERTY possessions that may be personal (movable), land or real estate, or securities (stocks and bonds)

PROSPERITY condition in which the economy of a country or a business enjoys a state of well-being

RECESSION period of temporarily reduced business activity

RENT income received by a land or property owner for the use of his or her land or property

RESOURCES natural and human assets that can be used to produce economic goods or provide services

REVENUE income from taxes and other sources that is available for use on behalf of the public

SAVINGS total money saved by an individual or a nation

SCAB employee of a business who continues to work during a strike against that business

SCARCITY gap between the supply of goods produced and human needs

SECURITIES documents, usually bonds or stock certificates, that are evidence of either indebtedness (bonds) or ownership (stocks)

SERVICES duties performed or work done for others that has economic value

SHOP if *open*, a business establishment where workers are employed regardless of union membership; if *union*, one in which labor and management agree that all employees must be union members

SLUM highly crowded area in which housing is rundown, sanitary conditions are poor, and poverty is widespread

SOCIALISM ownership and operation of the means of production and distribution by society rather than by private persons, with all members sharing in the work and the products

SOCIOECONOMIC STATUS position in society based on social and economic factors such as wealth

SPECULATION use of capital to buy and sell stocks, property, commodities, and businesses in situations where above-average risk is taken

STANDARD OF LIVING level of subsistence of a country or an individual that takes into account possession of the necessities and comforts of life

STOCK shares held by an individual in a corporation

STRIKE work stoppage carried out by workers to force the employer to improve working conditions and benefits and/or to increase wages

SUBSIDY sum of money given by a government to a private individual or business in the public interest

SUBSISTENCE lowest level of food, clothing, and shelter needed to sustain life

SUPPLY amount of goods and services available for sale, usually within a given price range at a given time

SURPLUS amount of goods over and above what is needed

SURTAX tax that is added to an already existing tax

TARIFF tax imposed by a country on imported goods

TAX sum that an individual or corporation is required by the government to pay on income or property or an object purchased

TECHNOLOGY use of scientific knowledge in industry and commerce

TRADE buying and selling of economic goods

TRUST combination of corporations in an industry to control prices and eliminate competition

UNDERDEVELOPED NATION country inadequately developed economically and industrially with a relatively low standard of living

UNEMPLOYMENT condition of being out of work

UNION organization of workers that seeks to protect and advance the interests of its members with respect to working conditions and wages, usually through collective bargaining

WAGES money paid to an employee for work done

WEALTH everything having economic value measurable in price

WELFARE referring to a state or nation in which government rather than private organizations assumes the primary responsibility for the well-being of its citizens

WILDCAT referring to a strike that takes place without the permission of the union representing the striking workers

GEOGRAPHY

ALTITUDE elevation of an object above sea level

ANTARCTIC relating to the region near the South Pole

ARCHIPELAGO group of many islands

ARCTIC relating to the region around the North Pole to approximately 65° N

BASIN body of water partly or fully enclosed

BAY inlet of the sea or other body of water, usually smaller than a gulf

BAYOU lake occupying the abandoned part of a stream channel

BLUFF steep rise of ground between bottom land and higher land on the shore of a river, sea, or lake

BUTTE steep-sided, round-topped hill or mountain

CANYON deep, narrow valley with steep sides cut by a river

CLIMATE average weather conditions at a given place over a period of years as evidenced by temperature, precipitation, and winds

CONSERVATION planned management of natural resources to prevent exploitation, destruction, or neglect

CONTINENT one of the great land areas of the earth

CYCLONE violent storm or system of winds rotating about a calm center of low atmospheric pressure, traveling at a speed of 20 to 30 miles per hour and accompanied by rain

DELTA triangular or fan-shaped area of low-lying land formed by deposits at the mouth of a river

DESERT dry, barren expanse of land unable to support normal plant and animal life

DROUGHT prolonged period of lack of rainfall

EARTHQUAKE shaking or trembling of the earth that is volcanic in origin or involves the earth's crust

ECOLOGY science concerned with the interrelationship of organisms and their environments

ELEVATION height above the level of the sea

ENVIRONMENT climatic, soil, and living factors that influence an organism or an ecological community

EQUATOR great circle of the earth that is equidistant from the North and South poles and divides the earth's surface into the Northern and Southern hemispheres

EQUINOX one of two times each year when day and night are everywhere of equal length

EROSION wearing away by the action of water, wind, or glacial ice of the surface features of the earth—mountains, plateaus, valleys, coasts

FAR EAST countries of east Asia, including China, Japan, and Korea, and southeast Asia and the Malay Archipelago

FAULT break in the earth's crust accompanied by a displacement of one side of the break with respect to the other

FAUNA animals or animal life of a region

FJORD narrow inlet of the sea between steep cliffs and extending far into the land

FLORA plants or plant life of a region or special environment

FRONT boundary between differing air masses that differ in temperature

GEYSER hot spring that, from time to time, violently ejects boiling water and steam

GLACIER large mass of ice and snow moving slowly down a mountain or valley

GLOBE spherical model of the earth

GRASSLAND area of grass or grasslike vegetation, such as a prairie

GULF large area of a sea or ocean partially enclosed by land

HABITAT region where a particular plant or animal naturally lives

HIGH center of high atmospheric pressure

HUMIDITY moisture or water vapor in the atmosphere

HURRICANE severe tropical cyclone having winds of over 75 miles per hour and usually involving heavy rains

ISLAND land mass, smaller than a continent, entirely surrounded by water

ISTHMUS narrow strip of land having water at each side and connecting two larger bodies of land

JUNGLE land densely overgrown with tropical vegetation and trees

LAKE relatively large inland body of water, usually fresh

LANDLOCKED surrounded by land, as a bay

LATIN AMERICA part of the Western Hemisphere south of the United States: Mexico, Central America, the West Indies and South America

LATITUDE distance north or south of the equator, measured in degrees

LEGEND title or key accompanying an illustration or map

LONGITUDE distance in degrees east or west of the prime meridian

LOW region of depressed barometric pressure

MAP representation on a flat surface of all or part of the earth

MARITIME on, near, or living near the sea

MEDITERRANEAN CLIMATE climate characterized by warm, dry summers and rainy winters

MERIDIAN any of the lines of longitude

MESA high, broad, and flat plateau bounded by a steep cliff

METROPOLIS any large, important city

MIDDLE EAST lands from the eastern shores of the Mediterranean and Aegean seas to India

MIGRATION movement of people from one region or country to another, with the intention to settle there

MONSOON seasonal wind that blows over the Indian Ocean from Australia to India

NATURAL RESOURCES forms of wealth supplied by nature, such as coal, oil, and water power

OASIS place in a desert that is fertile because of the presence of water

OCEAN any of the five main divisions of the body of salt water that covers over 70 percent of the earth's surface: Atlantic, Pacific, Indian, Arctic, or Antarctic

PARALLEL imaginary line parallel to the equator and representing degrees of latitude on the earth's surface

PENINSULA land area almost entirely surrounded by water and connected to the mainland by a narrow strip of land

PLAIN extent of level country

PLATEAU elevated tract of fairly level land

POLAR ICE CAP mass of glacial ice that spreads slowly out in all directions from the poles

POPULATION DENSITY number of people in a given area

POPULATION EXPLOSION very great and continuing increase in human population in modern times

PRAIRIE large area of level or slightly rolling grassland that occupies the region between the Ohio and the Mississippi-Missouri rivers

PRECIPITATION rain, snow, sleet deposited on the earth

PRIME MERIDIAN great circle on the earth's surface from which longitude is measured both east and west: 0° longitude

RAINFALL amount of water falling in the form of rain, snow, etc., over a given area in a given period of time

RAIN FOREST dense, evergreen forest occupying a tropical region that has abundant rainfall throughout the year

RANGE a series of connected mountains forming a single system

RAW MATERIAL material still in its natural or original state, before processing or manufacture

REGION large, indefinite part of the earth's surface

RELATIVE HUMIDITY amount of moisture in the air, expressed as a percentage, as compared with the maximum amount that the air could contain at the same temperature

REVOLUTION movement of a heavenly body, as a star or planet, in an orbit or circle

ROTATION turning of a body, such as the earth, around a center point or axis

SCALE proportion that the size of a feature on a map bears to the actual size of the feature it represents

SEA large body of salt water wholly or partly enclosed by land

SEASON any of four divisions of the year, characterized chiefly by differences in temperature, precipitation, amount of daylight, and plant growth

SOLSTICE either of two points on the sun's path at which it is farthest north or farthest south of the equator

SOUND wide channel or strait linking two large bodies of water or separating an island from the mainland

STEPPE in Europe and Asia, vast, usually level plain having few trees

STRAIT narrow waterway connecting two large bodies of water

SUBCONTINENT large subdivision of a continent

SUBTROPICAL referring to regions bordering on the tropical zone

TAIGA forests of cone-bearing trees in the far north of Europe, Asia, and North America

TEMPERATE ZONE one of two zones between the tropics and the polar circles

TERRACE any of a series of flat platforms of earth with sloping sides, rising one above the other, as on a hillside

TERRAIN natural or surface features of a tract of land

THUNDERSTORM storm accompanied by thunder and lightning

TIDAL WAVE unusually large wave sent inshore by an earthquake or a very strong wind

TIDES alternating rise and fall of the surfaces of oceans and of waters connected with them, caused by the attraction of the moon and sun and occurring twice in approximately 24 hours

TOPOGRAPHY surface features of a region, including hills, valleys, rivers, lakes, and man-made features: canals, bridges, roads, etc.

TORNADO violently whirling column of air, extending down from a mass of storm clouds, that usually destroys everything in its rapid advance along a narrow path

TORRID ZONE area of the earth's surface lying between the Tropic of Cancer and the Tropic of Capricorn and divided by the equator

TRIBUTARY stream or river flowing into a larger stream or river

TROPICS area between the Tropic of Cancer and and the Tropic of Capricorn, 23½° north and south of the equator

TUNDRA any of the vast, nearly level, treeless, and marshy plains of the arctic and extreme northern regions

TYPHOON violent tropical cyclone originating in the west Pacific, especially in the South China Sea, principally from July to October

VALLEY stretch of low land lying between hills or mountains and usually having a river or stream flowing through it

VOLCANO cone-shaped mountain built up around a vent to form a crater with lava, cinders, ashes, and gases escaping through the vent from the earth's interior when the volcano is active

WEATHER general condition of the atmosphere at a particular time and place with regard to temperature, moisture, cloudiness, etc.

WESTERLIES winds blowing primarily from the west

WIND air naturally in horizontal motion at the earth's surface, coming from any direction, with any degree of velocity

Social Studies Practice

Civics and Government

Read each of the following selections carefully. After each selection, there are questions to be answered or statements to be completed. Select the best answer.

Questions 1–3 are based on the following passage.

The American Revolution is the only one in modern history that, rather than devouring the intellectuals who prepared it, carried them to power. Most of the signatories of the Declaration of Independence were intellectuals. This tradition is ingrained in America, whose greatest statesmen have been intellectuals; Jefferson and Lincoln, for example. These statesmen performed their political function, but at the same time they felt a more universal responsibility, and they actively defined this responsibility. Thanks to them there is in America a living school of political science. In fact, it is at the moment the only one perfectly adapted to the emergencies of the contemporary world, and one which can be victoriously opposed to communism. A European who follows American politics will be struck by the constant reference in the press and from the platform to this political philosophy, to the historical events through which it was best expressed, to the great statesmen who were its best representatives.

1. This passage deals chiefly with
   (1) the causes of the American Revolution
   (2) Jefferson and Lincoln as ideal statesmen
   (3) the basis of political philosophy in the United States
   (4) democracy versus communism
   (5) a living school of political science

2. According to this passage, intellectuals who pave the way for revolutions are usually
   (1) honored
   (2) misunderstood
   (3) destroyed
   (4) forgotten
   (5) elected to office

3. Which statement is true according to the passage?
   (1) America is a land of intellectuals.
   (2) The signers of the Declaration of Independence were all well educated.
   (3) Jefferson and Lincoln were revolutionaries.
   (4) Adaptability is a characteristic of American political science.
   (5) Europeans are confused by American politics.

Question 4 is based on the following cartoon.

321

4. The cartoon indicates the foreign policy position of the United States in response to the

   (1) start of the League of Nations
   (2) collapse of the global economy
   (3) beginning of World War II
   (4) spread of communism to Eastern Europe
   (5) rise of Hitler

Question 5 is based on the following cartoon.

5. The main idea expressed by the cartoon is that

   (1) discipline has broken down in the U.S. military
   (2) a majority of the people must support the conflict before the United States enters a war
   (3) the president's use of military power depends on congressional cooperation
   (4) Congress often opposes presidential proposals for increased military spending
   (5) only the president can declare war

Question 6 is based on the following cartoon.

"Miss Jones, weren't there any founding MOTHERS?"

6. Which statement best expresses the main idea of the cartoon?

   (1) Women have increasingly difficult choices in a modern society.
   (2) Women are the dominant force in American education today.
   (3) Women made few significant contributions to society until the twentieth century.
   (4) Free public education in the United States was established primarily by women.
   (5) More emphasis should be placed on the role of women in U.S. history.

Questions 7–9 are based on the following passage.

The average citizen today is knowledgeable about "landmark" court decisions concerning such questions as racial segregation, legislative apportionment, prayers in the public schools, or the right of a defendant to counsel in a criminal prosecution. Too often, however, he thinks that these decisions settle matters once and for all. Actually, of course, these well-publicized court decisions are merely guideposts pointing toward a virtually endless series of vexing legal questions.

For example, this nation could hardly fail to agree that state-compelled racial segregation in the public schools is a denial of the equal protection of the laws guaranteed by the 14th amendment. The real difficulty lies in determining how desegregation shall be accomplished and how to solve the problem of de facto school segregation, perpetuated by the practical if unfortunate realities of residential patterns.

7. According to the author, the effect of many decisions in the courts has been to

   (1) make citizens study the law
   (2) lead to more legal complications
   (3) contradict the Constitution
   (4) deny states' rights
   (5) provide final solutions to many problems

8. The author implies that, so far as important court decisions are concerned, the public today is generally

   (1) disinterested
   (2) mystified
   (3) critical
   (4) well informed
   (5) disapproving

9. As used in the first line of the passage, the word *landmark* most nearly means

   (1) exciting
   (2) just
   (3) significant
   (4) publicized
   (5) legal

Questions 10–12 are based on the following passage.

Among the many effects of democracy's spread through much of the developing world in the last few decades is the birth of a new American industry, democracy promotion. Beginning in the early 1990's, Washington began a wide variety of programs worldwide to help third-world countries democratize, including training election observers, improving parliamentary libraries, persuading political parties to form coalitions, teaching citizens' groups how to lobby, and helping independent newspapers.

But one expert feels that no American democracy consultant can affect the underlying conditions of a country that really determine its democratic progress—concentrations of power and wealth, political traditions, the expectations of its citizens.

The right programs over the long term can do much in countries where a government genuinely wants democracy but lacks expertise—nations such as South Africa, Slovakia, or Chile. In dictatorships, aid to the opposition can keep hope alive. But in nations that enjoyed some democratic progress but fell into strongman rule—such as Peru, Haiti, Cambodia, Kazakhstan, or Zambia—democracy promotion efforts to reform government institutions have been thwarted by leaders who have little interest in sharing power.

10. Increased democracy in the developing world has been a result of

    (1) American democracy promotion
    (2) independent newspapers
    (3) American democracy consultants
    (4) concentrations of power and wealth
    (5) political traditions

11. American democracy promotion is *least* successful

    (1) where interested governments lack expertise
    (2) in dictatorships
    (3) in countries where some democracy exists
    (4) where there is strongman rule
    (5) where government institutions have been reformed

12. American help has included improving all of the following EXCEPT

    (1) elections
    (2) lobbying
    (3) the party system
    (4) government libraries
    (5) expectations of citizens

Economics

Read each of the following selections carefully. After each selection, there are questions to be answered or statements to be completed. Select the best answer.

Questions 13–15 are based on the following passage.

There are hundreds and thousands of homeless children in this nation—a fivefold increase in the years since 1981. Because they are scattered in a thousand different cities, they are easily unseen. Many of them will never live to tell their stories.

None of these children has committed any crime. They have done nothing wrong. Their only crime is being born poor in a rich nation.

Last year I met a homeless family in Los Angeles. The mother had come there from Ohio to search for rent that she could afford. The father—there was a father, none of these families fit the stereotypes; few people do—the father worked full time, for minimum wage, in a sweatshop making blue jeans, earning $500 a month. The parents couldn't pay their rent and feed their child in Los Angeles on $500. The child was with them in the street—38 days old. I shook my head and asked myself, "Is this the best the United States can do?"

Dr. Martin Luther King, Jr., told us, "I have been to the mountain." But almost every voice that we have heard for 20 years has counseled us to shut that mountain out of mind, and to direct our eyes instead to the attractive flatlands where careers are made, résumés typed, and profits maximized. Our culture heroes have been sleek and agile people; cynical and cold, streamlined for efficient malice, and unweighted by the excess burden of compassion.

"We owe a definite homage to the reality around us," Thomas Merton wrote, "and we are obliged at certain times to say what things are and to give them their right names." The right name for the willingness of a rich nation to leave half a million homeless children in its streets is sheer betrayal of ourselves and our best values.

It has been a long winter. But as with the seasons, so too with a nation: life renews itself.

I like to think another season of compassion is before us. We look to you who graduate this morning to renew this weary earth, to water the soil of the 1990s with the simple but forgotten values of the heart, to heal the ill, house the homeless, feed the hungry, and bring mercy to the frightened mother and her child.

It is not by standing tall, but by bending low—to reach a hand to those who are too frail to stand at all—that good societies are defined.

13. The author focuses on the plight of

    (1) cultural heroes
    (2) sleek people
    (3) homeless children
    (4) cynical and cold leaders
    (5) graduates of a university

14. The many homeless children are unseen because they

    (1) were born poor
    (2) are scattered
    (3) are decreasing in number
    (4) are sleek and agile
    (5) are cynical and cold

15. The author feels that the plight of the homeless is a result of

    (1) betrayal of our values
    (2) national poverty
    (3) obsession with résumés and careers
    (4) propaganda against the poor
    (5) maximized profits

Questions 16–18 are based on the following passage.

Child labor still exists in the United States. Experts say that it is a stubborn problem in every country and will take many years to solve. There are about 200 million children working all over the world. When people talk about child labor, they are talking about children who are being exploited, being forced to work long hours, often under dangerous conditions.

Child labor has been a problem for centuries. During the late 1800s and early 1900s, child labor was common in the United States and Europe. In 1900, more than two million children age 15 and under worked full time, many in dangerous jobs such as coal mining or factory work.

By the 1930s, the United States and other wealthy countries had made two important reforms that greatly reduced child labor. First, they passed and enforced tough laws against it. Second, they made schooling compulsory for all children. History shows that children who go to school have a better chance of becoming healthy adults.

Despite these measures, child labor remains a problem today, especially among poor people and illegal immigrants. Many illegal immigrants work in sweatshops, factories where people labor long hours under terrible conditions.

Even more common than sweatshop workers are migrant farm workers, who move from place to place. Hundreds of thousands of children do "stoop labor." This means they have to bend over all day picking vegetables and fruit.

16. Child labor includes all the children who work EXCEPT

    (1) as migrants
    (2) in sweatshops
    (3) in coal mines
    (4) as servants
    (5) in factories

17. Child labor refers to children who are exploited

    (1) only in the United States
    (2) only in Europe
    (3) in the United States and Europe
    (4) in wealthy countries
    (5) all over the world

18. Efforts to combat child labor have centered on

    (1) better working conditions
    (2) improved pay
    (3) shorter hours
    (4) legal prohibition
    (5) government inspectors

Questions 19–21 are based on the following passage.

Sparked by the debates of President John F. Kennedy's Commission on the Status of Women and by the birth of a new women's movement, a spate of legislation supports women's efforts to overcome job discrimination. In 1963, Congress passed a long-sought Equal Pay Act. The 1964 Civil Rights Act forbade discrimination on the grounds of sex and created an Equal Employment Opportunity Commission that workers could use to bring suit against employers who did not comply with the law. As a result, a small number of women managed to inch their way into better jobs. By the seventies, medical and law schools, corporate and financial institutions, and political bureaucracies had increased equal access for women.

Poor women, however, did not seem to benefit as much. Those who headed the expanding number of single-parent families searched for ways to combine family life with work. Many women found themselves confined to retail sales, clerical, and service jobs where low wages and part-time work carried no benefits. New immigrants could find jobs only in sweatshops. At the same time, the rising cost of living locked many

two-parent families into dual wage earning, with the problem of how to integrate work and family life. As attention shifted from workplace conditions, legislators increasingly advocated such reforms as subsidized child care, paid pregnancy and parental leaves, flextime, and more generous healthcare coverage. Most experts agreed that resolving these family-related issues would be the key to achieving equality in the workplace of the 21st century.

19. According to the passage, for many families equality for women in the workplace depends most on

    (1) the generosity of corporate and financial institutions
    (2) The Commission on the Status of Women
    (3) the rising cost of living
    (4) the ability to integrate work and family life
    (5) the improvement of workplace conditions

20. It can be inferred from the passage that efforts on behalf of women

    (1) had widely differing effects
    (2) improved the lot of most women
    (3) penalized employers
    (4) had little general effect
    (5) overcame conflict in the workplace

21. The major interest of legislators now is in

    (1) workplace conditions
    (2) family-related issues
    (3) better jobs for women
    (4) equal pay for women
    (5) job discrimination

Questions 22–25 are based on the following passage.

Most Americans look at the developing areas of the world without having the slightest idea of the difficulties with which they are faced. We must try to understand what life is like for the almost 4 billion human beings who live in developing nations.

Let us imagine how an American family, living in a housing development on a very low yearly income, could be changed into a family of the underdeveloped world.

Our first step is to strip our American home of its furniture. Everything from the living quarters goes—beds, chairs, tables, television set, lamps. Leave a few old blankets, a kitchen table, a wooden chair. For clothing, each member of the family may keep his oldest suit or dress, plus a shirt or blouse. Permit a pair of shoes for the head of the family, but none for the wife. In the kitchen the appliances have already been taken out, the water and the electric power shut off. The box of matches may stay, as well as a small bag of flour and some sugar and salt. We will leave a handful of onions and a dish of dried beans. All the rest must go—the meat, fresh vegetables, canned goods, crackers.

The house itself must go. The family can move into a small shack. It may be crowded, but they are fortunate to have any shelter at all.

Communication must go next—no more newspapers, magazines, books. They will not be missed, since we are not able to read. In our community, there will be only one radio.

Government services must go also. No more mail delivery or fire protection. There is a school, but it is three miles away and consists of two classrooms. It is not overcrowded, since only half the children in the neighborhood go to school. There are no hospitals or doctors nearby. The nearest clinic is ten miles away.

The human body requires a daily input of at least 2300 calories to make up for the energy used by the body. If we do no better than the Latin American peasant, we will average not more than 2000 to 2100 calories per day and our bodies will run down.

So we have brought our American family down to the very bottom of the human scale. When we are told that more half the world's population enjoys a standard of living of less than 100 dollars a year, this is what that figure means.

22. The purpose of the author is to describe

    (1) American family life
    (2) the comforts of civilization
    (3) life in developing nations
    (4) the American home
    (5) changes in the family

23. Over half the world's population has

    (1) a daily input of 2300 calories
    (2) crowded classrooms
    (3) kitchen appliances
    (4) a poor living standard
    (5) high-tech machinery

24. The passage implies that Americans

    (1) are well informed
    (2) lack understanding of life in developing nations
    (3) contribute to the problems of developing nations
    (4) distort the realities of life
    (5) provide help to those less fortunate

25. With which of the following necessities is a family in an underdeveloped nation left?

    (1) a house
    (2) a local hospital
    (3) electric power
    (4) government services
    (5) food

History

Read each of the following selections carefully. After each selection, there are questions to be answered or statements to be completed. Select the best answer.

Questions 26–28 are based on the following passage.

The early Europeans imagined that the natives of the New World were rovers, who lived and hunted at random wherever they pleased. They were mistaken: the tribes had their separate tracts that were marked off by definite boundaries. But the fundamental difference between the European conception of property and that of the Native Americans was that the Native Americans' property was held in common. The Native Americans had no idea of legal title, of the individual ownership of land, and the Europeans were incapable of thinking in any other terms. In 1879, a General Allotment Act was introduced in Congress. The object, or ostensible object, was to encourage the Native Americans to engage in farming by breaking up the reservations.

The fragments were to be allotted, a hundred and sixty acres to heads of families and eighty to single persons. The remainder could be bought by the government, and the individual owners, after twenty-five years, were authorized to sell their land.

The bill encountered opposition, but the act was passed in 1887 and had the effect of depriving the Native Americans of ninety million of their hundred and forty million acres. Few of them had taken to farming. Even if they had been eager to farm, they had no money to invest in equipment or livestock, and since their allotments were held in trust, they were unable to get commercial credit. If they did not dispose of their property, and it was divided among their descendants, there was soon very little left for anybody.

—adapted from Edmund Wilson

26. According to the passage, early Europeans believed natives of the New World to be

    (1) agrarian
    (2) uncivilized
    (3) nomadic
    (4) disorganized
    (5) unprogressive

27. According to the passage, the essential difference between the Native American and European concepts of property is that Europeans believed in

    (1) individual ownership of the land
    (2) governmental control of the land
    (3) breaking up large tracts of land
    (4) farming the land instead of hunting on it
    (5) handing it down to descendants

28. The official purpose of the General Allotment Act of 1879 was to

    (1) introduce new methods of hunting
    (2) encourage Native Americans to pursue a different way of life
    (3) allow the Native Americans to move about more freely
    (4) sell large tracts of land
    (5) consolidate ownership of land

Questions 29–31 are based on the following passage.

Foreign propagandists have a strange misconception of our national character. They believe that we Americans must be hybrid, mongrel, undynamic; and we are called so by the enemies of democracy because, they say, so many races have been fused together in our national life.

They believe we are disunited and defenseless because we argue with each other, because we engage in political campaigns, because we recognize the sacred right of the minority to disagree with the majority and to express that disagreement even loudly. It is the very mingling of races, dedicated to common ideals, which creates and recreates our vitality. In every representative American meeting there will be people with names like Jackson and Lincoln and Isaacs and Schultz and Kovacs and Sartori and Jones and Smith. These Americans with varied backgrounds are all immigrants or the descendants of immigrants. All of them are inheritors of the same stalwart tradition of unusual enterprise, of adventurousness, of courage—courage to "pull up stakes and git moving." That has been the great compelling force in our history.

29. According to the paragraph, our national character thrives because we have

    (1) few disagreements
    (2) majority groups
    (3) shared our wealth
    (4) common ideals
    (5) minority rights

30. Foreign propagandists believe that Americans

    (1) are enemies of democracy
    (2) lack a common heritage
    (3) have a unified national character
    (4) refuse to argue with each other
    (5) are ashamed of foreign descent

31. Foreign propagandists and the author agree that Americans

    (1) are disunited
    (2) have no common tradition
    (3) come from varied backgrounds
    (4) have the courage of their convictions
    (5) are deeply religious

Questions 32–34 are based on the following passage.

Underlying historical events which influenced two great American peoples, citizens of Canada and of the United States, to work out their many problems through the years with such harmony and mutual benefit constitute a story which is both colorful and fascinating. It is a story of border disputes, questions and their solutions, for certainly the controversies and wars of the early years of Canada and the northern colonies of what now is the United States, and after 1783 their continuation through the War of 1812, scarcely constituted a sound foundation for international friendship.

Yet it is a fact that solutions were found for every matter of disagreement that arose, and the two nations have been able to work out peaceful results from the many difficulties naturally arising in connection with a long and disputed boundary line, in many cases not delineated by great natural barriers.

32. The title that best expresses the ideas of this passage is

   (1) "A Proud Record"
   (2) "Our Northern Neighbor"
   (3) "Cooperation with Canada"
   (4) "Our Northern Boundary Line"
   (5) "The Role of the Loyalists in Canada"

33. Disagreements between Canada and the United States

   (1) did not occur after 1800
   (2) have been solved in every case
   (3) constituted a basis for friendship
   (4) were solved principally to America's advantage
   (5) resulted from the presence of natural barriers

34. The writer considers the period before 1812

   (1) an insurmountable barrier
   (2) a time of geographical disputes
   (3) the definer of our differences
   (4) a cementer of our Canadian friendship
   (5) the period that settled our northern boundary

Questions 35–37 are based on the following passage.

The gradual loss of Indian tribal authority was suddenly reversed in 1934 with the passage of the Indian Reorganization Act, which addressed the strengthening of tribal life and government with federal assistance. The act, the product of the thinking of John Collier, commissioner of Indian affairs, put Indian communities then nearing political and cultural dissolution on the road to recovery and growth. Collier, struck by the strength and viability of Indian communal societies in the Southwest (e.g., the Hopis) and appalled by the destructive effects on tribal societies of the allotment system, sought to restore tribal structures by making the tribes instrumentalities of the federal government. In this way, he asserted, tribes would be surrounded by the protective guardianship of the federal government and clothed with the authority.

Indian tribal governments, as Collier foresaw, now exist on a government-to-government basis with the states and the federal government. Although they are financially and legally dependent upon the federal government, they have been able to extend their political and judicial authority in areas nineteenth-century politicians would have found unimaginable.

American Indians, now a rapidly growing minority group, possess a unique legal status (based on treaties and constitutional decisions) and are better educated, in better health, and more prosperous than ever before (despite the persistence of high levels of unemployment, poverty, and disease).

35. The Indian Representative Act was the result of

   (1) Indian tribal authority pressure
   (2) the allotment system
   (3) action by the states
   (4) legislation by nineteenth-century politicians
   (5) action by a federal employee

36. The Indian Reorganization Act sought to

   (1) strengthen tribal government
   (2) dissolve Indian communities
   (3) widen the allotment system
   (4) make tribes independent
   (5) give states a more important role

37. Indian tribal governments are now

    (1) stronger politically and judicially
    (2) stronger financially and legally
    (3) weaker communally and culturally
    (4) weaker in tribal structure
    (5) weaker in government relations

Questions 38–40 are based on the following photograph.

Photo © Alfred Eisenstaedt/LIFE

38. This photograph was taken in

    (1) London
    (2) Boston
    (3) New York City
    (4) St. Louis
    (5) Los Angeles

39. What is the subject of the photograph?

    (1) a newlywed couple celebrating their marriage
    (2) a sailor's desire for romance at the end of the war
    (3) a couple celebrating the new year
    (4) accepted public displays of affection were in the 1940s
    (5) a famous movie scene

40. What is the purpose of the photograph?

    (1) to show the jubilation at the end of the World War II
    (2) to show the jubilation at the end of World War I
    (3) to show the excitement of the soldiers at the end of the Vietnam War
    (4) to show that it was acceptable for people to be affectionate in public
    (5) to show the relationship between soldiers and nurses

Geography

Read each of the following selections carefully. After each selection, there are questions to be answered or statements to be completed. Select the best answer.

Questions 41–43 are based on the table below.

41. From the table, it can be inferred that population growth is

   (1) greatest in Europe
   (2) greatest in developed countries
   (3) led by the United States and Japan
   (4) greatest in the Middle East
   (5) greatest in India

42. The country that will have the largest increase in population density by the year 2000 is

   (1) India
   (2) China
   (3) Japan
   (4) Brazil
   (5) the United States

43. It can be inferred from the table that

   (1) Africa is more densely populated than the United States
   (2) Canada has primarily a favorable environment
   (3) Japan is highly industrialized
   (4) India has an unhealthy climate
   (5) the population of North America is growing at a greater rate than that of Latin America

SIZES, POPULATIONS, AND DENSITIES OF THE WORLD'S LARGEST NATIONS AND REGIONS

Country	Size (sq. mi.)	Population (UN Estimate)* (millions)		People per Square Mile	
		1992	2000	1992	2000
Canada	3,850,000	27.36	30.42	7.1	7.9
China	3,700,000	1,187.99	1,309.74	321.1	353.98
USA	3,600,000	255.16	257.32	70.88	76.48
Brazil	3,300,000	154.11	172.77	46.7	52.36
India	1,200,000	879.55	1,018.67	732.96	848.89
Japan	143,000	124.49	128.06	870.57	895.57
Southeast Asia	1,692,000	461.5	531.01	272.75	313.83
Western Asia	1,830,817	139.27	171.43	76.07	93.64
Africa	11,700,000	681.69	836.15	58.26	71.47

*(Note the estimated increase of population in the eight years that separate the two sets of figures. Scientists estimate that the earth's population will double in less than 50 years.)

Current annual population growth rates for world regions

Africa	2.9%	Latin America	2.0%	Oceania	1.6%
Asia	1.9%	Europe	0.4%	World	1.7%
North America	1.0%	Former Soviet Union	0.8%		

Questions 44–46 are based on the following passage.

Green Seal, a nonprofit organization based in the nation's capital, helps shoppers single out honest environmental claims. The organization develops stringent environmental standards for products ranging from toilet tissue to re-refined motor oil, and then invites companies to let Green Seal test their products. Goods that equal or exceed the standards can print Green Seal's logo—a blue globe overlaid with a green check-mark—on product packaging. Dean says green labeling rewards companies that make environmentally sound products by giving them a presumed competitive edge and encourages more companies to jump on the green wagon.

Launched in 1990, Green Seal is modeled after eco-labeling programs in Germany, Canada, Japan, and nearly 15 other nations. However, most of these programs are government run, while money from foundations and individual donors bankrolls Green Seal. Dean, formerly director of the National Wildlife Federation's Environmental Quality Division, says that private financing frees Green Seal from the political problems that would arise with federal funding: "The 80 percent of the companies that aren't getting certified would be placing pressure on their members of Congress to squeeze the organization to become more lenient."

Green Seal develops technical standards for various categories of products. The staff considers how raw materials used to manufacture a product are obtained and monitors the product's role in the environment throughout its use and disposal. "We ask, where are the key impacts, and what can be done in these areas to make the product less damaging?" explains Dean.

For products such as bathroom and facial tissue, impacts include logging to get the wood used in paper pulp, discharge of chlorine and other toxic chemicals from paper mills into rivers, dumping of waste paper in landfills and air pollution from paper incineration.

Green Seal has set standards for roughly 40 categories of consumer products and has put its label on 23 products from eight companies.

44. Green Seal's logo would be most likely influential with shoppers who are

    (1) seeking bargains
    (2) honest
    (3) interested in politics
    (4) concerned about the environment
    (5) influenced by packaging

45. According to the passage,

    (1) companies seek out Green Seal
    (2) Green Seal is generous in its testing
    (3) Green Seal sets standards for products
    (4) environmental claims are honest
    (5) Green Seal profits from its services

46. Green Seal's staff is most concerned with a product's

    (1) environmental impact
    (2) profitability
    (3) utility
    (4) performance
    (5) cost

Questions 47–49 are based on the following map and passage.

THE MIDDLE EAST AND NORTH AFRICA

It is important to know about the Middle East for many reasons.

1. The Middle East is very rich in oil. It is believed that two-thirds of the world's total oil reserves lie in the Middle East. Oil is vital to industry throughout the world.

2. The Middle East has always been of great importance because it is located at the crossroads of three continents. Trade between Asia, Africa and Europe has had to pass through the Middle East, and its waterways have been used as trade routes since the beginning of civilization....

3. Some of the earliest civilizations developed in the Middle East....

4. Three of the world's great religions—Judaism, Christianity, and Islam—began in this part of the world. Many places in Israel, Jordan, and Saudi Arabia are thought of as holy by Christians, Moslems, and Jews.

5. Finally, the Jewish state of Israel stands in the middle of the Arab countries of the area. Israel is a democracy in a part of the world where most people have very little voice in their own government....

47. The map reveals that among the following the country with the smallest area is

(1) Egypt
(2) Saudi Arabia
(3) Iran
(4) Jordan
(5) Israel

48. Of the reasons given for knowing about the Middle East, the most important are

(1) political
(2) economic
(3) historical
(4) religious
(5) cultural

49. According to the map and the text, the bodies of water accessible for trade from the Mediterranean Sea include all of the following EXCEPT the

(1) Black Sea
(2) Caspian Sea
(3) Persian Gulf
(4) Arabian Sea
(5) Red Sea

Questions 50–52 are based on the following passage.

The initial impetus for the environmental movement was the growing interest in outdoor recreation in a more natural environment. This led to the creation of the National Preservation System (1964), the National Trails System (1968), and the National Wild and Scenic Rivers System (1968) and to a public purchase program in the Land and Water Conservation Act (1964). By 1989 the wilderness system, the most dramatic result of these measures, had reached 90 million acres.

These programs set a direction in resource management different from the conservation focus on efficient development of material resources. In wilderness areas, no timber was to be cut and no roads built. Wild and scenic rivers were to remain free-flowing with no dams built in them. The programs meant that resources were now prized for their aesthetic rather than their material value.

The environmental movement gave rise to a new appreciative use of wildlife as an object of observation rather than of hunting. This led to a federal endangered species program, nongame wildlife programs fostered by the states, a heightened interest in habitat for wild plants and animals, and a focus on biological diversity of wild resources.

In the environmental era, a new interest arose in curbing pollution—first air and water pollution in the 1950s and 1960s and then pollution from toxic wastes in the 1970s and thereafter.

50. The environmental movement arose from a desire for

    (1) conservation of natural resources
    (2) civilizing the wilderness
    (3) more hunting and fishing
    (4) resource management
    (5) outdoor recreation

51. The most recent efforts in the environmental field have focused on

    (1) curbing toxic chemical wastes
    (2) obtaining profit from natural resources
    (3) land and water conservation
    (4) reducing air and water pollution
    (5) controlling wildlife

52. New appreciation of wildlife has led to

    (1) increased hunting
    (2) increased profits from the sale of furs
    (3) conservation in resource management
    (4) efficient development of material resources
    (5) a federal endangered species program

Questions 53–55 are based on the following passage.

Puerto Rican migration to the city has constituted the largest influx since the great waves of European immigration in the 19th century.

The islander soon found out what early immigrants had learned. Wages were better but prices were higher; houses were dilapidated; crime was rampant; the weather was cold and damp; and the society at large was strange and different.

How to keep one's family together and preserve one's identity were problems faced by every immigrant group, and they are problems faced by New York Puerto Ricans today. Life in the city was not easy, but there was little to return to.

Unlike many other non-English-speaking newcomers to the city, Puerto Ricans are American citizens. As Americans, they have the right to come and go as they please. Also, unlike previous immigrants, Puerto Ricans did not have to sever their ties to the homeland once they arrived in the city. Thus they could maintain, and even constantly renew, contact with their culture.

53. Puerto Rican immigrants differ from other non-English-speaking new-comers to New York City in that they

    (1) have no language problems
    (2) are needed in the factories
    (3) came with high hopes
    (4) are already American citizens
    (5) were unprepared for migration

54. Puerto Ricans faced all the following problems previous immigrant groups faced EXCEPT

    (1) prices outdistancing wages
    (2) inadequate housing
    (3) poor climate
    (4) crime being prevalent
    (5) broken cultural ties

55. The passage implies that, once they immigrated to New York City, Puerto Ricans

    (1) were just like other immigrant groups
    (2) remained outside the normal course of daily life
    (3) had little alternative but to remain
    (4) returned to Puerto Rico in large numbers
    (5) eventually solved the problem of identity

ANSWER KEY

Civics and Government

1. **3**	3. **4**	5. **3**	7. **2**	9. **3**	11. **4**
2. **3**	4. **3**	6. **5**	8. **4**	10. **1**	12. **5**

Economics

13. **3**	16. **4**	18. **4**	20. **1**	22. **3**	24. **2**
14. **2**	17. **5**	19. **4**	21. **2**	23. **4**	25. **5**
15. **1**					

History

26. **3**	29. **4**	32. **3**	35. **5**	37. **2**	39. **2**
27. **1**	30. **2**	33. **2**	36. **1**	38. **3**	40. **1**
28. **2**	31. **3**	34. **2**			

Geography

41. **5**	44. **4**	47. **5**	50. **5**	52. **5**	54. **5**
42. **1**	45. **3**	48. **2**	51. **1**	53. **4**	55. **3**
43. **3**	46. **1**	49. **2**			

ANSWER ANALYSIS

Civics and Government

1. **3** The theme of the passage is expressed in the fourth sentence. The American statesmen are described as not only performing their political function, but also expressing a more universal responsibility. This is the basis of American political philosophy.

2. **3** The opening words of the passage indicate that intellectuals who lead the way for a revolution are usually devoured, or destroyed, by the forces that are unleashed.

3. **4** The middle part of the passage states that American political science is the only one perfectly adapted to the emergencies of the contemporary world.

4. **3** The cartoon shows that the United States adopted a foreign policy of neutrality in 1939 (see the license plate of the car), the start of World War II.

5. **3** Although a president as commander-in-chief can use military power, he is limited by law in his power to send troops into combat in foreign lands.

6. **5** The point of the pupil's question is the role of women in the founding of the United States, indicating that more attention should be given the role of women in U.S. history.

7. **2** The passage states that court decisions often lead to "virtually endless series of vexing legal questions."

8. **4** The opening sentence indicates that the average citizen is knowledgeable about important court decisions.

9. **3** *Landmark* refers to a distinguishing feature that guides someone on his or her way. It is, therefore, "significant."

10. **1** The passage calls democracy promotion a new American industry.

11. **4** Democratic progress has been most difficult in nations that fell into strongman rule.

12. **5** It is stated that no democratic consultant can affect the expectations of people.

Economics

13. **3** The author centers his remarks on the "hundreds and thousands of homeless children in this nation."

14. **2** The children are unseen because they are "scattered in a thousand different cities."

15. **1** He calls our leaving a half-million homeless children on our streets a sheer betrayal of ourselves and our best values.

16. **4** Migrants, sweatshops, coal mines, and factories are mentioned. Servants are not.

17. **5** The passage mentions that "there are about 200 million children working all over the world."

18. **4** Tough laws against child labor are mentioned as an important reform.

19. **4** The passage refers to the problem, for dual wage-earning parents, of finding ways to integrate work and family life.

20. **1** Poor women did not benefit as much as a small number of more fortunate women who managed to get better jobs.

21. **2** Legislators are now interested in family-related issues such as paid pregnancy, child care, and health care.

22. **3** The author wants the reader to understand what life is like in developing nations. For this purpose he imagines that a poor American family is transformed into "a family of the underdeveloped world."

23. **4** The article states that over half of the world's population has a standard of living of less than $100 a year.

24. **2** The author implies that most Americans do not understand the life of almost 4 billion persons living in underdeveloped nations. To help them do so, he creates an imaginary family.

25. **5** Families in underdeveloped nations lack houses, nearby hospitals, electric power, and government services. They have a daily food input of 2000 to 2100 calories, but that is not enough to sustain health.

History

26. **3** "The early Europeans imagined that the natives of the New World were rovers...."

27. **1** The author states that the Native Americans had "no idea of...the individual ownership of land, and the Europeans were incapable of thinking in any other terms."

28. **2** According to the author, the object of the General Allotment Act was to "encourage the Native Americans to engage in farming by breaking up the reservations."

29. **4** The passage refers to a "the mingling of races, dedicated to common ideals..."

30. **2** The words *hybrid* and *mongrel* indicate the lack of a common heritage.

31. **3** The author concedes that the "mingling of races," which foreign propagandists believe to be true of America, is a fact.

32. **3** The passage emphasizes the fact that Canada and the United States have cooperated to solve many problems.

33. **2** The passage states that solutions have been found for every matter of disagreement.

34. **2** The passage mentions border disputes that occurred through the War of 1812.

35. **5** The passage states that the Indian Reorganization Act was the work of John Collier, the commissioner of Indian affairs.

36. **1** The act sought to restore tribal authority; it "addressed the strengthening of tribal life and government."

37. **2** The passage refers both to the American Indian's unique legal status and his or her being more prosperous than ever before.

38. **3** The photograph was taken in Times Square, in New York City. Notice the landmark buildings behind the couple.

39. **2** The obvious subject of the photograph is a sailor's desire for romance at the end of the war; the photograph shows his excitement to be home.

40. **1** The purpose of this famous photograph was to show that the soldiers were jubilant about the end of the war.

Geography

41. **5** From 1992 to 2000, population growth in India will be over 139 million. China is second with over 121 million.

42. **1** In 2000, India's density per square mile will have had the largest increase: from 732.96 to 848.89.

43. **3** Since Japan has the largest number of people per square mile and high population densities frequently occur in areas of heavy industrialization, it can be inferred that Japan is highly industrialized.

44. **4** Since Green Seal "helps single out honest environmental claims," it would influence shoppers who are concerned about the environment.

45. **3** The article indicates that "the organization develops stringent environmental standards for products."

46. **1** The staff "monitors the product's role in the environment."

47. **5** Israel, about the size of the state of New Jersey, is by far the smallest with an area of 7,992 square miles, less than one quarter the size of Jordan, one fiftieth the size of Egypt, one eightieth the size of Iran, and one hundredth the size of Saudi Arabia.

48. **2** Oil and trade are mentioned first.

49. **2** The Caspian Sea is an inland sea.

50. **5** The initial impetus was a "growing interest in outdoor recreation in a more natural environment."

51. **1** In the 1970s and thereafter, a new interest arose in curbing pollution from toxic chemical wastes.

52. **5** Wildlife was seen as existing, not for being hunted, but for observation so a federal endangered species program was created.

53. **4** Unlike other newcomers to New York City, Puerto Ricans are already American citizens when they arrive.

54. **5** The first four responses are problems all newcomers faced. The exception is Choice 5; Puerto Ricans could maintain and renew contact with their culture.

55. **3** The passage states that, while life in the city was difficult, there was little in Puerto Rico for the immigrants to return to.

SCIENCE
TEST 3

CHAPTER 13: Reading and Interpreting Science Questions

Science questions on the GED Examination may be based on reading passages, graphs, diagrams, or tables. Test-taking tactics are presented through the use of 31 explained examples and step-by-step explanations. These examples represent the types of questions that you are likely to see on the actual GED exam. There is a heavy emphasis on analyzing and interpreting data and applying information, because the new GED exam places a much greater emphasis on these skills than the old GED exam. In this and subsequent chapters, in short, you'll find many questions based on graphs, tables, and diagrams, just like you'll see on the actual exam.

CHAPTER 14: Handling Science Skills Questions

Comprehension, application, analysis, and evaluation of science material are four skills on which you will be tested when you take the GED Examination. Twenty examples of typical questions are included in this chapter. The answers are briefly analyzed for you. Also, to help you with unfamiliar vocabulary, a handy "Glossary of Scientific Terms" is included.

CHAPTER 15: Science Practice

In this chapter 150 questions are arranged by subject (biology, earth science, chemistry, and physics). Articles, tables, graphs, and diagrams are presented in the actual GED format. Conveniently placed answer keys and full explanations follow the exercises in each subject.

13

Reading and Interpreting Science Questions

There are several types of questions on the Science Test, and each calls for a specific plan of attack.

Single-Item Questions

In this type, a short paragraph is followed by a single question. Your first task in dealing with this kind of question is to identify the main idea or ideas presented. The best way to do this is to start by reading the paragraph and the question quickly, without stopping to be sure you understand every point. This will give you some sense of the content of the question and of the kind of information you will need to answer it. Fix in your mind the main idea of the paragraph.

Next, reread the question carefully. You may be able to select the correct answer at once. If you have any doubt, go back to the paragraph and reread it carefully, searching for the answer to the question.

Practice this technique on the following question:

QUESTION

Growing plants will not develop their green color, caused by the chlorophyll in their leaves, unless they have both sunlight and the necessary genetic system.

If a seedling growing in dim light turns out to be colorless, what could be done to find out why?

(1) Give it a new set of genes.
(2) Add chlorophyll to the soil.
(3) Graft it onto a green plant.
(4) Move it into the sunlight.
(5) Add fertilizer to the soil.

ANSWER AND ANALYSIS

A quick reading tells you that the main idea deals with the factors involved in the development of a plant's green color. Now go back to the paragraph and read it again. After rereading, you know that the crucial factors are sunlight and genes. This narrows the answer possibilities to Choices 1 and 4. Since there is no way to give the plant a new set of genes, the answer is Choice 4.

Here is another sample of this kind of question:

QUESTION

Carbon dioxide (CO_2) gas is dissolved in soda water. The molecules of gas dissolve and are invisible while the bottle is sealed. When the cap is removed, however, the liquid foams up with the release of bubbles of CO_2 gas. If the soda water is warm, the bubbling is even more violent.

What general rule would explain these observations?

(1) Warm water tends to lower the pressure of the dissolved gas.
(2) CO_2 gas is more soluble at low temperature and high pressure.
(3) CO_2 gas does not dissolve in water when the pressure is too high.
(4) CO_2 gas is not as soluble when the pressure and temperature are too high.
(5) High pressure tends to keep the temperature low.

ANSWER AND ANALYSIS

A quick reading tells you that the main idea concerns the solubility of gases and its dependence on pressure and temperature. Now you have to reread carefully to find out just what this dependence is.

This question introduces a type of difficulty that you may meet often—the *unstated assumption*. To get the answer to this question, you will have to realize that the pressure in a sealed soda bottle is high. This should be obvious: when you remove the cap from the bottle of soda, gas rushes out. You will often be expected to supply, for yourself, bits of information that are commonly and widely known.

Adding this piece of information, you can now go back to the passage to find out how temperature and pressure affect the solubility of the gas in the soda. When you take the cap off, you reduce the pressure and the gas comes out of solution, so it is clear that the gas is more soluble when the pressure is high. Since there is more foaming when the soda is warm, the gas is more soluble at lower temperatures. Thus the answer is Choice 2.

Multiple-Item Questions Based on Readings

Some questions require you to read a passage consisting of several paragraphs and then to answer a number of questions about the material. In this case, you need to study the passage carefully *before* you look at the questions. As you read, note two or three main ideas.

To find the main ideas in the passage, look for key words. These are words such as *aorta* and *nucleus* and *ecosystem* that are normally used in a scientific context. Once you have found these words, they should lead you to one or more of the main ideas in the passage.

EXAMPLE

The annual migration of birds is a complex process that is only partly understood. Some birds that hatch in the Arctic fly thousands of miles to South America each winter, and then return to the place where they were born. The adults make these trips separately from their offspring. The young birds, however, find their way to the correct wintering grounds even though no adult bird shows them the way. No one knows how they are able to do this.

Biologists do understand, however, that in temperate zones the urge to migrate is prompted by a change in the length of daylight. As days grow shorter in the fall, certain physical changes occur in the birds, such as degeneration of the ovaries or testes. These changes are accompanied by restlessness and the urge to fly south.

There is some evidence that birds navigate using many clues, including the earth's magnetic field, the position of the sun in the sky, visible land forms, and even the pattern of the stars at night. How they know the route, however, is a complete mystery. It can be called instinct, but that is simply a word that explains little.

As you read this passage through for the first time, you should identify several key words, such as *migration, degeneration, ovaries, testes, navigate, magnetic field*. Now use these words to locate the main ideas in the passage. They will probably lead you to three main ideas: (1) the changing length of daylight is the signal that prompts migration; (2) birds use a number of clues to navigate; and (3) how they know the route is completely unknown.

Once you have these main ideas firmly fixed in your mind, you are ready to read the questions. Refer to the passage as needed to find the answers.

QUESTION

What is the most probable factor that prompts birds to migrate north in the spring?

(1) depletion of the food supply during the winter
(2) the disappearance of snow from the ground
(3) the coming of warmer weather
(4) the increase in the amount of daylight
(5) the instinct to fly north

ANSWER AND ANALYSIS

One of the main ideas tells you that, in the fall, migration is prompted by the decreasing length of daylight. It is surely reasonable to suppose that the reverse is true in the spring, so the answer is Choice 4.

QUESTION

In an experiment, the testes are removed from birds in the Arctic in the summertime. It is found that the birds then show the typical restlessness that precedes migration. What hypothesis does this suggest?

(1) Early migration causes the testes to degenerate.
(2) The length of the day has nothing to do with migration.
(3) The immediate physiological factor that initiates migration is degeneration of the testes.
(4) Increasing length of daylight causes the testes to degenerate.
(5) Restlessness is not a sign that migration is about to begin.

ANSWER AND ANALYSIS

This question requires you to analyze a cause-and-effect relationship. Since it deals with the factors that initiate migration, your attention is drawn to the second paragraph, where you find that degeneration of the testes (or ovaries) always precedes migration. The experiment tests whether loss of the testes is an actual cause of the urge to migrate. When it is found that removal of the testes produces premigratory restlessness, the cause-and-effect relationship is established; the answer is Choice 3. Choice 1 is wrong because a cause cannot come after an effect. Choice 2 is wrong because it introduces a factor not tested for in the experiment. Choice 4 is wrong because the length of daylight decreases, not increases, as the summer advances toward fall. Choice 5 is wrong because it violates one of the assumptions on which the experiment was based.

QUESTION

What has the study of migration revealed about how birds know what route to follow?

(1) Young birds learn by following their parents.
(2) Birds are born with an instinct that tells them the route.
(3) Birds use several different means of navigation.
(4) The changing length of daylight gives birds the necessary clues.
(5) So far, investigation has not given any answers to the question.

ANSWER AND ANALYSIS

One of the main ideas, already extracted from the passage, is Choice 5—the answer. The passage says that Choice 1 is not true, and Choice 2 offers a word, *instinct,* but not an explanation. Choices 3 and 4 are true, but irrelevant to this particular question. Choice 4 deals with the timing of migration, not the route.

QUESTION

In the tropics, some birds migrate short distances between wet and dry seasons. How do we know that they do not use the same seasonal clues as temperate-zone birds?

(1) There is no marked temperature variation between winter and summer in the tropics.
(2) Food is available all year round in the tropics.
(3) The testes and ovaries of tropical birds do not change cyclically during the year.
(4) In the tropics, the length of daylight is much the same all year.
(5) Since it is always warm in the tropics, the birds have no definite nesting season.

ANSWER AND ANALYSIS

The seasonal clue used by migrating birds in temperate zones is the change in the amount of daylight. Since there are no seasons to change in the tropics, the correct answer is choice 4. Choices 1, 2, and 5 may be correct statements, but the question concerns seasonal changes, not temperature or the availability of food. Choice 3 may also be true, but

it is not a valid answer because the statement cannot be verified with information presented in the passage.

Here is another passage for you to practice on:

EXAMPLE

Sickle cell anemia is a hereditary disease of the erythrocytes (red blood cells) that is found chiefly in the people of tropical Africa and their descendants in America. It is characterized by abnormal hemoglobin, the oxygen carrying erythrocytes.

People afflicted with this condition are subject to repeated attacks, brought on by conditions in which the erythrocytes receive insufficient oxygen in their passage through the lungs. This may happen during periods of intense physical exertion, or at high altitudes where the oxygen pressure is low. Under these conditions, the abnormal hemoglobin gels, distorting the erythrocytes into a rigid sickle shape. They are then unable to pass through the capillaries. Blockage of the circulation produces a variety of severe symptoms and may result in death.

The gene that produces the abnormal hemoglobin confers a certain benefit on its carriers. Children of a mating between a person with sickle cell anemia and one with normal hemoglobin have some damaged erythrocytes, but not enough to make them ill except under very severe conditions. They benefit by being immune to malaria, which is a devastating and often fatal disease common in Africa and Asia.

This is a complex passage containing many key words: *sickle cell anemia, Africa, erythrocyte, hemoglobin, hereditary, oxygen, capillary, malaria.* Some of these words may be unfamiliar, but you should note that three of them are defined for you. You are told that erythrocytes are red blood cells, hemoglobin is the oxygen carried in these cells, and malaria is a devastating disease. Sickle cell anemia is described in detail through the passage. You are expected to know the meaning of *Africa, hereditary, oxygen,* and *capillary.*

Using these words, you should find the following key ideas: (1) sickle cell anemia is hereditary; (2) it occurs in Africa, where malaria is common; (3) it involves abnormal hemoglobin; (4) attacks occur in conditions of low oxygen supply; (5) sickle cell anemia provides protection against malaria.

Now you are ready to look at the questions.

QUESTION

Which of the following might be an appropriate treatment for a person suffering an acute attack of sickle cell anemia?

(1) Administer antimalarial medication.
(2) Move the person to a high altitude.
(3) Administer oxygen.
(4) Make the person exercise strenuously to open the capillaries.
(5) Remove the sickled erythrocytes.

ANSWER AND ANALYSIS

One of the key ideas tells you that attacks are provoked by shortage of oxygen in the blood, so the answer is Choice 3. It should not be necessary to refer to the passage to get this answer.

QUESTION

Why does sickle cell anemia produce some benefit in Africa, but not in the United States?

(1) There is no malaria in the United States.
(2) The United States has a temperate climate.
(3) There is more oxygen in the air in the United States.
(4) The gene for sickle cell anemia is not found in the United States.
(5) The United States has a lower altitude than Africa.

ANSWER AND ANALYSIS

The last paragraph of the passage details the only benefit of sickle cell anemia: protection against malaria in the carriers of the gene. Where there is no malaria, this benefit disappears, and the answer is Choice 1. Choices 3, 4, and 5 are not true, and Choice 2 is irrelevant.

QUESTION

Of the following, in which group is sickle cell anemia likely to appear most frequently?

(1) Americans living in Africa
(2) Americans of African descent
(3) people who have been exposed to malaria
(4) all people living in the tropics
(5) people who have been in close contact with individuals who have sickle cell anemia

ANSWER AND ANALYSIS

One of the key points is that sickle cell anemia is hereditary; another is that it is common in Africa. It follows that people of African descent are most liable to get it. The answer is Choice 2.

QUESTION

A test is available to determine whether an individual is a carrier of sickle cell anemia. Someone might take such a test to help him or her decide whether to

(1) move to a tropical climate
(2) take an office job
(3) work at manual labor at a high altitude
(4) go to a hospital for treatment
(5) travel to Africa

ANSWER AND ANALYSIS

This is a difficult question, which cannot be answered except by careful reading of the passage. The last paragraph tells you that under severe conditions a carrier may become ill. In the second paragraph you learned that severe conditions mean a limited supply of oxygen, brought on by hard physical exertion or high altitude. The answer is Choice 3, a combination of both these factors.

QUESTION

Natural selection tends to eliminate genes that produce serious illness and no benefit. Which of the following would result in long-range reduction of the amount of sickle cell anemia in the world?

(1) improved sanitation in tropical countries
(2) a new vaccine against the disease
(3) restriction of immigration from Africa
(4) quarantine of affected individuals
(5) complete elimination of malaria in the world

ANSWER AND ANALYSIS

Since the disease is hereditary rather than infectious, Choices 1, 2, and 4 would have no effect. Choice 3 would have no effect in Africa. The only choice left is 5. The question states that natural selection eliminates genes that cause serious illnesses and no benefit. Since the only benefit of sickle cell anemia is immunity to malaria, elimination of malaria should cause the elimination of sickle cell anemia as well.

Questions Based on Graphs, Diagrams, and Data Tables

LINE GRAPHS

A line graph is a common way of showing how something changes or to show the relationship between two or more things. This kind of graph uses two scales, one going up the left side of the graph, called the vertical, or y, axis, and another along the bottom of the graph, called the horizontal, or x, axis.

If you are given a line graph on the GED test, read it carefully. Note the title, the labels on the vertical and horizontal axes, and the legend or key if there is one. Take your time, and pay attention to all of the printed material as well as the lines and the scales. Only then will you be ready to answer questions based on the line graph.

Here is a sample for you to work on:

EXAMPLE

The graph below represents the temperatures of a white sidewalk and a black asphalt driveway on a sunny day. The surfaces are side by side, and the measurements were made during a 24-hour period.

Legend: --- Driveway
       —— Sidewalk

What are the features of this graph? The vertical axis represents temperatures between 20 and 40 degrees Celsius. It does not matter whether you are familiar with the Celsius scale of temperature or not. All you need to be able to do is recognize the changes and the intervals from one temperature to another.

The horizontal axis represents the time of day. It is divided into 4-hour intervals for a 12-hour period.

According to the legend, the solid line on the graph represents the temperature of the sidewalk and the dash lines represents the temperature of the driveway. Note that both temperatures increase during daylight hours and start to decrease in the late afternoon or early evening. Note that a graph does not need to begin at 0.

Now you are ready for the questions.

QUESTION

At noon, what was the temperature of the driveway?

(1) 22°C
(2) 26°C
(3) 28°C
(4) 30°C
(5) 32°C

ANSWER AND ANALYSIS

Noon is halfway between 10 A.M. and 2 P.M., so start by placing the point of your pencil halfway between these two points on the horizontal scale. Move it straight up until it meets the dashed line, which represents the driveway. Now move the pencil point to the left; it meets the temperature scale at 26°. The answer is Choice 2.

QUESTION

What is the difference in the times when the two surfaces reach their maximum temperatures?

(1) The driveway reaches its maximum about 4 hours before the sidewalk.
(2) The sidewalk reaches its maximum about 4 hours before the driveway.
(3) The driveway reaches its maximum about 2 hours before the sidewalk.
(4) The sidewalk reaches its maximum about 2 hours before the driveway.
(5) Both surfaces reach their maximums at the same time.

ANSWER AND ANALYSIS

The dashed line (driveway) peaks at about 4 P.M. halfway between 2 P.M. and 6 P.M. The solid line (sidewalk) peaks a little before 8 P.M. The difference is fairly close to 4 hours, so the answer is Choice 1.

QUESTION

Where and when does the temperature increase most rapidly?

(1) the driveway at 4:30 P.M.
(2) the sidewalk at 5 P.M.
(3) the sidewalk at 7:30 P.M.
(4) the driveway at noon
(5) the driveway at 3 P.M.

ANSWER AND ANALYSIS

The most rapid change is shown as the steepest slope of the graph. This occurs on the dashed line at about 3 P.M., so the answer is Choice 5.

QUESTION

How do the temperature patterns of the two surfaces compare?

(1) The driveway is always warmer than the sidewalk.
(2) The sidewalk is warmer than the driveway at night and cooler in the afternoon.
(3) The two surfaces are never at the same temperature.
(4) The sidewalk changes temperature faster than the driveway.
(5) The driveway is always cooler than the sidewalk.

ANSWER AND ANALYSIS

Choices 1 and 5 are wrong by inspection of the graph. Choice 2 is right, because the graph for the driveway rises above the one for the sidewalk at about 1:30 P.M. and falls below it at midnight. Choice 3 is wrong because the two lines coincide at two times. Choice 4 is wrong because the line for the driveway is always steeper than that for the sidewalk.

QUESTION

What hypothesis might be advanced on the basis of this graph?

(1) Radiant heat flows in either direction more easily through a black surface than through a white one.
(2) Black objects tend to retain heat, while white ones lose it more easily.
(3) White objects tend to absorb heat more rapidly than black objects do.
(4) Black objects are always cooler at night than in the daytime.
(5) White objects are usually cooler than black ones.

ANSWER AND ANALYSIS

Since the black surface both warms up and cools down faster than the white one, the answer is Choice 1. Choice 2 is wrong because the black surface cools down faster than the white one. Choice 3 is wrong because the white surface warms up more slowly than the black one. Choices 4 and 5 are wrong because they do not take into account the conditions on which the graph was based, namely, that the two surfaces were in sunlight during the day.

BAR GRAPHS

Whereas a line graph is used to show how something changes, a bar graph is used to compare several quantities. Like a line graph, a bar graph has a vertical axis marked off as a kind of scale. The horizontal axis is used to indicate the different quantities that are being compared.

Look at a bar graph the same way you would a line graph. Read the title and the legend (if any). Then note the information given on the horizontal axis and on the vertical axis.

EXAMPLE

The following bar graphs show the percentages by volume of the sediment sizes found in four different sediment deposits, *A*, *B*, *C*, and *D*.

DEPOSIT A

DEPOSIT B

DEPOSIT C

DEPOSIT D

QUESTION

What is the total percentage of silt in deposit *B*?

(1) 7%
(2) 17%
(3) 27%
(4) 37%
(5) 47%

ANSWER AND ANALYSIS

In deposit *B* there are three bars representing silt. Each deposit is 10% or slightly less. Adding the three deposits of silt together produces a total of a little less than 30%, Choice 3.

QUESTION

Glaciers carry a wide range of particles. When glacier ice melts, this mixture of material is deposited. In which bar graph(s) is the material most likely deposited by a glacier reflected?

(1) deposit *A*
(2) deposit *B*
(3) deposit *C*
(4) deposit *D*
(5) deposits *A* and *D*

ANSWER AND ANALYSIS

The only graph that reflects the entire range of particles—pebbles, sand, silt, and clay—carried by a glacier is *B*, Choice 2.

QUESTION

Smaller particles tend to remain in suspension. In which deposit(s) is there the highest percentage of sediments that would stay in suspension for the longest time before settling?

(1) deposit *A*
(2) deposit *B*
(3) deposit *C*
(4) deposit *D*
(5) deposits *A* and *D*

ANSWER AND ANALYSIS

Deposit *C* contains mostly silt and clay, which are the smallest particles. The materials in deposit *C* would therefore tend to remain in suspension for the longest period of time. Choice 3 is the answer.

EXAMPLE

The following graph represents the counts of three kinds of leukocytes (white blood cells) in an animal that was administered a standard dose of a drug starting on day 4.

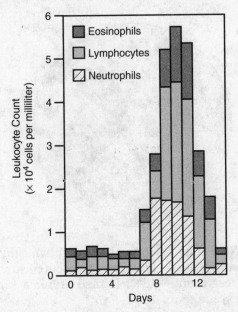

Note that the numbers of the three different kinds of leukocytes are indicated by using different patterns in the bars. Note also that the effect is short lived.

QUESTION

How long did the medication take to produce its maximum effect?

(1) 4 days
(2) 6 days
(3) 8 days
(4) 10 days
(5) 12 days

ANSWER AND ANALYSIS

Remember that the drug was started on day 4. The peak of leukocyte production was reached on day 10. Day 10 – Day 4 equals 6 days from the time the drug was administered to peak effect, Choice 2.

QUESTION

In regard to amount of increase, how did the three different kinds of leukocytes react to the medication?

(1) All three increased in roughly the same proportion.
(2) The neutrophils increased proportionally more than the others.
(3) The eosinophils increased proportionally more than the others.
(4) There was proportionally less increase in the eosinophils.
(5) There was proportionally less increase in the lymphocytes.

ANSWER AND ANALYSIS

At the peak, the ratios were about 1/4 neutrophils and 1/5 eosinophils, which were not much different from the starting ratios. The answer is Choice 1.

QUESTION

What do the data suggest as to the potential usefulness of this drug?

(1) It might be used to produce an increase in the leukocyte count in someone suffering from a long-time shortage of leukocytes.
(2) It is completely useless because the improvement is temporary.
(3) It is too dangerous because the increase in the leukocyte count is so great.
(4) It might be useful in producing a large, temporary increase in the availability of leukocytes.
(5) It is dangerous because, after the effect wears off, the leukocyte count is extremely low.

ANSWER AND ANALYSIS

In some condition, perhaps a systemic infection, in which the body has a sudden demand for an exceptionally large, temporary supply of leukocytes, this drug might be useful. The answer is Choice 4.

QUESTION

What is the probable reason that the drug was administered from day 4 instead of at the very start of the experiment?

(1) The delay allowed the animal to become used to its cage and the other conditions of its surroundings.
(2) The drug was not available for the first 3 days.
(3) The delay allowed the animal's leukocyte count to rise to normal levels before the experiment was begun.
(4) The experimenter needed this time to determine the correct dosage.
(5) The first three days served as a control to establish the pattern of leukocyte count before the drug was given.

ANSWER AND ANALYSIS

Before beginning the experiment, the scientist had to make sure that any changes in the leukocyte count were the result of the medication, and not some other factor. The answer is Choice 5.

PIE CHARTS

A pie chart is a circular graph in which the circle is divided into sections. Pie charts are useful when a particular item of information is a part, that is, a fraction or percentage, of a whole.

The first thing to notice on a pie chart is the labels, which tell you what the various segments represent. Each label is usually accompanied by a number that indicates what part of the whole this segment represents. Next you should note the sizes of the segments to get some idea of which are largest and which are smallest.

EXAMPLE

The pie chart below indicates the average numbers of macroscopic (large) organisms in one area.

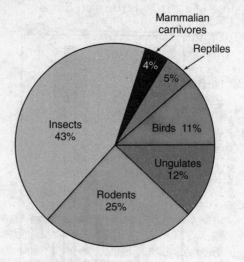

Note that insects, although physically the smallest of the animals represented, are the largest group—43%. Hoofed animals (ungulates) make up 12%.

QUESTION

Which statement is supported by the chart?

(1) Birds eat either insects or seeds.
(2) Most reptiles are carnivores.
(3) Eighty percent of the ecosystem consists of herbivores.
(4) The ecosystem in this study was a savannah.
(5) Insects are important because they are plant pollinators.

ANSWER AND ANALYSIS

Although Choices 1 and 2 are true statements, nothing on the chart indicates what birds or reptiles eat. Choice 4 is an excellent assumption, but noting on the chart proves this statement conclusively. Choice 5 is partly true, but again is not supported by the chart. The best answer is Choice 3. If you know that a great many insects, ungulates (hoofed animals), and rodents eat plants, and if you add up the number represented by their portions of the chart, the total is 80%.

QUESTION

If the population of carnivores increased by 10%, what would be the result?

(1) Rodents would increase.
(2) Ungulates and rodents would decrease, then carnivores would decrease.
(3) Birds and reptiles would increase, then decrease.
(4) Ungulates would decrease.
(5) Ungulates and rodents would increase, then decrease.

ANSWER AND ANALYSIS

There is no reason to suspect that any other population would increase because carnivores did so; therefore Choices 1, 3, and 5 cannot be correct. Choice 4 is a possible answer; however, Choice 2 is more specific and likely as a result of the increase in the population of carnivores. Carnivores feed on ungulates and rodents, and occasionally on some insects. If their population increased, carnivores would need more food, so the number of prey animals would decrease. When the food level dropped to a point where it could not support such a large population of consumers, however, the number of carnivores would also begin to decline.

DIAGRAMS

Diagrams, sometimes called graphics, show the relationships among the various parts of an object. Some parts may be inside others, be connected to others, or even be completely separate. When you see a diagram, the first things to look for are the connections between parts. Be sure to read all of the labels.

EXAMPLE

The following diagram represents the human ear. Empty spaces are shown in black.

You should see at once that the external auditory meatus is an empty space separated from the middle ear cavity by the tympanic membrane. The middle ear cavity contains three bones.

QUESTION

The incus is inside the

(1) malleus
(2) middle ear cavity
(3) tympanic membrane
(4) round window
(5) auditory tube

ANSWER AND ANALYSIS

The label "Incus" points to something white, a bone. The label "Middle ear cavity" indicates a black area, a cavity. The answer is Choice 2.

QUESTION

For a sound wave to get from the external auditory meatus into the pharynx, it would have to go through

(1) the malleus, incus, and stapes only
(2) the tympanic membrane, malleus, and middle ear cavity only
(3) the tympanic membrane, middle ear cavity, and auditory tube only
(4) the middle ear cavity, round window, and cochlea only
(5) the tympanic membrane and auditory tube only

ANSWER AND ANALYSIS

The path to the pharynx leads through the auditory tube, so that part must be included. Since there is no way to reach the auditory tube without passing through the tympanic membrane and middle ear cavity, the answer is Choice 3.

QUESTION

Ear wax is deposited in the

(1) auditory tube
(2) auricle
(3) middle ear cavity
(4) pharynx
(5) external auditory meatus

ANSWER AND ANALYSIS

The canal from the outside through the auricle leads into the external auditory meatus, where ear wax is found. The answer is Choice 5.

DATA TABLES

When a series of objects or situations, each having a certain value, is under consideration, a data table is used to make comparison easy. The table is in columns, each column headed by a label that tells what the column contains. If there are numerical data, the column head will also indicate the unit of measure, usually in parentheses. There are no special precautions in reading a data table; just be sure you know what the headings mean.

EXAMPLE

The following table gives the symbols, atomic numbers, and average atomic weights of the most common elements in the Earth's crust. The atomic number is the number of protons in the atom.

Element	Symbol	Atomic Number	Average Atomic Weight (daltons)
Aluminum	Al	13	27.0
Calcium	Ca	20	40.1
Carbon	C	6	12.0
Iron	Fe	26	55.8
Magnesium	Mg	12	24.3
Oxygen	O	8	16.0
Potassium	K	13	39.1
Silicon	Si	14	28.1
Sodium	Na	11	23.0

QUESTION

How many protons are there in a formula unit of magnesium oxide (MgO)?

(1) 4
(2) 8
(3) 12
(4) 16
(5) 20

ANSWER AND ANALYSIS

Just add the 12 in magnesium to the 8 in oxygen; the answer is Choice 5.

QUESTION

Which of the following groups is arranged in order of increasing atomic weight?

(1) calcium, iron, potassium
(2) carbon, oxygen, silicon
(3) aluminum, carbon, magnesium
(4) iron, silicon, sodium
(5) oxygen, calcium, silicon

ANSWER AND ANALYSIS

Choice 2 gives carbon, at 12.0 daltons (D); oxygen, at 16.0 D; and silicon at 28.1 D, and is the answer.

OTHERS

There is no limit to the inventiveness of a scientist who sets out to present data. You must expect to meet on the GED Examination an unfamiliar form of graph, table, or diagram. Study it carefully, and make sure you understand the information presented before you tackle the questions based on it.

Handling Science Skills Questions

The makers of the GED Examination try to test a wide range of skills. You can be asked to do something as simple as restating an idea from the passage, or something as complex as evaluating the scientific validity of an experiment. The questions are generally grouped into four levels of skill.

The Four Skills

It is not worth your while to try to determine to which of the four levels any one question belongs, or to develop special strategies for each of the four levels. In taking the test, this sort of approach would consume valuable time and require you to use a part of your thinking ability that is best reserved for answering questions. Nevertheless, it is a good idea to become familiar with the four levels of skill that are investigated in the test.

COMPREHENSION

Comprehension is the simplest level. What it comes down to is this: Do you understand the passage, graph, or diagram? Can you rephrase some of the information in it? Can you summarize it? Can you identify a simple implication of the information given?

Here are some examples of the simple comprehension type of question:

QUESTION

Elements can be either mixed mechanically to form a mixture, or combined chemically to form a compound. In a mixture, the properties of each of the elements present are recognizable. A mixture is rather like a stew in which the carrots, potatoes, and tomatoes are all identifiable. In a compound, however, the original elements are no longer recognizable as themselves, and another form of matter with its own characteristics has been produced.

Which of the following is NOT a mixture?

   (1) iron filings in sawdust
   (2) sugar water
   (3) vegetable soup
   (4) rust
   (5) soda water

ANSWER AND ANALYSIS

If you understood the passage, you know that the components of a mixture remain separate and identifiable, while the components of a compound are changed into a new form of matter. The only answer in which the elements have been completely altered is Choice 4, rust, the chemical combination of iron and oxygen. All of the other substances can be separated into their original parts.

QUESTION

The scientific name of an animal is printed in italic type and has two parts. The first word (capitalized) is the name of the genus to which the animal belongs. The second word (lower case) is the name of its species within the genus. Here are the English and scientific names of five birds:

A. American robin, *Turdus migratorius*
B. European robin, *Erithacus rubecula*
C. European blackbird, *Turdus merula*
D. Military macaw, *Ara militaris*
E. Red-breasted blackbird, *Sturnella militaris*

Of the following pairs, which belong to the same genus?

(1) A and B only
(2) D and E only
(3) B and C only
(4) A and C only
(5) C and E only

ANSWER AND ANALYSIS

Since the passage deals only with scientific names, you can ignore the English names. The first word of the scientific name is the same for two birds in the same genus, so the answer is Choice 4.

QUESTION

When you place a solution in a test tube and then spin the test tube very rapidly in a machine called a centrifuge, the materials in the solution will separate, with the densest ones on the bottom and the least dense ones on top.

The following diagram represents the result of spinning a suspension of broken cells in a centrifuge. Which is the correct conclusion?

(1) Ribosomes are more dense than mitochondria.
(2) Nuclei are more dense than mitochondria.
(3) Mitochondria and ribosomes are equal in density.
(4) The cell consists of only solid components.
(5) Nuclei are less dense than mitochondria.

Cell fluid (nearly clear)
Ribosomes and parts of reticulum
Mitochondria
Nuclei

Ultracentrifuge Tube, Showing Various Layers

ANSWER AND ANALYSIS

The correct choice is 2 because the most dense particles settle at the bottom after spinning.

QUESTION

The soft body feathers of a bird are useful as insulation, while the stiff feathers of the wings and tail form airfoil surfaces, like those of an airplane wing. If a new species of bird is found that has no stiff feathers, it is safe to assume that it

(1) cannot fly
(2) lives in a tropical country
(3) migrates south in winter
(4) lives mainly in the water
(5) is able to run rapidly

ANSWER AND ANALYSIS

This question calls for you to make a simple deduction. If the stiff feathers are used in flight, a bird without them cannot fly, so the answer is Choice 1.

QUESTION

The table below gives the densities of four kinds of materials found in the Earth:

Substance	Density (g/cm³)
Water	1.00
Petroleum	0.86
Wood chips	0.75
Sand	2.10

If a mixture of all four materials is placed in a cylinder, shaken, and allowed to stand, the materials will settle out with the most dense on the bottom. What will the cylinder look like?

(1) The sand and wood chips will be mixed together on the bottom, and the water will be on top of the petroleum.

(2) The sand will be on the bottom; above will be the water with the wood chips in the layer between the petroleum and the water.

(3) The wood chips will form a layer above the sand on the bottom, and the water will form a layer over the petroleum.

(4) The sand will be on the bottom; the petroleum will form a layer over the water, with the wood chips floating on top.

(5) The water will be on the bottom, with the wood chips floating on it; the petroleum and sand will be mixed above the water.

ANSWER AND ANALYSIS

The materials, top to bottom must be in the sequence of increasing density—wood chips, petroleum, water, sand—so the answer is Choice 4.

APPLICATION

If you have thoroughly understood the information provided in the passage, graph, diagram, or table, you should be able to apply what you have learned. The application questions ask you to use the general principle contained in the information, but to apply that principle to a different situation.

Here are some examples:

QUESTION

Study the graph below, which shows the percentage distributions of the Earth's surface elevation above, and depth below sea level.

Approximately what total percentage of the Earth's surface is below sea level?

(1) 30%
(2) 50%
(3) 70%
(4) 80%
(5) 90%

ANSWER AND ANALYSIS

There are more shaded bars below than above sea level on the graph. Adding up the lengths of all the shaded bars below sea level yields a total of about 70%. This represents the total percentage of the Earth's surface below sea level. The correct answer is Choice 3.

QUESTION

High-energy sound waves are known to produce long-term damage to the ears, resulting in loss of ability to hear high frequencies. Which of the following individuals is most likely to have good high-frequency hearing after many years of work?

(1) a rock musician
(2) an aircraft mechanic
(3) a riveter
(4) an accountant
(5) a sawmill operator

ANSWER AND ANALYSIS

Again, you cannot get the answer just by looking back at the information. You have to look at the list of choices to figure out who is least likely to have been exposed to loud noise. The answer is Choice 4. All the other occupations involve continuous, loud noises.

QUESTION

A 20-watt fluorescent lamp produces as much light as a 100-watt incandescent bulb. The lighting in a factory is redesigned to provide the same amount of light when half of the incandescent lamps are replaced with fluorescents. What fraction of the cost of lighting is saved?

(1) 10%
(2) 20%
(3) 30%
(4) 40%
(5) 80%

ANSWER AND ANALYSIS

A complete change to fluorescents would save 80 of every 100 watts. Since only half of the lamps are changed, the saving is half this, 40%; the answer is Choice 4.

QUESTION

When an animal eats another that contains PCB pollutants, the PCB concentrates in the predator's liver. The following food relationships exist in a certain ecosystem:

Big fish eat little fish.
Little fish eat plankton.
Wolves eat otters.
Otters eat big fish.

If the water of a pond contains PCB, which of the following will have the greatest concentration of PCB?

(1) otters
(2) wolves
(3) big fish
(4) plankton
(5) little fish

ANSWER AND ANALYSIS

The concentration of PCB must increase in the sequence plankton, little fish, big fish, otters, wolves, so the answer is Choice 2.

QUESTION

Many foods, such as bread, potatoes, and spaghetti, contain a great deal of starch. An enzyme in saliva, known as amylose, converts starch to sugar. Which of the following statements is most probably true?

(1) A piece of bread held in the mouth for a long time becomes sweet.
(2) Spaghetti in the mouth causes an increase in the flow of saliva.
(3) If you eat a potato, the enzyme is in your saliva.
(4) If you eat sugar, it can turn to starch in the mouth.
(5) A cookie tastes sweet because it contains starch.

ANSWER AND ANALYSIS

If the saliva in the mouth changes the starch in the bread to sugar, you might expect that the bread would begin to taste sweet. Choice 1 is correct. None of the other choices is suggested by the information given.

ANALYSIS

These questions are more complicated. To answer them, you will have to find the relationships among several different items of information. Some of these items will not be given; you will be expected to know things that are general knowledge. It is possible to identify five somewhat different kinds of skills that belong to the general category of analysis:

- Recognizing unstated assumptions
- Using several related pieces of information
- Distinguishing fact from opinion
- Distinguishing cause from effect
- Drawing conclusions from data

Here are some examples of questions requiring analysis:

QUESTION

A doctor discovers that a patient has blood pressure of 170/110. He tells the patient that medication, accompanied by a reducing diet and limited exercise, will bring the blood pressure down. What has the doctor assumed without actually stating it?

(1) Blood pressure of 170/110 is dangerous to the health of the patient.
(2) Medication can bring down blood pressure.
(3) Medication will reduce the patient's weight.
(4) The patient has not been exercising at all.
(5) Blood pressure varies greatly in the population at large.

ANSWER AND ANALYSIS

Surely the doctor would not bother with the problem if he did not assume that the patient's blood pressure is too high for continued good health, so the answer is Choice 1. Choice 2 is true, but it is not unstated; the doctor told the patient that medication would work. Since there is no reason to believe that the medication is used for weight reduction, Choice 3 is wrong. Choice 4 is wrong because the prescription for limited exercise might just as easily mean that the patient has been exercising too much. Choice 5 is true, but irrelevant.

If you are asked to find an unstated assumption, do *not* select one that is (a) stated in the information given; (b) untrue; (c) ambiguous; or (d) irrelevant.

QUESTION

Corals are tiny animals that obtain their energy from their close association with green algae. Fish that eat corals do not live in deep water because

(1) the pressure is too great in deep water
(2) the fish that live in deep water eat them
(3) sunlight does not penetrate into deep water
(4) there are no currents in deep water to carry nutrients to them
(5) it is too cold in deep water

ANSWER AND ANALYSIS

This is one of the questions in which you are expected to know a few facts and to put some ideas together. You should know that green algae need sunlight to grow, and that corals use energy for growth. The answer is Choice 3. Some of the other answers may be true, but they are irrelevant.

QUESTION

Someone sees a high waterfall on the side of a cliff and comments about it. Which of the following comments is probably based on opinion rather than fact?

(1) The waterfall is about 30 meters high.
(2) The valley into which it falls was carved by a glacier.
(3) The rock in the mountain is a form of granite.
(4) The speed of the water at the bottom of the fall is about 25 meters per second.
(5) A photograph of the fall would be really beautiful.

ANSWER AND ANALYSIS

"Based on fact" is not the same as "factual." A statement is probably based on fact if it can be derived from one or more facts. Choices 1 and 4 could be determined by measurement or calculation—facts. Choices 2 and 3 could be determined from facts by any competent geologist. Since beauty is in the eye of the beholder, Choice 5 is an opinion.

QUESTION

It is found that when a stream becomes more muddy, the population of catfish increases. Three possible explanations are offered:

A. More catfish tend to make the water muddy.
B. Catfish thrive on invertebrates that live in mud.
C. Other fish cannot live in muddy water, so catfish have less competition.

Which of these explanations is (are) feasible?

(1) A only
(2) B only
(3) C only
(4) A and B only
(5) B and C only

ANSWER AND ANALYSIS

This question requires you to tell the difference between cause and effect. Is it possible that explanation A is true? No; the water became muddy before the catfish population increased, and a cause can never come after its effect. In both explanation B and explanation C, the water is already muddy, and both are reasonable hypotheses, so the answer is Choice 5.

This type of question can be tricky. If one event follows another, the one that occurs first may or may not be the cause of the second, even if the second invariably follows the first. The crowing of the rooster does not make the sun rise. In the example given, the sequence of the two events stated in the question establishes only that B and C are possible explanations, not that they must necessarily be true.

QUESTION

A chemical factory manufacturing a detergent discovers that its product contains a material that is considered a biohazard. Of the following, which can be considered a conclusion based on data?

(1) The amount of reactant *A* is twice as great as that of reactant *B*.
(2) The temperature of the reaction is 140°C.
(3) The pH of the reaction mixture is 5.4.
(4) The problem can be solved by adding an alkali.
(5) There is a contaminant in reactant *A*.

ANSWER AND ANALYSIS

Fact or conclusion? All the statements except Choice 4 are data, testable and presumably confirmed by measurement. Putting all the known facts together, the engineer might use his knowledge of the process to obtain an overall picture of what is happening. He can then draw the conclusion in Choice 4.

A conclusion is a general statement that is not obtained from direct observation. It comes from intelligent application of known principles to measurement data.

EVALUATION

We all have our own beliefs and ideas, and most of our beliefs and general thought processes are not scientific. But then, this is how it should be. Science cannot tell you what career to choose or whom to marry, or whether to go to church on Sunday, or who to vote for, or what kind of music to listen to. What science can do, however, is provide highly reliable and accurate answers to specific questions.

On the GED Examination, evaluation questions test your ability to apply the rules of scientific analysis to questions. Before you can do this, though, you need to understand a little about some of the many different kinds of statements that you will encounter.

FACT OR DATUM

A fact (datum) is something that can be observed and proved to be true.

EXAMPLE

If you measure a piece of wood and it is precisely 8 feet long, you have established a fact. If, however, someone estimates and tells you that the piece is 8 feet long even though it has not been measured, then you have an estimation, not a fact. Another kind of statement is an opinion, as when someone remarks that the piece of wood is an attractive color. Again, you do not have a fact.

You may be asked to determine whether a statement is a valid fact. Sloppy techniques can produce a statement that looks like a fact, but which cannot be supported by evidence or by the experimental process. You will need to be able to identify such statements.

HYPOTHESIS

A hypothesis is an educated guess, the possible answer to a question. It is a purely tentative statement that may be modified or even disproved when more information becomes available.

EXAMPLE

If you find that a type-A shrub in the sunlight grows better than another type-A shrub in the shade, you might propose the hypothesis that type-A shrubs need sunlight for optimum growth. This hypothesis can be tested by a controlled experiment. The most common mistake that people make is to accept a hypothesis as a fact without realizing the need for an experiment to provide proof.

You may have to distinguish between a fact and a hypothesis.

CONCLUSION

A conclusion may be the result of a controlled experiment. A hypothesis becomes a conclusion when you have tested and verified the initial statement.

EXAMPLE

If the type-A shrub really does grow better in the sunlight during a carefully designed experiment, then it is a reasonable conclusion that this particular plant should be grown in the sun.

You may be asked whether it is reasonable to draw a certain conclusion from a given set of data. You will have to be able to distinguish between a hypothesis and a conclusion.

GENERALIZATION

A generalization is a conclusion that can apply to a wide variety of situations.

EXAMPLE

Many experiments with green plants have indicated that all of them, whether a tiny alga cell or an enormous redwood tree, need some sunlight in order to live.

If you are asked whether a certain generalization is reasonable, look to see if it applies to many situations.

VALUE JUDGMENT

A value judgment is an opinion based on cultural or emotional factors rather than on scientific evidence. Opinions have an important place in our lives, but they cannot be allowed to affect the process of arriving at a scientific conclusion.

EXAMPLE

A certain landowner decided that he should kill every snake on his property because he didn't like snakes. He also killed squirrels and chipmunks for the same reason—he didn't like them.

You will be asked to distinguish value judgments from scientifically valid statements.

LOGICAL FALLACY

A fallacy is a wrong conclusion that results when you use information incorrectly. The most common logical fallacy goes by the imposing name *post hoc ergo propter hoc*, which means "followed by, therefore caused by."

EXAMPLE

I drink a glass of milk for breakfast every morning, and I always get sleepy. Does the milk make me sleepy? Maybe. Or maybe I would become sleepy even if I didn't drink the milk. The way to avoid this kind of fallacy is to perform a controlled experiment and test the possible relationship.

The examples below will give you some idea of the sorts of questions that will test your ability to evaluate scientific statements.

QUESTION

A proposal to build a dam on a river is opposed by a group of citizens, offering various reasons. Which of the following reasons is based on a value judgment rather than scientific information?

(1) The river should be preserved because it is a habitat for much beautiful wildlife.
(2) The cost of the dam will be too high for the amount of electricity it produces.
(3) It is not possible to dam the river at the site selected because of the surface features of the land.
(4) The proposed site is on a fault, and the dam could be destroyed by an earthquake.
(5) The river carries so much silt that the lake formed by it would soon fill up and render the dam useless.

ANSWER AND ANALYSIS

The word *beautiful* in Choice 1 is a giveaway, specifying a value judgment. Whoever makes that argument sees an esthetic value in the preservation of wildlife. All the other objections are based on arguments that can be subjected to rigid testing, using established scientific principles.

QUESTION

The following graph shows the average growths of two groups of rats. The solid line represents a group raised under standard conditions by a supplier of laboratory animals; the dashed line, a group raised in a laboratory and treated with pituitary extract.

— Average growth of 38 untreated rats (control)
---- Average growth of 38 rats injected with anterior pituitary extract (experimental)

What is a proper conclusion from the experiment?

(1) It is known that pituitary extract stimulates growth, and the experiment confirms it.
(2) The difference between the control group and the experimental group is so clear that it can be concluded that pituitary extract stimulates growth.
(3) The growths of the two groups are too similar to show that there is any difference in average growth.
(4) The experiment is useless because there is no reason to believe that the same result would be obtained with human beings.
(5) The experiment is inconclusive because there was no attempt to control the heredity of the animals or the conditions of their nurture.

ANSWER AND ANALYSIS

Whether an experiment should have some obvious use is a value judgment that is not at issue here, so Choice 4 is wrong. Choice 1 is wrong because it suggests that the outcome of the experiment was prejudiced in advance. At first this looks like a nice, neat experiment; the difference in growth is marked, and so Choice 3 is wrong. However, Choice 2 is wrong because the controls are inadequate. The rats were not necessarily of the same breed, nor were they raised in the same place. They could differ also in their hereditary endowments, their feeding, and any number of other factors. The results of this experiment could lead to a hypothesis, but not a conclusion, so the answer is Choice 5.

QUESTION

Over the last hundred years, people have been burning more and more fossil fuel, which releases carbon dioxide into the atmosphere. This excess CO_2 is a cause of global warming, which, according to ecologists, is one of the most serious problems facing us today. Carbon dioxide in the upper atmosphere traps the Sun's heat, in much the same way that the panes of glass hold heat in a greenhouse.

Which graph best represents what most likely happens to the temperature of the Earth's atmosphere as the amount of carbon dioxide in the atmosphere increases over a period of many years?

ANSWER AND ANALYSIS

Graph (2) shows that, as the amount of carbon dioxide increases, the average temperature of the atmosphere also increases.

QUESTION

Which of the following advertising claims for a toothpaste cannot be confirmed or contradicted by laboratory or clinical tests?

(1) It contains 2% stannous fluoride.
(2) It removes plaque.
(3) It has a fresh taste.
(4) It is not abrasive.
(5) It prevents cavities.

ANSWER AND ANALYSIS

Taste is a highly subjective value judgment, and what is a fresh taste for one person may be revolting to another, so the answer is Choice 3.

QUESTION

A field biologist finds that for three successive winters the beavers in a pond were unusually active and the water level in the pond was exceptionally high in the following spring.

Which of the following is an appropriate response?

(1) She concludes that the winter activity of the beavers raises the water level.
(2) She decides to see what happens to the water level in years in which the beavers are less active.
(3) She suggests the possibility that the high water level makes the beavers more active.
(4) She proposes limiting the winter activity of the beavers so as to avoid flooding.
(5) She suggests that there is no connection between the water level and the activity of the beavers.

ANSWER AND ANALYSIS

Choice 1 is wrong because the evidence is insufficient for a conclusion; the fact that the rising water level followed the activity does not prove a cause-and-effect relationship. Choice 3 is wrong because an effect can never come before a cause. Choice 4 is wrong because there has been no suggestion that flooding is a problem, or that limiting the activity of the beavers will prevent it. Choice 5 is wrong because the evidence is sufficient to suggest the hypothesis that winter activity of beavers raises the water level. More investigation is called for, and Choice 2 is a good idea.

Glossary of Scientific Terms

In your preparation for the Science test you may on occasion find a term, an expression, or a reference that is not familiar to you. This handy glossary may save you trips to another source of reference. On some occasions your idea of a term may be hazy; you may have known the meaning of it well in the past but have now forgotten. Make it a habit to turn to this glossary to locate clear, succinct definitions. Some students have also used the glossary as a tool for checking up on science information. Your science background will greatly improve if you can find time to develop this habit.

ABIOGENESIS belief that living things may develop from lifeless matter

ACID a compound that dissociates in water to produce hydrogen ions; usually tastes sour; pH less than 7

ACID RAIN rain with an excessively acidic composition that has a harmful effect on fish and other animal and plant life

ALLOY homogenous mixture composed of two or more metals (e.g., bronze, steel, brass)

AMOEBA a type of protozoan that has no permanent shape

AMORPHOUS without definite shape

AMPLITUDE the maximum value of a wave or vibration

ANAEROBIC RESPIRATION fermentation, or respiration in the absence of oxygen

ANEMIA condition in which the blood has insufficient red blood cells

ANODE positive electrode of an electrolytic cell; negative terminal of a battery; negative plate of a vacuum tube; site where oxidation occurs

ANTIBIOTIC substance made by a microorganism that kill bacteria.

ANTIBODY a protein, usually in the blood of an organism, that serves to counteract the effects of disease-producing bacteria or viruses

ANTIDOTE a substance used to counteract the effects of poison

ANTISEPTIC a substance that prevents the growth or activity of bacteria

ANTITOXIN substance in the body that neutralizes toxins

APPENDIX wormlike, narrow part of the alimentary canal, in the lower right-hand part of the human abdomen

ARMATURE a piece of metal or a coil of wire that moves back and forth, or rotates, in a magnetic field

ARTERY a muscular vessel carrying oxygenated blood away from the heart to the periphery of the body

ARTHROPODS the phylum consisting of animals with nonliving external skeletons and jointed appendages; insects, spiders, crustaceans

ASCORBIC ACID vitamin C; found in citrus fruits, tomatoes, and green vegetables

ASEPTIC free of live bacteria

ASEXUAL REPRODUCTION producing offspring without union of individuals or germ cells

ASSIMILATION process by which digested food is utilized by the body to build up or repair cells

ASTEROID one of a group of "minor planets" between Mars and Jupiter, of which about 1,500 are known

ATMOSPHERE the whole mass of gases surrounding a planet

ATOM smallest unit of an element, consisting of a nucleus surrounded by electrons

ATOMIC FISSION the breaking down of an atomic nucleus, into two or more parts, with a great release of energy

ATOMIC FUSION the joining of atomic nuclei to form heavier nuclei, such as deuterium (heavy hydrogen) and tritium (another isotype of hydrogen) to make helium, resulting in the release of enormous quantities of energy

AURICLE an upper chamber of the heart that receives blood from the veins—also called the atrium

AUTONOMIC NERVOUS SYSTEM part of the human nervous system that regulates the involuntary activities of the body

AUTOTROPH organism (e.g., a green plant) that nourishes itself by making organic materials out of inorganic

AUXIN a plant hormone

BACILLUS a rod-shaped bacterium

BACTERIA the smallest one-celled organisms, having neither nucleus nor other organelles

BALANCE IN NATURE the interdependence of all plants and animals with their environment

BAROMETER an instrument that measures air pressure

BASAL METABOLISM the rate at which the body's activities are carried on when the body is at rest

BASE chemical compound that produces a salt when it reacts with an acid; an alkali; pH more than 7

BEDROCK the solid surface of the Earth's crust, often overlaid by soil or sediments

BENIGN TUMOR a growth that, although abnormal, does not spread and does no particular harm unless it presses a vital organ

BILE a fluid that is secreted by the liver and passes into the small intestine, where it aids in the digestion of fats

BINOMIAL NOMENCLATURE double name used to identify a living organism by genus and species

BIOME a community of plants and animals

BIOPSY the removal of a small part of living tissue for microscopic examination

BRAIN main center of the human nervous system, consisting of cerebrum, cerebellum, and medulla

BRONCHIAL TUBE one of the two branches of the windpipe

CALORIE a unit of measure of heat or other forms of energy (not metric)

CANCER an abnormal growth that, if not detected early and removed or destroyed, will usually, in time, spread widely throughout the body and ultimately cause death

CAPACITOR device that stores electric charge

CAPILLARY a thin-walled tube; one of the tiny blood vessels in the network connecting the arteries and the veins

CARBOHYDRATE a compound consisting of carbon, hydrogen, and oxygen (e.g., starch, sugar)

CARBON DIOXIDE colorless, odorless gas present in the air in small amounts; breathed out from the lungs

CARBON MONOXIDE poisonous gas that prevents oxygen from entering the red blood cells; produced when gasoline is not completely burned

CARCINOMA cancerous growth

CARNIVORE a flesh-eating mammal with long eyeteeth and sharp claws (e.g, cat, lion, dog)

CARTILAGE an elastic, yet hard, tissue composing most of the skeleton of the very young of all vertebrates and the breastbone of adults

CATALYST a substance that speeds up the rate of a chemical reaction without any change in itself

CATHODE negative electrode of an electrolytic cell; positive terminal of a battery; site where reduction occurs

CELL basic unit of plant and animal life, consisting of a small mass of protoplasm, including a nucleus, surrounded by a semipermeable membrane

CELL MEMBRANE the thin outer layer of lipid and protein acting as a cell boundary

CELLULOSE a complex carbohydrate found in the wall of plant cells

CELL WALL the nonliving, rigid wall surrounding the cells of plants, algae, fungi, and bacteria

CELSIUS temperature scale on which 0° is the freezing point of water and 100° is the boiling point; this term has replaced "centigrade"

CHEMOTHERAPY treatment of illness by the use of chemicals (drugs)

CHITIN material forming the exoskeleton of anthropods

CHLOROPHYLL a green pigment that enables green plants to make glucose by the process of photosynthesis

CHLOROPLAST a small green body that contains chlorophyll

CHOLESTEROL fatty substance found in animal fats

CHROMOSOME one of several small, more or less rod-shaped bodies in the nucleus of a cell; contains the hereditary factors (genes)

CLAY finely ground quartz, feldspar, and mica resulting from the erosion of rocks

CLIMATE a composite of weather conditions over a long period of time

COMET heavenly body having a head and tail and traveling in a long, oval orbit around the Sun

COMPOUND substance composed of two or more chemically united elements

CONDENSATION process by which a liquid or solid is formed from a vapor or gas

CONDUCTOR a material (e.g., copper wire) that carries a flow of electrons (electricity)

CONGLOMERATE sedimentary rock made up of a mixture of rounded fragments cemented together by natural substances such as clay

CONSERVATION wise and careful use of natural resources

CONSTELLATION any of the groups of stars and the area of the sky in the group's vicinity to which a definite name has been given (e.g., Ursa Major, the Great Bear)

CORNEA transparent tissue in front of the iris and the pupil of the eye

CORONARY pertaining to the blood vessels of the heart muscle

CORPUSCLE red or white cell in the blood

CORROSION the weakening of a metal by chemical action, such as oxidation

CYCLONE storm or system of winds blowing counterclockwise about a nearly circular region of low air pressure in the Northern Hemisphere and extending over an area covering thousands of square miles

CYCLOTRON instrument used to study the properties of atoms by increasing the speed of atomic particles

CYTOPLASM that part of the cell that lies outside the nucleus; carries on all life activities except reproduction

DECIBEL unit for measuring the relative loudness of a sound

DECIDUOUS vegetation that regularly loses its leaves with the change in seasons

DEHYDRATION loss of water

DEOXYRIBONUCLEIC ACID (DNA) nucleic acid that controls the metabolism of the cell and stores the hereditary information of the cell

DESALINATION removal of salt from a solution, as in the purification of seawater

DIABETES a disease in which the body cannot utilize sugar because of lack of insulin or an inability to properly use insulin

DIAPHRAGM a sheet of muscle that separates the chest cavity from the abdomen and by its movement helps in breathing; also, the vibrating disk of metal in a telephone

DIFFUSION movement from high to low concentration

DIGESTION a process of chemical change that prepares food for absorption by breaking down complex molecules into simpler ones

DISINFECTANT a chemical that kills microbes

DISTILLATION the process of heating a substance until it turns into a gas and then condensing this gas by cooling, usually used to separate substances from a mixture; distillation is a physical change

EBB TIDE outgoing tide

ECHO a reflected sound wave

ECLIPSE cutting off of light from one celestial body by another

ECOLOGY study of the relationships of living things with each other and with their environment

ELECTRIC CURRENT flow of electric charge (e.g., electrons in a wire, ions in a solution)

ELECTROLYSIS chemical breakdown of a compound due to the passage of an electric current through it

ELEMENT a chemical substance made up of one kind of atom; cannot be decomposed by ordinary means (e.g., hydrogen, sodium)

EMBRYO organism in an early stage of development

EMULSIFIER a substance (e.g., soap) that can break large fat droplets into many smaller droplets suspended in water

ENZYME protein that speeds up the reaction of chemicals without change to itself

EROSION wearing away of the Earth's surface by water, ice, and winds

ESOPHAGUS (gullet) tube that connects the mouth with the stomach

ESTROGEN female hormone secreted by the ovaries

EVAPORATION escape of molecules from the surface of liquids

EVOLUTION the process by which living things change into other kinds over time

EXCRETION elimination of the wastes of metabolism

FALLOUT radioactive particles that fall to Earth as the result of a nuclear explosion

FARSIGHTEDNESS defect of the eye in which sharper images of objects at a distance are formed than of things nearby

FATTY ACID organic substance whose molecule is a long hydrocarbon chain with a carboxyl group at the end; component of molecules of fats and oils

FAUNA animal life typical of a particular region

FERMENTATION chemical change brought about by enzymes produced by microbes; in the making of beer or wine, yeasts ferment sugars into alcohol and carbon dioxide

FERTILIZATION process that occurs in sexual reproduction when the gametes, a sperm and an egg, unite

FILAMENT fine wire inside an electric light bulb that gives off light and heat when electricity is passed through it

FISSION splitting of the nucleus of an atom with the release of tremendous amounts of energy

FJORD a narrow inlet of the sea between cliffs or steep slopes

FOG a cloud of condensed water vapor formed on or near the ground

FOOD CHAIN pathway of energy through an ecosystem from producers to consumers

FOOD WEB complex feeding relationships within a biological community

FOSSIL remains or impression, in rock or amber, of a plant or animal that lived long ago

FOSSIL FUEL remains of organisms that lived hundreds of millions of years ago; used to release energy on burning (e.g., coal, oil, natural gas)

FRATERNAL TWIN one of two individuals that result from the fertilization of two ova simultaneously by two different sperm

FUNGUS kingdom of plantlike organisms that lack chlorophyll and therefore cannot make their own food

FUSION atomic reaction in which the nuclei of atoms combine and energy is released

GALAXY a large group of billions of stars

GALLBLADDER sac attached to the liver that stores bile

GAMETE one of the two cells that unite in sexual reproduction (e.g., egg or sperm)

GAS phase of matter in which the substance spreads out to fill all the space in its container

GASOHOL a motor fuel that consists of nine parts gasoline and one part ethanol

GASTRIC JUICE acid digestive fluid produced by the glands in the walls of the stomach

GENE a part of a DNA molecule that controls the manufacture of a specific protein. Since it is copied and passed on in every cell division, it forms the unit of heredity

GEOTHERMAL ENERGY heat produced in the Earth's interior

GESTATION the period of time necessary for embryo development; pregnancy

GLUCOSE a simple sugar oxidized in the body to give energy

GROUND WATER water that saturates the soil, filling all the space between particles

HALF-LIFE time required for half of any sample of a radioactive material to undergo transformation into other nuclei

HARD WATER water containing a large quantity of dissolved mineral salts (usually calcium and magnesium salts)

HEMOGLOBIN an iron-rich chemical, found in the red blood cells, which carries oxygen to cells

HEMOPHILIA physical condition in which blood fails to clot properly

HEREDITARY the tendency of offspring to resemble parents due to the passage of genes in the reproduction process

HETEROTROPH organism that cannot synthesize food from inorganic material

HIBERNATION torpid or resting state of an organism throughout some or all of the winter season

HOMEOSTASIS maintenance of a stable internal environment in an organism

HOMOGENIZE to distribute the solute in a solution to form a permanent emulsion

HOMO SAPIENS scientific name for a human being

HORMONE chemical messenger, produced by an endocrine gland, that helps to control and coordinate the activities of the body (e.g., insulin)

HORSEPOWER a unit for measuring the rate of work, equal to 550 foot-pounds per second

HUMIDITY amount of water vapor in the air

HUMUS dead and decaying organic matter found in the soil

HURRICANE a cyclone with winds of at least 74 miles per hour

HYBRID a cross between species; an organism with dissimilar genes for a trait

HYDROCARBON compound containing only hydrogen and carbon atoms

HYDROELECTRIC referring to the generation of electric energy from falling water

HYDROGEN BOMB a bomb consisting of deuterium and tritium (isotopes of hydrogen), which are fused into helium, releasing a great deal of energy

HYDROPONICS soilless growth of plants

HYPOTHESIS assumption made as a basis for further investigation or research

IDENTICAL TWIN one of two individuals that result from the division of a single fertilized egg

IMMUNITY ability of the body to resist or overcome infection

INERTIA property by which a body at rest remains at rest or a body in motion remains in motion, unless acted upon by a force

INFECTIOUS DISEASE illness caused by microorganisms

INGESTION taking in of food

INHALATION phase of breathing in which air is drawn into the lungs

INSTINCT complex inborn pattern of involuntary responses

INSULATION material used to reduce the transfer of heat or to shield a conductor of electricity

INSULIN hormone secreted by the pancreas that enables cells to use glucose

INTERNAL-COMBUSTION ENGINE an engine in which the fuel is burned inside the cylinders

INTESTINE a section of the digestive system below the stomach in which digestion and absorption of nutrients take place

INVERTEBRATE animal without a backbone

IONOSPHERE the part of the atmosphere 40–300 miles above the Earth

IRIS muscular, colored part of the eye, surrounding the pupil

IRRIGATION supplying of land with water by means of canals and ditches

JET STREAM swift, high-altitude wind at a height of about 35,000 feet

KIDNEY one of a pair of bean-shaped organs in the back part of the abdomen that collect the wastes of metabolism from the blood

KILOMETER unit of distance, equal to about 5/8 mile (1,000 meters)

KINETIC ENERGY energy possessed by an object because of its motion, depending on its mass and velocity

LACTATION secretion of milk by the mammary glands

LAGOON shallow body of water near or communicating with a larger body of water

LARVA young, usually wormlike stage of an invertebrate

LARYNX the voice box, located in the upper part of the windpipe, in which the vocal cords are found

LASER device in which atoms, when stimulated by focused lightwaves, amplify and condense these waves and then emit them in a narrow, intense beam

LATEX a milky substance from which rubber is made

LATITUDE the distance due north or south from the Equator, measured in degrees and marked by an imaginary line parallel to the equator

LAVA liquid rock material that flows out on the surface of the earth from underground sources

LEGUME a member of the pea family: peas, beans, clover, alfalfa; roots contain nodules with nitrogen-fixing bacteria

LEUKEMIA a disease of the blood-forming organs: bone, lymph glands, spleen, etc.; characterized by uncontrolled multiplication of white blood cells

LEVER a rigid rod turning around a fulcrum to increase the force or distance moved of the work input

LICHEN a complex organism composed of a fungus and an alga in intimate connection, able to live in highly unfavorable conditions

LIGAMENT tissue joining two or more bones

LIGHT-YEAR distance that light, traveling at about 186,000 miles each second, travels in one year

LIMESTONE a type of sedimentary rock, rich in calcium carbonate, that yields lime when heated

LIPID a fat, oil, or wax

LIVER largest gland in the body; makes bile, stores extra sugar as glycogen

LOAM ordinary garden soil; a loose soil made up mainly of clay and sand and a small amount of humus

LODESTONE natural rock magnet occurring in the Earth

LONGITUDE distance on the Earth's surface measured in degrees east or west of the Greenwich meridian

LUNAR ECLIPSE an eclipse that occurs when the full Moon crosses the plane of the Earth's umbra

LYMPH a nearly colorless liquid containing proteins, found in the lymphatic vessels of the body

LYMPHOCYTE type of white blood cell involved in immunity

MAGGOT larva of a fly

MAGMA molten material from which igneous rocks are derived

MALARIA a disease of the blood caused by a protozoan and transmitted by the female *Anopheles* mosquito

MALIGNANT TUMOR a cancerous growth

MAMMAL a vertebrate that suckles its young

MARINE referring to saltwater environments

MARSUPIAL mammal whose young continue development in a pouch after birth

MATTER substance that occupies space and has mass

MEMBRANE a thin sheet of tissue; also the outer edge of the cytoplasm of a living cell

METABOLISM sum total of all chemical activity in an organism

METAMORPHOSIS the change from larval to adult form, as in insect and amphibian development

METEOR streak of light in the sky caused by the burning of a meteoroid as it enters the Earth's atmosphere

METEOROID a small stony or metallic body in outer space

METEORITE a meteoroid that strikes the Earth's surface

METER a unit of length in the metric system, equal to 39.37 inches (1 m = 100 cm)

MINERAL chemical element or compound occurring free or found in rocks

MIXTURE two or more substances mixed together in no definite proportions and not chemically united

MOLD a filamentous fungus

MOLECULE smallest unit, composed of one or more atoms, of any pure chemical substance

MOLLUSK a soft-bodied invertebrate; usually has a shell outside the body (e.g., snail, octopus, clam)

MOLTING the process by which an animal sheds its shell, skin, feathers, or other outer covering and grows a new one

NATURAL IMMUNITY resistance to disease produced without medical intervention, as by exposure to the causative organism or by passage of antibodies from mother to offspring

NATURAL SELECTION survival of organisms that are best adjusted to the conditions in which they live

NEARSIGHTEDNESS a defect of the eye in which sharper images of things nearby are formed than of things at a distance

NERVE bundle of nerve fibers held together by connective tissue

NIGHT BLINDNESS a condition in which a person does not see well in dim light, sometimes due to a deficiency of vitamin A

NOVA a star that suddenly becomes brighter than normal and then fades again

NUCLEAR FISSION breakup of a larger nucleus of an atom into two or more smaller nuclei

NUCLEAR FUSION joining of two or more atomic nuclei

NUCLEAR REACTOR device for splitting an atom in order to produce useful energy or valuable radioactive materials

NUCLEUS (BIOLOGY) specialized chromosome-containing portion of the protoplasm of cells; coordinates cell activities

NUCLEUS (PHYSICAL SCIENCE) positively charged, dense part of an atom containing protons and neutrons

NUTRIENT one of a group of substances in food used to nourish and repair body tissue

OPTIC NERVE nerve that carries impulses from the eye to the brain

ORE rock from which one or more minerals can be extracted

ORGAN group of tissues performing a special function in a plant or an animal

ORGANIC COMPOUND compound containing carbon and hydrogen

ORGANISM any individual living animal or plant

OXIDATION reaction involving the loss of electrons from an atom

OXYGEN colorless, odorless gas that makes up 20% of the air; needed by cells to burn food for energy

OZONE a form of oxygen (O_3), usually formed by an electrical charge

PALEONTOLOGY the study of fossils

PANCREAS a dual gland, near the beginning of the small intestine, that makes the pancreatic juice; also produces the hormone insulin in the cells of the islets of Langerhans

PARASITE animal or plant that obtains its food by living inside or on another living thing (e.g., tapeworm, hookworm, louse, ringworm, many harmful bacteria)

PASTEURIZATION process of heating to kill pathogenic microorganisms

PATHOGEN organism that causes an infectious or parasitic disease

PAYLOAD the contents of an earth satellite or rocket

PENICILLIN antibiotic obtained from a type of mold; used effectively in the treatment of many bacterial diseases

PETRIFIED referring to plant or animal remains that have become like stone

PHARYNX (THROAT) common passageway for air and food

PHOSPHORESCENCE capacity of a substance to emit visible light when stimulated by electrons

PHOTON particle of light

PHOTOSYNTHESIS process by which, in the presence of light, a green plant makes sugar from water and carbon dioxide

PLACENTA structure by which the young are nourished in the body of a mammal

PLANET one of the bodies orbiting the Sun (e.g., Earth, Mars)

PLANETOID one of the many small bodies between the orbits of the planets Mars and Jupiter

PLANKTON minute floating organisms that live at the surface of the ocean and serve as food for large animals

PLASMA the liquid part of the blood; contains antibodies, hormones, and digested foods

PLASTIC synthetic polymer capable of being molded (e.g., cellophane)

POLIO a viral disease that injures the nerve cells in the brain or spinal cord; may result in paralysis of the diaphragm or other muscles

POLLINATION transfer of pollen from the stamen of a flower to a pistil

POLLUTANT substance that contaminates air, water, or soil

POLLUTION accumulation of harmful substances in air, soil, or water

POLYMER giant molecule formed when smaller molecules join together

PRECIPITATION all forms of moisture falling from the sky: hail, snow, rain, and sleet

PREVAILING WIND wind that almost always blows from one direction

PRIMARY LIGHT COLOR one of a group of colors, red, green, and blue, that can be combined to produce all the colors visible to the human eye

PRIMATES order of mammals that includes lemurs, monkeys, apes, and humans

PROGESTRONE hormone produced by the ovaries that regulates the menstrual cycle and the uterus during pregnancy

PROTEIN one of a group of nitrogen-containing organic compounds of large molecular size; important constituent of protoplasm

PROTON positively charged particle found in the nuclei of all atoms

PROTOPLASM all the living substance of a cell

PSYCHIATRIST medical doctor who specializes in mental health

PSYCHOLOGY the study of behavior and learning

PTOMAINE poisonous substance formed by the action of certain bacteria

PULLEY a wheel with a grooved rim, used with a rope or chain to change direction of a pulling force; simple machine

PULSE beat of an artery, produced by the surging of blood out of the heart

PUS yellowish white matter consisting of dead tissue, white blood cells, and bacteria, present in an abscess or boil

QUARANTINE isolation of an individual carrying a contagious disease

QUININE drug once used to prevent and treat malaria

RABIES (HYDROPHOBIA) a dangerous disease of the nervous system caused by a virus; transmitted in the saliva when an infected dog, fox, or similar animal bites a victim

RADAR acronym for radio detection and ranging; device used for the detection of objects by radio waves

RADIANT ENERGY energy in the form of light or other kinds of radiation

RADIANT HEATING a heating system in which hot water or steam pipes set in floors or walls send out heat into rooms

RADIATION process by which energy is transferred in a vacuum

RADIOACTIVITY property of large atomic nuclei that are unstable and break down spontaneously, emitting particles and/or energy

RECYCLE to save and return material so that it can be used again

REFLEX an inborn, immediate response to a stimulus, made without thinking

REFRIGERANT a liquid (e.g., freon) that evaporates easily and therefore is useful in the cooling coils of a refrigerator

REGENERATION regrowth of lost body parts

RELATIVE HUMIDITY ratio of the amount of water vapor actually present in the air to the greatest amount that would be possible at a given temperature

Rh FACTOR a blood protein present in most people; incompatible Rh factors from the parents cause damage to the blood of newborns

ROTATING CROPS farming method in which different plants are sown in the same soil in succeeding years

ROUGHAGE coarse, fibrous food (e.g., bran) that adds bulk to the diet and prevents constipation

RUNOFF surface water that runs to the sea without entering the underground water supply

RUST a fungus related to the smuts; different forms cause plant diseases, such as wheat rust

SALINITY degree of saltiness

SALIVA a secretion produced by three pairs of glands near the tongue; contains an enzyme that changes starch into sugar

SALT a compound composed of a positive (metallic) ion and a negative ion other than OH^-

SATELLITE natural or artificial body circling the Earth or another planet

SCURVY a disease characterized by weakness of the capillaries, caused by vitamin C deficiency

SEED a developed ovule consisting of a protective coat, stored food, and an embryo plant

SHORT CIRCUIT an accidental direct connection between the two sides of an electric circuit, producing a destructive surge of current

SILT soil particles intermediate in size between clay particles and sand grains

SMOG layer of fog that contains smoke and irritating gases

SOFT WATER water that is relatively free of dissolved mineral salts

SOLAR CELL a device that produces electricity from the energy of sunlight

SOLAR SYSTEM the Sun with the group of bodies in space that, held by gravitational attraction, revolve around it

SOLID phase of matter in which the substance has a definite shape and volume

SOLSTICE time when the sun seems to reverse its apparent movement north or south of the equator

SOLUBLE capable of being dissolved

SOLUTION a mixture in which molecules or ions of a substance are evenly or uniformly dispersed in a liquid

SOLVENT liquid part of a solution in which a substance is dissolved

SOUND BARRIER the speed at which an airplane overtakes its own sound waves, resulting in violent vibration

SPAWNING the shedding of eggs and milt into the water during the reproductive process of fish

SPECIES a group of similar organisms, consisting of populations that can interbreed freely

SPECTRUM the array of colors or wavelengths into which light is divided, usually by the action of a prism or diffraction grating

SPONTANEOUS COMBUSTION bursting into flame of a substance because of the accumulated heat of slow oxidation

STATIC ELECTRICITY electric charge accumulated on an object

STERILITY complete absence of microscopic life; also, inability to have offspring

STIMULUS any form of energy to which protoplasm is sensitive

STREPTOMYCIN antibiotic used to combat infections, such as tuberculosis

SUBATOMIC PARTICLE particles that make up the atom

SUBLIMATION change from solid to gas or gas to solid without going through the liquid phase

SULFA DRUG synthetic drug used to combat certain bacterial infections

SUSPENSION a cloudy mixture composed of a finely divided solid in a liquid

SWEAT GLAND gland in the skin that excretes onto the skin surface a fluid consisting of water, salts, and urea

SYMBIOSIS beneficial relationship between organisms living closely together

SYNTHESIS building up of compounds from simpler compounds or elements

SYSTEM group of organs in an organism that deal with the same function

THEORY scientific principle, more or less acceptable, that is offered in explanation of observed facts

THERMODYNAMICS study of laws governing heat and energy, and their movement

THERMOMETER instrument for measuring temperature

THERMONUCLEAR referring to a nuclear reaction that requires heat in order to occur

THERMOSTAT device on a heating system that automatically controls temperature

THUNDER sound following a flash of lightning and caused by the sudden expansion of air in the path of the discharge

THYROID large ductless or endocrine gland in front of and on either side of the trachea in the lower part of the neck

TIDES regular movement of the oceans caused by the gravitational pull of the Moon and Sun

TISSUE group of similar cells and intercellular material that perform similar work

TOPSOIL upper fertile layer of soil, containing humus, that is necessary to plant life

TORNADO one of the most violent of windstorms, noted for its funnel-shaped clouds, high-speed winds, and great destructiveness over a short path and a small area

TOTAL ECLIPSE complete hiding of one heavenly body by another or by the umbra of the shadow cast by another

TOXIN poisonous substance of microbial origin

TRAIT distinguishing quality of a person or thing

TRANSFORMER device for transforming high voltage to low voltage, or low voltage to high voltage

TUBER underground storage stem that produces new plants (e.g., the white potato)

TUMOR an abnormal swelling or enlargement, either benign or malignant

TUNDRA far-northern type of ecological community; water soaked, with permanently frozen ground, bogs, and low plants

TURBINE rotary engine powered by steam, water, or gas

ULTRASONIC SOUND high-pitched sound above the range of human hearing

ULTRAVIOLET RAY electromagnetic radiation with wavelengths too short to be seen

UMBILICAL CORD structure that connects a mammalian embryo with the placenta

URANIUM heavy, radioactive element present in an ore called pitchblende

VACCINATE to inoculate with dead or weakened germs of a disease, such as smallpox, thereby causing a light attack of the disease but conferring future immunity

VACCINE a substance consisting of dead or weakened bacteria or viruses; used to produce immunity

VEIN a blood vessel that drains the other organs of the body and carries blood toward the heart

VELOCITY the time rate to traverse a distance in a particular direction

VENEREAL DISEASE disease transmitted through sexual intercourse (e.g., syphilis)

VENTRICLE one of the two muscular chambers of the heart that pump blood to parts of the body

VERTEBRATE animal having a backbone (e.g., bird, reptile, fish, dog)

VIRUS submicroscopic disease-causing organism, consisting of a DNA or RNA molecule surrounded by a protein coat

VITAMIN chemical found in foods and needed in small quantities for special body functioning

VOLCANO an opening in the Earth's crust from which molten rock and steam are ejected

VOLT unit of electric potential, equal to 1 joule of energy per coulomb of charge

WARM FRONT boundary between a mass of advancing warm air and a retreating mass of relatively cooler air

WATERSHED area from which a river or lake draws its water

WATER TABLE level below which the soil is saturated with water

WATT unit of power, equal to a joule per second

WAVELENGTH the distance between two points in the same phase on a wave, such as from one crest to the next

WEIGHT measure of the effect of gravity on the mass of an object

WHITE BLOOD CELL leukocyte; blood cell that helps destroy bacteria and other foreign particles that enter the body

YEAST a single-celled fungus, responsible for many kinds of fermentation and certain infections

Science Practice

Biology

Questions 1–3 refer to the following figure.

The figure above shows the range of hearing of various animals. Sounds that have a higher pitch or frequency than can be heard are called ultrasonic, whereas those that have a lower pitch or frequency than can be heard are called subsonic. The y axis (horizontal axis) shows the range of frequencies that an animal can hear. Note that the scale is by steps of 10 to accommodate the wide variation in hearing ranges.

1. What is the range of human hearing?

   (1) 10–10,000 Hz
   (2) 20–20,000 Hz
   (3) 10–20,000 Hz
   (4) 20–10,000 Hz
   (5) 10–100,000 Hz

2. Which of the following frequencies would be within the hearing range of both a dolphin and a dog?

   (1) 20 Hz
   (2) 200 Hz
   (3) 2,000Hz
   (4) 20,000 Hz
   (5) 200,000 Hz

3. Which animal's range of hearing covers the widest variation in frequencies?

   (1) moth
   (2) dog
   (3) human
   (4) frog
   (5) crocodile

Questions 4–7 refer to the following graph.

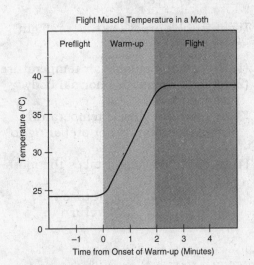

The graph above shows the temperature of flight muscles of a sphinx moth before flight, during a warm-up period, and during flight.

4. About how many minutes does it take the sphinx moth to warm up in order to fly?

(1) 1 minute
(2) 2 minutes
(3) 3 minutes
(4) 4 minutes
(5) 5 minutes

5. What temperature must the flight muscles be in order for the sphinx moth to be able to fly?

(1) 24°C
(2) 30°C
(3) 35°C
(4) 38°C
(5) 42°C

6. Why does the sphinx moth need a warm-up period to get ready for flight?

(1) It is a cold-blooded animal, and its muscles are not warm enough to generate enough energy when cold.
(2) It has large wings.
(3) The muscles need more blood supply to allow them to carry more oxygen to the muscle cells.
(4) The muscles generally move too slowly to allow the moth to fly.
(5) Muscle contraction requires a great deal of energy.

7. What is the purpose of the "preflight" section of the graph?

(1) to show the outside air temperature
(2) to show the moth's normal body temperature
(3) to show the muscle temperature when the moth is not preparing to fly
(4) to show how long it takes the moth to decide to fly
(5) to show what temperature the moth's muscles will return to

Questions 8–10 refer to the following information.

When a new individual is produced from a single parent cell or from two parent cells, the process of reproduction occurs. This life function differs from all other life processes in that it preserves the species rather than ensuring the survival of the individual. To understand how a cell divides, one must consider the behavior of the nuclear material and the cytoplasm. Mitosis is the process by which the hereditary material of the nucleus is doubled and then distributed into the daughter cells. This is accompanied by the division of the cytoplasmic material so that, as a result of cell division, normally two cells similar to the parent cell are produced. This is the basis of all forms of asexual reproduction, in which a single parent is involved, as is the case in binary fission in single-celled organisms such as amoebas, paramecia, and bacteria, or in the process of budding in yeast cells or sporulation in bread mold.

8. Which life function is more important to the species than the individual?

(1) growth
(2) movement
(3) food manufacture
(4) reproduction
(5) protection

9. Which of the following terms does NOT belong with the others?

(1) fertilization
(2) budding
(3) sporulation
(4) asexual reproduction
(5) binary fission

10. Which of the following processes is a part of all the others?

(1) binary fission
(2) asexual reproduction
(3) sporulation
(4) budding
(5) mitosis

Questions 11–13 refer to the following figures.

The figures above show a prokaryotic cell and a eukaryotic cell. The questions below ask you to describe some similarities and differences they have.

11. Which type of cell has a defined nucleus containing genetic information?

   (1) the eukaryotic cell
   (2) the prokaryotic cell
   (3) neither one
   (4) both the prokaryotic cell and the eukaryotic cell
   (5) it varies with the species from which the cell came

12. Which type of cell has chromosomes?

   (1) the prokaryotic cell
   (2) the eukaryotic cell
   (3) both the prokaryotic cell and the eukaryotic cell
   (4) neither one
   (5) it varies with the species from which the cell came

13. Prokaryotic cells were discovered much later than eukaryotic cells, even though they have been on earth for a much longer time. Which of the following would best explain why this is true?

   (1) Prokaryotic cells have no nucleus.
   (2) Eukaryotic cells have organelles, which are easy to see.
   (3) You can see only the nucleus
   (4) Prokaryotic cells are smaller and require better microscopes to see.
   (5) Eukaryotic cells have a cell membrane to help outline the cell.

Questions 14 and 15 refer to the following passage.

   Surprisingly, a fish's caudal (tail) fin, is not used for propulsion. Fins are used primarily for stability and steering. In order to swim, a fish needs to be able to flex its body back and forth very rapidly. To create this motion, a fish's muscles are arranged in a series of waves or segments called myomeres.
   Fish have two kinds of muscle fibers, white and red. White myomeres are used for short bursts of swimming. Groupers and other slow-moving fish have almost all white myomeres. Open-sea fish, such as the tuna and mackerel, are capable of cruising at high speed for long periods of time. The blood in their red muscle fibers is rich in a pigment called myoglobin, which can carry large amounts of oxygen. The oxygen nourishes muscle cells, enabling them to work harder for longer periods of time.

14. Cellular respiration requires the oxidation of fuel that is in the form of organic molecules. In the fish, which of the following is (are) responsible for carrying large amounts of oxygen?

    (1) caudal fins
    (2) myomeres
    (3) hemoglobin
    (4) myoglobin
    (5) red muscles

15. On dissecting a fish, a biologist saw that it had large quantities of red muscle fibers. From this observation he can assume that this fish

    (1) lived in a coral reef
    (2) would be good to eat
    (3) came from shallow waters
    (4) was usually slow moving
    (5) came from the open sea

Questions 16 and 17 refer to the following information.

It is well known that plants tend to grow toward the light, a process known as phototropism. Research with plant hormones, known as auxins, has disclosed the mechanisms at work. One such mechanism results in the bending of a stem toward the light. In the grass family, the tip of the growing stem produces an auxin. When light strikes one side of the tip, the auxin moves to the other side. It then diffuses down the stem, where it promotes the elongation of the cells below the tip. As the cells on the dark side elongate, the stem bends toward the light.

16. What causes a stem to turn toward the light?

    (1) phototropism
    (2) the need for light for photosynthesis
    (3) an auxin that controls cell elongation
    (4) the effect of light in stimulating growth
    (5) a plant hormone produced in the dark

17. Which of the following best describes auxins?

    (1) leaf structures
    (2) stem tips
    (3) tropisms
    (4) plant hormones
    (5) light filters

Questions 18–20 refer to the following passage.

If you were to cross two plants, one that carries only genes for tallness and one that carries only genes for shortness, the next generation of plants would be either all tall or all short. For this example let us say that all the second-generation plants were tall. The gene that causes a visible characteristic—here, tallness—is called dominant, and the gene for shortness is called recessive.

A small chart called a Punnett square is a useful way to illustrate how dominant and recessive genes may combine. On the assumption that each parent carries two genes for a certain characteristic, the square shows four possible combinations of the four parent genes.

For example, if a tall plant is crossed with a short plant, the Punnett square may look like this:

	Tall	Tall			T	T
short	Tall short	Tall short	or	s	Ts	Ts
short	Tall short	Tall short		s	Ts	Ts

Across the top of the square are one parent's two genes for tallness. Along the side are the other parent's two genes for shortness. Each square displays a possible combination of the four parent genes, one gene from each parent. As the Punnett square shows, the offspring from this breeding will be 100 percent hybrid, each carrying one dominant and one recessive gene.

18. If two of the hybrid offspring are mated, what is the possible combination of offspring?

    (1) 50% pure tall, 50% pure short
    (2) 75% pure tall, 25% hybrid
    (3) 75% pure short, 25% hybrid
    (4) 25% pure tall, 25% pure short, 50% hybrid
    (5) 50% pure tall, 25% pure short, 25% hybrid

19. Brown eye color is dominant over blue eye color. In a family, three of four children have brown eyes, and one has blue eyes. What is the most likely genetic makeup of the parents?

    (1) pure blue and pure brown
    (2) pure blue and hybrid brown
    (3) pure brown and pure brown
    (4) pure brown and hybrid brown
    (5) hybrid brown and hybrid brown

20. Any one of the brown-eyed children from the family described in question 19 could be

    (1) either 100% brown or hybrid
    (2) hybrid brown only
    (3) 100% brown only
    (4) hybrid blue/brown only
    (5) either 50% brown or hybrid

Questions 21–25 refer to the following article.

The timber wolf occupies an important position in the food chain. Like any other large carnivore, it plays a major role in keeping populations of smaller animals in balance. Its diet includes many rodents. Even as a deer killer, it is more helpfully selective than its rival predator, the human.

The human hunter kills for sport and pride, most often shooting the finest member of the deer herd, but the wolf kills for food alone, picking off the weakest, the oldest, and the sickliest. Thus, humans lower the quality of the herd, but the wolf preserves its health and keeps its numbers geared to the sustaining support of the land. The result is good for the deer, good for the wolf, and good for the browsing area.

Recently a project was launched in Minnesota to extend the range of the wolf. The plan is to trap a small pack of wolves there and then transplant them to a new wild environment in northern Michigan. At one time wolves inhabited this area but are now almost extinct there. The purpose of the project is to have the wolves breed and preserve the species. In this way, Northern Michigan University and several wildlife organizations that are sponsoring the experiment will be doing a service to preserve a creature that is useful in the natural environment. They hope also to explode the myth of the wolf's wickedness.

21. Which deer are killed by the wolf?

    (1) weakest
    (2) strongest
    (3) best specimens
    (4) those that eat rodents
    (5) fastest

22. In connection with deer population why is the human race more destructive than the wolf?

    (1) The wolf destroys only browsing areas.
    (2) The hunter preserves the health of the herd.
    (3) The hunter shoots deer for food alone.
    (4) The hunter shoots the weakest, the oldest, and the sickliest deer.
    (5) The hunter shoots the finest members of the herd.

23. What is the purpose of the Northern Michigan University Project?

    (1) trap the wolves in Michigan and export them to Minnesota
    (2) increase the range of the wolf in Michigan
    (3) increase the number of deer in Michigan
    (4) keep wolves out of Michigan
    (5) prove the wolf's wickedness

24. Which of the following best describes the wolf's position in the food chain?

    (1) important because it keeps the population of its prey in balance
    (2) unimportant because it preys mostly on rodents
    (3) unimportant because it is a large carnivore
    (4) unimportant because it leaves healthy deer alone
    (5) important because it lives in the midst of tall timber

25. Two examples of predators mentioned in the selection are

    (1) wolf and man
    (2) wolf and deer
    (3) man and deer
    (4) wolf and rodent
    (5) rodent and deer

Questions 26–28 refer to the figure below.

The figure below shows the approximate amount of energy used (kilocalories burned) by doing the illustrated activities for one hour. As a rough rule of thumb, burning 3,500 kilocalories is the equivalent of 1 pound of body weight.

26. To lose 1 pound of body weight, a person would have to run for how many hours?

    (1) 1 hour
    (2) 2 hours
    (3) 3 hours
    (4) 4 hours
    (5) 5 hours

27. Bicycling burns calories at about what rate compared to swimming?

    (1) twice as fast
    (2) half as fast
    (3) at the same rate
    (4) at triple the rate
    (5) at one third the rate

28. Arrange the following from activities that burn the most calories per hour to those that burn the fewest per hour

    (1) swimming, running, writing
    (2) writing, running, swimming
    (3) writing, swimming, running
    (4) running, swimming, writing
    (5) running, writing, swimming

Questions 29–33 refer to the following information.

The higher forms of plants and animals, such as seed plants and vertebrates, are similar or alike in many respects but decidedly different in others. For example, both of these groups of organisms carry on digestion, respiration, reproduction, transport, and growth and exhibit sensitivity to various stimuli. On the other hand, a number of basic differences are evident. Plants have no excretory systems comparable to those of animals. Plants have no heart or similar pumping organ. Plants are very limited in their movements. Plants have nothing similar to the animal nervous system. In addition, animals cannot synthesize carbohydrates from inorganic substances. Animals do not have special regions of growth, comparable to terminal and lateral meristems in plants, which persist throughout the life span of the organism. And finally the animal cell has no wall, only a membrane, but plant cell walls are more rigid, usually thicker, and may be composed of such substances as cellulose, lignin, pectin, cutin, and suberin. These characteristics are important to an understanding of living organisms and their functions and should, consequently, be carefully considered in plant and animal studies.

| 0 | 100 | 200 | 300 | 400 | 500 | 600 | 700 | 800 | 900 | 1000 |

29. Which of the following do animals lack?

    (1) ability to react to stimuli
    (2) ability to conduct substances from one place to another
    (3) reproduction by gametes
    (4) a cell membrane
    (5) a terminal growth region

30. Plants have rigid cell walls, but animals do not. This is probably related to the difference between animals and plants in the function of

    (1) respiration
    (2) photosynthesis
    (3) excretion
    (4) responsiveness
    (5) locomotion

31. Which of these do only plants possess?

    (1) specialized organs for circulation
    (2) excretory organs
    (3) organs of locomotion
    (4) the ability to manufacture carbohydrates from inorganic materials
    (5) specialized nerve tissue

32. Which of the following do plants lack?

    (1) rigid cell walls
    (2) pumping structures
    (3) special regions of growth
    (4) structures for reproduction
    (5) a digestive process

33. Which of these processes are carried on by plants and animals?

    (1) the synthesis of carbohydrates
    (2) transport
    (3) the manufacture of cellulose
    (4) the production of cutin
    (5) excretion through excretory organs

Questions 34–36 refer to the following figure.

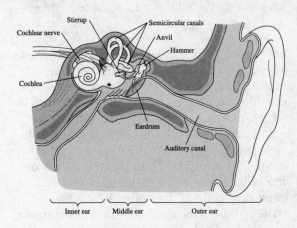

The figure above shows a diagram of the human ear.

34. Which of the following structures are in the middle ear?

    (1) the anvil
    (2) the hammer
    (3) the cochlea
    (4) the anvil and the hammer
    (5) the anvil, the hammer, and the cochlea

35. Which of the following structures would carry information directly to the brain?

    (1) the eardrum
    (2) the cochlea
    (3) the cochlear nerve
    (4) the semicircular canals
    (5) the stirrup

36. A sound wave's signal would be transmitted through structures in which order?

    (1) auditory canal, eardrum, cochlea, hammer
    (2) cochlea, eardrum, hammer, stirrup
    (3) hammer, anvil, cochlea, stirrup
    (4) cochlear nerve, cochlea, eardrum, hammer
    (5) auditory canal, eardrum, stirrup, cochlea

Questions 37–39 refer to the following article.

Plant cells contain specialized chlorophyll containing structures known as chloroplasts. These chloroplasts contain the pigment chlorophyll, which allows the cell to carry out photosynthesis, which is the process by which plants capture and use the sun's energy to sustain themselves. Some plants cells, such as those in *Spirogyra*, contain a single chloroplast. When these cells divide, the chloroplast must divide also, so that each new cell still has one chloroplast. Other plant cells, such as grasses or grains, may have as many as 40 or 50 chloroplasts.

Cells that do not have their chlorophyll stored in well-defined organelles such as chloroplasts are more accurately defined as algae. Many blue-green algae have chlorophyll scattered on specialized membranes throughout the cell, rather than stored in one specialized structure. These specialized membranes are known as chromatophores.

Algae and photosynthetic bacteria that are not exposed to light will rapidly lose their chromatophores and with them the ability to carry out photosynthesis.

37. The main function of chloroplasts in plant cells is to allow the cells to carry out

(1) cell division
(2) algal growth
(3) *Spirogyra*
(4) photosynthesis
(5) chromatophores

38. Which of the following statements is correct?

(1) All chlorophyll in cells is stored in chloroplasts.
(2) Algae can carry out photosynthesis under all conditions.
(3) Chromatophores are sites where photosynthesis is carried out.
(4) Chloroplasts must divide when cells divide.
(5) Plant cells generally have the same number of chloroplasts.

39. According to the passage, which of the following do not have chloroplasts?

(1) wheat
(2) *Spirogyra*
(3) grass
(4) blue-green algae
(5) brown algae

Questions 40–46 refer to the following article.

Whenever microorganisms have successfully invaded the body and are growing at the expense of the tissues, the process is called an infection. The term *infection* should always imply the existence of an abnormal state or unnatural condition resulting from the harmful action of microorganisms. In other words, the simple presence of an organism is not sufficient to cause disease.

Infection may arise from the admission of microorganisms to the tissues through the gastrointestinal tract, through the upper air passages, through wounds made by the contaminated teeth or claws of animals or by contaminated weapons, and by the bite of suctorial insects. Another type of infection sometimes occurs when for some reason the body has become vulnerable to the pathogenic action of bacteria whose normal habitat is the body.

The reaction of the body to the attack of an invading organism results in the formation of substances of a specific nature. The reacting substances that circulate mainly in the blood serum are known as antibodies and are classified according to their activities. Some, known as antitoxins, neutralize poisonous substances produced by the infecting organism. Others, called bacteriolysins, destroy bacteria by dissolving their cell walls. Opsonins or bacteriotropins prepare the bacteria for destruction by phagocytes; precipitins and agglutinins have the property of grouping the invading agents into small clumps of precipitates. The formation of defensive substances is specific for each organism.

40. Which of the following conditions illustrates an infection?

    (1) A guinea pig is exposed to diphtheria toxin.
    (2) A nurse taking care of a tubercular patient inhales some tuberculosis bacilli.
    (3) A man cuts his finger with a dirty knife. He uses no antiseptic.
    (4) A student examines his saliva with a microscope. Under high power he observes some streptococci.
    (5) Malaria parasites in the blood cause chills and fever.

41. Since each antibody is specific for the invading organism, it follows that

    (1) the body can produce only a small number of different kinds of antibodies
    (2) the antidiphtheria antibody will not protect against tetanus
    (3) there are many kinds of invading organisms that cannot be attacked by antibodies
    (4) an individual cannot be immune to more than one kind of disease organism at a time
    (5) immunity to some diseases weakens the body's ability to protect itself against others

42. Which of the following statements is true of phagocytes?

    (1) Opsonins are also called phagocytes.
    (2) Opsonins prepare bacteria for destruction by phagocytes.
    (3) Phagocytes destroy opsonins.
    (4) Bacteriotropins destroy phagocytes.
    (5) Phagocytes prepare bacteria for destruction by opsonins.

43. Which of the following is a correct statement?

    (1) The white blood corpuscles help ward off infection by distributing antibodies to all parts of the body.
    (2) A disease organism that lives in the body of a person always has a bad effect on the person.
    (3) Antibodies are classified according to the type of organism they attack.
    (4) Infection is accompanied by an abnormal state of the body.
    (5) Antitoxins are formed against every organism that enters the body.

44. All of the following are antibodies EXCEPT

    (1) phagocytes
    (2) antitoxins
    (3) bacteriolysins
    (4) opsonins
    (5) precipitins

45. All of the following might result in infection EXCEPT

    (1) inhalation of dust particles
    (2) a drink of contaminated water
    (3) a bite from a mosquito
    (4) a cut with a knife
    (5) a fly landing on the skin

46. By what process do agglutinins destroy invading organisms?

    (1) dissolving
    (2) neutralizing
    (3) clumping
    (4) engulfing
    (5) digesting

Questions 47–49 are based on the following information.

Relationships between organisms are classified according to the way they affect each other. Below are five types of relationships.

(1) parasitism—a relationship in which one organism lives on another organism and harms it
(2) commensalism—a relationship in which one organism is benefited and the other is neither harmed nor benefited
(3) saprophytism—a relationship in which an organism feeds on the dead remains or products of other organisms
(4) mutualism—a relationship between two organisms in which both organisms benefit from the association
(5) cannibalism—a relationship in which an organism feeds on the flesh of its own kind

Each of the following statements describes a relationship that refers to one of the categories just defined. For each item, choose the one category that best describes the relationship.

47. The relationship between athlete's-foot fungus and humans is best classified as

    (1) parasitism
    (2) commensalism
    (3) saprophytism
    (4) mutualism
    (5) cannibalism

48. Nitrogen-fixing bacteria enrich the soil by producing nitrates, which are beneficial to green plants. The bacteria live in nodules located on the roots of legumes. These nodules provide a favorable environment for the bacteria to grow and reproduce. The relationship between these bacteria and the leguminous plant is an example of

    (1) parasitism
    (2) commensalism
    (3) saprophytism
    (4) mutualism
    (5) cannibalism

49. Many bacteria or fungi decompose dead plants and animals, releasing ammonia into the environment. This relationship would best be described as

    (1) parasitism
    (2) commensalism
    (3) saprophytism
    (4) mutualism
    (5) cannibalism

Questions 50–55 refer to the following article.

At the beginning of the nineteenth century, it was generally believed that any features of an individual would be passed on to offspring. Thus, if a man lifted weights and had huge muscles, it was believed his children would have huge muscles as well. Jean Lamarck developed a theory of evolution, called the theory of use and disuse, in which this inheritance of acquired characteristics was considered to be the reason for the change in any organism through the generations.

Although Charles Darwin accepted the concept of inheritance of acquired characteristics, he believed that it played only a minor role. The main driving force of evolution, he said, is natural selection. This means that the only individuals that can survive long enough to reproduce are the ones that are optimally adapted to their environment. These adaptations improve generation after generation because only the best adapted individuals pass on the favorable traits to their offspring.

Later, August Weismann's theory suggests that acquired characteristics cannot be inherited because genes are somehow isolated from the rest of the body. Modern genetics has substantiated this theory; the information in the genes is already coded when the organism is born, and nothing that happens to it thereafter can change this coding. Today the theory of inheritance of acquired characteristics is dead, and Darwin's idea of natural selection remains a cornerstone of all theories of evolution.

50. Why was Darwin able to accept the theory of inheritance of acquired characteristics?

    (1) He did not know of Lamarck's work.
    (2) He had not gathered enough information.
    (3) There was good experimental evidence for it.
    (4) There was then no knowledge of the gene.
    (5) Weismann had developed a theory to explain it.

51. How would someone using Lamarck's theory of evolution probably explain the development in South American monkeys of a strong prehensile tail?

    (1) There was a mutation that made the tails strong.
    (2) The gene for a strong tail was dominant.
    (3) The monkeys interbred with other kinds.
    (4) The tail muscles were strengthened by use.
    (5) Strong-tailed monkeys left more offspring.

52. Which of these theories has been discredited by the development of modern genetics?

    (1) There is variation within a species.
    (2) The best adapted individuals survive.
    (3) Inherited features are passed on to offspring.
    (4) Acquired characteristics are inherited.
    (5) Development is controlled by genes.

53. Why have certain strains of bacteria that were susceptible to penicillin in the past now become resistant?

    (1) The mutation rate must have increased naturally.
    (2) The strains have become resistant because they needed to do so for survival.
    (3) A mutation was retained and passed on to succeeding generations because it had high survival value.
    (4) The principal forces influencing the pattern of survival in a population are isolation and mating.
    (5) Penicillin strains became less effective.

54. Which of the following statements is a modern expression of the theory of the continuity of the germ plasm?

    (1) Acquired characteristics may be inherited.
    (2) Genes are not altered to suit environmental demands.
    (3) Natural selection is an important factor in evolution.
    (4) Evolution produces better adapted forms.
    (5) Heredity changes by gene mutation.

55. In any species, which organisms are most likely to survive and reproduce?

    (1) the largest
    (2) the strongest
    (3) the best adapted
    (4) the most prolific
    (5) the most intelligent

Questions 56–60 refer to the following passage.

Most of us are familiar with the role of fats and cholesterol in health. Cholesterol is a white, fatty substance made by animals but not plants. Cholesterol is made by the liver and is essential for proper cell function. In general, the amount of cholesterol in a person's blood is regulated by two types of proteins that transport the cholesterol in the blood.

High Density Lipoprotein, or HDL, is considered "good" in that it tends to promote the removal of fatty deposits from blood vessels, thus decreasing the risk of heart attacks and strokes. Low Density Lipoprotein, or LDL, tends to promote the build-up of fatty deposits within the walls of blood vessels, thus tending to increase the risk of heart attacks and strokes. Fats and oils from animals not only contain cholesterol, but also raise LDL levels. Animal fats also are often saturated, and this too is associated with increased buildup of fatty deposits in blood vessels. Saturated fats from plants (including palm and coconut), while not containing cholesterol, also raise LDL levels. Among the habits that promote HDL level increases are exercise, eating less animal fat, and eating unsaturated or monounsaturated fats and oils such as olive oil or canola oil.

56. Which of the following would likely lower LDL levels in the blood?

    (1) eating bacon
    (2) eating foods cooked in coconut oil
    (3) eating beef
    (4) eating foods cooked in olive oil
    (5) eating lots of cheese and eggs

57. What is the risk caused by high blood levels of cholesterol?

    (1) failure to exercise
    (2) obesity
    (3) heart attacks and strokes
    (4) lack of sufficient HDL
    (5) improper balance of the amounts of HDL and LDL

58. A person who had a history of heart disease in her family would most likely be instructed to eat less of which of the following?

    (1) olive oil
    (2) canola oil
    (3) carrots
    (4) eggs
    (5) soybeans

59. Which of the following is least likely to be a sound medical reason for eating less saturated fat?

    (1) Eating large amounts of saturated fats increases the risk of strokes.
    (2) Eating large amounts of saturated fats increases the risk of heart attacks.
    (3) Saturated fats are components of deposits that block blood vessels.
    (4) People who eat large amounts of saturated fat often don't exercise enough.
    (5) Saturated fats are associated with high blood cholesterol levels.

60. What role does exercise play in benefiting the walls of blood vessels?

    (1) It lowers cholesterol.
    (2) It helps people lose weight.
    (3) It increases LDL levels.
    (4) It increases HDL levels.
    (5) It makes the walls of the blood vessels stronger and less likely to burst.

61. Homologous structures are those that have the same basic structure, but do not necessarily share the same function. They may, however, be indicators of some common ancestor far back on the evolutionary tree. Which of the following are homologous structures?

    (1) the foreleg of a horse and the arm of a human
    (2) the wings of a bee and the wings of a bird
    (3) the legs of a kangaroo and the legs of a grasshopper
    (4) the fins of a fish and the flipper of a whale
    (5) the wings of a bat and the wings of a butterfly

62. The term *metamorphoses* refers to a series of changes undergone from birth to adult. This is a common process in a number of organisms that change from one shape to another as they grow. Which of the following is NOT considered a metamorphosis?

    (1) The eggs of a frog hatch in the water, where the tadpoles must live and go through a series of physical changes before they can move onto the land.
    (2) A trout hatches from an egg and lives for a time as fry before growing into a mature fish.
    (3) A butterfly emerges from a chrysalis after spending the spring as a caterpillar.
    (4) It is much easier to kill flea larvae, with their soft bodies, before they become armored in chitin as adults.
    (5) During an early stage in its life, the jellyfish is attached to the ocean floor and looks rather like a plant. Only later does it become a free-swimming medusa.

63. Which assumption is the basis for the use of the fossil record as evidence for evolution?

    (1) Fossils have been found to show a complete record of the evolution of all mammals.
    (2) In undisturbed layers of the Earth's crust, the oldest fossils are found in the lowest layers.
    (3) All fossils can be found embedded in rocks.
    (4) All fossils were formed at the same time.
    (5) All fossils are found in sedimentary rock.

64. The graph shows the relationship between the number of cases of children with Down syndrome per 1,000 births and maternal age.

According to the graph, the incidence of Down syndrome

    (1) generally decreases as maternal age increases
    (2) is about nine times less at age 45 than at age 30
    (3) stabilizes at 2 per 1,000 births after age 35
    (4) is greater at age 15 than at age 35
    (5) is about ten times greater at age 45 than at age 30

65. The data presented in the graph suggest that

    (1) women over the age of 34 should not have children
    (2) older women should consider genetic counseling before planning a pregnancy
    (3) only younger women should have children
    (4) genetic counseling may be a good idea if there is reason to suspect that your baby has Down syndrome
    (5) children with Down syndrome need special care and training

Questions 66 and 67 are based on the following information.

People who want to stay healthy need to keep themselves well nourished. One important fact to remember is to eat moderate portions from each of the four food groups every day.

BASIC FOOD GROUPS			
(1) Meat	**(2) Dairy**	**(3) Fruits and Vegetables**	**(4) Grains (Cereal, Breads)**
2–3 servings	2 servings for adults 3 for children and pregnant women 4 for nursing mothers	4 servings	3–4 servings
Source of Protein B vitamins Minerals Fats	Source of Calcium Protein Phosphorus Vitamin A	Source of Vitamins A and C Minerals Fiber	Source of Fiber Starch Protein Vitamins Minerals

66. A person wanting to eliminate fats but still eat a high-protein diet might do which of the following?

    (1) Eat only from groups 2 and 4 and not from group 1.
    (2) Eat all the groups except 1.
    (3) Choose from group 4 only.
    (4) Choose mostly from groups 2, 3, and 4 and sparingly from group 1.
    (5) Eat only from groups 2 and 4.

67. From the information given in the table you can conclude that

    (1) citrus fruits are a good source of vitamin C
    (2) active people should eat a lot of protein
    (3) junk foods contain the most fats
    (4) nursing mothers should drink more milk than other adults
    (5) spinach is a good source of fiber

Questions 68–70 are based on the following graphs.

The graphs show data on some environmental factors acting in a large lake.

68. Which relationship can be correctly inferred from the data presented?

    (1) As oxygen content decreases, the carp population decreases.
    (2) As oxygen content decreases, the trout population increases.
    (3) Sewage waste and oxygen content are not related.
    (4) As sewage waste increases, oxygen content increases.
    (5) As sewage waste increases, oxygen content decreases.

69. Between what years did the greatest change in the lake's whitefish population occur?

    (1) 1970 and 1975
    (2) 1975 and 1980
    (3) 1980 and 1982
    (4) 1983 and 1985
    (5) 1986 and 1990

70. Which fish species appear(s) able to withstand the greatest degree of oxygen depletion?

    (1) trout
    (2) trout and walleye
    (3) walleye
    (4) whitefish
    (5) carp

Question 71 is based on the following information.

A green plant was placed in a test tube. A light, placed at varying distances from the plant, illuminated the plant. The bubbles of O_2 given off by the plant were counted. The table shows the data collected during this experiment.

Distance of Light from Plant (cm)	Number of Bubbles per Minute Produced by Plant
10	60
20	25
30	10
40	5

71. Which conclusion can be drawn from this investigation?
    (1) As the distance from the light increases, the number of bubbles produced decreases.
    (2) As the distance from the light increases, the number of bubbles produced increases.
    (3) As the distance from the light decreases, the number of bubbles produced decreases.
    (4) As the distance from the light decreases, the number of bubbles produced stays constant.
    (5) There is no relationship between the number of bubbles produced and the distance of the plant from the light.

Questions 72 and 73 are based on the following passage.

A consistent method is used by all scientists to design and conduct an experiment. If the experiment was performed correctly, the system allows any scientist anywhere in the world to duplicate the results. This procedure is called the Scientific Method.

The steps of the Scientific Method are as follows:

1. State the problem or ask a question.
2. Research the subject to see what others have found that might apply to the problem or question.
3. Form a hypothesis; based on the information acquired in step 2, attempt to predict a likely solution to the problem or an answer to the question.
4. Design and perform an experiment. In most situations, two groups of test subjects are used; an experimental group, which will test the factor in question (called the variable), and a control group, which will provide background information about the experimental group if the members of the control group are not exposed to the variable.
5. Observe, measure, and record as the experiment proceeds.
6. Draw conclusions based on the data from the experiment.
7. Repeat the experiment.

72. A botanist was experimenting with two groups of plants. Group 1 was watered with a solution containing a new plant food. Group 2 received plain water with no plant food of any kind. The plant food received by group 1 was the

(1) control
(2) variable
(3) experimental group
(4) data
(5) hypothesis

73. A drug company tested a new medication before putting it on the commercial market. Pills without the medication were given to 500 test subjects in group A, and pills containing the medication were given to 500 test subjects in group B. In this experiment, the individuals in group A served as the

(1) host
(2) variable
(3) control
(4) hypothesis
(5) generalization

WHAT'S YOUR SCORE?

_____right,	_____wrong
Excellent	65–73
Good	48–64
Fair	37–47

If your score is low, don't get discouraged. Perhaps biology is a difficult subject for you. Try to find out why you failed. The analysis of correct answers that follows will help you to pinpoint your errors. If your mistake was lack of information, turn to the "Glossary of Scientific Terms" (page 360) and look up the meanings of the words you did not understand. If it was a mistake in interpretation, review the analysis of the question.

Answer Analysis

1. **2** The graph shows that the range of human hearing extends from above 10 Hz to above 10,0000 Hz. The only choice that covers this range is Choice 2. Note that the scale on the vertical axis is based on orders of 10 (a logarithmic scale), so you have to do a little estimating.

2. **4** The only choice that falls within the hearing range of a dolphin (8,000–100,000 Hz) and a dog (20–60,000 Hz) is 20,000 Hz. Notice that even if your estimation was a bit off, the spacing of the choices would allow you to still get the right answer. Sometimes when you look at a graph it is not necessary to get all of the details. Often the "big picture" is sufficient.

3. **2** Of the choices provided, the widest range of hearing (the longest bar) belongs to the dog.

4. **2** The part of the graph labeled "warm up" extends from 0–2 minutes, and thus lasts 2 minutes.

5. **4** After the warm-up period, and during the flight period, the temperature is above 35°F, but clearly below 40°F. Only Choice 4 fits this range. Notice that if you had thought the correct answer should have been 37°F, you still would have picked Choice 4, because it is the closest.

6. **1** Moths are cold-blooded animals, and their body temperatures mimic their surroundings. By moving its muscles, the moth can generate heat to reach the proper muscle temperature for flight.

7. **3** The preflight part of the graph shows the temperature of the moth's muscles when it is not preparing to fly. This serves as a baseline for reference.

8. **4** Reproduction preserves the species.

9. **1** Fertilization is a sexual process, while all the others are asexual.

10. **5** All reproductive processes must include the division of cells by mitosis.

11. **1** The picture of the eukaryotic cell clearly shows a nucleus, whereas that of the prokaryotic cell does not. This is one of the primary distinctions between the two types of cells.

12. **3** Both types of cells show chromosomes. The prokaryotic cell has chromosomes in the nucleus, whereas the eukaryotic cell does not, but both cell types have genetic material on chromosomes.

13. **4** The figures do not tell you much about what it takes to see the cells. The pictures do indicate that eukaryotic cells are about ten times as large, which should make them easier to see. Smaller cells need better microscopes to be seen. The fact that one type of cell has been on earth longer is irrelevant, even though it is true.

14. **4** According to the passage, a red pigment called myoglobin carries large amounts of oxygen to the muscle cells.

15. **5** Open-sea fish have large quantities of red muscle fibers, which make it possible for these fish to cruise at high speeds for long periods of time.

16. **3** An auxin that controls cell elongation causes the cells on the dark side to elongate, and the stem turns toward the light. Choice 1 is merely the name of the process, not a statement of causation. Choice 2 tells why the bending is useful, but does not explain how it happens.

17. **4** An auxin is a chemical substance that moves through the plant and carries instructions for growth. This is a hormone. Auxim is specifically mentioned as a plant hormone.

18. **4**

TT = pure tall—25%
ss = pure short—25%
Ts = hybrid tall—50%

19. **5**

B = brown
b = blue
BB = pure brown
Bb = hybrid brown
bb = pure blue
Hybrid blue is not possible.

20. **1** Either pure brown or hybrid. Brown will dominate over the blue gene, so a hybrid child's eyes will be brown even though he or she carries a blue gene.

21. **1** The wolf kills only for food and eliminates the weakest, the oldest, and the sickliest deer.

22. **5** Humans kill for sport and pride and try to pick off the finest specimen of the herd.

23. **2** The project is aimed at exporting wolves from Minnesota into northern Michigan to preserve the species and extend the wolf's range there.

24. **1** The wolf occupies an important position in the food chain by keeping populations of smaller animals in balance. In addition, the wolf keeps the number of deer geared to the sustaining support of the land.

25. **1** The end of the first paragraph compares the wolf to its rival predator, the human. It thus identifies both as predators.

26. **4** One pound is the equivalent of 3,500 kilocalories. Because running uses up 900 kilocalories per hour 3,500/900 = 3.9, or just about 4 hours.

27. **1** Swimming burns calories at the rate of 300 kilocalories per hour, whereas bicycling burns calories at the rate of 600 kilocalories per hour. This means that bicycling burns kilocalories at double the rate. It does not matter if you think that bicycling only falls at 575 kilocalories per hour instead of 600. The value for bicycling will still be closer to double than any of the other choices.

28. **4** Choice 4 is the only one that shows the activities in the order from most to least (or top to bottom as shown on this figure).

29. **5** Animals do not have special regions of growth, comparable to terminal and lateral meristems in plants, that persist throughout the life span of the organism.

30. **5** The rigid cell walls severely limit the flexibility of the plant body, so that it is unable to move freely.

31. **4** Green plants have the ability to synthesize carbohydrates from inorganic substances (carbon dioxide and water) in the presence of light.

32. **2** Plants have no heart or similar pumping organ.

33. **2** Food, wastes, and other substances are conducted from one part of a plant or animal to another.

34. **4** The figure clearly shows that the anvil and the hammer are in the middle ear, whereas the cochlea is in the inner ear. It does not matter that not every structure in the middle ear is listed.

35. **3** Nerves are structures that transmit information.

36. **5** Only Choice 5 shows an order from outer ear, through middle ear, and then to inner ear.

37. **4** The first sentence of the passage spells out the role of chloroplasts. Other terms may be mentioned in the passage, but they are not what this particular question asks you for.

38. **3** Choices 1, 2, and 4 refer to situations that may be true, but are not true in all cases. Words like *all* and *must* mean that there can be no exceptions, and these words can serve as helpful clues in looking for the best answer to a question.

39. **4** Blue-green algae are specifically mentioned as not having chloroplasts. Brown algae (Choice 5) are not mentioned in the passage so that can not be the correct answer.

40. **5** Only in this choice is there evidence that the invading organism has produced a disease process.

41. **2** An antibody is produced in response to a specific invading organism, and will protect only against that one. The body can produce an unlimited variety of antibodies, and the blood usually has many of them.

42. **2** Opsonins prepare bacteria for destruction by phagocytes.

43. **4** Microorganisms that cause an infection produce an abnormal state or unnatural condition. Notice the term is in italics.

44. **1** Phagocytes are white blood cells that destroy bacteria by engulfing them.

45. **5** Unbroken skin is an excellent barrier against the invasion of microorganisms. In some cases, microorganisms may enter through normal body openings; in other cases, through wounds or bites.

46. **3** Agglutinins group or clump invading organisms.

47. **1** The relationship between athlete's-foot fungus and humans is known as parasitism. A parasite is an organism that lives in or on another organism and harms it.

48. **4** The relationship between nitrogen-fixing bacteria and the leguminous plant is an example of mutualism. Mutualism is an association between two organisms that benefits both. In this case, the plant gets nitrogen and the bacteria have a place to live.

49. **3** In a saprophytic relationship, an organism feeds on the dead remains of other organisms.

50. **4** After Darwin's day, the work of Weismann and others showed that genes (unknown to Darwin) pass unchanged by environmental influences from generation to generation.

51. **4** The theory of use and disuse said that any organ that is used becomes stronger. Although this is true of some organs, the changes are not hereditary and thus have no effect on evolution.

52. **4** With the discovery that heredity is controlled by genes that are sequestered in the germ cells, it became clear that there is no mechanism by which acquired characteristics can be inherited. See that last sentence of the passsage.

53. **3** Bacteria resistant to penicillin developed as a result of mutation. Organisms that did not receive the mutated gene were killed by the antibiotic. Those in which gene mutation occurred survived and passed the mutation on to succeeding generations.

54. **2** Continuity of the germ plasm occurs because no environmental influence affects the genes.

55. **3** Being larger, stronger, more prolific, or more intelligent may or may not promote survival. The general statement in Choice 3 is the only one that applies universally.

56. **4** The other choices all involve animal fats or fats that are saturated. The last sentence of the passage specifically tells you about the benefits of olive oil.

57. **3** The main risk of high levels of cholesterol is heart attacks and strokes. The other things mentioned may be associated (people with high cholesterol often do not get enough exercise) but the cause is the cholesterol levels in the blood.

58. **4** All of the other choices are vegetable products. Only eggs are an animal product and contain cholesterol. A person with a family history of heart disease would want to reduce animal fat intake.

59. **4** All of the statements given are correct, but only Choice 4 is not a direct result. This is an example of a correlation, not a cause and effect. People who eat lots of saturated fat may well not get enough exercise, but the fat intake is not causing them to get too little exercise.

60. **4** The last sentence of the passage states that exercise increases HDL levels.

61. **1** The foreleg of a horse is homologous to the arm of a human. In Choices 2, 3, and 5, a bird or mammal is compared to an insect, which is structurally quite different. In Choice 4, although both a fish and a whale are aquatic, the whale is a mammal.

62. **2** When a trout hatches from an egg, it looks very much like a little trout. All the other answers describe organisms that go through distinct stages as they mature.

63. **2** *Fossils* are the remains of organisms of the past. When an organism dies, it may be covered by sediment. Sediments are deposited in layers. The layers are compacted into rock. The oldest fossils are found in the lowest layers.

64. **5** According to the graph, the maximum number of Down syndrome cases occurs at age 45: 20 cases per 1,000 births. At age 30, there are 2 cases per 1,000 births. Therefore at age 45, there are ten times as many cases as at age 30.

65. **2** Choices 1 and 3 are opinions. Choice 5 is true, but has noting to do with the question. Genetic counseling is useful before planning a pregnancy, not after a baby is born, so Choice 4 is meaningless.

66. **4** According to the passage it is recommended that we eat something from all four groups. Cutting back on fats would mean eating less from group 1 and making up for the lost protein by eating a bit more from groups 2 and 4. The fiber and vitamins from group 3 remain important.

67. **4** The fact that the table does not mention specific foods eliminates Choices 1, 3, and 5. Although it may be true that active people need more protein (Choice 2), there is nothing to support this view in either the passage or the table. The table does say, however, that nursing mothers need more servings of dairy foods than others.

68. **5** According to the graph, oxygen content decreases as sewage waste increases. The organisms that decompose sewage are aerobic organisms, which consume oxygen.

69. **2** There was the greatest change in the whitefish population between 1975 and 1980. The whitefish population disappeared from the lake by 1980.

70. **5** The carp appears to be able to withstand oxygen depletion. The number of carp increased as the oxygen content decreased.

71. **1** According to the table of results, the number of bubbles produced by the plant decreases as the distance from the light increases. The results indicate that there is a relationship between the number of bubbles produced and the distance of the plant from the light.

72. **2** According to the passage, the variable is the part of the experiment that is being tested. In this case, the variable is the plant food.

73. **3** A control is a part of an experiment in which no changes have been made. Group *A* was the control. The individuals in this group received pills that did not contain the medication.

Earth Science

Questions 1–3 refer to the following passage.

It is often convenient to classify energy sources as either renewable or nonrenewable. Renewable resources are those that either grow back (such as trees) or that do not get used up, such as wind power, solar power, or hydroelectric power. Nuclear power is also considered renewable, even though the supplies can potentially be depleted. Nonrenewable resources are those that are not replaced by natural processes once they are used up. Fossil fuels, such as coal, petroleum, and natural gas fall into this category. These energy sources were formed over millions or billions of years from the action of great pressure on decayed animal and vegetable matter, such as decayed animals or plants. Our dependence on nonrenewable resources has often meant that we must pay more than we want to for these limited energy sources.

1. Which of the following are nonrenewable resources mentioned in the article?

   (1) coal, natural gas, and wind
   (2) solar energy and nuclear energy
   (3) coal and petroleum
   (4) petroleum and nuclear energy
   (5) solar power and hydroelectric power

2. Which of the following statements is not directly supported by the passage?

   (1) It takes a great deal of time for coal to be formed.
   (2) Fossil fuels are formed from the decayed remains of plants and animals.
   (3) Trees are considered renewable resources.
   (4) Natural gas is a fossil fuel.
   (5) We may have to go to war to be sure of our oil supplies.

3. Which of the following energy sources will likely become scarcer and more costly in the future?

   I. coal
   II. hydroelectric power
   III. natural gas

   (1) I only
   (2) II only
   (3) I and II only
   (4) II and III only
   (5) I, II and III

4. The Moon is approximately 240,000 miles from Earth. How long would a spacecraft launched from the Moon and traveling at an average velocity of 24,000 miles per hour, take to reach Earth?

(1) 10 hours
(2) 24 hours
(3) 10 days
(4) 100 days
(5) 240 days

Questions 5–7 refer to the following information.

The Moon goes through a cycle of four major phases in a period of 4 weeks. As it revolves around the Earth, its orbit takes it first between the Sun and the Earth and then to the other side of the Earth away from the Sun. When the Moon is in the area between the Earth and Sun, the side of the Moon toward us is not lighted directly by the Sun. However, the Moon is slightly visible because of sunlight reflected by the Earth. The light is called earthshine.

APPEARANCE OF THE MOON FROM THE EARTH

| New | First Quarter | Full | Third Quarter |

Tides are the result of the gravitational pull of the Moon and the Sun on the freely moving waters of the Earth. Since the Moon is so much closer to the Earth than is the Sun, the Moon has a much greater effect on the tides than does the Sun. The effect is greatest during the periods of the full and new Moon when the Moon and Sun are in

direct line with the Earth and exert a pull in the same direction. The result is a *spring tide*, or tide of great range. At the periods of the first and third quarters, the Sun and the Moon pull at right angles and thus oppose each other. Thus the pull of the Moon is lessened, the result being a *neap tide*, or tide of small range.

5. Earthshine is illumination seen during which phase of the Moon?

(1) full
(2) new
(3) first quarter
(4) crescent
(5) last quarter

6. Why is it possible for an observer on Earth to see the phases of the Moon?

(1) The Moon revolves around the Sun.
(2) The Moon rotates on its axis.
(3) The Earth revolves around the Sun.
(4) The Earth rotates on its axis.
(5) The Moon revolves around the Earth.

7. During what phase(s) of the Moon do we have a very high tide and a very low tide?

A. new Moon
B. full Moon
C. first quarter
D. third quarter

(1) A only
(2) B only
(3) A and B
(4) C only
(5) D only

Questions 8–10 refer to the following information.

According to geological evidence, Africa was once a continent of ice, while the Antarctic was a tropical jungle. Paleontologists have also found fossil remains from the same organisms on different continents far apart from each other. For example, the fossil of a medium-sized dinosaur called Kannemyerid has been found in North America, South America, Asia, and India.

Attempts to explain such discoveries have led to the theory of continental drift and plate tectonics. This theory states that the continents of Earth once formed one vast landmass, but later broke away from each other and are still drifting farther apart. Sometimes the geological plates carrying landmasses collide with one another, and we have an earthquake.

Evidence for continental drift lies in a chain of undersea mountains circling the globe. When marine geologists took the temperature in a deep valley running through the middle of this mountain range, they discovered that the valley was much warmer than the surrounding sea. Scientists believe that this is where molten rock is pushed up from within the Earth. As this new rock rises, it spreads out the seafloor, pushing the continents farther apart. More evidence to support this theory was discovered when core samples indicated that the rock nearest the mountains was much younger than rock farther away from the mountains.

8. From the evidence in the article we can infer that a paleontologist

    (1) collects rocks
    (2) studies volcanoes
    (3) maps the ocean floor
    (4) studies fossil remains
    (5) studies plate tectonics

9. The theory that the landmasses of Earth ride on huge geological plates is supported by the occurrence of

    (1) hurricanes
    (2) tidal waves
    (3) continental drifts
    (4) volcanoes
    (5) earthquakes

10. A prehistoric species could range over a number of continents with no problem because at that time

    (1) the continents formed one large landmass
    (2) there were land bridges between the continents
    (3) the oceans were much shallower
    (4) the creatures were excellent swimmers
    (5) large numbers of the animals evolved separately on each continent

Questions 11–13 refer to the following article.

Toward the end of the year 1973, the comet Kohoutek began to make newspaper headlines as it moved toward the Sun at great speed. Predictions were made that it would be more spectacular than Halley's comet, which was last seen in 1910, as well as Ikeya-Seki of 1965 and Bennett's comet of 1970. Kohoutek was first discovered in March 1973 by a Czech astronomer Dr. Lubos Kohoutek, when it was still more than 500 million miles from the Sun. Astronomers reasoned that if it was visible that far away, it would probably prove to be spectacular when it streaked to within 13 million miles of the Sun on December 28. Thus, it was expected to be the third brightest object in the sky, after the Sun and the Moon.

Measurements indicated that Kohoutek's nucleus was 20–25 miles across, its coma about 10,000 miles in diameter, and its tail about 20 million miles in length. The nucleus of a comet is thought to be composed of a clump of "dirty ice"—dust particles, stony matter, and frozen gases, such as water, methane, and ammonia. The coma is a large, hazy cloud formed when the Sun's heat liberates dust and gases from the nucleus as the comet enters the inner part of the solar system. The tail is a long cloud of ions and molecules that may become fluorescent under the influence of the solar wind.

Despite the predictions made for it, the comet Kohoutek turned out to be of such minimum brightness that few people were actually able to see it. The reason for its disappointing appearance may be traced to the fact that it was not the typical "dirty snowball" astronomers had predicted. Whereas the icy head of Halley's comet released streams of dust particles on melting as it approached the Sun, catching the sunlight and reflecting it in orange and yellow bands, Kohoutek turned out to be a relatively clean, blue-white comet.

Astronomers have identified in Kohoutek the molecule methyl cyanide, which is believed essential in star formation; this substance was previously detected only in the vast dust clouds toward the center of the galaxy. Consequently, the conclusion is drawn by some astronomers that comet Kohoutek originated in a dust cloud outside the solar system.

11. What is the composition of the comet Kohoutek?

    (1) a nucleus, a coma, and a tail
    (2) a nucleus, a comet, and a tail
    (3) only a nucleus and a tail
    (4) only a tail
    (5) star dust

12. Why was Kohoutek not as bright as predicted?

    (1) It originated within the solar system.
    (2) It originated outside the solar system.
    (3) It originated in a dust cloud.
    (4) It did not release streams of dust particles on approaching the Sun.
    (5) It contained too much ice.

13. Why was Kohoutek expected to be spectacularly bright?

    (1) Its appearance coincided with the Christmas season.
    (2) It would pass within 13 million miles of the Sun.
    (3) It was first visible when more than 500 million miles from the Sun.
    (4) It was the third brightest object in the sky.
    (5) Its nucleus was very large, about 10,000 miles in diameter.

Questions 14–18 refer to the following article.

One of the contributions of the space age has been a new vantage point for viewing the Earth's surface from distant heights. The Earth can now be viewed by remote sensing, which can be defined as detecting an object from afar without direct contact. All our lives could be influenced by the results of the new era of accomplishment that makes possible such activities as immediate observation of natural and human-made disasters; continuous study of the ocean; monitoring and more efficient management of land, food, and water resources; discovery of additional natural resources; identification of pollution; tracing current flow along coastlines; studying the distribution of fish; and mapmaking.

In July 1972, the Earth Resources Technology Satellite (ERTS-1) was launched to make a systematic surveillance of North America and other areas from space. This unmanned satellite follows a near-polar orbit at an altitude of 920 kilometers and circles the Earth 14 times daily. As it passes overhead, images are transmitted through its various cameras to a number of receiver stations. It also collects and relays information dealing with water quality, snow depth, rainfall, and earthquake activity from about 100 stations located in remote parts of the continent.

In addition to the advantages of viewing the Earth's surface from high altitudes is the value of using infrared photography to study features that would not be visible with ordinary photography. These include plant growth, fungus infections of plants, circulation of sewage in lakes, spread of oil slicks, spawning grounds of sea life, identification of bedrock, surveys of mineral deposits, volcanic activity, and temperature differences in warm water currents, such as the Gulf Stream. It is highly probable that the ultimate benefits to be derived from this program will far exceed the original cost.

14. Which of the following best defines the term *remote sensing*?

    (1) study of fish distribution by the use of sensitive currents
    (2) release of a rowboat to see its path in an ocean current
    (3) study of the Earth's features without direct contact
    (4) measurement of the effect of an atom bomb in causing an earthquake
    (5) measurement of the depth of snow without the use of snowshoes

15. The space age has contributed all of the following values of remote sensing in viewing the Earth's surface EXCEPT

    (1) immediate observation of natural disasters
    (2) continuous surveillance of the oceans
    (3) identification of pollution
    (4) monitoring of food resources
    (5) making accurate observations of the land features of the planet Mars

16. Which of the following describes the orbit of ERTS?

    (1) 14 times daily, at an altitude of 920 kilometers
    (2) 14 times daily, at an altitude of 920 miles
    (3) 41 times daily, at an altitude of 290 miles
    (4) 290 times daily, at an altitude of 41 kilometers
    (5) It is an orbit around the Equator.

17. What can be accomplished by infrared photography?

    (1) Fungus infections of plants can be sterilized.
    (2) Circulation of sewage in lakes can be speeded up.
    (3) The spread of oil slicks can be absorbed.
    (4) The location of mineral deposits can be surveyed.
    (5) The direction of the Gulf Stream can be influenced.

18. Which statement gives correct information about the Earth Resources Technology Satellite?

    (1) The Russians were the first to launch their ERTS in 1954.
    (2) The ERTS was launched in 1972 to make a study of North America.
    (3) In 1972, the Soviet Union applied for permission to survey North America with its ERTS.
    (4) The Apollo project to the Moon was equivalent to the use of the ERTS around the Earth.
    (5) The next use of ERTS is to study the surface of the planet Venus.

Questions 19–23 are based on the following information.

The diagrams show the general effect of the Earth's atmosphere on solar radiation at middle latitudes during the clear-sky and cloudy-sky conditions. The graph shows the percentage of sunlight reflected by the Earth's surface at different latitudes in the Northern Hemisphere in winter.

SUNLIGHT IN THE ATMOSPHERE

Earth's Surface (45° North Latitude)

19. Approximately what percentage of the sunlight actually reaches the ground at 45° North latitude on a clear day?

   (1) 100%
   (2) 80%
   (3) 60%
   (4) 40%
   (5) 20%

20. Which factor keeps the greatest percentage of sunlight from reaching the Earth's surface on cloudy days?

   (1) absorption by cloud droplets
   (2) reflection by cloud droplets
   (3) absorption by clear-air gas molecules
   (4) reflection by clear-air gas molecules
   (5) refraction by cloud droplets

21. According to the graph, on a winter day at 70° North latitude, what approximate percentage of the sunlight is reflected by the Earth's surface?

   (1) 55%
   (2) 65%
   (3) 75%
   (4) 85%
   (5) 95%

22. Which statement best explains why, at high latitudes, reflectivity of sunlight is greater in winter than in summer?

   (1) The North Pole is tilted toward the Sun in winter.
   (2) Snow and ice reflect almost all sunlight.
   (3) The colder air holds much more moisture.
   (4) Dust settles quickly in cold air.
   (5) Snow and ice absorb all sunlight.

23. The radiation that passes through the atmosphere and reaches the Earth's surface has the greatest intensity in the form of

   (1) visible-light radiation
   (2) infrared radiation
   (3) ultraviolet radiation
   (4) radio-wave radiation
   (5) invisible light radiation

Questions 24–27 refer to the following data table and information.

Mineral	Color	Luster	Streak	Hardness	Density (g/mL)	Chemical Composition
Biotite mica	black	glassy	white	soft	2.8	$K(Mg,Fe)_3(AlSi_3O_{10})(OH_2)$
Diamond	varies	glassy	colorless	hard	3.5	C
Galena	gray	metallic	gray-black	soft	7.5	PbS
Graphite	black	dull	black	soft	2.3	C
Kaolinite	white	earthy	white	soft	2.6	$Al_4(Si_4O_{10})(OH)_8$
Magnetite	black	metallic	black	hard	5.2	Fe_3O_4
Olivine	green	glassy	white	hard	3.4	$(Fe,Mg)_2SiO_4$
Pyrite	brass yellow	metallic	greenish-black	hard	5.0	FeS_2
Quartz	varies	glassy	colorless	hard	2.7	SiO_2

Definitions

Luster: a description of the general appearance of a material's surface

Streak: the color the powdered form of a mineral makes on a piece of white tile

Hardness: a general classification of the ease of a mineral at being scratched by other minerals (soft = easily scratched; hard = not easily scratched)

Chemical Symbols

Al	— Aluminum	Mg	— Magnesium
C	— Carbon	O	— Oxygen
Fe	— Iron	Pb	— Lead
H	— Hydrogen	S	— Sulfur
K	— Potassium	Si	— Silicon

24. A soft mineral is known to have a density greater than 3.0 g/ml and a metallic luster. Which of the following is it most likely to be?

(1) galena
(2) graphite
(3) magnetite
(4) pyrite
(5) quartz

25. Which mineral(s) on the chart is (are) composed of a single type of atom?

I. diamond
II. graphite
III. pyrite

(1) I only
(2) II only
(3) III only
(4) I and II only
(5) II and III only

26. A hard glassy mineral comprised of only two different elements could be which of the following?

(1) biotite mica
(2) diamond
(3) olivine
(4) pyrite
(5) quartz

27. Which mineral exists as a different color in powdered form than it does as a solid piece?

(1) galena
(2) graphite
(3) kaolinite
(4) magnetite
(5) pyrite

Questions 28 and 29 refer to the following information.

Since land heats up more rapidly than water, the air pressure over the land is lower. As the heated air rises, it moves out to the ocean and is replaced by the cooler air blowing in from the ocean. The diagram represents a coastal region with daytime wind direction as indicated.

28. Which of the following best explains the direction of the wind?

    (1) the land being cooled during a clear night
    (2) more water vapor in the air over the ocean than in the air over the land
    (3) low pressure over the land and high pressure over the ocean
    (4) warm ocean currents
    (5) high pressure over the land and low pressure over the ocean

29. According to the prevailing wind direction shown in the diagram, which location probably records the highest annual precipitation?

    (1) *A*
    (2) *B*
    (3) *C*
    (4) *D*
    (5) *E*

Questions 30–33 are based on the following information.

A cold air mass is more dense than a warm air mass. Since two air masses do not mix, when they meet, the more dense air mass will lift the less dense mass. The boundary between two air masses is called a front.

On Wednesday, the weather service predicted that a cold front was coming and that the warm weather would end by Thursday night. The following graph describes the weather at 6-hour intervals for 3 days.

30. What is the lowest temperature indicated on the graph?

    (1) 30°F
    (2) 35°F
    (3) 40°F
    (4) 45°F
    (5) 50°F

31. During which interval of time did the temperature vary LEAST?

    (1) 6 P.M. Wednesday to 6 A.M. Thursday
    (2) 6 A.M. to 6 P.M. Thursday
    (3) 6 P.M. Thursday to 6 A.M. Friday
    (4) 6 A.M. to 6 P.M. Friday
    (5) 6 A.M. to noon on Thursday

32. On Thursday, from 9 A.M. to 6 P.M., the approach of which of the following was most probably responsible for the change in temperature?

    (1) warm front
    (2) cold front
    (3) stationary air
    (4) warm air mass
    (5) combination of any of these

33. On Wednesday what was the difference in the temperature from 3 A.M. to noon?

    (1) 4°
    (2) 9°
    (3) 14°
    (4) 19°
    (5) 24°

Questions 34–37 are based on the following graph.

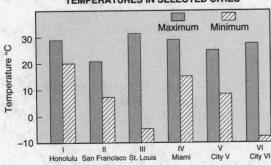

MAXIMUM & MINIMUM AVERAGE MONTHLY TEMPERATURES IN SELECTED CITIES

The graph represents data collected from six cities showing the average maximum and the average minimum temperatures for a 12-month period.

34. Of the following, which location has the highest average maximum monthly temperature?

    (1) I
    (2) II
    (3) III
    (4) IV
    (5) V

35. Of the following, which location has the greatest difference in average monthly temperatures?

    (1) I
    (2) II
    (3) IV
    (4) V
    (5) VI

36. Between San Francisco and what other city is the variation in temperature extremes greatest?

    (1) Honolulu
    (2) Miami
    (3) St. Louis
    (4) city V
    (5) any of the above

37. To the climate of which city is the climate of city Vl most similar?

    (1) I
    (2) II
    (3) III
    (4) IV
    (5) V

Questions 38 and 39 are based on the following graph.

This graph shows the measurements of air pollutants as recorded in a large city for a 2-day period—July 10 and 11.

38. What is a probable cause for the increase in pollutants at 8 A.M. and 5 P.M. on the two days?

    (1) change in amount of sunlight
    (2) occurrence of precipitation
    (3) high wind velocity
    (4) heavy automobile traffic
    (5) any of the above

39. On the basis of the trends indicated by the graph, at what time on Thursday, July 12, will the greatest amount of pollutants probably be observed?

    (1) 12 noon
    (2) 5 P.M.
    (3) 3 A.M.
    (4) 8 A.M.
    (5) midnight

40. An explosion occurs at the upper surface of an ocean. The sound returns to the original site of the explosion 4 seconds later, after having been reflected from the ocean bottom. If the speed of sound in ocean water is 4,800 feet per second, how deep is the water?

    (1) 4,800 ft.
    (2) 9,600 ft.
    (3) 14,400 ft.
    (4) 19,200 ft.
    (5) 96,000 ft.

WHAT'S YOUR SCORE?

	right,		wrong
Excellent			35–40
Good			25–34
Fair			20–24

If your score is low, don't get discouraged. Perhaps earth science is a difficult subject for you. Try to find out why you failed. The analysis of correct answers that follows will help you to pinpoint your errors. If your mistake was lack of information, turn to the "Glossary of Scientific Terms" (page 360) and look up the meanings of the words you did not understand. If it was a mistake in interpretation, review the analysis of the question.

ANSWER ANALYSIS

1. **3** Since each choice consists of two or more resources, each resource must be a nonrenewable resource in order for that to be the correct choice. Choices with one nonrenewable resource and one renewable resource can not possibly be the correct answers. Only Choice 3 meets the criteria for the correct answer.

2. **5** Statement five is an opinion, not a fact, as no mention is made of war or what we may have to do as a result of political changes that affect oil. Make sure that you distinguish facts in an article from opinions, no matter how much they may seem sensible.

3. **3** The question is asking for resources that will get more costly in the future. From reading the passage, you should know that this means nonrenewable

resources. Both coal and natural gas are nonrenewable, and Choice 5 includes both of them. Choice 1 includes one of the nonrenewable answers but is not the best choice.

4. **1** This question involves a basic mathematical formula:
    distance ÷ rate = time.
    The question tells us that the average distance from the Moon to Earth is 240,000 miles, and that the average velocity of the spacecraft is 24,000 miles per hour (mph). Substitute these values in the formula:

$$\frac{240,000 \text{ miles}}{24,000 \text{ mph}} = 10 \text{ hours}$$

5. **2** In discussing the new Moon phase, earthshine is explained.

6. **5** The diagram illustrates that the phases of the Moon result from the illumination of the Moon's surface by the Sun. Note that about half of the Moon's surface is always facing the Sun. Since the Moon revolves around the Earth, the angle between the Sun, Earth, and Moon changes, resulting in the different phases of the Moon.

7. **3** This question refers to the spring tide, when the gravitational pulls of the Moon and the Sun cause tides of great range.

8. **4** The article states that "paoleontologists have found fossil remains," implying that these scientists study fossils.

9. **5** The second paragraph states that occasionally the plates carrying landmasses collide with each other, causing an earthquake.

10. **1** This answer is given in the second paragraph. There is no mention of land bridges (Choice 2), the depth of the ocean (Choice 3), the creatures' swimming ability (Choice 4), or the animals' evolution on separate continents (Choice 5).

11. **1** A comet consists of three parts—a tightly packed nucleus consisting of frozen gases, dust particles, and stony matter, about 20–25 miles across; a hazy coma around the nucleus, composed of dust transformed into a glowing vapor under the Sun's influence, and 10,000 miles or more in diameter;

and the tail, composed of ions and molecules, which stretches out millions of miles in length.

12. **4** A comet with lots of dust is spectacularly visible to the naked eye when it is near the Sun. Light and electrified particles from the Sun blast the dust out of the comet's head, and the dusty tail reflects the yellow sunlight. Apparently Kohoutek did not release much dust.

13. **3** Astronomers reasoned that since comet Kohoutek was already visible at such a great distance from the Sun in March, it would be spectacular by the time it streaked to within 13 million miles of the Sun on December 28.

14. **3** *Remote sensing,* the ability to view the Earth's surface from the vantage point of heights, is a contribution of the space age.

15. **5** No mention is made of studying other planets in this project.

16. **1** The ERTS (Earth Resource Technology Satellite) follows a near-polar orbit at an altitude of 920 kilometers and circles the Earth 14 times daily.

17. **4** The use of infrared photography permits the study of features of the Earth's surface that would not be visible with ordinary photography.

18. **2** ERTS was launched to make a systematic surveillance of North America and other areas from space.

19. **2** The left-hand diagram shows that, when there is a clear sky, 80% of the sunlight reaches the ground.

20. **2** The right-hand diagram indicates that, when the sky is cloudy, cloud reflection returns 30% to 60% of the sunlight. This is greater than the percentage scattered and reflected by the atmosphere (6%), absorbed by gas molecules and dust (14%), or absorbed in clouds (5% to 20%).

21. **4** Find 70° North latitude on the horizontal axis of the graph. Trace upward until you reach the curve. The average reflectivity of sunlight (vertical axis) is 85% for this latitude.

22. **2** Compared to other darker surfaces, snow and ice are both very good reflectors of sunlight. This fact explains why surfaces covered with snow or ice do not heat up as quickly.

23. **1** The atmosphere is a better absorber of infrared, ultraviolet, or radio-wave radiation than of visible light. As a result, the greatest intensity of sunlight passing through the atmosphere and reaching the Earth's surface represents the visible part of the electromagnetic spectrum.

24. **1** Of the minerals listed in the choices, only galena, magnetite, and pyrite have densities greater than 3.0g/ml. This lets you eliminate two of the choices. Of the three choices with a density above 3.0g/ml, only galena is soft. In a question that asks you to analyze more than one thing, it can be helpful to deal with those items one at a time (in this case, density, then luster, then hardness).

25. **3** Both diamond and graphite are comprised of carbon atoms, as the last column in the chart tells you. Notice that the choice that includes both of these minerals is better than just diamond or graphite alone, since it is a more compete answer.

26. **5** Here is another case where you are asked to analyze more than one factor. You are looking for a mineral that is hard, glassy, and composed of only two different elements. Of the choices listed, diamond, olivine, and quartz are hard and glassy. The chart tells you that diamond is made of a single type of atom (carbon), while olivine is made of several types of atoms. Only quartz fits all the criteria for the question.

27. **5** This questions is asking you to look for a mineral with a different streak than its original color. You do not need to look at minerals on the table that are not choices for this question. Among the five choices, only pyrite has a different streak than color.

28. **3** As the air above the land heats up, its pressure becomes lower than that of the air above the water. This difference in pressure explains the direction of wind, which moves from high to low pressure.

29. **2** As the air blowing in from the ocean reaches the mountainous area, it tends to rise. As it rises, it cools, causing moisture in the air to condense. This condensation would probably cause

location *B* to record the highest annual precipitation.

30. **2** The lowest temperature occurred during the period of time between 6 P.M. Thursday and 6 A.M. Friday. At this time, the temperature remained fairly constant (at about 35°F).

31. **3** The temperature remained almost constant from 6 P.M. Thursday to 6 A.M. Friday, as indicated by the horizontal line on the graph.

32. **2** On Thursday from 9 A.M. to 6 P.M. the temperature dropped steadily. This may have been caused by the approach of a cold front. As the cold front approached, it brought cold air to replace the warm air.

33. **2** On Wednesday at 3 A.M., the temperature was 52°F. By noon, the temperature had risen to 61°F. The temperature, therefore, rose 9°F over a period of 9 hours.

34. **3** The solid bar is tallest for St. Louis, indicating that it has the highest average maximum monthly temperature.

35. **5** In city I, the average maximum temperature is about 29° and the average minimum is about 20°: 29° − 20° = 9°. In city II, the average maximum temperature is about 20° and the average minimum is about 7°: 20° − 7 ° = 13°. In city IV, the average maximum temperature is about 30° and the average minimum is about 15°: 30° − 15° = 15°. In city V, the average maximum temperature is about 26° and the average minimum is about 9°: 26° − 9° = 17°. City VI has the greatest difference since the average maximum temperature is about 29° and the average minimum is − 8°: 29° − (− 8°) = 37°.

36. **3** Except for city VI (which is not one of the choices), the difference between the length of the two bars is greatest for St. Louis.

37. **3** Cities III and VI have similar maximum and minimum temperatures and would therefore probably have similar climates. However, since climate also depends upon the amount of moisture, it is possible that the two cities have some differences in climates.

38. **4** Automobile emission adds pollutants to the atmosphere. Traffic is heaviest at 8 A.M. and 5 P.M. in most large cities. Changes in the amount of sunlight generally have little or no effect on pollution levels. Precipitation tends to remove some pollutants, such as particulate matter. High winds decrease pollution levels by blowing away polluted air and replacing it with fresh, clean air.

39. **2** Since the pattern indicates that the highest pollution level occurs at 5 P.M., it is reasonable to assume that the highest level will also be reached at that time on the following day.

40. **2** One-half of the 4 seconds is the time that the sound vibrations took to reach the bottom of the ocean:

$$(2 \text{ sec}) (4{,}800 \text{ ft/sec}) = 9{,}600 \text{ ft.}$$

Chemistry

Questions 1–4 refer to the following information.

A student placed a candle on a tabletop. For the first trial in her experiment, she carefully inverted a 500 ml jar over the candle and measured the time it took for the flame to go out. In trial #2, she repeated the experiment, only this time she filled the jar with exhaled air, rather than room air. For trial #3, she again filled the jar with exhaled air, but only after she had run in place for five minutes. Again, she noted and recorded the time for the flame to go out.

1. The main goal of the experiment was to show which of the following?

   (1) Exhaled air stops the process of combustion.
   (2) Candles go out when covered by jars.
   (3) The composition of exhaled air can vary depending on activity level.
   (4) Exhaled air extinguishes flames effectively.
   (5) Inhaled air has little effect on combustion.

2. Arrange in order from shortest to longest, the length of time the flame would last in each trial.

   (1) 1,3,2
   (2) 1,2,3
   (3) 3,2,1
   (4) 3,1,2
   (5) 2,3,1

3. Which trial served as the control for the experiment?

   (1) one only
   (2) two only
   (3) three only
   (4) one and two only
   (5) two and three only

4. What caused the flame to go out in each trial?

   (1) an increase in carbon dioxide levels
   (2) lack of combustion product levels
   (3) a decrease in carbon dioxide levels
   (4) an increase in oxygen levels
   (5) a decrease in oxygen levels

Questions 5–9 refer to the following figure.

The figure above shows the pH scale and the range of pH values for some common substances. By definition, the lower the pH the more acidic a substance is, and the higher the pH the more basic it is. Neutral substances have a pH of 7. Acids and bases often react to form salts.

5. Which of the following substances is the most basic?

   (1) detergent
   (2) ammonia
   (3) milk
   (4) lemon juice
   (5) club soda

6. Which of the following substances is likely to have a neutral pH?

   (1) human saliva
   (2) tap water
   (3) human urine
   (4) tape water and human urine
   (5) tap water, human urine, and human saliva

7. Which of the following combinations could produce a salt?

   (1) lemon juice and vinegar
   (2) tomato juice and lemon juice
   (3) ammonia and lemon juice
   (4) sea water and ammonia
   (5) detergent and ammonia

8. Which of the following has an acidic pH?

   (1) clear rain
   (2) acid rain
   (3) neither acid rain nor clear rain
   (4) both acid rain and clear rain
   (5) either depending on where the rain falls

9. Which of the following lists shows substances that increase in basicity?

   (1) milk, sea water, tomato juice
   (2) club soda, ammonia, human blood
   (3) acid rain, vinegar, detergent
   (4) milk, human blood, ammonia
   (5) sea water, detergent, lemon juice

10. The three phases of matter are the three states in which matter can exist—as a solid, a liquid, or a gas. Substances change from one to another phase as their temperatures change. Temperature reflects the rate of molecular movement, slow movement indicating colder temperature, and fast movement warmer temperature. For most substances, the freezing temperature and the melting temperature are the same, as are the boiling point and the condensation point.

    Antifreeze is added to the water-filled cooling system of an automobile engine to protect it from the effects of both overheating and freezing. This is possible because antifreeze

    (1) doesn't freeze
    (2) has a much lower freezing temperature than water and a higher boiling point
    (3) consists of alcohols that resist corrosion and can get to all parts of the car's cooling system
    (4) has slower moving molecules than water
    (5) can be used in various amounts to protect against a variety of temperatures

Questions 11–14 refer to the following graph.

The solubility curves on the graph above show the amount of a salt that can dissolve in 100 mL of water at a given temperature.

11. Which is the only substance shown that gets less soluble as the temperature increases?

    (1) $Ce_2(SO_4)_3$
    (2) NaCl
    (3) KBr
    (4) $NaNO_3$
    (5) $NaClO_3$

12. How many grams of KBr can dissolve in 100 mL of water at 10°F?

    (1) 20 grams
    (2) 40 grams
    (3) 60 grams
    (4) 80 grams
    (5) 100 grams

13. How many grams of $NaClO_3$ can dissolve in 200 grams of water at 15°F?

    (1) 75
    (2) 100
    (3) 150
    (4) 200
    (5) 250

14. The abbreviation KBr stands for potassium bromide and NaCl for sodium chloride. What is does NaBr stand for?

    (1) potassium bromate
    (2) sodium chlorate
    (3) sodium bromide
    (4) potassium chloride
    (5) bromide potassium

Questions 15–20 refer to the following article.

Nature has her own ways of purifying water. These methods can be physical, chemical, or biological. As a stream flows, the water becomes cleaner because sediments, for example, are diminished by the addition of more and more water, and they may be deposited along the banks of the stream.

Today, however, in our technologically complex civilization, human activity may cause some dangerous components to remain in stream water. Communities that wish to utilize water from "self-purified" streams have to use precautions, including filtration and chlorination.

Aeration, which may be accomplished in nature by wind action, turbulent flow, and waterfalls, causes an exchange of gases between the atmosphere and the water. In this way hydrogen sulfide, carbon dioxide, and methane are liberated from the water, and oxygen is absorbed from the atmosphere.

Light has an important effect on water. Light stimulates photosynthesis in aquatic plant life, and by this process carbon dioxide is absorbed and oxygen is liberated. Furthermore, the plants remove and use organic material that may be dissolved in the water. Light also has a germicidal effect on the surface of the water, although this effect below the surface is minimal.

A process called sedimentation removes organic bacterial food from water. Sedimentation, which is caused by gravity, occurs when the water is filtered through some fine material such as sand. Sedimentation is most effective in quiet waters.

Some bacteria help clean the water by oxidizing organic material, converting it into basic mineral substances. In the absence of oxygen, other organisms, known as anaerobic bacteria, can split organic compounds and prepare the way for subsequent oxidation. These anaerobic bacteria thrive at the bottom of bodies of water where there is a great deal of concentrated pollution.

Biological cycles also purify water. Protozoa, one-celled animals, thrive on bacteria. As the bacteria are reduced in population, green algae appear. They in turn consume carbon dioxide, nitrates, and ammonia and produce oxygen. Large invertebrate animals, such as worms and mollusks, appear and feed on the deposits at the bottom.

15. Which of the following prevents streams from purifying themselves?

    (1) human activity
    (2) evaporation
    (3) condensation
    (4) filtration
    (5) chlorination

16. What is accomplished by aeration of water?

    (1) loss of oxygen and carbon dioxide
    (2) loss of methane and gain of oxygen
    (3) gain of carbon dioxide and methane
    (4) gain of hydrogen and oxygen
    (5) gain of carbon dioxide and oxygen

17. Which of these causes sedimentation?

    (1) wind action
    (2) bacterial residue
    (3) turbulent water
    (4) gravity
    (5) organic material

18. Which of the following statements is correct in regard to the process of photosynthesis?

    (1) It is carried on by all protozoa.
    (2) Oxygen is necessary for this process to occur.
    (3) Light is necessary for this process to occur.
    (4) Carbon dioxide is given off during this process.
    (5) This process has a germicidal effect on deep stagnant water.

19. Which of these would best remove wastes at the bottom of ponds?

    (1) fish
    (2) aerobic bacteria
    (3) green plants
    (4) anaerobic bacteria
    (5) algae

20. All of the following tend to purify water EXCEPT

    (1) sedimentation
    (2) aeration
    (3) light
    (4) aquatic plants
    (5) bacteria

WHAT'S YOUR SCORE?

	right,		wrong
Excellent	16–20		
Good	13–15		
Fair	10–12		

If your score is low, don't get discouraged. Perhaps chemistry is a difficult subject for you. Try to find out why you failed. The analysis of correct answers that follows will help you to pinpoint your errors. If your mistake was lack of information, turn to the "Glossary of Scientific Terms" (page 360) and look up the meanings of the words you did not understand. If it was a mistake in interpretation, review the analysis of the question.

ANSWER ANALYSIS

1. **3** The experiment showed that exhaled air can have different effects on a flame, depending on its composition. The composition of the air changed as the student's activity level changed. Since the student varied the air composition by exercising at different levels, studying this must have been the purpose of the experiment.

2. **3** The candle would burn the shortest amount of time in the air after the vigorous exercise, a bit longer when filled with exhaled air, and longer still when filled with inhaled air. Notice that the question asked you to arrange from shortest to longest.

3. **1** A control is a part of the experiment used as a reference point, for comparison. In this case, nonexhaled room air was the starting point for the experiment and was the reference used for comparison.

4. **5** The flame was extinguished by a lack of oxygen. While it is true that there was also an increase in carbon dioxide levels, that alone is not enough to put out a flame. It is the lack of oxygen that caused the flame to go out.

5. **2** 5. The pH scale is set up so that the higher the pH value, the more basic (and less acidic) something is. Ammonia has the highest pH value and thus is the most basic.

6. **5** All of these substances have a pH range, rather than one specific value. All cover a range that includes the neutral pH value, 7.

7. **3** A salt is the product of the reaction of an acid and a base. Thus, you need to find a substance with a pH of less than 7 and with a pH of more than 7. Only Choice 3 meets these criteria.

8. **4** It most likely comes as no surprise that acid rain is acidic, but clear rain is also acidic, although much less so. Clear rain has a pH of about 6, which is just slightly acidic.

9. **4** To find a list that shows increasing basicity, you need to find substances listed from low pH to high pH. Only Choice 4 fits.

10. **2** The answer to this question must be derived by analyzing the information and realizing that, to keep something—in this case, water—from freezing, you have to add a substance that has a much lower freezing point than water. Similarly, to protect the same engine from overheating, you have to add a substance that has a higher boiling point than water. Antifreeze, in combination with water, can accomplish these purposes. Antifreeze and water will freeze at a low enough temperature, so Choice 1 is not valid. Choice 3 is not a good answer because resistance to corrosion is not the subject. If anything, the molecules in antifreeze have to move faster than water molecules, so Choice 4 is incorrect. Choice 5 may or may not be true, but it is not as logical an answer as Choice 2.

11. **1** Only $Ce_2(SO_4)_3$ shows a decrease in solubility as the temperature of the water increases. The line for NaCl is relatively flat but does not slope downward.

12. **3** At 10°F, the graph for KBr reads a value of 60 grams, so the solubility would be 60 grams KBr per 100 mL water. Note that the spacing of the choices (in increments of 20) allows you a bit of leeway in interpreting the graph. This can be valuable when a value is in between two lines and you have to estimate.

13. **4** At 15°F, the graph shows a solubility for $NaClO_3$ of 100 grams. Notice that the y axis of the graph is based on 100 mL of water. If you were dissolving in twice as much water, twice as much solid could be dissolved.

14. **3** In naming these compounds, the first part of the formula is written first and the second part comes last. Thus, only sodium bromide can be the correct answer. Using this approach KCl, would be potassium chloride.

15. **1** Humans are responsible for many forms of water pollution, including those due to industrial processes.

16. **2** During aeration of water, methane and carbon dioxide are liberated, and oxygen is absorbed from the air.

17. **4** Objects heavier than water will drop to the bottom of the water. This is an effect of gravity.

18. **3** Green plants absorb carbon dioxide and liberate oxygen during photosynthesis. The plants need light in order to carry on the process.

19. **4** Anaerobic bacteria thrive in environments, such as the bottom of ponds, where there is little oxygen.

20. **5** While bacteria of decay may at times decompose organic wastes, in this question the other four choices are definite methods of water purification. Another justification for Choice 5 is that bacteria may be pathogenic.

Physics

Questions 1 and 2 refer to the following information.

As you break a beam of light, in one case you may be operating an automatic door opener and in another case you may be setting off a burglar alarm system. Actually your body is breaking a beam of light that is focused on a photoelectric cell.

That beam has been producing a flow of electrons from the photoelectric cell. When your body interrupts the beam, the current stops. The result is to close a relay that starts a motor.

Almost a hundred years ago Heinrich Hertz found that certain substances give off a weak electric current when struck by a beam of light. This is the basis for the electric eye, in which light energy is changed into electricity.

1. Which of the following illustrates a change from mechanical energy to electrical energy?

   (1) electric iron
   (2) steam engine
   (3) fluorescent lamp
   (4) electric eye
   (5) electric generator

2. A photoelectric cell is a device that

   (1) opens doors
   (2) sets off burglar alarms
   (3) breaks a beam of light
   (4) produces electric energy from light
   (5) starts a motor

Questions 3–6 refer to the following chart.

Medium	Speed of sound (m/s)
Gases	
air (0°C)	331
air (25°C)	346
air (100°C)	386
helium (0°C)	972
hydrogen (0°C)	1,290
oxygen (0°C)	317
Liquids at 25°C	
water	1,490
sea water	1,530
Solids	
copper	3,813
iron	5,000

The chart above shows the speed of sound in different materials. Where appropriate, the temperature is specified.

3. What happens to the speed of sound in denser materials?

   (1) It is slower as the density increases.
   (2) It is faster as the density increases.
   (3) Density has no effect on it.
   (4) It is faster in warmer solids.
   (5) It is faster in colder liquids.

4. What would be a likely speed of sound in meters per second (m/s) in 50°C air?

   (1) 326 m/s
   (2) 336 m/s
   (3) 346 m/s
   (4) 366 m/s
   (5) 396 m/s

5. Lead is a dense solid. What might be a likely speed of sound for lead in m/s?

   (1) 1,000 m/s
   (2) 1,200 m/s
   (3) 3,000 m/s
   (4) 300 m/s
   (5) 500 m/s

6. Hydrogen gas has a molar mass of 2, helium gas has a molar mass of 4, and oxygen gas has a molar mass of 32. Based on the speeds of sound given in the table, what is the most likely speed of sound for neon gas (molar mass = 20)?

   (1) 50 m/s
   (2) 100 m/s
   (3) 200 m/s
   (4) 300 m/s
   (5) 400 m/s

Questions 7 and 8 refer to the following information.

Energy can take two forms, potential and kinetic. Potential energy is typically exemplified by an object at rest, its energy ready and waiting to be expressed. Kinetic energy is exemplified by an object in motion. An example of potential energy is a parked car. Kinetic energy is the car in motion.

7. Which of the following is NOT an example of potential energy?

   (1) a runner at the starting point
   (2) a bag of golf balls
   (3) an exercise bicycle
   (4) a sleeping child
   (5) a falling book

8. As a child on the swing shown in the diagram reaches the highest point (*A*), the swing seems to hesitate an instant before it begins to fall back. This hesitation is repeated at the other end of the arc (*D*). How is the energy of this motion expressed in the diagram at the points marked *A* through *D*?

   (1) potential, kinetic, potential, kinetic
   (2) kinetic, potential, kinetic, potential
   (3) potential, kinetic, potential, potential
   (4) potential, kinetic, kinetic, potential
   (5) kinetic, kinetic, potential, potential

Questions 9–11 refer to the following article.

The study of sounds outside the range of normal human hearing is known as ultrasonics. Most people are capable of hearing sounds with a vibrational range of between 20 and 20,000 hertz (vibrations per second). Bats use sounds with a range of greater than 50,000 hertz to help them "see." A bat sends out a sound and it bounces off walls and other objects, returning to the bat's ear. The bat's brain then processes these echoes and determines the location of objects around the bat. In this way, bats can catch food and avoid hidden objects no matter how little light there is.

Sound waves usually reflect back off a hard smooth surface, much like light reflecting off a mirror. Softer materials tend to absorb sounds. Submarines use sonar (sound navigation and ranging) to detect objects in the sea around them. Sound waves are sent out from the submarine and the time it takes the echo to return to the boat can be used to determine the depth of the water, or the distance to an object.

9. Which of the following would be an ultrasonic sound?

   (1) 20 hertz
   (2) 200 hertz
   (3) 2,000 hertz
   (4) 20,000 hertz
   (5) 200,000 hertz

10. What is a possible way to help reduce echoes in a room?

    (1) Use insulated glass for the windows.
    (2) Have people talk softly.
    (3) Raise the height of the ceiling.
    (4) Hang soft drapes and curtains.
    (5) Use reflective paints.

11. What is the proper name for a reflected sound?

    (1) frequency
    (2) ultrasonic
    (3) echo
    (4) vibration
    (5) Hertz

Questions 12–17 refer to the following information.

Although both a jet engine and a rocket engine operate on the principle of Newton's third law, they differ in that a jet must take in oxygen from the air to burn its fuel, but a rocket must carry its own oxygen. In both engines gases escaping under great pressure in one direction exert a push on the engine in the opposite direction. According to Newton's third law, to each action there is an equal and opposite reaction. You can illustrate the principle by blowing up a rubber balloon and then letting it go as you allow the air to escape. Notice that the balloon moves forward as the air escapes in the opposite direction.

12. Which of the following describes Newton's third law?

    (1) an object at rest
    (2) gravitational force
    (3) objects in uniform motion
    (4) falling bodies
    (5) action force equals reaction force

13. What characteristic of rocket engines is NOT characteristic of jet engines?

    (1) method of obtaining oxygen
    (2) method of using oxygen
    (3) reaction to the escaping gases
    (4) application of Newton's third law
    (5) methods involved in the burning process

14. Which of the following would be best explained by Newton's third law?

    (1) A balloon with a lower density than air rises.
    (2) A bat strikes a ball and the bat breaks.
    (3) A sled accelerates while sliding downhill.
    (4) A boat slows down when its engines are turned off.
    (5) A rock, thrown horizontally, falls to the ground.

15. Which of the following is (are) NOT found in an airplane with a jet engine?

    (1) ailerons
    (2) a fuselage
    (3) propellers
    (4) rudders
    (5) flaps

16. What propels jet planes?

    (1) the thrust of hot gases
    (2) propeller blades
    (3) rocket motors
    (4) steam turbines
    (5) any of these

17. Imagine that you are standing on a frictionless ice rink, holding a large, heavy ball. What will happen if you throw the ball forward?

    (1) You will move backwards.
    (2) You will move forward, following the ball.
    (3) You will not move at all.
    (4) How you move depends on how you are standing.
    (5) How you move depends on how heavy the ball is.

Questions 18–20 refer to the following figure.

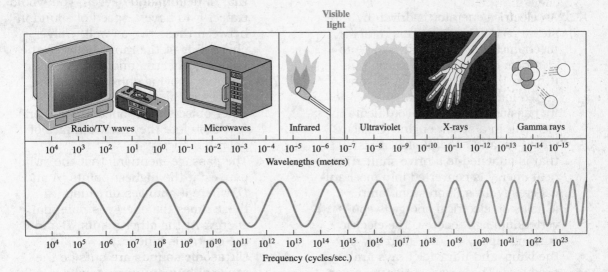

The figure above shows the range of electromagnetic energies known as the electromagnetic spectrum. Each part of the spectrum is characterized by its own wavelength (specified here in meters) and frequency (described here as cycles/sec). A key feature of the spectrum is that the higher the frequency the greater the energy. Notice that each part of the spectrum covers a range.

18. What is the most energetic part of the electromagnetic spectrum?

    (1) microwaves
    (2) gamma rays
    (3) visible light
    (4) radio and TV waves
    (5) x-rays

19. What is the least energetic part of the electromagnetic spectrum?

    (1) blue light
    (2) red light
    (3) radio and TV waves
    (4) gamma rays
    (5) microwaves

20. Violet light is more energetic than red light. Which of the following statements about violet light and red light is true?

    (1) Violet light has a longer wavelength than red light.
    (2) Violet light has a lower frequency than red light.
    (3) Violet light has a higher frequency than red light.
    (4) Violet light and red light both have the same frequency, so we see them both equally well.
    (5) Red light is close to infrared light on the spectrum.

WHAT'S YOUR SCORE?

_____right, _____wrong
Excellent   16–20
Good   13–15
Fair   10–12

If your score is low, don't get discouraged. Perhaps physics is a difficult subject for you. Try to find out why you failed. The analysis of correct answers that follows will help you to pinpoint your errors. If your mistake was lack of information, turn to the "Glossary of Scientific Terms" (page 360) and look up the meanings of the words you did not understand. If it was a mistake in interpretation, review the analysis of the question.

ANSWER ANALYSIS

1. **5** An electric generator is driven by steam or water power. This rotary mechanical energy is converted into electrical energy. In an electric iron (Choice 1), electrical energy is converted into heat energy when electricity passing through the core heats the element. In a steam engine (Choice 2), steam expands and pushes a piston that is attached to a drive shaft. Thus, heat energy is converted into mechanical energy. In a fluorescent lamp (Choice 3), electrical energy is converted into light energy. The electric current vaporizes some mercury in the lamp, and ultraviolet rays are produced. These rays strike the inner coating of the lamp and cause the chemical phosphorus in it to glow. The electric eye (Choice 4) or photoelectric cell and its operation are described in the selection. Light energy is converted into electric energy.

2. **4** All of the events in the choices do occur, but the photoelectric cell does nothing but produce electricity when light strikes it.

3. **2** Solids are generally denser than liquids, which are denser than gases. Notice that the speed of sound in solids is generally above that of liquids and well above that of gases.

4. **4** The speed of sound in 50° air must be between the speed of sound in 25°air and in 100° air. The speed of sound at 25° is 346 m/s and at 100° is 386 m/s. Only Choice 4 is in between those two values, so it must be the correct value. This is an example of a question that at first glance looks as if it requires a calculation but actually does not.

5. **3** Because lead is a solid, you would expect sound to travel at a high speed in lead. Only Choice 3 is in the range of the speed of sound in other solids. Don't let problems with numerical answers make you think you need to do a lot of calculations. Look for patterns and trends to help you think through a question.

6. **5** The pattern shown to you is that the greater the molar mass of the gas, the slower the speed of sound is. Because neon has a molar mass in between that of helium and oxygen, you would expect it to have a speed of sound in between those two as well. Only choice 5 is in the range between the values for helium and oxygen.

7. **5** The only moving object among the choices is the falling book. All the other objects mentioned are stationary; therefore they are examples of potential energy.

8. **4** The passage mentions that the swing pauses at the highest points, *A* and *D*, where it changes direction. At those times the energy is potential energy. At the other points, *B* and *C*, the energy is kinetic.

9. **5** Ultrasonic sounds are outside the range of human hearing, which is 20 hertz to 20,000 hertz. Choices 1 to 4 are all within that range.

10. **4** Echoes are caused by reflected sound waves and sounds reflect best off hard smooth surfaces. If you wanted to reduce echoes, you would reduce hard smooth surfaces. Drapes and curtains reduce the amount of flat wall space a sound wave could bounce off.

11. **3** The passage gives you the definition of an echo as being a reflected sound wave.

12. **5** To each action there is an equal and opposite reaction.

13. **1** The passage mentions that a rocket must carry its own oxygen supply, but the jet uses the oxygen of the air.

14. **2** When the bat strikes the ball, the ball strikes the bat, causing it to break.

15. **3** In jet engines the force of hot, expanding gases provides the energy that drives the plane forward. In other engines, the blades of the propeller pull against the air as they whirl. Ailerons (Choice 1) are flaps on the rear edge of the wing of the plane that help change the direction of the plane in flight. The fuselage (Choice 2) is the body of the plane. Rudders (Choice 4) are the part used to swing the nose of the plane and prevent it from slipping when making a turn. The flaps (Choice 5) act as brakes in the air and slow down the motion for a smooth landing.

16. **1** According to Newton's third law, the action of the ejected gases produces a reaction that thrusts the plane forward.

17. **1** If you push the ball forward, the ball will push you backward.
18. **2** The figure shows you frequencies and wavelengths for various parts of the electromagnetic spectrum. The information given in addition to the figure tells you that the greater the frequency, the greater the energy. So to find the most energetic part of the electromagnetic spectrum, you would look for the part with the greatest frequency.

19. **3** Use the same approach as in question 18, but in this case you are looking for the least energetic part of the electromagnetic spectrum. This is the section with the smallest frequency or the largest wavelength, which is radio/TV waves.
20. **3** Because violet light is more energetic than red light it must have a higher frequency and a shorter (or smaller) wavelength. Choice 5 is correct but has nothing to do with answering this question.

LANGUAGE ARTS, READING
TEST 4

CHAPTER 16: Reading and Interpreting Literature and the Arts

The three basic reading skills, presented here, are finding the main idea, finding details, and making inferences. Basic reading skills are applied to reading of prose, poetry, and drama selections. Reading commentary on the arts and business documents is also treated. The Glossary of Literary Terms is a mini-dictionary with definitions and illustrations of each.

CHAPTER 17: Language Arts and Reading Practice

There are 125 questions on interpreting literature and the arts. All of the arts are tested—literature, art, music, theater, dance, film, and television. One business document is also tested.

Reading and Interpreting Literature and the Arts

Basic Reading Skills

Reading consists of a complex combination of skills. The writer sets forth his or her ideas using the medium of language consisting of printed words. If the writer has stated the ideas clearly, they have been well organized and well developed. You, the reader, must draw meaning from the ideas expressed on the printed page. In addition, there may be ideas that are implied rather than openly stated. For example, a woman dressed in black is described as *grieving*. The implication is that she has lost a loved one, even if this fact is not stated in so many words.

Reading requires the use of a number of skills so you can decode or derive from the language used the meaning intended by the writer, whether it is explicitly stated or suggested by implication.

These skills are basically three in number.

You read to find the main idea of the selection.

You find the main idea in a variety of places. It may be stated directly in the first sentence (easy to find). It may be stated in the final sentence to which the others build up (a bit harder to find). It may have to be discovered within the passage (most difficult); an example (note the underscored words) occurs in the following paragraph:

> Several students were seriously injured in football games last Saturday. The week before, several more were hospitalized. <u>Football has become a</u>
> (5) <u>dangerous sport.</u> The piling up of players in a scrimmage often leads to serious injury. Perhaps some rule changes would lessen the number who are hurt.

You may also find that the main idea is not directly expressed, but can only be inferred from the selection as a whole.

> The plane landed at 4 P.M. As the door opened, the crowd burst into a long, noisy demonstration. The waiting mob surged against the police
> (5) guard lines. Women were screaming. Teenagers were yelling for autographs or souvenirs. The visitor smiled and waved at his fans.

The main idea of the paragraph is not expressed, but it is clear that some popular hero, movie or rock star is being welcomed enthusiastically at the airport.

> ***To find the main idea of a***
> ***passage,*** ask yourself any or all of
> these questions:
>
> 1. What is the *main idea* of the passage? (Why did the author write it?)
> 2. What is the *topic sentence* of the paragraph or paragraphs (the sentence that the other sentences build on or flow from)?
> 3. What *title* would I give this selection?

You read to find the details that explain or develop the main idea.

How do you do this? You must determine how the writer develops the main idea. He or she may give examples to illustrate that idea, or may give reasons why the statement that is the main idea is true, or may give arguments for or against a position stated as the main idea. The writer may define a complex term and give a number of aspects of a complicated belief (such as democracy). He or she may also classify a number of objects within a larger category. Finally, the writer may compare two ideas or objects (show how they are similar) or contrast them (show how they are different).

In the paragraph immediately above, you can see that the sentence "You must determine how the writer develops the main idea" *is* the main idea. Six ways in which the writer can develop the main idea follow. These are the details that actually develop the main idea of the paragraph.

> ***To find the main details of a***
> ***passage,*** the questions to ask yourself
> are these:
>
> 1. What examples illustrate the main point?
> 2. What reasons or proof support the main idea?
> 3. What arguments are presented for or against the main idea?
> 4. What specific qualities are offered about the idea or subject being defined?
> 5. Into what classifications is a larger group broken down?
> 6. What are the similarities and differences between two ideas or subjects being compared or contrasted?

You read to make inferences by putting together ideas that are expressed to arrive at other ideas that are not.

In other words, you draw conclusions from the information presented by the author. You do this by locating relevant details and determining their relationships (time sequence, place sequence, cause and effect).

How do you do this? You can put one fact together with a second to arrive at a third that is not stated. You can apply a given fact to a different situation. You can predict an outcome based on the facts given.

> ***To make inferences from a***
> ***passage,*** ask yourself the following
> questions:
>
> 1. From the facts presented, what conclusions can I draw?
> 2. What is being suggested, in addition to what is being stated?
> 3. What will be the effect of something that is described?
> 4. What will happen next (after what is being described)?
> 5. What applications does the principle or idea presented have?

READING LITERATURE

There are three periods of literature on the GED examination: pre-1920, 1920–1960, and post-1960. The basic reading skills apply to all types of literature.

Literature after 1960 is easier to read because you are more likely to have shared some of the same experiences as the writer. Also, you are generally more familiar with the language of the writer. Because the selections are drawn from sources that you read quite frequently—newspapers and magazines, for example—they should be no more difficult than the usual materials geared to the high school graduate.

Literature before 1960 differs from the more current literature in a number of ways. The settings are certainly different because they go back at least 40–200 years. Also, the style of writing is more complicated. The vocabulary is less familiar. Some of the subject matter may be dated for today's reader. On the other hand, this type of literature deals with the eternal emotions of love, hate, greed, loyalty, self-sacrifice, joy, fear, among others.

And many of the themes are eternal—the relationship of man to his fellow man and woman, of man to God, of man to nature, of man to his family, of man to his country.

Reading literature before 1960 requires patience, but it can be greatly rewarding. Try to imagine the unfamiliar setting. Reread the difficult sentences. Get the meaning of the unfamiliar word from its context. Find the application to life today of the theme of the selection. Continued practice will make these worthwhile tasks easier and the literature more satisfying.

Reading Prose, Poetry, and Drama

In addition to the reading skills required in general reading, to read literary material, additional special skills are necessary, namely the ability to: recognize the mood of the selection and the purpose for which it was written; deal with involved sentences and sentence structure; figure out unusual word meanings from the sentences in which they appear; interpret figures of speech. (See the Glossary of Literary Terms beginning on page 433.)

Read carefully the following treatment of these special skills and then go to the sample reading passages and the questions and analyzed answers based on them to get a feeling for these special, and necessary, skills.

LOCATING THE MAIN IDEA

Depending upon the type of passage—poetry, fiction, essay, drama—the technique of finding the main idea may vary. In the essay, for example, the main idea may very well appear as a straightforward statement, usually expressed in the topic sentence. In this particular case, the trick is to find the topic sentence. In works of fiction, poetry, or drama, the main idea might be found in a line of dialogue or exposition, or within a long, flowing line of verse.

PROSE

In reading *prose*, the main unit is the paragraph. Since all the paragraphs you will encounter on the GED examination have been chosen for their "loaded" content—that is, because they contain a number of ideas offering possibilities for questions—it is important that you learn how to locate the main idea. This, in turn, will enable you to understand many of the subordinate (less important) elements of the paragraph—all of which may also be the basis for examination questions.

The topic sentence containing the main idea is used in five standard patterns:

1. The topic sentence, expressing the main idea, may introduce the paragraph and be followed by sentences containing details that explain, exemplify, prove, or support the idea, or add interest.

EXAMPLE

In *Alice in Wonderland*, Lewis Carroll created a world of fantasy out of essentially real creatures, transformed into whimsy by the odd patterns of a dream. Sitting with her sister by a stream, Alice sees a rabbit; as she dozes off, the rabbit becomes larger, dons a waistcoat and a pocket watch, and acquires human speech.

2. The topic sentence may appear at the end of the paragraph, with a series of details leading to the main idea.

EXAMPLE

The small, darting rabbit on the riverbank becomes a huge White Rabbit, complete with waistcoat and pocket watch. The cards in a discarded deck become the Queen of Hearts and her court. <u>The real world of Alice Liddell becomes, through the odd patterns of the dream, the fantasy world of</u> *Alice in Wonderland.*

3. The selection may begin with a broad generalization (topic sentence) followed by details that support the main idea and lead to another broad generalization that is called the "summary sentence" (conclusion).

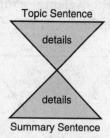

EXAMPLE

The elements of the real world <u>become, through the strange, shifting patterns of the dream, objects and creatures of curiosity and whimsy.</u> A scurrying rabbit becomes a humanized White Rabbit; a deck of cards becomes the court of the Queen of Hearts; a kitten becomes a chess Queen. In *Alice in Wonderland* reality becomes fantasy and, for a while, fantasy becomes reality.

4. The topic sentence may appear in the body of the paragraph.

EXAMPLE

When Alice goes through the looking glass, she enters a garden where the flowers speak. In a dark forest, a fawn befriends her. <u>The dream world reverses the events of the real world</u>. The Lion and the Unicorn come off their shield and do battle. The Red Queen, originally a kitten of Alice's pet cat Dinah, gives Alice instructions in etiquette.

5. The selection may contain *no expressed topic sentence* but consist of a series of sentences giving details and implying a central thought.

EXAMPLE

A deck of cards becomes a royal court. A kitten becomes a chess Queen. A scurrying wild creature becomes a sophisticated courtier, a White Rabbit in vest and pocket watch. A proper Victorian tea party becomes the setting for rude remarks and outrageous behavior.

POETRY

Poetry is a form of literature that is difficult to define. Dictionary definitions are very complicated. One states that a poem is a rhythmical composition, sometimes rhymed, expressing experiences, ideas, or emotions in a style more concentrated, imaginative, and powerful than that of ordinary speech or prose. Another dictionary defines poetry as writing that formulates a concentrated imaginative awareness in language chosen and arranged to create a specific emotional response through meaning, sound, and rhythm. A desk encyclopedia defines poetry as a meaningful arrangement of words into an imaginative emotional discourse, always with a strong rhythmic pattern.

All these definitions stress certain common elements.

1. The content is an experience of the poet, usually emotional, filtered through the poet's imagination.
2. The poet uses a special language that is concentrated, using words that suggest more than their exact meaning.
3. The poet creates rhythmic and sound patterns that contribute to the experience described. He or she frequently, but not necessarily, uses rhyme.

With these elements in mind, let us analyze the poem "Ozymandias" by Percy Bysshe Shelley.

WHAT REMAINS OF A ONCE POWERFUL KING

I met a traveler from an antique land
Who said: "Two vast and trunkless legs of stone
Stand in the desert... Near them, on the sand,
Half sunk, a shattered visage lies, whose frown
And wrinkled lip, and sneer of cold command,
Tell that its sculptor well those passions read
Which yet survive, stamped on these lifeless things,
The hand that mocked them, and the heart that fed;
And on the pedestal these words appear:
'My name is Ozymandias, king of kings:
Look on my works, ye Mighty, And despair!'
Nothing beside remains. Round the decay
Of that colossal wreck, boundless and bare
The lone and level sands stretch far away."

The poet meets someone who describes something seen in a desert. It is the colossal wreck of a statue of a powerful king that has decayed over time. The remains consist of several parts—two legs, a shattered face, and the pedestal on which the statue once stood. The poet wants to portray a scene of utter desolation. Only the shattered statue survives amidst the emptiness of the boundless, bare desert sands. The poem gains its power by means of irony—the opposite of what we expect for a powerful king, not a royal palace but a broken statue of a king, is described. The poet creates, in a few words, the character of the king—his frown, his wrinkled lip, his sneer of authority. All of these details lead to the lesson the poet wishes to teach the Mighty: life is brief; human desires are vain; power leads to despair. He does this in 14 lines and 111 words.

Technically the poem has faulty rhyme—*stone* and *frown*, *appear* and *despair*, and the word order in "Nothing beside remains" is unusual. Nevertheless, an emotional response from us results from the picture the poet creates and the message engraved on the pedestal: nothing lasts forever, not even the power of a mighty king.

FINDING DETAILS

Very often questions on reading passages will test your ability to locate relevant details. In a descriptive passage, the author may give a general impression of a scene. Take, as an example, Edgar Allan Poe's famous short story, "The Fall of the House of Usher." The narrator conveys his reaction on seeing the house with these words: "I know not how it was, but, with the first glimpse of the building, a sense of insufferable gloom pervaded my spirit." Two sentences later you learn the details that made him feel that way.

Or, in a passage dealing with the character of the subject of a biography, details will document the point the author is making. Sandburg's biography of Abraham Lincoln contains many passages that follow this pattern. To show the industriousness of Lincoln, Sandburg writes: "Abe knew the sleep that comes after long hours of work outdoors...." You feel almost certain that the "work" that is mentioned will be described in detail, and it is. Among the jobs listed are "clearing timberland," "splitting rails," "harrowing," "planting," "pulling fodder," "helping...house raisings, log-rollings, corn-huskings."

Details are also used to move the plot or story interestingly and smoothly along the way. In Hawthorne's "The Ambitious Guest," there is the sentence, "The simplest words must intimate, but not portray, the unutterable horror of the catastrophe." Immediately there follow the details that tell just how horrible the catastrophe was.

Finally, details are often used to provide reasons for a conclusion that has been reached. Sherlock Holmes, in talking to Dr. Watson about his solution of the case entitled, "The Adventure of the Speckled Band," says, "I had come to these conclusions before ever I had entered his room." Then Holmes proceeds to give the details of why he reached the conclusions.

How do you locate a detail? It may be necessary for you to return to the reading passage many times to dig out the particular detail required to answer a given question. In your search, a number of clues may help you. These involve what are called **transitional words**, words that point out the purpose of the details presented. (See "Chapter 6: Organization" for a complete list of transitions.)

DETERMINING TONE AND MOOD

Tone is the aspect of the author's style that reveals attitude toward the subject. *Mood* is the atmosphere, or emotional effect, created by the manner in which the author presents the material.

To determine the tone or mood of a passage, consider the feelings or attitudes that are expressed. Examine, for example, the following passages:

EXAMPLE

The room was dark—so dark that even after giving her eyes a while to accustom themselves to the blackness, she could still see nothing. Something soft—she hoped it was only a cobweb—brushed her lip. And the throbbing sound, attuned to her own heavy heartbeat, became stronger and faster.

EXAMPLE

The room was dark—not dark as it is when your eyes are just not used to blackness, but really *dark* dark. Then some soft creepy thing brushed her lip, and she found herself hoping very hard that it was only a cobweb. And then there was that sound—baBoom, baBoom, baBoom—getting faster and louder all the time like her own heart going thump, thump, thump.

Consider the contrasting moods of the two passages above. The first passage presents a sustained mood of suspense and fear. The woman in the room can see nothing; something strange touches her; she hears a heavy and mysterious sound. We have the feeling that something is going to happen; the indication is that what will happen is dangerous, evil, or deadly.

The second paragraph relates essentially the same event. But we are distracted somewhat from what is happening by several devices. First, we are brought informally into the story—we know what a room is like when it's *really* dark. And the quality of darkness is also expressed informally—it is not pitch dark, or night dark, but "dark dark." "Then something creepy" is felt, and the sounds of the noise and the woman's heart are described—baBoom. The feeling conveyed by these devices is somehow made less frightening by the familiarity of the language, and the general impression is less one of total

fear than of "scariness"—an easier emotion to deal with. Thus we have the impression from this second passage that whatever happens will probably not be all that bad or, if it is, it will somehow be easier to overcome.

INFERRING CHARACTER

Character is often implied by a person's words or actions, rather than by direct description. This has always been particularly true of drama, where the reader of a play is often called upon to interpret a character's personality without benefit of stage directions or other descriptive material. In the modern novel, too, the trend has been away from utilizing long descriptive passages and more toward allowing the characters' actions, speech, or thoughts (often called "inner dialogue") to reveal their personalities. The reader must rely, therefore, on the hints offered by the playwright or novelist to interpret character—and even then, a wide range of interpretation may be possible.

The following scene from *Life with Father* features Father and his son Clarence.

CLARENCE (desperately): I have to have a new suit of clothes—you've got to give me the money for it.
(Father's *account book reaches the table with a sharp bang as he stares at* Clarence *with astonishment.*)
FATHER: Young man, do you realize you're addressing your father?
(Clarence *wilts miserably and sinks into a chair.*)
CLARENCE: I'm sorry, Father—I apologize—but you don't know how important this is to me. (Clarence's *tone of misery gives* Father *pause.*)
FATHER: A suit of clothes is so—? Now, why should a —? (*Something dawns on* Father *and he looks at* Clarence.) Has your need for a suit of clothes anything to do with the young lady?
CLARENCE: Yes, Father.
FATHER: Why, Clarence! (*Suddenly realizes that women have come into* Clarence's *emotional life and there comes a yearning to protect this inexperienced and defenseless member of his own sex.*) This comes as quite a shock to me.
CLARENCE: What does, Father?

FATHER: Your being so grown up! Still, I might have known that if you're going to college this fall—yes, you're at an age when you'll be meeting girls. Clarence, there are things about women I think you ought to know! (*He goes up and closes the doors, then comes down and sits beside* Clarence, *hesitating for a moment before he speaks*.) Yes, I think it's better for you to hear this from me than to have to learn it for yourself. Clarence, women aren't the angels that you think they are! Well, now—first, let me explain this to you. You see, Clarence, we men have to run this world and it's not an easy job. It takes work, and it takes thinking. A man has to be sure of his facts and figures. He has to reason things out. Now, you take a woman—a woman thinks—I'm wrong right there—a woman doesn't think at all! She gets stirred up! And she gets stirred up over the damnedest things! Now I love my wife just as much as any man, but that doesn't mean I should stand for a lot of folderol! By God! I won't stand for it!

CLARENCE: Stand for what, Father?

FATHER (to himself): That's the one thing I will not submit myself to. (*Has ceased explaining women to* Clarence *and is now explaining himself*.) Clarence, if a man thinks a certain thing is wrong to do he shouldn't do it. Now that has nothing to do with whether he loves his wife or not.

What action is taking place? A son is asking his father for money to buy a suit. What is the relationship between father and son? Father scolds his son for doing so; the son is miserable and apologizes. Obviously, the first thing we learn about Father is his lack of understanding of his son's needs. He acts like a dictator and causes his son to "wilt miserably." Next, after realizing his son's newly found interest in girls, he takes it upon himself to teach Clarence about women. Father acts like a know-it-all. "It's better for you to hear this from me than to have to learn it yourself." Then he reveals his prejudices against women: "a woman doesn't think at all!" Finally, his thinking becomes disorganized, he starts telling Clarence about women and ends up trying to convince himself how *he* should deal with them. The conversation,

which started out as a request for money from a son to his father, ends in a useless discussion that reveals Father's prejudices.

We are left with a devastating picture of Father's character—a person who is dictatorial, lacking in understanding of his son's needs, filled with prejudices, self-deceptive, and disorganized, who regards himself as all knowing.

We learn all this from a cleverly written page of dialogue between father and son.

INFERRING SETTING

A number of factors are involved in the setting of a selection. These include not only *place* (physical location, type of locale—noisy, crowded, tranquil, etc.), but *time* (of day, of season, of historical period). See what clues to the setting you can find in the following passage.

EXAMPLE

He knew she would be late, but he could not keep himself from hurrying, pushing his way impatiently through the strolling, multilingual crowd. The Germans, their sunburned necks garlanded with camera straps, bargained gutturally with the indifferent women at their stalls, thinking to strike a sharp bargain on the price of a straw handbag or a painted box. The women let them struggle with the unfamiliar numbers, knowing exactly how much they would ultimately settle for. Three American girls, distinguishable by their short hair and madras skirts above sandalled feet and bare legs, dawdled along, giggling at the pleadings of two persistent *pappagalli* who seemed determined to improve international relations at all costs.

The sidestreet leading to the Signoria was hardly less busy, and he found it easier to dodge the small motorbikes bouncing noisily along the cobbled roadway than to struggle against the crowds pouring out of the great museum and onto the narrow sidewalks. He hated these annual floods of holiday-makers and culture-seekers who jammed the streets, the hotels, and the small restaurants so that the year-round residents found it necessary to retreat more than ever to the interiors of their cool, stone houses and their small, closed social circles. The more fortunate natives, of course, headed for Viareggio or the beaches of the South or the Riviera.

He finally found a table at the back of the cafe—a little too close to the bar but partially screened by a box hedge—and ordered a drink. The ancient *piazza* was mostly in shade now, except for the very tops of the towers which had been turned by the sun from the faded buff of the old stone to a rich gold against the blue sky.

What can we tell of the setting described?
Place: We can immediately pick up a number of clues. Obviously the setting is a city (crowds, sidewalks, a market, a museum). It is also not in the United States, since American girls are particularly distinguishable. By the mention of the Riviera as a nearby vacation spot, we know that we are somewhere in western Europe—but not Germany (the Germans are not familiar with the language). We can narrow the location down even further (although you are not expected to have all this extra information): two foreign words, *pappagalli* and *piazza*, might lead to the educated guess that the country is Italy.

Time: (1) Period—although the city itself is old (cobbled streets, narrow sidewalks, towers in an ancient piazza), the period is more recent. Motorbikes, barelegged girls, camera-carrying tourists all indicate the modern era. (2) Season—we can assume by the dress of the tourists, and by the fact that the natives usually head for the beach during this season, that it is summer. (3) Time of day—The piazza is in shade, except for the tops of the towers. It is unlikely, therefore, to be midday. Since the main character orders a drink in a cafe-bar, and since we have nowhere been given to understand that he has a drinking problem, we can assume it is late afternoon (cocktail time) and he has an appointment with someone for a predinner drink.

You should be made aware that the above passage was prepared solely to give you practice in inferring setting, and that you are not likely to find too many passages on the actual examination that concentrate on such description. However, you should learn to pick up small clues here and there that will give you an idea of the setting in a descriptive passage. Remember that, more often than not, the locale will be inferred rather than actually stated.

READING PROSE

Now let us turn to two representative passages from prose literature. Read these carefully; answer the six questions based on each; compare your answers with those in the answer key; then study the analysis of the answers, particularly for questions those that you answered incorrectly.

PRACTICE IN READING
POPULAR AND CLASSICAL PROSE

WHAT IS ABOUT TO HAPPEN TO BORIS?

The light carriage swished through the layers of fallen leaves upon the terrace. In places, they lay so thick that they half covered the stone balusters and reached the knees of Diana's stag. But the trees were bare; only here and there a single golden leaf trembled high upon the black twigs. Following the curve of the road, Boris's carriage came straight upon the main terrace and the house, majestic as the Sphinx herself in the sunset. The light of the setting sun seemed to have soaked into the dull masses of stone. They reddened and glowed with it until the whole place became a mysterious, a glorified abode, in which the tall windows shone like a row of evening stars.

Boris got out of the britska in front of the mighty stone stairs and walked toward them, feeling for his letter. Nothing stirred in the house. It was like walking into a cathedral. "And," he thought, "by the time that I get into that carriage once more, what will everything be like to me?"

1. The title that expresses the main idea of this passage is

(1) "The Lure of Autumn"
(2) "Sphinx in the Sunset"
(3) "A Mysterious Cathedral"
(4) "A Terrifying Surprise"
(5) "An Important Visit"

2. From the description of the house, we may most safely conclude that the house

    (1) is sometimes used as a place of worship
    (2) is owned by a wealthy family
    (3) was designed by Egyptian architects
    (4) is constructed of modern brick
    (5) is a dark, cold-looking structure

3. This story probably takes place in

    (1) the British Isles
    (2) the Far East
    (3) eastern Europe
    (4) southern United States
    (5) the Mediterranean

4. We may most safely conclude that Boris has come to the house in order to

    (1) secure a job
    (2) find out about his future
    (3) join his friends for the holidays
    (4) attend a hunting party
    (5) visit his old family home

5. In this passage, which atmosphere does the author attempt to create?

    (1) pleasant anticipation
    (2) quiet peace
    (3) carefree gaiety
    (4) unrelieved despair
    (5) vague uncertainty

6. From this passage, which inference can most safely be drawn?

    (1) The house was topped by a lofty tower.
    (2) Boris is tired from his journey.
    (3) There is only one terrace before the house is reached.
    (4) The most imposing feature of the house is the door.
    (5) Boris intends to stay at the house for only a short time.

ANSWER KEY

1. **5**   2. **2**   3. **3**   4. **2**   5. **5**   6. **5**

ANSWER ANALYSIS

1. **5** Boris has come to the house and as he enters, he wonders what changes may take place for him as a result of his visit. To Boris, this will be "an important visit." Choice 1 cannot be correct. Going back to the passage, we find "the trees were bare; only here and there a single golden leaf trembled high upon the black twigs." This and a reference to "layers of fallen leaves" in line 2 are the only indications of season, and "the lure" of the season is not even mentioned. We reject this choice because it states only the setting for the main idea of the selection and background detail at best. It is not the *main* idea. Choices 2 and 3 are incorrect for similar reasons. In each case, a *detail* has been picked out of the selection and offered as the *main* idea. Choice 2 refers to the house, compared in majesty to the Sphinx. Choice 3 also involves a comparison—this time of the house with a cathedral. Choice 4 is completely incorrect. There is no surprise, nor is the selection's mood one of terror. There is anticipation of something about to happen, rather than something surprising that has happened.

2. **2** We can conclude that the house is owned by a wealthy family because there are several terraces, the stone stairs are "mighty," the windows are tall, and there are "masses of stone." Of the possibilities offered, this is the one we may most safely conclude is correct. Choices 1 and 3 are both incorrect, for similar reasons. Each is based on a figure of speech used in the passage, an implied comparison between the house and a cathedral and the stated comparison of the house to the sphinx. These are comparisons in the mind of the writer. Choice 4 is incorrect because it flatly contradicts the passage; the house is built of stone. Choice 5 is incorrect because it, too, contradicts the selection. The stone is not dark; it glows with the light of the setting sun.

3. **3** This question calls on you to draw an inference. The chief character has a Russian name, Boris. He gets out of a

britska, and, even if you don't know that this is a kind of open carriage used in eastern Europe, the word suggests a conveyance that immediately eliminates "the British Isles" and "southern United States." It is safe to conclude, because of the name Boris, that the story "probably takes place in eastern Europe."

4. **2** The purpose of the question is to see whether you can determine the purpose of Boris's visit from the *evidence given*. While Choices 1, 3, and 4 may possibly be correct, there is no evidence in the passage to support them. Choice 5 must be considered along with Choice 2. If the selection ended just before the final sentence, the two choices would be equally plausible. But Boris is not merely making a visit. The question he asks himself in the final sentence makes it clear that the visit promises to change his future. Therefore, Choice 2 is the better of the two.

5. **5** Usually this type of question can be quite difficult. It involves not only locating details but also deciding what feeling the author wishes these details to create in you, the reader. Choices 5 and 2 remain possibilities. While "quiet peace" could describe the atmosphere, "vague uncertainty," Choice 5, is clearly superior as the answer. The whole place became "mysterious." Boris feels for his letter, the contents of which we are forced to guess. The uncertainty is climaxed by Boris's question, which asks, in effect, "What will become of me?" Choices 1, 3 and 4 involve some indication of Boris' feelings—of pleasure, of gaiety, of despair, but the passage contains no such indications.

6. **5** This question again calls for an inference, a conclusion that you, the reader, must draw from the facts that are presented. Choice 5 is correct because it represents the inference that "can most safely be drawn." Boris mentions getting back into the carriage. From this *fact* in the passage, we can *infer* that he intends to stay at the house for only a short time. Choices 1, 2, and 4 are not based on any facts in the passage: no tower is mentioned, nor is the door, and Boris's feelings are not described. Choice 3

contradicts the facts in the passage; one terrace is mentioned at the beginning and a main terrace is mentioned later. Clearly there are two terraces.

WHAT IS A CAMP OF WAR-WOUNDED LIKE?

Then the camps of the wounded—O heavens, what scene is this?—is this indeed humanity—these butchers' shambles? There are several of them. There they lie, in the largest, in an open space in the woods, from 200 to 300 poor fellows—the groans and the screams—the odor of blood, mixed with the fresh scent of the night, the grass, the trees—that slaughter-house! O well is it their mothers, their sisters cannot see them—cannot conceive, and never conceiv'd these things. One man is shot by a shell, both in the arm and leg—both are amputated—there lie the rejected members. Some have their legs blown off—some bullets through the breast—some indescribably horrid wounds in the face or head, all mutilated, sickening, torn, gouged out—some in the abdomen—some mere boys—many rebels, badly hurt—they take their regular turns with the rest, just the same as any—the surgeons use them just the same. Such is the camp of the wounded—such a fragment, a reflection afar off of the bloody scene—while all over the clear, large moon comes out at times softly, quietly shining. Amid the woods, that scene of flitting souls—amid the crack and crash and yelling sounds—the impalpable perfume of the woods—and yet the pungent, stifling smoke—the radiance of the moon, looking from heaven at intervals so placid—the sky so heavenly—the clear-obscure up there, those buoyant upper oceans—a few large placid stars beyond, coming silently and languidly out, and then disappearing—the melancholy, draperied night above, around. And there, upon the roads, the fields, and in those woods, that contest, never one more desperate in any age or land— both parties now in force—masses—no fancy battle, no semi-play, but fierce and savage demons fighting there— courage and scorn of death the rule, exceptions almost none.

—Walt Whitman

1. The author's main purpose in writing this selection is to

   (1) express his sympathy for the wounded
   (2) point out the brutal treatment of the rebels
   (3) praise the courage of the fighters
   (4) deplore the horrors of war
   (5) describe the camps of the wounded

2. The author shows his emotions in all of the following ways EXCEPT by

   (1) asking unanswerable questions
   (2) effective use of epithets
   (3) contrasting the battle with its peaceful setting
   (4) including gruesome details
   (5) sympathizing with the surgeons

3. All of the following relate to our sense of smell EXCEPT

   (1) "fresh scent of the night"
   (2) "the odor of blood"
   (3) "the radiance of the moon"
   (4) "the pungent, stifling smoke"
   (5) "the impalpable perfume of the woods"

4. The soldiers are referred to by all of the following EXCEPT

   (1) butchers
   (2) poor fellows
   (3) mere boys
   (4) flitting souls
   (5) savage demons

5. The reader can infer from the final sentence that, for the soldiers, the author has a feeling of

   (1) pity
   (2) contempt
   (3) indifference
   (4) admiration
   (5) resignation

6. That the author is also a poet may be inferred from his

   (1) description of the wounded
   (2) comments on the camps
   (3) conclusions about war
   (4) awareness of the night's beauty
   (5) indignation at what he sees

ANSWER KEY

1. **4**   2. **5**   3. **3**   4. **1**   5. **4**   6. **4**

ANSWER ANALYSIS

1. **4** The key word in the question is *main*. The question calls for you to identify the "main purpose" of the author. Although it is true that the author expresses his sympathy for the wounded ("poor fellows") and he does describe the camps of the wounded, his main purpose is to use these camps as "a reflection" of the "bloody scene" to express his disgust at the horrors of war. Therefore, Choices (1) and (5) are incorrect. Choice 2 is obviously wrong since the author indicates that the rebel soldiers got the same treatment as the rest. He mentions the courage of the fighters almost incidentally in the last sentence of the selection, so Choice 3 cannot be the main purpose of the author.

2. **5** This question requires you to go back to the selection and to ferret out the details that the possible answers identify. Choice 5 is correct because the one thing the author does *not* do is sympathize with the surgeons, although he does refer to the impartiality with which they treat soldiers on both sides. In the first two lines, the author asks unanswerable questions.

   Epithets describe significant qualities of the nouns they modify. We find "horrid" wounds and "desperate" contest, "fierce and savage" demons, as well as such poetic epithets as "melancholy, draperied" night. The bloody battle is indeed contrasted with the "placid," moon and "heavenly" sky. Gruesome detail abounds in the selection.

3. **3** This relatively easy question contains many clues to the answer. *Scent* and *odor* are synonyms of *smell*. While *pungent* may refer to both taste and smell, it is the smell of smoke, rather than its taste, that is obviously referred to here. Perfume, of course, is something that is smelled. The correct choice is 3 because "the radiance of the moon" refers to the sense of sight, not the sense of smell.

4. **1** Careful attention to the details of the passage reveals that the soldiers are referred to as "poor fellows," "some mere boys," "flitting souls," and "fierce and savage demons." The term *butchers' shambles* compares the camp of the wounded with a butchers' slaughterhouse and does not refer at all to the soldiers.

5. **4** The question identifies the specific place where the answer may be found—the final sentence. Study of that sentence gives us two clues to the author's feeling for the soldiers. They are "fierce and savage demons." "Courage and scorn of death" is typical of their fighting. The author does not pity the soldiers in this sentence, nor does he show any indifference to their "desperate" plight. There is no evidence that he is resigned to their having to continue the battle. While he does allude to their ferocity and savagery, he does not show contempt or scorn for the soldiers. Rather, he emphasizes their courage, since it is true that almost all display this quality in the fierce battle. Therefore, his feeling is one of admiration.

6. **4** What details would lead you, the reader, to conclude that any writer has the qualities of a poet? The "Glossary of Literary Terms" beginning on page 433 defines a poem as literature that has "deep emotion; highly imaginative language with figures of speech; distinctive rhythm;... words that mean more than they apparently say" among others. Mere description, comment, and conclusion are not poetic qualities. The writing of a good reporter has all of these features. Anger, while it is a deep emotion, is not as good a clue to the fact that the author is a poet as is his unusual sensitivity to the night's beauty: "the radiance of the moon," "those buoyant upper oceans" (referring to the sky), "the melancholy, draperied night above." The scene is viewed by the light of the moon, the sky is compared to a sea, and the night is compared to a hanging curtain in a way that only a poet could succeed in doing.

SUMMARY OF PROSE INTERPRETATION

Thus far, what have you learned, with respect to skills of interpretation, from the study of prose?

You should:

1. *Read the selection carefully.*
2. *In **selecting a title** that expresses the main idea, go back to the selection constantly. Arrive at the correct answer by a process of elimination. Eliminate the one or more possibilities that are clearly incorrect. Eliminate the possibilities that are based on minor details; there will be one or two of these. From the remaining choices, you must select the one that expresses the main rather than the subordinate idea.*
3. *In **drawing inferences**, find the clues in the passage from which you can draw the proper conclusion. The clue may be a name, a place, an adjective, an object, an unusual word. You may have to reread the selection a few times before you locate the clue or the two details that can be linked to make a clue.*
4. *In **determining purpose**, ask yourself why the author wrote the passage; what he or she wanted you, the reader, to understand or feel. After you have read the passage several times, try to define the total impression you get from your reading. The purposes of authors at various times may be to inform, to arouse anger, to poke fun at, to evoke pity, to amuse, and to urge to action, among others. Which of these predominates?*
5. *In **determining mood**, try to find words that either create an atmosphere or evoke an emotion. This is related to the author's purpose but may not necessarily be his or her main purpose. There are two main guides to determining atmosphere: selection of details and use of adjectives and adverbs.*

READING POETRY

Reading poetry requires a special set of skills because the poet uses both a special language and special writing techniques.

In poetry, words are not used in their normal, literal senses. Rather, they are used in such a way that you, the reader, must call on your imagination to fully understand them. Let's consider an example.

"I almost blew my top."

Here the words *blew* and *top* do not have their regular meanings, but are used figuratively to express the idea "I almost went crazy."

> **Skill One.** In poetry, words are often used in a figurative sense. Do not take these words literally. Use your imagination in order to understand them as the poet uses them.

In poetry, meaning is frequently compressed into a few words by the use of figures of speech such as metaphors. (See the "Glossary of Literary Terms," page 433.)

"The road was a ribbon of moonlight."

In seven words, the poet Walter de la Mare tells us that the time is night, the moon was shining, and the road is a lighted area surrounded by darker ones.

"The moon was a ghostly galleon."

In six words, the poet tells us that the moon is like a ship, the sky is like an ocean, and the moon creates an eerie, supernatural feeling as it moves across the sky.

> **Skill Two.** In poetry, words often compress or condense extended meanings and pictures into a few words, usually by the use of figures of speech such as metaphors. Add to the words you read the implied meanings and pictures they create.

In poetry, meaning is closely related to rhythm. For this reason it helps to read poetry aloud.

> **Skill Three.** Read the poem aloud paying attention to the rhythm, because the rhythm of the poem will help you understand its meaning.

In poetry, in addition to rhythm, which is always present, you will frequently encounter rhyme. Rhyme, too, often helps to convey meaning. In Edgar Allan Poe's poem "The Raven," the rhyme is repeated in *door, more, Lenore, forevermore,* and *nevermore.*

"'Tis some visitor,' I muttered, 'tapping at my chamber door: Only this and nothing more.'"

The sound itself adds to the atmosphere of mystery.

> **Skill Four.** As you read the poem aloud, note the rhyme as well as the rhythm, since both add to the meaning and feelings expressed.

In poetry, the poet uses sounds in addition to rhyme to help convey meaning. The poet John Masefield describes the effect of the wind with a series of "w" and "wh" sounds. He wants to return

"To the gull's *w*ay and the *wh*ales's *w*ay *wh*ere the *w*ind's like a *wh*etted knife."

This technique is known as alliteration. (See the "Glossary of Literary Terms," page 433.)

Another technique is the use of words whose sounds correspond to their meaning. Here is the way one poet describes the movement of the waters of a river:

"And rushing and flushing and brushing and gushing,

And flapping and rapping and clapping and slapping..."

> **Skill Five.** As you read the poem aloud, note the sounds of the words as well as their rhyme and their rhythm, since each adds to the meaning and feelings expressed by the poet.

In poetry, the poem itself has a certain shape or form. The poem can be in a very definite form, such as the sonnet, or in a very loose form. "The New Colossus," by Emma Lazarus, which follows below, is a sonnet with a definite rhythm and a definite rhyme scheme. The form of "The New Colossus" is appropriate because it lends itself to the main ideas expressed in each of the two stanzas of the poem.

> **Skill Six.** As you read the poem, study its form and structure. If it is divided into stanzas or paragraph units, try to determine what each stanza adds to the meaning of the poem. The poem's form is another aid to your understanding its meaning. Consult the "Glossary of Literary Terms," page 433, for *sonnet* and *stanza*, terms that relate to poetic form and structure.

Read the following poem carefully and answer the questions based on it. Compare your answers with the answer key: then study the analysis of the answers, particularly for questions that you have answered incorrectly.

PRACTICE IN READING POETRY

WHAT DOES THE NEW STATUE REPRESENT?

The New Colossus

Not like the brazen giant of Greek
  fame,
With conquering limbs astride from
  land to land;
Here at our sea-washed, sunset gates
  shall stand
A mighty woman with a torch, whose
  flame
Is the imprisoned lightning, and her
  name
Mother of Exiles. From her beacon-
  hand
Glows world-wide welcome; her mild
  eyes command
The air-bridged harbor that twin
  cities frame.

"Keep, ancient lands, your storied
  pomp!" cries she
with silent lips. "Give me your tired,
  your poor,
Your huddled masses yearning to
  breathe free,
The wretched refuse of your teeming
  shore.
Send these, the homeless, tempest-
  tost, to me.
I lift my lamp beside the golden
  door!"

            —Emma Lazarus

1. The main idea of the poem is that

  (1) the ancient lands of Europe should serve as a beacon to America
  (2) the Greek statue serves as a model for the American statue
  (3) the mighty are asked to come to these shores
  (4) America welcomes all persecuted freedom-lovers
  (5) the lamp guides those who come to the golden door

2. In the choices below, the incorrectly paired words are

  (1) brazen—of brass
  (2) sunset—east
  (3) beacon—guiding light
  (4) refuse—trash
  (5) pomp—splendor

3. The "mighty woman" and "Mother of Exiles" is the

  (1) United States of America
  (2) city of New York
  (3) Statue of Liberty
  (4) Plymouth Rock
  (5) Golden Gate

4. The title of this poem, "The New Colossus," implies

  (1) similarity to the old
  (2) replacement of the old
  (3) difference from the old
  (4) inferiority to the old
  (5) acceptance of the old

5. The *incorrectly* matched phrase from the poem with the figure of speech or poetic device it demonstrates is

(1) "Her mild eyes"—epithet
(2) "Keep, ancient lands, your storied pomp!" cries she—personification
(3) "shall stand a mighty woman"—inversion
(4) "world-wide welcome"—alliteration
(5) "flame is the imprisoned light-ning"—simile

6. The form of the poem is that of

(1) a ballad
(2) an octet
(3) an ode
(4) a sestet
(5) a sonnet

ANSWER KEY

1. **4**   2. **2**   3. **3**   4. **3**   5. **5**   6. **5**

ANSWER ANALYSIS

1. **4** Choice 1 is not correct because the reverse is actually true; America's "beacon-hand" as represented in the statue is a beacon to the exiles from the ancient lands of Europe. Nor is Choice 2 correct since the opening line begins "Not like" the Greek statue is the American statue. Choice 3 is incorrect; it is the "tired," "poor," and "homeless" who are welcomed to these shores. While Choice 5 is true as far as it goes, it is not the main idea. Choice A is correct.

REMEMBER: You must read the selection carefully. **In selecting the main idea**, *you must go back to the selection several times. Arrive at the correct answer by a process of elimination.*

2. **2** While this question is seemingly a vocabulary question that requires you to recall the meanings of the words in the five possible answers, the poem does provide hints or context clues to the meanings of several of the words. "From her *beacon*-hand glows world-wide welcome" indicates that light is going forth. The *refuse* is described as *wretched*. Pomp is contrasted with the *poor* and the *refuse*. Therefore, you can conclude that these words are correctly paired. If you deduce from the first verse that an ancient statue is being described, the meaning of *brass* for *brazen* seems logical. But even if you can't, "our"—meaning America's—"sunset gates" must be located in the west, where the sun sets. Choice 2 is the correct answer because sunset is always associated with the west rather than the east.

REMEMBER: Never give up on a question. **Where the meaning of words is involved**, *carefully study the clues to their meaning given by other nearby words in the passage.*

3. **3** To answer this question, you must draw an inference or conclusion from what is stated indirectly in the poem. What does the poem tell us about the "mighty woman" and "Mother of Exiles"? We learn that she stands "with a torch"; we also learn that "her mild eyes command the...harbor." These facts rule out all possible answers except Choice 3. The United States of America and the city of New York do not, even symbolically, stand "with a torch." Neither Plymouth Rock (a rock) nor the Golden Gate (a bridge) fits the clues contained in the poem.

REMEMBER: **In drawing inferences or making deductions** *from the text, find the clues that can help you. You may have to reread the selection a few times before you find them.*

4. **3** This is not a difficult question if you read the poem with care from the very beginning. The new colossus is "not like" the old, according to the very first verse, so Choices 1 and 2 are immediately ruled out. To find the correct answer, you must determine how the poet feels about this new colossus. Since she is "mighty" and since her eyes are "mild," it is obvious that the poet admires the new colossus and finds it superior to the old (which the poet rejects). Therefore, Choices 4 and 5 are also incorrect. It is the "difference" and the fact that the new is "not like" the old that are stressed. Therefore, Choice 3 is correct.

5. **5** It is important for you to refer to the "Glossary of Literary Terms" on page 433 if you haven't mastered the definitions already because all five possible answers are defined in that vocabulary. *Epithet*, an adjective or phrase that identifies a significant quality of the noun it describes, is exemplified by her *mild* eyes, so Choice 1 contains a correctly matched pair. *Personification*, the act of attributing human qualities to a "thing" (in this case the power of speech to a statue), is correctly paired with the quotation from the poem. *Inversion*, reversal of normal word order, applies to "shall stand a mighty woman" because the normal order is "a mighty woman shall stand." "Worldwide welcome" is a perfect example of *alliteration* since the same consonant sound, "w," is repeated at the beginning of two words that follow one another. By elimination, Choice 5 is correct since *simile* is *incorrectly* paired with "flame is the imprisoned lightning." *Like* or *as* is *not* used to make the comparison, so "flame is the imprisoned lightning" is properly called a *metaphor*.

6. **5** Where the form of a poem is required to answer a question, first count the number of lines. Then figure out the rhyme scheme. Here there are 14 lines with a rhyme scheme as follows:

fame	—a
land	—b
stand	—b
flame	—a
name	—a
hand	—b
command	—b
frame	—a
she	—c
poor	—d
free	—c
shore	—d
me	—c
door	—d

If you consult the "Glossary of Literary Terms" beginning on page 433, you will find that this form cannot fit the definitions of a ballad (which deals with a simple story) or an ode (which is a lengthy lyric poem). Since the poem has 14 lines, it cannot be an octet (eight lines) or a sestet (six lines). The correct answer must be Choice 5, a sonnet. This poem is actually only a fairly good example of an Italian sonnet. The octet or first eight lines present the main idea—the contrast between the new colossus, which represents a welcome to the exiles, and the old colossus, which symbolized conquest—and is in the exact rhyme scheme required. The sestet or second six lines expands the idea by stressing the freedom and opportunity offered to the exiles in contrast to their rejection by the countries from which they came. The rhyme scheme, instead of rigidly following the *c d e c d e* of the Italian sonnet, confines itself to *c d c d c d*, one of the possible combinations.

It should be noted that the sestet of this famous sonnet is inscribed on the base of the Statue of Liberty and is one of the most frequently quoted American poems.

SUMMARY OF INTERPRETATION OF POETRY

The skills needed in reading and interpreting poetry call for you to:

1. Try to get the extended meaning of words used figuratively by using your imagination to add to the usual meanings of the words.
2. Since poetry compresses meaning and description into a few words, fill in the

suggested meanings and pictures they create by studying the figures of speech used, such as similes and metaphors.

3. Read the poem aloud, since the rhythm will help you determine its meaning.
4. Note the rhymes used, since they will also help you get meaning and feeling from the poem.
5. Note the sounds of the words, since they reinforce meaning.
6. Study the form of the poem, since its subdivisions (stanzas) can help you understand it better.

Note: First, read the poem through quickly to get an overall idea of its meaning and feeling. Then read it more slowly and carefully after you have read the questions based on it.

READING DRAMA

The playwright does not speak directly to the reader in modern drama, as do the novelist and short story writer. Sometimes the playwright sets the scene for those who produce or read the play, and sometimes he or she includes instructions to the actors about mood or action. For the most part, however, the playwright leaves it to the actor and the reader to figure out appearance, character, actions, and feelings. The only real help the playwright should and must give is through the dialogue, the conversation between the characters. From this dialogue alone, you must *imagine the setting, visualize the action,* including "hearing" the speech of the actors, and *draw conclusions about their character and motives.* In addition, you must understand the nature of the essence of drama, which is conflict between ideas or characters. This is made clear only through the dialogue. A final point: you may also be asked to predict what is likely to happen on the basis of what you have read.

An analysis of the following scene from a modern American play will illustrate the skills you need to read and understand drama. Reading it aloud will help.

HOW DOES WILLY LOMAN'S FAMILY REACT TO HIS DEATH?

REQUIEM

CHARLEY: It's getting dark, Linda.
(Linda doesn't react. She stares at the grave.)
BIFF: How about it, Mom? Better get some rest, heh! They'll be closing the gate soon.
(Linda makes no move. Pause.)
HAPPY *(deeply angered)*: He had no right to do that. There was no necessity for it. We would've helped him.
BIFF: Come along, Mom.
LINDA: Why didn't anybody come?
CHARLEY: It was a very nice funeral.
LINDA: But where are all the people he knew? Maybe they blame him.
CHARLEY: Naa. It's a rough world, Linda. They wouldn't blame him.
LINDA: I can't understand it. At this time especially. First time in thirty-five years we were just about free and clear. He only needed a little salary. He was even finished with the dentist.
CHARLEY: No man only needs a little salary.
LINDA: I can't understand it.
BIFF: There were a lot of nice days. When he'd come home from a trip, or on Sundays, making the stoop, finishing the cellar, when he built the extra bathroom, and put up the garage. You know something, Charley, there's more of him in that front stoop than in all the sales he ever made.
CHARLEY: Yeah, he was a happy man with a batch of cement.
LINDA: He was so wonderful with his hands.
BIFF: He had the wrong dreams. All, all, wrong.
HAPPY: *(almost ready to fight Biff)*: Don't say that.
BIFF: He never knew who he was.
CHARLEY *(stopping Happy's movement and reply. To Biff)*: Nobody dast blame this man. You don't understand. Willy was a salesman. And for a salesman, there is no rock bottom to the life. He don't put a bolt to a nut, he don't tell

you the law or give you medicine. He's the man way out there in the blue riding on a smile and a shoeshine. And when they start not smiling back—that's an earthquake. And then you get yourself a couple of spots on your hat, and you're finished. Nobody dast blame this man. A salesman has got to dream, boy. It comes with the territory.

BIFF: Charley, the man didn't know who he was.

HAPPY *(infuriated)*: Don't say that.

BIFF: Why don't you come with me, Happy?

HAPPY: I'm not licked that easily. I'm staying right here in this city, and I'm gonna beat this racket! *(He looks at Biff, his chin set.)* The Loman Brothers!

BIFF: I know who I am, kid.

HAPPY: All right, boy. I'm gonna show you and everybody else that Willy Loman did not die in vain. He had a good dream. It's the only dream you can have—to come out number-one man. He fought it out here, and this is where I'm gonna win it for him.

1. "Requiem" most closely means

   (1) prayer
   (2) regret
   (3) argument
   (4) repetition
   (5) request

2. What has happened prior to this scene?

   (1) The Lomans had an unhappy marriage.
   (2) The brothers did not get along.
   (3) Willy Loman had many friends.
   (4) The Loman family had an easy life.
   (5) Willy Loman was buried.

3. From the dialogue, we can conclude that

   (1) the members of the family differed in their view of Willy Loman.
   (2) the brothers will stick together.
   (3) the family was not tightly knit.
   (4) there was a generation gap in the family.
   (5) everyone blames Willy for his action.

4. Happy defends Willy by saying

   (1) he wanted to be popular.
   (2) he was a family man.
   (3) he wanted to be a top salesman.
   (4) he wanted to build his house.
   (5) he didn't care for himself.

5. The member of the family who differs from the rest is

   (1) Linda
   (2) Biff
   (3) Charley
   (4) Happy
   (5) Willy

6. The irony of the situation is that, at the time of Willy's death, the family is

   (1) splitting up
   (2) united in tragedy
   (3) appreciative of Willy
   (4) in good shape financially
   (5) mutually supportive

ANSWER KEY

1. **1**   2. **5**   3. **1**   4. **3**   5. **2**   6. **4**

ANSWER ANALYSIS

1. **1** A requiem is a prayer, a Mass for a deceased person, in this case Willy Loman. In this instance, it is a tragic and solemn moment for the family of Willy Loman and, although a prayer is not involved, the Lomans remember and evaluate Willy's life.

2. **5** The clues to the locale of the scene, a cemetery, are: "They'll be closing the gate soon" and "It was a very nice funeral."

3. **1** The brothers differed in their view of their father. Biff criticizes him: "He had the wrong dreams." Happy answers, "Don't say that." Charley adds, "Nobody dast blame this man." The other choices are not true of the family. For example, Charley does not blame Willy at all.

4. **3** Happy defends Willy by saying, "He had a good dream. It's the only dream you can have—to come out number-one man." None of the other choices is supported by the dialogue although Willy was "a happy man with a batch of cement."

5. **2** It is Biff, and Biff alone, who criticizes Willy: "He had the wrong dreams" and "He never knew who he was." It is he who leaves his family and goes off to the city.

6. **4** Linda says, "At this time especially. First time in thirty-five years we were just about free and clear." Dramatic irony is a combination of circumstances or is a result that is the opposite of what might be expected, in this case, death instead of a happier life.

SUMMARY OF INTERPRETATION OF DRAMA READING

The skills needed in reading and interpreting drama call for you to:

1. Try to imagine the setting. If no stage directions are given, deduce from the speech and dialogue of the characters where the action is taking place.

2. Visualize the action. As the characters speak, figure out *what they are doing* while they are speaking.

3. Determine their motives. Why are the characters speaking as they do? *Why are they doing what they do?*

4. Determine their character and personality. What sort of person talks and acts the way he does? Why?

5. Determine the conflict that is taking place. Since the essence of drama is conflict, who or what is in conflict with whom or what? Is the conflict physical? Is it emotional? Is it a conflict of ideas?

6. Try to predict on the basis of all of the above what is most likely to happen next.

7. Read the scene aloud, trying to project yourself into the character of each of the roles.

Reading Commentary on the Arts

Selections that fall under the term *commentary* are limited to the aspects of contemporary writing that deal with the arts—music, art, theater, movies, television, literature, and dance. They are further limited to selections in which the author comments critically on the arts, discussing the value of the content and the style of these means of expression.

In reading commentaries, try to determine the point of view of the writer and whether his or her evaluation of the artist, the musician, the author, the playwright, the film, the television program, or the dancer is favorable or unfavorable. Also look for the insights of the critic into the meaning and emotion conveyed by the artist or the medium.

The writing style will be that of the author of a piece of popular literature, so sentence structure and vocabulary will be relatively simple. *Here is a helpful hint.* Since critics who comment on the arts are describing their reactions, they resort to many adjectives that express their judgment. Here are a couple of dozen of such adjectives: *adept, authentic, candid, credible, dynamic, eloquent, exquisite, graphic, inane, inept, laudable, lucid, naive, poignant, prosaic, spontaneous, superb, superlative, tedious, timeless, tiresome, trite, vivacious, witty.*

PRACTICE IN READING COMMENTARY ON THE ARTS

WHAT DID THE CREATOR OF THE MUPPETS CONTRIBUTE TO CHILDREN'S TELEVISION?

He built an empire on a discarded green coat and a Ping-Pong ball. Jim Henson, creator of Kermit the Frog and a menagerie of other furry creatures known as the Muppets, revolutionized puppetry and reinvented children's television.

The Muppets charmed audiences of all ages on *Sesame Street*, possibly the most influential children's show ever, and later on *The Muppet Show*, which became the mostly widely watched TV program in the world, attracting 135 million viewers in 100 countries.

Henson succeeded with craftsmanship and showmanship and salesmanship. But above all, he constantly challenged the status quo.

Henson was one of the first producers to use television not merely as a medium but as a tool to enhance his performances.

While earlier puppet programs, such as *Kukla, Fran, and Ollie*, simply pluncked a camera in front of a traditional stage, Henson used a variety of camera lenses to create illusions which made his Muppets more agile and antic.

He also taught his puppeteers to work while using a TV monitor. For the first time, they could see not only their performances as they were unfolding, but also what the viewers could see.

That insight led Henson to create a new, softer-looking style of puppet that was extremely expressive in TV closeups.

Henson's unconventional approach to life came through in his Muppets—a word he coined for the crossbreed of marionettes and puppets he developed in the mid-50s.

While companies like Disney were creating model characters that lived up to the era's model of perfection, such as Bambi, Henson's creatures, such as the proud Miss Piggy, the grumpy Oscar the Grouch, and the uncontrollable Animal, were wildly irreverent.

Henson also applied this irreverent approach to his work. He promoted productivity, not by demanding results, but by encouraging his associates to have fun. He promoted silliness, even chaos, on the set. In fact, he was most satisfied with a scene when it had grown so funny that no one could perform it without busting up, former associates say.

Despite his childlike enthusiasm, Henson was also a pragmatist who tackled situations by approaching them from new angles. He was a problem solver and had a knack for sidestepping complexity and finding a simpler, purer way of doing things.

1. The contributions of Jim Henson, according to the article,

   (1) retained earlier approaches
   (2) added little to current programming
   (3) climbed on the bandwagon of children's television
   (4) imitated Kukla, Fran, and Olllie
   (5) broke new ground in puppetry

2. The reinventing of children's TV was exemplified by the worldwide success of

   (1) *Sesame Street*
   (2) *The Muppet Show*
   (3) *Kukla, Fran, and Ollie*
   (4) Kermit the Frog
   (5) the status quo

3. The most important reason for the success of Jim Henson was

   (1) his craftsmanship
   (2) his showmanship
   (3) his salesmanship
   (4) his unconventional approach
   (5) his charm

4. Henson pioneered in using television

   (1) as a medium
   (2) to improve performance
   (3) as a traditional stage
   (4) to teach tried-and-true methods
   (5) to preserve the familiar puppets

5. Henson's Muppets

   (1) sought perfection
   (2) imitated Disney's creations
   (3) were disrespectful
   (4) were ideal role models
   (5) were static and serious

6. Jim Henson was all of the following EXCEPT

   (1) a man of childlike enthusiasm
   (2) a searcher for simple solutions
   (3) a pragmatist
   (4) an irreverent innovator
   (5) a conformist

1. **5**   2. **2**   3. **4**   4. **2**   5. **3**   6. **5**

ANSWER ANALYSIS

1. **5** The author stresses Henson's challenging of the status quo and his revolutionizing of puppetry. Since Henson rejected earlier approaches, Choice 1 is wrong. Being dissatisfied with current programming, he searched for something new and came up with Kermit the Frog, adding much to current programs. He didn't climb on the children's TV bandwagon (Choice 3); he reinvented children's TV. Whereas the progam *Kukla, Fran, and Ollie* was static and traditional, Henson injected movement into his characters by new uses of the camera.

2. **2** The audience for Choice 1 is not identified; but for Choice 2, *The Muppet Show*, its worldwide success is mentioned and its domination by the numbers of millions of viewers in a hundred countries. None of the other choices deals directly with the *success* of the Muppets.

3. **4** While Henson's craftsmanship, showmanship, and salesmanship are mentioned, his unconventional approach and unusual characters are stressed. The charm of the Muppets is subordinate to their unusual character.

4. **2** Henson used television not only as a medium but also as a tool to enhance performance. He opposed the tradtional, the tried and true, and the familiar.

5. **3** Henson's Muppets were unlike Disney's characters because they were not perfect, not ideal. They were proud, grumpy, and disrespectful.

6. **5** Henson's childlike enthusiasm, his search for simple solutions, and his irreverence are mentioned, but the major point of the article is Henson's nonconformism, his *not* acting in traditional ways.

Reading Business Documents

A new component to the GED examination, reading business documents, requires logical thinking. The types of documents you will find on the examination are business memorandums, company and college handbooks and policies, E-mail messages, letters of recommendation, and so on.

First read the document presented. Then determine the main purpose of the document. Note the topic sentences and the organization of each paragraph. Sometimes you will be asked to determine inferences or meanings that are not directly stated in the text. Because these are everyday types of documents, the language is fairly simple and straightforward. Nonetheless, pay close attention to the details referred to in the questions.

Review the basic reading skills presented at the beginning of this chapter for more practice of the skills involved.

Glossary of Literary Terms

This list includes words used frequently in discussing literature.

ACCENT   emphasis given to a syllable or to syllables of a word; used primarily with reference to poetry and also used for the mark (') that shows this emphasis

ALLITERATION   repetition of the same consonant sound at the beginning of two or more words in close proximity ("The fair *b*reeze *b*lew, the white *f*oam *f*lew…")

ALLUSION   offhand reference to a famous figure or event in literature or history ("He opened a Pandora's box.")

AUTOBIOGRAPHY   story of a person's life written by him- or herself (Franklin's *Autobiography*)

BALLAD   verse form that presents in simple story form a single dramatic or exciting episode and stresses such feelings as love, courage, patriotism, and loyalty ("Sir Patrick Spens")

BIOGRAPHY story of a person's life written by someone else (Boswell's *Life of Johnson*)

CLIMAX high point in the telling of a story, be it in fictional, poetic, or dramatic form (the appearance of Banquo's ghost in *Macbeth*)

COMEDY light form of drama that aims to amuse and/or instruct us and that ends happily (*All's Well That Ends Well*)

DIALOGUE conversation between people in a play

ELEGY lyric poem expressing a poet's ideas concerning death (Gray's "Elegy Written in a Country Churchyard")

EPIC long poem that tells a story about noble people and their adventures centering around one character who is the hero

EPITHET word, such as an adjective, or phrase that effectively identifies a significant quality of the noun it describes (Alexander the *Great*)

ESSAY prose writing that can be recognized by its treatment of any topic, no matter how unimportant, and by its approach— *formal* (containing an analysis with a moral) or *informal* (revealing the personality of the author through his or her humor, bias, and style)

FIGURE OF SPEECH expression used to appeal to the reader's emotions and imagination by presenting words in unusual meaning or context ("My love's like a red, red rose...")

FOOT certain number of syllables making up a unit in a verse of poetry

IMAGE figure of speech, especially a simile or a metaphor

INVERSION reversal of the normal order of words in a sentence ("A king of men am I.")

IRONY figure of speech in which the writer or speaker uses words meaning the exact opposite of what he really thinks (In *Julius Caesar*, Antony attacks Brutus with the words, "Brutus is an honorable man.")

LIMERICK jingle in verse containing five lines, with lines 1, 2, and 5 rhyming and lines 3 and 4 rhyming

LYRIC short poem expressing deep emotion in highly melodic and imaginative verse ("The Daffodils")

METAPHOR figure of speech that compares two things, or a person and a thing, by using a quality of one applied to the other. *Like* or *as* is omitted. ("All the world's a stage.")

METER rhythm patterns in verse

MYTH story of unknown origin, religious in character, that tries to interpret the natural world, usually in terms of supernatural events (the story of Atlas)

NARRATIVE story of events or experiences, true or fictitious. A poem may be narrative, as "The Rime of the Ancient Mariner."

NOVEL lengthy prose story dealing with imaginary characters and settings that creates the illusion of real life (Scott's *Ivanhoe*)

ODE lyric poem of particularly serious purpose written in language that is dignified and inspired (Keats' "Ode on a Grecian Urn")

ONOMATOPOEIA use of words whose sounds resemble and/or suggest their meanings (*buzz*, *hiss*)

PARADOX statement that seems contradictory, but that may, in fact, be true (In *The Pirates of Penzance*, the hero had only five birthdays although he was 21 years old. He was born on February 29th of a leap year!)

PARODY writing that pokes fun at a serious work by using exaggeration or broad humor in imitation of the serious work

PERSONIFICATION figure of speech wherein an idea or a thing is given human qualities ("Death, be not proud...")

POEM literature that has any or all of the following qualities to a high degree: deep emotion; highly imaginative language with figures of speech; distinctive rhythm; compression of thought; use of the familiar in a symbolic sense; rhyme scheme; words that mean more than they apparently say

REFRAIN word or group of words repeated regularly in a poem, usually at the end of a stanza (*nevermore* in "The Raven")

REPETITION restating of a phrase or line for emphasis
("And miles to go before I sleep
And miles to go before I sleep.")

RHYME in poetry, agreement in the final sounds of two or more words at the ends of lines (*June, moon*)

RHYTHM in poetry and certain kinds of prose, patterns of stress or accent in the units that make up the verse or sentence.

SARCASM figure of speech that is harsh in tone and expresses meaning by use of the opposite ("Excellent" said when a mistake is made.)

SATIRE work that makes fun of a person, an idea, or a social custom or institution by stressing its foolishness or lack of reasonableness (Swift's *Gulliver's Travels*)

SHORT STORY short prose narrative dealing with imaginary characters usually in a single setting, often relating a single incident, and striving for a single effect (Poe's "The Pit and the Pendulum")

SIMILE figure of speech in which two things essentially unlike are compared, with *like* or *as* being used to make the comparison ("...a poem lovely as a tree")

SOLILOQUY speech of a character in a play, uttered when alone on the stage, in which the speaker informs the audience of his or her thoughts or of knowledge the audience needs to follow the action of the play. (Hamlet's "To be or not to be...")

SONNET form of poetry consisting of fourteen verses in which two aspects of an idea are presented

In the *Italian* or *Petrarchan sonnet*, the first aspect of the idea or theme is presented in the first eight lines, which rhyme *a b b a a b b a*; the second aspect of the idea or commentary on the theme is presented in the second six lines, which rhyme (in various combinations) *c d e c d e*. The first eight lines are the *octet*; the second six lines the *sestet*.

In the *Shakespearean sonnet*, the first aspect is presented in the first twelve lines, which rhyme *a b a b c d c d e f e f*; the second aspect is presented in the last two lines, which rhyme *g g*.

STANZA unit in a poem, similar to a paragraph in prose writing, usually consisting of four or more lines

SYMBOL object that represents an idea, either psychological, philosophical, social, or religious (The cross represents Christianity; the Star of David is the symbol of Judaism.)

TRAGEDY form of drama that has any or all of the following qualities: conflict of character that ends unhappily; a person of great and noble character who meets with a sudden fall because of his or her own weakness; a theme that appeals to our emotions of pity and fear (*Othello*)

VERSE single line of poetry

Language Arts and Reading Practice

The Language Arts and Reading Practice test consists of excerpts from pre-1920 literature, 1920–1960 literature, and literature after 1960, as well as poetry, drama, commentary on the arts, and business documents. Each excerpt is followed by multiple-choice questions about the reading material. Read each excerpt first and then answer the questions following it. Refer to the reading material as often as necessary to answer the questions.

Each excerpt is preceded by a "purpose question," which gives a reason for reading the material. Use these purpose questions to help focus your reading. You are not required to answer these purpose questions. They are given only to help you concentrate on the main idea presented in a particular selection.

Literature (Prose, Poetry, and Drama)

Questions 1–5 refer to the following selection.

WHAT DO WE LEARN ABOUT SWANS?

On Lake Budi some years ago, they were hunting down the swans without mercy. The procedure was to approach them stealthily in little boats and then rapidly—very rapidly—row into their midst. Swans have difficulty in flying; they must skim the surface of the water at a run. In the first phase of their flight they raise their big wings with great effort. It is then that they can be seized; a few blows with a bludgeon finish them off.

Someone made me a present of a swan: more dead than alive. It was of a marvelous species I have never seen anywhere else in the world: a black-throated swan—a snow boat with a neck packed, as it were, into a tight stocking of black silk. Orange-beaked, red-eyed.

They brought it to me half-dead. I bathed its wounds and pressed little pellets of bread and fish into its throat; but nothing stayed down. Nevertheless the wounds slowly healed, and the swan came to regard me as a friend. At the same time, it was apparent to me that the bird was wasting away with nostalgia. So, cradling the heavy burden in my arms through the streets, I carried it to the river. It paddled a few strokes, very close to me. I had hoped it might learn how to fish for itself, and pointed to some pebbles far below, where they flashed in the sand like silvery fish. The swan looked at them remotely, sad-eyed.

For the next 20 days I carried the bird to the river and toiled back with it to my house. One afternoon it seemed more abstracted than usual, swimming very close and ignoring the lure of insects with which I tried vainly to tempt it to fish again. It became very quiet; so I lifted it into my arms to carry it home again. It was breast high, when I suddenly felt a great ribbon unfurl, like a black arm encircling my face: it was the big coil of the neck, dropping down.

It was then that I learned swans do not sing at their death, if they die of grief.

—Pablo Neruda

1. The swan's wounds healed in spite of its lack of

   (1) courage
   (2) nourishment
   (3) intelligence
   (4) shelter
   (5) companionship

2. The narrator implies that the swan's feeling toward him was one of

   (1) apprehension
   (2) trust
   (3) indifference
   (4) compassion
   (5) skepticism

3. The narrator realized that the swan was

   (1) eager to recover its strength
   (2) suspicious of human contact
   (3) angry at its imprisonment
   (4) homesick for its former life
   (5) devoid of feeling

4. What was the swan's reaction to the narrator's attempts to teach it to fish?

   (1) fear
   (2) antagonism
   (3) apathy
   (4) stubbornness
   (5) eagerness

5. According to the narrator, the swan songs of legends do not apply to death caused by

   (1) bludgeoning
   (2) starvation
   (3) heartbreak
   (4) neglect
   (5) exposure

Questions 6–10 refer to the following selection.

WHAT WAS A PARTY GIVEN BY CHINESE WOMEN LIKE?

My idea was to have a gathering of four women, one for each corner of my mah-jongg table. I knew which women I wanted to ask. They were all young like me, with wishful faces. One was an army officer's wife like myself. Another was a girl with very fine manners from a rich family in Shanghai. She had escaped with only a little money. And there was a girl from Nanking who had the blackest hair I had ever seen. She came from a low-class family, but she was pretty and pleasant and had married well, to an old man who died and left her with a better life.

Each week one of us would host a party to raise money and to raise our spirits. The hostess had to serve special *dyansyin* foods to bring good fortune of all kinds— dumplings shaped like silver money ingots, long rice noodles for long life, boiled peanuts for conceiving sons, and of course, many good luck oranges for a plentiful, sweet life.

What fine food we treated ourselves to with our meager allowances! We didn't notice that the dumplings were stuffed mostly with stringy squash and that the oranges were spotted with wormy holes. We ate sparingly, not as if we didn't have enough, but to protest how we could not eat another bite, we had already bloated ourselves from earlier in the day. We knew we had luxuries few people could afford. We were the lucky ones.

6. From the passage, we can conclude that the narrator is

   (1) a young army officer's wife
   (2) a rich girl from Shanghai
   (3) a low-class widow
   (4) a black-haired girl from Nanking
   (5) a girl with fine manners

7. The food incorrectly matched with its happy good fortune is

    (1) noodles—long life
    (2) peanuts—male children
    (3) dumplings—sweet life
    (4) oranges—abundant life
    (5) *dyansyin* foods—good fortune

8. It can be concluded from the passage that the four women

    (1) came from low-class families
    (2) were well off
    (3) were lonely
    (4) were married
    (5) were depressed

9. The approach of the group toward food was that of

    (1) indifference
    (2) resignation
    (3) disinterest
    (4) disgust
    (5) self-deception

10. That these were hard times in China is indicated by all of the following EXCEPT

    (1) they had little money
    (2) they were depressed
    (3) they had meager allowances
    (4) they ate sparingly
    (5) they had fine food

Questions 11–15 refer to the following selection.

WHAT ARE SOME OF THE EFFECTS OF THE HOLOCAUST?

She walked along the river until a policeman stopped her. It was one o'clock, he said. Not the best time to be walking alone by the side of a half-frozen river. He smiled at her, then offered to walk her home. It was the first day of the new year, 1946, eight and a half months after the British tanks had rumbled into Bergen-Belsen.

That February, my mother turned twenty-six. It was difficult for strangers to believe that she had ever been a concentration camp inmate. Her face was smooth and round. She wore lipstick and applied mascara to her large dark eyes. She dressed fashionably. But when she looked into the mirror in the mornings before leaving for work, my mother saw a shell, a mannequin who moved and spoke but who bore only a superficial resemblance to her real self. The people closest to her had vanished. She had no proof that they were truly dead. No eyewitnesses had survived to vouch for her husband's death. There was no one living who had seen her parents die. The lack of confirmation haunted her. At night before she went to sleep and during the day as she stood pinning dresses she wondered if, by some chance, her parents had gotten past the Germans or had crawled out of the mass grave into which they had been shot and were living, old and helpless, somewhere in Poland. What if only one of them had died? What if they had survived and had died of cold or hunger after she had been liberated, while she was in Celle dancing with British officers?

She did not talk to anyone about these things. No one, she thought, wanted to hear them. She woke up in the mornings, went to work, bought groceries, went to the Jewish Community Center and to the housing office like a robot.

11. The policeman stopped the author's mother from walking along the river because

    (1) the river was dangerous
    (2) it was the wrong time of day
    (3) it was still wartime
    (4) it was too cold
    (5) it was forbidden to do so

12. The author states that her mother thought about her parents when she

    (1) walked along the river
    (2) thought about death
    (3) danced with the officers
    (4) was at work
    (5) looked into the mirror

13. When the author mentions her mother's dancing with British officers, she implies that her mother

    (1) compared her dancing to the suffering of her parents
    (2) had clearly put her troubles behind her
    (3) felt it was her duty to dance with the officers
    (4) felt guilty about dancing
    (5) wanted to escape from her past

14. The mother did not discuss her concerns about her loved ones with anyone because she

    (1) thought no one was interested
    (2) felt it was no one's business
    (3) was too shy
    (4) did not know anyone
    (5) didn't want to hurt anyone

15. The author's purpose in writing this selection is most likely to

    (1) inform people about atrocities in the concentration camp
    (2) explain the long-range effects of a traumatic emotional experience
    (3) enlist active participation in refugee affairs
    (4) encourage people to prosecute former concentration camp guards
    (5) gain sympathy from her readers

Questions 16–20 refer to the following selection.

HOW HAVE HUMAN BEINGS CORRUPTED THEIR ENVIRONMENT?

I turned on my back and floated, looking up at the sky, nothing around me but cool clear Pacific, nothing in my eyes but long blue
(5) space. It was as close as I ever got to cleanliness and freedom, as far as I ever got from all the people. They had jerrybuilt the beaches from San Diego to the Golden Gate, bulldozed
(10) superhighways through the mountains, cut down a thousand years of redwood growth, and built an urban wilderness in the desert. They couldn't touch the ocean. They
(15) poured their sewage into it, but it couldn't be tainted.

There was nothing wrong with Southern California that a rise in the ocean level wouldn't cure. The sky
(20) was flat and empty, and the water was chilling me. I swam to the kelp-bed and plunged down through it. It was cold and clammy like the bowels of fear. I came up gasping and
(25) sprinted to shore with a barracuda terror nipping at my heels.

I was still chilly a half-hour later, crossing the pass to Nopal Valley. Even at its summit, the highway was
(30) wide and new, rebuilt with somebody's money. I could smell the source of the money when I slid down into the valley on the other side. It stank like rotten eggs.
(35) The oil wells from which the sulphur gas rose crowded the slopes on both sides of the town. I could see them from the highway as I drove in: the latticed triangles of the derricks where
(40) trees had grown, the oil-pumps nodding and clanking where cattle had grazed. Since 'thirty-nine or 'forty, when I had seen it last, the town had grown enormously, like a tumor.

16. In the first paragraph, the ocean is a symbol of nature's

    (1) inability to adapt
    (2) resistance to humanity's endeavors
    (3) submission to a mechanized society
    (4) attack on technology
    (5) constant change

17. What are the dominant images in lines 19–23?

    (1) light and dark
    (2) cold and heat
    (3) terror and fear
    (4) death and defeat
    (5) ugliness and hopelessness

18. In this passage, the narrator apparently is trying to

    (1) appeal to legislators for environmental action
    (2) inform readers of what Southern California looks like
    (3) indicate his disapproval of what has been done
    (4) show the potential beauty of the area
    (5) celebrate human progress

19. In the last paragraph, the main idea is developed through the use of

    (1) cause and effect
    (2) contrast
    (3) analogy
    (4) incident
    (5) comparison

20. In the last paragraph, the narrator feels that the growth of the town is

    (1) detrimental
    (2) inevitable
    (3) progressive
    (4) hasty
    (5) necessary ·

Questions 21–25 refer to the following selection.

HOW DOES THE HAWK'S JOYOUS CRY AFFECT THE WRITER?

 I saw him look that last look away beyond me into the sky so full of light that I could not follow his gaze. The little breeze flowed over me

(5) again, and nearby a mountain aspen shook all its tiny leaves. I suppose I must have had an idea then of what I was going to do, but I never let it come up into consciousness. I just
(10) reached over and laid the hawk on the grass.

 He lay there a long minute without hope, unmoving, his eyes still fixed on that blue vault above him. It must
(15) have been that he was already so far away in heart that he never felt the release from my hand. He never even stood. He just lay with his breast against the grass.

(20) In the next second after the long minute he was gone. Like a flicker of light, the head vanished with my eyes full on him, but without actually seeing even a premonitory wing beat.
(25) He was gone straight into that towering emptiness of light and crystal that my eyes could scarcely bear to penetrate. For another long moment there was silence. I could
(30) not see him. The light was too intense. Then from far up somewhere a cry came ringing down.

 I was young then and had seen little of the world, but when I heard
(35) that cry my heart turned over. It was not a cry of the hawk I had captured; for, by shifting my position against the sun, I was now seeing further up. Straight out of the sun's
(40) eye where she must have been soaring restlessly above us for untold hours hurtled his mate. And from far up, ringing from peak to peak of the summits over us, came a cry of such
(45) unutterable and ecstatic joy that it sounds down across the years and tingles among the cups of my quiet breakfast table.

21. In line 1, "that last look" suggests that the hawk

    (1) has been blinded
    (2) expects to be rescued
    (3) believes that his death is near
    (4) cannot understand what is happening
    (5) is looking for sympathy

22. In line 8, the clause "I never let it come up into consciousness" suggests that the freeing of the hawk is

    (1) premeditated
    (2) impulsive
    (3) impossible
    (4) accidental
    (5) an afterthought

23. In line 12, the minute is "long" to the narrator because he

    (1) is thinking of changing his mind
    (2) is young and inexperienced
    (3) regrets the action he is taking
    (4) is not sure what the hawk will do
    (5) is impatient

24. In this selection, the natural phenomenon the narrator seems most impressed by is the

    (1) deathlike silence
    (2) intense light
    (3) steady breeze
    (4) blue sky
    (5) quaking aspen

25. The narrator's most lasting memory is of the

    (1) hawk's eyes
    (2) bright light
    (3) complete stillness
    (4) joyous call of the hawk
    (5) beauty of the soaring hawk

Questions 26–30 refer to the following selection.

WHAT DANGEROUS MISTAKE WAS NEARLY MADE?

I was vainly trying to go to sleep that evening when I became aware of unfamiliar sounds. Sitting bolt upright, I listened intently.

(5) The sounds were coming from just across the river, and they were a weird medley of whines, whimpers and small howls. My grip on the rifle slowly relaxed. If there is one thing at which
(10) scientists are adept, it is learning from experience; I was not to be fooled twice. The cries were obviously those of a husky, probably a young one, and I deduced that it must be one of Mike's
(15) dogs (he owned three half-grown pups not yet trained to harness, which ran loose after the team) that had got lost, retraced its way to the cabin, and was now begging for someone to come and
(20) be nice to it.

I was delighted. If that pup needed a friend, a chum, I was its man! I climbed hastily into my clothes, ran down to the riverbank, launched the
(25) canoe, and paddled lustily for the far bank.

The pup had never ceased its mournful plaint, and I was about to call out reassuringly when it occurred
(30) to me that an unfamiliar human voice might frighten it. I decided to stalk it instead, and to betray my presence only when I was close enough for soothing murmurs.

(35) I had assumed the dog was only a few yards away from the far bank, but as I made my way over boulders and gravel ridges, the sounds seemed to remain at the same volume while I
(40) appeared to be getting no closer. I assumed the pup was retreating, perhaps out of shyness. In my anxiety not to startle it away, I kept quiet, even when the whimpering stopped,
(45) leaving me uncertain about the direction to pursue. However, I saw a steep ridge looming ahead of me and I suspected that, once I gained its summit, I would have a clear enough
(50) view to enable me to locate the lost animal. I got down on my stomach (practicing the fieldcraft I had learned in the Boy Scouts) and cautiously inched my way the last few feet.

(55) My head came slowly over the crest — and there was my quarry. He was lying down, evidently resting after his mournful singsong, and his nose was about six feet from mine. We stared at
(60) one another in silence. I do not know what went on in his massive skull, but my head was full of the most disturbing thoughts. I was peering straight into the amber gaze of a fully
(65) grown arctic wolf, who probably weighed more than I did, and who was certainly a lot better versed in close-combat techniques than I would ever be.

—Farley Mowat

26. What made the sounds so unusual?

    (1) They were very loud.
    (2) They were a strange mixture.
    (3) They were inhuman.
    (4) They were coming from across water.
    (5) They were persistent.

27. The expression "not to be fooled twice" (lines 11–12) implies that the

    (1) narrator was annoyed by a previous mistake
    (2) sounds were made by an echo
    (3) sounds were a trick
    (4) narrator had dealt with canines before
    (5) narrator was stubborn

28. The inference in the second paragraph is that Mike is

    (1) a forest ranger
    (2) a hunter
    (3) a dogsled owner
    (4) a child
    (5) a wildlife biologist

29. What do lines 22 and 23 suggest about the narrator?

    (1) He is an animal lover.
    (2) He is a clever man.
    (3) He is an excellent athlete.
    (4) He is a nervous individual.
    (5) He is restless.

30. What caused the narrator to lose track of the pup?

    (1) the terrain
    (2) the darkness
    (3) the silence
    (4) the distance
    (5) the lack of experience

Questions 31–35 refer to the following selection.

HOW CAN YOU IDENTIFY TWO TYPES OF PEOPLE—A AND Z?

There are only two types of people in the world. Type A and Type Z. It isn't hard to tell which type you are.

(5) How long before the plane leaves do you arrive at the airport? Early plane catchers, Type A, pack their bags at least a day in advance, and they pack neatly. If they're booked on a flight that leaves at four in the afternoon,
(10) they get up at five-thirty that morning. If they haven't left the house by noon, they're worried about missing the plane.

Late plane catchers, Type Z, pack
(15) hastily at the last minute and arrive at the airport too late to buy a newspaper.

What do you do with a new book? Type A reads more carefully and finishes every book, even though it
(20) isn't any good.

Type Z skims through a lot of books and is more apt to write in the margins with a pencil.

Type A eats a good breakfast. Type Z
(25) grabs a cup of coffee.

Type A's turn off the lights when leaving a room and lock the doors when leaving a house. They go back and make sure they've locked it, and they
(30) worry later about whether they left the iron on or not. The didn't.

Type Z's leave the lights burning and, if they lock the door at all when they leave the house, they're apt to
(35) have forgotten the keys.

Type A sees the dentist twice a year, has an annual physical checkup, and thinks he may have something. Type Z has been meaning to see a doctor.

(40) Type A squeezes a tube of toothpaste from the bottom and rolls it very carefully as he uses it, and puts the top back on every time.

Type Z squeezes the tube from the
(45) middle, and he's lost the cap under the radiator.

Type Z's are more apt to have some Type A characteristics then Type A's are apt to have any Type Z characteristics.

(50)   Type A's always marry Type Z's.
Type Z's always marry Type A's.

31. Type A is all of the following EXCEPT

(1) neat
(2) prompt
(3) hasty
(4) early
(5) worried

32. Type Z is all of the following EXCEPT

(1) late
(2) careful
(3) clumsy
(4) prompt
(5) foregetful

33. The author uses all of the following situations to differentiate Type A from Type Z EXCEPT

(1) catching a plane
(2) getting enough sleep
(3) reading a book
(4) getting a physical checkup
(5) leaving a house

34. It can be concluded from the passage that

(1) Type A and Type Z never change their habits
(2) Type A becomes more like Type Z
(3) Type A and Type Z are hardly distinguishable
(4) Type A is superior to Type Z
(5) Type A is more likely to copy Type Z

35. It can be concluded from the passage that

(1) Type A and Type Z are more alike than different
(2) the two types like each other
(3) to two are complete opposites
(4) the two types compete with each other
(5) the two types resemble each other

Questions 36–40 refer to the following selection.

WHAT ARE THE POET'S THOUGHTS ABOUT LIFE?

Alone

Lying, thinking
Last night
How to find my soul a home
Where water is not thirsty
(5)   And bread loaf is not stone
I came up with one thing
And I don't believe I'm wrong
That nobody,
But nobody
(10)   Can make it out here alone.

Alone, all alone
Nobody, but nobody
Can make it out here alone.

There are some millionaires
(15)   With money they can't use
Their wives run round like banshees
Their children sing the blues
They've got expensive doctors
To cure their hearts of stone.
(20)   But nobody
No nobody
Can make it out here alone.

Alone, all alone
Nobody, but nobody
(25)   Can make it out here alone.

Now if you listen closely
I'll tell you what I know
Storm clouds are gathering
The wind is gonna blow
(30)   The race of man is suffering
And I can hear the moan,

Cause nobody,
But nobody
Can make it out here alone.

(35)   Alone, all alone
Nobody, but nobody
Can make it out here alone.
—Maya Angelou

36. The main idea of the poem is that

    (1) a soul needs a home
    (2) a person needs bread and water
    (3) any individual can achieve success
    (4) people need people
    (5) no one need be lonely

37. The poet comes to her conclusion out of her

    (1) bitter experience
    (2) thoughts
    (3) need for recognition
    (4) envy of others
    (5) fear of loneliness

38. The poet's idea of some wealthy persons is that

    (1) they spend money wastefully
    (2) their families live well
    (3) they are unfeeling
    (4) they are well adjusted
    (5) they have physical ailments

39. The poet mentions "storm clouds" and "the wind" because

    (1) she foresees conflict
    (2) some people are wealthy
    (3) people are impatient
    (4) the future is uncertain
    (5) nature is unfriendly

40. The poem derives its power from effective use of

    (1) metaphor
    (2) rhyme
    (3) rhythm
    (4) repetition
    (5) irony

Questions 41–45 refer to the following selection.

**WHAT IS THE POET
DETERMINED TO DO?**

I've come this far to freedom and I
  won't turn back.
I'm climbing to the highway from my
old dirt track.
    I'm coming and I'm going
    And I'm stretching and I'm growing
And I'll reap what I've been sowing or
  my skin's not black.
I've prayed and slaved and waited and
  I've sung my song.

You've bled me and you've starved me
  but I've still grown strong,
    You've lashed me and you've treed
    me
    You've everything but freed me
But in time you'll know you need me
  and it won't be long.
I've seen the daylight breaking high
  above the bough.
I've found my destination and I've
  made my vow;
    So whether you abhor me
    Or deride me or ignore me
Mighty mountains loom before me and
  I won't stop now.

                          —Naomi Long Madgett

41. The poem is a poem of

    (1) praise
    (2) regret
    (3) resignation
    (4) determination
    (5) submission

42. The "destination" is

    (1) freedom
    (2) the highway
    (3) the old dirt track
    (4) the daylight
    (5) mighty mountains

43. The poet has done all of the following EXCEPT

    (1) reaped
    (2) prayed
    (3) slaved
    (4) waited
    (5) sowed

44. The poet will reach her goal because she

    (1) has stretched
    (2) has grown
    (3) will be needed
    (4) is abhorred
    (5) has been beaten

45. The rhyme scheme of the poem in each stanza is

    (1) abbaa
    (2) abbba
    (3) aabba
    (4) ababa
    (5) aaabb

Questions 46–50 refer to the following passage from a work of literature.

WHAT WAS A DAUGHTER'S HERITAGE FROM HER MOTHER?

...(M)y mother adorned with flowers whatever shabby house we were forced to live in. And not just your typical straggly country stand of zinnias, either. She planted ambitious gardens—and still does—with over fifty different varieties of plants that bloom profusely from early March until late November. Before she left home for the fields, she watered her flowers, chopped up the grass, and laid out new beds. When she returned from the fields she might divide clumps of bulbs, dig a cold pit, uproot and replant roses, or prune branches from her taller bushes or trees—until night came and it was too dark to see.

Whatever she planted grew as if by magic, and her fame as a grower of flowers spread over three counties. Because of her creativity with her flowers, even my memories of poverty are seen through a screen of blooms—sunflowers, petunias, roses, dahlias, forsythia, spirea, delphiniums, verbena...and on and on.

And I remember people coming to my mother's yard to be given cuttings from her flowers; I hear again the praise showered on her because whatever rocky soil she landed on, she turned into a garden. A garden so brilliant with colors, so original in its design, so magnificent with life and creativity, that to this day people drive by our house in Georgia—perfect strangers and imperfect strangers—and ask to stand or walk among my mother's art...

Her face, as she prepares the Art that is her gift, is a legacy of respect she leaves to me, for all that illuminates and cherishes life. She handed down respect for the possibilities—and the will to grasp them.

For her, so hindered and intruded upon in so many ways, being an artist has still be a daily part of her life. This ability to hold on, even in very simple ways, is work Black women have done for a very long time.

Guided by my heritage of a love of beauty and a respect for strength—in search of my mother's garden, I found my own.

46. The author's mother demonstrated her creativity by

   (1) working in the fields
   (2) chopping grass
   (3) dividing bulbs
   (4) digging a cold pit
   (5) growing flowers

47. Her garden is described as

   (1) straggly
   (2) ambitious
   (3) an evidence of poverty
   (4) magical
   (5) specializing in zinnias

48. Evidence of her mother's hardship is

   (1) varieties of plants
   (2) a screen of blooms
   (3) her famous garden
   (4) her shabby house
   (5) her garden design

49. In enduring hardships, the author's mother

   (1) was carrying on a tradition
   (2) remembered poverty
   (3) limited her originality
   (4) gave in to her poverty
   (5) was pessimistic about the future

50. The author's heritage from her mother included all of the following EXCEPT

   (1) love of beauty
   (2) respect for strength
   (3) respect for life
   (4) respect for possibilities
   (5) regret for being hindered and intruded upon

Questions 51–55 refer to the following passage from a play.

ABOUT WHAT WAS THE AUTHOR EXCITED?

That one, Platero, was in the shape of a watch. You opened the small silver box and it appeared, pressed against the cloth filled with purple ink like a bird in its nest. How exciting when, after pressing it a minute against the fine white and rose of my hand, there appeared the stamp

FRANCISCO RUIZ
MOGUER

How often I dreamed of that stamp belonging to my friend at Don Carlos' school! With a little printing press which I found upstairs in the old office writing desk in my house, I tried to assemble one with my name. But it did not come out well. . .

One day a salesman for office equipment came to my house with Arias, the silversmith from Seville. What a delightful array of rulers, compasses, colored inks, stamps. They were all shapes and sizes. I broke my money bank and with the five pesetas I found, ordered a stamp with my name and town. What a long week that was! How my heart would beat when the mail coach arrived! What a sweat I was in and how sad, when the mailman moved away in the rain! Finally one night he brought it to me. . . When one pressed on a spring, the stamp appeared, new and resplendent.

Was there anything in the whole house which went unstamped? What was there which did not belong to me that day? . . . The next day with what happy haste I took everything to school: my books, shirt, hat, boots and hands marked with the words

JUAN RAMON JIMENEZ
MOGUER

51. The name of the author is

(1) Francisco Ruiz
(2) Don Carlos
(3) Arias
(4) Platero
(5) Juan Ramon Jimenez

52. The author got the idea for his rubber stamp from

(1) Francisco Ruiz
(2) Don Carlos
(3) Arias
(4) Platero
(5) Juan Ramon Jimenez

53. The author addresses his story of the rubber stamp to

(1) Francisco Ruiz
(2) Don Carlos
(3) Arias
(4) Platero
(5) Juan Ramon Jimenez

54. The author got the money to pay for the stamp from

(1) Don Carlos' school
(2) Arias, the silversmith
(3) his friend Francisco Ruiz
(4) his old office writing desk
(5) his money bank

55. We know that the author lives in Spain because of

(1) the small silver box
(2) the little printing press
(3) the name of the coins of money
(4) the mail coach
(5) the salesman of office equipment

Questions 56–60 refer to the following selection.

HOW DID RIP VAN WINKLE SEEK COMFORT?

Rip Van Winkle was one of those happy mortals, of foolish, well-oiled dispositions, who take the world easy, eat white bread or brown, which ever can be got with least thought or trouble, and would rather starve on a penny than work for a pound. If left to himself, he would have whistled life away, in perfect contentment; but his wife kept continually dinning in his ears about his idleness, his carelessness, and the ruin he was bringing on his family. Morning, noon, and night, her tongue was incessantly going, and everything he said or did was sure to produce a torrent of household eloquence. Rip had but one way of replying to all lectures of the kind, and that, by frequent use, had grown into a habit. He shrugged his shoulders, shook his head, cast up his eyes, but said nothing. This, however, always provoked a fresh volley from his wife, so that he was fain to draw off his forces, and take to the outside of the house—the only side which, in truth, belongs to a henpecked husband.

Rip's sole domestic adherent was his dog Wolf, who was as much henpecked as his master; for Dame Van Winkle regarded them as companions in idleness, and even looked upon Wolf with an evil eye as the cause of his master's going so often astray....

...For a long while he used to console himself, when driven from home, by frequenting a kind of perpetual club of the sages, philosophers, and other idle personages of the village, which held its sessions on a bench before a small inn, designated by a rubicund portrait of His Majesty George the Third. Here they used to sit in the shade through a long, lazy summer's day, talking listlessly over village gossip, or telling endless, sleepy stories about nothing....How solemnly they would listen to...Derrick Van Brummel, the schoolmaster.

—Washington Irving

56. The story takes place about

    (1) 1660
    (2) 1770
    (3) 1800
    (4) 1812
    (5) 1848

57. An example of the author's sense of humor may be found in sentences

    (1) 2
    (2) 3
    (3) 4
    (4) 5
    (5) 6

58. The blame for Rip's conduct was placed by Dame Van Winkle on

    (1) Wolf
    (2) George the Third
    (3) Derrick Van Brummel
    (4) the club of sages
    (5) other idle villagers

59. Rip may be described by *all* of the following adjectives EXCEPT

    (1) henpecked
    (2) easygoing
    (3) happy
    (4) complaining
    (5) resigned

60. Rip's only problem was his

    (1) poverty
    (2) idleness
    (3) wife's nagging
    (4) wife's evil eye
    (5) village companions

Questions 61–65 refer to the following selection.

WHY DID THE AUTHOR GO TO THE WOODS?

I went to the woods because I wished to live deliberately, to front only the essential facts of life, and see if I could not learn what it had to teach, and not, when I came to die, discover that I had not lived. I did not wish to live what was not life, living is so dear; nor did I wish to practise resignation, unless it was quite necessary. I wanted to live deep and suck out all the marrow of life, to live so sturdily and Spartan-like as to put to rout all that was not life, to cut a broad swath and shave close, to drive life into a corner, and reduce it to its lowest terms, and, if it proved to be mean, why then to get the whole and genuine meanness of it, and publish its meanness to the world; or if it were sublime, to know it by experience, and be able to give a true account of it in my next excursion. For most men, it appears to me, are in a strange uncertainty about it, whether it is of the devil or of God, and have *somewhat hastily* concluded that it is the chief end of man here to 'glorify God and enjoy him forever.'

Still we live meanly, like ants; though the fable tells us that we were long ago changed into men; like pygmies we fight with cranes; it is error upon error, and clout upon clout, and our best virtue has for its occasion a superfluous and evitable wretchedness. Our life is frittered away by detail. An honest man has hardly need to count more than his ten fingers, or in extreme cases he may add his ten toes, and lump the rest. Simplicity, simplicity, simplicity! I say, let your affairs be as two or three, and not a hundred or a thousand; instead of a million count half a dozen, and keep your accounts on your thumb-nail.

—Henry D. Thoreau

61. The best statement of why the author went to the woods is that he went to

    (1) discover that he had not lived
    (2) live meanly, like ants
    (3) practice resignation
    (4) reduce life to its simplest terms
    (5) glorify God

62. The author thinks that life should be *all* of the following EXCEPT

    (1) Spartan-like
    (2) complicated
    (3) creative
    (4) noble
    (5) moral

63. All of the following words as used in this selection are correctly defined EXCEPT

    (1) *deliberately*—unhurriedly
    (2) *front*—confront
    (3) *swath*—space
    (4) *mean*—nasty
    (5) *frittered*—wasted

64. The tone of the selection is

    (1) bitter cynicism
    (2) moral indignation
    (3) flippant humor
    (4) quiet resignation
    (5) self-congratulation

65. The author

    (1) wishes to learn from nature
    (2) is afraid of death
    (3) has little regard for life
    (4) seeks reconciliation with God
    (5) celebrates the human life-style

Questions 66–70 refer to the following selection.

WHY DID THE GIRL CLIMB THE TREE?

There was the huge tree asleep yet in the paling moonlight, and small and hopeful Sylvia began with utmost bravery to mount to the top of it, with
(5) tingling, eager blood coursing the channels of her whole frame, with her bare feet and fingers that pinched and held like bird's claws to the monstrous ladder reaching up, up, almost to the
(10) sky itself. First she must mount the white oak tree that grew alongside, where she was almost lost among the dark branches and the green leaves heavy and wet with dew; a bird
(15) fluttered off its nest, and a red squirrel ran to and fro and scolded pettishly at the harmless housebreaker. Sylvia felt her way easily. She had often climbed there and knew that higher still one of
(20) the oak's upper branches chafed against the pine trunk, just where its lower boughs were set close together. There, when she made the dangerous pass from one tree to the other, the
(25) great enterprise would really begin.

She crept out along the swaying oak limb at last and took the daring step across into the old pine tree. The way was harder than she thought; she must
(30) reach far and hold fast. The sharp dry twigs caught and held her and scratched her like angry talons; the pitch made her thin little fingers clumsy and stiff as she went round and
(35) round the tree's great stem, higher and higher upward. The sparrows and robins in the woods below were beginning to wake and twitter to the dawn, yet it seemed much lighter there
(40) aloft in the pine tree, and the child knew that she must hurry if her project were to be of any use.

The tree seemed to lengthen itself out as she went up and to reach farther
(45) and farther upward. It was like a great mainmast to the voyaging earth; it must truly have been amazed that morning through all its ponderous frame as it felt this determined spark of
(50) human spirit creeping and climbing from higher branch to branch. Who knows how steadily the least twigs held themselves to advantage this light, weak creature on her way! The old pine
(55) must have loved his new dependent. More than all the hawks and bats and moths and even the sweet-voiced thrushes was the brave, beating heart of the solitary gray-eyed child. And the
(60) tree stood still and held away the winds that June morning while the dawn grew bright in the east.

—Sarah Orne Jewett

66. The girl's blood was tingling (line 5) because she was

    (1) cold
    (2) frightened
    (3) excited
    (4) ill
    (5) clumsy

67. Why did Sylvia climb the oak tree?

    (1) to observe the birds
    (2) to get closer to the pine tree
    (3) to get to the ladder
    (4) to chase a squirrel
    (5) to observe the sunset

68. Why was the first part of Sylvia's climb easy for her?

    (1) The branches were close together.
    (2) It was almost daylight.
    (3) There was a ladder nearby.
    (4) She had climbed the tree before.
    (5) She was in good physical shape.

69. In line 45, the tree is compared to

    (1) a giant's hand
    (2) the earth's axis
    (3) a part of a ship
    (4) a space shuttle
    (5) a monument

70. In lines 55 through 63, the pine tree is portrayed as a

    (1) kindly protector
    (2) solitary sentinel
    (3) stern parent
    (4) brave soldier
    (5) human spirit

Questions 71–75 refer to the following selection.

WHAT ARE FEUDS?

"Don't you know what a feud is?"

"Never heard of it before—tell me about it."

"Well," says Buck, "a feud is this way: A man has a quarrel with another man, and kills him; then that other man's brother kills *him*; then the other brothers, on both sides, goes for one another; then the *cousins* chip in—and by and by everybody's killed off, and there ain't no more feud. But it's kind of slow, and takes a long time."

"Has this one been going on long, Buck?"

"Well, I should *reckon*! It started thirty years ago, or some'ers along there. There was trouble 'bout something, and then a lawsuit to settle it; and the suit went agin one of the men, and so he up and shot the man that won the suit—which he would naturally do, of course. Anybody would."

"What was the trouble about, Buck—land?"

"I reckon maybe—I don't know."

"Well, who done the shooting? Was it a Grangerford or a Shepherdson?"

"Laws, how do *I* know? It was so long ago."

"Don't anybody know?"

"Oh, yes, pa knows, I reckon, and some of the other old people: but they don't know

now what the row was about in the first place."...

"Has anybody been killed this year, Buck?"

"Yes; we got one and they got one. 'Bout three months ago my cousin Bud, fourteen year old, was riding through the woods...and sees old Baldy Shepherdson a-linkin' after him with his gun in his hand and his white hair a-flying in the wind;...so at last Bud seen it warn't any use, so he stopped and faced around so as to have the bulletholes in front, you know, and the old man he rode up and shot him down. But he didn't git much chance to enjoy his luck, for inside of a week our folks laid *him* out."

Next Sunday we all went to church, about three mile, everybody a-horseback. The men took their guns along, so did Buck, and kept them between their knees or stood them handy against the wall. The Shepherdsons done the same. It was pretty ornery preaching—all about brotherly love...

—Mark Twain

71. The main purpose of this selection is to

   (1) write humorously of Southern mountainfolk
   (2) tell the story of the Grangerfords and the Shepherdsons
   (3) preach the importance of brotherly love
   (4) extol the courage of the narrator
   (5) satirize feuds

72. All of the following are true of the Grangerford-Shepherdson quarrel EXCEPT that it

   (1) was of long duration
   (2) was started by a Grangerford
   (3) had an unknown cause
   (4) involved courageous people
   (5) involved children as well as adults

73. Buck is

   (1) the author
   (2) a stranger
   (3) a Grangerford
   (4) a Shepherdson
   (5) an impartial observer

74. The church incident is mentioned to

   (1) bring out the importance of brotherly love
   (2) reaffirm the author's faith
   (3) place the blame on neither the Grangerfords nor the Shepherdsons
   (4) point up the hypocrisy of those who attended
   (5) present the author's view on grace and predestination

75. The attitude of Buck toward feuds is

   (1) impartial
   (2) critical
   (3) unquestioning
   (4) regretful
   (5) bitter

Poetry

Questions 76–80 refer to the following poem.

WHAT CAN WE LEARN ABOUT OPPORTUNITY?

Opportunity

This I beheld, or dreamed it in a dream:—
There spread a cloud of dust along a plain;
(5) And underneath the cloud, or in it, raged
A furious battle, and men yelled, and swords
Shocked upon swords and shields. A prince's banner
(10) Wavered, then staggered backward, hemmed by foes.
A craven hung along the battle's edge,
And thought, "Had I a sword of keener
(15) steel—
That blue blade that the king's son bears—but this
Blunt thing!" he snapped and flung it from his hand,
(20) And lowering crept away and left the field.
Then came the king's son, wounded, sore bestead,
And weaponless, and saw the broken
(25) sword,

Hilt-buried in the dry and trodden sand,
And ran and snatched it, and with battle-shout
(30) Lifted afresh he hewed his enemy down,
And saved a great cause that heroic day.
—Edward Roland Sill

76. The main purpose of the poem is to

(1) tell what happened in a dream
(2) relate an act of cowardice
(3) applaud an act of bravery
(4) teach a lesson in conduct
(5) tell an interesting story

77. The most logical words to continue the quotation that begins on line 14 are

(1) "...I could defend myself better."
(2) "...but I cannot have the blue blade."
(3) "...I could safely escape."
(4) "...I could help defeat the enemy."
(5) "...but what good would it do."

78. The word *craven* as used in this poem means a person who is best described as

(1) envious
(2) desirous
(3) cowardly
(4) traitorous
(5) angry

79. Lines 8 and 9 are an example of

(1) personification
(2) irony
(3) metaphor
(4) simile
(5) alliteration

80. The poem derives its power by presenting

(1) a graphic picture of nature
(2) a stark contrast in behavior
(3) a description of battle
(4) an effective use of rhyme
(5) a human tragedy

Questions 81–85 refer to the following poem.

HOW IS GRIEF AT THE LOSS OF A LOVED ONE EXPRESSED?

Stop All the Clocks

Stop all the clocks, cut off the telephone,
Prevent the dog from barking with a juicy bone,
(5) Silence the pianos and with muffled drum
Bring out the coffin, let the mourners come.

Let aeroplanes circle moaning overhead
(10) Scribbling on the sky the message He Is Dead,
Put crepe bows round the white necks of the public doves,
Let the traffic policemen wear black
(15) cotton gloves.

He was my North, my South, my East and West,
My working week, and my Sunday rest,
My noon, my midnight, my talk, my
(20) song:
I thought that love would last for ever: I was wrong.

The stars are not wanted now; put out every one:
(25) Pack up the moon and dismantle the sun;
Pour away the ocean and sweep up the woods;
For nothing now can ever come to any
(30) good.
—W.H. Auden

81. In line 1, the effect of using the one-syllable words *stop* and *cut* is to

(1) conceal the speaker's grief
(2) create an instant picture for the reader
(3) fill the reader with similar suffering
(4) emphasize the shock the speaker has suffered
(5) simplify a complex feeling

82. In line 10, which poetic device is used in the phrase "Scribbling on the sky"?

    (1) onomatopoeia
    (2) pun
    (3) alliteration
    (4) simile
    (5) metaphor

83. Which statement best summarizes the third stanza?

    (1) He was everything to me, but I lost him.
    (2) He was with me everywhere I went.
    (3) He was always talking or singing.
    (4) He was my life, my everything.
    (5) He was place and time for me.

84. In which line(s) does the climax of the poem occur?

    (1) lines 8 and 9
    (2) lines 14 and 15
    (3) lines 19 and 20
    (4) lines 21 and 22
    (5) lines 25 and 26

85. Although the title of the poem is "Stop All the Clocks," the speaker really wants to stop everything that

    (1) records time
    (2) reflects love
    (3) causes grief
    (4) continues life
    (5) makes sounds

Drama

Questions 86–90 refer to this excerpt from a play.

HOW DO MOTHER AND DAUGHTER DIFFER?

DAUGHTER (*gently*): Ma, you worked all your life. Why don't you take it easy?
OLD LADY: I don't want to take it easy. Now that your father's dead and in the grave I don't know what to do with myself.
DAUGHTER: Why don't you go out, sit in the park, get a little sun like the other old women?

OLD LADY: I sit around here sometimes, going crazy. We had a lot of fights in our time, your father and I, but I must admit I miss him badly. You can't live with someone 41 years and not miss him when he's dead. I'm glad that he died, for his own sake—it may sound hard of me to say that—but I am glad. He was in nothing but pain the last few months, and he was a man who could never stand pain. But I do miss him.
DAUGHTER (*gently*): Ma, why don't you come live with George and me?
OLD LADY: No, no, Annie, you're a good daughter.
DAUGHTER: We'll move Tommy into the baby's room, and you can have Tommy's room. It's the nicest room in the apartment. It gets all the sun.
OLD LADY: I have wonderful children. I thank God every night for that. I...
DAUGHTER: Ma, I don't like you living here alone...
OLD LADY: Annie, I been living in this house for eight years, and I know all the neighbors and the store people, and if I lived with you, I'd be a stranger.
DAUGHTER: There's plenty of old people in my neighborhood. You'll make friends.
OLD LADY: Annie, you're a good daughter, but I want to keep my own home. I want to pay my own rent. I don't want to be some old lady living with her children. If I can't take care of myself, I'd just as soon be in the grave with your father. I don't want to be a burden on my children.

86. The daughter's attitude toward the mother is one of

    (1) indifference
    (2) antagonism
    (3) caring
    (4) disrespect
    (5) conciliation

87. The mother's attitude toward the daughter is one of

    (1) antagonism
    (2) disrespect
    (3) indifference
    (4) bitterness
    (5) appreciation

88. The mother wants to

    (1) enjoy her leisure
    (2) forget her past life
    (3) retain her independence
    (4) criticize her children
    (5) forget her husband

89. The mother wants to live alone because

    (1) she wants an easy life
    (2) she doesn't get on well with her children
    (3) she is undecided what to do
    (4) she knows the neighborhood
    (5) she can't take care of herself

90. The daughter offers the mother all of the following EXCEPT

    (1) a sunny room
    (2) a friendly neighborhood
    (3) potential friends of the same age
    (4) independence
    (5) old companions

Commentary on the Arts

Questions 91–95 deal with the following selection on the theater.

WHAT IS THE ROLE OF SETTING IN A PLAY'S SUCCESS?

Rain pounds the cobblestone streets—empty except for a handful of urchins hovering around an enormous and imposing mansion. Then come the sounds of laughter and the clinking of champagne glasses. Cut to a shadowy figure in trench coat and snap-brim hat.

The scene is from a recent Broadway hit. It's not so much *An Inspector Calls* competent 50-year-old script or the solid acting that has excited critics and audiences. It's the remarkably inventive and surprising set designed by Ian MacNeil, who, with director Stephen Daldry, has transformed J. B. Priestly's sometimes preachy whodunit into first-rate theater.

MacNeil attributes the triumph of British set design not to artistic superiority but to the art-comes-first atmosphere of England's state-subsidized theaters. "At home, there aren't producers around who second-guess whether audiences want to pay to see it."

The play's most powerful moment is actually a set change: the fall, quite literally, of the house of the family in the play. Not everybody is happy with the fact that the set, not the play, is the thing. From an actor's point of view, says one cast member, "these sets are disturbing and a hindrance. It's not my particular cup of tea."

91. The review indicates that *An Inspector Calls* is good theater because of its

    (1) script
    (2) acting
    (3) direction
    (4) sound effects
    (5) set

92. *An Inspector Calls* is

    (1) a comedy
    (2) musical theater
    (3) a new play
    (4) a mystery
    (5) an American play

93. J. B. Priestly is the

    (1) author
    (2) director
    (3) set designer
    (4) producer
    (5) featured actor

94. The success of the set design for the play is due to

    (1) artistic superiority
    (2) British producers
    (3) union regulations
    (4) government assistance
    (5) experimentation

95. The reaction of some cast members to the set is

    (1) enthusiastic
    (2) indifferent
    (3) negative
    (4) dismissive
    (5) predictable

Questions 96–100 refer to the following play.

WHY DO POOR PEOPLE MAKE SUCH EXPENSIVE FUNERALS?

SALESMAN: [*Chewing*] I really don't understand...wherever you look, in all the newspapers, you read the most horrible stories about conditions among the weavers, and you get the impression that all the people here are half-starved. And then you see such a funeral! Just as I came into the village, there were brass bands, school-teachers, children, the pastor, and a whole string of people; my God, you'd think the Emperor of China was being buried. If these people can pay for that...! [*He drinks his beer. Then he puts his glass down and suddenly speaks in a friovolous tone.*] Isn't that so, Miss? Don't you agree with me?

[ANNA *smiles, embarassed, and continues busily with her embroidery.*]

SALESMAN: Those must be slippers for Papa.

WELZEL: Oh, I don't like to wear them things.

SALESMAN: Just listen to that! I'd give half my fortune if those slippers were for me.

MRS. WELZEL: He just don't appreciate such things.

WIEGAND: [*After he has coughed several times and moved his chair about, as if he wanted to speak*] The gentleman has expressed himself mighty well about the funeral. Now tell us, young lady, isn't that just a small funeral?

SALESMAN: Yes, I must say...That must cost a tremendous amount of money. Where do these people get the money for it?

WIEGAND: You'll forgive me for sayin' it, sir, there is no such folly among the poorer classes hereabouts. If you don't mind my sayin' so, they have such exagerated ideas of the dutiful respect and the obligations that's due the deceased and the blessed dead. And when it's a matter of deceased parents, they are so superstitious that the descendants and the next of kin scrape together their last penny. And what the children can't raise, they borrow from the nearest moneylender. And then they're in debts up to their necks; they'll be owing His Reverence the Pastor, the sexton, and every-body else in the neighborhood. And drinks and victuals and all the other necessary things. Oh, yes, I approve of respectful duty on the part of children toward their parents, but not so that the mourners are burdened down the rest of their lives by such obligations.

SALESMAN: I beg your pardon, but I should think the pastor would talk them out of it.

WIEGAND: Beggin' your pardon, sir, but there I would like to interpose that every little congregation has its ecclesiastcal

house of worship and must support its reverend pastor. The high clergy get a wonderful revenue and profit from such a big funeral. The more elaborate such a funeral can be arranged, the more profitable is the offeratory that flows from it. Whoever knows the conditions of the workers here-abouts can, with unauthoritative certainty, affirm that the pastors only with reluctance tolerate small and quiet funerals.

96. Which character in the passage seems to see things most clearly?

(1) The salesman
(2) Mrs. Welzel
(3) Welzel
(4) Wiegand
(5) Anna

97. What do the italicized portions in the passage signify?

(1) Directions to the actors
(2) Asides to the actors
(3) Directions to the cameraman
(4) Important parts of the dialogue
(5) Comments by the playwright

98. Why do the townspeople apparently have such elaborate funerals?

(1) They have more money than the public has been led to believe.
(2) They have strong ideas of the respect due to the dead.
(3) They look upon the funerals as holiday occasions.
(4) They wish to impress their neigh-bors.
(5) They wish to defy the advice of their parents.

99. Wiegand's speech about the church suggests that he views it as an insti-tution that is

(1) sympathetic to the weavers' needs
(2) interested only in formal worship
(3) in favor of small and quiet funer-als, rather than large, boisterous ones
(4) organized to do God's work on Earth
(5) interested in making money from the people

100. From this passage, the reader can most safely conclude that Anna is

    (1) Weigand's wife
    (2) Welzel's daughter
    (3) the salesman's friend
    (4) a worker in the weaving mills
    (5) a servant

Questions 101–105 refer to the following passage on film.

WHAT IS HOLLYWOOD REALLY LIKE?

Like other forms of American popular culture, Hollywood is a little world in itself—a subculture of the larger society, but with marked mirror distortions. It has strata of prestige and power, narrowing to a small top group who sit at the peak of the pyramid. They are the studio executives in charge of production. A mass of legendry clings to each of them, and what passes for conversation in Hollywood is likely to be anecdotes, gossip, and malice about them. Their royal position casts a deep shadow on Hollywood, for independent critical judgment is impossible where the employee must also be a courtier. A Hollywood "big shot" is surrounded by yes-men whose function is to give Number One the heady sense of being right. Where one man has the power of life and death there can be none of that responsibility which must mean taking risks in order to make independent choices. No one feels secure in his tenure—not even the top executives, who fear the intrigues of their rivals and the power of the bankers, and these in turn fear the whims and hostility of the movie audience.

The final decisions that affect creativeness are made in the "front office" with an eye on picture budgets that may run into millions of dollars. Everyone connected with a picture, including the director and script writers, knows that two or three million dollars may be at stake: as a result, no one takes risks with ideas, theme, treatment. The phrase "venture capital" has an ironic meaning when applied to Hollywood: since the capital being ventured is big, nothing else can be ventured. This is the nub of Hollywood's timidity. And timidity joins with bureacracy and the money yardstick to form Hollywood's deadly trinity.

The movie colony is always in feverish motion, always coming up with "terrific" ideas for "colossal" successes; yet for all its febrile quality, it is always in danger of becoming stagnant. It isn't a metropolis, yet it feels too important to be content with the life of a small town—nor could it even if it wished, since it is torn away from all the normal activities of a town. Thus Hollywood is one of the loneliest places in the world.

101. The attitude of the author to Hollywood is

    (1) objective
    (2) critical
    (3) admiring
    (4) even-handed
    (5) traditional

102. The structure of Hollywood society

    (1) makes for security
    (2) stifles independent thinking
    (3) encourages risk-taking
    (4) results in group tensions
    (5) reflects the larger society

103. The author implies that the ultimate authority rests with

    (1) the studio executive
    (2) the Hollywood employee
    (3) rivals of the top executives
    (4) the bankers
    (5) the movie audience

104. The word that best describes Hollywood movie-making is

    (1) legendary
    (2) responsible
    (3) venturesome
    (4) independent
    (5) fearful

105. The author points up a contradiction in Hollywood's

    (1) size
    (2) bureaucracy
    (3) success
    (4) creativeness
    (5) conversation

Questions 106–110 refer to the following passage.

WHAT IS THE SECRET OF A MOVIE DIRECTOR'S SUCCESS?

Orson Welles was once asked which director's work he admired. Welles, who had himself made cinematic history on a few occasions, responded: "The old masters, by which I mean John Ford, John Ford, and John Ford."

Welles wasn't alone in his admiration of Ford. His fellow directors awarded Ford Oscars for best director on four different occasions. While a few directors have produced individual films that equal, or perhaps even surpass, Ford's best, no one can match his total body of work.

Over a career spanning five decades, Ford directed 112 feature films, with only a couple of outright failures. Dozens of his films are recognized by critics as classics. The vast majority of the rest remain eminently watchable. *Stagecoach, Young Mr. Lincoln, The Grapes of Wrath, How Green Was My Valley, The Searchers, The Quiet Man, She Wore a Yellow Ribbon*—these are just a few of the classics he made.

Ford, who always protested that he did not aspire to make great art, only entertaining films, shrugged off the praise. He told anyone that would listen that he filled the set with mist and kept the actors in shadows because he didn't have a budget big enough for good sets.

This frugality was a trait that Ford did not abandon even at the height of his success. Another trait that distinguished Ford's filmmaking was his speed. The cavalry film, *She Wore a Yellow Ribbon*, for example, was shot in just 28 days. Most films have a shooting schedule of at least 60 days. His speed and frugality grew out of his character. Ford believed in hard work and was tight with a buck even in his private life. But these traits also seemed to be part of a deliberate strategy on Ford's part.

Because his films were so inexpensive, few of them failed to at least break even. Because he was so prolific, Ford could be certain that, even when one of his films was less-than-successful, he would be back in theaters just a few months later with one that would likely be a hit.

106. Ford's honors came from

   (1) his audiences
   (2) his actors
   (3) his choice of subjects
   (4) his critics
   (5) his fellow directors

107. The reader can infer from his reaction to praise that Ford was

   (1) hungry for recognition
   (2) antisocial
   (3) egocentric
   (4) proud
   (5) modest

108. The reader can infer from Ford's filling the set with mist that he

   (1) didn't have good actors
   (2) didn't have an adequate budget
   (3) had a love for the mysterious
   (4) valued a good set
   (5) was lavish in his direction

109. Ford's speed and frugality were a result of

   (1) necessity
   (2) poor planning
   (3) pressure to succeed
   (4) a purposeful plan
   (5) an unfortunate inefficiency

110. Ford's films were profitable because they were

   (1) made inexpensively
   (2) produced on lavish sets
   (3) made in foreign countries
   (4) notable for artistic quality
   (5) based on classics

Questions 111–115 are based on the following selection.

WHAT IS THE SURPRISING FINDING ABOUT KIDS AND READING?

A new study on how kids use different media could give a parent both apoplexy and cause for joy. The study, titled "Kids and Media at the New Millennium," found that the technology-savvy generation of 2- to 18-year-olds knows all too well the delights of TV, compact discs, video

(5)

games and video cassettes—all the
(10) latest cyber-gadgetry. But, and here
is the silver lining, reading is still
among the youthful set's top three
interests despite the glittery allure
of fancy electronics.
(15)   Watching television is still the most
popular pastime. On average, youngsters
spend 2 hours and 46 minutes in
front of the tube a day. Second comes
listening to music which takes up an
(20) average of 1 hour and 27 minutes a
day. Reading is 44 minutes a day but
it is third, above watching videos,
using a computer for fun, playing
video games, and going online.
(25)   The phenomenal popularity of the
Harry Potter books by J. K. Rowling
gave adults one major clue that
reading could entice children and
make them forget Nintendo and "The
(30) Simpsons" for a while.
      The study offers hope that reading
is here to stay. The challenge is to
figure out how to move it to the top
of the charts. Parents can have a
(35) significant influence on TV watching.
Just turning off the dial and having a
conversation during mealtime could go
a long way toward moving television
down and reading up on the popularity
(40) scale and families can set aside
nightly reading times for everyone
in the house.

111. The most encouraging finding of the
study is that, for youngsters, a top
interest is

    (1) video games and cassettes
    (2) television
    (3) music
    (4) reading
    (5) family electronics

112. The study found that this generation
of youngsters is

    (1) knowledgeable about technology
    (2) a source of disappointment to
        parents
    (3) wasting time on cyber-gadgetry
    (4) reading-illiterate
    (5) a cause of concern to parents

113. The study showed that reading is still
attractive to youngsters because of

    (1) Nintendo
    (2) "the Simpsons"
    (3) computer games
    (4) the delights of television
    (5) the Harry Potter books

114. The task for the future according to
the study is to

    (1) educate them in technology
    (2) increase interest in reading
    (3) expose them to music
    (4) increase family electronics
    (5) improve relationships with
        parents

115. The results of the study are

    (1) cause for disappointment
    (2) basically negative
    (3) inconclusive
    (4) hopeful
    (5) worrisome

Questions 116–120 refer to the following
selection on art.

WHAT WERE LEONARDO DA VINCI'S TALENTS?

Leonardo carried on his studies in
mathematics and physics, botany and
anatomy, not in addition to his art but as
a part of it. To him there was no essential
difference between art and science. Both
are ways of describing God's one universe.
He poured scorn on artists who wish to
improve on Nature. Let them improve on
themselves; Nature can't be wrong!

But when he came to paint, Leonardo
flung over chill, naked fact the glowing
cloak of beauty. His knowledge, his
technique, his peerless draftsmanship,
were concealed like a conjuror's sleight,
and he painted like a man in love with life.
How he loved it can be seen by turning
over his sketchbooks' pages—hundreds of
them. Here on one sheet may be seen the
dimples and creases in a baby's knee,
together with the contorted features of
soldiers dying and killing. Here are naked
laborers straining, there is a young woman
kneeling in prayer. Now he draws the
nervous anxiety in the neck tendons of an
old pauper, and here he has captured the
gaiety of a playing child. It is said that he

would follow beautiful or grotesque people around all day to study them. He visited the hospitals to watch old men die, and hastened to see a criminal hanged. Conspicuous for his golden locks topped with a little round black cap, and for his rose-colored cloak streaming like an anemone in the gusty streets, he loitered to watch the innocent greed of a baby at its mother's breast; then secretly, for it was frowned on, he hurried and dissected a human body that his brush might accurately paint "the divine proportion."

Indeed on no science did Leonardo spend so much time as on anatomy. Our muscles he demonstrated to be the levers they are, and he revealed the eye to be a lens. The heart he proved to be a hydraulic pump, and showed that the pulse is synchronized with the heart beat. He was the first discoverer, too, of the moderator bands involved in the contraction of the heart muscles. His many observations in the hospitals led him to the discovery of hardening of the arteries as a cause of death in old age.

116. According to the article, Leonardo da Vinci's life combined interests in

   (1) nature and science
   (2) technique and inspiration
   (3) God and art
   (4) science and art
   (5) nature and the universe

117. The contradiction in Leonardo implied by the writer found expression in his

   (1) scorn of artists
   (2) painting
   (3) distrust of nature
   (4) morbid curiosity
   (5) conspicuous clothing

118. The writer admires all of the following about Leonardo EXCEPT his

   (1) improvements on nature
   (2) technique
   (3) knowledge
   (4) draftsmanship
   (5) painting

119. His sketches of babies, soldiers, and laborers are cited as examples of Leonardo's

   (1) concealed technique
   (2) love of life
   (3) versatility
   (4) curiosity
   (5) realism

120. Leonardo's scientific studies led to discoveries regarding all of the following EXCEPT the

   (1) muscles
   (2) eye
   (3) heart
   (4) pulse
   (5) blood

Business Documents

Questions 121–125 refer to the following company memorandum.

Vehicle Expense Reimbursement

TO: Ms. Gratz
FROM: Accounting
RE: Vehicle Expense Reimbursement
DATE: December 2002

Dear Ms. Gratz,

It is essential that any of our personnel who drive company and personal vehicles in connection with company business maintain a detailed record of expenses incurred. It is our desire to be certain that you are reimbursed for any expenditures that you make in this regard, and your good record keeping will make this possible.

Receipts must be submitted for gasoline purchases, parking expenses, and repairs. In addition, we will require your daily record of the number of miles driven, the odometer reading, before and after, and the amount of time spent driving. This information should be included in your weekly report to Mr. Edward Hutson. Please use the attached form for your convenience.

Thank you very much for your cooperation in this matter.

Sincerely,
Gregory Snells

Gregory Snells
Director of Accounting

121. What is the purpose of the letter?

    (1) to reprimand an employee for not following the proper procedure for reporting vehicle expenses
    (2) to reward an employee for correctly submitting a vehicle expense report
    (3) to give reasons for submitting receipts for gasoline
    (4) to request a record of mileage
    (5) to outline the procedure for submitting reimbursed expenditures

122. All of the following are reimbursed expenditures EXCEPT

    (1) parking receipts
    (2) food
    (3) repairs
    (4) gasoline
    (5) auto services

123. Gregory Snells is writing to

    (1) persuade an employee
    (2) inform an employee
    (3) describe or narrate to an employee
    (4) explain to a customer
    (5) persuade a customer

124. Ms. Gratz is probably requesting

    (1) receipts for car repairs
    (2) a raise
    (3) money for expenses she incurred
    (4) a company car
    (5) a leave of absence

125. All employees at this company probably

    (1) enjoy taking a vacation
    (2) have company cars
    (3) don't travel much
    (4) do company business and travel while using their own cars
    (5) request money for extra expenses

ANSWER KEY

Literature/Page 436

1. 2	14. 1	27. 4	40. 4	53. 4	66. 3
2. 2	15. 2	28. 3	41. 4	54. 5	67. 2
3. 4	16. 2	29. 1	42. 1	55. 3	68. 4
4. 3	17. 3	30. 3	43. 1	56. 2	69. 3
5. 3	18. 3	31. 3	44. 3	57. 5	70. 1
6. 1	19. 2	32. 1	45. 3	58. 1	71. 5
7. 3	20. 1	33. 2	46. 5	59. 4	72. 2
8. 5	21. 3	34. 1	47. 2	60. 3	73. 3
9. 5	22. 2	35. 2	48. 4	61. 4	74. 4
10. 5	23. 4	36. 4	49. 1	62. 2	75. 3
11. 2	24. 2	37. 2	50. 5	63. 4	
12. 4	25. 4	38. 3	51. 5	64. 2	
13. 4	26. 2	39. 1	52. 1	65. 1	

Poetry and Drama/Pages 450/452

76. 4	79. 5	82. 3	85. 4	87. 5	89. 4
77. 4	80. 2	83. 1	86. 3	88. 3	90. 4
78. 3	81. 4	84. 4			

Commentary on the Arts/Page 453

91. 5	96. 4	101. 2	106. 5	111. 4	116. 4
92. 4	97. 1	102. 2	107. 5	112. 1	117. 2
93. 1	98. 2	103. 5	108. 2	113. 5	118. 1
94. 4	99. 5	104. 5	109. 4	114. 2	119. 2
95. 3	100. 2	105. 1	110. 1	115. 4	120. 5

Business Documents/Page 458

121. 5 122. 2 123. 2 124. 3 125. 4

WHAT'S YOUR SCORE?	
_____right,	_____wrong
Excellent	108–120
Good	96–107
Fair	84–95

If your score was low, the explanation of the correct answers that follows will help you. Analyze your errors. Then, reread the section on Basic Reading Skills (beginning on page 413), Reading Prose, Poetry, and Drama (page 415), and Reading Business Documents (page 433).

ANSWER ANALYSIS

Literature/Page 436

1. **2** The passage states that, despite the fact that no food stayed down, "the wounds slowly healed."

2. **2** The swan "came to regard me as a friend."

3. **4** The narrator felt "the bird was wasting away with nostalgia."

4. **3** The swan looked at the pebbles (fish) "remotely."

5. **3** In the last sentence, the narrator says, "Swans do not sing at their death if they die of grief."

6. **1** The author states that one of the women is an officer's wife, *like myself.*

7. **3** The passage does not link dumplings with bringing any specific piece of good fortune. Oranges are associated with sweet life.

8. **5** The author states they had parties "to raise their spirits."

9. **5** They did not notice the poor stuffing of the dumplings and the spotted oranges.

10. **5** The food they ate really wasn't fine. They didn't notice how poor it was.

11. **2** The selection states it was "not the best time to be walking alone by the side of a half-frozen river."

12. **4** The words "during the day as she stood pinning dresses" indicate that this activity took place regularly. Pinning dresses, therefore, must have been her work.

13. **4** The sentence "What if they...had died of cold or hunger...while she was...dancing with British officers?" communicates a sense of guilt.

14. **1** The sentence "No one, she thought, wanted to hear them" indicates that the woman believed others were not interested, not that she did not want to tell them. The fact that she continued to go to the Jewish Community Center proves that answer Choices 3 and 4 are incorrect.

15. **2** The last paragraph describes the long-range effects of the Holocaust. That is what the reader is meant to remember and to understand.

16. **2** The fact that "They poured their sewage into it, but it couldn't be tainted" means that, no matter what else happened around the ocean, nothing could taint it.

17. **3** Terror and fear are indicated by such words and phrases as *chilling, clammy,* and *bowels of fear.*

18. **3** The narrator wishes to show how the area has been ruined by the changes he describes.

19. **2** The contrasts are derricks instead of trees and oil-pumps instead of cattle.

20. **1** The clue is found in the last phrase, "like a tumor."

21. **3** "Taking a last look" is an expression that is often used in relation to death or a catastrophic event.

22. **2** To do something "consciously" is to do it "with deliberate thought or awareness." That the speaker did not let the freeing of the hawk "come into consciousness" would mean that it was never planned.

23. **4** The passage states that "He lay there a long minute without hope...his eyes still fixed on that blue vault above him." A minute may seem longer than a minute if it is filled with suspense and uncertainty.

24. **2** We are told the sky is "so full of light that I could not follow his gaze." Later, we are told that the "light was too intense."

25. **4** The passage refers to "a cry of such unutterable and ecstatic joy that it sounds down across the years and tingles...."

26. **2** The sounds were unusual because "...they were a weird medley of whines, whimpers and small howls."

27. **4** The narrator has learned "from experience.... The cries were obviously those of a husky."

28. **3** Mike "owned three half-grown pups not yet trained to harness..."

29. **1** The narrator states, "If that pup needed a friend...I was its man!"

30. **3** In the fifth paragraph, the narrator "kept quiet, even when the whimpering stopped, leaving me uncertain about the direction...."

31. **3** Type A is careful.

32. **1** Type Z is not late. He arrives just on time.

33. **2** Getting enough sleep is not mentioned.

34. **1** Nowhere is any change indicated. The other choices are either untrue or unlikely.

35. **2** That they like each other is evidenced by the observation that they always marry each other.

36. **4** The poet says repeatedly that "nobody can make it out here alone."
37. **2** The poet writes that "thinking last night" she came to her conclusion.
38. **3** The poet states that some millionaires have "hearts of stone."
39. **1** The poet says "Storm clouds are gathering" and "The wind is gonna blow" because "the race of man is suffering."
40. **4** Line 10 is repeated in lines 22 and 34.
41. **4** The poet says she "won't stop now."
42. **1** She says "she's come this far to freedom."
43. **1** The poet writes "I'll reap some time in the future."
44. **3** She states, "in time you'll know you need me."
45. **3** The rhyme scheme is a a b b a—in the first stanza back, track, going, growing, black.
46. **5** The passage mentions her creativity with flowers.
47. **2** The garden is described as ambitious and not a straggly country stand.
48. **4** A shabby house in which the author is forced to live in is mentioned.
49. **1** The passage states "holding on," which is work Black women have done for a very long time.
50. **5** Regret concerning her past is not mentioned about the author's mother.
51. **5** The stamp bore the author's name and town.
52. **1** The author got the idea from his school friend Francisco Ruiz.
53. **4** The passage starts, "That one, Platero," so the author is addressing Platero.
54. **5** The author broke his money bank to get the five pesetas to pay for the rubber stamp.
55. **3** The peseta is the unit of currency in Spain.
56. **2** See the section "Inferring Setting" (page 419). The reference to the portrait of George III, the reigning monarch at the time just prior to the American Revolution, implies a date of about 1770.
57. **5** The author refers to the outside of the house as "the only side which, in truth, belongs to a henpecked husband."
58. **1** Dame Van Winkle looked upon Wolf with "an evil eye as the cause of his master's going so often astray."
59. **4** The author says that Rip never said anything in response to his wife's nagging.
60. **3** He would be content were it not for his wife's "dinning in his ear."
61. **4** The author states "I went to the woods...to front only the essential facts of life...."
62. **2** The author says, "Our life is frittered away by detail... "Simplicity, simplicity, simplicity!... keep your accounts on your thumb-nail."
63. **4** *Mean* is used here to imply the opposite of *sublime* (used in the next clause), that is, as in the sentence "Still we live meanly, like ants."
64. **2** The author implies that people do not know how to live properly, but they should learn.
65. **1** The author went to the woods to see if he "could not learn what it had had to teach."
66. **3** "Small and hopeful Sylvia" climbed the tree with "tingling, eager blood coursing" through her body.
67. **2** Sylvia "knew that higher still one of the oak's upper branches chafed against the pine trunk...."
68. **4** The first part of Sylvia's climb was easy because "She had often climbed there...."
69. **3** "It was like a great mainmast...." A ship's mast supports its sails.
70. **1** "The old pine must have loved his new dependent."
71. **5** The feud has been going on for years and nobody knows what it is about. The author implies that a trivial event has been blown out of proportion.
72. **2** Buck doesn't know, so we aren't told, who started the feud; only a few old men remember.
73. **3** Buck talks of his cousin Bud's being ambushed by Baldy Shepherdson; we can, therefore, assume that Buck is a Grangerford.
74. **4** To hear a sermon about brotherly love, all the men arrive armed.
75. **3** Buck states, in answer to two questions, "I don't know" and "how do *I* know?"

Poetry and Drama/Pages 450/452

76. **4** The main purpose of the poem is to teach us a lesson in conduct—that, regardless of our station in life, we must make our own opportunities with the resources we have at hand.

77. **4** "I could help defeat the enemy" follows logically from the incomplete thought, "Had I a sword of keener steel."

78. **3** The "craven" hangs along the edge of the battle and creeps away, both actions of a cowardly person.

79. **5** The words "...swords shocked upon swords and shields" provide an example of alliteration, that is, repetition of the same sound.

80. **2** The bravery of the king's son is contrasted with the cowardly behavior of the craven soldier.

81. **4** *Stop* and *cut* are short, sharp words, just as *shock* is, both in sound and meaning.

82. **3** See the "Glossary of Literary Terms" (page 433) for a definition of alliteration. Here the letter *s* is repeated at the beginning of two or more words in close proximity— "scribbling" and "sky."

83. **1** The first three verses establish the importance of the poet's love. The last verse stresses the effects of the loss of that love.

84. **4** All of the emotion that follows from the loss of a loved one is indicated in lines 21 and 22.

85. **4** To the poet, none of the elements mentioned in the final stanza that represent life serve any purpose.

86. **3** The daughter cares; she doesn't like her mother living alone.

87. **5** The mother appreciates her daughter's caring and says, "Annie, you're a good daughter."

88. **3** The mother wants to be independent. She says, "I want to keep my own home."

89. **4** The mother wants to stay where she knows "all the neighbors and the store people."

90. **4** The daughter mentions everything except independence. Her mother doesn't want to be "some old lady living with her children."

Commentary on the Arts/Page 453

91. **5** The review refers to "the remarkably inventive and surprising set."

92. **4** The play is referred to as a whodunit," that is, a mystery.

93. **1** The play's author is J.B. Priestly.

94. **4** The success of the set design is attributed to "the art-comes-first atmosphere of England's state-subsidized theaters."

95. **3** One cast member says the sets are not his "particular cup of tea."

96. **4** Wiegand is the only character who can clarify matters for the salesman. The others hardly talk.

97. **1** These portions call for actions by the actors.

98. **2** Wiegand refers to their "exaggerated ideas of the dutiful respect" for the dead.

99. **5** Wiegand mentions that the clergy get revenue and profit from big funerals.

100. **2** Anna is embroidering slippers for Papa and Welzel says he doesn't like to wear them.

101. **2** The author refers to Hollywood's "marked mirror distortions" of society and its timidity, among other criticisms.

102. **2** It is stated that the position of the studio executives at the top of a pyramid makes independent critical judgment impossible.

103. **5** Executives fear rivals and bankers, who, in turn, fear the movie audience.

104. **5** The author refers to Hollywood's timidity or fearfulness.

105. **1** Hollywood, according to the article, isn't a metropolis nor is it a small town.

106. **5** Ford's fellow directors awarded him Oscars for best director.

107. **5** Ford shrugged off praise (fourth paragraph).

108. **2** Ford filled the set with mist "because he didn't have a budget big enough for good sets."

109. **4** Ford's speed and frugality were "part of a deliberate strategy on [his] part."

110. **1** The author of the article claims that, "Because his films were so inexpensive, few of them failed to at least break even."

111. **4** The passage states that reading is among the youngsters' top three interests.
112. **1** The study found the 2- to 18-year-olds "technology savvy."
113. **5** The popularity of the Harry Potter books indicated that reading could attract children.
114. **2** The challenge for the future is to move reading from third place up to the top, past watching TV and listening to music.
115. **4** It is stated that the study offers hope that reading is here to stay.
116. **4** Leonardo saw no essential difference between art and science.
117. **2** His painting resulted in the contradiction of art disguising reality (nature).
118. **1** Da Vinci hated artists who tried to improve on nature.
119. **2** These sketchbooks' pages show how Leonardo loved life.
120. **5** All are mentioned *except* circulation of the blood, which was discovered later.

Business Documents/Page 458

121. **5** The whole memo outlines the procedure for submitting reimbursed expenditures.
122. **2** The memo does not mention anything about food being reimbursed.
123. **2** Gregory Snells is writing to inform an employee of the procedures for submitting vehicle expense reports.
124. **3** The letter implies that Ms. Gratz has requested money for expenses she incurred while traveling.
125. **4** The employees at this company probably do business and travel while using their own cars, thus prompting the manager to write this memo.

Overview

Basic Facts

The Mathematics section of the GED test is divided into two 45-minute examination periods, each containing 25 questions. Before Part I, you will be given a Casio fx-260SOLAR calculator, which you may use only for this section of the examination. Part II is to be completed without a calculator. The kinds of questions you'll be asked are virtually the same in both parts, as is their level of difficulty, which ranges from easy to challenging. Most problems offer multiple-choice answers, but about 10 of the 50 questions require you to calculate answers on your own and then "bubble in" those answers on a grid. You are not required to show your work for either part.

THE "FORMULAS" SHEET

Students are usually relieved when they first hear the testing service provides a 1-page collection of mathematical formulas with every test booklet (see page 81). That is, until they actually examine the sheet and see how complicated-looking the information appears. The sheet can be a worthwhile aid, but first you must learn how and when to apply the information listed there. Such learning is only accomplished through hard work and dedication. Once it's done, however, you'll be pleasantly surprised to find you won't even need the sheet—much of it will already be committed to memory. You'll be able to move through the test more quickly and confidently.

HOW TO USE THIS SECTION

The section is designed to instruct self-motivated learners of varying abilities. The concepts and exercises within each chapter progress from easy to difficult, and the chapters, as a whole, move from simple (Chapter 19—Numbers and Basic Operations) to challenging (Chapter 24—Geometry).

If you're confident of your knowledge in a particular area, go directly to the Chapter Review exercises at the end of each chapter to test yourself. If you get all questions in the Review right, move on to the next chapter.

If you know that your math skills are pretty rusty, start at the beginning and carefully work your way through all the instruction, examples, and exercises. When you've completed all the review chapters, you're ready for the practice tests and exams at the end of the section.

This section includes a chapter on test-taking strategies specific to the Mathematics part of the GED. However, shortcuts and tips on how to handle operations and problems can be found throughout. Though it's best to save Chapter 25 (Test-taking Strategies) for the end of your study, those students who are especially pressed for time should review it before taking the GED, regardless of how far they've gone in the Mathematics section.

USING THE CASIO FX-260SOLAR CALCULATOR

Before taking Part I, you will be issued a Casio fx-260SOLAR calculator and then given a few minutes to practice using it. You don't have to use the calculator, but it is strongly recommended that you do so. It can really help you to avoid computational errors that lead to incorrect answers and can dramatically reduce the time it takes to solve certain problems, giving you more time to spend on the tougher questions.

If you have had some past experience using a calculator, it will help you in operating the Casio fx-260, which works like virtually all hand-held calculators. If you have never used a calculator, however, it is a good idea to purchase or borrow one to practice on prior to taking the GED. The most effective way to practice is to use the fx-260, which is available in retail stores for about $10 or can be ordered from the GED Fulfillment Center by calling (301) 604-9073.

As you do the exercises in the following chapters, use your calculator only occasionally or where indicated by a calculator icon and for Part I sections of Practice Tests. Because you will still be required to do your own calculations for many of the questions, it's important to keep your computational skills strong and avoid overdependence on the calculator.

Above is a basic diagram of the Casio fx-SOLAR calculator that will be issued to you. Please note that the calculator has a lot more function keys than you will need to use on the test.

Here are some basic rules to keep in mind when using a calculator:

- Press the keys firmly, checking the display window to make sure you have entered numbers accurately.
- Press **AC** (or similar key) after completing each problem to completely clear it. Pressing **C** will erase just the last number entered.
- Numbers and the decimal point will appear on the display window, but operations signs (like **+** or **×** or **÷**) will not.

Example One (Basic Operations)

28.3 ft.

52 ft.

How many square feet of carpet are required to cover the entire office floor in the diagram above?

PRESS **28.3,** then ☒ , then **52,** then =

Answer: 1471.6 sq. ft.

Example Two (Working with Parentheses)

Find: 12(117 + 13) – 68

PRESS *12* ☒ [[(··· *117* ⊞ *13* ···)]] ⊟ *68* =

Answer: 40

Note: The fx-260 has parentheses keys, but some other calculators don't.

Example Three (Working with Fractions)

Broadway	3/4 mile
Alice Avenue	2 1/2 miles
Stockton Street	4 miles

According to the highway exit sign above, how much further past Broadway is Alice Avenue?

PRESS *2* a b/c *1* a b/c *2* ⊟ a b/c *3* a b/c *4* =

Answer: 1 3/4 miles

Note: Not all calculators are able to compute fractions.

Example Four (Working with Signed Numbers)

What is the value of the following expression?

–3(–6 + 8) – (–12)

PRESS *3* +/– ☒ [[(··· *6* +/– ⊞ *8* ···)]] ⊟ *12* +/– =

Answer: 6

Note: Some calculators allow you to enter negative numbers using the ⊟ key.

Example Five (Working with Exponents)

A container that holds crushed gravel is in the shape of a cube, with each side measuring 17 feet. What is the volume of the container?

PRESS *17* X'' *3* =

Answer: 4,913 cu. ft.

Example Six (Working with Square Roots)

The square root of 138 is between what two whole numbers?

PRESS **138** [SHIFT] [X²]

Answer: between 11 and 12

FILLING IN ANSWER GRIDS

On 10 questions out of the 50 on the test, multiple-choice answers will not be provided. You must come up with an answer yourself and then record it on a grid (see illustration).

Example One (Recording Whole Numbers)

What is the measure in degrees of ∠*ACB*?

(Using what you will learn about triangles and supplemetary angles in Chapter 24, you calculate the correct answer to be 42°.)

Answer: 42°

You can fill in the answer grid for this response in four different ways; all are correct (see below). Make sure to write the answer in the top horizontal row of boxes and then "bubble in" the corresponding numbers below. Don't worry about including the degrees sign (°); it's unnecessary.

Example Two (Recording Numbers with Decimals)

Sharon and her coworkers want to purchase a portable CD player as a going-away present for their boss. The player costs $86.99. Sharon collects $47.35 from her coworkers and contributes $20 herself. How much more does she need to make the purchase?

Answer: $19.64

Here, there is only one way to complete the grid. Note that the decimal point *must* be recorded and takes up an entire column. Recording the $ sign is unnecessary.

Example Three (Recording Fractions)

A plumber measures a piece of pipe to be 1 5/8 inches. How much does he need to trim from the pipe to make it fit a connection that is 1 3/8 inches long?

Answer: 2/8 or 1/4

The grid can be completed in the following ways, all of which are correct.

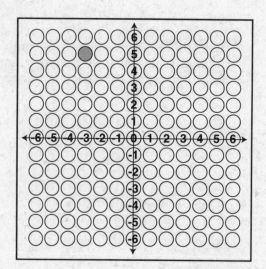

Example Four (Recording Points on a Coordinates Plane Grid)

Two lines intersect at a point with coordinates of (5, −3). Show the location of the intersecting point on the grid below.

Answer: see grid

Note: The coordinate plane grid illustrated is just like the rectangular coordinate grid in Chapter 23. However, the *x* and *y* axes are not labeled, so it's essential that you memorize which is which. There will most probably be only two questions out of the 50 requiring you to fill in this type of grid.

Numbers and Basic Operations

19

Place Values

Say this number out loud to yourself:

47,182

You should have said, "Forty-seven thousand, one hundred and eighty two." Each **digit** (another word for single numbers between 0 and 9) has its own separate value depending on the place it occupies. Study the chart of place values below until you know it by heart.

| _____ , | 100 | 10 | thousands | hundreds | tens | ones |
| millions | thousands | thousands | | | | |

PRACTICE—PLACE VALUES

Write each number out in word form—don't worry about spelling.

1. 734
2. 9,008
3. 12,615
4. 7,814,015

ANSWERS

1. **seven hundred thirty four**
2. **nine thousand and eight**
3. **twelve thousand, six hundred fifteen**
4. **seven million, eight hundred fourteen thousand, fifteen**

PRACTICE—IDENTIFYING PLACE VALUES

Find the value of the digit "7" in each of these numbers and state its value. (For example, in the number 17,412, the "7" has a value of 7,000)

1. 472,812
2. 31,174
3. 789,118
4. 7,018,111

ANSWERS

1. **70,000**
2. **70**
3. **700,000**
4. **7,000,00**

Addition

Choose the correct setup for adding these three numbers:

87   162   38

(a) 87   (b) 38
      162   162
    + 38   + 87

(c) 162   (d) 162
      38   38
    + 87   + 87

Answer: (d)

When it comes to addition, you must try your best to be neat and accurate in setting up problems. The place values of all the

473

numbers should be lined up precisely so that your answer will be correct. You chose (d) because the digits in the ones column (2,8,7) were lined up directly on top of each other, as were the digits in the tens column (6,3,8). The digit in the hundreds column (1) can stand by itself. The actual computation looks like this:

Step one: Setup

$$
\begin{array}{r}
162 \\
38 \\
+\ 87 \\
\end{array}
$$

Step two: Add

Ones Column

You always begin an addition problem at the top digit furthest to the right. Here, it's 2. Move down, adding each number in the ones column (2 + 8 + 7 = 17). You can't put the two-digit number 17 directly below the 7 in 87 because there's room for only one digit. Just write down the 7 from the 1<u>7</u> and carry the 1 to the top of the tens column.

Tens Column

Now add the 1 that you carried in with the three numbers from that column (1 + 6 + 3 + 8 = 18). Put the 8 from 1<u>8</u> under the 8 and carry the 1 to the top of the hundreds column.

Hundreds Column

Add that column (1 + 1 = 2). The **sum** is 287. **Sum** means the answer to an addition problem.

$$
\begin{array}{r}
^{1\ 1} \\
162 \\
38 \\
+\ 87 \\
\hline
287 \\
\end{array}
$$

Answer: 287

Practice—Addition

Find the sum for the following addition problems.

1.
$$
\begin{array}{r}
168 \\
402 \\
+\ 43 \\
\end{array}
$$

2.
$$
\begin{array}{r}
9,104 \\
586 \\
+\ 720 \\
\end{array}
$$

3.
$$
\begin{array}{r}
72,416 \\
4,803 \\
+\ 92 \\
\end{array}
$$

4.
$$
\begin{array}{r}
786 \\
412 \\
853 \\
+\ 971 \\
\end{array}
$$

Answers

1. **613**
2. **10,410**
3. **77,311**
4. **3022**

Do you know your basic addition facts?

Pay attention to how you're adding and be honest with yourself. Are you using your fingers to count? Are you using "half-steps"?

For example, when you come to a problem like 6 + 7, do you say, "Well, I know 6 + 6 = 12, so add one more on...."? Many GED students begin their study this way, but the successful ones soon realize these methods take too long and cause errors in computation.

The only answer is to memorize these addition facts. Buy some flashcards at a toy store or bookstore, or make your own from index cards, with the help of someone who really knows the facts. Practice until you've got it.

Subtraction

EXAMPLE ONE

Choose the correct setup for the following problem and solve:

$$168 - 42$$

a)
$$
\begin{array}{r}
168 \\
-\ 42 \\
\end{array}
$$

b)
$$
\begin{array}{r}
168 \\
-\ 42 \\
\end{array}
$$

c)
$$
\begin{array}{r}
168 \\
-\ 42 \\
\end{array}
$$

d)
$$
\begin{array}{r}
42 \\
-\ 168 \\
\end{array}
$$

As with addition, accurate place-value arrangement is essential to subtraction. But with subtraction, you must also remember that the larger number goes on top—at least, for now. The correct setup is (b). Here's how to solve it.

Step one: Setup
$$168 - 42$$

Subtract using the same "column" method you learned in addition.

Step two: Subtract
$$\begin{array}{r} 168 \\ -\ 42 \\ \hline 126 \end{array}$$

Answer: 126 The answer to a subtraction problem is called **the difference**.

Subtraction Using Borrowing

Subtraction gets a bit more complicated when the process of "borrowing" becomes necessary—that is, when the digit on top is smaller than the digit on the bottom. Consider this example below.

EXAMPLE TWO

$$724 - 486$$

Step one: Set-up with larger number on top.

$$\begin{array}{r} 724 \\ -\ 486 \end{array}$$

Step two: Subtract using borrowing.

Ones Column

The number 4 is smaller than 6, so you need to borrow 1 from the next column over, making 4 in the ones place now worth 14. Subtract the 1 borrowed from the 2 in the tens' place, so it now becomes 1. Since 14 – 6 = 8, put the 8 under the 6 as the first digit in your answer.

Tens Column

You can't subtract 8 from 1 (tens place) so you must borrow from the digit to its left, the 7. Now, 1 becomes 11 and you can subtract 11 – 8 = 3. Enter the 3 as the second digit of your answer. Do the final subtraction in the hundreds column—6 – 4 = 2 and enter the answer.

$$\begin{array}{r} \overset{6\ 11}{7\ 2\ 4} \\ -\ 486 \\ \hline 238 \end{array}$$

Answer: 238

Step three: Check. To check subtraction, **add** the answer to the second of the two numbers in the subtraction problem. The sum should equal the top number.

$$\begin{array}{r} 238 \\ +\ 486 \\ \hline 724 \end{array}$$

Borrowing and Zeros

Subtraction gets even more complicated when you have to borrow across two or more numbers. Consider the example below.

EXAMPLE

Find the difference between 7003 and 468.

Step one:
$$\begin{array}{r} 7003 \\ -\ 468 \end{array}$$

Step two: Subtract using borrowing.

Notice how you need to move two places over to the 7 to borrow. Then the 1 that was borrowed gets moved to the right *one digit at a time*: first, to the hundreds place, making the 0 a ten and the 7 a 6, then you borrow 1 from that 10 and move it to the 0 in the tens place. Then you borrow 1 from *that* 10, moving it finally to the ones place, making the 3 a 13. Only then can you subtract.

$$\begin{array}{r} \overset{6\ 9\ 9\ 1}{7\ 0\ 0\ 3} \\ -\ 468 \\ \hline 6{,}535 \end{array}$$

PRACTICE—SUBTRACTION

Subtract and find the difference for the following. Check.

1. $\begin{array}{r} 475 \\ -\ 62 \end{array}$

2. $\begin{array}{r} 806 \\ -\ 294 \end{array}$

3. $\begin{array}{r} 1413 \\ -\ 962 \end{array}$

4. $\begin{array}{r} 10{,}024 \\ -\ 8{,}751 \end{array}$

5. $\begin{array}{r} 62{,}400 \\ -\ 18{,}519 \end{array}$

ANSWERS

1. **413** 2. **512** 3. **451**
4. **1273** 5. **43,881**

Multiplication

Take a look at how to multiply using this example:

EXAMPLE ONE

$$306 \times 42$$

$$
\begin{array}{r}
306 \\
\times\ 42 \\
\hline
\end{array}
$$

$2 \times 306 = \rightarrow\quad 612$
$4 \times 306 = \rightarrow\quad \underline{1224}$
$\qquad\qquad\qquad 12{,}852 \quad \leftarrow \textbf{product}$

Answer: 12,852

The answer to a multiplication problem is called a **product**.

Step one: Arrange the problem with the larger number on top.

Step two: Begin multiplying with the bottom number using the digit furthest to the right—in this case, the 2 in 42. Moving from right to left, multiply each of the top digits by 2: $306 \times 2 = 612$

Step three: Repeat *step two* using the 4 in 42: $306 \times 4 = 1{,}224$. Actually, it's 306×40, which equals 12,240, but it's common practice to leave off the last zero and shift the entire answer one place to the left. Notice how the 4 in 1,224 is in the tens place.

Step four: Add the two numbers—612 and 1,224—to find the product.

EXAMPLE TWO

$$406 \times 312$$

$$
\begin{array}{r}
406 \\
\times\ 312 \\
\hline
\end{array}
$$

$2 \times 406 = \rightarrow\quad 812$
$1 \times 406 = \rightarrow\quad 406 \qquad$ 1-digit shift
$3 \times 406 = \rightarrow\quad \underline{1218} \qquad$ 2-digit shift
$\qquad\qquad\qquad 126{,}672$

Find the product of the following.

1. $\begin{array}{r} 46 \\ \times\ 13 \\ \hline \end{array}$

2. $\begin{array}{r} 892 \\ \times\ 27 \\ \hline \end{array}$

3. $\begin{array}{r} 404 \\ \times\ 95 \\ \hline \end{array}$

4. $\begin{array}{r} 724 \\ \times\ 106 \\ \hline \end{array}$

5. $\begin{array}{r} 4302 \\ \times\ 950 \\ \hline \end{array}$

ANSWERS

1. **598**   2. **24,084**   3. **38,380**
4. **76,744**   5. **4,086,900**

If you understand the steps to multiplication but find you're still getting the wrong answers, you may need to brush up on your multiplication facts. Use flashcards or some other means to help you memorize the multiplication tables up to 12.

Division

Many beginning GED students find division to be the most difficult of the four basic operations. It requires accuracy, neatness, and careful attention to a sometimes complicated step-by-step process.

EXAMPLE ONE

$$524 \div 4$$

$$
\begin{array}{r}
131 \\
4\overline{)524} \\
\underline{4\downarrow} \\
12 \\
\underline{-12} \\
04 \\
\underline{-4} \\
0
\end{array}
$$

Answer: 131. The answer to a division problem is called a **quotient**.

Here's the above process in steps.

Step one: 5 ÷ 4
Step two: 1 × 4
Step three: 5 − 4 = 1
Step four: Bring down the next number, 2

Repeat steps 1–4 until all the numbers are brought down.

Often, there is more than one digit in the **divisor** (the number used to divide). Consider the following example.

EXAMPLE TWO

$$1{,}170 \div 26$$

$$
\begin{array}{r}
45 \leftarrow \text{quotient} \\
\text{divisor} \rightarrow 26\overline{)1170} \leftarrow \text{dividend} \\
-\,104 \\
\hline
130 \\
-\,130 \\
\hline
0
\end{array}
$$

Of course, 26 doesn't go into 1, so you include the next digit in the dividend. But 26 doesn't go into 11 either. Include the 7, and now you can begin the problem because 26 *does* go into 117. You're not supposed to know, off the top of your head, the answer to 117 ÷ 26. Make an educated guess and do some multiplication on scrap paper to get 4. Notice that the 4 in the quotient goes directly above the 7 in the dividend.

Check: Multiply the quotient by the divisor. The answer should be equal to the dividend. For the last problem, the check would look like this:

$$
\begin{array}{r}
45 \\
\times\ 26 \\
\hline
270 \\
90 \\
\hline
1{,}170
\end{array}
$$

Sometimes, numbers don't divide evenly, and there is an amount "left over" called a **remainder**.

EXAMPLE THREE

$$75 \div 4$$

$$
\begin{array}{r}
18 \\
4\overline{)75} \\
-\,4 \\
\hline
35 \\
-\,32 \\
\hline
3 \leftarrow \text{remainder}
\end{array}
$$

There are no more numbers in the dividend to bring down. The **remainder**, then, is 3 and the answer would be expressed: 18r3 or 18 remainder 3.
Note: There is a more complete way of dealing with remainders that will be later taught in Chapter 19, Decimals.

Ways of Writing Division

There are a few ways in which division can be expressed. The problem of dividing 96 by 6 can be written:

$$96 \div 6 \quad \text{or} \quad 6\overline{)96} \quad \text{or} \quad \frac{96}{6}$$

In the last of these, $\frac{96}{6}$, the fraction bar (—), means "divided by." Read it from top to bottom, and it will soon sound and look like the other two more familiar expressions of division.

PRACTICE—DIVISION

Find the quotient and check.

1. $5\overline{)95}$
2. $14\overline{)532}$
3. $\dfrac{1680}{21}$
4. $\dfrac{156}{6}$
5. $32\overline{)933}$
6. $\dfrac{2142}{21}$
7. $92\overline{)21{,}528}$

ANSWERS

1. **19** 2. **38** 3. **80** 4. **26**
5. **29r5** 6. **102** 7. **234**

Word Problems Using Basic Operations

Almost all of the questions on the GED will be word problems. Read carefully and rely on your common sense to tell you what operations to use. Be aware of certain words and phrases that tell you what to do:

- **Sum, total,** and **all together** usually mean addition.
- **How much more, how much less, find the difference,** and **deduct** indicate subtraction.

EXAMPLE ONE

Carl purchased a computer for $589. In addition, he chose to buy a two-year service contract for $75 and a tech-support option for $35. What is the total cost of Carl's computer purchase?

The words **total** and **in addition** should clue you in to the fact that this is an addition problem:

```
  589   for the computer
   75   for the service contract
+  35   for tech-support option
$699    for the computer purchase
```

EXAMPLE TWO

The Glenridge Elementary School had an enrollment of 352 first-graders and 413 second-graders. How many more second-graders were there than first-graders?

```
  413   second-graders
- 352   first-graders
   61   more second-graders
```

Multiplication is not often associated with particular words or phrases. Rely on your mathematical sense to determine whether to multiply.

EXAMPLE THREE

Karen can type 65 words per minute. At this rate, find how many words she can type in 15 minutes.

```
    65   words per one minute
×   15   total minutes
   325
   65
   975   words in 15 minutes
```

Division is often indicated by words and phrases like **share, split, per, average,** and **grouped into.**

EXAMPLE FOUR

A bagging machine packages 28 oranges per bag. If the machine is loaded with 1,400 oranges, how many full bags will it produce?

```
                        50   number of full bags
Oranges per bag  28)1400     total oranges
                  − 140
                     0
```

PRACTICE—SOLVING WORD PROBLEMS

1. Geri cycled a 36-mile loop every day for two weeks. What is the total number of miles she rode during that period?

2. In 1939 there were 4,212 people who lived in the town of Twin Forks. By 1999 there were 32,118 people residing there. What is the difference between Twin Forks' population in 1999 and 1939?

3. Sonia's annual salary is $41,190 and she receives a holiday bonus of $2,670. She also receives $3,219 in stock-option benefits. What are her total earnings for the year?

4. Sean bought 7 CDs, each the same price, for a total of $98. Find the cost for one of the CDs.

5. Shirley was born in 1927. Find her age in 2001.

6. Rob's compact car gets 22 miles per gallon of gas. How far can he travel using 13 gallons of gas?

ANSWERS

1. **504**   2. **27,906**   3. **$47,079**
4. **$14**   5. **74**   6. **286**

MULTISTEP WORD PROBLEMS

Multistep problems ask you to use more than one operation to find an answer. You might, for example, need to add a set of numbers, then multiply the sum by another number.

EXAMPLE

The Wilson children were each given a weekly allowance. Tanya, the oldest, received $15, Ed got $10, and Lakisha, the youngest, got $8. Find the total amount the children received after four weeks.

Step one: Find the total allowance for **one** week by adding the amounts of each child.

$$\begin{array}{r} 15 \\ 10 \\ + \ 8 \\ \hline \$33 \end{array} \text{ for one week}$$

Step two: Multiply one week's total allowance by 4 (for 4 weeks)

$$\begin{array}{r} 33 \\ \times \ 4 \\ \hline \$132 \end{array} \text{ combined allowance for 4 weeks}$$

Gross and **net** are two words you will encounter frequently.

Gross is a total amount **before** deducting taxes, expenses, etc.

Net is the amount remaining **after** deducting taxes, expenses, etc.

EXAMPLE

Tracy's **gross** salary is $450 per week. After her employer deducts $150 for taxes and medical insurance, her **net** salary is $300.

PRACTICE—MULTISTEP WORD PROBLEMS

1. Each month, the Bluesteins pay a home mortgage of $860 and a $218 payment on their car loan. What is the cost of these expenses for one year?

2. Sue is an endurance athlete who likes to run and bike. She can run 6 miles per hour and can bike at 22 miles per hour. In three hours, how much farther can she travel biking than running?

3. Jim's Car Wash grossed $18,230 for one week of operation. However, Jim had the following expenses: $1,205 for workers' salaries, $560 for water and electrical use and $1,582 for supplies and other expenses. What is Jim's *net* profit for the week?

4. The Bevco Bottling Plant produces 192 bottles of soda per minute, which are then packed in cases of 24. How many cases are produced in 10 minutes?

5. Three relatives inherited $86,000. After paying $32,540 in taxes and legal fees necessary to claiming the inheritance, they decided to split the remainder equally among themselves. How much is each of the three relatives' share of the inheritance?

ANSWERS

1. **$12,936**   2. **48**   3. **$14,883**
4. **80**   5. **$17,820**

Setups

Throughout the GED, you will have to respond to setup questions. You won't have to find an answer to the problem, but, instead, will be asked to choose the setup of operations that will allow you to solve it. Setups are usually "friendly" questions; since you don't need to do any calculation to answer them, they take up less time.

EXAMPLE ONE

Bill, Jodi, and Sue decided to share evenly the cost of a computer package that includes the following items: computer and keyboard—$724, monitor—$212, and printer—$159. Which expression below represents what each person had to contribute to the purchase?

(1) ($724 + $212 + $159) + 3

(2) $\dfrac{3}{(\$724 + \$212 + \$159)}$

(3) 3($724 + $212 + $159)

(4) $\dfrac{(\$724 + \$212 + \$159)}{3}$

(5) (3 + $724) + (3 + $212)

The answer is (4) because it's the only one that adds the cost of the computer components together, then divides them among the three people sharing the expense.

Parentheses

Parentheses ( ) are a very important part of setups and mathematical computation, in general. They serve to enclose and isolate parts of mathematical sentences. *Do the operations in parentheses first.* Here are some examples of how parentheses work:

$$3(26 + 41)$$

tells you to add 26 + 41, then multiply the sum (67) by 3.
    Answer: 201

$$(95 + 26) - (81 + 14)$$

tells you, **first**, to add 95 + 26 = 121 and 81 + 14 = 95
then, **second**, to subtract 121 - 95
    Answer: 26

PRACTICE—SETUPS AND PARENTHESES

1. Find the value of 4(46 + 23 - 8)

2. Find the value of $\dfrac{5(19 + 3)}{11}$

3. Serena took her family out to a fast-food restaurant. The bill was $18.24 and the tax was $3.11. Serena gave the cashier $25 to pay the bill. Which of the following expression represents the change Serena received?

    (1) (20 + 5) + (18.24 - 3.11)

    (2) $\dfrac{(18.24 - 3.11)}{25}$

    (3) 25 - (18.24 + 3.11)

    (4) (18.24 - 3.11) - 25

4. A one-way plane ticket from Chicago to Los Angeles is $209 for adults and $159 for children under 10. If the round-trip fare is twice the price of the one-way fare, find the expression that represents a round-trip fare for one adult and one child under 10.

    (1) $\dfrac{(159 + 209)}{2}$

    (2) 2(209 - 159)

    (3) (159 × 1) + (209 × 1)

    (4) 2(159 + 209)

ANSWERS

1. **244**   2. **10**   3. **3**   4. **4**

Multiple Questions on One Topic

At some time on the GED, you will be asked two, three, or four questions having to do with one topic or situation.

EXAMPLE

Questions 1–3 are based on the following:

Jean is considering whether to join a work-out gym in her neighborhood. The gym offers three different payment options for membership:

Plan A: A monthly fee of $90
Plan B: A one-time fee of $650 at the beginning of membership, which is good for one year.
Plan C: Two payments of $370 each—one at the beginning of the membership and one six months later, also good for one year.

1. How much more would Jean pay annually (for one year) if she chose Plan C over Plan B?

    Simple multistep. Find the difference between the two plans using subtraction.

$$2(370) = \quad 740 \text{ (plan C)}$$
$$\underline{- 650} \text{ (plan B)}$$

Answer: $ 90

2. Which expression represents the difference between Plans A and C if Jean were to use the gym for one year?

    (1) $\dfrac{450}{12} - 12(52)$

    (2) (90 × 12) - 2(370)

    (3) 12(90 + 52)

    (4) $\dfrac{90}{12} + \dfrac{52}{12}$

Setup of Plan A has to be 90 × 12—only answers (2) and (3) have it. "Difference" means subtraction and only (2) has it.

Answer: 2   (90 × 12) - 2(370)

3. Jean's net monthly income is $1,940. All her living expenses total $1,182. If Jean decides to join the gym using Plan A, what will be the amount remaining from her net income at the end of the month?

Step one: Calculate remaining money *before* joining gym.

$$1940 - 1182 = 758$$

Step two: Subtract monthly gym payment from answer to above step.

$$758 - 90 = \$668$$

Answer: $668

PRACTICE—MULTIPLE QUESTIONS

Questions 1–3 are based on the following:

Walter has an A.M. newspaper route. He drives 88 miles Monday to Friday, 73 miles on Saturday, and 103 miles on Sunday. His van gets 20 miles per gallon of gas.

1. Which of the following represents the number of gallons of gas Walter uses for the weekend?

    (1) $73 + 103 + 88$

    (2) $(73 + 103) + 20$

    (3) $20(73 + 103)$

    (4) $\dfrac{103 + 73}{20}$

    (5) $20 \div (73 + 103 + 88)$

2. Find the total number of miles Walter drives per week.

3. How many more miles does Walter drive during the week compared with the miles he drives on the weekend?

ANSWERS

1. **4**   2. **616**   3. **264**

Exponents

Consider this number: 6^3

The little ^{3} that seems to be floating in the air is called an **exponent**. 6 is called the **base number**. What you're being told to do here is multiply **6 × 6 × 6**. It can also be stated as "6 to the third power."

$$6^3 = 6 \times 6 \times 6$$
$$6 \times 6 = 36 \times 6 = 216$$
$$6^3 = 216$$

Any number to the first power is equal to itself.

EXAMPLE

$$18^1 = 18$$

Sometimes on the GED, you might have to deal with more complex exponent problems like this one:

$$5^4 + 6^2 - 8^1 =$$

Convert each base/exponent pair into a separate number and then perform the operations.

$$5^4 = 5 \times 5 \times 5 \times 5 = 625$$
$$6^2 = 6 \times 6 = 36$$
$$8^1 = 8$$
$$625 + 36 - 8 = 653$$

PRACTICE—EXPONENTS

Find the value of the following.

1. 7^3 5. 30^2

2. 10^4 6. $17^3 + 19^2$

3. 16^3 7. $24^2 - 8^3$

4. 28^1 8. $20^2 - 5^3 + 2^5$

ANSWERS

1. **343**   2. **10,000**   3. **4096**   4. **28**
5. **900**   6. **5,274**   7. **64**   8. **307**

Square Roots

The square root sign $\sqrt{}$ looks like a cross between a checkmark and a division sign. When you see this: $\sqrt{49}$, you're being asked to find a number that, *multiplied by itself*, will equal 49. Since $7 \times 7 = 49$, 7 is the square root of 49 or $\sqrt{49} = 7$.

Here's how to find square roots of larger numbers.

EXAMPLE ONE

Find $\sqrt{441}$

Step one: Narrow down using multiples of 10.

You know that $10 \times 10 = 100$, but that's too low. Next, try $20 \times 20 = 400$—very close to 441. $30 \times 30 = 900$, which is way over. The square root of 441 must be a number more than 20 and less than 30. So we know $\sqrt{441} = 2\_$

Step two: Find the exact number for the ones digit.

441 ends in a "1." Therefore, the number you choose to accompany your 20, when multiplied by itself, *must end in one*. For example, $1 \times 1 = 1$ (that works, so it could be 21.) $2 \times 2 = 4$ (no) $3 \times 3 = 9$ (no), $4 \times 4 = 1\underline{6}$ (ends in "6"—no) and so on—up to $9 \times 9 = 8\underline{1}$ (ends in "1"—yes). You have two numbers to choose from—21 or 29. Which one is a better guess? 21, of course, because 29 is so close to 30 and you've already seen that 30^2 is 900, which is way over.

Step three: Try it. $21 \times 21 = 441$

Answer: $21 = \sqrt{441}$

EXAMPLE TWO

The value of $\sqrt{34}$ is between what pair of whole numbers?

(a) 16 and 17   (d) 9 and 10
(b) 5 and 6   (e) 6 and 7
(c) 2 and 3

This can be done in your head. Since $5 \times 5 = 25$ is too low and $6 \times 6 = 36$ is just a bit too high, the number has to be between the two. The actual $\sqrt{34}$ is 5.830518... but (b) will answer this question.

Answer: (b)

PRACTICE—SQUARE ROOTS

Solve.

1. $\sqrt{121}$
2. $\sqrt{289}$
3. $\sqrt{529}$
4. $\sqrt{256}$
5. $\sqrt{2704}$
6. $\sqrt{4489}$
7. The value of $\sqrt{28}$ is between what pair of whole numbers?

ANSWERS

1. **11**   2. **17**   3. **23**   4. **16**
5. **52**   6. **67**   7. **5** and **6**

Finding Square Roots with a Calculator

The calculator makes finding square roots much easier. For Part I square root problems, follow this procedure:

Enter the number whose square root you need to find—for example, 6,084. Then press the "Shift" key in the upper-left corner of the keypad, then press the "x^2" key. The answer will read 78.

Order of Operations

Do you remember learning *PEMDAS* or "Please Excuse My Dear Aunt Sally?" This is a way of remembering the order of operations for solving complicated mathematical sentences.

PEMDAS or "Please Excuse My Dear Aunt Sally"

1st—**P** stands for **parentheses**
2nd—**E** stands for **exponents**
3rd—**M** stands for **multiplication**
4th—**D** stands for **division**
5th—**A** stands for **addition**
6th—**S** stands for **subtraction**

If you have a problem that asks you to do addition, multiplication, and some work in parentheses, first you would do the work in parentheses, then the multiplication, and finally, the addition. Memorize the order and follow it.

EXAMPLE

Solve: $\dfrac{(5+3)^2}{4} + 27$

Step one: **P** (parentheses) always comes first, so do all work in parentheses.

5 + 3 = 8. Now the problem looks like this:

$$\dfrac{8^2}{4} + 27$$

Step two: **E** (exponents) comes second, so do 8 × 8 = 64

$$\dfrac{64}{4} + 27$$

Step three: **D** (division) is the next operation in the order that has to be performed in this particular problem, so do 64 ÷ 4 = 16

16 + 27

Step four: **A** (addition) is the last step for this problem. So do 16 + 27 = 43

Answer: 43

PRACTICE—ORDER OF OPERATIONS

Evaluate using order of operations.

1. (43 – 19) + (16 – 14)(4)

2. $\dfrac{48}{3} - 6$

3. $\dfrac{(6 + 7 + 2)^3}{3}$

ANSWERS

1. **32**   2. **10**   3. **1125**

Mean and Median

Finding the *mean* and *median* of a group of numbers are two operations you must learn for the GED. They both tell you to find the *average* for a group of numbers, but each is a bit different from the other.

> **Mean** is interchangeable with the word **average**. Add all of the numbers given, then divide by the amount of numbers.

EXAMPLE

Tanya is a waitress at the Mercer Street Café. Last week, she worked five days and earned the following tips:

Monday: $26
Tuesday: $32
Wednesday: $18
Thursday: $40
Friday: $39

Find the mean (average) amount of her daily tips for the five days she worked.

Step one: Add all of the numbers

(26 + 32 + 18 + 40 + 39) = 155

Step two: Count how many numbers you just added and divide by the amount of the numbers.

$$5\overline{)155} = 31$$

Answer: Mean amount of tips for the days worked that week is $31. It's true that Tanya never earned $31 on any of the given days she worked that week. The mean indicates that an **average** day's tips for her comes to about **$31**.

Median is the middle number in a group of numbers arranged in order. Sometimes this is a very simple operation—just line the numbers up in order and pick the one in the middle. Other times, it's a bit more complicated.

EXAMPLE ONE

For the marking period, Joe's test scores are 86, 66, 75, 81, and 68. What is his median score for the marking period?

Step one: Line the numbers up in order:

    66   68   75   81   86

Step two: Choose the middle number: 75

EXAMPLE TWO

For the next marking period, Joe's test scores are 62, 88, 90, 85, 75, and 83. What is his median score for the marking period?

Step one: Line the numbers up in order:

    62   75   83   85   88   90

Step two: Choose the middle number—but there's a problem. There *is* no middle number because there are an *even* amount of numbers. In these situations, *choose the two middle numbers* and average those two:

    62   75   83   85   88   90

The two middle numbers are 83 and 85.

Sub-step one: 83 + 85 = 168

Sub-step two: 168 ÷ 2 = 84

Answer: Joe's median score for the marking period is **84**.

1. Kwan is a bike messenger who works three days a week. On Wednesday, he pedaled 32 miles, on Thursday 48 miles, and on Friday 34 miles. What is the mean distance he pedaled during those days?

2. Cara is a real estate broker who does a survey of properties for sale on Beach Street. The prices for four homes are $96,000; $92,900; $101,500; and $91,000. Find the mean sale price for the homes on Beach Street.

3. Competing for the league championship, the Thompson Tigers bowling team members bowl individual games of 189, 207, 217, and 199. What is the mean bowling score for the team?

ANSWERS

1. **38**   2. **$94,450**   3. **203**

Not Enough Information Is Given

Sometimes, a question is purposely misleading. It fails to provide enough information for you to calculate the answer.

EXAMPLE

Forestry workers plant trees at the rate of 12 per hour. At that rate, how long will it take two workers to plant 8 acres of cleared land?

(a) 86 hours
(b) 14 hours
(c) 43 hours
(d) 16 hours
(e) not enough information given

The answer is (e). You would need to know how many trees need to be planted in order to calculate an answer. The size of the land is not relevant information.

Note: Don't be frequently tempted by the "not enough information is given" response. It is used on only a few occasions during the course of a GED Math section.

One of the following questions does *not* provide enough information; another does.

1. Gerald works at his uncle's restaurant 3 days a week, and gets paid $115 a day plus tips. He works two days a week delivering lumber for $90 a day. What is his average daily pay for a typical week?

   (1) $525
   (2) $105
   (3) $185
   (4) $95
   (5) not enough information is given

2. A plumber buys pipe at $1 a foot. From a 15-foot pipe, he cuts a piece 9 feet long to be used on a job. What is the value of the unused portion?

   (1) $16
   (2) 15 – 11
   (3) $6
   (4) $8
   (5) not enough information is given

ANSWERS

1. **5**   2. **3**

Basic Geometry

In this unit, you will deal with the rectangle, square, rectangular container, and cube. The triangle will be mentioned but will be more thoroughly dealt with in Chapter 20. Circles will be dealt with in Chapter 21. Chapter 24 will deal with more advanced geometric concepts.

PERIMETER

The perimeter is the distance around a figure. It's the sum of the lengths of all its sides.

EXAMPLE ONE

Find the perimeter of the triangle below.

To find perimeter, add the sum of all sides: 27 + 36 + 45 = 108 ft.
Note: Always be aware of the units named in the diagram or asked for in the problem. If it's *feet*, make sure your answer is in *feet*.

EXAMPLE TWO

Find the perimeter of the rectangle below.

The formula for finding the perimeter of a rectangle is:

$$P = 2(l) + 2(w)$$
l = length and w = width

The *length* of the rectangle is the longer side and the *width* is the shorter side.

You can easily see that a rectangle has two lengths and two widths—two pair of opposite sides—and those opposite sides are equal to each other.

In the rectangle above, the length = 14 in. and the width = 4 in. Now you can use the formula for perimeter:

$$P = 2(l) + 2(w)$$
$$P = 2(14) + 2(4)$$
$$P = 28 + 8$$
$$P = 36 \text{ in.}$$

Answer: Perimeter = 36 in.

EXAMPLE THREE

Find the perimeter of the square below.

The formula for finding the perimeter of a square is:

$$P = 4(s)$$
$$s = \text{side}$$

Unlike a rectangle, all four sides of a square are equal. So, to find a square's perimeter, multiply the one side × 4.

$$P = 4(s) \qquad P = 4(10) \qquad P = 40$$

Note how there is no unit of measure next to the 10. 10 what? You will sometimes see this on the GED. Simply express the answer in terms of a number without a unit of measure.

Answer: P = 40

Find the perimeter of the following figures.

1.

2.

3.

ANSWERS

1. **82 in.** 2. **44 yds.** 3. **164**

AREA

The area of a figure is the measure of flat surface inside its perimeter.

EXAMPLE ONE

A bedroom is 10 ft. long and 12 ft. wide. How many square feet of carpet will be needed to cover its floor?

The bedroom above is rectangular. The formula for the area of a rectangle is:

$$A = l(w) \qquad \text{or} \qquad A = lw$$

Note: When letters are pushed right next to each other it means multiply. In this case, ***lw*** means **length × width**

Step one: Draw a diagram. It's always a good idea to draw a diagram from a word problem about geometry to help visualize what you need to solve.

10 ft.

12 ft.

Step two: Using the formula for the area of a rectangle, find the area.

$$A = lw$$
$$A = 10(12)$$
$$A = 120 \text{ } square \text{ feet.}$$

Note: The word **square (sq.)** must always accompany an answer involving area, regardless of the shape of a figure. There are three ways to express **square**, all of which are correct.
1. 120 **sq.** ft.
2. 120 ft. **sq.**
3. 120 ft.^{2}

EXAMPLE TWO

Find the area of the square below.

17 miles

Since all the sides of a square are equal, the formula for the area of a square is:

$$A = s^2$$

$$A = s^2$$
$$A = 17^2$$
$$A = 17 \times 17$$
$$A = 289$$

Answer: A = 289 sq. miles

1.

23 in.

41 in.

(a) find perimeter
(b) find area

2.

14 ft.

(a) find perimeter
(b) find area

3. How many 1-ft. by 1-ft. square blocks would be required to pave a patio with a length of 20 ft. and a width of 12 ft.?

ANSWERS

1. (a) **128 in.**   (b) **943 sq. in.**
2. (a) **56 ft.**   (b) **196 sq. ft.**
3. **240**

VOLUME

Volume is the measure of the amount of space inside a three-dimensional figure such as a rectangular container, cube, or sphere. It tells how much these figures can hold.

EXAMPLE ONE

Find the volume for the rectangular container below.

4 ft.

8 ft.

25 ft.

The formula for volume of a rectangular container is:

$$V = lwh$$
$$V = \text{volume}$$
$$l = \text{length}$$
$$h = \text{height}$$
$$w = \text{width}$$
$$(V = l \times w \times h)$$

$V = 25 \times 8 \times 4 = 800$ **cubic** ft. or 800 ft. **cu.** or 800 ft.^{3}

Note: A rule in math called the **associative property** states that it doesn't matter in what order you multiply any three numbers together, the answer will always be the same. So, for finding volume, don't worry about which is the height, length, or width. Just multiply three numbers in any order.

EXAMPLE TWO

A cube-shaped container holds sand. How many cubic feet of sand will it hold if one of its sides is 8 feet?

The formula for volume of a cube is:

$$V = s^3 \qquad v = \text{volume} \qquad s = \text{side}$$

Since all sides of a cube are equal, there is no difference between its length, width, and height. Just multiply any side to the third power.

Step one: Draw a diagram.

8 ft.
8 ft.
8 ft.

Step two: Do the multiplication.
$8 \times 8 \times 8 = 512$ cu. ft.

PRACTICE—VOLUME

1. Find the volume of the figure below.

14 in.

8 in.

8 in.

2. What is the difference in volume between a 13-ft. cube and a 10-ft. cube?

ANSWERS

1. **896 cu. in.**   2. **1,197 cu. ft.**

PRACTICE—REVIEW OF GEOMETRIC FORMULAS

Match the formula used to calculate the following measurements, marking P for perimeter, A for area, and V for volume on the corresponding lines.

1. _____ The amount of wallpaper needed to cover the walls of a room.
2. _____ The amount of water needed to fill a swimming pool.
3. _____ The amount of fencing needed to enclose a yard.
4. _____ The amount of trunk space in a car.
5. _____ The amount of molding need to trim a ceiling.
6. _____ The amount of grass seed needed to plant a new lawn.

ANSWERS

1. **A**   2. **V**   3. **P**   4. **V**   5. **P**   6. **A**

CHAPTER REVIEW

Fill in the answer grids, and use a calculator where indicated.

1. What value does the "6" have in 462,103?

   (1) 600,000
   (2) 60
   (3) 62,000
   (4) 60,000
   (5) 16,000

Questions 2–4 are based on the following:

Jacqueline flies 730 miles on Tuesday, 1,250 miles on Thursday and 681 miles on Friday.

2. Find the total number of miles she flew for the three days.

3. What is the median number of miles Jacqueline flew?

4. What is the mean number of miles she flew?

5. There are 454 balloons that need to be blown up for the Homecoming Dance. If there are 19 volunteers, how many balloons does each person have to blow up? How many will be left over?

6. For each of its 38 municipal employees, the city of Irvington pays $720 per year to a health insurance provider. What is the total the city pays to purchase its employees' health insurance?

7. A jewelry store sells gold necklaces for $135 each. On Friday, there is a sale on the necklaces, reducing their price by $30. Which expression represents the price of five necklaces and a diamond pendant?

   (1) 5(135)
   (2) 5(135 − 30)
   (3) 5(135 − 30) + 200
   (4) $\dfrac{135 - 30}{5}$
   (5) not enough information given

8. There are three classes of second graders at Rockford Elementary School. One class has 21 students, another has 26, and the last has 25. The principal would like to split the second-grade population into two groups for lunch periods. Which expression represents the separation of the second grade into two groups?

(1) $2(21 + 26 + 25)$

(2) $\dfrac{21 + 26 + 25}{2}$

(3) $(21 + 26) - (25 + 2)$

(4) $\dfrac{2}{21 + 26 + 25}$

(5) not enough information is given

9. Traveling at 65 miles per hour, approximately how long will it take Angela to drive 310 miles?

(1) between 2 and 3 hours
(2) between 3 and 4 hours
(3) between 4 and 5 hours
(4) between 5 and 6 hours
(5) very close to seven hours

10. Evaluate the following: $5(8^3 - 4^3)$

(1) 60
(2) 620
(3) 2,240
(4) 1,860
(5) 185

11. The value of $\sqrt{26}$ is between which of the following pairs of numbers?

(1) 2 and 13
(2) 12 and 13
(3) 4.4 and 4.5
(4) 5 and 6
(5) 8 and 9

Questions 12 and 13 are based on the following:

The Smithville Auto Parts Store is open Monday–Friday from 9 A.M. to 6 P.M. and Saturday from 9 A.M. to 4 P.M. Tom, the cashier, earns $8 per hour, and Susan, the manager, earns $12 per hour.

12. Which expression represents the total number of hours the store is open during a four-week period?

(1) $4(9 + 7)$
(2) $4(9 \times 5) + 4\,(7)$
(3) $(4 + 12) + (5 \times 45)$
(4) $45 + 7 + 4$
(5) not enough information is given

13. How much more does Sue make than Tom during a Monday–Saturday work-week?

(1) $208
(2) $126
(3) $52
(4) $108
(5) $114

14. Dave operates a snack truck five days a week and uses crushed ice to cool his soft drinks. The following information indicates his ice use by the bucket for each of the days.

Monday—16
Tuesday—14
Wednesday—19
Thursday—21
Friday—15

If the supply house where Dave buys his ice charges him $1.50 per bucket, find the average cost he must pay for ice per day.

(1) $14.50
(2) $26.50
(3) $127.50
(4) $25.50
(5) $19.50

15. The diagram below represents a floor plan for an office and storeroom. If both floors are to be covered with 1 sq. ft. vinyl tiles that cost $2 per tile, how much would it cost in dollars to purchase the tiles for both rooms?

16. The diagram below shows the dimensions of a backyard swimming pool. Which expression represents the maximum volume in cubic ft. of water it can hold?

(1) 3(40 + 20 + 8)
(2) 3(8) + 3(40) + 3(20)
(3) (40 × 8) + (40 + 20)
(4) 8 × 20 × 40
(5) not enough information is given

ANSWERS

1. **4**	5. **23r17**	9. **3**	13. **1**
2. **2,661**	6. **$27,360**	10. **3**	14. **4**
3. **730**	7. **5**	11. **4**	15. **$920**
4. **887**	8. **2**	12. **2**	16. **4**

Fractions and Measurements

Writing Fractions

A **fraction** of something means a part of that thing; for example, a pizza pie has eight slices. If you take one slice, that equals $\frac{1}{8}$ (one eighth) of the pie. Two slices equals $\frac{2}{8}$ (two eighths), three slices equals $\frac{3}{8}$ (three eighths), and so on.

In the fraction $\frac{3}{8}$, the top number (3) is called the **numerator**. It tells how many parts you have. The bottom number (8) is called the **denominator** and tells you how many equal parts there are in the whole.

$$\frac{3}{8} \leftarrow \text{numerator} \atop \leftarrow \text{denominator}$$

Consider the square below:

It's one whole divided into nine equal parts. If four of those parts are shaded, as in the diagram above, the shaded area represents $\frac{4}{9}$ of the square.

What fraction of the square is shaded below?

7/9
(seven ninths)

If the entire square is shaded, the fraction represented is $\frac{9}{9}$ or **1**. Any fraction whose numerator and denominator are the same *is equal to one*.

$$\frac{9}{9} = 1 \qquad \frac{12}{12} = 1 \qquad \frac{181}{181} = 1$$

FRACTION TYPES

There are three types of fractions you need to become familiar with: proper fractions, improper fractions, and mixed numbers.

- *Proper fractions* have numerators that are smaller than their denominators and are always less than one. $\frac{1}{3}$, $\frac{5}{6}$ and $\frac{11}{12}$ are proper fractions.

- *Improper fractions* have numerators that are larger than or equal to their denominators. $\frac{7}{3}$, $\frac{9}{6}$ and $\frac{12}{12}$ are improper fractions.
  (**Note:** There's nothing wrong or "improper" about improper fractions. That's just a mathematical name given to them to distinguish them from proper fractions.)

- *Mixed numbers* have a whole number included to the left of the fraction.

$3\frac{1}{2}$ (three and one-half)

$5\frac{5}{6}$ (five and five-sixths) are mixed numbers

PRACTICE—WRITING FRACTIONS

Put an I for improper fraction, P for proper fraction, and M for mixed number on the blank lines next to each number below.

1. ___ $\frac{3}{8}$

2. ___ $\frac{8}{5}$

3. ___ $9\frac{3}{11}$

4. ___ $\frac{6}{6}$

5. ___ $\frac{1}{2}$

6. ___ $12\frac{1}{2}$

ANSWERS

1. **P**   2. **I**   3. **M**   4. **I**   5. **P**   6. **M**

Equivalent Fractions and Reducing to Lowest Terms

Four slices of pizza make up $\frac{4}{8}$ of a pie, which happens also to be $\frac{1}{2}$ the pie. Therefore, we say $\frac{4}{8}$ is **equivalent** (equal) to $\frac{1}{2}$. Even though the numbers in both the numerator and denominator are higher, the value of $\frac{4}{8}$ and $\frac{1}{2}$ are the same. Notice in the fraction $\frac{4}{8}$ that both numerator and denominator can be divided by 4.

$$\frac{4 \div 4 = 1}{8 \div 4 = 2}$$

This process is called **reducing to lowest terms**. Simply find the largest number that

can be used to divide both numerator and denominator, then divide.

EXAMPLE

Reduce the following fractions to lowest terms.

$$\frac{5}{25} \qquad \frac{6}{9}$$

$$\frac{5 \div 5 = 1}{25 \div 5 = 5} \qquad \frac{6 \div 3 = 2}{9 \div 3 = 3}$$

PRACTICE—REDUCING TO LOWEST TERMS

Reduce the following fractions to lowest terms.

1. $\frac{4}{8}$

2. $\frac{12}{16}$

3. $\frac{40}{50}$

4. $\frac{27}{36}$

5. $\frac{16}{48}$

6. $\frac{14}{14}$

7. $\frac{51}{85}$

ANSWERS

1. $\frac{1}{2}$

2. $\frac{3}{4}$

3. $\frac{4}{5}$

4. $\frac{3}{4}$

5. $\frac{1}{3}$

6. $\frac{1}{1}$

7. $\frac{3}{5}$

Raising Fractions to Higher Terms

When solving problems with fractions, the **answer** must be expressed in lowest terms. However, when working with fractions to solve a problem, you will often have to do the exact opposite—raise them to higher terms while keeping them equivalent. To do this, multiply both the numerator and denominator by the same number.

In virtually all situations where you will raise to higher terms, the denominator will already be determined. You'll just need to figure out the numerator.

EXAMPLES

Convert $\frac{2}{3}$ to sixths

$$\frac{2}{3} = \frac{?}{6} \qquad \frac{2 \times 2}{3 \times 2} = \frac{4}{6}$$

Convert $\frac{5}{8}$ to twenty-fourths

$$\frac{5}{8} = \frac{?}{24} \qquad \frac{5 \times 3}{8 \times 3} = \frac{15}{24}$$

PRACTICE—RAISING TO HIGHER TERMS

Add the appropriate numerator so that the fractions will be equivalent.

1. $\frac{5}{8} = \frac{}{24}$

2. $\frac{3}{8} = \frac{}{16}$

3. $\frac{4}{5} = \frac{}{20}$

4. $\frac{9}{6} = \frac{}{18}$

5. $\frac{7}{8} = \frac{}{56}$

ANSWERS

1. **15**   2. **6**   3. **16**   4. **27**   5. **49**

Converting Improper Fractions to Mixed Numbers

Sometimes the solution to a problem will be expressed as an improper fraction, which then must be converted to a mixed number.

EXAMPLE

$$\frac{11}{4} = 2\frac{3}{4}$$

Remember that fractions are division problems, so $\frac{11}{4}$ can be written as $11 \div 4$ or $4\overline{)11}$.

$$4\overline{)11} \quad \overset{2\ r3}{} \qquad 2\ r3 \text{ is the same as } 2\frac{3}{4}$$

PRACTICE—CONVERTING IMPROPER FRACTIONS TO MIXED NUMBERS

Convert the following improper fractions to mixed or whole numbers. Reduce where necessary.

1. $\frac{15}{2}$

2. $\frac{27}{3}$

3. $\frac{26}{4}$

4. $\frac{56}{7}$

5. $\frac{31}{10}$

6. $\frac{46}{12}$

7. $\frac{33}{9}$

ANSWERS

1. $7\frac{1}{2}$

2. **9**

3. $6\frac{1}{2}$

4. **8**

5. $3\frac{1}{10}$

6. $3\frac{5}{6}$

7. $3\frac{2}{3}$

Adding and Subtracting Fractions

Adding and subtracting fractions when the denominators are the same is a simple process. It looks like this:

$$\frac{1}{5} + \frac{3}{5} = \frac{4}{5} \qquad \frac{5}{7} - \frac{3}{7} = \frac{2}{7}$$

Notice the denominators stay the same and the numerators either increase or decrease.

PRACTICE—ADDING AND SUBTRACTING FRACTIONS WITH SAME DENOMINATOR

Solve the following and, where necessary, reduce to lowest terms.

1. $\frac{5}{8} - \frac{3}{8}$

2. $\frac{1}{6} + \frac{3}{6}$

3. $\frac{3}{11} + \frac{5}{11}$

4. $\frac{18}{21} - \frac{4}{21}$

5. $\frac{3}{5} + \frac{4}{5}$

ANSWERS

1. $\frac{1}{4}$ 4. $\frac{2}{3}$

2. $\frac{2}{3}$ 5. $1\frac{2}{5}$

3. $\frac{8}{11}$

Lowest Common Denominator

When denominators **differ**, however, fractions can't be added or subtracted until all the denominators are converted to the same number, known as the **lowest common denominator** or **LCD**.

EXAMPLE ONE

Find $\frac{5}{8} + \frac{1}{4}$

The two fractions have different denominators so you can't add them in their present state. Since $\frac{5}{8}$ can't be reduced to quarters, the lowest common denominator that can be used for both fractions is eighths. Both four and eight can divide eight evenly.

Step one: Choose the LCD. Here, it's eighths.

Step two: Convert $\frac{1}{4}$ to $\frac{2}{8}$ by raising to higher terms.

Step three: Add $\frac{5}{8} + \frac{2}{8}$

Answer: $\frac{7}{8}$

EXAMPLE TWO

Find $\frac{1}{2} + \frac{1}{6} + \frac{1}{8}$

Step one: Choose the LCD.
This is a bit more difficult here. None of the denominators in the problem ($\overline{2}$, $\overline{6}$, or $\overline{8}$) can be used as an LCD. You can convert $\frac{1}{2}$ to $\frac{4}{8}$ but you can't convert $\frac{1}{6}$ to eighths ($\overline{8}$) because six doesn't divide evenly into eight—there's a remainder of

two. And $\frac{1}{2}$ can be converted to $\frac{3}{6}$, but, eighths can't be converted to sixths. You must choose the lowest number all three denominators ($\overline{2}$, $\overline{6}$, and $\overline{8}$) can divide into evenly. This is often a trial-and-error process. You already know 6 and 8 don't work. How about 10? 2 divides 10 evenly, but neither 6 nor 8 does so. How about 12? Both 2 and 6 divide it evenly, but 8 doesn't. How about 16? Both 2 and 8 work, but 6 doesn't. Eventually, you will reach **24**. It is the **lowest** number that all three denominators can divide equally. Therefore, 24 is the **LCD** used for solving the problem. This may seem like a long process, but with some practice, finding the LCD will come more quickly to you.

Step two: Convert $\frac{1}{2}$ to $\frac{12}{24}$, $\frac{1}{6}$ to $\frac{4}{24}$, and $\frac{1}{8}$ to $\frac{3}{24}$

Step three: Add $\frac{12}{24} + \frac{4}{24} + \frac{3}{24}$

Answer: $\frac{19}{24}$

PRACTICE—ADDING AND SUBTRACTING USING LCD

Find the LCD, then add or subtract. Reduce answers to lowest terms where necessary.

1. $\frac{2}{7} + \frac{3}{21}$ 5. $\frac{3}{16} + \frac{1}{12} + \frac{1}{4}$

2. $\frac{5}{6} \pm \frac{1}{3}$ 6. $\frac{8}{15} \pm \frac{1}{3}$

3. $\frac{1}{4} + \frac{1}{6}$ 7. $\frac{7}{10} \pm \frac{1}{3}$

4. $\frac{5}{7} + \frac{3}{4}$ 8. $\frac{2}{3} + \frac{1}{6} \pm \frac{4}{9}$

ANSWERS

1. $\frac{3}{7}$ 5. $\frac{25}{48}$

2. $\frac{1}{2}$ 6. $\frac{1}{5}$

3. $\frac{5}{12}$ 7. $\frac{11}{30}$

4. $1\frac{13}{28}$ 8. $\frac{7}{18}$

Comparing and Ordering Fractions

To compare and order fractions with different denominators: (1) find the LCD, (2) convert fractions by raising to higher terms, where necessary, (3) compare the numerators.

EXAMPLE ONE

Find the larger of the two fractions:

$$\frac{2}{5} \qquad \frac{1}{3}$$

Step one: Find the LCD: $\overline{15}$

Step two: Convert: $\frac{2}{5} = \frac{6}{15} \qquad \frac{1}{3} = \frac{5}{15}$

Step three: Compare: $\frac{6}{15}\left(\frac{2}{5}\right)$ is larger than $\frac{5}{15}\left(\frac{1}{3}\right)$ by $\frac{1}{15}$

Answer: $\frac{2}{5}$ is larger

EXAMPLE TWO

Arrange the following fractions in order from greatest to least:

$$\frac{7}{8} \qquad \frac{5}{6} \qquad \frac{7}{12} \qquad \frac{3}{4}$$

Step one: Find the LCD: use $\overline{24}$

Step two: Convert: $\frac{7}{8} = \frac{21}{24} \qquad \frac{5}{6} = \frac{20}{24}$

$\frac{7}{12} = \frac{14}{24} \qquad \frac{3}{4} = \frac{18}{24}$

Step three: Compare and arrange in order:

$$\frac{7}{8}\left(\frac{21}{24}\right) \quad \frac{5}{6}\left(\frac{20}{24}\right) \quad \frac{3}{4}\left(\frac{18}{24}\right) \quad \frac{7}{12}\left(\frac{14}{24}\right)$$

PRACTICE—COMPARING AND ORDERING FRACTIONS

Choose the larger fraction in each pair.

1. $\frac{5}{8}$ $\frac{9}{16}$

2. $\frac{5}{12}$ $\frac{4}{9}$

3. $\frac{1}{3}$ $\frac{2}{7}$

4. Arrange the following in order from heaviest to lightest:

$$\frac{1}{4} \text{ lb.} \qquad \frac{3}{8} \text{ lb.} \qquad \frac{3}{5} \text{ lb.} \qquad \frac{3}{10} \text{ lb.}$$

5. Arrange the following in order from shortest to longest:

$$\frac{5}{8} \qquad \frac{7}{32} \qquad \frac{9}{16} \qquad \frac{3}{4}$$

ANSWERS

1. $\frac{5}{8}$

2. $\frac{4}{9}$

3. $\frac{1}{3}$

4. $\frac{3}{5}, \frac{3}{8}, \frac{3}{10}, \frac{1}{4}$

5. $\frac{7}{32}, \frac{9}{16}, \frac{5}{8}, \frac{3}{4}$

Working with Mixed Numbers

ADDITION

EXAMPLE ONE

$$\frac{7}{8} + \frac{5}{8} = \frac{12}{8}$$

This is simple enough. But $\frac{12}{8}$ must be converted to a mixed number.

$$\frac{12}{8} = 1\frac{4}{8} = 1\frac{1}{2}$$

$$\frac{7}{8} + \frac{5}{8} = 1\frac{1}{2}$$

EXAMPLE TWO

$$14\frac{3}{4} + 2\frac{3}{5}$$

Step one: Using LCD, convert the fractions so they can be added.

$$14\frac{3}{4} = 14\frac{15}{20}$$

$$+ 2\frac{3}{5} = 2\frac{12}{20}$$

$$16\frac{27}{20}$$

Step two: Convert the fraction to a mixed number

$$\frac{27}{20} = 1\frac{7}{20}$$

and carry the whole number 1 over to the whole-number column, adding it to the 16.

$$16 + 1\frac{7}{20} = 17\frac{7}{20}$$

SUBTRACTION AND "BORROWING"

To subtract mixed numbers, you must be able to "borrow." Here's how to do it.

EXAMPLE

$$5\frac{1}{6} - 2\frac{5}{6}$$

$$5\frac{1}{6}$$
$$-2\frac{5}{6}$$

The problem here is that you can't subtract 5 from 1. You need to borrow from the column to the left, just as you do in working with whole numbers. You borrow 1 from 5, which then becomes 4. Then convert the borrowed one into 6ths. Remember: $1 = \frac{6}{6}$. Add those borrowed $\frac{6}{6}$ to the $\frac{1}{6}$, which now becomes $\frac{7}{6}$.

$$^{4}5\frac{1}{6} + \frac{6}{6} = 4\frac{7}{6}$$
$$-2\frac{5}{6}$$
$$2\frac{2}{6} = 2\frac{1}{3}$$

Always convert the borrowed 1 into whatever the denominator specifies. If it's 8ths, add $\frac{8}{8}$, or if it's 12ths, add $\frac{12}{12}$ to the existing fraction.

PRACTICE—ADDING AND SUBTRACTING WITH MIXED NUMBERS

Add or subtract. Express answers as mixed numbers where appropriate. Reduce to lowest terms.

1. $\frac{7}{9} + \frac{5}{9}$

2. $12\frac{1}{8} - 5\frac{5}{8}$

3. $\frac{3}{4} + \frac{5}{6}$

4. $41\frac{1}{3} - 18\frac{5}{9}$

5. $16\frac{7}{8} + 12\frac{9}{16}$

6. $36\frac{5}{12} - 19\frac{17}{24}$

7. $9\frac{2}{5} + 8\frac{2}{3} + 7\frac{11}{15}$

ANSWERS

1. $1\frac{1}{3}$ 5. $29\frac{7}{16}$

2. $6\frac{1}{2}$ 6. $16\frac{17}{24}$

3. $1\frac{7}{12}$ 7. $25\frac{4}{5}$

4. $22\frac{7}{9}$

MULTIPLICATION

In one important way, multiplication is a much easier process than adding and subtracting fractions. You don't need to worry about finding a common denominator—simply multiply the numerators of the fractions by each other and then do the same for the denominators. Reduce to lowest terms where necessary.

EXAMPLE ONE

Find $\frac{5}{8} \times \frac{1}{3}$

$$\frac{5 \times 1}{8 \times 3} = \frac{5}{24}$$

When multiplying fractions, all mixed numbers must be converted to improper fractions, and all whole numbers must use $\frac{}{1}$ as a denominator. See the following example.

EXAMPLE TWO

Find $5\frac{3}{4} \times 7$

Step one: Convert to improper fractions

$$5\frac{3}{4} = \frac{23}{4} \qquad 7 = \frac{7}{1}$$

Step two: Multiply

$$\frac{23}{4} \times \frac{7}{1} = \frac{161}{4}$$

Step three: Divide and convert to a mixed number

$$\frac{161}{4} = 40\frac{1}{4}$$

CONVERTING MIXED NUMBERS TO IMPROPER FRACTIONS

How did we get $\frac{23}{4}$ from $5\frac{3}{4}$ in Step one above? Here's how.

Step one: Multiply the denominator of the fraction by the whole number to its left.

$$5\frac{3}{4} \quad (5 \times 4 = 20)$$

Step two: Take the product of Step one (20) and add it to the numerator.

$$(20 + 3 = 23)$$

Step three: Place the "new" numerator (23) over the same denominator (4).

$$5\frac{3}{4} = \frac{23}{4}$$

PRACTICE—CONVERTING MIXED NUMBERS TO IMPROPER FRACTIONS

Convert the following to improper fractions.

1. $2\frac{3}{8}$

2. $14\frac{1}{2}$

3. $9\frac{6}{7}$

4. $11\frac{3}{4}$

5. $20\frac{13}{16}$

ANSWERS

1. $\frac{19}{8}$

2. $\frac{29}{2}$

3. $\frac{69}{7}$

4. $\frac{47}{4}$

5. $\frac{333}{16}$

USING CROSS-CANCELING IN MULTIPLICATION

This process reduces the size of the numerators and denominators, making multiplication easier. Here's how to do it:

Look at the the numerator and its diagonal denominator. See whether there is a number that divides evenly into both. Choose the **highest** number common to both, then divide them by that number. Cross the old numbers out and replace them with the newer (smaller) numbers. Then multiply horizontally (across) to find the answer.

EXAMPLE

Find $\frac{5}{18} \times \frac{9}{20}$

Step one: Look for diagonal relationships. Both 18 and 9 can be divided evenly by 9; both 20 and 5 can be divided evenly by 5.

Step two: Cross out the old numbers and replace them with the new ones.

$$\frac{\overset{1}{\cancel{5}}}{\underset{2}{\cancel{18}}} \times \frac{\overset{}{\cancel{9}}^{1}}{\underset{4}{\cancel{20}}}$$

Step three: Multiply across using the new numbers.

$$\frac{1}{2} \times \frac{1}{4} = \frac{1}{8}$$

PRACTICE—MULTIPLICATION OF FRACTIONS

Solve, using cross-canceling where possible. Reduce where necessary.

1. $\frac{1}{4} \times \frac{5}{8}$

2. $\frac{5}{6}\left(\frac{8}{15}\right)$

3. $\frac{1}{8}\left(4\frac{2}{3}\right)$

4. $9 \times 5\frac{1}{4}$

5. $\frac{3}{15} \times \frac{5}{18} \times \frac{6}{7}$

6. $11\frac{3}{4} \times \frac{8}{94}$

ANSWERS

1. $\frac{5}{32}$ 4. $47\frac{1}{4}$

2. $\frac{4}{9}$ 5. $\frac{1}{21}$

3. $\frac{7}{12}$ 6. **1**

DIVISION OF FRACTIONS

Division of fractions is not often seen on the GED. The numerator and denominator of the second fraction in the problem (the divisor) is inverted or flip-flopped. Then, you multiply.

EXAMPLE

$$\frac{5}{8} \div \frac{1}{4}$$

Step one: Invert (flip-flop) the second fraction $\frac{1}{4}$ becomes $\frac{4}{1}$.

Step two: Convert to a multiplication problem $\frac{5}{8} \times \frac{4}{1}$

Step three: Cross-cancel and multiply

$$\frac{5}{{}_2 8} \times \frac{4^1}{1} = \frac{5}{2}$$

Step four: Reduce $\frac{5}{2} = 2\frac{1}{2}$

Answer: $\frac{5}{8} \div \frac{1}{4} = 2\frac{1}{2}$

PRACTICE—DIVISION OF FRACTIONS

Solve.

1. $\frac{3}{8} \div \frac{3}{4}$ 3. $26 \div \frac{2}{5}$

2. $5\frac{1}{3} \div \frac{4}{15}$ 4. $9 \div 1\frac{1}{4}$

ANSWERS

1. $\frac{1}{2}$ 3. **65**

2. **20**   4. $7\frac{1}{5}$

REVIEW EXERCISE—BASIC OPERATIONS WITH FRACTIONS

Solve the following.

1. $\frac{3}{8} + \frac{7}{8}$

2. $\frac{8}{11} \pm \frac{5}{11}$

3. $4\frac{1}{4} + 3\frac{5}{8}$

4. $19\frac{1}{3} + 5\frac{5}{6} + \frac{2}{9}$

5. $8\frac{1}{5} \pm 3\frac{3}{5}$

6. $\frac{1}{3} \times \frac{9}{17}$

7. $\frac{5}{8}\left(\frac{1}{3} + \frac{3}{5}\right)$

8. $1\frac{3}{4}\left(\frac{8}{11}\right)$

9. $\left(3\frac{1}{4} + \frac{1}{8}\right) \pm \left(\frac{5}{16} + \frac{1}{4}\right)$

10. $2\frac{5}{8} \div 1\frac{1}{4}$

11. Arrange in order from shortest to longest:

    $\frac{1}{2}$ mile, $\frac{5}{12}$ mile, $\frac{3}{4}$ mile, $\frac{4}{9}$ mile

ANSWERS

1. $1\frac{1}{4}$ 7. $\frac{1}{2}$

2. $\frac{3}{11}$ 8. $1\frac{3}{11}$

3. $7\frac{7}{8}$ 9. $2\frac{13}{16}$

4. $25\frac{7}{18}$ 10. $2\frac{1}{10}$

5. $4\frac{3}{5}$ 11. $\frac{5}{12}, \frac{4}{9}, \frac{1}{2}, \frac{3}{4}$

6. $\frac{3}{17}$

Using a Calculator for Fractions

A calculator can be a big help with all basic operations involving fractions. There is no need to find the LCD—the calculator does that automatically. It also gives answers in "mixed number" form.

EXAMPLE ONE

$\frac{3}{4} + 1\frac{5}{7}$

Press: ☐3☐ ☐a b/c☐ ☐4☐ ☐+☐ ☐1☐ ☐a b/c☐ ☐5☐ ☐a b/c☐ ☐7☐ ☐=☐

Answer: **2 ⌐ 13 ⌐ 28**   or   **$2\frac{13}{28}$**

A calculator can also convert improper fractions to mixed numbers.

EXAMPLE TWO

Convert $\frac{43}{3}$ to a mixed number.

Press: ☐43☐ ☐a b/c☐ ☐3☐ ☐=☐

Answer: $14\frac{1}{3}$

Fractions and the Answer Grid

It's important to remember that mixed numbers **cannot** be entered on the answer grid.

Let's say the answer to a problem is $4\frac{1}{4}$. You must enter it either as $\frac{17}{4}$ or in its decimal form, 4.25. Converting fractions to decimals will be further discussed in Chapter 21.

Any of these is correct:

Triangles

You already know how to calculate the perimeter of a triangle by adding up its sides. Finding its area is a bit more complicated. First, you must be able to identify two parts of the triangle—the base and the height.

The base is usually the "bottom" of the triangle, the side perpendicular to its height. The corner where the base and height lines meet make a 90-degree angle or square corner.

The height is almost always indicated by a vertical (up and down) dotted line. Only when the triangle is a **right triangle** is the height not marked by a dotted line. Study the diagrams below to become acquainted with base and height.

AREA OF A TRIANGLE

The formula for area of a triangle is

$$A = \frac{1}{2}\,bh$$

It's easier to separate this formula into two steps so that is looks like this:

$$\frac{1}{2}\,(b \times h)$$

Do the work in parentheses first by finding the product of the base times the height, then multiply the product by $\frac{1}{2}$.

EXAMPLE

Find the area of the following triangle.

$A = \frac{1}{2}\,(b \times h)$ $A = \frac{1}{2}\,(8 \times 11)$ $A = \frac{1}{2}\,(88)$

$A = 44$ sq. ft. (remember that area is always expressed in **square** units).

PRACTICE—AREA OF A TRIANGLE

Find the area of the following triangles.

1.

2.

8 ft.

6 ft.

3.

35 yds.

32 yds.

4.

17

10

Which expression represents the area of the triangle above?

(a) $17(10 + 2)$

(b) $\dfrac{17}{2} \times \dfrac{1}{10}$

(c) $\dfrac{1}{2}(17 + 10)$

(d) $\dfrac{17 \times 10}{2}$

(e) $\dfrac{1}{2}(17 - 10)$

ANSWERS

1. **54 sq. in.** 3. **560 sq. yds.**
2. **24 sq. ft.** 4. **(d)**

Parallelograms

Parallelograms are similar to rectangles. They have four sides, and each pair of opposite sides is parallel and equal. The formula for the area of a parallelogram is:

$$A = bh \text{ (area = base} \times \text{height)}$$

EXAMPLE

Find the area of the parallelogram below.

$A = bh$
$A = 6(14)$
$A = 84$ sq. ft.

6 ft.

14 ft.

PRACTICE—PARALLELOGRAMS

9 ft.

12 ft.

1. Find the area of the above parallelogram.

7 in.

2. If the area of the above parallelogram is 56 sq. in., find its base.

ANSWERS

1. **108 sq. ft.** 2. **8 in.**

Standard Measurements

Many of the GED math questions will test your knowledge of measurement conversions. You should make yourself very familiar with those listed below.

Time
1 year = 12 months = 52 weeks = 365 days
1 week = 7 days
1 day = 24 hours
1 hour = 60 minutes
1 minute = 60 seconds

Liquid Measure
1 pint = 16 ounces (oz.)
1 quart = 32 oz.
1 gallon = 4 quarts

Length
1 ft. = 12 in.   1 yd = 3 ft. = 36 in.

Weight
1 lb. = 16 oz.   1 ton = 2,000 lbs.

Sometimes, you'll need to convert larger units of measure to smaller ones, and vice versa. Some terms can be expressed in two different ways: (1) In two units of measure, and (2) as a fraction or mixed number. Become familiar with both.

EXAMPLE ONE

Convert 40 ounces to quarts.

Answer 1: 40 oz. = 1 qt. 8 oz. (32 oz. is one quart—8 oz. is the "remainder")

Answer 2: 40 oz. = $1\frac{1}{4}$ qts. (32 oz. is one quart—$\frac{8}{32}$ is $\frac{1}{4}$ qt.)

EXAMPLE TWO

Convert $2\frac{1}{2}$ days to hours.

$$2\frac{1}{2}(24) = \frac{5}{2} \times \frac{24}{1} = 60 \text{ hours}$$

PART-TO-WHOLE RELATIONSHIPS

A fraction is representative of a part-to-whole relationship. When converting units of measure this $\frac{\text{part}}{\text{whole}}$ setup is useful.

EXAMPLE

Convert 45 minutes to hours

You know that 45 minutes is less than one hour; therefore, it's going to be a fraction (or part) of the whole hour, which is made up of 60 minutes. To solve, set up a fraction with the part (45) as numerator and the whole (60) as denominator. Then reduce.

$$\frac{45}{60} = \frac{3}{4} \text{ hour}$$

PRACTICE—STANDARD UNITS OF MEASURE

1. Convert 6,500 lbs. to: (a) tons (b) tons and lbs.
2. Convert 18 months to: (a) years (b) years and months
3. Convert 260 seconds to: (a) minutes (b) minutes and seconds
4. Convert 17 ft. to: (a) yards (b) yards and feet

Using the *part* relationship, convert each of the following measures to a fraction of the whole units indicated.

5. 1 qt. = _____ gallons
6. 28 in. = _____ yd.
7. 18 hrs. = _____ day
8. 9 months = _____ yr.

Using multiplication, convert the following.

9. $6\frac{1}{2}$ tons = _____ lbs.
10. 5 years = _____ months
11. $8\frac{3}{4}$ ft. = _____ inches
12. $19\frac{1}{2}$ qts. = _____ ozs.

ANSWERS

1. (a) $3\frac{1}{4}$ **tons**   (b) **3 tons, 500 lbs.**
2. (a) $1\frac{1}{2}$ **years**   (b) **1 year, 6 months**
3. (a) $4\frac{1}{3}$ **minutes** (b) **4 min. 20 seconds**
4. (a) $5\frac{2}{3}$ **yds.**   (b) **5 yds, 2 ft.**
5. $\frac{1}{4}$
6. $\frac{7}{9}$
7. $\frac{3}{4}$
8. $\frac{3}{4}$
9. **13,000**
10. **60**
11. **105**
12. **624**

THE METRIC SYSTEM OF MEASURE

On the GED, you won't be asked to make precise conversions from the standard system to the metric system. But you should familiarize yourself with the following:

Liquid Measure

liter: about 1 qt.

milliliter: $\frac{1}{1000}$ of a liter

Weight

gram: $\frac{1}{28}$ of an ounce

milligram: $\frac{1}{1000}$ of a gram

kilogram: 1000 grams (2.2 lbs)

Length

meter: 39 inches

millimeter: $\frac{1}{1000}$ of a meter

kilometer: 1000 meters ($\frac{6}{10}$ of a mile)

Word Problems with Fractions

PART-TO-WHOLE RELATIONSHIP

The part-to-whole relationship is an important part of setting up solutions to word problems. Here's how to use it.

EXAMPLE ONE

There were 42 people taking the GED exam at Grovesville Center, 28 of whom were men. Find the fractional part of men taking the test.

The **part** you're seeking is the number of men taking the test—28. The **whole** is the total number of people taking the test—42.

$$\frac{\text{part}}{\text{whole}} = \frac{28}{42} = \frac{2}{3}$$

Answer: $\frac{2}{3}$ of those taking the test were men.

Sometimes, the **whole** won't be stated; you'll have to figure it out by adding the parts.

EXAMPLE TWO

Jerry packed his suitcase with 10 pairs of black socks, 12 pairs of white socks, and 2 pairs of striped socks. What fractional part of the socks he packed was white?

The **part** is 12, but the **whole** isn't stated. You must add 10, 12 and 2 to get it.

$$\frac{12}{10 + 12 + 2} = \frac{12}{24} = \frac{1}{2}$$

Solve.

1. The Kingsford field hockey team consisted of 27 girls, 18 of whom were seniors. What fractional part of the team was comprised of seniors?

2. Of the 736 registered voters in Youngstown, 552 turned out to vote in the most recent election. What fractional part of the population did *not* vote?

3. A fourth-grade class at Bucksville Elementary School took a poll regarding its favorite ice cream flavors. Fifteen class members chose chocolate as their favorite, 8 chose vanilla, 2 chose pistachio and 5 chose various other flavors. Which expression can be used to find the fractional part of the class favoring chocolate?

   (a) $\frac{15}{4} + \frac{(8 + 5 + 2)}{4}$

   (b) $\frac{30}{15}$

   (c) $\frac{15}{15 + 8 + 2 + 5}$

   (d) $\frac{(8 + 2 + 15) - 15}{4}$

ANSWERS

1. $\frac{2}{3}$ 2. $\frac{1}{4}$ 3. **(c)**

"OF" MEANS "MULTIPLY"

This may sound strange, but it's an important thing to remember. The word "of," especially when it appears in a fraction problem, almost always means you need to multiply.

EXAMPLE

At a free concert, $\frac{1}{6}$ of the 636 people who attended were senior citizens. How many senior citizens attended?

$$\frac{1}{6} \text{ of } 636 = \frac{1}{6} \times \frac{636}{1} = \frac{636}{6}$$

$$= 106 \text{ senior citizens}$$

PRACTICE—"OF" MEANS "MULTIPLY"

Solve.

1. The Granville PTA spends $\frac{1}{4}$ of its annual budget on scholarship funds. If the PTA's budget is $18,240, what fractional part is contributed to scholarship funds?

2. LeeAnn took a history test consisting of 75 questions, $\frac{2}{5}$ of which were multiple choice while the rest were short-answer. How many questions were short-answer?

ANSWERS

1. **4560**   2. **45**

RATIO

Ratio is just another way to express a fractional part of something. It looks a little different (example: the ratio 1:3 is actually $\frac{1}{3}$) and sounds different (you would say 1:3 as "a ratio of one to three") but it acts just like a fraction.

EXAMPLE

There are 54 workers in an office, 18 of whom are men. What is the ratio of men to women in the office?

Step one: The number of women is not stated, so it must be figured out.

54 (total) – 18 men = 36 women

Step two: Set the ratio up in the order it was asked for (men : women) or 18 : 36

Step three: Convert the ratio to a fraction and reduce $\frac{18}{36} = \frac{1}{2}$

Step four: Change back to a ratio when expressing the answer

Answer: 1 : 2 is the ratio of men to women.

PRACTICE—RATIO

1. A computer printer is $119 and its ink cartridge is $17. What is the ratio of the price of the cartridge to the printer?

2. A student takes an exam with 100 questions on it and answers five questions incorrectly. What is the ratio of the number of questions he answered correctly to the number he answered incorrectly?

ANSWERS

1. **1 : 7**   2. **19 : 1**

PROBABILITY

The probability of rolling a 3 using one die (one cube of dice) is said to be 1 in 6 or $\frac{1}{6}$. The numerator represents how many chances there are that a certain event will happen (in this case, rolling a 3) and the denominator represents the total number of possiblities. In this case, there are six different numbers (including the 3) that could come up. It's another use of the part-to-whole relationship.

EXAMPLE

A cooler is packed with 8 cans of ginger ale, 4 cans of root beer, and 12 cans of cola. What is the probability that a person reaching into the cooler will pull out a cola?

Step one: Get a denominator by calculating the total number of possibilities.

$$8 + 4 + 12 = 24$$

use $\frac{}{24}$ as a denominator

Step two: Get a numerator that represents the number of colas there are in the cooler.

$$\frac{12}{24} = \frac{1}{2}$$

Answer: The probability of pulling out a cola is $\frac{1}{2}$.

A root beer?

Step one: Get a denominator $\frac{}{24}$

Step two: Get a numerator $\frac{4}{24} = \frac{1}{6}$

Answer: The probability of pulling out a root beer is $\frac{1}{6}$.

A ginger ale?

$$\frac{8}{24} = \frac{1}{3}$$

Answer: The probability of pulling out a ginger ale is $\frac{1}{3}$.

PRACTICE—PROBABILITY

1. There are 6 limes, 5 lemons, and 4 tangerines in a bag. What is the probability of choosing a lemon the first time?

2. There are ten "number" keys on a computer keyboard and 36 "letter" keys. If a person presses a key at random, what is the likelihood that it will be the number 7?

3. You are trying to guess a person's birth date. What is the probability that the person was born in a month beginning with the letter "J?"

ANSWERS

1. $\frac{1}{3}$ 2. $\frac{1}{46}$ 3. $\frac{1}{4}$

CHAPTER REVIEW

Fill in the answer grids, and use a calculator where indicated.

1. Wuanlee buys Acme stock at $53\frac{1}{4}$ per share. The stock increases $1\frac{3}{8}$. How much is it now worth per share?

(1) $55\frac{1}{4}$

(2) $52\frac{7}{8}$

(3) $54\frac{5}{8}$

(4) $56\frac{1}{4}$

(5) $54\frac{1}{4}$

2. According to the pie chart below, what fractional part of Sally's monthly expenses goes to rent?

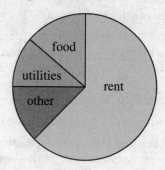

(1) $\frac{1}{3}$

(2) $\frac{5}{6}$

(3) $\frac{1}{2}$

(4) $\frac{2}{3}$

(5) $\frac{7}{8}$

3. Ted has the following open-ended wrenches:

$$\frac{5}{8}, \frac{1}{2}, \frac{15}{32}, \frac{9}{16}$$

Which represents the correct order, if he wishes to arrange them from smallest to largest?

(1) $\frac{5}{8}, \frac{15}{32}, \frac{9}{16}, \frac{1}{2}$

(2) $\frac{1}{2}, \frac{15}{32}, \frac{9}{16}, \frac{5}{8}$

(3) $\frac{9}{16}, \frac{15}{32}, \frac{1}{2}, \frac{5}{8}$

(4) $\frac{15}{32}, \frac{1}{2}, \frac{9}{16}, \frac{5}{8}$

4. From a 16-inch length of tubing, Rob cut a piece $4\frac{5}{8}$ inch long. How much is now left from the original piece?

(1) $12\frac{1}{8}$ inches

(2) $13\frac{3}{8}$ inches

(3) $11\frac{3}{8}$ inches

(4) $11\frac{1}{4}$ inches

(5) $12\frac{1}{4}$ inches

5. The five members of the Sanford family picked a total of $8\frac{1}{3}$ cartons of blueberries. Which expression would allow the berries to be distributed evenly among each family member?

(1) $\frac{25}{3} \times \frac{1}{5}$

(2) $\frac{3}{25} \div \frac{1}{5}$

(3) $5 \div \frac{25}{3}$

(4) $5\frac{1}{3} \times \frac{5}{1}$

(5) $8\frac{1}{3} \times \frac{5}{1}$

6. Find the area of the rectangle below:

$8\frac{2}{3}$ ft.

$14\frac{1}{2}$ ft.

(1) $125\frac{2}{3}$ sq. ft.

(2) $46\frac{1}{3}$ ft.

(3) $138\frac{1}{6}$ sq. ft.

(4) $408\frac{1}{3}$ sq. ft.

(5) $126\frac{1}{4}$ sq. ft.

7. Laura buys 4 yards of fabric at $3.20 a yard. She is making banners that are each 16 inches long. Which expression tells how many banners Laura can cut from the fabric?

(1) $\frac{(4 \times 12)3.20}{16}$

(2) $\frac{12(4 \times 2)}{4}$

(3) $\frac{4(36)}{16}$

(4) $\frac{4(3.20)}{2(16)}$

(5) $3.20\,(16)$

8. There are 132 members of the Otis Volunteer Fire Department. At a recent alarm, $\frac{1}{4}$ of the volunteers responded. How many volunteers did *not* respond?

9. Joan's commute to work is $27\frac{1}{4}$ miles each way. Her car averages 26 miles per gallon of gas. Which expression indicates how much gas Joan's car consumes for commutation during a 5-day work week?

(1) $\frac{27\frac{1}{4}}{26} \times \frac{1}{5}$

(2) $\frac{54\frac{1}{4} \times 5}{1}$

(3) $\frac{2\left(27\frac{1}{4}\right)}{26} \times \frac{5}{1}$

(4) $\frac{\left(27\frac{1}{4}\right)5}{13}$

(5) not enough information is given

10. Hector has a summer house where he resides for the months of June, July, and August. Over a three-year period, he followed this schedule, except for one year in which he stayed only in July and August. What fractional part of these three years did Hector reside in his summer house?

11. Greta planted a triangular garden shown below. She needs to spread fertilizer at the rate of $\frac{3}{4}$ lb. per sq. ft. Which expression shows how much fertilizer Greta needs to cover the garden?

43 ft.

36 ft.

(1) $\frac{1}{2} \times \frac{36(43)}{1} \times \frac{3}{4}$

(2) $\frac{36 + 43}{1} \times \frac{3}{4}$

(3) $\frac{1}{2} \times \frac{36 + 43}{1} \div \frac{3}{1}$

(4) $36 \times 43 \div \frac{3}{4}$

(5) $\frac{\frac{1}{2}}{x} \times 36(43)$

12. It takes a machine 2 minutes and 15 seconds to assemble one chair. If the machine runs continuously for 6 hours, how many chairs will it produce?

13.

42 ft.

14 ft.

If the length of ▭ *ABCD* is 42 ft. and the length of ▭ *AEFD* is 14 ft., what is the ratio of the area of ▭ *ACD* to the area of ▭ *AEFD*?

(1) $\frac{1}{3}$

(2) 5 : 1

(3) 3 : 1

(4) 2 : 1

(5) 3 : 2

14. A traffic light is red for 38 seconds, yellow for 10 seconds, and green for one minute and twelve seconds in a constantly repeating cycle. What is the probability that at the moment a passing pedestrian glances at it, the light will be green?

ANSWERS

1. **3**	6. **1**	11. **1**
2. **4**	7. **3**	12. **160**
3. **4**	8. **99**	13. **3**
4. **3**	9. **3**	14. **3/5 or .6**
5. **1**	10. **2/9 or .22**	

Decimals and Percents

Decimals are just like fractions—they are a way of showing part of a whole number. For example, $\frac{7}{10}$ is written as .7 or 0.7. You can read .7 as "seven tenths," but, more commonly, it is read as "point seven."

Actually, you've been using the decimal system for a long time, perhaps without realizing it. If you have a quarter, two dimes, and three pennies, you know you have $.48 or 48 cents. This .48 represents 48 cents out of one dollar, or $\frac{48}{100}$ or **.48 out of 1.00.**

Decimal Places

An important part of working effectively with decimals is understanding the **decimal place-value system**. As you move further to the right of the decimal point, the value of the numbers grows smaller. Study the chart below and memorize the values for each place to the right of the decimal point.

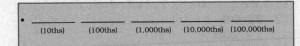

Of course, the place-value system could keep moving to the right forever, generating increasingly smaller numbers, but for the purposes of preparing for the GED, we need only worry about working effectively with numbers to the fifth decimal place (100,000ths).

Decimals and Fractional Equivalents

Study these fractional equivalents of decimals to better understand the system.

$$.1 = \frac{1}{10} \qquad .7894 = \frac{7894}{10,000}$$

$$.14 = \frac{14}{100} \qquad .90023 = \frac{90023}{100,000}$$

$$.235 = \frac{235}{1,000}$$

PRACTICE—WRITING DECIMAL EQUIVALENTS TO FRACTIONS

Write the following fractions as decimals. Refer to the place-value chart above if necessary.

1. $\frac{9}{10}$

2. $\frac{33}{100}$

3. $\frac{507}{1,000}$

4. $\frac{1286}{10,000}$

5. $\frac{17}{100}$

ANSWERS

1. **.9** 2. **.33** 3. **.507** 4. **.1286** 5. **.17**

Using Zeros with Decimals

Putting a zero to the **right** of a decimal number does not change its value at all. For example, .7 is equal to .70 or .700 or even .70000000! Which is worth more, seven dimes (.7 or $\frac{7}{10}$) or seventy cents (.70 or $\frac{70}{100}$)? Of course, their value is equal.

However, putting a zero to the left of a number (in between the number and the decimal point) **changes** its value by making it ten times smaller. For example, .07 is ten times smaller than .7. Which is larger, seven dimes (.7) or seven pennies (.07)? Seven dimes (.70) is larger than seven pennies (.07).

Which is larger, .4 or .396? Clearly, .4 is larger. This is often confusing to GED students at first. Try setting these decimals up as fractional equivalents and then compare.

$$.4 = \frac{4}{10} \qquad .396 = \frac{396}{1,000}$$

If you raise to higher terms for purposes of comparing fractions, you will see that:

$\frac{4}{10} = \frac{400}{1,000}$ is larger than $\frac{396}{1,000}$ **or** .400 is larger than .396

Study these fractional equivalents and decimal comparisons:

> $.06 = \frac{6}{100}$
>
> $.006 = \frac{6}{1,000}$
>
> $.6 = .600$ $(\frac{6}{10} = \frac{600}{1,000})$
>
> $5.6 = 5\frac{6}{10}$
>
> .3 is the same as .300
> .3 is larger than .299
> .3 is much larger than .039
> .33 is larger than .3

Write the decimal equivalent of the following fractions.

1. $\frac{5}{1,000}$

2. $\frac{60}{100}$

3. $\frac{47}{100}$

4. $\frac{71}{100}$

5. $\frac{408}{10,000}$

Write "L" if the first decimal of the pair is larger, "S" if it is smaller, and "E" if the pair is equal.

6. .703   .0788
7. .493   .6
8. 1.08   2.003
9. .52   .5200
10. .01030   .0103

Arrange the following sets of decimals in size order from smallest to largest.

11. 1.8, 1.743, .992, 1.089, 1.81
12. 71.049, 71.2, 70.98, 71.203, 71.0491

ANSWERS

1. **.005**   6. **L**
2. **.6**   7. **S**
3. **.47**   8. **S**
4. **.71**   9. **E**
5. **.0408**   10. **E**
11. **.992, 1.089, 1.743, 1.8, 1.81**
12. **70.98, 71.049, 71.0491, 71.2, 71.203**

Adding and Subtracting Decimals

ANSWERS

1. **65.059**   2. **113.18**   3. **1003.243**

These operations are the same as working with whole numbers. Here's what it looks like.

EXAMPLE ONE

5.04 + 12.62 + .88   23.214 – 8.906

```
  12.62              23.214
   5.04            –  8.906
+   .88              14.308
  18.54
```

Notice: (1) how the place-value columns are perfectly aligned
(2) that the decimal points are moved directly below in the answers.

The only complication with addition and subtraction is this:

EXAMPLE TWO

3.9 + 5 + 4.007

It might be set up: 5
4.007
+ 3.9

It **should** be set up:
```
   5.000
   4.007
+  3.900
  12.907
```

Notice how the zeros are added to keep the place–value columns looking aligned to eliminate confusion and to help when there is carrying. This is especially true for subtraction when there is borrowing.

EXAMPLE THREE

5 – 3.03

It **should** be set up:
```
   5.00
–  3.03
   1.97
```

PRACTICE—ADDING AND SUBTRACTING DECIMALS

Solve the following.

1. 4.09 + 55.369 + 5.6
2. 300 – 186.82
3. 88 + 903.01 + .06 + 12.173

Multiplying Decimals

You learned in basic operations that it is best to arrange the larger number on top when multiplying, but when working with decimals this is not always the case. Place the number with the *most* digits on top—there's less work to do.

EXAMPLE ONE

Solve   5.4 × 2.13

The number 5.4 is clearly larger than 2.13, but 2.13 has more digits. The problem should be set up this way, then solved using the following steps.

Step one: Don't align the decimals here. Just multiply.
```
    2.13
×   5.4
    852
  1065
  11502
```

Step two: Count the number of digits to the right of the decimal point in both multiplying numbers. Here, there are three (1 and 3 from 2.13 and 4 from 5.4).

Step three: Put your pen just past the last digit to the right. Here, it's the two. Now move the decimal point to the left the number of digits you counted in Step two (here, it's three). Place the decimal point there.

Answer: 11.502.

PRACTICE—MULTIPLYING DECIMALS

Solve.

1. 4.65(38)
2. .913(4.4)
3. 10.04(.03)
4. (9)1.13
5. 24.28(.01)

Dividing Decimals

When the decimal is in the dividend, all that's needed to be done is to duplicate it (carefully and precisely) directly above to the "shelf" of the dividing sign. Then, divide as you normally would. The decimal is already placed correctly in the answer.

EXAMPLE ONE

91.8 ÷ 54

$$
\begin{array}{r}
1.7 \\
54\overline{)91.8} \\
-54 \\
\hline
378 \\
-378 \\
\hline
0
\end{array}
$$

quotient ←
shelf ←
dividend ←
divisor →

When the decimal is in the divisor, the process becomes a bit more complicated. You cannot proceed with decimals there. Follow the steps below.

EXAMPLE TWO

30.176 ÷ 7.36

$$
\begin{array}{r}
4.1 \\
7.36\overline{)30.17.6} \\
-2944 \\
\hline
736 \\
-736 \\
\hline
0
\end{array}
$$

Step one: Move the decimal point in the divisor all the way to the right, making it a whole number. Count the number of places you've moved it. Here, it would be two.

Step two: Now move the decimal in the dividend the same number of spaces as you moved it in Step one.

Step three: Place a decimal on the "shelf" of the dividend just as you did in Example One above. Divide.

Note: Sometimes, you will need to move the decimal point in the dividend, but you will already be at the right end of the number. When this happens, create places to the right by adding zeros. See the following example.

EXAMPLE THREE

62 ÷ 1.25

$$
\begin{array}{r}
49.6 \\
1.25\overline{)62.00.0} \\
-520 \\
\hline
1200 \\
-1125 \\
\hline
750 \\
-750 \\
\hline
0
\end{array}
$$

The example above also illustrates another very important concept in division. Previously, you would have ended the division at the second zero in 6200 and expressed the answer as 49 r75. But now that you know how to work with decimals, this rough method of dividing is no longer necessary. Simply add zeros to the right side of the dividend until either:

(1) the dividend divides evenly (as it did in Example Three)
or
(2) you have carried out the division to the decimal place specified by the question and the answer can then be **rounded off**. See the example below.

EXAMPLE FOUR

Solve and round to the nearest hundredth.

$$\frac{154}{13}$$

$$
\begin{array}{r}
11.846 \\
13\overline{)154.000} \\
-13 \\
\hline
24 \\
-13 \\
\hline
110 \\
-104 \\
\hline
60 \\
-52 \\
\hline
80 \\
-78 \\
\hline
2
\end{array}
$$

To **round off**, always divide one place **past** the place value you were instructed to round. Division was done to the thousandths place, which is one place beyond the hundredths.

Examine the last place to the right. Is the number **5 or higher**? If so, round the next number to the left **up one**. In this example the last number is higher than 5.

Therefore, 11.846 rounded to the nearest hundredth is 11.85. If the number is **lower than 5,** simply leave the last number off and leave the number as it is. See the following examples.

EXAMPLE FIVE

Round the following numbers off to the nearest hundreth.

142.654 becomes 142.65
4.019 becomes 4.02
13.135 becomes 13.14

PRACTICE—DIVIDING DECIMALS

Solve using division. Round off answers to the nearest hundredth, where necessary.

1. $223.2 \div 12$
2. $34.44 \div 32.8$
3. $129 \div 5.14$
4. $\dfrac{67}{14}$

ANSWERS

1. **18.60**
2. **1.05**
3. **25.10**
4. **4.79**

CONVERTING DECIMALS TO FRACTIONS

This is a fairly simple operation. Set the decimal up as a fraction and reduce where necessary.

EXAMPLE

Convert .75 to a fraction

$$.75 = \frac{75}{100} = \mathbf{\frac{3}{4}}$$

CONVERTING FRACTIONS TO DECIMALS

This is a bit more complicated. Remember, once again, that every fraction is a division problem, so that $\frac{1}{4}$ really means $1 \div 4$. Dividing a smaller number by a larger one may look unfamiliar, but it's a very important operation to know. Here's how to do it:

EXAMPLE ONE

Convert $\frac{1}{4}$ to a decimal

Step one: Set $\frac{1}{4}$ up as a division problem and try to divide.

$$4\overline{)1}$$

Step two: You realize you can't divide 4 into 1. You must add a decimal point and a zero to the dividend.

$$4\overline{)1.0}$$

Step three: Transfer the decimal point in the dividend to the "shelf," then divide.

$$\begin{array}{r} .2 \\ 4\overline{)1.0} \\ -8 \\ \hline 2 \end{array}$$

Step four: Add another zero to the dividend and finish the problem.

$$\begin{array}{r} .25 \\ 4\overline{)1.00} \\ -8 \\ \hline 20 \\ -20 \\ \hline 0 \end{array}$$

Sometimes, when converting fractions to decimals, you will encounter a never-ending division problem, the answer to which is called a **repeating decimal**. In this situation, carry out division to the nearest thousandth (or whatever the directions indicate) and round off.

EXAMPLE TWO

Convert $\frac{1}{3}$ to a decimal—rounded off to the nearest hundredth.

Step one: $\frac{1}{3} = 3\overline{)1}$

Step two: $\begin{array}{r} .3 \\ 3\overline{)1.0} \end{array}$

Step three: $\begin{array}{r} .333 \\ 3\overline{)1.000} \\ -9 \\ \hline 10 \\ -9 \\ \hline 10 \\ -9 \\ \hline 1 \end{array}$

Step four: .333 = .33 rounded to the nearest hundredth

PRACTICE—CONVERTING DECIMALS AND FRACTIONS

Convert the following decimals to fractions and reduce, where necessary.

1. .50
2. .065
3. 2.25
4. .125
5. .367

Convert the following fractions to decimals and round to the nearest hundredth, where necessary.

6. $\frac{4}{5}$

7. $\frac{9}{4}$

8. $\frac{5}{8}$

9. $\frac{3}{32}$

10. $\frac{2}{3}$

ANSWERS

1. $\frac{1}{2}$

2. $\frac{13}{200}$

3. $2\frac{1}{4}$

4. $\frac{1}{8}$

5. $\frac{367}{1,000}$

6. **.80**

7. **2.25**

8. **.63**

9. **.09**

10. **.67**

The conversions in the chart below frequently appear on the GED. Memorize as many as you can.

$\frac{1}{3}$ = .333	$\frac{3}{5}$ = .6
$\frac{2}{3}$ = .666 or .67	$\frac{4}{5}$ = .8
$\frac{1}{4}$ = .25	$\frac{1}{8}$ = .125
$\frac{3}{4}$ = .75	$\frac{3}{8}$ = .375
$\frac{1}{5}$ = .2	$\frac{5}{8}$ = .625
$\frac{2}{5}$ = .4	$\frac{7}{8}$ = .875

Scientific Notation

Scientific notation is a method used by scientists to convert very large or very small numbers to more manageable ones. You will almost certainly be required to do one conversion to scientific notation on the GED. It's an easy operation.

EXAMPLE ONE

A space satellite can transmit from a distance of 46,000,000 miles away. What is the number written in scientific notation?

Step one: Starting at the "imaginary" decimal point to the *right* of the last zero, move the decimal point until only one digit remains to its *left*.

46,000,000 becomes 4.6

Step two: Count the number of places the decimal was moved left. It's 7 places, which is expressed this way:

10^7

Step three: Express the full answer in scientific notation this way:

46,000,000 miles = **4.6 × 10⁷**

EXAMPLE TWO

A microorganism is .000056 inch long. What is its length in scientific notation?

Step one: Move the decimal point to the *right* until there is one digit other than zero to the *left* of the decimal.

.000056 becomes 5.6

Step two: Count the number of places moved to the right—it's 5, which is expressed this way, using a *negative sign* with the exponent:

10^{-5}

Step three: Express the full answer in scientific notation this way:

.000056 = **5.6 × 10⁻⁵**

Consider these other examples to help you get the concept:

$$783,000,000 = 7.83 \times 10^8$$
$$500,000,000 = 5 \times 10^8$$
$$.00000923 = 9.23 \times 10^{-6}$$
$$.0005134 = 5.134 \times 10^{-4}$$

Express in scientific notation.

1. 83,000,000
2. .000012
3. 5,160,000,000
4. .0000006

ANSWERS

1. **8.3 × 10⁷**
2. **1.2 × 10⁻⁵**
3. **5.16 × 10⁹**
4. **6 × 10⁻⁷**

Circles and Cylinders

Now that you know how to multiply decimals, you can work with circles. First, there are important concepts you must understand and vocabulary you must memorize.

- The **circumference (c)** is the distance around the circle. It's another word for "perimeter."
- The **center** of a circle is its exact middle.
- The **radius (r)** of a circle is a straight line that runs from the exact center of the circle to its circumference.

- The **diameter (d)** is the distance across the circle from a point on the circumference to its opposite side, passing through the center. It is **twice the length of the radius** or **d = 2r**.

CALCULATING RADIUS, DIAMETER, AND CIRCUMFERENCE OF A CIRCLE

Learn the following:

> **radius = $\frac{d}{2}$** (radius = diameter ÷ 2)
>
> **diameter = 2r**
> **c = πd** (pi × diameter)

π = **pi** (pronounced "pie"). It is a letter from the Greek alphabet. It represents the number **3.14** and is essential for working with circles. Memorize it.

EXAMPLE

Calculate the radius, diameter, and circumference of the above circle.

- radius = 4 ft. (this is stated in the diagram—no calculation is necessary)
- diameter = 2r or 2(4) = 8 ft.
- circumference = πd or 3.14(8) = 25.12 ft.

CALCULATING THE AREA OF A CIRCLE

The formula for calculating the area of a circle is

$$A = \pi(r^2) \text{ or } \pi \times r^2$$

EXAMPLE

Find the area of the following circle.

Step one: Find the radius. If $d = 12$ inches then $r = \frac{d}{2}$ or 6 inches

Step two: Square the radius (r^2) 6 × 6 = 36 inches

Step three: Multiply $\pi \times r^2$
3.14 × 36 = 113.04 **square** inches (even though a circle is round, area is still expressed in terms of **square** units.)

PRACTICE—CALCULATING THE DIMENSIONS OF CIRCLES

Find the radius (*r*), diameter (*d*), circumference (*c*), and area (*a*) of the following circles. Round to the nearest hundredth, where necessary.

1.

2.

ANSWERS

1. **r = 30 inches, d = 60 inches, c = 188.4 inches, a = 2826 sq. inches**
2. **r = 24.1 feet, d = 48.2 feet, c = 151.35 feet, a = 1823.74 sq. feet**

CALCULATING THE VOLUME OF CYLINDERS

Like cubes and rectangular containers, cylinders are three-dimensional figures, which are measured by volume. The formula for volume of a cylinder is:

$$V = (\pi\, r^2)\, h \quad \text{or}$$
$$\text{volume} = (\pi \times \text{radius}^2) \times \text{height}$$

EXAMPLE

Find the volume of the above cylinder.

Step one: Find the area on the top (or bottom) circle of the cylinder.
$$A = \pi r^2 = 3.14 \times 10^2 = 314$$

Step two: $A \times h = 314 \times 46.3 = 14{,}538.2$ cubic (cu.) ft. (Always express a volume answer in **cubic** units.)

PRACTICE—VOLUME OF CYLINDERS

Find the volume for the following cylinder.

ANSWER

4615.8 cubic feet

Percents

Working with percents is one of the more frequently tested skills on the GED, so it's essential that you become familiar with it.

The percent sign (%) following a number means that the number is a fraction of 100. For example, if you read about the construction of a bridge and the newspaper says, "The project is 60% complete," it means that if the entire bridge-building job were divided into 100 equal parts, 60 of them are complete *or* $\frac{60}{100}$ of the project is complete *or* $\frac{3}{5}$ of the project is complete.

Changing Percents to Decimals

This is a simple procedure. Replace the % sign with a decimal point and move it two places **to the left**.

EXAMPLE ONE

Change 52% to a decimal (move two places to the left)—52% = .52

EXAMPLE TWO

Change 3% to a decimal (move two places to the left)—3% = .03 (add a zero to occupy the place)

EXAMPLE THREE

Change 90% to a decimal (move two places to the left)—90% = .90 = .9 (drop the zero—it has no value)

EXAMPLE FOUR:

Change 12.5% to a decimal (move two places to the left)—12.5% = .125

Notice that when there is a decimal point already included in the percent, begin at the decimal point and move it two places to the left.

EXAMPLE FIVE

Change 140% to a decimal (move two places to the left)—140% = 1.40

It's generally accepted that 100% means "all full up," but you can use numbers to express **more than 100%.**

Let's say that a boat-building shop constructs four boats in its first year of business, but the next year, the company gets busy, increases its work staff, and builds six boats.

The company has increased its production by 50%. It has built two more boats than the four built the first year—2 is 50% of 4. The next year, it builds eight boats. Now, the company has increased its production by 100% from the first year—4 is 100% or one whole of 4. In the fourth year, the company gets really busy and builds ten boats—that is six more boats than the first year. There is now an increase of 150% from the first year—6 is 150% or $1\frac{1}{2}$ of four. Don't panic if you see percents greater than 100; learn to work with them.

Likewise, it's possible to have less than 1%.

EXAMPLE SIX

Change .5% to a decimal (begin at the decimal point and move two places to the right)—.5% = .005 (it's $\frac{1}{2}$ of 1%)

Convert the following to decimals.

1. 23%
2. 6%
3. 138%
4. 8.5%
5. 70%
6. 8.25%
7. 238%
8. .6%

ANSWERS

1. **.23**
2. **.06**
3. **1.38**
4. **.085**
5. **.7**
6. **.0825**
7. **2.38**
8. **.006**

Changing Decimals to Percents

This is a much simpler process. Move the decimal place two places **to the right** and add a percent sign. See the following examples below:

.14 = 14%
1.23 = 123%
.03 = 3%

.4 = 40%
.825 = 82.5%
.025 = 2.5%

PRACTICE—CHANGING
DECIMALS TO PERCENTS

Convert the following decimals to percents.

1. .23
2. 5.03
3. .06
4. .7
5. .567
6. .0015

ANSWERS

1. **23%**
2. **503%**
3. **6%**
4. **70%**
5. **56.7%**
6. **.15%**

Converting Fractions and Percents

To change **percents to fractions**, simply convert the percent to a decimal and add the appropriate denominator, which would usually be 100, but not always (see last example). Reduce where necessary.

EXAMPLES

$$50\% = \frac{50}{100} = \frac{1}{2}$$

$$8\% = \frac{8}{100} = \frac{2}{25}$$

$$37\% = \frac{37}{100}$$

$$185\% = \frac{185}{100} = 1\frac{17}{20}$$

$$12.5\% = \frac{125}{1000} = \frac{1}{8}$$

To change **fractions to percents**, follow the same procedures as you would for converting fractions to decimals. Divide the numerator by the denominator to the 1000ths place. If the numbers don't divide evenly, round to the nearest 100th, then convert the decimal number to a percent.

EXAMPLE ONE

Convert $\frac{4}{9}$ to a percent.

Step one: Divide the numerator by the denominator:

$$9\overline{)4.000} \quad .444$$

Step two: Round to the nearest 100th:

$$.444 = .44$$

Step three: Convert decimal to a percent:

$$.44 = 44\%$$

EXAMPLE TWO

Convert $\frac{3}{8}$ to a percent.

$$8\overline{)3.000} \quad .375 \qquad .375 = 37.5\%$$

PRACTICE—CONVERTING FRACTIONS AND PERCENTS

Convert problems 1–4 to fractions and reduce where necessary. Convert problems 5–8 to percents.

1. 75%
2. 48%
3. 225%
4. .5%

5. $\frac{7}{10}$
6. $\frac{5}{8}$
7. $\frac{3}{16}$
8. $2\frac{8}{21}$

1. $\frac{3}{4}$
2. $\frac{12}{25}$
3. $2\frac{1}{4}$
4. $\frac{1}{200}$

5. **70%**
6. **63%**
7. **19%**
8. **238%**

Comparing and Ordering Fractions, Decimals, and Percents

This activity is a summary of all you've learned about conversions. Consider the following examples.

EXAMPLE ONE

Which of the following two numbers have the same value?

$$3\frac{3}{8} \qquad 33\% \qquad 37.5\% \qquad 3.33 \qquad \frac{3}{8}$$

(1) $3\frac{3}{8}$ and 3.33

(2) 33% and 3.33

(3) 37.5% and $3\frac{3}{8}$

(4) $\frac{3}{8}$ and 33%

(5) 37.5% and $\frac{3}{8}$

(1) $3\frac{3}{8}$ and 3.33 (no, but close, $3\frac{3}{8}$ = 3.375)

(2) 33% and 3.33 (no, 33% = .33)

(3) 37.5% and $3\frac{3}{8}$ (no, 37.5% = .375, $3\frac{3}{8}$ = 3.375)

(4) $\frac{3}{8}$ and 33% (no, 33% = $\frac{1}{3}$)

(5) 37.5% and $\frac{3}{8}$ (yes, both equal $\frac{3}{8}$ or .375 or 37.5%)

EXAMPLE TWO

The following table indicates what part of his or her 12 oz. bottle each infant drank.

Tina—60%

LaShaun—.7

Lina—$\frac{2}{3}$

Which of the following lists the infants according to how much they drank from *least to greatest*?

(1) Tina, Lina, LaShaun

CAR WASH

Lic #		Att.

WASH-LG ○ Van ○ Mini Van ○ Truck ○ Jeep

☐ Wash & Sealer Wax ☐ Ladies Special Day
☐ Wash & Polish Wax ☐ Mens Special Day
☐ Economy Wash ☐ Happy Hour
☐ Special Wash ☐ Senior Day Wash
☐ Super Wash ☐ Coupon Wash
☐ Magic Wash ☐ Hand Wash
☐ ☐ Mats Wash
☐ ☐ Wheels Clean

DRESSING

☐ Complete ☐ Tire ☐ Bumper
☐ Dash Board ☐ Door Panel ☐ Top

DETAILING SERVICE

☐ Hand Wax ☐ Polish & Buff Wax
☐ Eng. Steam Clean ☐ Interior Shampoo
☐ Complete ☐ Window Tinting

DISCLAIMER **NO CAR RELEASED WITHOUT A CLAIM CHECK EXCHANGE THE TICKET AT CASHIER'S WINDOW**

CAUTION: WE ARE NOT RESPONSIBLE FOR ITEMS LEFT IN YOUR CAR OR DAMAGES TO MODIFIED VEHICLES, CUSTOM WHEELS OR TIRES, POWER ANTENNAS NOT FULLY RETRACTED OR DAMAGE INCURRED PREVIOUS TO CAR WASH.

256198

SIR SPEEDY - ANAHEIM, CA 92801 714-527-3122 31076151 B-8

salary from commission. Juana gets $\frac{1}{5}$ of her salary from commission and Bill gets $\frac{3}{8}$ of his salary from commission. Which of the following lists the sales agents according to the size of their commissions from smallest to largest?

(1) Ed, Juana, Bill
(2) Bill, Ed, Juana
(3) Juana, Ed, Bill
(4) Bill, Juana, Ed
(5) Juana, Bill, Ed

3. Which expression could be used to compare 35% to $\frac{3}{7}$?

(1) 7 ÷ 3
(2) 7 ÷ 3 move decimal in the answer two places to the right and add a % sign
(3) 3 ÷ 7 move decimal in the answer two places to the right and add a % sign
(4) 7 × .03 move decimal in the answer two places to the left and add a % sign

ANSWERS

1. **3**   2. **1**   3. **3**

Solving Word Problems with Percents

All word problems that involve percents, no matter how complicated they may seem, can be reduced to one of these three operations:

> 1. Finding a percent of a number
>   30% of 86 = ?
>
> 2. Finding what percent one number is of another
>   40 is ?% of 100
>
> 3. Finding a number when a percent of it is given
>   30 is 40% of ?

GED students sometimes find it difficult to tell the difference among these three operations and when to apply each to a problem. An aid designed to help you with this difficulty is **the percent triangle**. Once it is understood and memorized, it will guide you through every operation with percents.

The Percent Triangle

Here's how to use it:

EXAMPLE ONE

What is 30% of 86?

Step one: Decode the problem by labeling its parts. In this problem, you have a **total (86)** and a **% (30%)**. 30% will become .30 (always convert percents to decimals in calculations).

Step two: Using the labeled parts, find the operation on the percent triangle. Notice that **total** and **%** are next to each other at the base of the triangle.

Step three: Perform the operation (either × or ÷) indicated by the separation line between the parts in Step two.

In this case, the × sign separates **total** and %.

$$86 \times .3 = 25.8$$

Answer: 30% of 86 = 25.8

EXAMPLE TWO

32 is what percent of 128?

Step one: Decode and label. 32 is a **part** and 128 is a **total**.

Step two: Find the operation on the triangle. The sign that separates **total** and **part** is a ÷ sign.

Step three: Perform the operation. **Be careful here!** In Example One, the operation was multiplication, so it makes no difference how the numbers are arranged, the answer will always be the same. But when it comes to division, there is a huge difference in the answer if you choose the wrong dividends and divisors. Follow this one simple rule and you shouldn't have problems: When dividing using the triangle, *always place the **part** first.*

Therefore, in this example, you would find 32 ÷ 128.

$$128\overline{)32.00}^{.25}$$

The problem asks for a percent. Simply convert .25 to 25%.

EXAMPLE THREE

30 is 40% of what number?

Step one: Decode and label. 30 is a **part** and 40% is a %.

Step two: Find the operation on the triangle. A ÷ sign separates part and %.

Step three: Perform the operation, remembering **part always comes first:** 30 ÷ .40

$$.40\overline{)30.00}^{75}$$

Answer: 30 is 40% of 75

PRACTICE—BASIC WORD PROBLEMS WITH PERCENTS

Label and solve.

1. 40% of 68 is ?
2. 90 is ? % of 135
3. 86 is 12.5% of ?
4. 125% of 80 is ?
5. 108.8 is ? % of 68
6. 30 is 2.5% of ?

ANSWERS

1. **27.2**   4. **100**
2. **67%**   5. **160%**
3. **688**   6. **1200**

Word Problems with Percents

Don't be intimidated by the length or complexity of percent word problems. Simply repeat the process you just learned. Reduce the sentences down to a short one, label, then perform the operations according to the triangle.

EXAMPLE ONE

Alan earns a salary of $1,420. The rent he pays on his apartment is 44% of his salary. How much is his rent?

Step one: Reduce—all this problem is asking you to find is: 44% of $1,420.

Step two: Label—% × **total**

Step three: Perform the operation—.44 × 1420 = $624.80

Answer: $624.80

EXAMPLE TWO

Lee and Huan went to dinner at the Riverside Restaurant. Not including tax, the bill came to $34.50. The sales tax on the meal was $2.07. What percent of the meal was the sales tax?

Step one: Reduce—$2.07 is ? % of $34.50?

Step two: **Part ÷ total**

Step three: Perform the operation—

$$34.00\overline{)2.07.00} \quad .06$$

Answer: .06 = 6%

EXAMPLE THREE

Karen has paid her father $2,640, which is 22% of the total she borrowed from him to purchase a car. How much money did Karen originally borrow?

Step one: $2,640 is 22% of ?

Step two: **part ÷ %**

Step three: 2,640 ÷ .22 = $12,000

Answer: $12,000

PRACTICE—BASIC WORD PROBLEMS II

Solve the following.

1. John bought 140 pieces of plywood for a construction job, but 40% of them were warped and had to be returned. How many pieces did John return?

2. Keira invested $43,608 in a mutual fund that paid $432.96 in interest at the end of the year. What was the percent of interest Keira earned from her initial investment?

3. The Baileys drove 280 miles during the first leg of a trip to visit their cousins. The distance represented 32% of the trip. How many miles is the entire trip?

ANSWERS

1. **56**   2. **1%**   3. **875**

Multistep Problems with Percents

Most of the problems involving percents on the GED Math section will be multistep. They require careful attention to wording, but they are usually not much more complicated than the problems in the last exercise.

EXAMPLE ONE

Michelle is a waitress who earns $7 per hour and receives 10% of all tips collected by her and the other waitresses by the end of the day. If she works a six-hour shift and $482.50 is the total collected by the end of the day, what are Michelle's total earnings for the day?

Step one: Calculate her hourly earnings—$7 × 6 = $42

Step two: Calculate her tips—10% of $482.50 = $48.25

Step three: Add $42 + $48.25 = $90.25

EXAMPLE TWO

A home-entertainment system, originally priced at $1,250, is on sale for 15% off. One week later, the price of the system is reduced an additional 20% off the discounted price. What is the final sale price of the system?

The "double discount" is a frequently-asked question. Avoid the temptation to add the two discounts together (35%) and then find 65% of $1,250. Here's the right way to do it.

Step one: Find the sale price of the first discount—$1,250 × .85 = $1,062.50

.85 is 100% (full price) – 15% (discount)

Step two: Find the sale price of the second discount—$ 1,062.50 × .80 = $850

Answer: $850

EXAMPLE THREE

There are 3,620 registered voters in Elizabethtown. In the last election, 1,267 did not vote. What percent of the town's registered voters *did* vote?

Step one: Reduce, label and perform the operation.
1,267 is ? % of 3,620, part ÷ whole, 1,267 ÷ 3,620 = .35 or 35%
35% is the percentage that represents those citizens that did not vote.

Step two: Easy. 100% – 35% = 65%
If 35% did *not* vote, then 65% *did* vote.

PRACTICE—MULTISTEP PERCENT PROBLEMS

Solve the following.

1. A businesswoman spends $\frac{1}{5}$ of her travel allotment on airfare and $\frac{3}{10}$ on hotel accommodations. What percent of her allotment is left?

2. Last year's Fourth of July parade was attended by 25,000 people, but this year attendance was only 21,000. What was the percentage of decrease in attendance?

3. A suit was on sale for $142.50, marked down 25% from its original price. What was the original price of the suit?

4. Sarah maintains a savings account of $1,658 that earns 8% annual interest. Dean has a mutual fund with $1,500 that earns 16% interest annually. At the end of one year, which account is worth more and by how much?

ANSWERS

1. **50%**   3. **$190**
2. **16%**   4. **Dean—$107.36**

Percent of Increase or Decrease

In these types of multistep word problems, you need to compare two numbers to find the percent of change.

EXAMPLE ONE

Errol bought stock for $25 per share. In three months, it rose to $49 dollars per share. Find the percent of increase of the stock.

Step one: Find the amount of the increase.
    49 – 28 = 21
The stock increased by $21.

Step two: Find the percent of increase by setting up a proportion;

$$\frac{\text{amount of increase}}{\text{original amount}} = \frac{21}{28}$$

Step three: Convert the proportion to a percent by dividing, as indicated in step 2.
    21 ÷ 28 = .75 = 75%

Answer: 75%

EXAMPLE TWO

A college's enrollment drops from 9,152 to 3,520 over the course of ten years. What is the percentage of decrease in enrollment?

Step one: Find the amount of decrease.
    9,152 – 3,520 = 5,632

Step two: $\dfrac{\text{amount of decrease}}{\text{original amount}} = \dfrac{5,632}{9,152}$

Step three: 5,632 ÷ 9,152 = .615 or 62%

Answer: 62%

PRACTICE—PERCENT INCREASE OR DECREASE

1. At eight years old, Susanna was 4'2" tall. At fourteen, she is 5'5". Find the percentage of increase in Susanna's height.

2. Harris buys a car for $8,200. He drives it for six years, then sells it for $1,400. By what percentage has the value of the car decreased?

ANSWERS

1. **30%**   2. **83%**

CHAPTER REVIEW

Fill in the answer grids, and use a calculator where indicated.

1. Tom purchased the following items at the paint store for the prices shown:

3 gallons of paint—$12.17
1 wide paintbrush—$6.49
1 paint roller set—$3.29

What change did he receive if he gave the clerk $30?

2. A precision laboratory thermometer measures a certain liquid's temperature at 44.014° (degrees) Fahrenheit. If the temperature of that liquid drops by 3.78°, what then would the thermometer read?

(1) 40.324°
(2) 47.794°
(3) 40.234°
(4) 41.09°
(5) not enough information is given

3. What is the area in square miles of the property in the diagram below?

12.4 miles

9.5 miles

4. John orders $1\frac{3}{4}$ lb. of salami from the deli department. After the clerk places the meat on the digital scale, it reads 1.85 lbs. What must the clerk do to give John the amount he asked for?

(1) add .62 lb.
(2) remove .1 lb.
(3) remove .05 lb.
(4) add .03 lb.
(5) add .12 lb.

5. The following library books with their corresponding filing numbers are out of order.

Book A—913.3
Book B—913.31
Book C—913.304
Book D—913.034

What is their correct order from lowest to highest?

(1) A, D, B, C
(2) C, A, B, D
(3) D, B, A, C
(4) D, A, C, B
(5) A, D, C, B

6.

Which expression indicates the maximum volume of the waste can in the above diagram?

(1) $36(3.14 \times 7 \text{ in.}^2)$
(2) $3(3.14 \times 14 \text{ in.})$
(3) $(14 \text{ in.} \times 3 \text{ ft.})^2$
(4) $\dfrac{14 \text{ in.}^2 \times 3 \text{ ft.}}{3.14}$
(5) $14 \text{ inches} \times 3.14 \times 3$

7. Janey is training for an upcoming marathon. Her running schedule for the week is as follows:

Monday—6.4 miles
Tuesday—8.3 miles
Wednesday—off
Thursday—7.7 miles
Friday—6 miles
Saturday—10.1 miles
Sunday—off

What is the average distance she runs for the days she *does* train?

(1) between 5 and 6 miles
(2) close to 9 miles
(3) close to 6 miles
(4) close to 8 miles
(5) between 6 and 7 miles

8.

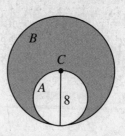

If C represents the center of circle B and the diameter of circle A is 8, which one of the expressions below indicates the area for the shaded portion of the diagram?

(1) $3.14(16 - 8)^2$
(2) $(3.14 \times 8^2) - (3.14 \times 4^2)$
(3) $(8 + 16^2) \, 3.14$
(4) $(3.14 \times 16) - (3.14 \times 8)$
(5) none of the above

9. Arrange in order from *largest to smallest*:

$\dfrac{9}{16}$ 54% $\dfrac{5}{8}$ .501   1.53

(1) $\dfrac{9}{16}$, 54%, $\dfrac{5}{8}$, .501, 1.53

(2) 1.53, .501, $\dfrac{5}{8}$, $\dfrac{9}{16}$, 54%

(3) 1.53, $\dfrac{5}{8}$, $\dfrac{9}{16}$, 54%, .501

(4) $\dfrac{5}{8}$, $\dfrac{9}{16}$, 54%, 1.53, .501

(5) 1.53, 54%, $\dfrac{5}{8}$, $\dfrac{9}{16}$, .501

10. Which of the following is not equal to 3.6?

(1) $3\dfrac{3}{5}$
(2) 360%
(3) 3.6%
(4) 3.600
(5) $3\dfrac{60}{100}$

11. Tom's gross salary is $760 per week. His salary is taxed at 16%. What is his net salary?

(1) $684
(2) $638.40
(3) $121.60
(4) $690.20
(5) $584

12. On a 56-question examination, Leslie answered 7 questions incorrectly. What percent of the questions did she answer correctly?

13. A delivery of 366 tons of sand to a construction site represents 60% of the sand needed to complete the job. How many more tons of sand need to be delivered?

14. There were 112 consumers who responded to a survey regarding laundry detergent. 38% preferred Brand A, 23% preferred Brand B, 19% preferred Brand C, and the rest were undecided. How many consumers were undecided?

(1) between 18 and 20
(2) between 15 and 18
(3) between 25 and 30
(4) between 24 and 26
(5) between 20 and 23

15. The Ortega family was looking to purchase a computer, originally priced at $940, which was discounted 25%. Later that month, it was reduced another 25% off the sale price. Since the Ortegas bought it for cash, they received an additional 5% discount. What was the final price they paid for the computer?

(1) around $460
(2) around $500
(3) around $530
(4) around $480
(5) around $600

16. The original price of a coffeemaker is ? dollars. If the price is discounted by 20%, which of the following expressions indicates the discounted price of *three* coffeemakers?

(1) ? × .80
(2) ? × .20
(3) $3\left(\dfrac{1}{3} \times ?\right)$
(4) 3(.20 × ?)
(5) 3(.80 × ?)

ANSWERS

1. **8.05**	5. **4**	9. **3**	13. **244**
2. **3**	6. **1**	10. **3**	14. **5**
3. **117.8**	7. **4**	11. **2**	15. **2**
4. **2**	8. **2**	12. **87.5**	16. **5**

Data Analysis

Many questions on the GED—not only in the Math section, but in the Science and Social Studies sections, as well—test your ability to read tables, charts, and graphs.

Tables

Tables are the simplest forms of graphic representation. Usually, you'll be asked to answer more than one question based on information in the table. Take care to read all the information provided.

SCHEDULE FOR TRAIN LEAVING CENTERVILLE AT 4:05 P.M.			
Destination	**Arrival Time**	**Departure Time**	**Fare**
Roxbury	4:20 P.M.	4:22 P.M.	$1.50
Lanesville	4:43 P.M.	4:45 P.M.	$2.10
Hampton	5:10 P.M.	5:12 P.M.	$4.50
Cheshire	5:31 P.M.	5:33 P.M.	$5.25

(double the fare for round-trip price)

EXAMPLE ONE

The following questions are based on the table.

1. Which is the least expensive destination to travel to from Centerville?

   Look at the "fare" column—it costs only $1.50 to travel to Roxbury.

   Answer: Roxbury

2. How long does it take to travel from Lanesville to Cheshire?

   This is a "clock" question. It's usually best to use an hour marker to help you

answer it. The train departs from Lanesville at 4:45, from 4:45 to 5:00 is 15 minutes, and from 5:00 to 5:31 (arrival time in Cheshire) is 31 minutes. Add the two sums together (15 + 31) to get 46 minutes.

Answer: 46 minutes

3. The fare to Roxbury is what percent of the fare to Hampton?

   This is a basic percent word problem. Just be careful to select the right numbers. When working with tables and charts, it can be helpful to use the straight edge of a piece of paper to read across a row.

Step one: Reduce—$1.50 is ? % of $4.50?

Step two: Solve—$1.50 ÷ $4.50 = .33 = 33%

Answer: 33%

4. James lives in Centerville and commutes to and from a job in Cheshire five days a week. What expression can be used to calculate the cost of his weekly commutation?

Always read "the fine print." In this case, it tells you that round trips are double the price listed in the "fare" column. Therefore the expression is: **5 (2 × $5.25)**—the "5" represents five days per week.

KINGSFIELD COMMUNITY RECREATION PROGRAM

Activity	Number of Participants	Enrollment Fee (per person)
Volleyball League	24	$30
Softball League	108	$10
Ballroom Dancing	32	$10
Cooking Class	15	$100
First Aid and CPR	25	$50

PRACTICE—TABLES

Use the chart above to answer the following questions.

1. Which activity attracted the smallest number of participants?

2. What is the difference in total enrollment fees between the cooking class and the softball league?

3. How many of the programs grossed over $1,000 in enrollment fees?

4. Which program netted the greatest profit for the Kingsfield Recreation Program?

5. What was the mean number of participants for the five classes listed?

ANSWERS

1. **Cooking**
2. **$420**
3. **3**
4. **not enough information is given**
5. **40.8 = 41**

Bar Graphs

Bar graphs use vertical (up and down) and horizontal (across) "bars" to represent quantities. It's essential that you read all labels and legends ("the fine print"), looking carefully at the base and sides of the graph to see what the bars are measuring and how much they're increasing or decreasing.

EXAMPLE ONE

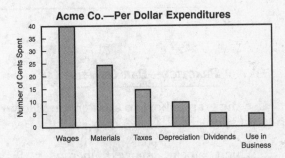

Before answering any questions, familiarize yourself with the graph and what it means. The Acme Co. may have gross income well over a million dollars, but the graph illustrates how much the company had to pay out *per dollar* in expenses, divided into six different categories. So, as an example, for every dollar the Acme Co. grossed, it had to pay out 15¢ in taxes.

1. How many cents of each dollar did the company use to pay for materials?

   Use the edge of a paper to line up the top of the "materials" bar with the numbers on the left side of the chart. It's very close to 25¢ spent.

   Answer: 25¢

2. How much are the combined expenses of taxes and "uses in business" equal to?

   Taxes = 15¢
   Use in business = 5¢
   15 + 5 = 20¢

   Answer: 20¢ spent per dollar

3. The combined expenses of depreciation, dividends, and use in business represent what percentage of the number of cents spent on wages?

   10 + 5 + 5 = 20   (combined expenses)
   20 is ? % of 40?   40 (wages)
   20 is half of 40 or 50%

   Answer: 50%

4. If the Acme Co. reduced its wage payroll by laying off five managers, what would be the new number of cents per dollar spent on wages?

   There is no indication of how much these managers are paid nor is there a dollar amount given that reflects total wages. The answer can't be calculated.

   Answer: not enough information is given

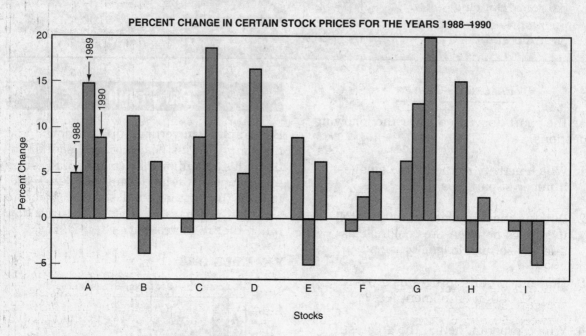

PERCENT CHANGE IN CERTAIN STOCK PRICES FOR THE YEARS 1988–1990

PRACTICE—BAR GRAPHS

Use the graph above to answer the following questions.

1. Which stocks showed *increases* for every year charted?

2. Which stock had the greatest percentage of change from one year to the next?

3. The percent of change for Stock G in 1990 was how much greater than the percent of change for Stock D in 1988?

4. How much was Stock F worth in 1990?

5. How much greater was Stock G's percent of increase than Stock F's during the three-year period?

   (1) twice as much
   (2) the same
   (3) three times as much
   (4) 1.5 times as much
   (5) not enough information is given

Answers

1. **C, F, G**
2. **H**
3. **15%**
4. **not enough information is given**
5. **1**

Line Graphs

Line graphs almost always measure how things increase or decrease over time.

There is often more than one line on a graph, which can cause some confusion. Proceed slowly and carefully.

EXAMPLE ONE

The graph below shows the conversion of farm and forest acreage to housing developments in Granite County.

1. How many acres of farm and forest were converted to housing developments in 1955?

   You can't tell **exactly** because the line crosses 1955 about one-third of the way between 50 and 60 acres. But an estimate of 70 acres would be correct.

   Answer: 70 acres

2. During which five-year period was there no increase in conversion?

   That's easy. Look for the place where the line runs horizontally for five years—between 1965 and 1970.

   Answer: 1965–1970

3. During which five-year period were conversions greatest?

   Look for the steepest rise in the line.

   Answer: 1970–1975

4. During which year were the most forest acres converted?

   Look carefully at the fine print. There is no special distinction between farm and forest conversion. Therefore, there is **not enough information** given to calculate the answer.

5. What is the difference between the number of acres converted in 1945–1950 and those converted in 1970–1975?

   The 1945–1950 conversions are approximately 45 acres, and the 1970–1975 conversions are approximately 125 acres. 125 − 45 = 80

   Answer: approximately 80 acres

PRACTICE—LINE GRAPH

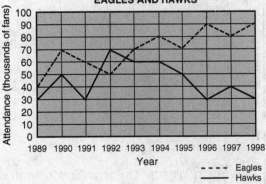

The Hawks and Eagles are minor-league baseball teams. The graph represents the paid attendance record of each team over a ten-year period. The following questions are based on information in the above graph.

1. During which year did the Hawks' attendance exceed that of the Eagles?

2. In 1996 how many more fans attended Eagles games than Hawks games?

3. By what percent did the Eagles' attendance increase from 1989 to 1993?

4. Between what years was the decrease in attendance the same for both teams?

5. What percent of the ten years covered by the graph did the Eagles' attendance exceed the Hawks'?

Pie Charts

Pie charts (sometimes called **circle graphs**) represent the way in which something is divided into parts. As always, try to get the big picture while paying attention to the fine print.

EXAMPLE ONE

Annual Expenses for the Golden Tree Landscaping Corp.

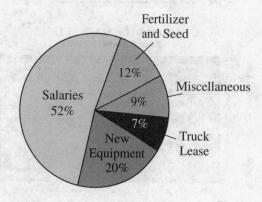

1. What part of Golden Tree's annual expenses does New Equipment and Fertilizer and Seed represent?

   (1) about $\frac{1}{2}$

   (2) about 20%

   (3) about $\frac{1}{3}$

   (4) about 40%

   First, add the two sections:
        20% + 12% = 32%.
   32% is very close to 33%. You know that 33% of anything is $\frac{1}{3}$.

   Answer: (3) about $\frac{1}{3}$

2. Golden Tree establishes a relationship with a new equipment sales company that gives them a 25% discount on all purchases. What would the recalculated percentage of expense be for new equipment using the new supplier?

   New equipment consumes 20% of expenses. If the company now gets a 25% (or $\frac{1}{4}$ off) discount on its purchases, then the percentage will be reduced by $\frac{1}{4}$. $\frac{1}{4}$ of 20% = 5% and 20 − 5 = 15%

   Answer: 15%

3. Which section of the chart accounts for equipment repair?

   Since none of the sections specify "Equipment Repair," it must be assumed that "Miscellaneous" (which means "other various unnamed items") accounts for it.

   Answer: Miscellaneous

4. If Golden Tree's expenses for one year total $62,000, how much does the company pay *per month* for the truck lease?

   Step one: Calculate the annual amount paid for the truck lease.
        $62,000 × .07 = $4,340

   Step two: Calculate the monthly amount of the lease.
        $4,340 ÷ 12 (for 12 months of the year) = $361.66

   Answer: $361.66

PRACTICE—PIE CHARTS

Distribution of $62,000 Grant for School Improvement

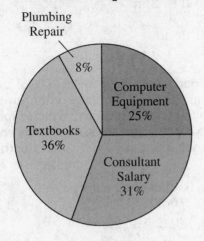

Plumbing Repair 8%

Computer Equipment 25%

Textbooks 36%

Consultant Salary 31%

Answer the following questions based on the information provided in the chart above.

1. How many dollars of the grant were spent on plumbing repair?

2. All of the money allotted to computer equipment went to the purchase of five of the same computer systems. How much did each system cost?

3. What expression represents the difference in dollars between money spent on textbooks and that spent on computer equipment?

4. If the grant increased by $21,500 for the following year, how much money would be allotted for consultant salary?

ANSWERS

1. **$4,960**
2. **$3,100**
3. **.11 (62,000)**
4. **$25,885**

CHAPTER REVIEW

Fill in the answer grids, and use a calculator where indicated.

THE EVENING POST—RATES FOR CLASSIFIED ADS	
Ads up to 15 words	$25
Ads up to 25 words	$35
Ads over 25 words	$1.50 per word
not including sales tax of 8%	

Use the information provided to answer the following questions.

1. How much does it cost to purchase an ad of 12 words, including sales tax?

2. How much more would it cost to purchase an ad of 36 words than two ads of 15 words each, not including tax?

(1) $4
(2) $2.75
(3) $12
(4) $4.25
(5) $15

3. *The Evening Post* offers its employees a "one-third off" discount on all classified ads. A worker there wishes to take out a 20-word ad. Including tax, what price will she pay for the ad?

(1) around $28
(2) around $20
(3) around $24
(4) around $25
(5) not enough information is given

Use the line graph above to answer the following question.

4. In miles per hour, what is the rate of travel represented by the diagonal line?

(1) between 60 and 70 mph
(2) between 85 and 90 mph
(3) between 55 and 60 mph
(4) between 75 and 80 mph
(5) not enough information is given

The graph above shows the average monthly snowfall for six consecutive months at a mountain ski resort.

5. How much more snow fell in January than in November?

(1) 2 ft. 11 in.
(2) 3 ft. 3 in.
(3) 2 ft.
(4) 25 in.
(5) 2 ft. 3 in.

6. A midwinter thaw melts 30% of the snow that accumulates from November to the end of January. Which expression represents the amount of snow accumulation left immediately *after* the thaw?

(1) $55 \times .30$
(2) $.30(20 + 42 + 55)$
(3) $.70(20 + 42 + 55)$
(4) $\dfrac{20 + 42 + 55}{.30}$
(5) $(.30 \times 55) + (20 + 42)$

7. By what percent does the snowfall increase from December to January?

How the Residents of Chambersville Heat Their Houses

Statistics based on survey of 3,216 households

8. If 10% of all households in Chambersville that heat with oil shifted to heating with wood, what percent would now heat with wood?

(1) 11.6%
(2) 18%
(3) 2%
(4) 18.3%
(5) 21%

9. How many households in Chambersville are dependent on gas and oil heat?

(1) 1,930
(2) 1,158
(3) 772
(4) 65%
(5) 1,479

ANSWERS

1. **27**	4. **4**	7. **31**
2. **1**	5. **1**	8. **1**
3. **4**	6. **3**	9. **1**

Algebra

The Number Line and Positive and Negative Numbers

Consider the number line above. The arrows at each end mean the line extends infinitely in each direction, so that any number imaginable can be found on it. Notice that 0 is at the midpoint of the line.

Up to this point, you have only dealt with positive numbers, but it's now time to introduce negative numbers, which are marked by a "–" sign. The further a number is to the **right** of the number line, the **greater** its value. For example, 3 > 0 (this symbol, >, means "is greater than") because it's further to the right on the number line. Likewise, 0 > –3 (0 is greater than –3) and –2 > –3.

FINDING POINTS ON THE NUMBER LINE

On the GED, you'll be asked to identify points on the number line.

EXAMPLE ONE

Which point represents 3.5?

Answer: *B*—it's halfway between 3 and 4.

EXAMPLE TWO

Which point represents –5?

Answer: *C*—it's right above the –5 marker.

EXAMPLE THREE

Which point approximates $\sqrt{28}$

$\sqrt{28}$ isn't a whole number. $5 \times 5 = 25$ and $6 \times 6 = 36$ Therefore, $\sqrt{28}$ has to be between 5 and 6.

Answer: *A* is between 5 and 6.

PRACTICE—FINDING POINTS ON THE NUMBER LINE

From the above number line, choose the correct letter for the following.

1. .5
2. –3.5
3. $\sqrt{16}$
4. $\sqrt{5}$
5. –6

ANSWERS

1. **E**   2. **D**   3. **C**   4. **A**   5. **B**

ADDING SIGNED NUMBERS

Here are the rules that tell how to add signed numbers. Memorize them.

- If the signs are the same (–,– or +,+) **add** the two numbers and label the answer with that sign.

EXAMPLES

7 + 3 = 10 (Both signs are positive, add, label answer positive.)

–5 + (–3) = –8 (Both signs negative, add, label answer negative.)

- If the signs are different (+,– or –,+), **subtract**. Forgetting for a moment the positive and negative signs, compare the numbers and choose **the larger of the two**. Label the answer with the sign of the "larger" number.

EXAMPLES

–6 + 5= –1 (Signs different, subtract, 6 – 5 = 1, compare, 6 is larger than 5, 6 has a negative sign, attach it to answer: –1).

12 + (–7) = 5 (Signs different, subtract, 12 – 7 = 5, 12 is larger and positive so attach sign to answer: +5 or 5).

- When adding **more than two** signed numbers, follow the above rules to get a sum for the first two numbers, then continue to use rules for adding subsequent numbers.

EXAMPLES

–5 + (–14) + (–6) = –25

Step one: –5 + (–14) = –19

Step two: –19 + (–6) = –25 (Same signs, add, label negative)

5 + (–12) + 7 = 0

Step one: 5 + (–12) = –7

Step two: –7 + 7 = 0 (Different signs, subtract 7 – 7 = 0 – 0 never takes a sign)

Add the following.

1. 12 + (–8)
2. –14 + (–6)
3. –40 + 13
4. –2 + (–19)
5. 36 + (–1)
6. –26 + 6 + (–15)
7. 8 + (–14) + 30

ANSWERS

1. **4**	5. **35**
2. **–20**	6. **–35**
3. **–27**	7. **24**
4. **–21**	

SUBTRACTING SIGNED NUMBERS

Here are the three steps that will help you to subtract signed numbers. Memorize them.

> *Step one:* Change the subtraction problem to an addition problem.
>
> *Step two:* Change the sign of the second number.
>
> *Step three:* Follow the rules of addition you just learned.

EXAMPLE ONE

–16 – 6 = –22

Step one: Change subtraction to addition.
–16 + 6

Step two: Change sign of second number.
–16 + (–6)

Step three: Follow rules of addition. (Same signs, add, 16 + 6 = 22, same sign, attach to answer)

Answer: –22

EXAMPLE TWO

12 – (–7) = 19

Step one: 12 – (–7) becomes 12 + (–7)

Step two: 12 + (–7) becomes 12 + 7

Step three: 12 + 7 = 19

Answer: 19

Solve.
1. −5 − 4
2. 16 − (−18)
3. 12 − 23
4. −20 − 16
5. −4 − (−18)
6. 26 − (−40)
7. 0 − 42
8. 42 − (−5) − 7

ANSWERS

1. **−9**   5. **14**
2. **34**   6. **66**
3. **−11**   7. **−42**
4. **−36**   8. **40**

MULTIPLYING AND DIVIDING SIGNED NUMBERS

Good news. The rules for these operations are much simpler than for addition and subtraction. They are:

> **1.** Signs **alike**—answer is **positive**
>
> **2.** Signs **different**—answer is **negative**

Look carefully at the following examples and see how the rules work.

$-3(5) = -15$ $3(-5) = -15$

$-3(-5) = 15$ $\dfrac{\pm 15}{3} = -5$

$\dfrac{15}{\pm 3} = -5$ $(3)(-5)(2) = -30$

$\dfrac{\pm 5}{\pm 3} = \dfrac{5}{3}$ $(3)(-5)(-2) = 30$

Solve.

1. $\dfrac{24}{\pm 8}$

2. $\dfrac{1}{4}(-3)$

3. $(-.5)(-6.1)$

4. $\dfrac{\pm 36}{\pm 6}$

5. $(9 - 20)(-18)(-3)$

ANSWERS

1. **−3**   4. **6**
2. $-\dfrac{3}{4}$ 5. **−594**
3. **3.05**

Use the +/− key on you calculator for negative numbers. It makes working with signed numbers much easier.

Working with Variables

In a mathematical sentence, a variable is a letter that represents a number. Consider this sentence: $x + 4 = 10$. Here, it's easy to figure out that x represents 6. However, problems with variables on the GED will become much more complex than that, and there are many rules and procedures that need to be learned.

Before you learn to solve equations with variables, you need to perform basic operations with them. Here's some vocabulary that will be helpful.

> $3y$ is called a **monomial**
>
> The 3 in $3y$ is called a **coefficient**
>
> The y is called a **variable**

ADDING AND SUBTRACTING WITH VARIABLES

Consider the following statements:

$x + x = 2x$ but $x + 1 = x + 1$
$3x + x = 4x$ but $3x + 1 = 3x + 1$
$4y + 3y = 7y$ but $4y + 3 = 4y + 3$
$3r - 6r = -3r$ but $3r - 6 = 3r - 6$
$3rx + 3rx = 6rx$ but $3r + 3rx = 3r + 3rx$

Remember: x is the same as $1x$

As you can see, only those monomials that have the same variables can be added to or subtracted from each other.

Sometimes, you'll see problems like this:

Evaluate: $a + 3b + 3a$

Answer: $4a + 3b$

Evaluate: $5b + 3c - 2b + c$

Answer: 3b + 4c

Do the addition and subtraction with like terms (the ones with exactly matching variables). Anything that stands alone, leave alone.

PRACTICE—ADDING AND SUBTRACTING WITH VARIABLES

Add or subtract the following. If the terms can't be added or subtracted, recopy them.

1. $5x + 12x$
2. $-14a - (-3a)$
3. $25 + 6a$
4. $12st + (-6st)$
5. $3y + 6$
6. $7xy + 8x$
7. $5p + p$
8. $14s - x$
9. $36x - x$
10. $25a + (-6a) - 7$
11. $6a - 3c + a + 2b$
12. $b + 2a + 3b - c$

ANSWERS

1. **17x**
2. **-11a**
3. **25 + 6a**
4. **6st**
5. **3y + 6**
6. **7xy + 8x**
7. **6p**
8. **14s - x**
9. **35x**
10. **19a - 7**
11. **7a - 3c + 2b**
12. **4b + 2a - c**

MULTIPLYING AND DIVIDING WITH VARIABLES

Once again, the rules are different with these operations. You *must* multiply and divide monomials with numbers as well as monomials with different variables. Carefully consider the following examples:

Multiplication

$3(4x) = 12x$ $3x(4y) = 12xy$

$3x(4yz) = 12xyz$ $\frac{1}{7}(5x) = \frac{5x}{7}$

$\frac{1}{2}(4a) = \frac{4a}{2} = 2a$

As you can see from the examples above, multiply the coefficients and include the variables.

Division

$\frac{12x}{4} = 3x$ $\frac{12x}{4x} = 3$ $\frac{12xy}{4x} = 3y$

(The variables cancel each other out.)

PRACTICE—MULTIPLYING AND DIVIDING WITH VARIABLES

Solve.

1. $5(5x) =$
2. $\frac{14s}{7} =$
3. $-5y(6x) =$
4. $\frac{72x}{9x} =$
5. $13x(5y) =$
6. $\frac{48xy}{6y} =$
7. $.36xy(4z) =$
8. $\frac{25abc}{5ac} =$
9. $\frac{1}{5}(15x) =$
10. $\frac{2}{7}(7a) =$

ANSWERS

1. **25x**
2. **2s**
3. **-30xy**
4. **8**
5. **65xy**
6. **8x**
7. **1.44xyz**
8. **5b**
9. **3x**
10. **2a**

VARIABLES AND EXPONENTS

Multiplication

Consider the following:

$x + x = 2x$ *but* $x(x) = x^2$ *and* $x^2(x^3) = x^5$
$2(4x) = 8x$ *but* $2x(4x) = 8x^2$
$2x^2(4x) = 8x^3$
$x(4x^3) = 4x^4$
$5x^3(4x^5) = 20x^8$
$4x^3y^2(5x^2y) = 20x^5y^3$
$3x^5y^3z^4(6x^3yz^2) = 18x^8y^4z^6$

What you *should* see from the above examples is that when multiplying variables with exponents, you *add* the exponents, as long as the bases are the same.

Division

Consider the following:

$\frac{12x^6y^4}{3x^3y^2} = 4x^3y^2$ $\frac{9a^8b^2c^7}{3a^5c} = 3a^3b^2c^6$

When dividing variables with exponents, **subtract** the exponents.

PRACTICE—VARIABLES AND EXPONENTS

Solve.

1. $x\,(x^3)$

2. $4x(5x)$

3. $\dfrac{16x^4}{4x}$

4. $\dfrac{25s^3}{s}$

5. $3x^3y^2\,(5x^2)$

6. $5ef^2\,(2y^3)$

7. $\dfrac{32a^5bc^3}{8a^4b}$

ANSWERS

1. x^4
2. $20x^2$
3. $4x^3$
4. $25s^2$

5. $15x^5y^2$
6. $10ef^2y^3$
7. $4ac^3$

WORKING WITH PARENTHESES

You already know that $5(6a)$ means $5 \times 6a$, but consider this more complicated statement:

$$5(6a + c)$$

It must be rewritten like this:

$$5(6a) + 5(c) \quad \text{which is} \quad 30a + 5c$$

Each term **inside** the parentheses must be multiplied by the one directly outside. Then the operation specified (in this case, addition) must be carried out.

Consider two more examples:

$$3b(6b - 2ac) \quad \text{becomes} \quad 18b^2 - 6abc$$

$$\tfrac{1}{3}(6x + 7) \quad \text{becomes} \quad \dfrac{6x}{3} + \dfrac{7}{3} = 2x + \dfrac{7}{3}$$

PRACTICE—PARENTHESES

Rewrite the following, as in the above examples.

1. $3(5a - 6)$
2. $2(2a + 7)$
3. $5(6r + 7s - t)$
4. $2a^2(5a + 6b)$
5. $3(8x - 5) + \dfrac{1}{8}(2x + z)$

ANSWERS

1. $15a - 18$
2. $4a + 14$
3. $30r + 35s - 5t$
4. $10a^3 + 12a^2b$
5. $(24x - 15) + \left(\dfrac{1}{4}x + \dfrac{z}{8}\right)$

FINDING VALUES WHEN VARIABLES ARE GIVEN

Consider the following:

EXAMPLE ONE

Find the value of z if $z = 3x + y^2$ where $x = 6$ and $y = -4$

Step one: Replace the variables with numbers

$$z = 3(6) + (-4)^2$$

Step two: perform the operations in proper order (remember PEMDAS from Chapter 19).

Answer: $z = 18 + 16$ or $z = 34$

EXAMPLE TWO

Find the value of c if $c = 3a^2(b - 5)$ where $a = 3$ and $b = 10$

Step one: $3(3)^2 \times (10 - 5)$

Step two: $(3)\,(9)\,(5) = 135$

Answer: $c = 135$

PRACTICE—FINDING VALUES WITH GIVEN VARIABLES

Solve.

1. $c = 4a - 3b$, if $a = 8$ and $b = 5$. Find c.

2. $s = 3q^2 + 2r$, if $q = 6$ and $r = .5$. Find s.

3. $z = 3x^2(y + 8)$, if $x = 10$ and $y = -12$. Find z.

4. $m = \dfrac{1}{4}n + 3o + 5p^2$, if $n = 16$ and $o = 12$ and $p = 3$. Find m.

5. $c = \dfrac{2a\left(b^2 - 8\right)}{a}$ if $a = 3$ and $b = -5$. Find c.

ANSWERS

1. **17**
2. **109**
3. **–1200**
4. **85**
5. **34**

ONE-STEP EQUATIONS

Here's an example of a one-step equation.

$$x + 5 = 29$$

Your goal is to figure out what number can replace x so that both sides of the equation will equal 29. The boundary line of each **side** of the equation is the = sign. So $x + 5$ is on the left side of this equation and 29 is on the right.

To reach your goal in any simple equation, you must reduce one side of the equation to just one variable and the other side to just one number. You accomplish this by performing any of the four basic operations to both sides of the equation. Just remember this:

> What you do to *one* side of the equation, you must do to the other side.

Here's how it works:

EXAMPLE ONE

$x + 5 = 29$ solve for x

$$x + 5 = 29$$

Step one: $\quad\underline{-\ 5\quad -5}$

Step two: $\quad x \quad\ = 24$

Step three: Check $24 + 5 = 29$

Step one: Since you want to reduce the left side of the equation to just x, you've got to get rid of the "+ 5" in "$x + 5$." The way to get rid of it is to perform its inverse (opposite) by subtracting 5 from that side of the equation. *Remember*, what you do to one side of the equation, you must do to the other side. Therefore, you do $29 - 5$.

Step two: Draw a line across the bottom of the entire equation and do the subtraction problems for each side. The result on the left is "$x + 0$." There is no need to write the 0. You have accomplished your goal of reducing one side of the equation to just one variable—x. The result on the right side is 24. Therefore, $x = 24$

Step three: Check. Simply replace the variable with the number, do the math, and make sure both sides of the equation are equal.

The procedure is the same for all other simple equations. Consider the following examples.

EXAMPLE TWO

$a - 19 = 12$ Solve for a.

$$\begin{array}{rl} a - 19 = & 12 \\ \underline{+\ 19} & \underline{+19} \\ a \quad\ = & 31 \end{array}$$ Check: $31 - 19 = 12$

EXAMPLE THREE

$5x = 45$ Solve for x

$$\frac{5x}{5} = \frac{45}{5}$$

$x\ =\ 9$ Check: $5(9) = 45$ $45 = 45$

Notice that this equation is a multiplication problem. Again, you do the inverse operation—division—to get rid of the number surrounding x. And, again, what you do to one side you must do to the other.

EXAMPLE FOUR

$$\frac{1x}{3} = 33$$

$$\frac{3}{1} \times \frac{1x}{3} = 33 \times \frac{3}{1}$$

$$x = 99$$

Check: $\frac{1}{3}(99) = 33$ $33 = 33$

In this division problem, once again, you must perform the inverse operation (multiplication) to get rid of the numbers attached to "x." Always multiply by the fraction's **reciprocal** to cancel it out. The reciprocal of $\frac{1}{3}$ is $\frac{3}{1}$—the reciprocal of $\frac{1}{6}$ is $\frac{6}{1}$, $\frac{1}{22}$ is $\frac{22}{1}$, $\frac{3}{8}$ is $\frac{8}{3}$, etc. When you multiply a number by its reciprocal, the product is **1**. Remember, **1x** is the same as **x**.

PRACTICE—ONE-STEP EQUATIONS

Solve for the variable.

1. $51 = x + 20$
2. $x - 43 = 12$
3. $38 = b + 14$
4. $r - 81 = 16$
5. $12t = 96$
6. $\frac{1}{5}p = 14$
7. $118 = 59s$
8. $21 = \frac{1}{3}h$

ANSWERS

1. $x = 31$
2. $x = 55$
3. $b = 24$
4. $r = 97$
5. $t = 8$
6. $p = 70$
7. $s = 2$
8. $h = 63$

MULTISTEP EQUATIONS

These equations are just a bit more complicated because they combine two or three of the procedures just learned into one problem. Consider the following:

EXAMPLE ONE

$$5m + 8 = 48$$

$$5m + 8 = 48$$
$$\underline{- 8 \quad -8}$$
$$\frac{5m}{5} = \frac{40}{5} \qquad m = 8$$

EXAMPLE TWO

$$\frac{3p}{8} + 17 = 38$$

$$\frac{3p}{8} + 17 = 38$$
$$\underline{\phantom{\frac{3p}{8}} - 17 = -17}$$
$$\frac{8}{3} \times \frac{3p}{8} = 21 \times \frac{8}{3}$$
$$p = 56$$

EXAMPLE THREE

$$\frac{x}{5} + 12 = 38$$

$$\frac{x}{5} + 12 = 38$$
$$\underline{\phantom{\frac{x}{5}} - 12 = -12}$$
$$\frac{x}{5} = 26$$
$$\frac{5}{1} \times \frac{x}{5} = 26 \times \frac{5}{1}$$
$$x = 130$$

EXAMPLE FOUR

$$3p + 7 = 10p$$
$$\underline{-3p \qquad\quad -3p}$$
$$\frac{7}{7} = \frac{7p}{7}$$
$$1 = p$$

What makes this equation different from the previous ones is that it has a variable on both sides. Notice how it's dealt with.

EXAMPLE FIVE

$$6(x - 4) = 36$$

$$6x - 24 = 36$$
$$\underline{ + 24 \quad +24}$$
$$\frac{6x}{6} = \frac{60}{6}$$
$$x = 10$$

Two final notes on solving equations—always do addition or subtraction first, if there is any to be done. *Do not* add or subtract so that one side of the equation equals 0. If it occurs, reexamine the equation and try inverse operation on another number.

PRACTICE—MORE COMPLEX EQUATIONS

Solve for the variable and check.

1. $12a + 6 = 42$
2. $7x - 14 = 14$
3. $\frac{r}{9} + 8 = 12$
4. $116 = 15c + 11$
5. $\frac{1}{8}m - 27 = 16$
6. $2(x - 9) = 46$
7. $14d = 18 + 8d$
8. $3h + 11 = 38$
9. $4(s + 6) = -28$

ANSWERS

1. $a = 3$
2. $x = 4$
3. $r = 36$
4. $c = 7$
5. $m = 344$
6. $x = 32$
7. $d = 3$
8. $h = 9$
9. $s = -13$

Inequalities

> means **is greater than** $\quad 5 > 4$
< means **is less than** $\quad 6 < 8$
≥ means **is greater than or equal to**
$\qquad 5 \geq 5$ and all positive numbers added to it
≤ means **is less than or equal to**
$\qquad 3 \leq 3$ and all positive numbers subtracted from it

Memorize the meanings of the inequality signs.

PRACTICE—SIMPLE INEQUALITIES

True or False.

1. $\frac{1}{4} > \frac{1}{8}$

2. $3(5) < 14$

3. $-.5 > 0$

4. $12(3) \geq 36$

5. $\frac{12}{7} \leq 1\frac{5}{7}$, 2, 3

ANSWERS

1. **True**
2. **False**
3. **False**

4. **True**
5. **True**

EQUATIONS WITH INEQUALITIES

On the GED, you will certainly have to solve equations with inequalities. Proceed exactly as you would with the equations just learned, replacing the = sign with whatever inequality sign is in the equation.

EXAMPLE

$$3s - 4 > 11$$
$$\underline{+ 4 \quad +4}$$
$$\frac{3s}{3} \quad > \quad \frac{15}{3}$$

Answer: s > 5

What this means is that s can be checked with any number **greater than** 5. It could be 5.1 or 5,000,000.

Let's use 6.

$3(6) - 4 > 11 = 18 - 4 > 11$

$14 > 11$ is a true statement. It works.

PRACTICE—EQUATIONS WITH INEQUALITIES

Solve and check.

1. $\frac{x}{3} < 12$

2. $5y - 2 > 23$

3. $18 > 3(a - 6)$

4. $12x - 5 \geq 4x + 1$

ANSWERS

1. $x < 36$

2. $y > 5$

3. $12 > a$

4. $x \geq \frac{3}{4}$

Multiplying Binomials

$x + 6$ is an example of a binomial. You won't be asked to identify one, nor define the difference between a monomial and a binomial, but you will need to know how to multiply two binomials. It's very much like multiplying regular numbers. Consider this example:

$$(x + 4) \ (x + 3)$$

Step one: Set up like a two-digit multiplication problem

$$x + 4$$
$$\underline{\times \quad x + 3}$$
$$+ 3x + 12$$
$$\underline{+ x^2 + 4x}$$
$$x^2 + 7x + 12$$

Step two: Starting with the lower right term (+3), multiply the two top terms, right (4) then left (x). Put the products to each computation in the column where they belong.

$$4 \times 3 = 12 \quad \text{and} \quad x \times 3 = 3x$$

Step three: Now do the same for the lower left term. Just as in numeral multiplication, skip a one-digit space at the far right when entering the second row of products.

$$4 \times x = 4x \quad \text{and} \quad x \times x = x^2$$

Step four: Again, as in numerical multiplication, add the results in columns going downward.

Carefully study the following additional examples of binomial multiplication:

$(x - 7) \ (x + 2)$

$$x - 7$$
$$\underline{x + 2}$$
$$2x - 14$$
$$\underline{x^2 - 7x}$$
$$x^2 - 5x - 14$$

$(x - 8) \ (x - 3)$

$$x - 8$$
$$\underline{x - 3}$$
$$- 3x + 24$$
$$\underline{x^2 - 8x}$$
$$x^2 - 11x + 24$$

$(x + 6) \ (x - 6)$

$$x + 6$$
$$\underline{x - 6}$$
$$- 6x - 36$$
$$\underline{x^2 + 6x}$$
$$x^2 + 0 - 36$$

Since the 0 is unnecessary, $x^2 - 36$.

PRACTICE—MULTIPLYING BINOMIALS

Solve.

1. $(x + 2)(x + 4)$ 4. $(x + 2)(x - 9)$
2. $(x - 6)(x + 3)$ 5. $(x + 9)(x - 9)$
3. $(x - 8)(x - 5)$

ANSWERS

1. $x^2 + 6x + 8$ 4. $x^2 - 7x - 18$
2. $x^2 - 3x - 18$ 5. $x^2 - 81$
3. $x^2 - 13x + 40$

PRACTICE—FACTORING QUADRATIC EXPRESSIONS

Factor the following.

1. $x^2 + 9x + 18$ 4. $x^2 + 9x - 36$
2. $x^2 - 7x + 10$ 5. $x^2 + x - 56$
3. $x^2 - 49$

ANSWERS

1. $(x + 3)(x + 6)$ 4. $(x + 12)(x - 3)$
2. $(x - 5)(x - 2)$ 5. $(x + 8)(x - 7)$
3. $(x + 7)(x - 7)$

Factoring Quadratic Expressions

This is the reverse operation of multiplying binomials. You will probably have one problem like this on the test, so it's best to be prepared. A quadratic expression looks like this:

$$x^2 + 10x + 16$$

Here's how to factor it.

EXAMPLE ONE

Factor $x^2 + 10x + 16$

$(x \quad)(x \quad)$ will always be your starting point because $x(x) = x^2$.

You now need to find **one set** of two numbers that, when multiplied, will equal +16 and when added will equal +10.

$16 \times 1 = 16$ but $16 + 1 = 17$—No
$4 \times 4 = 16$ but $4 + 4 = 8$—No
$8 \times 2 = 16$ *and* $8 + 2 = 10$—**Yes**

The factors for the quadratic expression $x_2 + 10x + 16$ are:

$$(x + 8)(x + 2)$$

A check will prove it.

EXAMPLE TWO

Factor $x^2 + 2x - 8$

$-8 \times 1 = -8$ but $-8 + -1 = -7$—No
$-4 \times 2 = -8$ but $-4 + (-2) = -2$—No
$4 \times -2 = -8$ *and* $4 + (-2) = +2$—**Yes**

Answer: $(x + 4)(x - 2)$

Quadratic Equations

The quadratic equation problems you'll see on the GED all look similar to this:

$$x^2 - 12x + 27 = 0 \qquad \text{Solve for } x$$

The key here is that you must come up with **two** different numbers for x that will make the equation work.

EXAMPLE

$$x^2 - 12x + 27 = 0 \qquad \text{Solve for } x$$

Step one: Factor the left side of the equation $(x - 9)(x - 3)$

Step two: Simply reverse the signs on the two numbers in each binomial factor. -9 becomes 9, -3 becomes 3

Answer: $x = 9, 3$

A check of both numbers replacing x is time-consuming. Know the process.

PRACTICE—QUADRATIC EQUATIONS

Solve for x.

1. $x^2 + 15x + 56 = 0$
2. $x^2 - 7x - 30 = 0$
3. $x^2 + 8x - 9 = 0$
4. $x^2 - 64 = 0$
5. $x^2 - 19x + 60 = 0$

ANSWERS

1. $(-7, -8)$ 4. $(8, -8)$
2. $(10, -3)$ 5. $(15, 4)$
3. $(-9, 1)$

Algebra and Word Problems

PROPORTIONS

This operation is the next logical step after "ratio," which you learned in Chapter 20, Fractions. In its simplest form, the idea is to make two ratios equal, when one of the four parts is unknown.

EXAMPLE ONE

$7 : 2 = x : 6$ solve for x

Step one: Set up ratios as fractions

$$\frac{7}{2} = \frac{x}{6}$$

Step two: Cross-multiply and set up the products as two numbers separated by an = sign:

$7 \times 6 = 42$ and $2 \times x = 2x$

Set up as $2x = 42$

Step three: Finish the equation by dividing

$$\frac{2x}{2} = \frac{42^{21}}{2^1}$$
$$7 : 2 = 21 : 6$$

Answer: $x = 21$

What this means is that 7 has the same numerical relationship to 2 as 21 does to 6.

Let's say you were baking a cake that required you to put in seven cups of milk to two cups of flour. If you wanted to bake a larger cake (in this case, three times larger), you would still follow the same recipe ratio of 7 parts to 2 parts by using 21 cups of milk and 6 cups of flour.

EXAMPLE TWO

The scale on a map is 1 inch to every 150 miles. How far apart in miles are two cities that are 6 inches apart on the map?

Step one: $1 : 150 = 6 : x$

Step two: $\dfrac{1}{150} = \dfrac{6}{x}$

Step three: $900 = x$, making *Step four* unnecessary

Answer: 900 miles

EXAMPLE THREE

In a hotel, the ratio of nonsmoking rooms to rooms where smoking is allowed is 5:2. If there are 350 rooms in the hotel, how many allow smoking?

Step one: Problem! The proportion can't be set up as it has been in the past two examples because the information doesn't match—5:2 gives you two parts (non-smoking:smoking) but 350 gives you a *total*. You need to compare total (350) to smoking (unknown or x).

The sum of the two parts (5 + 2) will give a total of 7. Now you have equal ratios to compare with.

$$\frac{\text{total}}{\text{smoking}} \qquad \frac{7}{2} = \frac{350}{x}$$

Step two: $7x = 700$

Step three: $\dfrac{7x}{7} = \dfrac{700}{7}$

Step four: $x = 100$

Answer: There are 100 rooms where smoking is allowed

PRACTICE—PROPORTIONS

1. On a construction job, a carpenter uses 26 feet of lumber to build 2 door frames. If he is going to build 5 door frames, how much lumber does he need?

2. The scale on a road map indicates that $\frac{1}{4}$ inch equals 20 miles. How far apart in miles are two towns that are $3\frac{1}{2}$ inches away on the map?

3. A photograph is 3 inches long by 5 inches wide. If Susan wants to enlarge it so that it is 12 inches long, how wide will the enlargement be?

ANSWERS

1. **65 feet**   2. **280 miles**   3. **20 inches**

Setups Using Variables

This is, perhaps, the most common type of problem seen on the GED, so understanding it is really important. Much like word problems in Chapter 19, Numbers and Basic Operations, you should rely on your common sense to guide you.

EXAMPLE ONE

Sally can plant x tomato seedlings per row and there are y rows in her garden. Write an algebraic expression that represents the total amount of seedlings that could be planted in the garden.

It should occur to you that this is very much like an "area" question ($l \times w$). What might help you to picture the solution is **to put numbers in place of the variables**. In this case, say Sally can plant 10 seedlings per row and there are 12 rows in the garden. The total number of seedlings would be represented by 10(12) or **xy**.

Answer: xy

EXAMPLE TWO

A class of fourth-graders voted for class president. P students voted for Jake, Q students voted for Ming, and R students voted for Louisa. What fractional part of the class voted for Louisa?

Fractional part is a good clue that this problem should be set up as a fraction and that you're looking for a part-to-whole relationship. Compute the *whole* or total of the class by adding each variable ($P + Q + R$). Remember that the *part* in a part-whole relationship goes on top.

Answer: $\dfrac{R}{P + Q + R}$

EXAMPLE THREE

A carpenter gets paid g dollars per hour and his assistant receives h dollars per hour. On Wednesday, they both worked j hours. Write an expression representing their combined earnings for the day.

If the solution doesn't come to you right away, try replacing variables with number amounts. Let's say the carpenter gets $20 per hour and the assistant gets $12 per

hour. They work a total of 7 hours. The phrase "combined earnings" suggests addition and the fact that they *both* worked the same number of hours suggests the use of parentheses. So, 7 hrs. (20 + 12) = combined earnings or:

Answer: $j(g + h)$

PRACTICE—SETUPS WITH VARIABLES

Choose the correct expression for each of the following.

1. A fisherman purchases two fishing rods at b dollars each and a lure for c dollars. He pays with a $20 bill. What is the amount of change returned?

   (1) $2b - c + 20$
   (2) $20 + (2b - c)$
   (3) $20 + 2(b - c)$
   (4) $20 - (2b + c)$
   (5) $\dfrac{2b + c}{20}$

2. Tom is b years old. How old will he be in 12 years?

   (1) $b - 12$
   (2) $b + 12$
   (3) $12b$
   (4) $b + 12 - x$
   (5) $12 - b$

3. The Wilsons need to drive 350 miles in y hours. How many miles per hour do they need to drive to reach their destination on time?

   (1) $\dfrac{350}{y}$
   (2) $350y$
   (3) $\dfrac{350 + y}{y}$
   (4) $4(350y)$
   (5) not enough information is given

4. A chest has four drawers, three of which contain x sweaters and a fourth that contains y sweaters. What is the total number of sweaters in the chest?

   (1) $3(x + y)$
   (2) $3 + x + y$
   (3) $3xy$
   (4) $x + 3y$
   (5) $3x + y$

5. Lina grosses $11,000 per month at her yogurt store. Each month she pays out f dollars for rental of the building, g for electric use, and h for other expenses. How much does she net per month?

    (1) $11(f + g + h)$
    (2) $11,000 - (f + g + h)$
    (3) $(f - g - h)11,000$
    (4) $(11,000 - h) - (f + g)$
    (5) not enough information is given

6. There are x girls on a volleyball team. One day, y girls were absent from practice. What fractional part of the team was absent that day?

    1) $\dfrac{x}{x + y}$
    2) $2x - y$
    3) $\dfrac{x - y}{x}$
    4) $(y + x) - y$
    5) $xy + x$

7. Alicia saves x dollars per month, Dean saves y dollars per month and Sarah saves z dollars per month. What represents their total savings for the year?

    (1) $12(x + y + z)$
    (2) $xyz - 12$
    (3) $30x + 30y + 30z$
    (4) $12 + (x - y - z)$
    (5) not enough information is given

8. Randy invests an equal amount of his salary in two different mutual funds. At the end of the year, Fund A's value increases by 22% but Fund B's value decreases by 6%. What is the total worth of his two funds at the end of the year?

    (1) $(.22 \times A) + (.06 \times B)$
    (2) $(.22 \times A) - (.06 \times B)$
    (3) $.84 (A + B)$
    (4) $.16(A + B) + (A + B)$
    (5) $(.22 \times A) - (.6 \times B)$

ANSWERS

1. **4**	3. **1**	5. **2**	7. **1**
2. **2**	4. **5**	6. **3**	8. **4**

Converting Words into Algebraic Equations

This is an important skill. To help master it, here is a list of commonly used phrases with numbers and their algebraic translations. Read the left-hand column and cover the right-hand column. Using x as a variable to replace the phrase "a number," predict what the right column will say.

Words	Algebraic Expression
5 plus a number	$5 + x$
12 decreased by a number	$12 - x$
The sum of a number and 6	$x + 6$
16 less than a number	$x - 16$
2.5 more than a number	$2.5 + x$
13 minus a number	$13 - x$
A number increased by 8	$x + 8$
The product of 13 and a number	$13x$
A number divided by 4	$\dfrac{x}{4}$
3 times a number	$3x$
18 divided by a number	$\dfrac{18}{x}$
5 times a number decreased by 7	$5x - 7$
A number times itself	x^2
The square root of a number less 6	$\sqrt{x} - 6$
14 increased by a number, all multiplied by 8	$8(14 + x)$
8 minus a number, all divided by that same number	$\dfrac{8 - n}{n}$

Converting Words to Equations and Solving

You've learned how to solve simple and complex equations. This operation asks you to convert sentences into equations and then solve them. Look for the words **is** or **equals**; they mark the place in the equation where the = sign belongs.

EXAMPLE

Three times a number increased by 14 is 23. Convert and solve.

Let $3x$ stand for "3 times a number"
Let $+ 14$ stand for "increased by 14"
Let $= 23$ stand for "is 23."
Put it all together and solve the equation.

$$3x + 14 = 23$$
$$\underline{- 14 \quad -14}$$
$$\frac{3x}{3} = \frac{9}{3}$$

Answer: $x = 3$

PRACTICE—SOLVING SIMPLE WORD EQUATIONS

Convert and solve for the variable.

1. A number decreased by 16 = 39.
2. 90 divided by a number is 18.
3. 48 equals a number increased by 6, and the sum, all multiplied by 5.
4. A number times itself and added to 23 is equal to 219.

ANSWERS

1. $x = 55$
2. $x = 5$
3. $x = 5\frac{3}{5}$
4. $x = 14$

Multistep Algebraic Word Problems

For some students, these are the most difficult questions on the GED. All these problems need to be converted to multistep equations that then need to be solved.

EXAMPLE ONE

Dolores and her brother Jim have a paper route. Dolores delivers twice as many papers as Jim does. Together, they deliver 117 papers. How many papers does Jim deliver? How many does Dolores deliver?

Step one: Build a box.

$$\boxed{\begin{array}{l} 2x = \text{Dolores} \\ x = \text{Jim} \end{array}}$$

We don't know how many papers either person delivered, but we *do* know Dolores delivered twice as many as Jim did. In virtually all of these problems, one of the unknowns, usually the smallest, will be represented by x.

Step two: Write an equation based on the information given.

$$2x + x = 117$$

Step three: Solve the equation.

$2x + x = 117$ becomes $\frac{3x}{3} = \frac{117}{3}$ $x = 39$

Step four: Return to the box and apply the information to the question asked.

Answer: Jim delivered **39** papers
Dolores delivered 2(39) or **78** papers

EXAMPLE TWO

Three soccer players led the Rhinos in scoring for the season. Henri scored twice as many goals as Fred, and Angelo scored 18 more goals than Fred. If the three combined to score 78 goals, how many did Henri score?

Step one: Build a box.

$$\boxed{\begin{array}{l} \text{Henri} = 2x \\ \text{Fred} = x \\ \text{Angelo} = x + 18 \end{array}}$$

Step two: $2x + x + (x + 18) = 78$

Step three:
$$4x + 18 = 78$$
$$\underline{- 18 \quad -18}$$
$$\frac{4x}{4} = \frac{60}{4}$$
$$x = 15$$

Step four: Henri scored 2(15) or **30** goals.

PRACTICE—MULTISTEP WORD PROBLEMS

Solve.

1. At Oasis College, three times as many freshmen live on campus as those who commute. If there are 988 freshmen, how many commute?

2. A soda vendor sold large sodas for $3 and small sodas for $2. If he sold 182 large sodas and his gross profit for the day was $894, how many small sodas did he sell?

3. Kelly is nine years older than her sister. Kelly's age is one more than twice her sister's age. What is Kelly's age?

4. Two cars were sold at auction to a buyer who paid a total of $2,000 for both cars. If the more expensive of the two cars was $240 less than three times the price of the cheaper car, how much was the more expensive car?

ANSWERS

1. **247**   2. **174**   3. **17**   4. **$1,440**

Coordinate Geometry

FINDING POINTS ON THE RECTANGULAR COORDINATE GRID

Study the diagram below.

Here, two number lines are set up perpendicular to each other. The horizontal line is the **x-axis** and the vertical line is the **y-axis**. Memorize that.

The diagram below is a more dressed-up version called a rectangular coordinate grid. You must learn to locate points on the grid using two numbers: the **x-coordinate** and the **y-coordinate**.

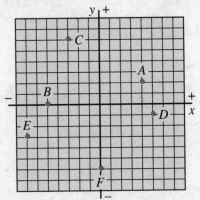

EXAMPLE ONE

Find the coordinates of Point *A*

Step one: Locate the *x*-coordinate (it comes first alphabetically and must be listed first in the answer). Using the darkened *x*-axis zero line as a guide, count the number of ticks (or boxes) on the number line you need to move horizontally (across) from the exact center (0,0) of the graph to the vertical line on which Point *A* is located. It's four horizontal ticks from the center, so the *x*-coordinate is **4**.

Step two: Find the *y*-coordinate. Again, start at dead center but move vertically (up) along the *y*-axis to the horizontal line on which Point *A* is located, counting the ticks as you go. It's two vertical ticks from the center, so the *y*-coordinate is **2**.

Answer: Coordinates for Point A (4,2)

EXAMPLE TWO

Find coordinates for Point *B*

Step One: Find the *x*-coordinate. Counting from dead center, *B* is five ticks away. Notice, though, that it is five steps to the **left** of 0, putting it on the negative side of the number line. The *x*-coordinate is –5.

Step two: Find the *y*-coordinate. Since Point *B* lies directly on the *x*-axis and does not rise above or sink below the 0 line, its *y*-coordinate is 0.

Answer: Coordinates for Point B (–5,0)

Here are coordinates for four more points on the above grid. Try to calculate the coordinates yourself first, and then check your accuracy.

Point *C* (–3,6)   Point *E* (–7, –3)
Point *D* (5, –1)   Point *F* (0, –6)

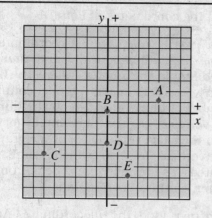

Identify the coordinates of the five points on the grid above.

1. Point A   4. Point D
2. Point B   5. Point E
3. Point C

ANSWERS

1. **(5, 1)**   3. **(–6, –4)**   5. **(2, –6)**
2. **(0, 0)**   4. **(0, –3)**

FINDING THE DISTANCE BETWEEN POINTS

This may look complicated, but it's a very simple operation.

EXAMPLE ONE

Find the distance between Points A and B

Don't worry because the grid is gone—you don't need it. Since y-coordinates of both points are +4, they both rest on that imaginary horizontal line parallel to the x-axis. To find the distance between the points, you just need to calculate how many ticks there are between the x coordinates. Disregard any + or – sign and **add the sum of the pair of coordinates that aren't the same**. In this

case, the pair of y-coordinates are the same (4,4) and the x-coordinates aren't the same (–2,5). Drop the signs and add: 2 + 5 = 7

Answer: The distance between Points A and B is 7

EXAMPLE TWO

Find the distance between Points C and D

These two points lie on the same imaginary line parallel to the y-axis (–3). The y-coordinates are the pair that's not the same, so drop the – sign and add 5 + 1.

Answer: The distance between C and D = 6

Using the graph below, find the distance between the following sets of points:

1. A and B   3. C and B
2. D and C   4. D and A

ANSWERS

1. **8**   2. **8**   3. **7**   4. **7**

FINDING THE SLOPE OF A LINE

This is another operation that looks complicated but isn't. The formula for calculating slope is included on the formula sheet (see pages 571–572) and looks like this:

slope of a line (m) $m = \dfrac{y_2 - y_1}{x_2 - x_1}$

Here's how to apply it.

EXAMPLE

What is the slope of the line that passes through A and B?

Step one: Write down the formula for slope.

$$m = \frac{y_2 - y_1}{x_2 - x_1}$$

Step two: Replace the letter symbols with the appropriate coordinates. There is no way to tell from the problem which are the $_2$'s and which are the $_1$'s. It's your choice, as long as you remain consistent by assigning one set of coordinates to a number and don't mix them. If, in this case, you decide A will be the $_2$'s and B will be the $_1$'s, then the slope solution will look like this:

$$m = \frac{6 - 2}{9 - 3} = \frac{4}{6} = \frac{2}{3}$$

Step three: Do the math and reduce.

Answer: slope is $\dfrac{2}{3}$

If you chose the coordinates for Point B as $_1$s and A as $_2$s, the answer would still be the same.

$$m = \frac{2 - 6}{3 - 9} = \frac{-4}{-6} = \frac{2}{3}$$

PRACTICE—FINDING THE SLOPE OF A LINE

Find the slopes of the lines passing through the following points on the graph.

1. *AC*
2. *AB*
3. *AD*
4. *BD*

ANSWERS

1. **–2**
2. $\dfrac{\mathbf{1}}{\mathbf{3}}$
3. $\mathbf{1\dfrac{4}{5}}$
4. **4**

FINDING A COORDINATE WHEN THE SLOPE IS GIVEN

This is a relatively simple algebra problem that won't be accompanied by a coordinate graph.

EXAMPLE

Find y if the slope of a line passing through points A ($5,y$) and B ($2,3$) is equal to 1.

Step one: Set up the formula for slope of a line:

$$m = \frac{y_2 - y_1}{x_2 - x_1}$$

Step two: Insert the slope and the given coordinates. Use y as a variable for the unknown. Again, it's your choice as to whether it's a y_1 or y_2. In this case, we'll make it a $_2$.

$$1 = \frac{y - 3}{5 - 2}$$

Step three: Solve as an equation.

$$1 = \frac{y-3}{5-2} = \frac{(3)}{1} \quad 1 = \frac{y-3}{3}\frac{(3)}{1} = \begin{array}{c} 3 = y-3 \\ +3 \quad\quad +3 \\ \hline 6 = y \end{array}$$

Answer: *y* = 6

PRACTICE—FINDING A COORDINATE WHEN SLOPE IS GIVEN

1. Find *x* if the slope of a line passing through Points *A* (4,3) and *B* (*x*,7) equals 4.

ANSWER

5

CHAPTER REVIEW

Fill in the answer grids, and use a calculator where indicated.

<u>Questions 1 and 2</u> are based on the following information:

1. The letter on the number line that best represents $\sqrt{32}$ is

   (1) A
   (2) B
   (3) C
   (4) D
   (5) E

2. The variable *x* in the expression $5x - 7 \geq 13$ is represented on the above number line by

   (1) point *B*
   (2) all points < *C*
   (3) point *A*
   (4) point *B* and all points > point *B*
   (5) all points < point *B*

3. Evaluate $(4x + y)(x^2 + 6)$ when $x = -3$ and $y = 5$

   (1) 59
   (2) –63
   (3) 80
   (4) 66
   (5) –105

4.

What is the perimeter of the above rectangle?

   (1) $6x + 3b + c$
   (2) $15x_2 + 5b + 2c$
   (3) $2x - b + c$
   (4) $8x + 4b = 2c$
   (5) $12x + 6b + 2c$

5. Given the equation $49 - x = 33$, find $3x$.

6. Given the equation $7a - 28 \geq 56$, find *a*.

   (1) all numbers < 12
   (2) all numbers > 12
   (3) all numbers ≤ 12
   (4) all numbers ≥ l2
   (5) 14

7. In the equation $x^2 - 8x - 48 = 0$, what are the solutions for *x*?

   (1) –12, 4
   (2) 6, –8
   (3) 12, –4
   (4) –8, 6
   (5) –6, –4

8. Find *x* if the slope of a line passing through points *A* (–2, *x*) and *B* (4,1) equals $\frac{-2}{3}$.

   (1) 3
   (2) $\frac{2}{3}$
   (3) 5
   (4) –6
   (5) –3

9. Tina and Simon visit an amusement park. Both children each pay x dollars for admission. All rides are the same price, represented by y. Tina goes on six rides and Simon goes on four. Which expression represents the total of what both children spent?

   (1) $\dfrac{6y + 4y}{2}$
   (2) $2(x + 10y)$
   (3) $(6y - 4y) + 2x$
   (4) $2x - 10y$
   (5) $(x + 6y) + (x + 4y)$

10. Nine times a number minus three is equal to five times that same number added to seven. What is the value of the number?

    (1) 2.5
    (2) 7
    (3) 6
    (4) 3
    (5) 13

11. Thomasville and Newtown are 260 miles apart. If the scale on a road map is $\dfrac{1}{2}$ inch : 40 miles, how far apart in inches will the two towns be on the map?

12. John owns three guitars. The most valuable is $25 less than three times the least valuable. The other guitar is worth $16 more than twice the least valuable. All together, the three guitars are worth $1,245. What is the value of the most expensive guitar?

    (1) around $500
    (2) between $650 and $700
    (3) around $600
    (4) around $4,700
    (5) around $550

13. Which point denotes the center of the circle?

    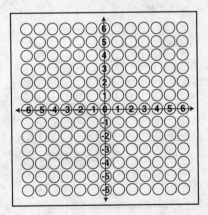

ANSWERS

1. **3**	5. **48**	9. **5**	13. **(2,–2)**
2. **4**	6. **4**	10. **1**	
3. **5**	7. **3**	11. **3.25**	
4. **5**	8. **3**	12. **3**	

Geometry

Angles

Learn the following vocabulary.

vertex of an angle

right angles
90° exactly

acute angles
less than 90°

obtuse angle
more than 90°
less than 180°

straight angle
exactly 180°

On the GED, angles might be referred to in a few different ways.

The angle above might be referred to as ∠CBA or ∠ABC. Notice how the letter B, the one that marks the vertex, is always in the middle of the three letters.

The angle above might be referred to as ∠x or m of ∠x, with **m** meaning **the measure of ∠x**.

PRACTICE—IDENTIFYING ANGLES

Refer to the above diagram to answer the following.

1. What is m ∠f? (How many degrees?)
2. What kind of angle is ∠ABC?
3. What kind of angle is ∠ABD?
4. What kind of angle is ∠EBC?

5. What is m ∠EBD + m ∠ABD?
6. What kind of angle is ∠ABE?
7. What is m ∠ABC if it is equal to
   $\frac{1}{2}$ m ∠EBF?

ANSWERS

1. **90°**
2. **acute**
3. **obtuse**
4. **obtuse**

5. **180°**
6. **straight angle**
7. **45°**

Complementary and Supplementary Angles

Two or more angles are *complementary* if their sum is equal to 90 degrees.

m ∠ABC = 33°
m ∠CBD = 57°
             90°

∠ABC and ∠CBD are *complementary*

Two or more angles are *supplementary* if their sum is equal to 180°.

m ∠x = 50°   m ∠y = 130°
       (130 + 50 = 180)
x and y are *supplementary*

Bisectors

Any line that *bisects* an angle divides the measure of the angle *in half.*

m ∠ABC = 180°
$\overline{BD}$ bisects ∠ABC

m ∠CBD = 90°   m ∠ABD = 90°

Vertical Angles

Vertical angles, the ones that appear *opposite* to each other, are equal.

∠a is vertical to ∠c and ∠b is vertical to ∠d

∠a = ∠c
∠b = ∠d

If, in the above diagram ∠a = 60°, then ∠b = 120° (supplementary) and ∠d = 120° (vertical) and ∠c = 60° (vertical).

These concepts will be tested over and over in various ways. Know them.

PRACTICE—ANGLES

To answer questions 1–3, refer to the diagram below.

1. What two angles, when separately added to ∠j, will equal 180°?

2. What is the sum of all angles in the diagram?

3. What other angle is equal to ∠i?

m ∠x = 39°

4. In the diagram above, what is m ∠y?

m ∠ABD = x
m ∠CBD = 4x

5. In the diagram above, what is m ∠CBD? (Hint: 4x + x = 180)

$\overline{BE}$ bisects $\angle ABD$

Questions 6 and 7 refer to the diagram above.

6. What is m $\angle CBG$?

7. Which *two* expressions are true?

    (1) m $\angle DBC = 2(\angle ABH)$

    (2) m $\angle DBH = \dfrac{\angle ABH}{2}$

    (3) m $\angle ABC =$ m of $2(\angle CBH)$

    (4) $2(\angle CBG) = \dfrac{\angle ABC}{2}$

ANSWERS

1. **I, K**	5. **144°**
2. **360°**	6. **45°**
3. **K**	7. **3, 4**
4. **141°**	

TRANSVERSALS

A **transversal** is a line that cuts across a set of parallel lines. You won't have to know a definition for this type of diagram, but you must thoroughly understand the concepts it illustrates.

In the above diagram, $\overline{AB} \parallel \overline{CD}$ ($\parallel$ means $\overline{AB}$ is parallel to $\overline{CD}$.) $\overline{EF}$ is the transversal.

We know that because of the rule of vertical (opposite) angles:

$$\angle c = \angle d \quad \text{and} \quad \angle a = \angle b$$
$$\angle e = \angle f \quad \text{and} \quad \angle g = \angle h$$

Also: $\angle b = \angle g$ and $\angle c = \angle f$

           $\angle c = \angle e$ and $\angle b = \angle h$

PRACTICE—TRANSVERSALS

In the above diagram, $\overline{AB}$ is $\parallel$ to $\overline{CD}$.

1. Name all other angles equal to $\angle h$.

2. Name all other angles equal to $\angle n$.

3. If m $\angle o = 36°$, what is m $\angle i$?

4. If m $\angle n = 117°$, what is m $\angle h$?

5. If m $\angle h = 63°$, then what is m $\angle h + \angle n + \angle o$?

6. If m $\angle h$ was expressed as x and m $\angle i$ was expressed as $3x$, which statement would be true?

    (1) $3x - x = 180°$

    (2) $3x + 2x = 180°$

    (3) $4x = 180°$

7. If the answer to question 6 is 3, what is m $\angle i$ in degrees?

8. If m $\angle h = 58°$ and a line is drawn that bisects $\angle n$, what are the measures of the two angles created by the bisection of $\angle n$?

ANSWERS

1. **K, L, O**	5. **243°**
2. **M, I, J**	6. **3**
3. **144°**	7. **135°**
4. **63°**	8. **61°**

TRIANGLES

There are four types of triangles you need to know about.

Equilateral triangle—All sides are equal. All angles equal 60°.

Isoceles triangle (pronounced *I-sosaleez*)— Two sides are equal. Two angles are equal.

Scalene triangle (pronounced *skayleen*)— No sides are equal. No angles are equal.

Right triangle—one of the angles is always 90°.
The other two angles can be equal to each other or different, but their sum will always equal 90°.

The two sides that make up the right angle *can* be equal but don't have to be.

The third side, the one opposite the right angle, is always longer than the other two and is called the *hypotenuse*.

> The sum of all angles of a triangle always add up to 180°.

This is a fact that will help you to solve several questions on the GED. Memorize it.

PRACTICE—TRIANGLES

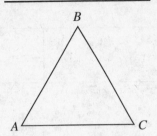

1. In △ABC above, ∠A = 70° and ∠B = 40°. What is the measure of ∠C?

2. What kind of triangle is △ABC?

3. What kind of triangle is △DEF if it has a hypotenuse?

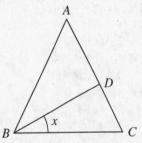

4. △ABC, above, is an equilateral triangle. $\overline{BD}$ bisects ∠ABC. What is m ∠x?

5. △ABC, above, is a scalene triangle. ∠B = 80°, $\overline{CD}$ bisects ∠ACB. What is m ∠x?

(1) 50°
(2) 25°
(3) 55°
(4) 35°
(5) not enough information is given

6. In the above diagram, $\overline{AB} \parallel \overline{CD}$, $\overline{GF} \perp$ $\overline{AB}$ and m $\angle G = 35°$. What is m $\angle AEG$?

7. In $\triangle ABC$, m $\angle a = 30°$, $\angle B = 60°$, $\angle C = 90°$.
   (a) What kind of triangle is $\triangle ABC$?
   (b) What is the ratio of $\angle A$ to $\angle C$?
   (1) 3:1　(2) 2:1　(3) 1:2
   (4) 1:3　(5) 4:3

8.

$AD \perp BD$. If m $\angle DAB = 40°$, what is m of $\angle BCD$? (Clue: Use $\triangle ABC$ to help figure this out. Don't be distracted by DB, which seems to bisect $\angle ABC$).

ANSWERS

1. **70°**　　　5. **5**
2. **isosceles**　6. **125°**
3. **right triangle**　7. (a) **right**　(b) **4**
4. **30°**　　　8. **50°**

RELATIONSHIPS BETWEEN SIDES AND ANGLES

In a triangle, **the sides opposite two equal angles are also equal.**

EXAMPLE ONE

Find $\overline{BC}$

$\overline{BC}$ is **opposite** $\angle A$　$\overline{AB}$ is **opposite** $\angle C$

m $\angle A = $ m $\angle C$　　Find $\overline{BC}$

m $\angle A = $ m $\angle C$, so $\overline{AB} = \overline{BC}$; if $\overline{AB} = 4$ ft., then $\overline{BC} = 4$ ft.

In a triangle, **the angles opposite two equal sides are equal.**

EXAMPLE TWO

Find x in both figures.

Figure One　　　　**Figure Two**

Where AB is the radius of the circle

In Figure One, $\overline{AB} = \overline{AC}$. Therefore, $\angle B$ (opposite $\overline{AC}$) = m $\angle C$ (opposite $\overline{AB}$).

Answer: $x = 45°$

In Figure Two, $\overline{AB}$ and $\overline{BC}$ are both radii (plural of "radius") of the circle. Therefore, $\overline{AB} = \overline{BC}$. So, m $\angle C$ (opposite $\overline{AB}$) = m $\angle A$ (opposite $\overline{BC}$).

Answer: $x = 65°$

In all triangles except the equilateral, **the longest side is opposite the largest angle and the shortest side is opposite the smallest angle.**

EXAMPLE THREE

In $\triangle ABC$, m $\angle A = x$, m $\angle B = 1.5x$, and m $\angle C = 2.5x$. Which *side* is the longest?

Step one: It might help to draw a diagram. Don't worry about where you place the angles or the scale of the drawing; it'll work out.

Since the longest side is opposite the largest angle, it has to be $\overline{AB}$.

Answer: $\overline{AB}$

1. In the triangle above, if $\overline{AB} = \frac{3}{4}(\overline{AC})$ and m $\angle A = \angle C$, what is the length of $\overline{AB}$?

2. In △ABC above, find m $\angle B$.

3. The perimeter of △ABC above = 29. Which angle is largest?

4. In △ABC above m $\angle B = 50°$ and $\overline{AB} = \overline{BC}$. What is m $\angle DAB$?

5. $\overline{BC}$ and $\overline{AB}$ are the radii of the circle above. If m $\angle C = 60°$, what kind of triangle is △ABC?

1. **12°**   4. **115**
2. **62°**   5. **equilateral**
3. **∠A**

SIMILAR TRIANGLES

Similar triangles are *not* equal in size—one could be tiny and one could be huge. What they do have in common is:

- All their corresponding angles are **equal**
- All their corresponding sides are **proportional**

EXAMPLE ONE

Is △ABC similar to △DEF?

You have the choice of establishing similarity by proving all corresponding angles are equal or all corresponding sides are proportional. In this case, since two angles are already given, go for all angles.

m $\angle B$ = m $\angle D$. That's given in the diagram. Since m $\angle C = 35°$ in △ABC, m $\angle A$ must equal 55° (35 + 55 + 90 = 180).

Likewise, since m $\angle E$ in △DEF = 55°, m $\angle F$ must equal 35°.

Now, all corresponding angles are equal: $\angle B = \angle D$, $\angle A = \angle E$, $\angle C = \angle F$.

Answer: △ABC and △DEF are similar.
(This would also mean all sides are proportional.)

EXAMPLE TWO

Is △GHI similar to △JKL?

It's easy to decide whether to prove similarity through equal angles or proportional sides here. Since you're given all sides, go for sides.

Set up a proportion for one pair of corresponding sides:

$$\overline{GH} : \overline{JK} = 3:9 = 1:3$$

A quick look at the lengths of the other pairs of corresponding sides tells you that they are both in the same 1:3 proportion to each other.

Answer: △GHI is similar to △JKL
(This also means their corresponding angles are equal)

EXAMPLE THREE

In the diagram below, $\overline{AB} \parallel \overline{DC}$. Find the length of $\overline{AB}$.

This may seem complicated, but it isn't. A very important fact is that $\overline{AB} \parallel \overline{DC}$, which means $\overline{BD}$ is a transversal.

Step one: Decide whether △DEC and △AEB are similar. Because of the rules governing transversals, you know that ∠D = ∠B and ∠C = ∠A. ∠DEC = ∠AEB because they're opposite angles. The two triangles are similar because all three angles are equal. And, their sides are **proportional**.

Step two: Find the length of $\overline{AB}$ using proportion.

$$\overline{DE} : \overline{EB} = 25:75 = 1:3 \quad \text{so} \quad \overline{DC} : \overline{AB} = 1:3$$

$$\frac{32}{x} = \frac{1}{3} \qquad x = 96$$

Answer: $\overline{AB}$ equals 96 feet.

PRACTICE—SIMILAR TRIANGLES

1. Are the triangles shown below similar.?

2. If the perimeter of △DEF = 18, are the triangles shown below similar.?

Questions 3 and 4 refer to the figure below.

3. $\overline{AB} \parallel \overline{DE}$. What is the length of $\overline{CD}$?

4. What is m ∠ACB?

ANSWERS

1. **No**　　2. **Yes**　　3. **21.9**　　4. **60°**

RIGHT TRIANGLES AND THE PYTHAGOREAN THEOREM

Using a formula known as the Pythagorean theorem can help you to figure out the length of unknown sides of right triangles. It's listed on the formula sheet, but you should memorize it anyway.

> Pythagorean theorem: $c^2 = a^2 + b^2$ where c always represents the hypotenuse and a and b represent the other sides of a right triangle.

EXAMPLE ONE

What is the length of EF?

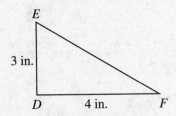

Step one: Replace the formula with numbers from the diagram.

$c^2 = a^2 + b^2$ becomes $c^2 = 3^2 + 4^2$ (it doesn't matter which side you use as a or b)

Step two: Continue the equation by solving the exponents.

$c^2 = 3^2 + 4^2$ becomes $c^2 = 9 + 16 = c^2 = \sqrt{25}$

Step three: Find the square root of c^2

$$\sqrt{25} = 5$$

Answer: $\overline{EF}$ = 5 in.

EXAMPLE TWO

What is the length of $\overline{AC}$?

Step one: $c^2 = a^2 + b^2$ becomes $45^2 = 27^2 + b^2$

Step two: $\begin{aligned} 2025 &= 729 + b^2 \\ -729 &\quad -729 \\ \hline 1296 &= \qquad b^2 \end{aligned}$

Step three: Find the square root of b^2

$$\sqrt{1296} = 36$$

Answer: $\overline{AC}$ = 36 ft.

EXAMPLE THREE

A carpenter needs to cut a diagonal support for the frame of a wall pictured below. How long should it be?

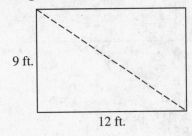

Step one: $c^2 = a^2 + b^2$ becomes $c^2 = 9^2 + 12^2$

Step two: $c^2 = 81 + 144 = c^2 = 225$

Step three: $c = \sqrt{225} = 15$

Answer: 15 feet

EXAMPLE FOUR

Kyla hikes .6 mile due north across a meadow. She then turns and hikes .8 mile due east. How far is she from her starting point?

The "due north" and "due east" phrases are immediate tip-offs that you're working with right triangles and the Pythagorean theorem. Remember that.

Step one: Draw a diagram.

Due east .8 mile

Due north .6 mile

Starting point

Step two: $c^2 = a^2 + b^2$ becomes $c^2 = .6^2 + .8^2$

$$c^2 = .36 + .64 = c^2 = 1$$

Step three: $c = \sqrt{1} = 1$

Answer: 1 mile

PRACTICE—PYTHAGOREAN THEOREM

1. What is the length of $\overline{BC}$ in the diagram below?

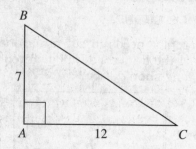

B

7

A   12   C

   (1) 15
   (2) 13.6
   (3) $\sqrt{193}$
   (4) 95
   (5) not enough information is given

2. A telephone pole is 40 ft. high and perpendicular to the ground. It needs to be supported by a wire staked into the dirt 30 ft. from the base of the pole and attached to its top. How long is the wire?

3. In the diagram below, what is the length of $\overline{DF}$?

E

35   21

D   F

4. A sailboat takes off from its mooring and sails due south for 12 miles, then due east for 16 miles and drops anchor. How far is it from its mooring?

ANSWERS

1. **3**   2. **50 ft.**   3. **28**   4. **20 miles**

Geometry and Proportion

These questions are frequently asked and each is somewhat different from the other. The solutions all rely on your knowledge of geometry and proportion.

EXAMPLE ONE

A   B   C

On line segment $\overline{AC}$, $\overline{BC}$ = 18 inches. $\overline{AB}:\overline{BC}$ = 2:3. What is the length, in inches, of $\overline{AB}$?

Step one: $x : 18 = 2:3$ or $\dfrac{x}{18} = \dfrac{2}{3}$

Step two; Cross-multiply, then solve the proportion.

$$3x = 36 \qquad \frac{3x}{3} = \frac{36}{3}$$
$$x = 12$$

Answer: $\overline{AB}$ = 12 inches

EXAMPLE TWO

A tree casts a shadow of 72 ft. at the same time that a 6-ft. man's shadow measures 8 ft. How tall is the tree?

Shadow questions are proportion questions. Set up the proportions in the correct order and solve.

Step one: height of tree : shadow of tree
   x :   72

   height of man : shadow of man
   6   :   8

Step two: Convert to fractional proportions, cross-multiply, and solve.

$$\frac{x}{72} = \frac{6}{8} \text{ (reduce) } \frac{x}{72} = \frac{3}{4}$$
$$\frac{216}{4} = \frac{4x}{4}$$
$$x = 54$$

Answer: 72 ft.

EXAMPLE THREE

Based on a survey answered by 900 people, the pie graph above shows where holiday shoppers buy the majority of their gifts. How many people surveyed purchased the majority of their gifts at small shops?

Be careful. The segments of the pie are represented by *degrees*, not percentages. There are 360° in a circle, so:

Step one: Create a proportion.

Small shop degrees : total degrees
40° : 360°

small shop buyers : total buyers
x : 900

Step two: Solve.

$$\frac{40}{360} = \frac{x}{900} \text{ (reduce) } \frac{1}{9} = \frac{x}{900}$$
$$\frac{9x}{9} = \frac{900}{9}$$
$$x = 100$$

Answer: 100 people

EXAMPLE FOUR

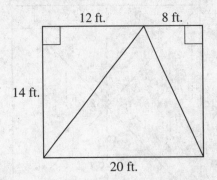

What is the ratio of the area of the triangle to the area of the rectangle?

This may look complicated, but it's quite simple. *Don't* be distracted by the 90° markers or the 12 ft. measurement. *Do* remember your formulas.

Area of a rectangle = *lw*

Area of a triangle = $\frac{1}{2}$ (*bh*)

In the diagram, the length and width of the rectangle are the same as the base and height of the triangle. Since the area of the triangle is *half* the length × width of the rectangle, its area would be half the size of the rectangle's. Therefore, the ratio would be 1:2.

Answer: 1:2

PRACTICE—*GEOMETRY AND PROPORTION*

1.

If line segment $\overline{AC}$ = 120 ft. and the ratio of $\overline{AB}:\overline{BC}$ = 3:5, what is the length of $\overline{AB}$?

2. A 35-foot telephone pole casts a shadow 21 ft. tall at the same time that a lamppost's shadow measures 12 ft. How tall is the lamppost?

3.

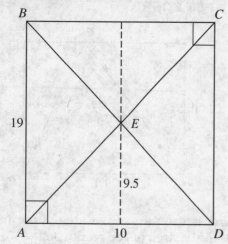

What is the ratio of the combined areas of △*AED* and △*BEC* to the area of ▭ *ABCD*?

4.

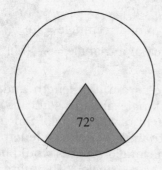

The shaded area of the chart represents the number of Acme employees who bring their children to day-care centers before work. If there are 465 employees at Acme, how many do *not* bring their children to day-care centers before coming to work?

ANSWERS

1. **45 feet**   3. **1 : 2**
2. **20 feet**   4. **372**

Geometry and Algebra

To answer these challenging problems, you must know facts, formulas and procedures from both disciplines.

EXAMPLE ONE

In the diagram above, find the measure of ∠*c*.

The key fact that will allow you to solve this problem is that a straight angle = 180°. You should recognize that $3x - 20$ and x are supplementary.

Step one: Set up an equation and solve for x.

$$3x - 20 + x = 180$$
$$4x - 20 \quad\ = 180$$
$$\underline{+\ 20 \qquad\ +\ 20}$$
$$\frac{4x}{4} = \frac{200}{4}$$
$$x = 50°$$

Step two: Find m ∠*c* based on the measure of ∠*x*
That's easy. The diagram is a transversal—
∠*c* = ∠*x*
    Answer: m ∠*c* = 50°

EXAMPLE TWO

In a triangle, the largest angle is 18 more than twice the smallest angle. The other angle is 18 more than the smallest angle. What is the size of the *largest* angle?

The key fact here is that the sum of all angles in a triangle is always 180°.

Step one: Build a box.

Largest ∠ = 2x + 18
Middle ∠ = x + 18
Smallest ∠ = x

Step two: Set up an equation and solve for *x*. Add all the angles together with their sum equaling 180°.

$2x + 18 + x + 18 + x = 180$ becomes

$$4x + 36 = 180$$
$$\underline{-36 \quad -36}$$
$$\frac{4x}{4} = \frac{144}{4}$$
$$x = 36$$

Step three: Find the measure of the largest angle. Go back to the box for the "largest angle" sentence: Largest $\angle = 2x + 18$ and replace *x* with 36.

Answer: largest angle is 90°

PRACTICE—GEOMETRY AND ALGEBRA

1. What is the perimeter of the figure above?

Questions 2 and 3 are based on the diagram below.

2. Solve for *x*. (Hint: set up equation using rules of transversals: $3x = x + 32$)

3. What is m $\angle y$?

4. If the area of the above rectangle equals 108 sq. ft., find both its length and width.

5. In a scalene triangle, the measure of the largest angle is four more than two times the smallest and the other angle is two more than the smallest. What is the measure of the largest angle?

ANSWERS

1. **12a + 8b**
2. **x = 16**
3. **y = 132**

4. **18, 6**
5. **91°**

CHAPTER REVIEW

Fill in the answer grids, and use a calculator where indicated.

1. In the diagram above, ∠ADB is a
   straight angle. If m ∠BDC = x and
   $\overline{DE}$ bisects ∠BDC, what is the measure of ∠y?

   (1) 29°
   (2) 58°
   (3) 60°
   (4) 26°
   (5) not enough information is given

2. In the diagram above, m ∠a = 2x.
   Which expression represents m ∠d?

   (1) 2x + 180°
   (2) 180° − 2x
   (3) 2x − 180°
   (4) $\dfrac{180}{2x}$
   (5) 2x(180°)

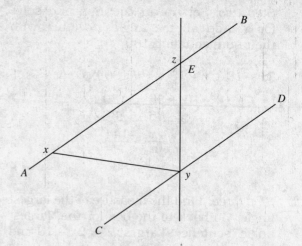

3. In the diagram above, $\overline{AB} \parallel \overline{CD}$ and
   m ∠E = 125°. Which of the following
   cannot be true?

   (1) △xyz is a right triangle
   (2) △xyz is a scalene triangle
   (3) △xyz is an equilateral triangle
   (4) m ∠z = m ∠y
   (5) △xyz is an isoceles triangle

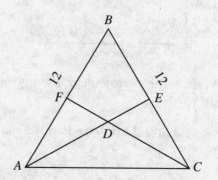

4. In the diagram above, $\overline{AB} = \overline{BC}$, $\overline{AE}$
   bisects ∠BAC, and $\overline{CF}$ bisects ∠ACB.
   If m ∠BAC = 70°, what is the measure
   in degrees of ∠D?

5.

In the above diagram, if $\overline{BE}$ = 18 ft. and $\overline{AC}$ = 6 ft., what is the length of $\overline{EC}$?

(1) $2x - 90°$
(2) $3x$
(3) $x + 18$
(4) $x + 11$
(5) $2x$

6. A bird flies due south from its nest for 5 miles, then due west for 12 miles. How far is the bird from its nest?

(1) 18 miles
(2) 16 miles
(3) 14 miles
(4) between 14 and 15 miles
(5) 13 miles

7. In the line segment $\overline{JL}$ above, the ratio of $\overline{JK} : \overline{KL}$ = 7:2. If $\overline{JK}$ = 35 inches, what is the length of $\overline{KL}$?

(1) $\frac{1}{2}$ ft.

(2) $\frac{3}{4}$ ft.

(3) $\frac{5}{6}$ ft.

(4) 1 ft.

(5) not enough information is given

8. If a building casts a shadow of 120 ft. and, at the same time, a tree's shadow measures 60 ft., how tall is the building?

(1) 100 ft.
(2) 240 ft.
(3) 200 ft.
(4) half the tree's size
(5) not enough information is given

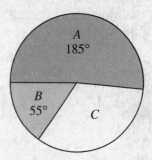

9. In the chart above, what *percent* of the pie is represented by *C*?

ANSWERS

1. **1**   6. **5**
2. **2**   7. **3**
3. **3**   8. **5**
4. **110**   9. **33.3**
5. **5**   10. **29**

10. In the diagram above, △*CDB* has an area of 58 sq. ft. What is the length in feet of $\overline{CD}$?

25

Test-taking Strategies

A sure strategy for success on the Mathematics section of the GED is to learn how to quickly solve every type of problem you might be likely to find there. That means familiarizing yourself with all concepts, formulas, and operations in the seven previous chapters.

Achieving that level of familiarity with the material is not always possible. Furthermore, it's certainly not necessary in order to pass the test. Though requirements vary from state to state, it's safe to say that if you answer at least 30 out of the 50 problems in the section correctly, you'll pass (check with the appropriate agency in your state or region to find out the exact requirements).

Though they are no replacement for knowing the material, here are some test-taking strategies specific to the Math section that should prove helpful.

The Two-step Evaluation

"What am I being asked to find?" and "How do I find it?" are the two most important questions you need to answer when approaching any math problem.

Step one: After reading each question, say to yourself,

"I need to find...."

It could be the value of x, the length of side $\overline{AB}$ in $\triangle ABC$, or the percent of questions Susan answered incorrectly on a test. Whatever it is, do *not* proceed with any calculations or attempt to eliminate any of the choices until you feel confident you know what you're being asked to find.

If you're in doubt, carefully reread the problem, paying special attention to the *last sentence*, which tells you specifically what you need to find. If you're still unsure, immediately skip to the next problem.

Step two: Once you are certain of what you need to find, say to yourself,

"I find the answer by doing this: ...."

Avoid reviewing the multiple choices before beginning calculation. There are four wrong answers there that can serve to mislead you. Instead, pause a moment and think carefully. Ask yourself the following:

- Is this a single- or multistep problem?
- What operations and formulas will I use?
- What information given in the problem will be useful?
- Is there a diagram, and, if so, how can it help?
- Do I need to draw my own diagram?
- Is there important information *missing* from the problem that can't be figured out? If so, immediately choose (5) *not enough information is given*, and move to the next problem.
- Is there unnecessary information that must be ignored?

With practice, the answers to these questions will come to you quickly. Begin working, doing your calculations on scrap paper. The scrap paper will *not* be collected, but get in the habit of writing neatly and precisely anyway. Neatness helps in avoiding errors and can aid in making you feel more confident about your work.

Come up with an answer and carefully compare it with the multiple choices. You should find a match among the five offered.

Quick review:
Step one: "I need to find...."
Step two: "I find the answer by doing this: ...."

Try using this way of approaching a problem in the example below.

EXAMPLE

Parking meters in Springfield read: "12 minutes for 5 cents. Maximum deposit—50 cents." What is the maximum time, in hours, that a driver may be legally parked at one of these meters?
(1) 1
(2) 1.2
(3) 120
(4) 2
(5) not enough information is given

Step one: What are you being asked to find?

"I need to find the maximum hours a driver can park."

Not maximum deposit—that's given. Not maximum minutes, even though the information is provided in minutes. You need to find the maximum hours a driver can park, using the information provided.

Step two: How do you find the answer?

"I find the maximum hours a driver can park by doing this:"

Now it's time to think, using the questions listed above. This is a multistep problem. You're given a maximum *deposit*, and from that information you can calculate a maximum *time*. You'll also need to convert maximum minutes to hours. You know 5 cents buys a driver 12 minutes of parking time, so:

(1) 12 min. × 10 (the number of 5-cent deposits in 50 cents) = 120 min.

Now, you need to convert 120 minutes to hours:

(2) $\frac{120 \text{ min.}}{60 \text{ min.}} = 2$ hours

Answer: (4) 2

If you'd reviewed the multiple choices first, you might have been misled. Choice (5) looks tempting because the problem doesn't mention a "maximum *time*" and choice (3) seems appealing because it's the correct number of minutes, not hours. Again, attempt to solve the problem before looking at the answer choices.

Try this two-step evaluation strategy with every problem on the Mathematics section. It should help to keep you focused during a time when anxiety tends to creep in.

Skipping and Returning

The questions on the Mathematics section do *not* increase in difficulty; more difficult questions alternate with easier ones in a random pattern throughout the test. It is a far better strategy to direct your time and attention to all the questions you feel confident in answering quickly and correctly than to spend excessive time trying to solve very difficult questions you have a greater chance of getting wrong. Therefore, you should be ready to make a quick judgment about each problem using the Two-step Evaluation.

If you

- are unsure of what you're being asked to find
  or
- you know what you have to find but are unsure how to proceed
  or
- you know what to find and how to proceed, but feel it will take a while to get a correct answer,

skip the problem and go to the next one.

You may find yourself skipping more than half the problems on the test your first time around. That's O.K.

Establish a system for recording your skips. On your answer grid, put a checkmark to the left of each problem you skip and be especially mindful of the problem numbers *at all times* whether skipping or entering answers. You don't want to make the discovery more than halfway through the section that you just entered an answer on the grid space (31) for problem (32)! Careful attention to the question numbers will avoid this problem.

After you finish the last question on your first time through, return to those questions you skipped. Now attempt the ones you know how to solve but initially judged to be too time-consuming. Do not obsess over any one problem. If you divide the 90 minutes allotted for the section by 50 problems, that allows you an average of about $1^{1}/_{2}$ minutes per question. If you feel two minutes have slipped away and you're still not even close to an answer, make your best guess and *move on*. Mark the answer grid with a different symbol—perhaps an X—and return to the question later, if you have time.

Plugging In

There will be a handful of occasions when, after doing a Two-step Evaluation, you decide it's quicker and easier to use the multiple choices to get an answer to the problem instead of calculating an answer on your own. *Plugging in* is a strategy in which you choose what looks like a correct answer from the multiple choices and plug it in to a formula or operation to see if it works.

EXAMPLE

Which of the following is a solution to the inequality:

$$3x + 7 > 23 ?$$

(1) 4
(2) 6
(3) 2
(4) 5
(5) 4.5

Using the Two-step Evaluation, you'd say to yourself, I need to find the value for "*x*," which can be gotten by setting up and solving this multistep equation,

or...

you could go directly to the multiple choices, pick what looks like a correct answer, and plug

it in to the inequality. Choice (1) looks good; try plugging it in on paper or in your head.

$$3(4) + 7 > 23 \ldots 12 + 7 > 23 \ldots 19 > 23?$$

Close, but wrong. Try another—choice (4). It's easy to do and you don't have to deal with the decimal that's in choice (5).

$$3(5) + 7 > 23 \ldots 22 > 23$$

Really close, but still not large enough to make the inequality a true statement. However, you now know the answer must be choice (2) because it's the only number larger than choice (5).

   Answer: (2) 6

Eliminating

Eliminating choices you *know* are wrong so that you can spend more time considering choices that *might* be right is a standard test-taking strategy. Consider this:

EXAMPLE

A hockey team won *x* games, lost *y* games, and tied *z* games. What fractional part of the games played were won?

(1) $\dfrac{x}{x + y + z}$

(2) $\dfrac{x}{xyz}$

(3) $\dfrac{x}{xy}$

(4) $\dfrac{x}{x + y}$

(5) $\dfrac{x}{x - y - z}$

Since *x* represents the number of games won, it has to be in the numerator. All choices have *x* as a numerator, so you can't eliminate any yet. But the denominator has to represent a **sum** of all the games, which means **addition** would have to be included. Therefore, choices (2), (3), and (5) can be eliminated. You've narrowed the possibilities down to only two possible choices and, by doing so, have more than doubled your chances of getting the answer correct, even if you have to guess between choices (1) and (4). The correct answer, of course is (1) because it represents the sum of *all* games.

Making an Educated Guess

It's important to remember that the penalty for a wrong answer is the same as it is for a blank answer. **You have nothing to lose by guessing; it's essential that you fill in every answer on the grid, leaving no blanks.** Sometimes, you might be unsure of how to reach a solution to a problem. In these situations, making an educated guess using common sense and elimination is the only logical strategy you can use.

EXAMPLE

Martin has a piece of lumber 9 ft. 8 in. long. He wishes to cut it into four equal lengths. How far from the edge should he make his first cut?

(1) 2.5 ft.
(2) 2 ft. 5 in.
(3) 2.9 ft.
(4) 29 ft.
(5) 116 in.

The wording in this problem might be confusing to some. "How far from the edge" is an overly complicated way of asking, "How long would the first of the four pieces be?" Also, there are numerous conversions to consider: feet to inches, feet to feet and inches, feet and inches to feet and inches in a decimal setup, etc. Even if you aren't quite sure this problem requires you to divide 9 ft. 8 in. by 4, you can eliminate choices (4) and (5). Common sense tells you that the board is just a bit less than 10 feet. Choice (4)—29 ft.—is almost three times longer than the board's length, and choice (5)—116 inches—is exactly equal to its length. It's impossible to make cuts anywhere on the board using these answers. All the other answers are close. A 60% chance of getting a correct answer (eliminating 2 out of 5 choices, then guessing) is better than a 20% chance (eliminating none and guessing). The correct answer is (**2**).

Using the Formula Page

Review the formula (pages 571–572) now. You will probably notice that most of the information provided there you've already memorized, especially the section on perimeter, area, and volume. If you haven't memorized these formulas but clearly understand when to apply each one, use the page as a study sheet to "lock in" your knowledge. Knowing them is a big time-saver and confidence booster. The same is true for the Pythagorean theorem.

The formulas for distance between points and slope of a line do not need to be committed to memory; use the page.

The formulas for mean and median are poorly written and confusing. If you don't already have these concepts committed to memory, use the explanations in Chapter 19, Numbers and Basic Operations, as your guide. The same can be said for interest, distance, and cost.

Using the Practice Exams

The Practice Test that immediately follows this chapter and the two Practice Exams at the end of the book provide excellent opportunities for you to apply what you have learned. It's important that you create a test-taking environment as similar as possible to the one in which you'll take the GED. Set aside two 45-minute blocks of uninterrupted time, use the answer grids provided and scrap paper, and keep an honest eye on the clock. Pace yourself, take mental note of the strategies mentioned that work for you, and notice successful strategies you come up with on your own.

The practice test and exams all have answers, answer explanations, and references to chapters and subsections in the book where you can find help with a particular problem.

Practice Mathematics Test

This test is designed to give you practice in taking the two sections of the Math part of the GED exam. When taking the test, give yourself the benefit of realistic conditions. Select a quiet place, and allow yourself two 45-minute periods for each part. Use a calculator only for the first section. If you finish in less than the allowed time, use the remaining minutes to check your work

After you have completed the test, use the answer key to find your score and then study the solutions and explanations. You may discover new ways to attack problems. Also you will obtain help on the questions that you could not answer, and you will be able to correct any errors that you have made.

Remember that you do not have to get a perfect score to pass the test. If you find that you are weak on a certain topic, review the material in the text on that topic.

FORMULAS

Description	Formula
AREA (A) of a:	
square	$A = s^2$; where s = side
rectangle	$A = lw$; where l = length, w = width
parallelogram	$A = bh$; where b = base, h = height
triangle	$A = \frac{1}{2} bh$; where b = base, h = height
trapezoid	$A = \frac{1}{2}(b_1 + b_2) h$; where b = base, h = height
circle	$A = \pi r^2$; where $\pi = 3.14$, r = radius
PERIMETER (P) of a:	
square	$P = 4s$; where s = side
rectangle	$P = 2l + 2w$; where l = length, w = width
triangle	$P = a + b + c$; where a, b, and c are the sides
circumference (C) of a circle	$C = \pi d$; where $\pi = 3.14$, d = diameter
VOLUME (V) of a:	
cube	$V = s^3$; where s = side
rectangular container	$V = lwh$; where l = length, w = width, h = height
cylinder	$V = \pi r^2 h$; where $\pi = 3.14$, r = radius, h = height
square pyramid	$V = \frac{1}{3}(\text{base edge})^2 h$
cone	$V = \frac{1}{3}\pi r^2 h$

FORMULAS (continued)	
Description	**Formula**
Pythagorean theorem	$c^2 = a^2 + b^2$; where c = hypotenuse, a and b are legs, of a right triangle
distance (d) between two points in a plane	$d = \sqrt{(x_2 - x_1)^2 + (y_2 - y_1)^2}$; where (x_1, y_1) and (x_2, y_2) are two points in a plane
slope of a line (m)	$m = \dfrac{y_2 - y_1}{x_2 - x_1}$; where (x_1, y_1) and (x_2, y_2) are two points in a plane
MEASURES OF CENTRAL TENDENCY	mean = $\dfrac{x_1 + x_2 + \ldots + x_n}{n}$; where the x's are the values for which a mean is desired, and n = number of values in the series
	median = the point in an ordered set of numbers at which half of the numbers are above and half of the numbers are below this value
simple interest (i)	$i = prt$; where p = principal, r = rate, t = time
distance (d) as function of rate and time	$d = rt$; where r = rate, t = time
total cost (c)	$c = nr$; where n = number of units, r = cost per unit

Practice Test Part I

You have 45 minutes to complete this part. You may use a calculator, if needed. Fill in the answer grids where they are provided.

1. In a theater audience of 650 people, 80% were adults. How many children were in the audience?

    (1) 130
    (2) 150
    (3) 450
    (4) 500
    (5) 520

2. On a certain map 1 inch represents 60 miles. If two towns are 255 miles apart, what is the distance, in inches, between the towns on the map?

3. A carpenter has a board 4 feet 3 inches in length. He cuts off a piece 2 feet 8 inches in length. The length of the piece that is left is

    (1) 1 ft. 5 in.
    (2) 2 ft. 7 in.
    (3) 2 ft. 5 in.
    (4) 1 ft. 7 in.
    (5) 2 ft. 3 in.

4. A cardboard crate is 5 feet long, 3 feet wide, and 2 feet tall. What is its holding capacity in cubic feet?

5. 50 kilometers =

   (1) 5,000 miles
   (2) 50,000 centimeters
   (3) 50,000 meters
   (4) 500,000 millimeters
   (5) 1,000 kilograms

6. If O is the center of the circle and m $\angle B$ = 52°, find m $\angle O$.

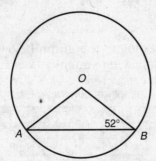

   (1) 52°
   (2) 76°
   (3) 80°
   (4) 94°
   (5) not enough information is given

7. On line segment $\overline{AC}$, $AB:BC = 3:5$ and BC = 20 inches.

   The length, in inches, of $\overline{AB}$ is

   (1) 3
   (2) 10
   (3) 12
   (4) 15
   (5) 16

8. The diagram below represents a cross section of a pipe. If the diameter of the outer circle is $7\frac{1}{2}$ inches and the diameter of the inner circle is $4\frac{1}{2}$ inches, what is the thickness of the pipe wall, represented by x?

   (1) 1 in.
   (2) $1\frac{1}{4}$ in.
   (3) $1\frac{1}{2}$ in.
   (4) 2 in.
   (5) 3 in.

9. Mr. Gray's weekly salary was increased from $400 per week to $500 per week. The percent increase in his salary was

   (1) 20%
   (2) 25%
   (3) 80%
   (4) 100%
   (5) 125%

10. A shopper buys a loaf of bread at x cents and 2 pounds of coffee at y cents per pound. If she pays with a $5.00 bill, the number of cents she receives in change is

    (1) $500 - x - y$
    (2) $500 - (x - y)$
    (3) $500 - x + y$
    (4) $500 - x - 2y$
    (5) $x + y - 500$

11. The area of a rectangular living room is 240 square feet. If the length of the room is 20 feet, what is the perimeter, in feet, of the room?

    (1) 12
    (2) 32
    (3) 50
    (4) 64
    (5) not enough information is given

12. A woman buys a Thanksgiving Day turkey weighing 19 pounds 6 ounces. If the turkey sells for $0.88 per pound, how much change does the woman receive from a $20 bill?
    (1) $1.95
    (2) $2.05
    (3) $2.95
    (4) $3.95
    (5) $4.15

13. A crew of painters can paint an apartment in $4\frac{1}{2}$ hours. What part of the apartment can they paint in $2\frac{1}{2}$ hours?

Question 14 refers to the chart below.

Planet	Distance from the Sun in Kilometers
Mercury	57,900,000
Venus	108,200,000
Earth	149,600,000
Mars	227,900,000

14. A small planet is discovered halfway between Venus and the sun. What is its distance from the sun in kilometers? Express the distance in scientific notation.
    (1) 54.1×10^6
    (2) 5.7×10^5
    (3) $.541 \times 10^8$
    (4) 1.082×10^9
    (5) 5.41×10^7

15. The expression $x^2 - 5x + 6$ may be written as
    (1) $(x + 3)(x + 2)$
    (2) $(x + 3)(x - 2)$
    (3) $(x - 3)(x - 2)$
    (4) $(x - 3)(x + 2)$
    (5) $x(5x + 6)$

16. Joshua earns $72 for typing 20 pages. At the same rate, how much does he earn for typing 15 pages?
    (1) $48
    (2) $54
    (3) $60
    (4) $72
    (5) $84

17. At Adams High School 402 students are taking Spanish and French. If twice as many students take Spanish as take French, how many students take Spanish?

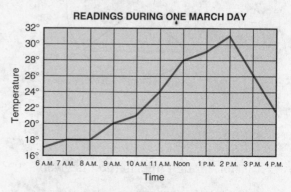

18. According to the graph below, which of the following statements is correct?

READINGS DURING ONE MARCH DAY

(1) The change in temperature between 7 A.M. and noon was 8°.
(2) The highest temperature reached during the day was 32°.
(3) The change in temperature between 8 A.M. and noon was –10°.
(4) The temperature did not change between 7 A.M. and 8 A.M.
(5) The temperature at noon was 30°.

19. A shipment of 2,200 pounds of sugar is packed in 40-ounce bags. How many bags will be packed?

    (1) 640
    (2) 750
    (3) 780
    (4) 800
    (5) 880

20. A ship sails 8 miles due east and then 15 miles due north. At this point, how many miles is the ship from its starting point?

21. A book salesman earns 12% commission on sales. Last month he sold a set of 300 textbooks at $20 per book, a group of 20 art books at $50 per book, and a shipment of 400 novels at $25 per book. What was his commission for the month?

    (1) $204
    (2) $1,700
    (3) $2,040
    (4) $17,000
    (5) $20,400

22. Mrs. Alvin bought 120 shares of RST Corporation at $32.75 per share and sold these shares a year later at $36.50 per share. Her profit before paying commission and taxes was

    (1) $400
    (2) $450
    (3) $480
    (4) $520
    (5) $560

23. Mr. and Mrs. Donato went on a vacation motor trip. When the trip started, the odometer reading in their car was 8,947 miles. When the trip was completed the odometer reading was 9,907 miles. How many gallons of gas, to the nearest gallon, were used on the trip?

    (1) 36
    (2) 38
    (3) 40
    (4) 41
    (5) not enough information is given

24. What is the area of the rectangle below?

    $3a^2b^3$

    $5a^3b^4$

    (1) $16a^{10}b^{14}$
    (2) $8a^5b^{12}$
    (3) $15a^5b^7$
    (4) $15a^6b^{12}$
    (5) $16a^6b^{12}$

25. The number of miles per hour needed to cover 120 miles in x hours may be expressed as

    (1) $\dfrac{120}{x}$
    (2) $\dfrac{x}{120}$
    (3) $120x$
    (4) $120 + x$
    (5) $x - 120$

END OF PART I

Practice Test Part II

You have 45 minutes to complete this part. You may not use a calculator. Fill in the answer grids where they are provided.

26. In 5 years the population of a town decreased from 3,500 to 2,800. The percent of decrease was

    (1) 20%
    (2) 25%
    (3) 30%
    (4) 40%
    (5) 70%

27. Mr. Fox's will provided that his wife receive $\frac{1}{2}$ of his estate, and his three sons divide the rest equally. If each son's share was $8,000, what was the value of the estate?

    (1) $24,000
    (2) $32,000
    (3) $40,000
    (4) $48,000
    (5) $50,000

28. A class has 32 students. On a certain day x students are absent. What fractional part of the class is present on that day?

    (1) $\dfrac{x}{32}$
    (2) $\dfrac{32-x}{x}$
    (3) $\dfrac{x}{32-x}$
    (4) $\dfrac{32-x}{32}$
    (5) $\dfrac{32-x}{32+x}$

29. The Shore Multiplex Theater charges $6 for matinee movies and $9 for evening shows. On one day, 267 matinee tickets and 329 evening tickets were sold. An expression that represents the total receipts, in dollars, for that day is

    (1) 9(267) + 6(329)
    (2) 6(267) + 9(329)
    (3) 15(267 + 329)
    (4) 6(267 + 329) + 9(267 + 329)
    (5) 9(267 + 329)

30. Frank had x dollars. He bought y articles for z dollars each. The number of dollars Frank had left was

    (1) $yz - x$
    (2) $yx - z$
    (3) $x - yz$
    (4) $x + yz$
    (5) $xy + z$

Questions 31 and 32 are based on the following information.

The fare schedule for Checker Taxi is shown below:

First one-fifth mile	1 dollar
Each one-fifth mile after the first	20 cents

31. How much would a 3-mile trip cost (not including tip)?

    (1) $2.00
    (2) $2.50
    (3) $3.00
    (4) $3.80
    (5) $5.00

32. If a passenger has exactly $10.00, how many miles can she ride and still be able to give the driver a tip of $1.00?

    (1) 7 or less
    (2) more than 7 but no more than 8
    (3) more than 8 but no more than 9
    (4) more than 9 but no more than 10
    (5) more than 10

33. In the diagram below, a semicircle surmounts a rectangle whose length is $2a$ and whose width is a. A formula for finding A, the area of the whole figure, is

2a

(1) $A = 2a^2 + \dfrac{1}{2}\pi a^2$

(2) $A = 2\pi a^2$

(3) $A = 3\pi a^2$

(4) $A = 2a^2 + \pi a^2$

(5) not enough information is given

34. The graph indicates the way a certain man spends his day. Which one of the following statements is correct?

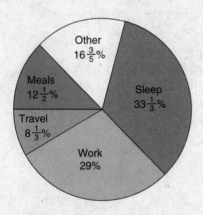

(1) The man works 8 hrs. per day.

(2) The man spends 1 hr. more on meals than he does on travel.

(3) The man sleeps 7 hrs. per day.

(4) The man spends half his time on work and travel.

(5) The man spends 4 hrs. on meals.

35. *ABCD*, shown in the diagram below, is a rectangle. The ratio of the area of $\triangle EDC$ to the area of the rectangle *ABCD* is

(1) $1:4$

(2) $1:3$

(3) $1:2$

(4) $3:5$

(5) $3:4$

36. If $y = 2x^2(z - 3)$, find the value of y if $x = 5$ and $z = 7$.

(1) 54

(2) 150

(3) 180

(4) 200

(5) 400

37. On a motor trip Mr. Shore covered $\dfrac{2}{7}$ of his total trip distance during the first day by driving 384 miles. The total distance to be covered, in miles, is

(1) 98

(2) 1,244

(3) 1,306

(4) 1,344

(5) 1,500

38. The table below gives the annual premiums for a life insurance policy taken out at various ages.

AGE IN YEARS	PREMIUM PER $1,000
22	$18
30	$22
38	$28
46	$38

If the policy is fully paid up after 20 years, how much is saved by taking out a $10,000 policy at age 30 rather than at age 46?

39. In a right triangle, the ratio of the two acute angles is $3:2$. The number of degrees in the larger acute angle is

    (1) 36
    (2) 54
    (3) 72
    (4) 90
    (5) not enough information is given

40. If $3x - 1 < 5$, then x must be

    (1) greater than 2
    (2) less than 2
    (3) greater than 3
    (4) less than 0
    (5) greater than 5

41. If $\overrightarrow{AB} \parallel \overrightarrow{GH}$, m $\angle BDE = 100°$, $\overrightarrow{DJ}$ bisects $\angle BDE$, $\overrightarrow{EJ}$ bisects $\angle DEH$, find m $\angle J$ in degrees.

42. A chair was marked for sale at $315. This was a discount of 25% off the original price. What was the original price of the chair?

    (1) $236.50
    (2) $390
    (3) $420
    (4) $450
    (5) $520

43. There are 48 couples at a dance. Each couple consists of 1 male and 1 female. Mr. Fowler selects a female dancing partner for the next dance at random. What is the probability that Mr. Fowler selects his wife?

    (1) $\dfrac{1}{50}$

    (2) $\dfrac{1}{48}$

    (3) $\dfrac{2}{48}$

    (4) $\dfrac{1}{2}$

    (5) $\dfrac{2}{3}$

44. Which inequality is true?

    (1) $\dfrac{4}{5} > \dfrac{2}{3} > \dfrac{5}{7}$

    (2) $\dfrac{5}{7} > \dfrac{2}{3} > \dfrac{4}{5}$

    (3) $\dfrac{4}{5} > \dfrac{5}{7} > \dfrac{2}{3}$

    (4) $\dfrac{2}{3} > \dfrac{4}{5} > \dfrac{5}{7}$

    (5) $\dfrac{5}{7} > \dfrac{4}{5} > \dfrac{2}{3}$

Question 45 refers to the following coordinate graph.

45. At what point on the graph will the line extending from point A intersect with the line extending from point B? Fill in the coordinate grid.

46. A family spent $\dfrac{1}{4}$ of its income for rent and $\dfrac{1}{5}$ of its income for food. What percent of its income remains?

    (1) 40%
    (2) 45%
    (3) 50%
    (4) 52%
    (5) 55%

47. A tree is 24 feet tall and casts a shadow of 10 feet. At the same time a tower casts a shadow of 25 feet. What is the height, in feet, of the tower?

    (1) 45
    (2) 60
    (3) 75
    (4) 80
    (5) 84

48. Mr. Capiello is on a diet. For breakfast and lunch together, he consumes 40% of his allowable number of calories. If he still has 1,200 calories left for the day, his daily calorie allowance is

    (1) 2,000
    (2) 2,200
    (3) 2,400
    (4) 2,500
    (5) 2,800

49. If $3x - y = 11$ and $2y = 8$, then $x =$

    (1) 3
    (2) 4
    (3) $4\frac{1}{2}$
    (4) 5
    (5) 6

50. On the number line below, $\sqrt{7}$ is located at point

    (1) A
    (2) B
    (3) C
    (4) D
    (5) E

Answer Key

1. **1**		26. **1**	
2. **¹⁷⁄₄, or 4.25**		27. **4**	
3. **4**		28. **4**	
4. **30**		29. **2**	
5. **3**		30. **3**	
6. **2**		31. **4**	
7. **3**		32. **3**	
8. **3**		33. **1**	
9. **2**		34. **2**	
10. **4**		35. **3**	
11. **4**		36. **4**	
12. **3**		37. **4**	
13. **⁵⁄₉, or .56**		38. **3,200**	
14. **5**		39. **2**	
15. **3**		40. **2**	
16. **2**		41. **90**	
17. **268**		42. **3**	
18. **4**		43. **2**	
19. **5**		44. **3**	
20. **17**		45. **(−4,4)**	
21. **3**		46. **5**	
22. **2**		47. **2**	
23. **5**		48. **1**	
24. **3**		49. **4**	
25. **1**		50. **3**	

WHAT'S YOUR SCORE?

_____right	_____wrong
Excellent	45–50
Good	39–44
Fair	34–38

If your score was low, the explanation of the correct answers that follows will help you. You may obtain additional help and practice by referring to the review material in Unit VII.

ANSWER ANALYSIS

Following the correct answer are the chapter and section containing the material covered in the question.

1. **1** Chapter 21 (Word Problems)
If 80% of the audience were adults,
100% − 80% = 20% were children.
20% = 0.20, and 0.20(650) = 130

2. **$^{17}/_4$, or 4.25** Chapter 20 (Ratio)
Let x = number of inches between the towns on the map.
Set up a proportion:
$$\frac{1 \text{ in.}}{60 \text{ mi.}} = \frac{x \text{ in.}}{225 \text{ mi.}}$$
$$60x = 255$$
$$x = \frac{255}{60} = 4\frac{1}{4} = 4.25$$

3. **4** Chapter 20 (Standard Measures)
$$\frac{4 \text{ ft. 3 in.}}{-2 \text{ ft. 8 in.}} = \frac{3 \text{ ft. 15 in.}}{-2 \text{ ft. 8 in.}}$$
$$1 \text{ ft. 7 in.}$$

4. **30** Chapter 19 (Basic Geometry and Volume)
v = lwh. The container is 5 ft. long × 3 ft. wide × 2 ft. high.
(5 × 3 × 2 = 30 cu. ft.)

5. **3** Chapter 20 (Standard Measures)
Since 1 km = 1,000 m,
50 km = 50,000 m.

6. **2** Chapter 24 (Triangles)

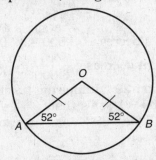

$OA = OB$, since each is a radius.
m∠A = m∠B = 52°
m∠A + m∠B + m∠O = 180°
52 + 52 + m∠O = 180
104 + m∠O = 180
m∠O = 180 − 104 = 76°

7. **3** Chapter 24 (Geometry and Proportion)

Let $x = AB$.
Then $\frac{3}{5} = \frac{x}{20}$, so $5x = 60$ and $x = 12$.

8. **3** Chapter 21 (Circles)

Let x = thickness of the pipe.
Then $x + x + 4\frac{1}{2} = 7\frac{1}{2}$
so $2x = 3$ and $x = 1\frac{1}{2}$ in.

9. **2** Chapter 21 (Percent Increase)
$$\text{Percent increase} = \frac{\text{actual increase}}{\text{original amount}}$$
Actual increase: $500 − $400 = $100
Percent increase: $\frac{100}{400} = \frac{1}{4}$ = 25%

10. **4** Chapter 23 (Setups and Variables)
The shopper gives the storekeeper $5.00, or 500 cents. From this amount the storekeeper takes out x cents for the bread and $2y$ cents for the coffee.
The result is $500 - x - 2y$.

11. **4** Chapter 19 (Basic Geometry)
Draw a diagram:

Since $A = lw = 240$, then $20w = 240$, and $w = 12$. Then
$P = 2(l + w) = 2(20 + 12) = 2(32) = 64$.

12. **3** Chapter 20 (Standard Measures)
6 oz. $= \frac{6}{16} = \frac{3}{8}$ lb.
19 lb. costs 19($0.88) = $16.72
$\frac{3}{8}$ lb. costs $\frac{3}{8}$($0.88) = $0.33
$19\frac{3}{8}$ lb. costs $16.72 + $.33 = $17.05
Change = $20.00 − $17.05 = $2.95.

13. **$^5/_9$, or .56** Chapter 20 (Word Problems)
The part of the apartment painted in $2\frac{1}{2}$ hours =
$$\frac{2\frac{1}{2}}{4\frac{1}{2}} = \frac{5}{2} \div \frac{9}{2} = \frac{5}{2} \times \frac{2}{9} = \frac{5}{9} = .56$$

14. **5** Chapter 21 (Scientific Notation)
To find the halfway mark between
Venus and the sun:

$$\frac{108,200,000}{2} = 54,100,000 \text{ km}$$

Then, count the number of places
moved to the left until the decimal is
at 5.4. That number is 7. Scientific
notation for the distance is 5.4×10^7.

15. **3** Chapter 23 (Multiplying Binomials)
The expression $x^2 - 5x + 6$ factors as
$(x - 3)(x - 2)$. If you can't factor, check
each choice by multiplying out.

16. **2** Chapter 20 (Ratio)
Let x = amount Joshua earns for
typing 15 pages.
Set up a proportion:

$$\frac{\text{pages typed}}{\text{dollars earned}} : \frac{20}{72} = \frac{15}{x}$$

$$20x = 15 \times 72 = 1,080, \text{ and}$$
$$x = 1,080 \div 20 = \$54.$$

17. **268** Chapter 23 (Word Problems)
Let x = number of students taking
French,
and $2x$ = number of students taking
Spanish.
$$x + 2x = 402$$
$$3x = 402$$
$$x = 402 \div 3 = 134$$
$$2x = 2(134) = 268$$

18. **4** Chapter 22 (Line Graphs)
Note on the graph that the
temperature neither rose nor fell, that
is, it did not change, between 7 A.M.
and 8 A.M.

19. **5** Chapter 20 (Standard Measures)
Since there are 16 oz. in 1 lb.
2,200 lb. = 2,200 × 16 = 35,200 oz.
35,200 ÷ 40 = 880

20. **17** Chapter 24 (Pythagorean Theorem)
Use the Pythagorean theorem.
$$x^2 = 8^2 + 15^2$$
$$= 64 + 225$$
$$= 289$$
$$x = \sqrt{289} = 17$$

21. **3** Chapter 21 (Word Problems)
Textbook sales: 300 × \$20 = \$6,000
Art book sales: 20 × \$50 = \$1,000
Novel sales: 400 × \$25 = \$10,000
Total sales = \$17,000
Commission: 12% of \$17,000 =
\$2,040

22. **2** Chapter 21 (Word Problems)
Profit per share:
\$36.50 – \$32.75 = \$3.75
Total profit: 120 × \$3.75 = \$450

23. **5** Chapter 19 (Word Problems)
You could subtract to find the
number of miles driven, but since the
number of miles per gallon is not
given, the problem cannot be solved.

24. **3** Chapter 22 (Multiplying Variables)
$A = lw$ Multiply the numbers (5 × 3),
but add the like exponents $a^3 + a^2 = a^5$
and $b^4 + b^3 = b^7$
$15a^5b^7$

25. **1** Chapter 23 (Setups with Variables)
Use the relationship
Rate × Time = Distance

$$\text{or Rate} = \frac{\text{Distance}}{\text{Time}}$$

In this case, distance = 120 mi. and
time = x
Therefore, the number of miles per
hour is $\dfrac{120}{x}$.

26. **1** Chapter 21 (Percent Decrease)

$$\text{Percent decrease} = \frac{\text{actual decrease}}{\text{original number}}$$

Actual decrease: 3,500 – 2,800 = 700

Percent decrease: $\dfrac{700}{3,500} = \dfrac{1}{5} = 20\%$

27. **4** Chapter 20 (Multiplying Fractions)
\$8,000 = 1 son's share
3 × \$8,000 = \$24,000, amount left to
three sons

$\$24,000 = \dfrac{1}{2}$ of the estate

2(\$24,000) = \$48,000, value of the
full estate.

28. **4** Chapter 23 (Setups with Variables)
If there are 32 students in the class
and x students are absent, then
$32 - x$ students are present.
The fractional part of the students
present is $\dfrac{32 - x}{32}$.

29. **2** Chapter 19 (Multistep Word Problems)
To find the total receipts, find the receipts of the matinee performances and add to these the receipts of the evening performances.
$6(267) + 9(329)$ = total receipts

30. **3** Chapter 23 (Setups with Variables)
Frank spent yz dollars.
Subtract yz from x. The result is $x - yz$.

31. **4** Chapter 20 (Word Problems)
Note that, after the first $\frac{1}{5}$ mi., the fare amounts to $1 per mile. Therefore, a 3-mi. trip would cost $2 for the second and third miles. The first $\frac{1}{5}$ mi. would cost $1, and each of the next $\frac{4}{5}$'s would cost 20 cents each, for a total of $1.80. The entire 3-mi. trip would cost $2.00 + $1.80 = $3.80.

32. **3** Chapter 20 (Word Problems)
Taking $1 tip from the $10 available leaves $9 for the actual travel. The first $\frac{1}{5}$ mi. costs $1, leaving $8. Since the fare is $1 per mile thereafter, the trip could be as long as $8\frac{1}{5}$ mi.

33. **1** Chapter 24 (Geometry and Algebra)
Area of rectangle = $(2a)(a) = 2a^2$.
Radius of semicircle = $\frac{1}{2}(2a) = a$.
The formula for the area of a circle is $A = \pi r^2$.
Area of semicircle = $\frac{1}{2}(\pi a^2)$.
Area of whole figure =
$2a^2 + \frac{1}{2}\pi a^2$.

34. **2** Chapter 21 (Percent)
The man spends 12½% (or .125) on meals in a 24-hour day.
$.125 \times 24 = 3$ hours
$.0833 \times 24 = 1.99$ or 2
The man spends an hour more a day on meals than on traveling. Some other choices can be eliminated by common sense; others must be multiplied as above before being eliminated.

35. **3** Chapter 24 (Geometry and Proportion)
Area of $\triangle EDC = \frac{1}{2}(DC)h$

Area of rectangle $ABCD = (DC)h$.
Thus, area of $\triangle EDC$ is equal to one-half area of rectangle $ABCD$. Ratio of area of $\triangle EDC$ to area of rectangle $ABCD = 1:2$.

36. **4** Chapter 23 (Finding Values with Given Variables)
$y = 2x^2(z - 3)$
$\quad = 2(5)(5)(7 - 3)$
$\quad = 2(5)(5)(4)$
$\quad = 200$

37. **4** Chapter 20 (Word Problems)
Let x = total distance to be covered.
$\frac{2}{7}x = 384$
$2x = 7(384) = 2,688$
$x = 2,688 \div 2 = 1,344$

38. **3,200** Chapter 22 (Tables)
At age 30, the policy costs $22(10) = $220 per year.
At age 46, the policy costs $38(10) = $380 per year.
Thus, $380 - $220 = $160 saved per year.
In 20 years, the savings is $160(20) = $3,200.

39. 2 Chapter 24 (Geometry and Proportion)

Let $3x$ = measure of the larger angle, and $2x$ = measure of the smaller angle.
$3x + 2x = 90$
$\qquad 5x = 90$
$\qquad x = 90 \div 5 = 18$
$\qquad 3x = 3(18) = 54°$

40. 2 Chapter 23 (Inequalities)
$\qquad 3x - 1 < 5$
$\qquad 3x < 6$
$\qquad x < 2$
x must be less than 2.

41. 90 Chapter 24 (Transversals, Triangles)

m∠BDE = 100°
Since $\overleftrightarrow{AB} \parallel \overleftrightarrow{GH}$, m∠$BDE$ + m∠DEH = 180°
100 + m∠DEH = 180
m∠DEH = 180 − 100 = 80°

m∠JDE = $\frac{1}{2}$m∠BDE = 50°

m∠DEJ = $\frac{1}{2}$m∠DEH = 40°

m∠J + 50 + 40 = 180
m∠J = 180 − 50 − 40 = 90°

42. 3 Chapter 21 (Word Problems)

25% = $\frac{1}{4}$. Selling price of chair

was $\frac{3}{4}$ of original selling price.

Let x = original selling price.

$\frac{3}{4}x = \$315$

$x = \$315 \div \frac{3}{4} = \$315 \times \frac{4}{3} = \$420$

43. 2 Chapter 20 (Probability)
Probability =
$\dfrac{\text{number of successful outcomes}}{\text{number of possible outcomes}}$

In this case, the number of successful outcomes is 1 since, of the 48 women present, only 1 woman is Mr. Fowler's wife. The number of possible outcomes is 48 since there are 48 possible women partners.

Probability = $\dfrac{1}{48}$

44. 3 Chapter 23 (Inequalities)

$\dfrac{4}{5} > \dfrac{5}{7}$ because $4 \times 7 > 5 \times 5$

$\dfrac{5}{7} > \dfrac{2}{3}$ because $5 \times 3 > 7 \times 2$

Thus, $\dfrac{4}{5} > \dfrac{5}{7} > \dfrac{2}{3}$ is correct.

Alternative Method:
Convert the three fractions to decimals, to the nearest hundredth.

$\dfrac{5}{7} = 0.71$, $\dfrac{4}{5} = 0.80$, $\dfrac{2}{3} = 0.67$

Therefore, $\dfrac{4}{5} > \dfrac{5}{7} > \dfrac{2}{3}$

45. (−4,4) Chapter 23 (Coordinates)

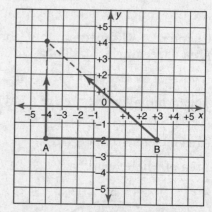

Line starting at point A stays right on the −4 coordinate for x. Use a straight edge (edge of a piece of paper) to trace the diagonal path of line, starting at point B. It intersects A at +4, which is the y coordinate.

46. 5 Chapter 21 (Converting Fractions to Percents)
Fractional part of income spent on

rent and food: $\dfrac{1}{4} + \dfrac{1}{5} = \dfrac{5}{20} + \dfrac{4}{20} = \dfrac{9}{20}$

$1 - \dfrac{9}{20} = \dfrac{11}{20}$, remaining income,

$\dfrac{11}{20} = 0.55 = 55\%$.

47. 2 Chapter 24 (Geometry and Proportion)

Let x = height of tower.
Set up a proportion.

$$\frac{\text{height of object}}{\text{length of shadow}}: \frac{x}{25} = \frac{24}{10}$$

$10x = 25(24) = 600$
$x = 600 \div 10 = 60$

48. 1 Chapter 21 (Word Problems)
If Mr. Capiello has consumed 40% of his allowable calories, he has 60% left.
Let x = his daily allowance of calories
$0.60x = 1,200$
$x = 1,200 \div 0.60 = 2,000$

49. 4 Chapter 23 (Working with Variables)
Since $2y = 8$, then $y = 4$.
$3x - y = 11$
$3x - 4 = 11$
$3x = 15$ and $x = 5$

50. 3 Chapter 23 (Points on a Number Line)
Since $2^2 = 4$ and $3^2 = 9$, $\sqrt{7}$ is between 2 and 3. On the number line, only point C lies between 2 and 3.

TWO PRACTICE EXAMINATIONS

Answer Sheet for the Practice Examination

TEST 1: LANGUAGE ARTS, WRITING, PART I

1. ① ② ③ ④ ⑤
2. ① ② ③ ④ ⑤
3. ① ② ③ ④ ⑤
4. ① ② ③ ④ ⑤
5. ① ② ③ ④ ⑤
6. ① ② ③ ④ ⑤
7. ① ② ③ ④ ⑤
8. ① ② ③ ④ ⑤
9. ① ② ③ ④ ⑤
10. ① ② ③ ④ ⑤
11. ① ② ③ ④ ⑤
12. ① ② ③ ④ ⑤
13. ① ② ③ ④ ⑤
14. ① ② ③ ④ ⑤
15. ① ② ③ ④ ⑤
16. ① ② ③ ④ ⑤
17. ① ② ③ ④ ⑤
18. ① ② ③ ④ ⑤
19. ① ② ③ ④ ⑤

20. ① ② ③ ④ ⑤
21. ① ② ③ ④ ⑤
22. ① ② ③ ④ ⑤
23. ① ② ③ ④ ⑤
24. ① ② ③ ④ ⑤
25. ① ② ③ ④ ⑤
26. ① ② ③ ④ ⑤
27. ① ② ③ ④ ⑤
28. ① ② ③ ④ ⑤
29. ① ② ③ ④ ⑤
30. ① ② ③ ④ ⑤
31. ① ② ③ ④ ⑤
32. ① ② ③ ④ ⑤
33. ① ② ③ ④ ⑤
34. ① ② ③ ④ ⑤
35. ① ② ③ ④ ⑤
36. ① ② ③ ④ ⑤
37. ① ② ③ ④ ⑤
38. ① ② ③ ④ ⑤

39. ① ② ③ ④ ⑤
40. ① ② ③ ④ ⑤
41. ① ② ③ ④ ⑤
42. ① ② ③ ④ ⑤
43. ① ② ③ ④ ⑤
44. ① ② ③ ④ ⑤
45. ① ② ③ ④ ⑤
46. ① ② ③ ④ ⑤
47. ① ② ③ ④ ⑤
48. ① ② ③ ④ ⑤
49. ① ② ③ ④ ⑤
50. ① ② ③ ④ ⑤

TEST 2: SOCIAL STUDIES

1. ① ② ③ ④ ⑤
2. ① ② ③ ④ ⑤
3. ① ② ③ ④ ⑤
4. ① ② ③ ④ ⑤
5. ① ② ③ ④ ⑤
6. ① ② ③ ④ ⑤
7. ① ② ③ ④ ⑤
8. ① ② ③ ④ ⑤
9. ① ② ③ ④ ⑤
10. ① ② ③ ④ ⑤
11. ① ② ③ ④ ⑤
12. ① ② ③ ④ ⑤
13. ① ② ③ ④ ⑤
14. ① ② ③ ④ ⑤
15. ① ② ③ ④ ⑤
16. ① ② ③ ④ ⑤
17. ① ② ③ ④ ⑤
18. ① ② ③ ④ ⑤
19. ① ② ③ ④ ⑤
20. ① ② ③ ④ ⑤
21. ① ② ③ ④ ⑤
22. ① ② ③ ④ ⑤

23. ① ② ③ ④ ⑤
24. ① ② ③ ④ ⑤
25. ① ② ③ ④ ⑤
26. ① ② ③ ④ ⑤
27. ① ② ③ ④ ⑤
28. ① ② ③ ④ ⑤
29. ① ② ③ ④ ⑤
30. ① ② ③ ④ ⑤
31. ① ② ③ ④ ⑤
32. ① ② ③ ④ ⑤
33. ① ② ③ ④ ⑤
34. ① ② ③ ④ ⑤
35. ① ② ③ ④ ⑤
36. ① ② ③ ④ ⑤
37. ① ② ③ ④ ⑤
38. ① ② ③ ④ ⑤
39. ① ② ③ ④ ⑤
40. ① ② ③ ④ ⑤
41. ① ② ③ ④ ⑤
42. ① ② ③ ④ ⑤
43. ① ② ③ ④ ⑤
44. ① ② ③ ④ ⑤

45. ① ② ③ ④ ⑤
46. ① ② ③ ④ ⑤
47. ① ② ③ ④ ⑤
48. ① ② ③ ④ ⑤
49. ① ② ③ ④ ⑤
50. ① ② ③ ④ ⑤

TEST 3: SCIENCE

1. ① ② ③ ④ ⑤
2. ① ② ③ ④ ⑤
3. ① ② ③ ④ ⑤
4. ① ② ③ ④ ⑤
5. ① ② ③ ④ ⑤
6. ① ② ③ ④ ⑤
7. ① ② ③ ④ ⑤
8. ① ② ③ ④ ⑤
9. ① ② ③ ④ ⑤
10. ① ② ③ ④ ⑤
11. ① ② ③ ④ ⑤
12. ① ② ③ ④ ⑤
13. ① ② ③ ④ ⑤
14. ① ② ③ ④ ⑤
15. ① ② ③ ④ ⑤
16. ① ② ③ ④ ⑤
17. ① ② ③ ④ ⑤
18. ① ② ③ ④ ⑤
19. ① ② ③ ④ ⑤

20. ① ② ③ ④ ⑤
21. ① ② ③ ④ ⑤
22. ① ② ③ ④ ⑤
23. ① ② ③ ④ ⑤
24. ① ② ③ ④ ⑤
25. ① ② ③ ④ ⑤
26. ① ② ③ ④ ⑤
27. ① ② ③ ④ ⑤
28. ① ② ③ ④ ⑤
29. ① ② ③ ④ ⑤
30. ① ② ③ ④ ⑤
31. ① ② ③ ④ ⑤
32. ① ② ③ ④ ⑤
33. ① ② ③ ④ ⑤
34. ① ② ③ ④ ⑤
35. ① ② ③ ④ ⑤
36. ① ② ③ ④ ⑤
37. ① ② ③ ④ ⑤
38. ① ② ③ ④ ⑤

39. ① ② ③ ④ ⑤
40. ① ② ③ ④ ⑤
41. ① ② ③ ④ ⑤
42. ① ② ③ ④ ⑤
43. ① ② ③ ④ ⑤
44. ① ② ③ ④ ⑤
45. ① ② ③ ④ ⑤
46. ① ② ③ ④ ⑤
47. ① ② ③ ④ ⑤
48. ① ② ③ ④ ⑤
49. ① ② ③ ④ ⑤
50. ① ② ③ ④ ⑤

TEST 4: LANGUAGE ARTS, READING

1. ① ② ③ ④ ⑤
2. ① ② ③ ④ ⑤
3. ① ② ③ ④ ⑤
4. ① ② ③ ④ ⑤
5. ① ② ③ ④ ⑤
6. ① ② ③ ④ ⑤
7. ① ② ③ ④ ⑤
8. ① ② ③ ④ ⑤
9. ① ② ③ ④ ⑤
10. ① ② ③ ④ ⑤
11. ① ② ③ ④ ⑤
12. ① ② ③ ④ ⑤
13. ① ② ③ ④ ⑤
14. ① ② ③ ④ ⑤
15. ① ② ③ ④ ⑤

16. ① ② ③ ④ ⑤
17. ① ② ③ ④ ⑤
18. ① ② ③ ④ ⑤
19. ① ② ③ ④ ⑤
20. ① ② ③ ④ ⑤
21. ① ② ③ ④ ⑤
22. ① ② ③ ④ ⑤
23. ① ② ③ ④ ⑤
24. ① ② ③ ④ ⑤
25. ① ② ③ ④ ⑤
26. ① ② ③ ④ ⑤
27. ① ② ③ ④ ⑤
28. ① ② ③ ④ ⑤
29. ① ② ③ ④ ⑤
30. ① ② ③ ④ ⑤

31. ① ② ③ ④ ⑤
32. ① ② ③ ④ ⑤
33. ① ② ③ ④ ⑤
34. ① ② ③ ④ ⑤
35. ① ② ③ ④ ⑤
36. ① ② ③ ④ ⑤
37. ① ② ③ ④ ⑤
38. ① ② ③ ④ ⑤
39. ① ② ③ ④ ⑤
40. ① ② ③ ④ ⑤

TEST 5: MATHEMATICS, PART I

1. ① ② ③ ④ ⑤
2. ① ② ③ ④ ⑤
3. ① ② ③ ④ ⑤
4. ① ② ③ ④ ⑤
5.

6. ① ② ③ ④ ⑤
7. ① ② ③ ④ ⑤
8. ① ② ③ ④ ⑤
9.

10. ① ② ③ ④ ⑤

11.

12. ① ② ③ ④ ⑤
13.

14. ① ② ③ ④ ⑤
15. ① ② ③ ④ ⑤
16. ① ② ③ ④ ⑤
17. ① ② ③ ④ ⑤
18. ① ② ③ ④ ⑤
19. ① ② ③ ④ ⑤
20. ① ② ③ ④ ⑤

21. ① ② ③ ④ ⑤
21. ① ② ③ ④ ⑤
23.

24.

25. ① ② ③ ④ ⑤

TEST 5: MATHEMATICS, PART II

26. ① ② ③ ④ ⑤
27. ① ② ③ ④ ⑤
28. ① ② ③ ④ ⑤
29. ① ② ③ ④ ⑤
30. ① ② ③ ④ ⑤
31.

32. ① ② ③ ④ ⑤
33. ① ② ③ ④ ⑤
34. ① ② ③ ④ ⑤
35.

36. ① ② ③ ④ ⑤
37. ① ② ③ ④ ⑤
38. ① ② ③ ④ ⑤
39. ① ② ③ ④ ⑤
40. ① ② ③ ④ ⑤
41. ① ② ③ ④ ⑤
42. ① ② ③ ④ ⑤
43.

44.

45. ① ② ③ ④ ⑤
46. ① ② ③ ④ ⑤
47. ① ② ③ ④ ⑤
48. ① ② ③ ④ ⑤
49. ① ② ③ ④ ⑤
50. ① ② ③ ④ ⑤

PRACTICE EXAMINATION ONE

TEST 1: LANGUAGE ARTS, WRITING, PART I

Directions

The Language Arts, Writing test is intended to measure your ability to use clear and effective English. It is a test of English as it should be written, not as it might be spoken. This test includes both multiple-choice questions and an essay. These directions apply only to the multiple-choice section; a separate set of directions is given for the essay.

The multiple-choice section consists of paragraphs with numbered sentences. Some of the sentences contain errors in sentence structure, usage, or mechanics (spelling, punctuation, and capitalization). After reading the numbered sentences, answer the multiple-choice questions that follow. Some questions refer to sentences that are correct as written. The best answer for these questions is the one that leaves the sentence as originally written. The best answer for some questions is the one that produces a sentence that is consistent with the verb tense and point of view used throughout the paragraph.

You should spend no more than 75 minutes on the multiple-choice questions and 45 minutes on your essay. Work carefully, but do not spend too much time on any one question. You may begin working on the essay part of this test as soon as you complete the multiple-choice section.

To record your answers, mark one numbered space on the answer sheet beside the number that corresponds to the question in the test.

FOR EXAMPLE:

Sentence 1: **We were all honored to meet governor Phillips.**

What correction should be made to this sentence?

(1) insert a comma after <u>honored</u>
(2) change the spelling of <u>honored</u> to <u>honered</u>
(3) change <u>governor</u> to <u>Governor</u>
(4) replace <u>were</u> with <u>was</u>
(5) no correction is necessary

① ② ● ④ ⑤

In this example, the word "governor" should be capitalized; therefore, answer space 3 would be marked on the answer sheet.

GO ON TO THE NEXT PAGE

TEST 1: LANGUAGE ARTS, WRITING, PART I

Questions 1–9 refer to the following paragraphs.

(A)

(1) Safe food must be planned and not left to chance, for the consumer, food safety begins in the marketplace. (2) All cooperative efforts made by states and the U.S. department of agriculture to make available a clean, safe, wholesome food supply will be in vain unless the consumer takes certain precautions to keep it that way. (3) The precautions to be taken by the consumer include care in buying, storing, handling, and cooking food.

(B)

(4) Shop for groceries last after all other errands has been run. (5) Take foods home immediately and don't leave them unattended for a long period of time. (6) Sufficient light in grocery stores is necessary to enable you to adequately view foods four proper selection. (7) Store personnel should make sure that foods are replaced frequently in order to keep it as fresh as possible.

(C)

(8) Under no circumstances buy swollen or leaking cans. (9) The food in a swollen or leaking can may be dangerous to eat or even to taste.

(D)

(10) Ask the checkout clerk to bag cold foods together so that they keep cold longer; interspersed with room-temperature foods, they may warm up quickly.

1. Sentence 1: **Safe food must be planned and not left to <u>chance, for</u> the consumer, food safety begins in the marketplace.**

   Which of the following is the best way to write the underlined portion of this sentence? If you think the original is the best way, choose option (1).

   (1) chance, for
   (2) chance: for
   (3) chance; for
   (4) chance, For
   (5) chance. For

2. Sentence 2: **All cooperative efforts made by states and the U.S. department of agriculture to make available a clean, safe, wholesome food supply will be in vain unless the consumer takes certain precautions to keep it that way.**

   What correction should be made to this sentence?

   (1) insert a hyphen in <u>cooperative</u>
   (2) capitalize <u>department</u> and <u>agriculture</u>
   (3) remove the comma after <u>clean</u>
   (4) change <u>it</u> to <u>them</u>
   (5) no correction is necessary

3. Sentence 3: **The precautions to be taken by the consumer include care in buying, storing, handling, and cooking food.**

   If you rewrote sentence 3 beginning with

   <u>Care in buying, storing, handling and cooking food</u>

   the next words should be

   (1) include
   (2) is
   (3) is among
   (4) would be among
   (5) will be among

4. Sentence 4: **Shop for groceries last after all other errands has been run.**

   What correction should be made to this statement?

   (1) insert a comma after <u>last</u>
   (2) remove the word <u>other</u>
   (3) change <u>run</u> to <u>ran</u>
   (4) change <u>has been</u> to <u>have been</u>
   (5) no correction is necessary

GO ON TO THE NEXT PAGE

TEST 1: LANGUAGE ARTS, WRITING, PART I

5. Sentence 5: **Take foods home immediately <u>and don't</u> leave them unattended for a long period of time.**

   Which of the following is the best way to write the underlined portion of this sentence? If you think the original is the best way, choose option (1).

   (1) and don't
   (2) also don't
   (3) but don't
   (4) however don't
   (5) nevertheless don't

6. Sentence 6: **Sufficient light in grocery stores is necessary to enable you to adequately view foods four proper selection.**

   What correction should be made to this sentence?

   (1) change the spelling of <u>four</u> to <u>for</u>
   (2) insert a comma after <u>stores</u>
   (3) change the spelling of <u>necessary</u> to <u>necessery</u>
   (4) insert a comma after <u>foods</u>
   (5) no correction is necessary

7. Sentence 7: **Store personnel should make sure that foods are replaced frequently in order to keep it as fresh as possible.**

   What correction should be made to this sentence?

   (1) change <u>it</u> to <u>them</u>
   (2) change the spelling of <u>personnel</u> to <u>personal</u>
   (3) change <u>should</u> to <u>might</u>
   (4) change <u>fresh</u> to <u>freshly</u>
   (5) no change is necessary

8. Sentences 8 and 9: **Under no circumstances buy swollen or leaking cans. The food in a swollen or leaking can may be dangerous to eat or even to taste.**

   The most effective combination of sentences 8 and 9 would include which of the following groups of words?

   (1) which contain food that may be
   (2) and the food in a swollen can
   (3) since the food in a swollen can
   (4) being dangerous to eat
   (5) that may be dangerous to eat

9. Which of the following is the thesis statement for the passage?

   (1) sentence 1
   (2) sentence 3
   (3) sentence 4
   (4) sentence 10
   (5) none; thesis statement is implied

Questions 10–18 refer to the following paragraphs.

(1) The traditional family grouping will remain dominant, although the people in the family may change because of divorce, separation, and remarriage. (2) The family with dual careers, both husband and wife working, will increase—particularly among the young. (3) The husband and wife family with no children will also increase.

(4) Some couples will choose to remain childless, others will spend the major part of their lifetime with no children present because of the possibilities for spacing and limiting family size.

(5) An increasing number of single-parent families will be formed as a result of divorce, death, abandonment, or the choice of the unwed to rear its children alone. (6) In most cases, the single-parent family will have an employed woman as its head.

GO ON TO THE NEXT PAGE

(7) Because of increased acceptability, more individuals may remain unmarried and establish single households. (8) The single adult living alone will establish close kin or simulated kin networks, relying upon and sharing with others economic and emotional resources to fulfill parentlike roles in an "aunt-uncle" capacity.

(9) These family forms will present different issues and problems for family members.

(10) Families will need information to select wisely the family pattern they want to pursue.

10. Sentence 1: **The traditional family grouping will remain <u>dominant, although</u> the people in the family may change because of divorce, separation, and remarriage.**

Which of the following is the best way to write the underlined portion of this sentence? If you think the original is the best way, choose option (1).

(1) dominant, although
(2) dominant, indeed
(3) dominant, so
(4) dominant, therefore
(5) dominant, nevertheless

11. Sentences 2 and 3: **The family with dual careers, both husband and wife working, will increase—particularly among the young. The husband and wife family with no children will also increase.**

The most effective combination of sentences 2 and 3 would include which of the following groups of words?

(1) as well as
(2) but
(3) although
(4) nevertheless
(5) therefore

12. Sentence 4: **Some couples will choose to remain <u>childless, others</u> will spend the major part of their lifetime with no children present because of the possibilities for spacing and limiting family size.**

Which of the following is the best way to write the underlined portion of this sentence? If you think the original is the best way, choose option (1).

(1) childless, others
(2) childless. others
(3) childless. Others
(4) childless; Others
(5) childless: others

13. Sentence 5: **An increasing number of single-parent families will be formed as a result of divorce, death, abandonment, or the choice of the unwed to rear its children alone.**

What correction should be made to this sentence?

(1) change <u>its</u> to <u>their</u>
(2) change the spelling of <u>families</u> to <u>familys</u>
(3) remove the comma after <u>abandonment</u>
(4) change <u>rear</u> to <u>raise</u>
(5) no correction is necessary

14. Sentence 6: **In most cases, the single-parent family will have an employed woman as its head.**

What correction should be made to this sentence?

(1) remove the comma after <u>cases</u>
(2) remove the hyphen in <u>single-parent</u>
(3) change <u>will have</u> to <u>has</u>
(4) change <u>its</u> to <u>it's</u>
(5) no change is necessary

GO ON TO THE NEXT PAGE

TEST 1: LANGUAGE ARTS, WRITING, PART I

15. Sentence 7: **Because of increased acceptability, more individuals may remain unmarried and establish single households.**

    What correction should be made to this sentence?

    (1) change the spelling of <u>acceptability</u> to <u>acceptibility</u>
    (2) remove the comma after <u>acceptability</u>
    (3) change <u>may remain</u> to <u>will remain</u>
    (4) insert a comma after <u>unmarried</u>
    (5) no correction is necessary

16. Sentence 8: **The single adult living alone will establish close kin or simulated kin networks, relying upon and sharing with others economic and emotional resources to fulfill parentlike roles in an "aunt-uncle" capacity.**

    What correction should be made to this sentence?

    (1) add a comma after <u>close kin</u>
    (2) remove the comma after <u>networks</u>
    (3) change the spelling of <u>resources</u> to <u>resourses</u>
    (4) change <u>to fulfill</u> to <u>fulfilling</u>
    (5) no correction is necessary

17. A new paragraph can

    (1) not be started
    (2) be started after sentence 2
    (3) be started after sentence 5
    (4) be started after sentence 6
    (5) be started before sentence 8

18. Sentence 10: **Families will need information to select wisely the family pattern they want to pursue.**

    What correction should be made to this sentence?

    (1) change <u>will need</u> to <u>will be needing</u>
    (2) change <u>select wisely</u> to <u>wisely select</u>
    (3) change the spelling of <u>pattern</u> to <u>pattren</u>
    (4) change the spelling of <u>pursue</u> to <u>persue</u>
    (5) no correction is necessary

GO ON TO THE NEXT PAGE

TEST 1: LANGUAGE ARTS, WRITING, PART I

<u>Questions 19–27</u> refer to the following paragraphs.

(A)

(1) Drug abuse is like a communicable disease. (2) It spreads—by example, by word of mouth, and by imitation. (3) Drug abuse is certainly increasing, but so is the number of young people who have tried drugs and want out. (4) As we provide treatment services for them, these young people become able to tell other youth that the drug scene is not as great as they thought it was before they got hooked. (5) And, of greater importance, they are believed by they're contemporaries before experimentation becomes habit.

(B)

(6) Parents can help prevent drug usage by setting an example, by knowledge, and by understanding. (7) If they are to talk to their children about drugs they must be informed. (8) usually they know far less about drugs than do their children. (9) Ideally, before their child is tempted to experiment, they will be able to explain to him the undesirability of the drugged life. (10) What is even more convincing to young people, they will have been able to communicate to him the actual damage that a drug abuser does to their body.

19. Sentences 1 and 2: **Drug abuse is like a communicable disease. It spreads—by example, by word of mouth, and by imitation.**

    The most effective combination of sentences 1 and 2 would include which of the following groups of words?

    (1) disease. it spreads
    (2) disease although it spreads
    (3) disease yet it spreads
    (4) disease that spreads
    (5) disease having spread

20. Sentence 3: **Drug abuse is certainly increasing, but so is the number of young people who have tried drugs and want out.**

    What correction should be made to this sentence?

    (1) remove the comma after <u>increasing</u>
    (2) change <u>but</u> to <u>and</u>
    (3) change <u>number</u> to <u>amount</u>
    (4) insert a comma after <u>people</u>
    (5) no correction is necessary

21. Sentence 4: **As we provide treatment services for them, these young people become able to tell other youth that the drug scene is not as great as they thought it was before they got hooked.**

    What correction should be made to this sentence?

    (1) change <u>As</u> to <u>Although</u>
    (2) remove the comma after <u>them</u>
    (3) change <u>become</u> to <u>became</u>
    (4) change <u>thought</u> to <u>think</u>
    (5) no correction is necessary

22. Sentence 5: **And, of greater importance, they are believed by they're contemporaries before experimentation becomes habit.**

    What correction should be made to this sentence?

    (1) remove the commas before <u>of</u> and after <u>importance</u>
    (2) change <u>they're</u> to <u>their</u>
    (3) insert commas before <u>by</u> and after <u>contemporaries</u>
    (4) change <u>becomes</u> to <u>will become</u>
    (5) no correction is necessary

GO ON TO THE NEXT PAGE

TEST 1: LANGUAGE ARTS, WRITING, PART I

23. Sentence 6: **Parents can help prevent drug usage by setting an example, by knowledge, and by understanding.**

    What correction should be made to this sentence?

    (1) change <u>can</u> to <u>could</u>
    (2) change <u>by setting an example</u> to <u>by example</u>
    (3) change the spelling of <u>knowledge</u> to <u>knowlege</u>
    (4) remove the comma before <u>and</u>
    (5) no correction is necessary

24. Sentence 7: **If they are to talk to their children about drugs they must be informed.**

    What correction should be made to this sentence?

    (1) change <u>are to</u> to <u>would</u>
    (2) change <u>their</u> to <u>they're</u>
    (3) insert a comma after <u>drugs</u>
    (4) change <u>informed</u> to <u>informative</u>
    (5) no correction is necessary

25. Sentences 7 and 8: **If they are to talk to their children about drugs they must be <u>informed. usually</u> they know far less about drugs than do their children.**

    Which of the following is the best way to write the underlined portion of this sentence? If you think the original is the best way, choose option (1).

    (1) informed. usually
    (2) informed usually
    (3) informed: usually
    (4) informed—Usually
    (5) informed. Usually

26. Sentence 9: **Ideally, before their child is tempted to experiment, they will be able to explain to him the undesirability of the drugged life.**

    What correction should be made to this sentence?

    (1) change the spelling of <u>ideally</u> to <u>idealy</u>
    (2) remove the comma before <u>before</u>
    (3) change <u>be able</u> to <u>have been able</u>
    (4) change the spelling of <u>undesirability</u> to <u>undesireability</u>
    (5) no correction is necessary

27. Sentence 10: **What is even more convincing to young people, they will have been able to communicate to him the actual damage that a drug abuser does to their body.**

    What correction should be made to this sentence?

    (1) move <u>even</u> to after <u>convincing</u>
    (2) remove the comma after <u>people</u>
    (3) change the spelling of <u>communicate</u> to <u>comunicate</u>
    (4) change <u>their</u> to <u>his</u>
    (5) no change is necessary

GO ON TO THE NEXT PAGE

TEST 1: LANGUAGE ARTS, WRITING, PART I

Questions 28–37 refer to the following paragraphs.

(A)

(1) Statistically, by far the most common type of home accidents are falls. (2) Each year thousands of americans meet death in this way, within the four walls of their home or in yards around their house. (3) Nine out of ten of the victims is over 65, but people of all ages experience serious injuries as a result of home falls. (4) It is impossible to estimate how many injuries result from falls, but it must run into the millions.

(B)

(5) Falls can be a problem for all ages. (6) In the process of growing up, children or teenagers often will fall. (7) Fortunately their bodies are supple, so they may suffer only skinned knees bumps, and bruises. (8) In an older person, however, the same fall may cause a broken arm, leg, or hip, or other injury that requires hospitalization or Medical care. (9) As you get older, you may not fall any more often but the results usually are more serious and may even be fatal.

(C)

(10) Adults fall because they don't look where they're going, are in a hurry, are careless, or thinking about something else. (11) A few inexpensive items such as a suction-type rubber mat or safety strips in the tub, a non-slip mat on the floor, and bathtub handholds can go a long way toward eliminating falls in the bathroom.

28. Sentence 1: **Statistically, by far the most common type of home accidents are falls.**

    What correction should be made to this sentence?

    (1) change the spelling of <u>Statistically</u> to <u>Statisticly</u>
    (2) remove the comma before <u>by</u>
    (3) insert a comma after <u>accidents</u>
    (4) change <u>are</u> to <u>is</u>
    (5) no correction is necessary

29. Sentence 2: **Each year thousands of americans meet death in this way, within the four walls of their home or in yards around their house.**

    What correction should be made to this sentence?

    (1) change <u>americans</u> to <u>Americans</u>
    (2) remove the comma after <u>way</u>
    (3) change <u>within</u> to <u>in</u>
    (4) insert a comma after <u>home</u>
    (5) no correction is necessary

30. Sentence 3: **Nine out of ten of the victims is over 65, but people of all ages experience serious injuries as a result of home falls.**

    What correction should be made to this sentence?

    (1) remove the comma after <u>65</u>
    (2) change <u>is</u> to <u>are</u>
    (3) change <u>but</u> to <u>and</u>
    (4) change <u>experience</u> to <u>experiance</u>
    (5) no correction is necessary

31. Sentence 4: **It is impossible to estimate how many injuries result from falls, but it must run into the millions.**

    What correction should be made to this sentence?

    (1) change <u>it must run</u> to <u>they must run</u>
    (2) change <u>result</u> to <u>results</u>
    (3) remove the comma after <u>falls</u>
    (4) change <u>but</u> to <u>since</u>
    (5) no correction is necessary

GO ON TO THE NEXT PAGE

TEST 1: LANGUAGE ARTS, WRITING, PART I

32. Sentences 5 and 6: **Falls can be a problem for all <u>ages. In</u> the process of growing up, children or teenagers often will fall.**

    Which of the following is the best way to write the underlined portion of this sentence? If you think the original is the best way, choose option (1).

    (1) ages. In
    (2) ages. in
    (3) ages: In
    (4) ages: in
    (5) ages; In

33. Sentence 7: **Fortunately their bodies are supple, so they may suffer only skinned knees bumps, and bruises.**

    What correction should be made to this sentence?

    (1) change the spelling of <u>Fortunately</u> to <u>Fortunitely</u>
    (2) remove the comma after <u>supple</u>
    (3) change <u>suffer only</u> to <u>only suffer</u>
    (4) insert a comma after <u>knees</u>
    (5) no correction is necessary

34. Sentence 8: **In an older person, however, the same fall may cause a broken arm, leg, or hip, or other injury that requires hospitalization or Medical care.**

    What correction should be made to this sentence?

    (1) remove the commas around <u>however</u>
    (2) change <u>Medical</u> to <u>medical</u>
    (3) insert a colon after <u>cause</u>
    (4) change <u>requires</u> to <u>require</u>
    (5) no correction is necessary

35. Sentence 9: **As you get older, you may not fall any more often but the results usually are more serious and may even be fatal.**

    What correction should be made to this sentence?

    (1) change <u>As</u> to <u>When</u>
    (2) change <u>get</u> to <u>will get</u>
    (3) insert a comma after <u>often</u>
    (4) change <u>more</u> to <u>most</u>
    (5) no correction is necessary

36. Sentence 10: **Adults fall because they don't look where they're going, are in a hurry, are careless, or thinking about something else.**

    What correction should be made to this sentence?

    (1) change <u>don't</u> to <u>doesn't</u>
    (2) change <u>they're</u> to <u>there</u>
    (3) remove the <u>comma</u> after <u>hurry</u>
    (4) insert <u>are</u> before <u>thinking</u>
    (5) no correction is necessary

37. A new paragraph can

    (1) be started after sentence 10
    (2) be started after sentence 8
    (3) be started after sentence 5
    (4) be started after sentence 3
    (5) not be started

GO ON TO THE NEXT PAGE

TEST 1: LANGUAGE ARTS, WRITING, PART I

Questions 38–46 refer to the following paragraphs.

(A)

(1) The only known cure for bikomania, a highly contagious fever sweeping the country from coast to coast, is to ride a bike. (2) Nearly 100 million happy victims, including mom and pop and the kids, now are taking this delightful treatment and pedaling their two-wheelers into an exciting new world of fun and adventure.

(B)

(3) Why buy a bike? Partly because riding a bike benefits both you and you're environment. (4) A bike doesn't foul up the air, makes no noise, keeps you in top physical shape, takes up little room on the road. and is easy to park in a small space. (5) With appropriate accessory's—such as saddle bags, luggage racks, or baskets—a bike can be used on shopping missions, picnic excursions, or bicycle tours.

(C)

(6) What kind of bike should you get? (7) Bewildered by the tantalizing display of racing models with 10-speed gearshifts and lots of fancy gimmicks, your apt to plunge into something you really don't need. (8) Best advice: buy the simplest model that meets your transportation requirements. (9) You need not invest in dropped handlebars, multigear ratios, and special frames that may be too complicated for your purposes.

(D)

(10) Try renting a bike before you buy one. (11) Spend a couple of weekends pedaling various makes over typical terrain in your area; this tryout will answer many of your questions.

38. Sentence 1 should be

    (1) left as it is
    (2) moved after sentence 8
    (3) moved after sentence 5
    (4) moved after sentence 3
    (5) omitted

39. Sentence 2: **Nearly 100 million happy victims, including mom and pop and the kids, now are taking this delightful treatment and pedaling their two-wheelers into an exciting new world of fun and adventure.**

    What correction should be made to this sentence?

    (1) remove the comma after <u>victims</u>
    (2) capitalize <u>mom, pop</u>
    (3) capitalize <u>kids</u>
    (4) change the spelling of <u>exciting</u> to <u>exsiting</u>
    (5) no correction is necessary

40. Sentence 3: **Why buy a bike? Partly because riding a bike benefits both you and you're environment.**

    What correction should be made to this sentence?

    (1) change <u>buy</u> to <u>by</u>
    (2) insert a comma after <u>and</u>
    (3) remove the question mark after <u>bike</u>
    (4) change <u>you're</u> to <u>your</u>
    (5) no correction is necessary

41. Sentence 4: **A bike doesn't foul up the air, makes no noise, keeps you in top physical shape, takes up little room on the <u>road. and</u> is easy to park in a small space.**

    Which of the following is the best way to write the underlined portion of this sentence? If you think the original is the best way, choose option (1).

    (1) road. and
    (2) road. And
    (3) road, and
    (4) road, And
    (5) road: and

GO ON TO THE NEXT PAGE

TEST 1: LANGUAGE ARTS, WRITING, PART I

42. Sentence 5: **With appropriate accessory's—such as saddle bags, luggage racks, or baskets—a bike can be used on shopping missions, picnic excursions, or bicycle tours.**

What correction should be made to this sentence?

(1) change <u>accessory's</u> to <u>accessories</u>
(2) remove the dashes before <u>such</u> and after <u>baskets</u>
(3) remove the comma after <u>bags</u>
(4) change the spelling of <u>excursions</u> to <u>excurshuns</u>
(5) no change is necessary

43. Sentence 7: **Bewildered by the tantalizing display of racing models with 10-speed gearshifts and lots of fancy gimmicks, your apt to plunge into something you really don't need.**

What correction should be made to this sentence?

(1) insert commas before <u>with</u> and after <u>gearshifts</u>
(2) remove the comma after <u>gimmicks</u>
(3) change the spelling of <u>your</u> to <u>you're</u>
(4) change the spelling of <u>really</u> to <u>realy</u>
(5) no correction is necessary

44. Sentence 8: **<u>Best advice: buy</u> the simplest model that meets your transportation requirements.**

Which of the following is the best way to write the underlined portion of this sentence? If you think the original is the best way, choose option (1).

(1) Best advice: buy
(2) Best advice; Buy
(3) Best advice; buy
(4) Best advice, Buy
(5) Best advice, buy

45. Sentence 9: **You need not invest in dropped handlebars, multigear ratios, and special frames that may be too complicated for your purposes.**

If you rewrote sentence 9 beginning with

<u>Nor need you</u>

the next words should be

(1) invest in
(2) dropped handlebars
(3) multigear ratios
(4) that may be
(5) for your purposes

46. A new paragraph can be

(1) started after sentence 9
(2) started after sentence 7
(3) started after sentence 4
(4) started after sentence 3
(5) not be started

GO ON TO THE NEXT PAGE

TEST 1: LANGUAGE ARTS, WRITING, PART I

<u>Questions 47–50</u> refer to the following paragraphs.

(A)

(1) At every stage of development, clothes can help establish a person's identity for himself and for those with who he interacts. (2) The childhood game of "dressing up" in parents' clothes provides an opportunity for the child to practice the roles he will be expected to play in adult life.

(B)

(3) The degree to which a person chooses clothes that fit the roles will affect his performance in those roles.

(C)

(4) Clothes are an important factor in developing feelings of self-confidence and self-respect. (5) When you look good, you feel good. (6) For most people, clothes are often a source of positive reaction from others, since in our culture we are more apt to compliment a person on his appearance than on other aspects of the "self."

(D)

(7) Most Americans also recognize that a proper appearance and proper dress are the keys to association with the right crowd, which in turn opens the door to job advancement increased income, and greater prestige.

(E)

(8) Our clothing needs are influenced by a multitude of circumstances. (9) Buying motives are seldom simple.

(F)

(10) The first step in the decision-making process is to make a conscious ordering of the things that are important to us. (11) If a person recognizes and accepts the priorities of his values—for example, that his status and prestige may be more important than his physical comfort—his choice of clothing is not only simplified, but more likely to bring him greater satisfaction.

47. Sentence 1: **At every stage of development, clothes can help establish a person's identity for himself and for those with who he interacts.**

What correction should be made to this sentence?

(1) change the spelling of <u>development</u> to <u>developement</u>
(2) remove the comma after <u>development</u>
(3) insert a comma after <u>himself</u>
(4) change <u>who</u> to <u>whom</u>
(5) no correction is necessary

48. A new paragraph can

(1) be started after sentence 8
(2) be started after sentence 5
(3) be started after sentence 4
(4) be started after sentence 1
(5) not be started

49. The thesis statement of the passage is

(1) sentence 1
(2) sentence 2
(3) sentence 7
(4) sentence 11
(5) implied

50. Sentences 4 and 5: **Clothes are an important factor in developing feelings of self-confidence and self-respect. When you look good, you feel good.**

The most effective combination of sentences 4 and 5 would include which of the following groups of words?

(1) self-respect, moreover, when
(2) self-respect, although, when
(3) self-respect, nevertheless, when
(4) self-respect, therefore, when
(5) self-respect, since, when

GO ON TO THE NEXT PAGE

TEST 1: LANGUAGE ARTS, WRITING, PART II

This part of the Language Arts, Writing test is intended to determine how well you write. You are asked to write an essay that explains something, presents an opinion on an issue, or concentrates on retelling a personal experience.

PROMPT

Throughout one's life there is usually someone who has influenced us in such a way that leaves a lasting postive impression. This may have been a family member, teacher, or special friend who may have helped you through a rough time. Because of this person's influence, you may feel that your life has become richer in ways of personal happiness or success.

DISCUSSION QUESTION

Think of one person in your life who has been an influence to you in such a way that your life is better today. Why has this person been such an influence on you?

Directions

Write an essay of about 250 words in which you present your reasons on this topic. Give supporting details and examples for each reason in your essay. You have 45 minutes to write on this topic.

CHECK YOURSELF

- Read carefully the prompt, discussion question, and directions.
- Decide if the prompt is expository, persuasive, or narrative.
- Plan your essay before you begin.
- Use scratch paper to prepare a simple outline.
- Write your essay on the lined pages of a separate answer sheet.
- Read carefully what you have written and make needed changes.
- Check for focus, elaboration, organization, conventions, and integration.

END OF EXAMINATION

TEST 2: SOCIAL STUDIES

Directions

The Social Studies test consists of multiple-choice questions intended to measure general social studies concepts. The questions are based on short readings that often include a graph, chart, photograph, or figure. Study the information given and then answer the question(s) following it. Refer to the information as often as necessary in answering the questions.

You should spend no more than 70 minutes answering the questions. Work carefully, but do not spend too much time on any one question. Be sure you answer every question. You will not be penalized for incorrect answers.

To record your answers, mark the numbered space on the answer sheet beside the number that corresponds to the question in the test.

FOR EXAMPLE:

Early colonists of North America looked for settlement sites that had adequate water supplies and were accessible by ship. For this reason, many early towns were built near

(1) mountains
(2) prairies
(3) rivers
(4) glaciers
(5) plateaus

① ② ● ④ ⑤

The correct answer is "rivers"; therefore, answer space 3 would be marked on the answer sheet.

GO ON TO THE NEXT PAGE

TEST 2: SOCIAL STUDIES

Questions 1–3 are based on the following passage.

The term *genocide*, a joining of the Greek *genos*, meaning race or tribe, and the Latin suffix *-cide*, or killing, was coined in 1946 by a distinguished international legal scholar, Professor Raphael Lemkin.

The mass murder of six million Jews by the Nazis was the most vivid, violent, and tragic expression of genocide. But this century alone has seen others—Armenians, Gypsies, Chinese, Slavs. Some 20 million people have been slaughtered because of their racial, religious, or ethnic backgrounds.

In the language of the United Nations Convention on the Prevention and Punishment of the Crime of Genocide, *genocide* means certain specifically defined acts *"committed with intent to destroy, in whole or in part, a national, ethnical, racial or religious group, as such."*

1. The word *genocide* literally means

   (1) mass murder
   (2) race killing
   (3) slaughter
   (4) convention
   (5) ratification

2. According to this passage, genocide involves intent to destroy *all* of the following EXCEPT

   (1) nations
   (2) races
   (3) ethnic groups
   (4) political groups
   (5) religious groups

3. All of the following have been subjected to genocide EXCEPT

   (1) Jews
   (2) Nazis
   (3) Slavs
   (4) Gypsies
   (5) Chinese

Questions 4–6 are based on the following passage.

We come then to the question presented: Does segregation of children in public schools solely on the basis of race, even though the physical facilities and other "tangible" factors may be equal, deprive the children of the minority group of equal educational opportunities? We believe that it does.

"Segregation of white and colored children in public schools has a detrimental effect upon the colored children. A sense of inferiority affects the motivation of a child to learn. Segregation with the sanction of law, therefore, has a tendency to [retard] the educational and mental development of Negro children and to deprive them of some of the benefits they would receive in a racial[ly] integrated school system."

Whatever may have been the extent of psychological knowledge at the time of *Plessy v. Ferguson*, this finding of the Kansas court is amply supported by modern authority. Any language in *Plessy v. Ferguson* contrary to this finding is rejected. We conclude that in the field of public education the doctrine of "separate but equal" has no place.

4. "We" (first paragraph) refers to

   (1) the plaintiff
   (2) the defendant
   (3) the Congress
   (4) the Supreme Court
   (5) Plessy and Ferguson

5. Segregation of children in grade or high school is rejected for

   (1) historical reasons
   (2) political reasons
   (3) physical reasons
   (4) psychological reasons
   (5) economic reasons

GO ON TO THE NEXT PAGE

TEST 2: SOCIAL STUDIES

6. The passage implies that *Plessy v. Ferguson*

   (1) called for integration
   (2) stated that separate facilities were unequal
   (3) was based on outmoded psychology
   (4) was constitutional
   (5) applied only to private schools

7. This photograph is known for how it

   (1) sparked additional protest against America's involvement in the Vietnam War
   (2) showed American soldiers murdering innocent civilians in Vietnam
   (3) showed the inhumane treatment of the Koreans by the Americans
   (4) showed the careless judgment of a soldier
   (5) falsely represented Americans who hated the Vietnam War

8. "Without our two great political parties cutting across economic and geographic interests, democracy as we know it could never have been made to function." The author of this statement probably meant to suggest that

   (1) political parties in the United States tend to represent sectional interests
   (2) each political party appeals to a different social class
   (3) there is no significant difference between the Democratic and Republican parties
   (4) an important feature of the U.S. political system is the broadly based appeal of the two political parties
   (5) only a two-party system can function in a democracy

Question 9 is based on the following cartoon.

9. What is the main idea of this 1994 cartoon?

   (1) White South Africans can no longer vote in their own country.
   (2) Free elections are the key to true democracy in South Africa.
   (3) People who fail to vote in South Africa's elections may be arrested.
   (4) Blacks can control elections by casting multiple votes.
   (5) Slavery has been abolished in South Africa.

GO ON TO THE NEXT PAGE

TEST 2: SOCIAL STUDIES

Questions 10–11 are based on the following graph.

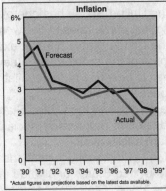

Source: *The New York Times*

Questions 12 and 13 are based on the following graph.

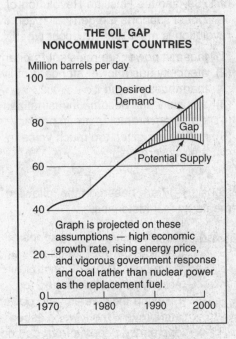

10. Forecasts of economic growth have consistently

   (1) overestimated economic growth from 1990–1998
   (2) underestimated economic growth from 1990–1998
   (3) overestimated economic growth from 1996–1999
   (4) underestimated economic growth from 1996–1999
   (5) forecast correctly economic growth from 1990–1999

11. Forecasts of economists have

   (1) overestimated inflation
   (2) underestimated inflation
   (3) generally been accurate on inflation
   (4) been less accurate than forecasts of economic growth
   (5) been as accurate as those for economic growth

12. Based on the information in the graph, the demand of noncommunist countries for oil will begin to exceed the supply of oil in about the year

   (1) 1980
   (2) 1985
   (3) 1990
   (4) 1995
   (5) 2000

13. A valid conclusion that can be drawn from the data in the graph is that the noncommunist countries (western Europe and Japan) would

   (1) have serious economic problems if alternative sources of energy are not developed
   (2) avoid any gap between oil supply and demand by increasing oil production
   (3) have until the year 2000 to make major changes in energy policies
   (4) be unable to solve their energy problems
   (5) use less oil because of its high price

GO ON TO THE NEXT PAGE

TEST 2: SOCIAL STUDIES

14. A study of the causes of the American Revolution of 1776, the French Revolution of 1789, and the Russian Revolution of 1917 best supports the generalization that revolution is most likely to occur when

    (1) those in power are resistant to change
    (2) a society has a lower standard of living than those around it
    (3) a society has become industrialized
    (4) stable governments are in power
    (5) people are given too much voice in their government

Questions 15–17 are based on the following statements by four historians.

Speaker A: American history is a series of conflicts between the haves and have-nots. Those in control of our society have always tried to maintain their wealth and power and prevent the lower classes and oppressed peoples from getting justice.

Speaker B: The American experience is unique in the story of nations. Due especially to the presence of a large, unused frontier during most of our history, we have been spared many of the problems and conflicts found in the rest of the world.

Speaker C: American history is a series of compromises between groups who have disagreed, but never over basic issues. From the writing of the Constitution to the decision to withdraw from Vietnam, extremists have represented only a minority view; the majority of the American people have usually favored compromise and moderate solutions to problems.

Speaker D: In every crisis of American history a great person, often a president, has risen above party politics and personal interest to lead the nation in the direction of greatness. We owe everything to those famous Americans who have governed us in the past.

15. Which speakers would be most likely to agree that the American Revolution cannot be compared with the French Revolution because the American Revolution did not involve a basic class struggle?

    (1) *A* and *D*
    (2) *B* and *C*
    (3) *B* and *D*
    (4) *C* and *D*
    (5) *A* and *C*

16. With which statement about the United States would Speaker *B* most likely agree?

    (1) The United States has one of the highest crime rates in the world.
    (2) The United States has not experienced some of the problems of other nations, mainly because of the availability of space.
    (3) Large cities in the United States tend to have more progressive social policies than small towns.
    (4) Many of the social institutions found in the United States originated in Europe.
    (5) The United States has few social problems.

17. The most valid inference to be drawn from the statements of the four speakers is that

    (1) all the facts should be known before a conclusion is drawn
    (2) historians must be free of personal bias
    (3) a study of history enables people to predict future events
    (4) historians disagree over interpretation of events
    (5) only one of the speakers is correct in his views

GO ON TO THE NEXT PAGE

TEST 2: SOCIAL STUDIES

Question 18 is based on the following chart.

18. Which is a valid conclusion that can be drawn from the information in the chart?

(1) The main purpose of the system illustrated was to benefit the colonies.
(2) Nationalism was the motivating factor in English colonization.
(3) The profit motive was a strong force in colonization.
(4) The opportunity to own land attracted many settlers to the colonies.
(5) Inducements were offered to prospective settlers.

Questions 19 and 20 are based on the following passage.

The task of economic policy is to create a prosperous America. The *unfinished task of prosperous Americans is to build a Great Society.*

Our accomplishments have been many; these tasks remain unfinished:
—to achieve full employment without inflation;
—to restore external equilibrium and defend the dollar;
—to enhance the efficiency and flexibility of our private and public economies;
—to widen the benefits of prosperity;
—to improve the quality of American life . . .

—Lyndon B. Johnson

19. Former President Lyndon B. Johnson felt that the most important first step in the war against poverty is

(1) full employment
(2) a sound dollar
(3) private and public economics
(4) our natural defense
(5) efficiency in government

20. The speech implies that America's prosperity

(1) is threatened
(2) is at its peak
(3) must be retained
(4) must be broadened
(5) threatened Johnson's war against poverty

Questions 21 and 22 are based on the following cartoon.

GO ON TO THE NEXT PAGE

TEST 2: SOCIAL STUDIES

21. Which aspect of the United States Government is best illustrated by the cartoon?

   (1) system of checks and balances
   (2) veto power of the president
   (3) congressional committee system
   (4) civilian control of the military
   (5) veto power of the Senate

22. The actions of the Senate are authorized

   (1) by the president
   (2) by popular vote
   (3) by the Constitution
   (4) by the Bill of Rights
   (5) by the House of Representatives

Questions 23–25 are based on the following chart.

Nations	Birthrate (per 1000 females)	Infant Mortality Rate (per 1000 births)
Uganda	51	104
Somalia	50	122
Angola	47	137
Cambodia	46	112
Ethiopia	46	110
Pakistan	40	109
Canada	14	6.8
France	13	6.7
Denmark	13	6.6
Italy	10	8.3
Germany	10	5.9
Japan	10	4.4

Source: Information Please Almanac, 1995
(est. mid-1994)

23. Which is a valid generalization based on the information in the chart?

   (1) In developing nations, the infant mortality rate decreases as the birthrate increases.
   (2) Industrialized nations have lower birthrates and infant mortality rates than developing nations.
   (3) Decreasing the infant mortality rate will limit population growth in developing nations.
   (4) Industrialized nations have higher population densities than developing nations.
   (5) Developing nations have ten times the infant mortality of industrialized nations.

24. According to the chart, the lowest birthrates are found mostly in

   (1) western Europe
   (2) Southeast Asia
   (3) North America
   (4) Africa
   (5) Latin America

GO ON TO THE NEXT PAGE

TEST 2: SOCIAL STUDIES

25. According to the chart, the highest infant mortality rates are in

    (1) western Europe
    (2) Southeast Asia
    (3) North America
    (4) Africa
    (5) Latin America

26. From the point of view of an environmentalist, which is probably the most significant argument against offshore drilling for oil?

    (1) There is little need to take such natural resources from the ocean waters.
    (2) Oil corporations are falsely advertising an oil shortage in order to expand their drilling operations.
    (3) The potential oil to be found is not worth the capital investment needed to extract it.
    (4) The possible harm to the balance of nature is more important than a gain in energy.
    (5) Coal is a preferable resource to oil.

27. Topography deals with surface features of a region, including its landforms and rivers, lakes, etc., and with man-made features such as canals, bridges, and roads. According to this definition, the topography of a region includes its

    (1) climate
    (2) plants
    (3) animals
    (4) mountains
    (5) inhabitants

Questions 28–30 are based on the following passage.

A Continental army and Congress composed of men from all the states, by freely mixing together, were assimilated into one mass. Individuals of both, mingling with the citizens, spread principles of union among them. Local prejudices lessened. By frequent contact, a foundation was laid for the establishment of a nation out of varied materials. Intermarriages between men and women of different states were much more common than before the war, and became an additional cement to the Union. Unreasonable jealousies had existed between the inhabitants of the eastern and of the southern states; but on becoming better acquainted with each other, these in a great measure subsided. A wiser policy prevailed. Men of liberal minds led the way in discouraging local differences, and the great body of the people, as soon as reason got the better of prejudice, found that their best interests would be best promoted by union.

28. The passage deals principally with the

    (1) prejudices in America at the time of the Revolution
    (2) frictions between the sections during the Revolution
    (3) positive social and political results of the Revolution
    (4) triumph of union over local differences
    (5) fear of the Church of England

29. Prior to the Revolution

    (1) a spirit of cooperation existed in the colonies
    (2) reason prevailed over prejudice
    (3) regional rivalry was present
    (4) most Americans knew one another
    (5) religious freedom was the general rule

GO ON TO THE NEXT PAGE

TEST 2: SOCIAL STUDIES

30. The passage implies that

    (1) self-interest has little to do with prejudice
    (2) social contact helps do away with prejudice
    (3) Americans were generally very much alike
    (4) trade discourages social contact
    (5) Congress was a divisive instrument

Questions 31–33 are based on the following passage.

Since the days when the fleet of Columbus sailed into the waters of the New World, America has been another name for opportunity, and the people of the United States have taken their tone from the possibilities of expansion open to them. But never again will such gifts of free land offer themselves. Each frontier did indeed furnish a new field of opportunity, a gate of escape from the bondage of the past. What the Mediterranean Sea was to the Greeks, breaking the bond of custom, offering new experiences, calling out new institutions and activities, that, and more, the ever-retreating frontier has been to the United States. And now, four centuries from the discovery of America, at the end of a hundred years of life under the Constitution, the frontier has gone, and with its going has closed the first period of American history.

31. The term *frontier* as used in this passage means

    (1) the New World
    (2) American energy
    (3) movement
    (4) the expansive nature of American life
    (5) the availability of free land

32. The attitude of the author to the frontier is one of

    (1) admiration
    (2) regret
    (3) indifference
    (4) restraint
    (5) suspicion

33. References in the passage lead to the conclusion that it was written approximately in the year

    (1) 1865
    (2) 1875
    (3) 1890
    (4) 1900
    (5) 1920

GO ON TO THE NEXT PAGE

TEST 2: SOCIAL STUDIES

Questions 34 and 35 are based on the following cartoon.

34. Which political system is referred to in the cartoon?

    (1) feudalism
    (2) monarchy
    (3) democracy
    (4) communism
    (5) fascism

35. The "giant lumbering creature" symbolized by the hammer and sickle is

    (1) NATO
    (2) OPEC
    (3) the USSR
    (4) OAS
    (5) the UN

36. Which statement best illustrates the principle of multiple causation of human behavior?

    (1) To each according to his or her needs.
    (2) Environment and heredity are constantly interacting.
    (3) Geographic differences account for variations in civilizations.
    (4) Wealth and power go together.
    (5) Habit results from repeated acts.

Questions 37 and 38 are based on the following passage.

Since 1750, about the beginning of the Age of Steam, the earth's population has more than tripled. This increase has not been an evolutionary phenomenon with biological causes. Yet there was an evolution—it took place in the world's economic organization. Thus 1,500,000,000 more human beings can now remain alive on the earth's surface, can support themselves by working for others who in turn work for them. This extraordinary tripling of human population in six short generations is explained by the speeded-up economic unification that took place during the same period. Thus most of us are now kept alive by this vast cooperative unified world society.

GO ON TO THE NEXT PAGE

TEST 2: SOCIAL STUDIES

37. The writer considers trade necessary for

    (1) travel
    (2) democracy
    (3) political unity
    (4) self-preservation
    (5) the theory of evolution

38. The basic change that led to the greatly increased population involves

    (1) new explorations
    (2) economic factors
    (3) biological factors
    (4) an increase in travel
    (5) the growth of world government

39. The number of Native American men and women in professional life has multiplied remarkably in the past generation. Movement back and forth from the Native American to the white world has become freer. At the same time, the long-standing conviction that sooner or later all Indians would become totally assimilated into the standardized stream of American life has steadily lost ground. Most experts today feel that Native American tribes and communities will retain separate identities for a long, long time into the future—and most experts believe that is good, not bad.

    There is a difference of opinion regarding Native Americans'

    (1) status as wards of the United States
    (2) status as citizens
    (3) assimilation into American life
    (4) property holdings
    (5) tribes and communities

40. "The parties agree that an armed attack against one or more of them in Europe or North America shall be considered an attack against them all. . . ."

    This quotation is most closely associated with which concept?

    (1) collective security
    (2) intervention
    (3) ultimatum
    (4) appeasement
    (5) aggression

41. Social mobility refers to a society in which an individual can and often does change in social status. Which best illustrates social mobility in the United States?

    (1) A midwestern farm family buys a farm in California.
    (2) The son of a president of a large manufacturing plant becomes a company executive.
    (3) The daughter of an unskilled immigrant worker becomes a teacher.
    (4) A woman whose parents are both college professors receives a graduate degree.
    (5) A New Yorker moves to Boston.

42. Cultural diversity, a variety of cultural patterns, is generally the result of

    (1) actions by the government of the area
    (2) the desire of the inhabitants to develop original ideas and styles
    (3) competition among the people for control of food sources
    (4) migrations to the area by various groups
    (5) reciprocal regional agreements

43. Culture shock is the confusion experienced by someone encountering unfamiliar surroundings, a strange community, or a different culture. Which situation is the best example of culture shock?

    (1) the refusal of the Amish to drive motor vehicles
    (2) the hippies' rejection of the "Establishment" in the 1960s
    (3) the difference in lifestyles between European and western American Indian tribal groups
    (4) the initial reaction of a U.S. Peace Corps participant arriving in a developing nation
    (5) the generation gap

GO ON TO THE NEXT PAGE

TEST 2: SOCIAL STUDIES

44. An extended family is a group of relatives by blood, marriage, or adoption living in close proximity or together, especially if three generations are involved.

Which is usually a characteristic of societies that have the extended family as their basic unit?

(1) The society tends to be highly industrialized.
(2) The roles of the family members are economically and socially interdependent.
(3) The government usually provides incentives to increase family size.
(4) The functions of the family unit are defined mainly by the government.
(5) The family becomes widely dispersed geographically.

45. Pluralism is the existence within a society of groups distinctive in ethnic origin, cultural patterns, or religion. Maintaining stability in a pluralistic society is difficult because

(1) individuals are often forced to deal with the views of others that may challenge their own ideas
(2) there is usually no well-defined order of governmental authority
(3) new members in the society are often unwilling to obey established laws of the society
(4) the wide variety of citizens' abilities hinders the management of labor resources
(5) there are differing degrees of respect for authority

Questions 46 and 47 are based on the following passage.

Adults who like to think of America's young as a bunch of lazy, cigarette-packing television addicts may be disappointed by a major new study that finds the adolescents in the United States smoke and watch television less than those in many other industrialized nations. The study, conducted by the World Health Organization, finds that American teenagers exercise less than their peers elsewhere. And they eat more junk food. But

American young people measure up rather well, certainly better than they are depicted in much of the mass media.

American children fared well, or at least in the middle, in at least two respects. Eleven-year-olds tried cigarettes at about the same rate as children in other countries. But the 15-year-old Americans smoked less than their counterparts, ranking 24th of 28 in the daily rate of smoking (about 12%). The highest rates were in Austria and France. American youths also watched a little less television than most of their counterparts: 15-year-olds ranked 20th and 11-year-olds ranked 6th.

46. American teenagers, according to the study, are much better than teenagers abroad in their

(1) food habits
(2) exercise habits
(3) smoking habits
(4) image in the mass media
(5) addiction to drugs

47. Fifteen-year-old Americans did better in the study than the 11-year-olds in

(1) exercising
(2) avoiding junk food
(3) avoiding smoking
(4) an addiction to TV
(5) avoiding smoking and watching TV

48. Mountains and coasts have served to restrict settlements; rivers and plains, to extend them. Each of these natural features has placed a characteristic imprint on the society that it dominated, largely fashioning its mode of life, its customs, morals, and temperament.

The passage implies that

(1) mountains and coasts are unfriendly to human beings
(2) mountains and rivers exert equal influences on society
(3) mountains and plains have similar effects on settlement
(4) natural features result from the society that evolves within them
(5) geographic features influence the society that develops

GO ON TO THE NEXT PAGE

TEST 2: SOCIAL STUDIES

<u>Questions 49 and 50</u> are based on the following tables.

TABLE *A*

Question: "Here are two suggestions that people have made to improve stability and order in this country. For each, would you favor or oppose such a step being taken?"

Suggestions	Percent of Public		
	Favor	Oppose	Not Sure
A law should be passed allowing police officers to search a home without a warrant in an emergency, as when they are looking for drugs.	32	65	3
The government should be given authority to use wiretaps and other electronic surveillance to gather evidence against citizens suspected of criminal activity, even if a court does not authorize such activity.	27	68	5

TABLE *B*

Question: "Do you feel the federal government should be allowed to engage in wiretapping and electronic surveillance if, in each case, it had to go to court beforehand to obtain court permission, or don't you feel the federal government should ever be allowed to engage in wiretapping or electronic surveillance?"

Response	Percent of Public
Should be allowed	63
Should not be allowed	28
Not sure	9

---

49. The information in Table *A* indicates that most people questioned

    (1) were undecided on the issues in question
    (2) supported the idea of a search without a warrant only in an emergency
    (3) favored protecting their privacy
    (4) favored permitting the government to investigate their lives
    (5) favored electronic eavesdropping over searches

50. A valid conclusion based on both tables is that the results of opinion surveys

    (1) tend to obscure the issues
    (2) are purposely biased by the pollsters
    (3) can vary according to the way the issue is presented
    (4) show that public attitudes are generally consistent
    (5) tend to be inconclusive

END OF EXAMINATION

TEST 3: SCIENCE

Directions

The Science test consists of multiple-choice questions intended to measure the general concepts in science. The questions are based on short readings that often include a graph, chart, or figure. Study the information given and then answer the question(s) following it. Refer to the information as often as necessary in answering the questions.

You will have 80 minutes to answer the questions. Work carefully, but do not spend too much time on any one question. Be sure you answer every question. You will not be penalized for incorrect answers.

To record your answers, mark the numbered space on the answer sheet beside the number that corresponds to the question in the test.

FOR EXAMPLE:

Which of the following is the smallest unit?

                                            ① ② ● ④ ⑤

(1) solution
(2) molecule
(3) atom
(4) compound
(5) mixture

The correct answer is "atom"; therefore, space 3 would be marked on the answer sheet.

GO ON TO THE NEXT PAGE

TEST 3: SCIENCE

<u>Questions 1–6</u> are based on the following article.

The study of ecology, the branch of biology that deals with the interrelations between living things and their environment, is most important today. The environment must be considered from the point of view of physical factors, such as temperature, soil, and water, and biotic factors, which are the living organisms.

Ecologists organize groups of living things into populations, communities, ecological systems, and the biosphere. A *population* consists of organisms of the same species living together in a given location, such as all the oak trees in a forest or all the frogs of the same species in a pond. A *community* consists of populations of different species, living together and interacting with each other.

The accompanying diagram illustrates a simple community. It pictures a large bottle with a layer of mud on the bottom. The bottle was filled with pond water, and several fish and some green plants were added. The bottle was then made airtight. The members of this community will thrive as long as the balance is maintained.

1. Which of the following consists of a single species?

   (1) biosphere
   (2) community
   (3) ecosystem
   (4) biome
   (5) population

2. The fact that living things can survive in an airtight bottle illustrates the

   (1) need for green plants in our environment
   (2) need for physical factors in a community
   (3) balance within a population
   (4) need for biotic factors in a community
   (5) interrelations between living things and the environment

3. When species of plants and animals are introduced into a new habitat, they often become pests there, even though they were not pests in their native habitats. The most probable reason for this is that in the new habitat they

   (1) have fewer natural enemies
   (2) have a much lower mutation rate
   (3) develop better resistance to the new climate
   (4) learn to use different foods
   (5) have more predators

4. If the airtight container and its contents were weighed each day for several days, it would be found that the total weight would

   (1) increase gradually
   (2) remain the same
   (3) decrease gradually
   (4) decrease for the first few days and then increase
   (5) increase for the first few days and then decrease

GO ON TO THE NEXT PAGE

TEST 3: SCIENCE

5. All of the following are biotic factors affecting the balance of the airtight container EXCEPT

    (1) the concentration of minerals in solution
    (2) the number of fishes in the water
    (3) the kinds of protozoa in the water
    (4) the kinds of plants in the bottle
    (5) the presence of crustaceans in the mud

6. Many different species of organisms interacting in a particular environment is an example of a

    (1) population
    (2) biosphere
    (3) community
    (4) biome
    (5) species

<u>Questions 7–10</u> refer to the following graph.

7. How many months out of the year are gray whales feeding in Arctic waters?

    (1) 1 month
    (2) 2 months
    (3) 3 months
    (4) 5 months
    (5) 8 months

8. At what age do gray whale calves first migrate south?

    (1) 2 months
    (2) 4 months
    (3) 6 months
    (4) 10 months
    (5) 12 months

9. About how many months after conception are gray whale calves born?

    (1) 1 month
    (2) 5 months
    (3) 7 months
    (4) 13 months
    (5) 16 months

10. In its first year of life, how many months will a gray whale calf spend in the waters of Baja California?

    (1) 1 month
    (2) 2 months
    (3) 5 months
    (4) 8 months
    (5) 9 months

    The graph above shows the gray whale's 2-year breeding cycle. Arrow one shows the peak period of fertilization for the whale. Arrow two shows the peak period for births of whale calves, and arrow three shows the period when the whale calves stop drinking milk from their mothers, also known as the weaning period.

GO ON TO THE NEXT PAGE

TEST 3: SCIENCE

Questions 11–15 refer to the following article.

The human brain is a truly amazing organ. It allows us to process signals coming in from our world, such as smells, tastes, sounds, and sights, and it controls our responses to the world around us. From actions we do not think about at all, such as reflexes, to the most complex thought patterns, such as creating music or solving difficult equations, the brain is in charge. All this is done by a 3-pound organ made of 10 billion specialized cells called neurons. The neurons use a combination of electrical and chemical signals to process information and elicit responses.

The brain is actually composed of two sides, or hemispheres, the left and the right. At first glance the two sides appear to be the same, but each has its own specialized areas of function. The left side of the brain is actually what controls the right side of the body, while the right side of the brain is responsible for the left side of the body. In addition, each side of the brain has specific functions it controls. They are summarized in the table below. The two halves of the brain can "communicate" with each other via the *corpus callosum*, a bundle of nerve fibers that connects the two sides. This allows information to pass from one side of the brain to the other.

11. A person who suffered an injury to the right side of her brain would likely have diminished abilities to do which of the following?

 (1) arrange a series of pictures in order
 (2) solve algebraic equations
 (3) keep track of time
 (4) use the right leg and foot
 (5) musical ability

12. Cells that make up the brain are called

 (1) neurons
 (2) hemispheres
 (3) ganglions
 (4) callosums
 (5) processors

13. The left side of the brain controls which of the following functions?

 (1) musical ability
 (2) mathematical reasoning
 (3) holistic thinking
 (4) intuition
 (5) imagination

LEFT HEMISPHERE	**RIGHT HEMISPHERE**
Right side of the body Spoken language Written Language Numerical and mathematical skills Scientific and logical reasoning Linear thinking—ordering and organizing Logic Sense of time	Left side of the body Imaginative thought and synthesis Insight and awareness Musical and artistic skills Three-dimensional thought and analysis Holistic thought Intuition Nonverbal communication

GO ON TO THE NEXT PAGE

TEST 3: SCIENCE

14. A person who suffers a stroke that damages part of her left hemisphere may be able to regain some use of that part of the brain. Which brain structure would probably be responsible for allowing information to pass from the undamaged hemisphere to the damaged one?

    (1) the neurons
    (2) the corpus callosum
    (3) the tissue cells
    (4) the nerve fibers
    (5) the Broca's region

15. Which of the following is/are involved in the transmission of nerve signals?

    I. chemical signals
    II. electrical signals
    III. hemisphere signals

    (1) I only
    (2) II only
    (3) III only
    (4) I and II only
    (5) II and III only

---

16. Scientists admit that they still have a great deal to learn about the human brain. What they do know so far is that the nervous system is composed of neurons that carry signals throughout the body. The junction between neurons is called a synapse. A long, thin part of the neuron, called an axon, actually carries the signal. Unlike the wires in an electrical circuit, which sends signals by movement of electrons, the biological circuit of the nervous system dispatches information by means of ions of potassium and sodium, called neurotransmitters.

    In the biological circuit of the nervous system, a signal passes from

    (1) transmitter to neuron to synapse
    (2) neuron to axon to synapse
    (3) axon across synapse to axon
    (4) neuron to neuron across axon
    (5) axon to synapse by way of neuron

Questions 17 and 18 refer to the following graph.

Changes in Soil Moisture

The graph above shows the relative moisture content of soil covered with mulch and soil not covered with mulch.

17. Which statement best summarizes the effects of mulch coverings on soil?

    (1) Mulch lowers the moisture content and increases the range of moisture content.
    (2) Mulch lowers the moisture content and decreases the range of moisture content.
    (3) Mulch raises the moisture content and increases the range of moisture content.
    (4) Mulch raises the moisture content and decreases the range of moisture content.
    (5) Mulch has no effect on moisture content, but it does decrease the range of moisture content.

18. Between which days was it most likely to have rained the most?

    (1) 0 and 5
    (2) 5 and 10
    (3) 10 and 15
    (4) 15 and 20
    (5) 20 and 25

GO ON TO THE NEXT PAGE

TEST 3: SCIENCE

<u>Questions 19–22</u> refer to the following information.

Scientists performed an experiment to determine whether there is a connection between learning ability and food. They took two groups of 20 mice each, all from the same purebred strain. The mice were deprived of food for 3 days and then given a standard learning session in running through a maze. They were trained by giving them a mild electric shock whenever they took a wrong turn. Immediately after each learning session, one group of mice was fed, but the other was not. A week later, all of the mice were tested to see whether they could still run the maze correctly. The group that had been fed had retained this ability, but the other group had not.

19. The probable reason that the scientists used only mice from the same pure-bred strain is so that

    (1) the mice would all be the same size
    (2) the mice would all be the same color
    (3) the experiment could be repeated with the same mice
    (4) genetic differences would not affect the outcome of the test
    (5) the experiment wouldn't cost as much

20. A finding is a proven result obtained as part of an experiment. Which of the following could be considered a valid finding?

    (1) Mice remember better if they are fed immediately after each training session.
    (2) Mice remember better if they are fed and then allowed some time to think about the training.
    (3) Experiments with mice have nothing to do with human learning processes.
    (4) Mice used in experiments have to be from the same purebred strain.
    (5) Mice do not need to be fed in order to learn.

21. The use of an electric shock in the teaching process is

    (1) necessary to keep the mice alert
    (2) cruel and should not be allowed
    (3) a way to show the mice that they have taken a wrong turn in the maze
    (4) designed to elicit a predetermined response
    (5) part of the variable

22. It was noted that the mice could learn to run the maze more readily if it was well illuminated. This information is

    (1) not relevant to their experiment
    (2) vital to the experiment
    (3) an assumption made by someone who observed the experiment
    (4) a result of the experiment
    (5) an important finding

<u>Questions 23–25</u> refer to the following passage.

As scientists plan longer and longer experiments to be carried out in space, the issues of long-term survival in space become much more significant. When trips to space lasted only a few days, it was comparatively easy to provide for all the needs of the crew. Now, however, we must develop long-term methods for maintaining proper air pressure in the cabin, providing clean, breathable air, providing protection from gamma and X-ray radiation emitted by the stars (and our own Sun), dealing with the unique problems of weightlessness, as well as providing food and removing waste products.

Air pressure can be maintained by using a series of air locks to connect the passenger cabin to the outside. A similar system is used in submarines, to keep air in and water out of the cabin.

Since humans can live only a matter of minutes without oxygen, the problem of a constant production of safe air is of major importance. One solution has been to use green plants, which take up the carbon dioxide waste products, and produce oxygen as a

GO ON TO THE NEXT PAGE

TEST 3: SCIENCE

by-product of photosynthesis. It is also possible, that if enough plants were grown, they could help with food as well. Another option is to use chemical oxygen generation systems. These are good in the short term, but eventually run out of materials.

We rarely think of needing protection from radiation. Our ozone layer does an excellent job of protecting us from ultraviolet radiation given off by the sun and from other forms of radiation as well. To date, we do not know if we can effectively shield astronauts from the high radiation doses they will likely receive in space over the long term.

Weightlessness is known to cause a loss of calcium from bones, making them weak and brittle, and to atrophy muscles. There are also documented weaknesses in blood vessels. One possible solution is to develop an artificial gravity.

Lastly, we must find ways to provide for basic food and water needs. Not only does a person use about 1 kilogram (2.2 pounds) of oxygen per day, but he or she also needs about .5 kilograms of food and 2 kilograms of water daily. While it is possible to transport compressed oxygen, water, and food for short trips, any efforts to establish long-term space colonies will require an ability to generate oxygen, food, and water in space as it will be impossible to transport them into space. Recycling will be a priority.

23. A five-minute loss of which of the following functions in a spaceship would have the greatest consequences?

   (1) loss of water production
   (2) loss of food
   (3) loss of oxygen generation
   (4) loss of artificial gravity
   (5) loss of gamma radiation shielding

24. A space station needs to provide for 10 people for 3 weeks. How much oxygen is needed?

   (1) 10 kilograms
   (2) 21 kilograms
   (3) 30 kilograms
   (4) 210 kilograms
   (5) 442 kilograms

25. Which of the following concerns for an astronaut in space is probably of the least concern to a person on Earth?

   (1) food loss
   (2) loss of gravity
   (3) weightlessness
   (4) air quality
   (5) exposure to ultraviolet radiation

Questions 26–31 refer to the following passage.

Acid rain, more properly known as acid precipitation, is a man-made environmental problem that is known to be escalating. The source of acid rain is oxides of sulfur and nitrogen that dissolve in water, lowering the pH to such an extreme that damage to living and nonliving things results. Often the source of acid rain is pollutants from factories or automobiles. The gases produced by fuel combustion react with water vapor in the air and produce acids such as sulfurous acid, sulfuric acid, and nitrous acid. Burning of coal, oil, and natural gas is especially likely to cause an increased amount of acid rain. In addition to man-caused sources of acid rain, volcanic eruptions and some bacterial decay also produce these acidic oxides which lower the pH of water.

Scientists measure the acidity of an object using the pH scale. The scale ranges from 0 to 14, with a pH of 7 being considered neutral. A pH less than 7 is acidic and one more than 7 is basic or alkaline. Normal rain has a pH of about 5.6. It is not neutral because rainwater naturally dissolves a small amount of carbon dioxide from the air and becomes slightly acidic.

Acid rain becomes a serious problem when the pH of the precipitation becomes less than 3.5. There have been reported pH's of 1.3 in some areas. These extremely acidic conditions kill fish and plants, and may render lakes and soil totally uninhabitable. Young fish not only are killed by such acidic waters, but any fish that may survive are usually not able to reproduce. Sometimes, nature provides a means of neutralizing these acidic waters via naturally alkaline ammonia compounds or calcium compounds such as limestone.

GO ON TO THE NEXT PAGE

TEST 3: SCIENCE

The table below gives the pH of some common substances:

pH	SUBSTANCE
1.1	Battery acid
2.8	Household vinegar
5.5	Normal rainwater
7.0	Distilled water
8.2	Baking soda
11.6	Household ammonia
13.9	Lye

26. Which of the following mineral formations would be most effective at neutralizing acid rain?

    (1) nitrogen
    (2) oxygen
    (3) calcium carbonate
    (4) magnesium acetate
    (5) baking soda

27. Which of the following is not a cause of acid precipitation?

    (1) automobile engines
    (2) gasoline-powered lawnmowers
    (3) burning of coal
    (4) hydroelectric plants
    (5) burning of natural gas

28. According to the passage, which of the following is the most basic?

    (1) ammonia
    (2) lye
    (3) distilled water
    (4) normal rainwater
    (5) battery acid

29. Which pair of substances would likely neutralize each other?

    (1) lye and ammonia
    (2) vinegar and battery acid
    (3) vinegar and ammonia
    (4) ammonia and calcium carbonate
    (5) distilled water and rainwater

30. Which of the following responses to an acid rain-caused fish kill would have the best chance of preventing the problem from reappearing?

    (1) restocking the lake with heartier fish
    (2) allowing the stronger fish to survive and then reproduce
    (3) seeding clouds so that the rain falls elsewhere
    (4) reducing the amount of air pollution created
    (5) adding large amounts of ammonia to the lake to neutralize the acid

31. Which of the following compounds does not dissolve in water and cause acid rain?

    (1) sulfur dioxide
    (2) sulfur trioxde
    (3) carbon dioxide
    (4) nitrogen dioxide
    (5) nitrogen monoxide

32. Chemical fertilizers stimulate plant growth; but if the concentration is too high, they may damage roots. What precautions concerning chemical fertilizers must a gardener take?

    (1) Use them only on some of his or her plants.
    (2) Use only the amount recommended.
    (3) Do not apply chemical fertilizers.
    (4) Apply as much as possible without damaging roots.
    (5) Give the plants only tiny amounts.

33. Amniote vertebrates are generally classified into three orders: Reptilia, Aves (birds), and Mammalia. Of the following, which group of three animals contains one member of each order?

    (1) ostrich, American robin, Norway rat
    (2) Beluga whale, black-footed ferret, box turtle
    (3) timber rattlesnake, fence lizard, leopard
    (4) African lion, sea otter, herring gull
    (5) house sparrow, garter snake, African elephant

GO ON TO THE NEXT PAGE

TEST 3: SCIENCE

34. As temperature rises, solids generally become more soluble in water, but gases become less soluble. If a soft drink contains high concentrations of sugar and carbon dioxide, which of the following may be expected to happen if it is cooled down?

A. Sugar may precipitate out.
B. Gas bubbles may form and produce foam.
C. Water may evaporate rapidly.

(1) B only
(2) B and A only
(3) A only
(4) C and B only
(5) A and C only

Question 35 is based on the following graph.

Pressure (mm Hg)

35. This graph represents the relationship of the pressure and volume of a given mass of a gas at constant temperature. When the pressure equals 8 millimeters of mercury (mm Hg), what is the volume, in milliliters (mL)?

(1) 1
(2) 2
(3) 4
(4) 8
(5) 16

Ions are electrically charged particles that are formed when certain compounds are dissolved in water. These solutions will conduct electricity. The Swedish scientist Svante Arrhenius coined the term *ion* (which means wanderer) to explain why solutions of electrolytes will conduct an electric current. When an electrolyte forms into a solution, it dissolves or dissociates into ions, a process called ionization. If a substance does not ionize, it will not conduct an electric current.

Electrolytes include most acids, bases, and salts. Some conductors include hydrogen and sodium chloride, copper sulfate, and potassium nitrate. Substances that are not electrolytes include distilled water, sugar water, and most organic compounds.

36. Which of the following is a nonelectrolyte?

(1) HNO_3 (nitric acid)
(2) HCl (hydrochloric acid)
(3) H_2SO_4 (sulfuric acid)
(4) C_3H_8 (propane gas)
(5) $NaCl$ (table salt)

37. Which of the following compounds in the liquid phase can be considered an electrolyte?

(1) H_2O (distilled water)
(2) CO_2 (carbon dioxide)
(3) $NaCl$ (sodium chloride)
(4) CuO (oxidized copper)
(5) H_2O_2 (hydrogen peroxide)

GO ON TO THE NEXT PAGE

TEST 3: SCIENCE

38. An object accelerates (changes its speed) only if the forces acting on it in one direction are greater than the forces in the opposite direction. All of the following objects will accelerate EXCEPT

    (1) a gas balloon in which the buoyant force is greater than its weight and air resistance
    (2) a man in a parachute when the air resistance is less than his weight
    (3) an airplane in horizontal flight when the thrust of the engine is equal to the drag of the air
    (4) a ball striking a wall, in which the force of the ball on the wall is equal to the force of the wall on the ball
    (5) a rocket fired straight up, when the engine thrust is equal to the air resistance

39. The four giant planets, Jupiter, Saturn, Uranus, and Neptune (in that order), are very far from the Sun; only the small planet Pluto is farther. The *Voyager* space explorer found that Neptune and Uranus are surrounded by rings like those of Saturn. What hypothesis would be suggested by the discovery that Pluto has no rings?

    (1) All large planets have rings, and small ones do not.
    (2) Rings are present around any planet that is far from the Sun.
    (3) Rings are distributed at random, regardless of the size or position of the planet.
    (4) Large planets may have rings, but small ones do not.
    (5) Pluto has lost its rings because it is so far from the Sun.

40. Wind can carry dry sand, blowing it against bedrock and eroding the rock into fantastic shapes. What kind of ecosystem is most likely to have wind-eroded rocks?

    (1) seashore
    (2) desert
    (3) prairie
    (4) tundra
    (5) deciduous forest

41. In a tank with water contaminated with bacteria, a surgical wound in a frog's skin heals much more rapidly than a similar wound on a fish. Any of the following might be a possible explanation EXCEPT

    (1) The bacteria in the tank are not harmful to frogs.
    (2) Some chemical in the frog's skin defends against bacteria.
    (3) The frog's immune system responds efficiently to the bacteria.
    (4) Frog skin has a much better ability to regenerate than the skin of a fish.
    (5) The water contains some chemical substance that promotes healing.

Questions 42 and 43 refer to the following information.

A student heated a sample of a hydrated mineral and removed the water from the sample. The data table below summarizes his data:

TIME (MINUTES)	MASS OF SAMPLE (GRAMS)
0	20.00
1	18.65
2	15.19
3	12.07
4	12.01
5	12.01
6	12.00

42. At the end of the heating process, what mass of water had been removed from the mineral?

    (1) 0.00 grams
    (2) 8.00 grams
    (3) 12.00 grams
    (4) 20.00 grams
    (5) 100.00 grams

GO ON TO THE NEXT PAGE

TEST 3: SCIENCE

43. What percentage of the sample was water at the start of the experiment?

    (1) 0.0%
    (2) 20.0%
    (3) 40.0%
    (4) 60.0%
    (5) 80.0%

---

44. In a reflex, an impulse starts at a sense organ, passes through sensory neurons to the brain or spinal cord, then goes through motor neurons to a muscle or a gland. What is the sequence of organs in the reflex that causes tears to flow when the cornea of the eye is irritated?

    (1) cornea–tear gland–brain–sensory neuron–motor neuron
    (2) cornea–brain–motor neuron–sensory neuron–tear gland
    (3) cornea–sensory neuron–brain–motor neuron–tear gland
    (4) tear gland–cornea–motor neuron–brain–sensory neuron
    (5) brain–cornea–sensory neuron–motor neuron–tear gland

45. In a certain area, DDT-resistant mosquitoes now exist in greater numbers than 10 years ago. What is the most probable explanation for this increase in numbers?

    (1) DDT causes sterility in mosquitoes.
    (2) Mosquito eggs were most likely to have been fertilized when exposed to DDT.
    (3) DDT acted as a reproductive hormone for previous generations of mosquitoes.
    (4) DDT serves as a new source of nutrition.
    (5) Genetic differences permitted some mosquitoes to survive DDT use.

46. A scientist studying fossils in undisturbed layers of rock identified a species that, he concluded, had changed little over the years. Which observation probably would have led him to this conclusion?

    (1) The simplest fossil organisms appeared only in the oldest rocks.
    (2) The simplest fossil organisms appeared only in the newest rocks.
    (3) The same kind of fossil organisms appeared in old and new rocks.
    (4) No fossil organisms of any kind appeared in the newest rocks.
    (5) Few fossil organisms appeared in the oldest rock.

47. In sexual reproduction, the original chromosome number must be reduced in order that members of the next generation will have the same chromosome number as their parents. For this reason, each reproductive cell—egg or sperm—has only half as many chromosomes as the other cells in the organism. The pollen grain of a wheat plant produces a sperm nucleus with 14 chromosomes. How many chromosomes will there be in the egg nucleus and in a leaf cell?

    (1) 14 in the egg nucleus, 28 in a leaf cell
    (2) 14 in both the egg nucleus and leaf cells
    (3) 28 in both the egg nucleus and leaf cells
    (4) 7 in the egg nucleus, 14 in a leaf cell
    (5) 7 in the egg nucleus, 28 in a leaf cell

48. A salmon will die after laying thousands of eggs, depositing them in the open water. A robin lays about 4 eggs and cares for the young when they hatch. It is reasonable to assume that

    (1) there are far more salmon than robins in the world
    (2) far more salmon than robins die before reaching adulthood
    (3) more food is available for growing salmon than for young robins
    (4) salmon do not reproduce until they are much older than adult robins
    (5) robins are better parents than salmon

GO ON TO THE NEXT PAGE

TEST 3: SCIENCE

49. Corn plants that are grown in the dark will be white and usually much taller than genetically identical corn plants grown in light, which will be green. The most probable explanation for this finding is that the

    (1) corn plants grown in the dark are all mutants for color and height
    (2) expression of a gene may be dependent on the environment
    (3) plants grown in the dark will always be genetically albino
    (4) phenotype of a plant is independent of its genotype
    (5) genotype is independent of its phenotype

50. Potatoes can be reproduced either by cuttings of the tubers or by seed formed sexually. Why would an agriculture specialist decide to go to the trouble of growing potatoes from seed?

    (1) to produce the largest possible crop
    (2) to try out a new fertilizer
    (3) to reduce the difficulty of planting
    (4) to produce new varieties
    (5) to protect the new plants from insects

END OF EXAMINATION

TEST 4: LANGUAGE ARTS, READING

Directions

The Language Arts, Reading test consists of excerpts from pre-1920, 1920–1960, and post-1960 literature; articles about literature or the arts; and at least one business document.

Read each excerpt first and then answer the questions following it. Refer to the reading material as often as necessary in answering the questions.

Each excerpt is preceded by a "purpose question." The purpose question gives a reason for reading the material. Use these purpose questions to help focus your reading. You are not required to answer these purpose questions. They are given only to help you concentrate on the ideas presented in the reading materials.

You should spend no more than 65 minutes answering the questions. Work carefully, but do not spend too much time on any one question. Be sure you answer every question. You will not be penalized for incorrect answers.

To record your answers, mark the numbered space on the answer sheet beside the number that corresponds to the question in the test.

FOR EXAMPLE:

It was Susan's dream machine. The metallic blue paint gleamed, and the sporty wheels were highly polished. Under the hood, the engine was no less carefully cleaned. Inside, flashy lights illuminated the instruments on the dashboard, and the seats were covered by rich leather upholstery.

The subject ("It") of this excerpt is most likely

(1) an airplane   ① ② ● ④ ⑤
(2) a stereo system
(3) an automobile
(4) a boat
(5) a motorcycle

The correct answer is "an automobile"; therefore, answer space 3 would be marked on the answer sheet.

GO ON TO THE NEXT PAGE

TEST 4: LANGUAGE ARTS, READING

Questions 1–5 refer to the following passage.

HOW DID A CHILD REACT TO AUGUST WEATHER?

I grew up near the Atlantic Ocean among marshes and estuaries, only a few miles back from a low-lying coast. I remember the month of August with a special kind of
(5) pleasure. At this time of year, mainland, marshland, and ocean would blend together into a grey, hot, humid haze. My mother would open all the windows, pull all the blinds, and hope to catch a sea breeze, but
(10) no breeze stirred. The dogs lay under the tables and panted; the cats lurked in the cool tunnels of the earth cellar. August was a time to do nothing and be proud of it.

But I also remember August with a bit of
(15) anxiety. August was the time of hurricanes and polio. Hurricanes and polio were different in many ways but were alike in that both were very bad things that usually happened to other people. During my
(20) childhood, I was lucky enough never to get polio. But we had bad hurricanes three times.

The hurricanes were pretty scary for the adults, but for a child, they were mostly a lot
(25) of fun. First, there was all the getting ready: buying candles and flashlight batteries and food, filling the car with gasoline, helping neighbors board up the only plate-glass window in the neighborhood, and making
(30) sure the buildings were closed up snug and everything loose was stashed away.

Then there was watching for the storm. I remember my father pointing out to me the eerie sky with its banners of cirrus clouds
(35) radiating out of the south, and I remember the strange feel of the air. The first breezes of the hurricane were so mild, so moist, so soft as to be barely distinguishable from the feel of one's own skin.

(40) The storm itself wasn't so bad, except I had to stay indoors. I remember peering through windows watching the water sheet down outside, the ocean tide creep up in the back marsh, and the trees lash back
(45) and forth. Every time the wind let up I would say, "Is this the eye of the hurricane? Can I go outside and see the eye?"

—Calvin Simonds

1. The mood in lines 1 through 13 is expressed chiefly through the use of

   (1) descriptive details
   (2) sequential order
   (3) figurative language
   (4) simple sentences
   (5) objective observation

2. Why was the narrator "proud" (line 13) to do nothing in August?

   (1) He was lazy.
   (2) It was easier to keep cool.
   (3) He was observing animals' actions.
   (4) It was proper August behavior.
   (5) He was afraid of hurricanes.

3. The narrator characterizes hurricanes and polio as reasons for

   (1) fearing the weather
   (2) being concerned in August
   (3) discussing misfortunes
   (4) helping the neighbors
   (5) staying indoors

4. In the fourth paragraph, the narrator suggests that the early stages of a hurricane are

   (1) unpredictable
   (2) obvious to the eye only
   (3) apparent in the atmosphere
   (4) felt before they are seen
   (5) frightening for children

5. Which words best describe the narrator's memories of August?

   (1) confusing events
   (2) conflict and danger
   (3) contrasting feelings
   (4) freedom and relaxation
   (5) expectancy and fulfillment

GO ON TO THE NEXT PAGE

TEST 4: LANGUAGE ARTS, READING

Questions 6–10 refer to the following passage.

WHO ARE THE MOST RECENT SEEKERS AFTER THE AMERICAN DREAM?

New immigrants are trying all over to integrate themselves into the system. They have the same hunger. On any given day, there are millions throughout the world who are applying to come to the United States and share the American Dream. The same battles.

Sometimes the whole family saves up and gives the bright young man or the bright young woman the family savings. It even goes in hock for a year or two. They pin all their hopes on this one kid, put him on a bus, let him go a thousand miles. He doesn't speak a word of English. He's only seventeen, eighteen years old, but he's gonna save that family. A lot rides on that kid, who's a busboy in some hotel.

He's gonna be the first hook, the first pioneer coming into an alien society, the United States. He might be in Chicago. He works as a busboy all night long. They pay him minimum or less, and work him hard. He'll never complain. If he makes a hundred a week, he will manage to send back twenty-five.

After the kid learns a bit, because he's healthy and young and energetic, he'll probably get another job as a busboy. He'll work at another place as soon as the shift is over. He'll try to work his way up to be a waiter. He'll work incredible hours. He doesn't care about union scale. He doesn't care about conditions, about humiliations. He accepts all this as his fate.

He's burning underneath with this energy and ambition. He outworks the U.S. busboys and eventually becomes the waiter. Where he can maneuver, he tries to become the owner and gives a lot of competition to the locals.

The only thing that helps me is remembering the history of this country. We've always managed, despite our worst, unbelievably nativist actions, to rejuvenate ourselves, to bring in new people. Every new group is scared of being in the welfare line or in the unemployment office. They go to night school. They learn about America. We'd be lost without them.

I see all kinds of new immigrants starting out all over again, trying to work their way into the system. They're going through new battles, yet they're old battles. They want to share in the American Dream. The stream never ends.

6. The attitude of the author toward the new immigrant is

   (1) critical
   (2) skeptical
   (3) cautious
   (4) enthusiastic
   (5) cynical

7. The approach to immigration by the immigrant family is to

   (1) come as a unified family
   (2) send a promising youth
   (3) borrow from relatives
   (4) expect the worst
   (5) bank on a senior member

8. From the passage, it can be inferred that

   (1) other family members will follow the pioneer
   (2) the family will be abandoned
   (3) the family will despair of achieving the American Dream
   (4) the family will give up their efforts
   (5) the family will be frightened by feeling alien

9. The American Dream, as illustrated in this article, allows newcomers to

   (1) make a lot of money
   (2) be exploited
   (3) move upward in society
   (4) be welcomed enthusiastically
   (5) be victims of exclusion

10. The history of America indicates that immigrants

    (1) benefit the United States
    (2) are losing faith
    (3) are easily discouraged
    (4) expect help
    (5) seek welfare

GO ON TO THE NEXT PAGE

TEST 4: LANGUAGE ARTS, READING

<u>Questions 11–15</u> are based on the following selection.

HOW DOES AN ELDERLY COUPLE CELEBRATE A SABBATH MEAL?

Both of them had eaten sparingly during the day so that they would have an appetite for the Sabbath meal. Shmul-Leibele said the benediction over the raisin wine and
(5) gave Shoshe the cup that she might drink. Afterwards, he rinsed his fingers from a tin dipper, then washed hers, and they both dried their hands with a single towel, each at either end. Shmul-Leibele lifted the
(10) Sabbath loaf and cut it with the bread knife, a slice for himself and one for his wife.

He immediately informed her that the loaf was just right, and she countered: "Go on, you say that every Sabbath."
(15) "But it happens to be the truth," he replied.

Although it was hard to obtain fish during the cold weather, Shoshe had purchased three-quarters of a pound of pike from
(20) the fishmonger. She had chopped it with onions, added an egg, salt and pepper, and cooked it with carrots and parsley. It took Shmul-Leibele's breath away, and after it he had to drink a tumbler of whiskey.
(25) When he began the table chants, Shoshe accompanied him quietly. Then came the chicken soup with noodles and tiny circlets of fat which glowed on the surface like golden ducats. Between the soup and the
(30) main course, Shmul-Leibele again sang Sabbath hymns. Since goose was cheap at this time of year, Shoshe gave Shmul-Leibele an extra leg for good measure. After the dessert, Shmul-Leibele washed
(35) for the last time and made a benediction. When he came to the words: "Let us not be in need either of the gifts of flesh and blood nor of their loans," he rolled his eyes upward and brandished his fists.

11. We know that Smul-Leibele is religious because

(1) he says a benediction
(2) he offers Shoshe a drink
(3) he washes his hands
(4) he slices the loaf
(5) he offers Shoshe a slice

12. We can deduce the relationship between husband and wife from

(1) his compliment to her
(2) his appetite
(3) his benedictions
(4) his hymns
(5) his drink of whiskey

13. The Sabbath rituals included all of the following EXCEPT

(1) blessing the wine
(2) rinsing fingers
(3) raising the loaf
(4) drinking whiskey
(5) singing hymns

14. Shmul-Leibele prayed that he could

(1) continue to be with Shoshe
(2) have food and drink
(3) be free of moneylenders
(4) need the gifts of flesh and blood
(5) be blessed with long life

15. The purpose of the selection is to

(1) describe the relationship between husband and wife
(2) stress the importance of prayer
(3) describe a Sabbath meal
(4) stress the couple's poverty
(5) stress the couple's loneliness

GO ON TO THE NEXT PAGE

TEST 4: LANGUAGE ARTS, READING

Questions 16–20 are based on the following selection.

WHAT HAPPENS AT THE REUNION OF TWO SISTERS?

"Oh, Lottie, it's good to see you," Bess said, but saying nothing about Lottie's splendid appearance. Upstairs Bess, putting down her shabby suitcase, said "I'll sleep
(5) like a rock tonight," without a word of praise for her lovely room. At the lavish table, top-heavy with turkey, Bess said, "I'll take light and dark both," with no marveling at the size of the bird, or that there was turkey for two elderly women, one of them too poor to
(10) buy her own bread.

With the glow of good food in her stomach, Bess began to spin stories. They were rich with places and people. . . Her face reflected her telling, above all, the love she lived by that enhanced the poorest place, the
(15) humblest person.

Then it was that Lottie knew why Bess had made no mention of her finery, or the shining room, or the twelve-pound turkey. She had not even seen them. Tomorrow she would see . . . Lottie as she really looked. Tonight
(20) she saw only what she had come seeking, a place in her sister's home and heart.

She said, "That's about enough for me. How have the years used you?"

"It was me who didn't use them," said Lottie wistfully. "I saved for them. I forgot the
(25) best of them would go without my ever spending a day or a dollar enjoying them. That's my life story in those few words, a life never lived. Now it's too near the end to try."

Bess said, "To know how much there is to know is the beginning of learning to live.
(30) Don't count the years that are left us. At our time of life it's the days that count. You've got too much catching up to do to waste a minute of a waking hour feeling sorry for yourself."

16. Bess

    (1) took note of her sister's appearance
    (2) envied her sister's finery
    (3) appreciated her welcome
    (4) was oblivious of her surroundings
    (5) was satisfied by what she saw

17. Bess was seeking

    (1) rich people
    (2) rich places
    (3) a place in her sister's home
    (4) a lavish table
    (5) an escape from poverty

18. Lottie looked back on her life

    (1) happily
    (2) regretfully
    (3) with satisfaction
    (4) with nostalgia
    (5) longingly

19. Bess will probably

    (1) take advantage of Lottie
    (2) teach Lottie how to live
    (3) feel sorry for herself
    (4) regret her past life
    (5) count her remaining years

20. Lottie will probably

    (1) change her way of life
    (2) be too old to change
    (3) continue to feel sorry for herself
    (4) count her remaining years
    (5) live in the past

Questions 21–25 refer to the following poem.

WHY DOES THE POET OBJECT TO A PHOTOGRAPH?

To a Photographer

I have known love and hate and work and fight;
I have lived largely, I have dreamed and planned,
And Time, the Sculptor, with a master hand
Has graven on my face for all men's sight
Deep lines of joy and sorrow, growth and blight,
Of labor and of service and command
—And now you show me this, this waxen, bland
And placid face, unlined, unwrinkled, white.
This is not I—this fatuous thing you show,
Retouched and smoothed and prettified to please.

GO ON TO THE NEXT PAGE

TEST 4: LANGUAGE ARTS, READING

Put back the wrinkles and the lines I know;
I have spent blood and tears achieving these,
Out of the pain, the struggle and the wrack
These are my scars of battle—put them back!
       —Berton Braley

21. It can be assumed from the poet that

 (1) the poet has taken a photograph
 (2) the poet has been shown a photograph of himself
 (3) a faithful photograph has been taken of him
 (4) the poet is still young
 (5) the poet is a dreamer

22. The poet wishes everyone to know that he has

 (1) led a quiet life
 (2) experienced hardships
 (3) been unsuccessful
 (4) maintains a youthful appearance
 (5) aged gracefully

23. The passage of time has left the poet with a face that is

 (1) lined
 (2) placid
 (3) ashen
 (4) smooth
 (5) bland

24. The poet is

 (1) content with his lot
 (2) resentful of time
 (3) proud of his scars
 (4) desirous of youth
 (5) untrue to himself

25. The poem is written in the form of a

 (1) ballad
 (2) dialogue
 (3) lyric
 (4) limerick
 (5) sonnet

Questions 26–30 refer to the following excerpt from a play.

WHY DOES A CANDIDATE DECIDE NOT TO RUN FOR OFFICE?

GRANT: I'm not going to kid anybody along. I never have.

KAY *(pleadingly)*: Grant, everybody here tonight was thinking of the future—which is how to get you elected. It's stupid right now to think in any other terms.

(Grant unbuttons his coat and takes it off. Kay turns to Conover in alarm.)

CONOVER *(going to Grant)*: I've got to talk to these people, and that means you've got to talk to me.

GRANT: I'm talking to a lot of people in my speech Thursday night. You'll be one of them. I promised myself when I went into this that I'd appeal to the best in the American people. The only advice I've ever had from any of you was to appeal to their worst. And that's what both parties are starting to do today. Let's end rationing. Who cares if Europe starves? Let's lift price ceilings—suppose it does bring inflation. Let's lower taxes and all get rich.

CONOVER: I see. You're the only honest man in politics.

GRANT: No, Jim! We have some good men. There are some wonderful men in the Senate and in the House, too—Democrats and Republicans. But, Jim, there aren't enough of them to shape party policies, so, to get votes, both parties are out to buy the American public. I can't do that, Jim. So I'm afraid I can't be of any use to you.

KAY: Well, Grant, I won't accept that decision. Oh, Grant, we've always talked these things out together. All right, we won't discuss it any more tonight. You're upset. I'll be in touch with you tomorrow. Come on, Jim. *(She exits.)*

CONOVER: I think Kay's right, Grant. You'd better sleep on it. I can stay over another day.

GRANT: No, Jim, I've made up my mind.

CONOVER: Grant, in this country we play politics—and to play politics you have to play ball . . . .*(He exits.)*

GO ON TO THE NEXT PAGE

TEST 4: LANGUAGE ARTS, READING

GRANT: Thank God that's settled. I hope they're all listening in Thursday night because I'm going to burn their ears off. Any candidate for any office who threatens world peace for a few votes—there's the international criminal for you. I'll take care of them Thursday night—and from now on.

26. You can deduce from what Kay and Conover are saying that

    (1) they disagree with each other
    (2) they agree with Grant
    (3) they agree with the American people
    (4) they disagree with Grant
    (5) they think well of Grant

27. Grant is implying

    (1) he won't play politics
    (2) he will lift price ceilings
    (3) he will lower taxes
    (4) he will buy the American public
    (5) he'll get rich

28. Grant is critical of

    (1) all Republicans
    (2) all Democrats
    (3) Congress
    (4) the American public
    (5) both political parties

29. Grant feels that the American public

    (1) can be bought
    (2) can be fooled
    (3) can be appealed to
    (4) plays politics
    (5) is cynical about politicians

30. Grant will

    (1) be a candidate for public office
    (2) compromise his principles
    (3) attack dishonest candidates
    (4) go along with Kay and Conover
    (5) drop out of politics

Questions 31–35 refer to the following passage.

WHAT IS THE MEANING OF THE FATHER'S ACT?

So it was with a heart full of longing and hope that my father led us to school on that first day. He took long strides in his eagerness, the rest of us running and hopping to keep up.

At last the four of us stood around the teacher's desk; and my father, in his impossible English, gave us over in her charge. . . . I venture to say that Miss Nixon was struck by something uncommon in the group we made. . . . My little sister was pretty as a doll, with her clear pink-and-white face, short golden curls, and eyes like blue violets when you caught them looking up. My brother . . . stood up straight and uncringing before the American teacher, his cap respectfully doffed. Next to him stood a starved-looking girl with eyes ready to pop out, and short dark curls that would not have made much of a wig for a Jewish bride.

All three children carried themselves rather better than the common run of "green" pupils that were brought to Miss Nixon. But the figure that challenged attention to the group was the tall, straight father, with his earnest face and fine forehead, nervous hands eloquent in gesture, and a voice full of feeling. This foreigner, who brought his children to school as if it were an act of consecration, was not like other aliens, who brought their children in dull obedience to the law; was not like the native fathers, who brought their unmanageable boys, glad to be relieved of their care. I think Miss Nixon guessed what my father's best English could not convey. I think she divined that by the simple act of delivering our school certificates to her he took possession of America.

—Mary Antin

31. The best title for this selection is

    (1) "Our First Day at School"
    (2) "America: Land of Opportunity"
    (3) "We Were Different"
    (4) "A Father's Faith in Education"
    (5) "Americanization of the Alien"

GO ON TO THE NEXT PAGE

TEST 4: LANGUAGE ARTS, READING

32. From their use in the passage, all of the following words are correctly paired EXCEPT

    (1) *charge*—care
    (2) *uncommon*—unusual
    (3) *doffed*—removed
    (4) *consecration*—dedication
    (5) *divined*—heavenly

33. The author's father regarded school in the United States as all of the following EXCEPT

    (1) an act of dedication
    (2) a parental responsibility
    (3) a legal obligation
    (4) a source of hope
    (5) a stake in America

34. The incorrect group of words describing the persons in the passage is

    (1) the author's sister—blonde and beautiful
    (2) the author's brother—erect and respectful
    (3) the author's father—calm and sincere
    (4) the author—observant and plain-looking
    (5) Miss Nixon—sensitive and understanding

35. As used in this passage, *green* means

    (1) inexperienced
    (2) frightened
    (3) disobedient
    (4) sallow-complexioned
    (5) immigrant

Questions 36–40 refer to the following letter of recommendation.

January 2003

To Whom It May Concern:

(A)
(1) This will confirm that Shawn Black has been employed by Smith Incorporated for approximately 4 years.

(B)
(2) During his tenure of employment, he has displayed a unique ability to identify and solve problems. (3) He has been instrumental in helping to streamline our marketing department. (4) His experience in the marketing and advertising area has been a valuable asset, one that can be of great value to any company using his services. (5) His ideas are fresh and unique, always on the cutting edge in his field.

(C)
(6) He is a loyal employee and always places the welfare of the company above all else. (7) His long hours and his patience with employees under him and with management make him an ideal employee. (8) If available, he can certainly count on reemployment with our firm, should the opportunity arise.

(D)
(9) Any company considering this individual for employment has my most enthusiastic recommendation. (10) If his performance here is any indication, he is destined to achieve new heights in his career and set new records for his future employer. (11) If you have any questions, please do not hesitate to contact me at (310) 555-9902.

Sincerely,

Kristoph Peterson

Kristoph Peterson
Marketing Manager

GO ON TO THE NEXT PAGE

TEST 4: LANGUAGE ARTS, READING

36. According to the letter, the employee, Shawn Black, is

    (1) unemployed and seeking unemployment insurance
    (2) requesting an application for employment with Smith Incorporated
    (3) writing a letter of recommendation for his employee, Kristoph Peterson
    (4) no longer working for Smith Incorporated, but seeking employment elsewhere
    (5) receiving a letter of reprimand for his behavior at Smith Incorporated

37. According to the letter,

    (1) Kristoph Peterson was not pleased with Shawn Black's performance on the job
    (2) Shawn Black is submitting his letter of resignation to Kristoph Peterson
    (3) Shawn Black is an excellent candidate for any job in the marketing or advertising field
    (4) Shawn Black was highly recommended for any job in the accounting department
    (5) Kristoph Peterson accepted Shawn Black's letter of resignation

38. The letter implies that Shawn Black

    (1) has excellent communication skills
    (2) has excellent accounting skills
    (3) has applied to Smith Incorporated
    (4) has not impressed his employer
    (5) has not worked to the best of his ability

39. The author feels that

    (1) he has been let down by Shawn Black because he is seeking employment elsewhere
    (2) Shawn Black is seeking a career in the accounting field
    (3) Shawn Black will not be loyal to his next company
    (4) Shawn Black will make an excellent employee for any company
    (5) he wants to hire Shawn Black next time he applies for the job

40. The letter implies that Kristoph Peterson felt what about Shawn Black's performance?

    (1) frustration
    (2) excitement
    (3) distrust
    (4) displeasure
    (5) pleasure

END OF EXAMINATION

TEST 5: MATHEMATICS

Directions

The Mathematics test consists of multiple-choice and alternate format questions intended to measure general mathematics skills and problem-solving ability. The questions are based on short readings that often include a graph, chart, or diagram.

You should spend no more than 45 minutes answering the questions. Work carefully, but do not spend too much time on any one question. Be sure you answer every question. You will not be penalized for incorrect answers.

Formulas you may need are given on pages 641–642. Only some of the questions will require you to use a formula. Not all the formulas given will be needed.

Some questions contain more information than you will need to solve the problem. Other questions do not give enough information to solve the problem. If the question does not give enough information to solve the problem, the correct answer is "Not enough information is given."

You may use a calculator on Part I.

To record your answers, mark the numbered space on the answer sheet beside the number that corresponds to the question in the test.

FOR EXAMPLE:
If a grocery bill totaling $15.75 is paid with a $20.00 bill, how much change should be returned?

(1) $5.26
(2) $4.75
(3) $4.25
(4) $3.75
(5) $3.25

① ② ● ④ ⑤

The correct answer is "$4.25"; therefore, answer space 3 would be marked on the answer sheet.

GO ON TO THE NEXT PAGE

TEST 5: MATHEMATICS

FORMULAS

Description	Formula
AREA (*A*) of a:	
square	$A = s^2$; where s = side
rectangle	$A = lw$; where l = length, w = width
parallelogram	$A = bh$; where b = base, h = height
triangle	$A = \frac{1}{2} bh$; where b = base, h = height
trapezoid	$A = \frac{1}{2}(b_1 + b_2) h$; where b = base, h = height
circle	$A = \pi r^2$; where π = 3.14, r = radius
PERIMETER (*P*) of a:	
square	$P = 4s$; where s = side
rectangle	$P = 2l + 2w$; where l = length, w = width
triangle	$P = a + b + c$; where a, b, and c are the sides
circumference (*C*) of a circle	$C = \pi d$; where π = 3.14, d = diameter
VOLUME (*V*) of a:	
cube	$V = s^3$; where s = side
rectangular container	$V = lwh$; where l = length, w = width, h = height
cylinder	$V = \pi r^2 h$; where π = 3.14, r = radius, h = height
square pyramid	$V = \frac{1}{3}(\text{base edge})^2 h$
cone	$V = \frac{1}{3}\pi r^2 h$
Pythagorean theorem	$c^2 = a^2 + b^2$; where c = hypotenuse, a and b are legs, of a right triangle
distance (*d*) between two points in a plane	$d = \sqrt{(x_2 - x_1)^2 + (y_2 - y_1)^2}$; where (x_1, y_1) and (x_2, y_2) are two points in a plane
slope of a line (*m*)	$m = \dfrac{y_2 - y_1}{x_2 - x_1}$; where (x_1, y_1) and (x_2, y_2) are two points in a plane

GO ON TO THE NEXT PAGE

TEST 5: MATHEMATICS

FORMULAS (continued)	
Description	**Formula**
MEASURES OF CENTRAL TENDENCY	mean = $\dfrac{x_1 + x_2 + \ldots + x_n}{n}$; where the x's are the values for which a mean is desired, and n = number of values in the series
	median = the point in an ordered set of numbers at which half of the numbers are above and half of the numbers are below this value
simple interest (*i*)	$i = prt$; where p = principal, r = rate, t = time
distance (*d*) as function of rate and time	$d = rt$; where r = rate, t = time
total cost (*c*)	$c = nr$; where n = number of units, r = cost per unit

GO ON TO THE NEXT PAGE

TEST 5: MATHEMATICS, PART I

Directions: You will have 45 minutes to complete this section. You may use a calculator.

1. Luisa worked 40 hours and earned $6.30 per hour. Her friend Joan earned $8.40 per hour at her job. How many hours did Joan have to work in order to equal Luisa's earnings for 40 hours?

   (1) 20
   (2) 25
   (3) 30
   (4) 252
   (5) Not enough information is given.

<u>Question 2</u> is based on the following figure.

2. △*ABC* is a right triangle, and $\overline{CD} \perp \overline{AB}$. If the measure of ∠*CAD* = 40°, what is the measure of ∠*DCB*?

   (1) 10°
   (2) 20°
   (3) 40°
   (4) 50°
   (5) 90°

3. The number of students in a class is *x*. One day 5 students were absent. What fractional part of the class was present?

   (1) $\dfrac{x}{5}$

   (2) $\dfrac{5}{x}$

   (3) $\dfrac{5}{x-5}$

   (4) $\dfrac{x+5}{5}$

   (5) $\dfrac{x-5}{x}$

4. The gasoline gauge shows that a gasoline tank is $\dfrac{1}{3}$ full. In order to fill the tank, 16 gallons of gasoline are added. How many gallons of gasoline does the tank hold when full?

   (1) 20
   (2) 24
   (3) 30
   (4) 32
   (5) 48

<u>Question 5</u> is based on the following figure.

5. What is the length in feet, of the ramp?

   Mark your answer in the circles on the grid on the answer sheet.

GO ON TO THE NEXT PAGE

TEST 5: MATHEMATICS, PART I

6. At a luncheon, 48 half-pints of fruit juice are served. What is the cost, at $3.50 per gallon, of these servings of fruit juice?

    (1) $6.00
    (2) $7.00
    (3) $10.50
    (4) $12.50
    (5) $15.00

7. If $5x - 1 = 34$, then $2\frac{1}{2}x$ is equal to

    (1) 7
    (2) 14
    (3) $16\frac{2}{3}$
    (4) 17
    (5) $17\frac{1}{2}$

Question 8 is based on the following figure.

8. If $AC = 18$ inches and $BC = 8$ inches, the ratio $AB:BC$ is equal to

    (1) 2:1
    (2) 4:5
    (3) 3:2
    (4) 5:4
    (5) Not enough information is given.

9. A rectangular living room has a floor area of 322 square feet. If the length of the room is 23 feet, what is the perimeter in feet?

    Mark your answer in the circles on the grid on the answer sheet.

10. Fatima saw a digital camera priced at $280 at the Triangle Store. She then saw an advertisement for the same camera at Computer Central, announcing 20% off on all merchandise. What additional information does Fatima need to make a wise buying decision?

    (1) The Triangle Store has a better reputation than Computer Central.
    (2) The sales tax on digital camera purchases is 5%.
    (3) Both stores have a $5 delivery charge.
    (4) The name of the manufacturer of the digital camera is Optomix.
    (5) The price of the digital camera at Computer Central is $280.

11. A crew can load a truck in 3 hours. What part of the truck can they load in 45 minutes?

    Mark your answer in the circles on the grid on the answer sheet.

12. Given the equation $x^2 + x - 6 = 0$, which of the following give(s) a complete solution of the equation?

    (1) 2
    (2) 2 and −3
    (3) −2 and 3
    (4) 2 and 3
    (5) 3 and −3

GO ON TO THE NEXT PAGE

TEST 5: MATHEMATICS, PART I

13. Mrs. Edwards buys 40 feet of woolen material to use for scarfs. How many scarfs each 3 feet 4 inches in length can she cut from this material?

    Mark your answer in the circles on the grid on the answer sheet.

14. Henry has $5 more than Bob, who has the same amount of money as Tom. Together, all three have $65. How much money does Bob have?

    (1) $10
    (2) $12
    (3) $15
    (4) $20
    (5) Not enough information is given.

15. A motel charges $68.00 per day for a double room. In addition, there is a 9.5% tax. How much does a couple pay for several days' stay?

    (1) $198.86
    (2) $208.20
    (3) $246.60
    (4) $288.95
    (5) Not enough information is given.

16. If the square of a number is added to the number increased by 4, the result is 60. If n represents the number, which equation can be used to find n?

    (1) $n^2 + 4 = 60$
    (2) $n^2 + 4n = 60$
    (3) $n^2 + n + 4 = 60$
    (4) $n^2 + 60 = 4n + 4$
    (5) $n^2 + n = 64$

17. Evaluate $(6 \times 10^5) \div (4 \times 10^3)$.

    (1) 20
    (2) 100
    (3) 150
    (4) 1,500
    (5) 2,000

18. The measures of the angles of a triangle are in the ratio 3 : 2 : 1. What is the measure of the largest angle of the triangle?

    (1) 65°
    (2) 70°
    (3) 72°
    (4) 80°
    (5) 90°

GO ON TO THE NEXT PAGE.

TEST 5: MATHEMATICS, PART I

Question 19 is based on the following figure.

19. If $m\angle 1 = 36°$ and $m\angle 2 = 2(m\angle 3)$, then $m\angle 3$ equals

    (1) 36°
    (2) 40°
    (3) 44°
    (4) 48°
    (5) Not enough information is given.

20. Mrs. Adams bought 4 pounds of beef and $3\frac{1}{2}$ pounds of chicken for $13.98. If the beef costs $2.76 per pound, what was the cost of the chicken per pound?

    (1) $0.72
    (2) $0.80
    (3) $0.84
    (4) $0.87
    (5) $0.92

21. A carpenter earns $16 per hour, and his assistant earns half as much. Which of the following expressions represents how many dollars both men earned on a job that took 9 hours?

    (1) $9(16) + 9(\frac{1}{2})$

    (2) $9(16) + 9(10)$
    (3) $16(8) + 9(9)$

    (4) $16(\frac{1}{2}) + 9(\frac{1}{2})$

    (5) $9(16) + 9(8)$

22. The difference in estimated weights between two asteroids is 63,150,000,000 tons. What is this number expressed in scientific notation?

    (1) 631.5×10^8
    (2) 63.15×10^9
    (3) 6315×10^7
    (4) 6.315×10^{10}
    (5) 6.315×10^{-10}

23. A lines passes through a point whose coordinates are (−4,−2). Show the location of the point.
    Mark your answer on the coordinate plane grid on the answer sheet.

24. Mr. Barnes has invested $12,000 in bonds that pay interest at the rate of 9% annually. What is Mr. Barnes's annual income expressed in dollars from this investment?
    Mark your answer in the circles on the grid on the answer sheet.

25. Which of the following numbers is a solution of the inequality $3x + 2 < 14$?

    (1) 3
    (2) 4
    (3) 5
    (4) 6
    (5) 7

END OF EXAMINATION

TEST 5: MATHEMATICS, PART II

Directions: You will have 45 minutes to complete questions 26–50. You may NOT use a calculator; otherwise, directions are the same as in Part I. You MAY refer to the *Formulas* sheet.

Question 26 is based on the following graph.

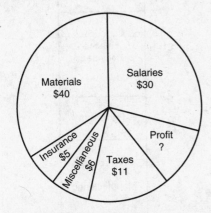

26. The graph shows what happens to each $100 taken in by a small business firm. How many dollars out of each $100 taken in represent profit?

    (1) $5
    (2) $6
    (3) $7
    (4) $7.5
    (5) $8

Question 27 is based on the following figure.

27. What is the perimeter of the figure?

    (1) $6a + b$
    (2) $5a + 5b$
    (3) $6a + 4b$
    (4) $4a + 4b$
    (5) $3a + 5b$

28. Ben scored 7 more points than Jack in a basketball game. Paul scored 2 points less than Jack in the same game. If the three boys scored a total of 38 points, how many points did Jack score?

    (1) 5
    (2) 9
    (3) 11
    (4) 14
    (5) 15

Question 29 refers to the following diagram.

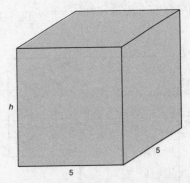

29. A commercial recycling bin (shown above) in the form of a rectangular solid has a square base 5 feet in length and a height of h feet. If the volume of the rectangular solid is 200 cubic feet, which of the following equations may be used to find h?

    (1) $5h = 200$
    (2) $5h^2 = 200$
    (3) $25h = 200$
    (4) $h = 200 \div 5$
    (5) $h = 5(200)$

GO ON TO THE NEXT PAGE

TEST 5: MATHEMATICS, PART II

Question 30 is based on the following figure.

30. Which point on the number line represents the closest approximation to the square root of 12?

    (1) A
    (2) B
    (3) C
    (4) D
    (5) E

Question 31 is based on the following figure.

31. The diagram represents a large living room. What is the area, in square feet, of the room?

    Mark your answer in the circles on the grid on the answer sheet.

Questions 32 and 33 are based on the following graph.

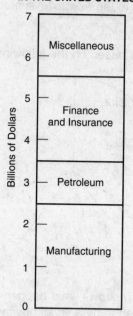

FOREIGN INVESTMENTS IN THE UNITED STATES

32. What Americans spend per year on video games is equal to 50% of foreign investment in finance and insurance. How much do Americans spend annually on video games?

    (1) $300 million
    (2) $1.5 billion
    (3) $1 billion
    (4) $2 billion
    (5) $.75 billion

GO ON TO THE NEXT PAGE

TEST 5: MATHEMATICS, PART II

33. How much more is invested in manufacturing than in petroleum?

    (1) $1\frac{1}{2}$ million

    (2) $3\frac{1}{2}$ million

    (3) $0.5 billion

    (4) $1\frac{1}{2}$ billion

    (5) $3\frac{1}{2}$ billion

---

34. Evaulate $y^2(4x - y)$ if $y = -2$ and $x = 8$

    (1) −18
    (2) 18
    (3) 86
    (4) 96
    (5) 136

35. On a road map, $\frac{1}{4}$ inch represents 8 miles of actual road distance. The towns of Alton and Waverly are represented by points $2\frac{1}{8}$ inches apart on the map. What is the actual distance, in miles, between Alton and Waverly?

    Mark your answer in the circles on the grid on the answer sheet.

36. At a certain time of day, a man 6 feet tall casts a shadow 4 feet in length. At the same time, a church steeple casts a shadow 28 feet in length. How high, in feet, is the church steeple?

    (1) 30
    (2) 32
    (3) 42
    (4) 48
    (5) 56

Question 37 and 38 are based on the following table.

Nutrition Facts for Tastee Chips	
Serving Size 1 oz. (10 chips)	
	% Daily Value
Total 6 g	**9%**
Saturated Fat 0.5 g	**3%**
Cholesterol 0 mg	**0%**
Sodium 110 mg	**5%**
Total Carbohydrates 19 g	**6%**
Dietary Fiber 1 g	**5%**

37. If Kristen eats 15 chips, what percent of the daily value of total carbohydrates has she consumed?

    (1) 9%
    (2) 12%
    (3) 3%
    (4) 33%
    (5) 28.5%

38. The Tastee Company introduces new Tastee Chips *Light,* claiming the product has "half the saturated fat" of the original, described above. How many grams of saturated fat should the *light* chips have for this claim to be true?

    (1) 1 gram
    (2) .05 gram
    (3) 1.5 grams
    (4) .2 gram
    (5) .25 gram

GO ON TO THE NEXT PAGE

TEST 5: MATHEMATICS, PART II

Question 39 is based on the following figure.

39. In the figure $\overrightarrow{AB}$ and $\overrightarrow{CD}$ are both parallel to the *x*-axis. The coordinates of *B* are (5,4) and the coordinates of *D* are (5,−3). The perpendicular distance between $\overrightarrow{AB}$ and $\overrightarrow{CD}$ is

    (1) −2
    (2) 5
    (3) 6
    (4) 7
    (5) 10

Question 40 is based on the following graph.

40. If the slope of $\overrightarrow{AB}$ is 1, what is the value of *y*?

    (1) 1
    (2) 2
    (3) 3
    (4) 4
    (5) 5

Questions 41–43 are based on the following graph.

The graph shows the number of gallons of paint sold by a local hardware store in 1 week.

41. How many gallons of paint were sold on Wednesday?

    (1) 3
    (2) 4
    (3) 5
    (4) 6
    (5) 7

42. By what percent did sales increase on Saturday compared with Tuesday?

    (1) about 50%
    (2) more than 300%
    (3) between 150% and 200%
    (4) 100%
    (5) 400%

43. What was the total amount, in gallons, of paint sold by the store that week?

    Mark your answer in the circles on the grid on the answer sheet.

GO ON TO THE NEXT PAGE

TEST 5: MATHEMATICS, PART II

Question 44 is based on the following figure.

44. *O* is the center of the circle, and the measure of ∠*O* is 70°. What is the measure in degrees of ∠*OAB*?
    Mark your answer in the circles on the grid on the answer sheet.

Question 45 is based on the following table.

Time	3:00 P.M.	4:00 P.M.	5:00 P.M.
Distance covered (miles)	80	124	168

45. Sylvia took an automobile trip. The table shows the mileage she covered during one afternoon. If she drove at a steady rate, how many miles had she covered at 4:15 P.M.?

    (1) 30
    (2) 132
    (3) 135
    (4) 140
    (5) Not enough information is given.

46. The following is a list of ingredients used in making cornmeal crisps:

    1 cup of yellow cornmeal

    $\frac{1}{2}$ cup of sifted flour

    $\frac{2}{3}$ teaspoon of salt

    $\frac{1}{4}$ teaspoon of baking powder

    2 tablespoons of melted shortening

    $\frac{1}{3}$ cup of milk

    If Joan decides to make a larger batch of cookies by using a full cup of milk, she will have to use

    (1) 1 cup of sifted flour
    (2) 2 teaspoons of salt
    (3) 3 teaspoons of baking powder
    (4) 3 tablespoons of melted shortening
    (5) $2\frac{1}{2}$ cups of yellow cornmeal

GO ON TO THE NEXT PAGE

TEST 5: MATHEMATICS, PART II

<u>Question 47</u> is based on the following graph.

Sharpee Shirt Manufacturing Co.
Production Record 1990–2000

47. In what year did Sharpee experience a $10,000 decrease in sales from the previous year?

(1) 1991
(2) 1994
(3) 1996
(4) 1997
(5) 2000

48. A house and a lot cost $120,000. If the house cost 3 times as much as the lot, how much did the house cost?

(1) $30,000
(2) $40,000
(3) $60,000
(4) $90,000
(5) $100,000

<u>Question 49</u> is based on the following figure.

49. If $\overrightarrow{AB}$ is parallel to $\overrightarrow{CD}$, each of the following is true EXCEPT

(1) $a = d$
(2) $b = f$
(3) $c = b$
(4) $f = c$
(5) $b = g$

<u>Question 50</u> is based on the following figure.

50. A flower bed is circular in shape with a concrete border. If the diameter of the flower section is 40 inches and the width of the concrete border is 4 inches, what is the area, in square inches, of the border? (Leave your answer in terms of π.)

(1) 16π
(2) 176π
(3) 180π
(4) 200π
(5) 240π

END OF EXAMINATION

Answer Keys, Summaries of Results, and Self-Appraisal Charts

TEST 1: LANGUAGE ARTS, WRITING, PART I/PAGE 593

I. CHECK YOUR ANSWERS, using the following answer key:

1.	**5**	12.	**3**	23.	**2**	34.	**2**	45.	**1**
2.	**2**	13.	**1**	24.	**3**	35.	**3**	46.	**5**
3.	**3**	14.	**5**	25.	**5**	36.	**4**	47.	**4**
4.	**4**	15.	**5**	26.	**3**	37.	**1**	48.	**5**
5.	**1**	16.	**5**	27.	**4**	38.	**1**	49.	**1**
6.	**1**	17.	**1**	28.	**4**	39.	**2**	50.	**5**
7.	**1**	18.	**5**	29.	**1**	40.	**4**		
8.	**1**	19.	**4**	30.	**2**	41.	**3**		
9.	**1**	20.	**5**	31.	**1**	42.	**1**		
10.	**1**	21.	**5**	32.	**1**	43.	**3**		
11.	**1**	22.	**2**	33.	**4**	44.	**1**		

II. SCORE YOURSELF:

Number correct:

Excellent	_____
	45–50
Good	_____
	40–44
Fair	_____
	35–39

III. EVALUATE YOUR SCORE: Did you get at least 35 correct answers? If not, you need more practice for the Language Arts, Writing, Part I test. In any event, you can improve your performance to Excellent or Good by analyzing your errors.

IV. ANALYZE YOUR ERRORS: To determine your areas of weakness, list the number of correct answers you had under each of the following categories (which correspond to the content areas of the Language Arts, Writing, Part I test), and compare your score with the average scores in the right-hand column. Review the answer analysis beginning on page 660 for each of the questions you got wrong, and give yourself more practice in your weak areas with the appropriate material in Unit II before attempting Practice Examination Two.

Content Areas	Items	Your Score	Average Score
Sentence Structure	1, 3, 5, 8, 10–12, 19, 25, 32, 35, 45, 50		8
Usage	4, 7, 13, 16, 23, 26–28 30–31, 36, 43, 47		8
Mechanics			
Spelling (homonyms, (contractions, possessives)	6, 22, 40, 42		3
Punctuation	24, 33, 41, 44		3
Capitalization	2, 29, 34, 39		3
Organization	9, 17, 37–38, 46, 48, 49		5
No correction	14–15, 16, 20–21		3

Total _____

TEST 2: SOCIAL STUDIES/PAGE 606

I. CHECK YOUR ANSWERS, using the following answer key:

1. **2**	14. **1**	27. **4**	40. **1**
2. **4**	15. **2**	28. **4**	41. **3**
3. **2**	16. **2**	29. **3**	42. **4**
4. **4**	17. **4**	30. **2**	43. **4**
5. **4**	18. **3**	31. **5**	44. **2**
6. **3**	19. **1**	32. **1**	45. **1**
7. **1**	20. **4**	33. **3**	46. **3**
8. **4**	21. **1**	34. **4**	47. **4**
9. **2**	22. **3**	35. **3**	48. **5**
10. **4**	23. **2**	36. **2**	49. **3**
11. **3**	24. **1**	37. **4**	50. **3**
12. **3**	25. **4**	38. **2**	
13. **1**	26. **4**	39. **3**	

II. SCORE YOURSELF:

Number correct:

Excellent _____
45–50

Good _____
40–44

Fair _____
35–39

III. EVALUATE YOUR SCORE: Did you get at least 35 correct answers? If not, you need more practice for the Social Studies test. In any event, you can improve your performance to Excellent or Good by analyzing your errors.

IV. ANALYZE YOUR ERRORS: To determine your specific weaknesses, list the number of correct answers you had under each of the following categories (which correspond to the content areas of the Social Studies test), and compare your score with the average scores specified in the right-hand column. Review the answer analysis section beginning on page 661 for each of the questions you got wrong, and give yourself more practice in your weak areas with the appropriate material in Unit IV (including the "Glossary of Social Studies Terms"), before attempting Practice Examination Two.

Content Areas	Items	Your Score	Average Score
Civics and Government	1–6, 8–9, 21–22, 34–35, 49–50		11
Economics	10–13, 19–20		4
History	7, 14–18, 28–33, 40		9
Geography	23–27, 37–38, 48		6

Total _____

TEST 3: SCIENCE/PAGE 619

I. CHECK YOUR ANSWERS, using the following answer key:

1. **5**	15. **4**	29. **3**	43. **3**
2. **5**	16. **3**	30. **4**	44. **3**
3. **1**	17. **4**	31. **3**	45. **5**
4. **2**	18. **4**	32. **2**	46. **3**
5. **1**	19. **4**	33. **5**	47. **1**
6. **3**	20. **1**	34. **3**	48. **2**
7. **3**	21. **3**	35. **2**	49. **2**
8. **1**	22. **1**	36. **4**	50. **4**
9. **4**	23. **4**	37. **3**	
10. **2**	24. **4**	38. **3**	
11. **5**	25. **4**	39. **4**	
12. **1**	26. **4**	40. **2**	
13. **2**	27. **4**	41. **5**	
14. **2**	28. **2**	42. **2**	

II. SCORE YOURSELF:

Number correct:

Excellent _____
44–50

Good _____
38–43

Fair _____
32–37

III. EVALUATE YOUR SCORE: Did you get at least 32 correct answers? If not, you need more practice for the Science test. In any event, you can improve your performance to Excellent or Good by analyzing your errors.

IV. ANALYZE YOUR ERRORS: To determine your specific weaknesses, encircle the number of each question you got wrong. This will reveal the specific science area that needs emphasis in planning your study program. After studying the answer analysis section beginning on page 664 for each of the questions you got wrong, list the terms that you feel need further explanation and study them in the "Glossary of Scientific Terms" beginning on page 360. Then give yourself more practice in your weak areas with the appropriate material in Unit V before attempting Practice Examination Two.

Content Areas	Items	Your Score	Average Score
Biology	1–22, 32, 33, 41, 44, 45, 47–50		22
Earth Science	23–25, 37, 39, 40, 46		3
Chemistry	26–31, 34, 36, 37, 42, 43, 51–57		10
Physics	35, 38,		7

Total _____

TEST 4: LANGUAGE ARTS, READING/PAGE 631

I. CHECK YOUR ANSWERS, using the following answer key:

1. **1**	10. **1**	19. **2**	28. **5**	37. **3**
2. **4**	11. **1**	20. **1**	29. **3**	38. **1**
3. **2**	12. **1**	21. **2**	30. **3**	39. **4**
4. **3**	13. **4**	22. **2**	31. **4**	40. **5**
5. **3**	14. **3**	23. **1**	32. **5**	
6. **4**	15. **3**	24. **3**	33. **3**	
7. **2**	16. **4**	25. **5**	34. **3**	
8. **1**	17. **3**	26. **4**	35. **5**	
9. **3**	18. **2**	27. **1**	36. **4**	

II. SCORE YOURSELF:

Number correct:

Excellent _____
36–40

Good _____
32–35

Fair _____
28–31

III. EVALUATE YOUR SCORE: Did you get at least 28 correct answers? If not, you need more practice for the Language Arts, Reading test. You can improve your performance to Excellent or Good by analyzing your errors.

IV. ANALYZE YOUR ERRORS: To determine your specific weaknesses, first list the number of correct answers you had under each of the following categories and compare your score with the average scores in the right-hand column. After studying the Answer Analysis section beginning on page 667 for each of the questions you answered incorrectly, study the material in the sections "Basic Reading Skills" and "Reading Prose, Poetry, and Drama" in Unit VI as well as the "Glossary of Literary Terms" (page 433) to strengthen your weak areas before attempting Practice Examination Two.

Reading Skills	Items	Your Score	Average Score
Locating the Main Idea	6, 15, 26, 28, 31		3
Finding Details	2–3, 7, 11, 13–14, 16–17, 25, 27–29, 33–34, 36–37, 40		12
Inferring Meaning	4–5, 12, 18–20, 22–23, 32, 35		6
Making Inferences	8–10, 17, 21, 24, 26–27, 38–39		7
Determining Tone and Mood	1, 13–14		2
Inferring Character	5		1

Total _____

Now to see how your scores in the content areas of Language Arts, Reading test compare with the average scores in the right-hand column, list your score for each of the following:

Literary Forms	Items	Your Score	Average Score
Prose Fiction	11–20		7
Prose Nonfiction	1–10, 31–40		15
Poetry	20–25		3
Drama	26–30		3

Total _____

Note: While Commentary on the Arts is a content area in itself, the commentary, as written, is in the form of prose nonfiction.

TEST 5: MATHEMATICS/PAGE 640

I. CHECK YOUR ANSWERS, using the following answer key:

Part I

1. **3**	21. **5**	31. **450**
2. **3**	22. **4**	32. **3**
3. **5**	23.	33. **4**
4. **2**		34. **5**
5. **20**		35. **68**
6. **3**		36. **3**
7. **5**		37. **1**
8. **4**		38. **5**
9. **74**		39. **4**
10. **5**		40. **5**
11. **1/4 or .25**		41. **4**
12. **2**		42. **2**
13. **12**	24. **1,080**	43. **60**
14. **4**	25. **1**	44. **55**
15. **5**	**Part II**	45. **3**
16. **3**	26. **5**	46. **2**
17. **3**	27. **3**	47. **5**
18. **5**	28. **3**	48. **4**
19. **4**	29. **3**	49. **5**
20. **3**	30. **4**	50. **2**

II. SCORE YOURSELF:

Number correct:

Excellent _____
40–50

Good _____
32–39

Fair _____
28–31

III. EVALUATE YOUR SCORE: Did you get at least 38 correct answers? If not, you need more practice for the Mathematics test. In any event, you can improve your performance to Excellent or Good by analyzing your errors.

IV. ANALYZE YOUR ERRORS: To determine your specific weaknesses, list the number of correct answers you had under each of the following categories, and compare your score with the average scores specified in the right-hand column. After studying the Answer Analysis section beginning on page 668 for each of the questions you got wrong, give yourself more practice in your weak areas with the appropriate material in Unit VII before attempting Practice Examination Two.

Content Areas	Items	Your Score	Average Score
Numbers and Basic Operations	1, 4, 9, 11, 13, 16, 17, 22, 34, 48		5
Fractions and Measurements	6, 20, 35, 46		2
Decimals and Percents	10, 15, 24		2
Data Analysis	26, 29, 30, 32, 33, 37 38, 41–43, 45, 47		7
Algebra	3, 7, 8, 12, 14, 21, 25 28, 36		5
Geometry	2, 5, 18, 19, 23, 27, 31 39, 40, 44, 49, 50		7

Total _____

YOUR TOTAL GED SCORE

The Language Arts, Writing Test _____

The Social Studies Test _____

The Science Test _____

The Language Arts, Reading Test _____

The Mathematics Test _____

Total _____

Answer Analysis

TEST 1: LANGUAGE ARTS, WRITING, PART I/PAGE 593

1. **5** This change is necessary to correct the run-on sentence.
2. **2** *Department of Agriculture* must be capitalized.
3. **3** The singular subject *Care* requires the singular verb *is*. *Among* is necessary because the verb *include* implies other precautions that are not mentioned.
4. **4** The correct verb to agree with the subject *errands* is *have*.
5. **1** The original is correct because two equally important ideas require two independent clauses connected by a coordinate conjunction. Since the clauses express similar, not opposing, ideas, *and*, rather than *but*, is the correct conjunction.
6. **1** The correct homonym is *for*; *four* is the number.
7. **1** The correct pronoun to agree with the noun *foods* is *they*.
8. **1** The use of the two adjective clauses *which contain food that may be* avoids the repetition of *swollen or leaking can*.
9. **1** The first sentence is the thesis statement because it is a general statement about food safety beginning in the marketplace; all other sentences relate to that one idea.
10. **1** The original is correct. The second idea, "the people in the family may change," is in opposition to the first, so *although* is necessary. The comma after *dominant* must be retained.
11. **1** This combination eliminates repetition of the words *will also increase*.
12. **3** This is necessary to avoid the run-on sentence.
13. **1** The correct pronoun to agree with the noun *families* is *their*, meaning "belonging to them."
14. **5** No correction is necessary.
15. **5** No correction is necessary.
16. **5** No correction is necessary.
17. **1** No new paragraph is needed in this passage.
18. **5** No correction is necessary.
19. **4** The sentences are best combined by an adjective clause, *that spreads*, which modifies *disease*.
20. **5** No correction is necessary.
21. **5** No correction is necessary.
22. **2** The correct homonym is *their*, meaning "belonging to them."
23. **2** To achieve parallelism with *knowledge* and *understanding*, a noun, *example*, must be used.
24. **3** A comma is needed after a lengthy introductory clause.
25. **5** This change is necessary to prevent a run-on sentence.
26. **3** The proper sequence of tenses requires the future perfect tense *will have been* since this action precedes *is tempted*.
27. **4** The pronoun, *his*, must agree in number with its antecedent, *drug abuser*.
28. **4** The verb, *is*, must be singular because its subject, *type*, is singular.
29. **1** *Americans* should be capitalized.
30. **2** The correct verb to agree with the subject *nine* is *are*.
31. **1** The correct pronoun to agree with the noun *injuries* is *they*.
32. **1** The correct pronoun to agree with noun *injuries* is *they*.
33. **4** A comma is used to separate items in a series.
34. **2** *Medical* should not be capitalized in the sentence because it is not a proper pronoun.
35. **3** The sentence is a run-on sentence and requires a comma before the conjunction *but*.
36. **4** The insertion of *are* is necessary to parallel *are in a hurry* and *are careless*.
37. **1** After sentence 10, a new topic begins; therefore, a new paragraph should be started.
38. **1** No correction is necessary.
39. **2** *Mom* and *Pop* should be capitalized since they are proper nouns.
40. **4** The proper homonym is *your*, meaning "belonging to you."
41. **3** A comma, not a period, is necessary before the final verb in the series, which cannot be a separate sentence.
42. **1** The correct spelling is *accessories*.
43. **3** *You're*, which is a contraction of *you are*, is required in this sentence.

44. **1** The original is the best way. The colon is used because it introduces the advice.
45. **1** *Invest in* is required by the sense of the sentence.
46. **5** No new paragraph is needed in this passage. All ideas have been clearly organized.
47. **4** *Whom* is necessary since this word is the object of the preposition *with* and must be in the objective case.

48. **5** No new paragraph is needed in this passage. All ideas have been clearly organized.
49. **1** Sentence 1 is the thesis statement because it generally states "clothes can help establish a person's identity. . . ." All other sentences relate to this one idea.
50. **5** *Since* would be required because the second idea is the result of the first.

TEST 1: LANGUAGE ARTS, WRITING, PART II/PAGE 605

SAMPLE ESSAY

I have known a great many people in my life, but the one person that has had the greatest influence on my life would be my father. He taught me that hard work really pays off, small things really matter, and love lasts more than a lifetime.

My father taught me that hard work really pays off. He worked day and night in a small mining company barely making enough to feed a family of seven. I never heard him complain as he brought home his weekly pay and handed it to my mother to buy food and necessities. I remember how hard and how long he had to work to be able to buy me a new coat for winter. It made me appreciate it all the more.

My father taught me that small things in life really matter. He didn't have a lot of material possessions to offer me, but would often save me back a part of his lunch. He knew that I met him at the end of the driveway every day to carry his lunchbox and I would always look in to see if there was something for me. There usually was.

My father taught me that love lasts more than a lifetime. I found this out when he passed away. I will never forget the love that he had for me and my family and I for him. His lunchbox remains on the shelf as a reminder of the times we shared.

My father was a wonderful person who influenced my life more than he will ever know. It was both a privilege and an honor to be his daughter.

TEST 2: SOCIAL STUDIES/PAGE 606

1. **2** As indicated in the first paragraph, the word *genocide* is the joining of the Greek *genos*, meaning race or tribe, and the Latin suffix *-cide*, meaning killing.
2. **4** The third paragraph gives the scope of the term *genocide* as including the intent to destroy a national, ethnical, racial, or religious group. It does not refer to political groups, as such.

3. **2** Genocide was practiced on a large scale by the Nazis in the destruction of six million Jews. Other groups that have been subjected to genocide, as mentioned in the second paragraph, are Armenians, Gypsies, and Chinese.
4. **4** This obviously is a ruling of a court. Therefore of the choices given, only Choice 4, the Supreme Court, could be correct. Incidentally, this selection is part of the important decision of

the Supreme Court on the subject of desegregation of schools.

5. **4** The passage indicates that to separate children in grade and high schools solely because of race is to generate a feeling of inferiority in minority children. This is a psychological reason for rejecting segregation.

6. **3** The first sentence of the final paragraph indicates that modern psychological knowledge does not support the *Plessy* v. *Ferguson* decision and, by implication, indicates that psychological knowledge at the time of *Plessy* v. *Ferguson* no longer applies.

7. **1** The photograph is a Pulitzer prize–winning photograph by Bill Pierce. His photo captured the American soldier's quick and brutal execution of a Vietcong soldier. His photograph sparked even more protest against America's involvement in the Vietnam War.

8. **4** Both the Democrats and Republicans include supporters from all sections of the nation and from various social and ethnic backgrounds. Each contains leaders and members whose political views range from conservative to moderate to liberal. To gain control of the government, a political party needs the support of a majority of the American voters, and thus must have broad appeal. The Democrats have usually drawn support from labor and minority groups; the Republicans, from businesspeople and wealthier farmers. Party differences have been greater on domestic issues (e.g., tax cuts and spending for social programs) than on foreign policy.

9. **2** The cartoon refers to the first free elections in South Africa, which took place in 1994, when a new constitution provided equal rights to vote for all South Africans. The shackle falling from the arm of the black voter symbolizes the freedom that came with the right to vote.

10. **4** In the graph of economic growth, the line for actual growth is much higher for 1996–1999, about 3.6%, than the forecast of about 2.4%.

11. **3** The lines for actual and forecast inflation nearly coincide, indicating the accuracy of the economists' forecasts.

12. **3** The gap between the fast-rising "desired demand" and the "potential supply," which levels off, is first noticeable on the graph at about 1990.

13. **1** Western European countries and Japan would lack fuel for their industries, and production would drop, with resultant unemployment and depression.

14. **1** Such resistance is often expressed by *denying* the formal methods for peaceful change. Failure to permit evolutionary change may result in revolution.

15. **2** Speaker *B* holds that the frontier made U.S. history unique; he would see only dissimilarities between the French and American revolutions. Speaker *C* stresses historical compromise between conflicting American groups.

16. **2** Speaker *B* would most likely agree that the existence of the American frontier provided a *safety valve* for those who wanted to leave the more crowded East. Such space was unavailable in the European countries from which most Americans or their forebears had come.

17. **4** The different historical perspective of each historian will assign differing causes and results to the same major events.

18. **3** The company's charter gave it a monopoly over colonization and trade in an area, with profits being shared by the shareholders and the King.

19. **1** President Johnson mentioned full employment as the first of America's unfinished tasks and the first goal that must be achieved in the national interest.

20. **4** President Johnson listed the widening of the benefits of prosperity as one of the tasks that remained unfinished.

21. **1** While the president is authorized to negotiate treaties, two-thirds of the Senate must ratify any treaty he negotiates. This is the system of checks and balances.

22. **3** The role of the Senate is authorized in Section 3 of Article 1 of the Constitution.

23. **2** A valid generalization from the chart is that industrialized nations have lower birth rates and infant mortality rates than developing nations. The first six nations of the chart are developing nations, whereas the last six are industrialized nations. The average birth rate of the developing nations is four times greater than that of the industrialized nations. The difference between infant mortality rates is even greater, from Uganda's, which is 12 times greater than Italy's, to Angola's, which is 31 times greater than Japan's.

24. **1** According to the chart, the lowest birthrates are found mostly in western Europe. Four of the six industrialized nations with low birthrates are in western Europe.

25. **4** Uganda, Somalia, Angola, and Ethiopia, four of the six countries with the highest infant mortality, are in Africa.

26. **4** Oil spills have repeatedly ruined the recreational value of beaches and destroyed fish and birdlife, causing both economic and ecological damage.

27. **4** The definition states that topography deals with the surface features of a region.

28. **4** The passage alludes to "principles of union," "cement to the Union," and "their best interests would be best promoted by union."

29. **3** The passage refers to "reasonable jealousies" between the people of the eastern and the southern states.

30. **2** Jealousies "subsided" when inhabitants of different states became better acquainted.

31. **5** The frontier's passing coincides with the end of gifts of free land.

32. **1** The author lists all the contributions of the frontier—escape from the past and opportunity for new experiences, among others.

33. **3** It was written one hundred years after the Constitution (1789) and four hundred years after the discovery of America (1492).

34. **4** The cartoon refers to the collapse of communism in the early 1990s. The hammer and sickle is a symbol of the Soviet Union. A series of symbols is arranged to look like the rib cage of the skeleton of a dinosaur, and the wording in the cartoon implies that communism, like the dinosaur, could not adapt to change.

35. **3** The hammer and sickle is the symbol of the former Union of Socialist Soviet Republics (USSR).

36. **2** Heredity and environment each represents various factors contributing to the behavior of individuals and groups. No *single* factor can be isolated and identified as determining human actions.

37. **4** It is trade that keeps us alive.

38. **2** Increased population was due to speeded-up economic unification.

39. **3** Two views regarding assimilation of Native Americans into American life are mentioned—a belief that total assimilation is inevitable, and a belief that Native Americans will keep separate identities for a long time into the future.

40. **1** Collective security calls for nations to coordinate their military strength to protect one another from aggression.

41. **3** Social mobility is the movement of individuals up or down in social and economic status in society, largely on ability and effort. Choice 3 is an example of social mobility.

42. **4** Cultural diversity, a variety of cultural patterns, exists where different peoples come together frequently and intermingle. Migration is a principal means of bringing this diversity about.

43. **4** Culture shock results from rapid social change—movement to a more developed society or movement to a less developed one. Choice 4 is an example of the latter.

44. **2** An extended family includes grandparents, uncles, aunts, and cousins. Out of economic necessity, they may live together and survive because of their dependence on one another.

45. **1** A pluralistic society encourages coexistence of peoples of various ethnic heritages, usually holding differing views on important issues.

46. **3** The study found that United States adolescents smoke less than those in many industrialized nations.

47. **4** The 15-year-olds ranked 20th, 14 places lower than 11-year-olds. They are less addicted to TV.

48. **5** The passage states that geographic natural features leave their imprint on society.

49. **3** In Table *A*, 65% opposed home searches without a specific warrant; 68% opposed electronic surveillance of citizens without a court order.

50. **3** Table *B* shows that 63% would allow the federal government to eavesdrop with specific court permission. When the same question was asked negatively in Table *A*, 68% opposed electronic eavesdropping without such permission.

TEST 3: SCIENCE/PAGE 619

1. **5** The article defines population as a group of organisms of the same species living together in a given location. An ecosystem (or ecological system) consists of the living community of a region and its nonliving environment. The biosphere is that portion of the earth in which ecosystems function. A community consists of populations of different species.

2. **5** The diagram illustrates a simple community consisting of populations of different species living together and interacting with each other.

3. **1** The factor that helps to keep a population in check is natural *predators*. Both predators and prey are adapted to each other and to the environment. If an organism is introduced into a new habitat, it will have few natural enemies or predators. Its population increases.

4. **2** In this simple community the plants carry on photosynthesis, whereby they give off oxygen and make food for themselves and the fish. The fish breathe and supply carbon dioxide to the plants, which they need for the process of photosynthesis. The wastes produced by the fish are acted upon by bacteria in the mud and produce nitrates for the plant. As long as these interrelationships are maintained, the total weight of the container and its contents will remain the same.

5. **1** A biotic factor is one concerned with living things. Minerals are not living.

6. **3** A *community* is a particular environment in which organisms of different species live and interact. A community is a self-maintaining unit in which energy and food materials are recycled.

7. **3** The chart shows a 2-year cycle, but for either year, the whales spend 3 months in Arctic waters.

8. **1** The whales are born in January (arrow 2) and by March they are migrating north. This is a span of 2 months.

9. **4** Gray whales conceive in December (arrow 1), and calves are born in January, 13 months later. Keep in mind that this figure shows a 2-year cycle.

10. **2** In its first year of life, only the first 2 months are spent in the waters off Baja California. The rest of that year is spent living in Arctic waters or migrating to and from those waters.

11. **5** This question is asking you to find a function that is specific to the right

side of the brain. Choices 1 to 4 are all found in the list of left-brain functions, while musical ability, Choice 5, is a right-brain function and is the correct answer.

12. **1** Nerve cells, such as those that make up the brain are known as neurons. Notice that the term is defined for you near the end of the first paragraph. As is often the case with a GED question, the information you need is given in the passage.

13. **2** The left side of the brain is responsible for mathematical reasoning, as the table tells you.

14. **2** In order for functions to move from one side of the brain to the other, there must be some communication between the two sides. The passage explains that the *corpus callosum* is responsible for this.

15. **4** Both chemical and electrical signals are mentioned in the passage. Hemisphere signals are not mentioned at all.

16. **3** The passage says that the axon is the part of the neuron that carries the signal from neuron to neuron, and that the synapse is the junction between neurons. Each of the other choices contains an error.

17. **4** The graph shows that soil covered with mulch has a higher moisture content and less range (variation) of moisture content than soil not covered with mulch.

18. **4** Rain would probably increase the moisture content, so look for the part of the graph where moisture content increased the most, which is days 15–20. Note that this is true for both soil covered by mulch and soil not covered by mulch.

19. **4** Neither size nor color was a factor in this experiment, nor was the cost an issue. The same mice could not be reused; the variable in this experiment is learning, and the mice had already been influenced. Choice 4 is the best answer.

20. **1** This choice is a conclusion that can be drawn from the experiment. All the other choices are irrelevant or erroneous.

21. **3** This answer is given in the passage.

22. **1** The issue of illumination was not part of the experiment and is therefore irrelevant.

23. **3** As important as the other functions are, losing oxygen would have the most immediate damage. Humans can live only a matter of minutes without oxygen, but can go much longer without food or water.

24. **4** Each person needs a kilogram of oxygen a day. Multiply 1 kilogram per person per day times 10 people times 21 days to get 210 kilograms.

25. **3** Weightlessness would not be concern for people on Earth.

26. **4** The passage specifically mentions calcium compounds as being natural neutralizers of acid rain.

27. **4** Hydroelectric plants do not burn fossil fuels to generate electricity. All of the other choices are specifically mentioned as contributing to acid rain.

28. **2** The chart chows that the highest pH substance listed is lye, the most basic. The information is almost always provided to you. Your job is to take the information given in the passage and use it to answer the questions.

29. **3** Neutralization requires an acid and a base. The only combination listed among the choices that has an acid and a base is Choice 3. Choice 1 consists of two acids, and Choice 2 of two bases. Choice 4 also contains two bases. Distilled water is neutral and will not be involved in a neutralization.

30. **4** The best approach would be to reduce or stop the problem at its source. The other choices would do nothing to prevent the same problems from reappearing again.

31. **3** The passage specifically mentions that carbon dioxide dissolving in water does not cause acid rain. It also tells you that oxides of nitrogen and sulfur are leading causes of acid rain. Choice 1, 2, 4, and 5 are oxides of nitrogen and sulfur.

32. **2** The only way the gardener can know how much to use is to follow the instructions given.

33. **5** Reptilia: garter snake; Aves: house sparrow; Mammalia: African elephant.

34. **3** The sugar becomes less soluble, and may come out of solution as a solid. The gas becomes more soluble and will remain in solution. If anything, the water will evaporate more slowly at lower temperatures.

35. **2** Locate the given pressure, 8 mm, along the horizontal axis. Move up the 8 mm line until the graph curve is reached. On the vertical axis at the left, you will find that the volume at this point is approximately 2 mL.

36. **4** Propane (C_3H_8) is an organic compound. HNO_3, H_2SO_4, and HCl are acids. NaCl is a salt.

37. **3** The only solution among the answers that is specifically identified in the passage as an electrolyte is sodium chloride.

38. **3** In horizontal flight, the engine thrust pushes the plane forward and air drag holds it back; if they are equal, there will be no change in speed. In Choices 1 and 2 one of the vertical forces is greater than the other. Choice 4 is wrong because the force acting on the wall has nothing to do with the speed of the ball. Choice 5 is wrong because it takes no account of the pull of gravity.

39. **4** No small planets have rings, but all the large planets except Jupiter have them. Choice 1 is wrong because Jupiter has no rings. Choice 2 is wrong because Pluto has no rings. Choice 3 is wrong because a definite trend is apparent. Choice 5 is wrong because there is no reason to believe that Pluto ever had rings.

40. **2** Only in deserts is dry sand on the surface, where it can be picked up and carried by the wind.

41. **5** If some such substance is present, there is no reason to suppose that it would affect frogs differently from fish.

42. **2** The original sample had 20.00 grams total. At the end of the heating process, 12.00 grams were left; thus, 8.00 grams must have been water that evaporated away.

43. **3** The percentage that was water was 8.00 grams water/20.00 grams total or .4 which is 40%.

44. **3** The impulse starts with irritation of the cornea, goes through a sensory neuron to the brain, and then passes through a motor neuron to the tear gland.

45. **5** That DDT-resistant mosquitoes now exist in greater numbers than 10 years ago means that genetic differences permitted some mosquitoes to survive DDT use. Mosquitoes that did not survive DDT use died off. Those with survival power lived and reproduced others with similar survival power. The result was an increase in the numbers of DDT-resistant mosquitoes in the species.

46. **3** Fossils are found in sedimentary rocks, which are laid down in layers. The oldest layers are closest to the Earth's crust, and the youngest layers are near the surface. To conclude that a species had not changed very much over the years, the unchanged fossils of that species must have been distributed throughout the layers.

47. **1** Gametes—eggs and sperms—have half as many chromosomes as somatic cells, such as leaf cells. The somatic cell number is produced at fertilization.

48. **2** Under normal circumstances, the total number of adult robins or of adult salmon does not change rapidly. Each adult pair, on the average, produces enough eggs to replace itself, so only two eggs survive to adulthood for each adult pair.
49. **2** Corn plants grown in the dark are white. The most probable explanation is that the expression of the gene

for color may depend on the environment. That these plants have the genetic information for chlorophyll production can be assumed because they are genetically identical to the plants grown in the light. Light is needed to activate the chlorophyll gene.
50. **4** In sexual reproduction, new properties can be produced by recombination of the genes of the two parents.

TEST 4: LANGUAGE ARTS, READING/PAGE 631

1. **1** In the first paragraph, the writer describes "the hot, humid haze" and other details of August in his surroundings.
2. **4** The writer states that "August was a time to do nothing and be proud of it."
3. **2** The writer remembers August "with a bit of anxiety because it "was the time of hurricanes and polio."
4. **3** ". . . I remember the strange feel of the air. The first breezes of the hurricane were so mild, so moist, so soft as to be barely distinguishable from the feel of one's own skin."
5. **3** August is remembered as a time of both pleasure and anxiety. The hurricanes were scary for adults, but they were "a lot of fun" for the narrator.
6. **4** The author states "we'd be lost without" new groups.
7. **2** The family sends a bright young man or woman.
8. **1** Other family members will come with the money the youth is sending back.
9. **3** The newcomer progresses from busboy to waiter and then tries to become the owner.
10. **1** The United States rejuvenates itself by bringing in new people.
11. **1** As a religious person, Shmul-Leibele blesses the Lord for his food.
12. **1** Shmul-Leibele compliments Shoshe, saying, "the loaf is just right."
13. **4** Whiskey was not part of the ritual. Shmul-Leibele drank it because the fish course took his "breath away."

14. **3** He prayed "not to be in need . . . of their loans."
15. **3** Its purpose is to describe the Sabbath meal of an elderly Jewish couple.
16. **4** Lottie realizes Bess hadn't "seen" her shining room.
17. **3** Bess saw only a place in her sister's home and heart.
18. **2** Lottie felt that she had not really lived.
19. **2** Lottie says to Bess that she's going to let her show her how to live.
20. **1** Lottie is going to try to catch up with life.
21. **2** The poet is reacting to a "fatuous thing" (a photograph of himself) that he has been shown by a photographer.
22. **2** The poet has "spent blood and tears" and experienced "pain, the struggle and the wrack."
23. **1** Time "has graven . . . deep lines of joy and sorrow" on his face.
24. **3** The poet wants his "scars of battle" to be put back into the photograph.
25. **5** The 14-line poem is a sonnet with the rhyme scheme *a b b a a b b a c d c d e e.*
26. **4** Kay says to Grant, "I won't accept that." Conover says, "I think Kay's right."
27. **1** Grant implies that he won't play ball and states that he will go ahead with his speech.
28. **5** Grant says that "to get votes, both parties are out to buy the American people."
29. **3** Grant promises himself that he would appeal to the best in the American people.

30. **3** Grant says he'll take care of any candidate who threatens peace from now on.

31. **4** See the section "Locating the Main Idea." The opening and closing lines refer to the father's devotion to education.

32. **5** *Divined* means "guessed," not "heavenly."

33. **3** The father is described as "not like other aliens, who brought their children in dull obedience to the law . . . ."

34. **3** The author's father is described as "eager," with "nervous hands eloquent in gesture, and a voice full of feeling." He is evidently sincere, but not in the least calm.

35. **5** Here *green* means immigrant, new to the United States.

36. **4** According to the letter, Shawn Black is mentioned as an employee who performed well at Smith Incorporated, but is "destined to achieve new heights in his career and set new records for his future employer"; thus, he is seeking employment with a different company.

37. **3** According to the letter, many of Shawn Black's positive qualities are mentioned, implying that he is an excellent candidate in the marketing field.

38. **1** The letter saying that Shawn Black's "patience with employees under him and with management make him an ideal employee" implies that he has great communication skills.

39. **4** The author of the letter states that "any company considering this individual for employment has my most enthusiastic recommendation."

40. **5** The letter states that the author gives his "most enthusiastic recommendation" for Shawn Black, implying that he is pleased with his job performance at Smith Incorporated.

TEST 5: MATHEMATICS/PAGE 640

Part I

1. **3** Luisa earned a total of 40($6.30) = $252. To find the number of hours Joan would take to earn $252, divide $252 by $8.40:
$252.00 \div 8.40 = 30$

2. **3** Since $m\angle ACB = 90°$ and $m\angle CAD = 40°$, then $m\angle B = 180° - 90° - 40° = 50°$.
In $\triangle BCD$, $m\angle CDB = 90°$ and $m\angle B = 50°$.
Therefore,
$m\angle DCB = 180° - 90° - 50° = 40°$.

3. **5** If the class has x students and 5 students are absent, then $x - 5$ students are present:
$$\frac{x - 5}{x}$$

4. **2** If the tank is $\frac{1}{3}$ full, it is $\frac{2}{3}$ empty.
Let x = capacity of tank.
$\frac{2}{3}x = 16$, so $x = 16 \div \frac{2}{3} = 16 \times \frac{3}{2} = 24$.

5. **20** Let x = length of ramp.
Use the Pythagorean theorem to obtain the equation:
$x^2 = 12^2 + 16^2 = 144 + 256 = 400$
$x = \sqrt{400} = 20$

6. **3** 48 half-pints = 24 pt.
Since 2 pt. = 1 qt.,
24 pt. = 12 qt.
Since 4 qt. = 1 gal.,
12 qt. = 3 gal.
3($3.50) = $10.50

7. **5** You do not need the value of x, you need the value of $2\frac{1}{2}x = \frac{5}{2}x = \frac{5x}{2}$.
Since $5x - 1 = 34$, then $5x = 35$, and
$\frac{5x}{2} = \frac{35}{2} = 17\frac{1}{2}$.

8. **4** If $AC = 18$ and $BC = 8$ then
$AB = 18 - 8 = 10$.
The ratio $AB:BC = 10:8$, or $5:4$.

9. **74** Let x = width of room.
   $23x = 322$
   $x = 332 \div 23 = 14$
   Perimeter =
   $23 + 14 + 23 + 14 = 74$ ft.

```
+---------------------------+
|                           |
|      AREA = 322          | x
|      sq. ft.             |
|                           |
+---------------------------+
            23'
```

10. **5** To determine the price that Computer Central charges for the digital camera, Fatima must know the price from which the store deducts 20%.

11. **1/4 or .25** If a crew can load a truck in 3 hrs., it can load $\frac{1}{3}$ of the truck in 1 hr. In 45 min., or $\frac{3}{4}$ hr., the crew can load $\frac{3}{4} \times \frac{1}{3} = \frac{1}{4} = .25$ of the truck.

12. **2** $\quad x^2 + x - 6 = 0$
   $(x + 3)(x - 2) = 0$
   $x + 3 = 0$ or $x - 2 = 0$
   $x = -3$ or $x = 2$
   The correct choice is (2).

13. **12** 40 ft. $= 40 \times 12 = 480$ in.
   3 ft. 4 in. $= 3(12) + 4 = 36 + 4 = 40$ in.
   $480 \div 40 = 12$ scarfs

14. **4** Let x = amount of money Bob has. Then x is also the amount that Tom has, and $x + 5$ = amount that Henry has.
   Since $65 = x + x + x + 5 = 3x + 5$, then $3x = 60$, and $x = \$20$.

15. **5** You cannot compute the cost unless you are told the number of days that the couple stays at the motel. This information is not given.

16. **3** Let $\quad n$ = number.
   Then $\quad n^2$ = square of number,
   and $n + 4$ = number increased by 4.
   The equation is $n^2 + n + 4 = 60$.

17. **3** $6 \times 10^5 = 600,000$
   $4 \times 10^3 = 4,000$
   $600,000 \div 4,000 = 600 \div 4 = 150$

18. **5** Let x, $2x$, and $3x$ be the measures of the three angles. Then:
   $3x + 2x + x = 180$
   $6x = 180$
   $x = 180 \div 6 = 30$
   $3x = 3(30) = 90°$.

19. **4** Let $x = m\angle 3$,
   and $2x = m\angle 2$.
   $m\angle 1 + m\angle 2 + m\angle 3 = 180°$
   $36 + 2x + x = 180$
   $3x + 36 = 180$
   $3x = 180 - 36 = 144$
   $x = 144 \div 3 = 48°$

20. **3** The beef costs $4(\$2.76) = \$11.04$.
   The chicken costs $\$13.98 - \$11.04 = \$2.94$.

   To find the cost per pound of chicken, divide $\$2.94$ by $3\frac{1}{2}$, or by $\frac{7}{2}$.

   $2.94 \div \frac{7}{2} = 2.94 \times \frac{2}{7} = 0.84$

   The chicken cost $\$0.84$ per pound.

21. **5** The carpenter earns $\$16$ per hour or $9(16)$ dollars for 9 hrs. of work.
   The assistant earns $\$8$ per hour or $9(8)$ for 9 hrs. of work.
   Together they earned $9(16) + 9(8)$ dollars.

22. **4** To express a number in scientific notation, express it as the product of a number between 1 and 10 and a power of 10. In this case, the number between 1 and 10 is 6.315. In going from 6.315 to $63,150,000,000$, you move the decimal point 10 places to the right. Each such move represents a multiplication by 10. Thus, the entire movement of the decimal point represents multiplication by 10^{10}, and, $63,150,000,000 = 6.315 \times 10^{10}$.

23. **(-4,-2)** For the x coordinate (-4), count four places to the right of dead center (where the x and y lines intersect), then, for the y coordinate (-2), count two places down. Bubble in the appropriate grid.

24. **1,080** $\$12,000 \times 0.09 = \$1,080$

25. **1** $3x + 2 < 14$
   $3x < 12$
   $x < 4$
   The only choice less than 4 is 3.

Part II

26. **5** Add the amounts given:
   $11 + 6 + 5 + 40 + 30 = \$92$
   $\$100 - \$92$ leaves $\$8$ for profit.

27. **3** To find the perimeter of the figure, find the sum of the lengths of its sides.
   $2a + a + b + 2a + b + a + 2b = 6a + 4b$

28. **3** Let x = number of points scored by Jack,

$x + 7$ = number of points scored by Ben, and

$x - 2$ = number of points scored by Paul.

$$x + x + 7 + x - 2 = 38$$
$$3x + 5 = 38$$
$$3x = 38 - 5 = 33$$
$$x = 33 \div 3 = 11$$

29. **3** Use the formula $V = lwh$.

In this case, $l = 5$, $w = 5$, and $h = h$.

Therefore, $V = 5 \times 5 \times h = 25h$ and $25h = 200$.

5' h

5'

30. **4** Since $3^2 = 9$ and $4^2 = 16$, $\sqrt{12}$ is between 3 and 4. Only point D lies between 3 and 4.

31. **450** Divide the floor space into 2 rectangles by drawing line segment NM.

Area of a rectangle = lw

Area of large rectangle =
$20 \times 15 = 300$ sq. ft.

Area of small rectangle =
$10 \times 15 = 150$ sq. ft.

Total area of floor space =
$150 + 300 = 450$ sq. ft.

15' N 10'

20'   15'

M 10'

32. **3** Foreign investment on finance and insurance = $2 billion. If Americans spend 50% (or half) of that on video games, then they spend $1 billion.

33. **4** Foreign investment in manufacturing =
$2\frac{1}{2}$ billion

Foreign investment in petroleum =
$1 billion

Difference = $1\frac{1}{2}$ billion

34. **5** Replace the variables with their given values.

$-2^2(32 - (-2)) = 4(34) = 136$

35. **68** Since $\frac{1}{4}$ in. represents 8 mi., 1 in., represents $4 \times 8 = 32$ mi., and 2 in. represents $2 \times 32 = 64$ mi. $\frac{1}{8}$ in. = $\frac{1}{2}$ of $\frac{1}{4}$ in., so $\frac{1}{8}$ in. represents 4 mi. Then $2\frac{1}{8}$ in. represent $64 + 4 = 68$ mi.

36. **3** Let x = height of steeple. Set up a proportion:

$$\frac{\text{height of object}}{\text{length of shadow}} : \frac{x}{28} = \frac{6}{4}.$$

$4x = 6(28) = 168$

$x = 168 \div 4 = 42$ ft.

x

28'   6'

4'

37. **1** Ten chips is equal to 6% of total carbohydrates. Therefore, 5 chips would be half of that—or 3%.

$10 + 5 = 15$ chips, and
$6\% + 3\% = 9\%$

38. **5** Half of .5 g is .25 g.

39. **4** To find the distance between two points on the same vertical line, subtract their y-coordinates: $4 - (-3) = 4 + 3 = 7$.

40. **5** Slope $= \dfrac{y_1 - y_2}{x_1 - x_2}$

In this case, $y_1 = y$, $y_2 = 2$, $x_1 = 4$, and $x_2 = 1$.

Therefore, $\dfrac{y - 2}{4 - 1} = 1$

$$\dfrac{y - 2}{3} = 1$$

$$y - 2 = 3$$

$$y = 3 + 2 = 5.$$

41. **4** The top of the bar for Wednesday is at 6 on the vertical scale.

42. **2** Saturday's sales were more than 16 gallons, and Wednesday's sales were 6 gallons. For percent increase, find the actual amount of increase $(16 - 4 = 12)$, and divide it by the original amount, $\dfrac{12}{4} = 3 = 300\%$. Because Saturday's sales were more than 16 gallons, the answer is 2.

43. **60** The tops of the bars for Monday through Sunday are at 5, 4, 6, 5, 14, 17, and 9. These add up to 60.

44. **55** Let $x = m\angle OAB$
$OA = OB$ since radii of the same circle have equal measures.
Therefore, $m\angle OAB = m\angle OBA$.
$$x + x + 70 = 180$$
$$2x + 70 = 180$$
$$2x = 180 - 70 = 110$$
$$x = 110 \div 2 = 55$$

45. **3** Between 3:00 P.M. and 4:00 P.M., Sylvia drove $124 - 80 = 44$ mi. Since she was driving at a steady rate for the entire trip, in the $\frac{1}{4}$ hr. from 4:00 to 4:15 she drove another $\frac{1}{4}(44) = 11$ mi.

Therefore, at 4:15 P.M. she had driven $124 + 11 = 135$ mi.

46. **2** If Joan uses a full cup of milk instead of $\frac{1}{3}$ cup, she must multiply the measure of each ingredient by 3.
$3\left(\dfrac{2}{3}\right) = 2$ teaspoons of salt.

47. **5** This information can be read directly on the graph.

48. **4** Let $x =$ cost of lot, and
$3x =$ cost of house.
$$x + 3x = 120{,}000$$
$$4x = 120{,}000$$
$$x = 120{,}000 \div 4 = 30{,}000$$
$$3x = 3(30{,}000) = \$90{,}000$$

49. **5** In the figure below, the four obtuse angles all have the same measure, and the four acute angles also have the same measure:

$$a = d = e = g \quad b = c = f = h$$

Checking the choices, you see that they are all correct except (5): $b \neq g$

50. **2** Radius of outer circle $= \dfrac{1}{2}(48) = 24$ in.
Radius of inner circle $= 20$ in.
Use the formula $A = \pi r^2$.
Area of outer circle $=$
$\pi \times 24 \times 24 = 576\pi$
Area of inner circle $=$
$\pi \times 20 \times 20 = 400\pi$
Area of border $= 576\pi - 400\pi = 176\pi$

Answer Sheet for the Practice Examination

TEST 1: LANGUAGE ARTS, WRITING, PART I

1. ① ② ③ ④ ⑤
2. ① ② ③ ④ ⑤
3. ① ② ③ ④ ⑤
4. ① ② ③ ④ ⑤
5. ① ② ③ ④ ⑤
6. ① ② ③ ④ ⑤
7. ① ② ③ ④ ⑤
8. ① ② ③ ④ ⑤
9. ① ② ③ ④ ⑤
10. ① ② ③ ④ ⑤
11. ① ② ③ ④ ⑤
12. ① ② ③ ④ ⑤
13. ① ② ③ ④ ⑤
14. ① ② ③ ④ ⑤
15. ① ② ③ ④ ⑤
16. ① ② ③ ④ ⑤
17. ① ② ③ ④ ⑤
18. ① ② ③ ④ ⑤
19. ① ② ③ ④ ⑤

20. ① ② ③ ④ ⑤
21. ① ② ③ ④ ⑤
22. ① ② ③ ④ ⑤
23. ① ② ③ ④ ⑤
24. ① ② ③ ④ ⑤
25. ① ② ③ ④ ⑤
26. ① ② ③ ④ ⑤
27. ① ② ③ ④ ⑤
28. ① ② ③ ④ ⑤
29. ① ② ③ ④ ⑤
30. ① ② ③ ④ ⑤
31. ① ② ③ ④ ⑤
32. ① ② ③ ④ ⑤
33. ① ② ③ ④ ⑤
34. ① ② ③ ④ ⑤
35. ① ② ③ ④ ⑤
36. ① ② ③ ④ ⑤
37. ① ② ③ ④ ⑤
38. ① ② ③ ④ ⑤

39. ① ② ③ ④ ⑤
40. ① ② ③ ④ ⑤
41. ① ② ③ ④ ⑤
42. ① ② ③ ④ ⑤
43. ① ② ③ ④ ⑤
44. ① ② ③ ④ ⑤
45. ① ② ③ ④ ⑤
46. ① ② ③ ④ ⑤
47. ① ② ③ ④ ⑤
48. ① ② ③ ④ ⑤
49. ① ② ③ ④ ⑤
50. ① ② ③ ④ ⑤

TEST 2: SOCIAL STUDIES

1. ① ② ③ ④ ⑤
2. ① ② ③ ④ ⑤
3. ① ② ③ ④ ⑤
4. ① ② ③ ④ ⑤
5. ① ② ③ ④ ⑤
6. ① ② ③ ④ ⑤
7. ① ② ③ ④ ⑤
8. ① ② ③ ④ ⑤
9. ① ② ③ ④ ⑤
10. ① ② ③ ④ ⑤
11. ① ② ③ ④ ⑤
12. ① ② ③ ④ ⑤
13. ① ② ③ ④ ⑤
14. ① ② ③ ④ ⑤
15. ① ② ③ ④ ⑤
16. ① ② ③ ④ ⑤
17. ① ② ③ ④ ⑤
18. ① ② ③ ④ ⑤
19. ① ② ③ ④ ⑤
20. ① ② ③ ④ ⑤
21. ① ② ③ ④ ⑤
22. ① ② ③ ④ ⑤

23. ① ② ③ ④ ⑤
24. ① ② ③ ④ ⑤
25. ① ② ③ ④ ⑤
26. ① ② ③ ④ ⑤
27. ① ② ③ ④ ⑤
28. ① ② ③ ④ ⑤
29. ① ② ③ ④ ⑤
30. ① ② ③ ④ ⑤
31. ① ② ③ ④ ⑤
32. ① ② ③ ④ ⑤
33. ① ② ③ ④ ⑤
34. ① ② ③ ④ ⑤
35. ① ② ③ ④ ⑤
36. ① ② ③ ④ ⑤
37. ① ② ③ ④ ⑤
38. ① ② ③ ④ ⑤
39. ① ② ③ ④ ⑤
40. ① ② ③ ④ ⑤
41. ① ② ③ ④ ⑤
42. ① ② ③ ④ ⑤
43. ① ② ③ ④ ⑤
44. ① ② ③ ④ ⑤

45. ① ② ③ ④ ⑤
46. ① ② ③ ④ ⑤
47. ① ② ③ ④ ⑤
48. ① ② ③ ④ ⑤
49. ① ② ③ ④ ⑤
50. ① ② ③ ④ ⑤

TEST 3: SCIENCE

1. ① ② ③ ④ ⑤
2. ① ② ③ ④ ⑤
3. ① ② ③ ④ ⑤
4. ① ② ③ ④ ⑤
5. ① ② ③ ④ ⑤
6. ① ② ③ ④ ⑤
7. ① ② ③ ④ ⑤
8. ① ② ③ ④ ⑤
9. ① ② ③ ④ ⑤
10. ① ② ③ ④ ⑤
11. ① ② ③ ④ ⑤
12. ① ② ③ ④ ⑤
13. ① ② ③ ④ ⑤
14. ① ② ③ ④ ⑤
15. ① ② ③ ④ ⑤
16. ① ② ③ ④ ⑤
17. ① ② ③ ④ ⑤
18. ① ② ③ ④ ⑤
19. ① ② ③ ④ ⑤

20. ① ② ③ ④ ⑤
21. ① ② ③ ④ ⑤
22. ① ② ③ ④ ⑤
23. ① ② ③ ④ ⑤
24. ① ② ③ ④ ⑤
25. ① ② ③ ④ ⑤
26. ① ② ③ ④ ⑤
27. ① ② ③ ④ ⑤
28. ① ② ③ ④ ⑤
29. ① ② ③ ④ ⑤
30. ① ② ③ ④ ⑤
31. ① ② ③ ④ ⑤
32. ① ② ③ ④ ⑤
33. ① ② ③ ④ ⑤
34. ① ② ③ ④ ⑤
35. ① ② ③ ④ ⑤
36. ① ② ③ ④ ⑤
37. ① ② ③ ④ ⑤
38. ① ② ③ ④ ⑤

39. ① ② ③ ④ ⑤
40. ① ② ③ ④ ⑤
41. ① ② ③ ④ ⑤
42. ① ② ③ ④ ⑤
43. ① ② ③ ④ ⑤
44. ① ② ③ ④ ⑤
45. ① ② ③ ④ ⑤
46. ① ② ③ ④ ⑤
47. ① ② ③ ④ ⑤
48. ① ② ③ ④ ⑤
49. ① ② ③ ④ ⑤
50. ① ② ③ ④ ⑤

TEST 4: LANGUAGE ARTS, READING

1. ① ② ③ ④ ⑤
2. ① ② ③ ④ ⑤
3. ① ② ③ ④ ⑤
4. ① ② ③ ④ ⑤
5. ① ② ③ ④ ⑤
6. ① ② ③ ④ ⑤
7. ① ② ③ ④ ⑤
8. ① ② ③ ④ ⑤
9. ① ② ③ ④ ⑤
10. ① ② ③ ④ ⑤
11. ① ② ③ ④ ⑤
12. ① ② ③ ④ ⑤
13. ① ② ③ ④ ⑤
14. ① ② ③ ④ ⑤
15. ① ② ③ ④ ⑤

16. ① ② ③ ④ ⑤
17. ① ② ③ ④ ⑤
18. ① ② ③ ④ ⑤
19. ① ② ③ ④ ⑤
20. ① ② ③ ④ ⑤
21. ① ② ③ ④ ⑤
22. ① ② ③ ④ ⑤
23. ① ② ③ ④ ⑤
24. ① ② ③ ④ ⑤
25. ① ② ③ ④ ⑤
26. ① ② ③ ④ ⑤
27. ① ② ③ ④ ⑤
28. ① ② ③ ④ ⑤
29. ① ② ③ ④ ⑤
30. ① ② ③ ④ ⑤

31. ① ② ③ ④ ⑤
32. ① ② ③ ④ ⑤
33. ① ② ③ ④ ⑤
34. ① ② ③ ④ ⑤
35. ① ② ③ ④ ⑤
36. ① ② ③ ④ ⑤
37. ① ② ③ ④ ⑤
38. ① ② ③ ④ ⑤
39. ① ② ③ ④ ⑤
40. ① ② ③ ④ ⑤

TEST 5: MATHEMATICS, PART I

1. ① ② ③ ④ ⑤
2. ① ② ③ ④ ⑤
3. ① ② ③ ④ ⑤
4.

5.

6. ① ② ③ ④ ⑤
7.

8. ① ② ③ ④ ⑤
9. ① ② ③ ④ ⑤
10. ① ② ③ ④ ⑤
11. ① ② ③ ④ ⑤
12. ① ② ③ ④ ⑤
13.

14. ① ② ③ ④ ⑤
15. ① ② ③ ④ ⑤
16.

17. ① ② ③ ④ ⑤
18. ① ② ③ ④ ⑤
19. ① ② ③ ④ ⑤
20. ① ② ③ ④ ⑤

21. ① ② ③ ④ ⑤
21. ① ② ③ ④ ⑤
23. ① ② ③ ④ ⑤
24.

25.

TEST 5: MATHEMATICS, PART II

26. ① ② ③ ④ ⑤
27. ① ② ③ ④ ⑤
28. ① ② ③ ④ ⑤
29. ① ② ③ ④ ⑤
30. ① ② ③ ④ ⑤
31. ① ② ③ ④ ⑤
32. ① ② ③ ④ ⑤
33. ① ② ③ ④ ⑤
34. ① ② ③ ④ ⑤
35.

36. ① ② ③ ④ ⑤
37. ① ② ③ ④ ⑤
38. ① ② ③ ④ ⑤

39.

/	/	/	
.	.	.	.
0	0	0	0
1	1	1	1
2	2	2	2
3	3	3	3
4	4	4	4
5	5	5	5
6	6	6	6
7	7	7	7
8	8	8	8
9	9	9	9

40. ① ② ③ ④ ⑤
41. ① ② ③ ④ ⑤
42.

/	/	/	
.	.	.	.
0	0	0	0
1	1	1	1
2	2	2	2
3	3	3	3
4	4	4	4
5	5	5	5
6	6	6	6
7	7	7	7
8	8	8	8
9	9	9	9

43. ① ② ③ ④ ⑤
44. ① ② ③ ④ ⑤
45. ① ② ③ ④ ⑤
46. ① ② ③ ④ ⑤
47. ① ② ③ ④ ⑤
48. ① ② ③ ④ ⑤
49. ① ② ③ ④ ⑤
50. ① ② ③ ④ ⑤

PRACTICE EXAMINATION TWO

TEST 1: LANGUAGE ARTS, WRITING, PART I

Directions

The Language Arts, Writing test is intended to measure your ability to use clear and effective English. It is a test of English as it should be written, not as it might be spoken. This test includes both multiple-choice questions and an essay. These directions apply only to the multiple-choice section; a separate set of directions is given for the essay.

The multiple-choice section consists of paragraphs with numbered sentences. Some of the sentences contain errors in sentence structure, usage, or mechanics (spelling, punctuation, and capitalization). After reading the numbered sentences, answer the multiple-choice questions that follow. Some questions refer to sentences that are correct as written. The best answer for these questions is the one that leaves the sentence as originally written. The best answer for some questions is the one that produces a sentence that is consistent with the verb tense and point of view used throughout the paragraph.

You should spend no more than 75 minutes on the multiple-choice questions and 45 minutes on your essay. Work carefully, but do not spend too much time on any one question. You may begin working on the essay part of this test as soon as you complete the multiple-choice section.

To record your answers, mark the numbered space on the answer sheet beside the number that corresponds to the question in the test.

FOR EXAMPLE:

Sentence 1: **We were all honored to meet governor Phillips.**

What correction should be made to this sentence?

(1) insert a comma after <u>honored</u>
(2) change the spelling of <u>honored</u> to <u>honered</u>
(3) change <u>governor</u> to <u>Governor</u>
(4) replace <u>were</u> with <u>was</u>
(5) no correction is necessary

① ② ● ④ ⑤

In this example, the word "governor" should be capitalized; therefore, answer space 3 would be marked on the answer sheet.

GO ON TO THE NEXT PAGE

TEST 1: LANGUAGE ARTS, WRITING, PART I

<u>Questions 1–10</u> refer to the following paragraphs.

(1) Each year more young men and young women are recognizing the rewards in nursing and enroll in nursing programs, but the demand for nurses continues to outstrip the supply.
(2) If you join the personnel of a hospital you can choose among absorbing fields. (3) You can concentrate on work with children, in obstetrics, in surgery, or on the fascinating new techniques of orthopedics, which calls so heavily for a nurse's skill and imagination.
(4) Since Florence Nightingale went to the crimea over a hundred years ago, nurses have been an enormously mobile group. (5) If one wants to travel, many posts are open to you, both in this country and abroad. (6) You can choose foreign service with the World Health Organization, with our own goverment's foreign operations or with one of our armed services.
(7) Schools need nurses. (8) Many married nurses who want time in the afternoon with her own children find part-time positions ideal and easy to get. (9) Private practice bring its special rewards in choice of hours and cases.
(10) Opportunities in community and public health programs that require a bachelor's degree from an accredited school are growing rapidly. (11) A visiting nurse has a fascinating career, moving through many homes each day and leaving order and comfort behind.

1. Sentence 1: **Each year more young men and young women are recognizing the rewards in nursing and enroll in nursing programs, but the demand for nurses continues to outstrip the supply.**

   What correction should be made to this sentence?

   (1) change the spelling of <u>recognizing</u> to <u>reconizing</u>
   (2) change <u>enroll</u> to <u>are enrolling</u>
   (3) remove the comma before <u>but</u>
   (4) change <u>but</u> to <u>and</u>
   (5) no correction is necessary

2. Sentence 2: **If you join the personnel of a hospital you can choose among absorbing fields.**

   What correction should be made to this sentence?

   (1) change <u>join</u> to <u>will join</u>
   (2) change the spelling of <u>personnel</u> to <u>personel</u>
   (3) insert a comma after <u>hospital</u>
   (4) change the spelling of <u>choose</u> to <u>chose</u>
   (5) no correction is necessary

3. Sentence 3: **You can concentrate on work with children, in obstetrics, in surgery, or on the fascinating new techniques of orthopedics, which calls so heavily for a nurse's skill and imagination.**

   What correction should be made to this sentence?

   (1) change the spelling of <u>concentrate</u> to <u>consentrate</u>
   (2) change the spelling of <u>children</u> to <u>childern</u>
   (3) remove the comma after <u>surgery</u>
   (4) change <u>calls</u> to <u>call</u>
   (5) no correction is necessary

4. Sentence 4: **Since Florence Nightingale went to the crimea over a hundred years ago, nurses have been an enormously mobile group.**

   What correction should be made to this sentence?

   (1) change <u>went</u> to <u>had gone</u>
   (2) capitalize <u>crimea</u>
   (3) remove the comma after <u>ago</u>
   (4) change the spelling of <u>enormously</u> to <u>enormusly</u>
   (5) no correction is necessary

GO ON TO THE NEXT PAGE

TEST 1: LANGUAGE ARTS, WRITING, PART I

5. Sentence 5: **If one wants to travel, many posts are available to you, both in this country and abroad.**

   What correction should be made to this sentence?

   (1) change <u>one wants</u> to <u>you want</u>
   (2) remove the comma after <u>travel</u>
   (3) change the spelling of <u>available</u> to <u>availible</u>
   (4) remove the comma after <u>you</u>
   (5) no correction is necessary

6. Sentence 6: **You can choose foreign service with the World Health Organization, with our own goverment's foreign operations, or with one of our armed services.**

   What correction should be made to this sentence?

   (1) change the spelling of <u>foreign</u> to <u>forign</u>
   (2) remove the capitals from <u>World Health Organization</u>
   (3) remove the comma after <u>Organization</u>
   (4) change the spelling of <u>goverment's</u> to <u>government's</u>
   (5) no correction is necessary

7. Sentence 8: **Many married nurses who want time in the afternoon with her own children find part-time positions ideal and easy to get.**

   What correction should be made to this sentence?

   (1) change <u>who</u> to <u>whom</u>
   (2) insert a comma after <u>nurses</u>
   (3) remove the hyphen from <u>part-time</u>
   (4) change <u>her</u> to <u>their</u>
   (5) no correction is necessary

8. Sentence 9: **Private practice bring its special rewards in choice of hours and cases.**

   What correction should be made to this sentence?

   (1) insert a comma after <u>hours</u>
   (2) change <u>its</u> to <u>it's</u>
   (3) change the spelling of <u>special</u> to <u>speshal</u>
   (4) change <u>bring</u> to <u>brings</u>
   (5) no correction is necessary

9. Sentence 10: **Opportunities in community and public health <u>programs that require</u> a bachelor's degree from an accredited school are growing rapidly.**

   Which of the following is the best way to write the underlined portion of this sentence? If you think the original is the best way, choose option (1).

   (1) programs that require
   (2) programs who require
   (3) programs that do require
   (4) programs that are requiring
   (5) programs that will require

10. Sentence 11: **A visiting nurse has a fascinating career, moving through many homes each day and leaving order and comfort behind.**

    What correction should be made to this sentence?

    (1) change the spelling of <u>fascinating</u> to <u>fasinating</u>
    (2) remove the comma after <u>career</u>
    (3) change the spelling of <u>through</u> to <u>thorough</u>
    (4) insert a comma after <u>order</u>
    (5) no correction is necessary

GO ON TO THE NEXT PAGE

TEST 1: LANGUAGE ARTS, WRITING, PART I

<u>Questions 11–19</u> refer to the following paragraphs.

(1) Nutritional food buying emphasizes the "Basic Four." (2) Backpacking also has its basic four, these being, in order of importance, hiking shoes, the backpack, sleeping gear, and shelter. (3) Selection of hiking shoes should be your first concern. (4) Even a one-day hike can be misery without comfortable shoes. (5) Today's hikers prefer a shoe that is six inches high, is made of leather, and thick sturdy composition soles. (6) Break the shoes in thoroughly on short walks before going on any extended hike. (7) When purchasing a backpack, you will find an almost bewildering array of makes, styles, and materiels to choose from. (8) The backpacking frame must have both shoulder straps and a waist strap. The latter strap being of such design as to permit much of the weight of the pack to rest on the sturdy hip bones rather than on the more fragile shoulder bones. (9) The sleeping bag and its two accessories (ground cloth and mattress) are next on the list of basics. (10) The fourth and last of the basic four is the tent or other emergency shelter. (11) An inexpensive shelter is the plastic tube tent.

11. Which sentence is the topic sentence?

    (1) sentence 11
    (2) sentence 7
    (3) sentence 3
    (4) sentence 2
    (5) sentence 1

12. Sentence 2: **Backpacking also has its basic four, these being, in order of importance, hiking shoes, the backpack, sleeping gear, and shelter.**

    What correction should be made to this sentence?

    (1) change <u>its</u> to <u>it's</u>
    (2) change the colon to a semicolon
    (3) change <u>being</u> to <u>are</u>
    (4) remove the comma after <u>gear</u>
    (5) no correction is necessary

13. Sentences 3 and 4: **Selection of hiking shoes should be your first concern. Even a one-day hike can be misery without comfortable shoes.**

    The most effective combination of sentences 3 and 4 would include which of the following groups of words?

    (1) concern, also even
    (2) concern, although even
    (3) concern, because even
    (4) concern, if even
    (5) concern, whereas even

14. Sentence 5: **Today's hikers prefer a shoe that is six inches high, is made of leather, and thick sturdy composition soles.**

    What correction should be made to this sentence?

    (1) remove the apostrophe from <u>today's</u>
    (2) insert a comma after <u>shoe</u>
    (3) remove the comma after <u>high</u>
    (4) insert <u>has</u> before <u>thick</u>
    (5) no correction is necessary

15. Sentence 6: **Break the shoes in thoroughly on short <u>walks before</u> going on any extended hike.**

    Which of the following is the best way to write the underlined portion of this sentence? If you think the original is the best way, choose option (1).

    (1) walks before
    (2) walks, before
    (3) walks: before
    (4) walks. before
    (5) walks. Before

GO ON TO THE NEXT PAGE

TEST 1: LANGUAGE ARTS, WRITING, PART I

16. Sentence 7: **When purchasing a back-pack, you will find an almost bewildering array of makes, styles, and materiels to choose from.**

    What correction should be made to this sentence?

    (1) remove the comma after <u>backpack</u>
    (2) change the spelling of <u>almost</u> to <u>allmost</u>
    (3) remove the comma after <u>makes</u>
    (4) change the spelling of <u>materiels</u> to <u>materials</u>
    (5) no correction is necessary

17. Sentence 8: **The backpacking frame must have both shoulder straps and a waist <u>strap. The</u> latter strap being of such design as to permit much of the weight of the pack to rest on the sturdy hip bones rather than on the more fragile shoulder bones.**

    Which of the following is the best way to write the underlined portion of these sentences? If you think the original is the best way, choose option (1).

    (1) strap. The
    (2) strap. the
    (3) strap, The
    (4) strap, the
    (5) strap: the

18. Sentence 9: **The sleeping bag and its two accessories (ground cloth and mattress) are next on the list of basics.**

    If you rewrote sentence 9 beginning with

    <u>Next on the list of basics</u>

    the next word(s) should be

    (1) the sleeping bag
    (2) its two accessories
    (3) ground cloth and mattress
    (4) are
    (5) is

19. Sentences 10 and 11: **The fourth and last of the basic four is the tent or other emergency shelter. An inexpensive shelter is the plastic tube tent.**

    The most effective combination of sentences 10 and 11 would include which of the following groups of words?

    (1) shelter of which an inexpensive shelter is
    (2) shelter such as the inexpensive plastic tube tent
    (3) shelter whose inexpensive shelter is
    (4) shelter: an inexpensive shelter is
    (5) shelter; an inexpensive shelter is

Questions 20–27 refer to the following paragraphs.

(A)

(1) We were born to be creative in a world rich in creative design rich in natural resources rich with innovative people who consider creativity fun and a responsibility, in a world of rich endowments from nature and man's creative urge. (2) Crafts is one of the rich heritages of our nation. (3) In pioneer days the itinerant craftsman traveled from home to home, selling his wares and earning his bed and board by weaving fabric or a coverlet or hand carving wooden items for the kitchen or barn.

(B)

(4) If people become involved in these early crafts, they may become interested in "trying their hands." (5) They have not only all the rich natural resources and related contemporary subject matter, but they also have man-made materials and efficient, fast equipment to aid them in their creativity. (6) Their products are limited only by their imagination, skill, and knowledge of design.

(C)

(7) If they live in a wooded area and like to collect the unusual from nature's wonders, they may begin to reproduce the pine and nut "kissing balls" and christmas wreaths. (8) If the male member of their family loves to hunt, they may create with feathers. (9) Feather wreaths were made at an early date.

GO ON TO THE NEXT PAGE

TEST 1: LANGUAGE ARTS, WRITING, PART I

20. **Sentence 1: We were born to be creative in a world rich in creative design rich in natural resources rich with innovative people who consider creativity fun and a responsibility, in a world of rich endowments from nature and man's creative urge.**

    What correction should be made to this sentence?

    (1) insert commas after <u>design</u> and <u>resources</u>
    (2) change the spelling of <u>innovative</u> to <u>inovative</u>
    (3) remove the comma after <u>responsibility</u>
    (4) insert a comma after <u>nature</u>
    (5) no correction is necessary

21. **Sentences 2 and 3: Crafts is one of the rich heritages of our nation. In pioneer days the itinerant craftsman traveled from home to home, selling his wares and earning his bed and board by weaving fabric or a coverlet or hand carving wooden items for the kitchen or barn.**

    What correction should be made to this sentence?

    (1) change <u>Crafts is</u> to <u>Crafts are</u>
    (2) insert a hyphen between <u>hand</u> and <u>carving</u>
    (3) insert a comma after <u>fabric</u>
    (4) remove the comma after <u>home</u>
    (5) no correction is necessary

22. **Sentence 3 should be**

    (1) omitted
    (2) placed first
    (3) placed after sentence 5
    (4) placed last
    (5) left as it is

23. **Sentence 4: If people become involved in these early crafts, they may become interested in "trying their hands."**

    What correction should be made to this sentence?

    (1) change <u>become</u> to <u>became</u>
    (2) change <u>they</u> to <u>one</u>
    (3) change <u>may</u> to <u>might</u>
    (4) change <u>hands."</u> to <u>hands"</u>.
    (5) no correction is necessary

24. **Sentence 5: They have not only all the rich natural resources and related contemporary subject matter, but they also have man-made materials and efficient, fast equipment to aid them in their creativity.**

    What correction should be made to this sentence?

    (1) place <u>not only</u> before <u>have</u>
    (2) change the spelling of <u>contemporary</u> to <u>contemperary</u>
    (3) change <u>but</u> to <u>although</u>
    (4) change the spelling of <u>equipment</u> to <u>equiptment</u>
    (5) no correction is necessary

25. **Sentences 5 and 6: They have not only all the rich natural resources and related contemporary subject matter, but they also have man-made materials and efficient, fast equipment to aid them in their <u>creativity Their</u> products are limited only by their imagination, skill, and knowledge of design.**

    Which of the following is the best way to write the underlined portion of this sentence? If you think the original is the best way, choose option (1).

    (1) creativity Their
    (2) creativity, their
    (3) creativity. their
    (4) creativity. Their
    (5) creativity: Their

GO ON TO THE NEXT PAGE

TEST 1: LANGUAGE ARTS, WRITING, PART I

26. Sentence 7: **If they live in a wooded area and like to collect the unusual from nature's wonders, they may begin to reproduce the pine and nut "kissing balls" and christmas wreaths.**

    What correction should be made to this sentence?

    (1) change <u>live</u> to <u>lived</u>
    (2) change <u>like</u> to <u>would like</u>
    (3) remove the comma after <u>wonders</u>
    (4) capitalize <u>christmas</u>
    (5) no correction is necessary

27. Sentences 8 and 9: **If the male member of the family loves to hunt, they may create with feathers. Feather wreaths were made at an early date.**

    The most effective combination of sentences 8 and 9 would include which of the following groups of words?

    (1) feather and feather wreaths
    (2) feathers because feather wreaths
    (3) feathers although feather wreaths
    (4) feathers, which were made into wreaths
    (5) feathers made at an early date

<u>Questions 28–36</u> refer to the following paragraphs.

(A)

(1) Housing is the hub of the family's private world, the nature of housing has a direct effect on the quality of family life. (2) It effects the health, time, and energy required to rear a family and care for its members, self-related attitudes, morale, and satisfaction with one's station in life. (3) It also affects the way in which one family relates to another, to the neighborhood, and to the community.

(B)

(4) Families do not want, expect, or require dwellings that is identical. (5) Families with limited means are more interested in securing clean, safe, and reasonably comfortable housing than to find quarters that are especially psychologically stimulating. (6) At the same time

many families having greater incomes can take basic shelter for granted and proceed to satisfy higher level needs in housing.

(C)

(7) Nevertheless, as a nation we are being more and more concerned with housing that does far more than support physical survival. (8) In other words, essentially all American families are upgrading their housing goals and expectations. (9) And the dominant housing image remains the single-family house.

(D)

(10) Only when families are more articulate in identifying their needs and when builders and public policy become more sensitive to human needs will the nation have a variety of good housing designed, built, and serviced in line with family purposes.

28. Sentence 1: **Housing is the hub of the family's private <u>world, the</u> nature of housing has a direct effect on the quality of family life.**

    Which of the following is the best way to write the underlined portion of this sentence? If you think the original is the best way, choose option (1).

    (1) world, the
    (2) world. the
    (3) world; The
    (4) world: The
    (5) world. The

29. Sentence 2: **It effects the health, time, and energy required to rear a family and care for its members, self-related attitudes, morale, and satisfaction with one's station in life.**

    What correction should be made to this sentence?

    (1) change the spelling of <u>effects</u> to <u>affects</u>
    (2) change the spelling of <u>its</u> to <u>it's</u>
    (3) remove the comma after <u>members</u>
    (4) change the spelling of <u>morale</u> to <u>moral</u>
    (5) no correction is necessary

GO ON TO THE NEXT PAGE

30. Sentence 3: **It also affects the way in which one family relates to another, to the neighborhood, and to the community.**

What correction should be made to this sentence?

(1) change <u>also</u> to <u>nevertheless</u>
(2) insert a comma after <u>way</u>
(3) remove the comma after <u>another</u>
(4) change the spelling of <u>neighborhood</u> to <u>nieghborhood</u>
(5) no correction is necessary

31. Sentence 4: **Families do not want, expect, or require dwellings that is identical.**

What correction should be made to this sentence?

(1) change the spelling of <u>families</u> to <u>family's</u>
(2) remove the comma after <u>want</u>
(3) change <u>is</u> to <u>are</u>
(4) change the spelling of <u>identical</u> to <u>identicle</u>
(5) no correction is necessary

32. Sentence 5: **Families with limited means are more interested in securing clean, safe, and reasonably comfortable housing than to find quarters that are especially psychologically stimulating.**

What correction should be made to this sentence?

(1) remove the comma after <u>clean</u>
(2) change <u>to find</u> to <u>in finding</u>
(3) change the spelling of <u>especially</u> to <u>especialy</u>
(4) change the spelling of <u>psychologically</u> to <u>phsycologically</u>
(5) no correction is necessary

33. Sentence 6: **At the same time many families having greater incomes can take basic shelter for granted and proceed to satisfy higher level needs in housing.**

What correction should be made to this sentence?

(1) insert a comma after <u>incomes</u>
(2) change <u>can</u> to <u>must</u>
(3) insert a comma after <u>granted</u>
(4) change the spelling of <u>proceed</u> to <u>procede</u>
(5) no correction is necessary

34. Sentence 7: **Nevertheless, as a nation we are being more and more concerned with housing that does far more than support physical survival.**

If you rewrote sentence 7 beginning with

<u>Housing that does far more than support physical survival</u>

the next words would be

(1) as a nation
(2) we are being
(3) we, as a nation,
(4) concerns us, as a nation,
(5) we are concerned

35. Sentences 8 and 9: **In other words, essentially all American families are upgrading their housing goals and expectations. And the dominant housing image remains the single-family house.**

The most effective combination of sentences 8 and 9 would include which of the following groups of words?

(1) expectations but the single-family house remains
(2) expectations since the single-family house remains
(3) expectations although the single-family house remains
(4) expectations with the single-family house remaining
(5) expectations despite the single-famiy house remaining

GO ON TO THE NEXT PAGE

TEST 1: LANGUAGE ARTS, WRITING, PART I

36. Sentence 10: **Only when families are more articulate in identifying their needs and when builders and pubic policy become more sensitive to human needs will the nation have a variety of good housing designed, built, and serviced in line with family purposes.**

    If you rewrote sentence 10 beginning with

    The nation

    the next words should be

    (1) are more articulate
    (2) identifying their needs
    (3) become more sensitive
    (4) will have
    (5) serviced in line

Questions 37–45 refer to the following paragraphs.

(A)

(1) Auto insurance can be bought in the form of a bundle of coverage, or each section in the bundle can be bought seperately.

(B)

(2) Liability, the core of an auto policy, pays for bodily injury and property damage to others when you are legally responsible for the accident. (3) Liability coverage, stated separately for bodily injury and property damage, pay for other people's injuries—not yours.

(C)

(4) Medical payments cover you and your passengers' medical fees regardless of who was to blame for the accident. (5) The uninsured motorist coverage offers protection to you, your spouse, and resident children if you are stricken by an uninsured motorist or a hit and run driver while driving or walking.

(D)

(6) Collision pays for damage to your car when you hit another vehicle or an object like a tree, telephone pole, etc. (7) Collision coverage is usually sold in the form of a deductible. (8) The larger the amount of the deductible, the less the premium.

(E)

(9) Losses caused by fire, wind, theft, vandalism, collision with animals, explosions, flood, and lightning are covered by the comprehensive coverage feature.

(F)

(10) Accidental Death and Dismemberment coverage pays a lump sum for death in a car accident, loss of a limb, blindness, fractures, and dislocations, plus a disability benefit each week.

37. Sentence 1: **Auto insurance can be bought in the form of a bundle of coverage, or each section in the bundle can be bought seperately.**

    What correction should be made to this sentence?

    (1) change the spelling of <u>insurance</u> to <u>insurence</u>
    (2) insert a comma after <u>bought</u>
    (3) change <u>or</u> to <u>and</u>
    (4) change the spelling of <u>seperately</u> to <u>separately</u>
    (5) no correction is necessary

38. Which transitional word(s) could be added to sentence 2?

    (1) First of all,
    (2) However,
    (3) In addition to,
    (4) Nevertheless,
    (5) On the other hand,

39. Sentence 3: **Liability coverage, stated separately for bodily injury and property damage, pay for other people's injuries—not yours.**

    What correction should be made to this sentence?

    (1) remove the comma after <u>coverage</u> and <u>damage</u>
    (2) change <u>pay</u> to <u>pays</u>
    (3) change <u>people's</u> to <u>peoples</u>
    (4) remove the dash after <u>injuries</u>
    (5) no correction is necessary

GO ON TO THE NEXT PAGE

TEST 1: LANGUAGE ARTS, WRITING, PART I

40. Sentence 4 should be

    (1) placed first
    (2) placed last
    (3) left as it is
    (4) placed after sentence 10
    (5) omitted

41. The main idea of this passage is

    (1) stated in sentence 1
    (2) stated in sentence 10
    (3) stated in sentence 3
    (4) stated in sentence 2
    (5) not stated; it's implied

42. A new paragraph can be

    (1) started after sentence 7
    (2) started after sentence 6
    (3) started after sentence 4
    (4) started after sentence 2
    (5) not started

43. Sentences 7 and 8: **Collision coverage is usually sold in the form of a** deductible. **The larger the amount of the deductible, the less the premium.**

    Which of the following is the best way to write the underlined portion of this sentence? If you think the original is the best way, choose option (1).

    (1) deductible. The
    (2) deductible. the
    (3) deductible; The
    (4) deductible; the
    (5) deductible, The

44. Sentence 9: **Losses caused by fire, wind, theft, vandalism, collision with animals, explosions, flood, and lightning are covered by the comprehensive coverage feature.**

    If you rewrote sentence 9 beginning with

    The comprehensive coverage feature

    the next word(s) would be

    (1) losses caused
    (2) causes losses
    (3) collision
    (4) explosions
    (5) covers

45. Sentence 10: **Accidental Death and Dismemberment coverage pays a lump sum for death in a car accident, loss of a limb, blindness, fractures, and dislocations, plus a disability benefit each week.**

    What correction should be made to this sentence?

    (1) change benefit to benifit
    (2) remove the comma after dislocations
    (3) change pays to pay's
    (4) change Accidental Death and Dismemberment to Accidental death and dismemberment
    (5) no correction is necessary

GO ON TO THE NEXT PAGE

TEST 1: LANGUAGE ARTS, WRITING, PART I

<u>Questions 46–50</u> refer to the following paragraphs.

(A)

(1) How do you find help, when you require it, in your community, assuming that you or your family just cannot meet your own needs or solve your own problems.

(B)

(2) It's not easy, but it can be done. (3) Most Americans, in most communities, can find most of the kinds of help they may need within their local area.

(C)

(4) In just about every city in the Nation, there is a classified phone directory called the Yellow Pages and, if any public, voluntary, or private (for profit) services agencies exist, they will be listed under the heading: "Social Services Organizations."

(D)

(5) In the Washington, D.C., directory, for example, the organizations under this heading number in the hundreds and ranges from Big Brothers through Family Service to Young Adult Rehabilitation Council. (6) In your phone book there may be only four agencies listed where he can call for help, or there may be 400. (7) The longer the list, unfortunately, the more difficult it is to decide from organization names which one can help you with your particular problem.

(E)

(8) Strangely enough, the best place to call or see is your county or local public welfare office (in some areas called social services or public assistance), whether you can or cannot afford to pay for the help you need. (9) Under the Social Security Act, all Federally funded local welfare agencies provide information and referral services without regard for welfare eligibility by reason of poverty, etc.

(F)

(10) Just a word about a very special problem: the problem of where a non-English-speaking person can be sent for help. (11) Because of the increasing awareness of this problem, a number of self-help organizations have recently come into existence in communities where there are significant numbers of ethnic minorities.

46. Sentence 1: **How do you find help, when you require it, in your community, assuming that you or your family just cannot meet your own needs or solve your own problems.**

    What correction should be made to this sentence?

    (1) remove the comma after <u>help</u>
    (2) remove the comma after <u>it</u>
    (3) remove the comma after <u>community</u>
    (4) place a question mark after <u>problems</u>
    (5) no correction is necessary

47. Sentence 2 should be

    (1) placed first
    (2) placed last
    (3) omitted
    (4) moved after sentence 10
    (5) left as it is

48. Sentence 4: **In just about every city in the Nation, there is a classified phone directory called the Yellow Pages and, if any public, voluntary, or private (for profit) services agencies exist, they will be listed under the heading: "Social Services Organizations."**

    What correction should be made to this sentence?

    (1) remove the capital in <u>Nation</u>
    (2) change the spelling of <u>directory</u> to <u>directry</u>
    (3) remove the capitals in <u>Yellow Pages</u>
    (4) change the colon to a semicolon after <u>heading</u>
    (5) no correction is necessary

GO ON TO THE NEXT PAGE

TEST 1: LANGUAGE ARTS, WRITING, PART I

49. Sentence 5: **In the Washington, D.C., directory, for example, the organizations under this heading number in the hundreds and ranges from Big Brothers through Family Service to Young Adult Rehabilitation Council.**

    What correction should be made to this sentence?

    (1) remove the capital from <u>Brothers</u>
    (2) remove the comma after <u>D.C.</u>
    (3) change <u>ranges</u> to <u>range</u>
    (4) remove the comma after <u>Washington</u>
    (5) no correction is necessary

50. Sentence 6: **In your phone book there may be only four agencies listed where he can call for help, or there may be 400.**

    What correction should be made to this sentence?

    (1) change <u>your</u> to <u>their</u>
    (2) change <u>he</u> to <u>you</u>
    (3) change <u>there</u> to <u>they're</u>
    (4) remove the comma after <u>help</u>
    (5) no correction is necessary

GO ON TO THE NEXT PAGE

TEST 1: LANGUAGE ARTS, WRITING, PART II

This part of the Language Arts, Writing test is intended to determine how well you write. You are asked to write an essay that explains something, presents an opinion on an issue, or concentrates on retelling a personal experience.

PROMPT

Each year in the United States thousands of immigrants are allowed into the country and are naturalized to become citizens. These immigrants come to the United States from many different countries. They come here for many reasons such as religious freedom, political reasons, or opportunities.

DISCUSSION QUESTION

What is your opinion on this issue? Do you feel that the United States should put a limit on the number of immigrants that come into the United States or should we continue allowing people to enter and become citizens?

Directions

Write an essay of about 250 words in which you present your reasons on this topic. Give supporting details and examples for each reason in your essay. You have 45 minutes to write on this topic.

CHECK YOURSELF

- Read carefully the prompt, discussion question, and directions.
- Decide if the prompt is expository, persuasive, or narrative.
- Plan your essay before you begin.
- Use scratch paper to prepare a simple outline.
- Write your essay on the lined pages of a separate answer sheet.
- Read carefully what you have written and make needed changes.
- Check for focus, elaboration, organization, conventions, and integration.

END OF EXAMINATION

TEST 2: SOCIAL STUDIES

Directions

The Social Studies test consists of multiple-choice questions intended to measure general social studies concepts. The questions are based on short readings that often include a graph, chart, photograph, or figure. Study the information given and then answer the question(s) following it. Refer to the information as often as necessary in answering the questions.

You should spend no more than 70 minutes answering the questions. Work carefully, but do not spend too much time on any one question. Be sure you answer every question. You will not be penalized for incorrect answers.

To record your answers, mark the numbered space on the answer sheet beside the number that corresponds to the question in the test.

FOR EXAMPLE:

Early colonists of North America looked for settlement sites that had adequate water supplies and were accessible by ship. For this reason, many early towns were built near

(1) mountains
(2) prairies
(3) rivers
(4) glaciers
(5) plateaus

The correct answer is "rivers"; therefore, answer space 3 would be marked on the answer sheet.

GO ON TO THE NEXT PAGE

TEST 2: SOCIAL STUDIES

Questions 1–3 are based on the following passage.

The true principle of a republic is that the people should choose whom they please to govern them. . . . This great source of free government, popular election, should be perfectly pure, and the most unbounded liberty allowed. Where this principle is adhered to; where, in the organization of the government, the legislative, executive, and judicial branches are rendered distinct; where, again, the legislature is divided into separate houses, and the operations of each are controlled by various checks and balances, and, above all, by the vigilance and weight of the state governments, —to talk of tyranny, and the subversion of our liberties, is to speak the language of enthusiasm. This balance between the national and state governments . . . is of the utmost importance. . . . I am persuaded that a firm union is as necessary to perpetuate our liberties as it is to make us respectable. . . .

—Alexander Hamilton

1. According to the passage, which one of the following did Mr. Hamilton believe?

   (1) States should determine voting qualifications.
   (2) Suffrage should be granted to all adult males.
   (3) Suffrage should be limited.
   (4) Suffrage should be unrestricted.
   (5) United States senators should be appointed by the state legislatures.

2. Hamilton considered all of the following as safeguards of free government EXCEPT

   (1) popular elections
   (2) separation of the branches of government
   (3) separate legislative houses
   (4) checks and balances
   (5) sovereignty of state governments

3. Hamilton believed that the most important characteristic of a republic is

   (1) popular election
   (2) states' rights
   (3) national militia
   (4) federal taxation
   (5) checks and balances

Questions 4–6 are based on the following passage.

The political party organization is designed to influence voters to support its candidates. Its base of direct operations is, therefore, the voting district, where approximately 700 citizens cast their ballots.

Ordinarily, the enrolled party members choose two committeepersons at the annual fall primary in September, but in presidential election years this action is taken at the spring primary in June. This county committee may by rule, however, set the term at two years; it may demand equal representation of the sexes so that there will be one committeeman and one committeewoman in each district; it can provide for as many as four committee members from a large district as long as the representation is proportional. The important point is that the primary is, for each party, an election for its own officers.

4. All of the following statements about committeepersons are true EXCEPT that

   (1) two are chosen at the September primary
   (2) the elections take place at the June primary during a presidential election year
   (3) the term of office may be set at two years by the county committee
   (4) a large district may have four committee members
   (5) women may not serve on the committee

GO ON TO THE NEXT PAGE

TEST 2: SOCIAL STUDIES

5. The purpose of the primary election is

   (1) to designate the primary candidate
   (2) to ensure proportional representation
   (3) to equalize the vote of the sexes
   (4) for each party to elect its own officers
   (5) for the nomination of four committeepersons per district

6. It can be inferred from the passage that

   (1) the role of committeepersons is relatively unimportant
   (2) each committeeperson represents about 350 voters
   (3) committeepersons serve for two years
   (4) the county committees consist of equal numbers of men and women
   (5) all candidates for committeeperson have equal chances for election

Questions 7 and 8 are based on the following cartoon.

7. The U.S. involvement in Europe indicated in the cartoon most probably refers to the role of the United States in the

   (1) Alliance for Progress
   (2) Common Market
   (3) Nuclear Test-Ban Agreement
   (4) North Atlantic Treaty Organization
   (5) Helsinki Agreement

8. On the basis of the cartoon, it can be concluded that the cartoonist

   (1) questions the U.S. role of "world policeman"
   (2) favors U.S. imperialism
   (3) supports the foreign policy of the United States
   (4) opposes a return to an isolationist policy
   (5) is expressing concern for world survival

Question 9 refers to the following photograph.

9. Where are these people being searched?

   (1) at a train station
   (2) at a border crossing
   (3) in a Nazi war camp
   (4) in a local market place
   (5) outside their homes

GO ON TO THE NEXT PAGE

TEST 2: SOCIAL STUDIES

Questions 10–12 refer to the following graph.

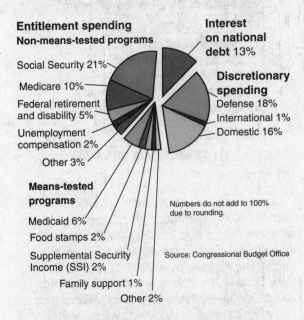

Entitlement spending
Non-means-tested programs

Social Security 21%
Medicare 10%
Federal retirement and disability 5%
Unemployment compensation 2%
Other 3%

Interest on national debt 13%

Discretionary spending
Defense 18%
International 1%
Domestic 16%

Means-tested programs

Medicaid 6%
Food stamps 2%
Supplemental Security Income (SSI) 2%
Family support 1%
Other 2%

Numbers do not add to 100% due to rounding.

Source: Congressional Budget Office

10. Entitlements are government programs providing benefits to members of certain groups. Members of some groups have to be examined (means test) before they can receive benefits. According to the graph, the largest single item of federal spending is

(1) Social Security
(2) defense
(3) interest on the national debt
(4) Medicare
(5) Medicaid

11. Of the means-tested programs, the largest is

(1) Medicaid
(2) Social Security
(3) food stamps
(4) family support
(5) other

12. The percentage of federal spending going to entitlements is

(1) 87%
(2) 54%
(3) 41%
(4) 35%
(5) 13%

Question 13 is based on the following cartoon.

Give me your scientists, your doctors, your teachers, but keep your huddled masses to yourselves.

Adapted from *World Press Review*. November 1980

13. The above cartoon, which appeared in a newspaper published in India, is using the statement attributed to the Statue of Liberty to

(1) convince the reader of the value of education in the United States
(2) criticize the United States for not accepting poor immigrants
(3) deplore the immigration policies in less developed countries
(4) publicize the need for professionals in the United States
(5) support the imposition of immigration quotas for professionals

GO ON TO THE NEXT PAGE

TEST 2: SOCIAL STUDIES

Questions 14–16 are based on the following passage.

It is said that growth by merger adds nothing to the economy in the way of new investment, whereas so-called "grass roots" growth does. This, too, is not necessarily so. In many cases, a company has the available capital and several other ingredients of success for a new venture, but can only get some missing ingredient—such as qualified technical manpower—by acquiring another company. In such a case the merging of two companies means a new investment which would not have taken place by the "grass roots" method.

Actually, corporate diversification in the past has served to enhance competition, and it will continue to do so. No company today can confidently look upon its established competitors as being its only future competitors. Tomorrow their ranks may be joined by others now in wholly unrelated industries. If new competitors do enter by acquisition or otherwise, it will be only because they think in the long run they can market a better product, or sell at a lower price, and make a profit by doing so.

14. A reason that is offered for the need to merge is to

    (1) meet new competition
    (2) increase diversification
    (3) increase available capital
    (4) provide for "grass roots" growth
    (5) extend consumer choice

15. The author maintains that growth by merger is sometimes necessary to

    (1) acquire capital
    (2) reduce competition
    (3) make a new investment
    (4) gain technically qualified personnel
    (5) add to the economy

16. Motivations for merger mentioned in this passage include all of the following EXCEPT

    (1) marketing a better product
    (2) selling at a lower price
    (3) making a profit
    (4) getting a missing ingredient
    (5) meeting current competition

Questions 17–19 are based on the following passage.

Americans are the western pilgrims, who are carrying along with them the great mass of arts, sciences, vigor, and industry which began long since in the East. They will finish the great circle. The Americans were once scattered all over Europe. Here they are incorporated into one of the finest systems of population which has ever appeared and which will hereafter become distinct by the power of the different climates they inhabit. The American ought therefore to love this country much better than that in which either he or his forefathers were born. Here the rewards of his industry follow with equal steps the progress of his labor. His labor is founded on the basis of nature, *self-interest*. Can it want a stronger allurement?

17. The attitude of the author toward the American is one of

    (1) caution
    (2) inquiry
    (3) enthusiastic approval
    (4) self-interest
    (5) prejudice

18. The author predicts that Americans will be unique because of

    (1) a new way of life
    (2) a new government
    (3) a different environment
    (4) their own labors
    (5) self-interest

GO ON TO THE NEXT PAGE

TEST 2: SOCIAL STUDIES

19. The American should be loyal to his new country, according to this passage, because he

    (1) is a new man
    (2) has a new alma mater
    (3) is a western pilgrim
    (4) fled Europe
    (5) benefits from his own labors

---

20. Which has been an important result of improved means of communication and travel?

    (1) Changes in one part of the world can greatly affect other parts of the world.
    (2) Countries have become more nationalistic.
    (3) Barriers to international trade have been abolished.
    (4) There is less need for international organizations.
    (5) Isolationism has been eradicated.

Question 21 is based on the following cartoon.

21. According to the cartoon, a problem of political elections in the United States is that

    (1) candidates have few serious issues to consider
    (2) candidates offer simplistic solutions in television campaigning to gain votes
    (3) most voters demand quick solutions to national problems
    (4) television reporting of candidates and their campaigns is biased
    (5) these television viewers believe what they are seeing and hearing

Questions 22 and 23 are based on the following graph.

DISTRIBUTION OF WORLD POPULATION BY MAJOR REGIONS 1990 AND 2025 (PROJECTED)

1990
5,292 million

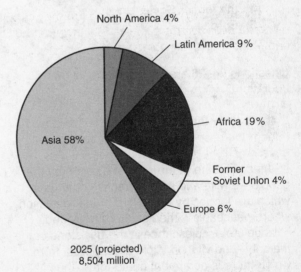

2025 (projected)
8,504 million

GO ON TO THE NEXT PAGE

TEST 2: SOCIAL STUDIES

22. According to the graph, which of the following statements is correct?

    (1) The population of the world will double between 1990 and 2025.
    (2) The distribution of the world's population by regions will remain the same between 1990 and 2025.
    (3) By 2025, there will be a major shift in population from the former Soviet Union to Europe.
    (4) By 2025, Africa's percentage of the world's population will increase more than any other region's percentage.
    (5) By 2025, the former Soviet Union's population will lose the most.

23. The greatest decrease in population from 1990 to 2025 will be in

    (1) North America
    (2) Latin America
    (3) Asia
    (4) the former Soviet Union
    (5) Europe

Questions 24–26 are based on the following quotation.

   It is proper that you should understand what I deem the essential principles of our government. . . .
   a jealous care of the right of election by the people—a mild and safe corrective of abuses which are lopped by the sword of the revolution where peaceable remedies are unprovided;
   absolute acquiescence in the decisions of the majority—the vital principle of republics, from which there is no appeal but to force, the vital principle and immediate parent of despotism;
   a well-disciplined militia—our best reliance in peace and for the first moments of war, till regulars may relieve them;
   the supremacy of the civil over the military authority;
   economy in the public expense, that labor might be lightly burdened;
   the honest payment of our debts and sacred preservation of the public faith;
   . . . freedom of religion;
   freedom of the press;
   freedom of person under the protection of the *habeas corpus*;
   and trial by jury impartially selected. . . .

   —Thomas Jefferson, Inaugural Address

24. All of the following principles mentioned by Jefferson are found in the Bill of Rights EXCEPT

    (1) freedom of religion
    (2) freedom of the press
    (3) the right of election by the people
    (4) a well-disciplined militia
    (5) trial by jury

25. An example of the "supremacy of the civil over the military authority" is the

    (1) operation of the National Guard
    (2) Pentagon
    (3) President as Commander-in-Chief
    (4) National Security Agency
    (5) National Security Council

26. The alternative to the "right of election by the people," according to the passage, is

    (1) force
    (2) despotism
    (3) war
    (4) peaceable remedies
    (5) revolution

GO ON TO THE NEXT PAGE

TEST 2: SOCIAL STUDIES

<u>Questions 27 and 28</u> are based on the following passage.

A map is a presentation on flat surface of all, or a part of, the earth's surface, drawn to scale. A map, in order to accomplish fully the objectives for which it was intended, should generally possess certain essentials. These are a title, a legend, direction, scale, latitude and longitude, and a date. . . .

A legend should define the symbols used on a map to explain the colors or patterns employed.... Since a legend unlocks map details, key is probably an appropriate synonym.

Scale may be defined as the ratio between map distance and earth distance. Scale may be shown as a fraction, for example, $\frac{1}{62,500}$, that is, one unit on the map represents 62,500 units on the earth's surface . . .

A compass rose showing direction is a desirable feature on every map. This directional feature can be eliminated on certain maps where both parallels indicating latitude and meridians indicating longitude are straight lines at right angles to each other.

27. "Drawn to scale" as used in this passage means

    (1) the direction of the parallels and meridians
    (2) the relationship between map distance and earth distance
    (3) linear scales
    (4) verbal scales
    (5) latitude and longitude

28. A compass rose is associated with

    (1) a map title
    (2) a legend
    (3) scale
    (4) direction
    (5) latitude and longitude

29. Which statement best supports the argument for expansion of federal power at the expense of state power in the United States?

    (1) The economic interdependency of all sections of the United States has increased the number and complexity of national problems.
    (2) A uniform penal code is needed in order to insure equal enforcement of the law.
    (3) The federal government with its system of checks and balances is a better guarantee of individual freedom than state governments.
    (4) Increases in population have made it almost impossible for state governments to function efficiently.
    (5) Corruption is more likely to take place at the state governmental level.

30. ". . . the words used are used in such circumstances and are of such a nature as to create a clear and present danger that they will bring about the substantive evils that Congress has a right to prevent . . . . The most stringent protection of free speech would not protect a man in falsely shouting 'fire' in a theatre and causing a panic."

This quotation best reflects the view that freedom of speech is

    (1) guaranteed by the Constitution
    (2) subject to limitations
    (3) clearly dangerous and evil
    (4) likely to cause panic
    (5) impossible to protect

GO ON TO THE NEXT PAGE

TEST 2: SOCIAL STUDIES

31. ". . . it necessarily became the great object of political economy to diminish as much as possible the importation of foreign goods for home consumption and to increase as much as possible the exportation of the produce of domestic industry."

    Although these words were written in 1776, they apply as well to current U.S. efforts to deal with the problem of the

    (1) decline in the gross national product
    (2) increase in the tariff rates
    (3) surplus in the federal budget
    (4) deficit in the balance of payments
    (5) cost of living

Question 32 is based on the following cartoon.

32. According to the cartoonist, which is a likely result of permitting the Energy Mobilization Board to determine government policy?

    (1) a massive rebuilding program to aid urban areas
    (2) nullification of the benefits of current environmental laws
    (3) an increase in off-shore drilling to lessen our dependence on foreign oil
    (4) land-clearing and home building projects to relieve unemployment among construction workers
    (5) government-sponsored work projects to combat inflation

Questions 33 and 34 are based on the following graph, which shows the relationship of supply and demand for consumer goods and services in five model economies.

33. If model B were representative of the economy of the United States, which government action would most likely lead to a balance between supply and demand?

    (1) freeze on wages
    (2) limits on consumer credit
    (3) decrease in income tax rates
    (4) increase in sales taxes
    (5) increase in interest rates

34. Which model economy is most similar to the economic situation in the United States during the years 1929–1939?

    (1) A
    (2) B
    (3) C
    (4) D
    (5) E

GO ON TO THE NEXT PAGE

TEST 2: SOCIAL STUDIES

<u>Questions 35 and 36</u> refer to the following passage.

Latin America has a rich and varied cultural heritage. It was brought into world history by Columbus, was colonized and made a part of Western culture by European powers, and was successful (with a few exceptions) in securing independence during the revolutionary era of George Washington and Simon Bolivar. Latin America differs, however, from the United States in carrying over from pre-Columbian times an Indian population whose cultural influence has intermingled with that of the European. Latin America was colonized primarily by Spanish and Portuguese. They brought to the area a Catholic religious tradition, an agricultural way of life with a land-owning wealthy class, and an influential military class. Independence resulted in twenty separate countries, the Spanish-speaking portion alone being divided into eighteen states, the Portuguese portion being represented by Brazil, and Haiti, which emerged from a long period of French rule.

35. The countries that colonized Latin America brought with them all of the following EXCEPT

    (1) a religious tradition
    (2) an agricultural way of life
    (3) a military class
    (4) a largely Spanish-speaking population
    (5) an Indian population

36. All of the following peoples are represented in the population of Latin America EXCEPT

    (1) Spanish
    (2) Portuguese
    (3) United States
    (4) French
    (5) Indian

<u>Questions 37–39</u> are based on the following graphs.

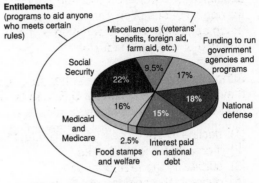

Source: *U.S. Office of Management and Budget*

Source: *U.S. Office of Management and Budget*

37. The largest jump in the national debt occurred between

    (1) 1970–1975
    (2) 1975–1980
    (3) 1980–1985
    (4) 1985–1990
    (5) 1990–1995

38. Of the budgeted money as depicted in the pie graph, entitlements received about

    (1) $\frac{3}{4}$

    (2) $\frac{2}{3}$

    (3) half

    (4) $\frac{1}{3}$

    (5) $\frac{1}{4}$

GO ON TO THE NEXT PAGE

TEST 2: SOCIAL STUDIES

39. The largest part of federal spending is for

    (1) national defense
    (2) Social Security
    (3) interest on the national debt
    (4) Medicare and Medicaid
    (5) veterans' benefits

40. Which situation in the United States is an illustration of lobbying, that is, attempting to influence legislators to support bills that favor a special group?

    (1) A defeated candidate for the Senate is appointed a member of the president's cabinet.
    (2) A corporation hires a person to present its views to certain members of Congress.
    (3) Federal public works projects are awarded to a state in return for certain political actions by that state's senators.
    (4) Two members of Congress agree to support each other's bills.
    (5) A member of Congress prevents a bill from coming to a vote.

41. The Monroe Doctrine states that any attempt by European powers to interfere with their old colonies or with the independence of a republic in the Western Hemisphere would not be tolerated by the United States, nor would any attempt by them "to extend their system to any portion of this hemisphere."

    Which event best illustrates the application of the Monroe Doctrine in United States foreign policy?

    (1) the United States joining the North Atlantic Treaty Organization (NATO)
    (2) President Truman's involving the United States in the Berlin airlift
    (3) President Kennedy's response to the Cuban missile crisis
    (4) Congress' declaration of war against Germany in World War II
    (5) the sale by the United States of AWACs to Saudi Arabia

42. In the United States, changes in occupational titles from busboy to dining room attendant and stewardess to flight attendant illustrate an attempt to deal with the problem of

    (1) racism
    (2) ethnocentrism
    (3) sexism
    (4) age bias
    (5) unionism

Question 43 is based on the following chart.

Income and Management Level of Men and Women Managers*		
Income	**Men**	**Women**
Income in early career	$ 68,480	$57,210
Income in midcareer	102,540	83,370
Management level		
Top level management	23%	9%
Upper-middle management	33	43
Lower-middle management	21	22
Supervisory management	8	10
Nonmanagement	15	16

Source: "The Impact of Gender as Managerial Careers Unfold," by Joy A. Schneer, Rider University, and Frieda Reitman, Pace University, *Journal of Vocational Behavior.*
*Excludes self-employed.

43. The data in the table show that

    (1) women earn less than men at every managerial level
    (2) men outnumber women on every managerial level
    (3) income in midcareer is comparable for men and women
    (4) fewer women than men become supervisors
    (5) fewer women than men become top-level managers

GO ON TO THE NEXT PAGE

TEST 2: SOCIAL STUDIES

<u>Questions 44–46</u> are based on the following passage.

The numbing row upon row of identical houses, the busy highways leading up to those houses clogged with cars, gas stations, fast-food restaurants, and strip malls are all features of America's suburbs. Traffic jams are all too common since most suburban areas are miles away from good public transportation.

All these things added together have a name: suburban sprawl. Sprawl happens when too many homes, businesses, and shopping centers are built on the fringes of metropolitan areas too quickly.

The costs and consequences of poorly planned development are clear and common. Alarmed by the loss of green space, voters approved nearly 200 state and local ballot initiatives to buy $7 billion of open space. Sprawl is also a major source of traffic congestion and air pollution. It also destroys water quality. The Chesapeake Bay is rapidly being lost to development. Sprawl threatens more than the environment. It also helps destroy older cities and suburbs.

Most Americans want to control sprawl by saving green spaces, redeveloping urban areas, and investing more money in mass transit.

44. Suburban sprawl is caused by all of the following EXCEPT

    (1) housing
    (2) cars
    (3) businesses
    (4) mass transit
    (5) shopping malls

45. Sprawl is chiefly the result of

    (1) increased population
    (2) poor development planning
    (3) public transportation
    (4) inadequate housing
    (5) family travel

46. Efforts to control sprawl include

    (1) more gas stations
    (2) more fast-food restaurants
    (3) more green space
    (4) more highways
    (5) more strip malls

<u>Question 47</u> is based on the following table.

TAX TABLE	
Income	**Tax Percentage Rate**
$0– 3,000	0
3,001– 8,000	10
8,001–14,000	20
14,001–20,000	25

47. The income tax shown in the table above is best described as

    (1) graduated
    (2) negative
    (3) proportional
    (4) regressive
    (5) universal

48. "We must bring the benefits of Western civilization and Christianity to the less fortunate."

This idea has been used to justify

    (1) imperialism
    (2) nationalism
    (3) socialism
    (4) feudalism
    (5) regionalism

49. "Nations strive to prevent any one country from becoming all-powerful and domineering."

Which concept is referred to by this statement?

    (1) militarism
    (2) imperialism
    (3) national sovereignty
    (4) balance of power
    (5) appeasement

GO ON TO THE NEXT PAGE

TEST 2: SOCIAL STUDIES

<u>Question 50</u> is based on the following chart.

ACTUAL AND PROJECTED POPULATIONS OF WORLD REGIONS

Region	1980	1990	2000 (est.)
Asia	2,583,477,000	3,112,695,000	3,712,542,000
Africa	477,231,000	642,111,000	866,585,000
Europe*	749,973,000	786,966,000	818,378,000
Latin America**	362,685,000	448,076,000	538,439,000
North America	251,909,000	275,866,000	294,712,000
Oceania	22,800,000	26,481,000	30,144,000
World	4,448,048,000	5,292,195,000	6,260,800,000

*Includes the former USSR
**Includes Mexico, Central America, and the Caribbean

50. The chart reveals that

    (1) over half of the 1990 population and of
        the projected world population in 2000
        lives in Asia
    (2) most of the world's population lives in
        the Americas
    (3) the largest population growth is in
        North America
    (4) the smallest population growth is in
        Latin America
    (5) the population growth is steadiest in
        Africa

END OF EXAMINATION

TEST 3: SCIENCE

Directions

The Science test consists of multiple-choice questions intended to measure the general concepts in science. The questions are based on short readings that often include a graph, chart, or figure. Study the information given and then answer the question(s) following it. Refer to the information as often as necessary in answering the questions.

You will have 80 minutes to answer the questions. Work carefully, but do not spend too much time on any one question. Be sure you answer every question. You will not be penalized for incorrect answers.

To record your answers, mark one numbered space on the answer sheet beside the number that corresponds to the question in the test.

FOR EXAMPLE:

Which of the following is the smallest unit?

(1) solution
(2) molecule
(3) atom
(4) compound
(5) mixture

① ② ● ④ ⑤

The correct answer is "atom"; therefore, space 3 would be marked on the answer sheet.

TEST 3: SCIENCE

Questions 1–3 refer to the following figure.

The figure above shows the cell cycle. It shows the typical amount of time spent in each stage of the cell cycle.

1. Mitosis, or cell division, is the time when cells divide to create new cells. About what percentage of the cell cycle is devoted to mitosis?

   (1) 5%
   (2) 20%
   (3) 40%
   (4) 60%
   (5) 75%

2. Which stage of the cell cycle is further subdivided into more stages?

   (1) G1 (first growth phase)
   (2) G2 (second growth phase)
   (3) S (synthesis phase)
   (4) Mitosis
   (5) All of the stages are subdivided

3. Interphase is another name for the time in the cell cycle that is not devoted to mitosis. In a typical cell cycle, how many hours long is the interphase?

   (1) 9 hours
   (2) 10 hours
   (3) 12 hours
   (4) 19 hours
   (5) 21 hours

Questions 4–7 refer to the following article.

Vertebrate blood, which consists of red and white blood cells and plasma, can be broken down even further into its chemical constituents. The largest mineral ingredient of blood is sodium chloride or salt. This mineral is important because it regulates water exchange within the organism. This exchange, as some scientists have emphasized, is more extensive and more important than may at first been thought. Cannon points out that "there are a number of circulations of the fluid out of the body and back again without loss."

For example, it is estimated that from a quart to a quart and one-half of water daily "leaves the body" when it enters the mouth as saliva. Another one or two quarts are passed out as gastric juice, and perhaps the same amount is contained in bile and the secretions of the pancreas and the intestinal wall.

This large volume of water enters the digestive processes, and practically all of it is reabsorbed through the intestinal wall, where it performs the equally important function of carrying in the digested foodstuffs. These and other instances of what Cannon calls "the conservative use of water in our bodies" involve osmotic pressure relationships in which the concentration of sodium chloride plays an important part.

GO ON TO THE NEXT PAGE

TEST 3: SCIENCE

4. This passage implies that

    (1) substances can pass through the intestinal wall in only one direction
    (2) water cannot be absorbed by the body unless it contains sodium choloride
    (3) every particle of water ingested is used over and over again
    (4) sodium chloride does not actually enter the body
    (5) regulation of water exchanges in the organism is controlled by the concentration of sodium chloride

5. The main point of this passage is that

    (1) we should drink large quantities of water daily
    (2) water is needed to digest our food completely
    (3) we need to consume large amounts of salt
    (4) salt is important in the regulation of water
    (5) the reuse of body water is an automatic function

6. Sodium chloride is an important constituent of

    (1) gastric juice
    (2) bile
    (3) pancreatic juice
    (4) intestinal juice
    (5) blood

7. Water is important in the intestine because of its ability to

    (1) form saliva
    (2) dilute the gastric juice
    (3) form bile
    (4) act as a vehicle for digested food
    (5) dissolve sodium chloride

Questions 8–11 refer to the following graph.

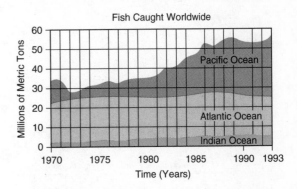

The graph above shows the number of fish caught (based on weight in millions of metric tons) from 1970–1993 in three major fishing regions of the world.

8. In which region or regions of the world has the number of metric tons remained constant?

    (1) The Atlantic Ocean
    (2) The Indian Ocean
    (3) The Pacific Ocean
    (4) The Atlantic Ocean and the Indian Ocean
    (5) The Pacific Ocean and the Indian Ocean

9. Approximately how many metric tons of fish were taken from all three oceans in 1980?

    (1) 5
    (2) 20
    (3) 25
    (4) 35
    (5) 50

10. What percentage of fish was obtained from the Pacific Ocean in 1970?

    (1) 5%
    (2) 10%
    (3) 30%
    (4) 50%
    (5) 70%

GO ON TO THE NEXT PAGE

TEST 3: SCIENCE

11. In what year did the Pacific Ocean first become the major source of fish?

    (1) 1974
    (2) 1978
    (3) 1982
    (4) 1986
    (5) 1990

<u>Questions 12–14</u> refer to the following graph.

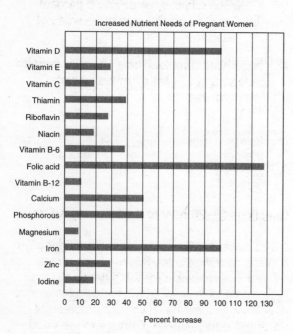

Increased Nutrient Needs of Pregnant Women

Percent Increase

Pregnant women need much higher amounts of many vitamins and minerals to support changes in their bodies and the developing fetus. This graph shows the percentage increase in several vitamins and minerals during pregnancy.

12. What three vitamins and minerals undergo the greatest percentage increase during pregnancy?

    (1) Vitamin D, iron, and folic acid
    (2) Iron, folic acid, and calcium
    (3) Iron, folic acid, and vitamin D
    (4) Vitamin D, iron, and calcium
    (5) Iodide, iron, and niacin

13. The normal recommended amount of vitamin C is 1,000 milligrams (mg) per day. During pregnancy, how much vitamin C does a woman need?

    (1) 20 mg
    (2) 200 mg
    (3) 1,200 mg
    (4) 2,000 mg
    (5) 2,400 mg

14. What is the percent increase in dietary calcium needs during pregnancy?

    (1) 10%
    (2) 30%
    (3) 50%
    (4) 70%
    (5) 150%

GO ON TO THE NEXT PAGE

TEST 3: SCIENCE

Questions 15–17 refer to the following information.

Water will change from one phase to another as its temperature changes. In its gaseous form, steam, water has its highest temperature. Water in this form will not change into liquid unless a certain amount of heat is removed. An example is the condensation of water on a bathroom mirror while someone takes a shower. The surface of the mirror is a lot cooler than the warm, steamy bathroom. Water vapor in the air turns into drops of liquid when it touches the cold surface of the mirror. This occurs because the cool mirror cools the air, and cool air cannot hold as much water as warm air.

The diagram represents a sealed plastic container with two Celsius thermometers, one of which is in a glass cup containing ice and water. The purpose of this demonstration is to study the behavior of water vapor and the temperature at which air becomes saturated by water (the dew point).

15. What is the temperature of the air in the box?

    (1) 23.0°C
    (2) 25.0°C
    (3) 26.0°C
    (4) 28.0°C
    (5) 30.0°C

16. Why have droplets of water formed on the outside of the glass cup?

    (1) Glass cups always accumulate water droplets on the outside when they are filled with water.
    (2) The air near the glass cup has become saturated with water.
    (3) Water has seeped through the pore spaces in the glass cup.
    (4) The relative humidity of the air near the glass cup is approaching 0 percent.
    (5) The dew point temperature was not reached.

17. If the water droplets have just appeared on the glass cup, what is the dew point temperature?

    (1) 5.0°C
    (2) 23.0°C
    (3) 28.0°C
    (4) 29.0°C
    (5) 30°C

Questions 18–20 refer to the following article.

Although we often observe the condensation of water vapor on cold surfaces, we seldom think of solid substances going directly to the vapor state. It is possible to change some solids directly to gases by heating them. Instead of melting, these solids go directly into the vapor state because the connections between molecules in these substances are very weak, allowing them to evaporate readily. A good example of such a substance is naphthalene (mothballs). You may have noticed that, over time, mothballs slowly decrease in size. This occurs because of the weak intermolecular forces. The process in which a solid passes directly to the gaseous phase without melting or changing back to the solid state is called sublimation.

18. Condensation is a change from the

    (1) gaseous phase to the solid phase
    (2) gaseous phase to the liquid phase
    (3) liquid phase to the gaseous phase
    (4) liquid phase to the solid phase
    (5) solid phase to the liquid phase

GO ON TO THE NEXT PAGE

TEST 3: SCIENCE

19. Some substances evaporate more easily than others because they

    (1) condense on cold surfaces
    (2) can be heated at atmospheric pressure
    (3) do not change from solid to liquid
    (4) pass from solid state to vapor state
    (5) have weak intermolecular forces

20. Sublimation is a change directly from the

    (1) solid phase to the gaseous phase
    (2) solid phase to the liquid phase
    (3) liquid phase to the gaseous phase
    (4) gaseous phase to the liquid phase
    (5) liquid phase to the solid phase

Questions 21–23 refer to the following article.

Most of us accept the common changes of melting and freezing as being "everyday"—and perfectly understandable. Most of also think little of seeing drops of condensation that appear overnight from condensed water vapor in the air. One physical change we rarely observe and thus hardly ever think about is the change directly from a solid to a gas. Admittedly, this is not a common occurrence at normal air pressures, but there are a few substances that do this. Naphthalene (used in mothballs or moth flakes) is one such substance. A block of solid naphthalene, left in a room, will slowly change to naphthalene vapors in the air, without melting and passing through the liquid state of matter. The reason this can happen is that the forces that hold individual molecules of naphthalene together are very weak, allowing the molecules to separate from each other quite easily. This change from a solid directly to a gas is known as sublimation.

Iodine crystals can also undergo this process, but at temperatures above 100°C. The solid dark crystals change into a purple gas that fills its container. Interestingly, some of the molecules of iodine in the gas phase will eventually attract each other enough to reform the solid. This shows that this phase change, like others, is reversible.

21. Condensation is the change from the

    (1) solid phase to the liquid phase
    (2) gas phase to the solid phase
    (3) liquid phase to the gas phase
    (4) gas phase to the liquid phase
    (5) solid phase to the gas phase

22. Which of the following phase changes is reversible?

    I. melting
    II. condensation
    III. sublimation

    (1) I only
    (2) II only
    (3) III only
    (4) I and III only
    (5) I, II, and III

23. When solid iodine sublimes, which of the following is formed?

    (1) liquid iodine
    (2) iodine vapor
    (3) condensed iodine
    (4) iodine ice
    (5) solid iodine

GO ON TO THE NEXT PAGE

TEST 3: SCIENCE

Questions 24–26 refer to the following article.

Sound waves travel best through denser materials. The speed of sound in air is about 340 meters/second, while the speed of sound in water is about 1,500 meters/second. A rock hitting a solid surface underwater will be very loud, even at a large distance. This is because water, being denser than air, is a better conductor of sound waves. This property of sound waves has been used by navies around the world to identify enemy submarines. Using sensitive listening devices, it is possible to hear the sounds generated by propellers in the submarines at distances of many kilometers. In fact, each class of submarine makes its own unique sound and some detectors are so sensitive that they can tell the differences between the propellers of two nearly identical submarines. This makes the sound of the propeller almost like a fingerprint, allowing that submarine's path to be tracked. Such knowledge was of great value to our ships in World War II.

Sound waves are also used to determine distances to objects or to the bottom of the ocean. A sound wave is sent from the ship to the ocean floor, where it is reflected back. By knowing the speed of sound in water (1,500 meters per second) and the time it took to travel to the ocean floor and then back up, it is possible to calculate the distance to the ocean floor. If a signal took four seconds to travel to the ocean floor and bounce back to the ship, then one would know that it took two seconds to go down and two seconds to come back up. Since sound waves go 1,500 meters per second, the ocean floor would be calculated at 1,500 meters/second times 2 seconds = 3,000 meters (about 1.9 miles deep). A similar strategy is used to find the distance to objects such as schools of fish or ships.

24. The reason submarines can detect other underwater objects is largely due to which of the following?

   (1) Submarines can get very close to these objects.
   (2) Sound travels very well through water.
   (3) It is possible to determine the distance to objects using sound waves.
   (4) Sound waves are affected by propellers.
   (5) Our navy has used sound waves to detect enemy submarines.

25. A sound wave is sent out by a ship and the reflected wave is detected six seconds later. How deep is the ocean floor?

   (1) 1,500 meters
   (2) 3,000 meters
   (3) 4,500 meters
   (4) 6,000 meters
   (5) 9,000 meters

26. In which of the following materials would sound waves travel best?

   (1) air
   (2) helium gas
   (3) water
   (4) oil
   (5) steel

GO ON TO THE NEXT PAGE

TEST 3: SCIENCE

<u>Questions 27 and 28</u> refer to the following table.

APPROXIMATE SWIMMING SPEEDS OF SOME COMMON FISH

Common Name	Scientific Name	Length (in.)	Speed (mph)
Barracuda	*Sphyraena barracuda*	73	30
Cod	*Gadus callarius*	22	4.2
Eel	*Anguilla vulgaris*	24	2.8
Flounder	*Pleuronectes flesus*	11	2.4
Goldfish	*Carassius aurataus*	5	3.6
Lemon shark	*Negaprion brevirostris*	75	6
Lemon sole	*Pleuronectes microcephalus*	3.5	.26
Mackerel	*Scomber scombrus*	14	5.4
Rainbow trout	*Salmo irideus*	8	3.4
Sea trout	*Salmo trutta*	14	5.4

27. Which of the following statements is supported by information in the table?

(1) The larger the fish, the faster it swims.
(2) Some small fish can swim faster than larger fish.
(3) Sharks are predators and have to swim fast.
(4) The size of a fish is not related to its speed.
(5) Saltwater fish are faster than freshwater fish.

28. Other than the two species of trout, which of the following fish are probably related?

(1) flounder and mackerel
(2) goldfish and mackerel
(3) flounder and lemon sole
(4) lemon shark and lemon sole
(5) cod and mackerel

29. Commercial fishermen have all the advantages of technology to help them increase their catch. They use locators to find the largest schools and miles of nets to scoop the fish out of the water. Because of overfishing, among other reasons, fish populations all over the world are declining, and the average size of fish that are caught is smaller. This statement is also true of game fish. There are no longer spectacular swordfish of over 1,000 pounds, or giant sea bass weighing 500 pounds. Also, some other fish that were once quite common have become rare.

All of the statements below are opinions EXCEPT

(1) no one should be allowed to fish American waters except Americans
(2) there has to be some other explanation for the decline in game fish; no one could possibly catch enough of them to cause the populations to decline
(3) the oceans are big enough for everybody to take all the fish he or she wants
(4) if fishermen would allow enough larger breeder fish to go free, the populations might increase
(5) the U.S. Department of Fish and Game needs to tell fishermen how many fish they can catch

GO ON TO THE NEXT PAGE

TEST 3: SCIENCE

<u>Questions 30–32</u> are based on the following graphs.

AVERAGE MONTHLY TEMPERATURE

TOTAL MONTHLY PRECIPITATION

The two graphs represent average monthly temperature and total monthly precipitation from January through December for a city located near the center of a continent.

30. Between which two consecutive months is there the least change in the average temperature?

   (1) January and February
   (2) February and March
   (3) May and June
   (4) October and November
   (5) December and January

31. The average temperature and the total precipitation during the month of September (S on the horizontal axis of the graphs) were

   (1) 7°C; 60 mm
   (2) 15°C; 50 mm
   (3) 16°C; 68 mm
   (4) 21°C; 68 mm
   (5) 21°C; 80 mm

32. Which best describes the climate pattern of this location?

   (1) hotter and wetter in summer than in winter
   (2) hotter in summer than in winter, with no pronounced wet or dry season
   (3) wetter in summer than in winter, with fairly constant temperature throughout the year
   (4) dry and cold during the winter months
   (5) dry and warm during the summer months

<u>Questions 33 and 34</u> are based on the following graph.

The graph above shows the heating of ethylene glycol, the most common component of commercial antifreeze as it is heated for 12 minutes. Ethylene glycol is liquid at room temperature. At 198°C, it starts to boil.

33. In this experiment, how long did the ethylene glycol warm up before it started to boil?

   (1) 3 minutes
   (2) 6 minutes
   (3) 9 minutes
   (4) 12 minutes
   (5) 15 minutes

GO ON TO THE NEXT PAGE

TEST 3: SCIENCE

34. Suppose a similar experiment was done with water. Water boils at 100°C. What would the temperature of boiling water be after boiling for 5 minutes?

    (1) 20°C
    (2) 95°C
    (3) 100°C
    (4) 105°C
    (5) 198°C

35. Pure water has a pH of 7. Acids have pH values lower than 7, and alkalis or bases have values higher than 7. A gardener knows that the plants she grows need soil with a pH of 7.5. If the pH of the soil is 6.5, what action might she take?

    (1) Use only pure water in watering the plants.
    (2) Add a mild acid to the soil.
    (3) Add a mild alkali to the soil.
    (4) Use tap water, which has a pH of 6.5.
    (5) Use an organic fertilizer that becomes acid when it decays.

Question 36 is based on the following diagram.

Plane Mirror

36. The arrow in the diagram represents an object in front of a plane mirror. The image formed in a plane mirror must obey the rule that every point on the image is just as far behind the mirror as the corresponding point on the object. Which of the following arrows represents the image?

(1) (2) (3) (4) (5)

Questions 37 and 38 are based on the following chart.

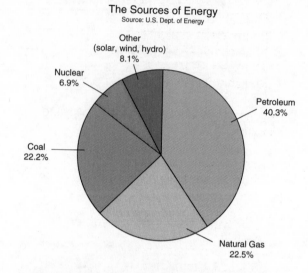

The Sources of Energy
Source: U.S. Dept. of Energy

Other (solar, wind, hydro) 8.1%

Nuclear 6.9%

Petroleum 40.3%

Coal 22.2%

Natural Gas 22.5%

The pie chart shown describes the percentage of energy sources in the United States in 1998.

37. Coal, natural gas, and petroleum are collectively known as fossil fuels. About what percentage of energy sources came from fossil fuels?

    (1) 22.2%
    (2) 22.5%
    (3) 40.3%
    (4) 62.8%
    (5) 85.0%

38. What was the largest energy source in 1998?

    (1) Nuclear
    (2) Petroleum
    (3) Coal
    (4) Hydroelectricity
    (5) Natural gas

GO ON TO THE NEXT PAGE

TEST 3: SCIENCE

39. If an opaque object is placed between a light bulb and a wall, the shadow on the wall is a faithful copy of the shape of the object. This is evidence that light

    (1) is a type of wave
    (2) travels in straight lines
    (3) is composed of photons
    (4) travels very fast
    (5) can travel in a vacuum

<u>Questions 40–49</u> are based on the following information.

Behavior in living organisms is the pattern of activities in response to stimuli of the environment. Below are five types of behavior.

(1) reflex act—a simple, inborn, automatic response
(2) instinct—a complex behavior pattern performed without learning
(3) conditioned behavior—a changed stimulus produces the original response
(4) habit—a conscious response becomes automatic after constant repetition
(5) learned behavior—a complex process involving reasoning and insight

Each of the following items refers to one of these types of behavior. For each item choose the category that best describes the one type of behavior. A category may be used more than once in answering the following questions.

40. In January, I find myself dating checks with the old calendar year. This type of behavior is best described as

    (1) reflex act
    (2) instinct
    (3) conditioned behavior
    (4) habit
    (5) learned behavior

41. Students are asked to write their names as many times as they can in 2 minutes. Then they are asked to do the same using the other hand. Comparisons are made regarding quality of performance and number of copies made. This type of behavior is best described as

    (1) reflex act
    (2) instinct
    (3) conditioned behavior
    (4) habit
    (5) learned behavior

42. The brain of a frog is destroyed in a painless fashion. Some absorbent cotton is dipped in vinegar (five percent acetic acid) and then placed on the frog's thigh. The leg reacts. This type of behavior is best described as

    (1) reflex act
    (2) instinct
    (3) conditioned behavior
    (4) habit
    (5) learned behavior

43. Joan holds a square of wire mesh closely to her face. Although Martin warns her that he is about to throw a wad of paper at her, when he throws the ball of paper she blinks. This type of behavior is best described as

    (1) reflex act
    (2) instinct
    (3) conditioned behavior
    (4) habit
    (5) learned behavior

44. Stanley and Lynda finish a difficult crossword puzzle in 60 minutes. Florence and Regina need more time to do the same puzzle. This type of behavior is best described as

    (1) reflex act
    (2) instinct
    (3) conditioned behavior
    (4) habit
    (5) learned behavior

GO ON TO THE NEXT PAGE

TEST 3: SCIENCE

45. A robin raised in an incubator builds a nest much like those of wild robins. This type of behavior is best described as

    (1) reflex act
    (2) instinct
    (3) conditioned behavior
    (4) habit
    (5) learned behavior

46. A newborn baby cries when it is uncomfortable, but an older baby will cry just to get attention. This type of behavior is best described as

    (1) reflex act
    (2) instinct
    (3) conditioned behavior
    (4) habit
    (5) learned behavior

47. A dolphin is rewarded with extra food each time it performs a trick. This type of behavior is best described as

    (1) reflex act
    (2) instinct
    (3) conditioned behavior
    (4) habit
    (5) learned behavior

48. After a passage is read to a class very slowly, it is read so that the class could copy what they hear but they are told NOT to cross the t's and NOT to dot the i's. Then the number of errors are reported. What is the kind of behavior that causes the errors?

    (1) reflex act
    (2) instinct
    (3) conditioned behavior
    (4) habit
    (5) learned behavior

49. Persons who have used this book to prepare for the GED have attained satisfactory scores on the test. This type of behavior is best described as

    (1) reflex act
    (2) instinct
    (3) conditioned behavior
    (4) habit
    (5) learned behavior

Questions 50 refers to the following information.

About 100 years ago, two German scientists studying the function of the pancreas as an organ of digestion removed the entire pancreas from several dogs. A short time later some assistants observed that swarms of flies hovered around the cages that housed these dogs. Many regard this as the initial, but accidental, step in diabetes research. However, it was not until 1922 that Banting and Best showed that the pancreas produces the hormone insulin, which is essential for the proper use of sugar by the body. They concluded that if insulin is lacking, diabetes results.

50. The cages around the group of dogs not given the pancreas surgery did not seem to attract as many flies. This statement should be classified as

    (1) the problem statement
    (2) a hypothesis
    (3) an observation
    (4) an assumption
    (5) irrelevant information

END OF EXAMINATION

TEST 4: LANGUAGE ARTS, READING

Directions

The Language Arts, Reading test consists of excerpts from pre-1920, 1920–1960, and post-1960 literature; articles about literature or the arts; and at least one business document.

Read each excerpt first and then answer the questions following it. Refer to the reading material as often as necessary in answering the questions.

Each excerpt is preceded by a "purpose question." The purpose question gives a reason for reading the material. Use these purpose questions to help focus your reading. You are not required to answer these purpose questions. They are given only to help you concentrate on the ideas presented in the reading materials.

You should spend no more than 65 minutes answering the questions. Work carefully, but do not spend too much time on any one question. Be sure you answer every question. You will not be penalized for incorrect answers.

To record your answers, mark the numbered space on the answer sheet beside the number that corresponds to the question in the test.

FOR EXAMPLE:

It was Susan's dream machine. The metallic blue paint gleamed, and the sporty wheels were highly polished. Under the hood, the engine was no less carefully cleaned. Inside, flashy lights illuminated the instruments on the dashboard, and the seats were covered by rich leather upholstery.

The subject ("It") of this excerpt is most likely

(1) an airplane   ① ② ● ④ ⑤
(2) a stereo system
(3) an automobile
(4) a boat
(5) a motorcycle

The correct answer is "an automobile"; therefore, answer space 3 would be marked on the answer sheet.

GO ON TO THE NEXT PAGE

TEST 4: LANGUAGE ARTS, READING

<u>Questions 1–5</u> refer to the following passage.

HOW SHOULD ONE HANDLE THE PROBLEM OF CORRECTING OTHERS?

Miss Manners is constantly besieged by people who want to know the tactful manner of pointing out their friends' and relatives' inferiorities. These people, their loved ones report to Miss Manners, chew with their mouths open, mispronounce words, crack their knuckles, spit, belch, and hum tunelessly to themselves. They have bad breath and runs in their stockings. They are too fat, dress badly, and do their hair all wrong.

How can those who love these people dearly, for reasons that are not clear, and who wish to help them, for reasons that unfortunately are clear, politely let them have it?

The answer is that they cannot, certainly not politely. There are times, in certain trusting relationships, when one can accomplish this impolitely. One can sometimes say, "Cracking your knuckles drives me up the wall, and if you do it one more time I'll scream," or "Have a mint— there's something wrong with your breath," or "What's that thing on your left front tooth?" No reasonable person should take offense at these remarks. Because they are so frank, they do not seem to carry a history of repulsion long predating the offense. Also they deal with matters that are more or less easily correctable (although Miss Manners knows some determined knuckle crackers she suspects aren't half trying to stop), and which it is plausible to assume the offenders hadn't noticed.

What is unacceptable is to criticize things a person cannot easily remedy or may not want to. People who you think are too fat either disagree about what too fat is, are trying to do something about it, or are not trying to do something about it. In no case is it helpful for them to know that other people consider them too fat.

It is admittedly difficult to arrest the pleasure of correcting and advising long enough to ask oneself who will feel better after the correction is delivered—the person issuing it, or the one who gets it full in the face? But it is well worth the effort, not only for kindness' sake, but because it is a law of nature that he who corrects others will soon do something perfectly awful himself.

1. The selection deals mainly with

   (1) correcting others
   (2) inferior people
   (3) unacceptable behavior
   (4) trusting relationships
   (5) forcing changes in behavior

2. Unattactive behavior includes all EXCEPT

   (1) bad breath
   (2) loud talk
   (3) cracking knuckles
   (4) inappropriate vocabulary
   (5) spitting

3. According to the passage, people who criticize do so out of

   (1) spite
   (2) revenge
   (3) feelings of superiority
   (4) repulsion
   (5) love

4. Those who correct others should focus on

   (1) matters offenders notice
   (2) matters offenders take offense at
   (3) matters indicating inferiority
   (4) easily correctable matters
   (5) matters carrying a history of repulsion

5. The one who criticizes should consider

   (1) politely letting them have it
   (2) things easily remedied
   (3) both the criticizer and the criticized
   (4) the pleasure of correcting
   (5) only those who agree on the behavior criticized

GO ON TO THE NEXT PAGE

TEST 4: LANGUAGE ARTS, READING

Questions 6–10 are based on this selection from a play.

WHAT IS THE TOWN OF GROVER'S CORNERS LIKE?

STAGE MANAGER: Mr. Webb is Publisher and Editor of the Grover's Corners *Sentinel*. That's our local paper, y'know.

MR. WEBB: Hm. . . I don't have to tell you that we're run here by a Board of Selectmen. All males vote at the age of 21. Women vote indirect. We're lower middle class, sprinkling of professional men. . .

STAGE MANAGER: Have you any comments, Mr. Webb?

MR. WEBB: Very ordinary town, if you ask me. Little better behaved than most. Probably a lot duller. But our young people here seem to like it well enough: 90% of 'em graduating from high school settle down right here to live—even when they've been away to college.

STAGE MANAGER: Thank you, Mr. Webb. Now, is there anyone in the audience who would like to ask Editor Webb anything about the town? . . .

TALL MAN: Is there no one in town aware of social injustice and industrial inequality?

MR. WEBB: Oh, yes, everybody is— somethin' terrible. Seems like they spend most of their time talking about who's rich and who's poor.

TALL MAN: Then why don't they do something about it?

MR. WEBB: Well, we're ready to listen to everybody's suggestion as to how you can see that the diligent and sensible'll rise to the top and the lazy and quarrelsome sink to the bottom. We'll listen to anybody. Meantime, until that's settled, we try to take care of those that can't help themselves, and those that can we leave alone. Are there any more questions?

LADY IN A BOX: Oh. Mr. Webb? Mr. Webb is there any love of beauty in Grover's Corners?

MR. WEBB: Well, ma'am, there ain't much—not in the sense that you mean. . . No, ma'am, there isn't much culture, but maybe this is the place to tell you that we've got a lot of pleasures of a kind here: we like the sun comin' up over the mountain in the morning, and we all notice a good deal about the birds. We pay a lot of attention to them, and trees and plants. And we watch the change of seasons: yes, everybody knows about them. . .

6. Grover's Corners is

(1) a modern town
(2) an active town
(3) an unusual town
(4) a progressive town
(5) an ordinary town

7. Grover's Corners is

(1) a conservative town
(2) a socially sensitive town
(3) an economically well-off town
(4) a constantly changing town
(5) an ill-behaved town

8. In Grover's Corners, the chief source of happiness is

(1) music
(2) art
(3) reading
(4) culture
(5) nature

9. The inhabitants of Grover's Corners are mostly

(1) professionals
(2) high school graduates
(3) upward mobile
(4) respectful of women's rights
(5) irreligious

10. The attitude of Grover's Corners to the poor is one of

(1) sympathy
(2) selective help
(3) intolerance
(4) impatience
(5) ignorance

GO ON TO THE NEXT PAGE

TEST 4: LANGUAGE ARTS, READING

<u>Questions 11–15</u> refer to the following passage.

HOW DID ONE VILLAGE BRING DISASTER ON ITSELF?

On a morning in early spring, 1873, the people of Oberfest left their houses and took refuge in the town hall. No one knows why, precisely. A number of rumors had raced through the town during recent weeks, were passed on and converted to news; predictions became certainties. On this particular morning, fear turned into terror, and people rushed through the narrow streets, carrying their most precious possessions, pulling their children and dashing into the great hall. The doors were nailed shut, and men took their turns watching out the window. Two days passed. When no disaster came, the fear grew worse, because the people began to suspect that the danger was already in the hall, locked inside. No one spoke to anybody else; people watched each other, looking for signs. It was the children who rang the great bell in the first bell tower—a small band of bored children found the bell rope and swung on it—set the bell clanging. This was the traditional signal of alarm, and in a moment the elders were dashing in panic to all the other bell towers and ringing the bells. For nearly an hour, the valley reverberated with the wild clangor—and then, a thousand feet above, the snow began to crack, and the avalanche began; a massive cataract of ice and snow thundered down and buried the town, silencing the bells. There is no trace of Oberfest today, not even a spire, because the snow is so deep; and, in the shadow of the mountains, it is very cold.

11. Which element is especially significant in this passage?

    (1) dialogue
    (2) setting
    (3) illustrations
    (4) levels of usage
    (5) rhythm

12. Which is the most valid conclusion regarding the theme of the passage?

    (1) It is a minor feature of the passage.
    (2) It is not related to the plot.
    (3) It is related to the topic sentence.
    (4) It is stated, rather than implied.
    (5) It is implied, but not stated.

13. That the alarm, traditionally sounded to avert danger, became the apparent cause of the avalanche is an example of

    (1) irony
    (2) simile
    (3) satire
    (4) personification
    (5) exaggeration

14. The effect of the last phrase of the passage, "it is very cold," depends mainly on

    (1) rhythm
    (2) rhyme
    (3) comparison
    (4) connotation
    (5) sound

15. Which word best expresses the main idea of the passage?

    (1) faith
    (2) suspicion
    (3) nostalgia
    (4) disaster
    (5) rumors

<u>Questions 16–20</u> refer to the following poem.

HOW DOES THIS POET FEEL ABOUT HIMSELF?

EVERY GOOD BOY DOES FINE

I practiced my cornet in a cold garage
Where I could blast it till the oil in drums
Boomed back; tossed free-throws till I
    couldn't move my thumbs;

GO ON TO THE NEXT PAGE

TEST 4: LANGUAGE ARTS, READING

(5) Sprinted through tires, tackling a headless
dummy.
In my first contest, playing a wobbly solo,
I blew up in the coda, alone on stage,
And twisting like my hand-tied necktie, saw
(10) the judge
Letting my silence dwindle down his scale.

At my first basketball game, gangling away
from home
A hundred miles by bus to a dressing
(15) room,
Under the showering voice of the coach, I
stood in a towel,
Having forgotten shoes, socks, uniform.

In my first football game, the first play
(20) under the lights
I intercepted a pass. For seventy yards, I
ran
Through music and squeals, surging, lifting
my cleats,
(25) Only to be brought down by the safety
man.
I took my second chances with less care,
but in dreams
I saw the bald judge slumped in the front
(30) row,
The coach and team at the doorway, the
safety man
Galloping loud at my heels. They watch
me
(35) now.

You who have always horned your way
through passages,
Sat safe on the bench while some came
(40) naked to court,
Slipped out of arms to win in the long run,
Consider this poem a failure, sprawling flat
on a page.

16. The "I," or speaking voice of the poem,
probably regards himself mainly as

(1) an athlete
(2) a musician
(3) a loser
(4) a wit
(5) a critic

17. In relation to the content of the poem, its
title is an example of

(1) personification
(2) allegory
(3) sensory language
(4) irony
(5) an epithet

18. In the final stanza, the reader is asked to

(1) make an improper judgment
(2) feel sorry for the poet
(3) feel superior to the poet
(4) agree with the poet
(5) admire the poet

19. In line 9, "twisting like my hand-tied
necktie" is an example of

(1) a striking contrast
(2) a vague reference
(3) an implied meaning
(4) an overused symbol
(5) a vivid comparison

20. With which group of words does the poet
address the reader directly?

(1) "I practiced my cornet" (line 1)
(2) "In my first contest" (line 7)
(3) "in dreams I saw the bald judge" (lines
28 and 29)
(4) "some came naked to court" (lines 37
and 38)
(5) "Consider this poem a failure" (line 40)

GO ON TO THE NEXT PAGE

TEST 4: LANGUAGE ARTS, READING

Questions 21–25 refer to the following poem.

HOW SHOULD WE LIVE OUR LIVES?

BARTER

Life has loveliness to sell—
All beautiful and splendid things,
Blue waves whitened on a cliff,
Climbing fire that sways and sings,
(5) And children's faces looking up
Holding wonder like a cup.

Life has loveliness to sell—
Music like a curve of gold,
Scent of pine trees in the rain,
(10) Eyes that love you, arms that hold,
And for your spirit's still delight,
Holy thoughts that star the night.

Spend all you have for loveliness,
Buy it and never count the cost.
(15) For one white singing hour of peace
Count many a year of strife well lost,
And for a breath of ecstasy
Give all you have been or could be.

—Sara Teasdale

21. The main idea of the poem is to urge us

    (1) to be cautious in life
    (2) to avoid strife
    (3) to despise the ugly part of life
    (4) to enjoy life's treasures
    (5) not to become involved

22. The beauty of nature is indicated in line

    (1) 3
    (2) 6
    (3) 10
    (4) 12
    (5) 16

23. There is a simile (comparison) in line

    (1) 2
    (2) 4
    (3) 7
    (4) 10
    (5) 16

24. The poet includes the spiritual in life with the words

    (1) "climbing fire"
    (2) "children's faces"
    (3) "arms that hold"
    (4) "holy thoughts"
    (5) "year of strife"

25. The word *barter* means exchange by trade without money. In the poem the exchange is

    (1) personal commitment for life's beauty
    (2) a year of strife for ecstasy
    (3) spirit's delight for peace
    (4) children's faces for wonder
    (5) music for a curve of gold

GO ON TO THE NEXT PAGE

TEST 4: LANGUAGE ARTS, READING

Questions 26–30 are based on the following document.

THE COMMONWEALTH OF VIRGINIA'S POLICY ON ALCOHOL AND OTHER DRUGS

The Commonwealth of Virginia's Policy 1.05 on Alcohol and Other Drugs states that the following acts by employees are prohibited:

(A)

I. the unlawful or unauthorized manufacture, distribution, dispensation, possession, or use of alcohol and other drugs in the workplace;

II. the impairment on the workplace from the use of alcohol or other drugs (except the use of drugs for legitimate medical purposes);

III. action which results in the criminal conviction for:

- a violation of any criminal drug law, based upon conduct occurring either on or off the workplace, or
- a violation of any alcoholic beverage control law, or law which governs driving while intoxicated, based upon conduct occurring in the workplace;

IV. the failure to report to their supervisors that they have been convicted of any offense, as defined in III above, within five calendar days of the conviction.

(B)

– Included under this policy are all employees in Executive Branch agencies, including the Governor's Office, Office of the Lieutenant Governor, and the Office of the Attorney General.

(C)

– The workplace consists of any state owned or leased property or any site where official duties are being performed by state employees.

(D)

– Any employee who commits any prohibited act under this policy shall be subject to the full range of disciplinary actions, including discharge, and may by required to participate satisfactorily in an appropriate rehabilitation program.

(E)

– A copy of the entire Commonwealth of Virginia's Policy on Alcohol and Other Drugs may be obtained from your agency human resource office.

(F)

CERTIFICATE OF RECEIPT

Your signature below indicates your receipt of this policy summary of Policy 1.05, Alcohol and Other Drugs. Your signature is intended only to acknowledge receipt; it does not imply agreement or disagreement with the policy itself. If you refuse to sign this certificate of receipt, your supervisor will be asked to initial this form indicating that a copy has been given to you.

26. ALL of the following are unacceptable according to the policy EXCEPT

(1) distribution of drugs on work site
(2) manufacturing of drugs on work site
(3) abuse of illegal drugs
(4) abuse of alcohol
(5) use of prescription drugs

27. The purpose of the policy is

(1) to arrest drug dealers
(2) to stop drinking on the job
(3) to discontinue manufacturing illegal drugs
(4) to allow prescription drugs in the workplace
(5) inform employees of the company's policy on alcohol and other drugs

GO ON TO THE NEXT PAGE

TEST 4: LANGUAGE ARTS, READING

28. According to the document, who is included in this policy?

    (1) some employees in Executive Branch agencies
    (2) just the Governor's Office employees
    (3) all of the workers at the Office of the Attorney General
    (4) all employees in Executive Branch agencies, including the Governor's Office, Office of the Lieutenant Governor, and the Office of the Attorney General.
    (5) all employees who receive a copy of this policy

29. Any employee caught committing any prohibited act under this policy may be subject to ALL of the following EXCEPT

    (1) discharge
    (2) disciplinary action
    (3) participation in a rehabilitation program
    (4) immediate release from the company
    (5) a review of the offense by a manager

30. If an employee refuses to sign the "certificate of receipt," then

    (1) he will be fired
    (2) his supervisor will file it without a signature
    (3) he will be arrested
    (4) he will receive a pay cut
    (5) his supervisor will initial the form as receipt for him

Questions 31–35 refer to the following passage.

HOW DOES THE AUTHOR FEEL ABOUT PRIZE FIGHT CROWDS?

The fight crowd is a beast that lurks in the darkness behind the fringe of white light shed over the first six rows by the incandescents atop the ring, and is not to
(5) be trusted with pop bottles or other hardware.

People who go to prize fights are sadistic.

When two prominent pugilists are
(10) scheduled to pummel one another in public on a summer's evening, men and women file into the stadium in the guise of human beings, and thereafter become a part of a gray thing that squats in the dark until, at
(15) the conclusion of the bloodletting, they may be seen leaving the arena in the same guise they wore when they entered....

As a rule, the mob that gathers to see men fight is unjust, vindictive, swept by
(20) intense unreasoning hatreds, proud of its swift recognition of what it believes to be sportsmanship. It is quick to greet the purely phony move of the boxer who extends his gloves to his rival, who has slipped or been
(25) pushed to the floor, and to reward this stimulating but still baloney gesture with a pattering of hands which indicates the following: "You are a good sport. We recognize that you are a good sport, and we
(30) know a sporting gesture when we see one. Therefore we are all good sports, too. Hurrah for us!"

GO ON TO THE NEXT PAGE

TEST 4: LANGUAGE ARTS, READING

The same crowd doesn't see the same boxer stick his thumb in his opponent's eye (35) or try to cut him with the laces of his glove, butt him or dig him a low one when the referee isn't in a position to see. It roots consistently for the smaller man, and never for a moment considers the desperate (40) psychological dilemma of the larger of the two. It howls with glee at a good finisher making his kill. The Roman hordes were more civilized. Their gladiators asked them whether the final blow should be (45) administered or not. The main attraction at the modern prize fight is the spectacle of a man clubbing a helpless and vanquished opponent into complete insensibility. The referee who stops a bout to save a slugged (50) and punch-drunken man from the final ignominy is hissed by the assembled sportsmen.

31. The writer of this passage is

   (1) disgusted
   (2) jovial
   (3) matter-of-fact
   (4) satiric
   (5) optimistic

32. As used in line 23, which action is referred to as a "baloney gesture"?

   (1) pushing the opponent to the floor
   (2) shaking hands with the opponent
   (3) touching gloves with the downed opponent
   (4) smiling at the opponent
   (5) digging the opponent a low blow

33. The "desperate psychological dilemma" of the bigger man (lines 39–40) is caused by the crowd's

   (1) rooting for the smaller man, but cheering a good finisher
   (2) cheering a good finisher, but hissing at the referee
   (3) applauding a friendly gesture, but rooting for the smaller man
   (4) hissing at the referee, but howling at a good finisher
   (5) applauding a friendly gesture, but cheering a helpless opponent

34. Which group of words best indicates the author's opinion?

   (1) *referee, opponent, finisher*
   (2) *gladiators, slugged, sporting gesture*
   (3) *stimulating, hissing, pattering*
   (4) *beast, lurks, gray thing*
   (5) *spectacle, psychological dilemma, sportsmen*

35. The author states that the prize fight audience is

   (1) sportsmanlike
   (2) fair
   (3) civilized
   (4) uninvolved
   (5) vengeful

GO ON TO THE NEXT PAGE

TEST 4: LANGUAGE ARTS, READING

Questions 36–40 refer to the following commentary on literature.

WHAT HERITAGE DID WILLA CATHER LEAVE TO US?

Willa Cather (1873–1947) grew up to be a major American writer, but today many people still do not know her face. Critics rank her with our great modern novelists—Faulkner, Hemingway, Fitzgerald—and she was certainly esteemed in her own time. Supreme Court Justice Oliver Wendell Holmes praised *My Antonia* as a book that "makes the reader love his country more."

Miss Cather wrote that novel and 11 others. Her books still have this effect on readers, for she had the power to elevate ordinary people and places. No one has described the American West with more passion and clarity. In every sentence, her feeling for the earth surges beneath a strong, disciplined prose. This is from *My Antonia:*

We were talking about what it is like to spend one's childhood in little towns like these, buried in wheat and corn, under stimulating extremes of climate: burning summers when the world lies green and billowy beneath a brilliant sky, when one is fairly stifled in vegetation, in the colour and smell of strong weeds and heavy harvests; blustery winters with little snow, when the whole country is stripped bare and grey as sheet-iron. We agreed that no one who had not grown up in a little prairie town could know anything about it. It was a kind of freemasonry, we said.

Willa Cather became the voice of an unsung people, the generation of immigrants who settled our western frontier. Today many writers regard that history as tragic, a paradise lost through careless greed. Cather believed that America's promise would endure: *We come and go, but the land is always here. And the people who love it and understand it are the people who own it—for a little while.*

36. The author implies impatience with

    (1) lack of modern recognition of Cather's work
    (2) lack of critical acclaim for Cather's work
    (3) lack of appreciation by her contemporaries
    (4) Cather's stature as a writer
    (5) Cather's patriotism

37. The author admires Cather's

    (1) huge output
    (2) popular success
    (3) unusual subject matter
    (4) objectivity
    (5) earthiness

38. In the excerpt from *My Antonia*, Cather stresses a childhood rooted in a small town's

    (1) repression
    (2) activity
    (3) passion
    (4) natural characteristics
    (5) brutal hardships

39. The author implies praise for all of the following characteristics of Cather's work EXCEPT her

    (1) style
    (2) passion
    (3) clarity
    (4) effect on her readers
    (5) unusual subjects

40. Cather's view of America was

    (1) cynical
    (2) resigned
    (3) tragic
    (4) optimistic
    (5) regional

END OF EXAMINATION

TEST 5: MATHEMATICS

Directions

The Mathematics test consists of multiple-choice and alternate format questions intended to measure general mathematics skills and problem-solving ability. The questions are based on short readings that often include a graph, chart, or diagram.

You should spend no more than 45 minutes answering the questions. Work carefully, but do not spend too much time on any one question. Be sure you answer every question. You will not be penalized for incorrect answers.

Formulas you may need are given on pages 726–727. Only some of the questions will require you to use a formula. Not all the formulas given will be needed.

Some questions contain more information than you will need to solve the problem. Other questions do not give enough information to solve the problem. If the question does not give enough information to solve the problem, the correct answer is "Not enough information is given."

You may use a calculator on Part I.

To record your answers, mark the numbered space on the answer sheet beside the number that corresponds to the question in the test.

FOR EXAMPLE:

If a grocery bill totaling $15.75 is paid with a $20.00 bill, how much change should be returned?

(1) $5.26   ① ② ● ④ ⑤
(2) $4.75
(3) $4.25
(4) $3.75
(5) $3.25

The correct answer is "$4.25"; therefore, answer space 3 would be marked on the answer sheet.

GO ON TO THE NEXT PAGE

TEST 5: MATHEMATICS

FORMULAS

Description	Formula
AREA (A) of a:	
square	$A = s^2$; where s = side
rectangle	$A = lw$; where l = length, w = width
parallelogram	$A = bh$; where b = base, h = height
triangle	$A = \frac{1}{2} bh$; where b = base, h = height
trapezoid	$A = \frac{1}{2}(b_1 + b_2) h$; where b = base, h = height
circle	$A = \pi r^2$; where π = 3.14, r = radius
PERIMETER (P) of a:	
square	$P = 4s$; where s = side
rectangle	$P = 2l + 2w$; where l = length, w = width
triangle	$P = a + b + c$; where a, b, and c are the sides
circumference (C) of a circle	$C = \pi d$; where π = 3.14, d = diameter
VOLUME (V) of a:	
cube	$V = s^3$; where s = side
rectangular container	$V = lwh$; where l = length, w = width, h = height
cylinder	$V = \pi r^2 h$; where π = 3.14, r = radius, h = height
square pyramid	$V = \frac{1}{3}(\text{base edge})^2 h$
cone	$V = \frac{1}{3} \pi r^2 h$
Pythagorean theorem	$c^2 = a^2 + b^2$; where c = hypotenuse, a and b are legs, of a right triangle
distance (d) between two points in a plane	$d = \sqrt{(x_2 - x_1)^2 + (y_2 - y_1)^2}$; where (x_1, y_1) and (x_2, y_2) are two points in a plane
slope of a line (m)	$m = \dfrac{y_2 - y_1}{x_2 - x_1}$; where (x_1, y_1) and (x_2, y_2) are two points in a plane

GO ON TO THE NEXT PAGE

TEST 5: MATHEMATICS

FORMULAS (continued)	
Description	**Formula**
MEASURES OF CENTRAL TENDENCY	mean = $\dfrac{x_1 + x_2 + \ldots + x_n}{n}$; where the x's are the values for which a mean is desired, and n = number of values in the series
	median = the point in an ordered set of numbers at which half of the numbers are above and half of the numbers are below this value
simple interest (i)	$i = prt$; where p = principal, r = rate, t = time
distance (d) as function of rate and time	$d = rt$; where r = rate, t = time
total cost (c)	$c = nr$; where n = number of units, r = cost per unit

GO ON TO THE NEXT PAGE

TEST 5: MATHEMATICS, PART I

Directions: You will have 45 minutes to complete this seciton. You may use a calculator.

1. A salesman earns $300 per week plus a 5% commission on all sales over $8,000. One week, his sales amounted to $15,000. What were his earnings that week?

   (1) $300
   (2) $450
   (3) $600
   (4) $650
   (5) $700

2. How much does Jane pay for 1 pound 12 ounces of apples at $1.29 per pound?

   (1) $2.26
   (2) $3.04
   (3) $3.57
   (4) $3.65
   (5) $3.75

3. One morning Martin drove 80 miles in 2 hours. After lunch, he covered 100 miles more in 3 hours. What was his average rate of speed, in miles per hour, for the 5 hours of driving?

   (1) 35
   (2) 36
   (3) 37
   (4) 45
   (5) Not enough information is given.

4. A picture 8 inches long and 6 inches wide is to be enlarged so that its length will be 12 inches. What is the width, in inches, of the enlarged picture?

   Mark your answer in the circles on the grid on the answer sheet.

5. A man bought ABC stock at $19.625 per share and sold it at $23.25 per share. What was his profit on 80 shares before deductions for commission and taxes?

   Mark your answer in the circles on the grid on the answer sheet.

6. A solution of the inequality $3x - 1 < 5$ is

   (1) 3
   (2) 2
   (3) 1
   (4) 5
   (5) $2\frac{1}{2}$

7. A theater has 850 seats, 60% of which are in the orchestra. How many seats are NOT in the orchestra?

   Mark your answer in the circles on the grid on the answer sheet.

8. In a right triangle, the ratio of the measures of the two acute angles is $4 : 1$. What is the measure, in degrees, of the larger acute angle?

   (1) 50
   (2) 54
   (3) 70
   (4) 72
   (5) Not enough information is given.

GO ON TO THE NEXT PAGE

TEST 5: MATHEMATICS, PART I

9. If 18 feet 10 inches is cut from a wire that is 25 feet 8 inches long, what is the length of the wire that is left?

    (1) 6 ft. 1 in.
    (2) 6 ft. 2 in.
    (3) 6 ft. 9 in.
    (4) 6 ft. 10 in.
    (5) 7 ft. 2 in.

10. Bill earns m dollars per month, and Angelo earns n dollars per month. How many dollars do both men earn in 1 year?

    (1) $12mn$
    (2) $12m + n$
    (3) $12(m + n)$
    (4) $12n + m$
    (5) $12n - m$

11. A boat travels due east for a distance of 15 miles. It then travels due north for a distance of 20 miles, at which point it drops anchor. How many miles is the boat from its starting point?

    (1) 23
    (2) 25
    (3) 29
    (4) 30
    (5) 35

12. Joan and Maria earn money by babysitting. If Joan earns twice as much as Maria and the two girls earn a total of $42, how much does Maria earn?

    (1) $8
    (2) $10
    (3) $12
    (4) $14
    (5) Not enough information is given.

Question 13 is based on the following table.

The table gives the instructions that accompany an income tax form.

If your taxable income is:		
At least	**But not more than**	**Your tax is**
0	$3,499	2% of the amount
$3,500	$4,499	$70 plus 3% of any amount above $3,500
$4,500	$7,499	$100 plus 5% of any amount above $4,500
$7,500		$250 plus 7% of any amount above $7,500

13. How much tax in dollars is due on a taxable income of $5,800?

    Mark your answer in the circles on the grid on the answer sheet.

GO ON TO THE NEXT PAGE

TEST 5: MATHEMATICS, PART I

14. Given the formula $x = 2a(b + 7)$, find x if $a = 3$ and $b = 5$.

    (1) 13
    (2) 72
    (3) 108
    (4) 120
    (5) 210

15. A school has 18 classes with 35 students in each class. In order to reduce class size to 30, how many new classes must be formed?

    (1) 2
    (2) 3
    (3) 5
    (4) 6
    (5) 8

16. A committee consists of 7 women and 4 men. If a member of the committee is chosen at random to act as chairperson, what is the probability that the choice is a woman?

    Mark your answer in the circles on the grid on the answer sheet.

17. A bag of potatoes weighing 5 pounds 12 ounces costs $2.07. What is the cost of 1 pound of potatoes?

    (1) $0.36
    (2) $0.38
    (3) $0.40
    (4) $0.45
    (5) $0.48

Question 18 is based on the following figure.

18. If $\overrightarrow{AC}$ is perpendicular to $\overleftrightarrow{CB}$ and $m\angle CBD = 125°$ then $m\angle A$ equals

    (1) 15°
    (2) 20°
    (3) 35°
    (4) 45°
    (5) Not enough information is given.

19. In a large class 80 students took a test. When the test papers were rated, it was found that 10% of the students had A papers, 25% had B papers, 30% had C papers, 15% had D papers, and the rest failed. How many students failed the test?

    (1) 10
    (2) 12
    (3) 15
    (4) 16
    (5) Not enough information is given.

20. A man invests $20,000 at an annual interest rate of 7%, and $12,000 at an annual interest rate of $7\frac{1}{2}$%. What was his annual income on the two investments?

    (1) $1,400
    (2) $1,500
    (3) $2,000
    (4) $2,300
    (5) $2,800

GO ON TO THE NEXT PAGE

TEST 5: MATHEMATICS, PART I

21. How many 4-inch by 8-inch bricks are needed to build a walk 6 feet wide and 24 feet long?

    (1) 54
    (2) 600
    (3) 648
    (4) 840
    (5) 1,000

22. Pete Rossini has just graduated from college with honors. He has been offered four jobs with the following pay provisions:

    A. $37,000 for the first year
    B. $870 per week for the first year
    C. $3,250 per month for the first year
    D. $3,000 per month for the first 6 months and an increase of 10% for the last 6 months

    Which of the above offers will give Pete Rossini the greatest income for the first year?

    (1) A
    (2) B
    (3) C
    (4) D
    (5) Not enough information is given.

23. A dealer bought two dozen jackets at $48 each. The next month she bought 15 more jackets at $48 each. Which of the following expressions gives the total number of dollars the dealer spent for the jackets?

    (1) $24 \times 48 + 15$
    (2) $(24 \times 48) \times 15$
    (3) $24 + 48 \times 15$
    (4) $48(24 + 15)$
    (5) $24 + (48 + 15)$

24. One car travels at an average speed of 48 miles per hour. A slower car travels at an average speed of 36 miles per hour. In 45 minutes how many more miles does the faster car travel than the slower car?

    Mark your answer in the circles on the grid on the answer sheet.

Question 25 is based on the following graph.

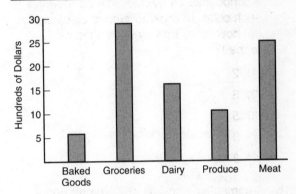

25. By how many dollars do the sales in the meat department exceed the sales in the dairy department?

    Mark your answer in the circles on the grid on the answer sheet.

END OF EXAMINATION

TEST 5: MATHEMATICS, PART II

Directions: You will have 45 minutes to complete questions 26–50. You may NOT use a calculator; otherwise, directions are the same as in Part I. You MAY refer to the *Formulas* sheet.

Question 26 is based on the following figure.

26. What is the perimeter of the figure?

    (1) $11x + 5y$

    (2) $10x + 5y$

    (3) $11x + 4y$

    (4) $9x - y$

    (5) $8x + 3y$

27. On January 1, a 280-gallon oil tank was $\frac{7}{8}$ full; on January 31 it was $\frac{1}{4}$ full. How many gallons of oil were used during the month?

    (1) 70

    (2) 105

    (3) 175

    (4) 210

    (5) Not enough information is given.

28. Express 2,750,389 in scientific notation.

    (1) 27.50389×10^5

    (2) 275.0389×10^3

    (3) 27.50389×10^6

    (4) 0.2750389×10^7

    (5) 2.750389×10^6

29. A basketball team has won 50 games of 75 played. The team still has 45 games to play. How many of the remaining games must the team win in order to win 60% of all games played during the season?

    (1) 20

    (2) 21

    (3) 22

    (4) 25

    (5) 30

Question 30 is based on the following diagram.

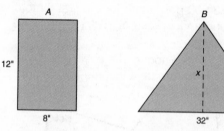

Area of ▭ A = Area of △ B

30. Which of the following expressions will provide the height (x) of $\triangle B$?

    (1) $\frac{1}{2}(32x) = 12(8)$

    (2) $(12 \times 2) + (8 \times 2) = 3(32) + x$

    (3) $\frac{1}{2}(32x) = 8x(24)$

    (4) $16x^2 = 96$

    (5) $\frac{1}{2}(32) = \frac{20}{2}$

GO ON TO THE NEXT PAGE

TEST 5: MATHEMATICS, PART II

31. The weights of the 11 men on the Panthers football team are 201, 197, 193, 212, 205, 207, 195, 214, 198, 203, and 184 pounds. What is the median weight, in pounds, of a player on this team?

    (1) 199
    (2) 200
    (3) 201
    (4) 203
    (5) 205

Question 32 is based on the following graph.

Distribution of Expenses for Sales of
$240,000 Triad Technologies Group

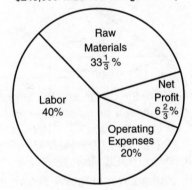

32. How many dollars were spent for labor?

    (1) $4,800
    (2) $9,600
    (3) $48,000
    (4) $96,000
    (5) $960,000

Question 33 is based on the following graph.

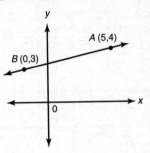

33. What is the slope of the line passing through points A (5,4) and B (0,3)?

    (1) $\dfrac{1}{10}$

    (2) $\dfrac{1}{5}$

    (3) $\dfrac{3}{5}$

    (4) $\dfrac{4}{5}$

    (5) 5

34. A relay team consists of three runners who each run a different distance around a 400-meter track. The first runner runs 4 laps around the track, the second runs 6 laps, and the third runs 2 laps. What is the total distance run by the relay team?

    1) 48,000 meters
    2) 4.8 kilometers
    3) 480 millimeters
    4) 9,600 meters
    5) 48 kilometers

GO ON TO THE NEXT PAGE

TEST 5: MATHEMATICS, PART II

<u>Question 35</u> is based on the following graph.

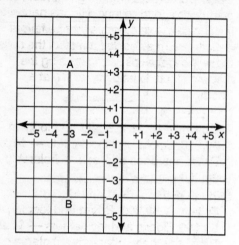

35. Line $\overline{AB}$ is the left side of a rectangle whose length is 7 units. If the rectangle's width is 6 units, at what point will the upper-right corner of the rectangle be located?

Mark your answer on the coordinate grid on your answer sheet.

36. If $3x - 1 = 11$, what is the value of $x^2 + x$?

   (1) 12
   (2) 15
   (3) 16
   (4) 18
   (5) 20

37. A bell rings every 2 hours, a second bell rings every 3 hours, and a third bell rings every 4 hours. If all 3 bells ring at 9:00 A.M., at what time will all 3 bells next ring?

   (1) noon
   (2) 6:00 P.M.
   (3) 9:00 P.M.
   (4) 10:00 P.M.
   (5) Not enough information is given.

38. A family spends 20% of its monthly income on food, 23% on rent, and 42% on other expenses and saves the balance. If the family saves $360 per month, what is its monthly income?

   (1) $2,000
   (2) $2,200
   (3) $2,400
   (4) $2,500
   (5) $28,800

<u>Question 39</u> is based on the following figure.

39. To measure the distance (DC) across a pond, a surveyor takes points A and B so that $\overleftrightarrow{AB}$ is parallel to $\overleftrightarrow{DC}$. If $AB = 60$ feet, $EB = 48$ feet, and $ED = 80$ feet, and $\triangle ABE$ is similar to $\triangle DEC$, find DC, in feet.

Mark your answer in the circles on the grid on the answer sheet.

GO ON TO THE NEXT PAGE

TEST 5: MATHEMATICS, PART II

40. A dozen eggs cost *x* cents. What is the cost, in cents, of 3 eggs at the same rate?

    (1) $\dfrac{x}{3}$

    (2) $\dfrac{x}{4}$

    (3) $\dfrac{3x}{4}$

    (4) $\dfrac{x}{12}$

    (5) $3x$

41. Each of the numbers below is a solution of the inequality $2x + 3 > 7$ EXCEPT

    (1) 10
    (2) 5
    (3) 4
    (4) 3
    (5) 0

Question 42 is based on the following figure.

42. What is the area, in square graph units, of the triangle?

    Mark your answer in the circles on the grid on the answer sheet.

43. David Gordon is a bright high school senior planning to go to college. He has narrowed his choice to two colleges that he favors equally. He has decided to select the college that will be less costly and is using the following facts to help him arrive at a decision.

    COLLEGE *A*
     Tuition — $9,480, Board and lodging — $6,320. Books and incidentals — $1,200. David has been offered a scholarship of $4,200 per year.

    COLLEGE *B*
     Tuition — $9,200, Board and lodging — $6,150. Books and incidentals — $1,200. David has been offered a scholarship of $3,200 per year.
     David has also been offered a part-time job working in the college library.

    What additional information does David need in order to make a choice?

    (1) how many miles he lives from each college

    (2) which college has the better reputation

    (3) how many scholarships each college grants

    (4) how much he can earn by working in the library at College *B*

    (5) which college has better athletic facilities

GO ON TO THE NEXT PAGE

TEST 5: MATHEMATICS, PART II

44. A room is 24 ft. long, 18 ft. wide, and 9 ft. high. Which of the following expressions represents the number of square yards of wallpaper needed to paper the four walls of the room?

(1) $\dfrac{(lwh)}{9}$

(2) $\dfrac{(lw) + (hw)}{3}$

(3) $\dfrac{8(lw) + 4h}{3}$

(4) $\dfrac{4(lw) + 4h}{3}$

(5) $\dfrac{2(lh) + 2(wh)}{9}$

45. A man drives x miles the first day, y miles the second day, and z miles the third day. The average mileage covered per day is

(1) $\dfrac{xyz}{3}$

(2) $\dfrac{xy + z}{3}$

(3) $x + y + z$

(4) $\dfrac{x + y + z}{3}$

(5) $3xyz$

46. A plumber must cut a pipe 64 inches long into two parts so that one part is 8 inches longer than the other part. Find the length, in inches, of the larger part.

(1) 28
(2) 30
(3) 36
(4) 40
(5) Not enough information is given.

47. After working 4 hours, Frank has made 21 machine parts. Which expression represents the number of parts he can make in 7 hours?

(1) $\dfrac{7(21)}{4}$

(2) $\dfrac{7(4)}{21}$

(3) $7(21)$

(4) $\dfrac{4(21)}{7}$

(5) $7(4)(21)$

48. A storage box in a form of a rectangular solid has a square base. If V represents the volume of the box, x represents the length of a side of the base, and y represents the height of the box, which of the following equations expresses the relationship among V, x, and y?

(1) $V = 2xy$
(2) $V = xy^2$
(3) $V = 2xy^2$
(4) $V = x^2y$
(5) $V = x + xy$

49. In his will, Mr. Adams left $\dfrac{1}{4}$ of his estate to his wife and divided the balance between his son and his daughter. If the son received $36,000 as his share, what was the total value of the estate?

(1) $45,000
(2) $72,000
(3) $80,000
(4) $90,000
(5) Not enough information is given.

GO ON TO THE NEXT PAGE

TEST 5: MATHEMATICS, PART II

Question 50 is based on the following information.

A 3-foot-wide walkway is built around a swimming pool that is 20 feet by 30 feet, as shown in the figure below.

50. In order to determine how much flagstone to buy, the homeowner needs to know the total area, in square feet, of the walkway.

    Which of the following expressions represents this area?

    (1) (23)(33)
    (2) (26)(36)
    (3) (23)(33) − (20)(30)
    (4) (26)(36) − (20)(30)
    (5) (26)(36) − (23)(33)

END OF EXAMINATION

Answer Keys, Summaries of Results, and Self-Appraisal Charts

TEST 1: LANGUAGE ARTS, WRITING, PART I/PAGE 677

I. CHECK YOUR ANSWERS, using the following answer key:

1. **2**	12. **5**	23. **5**	34. **4**	45. **4**
2. **3**	13. **3**	24. **1**	35. **4**	46. **4**
3. **4**	14. **4**	25. **4**	36. **4**	47. **5**
4. **2**	15. **1**	26. **4**	37. **4**	48. **1**
5. **1**	16. **4**	27. **4**	38. **1**	49. **3**
6. **4**	17. **4**	28. **5**	39. **2**	50. **2**
7. **4**	18. **4**	29. **1**	40. **3**	
8. **4**	19. **2**	30. **5**	41. **4**	
9. **1**	20. **1**	31. **3**	42. **3**	
10. **5**	21. **1**	32. **2**	43. **4**	
11. **4**	22. **5**	33. **5**	44. **5**	

II. SCORE YOURSELF:

Number correct:

Excellent	_____
	45–50
Good	_____
	40–44
Fair	_____
	35–39

III. EVALUATE YOUR SCORE: Did you get at least 35 correct answers? If not, you need more practice for the Language Arts, Writing, Part I test. In any event, you can improve your performance to Excellent or Good by analyzing your errors.

IV. ANALYZE YOUR ERRORS: To determine your areas of weakness, list the number of correct answers you had under each of the following categories (which correspond to the content areas of the Language Arts, Writing, Part I test), and compare your score with the average scores in the right-hand column. Review the answer analysis beginning on page 745 for each of the questions you got wrong, and give yourself more practice in your weak areas with the appropriate material in Unit II before attempting to take the actual GED Examination.

Content Areas	Items	Your Score	Average Score
Sentence Structure	13, 15, 17–19, 25, 27–28, 34–36, 43–44		8
Usage	1, 3, 5, 7, 8, 14, 21, 24 31–32, 39, 49–50		8
Mechanics			
Spelling (homonyms, (contractions, possessives)	6, 16, 29, 37		3
Punctuation	2, 20, 33, 46		3
Capitalization	4, 26, 45, 48		3
Organization	11, 22, 38, 40–42, 47		5
No correction	9–10, 12, 23, 30		3

Total _____

TEST 2: SOCIAL STUDIES/PAGE 690

I. CHECK YOUR ANSWERS, using the following answer key:

1. **4**	14. **1**	27. **2**	40. **2**
2. **5**	15. **4**	28. **4**	41. **3**
3. **1**	16. **5**	29. **1**	42. **3**
4. **5**	17. **3**	30. **2**	43. **5**
5. **4**	18. **3**	31. **4**	44. **4**
6. **2**	19. **5**	32. **2**	45. **2**
7. **4**	20. **1**	33. **3**	46. **3**
8. **1**	21. **2**	34. **1**	47. **1**
9. **2**	22. **4**	35. **5**	48. **1**
10. **1**	23. **5**	36. **3**	49. **4**
11. **1**	24. **3**	37. **5**	50. **1**
12. **2**	25. **3**	38. **2**	
13. **2**	26. **5**	39. **2**	

II. SCORE YOURSELF:

Number correct:

Excellent _____
　　　　　　　45–50

Good _____
　　　　　40–44

Fair _____
　　　　35–39

III. EVALUATE YOUR SCORE: Did you get at least 35 correct answers? If not, you need more practice for the Social Studies test. In any event, you can improve your performance to Excellent or Good by analyzing your errors.

IV. ANALYZE YOUR ERRORS: To determine your specific weaknesses, list the number of correct answers you had under each of the following categories (which correspond to the content areas of the Social Studies test), and compare your score with the average scores specified in the right-hand column. Review the answer analysis section beginning on page 746 for each of the questions you got wrong, and give yourself more practice in your weak areas with the appropriate material in Unit IV (including the "Glossary of Social Studies Terms"), before taking the actual GED Examination.

Content Areas	Items	Your Score	Average Score
Civics and Government	1–6, 9, 24–26, 29–30, 40		9
Economics	10–12, 14–16, 31, 33–34, 43, 47		8
History	7–8, 13, 17–19, 39, 41–42, 44–46, 48–50		11
Geography	20–23, 27–28, 32, 35–38		8

Total _____

TEST 3: SCIENCE/PAGE 703

I. CHECK YOUR ANSWERS, using the following answer key:

1. **1**	15. **4**	29. **4**	43. **1**
2. **4**	16. **2**	30. **1**	44. **5**
3. **5**	17. **2**	31. **3**	45. **2**
4. **5**	18. **2**	32. **2**	46. **3**
5. **4**	19. **5**	33. **3**	47. **3**
6. **5**	20. **1**	34. **3**	48. **4**
7. **4**	21. **4**	35. **3**	49. **5**
8. **4**	22. **5**	36. **3**	50. **3**
9. **4**	23. **2**	37. **5**	
10. **3**	24. **2**	38. **2**	
11. **4**	25. **3**	39. **2**	
12. **1**	26. **5**	40. **4**	
13. **3**	27. **1**	41. **4**	
14. **3**	28. **3**	42. **1**	

II. SCORE YOURSELF:

Number correct:

Excellent	_____ 44–50
Good	_____ 38–43
Fair	_____ 32–37

III. EVALUATE YOUR SCORE: Did you get at least 32 correct answers? If not, you need more practice for the Science test. In any event, you can improve your performance to Excellent or Good by analyzing your errors.

IV. ANALYZE YOUR ERRORS: To determine your specific weaknesses, encircle the number of each question you got wrong. This will reveal the specific science area that needs emphasis in planning your study program. After studying the Answer Analysis section beginning on page 749 for each of the questions you got wrong, list the terms that you feel need further explanation and study them in the "Glossary of Scientific Terms" beginning on page 360. Then give yourself more practice in your weak areas with the appropriate material in Unit V before taking the actual GED Examination.

Content Areas	Items	Your Score	Average Score
Biology	1–11, 27–29, 33, 34, 40–50		19
Earth Science	12–17, 30–32		8
Chemistry	18–20, 35		2
Physics	21–26, 36–39		8

Total _____

TEST 4: LANGUAGE ARTS, READING/PAGE 715

I. CHECK YOUR ANSWERS, using the following answer key:

1. 1	10. 2	19. 5	28. 4	37. 5
2. 4	11. 2	20. 5	29. 4	38. 4
3. 5	12. 5	21. 4	30. 5	39. 5
4. 4	13. 1	22. 1	31. 1	40. 4
5. 3	14. 4	23. 3	32. 3	
6. 5	15. 4	24. 4	33. 1	
7. 1	16. 3	25. 1	34. 4	
8. 5	17. 4	26. 5	35. 5	
9. 2	18. 1	27. 5	36. 1	

II. SCORE YOURSELF:

Number correct:

Excellent _____
 36–40

Good _____
 32–35

Fair _____
 28–31

III. EVALUATE YOUR SCORE: Did you get at least 28 correct answers? If not, you need more practice for the Language Arts, Reading test. You can improve your performance to Excellent or Good by analyzing your errors.

IV. ANALYZE YOUR ERRORS: To determine your specific weaknesses, first list the number of correct answers you had under each of the following categories and compare your score with the average scores in the right-hand column. After studying the answer analysis section beginning on page 751 for each of the questions you answered incorrectly, study the material in the section "Basic Reading Skills" and "Reading Prose, Poetry, and Drama" in Unit VI as well as the "Glossary of Literary Terms" (page 433) to strengthen your weak areas before taking the actual GED Examination.

Reading Skills	Items	Your Score	Average Score
Locating the Main Idea	6, 12, 15, 21, 25, 30		4
Finding Details	1–2, 5, 8–9, 13, 20, 22–24, 28, 32–33, 35, 37–39		11
Inferring Meaning	3, 7, 14, 19, 27–29		4
Making Inferences	4, 8–10, 13, 17–18, 26, 29–30, 34, 36, 40		9
Determining Tone and Mood	31		1
Inferring Character	16		1
Inferring Setting	11		1

Total _____

Now to see how your scores in the content areas of Language Arts, Reading test compare with the average scores in the right-hand column, list your score for each of the following:

Literary Forms	Items	Your Score	Average Score
Prose Fiction	11–20, 26–30		11
Prose Nonfiction	1–10, 31–40		13
Poetry	16–25		7
Drama	6–10		3

Total _____

Note: While Commentary on the Arts is a content area in itself, the commentary, as written, is in the form of prose nonfiction.

TEST 5: MATHEMATICS/PAGE 725

I. CHECK YOUR ANSWERS, using the following answer key:

Part I

1. **4**
2. **1**
3. **2**
4. **9**
5. **290**
6. **3**
7. **340**
8. **4**
9. **4**
10. **3**
11. **2**
12. **4**
13. **165**
14. **2**
15. **2**
16. **7/11 or .64**
17. **1**
18. **3**
19. **4**
20. **4**

21. **3**
22. **2**
23. **4**
24. **7.5**
25. **$1,000**

Part II

26. **1**
27. **3**
28. **5**
29. **3**
30. **1**
31. **3**
32. **4**
33. **2**
34. **2**
35.

36. **5**
37. **3**
38. **3**
39. **100**
40. **2**
41. **5**
42. **16**
43. **4**
44. **5**
45. **4**
46. **3**
47. **1**
48. **4**
49. **5**
50. **4**

II. SCORE YOURSELF:

Number correct:

Excellent _____
40–50

Good _____
32–39

Fair _____
28–31

III. EVALUATE YOUR SCORE:
Did you get at least 38 correct answers? If not, you need more practice for the Mathematics test. In any event, you can improve your performance to Excellent or Good by analyzing your errors.

IV. ANALYZE YOUR ERRORS:
To determine your specific weaknesses, list the number of correct answers you had under each of the following categories and compare your score with the average scores specified in the right-hand column. After studying the answer analysis section beginning on page 753 for each of the questions you got wrong, give yourself more practice in your weak areas with the appropriate material in Unit VII before attempting Practice Examination Two.

Content Areas	Items	Your Score	Average Score
Numbers and Basic Operations	3, 5, 9, 15, 21–24, 28 31, 37, 47		7
Fractions and Measurements	2, 16, 17, 27, 34, 49		3
Decimals and Percents	1, 7, 19, 20, 29, 38		3
Data Analysis	13, 25, 32, 39, 43, 44, 50		4
Algebra	4, 6, 10, 12, 14, 26, 36, 40, 41, 45, 46		6
Geometry	8, 11, 18, 30, 33, 35, 42 48		5

Total _____

YOUR TOTAL GED SCORE

The Language Arts, Writing Test _____

The Social Studies Test _____

The Science Test _____

The Language Arts, Reading Test _____

The Mathematics Test _____

Total _____

Answer Analysis

TEST 1: LANGUAGE ARTS, WRITING, PART I/PAGE 677

1. **2** *Are enrolling* is necessary to parallel *are recognizing*.
2. **3** A comma is used after an introductory clause.
3. **4** The plural verb *call* must be used to agree with the plural subject *techniques*.
4. **2** The name of a specific place such as Crimea is capitalized.
5. **1** You cannot shift pronouns that refer to the same person in the same sentence. Use either *you* or *one* throughout the sentence.
6. **4** The correct spelling is *government's*.
7. **4** The pronoun that agrees with the noun *nurses* is *their*.
8. **4** The subject *practice* agrees with the verb *brings*.
9. **1** The original is the best way.
10. **5** No correction is necessary.
11. **4** Sentence 2 states the *four basic elements*. All of the other sentences elaborate on that one idea.
12. **5** No correction is necessary.
13. **3** *Because* is correct since the second sentence states the reason for the first.
14. **4** *Has* must be inserted for parallel structure with *is six inches high, is made of leather*.
15. **1** The original is the best way.
16. **4** The correct spelling is *materials*.
17. **4** The comma is necessary to avoid the sentence fragment beginning with the *waist strap*.
18. **4** A plural verb is needed since the new subject, *the sleeping bag and its two accessories*, is plural.
19. **2** The second sentence names an example of the *tent* mentioned in the first sentence, so *such as* is used.
20. **1** Commas are used to separate items in a series.
21. **1** The plural subject *Crafts* agrees with the verb *are*.
22. **5** Sentence 3 follows a logical order within the passage.
23. **5** No correction is necessary.
24. **1** The correlatives *not only* and *but also* must be followed by parallel elements.
25. **4** The period is necessary to prevent a run-on sentence.

26. **4** Holidays, such as Christmas, are capitalized.
27. **4** The second sentence becomes an adjective clause modifying *feathers*.
28. **5** The period and capital are necessary to avoid a run-on sentence.
29. **1** The correct spelling in this sentence is *affects*.
30. **5** No correction is necessary.
31. **3** The plural verb *are* is needed to agree in number with *dwellings*, the antecedent of *that*.
32. **2** *In finding* is necessary for parallel structure with *in securing*.
33. **5** No correction is necessary.
34. **4** *Concerns* must follow since the new subject, *housing*, requires a verb.
35. **4** A participial phrase is used to describe *are upgrading*.
36. **4** The sense of the sentence requires the verb *will have* after the new subject, *nation*.
37. **4** The correct spelling is *separately*.
38. **1** The only transition word(s) that would fit with this sentence are *First of all* because that sentence is the first point in the passage.
39. **2** The singular subject *coverage* requires the verb *pays*.
40. **3** Sentence 4 should be left as it is, since it follows a logical order of organization.
41. **4** The main idea of this passage is that *liability pays for injury and property damage*. All of the other sentences are details supporting that thesis.
42. **3** A new paragraph can be started after sentence 4 because a new topic is introduced: *uninsured motorist coverage*.
43. **4** The semicolon is needed to prevent a sentence fragment starting with *The larger*.
44. **5** The new subject *feature* requires the verb *covers*.
45. **4** *Accidental death and dismemberment* is not a proper noun and should not be capitalized.
46. **4** A question mark is used after a sentence that asks a question.

47. **5** Sentence 5 should be left as it is because it follows a logical order in the passage.
48. **1** Only the names of specific countries are capitalized; *nation* is a common noun.
49. **3** The subject *organizations* agrees with the verb *range*.
50. **2** The pronoun *you* matches the first pronoun, *your*.

TEST 1: LANGUAGE ARTS, WRITING, PART II/PAGE 689

SAMPLE ESSAY

> *I feel very strongly that immigrants have a right to become citizens of the United States. There are several reasons why I believe this, but three of the reasons are: the United States is known as a culturally diverse society, we are in a sense all immigrants, and everyone should have the right to make choices.*
>
> *The United States is known as a culturally diverse society. The reason for this is because of the great diversity of people that have entered into the United States through the immigration process. People have been coming into the United States in waves for centuries.*
>
> *When we check our own ancestors we find that each of us has forefathers from other countries. Unless a person is one hundred percent native American, then somewhere through time an ancestor has come from another country to the United States.*
>
> *Everyone in the world should have a right to make choices. Some countries don't allow their citizens to make their own choices, which in turn creates a stalemate in society. People need to be allowed to follow their dreams.*
>
> *I'm glad no one told my ancestors they weren't allowed to come into the United States to become citizens. If they had, I might not be part of a culturally diverse society or be able to make my own choices.*

TEST 2: SOCIAL STUDIES/PAGE 690

1. **4** Hamilton believed in unrestricted suffrage, that is, right of voting, on the part of the people, as stated in his opening sentence.
2. **5** Rather than sovereignty of governments, Hamilton emphasized "balance between the national and state governments."
3. **1** Hamilton mentioned popular election as "this great source of free government" to be kept "perfectly pure."
4. **5** Women are permitted to serve. In fact, as stated in the middle of the second paragraph, the county committee may require equal representation of the sexes in each district.
5. **4** The end of the second paragraph contains the statement giving the purpose of the primary.
6. **2** If about 700 citizens cast their ballots in a voting district for two committee-persons, the inference can be drawn that each committeeperson represents half of the voters, or about 350.
7. **4** Of the choices given, the United States has direct involvement with Europe only in NATO, a military alliance created in 1949 as a shield against further Communist expansion or aggression. Under the North Atlantic Pact, a mutual defense agreement, an attack on any NATO member is considered an attack on all.

8. **1** The exaggerated, uncomfortable, and desperate position of Uncle Sam is meant to be critical. Note the arms stretched to reach Southeast Asia and South America, the left leg raised to touch Europe, and the outer lines beyond the globe and human figure, showing both to be unstable. The implication is that the United States cannot continue in this position.

9. **2** Typically, at border crossings, guards in uniform had travelers place their purchases in wooden bins to be searched.

10. **1** Social Security accounts for 21%, 3% more than defense, which is the second largest program.

11. **1** Of the means-tested programs, the largest is Medicaid, three times more in percentage than either food stamps or Supplemental Security Income.

12. **2** The total of entitlement spending, both means-tested and non-means tested, is 54%, slightly more than the interest on the national debt and discretionary spending combined.

13. **2** The quotation is a perversion of the original poem, which reads "Give me your tired, your poor, your huddled masses," that is inscribed on the Statue of Liberty. By changing it to welcome only the educated, the cartoonist is criticizing the United States for not accepting poor immigrants.

14. **1** The second paragraph points out that corporate diversification (by merger) will continue to be necessary to meet new competitors.

15. **4** The third sentence mentions that a company can sometimes get qualified technical manpower only by acquiring another company.

16. **5** The passage emphasizes future, rather than established, competitors as creating a motivation to merge.

17. **3** The author uses such terms as *finest* to describe the American population.

18. **3** He predicts that Americans will become "distinct" because of the "different climates" they inhabit.

19. **5** In America, the rewards of work are readily available.

20. **1** The world is becoming a "global village" according to Marshall McLuhan, as a result of this aspect of the Industrial Revolution.

21. **2** The cartoon indicates that candidates for office can afford only 30 seconds on TV because of the cost to propose simple solutions to very complicated problems. That is hardly enough.

22. **4** The graphs project that, by 2025, Africa's percentage of the world's population will increase by 7%, from 12% in 1990 to 19% in 2025 which is more than any other region's percentage.

23. **5** North America, the former Soviet Union, and Asia will each decrease by 1%; Latin America will increase 1%; Europe will have the largest decrease—3%.

24. **3** All of the others are mentioned in the Bill of Rights: freedom of religion—Amendment 1; freedom of the press—Amendment 1; a well-disciplined militia—Amendment 2; trial by jury—Amendment 7.

25. **3** "The President shall be Commander-in-Chief of the Army and Navy . . . and of the Militia" according to the United States Constitution.

26. **5** Elections by the people correct abuses that otherwise would have to be "lopped by the sword of revolution."

27. **2** Scale is the ratio between distance as shown on a map and the actual distance on the earth.

28. **4** The passage states that a compass rose shows direction.

29. **1** Problems like those of inflation, recession, and shortages of fuel or fertilizer cannot possibly be handled by individual state governments.

30. **2** This is the famous "clear and present danger" doctrine stated by Justice Oliver Wendell Holmes in the case of *Schenck v. U.S.* (1919). When the right to free speech endangers the common good, the common good prevails and free speech must be limited.

31. **4** The balance of payments involves all the economic transactions that a nation and its people have with the rest of the world, including the trade and investments of businesses, the tourism of citizens, and the economic and military grants and loans of

government. A deficit in the balance of payments reflects a net cash flow out of a nation as a result of all the above exchanges. The quotation says that such a deficit might be minimized or reversed by increasing exports and decreasing imports.

32. **2** Those who favor development of new energy sources tend to give a low priority to the need to protect our environment and to conserve our natural resources.

33. **3** Model *B* shows an economy that could lead to depression if supply and demand were not brought into balance. A balance could result from a decrease in income tax rates, which would increase consumer demand.

34. **1** In 1929–1939, the great depression in the United States was characterized by huge supply and little demand because of high unemployment. This situation is depicted in model *A*.

35. **5** The Indian population was carried over from the time before Columbus discovered the Americas.

36. **3** The United States had no role in settling or colonizing Latin America.

37. **5** The national debt jumped $1.75 trillion between 1990 and 1995, the largest jump for any period on the graph.

38. **2** Entitlements, including Social Security, Medicaid, and Medicare received 50% of the budgeted money, half of the pie.

39. **2** The largest single part of federal spending is for Social Security, 22%.

40. **2** Lobbying is the use of politically experienced persons to influence lawmakers by providing financial support, testifying at hearings, supplying information, and drafting legislation on behalf of interested parties.

41. **3** The Monroe Doctrine, a statement that any attempt by European powers to intervene in the Western Hemisphere would be regarded as dangerous to the peace and safety of the United States, was applied by President Kennedy to Russia's attempt in 1962 to establish a missile base in Cuba.

42. **3** Sexism, the exploitation and domination of one sex by the other, more traditionally of women by men, has been countered by the Women's Liberation Movement and by legislation. Women, on the basis of preference and ability, now enter occupations, previously closed to them.

43. **5** Top-level management has 23% men and only 9% women.

44. **4** Investing in mass transit is mentioned as one of the ways to control sprawl.

45. **2** Sprawl is mentioned as the result of poorly planned development.

46. **3** The passage mentions both buying open spaces and saving green space.

47. **1** The tax is graduated because it divides the taxed population into income groups with increasing tax percentage rates by stages for groups with increasing incomes.

48. **1** Imperialism is the policy of acquiring colonies or of establishing political and economic control of foreign areas.

49. **4** The cooperation of nations to prevent any one country from becoming dominant is a definition of the term *balance of power*.

50. **1** In 1990, Asia has approximately 31/53 of the world's population. In 2000 (est.), it is projected to have 37/63. Both are over 50%.

TEST 3: SCIENCE/PAGE 703

1. **1** The entire cell cycle is 22 hours, and only 1 hour is for mitosis. 1/22 is just under 5%, so this must be the correct answer.

2. **4** The figure shows that mitosis is subdivided into more stages, whereas the other phases of the cell cycle are not.

3. **5** The cell cycle is 22 hours long, as it is shown in the figure: 1 hour is for mitosis, and the rest, 21 hours, is for interphase

4. **5** The first sentence indicates that sodium chloride assumes special significance in the regulation of water exchange in the organism.

5. **4** According to the passage, the largest mineral component of blood is sodium chloride (salt); the purpose of this salt is the regulation of water within the organism.

6. **5** The opening sentence of the passage states that sodium chloride is the largest constituent of the mineral matter of the blood.

7. **4** The digested food is dissolved in water and is absorbed through the intestinal wall.

8. **4** The graph shows that the number of metric tons of fish from the Indian Ocean has not changed much over the time period shown. The same can be said about the Atlantic Ocean. There has been a large increase in the fish taken from the Pacific Ocean.

9. **4** The total number of millions of metric tons in 1980 is between 30 and 40 million metric tons, making choice 4 the best choice.

10. **3** In 1980, the total amount of fish from all three oceans was about 35 million metric tons. The catch from the Pacific Ocean was about 12 million metric tons, and 12/35 is about 30%. Notice how even if you had estimated a bit differently, choice 3 would have still been the best choice.

11. **4** It is not until after 1985 (in this case 1986) that the Pacific Ocean became the largest source of fish.

12. **1** The graph clearly shows that vitamin D, folic acid, and iron are the three nutrients that have the greatest increase. Notice how these three really stand out on the graph. Most questions of the GED ask you find clear distinctions. You should not expect to make a distinction of a 1% difference on a graph such as this.

13. **3** Vitamin C needs to increase by about 20%. This means that if a non-pregnant woman needs 1,000 mg, the increase will be 20% of 1,000 mg, or 200 mg. The total need will be 1,200 mg.

14. **3** The graph shows that the increase in calcium needs is 50%, making choice 3 the best choice.

15. **4** The temperature of the air is indicated on the thermometer marked *B*. The scale is marked in units of 10°, and the mercury has risen to the fourth subdivision between 20° and 30°. Therefore the reading is 28°.

16. **2** The temperature of the ice-water mixture (23°) is lower than the temperature of the air in the box (28°). Therefore, the air near the glass cup will be cooled below the temperature of the surrounding air. At this lower temperature, the amount of moisture the air can hold decreases. The droplets of water represent the excess moisture that has condensed out of the air.

17. **2** The dew point temperature is the temperature at which the air becomes saturated (as shown by the water droplets). Since the temperature of the air near the cup is the same as that of the ice-water mixture, the reading of 23°C on thermometer *A* is the dew point temperature.

18. **2** A change from the gaseous phase to the liquid phase is called condensation. A change from the liquid phase to the gaseous phase is called evaporation. A change from the solid phase to the liquid phase is called melting or fusion.

19. **5** The passage says that naphthalane, for example, vaporizes easily because of weak intermolecular forces.

20. **1** The definition of sublimation is given in the closing sentence of the passage.

21. **4** The second line of the passage tells you that condensation produces droplets that are formed from water vapor. The change from a solid to a liquid is called melting, from a liquid to a solid is called freezing, and from a liquid to a gas is called evaporation.

22. **5** The last line of the passage tells you that sublimation, like other phase changes, is reversible. Since melting and condensing are phase changes like sublimation, they too must be reversible.

23. **2** When any solid substance sublimes it changes to the vapor (or gas) phase of that same substance. Solid iodine sublimes to iodine vapor. Liquid iodine would be formed if iodine melted.

24. **2** The reason sound detection works so well underwater is that sound travels well in water, since water conducts sound well. Some of the other choices are true statements, but they are not the reason submarines can detect underwater objects.

25. **3** If it took six seconds for the sound wave to travel to the ocean floor and reflect back, then it must have taken half that time, or three seconds for the sound wave to travel in one direction. Multiply 1,500 meters per second times 3 seconds to get 4,500 meters. A very similar example is provided within the passage. Very often you will find worked-out sample problems for any calculations you need to do.

26. **5** Sound travels best in denser materials. Of the materials listed, steel is by far the densest and is the one in which sound would travel best.

27. **1** The largest fish on the chart swim faster than the smaller fish. In fact, the slowest fish, the lemon sole, is also the smallest. While size and speed may not actually be connected in this way, from the figures on the chart one may hypothesize that they are.

28. **3** The scientific names of the flounder and the lemon sole indicate that they belong to the same genus, *Pleuronectes*, and therefore are probably related.

29. **4** Being careful that enough breeders survive to replace the fish taken is a logical solution to the problem of declining populations. The other answer choices are opinions.

30. **1** Observe that there is almost no change in temperature between the months of January and February. The temperature in January is –5°C, and in February it is just above –5°C.

31. **3** In September the average temperature was just above 15°C and can be estimated to be 16°C. The precipitation for September was between 60 mm and 80 mm and can be estimated to be 68 mm.

32. **2** The graph for temperature shows a pronounced rise in the summer months, while the bars for moisture are all about the same size.

33. **3** It is not until 9 minutes have passed that the ethylene glycol reaches 198°C, at which time it will start to boil.

34. **3** The boiling ethylene glycol stays at 198°C. The temperature of a billing liquid does not change. Thus boiling water will stay at 100°C while it is boiling.

35. **3** Since alkalis have a high pH, adding an alkali will raise the pH of the soil. Choices 2 and 5 add acid, thus lowering the pH. Pure water could raise the pH, but never higher than pH 7. The tap water has the same pH as the soil, so it would make no change at all.

36. **3** For a plane mirror, every point of the image is as far behind the mirror as the corresponding point of the object is in front. This is indicated in the following sketch. Note that Choice 3 closely points in the same direction as the image. In addition, the angle of the incoming ray equal that of the outgoing ray.

37. **5** To get the total from the three sources that qualify as fossil fuels, petroleum, natural gas, and coal must be added together, giving the total of 85% and making choice 5 the best answer.

38. **2** The pie chart clearly shows petroleum to be the largest energy source in 1998.

39. **2** All of the listed properties of light are true, but only one explains why the shadow conforms to the shape of the object. Light waves traveling in straight lines from the lamp to the wall are blocked by the object to form the shadow.

40. **4** After the calendar year has been written on various documents for 365 days, writing these dates becomes automatic, and so, without thinking, the error is made in the early days of the new year.

41. **4** Habit formation leads to efficiency. This explains why the names were written more neatly and in greater number with the hand normally used.

42. **1** The brain is not involved in reflex acts. A reflex is a simple, quick, automatic act that involves the neurons and the spinal cord.

43. **1** See explanation for question 42.

44. **5** Solving a crossword puzzle involves the higher senses of memory and reasoning.

45. **2** Nest building is a complex activity, involving finding materials and constructing the nest. Through instinct, the incubator robin does things right the first time, even though it has never seen a nest.

46. **3** On previous occasions when the baby cried, adult attention was forthcoming. The infant cried in response to pain, but for the older baby crying was conditioned behavior.

47. **3** All training of animals is the result of conditioning. The dolphin associates the reward (food) with the performance of the trick.

48. **4** Dotting *i*'s and crossing *t*'s has been learned by extensive practice, forming a habit that is hard to disobey.

49. **5** The higher senses are involved in the studying and remembering necessary for satisfactory GED scores.

50. **3** This is an important observation that led to further research.

TEST 4: LANGUAGE ARTS, READING/PAGE 715

1. **1** Ways to correct others' behavior without hurting their feelings is the main subject of the article.

2. **4** All are mentioned except inappropriate vocabulary. This is different from mispronouncing words, which is one of the behaviors mentioned in the passage.

3. **5** The article refers to people who love those they correct dearly and work to help them.

4. **4** If it is unacceptable to criticize things a person cannot correct as the passage states, then it is acceptable to criticize behavior the person can correct.

5. **3** The article mentions the feelings of both the person receiving the criticism and the person giving it.

6. **5** Mr. Webb indicates that Grover's Corners is a "very ordinary town."

7. **1** Mr. Webb paints a picture of a "better behaved" "duller" town that leaves people who can take care of themselves alone.

8. **5** The pleasures that are mentioned are the sunrise, the birds, the trees, the plants and the change of seasons, all part of nature.

9. **2** Mr. Webb says that 90% of the young people are high school graduates.

10. **2** The town lets the "lazy and quarrelsome sink to the bottom" and it takes care only of those "that can't help themselves."

11. **2** The setting of Oberfest at the foot of the snow-covered mountains is especially significant because of its contribution to the tragic ending.

12. **5** Nowhere is any theme (the essential subject) of the incident stated. The theme—that people, through actions based on rumor and fear, bring about their own destruction—is left to the reader to deduce from the evidence presented by the author.

13. **1** In addition to the meaning given in the "Glossary of Literary Terms" on page 434, irony also refers to a combination of circumstances that results in the opposite of what might be expected to happen. That is true of this selection; the alarm, which should summon help, brings the opposite—destruction.

14. **4** The word *cold* has two meanings in this context: a literal or denotative meaning of very chilly as applied to climate, and an extended or connotative meaning, lifeless.

15. **4** Oberfest was buried beneath the snow without a trace.

16. **3** "I" failed as a cornetist, a basketball player, and a football player.

17. **4** The title, a way of remembering E, G, B, D, F—the notes of the musical staff, describes the opposite of what happened to the poet.

18. **1** The reader is asked to consider the poem a failure, which it definitely is not.

19. **5** The poet compares his physical posture on stage to his "hand-tied necktie."

20. **5** The poet says to the reader, "Consider this poem a failure."

21. **4** Lines 2–6 and 8–12 list life's treasures, which the poet urges us to enjoy.

22. **1** Line 3 refers to "blue waves whitened on a cliff."

23. **3** In line 7, music is compared to a curve of gold. Since the word *like* is used, this comparison is a simile.

24. **4** The poet indicates that "holy thoughts" will delight the spirit.

25. **1** The poet urges the reader to "give all you have been or could be" for life's loveliness.

26. **5** The policy states that the *use of drugs for legitimate medical purposes* is acceptable.

27. **5** The purpose of the policy is simply to inform employees of the company policy on alcohol and other drugs.

28. **4** The company states that *all employees in Executive Branch agencies, including the Governor's Office, Office of the Lieutenant Governor, and the Office of the Attorney General* are subject to its policy.

29. **4** The policy states nothing about immediate release from the company.

30. **5** The policy states that an employee who refuses to sign the "certificate of receipt" will have his supervisor initial the form, indicating that a copy of the form has been given to the employee.

31. **1** The author's negative feelings are indicated by the use of such words as *beast* and *sadistic*, and *vindictive*.

32. **3** The action referred to is "the purely phony move of the boxer who extends his gloves to his rival" on the floor.

33. **1** The passage states that the mob "roots consistently for the smaller man" and "howls with glee at a good finisher making his kill."

34. **4** The author's opinion is evident in the use of such words as *beast, lurks,* and *gray thing*.

35. **5** The author describes the mob (audience) as "vindictive."

36. **1** The word *still* indicates the author is surprised that many do not know this major American writer.

37. **5** The author refers to Cather's "feeling for the earth."

38. **4** The excerpt refers to the town's "burning summers" and "blustery winters."

39. **5** Cather "had the power to elevate ordinary people and places."

40. **4** "Cather believed that America's promise would endure," states the passage.

TEST 5: MATHEMATICS/PAGE 725

1. **4** $15,000 – $8,000 = $7,000 sales over $8,000
0.05 × $7,000 = $350 commission
$300 + $350 = $650 total salary

2. **1** 12 oz. = $\frac{12}{16}$ lb. of applies = $\frac{3}{4}$ lb. = .75

   Cost of 1.75 lbs. of apples:1.75 ($1.29) = $2.26

3. **2** To obtain the average rate of speed, divide the total distance covered by the total driving time.
Total distance = 80 + 100 = 180 mi.
Total time = 2 + 3 = 5 hr.
180 ÷ 5 = 36 mph.

4. **9** Let x = width of enlarged picture.
Set up a proportion:
$$\frac{\text{length of picture}}{\text{width of picture}} : \frac{8}{6} = \frac{12}{x}$$
$8x = 6(12) = 72$
$x = 72 ÷ 8 = 9$ in.

5. **290** 23.25 – 19.625 (use your calculator!) = 3.625

   3.625 is profit for 1 share
   × 80
   ___
   $290

6. **3** $3x – 1 < 5$
$3x < 6$
$x < 2$
Of the choices given, the only choice less than 2 is 1.

7. **340** 850 × 0.60 = 510 seats in orchestra
850 – 510 = 340 seats not in orchestra

8. **4** Let $4x$ = measure of larger acute angle, and x = measure of smaller acute angle.
$4x + x = 90$
$5x = 90$
$x = 90 ÷ 5 = 18$
$4x = 4(18) = 72°$.

9. **4** 25 ft. 8 in. = 24 ft. + 12 in. + 8 in.
= 24 ft. 20 in.
  24 ft. 20 in.
– 18 ft. 10 in.
_____
   6 ft. 10 in.

10. **3** Bill earns m dollars per month.
Angelo earns n dollars per month.
Together Bill and Angelo earn ($m + n$) dollars per month.
In 1 year, Bill and Angelo earn $12(m + n)$ dollars.

11. **2** Use the Pythagorean theorem.
$x^2 = (15)^2 + (20)^2$
$= 225 + 400 = 625$
$x = \sqrt{625} = 25$ mi.

12. **4** Let x = Maria's earnings, and $2x$ = Joan's earnings.
$x + 2x = 42$
$3x = 42$
$x = 42 ÷ 3 = 14

13. **165** $5,800 – $4,500 = $1,300
Tax is $100 + 5% of $1,300 =
$100 + 0.05(1,300) = 100 + 65 = $165

14. **2** $x = 2a(b + 7)$
$= 2(3)(5 + 7)$
$= 2(3)(12)$
$= 72$

15. **2** The number of students in the school is 18 × 35 = 630. If there are to be 30 students in a class, the number of classes needed is 630 ÷ 30 = 21. Therefore, the number of new classes needed is 21 – 18 = 3.

16. **7/11 or .64** Since there are 7 women among the 11 committee members, the probability of choosing a woman is $\frac{7}{11}$.

17. **1** 12 oz. = $\frac{12}{16} = \frac{3}{4}$ lb.

   5 lb. 12 oz. = $5\frac{3}{4} = \frac{23}{4}$ lb.

   If $\frac{23}{4}$ lb. cost $2.07, then 1 lb.

   costs $2.07 ÷ $\frac{23}{4}$.

   $2.07 ÷ \frac{23}{4} = 2.07 × \frac{4}{23} = 0.36

18. **3** m∠CBD = 125°
m∠ABC = 180° − 125° = 55°
m∠A + m∠ABC = 90°
m∠A + 55° = 90°
m∠A = 90° − 55° = 35°

19. **4** 10% + 25% + 30% + 15% = 80%, so
80% passed, and 20% failed.
20% of 80 = 0.20(80) = 16
20. **4** $20,000 × 0.07 = $1,400
$12,000 × 0.075 = $900
$1,400 + $900 = $2,300
21. **3** Width of walk is 6 ft., or 6 × 12 = 72 in.
Width of each brick is 4 in. Number of
bricks that can be fitted along the width
is 72 ÷ 4 = 18.
Length of walk is 24 ft., or
24 × 12 = 288 in. Length of each brick
is 8 in. Number of bricks that can be
fitted along the length is 288 ÷ 8 = 36.
18 × 36 = 648
22. **2** Calculate the yearly income for each
choice.
A. $37,000
B. $870 × 52 (weeks in a year) =
$45,240
C. $3,250 × 12 = $39,000
D. $3,000 × 6 = $18,000 (first half-year)
+
$3,000 × 1.10 (raise) = 3,300 × 6 =
$19,800 (second half-year)
$18,000 + $19,800 = $37,800
B or 2 is correct.
23. **4** First, the dealer bought 2(12) or 24
jackets at $48 each. The following
month, she bought 15 jackets at $48.
In all, she bought (24 + 15) jackets at
$48, spending a total of 48(24 + 15)
dollars.
24. **1** 45 min. = $\frac{45}{60}$, or $\frac{3}{4}$ hr.
At 48 mph, the faster car covers $\frac{3}{4}$ ×
48, or 36 mi.
At 36 mph, the slower car covers $\frac{3}{4}$ ×
36, or 27 mi.
36 − 27 = 9 mi.

25. **$1,000** Meat department sales = $2,500
Dairy department sales = $1,500
Difference = $1,000
26. **1** Perimeter of figure is
x + 2y + 3x − y + 2x + 3y + 5x + y =
11x + 5y.
27. **3** $\frac{7}{8} - \frac{1}{4} = \frac{7}{8} - \frac{2}{8} = \frac{5}{8}$
$\frac{5}{8} × 280 = 175$ gal. used
28. **5** To express a number in scientific
notation, express it as the product of a
number between 1 and 10 and a power
of 10. In this case, the number
between 1 and 10 is 2.750389. In
going from 2.750389 to 2,750,389,
you move the decimal point 6 places
to the right. Each move represents a
multiplication by 10 and 6 moves
represents a multiplication by 10^6.
Thus, 2,750,389 = 2.750389 × 10^6.
29. **3** The team has played 75 games and
will play 45 more games.
75 + 45 = 120
60% of 120 = 0.6 × 120 = 72
The team must win 72 games, and it
has already won 50 games.
Therefore, the team must win
72 − 50 = 22 more games.
30. **1** Because the areas of both figures are
equal to each other, write an equation
for both areas using an "equals" sign.
$\frac{1}{2} (b × h) = lw$

Then fill in the dimensions given in the
diagram:
$\frac{1}{2} (32x) = 12(8)$

31. **3** To find the median weight, arrange the
weights in increasing order and identify
the middle weight. In order of increasing
size, the weights are as follows:
184, 193, 195, 197, 198, 201, 203, 205,
207, 212, 214 lb.
The median (sixth) weight is 201 lb.

32. **4** 40% of the total expenses of $240,000 went for labor.
0.40($240,000) = $96,000

33. **2** Slope = $\dfrac{y_1 - y_2}{x_1 - x_2}$
In this case $y_1 = 4$, $y_2 = 3$, $x_1 = 5$, and $x_2 = 0$.
Slope = $\dfrac{4 - 3}{5 - 0} = \dfrac{1}{5}$

34. **2** First, find the sum of all laps around the track:
4 + 6 + 2 = 12
12 × 400 meters (1 lap) = 4,800 meters
1000 meters = 1 kilometer
$\dfrac{4,800}{1,000}$ = 4.8 kilometers

35. **(3,3)** Starting from the upper-left corner (point A) of what would be a rectangle, count 6 units (boxes) to the right on the same x plane. You will arrive at point 3,3 on the coordinate grid, as the answer key indicates.

36. **5** $3x - 1 = 11$
$3x = 11 + 1 = 12$
$x = 12 \div 3 = 4$
$x^2 + x = (4)^2 + 4 = 16 + 4 = 20$

37. **3** The first bell rings at 9:00 A.M., 11:00 A.M., 1:00 P.M., 3:00 P.M., 5:00 P.M., 7:00 P.M., 9:00 P.M.
The second bell rings at 9:00 A.M., 12:00 noon, 3:00 P.M., 6:00 P.M., 9:00 P.M.
The third bell rings at 9:00 A.M., 1:00 P.M., 5:00 P.M., 9:00 P.M.
All 3 bells will ring again at 9:00 P.M.

38. **3** Expenditures: 20% + 23% + 42% = 85%
Savings: 100% − 85% = 15%
Let x = family's monthly income. Then
0.15x = $360, so x = $360 ÷ 0.15 = $2,400

39. **100** Let $x = DC$.
Since $\triangle ABE$ is similar to $\triangle CED$, the lengths of their corresponding sides are in proportion.
$\dfrac{x}{60} = \dfrac{80}{48}$
$48x = 80(60) = 4800$
$x = 4800 \div 48 = 100$ ft.

40. **2** Since 12 eggs cost x cents, 3 eggs cost $\dfrac{3}{12}$, or $\dfrac{1}{4}$, as much: $\dfrac{1}{4}x = \dfrac{x}{4}$.

41. **5** Since $2x + 3 > 7$, then $2x > 4$, and $x > 2$. Of the choices listed, only 0 is *not* greater than 2.

42. **16** Use the formula for the area of a triangle:
$A = \dfrac{1}{2} bh$.
In this case, $b = 4$ and $h = 8$.
Area = $\dfrac{1}{2}(4)(8) = 16$

43. **4** To make a sound financial decision, David must know how much he can earn by working in the College *B* library.

44. **5** It always helps to draw a diagram when none is provided in the question. There are two pairs of walls, and each pair has a different area to be calculated then added.
Pair 1 = 2(24 × 9) or 2(*lh*)
+
Pair 2 = 2(18 × 9) or 2(*wh*)
The sum of the pairs provides the total square *feet* of wallpaper needed, but it must then be divided by 9 to get total square *yards*.
9 sq. ft. = 1 sq. yd.

45. 4 To find the average, divide the total mileage by the total time.

Total distance = $x + y + z$

Total time = 3 days

Average = $\dfrac{x + y + z}{3}$

46. 3 Let x = length of shorter part, and $x + 8$ = length of longer part.

$$x + x + 8 = 64$$
$$2x + 8 = 64$$
$$2x = 64 - 8 = 56$$
$$x = 56 \div 2 = 28$$
$$x + 8 = 28 + 8 = 36$$

47. 1 Let x = number of machine parts Frank can make in 7 hr.

Set up a proportion:

$$\dfrac{4}{21} = \dfrac{7}{x}$$
$$4x = 7(21)$$
$$x = \dfrac{7(21)}{4}$$

48. 4 Use the formula $V = lwh$.

In this case, $l = x$, $w = x$, and $h = y$

$$V = x(x)y \quad V = x^2 y$$

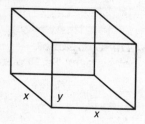

49. 5 To find the value of the estate, you need to know either the daughter's share or the fractional part of the estate received by the son. Neither item of information is given.

50. 4 As you can see from the figure below, to find the area of the white walkway, you need to subtract the area of the inner rectangle, (20)(30) sq. ft., from the area of the outer rectangle, (26)(36) sq. ft.:

(26)(36) – (20)(30) sq. ft.

ACKNOWLEDGMENTS

The authors gratefully acknowledge the kindness of all organizations concerned with the granting of permission to reprint passages, charts, graphs, and outlines. The test directions used in our diagnostic and practice examinations were adapted with permission from the "Official GED Practice Test" published by the GED Testing Service of the American Council on Education.

We are indebted to Scholastic Magazines, Inc. for their kind permission to reproduce passages from **Senior Scholastic** that formed the basis for original questions interpreting items to be analyzed in social studies. Sources and permissions for charts and graphs appear on the appropriate pages throughout the book courtesy of the following organizations: U.S. Department of Agriculture; U.S. Department of Health, Education, and Welfare—Office of Education; U.S. Bureau of the Budget; Social Security Administration; Census Bureau; and Bureau of Labor Statistics.

The copyright holders and publishers of quoted materials are listed below.

Page 73, Passage for Questions 11–15: Excerpt from **All God's Children Need Traveling Shoes,** by Maya Angelou. Copyright © 1975 by Maya Angelou. Reprinted by permission of Random House, Inc.

Page 75, Poem for Questions 21–25: from "Elegy for Jane," by Theodore Roethke. Copyright © 1950 by Theodore Roethke, in **Collected Poems of Theodore Roethke**. Reprinted by permission of Doubleday, a division of Random House, Inc.

Page 76, Passage for Questions 26–30: from **A Raisin in the Sun**, by Lorraine Hansberry. Copyright © 1958 by Robert Nemiroff, as an unpublished work. Copyright © 1959, 1966, 1984 by Robert Nemiroff. Reprinted by permission of Random House, Inc.

Page 77, Passage for Questions 31–35: from **Memoirs of Chief Red Fox**, by Chief Red Fox. Copyright © 1971. Reprinted by permission of The McGraw-Hill Companies.

Page 247, Passage from **Paths to the Present**, by Arthur M. Schlesinger, Sr. Reprinted by permission of Arthur Schlesinger, Jr.

Page 251, Passage from Arthur H. Doerr and J. L. Guernsey, **Principles of Geography—Physical and Cultural**, Second Edition Revised. Copyright © 1975 by Barron's Educational Series, Inc.

Page 270, Table for Questions 38–40: from **Let's Review Global Studies**, Second Edition. Copyright © 1994 by Barron's Educational Series, Inc.

Page 275, Cartoon for Question 3: from **The Atlanta Constitution**.

Page 275, Cartoon for Question 4: from **New York State June 1998 Global Studies Regents**.

Page 276, Cartoon for Question 5: from **USA Today**.

Page 276, Cartoon for Question 6: from **The Hartford Courant**.

Pages 280–282, Photographs for Questions 1–5: from Corbis-Bettmann Archive.

Page 323, Passage for Questions 13–15: from a speech by Jonathan Kozol, Boston College, May 1969.

Page 325, Passage for Questions 19–21: from **Women and the Work Force**, in **The Reader's Companion to American History**, edited by Eric Foner and John A. Garraty. Copyright © 1991 by Houghton Mifflin Company. All rights reserved.

Pages 325–326, Passage for Questions 22–25: from "What It Is Like to Be Underdeveloped," in **Global Studies, Vol. 1,** Second Edition. Copyright © 1993 by Barron's Educational Series, Inc.

Page 326–327, Passage for Questions 26–28: from "Apologies to the Iroquois," by Edmund Wilson. Copyright © 1992.

Page 328, Passage for Questions 35–37: from "Indians," in **The Reader's Companion to American History**, edited by Eric Foner and John A. Garraty. Copyright © 1991 by Houghton Mifflin Company. All rights reserved.

Page 331, Passage for Questions 44–46: from "Green Seal of Approval," by Michael Lipske, in *National Wildlife*, June–July 1994, pp. 22–23.

Page 332, Map and Passage for Questions 47–49: from Erwin Rosenfeld and Harriet Geller, *Afro-Asian Culture Studies*, Second Revised Edition. Copyright © 1976 by Barron's Educational Series, Inc.

Page 333, Passage for Questions 50–52: from "Conservation and Environmental Movements," in *The Reader's Companion to American History*, edited by Eric Foner and John A. Garraty. Copyright © 1991 by Houghton Mifflin Company. All rights reserved.

Pages 418–419, Passage from *Life With Father*, by Howard Lindsay, Russell Crouse, and Katherine B. Day.

Pages 429–430, Passage for Questions 1–6: from *Death of a Salesman*, by Arthur Miller. Copyright © 1949, 1977 by Arthur Miller. Used by permission of Viking Penguin, a division of Penguin Putnam, Inc.

Pages 431–432, Article for Questions 1–6: from *Investor's Business Daily*, December 1, 1997.

Page 437, Passage for Questions 6–10: from *The Joy Luck Club*, by Amy Tan. Copyright © by Penguin Putnam, Inc.

Pages 442–443, Passage for Questions 31–35: from *A Few Minutes with Andy Rooney*. Copyright © 1981 by Atheneum Publishers.

Page 443, Poem for Questions 36–40: from "Alone," by Maya Angelou, in *Oh Pray My Wings Are Gonna Fit Me Well*. Reprinted by permission of Random House, Inc.

Page 444, Passage for Questions 41–45: from *Star by Star*, by Naomi Long Madgett. Copyright © 1972 by Harlo Press.

Page 445, Passage for Questions 46–50: from *In Search of Mother's Garden*, by Alice Walker. Copyright © 1974 by Julian Bach Literary Agency, Inc.

Page 446, Passage for Questions 51–55: from *Platero and I*, by Juan Ramon Jimenez Moguer. Copyright © by Philip Duschenes.

Page 452, Passage for Questions 86–90: from "The Mother," in *Television Plays*, by Paddy Chayevsky. Copyright © 1955 by Simon and Schuster, Inc.

Page 453, Passage for Questions 91–95: from "Destruction Men," by Michael Goldstein, in *New York Magazine*, May 28, 1994, pp. 63–64.

Page 455, Passage for Questions 101–105: from *America as a Civilization*, by Max Lerner. Copyright © 1957, 1985 by Max Lerner. Reprinted by permission of Simon and Schuster, Inc.

Page 466, Passage for Questions 106–110: from "Hollywood's John Ford," by Charles Oliver, in *Investor's Business Daily*, April 21, 1994, pp. 1–2.

Page 608, Cartoon for Question 9: from *The Pittsburgh Post Gazette*, 1994.

Page 633, Passage for Questions 6–10: from "Literary Cavalcade," Lionel I. Castillo. Copyright © 1986 by Scholastic, Inc.

Pages 635–636, Poem for Questions 21–25: from "To a Photographer," by Berton Braley. Copyright © 1965 by Barton Braley.

Pages 636–637, Passage for Questions 26–30: from *State of the Union*, by Howard Lindsay and Russell Crouse. Copyright © 1946 by Random House, Inc.

Page 697, Passage for Questions 27–28: from *Principles of Geography—Physical and Cultural*, Second Revised Edition, by Arthur Doerr and J. L. Guernsey. Copyright © 1975 by Barron's Educational Series, Inc.

Page 717, Passage for Questions 6–10: from *Our Town*, by Thornton Wilder.

Page 724, Passage for Questions 36–40: from "Willa Cather: Voice of the Frontier," by William Howarth. Copyright © 1982 by National Geographic Society.

DOCUMENTATION

This book/disk package contains a CD-ROM. You should read the following documentation and instruction sections before you begin to use this CD-ROM.

System Requirements

This CD-ROM will run on either a PC or a Macintosh that is equipped with a CD-ROM drive.

Windows

A Pentium II processor or better is strongly recommended. Your PC must have either Windows 98, ME, NT4, 2000, or XP. It is suggested that you have at least 128 MB of installed RAM. Finally, your PC must have an 800 × 600 color display.

Macintosh

A Power Macintosh G3 processor or better is strongly recommended. Your Macintosh must have at least the Mac OS 8.6 operating system. It is suggested that you have at least 128 MB of installed RAM. Finally, your Macintosh must have an 800 × 600 color display.

Installation

Windows

Insert the CD-ROM into the CD-ROM drive. The CD-ROM should start up automatically. If it does not do so, double click on the My Computer icon on your desktop. Then, double click on the CD-ROM drive option, most commonly called the D:/ drive. Finally, double click on the GED.exe file from the CD-ROM.

Macintosh

Insert the CD-ROM into the CD-ROM drive. Then, double click on the GED CD-ROM icon on your desktop. Finally, double click on the GED file if you have OS X or GED_classic if you have OS 8.6 or better.

HOW TO USE THE PROGRAM

Examinations

This CD-ROM contains three full-length examinations: a diagnostic test and two practice tests, with all questions answered and explained. You can access all three exams from the Home Screen.

The diagnostic test should be taken before you work with the instructional material in the review section of this CD-ROM. Take one part of the exam and then review the answers and explanations in order to assess your strengths and weaknesses with regard to this part. Then, move on to the next part, repeating this process for all parts of the exam.

The practice tests should be taken after you have studied the instructional material in the review section. These tests may be taken in either "untimed" or "timed" mode. Untimed mode places no limit on the amount of time that you may spend working on a specific part of the test. Timed mode, on the other hand, limits the amount of time that you may spend on any part of the test to the amount of time you will have on that part of the actual GED exam. It is suggested that you take at least one full practice exam in timed mode in order to simulate actual test conditions. Also, make sure to consult the answers and explanations accompanying these practice tests, especially for questions that you did not get correct.

Instructional Material

This CD-ROM contains a complete review of each part of the GED exam. These reviews may be found by clicking on the review section of the Home Screen. As you work your way through these reviews, you should complete the interactive drills and exercises contained within them, consulting the answers and explanations, especially for questions that you did not get correct.

Screen Navigation

Use the buttons on the upper and lower panels to move back and forth among different screens and parts of the CD-ROM. The upper panel contains a convenient pull down menu that allows you to move anywhere in the CD-ROM by clicking on that location. The lower panel contains a "glossary" button that allows you to access a number of different lists of words or terms and their definitions. This panel also contains a "formulas" button on math screens that allows you to view important formulas. Use the up and down arrows on the right panel to view passages and illustrations that are too large to fit entirely on the screen. Some illustrations can be made larger by clicking directly on them. You can access answer explanations by clicking on the answer number on answer screens. Finally, buttons on the lower panel of the Home Screen allow you to access an overview of the GED exam as well as to quit the program entirely.

For Waldman

Great news!
MyEconLab **can help you improve your grades!**

With your purchase of a new copy of this textbook, you received a Student Access Kit for **MyEconLab** for Waldman. Your Student Access Kit looks like this:

DON'T THROW IT AWAY!

What is **MyEconLab** and how will it help you? **MyEconLab** is an extensive online learning environment with a variety of tools to help raise your test scores and increase your understanding of economics. **MyEconLab** includes the following resources:

- ■ *eText:* An online version of the textbook with narrated animations of key figures

- ■ *Interactive Quizzes:* With feedback and hotlinks to the *eText*

- ■ *MathXL for Economics:* A basic math-skills tutorial

- ■ *Research Navigator:* A one-stop resource for college research assignments

- ■ *eThemes of the Times:* Thematically related articles from the *New York Times* accompanied by critical-thinking questions

- ■ *Tutor Center:* Phone, fax, and email access to live tutors, five days per week

If you did not purchase a new textbook or cannot locate the Student Access Kit and would like to access the resources in **MyEconLab** for Waldman, you may purchase a subscription online with a major credit card at www.myeconlab.com/waldman.

To activate your prepaid subscription:

1. Locate the **MyEconLab** Student Access Kit that came bundled with your textbook.

2. Ask your instructor for your **MyEconLab** course ID.*

3. Go to www.myeconlab.com/waldman. Follow the instructions on the screen and use the access code in your **MyEconLab** Student Access Kit to register as a new user.

* If your instructor does not provide you with a Course ID, you can still access most of the online resources listed above. Go to www.myeconlab.com/waldman to register.

Microeconomics

The Addison-Wesley Series in Economics

Microeconomics

Don E. Waldman

Colgate University

PEARSON

Addison
Wesley

Boston San Francisco New York
London Toronto Sydney Tokyo Singapore Madrid
Mexico City Munich Paris Cape Town Hong Kong Montreal

To Lynn, Abigail, and Gregory

Editor-in-Chief: Denise Clinton
Acquisitions Editor: Adrienne D'Ambrosio
Development Editor: Jennifer Jefferson
Managing Editor: James Rigney
Design Manager: Regina Hagen Kolenda
Cover Design: Regina Hagen Kolenda
Interior Design: Leslie Haimes
Senior Production Supervisor: Katherine Watson
Executive Marketing Manager: Stephen Frail
Senior Media Producer: Melissa Honig
Digital Assets Manager: Jason Miranda
Supplement Production Coordinator: Diana Theriault
Senior Manufacturing Buyer: Hugh Crawford
Project Management and Composition: Argosy Publishing
Cover Image: Original painting "Paysage Sensation de Pasteque" by Giacomo Balla. ©2004 Swiss Institute, Rome, Italy / Peter Willi / Superstock.

Library of Congress Cataloging-in-Publication Data
Waldman, Don E.
Microeconomics / Don E. Waldman.
    p. cm.
  Various multi-media instructional aids, including web sites, are
    available to supplement the text.
  Includes index.
  ISBN 0-201-65877-1
  1. Microeconomics. I. Title.
HB172.W35   2003
338.5—dc22

                2003052391

ISBN: 0-201-65877-1

1 2 3 4 5 6 7 8 9 20—QWT—07 06 05 04 03

A woman walked into Mike's bagel bakery and asked, "How much are bagels?"
"$5.25 a dozen," came Mike's reply.
"That's awfully high," said the woman, "Sandler sells them for $4.25."
"So buy from Sandler."
"I can't; he's out of bagels," said the woman.
"Aha," said Mike. "When I'm out of bagels, I also sell them for $4.25."

Most prefaces to economics texts start out on a serious note and set that tone for the book. I started with a joke because there is a great deal of microeconomics in this joke. This might come as a surprise to some of you, but the joke itself plays off of an important element of microeconomics: supply and demand. At low prices, bagel bakeries will not be willing to sell bagels, but consumers will want to buy them. Furthermore, by introducing the book with a joke, I am signaling those who know little about this book, that it—unlike many others—attempts to be user-friendly, and perhaps even mildly entertaining. Signaling is used under circumstances where one individual has a great deal more information than another. In this case, I know the book, but you don't, so I am attempting to signal something important about the book. Signaling behavior is an important part of information theory, which is a relatively recent addition to courses on microeconomics. Like other recent additions to the field of microeconomics, signaling receives a good deal of attention in this text.

Why I Wrote this Book

Several years ago, I was talking with my colleagues about the problems we were all having teaching the required intermediate microeconomics course, which is a difficult course that requires a minimum grade of C in order to complete the economics major. One of my colleagues commented that he couldn't believe that no matter how many times he taught the course, the students made the same errors over and over again. I joked that it couldn't possibly be the quality of his teaching, so it must be the text. He responded, "The problem is that the text only presents the correct material; maybe we need a book that shows common errors that students make so they won't make them again. Yes, what the profession really needs is a book with all the incorrect material. Don, why don't you write one?" Intrigued by this idea, I began discussing possibilities with a publisher. Several discussions later with Addison-Wesley editors John Greenman and Denise Clinton, the basic outline of this book—including the use of common errors in each chapter—took shape.

No book's primary purpose could be to present a series of common errors, and in fact, this book was written for one purpose only: to help teach students microeconomic theory. I have incorporated all of the methods that worked best for me over the past 30 years. I have, for example, discovered that there is little room for shortcuts when teaching microeconomic theory, and therefore, this book uses many figures and equations to teach the major concepts. Unlike some other texts, if it requires two or three figures to adequately explain a topic, all the figures are presented. If one equation leads to an important result, all the steps along the way are presented carefully. I have worked hard to make the text an enjoyable read for both students and instructors, because as Leonardo da Vinci once stated, "Just as eating against one's will is injurious to health, so study without a liking for it spoils the memory, and it retains nothing." I think Leonardo had it right, and I hope that the large number of extended applications, many of which are relevant to students' lives, will keep the text flowing easily for readers.

Why This Text?

There are many microeconomics texts available, so why did I write this text, and what are the features that distinguish it from the other books on the market? Why will students learn better from this text than others? My basic principles for the book were to:

- Make it accessible by keeping the narrative flowing smoothly and the language structure informal.
- Make it relevant to students by using many current and historical real-world applications that students can readily relate to.
- Incorporate detailed Common Error boxes directly into the flow of the text to show the major pitfalls to avoid.
- Be rigorous without using calculus or other advanced mathematics (except in the footnotes and appendices), and use both algebra and geometry to explain basic theoretical principles, without skipping important steps in the mathematical analysis, even if it meant adding a few extra graphs and equations along the way.
- Give prominence to the most recent important additions to the field, such as game theory, decision-making under uncertainty, and information theory.
- Return to the core principles many times; for instance, the concept of economic efficiency is emphasized frequently from Chapter 1 onwards.
- Push the envelope of the analysis a bit; for example, by presenting some games in more detail than they are presented in other intermediate microeconomics texts.
- Supply lots of questions and problems at the end of each chapter.

Content Innovations

An Emphasis on the Modern Approach to Microeconomics: Game Theory, Uncertainty, and Information Theory. The field of microeconomics has expanded beyond the core requirements of teaching consumer theory, perfect competition, monopoly, and input markets. A modern year-long graduate course in microeconomics devotes one-third or more of the course material to decision-making under conditions of uncertainty, game theory, and information theory. Yet these topics have been relatively slow to make their way into the core of the undergraduate microeconomics course. This book allows—and indeed encourages—instructors to go beyond the core topics to explore uncertainty in Chapter 6, the basics of game theory in Chapter 13, and information theory in Chapter 20. While Chapter 13 provides an introduction to game theory that can be easily incorporated into most courses, Chapters 14 and 15 allow instructors to expand beyond the basics of game theory by presenting oligopoly models such as limit pricing and predatory pricing using elementary game theory. Furthermore, Chapter 20 presents the problems of asymmetric information mostly in a game-theoretic context, including the lemons model and principal-agent problems such as the separation of ownership and control in modern corporations and efficiency wage theory.

The Recurring Theme of Economic Efficiency. Students leaving a microeconomics course should understand the concept of economic efficiency and the many reasons why it is difficult to achieve. As a guiding principle, this book returns over and over again to the concept of Pareto efficiency, which is defined in Chapter 1. Furthermore, an entire chapter (Chapter 9) is devoted to the efficiency implications of the perfectly competitive model. While emphasizing modern topics, there is no skimping on the importance of learning the basics of microeconomic theory.

The Combining of the Theory of Production and Cost into One Chapter. Most instructors teach the theory of production and costs in a unified way in the classroom; that is, they emphasize the interrelationship between concepts such as diminishing marginal returns and the upward-sloping short-run marginal cost curve and between returns to scale and the economies and diseconomies of scale. Microeconomics texts, however, have consistently separated the topics into two chapters. The theoretical connection between the two is so close that they are combined in this chapter. Because it is often difficult to motivate students through this material, combining the topics into one chapter reinforces to students how intertwined these topics are.

Important Features

A Wealth of Applications. Microeconomics is laden with real-life applications that help students understand the technical analysis. In this text, there is an application in virtually every main heading, and if a main heading does not have an application, an extra application has been added in some other main heading in the chapter. Students will therefore come to expect that if a chapter is broken into five main sections, there will be at least five applications in the chapter. But those are not the only applications in the book. For each of the three major topics of consumer theory—perfect competition, monopoly, and oligopoly—there is an entire chapter devoted to extended applications. These applications go beyond the detail presented in the chapters' boxed applications and deal with some controversial social issues. For example, Chapter 5, "Using Consumer Theory," analyzes school voucher systems and the impacts of income tax cuts on work effort and savings; Chapter 10, "Using the Model of Perfect Competition," explores the impact of legalizing drugs and selling human organs; and Chapter 16, "Using the Models of Monopoly and Oligopoly," evaluates why trade policies aimed at protecting a domestic monopolist from foreign competition might end up hurting the monopolist, and why, for many years, the nation's leading universities conspired on the aid packages offered to accepted students. These extended application chapters give students vital insight into the important uses of microeconomics in evaluating public policies in a large variety of areas.

The Common Errors Features. This feature is unique to this book. Every chapter, except for the introductory Chapter 1, presents two Common Error boxes. These do not appear as icons in the margins warning students of potential problems, but as fully developed Common Error boxes that attempt to explain to students why it is reasonable to expect them to make these errors, and in the process, prevent them from making them. Incorrect graphs and incorrect algebra, juxtaposed with the correct material, aid students further. For example, students are shown that it is often incorrect to measure a competitive firm's profits graphically by using the minimum point on the average cost curve or to measure the elasticity of demand by the slope of a linear demand curve.

Table of Contents Flexibility

The text is primarily meant to be used in a one-semester undergraduate course on microeconomic theory by students who have already completed a course that includes introductory microeconomics. However, because of the wide variety of business applications, especially in Chapters 10–18, it can also serve as the basis of graduate business school microeconomics courses. Few instructors, if any, will cover the entire text in either a semester or quarter course. The book was written to have a great deal of flexibility, particularly with regard to applications, game theory, and information theory. The following outlines are meant only as suggestions; please note that the shaded boxes represent the applications-focused "Using" chapters, from which instructors will likely select their own favorites:

Chapter	Traditional Emphasis	Emphasis on Game and Theory	Emphasis on Specific Firm Behavior	Emphasis on Business	Emphasis on Public Policy
1. Introduction	•	•	•	•	•
2. Supply and Demand	•	•	•	•	•
3. Theory of Consumer Behavior	•	•	•	•	•
4. Further Topics in Consumer Theory	•	•	•		•
5. Using Consumer Theory	•	•			
6. Uncertainty	•	•	•	•	•
7. The Theory of Production and Costs	•	•	•	•	•
8. Perfectly Competitive Product Markets	•	•	•	•	•
9. The Invisible Hand at Work	•	•	•	•	•
10. Using the Model of Perfect Competition	•	•	•	•	•
11. Monopoly and Monopolistic Competition	•	•	•	•	•
12. Additional Monopoly Topics: Pricing Strategies and Public Policy			•	•	•
13. An Introduction to Game Theory	•	•	•	•	•
14. Oligopoly	•	•	•	•	
15. Strategic Behavior		•	•	•	•
16. Using the Models of Monopoly and Oligopoly	•	•	•	•	•
17. Factor Markets	•	•	•	•	•
18. Investment, Time, and Risk			•	•	
19. General Equilibrium and Efficiency	•	•	•		•
20. Asymmetric Information		•		•	
21. Externalities and Public Goods					•

Instructor and Student Supplementary Resources

INSTRUCTOR'S MANUAL

Written by David Huffman of Bridgewater College, this comprehensive manual integrates a broad array of tools for instructors. For each chapter of the main text, the manual provides chapter outlines, teaching tips, additional applications, answers to even-numbered end-of-chapter problems, and additional discussion questions and problems with answers. The Instructor's Manual is available on the password-protected portion of the *Microeconomics* Web site, as well as on an Instructor's Resource CD-ROM.

TEST BANK

Prepared by Della L. Sue of Marist College, the test bank provides instructors with approximately 100 additional questions for each chapter of the main text. Questions come in the form of multiple-choice, quantitative/graphing, and essay. Instructors can access the test bank on the *Microeconomics* Web site or through the Instructor's Resource CD-ROM.

STUDY GUIDE

Written by Mark Ashe of Westminster College, this supplement walks students through each chapter of the main text. Chapter outlines, summaries, lists of key terms, multiple-choice questions, quantitative/graphing problems, and essay questions give students the extra tools they need to succeed. The study guide is available on the student portion of the *Microeconomics* Web site.

POWERPOINT

Prepared by Vani Kotcherlakota of the University of Nebraska, Kearney, the Microsoft® PowerPoint presentation includes all figures and tables from the text, as well as complete chapter outlines. Outlines include learning objectives, key concepts, definitions, and equations for the main sections of each chapter. The PowerPoint presentation is available on the *Microeconomics* Web site and on the Instructor's Resource CD-ROM.

INSTRUCTOR'S RESOURCE DISK

Fully compatible with Windows and Macintosh operating systems, the CD-ROM provides access to the Instructor's Manual and PowerPoint presentation. It also includes the test bank, with easy-to-use testing software (Test-Gen EQ with QuizMaster-EQ for Windows and Macintosh) that allows instructors to view, edit, and add questions.

MYECONLAB

MyEconLab is an online, text-specific, customizable suite of tools that saves the instructor time and helps students come to class better prepared.

For students, *MyEconLab* offers the following features:

- The complete *Microeconomics* textbook online with Flash animated graphs so students can follow the shifts;
- Diagnostic quizzes with feedback and hotlinks to the online textbook page to which students should turn for review;
- Access to the Addison Wesley Economics Tutor Center, staffed by qualified, experienced college economics instructors; the Econ Tutor Center is open five days a week, seven hours a day, including evening and weekend hours, and tutors can be reached by phone, fax, e-mail, or White Board technology;
- Web links and suggested web resources;

- Internet Activities;
- Research Navigator, a research tool that helps students conduct research, and gives students access to a number of peer-reviewed journals, an archive of full-text articles from *The New York Times*, and a "Best of the Web" Link Library of peer-reviewed Web sites;
- *eThemes of the Times*, a set of articles from the *The New York Times*, accompanied by discussion questions, that are thematically related to the content of each chapter;
- *MathXL*, a self-paced tutorial to help students refresh their basic math and algebra skills.

For instructors, *MyEconLab* offers all the above as well as:

- Automatically graded homework capabilities;
- Communication tools such as e-mail, Chat, discussion boards and bulletin boards;
- Control over the content students see and when they see it;
- Online test generation software;
- An online gradebook.

THE ECON TUTOR CENTER EDITION

Staffed by qualified, experienced college economics instructors, the Econ Tutor Center is open five days a week, seven hours a day, including evening and weekend hours. Tutors can be reached by phone, fax, e-mail, or White Board technology. Students receive one-on-one tutoring on examples, related exercises, and problems. Your Addison-Wesley representative can help you make this service available to your students.

THE WALL STREET JOURNAL EDITION

Addison-Wesley is also pleased to provide your students with access to *The Wall Street Journal*, the most respected and trusted daily source for information on business and economics. For a small additional charge, Addison-Wesley offers your students a 10-week subscription to *The Wall Street Journal* and *WSJ.com*. Adopting professors will receive a complimentary one-year subscription to *The Wall Street Journal* as well as access to *WSJ.com*.

ECONOMIST.COM EDITION

Through an agreement between Addison-Wesley and *The Economist*, your students can receive a low-cost subscription to this premium Web site for 12 weeks, including the complete text of the current issue of *The Economist* and access to *The Economist*'s searchable archives. Other features include Web-only weekly articles, news feeds with current world and business news, and stock market and currency data. Professors who adopt this special edition will receive a complimentary one-year subscription to *http://economist.com*.

FINANCIAL TIMES EDITION

Featuring international news and analysis from FT journalists in more than 50 countries, *The Financial Times* edition will provide your students with a 15-week subscription to one of the world's leading business publications. Adopting professors will receive a complimentary one-year subscription to *The Financial Times* and access to *FT.com*.

Acknowledgments

Putting together a text such as this is an excellent economic example of specialization, and I have been aided by many excellent specialists. The project began with the encouragement of Denise Clinton, Editor-in-Chief at Addison-Wesley. As always, Denise provided exactly the right combination of good-humored positive reinforcement and constructive criticism to keep things moving forward. Sylvia Mallory, Director of Development, stepped in to deal admirably with the inevitable major crises that arose from time to time, serving the critical role of calming the nerves of an occasionally frazzled author. Rebecca Ferris, Senior Development Editor, did an outstanding job of coordinating all aspects of the project. Jennifer Jefferson, Assistant Development Editor, has been more efficient and good-natured in coordinating the project than I could have imagined possible. I suspect that Jenny knows the book as well as, if not better than, I do. Adrienne D'Ambrosio, Acquisitions Editor, joined the project with a sense of positive reinforcement and enthusiasm that was reinvigorating at just the right moment. Regina Kolenda, who served as the design supervisor, has put together a text that is not only easy to read and learn from, but extremely pleasing to the eye; not to mention creating a cover that was greeted with great enthusiasm by the entire Waldman household, an almost impossible task. I also wish to thank Joe Vetere, Senior Technical Art Specialist, for making the visual aspects of the text, especially the figures, tables, applications, and Common Errors, so easy to read and understand. Stephen Frail, Executive Marketing Manager, deserves great thanks for the innovative marketing effort put forward by Addison-Wesley. Without his efforts, far fewer people would have been introduced to the book. I also owe great thanks to Katherine Watson, Senior Production Supervisor; Michelle Neil, Executive Producer, Technology; Melissa Honig, Senior Media Producer; Jason Miranda, Digital Assets Manager; and Diana Theriault, Archive Specialist.

In addition to the people at Addison-Wesley, I wish to express my appreciation to Maxine Effenson Chuck of B. Czar Productions for her extensive editorial assistance; particularly her help in refining the informal writing style of the text. Edalin Michael of Argosy Publishing did an outstanding job of coordinating the final production stages of the text. The final fruit of her labor has been not only a more accurate text, but an aesthetically pleasing book as well.

Before thanking the many economists who have reviewed the manuscript and provided invaluable input, I want to mention several economists who have been particularly important. First, the basic outline for Chapters 1–4 and 6–9, as well as several of the applications and many of the questions in those chapters, owe a large debt to Geoffrey Jehle of Vassar College and Marc Lieberman of New York University. Elizabeth Jensen of Hamilton College provided important input and help in organizing and presenting the ideas in Chapters 12–15, which are partially derived from our industrial organization text. Rochelle Ruffer of Youngstown State University not only served as an excellent reviewer of the entire manuscript, but provided most of the end-of-chapter questions for Chapters 10–21. No matter how hard one tries, errors always remain in any manuscript, and surely some errors still remain in this one, however, many more errors would be there if it were not for the excellent efforts of Mark Ashe of Westminster College and Daniel Flores-Guri of Skidmore College, who carefully checked the final book for accuracy. In addition, Philip Heap of James Madison University and Caprice Knapp of the University of Florida checked the accuracy of the supplements written by Mark Ashe of Westminster College, David Huffman of Bridgewater College, and Della L. Sue of Marist College.

In addition, I want to the thank all of the other reviewers who read some or all of the manuscript and made helpful suggestions. Their important contributions have made the final manuscript better in hundreds of different ways, ranging from relatively minor stylistic changes to major content changes. Given the large number of reviewers, I was unable to incorporate every worthwhile suggestion, but all of the following reviewers made important contributions.

Ingela Alger, Boston College
Sam Allgood, University of Nebraska, Lincoln
Donna Anderson, University of Wisconsin, La Crosse
Lisa R. Anderson, College of William and Mary
Richard Anderson, Texas A&M University
Emrah Arbak, State University of New York, Albany
Mark Ashe, Westminster College
Djeto Assane, University of Nevada, Las Vegas
Tibor Besedes, Rutgers University
Michael Bognanno, Temple University
Donald Bumpass, Sam Houston State University
Bruce Caldwell, University of North Carolina, Greensboro
Leo Chan, University of Kansas
Joni Charles, Southwest Texas State University
Paul Comolli, University of Kansas
Steven Craig, University of Houston
Jerry Crawford, Arkansas State University
Ron Deiter, Iowa State University
Greg Delemeester, Marietta College
Daniel Flores-Guri, Skidmore College
Roger Frantz, San Diego State University
Mark Frascatore, Clarkson University
Abbas P. Grammy, California State University, Bakersfield
Ralph Gunderson, University of Wisconsin, Oshkosh
Simon Hakim, Temple University
Paul Hayashi, University of Texas, Arlington
Philip Heap, James Madison University
Erik C. Helm, University of Delaware
Paul Hettler, Duquesne University
Saul Hoffman, University of Delaware
Don Holley, Boise State University
Gary A. Hoover, University of Alabama, Tuscaloosa
David Huffman, Bridgewater College
Susumu Imai, Concordia University
Paul Jensen, Drexel University
Sumit Joshi, The George Washington University

Tim D. Kane, University of Texas, Tyler
Youn Kim, Western Kentucky University
Philip King, San Francisco State University
Vani V. Kotcherlakota, University of Nebraska, Kearney
Laura Marsiliani, University of Rochester
Jim McClure, Ball State University
Claudio Mezzetti, University of North Carolina, Chapel Hill
Hong Nguyen, University of Scranton
Kenneth Parzych, Eastern Connecticut State University
Genevieve Peters, University of California, San Diego
Robert Posatko, Shippensburg University
Daniel Primont, Southern Illinois University
Rati Ram, Illinois State University
Francesco Renna, University of Akron
Adam Rennhoff, University of Virginia
Michael Robinson, Mount Holyoke College
Jeffrey Rous, University of North Texas
Stephen Rubb, Bentley College
Rochelle Ruffer, Youngstown State University
Russell Sobel, West Virginia University
John Sondey, South Dakota State University
Dwight Steward, University of Texas, Austin
Gary Stone, Winthrop University
Leonie Stone, State University of New York, Geneseo
Della L. Sue, Marist College
Jane Sung, Truman State University
Valerie Suslow, University of Michigan
Janet Thomas, Bentley College
Theofanis Tsoulouhas, North Carolina State University
Stanton Ullerich, Buena Vista University
Adel Varghese, Saint Louis University
Eleanor von Ende, Texas Tech University
Mickey Wu, Coe College
Daching Yang, Ohio State University
Benjamin Yu, California State University, Northridge
Ernie Zampelli, The Catholic University of America

I also wish to thank my many students at Colgate University who were the guinea pigs for much of the early material in the book and also helped create some of the questions and applications. One outstanding student deserves particular thanks: Amanda Griffith, who spent a good deal of time and energy helping me draft questions for the first part of the book.

Finally, my greatest thanks go to my family: my wife, Lynn, and children, Abby and Greg. They had to put up with my occasionally short temper and sleep deprivation over many years as I worked through the manuscript. Without the three of them, none of the effort would be very meaningful. And as I promised my children, I also want to thank our cat Chloe and our late cat Rickie for just being there.

Brief Table of Contents

Table of Contents

Part 2 Consumer Behavior

10 Using the Model of Perfect Competition   259

Part 4 Imperfect Competition

√ 11 Monopoly and Monopolistic Competition   285

Chapter 1

Introduction

On September 11, 2001, the political, social, and economic worlds changed forever. As terrorists crashed planes into the World Trade Center, the Pentagon, and a field in Pennsylvania, these events created a human tragedy of almost unimaginable proportions, and set off a chain reaction of economic decisions throughout the world. We will never forget the great human cost of those awful events; sadly, the thousands of innocent lives lost that day can never be recovered. In addition to the heartrending loss of life, the terrorists' attacks caused thousands of households and business firms to reconsider their plans to buy and sell goods and services. Virtually every industry was affected. Companies had to decide whether to cut prices in anticipation of a decline in demand, whether to delay new advertising campaigns, and whether to make changes in their production lines; investors had to decide whether to buy or sell shares of stock in light of the terrorists' attacks.

Firms and individuals reacted immediately. Airline traffic plummeted, forcing most airlines to dramatically cut the number of daily flights. Because consumers stopped flying, they stopped traveling to distant vacation destinations such as Disney World and Las Vegas; therefore, hotel occupancy rates at such destinations also plummeted. Consumers also stopped taking cruises, in part because they refused to fly to the points of embarkation. As a result of this huge economic shock, investors sold shares in airline, hotel, and cruise line companies. For example, share values collapsed for American Airlines (AMR Corp), Hilton Hotels, and Princess Cruises. The day the stock market reopened, American Airlines and Hilton stock prices declined by more than 30 percent, and Princess Cruises stock declined by more than 45 percent.

Learning Objectives

After reading Chapter 1, you will have learned:

➤ To distinguish economics from other fields of study and to distinguish microeconomics from macroeconomics.

➤ To recognize the three fundamental problems of microeconomics: what, how, and for whom to produce goods and services.

➤ The alternative mechanisms for solving the problems of resource allocation.

➤ How economists build models by making assumptions about human behavior.

➤ The definition of a number of basic economic concepts, such as: an economic agent, a market, an equilibrium, and Pareto efficiency.

➤ What distinguishes positive economics from normative economics.

Featured Applications

➤ 1.1 Application The Opportunity Cost of Credit Card Debt

➤ 1.2 Application Economists as the Brunt of Jokes

➤ 1.3 Application Efficiency, Young Waldman, and Baseball Card Trading

Not all companies suffered from the events of September 11. In the month following September 11, 2001, the price of shares increased dramatically for Lockheed Martin, a major defense contractor; Armor Holdings, a supplier of security products and services such as bulletproof vests, tear gas and mace, and security services; and Blockbuster. Lockheed's shares rose in value by almost 30 percent, Blockbuster's by almost 50 percent, and Armor Holdings' a remarkable 75 percent. Furthermore, Thomas Nelson, Inc., a leading producer of Bibles and other religious books, saw its stock price rise by almost 30 percent. As a result of these changes in stock prices, many stockholders experienced significant changes in their wealth, and responded with new saving, investment, and spending plans.

All of these decisions made by individuals and firms as a result of the events of September 11 have something in common: they were *microeconomic* decisions. This book analyzes how such microeconomic decisions are made and what they mean to the economy. In particular, we will study how firms make decisions about output, prices, and employment; how households make decisions about working, spending, and saving; and the impact of these decisions on the overall functioning of the economy. We will also study government intervention in the marketplace, and learn to distinguish between government intervention that is likely to help or hurt our collective interests.

▼▼▼ 1.1 The Scope of Microeconomics

Few people other than economists have an accurate picture of what economics really is and what economists actually do. Tell someone you are studying economics, and more often than not they will ask you a question like, "So, what's going to happen in the stock market over the next few months?" or "Say, do you think you could help me with a little problem I've been having in my business?" Neither of these questions deals with the essence of economics. The question about the stock market deals with the field of *finance*, which is the specialized study of stock, bond, and commodity markets, and how one goes about making money in them. The question about a small firm relates to the subject area of *business*, which concerns specific actions firms can take to increase their profits. Economics is neither finance nor business, yet anyone hoping to master either of these fields had better understand quite a bit of economics. Moreover, the study of economics provides valuable insights into business and finance.

What Is Economics?

Economics begins with a huge problem: in any society, the combined desires of all individuals for food, clothing, computers, new cars, Broadway plays, and all other goods and services could not possibly be satisfied. We simply do not have the **resources**—the land, raw materials, labor, and machinery—to produce everything that everyone wants, and we must therefore make choices among competing desires. *Economics* is the study of these choices, where they originate, how they are made, and what they mean to our society as a whole.

Fundamentally, economics is the study of resource allocation under conditions of **scarcity**. In economics, *scarcity* refers to the common human condition under which the amount of a good or service available is insufficient to satisfy the desire for that good or service. Production requires resources, and resources are scarce. Therefore if we want to produce more of one thing, we must transfer resources away from the production of another thing. If we lived in the Garden of Eden, we would not be faced with making

resources

The land, labor, raw materials, and machinery used to produce goods and services.

scarcity

The fundamental economic problem that available resources are insufficient to satisfy human desires for goods and services.

choices under conditions of scarcity. But the Garden of Eden has long since disappeared, and all of us must decide how to spend our scarce resources, be they time or money, on an almost limitless number of possible choices. Do I study economics or biology tonight? Do I snack on pizza or chips tonight? Do I forget about studying tonight, and instead go to the movies? All of these decisions are economic decisions made under conditions of scarcity.

The field of economics is generally divided into two main branches. **Microeconomics** studies the behavior of individual decision-makers—households, business firms, and governments—and how they interact in *markets*. A **market** is the coming together of buyers and sellers with the actual or potential objective of exchanging goods or services. **Macroeconomics** studies the overall level of economic activity in a society, focusing on such topics as unemployment, inflation, and the rate of economic growth.

The distinction between microeconomics and macroeconomics can sometimes get confusing. After all, a macroeconomic event like a recession is a reflection of millions of collective individual decisions, such as firms deciding to decrease production, households deciding to decrease spending, banks deciding to decrease lending, and so on. For this reason, practitioners of either branch of economics must have a good grasp of the other.

Nevertheless, there are important differences between the two branches of economics concerning the types of questions asked and the methods used to answer these questions. Macroeconomists almost always focus on the broadest possible measures of economic activity, such as gross domestic product, unemployment rate, price level, and the general level of interest rates. Microeconomists, by contrast, like to break down the economy into smaller pieces—individual industries, individual firms, and even individual branches within a firm—and study how each of these pieces behaves and interacts with the other pieces.

For example, a macroeconomist studying economic growth might ask, "How do large budget deficits affect the overall level of investment spending in a nation, and how does investment spending, in turn, affect the growth rate of the gross domestic product?" A microeconomist studying growth, however, would ask, "How do individual business firms allocate scarce funds to research and development or the purchase of new machinery, and how do various government policies help or hinder growth within firms?" Both of these approaches are important for anyone wishing to understand and promote national economic growth, but the questions are notably different.

A Fundamental Microeconomic Problem

One of the most important concepts in economics is the concept of *opportunity cost*. The **opportunity cost** of any action is the value of the next best alternative action sacrificed. In order to produce this book, the author had to reduce his time spent on other activities he values, such as reading or playing golf. The Addison-Wesley publishing company had to purchase paper and ink and editorial services that could have been used to produce other textbooks. To Addison-Wesley, the opportunity cost of producing this book, then, is the value of the next best alternative good or service that could have been produced instead.

The fundamental economic problem facing every society is how to distribute its scarce resources among the millions of competing and desirable possible uses for them. This is the problem of **resource allocation**, which can be summarized by the following three questions:

1. What goods and services will be produced?
2. How will these goods and services be produced?
3. Who will get these goods and services?

microeconomics

The study of the behavior of individual economic decision-makers such as households, businesses, and governments.

market

The coming together of buyers and sellers with the potential of exchanging goods or services.

macroeconomics

The study of the overall level of economic activity in an entire economy, such as the level of output, unemployment, inflation, and growth.

opportunity cost

The economic cost of undertaking any action; equal to the value of the best alternative action sacrificed.

resource allocation

How society decides to distribute its scarce resources, in terms of what goods and services to produce, how to produce them, and for whom to produce them.

▲▲▲ 1.1 APPLICATION   The Opportunity Cost of Credit Card Debt

One of the most expensive ways to borrow is to fail to pay off your credit cards each month. Most credit card interest rates are much higher than rates for mortgages and car loans. For example, according to *http://www.bankrate.com*, in January 2003, the average fixed interest rate on a standard credit card was 13.5 percent. Yet some consumers save money by putting money into a passbook saving account each month while carrying a balance on their credit cards. In January 2003, the average passbook savings account paid approximately 1.00 percent.

Suppose a consumer carries a monthly balance on his credit cards of $2,000 per month at an annual interest rate of 13.5 percent. Each month, this consumer deposits $100 into a passbook savings account earning 1.00 percent per year. What is the opportunity cost of putting $100 into his savings account? The opportunity cost is 13.5 percent that the consumer could "earn" by paying off his credit card debt by $100. By paying off his debt by $100, the consumer would save $13.50 in interest charges in one year, which is much better than the $1.00 he earns in a year by putting $100 into his savings account. By "saving" the $100, he costs himself $12.50 over the course of the year.

Notice that merely determining what to produce among all the alternatives solves only part of the problem. In addition to the composition of production, society must also determine how to produce each item. Should we use complicated, expensive machinery to produce a shirt, in order to free up labor for some other use? Or should more labor be used, so we can economize on machinery and make it available elsewhere? Finally, there is the problem of distribution: how much output is each member of our society entitled to, and what mechanism should we use to distribute this output?

Surprisingly, in the long sweep of human history, only three general mechanisms for allocating resources have been used. In **command systems**, households and firms are told what to produce, how to produce it, and who will get it. In **traditional systems**, households and firms simply do things the way they've always been done. And in **market systems**, everyone is more or less free to pursue their own interests, and resources are allocated as a consequence—almost as a by-product—of their activities.

Of course, no society relies exclusively on just one of these three mechanisms. Until the 1990s, the former Soviet Union and Eastern Europe had primarily command economies, yet the market was used to some extent to allocate goods and services among households. In the United States—primarily a market economy—the government uses "command" in the form of compulsory taxation, and spending on goods such as national defense and national parks. Furthermore, in the United States, to a considerable extent, class "traditions" determine who among us will become doctors and lawyers, and who will become clerks and factory workers.

Determining how markets solve the resource allocation problem occupies a central place in microeconomics. This is so largely because most nations now use the market as the dominant mechanism for allocating resources. During the past 15 years, the central role of the market has been reinforced by the sudden and dramatic transformation of the Eastern European command economies into market economies. We will learn more about this transformation in Chapter 5.

command system

An economic system that solves the problem of resource allocation by having the government tell households and firms what goods to produce, how to produce them, and for whom to produce them.

traditional system

An economic system that solves the problem of resource allocation by having households and firms produce and distribute goods the way they have been produced and distributed in the past.

market system

An economic system that solves the problem of resource allocation by permitting households and firms to pursue their own self-interests and make individual decisions.

The Uses of Microeconomics

Microeconomics is a very practical field of study. It can help you understand how the world works, and also help you solve the economic problems faced by your family, your firm, your community, your country, and even the community of nations.

Why are countries often reluctant to reduce agricultural subsidies? Why do they form international cartels like the Organization of Petroleum Exporting Countries (OPEC), and why do these cartels almost inevitably break down? How would a national gasoline tax affect employment and profits in the automobile industry? Why do rent-control programs or usury laws often hurt the very groups of people they are designed to help? Which occupations will attract the highest salaries over the next several years? How will one firm's price cuts affect the sales and profits of competing firms? Should the government have bailed out the airline industry after September 11? Should the government have broken up Microsoft's monopoly over computer operating systems? These are all questions that microeconomists are routinely called upon to answer.

Microeconomics also provides valuable insights into a vast range of social problems beyond those you may consider purely economic. Microeconomic tools have been used to help prevent insurance fraud, optimize preventative medical care, reform teaching methods, improve driver safety, design national defense strategies, and study the voting behavior of legislators. In addition, microeconomics can provide insight into personal life decisions concerning how much time to spend studying or how to serve in tennis. All of these applications use the tools you will learn in this course.

▼▼▼ 1.2 The Methods of Microeconomics

Earlier, we learned that economics is the study of choice under conditions of scarcity. But this is only part of what economics is about, the *what* to produce question of economics. There is also the *how* to produce question. Economics distinguishes itself from other fields of study not only by the questions it traditionally asks, but also by the methods used to answer them. In this section, we discuss two central aspects of the methodology of economics: the use of mathematics and the distinction between assumptions and conclusions.

Models

model

A simplified and abstract representation of the real world.

Economists, like other scientists and social scientists, use models to help them understand the world. A **model** is an abstract representation of some aspect of the real world. The key word here is "abstract." A model does not include every detail of what it represents. Instead, a model abstracts or takes from the thing that it represents the characteristics that will enable us to understand it better. Models, therefore, are simplifications of the world.

A road map is a good example of a model. In the real world, a city street is large and three-dimensional, perhaps lined with houses and trees. A road map abstracts and simplifies the reality of streets by eliminating the third dimension, getting rid of the houses and the trees, and using tiny lines to represent the much larger streets.

Models come in many forms. Some are actually physical models, such as the road map or the astronomer's plastic replica of the solar system. Some are simply verbal statements, like: "Mean earnings of high school graduates in the United States vary positively with the number of years of post-secondary education. High school graduates earn a mean income of \$27,000 and for each year of post-secondary education, mean earnings increase by 10 percent." This verbal model could be converted to a mathematical model as follows:

$$I = \$27,000(1.1)^y \tag{1.1}$$

where I represents mean income for high school graduates and y represents the number of years of post-secondary education. We can also view the same model graphically as presented in Figure 1.1.

Figure 1.1 Years of Post-Secondary Education and Mean Earnings
This figure graphically models the relationship between the number of years of post-secondary education and mean earnings.

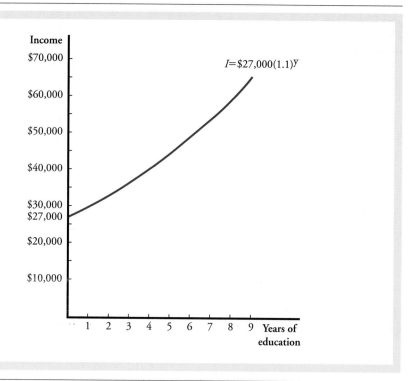

Each of these models represents something about the real world, but does so in a very simplified way. How much of the real world should we put into a model, and how much should we leave out? There is no automatic answer to this question, and this is why model building is as much an art as a science. There is, however, a useful guideline: a model should have just enough real-world details to fulfill its purpose, and no more. The proper level of detail, then, depends on our purpose in building the model in the first place.

Let's go back to the example of the road map. If we are using this model to determine the best route from Grand Central Station to the Empire State Building in New York City, we want a map that includes most of the city's streets. But if our purpose is to find the best route from New York to Washington, we want a map that shows major highways and ignores individual streets.

The same is true of economic models. Whether we are building a model of the global market for crude oil or a local market for olive oil, the fewer the details the better, as long as the model has enough detail to accomplish its purpose. With fewer details, it is easier to see the features of the real world we are interested in, and easier to communicate these features to others.

In economics, the models behind an idea typically rely almost exclusively on mathematics. These mathematical models often use either algebra, geometry, or calculus. The use of calculus, however, is not necessary to understand the major concepts in microeconomics, and therefore, in the main body of this text, we will confine our use of mathematics to algebra and geometry.

There are a number of reasons for this reliance on mathematics. Foremost among them is the old Chinese proverb that says a picture, or in our case, a graph or equation, is worth a thousand words. Often, a single graph or a simple algebraic equation can take the place of pages and pages of convoluted verbal exposition. For economists, using diagrams and equations makes a model easier to learn, and easier to remember and use.

COMMON ERROR 1.1   **Over-Thinking an Economic Problem**

This text presents a series of sections entitled "Common Errors." Each common error section presents an example of how *not* to think about an economic topic. *The material in these sections is wrong!* Be careful not to fall into the traps exposed in these common error sections.

One of the most common errors among undergraduate economics students is a failure to keep their analysis simple and to separate out primary economic forces from much less important secondary forces. We can refer to such thinking as *over-thinking*.

Here is an example of over-thinking. A student is asked: "What is the impact on the automobile market of a large increase in wages negotiated by the United Automobile Workers (UAW) union?" The student thinks for a second, and then responds, "Higher wages increase the costs of producing cars, which means the price of cars will increase and fewer cars will be sold; but higher wages for auto workers also mean that auto workers will buy more cars, which increases the price and number of cars sold. Therefore, higher auto worker wages result in an increase in the price of cars, but anything can happen to the quantity of cars sold; that is, the quantity may increase or decrease."

You might recognize that the primary, dominant impact of a significant increase in auto workers' wages is on the cost of producing cars, which results in an increase in price and a decrease in the number of cars sold. The impact of higher wages on auto workers' purchases of cars will therefore be trivial compared to the impact of higher wages on the costs of producing cars. So remember to keep your economic analysis simple and to the point, and don't over-think.

Another reason is that compared to verbal exposition, graphs and equations are less open to alternative interpretations.

Finally, economists are often asked to give not only qualitative conclusions such as "a rise in the minimum wage will cause an increase in teenage unemployment," but quantitative conclusions such as "a ten-percent rise in the minimum wage will cause the teenage unemployment rate to increase by between one and four percent." To come to such quantitative conclusions, economists must combine their economic models with real-world data using a set of statistical techniques known as **econometrics**. Only precise economic models lend themselves to econometric techniques, and this precision requires the use of mathematical equations.

econometrics

The branch of economics specializing in the use of statistical techniques to test the validity of economic models.

Assumptions and Conclusions

The foundation of any economic model is the set of assumptions behind it. In economics, the assumptions behind a model are always stated at the outset. In this way, an economic model and the conclusions that come from it can be subject to greater scrutiny and challenge, and disagreements can be more quickly resolved.

Suppose we are engaged in an argument with a friend about a third person, John. Our friend says that John is French, while we insist that John is not French. Our friend, who claims that John is French, might be making the following two assumptions:

1. "Anyone born in France is French."
2. "John was born in France."

If these two assumptions remain hidden, we might argue for quite some time without understanding why we disagree. But once the assumptions are revealed, our argument that John is not French becomes an argument that either 1 or 2 or both 1 and 2, are wrong. We might believe that being born in France does not necessarily make one French, or we might know that John was not born in France. In either case, since we agree about the rules of logic, the arena of battle moves to the more clearly arguable assumptions.

▲▲▲ **1.2 APPLICATION**   Economists As the Brunt of Jokes

Economists have a reputation for making many assumptions in creating their models of economic behavior. The truth is that economic models are typically based on relatively few assumptions. Occasionally, however, economists make assumptions that seem unrealistic to many people. This has led to a series of stories and jokes about economists such as this one:

Three professors—a chemist, a physicist, and an economist—are shipwrecked on an isolated island in the Pacific Ocean. The only item that survived the shipwreck and made it to shore was a carton of canned tuna fish. The three survivors have no tools, so they have to figure out a way to open the cans or face starvation. The chemist

suggests that they put the cans in the ocean until the salt water begins to oxidize the cans and they can open them. The physicist argues that the chemist's solution will take too long. She suggests climbing to the top of the highest tree on the island and dropping the cans to the ground so that gravity will bust them open. The economist speaks last and states simply: "Why would you bother with such difficult solutions to such a simple problem? First, assume we have a can opener."

There is a serious side to this amusing story: The implications of a model are no better than the assumptions underlying that model. If you start with poor assumptions, you end up with poor conclusions.

In later chapters, we will build models of the typical household, the typical business firm, and a variety of different types of markets. In each case, we will state our fundamental assumptions clearly at the outset.

▼▼▼   **1.3   Basic Principles of Microeconomics**

Every science or profession has its own way of organizing reality, of imposing order on the sometimes-chaotic world around us. A specialist in international affairs organizes the world by breaking it down into different nations and alliances. A chemist organizes physical reality by breaking it down into its basic elements and compounds. Similarly, microeconomists have their own way of organizing reality to guide them in their study of the economy. We now turn our attention to these organizing principles and the vocabulary associated with them.

Economic Agents

economic agent

A single decision-making unit, such as an individual consumer, a business firm, or a government.

In microeconomics, the term **economic agent** refers to any single decision-making unit. Part II of this book is devoted entirely to the study of economic agents. Every consumer, factory worker, and corporate board is an economic agent.

Economic agents can be categorized into three broad groups: households, business firms, and governments. Understanding how individual members of these groups behave, why they act the way they do, and how they can be expected to act in different circumstances is the starting point of microeconomic theory. Why does one household buy a Toyota and one buy a Ford? Why does Nieman Marcus charge twice the price of some other stores for the same brand of shoes? Why does one city government spend tax dollars improving parks, while another chooses to close its parks and reduce taxes instead? In each of these cases, agents have made a choice: a choice of car, a choice of pricing policy, a choice of city budgets. Presumably, each agent faced alternatives that could have been chosen but were not. As noted earlier, microeconomics is the study of choice, and all of microeconomics is built upon theories of how individual households, firms, and government agencies make choices.

All microeconomic theories of choice have several important common elements. When economic agents make choices, economists always assume they have clear objectives in mind; that is, that the agents know what they are trying to achieve. In the case of firms and households, it is assumed that self-interest is the overriding objective. For example, firms are usually assumed to have profit maximization as their primary objective. Governments, on the other hand, are supposed to act in accordance with the public interest. Whatever their goal may be, economists assume that when making choices, economic agents seek to achieve their goals as nearly as possible. At the same time, scarcity is a pervasive fact of economic life, and scarcity imposes constraints on what agents can do. To a microeconomist, economic choices are always the result of agents attempting to optimize their well-being in the face of constraints.

Markets

Markets are made up of individual economic agents, and microeconomics is as much the study of how individual economic agents behave when they come together in markets as how they behave separately. Parts III, IV, and V of this book are all devoted to the study of markets. You will see that when we study markets, we build from our theories of individual behavior to theories of market behavior.

From a very broad perspective, a market can be defined as any group of economic agents with the potential to exchange goods or services. The potential to trade, in turn, exists whenever economic agents have both an interest in trading with one another and the ability to trade with one another.

Agents have an interest in trading with one another when both believe they will gain from the trade. For example, business firms have an interest in selling goods and services in order to make a profit; households have an interest in buying goods and services for survival and/or pleasure. When firms and households come together so that the former can sell goods to the latter, they form a **product market**. The markets for oranges, automobiles, haircuts, computers, and banking services are specific examples of product markets. **Factor markets** exist when households sell factors of production such as land, labor, and capital to business firms. **Asset markets** exist when households trade valuable assets among themselves, usually with the help of intermediaries like stockbrokers or financial institutions.

Figure 1.2 illustrates the different types of markets that arise when economic agents come together to trade. Note that each type of market—product, factor, and asset—has a demand side, represented by arrows pointing inward, and a supply side, represented by the arrows directed outward. Also, each sector participates in each market. For example, factor markets demand resources from households, but also supply goods and services to households in product markets.

Figure 1.2 includes several simplifications. First, it ignores the flows of money that ordinarily accompany market trades. For example, when households supply factors of production, they receive **factor payments** from firms, in the form of wages, interest, rent, and profit. Similarly, when firms sell products, they receive payments from households and other buyers. We are ignoring these money flows in the diagram, concentrating instead on the flows of resources, products, and non-money assets.

LOCAL MARKETS So far, we have seen how an interest in trading can bring about different types of markets. We now take a closer look at the second prerequisite for a market to exist: the ability to trade. In order to have a market, economic agents must be able to communicate with each other and to exchange the goods and services they are trading. In many cases, this requirement places important geographic limits on a market. For

product market

The coming together of economic agents to buy and sell goods and services.

factor market

The coming together of households and other economic agents so that the households can sell their control over resources such as land, labor, and capital to the other economic agents.

asset market

The coming together of economic agents to buy and sell valuable assets such as stocks and bonds among themselves.

factor payments

The income received by households in the form of wages, interest, rent, and profit for the factors supplied to other economic agents.

Figure 1.2 Markets and the Market System
Each type of market—product, factor, and asset—has a demand side, represented by blue arrows pointing inward, and a supply side, represented by red arrows pointing outward. For example, firms demand factors of production from households in factor markets, and use these factors to supply products to households.

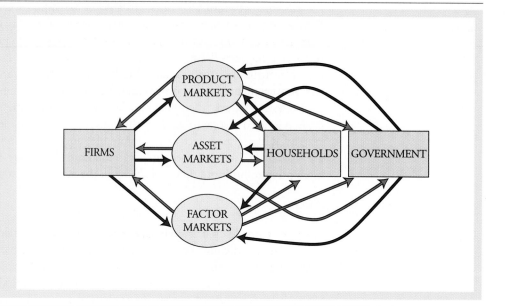

---

local market

A market that is restricted to a limited geographic area.

global market

A market that is not restricted to a limited geographic area.

equilibrium

A situation where every economic agent is doing the best it can, and therefore no economic agent wants to change its behavior.

---

example, it is not typically rational for an individual in Des Moines to fly to Denver to get a haircut, nor is it typically rational for a barber to fly from Denver to Des Moines to give one. It could be done, but few households or barbers would consider it worth the expense. Thus, the market for haircuts, like the market for most personal services, is a **local market**. Markets for restaurant meals, movies in theaters, and psychotherapy are other examples of local markets.

GLOBAL MARKETS Oil, on the other hand, is relatively cheap to transport across a country, or even from one country to another. Buyers in Tokyo can easily trade with sellers in Teheran. The market for oil, therefore, is a **global market**. Similarly, the markets for computer chips, oranges, and shares of corporate stock are global markets.

When we refer to the market for oil, or for restaurant meals, or haircuts, we will typically not specify explicitly whether the market is local or global. Instead, we assume that the geographic size of the market is implied. It is vitally important, however, to keep any geographic market limitations in mind, especially when analyzing the impact of regional economic events such as a natural disaster.

Equilibrium

Economists say that a market is in **equilibrium** if every agent in the market, whether buyer or seller, is doing the best he or she can given their own scope of action and given the actions of all other agents in the market. If under prevailing conditions there is nothing more an agent can do to make herself better off, then certainly that agent has no incentive to change what she is doing. If, simultaneously, every other agent in the market feels the same way, given their own circumstances and their own objectives, then no one will want to change their behavior. When no one has any incentive to change their behavior, there can be no pressure for change, so the market must truly be in a state of rest or equilibrium.

Parts III and IV of this text identify some important characteristics of different kinds of markets and study how those characteristics can affect the equilibrium market out-

market structure

The number and size distribution of the economic agents in a market.

inefficient

A situation where there is a way of reallocating resources to make at least one person better off without making anyone else worse off.

efficient

A situation where it is impossible to reallocate resources to make at least one person better off without making someone else worse off.

Pareto improvement

A reallocation of goods or services that makes at least one person better off without making anyone else worse off.

Pareto efficiency

An allocation of goods and services where it is impossible to reallocate the goods and services in a way that makes anyone better off without making someone else worse off.

come. One of those characteristics is **market structure**, or the number and relative size distribution of the economic agents that make up that market. In some markets, there are a great many individual buyers and a great many individual sellers. In other markets, there are relatively few buyers, or relatively few sellers, or both. While the notion of equilibrium remains the same despite differing market structures, market outcomes vary greatly depending on the market structure being analyzed.

Efficiency

Some market outcomes are efficient and others are inefficient. The terms "efficient" and "inefficient" have very precise meanings to economists. Economists are concerned about waste within individual firms and households, but they are also concerned about much more than this. Specifically, economists consider a situation to be **inefficient** if there is a way of re-allocating resources to make at least one person better off without making anyone else worse off. Conversely, economists consider a situation to be **efficient** if it is impossible to re-allocate resources to make at least one person better off without making someone else worse off.

Application 1.3 demonstrates the concept of efficiency by describing how each baseball card trade makes the traders better off as a group, because every trade makes someone better off without making anyone worse off. This type of reallocation is called a **Pareto improvement**, named after the late 19th- and early 20th-century Italian social scientist Vilfredo Pareto. A Pareto improvement is any change within society that makes at least one person better off and harms no one. To an economist, any potential Pareto improvement not undertaken represents a wasted opportunity to make someone better off. Anytime we can identify an unexploited Pareto improvement, therefore, we are operating inefficiently from society's point of view. The economist's definition of efficiency—called **Pareto efficiency**—incorporates this view: a Pareto efficient situation is one in which all possible Pareto improvements have been exhausted.

▲▲▲ 1.3 APPLICATION Efficiency, Young Waldman, and Baseball Card Trading

I grew up in Philadelphia and, to my great misfortune, was a big fan of the Philadelphia Phillies baseball team. Every summer I went to New Hampshire, where all of my friends were Yankees or Red Sox fans. I made sure that by the time I left for New Hampshire, I had collected as many Yankees and Red Sox baseball cards as I could in the spring; and my friends came to New Hampshire with as many Phillies cards as they could. When we arrived, we started with an economically inefficient situation where I had many Yankees and Red Sox cards and they had many Phillies cards. We immediately began trading cards: first I might trade a Whitey Ford card for a Robin Roberts card, and then I might trade a Carl Yastrzemski card for a Richie Ashburn card, and eventually we would get down to trades like Ralph Terry (Yankees pitcher) for Tony Taylor (Phillies second baseman).

By the end of a week, there were no more trades to be made, because each and every trade that could make one of us better off without hurting the other trader had been completed. At that point, the market for baseball cards among my summer friends was efficient. At the end of the summer, of course, my friends went home with many Mickey Mantle, Yogi Berra, Carl Yastrzemski, and Whitey Ford cards; and I went home with many Robin Roberts, Richie Ashburn, Seth Morehead (an awful pitcher), and Sparky Anderson (a weak second baseman, but later a Hall of Fame manager) cards. As an adult, I came to realize what an easy trading target I was for my friends during those summers, but at the time, the trading outcome was economically efficient.

Positive Versus Normative Economic Analysis

The beginning of this chapter discussed how the tragic events of September 11, 2001 reverberated throughout the world and caused a complex series of emotional and economic reactions. To most of the world's population, the events immediately following September 11 seemed chaotic and confusing. Most economists, however, saw significant order in the economy's reactions to September 11. Hopefully, you now can begin to understand how the study of economics, by asking a series of questions, attempts to create order out of almost any economic event, even a catastrophic one. Such questions include: Who are the optimizing agents making decisions? What are the agents trying to achieve? In which markets do they come together? How will the equilibrium be affected in each of these markets?

The process described here—where we look at events such as those of September 11 and ask what will happen to markets, to firms, and to individual agents as a result—is an example of **positive economic analysis**. This type of analysis is concerned solely with understanding events and predicting their consequences. But economists, as social scientists, do much more than this. They are interested not only in what will happen as the result of some event, but also in judging whether what happens will be "good" or "bad," and what, if anything, we might do to make things "better." When we move beyond merely predicting consequences and begin assessing them from a social point of view, we are performing **normative economic analysis**.

For example, as a result of September 11, there were economic winners and losers. Lockheed Martin was among the winners and American Airlines was among the losers. A normative analysis might ask: Is society better or worse off when resources are shifted from the airline industry to the defense industry? Are we closer or further away from a **social optimum**—a state of being where our society is as well off as it can be? This is a value judgment, and as such, is an example of normative analysis. The question concerning whether society is better or worse off after resources are transferred from the airline industry to the defense industry can only be answered in relation to some underlying system of values: political, social, or moral.

Economists, like everyone else, can and do disagree widely among themselves on a great many matters where value judgments are involved. Should we invest in electric cars to reduce our dependence on foreign oil? Should high-income households pay a higher percentage of their income in taxes, or should we have a flat tax, where everyone pays the same percentage? Should there be a lower minimum wage for teenagers than for adult workers? Should we eliminate the corporate profits tax? Economists are no more likely to agree on these issues than anyone else.

Economists do agree on one thing: a social optimum *requires* Pareto efficiency. If something can be done to make someone better off without making anybody worse off, all economists, regardless of their values, would agree that we should do it. This insight is why economists have a natural bias in favor of markets. We will see that under certain conditions, a market system where everyone is free to do what they want with what they've got leads to Pareto efficiency. We will also learn to recognize when these conditions are likely to be present, and when they are not.

But is Pareto efficiency enough? Most of us would argue that it is not. A situation where one member of society owns everything and everyone else has nothing may be Pareto efficient, in that there is no way to make anyone better off without harming the sole wealth-holder, but it is far from equitable or fair. Many of the economic issues that divide management from labor, Democrats from Republicans, and wealthy nations from poor ones are really issues of equity rather than efficiency.

positive economic analysis

Uses economic models to predict the actual consequences of actions.

normative economic analysis

The study of what should be, requiring the use of value judgments to determine whether the predicted outcomes of economic actions are positive or negative.

social optimum

A normative state where society is as well off as possible.

How can microeconomics help resolve what are essentially moral or political disagreements? While economic science alone cannot actually solve these problems, it can help us make decisions by outlining alternatives and identifying the consequences of different choices we might make.

Summary

1. Economics is the study of choice under conditions of scarcity. The field is divided into two major branches: microeconomics and macroeconomics. Microeconomics studies the behavior of individual economic agents and how they interact with each other in markets. Macroeconomics focuses on the overall level of economic activity in a society, studying such topics as unemployment, inflation, and the rate of economic growth.

2. Every society faces the difficult problem of deciding what will be produced, how it will be produced, and who will get what is produced. Together, these three problems constitute the fundamental microeconomic problem of resource allocation.

3. Three mechanisms have been used to solve the problem of resource allocation: command, tradition, and the market. Of these, the market plays a dominant role in most of the world's economies, and a central role in the thinking of microeconomists.

4. Economists rely heavily on graphical and mathematical models to understand the real-world economy. A model should contain just enough real-world detail to fulfill its purpose, and no more. There should also be a clear distinction between the assumptions behind a model and the conclusions derived from it.

5. Microeconomists understand and study economic events by organizing the world into optimizing economic agents who interact with each other in different markets, each of which tends toward a specific state of rest, or equilibrium. When economists use the word "efficiency," they mean Pareto efficiency, which is a much broader concept than the mere elimination of waste. A situation is Pareto efficient only when it is impossible to reallocate goods and services in a way that makes at least one person better off without making anyone else worse off.

6. Microeconomists are called upon to practice both positive economic analysis, which describes and predicts the consequences of economic events, and normative economic analysis, which considers whether a given set of consequences is positive or negative.

Self-Test Problems

1. Consider the following mathematical model of attendance at a national park on any given Sunday:
$$N = 10T - 15C - 20R$$
where:

N = attendance at the park, in thousands

T = temperature, in degrees Fahrenheit

C = percentage of the sky covered by clouds

R = rainfall, in inches

Construct a verbal model that conveys precisely the same information.

2. State whether each of the following is a Pareto improvement and briefly explain your answer.

   a. A mugger steals your wallet.

   b. Two children voluntarily trade baseball cards.

   c. All tariffs and quotas on foreign goods are removed.

   d. A city enacts a rent-control law.

   e. A city abolishes its rent-control law.

Questions and Problems for Review

1. How might a microeconomist and a macroeconomist differ in their approach to the problem of unemployment? In particular, state a positive and a normative question that might be asked of a microeconomist, and then do the same for a macroeconomist.

2. Is it theoretically possible to have a command economy and a democratically elected government? Explain.

3. "If we sign a free-trade agreement with Ecuador, the wages of American workers will fall relative to those of the typical Ecuadorian worker." Construct a set of assumptions that would, if correct, require us to accept this statement as true.

4. Is the market for used cars a local, national, or global market? Explain.

5. Suppose a firm is wasting electricity; that is, the same output could be produced with less electricity than is currently being used. Which of the following situations are ruled out?

   a. Market equilibrium

   b. Pareto efficiency

   c. Social optimality

6. In a market equilibrium, all agents are doing the best that they can possibly do, and all waste has been eliminated. How, then, can we say that some market equilibria are socially positive and some are negative?

Internet Exercises

Visit *http://www.myeconlab.com/waldman* for this chapter's Web exercises. Answer real-world economics problems by doing research on the Internet.

Chapter 2
Supply and Demand

In mid-1995, the average price of a single-family home in San Francisco was $250,450. Three years later, the average price was $330,000, and by 2000, it had reached a staggering $404,323, and that was for the "average" house![1] How could San Francisco housing prices increase by 61.4 percent in six years? The answer can be captured in three words: the Internet boom. From 1995 to1999, hundreds of Internet entrepreneurs became billionaires and settled in the Silicon Valley around San Francisco, which is one of the major technological capitals of the United States. Hundreds of thousands of highly educated people in the Silicon Valley became instant millionaires as they watched the value of their dot-com stocks soar. Furthermore, thousands more moved to the San Francisco Bay area in hopes of finding their Internet fortunes. With the number of housing units in San Francisco growing only slowly at best, these *nouveau riches* bid up the price of housing in San Francisco to previously unimaginable levels. When the dot-com bubble burst, and many Internet companies went bankrupt, housing prices in San Francisco declined by an estimated six percent in 2001.

The dramatic escalation of housing prices in San Francisco can be explained by using what is widely considered to be the most important of all economic models. That model—supply and demand—is so central to economists' thinking about world events that to the general public, the phrase "supply and demand" has become almost synonymous with economics.

Supply and demand is a model that predicts how buyers and sellers behave when they come together in markets and the likely results of that behavior. One of the most important outcomes of using the model of supply and demand is being able to predict the market price at which a good is bought and sold. Large price changes, such as the large price increases in the San Francisco housing market, can create serious social problems. For example, as the wealthy Internet

---

[1] "Hot and Cold Real Estate Markets in the San Francisco Bay Area," *Federal Reserve Bank of San Francisco Economic Letter*, August 6, 1999, and Elizabeth Razzi, "Sanity Returns to the Housing Market," *Kiplinger's Personal Finance*, January 2001.

15

entrepreneurs drove up the price of housing in San Francisco, blue-collar workers were displaced and had difficulty finding affordable housing in the Bay area. Large price changes have also created a crisis in the United States healthcare system; a need for wealthy nations to provide billions of dollars in foreign aid to Russia; and a powerful incentive for drug buyers and sellers to break the law.

This chapter introduces the essentials of the supply and demand model. We begin by studying the behavior of buyers—the demand side of the model. Next, we turn our attention to sellers' behavior—the supply side. Finally, we put supply and demand together and see how economists use this powerful tool to explain events in the real world.

2.1   Demand

market demand

The relationship that specifies the quantity of a good that all buyers in a market would like to buy at each possible price over a given period of time, holding constant all other factors except the price.

We begin our study of demand with a definition. The **market demand** for a good is the relationship that specifies the quantity of that good that all buyers in a market would like to buy at each possible price over a given period of time, given that all other factors except the price of the good remain constant.

There are a few important things to note about this definition. First, notice the words "would like to." Demand tells us how much individuals would like to buy (given the constraints they face) and the other opportunities available to them. Second, notice that demand always refers to a given period of time. In economics, it is crucial to know exactly what this time period is. The demand for bread is much greater "per year" than it is "per week." Finally, note that demand refers to "buyers in a market," and therefore it is vital to know the correct definition of the market; for example, whether it is local or global, and who the buyers are.

Consider the market for silver, and an arbitrary period of time of one day. The market could be narrowed to focus on the market for silver only in the United States or any other locality; however, because silver is easily transported and international trade in silver is largely unrestricted, the market will be considered global. On the buyers' side of the market, many different types of economic agents demand silver. Jewelers demand silver to produce rings, necklaces, and decorative objects. Manufacturers demand silver to produce electronic components and photographic film. Dentists demand silver for fillings. And finally, speculators demand silver as a form of financial investment. It is possible to narrow our focus and consider only the demand for silver jewelry or photographic silver powder, or to broaden our focus and consider all uses of silver together. If the broader approach is taken, then the demand for silver is the *total quantity* that all of these agents would like to buy in the global market for silver.

The Determinants of Demand

How exactly is the demand for silver determined? Philosophically, any event in the universe affects every other event, so that, for example, the alignment of the stars might be theorized to have some impact on the demand for silver. But recall from Chapter 1 our rule of thumb in building a model: to keep it as simple as possible. With this in mind, let's examine the factors that economists believe are the most important in determining the market demand for any good.

THE PRICE OF THE GOOD   In general, holding all other things constant, the higher the price of any good, the less of it consumers will want to buy. This inverse relationship between price and quantity demanded is so commonly observed that economists have identified it as **the law of demand**.

the law of demand

The inverse relationship between price and quantity demanded.

THE INCOMES OF BUYERS For silver and most goods, an increase in buyers' incomes can be expected to increase quantity demanded. Buyers' incomes increase when population increases or when individual consumers' incomes increase; for example, during an economic expansion. Such goods are called **normal goods**—goods whose demand is positively related to buyers' incomes. Automobiles, compact discs, and vacation trips to Europe are all examples of normal goods. If an increase in income decreases the quantity demanded of a good, the good is called an **inferior good**. For many individuals, ground beef, potatoes, rice, Spam, and public transportation are inferior goods.

normal goods

Goods or services that consumers purchase in larger quantities as consumers' incomes increase.

inferior goods

Goods or services that consumers purchase in smaller quantities as consumers' incomes increase.

THE PRICES OF RELATED GOODS A **substitute good** is a good that can be used in place of another good. In dentistry, both gold and porcelain are possible substitutes for silver in fillings. If the price of gold rises, some dental patients would be expected to request silver fillings instead. In general, the demand for any good will be *positively* related to the price of a substitute.

substitute goods

Two goods or services where an increase in the price of one good or service results in an increase in the quantity demanded of the other good or service.

When a dentist fills a tooth with silver, other goods—for example, mercury—are used along with the silver. An increase in the price of mercury, therefore, would be expected to cause an increase in the cost of silver fillings, and make at least some dental patients choose gold or porcelain fillings instead. Goods like silver and mercury that tend to be used together are called **complements**. The demand for any good should be *inversely* related to the price of a complement.

complement goods

Two goods or services where an increase in the price of one good or service results in a decrease in the quantity demanded of the other good or service.

TASTES Individuals differ in their tastes for metallic jewelry, patients differ in their tastes for different types of dental fillings, and speculators differ in their tastes for commodities with different risk characteristics. These tastes can shift for a number of reasons, including the effects of advertising, social fads, or even rumors. Each of these influences could be included as a separate variable in our list, but to do so would not gain us much. Instead, the word "tastes" encompasses all such influences on demand. Economists leave it to other professionals, such as psychologists, sociologists, and marketing specialists, to explain how tastes are formed. When tastes change, however, economists are equipped to analyze the consequences.

EXPECTATIONS Buyers' thoughts about the future often affect what they do today. For example, if speculators think the price of silver is about to increase, they will demand more silver today so they can profit by selling the silver at a higher price in the future. In some markets—for example, the markets for commodities, stocks, and bonds—changes in expectations can explain virtually all of the day-to-day changes in demand.

The Market Demand Curve

Many factors affect the demand for a good, and in the real world, all of these will be changing simultaneously. How then is it possible to study demand without getting hopelessly confused? In general, this is done by focusing on one determinant of demand at a time: by asking, for example, what would happen if all the variables affecting quantity demanded remained constant except for one variable that is allowed to change. This method of letting one variable change and holding all others constant is used so often in economic analysis that economists use a shorthand phrase, the Latin expression *ceteris paribus*, "all else the same," to describe it.

ceteris paribus

A Latin expression meaning "all else the same." Commonly assumed in economics when analyzing the impact of a change in one particular variable on another variable.

market demand curve

A graph showing the quantity of a good that buyers in the market would like to buy at different prices.

Let us return to the market for silver by exploring the relationship between the quantity demanded and the price of silver, *ceteris paribus*. Figure 2.1 illustrates this relationship.

The downward-sloping curve in Figure 2.1(a) is an example of a **market demand curve** that tells us the quantity of a good that buyers in the market would like to buy at different prices, *ceteris paribus*. In the case of silver, *ceteris paribus* means that as the price of silver changes, the prices of complements, such as mercury, and substitutes, such as gold and porcelain, are held constant. Furthermore, all buyers' incomes, expectations, and tastes are also held constant. Move along the demand curve in Figure 2.1(a); only the price of silver and the quantity of silver demanded are changing. A price decrease from p_1 to p_2 causes an increase in quantity demanded from q_1 to q_2. This is a graphical representation of the law of demand.

What happens when one of the variables that has been held constant changes? Suppose the price of gold, a substitute for silver, increases. *Ceteris paribus*, the demand for silver by dentists and jewelry-makers would be expected to increase, whatever the price of silver happens to be. In Figure 2.1(b), for a silver price of p_1, the demand might increase from q_1 to q_3, so that our demand curve would go through point C rather than point A. Similarly, if the price of silver were p_2, demand might be q_4 instead of q_2, and our demand curve would go through point E instead of B. No matter what price is assumed for silver, a rise in the price of gold will increase the demand for silver. In other words, a rise in the price of gold, a substitute, causes the demand curve for silver to shift to the right to D_2. Also note that a rightward shift in demand could also have been caused by a decrease in the price of a complementary good like mercury, an increase in buyers' incomes (because silver is a normal good), or a positive change in buyers' tastes for the good.

It is possible to summarize the impact of different variables on a demand curve with the following basic rules: *When the price of a good changes, we move along the market*

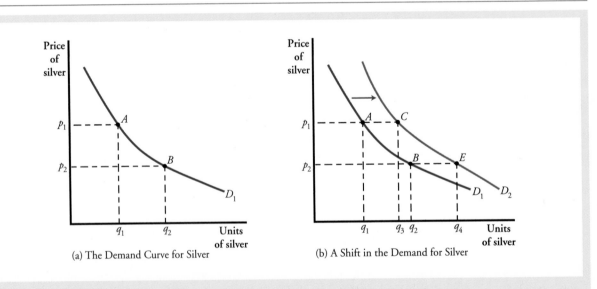

Figure 2.1 The Demand Curve for Silver and a Shift in the Demand for Silver
In panel (a), only the price of silver and the quantity of silver demanded change, and a price decrease from p_1 to p_2 causes an increase in quantity demanded from q_1 to q_2. In panel (b), suppose the price of a substitute, gold, increases. *Ceteris paribus*, the demand for silver increases at every price. For a silver price equal to p_1, the quantity demanded increases to q_3 instead of q_1; and for price equal to p_2, the quantity demanded increases from q_2 to q_4. In other words, a rise in the price of gold causes the demand curve for silver to *shift to the right* from D_1 to D_2.

▲▲▲ 2.1 APPLICATION Supermarket Wars in the United Kingdom

Supermarkets are not identical. They carry different combinations of products, different take-out foods, and different qualities of produce. Nevertheless, any supermarket in Great Britain is a very close substitute for any other supermarket. Just how close became clear in 1995 when Britain's leading supermarket chain, Tesco, initiated a policy of price cutting. Until Tesco began cutting prices, Sainsbury was the leading supermarket chain.

The graph shows Tesco's and Sainsbury's initial demand curves D_{T1} and D_{S1} for food before Tesco began cutting prices. Initially, a typical weekly market basket cost £100 at either store, so Tesco was at point A in panel (a) and sold q_{T1} market baskets of food, and Sainsbury was at point A' in panel (b) and sold q_{S1} market baskets of food. In 1995–96, Tesco lowered its prices by 20 percent, so a market basket cost £80. Fortunately for Tesco, Sainsbury, and virtually all other supermarkets in Britain, continued to charge £100 for an identical market basket of food. In the language of microeconomics, Tesco was permitted to change its price *ceteris paribus*, and the effect is shown in panel (a) as a movement along Tesco's demand curve D_{T1} from point A to point B, which shows an increase in *quantity demanded* from q_{T1} *to* q_{T2}.

From Sainsbury's point of view, Tesco's move was a decrease in the price of a substitute good, which caused a

leftward shift of Sainsbury's demand curve, a decrease in demand, from D_{S1} to D_{S2} in panel (b). As a result, Sainsbury, which initially refused to lower its prices, moved from point A' to point B'. Eventually, Sainsbury tried to get its customers back by cutting its prices to £80 per market basket. This caused a movement along Sainsbury's new demand curve, D_{S2}, from point B' to point C' as Sainsbury briefly reestablished its market share. This, in turn, caused a leftward shift of Tesco's demand curve, from D_{T1} to D_{T2} in panel (a). This new situation, with Sainsbury at point C' and Tesco at point C, did not last long. Almost immediately, Tesco cut its prices, and once again Sainsbury responded, prompting yet another response from Tesco. In each round, the price cuts caused a movement along the price-cutter's demand curve, and a shift of its competitor's demand curve.

In 1999, the price wars escalated as a result of Wal-Mart's purchase of Asda, the United Kingdom's third-largest supermarket chain. Tesco and Asda initiated price cuts in sequential rounds, and those two firms kept gaining market share at Sainsbury's expense. In September 2001, it was estimated that Tesco's prices were eight percent lower than Sainsbury's. As a result, Tesco's market share continued to increase and Sainsbury's continued to fall. Because Sainsbury was at first slow to cut its prices, it was unable to reestablish itself as the leading firm.

(a)Tesco

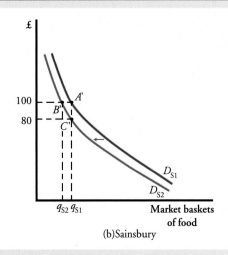
(b)Sainsbury

Application Figure 2.1 Initially, a typical weekly market basket cost £100 and Tesco was at point A and Sainsbury was at point A'. When Tesco lowered its price to £80, Sainsbury continued to charge £100 for a basket of food, so its demand decreased to D_{S2} and its quantity demanded decreased to q_{S2}. Tesco was permitted to change its price *ceteris paribus*, and it moved from point A to point B, an increase in the quantity demanded from q_{T1} *to* q_{T2}. Sainsbury then cut prices to £80, which caused a movement along Sainsbury's new demand curve from point B' to point C'. This caused a shift of Tesco's demand curve from D_{T1} to D_{T2}, and moved Tesco from point B to point C.

demand curve. When any variable affecting demand other than the price of the good changes, the market demand curve shifts.

It is important to distinguish between a movement along a demand curve and a shift in the entire curve. Vague phrases such as "demand goes up" or "people want less" can lead us astray. To avoid confusion, economists use the phrase "an increase in demand" to signify a rightward shift of the entire demand curve and the phrase "an increase in quantity demanded" to signify a rightward movement along the demand curve. We follow this convention throughout this book.

▼▼▼   2.2   Supply

market supply

The relationship that specifies the quantity of a good that all sellers in a market would like to sell at each possible price over a given period of time, holding constant all other factors except the price.

The **market supply** of a good is defined as the quantity of the good that all sellers in a market would like to sell at each possible price over a given period of time, *ceteris paribus*. Usually, sellers are thought of as firms engaged in the business of producing and then selling the good in question, but this is not always the case. In the market for silver, for example, some sellers are speculators who have bought silver in the past, hoping to sell it at a higher price in the future.

Supply, like demand, refers to a hypothetical quantity: the amount of the good that sellers would like to sell. And as with demand, some care must be taken to specify the time period, the size and location of the market, and the identity of the suppliers. In discussing the demand for silver, the market was specified as global, and the time period as a day, so these same parameters will be chosen for the supply of silver. The "supply of silver" means the quantity supplied per day by all sellers in the global market.

The Determinants of Supply

The following important variables affect the supply of any good.

THE PRICE OF THE GOOD   A higher price for a good, *ceteris paribus*, should cause self-interested producers to want to produce and sell more of it. It should also cause speculators and other suppliers to release more of the good for sale. In general, a higher price should increase the total quantity supplied.

THE PRICES OF INPUTS   Inputs are the goods and services that firms use to produce a specific output. In the production of silver, the inputs include land, mining equipment, labor, and refining equipment. If the price of an input rises, *ceteris paribus*, firms will find production of a good less profitable, and tend to decrease the supply.

THE PRICES OF ALTERNATE GOODS   An alternate good is some other good a firm could produce instead of the good in question. Because firms that produce and sell silver already have mining equipment, labor, and refining equipment, they might find it relatively easy to shift to mining other metals. Gold, nickel, and copper would be examples of alternate goods to produce instead of silver. In general, a higher price for an alternate good, like gold, induces firms to shift resources away from the good in question, silver, toward the alternate good, because the opportunity cost of continuing to produce silver increases. Consequently, there is an inverse relationship between the price of an alternate good and the supply of the good. If the price of gold increases, the supply of silver will decrease as mining companies shift to mining more gold.

technological improvement

A change in production technique that enables the same quantity of a good to be produced with fewer inputs.

TECHNOLOGY   A **technological improvement** is a change in production technique that enables the same quantity of a good to be produced with smaller quantities of inputs. A change in technology might result from a scientific discovery, the invention of a new machine, or a new way of organizing existing inputs such as labor. Technological improvements tend to increase the supply of a good.

EXPECTATIONS If sellers and speculators believe that the price of a good will soon decrease, they might want to sell more of it now. Expectations about future government regulations, future input prices, and future taxes can also affect supply. If the price of silver is expected to decrease in the future, producers will supply more silver today.

The Market Supply Curve

Sellers consider many factors when trying to decide how much of a good to supply, and in the real world, all of these things are changing constantly and simultaneously. Once again, all variables other than the price of the good itself are held constant. Continuing with our silver market example, let's explore what happens to the quantity of silver supplied when the price of silver changes.

market supply curve

A graph showing the quantity of a good that sellers in the market would like to sell at different prices.

The upward sloping curve in Figure 2.2(a) is an example of a **market supply curve**, which tells us the quantity of a good that sellers in the market would like to sell at different prices. Moving along the market supply curve for silver, the prices of alternate metals like gold and copper, the prices of inputs like labor and mining machinery, the state of technology, and sellers' expectations about the future are all held constant.

When any of the variables being held constant changes, the supply curve shifts. For example, suppose the price of mining equipment falls. At any given price for silver, more would be supplied, because it would be more profitable for producers to do so. Figure 2.2(b) shows this as a rightward shift of the supply curve. If the price of silver stayed constant at p_1, supply would rise from q_1 to q_3, and our supply curve would go through point C rather than point A. Similarly, if the price of silver stayed constant at p_2, sellers would

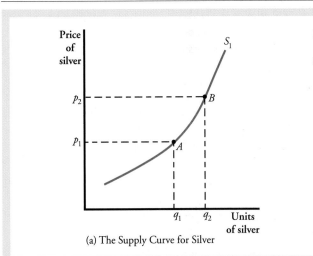

(a) The Supply Curve for Silver

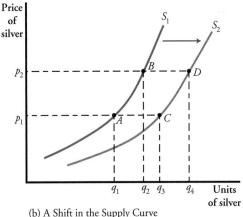

(b) A Shift in the Supply Curve

Figure 2.2 The Supply Curve for Silver and a Shift in the Supply Curve for Silver
The upward sloping curve in panel (a) is an example of a market supply curve, which identifies the quantity of a good that sellers in the market would like to sell at different prices, *ceteris paribus*. When any of the variables being held constant changes, the supply curve shifts. In panel (b), for example, if the price of mining equipment falls, then the supply curve for silver shifts from S_1 to S_2. If the price of silver stayed constant at p_1, the supply would rise from q_1 to q_3, and the supply curve goes through point C rather than point A.

supply more units and the supply curve would go through point D instead of B. No matter what price is assumed for silver, the supply will be greater, due to the decrease in the cost of mining equipment. More generally, when the price of any input decreases, the entire supply curve shifts to the right. Similar rightward shifts would be caused by a decrease in the price of an alternative good, a technological improvement, or an expectation that the price of the good is about to drop.

The impact of different variables on the supply curve is summarized with the following basic rules: *When the price of a good changes, we move along the supply curve. When any variable other than the price of the good changes, the entire supply curve shifts.* In this book, the phrase "increase in supply" signifies a rightward shift of the supply curve, while "increase in quantity supplied" signifies a rightward movement along the current supply curve.

2.3   Supply and Demand Together

The demand and supply curves identify the hypothetical quantities of silver that buyers would like to buy and sellers would like to sell at different hypothetical prices. But what will the price of silver be at any given moment? And how much will buyers and sellers actually buy and sell on any given day? To answer these questions, it is necessary to put the supply and demand curves together.

Market Equilibrium

Recall from Chapter 1 that an equilibrium is defined as a situation where, for the moment, no agents have any incentive to change their behavior. At any given moment, most markets, including the silver market, can be expected to be functioning at or near their equilibrium, so a search for the price and quantity of silver that actually prevails is really a search for the equilibrium price and quantity. Figure 2.3 puts the supply and demand curves for silver together so that the equilibrium price and quantity can be identified.

excess demand

The amount by which the quantity demanded exceeds the quantity supplied because the price of a good is below the equilibrium price.

Consider a price of \$3.50 per ounce and ask yourself whether this could be the equilibrium price. At this price, sellers want to supply only $q_s = 7$ million ounces per day, but buyers want to buy $q_d = 10$ million ounces per day. There is an **excess demand** for silver of $q_d - q_s = 3$ million ounces per day. At a price of \$3.50 per ounce, all available silver would be sold out quickly, and many customers would go unsatisfied. In the face of excess demand, sellers could raise their prices, still sell all the silver they are currently selling, and increase their profits. Also, some buyers would offer sellers a higher price rather than take a chance on ending up empty-handed. Because buyers and sellers have an incentive to change their behavior, a price of \$3.50 per ounce cannot possibly be our sought-after equilibrium price.

How about a price of \$3.90 per ounce? Now the situation is reversed: sellers would like to sell $q_s = 10$ million ounces per day, but buyers want to buy only $q_d = 7$ million ounces. There is an **excess supply** for silver of $q_s - q_d = 3$ million ounces per day. In this situation, some sellers would have an incentive to cut their prices, while buyers, finding sellers more willing to bargain, have an incentive to seek a lower price. Once again, the price changes, so \$3.90 cannot be our equilibrium price.

excess supply

The amount by which the quantity supplied exceeds the quantity demanded because the price of a good is above the equilibrium price.

Only at a price of \$3.70, where quantity supplied and quantity demanded are both equal at 8.5 million ounces per day, will the market be in equilibrium. At this price, there is neither an excess supply nor an excess demand, so no one has an incentive to change their behavior.

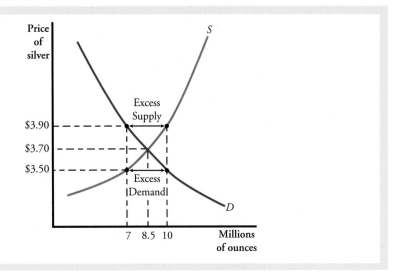

Figure 2.3 Supply and Demand for Silver
In equilibrium, the quantity supplied equals the quantity demanded, where the supply curve intersects the demand curve. In equilibrium, $q = 8.5$ million ounces of silver and $p = \$3.70$. At any price below the equilibrium price—for example, at $p = \$3.50$—there is an excess demand for silver; and at any price above the equilibrium price—for example, at $p = \$3.90$—there is an excess supply.

But is it certain that this equilibrium will actually be attained? This is an important question, and to answer it, let's begin by once again assuming an initial price of $3.50 per ounce. At this price, excess demand will cause the price to rise. Now, as the price of silver rises, two things happen that simultaneously work to eliminate the excess demand: (1) the rising price decreases the quantity demanded of silver, shown as an upward movement along the demand curve; and (2) the rising price increases the quantity supplied, shown as an upward movement along the supply curve. These two movements together reduce the excess demand, until at a price of $3.70 per ounce, the excess demand is gone and there is no reason for prices to rise further. The same logic would hold if the price were initially $3.90: price would continue to decrease until it hit $3.70, where it would stop.

In sum, once the supply and demand curves are drawn together, the equilibrium is easily spotted as the price and quantity where the two curves intersect. If price and quantity deviate from this equilibrium for any reason, the behavior of self-interested buyers and sellers will cause the price to change until the equilibrium is attained.

Endogenous and Exogenous Variables

exogenous variable

Variable in a model whose numerical value is determined outside the model and therefore is taken as given.

endogenous variable

Variable in a model whose numerical value is determined by the model.

Economists classify the variables in a model into two types, and the distinction is always important. An **exogenous variable** is one whose numerical value is determined "outside" the model. That is, the model is not intended to explain how the variable is determined, or to predict when or how it might change. Exogenous variables are simply given, and used as data. An **endogenous variable**, by contrast, is determined "inside" the model. Indeed, a key goal of building any model is to predict the values of endogenous variables and to explain when and how they might change.

In our model of supply and demand for silver, there are two endogenous variables: the price of silver and the quantity of silver. Every other variable in the model, whether it affects supply or demand or both, is exogenous. For example, the price of gold affects both the demand and the supply of silver, because gold is both a substitute in consumption and an alternate production good for the producers of silver. But our model of the silver market does not attempt to explain how the price of gold is determined. On the contrary, the price of gold is taken as given data. If and when the price of gold changes, there is a new piece of data to work with. Whether a particular variable is exogenous or

▲▲▲ 2.3 APPLICATION   The San Francisco Housing Market in the Late 1990s

This chapter began by noting the dramatic increase in housing prices in San Francisco in the late 1990s. Recall that in 1995, the equilibrium price of a typical single-family home in San Francisco was $250,450; in 1998, it was $330,000; and in 2000, the equilibrium price reached $404,323. In terms of supply and demand, the reason for the dramatic increase in the equilibrium price was a rapid increase in demand combined with a constant supply. Because there was little land available to build new housing in San Francisco, the quantity supplied did not increase much, despite the tremendous increase in price.

In the graph, the supply curve for housing is upward-sloping and very steep. In fact, the relatively fixed number of housing units is indicated by the almost vertical supply curve. Because of the large increase in buyers' incomes in the San Francisco area, the demand curve shifted dramatically to the right from D_{95} to D_{98} to D_{00} for the years 1995, 1998, and 2000 respectively. The combination of a relatively fixed quantity supplied and a rapid increase in demand resulted in a rapid escalation in housing prices.

Application Figure 2.3 In San Francisco, the quantity supplied of housing does not increase much with an increase in price, so the supply curve is close to vertical. As demand increased dramatically from D_{95} to D_{98} to D_{00}, the equilibrium price increased from $250 to $330 to $404 thousand dollars between 1995 and 2000. The quantity supplied, however, increased only slightly from q_{95} to q_{98} to q_{00}.

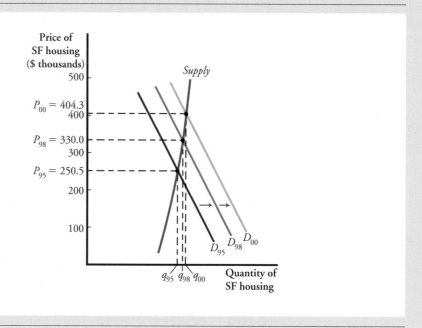

endogenous is not an intrinsic trait of the variable, but rather a consequence of how that variable is used in a particular model. A variable can be exogenous in one model, yet endogenous in another. In a model of the market for gold, some of the roles would be reversed: the price of silver would become an exogenous variable, while the price of gold would become endogenous.

Comparative Statics

comparative statics

The process of changing one exogenous variable and observing the effect on the equilibrium values of one or more endogenous variables.

A change in an exogenous variable causes the supply curve or the demand curve or both to shift, and the market equilibrium to change. **Comparative statics** is the process of changing a single exogenous variable and observing the effect on the equilibrium values of one or more endogenous variables. The term "comparative statics" comes from the fact that after an equilibrium changes, we find ourselves comparing two situations of stasis— the new equilibrium and the old one.

COMMON ERROR 2.1   Confusing a Shift in the Supply Curve with a Change in Quantity Supplied

Students often confuse a shift in the supply curve with a change in quantity supplied or a shift in the demand curve with a change in quantity demanded. The term "supply" refers to the entire supply curve relationship. For example, consider the market for lobsters. In the graph, suppose the supply curve for lobsters is $S_{correct}$, and because of a recession, consumers' incomes decline, causing a decrease in the demand for lobsters from D_1 to D_2. The decrease in the demand for lobsters results in a decrease in the price of lobsters from p_1 to p_2 and a decrease in the *quantity supplied* of lobsters from q_1 to q_2. However, there is *no change* in the supply curve of lobsters.

Many students mistakenly reason as follows: The decrease in demand for lobsters causes a decrease in the price of lobsters, and this decrease in price in turn causes a decrease in supply and a leftward shift in the supply curve for lobsters to the light red supply curve S_{wrong}. These students incorrectly believe that a decrease in price shifts the supply curve to the left. However, supply curves are drawn on the assumption that all *other things except price remain the same*, and therefore, a change in the price of a good by itself only results in a movement along the supply curve.

One way to prevent this confusion is to remember that the term "supply" refers to the entire supply curve relationship. Only factors that change this entire relationship—the prices of inputs, the prices of alternative goods, technology, and expectations—cause a shift in the supply curve. A change in the price of the good by itself causes a movement along the supply curve and a change in quantity supplied, not a new supply curve.

Common Error Figure 2.1 If the supply curve for lobsters is $S_{correct}$, a decrease in the demand for lobsters from D_1 to D_2 results in a decrease in the price of lobsters from p_1 to p_2 and a decrease in the *quantity supplied* of lobsters from q_1 to q_2. However, there is no change in the supply curve of lobsters. Do not make the mistake of shifting the supply curve to S_{wrong}.

Let us conduct a comparative statics experiment by observing what happens to the equilibrium in the silver market when there is a change in the incomes of buyers. Figure 2.4(a) begins with equilibrium at point A, where the supply and demand curves intersect at price p_1 and quantity q_1. Because silver is a normal good, when buyers' incomes increase, the demand curve shifts to the right to D_2. The new equilibrium is at point B, with price p_2 and quantity q_2. The generalized results of this comparative statics experiment are: *an increase in buyers' incomes causes an increase in the equilibrium price of a good, and an increase in equilibrium quantity as well.*

Figure 2.4(b) illustrates another comparative statics experiment. Here, the price of a chemical used in the process of refining silver increases, causing the supply curve to shift leftward to S_2. The equilibrium price rises from p_1 to p_2, and the equilibrium quantity falls from q_1 to q_2. This comparative statics experiment shows that *a rise in the price of an input will cause the equilibrium price of a good to rise, and the equilibrium quantity to fall.*

Figure 2.4 An Increase in Buyers' Incomes, an Increase in the Price of an Input, or a Decrease in the Price of a Good that is Both a Substitute and an Alternative Good

In panel (a), equilibrium is initially at point A. When buyers' incomes increase, the demand curve shifts to the right to D_2, and the new equilibrium is at point B, with price p_2 and quantity q_2. In panel (b), equilibrium is initially at point A. An increase in the price of an input causes the supply curve to shift to the left to S_2, and the new equilibrium is at point B with price p_2 and quantity q_2. In panel (c), a decrease in the price of gold, which is both a substitute good in consumption for silver and an alternative production good for mining companies, simultaneously shifts the supply curve for silver to the right and the demand curve for silver to the left. Here, the result is a lower equilibrium price for silver and a lower equilibrium quantity as well.

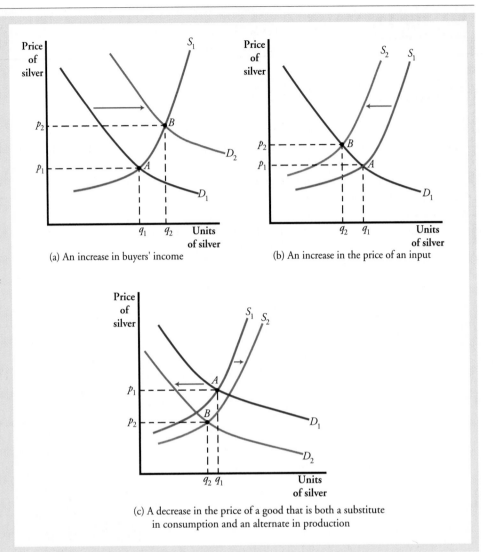

(a) An increase in buyers' income

(b) An increase in the price of an input

(c) A decrease in the price of a good that is both a substitute in consumption and an alternate in production

Finally, Figure 2.4(c) illustrates the case of a decrease in the price of gold, which is both a substitute good in consumption for silver and an alternative production good for mining companies. In this case, the supply curve shifts right and the demand curve shifts left. The result is a lower equilibrium price for silver, and, in the case shown here, a lower equilibrium quantity as well. Note, however, that if the supply curve is shifted farther to the right, the equilibrium quantity of silver might have increased or stayed constant. Thus, *a drop in the price of a good that is both a substitute in consumption and an alternative in production will decrease the equilibrium price of a good, and have an indeterminate effect on equilibrium quantity.*

It is possible to make the following general conclusion. Whenever some exogenous variable(s) changes that results in a simultaneous shift in *both* the supply and demand curves, it is always possible to determine the change in *either* price or quantity, but *not* the change in *both* price and quantity. For example, if *both* supply and demand increased, then the equilibrium quantity must increase, but the equilibrium price could increase, decrease, or remain constant, depending on the relative size of the shifts in supply and demand. Similarly, if supply decreased and demand increased, then the equilibrium price must increase, but the equilibrium quantity could increase, decrease, or remain constant, depending on the relative size of the shifts in supply and demand.

2.4 Government Intervention

We have seen how supply and demand work to determine equilibrium prices and quantities in a variety of markets. But sometimes governments and the constituents they represent find themselves dissatisfied with the market equilibrium, and attempt to interfere with the supply and demand mechanism in order to change it. For example, a government might view a particular good's price as too high, because many citizens are unable to afford it. Or it may view a particular price as too low, because suppliers of the good are unable to earn sufficient incomes by selling it. This section explores two common types of government market intervention: price ceilings and price floors.

Price Ceilings

price ceiling

A maximum legal price for a good established by a government.

When a government wants to keep a price low, the most straightforward procedure is to establish a **price ceiling**, or maximum legal price for a good. In Figure 2.5(a), when the price ceiling is set at p_{max}, quantity demanded is q_2 and quantity supplied is q_1, so there is an excess demand of $q_2 - q_1$. Ordinarily, the excess demand would drive the price up to p_e, but if the price ceiling is successfully enforced, the price will remain at p_{max}. What

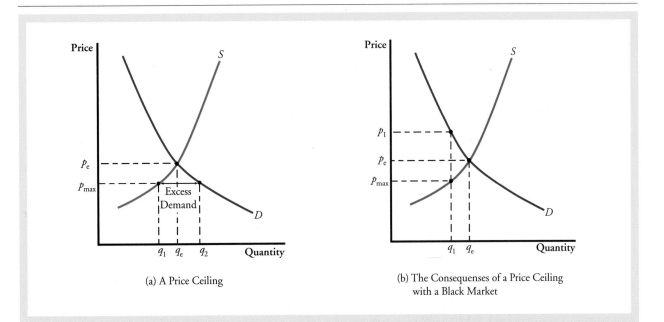

(a) A Price Ceiling

(b) The Consequenses of a Price Ceiling with a Black Market

Figure 2.5 A Price Ceiling and the Consequences of a Price Ceiling with a Black Market
In panel (a), if there is an effectively enforced price ceiling set at p_{max}, quantity demanded is q_2 and quantity supplied is q_1, so there is an excess demand of $q_2 - q_1$. In the extreme case shown in panel (b), where arbitrageurs buy up all q_1 units of the good available in the legal market and offer it for sale in the black market, the price in the black market increases to p_1 because at price p_1 buyers would buy the quantity q_1. After the imposition of a price ceiling, the price paid by all buyers except arbitrageurs rises from p_e to p_1, while the quantity purchased falls from q_e to q_1.

happens next is determined by a simple rule of markets: *when quantity supplied and quantity demanded are unequal, the lesser of the two determines the quantity actually exchanged.* This rule of markets follows from the voluntary nature of market exchanges. If quantity demanded is less than quantity supplied, demand prevails, because buyers cannot be forced to buy more than they want to. In the case of a price ceiling, however, it is the other way around: quantity supplied is less than quantity demanded. In this case, supply prevails, since sellers cannot be forced to supply more than they want to.

It follows immediately from this rule of markets that price ceilings, when they are effective, result in shortages and queuing. Because supply falls short of demand, goods disappear from store shelves long before demand is exhausted. As a consequence, people must get to the store early in order to ensure that the goods will still be there, and this accounts for the characteristic long lines that always seem to accompany price ceilings. For example, Application 2.4A shows that in the former Soviet Union, the prices of basic commodities such as meat and bread were kept far below the equilibrium prices and con-

▲▲▲ 2.4A APPLICATION Price Reform in Eastern Europe

We have seen how price ceilings lead to shortages, and how shortages lead to long lines and black markets where goods are sold at higher prices. For much of the 20th century, price ceilings were a routine part of life for millions of people in Eastern Europe and the former Soviet Union. In these nations, quantities and prices were set by central planning boards. For reasons of social policy, the prices of most goods were set too low; that is, at the official price, quantity demanded exceeded quantity supplied. In this sense, the official prices functioned very much like price ceilings in a market economy. Moreover, if there were a sudden increase in demand for some good, such as heating oil during an unusually cold winter, the price would not be permitted to rise, and the shortage would worsen.

In some cases, arbitrageurs would buy up scarce goods and sell them on the black market at high prices. But because extreme legal efforts were taken in these countries to suppress black-market activity, shortages manifested themselves in the classic long lines of weary shoppers waiting patiently, sometimes for hours, just to buy a loaf of bread.

The graph illustrates the situation in many typical East European markets. The supply curve is the perfectly inelastic vertical line, because no matter what the price, the quantity for sale would always remain at whatever quantity enterprises were ordered to produce by the central planning authority. Buyers, however, behaved according to the law of demand: *ceteris paribus*, the lower the price, the more they wanted to buy. Initially, the

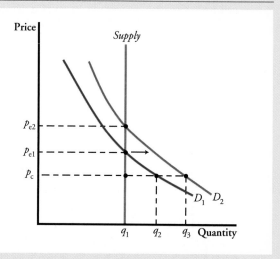

Application Figure 2.4A A Typical Market in Eastern Europe Prior to Price Reforms
In the typical East European market before price reforms, the supply curve for many goods was perfectly inelastic. Initially, the demand curve is D_1 and there is an excess demand, so consumers waited in long lines to get the available goods. As a result, the typical Eastern European family had more income than it could spend, and this increased income increased demand from D_1 to D_2, which made the shortages worse. After the demand shift, the price would have to rise to p_{e2} to clear the market.

demand curve is at D_1. If the government were to let the price float freely, it would rise to p_{e1}. At the official price, however, the characteristic shortage associated with price

(continued)

ceilings is shown, with buyers wanting to purchase q_2 but only able to buy q_1.

Because the markets for many goods were characterized by shortages of this type, the typical Eastern European family found itself in an ironic situation: it had more income than it could spend! As a result, households accumulated unspent cash, and by the 1980s, most households had stored up cash equal to several years' income. An increase in income tends to shift the market demand curve for any normal good rightward as depicted in the graph by the increase in demand from D_1 to D_2. This increase in demand exacerbates the shortage, since quantity demanded increases to q_3, but

quantity available remains constant at q_1. The demand shift also raises the price that must be reached in order to eliminate the shortage. Now, the price would have to rise to p_{e2}. By the 1990s, when these nations were ready for economic reform, their new leaders inherited an unpleasant legacy: households were awash in cash, and shortages were rampant. Keeping prices fixed meant continuing shortages; but freeing prices meant temporary hyperinflation, which threatened the reform process itself and the newly democratic government. In most cases, these new leaders had no choice but to let the prices rise and suffer the economic and political consequences.

sumers were forced to wait in long lines to attempt to purchase these goods. Despite these long waits, many Soviet consumers came away empty-handed. Another common example in the United States is the pricing of tickets to major rock concerts below the equilibrium level. Fans line up at ticket windows in advance to purchase tickets, and many fans go home disappointed because they were too far back in the line to get tickets.

The last paragraph noted that price ceilings result in shortages when they are effective. Price ceilings, however, are not always effective. Even though it may be illegal to charge more than p_{max}, there are usually enough individuals willing to break the law to create a thriving **black market** in which the goods are sold illegally in violation of the price ceiling law. In black markets, goods are sold according to the laws of supply and demand instead of the laws of the state. Often, those who sell goods in the black market obtain them in the legal market at the price p_{max}. Indeed, many of those waiting in line in the legal market are buying not for their own use, but rather to resell at the higher black-market price. People who buy a good at low prices and then resell them at higher prices are **arbitrageurs**. Arbitrageurs often serve a very important positive function in markets. In a black market, however, the arbitrageurs are serving an illegal function. Figure 2.5(b) shows what can happen in the extreme case where arbitrageurs buy up all of the good available in the legal market and offer it for sale in the black market.

In the face of the price ceiling, our rule of markets tells us that the quantity of the good available will be q_1. When arbitrageurs buy up this entire quantity and illegally offer it for sale, how much will they be able to charge? The answer is p_1, because according to our demand curve, at that price buyers would buy the quantity q_1. And here is one of the ironies of price ceilings: instead of bringing about a lower price as originally intended, the price ceiling may actually result in a higher price for buyers. In Figure 2.5(b), after the imposition of a price ceiling, the price paid by all buyers (other than arbitrageurs) rises from p_e to p_1, while the quantity purchased falls from q_e to q_1. Ironically, the very people the government tried to aid with the price ceiling have been hurt by it instead.

black market

A market in which goods are sold illegally in violation of a price ceiling law.

arbitrageurs

Economic intermediaries who buy a good at a low price in hopes of reselling it at a higher price.

price floor

A minimum legal price for a good established by a government.

Price Floors

In the United States and many West European nations, governments attempt to maintain high incomes for farmers by establishing a **price floor**, a minimum price below which

Figure 2.6
A Price Floor
If the price floor is set at p_{min} above the equilibrium price p_e, the excess supply equals $q_2 - q_1$.

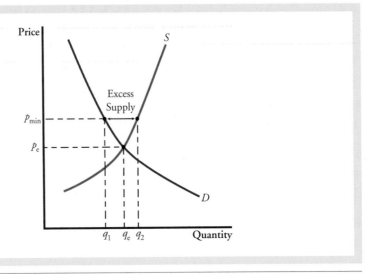

the government will not allow the price to drop. Another important example of a price floor is the establishment of a minimum wage for workers.

In Figure 2.6, the equilibrium price is p_e, but the price floor is set higher at p_{min}. At this price, the excess supply, equal to the distance $q_2 - q_1$, would ordinarily cause the price to decline. To maintain the price floor, a government must do one or more of the following things: (1) enforce the price floor, with credible threats to penalize those caught selling at a price below the floor; (2) shift the market demand rightward, by advertising the good or issuing special coupons for buying the good (like food stamps); (3) shift the market supply of the good leftward, by limiting imports or restricting domestic production; or (4) take the excess supply out of the market by purchasing it directly. In efforts to support the incomes of farmers, authorities in market economies regularly pursue policies 2, 3, and 4. Application 2.4B discusses one example of this kind of intervention in the United States.

▲▲▲ 2.4B APPLICATION   How the U.S. Government Keeps Milk Prices High

Since the 1930s, the United States Department of Agriculture (USDA) has used a variety of methods to maintain a price floor for milk and milk products above their equilibrium prices. By the 1980s, several methods were being used simultaneously. Imports of powdered milk, butter, and cheese were limited. The USDA each year bought several billion dollars worth of butter, cheese, and powdered milk directly. And when these efforts proved insufficient, the government began paying dairy farmers not to produce milk. A part of this effort was the "Dairy Termination Program," in which dairy farmers were paid if they slaughtered their cattle and

promised to stay out of the dairy business for five years. In fiscal year 1983, the government purchased 16.8 billion pounds of milk at a total cost of $2.5 billion, and during 1986–87, over 12.2 billion pounds were purchased at a cost of $1.8 billion. These programs significantly raised the price of milk and all other dairy products for American consumers.

In 1996, Congress passed the Agriculture Improvement and Reform Act in an attempt to reduce the problems associated with milk price supports. The new system consolidated 31 milk regulations into just 11 and reduced some of the wide disparity in regional price

(continued)

supports that discriminated against midwestern farmers. Under the new system, however, a farmer in Eau Claire, Wisconsin is guaranteed an extra $1.70 per hundred pounds of milk, while farmers in Knoxville, Tennessee are guaranteed $2.80, and farmers in Miami receive $4.30. The 1996 law also permitted New England farmers to fix the price of milk through a northeast dairy compact. As a result, the average retail price of a gallon of milk increased from $2.28 in 1995 to almost $3.00 in 1999. It was estimated that the 1996 law was still costing consumers billions of dollars in increased milk prices.

Note that the total cost of a price floor is generally greater than just the additional amount spent on a good. In the case of milk, health experts have expressed concerns that because of higher milk prices, households consume less milk than they otherwise would. Imperfect substitutes, like fruit juices and soft drinks, have been used instead. These experts are concerned that the higher price of milk has exacerbated the problem of calcium deficiency among children and elderly women. The resulting health problems (and the medical expenses to treat them) represent yet another cost of the milk price floors.

2.5 The Elasticity of Demand

elasticity

The percentage change in one variable associated with a one percent change in another variable.

price elasticity of demand

The percentage change in the quantity demanded of a good associated with a one percent change in the good's own price.

Sometimes it is not enough to know that an increase in one variable causes an increase or decrease in some other variable. For many purposes, it is necessary to know precisely *how much* one variable changes in response to another. For example, if the government wished to increase the minimum wage by 10 percent, it is extremely important to know how much the quantity demanded for minimum-wage workers will decrease as a result. For this type of analysis, economists use a measure called **elasticity**, which is calculated as the percentage change in one variable associated with a one percent change in another.

The elasticity most commonly used by economists is the **price elasticity of demand**, which measures the *percentage* change in the quantity demanded associated with a *one percent* change in price. The elasticity tells us how sensitive quantity demanded is to changes in a good's own price. The price elasticity of demand is represented by the symbol ε_p and defined mathematically as follows:

$$\varepsilon_p = -\frac{\%\Delta q_d}{\%\Delta p} \tag{2.1}$$

where q_d is the quantity of the good demanded, p is its price, and the Greek letter Δ (delta) stands for the change in a variable. Therefore, Δq_d represents the change in the quantity demanded and Δp represents the change in price.

Notice the minus sign in the formula. Without it, price elasticity of demand would almost always be negative, since price and quantity demanded almost always change in opposite directions. There is nothing wrong with a negative elasticity; indeed, many of the elasticities economists use often have negative values. However, since price elasticity is used so often, and since negative numbers sometimes create confusion when stating that one number is "larger" or "smaller" than another, most economists include the minus sign in the formula to convert the price elasticity of demand into a positive number. With this convention in mind, *the larger the price elasticity, the more sensitive the quantity demanded is to price.*

elastic

Refers to goods whose quantities demanded are sensitive to price changes; specifically, any market demand where a one percent change in price results in more than a one percent change in quantity demanded.

Price elasticity is used to classify goods according to their price sensitivity. If the quantity of a good demanded changes by a larger percentage than its price, the good is classified as price-sensitive. According to Equation 2.1, such goods will have $\varepsilon_p > 1$ and the demand for these goods is called **elastic**. If quantity demanded changes by a smaller

inelastic

Refers to goods whose quantities demanded are insensitive to price changes; specifically, any market demand where a one percent change in price results in less than a one percent change in quantity demanded.

unit elastic
or **unitary elastic**

Refers to any market demand where a one percent change in price results in a one percent change in quantity demanded.

percentage than price, the good is relatively insensitive to price changes. Such goods will have $\varepsilon_p < 1$ and the demand for these goods is called **inelastic**. Finally, if both price and quantity demanded change by the same percentage, then $\varepsilon_p = 1$. The demand for such goods is called **unit elastic** or **unitary elastic**.

Point Elasticity for a Linear Demand Curve

To simplify their analysis, it is quite common for economists to assume that demand curves are linear, and therefore, it is useful to be able to identify the elasticity of demand at any point on a linear demand curve. Fortunately, the exact value of the elasticity of demand at any point on a linear demand curve can be calculated using algebra.

Suppose the demand curve for silver depicted in Figure 2.7 is:

$$p_s = 100 - 2q_s$$

From Equation 2.1, the elasticity of demand for silver is:

$$\varepsilon_p = -\frac{\%\Delta q_s}{\%\Delta p_s} = -\frac{\dfrac{\Delta q_s}{q_s}}{\dfrac{\Delta p_s}{p_s}} = -\frac{\Delta q_s p_s}{\Delta p_s q_s} \tag{2.2}$$

The demand curve in Figure 2.7 has a constant slope $\Delta p_s/\Delta q_s$ equal to -2. The first term on the right-hand side of Equation 2.2 is the inverse of the slope of the demand curve, and therefore $\Delta q_s/\Delta p_s = -(1/2)$. This term remains constant along the entire demand curve in Figure 2.7. The value of ε_p can be determined by multiplying -1 times the inverse of the slope of the demand curve, which yields $-(\Delta q_s/\Delta p_s) = -(-1/2) = 1/2$, by the ratio of p_s/q_s. This calculation gives a precise measure of the elasticity of demand at any point on the

---

Figure 2.7 The Elasticity of Demand for a Linear Demand Curve

For any linear demand curve, demand is unit elastic at the midpoint, elastic above the midpoint, and inelastic below the midpoint. In this case, $\varepsilon_p = 1$ at point C; $\varepsilon_p > 1$ at all the dark-blue points; and $\varepsilon_p < 1$ at all the light-blue points.

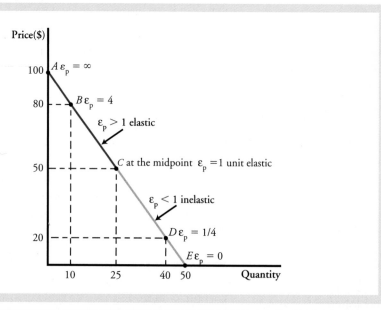

linear demand curve $p_s = 100 - 2q_s$. Moving down the demand curve from point A to point E, the ratio p_s/q_s decreases continuously, so ε_p decreases continuously as well.

Consider the elasticity at the points A and B in Figure 2.7. At point A, $p_s/q_s = 100/0 = \infty$, so demand is infinitely elastic. At point B, $p_s/q_s = 80/10 = 8$, so $\varepsilon_p = (1/2)(8) = 4$. At the midpoint C, $p_s/q_s = 50/25 = 2$, so $\varepsilon_p = (1/2)(2) = 1$. At the midpoint of any linear demand curve, p/q equals the absolute value of the slope of the demand curve.[2] Furthermore, from Equation 2.2, ε_p equals the absolute value of the inverse of the slope multiplied by p/q. At the midpoint, ε_p equals the absolute value of the inverse of the slope multiplied by the slope, and therefore, $\varepsilon_p = 1$. A linear demand curve is unit elastic at the midpoint; and because ε_p decreases continuously as we move down the demand curve, $\varepsilon_p < 1$ for all points below the midpoint, and $\varepsilon_p > 1$ for all points above the midpoint.

At point D, $p_s/q_s = 20/40 = 1/2$, so $\varepsilon_p = (1/2)(1/2) = 1/4$. Finally, at point E, $p_s/q_s = 0/50 = 0$, so $\varepsilon_p = (1/2)(0) = 0$. Notice that because the ratio p/q varies at every point on a linear demand curve, the elasticity of demand also varies at every point.

Summarizing the important implications of Equation 2.2, for any linear demand curve:

1. The elasticity of demand varies from ∞ at the price intercept to 0 at the quantity intercept.
2. The elasticity of demand at the midpoint equals 1.
3. The demand curve is elastic above the midpoint; that is, $\varepsilon_p > 1$.
4. The demand curve is inelastic below the midpoint; that is, $\varepsilon_p < 1$.

Given the equation of any linear demand curve, you should now be able to identify the precise elasticity of demand at any point.

Arc Elasticity

Suppose the demand curve is non-linear, or that only two points on the demand curve are known and nothing is known about the shape of the demand curve between these two points. In such cases, it is impossible to use the point elasticity of demand, because using the point elasticity would yield two different measures of elasticity, depending on which of the two points was used as the base point for calculating percentage changes in quantity demanded and price. Instead, the elasticity of demand must be estimated using a measure called the **arc elasticity of demand**. In calculating the arc elasticity of demand, the percentage changes in quantity and price are obtained by dividing the change in each variable by a value midway between the two points. By doing so, it is possible to avoid having to make a choice between which of the two points to use as the base point in calculating the elasticity.

The formula for the arc elasticity of demand between any two points (q_1, p_1) and (q_2, p_2) is:

arc elasticity of demand

A measure used to calculate the elasticity of demand between two points on a demand curve by dividing the change in quantity by the average of the two quantities and the change in price by the average of the two prices.

$$\varepsilon_p = -\frac{\%\Delta q}{\%\Delta p} = -\left(\frac{\dfrac{\Delta q}{q_1 + q_2}}{\dfrac{\Delta p}{p_1 + p_2}} \right) = -\left(\frac{\Delta q}{\Delta p} \right)\left(\frac{p_1 + p_2}{q_1 + q_2} \right) \tag{2.3}$$

[2] For any linear demand curve $p = a - bq$, the price intercept is a, and the quantity intercept is a/b. Therefore, at the midpoint, price equals $a/2$, and quantity equals $a/2b$; the ratio of $p/q = (a/2)/(a/2b) = b$.

For example, suppose only two points on a demand curve are known: point 1 is $(q_1 = 5, p_1 = 7)$ and point 2 is $(q_2 = 7, p_2 = 3)$. The arc elasticity between these two points is:

$$\varepsilon_p = -\left(\frac{\Delta q}{\Delta p}\right)\frac{p_1 + p_2}{q_1 + q_2} = -\frac{2}{-4}\frac{10}{12} = \frac{20}{48} = \frac{5}{12}$$

In this case, because $\varepsilon_p < 1$, demand is inelastic between these two points.

Elasticity and Total Expenditures

Suppose the supply curve for silver shifts to the right, and the equilibrium price of silver decreases from p_1 to p_2, as shown in Figure 2.8. The quantity of silver produced increases from q_1 to q_2. As a result of this shift in supply, will buyers spend more or less on silver?

On one hand, because more silver is purchased, consumers might spend more on it. On the other hand, each ounce of silver costs less than before, so perhaps less will be spent. It turns out that the crucial piece of information needed to answer this question is the price elasticity of demand for silver.

total expenditures

Total expenditures on any good or service are calculated by taking the product of the price and the quantity purchased.

To see why, note that the **total expenditures** (TE) on any good are given by the product of its price p and quantity purchased q: TE $= pq$. For example, in Figure 2.8, if quantity increases from q_1 to q_2, total spending on silver goes from $p_1 q_1$ to $p_2 q_2$. This change in total expenditures can be represented as:

$$\Delta \text{TE} = (q_2 - q_1)p_2 + (p_2 - p_1)q_1 = (\Delta q)p_2 + (\Delta p)q_1 \qquad (2.4)$$

If the change in quantity, Δq, is very small, the subscripts can be dropped, and the change in total expenditures can be represented as:

$$\Delta \text{TE} = (\Delta q)p + (\Delta p)q \qquad (2.5)$$

Figure 2.8 Elasticity and Total Expenditure
As output increases from q_1 to q_2, the red shaded area equal to $q_1(\Delta p)$ represents a loss in revenue because of the price decrease, and the green shaded area equal to $p_2(\Delta q)$ represents a gain in revenue because of the increase in quantity sold. If the red area is greater than the green area, total revenues decrease as quantity increases, and demand is inelastic. If the red area is smaller than the green area, total revenues increase as quantity increases, and demand is elastic. If the red area equals the green area, demand is unit elastic.

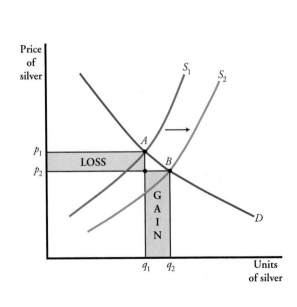

As quantity increases, $\Delta q > 0$, but $\Delta p < 0$. Therefore, as quantity increases, the first term on the right-hand side of Equation 2.5 is positive and the second term is negative.

Recall from Equation 2.1 that:

$$\varepsilon_{\mathrm{p}} = -\frac{(\Delta q)p}{(\Delta p)q} \tag{2.6}$$

The first term on the right-hand side of Equation 2.5, $(\Delta q)p$, is simply the numerator in Equation 2.6, and the second term, $(\Delta p)q$, is the denominator. Suppose that the positive first term in Equation 2.5 is greater than the negative second term. Then for $\Delta q > 0$, $(\Delta q)p > (\Delta p)q$, and $\Delta TE > 0$; so total expenditures increase. By logical extension, if the positive first term in Equation 2.5 is greater than the negative second term, the numerator in Equation 2.6 must be greater than the denominator, so $\varepsilon_{\mathrm{p}} > 1$, and demand must be elastic. To summarize, *if as the quantity demanded of a good increases (that is, $\Delta q > 0$) total expenditures also increase, then demand must be elastic.*

Similarly, if for $\Delta q > 0$, the positive first term in Equation 2.5 is less than the negative second term, then when quantity increases, $\Delta TE < 0$, and total expenditures decrease. In this case, the numerator in Equation 2.6 must be smaller than the denominator, $\varepsilon_{\mathrm{p}} < 1$, and demand must be inelastic. To summarize, *if as the quantity demanded of a good increases (that is, $\Delta q > 0$) total expenditures decrease, demand must be inelastic.*

Finally, if the positive first term in Equation 2.5 equals the negative second term, then when quantity increases, $\Delta TE = 0$, and total expenditures remain constant. In this case, the numerator in Equation 2.5 must equal the denominator, $\varepsilon_{\mathrm{p}} = 1$, and demand must be unit elastic. To summarize, *if as the quantity demanded of a good increases (that is, $\Delta q > 0$) total expenditures remain constant, then demand must be unit elastic.*

Another method of identifying whether demand is elastic, inelastic, or unit elastic, therefore, is to observe what happens to total expenditures as the quantity demanded of the good increases (or the price decreases). If as quantity demanded increases (or price decreases) total expenditures increase, demand is elastic. The corollaries to these three relationships are: If as quantity demanded decreases (or price increases) total expenditures decrease, demand is elastic. If as quantity demanded decreases (or price increases) total expenditures increase, demand is inelastic. If as quantity demanded decreases (or price increases) total expenditures remain constant, demand is unit elastic. Table 2.1 summarizes the relationship between elasticity and total expenditure.

What Determines the Elasticity of Demand?

Information about demand elasticities is valuable to managers, entrepreneurs, government officials, and economists. This is why millions of dollars are spent each year on

Table 2.1   Elasticity and Total Expenditure

	If $\varepsilon_{\mathrm{p}} > 1$ – Demand is Elastic	If $\varepsilon_{\mathrm{p}} < 1$ – Demand is Inelastic	If $\varepsilon_{\mathrm{p}} = 1$ – Demand is Unit Elastic
A price increase causes total expenditures to:	Decrease	Increase	Remain constant
A price decrease causes total expenditures to:	Increase	Decrease	Remain constant

▲▲▲ **2.5 APPLICATION**   The War on Drugs Versus the War on Crime

The United States and other Western nations spend billions of dollars each year to interdict supplies of illegal drugs, and billions more fighting crime against property and people. Yet the war on drugs and the war on crime may in some ways be competing with each other. Panel (a) in the graph shows the impact of a successful increase in drug interdiction by the government.

Before the increase in interdiction activities, the market for illegal drugs reaches equilibrium at point A, with equilibrium price p_1 and quantity q_1. Now, if significant increases occur in the quantity of illegal drugs confiscated as they enter the country, the supply curve shifts leftward, because a smaller quantity will be offered for sale at each price. The previous equilibrium price was p_1, but the new equilibrium price increases to p_2. The impact of interdiction is an increase in the price of drugs, and a decrease in the quantity purchased.

But what happens to total spending on drugs by users? That depends entirely on the price elasticity of demand. If, as economic studies suggest, the demand for illegal drugs is inelastic, then the price increase will cause total spending to increase as well. Because a high proportion of crimes can be traced to drug users who need money to support their habits, an increase in total spending on drugs suggests that more and/or bigger crimes will be committed by users to feed their habits.

Another drug-crime connection should also be noted: interdiction efforts, by raising total spending on drugs, increase the potential profits of those willing and able to break the law by selling drugs. As a consequence, drug territory—the exclusive rights to sell in an area—becomes more valuable, and more violence is needed to secure it.

For this and other reasons, a number of prominent economists, including Nobel Prize winners Milton Friedman and Lester Thurow and the former U.S. Secretary of State George Schulz, have suggested that the United States consider legalizing many currently illegal drugs. According to Friedman, "Legalizing drugs would

(a) Impact of Drug Interdiction

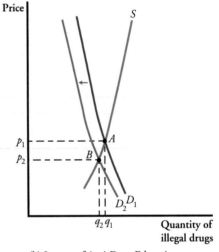

(b) Impact of Anti-Drug Education

Application Figure 2.5 The Impact of Drug Interdiction Compared to Anti-Drug Education
In panel (a), before the increase in interdiction activities, the market for illegal drugs is in equilibrium at point A. If more drugs are confiscated, the supply curve shifts leftward and the new equilibrium is at point B. As a result, price increases from p_1 to p_2. Because the demand for illegal drugs is inelastic, total spending on drugs will increase, and to support their drug habits, users will have to commit more and/or bigger crimes. In panel (b), a successful anti-drug education campaign decreases the demand for drugs. As a result, the price and quantity supplied of drugs both decrease and total expenditures decrease as well. In this case, drug-related crimes should decrease.

(continued)

reduce enormously the number of victims of drug use who are not addicts: people who are mugged, people who are corrupted, the reduction of law and order because of the corruption of law enforcement, and the allocation of a very large fraction of law enforcement resources to this one particular activity."*

Others have taken a less radical approach, recommending that the United States government shift the emphasis of anti-drug policies away from interdiction toward education and publicity. Panel (b) shows the impact of a successful anti-drug education campaign that decreases the demand for drugs at any given price. In this case, it is the demand curve that shifts. As a result, the drop in the quantity of drugs purchased is accompanied by a lower price. Total expenditures decrease, and drug-related crimes should decrease as well.

*Milton Friedman, "Stop Taxing Non-Addicts," *Reason Magazine*, October 1988.

research to determine the price elasticities of demand for different goods. But some important conclusions about elasticities can be obtained without actually gathering data.

In general, demand should be more elastic (more sensitive to price changes) if a good has one or more close substitutes. For example, oranges have several close substitutes, among them tangerines and grapefruits. If the price of oranges rises by 10 percent, *ceteris paribus*, we expect a relatively large decrease in quantity demanded as buyers switch to these substitutes. Thus, oranges should have a relatively large elasticity of demand. Wheat flour, on the other hand, has no close substitutes, given the tastes and diet patterns of the general public. We expect wheat flour to be less price-sensitive, and to have a relatively small elasticity of demand.

Whether a good does or does not have close substitutes depends to a large extent on how narrowly the market for the good is defined. The elasticity of demand for lettuce would be relatively small, because lettuce is such a basic salad ingredient that it is difficult to make salads without it. The elasticity of demand for red-leaf lettuce, however, should be relatively large, because a rise in its price, *ceteris paribus*, would lead consumers to switch to close substitutes such as green-leaf lettuce, Boston lettuce, or romaine lettuce. Indeed, if the market is defined even narrower as red-leaf lettuce grown in California, there is an even closer substitute: red-leaf lettuce grown anywhere else. In general, *the narrower the definition of the market for the good, the higher the elasticity of demand.*

The elasticity of demand is also affected by whether a good is a necessity or a luxury. Necessities have smaller price elasticities than luxuries. Consider the elasticity of demand for a necessity such as blood plasma. Blood plasma will have a very inelastic demand, because it is so important for individuals who need it that it is almost true that "price is no object." Few patients about to be wheeled into an operating room bother to ask the hospital, "By the way, what is the price of blood plasma today?" On the other hand, a luxury good such as boat cruises will have a highly elastic demand, because consumers will be very sensitive to price in deciding whether to take a cruise. Note that for both blood plasma and boat cruises, the number of substitutes also plays an important role in determining the elasticity of demand. Blood plasma has no close substitutes, while the number of substitutes for boat cruises is very large and includes airline flights to the same or alternative destinations, car travel to a vacation resort, or even staying home and building a swimming pool.

Another determinant of demand elasticity is the length of time that elapses after the price change, before the change in quantity demanded is measured. In general, *the longer the time interval, the greater the elasticity,* largely because buyers usually need time to adjust to a price change. Consider what happened in 1973–74 when OPEC quadrupled the price of a barrel of oil in just six short months following a Middle Eastern war. In the short run, consumers were stuck with their gas-guzzling cars and inefficient home heating systems, and businesses were stuck with their high-energy-consuming plants and equipment. Few consumers could afford to replace their cars and heating systems in response to the increase in the price of oil, and few businesses could replace their manufacturing plants and equipment, so the short-run demand for oil was highly inelastic. In the long run, however, consumers switched to much more fuel-efficient cars, many coming from Japan and Europe, and manufacturing plants switched to much more energy-efficient means of production. Furthermore, many consumers insulated their houses and switched to wood stoves to heat their homes. As a result, the demand for oil proved to be far more elastic in the long run than the short run.

This example shows why economists distinguish between a long-run elasticity and a short-run elasticity. Short-run elasticities generally measure the quantity response that occurs within a short period of time; say, a few months or a year after a price change, whereas long-run elasticities measure the quantity response after one, two, or even more years have elapsed. In one famous study, Houthakker and Taylor estimated both short-run and long-run elasticities for many consumer goods. Table 2.2 presents a number of their estimates. Notice that the long-run elasticities are consistently much larger than their short-run counterparts.

Another determinant of the elasticity of demand is the importance of the good in a buyer's budget. Other things being equal, the greater the portion of one's total budget spent on a good, the greater the elasticity of demand. Changing our buying patterns takes time and trouble, and is only worthwhile when our budget will be affected in some significant way. If automobiles were to double in price, we would expect a very large decline in quantity demanded, in part because the price change would have a major impact on our budgets. But if table salt doubled in price, hardly anyone would notice, because most people spend less than a dollar a year on table salt.

Some economists contend that the importance of a good in the consumer's budget is not a valid determinant of the elasticity of demand, and there is some technical truth to

Table 2.2 Some Short-Run and Long-Run Elasticities

Market	Short-Run Elasticity	Long-Run Elasticity
Alcohol	0.92	3.63
Local Bus Travel	0.77	3.54
International Air Travel	0.70	4.00
Natural Gas	0.15	10.74
Electricity (residential)	0.13	1.90
Newspapers	0.10	0.52
Radio and Television Repair	0.47	3.84
Fresh Salmon	2.47	
Cigarettes	0.23	
Chicken	1.67	
Gasoline	0.50	
Airline Vacation Travel	1.90	
Airline Business Travel	0.80	

this position. For example, if an item is the only item in a consumer's budget, then according to this argument, the price elasticity of demand for that item should be very high, because it takes up 100 percent of the consumer's spending. However, the actual elasticity of such a good must equal 1; that is, it must be unit elastic, because no matter what the price of the good, the consumer's total expenditures on the good are constant. This is, of course, an extreme case, and in most instances it is useful to recognize that as the importance of a good in a consumer's budget increases, so will the elasticity of demand.

Some Special Cases of Elasticity

Figure 2.9 shows three different demand curves, each illustrating a special case of price elasticity of demand. In panel (a), the demand curve is vertical, signifying that quantity demanded is the same at every price. In this case, price changes cause absolutely no change in quantity demanded. Using our formulas for either point or arc elasticity, the price elasticity of demand at every point or interval along this demand curve will be zero, and the demand for such a good is called **perfectly inelastic**. The demand for insulin, used by diabetics to control their blood sugar, might be perfectly inelastic over some price range, because it is needed for survival, and there are no substitutes.

In panel (b), the demand curve is horizontal. Here, even the tiniest change in price causes a huge quantity response, and in this case, demand is called **perfectly elastic**. When a good has perfect substitutes, it is likely to be characterized by perfectly elastic demand. The demand for the wheat produced by Farmer Smith, for example, is likely to be perfectly elastic, because wheat produced at other farms is a perfect substitute for Farmer Smith's wheat.

Finally, in panel (c), a demand curve is shown where elasticity is the same at every point. Such demand curves are often assumed in statistical work, so it is interesting to see what such curves look like. **Constant elasticity demand curves** have the general form:

$$q = bp^{-k} = \frac{b}{p^k} \qquad (2.7)$$

perfectly inelastic

Refers to a good with an elasticity of demand equal to zero that has a vertical demand curve.

perfectly elastic

Refers to a good with an elasticity of demand that is mathematically undefined (equal to infinity) and has a horizontal demand curve.

constant elasticity demand curve

Refers to a demand curve where the elasticity of demand is the same at each and every point.

Figure 2.9 Three Special Cases of Elasticity

In the case of a vertical demand curve such as that in panel (a), demand is perfectly inelastic. The demand for insulin is an example. If the demand curve is horizontal, as in panel (b), demand is perfectly elastic. In panel (c), the demand curve is of the mathematical form $q = b/p^k$ and has a constant elasticity equal to k.

COMMON ERROR 2.2   Confusing the Slope of a Demand Curve with Elasticity

Consider the following question: A student is asked which of the two demand curves in the graph is more inelastic—demand curve D_A, where $p = 100 - q$, or demand curve D_B, where $p = 100 - 2q$. Many students reason that because demand curve D_B is steeper, demand curve D_B must be *more* inelastic. These students are wrong!

The correct answer is that for any given price, the elasticity of demand is *equal* for these two demand curves. Consider any price between 0 and 100. Recall that the point elasticity of demand is defined as:

$$\varepsilon_p = -\left(\frac{\Delta q}{\Delta p}\frac{p}{q}\right)$$

For demand curve D_A, $-\Delta q/\Delta p = 1$, but for demand curve D_B, $-\Delta q/\Delta p = 1/2$. To calculate the point elasticity of demand for any price p, it is necessary to calculate only the ratio p/q. For demand curve D_A:

p	$-\Delta q/\Delta p$	p/q	$\varepsilon_p = -(\Delta q/\Delta p)(p/q)$
0	1	0	0
25	1	25/75 = 1/3	1/3
50	1	50/50 = 1	1 (midpoint)
75	1	75/25 = 3	3
100	1	∞	∞

For demand curve D_B:

p	$-\Delta q/\Delta p$	p/q	$\varepsilon_p = -(\Delta q/\Delta p)(p/q)$
0	1/2	0	0
25	1/2	25/37.5 = 2/3	1/3
50	1/2	50/25 = 2	1 (midpoint)
75	1/2	75/12.5 = 6	3
100	1/2	∞	∞

From the two tables, we see that for demand curves D_A and D_B, *the elasticity of demand is equal for any given price.* This common error is caused by the students' misconception that the slope of the demand curve measures the elasticity of demand. Because elasticity depends on percentage changes, while the slope of a linear demand depends on absolute changes, the slope and elasticity of a linear demand curve are clearly not equal. Do not confuse them!

More generally, we have seen that for any linear demand curve with a slope b between zero and infinity, the top half of the curve is elastic, the bottom half of the curve is inelastic, and the midpoint is unit elastic. This also shows the danger of assuming that any linear demand curve is elastic or inelastic, unless the demand curve is vertical (perfectly inelastic) or horizontal (perfectly elastic).

Common Error Figure 2.2
Do Not Think That Slope Equals Elasticity
Demand curve D_A is $p = 100 - q$ and demand curve D_B is $p = 100 - 2q$. Many students reason that because demand curve D_B is steeper, demand curve D_B must be *more* inelastic. However, at any given price, both of these demand curves have the same elasticity of demand.

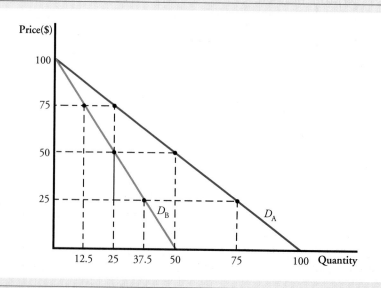

where b and k are positive constants. At every price and quantity, $\varepsilon_p = k$, so elasticity is constant at every point on the demand curve. In the special case where $k = 1$, demand is everywhere unit elastic, so total expenditures will be the same at every price and quantity along the demand curve.

▼▼▼ 2.6 Some Other Important Elasticities

In addition to the price elasticity of demand, economists often use many other important elasticities. Three of the most important are the income elasticity of demand, the cross-price elasticity of demand, and the elasticity of supply.

The Income Elasticity of Demand

income elasticity of demand

The percentage change in the quantity demanded of a good associated with a one percent change in income.

cross-price elasticity of demand

The percentage change in the quantity demanded of one good associated with a one percent change in the price of another good.

The demand for most goods is affected by the aggregate level of consumers' income. The **income elasticity of demand** is defined as the ratio of the percentage change in the quantity demanded to the percentage change in aggregate consumer income. The income elasticity of demand is represented by the symbol ε_I, and is defined as follows:

$$\varepsilon_I = \frac{\%\Delta q}{\%\Delta I} \tag{2.8}$$

where q is the quantity demanded, I is aggregate income, and the Greek letter Δ once again stands for the change in a variable. The income elasticity of demand measures the percentage change in the quantity demanded associated with a one percent change in income.

For most goods, such as automobiles, computers, higher education, clothing, and owner-occupied housing, consumers consume more as income increases and $\varepsilon_I > 0$. Goods with positive income elasticities are normal goods. There are, however, a smaller number of goods, such as starchy foods like potatoes and rice, fast-food hamburgers, and Spam, for which consumption decreases as income increases and $\varepsilon_I < 0$. Goods with negative income elasticities are inferior goods.

Table 2.3 presents a number of income elasticity estimates. Notice that in the table, some of the normal goods have values of $\varepsilon_I > 1$, while others have values of $0 < \varepsilon_I < 1$. Goods with income elasticities greater than one, like fresh fruits, computers, and transatlantic air travel, are economic luxury goods. Goods with income elasticities between zero and one, like eggs, milk, and a college education, are economic necessities.

Table 2.3 Some Income Elasticity Estimates

Good or Service	Income Elasticity
Fresh salmon	2.14
Cream	1.72
Computers	1.71
Peaches	1.43
Apples	1.32
Eggs	0.57
College education	0.55
Milk	0.50
Cigarettes, teenagers	-0.44
Cigarettes, adults	-0.10
Ground beef	-0.20

The Cross-Price Elasticity of Demand

The demand for a good depends not only on its own price and income, but on the prices of all available substitutes and complements. For example, the demand for chicken is affected by the price of substitutes like beef, pork, and fish. Similarly, the demand for automobiles is affected by the price of a critical complementary good: gasoline. The **cross-price elasticity of demand** measures the sensitivity of the demand for one good to a price change of another good.

The cross-price elasticity of demand is defined as the ratio of the percentage change in the quantity demanded of one good to the percentage change in the price of another good. For example, the cross-price elasticity of demand for good x with respect to a change in the price of good y is represented by the symbol ε_{xy} and is defined as follows:

$$\varepsilon_{xy} = \frac{\% \Delta q_x}{\% \Delta p_y} \qquad (2.9)$$

where q_x is the quantity demanded of good x and p_y is the price of good y. The cross-price elasticity of demand measures the percentage change in the quantity demanded of one good associated with a one percent change in the price of another good.

Table 2.4 presents a number of cross-price elasticity estimates. The sign of the cross-price elasticity tells us whether the two goods are substitutes or complements. If two goods are substitutes, like Coke and Pepsi, then when the price of one increases, the demand for the other increases, so $\varepsilon_{xy} > 0$. If two goods are complements, like

Table 2.4 Some Cross-Price Elasticities

Products	Cross-Price Elasticity
Fresh salmon with frozen salmon	1.12
Pepsi Cola with the price of Coca Cola	0.80
Coca Cola with the price of Pepsi Cola	0.61
Ground beef with the price of beef table cuts	0.41
Ground beef with the price of poultry	0.24
Electricity with the price of natural gas	0.20
Entertainment with the price of food	-0.72

▲▲▲ 2.6 APPLICATION The Natural Gas "Surprise" of 1990

During the 1980s, many of the small, liberal arts colleges on the East Coast purchased expensive equipment to enable them to switch more quickly from oil to natural gas as a source of heat and energy, thus increasing the cross-price elasticity of natural gas with respect to oil for these schools. With their new equipment in place, college administrators felt confident that the next time oil prices shot up, they would be able to switch easily to cheaper natural gas and save enough money to justify the expense of the equipment.

They didn't have to wait long. In August 1990, Iraq invaded Kuwait. Although oil supplies were not immediately disrupted, the invasion raised fears of future disruptions, especially as it became clear that the United States and its Western allies were prepared to go to war to force Iraq back to its original borders. If indeed Kuwaiti and/or Iraqi oil were removed from the market, the price of oil would rise. Thus, in August 1990, there was an *expectation* of future oil price increases, causing both an immediate rightward shift of the demand curve for oil and a leftward shift in the supply curve for oil. Both the increase in oil demand and the reduction in oil supply predicted an increase in price, and it did! The price of crude oil, which was around $20 per barrel on August 1, shot up to $28 within a week, and $38 per barrel within a month.

This was just the sort of event the East Coast colleges had prepared for. They happily put their new equipment to use, switching to the use of natural gas. Only something the colleges never thought would occur, happened: because of the high cross-price elasticity of demand of natural gas with respect to oil, the demand for natural gas increased and the price of natural gas shot up as well! Many college administrators accused their local natural gas distributors of "gouging" the public. The invasion of Kuwait did not threaten natural gas supplies, they argued, so there was no justification for the natural gas price hike.

To students of microeconomics, the rise in natural gas prices should come as no surprise. Natural gas and oil are substitutes, and therefore, have a high cross-price elasticity of demand. The predictable consequence of higher oil prices was higher natural gas prices. The local natural gas distributors had to pay more for natural gas themselves and simply passed the higher prices along to their consumers. Ironically, the new switching technology purchased by many institutions during the 1980s served only to increase the cross-price elasticity of demand and make the price of natural gas respond more quickly and more strongly to changes in the price of oil. The money might have been better spent insulating dorm rooms or on other energy-conserving projects.

food and entertainment, then when the price of one increases, the demand for the other decreases, so $\varepsilon_{xy} < 0$. Finally, if the goods are essentially unrelated, like fast food hamburgers and haircuts, then $\varepsilon_{xy} = 0$.

The Elasticity of Supply

elasticity of supply

The percentage change in the quantity supplied of a good associated with a one percent change in the good's own price.

The **elasticity of supply** is in many ways analogous to the elasticity of demand. The elasticity of supply is represented by the symbol ε_s, and is defined as follows:

$$\varepsilon_s = \frac{\%\Delta q_s}{\%\Delta p_s} \tag{2.10}$$

where q_s is the quantity of the good supplied and p is its price. The elasticity of supply tells us how sensitive quantity supplied is to changes in price. The elasticity of supply measures the percentage change in the quantity supplied associated with a one percent change in price. Because most supply curves slope upward, the value of the elasticity of supply is typically positive, and there is no need to add a minus sign in front of the elasticity of supply calculation.

Summary

1. The market demand for a good is the relationship that, *ceteris paribus*, specifies the quantity of that good that all buyers in a market would like to buy at each possible price over a given period of time. Demand depends on the price of the good, the prices of substitutes and complements, and the income, expectations, and tastes of buyers. The demand curve shows how the quantity demanded changes when only the price of the good is allowed to change. If any of the other determinants of demand changes, the demand curve will shift.

2. The market supply for a good is the relationship that, *ceteris paribus*, specifies the quantity of that good that all sellers in a market would like to sell at each possible price over a given period of time. Supply depends on the price of the good, the prices of inputs and alternate goods, technology, and expectations. The supply curve shows how the quantity supplied changes when only the price of the good is allowed to change. If any of the other determinants of supply changes, the supply curve will shift.

3. The actual quantity bought and sold tends toward equilibrium, where the demand and supply curves intersect. A change in an exogenous variable shifts the supply or demand curve and causes a change in the market equilibrium.

4. Governments often intervene in markets when they are dissatisfied with the market outcome. Two of the most common methods of intervention are price ceilings and price floors. Price ceilings tend to create shortages and encourage the formation of a black market. Price floors generate surpluses of production that are costly to society.

5. Price elasticity of demand measures the sensitivity of quantity demanded to price. Economists measure elasticity of demand in two ways: point elasticity, for very small price changes; and arc elasticity, for larger price changes. Elasticities help us classify goods according to their price sensitivity, and also enable us to predict changes in total expenditure. When demand is inelastic, price and total expenditures move in the same direction. When demand is elastic, price and total expenditures move in opposite directions.

6. In addition to the elasticity of demand, three other important elasticities are the income elasticity, the cross-price elasticity, and the elasticity of supply.

Self-Test Problems

1. Determine the effect of each of the following events on equilibrium price and quantity in the global market for silver. Support each of your answers with a diagram.
   a. A dramatic drop in the price of mining equipment.
   b. A technological discovery that enables more silver to be mined with the same labor and equipment.
   c. A rise in the price of mercury, used by dentists to fill teeth with silver.
   d. The invention of a new video technology that replaces standard cameras and photographs.
   e. A general expectation that the price of silver is about to rise.
   f. A discovery that gold fillings fall out after a few years.
   g. A new technological discovery that makes gold cheaper to produce.
   h. A decision by the Russian government to sell its official gold reserves on the open market.

2. Suppose that supply and demand curves for a good are described by the following equations:

$$q_s = 10 + \frac{1}{2}p$$
$$q_d = 100 - 2p$$

   where p is the dollar price of the good.
   a. Solve for equilibrium price and quantity.
   b. Calculate the point elasticity of demand at the equilibrium price.
   c. Starting at the equilibrium price, calculate the arc elasticities of demand for a $1.00 increase in price and a $1.00 decrease in price. Are your answers different? Why?

3. Price floors in the United States have been estimated to raise the price of fresh milk by about 30 percent. The elasticity of demand for fresh milk has recently been estimated at 0.63. What effect would the elimination of the price floor have on quantity demanded? What effect would it have on the total revenue of milk sellers?

Questions and Problems for Review

1. Diagram the effects of the following events on the supply and/or demand for raisin bran cereal:
   a. The price of raisins increases.
   b. The price of milk decreases.
   c. The price of corn flakes decreases.
   d. Drought kills off much of the nation's wheat crop.
   e. Researchers find that bran makes you live longer.
   f. Average family income increases.

2. Does a shift in the supply curve that lowers price increase demand? Why or why not?

3. Tickets at Fenway Park in Boston to Red Sox–Yankees games always sell out, and therefore have a price ceiling that is below the equilibrium market price. What effect does this have on the market? How does the black market play a hand in this market?

4. Why wouldn't the slope of the demand curve be a good measure of a good's price sensitivity? (Hint: What would happen to the slope of the demand curve for gasoline if we changed our unit of measurement from gallons to pints or liters?)

5. A single opening for a professor of English at an American college or university will generally attract thousands of qualified applicants. Is this market in equilibrium? Why or why not?

6. The Matsushita corporation observes that the price of one of its Panasonic cordless telephone models has risen every year for the last four years, and yet the quantity purchased has risen as well. Would it be correct to assume that this product disobeys the "law of demand?" Why or why not?

7. As East European nations transform from centrally planned to market economies, the prices of most goods are rising faster than the incomes of most

households. Yet many commentators assert that, even in the short run, most households are better off. How can this be?

8. Two facts about health care in the United States are often cited: (a) medical costs have risen dramatically over the past two decades; and (b) more and more Americans have obtained health insurance policies that pay most of their medical expenses. In the media, it is often stated that (a) has caused (b). Use supply and demand analysis to show how (b) could have caused (a).

9. Tropicana produces orange juice and sells it at the equilibrium price in the orange juice market. Suppose the price of grapefruit juice falls and consumers' incomes increase. To determine the equilibrium price for Tropicana in this model, what are the endogenous variables? What are the exogeneous variables?

10. For the following markets, list which is more price elastic and explain why:
   a. The market for orange juice or the market for flour?
   b. The market for airplane tickets in the short run or the long run?
   c. The market for Toyota Camrys or the market for cars?

11. Graph the following demand curves:

$$p = 100 - q \qquad p = 50 - q$$

At $p = 50$, what are the price elasticities of demand for both curves?

12. Graph the following demand curves:

$$p = 50 - q \qquad p = 50 - 2q$$

Are the price elasticities of demand for these two demand curves the same or different at any given price? Explain your reasoning.

13. Which would have a higher price elasticity of demand: studio apartments on the Upper West Side of Manhattan, or apartments in Manhattan? Why?

14. Suppose the income elasticity of hamburger is -0.7. What does this tell you about hamburger? If incomes see a 10 percent decrease, what effect would this have on the quantity demanded of hamburger?

15. Suppose a student only buys two things with her budget: Snickers and Cliffs Notes. She is currently purchasing five Snickers at $2 and four Cliffs Notes at $20. If her income elasticity of demand for Snickers is 1 (unit elastic), what is her income elasticity of demand for Cliffs Notes?

16. Suppose the price elasticity of demand for peanut butter is greater than 1. To raise total expenditures, would you raise prices, lower prices, or leave them the same? Explain.

17. Using the definition of the price elasticity of supply:
   a. Draw the supply curve for a good whose supply has zero price elasticity.
   b. Draw a supply curve for a good whose supply is "perfectly elastic."

18. Suppose a 10 percent reduction in the price of cheese causes a 20 percent increase in the quantity demanded of crackers. What is the cross-price elasticity of demand of crackers with respect to a change in the price of cheese? Are they complements, substitutes, or unrelated?

19. Using the definition of the cross elasticity of demand between goods x and y, what can you say about the relationship between goods x and y if the cross-elasticity of demand is:
   a. positive and very large
   b. positive and very small
   c. negative and very large
   d. negative and very small.

20. Greyhound Bus Lines and Peter Pan Bus Lines compete on the Boston to Albany route. The companies have been tracking their pricing competition for several years and have identified the following market data (see Problem 20 Table on page 46).
   a. What is the best estimate of the price elasticity of demand for both Greyhound and Peter Pan? What two years did you use for each to calculate these figures? Why?
   b. What is cross-price elasticity of Greyhound with respect to Peter Pan's price changes? What two years did you use? Why?

Problem 20 Table

Year	Price$_{Greyhound}$	Quantity$_{Greyhound}$	Price$_{Peter Pan}$	Quantity$_{Peter Pan}$	Income
1990	$50	110	$51	114	2,250
1991	$52	107	$52	112	2,500
1992	$56	101	$50	116	2,500
1993	$50	112	$48	121	2,250
1994	$56	102	$52	110	2,500

Internet Exercises

Visit *http://www.myeconlab.com/waldman* for this chapter's Web exercises. Answer real-world economics problems by doing research on the Internet.

Part 2 Consumer Behavior

Chapter 3
Theory of Consumer Behavior

On Thursday, December 20, 2001, the author made a business trip from Hamilton, New York to Boston to discuss plans for completing this text with a group of advisors at Addison Wesley. Before September 11, I would have gotten on an airplane in Syracuse on December 20 and arrived in Boston an hour later for a day of meetings. Instead, on Wednesday, December 19, 2001, I got into my car and drove six hours to Boston. I did this despite airfares from Syracuse to Boston that were lower on December 19 than they were on September 10, and despite having to sacrifice all day Wednesday and Friday traveling in a car. I was not alone; millions of travelers worldwide decided to forsake air travel after September 11, 2001, resulting in a huge decline in the number of airline passengers in September and October 2001.

The decline in air passenger traffic came about despite a large decline in fares following the events of September 11. Does this behavior violate the law of demand introduced in Chapter 2? Not at all; after September 11, the demand curve for air travel shifted left because of a shift in tastes of consumers away from air travel and in favor of automobile and train travel.

In this chapter, we will study the sources of market demand in detail. As noted previously, markets are made up of individual economic *agents* (consumers and sellers); our study of market demand begins with a study of the behavior of individual consumers. We will see that a person's demand for any single good, like air travel, cannot be properly understood if we focus too narrowly on that one good alone. Instead we must focus on the context of that consumer's demand for *all* of the goods and services she can purchase. With limited income and essentially unlimited desires, consumers must make difficult choices about how to allocate their available income among the goods and services they want and need.

▼▼▼ 3.1   An Outline of Consumer Theory

Consumer theory, like all theories of rational choice, has only a handful of basic ingredients. Because such theories will be encountered again in different guises when examining the behavior of firms, workers, and other types of economic agents, it is worthwhile to examine the common features of all these theories of rational choice.

Theories of choice view behavior as the outcome of a coherent, goal-directed process in pursuit of clear objectives. The structure of these theories consists of four distinct, basic components that contribute to our overall picture of the agent and the problem she faces. The four components are:

1. The agent's objects of choice
2. The agent's preferences
3. The agent's opportunities
4. The agent's objectives

The *objects of choice* are the things the agent is choosing among. *Preferences* involve such things as the agent's ability to make choices along with her tastes for the objects themselves. Our description of the agent's *opportunities* will take account of the circumstances under which she will be making her choices, as well as any economic realities she faces that tend to constrain those choices. Finally, in our description of the agent's *objectives*, it is necessary to lay out our assumptions about behavior, and be specific about what is assumed to motivate the agent. Tastes and circumstances alone are not enough information to predict the choices that will be made.

It is sometimes useful to think of this outline of modeling choice behavior as a checklist that a person might use when making an important decision. For example, you might be deciding between returning to school next year and taking a trip around the world. These are the objects of choice, or the alternatives you are considering. Next you will consider your preferences. "How do I feel about going to school?" "How do I feel about taking a trip around the world?" You must next answer different questions about your realistic opportunities. "Can I afford to go to school next year?" "Can I afford to take a trip around the world?" Finally, you'll have to clarify your objectives. The choice you eventually make will depend on the answers to all these questions, which guide your decision-making in a careful and deliberate way.

The model of consumer theory builds on reasonable assumptions in each of the four categories discussed. Out of that model of choice will evolve a theory of individual demand that is well suited to predicting the behavior of a typical consumer who operates within a typical economy.

In any market economy, the consumer can select from a variety of goods and services offered for sale. She can go into shops, or she can order by phone or over the Internet. There are, then, a truly enormous number of markets in which the consumer is at least a potential buyer. Yet in virtually all of them, the overwhelming majority of consumers are individually quite insignificant. How many shops consider you an important enough customer to offer you special discounts they don't offer everyone else? I suspect your answer is: "Not too many." Instead, you're much more likely to face a situation of "take it or leave it" at the going price. In effect, you have no more weight than a single atom in virtually every market you enter as a buyer.

These observations have two important implications for the theory of consumer behavior. First, our theory must recognize that consumers face a wide range of alternatives. Indeed, that is what makes the consumer's problem of choice both necessary and interesting. Second, it must reflect the fact that in most markets a typical consumer has absolutely no independent influence over the terms at which she may buy the goods and services she wants. The theory of consumer behavior builds on both these implications.

▼▼▼ 3.2 Preferences and Utility

Microeconomists describe consumer preferences by making certain assumptions about how a rational consumer behaves. In essence, this involves laying out all of the assumptions economists are prepared to make about an agent's ability to make choices, and about the agent's tastes for the goods and services she/he may want to consume. Should you want to challenge the predictions of the theory, you will have to find fault with one or more of these basic assumptions. The basic assumptions of consumer theory are quite simple, however, making them difficult to challenge.

Assumptions Concerning Consumer Preferences

It is useful to think of the consumer as choosing between baskets, or bundles, containing different amounts of different kinds of goods and services. The theory of consumer behavior builds on the following four simple assumptions about the consumer's preferences:

1. **Completeness.**
   The consumer is able to consider any two bundles A and B at a time and say one (and only one) of three things: either he prefers bundle A to bundle B, or he prefers bundle B to bundle A, or he is indifferent between the two bundles.
2. **Transitivity.**
   When considering three bundles A, B, and C, if the consumer prefers A to B, and prefers B to C, then he will prefer A to C. Similarly, if he is indifferent between A and B, and indifferent between B and C, he will be indifferent between A and C.
3. **Non-satiation.**
   Ceteris paribus, the consumer always prefers more goods to fewer goods. If A contains more of any good than B does, yet A contains no less of any good than B does, the consumer always prefers A to B.
4. **Convexity.**
   The rate at which a consumer is willing to give up one good, Y, in exchange for another, X, while always remaining indifferent after the exchange *decreases* as he gets more of one good, X, and less of the other, Y.

Assumption 1 states that the agent is able to make choices. When the consumer says he likes one bundle better than another, he is not required to also be able to identify *how much* better he likes one compared to the other. There is, in other words, no need to worry about the intensity of the agent's preferences.

Assumption 2 says that preferences must be logically consistent in a particular way. If someone tells you that he likes ice cream better than cake, and that he likes cake better than fruit, wouldn't you expect him to say that he likes ice cream better than fruit? Otherwise you'd think there was something very illogical or confused about that person's preferences.

The implication of combining assumptions 1 and 2 is a little surprising. Assumption 1 says the consumer can look at any two bundles at a time and tell us how he ranks the two relative to each other. Assumption 2 says all those pair-wise rankings

▲▲▲ 3.2 APPLICATION Moe, Larry, and Curly Attempt to Choose a Restaurant

Much of what is assumed about individual preferences does not necessarily characterize group preferences. A famous example is the so-called Condorcet Paradox, which can be related to a typical urban dilemma. Suppose three friends—Moe, Larry, and Curly—are trying to decide where to eat dinner. They have agreed to limit their choices to three possible cuisines: Chinese, Italian, or Mexican. The table shows how each individual ranks the three choices:

	Moe	**Larry**	**Curly**
1st Choice	Chinese	Italian	Mexican
2nd Choice	Italian	Mexican	Chinese
3rd Choice	Mexican	Chinese	Italian

The group decides on the following majority-rule process: two cuisines will be arbitrarily selected, and all three will vote on which of the two they prefer. The winning cuisine will then be compared to the remaining one, and everyone will vote again. The winner in this round is the type of food the group will eat.

Let the first choice be between Chinese and Italian. Note that Moe and Curly prefer Chinese to Italian, while only Larry prefers Italian to Chinese. Thus, according to majority rule, the group prefers Chinese to Italian. Next, the group compares Chinese with Mexican. This time, Larry and Curly prefer Mexican to Chinese, while only Moe prefers Chinese to Mexican. Thus, according to majority rule, the group prefers Mexican to Chinese. Mexican wins the last round, and the group will eat Mexican food.

But wait! Moe and Curly now bring up an interesting fact: they haven't compared Mexican with Italian. When this choice is put before the group, Italian gets two votes, while Mexican gets only one. Thus, the group prefers Italian to Mexican. Should they eat Italian? Not really, because it has already been determined that the group also prefers Chinese to Italian.

To summarize, the group prefers Italian to Mexican, Mexican to Chinese, and Chinese to Italian. As you can see, these three guys are probably not going to eat anywhere unless they change their method of determining group preferences. Even though each individual has *transitive* preferences, the preferences of the group as a whole are *intransitive*.

must be logically consistent with one another in a straightforward way. The combined effect of these two assumptions, however, is that the consumer can rank all of the bundles before him from the ones he likes best to the ones he likes least.

Preferences and Indifference Curves

To simplify the analysis, consumer choice is often analyzed for just two goods at a time, good X and good Y. This is done while recognizing that consumers are actually faced with a dizzying array of choices over a great many goods. The ordered pair of numbers (x,y) in Figure 3.1(a) stand for a bundle containing x units of good X and y units of good Y; the planes in Figures 3.1(a) and 3.1(b) can be thought of as representing all the different bundles over which the consumer's preferences may range. In panel (a), point A, for example, is a bundle containing 5 units of X and 22 units of Y; point B is a bundle containing 17 units of X and 12 units of Y, and so on.

When preferences satisfy assumptions 1 and 2—when the consumer can make choices that are logically consistent—we say the consumer is *rational*. The preferences of a rational consumer can be represented graphically with the use of indifference curves. In panel (b) of Figure 3.1, an **indifference curve** through some point such as A is the collection of all other bundles the consumer ranks the same as he ranks bundle A. That is, the indifference curve identifies all of the bundles he is indifferent to compared to bundle A. Similarly, the indifference curve through B is the collection of all bundles the con-

indifference curve

A curve depicting all of the possible market baskets that provide the consumer with a given level of utility or satisfaction.

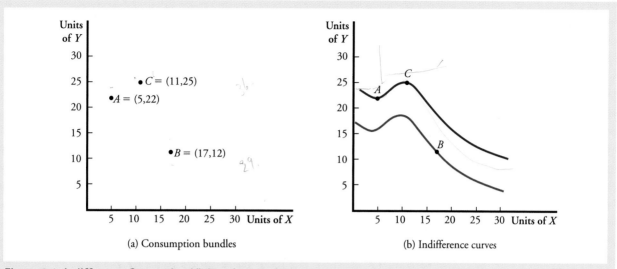

Figure 3.1 Indifference Curves that Violate Assumption 3
In panel (a), point A represents a bundle containing 5 units of good X and 22 units of good Y; point B represents a bundle containing 17 units of X and 12 units of Y, and point C represents a bundle containing 11 units of X and 25 units of Y. In panel (b), an indifference curve through the point A is the collection of all bundles the consumer supposedly ranks equal to bundle A. However, the consumer cannot possibly be indifferent between A and C, because bundle C contains more of both goods than bundle A, and therefore bundles A and C cannot be on the same indifference curve.

sumer ranks the same as bundle B, and so on. If the only requirement of the consumer is that he be rational, there is really no reason why his indifference curves could not look like just about anything. Only when some assumptions about the agent's tastes are imposed, as they are by assumptions 3 and 4, do indifference curves begin to assume some predictable shape.

Assumption 3 says more of any good is always preferred to less. When that is the case, can the consumer's indifference curves look like they do in panel (b) of Figure 3.1? Clearly not. Note that bundles A and C are on the same indifference curve in that figure. Bundle C, however, has strictly more X and more Y than bundle A does. Because of assumption 3, more goods are preferred to less goods, and therefore bundle C must be preferred to bundle A. The consumer cannot possibly be indifferent between A and C, and therefore bundles A and C cannot be on the same indifference curve. Put another way, *an indifference curve representing two goods that the consumer values cannot have a positive slope.*

How must indifference curves look when assumption 3 is added to the list of assumptions? Look at Figure 3.2. Under assumption 3, all bundles due north, due east, and northeast of A, must be preferred to A, because all of these contain either more Y, more X, or more of both than A does. In turn, A must be preferred to all bundles due south, due west, and southwest of A, because A contains more Y, more X, or more of both than do these other bundles. The indifference curve through A must therefore run from northwest of A, through A, and then southeast of A. In the previous paragraph you learned that indifference curves for two goods cannot have positive slopes, so picking any other bundle on that indifference curve running through point A, such as B or C, *the entire indifference curve must be negatively sloped.*

But that's not all. Assumption 3 also tells us that indifference curves further away from the origin contain bundles preferred to those on indifference curves closer toward

Figure 3.2 Indifference Curves are Negatively Sloped

Under assumption 3, all bundles in the red shaded area must be preferred to bundle A and bundle A must be preferred to all bundles in the blue shaded area. The indifference curve that includes bundle A, therefore, must run from the white area northwest of A, through A, and then through the white area southeast of A. The indifference curves for two goods cannot have positive slopes because more is better than less, so picking any other bundle on the indifference curve running through A, such as bundle B or C, the entire indifference curve must be negatively sloped.

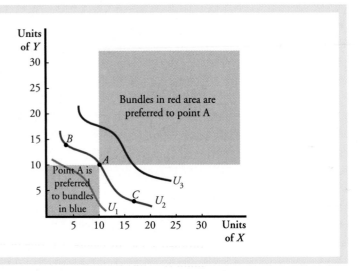

the origin. Thus, looking at the entire map containing all the indifference curves of some consumer, *the direction of increasing preference is always northeasterly as we move outwards on that map.* Finally, assumption 3 ensures that indifference curves cannot cross. To see why, it is only necessary to ask what would go wrong if they did, as in Figure 3.3. Because C and A are on the same indifference curve, the consumer must be indifferent between C and A. Because A and B are also on the same indifference curve, he must also be indifferent between A and B. By assumption 2 (transitivity) he must, therefore, also be indifferent between C and B. But C contains more of both goods than B does, so by assumption 3 he must prefer C to B. Can a consumer be both indifferent between B and C and at the same time prefer C to B? Not without running afoul of assumption 1, which requires the consumer either to prefer one bundle to another *or* to be indifferent between the two bundles, but not both at the same time. It is safe to conclude, therefore, that *indifference curves can never cross one another.*

Figure 3.3 Indifference Curves Cannot Cross

Because bundles C and A are on the same indifference curve, the consumer must be indifferent between C and A. Because bundles A and B are also on the same indifference curve, he must also be indifferent between A and B. By assumption 2, he must therefore also be indifferent between bundles C and B. But C contains more of both goods than B does, so by assumption 3 he must prefer C to B. But a consumer cannot be both indifferent between B and C and at the same time prefer C to B, because that would violate assumption 1. Therefore, two indifference curves can never cross.

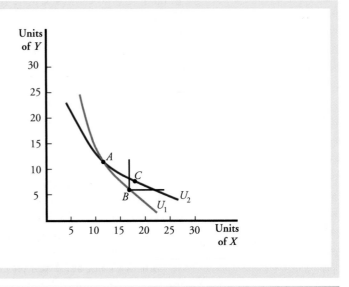

The Marginal Rate of Substitution

The first three assumptions ensure that consumer preferences can be represented by *negatively sloped, non-intersecting* indifference curves covering the plane. So far, though, nothing has been assumed about the *curvature* of indifference curves, or the way in which the slope of the indifference curves must behave moving down any given indifference curve from the top of the curve to bottom. Empirical studies (and only a little introspection) tend to confirm the old adage that "variety is the spice of life." In many cases, consumer preferences display a definite bias in favor of diversity and a bias against extremes in consumption. The final assumption about consumer tastes expresses this tendency and in so doing speaks to the issue of curvature.

To appreciate what assumption 4 says about tastes, suppose you like the Dave Matthews Band and the Allman Brothers Band. Specifically, suppose you'd be just as happy having a collection containing 15 Dave Matthews CDs and 6 Allman Brothers CDs as you would be having a collection containing 7 Dave Matthews CDs and 10 Allman Brothers CDs. In Figure 3.4, one of your indifference curves would pass through both point $A = (6,15)$ and point $C = (10,7)$. At A, when you have lots of Dave Matthews CDs and very few Allman Brothers CDs, you are likely to be quite willing to trade some of your Dave Matthews CDs to get another Allman Brothers CD. Figure 3.4 assumes that at point A you would be willing to give up 3 Dave Matthews CDs for one more Allman Brothers CD without feeling any worse off. On the other hand, at C on the same indifference curve, you've already got lots of Allman Brothers CDs but you've only got a few Dave Matthews CDs. When this is the case, you're likely to be less willing than before to give up your Dave Matthews CDs in exchange for more Allman Brothers CDs. As shown in Figure 3.4, you'd only be willing to give up 1 of your now relatively scarce Dave Matthews CDs to get that next Allman Brothers CD. Notice that when your tastes behave like this, the rate at which you are willing to give up one good in exchange for another—while always remaining indifferent after the exchange—always decreases as you get more of one good and less of the other. This is just what assumption 4 requires.

Economists use the term **marginal rate of substitution**, or MRS_{yx}, for the rate at which a consumer will exchange Y for X while remaining indifferent after the exchange. It will be

the marginal rate of substitution, MRS_{yx}

The rate at which a consumer is willing to sacrifice one good (y) in return for more of another good (x).

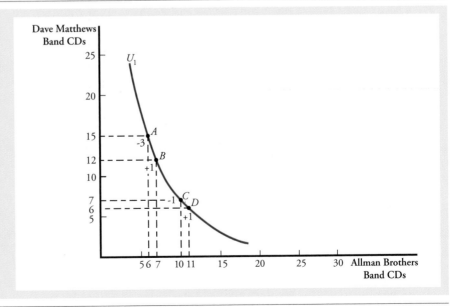

Figure 3.4 Convex Indifference Curves and Assumption 4
At point A, the consumer's utility remains constant if he gives up three Dave Matthews CDs for one more Allman Brothers CD. At point C on the same indifference curve, he is willing to give up only one Dave Matthews CD in exchange for one more Allman Brothers CD. Consistent with assumption 4, the rate at which he is willing to give up Dave Matthews CDs in exchange for Allman Brothers CDs while remaining indifferent decreases as he gets more Allman Brothers CDs and has fewer Dave Matthews CDs.

shown shortly that for very small changes (where the change approaches zero) in X, the MRS_{yx} is merely the absolute value of the slope of an indifference curve where X is on the horizontal axis and Y is on the vertical axis. The absolute value of the slope is used, rather than just the slope itself, so we can always speak of the MRS_{yx} as a positive number. For larger changes in X, the MRS_{yx} is equal to the absolute value of the slope of a line connecting the two points on the indifference curve. For example, in moving from point A to point B in Figure 3.4, the total change in Y involved is $\Delta y = -3$, and the total change in X is $\Delta x = 1$. By definition slope is "rise over run," or $\Delta y / \Delta x$. Thus, for the move from A to B:

$$MRS_{yx} \equiv \left| \frac{\Delta y}{\Delta x} \right| = \left| \frac{-3}{1} \right| = 3$$

Farther down the indifference curve in Figure 3.4, in moving from C to D, $\Delta y = -1$ and $\Delta x = 1$, so $MRS_{yx} = |-1/1|$. In moving from point A to point C, the MRS_{yx} has declined from 3 to 1. Assumption 4 therefore has a very simple geometric interpretation. It says that *when moving down any indifference curve from the top to the bottom, the absolute value of that curve's slope must be continuously declining.* This property of indifference curves is called the **principle of diminishing marginal rate of substitution**. In mathematical terms, for two goods this is the same thing as saying that negatively sloped indifference curves must be convex away from the origin (or bowed-in toward the origin) as they are in Figure 3.4. An indifference curve is *convex* if all the points on a straight line connecting any two points on the curve are preferred to the two points on the curve. By contrast, an indifference curve is *concave* if all the points on a straight line connecting any two points on the curve are *not* preferred to the two points on the curve. Because indifference curves are typically convex, assumption 4 is called the *convexity* assumption.

Modeling Non-Standard Tastes

Indifference curves are a powerful and versatile tool for modeling consumer preferences. They can be used to depict a variety of non-standard as well as standard kinds of tastes for the rational consumer, as shown in the four indifference maps in Figure 3.5. In each panel of the figure, the arrow indicates the direction of increasing preference through the map. The preferences depicted in panel (a) satisfy assumption 3, because having more of either good always enables the consumer to reach a higher indifference curve. However, those preference do not satisfy assumption 4, because the MRS is always constant (not diminishing) as X increases and Y decreases along any indifference curve. Indifference curves like these represent preferences for two goods that the consumer views as **perfect substitutes** for one another, such as two nickels and one dime.

Strictly speaking, the preferences in panel (b) satisfy neither assumption 3 nor assumption 4. Assumption 3 is not satisfied, because if the consumer has an equal number of right shoes and left shoes, additional right shoes alone (or left shoes alone) will not increase the consumer's utility. Assumption 4 is not satisfied because along any horizontal segment of an indifference curve in panel (b), the rate at which a consumer is willing to give up left shoes in exchange for right shoes, while always remaining indifferent after the exchange, remains constant and equal to zero. Therefore, it is not always the case that an extra unit of either good makes the consumer strictly better-off, nor does the MRS always diminish continuously. Indeed, in panel (b), the MRS takes only one of two values: either zero or infinity! With preferences like these, the consumer prefers more of either good *only if he can increase his consumption of both together.* Indifference curves like these represent preferences for goods the consumer views as **perfect complements**, like left shoes and right shoes.

---

principle of diminishing marginal rate of substitution

A rule stating that for any convex indifference curve when moving down the curve from the top (northwest) to the bottom (southeast), the absolute value of that curve's slope must be continuously declining.

perfect substitutes

Two goods where the marginal rate of substitution of one for the other is always constant, and therefore the indifference curves are straight lines.

perfect complements

Two goods where the marginal rate of substitution of one for the other is either infinite or zero, and therefore the indifference curves are right angles.

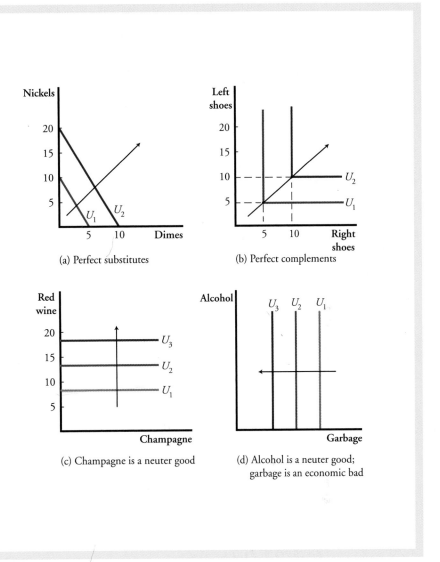

Figure 3.5 Indifference Maps for Some Non-Standard Tastes

In panel (a) more is better than less, because having more of either good always enables the consumer to reach a higher indifference curve. However, the indifference curves are not convex, because the MRS is constant along any indifference curve, and the two goods are perfect substitutes. In panel (b), more is not always better than less, because if the consumer has an equal number of right shoes and left shoes, additional right shoes alone or left shoes alone will not increase utility. The consumer prefers more of either good only if he can increase his consumption of both together, and the two goods are perfect complements. In panel (c), the consumer prefers more red wine to less, but is completely indifferent about champagne. In this case, champagne is called a *neuter good*. In panel (d), alcohol is a neuter good and garbage is an economic bad (explained in text), and therefore utility increases as the consumer moves toward the left.

(a) Perfect substitutes

(b) Perfect complements

(c) Champagne is a neuter good

(d) Alcohol is a neuter good; garbage is an economic bad

neuter good

A good that the consumer is completely indifferent about, and therefore, more of the good does not increase or decreases the consumer's utility; as a result, the indifference curves are either horizontal (if good X is a neuter good) or vertical (if good Y is a neuter good).

economic bad

A good for which marginal utility is negative, so the consumer prefers less of the good rather than more of the good. Pollution is a common example.

In panel (c), the consumer prefers more red wine to less, but he is completely indifferent to champagne. Take some champagne away from him or give him some more and he just moves horizontally along the same indifference curve. Champagne is called a **neuter good**. Preferences like this bring to mind the old Cole Porter lyric, "I get no kick from champagne…" and those in panel (d) complete the thought with "Mere alcohol doesn't thrill me at all." The difference in panel (d), of course, is that the direction of increasing preference is *toward* the left. This occurs because X is something the consumer prefers less of to more, like sacks of garbage! In this case, good X, sacks of garbage, is an **economic bad**. If an increase in consumption of a good or service reduces a consumer's utility, that good or service is an economic bad.

Our usual assumptions on preferences are appropriate for most things, but it should be recognized that non-satiation and convexity are merely two taste assumptions that can credibly be argued as typical of most consumers, most of the time, for most kinds of goods and services. There are exceptions, of course, but our theory of consumer behavior is usually quite capable of analyzing consumer choice in those exceptional cases as well.

3.3 Utility Functions

Sometimes working directly with the various assumptions on preferences can be confusing, and it is easier to summarize all of the information the assumptions give us about preferences in a single mathematical function. Doing so allows us to bring some standard mathematical methods to bear on our analysis of consumer choice. To see how consumer preferences can be summarized mathematically, remember that when preferences are complete and transitive, the consumer is be able to order all the alternatives before her from those she likes best to those she likes least. In effect, she can make up a list of bundles like the one in column 1 of Table 3.1. Numbers, or scores, can be assigned to each of these bundles by following some simple rules:

1. Whenever the consumer prefers one bundle to another, assign a higher number to the preferred bundle than to the other bundle.
2. Whenever the consumer is indifferent between two bundles, assign the same number to each bundle.

utility function

A mathematical formula that assigns numerical utility to bundles of goods in a way that guarantees that if the consumer prefers one bundle to another bundle, the preferred bundle is assigned a higher number; and if the consumer is indifferent between two bundles, both bundles are assigned the same number.

The numbers assigned to bundles in this way have no particular significance in and of themselves. They merely help to summarize information about the consumer's preferences in a simple numerical way, with bigger numbers denoting preferred bundles and equal numbers denoting indifferent bundles. In modern consumer theory, a **utility function** is a mathematical formula that assigns numbers to bundles following these two simple rules. When preferences are complete and transitive, there will always be some formula that can assign numbers to bundles in this way. Such a utility function, $u(x,y)$, represents the consumer's underlying preferences.

Column 2 of Table 3.1 uses a utility function, $u(x,y) = \sqrt{xy}$, to represent the consumer's preferences for the bundles listed in column 1. In column 2, preferred bundles are assigned larger numbers when those bundles are plugged into the utility function $u(x,y) = \sqrt{xy}$; and if the consumer is indifferent between bundles, the bundles receive the same number when plugged into $u(x,y) = \sqrt{xy}$. For example, in column 2, $u(10,7) = \sqrt{70} = 8.37$, while $u(8,5) = \sqrt{40} = 6.32$. Because $8.37 > 6.32$, the consumer prefers bundle $(10,7)$ to bundle $(8,5)$. Similarly, the consumer is indifferent between bundles $(8,5)$ and $(5,8)$, because $u(8,5) = u(5,8) = \sqrt{40} = 6.32$ for both bundles.

A utility function represents the consumer's ordering of bundles from best to worst, so we can ask no more of the utility function than that it properly reflect that ordering. Utility, then, has only a purely ordinal number significance in modern theory. That is, the utility numbers assigned to bundles do not pretend to say anything about the level of consumer satisfaction or happiness, nor do differences between utility numbers assigned to different bundles say anything about how intensely the consumer prefers one bundle to another.

Table 3.1 **A Utility Function Representing Preferences**

(1) Bundle	(2) $u(x,y) = \sqrt{xy}$
(14,6)	9.17
(10,7)	8.37
(8,5)	6.32
(5,8)	6.32
(6,6)	6.00
(4,5)	4.47

Utility Functions and Indifference Curves

Earlier, indifference curves were used to display consumer preferences graphically, and it was shown that an individual indifference curve represents a locus of points that the consumer ranks as indifferent. The utility function gives us another way to think about indifference curves. Because the consumer is indifferent between two bundles only if the utility he gets from both bundles is equal, *an indifference curve tells us all the bundles that give the consumer the same level of utility.*

In the language of mathematics, indifference curves are level curves of the utility function $u(x,y)$. They indicate in two dimensions, the (x,y) plane, what's happening in a third dimension, $u(x,y)$—much the same way that elevation contours are used to indicate points of equal height above sea level on two-dimensional maps. For any level of utility k, the equation:

$$u(x,y) = k$$

defines a *single* indifference curve. Larger values for k give us the equation for indifference curves farther out in the plane. In Figure 3.6, A and B are on the same indifference curve, so they each give rise to the same level of utility. There we've assumed that $u(5,10) = u(8,3) = 10$. Because the consumer is indifferent between *all* bundles on the indifference curve through A and B, all those bundles will satisfy the equation $u(x,y) = 10$. Bundles such as C and D on indifference curves farther out are preferred to A and B. Every bundle on the indifference curve through C will satisfy the equation $u(x,y) = 25$; those on the indifference curve through D will satisfy $u(x,y) = 42$.

Sometimes it is useful to think of the change or increment in utility that results when the consumer gets more (or less) of some good. For example, at point A in Figure 3.6, the consumer has 5 units of X and 10 units of Y, and the utility he gets is 10. When the consumer is given 2 more units of X, while keeping the amount of Y constant, he arrives at point C, where his utility is 25. As a result of increasing his consumption of X by 2 units, the consumer's utility increased by $25 - 10 = 15$. This is called the total change in utility for a total change in consumption of X of 2 units.

Generally it is more convenient to express these same ideas in terms of the rates of change involved. In our example, letting Δx stand for the change in consumption of X, then $\Delta x = 7 - 5 = 2$; and letting Δu stand for the associated increment in utility, then $\Delta u = 25 - 10 = 15$. The rate at which utility changes between points A and C would then be the ratio $\Delta u / \Delta x = 15/2 = 7.5$. By taking the ratio of the two total changes

Figure 3.6 Indifference Curves and the Utility Function

Bundles on the same indifference curve, like A and B, have the same level of utility, here identified as 10. Bundles on indifference curves farther away from the origin, such as C and D, have higher utility levels.

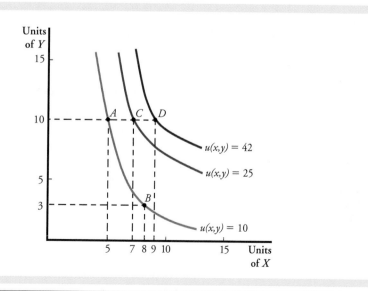

involved, we are in effect expressing the increment in utility that occurs *per unit change* in the consumption of *X*.

Marginal Utility

marginal utility

The extra utility (satisfaction) associated with consuming an extra unit of a good.

Economists call the incremental change in utility per unit change in the consumption of *X* the **marginal utility** of good *X*, or MU_x. Because the extra utility a consumer gets from an additional unit of some good depends on how much of all goods he has, marginal utilities will generally be different when the consumer is consuming different bundles. To remind ourselves of this, marginal utility is defined at a point (x,y). Letting Δx stand for any (small) change in *X* consumption, Δy for any (small) change in *Y* consumption, and $\Delta u(x,y)$ for the change in utility that results, it is possible to define the marginal utility of *X*, MU_x, and the marginal utility of *Y*, MU_y, at the point (x,y) as follows:

$$MU_x = \frac{\Delta u(x,y)}{\Delta x}$$ (3.1)

$$MU_y = \frac{\Delta u(x,y)}{\Delta x}$$ (3.2)

▲▲▲ 3.3 APPLICATION The Case of Airline Travel After 9/11/01

Economic shocks such as the terrorists' attacks of September 11, 2001 cause consumers' tastes to change dramatically, and these changes in tastes cause a change in consumers' utility functions and shifts in consumers' indifference curves. Panel (a) in the graph shows a typical consumer's indifference curves for two goods: airline miles traveled and other goods before September 11, 2001. The consumer's indifference curves were fairly steep, because

she was willing to give up a substantial quantity of other goods in exchange for an increase in airline miles traveled. In panel (b), after September 11, she is fearful of flying and much less willing to give up other goods in exchange for airline miles traveled. Each and every indifference curve, therefore, became flatter, indicating that she is willing to give up only a small amount of other goods in exchange for an increase in airline miles traveled.

Application Figure 3.3
Impact of September 11, 2001 on the Shape of a Consumer's Indifference Curves for Airline Travel
In panel (a), before September 11, 2001, this consumer was willing to sacrifice many other goods for an increase in airline travel. In panel (b), after September 11, she was willing to sacrifice only a few other goods for additional miles of airline travel.

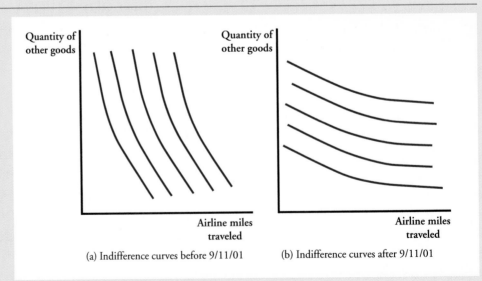

(a) Indifference curves before 9/11/01
(b) Indifference curves after 9/11/01

Often, the easiest and most intuitive way to describe tastes is by making assumptions about marginal utilities. For a typical good or service, the consumer prefers more to less, so the marginal utility of such goods is *positive*. Yet for some goods, the consumer would rather have less than more. For things like pollution, or dead bugs in your swimming pool, it is reasonable to suppose that marginal utility is *negative*, rather than positive. No matter what kind of tastes are being described, knowing something about the marginal utilities of the things involved tells us two very important things about the indifference curves representing those preferences. It tells the *slope* of the indifference curves and the *direction of increasing preference* through the entire map of indifference curves.

Figure 3.7 sketches an indifference curve through an arbitrarily chosen point, A. The slope of the indifference curve at A is given by the slope of the red line just tangent to the indifference curve there. Point B is another point on the same indifference curve. The slope of the blue chord connecting A and B is not the same as the slope of the tangent at A, but it is a rough approximation to the slope of that tangent. Clearly, the closer point B is picked to point A, the better that approximation will be. Now suppose the consumer moves from A to B by way of point C, which is not on the same indifference curve. This requires first taking some Y away from the consumer to go from A to C, and then giving the consumer some X to go from C to B. Let Δy and Δx be the necessary amounts of Y and X, respectively.

Consider what happens to the consumer's utility as these moves are made. In moving from A to C, utility changes by MU_y for every unit change in Y, so the total change in utility from A to C will be $MU_y(\Delta y)$. Similarly, in moving from C to B, utility changes by MU_x for every unit of change in X, so the total change in utility from C to B must be $MU_x(\Delta x)$. What is the overall change in utility for the complete movement from A to B by way of C? Clearly, no matter how she gets from A to B, her utility must end up being what it was originally at point A, because A and B are both on the same indifference curve, and therefore utility is the same at both points. Then for any Δy and Δx that takes us from one point on an indifference curve back to another point on the same indifference curve, it must be true that:

$$MU_y(\Delta y) + MU_x(\Delta x) = 0 \qquad (3.3)$$

Figure 3.7 The Slope of the Indifference Curve at a Point

The slope of the indifference curve, $\Delta y/\Delta x$, at point A equals the slope of the red tangent to the indifference curve at that point, which equals $-MU_x/MU_y$, and also equals the *MRS* at point A.

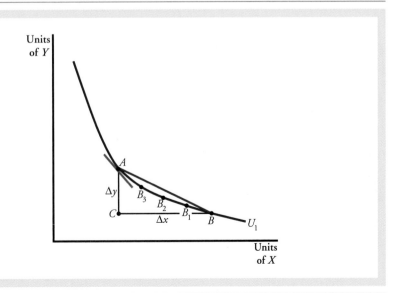

By rearranging Equation 3.3 a bit, an expression for the slope of the blue chord between A and B can be obtained. Because slope is just "rise" (Δy) over "run" (Δx), it follows that:

$$\text{slope of the chord } AB = \frac{\Delta y}{\Delta x} = -\frac{MU_x}{MU_y} \qquad (3.4)$$

Does it make any difference to our argument how far away point B is from point A, as long as the two points are on the same indifference curve? Not at all. Just imagine picking B closer and closer to A, say at B_1, B_2, B_3, and so on. Now imagine re-drawing the chord from A, and you'll see that it is possible to continue to make exactly the same argument and get the same kind of expression. The difference, of course, is that the closer B is to A, the closer the slope of the chord approximates the slope of the tangent at A. As B gets arbitrarily close to A, and as Δy and Δx involved get correspondingly smaller in size, the slope of the chord and the slope of the tangent at A will eventually become indistinguishable from one another. Using Equation 3.4, this procedure results in a perfectly general formula for the slope of *any* indifference curve at any point (x,y) in the plane:

$$\text{slope of the indifference curve at point } (x,y) = -\frac{MU_x}{MU_y} \qquad (3.5)$$

Equation 3.5 gives us a way to determine the slope of a consumer's indifference curves, which also equals the *MRS* at that point. Typically, the consumer prefers more of both goods to less, so $MU_x > 0$ and $MU_y > 0$ everywhere in the plane. In panel (a) of Figure 3.8, this will mean the direction of increasing preference through the indifference map is northeasterly. Using our formula for slope:

$$-\frac{MU_x}{MU_y} = \frac{-(+)}{(+)} < 0$$

so every indifference curve must be negatively sloped, which confirms our previous finding.

What if one of the commodities, X, is an economic bad, something the consumer would rather have less of, like sacks of garbage on her lawn? In panel (b) of Figure 3.8, good X is an economic bad so $MU_x < 0$, while good Y is a good so $MU_y > 0$, and in this case preference increases northwesterly through the indifference map and every indifference curve has a positive slope, because $-MU_x/MU_y = -(-)/(+) > 0$. Panels (c) and (d) illustrate other types of preferences.

▼▼▼   3.4   Budget Constraints

The next important building block in our theory of consumer choice is some description of the realistic opportunities the agent has when making her choices. In the words of Mick Jagger, "You can't always get what you want," and that is an unfortunate but important fact of life. In this section, we will account for the factors that constrain the consumer's freedom of choice.

Figure 3.8 Using Formula 3.5 for the Slope of an Indifference Curve
In panel (a), both X and Y are economic goods, so the direction of increasing preference is to the northeast, as indicated by the arrow, and the slope of the indifference curve is negative. In panel (b), X is an economic bad, and Y is an economic good, so the direction of preference is to the northwest and the slope of the indifference curves is positive. In panel (c), X is a neuter good and Y is an economic good, so the direction of preference is straight up and the slope of the indifference curves is zero. Finally, in panel (d), X is an economic good, but Y is an economic bad, so the direction of preference is to the southeast and the slope of the indifference curves is positive.

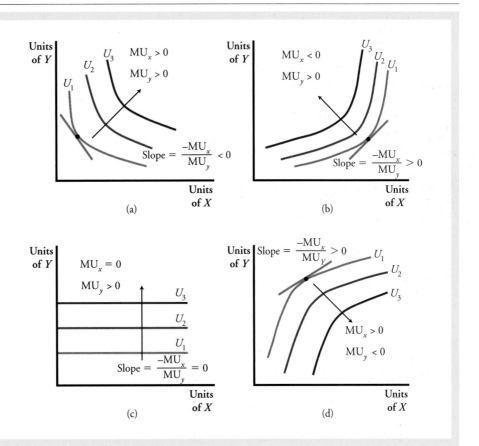

Standard Budget Constraints

To keep our focus simple, for now let's ignore the possibility of borrowing and lending. With only a limited income, the constraint the consumer faces is easily stated: *she may buy only what she can afford at fixed market prices from the income she has to spend.* That is, the consumer's total expenditure on all goods cannot exceed her income. To make this observation more precise, suppose the market price of good X is p_x dollars per unit, and the market price of Y is p_y dollars per unit. To buy x units of X requires expenditure of $p_x x$ dollars. To buy y units of Y requires expenditure of $p_y y$ dollars. To buy the bundle (x,y) containing x units of X and y units of Y requires a total expenditure of $p_x x + p_y y$ dollars. If the consumer has an income of I dollars to spend, she can only afford bundles (x,y) for which:

$$p_x x + p_y y \leq I \qquad (3.6)$$

budget constraint

A locus of points depicting all of the market baskets it is possible for the consumer to purchase.

Inequality 3.6 is called the consumer's **budget constraint**. In a compact and simple way, it expresses that the consumer cannot spend more on goods and services than she has available to spend. This constraint can be represented graphically by solving Inequality 3.6 for y as follows:

$$y \leq \frac{I}{p_y} - \frac{p_x}{p_y} x \qquad (3.7)$$

When this constraint holds with equality, it is simply a linear equation of the form $y = b + mx$. The y-intercept, b, is I/p_y and the slope, m, is $-p_x/p_y$. You can check that the x-intercept will be I/p_x. Figure 3.9 shows the budget constraint.

Keep in mind that there are many bundles that satisfy Inequality 3.6, and each one is a feasible choice for the consumer. To obtain any bundle on the green straight-line boundary in Figure 3.9, the consumer has to spend her entire income, because for all those bundles, condition 3.6 holds as an equality. Bundles inside the boundary are affordable, too, because they cost less than the consumer's income. Bundles outside the boundary are unattainable, because they cost more than the consumer's available income.

The intercepts of the budget constraint have their own economic significance. Money income, I, is called **nominal income**, which is simply the total number of dollars, euros, pesos, pounds, yen, or other currency the consumer has available to spend, and it is one measure of purchasing power. Economists, however, generally prefer to think of purchasing power as the consumer's true command over real goods and services. The consumer's command over real goods and services depends both on the consumer's nominal income and the prices he faces. A consumer's **real income** refers to the maximum number of units of real goods or services the consumer *could* buy, if he wanted to, with his available nominal income and given the prices he faces. In Figure 3.9, the horizontal intercept I/p_x measures the consumer's real income in units of good X. If nominal income is \$2,000 and the price of a unit of X is \$20, real income in units of X is I/p_x = \$2,000/\$20 = 100 units of X. Similarly, the vertical intercept I/p_y measures the consumer's real income in terms of Y. With the same nominal income of \$2,000, when the price of Y is \$4, the consumer's real income in units of Y is I/p_y = \$2,000/\$4 = 500 units of Y.

The slope of the budget constraint has economic significance as well. The ratio p_x/p_y is called the **relative price** of good X. This measures the number of units of good Y that

nominal income

The monetary value (in dollars, euros, pesos, pounds, yen, etc.) of what the consumer has available to spend.

real income

The maximum number of units of goods and services the consumer can buy.

relative price

The price of a good expressed as the number of units of another good that must be sacrificed to obtain one more unit of the good.

Figure 3.9
The Budget Constraint
Bundles on the green straight-line boundary between the blue and red areas require the consumer to spend his entire income. Bundles inside the boundary in the shaded blue area are affordable, because they cost less than the consumer's income. Bundles outside the boundary in the shaded red area are unattainable, because they cost more than the consumer's available income.

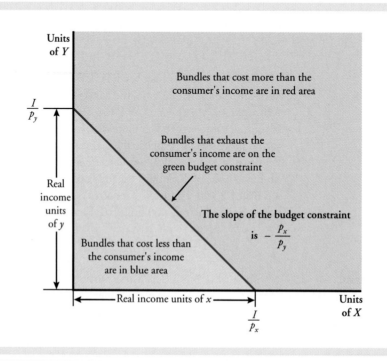

COMMON ERROR 3.1   The Slope of the Budget Constraint

A student is asked: What is the slope of the budget constraint in the (x,y) plane? The student pauses for a second and answers assuredly "$-(p_y/p_x)$." Ever since the student started to study mathematics, he has been taught that the slope of a line in the (x,y) plane is $\Delta y /\Delta x$, so surely the slope of the budget line must be the price of the good on the y-axis over the price of the good on the x-axis. There is a logical consistency to such thinking, but it is wrong in this case!

The slope of the budget constraint in the (x,y) plane is, indeed, $\Delta y/\Delta x$. However, the ratio $\Delta y/\Delta x$ is simply the ratio of the y-intercept over the x-intercept, or:

$$\frac{\Delta y}{\Delta x} = -\frac{\dfrac{I}{p_y}}{\dfrac{I}{p_x}} = -\frac{p_x}{p_y}$$

In this case, $\Delta y/\Delta x$ equals $-(p_x/p_y)$, that is, the slope of the budget constraint equals *minus* the price of the good on the x-axis over the price of the good on the y-axis. Do not fall into the common trap of inverting this ratio.

must be foregone in order to have one more unit of good X. In our previous example, the price of X was \$20 per unit and the price of Y was \$4 per unit. The relative price of X is therefore:

$$\frac{p_x}{p_y} = \frac{\$20}{\$4} = 5$$

Thus, when $p_x = \$20$ and $p_y = \$4$, the consumer must forego five units of Y for every unit of X he consumes. The ratio p_x/p_y measures the rate at which the consumer must trade off Y to get X in the marketplace. Just like our measures of real income, relative prices eliminate the "yardstick of money" and help us to focus on what truly matters, the rate at which one good can be exchanged for another good in the market.

What happens when the price of some good or the consumer's nominal income changes? This question can be answered by looking back at the rearranged budget constraint in Inequality 3.7. If the price of X decreases to $p_{x1} < p_{x0}$, there will be no change to the y-intercept of the boundary, but the absolute value of the slope will decrease to $p_{x1}/p_y < p_{x0}/p_y$. A decrease in the price of X also makes the x-intercept increase because, when $p_{x1} < p_{x0}$, the ratio I/p_{x1} is greater than the ratio I/p_{x0}. In panel (a) of Figure 3.10, the decrease in the price of X causes the budget constraint to pivot outward from the original y-intercept. When the price of X increases to $p_{x1} > p_{x0}$, the absolute value of the slope increases, the x-intercept decreases, and the budget constraint pivots inward from the original y-intercept, as in panel (b). Looking once again at Inequality 3.7, notice that a decrease in the price of Y will leave the x-intercept unaffected but will increase both the (absolute value of) slope and the y-intercept, causing the budget constraint this time to pivot outward from the x-intercept as in panel (c). An increase in p_y will cause the constraint to pivot inward from the x-intercept as in panel (d). Finally, notice that any change in the consumer's income, I, will have no effect on the slope of the budget constraint, because the slope depends only on relative prices. It will, however, affect *both* intercepts. An increase in income causes a *parallel outward shift*, while a decrease in income causes a *parallel inward shift*, as in panels (e) and (f).

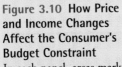

Figure 3.10 How Price and Income Changes Affect the Consumer's Budget Constraint
In each panel, areas marked with + signs indicate increased consumption possibilities for the consumer and areas marked with − signs indicate decreased consumption possibilities for the consumer. In panel (a), a decrease in the price of X causes the budget constraint to pivot outward from the original y-intercept. In panel (b), an increase in the price of X causes the budget constraint to pivot inward from the original y-intercept. In panel (c), a decrease in the price of Y causes the budget constraint to pivot outward from the original x-intercept. In panel (d), an increase in the price of Y causes the budget constraint to pivot inward from the original x-intercept. In panel (e), an increase in income causes a parallel shift outward in the budget constraint. Finally, in panel (f), a decrease in income causes a parallel shift inward in the budget constraint.

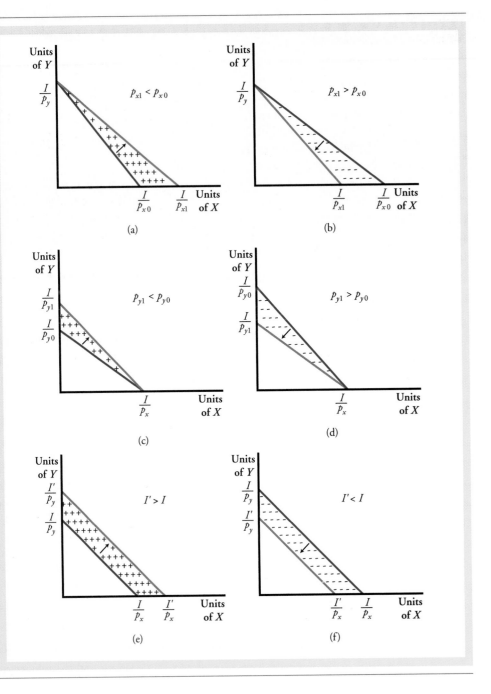

Some Non-Standard Constraints

At the height of the energy crisis in 1973–74, the U.S. federal government drew up plans to ration gasoline to consumers. Had these plans been implemented, they would have introduced an additional kind of constraint for consumers. Additional constraints like this can be incorporated into our description of the consumer's constraint.

In the simplest form of rationing, consumers are provided with a fixed number of coupons for their own use and may not sell their coupons to anyone else. Every time one

▲▲▲ 3.4 APPLICATION Kinko's "Kinky" Budget Constraint

Over the last two decades, Kinko's Copies, Inc. has grown from a single outlet photocopier to a 700-store, highly successful worldwide chain, providing a range of electronic services—primarily photocopies, faxes, Internet usage, and computer rentals. Kinko's has achieved its success by combining high-quality service with an aggressive pricing policy.

In February 2002, for orders placed over the Internet, Kinko's charged the following prices for color copies:

Number of color copies	Price per copy
1–149	0.99
150–249	0.89
250–349	0.79
350–399	0.69
400+	0.59

The price was $0.99 for the first 149 single-sided color copies, but only $0.89 for all color copies if the order was for 150–249 copies (including the first 149 copies). In other words, 149 copies cost $147.51, but 150 copies cost only $133.50, and 400 copies cost only $236.00. Suppose a consumer's income is $500 and the price of "all other goods" is $1.00. Then in a choice between "color copies" and "all other goods," Kinko's offers its customers the "kinky" budget constraint shown in the graph.

If Kinko's charged $0.99 for every copy, the customer's budget constraint would be a steep straight line with slope −0.99. If they charged $0.59 for each copy, the budget constraint would be the flatter line with slope −0.59. Because the price of all other goods is $1.00, the vertical intercept is $500/$1 = 500 units of other goods in either case. Under Kinko's quantity discount policy, a customer will be on the steepest line if they buy 149

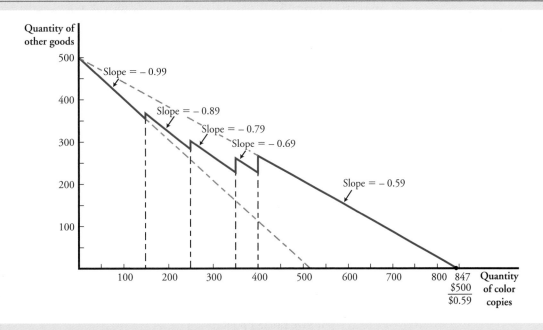

Application Figure 3.4AP Kinko's "Kinky" Budget Constraint
If Kinko's charged $0.99 for every copy, the customer's budget constraint would be a steep straight line with slope −0.99. If they charged $0.59 for each copy, the budget constraint would be the flattest line with slope −0.59. If the price of all other goods is $1.00, the vertical intercept is 500 units of other goods. Under Kinko's quantity discount policy, a customer will be on the steepest line if they buy 149 copies or fewer, and they will be on one of the four flatter line segments if they order 150 or more copies. The complete budget constraint is the "kinky" solid green line.

(continued)

copies or fewer, and then they will be on one of the four flatter line segments if they order 150 or more copies. The resulting overall budget constraint is the "kinky" solid green line.

It would be nice to claim that Kinko's got its name because its founder had taken microeconomics and

decided to name his firm after the shape of the budget constraint in the graph. In fact, however, the true origins of the name are much less academic: Paul Orfalea, who started Kinko's in 1973 with a single Xerox machine, has kinky hair.

unit of the good is purchased at the current price, one coupon must be presented to the seller, so the consumer can buy only as many units of the rationed good as she has coupons to spend. In effect, the consumer faces two constraints instead of just one. She cannot spend more than she has in income, *and* she cannot buy more than a certain number of units of the rationed good. If X is the rationed good, and if x_0 is the maximum number of units for which she has coupons, the consumer may only buy bundles (x, y) that satisfy the two constraints:

$$p_x x + p_y y \leq I \tag{3.8}$$

$$x \leq x_0 \tag{3.9}$$

In panel (a) of Figure 3.11, all bundles on or inside the consumer's ordinary budget constraint to the right of x_0 contain more X than the ration limit, so none of these can be purchased. Thus, the feasible alternatives that remain are only those inside or on the "truncated" portion of the original budget constraint. Panel (b) of Figure 3.11 shows the consumer's alternatives when Y is rationed, and panel (c) when both X and Y are rationed.

Sometimes buyers must pay different prices for the same good depending on how much they buy. For example, during periods when water is scarce, some localities in California will charge residential users one price per gallon up to a certain number of gallons, and then a higher (punitive) price for every additional gallon thereafter. Suppose a pricing scheme such as this is in effect for good X. If you buy no more than x_0 units of the good, you pay p_{x1}; if you buy more than x_0 units, you pay a higher price per unit, $p_{x2} > p_{x1}$, for each additional unit. If you could always pay the lower price p_{x1}, with a fixed income I and facing a fixed price of Y, your budget constraint would be the flatter of the two lines in Figure 3.12. However, because you can pay the lower price only until your consumption of X reaches x_0, and you must then pay the higher price for every unit beyond x_0, your overall budget constraint will consist of two separate segments: the flatter segment with a slope of $-(p_{x1}/p_y)$ up to x_0, and the steeper segment with a slope of $-(p_{x2}/p_y)$ beyond x_0. Consumption bundles on the flatter constraint beyond an output of x_0, which would normally be affordable at everyday prices, will not be affordable any longer under the punitive pricing policy.

3.5 Consumer Choice

To complete our theory of consumer choice, we need to make some assumptions about the agent's objectives by spelling out exactly what the consumer is after when he has to choose from among a number of mutually exclusive alternatives. Economists believe that self-interest

Figure 3.11
The Effects of Rationing on the Consumer's Budget Constraint

In panel (a), X is rationed and all bundles in the red areas that are on or inside the consumer's ordinary budget constraint but to the right of x_0 are beyond the consumer's reach. The feasible points of consumption are on the kinked green line. In panel (b), Y is rationed and all bundles in the blue areas are beyond the consumer's reach. The feasible points of consumption are on the kinked green line. Finally, in panel (c), both X and Y are rationed, and the feasible points are once again only those on the kinked green line.

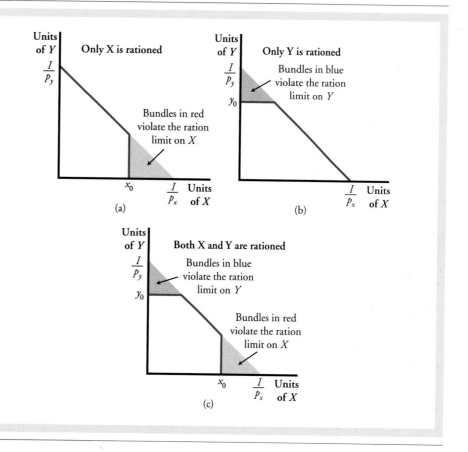

Figure 3.12
The Budget Constraint with Punitive Pricing on Good X

Suppose if you buy no more than x_0 units of the good you pay p_{x1}; if you buy more than x_0 units you pay a higher price per unit, $p_{x2} > p_{x1}$, for each additional unit. The budget constraint will then consist of two separate line segments: the flatter light-green segment with a slope of $-(p_{x1}/p_y)$ up to x_0, and the steeper dark-green segment with a slope of $-(p_{x2}/p_y)$ beyond x_0.

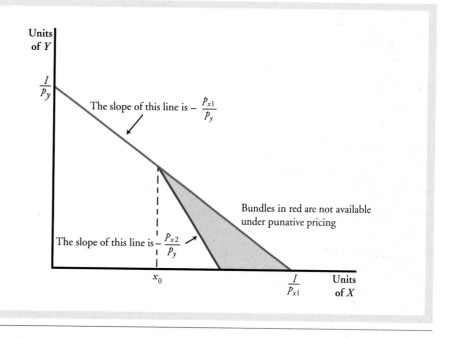

motivates the market decisions of all private agents. As disarmingly simple as such an assumption may be, self-interest is clearly not the only thing that motivates people in everything they do. People give money to charity, expecting little financial benefit in return. Some people don't smoke cigarettes in public out of consideration for how their second-hand smoke might offend (or even injure) others. However, for the average consumer who transacts in a range of large and impersonal markets, there is ample evidence suggesting that self-interest is what motivates most people, most of the time, in most of their market behavior.

Consumer Equilibrium

utility maximization

The condition of consumer equilibrium where the consumer chooses from all of the possible market baskets on the budget constraint, the basket that yields the highest level of utility (satisfaction).

When choosing among the various goods and services a consumer might buy, self-interest suggests that consumers always try to buy the bundle they prefer. Because one bundle of goods is preferred to another bundle only if the utility from that bundle is higher than the utility from the other, we will restate this as the assumption of **utility maximization**. Utility maximization states that *the consumer will always choose the bundle that maximizes utility from among all those bundles that are feasible.* Once this assumption about the agent's objectives is added to our descriptions of his preferences and his opportunities, all the pieces of our theory are in place to predict the consumer's equilibrium choice.

Figure 3.13 superimposes an indifference map representing a standard set of preferences over a budget constraint representing the ordinary type of market opportunities a consumer faces. To predict the consumer's choice, it is necessary to search among the feasible alternatives for the one that is preferred to all others. No bundle *inside* the boundary of the budget constraint, such as *A* or *B*, will be chosen, because there will always be some other bundle *on* the budget constraint, such as *D* or *E*, that contains more of both *X* and *Y*, and therefore will be preferred by the assumption of non-satiation. At the same time, not every bundle on the budget constraint is the best choice either. Neither *D* nor *E* could be best, because there are other bundles, such as *C* and *F*, which are also affordable, because they too lie on the budget constraint, but which are preferable over *D* and *E*, because they lie on higher indifference curves. With only a little bit of experimenting with different feasible bundles, you will see that (x^*, y^*) is the best choice. Because no other bundle inside or on the budget constraint can be found that will put the consumer

Figure 3.13 An Interior Solution to the Consumer's Choice Problem
Bundle (x^*, y^*) is the consumer's best choice, because no other bundle inside or on the budget constraint can be found that will put the consumer on a higher indifference curve. Therefore, the consumer is in equilibrium at the point (x^*, y^*).

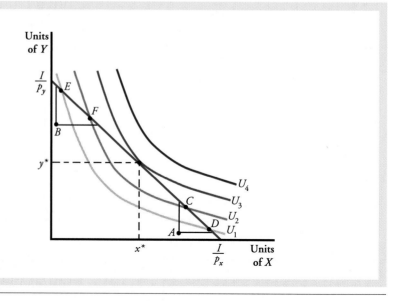

on a higher indifference curve, the bundle (x^*, y^*) maximizes the consumer's utility among his available options. The consumer is in equilibrium at (x^*, y^*), because as soon as she has located that bundle, she has no incentive to change her behavior or search any further. This is, therefore, the bundle the consumer will purchase in the marketplace.

INTERIOR SOLUTIONS When a consumer buys positive amounts of both X and Y, as in Figure 3.13, there is an **interior solution** to the consumer's choice problem, because equilibrium occurs somewhere between the end-points of the budget constraint, where the consumer consumes positive quantities of both goods. Under our usual assumptions on preferences, and facing fixed prices and income, an interior solution always involves a tangency between the budget constraint and the highest indifference curve the consumer can reach. Thus, two conditions characterize an interior consumer equilibrium:

interior solution

A consumer equilibrium where the consumer purchases positive amounts of all available goods.

1. The slope of the indifference curve and the slope of the budget constraint at the chosen point must be equal.
2. The chosen point must be on, rather than inside, the budget constraint.

It is useful to translate these two conditions into mathematical form to reinforce our understanding of the geometry in Figure 3.13. We've seen (1) that the MRS_{yx} is the absolute value of the slope of the indifference curve and (2) that the absolute value of the slope of the budget constraint is just the ratio of p_x over p_y. The first of our two conditions tells us that at equilibrium, the MRS_{yx} must equal the absolute value of the slope of the budget constraint. The second condition says that the budget constraint in Inequality 3.6 must hold with equality in equilibrium. Thus, when the consumer buys positive amounts of each good, the chosen bundle (x^*, y^*) will satisfy the following two mathematical conditions:

$$MRS_{yx} = \frac{p_x}{p_y} \qquad (3.10)$$

$$p_x x^* + p_y y^* = I \qquad (3.11)$$

Because a utility-maximizing consumer chooses some point on rather than inside the budget constraint, Equation 3.11 must hold. To see why Equation 3.10 must also hold, suppose that Equation 3.10 did *not* hold. For example, at point E in Figure 3.13, the $MRS_{yx} > p_x/p_y$ (the slope of the indifference curve is greater than the price ratio). When $MU_x > 0$ and $MU_y > 0$, our formula for the slope of an indifference curve in Equation 3.5 tells us that MRS_{yx} will be equal to the ratio of MU_x to MU_y. Thus, at point E:

$$MRS_{yx} = \frac{MU_x}{MU_y} > \frac{p_x}{p_y} \qquad (3.12)$$

or, rearranging a bit:

$$\frac{MU_x}{p_x} > \frac{MU_y}{p_y} \qquad (3.13)$$

This inequality states that the marginal utility the consumer can *gain* by spending an extra dollar on X exceeds the marginal utility he would *lose* by spending one less dollar on Y. By reducing his expenditure on Y by one dollar and increasing his expenditure on X by one dollar, total expenditure remains the same but total utility must increase by $[(MU_x/p_x) - (MU_y/p_y)] > 0$! Because moving down the budget constraint toward (x^*, y^*) will increase utility without the need to spend more money, no point like E can be the

▲▲▲ 3.5 APPLICATION   The Problem with College Meal Plans

Many colleges and universities require students to purchase "meal plans," in which students pay a fixed fee at the beginning of the year regardless of the number of meals they will eat. Students are often dissatisfied with this arrangement. They complain about poor quality food, lack of variety, inflexible meal hours, and more. Yet even if all these problems were solved, the theory of consumer choice suggests that students would remain dissatisfied.

To illustrate, assume that a meal costs $5.00, whether that meal is prepared by the college dining hall or purchased in an off-campus restaurant. Also assume that a student has $4,000 to spend on meals and all other goods, and the price of other goods is $1.00 per unit. In the absence of a meal plan, the student's budget constraint would be the line AB in panel (a) of the graph. For this student, utility is maximized at point F, where he consumes 500 meals at a cost of $2,500 and 1,500 units of other goods.

Now, suppose instead that this student is forced onto a meal plan that provides 600 meals during the academic year and charges $3,000 regardless of the number of meals the student chooses to consume. The budget constraint is now the kinked line segment DEB. The highest

level of utility this student can now achieve is at point E, with 600 meals consumed, and only 1,000 units of other goods. Because the indifference curve through E is lower than the one through F, forcing the student onto the meal plan makes him worse off. This will remain the case even if once on the meal plan, he chooses to eat every meal offered by the plan.

Not all students would be worse off under the meal plan. Suppose that in the absence of the meal plan some other student, with different tastes and indifference curves than those in panel (a), achieved tangency with the budget constraint at a point to the right of E. Panel (b) shows such a situation. Here a student with different preferences is in equilibrium at point C regardless of whether there is a meal plan. At point C, for example, this student buys 700 meals during the academic year, leaving only $500 to spend on other goods. Forcing this student onto the meal plan just changes *where* he purchased some of his meals, but does not change the total number of meals he purchases. Again assuming away issues of food quality, ambience, and convenience, this student would be neither worse nor better off under the meal plan.

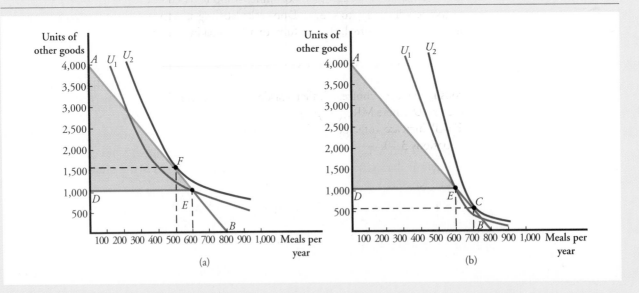

Application Figure 3.4 A College Meal Plan
In panel (a), in the absence of a meal plan, the student's budget constraint is the straight line AB. Equilibrium is at F, where the student consumes 500 meals and 1,500 units of other goods. If the student is forced onto a meal plan that provides 600 meals and charges $3,000 regardless of the number of meals the student consumes, the budget constraint is the kinked dark green line segment DEB. The highest level of utility this student can now achieve is at point E, with 600 meals consumed, and only 1,000 units of other goods. In panel (b), equilibrium is at C, where 700 meals and 500 units of other goods are consumed regardless of whether there is a meal plan.

COMMON ERROR 3.2   Taking Shortcuts in Labeling the *X*-Axis and *Y*-Axis

Students often try to take shortcuts with the labels in their graphs, and as a result create unnecessary problems. For example, in this graph, a student has labeled the consumer's initial equilibrium at point *A* on the budget line y_1x_1. Instead of labeling the intercepts as I/p_y and I/p_x, the student has used the shortcut labels of y_1 and x_1. Now the student is asked to show the effect of a decrease in the price of good *X*. The student instinctually thinks: "The price of good *X* has decreased and a decrease in *X* is measured by moving the intercept to the left toward the origin. The new budget line, therefore, is the line y_1x_2 and the new equilibrium is at point *B*." *This is entirely wrong!* Notice that because $x_2 < x_1$, the implication of this error is that the consumer purchases less of good *X* as the price of *X* decreases.

The correct answer is: A decrease in the price of good *X* increases I/p_x and shifts the *x*-intercept to the right, not the left. As a result, if good *X* is normal, the

Common Error Figure 3.2 A Shortcut Labeling Problem
To save time the initial quantities of *x* and *y* are labeled as x_1 and y_1. When the price of *x* decreases, the student instinctually shifts the *x* intercept left to x_2, but this is wrong.

consumer will purchase more *X* as the price decreases. Don't take labeling shortcuts. Label your graphs carefully to avoid making this common error.

---

consumer's best choice. Similar reasoning should convince you that from some point such as *D*, where $MRS_{yx} < p_x/p_y$, reallocating expenditure away from *X* and toward more *Y* will increase total utility. Thus, whenever the consumer buys some of each good, Equations 3.10 and 3.11 must be satisfied.

CORNER SOLUTIONS Of course, whether the consumer buys positive amounts of some good in his budget will depend on the prices of all goods and the consumer's income. Facing some prices and income, it is possible that a rational consumer, even one who prefers more of every good to less, will choose not to buy any amount of some goods in his budget. When this occurs, the consumer's equilibrium occurs at a **corner solution**. Figure 3.14 illustrates this possibility. In panel (a), the price of caviar is very high compared to the price of smoked salmon, so the budget constraint is very flat. Given the consumer's indifference curves, the consumer maximizes utility at point *A*, where she consumes only smoked salmon and no caviar. At point *A*, the $MRS_{CS} > (p_S/p_C)$, and therefore the condition in Equation 3.10 does not hold. Similarly, in panel (b), the price of a BIC ballpoint pen is very low (less than $1.00) compared to the price of a fine Parker Fourge fountain pen ($300.00!), so the budget constraint is very steep. Given the consumer's indifference curves, the consumer maximizes utility at point *B*, where she consumes only BIC pens and no Parker Fourge fountain pens. At point *B*, the $MRS_{BP} < (p_P/p_B)$, and therefore, the condition in Equation 3.10 once again does not hold.

corner solution

A consumer equilibrium where the consumer prefers to purchase a quantity equal to zero of some good or service.

Figure 3.14 Corner Solutions to the Consumer's Choice Problem
In panel (a), the consumer maximizes utility at point A on the quantity of smoked salmon axis and consumes only smoked salmon and no caviar. At point A, the $\mathrm{MRS}_{CS} > (p_C/p_S)$. In panel (b), the consumer maximizes utility at point B and consumes only BIC pens. At point B, the $\mathrm{MRS}_{BP} < (p_P/p_B)$.

(a) Corner Solution on the Horizontal Axis   (b) Corner Solution on the Vertical Axis

3.6   Consumer Demand

Our theory of consumer behavior tells us that the quantity of any single good a consumer buys will depend on income and the prices of all goods in the consumer's budget. Using the tools developed to this point, it is possible to explore in more detail just how consumer demand might respond to price and income changes. First we explore consumer behavior when all prices and the consumer's income change proportionally. Then we examine separately how demand responds to a change in a good's own price, a change in some other good's price, and a change in the consumer's income. Appendix 3.1 shows how the precise mathematical form of the demand curve can be derived from a utility function and budget constraint.

Proportional Changes in All Prices and Income

How do consumers respond to a general increase in the level of prices and incomes? To explore this question, suppose some consumer initially faces prices p_x and p_y, and has an income of I. Now suppose there is a simultaneous equal percentage change in both prices and the consumer's income. That is, suppose all prices and income are doubled, tripled, or just scaled upward by any common factor $t > 0$. Facing prices tp_x, tp_y, and having income tI, how will the consumer change his behavior? The answer is *not at all*! To understand why, notice that any equal percentage change in prices and income must leave relative prices and real income completely unchanged. Thus, the consumer's budget constraint before and after this kind of price and income change will be *exactly the same*. With no change in the consumer's opportunities, there is no change in his behavior.

money illusion

A situation where consumers believe they are better off when their nominal income increases, even if prices increase by an equal or greater percent.

This experiment illustrates that consumers do not suffer from **money illusion**. That is, rational utility-maximizing consumers will not be fooled by increases in income if prices of everything they consume go up at the same time in exactly the same proportion.

Own Price Changes

When the price of a good decreases, the consumer's purchasing power over all goods increases. Ordinarily, at least some of that increased purchasing power will go toward buying more of the good that has become relatively cheaper. Figure 3.15 illustrates such a case. In panel (a), as the price of X falls from p_{x0} to p_{x1} to p_{x2}, the consumer's equilibrium changes from point A to point B to point C. Panel (b) shows an x-axis parallel to the one above it and a vertical axis that measures different prices of X. If the quantity of good X that the consumer would buy is plotted against the price of X at which he would buy it, holding the price of Y and his income constant, the consumer's demand curve for good X can be traced out.

In panel (a) in Figure 3.15, at a price of p_{x0}, the consumer demands x_0 units of good X; at a price of p_{x1}, the consumer demands x_1 units of good X; and at a price of p_{x2}, the consumer demands x_2 units of good X. Each of these points is identified in panel (b), where the demand curve tells us how many units of good X the consumer will buy at every possible price of X, *ceteris paribus*. By holding income and the price of Y constant and varying the price of X, it is possible to analyze the effects on consumer demand of

Figure 3.15 Deriving the Demand Curve for Good *X*

In panel (a), as the price of X falls from p_{x0} to p_{x1} to p_{x2}, the consumer's equilibrium changes from point A to point B to point C. Points on the blue curve identify the price-consumption path showing all of the possible consumer equilibrium points associated with every possible price of X, *ceteris paribus*. In panel (b), the quantity of good X that the consumer would buy at different prices is plotted, and the consumer's demand curve for good X is identified. Each point on the demand curve corresponds to one unique point on the price-consumption path.

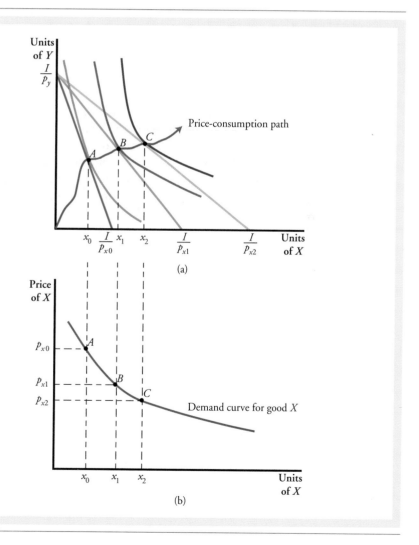

any change in the price of *X*. In panel (a), a solid blue curve connects successive points of consumer equilibrium at the different prices of *X*. Moving upward from the origin, the points on this blue curve identify the **price-consumption path**, which tells us how the demand for *X* changes as the price of *X* decreases.

In Figure 3.15, every price decrease causes an increase in the quantity of *X* demanded. This need not always be the case, however. In highly unusual cases, a price decrease might even cause a *decrease* in the quantity of some good a consumer buys. Goods like this are called **Giffen goods**, and the demand curve for a Giffen good is positively sloped. In Figure 3.16, at a price of p_{x0}, the consumer demands x_0 units of good *X*; at a lower price of p_{x1} the consumer demand declines to x_1 units of good *X*, and at a still lower price of p_{x2} the consumer demand declines further to x_2 units of good *X*. Panel (b) identifies each of these points. In the case of a Giffen good, demand is upward-sloping in this price range.

Some economists are skeptical of the existence of Giffen goods. Others believe that in the mid-nineteenth century in Ireland, potatoes were a Giffen good. Potatoes were the main staple of the Irish diet back then, and when the price of potatoes decreased, Irish consumers purchased fewer potatoes and used the income saved from the lower price of

price-consumption path

A curve showing all of the possible consumer equilibrium points associated with every possible price for one good, *ceteris paribus*.

Giffen good

A good with a positively sloped demand curve, because the consumer purchases more of the good as the price increases.

Figure 3.16 Demand for a Giffen Good
In panel (a), at a price of p_{x0}, the consumer demands x_0 units of good *X*; at a lower price of p_{x1}, the consumer demand declines to x_1 units of good *X*; and at a still lower price of p_{x2}, the consumer demand declines further to x_2 units of good *X*. Panel (b) identifies these points as resulting in an upward-sloping demand curve in this price range.

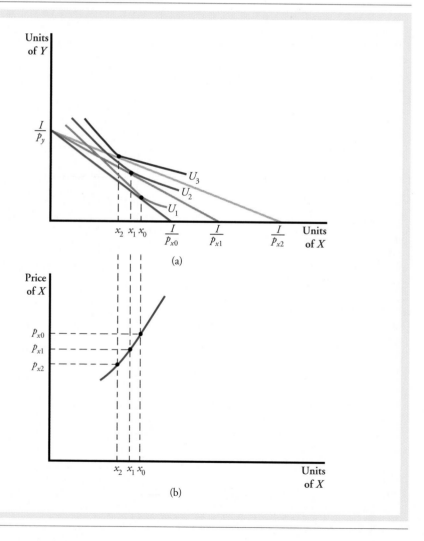

potatoes to purchase other goods such as beef or pork. As unusual as Giffen goods are, our theory of consumer behavior and demand can explain this type of behavior as the outcome of a rational decision-making process by a consumer with certain preferences and facing certain kinds of market circumstances.

Cross-Price Changes

cross-price effects

The change in quantity demanded of one good in response to a price change of another good.

Our theory predicts that demand for any one good will depend on the prices of all related goods, as well as on its own price. **Cross-price effects** tell us how the quantity demanded of one good responds to a change in the price of some other good. Figure 3.17 illustrates the three possible cross price effects on the demand for X that might occur in response to an increase in the price of Y. In the top portion of panel (a), an increase in p_y causes a decrease in the quantity of Y demanded and an increase in the quantity demanded of X from x_0 to x_1. When the quantity of one good increases after the price of another good increases, the two goods are substitutes for one another. Here, the increase in the price of Y to $p_{y1} > p_{y0}$ causes the quantity of X demanded to increase to $x_1 > x_0$. Because the demand curve for X is constructed for a given price of Y and a given level of income, an

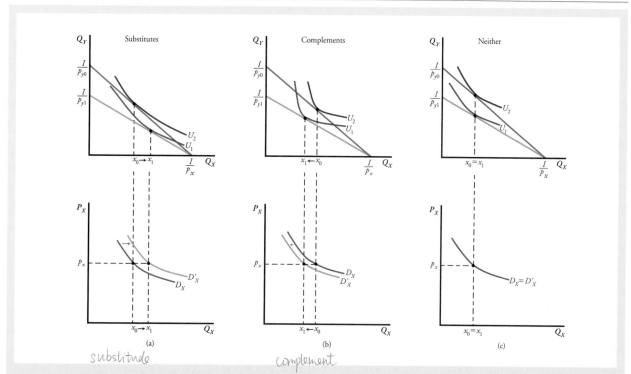

Figure 3.17 Cross-Price Effects on the Demand for Good X

In the top portion of panel (a), an increase in the price of Y to $p_{y1} > p_{y0}$ causes the quantity of X demanded to increase from x_0 to x_1. In the lower panel of (a), the increase in the price of Y causes the demand curve for X to shift to the right. In this case, X and Y are substitutes. In the top portion of panel (b), an increase in the price of Y to $p_{y1} > p_{y0}$ causes the quantity of X demanded to decrease from x_0 to x_1. In the lower panel of (b) the increase in the price of Y causes the demand curve for X to shift to the left. In this case, X and Y are complements. In the top portion of panel (c), an increase in the price of Y to $p_{y1} > p_{y0}$ does not cause a change in the quantity of X demanded, so the demand curve does not shift at all. In this case, X and Y are neither substitutes nor complements, but are essentially unrelated to each other.

increase in the price of a substitute good will cause the demand curve for X to shift to the right in the bottom portion of panel (a).

In panel (b) of Figure 3.17, an increase in the price of Y causes a decrease in the quantity of X demanded at every given price of X and income level. Here, X and Y are complements, and the price increase to $p_{y1} > p_{y0}$ causes the demand curve for X to shift to the left in the bottom portion of the panel. Finally, in panel (c) of Figure 3.17, an increase in the price to $p_{y1} > p_{y0}$ has no effect on the demand for X. In this case, X and Y are neither substitutes nor complements.

Income Changes

A change in income will also affect how much of all goods the consumer can afford. Once again, our theory of consumer demand allows us to explain a wide range of ways the consumer might respond to a change in income. Economists have developed a special vocabulary to help classify the different possibilities. Recall from Chapter 2 that a normal good is one that a person consumes more of as his income rises, *ceteris paribus*. If you buy more restaurant meals and theater tickets when your income increases, then both of these would be normal goods for you. By contrast, an inferior good is one a person consumes less of as income increases. If you buy fewer bags of Cheetos, choosing more exotic *hors d'oeuvres* instead as your income increases, then Cheetos are an inferior good for you.

By holding relative prices constant and varying the consumer's income, the effects on consumer demand of any change in income can be analyzed using the framework developed in this chapter. The top panels of Figure 3.18 illustrate a number of possibilities that might arise as a result of an increase in income from I_0 to I_1. In each case, a solid blue curve connects successive points of consumer equilibrium at the different levels of income. These blue **income-consumption paths** tell us how demand for both X and Y will change as income rises in each case.

In panel (a), an increase in income causes the quantity of both goods demanded to increase. When X and Y are both normal goods, the income-consumption path will be upward-sloping. In panel (b), an increase in income causes the consumer to buy more Y and less X, so in this case Y is a normal good but X is an inferior good. When one good is inferior and the other is normal, the income-consumption path will be negatively

income-consumption path

A curve showing all of the possible consumer equilibrium points associated with every possible level of income, *ceteris paribus*.

▲▲▲ **3.6 APPLICATION**   Income Effects and Charitable Giving

The year 2001 was a difficult economic year. The economy went into a recession beginning in March 2001, and the stock market continued the downward slide that began in March 2000. To make matters worse, on September 11, the world's economic stability was shattered. All of these negative effects had a great impact on the incomes of many individuals, including the world's wealthiest individuals. Charitable giving is a normal good with a high income elasticity of demand. As the incomes of the world's super-rich declined dramatically in 2001, so did their charitable giving.

Bill Gates, the chair of Microsoft Corporation and the world's wealthiest person, was the world's leading philanthropist in both 2000 and 2001. However, Gates's charitable contributions fell from $5 billion in 2000 to "just" $2 billion in 2001, a decline of 60 percent. In fact, the ten largest single charitable gifts in 2001 totaled only $4.6 billion, compared to $11.08 billion in 2000. These figures show that even the super-rich have budget constraints, and economic forces impact their households just as they do every other household.

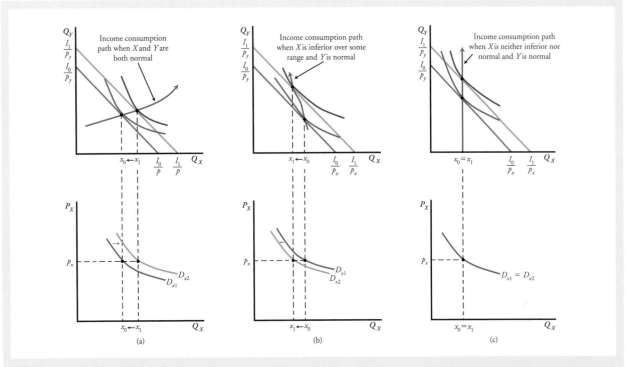

Figure 3.18 Income Changes and the Demand for Good X

In the top portion of panel (a), an increase in income from I_0 to I_1 causes the quantity of both X and Y to increase, and therefore both X and Y are normal goods and the income-consumption path is upward-sloping. In the lower panel of (a), the increase in income causes the demand curve for X to increase from D_{x1} to D_{x2}. In panel (b), an increase in income from I_0 to I_1 causes the consumer to buy more Y and less X, so in this case Y is a normal good but X is an inferior good. When one good is inferior and the other is normal, the income-consumption path will be negatively sloped. In the lower panel of (b), the increase in income causes the demand curve for X to decrease from D_{x1} to D_{x2}. In panel (c), Y is normal, but the demand for X is completely income-inelastic and the income-consumption path is a vertical straight line. In the lower panel of (c), the demand curve for X remains constant.

sloped. In panel (c), Y is normal, but X is neither normal nor inferior. In this case, the demand for X is completely income-inelastic and the income-consumption path is a vertical straight line.

The bottom panels illustrate how a change in income will affect the demand curve for X in each of these three cases. In panel (a), when X is normal, an increase in income, holding all prices constant, will cause an increase in the demand for X, so the demand curve for X at income $I_1 > I_0$ will lie to the right of the demand curve when income is I_0. In panel (b), when X is inferior, an increase in income to I_1 causes the quantity demanded at every price to decline and results in an inward shift in the demand curve for X. In panel (c), when X is completely income-inelastic, an increase (or decrease) in income has no effect on the demand curve for X.

Summary

1. The theory of consumer behavior has four separate components: a description of the objects of choice, the consumer's preferences, the consumer's opportunities, and the consumer's objectives. Preferences are described by four assumptions of rationality. Completeness and transitivity guarantee that the consumer can make choices that are logically consistent. The assumption of non-satiation says more of every good is better than less of it. The assumption of convexity ensures a diminishing marginal rate of substitution.

2. Preferences can be represented graphically by indifference curves. Under our four basic assumptions, indifference curves will be negatively sloped, non-intersecting, and convex away from the origin.

3. A utility function represents consumer preferences by assigning numbers to bundles in a particular way. When one bundle is preferred to another, a utility function assigns a larger number to the one that's preferred. When the consumer is indifferent between two bundles, the utility function will assign both bundles the same number. Because economists assume that consumers can rank only alternative bundles of goods and services from better bundles to worse bundles, but it is impossible to measure how much better or worse one bundle is compared to another, utility functions measure utility using ordinal measures.

4. The budget constraint reflects a consumer's inability to spend more than her available income. The intercepts of the budget constraint measure the consumer's real income in terms of purchasing power of the good measured on that axis. The slope of the budget constraint reflects relative prices. Any change in real income or relative prices will change the consumer's budget constraint.

5. A consumer maximizes utility by choosing a bundle on the budget constraint that gets her on the highest possible indifference curve. At an interior solution, this will involve a tangency between the budget constraint and the highest indifference curve, and the MRS equals the price ratio.

6. Consumer demand for any one good depends on the prices of all goods and the consumer's income. Any change in relative prices or real income will generally cause the quantity of every good demanded to change as well. The demand curve depicts how the utility-maximizing amount of one good varies as that good's own price varies, holding all other prices and income constant. The income-consumption path shows how the demand for all goods varies as real income changes, holding relative prices constant.

Self-Test Problems

1. Carefully plot the following bundles in the (x,y) plane: $A = (5,12)$; $B = (15,8)$; $C = (10,10)$; $D = (13,12)$; $E = (5,9)$. We know the consumer's preferences satisfy assumptions 1 through 4 given in the text, and we know the consumer is *indifferent* between bundles A and B.

   a. When comparing bundles A and E, which does the consumer prefer? Why?

   b. When comparing the following bundles, which does she prefer, and why? C and D? E and B? C and B? B and D?

   c. Indicate the consumer's preferences over all bundles A through E by making a list in descending order of preference, starting with the bundles she prefers to all others at the top, and ending with the bundle to which all others are preferred at the bottom. If she's indifferent between two bundles, put them side-by-side in your list.

2. Suppose a consumer has no money income. Instead, she owns 200 units of X and 100 units of Y. Suppose she can freely buy or sell X at a market price of $2, and freely buy or sell Y at a market price of $4.

   a. Write down an algebraic expression for the consumer's budget constraint in this case, summarizing her consumption possibilities over X and Y.

   b. Carefully sketch her budget constraint in the (x,y) plane.

3. A consumer's utility function is $u(x,y) = x + y$. Suppose the price of X is $4, the price of Y is $2, and the consumer's income is $12.

   a. Carefully sketch this consumer's indifference map. Briefly justify why slope and direction of increasing preference must be as you have depicted them.

   b. On the same axes, superimpose the consumer's budget constraint. Briefly justify why slope and intercepts must be as you have depicted them.

   c. How much X and how much Y will the consumer buy at these prices and income? Briefly justify your claim.

Questions and Problems for Review

1. Consider a person whose preferences are represented by the utility function $u(x,y) = xy$.

   a. For each pair of bundles A and B, indicate whether A is preferred to B, B is preferred to A, or A is indifferent to B:

   $$(0,1) \quad (1,0)$$
   $$(3,5) \quad (4,2)$$
   $$(3,10) \quad (4,8)$$
   $$(8,3) \quad (16,6)$$

   b. For this person, and for the eight bundles in (a), list the bundles in order of preference from most to least preferred. If two bundles are indifferent, put them side-by-side in your list.

   c. Consider any pair of bundles (x_0,y_0) and (x_1,y_1) between which this consumer is indifferent. Prove that with this utility function she will also be indifferent between the pair of bundles containing twice as much of each good as in the original pair of bundles.

   d. Can you suggest another utility function that will represent this same consumer's preferences? Briefly justify your suggestion.

2. Our model of consumer demand treats consumer preferences as exogenously given; that is, determined outside the model. Yet every year, firms spend hundreds of millions of dollars to advertise their products in the hope of increasing—or even creating—consumer demand for their products. Indeed, economist John Kenneth Galbraith (1977) has noted that:

   From early morning to late at night, people are informed of the services rendered by goods—of their profound indispensability. Every feature and facet of every product having been studied for selling points, these are then described with talent, gravity, and an aspect of profound concern as the sources of health, happiness, social achievement, or improved community standing. Even minor qualities of unimportant commodities are enlarged upon with a solemnity which would not be unbecoming in an announcement of the combined return of Christ and all the apostles.

   Are preferences "innate," or can they be "formed" by advertising? Is our practice of treating them as given in our theory of demand a strength or a weakness in our approach?

3. Suppose a new technique for teaching economics is introduced, and that it really "works;" that is, it really does increase a student's economics test grades for any given number of hours of studying. Show how a naive experimenter, focusing only on what happens to a student's test scores in economics and English, might actually observe a *decrease* in economics scores and incorrectly conclude that the new technique was a total disaster!

4. A woman I know has funny tastes. If she has more Y than X, she will always trade $2Y$ for $1X$ and be indifferent. If she has more X than Y, however, every time she gives up $1Y$ she requires $2X$ to remain indifferent after the exchange.

   a. Sketch this woman's indifference map.

b. What is her MRS_{yx} at any bundle (x_0, y_0) where $x_0 < y_0$?

c. What is her MRS_{yx} at any bundle (x_1, y_1) where $x_1 > y_1$?

d. Do her preferences satisfy assumption 4? Why or why not?

5. Some indifference curves for a consumer whose preferences are complete and transitive are sketched in the following figure. The figure has been divided into quadrants labeled I–IV relative to the point (x_0, y_0). The numbers to the right of each indifference curve are the numbers assigned to *all* bundles on the curve by the consumer's utility function. Notice that the direction of increasing preference is always *toward* the point (x_0, y_0).

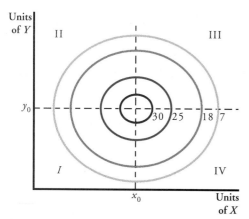

Figure Exercise 5

For each of the quadrants I-IV, answer each of the following questions:

a. Is MU_x positive, negative, or zero?

b. Is MU_y positive, negative, or zero?

c. Do the preferences satisfy the assumption of non-satiation in this quadrant? Why or why not?

d. Do the preferences satisfy the assumption of convexity in this quadrant? Why or why not?

6. Using a diagram like the one in the Kinko's application 3.4, sketch in some different preferences to show that:

a. By setting a higher price for the first 149 copies, Kinko's could get more money out of *some* customers who would never buy more than 149 copies.

b. Kinko's can induce *some* people to buy more copies—and spend more money at Kinko's—than they would have bought without the discount policy; that is, show a consumer who spends more and buys more with a discount policy.

7. A consumer has an income of $100 and faces fixed prices $p_x = \$5$ and $p_y = \$20$. Carefully draw this consumer's budget constraint. Assuming typical convex indifference curves and an initial interior equilibrium, on the same graph, illustrate the effects of:

a. a 20% increase in p_y

b. a 20% increase in p_x

c. a 20% increase in I

d. a 20% increase in both p_x and p_y

e. a 20% increase in p_x, p_y, and I

8. Answer *true* or *false*, and justify your answers:

a. If MU_x is positive, then X must be a normal good.

b. If MU_x is negative, then X must be an inferior good.

9. A student has an income of $100 and buys only two goods, pizza and books. Pizza costs $2 a slice and books cost $10 each. At the student's present level of consumption, his marginal utility of pizza is $MU_p = 4$ and his marginal utility of books is $MU_b = 2$. Is this student currently in consumer equilibrium? Why or why not? Draw a graph showing his current consumption point using indifference curves and his budget constraint. If he is not in equilibrium, show on your graph how this student could obtain his equilibrium.

10. Bill has an income of $60 per week. Gasoline is rationed at a maximum of 10 gallons a person per week at a price of $1.50/gallon. If the price of a composite other good is $1, draw Bill's budget constraint for gasoline and other goods per week. Using your graph, if Bill currently maximizes utility when he buys 10 gallons of gasoline per week, would he be better off if there were no rationing but the price of gasoline was $3.00/gallon?

11. Nikki buys two products, cheese and pretzels, with an income of $100. Her present level of consumption is 25 packages of cheese and 10 boxes of pretzels and her $MRS_{cp} = MU_p/MU_c = 5/2$. When Nikki's income increases to $150, she still buys 25 packages of cheese. Draw Nikki's income consumption path. Is cheese a normal or inferior good? How about pretzels? Explain your reasoning.

12. If chocolate is a normal good and a consumer's utility function is $u(C, OG)$, where C is units of chocolate and OG is units of other goods, derive the demand curve for chocolate from a series of indifference curves representing the consumer's tastes.

13. a. Emma tells her friend that she can eat a bag of tortilla chips only if she has a pint of salsa and she can eat a pint of salsa only if she has a bag of tortilla chips. Draw Emma's indifference curves for these two goods. What kinds of goods are tortilla chips and salsa for Emma?

b. Dan states that "I can eat either a plum or a peach with no preference for either." Draw his indifference curves. What kinds of goods are plums and peaches for Dan?

14. Mike considers sushi and hamburgers perfect substitutes. Draw his indifference curves. If the prices of sushi and hamburgers are both $3 and Mike's income is $30, show his budget constraint and consumption choice(s). If the price of sushi goes up to $5, show Mike's new point of consumption.

15. Alice likes green beans much more than peas, while Jessica prefers peas to green beans. The prices of green beans and peas are $3 and $2 respectively. If both women have an income of $30, show their budget constraints on two separate graphs. If the first graph is for Alice and the second graph is for Jessica, would you expect both women to consume the same combination of green beans and peas? Why or why not? In equilibrium, is Alice's MRS_{bp} larger, smaller, or the same as Jessica's? Explain your reasoning.

16. Two people have identical convex utility functions for steak and chicken. If they live in different parts of the country and face different price ratios for steak and chicken, is it reasonable to assume that they consume the same combination of steak and chicken? Is it possible for both to choose the same market basket at their optimal point of consumption? Why or why not? Explain, using graphs.

17. Draw a series of indifference curves for garbage and food. Draw a series of indifference curves for garbage and pollution. What are the shapes of the curves? Why?

18. Paul goes to the supermarket. He sees that bags of potato chips are labeled "buy 3 get 1 free." If the price of other goods is $1, he has an income of $30, and the price of a bag of chips is $2, draw Paul's budget line.

19. A man I know says, "X is all right, but I can take or leave Y. If you give me more X, my utility always goes up, but if you give me more Y, my utility stays the same."

a. Draw this man's indifference map for X and Y. Use it to derive his demand curve for X on a set of axes underneath his indifference map, as in Figure 3.15. In both panels of your diagram, be sure to illustrate what happens at two or more different prices of X.

b. What is the cross-elasticity, $\varepsilon_{xy} = \%\Delta q_x / \%\Delta p_y$, equal to for this man?

c. What is his income elasticity of demand for Y, $\varepsilon_I = \%\Delta y / \%\Delta I$?

d. What is his income elasticity of demand for X, $\varepsilon_I = \%\Delta x / \%\Delta I$?

e. What is his own-price elasticity of demand for X equal to?

20. Do not answer these questions unless you have read Appendix 3.1. Marginal utilities for a consumer are given by:

$$MU_x = \frac{0.5\sqrt{y}}{\sqrt{x}}$$

$$MU_y = \frac{0.5\sqrt{x}}{\sqrt{y}}$$

a. What is the MRS_{yx} for this consumer? What happens to the MRS_{yx} as the amount of X and Y this consumer has simultaneously doubles? triples? increases or decreases by any common factor $t > 0$?

b. Derive the consumer's demand functions for X and Y.

c. What fraction (share) of her total income does this consumer spend on X? What fraction does she spend on Y? Justify.

d. What is the own-price elasticity of demand for X for this consumer? Briefly justify.

e. Suppose relative prices remain fixed. Show that the ratio of Y consumed to X consumed remains constant as income changes. Sketch preferences and an income-consumption path that would produce this kind of behavior.

Internet Exercises

Visit *http://www.myeconlab.com/waldman* for this chapter's Web exercises. Answer real-world economics problems by doing research on the Internet.

Appendix 3.1

Deriving a Demand Curve from a Utility Function

This appendix shows how consumer demand functions can be derived from information about consumers' preferences in the form of mathematical utility functions. Suppose the utility function is:

$$u(x,y) = \sqrt{x} + \sqrt{y} = x^{\frac{1}{2}} + y^{\frac{1}{2}}$$

In this case, marginal utilities for the two goods will be:

$$\mathrm{MU}_x = \frac{\partial u}{\partial x} = \frac{1}{2}x^{-\frac{1}{2}} = \frac{1}{2\sqrt{x}} \quad \text{and} \quad \mathrm{MU}_y = \frac{\partial u}{\partial y} = \frac{1}{2}y^{-\frac{1}{2}} = \frac{1}{2\sqrt{y}}$$

The marginal rate of substitution will be the ratio of these two:

$$\mathrm{MRS}_{yx} = \left| -\frac{\mathrm{MU}_x}{\mathrm{MU}_y} \right| = \frac{\sqrt{y}}{\sqrt{x}}$$

The quantities of X and Y demanded will be the ones that solve the consumer's utility maximization problem. From Equations 3.10 and 3.11, utility maximization requires that the marginal rate of substitution be equal to the relative prices of good X and good Y, and that the consumer be on, rather than inside, the budget constraint. Thus, for this utility function, the utility-maximizing quantities x^* and y^* demanded must simultaneously solve the following two equations in two unknowns:

$$\frac{\sqrt{y^*}}{\sqrt{x^*}} = \frac{p_x}{p_y} \tag{A.1}$$

$$p_x x^* + p_y y^* = I \tag{A.2}$$

By squaring both sides of equation (A.1) and rearranging terms, we find that y^* must satisfy the following equation:

$$y^* = x^* \frac{p_x^2}{p_y^2} \tag{A.3}$$

Substituting from (A.3) into the budget constraint (A.2) and simplifying, we get:

$$p_x x^* + p_y \left(x^* \frac{p_x^2}{p_y^2} \right) = I$$

$$p_x x^* + x^* \frac{p_x^2}{p_y} = I$$

$$x^* \left(p_x + \frac{p_x^2}{p_y} \right) = I \tag{A.4}$$

$$x^* \left(\frac{p_x p_y + p_x^2}{p_y} \right) = I$$

$$x^* = \frac{p_y I}{p_x p_y + p_x^2}$$

Equation (A.4) is the demand for good X.

To get the demand for Y, substitute from (A.4) back into (A.3) and get:

$$y^* = x^* \frac{p_x^2}{p_y^2} = \left(\frac{p_y I}{p_x p_y + p_x^2} \right)\left(\frac{p_x^2}{p_y^2} \right)$$

$$y^* = \frac{p_y I p_x^2}{p_x p_y^3 + p_y^2 p_x^2} \tag{A.5}$$

$$y^* = \frac{I p_y}{p_x p_y + p_x^2}$$

Equations (A.4) and (A.5) are the consumer's demand functions for X and Y. They tell us exactly how the quantity demanded of each good depends on its own price, the price of the other good, and the consumer's income.

The demand curve tells us how the quantity demanded changes as the good's own price changes, *ceteris paribus*. To derive one of the demand curves for X, we would simply hold the price of Y and the consumer's income constant and plot the resulting relationship between x^* and p_x. For example, if $I=100$ and $p_y=5$, the demand for X in (A.4) will be:

$$x^* = \frac{500}{5p_x + p_x^2}$$

as shown in Figure A.1.

Figure A.1
The demand curve
$$x^* = \frac{500}{5p_x + p_x^2}$$

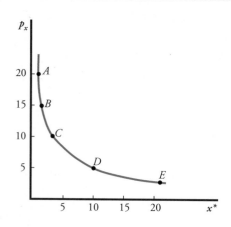

Chapter 4
Further Topics in Consumer Theory

The rate of personal savings in the United States declined dramatically during the 1990s, as the graph indicates. In fact, the savings rate actually became negative in 1999 and 2000: that is, American consumers spent more than their after-tax income during 1999 and 2000. The decline in savings occurred despite a decade of continuous economic growth, a boom in the stock market, and the growth of Internet firms. Intuitively you might assume that as Americans' incomes increased, they would save more of their income; yet the figures in the graph tell a far different tale. How can this decline in savings be explained in light of a large increase in consumers' incomes? As we will see in this chapter, by incorporating savings into our model of consumer demand developed in Chapter 3, and considering the impact of an increase in income on the rate of savings, we can explain this decline in the rate of savings.

In this chapter, we consider a range of demand-related topics that will deepen and extend our understanding of consumer behavior. First, we take a close look at how price changes affect consumer demand, analyzing in detail how and why consumers respond when prices change. Then we'll shift our attention from the individual consumer to the market, and learn how market data can be used to forecast consumer demand. Next we focus on how an understanding of demand can uncover surprising information about what

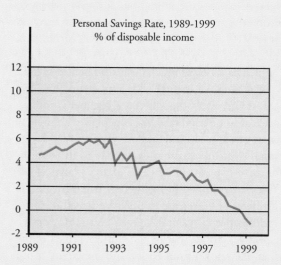

Personal Savings Rate, 1989-1999
% of disposable income

Learning Objectives

After reading Chapter 4, you will have learned:

> How to define substitution and income effects of price changes, and how to separate the substitution effect of a price change from the income effect both for own-price changes and cross-price changes.

> How to derive the market demand curve from the individual consumers' demand curves, and how economists attempt to estimate real-world demand curves.

> How to define and measure consumer surplus, and how to use consumer surplus as a measure of consumers' well-being.

> How to incorporate saving and borrowing into our model of consumer choice, and how consumers decide to spread out their consumption over time.

Featured Applications

> 4.1 Application Tax Deductions that Subsidize Vacation Stays

> 4.2 Application Estimating the Demand for Abortions

> 4.3 Application Why NFL Teams Force Season Ticket Holders to Purchase Tickets to Pre-Season Games

> 4.4 Application Borrowing for College

consumers will pay for goods and services, and how consumer welfare is affected when market conditions change. Finally, we broaden our view of the consumer's decision-making by analyzing how consumers allocate their budgets in the context of long-run priorities and learn why consumers sometimes save and sometimes borrow. The final section of the chapter will provide a framework for explaining why consumers might decrease their savings rate when their incomes increase.

▼▼▼ 4.1 Income and Substitution Effects

In the previous chapter, you learned how to derive the demand curve for a single good from information about consumer preferences, income, and market prices. Here we return to our analysis of the demand curve and consider more closely how and why a change in price can cause a change in buying behavior.

Effects of Price Changes on Consumer Behavior

When the Law of Demand was introduced in Chapter 2, it seemed quite reasonable to accept the proposition that when price falls, quantity demanded increases, so demand curves must be downward-sloping. However, we've really not proven that there is such a "law." Indeed, at the very end of the previous chapter, it became clear that distinctly different responses to a fall in price were at least theoretically possible within the theory of consumer behavior. For example, a quick look back at Figure 3.16 shows that nothing in the logic of consumer choice rules out the case of a Giffen good with an upward-sloping demand curve.

What then does our model of consumer behavior lead us to expect when a good's own price changes? Intuition tells us that when the price of some good falls, there are at least two distinctly different reasons for expecting some change in the consumer's purchases. First, that good immediately becomes cheaper than it was before relative to all other goods in the consumer's budget. Even if the consumer's total command over goods and services were to remain unchanged, this change in relative prices would be expected to lead the consumer to substitute more of the now relatively cheaper good for less of the ones that have become relatively more expensive. At the same time, however, whenever the price of one good changes, the consumer's command over goods and services in general changes. We've seen before, in Figure 3.10, that any price decrease will increase the consumer's command over all goods and services in the budget. Any time a good bought by the consumer becomes cheaper, she can always buy as much as she did before and still have income left over from her unchanged nominal income. She can spend this "leftover" income on any good she pleases. Thus, even though the consumer's nominal income remains unchanged when the price of some good falls, she experiences an increase in real income that can be allocated across goods as she sees fit.

We should be able to explain the total effect on quantity demanded as the result of these two separate effects. However, for these two categories to be of any analytical use, it is necessary to find a way to define these effects more formally. Let's begin by looking at Figure 4.1. In panels (a) and (b), the effects of a decrease in price are traced out from two perspectives simultaneously: the indifference curve and budget constraint perspective, and the simple demand curve perspective. Notice that in panel (a), as price declines from p_{x0} to p_{x1}, the optimal consumption plan moves from A to B and the quantity of X

Figure 4.1 The Total Effect of a Price Change
Before the price decrease consumer equilibrium is at point A in panel (a). After the price of X declines, the new equilibrium is at point B. The dashed hypothetical budget line is drawn tangent to the original indifference curve U_0 and parallel to the new budget constraint. The substitution effect, SE, is the movement from point A to point C, which results in an increase in the consumption of X equal to $(x_s - x_0)$. The income effect, IE, is the movement from point C to point B, which results in an increase in the consumption of X equal to $(x_1 - x_s)$.

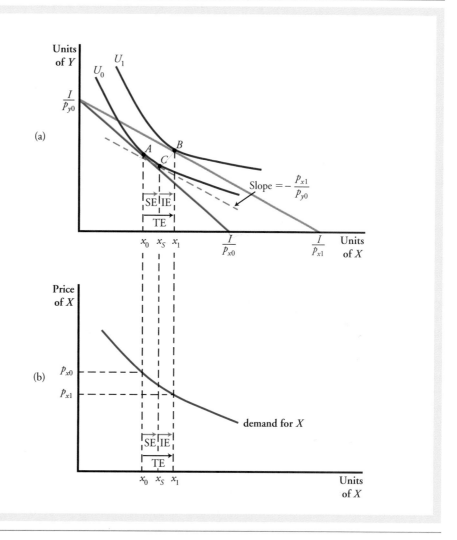

demanded increases from x_0 to x_1. In panel (b), the same change in X consumption is the movement along the demand curve that accompanies a change in price from p_{x0} to p_{x1}. This change in consumption is called the **total effect** on the quantity demanded for good X of a change in price from p_{x0} to p_{x1}. It is this total effect on quantity demanded that is observed in the consumer's market behavior: it is the amount by which his purchases of good X actually change, and it is the total effect that we would like to understand as having separate parts that can be attributed either solely to the change in relative prices, or solely to the change in real income or purchasing power.

total effect

The change in the quantity demanded of a good associated with a price change.

Identifying the Substitution Effect

Notice in Figure 4.1 that the consumer is always made better off by a fall in price. Before the price decrease, our consumer reaches a utility of U_0 at point A. After the price of X declines, she enjoys utility level U_1 at point B. To determine that part of the total effect that can be attributed to the change in relative prices, *ceteris paribus*, we ask the following hypothetical question: What is the change in X consumption that would have occurred had relative prices changed to their new level, but also had the consumer not been allowed

substitution effect

The change in the consumption of a good associated with a change in its relative price holding the consumer's level of utility constant.

to experience any change in her utility? The resulting hypothetical change in consumption is called the **substitution effect** on the demand for good X. The substitution effect is the change in the quantity consumed of a good that results entirely from a change in relative prices with utility held constant. At first it might strike you as strange to hold the consumer's utility level constant while performing this experiment. But remember that what we are trying to capture with the substitution effect is that part of the change in consumption attributable *exclusively* to the change in relative prices, *ceteris paribus*.

Next let's measure the substitution effect in Figure 4.1. Suppose the relative price of X falls from p_{x0}/p_{y0} to p_{x1}/p_{y0}. Now imagine confronting our consumer with a hypothetical budget constraint that reflects these new, post-price change relative prices that is just tangent to the original indifference curve that includes point A. The dashed line in Figure 4.1, which is drawn parallel to the actual post-price change budget constraint but tangent to the original indifference at point C, is such a constraint. If the consumer had been confronted with that budget constraint, she would have chosen point C to maximize utility and achieved utility U_0, the same utility level she began with when she consumed at point A. We measure the substitution effect of the price change by the change in consumption from point A to point C along the original indifference curve U_0. On the horizontal axis in the top panel, the substitution effect on X will be the change in consumption from x_0 to x_s. This, of course, is just the same as that part of the total effect from x_0 to x_s in the lower panel.

Identifying the Income Effect

The substitution effect captures the effect of the change in relative prices on the quantity demanded. Yet we still must identify that part of the total effect attributed solely to the change in purchasing power, or real income. The **income effect** is defined as whatever is left of the total effect after taking account of the substitution effect. The income effect is represented by a parallel shift in the budget constraint from the hypothetical budget constraint to the final budget constraint. When you identify a parallel shift in a budget line, you should always identify that shift with an income effect. The substitution effect and the income effect, taken together, fully explain the total effect of any price change.

income effect

The change in the consumption of a good associated with a change in the consumer's real income holding relative prices constant.

A glance back at panel (a) in Figure 4.1 should convince you that defining the income effect in this way makes good economic sense. Before, the substitution effect from x_0 to x_s was identified as the increase in X consumption due purely to the decrease in its relative price, with no change whatsoever in the consumer's well-being. Once consumption has increased from x_0 to x_s, only the portion from x_s to x_1 remains. Notice, though, that this is precisely the change in consumption that would occur if, after the substitution effect from A to C, the consumer were given an increase in real income sufficient to shift her budget line outward from the dashed one to the final, post-price change line tangent to U_1 at B. This hypothetical change in real income can be thought of as the increase in purchasing power caused by the price decrease. It is thus quite natural to think of the resulting change in consumption as that part of the total change in consumption attributable to the increase in purchasing power alone.

Taken together, the substitution effect, SE, and the income effect, IE, completely explain the total effect, TE, of any price change:

$$TE = SE + IE$$

It is also possible to separate the income effect from the substitution effect mathematically. This can be done by identifying the consumer's utility function and budget constraint and then changing the price of one good and adjusting income to bring the consumer's level of utility back to its original level. The appendix shows a commonly used mathematical example using a utility function of the general form $U(x,y) = x^a y^{(1-a)}$, where $a > 0$. Utility functions of this form are called **Cobb-Douglas utility functions**.

Cobb-Douglas utility function

A commonly used utility function of the general form $U(x,y) = x^a y^{(1-a)}$ where x is the quantity of good X, y is the quantity of good Y, and a is a positive constant.

Normal and Inferior Goods

Given convex indifference curves and an interior equilibrium, *the substitution effect always works to increase consumption of a good when its own price falls.* A look back at Figure 4.1 should convince you of this. As long as indifference curves are negatively sloped and convex, any time the relative price of X declines and the consumer is constrained to remain on the same indifference curve, point C must move down that indifference curve to the right, a movement that always involves an increase in the consumption of good X. Thus, with convex indifference curves, the direction of the substitution effect is always predictable.

Having determined that the substitution effect always causes an increase in the consumption of a good whose price decreases, let's turn our attention to the income effect. In Figure 4.1, the increase in real income that accompanies the decrease in the price of X causes an increase in consumption of X from x_s to x_1. In this case, X is a normal good, because an increase in real income, *ceteris paribus*, causes consumption to increase. Thus, whenever a good is normal, the income effect of a price decrease will work to increase the quantity demanded.

What we've learned so far about income and substitution effects suggests a better definition of the Law of Demand. When price declines, the substitution effect always works to increase quantity demanded. If the good is a normal good, the increase in real income that accompanies that price decrease will also work to increase quantity demanded. Because the two together completely explain the total effect on quantity demanded, we can confidently offer this final and most complete statement of the Law of Demand: *When the price of a normal good declines, quantity demanded will always increase.* Thus the demand curve for a normal good will always be negatively sloped, as in Figure 4.1.

Not all goods, however, are normal goods. Bus tickets and potatoes are things many consumers tend to buy fewer of as income increases. In the case of inferior goods such as these, we can say nothing as unequivocal as in the case of normal goods. Figure 4.2 illustrates what can happen to the demand for inferior goods as income increases.

The top panels of Figure 4.2 illustrate the effects of a decrease in the price of X from p_{x0} to p_{x1}, leading to a final change in consumer equilibrium from point A to B. In all three cases, as always, the substitution effect of that decrease in the relative price of good X, the movement from A to C, works to increase the quantity of X demanded. Notice that in each of those three panels, the income effect of the increase in real income that accompanies that price decrease—that is, the movement from C to B—works to reduce the quantity of X demanded. Thus, in each of those three panels, X is an inferior good. As you can see, whenever X is inferior, the income effect will always work against the substitution effect for the good X. What happens to the total effect, then, depends entirely on which of these two countervailing forces, the income effect or the substitution effect, is greater in magnitude.

In panel (a), the substitution effect outweighs the income effect, so the total effect of the price decrease is still some increase in the quantity of X demanded. In this case, the demand curve for an inferior good is downward-sloping, like that of a normal good. When the inferior good in question is one that occupies only a very small part of the consumer's total budget, such as bus tickets, the change in real income from any small price cut will itself be small and the resulting income effect will usually not be large enough to

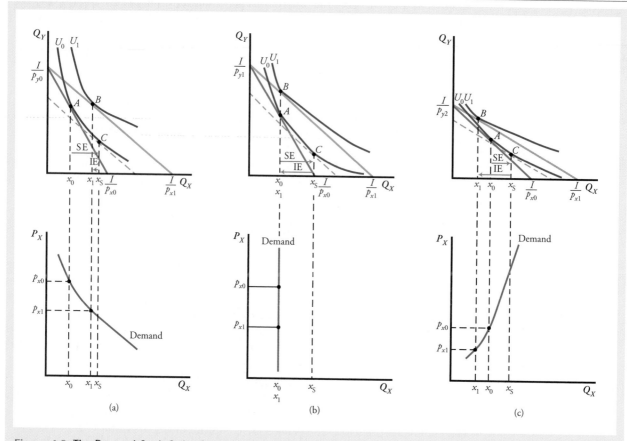

Figure 4.2 The Demand for Inferior Goods

If good X is an inferior good, the income effect is negative. In panel (a), the substitution effect of the price decrease from p_{x0} to p_{x1} dominates the income effect, so the demand for X is downward-sloping. In panel (b), the substitution effect of the price decrease exactly equals the income effect, so the demand for X is perfectly inelastic. Finally, in panel (c), the income effect of the price decrease dominates the substitution effect, so the demand for X is upward-sloping—the case of a Giffen good.

overwhelm the substitution effect. Thus as an empirical matter, most goods, whether normal or inferior, would be expected to have negatively sloped demand curves.

However, exceptions can arise, as in panels (b) and (c) of Figure 4.2. In panel (b), the income effect is opposing but *exactly equal* in size to the substitution effect, so the total effect on quantity demanded is zero. Because the substitution effect of a price decrease always works toward increased consumption, the only way demand can be perfectly inelastic—as it is in panel (b)—is if good X is an inferior good. Finally, in panel (c), we once again encounter the rather unique case of the Giffen good. This time, however, it is easy to understand how such a thing can arise, at least in theory. Once again, the substitution effect of a price decrease must work to increase the quantity demanded of X. If, as in panel (c), the total effect is a decrease in quantity demanded, then two things must be true: Good X must be inferior and the countervailing income effect must be larger in absolute size than the substitution effect. Empirically, Giffen goods are considered exceedingly rare. Indeed, few economists really believe that even one convincing example has ever been found. For income effects to be as large as they would have to be, the good

COMMON ERROR 4.1 Drawing the Hypothetical Budget Constraint Tangent to the New Indifference Curve

Often a student is asked to separate the income and substitution effects of a price change. The student knows that it is necessary to draw a line tangent to one of the indifference curves, but is unsure to *which* indifference curve.

Suppose, for example, that in the graph, the original budget constraint is tangent to U_0 at point A and the price of good X declines so that the new equilibrium is at point B on indifference curve U_1. The student draws the hypothetical dashed budget line tangent to U_1 at point C. She knows the substitution effect is measured by moving along an indifference curve from the solid budget line to the dashed budget line, so she concludes that the substitution effect is the movement from point B to point C resulting in a decrease in the consumption of good X by $(x_2 - x_1)$. She has concluded that the substitution effect of the price decrease results in a decrease in the consumption of X, which is backwards. Furthermore, she knows that the income effect is always due to a parallel shift in the

budget constraint, so she reasons that the income effect must be the movement from point C to the original equilibrium point A. She concludes, therefore, that the income effect results in a further decrease in the consumption of good X equal to $(x_1 - x_0)$ units. Her entire analysis is backwards and completely wrong!

The student has not identified the substitution effect of this price decrease, because in drawing the dashed budget line, she did not maintain the consumer's level of real income constant at U_0 on the original indifference curve. Always remember that the substitution effect abstracts from the impact of the price change on the consumer's level of real income. That simply means that to identify the substitution effect, you must always remain on the original indifference curve. To do this, always slide the budget constraint along the original indifference curve to identify the substitution effect. Then identify the income effect as the movement from the original indifference curve to the final indifference curve.

Common Error Figure 4.1 **The Common Error Associated with Identifying the Substitution and Income Effects**
Here the price has decreased from p_{x1} to p_{x2}, but the student has incorrectly drawn the hypothetical budget line tangent to the new indifference curve instead of the original indifference curve. As a result, the student measures the substitution effect from point B to point C as $(x_2 - x_1)$ and contends that when the price of X decreased, the substitution effect resulted in a decrease in the consumption of X, which makes no sense. The student compounds the error by claiming that the income effect further reduces the consumption of X by $(x_1 - x_0)$.

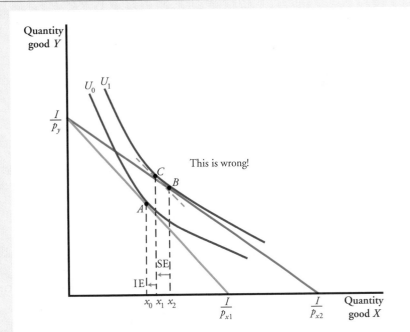

in question would have to occupy a very large portion of the consumer's budget. Yet goods that make up such a large portion of the consumer's budget, such as housing, are almost always normal goods.

Cross-Price Effects

Up to this point, we've focused on how quantity demanded of good X changes when the price of X changes. However, the demand for many other goods will also be affected by a change in the price of X. When one good becomes relatively cheaper because of a decline in its own price, all other goods become relatively more expensive. Just as the substitution effect causes the consumer to buy more of the good that has become relatively cheaper; the substitution effect on the demand for other goods would be expected to cause the consumer to buy less of the goods that have become relatively more expensive. Furthermore, there will be income effects on other goods. For normal goods, the increase in real income that comes with a decrease in any one price will, *ceteris paribus*, cause the consumer to buy either more or less, depending on whether the income or substitution effect dominates for the purchase of these "other goods."

Figure 4.3 reconsiders the impact of a decline in the price of X from p_{x0} to p_{x1}. As in Figure 4.1, consumer equilibrium moves from A to B. The only difference now is that attention is focused on what happens to the demand for the other good, good Y, following this change in the price of X. The total effect on the quantity of Y demanded from this cross-price effect is the decrease from y_0 to y_1. The substitution effect on Y is defined as the change in the demand for Y that would occur as the relative price of X falls from p_{x0}/p_{y0} to p_{x1}/p_{y0}, holding the level of consumer well-being constant. This is measured in Figure 4.3 by the decrease from y_0 at point A to y_s at point C, where the hypothetical budget line reflecting the new relative prices is tangent to the original indifference curve U_0. The income effect on Y is the remainder of the total effect on Y, and measures the change in the quantity of Y demanded that can be attributed to the increase in real income that accompanies the decrease in the price of X. Here, the income effect on Y is an increase in the quantity of Y demanded from y_s to y_1 that occurs as we move from

Figure 4.3 Cross-Price Effects

When the price of X decreases from p_{x0} to p_{x1}, the total effect on the quantity demanded of Y is the decrease from y_0 to y_1. The substitution effect is the decrease in Y consumption from y_0 at point A to y_s at point C. The income effect is an increase in the quantity of Y demanded from y_s to y_1 that occurs moving from point C to point B.

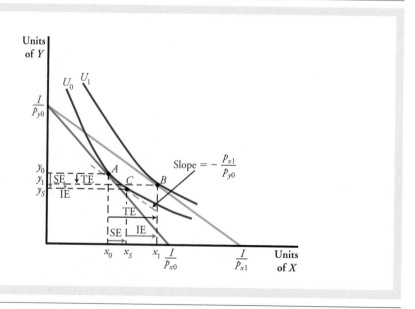

point C on the hypothetical budget line to point B on the new budget line that is tangent to U_1.

Now, step back a moment and look again at Figure 4.3. As the price of X falls from p_{x0} to p_{x1}, X becomes *relatively* cheaper and Y becomes *relatively* more expensive. Because indifference curves are convex, the substitution effects on X and Y show that the consumer will always substitute away from the good that has become relatively more expensive, good Y, and substitute into the good that has become relatively cheaper, good X, purely as a result of the change in relative prices. However, the increase in real income that comes with that decrease in price will have a separate effect on the demands for good X and good Y. In Figure 4.3, X and Y are both normal goods. Thus, the consumer allocates some part of the increase in real income toward greater consumption of both goods.

Greater insight into what makes some goods substitutes and others complements can be gained by analyzing the income and substitution effects of cross-price changes more carefully. Both panels of Figure 4.4 separate the total effect of a decrease in the price of X into its substitution and income effects on Y. In each case, the substitution effect causes consumption of Y to decline, as the consumer substitutes out of the now more expensive Y and into now cheaper X, *ceteris paribus*. In each case, too, Y is a normal good, as the

Figure 4.4 Substitutes and Complements
In panel (a), the substitution effect of the cross-price change on good Y dominates the income effect, so X and Y are substitutes and $\varepsilon_{yx} > 0$. In panel (b), the income effect of the cross-price change dominates the substitution effect, so X and Y are complements and $\varepsilon_{yx} < 0$.

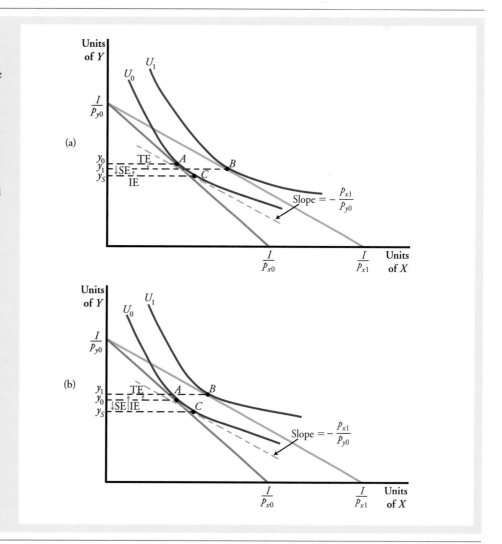

increase in real income shifting the dashed hypothetical budget line outward leads to increased consumption of Y, *ceteris paribus*. Yet in panel (a), the total effect is a decrease in the quantity of Y demanded from y_0 to y_1, while in panel (b), the total effect is an increase in the quantity of Y demanded from y_0 to y_1. In panel (a), then, Y is a substitute good for X and the cross-elasticity $\varepsilon_{yx} > 0$; while in panel (b), Y is a complement good to X with $\varepsilon_{yx} < 0$.

What accounts for the difference between the two cases? When the price of X falls and Y is normal, the substitution effect and the income effect on Y will always work in *opposite* directions, with the substitution effect working toward *reduced* consumption of Y, and the income effect working toward *increased* consumption of Y. The total effect, which determines whether good X and good Y will be substitutes or complements, is simply the sum of these two countervailing components. Thus, in panel (a), Y is a substitute for X, because the substitution effect of the cross-price change dominates, making the total effect on the quantity of Y demanded negative and $\varepsilon_{yx} > 0$. In panel (b), Y is a complement for X, because the income effect dominates, making the total effect on the quantity of Y demanded positive and $\varepsilon_{yx} < 0$. Thus, for normal goods, we have a rule of thumb: *the goods will be substitutes when the substitution effect of a cross-price change dominates, and they'll be complements when the income effect of a cross-price change dominates.*

▲▲▲ 4.1 APPLICATION   Tax Deductions That Subsidize Vacation Stays

The U.S. income tax laws permit a number of deductions from a taxpayer's before-tax income. Taxpayers do not pay any tax on income spent on tax-deductible items. The largest deduction for many taxpayers is for the mortgage interest and property taxes on their home. The objective of the tax deduction is to encourage home ownership.

The graph analyzes the impact of these tax deductions on two goods: the quantity of owner-occupied housing and vacation hotel stays. In the absence of any tax benefits for either good, the consumer's budget constraint is the dark-green line with intercepts I/p_{HT} and I/p_{OH}, and the consumer's equilibrium is at point O with OH_1 units of housing and HT_1 nights of vacation hotel stays.

Application Figure 4.1 Housing Tax Deduction Increases Vacation Nights
A tax deduction on owner-occupied housing decreases the price of owner-occupied housing from P_{OH} to $P_{OH}(1 - t)$, where t is the homeowner's income tax rate. As a result, the consumer increases the number of vacation nights in hotels from HT_1 to HT_2 nights because the income effect on vacation nights of the price reduction of owner-occupied housing dominates the substitution effect.

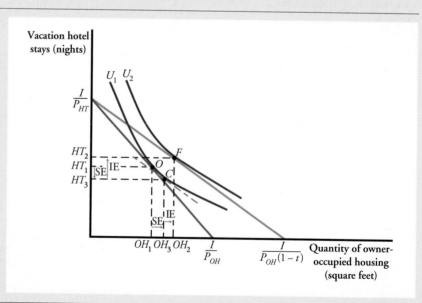

(continued)

With a tax deduction for housing, the price of housing declines to $p_{OH}(1 - t)$ where t is the taxpayer's combined federal and state income tax rate. For many high-income taxpayers, t is 33 percent or higher, so this price reduction is significant. With the deduction, the budget constraint shifts to the light green budget line with intercepts I/p_{HT} and $I/[p_{OH}(1 - t)]$, and the consumer's equilibrium is at point F with OH_2 units of housing and HT_2 nights of hotel stays. The tax deduction on housing has not only increased the quantity of housing, but has also increased the quantity of vacation hotel stays. To understand why the tax deduction on housing results in an increase on the consumer's vacation hotel stays, it is necessary to separate the income and substitution effects of the tax deduction. The dashed teal line is drawn tangent to the original indifference curve and parallel to the light green budget line with the deductions. The substitution effect results in an increase in housing from OH_1 to OH_3 and a *decrease* in vacation hotel stays from HT_1 to HT_3. The income effect results in an increase

in housing from OH_3 to OH_2 and an *increase* in vacation hotel stays from HT_3 to HT_2. In this case, because the positive income effect on vacation hotel stays dominantes the negative substitution effect, the two goods, owner-occupied housing and hotel stays, are complements, and the tax deduction on owner-occupied housing results in an increase in vacation hotel stays.

If the government tried to pass a law that permitted some taxpayers to deduct all of their vacation hotel stays, there would be a political uproar. Yet because of the income effect, the current tax laws effectively "subsidize" vacation hotel stays for a large number of high-income taxpayers. Of course, if—for a particular consumer—the substitution effect dominates the income effect on vacation hotel stays, then the tax deduction results in a reduction in vacation hotel stays. The higher the income elasticity of demand for vacation hotel stays, the more likely it is that the income effect will dominate the substitution effect and the deduction will result in an unintended increase in hotel stays.

4.2 Market Demand

Until now, we have concentrated on the theory of individual demand, and explored the connection between rational choice and an individual's market behavior. In this section, our perspective changes in two ways. First, we'll focus on the market demand that arises from all consumers of some good, rather than on the demand from one consumer alone. Second, we'll look at some of the ways firms and economists try to learn about and predict market demand in real-world situations.

From Individual Demand to Market Demand

The market demand schedule tells us how many units of a good all buyers together would demand at different market prices during some specified period of time. To illustrate how we might construct such a schedule, suppose there are only three potential buyers of good q. The first column of Table 4.1 lists various market prices. The next three columns list the quantities demanded by each individual buyer at each price. To find market demand, take the horizontal sum across the columns of Table 4.1. For example, when price is \$2, Buyer 1 demands 8 units, Buyer 2 demands 11 units, and Buyer 3 demands 12 units. Summing horizontally, total quantity demanded in the

Table 4.1 Market Demand Is the Horizontal Sum of All Individual Demands

Price	Demand for Buyer 1	Demand for Buyer 2	Demand for Buyer 3	Market Demand
2	8	11	12	31
4	6	7	6	19
6	4	3	0	7
8	2	0	0	2
10	0	0	0	0

market at a price of $2 will be $8 + 11 + 12 = 31$, as recorded in the final column. When price is $4, market demand is $6 + 7 + 6 = 19$, and so on.

market demand curve

The horizontal summation of all of the individual consumers' demand curves.

If we have graphs of the individual demand curves, we can graph the **market demand curve** using a similar process. Figure 4.5 plots the individual demand curves and the market demand curve from the data in Table 4.1. To find the market demand curve, we present each of the buyers with a price such as $p = 4$ and read off the quantity demanded by each. These quantities are then added together and the sum is plotted against price $p = 4$ on the market demand curve. We then do the same thing for every possible price. In this way, the market demand curve is obtained as the horizontal sum of the demand curves of all individual buyers in the market.

The summing can also be done algebraically. The equations for the individual demand curves in Figure 4.5 are as follows:

$$q_1 = 10 - p \text{ for } p \leq 10$$

$$q_2 = 15 - 2p \text{ for } p \leq 7.5$$

$$q_3 = 18 - 3p \text{ for } p \leq 6$$

where q_i denotes the quantity demanded by person i. The equation for the market demand curve for $p \leq 6$ in Figure 4.5 can be derived by adding these three equations together. Letting Q_m denote the market quantity demanded, we have:

$$Q_m = q_1 + q_2 + q_3$$

$$= (10 - p) + (15 - 2p) + (18 - 3p)$$

$$= (10 + 15 + 18) - (p + 2p + 3p)$$

$$= 43 - 6p \text{ for } p \leq 6$$

Plug a few of the prices less than or equal to 6 in Table 4.1 into this equation. You'll see that you get the corresponding quantity demanded listed in the final column of that table.

Figure 4.5 Horizontal Sum of Demand Curves
The market demand curve D_{total} is derived by horizontally summing the demand curves D_1, D_2, and D_3 for each individual consumer.

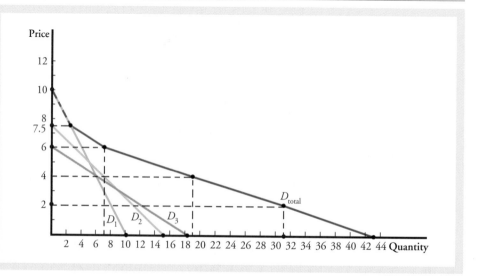

Even though we've focused here only on the good's own price, theory tells us that a person's demand for any good depends on the prices of all goods in the budget and on the consumer's income. In general, then, the **market demand function** for any one good will depend on the prices of all goods and every consumer's income. Technically, letting $q_i(p_1,\ldots,p_n,I_i)$ be Buyer i's demand for good q as a function of n different prices and i's income, the market demand function for good q is defined as:

$$Q_m = \sum_{i=1}^{m} q_i(p_1, \cdots ,p_n,I_i)$$

where m is the total number of potential buyers in the market, and the summation runs from 1 to m.

Although our theory of demand tells us quite a bit about how one person will allocate his purchases across a range of goods, it tells us very little about how *groups* of buyers will behave in the market for any one good. The fact is, individuals differ substantially from one another. They have different preferences, different incomes, and so forth. As a result, little can be said about how market demand should behave. Because of this, when applied economists, business executives, or policy-makers need to know more about the market demand for a particular good, they will generally try to supplement the lessons of economic theory with a look at some actual data. In the next sections, we consider some of the ways such data are used to learn about market demand.

Estimating Market Demand

In September 1993, President Clinton persuaded Congress to raise federal excise taxes on gasoline by 4.5 cents per gallon as part of an effort both to reduce the federal budget deficit and to encourage energy conservation. Before the figure of 4.5 cents was settled upon, administration economists made careful studies of the market demand for gasoline and so were able to give skeptical members of Congress a fairly accurate idea of just how much revenue the tax would bring in, and how much of a decrease in gasoline consumption the tax would cause. Accurate empirical information on market demand is just as important to businesses. Before Toyota decided to spend $200 million building an assembly plant in Kentucky, it had to reach a judgment that future demand for automobiles would be strong enough to justify such an outlay, and that decision required a hard look at the numbers. Analysts use many different approaches to uncover information about market demand. Among the most common are surveys and experiments, barometric methods, and statistical estimation. We'll take a brief look at each of these in turn.

SURVEYS AND EXPERIMENTS You might think that when you want to know how much of a good someone will buy at a certain price that you should simply go out and ask the person. Indeed, consumer surveys of this sort are often the first tactic of sales executives anxious to plan a sales campaign. The survey is a time-honored research technique in the social sciences. Psychologists and sociologists in particular make heavy use of these methods, and they have raised survey design and analysis to virtual art forms. Often, very useful information about consumer attitudes and buying behavior can be gleaned from a carefully administered and properly interpreted survey of the relevant population.

Economists are often skeptical about such surveys. The reason is simple: Talk is cheap! Someone might tell you that he'll keep buying your product even if you raise the price by 20 percent, but that doesn't mean he will behave that way. People sometimes lie to survey-takers or kid around: people usually have no good reason to take such surveys too seriously. Surveys are subject to an even more serious problem: People often do not

---

market demand function

The quantity demanded of a good in terms of the prices of all goods and income, such that if $q_i(p_1,\ldots,p_n,I_i)$ is consumer i's demand for good q as a function of n different prices and consumer i's income, the market demand function is:

$$Q_m = \sum_{i=1}^{m} q_i(p_1, \cdots ,p_n,I_i)$$

where m is the total number of consumers.

know how they would behave under circumstances they've never faced. Thus, even if a person is willing to be truthful, the answers given to a surveyor may have little real value.

Firms sometimes conduct survey market experiments. For example, perhaps a firm is contemplating a nationwide price hike and wants to know what effect this hike would have on demand. It might first choose a limited geographical area in which to raise prices. Experiments like this can give useful information about market demand. The situation is real, not artificial, and buyers are making real, not hypothetical, choices. Yet market experiments are also not without drawbacks. For one thing, they can be expensive. Sometimes buyers in the experimental market never return, even after the experiment is over and price returns to its previous level. In addition, such experiments are rarely as "controlled" as they should be. A competitor who ignores a local price cut by the firm conducting the experiment might respond aggressively to any nationwide price cut. Drawing lessons about overall market demand from experiments in isolated sub-markets can be very risky.

BAROMETRIC METHODS Ancient Phoenician traders posted runners on the Mediterranean coastline many miles north of their major trading centers. Their job was to make regular reports on the number of trading ships southward-bound. When the number of ships heading south increased or decreased, traders could forecast a corresponding increase or decrease in the demand for their products soon to follow.

Businesses and economists have long searched for such correlation between data. When changes in one variable (for example, the number of ships heading south) precede or lead to changes in another variable (for example, demand for products) in a regular and predictable way, the first variable can often be useful in forecasting the second variable in much the same way that changes in barometric pressure are used to forecast changes in the weather. The U.S. Department of Commerce reports monthly on a number of so-called **leading economic indicators** in its *Survey of Current Business*, and some of these are listed in Table 4.2. All of these data series and the composite indices constructed from them have been studied extensively and shown to provide some advance warning of short-run changes in overall business activity. Some of these data can also be useful in predicting demand changes for particular industries. For example, when the index of new building permits rises, the demand for building and construction material will usually increase soon afterward. Over time, firms learn what kind of events precede important changes in their own business. They will then construct formal or informal leading indicators of their own from publicly and privately available data, and track those series closely.

Time-honored as they may be, barometric methods of forecasting can give the firm only limited information. Even at their best, such measures can suggest only the likely direction of change, but never its magnitude. That limitation might be fine if all you need to know is whether sales will rise or fall next month. But if you need to know whether sales will rise by 2 percent or 200 percent, barometric methods are not much help, because they can provide only qualitative, not quantitative, forecasts. By their very nature, barometric techniques are of very limited help when management sits down to do the kind of "what if" analyses so important to real-world decision-making.

STATISTICAL ESTIMATION Firms can often get the answers they need by statistically estimating the demand relationship itself. Statistical estimation offers a number of advantages over the other

leading economic indicators

A group of data series and indices that provide advanced warning of short-run changes in the level of business activity.

Table 4.2 Leading Economic Indicators

Length of manufacturing workweek
First-time unemployment claims
New orders for consumer goods
Orders for investment goods
New building permits for private housing
Change in business inventories
Change in commodity prices
Stock market prices
Money supply
Consumer confidence

methods the firm can use to learn about market demand. Its primary advantage is that it does not rely on what people say, nor does it draw its conclusions from how people behave in artificial situations. Instead, it is based on the data to determine what people actually do in real markets. Once equipped with a properly estimated demand curve, it is a simple matter for the firm to pose "what if" questions like: "What will happen to consumer demand if price is raised by 15 percent?" "What will happen to sales if advertising expenditures are increased another 10 percent?" "How many production runs will we need next month if we're forced to cut price by $20?" and so on.

Econometrics is the branch of economics concerned with statistically estimating the theoretical relationships predicted by microeconomic and macroeconomic theory. In the hands of a skilled econometrician, appropriate statistical tools and careful analysis of the data can lead to accurate and useful estimates of important economic relationships.

econometrics

The field of economics that uses the application of statistics to estimate the theoretical relationships predicted by economic theory.

▲▲▲ 4.2 APPLICATION   Estimating the Demand for Abortions

Economists, policy-makers, and business managers often need to know how to obtain and interpret the results of econometric analysis. Consider, for example, the demand for abortion services in the United States. If policy-makers decrease or increase public funding for abortions, will it have a significant impact on the number of abortions? Furthermore, how does income impact the demand for abortion services? Do wealthy women demand more abortions than poor women? These are important issues that can be addressed only if we have some knowledge about the demand for abortion services.

In a 1997 paper, Marshall Medoff estimated the demand for abortion services in the United States by modeling the demand as:[*]

$$A = f(p_a, I, SNGL, LFP, M, CATH, WEST),$$

where A is the abortion rate, p_a is the price of abortion services, I is income, $SNGL$ is the percentage of women aged 15–44 who are unmarried, LFP is the labor force participation rate among women, M is a measure of a state's Medicaid abortion funding, $CATH$ is the percentage of Catholics in a state's population, and $WEST$ is a measure of whether a woman lives in one of the six western states of California, Oregon, Washington, Nevada, Arizona, or Hawaii. According to Medoff's model, these seven factors would be expected to influence the demand for abortion services.

Why did Medoff include controls for the last five variables? He included $SNGL$ because the opportunity cost of child rearing is greater for single women who cannot depend on their spouses' incomes than for married women. In addition, single women might still fear social sanctions if they have a child out of wedlock. Therefore, single women should statistically demand more abortions, *ceteris paribus*. LFP was included because working women have greater opportunity costs of raising children because they may need to sacrifice some or all of their work income. M was included because in 1977 Congress passed a law that prohibited federal Medicaid funding of abortions, but states still have a right to fund abortions through Medicaid. Medoff theorized that in states with Medicaid funding, poor women would obtain more abortions. $CATH$ was included because the Catholic church is opposed to abortion, and therefore states with larger percentages of Catholics should have fewer women obtaining abortions. Finally, Medoff included $WEST$ because the populations in those western states have more liberal attitudes toward abortion.

The equation Medoff estimated was:

$$A = b_0 + b_1 p_a + b_2 I + b_3 SNGL + b_4 LFP + b_5 M + b_6 CATH + b_7 WEST$$

This equation assumes that the percentage of women obtaining abortions is a linear function of each of the

---

[*]Marshall Medoff, "A Pooled Time-Series Analysis of Abortion Demand," *Population Research and Policy Review*, 16:597–605, 1997.

(continued)

variables on the right side of the equation. Using state data for the years 1982 and 1992, Medoff used econometrics to estimate the following demand equation:

$$A = -60.51 - 0.80\, p_a + 0.01\, I + 5.28\, SNGL$$
$$+ 2.04\, LFP + 51.46\, M + 1.33\, CATH + 42.24\, WEST$$

Most of Medoff's results are exactly what you would expect.[†] Of particular importance is $b_2 = -0.80$, so there is a negative relationship between the price of an abortion, p_a, and the quantity demanded of abortions, A, *ceteris paribus*. Specifically, because p_a is measured in dollars and A is measured in number of abortions per 1,000 pregnancies; $b_2 = -0.80$ suggests that for every $10 increase in the price of an abortion, there would be a reduction in the number of abortions by 8 per 1,000 pregnancies. In addition, abortions are a normal good, because $b_3 = 0.01$, so there is a positive relationship between income, I, and the quantity demanded of abortions. All of the other relationships are what Medoff expected, except for the percentage of Catholics. Surprisingly, in states with a larger percentage of Catholics, the quantity demanded for abortions *increased*. This suggests that there may be a big difference between the official position of the Catholic church on abortion and the actual practices of members of the church.

It is possible to determine the price elasticity of demand and income elasticity of demand for abortions from the estimated equation. For a given price or income, this can be done just as it can be done for any linear demand curve. Medoff estimated these elasticities at the mean price and mean income and found that the price elasticity of demand equaled -0.86 and the income elasticity of demand equaled 0.31. Therefore, the demand for abortions is price inelastic and abortions are a normal good.

According to Medoff, "[t]he finding that the demand for abortions is [price] inelastic suggests that any state restrictions on abortion that will presumably increase the cost of obtaining an abortion will have very little effect on the abortion rate."[‡] Furthermore, high-income women obtain more abortions than low-income women, suggesting that current public policies do not make it easy for poor women to obtain abortions.

[†]All of the variables on the right-hand side of the equation except *LFP* are statistically significant at a 5 percent level.

[‡]Medoff, "A Pooled Time-Series Analysis of Abortion Demand," p. 603.

▼▼▼ 4.3 Consumer Surplus

Consumers buy goods and services to make themselves better off. Indeed, utility maximizers engage in a market transaction only if what they purchase has greater value to them than what they must give up in exchange. From this observation, we can conclude that consumers would generally be willing to pay more than they do for the things they buy. How much would you pay for salt if you had to? For water? Wouldn't you have been willing to pay more for your cell phone service than you do, rather than go without it? We've seen how information about consumers' preferences can be used to derive the market demand curve. In this section, we'll see how information about the market demand curve can be used to uncover important information about consumers' preferences and their well-being. First, however, we want to see how information about an individual's preferences can be used to determine the consumer's well-being.

Using Indifference Curves to Calculate Consumer Surplus

Figure 4.6 illustrates the consumer's choice between a single good, X, and all other goods combined, represented by AOG. The analysis can be simplified by choosing the units in

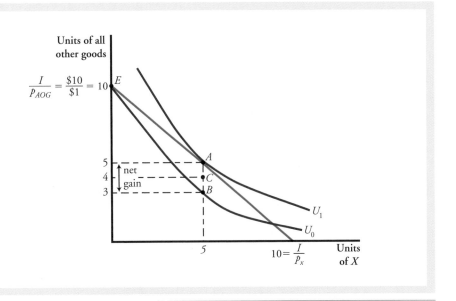

Figure 4.6 Total Value and Total Expenditure
Starting at point E, the consumer would be willing to sacrifice up to 7 units of all other goods to obtain 5 units of good X, but at current market prices, only has to sacrifice 5 units of all other goods to obtain 5 units of good X. The difference between the maximum amount of all other goods he would be willing to sacrifice, 7, and what he actually has to sacrifice, 5, measures his consumer surplus.

which to measure the price of AOG as one dollar per unit. If we set $p_{AOG} = \$1.00$, then the slope of the consumer's budget constraint will be $-p_x/1 = -p_x$, and the vertical intercept of the budget constraint will be $\$I/\$1 = \$I$, or just the consumer's income. For simplicity, in Figure 4.6, $p_x = \$1.00$ and $I = \$10.00$. At these prices and income, the consumer maximizes utility at point A buying 5 units of X and 5 units of all other goods. If $p_{AOG} = \$1.00$, the consumer spends $\$5.00$ on AOG. The remainder of his income of $\$10.00$ is spent on good X. Total expenditures on X can be measured down from the intercept of the budget constraint as the distance (10–5) along the vertical axis. The consumer therefore spends $\$5.00$ on good X and $\$5.00$ on all other goods.

One way to measure the total value of a good is to ask someone how much they would pay rather than go without the good entirely. If the consumer spent nothing on good X, consumed none of good X, and spent all his income on all other goods, he would consume at point E and receive utility of U_0. By giving up $\$5.00$ of possible spending on AOG for 5 units of good X, the consumer reaches point A and makes himself strictly better off, raising utility from U_0 to U_1.

But is $\$5.00$ the maximum amount of money this consumer would pay rather than go without good X altogether? Intuitively, if he can give up $\$5.00$ and be that much better off, he ought to be able to pay just a little more for those same 5 units of good X and still be better off. In Figure 4.6, for example, starting at point E with zero units of X and 10 units of AOG, we could take $\$6.00$ away from the consumer, give him the same 5 units of good X, and bring him to point C. Of course, the consumer prefers A to C, but that's not important. What's important is that he is still better off at point C than he would be at point E. How much more can we take from this consumer? We can take as much as $\$7.00$, or just enough to bring him to point B, where he is just indifferent between consuming his 5 units of good X at point B and going without good X altogether at point E.

It is appropriate for us to think of these $\$7.00$ as measuring, in dollar terms, the utility or total worth to this consumer of 5 units of good X, because the consumer would be willing to trade a maximum of $\$7.00$ to obtain 5 units of good X. Note, however, that this consumer need only spend $\$5.00$ in the marketplace to acquire something that has a dollar value to him of $7.00. The difference between the two, ($7.00 − $5.00) = $2.00, is a sort of excess or surplus in value that the consumer obtains from the exchange. That distance of $2.00 gives us a dollar figure for the consumer's net gain, or **consumer surplus**, from this market transaction.

consumer surplus

The difference between the maximum amount consumers are willing to pay for a given quantity of a good and what they actually have to pay to obtain that quantity of the good.

Receiving Unanticipated Consumer Surplus

Unless you are the unluckiest person on earth, you have experienced an unanticipated gain in consumer surplus many times in your life. Here's how. You walk into a store to buy a specific item such as a replacement cartridge for your computer's printer. Suppose you know that the replacement cartridge normally sells for $29.99. You grab a cartridge off of the shelf, take it to the cashier and expect to pay $29.99 plus 6 percent tax. The cashier scans the cartridge and says, "That will be $26.49 ($24.99 plus 6 percent tax)." You are quite happy, because you have just received unanticipated consumer surplus of $5.30 (a price reduction of $5.00 plus the $0.30 tax savings). You would have been willing to pay at least $31.79 ($29.99 plus 6 percent tax), but you only had to pay $26.49! What a great deal.

How much total consumer surplus did you receive from purchasing the cartridge? That depends on how much you would have been willing to pay rather than going entirely without the cartridge. One thing is certain, however: you must have received at least $5.30 in consumer surplus. You probably received a good deal more consumer surplus than $5.30, because you would be in really bad shape if you couldn't print at all. Any time you stumble upon an unexpected sale on an item you intended to purchase even if it was not on sale, you receive some unanticipated consumer surplus and you are better off as a result.

Using Demand Curves to Calculate Consumer Surplus

It would be difficult, indeed, to use the framework of Figure 4.6 to determine the consumer's net gain from a market transaction. For one thing, to measure the distance $7.00 − $5.00 = $2.00, we would need to be able to see the two indifference curves U_0 and U_1 and, unfortunately indifference curves are not directly observable. Consumer demand curves are observable, however. Because consumer demand curves are generated from the consumer's underlying utility maximization problem in Figure 4.6, and because every point on the demand curve represents a point of utility maximization, it is possible to work backwards from a consumer's *observable* demand curve to infer a great deal about his *unobservable*, underlying utility.

Look at panel (a) of Figure 4.7, which shows the demand curve for X derived from the consumer's indifference map in Figure 4.6. Normally when we "read" that demand curve, we pick a price like p_x, then read to the right and down to find out how many units the consumer would buy at that price per unit. We can, however, just as easily read that demand curve "up and over" from the bottom. Pick a quantity on the horizontal axis, then read up and to the left to find out the price per unit the consumer would pay if he could buy all of his units at the same price. Whenever the demand curve is presented or interpreted in this way, it is called the consumer's **inverse demand curve**.

inverse demand curve

The price of a good as a function of the quantity demanded; i.e., $p=f(q)$.

Now imagine that you own all of good X, and you're going to sell it for as much as possible. You decide to parcel each single unit out separately, making the consumer pay the very maximum he is willing to pay for every single unit. How much can you charge for the first unit? Reading his demand curve in Figure 4.7 up and over, it seems he is willing to pay up to P_1 for that first unit. Thus, $P_1 \times 1$, or the area of the light-purple rectangle with base width 1 unit and height P_1, is the *maximum* he would pay you for the first unit rather than

Figure 4.7 Total Value Two Ways: Saw-Toothed and Smooth
In panel (a), if the units of X are not divisible, the total value of five units of good X equals the sum of the five shaded rectangles. In panel (b), if the units are divisible into very small increments, the total value of the first five units equals the entire area under the demand curve; in this case, the shaded blue area.

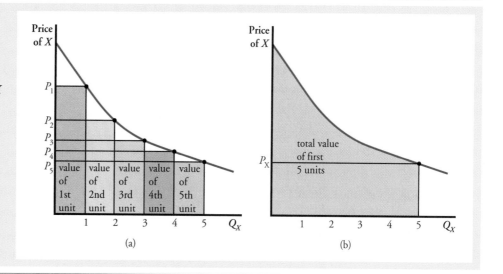

go without the good. But if, as before, we measure a good's worth to this consumer by his maximum willingness to pay for it, that same rectangular area must also measure the total worth or value to this consumer of having that very first unit of the good.

Proceeding in this same way, we can determine the value of the second unit. In Figure 4.7, the consumer will pay up to P_2 for the second unit once he has the first, so $P_2 \times 1$, or the light-green rectangular area with base width 1 and height P_2, gives us a measure of the total worth of the second unit of good X to this consumer. We can proceed to find the respective values of the third, fourth, and finally fifth unit in turn, each time finding it to be the appropriate rectangle with base width 1 unit and height given by the demand curve. We simply measure the marginal value of each incremental unit in turn.

To compute the total value to this consumer of having a total of five full units to consume, we add up all the separate rectangles. That saw-toothed area under the demand curve gives us a pretty good idea of the consumer's maximum willingness to pay for those five units when faced with the alternative of going without good X entirely. We could get an even better idea, however, if we parceled the good out by each half-unit, or each quarter, or each eighth of a unit, and charged the corresponding maximum price off the demand curve for each small fraction of the good we offered. The smaller we make the units that we parcel out, the closer the total area taken up by all the little rectangles together will get to the entire shaded area underneath the demand curve up to five units, as illustrated in panel (b) of Figure 4.7. Thus, as we make our units smaller and smaller, we discover the following general rule: *the entire area beneath a demand curve up to any given quantity is a measure of the consumer's total willingness to pay for that quantity*, and is therefore a measure of its total worth to the consumer. That entire area, then, is an *observable* counterpart to the *unobservable* distance $10 - 3 = 7$ in Figure 4.6.

Measuring Consumer Surplus

In a typical market transaction, the consumer will not be asked to pay the maximum that he is willing to pay. As we saw earlier, when consumers are free to choose how much or how little to buy at a fixed price per unit, the value of what they obtain in the transaction will generally be greater than what they have to give up. That excess or surplus that we measured by the unobservable distance $5 - 3 = 2$ between points A and B in Figure 4.6

has an observable counterpart in Figure 4.8. The entire area *Oabx* under the demand curve and up to the quantity 5 measures the total worth to our consumer of all five units of good *X*. At a fixed market price of p_x = $1.00, those five units cost the consumer 5($1.00) = $5.00, or an amount equal to the blue shaded total expenditure rectangle $Op_x bx$.

In Figure 4.8, the consumer surplus is the purple triangle abp_x = (1/2)(0.80)(5) = $2.00; that is, the area below the demand curve and above the price line. The consumer surplus triangular area measures the difference between the maximum value of five units of good *X* to the consumer, the entire area *Oabx* (which equals $7.00), and what he has to pay for it, the blue rectangular area $Op_x bx$ (which equals $5.00). Consumer surplus is the observable counterpart of the unobservable distance from point *A* to point *B* (5 − 3 = 2) in Figure 4.6. It is a dollar measure of how much better off the consumer is for being able to buy five units of this good at p_x = $1.00 per unit, rather than having to do without the good entirely.

But where does consumer surplus really come from? Looking up and over on the demand curve in Figure 4.8, notice that the maximum the consumer would pay for the first unit (that is, its marginal value) is greater than the marginal value of each succeeding unit. Indeed, the demand curve's negative slope suggests that each successive unit adds less and less to the consumer's well-being than the unit before it. When consumers are free to buy as many units as they want at the same fixed market price per unit, they tend to reap substantial surplus gains on the first few units consumed—the ones with the greatest marginal value to them. The size of that marginal gain diminishes as consumption increases, because each successive unit continues to cost the same as the first one did, but brings with it less and less extra satisfaction to the consumer.

But if those early units have such a high value to the consumer, why don't sellers charge more for them? The answer is that they would if they could. In most cases, however, it is simply impossible or not worthwhile for sellers to collect all of the massive information they would need to price each unit of their product at its full value to each consumer. In general, the larger the market is, the more insurmountable the task will be for individual sellers. Ironically, because each individual consumer is so anonymous in the marketplace and individually insignificant, individual consumers are able to reap consumer surplus on most of their market transactions.

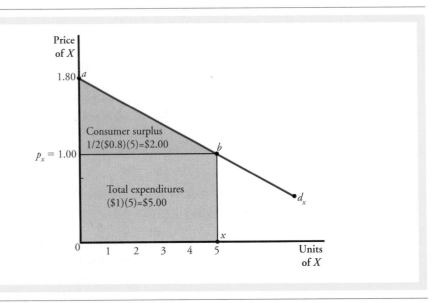

Figure 4.8 Consumer Surplus
When the units of good *X* are divisible into very small quantities, consumer surplus equals the purple triangle, which represents the difference between what consumers actually pay for 5 units of good *X*, shown by the blue shaded area, and the total value of five units, which equals the sum of the blue and purple shaded areas.

▲▲▲ 4.3 APPLICATION Why NFL Teams Force Season Ticket Holders to Purchase Tickets to Pre-Season Games

We've seen that in competitive market situations, consumers usually end up paying less than their maximum willingness to pay. When markets are not competitive, however, firms can often devise ways to extract some of that consumer surplus from their customers. One way that firms with some degree of market power can do this is by setting minimum order sizes.

Suppose that the only firm producing a perishable good X faces the linear demand curve in the figure from one of its customers. At the company's list price of $10, this customer will order 200 units per month, and the company will earn $10 × 200 =$2,000 per month in sales revenues when the customer is allowed to order as much or as little as she pleases at list price.

Now suppose the company introduces a new minimum order policy. It will continue to sell the product at a list price of $10, but from now on it will only fill orders of 300 units or more a month. Facing this new policy, will the customer increase the size of her order, or will she stop buying altogether?

In this graph, the 300 units she must now buy have a total worth to her equal to the area under her demand curve up to 300, the area $Oacfg$. At $10 apiece, those 300 units will cost her $3,000, or area $Obeg$. What she receives in the transaction has a value to her greater than what she is required to give up. That is, she continues to earn a *positive* amount of consumer surplus equal to the difference $Oacfg - Obeg$, which geometrically reduces to

the difference between the two triangles, $(\Delta abc - \Delta cfe) > 0$. Although positive, this surplus is less than the customer enjoyed when she was free to order as she pleased.

Is this as far as this customer can be pushed? Not at all. A utility-maximizing customer (with no alternative sources for this good) will keep on buying as long as she earns some consumer surplus—that is, as long as her *net gain* from transacting in this market is positive. Notice that in the graph, the total worth of 400 units, the area $Oaij$, is equal to what would have to be paid for 400 units at the list price, the area $Obhj$. In effect, the positive surplus the customer enjoys on the first 200 units, area abc, is offset by the negative surplus on the next 200 units, area chi. If the company sets its minimum order size at 400, then this customer would have a consumer surplus of zero and be indifferent between buying and not buying the good at all. To ensure that she buys, the firm can set a minimum just below 400—say at 399 units. At a list price of $10 and a minimum order size of 399, the customer will place the order, enjoy a very small positive consumer surplus, and the firm will have increased its revenues from this buyer from $2,000 with no minimum order requirement to $3,990 with a minimum order of 399 units.

Common examples of this behavior include professional football teams that require fans to purchase tickets for two or three pre-season games in order to buy season tickets, and vacation hotels in busy resort areas that require a minimum week-long stay during peak holiday seasons.

Application Figure 4.3 Why Firms Require Minimum Order Sizes

At a price of $10 with no minimum order requirements, the consumer purchases 200 units and consumer surplus equals the shaded blue area. If the company requires a minimum order size of 300 units, the consumer agrees to purchase 300 units and gains consumer surplus equal to the blue triangle abc on the first 200 units. However, the consumer pays more for the next 100 units, rectangle $dceg$, then the value of those units, area $dcfg$, the loss is represented by triangle cef. The consumer still purchases the good, because the gain of abc is greater than the loss cef. In fact, if the blue triangle equals the red triangle, the consumer will purchase any minimum order up to 400 units.

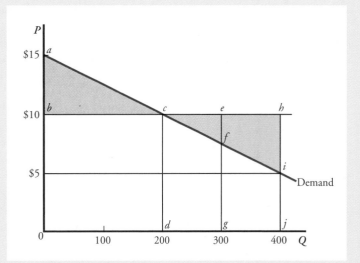

▼▼▼   4.4   Intertemporal Choice

So far it has been convenient to assume that consumers always "balance their books" by spending in every period all of their income received in that period. Yet consumers may sometimes want to spend a bit more than their income, and at other times spend a bit less. When a consumer borrows from a bank or uses a credit card, he is demanding loanable funds from the **financial sector**, which consists of banks, savings and loans, and other institutions that are in the business of borrowing funds from savers and lending funds to borrowers. When a consumer puts money away in a vacation account at a savings and loan institution, or when he buys a certificate of deposit from his bank, he is supplying loanable funds to the financial sector. Consumers are important players in many credit and debt markets, and it is impossible to understand events in those markets without first understanding what motivates and guides consumer behavior.

This section extends our analysis of consumer choice to account for decisions to borrow and save. When you borrow to increase consumption today, eventually you will have to pay back that money. When you do, you will have to reduce your consumption in the future below what it otherwise would have been. Similarly, when you reduce your consumption today in order to save, it is with a view toward spending that savings at some future date, thereby enabling you to increase your consumption later beyond what it would otherwise have been. Thus decisions to borrow and save can be modeled as the outcome of an agent's attempt to choose an optimal consumption path over time.

Intertemporal Preferences

Let's examine a simple case. Suppose there are only two time periods: period 1 and period 2. You can think of these as "this year" and "next year." In each period, the consumer expects with certainty to receive some fixed amount of income from his paycheck and other sources. Let these be Y_1 dollars in period 1 and Y_2 dollars in period 2, respectively. When borrowing and saving are possible, the overall level of consumption spending in any one period need not be the same as the consumer's income in that period. Let C_1 and C_2 represent dollar amounts of total consumption spending in periods 1 and 2 respectively. The ordered pair (C_1, C_2) consisting of total consumption spending in period 1 and total spending in period 2, represents a complete **intertemporal consumption plan** from the present into the future. The intertemporal consumption plan consists of the consumer's intended consumption pattern over time beginning in the present period and covering all future periods. In this case, utility is a function of consumption in both time periods, so $U = U(C_1, C_2)$. All borrowing or lending the consumer undertakes helps achieve the most desirable intertemporal consumption plan possible given the constraints she faces.

To model the consumer's intertemporal choice problem, let's recall the basic elements every model must have. First, we must identify the objects of choice, and provide some description of the agent's preferences for these objects. Next we have to describe the agent's opportunities, or constraints, and be clear about her objectives.

Here, the objects of choice are alternative intertemporal consumption plans. In the (C_1, C_2) plane of Figure 4.9, these will be represented by points on indifference curves like point A and point B. *Ceteris paribus*, a one-dollar increase in consumption spending today should make the consumer better off. Similarly, a one-dollar increase in spending tomorrow, *ceteris paribus*, will also make the consumer better off. When, as here, the marginal utility of an extra dollar's consumption today, MU_1, and the marginal utility of an

---

financial sector

In an economy, the banks, savings and loans, and other institutions that are in the business of borrowing funds from savers and lending those funds out to borrowers.

intertemporal consumption plan

The consumer's intended consumption pattern over time beginning in the present period and covering all future periods.

Figure 4.9 Indifference Curves in the Consumption Plane
The consumer's utility is a function of consumption in period 1, C_1, and consumption in period 2, C_2, so $U = U(C_1, C_2)$. The indifference curves are convex, because of a diminishing marginal rate of intertemporal substitution.

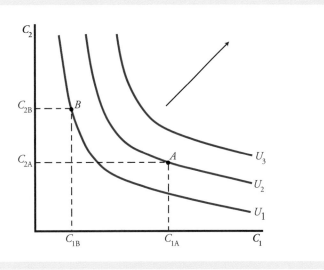

extra dollar's consumption next year, MU_2, are both always positive, indifference curves will be negatively sloped. To see this, we apply the formula for the slope of an indifference curve given in Equation 3.5 to obtain $-(MU_1/MU_2) < 0$.

The absolute value of the slope of an indifference curve between present and future consumption is called the **marginal rate of intertemporal substitution (MRIS)**, or:

marginal rate of intertemporal substitution (MRIS)

Measures the rate at which consumers are willing to trade future consumption for present consumption: It equals MU_p/MU_f, where MU_p is the marginal utility of present consumption and MU_f is the marginal utility of future consumption.

$$\text{MRIS} \equiv \left| \frac{-MU_1}{MU_2} \right| = \left| \frac{-MU_p}{MU_f} \right| \tag{4.1}$$

The MRIS identifies the rate at which the consumer would be willing to sacrifice future consumption spending for greater consumption today, while remaining indifferent after the adjustment. Given these assumptions about tastes and diminishing marginal utility for present and future consumption, the consumer's preferences can be represented by typical convex indifference curves with utility increasing as the consumer moves northeasterly, as in Figure 4.9.

The Intertemporal Budget Constraint

For the consumer, borrowing and saving are possible only at fixed terms determined in impersonal debt or credit markets. For the sake of simplicity, we will assume that the rate at which the consumer can borrow is equal to the rate at which she can save. Suppose $r > 0$ is that common interest rate per period for borrowing and saving in decimal terms. Then for every dollar borrowed in period 1, $(1 + r)$ dollars must be repaid in period 2; and for every dollar saved in period 1, $(1 + r)$ dollars will be received back in period 2.

What constraints limit the range of feasible consumption plans when one can both borrow and lend? Before, we required the consumer to spend no more at any time than she received in income. Yet when consumers can borrow and save, they don't have to balance their books in each and every period. They do, however, have to make sure they balance their books over the course of their lifetimes. Thus, in a two-period model, if the consumer borrows in the first period, she must repay that loan, with any interest due, during the second (and final) period. Likewise, if she saves during the first period, she receives any interest due during the second period.

▲▲▲ 4.4 APPLICATION   Borrowing for College

This table shows the average debt load assumed by students, excluding parents' debt, at various public and private colleges and universities according to the 2003 edition of the U.S. News & World Report's "America's Best Colleges" issue. The table shows what you likely know already: many students need to borrow a great deal of money to attend the college of their choice.

Suppose a student borrows $20,000 in student loans at 5 percent interest and agrees to pay back the loan over 10 years beginning the year he graduates. All interest on the loan is deferred until graduation; however, upon graduation, the student must begin to make monthly payments. From a standard loan payment table, we can see that the student will have to make a monthly payment of $212.13 for 120 months, or a total of $25,455.60 in payments. For each of the first ten years following graduation, the student's nominal income will be reduced by $2,545.56. Students who borrow to attend college make a choice to consume more than their income today and less than their nominal income for many years following graduation. In this section, we will discover why it is rational for so many utility-maximizing students to borrow money while attending college.

School	2001 Percent of Graduates With Debt	2001 Average Amount of Student Debt ($)
Pepperdine University	68	28,620
Rensselaer Polytechnic Institute	76	25,100
Union Institute	70	25,000
The George Washington University	55	24,894
Wesleyan University	46	24,448
Biola University	73	23,989
Austin College	69	23,892
University of San Diego	41	23,800
Nova Southeastern University	58	23,405
Whittier College	82	23,247
University of Miami	57	23,001
Albright College	77	23,000
University of Texas-Kingsville	78	23,000
Illinois Institute of Technology	53	22,733
Massachusetts Institute of Technology	56	22,669
University of Puget Sound	62	22,535
Brown University	39	22,530
Fisk University	85	22,500
University of Vermont	45	22,425
University of Notre Dame	55	22,270

Suppose the consumer decides to spend less than her income in the first period and saves $Y_1 - C_1 > 0$ dollars. If she lends that savings out at the interest rate r, she will receive back in period 2 that same amount plus interest earned, or $(Y_1 - C_1)(1 + r)$ in principal and interest repaid. Anticipated second period income of Y_2 will also be available to spend in period 2, so the overall constraint on second period consumption can be written as:

$$C_2 \leq Y_2 + (1 + r)(Y_1 - C_1) \tag{4.2}$$

Inequality 4.2 states that the second-period consumption can be no more than second-period income plus the principal and interest earned from any first-period savings.

What if, instead, this consumer had decided to spend more than her income on consumption in period 1? Any excess of desired consumption over available first-period income would have to be obtained by borrowing. If $C_1 - Y_1$ is the amount by which desired consumption exceeds income, then this is precisely the amount of borrowing required. When the consumer borrows in the first period, she must repay in the second. Because some of the anticipated income in period 2 will have to be used to repay that obligation, second period consumption will have to fall *below* second period income. In particular, the constraint on period 2 consumption will be:

$$C_2 \leq Y_2 - (1 + r)(C_1 - Y_1) \qquad\qquad (4.3)$$

The second-period consumption can be no more than second-period income *minus* the principal and interest that must be repaid for any first-period borrowing.

Notice the interesting similarity between inequalities 4.2 and 4.3. Let's rewrite Inequality 4.3 by multiplying through the second term on the right by the minus sign as follows:

$$C_2 \leq Y_2 + (1 + r)(-1)(C_1 - Y_1) \qquad\qquad (4.4)$$

or:

$$C_2 \leq Y_2 + (1 + r)(Y_1 - C_1) \qquad\qquad (4.5)$$

Inequality 4.5 is identical to Inequality 4.2! This is true because any amount borrowed in Inequality 4.3, $C_1 - Y_1 > 0$, can always be thought of as just *negative savings* of $Y_1 - C_1 < 0$ in Inequality 4.2. After a careful look at both inequalities, you should be able to convince yourself that the complete constraint the consumer faces on his choice of consumption path (C_1, C_2) can equally well be expressed by *either* Inequality 4.2 or 4.3. The two are exactly the same.

To represent the consumer's constraint graphically, let's focus on Inequality 4.2. Multiplying out $(1 + r)$ times $(Y_1 - C_1)$ on the right-hand side, Inequality 4.2 can be rewritten as:

$$C_2 \leq Y_2 + (1 + r)Y_1 - (1 + r)C_1$$

or:

$$C_2 \leq [Y_2 + (1 + r)Y_1] - (1 + r)C_1 \qquad\qquad (4.6)$$

From the consumer's point of view, Y_2, r, and Y_1 are *fixed*. Thus, the relationship between feasible levels of C_2 and C_1 is a simple linear one. When the consumer saves all of the income she receives in period 1, then $C_1 = 0$, and the intercept on the C_2-axis is $[Y_2 + (1 + r)Y_1]$, and the slope of the intertemporal budget constraint is $-(1 + r)$. Graphing Inequality 4.6 in Figure 4.10, this intertemporal budget constraint is bounded by a straight line going through the point (Y_1, Y_2) with a slope equal to $-(1 + r)$. This slope represents the rate at which the consumer can trade current consumption for future consumption by saving, and the rate at which she can trade future consumption for current consumption through borrowing, both of which depend on the market interest rate.

Because the consumer can always choose not to borrow or lend by choosing $C_1 = Y_1$ and $C_2 = Y_2$, *the intertemporal budget constraint must always pass through the point (Y_1, Y_2) in the plane.* That point labeled E in Figure 4.10 is called the **income endowment**

Figure 4.10 Intertemporal Budget Constraint
The consumer can always choose not to borrow or lend by choosing $C_1 = Y_1$ and $C_2 = Y_2$, so the intertemporal budget constraint must always pass through the income endowment point (Y_1, Y_2). Points on the blue segment below E, such as B, can be achieved only by borrowing. Points on the dark-green segment above E, such as A, can be achieved only by saving.

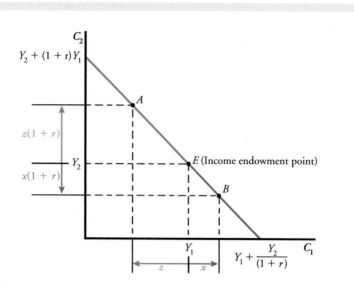

income endowment point

Identifies the consumption point if the consumer neither borrows nor saves.

future value of the income stream

Identifies the consumer's maximum future consumption if the consumer saves all current income.

point. The income endowment point identifies the consumption point if the consumer neither borrows nor saves. Points below E, such as B, can be achieved only by borrowing. To reach point B, the consumer borrows the amount x by which first-period consumption exceeds first-period income. At point B, second-period consumption must then be reduced below second-period income to repay that borrowing with interest. To reach points above E, such as A, the consumer must save. To reach A, the consumer saves an amount z, the excess of first-period income over first-period consumption at A. Second-period consumption at A will then be greater than second-period income by the amount of the principal and interest earned from first-period savings.

The intercepts in Figure 4.10 are also significant. The vertical intercept, $Y_2 + (1 + r)Y_1$, is called the **future value of the income stream** (Y_1, Y_2). It tells us what the consumer's available resources would be in the second period if she saved all of her first-period income at interest rate r. We can find the horizontal intercept by setting second-period consumption equal to zero in Inequality 4.6 and solving for C_1, as follows:

$$0 \leq [Y_2 + (1 + r)Y_1] - (1 + r)C_1$$

$$C_1(1 + r) \leq Y_2 + (1 + r)Y_1$$

$$C_1 \leq Y_1 + \frac{Y_2}{(1 + r)}$$

present value of the income stream

Identifies the value today of all current and future income.

That intercept $Y_1 + Y_2/(1 + r)$ is called the **present value of the income stream** (Y_1, Y_2). It measures the value today of all current and expected future receipts. Because the consumer must repay any first-period borrowing out of second-period income, the maximum possible level of first-period consumption spending can be no more than the present value of the consumer's entire income stream. The second term, $Y_2/(1 + r)$, is the present value of a promise to pay Y_2 in one year at interest rate r. It represents the amount a lender, such as a bank, would lend the borrower in year 1 if the borrower promised to repay Y_2 in year 2.

COMMON ERROR 4.2 Incorrectly Identifying the Intertemporal Budget Constraint

Students often make one of two errors when graphing the intertemporal budget constraint. The first error is to fail to identify the endowment point as a point in the plane and to instead identify the endowment point as two points at the intercepts of the axis. Panel (a) of the figure illustrates such an error. Here the consumer's endowment is (Y_1, Y_2) at point *EP*; however, the student has drawn a budget constraint with intercepts Y_1 and Y_2. If you make this error, you will be unable to analyze intertemporal choices in a reasonable way, because even the slope of the budget con-

straint is incorrect. When you use this budget constraint, all of your results will be wrong!

Panel (b) shows a second common error. Here the interest rate declines from r_0 to r_1 and the budget constraint should rotate to the left around the point *EP*. Instead, the student has shifted the intercept for consumption in period 2 down, because at a lower interest rate, savings yield a smaller future income. This budget constraint fails to recognize that at a lower interest rate, the consumer can also borrow and consume more in period 1. Once again, any analysis using this budget constraint will be wrong!

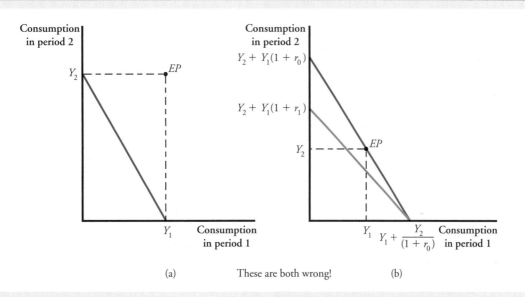

(a)　　　These are both wrong!　　　(b)

Common Error Figure 4.2
In panel (a) the budget constraint is incorrectly drawn because the components of the endowment point have been graphed on the intercepts. The budget constraint in panel (b) is also incorrect: when the interest rate falls, the budget constraint does not shift down from the dark-green to the light-green line, because the new budget constraint must still go through the endowment point, and therefore the new constraint must rotate around the endowment point.

The Effect of Interest Rate Changes

To complete the model of intertemporal choice, we need to describe the agent's objectives. We make our usual assumption that consumers seek to maximize utility; this time, however, in planning the course of their consumption stream over time. Even with given preferences and given income streams, most people are neither always borrowers nor always savers. How each of us chooses to allocate available resources between current and future consumption depends importantly on the interest rate. At some rates of interest, we find it worthwhile to save. At others, we find it worthwhile to borrow.

In Figure 4.11, when the interest rate is r, the individual with income endowment of Y_1 in period 1 and Y_2 in period 2 at point E maximizes utility by choosing consumption just equal to income in each period, and so follows the advice of Polonius in Hamlet, "Neither a borrower nor a lender be."[1] When the interest rate rises to $r' > r$, the intertemporal budget constraint becomes steeper and pivots through the income endowment point E. There are several ways of explaining why a rise in the interest rate will have this effect. One way is to recall that the slope of the constraint is always given by $-(1 + r)$ and that—regardless of the interest rate—it must always be possible for the consumer to choose not to borrow or lend. Thus, for any interest rate, the constraint must always go through E. Another way is to note that increases in r reduce the present value of the income stream $Y_1 + Y_2/(1 + r)$ (moving the horizontal intercept inwards), and increase the future value of the income stream $Y_2 + Y_1(1 + r)$ (moving the vertical intercept outwards), and therefore twist the constraint as shown in Figure 4.11.

Facing a higher market interest rate, this consumer now maximizes utility by consuming Y_{1H} in period 1 and Y_{2H} in period 2 at point A, being induced by the higher interest rate to save the amount indicated on the diagram. When interest rates fall below r, current consumption becomes relatively cheaper than future consumption, and the consumer finds it worthwhile to borrow to finance greater consumption today. In Figure 4.11, a decrease in the interest rate to $r'' < r$ causes the constraint to become flatter and once again pivot through E. The consumer maximizes utility by consuming Y_{1L} in period 1 and Y_{2L} in period 2 at point B, borrowing the amount indicated there to finance that choice.

To economists, the demand for borrowing and the supply of savings are both derived from the consumer's desire to maximize the utility of consuming goods and services over time. Neither saving nor borrowing themselves have any intrinsic utility or dis-utility.

Figure 4.11 Changes in the Interest Rate and Rotating the Budget Constraint through Point E

When the interest rate is r, the consumer maximizes utility at the endowment point E where the indifference curve U_0 is tangent to the dark-green budget constraint. If the interest rate increases to r', the budget constraint becomes the steeper teal line, and the consumer becomes a saver who maximizes utility at the point A. If the interest rate decreases to r'', the budget constraint becomes the flatter light-green line, and the consumer becomes a borrower who maximizes utility at the point B.

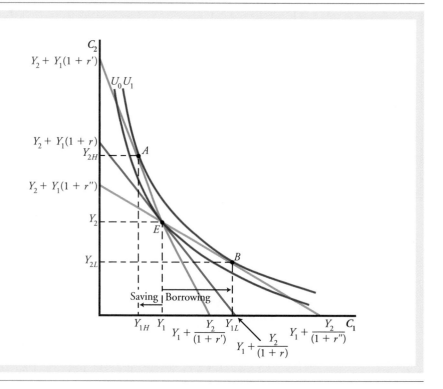

[1] Shakespeare, *Hamlet*, 1.3.75.

Each is only a means to an end, and that end is consumption. Often, however, it is useful to focus attention on how agents will behave when net savers encounter dis-savers in the financial markets. The framework developed so far can be used to observe a good deal about that market behavior.

Panel (a) of Figure 4.12 represents the situation of a typical saver. The top panel illustrates the intertemporal consumption problem the consumer must solve for three interest

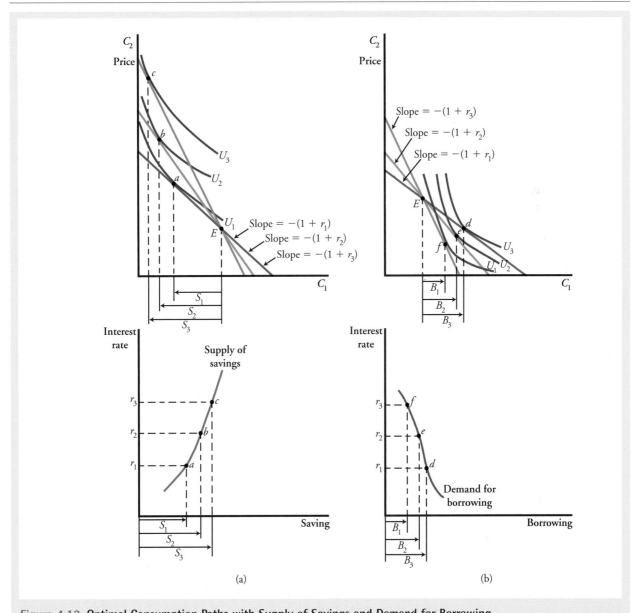

Figure 4.12 Optimal Consumption Paths with Supply of Savings and Demand for Borrowing
In the top of panel (a), as the interest rate increases from r_1 to r_2 to r_3, the saver's equilibrium moves from a to b to c and savings increase from S_1 to S_2 to S_3 respectively. In the bottom of panel (a), the supply curve of savings is derived from the top panel and is upward-sloping. In the top of panel (b), as the interest rate increases from r_1 to r_2 to r_3, the borrower's equilibrium moves from d to e to f, and borrowing decreases from B_3 to B_2 to B_1 respectively. In the bottom of panel (b), the demand curve for borrowing is derived from the top panel and is downward-sloping.

rates r_1, r_2, and r_3. The bottom panel measures the interest rate on the vertical axis and the equilibrium quantity of savings on the horizontal axis. In the top panel, as the interest rate rises from r_1 to r_2 to r_3, the optimal consumption point moves from a to b to c. In the bottom panel, as the quantity of savings supplied is plotted against the interest rate, the consumer's supply curve of savings is traced out. Here, that supply curve is upward-sloping. As the interest rate increases, the consumer increases his savings and, as a result, increases the quantity of loanable funds he supplies to financial markets.

Panel (b) of Figure 4.12 illustrates the situation of a typical borrower. The bottom panel once again measures the interest rate on the vertical axis. This time the horizontal axis measures the amount of borrowing the consumer undertakes. Here, as the interest rate rises from r_1 to r_2 to r_3, the optimal consumption choice moves from d to e to f. In the bottom panel, by plotting the quantity of borrowing demanded against the interest rate at which it is desired, this consumer's demand curve for borrowing can be traced out. Here, as we usually expect to find, that demand curve is downward-sloping. As the interest rate increases, the consumer decreases his borrowing and, as a result, decreases the quantity of loanable funds he demands from financial markets.

There are two differences between panel (a) and panel (b): the preferences of the two consumers and their initial endowment points. The consumer in panel (a) has a larger current endowment of income, but a smaller future endowment than the consumer in panel (b). Furthermore, the indifference curve mapping shows that the consumer in panel (a), the saver, is less willing to sacrifice future consumption for current consumption than the consumer in panel (b), the borrower. In a technical sense, the borrower has a higher MRIS of future for current consumption than the saver.

Summary

1. The total effect on quantity demanded can always be decomposed into a substitution effect and an income effect. The substitution effect captures the change in demand due purely to the change in relative prices. The income effect captures the change in demand due to changes in "real income" or purchasing power that accompany every price change. When a good's price increases, the substitution effect always works to decrease quantity demanded; when price decreases, the substitution effect always works to increase quantity demanded. For normal goods, the income effect of an own-price change reinforces the substitution effect, ensuring the demand curve will slope downward. For inferior goods, the income effect opposes the substitution effect. The demand curve for an inferior good can therefore have virtually any slope depending on which effect dominates.

2. To construct the market demand, we add together the quantities demanded by each buyer in the market at every possible price. Market demand for any single good depends on the prices of all goods in the consumers' budgets and their incomes. To learn about real-world market demand curves, analysts will use a variety of approaches. They may conduct surveys, market experiments, or even laboratory experiments. Sometimes, one or more data series may serve as leading indicators of important changes in overall or firm-specific business conditions. When appropriate and adequate data exist, economists will generally want to estimate market demand using econometric techniques.

3. The entire area under a demand curve up to a given quantity is a measure of the total worth or utility the consumer derives from consuming that quantity of the good. Consumer surplus is the difference between what a given quantity of a good is worth to the consumer and what she must pay to acquire it. When consumers are free to buy all units at the same fixed price, consumer surplus will be the area below the demand curve and above a horizontal line at the fixed price.

4. The consumer's demand for borrowing or supply of savings can be derived from the consumer's intertemporal consumption choice problem. When the consumer can borrow and save at the same rate of interest, r, if we graph current consumption on the x-axis, the intertemporal budget constraint will be a negatively sloped straight line passing through the income endowment point with slope equal to $-(1 + r)$. For interior solutions, the optimal intertemporal consumption plan will have a present value just equal to the present value of the income stream, and will equate the MRIS to $(1 + r)$. By varying the interest rate, we can trace out the demand for borrowing and the supply of savings by plotting the consumer's optimal levels of borrowing or saving against the interest rate.

Self-Test Problems

1. A consumer consumes two goods, X and Y. Illustrate the following using a separate, carefully drawn budget constraint and indifference curve map for each part. Be sure to identify the substitution, income, and total effect on the quantity demanded for *each good* on your diagram.

   a. A decrease in p_x when X and Y are both normal goods.

   b. An increase in p_x when X and Y are both normal goods.

   c. A decrease in p_y when X and Y are both normal goods.

   d. An increase in p_y when X and Y are both normal goods.

   e. An increase in p_x when X is inferior, but not a Giffen good, and Y is a normal good.

   f. An increase in p_y when X is inferior and Y is normal.

2. The demand for imported truffles by Harry's West-Side Truffle Bar in Kokomo is given by:

   $$p = 50 - 0.05\, q$$

   where p is price and q is ounces of truffles per month. Last month, Harry paid $20 an ounce for his truffles. This month, the government announced it will impose a new $5 per ounce tariff on truffles in retaliation for increases in French tariffs on American wines. Answer the following questions, assuming the price of truffles increases by the full $5 amount of the tariff:

   a. How many truffles did Harry buy before the new tariff and how many will he buy after the tariff?

   b. How much tariff revenue will the government collect from Harry?

   c. How much consumer surplus will Harry lose if the tariff is imposed?

   d. Harry knows a lobbyist in Washington who can fix things. For $2,700, the lobbyist can stop the tariff from being imposed. Will Harry hire the lobbyist? Why or why not?

3. You are offered a job that will take you two periods to complete. You have your choice of compensation plans. Under Plan A, you would be paid $5,000 now and $5,000 when the job is complete. Under Plan B, you would be paid nothing now, but would get $10,500 when the job was complete. If you can both borrow and lend at an interest rate of $r = 0.05$, which plan would you choose? Why?

Questions and Problems for Review

1. Regardless of the price of potatoes, Tom buys the same quantity of potatoes. Using indifference curve analysis, show the effect on Tom's consumption of potatoes and other goods of a decrease in the price of potatoes. Separate the substitution and income effects. Are potatoes a normal or inferior good for Tom? Explain.

2. Answer true or false and justify your answer: If X is normal and Y is inferior, a decrease in the price of X just *might* cause the consumer to buy more Y.

3. "Hey Doctor, a funny thing happens to my demand for good Y when there is a decrease in the price of good X. Even though I really like good Y—that is, I prefer more of it to less—it seems I'll only buy just so much of good Y. Whenever the price of good X goes down, enabling me to buy more good Y if I want to, I simply increase the quantity of good X I buy, but the quantity of Y just remains the same. Am I normal? Please explain what's going on."

4. Marc has an income of $100 and he has two goods to choose from, Wheat Thins and Triscuits. The price of Triscuits is $5 a box. If the price of Wheat Thins increases from $4 to $5 a box, how do you think this will affect Marc's consumption of Wheat Thins and Triscuits? Show using an indifference curve analysis. With regard to the cross-price effect of this price change, which dominates for Triscuits, the substitution effect or the income effect?

5. An increased tax on movie theatre tickets causes Zach's consumption of popcorn to decrease, but leaves his consumption of movies unchanged. How can this be? Explain using a graph and the concepts of income and substitution effects.

6. Suppose the nation decides to ration gasoline to a maximum of 10 gallons per week at a price of $1.50 per gallon. With rationing, Gavin purchases 10 gallons per week. If rationing is eliminated, the price would increase to $2.50 and Gavin would buy 15 gallons per week. Is it possible to tell for sure whether Gavin is better off with rationing? Show using a graph (or graphs).

7. Firms must have a good understanding of market demand for their product to guide decisions on product pricing, production scheduling, inventory control, and so on. As a manager, you have to decide whether to estimate a careful econometric model of your product's demand, or just rely on

"rules of thumb" that have been used in the past. What factors would you consider in reaching your decision concerning which method to use?

8. Firestone does a survey to determine the effect of a 20 percent price increase on snow tires in Minnesota and finds that the quantity demanded decreases very little. As a result, Firestone raises snow tire prices by 20 percent throughout the country. However, the quantity demanded for Firestone snow tires decreases significantly. Why are these market results different from the Minnesota survey results?

9. An economist is using econometrics to estimate the demand for wood stoves in the United States. She uses the following model:

$$q_{ws} = f(p_{ws}, p_w, p_{kh}, p_{eh}, I)$$

where q_{ws} is the quantity demanded of wood stoves, p_{ws} is the price of wood stoves, p_w is the price of a cord of firewood, p_{kh} is the price of kerosene heaters, p_{eh} is the price of electric room heaters, and I is per-capita consumer income. Does this model include all of the major factors you would expect to influence the demand for wood stoves? Would you expect this model to yield a good econometric estimate of the demand for wood stoves? Why or why not?

10. Suppose the market for rental housing in Hamilton, New York is characterized by the following monthly demand and supply curves:

$$p = 2000 - 2q$$
$$p = 200 + q$$

What is the current equilibrium price and quantity of rental housing in Hamilton? Suppose the village board of directors decides that rents are too high in Hamilton, so they impose an immediate price ceiling on rental housing equal to $600 per month. What is the impact of this price ceiling on consumer surplus in the rental housing market in Hamilton? Provide a numerical value for the change in consumer surplus. Do your consumer surplus calculations imply that rent control in Hamilton is a good or bad economic policy? Explain your reasoning.

11. Do consumers gain more *total* consumer surplus from their consumption of water or diamonds? Is

this conclusion consistent with the relative prices consumers pay for water and diamonds? Explain your reasoning.

12. Jen has an elasticity of demand for chocolate bars of 1.5, while Maggie's elasticity of demand for chocolate bars is 0.75. The price of a chocolate bar is initially $1.50. Jen and Maggie go to a store and discover that chocolate bars are on sale for $1.00. Who benefits most from this sale? Explain using a graph.

13. There are five people with identical individual demand curves for apples each equal to $p_a = 50 - (1/2)q_a$. Will the price elasticity of demand for apples at any given price be the same or different for the individual demand curves and market demand curve? Explain.

14. Consider an intertemporal choice model where Diane has an income of $5 million in period 1 and $7 million in period 2. She currently borrows $1 million, and the interest rate for both borrowing and saving is 10 percent. Assuming both present and future consumption are normal goods for Diane: if her income in period 2 decreases to $6 million, show the effect on Diane's consumption choice. Draw a graph showing how Diane's intertemporal consumption plan changes as a result of the decrease in income in period 2. Does Diane still borrow? Why or why not?

15. This chapter made the simplifying assumption that the interest rates at which the consumer can borrow and lend were the same. Typically, interest rates at which we can borrow are higher than those at which we can lend. On a piece of graph paper, carefully sketch the intertemporal budget constraint for a person who expects income this period of $100 and income next period of $120, if this person can lend at an interest rate of 5 percent but can only borrow at an interest rate of 10 percent. Be sure to label slopes, intercepts, and all important points clearly.

16. True or false? "An increase in the interest rate will generally make savers better off and borrowers worse off." Justify your answer and support your argument with appropriate and carefully drawn diagrams.

17. "A friend of mine used to pinch every penny till it cried. He just saved and saved. Then, one day, he saw his rich uncle's will and learned he was going to get a big inheritance someday. Now I hardly recognize my friend. If you can believe it, he now spends so much on consumption he has to borrow money to pay for it! What's come over him? Has he become irrational, or can you explain his behavior to me?"

18. Jillian can either save or borrow at an interest rate of 10 percent. Her current income is $6 million and her expected future income is $8 million. Currently Jillian saves $1 million. Show her current intertemporal consumption plan. If Jillian can no longer save at 10 percent, but instead must save at 5 percent, however, she must still borrow at 10 percent, how will this change in interest rates affect her budget constraint? How will this change her intertemporal consumption plan? Is future consumption a normal good for Jillian?

19. The supply curve of savings we derived in Figure 4.12 was upward-sloping everywhere. It is possible, however, that the supply of savings from a perfectly rational person might "bend backwards," or have a negative slope at higher rates of interest. This would suggest that further increases in the interest rate would actually cause the consumer to save less.

    a. In a diagram similar to the left-hand side of Figure 4.12, illustrate a case where an increase in the interest rate causes the consumer to save less. Sketch the corresponding section of the supply curve of savings below, as in Figure 4.12.

    b. Decompose the total effect of your interest rate change on consumption today and consumption tomorrow into substitution and income effects on the same diagram. Study your analysis carefully.

    c. Use your answers above to explain a backward-bending supply curve of savings.

20. In Japan, the rate of savings out of current income for the typical person is 15 percent, while in the United States that figure is about 5 percent. Based on the analysis in this chapter, what factors do you think might account for this difference?

Internet Exercises

Visit *http://www.myeconlab.com/waldman* for this chapter's Web exercises. Answer real-world economics problems by doing research on the Internet.

Appendix 4.1

Cobb–Douglas Utility Functions and Income and Substitution Effects

Economists often use a Cobb-Douglas utility function of the general form $U(x,y) = x^a y^{(1-a)}$ to analyze consumer behavior. Let's consider an example using a commonly used value for a of 1/2. The Cobb-Douglas utility function is then $U(x,y) = x^{1/2}y^{1/2}$, where x is the quantity of good X and y is the quantity of good Y. Using this function, it is possible to mathematically separate the income effect from the substitution effect of a price change on the quantity demanded of X. Suppose the consumer's income is I, and the price of good X is p_x and the price of good Y is p_y. The consumer wishes to maximize utility:

$$U(x,y) = x^{1/2}y^{1/2} \tag{A.1}$$

subject to the budget constraint condition that:

$$p_x x + p_y y = I \tag{A.2}$$

Utility maximization requires $\text{MRS} = \text{MU}_X/\text{MU}_y = p_x/p_y$, or:

$$\text{MRS} = \frac{\text{MU}_x}{\text{MU}_y} = \frac{\dfrac{\partial U(x,y)}{\partial x}}{\dfrac{\partial U(x,y)}{\partial y}} = \frac{\dfrac{1}{2}y^{\frac{1}{2}}x^{-\frac{1}{2}}}{\dfrac{1}{2}x^{\frac{1}{2}}y^{-\frac{1}{2}}} = \frac{y}{x} = \frac{p_x}{p_y}$$

Solving Equation A.2 for y yields:

$$y = \frac{I - p_x x}{p_y} \tag{A.4}$$

Substituting y from Equation A.4 into Equation A.3, we obtain:

$$\frac{\dfrac{I - p_x x}{p_y}}{x} = \frac{p_x}{p_y} \tag{A.5}$$

Simplifying yields:

$$I - p_x x = p_x x \text{ or } 2p_x x = I$$

Solving for x:

$$x = \frac{\dfrac{1}{2}I}{p_x} \tag{A.6}$$

Substituting Equation A.6 into Equation A.2 yields:

$$p_x\left(\frac{\frac{1}{2}I}{p_x}\right) + p_y y = \frac{1}{2}I + p_y y = I \tag{A.7}$$

Simplifying Equation A.7 and solving for y:

$$y = \frac{\frac{1}{2}I}{p_y} \tag{A.8}$$

Suppose $I_0 = 100$, $p_x = 5$ and $p_y = 5$, then from Equation A.6 and Equation A.8:

$$x = \frac{\frac{1}{2}(100)}{5} = 10$$

$$y = \frac{\frac{1}{2}(100)}{5} = 10$$

Given $x = 10$ and $y = 10$, $U(x,y) = 10^{1/2}10^{1/2} = \sqrt{10 \times 10} = 10$.

If the price of good X increases to $p_x = 10$, then from Equation A.6 and Equation A.8:

$$x = \frac{\frac{1}{2}(100)}{10} = 5 \tag{A.9}$$

$$y = \frac{\frac{1}{2}(100)}{5} = 10 \tag{A.10}$$

The new equilibrium quantity of X is 5, and utility is $U(x,y) = 5^{1/2}10^{1/2} = \sqrt{50} = 7.07$.

To determine the substitution effect, we calculate the hypothetical income level I_1 that would get the consumer back to utility level $U = 10$ at the new price ratio $p_x/p_y = 10/5$. Therefore, from Equations A.1, A.6, and A.8, the following equation must hold:

$$10 = \sqrt{\left(\frac{\frac{1}{2}I_1}{10}\right)\left(\frac{\frac{1}{2}I_1}{5}\right)} \tag{A.11}$$

Squaring Equation A.11 yields:

$$100 = \frac{\frac{1}{4}(I_1)^2}{50} = \frac{(I_1)^2}{200}$$

$$(I_1)^2 = 100(200) = 20,000$$

$$I_1 = \sqrt{20,000} = 141.42 \tag{A.12}$$

For the consumer to reach the original level of utility $U = 10$ at the new price ratio, income must be increased to $I_1 = 141.42$. With $I_1 = 141.42$, $p_x = 10$ and $p_y = 5$, the equilibrium quantities of x and y are:

$$x = \frac{\frac{1}{2}(141.42)}{10} = 7.07 \tag{A.13}$$

$$y = \frac{\frac{1}{2}(141.42)}{5} = 14.14 \tag{A.14}$$

Because the original equilibrium quantity of good X was $x = 10$, the substitution effect is $10 - 7.07 = 2.93$. Because the final equilibrium quantity of X at the new price ratio is 5, the income effect equals $7.07 - 5 = 2.07$. The total effect of the price increase for good X from $p_x = 5$ to $p_x = 10$, is $10 - 5 = 5$, which can be broken down into a substitution effect equal to 2.93 and an income effect equal to 2.07.

Chapter 5
Using Consumer Theory

▲▲▲

Between 1980 and 2000, the United States government's expenditures on food stamps varied from just over $9 billion in 1980 to over $24.6 billion in 1994. In the 1990s, expenditures on the food stamp program expanded considerably. In this chapter, we use the theory of consumer behavior to analyze whether food stamp recipients would have been better off with billions of dollars in cash payments instead of billions of dollars in food stamps.

When commercial cellular phone service was introduced in 1982 in the United States, the wireless providers priced their service on a per-minute-of-use basis. By 2001, however, the major cellular providers had introduced a pricing option that permitted a large number of minutes of calls for a fixed charge. This chapter uses consumer theory to help us understand why these firms changed their pricing strategies.

In the 2000 presidential election between George W. Bush and Al Gore, the candidates debated the pros and cons of across-the-board income tax cuts and school voucher programs, with Bush in favor and Gore opposed. In 1980, Ronald Reagan promised to cut income taxes in order to increase savings and work effort. In the former Soviet Union, it was common for the prices of basic commodities such as bread and chicken to be set below the equilibrium prices; and as a result, consumers had to wait in long lines to obtain these basic goods. In this chapter, we use the utility-maximizing model of consumer behavior developed in Chapters 3 and 4 to analyze how consumers might respond to each of these policies.

Learning Objectives

After reading Chapter 5, you will have learned:

➤ How to use consumer theory to show the comparative effects of different government welfare policies.

➤ How consumer theory can be used to analyze the impact of a school voucher system.

➤ How a business firm can use consumer theory to help select an optimal pricing strategy.

➤ How to use consumer theory to explain the impact of rationing.

➤ How the theory of income and substitution effects can explain the ways in which income tax reductions might affect consumer behavior.

➤ How the theory of income and substitution effects can be used to explain how consumers respond differently to income taxes and consumption taxes.

5.1   Welfare Grants in Kind Versus Monetary Grants

grants-in-kind

Government welfare programs that pay benefits in the form of goods or services instead of cash; for example, food stamp programs, housing subsidies, and Medicaid.

negative income tax

A program that would guarantee poor families a certain minimum level of income based on family size and certain other needs criteria. Instead of paying taxes, the government would send these families cash benefits.

The United States welfare system is a complex web of different programs. Qualified recipients receive benefits under one or more of the following **grants-in-kind** programs that pay benefits in the form of goods or services instead of cash: food stamps, housing subsidies, and medical benefits through the Medicaid program. From time to time, some economists have suggested that some or all of these need-based grants-in-kind programs should be eliminated in favor of a direct cash payment to poor families, who would then be free to spend the funds in whatever way they wished. As early as the 1950s, Nobel Laureates Milton Friedman and James Tobin suggested replacing the myriad of welfare programs with a **negative income tax** program for the poor. Under their negative income tax plans, the government would guarantee families a minimum level of dollar income based on family size and certain other criteria.

The Food Stamp Program

Would the poor be better off under a negative income tax that paid them the same value of benefits as the value of the current set of grants-in-kind? The use of consumer theory provides some interesting insights into this question. Consider the current food stamp program that provides qualified families with food stamps, which can be used only to purchase certain types of food. In Figure 5.1, we consider the impact of the food stamp program on a typical recipient whose utility function is $u = u(F, OG)$, where F represents units of food and OG represents units of all other goods. In the absence of any aid programs, the consumer's budget constraint would be the light-green budget constraint ae, with intercepts of I/P_{OG} and I/P_f, and a slope of $-P_f/P_{OG}$. The consumer maximizes utility at point X, and consumes F_1 units of food and OG_1 units of other goods.

Suppose the only government welfare program is one that provides the consumer with FS dollars worth of food stamps. These stamps can be used only to purchase food, so under the food stamp program, the new budget constraint would be the dark-green

Figure 5.1 A Consumer Who Is Indifferent Between Food Stamps and Cash

In the absence of a food stamp program, the budget constraint is the light-green line ae, and the consumer consumes at point X. With a food stamp program that offers the consumer FS dollars worth of food stamps, the budget constraint is the dark-green kinked constraint abc, and the consumer consumes at point Y. With a cash grant of FS dollars, the budget constraint is the line dbc, and the consumer consumes at point Y.

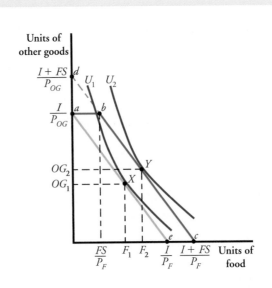

kinked line *abc*. The consumer can still purchase a maximum amount of other goods equal to I/P_{OG}, but now can purchase that amount of other goods and use food stamps to purchase FS/P_F units of food at point *b*. From point *b*, the consumer can purchase additional units of food at the market price P_F, so the food stamp program enables the consumer to purchase anywhere along the dark-green line running from point *b* to point *c*.

An Equivalent Cost Cash Grant Program

As an alternative to the food stamp program, the government could make a direct cash payment to qualified recipients equal to *FS* dollars. Such a cash grant would cost the government the same amount of dollars as the food stamp program. The cash grant would shift the budget constraint out parallel to the original budget constraint with the new other goods intercept at $(I + FS)/P_{OG}$. The new budget constraint is the straight line *dbc* and includes the teal dashed extension from point *b* to point *d*.

In the absence of any government aid, the consumer is in equilibrium at point *X* and consumes F_1 units of food and OG_1 units of other goods. With the food stamp program, the consumer consumes at point *Y* and consumes F_2 units of food and OG_2 units of other goods. Notice that the food stamp program enables the consumer to consume both more food and more other goods. For this consumer, a cash grant of *FS* dollars would have exactly the same impact. The two programs are therefore exactly equivalent for this consumer, and the consumer is completely indifferent between them.

Now consider Figure 5.2. Here a different consumer with different tastes (that is, with a different set of indifference curves) faces exactly the same choices. With a food stamp program, the consumer maximizes utility at point *X* and consumes FS/P_F units of food and I/P_{OG} units of other goods. She would spend all of her cash income on other goods and all of her food stamps on food. If this consumer were offered an equal cost cash grant of *FS* dollars, she would consume at point *Y*, and consume F_2 units of food and OG_2 units of other goods. She would be better off with a cash grant, because it would enable her to reach a higher level of utility, U_2 instead of U_1.

Figures 5.1 and 5.2 demonstrate that some consumers would be better off with a cash grant program, and some consumers would be indifferent between a cash grant program

Figure 5.2 A Consumer Who Prefers Cash to Food Stamps

With a food stamp program that offers the consumer *FS* dollars' worth of food stamps, the budget constraint is the dark-green kinked constraint *aXc* and the consumer consumes at point *X*. If the government gave this consumer *FS* dollars in cash instead of food stamps, the budget constraint would be the line *dYXc*, and the consumer consumes at point *Y*.

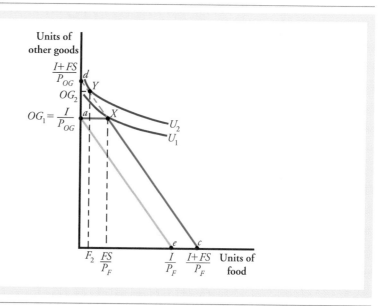

and an equal-benefit food stamps program. The important question to ask is: Could any consumer be better off with a food stamp program than a cash grant program? The answer is no. No matter what shape you draw the indifference curves, no consumer could possibly be better off with a food stamps program than a cash grant program. The reason is that the cash grant program adds an additional group of consumption opportunities (on the teal dashed segment of the budget constraint) that do not exist with a food stamp program.

Political Issues

If the previous positive economic analysis is correct, why does the government rely heavily on grants-in-kind instead of equal-cost cash grants? The answer is primarily political. Many politicians and citizens believe that numerous recipients would spend a cash grant on wasteful items such as illegal drugs, alcohol, lottery tickets, and fancy clothing. To guard against this type of spending, politicians have historically preferred to provide a significant percentage of aid to the poor in the form of grants-in-kind instead of cash.

This political argument against the use of cash grants instead of grants-in-kind might or might not be strong enough to override the economic argument against grants-in-kind and in favor of cash grants. These non-economic arguments against cash grants are *normative*; they depend on individual value judgments. Note, for example, that in Figure 5.1, the consumer consumes more other goods as a result of the current food stamps program, and some of this increase in other goods consumption could be in the form of illegal drugs, alcohol, lottery tickets, and fancy clothing. Under the current program, therefore, the consumption of wasteful items might increase as a direct result of the food stamp program.

By using positive economic analysis, we can conclude that recipients as a group will be better off with cash grants that cost the taxpayers an equal number of tax dollars. Many economists also believe that the administrative costs of a cash grant program would be significantly lower than the costs of the current food stamp programs and would help recipients become psychologically more self-reliant. The issue is far more complex than suggested by Figures 5.1 and 5.2, but many economists weighing all of the positive and normative arguments have concluded that Friedman and Tobin were on the right track with their concept of a negative income tax program to replace most of the current grants-in-kind programs. The negative income tax programs envisioned by Friedman and Tobin would provide all poor families a guaranteed minimum level of cash income.

The public debate over whether to replace grants-in-kind with cash grants continues, but in recent years, there has been another, more heated public debate concerning whether the government should offer parents vouchers for their children to attend private schools instead of public schools. The school voucher debate, to which we turn next, can also be analyzed using the basic tools of consumer theory.

▼▼▼   5.2   Public Schools Versus School Vouchers

school vouchers

Government grants that families can use to purchase education in either the public or private sector.

In the United States, one of the most hotly debated public issues in recent years has centered on the subject of school vouchers. **School vouchers** are government grants-in-kind that families can use to purchase education in either the public or private sector. Proponents of the voucher system argue that it would increase parental choice, especially for lower-income families that cannot currently afford to send their children to private schools. Opponents of vouchers argue that the system could destroy the public school system as we know it. Economics cannot provide all of the answers to the debate about school vouchers; however, as we will see, consumer theory can provide important insights into the ongoing debate.

The Current System of Education

To understand the school voucher debate, it is first necessary to understand how the current system of public education affects consumer behavior. Figure 5.3 shows the choices currently available to a typical consumer of education. The consumer's utility is a function of the units of educational services purchased, E, and the units of other goods purchased, OG, so utility $u = u(E, OG)$. Units of educational services E are measured in terms of spending per pupil, and therefore the price of an additional unit of educational services, P_E, equals $1.00. In a world with only private education, the family faces a straight-line budget constraint equal to *acdf*, with a slope equal to $-P_E/P_{OG} = -\$1.00/P_{OG}$. The family could exchange other goods for educational services at these relative prices.

A FAMILY THAT SENDS ITS CHILD TO A PUBLIC SCHOOL Currently, the government must offer to provide a public school education to every child. If the public school spends $4,000 per pupil, then a student in a public school consumes $\$4,000/P_E = \$4,000/\$1.00 = 4,000$ units of educational services. One possible consumption point on the family's budget constraint is b, where the student attends a public school and the family spends its entire after-tax income, I, on other goods. Income I is measured in after-tax dollars, because all families must pay school taxes regardless of which school their children attend; and therefore the maximum amount of other goods a family can consume is measured by the ratio of after-tax income I to the price of other goods, P_{OG}. If a family desires to purchase more than a public school education, it must send its child to a private school, where each family pays tuition to cover the entire cost of their child's education. A family that sends its child to a private school would consume somewhere on the linear budget constraint connecting points c and f, with a slope equal to $-P_E/P_{OG} = -\$1/P_{OG}$. The family's complete budget constraint, therefore, is the green kinked line connecting points a, b, c, d, and f. The family in Figure 5.3 maximizes utility at point b and sends its child to a public school.

Figure 5.3 A Family that Sends its Child to a Public School
Without a voucher system, the family budget constraint is the green kinked line *abcdf*. At point b, this family uses the public school system and consumes 4,000 units of educational services and $(I/P_{OG}) = OG_1$ units of other goods.

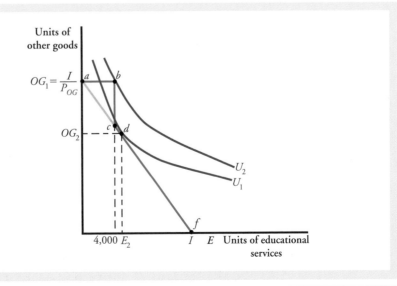

A FAMILY THAT SENDS ITS CHILD TO A PRIVATE SCHOOL   Figure 5.4 shows a different family with different tastes (and a different utility function), which would maximize utility at point *d*. This family consumes more education, E_2 units, than the 4,000 units offered in the public school system. So far, we have seen that some families choose a public education and some choose a private education. The different outcomes can result from differences in tastes and/or incomes. The family depicted in Figure 5.4 is willing to sacrifice more units of other goods for additional units of education than the family in Figure 5.3. Therefore, the family depicted in Figure 5.4 has a higher MRS of other goods for education and steeper indifference curves than the family depicted in Figure 5.3.

A Voucher System

Now suppose the government offers all families a $4,000-per-pupil voucher that can be spent on either public school or private school educational services. Panel (a) of Figure 5.5 shows the impact of the voucher system on the family from Figure 5.3. With the voucher, the family can pay the $4,000 voucher to the public school system and continue to consume at its former consumption point *b*, or it can use the $4,000 to pay part of the cost of a private education. The family could spend its entire after-tax income *I* plus $4,000 on education and consume at point *d*, or it could consume at any point on the teal budget line *bd* with a slope equal to $-\$1/P_{OG}$. The budget constraint with a voucher system is therefore the teal kinked line *abfd*. The family's equilibrium is now at point *f*, where the family consumes E_3 units of private educational services and OG_3 units of other goods. The family is better off at point *f* with a voucher system than at point *b* with a public school system without vouchers. The government voucher helps to cover the cost of a private education and causes the family depicted in panel (a) to switch from the public school system to the private school system. The switch increases the family's utility from U_2 to U_3.

   Opponents of vouchers sometimes suggest that a voucher system would destroy the public schools. Although it is likely that—at least initially—with the implementation of a voucher system many families would move their children out of the public schools,

Figure 5.4 A Family that Sends its Child to a Private School

Without a voucher system, the family budget constraint is the green kinked line *abcdf*. At point *d*, this family utilizes the private school system and consumes E_2 units of educational services and OG_2 units of other goods.

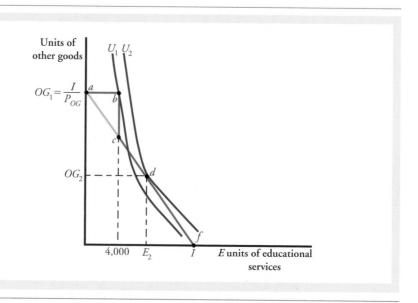

Figure 5.5 A Voucher System

In panel (a) with a $4,000 voucher, the budget constraint is the teal kinked line *abfd*. Without a voucher system, this family consumes at point *b* and uses the public school. With a voucher system, this family consumes at point *f*. In panel (b) with a $4,000 voucher, the budget constraint is the teal kinked line *abd*. Both with and without a voucher system this family consumes at point *b*.

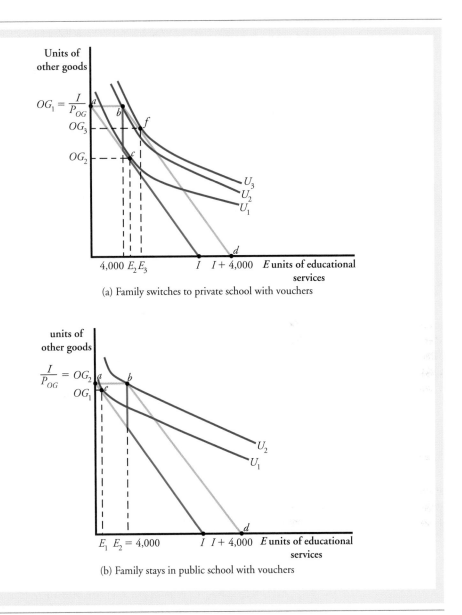

(a) Family switches to private school with vouchers

(b) Family stays in public school with vouchers

many others would not. In panel (b) of Figure 5.5, for example, we show a family that would use its voucher to send its child to a public school. This family prefers to spend the $4,000 voucher on the public school and consume a maximum possible amount of I/P_{OG} units of other goods. In this case, the relatively flat indifference curves indicate that the family is willing to trade relatively few units of other goods to obtain additional units of educational services and would consume only E_1 units of educational services at point *e* in the absence of a public school system.

Non–Economic Issues and Concerns

A voucher system would give all families more options with regard to their children's education, and therefore families as a group would be better off with a voucher system. Many families seem to understand this, and thus in polling done over the last decade, many consumers in all socio-economic groups favor some form of a voucher system. Roughly speaking, anywhere from 1/3 to 1/2 of Americans polled typically favor school vouchers.[1] Those with the strongest objections to a voucher system are often public school administrators and teachers, groups that fear vouchers would be used to fund parochial schools and weaken the constitutional guarantee of a separation of church and state, and those who believe that vouchers would leave the public schools to the poorest of the poor who do not have sufficient income to subsidize a private education even with a voucher system. These are very legitimate concerns and should not be taken lightly. However, positive economic analysis suggests that many families would be either better off or no worse off with a voucher system.

Our analysis suggests that some families will be better off with a voucher system because it provides more choices. Others will be no worse off. Like the food stamp example, consumer theory suggests that no family would be worse off with a voucher system. But is this really the case? In the short run, it might be; however, what if as a result of the voucher system, the quality of public school education declines dramatically, because only those families placing a relatively low value on education remain in the public schools? The students and their families left in the public schools might then suffer a loss of utility in the long run. Furthermore, the administrators and teachers in the public school system would almost certainly be worse off in the long run after the implementation of a voucher system, because of a loss of jobs to the private sector and perhaps a loss of teachers' tenure guarantees.

Thus far in this chapter, we have seen that government welfare and education policies affect consumer utility. In addition to analyzing the impact of government policies, we can use consumer theory to analyze the impact of firms' pricing strategies on consumer behavior and utility. It is important for business firms to have an understanding of consumer theory in order to determine their optimal pricing strategies. A change in a firm's pricing strategy shifts every consumer's budget constraint, and these changes can cause dramatic changes in consumer behavior and the demand for a firm's products. The next section analyzes the impact of one recent change in an industry's pricing strategy.

5.3   The Pricing of Wireless Cellular Phone Service

Wireless telephone service providers have dramatically changed their pricing strategies since the introduction of commercial wireless cellular phone service in the United States in 1982. When cellular phone service was introduced in the United States, providers charged a flat per-minute rate for service that typically ranged from $0.29 to $0.99. These charges were much higher than the per-minute charge for making a call from a home telephone, and as a result, many consumers chose not to use cellular service.

Pricing on a Per-Minute Basis Only

Panel (a) of Figure 5.6 shows a typical consumer's equilibrium when pricing was on a per-minute basis only. Here we assume that the consumer has an income of $5,000 per month, the price of other goods (p_{OG}) is $1.00, and the price per minute of wireless service is $p_{CELL} = \$0.40$. The budget constraint is the dark-green line ab with slope $-p_{CELL}/p_{OG} = -\$0.40/\$1.00 = -0.40$. Given this consumer's indifference curves, she maximizes utility at the corner solution equilibrium point a, where she consumes 5,000 units of other goods and zero units of cellular phone service.

---

[1] "Most Americans Oppose Vouchers," August 20, 2002, *http://CNN.com.*

Figure 5.6 The Demand for Wireless Cellular Phone Service
In panel (a), a consumer earning $5,000 per month faces a choice between paying $0.40 a minute for wireless service or $1.00 for a unit of other goods, and consumes at point *a*. In this case, the consumer has no demand for cellular phone service. In panel (b), the same consumer faces a wireless service option of paying either $0.40 per minute or $200 per month for up to 3,000 minutes and $0.25 for additional minutes, and the consumer is in equilibrium at point *c*. The new pricing option has increased the consumer's demand for wireless services.

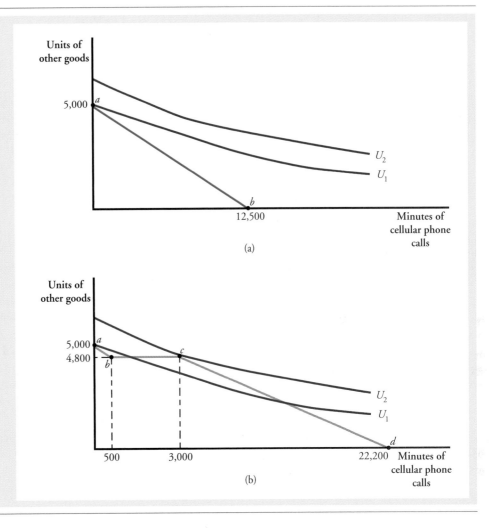

Pricing on an Optional Fixed–Fee Basis

Wireless providers such as Verizon Wireless and Cingular Wireless realized that a large potential market of subscribers were behaving like the consumer in panel (a) and not subscribing to cellular phone service, so these firms began to experiment with alternative fixed-fee plans. In June 2002, Cingular Wireless offered a plan with a monthly fixed payment of $200 for up to 3,000 minutes of calls anywhere at any time in the United States. Additional minutes beyond 3,000 cost $0.25 per minute. This plan gave consumers the option of paying a fixed charge each month in return for a fixed number of minutes of wireless service or paying a per-minute fee.

Panel (b) of Figure 5.6 shows the impact of this plan on our consumer in panel (a). Suppose Cingular charges either $0.40 per minute, or $200 per month for up to 3,000 minutes and $0.25 per minute for each additional minute beyond 3,000. The budget constraint is then the kinked light-green line *abcd*. The section from point *a* to point *b* consists of the segment where for $0.40 per minute, the consumer can make up to 500 minutes of calls for less than $200. The segment from point *b* to point *c* shows that if the consumer spends $200, she can make up to 3,000 minutes of calls. Finally, the segment from point *c* to point *d* represents the segment where a consumer can pay $0.25 per minute for additional minutes beyond 3,000 minutes per month. At point *d*, the consumer pays $200 for 3,000 minutes and her entire remaining income of $4,800 is used to purchase an additional 19,200 ($4,800/$0.25) minutes of cellular phone service for a maximum total of 22,200 minutes per month.

Given this budget constraint, the consumer in panel (b) maximizes utility at point c, where she consumes 3,000 minutes of cellular phone service and 4,800 units of other goods. The fixed-fee option has increased her utility from U_1 to U_2, and more importantly for Cingular, the fixed-fee option has created an increase in the demand for wireless service and an increase of $200 in Cingular's total revenues.

In a market economy, the pricing strategies of business firms have a significant impact on consumer utility. In a command economy, such as the economy of the former Soviet Union, government pricing strategies, such as price ceilings, often had an equally significant impact on consumer utility. We now turn our attention to the impact of these ceilings.

5.4 First-Come, First-Served Rationing in the Former Soviet Union

In the former Soviet Union, many basic necessities such as food and housing were purposely priced well below their equilibrium prices. This pricing policy was aimed at keeping the cost of basic necessities down to a relatively small percentage of a typical Soviet family's income. You might think that such a policy would benefit the typical Soviet worker, and this was undoubtedly the government's objective. But did the Soviet government achieve its objective? Let's consider the typical worker's choices under a command system where prices are fixed below their equilibrium levels and goods are allocated on a first-come, first-served basis.

Rationing by Waiting in Lines

Suppose there is only enough chicken available in the Soviet Union for the typical consumer to consume 10 kilograms per week, and that a typical Soviet worker could work a maximum of 50 hours a week at a wage of 10 rubles an hour and earn an income of $I = 500$ rubles per week. The government sets the price of chicken at 2 rubles per kilogram. The consumer's utility is $u = u(C, OG)$, where C represents kilograms of chicken and OG represents our now-familiar "all other goods." If $P_{OG} = 1$ ruble, the consumer might believe he faces a budget constraint equal to the solid and dashed green line cbe in Figure 5.7, with intercepts of $I/P_{OG} = 500/1 = 500$ units of OG and $I/P_C = 500/2 = 250$ kilograms of C. But this budget constraint assumes that there is enough chicken to satisfy demand at a price of 2 rubles. Assume that the reality is that to purchase one kilogram of chicken on a first-come, first-served basis, the consumer must wait in line for one hour. Furthermore, once the consumer gets to the front of the line, he can purchase only one kilogram of chicken at a time and then must return to the back of the line if he wants more than one kilogram. The opportunity cost of the hour in line is the 10 rubles he could earn working during that hour. The true price of a kilogram of chicken is, therefore, the retail price of 2 rubles plus the opportunity cost of waiting in line of 10 rubles, or 12 rubles per kilogram, and the true budget constraint is the solid light-green line caf with intercepts of 500 units of other goods, and $500/P_C = 500/12 = 41.67$ kilograms of chicken. Our typical consumer consumes at the equilibrium point a, where he waits in line for 10 hours and purchases 10 kilograms of chicken per week.

Surely there must be a better solution to the problem of allocating chicken than having consumers wait in line 10 hours a week to buy the limited supply. One possible solu-

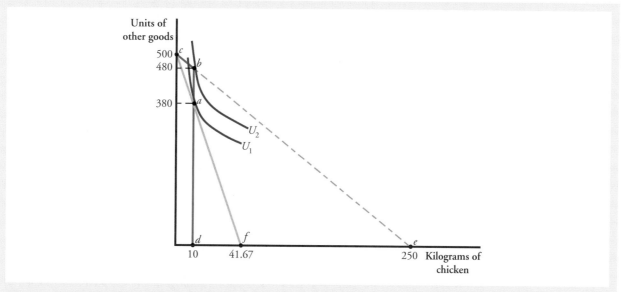

Figure 5.7 The Rationing of Chicken in the Former Soviet Union

If the government sets the price of chicken at $P_C = 2$ rubles per kilogram and the price of other goods is $P_{OG} = 1$ ruble, then with $I = 500$ rubles, the consumer believes he faces the solid and dashed green line *cbe* budget constraint. But the consumer must wait in line for an hour to purchase a kilogram of chicken, and the opportunity cost of an hour in line is 10 rubles. The true price of chicken is 12 rubles per kilogram, and the true budget constraint is the solid light-green line *caf.* Equilibrium is at point *a*. If the government maintains the price at 2 rubles per kilogram, but issues ration coupons permitting the consumer to purchase only 10 kilograms, the budget constraint is the green kinked line *cbad* and the consumer's equilibrium point is at *b*.

tion would be to charge the market-clearing price of 12 rubles per kilogram of chicken. The consumer would then face the light-green budget constraint line *caf* and consume at equilibrium point *a*. However, the consumer would avoid waiting in line, because at a price of 12 rubles per kilogram, the quantity supplied would equal the quantity demanded. Instead of waiting in line for 10 hours a week, the consumer would be able to work and produce some goods or services during those 10 hours. Society would be better off, because the consumer's utility would remain unchanged at U_1, but there would be a larger total output of goods and services in the Soviet Union.

Ration Coupons

An alternative solution to the problem of allocating chicken would be for the Soviet Union to maintain the price at 2 rubles per kilogram, but to issue ration coupons permitting the consumer to purchase 10 kilograms of chicken per week at a price of 2 rubles per kilogram. The budget constraint would then be Figure 5.7's dark-green kinked line *cbad.*

NON–TRANSFERABLE COUPONS If severe penalties prevented the development of a black market in coupons, so that consumers had to use their coupons and could not sell them, then with rationing in Figure 5.7, the consumer's equilibrium would be at point *b*. The consumer's utility is now higher, at U_2, and the consumer has more income to spend on other goods than at point *a*. Society is also better off with ration coupons, because the consumer is able to work instead of waiting in line for those 10 hours.

TRANSFERABLE COUPONS We saw in Chapter 2 that in the absence of an effective penalty for buying and selling coupons, arbitrageurs would enter the coupon market and drive the price of a coupon up to 10 rubles. If a black market developed, a consumer could buy and sell coupons at a price of 10 rubles per coupon, or alternatively they could buy and sell chicken at a price of 12 rubles per kilogram. In panel (a) of Figure 5.8, the budget constraint with a black market shifts out to the teal straight line *fbg*. If the consumer sold all 10 coupons for 10 rubles each, he could increase his consumption of other goods by 100 rubles to a maximum of 600 at point *f*. Alternatively, he could purchase as many kilograms of chicken as he desired at a price of 12 rubles, so the maximum number of kilograms he could consume would be 600/12 = 50 at point *g*. The price of a kilogram of chicken would include both 10 rubles to purchase a coupon *plus* 2 rubles to buy the kilogram in the store. The total price per kilogram, therefore, would be 12 rubles. The black market budget constraint is then a linear constraint with an other goods intercept of 600 and a slope of $-P_C/P_{OG} = -12/1 = -12$. In panel (a) of Figure 5.8, this consumer would want to purchase coupons and consume more than 10 kilograms of chicken at the equilibrium point *e*. Notice that the existence of a black market enables the consumer to increase his utility from U_1 to U_2.

Other consumers with different tastes might wish to purchase less than 10 kilograms of chicken and would offer their coupons for sale at 10 rubles. The consumer in panel (b) of Figure 5.8 wishes to consume less than 10 kilograms of chicken and can sell his remaining coupons for rubles. His equilibrium point is at *d*. The existence of a black market enables the consumer in panel (b) to increase his utility from U_1 to U_2. In panels (a) and (b), the existence of a black market makes both the buyers and sellers of coupons better off.

The leaders of the Soviet Union undoubtedly realized that a rationing plan based on *non-transferable* coupons would lead to a tremendous incentive for an illegal black market to develop. The government would then have to use police and judicial resources to prosecute black market transactions. To avoid these enforcement costs, the Soviet Union decided to go with a first-come, first-served form of rationing. This decision exacerbated

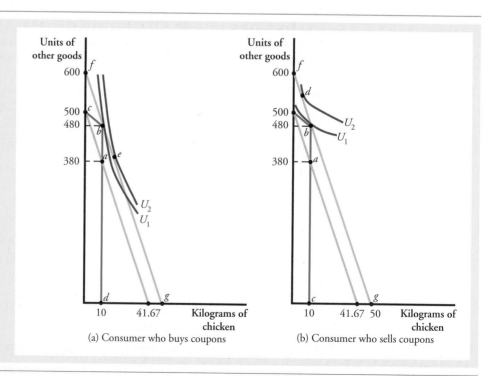

Figure 5.8 Rationing with Transferable Coupons
With a black market, arbitrageurs drive the price of a ration coupon up to 10 rubles and the price of chicken up to 12 rubles per kilogram. In panel (a), the budget constraint shifts to the teal line *fbg*, and the consumer purchases coupons and consumes more than 10 kilograms of chicken at point *e*. In panel (b), the budget constraint shifts to the teal line *fbg*, and the consumer sells coupons and consumes less than 10 kilograms of chicken at point *d*.

(a) Consumer who buys coupons

(b) Consumer who sells coupons

the nation's shortages, as consumers wasted hour after hour of potentially productive time waiting in lines. From an economic perspective, of all the possible allocation options, the Soviet government may have chosen the worst.

Like command economies, free market economies also sometimes adopt controversial economic policies. For example, we now turn our attention to the supply-side tax cuts aimed at increasing work effort and savings that the United States adopted in the early 1980s.

▼▼▼ 5.5   The Impact of Supply-Side Tax Cuts on Work Effort and Savings

Laffer curve

Shows how tax revenues are related to marginal tax rates.

In 1974, economist Arthur Laffer suggested that tax rates on income and savings were so high in the United States that they discouraged workers from working and consumers from saving. Figure 5.9 illustrates the **Laffer curve**, which shows how tax revenues are related to marginal tax rates. The key to maximizing tax revenues is to identify the marginal tax rate t^* in Figure 5.9. For some high tax rates, Laffer's argument holds. For example, a tax rate of 100 percent on additional income would obviously put an end to all rational consumer decisions to work more.

supply-side tax cuts

Income tax reductions aimed at increasing work effort and savings rates.

In the 1980 presidential campaign, Ronald Reagan picked up on Laffer's theory and suggested that large income tax reductions would result in more work effort and greater savings. These tax cuts, known as **supply-side tax cuts**, were passed by Congress and put into effect. In the 1996 presidential election, Republican vice-presidential candidate Jack Kemp (but not presidential candidate Bob Dole) also strongly advocated this theory. And in 2001, President George W. Bush supported and signed into law another large income tax cut.

Tax Cuts and the Work–Leisure Trade-Off

Using consumer theory, we can address the issue of whether a typical consumer would respond to a reduction in income tax rates by increasing his work effort and increasing his savings. First we analyze work effort.

Consider the following utility function:

$$utility = u(Leisure, Income) = u(L, I)$$

Figure 5.10 identifies a typical consumer's indifference curves for leisure and income as U_1 and U_2. Because the marginal rate of substitution (MRS) represents the rate at which

---

Figure 5.9 The Laffer Curve
The Laffer curve shows the theoretical relationship between marginal tax rates t and tax revenues. Here, a marginal tax rate t^* maximizes total revenues.

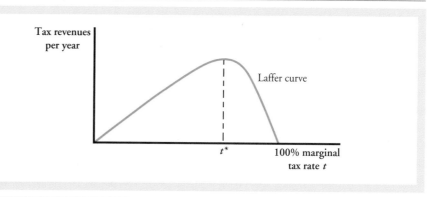

Figure 5.10 Income Tax Cut Results in More Work
Prior to the income tax reduction, the consumer's equilibrium is at point O and he takes L_1 hours of leisure and earns $(24 - L_1)w(1 - t_1)$ dollars of after-tax income. After the tax cut, his equilibrium is at point F and he takes L_2 hours of leisure and earns $(24 - L_2)w(1 - t_2)$ dollars of after-tax income. This consumer works more after the tax reduction, because for the good leisure, the substitution effect (SE) of the tax cut dominates the income effect (IE).

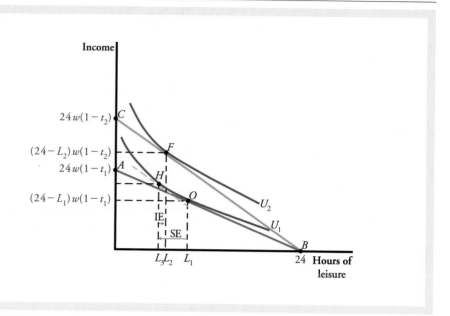

work–leisure trade-off

The rate at which consumers are willing to sacrifice additional income for leisure, typically represented by an indifference curve mapping.

the consumer is willing to trade income for leisure, economists refer to this indifference curve mapping as representing the consumer's **work–leisure trade-off**.

What is the consumer's budget constraint? One of the greatest constraints on our lives is our time constraint, and no matter how hard we try, we cannot possibly exceed 24 hours of leisure in a day. The leisure-axis intercept is, therefore, 24 hours, and point B cannot change. If the average tax rate on income is initially t_1, the maximum amount of after-tax income a consumer can earn by working 24 hours a day is represented by $24w(1 - t_1)$, where w is the consumer's wage. For example, if $t_1 = 0.30$ and $w = \$10$, then $24w(1 - t_1) = 24(\$10)(1 - 0.3) = \$168$ represents the maximum after-tax income a consumer could earn in a day. The slope of the dark-green budget constraint AB is $-[24w(1 - t_1)]/24 = -[w(1 - t_1)]/1 = -P_{Leisure}/P_{Income}$. Notice that the price of leisure is the opportunity cost of taking one extra hour of leisure, which equals $w(1 - t_1)$. For example, if $t_1 = 0.30$ and $w = \$10$, then the opportunity cost of one hour of leisure is $(\$10)(1 - 0.30) = \$7$; that is, the consumer sacrifices $7 in after-tax income by choosing to take an additional hour of leisure. The original consumer equilibrium is at point O on indifference curve U_1. The consumer chooses L_1 hours of leisure, works $(24 - L_1)$ hours, and earns $(24 - L_1)w(1 - t_1)$ dollars of income.

TAX CUTS THAT INCREASE WORK EFFORT Suppose that the government reduces income tax rates so that the average tax rate decreases to $t_2 < t_1$. The new, steeper light-green budget constraint CB has an income intercept of $24w(1 - t_2)$. Notice that the price of leisure now increases because the opportunity cost of taking one extra hour of leisure now equals $w(1 - t_2)$, which is greater than $w(1 - t_1)$. The final consumer equilibrium is at point F on indifference curve U_2. The consumer chooses L_2 hours of leisure, works $(24 - L_2)$ hours, and earns $(24 - L_2)w(1 - t_2)$ dollars of income. This consumer has indeed elected to increase his work effort. He now enjoys less leisure and works more hours. So far, the supply-side theory appears to be correct. But there is more to the analysis.

TAX CUTS THAT DECREASE WORK EFFORT Figure 5.11 analyzes the impact of the tax reduction on another consumer and assumes $w = \$10$, $t_1 = 0.30$, and $t_2 = 0.10$.

Figure 5.11 Income Tax Cut Results in Less Work
Prior to the income tax reduction, the consumer is at point O and takes 12 hours of leisure and earns $84. After the tax reduction, the consumer is at point F and takes 12.5 hours of leisure and earns $103.50. This consumer works one-half hour less after the tax reduction, because for the good leisure, the income effect (IE) of the tax cut dominates the substitution effect (SE).

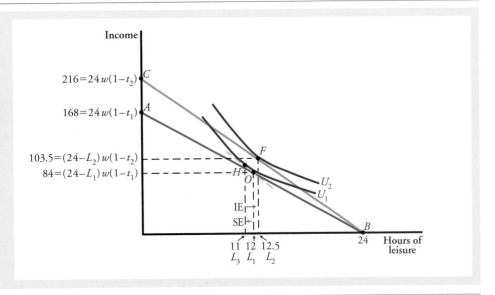

Most of the analysis is the same as Figure 5.10. However, in the final consumer equilibrium at point F, the amount of leisure has increased from $L_1 = 12$ hours to $L_2 = 12.5$ hours, and the amount of income has increased from $84 to $103.50. The consumer in Figure 5.11 has reduced his hours of *work* from $(24 - L_1) = 12$ hours to $(24 - L_2) = 11.5$ hours. In this case, the supply-side theory does not hold. The consumer works less, rather than more, when taxes are reduced.

Income and Substitution Effects on Leisure

Why are the results in Figure 5.10 and Figure 5.11 diametrically opposite each other? We can use our knowledge of substitution and income effects to answer this question. In Figure 5.10, we have separated the substitution and income effects on leisure by drawing our hypothetical budget line (the dashed line) tangent to the original indifference curve U_1 and parallel to the new budget line. When taxes are reduced, the opportunity cost of leisure increases, and the substitution effect causes the consumer to choose more income and less leisure. In this case, the substitution effect results in a movement from point O to point H, and a reduction in leisure of $(L_1 - L_3)$ hours. The reduction in taxes, of course, increases the consumer's real income, by enabling him to increase his utility from U_1 to U_2. The income effect results in a movement from point H to point F and an increase in leisure of $(L_2 - L_3)$ hours. In Figure 5.10, the substitution effect (SE) dominates the income effect (IE) and the consumer chooses less leisure and more work.

Figure 5.11 also separates the substitution and income effects. In this case, the substitution effect results in a movement from point O to point H, and a reduction in leisure of $(L_1 - L_3) = 1$ hour. The income effect results in a movement from point H to point F and an increase in leisure of $(L_2 - L_3) = 1.5$ hours. In Figure 5.11, the income effect dominates the substitution effect and the consumer chooses 1/2 hour more leisure and 1/2 hour less work. This result is the opposite of the result in Figure 5.10.

Recall that Laffer argued that tax cuts would reduce leisure and increase work effort. Laffer essentially assumed that either: (1) the income effect doesn't exist; or (2) there are far more consumers with tastes like those in Figure 5.10 than in Figure 5.11. Our knowledge of income and substitution effects, however, suggests that there are many people that fit into each of these categories, and therefore a reduction in income taxes might result in either more or less work effort.

EMPIRICAL EVIDENCE We cannot use economic theory to definitely answer the question regarding whether consumers as a group will increase or decrease their work effort in response to a decrease in tax rates. Only empirical testing of exactly how consumers respond to a reduction in income tax rates can provide any good insight into this issue. Many influential macroeconomists have tested this relationship over the past 15 years.

Economist Robert Barro concluded that there is some evidence that the tax payments of the richest 0.5 percent of American taxpayers increased after marginal rates were reduced in the 1980s. However, Barro went on to conclude that "[supply-side economists] contended that the average marginal tax rate on income exceeded the value [t^*], so that a general cut in rates would yield a larger volume of real tax revenues. There is, however, no evidence that the United States has reached high enough tax rates for this result to apply."[2] Similarly, economists Andrew Abel and Ben Bernanke concluded that "[t]he responses of labor supply to the revisions to the tax law in the 1980s are consistent with our analysis of the effects of average and marginal tax rates. However, contrary to the predictions of the supply-siders, the actual changes in labor supply were quite small."[3]

On the other side of the issue, supply-side economist Lawrence Lindsey found that the wages and salaries of high-income taxpayers increased by about 30 percent over projections as a result of the 1980s tax cuts; and that among taxpayers with incomes over $200,000 a year, the tax reductions in the 1980s increased tax revenues by 3 percent in 1982, 9 percent in 1983, and 23 percent in 1984.[4] Lindsey concluded that high-income earners were definitely operating on the downward-sloping portion of the Laffer curve before the supply-side tax cuts of the 1980s.

Tax Cuts, Savings, and Borrowing

Even if supply-side tax cuts fail to increase work effort, could they increase the rate of savings in the economy? To examine the impact of supply-side tax cuts on savings, we return to the model of intertemporal choice developed in Chapter 4. Recall that at any interest rate i, the slope of the intertemporal budget constraint with future consumption on the y-axis equals $-(1 + i)$. We begin our analysis by assuming that a consumer has a before-tax income endowment of Y_1 in period 1 and Y_2 in period 2. If the initial average tax rate is t_1, then the after-tax income endowment point in Figure 5.12 is the point $(Y_1(1 - t_1), Y_2(1 - t_1))$, identified as point ep_1. The initial budget constraint must go through point ep_1 and have a slope equal to $-(1 + i)$.

If the government reduces the average tax rate to $t_2 < t_1$, the new after-tax endowment point moves northeast to $(Y_1(1 - t_2), Y_2(1 - t_2))$, which we identify as point ep_2. The tax cut results in an *income effect* that shifts the budget constraint to the right, parallel to the original budget constraint. In Figure 5.12, the consumer's initial equilibrium point is at the endowment point ep_1, with utility equal to U_1. The consumer in this situation is neither a saver nor a borrower. After the tax decrease, the new equilibrium point is cp, and the consumer is a saver. Her savings have increased from zero to an amount designated by *savings* in Figure 5.12. So far, the supply-side argument seems correct:

---

[2] Robert J. Barro, *Macroeconomics*. Cambridge, MA: MIT Press, 1997, p. 495.

[3] Andrew B. Abel and Ben S. Bernanke, *Macroeconomics*. Boston: Addison Wesley, 2001, p. 578.

[4] Lawrence Lindsey, *The Growth Experiment: How Tax Policy Is Transforming the U.S. Economy*. New York: Basic Books, 1990; and Lawrence Lindsey, "Individual Taxpayer Response to Tax Cuts, 1982–84: With Implications for the Revenue Maximizing Tax Rate," *Journal of Public Economics*, 33, July 1987, pp. 173–206.

Figure 5.12 Income Tax Cut Results in More Savings

Prior to the income tax reduction, the consumer has an endowment at point ep_1 of $(Y_1(1 - t_1), Y_2(1 - t_1))$ and neither borrows nor saves. If the government reduces the average tax rate to $t_2 < t_1$, the new endowment point moves to $(Y_1(1 - t_2), Y_2(1 - t_2))$ at point ep_2 and the consumer saves the amount identified as *savings*.

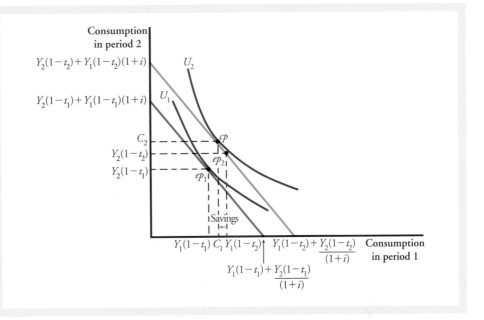

Decreasing income tax rates appears to increase the rate of savings. But once again, the analysis is incomplete.

INCOME ELASTICITY OF DEMAND FOR PRESENT AND FUTURE CONSUMPTION
To complete our analysis, consider the consumer depicted in Figure 5.13. In Figure 5.13, we assume $Y_1 = Y_2 = 100$, $t_1 = 0.30$, $t_2 = 0.15$, and $i = 0.10$, so $Y_1(1 - t_1) = 70$ and $Y_2(1 - t_2) = 70$. This consumer was initially in equilibrium at the endowment point ep_1 and was neither a saver nor borrower, with consumption in both period 1 and period 2

Figure 5.13 Income Tax Cut Results in Less Savings

Prior to the income tax reduction, the consumer has an income endowment at point ep_1 of $(70,70)$ and neither borrows nor saves. If the government reduces the average tax rate from 30 percent to 15 percent, the new after-tax endowment point moves to $(85,85)$ at point ep_2, and the consumer borrows 10.

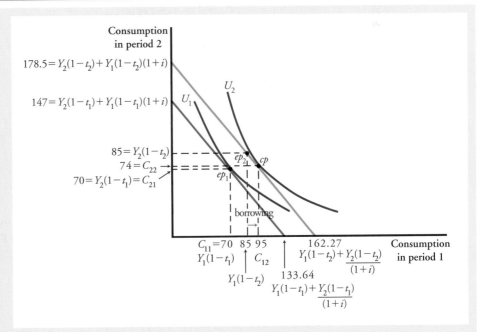

equal to 70. In this case, however, the reduction in tax rates moves the equilibrium point from ep_1 to cp, and after the tax cut, the consumer is a borrower. The consumer borrows $10 in period 1 in exchange for a reduction in consumption of $11 in period 2. Once again, our theoretical results are ambiguous. Some consumers save more as a result of a tax cut and some save less.

The result depends on the relative size of the income elasticity of demand for present and future consumption. In Figure 5.12, the consumer has an income elasticity of demand for future consumption that is greater than one; that is, a one percent increase in after-tax income results in *more* than a one percent increase in future consumption, and an income elasticity of demand for present consumption that is less than one; that is, a one percent increase in after-tax income results in *less* than a one percent increase in future consumption.

In Figure 5.13, the opposite is true. Recall from Chapter 2 that the income elasticity of demand is the percentage change in quantity demanded divided by the percentage change in income. Using the arc elasticity formula, in Figure 5.13, the calculations are:

$$\varepsilon_{IC_1} = \frac{\dfrac{\Delta C_1}{C_{11} + C_{12}}}{\dfrac{\Delta I_1}{Y_1(1 - t_1) + Y_1(1 - t_2)}} = \frac{\dfrac{25}{70 + 95}}{\dfrac{15}{70 + 85}} = \frac{0.152}{0.097} = 1.57$$

$$\varepsilon_{IC_2} = \frac{\dfrac{\Delta C_2}{C_{21} + C_{22}}}{\dfrac{\Delta I_2}{Y_2(1 - t_1) + Y_2(1 - t_2)}} = \frac{\dfrac{4}{70 + 74}}{\dfrac{15}{70 + 85}} = \frac{0.028}{0.097} = 0.29$$

The consumer has an inelastic income elasticity of demand for future consumption equal to 0.29, which is less than one; and an elastic income elasticity of demand for present consumption equal to 1.57, which is greater than one. In the case of savings incentives, supply-side economists assumed that consumers typically have a higher income elasticity of demand for future consumption than for present consumption.

EMPIRICAL EVIDENCE Much of the empirical evidence suggests that the 1980s tax cuts did not result in an increase in overall savings rates in the United States. In fact, according to economists Philip Arestis and Mike Marshall, the national savings rate declined in the 1980s after the large supply-side tax cuts.[5] Their results suggest that the income effect caused many people to consume more in the present period and save less. Of course, other economic factors were at work in the 1980s that may have resulted in a decrease in the savings rate. For example, the stock market was increasing in value and the economy was expanding; therefore, consumers may have felt wealthier and more confident in the future and were less willing to sacrifice current consumption for future consumption. Such a change in taste would make the slope of the indifference curves in Figures 5.12 and 5.13 steeper, because the marginal rate of substitution of future for present consumption would increase and result in reduced savings.

On the other hand, economist Lawrence Lindsey found that among high-income taxpayers, capital gains on investments doubled in the 1980s, suggesting a large increase

[6] Philip Arestis and Mike Marshall, "The New Right and the U.S. Economy in the 1980s: An Assessment of the Economic Record of the Reagan Administration," *International Review of Applied Economics*, Vol. 4, No. 1, January 1990, p. 53.

in investment activity among high-income Americans.[6] Once again, the empirical evidence is inconclusive.

In this section, we examined how tax cuts affect consumers' decisions to work and save. We consistently saw that, *ceteris paribus*, tax cuts increase consumer utility. Governments, however, must raise taxes in order to provide goods and services to their citizens. Different taxes affect consumer utility in different ways. We now turn our attention to a comparison of the impact on consumer behavior and utility of two common methods of taxation: excise taxes and income taxes.

5.6 Raising Government Revenues with Excise Taxes or Income Taxes

Federal, state, and local governments raise tax revenues in order to finance expenditures on many goods such as education, national defense, police and fire protection, and protection of the environment. Two of the most common types of taxes used to raise revenues are income taxes and excise taxes on goods, such as the federal excise taxes on cigarettes, liquor, and gasoline. An **excise tax** is a tax placed on one particular good, and should not to be confused with a **general sales tax** on all goods, such as a state sales tax.

excise tax

A tax placed on one particular good, such as the federal excise taxes on cigarettes, liquor, and gasoline.

general sales taxes

Taxes on all goods consumed, such as a state sales tax.

The Burden of Excise Taxes

Suppose the government wants to raise a certain amount of tax revenue. In terms of consumer utility, is an income tax preferable to a excise tax or vice versa? To answer this question, let us first consider the impact of an excise tax on gasoline. In Figure 5.14, the

Figure 5.14 Excise Tax on Gasoline
The initial budget constraint without any taxes is the dark-green line dg, and the consumer's initial equilibrium is at point a. With an excise tax on gasoline of t_g per unit, the new budget constraint is the light-green line dh, the new equilibrium is at point b, and the consumer purchases G_2 units of gasoline. The distance from point c to point b, which equals $OG_3 - OG_2$ units of other goods, represents the consumer's total tax payment in terms of other goods sacrificed.

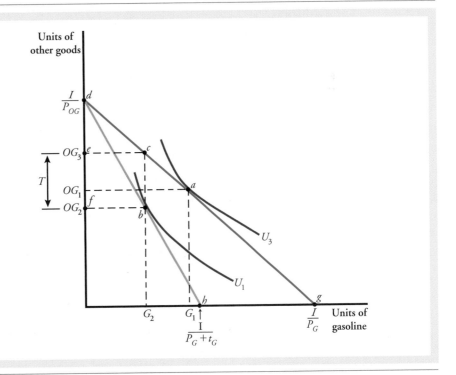

[7] Lawrence Lindsey, *The Growth Experiment: How Tax Policy Is Transforming the U.S. Economy.* New York: Basic Books, 1990.

consumer's utility function is $u = u(G, OG)$, where G represents units of gasoline and OG represents units of other goods. The initial budget constraint without any taxes is the dark-green line dg, with intercepts of I/P_{OG} on the other goods axis and I/P_G on the gasoline axis. The consumer's initial equilibrium is at point a.

Now consider the impact of an excise tax on gasoline of t_G per unit. The new budget constraint is the light-green line dh, with intercepts of I/P_{OG} on the other goods axis and $I/(P_G + t_G)$ on the gasoline axis. The new equilibrium is at point b. As a result of the excise tax, the consumer in Figure 5.14 consumes less gasoline and less of other goods.

How much tax does the consumer pay? At the after-tax equilibrium, b, the consumer purchases G_2 units of gasoline and OG_2 units of other goods. Prior to the imposition of the tax on gasoline, the consumer could have sacrificed other goods equal to the distance of the line segment from point d to point e and purchased G_2 units of gasoline and OG_3 units of other goods at point c on the budget constraint. After the tax, the consumer can consume only OG_2 units of other goods and G_2 units of gasoline. The distance from point c to point b, which equals $OG_3 - OG_2$ units of other goods, represents the extra units of other goods that must be sacrificed to consume G_2 units of gasoline because of the tax. This distance, therefore, represents the consumer's total tax payment to the government in terms of other goods sacrificed. In Figure 5.14, the distance T also represents this total tax payment.

An Equal–Yield Income Tax

Instead of an excise tax of t_G per unit on gasoline, the government could have raised the same amount of tax revenue by imposing an income tax equal to T units of other goods. What would be the effect of the imposition of such an equal yield income tax on the consumer's budget constraint and equilibrium? Figure 5.15 shows both the budget constraint

Figure 5.15 An Equal–Yield Income Tax

If the consumer is in equilibrium at point b with an excise tax, an equal-yield income tax shifts the original budget constraint down vertically by the amount of the tax, which equals T units of other goods. The new budget constraint is the dashed green line passing through point b. The consumer is better off at point g with an equal-yield income tax than at point b with an excise tax.

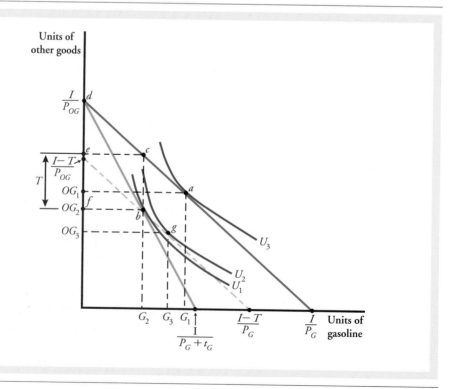

with the excise tax and the budget constraint with an equal-yield income tax. An equal-yield income tax shifts the original budget constraint down vertically by the amount of the tax, which equals T units of other goods. The budget constraint with an equal-yield income tax, therefore, is the dashed green line passing through point b and with intercepts of $(I - T)/P_{OG}$ on the other goods axis and $(I - T)/P_G$ on the gasoline axis. The equal-yield income tax budget constraint must pass through point b, because it is still possible to consume the combination of G_2 units of gasoline and OG_2 units of other goods after the imposition of an equal-yield income tax. The consumer's equilibrium with an equal-yield income tax is at point g on indifference curve U_2.

The Excess Burden of an Excise Tax

excess burden

A measure of how much more one tax reduces consumers' utility compared to another tax.

Comparing the two taxes, the consumer's utility is greater at point g with an income tax than at point b with an equal-yield excise tax. For consumers with convex indifference curves, this must be the case. We can conclude, therefore, that consumers with convex indifference curves are better off with an equal-yield income tax, than with an excise tax. This result is because with an income tax, there is no change in the relative prices of the goods compared to the initial equilibrium at point a. By comparison, the excise tax distorts the relative prices faced by the consumer and this distortion creates an **excess burden** compared to the income tax. The reduction in the consumer's utility from U_2 to U_1 that results from the excise tax compared to the income tax measures this excess burden.

Summary

1. The United States relies heavily on helping the poor through grants-in-kind such as food stamps and housing subsidies. Consumer theory shows that recipients would always be either better off or no worse off with an equal-cost cash payment. This conclusion has led some economists to call for a change in the current system of grants-in-kind.

2. School voucher systems provide consumers with greater choice and therefore result in greater utility for many families. Some families who currently send their children to public schools would send their children to private schools with a voucher system. However, not all families would remove their children from the public schools with a voucher system. The two systems would coexist.

3. By shifting from a charge per minute of cellular phone service to a fixed charge for a large number of minutes of service, wireless providers were able to increase their number of subscribers. This result suggests that firms must have an understanding of consumer theory in order to adopt optimal pricing strategies.

4. The former Soviet Union maintained prices for many necessities below their equilibrium prices, resulting in consumers waiting in long lines for many hours for these basic commodities. The true social cost of these commodities was much higher than their prices would indicate, because of the lost output that could have been produced during the hours consumers spent waiting in lines. The Soviet Union would have been better off either letting prices increase to clear the market or establishing a system of transferable coupons to ration necessities.

5. Supply-side economists suggest that income tax reductions result in greater work effort and increased savings. Consumer theory suggests that neither of those results is certain. Income tax reductions could result in consumers working either more or less and saving either more or less.

6. The government can raise tax revenues with either excise or income taxes. With regard to a consumer's choice between goods, an equal-yield income tax is preferable to an excise tax, because the income tax results in a higher level of utility. Therefore, there is an excess burden associated with the excise tax.

Self-Test Problems

1. Consider Figure 5.8. If the market-clearing price of a kilogram of chicken were 20 rubles instead of 12 rubles, what would be the price of a coupon? Would the typical consumer now be more likely to buy or to sell coupons? Why? What would happen to the typical consumer's budget constraint if the coupons were transferable? Is the social cost of a first-come, first-served policy now higher or lower? Explain.

2. Using the work–leisure trade-off diagram, derive a typical consumer's labor supply curve. Remember that the labor supply curve identifies the quantity of labor supplied at every possible wage rate w. Now show that it is possible to obtain a downward-sloping supply curve for labor. Which effect dominates for a downward-sloping supply curve for labor—the income effect or the substitution effect?

3. With an excise tax of $1.00 per movie ticket, Abby purchases five movie tickets per month. Assume the price of other goods is $1.00. If the government eliminates the excise tax on tickets and instead imposes a $5.00 per month lump-sum tax on Abby, how will Abby's consumption patterns change with regard to movies and other goods? Will Abby be better or worse off with the lump-sum tax?

Questions and Problems for Review

1. Given the economic advantages of cash grants over equal-cost grants-in-kind, why do you think that most governments continue to rely heavily on grants-in-kind? Do you think this makes sense?

2. If consumer theory suggests that vouchers are better for consumers than the current system of funding for public education, why have so few states made vouchers an option for school districts? Is something important missing from our analysis?

3. Using a graph, show that it is possible for a student who goes to a public school to consume more units of schooling if there were no public schools available at all. If education is a normal good, would this student consume more, less, or the same amount of education with a voucher system?

4. Economists recognize that it is generally very difficult to tax leisure, and therefore all taxes tend to distort the work–leisure trade-off. Can you suggest a way to tax leisure? How would your tax affect the typical consumer's work–leisure trade-off?

5. The Syracuse Skychiefs are a minor league baseball team. The Skychiefs charge $10 for a reserved seat ticket to any one of the 71 home games they play each year. In addition, only before the season begins, the team offers to sell one and only one ticket book to each fan. The ticket books contain 10 reserve seat tickets to any game for a total payment of $50. Using consumer theory, show why the Skychiefs sell the ticket books. If Skychiefs tickets are an inferior good, could a fan end up attending fewer games a year because of the ticket-book offer? If Skychief tickets are a normal good, could a fan end up attending fewer games a year because of the ticket book offer? What does this suggest about the team's belief concerning the income elasticity of demand for tickets?

6. Why do you think the former Soviet Union insisted on a first-come, first-served method of rationing goods? Today Russia uses a market system to allocate most goods and services. Do you think that some Russian citizens would like to see a return to the old system of rationing on a first-come, first-served basis? Who might want the old system back, and why?

7. With regard to the consumer's choice between goods, are excise taxes or income taxes preferable as a source of government revenue? Explain your reasoning.

8. In 1974, the United States was faced with rapidly escalating energy prices. Suppose that in order to reduce the negative impact on the poor of the increase in heating oil prices, the government insti-

tuted a policy that rebated all of the higher cost of heating oil to the poor. [Hint: If the price increases by $0.50 a gallon, and after the price increase, the consumer buys 100 gallons of heating oil, then the consumer receives a rebate of $50.00 ($0.50 × 100) to cover the higher price of the 100 gallons.] Would this make the poor consumers as well off as they were before the price increase? After the increase in price and rebate, would the consumers still consume as much heating oil as they did before the rise in the price of heating oil?

9. The government is considering a subsidy for the elderly to purchase prescription and non-prescription (over-the-counter) drugs. If George Williams is a typical elderly person, show how the subsidy would affect George's choice between drugs and other goods. If instead of the subsidy, the government gave George an equal-cost cash payment; would George be better or worse off? Would George purchase more or fewer drugs with a cash payment?

10. Ben has an income of $2,500 and the price of other goods is $1. He has two cellular phone plan options. Plan 1 is a $0.30-per-minute plan for all calls. Plan 2 offers up to 1,000 minutes for a flat fee of $100 with each minute after that costing $0.25. Draw his budget line. Is it possible for Ben to prefer Plan 1 to Plan 2? Explain, using a graph.

11. During the energy crisis of the mid-1970s, the U.S. rationed gasoline. Only people with certain license plate numbers could buy gas on certain days and the amount they could purchase at one time was limited. Under the plan, long lines developed at many gas pumps. What were the downsides of such a rationing program? Could the government have improved the situation by issuing tradable gas vouchers? Explain your reasoning carefully.

12. The amount of sulfur dioxide that factories can emit is limited by the Environmental Protection Agency (EPA). The EPA issues permits to companies that emit sulfur dioxide, which allow each company a certain legal amount of emissions. Should the EPA allow the buying and selling of these emission permits? Why or why not?

13. Suppose that the government places a tax on heating oil in order to conserve oil. However, for poor families, the government rebates enough income to ensure that poor consumers are able to achieve the same level of utility after the rebate that they had before the tax was imposed. That is, the poor are no

worse off after the tax and rebate than they were to begin with. Will the tax and rebate policy completely eliminate the conservation of oil by the poor?

14. Jake has a before-tax wage of $10 and pays an income tax of 20 percent, so $t = 0.20$. Show his budget constraint for work and leisure for one day. Suppose Jake's before-tax wage decreases to $8, but t remains constant; however, it turns out that Jake still consumes the same amount of leisure. Show this on a graph. Do these results seem reasonable? What do the results tell you about the relative size of the income and substitution effects for leisure for Jake?

15. Is it possible for a reduction in income taxes to decrease work effort? If so, show. If not, explain why not.

16. Sarah states: "I prefer an excise tax on gasoline to an equal-yield income tax, because it gives me a higher level of utility." If Sarah has normally shaped convex indifference curves, can this be true? Why or why not?

17. A town has a garbage collection program where residents pay per bag for garbage removal. If the town switches to a monthly flat fee, show the impact on the budget constraint for a typical consumer. Which program is better for the typical consumer? Is this true for all consumers?

18. Jane currently pays an excise tax of $1.00 per pack of cigarettes and consumes four packs a day. The government replaces the tax with a fixed daily tax of $4.00 per day. How will this change affect Jane's consumption patterns? Which tax would Jane prefer? Under which plan will she smoke more? Explain.

19. Jack participates in the food stamp program, currently receives $200 a month in food stamps, and has a cash income of $1,000 per month. If the food stamp program is replaced by a cash grant program paying Jack $200 per month, will Jack buy more or fewer other goods? What does this change mean for his consumption of food? Why might policy-makers worry about the effects of this policy change?

20. Kevin and Jill have two options for educating their children. The children can go to a public school for no charge, or they can use a government voucher for private school equal to the cost per pupil of the public school. Show their options using a graph. In your graph, which option do Kevin and Jill prefer? Would all families prefer the same option?

Internet Exercises

Visit *http://www.myeconlab.com/waldman* for this chapter's Web exercises. Answer real-world economics problems by doing research on the Internet.

Chapter 6
Uncertainty

The table on the next page shows the Las Vegas betting odds as of March 6, 2003, on teams' chances to win the 2004 Super Bowl and the 2003 World Series. These were the betting odds ten months before the Super Bowl and seven months before the World Series would be played. By the time you read this, you probably know who won these games. But those who bet on the winners on March 6, 2003, had no idea how the 2003 baseball and football seasons would play out. Would the Eagles win the Super Bowl, or would the Eagles' best player, quarterback Donovan McNabb, get hurt during the 2003 season as he did during the 2002 season? Would the Yankees win yet another championship, or would their team continue to show signs of age as the Yankees did during the 2002 season when the Anaheim Angels beat the Yankees on the way to the championship? Individuals placing bets on March 6, 2003, were betting under conditions of great *uncertainty*, because they had no real knowledge about what would happen during the upcoming baseball and football seasons; they had no idea what the probabilities really were of the Eagles winning the Super Bowl and the Yankees winning the World Series.

Until now, we have examined household decisions under conditions of certainty. That is, we have assumed that the household knows the contents of alternative consumption bundles and, once the household chooses a bundle, that it knows the contents with certainty. But many choices faced by households are characterized by uncertainty. Should you rent an expensive apartment in the safe part of town, or a cheaper apartment in a more dangerous neighborhood? Which college major—economics, political science, or English—will maximize your chance of getting into law school after you graduate? How should you invest the money you are saving for your down payment on a house? All of these decisions involve substantial elements of uncertainty.

In this chapter, we explore the techniques that economists use to analyze decision-making under uncertainty. Much of what we learned about choice under certainty applies here as well, but there is also much that is new. The

Team	Odds to Win the 2004 Super Bowl	Team	Odds to Win the 2003 World Series
Philadelphia Eagles	9:2	New York Yankees	5:2
Tampa Bay Buccaneers	5:1	Oakland Athletics	7:2
Oakland Raiders	6:1	Arizona Diamondbacks	5:1
St. Louis Rams	7:1	St. Louis Cardinals	6:1
Pittsburgh Steelers	8:1	Houston Astros	7:1
Miami Dolphins	10:1	Philadelphia Phillies	8:1
New York Jets	10:1	Boston Red Sox	9:1

special techniques we will learn in this chapter can be applied to a broad variety of situations. They can explain why political candidates pursue some campaign strategies and avoid others, why people hold their wealth in one form and not another, why companies build a plant in one location rather than another, why people obey certain laws and not others, and much more.

▼▼▼   6.1   Risky Situations

To help us establish a framework for exploring uncertain situations, we should first agree on what we are talking about. Two terms will be important to our understanding of decision-making in this chapter: *risk* and *uncertainty*. Economists often use these terms interchangeably. However, economist Frank Knight distinguished between the two terms as follows: **uncertainty** is a situation where there are many possible results, but there is no knowledge concerning the probabilities of the results.[1] **Risk** refers to a situation where there are many possible results and the probabilities of each result are known. Consider, for example, the following two situations. In the first, you can play a game where you draw one card from a fair deck of 52 cards with 26 red and 26 black cards. If you draw a red card, you win $1,000, and if you draw a black card, you lose $800. According to Knight, this game is played under conditions of risk, because the player knows that the probability of drawing a red card is 50 percent. In the second game, the player draws one card from a deck of 52 cards, but the player has no idea what cards are in the deck. It could consist of all spades or all hearts, 90 percent red cards or 90 percent black cards. This game is played under conditions of uncertainty because the player knows nothing at all about the probability of drawing a red card: in reality, it could be 100 percent or zero percent. Most of the time economists do not maintain Knight's distinction between risk and uncertainty, but instead use the terms interchangeably.

In this chapter, decision-making under uncertainty implies: (1) a decision must be made between alternative courses of action; (2) each course of action can lead to one or more results; and (3) for a given course of action, the likelihood or probability of each result is known. Using Knight's terminology, we are therefore analyzing risk rather than uncertainty.

uncertainty

A situation where an action has more than one possible result and the probability of each result is unknown.

risk

A situation where an action has more than one possible result and the probability of each result is known.

---

[1] Frank Knight, *Risk, Uncertainty, and Profit*. Boston: Houghton Mifflin, 1921.

Decision Trees

If you buy a pair of contact lenses, your optometrist will probably offer you an extended service contract that provides a substantial discount on new lenses to replace any that you lose during the year. Suppose that, without the service contract, it would cost you $100 for each replacement lens; with the service contract, each lens would cost $25. The contract itself costs $75 for the year. This is a decision involving uncertainty—you must decide whether to buy the contract before you know how many lenses you will lose during the year.

Figure 6.1 shows a **decision tree**, which shows the relationship between alternative courses of action and the various outcomes that might result from each action. A decision tree helps us to see the difference between a decision and a state of the world. An **outcome** is the combined result of a decision and a state of the world. In our contact lens example, there are two decisions to choose between: buy the service contract, or don't buy the service contract. There are three alternative states of the world that might come about during the year: you lose no lenses, you lose one lens, or you lose two lenses. When analyzing uncertainty, economists assume that economic agents can make decisions, but cannot determine the state of the world. Indeed, it is the inability to control the state of the world that causes the problem of uncertainty.

Note that there are six different dollar values in this decision tree. Each of these values is an outcome. For example, suppose you decide to buy the service contract and it turns out that you lose one lens. Then you will have paid $75 for the contract, plus $25 for the lens, so you are out a total of $100. The outcome for the decision "buy the contract" and state of the world "lose one lens" will therefore be −$100. In all, if you decide to buy the service contract, there are three possible outcomes: −$75, −$100, and −$125. If you do not buy the contract, the three possible outcomes are $0, −$100, and −$200. (Make sure you can see how each of these dollar outcomes results from a particular state of the world.)

decision tree

A schematic diagram showing how alternative actions result in different results.

outcome

The combined result of a decision and a state of the world.

Figure 6.1 Decision Tree for a Contact Lens Service Plan

If you buy a service contract for $75, you have to pay only $25 to replace a lost lens; and you have outcomes of −$75, −$100, or −$125, depending on whether you lose 0, 1, or 2 lenses respectively. If you do not buy a service contract; you have outcomes of $0, −$100, or −$200, depending on whether you lose 0, 1, or 2 lenses respectively. The probability of losing 0 lenses is 0.5, the probability of losing 1 lens is 0.3, and the probability of losing 2 lenses is 0.2.

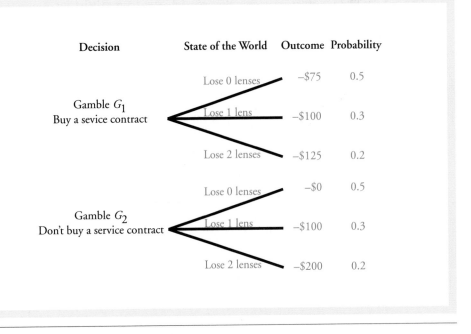

Decision	State of the World	Outcome	Probability
	Lose 0 lenses	−$75	0.5
Gamble G_1 Buy a sevice contract	Lose 1 lens	−$100	0.3
	Lose 2 lenses	−$125	0.2
	Lose 0 lenses	−$0	0.5
Gamble G_2 Don't buy a service contract	Lose 1 lens	−$100	0.3
	Lose 2 lenses	−$200	0.2

▲▲▲ **6.1 APPLICATION** Decision Trees and the Making of *The Last Action Hero*

Every branch of the film industry is plagued by high levels of uncertainty. No one knows in advance whether a particular film will be a blockbuster or a bust, so everyone—from executives at the biggest Hollywood studios to fledgling screenwriters trying to break into the business—must make decisions whose outcomes depend upon an unknown state of the world.

Consider the case of two young screenwriters, Zak Penn and Adam Leff. In 1993, these two writers, both in their early twenties, tried to break into the business with a screenplay in which a young boy literally walks into a movie-theater screen and becomes part of an action-adventure story. Because they were new writers, Penn and Leff wrote their screenplay "on spec," which means that they wrote it by themselves, with no input from the Hollywood studios, and no advance indication that a studio would buy it.

When executives at Columbia Pictures read the finished script, they loved it. In Hollywood, when executives love a script, it means they think the script has a chance of attracting a big star, which, in turn, means a high probability that the film will attract a large audience and make big profits. For this film, the star Columbia had in mind was Arnold Schwarzenegger. Columbia, however, faced a problem: they could not show the project to Schwarzenegger until they had secured the rights to the screenplay. But buying the screenplay for a large sum of money before Schwarzenegger had even seen it seemed too great a risk. In this situation, Columbia did what most Hollywood studios do: they offered Penn and Leff a smaller sum of money—$100,000—to option their script. This meant that Columbia would have the exclusive right to buy the script at any time over the next year. If Columbia chose to buy it, they would pay Penn and Leff an additional $250,000. If they chose not to buy it, Penn and Leff could keep the $100,000 and offer the script to another studio for $250,000.

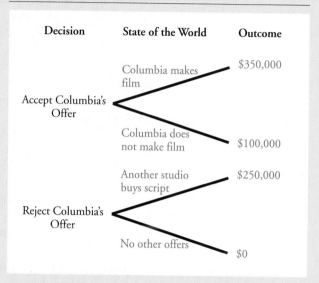

Application Figure 6.1 Decision Tree for Screenwriter Facing an Option

Columbia's offer to option their script confronted Penn and Leff with a difficult and risky decision. On one hand, if they accepted Columbia's offer, Columbia might decide to buy their script for the additional $250,000. But Columbia also might not buy it. On the other hand, if they turned down Columbia's offer, another offer might come their way from a different studio . . . or it might not.

The figure shows the decision tree facing Penn and Leff. Penn and Leff finally decided to take Columbia's offer. Columbia showed the script to Schwarzenegger, who decided to star in the picture. Columbia subsequently bought the script from Penn and Leff for the agreed-upon additional $250,000, and the movie *The Last Action Hero* opened in theaters across the country in the summer of 1993.

Outcomes, Probabilities, and Gambles

A decision tree can help clarify the choices an individual must make by giving a concise picture of the consequences of different decisions. But that is not enough. When facing a decision under uncertainty, we need to know not only what the outcomes are, but also the likelihood or probability of each outcome.

But how can we know these probabilities? In some situations, the probabilities of different outcomes can be determined *objectively* from past data. For example, suppose that over the last ten years, whenever the weather forecast predicted rain in Cincinnati, it was correct 70 percent of the time. Then we can say that the probability of rain in Cincinnati—when rain is the official forecast—is 0.7. Another way to arrive at an objective probability is to combine objective information with the mathematical laws of probability. If you buy ten raffle tickets to win a car and know that two million lottery tickets were sold, then you can calculate your probability of winning as ten in two million, or 0.000005.

Often, though, we must estimate probabilities *subjectively*. When buying a new stereo system, you may have no objective information on the likelihoods of defects among certain brands. Nevertheless, in order to decide which brand to purchase, you will implicitly determine such probabilities. Your subjective probability estimates might come from things you have heard about certain brands, or perhaps from a past experience with this or that brand. It is important to remember that individuals can and do differ in their estimates of probabilities, whether we are talking about objective or subjective probabilities. In the case of objective probabilities, individuals might differ in the way they interpret past data or current conditions. In the case of subjective probabilities, there is even more room for disagreement, because there is little or no common information available with which to estimate probabilities.

Let's go back to the example of the contact lens service contract. Suppose that, either objectively or subjectively, you attach the probabilities in the last column of Figure 6.1 to each state of the world. This additional information enables us to see that the decision to buy or to not buy the service contract boils down to a choice between gambles. In general, we define a **gamble** as a set of outcomes and their associated probabilities. Deciding to buy the service contract means, in effect, accepting a gamble in which you lose $75 with probability 0.5, lose $100 with probability 0.3, and lose $125 with probability 0.2. Not buying the contract, in turn, means choosing an alternative gamble in which you lose $0 with probability 0.5, $100 with probability 0.3, and $200 with probability 0.2.

When analyzing decisions under uncertainty, economists usually reduce the decision-maker's problem to a choice between alternative gambles, such as the choice between Gamble G_1, buy a service contract, and Gamble G_2, don't buy a service contract, in Figure 6.1. As we will see, this enables us to view the problem of choice under uncertainty in a way analogous, but not identical, to the way we dealt with choice under certainty in Chapter 3.

gamble

A set of possible outcomes combined with the probability of each outcome.

EXPECTED VALUE One important feature of a gamble with quantitative payoffs is the **expected value** of the gamble, which is the weighted average of a gamble's outcomes, where the weights are the probabilities associated with each outcome. If a gamble G has n possible outcomes $Y_1, Y_2, ..., Y_n$ with associated probabilities $p_1, p_2, ..., p_n$ respectively, then the expected value is defined as:

expected value

The weighted average of a gamble's outcomes, where each outcome is weighted by its probability.

$$E[G] = p_1 (Y_1) + p_2 (Y_2) + ... + p_n (Y_n) \qquad (6.1)$$

When each of the outcomes is equally likely with a probability of $1/n$, the expected value is the same as the simple average of the outcomes. To see this, just substitute $1/n$ for the probabilities in Equation 6.1:

$$E[G] = \frac{1}{n}Y_1 + \frac{1}{n}Y_2 + ... + \frac{1}{n}Y_n$$
$$= \frac{Y_1 + Y_2 + ... + Y_n}{n}$$

When some outcomes are more likely than others, however, the probabilities will differ and the expected value gives more weight to those outcomes that are more likely to occur.

Statisticians have shown that the expected value of a gamble is the average payoff you can expect to get if you repeat the gamble many times.

Let's calculate the expected value of each of the gambles in Figure 6.1. For Gamble G_1 and Gamble G_2, we have:

$$E[G_1] = 0.5 \ (-\$75) + 0.3 \ (-\$100) + 0.2 \ (-\$125) = -\$92.50$$

$$E[G_2] = 0.5 \ (\$0) + 0.3 \ (-\$100) + 0.2 \ (-\$200) = -\$70$$

These calculations tell us that if Gamble G_1 could be repeated many times, the *average* payoff would be $-\$92.50$. In other words, if you bought the service contract each year for many years, your average yearly cost would be about $92.50 per year. For Gamble G_2, your average cost would be $70 per year.

Looking at gambles G_1 and G_2 in Figure 6.1, we might be tempted to say that because G_2 has the greater (less negative) expected monetary value, we should always prefer it to G_1. But always preferring G_2 implies that when making choices under uncertainty, people care only about expected *monetary* value, which is not usually the case. In addition to a gamble's expected monetary value, people also care about the relative risks of gains and losses. In Section 6.2, we will explore how individuals' preferences with regard to the risks of gains and losses affect their final choices. First, however, we need to understand how risk affects those choices.

To see how the risk of gains and losses matters, let's first consider two simple gambles based on tossing a coin. In Gamble A, if the coin comes up heads, you win $5, tails; you lose $5. In Gamble B, heads wins you $5,000, but tails loses you $4,999. Table 6.1 shows the outcomes and probabilities associated with each of these gambles as well as with a third gamble, C.

The expected monetary values of each of Gambles A and B are:

$$E[G_A] = 0.5 \ (\$5) + 0.5 \ (-\$5) = \$0$$

$$E[G_B] = 0.5 \ (\$5,000) + 0.5 \ (-\$4,999) = \$0.50$$

If you had to choose between these two gambles, which one would you choose? There is no right or wrong answer, but many people would prefer Gamble A to Gamble B even though Gamble B has the higher expected monetary value. For many people, Gamble B

Table 6.1 Outcomes of Three Coin Toss Gambles

	State of the World	**Outcome**	**Probability**
Gamble A	Heads	$5	0.5
	Tails	−$5	0.5
Gamble B	Heads	$5,000	0.5
	Tails	−$4,999	0.5
Gamble C	Heads	$5,000	0.99
	Tails	−$494,950	0.01

would be too risky. Expected monetary value, then, is only part of what matters in choosing between gambles.

But how exactly can you evaluate the risk in Table 6.1? This question is not always easy to answer. The risk seems to reflect the old adage, "I can't tell you what it is, but I know it when I see it." Looking at Gambles A and B, we might all agree that Gamble B is more risky. But now, consider the third gamble in Table 6.1, Gamble C. The expected value of Gamble C is $(0.99)(\$5,000) + (0.01)(-\$494,950) = \$0.50$, which is the same as the expected value for Gamble B. But which gamble is more "risky," B or C? Some might say that B is more risky, since it has a greater probability of losing (50 percent, as opposed to 1 percent). But others might feel that Gamble C is more risky, since if you do lose, the loss is much greater ($494,950, as opposed to $4,999). But you should remember that evaluating risk remains a somewhat slippery concept.

COMPLEX DECISION TREES   Now we consider more complex decision trees. Suppose a freelance computer consultant is offered a temporary job by three different firms, but she can accept only one of the jobs. The job at Firm A pays $20,000; the one at Firm B pays $25,000; and the one at Firm C pays $43,000. If there are no additional job factors to consider, such as scheduling, committee work, and getting along with the project director, and if all the jobs are equally enjoyable, she should take the job at Firm C.

But let's suppose our consultant also knows that the job for Firm C is a dead-end job—it cannot lead to any additional consulting jobs in the future. However, once she has worked for Firm A or Firm B, she could be offered additional consulting jobs, depending on whether she gets along with the director of computer services at each firm. At Firm A, she knows she has a 75 percent chance of getting along with the director. Furthermore, if she does get along with the director, she would have a two-thirds chance (66 percent) of being awarded an additional consulting job worth $50,000. Prospects at Firm B are a bit more complicated. Here, she knows there is an 80 percent chance of getting along with the director, and in this case she would definitely be given an additional consulting job. But at Firm B, she can't be sure how much the additional consulting job is worth: there is a 50 percent chance it is worth $30,000, and a 50 percent chance it will pay only $10,000. Table 6.2 summarizes all of this information.

Decision trees are especially useful in sorting out different possible outcomes in complicated situations like this. Figure 6.2 summarizes the decision tree for this consultant. Note that the outcome of a decision, such as the decision "take the job at Firm B," can be a further gamble (the additional job may have a large or small payoff). Also note that each decision will lead to a single final outcome, but there is no way of knowing in advance what that outcome will be. Each potential final outcome has an associated probability, which we find by multiplying the probabilities of each branch along the way. For

Table 6.2 Outcomes of Three Job Opportunities

Firm	Payment for Initial Job	Probability of Getting Along with Director	Payment for Additional Job	Probability of Additional Job If Getting Along with Director
A	$20,000	0.75	$50,000	0.66
B	$25,000	0.80	$30,000	0.5
			$10,000	0.5
C	$43,000			

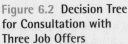

Figure 6.2 Decision Tree for Consultation with Three Job Offers

If the consultant takes the job at Firm A and gets along with the director, she earns $70,000 with probability 0.5; if she doesn't get along with the director, she earns $20,000. If the consultant takes the job at Firm B and gets along with the director, there is a 50 percent chance that she'll earn $55,000 and a 50 percent chance she'll earn $35,000; if she doesn't get along with the director, she earns $25,000. If she takes the job at Firm C, she earns $43,000 with certainty.

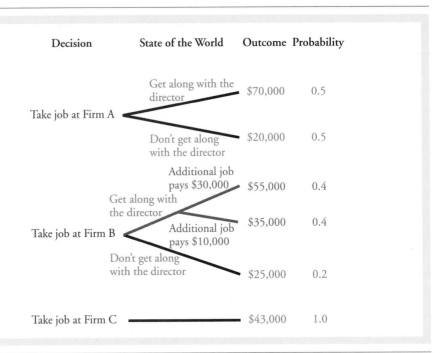

example, one possible monetary outcome of taking the job at Firm B is $55,000. In order for this final outcome to come about, the consultant would have to get along with the director (probability = 0.8) and then be offered the larger additional consulting job (probability = 0.5). Therefore, once the consultant makes the decision to work at Firm B, the probability of the final outcome of $55,000 is 0.8 × 0.5 = 0.40. We can calculate the probabilities of the other final outcomes in a similar fashion.

Once we know the final outcomes and associated probabilities for each decision, we can reduce the consultant's problem to the familiar one of a choice between gambles, as shown in Table 6.3. Here we see that the consultant must choose between Gamble A, a 50-50 gamble paying $20,000 or $70,000; Gamble B, with a 20 percent chance of earning $25,000, a 40 percent chance of earning $55,000, and a 40 percent chance of earning $35,000; and Gamble C, which pays $43,000 with certainty. Table 6.3 calculates the expected value of each gamble. In Section 6.2, we'll examine how to choose between these gambles.

Table 6.3 Expected Value of Three Job Opportunities

Decision (Gamble)	Final Outcome	Probability	Expected Value
Gamble A (Take job at Firm A)	$20,000	0.50	$45,000
	$70,000	0.50	
Gamble B (Take job at Firm B)	$25,000	0.20	
	$55,000	0.40	$41,000
	$35,000	0.40	
Gamble C (Take job at Firm C)	$43,000	1.00	$43,000

6.2 Preferences Under Uncertainty

We've seen that virtually any choice under uncertainty can be viewed as a choice between gambles. We've also seen that when a gamble has numerical outcomes, such as amounts of money to be won or lost—an important characteristic of the gamble is its expected monetary value—the average numerical result we could expect from repeating the gamble many times. Next, we'll explore how individuals decide between different gambles.

von Neumann–Morgenstern Utility Functions

Consider the problem of the consultant trying to decide between Gambles A, B, and C in Table 6.3. We can see that Gamble A has the highest expected monetary value ($45,000), followed by Gamble C ($43,000), and finally by Gamble B ($41,000). It might seem, therefore, that Gamble A would be the preferred choice, and the consultant should accept the job at Firm A. But this is not necessarily the case; Gamble A has a higher expected monetary value than Gamble C, but the consultant might also feel that Gamble A is more risky. With Gamble C, the consultant has a guarantee of earning $43,000, while with Gamble A, there is a 50-50 chance of earning $70,000 (which is $27,000 more than $43,000) or $20,000 ($23,000 less than $43,000). Will the consultant prefer such a gamble to the "sure thing" of $43,000? That depends on the consultant's preferences over gambles. But how can we model preferences over gambles?

In the 1940s, mathematician Jon von Neumann and economist Oskar Morgenstern demonstrated that under very general conditions, it is possible to attach utility values to the outcomes of gambles and use these utility values to predict how an individual will choose between gambles. In a sense, they reinterpreted a gamble for different outcomes (such as for amounts of money) into a gamble for different amounts of utility. They then calculated the **expected utility** of each gamble—the expected value of the different utilities we might get from the gamble. Finally, they predicted that the individual will always choose the gamble with the highest expected utility. A utility function with this expected utility property is called a **von Neumann–Morgenstern (VNM) utility function**.

Before we explore the implications of VNM utility functions, you should understand precisely what a VNM utility function is and how it is used. In reality, individuals choose between gambles based on their preferences for one gamble over another. By using a VNM utility function, we are attempting to find a way of assigning utility values to outcomes to help us predict how individuals choose between gambles involving those outcomes. We predict that the individual will always prefer gambles with larger expected utility to gambles with smaller expected utility.

Suppose that, for a particular individual, the von Neumann–Morgenstern utility function for assigning utility values to different sums of money Y is $U(Y) = Y^{1/2} = \sqrt{Y}$. Let's calculate the expected utility of Gamble A facing our consultant in the example in Table 6.3. The utility of $20,000 is $\sqrt{20,000} = 141.4$, and the utility of $70,000 is $\sqrt{70,000} = 264.6$. To find the expected utility of Gamble A, we multiply each utility-outcome by its probability and sum:

$$E[U(G_A)] = 0.5\,(141.4) + 0.5\,(264.6) = 203.0$$

In general, we define the expected utility of any gamble G with n outcomes $Y_1, Y_2, \ldots, Y_n$ and probabilities $p_1, p_2, \ldots, p_n$ as:

$$E[U(G)] = p_1\,U(Y_1) + p_2\,U(Y_2) + \ldots + p_n\,U(Y_n)$$

expected utility

Given a VNM utility function, the weighted average of a gamble's utility, where each utility is weighted by its probability.

von Neumann–Morgenstern (VNM) utility function

A utility function expressed as the expected value of utility of an uncertain event such that, if $U(c_i)$ represents the utility associated with event c_i, p_i represents the probability of event c_i, and there are n possible events; then the von Neumann–Morgenstern utility is $p_1\,U(c_1) + p_2\,U(c_2) + \ldots + p_n\,U(c_n)$.

Note carefully the difference between the expected utility of a gamble and the expected value of a gamble, which is defined as:

$$E(G) = p_1\,(Y_1) + p_2\,(Y_2) + \dots + p_n(Y_n)$$

Table 6.4 shows the expected utility as well as the expected value of all three gambles facing our consultant.

Here we see a rather interesting result: when ranked by the expected value of their monetary outcomes, $E(G_A) > E(G_C) > E(G_B)$. But when ranked by expected utility, $E[U(G_C)] > E[U(G_A)] > E[U(G_B)]$. If the utility function $U(Y) = Y^{1/2} = \sqrt{Y}$ is the correct VNM utility function for our consultant, then she will prefer the job at Firm C to jobs at either of the other two companies.

If we have chosen our VNM utility function correctly, our predictions of how the individual will rank gambles will be correct. If we have chosen our VNM function incorrectly, our predictions will not be correct. In our example, using the VNM utility function $U(Y) = Y^{1/2} = \sqrt{Y}$, the expected utility of Gamble C is higher than the expected utility of Gamble A. If our consultant still insists that she prefers Gamble A to Gamble C, then $U(Y) = Y^{1/2} = \sqrt{Y}$ is not the correct VNM utility function.

Attitudes Toward Risk

People differ from one another in their attitudes toward risk, and these differences help explain why some people start businesses of their own, while others become employees; why some people become artists or writers, while others with the same talents become accountants; and why some people insure against a variety of calamities, while others purchase the minimum insurance allowed by law. In this section, we explore some of the implications of differing attitudes toward risk. But before we do, we need a way of determining and describing what those attitudes are. We can do this by looking more closely at the VNM utility function that represents an individual's preferences over gambles.

Consider a choice between two gambles: One gamble, which we will call the "risky gamble," gives you a 50-50 chance of winning $500,000 or winning nothing. Note that the expected monetary value of this risky gamble is $(0.5)(\$500,000) + (0.5)(\$0) = \$250,000$. Now consider another gamble, which we will call the "sure thing," which guarantees you will receive $250,000. Which would you prefer—the risky gamble or the sure thing? If you are like most people, you would prefer the sure thing, even though both gambles have the same expected value.

Table 6.4 Expected Utility of Three Job Opportunities

Decision (Gamble)	Final Outcome	Probability	Expected Value	Expected Utility
Gamble A (Take job at Firm A)	$20,000	0.50	$45,000	203
	$70,000	0.50		
Gamble B (Take job at Firm B)	$25,000	0.20		
	$55,000	0.40	$41,000	200.3
	$35,000	0.40		
Gamble C (Take job at Firm C)	$43,000	1.00	$43,000	207.4

risk-averse

Term used to describe an individual always preferring a sure thing to a risky gamble with the same expected outcome as the sure thing.

risk-loving

Term used to describe an individual always preferring a risky gamble to a sure thing if the expected outcome of the gamble equals the outcome of the sure thing.

risk-neutral

Term used to describe an individual who is indifferent between a sure thing and a risky gamble with the same expected outcome as the sure thing.

When an individual faced with the choice between a sure thing and a risky gamble with the same expected value prefers the sure thing, we say that the individual is **risk-averse**. An individual who would prefer the risky gamble is **risk-loving**. Finally, we would call someone who is indifferent between the risky gamble and the sure thing **risk-neutral**. In this last case, all the individual cares about is the expected value of the gamble, and risk doesn't matter to the individual at all.

Each of these attitudes toward risk is associated with a particular shape of the VNM utility function for wealth. Suppose an individual's VNM utility function is: $U(Y) = 10\ln((Y + 1,000)/1,000)$. Given this VNM utility function, let us compute the expected utility of the risky gamble just discussed. To find this, we must first compute the utility value of each possible outcome. Table 6.5 presents this information.

Figure 6.3 graphs the VNM utility function $U(Y) = 10\ln((Y + 1,000)/1,000)$, measuring income Y along the horizontal axis, and VNM utility $U(Y)$ along the vertical axis. The utility for $Y = \$0$ is $10\ln((0 + 1,000)/1,000) = 10\ln(1) = 0$, given by point A. The utility for $Y = \$500,000$ is $10\ln((500,000 + 1,000)/1,000) = 10\ln(501) = 62.17$, as shown by point B. The expected utility of the risky gamble is thus $0.5(62.17) + 0.5(0) = 31.09$, the average of the two possible utilities that can result. We can find the expected utility value of a 50-50 gamble by drawing a chord that connects the utility values of the two outcomes. We then find the point midway on the chord, and its vertical height represents the average of the two utilities, or the expected utility of this 50-50 gamble. Figure 6.3 shows such a chord between points A and B; notice that the vertical height of its midpoint C is 31.09, the expected utility of the risky gamble.

Table 6.5 Expected Utility of a Risky Gamble and Sure Thing, If the VNM Utility Function Is: $U(Y) = 10\ln((Y + 1,000)/1,000)$

Gamble	Outcome	Utility	Probability	Expected Utility
Risky Gamble	\$0	0	0.50	$0.5(0) + 0.5(62.17) = 31.09$
	\$500,000	62.17	0.50	
Sure Thing	\$250,000	55.25	1.00	55.25

Figure 6.3 A Risk–Averse Utility Function

With the concave VNM utility function $U(Y) = 10\ln((Y + 1,000)/1,000)$, the expected utility of a 50-50 gamble that pays either \$0 or \$500,000 is 31.09, and the utility of a sure thing that pays \$250,000 is 55.25. The risk-averse individual prefers the sure thing to the gamble.

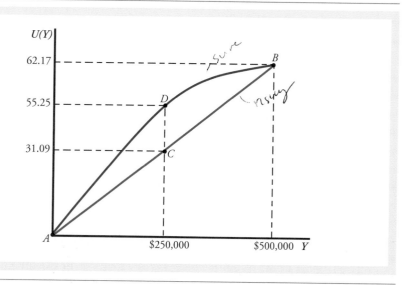

Now let us find the expected utility associated with the sure thing. Because the sure thing is a gamble that always pays $250,000, we can calculate its expected utility as $U(250,000) = 10\ln((250,000 + 1,000)/1,000) = 10\ln(251) = 55.25$. Note that the sure thing always pays the expected value of the risky gamble, $E(Y) = \$250,000$, which is the midpoint between the two payoffs of $0 and $500,000 on the horizontal axis. Thus, we can represent the utility of the sure thing as the vertical height of the VNM utility function for $Y = \$250,000$. In Figure 6.3, this vertical height is 55.25.

In Figure 6.3, the expected utility of the sure thing, 55.25, is greater than the expected utility of the risky gamble, 31.09, even though both have the same expected value. Because the individual prefers the sure thing to the gamble, we would call her risk-averse. She prefers the sure thing to the gamble because the chord between points A and B lies beneath the VNM utility function itself. The chord will lie below the VNM utility function whenever the VNM utility function is concave. Recall from Chapter 3 that a utility function is concave if a chord connecting any two points on the utility function lies everywhere below the utility function. Risk-averse preferences, then, are equivalent to having a concave VNM utility function.

When a utility function is concave, the *marginal utility* of wealth—the utility of an additional dollar—decreases as wealth increases. Mathematically, this is why the individual prefers the sure thing to the gamble in Figure 6.3. Suppose the individual already has the sure thing, and is considering trading it for the risky gamble. For a risk-averse individual with a concave VNM utility function, the additional $250,000 that could be won in the gamble is worth less than the $250,000 that could be lost in the gamble. Thus, the risky gamble would mean a 50-50 chance of winning something and losing something, but with a concave utility function, the individual values what could be lost more highly than what could be gained. Thus, she will never choose the gamble.

COMMON ERROR 6.1   Incorrectly Calculating the VNM Utility of a Risky Gamble

To find the expected VNM utility of a risky gamble, we must calculate the expected value of the VNM utility associated with the gamble. One common error is to calculate the VNM utility of the expected income, Y, instead of the expected VNM utility.

Suppose the VNM utility function is $U(Y) = Y^{1/2} = \sqrt{Y}$, and the risky gamble has a 90 percent probability of $Y = \$100$ and a 10 percent probability of $Y = \$2,000$. Students often incorrectly calculate the expected VNM utility as follows. First, they calculate the expected value of income Y:

$$E(Y) = 0.9(\$100) + 0.1(\$2,000) = \$209$$

Then they calculate the VNM utility for the expected value of income $E(Y) = \$209$:

$$U(Y) = \sqrt{209} = 14.46$$

Finally, the students conclude that 14.46 is the expected VNM utility of the gamble. This is wrong!

The students have calculated the VNM utility for a guaranteed income of $209, which is not the correct calculation.

We can correctly calculate the expected value of the VNM utility as follows:

$$U(100) = \sqrt{100} = 10 \text{ and}$$

$$U(2,000) = \sqrt{2,000} = 44.72$$

Therefore, the expected VNM utility of the gamble is:

$$0.9(10) + 0.1(44.72) = 9 + 4.472 = 13.472$$

The expected VNM utility equals 13.472 and is less than the VNM utility of a sure income of $209, which equals 14.46. According to the incorrect calculations of many students, however, all gambles will have the same VNM utility as a sure thing with the same income Y as the expected income $E(Y)$ of the gamble. Be careful not to make this common error.

Now consider a different VNM utility function: $U(Y) = (0.001Y)^2 - 0.2Y$. Table 6.6 recalculates the expected utilities of the risky gamble and the sure thing with this new VNM utility function. With this utility function, the expected utility of the risky gamble, 75,000, is greater than the utility of the sure thing, 12,500, even though both have the same expected value. Because here the individual prefers the gamble to the sure thing, we would call her risk-loving.

Now look at Figure 6.4. As before, the vertical height of the midpoint of the chord, 75,000, indicates the expected utility of the 50-50 gamble. The vertical height of the utility function above or below the chord's midpoint (12,500) gives the utility of the sure thing. In this case, the utility of the sure thing lies below the expected utility of the gamble, so the individual will prefer the gamble. As you can see in the diagram, the individual will prefer the gamble to the sure thing any time the chord connecting the payoffs (the chord between points A and B) lies above the VNM utility function itself. This, in turn, means that the VNM utility function is *convex*. Risk-loving preferences, then, are equivalent to having a convex VNM utility function. Intuitively, with a convex utility function, marginal utility increases with income, so that what might be won in the 50-50 gamble is valued more highly than what might be lost.

Finally, let us consider one last VNM utility function: the linear VNM utility function $U(Y) = 100 + 0.001Y$. Table 6.7 shows expected utility calculations with this new utility function. For this example, the expected utility of the risky gamble and the sure thing are equal. An individual with this utility function would be indifferent between a gamble and a sure thing with the same expected value, and we would call her risk-neutral.

Table 6.6 Expected Utility of a Risky Gamble and Sure Thing, If the VNM Utility Function Is: $U(Y) = (0.001Y)^2 - 0.2Y$

Gamble	Outcome	Utility	Probability	Expected Utility
Risky Gamble	$0	0	0.50	$0.5(0) + 0.5(150,000) = 75,000$
	$500,000	150,000	0.50	
Sure Thing	$250,000	12,500	1.00	12,500

Figure 6.4 A Risk-Loving Utility Function

With the convex VNM utility function $U(Y) = (0.001Y)^2 - 0.2Y$, the expected utility of a 50-50 gamble that pays either $0 or $500,000 is 75,000, and the utility of a sure thing that pays $250,000 is 12,500. The risk-loving individual prefers the gamble to the sure thing.

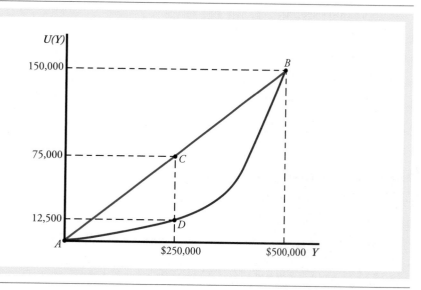

Table 6.7 Expected Utility of a Risky Gamble and Sure Thing, If the VNM Utility Function Is: $U(Y) = 100 + 0.001Y$

Gamble	Outcome	Utility	Probability	Expected Utility
Risky Gamble	$0	100	0.50	$0.5(100) + 0.5(600) = 350$
	$500,000	600	0.50	
Sure Thing	$250,000	350	1.00	350

Figure 6.5 illustrates this case of a risk-neutral utility function, which will always be linear. In this case, the chord whose midpoint represents the expected utility of the 50-50 gamble coincides with the VNM utility function itself. Therefore, the vertical height of the chord and the vertical height of the utility function are precisely equal at point B, the chord's midpoint. Point B therefore represents both the expected utility of the gamble and the expected utility of the sure thing, and there is no reason to prefer one over the other. With a linear, risk-neutral VNM utility function, the marginal utility of wealth remains constant as wealth changes.

Note that we have used a specific, 50-50 gamble to explore differing attitudes toward risk in this section. But our definitions hold for any type of gamble. When an individual prefers the sure thing to the gamble, she is risk-averse; when she prefers the gamble, she is risk-loving; and when she is indifferent between the two, she is risk-neutral. In this last case of risk neutrality, the individual cares only about the expected value of a gamble; she ignores risk.

Certainty Equivalent and Risk Premium

Suppose an individual faces a particular gamble G. Whether the individual is risk-averse, risk-loving, or risk-neutral, there will always be some amount of money—call it $\$C$—we could offer him that the individual would value as highly as the gamble. In other words, faced with a choice between gamble G or $\$C$ with certainty, the individual would be

Figure 6.5 Risk-Neutral Utility Function

With the linear VNM utility function $U(Y) = 100 + 0.001Y$, the expected utility of a 50-50 gamble that pays either $0 or $500,000 is 350, and the utility of a sure thing that pays $250,000 is 350. The risk-neutral individual is indifferent between the gamble and the sure thing.

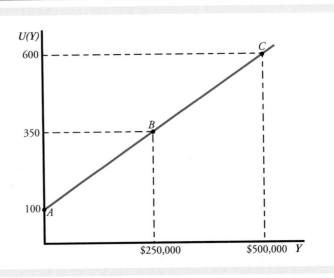

▲▲▲ 6.2 APPLICATION   Risk–Loving Preferences and Gambling

Most people purchase many different types of insurance, including automobile, fire, health, and life insurance. The purchase of insurance indicates that most individuals are risk-averse and have convex VNM utility functions. However, many of these same people also gamble from time to time. They make trips to Las Vegas and Atlantic City, buy state-sponsored lottery tickets, and bet on sporting events. Individuals with convex VNM utility functions would never gamble, because gambling is never a fair wager; that is, the gambler should always expect to end up with less income after the gamble, given the relatively small odds of winning and because all games of chance are set up to insure a profit for the house; or in the case of a state lottery, for the state. Despite the poor odds of winning, in 2000, in the United States, consumers spent almost $61.4 billion on gambling; including $26.3 billion at casinos, $17.2 billion on lotteries, $10.4 billion on Native American reservations, $3.8 billion on horse and dog racing, and $2.2 billion on Internet games.

How is it possible that so many consumers who purchase insurance also gamble? One possible explanation is that gambling is a consumer good that gives gamblers utility much like any other consumer good. According to this explanation, gambling is no different than attending a sporting event, concert, or movie. Consumers simply choose to substitute gambling for other forms of entertainment. In support of this theory, economist Melissa Kearney examined spending patterns on state lotteries and found that spending on state lotteries was financed completely by a reduction in other types of household spending. The introduction of a state lottery reduced average household non-gambling consumption by $460 a year. Kearney's results suggest that gambling substituted for other forms of spending, but did not reduce a household's overall income in the manner suggested by our theory of gambles. Kearney also found that among the poorest third of American households, the introduction of a state lottery significantly reduced alcohol consumption, suggesting that these households substituted gambling for alcohol consumption.

A second possible explanation for gambling is that while most individuals are risk-averse with regard to potentially large losses of income, they are risk-loving with regard to *very large* potential gains. For example, in the figure the consumer's current income is $100,000 at point B and he is risk-averse for incomes up to $200,000. With the gamble, the expected value of Y decreases by the

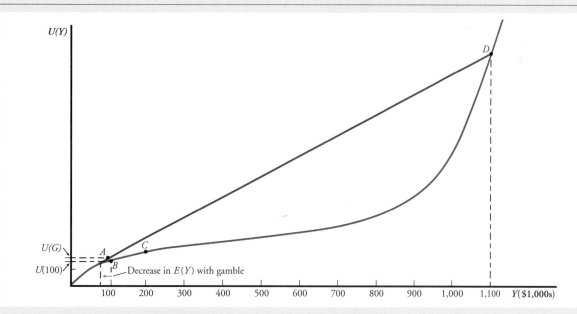

Application Figure 6.2 The VNM Utility Function for a Person Who Gambles
This consumer has an income of $100,000 at point B. He is risk-averse for losses and gains up to point C. However, for large gains in income, he is risk-loving. The expected utility with the gamble at point A is greater than the expected utility of the sure thing at point B.

(continued)

amount of the small red arrow. However, the consumer gains a great deal of utility if he hits the lottery and wins $1 million. This consumer would purchase a lottery ticket even though the chance of winning $1 million is small, because the expected utility with the gamble, $U(G)$ at point A, is greater than the utility of the sure thing, $U(100)$ at point B, and therefore, the consumer's expected VNM utility is greater with the gamble.

Evidence of this risk-loving behavior is provided by consumer conduct when the jackpot for a major lottery, such as Powerball or Mega Millions, reaches hundreds of millions of dollars. When this happens, sales of lottery tickets increase dramatically. Individuals who would never purchase a lottery ticket with a $10 million jackpot are willing to wait in line for hours to purchase tickets for a miniscule chance of winning $200 or $300 million.

certainty equivalent

The fixed income an individual would accept instead of taking a gamble, such that the individual would be indifferent between accepting this fixed income and taking the gamble; that is, the VNM utility of the fixed income equals the VNM utility of the gamble.

indifferent. If an individual is indifferent between a fixed amount of income, say C and a gamble G, then C is the **certainty equivalent** of gamble G. The certainty equivalent C of the gamble G will always satisfy the following equation:

$$U(C) = E[U(G)]$$

If gamble G is a lottery ticket you have just purchased, you can think of C as the minimum price you would accept to sell your lottery ticket.

Figure 6.6 shows the VNM utility function $U(Y) = Y^{1/3} = \sqrt[3]{Y}$, which is concave and therefore represents risk-averse preferences. Gamble G is a 50-50 gamble offering either $50,000 or $100,000. Its expected utility of 41.63 is the vertical height of the midpoint of the chord connecting points A and B. To find the certainty equivalent for this gamble, we ask: what amount of money received with certainty would provide a utility of 41.63? We find the answer by solving $U(C) = \sqrt[3]{C} = 41.63$, so $C = \$72,147$. Thus, the certainty equivalent to gamble G is $72,147. The individual with this VNM utility function will be indifferent between a 50-50 gamble that pays $50,000 or $100,000 on the one hand, or receiving $72,147 with certainty on the other hand.

Notice that although the expected value of this 50-50 gamble is $75,000, the certainty equivalent is only $72,147. For a risk-averse individual, the certainty equivalent of a gamble will always be less than the expected value of the gamble ($C < E[G]$). In gen-

Figure 6.6 Certainty Equivalent and Risk Premium with a VNM Utility Function

With a VNM utility function $U(Y) = Y^{1/3} = \sqrt[3]{Y}$, a 50-50 gamble of either $50,000 or $100,000 has an expected income of $75,000 and an expected VNM utility of 41.63 at point C. This is the same utility as the certainty equivalent of $72,147 at point D. The risk premium is the horizontal distance from point C to point D equal to $2,853.

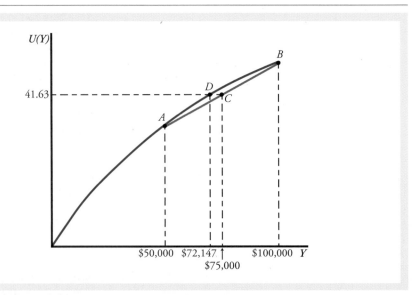

risk premium

The difference between the expected value of a gamble and the gamble's certainty equivalent.

eral, we define the **risk premium**, rp, of a gamble as the difference between its expected value and its certainty equivalent:

$$rp = E[G] - C$$

For a 50-50 gamble such as the one in Figure 6.6, the risk premium is the horizontal distance between the midpoint of the chord at point C and the utility function at point D. When an individual is risk-averse, the risk premium tells us the maximum amount of money she would be willing to pay to avoid taking a risk and to receive the gamble's expected value instead. We calculate the risk premium in our example as follows:

$$rp = E[G] - C = \$75,000 - \$72,147 = \$2,853$$

Thus, an individual with the VNM utility function $U(Y) = \sqrt[3]{Y}$ would be willing to pay up to \$2,853 in order to receive \$75,000 with certainty rather than a 50-50 gamble paying \$50,000 or \$100,000.

What about individuals who are not risk-averse? A risk-neutral individual cares only about a gamble's expected value; she would be indifferent between a gamble or receiving its expected value with certainty. Thus, for a risk-neutral individual, the certainty equivalent of a gamble is its expected value ($C = E[G]$), so we have $rp = E[G] - C = 0$. A risk-loving individual, however, would be indifferent between a gamble and a sure thing that paid more than the expected value of the gamble. For such an individual, we have $C > E[G]$, and $rp < 0$. When the risk premium is negative, its absolute value tells us the amount an individual would pay to take a risky gamble rather than receive the expected value of that gamble.

Although the cases of risk neutrality and risk loving are theoretically important and accurately describe the behavior of certain individuals under certain circumstances (particularly people who are gamblers), risk aversion is far more common for most individuals under most circumstances. As we have seen, risk-averse people are willing to pay to reduce risk and in some cases to avoid it entirely. But in the real world, how can individuals reduce their exposure to risk? The remainder of this chapter is devoted to answering this question.

6.3 Reducing Risk

Most individuals are risk-averse, and therefore try to avoid taking large risks. Risk-averse individuals can reduce risk in a variety of ways. They might purchase insurance that provides protection against large losses, or they might attempt to gather more information before undertaking a risky action. In addition, risk can be reduced by engaging in a number of different and unrelated gambles rather than only one gamble. For example, the risk of investment in the stock market can be reduced through *diversification*, or purchasing a small number of shares in many companies instead of a large number of shares in one company. Risk can also be reduced by creating opportunities to back out of a risky decision. In this section, we consider each of these possible methods of reducing risk, beginning with insurance.

Insurance

One way to reduce risk is to purchase insurance against unfavorable outcomes. Suppose, for example, that an individual has a \$100,000 home in an area where the risk of fire in a given year is known to be 2 percent. Let us suppose that in the event of a fire, the individual will suffer $100,000 in damage to his home. Without insurance, the individual faces a gamble where he loses $100,000 with probability 0.02, and loses nothing with probability 0.98. This gamble has an expected monetary value of $0.02(-\$100,000) + 0.98(\$0) = -\$2,000$. Suppose that the individual is able to buy insurance that covers all losses in the event of a fire. The yearly charge for the insurance is X, and for now we will leave X as an unknown. Buying insurance therefore implies a gamble that pays $-\$X$ with certainty. What is the greatest amount of money X this individual will pay for insurance? The answer depends on one's attitude toward risk.

Recall that information on an individual's attitude toward risk is contained in her VNM utility function. Suppose the individual is risk-averse, with the utility function $U(Y) = \sqrt{100 + 0.001Y}$. The gamble "don't buy fire insurance" has an expected utility of:

$$E(U) = 0.98\,U(0) + 0.02\,U(-100,000) = 0.98\,(10) + 0.02\,(0) = 9.8$$

The gamble "buy fire insurance" has expected utility of:

$$U(-X) = \sqrt{100 + 0.001(-X)}$$

To find the maximum value of X the individual would pay, we must find X such that the two gambles have the same expected utility, or:

$$\sqrt{100 + 0.001(-X)} = 9.8$$

Solving, we obtain $X = 3,960$. We conclude that an individual with the VNM utility function $U(Y) = \sqrt{100 + 0.001Y}$ would pay a maximum of $3,960 per year to insure his house against a 2 percent chance of $100,000 in damages.

Now let's ask a different question: what will it cost an insurance company to provide such insurance? If, for the moment, we ignore administration and other overhead costs, and assume that the insurance company can insure thousands of homes of similar value with similar fire risk, then in an average year it will have to pay a claim of $100,000 on 2 percent of the homes. Its average claim per insured home in a given year will thus be $2,000. This amount is often called the **actuarially fair insurance premium**, which is the amount the insurance company must charge each individual to break even.

Here we have an interesting result: our individual would be willing to pay up to $3,960 to insure his home, and an insurance company could break even charging such customers only $2,000. Clearly, there is a price somewhere between $2,000 and $3,960 at which both the insurance company and the homeowner could benefit. Figure 6.7 which shows the consumer's concave utility function $U(Y) = \sqrt{100 + 0.001Y}$, illustrates this situation. A chord connects points A and B, the utility of the two possible outcomes. Splitting the chord at a point 98 percent of the way from point A to point B gives us point C. The horizontal location of point C is the expected value of the "no insurance" gamble, $-\$2,000$. The vertical height of point C tells us the expected utility of this gamble. Point D on the utility function, which has the same vertical height as point C, tells us the amount of money that would have an equal value to the gamble. In this case, this sum of money is $-\$3,960$.

Will it always be the case that an insurance premium exists that will benefit both the insurance company and the insurer? Yes, as long as the individual is risk-averse. To demonstrate this, let us generalize from the preceding insurance problem. In the absence of insur-

actuarially fair insurance premium

The amount of money an insurance company must charge each insured to break even.

Figure 6.7 Insurance with a Concave VNM Utility Function

With VNM utility function $U(Y) = \sqrt{100 + 0.001Y}$, the gamble of not buying insurance is represented by a chord connecting points A and B, with a 2 percent probability of being at point A and a 98 percent chance of being at point B. The expected utility of the gamble at point C, with a $2,000 expected loss, is 9.8. With insurance, the consumer is willing to pay up to $3,960 and receive the same utility of 9.8 with certainty. The risk premium is the difference between the actuarially fair premium of $2,000 and certainty equivalent of $3,960, or $1,960.

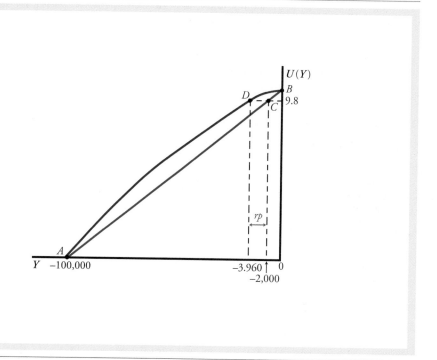

ance, an individual will face gamble G, which involves some probability of loss and has a negative expected value: $E[G] < 0$. In our example, $E[G]$ was $-$2,000. The certainty equivalent of gamble G is defined by $U(C) = E[U(G)]$; that is, it is the amount of money the individual could receive that would make him indifferent between the money or the gamble. If the individual is risk-averse, the individual is willing to pay to avoid the gamble, so that C will be a negative number, with $C < E[G]$ (C is "more negative" than $E[G]$, or $|C| > |E[G]|$). That is, with risk aversion, the individual will be willing to pay an amount greater than the expected loss in order to avoid the gamble. In our example, we now recognize $3,960 as the certainty equivalent of the "no-insurance" gamble. The insurance company, however, must charge each insured person $|E[G]|$ in order to break even. Thus, as long as the individual is risk-averse, so that $|C| > |E[G]|$, there exists an insurance premium that benefits both the insurance company and the consumer.

Recall that the risk premium, rp, is defined as $rp = E[G] - C$. As long as the individual is risk-averse, and the gamble has a negative expected value with an even more negative certainty equivalent, the risk premium will be a positive number. For instance, in our example, the individual's risk premium for the no-insurance gamble is $rp = -$2,000 $-$ ($-$3,960) $= -$2,000 $+$ $3,960 $=$ $1,960. Now we can see what the risk premium really tells us: it is the amount of money an individual would pay beyond the actuarially fair premium to insure against a gamble. As long as the individual is risk-averse, rp is positive, and we expect the individual to purchase insurance.

If the individual is risk-loving, we have $rp < 0$. In this case, he might want to purchase insurance, but only at a premium less than the actuarially fair premium. An insurance company would go broke offering insurance to risk lovers at this price. The same is true in the case of risk neutrality, where $rp = 0$. Here, the consumer would buy insurance only if the insurance company offered it at the actuarially fair premium. When we consider the administrative and other overhead costs the insurance company would have to bear, we see that an insurance company could not survive unless it could charge slightly more than the actuarially fair premium. We conclude, then, that insurance companies must be in the business of insuring risk-averse individuals who, by definition, possess concave VNM utility functions over the relevant range of wealth outcomes.

Practical difficulties plague insurance as a method of reducing risk. The two most serious problems are that more high-risk than low-risk individuals want to purchase insurance; and that once a person is insured, the individual has less incentive to behave carefully to avoid a loss. In the 1990s, such problems led to plans to restructure not only the health insurance industry, but the entire medical care industry. Microeconomists are well equipped to understand the practical difficulties of insurance as a method of reducing risk. In Chapter 20, we return to this topic and explore these two insurance-related problems in detail.

Information

Insuring against a potential loss is one way to deal with (and sometimes virtually eliminate) uncertainty, but it is not the only way. In many situations, insurance is either unobtainable or too costly, but we can still reduce or eliminate risk by obtaining information.

Suppose someone offers to sell you a painting by a well-known artist for $10,000. If the painting is authentic, you could resell it for $15,000 and turn a quick profit of $5,000. If the painting is fake, it will be worthless and you will have lost your $10,000 investment. Suppose you believe there is a 25 percent probability that the painting is fake. Then buying the painting means taking a gamble, G, that pays $5,000 with probability 0.75 and −$10,000 with probability 0.25. If your VNM utility function is the concave function $U(Y) = (50,000 + Y)^{1/2} = \sqrt{50,000 + Y}$, the expected utility of this gamble would be:

$$E[U(G)] = 0.75 \sqrt{50,000 + 5,000} + 0.25 \sqrt{50,000 - 10,000} = 225.89$$

The alternative, not taking the gamble, would yield an expected utility of $U(0) = \sqrt{50,000} = 223.60$, which is less than the expected utility of the gamble. If you had only two choices—to accept or not accept gamble G—you would accept the gamble and buy the painting. However, in a case like this, there may be a third option: obtaining information about the authenticity of the painting. In particular, suppose you can bring the painting to an appraiser who would be able to guarantee whether it was authentic or fake. How much would the appraisal be worth to you?

Note that once you obtain the information you will know for certain whether the painting is authentic or fake, and you will either buy or not buy the painting accordingly, so there is no uncertainty after you have the painting appraised. But before you get the painting appraised, you do not yet know what the appraiser will find. This is where the uncertainty lies. Because you think there is a 25 percent chance the painting is fake, you must also believe that there is a 25 percent chance the appraiser will find it to be fake. If this occurs, you will not buy the painting, and your payoff will be $0. On the other hand, there is a 75 percent chance the appraiser will find the painting to be authentic, in which case you will buy the painting and be guaranteed a $5,000 profit. Thus, the decision to go to the appraiser means accepting the new gamble G_{NEW}, with a 25 percent chance of gaining $0, and a 75 percent chance of gaining $5,000.

The expected utility of this new gamble is:

$$E[U(G_{NEW})] = 0.25 \sqrt{50,000} + 0.75 \sqrt{50,000 + 5,000} = 231.79$$

Note that going to the appraiser changes the gamble that you would choose from gamble G, with an expected utility of 225.89, to gamble G_{NEW}, with an expected utility of

231.79. Remember, too, that each of these gambles—G and G_{NEW}—has a certainty equivalent, an amount of money that you would value as highly as the gamble itself. For gamble G, with expected utility 225.89, you would find the certainty equivalent as follows:

$$U(C) = 225.89$$

$$\sqrt{50,000 + C} = 225,89$$

$$C = (225.89)^2 - 50,000 = 1,026.29$$

And for gamble G_{NEW}, with expected utility 231.79:

$$U(C_{NEW}) = 231.79$$

$$\sqrt{50,000 + C_{NEW}} = 231.79$$

$$C_{NEW} = (231.79)^2 - 50,000 = 3,726.60$$

Thus, obtaining the appraisal converts a gamble with a certainty equivalent of $1,026.29 into a gamble with a certainty equivalent of $3,726.60. The value of the information provided by the appraiser is thus $3,726.60 − $1,026.29 = $2,700.31. This is the maximum amount this individual would pay for the appraisal.

Let us retrace our steps and generalize from what we have done. You face a gamble, but have the opportunity to obtain information that will bear on your decision and thus change the nature of the gamble. The value of the information to you is simply the difference between two certainty equivalents: that of the original gamble and that of the new gamble faced with the information in hand.

In many situations, agents are able to acquire information, and that information has value. In our earlier example of the consultant who had to decide between three jobs, a trip to Firm A might have enabled her to determine whether she would get along with the director there. This information might have changed the gamble she faced. Of course, a trip to Firm A also has costs. At a minimum, it involves a sacrifice of time to travel to the firm and meet the director. There might also be significant travel expenses. Is the information worth it? Only if the value of the information—calculated as suggested earlier—is greater than the cost. That many people make good livings as appraisers, economic consultants, stock-market analysts, and industrial spies suggests that in many cases of decision-making under uncertainty, the perceived value of information exceeds its costs.

Diversification

diversification

The process of reducing risk by varying the collection of gambles.

In addition to purchasing insurance and obtaining information, we can also reduce risk through diversification. **Diversification** means to reduce one's risk by choosing an appropriate collection of gambles. A classic example is the small factory in a tourist town, where there is a 50-50 chance of either heavy rain or sun for the season, and no way to predict the weather in advance. The factory can manufacture either umbrellas or sunglasses. If the factory produces just sunglasses and the season turns out to be sunny, profit will be $50,000, but if it is rainy, profit will be zero. The decision to produce just sunglasses means the owner of the factory will face the 50-50 gamble G_S, which will pay either $50,000 or $0. If the factory owner has the VNM utility function $U(Y) = 10\ln(10 + Y)$, we find that $U(50,000) = 108.2$ and $U(0) = 23.03$, so that $E[U(G_S)] = 0.5(108.2) + 0.5(23.03) = 65.62$.

If the factory produces just umbrellas and there is rain, profit will be $50,000, but if there is sun, profit will be zero. The decision to produce just umbrellas implies that the factory owner will face gamble G_U, which is, once again, a 50-50 gamble that will pay either $50,000 or $0, so that $E[U(G_U)] = 65.62$, the same as $E[U(G_S)]$. With a 50-50 chance of rain or sun, and complete symmetry of profit and losses, producing only sunglasses or only umbrellas leads to a gamble with the same outcomes and the same associated probabilities, and so the same expected utility for the factory owner.

But what if we allow the owner to diversify—to produce umbrellas for half the year and sunglasses for half the year? We will assume that in this case, whether the season turns out to be rainy or sunny, profit is guaranteed to be $25,000. Note that the expected *value* of profit from producing only umbrellas, only sunglasses, or half of each is the same: $25,000. But the expected *utility* of this diversified approach yields the gamble G_D, which pays $25,000 with certainty, so that $E[U(G_D)] = 10\ln(10 + 25,000) = 101.27$.

Let's review what we've found: producing only umbrellas or only sunglasses implies a gamble for the factory owner where profit could be high or zero, with an expected utility of 65.62. Producing both goods together implies more modest profit, but no risk, and a greater expected utility of 101.27. Thus, through diversification, the factory owner is better off.

In the real world, individuals diversify in a number of ways. They maintain good relations with a variety of potential employers in addition to their current employer; they serve a variety of foods at dinner parties to ensure that everyone will find something they like; and they hold their wealth in a variety of forms (stocks, bonds, money, housing) rather than just one. Chapter 18 will have much more to say about this last type of diversification.

Flexibility

flexibility

A method of reducing risk by maintaining the ability to make a decision after the state of the world is known.

Perhaps the most commonly used method of reducing risk is **flexibility**—maintaining the ability to make a decision after the state of the world is known. It might seem at first glance that flexibility and insurance are the same things, because both usually require up-front payments to help reduce risk of unfavorable outcomes. There is, however, an important but subtle difference between them. Insurance provides compensation in the event of an unfavorable outcome, but does not reduce its probability. Flexibility, however, reduces the probability of the unfavorable outcome itself. It does this by allowing the

---

COMMON ERROR 6.2   Believing That Diversification Always Reduces Risk

Students often believe that diversification always reduces risk. However, this is not true. Consider diversification of stock investments. Suppose an investor who owns only one stock, Exxon Mobil, decides to diversify by purchasing shares in two other companies, Shell and Chevron Texaco. Because Exxon Mobil, Shell, and Chevron Texaco are all major oil companies, their stock market prices are likely to move in the same direction; that is, if Exxon Mobil's stock market value decreases, it is likely that the values of Shell and Chevron Texaco will decrease as well. Diversification

by purchasing shares in three oil companies instead of one is likely to have no significant effect on risk.

On the other hand, suppose an investor owns only Exxon Mobil shares, and diversifies by purchasing shares in General Mills and Starbucks. This diversification would reduce risk substantially, because the stock price movements of these three companies would not normally move together in the same direction. Remember that stock market diversification decreases risk only if the various stock prices are not positively related.

agent to postpone her decision until after the state of the world is known, or at least better known than at present.

We see flexibility in many areas of life. Tenured college professors who want to change jobs usually take a leave without pay while they try out the new job. If they don't like the job, they can return to their campus and resume their old job. In this way, professors do not really decide on the new job until after the state of the world (how much they will like the new job) is known. Couples who are thinking about marriage often live together for a while first. This reduces risk in two ways: (1) they obtain information on what marriage will be like before committing to the decision; and (2) they maintain flexibility, preserving an "easy out" if the relationship doesn't work.

Flexibility as a method of reducing risk works like the other methods we have discussed in Section 6.3: it can change the set of gambles faced by an economic agent and enable her to choose one with a higher expected utility than would otherwise be possible. Why, then, doesn't everyone maximize their flexibility? Because flexibility (like insurance, information, and diversification) usually has a cost. As with all methods of reducing risk, the gains in the form of higher expected utility must be balanced against the costs incurred.

▲▲▲ 6.3 APPLICATION   Information Versus Flexibility in Manufacturing

When a manufacturing firm wants to launch a new product, it faces a number of decisions about product design, marketing strategy, packaging, and advertising. All of these decisions must be made under conditions of uncertainty, because with a new product, there is no direct experience to rely upon. Traditionally, firms have tried to reduce their risk primarily by obtaining information. In manufacturing, this information comes from market research in which the firm builds a prototype of the product and then tests it on selected consumers, who are then interviewed about the product. In recent years, however, there has been growing dissatisfaction with the results of market research. The computer mouse, the telephone answering machine, and hair styling mousse were all judged as failures according to market research, yet all three have been phenomenal successes in the marketplace. Dissatisfaction with market research has led a number of firms to experiment with flexibility as a means to reduce risk. The following excerpt (taken from *The Wall Street Journal*, March 8, 1993) gives some examples of flexibility in practice. In each case, a firm has adopted a strategy that allows it to delay important decisions until the state of the world is better known.

…Sony obtains information from the actual sales of various Walkman models and then quickly adjusts its product mix to conform to those sales patterns. Specifically, the process design of each Walkman model is based on a core platform containing the essential technology. But the platform is designed to be flexible, which allows a wide range of models to be easily built on it, such as a beach model, a child's model, one that attaches to the arm, and so on.

Depending on which models sell, the models or features are changed, but the platform remains the same.

Similarly, without customer research, Seiko "throws" into the market several hundred new models of its watches. Those that customers buy, it makes more of; the others, it drops. Capitalizing on the design-for-response strategy, Seiko has a highly flexible design and production process that lets it quickly and inexpensively introduce products.

When creating a new magazine, Hearst Magazines also follows this approach. Hearst learned that it was almost impossible to customer-test the magazine's ideas and that it was better to launch the magazine and see what happens. To do this, Hearst has created a special group of editors with the talent and flexibility to launch almost any new magazine. Based upon the initial sales of the new magazine, they will either revise the content and format or drop the publication. Any new

(continued)

magazine that proves successful is spun off to run independently.

These examples represent a shift from information to flexibility as a method of reducing risk. Note that in each case, flexibility does not come free—different and possibly more expensive production technologies are required to take advantage of this strategy. But for these firms, the added cost seems to be well worth the reduced risk.

Summary

1. A decision tree can be used to represent choices under uncertainty by specifying the different possible outcomes and states of the world that can result from each decision. A choice under uncertainty can be represented succinctly as a choice between gambles. A gamble lists the possible outcomes of a decision and a probability for each outcome. An important way to characterize a gamble with quantitative outcomes is through its expected value, a probability-weighted average of all possible outcomes. The expected value of a gamble tells us the average result we could expect to obtain if the gamble were repeated many times.

2. A von Neumann–Morgenstern (VNM) utility function can be used to characterize preferences under uncertainty as well as different attitudes toward risk. The VNM utility function attaches a utility value to each possible outcome. If we have found the correct VNM utility function for an individual, he/she will always choose the gamble with the highest expected utility. An individual with a concave VNM utility function is risk-averse and will always prefer the expected value of a gamble with certainty to the gamble itself. An individual with a convex VNM utility function is risk-loving and will always prefer a gamble to its expected value with certainty. An individual with a linear VNM utility function is risk-neutral and will be indifferent between a gamble and its expected value with certainty. The certainty equivalent of a gamble is an amount of money that an individual would consider equally attractive to the gamble itself. The risk premium of a gamble is the difference between a gamble's expected value and its certainty equivalent.

3. The four methods individuals use to reduce risk are insurance, information, diversification, and flexibility. All of these methods can increase the expected utility of an economic agent facing a decision under uncertainty. Insurance can reduce risk by providing compensation in the event of an unfavorable outcome. The actuarially fair insurance premium is the price an insurance company must charge its customers in order to break even, not including overhead costs. A risk-averse individual will always purchase insurance when it is available at the actuarially fair price. In general, the value of information can be calculated as the difference between two certainty equivalents: that of the best gamble in the absence of information, and that of the best gamble after the information is obtained. Diversification allows agents to reduce risk by choosing a collection of different gambles. Flexibility reduces risk by permitting agents to postpone decisions until after the state of the world is known.

Self-Test Problems

1. Suppose you must decide whether to buy insurance to cover your personal possessions, which are worth $30,000. The insurance would cost you $800 per year, and you live in a neighborhood where the probability of a robbery is 2 percent in a given year.

   a. Draw the decision tree representing your options. Be sure to identify the decision, outcomes, and states of the world in your diagram.

   b. Present the decision you must make as a choice between two gambles: G_1 and G_2.

   c. Compute the expected value of each gamble.

2. An individual can make either of the following investments.

	Outcome (Earnings)	Probability
Investment A	$40,000	0.3
	$60,000	0.7
Investment B	$30,000	0.3
	$50,000	0.3
	$70,000	0.4

   a. Draw a decision tree for these investments.

   b. What is the expected value of earnings for each investment?

   c. If a consumer's VNM utility function is $U(Y) = 10 + \sqrt{Y}$, which investment will be chosen?

3. Suppose someone offers to sell you a Michael Jordan autographed jersey for $1,000. You think there is an 80 percent chance the jersey is authentic. If it is authentic, your friend who is a huge Michael Jordan fan has offered to buy the jersey from you for $3,000. If your VNM utility function is $U(Y) = \sqrt{Y + 2,000}$, what is the maximum amount you would be willing to pay a sports memorabilia expert to appraise the jersey, if the expert can tell you with 100 percent certainty whether the jersey is authentic?

Questions and Problems for Review

1. How could the concept of a VNM utility function help explain why some people become actors while others with equal acting talents become lawyers?

2. How do college students use flexibility at the beginning of a semester to reduce risk when scheduling classes?

3. Some people buy actuarially fair insurance for their homes, and yet take gambles with negative expected values in Las Vegas casinos. Could the shape of an individual's VNM utility function explain this behavior?

4. Consider the case of a college student who wants to insure against the possibility of not getting a job after graduation. Why is there no insurance for this unfavorable outcome? What other methods, besides insurance, do students actually use to reduce their risk?

5. In each of the following cases, identify the method(s) used to reduce risk:

   a. You try to find out everything you can about a neighborhood before buying a house there.

   b. You keep some of your money at home "just in case" your bank fails.

   c. You make reservations on more than one airline in case one airline cancels the flight.

   d. You look both ways before crossing the street.

   e. You make a small down payment on a gift for a friend to guarantee it will not be sold to someone else while you check to see if your friend already has it.

   f. You purchase a special service agreement for your personal computer that provides for free repairs if the computer malfunctions.

6. Does a risk premium always exist if you purchase fire insurance on your home?

7. Drivers often have to decide whether to speed on a highway. How can drivers reduce the risk of getting a speeding ticket?

8. Suppose that you have $10,000 to gamble at the races. A horse named Young Trustworthy has a 90 percent chance of winning, but your winnings would total only 10 percent of your bet. An alternative horse, Old Risky, has only a 10 percent chance of winning, but if she does, you would gain ten times your bet.

   a. If you must bet all $10,000 on one of the two horses, identify the two gambles (outcomes with payoffs and probabilities) that represent the choice you must make.

   b. What is the expected value of each gamble?

   c. Suppose your VNM utility function is $U(Y) = 10\ln(Y)$. Which horse would you bet on? Why?

   d. Calculate the certainty equivalent and the risk premium for each of the two gambles.

   e. Which horse would you bet on if your VNM utility function were $U(Y) = 0.0001Y^2$?

   f. Suppose you can bet $5,000 on each horse. Express this option as a third gamble, and compute the expected utility of this gamble using the VNM utility function in question c. Which of the three gambles would you prefer?

9. A friend gives you a stock tip that he says is "guaranteed" to double your original investment of $2,000. Based on past experience, you think there is a 60 percent chance that your friend is correct but there is also a 40 percent chance that the stock will halve your money—in other words, you will lose 50 percent. You know a stock broker who can investigate the stock and give you a guaranteed answer on whether your friend is right this time. Determine the maximum you would pay for the broker's investigation if your VNM utility function is:

   a. $U(Y) = 100\ln(Y)$

   b. $U(Y) = 100Y$

   c. $U(Y) = Y^3/1,000$

10. Would a risk-neutral individual faced with the service contract decision depicted in Figure 6.1 buy the contract? Explain your reasoning. Suppose the probabilities in Figure 6.1 were changed to the following: probability of losing 0 lenses equals 0.2; probability of losing 1 lens equals 0.5; and the probability of losing 2 lenses equals 0.3. Would a risk-averse individual buy a service contract?

11. Why can't consumers simply calculate the expected value of their income when making decisions under conditions of uncertainty? Are there any conditions under which this would be a valid method of decision-making under uncertainty?

12. How can the concept of marginal utility be used to explain the difference between risk-averse, risk-neutral, and risk-loving individuals?

13. Which of the following consumers would be most likely to buy lottery tickets every week?

   a. Consumer A with VNM utility function $U(Y) = Y^{1.5} = \sqrt{Y^3}$.

   b. Consumer B with VNM utility function $U(Y) = Y^{1/3} = \sqrt[3]{Y}$.

   c. Consumer C with VNM utility function $100 + 10Y$.

   Explain your reasoning.

14. Suppose a homeowner has the VNM utility function $U(Y) = \sqrt{100 + 0.0005Y}$. Without fire insurance, the homeowner faces a potential loss of $200,000 from a fire. If the probability of a fire is 1 percent per year, what is the actuarially fair insurance premium? What is the risk premium for this homeowner?

15. A homeowner owns a house worth $250,000. There is a 2 percent chance of a fire burning the house down in any given year. The homeowner's risk premium is $1,800 and he is offered an insurance policy for $750 above the actuarially fair insurance premium. Should the homeowner purchase this insurance policy? Explain your reasoning. Why is the insurance company willing to provide this insurance?

16. Abby has a VNM utility function $U(Y) = 1,000 - 100/Y$, where Y is her income. Abby just graduated from college and has a career choice for her first job of either working as a teacher and earning a guaranteed $40,000 or trying to become a theater lighting director and earning $70,000 if there is growth in the demand for theater next year, or $20,000 if there is no growth. There is a 50 percent probability of growth. A consulting firm guarantees Abby that it already knows whether there will be growth in the demand for theater next year. What is the maximum amount Abby should be willing to pay for this information?

17. Draw VNM utility functions for each of the following types of individuals:

    a. Greg never gambles under any circumstances.

    b. Kristin always takes any gamble no matter what her current level of income.

    c. Art never gambles unless the potential winnings are greater than $100 million.

18. Surveys consistently show that over half of all Americans are dissatisfied with their current jobs, yet the same surveys indicate that most Americans have no plans to leave their jobs or search for another job. What does this behavior suggest about working Americans' risk preferences and their VNM utility functions?

19. Two consumers, Jack and Jill, own homes worth $250,000. Jack's home was built of steel and bricks in the middle of a desert. Jill's home was built of wood in the middle of a forest. Which home will have a higher actuarially fair insurance premium? If all $250,000 homeowners must pay the same insurance premium, who is more likely to buy insurance? Explain your reasoning. Does your answer suggest a problem for insurance companies?

20. The parents of many college students pay the automobile insurance for their children. How does this affect the children's risk of having an automobile accident? Could this parental financial support affect the accident rate for the children?

21. Investors can invest in either stocks or bonds. Bonds tend to pay a fixed interest rate and United States government bonds are virtually risk-free. On the other hand, stocks tend to vary widely in value depending on a variety of economic conditions, but it is not unusual for a stock's price to increase or decrease by 10 percent or more in a month. Some investors put most of their funds into bonds, while others rely primarily on stocks. Do you think these two groups of investors would have the same VNM utility functions? Do you think that the expected earnings on bonds would be greater than, less than, or equal to the expected earnings on stocks? Explain your reasoning.

Internet Exercises

Visit *http://www.myeconlab.com/waldman* for this chapter's Web exercises. Answer real-world economics problems by doing research on the Internet.

Production and Costs and Perfect Competition

Chapter 7
The Theory of Production and Costs

An accurate accounting of a firm's production costs is crucial to its economic performance. In June 2002, a huge economic scandal broke when it was announced that WorldCom, then one of the world's largest telecommunications companies, had incorrectly reported its costs. Throughout 2001 and the first quarter of 2002, WorldCom identified many of its costs of using the services of other telecommunication companies as an investment cost to be incurred over time, instead of as an immediate cost. According to the *BBC News*, "It is as if a company pretended its outlay on paperclips and stationary—necessary, certainly, but by no means adding value—was in fact used to buy new equipment or build a new factory." In fact, WorldCom understated its cost so much that its profits were overstated by $3.8 billion. The result was a huge collapse in the value of WorldCom stock. On Monday, July 1, 2002, WorldCom's stock price fell from a high of $64 in 1999 to 6 cents a share! You will learn in this chapter that WorldCom's fraudulent accounting practice was to treat one type of economic cost, variable costs, as another type of cost, fixed costs. Rarely has there been a better example of how important it is for investors to have a complete understanding of the production costs of the firms they invest in.

In this chapter, we turn our attention to business firms as principal actors on the economic stage. Business firms have been called the "engines of prosperity" in a capitalist economy, and that is no hyperbole. Firms produce and market the goods and services that satisfy needs and wants of consumers. They provide employment, paying workers the wages they need to buy the goods and services they consume. Firms are owned by households, making them an important source of consumer wealth. During the 1980s, the market value of America's publicly held corporations more than tripled. Then, from 1990–1999, the value increased more than fivefold to over $19.5 trillion, before the stock market decline of 2000–2002 brought the values back down. The value of publicly held corporations, of course, is only the tip of the iceberg, since many of America's firms—both large and small—are privately held. In this chapter, we begin the study of firm behavior by learning the theoretical foundation of market supply: the theory of production and costs.

7.1   An Outline of Producer Theory

No doubt you have some idea what a firm is—after all, you encounter them every day. You may have worked for one or two in your life, and a few of you may even have started one. When asked this question in class, one very bright student once responded, "A firm is an organization that uses resources to produce output." Asked on follow-up to define "organization," the student continued, "… and an 'organization' is a collection of capital and labor." These are good answers, but they neglect to mention something very important. A firm is created by someone—and it is created for a purpose. What might that purpose be? Why do people go to the considerable trouble involved in starting and running a firm? Do they do it for the sheer joy of hard work? Do they do it to make society a better place in which to live? Maybe sometimes, but surely not most of the time. The overwhelming majority of firms are created for one overriding purpose: to make profits for their owners.

Those owners, in turn, have good reason to want the firm to make a profit: with a profit, they can buy goods and services to consume. To economists, consumption is the ultimate objective of most economic activity. If individual consumers seek to maximize utility from consumption, thens it is quite easy to see how those same individuals would want things done in their role as firm owners. They will want to maximize profit, because profit is income to the firm's owners, and greater income enables greater consumption and utility. This hypothesis of **profit maximization** is the fundamental behavioral assumption we will make about firms, and it is entirely consistent with our view of the consumer as a utility maximizer. With this perspective in mind, let's sketch an outline of the firm's activities.

profit maximization

The fundamental economic assumption that firms always attempt to make the largest profit possible by maximizing the difference between their total revenues and total costs.

1. The firm buys inputs at prices determined in input markets. The firm's expenditures on inputs are its cost of production.
2. The firm uses inputs to produce output according to what is possible, given the state of knowledge and technology.
3. The firm sells output in product markets, earning revenue from sales.
4. Owners of the firm keep as profit the difference between total revenue and the cost of production.

Take another look at this list and notice that in each of the first three stages, the firm is making decisions. How much of which inputs should it buy? At what prices? Can the firm affect the prices it pays? If so, how should it try to affect them? How should inputs be combined to make output? Where should the output be sold? At what price? How should it be marketed? Countless decisions of this sort have to be made when running a firm, and we will examine quite a few of them. Yet to predict what a firm will do in almost any situation, we need only ask one simple question: "What action would maximize profit?"

The Short Run and the Long Run

For analytical purposes, it is useful to classify the decisions a firm makes into two types: short-run decisions and long-run decisions. We define the **short run** as that period of time over which the firm must take as given one or more pre-existing (and unchangeable) commitments that affect production. For example, if the firm has a two-year unbreakable lease on its plant and equipment, it is committed to using that plant for that amount of time. Over the period of that lease, the decisions it makes with regard to how much labor to hire per month, how much heat and electricity to use per month, and so on, are all

short run

The time horizon over which at least one of the firm's inputs is fixed.

▲▲▲ 7.1 APPLICATION   WorldCom: Cooking the Books to Make Profits

Sometimes firms try to make their profits appear to be larger by misrepresenting their revenues or costs. In the WorldCom case, the firm's top managers knew exactly what they were doing when they misrepresented some costs to make their profits appear to be $3.8 billion larger than they actually were. Why would the managers risk going to prison to cook their books? The answer is the close connection between WorldCom's reported profits and the market value of the firm's stock. High profits increase the demand for a firm's stock, and thereby raise the price of a share of the company's stock. Because the top managers all owned a huge number of shares of WorldCom stock, they had a great deal to gain from an increase in the firm's stock price and, perhaps more importantly, they had a great deal to lose from any significant decline in the company's stock value. Ironically, WorldCom's efforts to artificially increase their profits caused a complete collapse in the firm's stock value and most of the managers lost their fortunes. In the end, honesty would have been a better policy for WorldCom.

long run

The time horizon over which the firm can change all of its inputs, and therefore all inputs are variable.

short-run decisions, because they must take as given the commitment to the plant of a specific size.

By contrast, we define the **long run** as that period of time over which the firm can plan with complete freedom of choice how much or how little of all productive inputs it will use. Over time, the firm in our example could let its lease expire and lease a smaller plant employing fewer workers; it could also construct a new plant of its own, expanding its labor force at the same time. Decisions such as this, in which the firm is free to plan changes in how it combines all its factors of production, are long-run decisions.

This distinction between the short run and long run is not one made on the basis of calendar time. The short run need not be a month; it might be years. The long run need not be decades; it could be weeks. What matters is how free the firm is to act in the circumstances of the decision. If it must contend with fixed amounts of one or more factors, then the decision is short-run. If the firm has complete freedom to plan how to deploy all the factors it requires, the decision is long-run.

▼▼▼ 7.2   Production

Production is the process of transforming inputs into output. As we noted in item (2) of our outline of the firm's activities, the state of technology determines what is feasible in production. Therefore, it may seem to you that the process of combining inputs to produce output is a purely mechanical matter—one requiring little, if any, decision-making on the part of the firm. This would be a mistaken impression, though, because there will almost always be different ways the firm can combine inputs to produce output. Because the inputs a firm buys are costly, how they are combined with one another and in what quantities directly determines the cost of production. Cost, in turn, has an obvious impact on profit. This is why production decisions are so important.

There is no hard and fast rule to define an input or an output, or what the difference is between them. Automobiles are an output of General Motors and Toyota, but they are inputs to Hertz and Avis. Defining inputs and outputs therefore depends on the context and the particular firm in question. What's more, the number of inputs required to make a unit of output also differs widely across firms. To make a gallon of ice cream, Ben and Jerry may need only some fresh Vermont milk, some sugar, and a freezer. An aircraft manufacturer like Boeing, however, can require literally hundreds of thousands of different inputs to produce just one plane. For most of our analysis, we'll usually keep

capital goods

Goods used to produce other goods, such as a firm's plant and equipment.

things simple and assume that output is produced from only two inputs: the services of human labor, and the services of some capital good. **Capital goods** can usually be thought of as goods used to produce other goods, such as the firm's physical plant and equipment.

In another effort to simplify our model, we assume that firms know the current state of the industry's technology, and that technology does not change during the period of our analysis. Furthermore, except when studying technological change, we assume the firm has access to the same technology in both the short run and the long run. What can change between the short run and the long run is what the firm can do with its technology, not the technology itself.

Production Functions

production function

The relationship between inputs and the maximum possible output that can be produced using those inputs over a given period of time and given the current state of technology.

The **production function** summarizes the technological relationship between the amount of inputs used and the maximum amount of output produced during some specified period of time given the current state of technology. Letting X_1 stand for the number of units of input 1 employed per month, X_2 stand for the number of units of input 2 employed, X_n stand for the number of units of input n employed, and Q stand for the units of output produced per month, the production function is written as:

$$Q = f(X_1, X_2, X_3, \ldots, X_n) \tag{7.1}$$

Here, the function f summarizes the state of technology for producing this good, and we interpret Q as the maximum number of units of output per month that it is technically possible to produce with the application of X_1 units of input 1, X_2 units of input 2, X_3 units of input 3, etc. Different amounts of inputs 1 through n enable the firm to produce different maximum amounts of output Q, and the production function in Equation 7.1 gives all such possibilities.

A HYPOTHETICAL PRODUCTION FUNCTION   Table 7.1 shows a hypothetical production function $Q_{corn} = f(L, A)$ relating the output of corn to the input of labor, L, and acres of land, A, for a small farmer. To simplify the analysis, we are holding the fixed quantities of all other inputs, such as seeds, pesticide, and fertilizer. Labor is measured in worker days and land in acres. In general, using more of any input enables the firm to produce more output. For example, look at Table 7.1, which shows the maximum output produced with various combinations of labor and land. As more labor is added to a

Table 7.1 **Output of Corn for a Hypothetical Production Function** $Q_{corn} = f(L, A)$ **(bushels of corn)**

		Acres of Land A			
	5	**10**	**15**	**20**	**25**
1	70	170	240	290	330
2	160	270	350	410	460
3	220	340	430	500	560
4	260	390	490	570	640
5	290	430	540	630	710
6	310	460	580	680	770

Labor L (worker-days) labels rows 1–6.

given amount of land, output increases. Similarly, read across any row: adding more acres of land to a fixed amount of labor also causes output to increase. Finally, look down any diagonal: increasing both labor and land together increases output.

There are two very useful measures of an input's contribution to output. The first is the **average product**, which is defined as the total output produced divided by the number of units of the input employed. The average product of labor, for example, is $AP_L = Q/A$. Similarly, the average product of land is total output divided by the number of acres employed, or $AP_A = Q/A$. Because the amount of output produced depends on how much of *both* factors the firm uses, both AP_L and AP_A will depend on how much of the other factor is being used. For example, look once more at Table 7.1. Going down any column, the AP_L is computed by dividing total output by the corresponding amount of labor.

Figure 7.1 graphs the AP_L for our hypothetical production function for three different amounts of land: 5 acres (the dark-blue curve), 15 acres (the medium-blue curve), and 25 acres (the light-blue curve). Notice that adding more labor to a fixed amount of land, causes the AP_L to rise, meaning that more land makes the firm's labor more productive, on average. $AP_L = Q/A. \quad AP_A = Q/A$

Often we want to know how much *extra* output can be produced if more of one factor is combined with fixed amounts of all the other factors. The **marginal product** of labor, MP_L, is the additional output obtained from a one-unit increase in the amount of labor employed, holding the amount of land constant. Similarly, the marginal product of an acre, MP_A, is the increment in output obtained from a one-acre increase in the amount of land used, holding the amount of labor constant. Formally, we define these marginal products as:

average product

For a given input, total output divided by the number of units of the input.

marginal product

For a given input, the additional output obtained from a one-unit increase in the amount of the input employed, holding the amounts of all other inputs fixed.

$$MP_L = \frac{\Delta Q}{\Delta L}$$

$$MP_A = \frac{\Delta Q}{\Delta A}$$

Because the MP_L is the ratio of the change in output to the change in labor input that causes it, you can think of the MP_L as the rate at which output changes per-unit change in L. Similarly, MP_A measures the rate of change in output as A changes.

Figure 7.1 Average Product of Labor

If workers have 5 acres of land to work on, the AP_L curve is the lowest dark-blue curve. If workers have 15 acres of land to work on, the AP_L curve is the higher medium-blue curve, and if workers have 25 acres of land to work on, the AP_L curve is the highest light-blue curve.

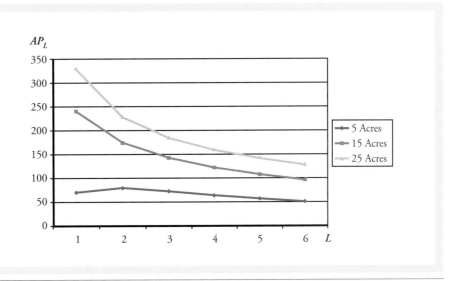

In all regions of a production function where firms might choose to produce, the marginal product of any input X_i, MP_{X_i} must be positive for all inputs i. The intuition behind this statement applies equally well to any factor in the production process: A firm will purchase additional inputs only if those inputs increase output. Thus, even if regions of zero or negative marginal product exist, we will never observe a profit-maximizing firm operating there.

In Table 7.1, both the MP_L and the MP_A depend on how much labor and land the firm uses. When land is fixed at 5 acres—that is, $A = 5$—adding the first unit of labor causes output to rise from zero to 70 bushels. Therefore, $\Delta Q = 70 - 0$, while $\Delta L = 1 - 0$, giving a marginal product for the first worker of $MP_L = \Delta Q / \Delta L = 70/1 = 70$ bushels. When land remains fixed at 5 acres, the second worker produces *more* additional output than the first worker, because the marginal product of the second worker is $MP_L = \Delta Q / \Delta L = 90/1 = 90$ bushels. The marginal product of the third worker, however, is smaller than the marginal product of the second worker. The third worker produces less additional output than the second worker, because the marginal product of the third worker is $MP_L = \Delta Q / \Delta L = 60/1 = 60$ bushels, which is less than the marginal product of 90 bushels for the second worker.

Table 7.2 computes the marginal product of labor for our hypothetical farmer for 5-acre, 15-acre, and 25-acre farms. Notice how the MP_L column changes down any column and across any row. Looking down the MP_L column for $A = 5$, the MP_L at first increases from 70 bushels for the first worker to 90 bushels for the second worker; however, beginning with the addition of the third worker, the MP_L declines continuously as the firm adds more labor to a fixed amount of land.

It is common for the MP_L to increase at first and then decrease. The initial increase in the MP_L results from the division of labor tasks among workers. For example, consider adding labor to our small 5-acre farm: The first worker must do all the jobs alone: tilling, sowing, fertilizing, reaping, and marketing. With the addition of a second worker, the two workers can divide the tasks. Perhaps the first worker does the tilling and reaping, while the second worker does the sowing and fertilizing, and they share the marketing task. As a result of this division of labor, they each become specialized and perform their tasks more efficiently than if they had to work alone. In the early stages of a production process, therefore, it is common for a production function to exhibit increasing marginal productivity for inputs.

In Table 7.2, with the amount of land held constant at $A = 5$, the MP_L declines continuously, beginning with the addition of the third worker; and holding land fixed at

Table 7.2 MP_L and AP_L for a Hypothetical Production Function $Q_{corn} = f(L, A)$ (bushels of corn) for Land Fixed at 5, 15, and 25 acres

| | | Land $A = 5$ Acres | | | Land $A = 15$ Acres | | | Land $A = 25$ Acres | | |
		Q_{corn}	MP_{Labor}	AP_{Labor}	Q_{corn}	MP_{Labor}	AP_{Labor}	Q_{corn}	MP_{Labor}	AP_{Labor}
	1	70	70	70	240	240	240	330	330	330
Labor L	2	160	90	80	350	110	175	460	130	230
(worker-days)	3	220	60	73.3	430	80	143.3	560	100	186.7
	4	260	40	65	490	60	122.5	640	80	160
	5	290	30	58	540	50	108	710	70	142
	6	310	20	51.6	580	40	96.7	770	60	128.3

either 15 acres or 25 acres, the MP_L declines continuously, beginning with the addition of the second worker. When an additional unit of labor contributes less to total output than the unit before it contributed, the production function is said to display **diminishing marginal returns** to labor. Sometimes economists say such production functions exhibit "diminishing returns," instead of the longer but more precise "diminishing *marginal* returns." Either way is fine, as long as you remember that we're talking about how *incremental* output behaves as more of one factor is added to fixed amounts of the other inputs.

All real-world production functions must eventually exhibit diminishing marginal returns in the short run. To understand why this must be true, consider any short-run production function $f(L, \overline{K})$, where labor L is the variable input, and the other input, capital, is fixed at $\overline{K}$. Initially, as the firm adds units of labor to a fixed quantity of capital $\overline{K}$, each worker has a great deal of capital to work with and the associated increments in output increase as workers are able to specialize in their production tasks. At some point, however, as the firm continues to add additional workers to the fixed supply of capital, and each worker has fewer units of capital to work with, the increment in output associated with an additional worker must decline. All short-run production functions display diminishing marginal returns; this is called the **law of diminishing returns**.

One of the ways to understand the law of diminishing returns is to consider the implications if the law of diminishing returns did not hold for short-run production functions. Suppose, for example, the law of diminishing returns did not hold with regard to food production, so that as additional units of variable inputs such as labor, fertilizer, pesticides, and seeds were added to a fixed amount of land, the increments in output never declined. How much land would be necessary to feed the entire world's population? According to economist George Stigler, if the law of diminishing marginal returns did not hold, you could feed the world's entire population with the food grown in one flowerpot! All you would need to do is continue to add increasing amounts of the variable inputs to the fixed amount of land in the flowerpot, and because the extra output associated with adding these variable inputs would never decline, you could grow an infinite amount of food in the flowerpot. This example illustrates why for any short-run production function, the law of diminishing marginal returns must hold.

THE MP_L CURVE, THE AP_L CURVE, AND THE RELATIONSHIP BETWEEN MARGINAL AND AVERAGE NUMERICAL CONCEPTS

Figure 7.2 graphs the marginal product of labor and average product of labor curves for a 5-acre farm based on the data in Table 7.2. The curves have been smoothed out because it is possible to hire a worker for a fraction of a day of labor. For example, a farmer can hire a worker for four hours a day—1/2 a worker-day; or two hours a day—1/4 a worker-day; or any fraction of a worker-day. The MP_L increases for the first and second worker, then decreases for additional workers. The AP_L increases up to L_1 units of labor, which is between 2 and 3 worker-days of labor. At point Z, the two curves intersect precisely at the maximum point of the AP_L curve.

Figure 7.2 illustrates the general relationship between marginal and average, a frequently used relationship in economics that is the same for all marginal and average curves. Consider the case when the MP_L is greater than the AP_L as the amount of labor increases. The AP_L reflects the output of *all* the workers employed in the production process, while the MP_L measures the additional output produced by the *last* worker hired. If the additional output produced by the last worker—that is, the MP_L—is greater than the AP_L, the average product must be pulled up by the addition of the last worker.

You can understand this relationship by thinking of your performance in a course. Suppose your average grade on two economics exams is 75. If the grade on your third

---

diminishing marginal returns

In the short run, diminishing marginal returns exist when an additional unit of a variable input contributes less to total output than the addition of the previous unit of the input contributed, holding all other inputs fixed.

law of diminishing returns

A relationship between inputs and outputs which states that as additional units of a variable input are added to a production process with at least one fixed input, eventually the increment in output associated with adding additional units of the variable input must decrease.

Figure 7.2 MP_L and AP_L with Land Fixed at $A = 5$ Acres

For a labor input less than L_1, the MP_L is greater than the AP_L, so the AP_L curve increases. For a labor input greater than L_1, the MP_L is less than the AP_L, so the AP_L curve decreases. For a labor input equal to L_1, the $MP_L = AP_L$, so the AP_L curve is at its maximum value.

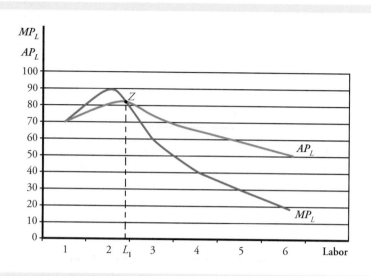

exam, the marginal grade, is an 85, the marginal exam pulls the course average up, but it doesn't pull the average grade up as high as the marginal grade of 85. Of course, if the marginal grade is 60, then the average grade decreases, but the average grade doesn't decrease to the level of the marginal grade of 60. Finally, if the marginal grade is 75, then the average grade remains constant at 75 and exactly equals the marginal grade. By analogous reasoning, the general relationship between marginal and average implies that as long as the MP_L is greater than the AP_L, the AP_L curve must be increasing. Furthermore, as long as the MP_L is less than the AP_L, the AP_L curve must be decreasing. Therefore, the MP_L curve equals the AP_L curve precisely at the maximum of the AP_L curve. This is shown in Figure 7.2: there the MP_L equals the AP_L at L_1, where the AP_L curve reaches its maximum value.

In the economically relevant regions of production, a production function $Q = f(L,K)$ will have positive marginal products for both factors; that is, $MP_L > 0$ and $MP_K > 0$. Furthermore, once diminishing returns set in, the marginal products will continuously

---

COMMON ERROR 7.1 Misunderstanding the Law of Diminishing Returns

Students often misinterpret the law of diminishing marginal returns by thinking that it is the law of *zero* marginal returns. What is the difference between "diminishing marginal returns" and "zero marginal returns"? The law of diminishing returns states that as you add more and more additional units of a variable input to a production function with at least one fixed input, eventually the marginal product of the variable input declines. However, even beyond the point of diminishing marginal returns, *total output continues to increase as more of the variable input is used.*

Many students mistakenly believe that diminishing returns implies that total output begins to decline. With at least one fixed input, it is true that eventually you will reach a maximum capacity that can be produced with that fixed input, and beyond that point, total output can indeed begin to decline. However, that point is of little or no interest to economists, because no rational firm would ever use a unit of a variable input that produced zero additional units of output. The point of diminishing marginal returns occurs far before the point of zero marginal returns in any short-run production function.

decrease as the quantities of the inputs increase, so an increase in L will cause the MP_L to decrease, while an increase in K will cause the MP_K to decrease. Finally, for most production functions, an increase in L will cause the MP_K to increase and an increase in K will cause the MP_L to increase.

Isoquants

isoquant

A level curve that identifies all of the input combinations that, when used as efficiently as possible, can produce a given level of output.

With only two factors of production, L and K, we can represent the production function graphically much the same way we represented the consumer's utility function with indifference curves. For any level of output Q_0, we define the Q_0-level **isoquant** as all input combinations that produce Q_0 units of output. An isoquant is thus a level-curve of the production function, just as an indifference curve is a level-curve of the utility function, and we represent isoquants much the same way we represented indifference curves in Chapters 3–5.

Figure 7.3 shows a typical isoquant drawn through some arbitrary combination of inputs (L_0, K_0) denoted by point A. It will be useful to have an analytical expression for the slope of the isoquant through such points, and we can derive one in much the same way we earlier derived the MRS for the slope of an indifference curve. To begin, note that the slope of the isoquant at point A is equal to the slope of the blue line tangent to it there. That slope can be approximated by the slope of a chord (the green line) drawn from point A to another point B on the same isoquant. Now imagine moving from point A to point B by way of point C. The movement from A to C requires that capital be reduced by $\Delta K < 0$, with no change in the amount of labor. If the marginal product of capital is MP_K, that movement from A to C must cause a change in total output equal to $Q_0 - Q_1 = (\Delta Q/\Delta K)(\Delta K) = (MP_K)(\Delta K) < 0$ units. Similarly, the move from C to B requires that labor increase by $\Delta L > 0$, with no change in capital. If the marginal product of labor is MP_L, the movement from C to B must cause a change in total output equal to $Q_1 - Q_0 = (\Delta Q/\Delta L)(\Delta L) = (MP_L)(\Delta L) > 0$. Multiplying this last expression by (-1), we can write $Q_0 - Q_1 = -(MP_L)(\Delta L) < 0$. It follows that:

$$Q_0 - Q_1 = (MP_K)(\Delta K) = -(MP_L)(\Delta L) = Q_0 - Q_1$$

Figure 7.3 Isoquants and the Marginal Rate of Technical Substitution
At any point on an isoquant, the slope of a tangent line equals the marginal rate of technical substitution, *MRTS*. In this case, at point A, output equals Q_1 and the *MRTS* equals the slope of the blue tangent line.

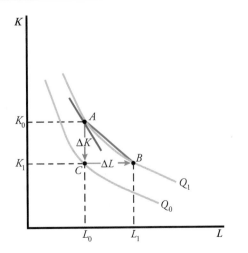

or:

$$(MP_K)(\Delta K) = -(MP_L)(\Delta L)$$

Therefore:

$$\frac{\Delta K}{\Delta L} = -\frac{MP_L}{MP_K}$$

Had we selected point B closer to point A on that same isoquant, the slope of the corresponding chord would have been an even better approximation to the slope of the tangent at point A. Now, imagine sliding point B up the isoquant closer and closer to point A. Eventually point B would be virtually on top of point A and the slope of the chord AB would converge to the slope of the tangent line at A. Thus, we can write a general expression for the slope of the isoquant through any point:

$$\text{slope of the isoquant at point } (L,K) = -\frac{MP_L}{MP_K} \qquad (7.2)$$

marginal rate of technical substitution

The rate at which one input can be substituted for another input while still producing the same level of output.

Curvature is another important characteristic of an isoquant. The absolute value of an isoquant's slope is called the **marginal rate of technical substitution**, or **MRTS**. The *MRTS* measures the rate at which more labor can be substituted for less capital while still producing the same level of output. In Figure 7.3 the isoquants are drawn with negative slopes and convex away from the origin. The convex shape results because the *MRTS* diminishes as we move down the isoquant from northwest to southeast. A diminishing *MRTS* indicates that the rate at which labor can be substituted for capital, with no effect on output, declines as the firm uses more labor and less capital. In effect, the more labor and the less capital the firm uses, the harder it is to substitute even more labor for even less capital.

The two panels of Figure 7.4 summarize two other possible isoquant mappings. In panel (a), the isoquants are parallel straight lines, so the *MRTS* is constant. Here, the

Figure 7.4 Two Isoquant Mappings: Perfect Substitutes and Perfect Complements

In panel (a), the two inputs, maple and oak, are perfect substitutes for each other in the production of lumber, so the isoquants are linear. In panel (b), the two inputs, steering wheels and oil filters, are perfect complements for each other in the production of automobiles. In this case, the inputs are used in fixed proportions, and the isoquants form right angles along a ray that represents those proportions.

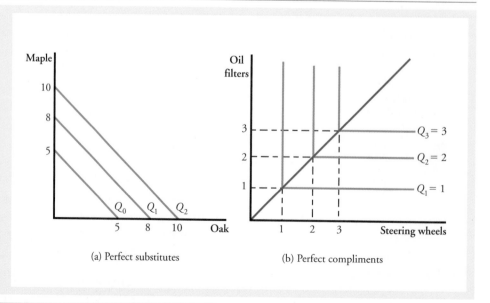

(a) Perfect substitutes   (b) Perfect compliments

inputs maple and oak are used to produce lumber, and they can always be substituted for each other at a fixed, unchanging rate. When this is the case, we say that the inputs are **perfect substitutes**. Notice in panel (b) that an increase in the number of steering wheels, with no increase in the number of oil filters, yields no increase in the number of automobiles whatsoever. For output to increase in panel (b), steering wheels and oil filters must be increased together in fixed proportions. In the extreme case when two inputs can be used together only in fixed proportions, the isoquants will be right angles, like those in panel (b). When this is so, we say that steering wheels and oil filters are **perfect complements**. Notice how the isoquant mappings for perfect substitutes and perfect complements are completely analogous to the indifference curve mappings for perfect substitutes and perfect complements.

Returns to Scale

The phrase **returns to scale** refers to how output behaves as all inputs are varied simultaneously, and in equal proportion. Because all inputs are changing simultaneously, returns to scale is a long-run concept. We want to know how output behaves as we simultaneously double, triple, or cut in half the amount of every input the firm uses.

If all inputs are increased by a common factor of t and output increases by that same factor of t, we say the production function exhibits **constant returns to scale**. Under constant returns to scale, doubling or tripling all inputs causes output to double or triple, respectively, and cutting the amount of all inputs by one-half causes output to fall by one-half. If all inputs are changed by a common factor of t and output increases by more than a factor of t, we say the production function exhibits **increasing returns to scale**. Thus, under increasing returns to scale, a doubling or tripling of all inputs leads to something more than a doubling or tripling of output, respectively. There is also a third possibility. If all factors are increased by a common factor of t, and the firm's output increases by less than a factor of t, the production function exhibits **decreasing returns to scale**. In this case, doubling or tripling all inputs causes output to less than double or triple, respectively. Or if $t = 0.5$, then a 50 percent increase in all inputs results in less than a 50 percent increase in output.

Figure 7.5 illustrates the isoquants for three different production functions. In panel (a), the input combination (L_0, K_0) produces 100 units of output. It takes twice as much of both inputs to produce 200 units of output and three times as much to produce 300 units, so this production function has *constant* returns to scale. In panel (b), something more than $2L_0$ and $2K_0$ is required to produce 200 units, and more than $3L_0$ and $3K_0$ is required to produce 300. This production function therefore displays *decreasing* returns to scale because doubling or tripling all inputs leads to something less than a proportionate increase in output. By contrast, in panel (c), doubling or tripling inputs L_0 and K_0 produce, respectively, more than twice or three times the output. That production function therefore displays *increasing* returns to scale.

Figure 7.5 also shows that when the production function displays constant returns to scale, isoquants giving equal increments in output must be equally spaced from one another as we move out along any ray from the origin. That is, in panel (a), the distance AB must be equal to the distance BC. In panel (b), there are decreasing returns to scale, and isoquants giving equal increments in output will be spaced further and further apart as we move out along a ray: the distance $A'B'$ will be smaller than the distance $B'C'$. Finally, under increasing returns to scale in panel (c), the distance $A''B''$ must be greater than the distance $B''C''$, so the isoquants giving successive equal increments in output become closer and closer together as we move out along any ray from the origin.

---

perfect substitutes

In production, two inputs are perfect substitutes if they can always be substituted for one another at a fixed rate.

perfect complements

In production, two inputs are perfect complements if they can be used only in fixed proportions.

returns to scale

A long-run production concept that refers to how output changes when all inputs are varied in equal proportions.

constant returns to scale

A production function where if when all inputs are increased (decreased) by a fixed proportion t, output increases (decreases) by the same proportion t.

increasing returns to scale

A production function where when all inputs are increased (decreased) by a fixed proportion t, output increases (decreases) by more than the proportion t.

decreasing returns to scale

A production function where when all inputs are increased (decreased) by a fixed proportion t, output increases (decreases) by less than the proportion t.

Figure 7.5 Returns to Scale and the Spacing of Isoquants
In panel (a), there are constant returns to scale, because any percentage increase in all inputs results in an equal percentage increase in output. In panel (b), there are decreasing returns to scale, because any percentage increase in all inputs results in a smaller percentage increase in output. In panel (c), there are increasing returns to scale, because any percentage increase in all inputs results in a larger percentage increase in output.

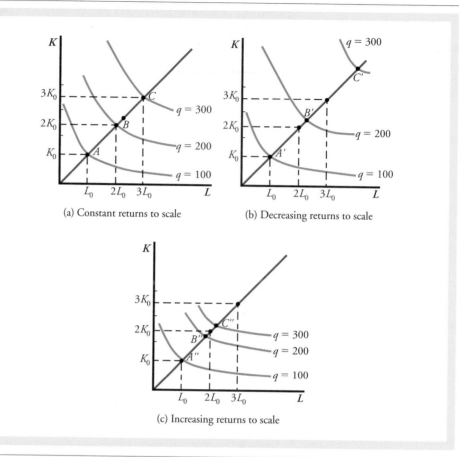

(a) Constant returns to scale

(b) Decreasing returns to scale

(c) Increasing returns to scale

SPECIALIZATION AND INCREASING RETURNS TO SCALE Increasing returns to scale can exist for a variety of reasons. The reason most commonly cited by economists is the **specialization** of input tasks. Consider the specialization of machinery. Firms can often reduce the time and resources needed to produce a unit of a good by investing in highly specialized machinery. The time required to learn how to operate such machinery, however, can be substantial. Firms expecting to produce small quantities of output, therefore, may discover that it is better to invest in more general types of machinery rather than highly specialized machinery. As output expands, firms find it increasingly attractive to invest in specialized machinery; so as the investment in highly specialized machinery increases, output expands rapidly.

Output also expands as labor becomes more specialized. As output increases, workers can be given more and more highly specialized tasks. Henry Ford recognized the benefits associated with the simultaneous specialization of labor and machinery, and took advantage of these when he introduced the production line to manufacture automobiles. Prior to Ford's innovation, automobiles were built by laying out all of the parts in front of the workers and having them put the car together like a giant Lego set. Each worker was required to do multiple tasks. Working on Ford's production line was completely different: each worker was trained to do one small task, such as mounting the steering wheel on the chassis or tightening the lug nuts on the wheels. As tasks became more and more narrowly defined, workers became more and more adept at their particular task and output increased substantially. Ford's production line combined highly specialized machin-

specialization

The narrowing of tasks performed by an input such as labor or machinery.

ery with highly specialized workers to produce a very large number of automobiles in a short amount of time.

LOSS OF MANAGERIAL CONTROL AND DECREASING RETURNS TO SCALE

Decreasing returns to scale may seem like an unlikely possibility, because even after a firm has exhausted all of the advantages associated with specialization, it might seem that the firm should be able to double the quantities of all its inputs and double output. Duplication of the production process should, therefore, result in a doubling of output, and constant returns to scale. Economists, however, have suggested one primary reason for the existence of decreasing returns to scale. Even in the long run, some inputs may be scarce, and therefore, the firm cannot increase these inputs proportionally with all other inputs. The most commonly cited scarce input is high quality managerial talent. Because of a shortage of managerial talent, organizational problems of control arise as the firm becomes larger. When firms become very large, some managers may have little, if any, idea about what's going on at lower organizational levels in their firms. The apparent loss of hierarchical control was mightily apparent in the collapse of the energy industry giant

---

▲▲▲ 7.2 APPLICATION   The Collapse of Enron

There are few better examples of a corporation's loss of managerial control than the case of the financial collapse of Enron. Enron was founded in the 1980s as a small gas-producing company, which later expanded into gas pipelines, and eventually into trading in the natural gas market. Apparently unbeknown to many of Enron's executives and most of its board of directors, in 2000, some managers began to set up a sophisticated scheme of partnerships to increase the company's reported accounting profits. The diagram on the right shows how the scheme worked. First, Enron set up a legal entity called a *partnership* using its own stock to fund the ostensibly independent new company. Second, the new partnership signed a contract with Enron whereby it agreed to pay Enron if Enron's stock price, and therefore, the company's value, decreased. Third, as the stock price of Enron declined, the partnership made a payment to Enron that was posted on Enron's books as "profit," even though the money used to make the payment was Enron's own money, which Enron had used to establish the partnership in the first place! When the illegal scheme was discovered, it ultimately led to Enron's bankruptcy. Virtually all of Enron's lower-level employees lost their jobs, and more importantly for many, lost their retirement savings that were forcibly tied up in Enron stock. Adding to the anger and resentment of these employees, some of the top executives had sold their Enron stock before the price collapsed from an all-time high of more than $90 per share to less than $1.

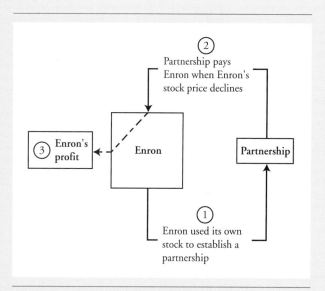

The scandal came to light in large part because Sherron Watkins, an Enron employee, became aware of what was going on and began to talk. According to Watkins, Enron's chief executive officer (CEO) Kenneth Lay had no knowledge of the scheme and was duped by two other executives, Jeffrey Skilling and Andrew Fastow. Testifying before Congress in May 2002, four members of Enron's board of directors also claimed to have had no knowledge of the partnership scheme. Here is a tragic example of what can happen when there is a loss of managerial control at the highest levels of a corporation.

Enron in 2001. In such cases, proportional increases in managerial inputs result in less-than-proportional increases in output and decreasing returns to scale.

Returns to Varying Proportions in the Short Run

Returns to scale are important in the long run, because only in the long run can the firm change *all* the factors it uses. As scale is changed—that is, as all inputs are doubled, or tripled, or expanded by any common factor—the proportions in which they are mixed remain unchanged. In the short run, however, at least one factor is fixed, so changing the scale of operations is never an option. Instead, the firm needs to know how output will respond when it changes some factors and holds others constant. Of course, as it does this, it necessarily changes the proportions in which the various factors are being combined. When we speak of the **returns to varying proportions**, we refer to how output responds when the firm applies inputs in different amounts and in different proportions. These are the most critical properties of the short-run production function.

Panel (a) of Figure 7.6 uses isoquants to illustrate a typical short-run situation with capital fixed at $\overline{K}$. To change output, the firm can change only the amount of labor it

returns to varying proportions

How output changes when inputs are varied in both their amounts and proportions.

Figure 7.6 Deriving the Short-Run Total Product Curve

In panel (a), capital is fixed at $\overline{K}$ units and output is 100 at point A and 200 at point B. In panel (b), the horizontal axis measures units of labor input and the vertical axis measures output, so at point A, output is 100 when L_0 units of labor are employed; and at point B, output is 200 when L_1 units of labor are employed. Continuing in this manner, it is possible to identify all of the points that make up the *SRTP* curve in panel (b).

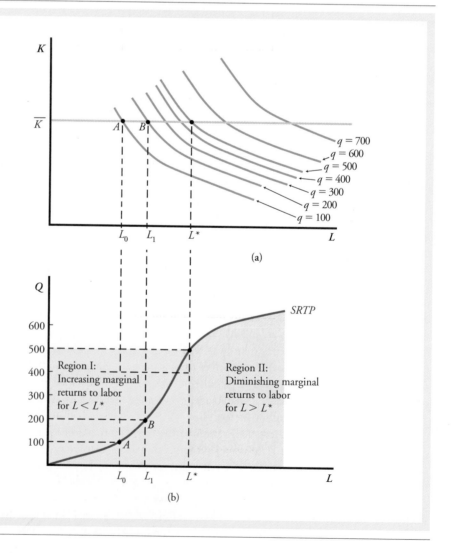

uses. As it does so, the proportion of capital to labor, $\overline{K}/L$, will also change, and the firm will move out along the horizontal line at $K = \overline{K}$. How the isoquants are shaped and how they are spaced as we move out through that isoquant map along such horizontal lines tells the firm everything it needs to know about production in the short run.

Now look at panel (b) of Figure 7.6. This panel shows a labor axis parallel to the one in panel (a), and a vertical quantity axis carefully marked off with equal 100-unit increments in output. Moving out the horizontal line at $K = \overline{K}$ in panel (a), we can plot against each quantity of labor the amount of output produced when that quantity of labor is combined with $\overline{K}$ units of capital. In panel (a), L_0 units of labor combined with $\overline{K}$ units of capital produce 100 units of output at point A. So, in panel (b), L_0 is plotted against 100 units of output on the vertical Q axis at point A. Similarly, in panel (a), L_1 units of labor together with $\overline{K}$ of capital produce 200 units of output at point B, so in panel (b), L_1 is plotted against 200 on the vertical Q axis, and so on. Proceeding in this way for each of the infinite possible amounts of labor input and output, we obtain the curve labeled *SRTP*. This **short-run total product curve**, derived from the isoquant map in panel (a), tells the firm precisely how much of the variable input, labor, it needs to use with the fixed capital, $\overline{K}$, to produce any level of output.

The *SRTP* curve conveys useful information. For example, recall that the marginal product of labor is the change in output per unit change in labor input, holding the amount of capital constant, or $MP_L = \Delta Q / \Delta L$. A look at the graph should convince you that this is precisely the definition of the slope of the *SRTP* curve. Thus, by looking at how the slope of the *SRTP* behaves as L increases, we see how the MP_L behaves as the firm adds more and more labor to its fixed capital.

The *SRTP* curve in panel (b) of Figure 7.6 has a fairly typical shape, reflecting typical behavior of the MP_L. Notice first that in the identified range, the slope is positive everywhere, so labor is always a productive factor. Now look at the curvature of the *SRTP* curve. When the firm starts adding the first few units of labor, the slope of the *SRTP* curve is positive and increasing. Region I in panel (b) of Figure 7.6 (shaded yellow) is therefore a region of increasing MP_L: as the firm adds more labor, the incremental output produced increases. Beyond L^*, however, when output exceeds 500, the curvature changes. The slope of the *SRTP* remains positive, but throughout Region II (shaded blue) it is everywhere declining. This is the region of diminishing marginal returns: as more and more labor is added to the fixed capital, the firm experiences continuously diminishing increments in output as each successive unit of labor has less and less of the fixed capital to work with.

Notice, though, that since the *SRTP* curve is derived from the isoquant map, all information we can glean from the *SRTP* curve should be available directly from the isoquant map—and indeed it is. Refer again to panel (a) of Figure 7.6, and look at the horizontal line drawn at $K = \overline{K}$ units of capital. Remember that in Figure 7.6 each successive isoquant indicates an *equal* 100-unit increment in output, so moving from one isoquant to another always involves a constant $\Delta Q = 100$. At the same time, the horizontal distance between successive isoquants measures the increment in labor, ΔL, needed to produce the next such increment in output. Moving along that horizontal line, it is clear that the extra labor it takes to produce equal 100 increments of output gets smaller and smaller up to a total output of 500 units, and then becomes larger and larger thereafter. With ΔQ held constant, the ratio $\Delta L / \Delta Q$ must follow the same pattern: first it gets smaller and smaller up to $Q = 500$, then it gets larger and larger thereafter. But that means its reciprocal, $\Delta Q / \Delta L = MP_L$, first gets larger and larger, and then gets smaller and smaller as output moves beyond 500 units. And there we have our insight! Holding capital fixed along a horizontal line in panel (a), when successive isoquants giving equal increments in output are spaced closer and closer together, the MP_L

short-run total product curve

A curve identifying how much output is produced when the amount of a variable input is changed, holding all other inputs fixed.

slope of $SRTP = MP_L = \Delta Q / \Delta L$

is increasing as in Region I of the *SRTP* curve. By contrast, when successive isoquants giving equal increments in output are spaced farther and farther apart as L increases, the MP_L is decreasing, and we have a region of diminishing marginal returns to labor, as in Region II of the *SRTP* curve.

The point to remember is this: The isoquant map is a complete representation of the production function, so it will always reflect every technological reality the firm must contend with in transforming inputs into output. What are the returns to scale? Where do diminishing marginal returns begin to set in? All of this and more is there for you to uncover.

▼▼▼   ## 7.3   Costs

Firms always complain about costs. Pick up the financial section of today's newspaper and chances are you will see at least one article in which some group of firms is complaining about its costs being too high. Maybe shifting demographics have made it more expensive to hire and train workers; or maybe the government is considering a new tax on some critical input, such as fuel oil or electricity. Firms care so much about their costs because controlling cost is fully half the battle in making profit.

Accounting Costs Versus Economic Costs

accounting costs

The costs reported by book-keepers in a firm's official financial statement.

economic cost

The value of an input in its best alternative employment; that is, the opportunity cost of using the input.

Before developing the theory of costs, we have to clarify what economists mean by "costs," distinguishing between accounting costs and economic costs. **Accounting costs** are the costs reported by firms in their financial reports following various book-keeping conventions. The **economic cost** of an input is the payment that input would receive in its best alternative employment. The definition of economic costs draws on the concept of the opportunity cost of a good: the value of the resources used to produce that good in their best alternative use.

It is the economic costs that are relevant for our purposes. A good way to understand the distinction between accounting and economic costs is to use each to measure the costs of various inputs. For some inputs, the cost as measured by accountants and economists are the same. An example is labor hired at some hourly wage. Consider a firm that hires four workers at the going wage of $15 per hour. An accountant would measure the cost of the four workers as the out-of-pocket expenditures of $60. To calculate the opportunity cost, an economist would assume that the going wage of $15 per hour is the amount that the labor services would earn in their best alternative employment. The economic cost of hiring four workers for one hour would thus also be $60.

rental rate

The amount that another firm would pay to use a unit of capital for a specified period of time—typically an hour or a day.

For other inputs, accounting costs and economic costs differ considerably. Two important categories are capital and labor inputs supplied by the owners of a firm. Consider a machine that is owned by a firm. An accountant would determine how much of the original price of the machine to charge to current costs by applying a standard accounting depreciation formula based on the original cost of the machine. Economists, however, want to know the opportunity cost of using that machine for one hour of production. This implicit cost is the **rental rate**: the amount that another firm would be willing to pay for the use of the machine for an hour. By continuing to use the machine, the firm is implicitly choosing to give up the rental income it could earn from another firm. A similar distinction between accounting cost and economic cost arises in the case of labor services supplied to a firm by its owner. An accountant would not count the value of any unpaid owner's services supplied to the firm as part of the firm's cost. An economist, however, would ask what an owner could have earned in her best alternative employment opportunity. This opportunity cost would be included as part of economic costs.

Because accounting and economic costs differ, accounting profits and economic profits differ. Economic profits are typically smaller than accounting profits, because accountants do not count the value of any labor and capital inputs supplied by the owners of the firm. Throughout this chapter, whenever we refer to costs, we mean economic costs, not accounting costs.

Sunk Costs

Most costs must be taken into account when firms make decisions about the future. There is, however, one type of cost that should not affect a firm's future decisions or actions: sunk costs. **Sunk costs** are costs that have already been incurred by the firm and can never be recovered. To distinguish non-recoverable sunk costs from recoverable costs, consider two types of fixed costs for a new restaurant owner: the $500,000 cost of building the restaurant and the $20,000 in advertising expenditures to announce the restaurant's opening. Both costs are fixed, because they are independent of the restaurant's output. If the restaurant fails and the owner decides to leave the market, he can sell the $500,000 building to another potential restaurant owner, and therefore can recover at least part of the cost of building the restaurant. Suppose he can sell the restaurant for the full $500,000 that it cost him to build it. The entire $500,000 cost of building the restaurant therefore is a recoverable fixed cost. However, if the owner leaves the market, he cannot recover any of the $20,000 in advertising expenditures, and therefore his advertising expenditures are a non-recoverable sunk cost. Signing bonuses paid to professional athletes are one common example of sunk costs. Because signing bonuses are a sunk cost, they are irrelevant to a team's future decision concerning whether to keep, trade, or release a player.

sunk costs

Costs that have already been incurred and cannot be recovered.

Costs in the Short Run

The firm must always make choices during the production process. How much labor should be used? How much capital will the labor need to work with? How large an inventory of materials should be kept? It's always possible that some firm might make foolish choices: it might hire more workers than it needs, leaving some workers to just stand around and watch; it might rent extra machines and let them stand idle. Often, when firms lament their "rising costs" and declare their determination to cut them by "eliminating waste," it is precisely this sort of inefficiency they intend to correct. Whenever more profit can be squeezed out by eliminating waste, firm owners would be expected to attempt to do so, because waste-reduction directly increases profit. Thus, cost-minimization goes hand-in-hand with profit-maximization, and economists assume that in every production decision the firm makes, it keeps these twin and inseparable goals firmly in mind.

The prices firms must pay to acquire the inputs they need are crucial to the goal of cost minimization. Few firms are large enough to affect the price they pay for inputs, and therefore, most firms, like most consumers, are price takers. If the firm must pay a fixed market wage, w, for every unit of labor, and a fixed market price, r, per unit of capital services, the total outlay it must make to acquire a combination of L units of labor and K units of capital is the sum of what the firm spends on labor, wL, and what the firm spends on capital, rK, so that:

$$\text{total outlay on factor bundle } (L,K) = wL + rK$$

In producing any level of output, the profit-maximizing firm chooses, from among all of the alternative efficient production plans on the firm's isoquants, the plan that minimizes its total outlay on factors of production. With two factors, L and K, therefore, the formal requirements for cost minimization when the firm faces factor prices w and r are:

$$\text{minimum cost of producing } Q \text{ units of output} = \min (wL + rK) \qquad (7.3)$$

$$\text{subject to } Q = f(L, K) \qquad (7.4)$$

Equations 7.3 and 7.4 say that the cost of producing output Q is the minimum total outlay on inputs $wL + rK$ that can be achieved by choosing from alternative input combinations for which $Q = f(L, K)$. This last condition in Equation 7.4, "subject to $Q = f(L, K)$," is our reminder that the chosen input combination must be capable of producing the output level Q we have in mind.

Because capital is fixed at $\overline{K}$ in the short run, the firm has fewer choices in the short run when deciding how it will produce its output. In terms of the conditions given in Equations 7.3 and 7.4, the *short-run total cost* (*SRTC*) of producing output level Q is:

$$SRTC = \min (wL + r\overline{K}) \qquad (7.5)$$

$$\text{subject to } Q = f(L, \overline{K}) \qquad (7.6)$$

As before, costs arise from the outlay the firm must make on the inputs it uses to produce Q. In the short run, however, the firm must use $\overline{K}$ units of capital. With only two factors, one of which is fixed, the only remaining choice the firm must make is how much labor to use.

The short-run production function $Q = f(L, \overline{K})$ not only identifies precisely how much output will be produced when labor L is applied to the fixed capital $\overline{K}$, but it also identifies how much labor is needed to produce an output of Q, given $\overline{K}$ units of capital. Mathematically, this amounts to *inverting* the short-run production function $Q = f(L, \overline{K})$ in Equation 7.6 to obtain $L = L(Q)$. Doing so presents the same information about how output is related to inputs in the short run, but it does so in a more convenient way by identifying labor input L as a function of output Q.

By substituting the inverse production function $L = L(Q)$ for L in Equation 7.5, we can rewrite short-run total cost as:

$$SRTC = \min(wL(Q) + r\overline{K}) \qquad (7.7)$$

short-run variable cost

The total cost of using all of the inputs whose levels vary with output.

short-run fixed cost

The total cost of using all of the inputs whose levels are fixed in the short run.

Here, the term $wL(Q)$ is the cost of the labor required to produce output Q. The costs of inputs such as labor, whose use varies with the level of output, are called **short-run variable costs**. The term $r\overline{K}$ is the cost the firm must bear for its fixed capital. The costs of fixed inputs, such as capital in the short run, are the firm's **short-run fixed costs**. Letting $VC = wL(Q)$ stand for short-run variable costs, and $FC = r\overline{K}$ stand for fixed costs, Equation 7.7 implies:

$$SRTC = VC + FC \qquad (7.8)$$

Equation 7.8 emphasizes that there are two very different types of cost in the short run: variable costs, or the cost of the firm's variable factors; and fixed costs, or the cost of the firm's fixed factors.

short-run marginal cost

The change in total cost (or total variable cost) associated with the production of one additional unit of output, holding at least one input fixed.

Often we want to know how costs change as a result of a small increase or decrease in the level of output. We define **short-run marginal cost**, *SRMC*, as the change in short-run total cost as output changes by a small amount. If ΔQ stands for a small change in output, and $\Delta SRTC$ stands for the resulting change in total cost, then we can interpret short-run marginal cost as the rate of change of short-run total cost:

$$SRMC = \frac{\Delta SRTC}{\Delta Q}$$

total fixed cost

The total cost of all of the inputs whose levels are fixed.

To gain a better understanding of the relationships between various short-run costs, let's work through the numerical example shown in Table 7.3. The second column gives **total fixed costs** (*FC*). In this example, the firm must pay $50 per month even if it produces no output. For example, perhaps the firm has leased a highly specialized piece of machinery, for which no other firm has any use, for $50 per month, and has signed a written agreement to pay the $50 regardless of how many units of output it produces. In this case, the $50 per month payment is a non-recoverable cost, so it is a sunk cost. Even if the firm shuts down, it still is legally obligated to pay the $50 per month.

total variable cost

The total cost of all of the inputs whose levels vary with output.

short-run total cost

The total cost of all inputs used to produce output in the short run.

The third column shows **total variable costs** (*VC*). To produce more output in the short run, the firm must use more variable inputs such as labor, electricity, and raw materials. Because the usage of variable inputs increases with the level of output, variable costs also increase. **Short-run total cost** (*SRTC*), shown in column 4, is the sum of fixed costs and variable costs.

The fifth column in Table 7.3 shows short-run marginal cost (*SRMC*). When output increases from 4 to 5 units, for example, total cost increases from $130 to $150. The marginal cost of the fifth unit of output is thus $20. Because variable cost is the only part

Table 7.3 An Example of Short-Run Costs of Production

Output	FC ($)	VC ($)	SRTC ($)	SRMC ($)	AFC ($)	AVC ($)	SRAC ($)
(1)	(2)	(3)	(4) = (2) + (3)	(5)	(6) = (2)/(1)	(7) = (3)/(1)	(8) = (4)/(1)
0	50	0	0	—	—	—	—
1	50	30	80	30	50.00	30.00	80.00
2	50	49	99	19	25.00	24.50	49.50
3	50	65	115	16	16.67	21.67	38.34
4	50	80	130	15	12.50	20.00	32.50
5	50	100	150	20	10.00	20.00	30.00
6	50	124	174	24	8.33	20.67	29.00
7	50	150	200	26	7.14	21.43	28.57
8	50	180	230	30	6.25	22.50	28.75
9	50	215	265	35	5.56	23.89	29.45
10	50	255	305	40	5.00	25.50	30.50
11	50	300	350	45	4.55	27.27	31.82
12	50	360	410	60	4.17	30.00	34.17

of total cost that changes with the level of output, we can also calculate marginal cost from variable cost. Notice, for example, that variable cost rises from $80 to $100 when output increases from 4 to 5 units, again giving marginal cost of the fifth unit as $20.

Table 7.3 also shows three important measures of average cost per unit of output. **Average fixed cost** (*AFC*) is fixed cost divided by output, or *FC/Q*. Because fixed cost is constant, average fixed cost falls continuously as output increases. **Average variable cost** (*AVC*), shown in column 7 of Table 7.3, is variable cost divided by output, or *VC/Q*. **Short-run average cost** (*SRAC*) (or **short-run average total cost**), shown in column eight, is total cost divided by output *SRTC/Q*. Dividing Equation 7.8 by *Q*, we can also define average total cost as the sum of average fixed cost plus average variable cost.

Figure 7.7 shows the short-run cost curves for a firm. The shapes of these curves are consistent with the data in Table 7.3 and in fact are the typical shapes for short-run cost curves. It is important to note first that the prices (*w* and *r*) of inputs are held constant in drawing these curves; we assume that the firm can hire any quantity of an input at a given price per unit. The *SRAC*, *AVC*, and *SRMC* curves would all shift up if the price of a variable input, such as the price of labor *w*, increased. However, because labor is a variable input, an increase in *w* would not cause the *AFC* curve to shift up.

The short-run marginal cost curve, *SRMC*, in Figure 7.7 is U-shaped. At first, the cost of additional units of output falls as the firm adds more units of labor, the variable input. In most short-run production functions, the firm benefits from specialization and division of labor up to the point of diminishing marginal returns to the variable inputs. In Table 7.3, for example, marginal cost falls until the firm is producing four units of output per month. Eventually, however, the point of diminishing marginal returns must be reached. At this point, short-run marginal cost starts to increase, because the firm must add more and more units of the variable input to obtain an additional unit of output.

In the curves in Figure 7.7, we once again observe the general relationship between marginal and average. As long as the *SRMC* is less than *SRAC*, the *SRAC* curve will decline; and as long as the *SRMC* is greater than *SRAC*, the *SRAC* curve will increase. Therefore, *SRMC* equals *SRAC* precisely at the minimum of the *SRAC* curve. This is shown in Figure 7.7: There, *SRMC* equals *SRAC* at point *B* for output q_2, the minimum

---

average fixed cost (*AFC*) $= FC/Q$

Fixed cost divided by output, or *FC/Q*.

average variable cost (*AVC*) $= VC/Q$

Variable cost divided by output, or *VC/Q*.

short-run average cost (*SRAC*) $= SRTC/Q$

Short-run total cost divided by output, or *SRTC/Q*.

Figure 7.7 Short-run Per Unit Costs for a Typical Firm

The short-run average fixed cost (*AFC*), average variable cost (*AVC*), average total cost (*SRAC*), and marginal cost curves (*SRMC*) have the general shapes depicted in this graph. The *SRMC* curve always intersects the *AVC* and the *SRAC* curves at the minimum points on those two curves, such as points *A* and *B* respectively. The *AFC* curve is always downward-sloping, because fixed costs remain constant as output expands.

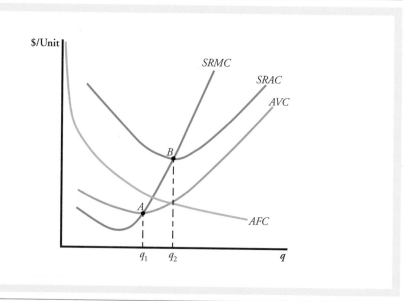

of the *SRAC* curve. Similarly, *SRMC* equals *AVC* at point *A* for output q_1, the minimum of the *AVC* curve.

Derivation of Short–Run Cost Curves from a Cobb-Douglas Production Function

Empirical work on production functions has shown that one special functional form often represents a firm's technology quite well. This is the **Cobb-Douglas production function:**

Cobb-Douglas production function

A commonly used production function of the general form $Q = AL^aK^b$ where Q is the quantity of output; L is the quantity of labor input; K is the quantity of capital input; and A, a, and b are positive constants.

$$Q = f(L,K) = AL^aK^b \qquad (7.9)$$

Here A, a, and b are positive constants. One reason that the Cobb-Douglas production function is so popular is that it is quite flexible. By merely changing the values of the constants A, a, and b, a variety of different technologies can be represented. We can use a specific Cobb-Douglas production function to see how economists derive cost curves directly from production functions. For example, let:

$$Q = L^{1/2}K^{1/2} = \sqrt{L}\sqrt{K} \qquad (7.10)$$

Suppose capital is fixed at $\overline{K} = 100$. Substituting $\overline{K} = 100$ gives us the short-run total product relation:

$$Q = 10L^{1/2} = 10\sqrt{L}$$

Squaring both sides:

$$Q^2 = 100L$$

and solving for L:

$$L = \frac{Q^2}{100} = (0.01)Q^2$$

For fixed factor prices w and r, variable and fixed costs are:

$$VC = wL = w(0.01)Q^2$$

$$FC = r\overline{K} = r(100)$$

Adding *VC* and *FC* together, we get the short-run total cost function:

$$SRTC = VC + FC = w(0.01)Q^2 + r(100)$$

Figure 7.8 graphs this cost function for $w = \$5$ and $r = \$2$. Notice that because fixed costs do not vary with the level of output, the *FC* curve is horizontal at $FC = r(100) = \$2(100) = \$200$. By contrast, variable costs rise with the level of output, and here they rise at an ever-increasing rate. Panels (b) and (c) illustrate the effect of increasing each of the factor prices r and w in turn. In panel (b), an increase in r, the price of the fixed factor, from $\$2$ to $\$4$ causes an upward parallel shift in the fixed cost and total cost curves.

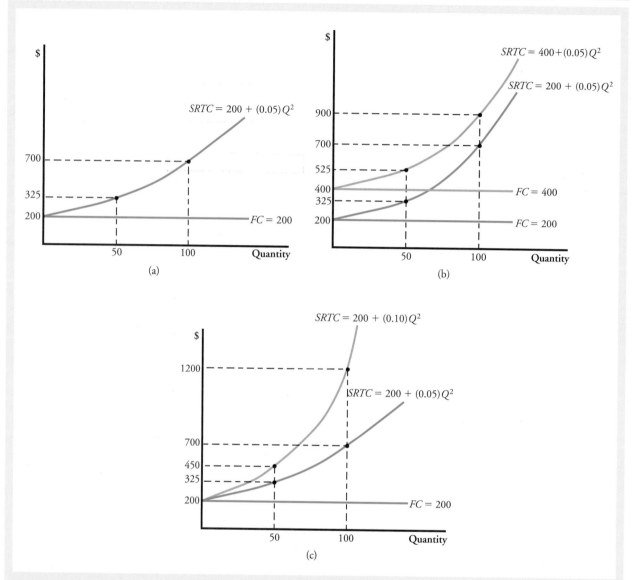

Figure 7.8 Short-Run Cost for the Cobb-Douglas Production Function
Panel (a) is the graph of the short-run total cost curve and fixed cost curve for the Cobb-Douglas production function
$Q = L^{1/2}K^{1/2} = \sqrt{L}\sqrt{K}$ when $w = \$5$ and $r = \$2$. Panel (b) shows the impact of an increase in the price of the fixed input
r from $2 to $4. Both curves shift upward, but the slope of the $SRTC$ curve remains the same for any given output. In panel (c),
$r = \$2$, but the wage increases from $5 to $10, resulting in an upward shift in the $SRTC$ curve, and the $SRTC$ curve becomes
steeper for any given output.

Panel (c) illustrates the effect of an increase in the price of the variable factor to $w = \$10$,
with $r = \$2$. Notice that an increase in w to $10 both shifts the $SRTC$ curve upward and
increases its slope at every level of output, but the FC curve does not shift.

Relationship Between $SRMC$ and MP_L

In the short run, some of the firm's factors are fixed, and so are all costs associated with
them. When the firm increases or decreases output, therefore, although we define $SRMC$

as the change in short-run total cost, only variable cost can be affected by a change in output, so marginal cost must also be equal to the rate of change in variable cost:

$$SRMC = \frac{\Delta VC}{\Delta Q} \qquad (7.11)$$

Let's explore these costs a bit. When labor is the sole variable factor, the only way a firm can increase output in the short run is by increasing the amount of labor it employs. Let ΔQ stand for a small increase in output, and let ΔL be the increase in labor required to produce it. What impact will a change in labor ΔL have on total variable costs? If the firm must pay each additional unit of labor the going wage w, then if labor increases by ΔL, variable cost must increase by $\Delta VC = w\Delta L$. Dividing both sides of this equation by ΔQ, we obtain:

$$SRMC = \frac{\Delta VC}{\Delta Q} = \frac{w(\Delta L)}{\Delta Q} = \frac{w}{\dfrac{\Delta Q}{\Delta L}} = \frac{w}{MP_L} \qquad (7.12)$$

The expression $\Delta L/\Delta Q$ tells us how much extra labor is required to produce an additional unit of output. Its reciprocal, $\Delta Q/\Delta L$, therefore tells us the extra output we could obtain from adding one more unit of labor, which is precisely the marginal product of labor, MP_L. The important relationship in Equation 7.12, therefore, is:

$$SRMC = \frac{w}{MP_L} \qquad (7.13)$$

Equation 7.13 gives us important insights into the very close connection between production and cost in the short run. First, marginal cost will always be positive as long as wages, w, and the marginal product of labor, MP_L, are positive. This confirms common sense: The firm's costs must increase whenever the firm produces more output. Second, by pointing to the reciprocal relationship between $SRMC$ and MP_L, Equation 7.13 tells us that marginal cost will be decreasing, constant, or increasing precisely as the marginal product of labor is increasing, constant, or decreasing, respectively.

▲▲▲ 7.3A APPLICATION   Reform of Fixed and Variable Costs in Hard–Rock Mining

". . . [A]fter eight years in this office, I have come to the conclusion that the most important piece of unfinished business on the nation's resource agenda is the complete replacement of the Mining Law of 1872."
— Stewart Udall, Letter of Resignation
from the Office of Interior Secretary, 1969

Thirty-four years after Secretary Udall made that statement in 1969, the Mining Law of 1872 is still on the books. The law allows miners and prospectors to stake claims on federal lands—and hold them indefinitely—merely by spending a minimum $100 per year on exploration expenses per 20-acre claim. The $100 required annual exploration cost is a fixed cost, because owners must pay this cost regardless of whether they extract any materials from the mine. If the claim holder finds an ore deposit, he or she can purchase, or "patent," the land for as little as $2.50 per acre, which is a fixed cost. Moreover, the claim holder is not required to pay the federal government any royalties or extraction fees, which are variable costs, on ore sold from the claim. The law was originally enacted to encourage miners to settle the West in the nineteenth century. By modern standards, these fixed and variable costs are well below the opportunity cost of using these federal lands.

Numerous problems with the law—commonly related to real estate speculation, increasing foreign ownership of mining companies, and pollution—led to Congressional

(continued)

calls for reform in 1992, 1997, and 2001. The calls for reform are all similar to the bill sponsored in 1992 by former Senator Dale Bumpers of Arkansas, which would have increased both the fixed and the variable costs of hard-rock mining on federal lands. Under the Bumpers bill, required exploration expenses, or fixed costs, per 20-acre claim would have increased from $100 a year to nearly $3,200 a year. Further, the Bumpers bill would have assessed royalties, or variable costs, of 5 percent on the market value of production from federal lands, where currently there are no such variable royalty charges. At a price of $383 per ounce for gold, this would mean a mining company would pay royalties of 0.05 × $383 = $19.15 for every ounce of gold produced. The impact of such a change on mining costs would be huge. For example, consider a company maintaining 30 separate 20-acre claims on federal land.

Suppose the company mines 2000 ounces of gold per year from these lands. Under the Bumpers proposal, this firm's total fixed cost would rise by the increase in required exploration costs equal to $3,100 × 30 = $93,000 per year. Its total variable cost would rise by the full extent of its royalty payments, or by $19.15 × 2000 = $38,300 per year. The impact on total mining cost would be an increase equal to the sum of these two, or $93,000 + $38,300 = $131,300 per year!

The Bumpers bill was never passed by Congress, due to strong lobbying efforts by mining companies. In 1997, however, the Clinton Administration placed a moratorium on the issuing of new patents on federal lands. In March 2001, the Bush Administration suspended the moratorium after a bill was introduced in Congress that would make the moratorium permanent.

Figure 7.9 illustrates the relationship between the MP_L and MC for a production function $Q = f(L,K)$. It shows a $SRMC$ curve that might be faced by a firm having the $SRTP$ curve in panel (b) of Figure 7.6. In panel (b) of Figure 7.6, the MP_L is increasing throughout Region I, and this gives rise to decreasing marginal cost up to an output of 500 units in Figure 7.9. From then on, there are diminishing returns to labor throughout Region II in panel (b) of Figure 7.6, and this gives rise to increasing marginal cost in Figure 7.9 beyond 500 units of output.

Cost in the Long Run

In the long run, there are no fixed inputs; therefore, firms have greater freedom in planning production than they do in the short run. Of course, a firm's goal remains profit

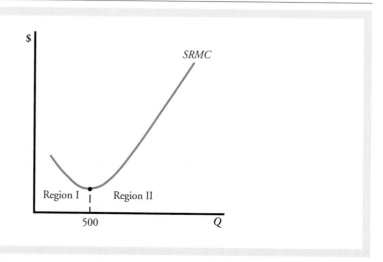

Figure 7.9 The Short-Run Marginal Cost Curve and the Marginal Product of Labor

For production function $Q = f(L,K)$, the $SRMC$ of production is decreasing up to 500 units of output, so we know that the MP_L is increasing up to 500 units of output. Beyond 500 units of output, the $SRMC$ is increasing, so the MP_L must be decreasing.

maximization, and as always, that requires cost minimization. With two factors of production, the long-run total cost (*LRTC*) of output level Q is defined as:

$$LRTC = \min(wL + rK) \tag{7.14}$$

$$\text{subject to } Q = f(L,K) \tag{7.15}$$

These conditions are essentially the same as the short-run total cost conditions introduced in Equations 7.3 and 7.4. They differ in one very important way, however. In the short run, the firm is constrained to use $\overline{K}$ units of the fixed factor. In the long run, the firm must choose how much of each factor it will use to produce its output. When capital and labor are good substitutes, there might be many ways to produce a given level of output; indeed, there could be an infinite number of ways. As a result, the firm faces a more complex cost minimization problem in the long run than it does in the short run. Its goal is still the same—to minimize cost—but its choices, and as a result its challenges, are greater.

To derive long-run total cost, we need to solve the cost-minimization conditions in Equations 7.14 and 7.15. With only two factors, that problem can be solved graphically, but it requires a new analytic tool. That tool, an **isocost curve**, shows all the different combinations of K and L that the firm can buy for a fixed amount of money at prevailing factor prices w and r. These curves can be defined for any level of total outlay. In general, letting C_0 be the dollar amount of total outlay, then every combination of K and L that costs C_0 dollars to buy must satisfy:

$$C_0 = wL + rK \tag{7.16}$$

Using algebra to rearrange Equation 7.16, K can be expressed as a function of L, C_0, w, and r, as follows:

$$K = \frac{C_0}{r} - \frac{w}{r}L \tag{7.17}$$

Equation 7.17 looks remarkably similar to the budget constraint in consumer theory. In the (L, K) plane of Figure 7.10, the graph of Equation 7.17 is a straight line with slope $-w/r$. Notice that $-w/r$ is always the slope, regardless of the level of outlay C_0. The intercepts, however, depend on the level of outlay: for an outlay of C_0, the vertical intercept is C_0/r, and the horizontal intercept is C_0/w. Isocost curves for greater total outlays, such as C_1 and C_2 in Figure 7.10, will have larger intercepts and lie farther out from the origin. Isocost curves giving less expensive input combinations lie closer in toward the origin.

Isocost curves, along with isoquants, can be used to solve the firm's cost-minimization problem. Suppose that output is Q_0. In Figure 7.11, any combination of K and L that lies along the Q_0-level isoquant is capable of producing Q_0 units of output. For example, the combination (L_0, K_0) at point A produces output Q_0, but it does not do so at the lowest total cost. We discover this fact by moving up that isoquant to the northwest, where we can find another combination, such as (L_1, K_1) at point B that also produces output Q_0. Point B, however, lies on a lower isocost curve than point A does, indicating that it requires a smaller total outlay to acquire the input combination (L_1, K_1) at point B. To find the least costly solution, it is necessary to find the combination of inputs that lies on the lowest possible isocost curve while still remaining on the

Figure 7.10 Identifying a Firm's Isocost Lines
There are an infinite number of isocost lines each with a slope equal to -1 times the input price ratio of the input measured on the horizontal axis over the input measured on the vertical axis; in this case, -1 times the price of labor over the price of capital, or $-w/r$. Along any one isocost line, the total cost of inputs is constant.

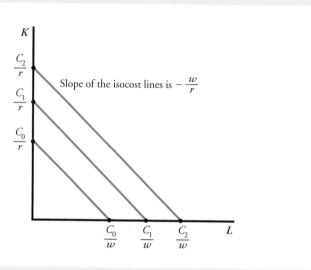

Q_0-level isoquant. That combination will be (L^*, K^*) at point C: the point of tangency between the isoquant in question and the lowest possible isocost curve.

The optimal long-run input choice (L^*, K^*) at point C in Figure 7.11 is distinguished from all the other possible choices because it is the only one that satisfies two conditions simultaneously: first, the slope of the isoquant and the slope of the isocost curve are equal; second, the point (L^*, K^*) lies on the Q_0-level isoquant. The slope of the isocost curve is always equal to $-w/r$, the (signed) ratio of factor prices. Recall that the slope of the isoquant at point $(L,K) = -MP_L/MP_K$; that is, the slope of the isoquant will be equal to the (signed) ratio of the marginal products of labor and capital. To be on the Q_0-level isoquant means that the input combination in question produces Q_0 units of

Figure 7.11 Long-Run Cost Minimization
For any given output, such as Q_0, long-run costs are minimized by using the input combination where the slope of the isoquant equals the slope of the isocost lines. In this case, the optimal input combination is at point C, using L^* units of labor and K^* units of capital with total costs equal to C_0.

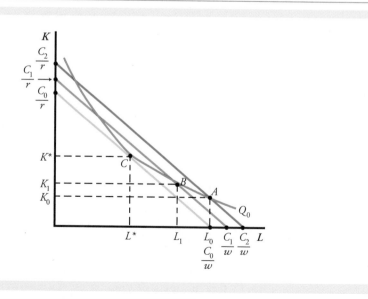

output. It is now possible to write expressions stating the necessary conditions for a solution to the cost-minimization problem. If (L^*, K^*) minimizes costs for output Q_0, then:

$$MRTS = \frac{MP_L}{MP_K} = \frac{w}{r} \tag{7.18}$$

$$f(L^*, K^*) = Q_0 \tag{7.19}$$

Equation 7.18 states that the slope of the isoquant must equal the slope of the isocost line. Equation 7.19 says (L^*, K^*) must produce the level of output, Q_0, in question.

How can we verify that these two equations determine exactly the right combination of capital and labor to produce Q_0 at minimum total cost? Equation 7.19 is straightforward enough. But like similar conditions encountered before, it's not crystal clear why Equation 7.18 is required. To see why, suppose Equation 7.18 did not hold. That is, suppose we were at a point such as A using (L_0, K_0) in Figure 7.11. There, Equation 7.19 is satisfied, but Equation 7.18 is not. Instead, the absolute value of the slope of the isoquant is less than the absolute value of the slope of the isocost curve, or:

$$\frac{MP_L}{MP_K} < \frac{w}{r}$$

which implies that:

$$\frac{MP_L}{w} < \frac{MP_K}{r} \tag{7.20}$$

What interpretation can we give to Inequality 7.20? At point A, the marginal product per dollar spent on labor is less than the marginal product per dollar spent on capital. If the firm substitutes one dollar more of capital for one dollar less of labor, it increases its total output at the same cost. It follows that to maintain its output at Q_0, the firm can substitute less than one dollar's worth of capital for exactly one dollar's worth of labor. If Inequality 7.20 holds, therefore, the firm can produce the output Q_0 at lower total cost by using more capital and less labor. Only when Equation 7.18 holds is it impossible for the firm to rearrange its input mix to lower cost, and only then will cost be minimized. This is the condition for long-run cost minimization.

▲▲▲ 7.3B APPLICATION The Use of Industrial Robots in United States Automobile Manufacturing

Many people were alarmed by Steven Spielberg's and Stanley Kubrick's futuristic view of the world presented in the movie *AI* (Artificial Intelligence), which suggested that machines might one day replace most workers, and, for that matter, most people. A more realistic present-day concern has been that of industrial robots taking over many human manufacturing jobs. The first wide-scale utilization of industrial robots in the United States occurred in the 1980s in the automobile industry. At the time, managers in automobile manufacturing expected the coming of robots to herald great changes in how cars were made. Indeed, during the 1980s, the chairman of General Motors, Roger B. Smith, remarked, "Every time the cost of labor goes up a dollar an hour, a thousand more robots become economical." Smith—like many others—apparently believed that human labor and

(continued)

robots were highly substitutable in production. For if small changes in the relative price of two inputs lead to large changes in the amounts of those inputs used, then the two inputs must be close substitutes.

Recent evidence suggests that Roger Smith may have been right. Average hourly earnings for production workers in the motor vehicle and equipment industry in the United States rose from $9.85 per hour in 1980 to $14.79 per hour in 1990, and to $19.58 per hour in 2000—an increase of 98.8 percent in twenty years. Conversely, the price of industrial robots fell by nearly 90 percent over roughly the same twenty-year period. These price changes resulted in a whopping 1,988 percent increase in the relative price of labor compared to robots. In 1999, orders for industrial robots increased by 60 percent in the United States; and in 2000, investment in robots increased by another 25 percent as 100,000 new robots were installed in American factories. A large percentage of these new robots were installed in American automobile plants. By 2001, approximately 750,000 robots were in use throughout the world, many in the United States automobile industry.

Some Comparative Statistics

So far we've seen that the amounts of capital and labor that minimize cost depend on the input prices and the level of output. The cost-minimizing amounts of labor and capital are therefore best viewed as *functions* of factor prices and the level of output, which can be written as $L^* = L(Q, w, r)$ and $K^* = K(Q, w, r)$. To explore how these functions behave when factor prices and the level of output change, take a look at Figure 7.12.

Panel (a) illustrates the effect of a change in relative input prices, holding output constant at Q_0. Notice that in choosing the least-cost input combination to produce Q_0, only *relative* input prices matter, not *absolute* price levels. In other words, the point of tangency between the Q_0-level isoquant and the lowest isocost curve remains at point A as long as relative input prices remain equal to w/r. Point A marks the optimal combination of capital and labor to use to produce Q_0 regardless of whether input prices are w and r, $2w$ and $2r$, or tw and tr for any $t > 0$.

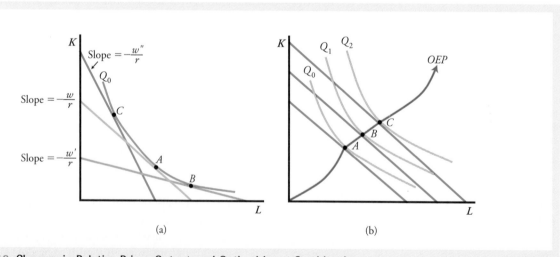

Figure 7.12 Changes in Relative Prices, Output, and Optimal Input Combinations

In panel (a), if the input prices are w and r respectively, the firm uses the input combination at point A to produce an output of Q_0. If the wage decreases to w', the optimal input combination to produce Q_0 is at point B. If the wage increases to w'', the optimal input combination is at point C. In panel (b), the blue input expansion path, OEP, represents all of the possible optimal input combinations for a given input price ratio.

When relative prices change, however, the firm will respond in sensible ways. If the price of labor decreases to $w' < w$; the relative price of labor falls from w/r to w'/r, the slope of the isocost curves falls, and the least-cost choice to produce Q_0 moves from A to B. As labor becomes relatively cheaper compared to capital, the firm responds by adopting more labor-intensive methods to produce any given level of output. By contrast, if the price of labor increases to $w'' > w$; the relative price of labor rises to $w''/r > w/r$, the slope of the isocost curves rises, and the least-cost input combination to produce Q_0 shifts to point C as the firm adopts more capital-intensive production methods at every level of output.

Panel (b) of Figure 7.12 depicts how the firm's choice of technique changes with changes in the level of output, holding relative factor prices constant. As output increases from Q_0 to Q_1 to Q_2, the firm's input choices follow the blue path labeled *OEP*. This **output expansion path** (*OEP*) for a given input price ratio w/r is the locus of all points of tangency between every possible isoquant and the corresponding lowest possible isocost curve. Because there are an infinite number of possible points of tangency between the isoquants and isocost curves, there are an infinite number of points that make up the *OEP*. The output expansion path traces out precisely how the firm should expand its use of capital and labor together as it expands output in the long run. Here, the firm always increases both labor and capital as output increases, but the optimal mix of these two inputs varies with the level of output.

Once we find the values of K^* and L^* that minimize the cost of Q_0—either graphically, by looking for the tangency, or analytically, by solving Equations 7.18 and 7.19—we can find the long-run total cost of producing Q_0 by solving Equations 7.14 and 7.15 for $L = L^*$ and $K = K^*$. The resulting *LRTC* is:

$$LRTC = wL^* + rK^* \qquad (7.21)$$

output expansion path (*OEP*)

The locus of points of tangency between every possible isoquant and the corresponding lowest possible isocost curve.

▼▼▼ 7.4 The Relationship Between Short- and Long-Run Cost

Long-run and short-run costs are closely related, although it can be difficult to see how without recalling the basic difference between the short run and the long run. In the long run, the firm may freely choose how best to combine all factors to produce its output. In the short run, by contrast, it must contend with fixed amounts of one or more inputs, and so the firm does not enjoy the same freedom of action as it does in the long run. The implication is that for any level of output, short-run cost will always be greater than or equal to long-run cost. In fact, for most output levels, long-run cost will be strictly lower than short-run cost, as the firm takes full advantage of the extra degrees of freedom it enjoys in the long run to minimize cost.

Figure 7.13 shows the general relationship between short-run and long-run costs. In the short run, the firm is constrained to use $\overline{K}$ units of capital. Facing factor prices w and r, the firm produces output Q_0 by operating at point A—it has no other choice in the short run. In the long run, however, facing those same factor prices, the firm economizes on capital, choosing to produce Q_0 with the less capital-intensive method at point B. Because B lies on a strictly lower isocost curve than A, the $LRTC < SRTC$ at output level Q_0. Similarly, to produce Q_3 in the short run the firm must operate at point C. In the long run, it chooses the more labor-intensive method at point D to minimize cost. Since D is on a lower isocost curve than C, once again $LRTC < SRTC$ for $Q = Q_3$.

Figure 7.13 Short-Run Versus Long-Run Expansion Paths and Costs

With capital fixed at $\overline{K}$ units, in the short run, the firm must operate along the green expansion path running from points A to E to C. In the long run, the firm can utilize any amount of capital and operates along the blue expansion path. Stuck with $\overline{K}$ units of capital in the short run, the firm's short-run costs of production are higher than its long-run costs of production for every output except Q_2, because the green short-run expansion path intersects the blue long-run expansion path only at point E.

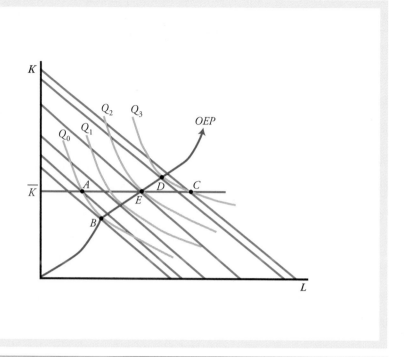

Checking virtually any other level of output, the story will be the same; in the long run, the firm's greater freedom of action enables it to achieve lower cost. For any fixed level of capital $\overline{K}$, there will always be one exception to this, though. For example, in Figure 7.13, the green horizontal line $K = \overline{K}$ and the blue output expansion path OEP intersect at point E. In the short run, the firm would be forced to operate at E to produce Q_2 units; in the long run, it would freely choose that same combination of capital and labor to produce Q_2 at minimum cost. Long-run and short-run costs will therefore be equal at point E, so $LRTC = SRTC$ at an output of Q_2.

The conclusion from this analysis is that given fixed input prices, $LRTC \leq SRTC$ for any level of output produced. Whenever we graph long-run and short-run cost curves on the same set of axes, this means the long-run total cost curve is the lower envelope curve of the various short-run total cost curves, each of which is derived assuming a different amount of the fixed input. An **envelope curve** is a curve that is derived entirely from a series of points taken from other curves.

envelope curve

A curve that is derived entirely from a series of points taken from other curves.

Figure 7.14 shows the relationship between long-run average cost and short-run average cost. Suppose there are only four plant sizes to choose from. Associated with each plant size is a short-run cost curve, shown as $SRAC_1$, $SRAC_2$, and so on. The optimal plant size depends on the output level being produced: the firm should use plant size 1 for output q_1, but plant size 2 for output q_2. The long-run average cost curve is the red portion of each of the short-run curves, because each of these segments shows the lowest possible average cost for the corresponding level of output.

Typically, a firm will have many more than four plant sizes to choose among. As the number of possible plant sizes increases, the long-run average cost curve becomes smoother. Eventually, it becomes a smooth envelope curve with each point on the curve associated with a different possible plant size. The orange envelope curve in Figure 7.14 is the long-run average cost curve.

Figure 7.14 The Relationship Between Short-Run and Long-Run Average Costs
If there were only four possible plant sizes to choose from and those plants could produce with short-run average costs $SRAC_1$, $SRAC_2$, $SRAC_3$, and $SRAC_4$ respectively, then in the long run, the firm would choose the lowest cost plant to produce any given output. The long-run average cost curve would therefore be the red portion of each of the four short-run curves. As the number of possible plant sizes becomes very large, the long-run average cost curve, LRAC, becomes the smooth orange envelope curve.

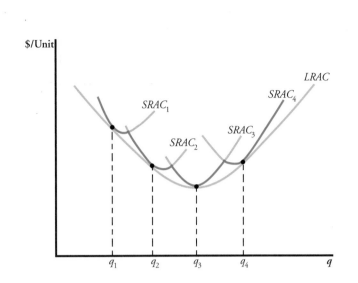

7.5 Returns to Scale and Long-Run Cost

Recall that returns to scale refers to how output behaves as all inputs are varied simultaneously and in equal proportion. Because all inputs are changing simultaneously, returns to scale is a long-run concept. Because the firm may vary all its inputs simultaneously in the long run, the production function's returns to scale will have an important influence on the firm's long-run costs. First, consider some of the unique properties of production functions with constant returns to scale. If a production function $Q = f(L,K)$ exhibits constant returns to scale, the following conditions must hold for any $a > 0$:

$$aQ = f(aL,aK) \tag{7.22}$$

Given fixed factor prices w and r, long-run average total costs for Q and aQ respectively, are:

$$LRAC(Q) = \frac{wL + rK}{Q} \tag{7.23}$$

$$LRAC(aQ) = \frac{waL + raK}{aQ} = \frac{a(wL + rK)}{aQ} = \frac{wL + rK}{Q} = LRAC(Q) \tag{7.24}$$

It follows directly from Equations 7.23 and 7.24 that long-run average total costs are constant for any production function that exhibits constant returns to scale.

Now suppose a production function exhibits increasing returns to scale, so:

$$f(L,K) = Q_0$$

$$f(2L,2K) = Q_1 > 2Q_0$$

For example, suppose $f(L, K) = f(50, 10) = 100$, so that 50 units of labor and 10 units of capital result in a maximum output of 100 units of output and $f(L, K) = f(100, 20) = 250$. This production function exhibits increasing returns to scale in the range of inputs because doubling all inputs more than doubles output. Therefore, given fixed factor prices w and r doubling all inputs exactly doubles total costs, but more than doubles output, so *LRAC* must decrease. In the case of increasing returns to scale, *LRAC* must be decreasing, and we say there are economies of scale in production. **Economies of scale** exist whenever there are increasing returns to scale in the production function and fixed factor prices resulting in a downward-sloping *LRAC* curve. In Figure 7.15 (a) economies of scale exist because the *LRAC* is entirely downward-sloping.

economies of scale

A term used to describe a long-run cost function where *LRAC* are decreasing so the *LRAC* curve is downward-sloping.

Figure 7.15 Long-run Average Cost with Economies and Diseconomies of Scale
In panel (a), the *LRAC* curve is sloping downward everywhere, and therefore, given fixed factor prices, the production function must exhibit economies of scale for all outputs. In panel (b), the *LRAC* curve is sloping upward everywhere, and therefore, the production function must exhibit diseconomies of scale for all outputs.

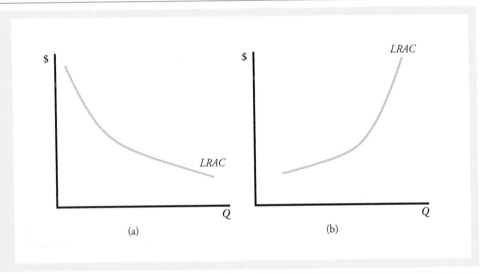

(a)   (b)

COMMON ERROR 7.2 Incorrectly Explaining the Existence of Economies of Scale

Here is a question I ask my students every semester. Holding relative factor prices constant, what do economists mean when they say that economies of scale exist? The answers I receive typically include one or all of the following, all of which are wrong:

1. "When price declines, output increases." I always find this one particularly interesting, because this is simply a slight misstatement of the law of demand!

2. "Increasing marginal returns exist." This answer relates to a *short-run* phenomenon in which before reaching the point of diminishing returns, marginal products increase and marginal costs decline. But economies of scale are a *long-run* concept, where all the inputs are changed by some fixed proportion.

3. "The average cost curve declines." This is getting closer, but which average cost curve is the student talking about, *SRAC* or *LRAC*? *SRAC* curves decline whenever short-run marginal costs are less than short-run average costs, holding at least one input fixed. This is not related to economies of scale, because once again, the student is referring to a short-run concept.

What is the correct answer? Economies of scale exist whenever (holding relative input prices constant) a production function exhibits increasing returns to scale, and therefore, the *LRAC* curve is downward-sloping. That's all there is to it! When you hear the term "economies of scale," you should immediately think of three things: the long run, increasing returns to scale, and a downward-sloping *LRAC* curve.

Finally, suppose that a production function exhibits decreasing returns to scale, so:

$$f(L,K) = Q_0$$

$$f(2L,2K) = Q_1 < 2Q_0$$

diseconomies of scale

A term used to describe a long-run cost function where $LRAC$ are increasing so the $LRAC$ curve is upward-sloping.

For example, suppose $f(L, K) = f(50, 10) = 100$, and $f(L, K) = f(100, 20) = 180$. This production function exhibits decreasing returns to scale, because doubling all inputs less than doubles output. Therefore, doubling all inputs exactly doubles total cost, but less than doubles output, so $LRAC$ must increase. In the case of decreasing returns to scale, $LRAC$ are increasing, and there are **diseconomies of scale** in production. In Figure 7.15 (b), diseconomies of scale exist and the $LRAC$ is entirely upward-sloping.

▲▲▲ 7.5 APPLICATION   Scale Economies in New York State Nursing Homes

Medicaid and Medicare often cover the nursing home expenses of needy and elderly citizens. Usually, the government reimburses nursing homes for the care they give at some fixed rate per patient-day. In setting that rate, the government needs to know a good deal about the long-run average cost of patient-days in nursing homes.

In one study of nursing home costs, Paul J. Gertler and Donald M. Waldman (no relation to the author of this text) used 1980 data on 279 nursing homes in the state of New York. Gertler and Waldman recognized that the quality of care in nursing homes differed widely, and that the costs of providing care at different levels of quality might well be different. The authors found that not only were the costs of high quality care higher, but there are also significant diseconomies of scale in providing

that level of care. Average costs for average quality care were lower, and roughly constant over the range of output considered. By contrast, Gertler and Waldman found noticeable economies of scale in providing only the lowest-quality (and least-expensive) care in a nursing home size of roughly 500 beds.

Recognizing that economies of scale exist only for the lowest quality of nursing home care complicates the government's problem in deciding upon reimbursement rates for Medicare and Medicaid patients. No matter what reimbursement rate the government sets, nursing homes face powerful incentives to provide only low-cost, low-quality care to take advantage of economies of scale. Good policy-making must acknowledge that there is a significant trade-off between quality and average cost of nursing home care.

Summary

1. According to the profit-maximization hypothesis, the desire to maximize profits guides all decisions of the firm.

2. The production function summarizes the technological relationship between different inputs and the maximum output obtainable. In the short run, one or more factors of production are fixed, and the firm must contend with this limitation in planning production. Specifically, the existence of at least one fixed factor means that diminishing marginal returns eventually set in for the variable factors of production and the law of diminishing returns must hold. The Q-level isoquant contains all input combinations capable of producing Q units of output. With only two inputs, the entire production function can be represented with a map of isoquants. Long-run production functions exhibit constant, increasing, or decreasing return to scale depending on whether output doubles, more than doubles, or less than doubles as all inputs are doubled.

3. The cost of output is the minimum achievable outlay on the inputs necessary to produce it. In the short run, fixed cost is the cost of fixed factors. Variable cost is the cost of variable factors. Before the point of diminishing returns sets in, short-run total costs increase, but at a decreasing rate; after the point of diminishing returns, short-run total costs increase at an increasing rate. To produce output at minimum cost in the long run, the amounts of capital and labor chosen must satisfy the condition $MP_L/MP_K = w/r$.

4. For any level of output the firm's short-run average cost must be greater than or equal to the firm's long-run average cost. Therefore, the firm's *LRAC* curve is an envelope curve that consists of a series of points derived from the firm's many *SRAC* curves.

5. If a firm's production function exhibits constant returns to scale, if factor prices are fixed, its long-run average cost is constant and its *LRAC* curve is a horizontal line. If a firm's production function exhibits increasing returns to scale with fixed factor prices, its long-run average cost is decreasing and its *LRAC* curve is a downward-sloping curve. If a firm's production function exhibits decreasing returns to scale with fixed factor prices, its long-run average cost is increasing and its *LRAC* curve is an upward-sloping curve.

Self-Test Problems

1. A firm purchases capital and labor at fixed input prices of $r = 5$ and $w = 10$, respectively. With the firm's current input mix, the marginal product of capital is $MP_K = 10$ and the marginal product of labor is $MP_L = 10$.

   a. Using an isoquant–isocost graph, show the firm's current input combination.

   b. Could this firm be in a short-run cost-minimizing equilibrium? If not, what should it do to achieve one? Explain carefully.

   c. Could it be in a long-run cost-minimizing equilibrium? If not, what should it do to achieve one? Explain carefully.

   d. Suppose the price of capital increased to 10. What happens to the output expansion path?

   e. Assume capital is a fixed input. When the cost of capital r increases from 5 to 10, what happens to the short-run marginal cost curve? What happens to the short-run average cost curve? What happens to the long-run average cost curve?

2. Pyramid Corporation is currently employing 20 tons of cement and 40 tons of steel to produce 50,000 square feet of shopping space in a mall. Cement costs $20 a ton and steel costs $60 a ton. At the input quantities employed, $MP_c = 12$ and the $MP_s = 6$. Show the situation in an isoquant–isocost diagram. Is Pyramid currently minimizing its long-run costs? If not, what should it do if it wants to produce 50,000 square feet of shopping space at minimum long-run cost? Explain, and show in the diagram. In the long run, what is the *MRTS*?

3. Do the following two production functions exhibit increasing, decreasing, or constant returns to scale? Explain.

$$Q = 0.5KL$$

$$Q = 2L + 3K$$

For one of the two production functions, the *MRTS* is constant. Which one is it, and why?

Questions and Problems for Review

1. Production takes place in a variety of settings, and in a variety of ways. Write down a list with three columns and title the first "Type of Firm," the second "Inputs," and the third "Outputs." Fill in your list indicating the inputs and outputs of about ten or fifteen operations. To get you started, universities use faculty, staff, classrooms, and libraries to produce educated students and research. Keep going.

2. In the first few pages of his book *Small is Beautiful*, E.F. Schumacher says that "[o]ne of the most fateful errors of our age is the belief that the 'problem of production' has been solved." He argues that mechanization and the techniques of mass production have advanced so far that workers have lost the sense of meaning in work and that the environment is being gravely injured as we use up the non-renewable resources of nature at an alarming rate. That is why "it is an absurd and suicidal error to believe that the problem of production has been solved." Schumacher argues that firms should adopt intermediate or so-called "appropriate technologies," ones that give greater regard to environmental and social consequences of production, as well as the economic ones. Do you agree or disagree?

3. True or False? "When MP_L and the MP_K are positive, isoquants can never cross."

4. Equation 7.13 showed that short-run marginal cost was equal to the wage divided by the marginal product of labor; that is, $SRMC = w/MP_L$. Show that average variable cost is equal to the wage divided by the average product of labor; that is, show that $AVC = w/AP_L$.

5. A Leontief production function is given by $Q = \min(L, K)$, which means that output is equal to the smaller or minimum of the two numbers L and K. Sketch a few isoquants for this production function. Are capital and labor substitutes or complements? Explain.

6. Marginal cost equals average cost when average cost is constant. Furthermore, if average cost is U-shaped, $MC = AC$ at the point of minimum average cost. Suppose that total cost is $TC(Q) = Q^2 + 4$. The associated marginal cost is $MC(Q) = 2Q$. Sketch the MC and AC curves on the same set of axes. At what output does average cost reach its minimum? Be precise.

7. Give an algebraic or geometric proof that given fixed factor prices, decreasing returns to scale in production leads to increasing long-run average cost.

8. Suppose the marginal product of labor is greater than the average product of labor at a firm's current level of employment. Is the average product of labor increasing, decreasing, or constant? Explain your answer using a graph. Is this firm's marginal cost greater than, less than, or equal to its average variable cost? Explain your reasoning.

9. Suppose that the current wage is $w = 10$ and the current cost of capital is $r = 10$.

   a. For a typical production function with convex isoquants, is the $MRTS$ constant or variable at points on the firm's long-run output expansion path (OEP)? Draw the long-run output expansion path for your hypothetical production function on a graph.

   b. Suppose the economy takes a downturn and wages decline by 50 percent to 5, but r remains constant at $r = 10$. Show graphically how this change would affect the firm's long-run output expansion path. For any given output, is the $MRTS$ constant or variable at points on the firm's new long-run expansion path?

   c. Does the decrease in wages change the $MRTS$ at any points on the original (before the decrease in w) long-run expansion path?

10. Consider the following set of isoquants for a production function $Q = f(L,K)$. If capital K is fixed at the level $\overline{K}$, carefully draw the short-run total product curve ($SRTP$) for this production function. Label your figure carefully.

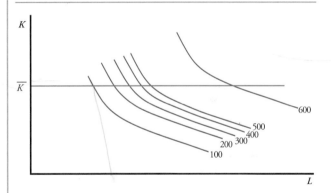

11. Letters Publishing has a production function $f(L,K)$. Currently the wage rate is $10 and the rental rate for capital is $5. Letters Publishing is producing at a point on an isoquant where $MRTS = 3K/1L$. Is the firm minimizing its long-run costs? If not, what should Letters Publishing do to minimize long-run costs? Could Letters Publishing be minimizing its short-run costs? Explain your reasoning.

12. Consider three corporations: Toyota, Applebee's Restaurants, and the Gap. Would the short-run time period be the same for each of these firms? Explain your reasoning.

13. Suppose a firm's production function exhibits constant returns to scale for all levels of output. If this firm is not currently operating at the minimum point on its *SRAC* curve, could it be currently operating on its *LRAC* curve? Explain your reasoning using a graph.

14. Suppose for the short-run production function $q = f(L, \overline{K})$ with capital fixed at $\overline{K}$ units, the MP_L is constant and equal to 5 for all L. Draw the AP_L curve. If the wage $w = \$10$, draw the *SRMC* and *SRAC* curves.

15. Consider the following three Cobb-Douglas production functions:

    a. $Q = 100 L^{1/2} K^{1/2}$

    b. $Q = 50 L^{1/3} K^{1/3} = \sqrt[3]{LK}$

    c. $Q = 10 L^2 K^2$

    What are the returns to scale for each of these production functions? What is the shape of each of the LRAC curves for these production functions?

    For any Cobb-Douglas production function $Q = AL^\alpha K^\beta$, where A, α, and β are positive constants, the sum of $\alpha + \beta$ tells us something important about returns to scale. Given your previous answers, what do you think is the relationship between $\alpha + \beta$ and returns to scale for a Cobb-Douglas production function $Q = AL^\alpha K^\beta$?

16. Complete the following table for Deb's TV Inc.

# Plants	Labor # Workers	Total TVs	AP_L	MP_L
1	0	0	—	—
1	1	20		
1	2		22	
1	3	66		
1	4			14
1	5		18	

After which worker do diminishing returns set in?

17. Suppose for the short-run production function $q = f(L, \overline{K})$ with capital fixed at $\overline{K}$ units, diminishing returns to labor sets in with the addition of the fiftieth unit of labor. Can *SRMC* and *AVC* be minimized at the same point for this production function? Explain your reasoning.

18. Draw isoquants for the following pairs of inputs for the following sandwiches:

    a. Big Macs: hamburger patties and slices of cheese.

    b. Subway foot-long subs: Swiss cheese and provolone cheese.

19. Complete the following table:

Q	FC	TVC	TC	MC	AFC	AVC	ATC
1	50	12					
2				10			
3						10	
4			90				
5							21

Internet Exercises

Visit *http://www.myeconlab.com/waldman* for this chapter's Web exercises. Answer real-world economics problems by doing research on the Internet.

Chapter 8
Perfectly Competitive Product Markets

In 1990, the United States Congress decided that an excellent way to raise additional revenues from wealthy Americans would be to place a large luxury tax on yachts purchased in the United States. The global market for yachts, however, proved to be far more competitive than Congress imagined. Wealthy Americans immediately stopped buying yachts in the United States and began purchasing yachts in foreign countries. In the end, the tax on yachts raised virtually no revenue and severely hurt the American yacht industry. Realizing its mistake, in 1993 Congress repealed the yacht tax. Even the most basic understanding of how competitive global markets work would have prevented Congress from enacting such a tax.

Someone once said, "Teach a parrot to say 'supply and demand,' and you've got yourself an economist." In defense of economists, there is more to supply and demand theory than many non-economists suspect. In this chapter, we study how prices are determined in perfectly competitive product markets. As we proceed, you'll see just how economists use the model of price-taking consumers and price-taking competitive firms to build a coherent model of supply and demand. Then we'll study how supply and demand together determine price. In doing so, it will be useful to distinguish between price determination in the short run and in the long run. We'll begin with a look at the basic assumptions of a competitive market and the logic of profit maximization, and then proceed to examine short-run and long-run equilibrium.

Learning Objectives

After reading Chapter 8, you will have learned:

> The basic assumptions of a perfectly competitive market and the logic of the profit-maximizing output rule for firms.

> How to derive the firm's short-run supply curve.

> How to measure producer surplus in the short run.

> How to derive an industry's short-run equilibrium in perfectly competitive markets.

> How to derive the long-run equilibrium in competitive markets and the long-run supply curves in constant-cost, increasing-cost, and decreasing-cost industries.

Featured Applications

> 8.1 Application Excessive Spending on Advertising

> 8.2A Application Short-Run Losses in the Airline Industry

> 8.2B Application The Costs of Producing Corn and Optimal Output

> 8.3 Application The Importance of Producer Surplus in the Commercial Aircraft Industry

> 8.5 Application The Slope of the Long-Run Industry Supply Curves

8.1 Perfectly Competitive Markets and Profit Maximization

A perfectly competitive product or input market must meet the following four specific assumptions:

1. *Many buyers and many sellers.* There are so many buyers and sellers that each one of them is an insignificant force on the market. Specifically, the amount that any one buyer might purchase is so small relative to the total quantity traded in the market that her purchases have no noticeable impact on the prevailing market price. Similarly, the amount that any one seller might sell is so small relative to the total traded that his sales have no noticeable impact on the prevailing market price.

2. *Homogeneity.* The output or factor of production sold by one seller must be indistinguishable from that of any other seller. This implies and ensures that no buyer has any reason to prefer dealing with one seller over another.

3. *Free entry and exit.* New firms are able to acquire the necessary technology and inputs to produce the product as easily as established firms. Exclusive patent rights, unusually large set-up costs, or any other such barriers to free entry into the market are incompatible with perfect competition. Buyers, too, are able to enter and depart the market at will, with no unusual financial penalties or legal restrictions to inhibit them.

4. *Perfect and freely available information.* All buyers and sellers are fully informed about all relevant characteristics of the good or service, and about market conditions. No seller or buyer can enjoy the advantage of inside information that is not readily available to everyone else.

price-takers

Economic agents who take the market price as fixed and beyond their control.

In a perfectly competitive market, market demand and market supply determine the equilibrium price and quantity traded. Because no single buyer or seller has any discernible impact on market price, all economic agents in competitive markets are **price-takers**—each takes the market price as fixed and beyond their control. This kind of price-taking behavior by buyers and sellers is important, and it is one of the factors that distinguishes perfect competition from other forms of market structure.

Many real-world markets largely satisfy the assumptions of perfect competition. National and world markets for most agricultural products—such as the markets for wheat, soybeans, hogs, and steers—are good examples. Other examples include markets for most national currencies and for many stocks and bonds. In many important markets, the models of perfect competition give us valuable insights and help us predict market outcomes with a good deal of accuracy.

Of course, even if a much smaller fraction of the world's trade were conducted in perfectly competitive markets, it would still be worthwhile to study them. As we proceed, keep in mind that perfect competition is one of the oldest, simplest, and most elegant paradigms in economics, and it is the one we can say the most about. You will see that what we learn from studying perfect competition gives us a useful benchmark against which to compare other, more complex market structures.

The Logic of Profit Maximization

In the early 2000s, top management in many of America's largest corporations found itself on the defensive as increasingly militant stockholder groups complained loudly and campaigned aggressively against what they perceived as excessive executive compensation schemes. Large institutional stockholders joined small individual investors to demand a greater role for performance-based pay at the top, and many of America's leading executives had their compensation reduced as a result. Those executives learned the hard way that in many corporations, managers who pursue goals other than profit do so at their peril. This section explains how all firms, not just perfectly competitive firms, go about maximizing profits and how economists analyze firms' profit-maximizing efforts.

Let's suppose there is some action a firm can take that will affect its profit. For example, the firm might increase its output, advertising expenditures, or its research and development budget. If by undertaking more of an action, profit increases, then the firm is not doing enough of that action and should do more. If by cutting back on an action, profit rises, then the firm is doing too much of that action and should do less if it wants to maximize profit. When is the firm engaged in just the right amount of an action to maximize profit? When it's doing neither too much, nor too little.

Let's imagine that π stands for the profit earned when the firm takes some action at level a. Suppose the relationship between profit π and a is as depicted in Figure 8.1. There, profit first increases, reaching its maximum at a^*, then declines with further increases in a. At point X, the rate of change of profit—the *slope* of the green profit-hill— is positive. This means that a small increase in a, past a_1, will increase the level of profit, so a_1 cannot be the profit-maximizing level of this activity. Thus, when the rate of change of profit is positive, the firm is doing too little and should do more. At point Z, the rate of change of profit (again the slope of the profit-hill) is negative. Here a small increase in a will reduce firm profit, but a small decrease in a will increase it. Thus, when the rate of change of profit is negative, the firm is doing too much and should do less.

A firm that maximizes profit will do neither too little nor too much: therefore, its rate of change of profit can be neither positive nor negative. This leaves only one possibility: When a profit-maximizing firm is in equilibrium, it will have chosen that level of activity at which the rate of change in profit just equals zero. In Figure 8.1, this occurs at a^*. At the very top of the profit-hill, at point Y, we have:

$$\frac{\Delta \pi}{\Delta a} = 0$$

(8.1)

Figure 8.1 The Profit-Hill
Undertaking the level of action a results in an increase in profit up to the level a^*, but profit decreases if any more of the action is undertaken beyond the level a^*. If the slope of the green profit-hill is positive, the firm should undertake more of the action; if the slope is negative, the firm should undertake less of the action. Therefore, the level of activity maximizes profit only when the slope of the profit-hill equals zero.

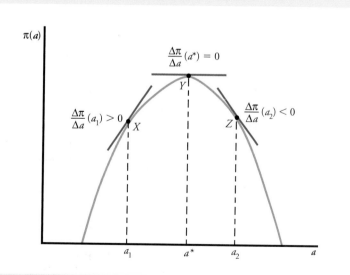

▲▲▲ **8.1 APPLICATION**   Excessive Spending on Advertising

One important activity aimed at increasing profit is advertising. In 2001, companies spent over $231 billion on advertising in the United States alone. General Motors led the way, spending almost $3.4 billion that year. Although increased advertising can and does sometimes increase profits, that result is not at all certain.

Consider the constant and often escalating advertising battles between Coca-Cola and Pepsi. Suppose Pepsi decides to engage in a major new advertising campaign. Pepsi's increased advertising is likely to cause three things to happen: first, the demand for all soft drinks, including Coca-Cola, is likely to increase as consumers are bombarded with messages encouraging them to drink soft drinks; second, Pepsi is likely to increase its share of the market in relation to its competitors as it extols the virtues of its soft drinks; and third, all of the other soft drink manufacturers, including Coca-Cola, are likely to increase their own advertising budgets in response to Pepsi's increased advertising. The increase in the demand for all soft drinks and the increase in the demand for Pepsi relative to other soft drinks should increase Pepsi's profits, but the third effect, especially the increase in advertising by Coca-Cola, is likely to reduce Pepsi's profits. It's certainly possible that in the end, Pepsi might find itself slipping *down* the profit-hill and spending too

much on advertising. Perhaps if Pepsi and Coca-Cola could call a truce and agree to reduce their levels of advertising, they would both earn higher profits.

Sometimes advertising wars get completely out of hand so that on top of the millions of dollars spent on advertising, companies can be faced with millions of dollars in legal expenses. Consider the somewhat bizarre advertising battle in the electric toothbrush industry between Gillette, the manufacturer of Oral-B toothbrushes, and Optiva, the manufacturer of Sonicare toothbrushes. Optiva not only claimed that Sonicare was less abrasive and more effective in attacking plaque than Oral-B, but in order to prove it, the company spent millions of dollars to do research brushing dead pigs' teeth! Gillette responded to Optiva's pigs' teeth claims by testing its toothbrushes on live pigs' teeth. When Optiva implied in its magazine advertising that using an Oral-B toothbrush might increase your risk of heart disease, stroke, and having low birth-weight babies, Gillette had had enough and sued for false advertising. In 1999, a federal district court jury awarded Gillette $2.5 million in damages, but the jury also ruled that *both* firms had engaged in false advertising. Optiva almost certainly would have earned higher profits if it had avoided making these wild and expensive advertising claims.

as required. Equation 8.1 is a necessary condition for profit maximization. In deriving it, *a* has purposely been left as a non-specific action to emphasize the broad applicability of this logic. Next, let's turn to one specific action: the firm's level of output, and show how the same logic can be used to determine the profit-maximizing level of output.

The Profit-Maximizing Output Choice

In choosing a level of output, the firm must take into account the separate effects of changing output on revenue and cost. At any output level, firm profit, π, is the difference between total revenue, TR, and cost, TC:

$$\pi = TR - TC$$

As the firm produces some small increment in output, Δq, it will incur some increment in cost, ΔTC. When it sells the additional output it has produced, there will be some impact on sales revenue, ΔTR. The resulting change in profit, $\Delta\pi/\Delta q$, will therefore be:

$$\frac{\Delta\pi}{\Delta q} = \frac{\Delta TR}{\Delta q} - \frac{\Delta TC}{\Delta q}$$

(8.2)

Equation 8.2 expresses the rate of change of profit as the difference between the rates of change in revenue and cost. The rate of change of profit with respect to a change in

marginal profit

The rate of change of profit with respect to a change in output.

marginal revenue

The rate of change of revenue with respect to a change in output.

output, $\Delta\pi/\Delta q$, is called **marginal profit**; the rate of change of revenue with respect to a change in output, $\Delta TR/\Delta q$, is called **marginal revenue**; and the rate of change of cost with respect to a change in output, $\Delta TC/\Delta q$, is *marginal cost*. According to Equation 8.2, marginal profit is the difference between marginal revenue and marginal cost. Letting MR stand for marginal revenue and MC for marginal cost, we can rewrite Equation 8.2 in the more familiar form:

$$\frac{\Delta\pi}{\Delta q} = MR - MC \qquad (8.3)$$

When marginal revenue exceeds marginal cost, marginal profit is positive and profit increases with an increase in output. When marginal cost exceeds marginal revenue, marginal profit is negative and profit will increase with a decrease in output.

Adapting our previous logic, the firm maximizes profit by choosing a level of output where marginal profit is zero, so that neither small increases nor small decreases in output increase profit. If q^* is the output that maximizes profit, then for $q = q^*$:

$$\frac{\Delta\pi}{\Delta q} = MR - MC = 0 \qquad (8.4)$$

as in Equation 8.1. Marginal profit equals zero only if marginal revenue equals marginal cost. This gives us the well-known and extremely important economic rule that for the profit-maximizing output:

profit-maximization $$\boxed{MR = MC} \qquad (8.5)$$

Thus far it hasn't been stated whether short-run or long-run marginal cost is involved in this "marginal revenue equals marginal cost" rule. This omission is intentional. It is first important to see that the logic of the optimal output rule is the same in both the short run and the long run: produce to the point where the extra revenue obtained from selling one more unit is just equal to the extra cost of producing that unit. In the short run, that extra cost will be what we called in Chapter 7 short-run marginal cost, or *SRMC*—the cost of acquiring the additional variable factors necessary to produce an additional unit of output. In the long run, all factors are variable, and long-run marginal cost, *LRMC*, is the relevant marginal cost in Equation 8.5. In the long run, *LRMC* will be the cost of acquiring *any* additional inputs the firm may need to produce an additional unit of output.

The Competitive Firm's Marginal Revenue Curve

To maximize profits, the competitive firm must equate marginal revenue to marginal cost. In Chapter 7, we derived the firm's costs from the production function. The marginal revenue curve is derived from the firm's demand curve, and therefore, to identify the marginal revenue curve for a perfectly competitive firm, we must first identify the firm's demand curve.

Panel (a) of Figure 8.2 shows the supply and demand curves for a perfectly competitive wheat market. The equilibrium price is $3.00 per bushel. In panel (b), a typical farmer is a price-taker for wheat, and therefore, the farmer takes the price of wheat as fixed at $3.00 per bushel. Because an individual farmer has no control over the price of wheat, the demand as viewed by any individual farmer is a horizontal line at the current market price of $3.00. An individual farmer, therefore, faces a perfectly elastic demand curve for wheat at the current price.

Given a perfectly elastic demand curve for wheat, what is a typical farmer's marginal revenue? If the price of wheat is constant at $3.00 per bushel, then the marginal revenue,

Figure 8.2 The Demand and Marginal Revenue Curves for a Perfectly Competitive Firm
In panel (a), equilibrium price is $3.00. The perfectly competitive firm takes the price of $3.00 as fixed and faces the horizontal and perfectly elastic demand curve in panel (b). The demand curve is also equal to the marginal revenue curve.

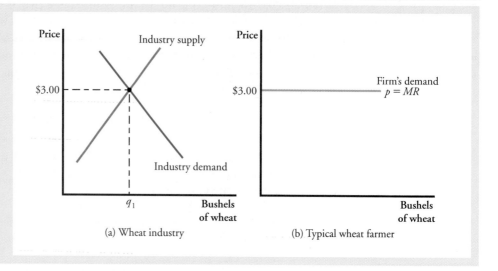

(a) Wheat industry

(b) Typical wheat farmer

$\Delta TR/\Delta q$, associated with selling another bushel of wheat always equals the price of $3.00 per bushel. Perfectly competitive firms therefore face perfectly elastic horizontal demand curves and marginal revenue always equals price; that is, $p = MR$. In Figure 8.2(b), the demand curve is horizontal and is also the marginal revenue curve.

▼▼▼   8.2   Firm Supply in the Short Run

short-run firm supply curve

A curve identifying the quantity of output the firm would offer for sale in the short run at each and every market price.

When output markets are perfectly competitive, demand and supply curves can summarize nicely the representative firm's behavior. The **short-run firm supply curve** tells us the quantity of output the firm would offer for sale in the short run at each and every market price that might prevail. When firms are profit-maximizers, profit determines the output they will offer. We can therefore refine our definition of the supply curve as follows: the short-run firm supply curve tells us the quantity of output that will maximize profit at every different market price that might prevail. Furthermore, we have just shown that to maximize profits, output must be chosen where marginal profit is zero or where marginal revenue equals marginal cost.

In the short run, at least one of the firm's inputs is fixed, and usually this input is the size and capacity of its plant. The firm can alter its output to maximize profit, but only by changing the quantity of variable inputs such as labor. The relevant marginal cost of output is therefore what we called short-run marginal cost, *SRMC*, in Chapter 7. Because *SRMC* measures the increment to short-run cost from a small increase in output, and because market price, p, measures the increment in revenue from the sale of any small increase in output, from Equation 8.3, we can express the rate of change of profit at any level of output, $\Delta\pi/\Delta q$, as the difference between the two:

$$\frac{\Delta\pi}{\Delta q} = MR - SRMC$$

$$= p - SRMC$$

From Equation 8.4, we know that profit maximization requires $\Delta\pi/\Delta q = MR - SRMC = 0$; which in a perfectly competitive market implies that $p = SRMC$. Thus, for the firm in a perfectly competitive product market, "marginal revenue equals marginal cost" becomes "price equals marginal cost" as the principle guiding selection of the profit-maximizing output.

Figure 8.3 illustrates these ideas. Suppose market price is p, and the firm produces output q_1. Can q_1 be the profit-maximizing output? To find out, consider what would happen if the firm increased output slightly. The vertical distance from point A to point C represents the marginal revenue the firm could earn by selling the next bit of output at price p. Producing that next bit adds the distance BC to costs. Clearly, producing and selling that additional output adds more to revenue than it does to cost. The difference between the two, the distance AB, is the net addition to total profit the firm would earn. Because this increment in profit is positive, some output levels greater than q_1 must earn higher total profit. Thus, q_1 cannot be the profit-maximizing choice. Notice we could make exactly the same argument for all output levels less than q^* in Figure 8.3.

By contrast, for outputs greater than q^*, such as q_2, we have a different situation. The distance DF measures the marginal cost of that unit, and EF measures the marginal revenue from selling it. We see that $DF > EF$, so producing and selling that unit actually decreases profit by an amount equal to distance DE. On the other hand, if this firm decreased output slightly, it would save more in costs (DF) than it would forego in revenue (EF), resulting in a net increase in profit (DE). This same argument applies to all outputs greater than q^*.

Marginal revenue equals marginal cost only at output q^*, and therefore, an output of q^* maximizes profits. There are however two important caveats to the "price equals marginal cost rule" for profit maximization. The first has to do with where price equals marginal cost; the second with whether it makes sense for the firm to produce any output at all.

Figure 8.3 Profit-Maximizing Level of Output

If price is p and the firm produces output q_1, it is not maximizing profit, because price is greater than marginal cost; so producing and selling additional output adds more to revenue than it does to cost. On the other hand, if price is p and the firm produces output q_2, it is not maximizing profit; because price is less than marginal cost; so producing and selling less output subtracts more from costs than it does from revenues. To maximize profit, the firm must produce the output q^*, where price equals marginal cost.

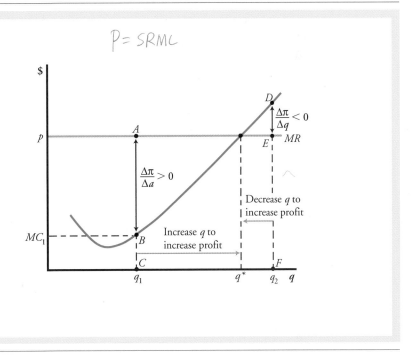

Profit Maximization When Price Equals Marginal Cost for Two Outputs

In Figure 8.4, when price is p, price equals marginal cost at two different outputs, q_1 and q^*. Which output maximizes profit? A close look can give us the answer. Notice that when the firm increases output a bit beyond q_1, marginal revenue stays constant at p, but marginal cost immediately falls below p. Because increasing output above q_1 adds more to revenue than it does to cost, profit increases. Therefore, output q_1 cannot maximize profit, even though price equals marginal cost for that output. By contrast, if you examine output q^*, you'll see that any small increase in output above q^* adds more to cost than it does to revenue, and so reduces profit; and any small decrease in output below q^* decreases revenue more than it decreases cost, and so also reduces profit. Output q^*, therefore, is the only one that maximizes profit. What we see here is a general principle at work: the "price equals marginal cost" rule does not apply if marginal cost is decreasing. A better statement of the rule would be: "Price equals marginal cost and marginal cost is not decreasing."

The Shut-Down Decision

normal or **zero economic profit**

Profit when total revenue equals total cost so the firm is exactly covering its opportunity cost of its investment; that is, it is doing as well as it could if it invested in the next best alternative investment.

The second caveat to the "price equals marginal cost rule" has to do with hard—often painful—business decisions, so it merits careful attention. Until now, we've been taking it for granted that firms can make at least a **normal economic profit** or **zero economic profit**. Unfortunately for firm owners, that is not always the case. Market circumstances can arise under which no matter what the firm does, it will sustain an economic loss. That is, the firm might not be able to cover the opportunity costs of all of the capital and labor the owners have invested in the business. When circumstances get this bad, the profit-maximizing firm must look for the *loss-minimizing* thing to do. Sometimes, the

Figure 8.4 Profit Maximization When Price Equals Marginal Cost for Two Outputs

At price p, price equals marginal cost at output levels q_1 and q^*. If the firm increases output a bit beyond q_1, marginal revenue is p, but marginal cost immediately falls below that level, so profit increases. It follows that output q_1 cannot maximize profit. At output q^*, any increase in output adds more to cost than it does to revenue, and therefore reduces profit. Output q^* therefore maximizes profit. The price equals marginal cost rule does not apply if marginal cost is decreasing.

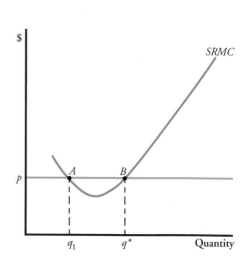

firm will minimize its loss by producing and selling some output; and in this case, it should produce where price equals marginal cost. Other times, it's better simply to shut the firm down and produce nothing at all.

To paraphrase Shakespeare, the firm always has two choices: to produce or not to produce. If it produces, it should produce the output where price equals marginal cost, because that output always maximizes profits, or minimizes losses, given that the firm produces at all. If q^* is the level of output where $p = SRMC$, profit equals:

$$\pi(q^*) = TR(q^*) - VC(q^*) - FC \qquad (8.6)$$

where $\pi(q^*)$ is the profit associated with an output q^*, $TR(q^*)$ is total revenue, $VC(q^*)$ is variable cost, and FC is fixed cost.

The firm's other option is to shut down. If it does not produce, its revenues equal zero. However, it still incurs fixed costs, because fixed costs continue to be borne in the short run regardless of whether the firm produces any output. Rent and interest on loans must be paid, a certain amount of heat and electricity may be needed merely to keep machinery from deteriorating, and so forth. With no revenue and no variable cost, the firm that shuts down will sustain an economic loss exactly equal to the amount it pays out in fixed cost. When the firm shuts down we know its economic loss will be:

$$\pi(q) = \pi(0) = -FC \qquad (8.7)$$

In choosing between its two options, producing and shutting down, the profit-maximizing firm chooses the one yielding the greatest profit. The economic profit from shutting down will be greater than the economic profit from producing q^* if and only if $\pi(0) > \pi(q^*)$. Substituting from Equations 8.6 and 8.7, this requires that if:

$$\pi(0) > \pi(q^*)$$

then:

$$-FC > TR(q^*) - VC(q^*) - FC$$

Adding $FC + VC(q^*)$ to both sides of the above equation, the firm will shut down in the short run if:

$$VC(q^*) > TR(q^*) \qquad (8.8)$$

Now that we've done the algebra, what's the logic and common sense behind this condition? Equation 8.8 says the firm should shut down whenever the total variable cost of producing the profit-maximizing output exceeds total revenue. And this makes sense: If the firm cannot collect enough total revenue to pay its total variable cost, it only increases its losses by continuing to produce, in which case it loses its entire fixed cost plus the portion of its variable cost that total revenue doesn't cover. In that case, it would be better simply to shut down in the short run, pay the fixed cost to which the firm is committed, and bear that painful but nonetheless smaller loss equal to its fixed cost. The logic of this argument applies equally well whether the firm is a competitive firm or not. Equation 8.8 therefore gives us a very general **shut-down rule** for the profit-maximizing firm: the firm should shut down to minimize its loss whenever total variable cost exceeds total revenue, regardless of the output produced.

shut down rule

A rule stating that a profit-maximizing firm should stop producing output whenever total variable cost exceeds total revenue, regardless of the output produced; or, stated differently, whenever price is less than average variable cost, regardless of the output produced.

For perfectly competitive firms, we can simplify this general rule even further. At a market price p, the price-taking competitive firm selling output q^* earns revenue $TR(q^*) = pq^*$. With this in mind, divide both sides of Equation 8.8 by output q^* and recall that $AVC(q^*) = VC(q^*)/q^*$. We can then express Equation 8.8 as the requirement that:

$$AVC(q^*) > p \qquad (8.9)$$

We can now state the shut-down rule for the perfectly competitive firm as follows: the firm should shut down to minimize its loss whenever average variable cost exceeds market price at the profit-maximizing (loss-minimizing) level of output.

It sometimes helps to see this rule graphically. Figure 8.5 shows two identical sets of cost curves for a typical competitive firm. In panel (a), the firm faces market price p_1. If it produces, it should produce q_1, where marginal cost equals price. Notice that p_1 is less than AVC_1, so by our rule, the firm should shut down rather than produce q_1. To confirm this, notice that when the firm produces q_1, total revenue pq, which equals the area of rectangle $EFHG$, minus total cost $q(ATC)$, which equals the area $ABHG$, leaves a negative profit equal to the sum of the shaded light- and dark-red areas $ABFE$. How does a loss of $ABFE$ compare to the loss the firm would bear if it shut down? We know that average fixed cost, AFC, at any level of output is equal to $ATC - AVC$; that is, the difference between average total cost and average variable cost. At output q_1, therefore, the vertical distance BD is average fixed cost, FC/q_1. By multiplying this by q_1, or by the horizontal distance CD, we can see that the shaded dark-red area of rectangle $ABDC$ exactly measures the firm's fixed cost FC. This, of course, represents the amount the firm would lose if it were to shut down. Because the loss it suffers by shutting down (shaded dark-red area $ABDC$) is less than the loss it suffers if it produces output q_1 (the sum of the light- and dark-red areas $ABFE$), the firm minimizes its economic loss by shutting down.

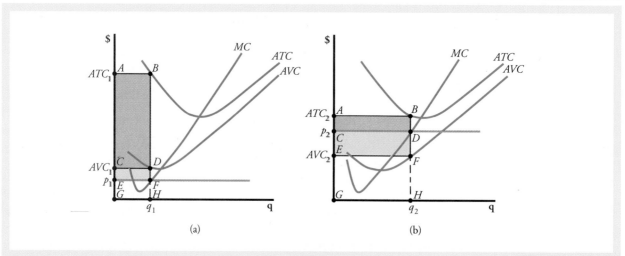

(a)   (b)

Figure 8.5 The Shut-Down Price

In panel (a), if the firm produces its profit-maximizing output q_1 at price p_1, the firm sustains an economic loss equal to area $ABFE$. However, if it shuts down, it only loses its fixed costs equal to area $ABDC$; and therefore, it should shut down, because price p_1 is less than AVC_1. In panel(b), if the firm produces its profit-maximizing output q_2 at price p_2, the firm sustains an economic loss equal to area $ABDC$. However, if it shuts down, it loses its fixed costs equal to area $ABFE$, and therefore is better off continuing to produce if price p_2 is greater than AVC_2.

▲▲▲ **8.2A APPLICATION**   Short–Run Losses in the Airline Industry

In 2002 American Airlines reported a loss of $3.5 billion, Delta Airlines a loss of $1.3 billion, and US Airways a loss of $1.65 billion. To make matters worse, in the aftermath of a recession and the events of September 11: in the year 2001, American Airlines reported a loss of $1.4 billion, Delta Airlines a loss of $1.2 billion, and US Airways a loss of $2.12 billion. These losses forced US Airways to file for bankruptcy protection in 2002. Despite these huge losses and the US Airways bankruptcy, American, Delta, and US Airways continued to fly throughout 2002 and into 2003. Congress helped the industry by passing a $5 billion emergency financial relief program, but even without this government bailout the industry would have continued to operate.

The years 2001 and 2002 were hardly the first years of losses for the airline industry. In 1992, American Airlines reported it lost $475 million, Delta Airlines reported a loss of $565, and US Airways reported a $601 million loss. To make matters worse, because of the eco-

nomic recession of the early 1990s, 1992 was the third consecutive year of large losses in the airline industry. The airline industry as a whole suffered losses not only from 2001–2002 and 1990–1992, but also from 1980–1982. Despite all of these years of consecutive economic losses, major carriers like American, Delta, and US Airways kept selling tickets and carrying passengers.

The major carriers did not shut down in 1982, 1992, or 2002, because they were able to more than cover their total variable costs. If they had shut down they would have lost their fixed costs. The largest fixed costs for the airlines were the interest payments on loans they made to purchase equipment such as airplanes and ground machinery. If the airlines could not resell these planes and equipment (and who would buy the planes in 2002–2003 when there were no profits to be earned in the industry?), then they would have to pay these fixed costs even if they closed down.

In Panel (b) of Figure 8.5, we have a different situation entirely. There the firm faces market price p_2 and, if the firm continues to produce in the short run, the profit-maximizing output is q_2. Here, p_2 exceeds AVC_2, so according to our rule, the firm should produce, even if an economic loss results. To confirm this, notice that if the firm produces q_2, total revenue, pq, of area $CDHG$ minus total cost, $q(ATC)$, of area $ABHG$ leaves an economic loss equal to the shaded dark-red area $ABDC$. We measure fixed cost by the sum of the light- and dark-red areas of rectangle $ABFE$, which in turn is the amount the firm would lose if it shut down. Here, however, the loss the firm suffers when it produces (dark-red area $ABDC$) is smaller than the one it suffers if it shuts down (light- and dark-red areas $ABFE$), so the firm minimizes its loss by producing output q_2 where price equals marginal cost.

A Fully Formed Supply Curve

We're now prepared to give a complete description of the short-run supply curve for a perfectly competitive firm. Remember that the short-run supply curve tells us the profit-maximizing output level the competitive firm would offer for sale at each and every possible market price. We've seen that at some market prices it makes sense to produce and at others it does not. When it does make sense to produce, the profit-maximizing choice at price p will always be the output q where $p = SRMC$, provided marginal cost is *not* decreasing there. When it does not make sense to produce, market price is so low that the firm cannot even cover the variable cost of producing, so its best recourse in the short run is to shut down, producing no output at all.

Figure 8.6 brings this analysis together and enables us to see what a typical firm's short-run supply curve looks like. The supply curve is vertical at an output of zero for all market prices that are less than minimum average variable cost, AVC_{min}. For market prices above AVC_{min}, the short-run supply curve is the heavy red curve that lies right on top of the firm's short-run marginal cost curve, $SRMC$.

Figure 8.6 The Firm's Short-Run Supply Curve
The firm's supply curve is vertical at an output of zero for all market prices less than AVC_{min}. For prices above AVC_{min}, the supply curve is identical to the firm's short-run marginal cost curve, $SRMC$.

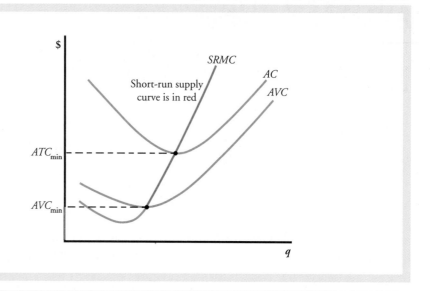

▲▲▲ 8.2B APPLICATION   The Costs of Producing Corn and Optimal Output

In 1996, the United States Department of Agriculture, or USDA, estimated that the marginal cost per acre of growing corn on a 500-acre farm in the United States was constant and equal to the average variable cost for production up to 65,000 bushels. However, to produce more than 65,000 bushels on a typical 500-acre farm, the USDA determined, required larger and larger increments of the variable inputs.

The USDA cost estimates resulted in the $SRMC$, AVC, and ATC curves depicted in the figure. Beyond 65,000 bushels, the MC curve slopes upward rapidly. The marginal cost of the 85,000th bushel was $2.50 and

Application Figure 8.2
Cost Curves for Corn Production
Up to an output of 65,000 bushels, $SRMC = AVC = \$1.26$ per bushel. Beyond 65,000 bushels $SRMC$ increases rapidly.

(continued)

the marginal cost of the 92,000th bushel was $3.50. At a price of $2.50/bushel, the farmer would produce 85,000 bushels and sustain an economic loss because $p < ATC$. However, because at a price of 2.50 $p > AVC$, the farmer would continue to stay in business in the short run and grow corn. At a price of $3.50/bushel, the farmer would produce 92,000 bushels and earn an economic profit, because $p > ATC$.

Notice that the supply curve for the farmer is the upward-sloping portion of the $SRMC$ curve for prices above $1.26/bushel. The firm's supply curve is very inelastic, with a 40 percent increase in price from $2.50/bushel to $3.50/bushel resulting in an increase in output of only 8.2 percent from 85,000 bushels to 92,000 bushels. The elasticity of supply, therefore, was only $\varepsilon_s = 8.2\%/40\% = 0.205 < 1$.

✳ Often, students will slip into the habit of thinking that the $SRMC$ curve and the short-run supply curve are identical. This is definitely not the case, and the importance of keeping these two curves distinct rests on more than semantics. We read the $SRMC$ curve up and over from the horizontal axis—it tells us the extra or incremental cost the firm must pay to produce one more additional unit of output. By contrast, we read the short-run supply curve over and down from the vertical axis—it tells us at any market price what the corresponding profit-maximizing output for the firm will be. The two curves are therefore different, so when you feel yourself letting the distinction between them become blurred, take another look at Figure 8.6 and notice how $SRMC$ and the supply curve diverge from one another when price falls sufficiently low.

At every point along the firm's supply curve, profit is maximized, given market price. But what is the relationship between the supply curve and the *level* of firm profit? Looking once more at Figure 8.6, remember that at all prices between zero and AVC_{min}, the firm's best course is to shut down and produce no output. At all these prices, profit will be the same—a loss just equal to its short-run fixed cost. For prices between AVC_{min} and ATC_{min}, profit is negative and the firm still suffers economic losses, but these losses are minimized by producing where price equals marginal cost. If price is just equal to ATC_{min}, the firm maximizes profit by producing where $p = SRMC = ATC_{min}$. As usual, the firm does its best by choosing output where price equals marginal cost. Here, and only here, because price equals average total cost simultaneously, the best it can do is earn zero economic profits or normal economic profits. At prices above ATC_{min}, however, producing where price equals marginal cost yields positive economic profit in the short run. In a perfectly competitive market, firms yearn for prices like these.

▼▼▼ 8.3 Producer Surplus

In Chapter 4, we learned about consumer surplus and identified it as a measure of how much better off the consumer is when he is able to buy some good rather than having to do without it entirely. There is an analogous concept to consumer surplus on the producer side of the market—producer surplus—that will help us understand how markets perform.

When we studied the notion of consumer surplus, we began by observing that no self-interested economic agent takes one course of action over another unless doing so makes him better off. This same idea applies as much to firms as it does to consumers. No self-interested firm owner sells output in the market unless doing so makes her better off than she would be staying out of the market entirely. Therefore, whenever a firm chooses to sell, we can infer that it must be earning a surplus over what it would obtain if it did not sell at all. Any such excess that is earned by the firm's factors of production, including

producer surplus

The excess earned by the firm's factors of production, including the owners of capital and labor, over and above what they would earn if the firm did not sell any output.

the owners of capital and labor—over and above what they would earn if the firm did not sell any output—is called **producer surplus**. When the firm is producing, it is precisely this surplus that is inducing it to do so. Therefore, we can also think of producer surplus as measuring the excess a firm's factors of production earn over and above what they minimally require in order to be just indifferent between producing and not producing.

Note that the concept of producer surplus is defined relative to a given set of alternatives the firm may have, so we'll have to be sensitive to those alternatives as we develop and apply the concept of producer surplus. In our theory of the firm, we've found it useful to distinguish between the short run and the long run, because each holds open different options and alternatives for the firm. As a result, we'll need to develop the notions of producer surplus in the short run and in the long run a little bit differently from one another. This section shows how to measure short-run producer surplus. Chapter 9 will show how to measure long-run producer surplus.

Producer Surplus in the Short Run

In the short run, the firm has two options: it can shut down or produce. Whenever total revenue exceeds total variable cost, the firm will produce; otherwise, it does better by shutting down. We can therefore think of any excess in total revenue over total variable cost as precisely the surplus we seek—the amount the firm's factors of production earn over and above what they would earn if the firm shut down. Algebraically, we define short-run producer surplus, PS, in just that way:

$$PS = TR - VC \qquad (8.10)$$

At first it can be difficult to accept that producer surplus, as we've defined it, is really a surplus at all. After all, TR can exceed VC, but still fall short of $SRTC$. In that case, producer surplus in Equation 8.10 would be positive ($PS > 0$) even though total economic profit would be negative ($\pi < 0$). How can it make sense to think of the firm as earning any kind of surplus when it's actually sustaining an economic loss; that is, when it's not covering its opportunity cost of production? We find the answer by remembering that the alternative to producing is shutting down. If the firm shuts down, its loss will equal its fixed cost, FC. Notice that $PS > 0$ if and only if total revenue exceeds total variable cost, thus enabling the firm to reduce the size of its loss below the level of FC by exactly the amount of PS. It is in this sense that we can—and should—view PS as defined in Equation 8.10 as truly a surplus.

PRODUCER SURPLUS, TOTAL VARIABLE COST, AND THE SHORT-RUN MARGINAL COST CURVE   Producer surplus can be represented graphically, but first we need to learn to see total variable cost by looking only at the firm's short-run marginal cost curve. The short-run marginal cost curve is closely related to the total variable cost curve. To discover this relationship, first remind yourself that marginal cost is the extra cost of producing one more unit of the good. In the short run, marginal cost coincides with the additional variable cost when one more unit is produced.

Next, look at the typical $SRMC$ curve in panel (a) of Figure 8.7, where three discrete units of the good have been marked off, along with the marginal cost associated with each of these units. Now notice that if you multiply c_1 by 1, you get c_1 again, but you also get the area of the blue shaded rectangle X in panel (a). We can therefore look to that area as a measure of the marginal cost of the first full unit. Similarly, the area of the red rectangle Y, and then the green rectangle Z, respectively measure the marginal cost of the second and then the third units of output the same way. Marginal cost c_1 measures

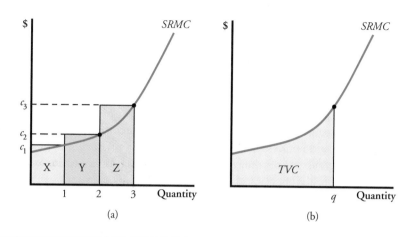

Figure 8.7 Total Variable Cost and the Marginal Cost Curve
In panel (a), output is produced in discreet unit increments and the total variable cost of producing the *first* unit equals the marginal cost of producing the first unit, which equals the area of the blue rectangle X. The total variable cost of producing three units is the sum of the blue, red, and green rectangles $X + Y + Z$. If the firm could make smaller equal-sized increments of one-half, or one-quarter, or one-eighth, or even one-hundredth or one-thousandth of a unit at a time, then the total variable cost equals the entire area under the marginal cost curve, which is shown by the blue shaded area in panel (b).

the addition to total variable cost from producing the very first unit. Because there can be no variable cost before that first unit is produced, this must also be the total variable cost of that very first unit. Thus,

$$VC_1 = c_1 = X$$

and we can see that the total variable cost of the first full unit of output is measured by the area of the blue shaded rectangle X in the figure.

Next, the total variable cost of two whole units, VC_2, can itself be thought of as the total variable cost of the first full unit *plus* the addition to total variable cost contributed by the second. Therefore:

$$VC_2 = VC_1 + c_2$$
$$= c_1 + c_2 = X + Y$$

so that this time the total variable cost of two full units is equal to the sum of the areas of the blue and red shaded rectangles, $X + Y$. In just the same way, we can think of the total variable cost of three full units as the total variable cost of the first two plus the addition to total variable cost contributed by the green rectangle Z, or:

$$VC_3 = VC_2 + c_3$$
$$= c_1 + c_2 + c_3 = X + Y + Z$$

From this equation we can see that by adding the area of all three rectangles in Figure 8.7(a), we measure the total variable cost of a *total* of three full units.

We could keep right on going like this, but by now you've gotten the idea. To measure the total variable cost of any level of output, we can sum the marginal cost of every unit of output up to that point. This sum in turn corresponds to adding the areas of appropriately formed rectangles in a marginal cost curve diagram like the one in panel (a) of Figure 8.7. There, we pretended that the firm could only produce whole incremental units and so we chose a base of one full unit for each of the rectangles. You can see that the total area that all three together contain approximates the area under the *SRMC* curve up to the third unit.

Now picture what would happen if we acknowledged that the firm could make smaller equal-sized increments, such as increments of one-half, one-quarter, one-eighth, or even one-hundredth of a unit at a time. For any such fraction of a unit, we could find its marginal cost off the curve and form our narrower rectangles. The total variable cost of three full units would still be approximated by the sum of all those little rectangles up to the third full unit, but this time there would be more of them and the difference between their total area and the area under the *SRMC* curve would be smaller. In fact, the smaller we take the width of our rectangles, the closer our measure of total variable cost and the area under the *SRMC* curve become. Mathematically, we can see that in the limit, as we consider smaller and smaller base increments in output, the approximation becomes exact. This leaves us with an interesting and useful geometrical fact worth remembering: the area underneath an *SRMC* curve up to any output q exactly measures the firm's total variable cost of q full units, $VC(q)$. Therefore, the shaded blue area in panel (b) of Figure 8.7 represents total variable cost for producing q units.

The Geometry of Short-Run Producer Surplus

Now let's return to producer surplus. Figure 8.8 reveals how we can see producer surplus on a familiar graph. It shows the short-run marginal cost curve *SRMC*. If the firm is a perfect competitor, we know its short-run supply curve will lie right on top of that marginal cost curve at all prices above minimum average variable cost.

When this firm faces market price p, it will produce at q and earn revenue equal to the sum of the orange and green shaded areas, *ABDO*. At the same time, we now know that the orange shaded area under the marginal cost curve up to q—the area *OCBD*—

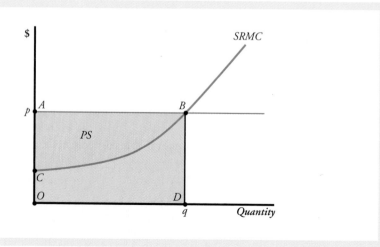

Figure 8.8 Short-Run Producer Surplus
If price equals p, the firm produces q and earns revenue equal to rectangular area *ABDO*. The orange shaded area under the marginal cost curve up to q, the area *OCBD*, measures the total variable cost of producing q units. Producer surplus is the excess of total revenue over total variable cost, which equals the shaded green area *ABC*.

▲▲▲ 8.3 APPLICATION   The Importance of Producer Surplus in the Commercial Aircraft Industry

In the 1960s, Boeing was a virtual monopolist in the commercial aircraft industry. In 1967, the British, French, and German governments provided subsidies to establish Airbus to compete against Boeing in the commercial aircraft industry. In 1974, the first European aircraft appeared on the market, but these aircraft were a commercial failure. The three governments then decided it was necessary to produce a complete line of different types of aircraft to compete successfully with Boeing. In order to produce a complete line of aircraft, the European governments decided to increase the subsidies paid to Airbus.

Economist Gernot Klepper analyzed the commercial aircraft industry to see whether the European subsidies improved welfare. The table presents one of his important results. If the Airbus entry is compared to an alternative market structure of a Boeing monopoly, total economic welfare worldwide decreases by over $73 billion as a result of the subsidies! The reason for the reduction is entirely the large decrease in producer surplus that results from Airbus's entry. Despite the increase in consumer surplus that results from the decline in aircraft prices, total surplus declines, because of the huge decline in Boeing's producer surplus.

Application Table 8.3 Effects of European-Supported Market Entry Into the Commercial Aircraft Industry (million 1986 $US)

	Producer Surplus	Consumer Surplus	Total Surplus
Europe	−2,826	10,544	7,718
North America	−107,582	12,631	−94,951
Rest of the world	0	13,630	13,630
Total	−110,408	36,795	−73,613

According to Klepper, because of the existence of large economies of scale in aircraft production, the optimal structure might be a world-wide monopoly. The entry of subsidized Airbus into a monopolized industry forces higher costs upon society and results in greatly reduced producer surplus.

measures the total variable cost of producing q units. From Equation 8.10, producer surplus is the excess of total revenue over total variable cost, $PS = TR - VC$. In Figure 8.8, revenue exceeds total variable cost by an amount just equal to the green area ABC. Therefore, it is precisely this green area above the marginal cost curve and below the price line that is our measure of short-run producer surplus.

▼▼▼ 8.4 Short-Run Equilibrium in Competitive Markets

In this section, we turn to the interaction between buyers and sellers in a market. Our first concern is to characterize and describe the short-run market equilibrium. First, we need to derive the short-run industry supply curve.

The Short-Run Industry Supply Curve

In competitive markets, the interaction of demand and supply determine the equilibrium market outcome. Remember from Chapter 4 that market demand tells us how many units of the good are demanded by all buyers together, at each and every market price over some period of time. Similarly, the short-run market supply curve tells us how many units of output will be supplied by all firms in the market together in the short run. Just as we formed the market demand curve by taking the horizontal sum of individual buyers' demand curves, we form the short-run market supply curve by taking the horizontal sum of the individual firms' supply curves.

To illustrate the derivation of the short-run industry supply, look at Figure 8.9, which shows the short-run supply curves of three competitive firms. To form the market supply curve in panel (a), we confront all three firms with the same market price and then sum the amount of output offered by all firms together. At a market price of $2, Firm 1 supplies 20 units of output as shown in panel (b). Because no other firm offers output for sale at that price, total quantity supplied at a price of $2 will be 20 units. For $2.00 \le p <$ $3.00, only Firm 1's supply curve is relevant, and it determines the entire market supply. As market price rises to $3.00, Firm 1 supplies 25 units, Firm 2 supplies 30, and Firm 3 supplies 15; total quantity supplied at $3 is therefore $25 + 30 + 15 = 70$. By the time the price rises to $4, Firm 1 supplies 30, Firm 2 supplies 40, and Firm 3 supplies 35 units. The quantity supplied at a price of $4 will therefore be $30 + 40 + 35 = 105$.

We can sum the firms' individual supply curves algebraically, too. In Figure 8.9, the industry contains three firms with the following respective supply curves:

$$\text{Firm 1's supply: } p = -2 + 0.20q_1 \quad \Rightarrow \quad q_1 = 10 + 5p \quad \text{for } p \ge 2$$
$$q_1 = 0 \quad \text{for } p < 2$$
$$\text{Firm 2's supply: } p = 0.10q_2 \quad \Rightarrow \quad q_2 = 10p \quad \text{for } p \ge 3$$
$$q_2 = 0 \quad \text{for } p < 3$$
$$\text{Firm 3's supply: } p = 2.25 + 0.05q_3 \quad \Rightarrow \quad q_3 = -45 + 20p \quad \text{for } p \ge 2$$
$$q_3 = 0 \quad \text{for } p < 3$$

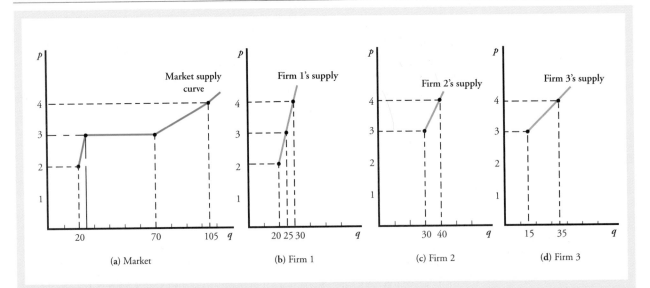

Figure 8.9 The Industry Supply Curve
The market supply curve in panel (a) is the horizontal summation of the firm supply curves. At a market price of $2, Firm 1 supplies 20 units of output and Firms 2 and 3 each supply zero units. As market price rises to $3, Firm 1 supplies 25 units, Firm 2 supplies 30, and Firm 3 supplies 15, and total quantity supplied is $25 + 30 + 15 = 70$. At $p = $4, the market quantity supplied is $30 + 40 + 35 = 105$.

We derive the equation for market supply, Q, by adding together the output of every firm over the relevant price range:

$$Q = q_1 + q_2 + q_3$$

for $p < 2$ $Q = 0$

for $2 \leq p < 3$ $Q = 10 + 5p + 0 + 0 = 10 + 5p$

for $p \geq 3$ $Q = (10 + 5p) + (10p) + (-45 + 20p) = -35 + 35p$

In general, if there are N firms in the market, and if firm i's supply curve is $q_i(p)$, short-run market supply Q_N will be the function:

$$Q_N = \sum_{i=1}^{N} q_i(p) \tag{8.11}$$

Whether we construct the market supply curve numerically or algebraically, we need to know how many firms to include in the sum. Recall that we define the short run as that period of time within which any given firm must contend with at least some fixed factor, such as the size of its plant. But if time is too short for any existing firm to change the size of its plant, it is too short to allow entrepreneurs or other firms not currently operating in the industry to enter the industry from scratch. Therefore, in the short run, the number of firms in the industry is fixed, and consists only of those firms that are currently producing.

The Industry and Firm in Short-Run Equilibrium

To find short-run equilibrium in a competitive market, we equate market demand and market supply, as shown in panel (a) of Figure 8.10. There, the short-run market supply curve with N firms in the industry, S_N, intersects the market demand curve at an equilibrium price of p_1. The total quantity demanded and supplied at p_1 is Q_1 units.

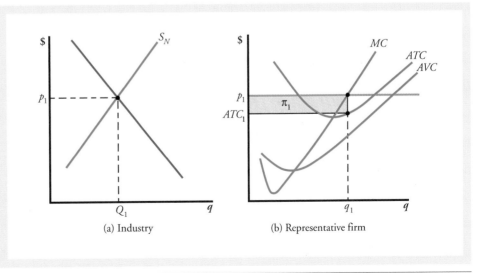

Figure 8.10 Short-Run Equilibrium in a Perfectly Competitive Industry
In panel (a), the industry equilibrium price is p_1. In panel (b), a representative firm takes the price p_1 as given and maximizes profit by producing output q_1, where price equals marginal cost. In the short run, price exceeds average total cost at output q_1, so the firm earns positive economic profit of $\pi_1 = q_1(p_1 - ATC_1)$, which equals the shaded green area.

(a) Industry

(b) Representative firm

In Figure 8.10, we correctly measured the firm's positive, or excess, economic profits as the green rectangle, which measures the area $q_1(p_1-ATC_1)$. Many students, however, measure this area incorrectly in the following manner. Consider this figure. Here, the industry equilibrium price is once again p_1. The firm takes the price as given and faces a horizontal demand curve at p_1. The firm, therefore, produces output q_1. When asked what are the firm's profits, many students answer: They are equal to the gray shaded area in this figure. These students are incorrectly forcing ATC to be equal to minimum ATC, but this is only true if the firm produces an output of q_2! At output q_1, the firm will have a higher ATC. Figure 8.10 shows the correct answer. Don't make this common error!

Common Error Figure 8.1
Incorrectly Measuring Profits
Profits are *not* equal to the gray shaded area. Many students incorrectly force ATC for producing output q_1 to be equal to minimum ATC.

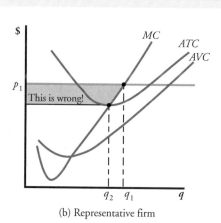

(a) Industry

(b) Representative firm

Panel (b) of Figure 8.10 illustrates the situation facing a representative firm in this market equilibrium: Each firm takes the market price p_1 as given and maximizes its own profit by producing output q_1, where price equals marginal cost. In the short run, price exceeds average total cost at the best level of output, so the representative firm earns positive economic profit of $\pi_1 = TR - TC = p_1q_1 - q_1(ATC_1) = q_1(p_1 - ATC_1)$, which equals the shaded green area in panel (b). In this case, the firm is more than covering its opportunity costs.

8.5   Long-Run Equilibrium in Competitive Markets

In the short run, a competitive market can be in equilibrium even though firms earn a positive economic profit or suffer an economic loss. As long as quantity demanded equals quantity supplied, and as long as existing firms are doing the best they can facing the fixed market price, the market will be in short-run equilibrium. In the long run, however, firms can make adjustments that they can't make in the short run. When firms earn short-run profit or suffer losses, we can expect market pressures to develop that will change the short-run market equilibrium.

There are two different types of economic forces at work in the long run. First, as we saw in Chapter 7, a firm that finds itself using sub-optimal amounts of one or more fixed inputs in the short run can change the amounts of those inputs over time. A plant that's too large or too small can be modified or replaced with one better suited to market conditions. Thus, how a firm produces output in the long run may differ significantly from how it produces output in the short run. Second, in the long run, firms can enter or exit a competitive industry in response to unusually good or unusually poor short-run profits. If economic profits are persistently above normal (positive) in one industry and below normal (negative) in another, entrepreneurs and investors will withdraw their capital from the latter and make new investments in the former. Thus, the number of firms can also be different in the long-run compared to the short run.

Entry and Exit

If firms can make positive short-run profit, entry into the industry will occur and the number of firms will increase over time. If the best firms can do is make short-run losses, some will exit the industry and the number of firms will decrease over time. When new firms enter an industry, market supply increases and equilibrium price falls; when firms exit, market supply decreases and price rises. When market price and the number of firms are changing, the industry can hardly be said to be in long-run equilibrium.

When will a competitive industry be in long-run equilibrium? There are three necessary conditions for long-run equilibrium:

1. All firms must be maximizing profit.
2. All firms must be earning zero economic profit.
3. Quantity demanded in the market must equal quantity supplied by all operating firms.

The first condition ensures that no firm has an incentive to change what it is doing, for if each produces a profit-maximizing output under the market conditions it faces, each is doing as well as it possibly can. The second condition says there must be no incentive for entry or exit. When economic profit is zero, firm owners earn normal returns on their investment and cover all opportunity costs of production, so those that are operating in the industry are doing as well as they can do anywhere else, while those outside the industry have no particular reason to be attracted to it. Finally, the third condition says the market must "clear," with every seller finding a buyer at the prevailing market price. When quantity demanded equals quantity supplied, there is no pressure on market price to either rise or fall; it is an equilibrium price.

To illustrate how an industry moves from short-run to long-run equilibrium, consider the situation depicted in Figure 8.11. For the moment, let's assume that input prices are fixed and independent of the level of industry output. In panel (a), suppose the demand curve is initially D_1. With 50 firms in the industry, the short-run supply curve is S_{50}, and short-run equilibrium is at point A with price equal to p_1. In panel (b), profit-maximizing firms produce output q_1 where marginal cost equals price. Because p_1 is greater than average cost at output q_1 by the distance between points E and F, firms earn short-run positive economic profit equal to the shaded green area π. This attracts entry in the long run because firms can earn profits that more than cover their opportunity cost of investing in industry. In panel (a), as firms enter, the short-run market supply shifts right, to S_N, where equilibrium is at point B and price equals p^*. Entry will continue until just enough firms have entered the industry so that market supply intersects market demand at p^*, insuring that p^* equals *minimum* average total cost and profits equal zero for the typical firm. Only when profits equal zero is there no longer any incentive for additional firms to enter the industry. This occurs with a total of N firms. This number, N, is therefore the long-run equilibrium number of firms in the industry.

Beginning from a long-run equilibrium at point B in panel (a), suppose that demand declined to D_2. In the short run, the new equilibrium would be at point C, and price

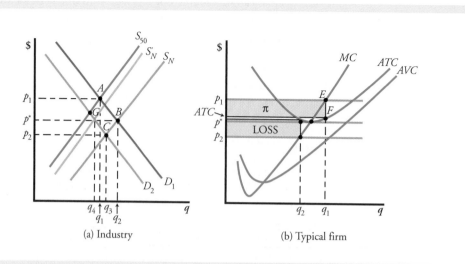

Figure 8.11 Long run Adjustments and Entry and Exit
In panel (a), if supply and demand intersect initially at the point A, price is p_1. In panel (b), firms earn positive economic profits equal to the green shaded area π. In panel (a), in the long run, the positive economic profits attract entry and shift the supply curve to S_N, so that price declines to p^* and economic profits are zero in panel (b). If demand then declines to D_2 in panel (a), price declines to p_2 and firms sustain an economic loss in panel (b) equal to the red shaded area. As a result, firms leave the market in the long run; and in panel (a), price rises back to p^*.

would decline to p_2. In panel (b), the representative firm produces q_2 units of output; and because $p_2 > AVC$, the firm continues to operate in the short run even though it is sustaining an economic loss equal to the shaded red area. In the long run, firms will leave the industry once they can get rid of their fixed costs. As firms leave, the short-run supply curve shifts to the left in panel (a) to supply curve S'_N. The new long-run equilibrium is at point G, where once again price equals p^*, $p^* = ATC_{min}$, and economic profits are zero for the typical firm.

A careful look at Figure 8.11 should convince you that only when market price is p^* will all three conditions for long-run equilibrium be satisfied simultaneously. At price p^*, price equals marginal cost, so each firm maximizes profit and condition 1, as listed earlier, is satisfied. At output q^*, price equals average cost, too, so every firm earns zero economic profit and condition 2 is also satisfied. Finally, at p^*, market demand equals market supply, satisfying condition 3.

In competitive markets like this, where all firms are identical, we can rewrite our three necessary conditions for long-run equilibrium in a particularly compact way. Translating each of these conditions in order, we can see that if p^* is the long-run equilibrium market price, q^* the output of each identical firm, and N^* the long-run equilibrium number of firms in the industry, the necessary conditions for long-run equilibrium can be written:

> 1. $p^* = LRMC_{q^*}$
> 2. $p^* = LRAC_{q^*}$
> 3. $Q^d_{p^*} = N^* q^*$

As before, the first condition states that each firm maximizes profit and the second, that maximum obtainable economic profits are zero. The third states that quantity demanded

COMMON ERROR 8.2 Too Many Firms Entering

Figure 8.11 shows how entry and exit bring about long-run industry equilibrium. Notice that if there is positive economic profit, firms enter until profits return to zero economic profit. Following is a common student error. Consider this figure. In panel (a), suppose initially the supply curve is S_{50} and the short-run equilibrium price is p_1. In panel (b), the firm earns a positive short-run economic profit equal to the shaded green area π. In the long run, entry will occur to eliminate these positive profits. But how much entry occurs? Theory is clear: Entry occurs until the supply curve shifts precisely to S_1 in panel (a) and profits are zero in panel (b). But for some reason, students often think that entry doesn't end there!

Instead, they argue that entry continues and the supply curve shifts farther to the right to a curve like S_2. Students then continue to argue that firms now sustain an economic loss equal to the shaded gray area in panel (b), and therefore, firms leave the market in the long run. But according to the model of perfect competition, there is no logic to this. Why would firms continue to enter the market after the supply curve has shifted to S_1? If they enter at that point, they are assured of economic *losses*! If you were asked whether it makes sense to enter an industry where you are guaranteed to sustain an economic loss, would you enter? Of course not. Keep this is mind and don't make this common error.

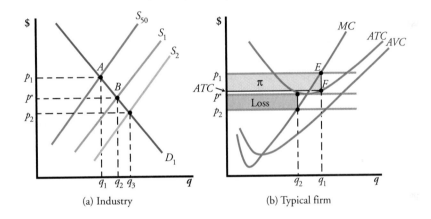

(a) Industry   (b) Typical firm

Common Error Figure 8.2 Too Many Firms Entering

In panel (a), initially the supply curve is S_{50} and the equilibrium price is p_1. In panel (b), the firm earns a positive economic profit equal to the shaded green area and entry will occur. Entry occurs until the supply curve shifts precisely to S_1 in panel (a) and profits are zero in panel (b). Firms do not continue to enter after the supply curve reaches S_1 in panel (a) because further entry will result in economic losses. If the supply curve shifts farther to the right to a curve like S_2, the price declines to p_2 and firms sustain an economic loss equal to the gray shaded area in panel (b).

at the equilibrium price, $Q_{p^*}^d$, is just equal to the quantity supplied by all N^* firms together, when market price is p^*.

Constant–Cost, Increasing–Cost, and Decreasing–Cost Industries

Until now, we've implicitly assumed that factor prices are independent of industry output, so input prices are unaffected as the industry expands or contracts output during adjustments from one long-run equilibrium to another. We refer to such an industry as

constant-cost industry

An industry in which factor prices are independent of industry output, so input prices are unaffected as industry output expands or contracts.

a **constant-cost industry.** What does the long-run supply curve look like in a constant-cost industry? In panel (a) of Figure 8.12, starting from an initial long-run equilibrium with supply equal to S_1, demand equal to D_1, and price of p_1, a permanent increase in market demand from D_1 to D_2 causes price to rise from p_1 to p_2 in the short run. At a price p_2, positive economic profits equal to the shaded green area in panel (b) exist, and entry occurs in response to those profits. If those new firms, with access to the same technology as the incumbent firms in the industry, can also acquire all the factors they need at the same existing factor prices, each will then have cost curves identical to those in panel (b). Entry must therefore continue to occur until the short-run market supply has shifted outward to S_2 in panel (a), and market price has returned to p_1, a price just equal to the minimum average cost of the representative firm so that each firm once again earns zero economic profit. In industries like this, in which factor prices are independent of the level of industry output, market price always returns to the same level in the long run, and therefore, the **long-run supply curve,** *LRS*, is horizontal. No matter how much short-run demand fluctuations result in price fluctuations above or below price p_1, in the long run, entry or exit always brings the price back to p_1.

long-run supply curve

All of the combinations of price and industry output that result in zero economic profit in the long run.

INCREASING COST INDUSTRIES You might question the assumption that factor prices are independent of total industry output. As industry output expands, there is often a significant increase in the demand for the factors of production in that industry, so that input prices increase. If, for example, production requires a certain amount of some rare mineral or some skilled labor that is in inelastic supply, the increased demand in the factor market will cause the price that every firm must pay for that factor to increase. Consider the recent rise in wages for workers in the information technology industry, or the increase in the price of lumber during boom periods in the home construction industry. In these markets, there is a positive relationship between factor prices

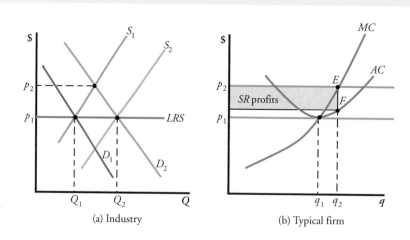

Figure 8.12 Long-Run Supply Curve in a Constant-Cost Industry
In a constant-cost industry, input prices are independent of industry output. In panel (a), initially the industry is in long-run equilibrium with short-run supply S_1, demand D_1, and equilibrium price p_1. In panel (b), economic profits are zero. If demand increases to D_2, the short-run price increases to p_2 and firms earn positive economic profits equal to the green shaded area in panel (b). In the long run, firms enter, the short-run supply curve shifts to S_2 in panel (a), and price returns to p_1, where economic profits are zero. In panel (a), the long-run supply curve, *LRS*, is the heavy red horizontal line at a price p_1.

increasing-cost industry

An industry in which factor prices are positively related to industry output, so input prices increase as industry output expands and decrease as industry output contracts.

and industry output. When industry output increases, so do factor prices; and when industry output decreases, so do factor prices. We refer to such industries as **increasing-cost industries.**

An increase in input prices has the effect of increasing firm costs, as Figure 8.13 illustrates. Initially, the long-run equilibrium is p_1, just equal to the representative firm's minimum long-run average cost on the curve AC_1 in panel (b). When demand for the product increases to D_2, price again rises to p_2, and in panel (b), firms increase their output to q_2 and make positive economic profits in the short run equal to the shaded green area, thus inducing long-run entry. This time, however, as new firms enter, they bid up the price of some factors, and every firm's costs increase in panel (b), shifting average cost and marginal cost upward to AC_2 and MC_2, respectively. Entry occurs only when there are excess profits to be earned, and excess profits cease to be possible once market price has fallen to p_3, just equal to the new higher level of minimum average cost on the curve AC_2 in panel (b). If further increases in market demand lead to further increases in factor prices, the long-run supply curve will be the upward-sloping curve LRS, as illustrated. The long-run supply curve consists of all the possible combinations of price and quantity that result in zero economic profit.

decreasing-cost industry

An industry in which factor prices are inversely related to industry output, so input prices decrease as industry output expands and increase as industry output contracts.

DECREASING COST INDUSTRIES There is one other possibility: as industry output expands, factor prices might decrease. We refer to such industries as **decreasing-cost industries.** Strange as this situation may seem, it is not unheard of. There can be economies of scale in the technology for producing some specialized input that results in a decline in the input price as more of the input is produced. If the price of that input declines as the number of units sold increases, the average cost for any firm that uses that

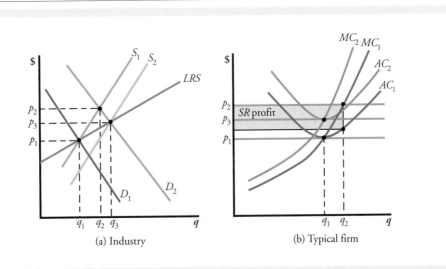

Figure 8.13 Long-Run Supply Curve in an Increasing Cost Industry
In an increasing-cost industry, there is a positive relationship between factor prices and industry output. Initially, in panel (a), the industry is in long-run equilibrium with short-run supply S_1, demand D_1, equilibrium price p_1, and economic profits are zero. If demand increases to D_2, the short-run price increases to p_2 and firms expand output in panel (b) from q_1 to q_2 and earn positive economic profits equal to the shaded green area. In the long run, firms enter, shifting the short-run supply curve to S_2. At the same time, the increase in industry output results in an increase in input prices and an upward shift in the MC and AC curves in panel (b). Eventually a new long-run equilibrium will be attained where price p_3 equals minimum average cost on the curve AC_2 in panel (b) and economic profits are zero. The long-run supply curve is the heavy red upward-sloping curve LRS.

factor will decline, and the result can be a downward-sloping long-run supply curve. For example, the personal computer market might be a decreasing-cost industry. As the output of personal computers increases, the demand for microprocessors increases and these microprocessors are produced, mostly by Intel, under conditions of large economies of scale. The more computers demanded by consumers from Dell, Gateway, Compaq, Hewlett Packard, and IBM, the more microprocessors are produced by Intel and the lower are Intel's average costs. If Intel lowers the price of its microprocessors as its costs decrease, the costs for the computer manufacturers will decrease as they produce and sell more computers.

▲▲▲ 8.5 APPLICATION   The Slope of the Long–Run Industry Supply Curves

So what does the slope of the typical long- run industry supply curve look like? Are there really such things as downward-sloping supply curves? Economist John Shea addressed these questions in a study of the supply curves in 26 manufacturing industries. Shea found that the most common type of supply curve was upward-sloping, exhibited by 16 of the 26 industries. Not surprisingly, the least common type of supply curve was downward-sloping,

exhibited by only three industries. The remaining seven industries appeared to have horizontal supply curves. Averaging over all 26 industries, the typical supply curve was upward-sloping with an elasticity of supply of 5.5, meaning that a 1 percent increase in price results in a 5.5 percent increase in quantity supplied in the long run.

Shea categorized supply curves in the 26 industries as follows:

Industries with Upward-Sloping Supply Curves	Industries with Horizontal Supply Curves	Industries with Downward-Sloping Supply Curves
Lumber	Animal and marine fats and oils	Prepared foods
Sawmills	Floor coverings	Construction equipment
Millwork and plywood	Synthetic fibers	Aircraft
Building paper and board	Metal barrels	
Drugs	Plumbing and heating products	
Paints	Structural metal	
Asphalt and paving materials	Lighting equipment	
Tires		
Stone, clay, glass, and containers		
Glass products, except containers		
Cement		
Structural clay		
Construction pottery		
Concrete and plaster		
Ordnance		
Electronic components		

Summary

1. Perfectively competitive markets are characterized by a large number of buyers and sellers, each one of which is a price taker; a homogeneous product; easy entry and exit; and perfect information. Firms maximize profits by undertaking any action to the point where the marginal cost of the action equals the marginal benefit of the action; therefore, with regard to output, firms maximize profits by producing at a level where the marginal cost of producing another unit equals the marginal revenue of selling the unit.

2. The short-run supply curve for the perfect competitor gives the profit-maximizing output at every market price. For prices below minimum AVC, the supply curve is vertical at zero units of output. At prices above minimum AVC, the supply curve lies directly on top of the $SRMC$ curve. A firm should shut down in the short run whenever TR falls below VC. For the perfect competitor, this occurs whenever market price is below AVC at the best level of output.

3. Producer surplus is any excess earned by the firm's factors of production, including the owners of capital and labor, over and above what they would earn if the firm did not sell any output. In the short run, producer surplus is the excess of total revenue over total variable cost.

4. The industry's short-run market supply curve is the horizontal sum of the supply curves for all firms in the short run. Short-run industry equilibrium is found where market demand intersects market supply with a fixed number of firms. In short-run equilibrium, every firm takes market price as given and sells the profit-maximizing output or shuts down. In the short run, firms can earn positive, zero (normal), or negative economic profit.

5. Short-run positive economic profit attracts entry, and short-run economic losses encourages exit. In long-rum equilibrium, all firms maximize profits, and maximum economic profit equals zero and market price $p^* = LRMC = LRAC$ for every firm. When factor prices paid by a competitive industry remain constant as the industry expands or contracts, the industry is a constant-cost industry and the long-run supply curve is horizontal. If industry expansion causes factor prices to rise, the industry is an increasing-cost industry and long-run supply will be upward-sloping. If increased demand for factors causes factor prices to fall, the industry is a decreasing-cost industry and the long-run supply curve will be downward-sloping.

Self-Test Problems

1. Questions *a* through *c* refer to the following data on the costs of a competitive firm:

Output	MC	AVC	ATC
1	2	2	18
2	4	3	11
3	6	4	9.333
4	8	5	9

Output	MC	AVC	ATC
5	10	6	9.2
6	12	7	9.667
7	14	8	10.286
8	16	9	11
9	18	10	11.778
10	20	11	12.6

a. On a piece of graph paper, plot this firm's *SRMC*, *AVC*, and *ATC* curves. On the same piece of graph paper, carefully draw the firm's short-run supply curve. Be sure to indicate the output supplied at every price.

b. For the firm in this table, what is the profit-maximizing level of output, and the level of maximum profit: when market price is $15? When it is $9? When it is $1?

c. Suppose market price is $9. Add two columns to this table. In the first, compute firm profit at the different levels of output. In the second, compute producer surplus, *PS*, at the different levels of output. Which level of output maximizes profit? Which maximizes producer surplus? What is the difference between profit and producer surplus at every level of output? What accounts for this difference?

2. A perfectly competitive industry is composed of a large number of firms, each with the total cost function:

$$SRTC = q^2 + 1$$

and the marginal cost function:

$$SRMC = 2q$$

The demand curve facing the industry is:

$$Q^d = 52 - p$$

a. What are the long-run equilibrium price, number of firms, and profit per firm in this industry?

b. If demand now shifts to

$$Q^d = 53 - p$$

what are the long-run price, equilibrium number of firms, and profit per firm?

3. Assume that the lumber industry is a perfectly competitive increasing-cost industry.

a. Explain the short-run impact of a $100 per-ton tax on the lumber industry and a typical lumber producer. Explain your answer using graphs for both a typical firm and the industry.

b. Explain the long-run impact of the tax on the lumber industry and a typical lumber producer. Explain your answer using graphs.

c. On your graph, indicate the total tax revenues generated by the tax on lumber in the long run.

d. Would the tax generate more tax revenue for the government if the lumber industry were a constant-cost industry? Explain, using a graph.

Questions and Problems for Review

1. Grade A winter wheat, corn, Saudi light crude, bananas, automobiles, pork bellies, wine, computers, video games: consider the market for each of these products. Can each be reasonably described as perfectly competitive? If so, explain how each market satisfies the requirements of perfect competition. If not, identify which requirements are not met.

2. "In long-run equilibrium, each firm in a perfectly competitive industry earns zero profit. Why, then, would anyone ever want to start a business in a perfectly competitive industry?" Discuss.

3. "Everybody knows price-taking behavior is irrational. In a perfectly competitive market, the firm that sets its *own* price below that of its rivals is sure to increase its sales, and so its profit. By regarding price as 'fixed,' the firm foregoes this profit opportunity." Comment.

4. Can there ever be more than one equilibrium price in a perfectly competitive market? Why or why not?

5. True or False? Justify Your Answer. "In the short run, a profit-maximizing perfectly competitive firm *might* choose an output in a region of its technology that exhibits increasing marginal returns to labor."

6. A student once remarked, "To maximize short-run profit, we've got to produce at minimum unit cost." Using a diagram with an ordinary U-shaped *SRAC* curve and upward-sloping *SRMC* curve, identify the output level the student thinks is best. If market price is fixed and above *SRAC* at this output, will profit be maximized there? Why or why not? If price is below *SRAC*, will profit be maximized there? Why or why not? Will profit ever be maximized there?

7. A competitive industry consisting of 100 firms produces good *X*. When firms have chosen the optimal size for the long run, their short-run costs are identical and given by:

$$SRTC = 2q^2 + 8$$
$$SRMC = 4q$$

Market demand is:

$$Q = 130 - p$$

Briefly justify your answers to the following:

a. What is the short-run equilibrium price in this market?

b. What is the long-run equilibrium price in this market?

c. How many firms must enter or exit this industry for the industry to be in long-run equilibrium?

8. A competitive industry is in long-run equilibrium. We know the following:

- Market demand is downward-sloping. The price elasticity of market demand is everywhere constant and equal to $\varepsilon_p = 2$.

- Current technology and input prices enable each firm to reach the lowest possible level of average total cost at an output of 10 units.

- The current market price is $100.

- There are currently 200 firms in the industry.

Suddenly, a technological innovation enables every firm in the industry to cut the average total cost of any level of output by 10 percent. Answer the following questions. Be sure to justify your answer.

a. What will be the new long-run equilibrium price in this market?

b. How much output will each firm produce in the new long-run equilibrium?

c. How many firms will there be in the industry in the new long-run equilibrium?

9. Many firms must pay a corporate profit tax, computed as a fixed percentage of total profit. Suppose a perfectly competitive industry is in long-run equilibrium before such a tax is imposed. The government then imposes one just on the one industry. Illustrate your answer to the following questions using a single carefully drawn set of diagrams for the industry and the representative firm.

a. Analyze and explain the short-run effects such a tax will have on market price and output, output per firm, and firm after-tax profit.

b. Analyze and explain the long-run effects such a tax will have on the number of firms in the industry, market price and output, output per firm, and firm after-tax profit.

10. Suppose an asparagus farmer is in long-run equilibrium in an increasing-cost perfectly competitive industry with $p^* = \$1.00$ per pound and $q^* = 10,000$ pounds. Suppose a large influx of immigrant labor from Mexico decreases wages for asparagus pickers by 15 percent. Show how this decrease in wages would impact the cost curves for the farmer. Also show how the asparagus industry would be impacted in the short run and the long run. What would you expect the asparagus farmer's political position to be regarding the immigration of workers from Mexico?

11. In this chapter, we have said that in the long-run equilibrium, firms receive zero economic profit. What incentive does this give firms to remain in the market? How can firms survive without earning profit in the long-run?

12. Just Juice is in a perfectly competitive long-run equilibrium, selling juice at a price of $5 per gallon. Demand falls and the price falls to $3 per gallon. At this new price, Just Juice produces 100 gallons of juice at an AVC of $3 per gallon. Will Just Juice continue to produce juice in the short run? What if AVC at 100 gallons of production was $3.25 per gallon? Explain your reasoning using a graph(s).

13. In a perfectly competitive widget market, demand and short-run supply are: $Q = 100 - 2p$ and $Q = 40 + p$.

a. What is the short-run equilibrium price and quantity in the widget market?

b. For the firm Perfect Widgets, $SRMC = AVC = 22$ when $q = 2$. What output will Perfect Widgets produce in the short run?

14. Suppose the movie theater industry in a city is a constant cost industry and is in long-run equilibrium when a per-ticket tax of $1.00 is placed on movie tickets.

a. Show the short-run impact of the tax on the movie theater industry.

b. In the short run, does the price of a theater ticket rise by $1.00? Explain using a graph.

c. Show the long-run impact of the tax on the movie theater industry. Does the price of a ticket rise by $1.00 in the long run? Explain using a graph.

15. Repeat question 8.14 for an increasing-cost movie theater industry. How do your answers change?

16. Identify a few industries in each of the following categories:

a. Constant-cost

b. Increasing-cost

c. Decreasing-cost

17. Suppose the 100 percent biodegradable diaper industry is a constant-cost perfectly competitive industry and is currently in long-run equilibrium. Now suppose the government decides that 100 percent biodegradable diapers have positive social impacts, so the government offers a subsidy (not a tax) of s dollars per unit to the producers of biodegradable diapers.

a. Explain the short-run impact of the subsidy on the biodegradable diaper industry and a typical biodegradable diaper producer. Explain your answer using graphs for both a typical firm and the industry.

b. Explain the long-run impact of the subsidy on the biodegradable diaper industry and a typical biodegradable diaper producer. Explain your answer using graphs.

c. On your graph indicate the cost of the subsidy to the government in the long run.

d. Would the subsidy cost the government more or less if the biodegradable diaper industry was an increasing-cost industry? Explain using a graph.

18. Downtown Philadelphia is famous for its soft pretzel stands. There are hundreds of such stands located on street corners. Suppose the Philadelphia soft pretzel retail market is a perfectly competitive constant-cost industry. If the manufacturers of Philadelphia soft pretzels (the wholesalers) increase the price of pretzels from $1.20 a dozen to $1.60 a dozen, use graphs to answer the following questions:

a. How will this input price increase affect the cost curves for a typical soft pretzel stand owner in the short run?

b. What will happen to the stand owner's price, output, and profit in the short run?

c. What happens to both consumer and producer surplus in the short run as a result of the increase in wholesale pretzel prices?

d. What will happen in the long run?

19. Consider a firm with the following production costs:

Output	Total Cost
0	50
1	100
2	128
3	148
4	162
5	180
6	200
7	222
8	260
9	305
10	360
11	425

a. Assuming a constant-cost perfectly competitive industry, what is the firm's profit-maximizing output if price equals $40? What is the firm's profit? What is the firm's producer surplus? Assume that the firm cannot produce fractional units of output.

b. Assuming a perfectly competitive industry, what is the firm's profit-maximizing output if demand declines and causes the price to fall to $35? What is the firm's profit? What is the firm's producer surplus?

c. Assuming a perfectly competitive industry, what is the firm's profit-maximizing output if demand declines further and causes the price to fall to $20? What is the firm's profit?

d. Assuming a perfectly competitive industry and a price equal to $40, what would be the firm's profit-maximizing output if fixed costs increased by $100 to a total of $150? What is the firm's profit?

20. "In long-run equilibrium, every firm in a competitive industry earns zero economic profit. Thus, if the price falls, all of these firms will be unable to stay in business and the industry will disappear." Using a graph(s), evaluate this statement.

Internet Exercises

Visit *http://www.myeconlab.com/waldman* for this chapter's Web exercises. Answer real-world economics problems by doing research on the Internet.

Chapter 9
The Invisible Hand at Work

Economic science was born in 1776, with the publication of Adam Smith's treatise *The Wealth of Nations*. A perceptive student of market economies, Smith drew attention to the crucial role self-interest plays in market performance. In his famous "invisible hand" passage, Smith wrote:

> As every individual endeavors as much as he can ... to employ his capital that its produce may be of greatest value; every individual necessarily labours to render the annual revenue of the society as great as he can. He generally, indeed, neither intends to promote the public interest, nor knows how much he is promoting it ... [B]y directing that industry in such a manner as its produce may be of the greatest value, he intends only his own gain, and he is in this, as in many other cases, led by an *invisible hand* to promote an end which was not part of his intention. Nor is it always the worse for the society that it was no part of it. By pursuing his own interest, he frequently promotes that of society more effectually than when he really intends to promote it.
>
> [Adam Smith, *The Wealth of Nations*.
> New York: Modern Library, 1994, p. 484-485.]

Today the invisible hand remains a powerful metaphor that can inspire us to think very differently than we have so far in this text. Until now, we have studied how agents behave alone and in groups. We have raised and answered questions such as: Which goods will the consumer purchase? How much will she buy? Which inputs will the firm employ? How much of each? How much output will be produced? How many firms will there be in long-run equilibrium? These and the many other questions we've studied so far are all questions of positive economics. Each asks "what is?" or "what will be?" given the circumstances of the problem. Recall from Chapter 1 that positive economics uses economic models to predict the actual consequences of actions.

Learning Objectives

After reading Chapter 9, you will have learned:

➤ How to use producer and consumer surplus as a measure of welfare.

➤ Why perfect competition maximizes total surplus and is Pareto-efficient.

➤ That Pareto efficiency in competitive markets does not take into account the distribution of goods and services among consumers.

Featured Applications

➤ 9.1 Application Adam Smith's "Folly and Presumption" of Market Intervention

➤ 9.2 Application The Case for Free Trade

➤ 9.3 Application The Distributional Consequences of the Proposed Bush Tax Cuts

Chapter 1 also introduced the concept of normative economics, which is the study of what should be, and requires the use of value judgments to determine whether the predicted outcomes of economic actions are good or bad. In this chapter, we broaden our perspective and take several steps into the world of normative economics. In normative economics, instead of asking "what is?" or "what will be?" we ask "what would be better?" or "what would be best?" or "how should things be?" While positive economic analysis can be value-free, normative economic analysis is inherently value-laden. This is because we cannot ask "what is better?" or "what is best?" except by reference to some standard of good and bad. Most of us draw our standards of good and bad from our religion or moral philosophy, not from economics. As a result, economics can never give us the "right" answer to normative questions. As you'll see, however, economics can help us to think systematically about normative questions, and that in itself can be quite an accomplishment.

9.1 Assessing Market Outcomes

In Chapter 8, we studied the theory of perfectly competitive markets. In this chapter, we assess the desirability of the perfectly competitive equilibrium. Consider the competitive market with demand and long-run supply curves as shown in Figure 9.1. We know that under ordinary circumstances, the forces of supply and demand will cause this market to come to rest at price p^* and quantity q^*. However, we can imagine alternative market outcomes when something interferes with the forces of supply and demand. For example, the government could mandate that the price of this good be p_1 and that no more than q_1 units may be produced and sold. Providing no one breaks the law, the market outcome would then be (q_1, p_1) at point A, rather than (q^*, p^*) at point B. Which outcome is better, point A or point B? Which outcome is best?

To make these judgments, we need some way to assess alternative market outcomes from a normative point of view. As noted, any method we devise to do this will inevitably involve ethical values, because the act of judging is an inherently value-laden activity. The

Figure 9.1 Different Market Outcomes
With perfect competition, price is p^* and quantity is q^*. We want to know whether society is better or worse off if the government mandates a price p_1 and quantity q_1.

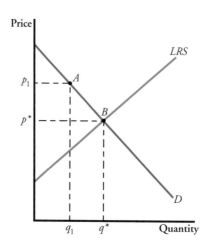

inclusion of value judgments should signal us to proceed with caution. But it need not prevent us from going forward, because most people will generally agree on certain broad ethical matters relevant to our task. For example, most people believe that the welfare of society is inseparably tied to the welfare of the individuals within that society. Today, this seems almost like a truism, but it has not always been so. In medieval Europe, people believed that the interests of society were inseparable from the interests of the king, or the church, and that the interests of very few others mattered. By contrast, most modern societies hold the view that the welfare of *all* individuals matters. Moreover, we generally believe that individuals themselves can best judge what is in their own interest, and we tend to reject the paternalistic view that someone else knows better than we do what is good for us. Finally, most people also accept the view that society is made better off when any one person is made better off, provided no one else is made worse off in the process. This is the concept of *Pareto efficiency*, introduced in Chapter 1, which is fundamental to the economist's view of social welfare. This chapter uses Pareto efficiency to analyze the efficiency of competitive markets. Chapters 11 and 12 use the concept of Pareto efficiency to analyze the economic problems associated with monopoly, and Chapter 19 undertakes a thorough analysis of Pareto efficiency.

Together, the commonly agreed-upon considerations argue for criteria of social welfare that depend on the welfare of each individual, as that individual sees it, and that give weight to the well-being of each individual. To satisfy the criteria of Pareto efficiency, our measure of welfare should also register an increase in society's welfare whenever the well-being of even one person increases, *ceteris paribus*. Economists have devised one such criterion of social welfare, called *total surplus*, that satisfies all these requirements, and that is also easy to apply.

Total Surplus and Social Welfare

The well-being of both buyers and sellers is important when analyzing the social welfare of a particular market outcome. As long as we maintain the viewpoint in which we suppose that conditions outside the market in question remain unchanged during our analysis, buyers and sellers in this one market are the relevant groups whose well-being we need to account for.

LONG–RUN PRODUCER SURPLUS In Chapter 4, we saw that consumer surplus could serve as a money-scaled measure of the individual buyers' well-being under alternative market conditions. In Chapter 8, we saw that producer surplus could serve as a money-scaled measure of the seller's well-being, and we derived a measure for short-run producer surplus. Having derived the long-run supply curve, we are now ready to derive a measure for long-run producer surplus. Producer surplus is always the excess earned by the firm's factors of production, including the owners of capital and labor, over and above what they would earn if the firm did not sell any output. Therefore, producer surplus measures the excess a firm's factors of production earn over and above what they minimally require in order to be just indifferent between producing and not producing. What changes between the short run and the long run is not the idea, but what the firm will "minimally require" in order to continue operating.

In long-run equilibrium at any point along a long-run supply curve, economic profit always equals zero. Long-run producer surplus therefore cannot refer to the long-run level of economic profit earned by firms, or it would always equal zero. To explain the distinction between short-run and long-run producer surplus, it is useful to return to the case of an increasing-cost industry with an upward-sloping long-run supply curve. Figure 9.2

Figure 9.2 Long-Run Producer Surplus in an Increasing-Cost Industry In a market with long-run supply $p = \$10 + \$1/2q$, and demand $p = \$100 - \$2q$, equilibrium quantity equals 36 and price equals $28.00. The area of the shaded green triangle, $1/2(\$28.00 - \$10.00)(36) = \$324$, represents the payments to factors of production above the minimally required payments to produce 36 units of output, and therefore equals producer surplus.

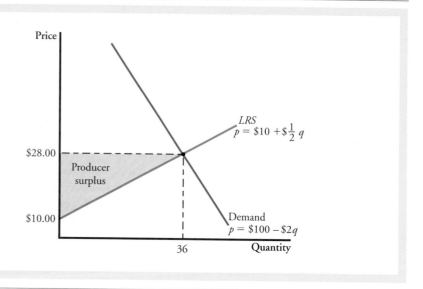

shows such a market with long-run supply curve, $p = \$10 + \$1/2q$, and demand, $p = \$100 - \$2q$. Setting supply equal to demand, the long-run equilibrium quantity is:

$$\$10 + \$\frac{1}{2}q = \$100 - \$2q$$

$$\$2.5q = \$90$$

$$q = 36$$

Equilibrium price is $p = \$100 - \$2q = \$100 - \$72 = \$28.00$.

To calculate producer surplus, we must determine what the firms' factors of production earn over and above what they minimally require in order to be just indifferent between producing and not producing 36 units of output. Given long-run supply $p = \$10 + \$1/2q$, in order to produce the first unit of output, the firms' factors of production would require a minimum price $p = \$10 + \$1/2(1) = \$10.50$. From the *LRS* curve, we know that at $p = \$10.50$, if the industry produced 1 unit of output, profits would be zero. Therefore, at any price lower than $10.50, the firms would sustain a loss and be unable to minimally compensate their factors of production. It follows that $10.50 measures what the firms' factors of production minimally require in order to be willing to produce one unit of output. Using the same reasoning, in order to produce the second unit of output, the firms' factors of production require a price $p = \$10 + \$1/2(2) = \$11.00$; and for the third unit, they require a minimum price $p = 10 + 1/2(3) = \$11.50$. For each additional unit produced, the firms' factors would minimally require a $0.50 increase in price.

In equilibrium, $q = 36$ and $p = \$28.00$, and in order to produce the 36th unit of output, the firms' factors would minimally require a price $p = \$10 + \$1/2(36) = \$28.00$. However, for each of the first 35 units produced, the price of $28.00 more than covers what the firms' factors of production would minimally require to produce each of those units, and therefore the factors earn some producer surplus on each of those first 35 units. Specifically: on the first unit, the firms' factors of production earn a producer surplus of $\$28.00 - \$10.50 = \$17.50$; on the second unit, they earn a producer surplus of $28.00 − $11.00 = $17.00; on the third unit, they earn a producer surplus of $28.00 − $11.50 = $16.50; and so forth. This analysis assumes that output can be produced only in discrete increments of one unit; however, if output can be subdivided into small fractions of a unit, producer surplus is measured by the green shaded triangle in Figure 9.2, or producer surplus = (1/2)($28.00 − $10.00)(36) = $324.

Who exactly gets this producer surplus? It's not economic profit to the firm, because anywhere along the *LRS* curve, including at a price of $28.00, economic profit equals zero. The producer surplus has gone to compensate some factor or factors of production over and above what they minimally would accept to produce 36 units of output. For example, suppose the supply curve for every factor of production except labor is perfectly elastic; that is, firms can obtain an unlimited supply of all inputs (except labor) at a fixed price. The supply curve for labor, however, is upward-sloping so that additional units of labor can be obtained only by paying a higher wage. As firms increase output, they must increase wages to attract more labor into the industry. In this case, the entire producer surplus measures the amount by which total wage payments exceed the minimal wage payments necessary to attract enough workers into the industry to produce 36 units of output.

Long-run producer surplus in an increasing-cost industry therefore measures the surplus to factors of production that have upward-sloping supply curves. Factors of production with horizontal supply curves receive no producer surplus. Furthermore, because in a constant-cost industry, all of the factors of production have horizontal supply curves, long-run producer surplus is zero.

CONSUMER SURPLUS, PRODUCER SURPLUS, AND TOTAL SURPLUS If we let *CS* denote aggregate consumer surplus and *PS* denote aggregate long-run producer surplus, we can construct a basic criterion of social welfare, called total surplus (*TS*) by adding the two together:

$$TS = CS + PS$$

total surplus

The sum of consumer surplus and producer surplus; often used as a measure of economic welfare.

Total surplus has all the desirable properties mentioned earlier of a welfare measure: it depends on the well-being of the individuals concerned, both buyers and sellers; it weighs the interests of each buyer and seller equally; and moreover, buyers' and sellers' own assessments of their own well-being. Notice also that *TS* increases whenever *CS* increases, *ceteris paribus*, and that *TS* increases whenever *PS* increases, *ceteris paribus*. The *TS* measure therefore satisfies Pareto efficiency, too: social welfare increases whenever the welfare of any one individual—whether buyer or seller—increases—other things equal.

There is one more reason economists like the *TS* measure of social welfare: it's easy to represent on a graph. Suppose, for example, we wanted to assess a market outcome like (q_1, p_1) at point *e* in Figure 9.3. In this figure, buyers all pay a fixed price p_1 per unit, and no more than q_1 units are sold. Consumer surplus, the purple area $abep_1$ underneath the demand curve and above the price line, is labeled *CS* in the figure. Producer surplus, *PS*, is the green area p_1ecd above the supply curve and below the price line. Total surplus, the sum of *CS* and *PS*, is therefore the entire purple and green areas between the demand curve and the supply curve at the output level q_1.

To compare alternative market outcomes, all we have to do is compare the relevant areas on the market demand and market supply diagram. In Figure 9.4, let's compare hypothetical market outcomes (q_1, p_1) and (q_2, p_2). Without some yardstick such as total surplus, it might be difficult to rank these two outcomes from a social point of view. The first one involves a low price, but low output as well. The second involves a higher price,

Figure 9.3 Assessing Market Outcomes with Total Surplus

If the market outcome is at point e with a price p_1 and quantity q_1, total surplus TS is the sum of the purple consumer surplus CS $abep_1$ and the green producer surplus PS p_1ecd.

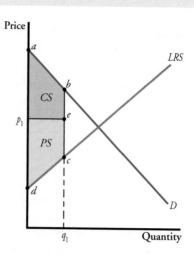

COMMON ERROR 9.1   Assuming That Long–Run Producer Surplus Always Equals Industry Profit

Students often confuse the concept of producer surplus with that of the firms' economic profits. In the long run, however, economic profits are zero at any point on the long-run supply curve, and therefore, if producer surplus is greater than zero, producer surplus cannot equal profit. Producer surplus is always the excess that the firm's factors of production earn over and above what they would earn if the firm did not sell any output. Producer surplus therefore measures the excess a firm's factors of production earn over and above what they minimally require to induce them to sell their services to the owner of the firm.

In an increasing-cost industry, long-run producer surplus is positive and greater than economic profit, because input prices, such as the wage and the rental rate for capital, increase as industry output increases. The increase in input prices is necessary to induce additional units of these inputs into the increasing-

cost industry. Long-run producer surplus in an increasing cost industry might more accurately be called "sellers' surplus," because it measures the surplus earned by the sellers of inputs rather than the surplus earned by firms.

In a constant-cost industry, long-run producer surplus does indeed equal industry profit, because input prices do not increase or decrease as industry output changes. With constant input prices and zero economic profits along the constant-cost industry's horizontal long-run supply curve, there is no producer surplus. In the case of a constant-cost industry, therefore, long-run producer surplus is equal to profit, which equals zero. But this is not the case in an increasing-cost industry, where long-run producer surplus is greater than industry profit. Don't make the common error of confusing long-run producer surplus with profit.

---

but a higher output as well. By computing TS in both cases, we see that (q_2,p_2) dominates (q_1,p_1) from a social point of view, because the total surplus generated under the outcome (q_2,p_2) exceeds that generated under (q_1,p_1) by an amount equal to the area of the shaded purple trapezoid.

In Figures 9.3 and 9.4, we chose "odd" market outcomes—ones lying on neither the market demand curve nor the market supply curve. Doing so illustrates the important point that TS can be used to evaluate any market outcome, not just conventional or ordinary ones. It is a flexible and very useful tool, as we will see throughout the remainder of the text.

Figure 9.4 Comparing the Total Surplus of Different Market Outcomes
Total surplus with output q_2 and price p_2 is greater than total surplus with output q_1 and price p_1 by the shaded purple trapeziod.

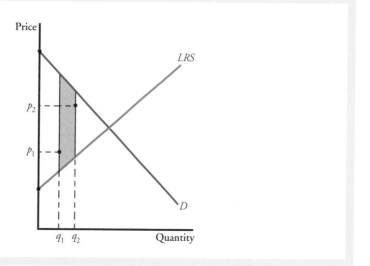

▲▲▲ **9.1 APPLICATION**   Adam Smith's "Folly and Presumption" of Market Intervention

As a champion of competition and market forces, Adam Smith was not very fond of politicians who proposed policies that distorted competitive market outcomes. For example, he wrote:

> The statesman, who should attempt to direct private people in what manner they ought to employ their capitals, would not only load himself with a most unnecessary attention, but assume an authority which could safely be trusted, not only to no single person, but to no council or senate whatever, and which would no-where be so dangerous as in the hands of a man who had folly and presumption enough to fancy himself fit to exercise it.
>
> [Adam Smith, *The Wealth of Nations.* New York: Modern Library, 1994, p. 485.]

By looking at two very common forms of government intervention in the marketplace—rent control and agricultural price supports—we can get a better idea of what Smith had in mind when he penned these words.

Suppose panel (a) of the figure illustrates the market demand and long-run supply of apartments in a metropolitan area. In the absence of government intervention, this market would come to rest at an equilibrium price of

p^*, with a total of q^* units rented. Well-meaning local governments from New York City to Berkeley, California, have tried to improve on this competitive outcome for the citizens in their communities. Many communities have passed rent-control laws establishing some maximum monthly rents that apartment owners can charge. Looking at the figure, suppose a city council passed a law stating that no apartment could rent for more than p_1 per month. At price p_1, owners will rent only q_1 units. People lucky enough to get one of these apartments pay less than they would have to pay at the market clearing price p^*, but is this good social policy?

By applying our *TS* measure of social welfare, we see that the answer is "no." This figure shows us that total social welfare is lower with rent control than with a competitive market equilibrium. Under rent control, the q_1 units rented at price p_1 give total surplus of the purple area *abcd*. By contrast, the greater number q^* that would be rented out at the higher price p^* with a competitive market equilibrium gives the larger total surplus of the purple and green areas *aed*. Rent control therefore lowers social welfare by the green area *bec* > 0.

You should not get the impression that governments enter markets only to keep prices low. For example, consider the U.S. government's agricultural policy. In the

(continued)

Application Figure 9.1
Rent Controls and Price Supports

In panel (a), with a rent ceiling of p_1, total surplus equals the shaded purple area *abcd*, which is less than the total surplus equal to the sum of the purple and green shaded areas *aed* with the competitive outcome at q^* and p^*. In panel (b), with output limited by the government to q_1, price is p_1; and total surplus equals the shaded purple area *abcd*, which is less than the total surplus equal to the sum of the purple and green shaded areas *aed* with the competitive outcome at q^* and p^*.

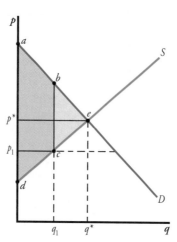

(a) Apartments market with rent control

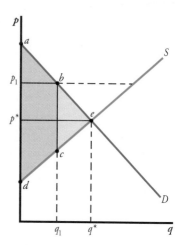

(b) Crop market with price supports

words of the 1992 Democratic party platform, America's agricultural policy has for many years and in many ways endeavored to "... ensure that family farmers get a fair return for their labor and investment." Over the years, many different programs have been devised to serve that goal. The Conservation Reserve Program (CRP) was one such program, under which the government paid farmers to keep part of their land out of production in order to keep crop prices artificially high.

Panel (b) of this figure shows market demand and market supply for some agricultural product eligible for the CRP, such as corn, soybeans, or wheat. In the absence of any government intervention, this market would come to rest at an equilibrium price p^* with q^* tons produced and consumed. Suppose, however, the government pays farmers not to produce, so that total output sold declines to q_1, while the price buyers pay rises to p_1. Even ignoring the cost to the government—and therefore to soci-

ety—of the CRP payments to farmers, is this scheme to raise prices above the market equilibrium good social policy?

Once again, under the criterion of social welfare we've been using, the answer is "no." Panel (b) illustrates that total social welfare is reduced by this program. Under the CRP, the q_1 units sold at price p_1 give total surplus of the purple area *abcd*. By contrast, the q^* units produced and consumed at the lower market equilibrium price p^* give a larger total surplus of the purple and green areas *aed*. The CRP program therefore lowers social welfare by the green area *bec* > 0, even ignoring the additional social costs of the CRP payments themselves.

So Adam Smith was providing valuable insight with his observation against "statesmen who should attempt to direct people in what manner they ought to employ their capitals."

9.2   Competition and Welfare

This chapter began with Smith's famous quote arguing that self-interest, harnessed by the invisible hand of competition, furthers society's interest. We're now equipped to examine that claim in detail to ask and answer the very important question, "What's so great about competition?" Here we'll focus on competition in the product market.

Competition and Total Surplus

Imagine a society of individuals wishing to produce and consume some good. Let the market demand curve in Figure 9.5 reflect buyers' preferences and willingness to pay for good X. Let the market supply curve reflect producers' technology and costs of production for good X. With enough cooperation among consumers and producers, or with enough coercion exerted upon one group by the other or by some outside force such as the government, we can imagine literally any (q,p) pair in the plane of Figure 9.5 as a possible market outcome. Take (q_1,p_1), for example. Buyers and sellers could agree among themselves that price would be p_1 and no more than q_1 units of the good would be produced and consumed. Or the government could require price to be p_1, leaving buyers the freedom to consume as much or as little as they chose. In this second case, sellers would want to sell more than q_1 units, but buyers would buy no more than q_1 at price p_1, so no more than q_1 would actually be sold. One way or another, we could contrive to arrange that, (q_1,p_1) be the market outcome.

By contrast, only one market outcome will arise here under perfect competition. If consumers take price as given, and worry only about maximizing their own utility from consumption, and if producers take price as given, and worry only about maximizing their own profit, then the only equilibrium market outcome under perfect competition will be the pair (q^*,p^*), where market demand intersects market supply at point e in Figure 9.5.

Which one of these outcomes is better for society? We can find the answer by measuring total surplus. At market outcome (q_1,p_1), total surplus is the purple area *abcd*. At (q^*,p^*), however, total surplus equals the sum of the purple and green areas *aed*. Since area *aed* exceeds area *abcd* by the green area *bec* > 0, the market outcome under perfect competition gives rise to greater total surplus, and so to greater social welfare.

Is there something special about the alternative (q_1,p_1) we contrasted with the competitive outcome (q^*,p^*)? Not really. In fact, it's the other way around: There's something special about the competitive market outcome (q^*,p^*). Specifically, the competitive outcome (q^*,p^*) is precisely the one that maximizes social welfare under the criterion we have employed. It will generate greater total surplus than any other market outcome we can imagine.

Figure 9.5 Maximization of Total Surplus Under Perfect Competition
The competitive equilibrium price equals p^* and quantity equals q^* and total surplus is maximized and equal to the sum of the purple and green areas *aed*. With any other price and quantity combination, total surplus is smaller. For example, with price p_1 and quantity q_1 total surplus equals the purple area *abcd*.

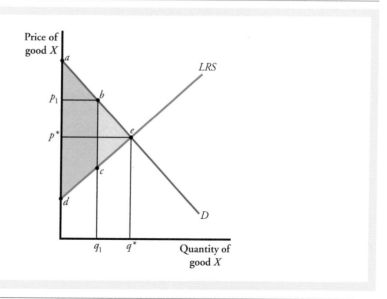

marginal social benefit

The extra contribution that an additional unit of a good makes to total social welfare, typically represented for an additional unit of output as the vertical distance from the quantity axis up to the demand curve.

marginal social cost curve

The extra social cost of producing an additional unit of output, typically represented for an additional unit of output as the vertical distance from the quantity axis up to the supply curve.

To further understand why the competitive outcome (q^*, p^*) in Figure 9.5 maximizes total surplus, notice that for any quantity of good X, the vertical distance from the quantity axis up to the demand curve measures the incremental or marginal addition to consumers' welfare from the consumption of that last unit of output. Under the welfare criterion we are employing, the ordinary market demand curve can therefore also be interpreted as a **marginal social benefit** curve, measuring at every quantity the marginal contribution that additional unit makes to total social welfare. Similarly, the vertical distance from the quantity axis to the market supply curve at any output measures the additional costs to some firm, or firms, of the last unit produced. Therefore the market supply curve can be interpreted as a **marginal social cost** curve, giving at every quantity the incremental cost to society of producing the last additional unit.

Now look again at Figure 9.5. When we consider together the marginal social benefit and the marginal social cost of output, we can see that all output levels less than q^* are "worthwhile" to society, and all those greater than q^* are not. Imagine beginning at an output of zero and, as you consider each successive unit of output in turn, ask yourself whether society should produce the unit. You'll see that every unit up to and including the q_1th unit is worthwhile—each offers a marginal social benefit that exceeds its marginal social cost. But social welfare can be increased still further if we move beyond q_1. Notice that every one of the units between q_1 and q^* is also worth it, so each adds something positive to the size of the social welfare pie. Should we increase output beyond q^*? No; for each unit of output beyond q^*, marginal social cost exceeds marginal social benefit, so total welfare would actually decline. The output q^* therefore does indeed maximize total social welfare.

Why, then, does a competitive market settle at the output that gives the greatest total social welfare? In a properly functioning competitive market, the social benefit of the last unit of output purchased coincides with the well-being buyers derive from it, while the social cost of the last unit produced coincides with the input costs sellers must pay to produce it. Whenever some buyer's willingness to pay for an additional unit exceeds the incremental costs of producing it, we can be sure some profit-seeking firm will produce and offer that unit for sale. When there is competition among such firms, we can be sure that buyers and sellers will exploit all such opportunities for mutual gain.

Adam Smith understood the welfare implications of competitive markets very well, and we are indebted to him for the vivid metaphor of the invisible hand, emphasizing as it does the value to society in the many self-interested actions of buyers and sellers that bring us output q^* in Figure 9.5. There may be other ways to arrive at an output of q^* in Figure 9.5; for example, careful planning and centralized control of production and consumption. But the important implication of what we've now discovered is that no other way of organizing production and consumption can ever do *better* than competition can. Indeed, perfect competition maximizes our criterion of social welfare, and unless some other way of producing and distributing goods happens by design or by chance to exactly reproduce the competitive market outcome, it must result in a lower level of social welfare.

Competition and Pareto Efficiency

Because market outcomes under perfect competition maximize total surplus, some economists have argued that perfect competition is a socially optimal way to organize economic activity. This is the position Adam Smith would have taken and, as long as you accept all the assumptions built into our total surplus criterion of social welfare, the argument has a great deal of logical force. However, there are some us who would question, and even object to, one or more of those many assumptions. Rejecting any one of them brings the optimality of perfect competition into question.

Are the virtues of perfect competition built on a shaky foundation of assumptions? The study of perfect competition would indeed hold less interest for economists if this were so. As it turns out, we can say much more about the optimality of perfect competition based on an understanding of Pareto efficiency. Recall that a Pareto improvement is defined as any change within society that makes at least one person better off and harms no one. A situation is Pareto-efficient if once in the situation, no subsequent Pareto improvements are possible.

Now think specifically about market outcomes. Are *all* market outcomes Pareto-efficient? No. Look, for example, at the hypothetical outcome (q_1, p_1) in Figure 9.6. We can see that (q_1, p_1) would not be Pareto-efficient. How do we know? Suppose output were increased just a bit beyond q_1. Such an increase in output has a marginal social value measured by the vertical distance from the quantity axis up to the demand curve that exceeds its social cost measured by the vertical distance from the quantity axis up to the supply curve, so adding a bit more output beyond q_1 makes the social welfare pie that much bigger. With a bigger pie to divide among a fixed number of people, there must be ways to divide the pie so that someone gets a slightly bigger slice while no one else has to get a slice any smaller than they had before. Because we could increase output beyond q_1 and make someone better off without hurting anyone else, market outcomes like (q_1, p_1) will not be Pareto-efficient.

Furthermore, we can see in Figure 9.6 that any increase in output beyond q^* has a marginal social value that is less than its marginal social cost, so adding a bit more output beyond q^* makes the social welfare pie smaller. With a smaller pie to divide among a fixed number of people, someone must receive a smaller slice than they had before. Because an increase in output beyond q^* makes someone worse off, it will not be a Pareto improvement.

By contrast, consider the competitive market equilibrium outcome (q^*, p^*). Precisely because that market outcome maximizes total surplus, we know it must be Pareto-efficient. Suppose to the contrary, that it were *not* Pareto-efficient. Starting from (q^*, p^*), there would have to remain some way to change output to make someone better off without

Figure 9.6 Market Equilibriums With and Without Pareto Efficiency With output q_1 and price p_1, a small increase in output increases total surplus because the marginal social benefit of additional output is greater than the marginal social cost; therefore, this combination is not Pareto-efficient. The competitive equilibrium with output q^* and price p^* maximizes total surplus and is Pareto-efficient because an increase or decrease in output reduces total surplus.

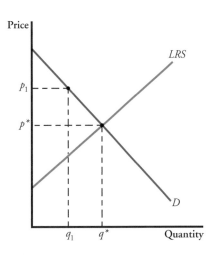

▲▲▲ 9.2 APPLICATION The Case for Free Trade

Economists almost always endorse free trade. In 1817, the English stockbroker and political economist David Ricardo wrote,

> Under a system of perfectly free commerce, each country naturally devotes its capital and labour to such employments as are most beneficial to each. This pursuit of individual advantage is admirably connected with the universal good of the whole. By stimulating industry, by rewarding ingenuity, and by using most efficaciously the peculiar powers bestowed by nature, it distributes labour most effectively and most economically; while, by increasing the general mass of productions, it diffuses general benefit, and binds together, by one common tie of interest and intercourse, the universal society of nations throughout the civilized world. ...
>
> [David Ricardo,
> *Principles of Political Economy and Taxation*,
> J M Dent & Sons, London, 1973, page 81.]

Following in Ricardo's tradition, the modern case for free trade is a case against tariffs, quotas, and other restrictions that governments impose on the free and unfettered flow of goods and services between nations. Over many years,

and through many rounds of multilateral negotiations, the major trading countries of the world have worked through the General Agreement on Trade and Tariffs (GATT) to lower tariff and non-tariff barriers to free trade.

This figure, which depicts market demand and supply in the perfectly competitive home country market for some good, explains GATT's efforts. The horizontal line at p^* indicates the (fixed) price at which this same good can be obtained from producers in the foreign country. Let's assume that home country buyers favor home country producers, *ceteris paribus*, but that they never are willing to pay a higher price for home-produced goods when they can get the same good cheaper from a foreign producer.

What does the market equilibrium look like under free trade? No home country buyer has to pay more than p^*, because the foreign producers stand ready to offer (an effectively unlimited amount of) the good at that price. In this figure, the free trade market equilibrium price is p^*, and q_1 units are produced and sold by home country producers, and q^* units purchased and consumed by home country buyers. The difference between home country consumption q^* and home country production q_1 measures the quantity of home country imports under free trade.

Now suppose the home country government imposes a tariff at the rate of t per unit of the value of the

---

Application Figure 9.2

The Effect of a Tariff

With free trade, the world price is p^*, domestic producers supply q_1 units, and $q^* - q_1$ units are imported. If a tariff of t is imposed, the price increases to $p^*(1 + t)$ and domestic producers supply q_2 units and $q_3 - q_2$ units are imported. The tariff increases producer surplus by the green area *abgh*, but decreases consumer surplus by the sum of the green, light-red, orange, and dark-red areas *acdh*. If the tariff revenues equal to the orange area *bcef* are returned to consumers, the welfare loss due to the tariff equals the sum of the light- and dark-red triangles *bfg* and *cde*.

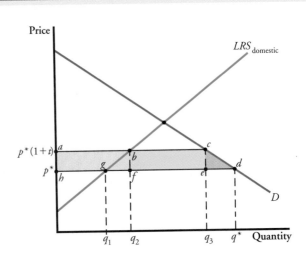

(continued)

imported good. Foreign goods can now enter the home country only at a total price of $p^*(1 + t)$, with foriegn producers keeping p^* and paying t to the home country government. With foreign goods now available only at the higher price, some buyers switch to cheaper domestic sources, and in so doing bid up the domestic price. Once again, the post-tariff equilibrium must have home country and foreign country goods trading at the same price to consumers, but now that price will be the higher price $p^*(1 + t)$. As prices rise, home country production expands from q_1 to q_2, while home country consumption shrinks from q^* to q_3. Domestic consumption still exceeds domestic production, but now only the units between q_2 and q_3 are imported.

What effect does the tariff of t per unit have on home country welfare? Producers in the protected domestic industry are better off, as producer surplus rises by the green area *abgh*. Domestic consumers, however, are very much worse off, because they now must pay the higher price $p^*(1 + t)$. In all, consumer welfare falls by the amount of the consumer surplus loss, or by the sum of the green, light-red, orange, and dark-red areas, *acdh*.

The government collects tariff revenue of $t(q_3 - q_2)$—an amount equal to the orange area of the rectangle *bcef*. Presumably, the government spends this money on something, so let's suppose it simply returns this money to consumers in an effort to minimize the impact this tariff has on them. To gauge the impact this process has on the whole of the domestic society, we must now sum everyone's gains and losses. When we do, notice an interesting and important fact: The loss to consumers, even after the tariff revenue rebate, exceeds the gain to producers by the amount of the two triangles: the light-red one *bfg*, and the dark-red one *ced*. A tariff thus not only redistributes welfare from consumers to producers; it also results in a loss of welfare for the domestic society.

Why does the impact of the tariff work out this way? Once again, it is because under competition, the free trade market equilibrium will always be Pareto-efficient. As a result, no tariff, even when combined with complex supplementary rebate and compensation schemes, can serve the interests of the protected industry without at the same time causing harm to consumers.

making anyone else worse off. But we have just seen that either an increase or a decrease in output from q^* reduces the size of the welfare pie. If the pie cannot be made bigger, it must have been maximized in the first place! This then leads us to the conclusion that equilibrium in a perfectly competitive market will always be Pareto-efficient.

If the logic of this argument for Pareto efficiency in competitive markets does not persuade you, try a more hands-on approach. Look carefully at (q^*, p^*) in Figure 9.6, and pencil in the resulting total surplus equal to the sum of the consumer and producer surplus areas. Now imagine a move that would drive this market away from the competitive outcome (q^*, p^*) to some other price and quantity. Check the size of producer and consumer surplus in your new hypothetical outcome. Did you find at least one (if not both) of those areas to be smaller? This should persuade you that once it is reached, any movement away from a competitive equilibrium may help someone, but it will always at the same time hurt someone else.

laissez-faire

An economic philosophy that argues for an absence of government intervention in the marketplace.

Competition can be a very powerful force working for society's benefit, but a policy of complete economic freedom, or **laissez-faire**, will not always be in society's interest. As we will see in subsequent chapters, market distortions of many different kinds can arise, and when they do, the laissez-faire market outcome will generally not be optimal. We'll see that when market structures are imperfect, when free and accurate information about products is not shared by buyers and sellers, and when by-products of consumption or production affect others, the pure laissez-faire market equilibrium will usually not provide the best social outcome. In cases like these, there will often be a good case in favor of some form of government intervention in the marketplace. Later, we'll see that when government intervention is well-designed and appropriate to the problem at hand, it can work to counter these distortions and further society's interests. Sometimes, when the invisible hand appears to be a bit shaky, the hand of government can usefully help it along.

▼▼▼   9.3   A Cautionary Note on Competition and Welfare

This chapter began by warning that normative judgments in economics, as in all endeavors, are inherently value-laden. Nonetheless, we've managed to come to some profound and rather sweeping conclusions about the role economic competition can play in benefiting society. Along the way, however, we've pushed quite a few important and controversial matters to one side. At this point, a few cautionary remarks on what we've learned about competition and welfare are necessary. The remarks fall into two broad categories: those having to do with the tools we fashioned to help us reach our conclusions, and those having to do with the scope of the conclusions themselves.

The first point is purely technical, but it does bear mentioning. This chapter has argued that the social assessment of any situation should depend on people's assessment of their own well-being; that is, on the utilities accruing to them. By aggregating utilities across individuals, we've also been taking it for granted that these utilities were measurable—and that they were comparable across different individuals. Both of these underlying assumptions are questionable, because they violate our assumption from Chapter 3 that an individual's utility can be measured only by an ordinal number; that is, the utility numbers assigned to consumption bundles do not tell us anything about the level of consumer satisfaction or happiness, nor do differences between utility numbers assigned to different bundles say anything about how intensely a consumer prefers one bundle to another. Yet most of the interesting choices society has to make involve having to weigh benefits that will flow to some against losses that will be suffered by others. If you believe we cannot measure those gains and losses, or that even if we can, we cannot then compare gains and losses accruing to different individuals, then there really is no point going forward at all with any analysis of alternative social policies. All we will ever be able to say is that every alternative involves benefits to some and losses to others. Most economists, if only for the sake of exploring the argument further, are usually willing to accept measuring utility in this non-ordinal way and some degree of interpersonal comparability of utility, because both are necessary to move welfare analysis forward.

Equity

utilitarians

A group of nineteenth century philosophers who believed the amount of satisfaction consumers received from consuming goods and services could be measured in terms of a number of pleasure units.

There is a more interesting issue that needs to be raised regarding our tools. As the simple sum of consumer and producer surplus, our total surplus index of social welfare, TS, is a decidedly utilitarian criterion of social welfare, named after a group of nineteenth century philosophers called **utilitarians**, because they believed that the way to maximize society's welfare was to maximize society's total utility. Many people think this makes very good sense, and utilitarianism has had many strong and persuasive defenders over the course of its long philosophical life. But there is one fact about using total surplus as a measure of welfare that we can't ignore: By focusing only on the size of the welfare pie, our total surplus measure completely ignores how that pie is divided.

To better understand the distributional issues we have ignored to this point, examine Figure 9.7, which looks a lot like other figures we've considered in this chapter. Imagine we had to choose between one set of polices that would result in market outcome (q, p_1) and another that would result in outcome (q, p_2) instead. In the former case, consumer surplus equals the purple triange abp_1, and producer surplus equals the sum of the blue and green areas p_1bcd. In the latter case, consumer surplus will be greater, and equal to the sum of the purple and blue areas $abcp_2$; producer surplus will be smaller, totaling only the green triangle p_2cd. We can see that consumers are much better off under market outcome (q, p_2) and that producers are much better off under (q, p_1). Notice, however, that when we apply our *TS* measure to compare them, both market outcomes would result in exactly the same total surplus, equal to the sum of the purple, blue, and green areas *abcd*. As a result, our *TS* measure will regard these two market outcomes as entirely equivalent from a social point of view, even though the distribution of the welfare pie is very different between them. If society has no reason to want to favor consumers over producers or producers over consumers, then either distribution should be acceptable from a social perspective.

But what if you feel you do have reason to favor one group over the other? Jules Dupuit, the French economist who originated consumer surplus analysis in the nineteenth century, argued that as a matter of basic fairness, producers should get any and all surplus because they are the ones who went to the trouble to produce the good in the first place. Modern-day consumer advocates like Ralph Nader would no doubt argue the opposite. In each of these cases, the argument being made is that how the welfare pie gets divided, not just how big it is, should sometimes matter in how we judge market outcomes from a social point of view. For better or worse, it is important to recognize that our *TS* measure does not allow us to build any kind of favoritism for one group over another into the social assessment of market situations.

The distribution consequences of market outcomes may seem like nothing more than a technical issue, but it is really more than that. We need to realize that the method we choose to use to measure welfare can affect the conclusions we make about policy outcomes, sometimes in ways we don't clearly perceive at the time we choose our welfare measure, and sometimes in ways that make us uncomfortable when we look back at our conclusions. For example, our earlier conclusions regarding whether the competitive equilibrium is socially optimal is a case in point. Let's do another experiment. Suppose everyone is completely identical in every way except one. People have identical physical and mental capabilities. They have identical tastes and preferences for all goods and services. The only way they differ is in the amount of income (or wealth) at their disposal.

Figure 9.7 Distributional Issues in Measuring Total Surplus

If the output q is sold at price p_1, consumer surplus is the purple triangle abp_1 and producer surplus is the sum of the green and blue areas p_1bcd. If the output q is sold at price p_2, producer surplus is the green triangle p_2cd and consumer surplus is the sum of the purple and blue areas $abcp_2$.

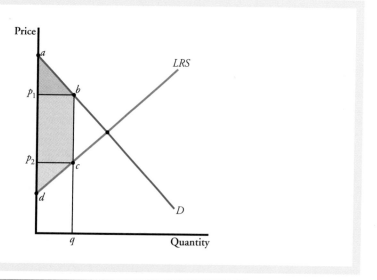

COMMON ERROR 9.2   Assuming That Consumer Surplus Is More Socially Desirable Than Producer Surplus

Students often assume that in competitive markets, increases in consumer surplus are more inherently fair and socially desirable than increases in producer surplus. Perhaps such reasoning results from the fact that all of us are consumers and only some of us consider ourselves producers. We have already seen, however, that long-run producer surplus does not accrue to the firm in the form of profits in competitive industries. Instead, long-run producer surplus accrues to the suppliers of inputs, including workers who supply labor.

The distributional issues surrounding consumer and producer surplus can become quite complicated depending on the industry. Consider, for example, the yacht industry. Consumer surplus in the yacht industry is primarily obtained by very wealthy individuals, while producer surplus is obtained by the owners of factors of production such as workers and small yacht retailers who are generally much less wealthy than yacht buyers. The same argument could be made for a wide variety of luxury goods, everything from diamonds and furs to first-class air travel and expensive wines. The important point to bear in mind is that all consumer and producer surplus is ultimately received by human beings. Don't make the common error of assuming that only poor people receive consumer surplus and only rich people receive producer surplus.

Now let's consider the competitive market for some good all people might like to buy. For simplicity, assume no one would ever need or buy more than one unit of this good. Think of the good as some large-ticket item, such as a house or a car.

For this good, every individual's demand curve is going to be a vertical line at one unit of the good, up to the person's maximum willingness-to-pay, or reservation price. Each consumer's **reservation price** is the highest price he or she is willing to pay for a good. Even though people are identical in every other way, their willingness to pay will be different, because their ability to pay is different. If we line up all these consumers in descending order of their willingness to pay, the market demand curve for this good might look something like the one in Figure 9.8. At each successive unit of the good, the heavy vertical black and green line is the individual demand curve of the person with the next lowest willingness to pay, and its height is the extent of that person's maximum willingness to pay.

Under perfect competition, our imaginary market will come to rest where demand and supply intersect, at a price of p^* and quantity q^*. Do the forces of competition give us something close to an ideal solution here? Many of us would say both yes and no. Competition does solve the problem of making the welfare pie as big as possible, as we saw earlier in the chapter, and that certainly is a very large part of the battle. The market outcome (q^*, p^*) once again gives rise to the largest possible welfare pie, *aed*. But there's that other part we don't yet really know how to describe very well, and that's how the pie gets divided. Left to themselves, the forces of competition will forge some solution; that is, the pie will get divided. The only question is what we think about the way that it's done.

Take another look at Figure 9.8 and, to make things even clearer, forget about how welfare is divided between consumers and producers. Instead, just focus on how it gets divided among consumers. Here, every consumer is identical to every other one, but each does not get the same share of the surplus. It is easy to see that those with a higher willingness-to-pay get a larger consumer surplus (as measured by the green vertical lines) in the final market equilibrium. Some consumers—the ones with the lowest willingness-to-pay— get none of the good, and therefore get no surplus at all. Because our consumers are

reservation price

The highest price a consumer is willing to pay for an additional unit of a good.

Figure 9.8 Differences in Consumer Surplus Across Consumers
At the competitive equilibrium, price is p^*. The green vertical lines above p^* measure the consumer surplus received by additional consumers. Consumers with higher incomes probably have higher reservation prices, and therefore receive more consumer surplus than poorer consumers. The poorest consumers have reservation prices below p^* and receive no consumer surplus.

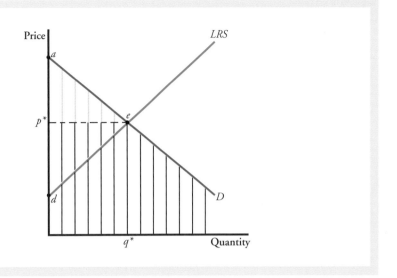

identical in every other way except income, it can be only differences in their incomes or wealth that account for these differences in what they receive. Here, in the end, it is the rich that get the largest share, while the poor get the smallest or no share at all.

If, on a personal level, you find that you do care about how the welfare pie is divided, what can you make of all we've learned about competition and welfare? Can Adam Smith still speak to you? Indeed he can. By drawing your attention to the very special properties of competitive market equilibrium, Smith tells you how to make the social welfare pie as big as it can possibly be. Once that's been done, you can search for and hopefully find creative ways of distributing that largest pie to everyone's benefit. This has more to do with the art of politics than it does with economics. But knowing the lessons of Adam Smith, you're better equipped for the job.

▲▲▲ **9.3 APPLICATION**   **The Distributional Consequences of the Proposed Bush Tax Cuts**

In 2003, President Bush proposed a $750 billion income tax reduction for United States citizens. The president argued that the tax cut was necessary to help end the economic slowdown that had begun in the spring of 2001. A majority of Democrats and some Republicans in Congress believed that the tax cuts were aimed too heavily toward the wealthiest Americans and would further increase the growing income gap between the rich and the poor in the United States. The debate was partly about positive economics: how much the tax cut would stimulate the economy versus how much it would increase the federal deficit and cause interest rates to rise and invest-

ment to fall. But it was also about normative economics: Is it fair to cut taxes in absolute dollars far more for the wealthiest Americans than the poorest Americans?

The debate was really over Pareto efficiency and equity: the president argued that the tax cut and associated growth in the economy would make some people better off and nobody worse off because of a larger economic pie. His political opponents argued that the tax cuts would result in higher long-term interest rates and leave many Americans worse off than they were before the tax cuts. In the end, the two sides compromised and passed a $330 billion tax cut.

Summary

1. In normative economics, we judge economic situations as good or bad for society as a whole. Normative judgments are inherently value-laden. Most economists agree that measures of social welfare should depend on the welfare of individuals as they see it themselves, that all people should be treated the same, and that the measure should satisfy Pareto efficiency. The total surplus social welfare measure is formed by summing consumer and producer surplus, $TS = CS + PS$. On an ordinary supply and demand diagram, TS at any level of output is the entire area below market demand and above long-run market supply at that output level. The market outcome under perfect competition maximizes total surplus, and therefore makes the social welfare pie as large as possible.

2. The competitive market outcome is Pareto-efficient, which means that it exhausts all opportunities for mutual gain between buyers and sellers in the market. From a competitive market equilibrium, there is no way to rearrange things to make one person better off without at the same time making some other person worse off.

3. Total surplus, TS, gauges social welfare by the overall size of the welfare pie and ignores how that pie is divided. When the distribution of welfare as well as its level are important, the TS measure should be applied with care.

Self-Test Problems

1. Governments sometimes restrict free trade with import quotas, rather than tariffs. Under a quota, foreign goods come into the home country without tariffs, but the quantity allowed to enter is limited. Re-draw Application Figure 9.2, and use your diagram to answer the following questions.

   a. If a government sets a quota to restrict total imports to $q_3 - q_2$ units—what they would have been under the tariff—what impact would this have on the product price for home country consumers and producers? Explain.

   b. Under a quota system, the government issues import licenses giving the holder the right to import one unit of the good. How much revenue can the government earn if it sells all $q_3 - q_2$ licenses to the highest bidder? Illustrate your answer on your diagram.

   c. What impact does this quota system have on home country welfare? Who gains, who loses, and by how much? Illustrate your answer on your diagram.

   d. Which is a better way to restrict free trade: quotas or tariffs? Is the welfare loss under this quota system larger or smaller than the loss under a tariff with identical effects on import volume? Explain your answer.

2. Consider the market depicted in the figure. It is composed of many buyers and many sellers.

No one is happy with the equilibrium price in this market, so consumers and producers have each decided to do something about it. Two plans have been proposed:

Plan 1—Fix the market price at p_1 and forbid firms from producing any more than q_1 in order to avoid a surplus.

Plan 2—Fix the market price at p_2 and require firms to produce q_2 in order to avoid a shortage. Answer the following questions and justify your answers carefully.

a. Which plan would consumers prefer?

b. Which plan would producers prefer?

c. Which of these two plans is better for society?

3. Market demand is the equation $p = 40 - q$ and market supply is $p = 10 + q$. Compute the 1aissez-faire equilibrium price and quantity in this market. Now suppose that government regulation restricts total output to only 10 units. Answer the following questions:

a. What price will buyers pay for the available goods after regulation?

b. To find out who gains and who loses, compute any change in consumer surplus and any change in producer surplus that result from this government intervention.

c. Does society as a whole gain or lose? Is there a welfare loss? If so, compute it. If not, explain why not.

 ## Questions and Problems for Review

1. Seeing how well the invisible hand can channel self-interest to the social good, some would argue that we must consequently view self-interest, even selfishness, as a virtue in our personal lives. Discuss.

2. How important is the social institution of private property to the work of the invisible hand of competition? If private property is legal and matters, does it matter how that property is divided among us?

3. The invisible hand ensures that competitive market outcomes are Pareto-efficient, but does it ensure that they are fair? What do you believe should go into our criterion of fairness?

4. According to nineteenth-century economist John Rawls and his followers, called Rawlsians, only the well-being of society's worst-off member matters. Rawlsians suggested that the preferred income distribution should maximize the utility of the individual with the lowest utility in society. Rawlsians therefore call for social policy to maximize the welfare of society's worst-off member. Compare and contrast this approach with the utilitarians' approach to social welfare. How does a competitive market outcome rate by the Rawlsian criterion?

5. Consider the following statement:

"In the short run, any per-unit tax imposed on firms in a perfectly competitive market must redistribute welfare from producers and consumers toward government. In addition, unless demand or supply is perfectly inelastic, such taxes must also always result in a social welfare loss."

Now answer the following questions, illustrating them with appropriate and carefully drawn diagrams.

a. If neither demand nor supply is perfectly inelastic, will a per-unit tax always result in a welfare loss? Explain.

b. What happens when demand is perfectly inelastic? How are consumers, firms, and the government affected by a per-unit tax in this case? Is there a welfare loss or not?

c. What happens when supply is perfectly inelastic? How are consumers, firms, and the government affected? Is there a welfare loss or not?

6. In thinking about what might constitute a "just" social welfare criterion, John Harsanyi, the 1994 Nobel Prize winner in economics, once suggested we consider how we'd view things from an "original position," behind a "veil of ignorance" through which we could not see who we might end up being in the society contemplated. Imagine, for example, a society with only two people in it, and let x and y represent alternative states we might be able to achieve in society through some policy choice. Let $U_1(x)$ be the utility you derive under state x if you end up being person 1, and let $U_2(x)$ denote the utility you'd derive if you end up being person 2. Let $U_1(y)$ and $U_2(y)$ be defined analogously. Now from behind the veil of ignorance, and by what he calls the "principle of insufficient reason," Harsanyi then argues that one would have to assign the same probability to the prospect of being person 1 as they'd assign to being person 2. If so, show that a

rational expected utility-maximizer facing the choice between state x and state y under uncertainty will always prefer the one under which the sum of utilities, $U_1 + U_2$, is highest.

7. A perfectly competitive constant-cost industry is in long-run equilibrium. Now suppose that the government imposes an excise (per-unit) tax on producers in the amount of $\$t$ for every unit sold. Carefully draw a diagram for the representative firm and another for the industry, and use them to answer the following questions.

   a. Describe the long-run effects of this tax on market price, market output, firm output, and the number of firms in the industry.

   b. Describe the long-run effects of this tax on consumer, producer, and social welfare. Who gains, who loses, and by how much in the long run?

   c. In the long run, and solely by reference to the TS criterion of social welfare, is this tax policy socially justified? How do the costs of this policy compare to its benefits in the form of tax revenue collected? Prove any claim you make as rigorously as possible.

8. What do you think Adam Smith meant by the term "invisible hand"? What is the relationship between Smith's invisible hand and Pareto efficiency?

9. The government is considering a policy that makes 95 out of every 100 people in society better off, but makes the remaining 5 percent of the population worse off. Is the policy a Pareto improvement? Should the government proceed with the policy? Is your answer an example of positive or normative economics? Explain.

10. What happens to total surplus if a group of firms in a perfectly competitive market get together and collude to set a price above the perfectly competitive equilibrium price? How can you be sure of your answer? Why might the firms want to engage in this type of behavior?

11. Suppose the government imposes a price ceiling below the equilibrium price in an increasing-cost perfectly competitive industry. Furthermore, suppose the government forces the firms in the industry to meet the quantity demanded at this price ceiling. Using a graph, show the impact of this policy on consumer surplus and producer surplus. What has happened to total surplus? What group might like this policy? What group would be opposed to this policy? Is the policy a Pareto improvement compared to the competitive equilibrium?

12. True or false? Explain your reasoning. "All per-unit taxes reduce total surplus; therefore, governments should never use per-unit taxes to raise revenues."

13. Are each of the following statements an example of positive or normative economics? Explain which ones fall into each category and why.

   a. An increase in the minimum wage will result in increased unemployment.

   b. A reduction in personal income tax rates will cause some individuals to work harder and save more, but will cause other individuals to work less and save less.

   c. An increase in unemployment benefits during a period of increasing unemployment will make society better off in the long run.

   d. The government tends to spend money inefficiently, and therefore reductions in government spending always improve economic welfare.

   e. All tariffs placed on competitive markets decrease total surplus.

14. Is producer surplus larger in a constant-cost or increasing-cost industry? Explain your answer using a graph or graphs.

15. Suppose the government provides a $\$10$ per-unit subsidy (the opposite of a per-unit tax) on a good produced in a perfectly competitive increasing-cost industry with demand curve $p = 50 - q$ and supply curve before the subsidy of $p = 20 + q$. Calculate the impact of the subsidy on consumer and producer surplus; that is, calculate the change in consumer and producer surplus resulting from the subsidy. What is the cost of the subsidy to the government? Who pays the cost of the subsidy? Calculate the following summation: (*the change in consumer surplus because of the subsidy*) + (*the change in producer surplus because of the subsidy*) − (*the cost of the subsidy to the government*). Is this summation positive or negative? What does this summation suggest to you about the government's decision to subsidize this industry?

Internet Exercises

Visit *http://www.myeconlab.com/waldman* for this chapter's Web exercises. Answer real-world economics problems by doing research on the Internet.

Chapter 10
Using the Model of Perfect Competition

▲▲▲

Between 1990 and 2000, there was a large and continuous growth in the number of marijuana—and heroin—related hospital emergency room episodes in the United States. During the same time period, the United States Drug Enforcement Administration (DEA) increased its budget by over 96 percent in real dollars (over 175 percent in nominal dollars) and almost doubled its workforce. This huge increase in resources spent fighting the war on drugs did not, however, result in an absolute decline in the number of serious drug incidents. Why is it that despite spending by the U.S. government of more than a billion dollars a year attempting to reduce the flow of illegal drugs into the country, these drugs continue to flow into the United States, and are available to most interested buyers? This chapter uses the perfectly competitive model to help us understand why we appear to be losing the war on drugs.

In this chapter, we use the theory of perfect competition to address some important economic issues. We expand greatly our analysis of some of the applications from Chapter 9, such as rent control and free trade, and consider some new examples as well. In addition to an examination of the market for illegal drugs, we will explore a number of other important policy issues. For example: Why is it that the great majority of economists support free trade agreements such as NAFTA (North American Free Trade Agreement), but many politicians and workers oppose them? Why do rent control laws often hurt the low-income people they are intended to help? Why do so many governments throughout the world place price floors on their agricultural products? Why do some economists argue that the sale of human organs and eggs should be legal? To address these questions, we need to remember the four major assumptions of a perfectly competitive market:

- There are many buyers and many sellers, all of whom are price takers.
- There is a homogeneous product.
- There is free entry and exit.
- Information must be perfect and freely available.

Learning Objectives

After reading Chapter 10, you will have learned:

➤ How to use the competitive model to analyze the impact of the war on drugs in the United States.

➤ How to use the competitive model to explain the impact of free trade on importing and exporting countries.

➤ How to use the competitive model to explain the economic impact of rent control programs designed to lower rents.

➤ How to use the competitive model to analyze the impact of government price supports aimed at increasing farmers' incomes.

➤ How the competitive model can provide insight into the ethical issue of whether to pay organ donors.

Although there are relatively few real-world markets where all four assumptions apply, many markets behave as if all four apply. This chapter analyzes markets that are nearly perfectly competitive. In each of these markets, the model of perfect competition can provide important insights into performance and efficiency. We begin with an example—illegal drugs—that we can analyze using the basic tools of supply and demand.

▼▼▼ 10.1 The Illegal Drug Market

Marijuana, cocaine, and heroin are illegal drugs in the United States and most other countries. Despite their illegality, these drugs are widely available in the United States. There is a substantial demand for such drugs, and suppliers are willing to supply them despite the risk of arrest, prosecution, and imprisonment. We can analyze the retail drug market using the perfectly competitive market because there are a large number of buyers and sellers of illegal drugs, and entry into the retail business is relatively easy. In contrast, relatively few large drug cartels control the wholesale market for illegal drugs, and therefore, the wholesale market could not be accurately analyzed using the competitive model.

The current American anti-drug policy focuses on restricting the supply of drugs by intercepting drug shipments to the United States and arresting domestic suppliers. Alternative policies aim to reduce demand by educating the public about the dangers of drug use and rehabilitating drug users. The opportunity cost of the current policy aimed primarily at restricting supply and preventing drugs from reaching users is very high. In 2002, for example, the United States Drug Enforcement Administration (DEA) had a budget of $1.8 billion. It had 9,388 employees and 4,625 special agents.[1] As a point of comparison, in 1990, the agency had a budget of $653.5 million ($908.4 million in 2002 dollars), and it had 6,274 employees and 3,191 special agents.

The United States government has claimed some major successes in the war on drugs. According to the DEA, in 2001 government officials seized 111 metric tons of cocaine, 1,211 metric tons of marijuana, and 2,506 kilograms of heroin.[2] Furthermore, the Department of Justice estimated that in 2000, of the 1.94 million people in prisons in the United States, 21 percent were imprisoned for selling or using drugs.[3]

Limiting the Supply of Drugs

Let's analyze the economic effectiveness of limiting the supply of drugs by using the perfectly competitive model and our knowledge of the elasticity of demand for illegal drugs. Consider a long-run equilibrium in the cocaine market. In Figure 10.1(a), the long-run equilibrium price is p_1. Initially, the short-run supply of drugs is S_1. With the market in long-run equilibrium, the typical dealer in panel (b) earns a zero, or normal, economic profit. Notice that the demand for drugs is inelastic; addicts must feed their habit even if the price becomes very high.

Let's consider how drug enforcement affects the short-run and long-run supply of drugs. In the short run, most of the high costs of drug dealing are related directly to law enforcement efforts. Increased law enforcement efforts drive up dealers' costs by increas-

---

[1] United States Drug Enforcement Agency, *http://www.usdoj.gov.*

[2] United States Drug Enforcement Agency, *http://www.dea.gov.*

[3] United States Department of Justice, *http://www.ojp.usdoj.gov.*

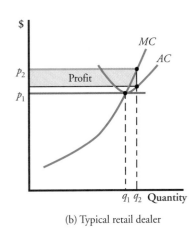

(a) Industry   (b) Typical retail dealer

Figure 10.1 The Illegal Market for Cocaine

In panel (a), the industry is in long-run equilibrium at price p_1. In panel (b), which shows output for a typical dealer as q_1, profits are normal. If the government increases its drug enforcement efforts and arrests some drug dealers, supply decreases from S_1 to S_2 in panel (a), and price increases to p_2. In the short run, a typical dealer who remains in business in panel (b) earns an economic profit equal to the shaded area. In the long run, profits result in the entry of new dealers, and the supply curve shifts back to S_1 in panel (a); as a result, the price declines back to p_1 and profits return to normal in panel (b).

ing their risk of arrest, fines, prison, and possibly death, as evidenced by "turf wars" and drive-by shootings. On the other hand, in the long run, the high percentage of youths in some neighborhoods who make a living selling drugs provides evidence that entry into the retail market is fairly easy. For example, a study by Reuter, et al. showed drug dealing to be widespread among Washington D.C. residents. The study found that in 1990, 16 percent of black males in Washington born in 1967 had been charged with selling drugs.[4] In detailed interviews with 186 drug dealers, they found that 37 percent of the dealers sold drugs on a daily basis, 40 percent sold drugs several days a week, and 23 percent sold drugs one day or less a week. In another study, Brounstein examined the perceived risks of drug dealing among 387 ninth and tenth graders in Washington.[5] Table 10.1 summarizes his findings. Frequent drug dealers had the lowest perceived risks associated with dealing. Infrequent dealers had the highest perceived risks of arrest or injury, and those who didn't deal at all had the highest perceived risk of imprisonment.

Suppose dealers know that enforcement efforts ebb and flow with temporary periods of severe crackdowns followed by periods of more lax enforcement. In light of this knowledge, the dealers' costs curves already include the expected risk of getting caught and the drug busts have little, if any, impact on the costs of doing business for a typical dealer. In the short run, a crackdown reduces the supply of illegal drugs, which in turn results in a higher price. Of course, a higher price is consistent with the overall objectives of the government's drug enforcement policy, because a high price reduces the quantity demanded.

[4] Peter Reuter, Robert J. MacCoun, P.J. Murphy, Allan F. Abrahamse, and Barbara Simon. *Money from Crime: A Study of the Economics of Drug Dealing in Washington, D.C.* Santa Monica: Rand, 1990.

[5] Paul J. Brounstein, et al. *Patterns of Substance Abuse and Delinquency Among Inner City Adolescents*, Washington, D.C.: The Urban Institute, 1989.

Table 10.1 Adolescents' Views of the Risks of Drug Dealing (percentage responding that the indicated outcome was highly likely after one year of drug dealing)

	Frequent Dealers $N = 32$	Infrequent Dealers $N = 18$	No Dealing $N = 337$
Arrest	38	56	48
Prison Sentence	25	33	37
Severe Injury or Death	50	65	61

Because of the inelastic demand for drugs, however, the quantity demanded is only insignificantly reduced.

Now let's explore how a period of increased enforcement would affect the market in the long run. Suppose that beginning with our long-run equilibrium in Figure 10.1, the government, with no increase in expenditures, makes several major drug busts, so in panel (a), the short-run supply of drugs decreases to S_2 and the price increases to p_2. In panel (b), the higher short-run equilibrium price primarily results in higher profits for the vast majority of drug dealers who were not busted. Each of the remaining dealers earns a positive economic profit equal to the green shaded area in panel (b). To determine whether the higher price is a new long-run equilibrium price, recall that the dealers have already fully incorporated the higher expected risks associated with arrest, fines, prison, and death into their costs. Consequently, the dealers' costs will not be affected by the temporary crackdown. The short-run excess profits meanwhile attract new entrants—that is, new dealers—into the market. Shortly after the drug busts, entry increases the short-run supply curve back to S_1, the price declines back to p_1, and profits return to normal. Even a successful law enforcement crackdown has little, if any, long-term impact on the price or supply of drugs.

The Economics of Drug Legalization

Does our analysis imply that current laws and enforcement have little impact on the illicit drug market? To answer that question, we must consider an alternative set of drug laws. To consider one extreme: What would happen, for example, if the U.S. government legalized drug use? Panels (a) and (b) of Figure 10.2 analyze the initial impact of the legalization of drugs in a constant-cost industry. Recall from Chapter 8 that the long-run supply curve is horizontal in a constant-cost industry. Before legalization, in panel (a), the long-run equilibrium price is p_1, and the long-run equilibrium industry quantity is Q_1. In panel (b), each dealer sells q_1 units and earns a normal economic profit.

After legalization, production costs drop dramatically. The most likely long-run scenario is that the major drug companies and perhaps the major tobacco companies would enter into drug production. These firms would not face the costs associated with arrest, fines, prison, and death; therefore, in panel (b) of Figure 10.2, the costs of production for a typical, now legal, seller would drop dramatically from the red MC_1 and AC_1 curves to the orange MC_2 and AC_2 curves. In the short run, the price would decrease (the graph does not show this decrease) due to the decrease in marginal cost, and sellers would earn positive short-run economic profits. In the long run, the excess profits attract entry. Panel (a) in Figure 10.2 shows that as new sellers enter, the short-run supply curve shifts to the right; in the long run, the short-run supply curve shifts to S_2, price decreases to p_2, and

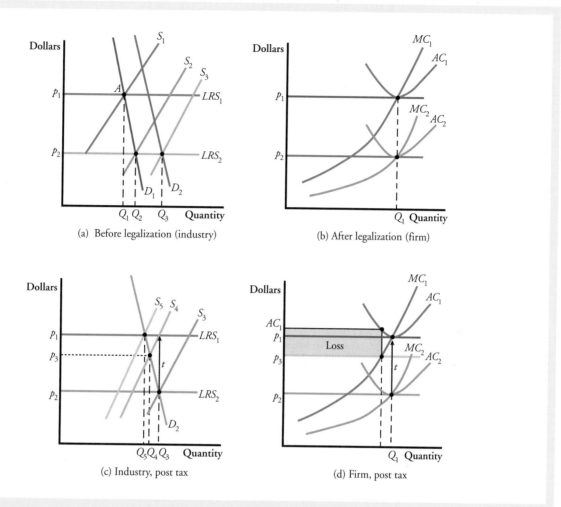

Figure 10.2 The Impact of the Legalization of Drugs with a Tax

Before legalization, in panel (a), the short-run supply curve is S_1, the long-run equilibrium price is p_1, and the long-run equilibrium industry quantity is Q_1. In panel (b), each dealer sells Q_1 units and earns a normal economic profit. With legalization, in panel (b), the marginal and average costs curves decline from MC_1 and AC_1 to MC_2 and AC_2. Furthermore, legalization increases the demand curve in panel (a) from D_1 to D_2. As a result, firms earn positive economic profits and firms enter. The long-run equilibrium is at price p_2, industry output increases to Q_3 in panel (a), and the typical dealer produces output Q_1 and earns a normal profit. In panels (c) and (d), the government combines legalization with a tax of t. In panel (d), the firm's costs increase back to MC_1 and AC_1; and in panel (c), the short-run supply curve decreases to S_4. Short-run price increases to p_3, and in panel (d), the typical firm sustains an economic loss equal to the shaded red area. In the long run, firms leave until price increases to p_1, the short-run supply is S_5 in panel (c), and the typical firm in panel (d) earns a normal profit. If anti-drug education spending decreases the demand curve to D_1 in panel (a), the final equilibrium is back at price p_1 and quantity equals Q_1.

each seller earns a normal economic profit. Assuming demand remains constant at D_1, the new long-run equilibrium price and quantity in the industry would be p_2 and Q_2. It is likely, however, that the demand for drugs would increase, because of the elimination of the legal risks to users. Suppose the demand curve increased to D_2. With the increase in demand, in the long run, additional entry increases supply to S_3, and the equilibrium quantity in panel (a) increases to Q_3. This outcome is exactly what the current policy is aimed at preventing—an increase in drug use.

Public Policy Toward Drugs after Legalization

Thus far, our analysis is incomplete, because we have ignored the likely changes in public policy that would probably accompany the legalization of drugs. Suppose, for example, the government imposes a significant excise tax on drugs, similar to the current taxes on alcohol and cigarettes. In panels (c) and (d) of Figure 10.2, suppose the government imposes an excise tax equal to t, so that when the tax t is added onto the production costs, the total costs are precisely equal to the costs of production in an illegal drug market. Beginning the analysis in panels (c) and (d) where we left off in panels (a) and (b), the long-run equilibrium price initially equals p_2 and industry quantity equals Q_3. The imposition of the tax causes the short-run supply curve in panel (c) to decrease from S_3 to S_4, and the short-run price to increase to p_3. Panel (d) shows that firms sustain a short-run economic loss equal to the shaded red area. Panel (c) shows that in the long run, firms leave, supply decreases to S_5, and price increases to p_1, which was the price when drugs were illegal in panel (a).

Looking at a final expected change in public policy resulting from legalization will complete our analysis. Suppose that in addition to the large tax, half of the DEA's budget of approximately $1.8 billion in 2002 was redirected toward drug education and information programs. You might be skeptical that such education and information campaigns can have an impact on drug use. However, consider the case of tobacco. According the U.S. Center for Disease Control (CDC), before the government began informing the public about the health risks associated with smoking in 1964, 52 percent of American men smoked. By 1994, that number had declined to only 28 percent. Furthermore, cigarette consumption has declined almost continuously in the United States since 1980. Information and education programs can, in fact, reduce demand, and if these programs are successful, demand might decline back to the level D_1 when drugs were illegal. In this scenario, the long-run equilibrium would be right back at point A in panel (a) of Figure 10.2 where the long-run supply curve LRS_1 intersects demand D_1, and the price, p_1, and quantity, Q_1, are the same regardless of whether drugs are legal or illegal. With legalization, an excise tax t, and expanded anti-drug education programs, the long-run equilibrium price and quantity are the same as they would be with an illegal drug market. However, legalization saves millions of dollars in police, judicial, and prison expenses, and perhaps more importantly, could save the lives of some police, dealers, users, and innocent by-standers currently caught in the middle of drug wars.

Consider some of the ramifications of legalization. There is the possibility that the combination of high taxes and education might result in less drug use. In fact, according to economist Susan Pozo, this outcome is quite possible.[6] Pozo studied price behavior in illegal drug markets by comparing the price of illegal drugs with the prices of alcohol and tobacco. Figure 10.3 shows Pozo's results for the period 1981–1991. Pozo adjusted the price of cocaine for both inflation and the purity of the drug. She also deflated the figures by the consumer price index (CPI) and normalized them. It is possible, therefore, to see how these prices behaved relative to each other, relative to their initial values, and relative to the CPI. To normalize the figures, Pozo divided each series by its initial value. This explains why each series starts at one on the y-axis in Figure 10.3.

Pozo's results are striking. The price of the illegal drug cocaine declined more than the price of the legal drug alcohol; the price of tobacco increased. There is also much more volatility in the price of cocaine than the prices of tobacco or alcohol. Pozo suggests

---

[6] Susan Pozo. *Price Behavior in Illegal Markets.* Aldershot, Hants, UK: Avebury Ashgate Publishing Limited, 1996.

Figure 10.3 The Change in the Relative Price of Legal and Illegal Substances

Between 1981 and 1991, the price of the illegal drug cocaine decreased more than the price of the legal drug alcohol. The price of the legal substance tobacco increased.

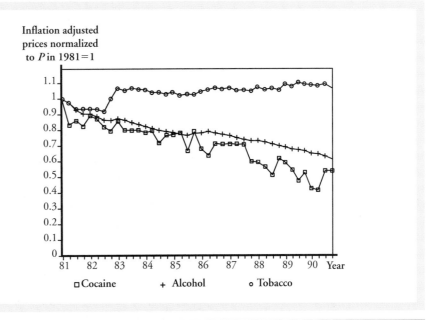

that this increased volatility in the cocaine market may result from misinformation in illegal markets and from variations in the level of law enforcement.[7]

Does it follow from this economic analysis that illegal drugs should be legalized? No. In fact, there are many factors that are absent from this analysis, including a great many important normative issues. Society may, for example, decide that legalization would cause new and unforeseen problems such as a less productive and more undisciplined workforce. Such problems already exist because of the widespread use of alcohol, and the legalization of drugs such as marijuana and cocaine might well exacerbate these problems. In the final analysis, the issue of drug legalization is extremely complex, and it is critical to consider all aspects of that complexity when discussing public policy options. In this section, we have primarily emphasized the positive economic analysis associated with legalization; however, the normative economic issues are extremely important as well.

10.2 The Gains from Trade

In 1993, the United States, Canada, and Mexico signed the North American Free Trade Agreement (NAFTA). NAFTA greatly reduced the barriers to trade between the three nations. The agreement, implemented on January 1, 1994, eliminated all non-tariff barriers to agricultural trade between the United States and Mexico. Furthermore, it eliminated many tariffs and established that other tariffs were to be phased out over 5 to 15 years. Predictions as to NAFTA's impact varied widely. Supporters argued that increased trade would benefit all three countries; opponents in the United States argued that a huge number of American jobs would be lost to Mexico, where wages were a small fraction of those in the United States.

Three years after the implementation of NAFTA, different groups still had vastly different opinions about the success or failure of the agreement. A study jointly authored by

---

[7] *Ibid.,* p. 45.

a number of groups including the Economic Policy Institute (a non-profit economic think tank) concluded that the U.S. trade deficits with Mexico and Canada had increased dramatically as a result of NAFTA and that NAFTA had cost the United States 420,208 jobs in its first three years.[8] According to CNN, after three years of NAFTA, a large number of manufacturing plants in El Paso, Texas had closed, while dozens of new plants had opened right across the border in Ciudad Juarez, Mexico.[9] The United Automobile Workers Union (UAW) estimated that by 2000, over 766,000 American workers had lost their jobs because of NAFTA.[10]

On the other hand, two detailed studies, one by the U.S. International Trade Commission (ITC) and the other by the North American Integration and Development Center (NAID) at UCLA, concluded that NAFTA had (if anything) a slightly positive impact on American jobs.[11] The ITC study generally found no statistically significant impact of NAFTA on American employment. The NAID study concluded that while NAFTA had a slightly positive impact on American employment, it had neither created the tens of thousands of jobs that some advocates of NAFTA suggested, nor had it caused any widespread dislocation of American workers as suggested by NAFTA's detractors. Which side is right? Did NAFTA have a negative or positive impact on the United States? We can use the competitive model to help answer these questions.

The Economics of Protectionism

By using the competitive model to analyze the general impact of reducing trade barriers, we can see why various political groups view NAFTA so differently. First, consider the general impact of trade liberalization on any market previously closed to trade. Assume, for example, that the United States initially prevents the importation of all tomatoes. Furthermore, assume that both the United States and the rest of the world produce in a perfectly competitive tomato market. Panel (a) in Figure 10.4 depicts the tomato market in the United States, and panel (b) depicts the tomato market in the rest of the world. In the absence of trade between the United States and the rest of the world, the equilibrium price is p_4 in the United States and p_2 in the rest of the world. Total consumer surplus in the United States equals the purple triangle A, and total producer surplus in the United States equals the sum of green and blue areas B and D.

THE MARKET WITH FREE TRADE   Suppose that the United States decides to permit free trade in tomatoes. Because the price of tomatoes in the United States, p_4, is greater than the price of tomatoes in the rest of the world, p_2, firms in the rest of the world want to export tomatoes to the United States. To determine how many tomatoes foreign firms will be willing to export to the United States at prices greater than p_2, calculate the horizontal difference between the supply curve in the rest of the world, S_{ROW}, and the demand curve in the rest of the world, D_{ROW}. For example, at a price of p_3, foreign firms are willing to export $q_3 - q_1$ tomatoes, represented by the distance between

---

[8] Economic Policy Institute, et al. *The Failed Experiment: NAFTA at Three Years.* Washington, DC: Economic Policy Institute, June 26, 1997.

[9] Charles Zewe, "Three Years Later, NAFTA's Effects Still Debated," *http://www.cnn.com.*

[10] "NAFTA's Hidden Costs: Trade Agreement Results in Job Losses, Growing Inequality," *http://www.uaw.org.*

[11] U.S. International Trade Commission. *The Impact of the North American Free Trade Agreement on the U.S. Economy and Industries.* Washington, D.C.: ITC Publication 3945, June 1997; and Raul Hinojosa Ojeda, et al. *North American Integration Three Years After NAFTA: A Framework for Tracking, Modeling and Internet Accessing the National and Regional Labor Market Impacts.* North American Integration & Development Center (NAID). Los Angeles: University of California, December 1996.

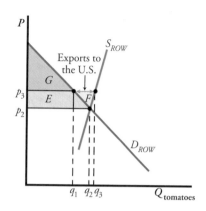

(a) Tomato market in the United States   (b) Tomato market in the rest of the world

Figure 10.4 The Impact of Trade Liberalization
Without free trade the initial prices are p_4 in the United States and p_2 in the rest of the world. With trade, imports flow into the United States, and the supply curve in the United States becomes $S_{US + FOR}$ in panel (a). The new equilibrium price in both the United States and the rest of the world is p_3. In panel (a), The United States imports $Q_3 - Q_1$ units; and in panel (b), the rest of the world exports $q_3 - q_1$ to the United States. With trade, in panel (a), consumer surplus in the United States increases by the sum of areas $B + C$, and producer surplus for U.S. producers decreases by area B; therefore, there is a net welfare gain equal to area C. In panel (b), with trade, consumer surplus in the rest of the world decreases by area E, and producer surplus increases by the sum of areas $E + F$; therefore, there is a net welfare gain equal to area F.

the orange arrowheads in Figure 10.4(b), to the United States. By adding the amount that foreign firms are willing to export to the United States at every price above p_2 to the United States supply curve for tomatoes without trade, S_{US}, we obtain the United States supply curve with trade, $S_{US + FOR}$. For prices below p_2, no foreign producers would want to sell in the United States—the price is too low. As the price rises above p_2, imports begin to flow into the United States.

Figure 10.4(a) shows that if trade is permitted, the price of tomatoes in the United States will decline to p_3, where the quantity supplied with trade equals the quantity demanded. In panel (a), American farmers supply Q_1 tomatoes to the American market, and foreign farmers export $Q_3 - Q_1$ tomatoes, which by construction must equal $q_3 - q_1$ tomatoes in panel (b). The equilibrium tomato price in the United States and the rest of the world must be equalized by free trade, or else there would be an incentive to sell more in the market with the higher price. As a result of free trade, total consumer surplus in the United States has increased by the sum of areas B and C, so total consumer surplus is equal to the sum of areas A, B, and C. Total producer surplus earned by American growers equals the green area D in Figure 10.4(a), and has declined by the blue area B.

WELFARE EFFECTS ON THE DOMESTIC ECONOMY What is the net welfare effect on Americans of the decision to permit trade? Consumer surplus increases by the areas B and C, but producer surplus among American tomato growers decreases by the blue area B. Because the area B represents a gain to American consumers *and* a loss to American producers, it has no net impact on American welfare. The gray area C, however, represents a net welfare gain to Americans. Therefore, the net impact on American

the gains from trade

The net increase in welfare that occurs to a country as a result of trade.

consumers and producers of permitting trade is positive. This increase in welfare from trade is called the **gains from trade**.

In the United States, American tomato growers stand to lose the most from a free trade policy, and American consumers are the big winners. Furthermore, because the American demand for farm workers decreases, the equilibrium farm worker wage and the equilibrium number of farm workers employed both decrease. Consequently, some farm workers in the United States lose their jobs, and those who are still working earn lower wages. As a result, tomato growers and farm workers will lobby to restrict the importation of tomatoes.

WELFARE EFFECTS ON THE REST OF THE WORLD Having analyzed the welfare effects of free trade on the United States, we turn our attention to the welfare impact of free trade on the rest of the world. According to Figure 10.4(b), in the rest of the world, with free trade, consumers pay a higher price for tomatoes, and consumer surplus declines by the green area *E*. Producer surplus in the rest of the world, however, increases by the sum of areas *E* and *F*. Because the area *E* represents both a loss to consumers and a gain for producers, it has no net effect on welfare in the rest of the world. Area *F*, however, represents a gain to producers and a net gain in welfare in the rest of the world.

Based on our discussion of the impact of free trade in the United States, it is possible to better understand the political positions of various groups toward free trade. American tomato growers and farm workers, the groups suffering losses as a result of free trade, will be opposed to trade liberalization, and American tomato consumers, who benefit, will favor free trade. On the other hand, tomato growers and farm workers in the rest of the world will be in favor of an American policy of free trade in tomatoes, and tomato consumers in the rest of the world will be opposed.

NAFTA and the American Tomato Market

Our tomato example is not hypothetical. The implementation of NAFTA resulted in a large increase in the export of Mexican tomatoes to the United States, which severely damaged profitability for American tomato growers. In fact, the damage to American growers was so severe that in the midst of the 1996 Presidential election, the Clinton Administration negotiated an agreement with Mexico that forced the Mexicans to set a minimum price on tomatoes exported to the United States. According to one administration official, "[t]he math was pretty simple: Florida has 25 electoral votes, and Mexico doesn't."[12]

real wages

The real buying power of wages measured as the ratio of the wage, *w*, to the consumer price index, *CPI*, or *w/CPI*.

The UAW and American workers in southern Texas strongly opposed NAFTA. Furthermore, because free trade caused the price of tomatoes to increase in Mexico, the Mexican consumer index, *CPI*, increased and Mexicans who did not work on tomato farms found their **real wages**, represented by the ratio of their dollar wage, *w*, to the *CPI*, or *w/CPI*, reduced by NAFTA. Despite political opposition and negative effects, economists were and still are overwhelmingly in favor of NAFTA. Microeconomic analysis suggests that the net welfare effects of trade liberalization are positive for all countries. In some countries, consumers win and producers lose; while in other countries, producers win and consumers lose. Assuming perfectly competitive markets, the net effect of trade liberalization is positive for all countries.

It is politically difficult to formulate rational trade agreements, because the costs and benefits of free trade agreements such as NAFTA affect different groups so differently.

---

[12] David E. Sanger, "President Wins Tomato Accord for Floridians: Mexico Agrees to End Low-Price Shipments," the *New York Times*, October 12, 1996, p. A1.

Furthermore, the groups of potential losers are often far more organized than the groups of potential winners. The organized groups of potential losers, U.S. tomato farmers and unionized farm workers, have a great incentive to lobby the government to protect their interests, whereas individual consumers who save a few cents a pound on tomatoes have much less incentive to spend time and/or money lobbying politicians about tomato trade policy. Therefore, it may be difficult to adopt trade policies that primarily help consumers by lowering prices when these policies also injure firms and their workers. In the case of tomatoes, the Clinton Administration elected to protect the organized interests of tomato growers rather than the interests of the nation's consumers. As a result, tomato prices increased and consumer surplus was reduced.

10.3   Rent Control

When governments reduce trade barriers, they enable the free market to operate more efficiently. Sometimes, however, governments take actions that prevent free market outcomes. The imposition of rent control, one of the most common types of price ceilings, is one such government action. Rent control has been implemented throughout the world, including in New York, London, Paris, and Hanoi.[13] Rent control first appeared in the United States in 1943 as part of the nation's wartime price controls imposed by the federal government. When the federal rent controls ended with the end of the war, some localities such as New York City maintained their controls. Eventually, localities around the country, including Boston, Santa Monica, Washington, San Francisco, Los Angeles, and 125 municipalities in New Jersey, were enforcing rent controls. Despite the widespread use of rent controls, surveys show that economists of all political persuasions almost unanimously oppose them. In a 1978 survey of 75 world famous economists published in the *American Economic Review*, there was almost unanimous agreement with the following statement: "A ceiling on rents will reduce the quality and quantity of housing."[14] A 1992 poll of economists resulted in the same opinion of rent control.[15]

Rent Control in the Short Run

We can use the competitive model to explain why economists have such a negative opinion of rent controls. Our analysis begins with the assumption that rent control freezes rents at their current equilibrium levels. Suppose the rental housing market is an increasing-cost industry, and therefore the long-run supply curve slopes upward. In Figure 10.5(a), for example, suppose that the market for rental housing in New York is in long-run equilibrium before the implementation of rent control, with the long-run supply curve, LRS_1, the short-run supply curve, S_1, and the demand curve, D_1, intersecting at point x with the equilibrium price p_c. In panel (b), with marginal costs MC_1 and average costs AC_1, the typical landlord provides output q_1; profits for the typical landlord are zero; and there is no economic inefficiency. If the government imposes a price ceiling at p_c, there is no immediate problem.

---

[13] Roger Leroy Miller, Daniel K. Benjamin, and Douglas C. North, *The Economics of Public Issues, 13th Edition*. Boston: Addison Wesley, 2003; and William Tucker, "How Rent Control Drives Out Affordable Housing," *Cato Policy Analysis* No. 274, Washington, D.C.: Cato Institute, May 21, 1997.

[14] J.R. Kearl, Clayne L. Pope, C. Whiting, and Larry T. Wimmer, "A Confusion of Economists," *American Economic Review*, Vol. 69, May 1979, pp. 26–37.

[15] "Survey of Members," *American Economic Review*, Vol. 82, December 1992.

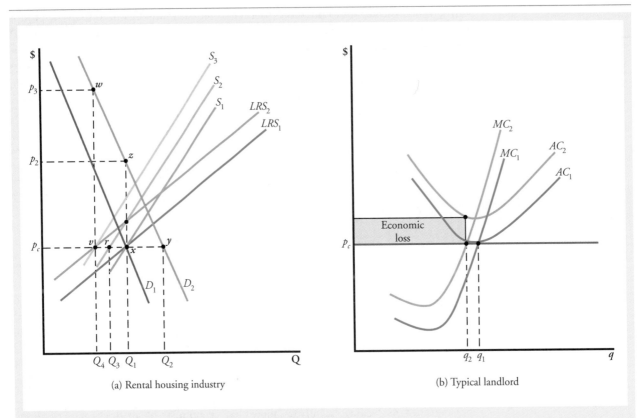

(a) Rental housing industry (b) Typical landlord

Figure 10.5 The Short-Run and Long-Run Impact of Rent Control
In panel (a), with rent control at price p_c, and initial demand equal to D_1, the short-run supply is S_1, and the long-run supply is LRS_1. If demand in panel (a) increases to D_2, excess demand equal to $Q_2 - Q_1$ develops. In panel (b), over time, costs increase for landlords from MC_1 and AC_1 to MC_2 and AC_2; and as a result, in panel (a), the short-run supply curve decreases to S_2 and the long-run supply curve decreases to LRS_2. In panel (b), landlords decrease output to q_2, and they sustain an economic loss equal to the shaded red area. In the long run, the losses cause landlords to withdraw rental units from the market, decreasing the short-run supply of rental housing to S_3. A new long-run equilibrium is achieved only when input prices decline, causing the cost curves in panel (b) to decline back to MC_1 and AC_1 so that profits are normal.

Problems arise when the demand for rental housing increases as the population increases. Suppose that a few years after the imposition of the price ceiling at p_c, demand increases to D_2. Figure 10.5(a) shows that at price p_c, there is now excess demand for rental housing equal to $Q_2 - Q_1$ units. Landlords are only willing to supply Q_1 units of rental housing at point x, but consumers demand Q_2 units at point y. With the quantity supplied fixed at Q_1, consumers would be willing to pay rents of p_2 for those Q_1 units at point z on demand curve D_2. Even though landlords could obtain rents of p_2 for Q_1 units of rental housing, they are prevented from doing so because of the price ceiling.

Given excess demand, the rental units must somehow be rationed. The landlords might simply permit the current tenants to stay in the units, or they might prefer to rent to tenants with the best chance of paying the rent. Ironically, the tenants with the best chance of paying the rent are middle- and upper-income families. Under rent control, landlords have an economic incentive to discriminate against low-income families, despite the fact that low-income families are precisely the families that rent control programs were originally intended to help. For example, despite the fact that Santa Monica's tight rent controls loosened considerably in 1999 when the state of California mandated that rents could be increased when an apartment became vacant, most rental housing in Santa Monica is still subject to rent control. In affluent Santa Monica, landlords can essentially pick and choose to rent only to upper-income professional families. Economists Miller, Benjamin, and North have noted that as a result, "There is no disputing that Santa Monica has become younger, whiter, and richer under rent control."[16] It's unlikely this result was the objective of Santa Monica's original rent control laws.

Rent Control in the Long Run

Thus far, we have limited our analysis to the short run. But the long-run consequences of rent control are quite different from the short-run consequences. Returning to Figure 10.5: over time, due to inflation, the price of inputs—such as labor and the cost of materials to maintain and improve rental housing units—would increase, resulting in an increase of the price of these inputs. The increase in input prices would increase the landlords' maintenance costs. If marginal and average costs increased to MC_2 and AC_2 in panel (b); the short-run and long-run supply curves in panel (a) both shift up vertically the same distance that the marginal and average cost curves shifted up in panel (b). Therefore, the supply curves shift up vertically to LRS_2 and S_2. The typical landlord is stuck with a rent of p_c, reduces output to q_2 in panel (b), and sustains a short-run economic loss equal to the light-red shaded area. Figure 10.5(a) shows that in the short run, the number of rental units available declines to Q_3 at point r. In the long run, landlords exit the industry either by closing down or converting their rental units to other uses such as condominiums or commercial property, and the short-run supply shifts further left to S_3. As a result, the number of rental units available declines much further to Q_4 at point v. Because the industry is an increasing-cost industry, as industry output declines, the landlords' costs decline too, and eventually the industry achieves a new long-run equilibrium where costs have declined to their original levels MC_1 and AC_1. Notice that the excess demand of $Q_2 - Q_4$ is much larger than it was before.

There now exists a huge excess demand for rental housing. Landlords are only willing to supply Q_4 units of rental housing at point v, but consumers demand Q_2 units at point y. With the quantity supplied fixed at Q_4, consumers would now be willing to pay rents of p_3 for those Q_4 units at point w on demand curve D_2. Even though landlords could obtain rents of p_3 for Q_4 units of rental housing, the price ceiling prevents them from doing so. Landlords will undoubtedly try to figure out a legal (or illegal) way of obtaining higher rents. In New York, for example, landlords often charge so-called "key money," a large advanced payment that the tenant must pay before moving in. Furthermore, landlords in New York often refuse to pay for any improvements not legally required, so tenants must pay costs of repairs and maintenance such as painting and plumbing that the landlord would usually pay.

A final additional long-run effect of rent control is the large cost of maintaining a bureaucracy to enforce all of the rules and regulations. For example, Santa Monica's rent control board, which began with a budget of $745,000 in 1979, had a nominal budget of close to $5 million in the 1990s (approximately $2.7 million in deflated 1979 dollars).[17] Such regulatory boards are necessary because the laws typically provide little incentive for landlords to make even the most necessary repairs. Because the laws often only permit landlords to raise rents when old tenants move out and new tenants move

---

[16] Miller, Benjamin, and North, *op. cit.*, p. 71.

[17] *Ibid.*, p. 72.

in, landlords have an incentive to make their current tenants' lives so intolerable that they voluntarily move out. If this doesn't work, however, it is almost impossible for landlords to evict tenants even if they violate the terms of their lease; in fact, it is even difficult to evict a tenant for non-payment of rent. This helps explain why New York landlords insist on receiving thousands of dollars in key money before they rent to a new tenant.

The Distributional Impacts of Rent Control

In the end, who really benefits from rent control? The largest beneficiaries are the tenants who are fortunate enough to find a rent-controlled apartment. In addition, the bureaucrats who work for the rent control boards are winners. Conversely, the losers are the landlords and all of the low-income families who are unable to find housing and end up in shelters, on the streets, or in other communities. Families living in surrounding communities without rent control are also losers, because those displaced by rent control look to the surrounding communities for housing, thereby increasing demand and rent in those communities.

Despite these problems, rent control programs continue to exist for political reasons: many politicians believe that supporting rent control will gain more votes than it will lose. In recent years, however, many communities, including the Commonwealth of Massachusetts, have eliminated rent control. In Hanoi, Vietnam, the government is rethinking its policy of rent control. The foreign minister of Vietnam, Nguyen Co Thach, stated that, "The Americans couldn't destroy Hanoi, but we have destroyed our city by very low rents."[18] Many economists suggest that if the problem is a lack of low-priced housing for the poor, society and the poor would be better off forgetting about rent control and instead redistributing income so that the poor have higher incomes and can afford better housing without rent control.

▼▼▼   10.4   Agricultural Price Supports

price supports

Laws that prevent prices from falling below legally set limits.

In addition to price ceilings, governments can also institute *price floors*, which prevent prices from falling below legal limits. Among the most common price floors throughout the world are **price supports** on agricultural products. The United States, the European Union, and Japan make extensive use of price supports. In recent years, however, the United States has increased its effort to reduce the dependence of American farmers on agricultural price supports. Furthermore, the World Trade Organization (WTO) has attempted to reduce price supports throughout the world and make agricultural markets behave more in line with their competitive market structures. To understand why the United States government and the WTO have taken these steps, we begin with an explanation of how these supports came into being in the United States.

The History of Price Supports in the United States

In the United States during the late 1920s, farmers were not reaping the benefits from the booming economy. In fact, large increases in agricultural production resulted in falling prices. Farm prices fell to such low levels that in 1927, Congress twice passed agricultural price support bills aimed at increasing agricultural prices, only to have President Coolidge veto them. In 1929, however, President Hoover signed an agricultural price

---

[18] *Ibid.*, p. 73.

Agricultural Marketing Act

A 1929 U.S. law that first established a fund to support farm prices.

Agricultural Adjustment Act

A 1933 U.S. law that established the nation's first price supports on major crops.

parity price

A price support established with the objective of insuring that farmers' real incomes remain comparable to the incomes earned by manufacturing workers.

Commodity Credit Corporation (CCC)

A government agency established to make loans to farmers in return for the farmer's crops as collateral.

support bill, the **Agricultural Marketing Act**, which established a $500 million fund to support farm prices. In 1933, in the midst of the Great Depression, Congress went one step further and passed the **Agricultural Adjustment Act** (AAA). The AAA was the beginning of modern price support policies in the United States. The key feature of this bill was to set price floors on the major crops, in an attempt to stabilize prices at so-called *parity prices*. The **parity price** was originally set to insure that farmers' real incomes would remain more or less equal to the high farm incomes that existed during the prosperous period for farmers between 1909 and 1914. Later parity prices were intended to ensure that farmers' incomes remained comparable to manufacturing workers' incomes.

Another key element of the 1933 bill was the establishment of the United States **Commodity Credit Corporation** (CCC). The CCC loaned money to farmers and in return received the farmer's crops as collateral. The official loan price was simply the support price. When a loan became due, usually after nine months, the farmer had a choice of either not repaying the loan and allowing the government to keep the crops, or buying back his crops by repaying the loan with a small interest charge and then selling the crops on the open market. The decision whether to default on the loan was entirely dependent on whether the market price was above or below the loan price.

The Economic Impact of Price Support Programs

The United States government has used three different types of price support programs: CCC loans, acreage limitation, and deficiency payments. Each of these programs results in an increase in farm income, but each accomplishes this objective in somewhat different ways. We begin by analyzing the original CCC loan program.

CCC LOAN PROGRAMS Figure 10.6 depicts the impact of the CCC loan policy on the wheat market. In Figure 10.6(a), the equilibrium price is $2.50, but the loan price or parity price is $3.00. Farmers sell Q_d bushels and turn over $(Q_s - Q_d)$ units to the CCC in return for loans equal to $3.00(Q_s - Q_d)$. Because the equilibrium price of $2.50 is less than the loan price of $3.00, the CCC would end up purchasing $(Q_s - Q_d)$ bushels of wheat at a price of $3.00. The total cost to taxpayers, $3.00(Q_s - Q_d)$, is represented by the orange shaded area in panel (a). The surplus wheat $Q_s - Q_d$ would typically be stored by the farmer, but owned by the government.

Figure 10.6 The Impact of Guaranteed Loans to Farmers.
In panel (a), if the government guarantees farmers a price of $3.00, farmers supply Q_s bushels; Q_d bushels are sold to consumers and the government purchases $Q_s - Q_d$ bushels for a total cost equal to the shaded orange area. In panel (b), individual farmers earn a normal economic profit.

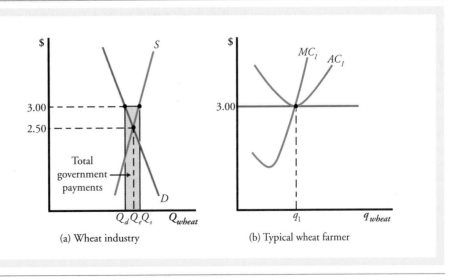

(a) Wheat industry (b) Typical wheat farmer

As shown in Figure 10.6(b), for the typical farmer, the price support program results in zero economic profit rather than excess profit. Zero economic profit existed in the long run for two reasons. First, easy entry insured that farmers would enter the wheat market if excess profit existed. Second, the existence of the price support program increased the opportunity cost of farm acreage by increasing the rental value of an acre of farmland: therefore, the average cost curve, AC_1, increased until only normal profit could be earned.

ACREAGE LIMITATION PROGRAMS A second policy intended to raise crop prices was the federal government's acreage limitation program, aimed at reducing the supply of agricultural commodities. Under the Agricultural Adjustment Act's original price support program, the government's grain holdings were large and growing. To reduce the surplus, the government tried to limit the number of acres farmers would put into production. For example, the federal government made the receipt of CCC loans contingent on limiting the number of acres cultivated. The government also used direct payments to induce output reductions. The result of these programs was a reduction in the supply of agricultural goods and an increase in their prices. The program reduced the size of the government's grain storage holdings by reducing production. Of the approximately one billion acres devoted to farming in the United States, these acreage limitation programs reduced production, on average, by about 66 million acres in the late 1980s.[19]

THE DEFICIENCY PAYMENT PROGRAM The third major federal price support is a program of *target pricing* and *deficiency payments*. This program was first proposed—but not adopted—in 1949 by Charles Brannan, President Truman's secretary of agriculture. It was not fully implemented until 1973. The program works by first setting a **target price**. This target price is supposed to cover the full costs of production, including a normal profit. If the target price is above the market price, the government pays the farmer a **total deficiency payment** or *TDP*. The **TDP** is a lump sum payment that was calculated according to the following formula:

$$TDP = [(\text{target price} - \text{market price})/\text{bushel}] \times (\text{base acreage})$$
$$\times (\text{program yield in bushels per acre})$$

The base acreage is purposefully not determined by current production, but on the farmer's historical production. The base acreage is typically a five-year moving average of the acreage planted by the farmer.[20] The secretary of agriculture sets the program yield. Since 1985, this figure has been based primarily on historical yields in the area. Note that the total deficiency payment is independent of the actual number of acres planted during the current year.

Consider a hypothetical example for Farmer Jones. Suppose the target price for wheat is $3.75/bushel, the equilibrium market price is $3.25, Farmer Jones's base acreage is 400 acres, and the program yield is 40 bushels/acre. Farmer Jones would sell his entire output of wheat at $3.25 and also receive a payment of ($3.75 − $3.25)(400)(40) = $8,000. By making the payment independent of this year's production and allowing Farmer Jones to sell his wheat on the open market, the program eliminates government surpluses in grain storehouses.

target price

A price established by a government agency calculated to cover the full costs of production, including a normal profit.

total deficiency payment (TDP)

A lump sum payment to a farmer that guarantees a minimum price per bushel based on the farmer's historical number of planted acres and the yield per acre.

---

[19] F.M. Scherer. *Industry, Structure, Strategy, and Public Policy.* New York: Harper Collins Publishers, 1996, p. 40.

[20] The five-year moving average in the year t was calculated as follows:

$$average = \frac{A_t + A_{t-1} + A_{t-2} + A_{t-3} + A_{t-4}}{5}$$

where A_t is the base acreage in the year t.

Figure 10.7 shows roughly how the target pricing and deficiency payments program works. Multiplying the base acreage by the program yield per acre results in Q_1 bushels that qualify for the deficiency payments. The government pays the difference between the target price $3.75 and the market equilibrium price of $3.25 that the farmers receive for selling the first Q_1 bushels they produce. The major difference between Figures 10.6(a) and 10.7 is that there is a large surplus produced by farmers and owned by the government in Figure 10.6(a), but there is no surplus owned by the government in Figure 10.7. Relative program costs depend on the parameters of the programs, such as the CCC loan price, the target price, and the program yield.

DISTRIBUTIONAL IMPACTS Regardless of which price floor program is adopted, most of the government payments, whether loans or deficiency payments, go to the largest farmers. Table 10.2 shows how government payments were distributed by farm size in 1991. The average government payment per farm increased incrementally up to farms with sales of between $500,000 and $999,999. In 1991, the majority of the 2,105,000 farms were small, with less than $20,000 in sales revenues. These small farmers received an average of only $651 per farm. Compare this payment with the average payment of $30,769 per farm for farms with sales between $500,000 and $999,999, and the $25,000 average payment to farms with over $1,000,000 in sales. The distributional impact of the government support program is of little help to the small farmer. In fact, the irony of this particular program is that the largest absolute dollar payments go to the farmers who need it least.

The Impact of Eliminating Price Supports

An analysis of government price support programs leads us to the question: What is the impact of eliminating these programs? Figure 10.8 shows the long-run impact of removing all price supports from the wheat market analyzed in Figure 10.6. Recall that the loan price is $3.00 and the short-run equilibrium price is $2.50. Initially, the marginal and average cost curves are MC_1 and AC_1, as shown in Figure 10.8(b), and the typical farmer

Figure 10.7 The Impact of the Deficiency Payment Program
With a deficiency payment program, if the target price is $3.75 and the base acreage times the program yield per acre equals Q_1 bushels, the government pays farmers $Q_1($3.75 − $3.25)$, which equals the shaded orange area. Farmers, however, sell their entire output Q_e at the market equilibrium price $3.25, so there is no surplus production.

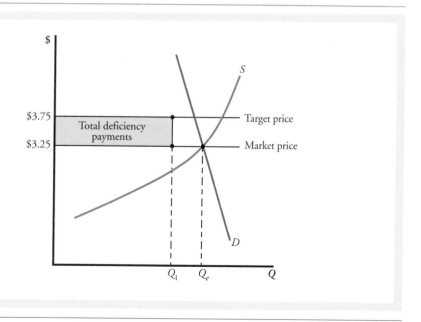

Table 10.2 Distribution of Farm Income and Direct Government Payments by Farm Size Class, 1991

1991 Farm Product Sales	Number of Farms (thousands)	Net Cash Income per Farm ($)	Average Government Payment per Farm ($)	Percent of Total Government Payments	Government Payments As a percent of Farms' Cash Receipts
Less than $20,000	1,229	−81	651	9.8	11.6
$20,000–$39,999	240	9,167	2,500	7.3	8.7
$40,000–$100,000	309	24,595	6,796	25.6	10.4
$100,000–$249,000	215	60,465	10,698	28.0	6.9
$250,000–$499,999	69	131,884	17,391	14.6	5.0
$500,000–$999,999	26	250,000	30,769	9.8	4.4
$1,000,000 and over	16	1,225,000	25,000	4.9	0.7
Total	2,105	27,553	3,895	100.0	4.9

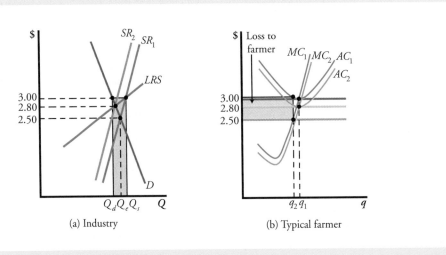

(a) Industry

(b) Typical farmer

Figure 10.8 The Elimination of Price Supports in Agricultural Markets
In panel (a), if the $3.00 price support is eliminated, in the short run, the price decreases to $2.50 and output decreases to Q_e. In panel (b), in the short run, output decreases from q_1 to q_2, and the typical farmer sustains an economic loss equal to the red shaded area. In the long run, in panel (a), farmers leave the market, which shifts the short-run supply to SR_2; and because the industry is an increasing-cost industry and industry output decreases, costs decrease to MC_2 and AC_2. In the new long-run equilibrium, price is $2.80, and farmers earn a normal economic profit in panel (b).

earns a normal profit. If the price supports were eliminated, the short-run effect would be a decline in the price to $2.50. In the short run, the typical farmer would reduce output from q_1 to q_2 in panel (b) and sustain an economic loss equal to the shaded red area. The elimination of price supports, therefore, would result in a large short-run negative impact on the typical farmer.

Now consider the long-run impact of eliminating the price supports. Assuming that wheat farming is an increasing-cost industry, the long-run supply curve is the upward-sloping *LRS* curve in Figure 10.8(a). In the long run, economic losses would result in some wheat farmers leaving farming, and the short-run supply curve would shift to the left to SR_2. Because the industry is an increasing-cost industry, as the industry output declines, the costs of production also decline. This would mean that the opportunity cost of farm acreage would decline once the government stops guaranteeing a minimum price. In Figure 10.8(b), the long-run equilibrium price is $2.80, and the long-run marginal and average costs have declined to MC_2 and AC_2. This means that the typical farmer earns a normal profit only when the price reaches $2.80.

This analysis leaves us asking: Who are the winners and losers from the elimination of the price supports? In general, the winners are consumers, who pay lower prices for agricultural goods, and taxpayers, who no longer have to pay for the price supports. Those small farmers who are forced to leave farming are the losers. Of course, all farmers sustain short-run losses as they are weaned off price supports. In the long run, however, the remaining farmers would earn exactly the same economic profits they earn now; that is, normal economic profits.

The Agricultural Market Transition Act of 1996

Agricultural Market Transition Act

A 1996 U.S. law that ended direct price supports for wheat, corn, barley, cotton, rice, sorghum, and oats, but continued paying farmers who agreed to use their land exclusively for agricultural purposes subject to certain land-conservation requirements.

The common problems of high prices and excess production associated with price supports in the United States led to the passage of the **Agricultural Market Transition Act** in 1996. The new policy ended direct price supports for seven commodities: wheat, corn, barley, cotton, rice, sorghum, and oats. However, farmers continue to receive direct government transition payments for agreeing to use land exclusively for agricultural purposes and to follow certain conservation measures. The payments were originally scheduled to decline from $5.6 billion in 1996 to $4.0 billion in 2002.[21] One of the most important provisions of the act was to limit the payment to any one farm to a maximum of $75,000 per year.

In 1996 and 1997, the new policy worked well, because world agricultural prices were high. However, when world agricultural prices declined dramatically in 1998 and 1999, farmers ran to Washington for financial help, and Congress responded by granting billions of dollars of emergency farm aid. In 1999, the emergency aid reached $8.7 billion.[22] Three years later, in 2002, elections in major farm states in the Midwest continued to be fought largely over which candidate could guarantee the most government farm aid. In the end, dismantling agricultural price supports may prove to be politically impossible.

Common Agricultural Policy (CAP)

The price support system used by the European Union (E.U.).

Despite the passage of the Agricultural Market Transition Act, the United States continues to provide price supports for peanuts, tobacco, citrus fruits, and milk. The United States is not alone in its continued use of price support programs. One study estimated that in 1999, the E.U.'s **Common Agricultural Policy** (CAP), which sets minimum prices on most European agricultural products, cost the world economy $75 billion, of which $49 billion was borne by E.U. members and another $26 billion was borne by other countries.[23] According to the study, the CAP increased milk production and livestock production in the E.U. by more than 50 percent over competitive levels. Truly, competitive agricultural markets are still far from a reality—not only in the United States, but in the rest of the world as well.

---

[21] Walter Adams and James Brock, *The Structure of American Industry*. Upper Saddle River, N.J.: Prentice Hall, 2001, p. 22.

[22] *Ibid.*, p. 23.

[23] Brent Borrell and Lionel Hubbard, "Global Economic Effects of the E.U. Common Agricultural Policy," *Journal of the Institute of Economic Affairs*, Vol. 20, June 1, 2000.

10.5 The Market for Human Eggs and Organs

On October 23, 1999, the *New York Times* reported the following story:[24]

> To the horror and disgust of mainstream infertility groups, a longtime photographer has begun offering up models as egg donors to the highest bidders, auctioning their ova via the Internet to would-be parents willing to pay up to $150,000 in hopes of having a beautiful child.

Now compare the *New York Times* story to the following story published in the journal *Diseases and Conditions:*[25]

> On average, 11 people die every day while waiting for the death of a stranger to give them a second birth. Last year, 4,300 people died while waiting on organ donation lists, and that number is expected to increase by another 300 to 500 this year, according to the United Network for Organ Sharing.... Such huge demand in the face of such short supply has challenged doctors, politicians and organ donation advocates to come up with strategies that will increase organ donation. One of the most controversial ideas makes what has traditionally been a difficult and delicate issue for Americans even more discomforting: offering money to people who sign over their relative's organs.

Is the auctioning of human eggs and organs to the highest bidder ethical or unethical? Although economists can add little, if any, insight into this normative moral question, they can analyze the positive economics of permitting a free market for human eggs and organs. In the United States, there is one major legal difference between selling human eggs and selling human organs: The sale of human eggs is legal, while the sale of organs is illegal.

The Welfare Effects of Banning Organ Sales

We begin by examining the illegal market for human organs. Consider the market for human kidneys, by far the largest human organ transplant market. In 2002, it was estimated that nearly 53,000 Americans were on kidney transplant waiting lists, and that less than 15,000 transplant operations would be performed.[26] Furthermore, 2,800 people on kidney transplant waiting lists would die in 2002. Panels (a) and (b) in Figure 10.9 identify two possible supply and demand curve conditions for kidneys. In both panels, if the sale of organs is illegal, organ donors are willing to supply q_s kidneys, so the quantity supplied of kidneys at a price of zero is equal to q_s. Additional kidneys can be received, but only by paying increasingly higher prices to donors or donor families. Kidneys differ from other types of transplanted human organs such as hearts and livers in that donors can survive and live a perfectly normal life with just one kidney. Therefore, although hearts and livers can be donated only after death, living donors can donate kidneys. In terms of economic analysis, this makes the human kidney market more comparable to the human egg market than either the human heart or human liver markets.

---

[24] Carey Goldberg, "Eggs for Sale!! Selling Human Eggs to the Highest Bidder," the *New York Times*, October 23,1999, Section A, p. 11.

[25] Katrina Woznicki, "Demand Pushes Debate About Organs for Sale," *Diseases and Conditions*, September 2, 1998.

[26] "Research May Ease Shortage of Kidney Donors," *USA Today*, July 25, 2002.

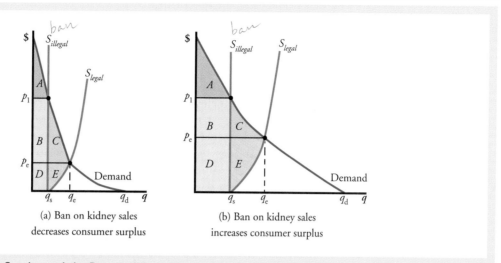

Figure 10.9 Consumer Surplus and the Ban on Kidney Sales
In panel (a), if the sale of kidneys is illegal, the supply is fixed at $S_{illegal}$. Total consumer surplus equals the sum of areas $A + B + D$ and there is no producer surplus. If the sale of kidneys is legal, the supply is S_{legal} and the equilibrium price is p_e. Consumer surplus equals the sum of areas $A + B + C$, and producer surplus equals the sum of areas $D + E$. Total surplus increases with legalization by the sum of areas $C + E$. In panel (a), the ban on sales decreases consumer surplus because area C is larger than area D. In panel (b), total surplus increases with legalization by the sum of areas $C + E$, but the ban on sales increases consumer surplus, because area D is larger than area C.

In panel (a), in the absence of government restrictions on the sale of organs, the equilibrium price of kidneys would be p_e and the equilibrium quantity supplied would be q_e. With a ban on sales, there is a large excess demand for kidneys equal to $q_d - q_s$ at the mandated price ceiling of zero. If we assume that the q_s donated kidneys are supplied at $p = 0$ to recipients with the highest reservation prices, then the total consumer surplus associated with the transplants equals the sum of the purple, yellow, and blue areas (areas $A + B + D$). If there were no government restrictions on the sale of kidneys, $p = p_e$, and total consumer surplus would equal the sum of the purple, yellow, and orange areas (areas $A + B + C$). If area C is greater than area D, as it appears to be in panel (a), then consumer surplus decreases as a result of the ban on kidney sales. However, if area C is less than area D, as it appears to be in panel (b), then consumer surplus increases as a result of the ban on kidney sales. The result depends on the relative price elasticities of the demand and supply curves.

Although in panel (b), consumer surplus is greater with a ban on sales, and therefore consumers appear to benefit from the ban on organ sales, donors (or their families in the case of a donation after death) are worse off. In panel (b), if kidney sales were permitted, all kidneys would be sold at a price equal to p_e, and the q_s individuals willing to donate kidneys at a price of zero would receive total payments equal to the blue rectangle D for those q_s kidneys. The ban on kidney sales therefore results in a transfer equal to the blue area D from donors and their families to recipients. ?

Welfare with Legal Organ Sales

Under the current system, q_s kidney recipients benefit from having the price set at zero. However, our analysis is far from finished. Let's consider what would happen if there were a legal market for kidneys. In both panels of Figure 10.9, with legalization, more kidneys would be supplied and recipients would receive q_e kidneys at a price of p_e. Total consumer surplus would equal the sum of areas $A + B + C$. Donors' surplus, or producer surplus, would equal the sum of areas $D + E$. The market solution therefore increases total surplus by the sum of areas $C + E$. Notice that the areas $C + E$ equal the deadweight loss associated with banning kidney sales.

Our analysis, to this point, has actually underestimated the likely deadweight loss associated with preventing the sale of kidneys, because we have assumed that the q_s donated kidneys are supplied at $p = 0$ to the recipients with the highest reservation prices. With $p = 0$, however, there is no guarantee that patients with the highest reservation prices will receive kidneys because all q_d potential recipients have reservation prices above zero. If kidney sales were permitted, only those recipients for whom doctors and insurance companies were willing to pay a price greater than p_e would receive kidneys. This means that most likely, the most seriously ill potential recipients would receive kidneys, while those individuals who were less seriously ill and who could still survive on dialysis would probably have to wait for a kidney.

Regardless of whether payments for organs are legal or illegal, many normative issues are involved in the allocation of transplanted organs. With legalization, society would probably want to be cautious about how to consider factors such as income, insurance coverage, and/or fame when deciding who would receive a new kidney. For example, under the current system, former Yankee and Hall of Fame baseball player Mickey Mantle was able to obtain a new liver despite being extremely ill with liver cancer. Mr. Mantle died shortly after the operation. The decision to perform a liver transplant on Mickey Mantle was severely criticized by some medical professionals, because of the low probability of success. The opportunity cost of performing Mickey Mantle's transplant may have been an early death for some other potential recipient. Legalizing payments for transplanted organs would not solve the moral and ethical issues involved in decisions regarding who receives an organ transplant.

Suppose that under the current voluntary donor system, some of the recipients who receive the q_s kidneys are recipients with reservation prices below p_1. This would reduce the consumer surplus associated with q_s kidney donations below the sum of areas $A + B + D$. The reduction in consumer surplus would depend on who receives the kidneys. Many outcomes are possible. Doctors and insurance companies might be able to screen patients in a manner that insures that only seriously ill patients with a high probability of health following surgery would receive kidneys, in which case the reduction in consumer surplus would be fairly small. However, it is also possible that poor screening techniques might result in a larger number of less ill patients with low reservation prices well below p_1 receiving kidneys. In this case, consumer surplus would be reduced substantially below its maximum possible level and the deadweight loss associated with the voluntary donor system would be much larger.

Under the current system, consumer surplus will also be reduced if a portion of the maximum potential consumer surplus (equal to areas $A + B + D$) is transferred to doctors, hospitals, and middlemen (those who harvest the kidneys from donors). These three groups have the ability to charge higher prices for their services, because the recipients receive their kidneys for free. If recipients or their insurance companies had to pay for their kidneys, they would have less income left after paying for them, and therefore would be willing to pay less for the services of the doctors, hospitals, and middlemen.

By now you might be thinking that we have ignored the largest social cost of a voluntary donor system: More people with kidney disease will die with a voluntary donor system than with a market-driven system. A large number of potential recipients, equal to $q_e - q_s$, who do not receive kidneys with a voluntary donor system would receive kidneys with a market system. With a ban on sales, some of these recipients will not be able to survive long enough on dialysis to receive a transplant. The bottom line is that all of our calculations in Figure 10.9 fail to measure the true social cost of preventing the sale of kidneys and other human organs.

The Legal Market for Human Eggs

Having analyzed the impact of a ban on organ sales, you may have a somewhat different reaction to the story about models selling their eggs to the highest bidders on the Internet. As previously noted, the sale of human eggs (and sperm) is legal in the United States. Fertility clinics typically pay $2,500–$5,000 for a collection of eggs. This compensates the donors for their time and discomfort. In 1996 Resolve, the National Infertility Association, estimated that approximately 1,700 babies were born to infertile couples using donated eggs. Insurance generally does not cover the expenses of this type of infertility treatment, so the parents must pay all of the costs, including the costs of obtaining the eggs.

Should a buyer be willing to pay $150,000 for the eggs of a Harvard-educated beautiful woman when the going market price is $5,000 for average eggs? This is a classic decision made under uncertainty, similar to those cases analyzed in Chapter 6. Although it might be true that there is a higher probability of creating a beautiful brilliant child from a beautiful brilliant donor's eggs, there is no guarantee. Harvard Medical School psychologist Nancy Etcoff responded to the story about the egg auctions on the Web by noting that "[t]he way that we inherit features is sort of a genetic roll of the dice. ... Clearly, these offspring might not be beautiful at all."[27]

As of March 2001, none of the models had received an Internet bid matching their asking price for their eggs. Despite the fact that the Web site had received millions of hits, no transactions took place. This led to speculation that the real economic reason for the creation of the egg auction Web site was for its creator to make a huge profit by having curious Web surfers visit the site for $24.95 a hit. Some commentators suggested that the Web site was little more than a hoax aimed at luring voyeurs to the site.

The lack of auction activity suggests that buyers are rational and realize that the expected value of a model's eggs is probably not much higher than the expected value of any other medically screened donor's eggs. Until science is able to determine the exact genetic quality of a particular human egg, it is doubtful that egg auctions will generate high prices for any donor's eggs. By then, science may be able to successfully clone a human baby, and that will create an even more serious ethical and perhaps economic dilemma.

A Cautionary Note

One major medical caution is necessary: The suppliers of purchased organs might be less healthy than the suppliers of donated organs. This has proven to be a problem in the blood market, where donated blood tends to be of a generally higher quality than sold blood. The economic explanation is that many people who sell their blood are low-income individuals, including many homeless individuals. These low-income donors receive little, if any, routine medical care and often have serious diseases. The sellers of organs therefore would have to be carefully screened to make sure that they were in good health.

There are many normative issues involved with permitting human organ and egg sales. Positive economic analysis, however, can once again help us to understand the costs and benefits of laws either banning or permitting such sales in free and open markets.

---

[27] "Beautiful Harvest? Controversial Web Auction of Models' Eggs Logs a Million Visitors," *http://abcnews.com.*

Summary

1. Using the competitive model, the war on drugs primarily reduces the supply of drugs. However, because entry into drug retailing is easy, successful efforts to reduce the supply tend to have only short-run effects. Drug legalization combined with high taxes on drugs and extensive anti-drug education might be as successful at combating the drug problem for much lower social costs. These arguments do not imply that society should legalize drugs, because legalization could cause new and unforeseen problems, such as more drug use and a less productive and more undisciplined workforce.

2. In competitive markets, free trade agreements such as NAFTA result in net gains for all the trading partners. However, free trade results in a shift in production of some goods from one country to another, and as a result, consumers and producers in some countries suffer losses. However, the losses are more than balanced by gains to consumers and producers, and therefore free trade results in a net gain for the trading partners.

3. Rent controls place a price ceiling below the equilibrium price. In the short- and long run, rent control results in a decrease in the quantity and quality of housing. Rent control programs tend to have unintended consequences and often hurt the low-income individuals the programs are intended to help.

4. Agricultural price supports place a floor on prices above equilibrium prices. Governments around the world are deeply invested in price support programs to increase farmers' incomes. Consumers, who pay higher prices for agricultural goods, and taxpayers, who pay for the price supports, are the losers; farmers are the winners.

5. Assuming a competitive market for human organs, lives could be saved if organ donors were paid the way human eggs donors are paid. Paying for organ donations would increase the quantity supplied of organs, and as a result, more transplant operations would be performed. Careful medical screening of the quality of sold organs would be necessary to make the policy work effectively.

Self-Test Problems

1. Consider the United States supply for a good: $P = 20 + Q_{US}$. The United States demand is: $P = 80 - Q_{US}$. The demand and supply in the rest of the world are: $P = 79 - Q_{row}$ and $P = -26 + 2Q_{row}$.

   a. Solve for the equilibrium price and output in the United States market and the rest of the world in the absence of trade.

   b. Suppose the U.S. decides to permit free trade. If trade is permitted, solve for the equilibrium price. How much output will be demanded in the United States? Of this output, how much will be supplied by the United States and how much will be imported (exported by the rest of the world)?

   c. Calculate the gains from trade in both the United States and rest of the world.

2. Suppose the demand curve for wheat is: $P = 150 - Q$ and the long-run supply for wheat is: $P = 30 + 1/2Q$.

   a. Without government intervention, what is the equilibrium price and quantity of wheat?

   b. Suppose the government imposes a price support on wheat equal to $85. How much wheat will farmers supply in the long run? Calculate the wheat surplus as a result of this policy and the cost to the government of purchasing the surplus.

   c. Now suppose the government lets the market clear, but also guarantees a target price of $80. If the base acreage multiplied by the program yield equals 80, calculate the total deficiency payment under this plan.

Questions and Problems for Review

1. In what ways does the analysis in Figure 10.2 support drug legalization? What pieces are missing from the analysis? Discuss the differences in the expected results when significant money is spent on drug education and information programs compared to when no money is spent on education and information.

2. Consider the three possible types of long-run industries: constant-cost, decreasing-cost, and increasing-cost.

   a. Which most likely describes the drug market discussed in Section 10.1?

   b. In Figure 10.2, it is assumed that the drug market is a constant-cost industry. Is this assumption reasonable? Why or why not?

   c. How might the analysis in Figure 10.2 change if the drug industry is an increasing-cost industry? Decreasing-cost industry?

3. Despite an overwhelming majority of economists who favor free trade, policies such as NAFTA have been incredibly controversial. Explain why there has been so much controversy. Who typically would oppose free trade agreements such as NAFTA?

4. Pozo argues that drug use may fall as a result of legalization yet this result isn't supported in Figure 10.2. Consider a new analysis of drug legalization that results in a decrease in consumption of the drug with legalization. Show the changes on a graph similar to Figure 10.2. Be sure to explain the movements in your graph that lead to this conclusion.

5. Consider the U.S. supply for a good: $P = 10 + 2Q$. The U.S. demand is: $P = 130 - Q$. The demand and supply in the rest of the world is given by: $P = 180 - 2Q$ and $P = Q$.

   a. Solve for the equilibrium price and output in the U.S. market and the rest of the world in the absence of trade.

   b. Suppose the United States decides to permit free trade. If trade is permitted, solve for the equilibrium price. How much output will be demanded in the United States? Of this output, how much will be supplied by the United States and how much will be imported (exported by the rest of the world)?

   c. Calculate the gains from trade in both the United States and the rest of the world.

6. Why do rent controls inevitably produce larger shortages in the long run than in the short run? Suppose that New York City imposes rent controls, but nearby New Jersey does not. What would be the effect of the rent control law in New York City on rents in nearby New Jersey?

7. In 2002, many retail stores went out of business due to falling demand and prices. Yet the U.S. government did not choose to impose price supports on these goods. Why do you think President Hoover felt compelled to impose price supports on "major crops," while so many other goods never received price supports?

8. Consider the demand and supply for milk: $P = 5.5 - (1/10)Q$ and $P = 0.5 + (1/40)Q$.

   a. Without government intervention, what is the equilibrium price and quantity of milk?

   b. Suppose the government imposes a price support on milk equal to $2. How much milk will farmers supply? Calculate the surplus as a result of this policy and the cost for the government to purchase the surplus.

   c. How much output would the government have to encourage farmers not to produce in order to guarantee a market price of $2?

   d. What would be the short-run effects of the complete elimination of the price support? What would we expect to happen in the long run?

9. Consider Figure 10.9. The figure shows that a ban on kidney sales can either increase or decrease consumer surplus. The book states "the result depends on the relative price elasticities of the demand and supply curves." Discuss this relationship. For example, if demand is more elastic than supply, will the ban on kidney sales increase or decrease consumer surplus? What if supply is more elastic than demand?

Internet Exercises

Visit *http://www.myeconlab.com/waldman* for this chapter's Web exercises. Answer real-world economics problems by doing research on the Internet.

Part 4 Imperfect Competition

Chapter 11
Monopoly and Monopolistic Competition

Learning Objectives

After reading Chapter 11, you will have learned:

> The primary sources of monopoly power, which include both structural and strategic barriers to entry.

> How a monopolist sets its profit-maximizing output and price, and how to measure the degree of monopoly power in an industry.

> The impact of monopoly power on economic efficiency.

> The model of monopolistic competition and how it differs from the models of monopoly and perfect competition.

Featured Applications

> 11.1A Application Microsoft's Absolute Cost Advantage

> 11.1B Application U.S. Firms with the Highest Advertising-to-Sales Ratios

> 11.2 Application Using the Lerner Index to Measure Market Power

> 11.3 Application Rent-Seeking Lobbying and Campaign Contributions by Drugs Companies

> 11.4 Application "It's Not Delivery, It's DiGiorno": Monopolistic Competition in the Frozen Pizza Market

In November 1999, in an eagerly anticipated antitrust ruling, District Judge Thomas Penfield Jackson decreed that Microsoft had illegally monopolized the market for Intel-compatible PC operating systems. Judge Jackson ordered that Microsoft should be broken up into two independent companies. His decision declared in part:

> Through its conduct toward Netscape, IBM, Compaq, Intel, and others, Microsoft has demonstrated that it will use its prodigious market power and immense profits to harm any firm that insists on pursuing initiatives that could intensify competition against one of Microsoft's core products. Microsoft's past success in hurting such companies and stifling innovation deters investment in technologies and businesses that exhibit the potential to threaten Microsoft. The ultimate result is that some innovations that would truly benefit consumers never occur for the sole reason that they do not coincide with Microsoft's self-interest.[1]

In June 2001, the United States Court of Appeals for the District of Columbia unanimously upheld Judge Jackson's conclusion that Microsoft had monopolized the market for Intel-compatible PC operating systems. However, the appeals court reversed many of Judge Jackson's other rulings; most importantly, it reversed the ruling that Microsoft should be broken up into two companies. In October 2001, the United States Supreme Court refused to hear Microsoft's appeal of the appeals court ruling, thereby making the appeals court decision final. In 2002, Microsoft agreed to an out-of-court settlement with the

---

[1] *United States v. Microsoft Corporation*, Civil Action No. 98-1232; June 2, 2000, District Court for the District of Columbia.

Department of Justice and most of the states involved in the case. The settlement limited Microsoft's anti-competitive behavior without breaking up the company.

According to the strict definition of monopoly, it is difficult to identify many real-world monopolists. Many of you would probably agree with Judge Jackson's 1999 statement that identified Microsoft as a monopolist in the personal computer operating systems market, in which it has more than 90 percent market share. Beyond Microsoft, however, how many firms can you label as monopolists according to the strict economic definition of a monopolist? Perhaps you would identify your local cable television supplier as such, including Viacom, TCI, Time Warner, or Comcast, because in each geographic region, consumers have a choice of only one cable television provider. But these cable companies do compete with a substitute service, satellite television providers such as DirecTV and the Dish Network. Furthermore, in a few years you might be able to obtain your cable television over the Internet. Twenty-five years ago, students would have identified AT&T as a monopolist in the provision of telecommunication services. Today, however, AT&T competes with many telecommunications firms for consumers' dollars. Your local supplier of telecommunication services, such as Verizon or SBC Communications, has some monopoly power, but your local telephone company faces competition from cellular companies and Internet chat rooms. If you heat your home with natural gas, there is only one company that runs a pipeline directly to your house and this company is a monopolist, as is the company that runs the electric wires to your home. Beyond these examples, however, you may have difficulty identifying firms with monopoly power according to the strict economic definition of monopoly.

Despite relatively few real-world pure monopolists, it is extremely important to understand the economic theory of monopoly. Many firms possess some degree of market power or an ability to have some control over the price of their goods or services. Unlike perfectly competitive firms, firms with monopoly power face downward-sloping demand curves, and therefore are not price takers. By understanding how firms facing downward-sloping demand curves determine their optimal output and price, we can go a long way toward understanding the behavior of many real-world firms.

11.1 Sources of Monopoly Power

monopoly

A market where there is only one seller and there are no close substitute products.

monopolist

The only seller in a monopoly market.

barrier to entry

Any market condition that enables established firms to increase their prices above perfectly competitive long-run levels for an extended period of time without attracting entry.

A **monopoly** is a market where there is only one seller and there are no close substitute products; and a **monopolist** is the only seller in a monopoly market. Monopoly power is dependent upon the existence of one or more barriers to entry. **Barriers to entry** are market conditions that permit established firms to increase their prices above perfectly competitive long-run levels for an extended period of time without attracting entry. In the absence of barriers to entry, positive economic profits attract entry, and economic profits return to normal in the long run. If entry barriers exist, however, excess profits may be sustainable for long periods of time without inducing significant entry. We divide entry barriers into several broad categories including structural barriers, strategic barriers, and government imposed barriers.

Structural entry barriers include any of the basic elements of market structure that act to deter entry: economies of scale, absolute cost advantages, high capital cost requirements, and product differentiation. **Strategic entry barriers** include behavioral barriers such as limit pricing, predatory pricing, and building excess capacity. Strategic barriers to entry are based

structural entry barriers

The basic elements of market structure that may act to deter entry: economies of scale, absolute cost advantages, high capital cost requirements, and product differentiation.

strategic entry barriers

Market conduct by established firms aimed specifically at reducing the probability of entry.

government-imposed entry barriers

Government regulations that prohibit or limit entry.

minimum efficient scale (MES)

The smallest level of output for which long-run average cost is at its minimum.

on the notion that existing firms deliberately behave in ways that decrease the probability of entry. Chapter 15 analyzes strategic behavior to deter entry in detail. **Government-imposed entry barriers** refer to government regulations that prohibit or limit entry. Thirty years ago, government regulations either restricted or prohibited entry into many industries including airlines, trucking, banking, and telecommunications. Deregulation, however, has greatly reduced the number of government-imposed barriers to entry.

Structural Barriers to Entry

As mentioned earlier, the major structural entry barriers are economies of scale, absolute cost advantages, high capital cost requirements, and product differentiation. We begin with an expansion of our earlier analysis of economies of scale, and then proceed to define and examine the other structural barriers.

ECONOMIES OF SCALE   Economies of scale are perhaps the most important barrier to entry. Recall from Chapter 7 that economies of scale exist if long-run average costs decline as output increases. For fixed input prices, economies of scale exist when the production function exhibits increasing returns to scale. Figure 11.1 illustrates this relationship for output levels less than q_1. In this figure, q_1 is the **minimum efficient scale** (**MES**). This is the smallest level of output for which average cost is at its minimum. Figure 11.1 also illustrates two additional theoretical possibilities discussed in Chapter 7: constant long-run average costs, or constant returns to scale, for $q_1 < q < q_2$; and diseconomies of scale, or decreasing returns to scale, for $q > q_2$.

How do economies of scale act as a structural barrier to entry? If each firm has the long-run average cost curve shown in Figure 11.1, it must produce and sell at least q_1 units of output to produce at the lowest possible cost. The number of firms producing at MES that can exist in an industry depends on the position of the market demand curve in relation to the *LRAC* curve.

Figure 11.2 shows three possible demand and long-run average cost curve relationships. In Figure 11.2(a), demand is sufficiently low so that one firm can satisfy demand and still not reach MES. In Figure 11.2(b), a few firms producing at MES could satisfy the entire demand. Figure 11.2(c) shows a situation in which the MES is small relative to industry demand. Thus, economies of scale are a more significant barrier to entry in the

Figure 11.1 Economies of Scale, Constant Returns to Scale, and Diseconomies of Scale
This *LRAC* curve exhibits economies of scale up to q_1 units of output because long-run average costs are decreasing. For outputs between q_1 and q_2, the production function exhibits constant returns to scale, so long-run average costs are constant. Beyond an output of q_2, diseconomies of scale exist because the long-run average costs are increasing.

Figure 11.2 Different Demand Curves in Relation to *LRAC* Curves
In panel (a), the demand curve is downward-sloping where it meets the *LRAC* curve, so one firm can meet the entire demand before reaching MES. In this case, economies of scale are a very significant barrier to entry. In panel (b), MES is a large percentage of total demand, so economies of scale would be an important barrier to entry. In panel (c), MES is a small percentage of total industry demand, so economies of scale would not be as significant a barrier to entry.

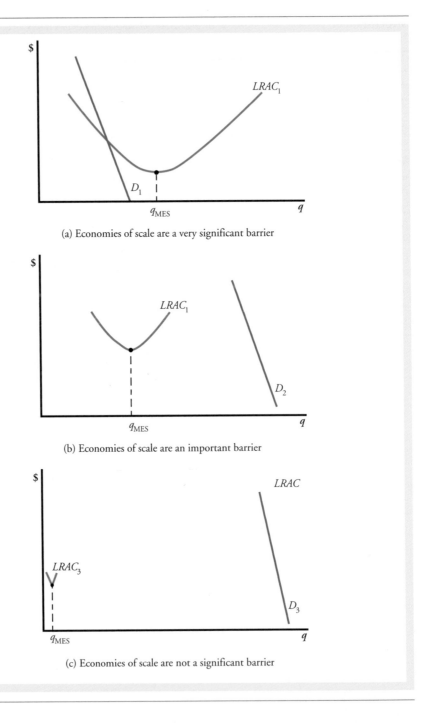

(a) Economies of scale are a very significant barrier

(b) Economies of scale are an important barrier

(c) Economies of scale are not a significant barrier

first case than in the second. The third case depicts a much more competitive market, because MES is a small percentage of output in relation to the industry demand curve.

ABSOLUTE COST ADVANTAGES A second barrier to entry is an *absolute cost advantage* enjoyed by existing firms. An **absolute cost advantage** exists if one firm can produce any given level of output at lower average cost than another firm. Figure 11.3 illustrates this advantage. For simplicity, we assume that long-run average cost is constant for both incumbent firms and potential entrants, but that a typical established firm can produce

absolute cost advantage

A situation where some firm or firms can produce any given level of output at lower average cost than other firms.

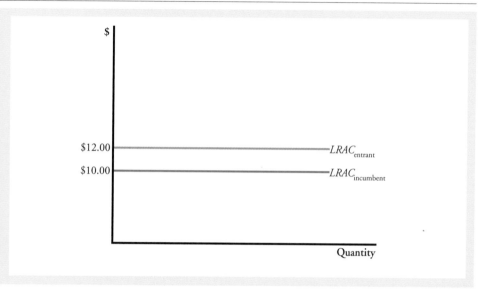

Figure 11.3 An Absolute Cost Advantage
An incumbent firm can produce output at long-run average costs of $10, or $LRAC_{incumbent}$. However, a potential entrant can only produce at long-run average costs of $12, or $LRAC_{entrant}$.

at a lower long-run average cost for any given level of output. In Figure 11.3, at any price between $10 and $12, an established firm makes positive economic profits. Because potential entrants have higher average costs, they cannot make a positive profit unless price rises above $12. Thus, the incumbent firms' absolute cost advantage acts as a barrier to entry for prices between $10 and $12.

What factors could lead to a gap between the average costs of established firms and potential entrants? Firms with an absolute cost advantage might control a crucial input or technology; or they might be able to borrow investment funds at lower interest rates than potential entrants. Effective patent protection can provide an excellent absolute cost advantage.

 11.1A APPLICATION Microsoft's Absolute Cost Advantage

Patents create an absolute cost advantage by enabling patent holders to produce at lower costs or with superior technology. Patents have been the basis of monopoly power for many of the world's most important companies and their famous founders, including General Electric (Thomas Edison) in electric light bulbs, American Telephone & Telegraph (Alexander Graham Bell) in telephone service, Xerox (George Carlson) in copying, Kodak (George Eastman) in photographic equipment and film, IBM (Thomas Watson) in computers, and Microsoft (Bill Gates) in PC operating systems.

Microsoft's monopoly began with the development and patenting of the source code for the MS-DOS operating system that Microsoft developed to run IBM's personal computers in the 1980s. What is perhaps most remarkable about Microsoft's monopoly is that the basic technology for MS-DOS was developed by another company, Seattle Computer Products. When IBM hired Microsoft to develop an operating system for the first IBM PC, Microsoft did not have time to develop an operating system from scratch, so Bill Gates and his partner Paul Allen purchased the patent rights to an operating system called QDOS (quick and dirty operating system) from Tim Patterson of Seattle Computer Products for $75,000. Microsoft put many hours into revising and expanding QDOS to create MS-DOS, which became the basis of Microsoft Windows. For its small investment in the patent rights to QDOS, Microsoft built a financial empire that created billions of dollars of wealth for Gates and Allen.

capital markets

All of the markets for obtaining investment funds, such as the stock market, the bond market, and banks and other lending institutions.

HIGH CAPITAL COST REQUIREMENTS   In general, the higher the capital costs associated with efficient entry into an industry, the less likely it is that potential entrants can finance entry. Potential entrants into an industry with capital cost requirements running into the hundreds of millions or billions of dollars must therefore turn to the *capital market* for funds. **Capital markets** include all of the markets for borrowing investment funds, including the stock market, the bond market, and banks and other lending institutions.

There is a connection between high capital cost requirements and an absolute cost advantage: if new firms have to pay a higher interest rate to borrow investment funds than established firms do, they face a barrier to entry. Furthermore, the effect of this differential in interest rates will be greater the more capital investment a firm needs to finance in order to enter. The capital barrier to entry, for example, is much greater in the oil refining industry than the fast food restaurant industry, because building a new efficient oil refinery requires an investment of a billion dollars or more, while building a new fast food restaurant requires an investment of a couple hundred thousand dollars.

transaction costs

The costs of gathering information and using a market to make a transaction.

Economists have identified at least three reasons why new firms have to pay more than established firms to borrow funds: risk, transactions costs, and loan market imperfections. Creditors may charge new firms a higher interest rate in order to compensate for a higher risk of bankruptcy and default on loans. **Transaction costs** refer to the costs of gathering information and using a market to make a transaction. The transaction costs of using the capital market are related to firm size. Because there are fixed transaction costs associated with issuing a new loan (for example, fixed legal expenses) and because large firms tend to borrow in relatively large amounts, large firms can spread these fixed costs over a larger volume of funds. For example, spreading fixed transaction costs over a larger dollar loan reduces the per dollar cost. Finally, empirical studies of the banking industry support the conclusion that small firms pay more to borrow investment funds than large firms *even after adjusting for risk differentials between large and small firms.*[2] *Ceteris paribus*, the more market power local lenders have, the higher the interest rate the small local borrowers pay. The bottom line is that small firms pay a higher interest rate on business loans than large firms, even after adjusting for risk differentials, and this creates a barrier to entry for small firms entering industries with high capital cost requirements.

PRODUCT DIFFERENTIATION   The final structural barrier to entry is product differentiation. Consumers view new products as imperfect substitutes for a variety of reasons, including differences in quality, performance, or reputation. In addition, there may be costs associated with switching from one brand to another, in which case products that are initially seen as identical become differentiated once a consumer has purchased a particular brand. For example, suppose a consumer uses Microsoft Word for word processing on his computer and is reasonably happy with its performance. If he decides to switch to Corel WordPerfect, there would be considerable switching costs because he would have to spend time learning to use the new program. These switching costs might keep him loyal to Microsoft Word.

advertising-to-sales ratio

The ratio of the firm's advertising expenditures to sales; a common measure of the intensity of a firm's advertising.

Product differentiation gives an established producer some market power, because it can raise its price without losing all of its customers. Product differentiation activities by firms can take many forms, including advertising, sales force efforts, service contracts and warranties, and style changes. Economists measure the intensity of a firm's advertising by measuring the ratio of the firm's advertising expenditures to sales, which is called the firm's **advertising-to-sales ratio**.

---

[2] F.R. Edwards, "Concentration in Banking and Its Effects on Business Loan Rates," *Review of Economics and Statistics*, Vol. 46, August 1964, pp. 294–300; and Paul A. Meyer, "Price Discrimination, Regional Loan Rates, and the Structure of the Banking Industry," *Journal of Finance*, March 1967, pp. 37–48.

▲▲▲ 11.1B APPLICATION   U.S. Firms with the Highest Advertising-to-Sales Ratios

The average advertising-to-sales ratio for manufacturing firms in the United States is approximately 2 percent. In some industries, however, the ratio is much greater. The table lists some of the top 100 advertisers in the United States according to advertising expenditures in 2001, and also ranks these firms according to their 2001 advertising-to-sales ratios.

All of the firms' advertising-to-sales ratios are at least four times the national average. Four firms, including L'Oreal, Estee Lauder, and McDonald's, spent over 20 percent of their sales revenues on advertising; Procter & Gamble, PepsiCo, and Pfizer spent over $2 billion on advertising. What is striking about the table is the relatively small number of industries (eleven) represented on the list,

Application Table 11.1B **Leading United States Advertisers in 2001 (advertising/sales in percent)**

Rank	Company	Industry	Advertising/Sales (percent)	Advertising Expenditures ($ millions)
1	L'Oreal	Cosmetics	27.0	1,041
2	Estee Lauder	Cosmetics	27.0	766
3	McDonald's	Fast food	22.2	1,195
4	Reckitt Benckiser*	Cleaners	20.4	316
5	Coors	Beer	18.2	430
6	Wendy's	Fast food	18.2	312
7	Mattel	Toys	13.6	449
8	General Mills	Cereals	13.2	884
9	Unilever	Health & beauty	13.2	1,484
10	Diageo[†] (Burger King)	Fast food	12.8	1,181
11	Procter & Gamble	Health & beauty	12.5	2,541
12	Gillette	Health & beauty	12.3	463
13	Colgate-Palmolive	Heath & beauty	12.3	355
14	PepsiCo	Soft drinks	12.2	2,210
15	Coca-Cola	Soft drinks	12.0	903
16	Nike	Athletic shoes	11.9	577
17	Pfizer	Drugs	11.0	2,189
18	Clorox	Cleaners	10.2	338
19	Hilton Hotels	Hotels	9.7	296
20	Wyeth[‡]	Drugs	8.5	771

*British producer of cleaners, including Lysol, Electrosol, Jet Dry, and Calgon.

[†]British producer of liquor, beer, and wine; owned Burger King until July 2002.

[‡]U.S. producer of drugs, including Advil, Anacin, Anbesol, Chap Stick, Preparation H, and Robitussin.

(continued)

and the large number (seven) of industries with more than one firm represented. The top two firms, L'Oreal and Estee Lauder, compete against each other in the highly profitable cosmetics industry. McDonald's, Wendy's, and Burger King (Diageo) compete in the fast food industry; Coca-Cola and PepsiCo compete in the soft drink market; and Unilever, Procter & Gamble, Gillette, and Colgate-Palmolive compete in the heath and beauty aids market.

If a new firm wanted to enter any of these industries, it would be faced with the daunting task of having to risk millions of dollars on advertising to match the advertising expenditures of these firms. Furthermore, if the entrant failed, these millions of dollars would be lost, because advertising expenditures are a sunk cost. Raising such large sums may prove to be impossible for all but the largest multinational corporations. Large advertising expenditures can therefore greatly limit the number of potential entrants into a market, and prevent most firms from seriously considering entry.

Strategic Barriers to Entry

In addition to structural barriers to entry, monopoly power may persist because monopolists engage in strategic behavior to deter entry. Chapter 15 analyzes some of the main types of strategic behavior in detail. Here we briefly introduce three types of entry-deterring behavior: limit pricing, predatory pricing, and building excess capacity.

LIMIT PRICING Monopolists might recognize that charging high short-run profit-maximizing prices will result in large positive economic profits and entry, which would eventually eliminate their monopoly power. An alternative strategy is to charge a price below the short-run profit-maximizing price in order to deter entry. By charging a price below the profit-maximizing price, the monopolist will earn lower short-run profits, and therefore, there is less incentive for new firms to enter the market. We call such a strategy aimed at limiting entry a **limit pricing** strategy.

PREDATORY PRICING Another strategy for an entry-deterring monopolist is to maintain a short-run profit-maximizing strategy until entry occurs and then use **predatory pricing**, in which a firm aggressively expands output and cuts prices with the objective of driving the entrant out of the market. By responding to entry using this aggressive strategy, the monopolist sends potential entrants the message that it would respond aggressively to all entry. As a result, potential entrants tend to stay out. By establishing a reputation for being tough early, the incumbent can prevent later entry.

EXCESS CAPACITY If a firm has more capacity than is required to meet its demand, it has **excess capacity**. If a firm is already producing at its maximum capacity, then it cannot respond to entry by expanding output. Building excess capacity well in advance of entry provides a credible threat to potential entrants, by making it easier for incumbents to respond aggressively to entry by dramatically increasing output and lowering price.

Government-Imposed Entry Barriers

Government mandated monopolies exist in markets in which the government decides that it is preferable to have only one supplier of a good or service. The government sometimes regulates prices and profits in such industries, but the regulated firms may have a good deal of price discretion. Examples of government mandated monopolies include: the United States Postal Service in the market for first-class mail delivery, local cable television service, the local distribution of electricity and natural gas, taxicab service in some cities, and food and lodging in National Parks.

limit pricing

A strategy of charging a price below the short-run profit-maximizing price in order to deter entry.

predatory pricing

A strategy of aggressively lowering price with the objective of driving entrants out of the market and preventing potential entrants from entering.

excess capacity

As an entry barrier, the decision to build large amounts of capacity so that incumbents can respond aggressively to entry by dramatically increasing output and lowering price.

11.2 The Theory of Pure Monopoly

Monopolists have the same primary objective as competitive firms—to maximize profits. Because of the existence of entry barriers, however, a monopolist has control over price and can set its price anywhere along its downward-sloping demand curve. As a result, a monopolist's marginal revenue curve differs from a perfectly competitive firm's marginal revenue curve. This section shows how this difference in the monopolist's marginal revenue curve results in differences in the monopolist's output and price compared to a perfectly competitive firm.

The Monopolist's Marginal Revenue Curve

The primary theoretical difference between a monopolist and a competitive firm is that a monopolist faces a downward-sloping demand curve, whereas a perfectly competitive firm faces a horizontal or perfectly elastic demand curve. Because all firms want to maximize profits, all firms produce the output at which marginal revenue equals marginal cost. However, because the perfectly competitive firm faces a horizontal demand curve, its marginal revenue curve is identical to its demand curve; that is, $p = MR$ for a perfectly competitive firm. On the other hand, a monopolist faces a downward-sloping demand curve, which results in a very different relationship between marginal revenue and price, where $MR < p$. Let's examine why this difference occurs.

Marginal revenue is the extra revenue a firm obtains from selling one additional unit of output. Due to the fact that a monopolist faces a downward-sloping market demand curve, the only way it can sell an additional unit of output is by lowering its price on *all* units. We should note that this argument assumes that the monopolist is unable to practice price discrimination and charge different buyers different prices for the same good. Chapter 12 will consider the pricing behavior of a price discriminating monopolist. Although the monopolist gains revenue from selling an additional unit of output, it loses revenue on those units previously sold at a higher price. Figure 11.4 shows the tradeoff faced by a monopolist. At p_1, the monopolist sells q_1 units, and total revenue is the area of rectangle Op_1Aq_1. To sell $q_1 + 1$ units, the monopolist must lower price to p_2; total revenue becomes the area $Op_2B(q_1 + 1)$. The monopolist gains the green area, $q_1CB(q_1 + 1)$, in total revenue. The width of this rectangle is 1 and its height is p_2, so the area of the gain in revenue equals p_2. However, by lowering price, the monopolist also loses the orange area p_1ACp_2, which is the original quantity sold, q_1, times the change in price. Marginal revenue equals the green "Gain" area, which equals the new price p_2 minus the orange "Loss" area. Thus, for a monopolist, marginal revenue is *always* less than price.

MR = Gain - Loss = Green - orange.

The Relationship Between the Monopolist's Marginal Revenue and Elasticity of Demand

We can derive a more precise measure of marginal revenue in terms of the elasticity of demand for any demand curve as follows. Begin with total revenue $TR = pq$. Imagine in Figure 11.4 that the change in quantity Δq is not 1, but is extremely small such that the increase in quantity of Δq approaches zero (*i.e.,* $\Delta q \rightarrow O$). We could then identify the change in total revenue ΔTR, associated with the very small increase in quantity as:

$$\Delta TR = p(\Delta q) + q(\Delta p) \tag{11.1}$$

Figure 11.4 Marginal Revenue for a Downward-Sloping Demand Curve

If output increases by one unit from q_1 to $q_1 + 1$, the monopolist gains extra revenue equal to the green shaded "Gain" rectangle, which equals $p_2(\Delta q) = p_2(1) = p_2$. However, on the units produced up to q_1, the price reduction results in a revenue loss equal to the orange "Loss" rectangle $q_1(\Delta p)$. Marginal revenue is equal to the green area minus the orange area, or $p_2 - q_1(\Delta p) < p_2$. Therefore, marginal revenue is less than price.

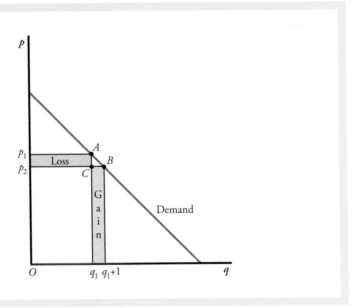

We obtain marginal revenue by dividing both sides of Equation 11.1 by Δq:

$$MR = \frac{\Delta TR}{\Delta q} = p\frac{\Delta q}{\Delta q} + q\frac{\Delta p}{\Delta q} = p + q\frac{\Delta p}{\Delta q} \qquad (11.2)$$

The second term on the right side of Equation 11.2, $q(\Delta p)/\Delta q$, must be negative for a downward-sloping demand curve, because if q increases (decreases) p must decrease (increase). Therefore, from Equation 11.2, we know that marginal revenue is less than price for a monopolist.

Using an algebraic transformation, Equation 11.2 is used commonly to relate marginal revenue to the elasticity of demand as follows. Factoring out a p from the right side of Equation 11.2 yields:

$$MR = p + q\frac{\Delta p}{\Delta q} = p\left(1 + \frac{q}{p}\frac{\Delta p}{\Delta q}\right) \qquad (11.3)$$

Because $\varepsilon_p = (\Delta q/\Delta p)(q/p)$, the second term in parentheses is the *inverse* of the elasticity of demand. Therefore, we have:

$$MR = p\left(1 + \frac{1}{\varepsilon_p}\right) = p\left(1 - \frac{1}{|\varepsilon_p|}\right) \qquad (11.4)$$

where ε_p is the price elasticity of demand.

MARGINAL REVENUE FOR A LINEAR DEMAND CURVE We can derive the marginal revenue curve for the special case of a linear demand curve.[3] From Equation 11.2:

$$MR = p + q\frac{\Delta p}{\Delta q} \qquad (11.5)$$

---

[3] Using calculus, the derivation of marginal revenue for a linear demand curve of the form $p = a - bq$ is:
$$TR = (a - bq)q = aq - bq^2 \text{ so } MR = (d\,TR)/(dq) = a - 2bq.$$

For any linear demand curve, $p = a - bq$, so substituting for p in Equation 11.5:

$$MR = (a - bq) + q\frac{\Delta p}{\Delta q}$$

Because $\Delta p / \Delta q$ is the slope of the linear demand curve, $\Delta p / \Delta q = -b$ and:

$$MR = (a - bq) + q(-b) = a - 2bq \tag{11.6}$$

For any linear demand curve, the marginal revenue curve always has the same vertical intercept but is twice as steep.

Figure 11.5 illustrates the relationship between the elasticity of demand and marginal revenue for the linear demand curve $p = 100 - q$. The marginal revenue curve has the same vertical intercept as the linear demand curve, 100, but is twice as steep with a slope equal to -2, so that the horizontal intercept of the marginal revenue curve, 50, is half the horizontal intercept of the demand curve. Later chapters refer to this relationship between a linear demand curve and marginal revenue as the *twice as steep rule*.

We know from Equation 11.4 the following relationship between marginal revenue and the elasticity of demand:

$$MR = p\left(1 - \frac{1}{|\varepsilon_p|}\right) \tag{11.7}$$

where $|\varepsilon_p|$ is the absolute value of the price elasticity of demand. Recall from Chapter 2 that for a linear demand curve, $|\varepsilon_p| = 1$ at the midpoint, $|\varepsilon_p| > 1$ for all points above the midpoint, and $|\varepsilon_p| < 1$ for all points below the midpoint. It follows from Equation 11.7 that at the midpoint of the linear demand curve in Figure 11.5:

$$MR = 50\left(1 - \frac{1}{1}\right) = 50(0) = 0$$

Figure 11.5 Marginal Revenue and the Elasticity of Demand for a Linear Demand Curve
At the midpoint of a linear demand curve—in this case, for $p = 50$—marginal revenue equals zero and demand is unit-elastic. For all prices above the midpoint—that is, above $p = 50$, marginal revenue is positive and demand is elastic; for all prices below the midpoint—that is, below $p = 50$—marginal revenue is negative and demand is inelastic.

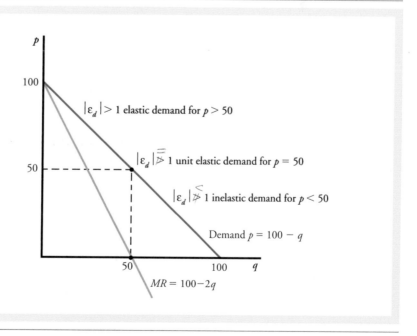

Therefore, we see once again that $MR = 0$ at the midpoint of a linear demand curve. For all prices *above* 50, $|\varepsilon_p| > 1$, so:

$$MR = p\left(1 - \frac{1}{|\varepsilon_p > 1|}\right) > 0$$

and therefore marginal revenue is positive when demand is elastic ($MR > 0$ for $|\varepsilon_p| > 1$). For all prices *below* 50, $|\varepsilon_p| < 1$, so:

$$MR = p\left(1 - \frac{1}{|\varepsilon_p < 1|}\right) < 0$$

and therefore marginal revenue is negative when demand is inelastic ($MR < 0$ for $|\varepsilon_p| < 1$).

The Monopolist's Profit–Maximizing Output and Price

To maximize profit, a monopolist, like a profit-maximizing competitive firm, produces the output at which marginal revenue equals marginal cost. Figure 11.6 illustrates how a monopolist maximizes profit for the case of linear demand and linear marginal cost. The demand curve is $p = 100 - q$; the total cost curve is $TC = \$200 + 20q$; and $MC = \$20$. Average cost is therefore:

$$AC = \frac{TC}{q} = \frac{\$200}{q} + \frac{\$20q}{q} = \$20 + \frac{\$200}{q}$$

Equating marginal revenue to marginal cost:

$$MR = 100 - 2q = 20 = MC$$
$$2q = 80, \text{ so } q = 40$$

and:

$$p = 100 - 40 = \$60$$

The monopolist maximizes profit by producing 40 units of output and charging a price of $60. To calculate profit:

$$\pi = TR - TC = q(p - AC) = 40(\$60 - \$25) = \$1,400$$

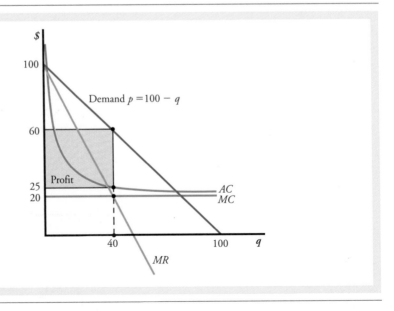

Figure 11.6 Profit Maximization for a Monopolist
With demand of $p = 100 - q$, $TC = \$200 + 20q$, and MC constant at $20, the profit-maximizing output and price are $q = 40$ and $p = \$60$. Profit is represented by the green area $q(p - AC) = 40(\$60 - \$25) = \$1,400$.

Demand $p = 100 - q$

Profit

AC
MC

MR

The green shaded rectangle in Figure 11.6 identifies profit.

How can we be certain $q = 40$ maximizes profit? Because $MR > MC$ for any value of $q < 40$, and $MR < MC$ for any value of $q > 40$. That is all we need to know. These conditions ensure that if we were to expand output beyond 40, the extra revenue we would obtain from selling extra units would be *less* than the marginal cost of producing these units, and therefore profit would decline. Similarly, if the monopolist reduced output below 40 units, it would find its profit reduced, because it would be sacrificing more in extra revenue than the extra cost of producing those units. To verify this assertion, consider what happens to profit if our monopolist produces either 39 or 41 units. For $q = 39$: $\pi = q(p - AC) = 39(\$61 - \$25.13) = \$1,398.93$. For $q = 41$; $\pi = q(p - AC) = 41(\$59 - \$24.88) = \$1,398.92$.

Table 11.1 summarizes the general relationship between output and profits for our monopolist. Figure 11.7 graphs our monopolist's total revenue, total cost, and profit functions. We obtain the profit function by calculating the vertical distance between the total revenue and the total cost curves. Profit is maximized at $q = 40$, where $MR = MC$. Notice that at the profit-maximizing output, the slope of the total revenue curve, MR, equals the slope of the total cost curve, MC. Economic profit equals zero when $p = AC$. Using the quadratic formula, profit equalss zero for $q = 2.58$ and $q = 77.42$.[4]

Figure 11.8(a) illustrates the monopoly equilibrium using the classic U-shaped long-run marginal cost and long-run average cost curves. Given typical cost curves, the monopolist maximizes profit by selecting the output, q_m, where $MR = LRMC$. To obtain price p_m, go up vertically to the demand curve D. Profit is identified by the green

Table 11.1 **The Monopolist's Total Revenue, Total Cost, and Profit**

Quantity	Price	TR	TC	MC	AC	Profits
0	100	0	200	—	—	−200
10	90	900	400	20	40.00	500
20	80	1,600	600	20	30.00	1,000
30	70	2,100	800	20	26.67	1,300
40	60	2,400	1,000	20	25.00	1,400
50	50	2,500	1,200	20	24.00	1,300
60	40	2,400	1,400	20	23.33	1,000
70	30	2,100	1,600	20	22.86	500
80	20	1,600	1,800	20	22.50	−200
90	10	900	2,000	20	22.22	−1,100
100	0	0	2,200	20	22.00	−2,200

---

[4] Profit equals zero where $p = AC$; or where $p = 100 - q = 200/q + 20 = AC$.

It follows that: $100q - q^2 = 200 + 20q \Rightarrow q^2 - 80q + 200 = 0$. Using the quadratic formula:

$$q = \frac{-b \pm \sqrt{b^2 - 4ac}}{2a} = \frac{-(-80) \pm \sqrt{(-80)^2 - 4(1)(200)}}{2(1)} = \frac{80 \pm \sqrt{5600}}{2}$$

$$q = 2.58 \quad \text{and} \quad q = 77.42$$

Figure 11.7 The Total Revenue, Total Cost, and Total Profit Curves for a Monopolist

Profits are maximized where $MC = MR$. In this case, the slope of the TR curve, which equals MR, equals \$20, which equals marginal cost, for $q = 40$. This is the output that maximizes the vertical distance between TR and TC. The green curve represents the profit curve and reaches its maximum at $q = 40$. For $q = 2.58$ and $q = 77.42$, $TR = TC$, and therefore profit equals zero.

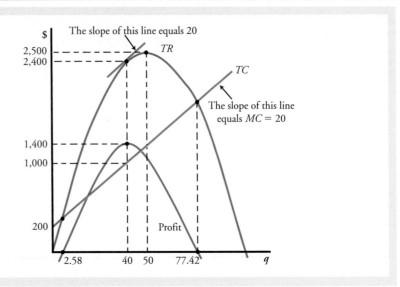

Figure 11.8 The Classic Long-Run Monopoly Equilibrium

In panel (a), given the typical U-shaped $LRMC$ and $LRAC$ curves, the monopolist maximizes profit by setting $LRMC = MR$, producing output $q = q_m$, charging price $p = p_m$, and earning profit equal to the green shaded area $q_m(p_m - AC_M)$. In panel (b), the green profit function reaches its maximum at $q = q_m$; and total revenues are maximized where $MR = 0$ at $q = q_2$.

(a)

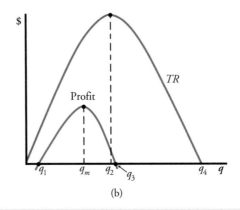

(b)

area $p_m XY(AC_m)$, which represents economic profit $\pi = q(p - LRAC)$. In panel (b), notice that the green profit function reaches a maximum at q_m, and profit equals zero at q_1 and q_3, where demand equals average cost. Total revenue is maximized at q_2, where $MR = 0$.

COMMON ERROR 11.1 **Believing That Monopolists Always Earn Short-Run Positive Economic Profits**

Many students mistakenly assume that a monopolist must earn a positive economic profit in the short run. As a result, these students always draw a monopolist's equilibrium to look like the equilibrium in panel (a) of Figure 11.8, where $p > AC$. Panel (a) of the graph below shows that a monopolist will sustain a short-run economic loss if the short-run average cost curve is completely above the demand curve, but price is above the average variable cost curve. For example, consider the New York City subway system's economic plight. The New York City subway is a monopolist in the market for subway transportation in New York,

but no matter what fare the subway charges it will not attract enough riders to cover its costs.

In the short run, monopolists might earn an economic profit, sustain an economic loss, or even earn a normal economic profit. In panel (b) of the graph, the profit-maximizing monopolist exactly covers its short-run average costs, because $p = AC$. In this case, economic profits equal zero. Don't make the common error of assuming that such outcomes are impossible because a firm with monopoly power must earn large economic profits.

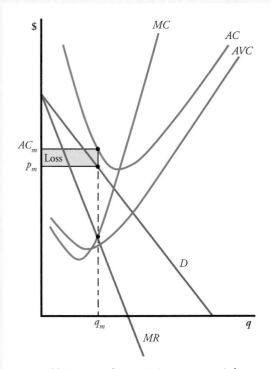

(a) A monopolist sustaining an economic loss

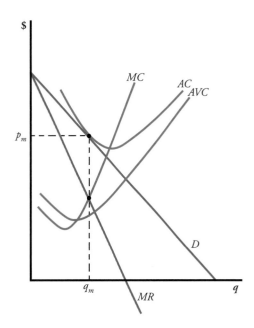

(b) A monopolist earning a normal economic profit

Common Error Figure 11.1 A Monopolist Can Sustain an Economic Loss or Earn a Normal Economic Profit
There is nothing wrong with either of these graphs! In panel (a), a monopolist sustains an economic loss, and in panel (b), a monopolist earns a normal economic profit.

The Multiplant Monopolist

The monopolist's profit-maximizing output decision is complicated if the monopolist produces with multiple plants that use different technologies. An example is an electric utility that generates electricity using each of the following technologies: hydroelectric, nuclear, oil, and coal. These technologies generate a kilowatt-hour of electricity at vastly different marginal costs. The marginal cost of hydroelectric generation is lower than the marginal cost of nuclear generation, which in turn is lower than the marginal cost of oil or coal generation.

The first decision the monopolist needs to consider is how much output to produce from each facility in order to maximize profit. To determine output, first we derive the marginal costs of production from the two plants combined. To minimize costs, the firm must always produce an additional unit of output from the plant with the lower marginal cost, or else it could lower its costs by switching production from the plant with the higher marginal cost to the plant with the lower marginal cost. To minimize costs, therefore, *the marginal cost of production must be equal in both plants.*

Figure 11.9 depicts the situation for a multi-plant monopolist. Suppose plant A is a low-marginal-cost production facility with $MC_A = 10 + 2q_A$, perhaps a hydroelectric power plant, and plant B is a high-marginal-cost facility with $MC_B = 30 + 2q_B$, perhaps an oil generation plant. Industry demand is given by:

$$P = 100 - \frac{1}{2}Q$$

Figure 11.9 The Profit-Maximizing Output for a Multiple-Plant Monopoly
If a monopolist can produce in two plants with marginal costs $MC_A = 10 + 2q_A$ and $MC_B = 30 + 2q_B$, respectively, it minimizes costs by producing each additional unit at the lowest possible marginal cost. In equilibrium, marginal cost must be equal in both plants. The marginal cost of production from both plants is the horizontal summation of the two marginal costs curves, which is $MC = 20 + Q$. If demand is $p = 100 - (1/2)Q$, marginal revenue is $MR = 100 - Q$; and $MC = MR$ for $Q = 40$ and $p = \$80$, and marginal cost is $\$60$ in each plant. Fifteen units are produced in the high-cost plant and 25 units in the low-cost plant.

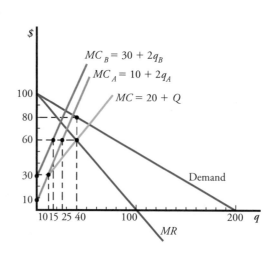

Therefore, by the twice as steep rule in Equation 11.6, marginal revenue is:

$$MR = 100 - Q$$

We derive the firm's marginal cost curve by adding the two individual marginal cost curves horizontally, not vertically. For example, in Figure 11.9, the firm can produce up to 25 units of output at marginal costs less than \$60 in plant A, and it can produce up to 15 units of output at marginal costs less than \$60 in plant B. Therefore, in the two plants combined, the firm can produce up to $25 + 15 = 40$ units at marginal costs less than \$60. The marginal cost of the 40th unit, therefore, is \$60. For marginal costs between \$10 and \$30 only the low-cost plant A is relevant, because all output produced at $MC < \$30$ must come from plant A. For outputs between 0 and 10 in Figure 11.9, therefore, the marginal cost curve is $MC = 10 + 2Q$. For outputs greater than 10, we define the firm's marginal cost curve by adding the quantities for any given marginal cost as follows:

$$MC_A = 10 + 2q_A \text{ or } q_A = \frac{1}{2}MC - 5$$

$$MC_B = 30 + 2q_B \text{ or } q_B = \frac{1}{2}MC - 15$$

$$Q = q_A + q_B = \frac{1}{2}MC - 5 + \frac{1}{2}MC - 15 = MC - 20$$

or:

$$MC = 20 + Q$$

Summarizing:

$$MC = 10 + 2Q \text{ for } 0 < Q \le 10$$

$$MC = 20 + Q \text{ for } Q > 10$$

For profit maximization, set $MC = MR$:

$$MC = 20 + Q = 100 - Q = MR$$

$$2Q = 80 \text{ or } Q = 40$$

Substituting the profit-maximizing output $Q = 40$ back into the demand curve yields $P = 100 - (1/2)(40) = 80$. Furthermore, for $Q = 40$, $MR = 100 - Q = 100 - 40 = 60 = MC$

With total industry output equal to 40, the division of output between plant A and plant B must insure that the marginal cost of production in each plant is equal to \$60. For plant A, this implies that:

$$MC_A = 10 + 2q_A = 60$$

or:

$$q_A = 25$$

For plant B, this implies that:

$$MC_B = 30 + 2q_B = 60$$

or:

$$q_B = 15$$

Profit maximization requires significantly different outputs from each plant with more output produced in the lower-cost plant A. However, in equilibrium the marginal cost is equal in both plants.

Important Implications of the Monopoly Model

Having examined the basic theory of monopoly, it is useful to point out a few important implications of the model.

1. A MONOPOLIST DOES NOT HAVE A SUPPLY CURVE Recall the definition of the market supply curve of a good from Chapter 2: "The quantity of the good that all sellers in a market would like to sell at each possible price over a given period of time." There are some serious problems trying to apply this definition to a monopoly. First, "all sellers" in the context of a monopoly means "one seller." Second, and more significantly, given any demand and marginal cost curves, a monopolist will only produce *one* quantity and sell it at *one* price. To ask how much of the good the monopolist would sell at any other price *at that moment in time* is meaningless. For example, refer to Figure 11.8(a) and ask yourself: What output would this monopolist produce at a price equal to 80 percent of p_m? The answer: The monopolist in Figure 11.8(a) would never sell any output at any price other than p_m. Think of the monopolist's supply curve as a single point. In Figure 11.8(a), this point is X where $q = q_m$ and $p = p_m$.

2. NO PROFIT-MAXIMIZING MONOPOLIST WOULD EVER CHARGE A PRICE WHERE DEMAND IS INELASTIC Students often incorrectly believe that monopolists who face highly inelastic demand curves have the ability to raise price almost without limit. Following is the proof that such unlimited price increases are impossible unless demand is perfectly inelastic.

From Equation 11.4, marginal revenue is defined as:

$$MR = p\left(1 - \frac{1}{|\varepsilon_p|}\right)$$

Marginal cost must be greater than or equal to zero, and therefore profit-maximization requires:

$$MR = p\left(1 - \frac{1}{|\varepsilon_p|}\right) = MC \geq 0$$

Because $p > 0$, it follows that:

$$1 - \frac{1}{|\varepsilon_p|} \geq 0$$

$$1 \geq \frac{1}{|\varepsilon_p|}$$

$$|\varepsilon_p| \geq 1$$

The monopolist, therefore, must produce an output where demand is either *elastic* or *unit elastic.*

If demand is inelastic, total revenue increases if price increases. Any monopolist who is pricing on the inelastic portion of its demand curve therefore can increase its total revenue by reducing output and raising price. Furthermore, any reduction in output must reduce total costs. If demand is inelastic, a reduction in output always increases total revenue *and* decreases total costs; therefore, profit has to increase.

The monopolist's economic power is essentially limited by its demand curve. If it tries to increase price too much, eventually, its demand curve will become elastic, and its total revenues will decline with further price increases. When the monopolist's price reaches a high enough level that further decreases in output *reduce* total revenues more than they reduce total costs, it makes no sense for the monopolist to increase price any further. The monopolist has then reached its profit-maximizing output.

3. AN INCREASE IN DEMAND MAY OR MAY NOT INCREASE PRICE In perfectly competitive markets with upward-sloping supply curves, an increase in demand results in an increase in price and quantity. In a monopoly, an increase in demand can result in an increase, decrease, or no change in price. In Figure 11.10, the monopolist originally faces the dark-blue demand curve, D_1. The profit-maximizing price is p_1. If demand increases to the light-blue demand curve, D_2, the profit-maximizing price is p_2, which is less than p_1. An increase in demand has resulted in a decrease in price. This outcome is because curve D_2 is more elastic at point B than the demand curve D_1 is at point A.

Monopolist manufacturers introduced many technologically advanced products such as DVD players, digital cameras, and DSS satellite television receivers at very high prices. As demand increased, prices declined dramatically in all three markets. Without ignoring the importance of economies of scale in production in lowering prices, as demand increased for DVDs, digital cameras, and satellite dishes, demand also became more elastic. In the first few years, demand was limited to a relatively small number of high-income buyers who were willing to try these risky new technologies. Demand was, therefore, highly inelastic. As these new technologies were perfected, a large number of middle and lower-middle income buyers were drawn into these markets. Many of these

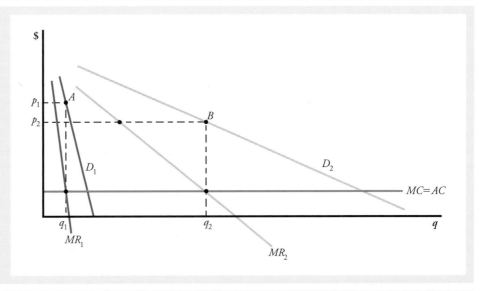

Figure 11.10 An Increase in Demand in a Monopoly When demand increases from D_1 to D_2, it becomes much more elastic. In this case, the increase in demand results in a decrease in price from p_1 to p_2.

second generation buyers had much lower reservation prices than the first group of high-income buyers. Demand, therefore, became more elastic as the huge second wave of buyers entered these markets. As the elasticity of demand increased, the monopolists lowered prices.

Be careful not to misinterpret this explanation. It states that in a monopoly, an increase in demand *may* result in a decrease in price. It does *not* state that an increase in demand *will* result in a decrease in price. The effect of an increase in demand on a monopolist's price depends on the characteristics of the product and the demand curve. With constant marginal costs, an increase in demand for a monopolist's product causes price to decrease, increase, or remain constant, depending on whether the elasticity of demand increases, decreases, or remains constant.

Measuring the Extent of Monopoly Power: The Lerner Index

Few firms have monopoly power that is unchecked by market forces. Instead, most firms with market power face some degree of competition from firms producing close substitute products. Any firm that has the ability to set price above marginal cost, however, has some degree of monopoly power. Although we know that the monopolist will choose the profit-maximizing price-quantity combination, we do not know how high the price will be in relation to marginal cost. The monopolist must also determine what constraints it faces from raising price higher and higher above marginal cost. To do this, monopolists use the relationship between marginal revenue and price introduced previously, that is:

$$MR = p\left(1 - \frac{1}{|\varepsilon_p|}\right)$$

Lerner Index

A measure of market power as:

$$\frac{p - MC}{p} = \frac{1}{|\varepsilon_p|}$$

The Lerner Index ranges from zero to one.

Combining this formula for marginal revenue with the fact that marginal revenue equals marginal cost at the profit-maximizing quantity and rearranging terms yields a measure of the degree of market power called the **Lerner Index**. To derive the Lerner Index, begin by noting that $MR = MC$ so that:

$$MR = p\left(1 - \frac{1}{|\varepsilon_p|}\right) = MC$$

which implies:

$$p - \frac{p}{|\varepsilon_p|} = MC$$

$$p - MC = \frac{p}{|\varepsilon_p|}$$

$$\frac{p - MC}{p} = \frac{1}{|\varepsilon_p|}$$

The last equation states that for a profit-maximizing monopolist, the price-cost margin, $(p - MC)/p$, is inversely related to the elasticity of demand. The less elastic demand, the greater is the markup of price over marginal cost, and the greater is the degree of monopoly power. To summarize:

$$\text{Lerner Index} = \frac{p - MC}{p} = \frac{1}{|\varepsilon_p|} \qquad (11.8)$$

▲▲▲ 11.2 APPLICATION Using the Lerner Index to Measure Market Power

Over the past 25 years, economists have attempted to measure the degree of market power in many industries by using statistical estimates of the Lerner Index. In one of the important early studies, for example, economist Elie Appelbaum estimated the Lerner Index to be 0.049 in rubber, 0.072 in textiles, 0.198 in electrical machinery, and 0.648 in tobacco.[5] These estimates were consistent with expectations that the rubber and textile markets, with low Lerner Indexes, are more competitive than the electrical machinery and tobacco markets, with much

Application Table 11.2 **Estimates of Lerner Indexes**

Author	Year	Industry	Lerner Index	Elasticity of Demand
Breshnahan	1981	Automobiles	0.100–0.340	2.94–10.00
Appelbaum	1982	Rubber	0.049	20.41
		Textiles	0.072	13.89
		Electrical machinery	0.198	5.05
		Tobacco	0.648	1.54
Porter	1983	Railroads (colluding)	0.400	2.50
Lopez	1984	Food processing	0.504	1.98
Roberts	1984	Coffee roasting— leading firm	0.055	18.18
		Coffee roasting— second-largest firm	0.025	40.00
Spiller, Favaro	1984	Banks—large regulated	0.88	1.14
		Banks—large deregulated	0.40	2.50
		Banks—small regulated	0.21	4.76
		Banks—small deregulated	0.16	6.25
Suslow	1986	Aluminum	0.590	1.69
Slade	1987	Retail gasoline	0.10	10.00
Gasmi, Laffont, and Vuong	1992	Soft drinks—Coke	0.64	1.56
Ellison	1994	Railroads (colluding)	0.472	2.12
Deodhar and Sheldon	1995	Bananas (in Germany)	0.26	3.85
Nebesky, McMullen, and Lee	1995	Trucking (under regulation)	0.262	3.82
		Trucking (deregulated)	0.019	52.63

(continued)

[5] Elie Appelbaum, "The Estimation of the Degree of Oligopoly Power," *Journal of Econometrics*, Vol. 19(1982): pp. 287–299.

higher Lerner Indexes. In particular, the tobacco industry with its high Lerner Index was controlled in 1982 by a handful of large firms including Philip Morris, R.J. Reynolds, Brown and Williamson, P. Lorillard, and Liggett & Myers. Appelbaum's study confirmed that these tobacco companies were able to raise price considerably above marginal cost.

The table summarizes the findings of several important studies that estimated Lerner Indexes. Two of these studies, Spiller and Favaro's study of the banking industry, and Nebesky, McMullen, and Lee's study of the trucking industry, compared the Lerner Indexes in these industries before and after deregulation. Under regulation, entry was generally prohibited into the banking and trucking indus-

tries, whereas after deregulation, entry was permitted. The theory of monopoly suggests the Lerner Index should be significantly higher under regulation when entry was prohibited. As the table shows, this was the case in both industries. In trucking, the Lerner Index decreased from 0.262 to 0.019 after deregulation. Because the trucking industry is structurally competitive with a large number of trucking companies and easy entry, this result is fully consistent with theory. In the banking industry, Spiller and Favaro found that deregulation resulted in a large decrease in the Lerner Index for both large and small banks. Furthermore, they found that large banks had significantly higher Lerner Indexes than small banks regardless of whether the banks were regulated.

The Lerner Index ranges from zero to one. A value of zero indicates that the firm has no market power because $p = MC$. Firms in perfectly competitive industries face perfectly elastic demand curves with $|\varepsilon_p| = \infty$, and therefore have Lerner Indexes equal to zero. In the previous section, we saw that for a profit-maximizing monopolist, demand is elastic and $|\varepsilon_p| > 1$. The Lerner Index, therefore, will be less than or equal to one.

The Lerner Index indicates that even a monopolist has only limited ability to raise price. If a monopolist faces competition from close substitute products, its price elasticity of demand will be relatively large, and the monopolist's profit-maximizing price will be relatively close to its marginal cost. A less elastic demand curve results in a larger monopoly markup. If the elasticity equals 10, for example, the Lerner Index equals 0.10 and the gap between price and marginal cost is quite low. If the elasticity equals 1.5, however, then the Lerner Index is 0.67 and the gap is considerably larger.

▼▼▼ 11.3 The Efficiency Effects of Monopoly

Recall from Chapter 9 that in order to make judgments about the efficiency of various market outcomes, we need a method of assessing alternative market equilibriums from a social point of view. To this end, we used the concept of Pareto efficiency to see that the perfectly competitive equilibrium maximizes social welfare. In this section, we return to the concept of Pareto efficiency to analyze the social welfare implications of monopoly.

Pareto Efficiency and Allocative Efficiency

Recall that we achieve Pareto efficiency if it is impossible to make one person better off without making someone else worse off. Let's consider the monopoly equilibrium in this context. In Figure 11.11, we see that the monopoly equilibrium with quantity equal to q_m and price equal to p_m is *not* Pareto-efficient. Suppose output were increased just a bit beyond q_m. We see that additional units beyond q_m have a marginal social value as measured by price that is greater than their marginal social cost MC. Therefore, expanding output beyond q_m makes the social welfare pie larger. With a larger pie to divide among a fixed number of people, there are ways to divide the pie so that someone gets a slightly bigger "slice" while no one else gets a smaller slice than they had before. Because this

Figure 11.11 Pareto Inefficiency and Dead-weight Loss Associated with Monopoly

Pareto efficiency requires $p = MC$ or production at $q = q_{so}$ and $p = p_{so}$. With Pareto efficiency, consumer surplus equals the sum of the purple, yellow, and orange areas $(A + B + D)$ and producer surplus equals the sum of the blue and green areas $(C + E)$. With monopoly, $q = q_m$, and $p = p_m$; consumer surplus equals the purple area A and producer surplus equals the blue plus yellow areas $(C + B)$. Monopoly, therefore, reduces total surplus by the sum of the orange and green areas $(D + E)$, which represents the deadweight loss due to monopoly.

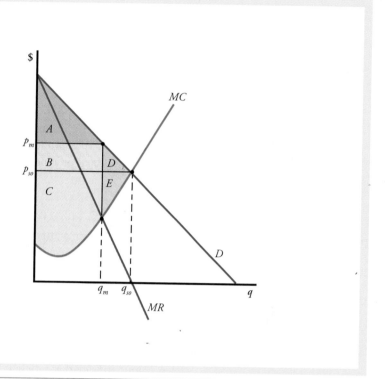

allocative efficiency

The socially optimal amount of a good to produce where the marginal benefit of producing another unit equals its marginal cost.

scenario could succeed in making someone better off without hurting anyone else, the monopoly outcome is not Pareto-efficient. In fact, only the outcome that exhausts all Pareto improving moves maximizes total social welfare. This occurs when price equals marginal cost at the *allocatively efficient* output q_{so}. We achieve **allocative efficiency** by producing the socially optimal amount of the good, which requires that the marginal benefit of producing another unit of output equals its marginal cost. If marginal benefit is greater than marginal cost, too little of the good is being produced; if marginal benefit is less than marginal cost, too much is being produced. We should continue to expand output and increase welfare as long as the price some consumer is willing to pay for an additional unit of the good is greater than the marginal cost to society of producing that additional unit.

Using this train of thought, consider carefully the equilibrium in Figure 11.11 where price equals marginal cost; and identify the resulting total consumer and producer surplus areas. Consumer surplus equals the shaded areas $A + B + D$ and producer surplus equals the shaded areas $C + E$. Chapter 9 showed that if we change output by moving this market away from the outcome where $p = p_{so}$ and $q = q_{so}$ to any other price and quantity, the total size of producer and consumer surplus will be smaller. This result should persuade you that *any* movement away from the output q_{so} reduces total surplus. We achieve Pareto efficiency, therefore, when $q = q_{so}$ and $p = p_{so}$. We also achieve allocative efficiency only at this output.

Let's now calculate total welfare in a monopolized market. If $q = q_m$, consumer surplus equals area A and producer surplus equals areas $B + C$. Total surplus therefore equals the sum of areas $A + B + C$. With the Pareto-efficient outcome, consumer surplus equaled $A + B + D$, producer surplus equaled $C + E$, and total surplus equaled $A + B + C + D + E$. The monopoly equilibrium therefore reduces total surplus by the sum of the

deadweight loss

Losses of consumer and producer surplus that are not transferred to other parties, and therefore, measure the misallocation of resources.

orange and green areas $D + E$. The sum of areas $D + E$ is called the **deadweight loss** due to monopoly. The deadweight loss measures the difference between what consumers would be willing to pay for the extra units between q_m and q_{so} and the opportunity costs of producing those extra units.

From a social welfare perspective, any time a consumer is willing to pay more for an additional unit of a good or service than the marginal social cost of producing that unit, welfare increases if that good or service is produced. In other words, as long as $p > MC$, welfare is increased by expanding output. By restricting output to q_m, a level well below where $p = MC$, the monopolist fails to produce all of the socially optimal units between q_m and q_{so}. Therefore, the profit-maximizing monopolist *always* produces an output below the socially optimal or allocatively efficient output.

Productive Efficiency

productive efficiency

Producing any level of output at the lowest possible long-run average cost (lowest opportunity costs) for that output.

In addition to allocative efficiency, Pareto efficiency requires that firms minimize their costs of production. A firm achieves **productive efficiency** if it produces its output at the lowest possible long-run average cost. Productive efficiency is necessary for survival in a perfectly competitive industry. Consider a farmer who produces corn in a competitive market. The farmer must minimize long-run average costs or be driven out of the market. He can't charge a higher price for his corn than other farmers, and unless he can figure out how to produce at minimum costs, he will sustain economic losses and leave the market in the long run. The perfectly competitive market disciplines inefficient firms by eliminating them.

In less competitive markets, there is far less pressure on firms to use inputs efficiently. In fact, even highly inefficient monopolists may not be driven out of the market. Figure 11.12 illustrates the welfare implications of an inefficient monopolist. Suppose a firm monopolizes good X and produces under conditions of constant returns to scale. The horizontal cost curves $LRMC_e = LRAC_e = \$20$ represent the minimum long-run marginal and long-run average costs of producing good X. Our inefficient monopolist, however, is producing good X with higher costs $LRMC_X = LRAC_X = \$25$. If the demand for good X is $p = 100 - q$, an inefficient monopolist maximizes profits by producing an output of 37.5 and charging a price of \$62.50. Profit equals the sum of the green and blue rectangle areas $A + B$:

$$\pi = 37.5(\$62.5 - \$25) = \$1,406.25$$

An efficient monopolist, on the other hand, would produce with minimum costs. Its profit would equal the sum of the blue and red areas $B + C$:

$$\pi = 40(\$60 - \$20) = \$1,600$$

Profit is significantly smaller if the firm does not minimize costs. In a competitive market, if a firm elevates its costs by 25 percent above minimum costs, that firm would be forced out of the market. Because of the existence of significant barriers to entry, however, nothing happens to the monopolist in this case. The monopolist simply earns lower profit and continues to monopolize the market.

THE SEPARATION OF FIRM OWNERSHIP AND CONTROL Although the inefficient monopolist sacrifices a great deal of profit by not minimizing costs, there can be logical reasons for not minimizing costs. Keep in mind that large corporations account for the vast majority of today's global sales. If we look closely at the corporate structure,

Figure 11.12 The Profit Loss of an Inefficient Monopolist

Suppose minimum marginal and average costs are $LRMC_e$ $= LRAC_e = \$20$, but an inefficient monopolist has higher costs $LRMC_x = LRAC_x = \$25$. The inefficient monopolist produces $q = 37.5$ and charges $p = \$62.50$. The inefficient monopolist's profits equal the sum of the green and blue areas $A + B$, or $\pi = 37.5(\$62.50 - \$25) = \$1,406.25$. If the monopolist produced with minimum costs, its profits would equal the sum of the blue and light red areas $B + C$, or $\pi = 40(\$60 - \$20) = \$1600$.

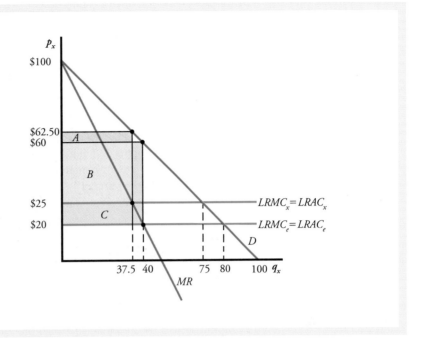

we see that a corporation is a separate legal entity, created by government charter and given certain powers, privileges, and liabilities. An important advantage of a corporation is that its owners have limited liability. Ownership of a corporation involves holding of shares of stock that can be bought or sold. The owners, who are also the shareholders, are liable only for the amount they paid to buy the shares of stock initially.

Prior to the 1900s, when most firms were organized as sole proprietorships or partnerships, ownership and control of the firm were in the hands of one or a few people. The people who made the day-to-day decisions were also the people who received any profit from the firm's operations. As corporations developed, however, ownership and control became separate, so the individuals in charge of day-to-day operations were not necessarily the people receiving profits. Today, professional managers, instead of their stockholder owners, run most corporations, which is relevant when taking into consideration the managers' key motivation. Let's start by accepting a central assumption of microeconomic theory: individuals try to maximize their own utility. This applies both to people who operate firms as well as to consumers. The people who run firms will maximize profits—as long as profit maximization is in their best interest. When owners run the firm, profit maximization and utility maximization are consistent goals, because the main source of income for the owners is the firm's profit.[6] When ownership and control are separate, however, profit maximization and utility maximization might conflict as managers pursue objectives other than maximizing profit.

Economist Oliver Williamson, who analyzed the implications of utility-maximizing managers,[7] theorized that managers maximize their utility by obtaining many executive

---

[6] R. Joseph Monsen, Jr. and Anthony Downs, "A Theory of Large Managerial Firms," *Journal of Political Economy*, Vol. 73 (June 1965), pp. 221–236.

[7] Oliver E. Williamson, *The Economics of Discretionary Behavior: Managerial Objectives in a Theory of the Firm*, Chicago: Markham, 1967.

perquisites or "perks," such as fancy offices, executive jets, an excessive number of administrative assistants, and "power breakfasts." Thus costs are higher than in the profit-maximizing model, because the firm spends resources on nice carpeting and art for fancy corner offices. More recently, economists have observed how managers' and owners' interests may diverge by studying the financial scandals in firms such as Enron and WorldCom, in which managers took actions that were clearly not in the stockholders' long-run interests.

X-inefficiency

A situation in which less than the maximum output is produced from a given set of inputs because managers have objectives other than profit maximization.

In a world in which managers have some discretion over costs, costs may also be higher due to what economist Harvey Leibenstein coined **X-inefficiency**, meaning "the extent to which a given set of inputs do not get to be combined in such a way as to lead to maximum output."[8] If managers are most interested in living a quiet, peaceful life, they may not continually strive to find the least costly way of organizing production, handling materials, and doing business in general. As a result, production costs are higher than necessary.

If monopolization raises costs, it also reduces output further below the allocatively efficient level, and therefore increases the deadweight loss due to monopoly. It follows that if increasing competition in monopolized markets leads to lower costs, then estimates of the welfare losses due to monopoly based on measured costs will be too low.[9]

Rent-Seeking Activities

economic rent

The difference between the total payments to a given quantity of a factor of production and the minimum payments necessary to obtain that quantity of the factor.

Economic rent is the difference between the total payments to a given quantity of a factor of production and the minimum payments necessary to obtain that quantity of the factor. We will analyze economic rent in detail in Chapter 17; however, the concept is relevant here because economists have identified rent-seeking activities as another important cost of monopolization in addition to deadweight losses and X-inefficiencies. Monopolists often engage in rent-seeking activities to try to gain and maintain monopoly power. For example, a monopolist may spend too much on advertising, product differentiation, or investments in excess capacity in order to protect its economic rents. Furthermore, Economist Gordon Tullock and Judge Richard Posner have argued that the welfare costs of monopoly include lobbying and campaign contributions intended to obtain tariff protection, patent protection, and other preferential government treatment.[10] In an extreme case, a firm would be willing to spend an amount up to the potential monopoly profits available in order to protect its monopoly or become a monopolist. Such rent-seeking activities increase the welfare costs of monopoly.

Dynamic Efficiency

To this point you might believe that we have been engaged in a game of monopoly bashing. The monopolist is Pareto-inefficient, may not minimize costs, may earn excess profit, and may waste social resources on rent-seeking activities. You might therefore believe that public policy should try to eliminate all vestiges of monopoly power. Not so. It is also important to pay attention to the possible positive effect of monopoly power with regard to the rate of technological change.

---

[8] Harvey Leibenstein, "Competition and X-Efficiency," *Journal of Political Economy,* May 1973, p. 766.

[9] Comanor and Leibenstein (William S. Comanor and Harvey Leibenstein, "Allocative Efficiency, X-Efficiency and the Measurement of Welfare Loss," *Economica,* Vol. 36 (August 1969), pp. 304–9) estimate that the pure X-inefficiency effect of monopoly may be as high as 9 percent of net national product.

[10] Gordon Tullock, "The Welfare Costs of Tariffs, Monopolies and Theft," *Western Economic Journal,* Vol. 5 (June 1967), pp. 224–32, and Richard A. Posner, "The Social Costs of Monopoly and Regulation," *Journal of Political Economy,* Vol. 83 (August 1975), pp. 807–27.

▲▲▲ 11.3 APPLICATION   Rent-Seeking Lobbying and Campaign Contributions by Drug Companies

In 2002, Congress was considering the Greater Access to Affordable Pharmaceuticals (GAAP) Act intended to make it easier for generic drugs to compete with brand-name patented drugs. The GAAP Act aimed to limit the brand-name drug companies' patent protection and reduce their monopoly power. The brand-name drug companies had been gearing up for years for this Congressional fight by lobbying Congress and making large campaign contributions to both Republicans and Democrats. The table shows a comparison of spending by the brand-name drug companies and the generic drug companies to influence the members of Congress between 1997–2001.

The brand-name companies outspent the generic companies on lobbying by $388.8 million to $6.7 million, or by more than $58 for every dollar spent by generic manufacturers between 1997 and 2001. What exactly were the brand-name companies trying to buy with these millions of dollars in expenditures? In 1999,

the brand-name companies fought a proposal from the Clinton Administration to create a Medicare prescription drug benefit that would have lowered payments for prescription drugs. In 2000 and 2001, the companies tried to extend their patent protection by getting Congress to establish a patent review board. The review board would consider requests to extend a drug's patent life by up to three additional years if the company could convince the board that too much patent protection had been lost due to extended Federal Drug Administration (FDA) testing of the drug's safety and efficacy. The companies succeeded in their fight against a Medicare prescription drug benefit, but they failed to persuade Congress to set up a patent review board.

The millions of dollars spent on lobbying could have been spent instead on the research and development of new drugs. And in the end, the millions spent attempting to prevent the establishment of a patent review board went for naught and were a complete welfare loss.

Application Table 11.3 **Lobbying and Campaign Contributions by Drug Companies 1997–2001 ($millions)**

Drug makers	1997	1998	1999	2000	2001	Total
Brand-name drug companies	72.6	69.3	82.5	89.0	75.4	388.8
Generic drug companies	0.8	1.1	1.1	1.3	2.4	6.7
Total	73.4	70.4	83.6	90.3	77.8	395.5

static model

A model that deals with viewing the world at a precise moment in time.

static efficiency

Efficiency at a precise moment in time; requiring price to equal marginal cost among other conditions.

dynamic model

A model that deals with changes over time.

dynamic efficiency

Efficiency over time; requiring an optimal rate of technological advance.

Microeconomics courses primarily emphasize **static models**, which deal with a moment in time. When short-run marginal and average cost curves are drawn in this textbook, the curves take a snapshot of the industry at a precise moment in time. **Static efficiency** refers to efficiency at a moment in time and requires price to equal marginal cost. **Dynamic models**, on the other hand, deal with changes over time. Dynamic models are strategic and emphasize research and development expenditures and the rate of technological change. **Dynamic efficiency** requires an optimal rate of technological change, and it can exist even if price exceeds marginal cost. Even if an industry achieves static efficiency, its performance may be poor if it fails to achieve dynamic efficiency.

According to microeconomic theory, firms possessing market power may be more innovative than perfectly competitive firms. In 1942, economist Joseph Schumpeter argued that dynamic efficiency, as opposed to static efficiency, drives capitalism.[11] Schumpeter theorized that only large powerful monopolists could invest sufficiently in

[11] Joseph A. Schumpeter, *Capitalism, Socialism, and Democracy*, New York: Harper & Brothers, 1942.

research and development to ensure that an economy would progress at an optimal rate of technological advance. Schumpeter's arguments may have been a bit overstated, but his basic point holds true today. Perfectly competitive firms, for example, may lack the resources necessary to invest in R&D. Consider farmers, who do not typically do agricultural research. Monopolists such as Microsoft, on the other hand, have plenty of funds available to invest in research and development. If there is a positive relationship between market power and the rate of innovation, society might willingly accept some deadweight loss today in return for the considerable benefits associated with new products and new production techniques in the future. Recent American public policy toward monopoly power has given increasing weight to concerns about technological change.

Equity

Thus far we have observed that monopoly always results in Pareto inefficiency and allocative inefficiency. Our analysis has been strictly *positive economic analysis,* concerned with understanding and predicting the consequences of monopoly. This analysis might lead us to ask: Is the monopoly outcome "equitable" or "fair"? As soon as we attempt to answer this question, we are engaging in *normative economic analysis,* because we are assessing whether a particular outcome is "good" or "bad." As social scientists, economists ask such questions all the time.

Figure 11.13 compares the equity implications of the monopoly result with the competitive and Pareto efficient result in a market with linear demand and costs. The monopoly output is 40 and the monopoly price is $60. The Pareto efficient output is 80 and the efficient price is $20. With the Pareto-efficient result, consumer surplus is the sum of the purple, green, and red areas A, B, and C equal to $(1/2)(80)($80) = $3,200$; economic profit is zero or normal. With monopoly, the purple triangle A represents consumer surplus of $(1/2)(40)($40) = 800, the green rectangle B represents monopoly profits equal to $(40)($40) = $1,600$, and the red triangle C represents the deadweight loss of $(1/2)(40)($40) = 800.

Figure 11.13 Equity Impacts of Monopoly
With the Pareto-efficient result, $q = 80$ and $p = 20. Consumer surplus equals the sum of the purple, green, and red areas $(A + B + C)$, and economic profit is zero. With monopoly, $q = 40$ and $p = 60$. Consumer surplus equals the purple area A and economic profit equals the green area B. The red area C represents a deadweight loss. Monopoly results in a transfer of the green area B from consumer surplus to economic profits.

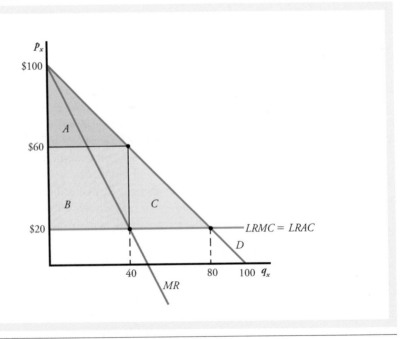

Monopoly results in a transfer of the green square B from consumer surplus to monopoly profit. Although it is a normative issue, many individuals will think this transfer is less fair and equitable than the efficient result in Figure 11.13 in which $p = LRMC = \$20$, consumer surplus is much larger (equal to the sum of areas $A + B + C$), and profit is much smaller (equal to zero). The monopolist is able to earn excess economic profit that more than compensates it for the opportunity costs of all of its invested resources. In deciding whether this transfer from consumers to the monopolist is fair, think of yourself as a consumer who purchases the monopolist's product, but does not own stock in the monopoly. In this case, you are likely to think it is unfair. If you own stock in the monopoly, however, you might think it is perfectly fair.

Most economists would agree that it is important to consider the equity implications of monopoly power in making a complete assessment of the pros and cons of monopoly. The existence of above-normal monopoly profit in and of itself is not a sufficient reason to condemn a monopolist, but the long-run existence of above-normal profit may suggest the existence of large entry barriers that lead to allocative and productive inefficiency. In this sense, above-normal profit, while not a problem in and of itself, may serve as a warning of possible economic problems.

11.4 The Economics of Monopolistic Competition

monopolistically competitive market

A market where there are no significant entry barriers, but firms face downward-sloping demand curves because of the existence of some product differentiation.

We have distinguished firms with monopoly power from competitive firms by the height of entry barriers and the shape of their respective demand curves. A monopolist faces a downward-sloping demand curve, and one or more entry barriers protect it from entry. A competitive firm faces a perfectly elastic or horizontal demand curve in a market with no entry barriers. Some firms exist in markets that are hybrids between monopoly and competition. In these markets, called **monopolistically competitive markets**, there are no significant entry barriers, but firms face downward-sloping demand curves because of the existence of some product differentiation. Examples are fairly common and include furniture, costume jewelry, toiletries, many food products, and most retailing.

The Monopolistically Competitive Equilibrium

Product differentiation gives each monopolistically competitive firm some degree of market power. Figure 11.14(a) shows a possible short-run equilibrium for a monopolistically competitive firm. The firm achieves its profit-maximizing equilibrium at quantity q_{SR}, where marginal revenue equals marginal cost. The corresponding price, P_{SR}, is greater than average cost, and thus the firm earns a positive economic profit.

As in perfect competition, positive economic profit cannot persist in the long run. Attracted by positive economic profit, new firms enter the industry. Entry shifts the firm's demand curve to the left, as shown in Figure 11.14(b). Entry continues until economic profit equals zero. In long-run equilibrium in panel (b), the firm produces q_{LR}, where marginal revenue equals marginal cost *and* where price equals average cost. Even though each firm has market power, the ease of entry drives economic profit to zero.

Efficiency Problems in Monopolistically Competitive Industries

Economists have identified two sources of inefficiency in a monopolistically competitive market. First, at the firm's profit-maximizing choice of output in both the short and long run, price is greater than marginal cost. Therefore, as in a monopoly, there is a deadweight

Figure 11.14 The Monopolistically Competitive Equilibrium
In panel (a), short-run equilibrium is at quantity $q = q_{SR}$, and $P = P_{SR}$. The firm earns a positive economic profit. The economic profit attracts entry and the firm's demand curve decreases. The firm achieves long-run equilibrium when new firms enter and economic profit equals zero, as shown in panel (b), where price equals average cost.

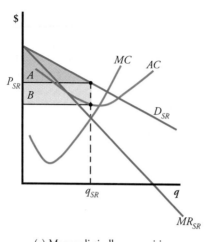

(a) Monopolistically competitive firm's short-run equilibruim

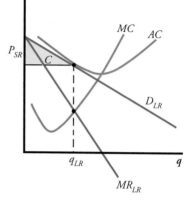

(b) Monopolistically competitive firm's long-run equilibruim

▲▲▲ 11.4 APPLICATION   "It's Not Delivery, It's DiGiorno": Monopolistic Competition in the Frozen Pizza Market

In 1995, Kraft Foods introduced a new type of frozen pizza: a rising-crust pizza with the brand name DiGiorno. Up until the introduction of DiGiorno, the frozen pizza market had experienced little growth in recent years. The introduction of DiGiorno dramatically changed that trend. In its first year, sales of DiGiorno were $382 million in 1995. DiGiorno was an entirely different product from the traditional cardboard-tasting frozen pizzas of the past, including Kraft's former top frozen brand Tombstone. Prior to the introduction of DiGiorno, frozen pizzas sold for between $2 and $3 and were never marketed as a close substitute for take-out and delivery pizza from large chains such as Pizza Hut, Domino's, and Little Caesar's. Kraft, however, decided to market DiGiorno as a close substitute for take-out and delivery pizza, and priced DiGiorno pizza at $5–$6, about half the price of take-out or delivery pizza. The result was an economic phenomenon: Sales skyrocketed and DiGiorno became known for its humorous advertisements claiming "It's Not Delivery, It's DiGiorno."

Kraft had a problem, however: It's not difficult to make frozen pizza. There are relatively low entry barriers into the frozen pizza business, especially for the many companies already making the awful-tasting cardboard pizzas. It didn't take long for entrants to be attracted by DiGiorno's profit. In 1996, one year after DiGiorno's introduction, Freschetta introduced its version of rising-crust frozen pizza, claiming, "It was the culmination of a great deal of research and study as we worked to create something unlike anything else: pizza with a crust that smells and tastes like fresh-baked bread. We traveled the small towns of Italy and France to sample the breads of local artisans and learn about the art of baking."* Freschetta pizza was also a commercial success, and eliminated DiGiorno's monopoly in the rising-crust frozen pizza market.

Freschetta's entry was just the beginning of a flood of entrants. By 2002, Rossini's Self-Rising Gourmet Pizza, Bravissimo! All-Natural Rising Cheese Pizza, Jack's Naturally Rising Pizza, Palermo's Crust that Rises Pizza, and Red Baron Bake to Rise Pizza joined DiGiorno and

http://www.freschetta.com.

(continued)

Freschetta. Meanwhile, Freschetta's parent company introduced Tony's Rise Crust Pizza, and Kraft introduced Tombstone Oven Rising Crust Pizza. Furthermore, the major chain supermarkets, such as Safeway, Kroger, Winn Dixie, and Wegman's, introduced their own versions of rising crust frozen pizza. Independent food groceries also introduced their versions produced by independent manufacturers such as Western Family.

By 2001, total frozen pizza sales had reached $2.6 billion, and the rising-crust frozen pizza industry had behaved exactly as a monopolistically competitive industry. Initially, DiGiorno had a monopoly. However, because of easy entry, a growing market, and the existence of economic profits, many entrants followed DiGiorno into the market. DiGiorno remains the leader, but it now faces many competitors.

loss in a monopolistically competitive market. Second, note that in long-run equilibrium, the firm does not operate at the minimum of its average cost curve as shown in Figure 11.14(b). This situation, in which the monopolistically competitive firm produces a smaller output level than that which minimizes average cost, is often described as "excess capacity." If there were fewer firms in the industry, each could operate at a larger scale and a lower average cost. Note, however, that consumers value the opportunity to choose among a variety of products with different characteristics.

To measure the benefits of variety in a monopolistically competitive market, we must initially assume that there is one firm in the industry and that this firm is in short-run equilibrium as shown in Figure 11.14(a). In other words, this firm is the founding parent firm of the industry, such as Kraft with its introduction of DiGiorno in the rising-crust frozen pizza industry. As additional firms enter the industry, the demand curve for the first firm shifts to the left and its profits decline until, in the long run, equilibrium economic profits are zero. In long-run equilibrium, all firms earn zero economic profits, as depicted in Figure 11.14(b).

As each additional firm enters the industry, profit *per firm* declines, so there is a *negative* relationship between the number of firms in the industry and the profit earned by each firm. The purple function $\pi(n)$ in Figure 11.15, where n is the number of firms in the industry, shows this relationship. The long-run equilibrium number of firms is n_{eq}, where $\pi(n_{eq}) = 0$. In long-run equilibrium, economic profit equals zero for each firm.

The optimal number of firms must maximize *total surplus*, which equals the sum of consumer surplus and total producer profits. Note that we are simplifying the analysis by assuming that the equilibrium number of firms has no impact on the producer surplus of input suppliers, so that the firms' profits measure the producer surplus. We calculate total profit by multiplying the number of firms, n, by the profits per firm, $\pi(n)$. Figure 11.15 shows the total profit function, $n \times \pi(n)$, in green.

Total consumer surplus, *CS*, is also a function of the number of firms, $CS(n)$. In Figure 11.14(a), consumer surplus with one firm is equal to the purple triangle A, and in Figure 11.14(b), consumer surplus per firm with n_{eq} firms is equal to the teal triangle C. With n_{eq} firms, total consumer surplus equals [$n_{eq} \times$ (area of the teal triangle C in Figure 11.14(b)]. Generally, total consumer surplus will increase for two reasons as the number of firms increases: entry causes total industry output to increase and prices to decline; and new firms increase variety and increase the likelihood that a particular consumer will find a product that exactly matches her tastes. Figure 11.16 shows $CS(n)$ as a positively sloped curve. It is unlikely, but conceivable, that $CS(n)$ could decrease with increases in n if increased variety enables each firm to cater very closely to the demands of a select group of consumers, thereby enabling firms to dramatically increase prices as variety increases. For simplicity, our analysis ignores this possibility.

Figure 11.15 The Number of Firms and Profits in a Monopolistically Competitive Industry
The purple function $\pi(n)$ shows the relationship between each firm's profit and the number of firms in the industry. Long-run equilibrium is reached when n_{eq} firms are in the industry and each firm earns a normal economic profit. We obtain total industry profits, represented by the green curve $n \times \pi(n)$, by multiplying the number of firms by profits per firm.

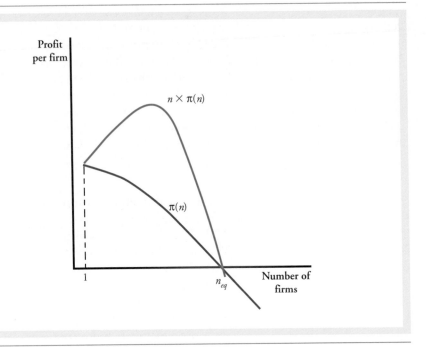

Figure 11.16 Consumer Surplus as a Function of the Number of Monopolistically Competitive Firms
Total consumer surplus increases as the number of firms in the monopolistically competitive industry increases. The function $CS(n)$ shows the relationship between the number of firms in the industry and total consumer surplus.

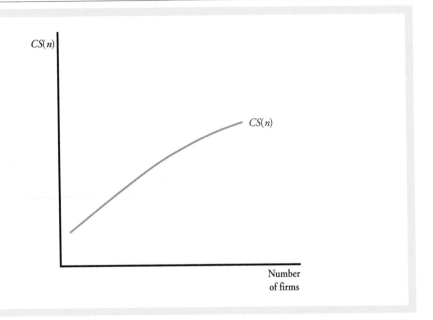

To determine total surplus, we add the total producer profits and total consumer surplus:

$$\text{total surplus}(n) = [n \times \pi(n)] + CS(n)$$

Figure 11.17(a) derives the total surplus curve from the vertical sum of the $[n \times \pi(n)]$ curve in Figure 11.15 and the $CS(n)$ curve in Figure 11.16. The socially optimal number of firms is n^*. Only with n^* firms does the industry maximize total surplus. In Figure 11.17(a), the

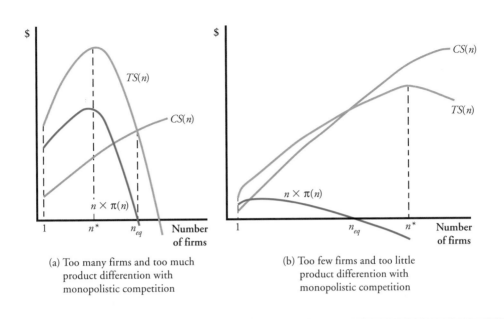

Figure 11.17 Variety and the Number of Firms in a Monopolistically Competitive Industry
The socially optimal number of firms, n^*, maximizes total surplus. In panel (a), the socially optimal number of firms is less than the equilibrium number of firms n_{eq}, so there are too many firms in the industry and too much variety. In panel (b), the socially optimal number of firms n^* is greater than the equilibrium number of firms n_{eq}, so there are too few firms in the industry and too little variety.

COMMON ERROR 11.2 Believing That Monopolistic Competition Is Always Inefficient

When analyzing the monopolistically competitive model, students often conclude that monopolistic competition always results in economic inefficiency because price is greater than marginal cost, and that each firm faces excess capacity because they are producing on the downward-sloping portion of their average cost curves. By producing an output on the downward-sloping portion of their average cost curves, the firms cannot possibly be minimizing their average costs. This reasoning, however, is wrong!

The source of this common error lies in the difference between the *private* benefits and the *social* benefits associated with entry. As long as there is some positive economic profit associated with entry, additional firms enter the industry. Entry reduces the profit of each of the incumbent firms. The total change in profit for society resulting from entry is

therefore *always* less than the private profit of the entering firm, so from a social viewpoint, the firm has too much incentive to enter. This profit effect tends to result in too many firms and too much product differentiation.

On the other hand, entry results in an increase in consumer surplus. The entrant, however, ignores this increase in consumer surplus and considers only the positive economic profit associated with entry. Because entrants ignore the increase in consumer surplus, too few firms enter, and there is too little product differentiation.

The profit effect results in too much entry; however, because entrants ignore the increase in consumer surplus, there is too little entry. The net effect depends on which factor is dominant. An industry will achieve the socially optimal level of product differentiation optimal number of firms n^* is less than the equilibrium number of firms n_{eq}. In this case, the monopolistically competitive industry will have too many firms and provide too large a variety of goods. As a result, there will be excessive product differentiation.

Figure 11.17(b) shows a different monopolistically competitive industry, where $n^* > n_{eq}$. In this case, the industry provides too little variety. There is, therefore, too little product differentiation in the industry represented in Figure 11.17(b). There is a third possible scenario, in which $n^* = n_{eq}$ and the industry provides the optimal level of product differentiation. It follows that in a monopolistically competitive industry, product differentiation may be greater than, less than, or equal to the socially optimal level of product differentiation.

▼▼▼ Summary

1. The major sources of monopoly power include structural barriers to entry, such as economies of scale, absolute cost advantages, high capital requirements, and product differentiation; strategic barriers to entry, such as limit pricing, predatory pricing, and the building of excess capacity; and government-imposed barriers to entry, such as government-mandated monopolies.

2. Like a competitive firm, a monopolist sets its profit-maximizing output and price by equating marginal revenue to marginal cost; however, because price is greater than marginal revenue for a monopolist, the monopolist's price is greater than marginal cost. The Lerner Index, which is equal to the inverse of the monopolist's elasticity of demand, measures the degree to which the monopolist's price is greater than marginal cost. The higher the Lerner Index, the greater the degree of monopoly power.

3. Because a monopolist's price is greater than marginal cost, the monopolist is always allocatively inefficient and fails to achieve Pareto efficiency. A monopolist may also survive even if it fails to minimize its costs, and therefore may be productively inefficient. A monopolist can also earn large economic profit in the long run, and this may create an equity problem for society. On the other hand, the monopolist may invest its profit in research and development, which may improve dynamic efficiency.

4. In a monopolistically competitive industry, product differentiation exists but entry is easy. As a result, in long-run equilibrium, monopolistically competitive firms earn zero economic profits but produce on the downward-sloping portion of their long-run average cost curves. The monopolistically competitive industry may maximize total economic surplus and be efficient; however, it is possible that either too few or too many firms may enter the industry and the industry would then be inefficient.

▨▨ Self-Test Problems

1. Consider a monopolist with the following demand: $P = 480 - 5Q$. Assume $TC = 400 + 20Q$, so $MC = 20$.

   a. Solve for the price and quantity that will maximize profit.

   b. Calculate the monopolist's profit.

   c. Draw a graph labeling price, quantity, and profit of the monopolist.

2. Consider a monopolist with two plants with the following marginal cost functions: $MC_a = 9 + 3q_a$

and $MC_b = 21 + 3q_b$. The demand function is: $P = 335 - (1/4)Q$.

a. Solve for the profit-maximizing level of output for each plant.

b. Calculate the profit-maximizing price to charge.

c. Draw a graph showing the profit-maximizing level of output at each plant, total output, and price charged.

3. Consider a monopolist with the following demand function: $P = 400 - (3/4)Q$. $MC = 40 + (1/2)Q$.

a. Solve for the price and quantity that will maximize profit.

b. Draw a graph labeling q_m, p_m, consumer surplus, and producer surplus.

c. Calculate consumer and producer surplus under a monopoly.

d. Find the socially optimal level of output and price and label these on your graph, q_{so} and p_{so}.

e. Calculate the producer surplus and consumer surplus at the socially optimal level of output. Label producer surplus and consumer surplus in this situation on the graph in part b.

f. Calculate deadweight loss. Explain what portion of the deadweight loss is a loss in consumer surplus and what portion is a loss in producer surplus.

Questions and Problems for Review

1. A monopolist is currently operating at a point on its *LRAC* curve where significant diseconomies of scale exist. Discuss the likelihood of this industry remaining a monopoly over time. Explain using a graph.

2. Using the table in Application 11.1B on page 291, discuss some of the difficulties that a potential entrant into the cosmetics market might face.

3. Consider the following scenarios. For each scenario, identify the most likely source of monopoly power.

a. A firm is meeting all of its demand, but is producing an output below its minimum efficient scale (MES).

b. Drug company A receives a patent on a drug to cure breast cancer.

c. Company A is a Fortune 500 company, has been in business for 100 years, and has a solid reputation in the business community. They recently received a low-cost loan to expand production to meet increasing demand.

d. Firm A has advertised during the SuperBowl game for the past 10 years. Studies have shown that consumers remember the ads from the previous years and the ads encourage the present consumption of Firm A's product.

e. A local gas station has managed to drive its only competitor out of business by constantly lowering price.

f. Harry visits a national park in Wyoming and has only one choice of where to eat while on park premises.

4. The demand curve for a monopolist is: $P = 100 - (1/4)Q$. The total cost curve $(TC) = \$500 + 10Q$. Thus, marginal cost is equal to 10.

a. Solve for the profit-maximizing level of output and price for the monopolist. What is the profit at that point?

b. Draw a graph showing the profit-maximizing level of output and price. Label profit.

c. Following the example in Figure 11.7, draw a graph of *TR*, *TC*, and profit. Label the points of zero profit as well as the total revenue-maximizing point and the profit-maximizing point.

5. The demand curve for a monopolist is: $P = 490 - 2Q$. $TC = 20 + 10Q + 2Q^2$. Thus, $MC = 10 + 4Q$.

a. Solve for the profit-maximizing level of output and price for the monopolist. Calculate profit.

b. Draw a graph labeling the profit-maximizing level of output and price. Label profit on the graph as well.

6. Graph the total revenue curve for a monopolist whose demand curve is given by $P = 400 - 2Q$. On a separate graph, draw the demand and marginal curves for the monopolist. What is the equation for marginal revenue?

7. In Chapter 11, we learned that increases in demand do not necessarily increase price. Consider the demand for a newly developed product: $P = 620 - 25Q$ and $MC = AC = 20$.

a. Solve for the profit-maximizing quantity and price.

b. Now assume the demand for the product increases dramatically to $P = 520 - 2Q$. MC stays the same. Solve for the new profit-maximizing quantity and price.

c. In Chapter 11, the explanation for why price falls with an increase in demand is that the higher demand is more elastic at the price charged than the original demand curve. Calculate the elasticity of demand for both the original demand curve and the new demand curve at the equilibrium price in part a. Is this example consistent with the explanation in the text?

8. Consider a monopolist with two plants with the following marginal cost functions: $MC_a = 18 + (1/2)q_a$ and $MC_b = 6 + (1/2)q_b$. The demand function is: $P = 30 - (1/4)Q$.

   a. Solve for the profit-maximizing level of output for each plant.

   b. Calculate the monopolist's profit-maximizing price.

   c. Draw a graph showing the profit-maximizing level of output for each plant, total output, and price.

9. Consider a monopolist with the following demand function: $P = 152 - 3Q$. $MC = 2$.

   a. Solve for the profit-maximizing price and quantity, p_m and q_m respectively.

   b. Draw a graph labeling q_m, p_m, consumer surplus, and producer surplus.

   c. Calculate total welfare under a monopoly.

   d. Now, find the socially optimal level of output and price and label these on your graph as q_{so} and p_{so} respectively.

   e. Calculate the total welfare at the socially optimal level of output (notice it is entirely made up of consumer surplus, because marginal cost is constant here).

   f. Calculate the deadweight loss. Label the deadweight loss on the graph you drew in part b.

10. Consider a monopolist with the following demand function: $P = 304 - (1/2)Q$. $MC = 4 + 2Q$.

    a. Solve for the profit-maximizing price and quantity, p_m and q_m respectively.

    b. Draw a graph labeling q_m, p_m, consumer surplus, and producer surplus.

    c. Calculate the monopolist's consumer surplus and producer surplus.

d. Now, find the socially optimal level of output and price and label these on your graph as q_{so} and p_{so}.

e. Calculate the producer surplus and consumer surplus at the socially optimal level of output. Label producer surplus and consumer surplus in this situation on the graph you drew in part b.

f. Calculate the deadweight loss. Explain which portion of the deadweight loss is a loss in consumer surplus and which portion is a loss in producer surplus. Label the deadweight loss on the graph you drew in part b.

11. Consider a monopolist with the following demand function: $P = 180 - 2Q$. The minimum long-run marginal and long-run average costs of producing the good are $LRMC_e = LRAC_e = 20$, but this monopolist is inefficient and operating with $LRMC = LRAC = 28$.

    a. Solve for the profit-maximizing price and quantity for the inefficient monopolist. Calculate profit for the inefficient monopolist.

    b. Solve for the profit-maximizing price and quantity if the monopolist produced the good efficiently. Calculate profit for an efficient monopolist.

    c. Assume an economist believes that the monopolist is minimizing its costs when it produces with $LRMC = LRAC = 28$. In this case, what would be the economist's estimate of the monopolist's deadweight loss?

    d. We know that the monopolist is not minimizing its costs when it produces at $LRMC = LRAC = 28$. What is the true deadweight loss for an inefficient monopolist if a cost-minimizing monopolist would produce with lower costs $LRMC_e = LRAC_e = 20$?

12. Consider the table in Application 11.2 on page 305.

    a. Assume that for some reason (perhaps an increase in the number of available substitutes), the price elasticity of demand for automobiles increases to 12. Calculate how the Lerner Index would change from the estimates in the table.

    b. Assume that the negative publicity about how smoking is bad for health has caused the demand curve to shift left and become more inelastic. Thus, the new elasticity of demand is estimated at $|-1.1|$ for tobacco. Calculate how the Lerner Index would change from the estimates in the table.

13. Microsoft typically spends approximately 11–15 percent of its revenues on R&D. Given this information, provide an argument for why we might be willing to accept some of the current inefficiencies as a result of its monopoly power.

14. Consider a monopolist who produces a highly specialized machine that is used in the canning industry. Assume that this monopolist is run by its managers. Would you expect the monopolist to minimize its costs? Explain your reasoning.

15. Consider Application 11.4 in the text. On a graph, show how the demand for DiGiorno's frozen pizza would change as more and more firms enter the rising-crust frozen pizza industry. Would the demand for DiGiorno's pizza become more or less elastic?

16. Think about the products sold in a grocery store. Name at least three products that are manufactured in monopolistically competitive markets.

17. This chapter uses rising-crust frozen pizza as an example of a monopolistically competitive market.
    a. What characteristics of this market make it monopolistically competitive, rather than perfectly competitive?
    b. Consider the two scenarios depicted in Figure 11.17. Do you think that the DiGiorno application is best represented by Figure 11.17(a) or Figure 11.17(b)? Explain.

18. Assume the rising-crust frozen pizza market becomes oversaturated so that a typical firm is earning economic losses. On a graph, draw a picture of a monopolistically competitive firm sustaining eco-nomic losses. Label the losses on your graph. Explain how this industry will adjust to long-run equilibrium. As the industry adjusts to its new long-run equilibrium, what should happen to profit per firm?

19. **Do not answer this question unless you have read Appendix 11.1.** Consider the linear demand curve $P = 160 - 4Q$.
    a. Solve for the elasticity of demand at $P = 120$, $P = 80$, and $P = 60$.
    b. Using calculus or the twice-as-steep rule, solve for the MR of this firm.
    c. Verify the formula $MR = p(1 + 1/\varepsilon_p) = p(1 - 1/|\varepsilon_p|)$.

20. Consider a monopolist facing a demand curve of $P = 175 - Q$ and $LRMC = LRAC = 25$.
    a. Solve for the profit-maximizing output and price.
    b. Calculate consumer surplus and producer surplus at the monopoly output and price.
    c. Solve for the competitive and Pareto-efficient level of output and price.
    d. Calculate consumer surplus and producer surplus at the competitive level of output.
    e. Calculate the deadweight loss due to monopoly.
    f. Discuss the fairness of the monopoly result with the competitive and Pareto-efficient result. In your discussion, be sure to consider the answer in two ways: if you are a consumer purchasing the monopoly product, and if you own substantial stock in the monopoly.

Internet Exercises

Visit *http://www.myeconlab.com/waldman* for this chapter's Web exercises. Answer real-world economics problems by doing research on the Internet.

Appendix 11.1

Deriving the Relationship Between *MR* and the Elasticity of Demand

Using calculus, marginal revenue, *MR*, is calculated as follows:

$$TR = pq$$

$$MR = \frac{dTR}{dq} = p\frac{dq}{dq} + q\frac{dp}{dq} = p\left(1 + \frac{q}{p}\frac{dp}{dq}\right)$$

Mathematically, the elasticity of demand ε_p is defined as:

$$\varepsilon_p = \frac{dq}{dp}\frac{p}{q} < 0$$

Therefore:

$$\frac{dp}{dq}\frac{q}{p} = \frac{1}{\varepsilon_p} < 0$$

Marginal revenue therefore equals:

$$MR = p\left(1 + \frac{1}{\varepsilon_p}\right) = p\left(1 - \frac{1}{|\varepsilon_p|}\right)$$

Chapter 12
Additional Monopoly Topics: Pricing Strategies and Public Policy

Most readers of this book are college students currently paying tuition. Many students have their tuition bills reduced because they receive some form of financial aid, such as a need-based, academic merit, or athletic scholarship. Furthermore, students who accept an early decision admission in December generally receive less generous financial aid packages than students who are regular springtime admissions to the same school. Many other students receive no financial aid and must pay the full tuition bill. Students at the same school therefore pay vastly different prices to attend. As we will learn in this chapter, colleges are able to charge different students different tuitions because they have a good deal of monopoly power over their students, particularly after a student has committed to attending the school. For example, colleges know that students accepting early decision admissions will attend the school regardless of the financial aid packages they are offered and that therefore they have a great deal of monopoly power over those students. Because colleges charge different students different prices for the same good, colleges engage in a practice known as *price discrimination*. In this chapter, we examine the reasons why firms practice price discrimination and the impact of discrimination on buyers and sellers.

In Chapter 11, we explored the basic theory of monopoly pricing. The welfare implications presented in Chapter 11 were a bit simplistic, though, because throughout Chapter 11, we assumed that monopolists always charge a uniform price to all buyers and the monopoly power is not regulated by the government. In Chapter 11, the monopolist (like a competitive firm) maximized profit by producing the output at which marginal revenue equaled marginal cost. This resulted in a uniform profit-maximizing price charged to all consumers. Although some monopolists charge uniform prices to all consumers, many firms with market power, like colleges and universities, are able to increase their profits by separating consumers into different groups with different elasticities of demand and setting their prices accordingly. In this chapter, we consider the various methods of price discrimination that monopolists use to increase their profits.

Learning Objectives

After reading Chapter 12, you will have learned:

> How firms with market power use price discrimination to increase profits, how to identify the three different types of price discrimination, and how each type affects welfare.

> How firms with market power use two-part tariffs, bundling, and tying arrangements to increase profits.

> How the United States government uses antitrust policy and direct price regulation to address problems created by monopoly power.

Featured Applications

> 12.1 Application Third-Degree Price Discrimination at Disney World

> 12.2 Application Changing Pricing Strategies at Disneyland and Disney World

> 12.3 Application The California Electricity Crisis

The potential allocative and productive efficiency problems associated with monopoly have led governments to try to minimize the negative impacts of monopoly power through a variety of legal mechanisms. The two most important methods of limiting monopoly power in the United States are antitrust policy and direct regulation. In the second part of this chapter, we analyze the rationale behind these public policies.

▼▼▼   12.1   The Price-Discriminating Monopolist

price discrimination

The practice of charging different consumers different prices for the same product.

Price discrimination, which exists when firms charge different consumers different prices for the same product, is a telltale sign that market power exists. If two sellers in a perfectly competitive market charge different prices for the same good, consumers will buy only from the lower-priced seller. Monopolists, on the other hand, use various methods of price discrimination to increase profits.

Price discrimination also requires an ability to separate consumers into different groups, each with a different elasticity of demand. For example, movie theaters separate senior citizens from other adults because they know that seniors have a more elastic demand; and the publishers of professional journals separate libraries from other buyers because they know that the libraries must subscribe to their journals and therefore the libraries have a very inelastic demand for their journals.

Finally, for price discrimination to be effective, the monopolist must be able to prevent the transfer of the good from one group to another. Consider, for instance, that although movie theaters discriminate in ticket prices between adults and children, they do not charge children lower popcorn prices, because if they did, children would buy virtually all the popcorn consumed at theaters.

first-degree price discrimination

The practice of charging each consumer the maximum price they are willing to pay to purchase a good.

perfect discrimination

Another term for first-degree price discrimination.

reservation price

The highest price a consumer is willing to pay for an additional unit of a good.

second-degree price discrimination

The practice of offering all consumers the same price schedule and permitting consumers to self-select into the different price categories of the schedule.

third-degree price discrimination

The practice of separating consumers into different groups, each with a different elasticity of demand and charging a higher price to consumers in the group with a more inelastic demand.

Types of Price Discrimination

Economists divide price discrimination into three general categories: *first-degree, second-degree,* and *third-degree price discrimination*. In **first-degree price discrimination**, which is often referred to as **perfect discrimination**, each consumer pays his or her *reservation price* for the good. Each consumer's **reservation price** is the highest price he or she is willing to pay for the good. With **second-degree price discrimination**, a firm offers all consumers the same price schedule, and then consumers self-select into the different price categories. **Third-degree price discrimination** depends on the firm's ability to effectively separate consumers into two or more groups according to their elasticities of demand. Unlike second-degree price discrimination, in third-degree discrimination, consumers are put into a group by the firm and cannot self-select into another group. In this section, we consider output and price under each type of price discrimination and pay close attention to the welfare implications of each type of discrimination.

FIRST-DEGREE PRICE DISCRIMINATION   With first-degree price discrimination, each consumer pays the highest price they are willing to pay for the monopolist's good, therefore, monopolists prefer to use first-degree discrimination whenever possible. Let's see why. Figure 12.1 shows a market with a demand curve of $P = 10 - Q$ and production costs of $MC = AC = 2$. In such a market, first-degree discrimination would require the first unit of the good to be sold at a price of $9, the second unit at $8, the third at $7, and so on, until the eighth unit was sold at $P = MC = \$2$. First-degree discrimination results in total revenue of $44 ($9 + $8 + $7 + $6 + $5 + $4 + $3 + $2 = $44) on the sale of eight units. The ninth unit would not be sold, because the consumer's reservation price of $1.00 is less than marginal cost.

Figure 12.1 First-Degree Price Discrimination

With first-degree price discrimination, each unit is sold for the maximum price some consumer is willing to pay. With demand $P = 10 - Q$, the first unit is sold for $9, the second unit for $8, the third for $7, until the eighth unit is sold for $2. Total revenue equals $9 + $8 + $7 + $6 + $5 + $4 + $3 + $2 = $44. There is no consumer surplus, but producer surplus equals the sum of the purple, blue, and green shaded areas $X + Y + Z$.

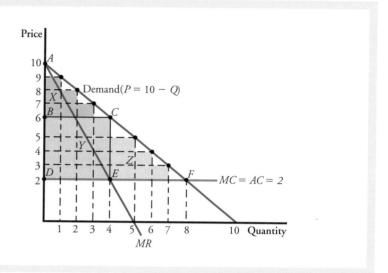

To determine the welfare effects of price discrimination, it is necessary to compare the total consumer surplus plus producer surplus with price discrimination versus the total consumer surplus plus producer surplus without price discrimination. With first-degree discrimination, in Figure 12.1, consumer surplus is zero, but producer surplus is the entire shaded area, consisting of the sum of the shaded purple, blue, and green areas $X + Y + Z$. If a firm does not discriminate and charges one price to all buyers, then the profit-maximizing quantity is 4 and price is $6, and therefore, total revenue equals $24. With a one-price policy, consumer surplus is equal to the shaded purple area X and producer surplus is equal to the shaded blue area Y. There is a welfare loss equal to the shaded green area Z. Because the elimination of price discrimination results in a welfare loss equal to the green area Z, first-degree price discrimination improves welfare. In fact, in the case of first-degree discrimination, allocative efficiency is achieved, because price equals marginal cost for the last unit purchased. Consequently, every consumer who is willing to pay a price greater than or equal to marginal cost receives the good. Pareto efficiency is also achieved with first-degree discrimination, because there is no way to exchange goods in a way that helps one consumer without hurting another.

SECOND–DEGREE PRICE DISCRIMINATION Recall that with second-degree discrimination, all consumers are offered the same price schedule, and then consumers self-select

---

COMMON ERROR 12.1 **Believing that Any Reduction in Consumer Surplus Reduces Welfare**

Students sometimes incorrectly believe that first-degree price discrimination reduces welfare because it eliminates all consumer surplus. In Figure 12.1, without discrimination, price equals $6.00 and consumer surplus equals the purple shaded area X, which also equals $6.00. First-degree price discrimination transfers all of the consumer surplus to producer surplus and also eliminates the green deadweight loss area Z,

which also equals $6.00. First-degree discrimination improves welfare, because the green deadweight loss area Z is eliminated. From an equity perspective, the transfer of consumer surplus to profit might concern society; however, this is a normative economic problem and not a positive economic problem. Positive economic analysis is unambiguous in this case; welfare is improved by first-degree price discrimination.

into different price categories. Although consumers pay different prices, every consumer who buys within the same price category pays the same price. Firms use second-degree discrimination when they know there are different groups of consumers with different reservation prices, but they are unable to identify, or it is too costly to identify, each type of consumer. Price discrimination in the airline industry is one common example of second-degree discrimination. Airlines typically offer all buyers a large variety of different fares on the same flight depending on a number of restrictions, including when the ticket is purchased and how long the passenger stays at his destination before taking a return flight. Pizza Hut, which often charges $10 for the first large pizza but only $5 for the second large pizza, provides another example of second-degree price discrimination. In this case, consumers buying one pizza pay $10 and those buying two pizzas pay only $7.50 per pizza.

Figures 12.2(a) and 12.2(b) illustrate another example of second-degree price discrimination—quantity discounts. Suppose Ralph Lauren produces a pair of designer jeans for $MC = AC = 20 and offers the following quantity discount. Consumers can

Figure 12.2 Second-Degree Price Discrimination

In panel (a), consumers purchase one pair of jeans for $80, a second pair for $60, a third pair for $40, and a fourth pair for $20. A total of 100 pairs are sold and total revenue equals the sum of the shaded areas $A + B + C + D$, or $6,000. In panel (b), consumer surplus is the sum of the four purple shaded areas $W + X + Y + Z$, and producer surplus is the sum of the three shaded rectangles $A + B + C$, which equals $4,000.

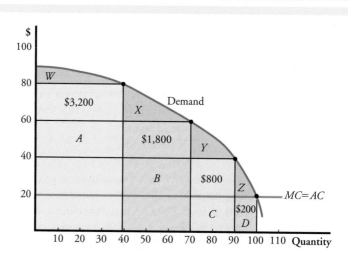

(a) Total revenue with second-degree price discrimination

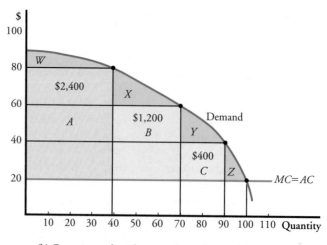

(b) Consumer and producer surplus with second-degree price discrimination

Table 12.1 The Demand for Ralph Lauren Jeans Using Second-Degree Price Discrimination

Price	Quantity at that Price	Total Quantity Sold
$80	40	40
$60	30	70
$40	20	90
$20	10	100

purchase one pair for $80, a second pair for $60, a third pair for $40, and a fourth pair for $20. Given this pricing structure, suppose a Ralph Lauren store sells jeans to 10 consumers in each of the four categories each day. All 40 buyers purchase the first pair at $80; 30 buyers purchase the first pair at $80 and a second pair at $60; 20 buyers purchase a first pair at $80, a second pair at $60, and a third pair at $40; and 10 buyers purchase the first pair at $80, a second pair at $60, a third pair at $40, and a fourth pair at $20.

Table 12.1 shows the daily demand for jeans. A total of 100 pairs are sold and total revenue is $6,000 ($3,200 + $1,800 + $800 + $200). Figure 12.2(a) shows the demand curve for Ralph Lauren's designer jeans using second-degree price discrimination. The sum of the shaded areas $A + B + C + D$ represents total revenue and equals $6,000.

Bear in mind that the demand curve in Figure 12.2(a) is not comparable to the demand curve for jeans that would exist without price discrimination. Without price discrimination, if Ralph Lauren charged a uniform price of $20 for all of its jeans, the company would sell more than 100 pairs. A demand curve without price discrimination, therefore, would typically lie well to the right of the demand curve in Figure 12.2(a). This makes welfare comparisons in the case of second-degree discrimination difficult.

Figure 12.2(b) identifies the consumer and producer surplus associated with second-degree price discrimination in the Ralph Lauren example. Figure 12.2(b) reproduces Figure 12.2(a), but here the shaded areas have been changed. In Figure 12.2(b), consumer surplus equals the sum of the four shaded purple areas $W + X + Y + Z$ while producer surplus equals the sum of the three shaded rectangles $A + B + C$. Unlike first-degree discrimination, in the case of second-degree discrimination, there is some consumer surplus. Because the seller cannot identify precisely the demand for each and every consumer, he or she is unable to extract the entire consumer surplus from the market.

THIRD–DEGREE PRICE DISCRIMINATION With third-degree price discrimination, firms are able to separate consumers into two or more groups according to their different elasticities of demand. With third-degree discrimination, consumers are put into a group by the firm and cannot self-select into another group. As long as the firm can distinguish the groups by their different elasticities at any given price, practicing price discrimination increases profit. For example, suppose a large multiplex movie theater in Fort Lauderdale, Florida, recognizes that it faces two distinct demand curves: one for senior citizens over age 65 and another for adults under age 65. Panel (a) of Figure 12.3 shows the demand curve for adults under age 65 to be $p_a = \$10.00 - (\$1/10)q_a$, where q_a is measured in thousands of tickets. Panel (b) shows the demand curve for senior citizens to be $p_s = \$5.00 - (\$1/30)q_s$, where q_s is measured in thousands of tickets. For any $p > 0$, the demand for adults is more inelastic than the demand for senior citizens. To simplify the analysis, we assume $MC = AC = \$1.00$.

To maximize profit, the theater sets marginal revenue equal to marginal cost for each consumer group. For adults in Figure 12.3(a), $MR_a = MC$ implies that $\$10.00 - (\$1/5)q_a =$

Figure 12.3 The Demand for Movies for Adults and Senior Citizens

To maximize profit, the theater equates marginal revenue to marginal cost in each market and charges a price of $5.50 per ticket to adults in panel (a) and $3.00 per ticket to seniors in panel (b). Total consumer plus producer surplus in both markets is the sum of areas $A + B + C + D$, which equals $483.75.

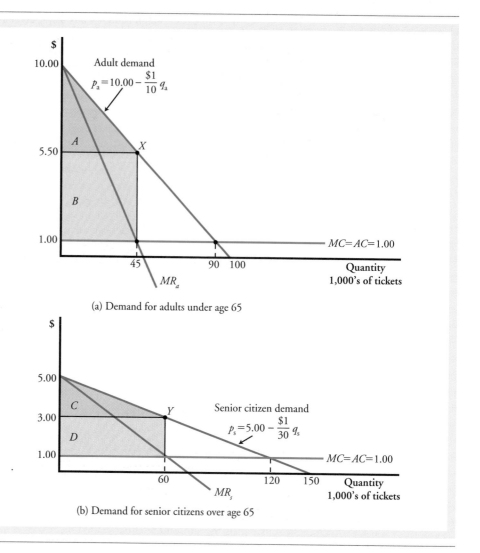

(a) Demand for adults under age 65

(b) Demand for senior citizens over age 65

$1.00, so $q_a = 45$ and p = $5.50. For senior citizens in panel (b), $MR_s = MC$ implies that $5.00 − ($1/15)q_s = $1.00, so $q_s = 60$ and p = $3.00. With price discrimination, adults 65 and under pay $5.50 per ticket and purchase 45,000 tickets and seniors over 65 pay $3.00 per ticket and purchase 60,000 tickets. The theater sells a total quantity of 105,000 tickets. At their respective equilibrium points, the elasticity of demand for adults is $\varepsilon_p = (\Delta q/\Delta p)(p/q) = 10(5.5/45) = 1.22$ at point X, and the elasticity of demand for seniors is $\varepsilon_p = (\Delta q/\Delta p)(p/q) = 30(3/60) = 1.5$ at point Y. With third-degree price discrimination, the price is lower in the senior citizen market with the more elastic demand.

WELFARE IMPLICATIONS OF THIRD-DEGREE PRICE DISCRIMINATION Third-degree price discrimination has the most complicated welfare implications of the three types of discrimination. However, we can draw a few basic points concerning welfare from our Fort Lauderdale theater example. With third-degree price discrimination, we can derive from Figure 12.3 consumer plus producer surplus in each market. In panel (a), consumer surplus for adults equals the area of the purple triangle A, which equals $(1/2)(45)($10.00 − $5.50) = (1/2)(45)($4.50) = 101.25, and in panel (b), consumer surplus for seniors equals the area of the purple triangle C, which equals $(1/2)(60)($5.00 − $3.00) = 1/2(60)($2.00) = 60. Therefore, the sum of consumer surplus in both markets equals the sum of areas $A + C$ or $\$101.25 + \$60 = \$161.25$. In panel (a), producer surplus equals the area of the green rectangle B equal to $45(\$4.50) = \$202.50$, and in panel (b), producer surplus equals the area of the green rectangle D equal to $60(\$2.00) = \$120$. Therefore, the sum of producer surplus in both markets equals $\$202.50 + \$120 = \$322.50$. The sum of consumer and producer surplus with discrimination equals $\$161.25 + \$322.50 = \$483.75$.

Now suppose the theater was forced by law to charge a uniform price to all buyers. What price would the theater charge? In Chapter 4, we learned how to add individual demand curves horizontally to derive the market demand curve. Using this technique, we can derive the market demand for theater tickets by adding the two group demand curves horizontally. Figure 12.4 shows the result of the horizontal addition of the two demand curves. For prices between $\$5.00$ and $\$10.00$, only the demand for adults under 65 is relevant, so in that price range, the combined demand is $p = \$10.00 - (1/10)q$. For prices between $\$0$ and $\$5.00$, both demands are relevant and the combined demand is the horizontal summation of the two demand curves, which yields the demand curve segment BC. The demand curve becomes much more elastic for prices below $\$5.00$, as the more elastic senior citizen demand is added to the less elastic adults-under-65 demand. The complete demand curve, therefore, is the kinked demand curve ABC.

We can derive the equation of the more elastic portion of the demand curve between points B and C by noting three facts about this segment of the demand curve: (1) the addition of two lines always results in a line, (2) the slope of line BC equals $5.00/200 = 1/40$, and (3) the line goes through the point $q = 250$, $p = 0$. Substituting $q = 250$ and $p = \$0$ into the general linear equation $p = K - (\$1/40)q$, yields $0 = K - (\$1/40)(250)$, so $K = \$250/40 = \$6.25$. The equation of the demand curve between points B and C, therefore, is $p = \$6.25 - (\$1/40)q$.

In Figure 12.5, we derive the profit-maximizing uniform price for a non-discriminating theater. For outputs up to 50, the demand curve is the demand curve for adults under 65: $p_a = \$10.00 - (\$1/10)q_a$, so the marginal revenue curve is $MR_a = \$10.00 - (\$1/5)q_a$. For outputs greater than or equal to 50, the demand curve is $p = \$6.25 - (\$1/40)q$, so the marginal revenue curve is $MR = \$6.25 - (\$1/20)q$.

In Figure 12.5, $MC = \$1.00$ intersects marginal revenue twice: first at $q = 45$ along the first segment of the marginal revenue curve; and again at $q = 105$ along the second

Figure 12.4 Combined Demand for Movie Tickets

The sum of the adult and senior demand curves for movie tickets is the horizontal summation of the two demand curves. For prices above $\$5.00$, this consists of only the adults-under-65 demand $p = \$10.00 - (1/10)q$. For prices below $\$5.00$, the demand $p = \$6.25 - (\$1/40)q$. The complete demand curve is the kinked dark-blue curve ABC.

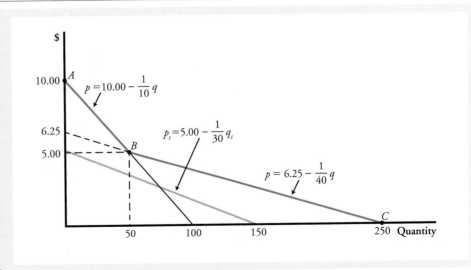

Figure 12.5 The Profit-Maximizing Uniform Price
To maximize profit, the theater equates marginal revenue to marginal cost on the second segment of the MR curve at $q = 105$ and sets the price at $3.625. Producer surplus equals the green shaded area C and consumer surplus equals the sum of the purple and blue shaded areas $A + B$. The sum of consumer and producer surplus equals 507.1875.

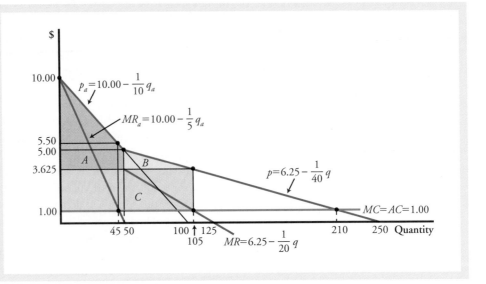

segment. Which output, 45 or 105, maximizes profit? If $q = 45$, the theater sells tickets only to adults under 65 at $p = \$5.50$, and profit equals $45(\$5.50 - \$1.00) = \$202.50$. If the theater sells 105 tickets, price equals $p = \$6.25 - (\$1/40)(105) = \$3.625$, and profit equals $105(\$3.625 - \$1.00) = \$275.625$. The theater therefore maximizes profits by expanding output to 105. Recall from Figure 12.3 that without discrimination, adults under 65 purchased 45,000 tickets and seniors purchased 60,000 tickets for a total of 105,000 tickets; therefore, the total output of 105,000 tickets is exactly the same both with and without price discrimination. This is a basic result of price discrimination with linear demand and linear marginal cost curves.[1]

To determine the welfare impact of price discrimination, we compare the total surplus without price discrimination in Figure 12.5 with the total surplus with discrimination in Figure 12.3. In Figure 12.5, total surplus is measured by the sum of consumer surplus equal to the purple and blue areas $A + B$ plus producer surplus equal to the green area C. Geometrically, the purple area A is a trapezoid, which has an area equal to one-half the altitude times the sum of the bases, or $(1/2)(50)(\$6.375 + \$1.375) = \$193.75$. The blue triangle B has an area equal to $(1/2)(55)(\$1.375) = \$37.8125$. Therefore, consumer surplus equals $\$193.75 + \$37.8125 = \$231.5625$. Producer surplus equals the area of the green rectangle C, or $105(\$2.625) = \$275.625$. The sum of consumer and producer surplus without discrimination equals $\$231.5625 + \$275.625 = \$507.1875$.

Table 12.2 shows the welfare comparison with and without price discrimination. Price discrimination increases producer surplus by $46.875. However, price discrimination reduces consumer surplus by $70.3125, and therefore, third-degree price discrimination results in a net reduction in total surplus and welfare of $23.4375. *Generally, with linear demand and linear marginal cost curves, price discrimination reduces welfare.* There is, however, one important exception to this rule: If one group(s) does not consume the good *without* price discrimination, then price discrimination increases total output and results in a net welfare gain.

---

[1] Joan Robinson first identified this result. See Joan Robinson, *The Economics of Imperfect Competition* (London: Macmillan, 1933).

▲▲▲ 12.1 APPLICATION Third-Degree Price Discrimination at Disney World

Families from all over the world travel to Disney World. Once a family has invested in the trip to Disney World, there is then the expense of the four theme parks: Magic Kingdom, Epcot, Disney MGM Studios, and the Animal Kingdom. The family's demand to enter the theme parks at this point is inelastic. They have already spent a thousand dollars or more on transportation and lodging, and therefore most families are unlikely to let a few hundred more dollars in admission fees prevent them from visiting the theme parks. For these families, the cost of admissions is a relatively small percentage of the total cost of the trip.

By comparison, many local families from Orlando, or elsewhere in Florida, have probably been to Disney World several times and can go for a day trip to the theme parks. For such Florida families, the cost of entering a theme park is a large percentage of the total cost of a day trip to Disney World. These Florida families would have much more elastic demands for theme park entry.

Recognizing these different elasticities, Disney charges Florida residents much less to enter the parks. To ensure that Florida resident tickets are not resold to non-residents, Disney issues photo IDs with Florida resident passes and they check IDs upon entry. Consider the following examples of some of the pricing schemes that were in effect in 2003:

Type of Admission for Adults	Non-Florida Residents	Florida Residents
Premium annual pass to all theme parks, water parks, and Pleasure Island	$489.00	$399.00
Annual pass to all four theme parks	$369.00	$299.00
Florida resident seasonal pass to all four theme parks during low-demand periods	Not Available	$189.00
4-day Park Hopper ticket	$208.00	$109.00
1-day, 1-park pass	$52.00	$52.00

According to the chart, an Orlando resident could visit a theme park every week for a year for a total of $299.00 or about $5.75 per visit. A non-resident, on the other hand, would have to pay $369.00 for an annual theme park pass and would be less likely to use it as often. Even to visit each park once, the Florida resident is able to spend $27.25 per visit with a $109.00 pass, compared to $52.00 per visit for non-residents. The price–cost margins are much higher for non-residents, who have the more inelastic demand. It is also apparent from the different types of admissions listed here that Disney also uses various methods of second-degree price discrimination by offering both Florida residents and non-residents many different types of passes. In fact, the options listed are a relatively small sample of all the various pricing options available.

Table 12.2 Welfare Comparison With and Without Third-Degree Price Discrimination

	Consumer Surplus	Producer Surplus	Total Surplus
Without Price Discrimination Figure 12.5	$231.5625	$275.625	$507.1875
With Price Discrimination Figure 12.3	$161.25	$322.50	$483.75
Net Gain (+) or Loss (−) With Price Discrimination	−$70.3125	$46.875	−$23.4375

<table>
<tr><td></td><td>

12.2 Two–Part Tariffs, Bundling, and Tying

</td></tr>
</table>

two-part tariff

A pricing policy consisting of a fixed or lump sum payment for a good or service combined with a per-unit user charge.

tie-in sales

A pricing policy that requires consumers to purchase one good in order to be permitted to purchase another good.

bundling

A special case of a tie-in sale where the two goods are purchased in fixed proportions.

requirements tie-in sales

A special case of a tie-in sale where the two goods are purchased in variable proportions; typically, the buyer agrees to purchase its entire requirements of one good in order to be permitted to purchase the other good.

Among the most common forms of second-degree price discrimination are *two-part tariffs*, *bundling*, and *tying*. Although the three concepts are closely related, they are technically different. A **two-part tariff** consists of *a lump sum* payment for a good or service combined with a per-unit user charge. Common examples include: a rental charge for a copier and a per-copy fee; a golf club that charges a membership fee and a greens fee per round; and an amusement park that charges an entrance fee and a per-attraction charge.

Under a **tie-in sales** agreement, consumers can purchase one good only if they agree to purchase another good. Tie-in sales agreements are subdivided into two types: *package tie-in sales*, typically called *bundling*, and *requirements tie-in sales*. **Bundling** is a tying agreement in which the goods are purchased in fixed proportions, meaning that if a unit of good X is purchased, a fixed number of units of good Y must also be purchased. A recent example of bundling is the combination of Microsoft's Windows operating system with Microsoft's Internet Explorer browser. When you purchase a PC computer, good X, you also purchase one installed copy of Microsoft's Internet Explorer, good Y. Another important example is a restaurant that serves only a fixed-price menu including an appetizer, salad, entrée, and dessert for a single price.

Requirements tie-in sales consist of an agreement in which goods are purchased in variable proportions. For example, if a buyer purchases a unit of good X, the buyer must also purchase a variable number of units of good Y. The number of units of Y typically varies greatly from one buyer to the next. For example, aluminum can manufacturers once leased their can-closing equipment, good X, only to customers who agreed to purchase all of their cans, good Y, from the can-closing equipment manufacturer. Each buyer who used can-closing equipment purchased a different number of cans. McDonald's is another example; it requires its franchisees to purchase all of their ingredients and paper goods from McDonald's.

Two–Part Tariffs

If a monopolist uses a two-part tariff, its pricing behavior will depend on whether all buyers have identical or different demands. Therefore, we first consider the case of a two-part tariff in a market in which all consumers have identical demands, and then we generalize the analysis to the more common case of consumers with different demands.

IDENTICAL DEMANDS Suppose all consumers have the demand for copies depicted by the demand curve D in Figure 12.6. The monopolist producer of copying machines is deciding what monthly rental fee and per-copy price to charge its customers. If the monopolist charges a price per copy p_1 equal to marginal cost and does not charge a fixed fee, each of the identical consumers will obtain consumer surplus equal to the sum of the three shaded areas $A + B + C$. If instead the monopolist charges a fixed fee equal to the entire consumer surplus area, $A + B + C$, and a per-copy charge of $p_1 = MC$, all of the potential consumer surplus will be transferred to the monopolist, and the monopolist earns no profit from the page charges. If FC (note: FC is not identified anywhere in Figure 12.6) represents the fixed cost of supplying one copying machine to a buyer, the monopolist's profits per machine equals $(A + B + C) - FC$. In this case, the monopolist's profit comes entirely from the fixed fee.

Why doesn't the monopolist raise the per-copy charge above marginal cost, so that it can earn some profit from the per-copy charge? In Figure 12.6, if the monopolist raises the per-copy charge to p_2, the monopolist earns a profit equal to the area of the green rec-

Figure 12.6 A Two-Part Tariff with Identical Demands for All Consumers

If the monopolist uses a two-part tariff and charges a fixed fee equal to the sum of the shaded areas $A + B + C$ and a per-copy charge $p_1 = MC$, then if FC represents the fixed costs of supplying one copier to a buyer, profit equals $(A + B + C) - FC$. If the monopolist charges a per-copy charge p_2, profit from the per-copy charges equals the green rectangle B, but the maximum fixed fee the monopolist could charge equals the shaded light-blue triangle A. When the per-copy price is increased from p_1 to p_2, profit is reduced by the purple triangle C.

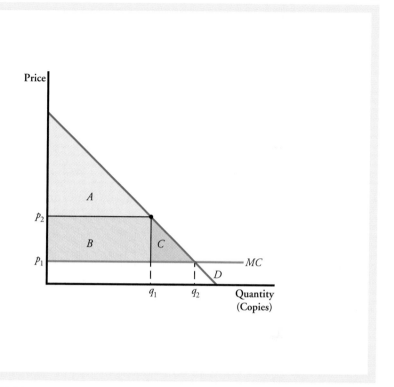

tangle B from the per-copy charges, but consumer surplus is reduced to the area of the blue triangle A. Therefore, the maximum fixed fee the monopolist could charge with a per-copy price, p_2, equals area A. Total profit per copier, if the monopolist charges a fixed fee equal to the area of the blue triangle A and a per-copy charge p_2, equals $(A + B) - FC$. When the per-copy price is raised from p_1 to p_2, profit is reduced by the area of the purple triangle C. No matter how slightly the price is increased above marginal cost, this logic holds and profit is reduced because the monopolist extracts the most profit out of consumer surplus by charging a per-copy fee equal to marginal cost. We can conclude that *when all consumers have identical demands, profit is maximized by charging a per-copy fee equal to marginal cost and a fixed fee equal to consumer surplus.*

DIFFERENT DEMANDS Having just explored the case of a two-part tariff with identical demands, now we consider the case of two different consumers with different demands. Figure 12.7 shows that one consumer is a light user of the copier with demand D_1 and the other is a heavy user with demand D_2. If the monopolist charges a per-copy fee equal to MC, the maximum fixed fee the low-volume user will pay equals the sum of areas $A + B + C$ and the maximum fixed fee the high-volume user will pay equals the sum of areas $A + B + C + D + E + F$. With a per-copy charge $p_1 = MC$, if the monopolist wants to keep the low-volume user in the market, it can charge both consumers a fixed fee no higher than $A + B + C$. If the fixed cost per copier is once again FC (note: FC is again not shown in Figure 12.7) and the monopolist charges both consumers a fixed fee equal to $A + B + C$ and a per-copy charge $p_1 = MC$, then the monopolist's profits equal $2(A + B + C) - 2FC$.

Now suppose the monopolist increases the per-copy charge to $p_2 > MC$. The maximum fixed fee it can charge is reduced to triangle A, the consumer surplus earned by the

Figure 12.7 A Two-Part Tariff with Different Demands
If the monopolist charges a per-copy fee equal to MC, the maximum fixed fee the low-volume user will pay equals the sum of the shaded areas $A + B + C$. If fixed costs are FC per copier and the monopolist charges both consumers a fixed fee equal to $A + B + C$ and a per-copy charge $p_1 = MC$, then profit equals $2(A + B + C) - 2FC$. If the per-copy charge increases to p_2, the maximum fixed fee is reduced to triangle A, profit from the low-volume user is reduced by the area of triangle C, and profit from the high-volume user equals $(A + B + C + E) - FC$. The increase in the per-copy charge increases profit from the high-volume user by the area E and reduces profits from the low-volume user by area C.

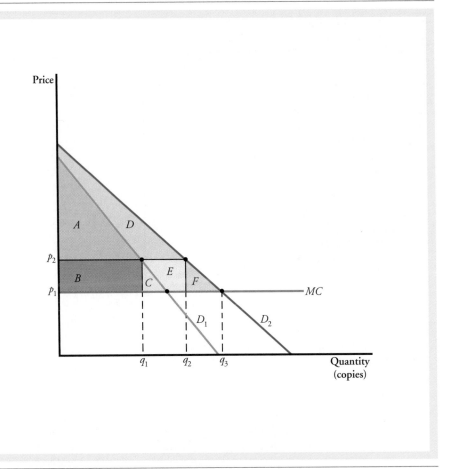

low-volume user. As we discovered in the case of identical demands in Figure 12.6, profit earned from the low-volume user is reduced by the area of the triangle C.

To complete the analysis, we need to compare what happens to the profit earned from the high-volume user when the per-copy charge is increased from p_1 to p_2. With a per-copy price equal to marginal cost and a fixed fee equal to $A + B + C$, profit earned from the high-volume user equals $(A + B + C) - FC$. With a per-copy charge equal to p_2 and a fixed fee equal to area A, profit earned from the high-volume user equals $(A + B + C + E) - FC$. Therefore, the increase in the per-copy charge combined with a reduction in the fixed fee increases the profit earned from the high-volume user by the area E.

Recall from Figure 12.7 that profit earned from the low-volume user was reduced by the area C when the per-copy charge was increased from p_1 to p_2 and the fixed fee was reduced to A. It follows that reducing the fixed fee to equal the shaded area A and increasing the per-copy charge to p_2 increases profit if and only if area E is larger than area C. In Figure 12.7, the area E is greater than the area C, so profit is increased when the per-copy charge is increased to p_2.

In Figure 12.7, the two demand curves are relatively close together and profit maximization calls for the monopolist to charge a per-copy fee above marginal cost and a fixed fee equal to triangle A. In Figure 12.8, however, the demand curve for the high-volume user is much greater than the demand curve for the low-volume user. In this case, profit maximization calls for a different strategy. In Figure 12.8, the monopolist maximizes profit by charging a per-copy charge equal to marginal cost, that is, $p_1 = MC$, and a large

Figure 12.8 A Two-Part Tariff With Different Demands That Eliminates the Low-Volume User from the Market
The demand curve for the high-volume user, D_2, is much greater than the demand curve for the low-volume user, D_1. The monopolist maximizes profit by charging a per-copy charge equal to marginal cost p_1 and a large fixed fee equal to the sum of all the shaded areas $A + B + C + D$. The low-volume user chooses to do without the machine.

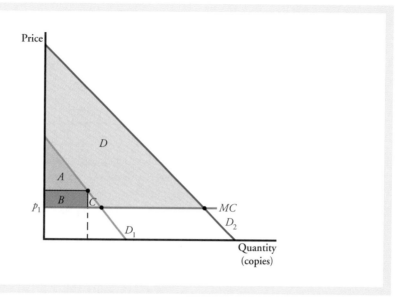

fixed fee equal to the sum of areas $A + B + C + D$. The high-volume user is willing to pay this large fixed fee, but the low-volume user chooses to do without the machine. The high fixed fee forces the low-volume user out of the market. If the potential consumer surplus that can be extracted from the high-volume user is much greater than the potential consumer surplus that can be extracted from the low-volume user, the profit-maximizing strategy for the monopolist is to charge a high fixed fee and eliminate the low-volume user from the market.

Bundling

Recall that bundling is a tying arrangement in which the goods are purchased in fixed proportions. One common example of bundling occurs in professional football, where NFL teams sell season tickets packages that include tickets to all eight regular season games plus two pre-season games in a 10-ticket package. The teams force fans to purchase tickets for the two pre-season games in order to be able to purchase season tickets for the regular season. For example, for the 2002 season, the Buffalo Bills sold their best seats to season ticket holders for all 10 games, including the pre-season games, for $360. The same seats were priced at $42 per game on an individual game basis. In theory, a fan could purchase eight regular season game tickets for $336 (8 × $42), but chances are that all of the good seats will be sold to season ticket holders.

To understand why the NFL teams have adopted this strategy, consider the Bills' ticket options. Table 12.3 shows the maximum price that two fans, Waldman and Kelly, are willing to pay for Bills season tickets. Waldman lives near Buffalo, but is a Philadelphia Eagles fan, and the Eagles are playing a pre-season game in Buffalo in 2002, so Waldman is willing to pay a relatively high price for pre-season tickets to see the Eagles. Waldman is willing to pay $280 for the regular season package and $100 for the pre-season package or $380 for the bundle. Kelly, on the other hand, cares little about the pre-season, but is willing to pay more than Waldman for the regular season package. He is willing to pay $60 for the pre-season games, but $300 for the regular season package, or $360 for all 10 bundled tickets. If the Bills could use first-degree discrimination,

Table 12.3 **Maximum Prices for Buffalo Bills Season Tickets for Waldman and Kelly with Negatively Correlated Demands**

| Fan | Maximum Price for Tickets | | |
	Regular Season Tickets	Pre-Season Tickets	Bundled Price
Waldman	$280	$100	$380
Kelly	$300	$60	$360

the team would love to charge each fan the maximum price they would be willing to pay for each package; the Bills' revenues would then be:

$$TR = \$280 + \$100 + \$300 + \$60 = \$740$$

The reality is that the Bills must charge the same ticket prices to all their fans. The team's options are either not to bundle and charge $280 for the regular season package and $60 for the pre-season package, or to bundle and charge $360 for all 10 tickets. Without bundling, the Bills' revenues equal:

$$TR = 2(\$280) + 2(\$60) = \$680$$

With bundling, the Bills' revenues equal:

$$TR = 2(\$360) = \$720$$

From this comparison, we see that the Bills are better off with bundling.

Why is bundling a form of price discrimination? With bundling, Waldman is effectively paying less for regular season tickets (he is actually paying only $260 for the regular season tickets, because he was willing to pay $100 for the pre-season tickets and $360 − $100 = $260) than Kelly, and Kelly is paying less ($60) for pre-season tickets than

---

▲▲▲ **12.2 APPLICATION** Changing Pricing Strategies at Disneyland and Disney World

When Disneyland opened in Anaheim, California, in 1955, the company used a two-part tariff that included both a fixed fee and a per-ride charge. After paying a fixed fee admission to enter the park, customers were required to purchase ticket books for the rides. When Disney World opened in Orlando, Florida, in 1971, Disney adopted the same pricing policy for the Magic Kingdom theme park.

By the mid-1970s, Disney decided to change its pricing strategy and began to charge a much higher fixed fee admission price, but no fee per ride. Disney eliminated the ticket books and replaced them with passports, which entitled the holder to one day of admission that included unlimited rides and attractions. Because the

marginal cost to Disney of putting one more customer on a ride is essentially zero, Disney moved from a policy like the one depicted in Figure 12.7, where the price per ride was greater than marginal cost and low-ride and high-ride volume consumers were encouraged to enter the parks by a relatively low fixed admission fee, to a policy like the one depicted in Figure 12.8, where the price per ride was set at $MC = 0$ and the fixed fee was set at a high level that prevented low-ride-volume consumers from entering the theme parks. Disney has maintained this pricing policy for over 25 years now, so it is reasonable to assume that high-ride-volume consumers have a much greater demand for rides than low-ride-volume consumers.

Waldman ($100). In this case, bundling works to increase profit because there is a difference in the *relative valuations* of the regular season tickets and the pre-season tickets for Waldman and Kelly. **Relative valuation** refers to how different consumers value different goods in relation to each other. In this case, even though both fans are willing to pay more for the eight regular season tickets, Kelly is willing to pay more for the regular season tickets than Waldman, while Waldman is willing to pay more for the pre-season tickets than Kelly. Therefore, there is a difference in the relative valuations of Waldman and Kelly for Bills tickets. In the case of different relative valuations, the demands are said to be negatively correlated, meaning that the consumer willing to pay the most for one good is willing to pay the least for the other good.

If the demands were positively correlated, one consumer would be willing to pay more for both goods, and bundling would not increase total revenues. Consider, for example, Table 12.4, which shows Kelly as willing to pay more for *both* regular season tickets and pre-season tickets. The bundled price is $380 and total revenue equals 2($380) = $760 with bundling. Without bundling, the Bills charge $280 for the regular season ticket package and $100 for the pre-season package and total revenues equal: 2($280) + 2($100) = $760. With positively correlated demands, total revenues are the same with individual pricing and bundling.

MIXED BUNDLING The example of Bills' season ticket pricing was an illustration of *pure bundling* because the team offered *only* season tickets that included both regular season and pre-season games. **Pure bundling** is a pricing policy where firms sell two goods only together. Waldman and Kelly had no other season ticket options available such as purchasing season tickets just for the regular season or just for the pre-season. A more common form of bundling exists when firms give consumers the choice of paying for products either separately or bundled together in packages, a practice known as **mixed bundling**. Perhaps the most common example of mixed bundling is at fast food restaurants, such as McDonald's, Taco Bell, or Subway. All American fast food restaurants offer an *à la carte* menu from which you can order just a sandwich or just fries, and they also offer a bundled combo meal such as a burger, fries, and a soft drink. Another example of mixed bundling is Microsoft's bundling of its software programs Word, Excel, PowerPoint, and Access, which it sells separately or as a bundle called Microsoft Office.

Table 12.5 considers the fast food example and identifies the maximum prices that Homer and Marge are willing to pay for a Big Mac double-patty hamburger and fries at McDonald's bought either separately or bundled. Notice that Homer and Marge have negatively correlated preferences; Marge is willing to pay more for a Big Mac than Homer and Homer is willing to pay more for fries than Marge. Suppose McDonald's can produce either a Big Mac or an order of fries for a marginal cost of $1.00. If McDonald's offers only single-item pricing, the profit-maximizing pricing policy calls for setting the price of a Big Mac at $3.25 and the price of fries at $1.50. Marge buys only a Big Mac and Homer buys only fries, and McDonald's earns a profit equal to $\pi = TR - TC = \$4.75 - \$2.00 = \$2.75$.

relative valuation

The way that different consumers value different goods in relation to each other: for example, if Smith and Jones are both willing to pay more for good *A* than good *B*, but Smith is willing to pay more than Jones for *A*, while Jones is willing to pay more than Smith for *B*, then Smith has a higher relative valuation of good *A* and Jones has a higher relative valuation of good *B*.

pure bundling

A pricing policy where firms will sell two goods only if they are sold together; that is, consumers cannot buy either good by itself.

mixed bundling

A pricing policy where firms give consumers a choice of paying for more than one good either separately or bundled.

Table 12.4 Maximum Prices for Buffalo Bills Season Tickets for Waldman and Kelly with Positively Correlated Demands

| Fan | Maximum Price for Tickets | | |
	Regular Season Tickets	Pre-Season Tickets	Bundled Price
Waldman	$280	$100	$380
Kelly	$300	$120	$420

Table 12.5 Maximum Prices for Big Macs and Fries for Homer and Marge

| | Maximum Price | | |
	Big Mac	Fries	Bundled Price
Homer	$2.00	$1.50	$3.50
Marge	$3.25	$0.25	$3.50

Because Homer and Marge have negatively correlated preferences, total profit can be increased with a bundling-only policy, under which McDonald's charges $3.50 for the bundle of a Big Mac and fries. Homer and Marge each buy the bundle and profit equals $\pi = TR - TC = \$7.00 - \$4.00 = \$3.00$. A bundling-only policy increases profit from $2.75 to $3.00.

Now consider the following mixed bundling policy. McDonald's offers a Big Mac for $3.20, an order of fries for $1.50, or the bundle of a Big Mac and fries for $3.50. Homer and Marge want to maximize their consumer surplus and accomplish this when Homer purchases the bundle for $3.50 (yielding a consumer surplus of $0.00) and Marge purchases only a Big Mac for $3.20 (yielding a consumer surplus of $0.05). McDonald's profit with mixed bundling equals $\pi = TR - TC = (\$3.50 + \$3.20) - \$3.00 = \$3.70$. Mixed bundling maximizes McDonald's profit at $3.70 compared to $3.00 with pure bundling and $2.75 with individual pricing only. Despite the fact that McDonald's sells more fries with a pure bundling policy, profit is higher with mixed bundling. Profit is lower with a pure bundling policy, because McDonald's is selling fries to Marge, who has a reservation price for fries of $0.25, which is below McDonald's marginal cost of $1.00 for producing fries. With a pure bundling policy, McDonald's earns $1.50 on its sale of the bundle to Homer and $1.50 on its sale of the bundle to Marge; but with mixed bundling, McDonald's earns $2.20 on its sale of one Big Mac to Marge and $1.50 on its sale of the bundle to Homer. Mixed bundling enables McDonald's to capture more of Homer's and Marge's total available consumer surplus, and therefore results in increased profit.

Depending on consumer tastes and the costs of production, any of the various pricing schemes, including single-item pricing only, pure bundling, or mixed bundling, can maximize profits. Because all of the major fast food chains have adopted a mixed bundling strategy, it is reasonable to conclude that in the fast food industry, a mixed bundling policy maximizes profits.

Requirements Tie-in Sales

Recall that requirements tie-in sales consist of a tying agreement in which the goods are purchased in variable proportions. In a typical requirements tie-in, a firm with market power over good X requires its buyers to purchase all of their requirements of a complementary good, good Y, in order to obtain good X. Requirements tie-ins are common in the world of franchising, where good X is the franchise trademark and good Y represents the ingredients and equipment used by the restaurant. To obtain a franchise, the franchisee pays a fixed franchise fee and agrees to purchase many, if not all, of its inputs from the franchisor. For example, obtaining a Taco Bell franchise in 2000 required a fixed franchise fee of $45,000 plus an agreement to purchase all of the franchise restaurant's major ingredients from Taco Bell. Because Taco Bell charges its franchisees a price for ingredients above average cost, Taco Bell earns a profit on every unit of franchised sales. Furthermore, larger-volume Taco Bell franchise restaurants purchase more ground beef, shredded chicken, and taco shells, and therefore pay Taco Bell more profit than smaller-

---

COMMON ERROR 12.2 | **Believing That With a Single–Item Pricing Policy Selling the Largest Total Number of Goods Always Maximizes Profit**

Students sometimes incorrectly conclude that the best single-item pricing policy is the one that maximizes the number of units sold. This is incorrect! Be careful not to conclude that McDonald's should set its single-unit pricing policy to sell the largest number of Big Macs and fries possible. For example, if McDonald's charges a price of $2.00 for a Big Mac and $0.25 for fries, Homer and Marge both buy Big Macs and fries, but profit is $\pi = TR - TC = \$4.50 - \$4.00 = \$0.50$.

Two other single-item pricing policies result in the sale of more units but lower profit than the profit-maximizing single-item pricing policy of $3.25 for a Big Mac and $1.50 for fries. For example, if McDonald's charges a price of $2.00 for a Big Mac and $1.50 for fries, Homer and Marge both buy Big

Macs, but only Homer buys fries, and profit is $\pi = TR - TC = \$5.50 - \$3.00 = \$2.50$. Finally, if McDonald's charges a price of $3.25 for a Big Mac and $0.25 for fries, Homer and Marge both buy fries, but only Marge buys a Big Mac, and profit is $\pi = TR - TC = \$3.75 - \$3.00 = \$0.75$.

All of these alternative single-item pricing policies yield more unit sales but lower profit than the profit-maximizing policy of charging $3.25 for a Big Mac and $1.50 for fries—in which case Marge buys only a Big Mac, Homer buys only fries, and McDonald's earns a profit equal to $\pi = TR - TC = \$4.75 - \$2.00 = \$2.75$. Don't make the common error of assuming that a larger volume of sales always increases profit.

---

volume franchises. In order to obtain the monopolized good, the Taco Bell trademark, the franchisees must pay above-average prices for many non-monopolized goods such as ground beef, taco shells, and guacamole.

Franchise agreements act as an effective form of price discrimination, because each franchisee pays Taco Bell a different amount for their franchise depending on their volume of sales. In this case, high-volume franchisees pay more for their Taco Bell trademark than low-volume franchisees.

▼▼▼ 12.3 Dealing with the Problems of Monopoly Power

We learned in Chapter 11 that market power can lead to Pareto inefficiency, because price is greater than marginal cost; it can also lead to X inefficiencies that result in wasted resources. Because of the potential problems associated with monopoly, federal and state governments have attempted to limit the negative effects of market power through legislation. In the United States, these attempts have been centered primarily on two broad policies: antitrust and direct regulation.

Antitrust Policy in the United States

Monopoly first became an important political issue in the United States during the last quarter of the nineteenth century. After the Civil War, the face of American industry changed dramatically. The rapid growth of national markets developed as a result of a combination of mass production, a national railroad system, the development of modern capital markets that enabled firms to raise large amounts of capital, and the liberalization of the laws of incorporation in many states. The larger national firms, which took advantage of economies of scale, were often able to invade local markets that were formerly insulated from competition and to charge significantly lower prices. As the national producers captured a larger and larger share of many local markets, they threatened to eliminate

Sherman Act

The first federal antitrust law passed in 1890; it made price fixing and monopolization illegal.

many local producers. As a result of this growing monopoly power, on July 2, 1890, President Harrison signed the **Sherman Act** into law. The major provisions of the Sherman Act were Sections 1 and 2, which read in part:

- **Section 1**: Every contract, combination in the form of a trust or otherwise, or conspiracy, in restraint of trade or commerce among the several states, or with foreign nations, is hereby declared to be illegal.
- **Section 2**: Every person who shall monopolize, or attempt to monopolize, or combine or conspire with any other person or persons to monopolize any part of the trade or commerce among the several States, or with foreign nations, shall be deemed guilty of a misdemeanor.

In 1914, President Wilson signed two other important pieces of antitrust legislation: the **Clayton Act** and the **Federal Trade Commission (FTC) Act**. The Clayton Act was aimed at preventing certain types of specific anticompetitive behavior, including price discrimination, tie-in sales, and anticompetitive mergers. The FTC Act created an independent, non-political agency to enforce the Clayton Act and prevent "unfair methods of competition." Subsequent antitrust legislation has amended these three laws to make it easier for the courts to interpret Congress's intent.

Clayton Act

An antitrust law passed in 1914 that outlawed certain specific types of firm behavior.

Federal Trade Commission (FTC) Act

A law, passed in 1914, establishing the Federal Trade Commission as an independent government agency to control business behavior.

The objective of the antitrust laws is to limit the negative economic consequences of monopoly power. Although monopoly power is often associated with inefficiencies, monopoly may be economically justified if it is based on economies of scale or necessary for invention and innovation. Policymakers therefore face the difficult task of trying to distinguish cases of justified monopoly power from cases of unjustified monopoly power. Enforcement has ebbed and flowed with political trends. Next, we explore briefly a few of the major precedent-setting cases.

MONOPOLIZATION CASES   The *Standard Oil* case[2] of 1911 is unquestionably one of America's most famous legal cases. Standard Oil managed to maintain a 90 percent share of the oil market for a long period by acquiring over 100 competitors through mergers and by controlling the major oil pipelines, acquisitions that permitted it to cut off crude oil supplies from its competitors. Standard Oil also obtained freight rebates from railroads on not only its own shipments, but its *competitors'* shipments as well. Using localized price discrimination, Standard Oil managed to drive its more stubborn competitors out of the market.

Rule of Reason

An important legal precedent establishing that only unreasonable attempts to monopolize violate the Sherman Act.

In October 1911, the Supreme Court ruled unanimously that Standard Oil had violated the Sherman Act and the court dismantled the firm. In his landmark decision, Chief Justice White laid down his famous **Rule of Reason** doctrine, which declared that only *unreasonable* attempts to monopolize violated Section 2. Justice White emphasized Standard's intent and positive drive as being the key elements necessary to any conviction under Section 2. The decision firmly established the precedent that market power, in and of itself, is insufficient to condemn a firm under the Sherman Act. Power must be combined with some effort to obtain and abuse that power. Standard Oil violated Section 2 not simply because it controlled 90 percent of the market, but because it went beyond the use of "normal methods of industrial development" to maintain control.

The next major monopoly precedent was set in the 1945 *Aluminum Company of America* (Alcoa) case. In the *Alcoa* case, there was little evidence of aggressive practices such as existed in the *Standard Oil* case. In fact, Alcoa's market power originated from a cost advantage associated with patents rather than aggressive behavior towards its competitors. Judge Learned Hand of the New York Circuit Court of Appeals ruled that once

---

[2] *United States v. Standard Oil Co. of New Jersey, et.al.* 221 U.S. 1 (1911).

the government had proven that Alcoa had a monopoly, that was sufficient grounds for Sherman Act action unless Alcoa could prove that the monopoly was "thrust upon it." Hand went on to state that, "unchallenged economic power deadens initiative, discourages thrift and depresses energy; that immunity from competition is a narcotic, and rivalry is a stimulant, to industrial progress; that the spur of constant stress is necessary to counteract an inevitable disposition to let well enough alone."[3] The *Alcoa* decision set a new precedent: A monopolist with an overwhelming market share violated Section 2 unless market power was virtually unavoidable.

The Justice Department filed major suits against International Business Machines (IBM) in 1969, and American Telephone and Telegraph (AT&T) in 1974; however, during the 1970s and 1980s, a series of court decisions generally favoring fairly aggressive actions by dominant firms seemed to put an end to the *Alcoa* precedent. On January 8, 1982, the Justice Department simultaneously announced that it was dismissing its case against IBM and settling its case against AT&T out of court. The AT&T settlement resulted in the break-up of the then-largest private corporation in the world. In 1981, AT&T had assets exceeding $130 billion, and a market share of 83 percent of all telephones in the United States. AT&T owned 22 local distribution telephone companies, Bell Long Lines Division, Western Electric (the equipment manufacturing company), and Bell Labs. AT&T's control of the telecommunications industry was built on a combination of government regulation and aggressive practices. Under the settlement, AT&T was permitted to keep Western Electric, Long Lines, and Bell Labs (later changed to Lucent Technologies), but agreed to divest its 22 local operating companies. When the decree was carried out, it resulted in the largest divestiture in antitrust history—over $87 billion in assets.

The most recent important Sherman Act case is *Microsoft*. On May 18, 1998, the Justice Department filed an antitrust action charging Microsoft with attempting to monopolize the market for PC computer operating systems. The trial received a tremendous amount of national attention. Among the more compelling evidence against Microsoft was a series of 150 e-mails provided by Microsoft's competitor Netscape, showing how Microsoft attempted to force Internet users to use Microsoft's Internet Explorer instead of Netscape's Navigator.[4] In June 2000, District Court Judge Thomas Penfield Jackson ruled that Microsoft was a monopolist in the market for Intel-compatible PC operating systems and should be broken up into two companies. Upon appeal, in August 2001, the Circuit Court of Appeals for the District of Columbia affirmed Jackson's ruling that Microsoft had illegally monopolized the PC operating system market, but overturned his ruling that the company should be broken up. In a highly unusual decision, the Appeals Court disqualified Judge Jackson from any further consideration of the case, because he had violated ethical guidelines by making public comments about the case while the appeal was pending. The Appeals Court then sent the case back to a new District Court Judge, Colleen Kollar-Kotelly, to consider appropriate remedies against Microsoft. In November 2002, the DOJ reached a final settlement agreement with Microsoft. The settlement limits Microsoft from practicing price discrimination and using tie-in sales agreements, including a prohibition on tying Microsoft's Internet Explorer to Windows. It also requires Microsoft to disclose more information to competitive software developers, and forbids it from retaliating against any firm that refuses to abide by Microsoft's demands.

---

[3] *United States v. Aluminum Company of America, et.al.* 148 F. 2nd 416(1945).

[4] "U.S. Releases E-Mail to Back Up Testimony," *Washington Post*, October 24, 1998, p. D4.

Regulation

Antitrust policy was established to set acceptable rules of competitive behavior and to level the playing field between competitors. However, sometimes it is impossible to establish viable competition in a market because of the existence of large economies of scale. In such cases, the government sometimes relies on direct price regulation of an industry to limit monopoly power.

natural monopoly

A market where it is most efficient for one firm to supply the entire output in that market.

THE RATIONALE FOR DIRECT PRICE REGULATION The United States first adopted a policy of direct price regulation in the late 1800s, in large part because the railroads in the western United States were *natural monopolies*. A **natural monopoly** is a market where because of large economies of scale, one firm can serve the market more efficiently than multiple firms. Figure 12.9 depicts a natural monopoly. The $LRAC$ curve in Figure 12.9 is sloping downward where it intersects the demand curve at an output of q_1. Because the $LRAC$ curve is sloping downward at q_1, $LRMC$ must lie *below* $LRAC$ for q_1. Pareto efficiency requires that output be expanded as long as price is above $LRMC$, or in Figure 12.9 until output equals q_2. If a private firm were forced to expand output to q_2 and charge price p_2, price would be below $LRAC$ and the firm would sustain an economic loss equal to the red area c_2ABp_2. This is not a viable pricing option for a private profit-maximizing firm, because no firm would charge a price that would guarantee an economic loss. If the government tried to force such an outcome, nobody would enter the industry.

Alternatively, the government could stay out of the market altogether and permit a profit-maximizing firm to set the price. If a firm were free to maximize profit, the firm would produce the output q_m, where $MR = LRMC$, and charge the profit-maximizing price p_m. The firm would earn a large positive economic profit equal to the shaded green area p_mCDc_m. If entry were possible, this large economic profit would attract entry and price would decline. However, given the cost structure in Figure 12.9, entry would be virtually impossible, because the natural monopolist could quickly expand output beyond q_m if threatened with entry. For example, to drive a new entrant out of the market, the

Figure 12.9 Natural Monopoly as a Justification for Regulation

If the monopolist charges the socially efficient price p_2, the firm sustains an economic loss equal to the red area c_2ABp_2. If the monopolist charges the profit-maximizing price p_m, it earns an excess economic profit equal to the green area p_mCDc_m. The regulated price, p_r, is a compromise between these two extremes.

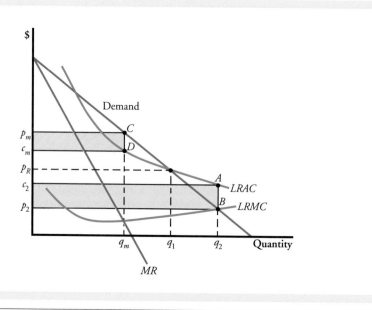

natural monopolist could expand output beyond q_1 and produce at an economic loss until the new firm decided to leave the industry. Because potential new entrants realize that the natural monopolist could drive them out of the market if they enter, they stay out of the market and the natural monopolist maintains its monopoly power. With no threat of entry, the natural monopolist could earn positive economic profit for a long time. In fact, unless there is some fundamental change in the cost structure or demand of the industry, they could maintain this profit indefinitely.

Direct price regulation attempts to find a compromise solution to this problem. Under direct price regulation, regulators attempt to set the price at p_R, where $p = LRAC$, or where the demand curve intersects the long-run average cost curve. With price equal to p_R, price equals average cost, so economic profit is zero. Investors can cover their opportunity costs of investing in the industry, so they will enter. Furthermore, while output is less than the socially optimal output q_2, it is considerably greater than the profit-maximizing output of q_m. The price p_R is known as a *Ramsey price*. The **Ramsey price** is the unit price that maximizes total social benefits subject to the requirement that profit cannot be negative. From a welfare perspective, p_R is significantly better than the profit-maximizing price, because it brings us closer to the socially optimal output q_2, but it is still significantly worse for welfare than actually reaching this optimal output.

Ramsey price

A price that maximizes total social benefits in a market subject to the constraint that profits cannot be negative.

Potential Problems Associated with Regulation

In theory, the regulated price appears to be a reasonable and workable economic and political compromise. In practice, however, there are serious problems associated with such a compromise price. Federal and state public utility commissions are charged with the complex task of regulating natural monopolies. The commissions have to simultaneously set the permitted rate of profit and the price structure. The objective is to make sure that investors earn a normal economic profit, one that is high enough to attract investment but low enough that prices will be fair to consumers. This type of regulation is called **rate-of-return regulation**.

rate-of-return regulation

A regulatory pricing policy that attempts to set the price of a regulated good at a level that results in zero or normal economic profit.

rate base

The total value of invested capital in the regulated portion of a company.

The commission sets the permitted rate of return by using the following formula:

$$r = \frac{TR - TC}{K} \tag{12.1}$$

where r represents the rate of return on invested capital, TR represents total revenue, TC represents total costs, and K represents the value of the firm's invested capital or the **rate base**. If r turns out to be less than the commission's target, investors might stay away from the utility's stocks and bonds, and capacity might lag behind demand requirements. Insufficient capacity could cause a regulator's worst nightmare—service interruptions, like those in California in the year 2001. On the other hand, if r turns out to be too high, output will be restricted below a more socially optimal level, and high profit might cause a public outcry against both the commission and the utility.

In addition to the problem of finding the correct rate of return, r, regulation can cause serious productive efficiency problems. With r guaranteed, there is little incentive for the utility to minimize costs, and this can encourage X inefficiency. In Equation 12.1, if X inefficiencies develop, TC increases, and r decreases below the permitted level set by the commission. The utility will then complain that the rate of return is too low and ask for the commission to permit an increase in price to raise total revenue. Although it is possible for a commission to deny a price hike if it determines that X inefficiencies exist, until fairly recently, most price increase requests were approved.

▲▲▲ 12.3 APPLICATION   The California Electricity Crisis

The California experience in 2001 provides an example of what can go wrong when regulation and deregulation policies are carried out improperly. In the spring of 2001, rolling electrical blackouts peppered the state of California, because the major state utilities were unable to meet the demand for electricity. In April 2001, the nation's largest electric utility, Pacific Gas & Electric, declared Chapter 11 bankruptcy in order to receive protection from its creditors. This led to a political as well as an economic crisis in California, with electricity shortages causing havoc for the states' citizens and businesses alike.

When California restructured, or deregulated its electricity industry in the mid-1990s, it made several critical errors. First, it encouraged its utilities to divest their generation facilities. This meant that most of the power plants that were owned by the utilities were sold to independent companies, many of which were from outside California. Consequently, the utilities became almost totally dependent on their distribution of electricity for their earnings. Second, the California Public Utility Commission (CPUC) prevented the utilities from entering into long-term supply contracts with electricity-generating companies. The result was that in periods of high demand, the California utilities were forced to purchase electricity at current high prices from distant suppliers in surrounding states, the entire northwestern United States, and western Canada. Third, the CPUC froze retail electricity prices, and therefore, the utilities could not pass their higher costs on to their consumers.

Initially, the CPUC froze prices at levels that covered average costs, so the utilities were able to make a normal profit in 1997–1999. Then demand increased and the marginal cost of purchasing electricity increased tremendously. As a result, the utilities' average costs soared above their permitted prices and they began sustaining economic and accounting losses. The only short-run solution in this situation was to raise prices in order to encourage conservation and cover average costs. The long-run solution, however, is to build more generation facilities in California and to grant permission for long-term supply contracts with electricity-generating companies.

In Equation 12.1, if the rate base K increases, then TC increases, r decreases, and once again the utility can request a price increase to raise r back up to the permitted level. Notice that if K increases, the utility has to earn a larger profit ($TR - TC$) to increase r back to permitted levels. The utility, therefore, has a strong incentive to try to raise its rate base K. Because only capital investments count as part of the rate base, the way to raise K is to increase the amount of capital the firm uses relative to other inputs. This distorts the firm's choice of inputs. For example, the firm might use too much capital and too little labor to produce any given output.

These potential problems are quite serious, and in recent years have persuaded many economists that the gains from direct price regulation are limited. This helps to explain why there has been a recent trend away from direct price regulation. This trend has been greatly accelerated by the development of new technologies that have reduced the incidence of natural monopoly in the modern economy. For example, before the widespread use of wireless telecommunications, your local telephone company was a natural monopolist. Today the local phone company can be replaced by any one of a number of wireless telecommunications providers. As a result of changing technology, the number of justified areas for direct price regulation has decreased dramatically. Deregulation has taken place in all of the regulated industries including transportation, telecommunications and broadcasting, natural gas, and even electricity.

Summary

1. Firms with market power often use various types of price discrimination to increase profits. In first-degree discrimination, each consumer pays his/her reservation price for each unit of the good, and therefore there is no consumer surplus. With second-degree discrimination, all consumers are offered the same price schedule and consumers self-select into different categories. With third-degree discrimination, firms separate consumers out into different groups according to their elasticities of demand, and groups with more inelastic demands pay higher prices.

2. Two-part tariffs, bundling, and tying are each different forms of second-degree price discrimination. A two-part tariff consists of a lump sum payment for a good combined with a per-unit charge. Bundling is a form of tie-in sales agreement in which the two goods are purchased in fixed proportions. Tie-in sales agreements require consumers to purchase one good in order to be permitted to purchase another good. If consumers have identical demands, the profit-maximizing two-part tariff requires the firm to charge a per-unit fee equal to marginal cost and a lump sum payment that eliminates all consumer surplus. With different demands, the optimal per-unit charge is often greater than marginal cost. Bundling makes economic sense for the monopolist only if consumers have negatively correlated demands for the different goods.

3. The United States government controls monopoly power by using antitrust policy and direct price regulation. An antitrust violation requires both the existence of monopoly in a clearly defined market and abusive conduct in that market. Direct price regulation is most common in cases of natural monopoly in which economies of scale are very significant, and therefore, it is more efficient to permit only one firm to supply the good.

Self-Test Problems

1. Suppose adults have the following demand curve for a local community theater: $P_a = 30 - (1/5)q_a$. Children have the demand: $P_c = 10 - (1/10)q_c$. Furthermore, $MC = AC = 2$.

   a. Solve for the price charged and number of tickets sold in each separate market. Draw a graph.

   b. Solve for total consumer surplus, total producer surplus, and monopoly profit. Label these areas on your graph from question 1(a).

   c. Now assume that the theater wants to charge a single, uniform price in both markets. Solve for the combined demand curve (remember: it will have a kink).

   d. Calculate the uniform price charged and the total number of tickets sold. Draw a graph of the combined demand, and show the uniform price charged and total amount sold on the graph.

   e. Solve for consumer surplus, producer surplus, and monopoly profit with a uniform price. Label these areas on your graph from question 1(d).

   f. Compare profits in question 1(b) to that in question 1(e). Which pricing method does the producer prefer?

   g. Prove that, in this case, third-degree price discrimination decreases total welfare.

2. Consider a golf course where each golfer has an identical annual demand function: $P = 200 - 4Q$, where P is price per round and Q is rounds per year. Furthermore, $MC = AC = 8$. Assume for simplicity that $FC = 0$.

a. What is the profit-maximizing single price and output the course should charge each golfer? Calculate profit per golfer.

b. Show that the monopolist can make more profit using a two-part tariff with $P = MC$. Solve for the fixed fee and profit per golfer.

c. Show that even a $1 increase in price (per round to $9) would cause profit per golfer to fall from those in question 2(b).

3. Consider a monopolist facing two consumers with the following two demand curves for its product: $P_1 = 200 - 4Q_1$ and $P_2 = 122 - 6Q_2$. Assume $FC = 0$ and $MC = 8$.

a. The monopolist decides to use a two-part tariff that permits both consumers to stay in the market. Assume they price at marginal cost. Solve for each consumer's output and fixed fee under this scenario. What is the monopolist's profit?

b. Show that the monopolist is better off eliminating the low-volume consumer from the market. Solve for the output, the fixed fee, and the monopolist's profit, if the low-volume consumer is eliminated.

Questions and Problems for Review

1. Consider a monopolist with the demand curve: $P = 120 - Q$. The monopolist's marginal cost (MC) is constant and equal to $4.

   a. Solve for the non-discriminating monopolist's price and quantity.

   b. Now assume that the monopolist practices first-degree price discrimination. What is the total number of goods sold under this pricing policy? What is the lowest price charged for the good?

   c. Figure 12.1 assumes a discrete number of units of the good to show consumer surplus and producer surplus (thus, consumer surplus is a collection of the areas of a number of rectangles rather than the area of one big triangle). Instead, assuming a continuous demand curve (similar to the analysis in Figure 4.7(b)), calculate total welfare under the two pricing schemes calculated in questions 1(a) and 1(b). In which pricing policy is total welfare higher?

   d. Is consumer surplus higher using the pricing method in which total welfare is higher or lower? Explain.

2. Consider a monopolist with the demand curve $P = 200 - 2Q$. The monopolist's marginal cost (MC) is equal to 2.

   a. Solve for the non-discriminating monopolist's price and quantity.

   b. Now assume that the monopolist practices first-degree price discrimination. What is the total number of goods sold under this pricing policy? What is the lowest price charged for the good?

   c. Figure 12.1 assumes a discrete number of units of the good to show consumer surplus and producer surplus (thus, consumer surplus is a collection of rectangles rather than one big triangle). Instead, assuming a continuous demand curve (similar to the analysis in Figure 4.7(b)), calculate total welfare under the two pricing schemes calculated in questions 2(a) and 2(b). In which pricing policy is total welfare higher?

   d. Is consumer surplus higher using the pricing method in which total welfare is higher or lower? Explain.

3. Consider a pizza shop with the following pricing schemes: Buy the first sheet pizza for $20, the second for $15, the third for $10, and the fourth for $5. Let's assume that on a given day, 100 consumers buy the first pizza, 60 buy the second pizza, 30 buy the third pizza, and 10 buy the fourth pizza. $MC = $5.

   a. Draw the daily demand for sheet pizzas at the pizza shop.

   b. Calculate total revenue for the pizza shop.

   c. Calculate producer surplus. In your graph from question 3(a), label both consumer surplus and producer surplus carefully.

4. Adults have the following demand curve for Broadway show tickets: $P_a = 200 - q_a$ and children have the demand: $P_c = 100 - (1/2)q_c$. $MC = AC = 20$.

   a. Solve for the price charged and number of tickets sold in each market with third-degree price discrimination.

b. Solve for the elasticity of demand for adults and children at their respective equilibrium points with third-degree price discrimination. In which market is demand more elastic at the equilibrium price/quantity combination?

c. Solve for total consumer surplus, total producer surplus, and monopoly profit with third-degree price discrimination.

5. Consider the same demand functions as those in question 4. Assume that the Broadway theaters want to charge a single uniform price in both markets.

a. Solve for the combined demand curve (remember that it will have a kink).

b. Calculate the uniform price charged and the total number of tickets sold. Draw a graph of the combined demand and show the uniform price charged and total number of tickets sold.

c. Solve for consumer surplus, producer surplus, and monopoly profit. Label these areas on your graph from question 5(b).

d. Compare monopoly profit with price discrimination from question 4 with profit in question 5(c). Which pricing method will the theaters prefer?

e. Does price discrimination increase or decrease total welfare?

6. For each of the following scenarios, identify which type of second degree price discrimination is described (two-part tariff, bundling, or a requirement tie-in sale).

a. A national copier producer requires that any business buying a copier must also buy their brand of paper to use in the copier.

b. My brother rents an apartment in New York City. His lease requires him to also rent one parking space for an additional fee per month.

c. The local YWCA has a yearly membership fee. There is an additional fee for each exercise class a member attends.

7. The Cold Trucking Company is a monopolist and rents its fleet of refrigerated trucks to food distributors. Each food distributor has the same demand on a yearly basis: $P = 605 - 5Q$ where P is the daily rental rate and Q is the number of rental days. The MC of a days' rental is $5. The fixed cost ($FC$) of a truck per year equals $30,000.

a. Assume that Cold Trucking uses a two-part tariff and decides to maximize the fixed fee by charging a price equal to marginal cost. Solve for each

food distributor's output, price, and fixed fee in this case. What is the monopolist's profit?

b. Show that even a $1 increase in price will decrease Cold Trucking's profit.

8. Comment on this statement: Third-degree price discrimination always decreases welfare.

9. For each of the following scenarios, identify which type of price discrimination is described (first-degree, second-degree, or third-degree).

a. Although illegal, a local car dealership researches the income, number of children, and debt load of each consumer before negotiating on price. They then offer a price for the car based on each consumer's characteristics.

b. A local retail store has a "buy one, get the second one at half price" deal on all remaining seasonal clothing items.

c. A phone company charges different rates based on the time of day the phone call is placed (lower prices in the evening and on weekends than during the weekday).

10. A local department store offers 10 percent discounts on Tuesdays for all senior citizens for any purchase they make. As an economist, you are perplexed by this policy, because you do not believe their method of price discrimination is effective (increases the store's profit). You recommend that they stop the price discrimination policy. Explain why.

11. Consider a monopolist facing the following two demand curves for its product:

$$P_1 = 200 - q_1$$
$$P_2 = 171 - 0.95q_2$$

For simplicity's sake, assume the fixed cost (FC) is equal to 0 and MC is equal to 4.

a. The monopolist decides to price using two-part tariff. Assume that price equals marginal cost. Solve for output in each market (round q_2 to two decimal places), the fixed fee, and monopoly profit under this scenario.

b. Now consider an increase in the per-unit price from $4 to $5. Calculate the total output sold in each market under this scenario and the fixed fee charged. What is monopoly profit?

c. Does pricing at $MC = 4$ and maximizing the fixed fee maximize profit? Explain using your numbers from questions 11(a) and 11(b).

12. Consider a monopolist facing the following two consumer demand curves for its product:

$$P_1 = 200 - Q_1$$
$$P_2 = 120 - 2Q_2$$

Assume FC is equal to 0 and MC is equal to 4.

a. If the monopolist uses a two-part tariff that permits both types of consumers to remain in the market, solve for output, the fixed fee, and monopoly profit.

b. Now show that the monopolist is better off eliminating the low-volume consumer. Solve for the output, fixed fee, and monopoly profit, if the low-volume consumer is eliminated.

13. Nathaniel and Jonathan both love baseball. The minor league team in their town is almost guaranteed to make it to the playoffs. Thus, the following table represents the maximum prices that Nathaniel and Jonathan will pay for regular season tickets and playoff tickets.

| | Maximum Price | | |
	Regular Season	Playoffs	Bundled Price
Nathaniel	$240	$60	$300
Jonathan	$300	$40	$340

a. Compare total revenue for the baseball team under a separate pricing policy and a pure bundled price.

b. Which pricing scheme should the team pick?

c. In what way does your result depend on the way the two demands are correlated? How are Nathaniel and Jonathan's demand curves correlated? Explain.

14. Consider a situation similar to question 13, but this time, Nathaniel and Jonathan's maximum prices look like this:

| | Maximum Price | | |
	Regular Season	Playoffs	Bundled Price
Nathaniel	$200	$40	$240
Jonathan	$240	$48	$288

a. Compare total revenue for the baseball team under a separate pricing policy and a pure bundled price.

b. Which pricing scheme should the team pick? Explain how your answer is a result of the correlation of the demand curves. How are Nathaniel and Jonathan's demand curves correlated in this example? Explain.

15. Consider a local fast food restaurant. The following table shows the maximum price that Alex and Anna will pay for two products: chicken nuggets and fries.

| | Maximum Price | | |
	Chicken Nuggets	Fries	Bundled Price
Alex	$1.50	$1.50	$3
Anna	$2.55	$0.45	$3

Assume that the marginal cost of chicken nuggets is $1 and the marginal cost of fries is $0.50.

a. Are Alex and Anna's demands negatively or positively correlated? Explain.

b. Compare all four possible single-item pricing policies to find the profit-maximizing single-item pricing policy.

c. Solve for profit if the restaurant engages in pure bundling.

d. Assume the restaurant engages in mixed bundling and charges $3 for a bundle, $2.52 for chicken nuggets, and $1.50 for fries. Show that the profit obtained under mixed bundling will be higher than that under pure bundling or single-item pricing.

16. Consider a local fast food restaurant. The following table shows the maximum price that Alex and Anna will pay for two products, chicken nuggets and fries. Assume that the marginal cost of chicken nuggets is $1 and the marginal cost of fries is $0.50.

| | Maximum Price | | |
	Chicken nuggets	Fries	Bundled price
Alex	$1.50	$2	$3.50
Anna	$2.50	$1	$3.50

a. Compare all four possible single-item pricing policies to find the profit-maximizing policy.

b. Solve for profit if the restaurant engages in pure bundling.

c. Assume that the restaurant engages in mixed bundling and changes $3.50 for a bundle, $2.45 for chicken nuggets, and $2 for fries. Show that the profit obtained under mixed bundling is not higher than that under pure bundling.

d. Explain why mixed bundling does not yield higher profit in this case.

17. Consider a natural monopolist with the following total cost function: $LRTC = 0.1Q^3 - 10Q^2 + 275Q$. This implies that the $LRMC = 0.3Q^2 - 20Q + 275$ and $LRAC = 0.1Q^2 - 10Q + 275$. The product demand is: $P = 500 - 10Q$. Given these conditions, the demand curve cuts the $LRAC$ curve at a point where the $LRAC$ curve is downward-sloping. Without drawing a graph, use algebra to answer the following questions.

a. Solve for the profit-maximizing unregulated single-price monopolist price and output. What is profit?

b. Now assume this monopolist is regulated. Solve for the output that the monopolist would charge if Ramsey pricing were enforced. What is the price? What is profit to the monopolist?

c. Calculate the increase in consumer surplus that results from regulation.

18. In your opinion, which ruling, Judge Jackson's or Judge Kollar-Kotelly's, made more *economic* sense in the Microsoft case? Explain the potential advantages and disadvantages of both rulings.

19. Explain what we mean by "X inefficiencies." In what way does direct price regulation help to cause X inefficiencies? What other problems are there with price regulation?

20. Consider the following questions regarding natural monopoly:

a. Explain "natural monopoly" in terms of the relationship between cost curves and the demand curve. Draw a graph depicting this situation.

b. If a natural monopolist is unregulated, what price and output will result? Label these points on your graph from question 20(a).

c. Label the allocatively efficient output for the natural monopolist. What problem would result if the government forced the natural monopolist to charge this price?

d. Label the price the government would most likely try to set in this regulated market.

e. How might the use of second-degree price discrimination help solve the allocative inefficiency problem associated with a regulated monopolist?

 Internet Exercises

Visit *http://www.myeconlab.com/waldman* for this chapter's Web exercises. Answer real-world economics problems by doing research on the Internet.

Chapter 13
An Introduction to Game Theory

In the television show "Malcolm in the Middle", Malcolm is an academically gifted student living with, to say the least, a non-gifted family. Despite his objections, Malcolm is placed in a class of academically gifted students known as the Krelboyne class, which is named after the social misfit Seymour Krelboyne from the1960 cult hit movie *The Little Shop of Horrors*. In one episode, a new teacher, Mr. Herkabe, arrives to teach the Krelboyne class and establishes a ranking system that pits the students against each other in a Darwinian survival of the fittest academic competition. The competition forces them to work around the clock to keep up their class standing, and drives the entire class to the brink of insanity. Malcolm comes up with a plan to thwart Mr. Herkabe: The entire class agrees to stop working and to start failing their exams. Malcolm reasons that if they all fail together, they will all have the same class rank. Malcolm's conspiratorial plan makes complete sense. When the day to carry out the conspiracy arrives, Malcolm dutifully fails his exam. However, when the exams are returned, Mr. Herkabe goes around the class congratulating all of the other students for their excellent grades and then stops in front of Malcolm to purposefully embarrass him by stating that Malcolm received an F. Even Malcolm's best friend, Stevie, defected! Malcolm is humiliated and his class rank drops to dead last. Malcolm might be gifted, but as we will learn shortly, he had no sense of a classic application of game theory, the Prisoner's Dilemma. All of the other students behaved rationally and defected from the agreement leaving Malcolm out to dry by himself. What Malcolm failed to understand, but the rest of the class did, was that no matter how many other students failed, it would be in his interest to do well.

In the Krelboyne class's academic competition, each student knew that his/her performance had a direct impact on each of the other students' class rank. This is far different from the competition that takes place in a perfectly competitive market, in which no one firm's actions have any impact on any

Learning Objectives

After reading Chapter 13, you will have learned:

➤ How economists use game theory to analyze the actions of economic agents, and why a Nash equilibrium is one of the most important concepts in game theory.

➤ How to identify and use the information structure of a game.

➤ The Prisoner's Dilemma game and its relationship to price fixing and collusion.

➤ The difference between simultaneous move and sequential move games.

➤ How to identify a game with a mixed-strategy equilibrium, and how to solve for that equilibrium in a simple mixed-strategy game.

Featured Applications

> 13.1 Application Lester Thurow's Zero-Sum Society and the Nature of Political Decisions

> 13.2 Application Did the Giants Steal the Pennant in 1951?

> 13.3 Application Low-Price Guarantees at Office Depot, Staples, and OfficeMax

> 13.4 Application NATO and How to "Win" the Game of Nuclear Deterrence

> 13.5 Application The Effect of Drug Testing in Baseball

other firm. It is also far different from monopoly, which in its pure form is even less prevalent than perfect competition. Structurally, most markets are neither perfectly competitive nor monopolistic, but somewhere in-between. These markets in which a relatively small number of interdependent firms control the market are *oligopolies*.

Because there are many different types of oligopoly market structures, for many years economists had a great deal of trouble developing models of oligopoly that could be generalized to more than a few markets. Over the past 20 years, however, a good deal more consensus has developed among economists who specialize in the study of oligopoly. The basis for much of this consensus is the application of *game theory* to models of oligopoly behavior.

▼▼▼ 13.1 What Is Game Theory?

game theory

The study of how interdependent economic agents make decisions fully aware of the fact that their actions affect each other.

Game theory is the study of how interdependent decision-makers make choices. The game's outcome depends on the game's assumptions, and economists have attempted to devise oligopoly games that come ever closer to approximating the real world. For more than 100 years, one point has been apparent to economists: Oligopolists recognize their interdependencies. For example, General Motors understands that its actions affect Ford, Daimler-Chrysler, Toyota, Nissan, and all other automobile manufacturers. When the number of competitors is relatively small, each firm realizes that any significant move on its part is likely to result in countering moves by its competitors. In this sense, oligopolistic competition can be viewed as a "game," where one move results in a counter-move by competitors. Most of the games presented in this chapter will be played by two firms. Duopolists are the two firms in an oligopoly market with only two firms. The implications of most of the results, however, are applicable even when the number of players is greater than two.

duopolists

The two firms in an oligopoly market with only two firms.

Game theory can provide insight into many types of decision-making besides oligopoly behavior. It can be used to analyze everything from political decisions, such as voting, to sports decisions, such as whether a baseball pitcher throws a fastball or a curve. In the last two decades, economists have used game theory to analyze a wide variety of economic agents' behaviors.

Some Important Game Theory Terms

players

The economic agents that make decisions in a game.

Before proceeding further, it is useful to define a number of important terms used by game theorists. All games must include *players*, *actions*, *information*, *strategies*, *payoffs*, *outcomes*, and an *equilibrium*. Together, the *players*, *actions*, and *outcomes* define the rules of the game. Understanding the following definitions will help you to learn the basics of game theory.

actions

All of the possible moves a player can make in a game.

information

How much each player knows at each point in a game.

strategies

A set of rules telling the players which actions to select at a given point in a game.

payoffs

The profit or utility the players expect to receive after taking actions in a game.

1. The **players** are the decision-makers. In most of our games, the players will be two or more oligopolists, or a monopolist and a potential entrant.
2. The **actions** include all possible moves a player can make.
3. **Information** is modeled by the game theorist, who defines how much each player knows at each point in the game.
4. **Strategies** are rules telling each player which action to choose at each point in the game.
5. **Payoffs** usually consist of the profit, expected profit, or utility the players receive after all of the players have picked strategies and the game has been played out.

outcomes

All of the possible results of the strategies that the players can select in a game; that is, the set of all possible game payoffs.

equilibrium

A strategy combination consisting of the best strategy for each player in a game.

zero-sum game

A game in which one player's gain is exactly matched by another player's loss.

6. The game's **outcomes** consist of all the possible results of the strategies that the players can select; that is, the set of all possible game payoffs.

7. An **equilibrium** is a strategy combination that consists of the best strategy for each player in the game.

Consider these definitions in the context of a game of chess. Chess has two players. The two players can take any action based on the permitted movements of the pieces. Before taking any action, both players have information about all of the previous moves. The strategies consist of each player's overall plan of attack to capture their opponent's king. The outcomes of the game consist of the winner capturing the loser's king or both players agreeing to a draw (tie). Finally, the game's equilibrium is the outcome that actually occurs: either the capture of a king or a draw. Notice that there are many possible outcomes in a game of chess, but only one equilibrium in a particular game.

Simple Zero–Sum Games and Nash Equilibrium[1]

We begin by analyzing one of the simplest types of games, called a *zero-sum game*. A **zero-sum game** is a game in which one player's gain is exactly matched by another player's loss. Consider the following game that was actually played by ice cream truck driver Don Waldman on July 4, 1968, and repeated on July 4, 1969. On those two holidays, I was driving a Good Humor ice cream truck in Willingboro, New Jersey, a suburb of Philadelphia, which held an annual Fourth of July parade. Unfortunately for me, Willingboro also had one other ice cream truck, Mr. Softee. The two drivers, Mr. Softee and myself, had to decide where to park during the parade. The parade route was about one-half mile long, and the trucks were free to park anywhere along the route. Parade watchers—potential ice cream customers—were equally spaced along the entire parade route. Where did the trucks locate?

Consider three possible locations: the beginning, middle, or end of the route. Table 13.1 presents the possible sales payoffs in matrix form for Good Humor and Mr. Softee. If both locate at the same point, assume that they divide total demand equally, so the trucks split sales 50-50. But what happens if one locates at the middle while the other locates at the beginning or end? Suppose, for example, that Mr. Softee locates at the middle and Good Humor locates at the end of the parade route. Because it is a shorter walk to the Mr. Softee truck for all consumers between the beginning and middle of the parade, Mr. Softee would gain 100 percent of the sales for consumers located between the middle and the beginning and divide the sales between the middle and the end 50-50, with the consumers walking to the closer truck. Therefore, overall, Mr. Softee would obtain 75 percent of the total available sales. Good Humor would obtain the remaining 25 percent, which would consist of the half of the consumers located between middle and end who were closer to the Good Humor truck. It follows that if one truck locates in the middle while the other locates at the beginning or end, the truck in the middle obtains 75 percent of total sales.

Table 13.1 shows all of the options. For example, in the upper-left corner entry, both trucks are located at the beginning of the parade route, and Good Humor and Mr. Softee each sell 50 percent of the ice cream sold as indicated by the entries in the green and blue triangles for Good Humor and Mr. Softee respectively. In the next cell down, Good Humor is located at the middle and Mr. Softee is located at the beginning. In this case, the entry in the green triangle shows that Good Humor receives 75 percent of sales compared to the

---

[1] For a good, simple treatment of zero-sum games, see J.D. Williams, *The Complete Strategist* (New York: McGraw-Hill, 1966).

Table 13.1 **A Simple Zero-Sum Game: Sales of Ice Cream (% Good Humor sales, % Mr. Softee sales)**

		Mr. Softee Location		
		Beginning	Middle	End
Good Humor Location	Beginning	50 \ 50	25 \ 75	50 \ 50
	Middle	75 \ 25	50 \ 50	75 \ 25
	End	50 \ 50	25 \ 75	50 \ 50

dominant strategy

A strategy that is always the best strategy, no matter what strategy choices are made by opponents.

entry in the blue triangle for Mr. Softee of only 25 percent. Each of the nine possible cells shows a possible outcome of the game given the location choices of the two trucks.

Both truck drivers knew all the information in Table 13.1. I solved the game by reasoning as follows: If Mr. Softee locates at the beginning of the parade, it is better for me to locate in the middle and gain 75 percent. If Mr. Softee locates in the middle, it is still better for me to locate in the middle and gain a 50-50 split. Finally, if Mr. Softee locates at the end of the parade, I should still locate in the middle. No matter what Mr. Softee does, I should locate in the middle. In this game, middle is my *dominant strategy*. A **dominant strategy** outperforms any other strategy *no matter what strategy an opponent selects*. Naturally, I decided to park in the middle. Mr. Softee's driver had reasoned exactly as I had and played his dominant strategy as well—middle. When I arrived at the middle, Mr. Softee was already parked there.

Looking at Table 13.1, you might ask why the trucks immediately selected middle-middle as the solution instead of beginning-beginning, end-end, beginning-end, or end-beginning. Closer inspection reveals that only middle-middle is a stable solution to the game. Suppose that due to an early morning traffic jam, both trucks were initially located at the beginning in the upper-left corner of the game payoff matrix. The split at the start is 50-50. However, if I believe that Mr. Softee will remain at the beginning of the parade, then I should move to the middle and gain a 75-25 split, which is shown in the cell directly below the upper-left corner cell. Mr. Softee should reason exactly the same way and would want to move to the cell immediately to the right of the upper left corner cell, so there is no stability to the solution beginning-beginning. Even though the result in terms of sales split is identical at beginning-beginning and middle-middle, only middle-middle is stable, because only when both trucks locate at the middle is it true that neither has an incentive to move to another location.

Nash equilibrium

An equilibrium in a game where all players are doing the best they can given the choices of their opponents.

Middle-middle has one unique characteristic compared to any of the other eight cells in Table 13.1: It is a *Nash equilibrium*. A **Nash equilibrium** is an equilibrium where both players are doing the best they can *given the choice of their opponent*. A Nash equilibrium is named after mathematician John Nash, who first devised this concept, and whose life was portrayed in the 2001 Oscar-winning film and the novel *A Beautiful Mind*.[2] A Nash equilibrium is one of the most important concepts to understand about the application of game theory to economic behavior.

The game depicted by Table 13.1 has another important characteristic that makes it a zero-sum game: In each and every cell, the combined sales of the two trucks adds up to 100 percent. It follows logically, then, that for every 1 percent increase in Good Humor

---

[2] John Nash, "Noncooperative games," *Annals of Mathematics*, Vol. 54 (September, 1951), pp. 286–295.

▲▲▲ **13.1 APPLICATION** **Lester Thurow's Zero–Sum Society and the Nature of Political Decisions**

In his 1980 book *The Zero-Sum Society*, MIT economist Lester Thurow argued that many of the most difficult decisions facing the United States are essentially zero-sum games where the benefits of any policy action for one group or individual are often offset by losses for another group or individual. Thurow suggested that effective policies to deal with the social problems of inflation, economic growth, environmental quality, and the redistribution of income all have strong elements of a zero-sum game associated with them and the zero-sum nature of political choices makes it difficult, if not impossible, to enact the necessary legislation to deal with these pressing problems. According to Thurow:

> Our economic problems are solvable. For most of our problems, there are several solutions. But all these solutions have the characteristic that someone must suffer large economic losses. No one wants to volunteer for this role, and we have a political process that is incapable of forcing anyone to shoulder this burden. Everyone wants someone else to suffer the necessary economic losses and as a consequence none of the possible solutions can be adopted …
>
> To protect our own income, we will fight to stop economic change from occurring or fight to prevent society from imposing the public policies that hurt us … (Thurow, pp. 11–12)

Consistent with Thurow's argument that the political system is incapable of dealing with important social problems, consider the zero-sum game depicted in the table's matrix. The two players are two presidential candidates, Mr. Bartlett and Mr. Whitmore. Suppose both candidates know that there is a crisis in the Social Security system and that the only way to deal with the crisis is to reduce benefits for current and future recipients. If both candidates support Social Security benefit reductions, the game outcome is the upper-left cell and Mr. Bartlett wins the election 52 percent to 48 percent. If both candidates oppose the Social Security cuts, the game outcome is the lower-right cell and Mr. Whitmore wins the election 51 percent to 49 percent. If one candidate opposes the cuts while the other supports them, the candidate opposed wins the election. This is a classic zero-sum game: any percentage increase in Bartlett's vote is matched by an identical percentage decrease in Whitmore's vote. Both candidates have a dominant strategy: to oppose reducing Social Security benefits. The Nash equilibrium is in the lower-right cell, with Mr. Whitmore winning the election 51 to 49 percent, but more important than who is elected president, is that the zero-sum nature of the election game guarantees that the necessary Social Security benefit reductions will not be made.

Application Table 13.1 **Zero-Sum Political Campaign (% Mr. Bartlett's vote, % Mr. Whitmore's vote)**

		Mr. Whitmore's Campaign Position	
		Support Social Security cuts	Oppose Social Security cuts
Mr. Bartlett's Campaign Position	Support Social Security cuts	52 48	43 57
	Oppose Social Security cuts	55 45	49 51

sales, there will be a 1 percent reduction in Mr. Softee sales. As noted previously, in all zero-sum games, one player's gain is exactly matched by another player's loss.

▼▼▼ **13.2 The Information Structure of Games**

In the ice cream truck example, each player knew all of the information presented in Table 13.1. They also knew that the other player knew the same information. When both

common knowledge

Description of a game in which all players know all the information and they know that all the other players also know all the information.

information structure

A description of how much information each player has at different points in a game.

perfect information

Description of a game in which each player knows all of the actions taken by all of the other players before taking an action.

players know all of the information in a game and they know the other player does as well, we refer to this as a game with **common knowledge**.

There are several other useful ways of categorizing who knows what and when they know it during a game, or the **information structure** of a game. Here are five important and useful terms used to identify the information structure of games:

1. **Perfect information.** In a game with **perfect information**, each player knows every move that has been made by the other players before taking any action. Therefore, all games where the players move simultaneously are games of **imperfect information**, because the players do not know the simultaneous moves of the other players. The ice cream truck game was an example of a simultaneous move game with imperfect information.

2. **Nature, a player of random actions.** Many games modeled by economists require a pseudo-player who game theorists call **nature** to take random actions

---

▲▲▲ 13.2 APPLICATION   Did the Giants Steal the Pennant in 1951?

"The Giants win the pennant! The Giants win the pennant!" These are the famous words of New York Giants radio announcer Russ Hodges as he called one of the most famous, if not the most famous, home runs in baseball history: Bobby Thomson's three-run homer in the bottom of the ninth inning of the third and deciding playoff game that gave the New York Giants a 5–4 win over the Brooklyn Dodgers and the 1951 National League championship. Almost 50 years later, in February 2001, the Associated Press broke a story claiming that during the last two months of the 1951 season, the Giants had been stealing signs from visiting catchers at the Polo Grounds (the home of the New York Giants). According to Hall of Fame outfielder Monte Irvin, catcher Sal Yvars, and pitcher Al Gettel, the Giants had managed to overcome a 13.5 game Dodger lead on August 11 by stealing signs when they played home games.

Stealing signs breaks the rules of baseball and completely changes the information structure of the game. In baseball, pitchers throw many different types of pitches, such as fastballs that go 90 plus miles per hour and curveballs that go slowly but curve sharply. The catcher signals the pitcher what type of pitch to throw by flashing a number of fingers down toward the ground. From time to time, teams playing at home have placed individuals in the outfield with binoculars aimed at the visiting team's catcher, so that they can steal the signals and then signal the hitter what pitch is coming next. If a team successfully steals signs, the hitter knows exactly what pitch is coming next, and this significantly increases the chance that the batter will get a hit.

If teams are not stealing signs, then there is asymmetric information before every pitch. The pitcher knows what pitch he is going to throw, but the batter does not. For example, the Dodger pitcher who threw the ball to Thomson, Ralph Branca, had both a good fastball and a good curveball. With asymmetric information, Thomson would have had to guess whether Branca was going to throw a fastball or a curve. Suppose that if Thomson guessed correctly, there was a 40 percent chance he'd get a hit. However, if Thomson guessed incorrectly, there was only a 10 percent chance he'd get a hit. If the Giants did steal the catcher's signs, then the information structure of the game became one of symmetric information, because both the pitcher and batter knew exactly what pitch was coming. Suppose that if Thomson knew what pitch was coming, there was a 60 percent chance he'd get a hit, regardless of what pitch was thrown. If the Giants stole the signs during Thomson's famous at-bat, the information structure of the game really did change, and it changed the outcome as well. If there was a 50 percent chance that Branca was going to throw a fastball and a 50 percent chance he was going to throw a curve, then by changing the information structure of the game, Thomson went from having a 25 percent chance of getting a hit (a .250 hitter) with legal asymmetric information, to a 60 percent chance (a .600 hitter) with illegal symmetric information. Perhaps Russ Hodges should have been screaming, "The Giants steal the pennant! The Giants steal the pennant!"

imperfect information

Description of a game in which at least one player is unaware of some action or actions taken by some other player or players before taking an action.

nature

A pseudo-player added by the game theorist to take random actions at some point or points in a game.

incomplete information

Description of a game in which some players have more information than other players at the beginning of the game, because nature moves first and nature's move is unobserved by at least one of the players.

complete information

Description of a game in which either nature does not take the first action or nature takes the first action and all of the players observe that action.

at some point or points in a game. Nature's random actions have well-defined probabilities. For example, in some games, nature randomly determines at the beginning of the game whether one of the players will always take the same action (for example, an established firm might always behave aggressively toward new firms), or vary its actions (for example, an established firm might sometimes behave aggressively toward new firms and sometimes behave passively). In a game of entry played between a monopolist and a potential entrant, for example, nature might randomly determine whether the monopolist is a high-cost or low-cost producer at the start of the game. Perhaps nature selects the monopolist to have high costs with probability of 0.30 and low costs with probability of 0.70. Because it is much easier for the potential entrant to compete against a high-cost monopolist than a low-cost monopolist, the potential entrant would behave very differently depending on how large or small the probability is that the monopolist is a high-cost producer.

3. **Incomplete information.** In games with **incomplete information**, some players have more information than other players at the beginning of the game. Nature is always an important player in games of incomplete information, because nature always moves first in such games, and nature's first move is unobserved by at least one of the players. By comparison, in a game with **complete information**, either nature does not take the first move, or nature's first move is observed by all the players.

COMMON ERROR 13.1   **Failing to Recognize the Information Gained in the Course of a Game**

Here's a classic gambling game in which the players often fail to realize all the information they possess. Two players, Abby and Greg, each receive an envelope filled with cash. They know that the envelopes contain an amount of money, either $100, $200, $400, $800, $1,600, or $3,200. They also know that one envelope contains exactly twice as much as the other. Abby opens her envelope and finds $400. A trade takes place only if both players agree to the trade. Should she trade with Greg? Abby reasons that she has a 50 percent chance of obtaining an envelope from Greg with $800 and a 50 percent chance of obtaining an envelope with $200; therefore, her expected value of making a trade is 0.5($800) + 0.5($200) = $400 + $100 = $500. Assuming for simplicity's sake that she is risk-neutral, her expected payoff from the trade is greater than $400, so she is willing to trade. Meanwhile, by similar reasoning, regardless of whether Greg has $200 or $800 in his envelope, he is also willing to trade. They are both making a mistake. They are both ignoring the information that is gained by observing whether their opponent is willing to trade.

How should Abby analyze the game? First, she should realize that if she had opened her envelope and found $3,200, she would have refused to trade. The next step is for Abby to realize that if Greg opened his envelope and found $1,600, then Greg would not trade because he would realize that if Abby had $3,200, she would not trade, and therefore, she would only trade if she had $800, which would make Greg worse off. But if Greg refuses to trade if he has $1,600, then Abby should refuse to trade if she has $800, which means that Greg should refuse to trade if he has $400, which means that Abby should refuse to trade if she has $200. Greg would be willing to trade if he had $100 in the envelope, but Abby would then have $200 and she would refuse to trade. Therefore, no trade should ever take place. Consequently, neither Abby nor Greg should ever be willing to trade if they have more than $100 in their envelope. Don't make the common error of ignoring important information while playing a game.

certain information

Description of a game in which nature never takes an action after any other player has taken an action.

uncertain information

Description of a game in which nature takes an action after another player has taken an action.

4. **Certain information.** In games including nature, if nature *never* moves after any other player moves, then the game is said to be of **certain information**. On the other hand, if nature moves after another player has taken a move, the game is said to be of **uncertain information**.

5. **Symmetric information.** If all players have exactly the same information when each player moves, the game is said to be of **symmetric information**. If some players have different information than other players, then the game is played with **asymmetric information**.

13.3 Prisoner's Dilemma Games[3]

symmetric information

Description of a game in which all the players have the same information when each player takes an action.

asymmetric information

Description of a game in which different players have different amounts of information when players take actions, with some players knowing more than other players.

non-zero-sum game

A game in which the combined payoffs in each cell of the payoff matrix vary, so one player's loss is not always equal to the other player's gain.

As discussed in section 13.1, zero-sum games, in which one player's loss equals the other player's gain, have fairly straightforward solutions. What happens, however, when we move into the realm of *non-zero-sum games*, such as oligopoly games in which the firms attempt to fix prices? **Non-zero-sum games** are games where the combined payoffs in each cell of the profit matrix vary, so one player's loss is not always equal to the other player's gain. Consider a collusive agreement between two duopolists, Kodak and Fuji, who agree to keep the price of film at the joint profit-maximizing level. Table 13.2 represents a possible profit matrix for such a game. Note that the *combined* profits vary from cell to cell, from a minimum of $600 million if they both defect and charge a low price to a maximum of $1 billion if they successfully collude. If Kodak and Fuji abide by an agreement to charge a high price, they each earn $500 million. If they both break the agreement, they each earn only $300 million. If only one breaks the agreement and cheats, the low-price cheater captures most of the market and earns $600 million, leaving the high price non-cheating firm with only a few customers and only $100 million. The game is of imperfect information because Kodak and Fuji simultaneously select prices.

Non-Repeated Prisoner's Dilemma Games

Suppose the game in Table 13.2 is played one time and one time only. Start by considering whether there is a dominant strategy for Kodak. If Fuji colludes and charges a high

Table 13.2 A Prisoner's Dilemma Game of Collusion ($millions Kodak's profit, $millions Fuji's profit)

		Fuji Action	
		Collude high price	Defect low price
Kodak Action	Collude high price	500 / 500	500 / 600 ... 100
	Defect low price	600 / 100	100 ... 300 / 300

[3] The Prisoner's Dilemma is usually attributed to R. Duncan Luce and Howard Raiffa, *Games and Decisions.* (New York: John Wiley and Sons, 1957), p. 94. For an easy-to-follow treatment, see Avinash Dixit and Barry Nalebuff, *Thinking Strategically* (New York: Norton, 1991), pp. 89–118. For more on the Prisoner's Dilemma, see Robert Axelrod, *The Evolution of Cooperation* (New York: Basic Books, 1984).

COMMON ERROR 13.2 Why Don't Firms Just Charge High Prices?

When students are first asked the solution to the game in Table 13.2, many argue that both Kodak and Fuji should collude because the top-left solution (*Collude, Collude*) maximizes joint profit. Typically, students argue that by colluding now, the firms can convince each other to collude in the future. The problem with this reasoning is that this is a non-repeated game, and according to the way we have defined such games, *there is no future!* The game is played once and then it ends, never to be repeated again. The students want to change the rules of the game. They want the game to continue beyond its mandated ending. Always remember to carefully understand the rules of every game, particularly when a game ends. Just as in chess or monopoly, there are rules that cannot be broken. That is also true of games developed and played by game theorists. Given that an explicit rule for the game in Table 13.2 is that it will be played only once, the only logical choice for both Kodak and Fuji is to defect. In a one-time-only game, defecting maximizes profit regardless of an opponent's action.

price, then Kodak should defect and charge a low price and earn $600 million. If Fuji defects and charges a low price, Kodak should still defect and earn $300 million. No matter what strategy Fuji adopts, Kodak should defect and charge a low price. Defect is a dominant strategy for Kodak. Furthermore, because the matrix is perfectly symmetric, Fuji's dominant strategy is also defect. Both firms should defect, which would result in each earning $300 million. Note that the bottom-right (*Defect, Defect*) equilibrium is a Nash equilibrium, because when Kodak and Fuji defect, both are doing the best they can given the choice of their opponent. Yet something seems amiss with this result. Wouldn't they both be much better off if they were to abide by an agreement to collude and charge a high price?

Prisoner's Dilemma

A game in which all the players have a dominant strategy that results in a worse outcome than if they pursued some other strategy or strategies.

The basic form of this game is known as the **Prisoner's Dilemma**. Why is this game called the Prisoner's Dilemma? Suppose two members of the mob, Tony and Paulie, have just been arrested for drug dealing. The District Attorney knows that she needs a confession from at least one of them to get a strong conviction and a stiff sentence. Agent Harris puts them in separate rooms for interrogation, where both are offered the same deal. If either confesses and turns state's evidence, he will receive a lighter sentence than if he didn't turn state's evidence. If both confess, there is no need to use either of them in court; in return for their confession, they will receive a somewhat smaller sentencing break.

Table 13.3 shows the game matrix. Both Tony and Paulie have a dominant strategy. No matter what the other does, both are better off confessing. If Paulie confesses, Tony reduces his own sentence by four years by also confessing. If Paulie stays quiet, Tony

Table 13.3 A Classic Prisoner's Dilemma Game (Tony's sentence, Paulie's sentence)

		Paulie's Action	
		Confess	Don't confess
Tony's Action	Confess	6 years / 6 years	10 years / 1 year
	Don't confess	1 year / 10 years	3 years / 3 years

reduces his sentence by two years by confessing. Clearly, both Tony and Paulie should confess. Given this payoff matrix, confession is a dominant strategy. This is the classic form of the Prisoner's Dilemma.

The mob has a major problem here: both arrested criminals have a dominant solution of confessing and talking to the authorities. The mob will work hard to find a solution to this problem. One solution is to slightly alter the payoff matrix so that it is known with certainty that all squealers will be killed. This alteration in the game changes Table 13.3 into Table 13.4, and as a result, changes the outcome. The dominant solution is now to play *Don't confess*. The death threat actually reduces both Tony's and Paulie's sentences; therefore, it's an excellent solution to the mob's problem.

Repeated Prisoner's Dilemma Games[4]

repeated game

The same game played over and over again by the same players.

The classic Prisoner's Dilemma game is played only once; however, most oligopoly games are played repeatedly. Kodak and Fuji compete not only in the current time period, but in many future time periods as well. The repeated nature of oligopoly games makes it possible for a player's current action to affect future outcomes. Suppose Kodak and Fuji expect to compete in the film market for a finite number of periods. Perhaps Fuji and Kodak anticipate that they will sell their film operations in 10 years, which means that they expect to compete for another 40 quarters. How should they play the game in each quarter for the next ten years? In a **repeated game** like this one, a simple one-period simultaneous-move game is repeated over and over again. In each round, the firms know the previous actions undertaken by the other firm.

Consider Kodak's strategy in the last quarter, the 40th, which occurs in 10 years. In the 40th quarter, Kodak has nothing to worry about regarding the future playing of the game. Therefore, in the last period (the 40th quarter), Kodak plays its dominant strategy—defect. This is in its best interest in the last period, no matter what Fuji does. Fuji plays its dominant strategy—defect—in the 40th quarter as well, so the 40th quarter results in a payoff of *Defect, Defect*, or $300 million each.

Table 13.4 **A Modified Prisoner's Dilemma Game (Tony's sentence, Paulie's sentence)**

		Paulie's Action	
		Confess	Don't confess
Tony's Action	Confess	death / death	death / 10 years
	Don't confess	10 years / death	3 years / 3 years

---

[4] For a basic explanation of repeated games, see Dixit and Nalebuff, *supra* note 3, pp. 95–118; Robert Gibbons, *Game Theory for Applied Economists* (Princeton, NJ: Princeton University Press, 1992), pp. 83–99; and Axelrod, *supra*, note 3. See also James W. Friedman, *Oligopoly and the Theory of Games* (Amsterdam: North-Holland, 1977); Richard Selten, "The Chain Store Paradox," *Theory and Decision*, April 1978, pp. 127–159; Drew Fudenberg and Eric Maskin, "The Folk Theorem in Repeated Games with Discounting or with Incomplete Information," *Econometrica*, May 1986, pp. 533–554; and Drew Fudenberg and Jean Tirole, "Game Theory for Industrial Organization: Introduction and Overview," in Richard Schmalensee and Robert Willig, eds., *Handbook of Industrial Organization* (Amsterdam: North Holland, 1989).

What should Kodak do in the 39th quarter? Because the result in the 40th quarter is known with certainty, Kodak's action in the 39th quarter will not affect the 40th quarter outcome, and Kodak should play the 39th quarter as if it were the last quarter. This means it should play its dominant strategy in the 39th quarter—defect. Fuji does the same, and the 39th quarter results in an equilibrium of *Defect, Defect*. But now the 38th quarter becomes the last, and the actions undertaken in the 38th quarter will have no effect on the outcome in the 39th or 40th quarters. The equilibrium in the 38th quarter, therefore, must also be *Defect, Defect*. By simply continuing to work backwards through time, it is obvious that the equilibrium play in every quarter is the dominant strategy—*Defect, Defect*. This will be true for any finite game: because there is no incentive to collude in the last round, there will be no incentive to collude in any earlier round.

To complicate matters, it is important to realize that most games played by oligopolists are *infinite games*. If there are no plans to sell their film operations, Kodak and Fuji probably expect to play this game forever. In any infinite game, there is no known last round; consequently, players can undertake early actions in the hopes of affecting their competitors' future strategies. In an infinite game, Kodak might believe that if it chooses an early play of colluding then that might encourage Fuji to collude in future rounds. The optimal strategy in an infinite game might be very different from the optimal strategy in a finite game. Application 13.3 explains how in the real world, Office Depot, Staples, and OfficeMax (the three leading office supplies superstores) have used **low-price guarantees**—that is, promises made by each seller to match or more than match any competitors' lower price—to solve their Prisoner's Dilemma in what each firm views as an infinite game.

low-price guarantee

A promise made by a seller to match or beat a competitor's lower price.

▲▲▲ **13.3 APPLICATION**   *Low-Price Guarantees at Office Depot, Staples, and OfficeMax*

Retailers play repeated Prisoner's Dilemma games every day. Consider the game played by Office Depot, Staples, and OfficeMax, the nation's three office supplies superstore chains. If OfficeMax and Staples compete against each other in a local market, then the store with lower prices will sell more products. Regardless of whether Staples charges high prices or low prices, OfficeMax's dominant strategy is to charge low prices, and vice versa for Staples. Office Depot, Staples, and OfficeMax, however, have discovered a solution to their Prison's Dilemma that at first sounds counter-intuitive: All three retailers offer low-price guarantees. Customers who believe that such guarantees ensure the lowest possible prices in a highly competitive market should think again.

Anyone who has shopped at one of these stores is probably familiar with the large signs that proclaim a low-price guarantee as you enter. For example, in May 2003, OfficeMax advertised, "115% Low Price Guarantee: If you find a lower price at any office product superstore on a new identical item, just show us the lower price when you buy the item at OfficeMax or within 14 days after your OfficeMax purchase and we'll give you 115% of the difference." Suppose that both OfficeMax and Staples charge $600 for a particular computer printer. One day Staples cuts the price to $500. Will this attract customers to Staples? Quite the contrary: The price cut actually drives customers to OfficeMax, where they can now buy the same printer for $485 ($600 minus 115 percent of the $100 difference between OfficeMax's price of $600 and Staples's price of $500). As a result of the low-price guarantee, the only policy that makes sense is for both OfficeMax and Staples to maintain the price at $600. Despite their low-price guarantee claims, these stores are in fact not charging very low prices or engaging in aggressive price competition. In this retail market, the use of low-price guarantees is an effective method of solving the repeated Prisoner's Dilemma facing the large office superstore chains.

▼▼▼   ## 13.4 Sequential Games[5]

normal form

The presentation of a game in the form of a matrix consisting of all the game's possible strategy combinations.

sequential games

Games where players take turns moving.

game tree

A method of describing a sequential game by showing the actions available to each player at every point in the game as a series of branches from that point.

extensive form

An alternative term used to describe a game tree. Technically, the extensive form has a somewhat broader meaning, because it describes all the payoffs in a game, while a game tree describes only the outcomes.

Up to this point, all of our games have been those in which both players move simultaneously, or what game theorists call the *normal form* of a game. The **normal form** of a game consists of all the possible strategy combinations typically presented in the form of a matrix. Many oligopoly games, however, are sequential, where firm 1 moves, then firm 2 responds, then firm 1 responds to firm 2's response, and so on. **Sequential games** are games where players take turns moving. If one player moves first, then it is misleading to represent the game as a matrix, because one player does, in fact, know the other player's choice before making a move. Because the next player to move knows its competitor's previous move, sequential games of this type are games of perfect information. Sequential games are represented by *game trees*, which are also known as the *extensive form* of the game. A **game tree** is a method of describing a sequential game by showing the actions available to each player at each point in the game as a series of branches from that point. The **extensive form** of a game is an alternative term used to describe a game tree.

To illustrate why it is important to represent sequential games in their extensive form, consider Table 13.5 and Figure 13.1. Both Table 13.5 and Figure 13.1 may appear to represent the same game, but the outcomes may be quite different. If the game is represented in its normal form as a simultaneous-move game such as Table 13.5, then there are two Nash equilibria, (*Top, Left*) and (*Bottom, Right*), because in each of those cells, neither player has an incentive to move, given the choice of his opponent.

Now consider the extensive form of the same game as shown in Figure 13.1. In the extensive form of the game, each player gets only one move and then the game ends. Ben has been given the first move. Ben must choose either *Right* or *Left*. As economists Avinash Dixit and Barry Nalebuff have noted, the first rule of game theory is to "look ahead and reason back."[6] By playing a game backwards, a player is trying to predict how a rational opponent would respond to any earlier moves in the game. Suppose Ben does just that. Ben knows that choosing *Left* will definitely result in a profit of $1 million no matter what Jerry does. However, choosing *Right* means that the only sensible thing for Jerry to do is play *Bottom*, because obviously, given a choice between earning $0 or $4 million, Jerry will select $4 million. Ben knows that playing *Right* will result in a profit of $4 million, and playing *Left* results in a profit of only $1 million. The choice for Ben is clear—play *Right*.

Table 13.5 The Normal Form of a Game Played Between Ben and Jerry ($millions Jerry's profit, $millions Ben's profit)

		Ben's Action	
		Left	Right
Jerry's Action	Top	10 \ 1	0 \ −2
	Bottom	10 \ 1	4 \ 4

---

[5] See Dixit and Nalebuff, *supra* note 3, chapter 5, pp.119–141. Also Jean Tirole, *The Theory of Industrial Organization* (Cambridge, MA: MIT Press, 1988), pp. 439–441; and Gibbons, *supra* note 4, pp. 55–82.

[6] Dixit and Nalebuff, *supra* note 3, p. 34.

Figure 13.1 The Extensive Form of the Game in Table 13.5 ($millions Ben's profit, $millions Jerry's profit)

Ben moves first and can go right or left. Given Ben's move, Jerry selects *Top* or *Bottom* to maximize his profit. Because Ben knows that he will earn $1 million if he goes *Left*, but $4 million if he goes *Right* and Jerry maximizes his profit, Ben goes *Right*, and Jerry then chooses *Bottom*. The only equilibrium is Ben, *Right*; Jerry, *Bottom*.

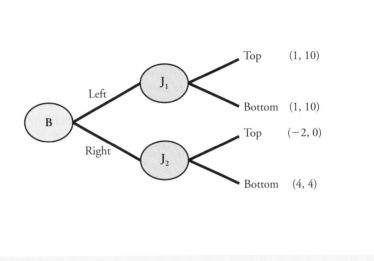

Once Ben has played *Right*, Jerry will play *Bottom* and also earn $4 million. In the extensive form of the game there is only one equilibrium: Ben, *Right*; Jerry, *Bottom*.

Although this scenario ensures that no one has to settle for a mere $1 million, why should Jerry settle for just $4 million, when he could earn $10 million if Ben would just play *Left*? Jerry could threaten to play *Top* if Ben plays *Right*, but is the threat credible? After all, once Ben selects *Right*, Jerry's choice is to earn $0 or earn $4 million. Given those choices, a rational player would select $4 million.

Are there ways that Jerry could convince Ben that he would play *Top* if Ben played *Right*? Probably. Jerry could hire an impartial agent, perhaps a lawyer or a firm in another industry, and publically sign a contract that states: "If Ben ever plays *Right*, my agent will make my move for me and play *Top*." By publically giving up the option of making the choice for himself, Jerry might convince Ben that a play of *Right* will result in a loss for Ben of $2 million.

The game depicted in Figure 13.1 can be related directly to an economic game between a monopolist, Jerry, and and a potential entrant, Ben, into the market monopolized by Jerry. The game can be reinterpreted if *Left* is Ben *Stays Out*, *Right* is Ben *Enters*, *Top* is Jerry *Responds aggressively if Ben enters*, and *Bottom* is Jerry *Maintains price at the current level*. The game tree in Figure 13.2 shows these changes. The game is now an entry

Figure 13.2 A Game of Entry ($millions Ben's profit, $millions Jerry's profit)

Ben moves first and can either enter or stay out. Given Ben's move, Jerry selects *Aggressive* or *Maintain price* to maximize his profit. Because Ben knows that he will earn $1 million if he stays out, but $4 million if he enters, Ben enters, and Jerry maintains price.

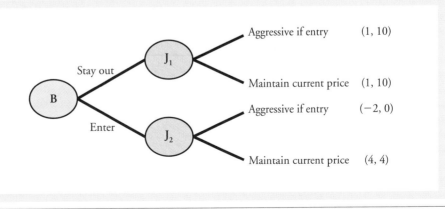

choice for Ben, followed by a response to entry choice for Jerry. Given the preceding analysis, the only equilibrium in this game is for Ben to enter and Jerry to maintain his current price. However, this is not always realistic. Many monopolists like Jerry have attempted to change this game tree to make Ben believe that in response to entry, the monopolist would choose *Aggressive if entry*. In Chapter 15, we consider some credible methods that Jerry might adopt to convince Ben of his serious intention to play *Aggressive if entry*. Application 13.4 examines a far more serious but closely related game: the game of potential nuclear war played by NATO and the Soviet Union between 1945 and 1989.

▲▲▲ 13.4 APPLICATION　NATO and How to "Win" the Game of Nuclear Deterrence

For 45 years after World War II, the greatest threat to world stability existed in Eastern Europe along the front between the countries that were members of the North Atlantic Treaty Organization (NATO) and the countries under the control of the former Soviet Union. The members of NATO feared that because of the large numerical superiority of the Soviet Union in terms of troops and conventional equipment, the Soviet Union could overrun Western Europe and win a conventional war. NATO could respond to a Soviet invasion either by using conventional weapons or tactical nuclear weapons.

Consider the serious game that NATO and the Soviet Union played from 1945–1989. In Application Figure 13.4A, the Soviet Union has the first move and must decide whether to attack NATO or maintain the status quo along the front line. The payoffs in parentheses are the Soviet Union's utility and NATO's utility, respectively. If the Soviet Union moves first and attacks using conventional forces, NATO could respond either with conventional weapons, in which case Western Europe would be overrun and NATO's utility would be

−100,000 and the Soviet Union's utility would be 100,000; or with nuclear weapons, in which case there is a nuclear catastrophe and both the Soviet Union and NATO suffer a cataclysm causing both to have utilities of −1,000,000. If the Soviet Union chooses not to attack, then the status quo in Europe is maintained and the relatively poor Soviet Union has utility of 50,000, while the relatively rich members of NATO have utility of 200,000. The Soviet Union should reason that once it has attacked, NATO has a choice between a conventional response resulting in utility of −100,000 or a nuclear response resulting in utility of −1,000,000. Given these options, NATO should not use nuclear weapons, and the Soviet Union should attack Western Europe.

How was NATO able to avoid this outcome for 45 years? The nations of Western Europe decided to hand over the response decision to the United States and insisted that the United States commit to a nuclear response to any Soviet attack, conventional or nuclear, on Western Europe. Consider the impact of this change in the game. In Application Figure 13.4B, the United States

---

Application Figure 13.4A Soviet Union–NATO Deterrence Game with the Soviet Union Moving First (USSR utility, NATO utility)

The Soviet Union gets the first move and can either attack NATO or not attack. After the Soviet Union attacks, NATO can use either conventional weapons or nuclear weapons to resist. If NATO uses nuclear weapons, its utility is −1,000,000 and if it uses conventional weapons, its utility is −1,000,000. Therefore, NATO will respond with conventional weapons. The Soviet Union now has utility of 50,000 if it doesn't attack and 100,000 if it attacks, so it will attack.

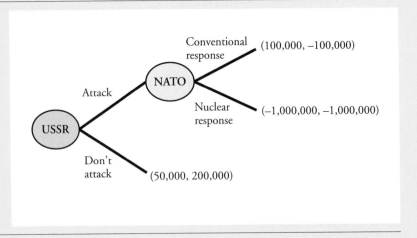

(continued)

is the player with the first move, and commits to a full nuclear response to any attack on any NATO member by the Soviet Union. This takes the conventional response action out of the game. Now the Soviet Union is faced with either attacking and having utility of −1,000,000 or not attacking and having utility of 50,000. The choice is clear: *Don't attack* is the Soviet Union's only rational play.

The key to the outcome is that the United States moves first to put its threat and commitment in place *before* the Soviet Union has an opportunity to make the first move. Waiting until after the Soviet Union invades to make the commitment would have failed to prevent a Soviet invasion of Western Europe.

In 2002, India and Pakistan played the same game. Along the India-Pakistan border, India had a far greater number of troops and equipment and could have almost certainly won a conventional war. Pakistan was able to prevent an invasion by moving first and refusing to state in advance that it would not use nuclear weapons first in any confrontation with India. As in the NATO-Soviet equilibrium, nuclear deterrence was able to prevent a full-scale war between India and Pakistan in 2002.

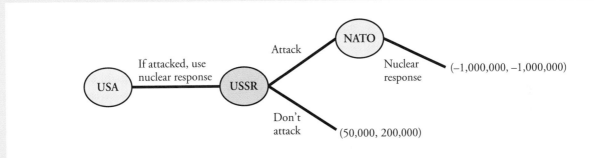

Application Figure 13.4B Soviet Union–NATO Deterrence Game with the USA Moving First (USSR utility, NATO utility)
Suppose the United States gets the first move and commits to a nuclear response to any Soviet Union attack. If the Soviets attack, NATO will definitely use nuclear weapons. The Soviet Union now has utility of 50,000 if it doesn't attack and utility of −100,000,000 if it attacks, so it will not attack.

13.5 Games of Mixed Strategies[7]

So far, all of the games in this chapter have resulted in one or more Nash equilibria. Some games, however, fail to produce even one pure strategy Nash equilibrium. Take the game depicted by the payoff matrix in Table 13.6 involving Coke and Pepsi. No matter what their current actions, there is an incentive for at least one company to change its action. If Coke's current action is *Low price* and Pepsi's action is *Heavy advertising*, then Coke has an incentive to change its action to *Heavy advertising*. In the cell *Heavy advertising, Heavy advertising*, Pepsi has an incentive to play *Low price*. Once Coke's play is *Heavy advertising*, and Pepsi's is *Low price*, Coke has an incentive to play *Low price* as well, but then Pepsi has an incentive to play *Heavy advertising* and we are right back where we started!

mixed strategy

A game in which the players' optimal strategies are to choose their actions randomly.

There is no pure strategy Nash equilibrium in this game; Coke and Pepsi instead play a *mixed strategy*. A **mixed strategy** exists in a game when the players' optimal strategy is to choose their actions randomly. In an optimal mixed-strategy equilibrium, each player

---

[7] For a basic explanation of mixed-strategy equilibria, see Eric Rasmusen, *Games and Information* (Oxford: Basil Blackwell, 1989), Chapter 3, pp. 69–82. See also Dixit and Nalebuff, *supra* note 3, Chapter 7, pp. 168–198; and Jean Tirole, *The Theory of Industrial Organization* (Cambridge: MIT Press, 1988), pp. 423–425.

Table 13.6 A Low Price-Heavy Advertising Game Played by Coke and Pepsi ($millions Coke's profit, $millions Pepsi's profit)

		Pepsi's Action	
		Low price	Heavy advertising
Coke's Action	Low price	600 \ 350	560 \ 450
	Heavy advertising	580 \ 500	600 \ 400

randomly selects its actions with given probabilities that maximize their expected profit, given the randomly selected strategy being played by their opponent. An optimal set of probabilities always exists to solve such problems.[8] Appendix 13.1 shows that for the payoff matrix presented in Table 13.6, the optimal strategy for Coke is to play *Low price* half the time and *Heavy advertising* half the time, and the optimal mixed strategy for Pepsi is to play *Low price* two-thirds of the time and *Heavy advertising* one-third of the time.

It is useful and important to understand the following characteristic of all mixed-strategy equilibria: Once a mixed-strategy equilibrium is obtained, both players are indifferent to whether they play their equilibrium mixed strategy or any other strategy. For example, in Table 13.6, notice that if Coke plays its optimal mixed strategy of 50 percent *Low price* and 50 percent *Heavy advertising*, then Pepsi's expected profit is $425 million no matter what strategy Pepsi selects.

It is possible to check the result for the case where Coke and Pepsi play their optimal mixed strategies. In this case, there is a 1/3 chance ((2/3) × (1/2) = (2/6) = (1/3)) of being in the top-left or bottom-left cells in Table 13.6 and a 1/6 chance ((1/3) × (1/2) = (1/6)) of being in the top-right or bottom-right cells in the payoff matrix. Pepsi's expected profit, therefore, equals (1/3)($350) + (1/3)($500) + (1/6)($450) + (1/6)($400) = $116.6666 + $166.6666 + $75.00 + $66.6666 = $424.9998 ≈ $425. If Pepsi plays *Low price* 100 percent of the time, its expected profit is 0.5($350) + 0.5($500) = $175 + $250 = $425. If Pepsi plays *Heavy advertising* 100 percent of the time, its expected profit is 0.5($450) + 0.5($400) = $225 + $200 = $425. No matter what Pepsi plays, its profits equal $425 million if Coke plays its optimal mixed strategy. Similarly, if Pepsi plays its optimal mixed strategy of *Low price* two-thirds of the time and *Heavy advertising* one-third of the time, then Coke's expected profit will equal $586.67 regardless of Coke's choice of actions.

The characteristic that given a mixed-strategy equilibrium, both players are indifferent between playing their optimal mixed strategy and any other strategy may at first seem surprising. However, it actually makes a great deal of intuitive sense if the optimal mixed strategy is envisioned as the strategy that makes your opponent's strategy selection irrelevant to your opponent's outcome. By playing your optimal mixed strategy, you have placed your opponent in a weak position where it simply doesn't matter what your opponent does.

Once this important characteristic of all mixed-strategy equilibria is understood, it is possible to solve for the mixed-strategy equilibrium in the special case of a game with only two players, where each player has only two possible actions. In this case, we can use

---

[8] Gibbons, *supra* note 4, pp. 29–33.

algebra to derive the equilibrium. Again, consider the game depicted in Table 13.6. Coke's optimal profit-maximizing mixed strategy is the one that takes all choice away from Pepsi. In other words, Coke's optimal strategy results in equal profit for Pepsi regardless of whether Pepsi plays *Low price* 100 percent of the time, *Heavy advertising* 100 percent of the time, or any other strategy. Let θ represent the optimal mixed-strategy probability for Coke to play *Low price*, then $(1 - \theta)$ represents the optimal mixed-strategy probability for Coke to play *Heavy advertising*. If Coke plays its optimal mixed-strategy, Pepsi must have the same expected value of profits regardless of whether Pepsi always plays *Low price* [expected profit = $350\theta + 500(1 - \theta)$] or always plays *Heavy advertising* [expected profit = $450\theta + 400(1 - \theta)$]. Mathematically, the following condition must therefore hold:

$$350(\theta) + 500(1 - \theta) = 450(\theta) + 400(1 - \theta)$$

Using algebra:

$$350\theta + 500 - 500\theta = 450\theta + 400 - 400\theta$$

$$500 - 150\theta = 400 + 50\theta$$

$$100 = 200\theta \Rightarrow \theta = \frac{1}{2} \Rightarrow (1 - \theta) = \frac{1}{2}$$

Coke's optimal mixed strategy is to play *Low price* half of the time and *Heavy advertising* half of the time.

Pepsi's optimal profit-maximizing mixed strategy is the strategy that makes Coke indifferent about its own choice of strategy. If Pepsi plays its optimal strategy, Coke will earn equal profit regardless of whether Coke plays *Low price* 100 percent of the time, *Heavy advertising* 100 percent of the time, or any other strategy. Let ρ represent the optimal mixed-strategy probability for Pepsi to play *Low price*, then $(1 - \rho)$ represents the optimal mixed-strategy probability for Pepsi to play *Heavy advertising*. If Pepsi plays its optimal mixed strategy, Coke must have the same expected value of profit regardless of whether Coke always plays *Low price* or always plays *Heavy advertising*. Mathematically, the following condition must therefore hold:

$$600(\rho) + 560(1 - \rho) = 580(\rho) + 600(1 - \rho)$$

Once again, using algebra:

$$600\rho + 560 - 560\rho = 580\rho + 600 - 600\rho$$

$$560 + 40\rho = 600 - 20\rho$$

$$40 = 60\rho \Rightarrow \rho = \frac{2}{3} \Rightarrow (1 - \rho) = \frac{1}{3}$$

Pepsi's optimal mixed strategy is to play *Low price* two-thirds of the time and *Heavy advertising* one-third of the time.

In this game, the mixed-strategy equilibrium where Coke plays *Low price* 50 percent of the time and *Heavy advertising* 50 percent of the time and Pepsi plays *Low price* 66.7 percent of the time and *Heavy advertising* 33.3 percent of the time is called a **mixed-strategy Nash equilibrium**.

mixed-strategy Nash equilibrium

An optimal set of random actions that maximize the players' expected outcomes in a game.

▲▲▲ **13.5 APPLICATION** The Effect of Drug Testing in Baseball

In May 2002, former major league baseball star José Canseco contended that 85 percent of major league baseball players used illegal steroids to boost performance. Canseco said, "It's completely restructured the game as we know it. That's why guys are hitting 50 or 60 or 75 home runs." A few days later, another retired star, Ken Caminiti, revealed that he had taken steroids during the 1996 season when he won the National League Most Valuable Player award. According to Caminiti, "At least half the guys are using steroids. They talk about it. They joke about it with each other." Unlike baseball, the National Football League (NFL) and the National Basketball Association (NBA) have random drug testing policies aimed at reducing drug use.

The decision whether to use random drug testing in baseball can be viewed as a game between the league and the players. Because it would be prohibitively expensive to test every player before every game, Major League Baseball (MLB) must devise an alternative random drug testing policy. Under a random drug testing policy, players using drugs are willing to risk being caught, but realize that it's possible they might not be caught. Consider the game depicted in Application Table 13.5 where the numbers in each cell represent the utility payoffs for MLB and a hypothetical player, Joe Hardy, respectively.

Joe prefers the current baseball policy of no testing, in which case his utility is maximized at 200 and he uses drugs. Under the current system, if Joe does not use drugs, he is competing mostly against players who do; therefore, his relative performance declines along with his income and utility. With drug testing, MLB's utility is lower if the players don't use drugs because the league is wasting resources on testing and the games have fewer home runs. If a drug testing policy is added to the game, there is no Nash equilibrium. Analyzing the game by beginning in the lower-left cell with no testing and Joe using drugs, MLB prefers to move to a testing policy in the upper-left cell. However, from the upper-left cell, Joe prefers to move to the upper-right cell with testing and no drug use. But once drug use is eliminated in the upper-left cell, MLB prefers to save resources by moving to the lower-right cell. But from the lower-right cell, Joe

prefers to return to the lower-left, which brings the game right back to where it began, and the cycle would start all over again.

There is no Nash equilibrium, but there must exist a mixed-strategy equilibrium. Suppose ρ represents the probability that MLB tests for drugs, $1 - \rho$ represents the probability that MLB does not test for drugs, θ represents the probability that Joe Hardy uses drugs, and $(1 - \theta)$ represents the probability that Joe does not use drugs. In any mixed-strategy equilibrium, Joe and MLB are indifferent between playing their optimal mixed strategy and any other strategy. If MLB plays its optimal mixed strategy, Joe's utility must be the same regardless of whether he always uses drugs or never uses drugs, and therefore:

$$-400(\rho) + 200(1 - \rho) = 150(\rho) + 50(1 - \rho)$$
$$-400\rho + 200 - 200\rho = 150\rho + 50 - 50\rho$$
$$-600\rho + 200 = 100\rho + 50$$
$$700\rho = 150 \Rightarrow \rho = \frac{150}{700} = \frac{3}{14} \Rightarrow (1 - \rho) = \frac{11}{14}$$

The optimal mixed strategy for MLB is to randomly test for drugs 21.4 percent of the time and not test 78.6 percent of the time.

If Joe plays his optimal mixed strategy, MLB's utility must be the same regardless of whether MLB always tests for drugs or never tests for drugs, and therefore:

$$200(\theta) + 100(1 - \theta) = -200(\theta) + 200(1 - \theta)$$
$$200\theta + 100 - 100\theta = -200\theta + 200 - 200\theta$$
$$100\theta + 100 = -400\theta + 200$$
$$500\theta = 100 \Rightarrow \theta = \frac{1}{5} \Rightarrow (1 - \theta) = \frac{4}{5}$$

The optimal mixed strategy for Joe Hardy is to use drugs 20 percent of the time and not use drugs 80 percent of the time. There is a 4.3 percent ($0.214 \times .20 = 0.043$) chance that Joe uses drugs *and* gets caught. The use of random

(continued)

drug testing reduces Joe's drug use by 80 percent and requires testing on a random basis only 21.4 percent of the time. We can understand why the NFL and NBA have adopted random drug testing policies: Random testing greatly reduces drug use, for a relatively modest cost.

The next two chapters will use the basics of game theory introduced in this chapter to examine a number of important models of oligopoly. As you work your way through the next two chapters, you may want to return to this chapter to recall the basics of game theory.

Table Application 13.5 A Drug Testing Game (Major League Baseball's utlity, Joe Hardy's utility)

		Joe Hardy	
		Use drugs	Don't use drugs
Major League Baseball	Drug testing	200 ╲ −400	100 ╲ 150
	No drug testing	−200 ╲ 200	200 ╲ 50

Summary

1. Game theory is the study of how interdependent decision-makers make choices. It is used to analyze many economic situations and, particularly, to analyze oligopoly behavior. A Nash equilibrium is an important concept in game theory and exists if every player in a game is doing the best they can given the actions of all the other players.

2. The information structure of a game can greatly affect the game's outcome. Information is perfect if each player knows every move that has been made by the other players before they move. A pseudo-player, nature, adds a random element to many games. If nature moves first in a game and nature's move is not observed by all of the players, then the game is said to be of incomplete information. If nature never moves after any other player has moved, then the game is of certain information. If all players have exactly the same information, the game is of symmetric information.

3. The Prisoner's Dilemma refers to a classic game of collusion in which the dominant strategy for all players is to defect rather than collude. In any finite Prisoner's Dilemma game, no matter how many times the game is repeated, the equilibrium is always for the players to defect.

4. Sequential games are games in which players alternate moves. With perfect, complete, certain, and symmetric information, the sequential game of entry results in entry every time the game is played. The outcome of a sequential game can depend on which player moves first.

5. Some games have no Nash equilibrium, but instead have a mixed-strategy equilibrium in which players take random actions with fixed probabilities. If all players in a game play their optimal mixed strategy, then no one firm can take an action to improve its outcome. Instead, no matter what action a player undertakes, its outcome will remain the same.

Self-Test Problems

1. There are two movie theaters in town. They agree to charge $9 per ticket in order to maximize joint profit. However, each theater must consider whether to cheat on the agreement and offer a "2-for-1" ticket price to its customers. Consider the payoff matrix depicting their payoffs in a game played once. The payoffs are as follows: (profit to Movie Theater Y, profit to Movie Theater X)

		Movie Theater X's actions	
		Charge $9	Offer 2 for 1" deal
Movie Theater Y's actions	Charge $9	(4000, 4000)	(1000, 6000)
	Offer "2 for 1" deal	(6000, 1000)	(3000, 3000)

   a. Determine if either theater has a dominant strategy. Solve for the Nash equilibrium of the game.

   b. Is this game a Prisoner's Dilemma? Why or why not?

2. Consider the extensive form of the following sequential entry game that is played once. The incumbent (I) has threatened to fight entry if the entrant (E) decides to enter. See Figure 13A.1.

   a. What is the Nash equilibrium of the game? Explain.

   b. Is the incumbent's threat to fight entry credible? Explain.

3. Consider the actions of Coke and Pepsi to either offer a low price or heavy advertise. Following are the payoff matrices associated with their choice of actions. Payoffs are (profit to Coke, profit to Pepsi):

		Pepsi's actions	
		Low price	Heavy advertising
Coke's actions	Low price	(500, 600)	(700, 400)
	Heavy advertising	(800, 400)	(500, 500)

   a. Does either firm have a dominant strategy? If so, to do what?

   b. Solve for the Nash equilibrium of the game.

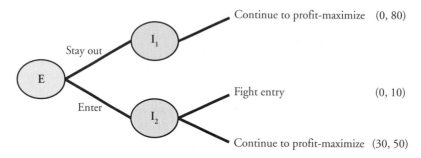

Figure 13A.1 ($millions entrant's profit, $millions incumbent's profit)

Questions and Problems for Review

1. Joe and Jerry are the only two hot dog vendors on the beach each summer. Each summer, they must decide where to locate on the mile-long beach. They have three choices of locations: at the beginning, halfway, and at the end. The game is a zero-sum game, because Joe and Jerry are competing for percentage of sales of hot dogs on the beach.

   a. Derive a payoff matrix that will reflect the payoffs (in terms of percentage of sales) for Joe and Jerry.

   b. Does either Joe or Jerry have a dominant strategy? If so, to do what?

   c. What is the Nash equilibrium of this game?

2. According to Thurow, in what ways are economic problems zero-sum games? What are some other policies, other than Social Security, that are likely to have zero-sum political implications? Explain.

3. Consider the following matrix of two firms competing for local sales of motorboats. They've each

developed two strategies: advertise big and give free stuff away to help increase sales. Payoffs are in terms of (Firm A's percentage of sales, Firm B's percentage of sales).

		Firm B's actions	
		Advertise big	Give free stuff away
Firm A's actions	Advertise big	(60, 40)	(45, 55)
	Give free stuff away	(50, 50)	(40, 60)

a. Does either firm have a dominant strategy? If so, what is it?

b. Solve for the Nash equilibrium of the game.

4. Consider the following matrix of two local grocery stores in a small town. They've each developed two strategies: offer double coupons or stay open 24 hours to help increase sales. Payoffs are in terms of (Firm A's percentage of sales, Firm B's percentage of sales).

		Firm B's actions	
		Double coupons	Stay open 24 hours
Firm A's actions	Double coupons	(40, 60)	(55, 45)
	Stay open 24 hours	(45, 55)	(60, 40)

a. Does either firm have a dominant strategy? If so, what is it?

b. Solve for the Nash equilibrium of the game.

5. George and Henry sell wool sweaters during the winter in front of the student union of a remote college in upstate Minnesota. Because their sweaters are similar, they have developed the following tactics to increase their sales. Payoffs are (percentage of sales to George, percentage of sales to Henry).

		Henry's actions		
		Shout insults	Post a big sign	Give away free balloons
George's actions	Shout insults	(50, 50)	(60, 40)	(55, 45)
	Post a big sign	(40, 60)	(50, 50)	(45, 55)
	Give away free balloons	(40, 60)	(45, 55)	(50, 50)

a. Does George have a dominant strategy? To do what?

b. Does Henry have a dominant strategy? To do what?

c. Solve for the Nash equilibrium of the game.

6. Star and Freedom sell surfboards on the beach in Santa Cruz, California. They have both developed the three same tactics to increase their sales. Payoffs are (percentage of sales to Star, percentage of sales to Freedom).

		Freedom's actions		
		Shout insults	Post a big sign	Give away free balloons
Star's actions	Shout insults	(60, 40)	(65, 35)	(40, 60)
	Post a big sign	(40, 60)	(50, 50)	(30, 70)
	Give away free balloons	(55, 45)	(60, 40)	(35, 65)

a. Does Star have a dominant strategy? To do what?

b. Does Freedom have a dominant strategy? To do what?

c. Solve for the Nash equilibrium of the game.

7. Stacey and Betsy are contestants on a game show. They each select a wrapped box from four choices. They know that one box contains $100, one contains $1,000, one contains $10,000, and one contains $100,000. They each then unwrap their chosen box and look inside. They then have a choice of whether to trade with one another. Stacey uses all the information in the game correctly. Betsy's husband has advised her to trade if she has the box with anything less than $100,000 inside. Betsy's box has $1,000 inside. She offers to trade with Stacey. Stacey agrees to trade. Did Betsy's husband give her good advice? What was in Stacey's box? Explain.

8. Two local department stores in town (Store K and Store D) both advertise their upcoming sales each week in the Thursday newspaper. They must turn in their advertisements no later than noon on Tuesday. However, Store K has a "spy" who works in Store D's advertising department and reports the information to Store K's advertising department. What type of information is represented in this game?

9. Consider the following game. Assume it is played one time and one time only. The game represents the collusive agreements of two countries who agree to fix output of oil. Payoffs to the two countries are represented as (profit to Saudi Arabia, profit to Venezuela).

		Venezuela's actions	
		Collude: limit output	Defect: increase output
Saudi Arabia's actions	Collude: limit output	(900, 600)	(700, 800)
	Defect: increase output	(1,100, 300)	(800, 400)

a. Does Venezuela have a dominant strategy? If so, to do what? Does Saudi Arabia have a dominant strategy? If so, to do what?

b. Solve for the Nash equilibrium of the game.

c. Is this game a Prisoner's Dilemma? Explain why or why not.

10. Consider the following game: Assume it is played one time and one time only. The payoffs are (profit to Firm A, profit to Firm B).

		Firm B's actions	
		Collude	Defect
Firm's A's actions	Collude	(900, 700)	(400, 900)
	Defect	(1,00, 400)	(500, 600)

a. Does Firm A have a dominant strategy? To do what? Does Firm B have a dominant strategy? To do what?

b. Solve for the Nash equilibrium of the game.

c. Is this game a Prisoner's Dilemma? Explain why or why not.

11. In question 9, the game was only played once, and thus the Nash equilibrium was for each country to defect. In the real world, these two countries are part of a group of countries, OPEC, that manages to successfully collude on oil production. What is the difference between real life and the situation in question 9? Given that collusion often works for OPEC, do you think OPEC is playing a finite or infinite game? Explain your reasoning. What other factors do you think come into play over time that are not depicted in question 9?

12. In Nathaniel's town, two competing stores advertise that they will "match any competitor's advertisement" plus give a free gift of some value. Nathaniel's mom thinks it's great how much competition there is in town. Nathaniel disagrees with his mom's assessment of the situation and thinks there is little competition. You are brought in as an outside economic consultant. As an economist, which person do you agree with and why?

13. Historically, Coke has been the leader in the carbonated beverage market. In that sense, Coke might be considered to play first in any games that Coke and Pepsi play. Consider the following sequential game. Coke is trying to decide whether to develop a new product. The payoff situation (in profit) is the following: If Coke does develop the product, Coke will get $600 million if Pepsi develops a new product too and $800 million if Pepsi chooses not to develop a new product. If Coke doesn't develop a new product, Coke will get $200 million if Pepsi

does develop a new product and $400 million if Pepsi doesn't develop a new product. If Coke does develop a new product, then Pepsi will get $600 million if it develops one too and only $200 million if it doesn't develop one. If Coke does not develop a new product, then Pepsi will get $800 million if it develops a new product and only $400 million if it doesn't develop a new product.

a. Create an extensive form of this game that represents this situation.

b. Solve for the Nash equilibrium of the game.

14. Harvey's wife, Martha (M), is always the one to decide their social schedule. She decides what to do and then Harvey (H) decides whether to go. Harvey loves spending time with his wife, but he is tired of going to the symphony. Tonight Harvey says: "I'm not going to go to the symphony again." Consider the extensive

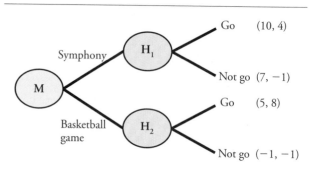

Figure 13P.1 (Martha's utility, Harvey's utility)

form of the game (Figure 13P.1). The payoffs of this game are (Martha's utility, Harvey's utility).

a. Solve for the Nash equilibrium of the game.

b. Is Harvey's threat credible?

15. Consider Harvey and his wife. This time, they decide simultaneously what to do and can both go their own way if they would like. The table depicts the payoff matrix of (Harvey's utility, Martha's utility) is depicted in the table below.

		Martha's actions	
		Attend symphony	Attend basketball game
Harvey's actions	Attend symphony	(4, 10)	(3, 3)
	Attend basketball game	(1, 1)	(8, 5)

a. Does Martha have a dominant strategy? If so, what is it?

b. Does Harvey have a dominant strategy? If so, what is it?

c. Solve for the Nash equilibrium (equilibria) of the game.

16. Coke and Pepsi are each simultaneously deciding whether to engage in a heavy advertising campaign to increase consumers' demand for carbonated beverages. The following payoff matrix shows (profit to Coke, profit to Pepsi).

		Pepsi's actions	
		Advertise campaign	Don't advertise
Coke's actions	Advertise campaign	(400, 400)	(500, 600)
	Don't advertise	(500, 800)	(300, 200)

a. Does Coke have a dominant strategy? If so, what is it?

b. Does Pepsi have a dominant strategy? If so, what is it?

c. Solve for the Nash equilibrium (equilibria) of the game.

17. Consider two firms, Firm A and B. Firm A is considering whether to offer a sale. Firm B is considering whether to develop a new product. The payoff matrix shows (profit to Firm B, profit to Firm A).

		Firm A's actions	
		Offer a sale	Don't offer a sale
Firm B's actions	Develop a new product	(1,200, 800)	(1,600, 600)
	Don't develop a new product	(800, 400)	(1,000, 600)

a. Does firm A have a dominant strategy? If so, what is it?

b. Does firm B have a dominant strategy? If so, what is it?

c. Solve for the Nash equilibrium of the game.

d. Is this game a Prisoner's Dilemma?

18. Consider two firms, Firm A and B. Firm A is considering whether to develop a new product. Firm B is considering whether to offer a sale. The payoff matrix shows (profit to Firm B, profits to Firm A).

		Firm A's actions	
		Develop new product	Don't develop new product
Firm B's actions	Offer a sale	(800, 1,000)	(1,000, 900)
	Don't offer a sale	(900, 1,400)	(800, 1,000)

a. Does firm A have a dominant strategy? If so, what is it?

b. Does firm B have a dominant strategy? If so, what is it?

c. Solve for the Nash equilibrium of the game.

19. Consider Coke and Pepsi and the simultaneous game depicted in the following payoff matrix. Payoffs are (Coke's profit, Pepsi's profit).

		Pepsi's actions	
		Advertise heavily	Lower price
Coke's actions	Develop new product	(1,000, 1,200)	(1,200, 800)
	Don't develop new product	(1,200, 1,200)	(1,000, 1,600)

a. Does Pepsi have a dominant strategy? If so, what is it?

b. Does Coke have a dominant strategy? If so, what is it?

c. Solve for the Nash equilibrium of the game (mixed-strategy equilibrium).

20. Consider Coke and Pepsi and the simultaneous game depicted in the following payoff matrix. Payoffs are (Coke's profit, Pepsi's profit).

		Pepsi's actions	
		Advertise heavily	Advertise lightly
Coke's actions	Advertise heavily	(60, 100)	(80, 60)
	Advertise lightly	(80, 40)	(40, 60)

a. Does Pepsi have a dominant strategy? If so, what is it?

b. Does Coke have a dominant strategy? If so, what is it?

c. Solve for the Nash equilibrium of the game (mixed-strategy equilibrium).

Internet Exercises

Visit *http://www.myeconlab.com/waldman* for this chapter's Web exercises. Answer real-world economics problems by doing research on the Internet.

Appendix 13.1

Using calculus, the solution to the game represented in Table 13.6 is obtained in the following manner. In the analysis, π represents profit, θ represents the probability that Coke plays *Low price*, $(1 - \theta)$ represents the probability that Coke plays *Heavy advertising*, ρ represents the probability that Pepsi plays *Low price*, and $(1 - \rho)$ represents the probability that Pepsi plays *Heavy advertising*. The problem for both Coke and Pepsi is to maximize their expected value of profit.

For Coke, the problem is to maximize expected profit $E(\pi)$, where:

$$E(\pi) = \theta[600\rho + 560(1 - \rho)] + (1 - \theta)[580\rho + 600(1 - \rho)]$$

After some algebraic manipulation:

$$E(\pi) = 600\theta\rho - 40\theta - 20\rho + 600$$

Assuming the existence of an interior solution, profit maximization requires:

$$\frac{\partial E(\pi)}{\partial \theta} = 60\rho - 40 = 0 \text{ or } \rho = \frac{40}{60} = \frac{2}{3} \text{ and } (1 - \rho) = \left(1 - \frac{2}{3}\right) = \frac{1}{3}$$

The optimal strategy for Pepsi is to play *Low price* 66.7 percent of the time and *Heavy advertising* 33.3 percent of the time.

For Pepsi, the problem is to maximize expected profit $E(\pi)$, where:

$$E(\pi) = \rho[350\theta + 500(1 - \theta)] + (1 - \rho)[450\theta + 400(1 - \theta)]$$

After some algebraic manipulation:

$$E(\pi) = -200\rho\theta + 100\rho + 50\theta + 400$$

Assuming the existence of an interior solution, profit maximization requires:

$$\frac{\partial E(\pi)}{\partial \rho} = -200\theta + 100 = 0 \text{ or } \theta = \frac{1}{2} \text{ and } (1 - \theta) = \left(1 - \frac{1}{2}\right) = \frac{1}{2}$$

The optimal strategy for Coke is to play *Low price* 50 percent of the time and *Heavy advertising* 50 percent of the time.

Chapter 14
Oligopoly

In May 1999, two of the world's largest pharmaceutical companies, the Swiss firm Roche Holding and the German firm BASF, agreed to pay criminal fines totaling $725 million to settle a U.S. Department of Justice price-fixing antitrust case that charged the two with conspiring to raise the price of vitamins. Between 1996 and 1999 the U.S. Department of Justice imposed its ten largest fines for price fixing on firms in the following markets: vitamins, electricity conductors, feed supplements, food additives, offshore oil construction, and industrial cleaners. These firms all have one thing in common: They are all *oligopolies*, or markets where a few large firms supply virtually all of the industry's output. Why did these firms conspire to fix prices, despite the risk of large fines and bad publicity? And why were other firms in oligopolies able to set their prices without entering into illegal price-fixing agreements with their competitors? In this chapter, we examine how firms behave in oligopolies.

Oligopoly market structures can result in a wide variety of firm behavior and industry performance. Consider the following examples of oligopolistic behavior:

- In 1995, an upstart airline, Spirit Airlines, entered the Detroit market and offered a one-way Detroit-Philadelphia fare of $49. At that time, Northwest Airlines, the dominant carrier out of Detroit, was charging an average Detroit-Philadelphia fare of $170. After Spirit entered, Northwest reduced its Detroit-Philadelphia fare to $49 for most seats.

- In 1967, a British, French, and German government consortium provided subsidies to enable the Europeans to enter the commercial aircraft industry and compete with Boeing. In 1974, the first European aircraft appeared on the market, but it was a commercial failure. The three governments then decided it was necessary to produce a complete line of aircraft to compete with Boeing. This goal was finally achieved when a European-subsidized company, Airbus, emerged. Initially, because of its small size relative to Boeing, Airbus faced a significant

Learning Objectives

After reading Chapter 14, you will have learned:

> How to derive the Cournot-Nash equilibrium using reaction functions and how the Cournot-Nash equilibrium compares to the competitive and monopoly equilibriums.

> How to derive the Stackelberg equilibrium and how the Stackelberg equilibrium differs from the Cournot-Nash equilibrium.

> How to derive the Bertrand equilibrium using reaction functions for a homogeneous product and for a heterogeneous product.

> The dominant firm model for the case of an oligopoly market dominated by one large firm that competes with a group of small fringe firms.

> Why the Prisoner's Dilemma typically makes collusion difficult and how firms try to solve the Prisoner's Dilemma by developing methods of coordinated behavior.

Featured Applications

> 14.1 Application Experimental Games and the Cournot-Nash Model

> 14.2 Application Fuji's Purchase of Wal-Mart's Photo-Processing Plants

> 14.3 Application Bertrand Pricing in the Airline Industry

> The Decline of Dominant Firms

> Price Fixing in the World Vitamin Market

> Price Leadership in Cyberspace: The Airlines Case

cost disadvantage that resulted in a need for the European governments to supply ever-larger subsidies. Today, however, after decades of large subsidies, Airbus competes effectively with Boeing.

- In the days when most gasoline contained lead, only a few firms produced lead-based anti-knock gasoline additives. From 1920 to 1948, Ethyl Corporation was the only American producer. DuPont entered in 1948, followed by PPG Industries and Nalco Chemical in the early 1960s. From 1974 to 1979, there were 24 price changes in the market. In 20 of these cases, all four companies changed price on the same day. In the other four cases, all four firms set identical prices within a day or two.

Each of these examples of an oligopoly market illustrates a different type of competitve behavior. In the Northwest Airlines example, prices are highly competitive. In the case of the Airbus consortium, several leading European nations spent billions of their taxpayers' euros and pounds to compete with an American worldwide-dominant firm—Boeing. In the lead-based anti-knock gasoline additives market, the firms found a method of eliminating price competiton. These disparate competitive outcomes show that in oligopoly markets, the possibilities range from successful agreements to keep prices high to competition that drives prices down toward marginal cost. This spectrum of possibilities makes it impossible for economists to explain oligopoly behavior using one model.

In this chapter, we explore a number of models of oligopoly behavior: the Cournot-Nash model, the Stackelberg model, the Bertrand model, the dominant firm model, and models used to explain successful collusion. Of the chapter's five sections, the first two deal with quantity-based models, the third and fourth with price-based models, and the fifth with models of successful collusion.

▼▼▼   14.1   The Cournot–Nash Model

The 19th-century French philosopher, mathematician, and economist Augustin Cournot made the first formal attempt to model oligopoly behavior in 1838.[1] Cournot considered the case of a duopoly market with two identical firms. The firms face identical costs and there is no product differentiation. Under these conditions, price is a simple function of the total quantity that the two firms produce. The driving force behind the Cournot model is one additional assumption: Both firms assume that their opponent will maintain its output at the current level *forever*. This is a rather unrealistic assumption that is inconsistent with most real-world situations. For example, suppose that your economics professor is ten minutes late for the first class of the semester. According to Cournot's assumption, you should assume he will be ten minutes late for every class for the entire semester. Furthermore, if he is five minutes late for the second class, you then assume he will be five minutes late for all the remaining classes. Later in this chapter, we return to the unrealistic nature of Cournot's output maintenance assumption.

---

[1] Augustin Cournot. *Recherches sur les principes mathematiques de la theorie des richesses*. Paris: M. Riviere & Cie., 1838. Translated in *Researches Into the Mathematical Principles of Wealth* (New York: A.M. Kelly, 1960).

In his original paper, Cournot began by assuming that one firm has a monopoly in a market in which a second firm is about to enter. Suppose, for example, that initially Kodak is a monopolist in the American photographic film industry and Fuji is considering entering. The demand for film in the United States is:

$$p = 10.00 - Q$$

where p is price in dollars and Q is output in millions of rolls of film. Assume further that Kodak's marginal cost and average cost equal $1.00 per roll; that is, $MC = AC = \$1.00$. Figure 14.1(a) shows Kodak's current monopoly equilibrium. Setting $MR = MC$, Kodak's profit-maximizing output is 4.5 million rolls of film, and the monopoly price is $5.50 per roll. Kodak's monopoly profit is $\pi = pq - (AC)q = \$5.50(4,500,000) - \$1.00(4,500,000) = \$24,750,000 - \$4,500,000 = \$20,250,000$, or $20.25 million.

Next Cournot turned his attention to the behavior of the firm entering the market—in our example, Fuji. If the second firm, Fuji, assumes that Kodak will produce 4.5 million rolls of film per year forever, what output should Fuji produce? Recall that the industry's demand curve is $p = 10.00 - Q$, which can also be written as $p = (10.00 - q_K) - q_F$, where q_K is Kodak's output and q_F is Fuji's output. Given Fuji's assumption that Kodak produces 4.5 million rolls, then Fuji's demand curve is $p = (10.00 - 4.5) - q_F = 5.50 - q_F$. Fuji's demand curve is depicted in Figure 14.1(b), and is referred to as a **residual demand curve**, because it is derived by assuming that Fuji faces a demand curve that is left over, or residual, after Kodak has chosen its output.

To better understand the concept of a residual demand curve, consider what happens to price if Fuji begins to produce any output greater than zero and Kodak produces $q_K = 4.5$. Note that for each 1 million rolls of film that Fuji sells, the price declines by one dollar below $5.50. If Fuji produces 1 million rolls, total industry output equals 5.5 million rolls and $p = \$4.50$. If Fuji sells 1 million rolls, price equals $4.50, so one point on Fuji's residual demand curve is ($q_F = 1$ million, $p = \$4.50$). What if Fuji sells 2 million rolls? Then $Q = q_K + q_F = 6.5$ million rolls, and $p = \$3.50$, so a second point on Fuji's residual

residual demand curve

A demand curve that is the leftover portion of an industry demand after a group of firms in the industry have chosen their outputs.

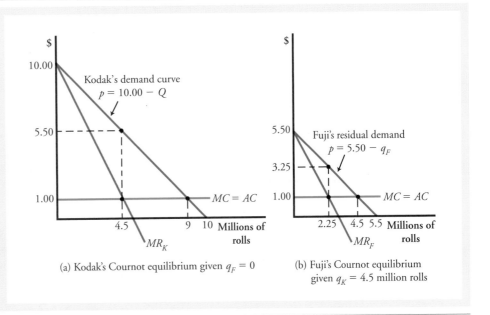

Figure 14.1 Kodak's Initial Monopoly and Fuji's Equilibrium When $q_K = 4.5$
In panel (a), Kodak is a monopolist that maximizes profit by producing 4.5 million rolls of film and charging $5.50 per roll. In panel (b), Fuji assumes that Kodak will produce 4.5 million rolls forever, and therefore faces a residual demand $p = 5.50 - q_F$ and maximizes profit by producing 2.25 million rolls of film and charging $3.25. Total industry output is now 6.75 million rolls, so the new equilibrium price is $3.25.

(a) Kodak's Cournot equilibrium given $q_F = 0$

(b) Fuji's Cournot equilibrium given $q_K = 4.5$ million rolls demand curve is (q_F = 2 million, p = \$3.50). Fuji's residual demand curve is, therefore, p = \$5.50 − q_F.

Figure 14.1(b) shows how to derive Fuji's profit-maximizing output. With identical costs to Kodak's, MC = \$1.00. Recalling that the MR curve bisects a linear demand curve, Fuji maximizes profit by producing where MR_F = \$5.50 − \$2q_F = \$1.00 = MC, so q_F = 2.25 million rolls. Total industry output is $Q = q_K + q_F$ = 4.5 + 2.25 = 6.75 million rolls, so p = \$3.25.

Now it's Kodak's turn to respond to Fuji's output. According to Cournot, Kodak assumes that Fuji will maintain an output of 2.25 million rolls per year forever. Figure 14.2(a) depicts Kodak's new equilibrium, given that Fuji is selling 2.25 million rolls of film per year. With q_F = 2.25, Kodak's residual demand curve is p = (10.00 − 2.25) − q_K = 7.75 − q_K, and its marginal revenue curve is MR_K = 7.75 − 2q_K. Kodak maximizes profit by producing where MR_K = 7.75 − 2q_K = 1.00 = MC, so q_K = 3.375 million rolls. Total industry output is 2.25 + 3.375 = 5.625 million rolls, and p = \$4.375 per roll.

Fuji now realizes that its strategy was wrong. After Fuji entered, Kodak did not maintain its output at 4.5 million rolls, but instead reduced its output to 3.375 million. Once Fuji observes that Kodak has changed its output, should Fuji drop its assumption that Kodak will maintain its output forever? Not according to Cournot. Instead, Cournot argued that Fuji would now assume that Kodak would maintain its output at 3.375 million rolls forever. As shown in Figure 14.2(b), Fuji's residual demand curve becomes p = (10.00 − 3.375) − q_F = 6.625 − q_F. Fuji equates its new MR_F curve to MC = 1.00 and produces 2.8125 million rolls. Industry output is now 2.8125 + 3.3750 = 6.1875 million rolls, and p = \$3.8125.

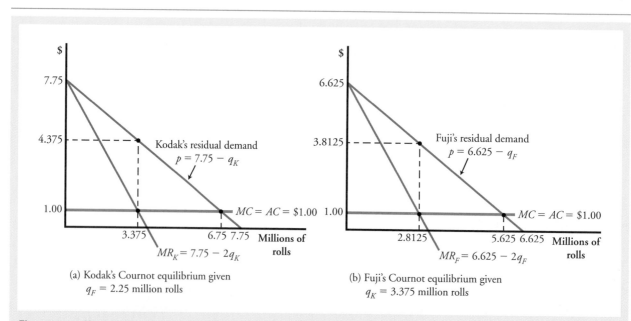

(a) Kodak's Cournot equilibrium given
q_F = 2.25 million rolls

(b) Fuji's Cournot equilibrium given
q_K = 3.375 million rolls

Figure 14.2 Kodak's Equilibrium When q_F = 2.25 and Fuji's Equilibrium When q_K = 3.375
In panel (a), Kodak assumes that Fuji will produce 2.25 million rolls per year forever, and therefore, Kodak faces a residual demand p = 7.75 − q_K and maximizes profit by producing 3.375 million rolls of film and charging a price of \$4.375. In panel (b), Fuji assumes Kodak will produce 3.375 million rolls forever, and therefore, Fuji faces a residual demand of p = 6.625 − q_F, and maximizes profit by producing 2.8125 million rolls of film and charging a price of \$3.8125.

Now Kodak's assumption that Fuji will maintain its output at 2.25 million rolls has been violated, because Fuji has increased its output to 2.8125 million rolls. Kodak responds by changing its output yet again. This in turn results in yet another output response by Fuji, which causes Kodak to change its output again, and so on. When does all of this end? Because of our assumption of symmetric costs and demands, only when both Kodak and Fuji face identical residual demand curves, and therefore both produce the same output, will this back-and-forth series of responses end. Figures 14.1–14.3 illustrate how the residual demand curves converge until they are identical when Kodak and Fuji face identical residual demand curves of $p = (10.00 - 3.00) - q_K = 7.00 - q_K$ and $p = (10.00 - 3.00) - q_F = 7.00 - q_F$, respectively. Figure 14.3 shows this equilibrium. Only when each firm produces 3 million rolls will each firm's assumption regarding the other's output be correct. In equilibrium, total industry output is 6 million rolls of film and $p = \$4.00$ per roll. One of the important implications of the Cournot equilibrium is that duopolists produce an equilibrium output between the profit-maximizing monopoly output of 4.5 million and the perfectly competitive output of 9 million, where $p = MC = \$1.00$.

Reaction Functions and the Cournot–Nash Equilibrium

We can find the Cournot equilibrium using algebra; however, first we need to understand an important new concept—a firm's *reaction function*.[2] In a duopoly Cournot game, a firm's **reaction function** identifies the profit-maximizing output that one firm produces in response to its competitor's output. More generally, in the context of other models, a reaction function might identify the profit-maximizing price that one firm would charge in response to any price that a competitor charged, or the profit-maximizing level of advertising expenditures that one firm would make in response to the level of advertising expenditures of its competitors.

To derive Kodak's and Fuji's reaction functions, we begin with Cournot's key assumption: Kodak assumes that Fuji's level of output will remain constant, and Fuji

reaction function

A function identifying one firm's optimal output (price) response to every possible output (price) produced (charged) by competitors.

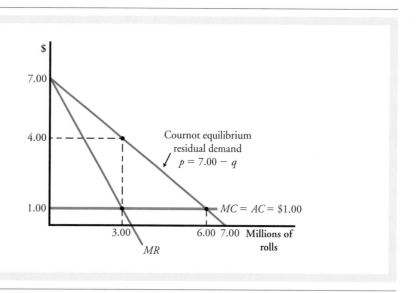

Figure 14.3 Final Cournot Equilibrium When $q_K = q_F = 3.0$
In the final Cournot equilibrium, Fuji and Kodak each assume the other firm will produce 3.0 million rolls per year forever, and therefore both firms face a residual demand $p = 7.00 - q$, and maximize profit by producing 3.0 million rolls of film and charging a price of \$4.00 per roll.

---

[2] The concept was introduced by Arthur L. Bowley, *The Mathematical Groundwork of Economics* (Oxford: Oxford University Press, 1924).

assumes that Kodak's level of output will remain constant. Given these assumptions, there exists a profit-maximizing output response for Kodak associated with any given output produced by Fuji, and vice versa. These functional relationships can be written as:

$$q_K = f(q_F) \text{ and } q_F = g(q_K) \tag{14.1}$$

To derive Kodak's reaction function, $q_K = f(q_F)$, we use the twice-as-steep rule from Chapter 11, which states that for a linear demand curve, the marginal revenue curve has the same price intercept and twice the slope of the demand curve. This rule permits us to derive the reaction functions using algebra. (Appendix 14.1 uses calculus to derive these reaction functions in a more precise mathematical way.) For industry demand curve $p = 10.00 - q_K - q_F$, Kodak's residual demand curve can be identified by noting that for any given level of Fuji's output, q_F, Kodak assumes that the quantity $(100 - q_F)$ is constant. It follows that for any given q_F, Kodak's demand curve is:

$$p_K = (10.00 - q_F) - q_K. \tag{14.2}$$

Equation 14.2 is a linear demand curve, with constant intercept $\$(10.00 - q_F)$ and slope -1, and therefore Kodak's marginal revenue is:

$$MR_K = (10.00 - q_F) - 2q_K$$

To obtain Kodak's reaction function, set $MR_K = MC$ for profit maximization:

$$MR_K = (10.00 - q_F) - 2q_K = 1.00 = MC \tag{14.3}$$

or:

$$2q_K = 9.00 - q_F \tag{14.4}$$

Solving Equation 14.4 for q_K, Kodak's reaction function is:

$$q_K = 4.5 - (1/2)q_F \tag{14.5}$$

Because Fuji faces identical demand and cost conditions, Fuji's reaction function is then:

$$q_F = 4.5 - (1/2)q_K \tag{14.6}$$

Figure 14.4 illustrates both reaction functions (Equations 14.5 and 14.6) on the same graph. The Cournot equilibrium occurs at the intersection of the two reaction functions, because only at that point are both firms making the correct assumption concerning the output of the other. We can derive the intersection by substituting the value of q_F from Equation 14.6 into Equation 14.5 and solving for q_K as follows:

$$q_K = 4.5 - \frac{1}{2}\left(4.5 - \frac{1}{2}q_K\right) = 4.5 - 2.25 + \frac{1}{4}q_K$$

$$\frac{3}{4}q_K = 2.25 \Rightarrow q_K = \frac{4(2.25)}{3} = \frac{9}{3} = 3$$

Figure 14.4 The Cournot Equilibrium Using Reaction Functions
Kodak's reaction function is $q_K = 4.5 - (1/2)q_F$, and Fuji's reaction function is $q_F = 4.5 - (1/2)q_K$. Only at the Cournot equilibrium where the two reaction functions intersect and $q_K = q_F = 3.0$ million rolls is there no incentive for either firm to change its output. The Cournot equilibrium is not on the red collusion curve where the firms produce a combined output of 4.5 million rolls and maximize joint profits.

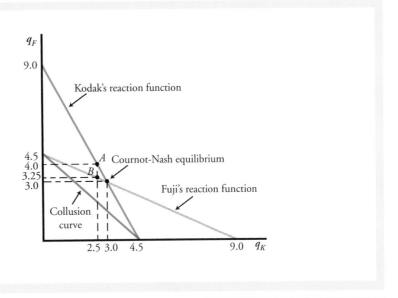

Substituting $q_K = 3$ into Equation 14.6:

$$q_F = 4.5 - \frac{1}{2}q_K = 4.5 - \frac{1}{2}(3) = 4.5 - 1.5 = 3$$

When each firm produces 3 million rolls, neither firm has an incentive to change output; therefore, Cournot's assumption that the other will maintain output is correct.

THE COURNOT EQUILIBRIUM AS A NASH EQUILIBRIUM In Figure 14.4, no other output combination can be sustained. Suppose Fuji produces 4 million rolls; then Kodak should produce at the point A on its reaction function, $q_K = 4.5 - (4/2) = 2.5$ million rolls. However, if Kodak produces 2.5 million rolls, then Fuji should operate at point B on its reaction function and produce $q_F = 4.5 - (2.5/2) = 3.25$ million rolls. However, that would result in a Kodak response, which would result in a Fuji response, and so on. A stable equilibrium is achieved only when the two reaction functions intersect and each firm produces the Cournot equilibrium quantity of 3.0 million rolls.

The Cournot equilibrium in Figure 14.4 has the characteristic that both players are doing the best they can, given the choice of their opponent. Recall from Chapter 13 that this is precisely the definition of a Nash equilibrium. Figure 14.4 reveals that there is one, and only one, Nash equilibrium, where $q_K = q_F = 3$ million. If both firms produce 3 million rolls, then a unilateral move to produce more or less than 3 million *always* reduces profits for the firm making the move. For example, if Fuji unilaterally reduces its output from 3 million to 2 million rolls, but Kodak maintains its output at 3 million rolls, then Fuji's profits decline from $9 million [$\pi = pq_F - AC(q_F) = \$(10.00 - 3 - 3)(3) - (\$1.00)(3) = \$4(3) - \$3 = \$9$ million] to $8 million [$\pi = pq_F - AC(q_F) = \$(10.00 - 2 - 3)(2) - (\$1.00)(2) = \$5(2) - \$2 = \$8$ million]. If Kodak unilaterally moves to produce 5 million rolls, but Fuji maintains its output at 3 million, Kodak's profit declines from $9 million to $5 million ($\pi = pq_K - AC(q_K) = \$(10.00 - 5 - 3)(5) - (\$1.00)(5) = \$2(5) - \$5 = \$5$ million). Given any combination of outputs produced by the two firms *except* $q_K = q_F = 3$ million, it is always possible for at least one of the firms to

Cournot-Nash equilibrium

The equilibrium outcome in a simultaneous move game where all the firms assume that the outputs of all the other firms in the industry will remain constant.

increase its profit through a unilateral move. Because the Cournot equilibrium is also a Nash equilibrium, the equilibrium is called a **Cournot-Nash equilibrium**.

THE COLLUSION CURVE   Does the Cournot-Nash equilibrium maximize the two firms' joint profits? If the firms arrive at the Cournot-Nash equilibrium, each firm earns $9 million, so joint profits are $18 million. But there are many output combinations that result in a larger joint profits. For example, if each firm produces 2 million rolls, then each earns $10 million [$\pi = pq - AC(q) = \$(10.00 - 2 - 2)(2) - (\$1.00)(2) = \$6(2) - \$2 = \$10$ million], and combined profits are $20 million. Better yet for Kodak and Fuji, if they each produce 2.25 million rolls, they combine to produce the monopoly output of 4.5 million rolls at $p = \$5.50$ per roll, and each earns profit of $10.125 million [$\pi = pq - AC(q) = \$(10.00 - 2.25 - 2.25)(2.25) - (\$1.00)(2.25) = \$5.50(2.25) - \$2.25 = \$10.125$ million] and joint profits are maximized at $20.25 million. In fact, if Kodak's and Fuji's combined output equals the monopoly output of 4.5 million rolls of film, combined profits equal $20.25 million, no matter how the output is divided between the two firms.

We have already established that the Cournot equilibrium is based on the questionable assumption that both firms assume the other firm will maintain its current level of output forever; we have also just discovered that the Cournot equilibrium is also a Nash equilibrium in a simple two-player game. The Cournot-Nash game is a simultaneous move, quantity-choice game with homogeneous products. The information structure of the Cournot-Nash game is *imperfect* (because the firms move simultaneously), *complete*,

▲▲▲ **14.1 APPLICATION**   Experimental Games and the Cournot–Nash Model

Empirical evidence on the likelihood of Cournot-Nash behavior is difficult to obtain, because it requires showing that oligopolists select prices between the competitive price and the monopoly price. Because of this difficulty, economists have turned to the use of experimental games to try to determine the likelihood of the Cournot-Nash outcome. These games are played typically by college students who receive information concerning their profit payoffs after making an output decision that is similar to the information in a Prisoner's Dilemma game. For example, the students know that if they charge a lower price than their opponent, they sell more units and are likely to earn a larger profit (unless the price is too low), and they know that if they charge a higher price than their opponent, they sell fewer units and are likely to sustain an economic loss. The student participants are often allowed to keep some of the profits they earn, so there is a strong incentive to do well.

In one experiment run by economists Lawrence Fouraker and Signey Siegel, 16 pairs of student duopolists played a game for 25 rounds.[3] The results showed that the Cournot-Nash solution was the most common outcome occurring in 7 of the 16 games, compared to 5 competitive outcomes, 3 joint profit-maximizing outcomes, and 1 outcome between the Cournot-Nash and joint profit-maximizing outcome. The mean outcome was also the Cournot-Nash outcome. When three students instead of two played the game, the competitive outcome became the most common. In another experiment, economist Charles Holt, Jr. found that the Cournot-Nash result was the most common outcome under a variety of different game structures.[4] A survey of experimental results by economist Charles Plott also found evidence of the Cournot-Nash outcome to be fairly common.[5]

---

[3] Lawrence Fouraker and Signey Siegel. *Bargaining Behavior.* New York: McGraw-Hill, 1963.

[4] Charles A. Holt, Jr., "An Experimental Test of the Consistent-Conjectures Hypothesis," *American Economic Review*, 1985, pp. 314–325.

[5] Charles R. Plott, "Industrial Organization Theory and Experimental Economics," *Journal of Economic Literature*, 1982, pp. 1485–1527.

certain, and *symmetric* (see Chapter 13). In such a game, both firms realize that it makes sense to produce the Nash equilibrium immediately without the back-and-forth jockeying for output position described by Cournot. Although the final outcome is the same, the Nash equilibrium is based on a much more reasonable set of behavioral assumptions than the Cournot equilibrium. The realization that Cournot's original equilibrium is also a Nash equilibrium resurrected Cournot's model, which has become one of the most widely used models of economic behavior.

We know that to maximize total industry profits at $20.25 million, Kodak and Fuji must produce together 4.5 million rolls of film, regardless of how output is distributed between the firms. In Figure 14.4, the red line where $q_K + q_F = 4.5$ million is called the *collusion curve*. The **collusion curve** identifies all the combinations of q_K and q_F that maximize joint profits. If the two firms combine to produce 4.5 million rolls, however, the combination will not be a Nash equilibrium. Each firm could, for example, produce 2.25 million rolls and earn a profit of $10.25 million, but then each firm would have an incentive to unilaterally increase output. For example, if Fuji unilaterally increased output to 3.5 million rolls, it would earn a profit of $11.375 million ($\pi = pq_F - AC(q_F)$) = $(10.00 - 2.25 - 3.5)(3.5) - (\$1.00)(3.5) = (\$4.25)(3.5) - \$3.5 = \$14.875 - \$3.5 = \$11.375$ million). None of the points on the collusion curve are Nash equilibria. In Section 14.5, we explore how Kodak and Fuji might attempt to reach a point on the collusion curve where joint profits are maximized.

collusion curve

A curve identifying all the output combinations that firms can produce to maximize joint industry profits.

14.2 The Stackelberg Model

You just learned that the Cournot-Nash model is a one-period simultaneous move game in which both players assume that their opponent's output is constant even after their opponent changes its output. In 1934, economist Heinrich von Stackelberg questioned Cournot's assumption that both firms take their opponent's output as given, by considering what would happen if only one of the two firms, known as the **Stackelberg follower**, assumed its opponent would maintain its output, while the other firm, known as the **Stackelberg leader**, used this knowledge about its opponent to select an output that maximized its profit.[6] In the Stackelberg model, the leader makes a more logical assumption than the follower, and as a result, the game's equilibrium changes.

Stackelberg follower

The firm that moves second in the Stackelberg game.

Stackelberg leader

The firm that moves first in the Stackelberg game.

Firms with Identical Costs and Demand

The Stackelberg model is a sequential game where the Stackelberg leader moves first, and the Stackelberg follower moves second. Returning to our Kodak-Fuji game, suppose Kodak is the leader and moves first; then Fuji, the follower, moves; and then the game ends. The demand and cost conditions are the same as they were before: demand is $p = 100 - q_K - q_F$ and costs are $MC = AC = \$1.00$ for both firms. As an initial simplifying assumption, suppose Kodak can select only from eight possible quantities: 2.0, 2.5, 3.0, 3.5, 4.0, 4.5, 5.0, or 5.5 million rolls. Fuji observes Kodak's quantity and then selects its quantity. The game tree in Figure 14.5 identifies some of the possible outcomes of such a game; it is only a partial depiction of the game, because it identifies only Fuji's profit-maximizing responses—as opposed to all of Fuji's possible responses—to Kodak's move. Once Kodak selects an output, Fuji chooses its profit-maximizing output by

---

[6] The original work was in Heinrich von Stackelberg, *Marktform und Gleichgewicht* (Vienna: Springer, 1934).

Figure 14.5 The Extensive Form of the Stackelberg Game ($millions Kodak profit, $millions Fuji profit)
If Kodak can produce only eight possible outputs between 2.0 and 5.5 million rolls, Fuji responds to Kodak's output by producing an output that maximizes Fuji's profit. Kodak moves first and selects $q_K = 4.5$ million rolls, knowing that Fuji will respond by producing 2.25 million rolls. Kodak produces 4.5 million rolls, because that output maximizes Kodak's profit at $10.125 million.

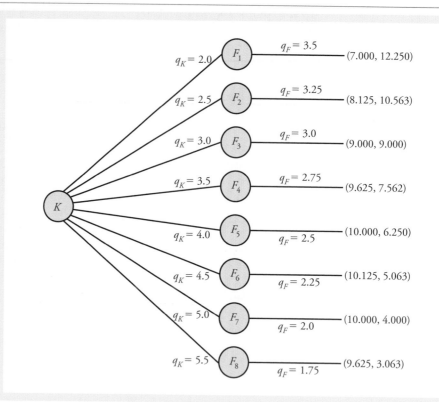

substituting Kodak's quantity for q_K in Equation 14.6. If Kodak produces 2.0 million rolls, Fuji produces $q_F = 4.5 - (1/2)q_K = 4.5 - 1.0 = 3.5$ million rolls; if Kodak produces 2.5 million rolls, Fuji produces $q_F = 4.5 - (1/2)q_K = 4.5 - 1.25 = 3.25$ million rolls; and so on. In Figure 14.5, the numbers in parentheses show Kodak's and Fuji's profits in millions of dollars, respectively.

What is Kodak's optimal move? Kodak knows that if it produces 2.0 million rolls, Fuji produces 3.5 million rolls and Kodak's profit equals $7 million; if Kodak produces 2.5 million rolls, Fuji produces 3.25 million rolls and Kodak's profit equals $8.125 million, and so on. Kodak selects the output that maximizes its profit, or 4.5 million rolls. Fuji responds by producing 2.25 million rolls. Kodak earns profit of $10.125 million, and Fuji earns $5.063 million. Then the game ends. Figure 14.5 shows the Cournot-Nash equilibrium at F_3 where Kodak and Fuji both produce 3.0 million rolls, and Kodak's profit is $9.0 million. By moving first, Kodak is able to "force" Fuji to its reaction function, and as a result, Kodak earns a larger profit than in the Cournot-Nash equilibrium.

Next, we eliminate the simplifying assumption that Kodak can produce only eight possible outputs, and consider the more realistic game where Kodak can produce any output. While Kodak can select any output in this new version of the game, Fuji must be on its reaction function when it takes the second move. This restriction is placed on Fuji by substituting Fuji's reaction function, $q_F = 4.5 - (1/2)q_K$, directly into Kodak's demand curve, which yields:

$$p = (10.00 - q_F) - q_K = \left(10.00 - \left(4.5 - \frac{1}{2}q_K\right)\right) - q_K = 5.5 + \frac{1}{2}q_K - q_K$$

$$p = 5.5 - (1/2)q_K \tag{14.7}$$

Equation 14.7 is Kodak's demand curve. Using the twice-as-steep rule, Kodak's marginal revenue is:

$$MR_K = 5.5 - q_K \qquad (14.8)$$

To maximize profit, Kodak sets $MR_K = MC$:

$$MR_K = 5.5 - q_K = 1.00$$

or:

$$q_K = 4.5$$

Kodak's profit-maximizing output is 4.5 million rolls. (Appendix 14.2 derives this result using calculus.)

Once Kodak produces 4.5 million rolls, we know from Figure 14.5 that Fuji's optimal response is to substitute $q_K = 4.5$ into its reaction function and produce 2.25 million rolls ($q_F = 4.5 - (1/2)q_K = 4.5 - 2.25 = 2.25$). Total industry output is $Q = q_K + q_F = 4.5 + 2.25 = 6.75$ million rolls, and price is $p = 10.00 - 6.75 = \$3.25$ per roll. The Stackelberg equilibrium thus yields a greater total industry output and lower price than the Cournot-Nash equilibrium.

Firms with Different Costs

Having identified the Stackelberg equilibrium in the case of completely symmetric duopolists, it is useful to address one common question: Why is Kodak, and not Fuji, the Stackelberg leader? The truth is, if both firms are symmetric, there is no theoretical reason why one firm should be the leader and the other the follower. Complete symmetry, however, is rare in real-world oligopolies. For example, General Motors and Toyota are not completely symmetric in terms of production costs or product demands. The same is true for Coca-Cola and Pepsi, Dell and Gateway, Boeing and Airbus, and Kodak and

---

COMMON ERROR 14.1 **Failing to Correctly Substitute the Follower's Reaction Function into the Leader's Demand Curve**

To correctly determine the Stackelberg equilibrium, it is necessary to substitute the follower's reaction function into the leader's demand curve. Many students mistakenly substitute the follower's reaction function into the leader's reaction function instead. However, one of the key points about the Stackelberg equilibrium is that in equilibrium, the leader is not on its own reaction function. Ironically, by constraining both firms to their reaction functions, this error results in finding the Cournot-Nash equilibrium. For example, if you substitute the follower Fuji's reaction function into the leader Kodak's reaction function, it yields:

$$q_K = 4.5 - \frac{1}{2}\left(4.5 - \frac{1}{2}q_K\right) = 2.25 + \frac{1}{4}q_K$$

$$\frac{3}{4}q_K = 2.25$$

$$q_K = \frac{4(2.25)}{3} = \frac{9}{3} = 3$$

This is Kodak's Cournot-Nash equilibrium output of 3 million rolls. As the Stackelberg leader, however, Kodak's equilibrium output is 4.5 million rolls, or 50 percent greater. Don't make this common error!

Fuji. In each of these oligopolies, there is some variation between the firms in terms of costs and demands.

Consider a case where one of the duopolists has an advantage because of lower production costs and/or greater demand. In this case, it is logical to assume that the firm with the advantage is the Stackelberg leader. Suppose, for instance, that Kodak's costs are $MC_K = AC_K = \$1.00$ per roll, but Fuji's costs are 10 percent higher, so $MC_F = AC_F = \$1.10$ per roll. Under these cost conditions, it makes sense to assume that Kodak, the low-cost firm with the theoretical ability to drive Fuji from the market by charging a price below $\$1.10$, controls the game by moving first.

Fuji's higher costs change its reaction function and the Stackelberg equilibrium. Kodak's reaction function, however, remains unchanged, because its costs and demand have not changed. To calculate the new Stackelberg equilibrium, it is necessary to first identify Fuji's new reaction function and then substitute the new reaction function into Kodak's demand curve. To derive Fuji's new reaction function, we start with Fuji's demand curve:

$$p_F = (10.00 - q_K) - q_F \tag{14.9}$$

According to the twice-as-steep rule, Fuji's marginal revenue is:

$$MR_F = (10.00 - q_K) - 2q_F$$

To obtain Fuji's reaction function, set $MR_F = MC = \$1.10$:

$$MR_F = (10.00 - q_K) - 2q_F = 1.10 = MC_F \tag{14.10}$$

or:

$$2q_F = 8.90 - q_K \tag{14.11}$$

Solving Equation 14.11 for q_F, Fuji's new reaction function is:

$$q_F = 4.45 - (1/2)q_K \tag{14.12}$$

Substituting $q_F = 4.45 - (1/2)q_K$ from Equation 14.12 into Kodak's demand curve yields:

$$p = (10.00 - q_F) - q_K = \left(10.00 - \left(4.45 - \frac{1}{2}q_K\right)\right) - q_K = 5.55 + \frac{1}{2}q_K - q_K$$

$$p = 5.55 - (1/2)q_K \tag{14.13}$$

Equation 14.13 is Kodak's new demand curve, so Kodak's marginal revenue is:

$$MR_K = 5.55 - q_K \tag{14.14}$$

To maximize profit, Kodak equates marginal revenue to marginal cost:

$$MR_K = 5.55 - q_K = 1.00$$

so:

$$q_K = 4.55$$

▲▲▲ **14.2 APPLICATION** Fuji's Purchase of Wal-Mart's Photo-Processing Plants

In the market for wholesale photofinishing, Kodak is by far the leading firm, controlling more than 60 percent of the market. Fuji is the second-largest wholesale photofinisher. In 1993 and 1994, Kodak began to expand its photofinishing capacity by purchasing two photofinishing labs from Walgreen's, which owns a large chain of drugstores. In 1995, Kodak also signed an agreement with Kmart to run all 320 of Kmart's in-store photofinishing mini-labs. In 1996, Kodak continued expanding its output, when it gained control of all seven of Eckard Drugs's photofinishing labs. The Eckard acquisition pushed Kodak's market share beyond 80 percent.

In early 1996, Fuji controlled 15 photofinishing labs in the United States and its market share was between five and six percent. After observing Kodak's output

expansion from 1993 to 1996, Fuji responded in July 1996 by purchasing all six of Wal-Mart's large wholesale photofinishing labs. Furthermore, Fuji gained control over all of Wal-Mart's out-of-store photofinishing services. The acquisition of Wal-Mart's labs, which followed Fuji's building of a large photofinishing lab in South Carolina earlier in the year, increased Fuji's market share to 16 percent in 1997.

In the context of the Stackelberg model, Kodak moved first and expanded its photofinishing operations, then Fuji, after observing Kodak's expansion, expanded its photofinishing capacity to a level it considered optimal, given Kodak's capacity. As expected, after Fuji's capacity expansion, photofinishing prices declined dramatically, as did Kodak's market share.

To obtain Fuji's profit-maximizing output, substitute $q_K = 4.55$ into Equation 14.12:

$$q_F = 4.45 - \frac{1}{2}q_K = 4.45 - \frac{1}{2}(4.55) = 4.45 - 2.275 = 2.175$$

If Fuji's costs are 10 percent higher than Kodak's, Kodak is the Stackelberg leader and produces 4.55 million rolls of film, while Fuji is the follower and produces 2.175 million rolls. Total output is $4.55 + 2.175 = 6.725$ million rolls and $p = 10.00 - 6.725 = \$3.275$. A 10 percent increase in Fuji's costs results in the following:

- A 1.1 percent increase in Kodak's output from 4.5 million rolls to 4.55 million
- A 3.3 percent decrease in Fuji's output from 2.25 million rolls to 2.175 million
- A 0.37 percent decrease in total output from 6.75 million rolls to 6.725 million
- A 0.80 percent increase in price from \$3.25 to \$3.275

14.3 The Bertrand Model

In 1883, Joseph Bertrand criticized Cournot's equilibrium by showing that if each duopolist assumes that its opponent holds constant its price (instead of its quantity), Cournot's logic results in an entirely different equilibrium.[7] Betrand considered the case where the two firms produce a homogeneous product. Later theorists expanded the model to include cases where the firms produce differentiated products. We will consider both cases, beginning with the simpler but less-realistic case of homogeneous products.

The Betrand Model with Homogeneous Products

Because most consumers consider a seat on any non-stop flight between the same two cities a homogeneous product, consider a game that Southwest Airlines and US Airways play on flights between Albany, New York and Baltimore, Maryland. Suppose the

---

[7] Bertrand's model was developed in a critical review of Cournot published 45 years after the original article in Joseph Bertrand, book review of *Recherches sur les principes mathematiques de la theorie des richesses*, in *Journal de Savants*, Vol. 67, 1883, pp. 499–508.

demand for seats is $p = 1,000 - Q$ and the marginal cost of adding an additional passenger on a one-way flight is $70. If Southwest assumes that US Airways always maintains its price at its current level, p_{US}, then Southwest's demand is dependent upon the current relationship between Southwest's price, p_S, and the US Airways price, p_{US}. Because seats on any flight are a homogeneous product, passengers always purchase a ticket on the less-expensive airline. If Southwest's price is greater than the US Airways price, US Airways captures the entire market, and $q_S = 0$. If Southwest's price is less than the US Airways price, Southwest captures the entire demand, and $q_S = 1,000 - p_S$. Finally, if $p_S = p_{US}$, the two firms split the market, in which case each obtains one-half of the total industry demand, and Southwest's demand curve is:

$$q_S = \frac{1}{2}(1,000 - p_S)$$

$$q_S = 500 - \frac{1}{2}p_S \text{ for } p_S = p_{US} \quad (14.15)$$

Southwest's demand curve can therefore be identified as:

$$q_s = \begin{bmatrix} 0 \text{ if } p_S > p_{US} \\ 500 - \frac{1}{2}p_S \text{ if } p_S = p_{US} \\ 1,000 - p_S \text{ if } p_S < p_{US} \end{bmatrix} \quad (14.16)$$

Bertrand model

A model developed by Joseph Bertrand that criticized Cournot's model by arguing that if firms assume that all other firms hold their prices constant, Cournot's logic results in an entirely different outcome, with price equal to marginal cost.

The **Bertrand model** with a homogeneous product is driven by the assumption that one of the airlines can capture the entire market if it charges a lower fare than its competitor. Given this assumption, if Southwest charges a fare just slightly less than p_{US}, it will virtually double its output and profit. This implies that if $p_S = p_{US} - \varepsilon$, where ε represents a number that is *infinitesimally* greater than 0, Southwest captures the entire market. Of course, if $p_{US} = p_S - \varepsilon$, then US Airways captures the entire market.

Figure 14.6 identifies Southwest's demand curve if US Airways charges a fare of $400 for a one-way ticket. If Southwest charges any fare greater than $400, US Airways sells all the tickets, Southwest sells no tickets, and Southwest's demand curve is the vertical blue line along the price axis. If Southwest matches the US Airways fare and charges $400, the airlines divide the total demand of 600 tickets, and Southwest sells 300 tickets at point A. Finally, if Southwest charges any fare less than $400, US Airways sells no tickets, Southwest sells all the tickets, and Southwest's demand curve is identical to the industry's demand curve $p = 1,000 - q_S$.

What is Southwest's optimal pricing strategy? If Southwest assumes US Airways maintains its price at $400, then Southwest can charge a fare *slightly* less than $400 and capture the entire market. To simplify the analysis, we assume that fares can be quoted only in whole dollar amounts. If Southwest lowers its fare by $1.00 to $399, its output will more than double, from 300 to 601 tickets. Southwest's marginal revenue associated with a fare reduction from $400 to $399 is calculated as follows. First, calculate the change in total revenue associated with the fare reduction: At $p_S = \$400$, $TR_S = pq_S = \$400(300) = \$120,000$, and at $p_S = \$399$, $TR_S = pq_S = \$399(601) = \$239,799$. Next, calculate Southwest's marginal revenue:

$$MR_S = \frac{\Delta TR_S}{\Delta q_S} = \frac{\$239,799 - \$120,000}{601 - 300} = \frac{\$119,799}{301} = \$398.00$$

Because marginal revenue is $398 and marginal cost is $70, Southwest is better off if it reduces its fare from $400 to $399.

Figure 14.6 The Southwest Airlines Demand Curve if US Airways Charges $400 for a Ticket
If Southwest Airlines assumes that US Airways will maintain its fare at $400, its demand curve consists of three segments. If Southwest charges a fare higher than $400, it sells zero tickets. If Southwest charges a fare equal to $400, it sells half the 600 tickets demanded or 300 tickets at point A. If Southwest charges a fare below $400, it sells all the tickets demanded.

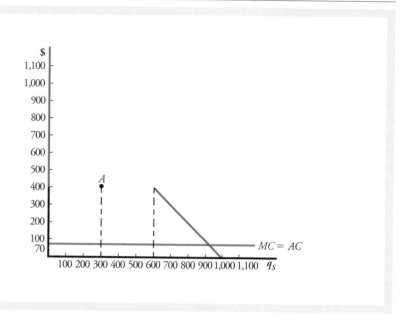

Should Southwest reduce its fare further in order to sell more tickets? To sell one additional ticket to the 602nd passenger, Southwest must reduce its fare to $398. The marginal revenue of reducing its fare from $399 to $398 is:

$$MR_S = \frac{\Delta TR_S}{\Delta q_s} = \frac{\$239{,}596 - \$239{,}799}{602 - 601} = \frac{-\$203}{1} = -\$203$$

Marginal revenue is negative (notice that Southwest is operating on the bottom half of a linear demand curve, where demand is inelastic), and therefore, any further fare reductions reduce Southwest's total revenues and profit. Southwest's optimal policy is to lower its fare to $399.

But surely, from US Airways's perspective, the game cannot end there. After Southwest lowers its fare to $399, what is US Airways' optimal pricing strategy? If US Airways assumes that Southwest will maintain its fare at $399, then US Airways can charge a fare slightly less than $399 and capture the entire market. If US Airways lowers its fare to $398, its output increases from zero at a fare of $400 to 602 at a fare of $398. US Airways' marginal revenue associated with this price reduction is:

$$MR_{US} = \frac{\Delta TR_{US}}{\Delta q_{US}} = \frac{\$239{,}596 - \$0}{602 - 0} = \frac{\$239{,}596}{602} = \$398.00$$

Because US Airways' marginal revenue is $398 and marginal cost is $70, US Airways is better off if it reduces its fare to $398.

But now Southwest is left out of the market, unless it lowers its fare to $397, in which case US Airways will respond by lowering its fare to $396. When does the game end? Any fare greater than $MC = \$70$ will result in one airline reducing fares, which in turn will result in a fare reduction by the other, and so on. Equilibrium occurs only when both fares equal $MC = \$70$, because only then will neither firm have an incentive to reduce its fare further.

Figure 14.7 identifies the reaction functions for Southwest and US Airways. Southwest's reaction function goes through the point ($70, $70), but is not identified for

Figure 14.7 A Bertrand Equilibrium with Homogeneous Products

If Southwest charges a fare above $MC = \$70$, US Airways responds by charging a fare \$1.00 less than Southwest's fare, and the US Airways reaction function lies at a distance \$1.00 below the 45-degree line. By the same reasoning, Southwest's reaction function lies at a distance \$1.00 to the left of the 45-degree line. The Bertrand equilibrium is the Nash equilibrium at the intersection point (\$70, \$70).

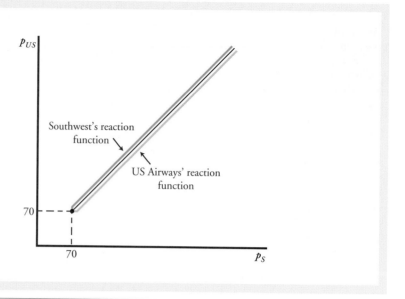

fares below \$70, because a fare cut below \$70 would result in economic losses; the fare would be below average cost. For all $p_{US} > \$70$, Southwest charges a fare $p_S = (p_{US} - \$1.00)$; therefore, for $p_{US} > \$70$, Southwest's reaction function lies at a distance \$1.00 to the left of the 45-degree line. Similarly, the US Airways reaction function lies at a distance \$1.00 below the 45-degree line. For $p > \$70$, the two reaction functions will be parallel to each other and also parallel to the 45-degree line where $p_S = p_{US}$. The Nash equilibrium occurs at the intersection point (\$70, \$70), because this is the only point where both firms are doing the best they can given the choice of their competitor.

We can interpret the Bertrand model as a simultaneous move game. Both firms reason: "If we set our fare at any $p > MC$, then our opponent will set its fare at $p - \varepsilon$, where ε is a number infinitesimally greater than zero, and we will sell nothing. But, if we set our fare at $p = MC = \$70$, then we either capture the entire market or split the market 50-50. We should, therefore, set our fare equal to MC."

The Bertrand Model with Product Differentiation

In the Bertrand duopoly model with a homogeneous product, price equals MC, the perfectly competitive price. In many oligopolies, however, firms produce differentiated products. Let's analyze the Bertrand model in the case where duopolists Ben & Jerry's and Häagen Dazs produce differentiated premium ice cream.[8]

Suppose that because of consumer brand loyalty, Ben & Jerry's and Häagen Dazs face the following symmetric demand curves for pints of ice cream:

$$q_B = 9.60 - 2p_B + p_H \qquad (14.17)$$

$$q_H = 9.60 - 2p_H + p_B \qquad (14.18)$$

---

[8] For a fairly simple treatment of the introduction of product differentiation into the Bertrand model, see Eric Rasmusen, *Games and Information: An Introduction to Game Theory* (Oxford: Basil Blackwell, 1989), pp. 267–269.

▲▲▲ 14.3 APPLICATION Bertrand Pricing in the Airline Industry

Pricing behavior in the airline industry has often been consistent with Bertrand price behavior. Many airlines have followed a policy of pricing at near-marginal cost on routes where they face competition, especially from low-price carriers such as Southwest Airlines or JetBlue. The carriers' rationale for this behavior is consistent with the Bertrand model assumptions. Each carrier fears that if its fares are even slightly higher than the competition, it will lose nearly its entire market share.

Consider the following fares offered by US Airways over the Internet on August 28, 2002. The distance from Syracuse to Baltimore is almost identical to the distance from Albany to Baltimore.

US Airways competed against Southwest Airlines in the Albany market, but not in the Syracuse market. In the Albany market, US Airways essentially matched Southwest's low fares. In the Syracuse market, US Airways was a virtual monopolist on flights to Baltimore and Raleigh-Durham. US Airways' lowest advanced-purchase fare from Syracuse to Baltimore was 50.4 percent higher than its lowest advanced-purchase fare from Albany to Baltimore, and its lowest fare from Syracuse to Raleigh-Durham was 22.7 percent higher than its lowest fare from Albany to Raleigh-Durham. If Southwest charged fares close to marginal cost, then the Albany fares can be interpreted as Bertrand equilibrium fares. US Airways reasoned that if its Albany fares were higher than Southwest's, it would fly mostly empty planes out of Albany to Baltimore or Raleigh-Durham.

Route	US Airways Lowest Round-Trip Advanced Fare	Southwest Lowest Round-Trip Advanced Fare
Syracuse, NY to Baltimore, MD	$173.00	No flights
Albany, NY to Baltimore, MD	$115.00	$120.00
Syracuse, NY to Raleigh-Durham, NC	$216.00	No flights
Albany, NY to Raleigh-Durham, NC	$167.00	$172.00

where q_B, $q_H \geq 0$ and p_B, $p_H \leq \$4.80$. Quantities are measured in millions of pints and price is measured in dollars. The restrictions that q_B and $q_H \geq 0$ prevent quantities from becoming negative, and the restrictions that p_B and $p_H \leq \$4.80$ prevent output from becoming infinite as an opponent's price increases. In Equation 14.17, Ben & Jerry's demand is a negative function of its own price p_B, and a positive function of Häagen Dazs' price p_H. Unlike the case of a homogeneous product, even if the price of Ben & Jerry's is greater than the price of Häagen Dazs—that is, $p_B > p_H$—Ben & Jerry's still sells some ice cream. Some consumers buy Ben & Jerry's ice cream because of its unique taste or certain flavors it produces, even if it is more expensive than Häagen Dazs. Furthermore, an increase in p_H results in an increase in q_B; that is, an increase in the price of Häagen Dazs increases the quantity demanded of Ben & Jerry's.

Assume $MC_B = MC_H = \$1.20$ per pint, so that in the absence of product differentiation, the Bertrand equilibrium price equals $1.20. In the following derivation of Ben & Jerry's reaction function, remember that the reaction function $p_B = f(p_H)$ is in terms of price, not quantity, and p_H is assumed to be constant throughout. We first solve Equation 14.17 for p_B:

$$2p_B = 9.60 + p_H - q_B$$

Dividing both sides of the equation by 2 yields:

$$p_B = \left(4.80 + \frac{1}{2}p_H\right) - \frac{1}{2}q_B \qquad (14.19)$$

Because p_H is assumed to be constant, using the twice-as-steep rule, MR_B is:

$$MR_B = \left(4.80 + \frac{1}{2}p_H\right) - q_B \qquad (14.20)$$

Using Equations 14.19 and 14.20, it is possible to calculate all the points on Ben & Jerry's reaction function. First, from Equation 14.20, we compute Ben & Jerry's profit-maximizing quantity for any given price of Häagen Dazs p_H. Then from Equation 14.19, we calculate Ben & Jerry's price. For example, if the price of Häagen Dazs is $p_H = \$2.00$ per pint, we compute Ben & Jerry's profit-maximizing quantity by setting $MR_B = MC$ and substituting $p_H = \$2.00$ into Equation 14.20, which yields $MR_B = (4.80 + (1/2)(2.00)) - q_B = 1.20 = MC$. Solving for q_B, $q_B = (4.80+1.00) - 1.20 = 4.60$ million pints. Once we know that Ben & Jerry's profit-maximizing quantity is 4.60 million pints, we calculate Ben & Jerry's price from Equation 14.19: $p_B = (4.80 + (1/2)(2.00)) - (1/2)(4.60) = (4.80+1.00) - 2.30 = \$3.50$ per pint. This identifies one point on Ben & Jerry's reaction function: When Häagen Dazs charges $p_H = \$2.00$, Ben & Jerry's maximizes its profit by charging $p_B = \$3.50$. If the price of Häagen Dazs is $p_H = \$4.00$, then $MR_B = (4.80 + (1/2)(4.00)) - q_B = 1.20 = MC$; $q_B = (4.80+2.00) - 1.20 = 5.60$ million pints; and $p_B = (4.80 + (1/2)(4.00)) - (1/2)(5.60) = (4.80+2.00) - 2.80 = \$4.00$. This identifies a second point on Ben & Jerry's reaction function: When Häagen Dazs charges $p_H = \$4.00$, Ben & Jerry's charges $p_B = \$4.00$.

Generalizing these results for any price of Häagen Dazs, Ben & Jerry's maximizes its profit by equating MR_B to MC from Equation 14.20:

$$MR_B = \left(4.80 + \frac{1}{2}p_H\right) - q_B = 1.20 = MC \qquad (14.21)$$

Solving Equation 14.21 for q_B:

$$q_B = 3.60 + \frac{1}{2}p_H \qquad (14.22)$$

To obtain Ben & Jerry's reaction function $p_B = f(p_H)$, substitute q_B from Equation 14.22 into Equation 14.19:

$$p_B = \left(4.80 + \frac{1}{2}p_H\right) - \frac{1}{2}q_B = \left(4.80 + \frac{1}{2}p_H\right) - \frac{1}{2}\left(3.60 + \frac{1}{2}p_H\right)$$

$$p_B = \left(4.80 + \frac{1}{2}p_H\right) - 1.80 - \frac{1}{4}p_H$$

$$p_B = 3.00 + \frac{1}{4}p_H \qquad (14.23)$$

Equation 14.23 is Ben & Jerry's reaction function. Because both firms face symmetric demand and costs, Häagen Dazs' reaction function is derived the same way:

$$p_H = 3.00 + \frac{1}{4}p_B \qquad (14.24)$$

Figure 14.8 shows the two reaction functions and the Nash equilibrium. To obtain the Nash equilibrium, we find the intersection point of the two reaction functions by sub-

Figure 14.8 A Bertrand Equilibrium with Product Differentiation

With product differentiation, each firm's profit-maximizing response to a price increase by its opponent is to increase price. If Häagen Dazs charges a price of $2.00, Ben & Jerry's profit-maximizing response is to charge a price of $3.50 at point A. If Häagen Dazs charges a price of $4.00, Ben & Jerry's response is also to charge a price of $4.00 at the intersection of the two reaction functions at point B. Point B is the Bertrand equilibrium.

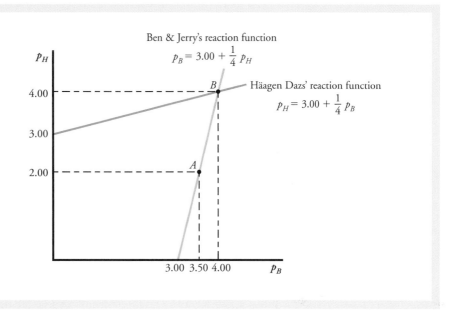

stituting Häagen Dazs' reaction function $p_H = 3.00 + (1/4)p_B$ from Equation 14.24 into Ben & Jerry's reaction function from Equation 14.23, and then solving for p_B as follows:

$$p_B = 3.00 + \frac{1}{4}\left(3.00 + \frac{1}{4}p_B\right) = 3.75 + \frac{1}{16}p_B$$

or:

$$\frac{15}{16}p_B = 3.75 \Rightarrow p_B = \frac{16(3.75)}{15} = 4.00$$

By analogous reasoning, $p_H = \$4.00$.

The Bertrand equilibrium with product differentiation yields a price of $4.00 per pint. In the absence of product differentiation, the Bertrand equilibrium is $p_B = p_H = MC = \$1.20$ per pint. The introduction of product differentiation has resulted in a dramatically increased price, and a price that is well above marginal cost.

14.4 The Dominant Firm Model

The Cournot-Nash, Stackelberg, and Bertrand games are played by large firms. These models are therefore best applied to real-world markets in which large firms compete against each other. Some markets, however, are characterized by one dominant firm that controls a large percentage of total industry output and a significant number of relatively small fringe firms that compete with the dominant firm.[9] Such markets are structured like the personal computer market in the 1980s, which was dominated by IBM, but also included many smaller PC manufacturers such as Compaq, Hewlett-Packard, Digital

[9] This model is sometimes referred to as the Forchheimer Model, because it was derived in Karl Forchheimer, "Theoretisches zum unvollstandegen Monopole," *Schmollers Jahrbuch*, 1908, pp. 1–12; A. J. Nichol, *Partial Monopoly and Price Leadership* (Philadelphia: Smith-Edwards, 1930). See also Dean A. Worcester, "Why Dominant Firms Decline," *Journal of Political Economy*, August 1957, pp. 338–347.

Equipment, Epson, Dell, and Gateway. In markets dominated by one large firm, we can assume that the dominant firm is able to set the industry price, and that the fringe firms then take the dominant firm's price as given and set their prices to maximize profits, given the dominant firm's price.

Figure 14.9 illustrates the dominant firm model. The industry demand curve, D_I, is the linear demand curve ABC and the fringe firms' supply curve is S_f. The dominant firm's demand curve, D_D, is a residual demand curve that is obtained by subtracting the fringe's supply curve S_f from the total industry demand curve D_I. For example, if price is p_4, total industry quantity demanded equals q_2 units, and the fringe would supply the entire industry demand of q_2 units. Therefore, if $p = p_4$, the residual quantity demanded for the dominant firm would be zero at point E. If price is p_1, total industry quantity demanded equals q_5 units, the fringe would supply zero, and the residual demand for the dominant firm equals q_5 units. If $p = p_2$, then total industry quantity demanded equals q_4 units, the fringe firms supply q_1 units, and the residual demand for the dominant firm equals $q_3 = q_4 - q_1$ units. Similar calculations can be done to obtain the dominant firm's residual demand for any price between p_1 and p_4. Such calculations yield the dominant firm's demand curve D_D, which is the dark-blue kinked line $EGIBC$. The dominant firm's marginal revenue curve for quantities less than q_5 is MR_D and bisects the segment $EGIB$ of the demand curve D_D. Recall from Chapter 11 that a profit-maximizing monopolist always prices where demand is elastic; therefore, the segment of the marginal revenue curve for quantities greater than q_5, that is, for the highly inelastic segment BC of the kinked demand curve $EGIBC$, is not shown in Figure 14.9.

If the dominant firm's marginal cost curve is MC_D, the dominant firm maximizes profit by setting $MR_D = MC_D$ at point F and by producing q_D units of output, which it sells at price p_3 taken from its demand curve at point G. The fringe firms take the price p_3 as given, respond as perfectly competitive firms, and produce q_f units at point K. Total industry demand equals $q_T = q_D + q_f$ at point L.

A major implication of the dominant firm model is that the dominant firm's market share often declines over time. If the competitive fringe firms earn positive economic

Figure 14.9 Equilibrium in the Dominant Firm Model

Industry demand D_I is the straight line $ALJBC$. The fringe firms' supply curve is S_f. To obtain the dominant firm's residual demand curve, subtract S_f from D_I, which yields the dark-blue demand curve $EGIBC$. The dominant firm equates its marginal cost, MC_D, to marginal revenue, MR_D, and produces output q_D and sets the price at p_3. The fringe firms take the price p_3 as given and produce an output of q_f units. Total output is $q_T = q_D + q_f$.

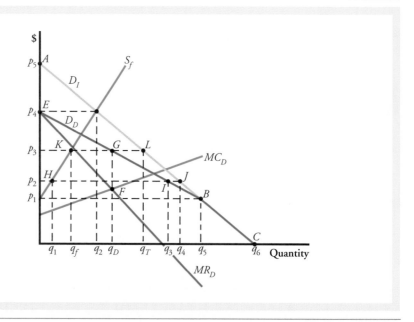

COMMON ERROR 14.2 Incorrectly Identifying the Price in the Dominant Firm Model

Because of the complexity of Figure 14.9, students often get confused and misidentify the dominant firm's equilibrium price. For example, in this figure, the dominant firm's residual demand curve D_D, and marginal cost curve MR_D, are correctly identified; however, the price p is taken from point B, where $MC_D = MR_D$. Students often fail to go up to the demand curve to obtain the price at which the dominant firm would sell the q_D units it produces. Given price p, the fringe firms supply q_f. Therefore, according to these mistaken students, total output $q_T = q_f + q_D$, which is wrong. By construction of the residual demand curve, we know that $q_T = q_f + q_1$, not $q_f + q_D$. Be careful not to make this common error when analyzing the dominant firm model.

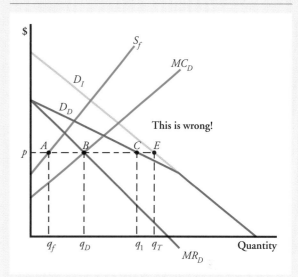

Common Error Figure 14.2 The dominant firm's demand curve is D_D and marginal revenue is MR_D, but the price is not p.

(continued)

▲▲▲ 14.4 APPLICATION   The Decline of Dominant Firms

There is considerable empirical evidence providing support for the dominant firm model. This evidence suggests that dominant firms' market shares often decline substantially over time. U.S. Steel is a case in point. A classic dominant firm after its formation in 1902, U.S. Steel's market share was 65 percent at the time of its creation. U.S. Steel charged high prices and earned high profits during the first twenty years of its existence. As a result, new competitors entered and established competitors expanded their outputs. By 1920, U.S. Steel's market share had declined to 50 percent.

In the low-volume segment of the copier industry, Xerox behaved as a classic dominant firm price leader. Xerox set high profit-maximizing prices in this sector and conceded market share to its smaller rivals. Between 1961 and 1967, more than twenty-five firms entered the low-volume segment of the market, and by the mid-1970s, copier prices had declined and Xerox had lost its dominant position.

Reynolds International Pen Corporation is one of the most dramatic examples of a dominant firm's decline. Reynolds invented an improved ballpoint pen that enabled the ink to flow much more smoothly to the pen's ball point. It began selling these pens in 1945. Initially, the pens cost approximately $0.80 each to produce and Gimbel's department stores sold them for $12.50. Gimbel's sold 10,000 pens the first day they went on sale. By early 1946, Reynolds was producing 30,000 pens a day and earning large economic profit. Reynolds's high prices encouraged large-scale entry. By Christmas of 1946, many firms were in the industry and prices had fallen to as low as $0.88. By 1948, competitors had managed to greatly reduce the average cost of producing pens, and prices declined to $0.39. In 1951, prices declined further and reached a low of $0.19. By then, Reynolds, which had lowered its prices as entry occurred, was long gone from the industry. Reynolds came and went quickly, but for one brief moment it was a dominant firm price leader and earned very large economic profit. This example points out the risks associated with dominant firm price leadership. By being completely passive toward its competitors, Reynolds found itself knocked out of the market in just a few years.

There are many more examples of dominant firm price leaders—International Harvester in farm equipment, Goodyear in tires, RCA in color televisions, General Electric in appliances, and IBM in computers—all of these firms lost significant market share to competitors as a result of a high price policy and passivity. With too little concern for competitors' entry, these companies stood by while they tumbled from positions of complete prominence.

profit at price p_3 in Figure 14.9, there will be an incentive for the fringe supply S_f to increase over time as new firms enter and as existing fringe firms expand their outputs. An increase in the fringe supply curve causes the market share of the fringe to increase. Furthermore, as the fringe supply S_f increases, the residual demand for the dominant firm D_D shifts to the left (decreases), and the dominant firm's relative share of output declines.

The dominant firm is remarkably passive in this model. This passivity is often cited as a major weakness of the dominant firm model. As we will see in Chapter 15, there are strategies that a dominant firm can adopt to try to maintain its market power in the face of competition from the competitive fringe.

▼▼▼   14.5   Collusion: The Great Prisoner's Dilemma

Recall from Chapter 13 that the basic lesson of the Prisoner's Dilemma is that defecting is a dominant strategy, which makes it difficult for oligopolists to collude effectively. In this section, we consider how firms attempt to solve the Prisoner's Dilemma. We begin by analyzing the case of firms with identical demand and cost curves and then proceeding to the case of differing demand and cost curves.

Collusion with Identical Demand and Cost Conditions

Table 14.1, which reproduces Table 13.2, shows Kodak and Fuji as completely symmetric firms that face identical demands and produce with identical costs. Regardless of whether this game is played once or any finite number of times, defecting is the dominant strategy for Kodak and Fuji. The companies, however, would be better off if they

Table 14.1 A Prisoner's Dilemma Game of Collusion ($millions Kodak's profit, $millions Fuji's profit)

		Fuji Action	
		Collude high price	Defect low price
Kodak Action	Collude high price	500 / 500	600 / 100
	Defect low price	100 / 600	300 / 300

could successfully collude and charge a high price. There is a great incentive for Kodak and Fuji to find a method of achieving the high price outcome. In the United States, overt collusion is illegal because of the antitrust laws, and therefore firms often look for alternative methods of coordination.

Suppose Kodak and Fuji believe that the game in Table 14.1 will go on forever; that is, that the game is an **infinite game**. If the firms are going to successfully solve the Prisoner's Dilemma, they must establish an environment where each believes the other will abide by a collusive agreement. To establish such a trusting environment, Kodak and Fuji must first figure out a way to signal each other their willingness to abide by a collusive agreement. Second, they must develop a system for detecting any defections from the agreement. And third, defections must be punished in order to deter future defections. Signaling, detection, and punishment: In the absence of these three conditions, Kodak and Fuji have such a strong incentive to defect that the outcome of the game will almost certainly be the dominant strategy of: *Defect, Defect.*

One possible strategy that incorporates signaling, detection, and punishment is the following:

1. Start in the first round by colluding and charging a high price.
2. In every subsequent round, adopt your opponent's strategy in the previous round: that is, in round N, adopt your opponent's strategy in round $N - 1$.

Suppose Kodak adopts this strategy. In the first round, Kodak charges a high price. If Fuji also charges a high price in round 1, then Kodak charges a high price in round 2. However, if Fuji charges a low price in round 1, Kodak punishes Fuji's behavior in round 1 by charging a low price in round 2. If Kodak and Fuji both adopt this strategy, then both charge a high price in round 1 *and* in every subsequent round. This simple two-part strategy incorporates signaling, detection, and punishment, and is known as **tit-for-tat**. By setting a high price in round 1, Kodak and Fuji signal to each other their willingness to collude. Furthermore, any future defection is quickly detected when prices are announced, and all defections are punished in the next round.

Tit-for-tat became a famous solution to the Prisoner's Dilemma when political scientist Robert Axelrod invited a group of world-renowned game theorists to enter a competition to try to solve the Prisoner's Dilemma.[10] In Axelrod's competition, 14 invited experts submitted computer programs to solve the Prisoner's Dilemma. Each program was run a total of 15 times: once in head-to-head competition against each of the other 13 programs, once against a random computer-generated program, and once against itself. The entrants knew that the game would last 200 rounds. To the surprise of many, the winner of the competition was Anatol Rapoport, who used the simple tit-for-tat strategy. At the end of the competition, Axelrod concluded that tit-for-tat won because it exhibits three important characteristics: It is nice toward competitors; it punishes all defections; and it forgives defectors who return to the fold. Tit-for-tat is "nice" in the sense that it never initiates an aggressive action. Yet it is "aggressive" in the sense that it punishes all aggressive moves, even first-time defections. It is "forgiving" in that it rewards defectors who revert to collusion by also reverting to collusion. Virtually all of the highly rated strategies submitted to Axelrod exhibited the characteristic of "niceness." In fact, each of the top eight ranking strategies was nice in the sense that a player using any of these strategies was never the first player to defect, and never defected until very close to the end of the game.

---

[10] Robert Axelrod. *The Evolution of Cooperation.* New York, Basic Books, 1984.

infinite game

A static game that is repeated forever.

tit-for-tat

A strategy in a Prisoner's Dilemma game in which a player starts off cooperating in the first round, and in every subsequent round adopts its opponent's strategy in the previous round.

▲▲▲ 14.5A APPLICATION   Price Fixing in the World Vitamin Market

At the beginning of this chapter, we learned that Roche Holding and BASF were fined a combined $725 million for fixing the prices of vitamins in violation of the Sherman Act (see Chapter 12). The vitamin price-fixing conspiracy lasted from January 1990 through February 1999—almost the entire decade of the 1990s. It included not only the Swiss firm Roche and the German firm BASF but Aventis (France), Solvay Pharmaceuticals (Netherlands), Merck (Germany), Daiichi (Japan), Esai (Japan), and Takeda Chemical (Japan). In all, the conspiracy included eight large companies in five different countries. If you used vitamin A, E, B1, B2, B5, B6, C, D3, biotin, folic acid, or beta carotene during the 1990s, you paid a price that was set by a world-wide price-fixing conspiracy at artificially high levels well above the average cost of producing these vitamins. Furthermore, even if you never took a vitamin in the 1990s, if you ate beef, chicken, or pork, you paid a price that was elevated, because the vitamin additives given to cattle, chickens, and pigs were sold at artificially high prices.

How did these eight companies solve the Prisoner's Dilemma? First, consistent with Axelrod's conclusion, they were extremely nice to each other. They held numerous meetings to fix prices and divide the world vitamin market. At these meetings, they allocated sales volumes and market shares. They went so far as to allocate specific customers and rig bids to specific buyers. The meetings signaled a strong desire to set a high collusive price. Second, they worked out a formalized method of detecting defectors. Meetings and conversations were held to ensure compliance with the agreements, and the firms exchanged their sales and pricing data with each other. Finally, a method of punishment was available for any firm that violated the agreement by selling too many units or by charging too low a price: that firm's market share could be reduced at a later meeting.

The vitamin conspiracy shows that it is possible for firms to overcome the Prisoner's Dilemma through direct collusion. To emphasize this point, when Assistant U.S. Attorney General Joel Kline announced that Roche and BASF had agreed to plead guilty and pay the largest antitrust fines in U.S. history, he stated:*

> Let me be clear about this: contrary to what some have suggested, these kinds of cartels are by no means transient or unstable. They are powerful and sophisticated and, without intervention by antitrust authorities, will often go on indefinitely.

*Statement of Assistant Attorney General Joel I. Kline, May 20, 1999, *http://www.usdoj.gov*.

Collusion with Differing Costs or Demand Conditions

As difficult as it is for firms with identical costs and demands to successfully solve the Prisoner's Dilemma, it is even more difficult for firms with differing costs or demands to successfully collude. Economists have developed many models of oligopoly behavior under conditions of differing demands and costs. In this section, we explore briefly two of those models: the *kinked demand curve* and *price leadership* models.

THE KINKED DEMAND CURVE MODEL   In Figure 14.10(a), duopolists produce a homogeneous product with different marginal costs. Assume that if the firms charge the same price, they divide the demand equally, so demand curve D represents one-half of the total industry demand curve. One firm has low marginal costs, MC_l, and the other firm has higher marginal costs, MC_h. The low-marginal-cost firm prefers an industry price of p_l; the high-cost firm prefers a higher price, p_h.

Suppose the two firms play a sequential game. The low-cost firm moves first and sets the price at p_l. The high-cost firm moves next. Before moving, the high-cost firm makes two assumptions: (1) If it charges a price greater than p_l, the low-cost firm maintains its price at p_l, and the high-cost firm loses many sales; and (2) If it charges a price equal to

Figure 14.10 The Kinked Demand Curve Model
In panel (a), two firms have identical demands but different marginal costs. The high-cost firm prefers a price p_h, and the low-cost firm prefers a price p_l. In panel (b), the high-cost firm faces a kinked demand curve ABC. As a result, the high-cost firm faces a gap in its marginal revenue curve between points E and F. Even if the high-cost firm's marginal cost increased to MC_h^2, it maintains a price of p_l.

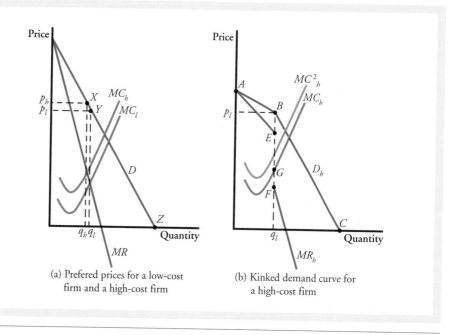

(a) Prefered prices for a low-cost firm and a high-cost firm

(b) Kinked demand curve for a high-cost firm

kinked demand curve model

An oligopoly model in which a firm's demand curve is based on the assumptions that if it independently raises price, its competitors maintain their prices, whereas a price decrease will be matched. As a consequence, the firm's demand curve is highly elastic for price increases but highly inelastic for price decreases.

price leadership

A model of oligopoly behavior in which the firms depend on one firm to signal price changes to the other firms, who then decide whether to follow the changes.

or less than p_l, the low-cost firm matches its price. Figure 14.10(b) shows the demand curve for the high-cost firm given these assumptions. If the high-cost firm increases its price above p_l, its demand is highly elastic, as indicated by the segment AB. If the high-cost firm charges a price less than or equal to p_l, the low-cost firm matches the price and the two firms continue to share the demand curve along the less-elastic segment BC, which is identical to the segment YZ in panel (a). The demand curve in panel (b) has a kink at point B, and as a result, the marginal revenue curve has a gap between points E and F. The elastic segment of the demand curve between points A and B has a marginal revenue curve equal to the line segment AE, and the more inelastic segment of the demand curve between points B and C has a marginal revenue curve equal to the line segment below point F. The dramatic decrease in elasticity at point B results in a large decrease in marginal revenue if the high-cost firm reduces its price below p_l. The high-cost firm maximizes profit by equating marginal cost to marginal revenue at point G, which is in the gap between points E and F, produces output q_l, and charges a price p_l. In fact, if the high-cost firm's marginal cost curve lies anywhere in the gap between points E and F, it will charge a price p_l. For example, if the high-cost firm's marginal cost increased to MC_h^2, its profit-maximizing price is still p_l.

The preceding model is the **kinked demand curve model**, which economist Paul Sweezy developed in the 1930s to explain why prices are often inflexible or rigid in oligopolistic markets. Sweezy's model explained price rigidity well, but provides no explanation for how the price, p_l, was set in the first place. Instead, the model assumed that once the price was set in an oligopoly, all the firms faced a kinked demand curve at that price, and therefore the firms maintained the current price.

PRICE LEADERSHIP The preceding analysis of the kinked demand curve combined Sweezy's original theory with another theory, the theory of *price leadership*. **Price leadership** is a model of oligopoly behavior where the oligopolists depend on one firm to signal price changes to the other firms, who then decide whether to follow the changes. Oligopolists often use price leadership to help solve the Prisoner's Dilemma. When price

price leader

The firm in an oligopoly that is first to change price in response to a change in an industry's underlying demand or cost conditions.

leadership works, all the firms rely on the **price leader** to signal the "correct" price to the other firms. The price leader is expected to understand the industry's underlying demand and cost conditions, and if those conditions change, to change the price. For example, if demand increases, the price leader increases the price and waits to see whether the other firms follow suit. If they do, the price increase sticks. If they don't, the leader rescinds the price increase and the price returns to its former level. If costs decrease because of a new technological advance, the price leader decreases price and waits to see whether the other firms follow the price decrease. Once again, if they do, the price decrease sticks. If they don't, the leader rescinds the price decrease.

In some industries, the same firm plays the role of the price leader for years or decades, while in other industries, different firms serve as the price leader from one price-changing episode to the next. The system works well as long as all the firms recognize the price leader's role as a signaling agent rather than viewing the price leader as a breakaway maverick trying to destroy the industry's pricing discipline. Price leadership has been common in many American industries, from automobiles and cigarettes to gasoline retailing and electric turbines.

In the models presented in this chapter, the firms shared power in their respective markets and there were no attempts to eliminate existing firms or to prevent new firms from entering the market. The next chapter considers cases in which dominant firms attempt to maintain their market power by taking strategic actions against their competitors or potential competitors.

▲▲▲ 14.5B APPLICATION   Price Leadership in Cyberspace: The Airlines Case

Successful price leadership requires that firms signal price changes to each other. Before the advent of the Internet, this signaling typically took place in a public forum such as a newspaper or a private forum such as a trade association. The signaling of price information through a newspaper might still work, but it is very slow compared to the instantaneous signaling of information that takes place over the Internet. In December 1992, the U.S. Department of Justice filed an antitrust case against eight major airlines (Alaska, American, Continental, Delta, Northwest, TWA, United, and USAirways) and the Airline Tariff Publishing Company (ATPCO), charging that the nine entities had used information exchanged over the Internet through ATPCO to fix fares.

ATPCO is an information clearinghouse for the airlines. The airlines inform ATPCO of all fare changes: new fares to be added, old fares to be deleted, and existing fares to be changed. Each day ATPCO produces an electronic list of all the fares and distributes the list to all the major airlines and the four major computer reservations systems, which make the list available to travel agents and airlines throughout the world. Included in this information is the fare, the first and last dates to sell tickets at that fare, the first and last dates that travel is permitted at that fare, and any restrictions on the fare such as a seven-day advanced purchase requirement or a Saturday night stay-over requirement. Because the fares submitted to ATPCO always included a first-ticket sale date, it was possible for an airline to announce a fare increase but delay its implementation until a future date. The ability to pre-announce a fare increase became a crucial issue in the antitrust case because it gave firms the ability to rescind a pre-announced price increase if the other airlines failed to follow the fare increase.

The government charged the eight airlines with using information exchanged through ATPCO to fix fares by linking fares on different routes. For example, Northwest Airlines (NW) and American Airlines (AA) compete on flights to and from Boston, Detroit, Chicago, and Los Angeles. Northwest has a hub at Detroit and American has a hub at Chicago. Northwest flies non-stop from Detroit to LA, but American only flies from Detroit

(continued)

to LA with a change of planes in Chicago. American flies non-stop from Chicago to Boston, but Northwest only flies from Chicago to Boston with a change of planes in Detroit. Consumers prefer non-stop flights and are often willing to pay a price premium for a non-stop flight. Suppose that before the price signaling began, American competed on the Detroit–LA route by charging a lower fare than Northwest, and Northwest competed on the Chicago–Boston route by charging a lower fare than American. One possible price-fixing agreement would be for American to raise its fare from Detroit to LA in return for an agreement from Northwest to raise its fare from Chicago to Boston. But how can American signal its intentions to Northwest? According to the Justice Department, American might signal Northwest through ATPCO as follows:

1. American sends a message to ATPCO lowering its fare from Detroit to LA. The new fare has the same set of restrictions as Northwest's lowest fare from Chicago to Boston. American is using this fare change to signal Northwest of the linkage between American's Detroit–LA fare and Northwest's Chicago–Boston fare. The last-ticket date (the last day to sell this type of ticket) for this low fare is two weeks from today.

2. At the exact same time, American also sends a message to ATPCO setting a Detroit–LA fare matching Northwest's current non-stop fare, but with a first-ticket date (the first day to buy this type ticket) of two weeks from today.

3. American then waits to see whether Northwest receives the signal. If Northwest gets the message, it puts a last-ticket date of two weeks from today on its *current* low fare from Chicago to Boston, and at the same time, institutes a new higher fare matching American's fare from Chicago to Boston, but with a first-ticket date of two weeks from today.

4. Two weeks from today, American's Detroit–LA fare and Northwest's Chicago–Boston fares will increase to match their competitors' non-stop fares and the lower fares will be eliminated.

On May 17, 1994, the eight airlines and ATPCO settled the antitrust case out of court by agreeing to eliminate the use of first-ticket dates, which effectively eliminated the pre-announcement of price increases. The defendants also agreed to eliminate the use of last-ticket dates except in public advertising campaigns. The idea behind permitting last-ticket dates in public advertising campaigns was to encourage discount sales in newspaper, television, and radio advertising. Finally, the airlines agreed to eliminate signaling each other through subtle messages passed back and forth in the footnotes to their listed fare restrictions.

Summary

1. The Cournot model is built upon the questionable assumption that firms' competitors maintain their current outputs. The Cournot equilibrium is also a Nash equilibrium, because all the firms are doing the best they can given their opponents' choices; therefore, this equilibrium is called a Cournot-Nash equilibrium. The Cournot-Nash equilibrium results in a greater output and lower price than monopoly, but a lower output and higher price than perfect competition.

2. The Stackelberg model consists of a leader and follower. The leader moves first and assumes that the follower will respond to the leader's output choice by producing on its reaction function. The leader selects a quantity that maximizes its profit, given the follower's decision to remain on its reaction function. The Stackelberg leader produces a greater output than a Cournot-Nash equilibrium would have it produce, while the Stackelberg follower produces less output than it would with a Cournot-Nash equilibrium.

3. In the Bertrand model, firms take their competitors' prices, not quantities, as fixed forever. With a homogeneous product, this assumption results in a price equal to

marginal cost. The Bertrand outcome is therefore identical to the perfectly competitive outcome. When product differentiation is added to the Bertrand model, the equilibrium price increases and is well above marginal cost.

4. In the dominant firm model, an industry is characterized by one large dominant firm and a group of small fringe firms. The dominant firm sets the price and the competitive firms take the price as given and behave as firms in a perfectly competitive industry. In the long run, if the fringe firms earn positive economic profits, entry tends to increase the fringe supply and decrease the dominant firm's market share.

5. The Prisoner's Dilemma makes it difficult for firms to collude successfully. Solutions to the Prisoner's Dilemma require that firms signal their intentions to each other, detect any defections, and punish defectors. Successful solutions often require all the firms to exhibit nice behavior toward their competitors. Tit-for-tat is one possible solution to the Prisoner's Dilemma, in which the firms are nice. Differences in demand and cost conditions across firms make it more difficult to solve the Prisoner's Dilemma and may result in the industry using a price leader to signal when it is time to change price. Firms other than the price leader may face a kink in their demand curves that results in maintaining price at the current level. Oligopolists may use price leadership to maintain industry discipline and prevent price competition.

Self-Test Problems

1. Consider a market with two identical firms. The market demand is $P = 100 - 4Q$, where $Q = q_a + q_b$. $MC_a = MC_b = AC_a = AC_b = 4$.

   a. Solve for the Cournot reaction functions of each firm.

   b. Solve for the Cournot-Nash equilibrium. Calculate the quantity, price, and profit for each firm.

   c. Solve for output and price with collusion and identify the collusion curve. Because costs are the same, assume the firms evenly divide the collusive output. Show that Firm A has an incentive to increase its collusive output by 1 unit.

   d. Now assume this market has a Stackelberg leader. Assume Firm A is the Stackelberg leader. Solve for each firm's quantity and price and profit.

   e. Compare the Stackelberg result to the Cournot result. Which outcome is more allocatively efficient?

2. Harvey (h) and Kim (k) both sell home-made decorated T-shirts on a college campus. They each produce a differentiated product, and because of brand loyalty, they face the following symmetric demand curves:

$$q_h = 5 - (1/5)p_h + (1/10)p_k \text{ and}$$

$$q_k = 5 - (1/5)p_k + (1/10)p_h$$

In addition, $MC_h = MC_k = 1.5$.

   a. Using the Bertrand model, if there were no product differentiation, what would be the price of the T-shirts?

   b. Assuming product differentiation, using the Bertrand model, solve for Harvey's reaction function $p_h = f(p_k)$ and for Kim's reaction function $p_k = f(p_h)$. What is the price in the market? How many T-shirts will Harvey sell? How many T-shirts will Kim sell?

3. Consider an industry that is characterized by a dominant firm (d) and a fringe (f). The market demand curve is: $P = 208 - 4Q$, where Q represents the total industry output ($q_d + q_f$). The supply of the fringe (S_f) is $P_f = 10 + 2q_f$, and the marginal cost of the dominant firm is $MC_d = 4 + (1/3)q_d$.

   a. Solve for the residual demand curve for the dominant firm.

   b. What output will the dominant firm produce? What price will it charge?

   c. What is the fringe's output?

   d. Show your results on a graph.

Questions and Problems for Review

1. Consider a market with two identical firms. The market demand is $P = 26 - 2Q$, where $Q = q_a + q_b$. $MC_a = MC_b = AC_a = AC_b = 2$.

   a. Solve for the Cournot reaction functions of each firm.

   b. Solve for the Cournot-Nash equilibrium. Calculate the quantity, price, and profit for each firm.

2. Consider a market with two identical firms. The market demand is $P = 93 - 3Q$, where $Q = q_a + q_b$. $MC_a = MC_b = AC_a = AC_b = 3$.

   a. Solve for the Cournot reaction functions of each firm.

   b. Solve for the Cournot-Nash equilibrium. Calculate the quantity, price, and profit for each firm.

3. Consider a market with two identical firms. The market demand is $P = 26 - 2Q$, where $Q = q_a + q_b$. $MC_a = MC_b = AC_a = AC_b = 2$. (Same equations as question 1.)

   a. Solve for output and price with collusion and identify the collusion curve.

   b. Assume that the firms initially evenly split the collusive output. Show that Firm A has an incentive to increase output by 1 unit. Does Firm B also have an incentive to increase output?

4. Consider a market with two identical firms. The market demand is $P = 93 - 3Q$, where $Q = q_a + q_b$. $MC_a = MC_b = AC_a = AC_b = 3$. (Same equations as question 2.)

   a. Solve for output and price with collusion and identify the collusion curve.

   b. Assume that the firms initially evenly split the collusive output. Show that Firm A has an incentive to increase output by 1 unit.

5. Consider a market with two identical firms. The market demand is $P = 26 - 2Q$, where $Q = q_a + q_b$. $MC_a = MC_b = AC_a = AC_b = 2$. (Same equations as question 1.) Now assume this market has a Stackelberg leader, Firm A. Solve for the quantity, price, and profit for each firm.

6. Consider a market with two identical firms. The market demand is $P = 93 - 3Q$, where $Q = q_a + q_b$. $MC_a = MC_b = AC_a = AC_b = 3$. (Same equations as question 2.) Now assume this market has a Stackelberg leader, Firm A. Solve for the quantity, price, and profit for each firm.

7. Consider a market with two firms. The market demand is $P = 26 - 2Q$, where $Q = q_a + q_b$.

Assume Firm A has a lower MC than Firm B. $MC_a = AC_a = 2$ and $MC_b = AC_b = 2.5$. This difference in cost functions provides better justification for the existence of a Stackelberg leader.

   a. Which firm would you expect to be the Stackelberg leader? Why?

   b. Solve for Firm B's Cournot reaction function.

   c. Solve for Firm A's demand curve.

   d. Solve for the Stackelberg quantity, price, and profit for each firm.

8. Consider a market with two firms. The market demand is $P = 93 - 3Q$, where $Q = q_a + q_b$. Assume Firm A has a lower MC than Firm B. $MC_a = AC_a = 3$ and $MC_b = AC_b = 3.5$. This difference in cost functions provides better justification for the existence of a Stackelberg leader.

   a. Which firm would you expect to be the Stackelberg leader? Why?

   b. Solve for Firm B's Cournot reaction function.

   c. Solve for Firm A's demand curve.

   d. Solve for the Stackelberg quantity, price, and profits for each firm.

9. Consider a market with two identical firms. The market demand is $P = 26 - 2Q$, where $Q = q_a + q_b$. $MC_a = MC_b = AC_a = AC_b = 2$. (Same equations as question 1) Assume there is no product differentiation in this case and the firms follow a Bertrand pricing model. Solve for the Bertrand equilibrium: Calculate output for each firm, and price and profit as well.

10. Consider a market with two identical firms. The market demand is $P = 93 - 3Q$, where $Q = q_a + q_b$. $MC_a = MC_b = AC_a = AC_b = 3$. (Same equations as question 2.) Assume there is no product differentiation in this case and the firms follow a Bertrand pricing model. Solve for the Bertrand equilibrium: Calculate output, price, and profit for each firm.

11. In questions 1, 3, 5, 7, and 9, we have used the same demand function to solve for the Cournot, collusive, Stackelberg, Stackelberg with different costs, and the Bertrand outcomes. Compare the results of these five different models in terms of price, output for each firm, total market output, profit for each firm, and total industry profits. Comment on the differences. Which outcomes are best from an economic perspective? Which are worst?

12. In questions 2, 4, 6, 8, and 10, we have used the same demand function to solve for the Cournot, collusive, Stackelberg, Stackelberg with different costs, and the Bertrand outcomes. Compare the results of these five different models in terms of price, output for each firm, total market output, profit for each firm, and total industry profits. Comment on the differences. Which outcomes are best from an economic perspective? Which are worst?

13. Consider two firms (A and B) that price using the Bertrand model and produce the same good, but with product differentiation. Because of brand loyalty, they face the following symmetric demand curves:

$$q_a = 21 - 3p_a + 2p_b \text{ and } q_b = 21 - 3p_b + 2p_a$$

In addition, $MC_a = MC_b = 1$.

   a. If there were no product differentiation, what would be the Bertrand equilibrium price in this market?

   b. Assuming product differentiation, solve for Firm A's reaction function $p_a = f(p_b)$ and for Firm B's reaction function $p_b = f(p_a)$. What is the price in the market?

   c. Compare the price with product differentiation in question 13(b) to the price without product differentiation in question 13(a).

14. Consider two firms (A and B) that produce the same good, but with product differentiation. Because of brand loyalty, they face the following symmetric demand curves:

$$q_a = 12 - 2p_a + p_b \text{ and } q_b = 12 - 2p_b + p_a$$

In addition, $MC_a = MC_b = 2$.

   a. If there were no product differentiation, what would be the Bertrand equilibrium price in this market?

   b. Assuming product differentiation, solve for Firm A's reaction function $p_a = f(p_b)$ and for Firm B's reaction function $p_b = f(p_a)$. What is the price in the market? Calculate output for each firm.

   c. Compare the results with no product differentiation in question 14(a) to those with product differentiation in question 14(b).

15. Consider an industry that is characterized by a dominant firm (d) and a fringe (f). The market demand

curve is: $P = 486 - 2Q$, where Q represents the total industry output $(q_d + q_f)$. The supply of the fringe (S_f) is $P_f = 6 + q_f$, and the marginal cost of the dominant firm is $MC_d = 4 + (2/3)q_d$.

   a. Solve for the residual demand curve for the dominant firm.

   b. What output will the dominant firm produce? What price will it charge?

   c. What is the fringe's output?

   d. Show your results on a graph.

16. Consider an industry that is characterized by a dominant firm (d) and a competitive fringe (f). The market demand curve is: $P = 200 - 2Q$ where Q represents the total industry output $(q_d + q_f)$. The supply of the fringe (S_f) is $P_f = 11 + q_f$, and the marginal cost of the dominant firm is $MC_d = 2 + (2/3)q_d$.

   a. Solve for the residual demand curve for the dominant firm.

   b. What output will the dominant firm produce? What price will it charge?

   c. What is the fringe's output?

   d. Show your results on a graph.

17. Consider a duopoly game of collusion with a different form of punishment where if one firm cheats, the other firm is "triggered" into playing its Cournot equilibrium outcome forever. Consider Axelrod's three important characteristics of successful punishment strategies. Compare the features of the punishment strategy described in this question to tit-for-tat.

18. The kinked demand curve model has been highly criticized as unrealistic. Describe its assumptions. Do you think the kinked demand curve model is realistic? Explain.

19. How is the price leadership model different from the dominant firm model? Explain. How are the two models similar?

20. Consider three of the models presented in this chapter: Cournot, Stackelberg, and Bertrand.

   a. Discuss the assumptions of each model.

   b. Discuss the realistic nature of each model.

   c. How did the development of the concept of a Nash equilibrium help to resurrect the Cournot model?

 Internet Exercises

Visit *http://www.myeconlab.com/waldman* for this chapter's Web exercises. Answer real-world economics problems by doing research on the Internet.

Appendix 14.1

Deriving Reaction Functions Using Calculus

Using calculus, Kodak's reaction function can be derived as follows. To maximize profit, Kodak must set $MR = MC$ for any given level of Fuji's output. Total revenue for Kodak, TR_K, is:

$$TR_K = q_K p = q_K(100 - q_F - q_K)$$

or:

$$TR_K = 100q_K - q_K^2 - q_K q_F$$

Marginal revenue, MR_K, is simply the partial derivative of TR_K with respect to q_K; therefore:

$$MR_K = \frac{\partial TR_K}{\partial q_K} = 100 - 2q_K - q_F$$

Because $MC = 10$, we set $MR_K = 10$ and obtain:

$$100 - 2q_K - q_F = 10$$

or:

$$q_K = \frac{90 - q_F}{2} = 45 - \frac{1}{2}q_F$$

Appendix 14.2

Deriving the Stackelberg Equilibrium Using Calculus

Using calculus:

$$TR_K = pq_K = \left[100 - \left(45 - \frac{1}{2}q_K \right) - q_K \right] q_K = 55q_K - \frac{1}{2}q_K^2$$

and:

$$MR_K = \frac{dTR_K}{dq_K} = 55 - q_K$$

Setting $MR = MC$:

$$55 - q_K = 10 \text{ or } q_K = 45$$

Chapter 15
Strategic Behavior

Between the years 1997–2001, Amazon.com's sales increased dramatically every year, from $114.76 million in 1997 to $3.12 billion in 2001. Yet, despite these incredible sales increases, Amazon's net income, or profit, was negative every year. In fact, accounting losses increased from $27.59 million in 1997 to $1.41 billion in 2000; the losses decreased to $567.27 million in 2001. What rational business could be run with sales increasing dramatically every year, yet huge annual losses piling up one upon another? Despite the appearance of irrational behavior, Amazon has had a long-term growth strategy that has recognized the necessity of short-term economic losses. In this chapter, we analyze a number of models of strategic behavior that can provide insight into Amazon's competitive strategy and economic performance.

In addition to Amazon's strategy, this chapter will help us understand a number of other strategies that firms with market power use to maintain or increase their power. For example, in the first half of the twentieth century, Alcoa had a virtual monopoly of American aluminum production, yet its economic profit was normal, by any reasonable measure. In the 1980s, the government deregulated the airline industry, and as a result, many new airlines entered. Whenever a new carrier entered one of their markets, American Airlines and Northwest Airlines followed a policy of slashing fares. In 2001, General Motors spent $3.4 billion to advertise its cars, and Procter & Gamble spent $2.5 billion to advertise its various consumer products. Kellogg's and General Mills produce a huge variety of different cereals, many seemingly aimed at relatively small market segments. Each of these huge corporations is engaged in a strategic battle to maintain its market share through a variety of different competitive strategies. In this chapter, we develop a number of models to explain why these firms adopted these various strategies.

In the models presented in Chapter 14, firms shared power in their respective markets. In this chapter, we consider cases where dominant firms attempt to maintain their market shares by taking strategic actions to deter entry. Dominant firms might use price or non-price methods to deter entry. We first consider how firms can use price to deter entry and then turn our attention to non-price methods of deterring entry.

15.1 Pricing to Deter Entry: Limit Pricing

limit pricing

Charging a low price with the specific purpose of deterring entry.

limit price

The highest possible price a monopolist can charge and still prevent entry.

The models presented in Chapter 14 dealt with the pricing decisions of firms with market power aimed at maximizing current profits. Current pricing decisions, however, can affect the future behavior of competitors and potential competitors. For example, a monopolist may be able to choose between: (1) charging a high price today and attracting entry; or (2) charging a low price today in an attempt to deter entry. The second policy, charging a low price to deter entry, is known as **limit pricing**. Furthermore, the highest possible price the monopolist can charge and still prevent entry is called the **limit price**. In this section, we develop a model to explain why rational firms sometimes adopt a limit pricing policy.

Consider a monopolist facing the hypothetical demand and cost conditions depicted in Figure 15.1(a). Total industry demand is $p = 100 - q$; the monopolist produces with constant marginal and average costs $MC_M = AC_M = \$40$. Given these demand and cost conditions, the monopolist maximizes short-run profit by setting $MR_M = MC_M$, selling a quantity of 30 at a price of $70.00, and earning profit equal to $q(p - AC_M) = 30(\$70 - \$40) = \$900$.

Suppose a potential entrant is considering entering the industry; however, the potential entrant faces a cost disadvantage, because the monopolist holds a patent. As a result of the patent, the potential entrant can produce only at higher costs $MC_{PE} = AC_{PE} = \$50$. As you learned in Chapter 14, if the monopolist is currently maximizing short-run profit and charging price $p = \$70$, the residual demand curve faced by the potential

Figure 15.1 The Monopolist's and Potential Entrant's Demand and Costs
In panel (a), the monopolist has lower costs than the potential entrant and maximizes profit by setting $MC_M = MR_M$ at $q = 30$ and $p = \$70$. A potential entrant then faces the residual demand curve equal to the line segment AC. In panel (b), the residual demand curve for a potential entrant is drawn as the line segment XZ. Given the potential entrant's costs, the potential entrant maximizes profit by setting $q = 10$, and the price falls to $60.

(a) The monopolist's demand

(b) The potential entrant's residual demand

entrant is $p = (100 - q_M) - q_{PE} = (100 - 30) - q_{PE} = 70 - q_{PE}$, which equals the line segment AC in panel (a) and the also the line segment XZ in panel (b).

Assume the potential entrant makes the Cournot assumption that the monopolist will maintain its current output *forever*. Given this assumption, if the potential entrant enters, it maximizes profit in panel (b) by setting $MR_{PE} = MC_{PE} = \$50$, selling a quantity of 10 at a price of \$60, and earning profit equal to $q(p - AC_{PE}) = 10(\$60 - \$50) = \$100$. The monopolist must now match the entrant's price of \$60; as a result, the monopolist's profit declines to $q(p - AC_M) = 30(\$60 - \$40) = \$600$. The arrival of a new entrant has resulted in a 33 percent reduction in the monopolist's profit.

Given the Cournot output maintenance assumption, in order to deter entry, the monopolist must lower its price sufficiently to ensure that the potential entrant's residual demand curve lies everywhere below the potential entrant's average cost curve. In Figure 15.1, let's determine the limit price for our monopolist. If the monopolist charges any price greater than \$50, the residual demand curve will have a segment that is above the potential entrant's average cost. However, if the monopolist increases output to 50 and charges a price $p = \$50$, the residual demand curve faced by potential entrants will be $p = (100 - q_M) - q_{PE} = (100 - 50) - q_{PE} = 50 - q_{PE}$, which equals the line segment BC in Figure 15.1(a).

Figure 15.2 shows this residual demand curve in relation to the potential entrant's costs. The AC_{PE} curve is now everywhere below the demand curve, except for an output of zero. Therefore, in Figure 15.2, if the potential entrant produces any output greater than zero, it will sustain an economic loss. A monopoly price $p = \$50$ therefore completely deters entry. The price of \$50 is the limit price, because it is the highest possible price the monopolist can charge and still prevent entry.

Game Theorists' Critique of Limit Pricing

Game theorists sharply criticized this basic limit pricing result. To understand their criticism, consider the situation depicted in Figures 15.1 and 15.2 as a sequential game. The game is two periods long with the potential entrant moving in period 1. The monopolist then responds in period 2, and then the game ends; it is not repeated. The information structure is *perfect, complete, certain*, and *symmetric* (see Chapter 13). Figure 15.3 shows

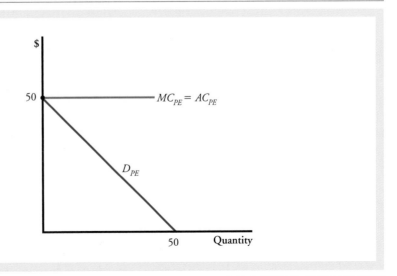

Figure 15.2 The Potential Entrant's Residual Demand Curve and Costs, If the Monopolist Sets Price Equal to \$50
If the monopolist lowers its price to \$50, the potential entrant's residual demand curve is $p = 50 - q$, which lies everywhere below the potential entrant's costs. Therefore, if the monopolist is assumed to maintain its output after entry, the entrant will sustain an economic loss and entry is impossible.

Figure 15.3 A Game of Entry ($millions Entrant's Profit, $millions Monopolist's Profit)
The potential entrant firm realizes that by staying out, it earns a normal profit; however, if it enters, the only rational response for the monopolist is to accommodate entry, and the entrant will earn $100 million. The equilibrium is for the entrant to enter and the monopolist to accommodate entry by producing an output of 30.

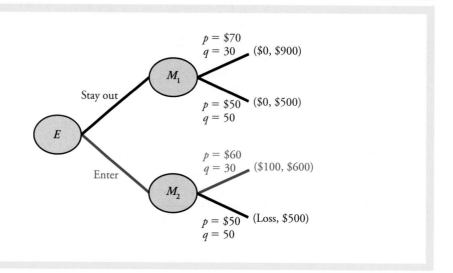

the sequential game. Recalling from Chapter 13 that sequential games must be solved backwards, we find only one solution to the game in Figure 15.3, as depicted by the green path. A potential entrant uses the following reasoning:

1. If I stay out, I earn $0.
2. If I enter and the monopolist produces the limit price quantity of 50, I sustain an economic loss and the monopolist earns $500.
3. If I enter and the monopolist maintains its output at 30, I earn $100 and the monopolist earns $600.
4. If I enter, the monopolist has a choice between producing 30 and earning $600 or producing 50 and earning $500. *Given these choices, the monopolist's only rational choice is to produce 30 and earn $600.*
5. I will enter and earn $100, which is much better than staying out and earning $0.

The game has only one solution: The entrant will enter and the monopolist will maximize its post-entry profit by maintaining output at 30. If the monopolist threatens in advance of entry to produce 50 if the potential entrant actually entered, it would simply not be a credible or believable threat, because such a response to entry would reduce the monopolist's profit. But suppose that for some unexplained reason, there is a small probability that the potential entrant makes a mistake and chooses not to enter. The small probability of such a mistake (or any mistake in these games) is called a **tremble**. The game is then reduced to the monopolist's choice of either maximizing short-run profits or employing limit pricing. Figure 15.3 reveals that the monopolist has only one rational choice. If the entrant stays out because of trembling, the monopolist's choices are to earn $900 or earn $500. Given this choice, the monopolist's only rational choice is to maximize profit and earn $900. A limit pricing policy would not be reasonable, because it reduces the monopolist's profit without credibly deterring entry. Even if the game were repeated, the entrant knows that the monopolist will share the market after entry occurs. There is no reason for the entrant to stay out, even if the monopolist charges the limit price.

tremble

The small probability that a player will make a mistake and choose the wrong action in a game.

Limit Pricing with Asymmetric Information

In the preceding game, the information structure is perfect, complete, certain, and symmetric. Given this information structure, limit pricing is not a viable strategy. However, if we change the information structure of the entry game to be *imperfect, incomplete, certain,* and *asymmetric,* limit pricing can be a reasonable profit-maximizing strategy.[1]

Figure 15.4 shows such a game with three players, nature (the pseudo-player introduced in Chapter 13), a monopolist, and a potential entrant. Both firms know the profit payoffs. The game is played as follows. First, nature, identified by N, moves first and selects the monopolist to be either a high-cost or a low-cost firm. Only the monopolist knows nature's move. The game is, therefore, a game of incomplete information, because nature moves first and nature's move is unobserved by at least one of the players. In this case, nature's move is unobserved by the potential entrant. The probability that the monopolist is a high-cost producer is ρ, and the probability that the monopolist is a low-cost producer is $(1 - \rho)$. Because the monopolist has information that is unavailable to the potential entrant, the game is also a game of asymmetric information. In the absence of a threat of entry, a high-cost monopolist prefers to charge a high price, and a low-cost monopolist prefers to charge a low price.

Figure 15.4 A Game of Entry with Asymmetric Information ($millions Entrant's Profit, $millions Monopolist's Profit)

The potential entrant knows only the probability ρ that nature selects the monopolist to be high-cost, whereas the monopolist knows whether it is a high-cost or low-cost firm. A high-cost monopolist may play low price at the node M_1, because then the potential entrant does not know whether the game has moved to the node E_1 or E_3. The potential entrant's expected profit is therefore $E(\pi) = \rho(200) + (1 - \rho)(-150)$. If $\rho < 0.429$, then $E(\pi) < 0$, and the potential entrant's expected profit is negative, so the potential entrant stays out at node E_1. By charging a low price, a high-cost monopolist can deter entry.

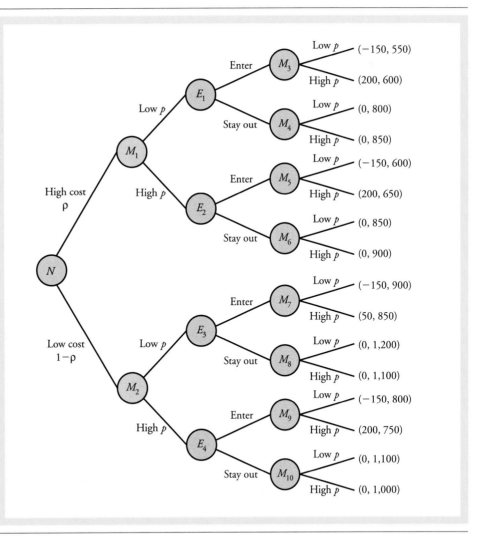

[1] P. Milgrom and J. Roberts, "Limit Pricing and Entry Under Conditions of Incomplete Information and Equilibrium Analysis," *Econometrica* 50, March 1982, pp. 443–460.

node

A point in an extensive form of a game at which a player or nature takes an action, or the game ends.

After nature moves, the monopolist, identified by M, selects either a low price (high output) or a high price (low output). The potential entrant, identified by E, then decides either to enter or to stay out. After the entrant makes its decision, the monopolist moves again and sets the price either low or high.

Suppose nature selects the monopolist to be a low-cost producer, so the monopolist's first move is from the red circle point M_2. A point such as M_2 is known as a **node**, which is a point in an extensive form of a game at which a player or nature takes an action or the game ends. If we look at only the bottom half of the game beginning at node M_2, we see a low-cost monopolist's dominant solution of always playing low price. If the low-cost producer is at node M_2 and plays low p, then the game moves to node E_3. If the entrant enters, the game moves to node M_7, and the monopolist maximizes profit at $900 million by playing low p once again. Unfortunately for the entrant, this results in a $150 million loss. If at node E_3, the entrant instead stays out, the monopolist still plays low p at node M_8, because low p maximizes the monopolist's profit at $1,200 million. A low-cost monopolist would *never* play high p at node M_2, because that would move the game to node E_4, and from that node, no matter what the entrant decided to do, the monopolist would always be better off if it had played low p at node M_2. In other words, the monopolist is better off if the game moves to node M_7 and it plays low p and earns $900 million than if the game moves to M_9 and it plays low p and earns $800 million. Similarly, the monopolist is better off if the game moves to node M_8 and it plays low p than if the game moves to node M_{10} and it plays low p.

If the potential entrant knows with certainty that the monopolist is a low-cost producer—that is, if $\rho = 0$—then there is only one solution to the game from node M_2: the monopolist plays low p, and because the entrant knows that if it enters it will sustain a $150 million loss, it stays out and earns a normal profit of $0. The equilibrium, therefore, would be "low p, stay out, low p," which maximizes the low-cost monopolist's profits at $1,200 million. Consequently, if the potential entrant knows that the monopolist is a low-cost producer, it stays out.

Now suppose that nature selects the monopolist to have high costs, so the game moves to node M_1. The potential entrant, however, does not know whether the game is at node M_1 or node M_2. If the high-cost monopolist plays high p at node M_1, it immediately reveals that the monopolist is a high-cost producer, because the potential entrant knows that if the monopolist were a low-cost producer at node M_2, it would never play high p. Therefore, if the monopolist plays high p at node M_1, the entrant knows the game is at node E_2. From node E_2, if the potential entrant enters, the monopolist plays high p and the entrant earns $200 million, which is better than the normal profit the potential entrant earns if it stays out. Therefore, from node M_1, if the monopolist plays high p, the game has only one solution: "high p, enter, high p."

There is another option for the high-cost monopolist at node M_1: it can play low p. If the monopolist plays low p, the potential entrant cannot tell whether the game has moved to node E_1 or node E_3. The potential entrant, however, knows that there is a probability ρ of being at node E_1 and a probability $1 - \rho$ of being at node E_3. We've already seen that if the potential entrant enters at node E_3, it sustains an economic loss of $150 million. On the other hand, if it enters at node E_1, then the game moves to node M_3 and the high-cost monopolist maximizes profit by playing high p, while the entrant earns $200 million in profit. The outcome of the game is determined entirely by the value of ρ. The larger ρ, the more likely the entrant is to earn $200 million; and the smaller ρ, the more likely the entrant is to lose $150 million. The entrant's expected profit is:

$$E(\pi) = \rho(200) + (1 - \rho)(-150)$$

If $\rho < 0.429$, then $E(\pi) < 0$, and the potential entrant's expected profit is negative, so the potential entrant stays out at node E_1. If the potential entrant stays out at node E_1, the game moves to node M_4, and the high-cost monopolist's final move is high p. The high-cost monopolist earns \$850 million, which is considerably greater than the \$650 million the monopolist would earn if it played high p at node M_1.

Suppose, for example, the potential entrant believes the probability that the monopolist is a high-cost producer is 30 percent; that is $\rho = 0.30$. If the potential entrant enters, expected profit is $0.3(\$200) + 0.7(-\$500) = \$60 - \$350 = -\$290$. If nature selects high-cost and the game moves to node M_1, the optimal play for the high-cost monopolist is low p, and the game's outcome is "low p, stay out, high p." The high-cost monopolist

---

▲▲▲ 15.1 APPLICATION   Limit Pricing in the Antihistamine Market

Millions of allergy sufferers in the United States used to walk around half-asleep for much of the year because of treatment with antihistamine drugs such as Benadryl and Chlortrimiton. Then, in the 1980s, the introduction of three drugs—Seldane, Hismanol, and Claritin—changed the world for many allergy sufferers. These non-sedating antihistamines made it possible to stop sneezing without falling asleep. In the early 1990s, when Seldane and Hismanol were found to increase the risk of heart problems and heart attacks, Schering-Plough's Claritin became the dominant drug in the non-sedating antihistamine market. A few years later, two other non-sedating antihistamines appeared: Pfizer's Zyrtec and Aventis's Allegra.

Claritin, Zyrtec, and Allegra remained patented prescription-only drugs in the United States until the fall of 2002, when Claritin lost its U.S. patent protection and became a non-prescription over-the-counter drug. In Canada, however, these antihistamines lost their patent protection and became over-the-counter drugs in the 1990s. According to *Pillbot.com*, in September 2002, the lowest prices for a one-month supply of the three prescription drugs in the United States were: \$88.99 for Claritin, \$65.77 for Allegra, and \$58.51 for Zyrtec. In September 2002, if you were fortunate enough to live in the United States close to the Canadian border, you could drive across the border, stop at the first Shopper's Drug Mart you came upon, and purchase a one-month supply of the same drugs for the following prices: \$22.22 (Can\$33.33) for Claritin, \$24.31 (Can\$36.47) for Allegra, and \$19.99 (Can\$29.99) for Zyrtec (sold in Canada under the brand name Reactine).

It's not surprising that these drugs were much less expensive in Canada, due to a lack of patent protection and their over-the-counter status. What is surprising, however, is that there were few generic alternatives to Claritin, Zyrtec, and Allegra available in Canadian drug stores. For example, in September 2002, Shopper's Drug Mart in Niagara Falls, Ontario, offered one generic alternative to Claritin and no alternatives to Zyrtec or Allegra. Furthermore, on the day the Shopper's Drug Mart price data was collected, the chain was offering a "two-boxes-for-the-price-of-one special" for Claritin, and as a result, the generic drug, Loratadine, was more expensive. By comparison, Shopper's Drug Mart offered many generic alternatives to analgesics such as Bayer aspirin, Tylenol, Advil, and Motrin, and to the most popular decongestant, Sudafed. In each of these markets, the generic drugs were much cheaper than the brand-name drugs.

Limit pricing theory can explain Schering-Plough's, Pfizer's, and Aventis's Canadian pricing behavior. In the United States, patent protection and the prescription drug status of Claritin, Zyrtec, and Allegra eliminated the threat of entry. However, in Canada, without patent protection or prescription drug status, if Schering-Plough, Pfizer, and Aventis charged high prices, there would be a tremendous threat that other drug manufacturers would enter the generic antihistamine market. To prevent large-scale entry, the three manufacturers charged very low prices in Canada compared to those in the United States. By charging low prices, the companies signaled their ability to earn economic profits even at low prices, and therefore, they signaled that they could produce these drugs at low costs. Schering-Plough, Pfizer, and Aventis could have charged high prices in Canada when Claritin, Zyrtec, and Allega first became available over the counter, but they choose not to. Instead, they slashed prices. This policy succeeded in limiting entry into the generic antihistamine market.

earns $850 million, which is much better than the alternative outcome of "high p, enter, high p," which results in a profit of $650 million. The high-cost monopolist charges a low price in order to deter entry: In other words, it is using limit pricing.

Intuitively, the game can be summarized as follows. A monopolist knows with certainty whether it is a low-cost or a high-cost producer; however, potential entrants can determine only the probability that the monopolist is a high-cost producer. A high-cost monopolist therefore may find it profitable to charge a low price in order to prevent potential entrants from gaining any information regarding the monopolist's true costs. As a result, potential entrants can calculate their expected profits only after entry, based on the probabilities that the monopolist is a low-cost or high-cost producer. If the probability that the monopolist is a low-cost producer is high enough, the potential entrant's expected profit is negative. Consequently, the potential entrant is deterred from entering if the high-cost monopolist charges a low price.

▼▼▼ 15.2 Pricing to Deter Entry: Predatory Pricing

predatory pricing

A strategy of expanding output aggressively and cutting price so that competitors sustain economic losses, with the intention of driving competitors from the market.

Limit pricing requires the monopolist to maintain a low price before entry occurs. By comparison, **predatory pricing** assumes that a monopolist maximizes profit until entry occurs, and that after entry, the monopolist expands output aggressively and cuts price, so that the entrant sustains an economic loss, even if this requires the monopolist to sustain an economic loss as well. What happens if a monopolist plays this predatory pricing strategy in response to every entry? It seems likely that potential entrants would eventually get the message and assume that the monopolist would respond aggressively to all entry, and, as a result, future potential entrants would stay out. By establishing a reputation for being aggressive early, the monopolist prevents later entry. Such a result depends, however, on the information available to the monopolist and potential entrants.

Predatory Pricing with Perfect, Certain, Complete, and Symmetric Information

At the end of Chapter 13, we analyzed the basic predatory pricing game using perfect, certain, complete, and symmetric information, and concluded that entry could not be deterred. Figure 15.5 presents a slight variation of that game. Both players know all of the information in Figure 15.5. As you learned in Chapter 13, if this game is played once, there is only one equilibrium: the potential entrant enters and the monopolist accommodates entry. Once the potential entrant enters, it is irrational for the monopolist to fight, because fighting results in an economic loss of $1 million, whereas accommodation results in an economic profit of $4 million.

Suppose the game is repeated any finite number of times. For example, the game is repeated N times sequentially from round 1 through round N. It may seem logical to presume that a rational monopolist would fight in early rounds in order to build an aggressive reputation and deter entry in later rounds. But, as Chapter 13 showed, that is not the equilibrium outcome in this game. The equilibrium is obtained by playing the game backwards from round N (the last round) through round 1. In the last round, round N, the monopolist has no incentive to fight, because fighting cannot possibly deter entry in later rounds, because there are no later rounds. The monopolist, therefore, accommodates the entrant in the last round and earns a profit of $4 million. The potential entrant into the last round knows this and enters. The potential entrant in round $N - 1$ knows that the monopolist will accommodate entry in round N, and therefore knows that the

Figure 15.5 A Game of Entry ($millions Potential Entrant's Profit, $millions Potential Monopolist's Profit)
If this game is played with perfect, certain, complete, and symmetric information, the only equilibrium is for the potential entrant to enter and the monopolist to accommodate entry. Both firms earn profits of $4 million.

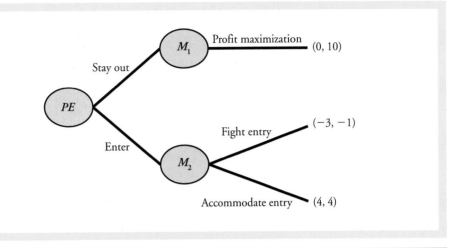

chain store paradox

A model developed by Richard Selton that argues that in any finite game, entry will always be accommodated in a game with perfect, certain, complete, and symmetric information, because fighting in early rounds cannot deter entry in later rounds.

monopolist has no incentive to establish an aggressive reputation in round $N - 1$. Why bother sustaining an economic loss of $1 million in round $N - 1$ when it does nothing to deter entry in the next round? In a sense, round $N - 1$ is now the last round of the game, so the potential entrant enters, and the monopolist accommodates entry in round $N - 1$. Regardless of the number of rounds, by reasoning backwards to the first round, the monopolist *never* fights; instead, it accommodates entry in each and every round from 1 through N. Economist Richard Selten first identified this result in 1978 and called it the **chain store paradox**.[2] Selten described it as a "paradox," because even with hundreds or thousands of rounds, the implication is that entry will be accommodated in each and every round, a somewhat counterintuitive result.

The chain store paradox is consistent with an economic theory developed in 1958 by economist John McGee.[3] McGee argued that predatory pricing almost never makes economic sense, because the profit losses associated with predatory pricing can almost never be recouped by raising prices later. McGee developed his theory after studying the behavior of John D. Rockefeller's Standard Oil monopoly in the last quarter of the nineteenth century. Before McGee's analysis, the common belief among scholars was that Standard Oil used predatory pricing on many occasions to eliminate its competitors. McGee found, however, that while Standard Oil indeed eliminated many competitors, it almost always eliminated them through merger. Furthermore, McGee discovered that Standard Oil typically paid a price for its competitors' assets that was greater than the assets' market value. Rather than engage in a drawn out and costly period of predatory pricing, Standard Oil eliminated competitors by buying them out at highly attractive prices. In most cases, the cost of acquiring competitors through merger was far less than the cost of driving them out by using predatory pricing. McGee generalized his findings by suggesting that predatory pricing is rarely used to eliminate competitors. In a world of perfect, certain, complete, and symmetric information, McGee's analysis makes a great deal of sense.

[2] Richard Selton, "The Chain Store Paradox," *Theory and Decision*, Vol. 9, April 1978, pp. 127–159.

[3] John S. McGee, "Predatory Price Cutting: The Standard Oil Case," *Journal of Law & Economics*, Vol. 1, October 1958, pp. 1327–169.

COMMON ERROR 15.1　Playing Games Forwards Instead of Backwards

To understand the chain store paradox, students must play the game of entry backwards, not forwards. Unfortunately, students often play the game forwards and reason that by being aggressive in response to entry in all early rounds, the monopolist can convince future potential entrants that it will behave aggressively toward all future entry. But does such reasoning make sense?

Consider the game depicted in Figure 15.5. The game is played with perfect, certain, complete, and symmetric information. The potential entrants know every aspect of Figure 15.5 just as well as the monopolist. Suppose in a game with N rounds, the student incorrectly plays the game forwards and reasons as follows. In the first round, the potential entrant enters, and the monopolist fights entry in order to deter later entry. Therefore, in the first round, the monopolist sustains an economic loss of $1 million. What happens in the second round? A rational potential entrant would reason: If I enter and the monopolist fights, the monopolist sustains an economic loss of $1 million *again*. Surely no rational monopolist would fight again; therefore, to accommodate is the only logical choice,

and I will enter. Now if the monopolist irrationally plays fight again, it loses $1 million again! But in the third round, it doesn't affect the potential entrant's thinking, because in the third round, the potential entrant would rationally believe that no monopolist would elect to sustain an economic loss of $1 million a third straight time when it could earn $4 million instead. If the student continues to use a strategy of having the monopolist fight entry in every round, the monopolist will sustain an economic loss of $1 million in every one of the first $N - 1$ rounds in the game. Furthermore, no monopolist would fight entry in the last round, round N, because it can't possibly deter future entry. So, in the final outcome of such a game, the monopolist's profit is ($4 - $($N - 1$)) million. If the game consists of 50 rounds, the monopolist sustains an economic loss of ($4 - $49) million, or $45 million!

If instead, the student played the same 50-round game *backwards*, the monopolist accommodates entry in all 50 rounds. The monopolist then earns an economic profit of 50($4) million, or $200 million. It simply makes no sense to play the game forward with perfect, certain, complete, and symmetric information.

Predatory Pricing with Imperfect, Certain, Incomplete, and Asymmetric Information

strong monopolist

In a predatory pricing game, a monopolist that is always predatory.

weak monopolist

In a predatory pricing game, a monopolist that is only predatory if it believes it will increase its future profit in other markets to at least compensate for its lower current profit.

Let's change the information structure of the predatory pricing game in Figure 15.5. In this new game, information is imperfect, certain, incomplete, and asymmetric. Now suppose nature first selects the monopolist to be either: (1) a **strong monopolist**, which enjoys being predatory and is always predatory; or (2) a **weak monopolist**, which is predatory in one market only if it believes it will increase its future profit in other markets to at least compensate for its lower current profit. Nature selects the monopolist to be strong with probability ρ and weak with probability $(1 - \rho)$. The monopolist knows whether it is strong or weak; however, the potential entrant only knows the value of ρ, the probability that the monopolist is strong. Potential entrants gain some information from observing the behavior of the monopolist, but initially, potential entrants do not know whether they are facing a strong or weak monopolist. Such a game is one of *incomplete* information, because nature moves first and nature's move is unobserved by the potential entrant. It is also a game of *asymmetric* information, because one player, the monopolist, knows more information than the other player, the potential entrant.

If the game is repeated many times, a weak monopolist may engage in predatory pricing in early rounds in order to create the impression that it is a strong firm. In this case, the weak monopolist is attempting to convince future potential entrants that it is strong. Because strong monopolists never permit entry, if a weak monopolist accommodates entry in any round, it reveals itself to be weak. Once the monopolist is revealed to be weak, the game transforms into a game with perfect, certain, complete, and symmetric information, because all future potential entrants know that $\rho = 0$. From that point onward, all potential entrants will enter and the weak monopolist will accommodate them.

Now suppose this version of the predatory pricing game, with imperfect, incomplete, and asymmetric information, is repeated N times sequentially from round 1 through round N. Figure 15.5 gives the profit payoffs. Assume that nature selects the monopolist to be weak. In the early rounds of the game, a rational weak monopolist responds to entry by fighting entry and sustaining an economic loss of $1 million. As a result, if a potential entrant enters, it will sustain an economic loss of $3 million. By fighting entry, the monopolist increases the probability in the minds of future potential entrants that it is actually a strong monopolist and is likely to fight all entry—even entry in the last, Nth

▲▲▲ **15.2 APPLICATION   Does Wal-Mart Use Predatory Pricing?**

Does Wal-Mart use predatory pricing to drive competitors out of the market and prevent new competitors from entering? If you asked Wal-Mart's competitors, from the small local drug store to giant Kmart, they would probably contend that Wal-Mart's pricing behavior is predatory. Wal-Mart's advertising slogan professes: "Always Low Prices *Always*." But are Wal-Mart's prices so low as to eliminate the competition? In 1991, three local pharmacies in Faulkner County, Arkansas, thought so, and took legal action to prove that Wal-Mart used predatory pricing in its Faulkner County store.

Wal-Mart entered Faulkner County by building a store in Conway. The Conway Wal-Mart began selling prescription drugs in 1987. Its main competitors were a dozen small local pharmacies and several large supermarkets. Wal-Mart admitted it sold many health and beauty items and pharmaceuticals below invoice cost; that is, below the cost of the items to Wal-Mart. In fact, evidence showed that up to 30 percent of the Conway Wal-Mart's health and beauty aids and pharmaceuticals were sold below invoice cost for extended periods of time. The products sold below cost included some of the most widely used pharmaceuticals and health and beauty aids including: the acid reducer Tagament, Efferdent, Mylanta, Oil of Olay, and Crest toothpaste. In addition to charging prices below cost, the Conway Wal-Mart monitored its competitors' prices and displayed a "scorecard" in the front of the store showing that its prices were lower than its competitors' prices. In addition, Wal-Mart advertised these comparison price advantages extensively throughout Faulkner County. Prices at the Conway Wal-Mart were substantially lower than in nearby Wal-Mart stores that faced less competition. This was consistent with the company's philosophy to "meet or beat" competitors' prices for all "highly competitive, price-sensitive merchandise."

On October 14, 1993, Judge David Reynolds of the Chancery Court of Faulkner County ruled that Wal-Mart's behavior violated the Arkansas Unfair Trade Practices Act. Specifically, the Judge wrote:

"The act" makes it unlawful for a business to sell, or advertise for sale "any article or product" at less than the "cost thereof." "Cost" in this instance is defined as the "invoice or replacement cost of the article to the distributor or vendor plus the cost of doing business."

The Judge ordered Wal-Mart to pay $396,469 in damages to the three plaintiffs.

Wal-Mart appealed Judge Reynolds's ruling, and on January 9, 1995, the Arkansas Supreme Court by a 4-3 decision overturned the lower court's judgment. The majority accepted Wal-Mart's defense that it was simply using below-cost pricing on a few products to entice customers into the Conway store where they would buy other items priced above cost. Wal-Mart contended that the pharmaceuticals and health and beauty aids departments in the Conway store always made a profit, proving that most items were sold above Wal-Mart's invoice costs.

Did Wal-Mart practice predatory pricing in Conway? Legally, it depends on which court and set of judges is writing the decision. From an economic standpoint, it is certainly consistent with Wal-Mart's overall pricing philosophy that prices were set below cost on many items for extended periods of time. Wal-Mart's pricing policies have established its reputation as an aggressive competitor that will stop at nothing to ensure that it has the lowest prices throughout the United States. That aggressive reputation has almost certainly made other firms hesitant to enter markets where Wal-Mart competes.

round of the game. If the monopolist can prevent entry in a few future rounds, it can earn a profit of $10 million in each of those rounds, which is 150 percent higher than the $4 million it earns by accommodating entry. Essentially, the weak monopolist decides that it is willing to accept a few $1 million losses early in the game in order to earn a few extra $10 million gains later.

Suppose, for example, that initially $\rho = 0.01$; that is, there is a one percent probability that the monopolist is strong and a 99 percent probability that the firm is weak. Given $\rho = 0.01$, potential entrants can be fairly confident that the monopolist will accommodate entry. Now suppose in the tenth round of the game, a potential entrant enters, and the monopolist fights, so the entrant sustains an economic loss of $3 million. As a result, the potential entrant into the eleventh round is likely to increase its estimate of ρ, the probability that the monopolist is strong. In round N, the last round, the monopolist still has no incentive to fight, because fighting cannot possibly deter entry in later rounds. Furthermore, as the game approaches the last, Nth round, a weak monopolist has progressively less and less incentive to fight entry, because there are fewer and fewer rounds available in which to earn $10 million. A weak monopolist is trying to trick potential entrants into believing that it is a strong monopolist and would always fight entry. One implication of the predatory pricing game with asymmetric information is that even a very small probability that a monopolist is strong—that is, a small ρ—might deter entry for a substantial period of time, especially if the monopolist fights entry in early rounds.

15.3 Non-Pricing Strategic Behavior: Raising Rivals' Costs

Dominant firms can use limit pricing or predatory pricing to maintain their market power, but such policies leave firms susceptible to charges of violating the antitrust laws discussed in Chapter 12. For these legal reasons dominant firms might prefer to use non-pricing strategies to maintain their power. One strategy to which economists have devoted a great deal of attention over the last 20 years is the possibility that firms attempt to deter entry by raising their rivals' fixed costs of entry.

Consider Figure 15.5 from the predatory pricing game analyzed in Section 15.2. With perfect, complete, certain, and symmetric information, there is no credible way of deterring entry in Figure 15.5. In this situation, the only Nash equilibrium is for the entrant to enter and for the monopolist to accommodate. Both firms earn an economic profit of $4 million. There may be another strategic alternative available to the monopolist, however. Figure 15.6 depicts the monopolist's game tree if it undertakes a strategic action that increases both the potential entrant's costs and the monopolist's costs by $4.1 million. Because the potential entrant now sustains an economic loss no matter what action the monopolist takes in response to entry at node M_2, the potential entrant stays out. Because the potential entrant stays out, the game moves to node M_1, and the monopolist earns an economic profit of $5.9 million, which is 47.5 percent larger than the $4 million profit it earns in equilibrium in Figure 15.5.

The monopolist may have an even better possible outcome. It might be able to spend $1.00 to increase the potential entrant's costs by more than $1.00; perhaps, for example, it can spend $1.00 to increase the potential entrant's costs by $2.00, or $5.00, or $100.00. How can a monopolist raise its rivals' costs? Economists have suggested three primary methods: (1) lobbying the government to erect barriers to entry, (2) increasing advertising expenditures to force entrants to increase their advertising expenditures, and (3) providing complementary goods and services to force entrants to also provide complementary products.

Figure 15.6 Raising Rivals' Cost(s) in a Game of Entry ($millions Potential Entrant's Profit, $millions Potential Monopolist's Profit)
If the monopolist in Figure 15.5 takes an action that increases both the potential entrant's costs and its own costs by $4.1 million, the profit payoffs change to those depicted here. The equilibrium outcome: the potential entrant stays out and earns a normal profit. If the potential entrant enters, it sustains an economic loss.

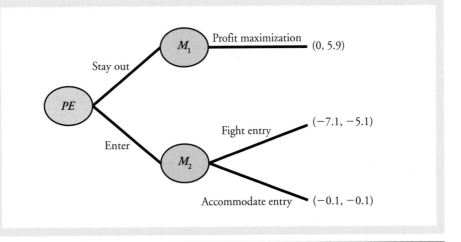

Lobbying to Increase Barriers to Entry

In New York City, only taxicabs displaying a city-issued taxicab medallion can legally cruise the streets. To limit entry, current medallion owners lobby city officials to prevent New York City from issuing more medallions. Potential entrants are forced to purchase one of the existing medallions in order to drive a cab. What's the fixed cost of a medallion? In 1998, the price of a medallion was $227,000 per taxicab, making it very expensive to enter the New York City taxicab market and increasing significantly the capital costs requirements of entry. Recall from Chapter 11 that increases in the capital requirements to enter an industry increase barriers to entry. Periodically, some city politicians suggest either eliminating the taxicab medallion requirement or having New York City offer a large supply of new medallions at a relatively low price. The group that has been most opposed to such a policy change is the organized group of current taxicab medallion owners who want to keep the capital requirements of driving a cab high. Like the taxicab owners, organized groups of doctors, dentists, lawyers, plumbers, electricians, and morticians have also lobbied to raise the cost of entry by establishing educational and licensing standards to enter their respective markets. There is an almost endless list of successful and unsuccessful lobbying efforts aimed at increasing the costs of entry.

Increasing Advertising

An increase in advertising is probably the most common method used to raise rivals' costs. Because increased advertising increases both demand and costs, increased advertising can theoretically have either a positive or negative effect on profit. Analyzing the direct effects of advertising can be complicated. Intuitively, increased advertising creates brand loyalty and makes demand more inelastic. These factors limit the likelihood of a net negative effect of increased advertising on dominant firms' profits. If the leading firms in an industry increase their advertising expenditures, this increase can deter potential entrants from entering by forcing them to at least match funds spent on advertising.

Economist John Sutton studied the impact of increased advertising expenditures on sunk costs and entry in many industries and in many countries.[4] Sutton concluded that increased advertising expenditures deterred entry by increasing sunk costs in many

---

[4] John Sutton, *Sunk Costs and Market Structure: Price Competition, Advertising, and the Evolution of Concentration*, Cambridge, MA: MIT Press, 1991.

▲▲▲ 15.3 APPLICATION Raising Rivals' Costs in Canned Soups

Sutton's study compared the history of the canned soup industry in the United States and Britain. His findings supported his belief that advertising is an effective method for raising rivals' costs and deterring entry. In the United States, Sutton observed that Campbell's entered the soup market first in 1869 and adopted a strategy of heavy advertising. That strategy has never changed; Campbell's spent $397 million on advertising in 2001. Heinz was a late entrant, and despite heavy advertising, was unable to make a significant dent into Campbell's domination. At one point, Heinz's promotional costs exceeded 33 percent of its sales revenues, yet it could not gain a major market share. In 2001, Campbell's still held a huge 70 percent share.

By comparison, Sutton noted that in Great Britain, Heinz entered first and Campbell's second, and the same scenario played out, except in Britain, Heinz became the leader. Heinz entered the British market in 1930 with ready-to-eat canned soups, as opposed to Campbell's condensed soups. Heinz used heavy advertising in Britain to establish its market dominance. Campbell's entered the British market 20 years later with a full line of condensed soups, which it advertised heavily. Heinz's initial reaction was to offer its own line of premium-priced condensed soups, but when these soups failed to gain a significant market share, Heinz quickly switched to a low-price policy on these new condensed soups. Heinz's low-price strategy apparently led British consumers to view all condensed soup as a poor-quality alternative to ready-to-eat soups, and Heinz consequently forced Campbell's into the role of a minor player in the British market. In 2001, Heinz held a 55 percent market share in the United Kingdom.

In the United States, Campbell's forced Heinz out of the premium brand market; and in Britain, Heinz forced Campbell's out. The two comparative histories suggest that the first firm into a heavily advertised consumer goods market can raise rivals' costs through advertising and deter entry not only of small potential entrants, but also of large well-financed multinational corporations.

markets. Leading examples included coffee, ready-to-eat cereals, biscuits, beer, prepared soups, margarine, soft drinks, chocolate candy, and baby foods.

Providing Complementary Goods and Services

A third method of raising rivals' costs is to provide complementary goods or services to consumers. Few markets have been more inundated with complementary services than the Internet service providers (ISP) market. First, America On-Line (AOL) offered 50 free minutes of Internet access for first-time AOL users, to entice consumers to sign up for its Internet services. It then provided 100 minutes, then 500, then 700, until in 2002, AOL was offering 1,000 free minutes—that's almost 42 free days of service to convince consumers to try AOL. By giving away so many free minutes of service, AOL made it difficult for smaller ISPs to enter the market, because the new entrants would also have to offer hundreds of hours of free access. But ISPs are not the only high-tech market where firms are providing complimentary goods and services. Wireless telecommunications firms constantly offer free cellular telephones, free minutes, and free premiums to entice consumers to try their service. Airlines also offer free travel through their frequent-flyer programs. Each of these programs increases the cost of entering the market.

▼▼▼ 15.4 Non-Pricing Strategic Behavior: The Optimal Level of Advertising

We've seen that advertising can be used to deter entry by raising rivals' costs. Yet a far more common strategic decision for a monopolist or oligopolist is to determine its profit-maximizing level of advertising. While the objective of increased advertising is to increase the firm's demand and total revenue, advertising also increases costs, and therefore additional advertising expenditures increase profit only if they increase total revenues more than total costs.

The Monopolist's Optimal Level of Advertising

Suppose that a monopolist initially does not advertise, and faces the demand curve D_1 in Figure 15.7 equal to $p = 100 - Q$. The firm produces with constant marginal and average production costs equal to $20. Given these conditions, the profit-maximizing output is $Q = 40$, and the profit-maximizing price is $p = \$60$. The purple-shaded area X represents the monopolist's profit, which equals $\pi_1 = Q(p - AC) = 40(\$60 - \$20) = \$1,600$.

Now suppose the monopolist decides to spend A_1 dollars on an advertising campaign that increases its demand curve to D_A equal to $p = 120 - Q$. Advertising expenditures, A_1, are a sunk cost, and therefore, like all fixed costs, they do not affect the marginal cost curve, so marginal cost remains constant and equal to $20. Ignoring for the moment the direct advertising expenditures A_1, the new profit-maximizing output is $Q = 50$ and the profit-maximizing price is $70. To calculate profit, it is necessary to incorporate the direct cost of advertising into the analysis. Total costs include all production costs plus advertising expenditures A_1. Therefore, profit equals:

$$\pi_2 = Q(p - AC) - A_1 = 50(\$70 - \$20) - A_1 = \$2,500 - A_1$$

Profit now equals the sum of the shaded purple area X plus the shaded green area Y minus the sunk costs of advertising A_1, which equals $2,500 minus A_1 (note that the sunk cost of adverting, A_1, is not shown in Figure 15.7). The shaded green area Y represents the increase in profit, ignoring the direct cost of advertising. Before the monopolist began advertising, its profit equaled $1,600. In this case, if $A_1 < \$900$, advertising increases the

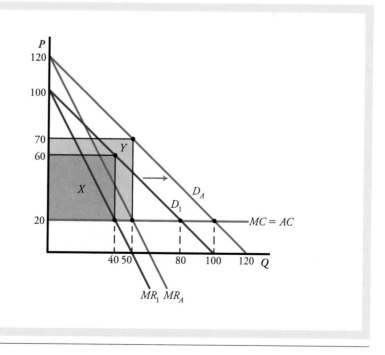

Figure 15.7 The Effect of Advertising on a Monopolist
Initially, the monopolist does not advertise and demand is D_1. Profit is maximized by producing $Q = 40$ and by charging a price $p = \$60$, and profit equals the shaded purple area X, which equals $\pi_1 = \$1,600$. If the monopolist spends A_1 dollars on advertising, demand increases to D_A, and profit is maximized by producing $Q = 50$ and setting price at $70. Profit equals: $\pi_2 = Q(p - AC) - A_1 = 50(\$70 - \$20) - A_1 = \$2,500 - A_1$; or the sum of the shaded purple area X plus the shaded green area Y minus the sunk costs of advertising A_1 (which is not shown on the graph), which equals $2,500 minus A_1. Advertising increases the monopolist's profit if—and only if—$A_1 < \$900$.

monopolist's profit. However, if $A_1 > \$900$, advertising decreases the monopolist's profit, and if $A_1 = \$900$, advertising has no effect on the monopolist's profit.

The monopolist's decision of whether to spend more or less than A_1 dollars on advertising depends on whether additional advertising expenditures increase the green shaded area Y, and therefore profit, by more or less than the additional direct costs of the advertising. More generally, the monopolist increases its advertising expenditures to the level where additional revenues generated by the additional advertising—that is, the marginal revenue of advertising—equal the marginal cost of advertising. The marginal cost of advertising consists of two components: (1) the production costs associated with the additional output sold because of the increased advertising, and (2) the direct advertising costs associated with the increased advertising. Formally, profit maximization requires:

$$MR_A = \frac{\Delta TR}{\Delta A} = \frac{\Delta TC}{\Delta A} = MC_A \tag{15.1}$$

where MR_A represents the marginal revenue generated by additional advertising and MC_A represents the marginal cost of advertising.

The Dorfman–Steiner Model of Advertising

In 1954, economists Robert Dorfman and Peter Steiner developed a model to explain the relationship between monopoly power and advertising expenditures.[5] The Dorfman-Steiner model assumes that a monopolist faces a demand curve that is a function of price and advertising expenditures, so:

$$Q = Q(p,A) \tag{15.2}$$

where Q represents the quantity demanded, p represents price, and A represents advertising expenditures. This demand curve assumes that advertising affects the quantity sold, but not the price of the product. From Equation 15.2, we can write MR_A as:

$$MR_A = \frac{\Delta TR}{\Delta A} = p\frac{\Delta Q}{\Delta A} \tag{15.3}$$

Equation 15.3 states that marginal revenue is the product of price (which is not affected by advertising in our model) and the change in quantity that results from a change in advertising expenditures.

The marginal cost of advertising, MC_A, is:

$$MC_A = \frac{\Delta TC}{\Delta A} = \frac{\Delta TC}{\Delta Q}\frac{\Delta Q}{\Delta A} + \frac{\Delta A}{\Delta A}$$

$$MC_A = \frac{\Delta TC}{\Delta Q}\frac{\Delta Q}{\Delta A} + 1 \tag{15.4}$$

The first term on the right side of Equation 15.4 represents the change in total costs associated with the change in output brought about by a change in advertising expenditures. The second term represents the direct cost of additional advertising.

---

[5] Robert Dorfman and Peter O. Steiner, "Optimal Advertising and Optimal Quality," *American Economic Review*, Vol. 44, December 1954, pp. 826–836.

Profit maximization requires setting $MR_A = MC_A$, or setting Equation 15.3 equal to Equation 15.4:

$$p\frac{\Delta Q}{\Delta A} = \frac{\Delta TC}{\Delta Q}\frac{\Delta Q}{\Delta A} + 1 = MC\frac{\Delta Q}{\Delta A} + 1$$

or:

$$1 = (p - MC)\frac{\Delta Q}{\Delta A} \tag{15.5}$$

Multiplying both sides of Equation 15.5 by the *advertising-to-sales ratio* (the ratio of a firm's advertising expenditures to its total revenues, or $A/(pQ)$) yields:

$$\frac{A}{pQ} = \left(\frac{A}{pQ}\right)(p - MC)\frac{\Delta Q}{\Delta A}$$

or:

$$\frac{A}{pQ} = \left(\frac{(p - MC)}{p}\right)\left(\frac{\Delta Q}{\Delta A}\frac{A}{Q}\right) \tag{15.6}$$

The first term on the right side of Equation 15.6, $(p - MC)/p$, should look familiar from Chapter 11: It is the Lerner Index of monopoly power, which can be written simply as $1/|e_d|$, the absolute value of the *inverse* of the elasticity of demand. The second term on the right side represents the **advertising elasticity of demand**, commonly denoted by e_A, which is the percentage change in quantity demanded associated with a 1-percent change in advertising expenditures. We can therefore rewrite Equation 15.6 as:

$$\frac{A}{PQ} = \frac{e_A}{|e_d|} \tag{15.7}$$

Equation 15.7 shows the major result of the Dorfman-Steiner model: A profit-maximizing monopolist sets its advertising-to-sales ratio equal to the ratio of its advertising elasticity of demand to its price elasticity of demand.

What does Equation 15.7 mean in practice, and how could a monopolist use it to determine its optimal level of advertising? First, Equation 15.7 suggests a positive link between market power and advertising: As the Lerner Index of market power increases, so does the advertising-to-sales ratio. Second, the equation provides a rule of thumb for determining the optimal level of advertising for a monopolist.

The Oligopolist's Optimal Level of Advertising

We've just derived a rule for determining the optimal level of advertising for a monopolist. But what happens in a world of oligopoly with product differentiation, where increased advertising by one firm can be matched or exceeded by its competitors? For example, if McDonald's increases its advertising budget, it's likely that Burger King, Wendy's, and Jack in the Box will also increase their advertising budgets. McDonald's increased advertising might even generate an advertising war of sorts. Such a reaction could counterbalance the positive impact of McDonald's advertising on McDonald's market share. Furthermore, even if McDonald's alone increases its advertising budget, it is likely to increase the demand for all fast food products, not just McDonald's products. For example, when McDonald's advertised "you deserve a break today," consumers could decide to take that fast food break at Burger King, Wendy's, Subway, Taco Bell, or KFC.

advertising elasticity of demand

The percentage change in quantity demanded associated with a 1-percent change in advertising expenditures.

McDonald's increased advertising is likely to have three separate effects. It should: (1) increase the generic demand for all fast food; (2) increase McDonald's share of the fast food business relative to other fast food products; and (3) result in a competitive response by other fast food companies in the form of increased advertising for their products. The first two of these effects should increase McDonald's sales and profit, but the third effect, the competitive response, should reduce McDonald's market share and profit.

This reasoning raises the possibility of a Prisoner's Dilemma associated with oligopolistic advertising that could result in excessive advertising beyond the profit-maximizing level. Table 15.1 depicts a possible Prisoner's Dilemma payoff matrix for high and low levels of advertising by McDonald's and Burger King. There is a dominant solution to this game. Regardless of a competitor's choice, it always pays to choose a high level of advertising expenditures: each firm will earn an economic profit of $100 million. If the two firms could solve the dilemma, they would reduce their advertising expenditures to a low level and earn a profit of $120 million each. Overspending on advertising costs each firm $20 million in profit.

Table 15.1 **Oligopolistic Advertising and the Prisoner's Dilemma ($millions McDonald's Profit, $millions Burger King's Profit)**

		Burger King's Action	
		High advertising	Low advertising
McDonald's Action	High advertising	100 / 100	80 / 130
	Low advertising	130 / 80	120 / 120

COMMON ERROR 15.2 **Believing That When a Firm Increases Its Advertising, Its Market Share Also Increases**

Students often have the misconception that when a firm increases its advertising, the increased advertising always increases its demand curve and relative market share. However, in oligopolies, a firm's increased advertising can result in a *decrease* in the firm's market share. In an oligopoly with a high degree of product differentiation, a firm's increased advertising increases the demand for its product, but can also increase both the demand for the generic product and its competitors' advertising expenditures. The increase in demand for the generic product combined with the increase in competitors' advertising can increase the demand for competitors' products enough to decrease the market share of the firm that initiated the increase in advertising spending.

For example, suppose General Foods runs an expensive new advertising campaign for its Maxwell House coffee showing the great pleasure consumers get from drinking Maxwell House coffee. As a result, some consumers may have an increased desire to drink coffee, but not necessarily Maxwell House coffee. Furthermore, Procter & Gamble, the manufacturer of Folger's coffee, may respond to General Foods' advertising campaign for Maxwell House by increasing its advertising expenditures on Folger's. As a result of the ad campaigns by General Foods and Procter & Gamble, consumers may increase their consumption of Folger's, Starbuck's, Seattle's Best, and Green Mountain coffee more than they increase their consumption of Maxwell House. In the end, it's possible that consumers would decrease their purchases of Maxwell House relative to other coffees. Increased advertising of Maxwell House coffee, therefore, can ultimately decrease Maxwell House's market share.

▲▲▲ **15.4 APPLICATION**   The Variability of the Advertising–to–Sales Ratio Across Industries

The Dorfman-Steiner model suggests that firms with little market power should have lower advertising-to-sales ratios than firms with significant market power and that firms with high advertising elasticities of demand should advertise more than firms with low advertising elasticities of demand. Furthermore, because of the Prisoner's Dilemma, oligopolists in markets with significant product differentiation may advertise beyond the profit-maximizing level. Putting these theoretical results together, oligopolists in less competitive industries with significant product differentiation should have the highest advertising-to-sales ratios. Furthermore, because competitive conditions, including the advertising elasticity of demand, vary widely across industries, the advertising-to-sales ratio should vary more *across* industries than *within* industries.

Each year *Advertising Age* magazine collects data on the leading 100 advertisers ranked by advertising expenditures in all media in the United States. The following table shows a sub-sample of the 2001 rankings. The leading 100 advertisers competed in only the 16 markets identified in the table. The table shows the leading two advertisers in each market and the last column identifies the advertising-to-sales ratio for each company.

Comparing the leading two advertisers in each of these 16 industries, with few exceptions, there was far more variability in the advertising-to-sales ratio *across* industries than there was *within* industries (as expected). For example, in automotives, General Motors' advertising-to-sales ratio was 2.6 percent and Ford's was 2.2 percent,

and in retailing, Sears's ratio was 4.0 percent and J.C. Penney's was 3.4 percent, whereas in soft drinks, PepsiCo's advertising-to-sales ratio was 12.2 percent and Coca-Cola's was 12.0 percent, and in personal care products, Procter & Gamble's advertising-to-sales ratio was 12.5 percent and Unilever's ratio was 13.2 percent. Among the other industries, the following had relatively low advertising-to-sales ratios: computers and software, financial services, and telecommunications. Other industries with relatively high advertising-to-sales ratios included: cleaners, drugs, miscellaneous, and restaurants. The beer industry was the only industry with a wide variation in the advertising-to-sales ratio across the leading two advertisers, with Anheuser-Busch having a ratio of 5.3 percent compared to Coors' ratio of 18.2 percent.

Finally, in several industries, such as restaurants and soft drinks, it is hard to imagine that advertising has not exceeded the profit-maximizing level. In 2001, McDonald's spent 22.2 percent of its sales, or almost $1.2 billion, on advertising; Diagio (Burger King's parent company in 2001) matched that spending. In all, they spent almost $2.4 billion in advertising. It seems unlikely that those huge advertising expenditures could increase the demand for hamburgers enough to increase McDonald's and Burger King's combined profits. A more likely scenario is that much of McDonald's and Burger King's advertising canceled each other out, and had little impact on either the total demand for fast food or the relative market shares of McDonald's and Burger King.

Application Table 15.4 Advertising-to-Sales Ratios of Leading Advertisers by Industry ($millions)

Industry	Company	Advertising Rank (Among Top 100)	2001 Advertising ($millions)	2001 Advertising/Sales (percent)
Automotive	General Motors	1	3,374	2.6
	Ford	3	2,408	2.2
Beer	Anheuser-Busch	48	656	5.3
	Coors	69	430	18.2
Candy	Mars	49	615	NA
	Hershey	78	366	8.0

(continued)

Application Table 15.4 Continued

Industry	Company	Advertising Rank (Among Top 100)	2001 Advertising ($millions)	2001 Advertising/Sales (Percent)
Cleaners	S.C. Johnson & Son	63	479	13.5
	Clorox	82	338	10.2
Computers & Software	IBM	26	994	2.8
	Microsoft	31	920	5.8
Drugs	Pfizer	5	2189	11.0
	Johnson & Johnson	10	1618	8.0
Entertainment & Media	AOL Time Warner	7	1885	5.8
	Walt Disney	9	1757	8.4
Financial Services	American Express	67	444	2.5
	Morgan Stanley	77	385	2.3
Food	Philip Morris	8	1816	3.5
	Nestlé	28	967	6.1
Hotels	Cendant	59	527	6.7
	Hilton	89	296	9.7
Miscellaneous	Nike	53	577	11.9
	Mattel	66	449	13.6
Personal Care	Procter & Gamble	2	2541	12.5
	Unilever	11	1484	13.2
Restaurants	McDonald's	18	1195	22.2
	Diagio (owners of Burger King)	19	1181	12.8
Retail	Sears	12	1480	4.0
	J.C. Penney	23	1086	3.4
Soft Drinks	PepsiCo	4	2210	12.2
	Coca-Cola	32	903	12.0
Telecommunications	Verizon	13	1462	2.3
	AT&T	15	1372	2.6

15.5 Non-Pricing Strategic Behavior: Product Proliferation

Product proliferation refers to the strategic decision to preempt potential entrants by cre-ating brands to fill every available product niche. For example, have you ever wondered why there are so many different varieties of cereal, almost all produced by Kellogg's,

▲▲▲ 15.5 APPLICATION   Product Proliferation in Ready-to-Eat Cereals

In a 1972 antitrust case, the Federal Trade Commission (FTC) staff charged that Kellogg's, General Mills, and General Foods (Post brand) had used product proliferation to maintain a shared monopoly in the ready-to-eat cereal market. According to the FTC's theory, the three leading producers had "tactically colluded and co-operated to maintain and exercise monopoly power." The case relied heavily on the use of product proliferation to deter entry. The FTC's evidence showed that the five leading manufacturers in the 1950s (Kellogg's, General Mills, General Foods [Post], Quaker, and Ralston) increased the number of brands from 26 in 1950 to 80 in 1973. During that twenty-three-year period, 84 new brands were introduced, but 30 did not survive. Furthermore, despite the fact that the cereal industry's profits were among the highest of any manufacturing industry in the United States, there was virtually no entry.

The rate of introduction of new brands increased somewhat over time. Product proliferation typically took market share away from older, established brands. Cornflakes, which accounted for 33 percent of sales in 1940, accounted for only 10.8 percent in 1972, and only 6.8 percent in 1982. Furthermore, the average market share per cereal brand declined from 4 percent in 1950 to just

1.3 percent in 1972. Between 1950 and 1972, Kellogg's introduced 24 new brands, General Mills introduced 34, and General Foods introduced 21. Most of these new brands achieved only small market shares. In fact, only seven new brands ever achieved market shares exceeding 2 percent.

Period	New Brands Introduced
1950–1955	8
1956–1960	15
1960–1965	22
1966–1970	19
1971–1973	20

In 1981, the FTC's antitrust case was dismissed when the Commission accepted a judge's ruling that product proliferation is not illegal under the antitrust laws, but is "a legitimate means of competition." The judge also rejected the notion that a group of firms could be charged with a "shared monopoly" under the existing antitrust laws.

product proliferation

The strategic decision to preempt potential entrants by creating brands to fill every available product niche.

General Mills, or General Foods (Post); or so many different varieties of beer, most produced by Anheuser-Busch or Miller? Economists theorize that by filling many different niches in the market for cereal or beer, the dominant firms are able to prevent potential entrants from gaining even a small foothold in these industries.

The strategy behind the use of product proliferation is best understood from the viewpoint of a dominant firm such as Nabisco in the cookie and cracker market. The optimal strategy for the dominant firm is to enter a new niche; for example, Nabisco might enter the "orange cream–filled chocolate cookie" market, just before it becomes profitable for a potential entrant to enter that niche. By entering at precisely that moment, the dominant firm is able to preempt entry and earn greater long-run profit than it would earn if it permitted entry.

▼▼▼   15.6   Non-Pricing Strategic Behavior: Excess Capacity

Another non-pricing method of deterring entry is to build a large amount of excess production capacity, even though this level of capacity is greater than the capacity that maximizes short-run profit. Models of entry deterrence based on the building of excess capacity are models in which the monopolist moves first and selects a level of capacity, then the potential entrant decides whether to enter, then the monopolist selects a capacity level and an output. The potential entrant produces a quantity of zero if it stays out.

In Figure 15.8(a), a monopolist faces a market demand $p = 100 - q$ and currently can produce up to 40 units of output at a constant marginal cost of $20. Assuming that all of the monopolist's fixed costs were sunk costs and paid many years ago, the monopolist's current fixed costs, FC_M, equal zero. Because the monopolist has sufficient capacity to produce a maximum of just 40 units, the marginal cost of producing more than 40 units is infinite, so the MC_1 curve is vertical at $q = 40$. In the absence of a threat of entry, the monopolist maximizes profit by producing $q = 40$, setting price $p = \$60$, and earning profit:

$$\pi = q(p - MC) - FC_M = 40(\$60 - \$20) - \$0 = \$1,600 \qquad (15.8)$$

Now suppose that a potential entrant appears on the scene. For a sunk cost of $575, the potential entrant can build a plant capable of producing output at constant marginal

Figure 15.8 Excess Capacity as a Deterrent to Entry

In panel (a), a monopolist can produce a maximum of 40 units of output at constant marginal cost of $20. In the absence of entry, the monopolist produces $q = 40$ at $p = \$60$ and earns profit $\pi_M = \$1,600$. In panel (b), an entrant produces $q_{PE} = 20$, so the residual demand curve is $p = 80 - q$, and the monopolist produces $q = 30$ at $p = \$50$ and earns profit $\pi_M = \$900$. In panels (c) and (d), a monopolist invests $575 in new capacity and can produce a maximum of 60 units of output at constant marginal cost of $15. In panel (c), an entrant produces $q_{PE} = 20$, so the residual demand curve is $p = 80 - q$; and the monopolist produces $q = 32.5$ at $p = \$47.5$ and earns profit $\pi_M = \$481.25$. In panel (d), in the absence of entry, the monopolist produces $q = 42.5$ at $p = \$57.5$ and earns profit $\pi_M = \$1,231.25$.

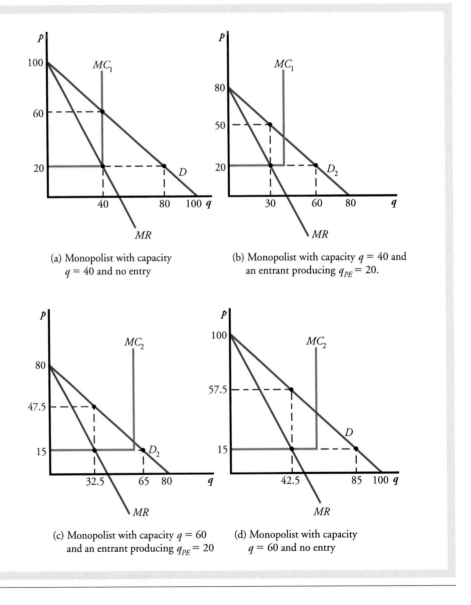

(a) Monopolist with capacity $q = 40$ and no entry

(b) Monopolist with capacity $q = 40$ and an entrant producing $q_{PE} = 20$.

(c) Monopolist with capacity $q = 60$ and an entrant producing $q_{PE} = 20$

(d) Monopolist with capacity $q = 60$ and no entry

cost of $20 up to a maximum capacity of 20 units. Assume that if the potential entrant builds the plant and enters, it produces at capacity and sells 20 units. Therefore, if entry occurs, the monopolist faces the residual demand curve (see Chapter 14) $p = 80 - q$ in panel (b). Given this residual demand curve, the monopolist maximizes profit by setting $MR = MC$, producing $q_M = 30$, and setting $p = \$50$. Profits for the two firms are:

$$\pi_M = q(p - MC_1) - FC_M = 30(\$50 - \$20) - 0 = \$900 - 0 = \$900 \qquad (15.9)$$

$$\pi_{PE} = q(p - MC_{PE}) - FC_{PE} = 20(\$50 - \$20) - \$575 =$$

$$\$600 - \$575 = \$25 \qquad (15.10)$$

where π_M represents the monopolist's profit and π_{PE} represents the potential entrant's profit.

Alternatively, in response to entry, the monopolist can increase its capacity by expanding its current production facilities. Suppose that for a sunk cost of $575, the monopolist can expand its plant so that it can produce up to a maximum of 60 units at a lower marginal cost of $15 per unit. Figure 15.8(c) shows the monopolist's new marginal cost curve, MC_2. If the monopolist builds this additional capacity in response to entry, it faces the residual demand curve $p = 80 - q$ in panel (c). Given this residual demand curve, the monopolist maximizes profit by setting $MR = MC$, producing $q_M = 32.5$, and setting $p = \$47.5$. With lower marginal costs, the monopolist charges a lower price $p = \$47.5$ and the total quantity demanded by consumers is $q = q_M + q_{PE} = 32.5 + 20 = 52.5$. Profit is:

$$\pi_M = q(p - MC_2) - FC_M = 32.5(\$47.5 - \$15) - \$575 =$$

$$\$1,056.25 - \$575 = \$481.25 \qquad (15.11)$$

$$\pi_{PE} = q(p - MC_{PE}) - FC_{PE} = 20(\$47.5 - \$20) - \$575 =$$

$$\$550 - \$575 = -\$25 \qquad (15.12)$$

If the potential entrant elects not to enter, and the monopolist builds the extra capacity, it faces the market demand curve $p = 100 - q$ in panel (d), and the monopolist maximizes profit by setting $MR = MC$, producing $q_M = 42.5$, and setting $p = \$57.5$. The monopolist's profit is:

$$\pi_M = q(p - MC_2) - FC_M = 42.5(\$57.5 - \$15) - \$575 =$$

$$\$1,806.25 - \$575 = \$1,231.25 \qquad (15.13)$$

Beginning at node PE_2 in Figure 15.9, the bottom part of the game tree summarizes the game just described. Initially, the monopolist has a capacity of 40. If the potential entrant enters, the game moves to node M_4. If the monopolist maintains its current capacity of 40 as shown in Figure 15.8(b), Equations 15.9 and 15.10 identify the firms' profits: the monopolist earns a profit of $900 and the entrant earns a profit of $25. If the potential entrant stays out, the game moves to node M_5, as in Figure 15.8(a), and Equation 15.8 identifies the monopolist's profit: the monopolist earns a profit of $1,600 and the entrant earns a normal profit of $0. Suppose the monopolist responds to entry at node M_4 by expanding its capacity to 60, as shown in Figure 15.8(c), in which case Equations 15.11 and 15.12 identify the firms' profits: the monopolist earns a profit of $481.25 and the

Figure 15.9 The Game of Excess Capacity to Deter Entry (Monopolist's Profit, Potential Entrant's Profit)
The monopolist moves first and selects a level of capacity either large ($q = 60$), or small ($q = 40$). The entrant then decides to enter or stay out. If the monopolist selects a large capacity, the game moves to node PE_1, and the entrant sustains an economic loss if it enters; so the entrant stays out and the monopolist earns a profit of $1,231.25. If the monopolist selects a small capacity at node M_1, the game moves to node PE_2: The entrant enters, the monopolist maintains a small capacity at node M_4, and the entrant earns profit of $25, while the monopolist earns a profit of $900. In the Nash equilibrium, the monopolist selects a large capacity and the potential entrant stays out.

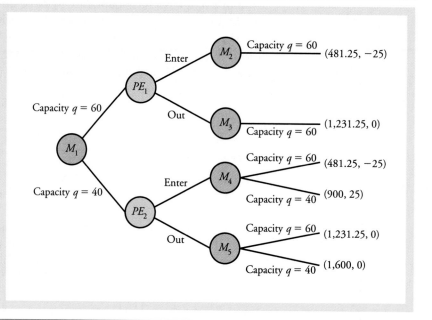

entrant sustains an economic loss of −$25. Finally, suppose the potential entrant stays out, but the monopolist expands its capacity to 60, as in Figure 15.8(d). The monopolist's profit is identified in Equation 15.13 as $1,231.25.

Look carefully at the game beginning at node PE_2 in Figure 15.9. If the game begins at node PE_2, the only equilibrium is when the potential entrant enters and the monopolist maintains its capacity at 40. The potential entrant knows that if it stays out, it earns a normal economic profit of $0; but if it enters, the monopolist will maximize profit by maintaining its capacity at 40. Therefore, the potential entrant enters. The monopolist earns a profit of $900 and the entrant earns a profit of $25. The monopolist can threaten to build the extra capacity after the potential entrant has already entered, however, such a threat is not credible. Once the entrant has entered, the monopolist earns $900 if it maintains its capacity or $481.25 if it expands its capacity to 60. At this point in the game, it is too late to build extra capacity. Instead, the monopolist maintains its capacity at 40 and earns $900.

The monopolist, however, is not forced to accept this outcome. Instead, the monopolist can build the extra capacity in advance of the potential entrant's decision of whether to enter. The game then moves to node PE_1 in Figure 15.9. The monopolist's early expansion of capacity would affect the profit payoffs for the two firms. If the monopolist builds the extra capacity, and the potential entrant enters, the game moves to node M_2, and the monopolist is in the situation depicted in Figure 15.8(c). Equations 15.11 and 15.12 identify the firms' profits: the monopolist earns a profit of $481.25 and the entrant sustains an economic loss of −$25. If the potential entrant stays out, the game moves to node M_3, and the monopolist is in the situation depicted in Figure 15.8(d). Equation 15.13 identifies the monopolist's profit as $1,231.25.

Viewing the entire game in Figure 15.9 beginning at node M_1, there is one Nash equilibrium: The monopolist expands capacity to 60 and the potential entrant stays out. The monopolist charges $p = $57.5 in Figure 15.8(d) and earns a profit of $1,231.25. The entrant stays out and earns a normal profit of $0. Because the monopolist has *pre-committed* to the expansion of capacity, it responds to entry by charging a low price $p = $47.5 in

▲▲▲ 15.6 APPLICATION   Safeway's Capacity Expansion in Edmonton, Alberta, Canada

Between 1959 and 1982, Safeway was the dominant supermarket in western Canada. Economists Douglas West and B. Von Hohenbalken examined the supermarket industry in Edmonton, Alberta during this period and hypothesized that "[i]f [Safeway] want[ed] to maintain its dominance, it w[ould] be forced to open new stores on its own before it would pay incipient rivals to enter. In other words, it would need to preempt the market and carry excess capacity as a result." When three of Safeway's competitors, Dominion, Tom Boy, and Loblaws, expanded rapidly into the Edmonton market in the early 1960s, Safeway responded by building many new stores. Safeway built these new stores either near the entrants' stores or in new geographic areas where the entrants were likely to enter. Between 1968 and 1973, Safeway opened ten new stores and only closed two in Edmonton.

Safeway's behavior resulted in the filing of a monopolization case against the firm in 1972. In 1973, Safeway signed a consent decree that prohibited it from expanding its total square footage in Edmonton for three and a half years. After signing the decree, Safeway opened only four new stores and closed seven old stores between 1974 and 1977. After the decree expired, Safeway opened five new stores and closed only two between 1978 and 1982, and therefore ultimately had as many stores in 1982—thirty-five—as it did in 1973. By comparison, the number of stores operated by Dominion, Tom Boy, and Loblaws declined from twenty-one in 1967 to twelve in 1973, and to just six in 1982. West and Von Hohenbalken also observed that "Safeway stores, on average, had market area populations greater than the break-even level, while [Dominion, Tom Boy and Loblaws] had smaller ones, a result that is consistent with the implications of the reputation hypothesis." In their final analysis, West and Von Hohenbalken concluded that Safeway engaged in capacity expansion to deter entry by its three large potential rivals.

Figure 15.8(c), which would result in a loss for the entrant. The monopolist has increased its profit from $900 if it elected not to increase its capacity at node M_1 to $1,231.25 at the Nash equilibrium. By investing a fixed cost of $575 early on to increase its capacity, the monopolist has maintained its monopoly and increased its profit by 36.8 percent.

We have seen in this chapter that there are many different types of strategic actions oligopolists can use in order to protect their market shares. Some of these models of strategic behavior (for example, limit pricing and predatory pricing) were based on economic models of asymmetric information, where dominant firms know more information than potential entrants and this information advantage enables the dominant firm to limit entry. In other models, even with symmetric information (for example, raising rivals' costs, product proliferation, and building excess capacity), oligopolists may be able to undertake strategic actions to deter entry. Because of the complexity of oligopolistic competition, economists have a great deal more to learn about behavior and performance in oligopoly markets.

Summary

1. Under conditions of perfect, complete, certain, and symmetric information, firms never use limit pricing to deter entry. However, under conditions of imperfect, incomplete, and asymmetric information, firms with high costs may charge a low price to deter entry; in other words, they may use limit pricing.

2. Under conditions of perfect, complete, certain, and symmetric information, firms never use predatory pricing to deter entry, because of the chain store paradox. However, under conditions of imperfect, incomplete, and asymmetric information, a weak firm may use predatory pricing to try to convince potential entrants that it is strong, and thereby deter future entry.

3. In order to deter entry, dominant firms may increase their rivals' sunk costs by lobbying the government, investing in advertising, or providing consumers with complementary goods. Such actions might also increase the dominant firm's costs, but they increase entrants' costs sufficiently to prevent entry.

4. In the Dorfman-Steiner model of advertising where price is not a function of the level of advertising, the optimal advertising-to-sales ratio for a monopolist is $A/(pq) = e_A/|e_d|$. Furthermore, because of the Prisoner's Dilemma, oligopolists may advertise beyond the profit-maximizing level of advertising, to the point where all the oligopolists could increase their profits by reducing their advertising.

5. Dominant firms in industries with a high degree of product differentiation might attempt to preempt potential entrants from every possible market niche by entering these niches before it is profitable for potential entrants to enter.

6. Monopolists sometimes build excess capacity in order to deter entry. The excess capacity creates an incentive for the monopolist to charge a low price in response to entry, and prevents potential entrants from entering the market, because the potential entrants know that if they enter, the monopolist will lower its price and thereby ensure that the entrant will sustain an economic loss.

Self-Test Problems

1. Consider a monopolist with the following demand curve: $P = 180 - 2Q$. The monopolist faces $MC_m = AC_m = 20$.

   a. Solve for the profit-maximizing level of monopoly output, price, and profit.

   b. Suppose a potential entrant is considering entering, but the monopolist has a cost advantage. The potential entrant faces costs: $MC_{pe} = AC_{pe} = 30$. Assuming that the monopolist continues to profit maximize, solve for the residual demand curve for the entrant.

   c. Assume the potential entrant follows the Cournot assumption about the monopolist output. Solve for the potential entrant's output, price, and profit in this scenario. What is the new monopoly profit?

   d. Is there a price the monopolist could charge to deter entry? Solve for the limit price and output that will completely deter entry. What is monopoly profit at this point?

   e. Make an extensive form of the game described in questions 1(a)–1(d).

   f. Solve for the Nash equilibrium of the game. If the monopolist threatens ahead of time to limit price, is the threat credible? Explain.

   g. What if the potential entrant trembled? What would the monopolist choose to do? Explain.

2. Consider a monopolist with the following demand curve: $P = 200 - 2Q$ and $MC_m = AC_m = 20$.

   a. Solve for the profit-maximizing level of output, price, and profit for the monopolist.

   b. Suppose the monopolist has the opportunity to spend $\$A$ on advertising to raise its demand to $P = 240 - 2Q$. Solve for the most that the monopolist would spend on advertising in this situation.

   c. Calculate elasticity of demand at the price and quantity in question 2(b).

   d. Given the elasticity of demand in question 2(c), suppose that the advertising elasticity of demand is estimated to be 0.2. Using the Dorfman-Steiner Model, what is the optimal level of money the monopolist should spend on advertising?

Questions and Problems for Review

1. Consider a monopolist with the following demand curve: $P = 390 - 2Q$. The monopolist faces $MC_m = AC_m = 30$.

   a. Solve for the profit-maximizing level of monopoly output, price, and profit.

   b. Suppose a potential entrant is considering entering, but the monopolist has a cost advantage. The potential entrant faces costs: $MC_{pe} = AC_{pe} = 40$. Assuming the monopolist continues to maximize profit, solve for the residual demand curve for the entrant.

   c. Assume the potential entrant follows the Cournot assumption about the monopolist output. Solve for the potential entrant's output, price, and profit in this scenario. What is the new monopoly profit?

   d. Is there a price the monopolist could charge to deter entry? Solve for the limit price and output that will completely deter entry. What is monopoly profit at this point?

2. Consider a monopolist with the following demand curve: $P = 1,000 - 10Q$. The monopolist faces $MC_m = AC_m = 100$.

   a. Solve for the profit-maximizing level of monopoly output, price, and profit.

   b. Suppose a potential entrant is considering entering, but the monopolist has a cost advantage. The potential entrant faces costs: $MC_{pe} = AC_{pe} = 150$. Assuming the monopolist continues to maximize profit, solve for the residual demand curve for the entrant.

   c. Assume the potential entrant follows the Cournot assumption about the monopolist output. Solve for the potential entrant's output, price, and profit in this scenario. What is the monopolist's new profit?

   d. Is there a price the monopolist could charge to deter entry? Solve for the limit price and output that will completely deter entry. What is monopoly profit at this point?

3. Consider the problem described in question 1.

   a. Make an extensive form of the game based on your solutions to question 1.

   b. Solve for the Nash equilibrium of the game. If the monopolist threatens ahead of time to limit price, is the threat credible? Explain.

   c. What if the potential entrant trembled? What would the monopolist choose to do? Explain.

4. Consider the problem described in question 2.

   a. Make an extensive form of the game based on your solutions to question 2.

   b. Solve for the Nash equilibrium of the game. If the monopolist threatens ahead of time to limit price, is the threat credible? Explain.

   c. What if the potential entrant trembled? What would the monopolist choose to do? Explain.

5. Explain the difference between limit pricing and predatory pricing.

6. What is the difference between sunk costs and recoverable fixed costs? Give an example of each.

7. Explain how the existence of asymmetric information helps to justify the theoretical possibility of limit pricing.

8. In my town, there have been three new drugstores built by different companies along a two-mile stretch of road in the past six months. How might you explain this continual entry using the theory of the chain store paradox?

9. Consider the entry game from Self-Test Problem 2 in Chapter 13. We played the game once and found that the Nash equilibrium there predicted that the entrant would enter and the incumbent would continue to maximize profit (accommodate entry). What would be the result of this game if it were played N times?

10. Again consider the entry game for Self-Test Problem 2 in Chapter 13. How might the existence of asymmetric information change the outcome of the game? For example, assume that nature selects the incumbent to be either weak or strong, but only the monopolist knows the selection. Discuss in what ways the result of the game might be altered under this situation.

11. Discuss the different types of strategic behavior an incumbent might be able to use to deter entry.

12. Application 15.2 discusses the behavior of Wal-Mart.

    a. What incentive does Wal-Mart have to price below cost for so many products? Does Wal-Mart play a finite or infinite game with its competitors?

    b. Recently a new discount store, Target, was built in my town. Many people describe Target as an upscale version of Wal-Mart. The Target store is less than one mile from the Wal-Mart. Given the information in Application 15.2, what type of behavior might you expect from Wal-Mart, given the new competitor in town? Are there issues of product differentiation that might affect Wal-Mart's behavior?

13. Consider a monopolist with the following demand curve: $P = 360 - 3Q$ and $MC_m = AC_m = 60$.

    a. Solve for the profit-maximizing level of output, price, and profit for the monopolist.

    b. Suppose the monopolist has the opportunity to spend $\$A$ on advertising to raise its demand to $P = 420 - 3Q$. Solve for the largest amount that the monopolist would spend on advertising in this situation.

    c. Calculate the elasticity of demand at the price and quantity in question 13(b).

    d. Suppose the advertising elasticity of demand is estimated to be 0.25. Using the Dorfman-Steiner model, what is the optimal amount of money the monopolist should spend on advertising?

14. Application Table 15.4 gives advertising/sales figures for many industries. Although none of these industries match exactly, we learned from Table 2.2 in Chapter 2 that the elasticity of demand for airline vacation travel was 1.90. Let's assume, similarly, the elasticity of demand for hotels is 1.90.

    a. Following Dorfman and Steiner, if we are to presume that Cendant and Hilton are each profit-maximizing, what does their behavior imply about the value of their advertising elasticities of demand?

    b. Interpret the values of the advertising elasticities of demand calculated in question 14(a).

    c. Why might the Dorfman-Steiner model not be the most appropriate to use in this example? Can you think of some other effects of advertising that the basic Dorfman-Steiner model ignores?

15. Application Table 15.4 gives advertising/sales figures for many industries. Although none of these indus-

tries match exactly, we learned from Table 2.2 in Chapter 2 that the elasticity of demand for chicken is 1.67 and for salmon is 2.47. Let's assume, similarly, the elasticity of demand for "food" as defined in Application Table 15.4 falls somewhere in between these two numbers, at 2.0.

    a. Following Dorfman and Steiner, if we are to presume that Philip Morris and Nestlé are each profit-maximizing, what does their behavior imply about the value of their advertising elasticities of demand?

    b. Interpret the values of the advertising elasticities of demand calculated in question 15(a).

    c. Why might the Dorfman-Steiner model not be the most appropriate to use in this example? Can you think of some other effects of advertising that the Dorfman-Steiner model ignores?

16. In Application Table 15.4 we see that the advertising to sales ratio for McDonald's is 22.2 percent. Assume McDonald's can expect an advertising elasticity of demand of 0.20. Using the Dorfman-Steiner model, what does their behavior imply about the value of McDonald's price elasticity of demand? As an economist, what do you advise McDonald's to do?

17. A recent perusal of the Coca-Cola Web site found a minimum of 17 different types of carbonated beverages that Coca-Cola produces (not to mention bottled water, Minute Maid products, etc.). On February 25, 2003, Coca-Cola announced its launch of Sprite Remix, which was introduced in late spring 2003. The press release stated "Sprite Remix features a new tropical version of the great taste of Sprite and will be launched with a unique graphic treatment of the signature Sprite logo." Sprite Remix was likely a response to the incredible popularity of Pepsi's Sierra Mist. Discuss the non-price strategic behavior depicted in this example.

18. The beginning of Chapter 15 lists a number of examples of firms engaging in strategic behavior: *Amazon.com*, Alcoa, American and Northwest Airlines, General Motors, Procter & Gamble, and Kellogg's and General Mills. Now that you have read the chapter, go back and re-read the first two paragraphs. Try to identify in what type of strategic behavior each of the firms is engaged.

19. Consider a monopolist with the following demand curve: $P = 210 - Q$. Assume the fixed costs of the monopolist are equal to 0 ($FC_m = 0$), because the

monopolist has been in business so long. The monopolist has a constant $MC_m = 30$ for levels of output ≤ 90. If $q_m > 90$, MC_m is infinite.

a. Solve for the profit-maximizing level of output, price, and profit for the monopolist.

b. Suppose that a potential entrant has an option to enter the market for a sunk cost of $3,000. If it enters, the potential entrant's $MC_{pe} = 30$ for output ≤ 45 units. If $q_{pe} > 45$, MC_{pe} is infinite. If the potential entrant does enter, it produces $q_{pe} = 45$. Assuming that the monopolist accommodates entry, solve for the output and profits to the monopolist and the potential entrant.

c. Suppose the monopolist has the option to increase its capacity up to a maximum of 135 units and lower its $MC_m = 25$ (infinity after $q_m = 135$) for a sunk cost of $1,600. If the monopolist chooses to make this investment and then accommodates entry of the potential entrant with $q_{pe} = 45$, solve for the output, price, and profits to the monopolist and the potential entrant.

d. Assume that the entrant chooses not to enter and earns a normal profit, but the monopolist spends the $1,600 to expand as described in question 19(c). Solve for the monopolist's output and profit.

e. Consider the game just described. Construct a game tree depicting this situation. What is the Nash equilibrium of the game?

20. Consider a monopolist with the following demand curve: $P = 140 - 2Q$. Assume the fixed costs of the

monopolist are equal to 0 ($FC_m = 0$), because the monopolist has been in business so long. The monopolist has a constant $MC_m = 20$ for levels of output ≤ 30. If $q_m > 30$, MC_m is infinite.

a. Solve for the profit-maximizing level of output, price, and profit for the monopolist.

b. Suppose a potential entrant has an option to enter the market for a sunk cost of $775. If it enters, the potential entrant's $MC_{pe} = 20$ for output ≤ 15 units. If $q_{pe} > 15$, MC_{pe} is infinite. If the potential entrant does enter, it produces $q_{pe} = 15$. Assuming that the monopolist accommodates entry, solve for the output and profits to the monopolist and the potential entrant.

c. Suppose that the monopolist has the option to increase its capacity up to a maximum of 45 units and lower its $MC_m = 15$ (infinity after $q_m = 45$) for a sunk cost of $400. If the monopolist chooses to make this investment and then accommodates entry of the potential entrant with $q_{pe} = 45$, solve for the output, price, and profits to the monopolist and the potential entrant.

d. Assume that the entrant chooses not to enter, but the monopolist spends the $400 to expand as described in question 20(c). Solve for the monopolist's output and profit.

e. Consider the game just described. Construct a game tree depicting this situation. What is the Nash equilibrium of the game?

 ## Internet Exercises

Visit *http://www.myeconlab.com/waldman* for this chapter's Web exercises. Answer real-world economics problems by doing research on the Internet.

Chapter 16
Using the Models of Monopoly and Oligopoly

▲▲▲

In the early 1980s, the United States negotiated a series of "voluntary" export restrictions on automobiles produced in Japan and sold in the U.S. The restrictions greatly reduced the number of cars that the Japanese automakers could ship to the United States. Ironically, by restricting imports from Japan, the policy served to encourage the Japanese automakers to build plants in the U.S.; and as a result, the Japanese were able to increase their market share in America.

In this chapter, we use the theories of monopoly and oligopoly behavior developed in Chapters 11–15 to gain a better understanding of many types of real-world firm behavior such as the voluntary export restraints placed on Japanese cars exported to the United States. In addition to the voluntary export restraints on Japanese cars, we explore the impacts of consumption taxes and profit taxes on monopolists and how these different impacts might affect government tax policies. We also use the models of competition and monopoly to explain why many mergers both reduce costs and increase monopoly power, and why artists often produce limited editions of their work. In previous chapters, we have seen that economists argue typically in favor of the virtues of free trade; however, in this chapter, we will discover that under conditions of oligopoly, it is possible for trade restrictions to increase domestic welfare. We will also discover why the nation's top universities believed it was in their best interests to violate the antitrust laws in order to fix the aid packages offered to individual students. Finally, we will try to determine whether some airlines used predatory pricing during the 1990s to maintain control of their markets. After reading this chapter, you should have a better appreciation of why economists have increasingly come to realize that many markets cannot be analyzed effectively using the perfectly competitive model.

Learning Objectives

After reading Chapter 16, you will have learned:

➤ How to use the theory of monopoly to explain the impacts of consumption taxes and profit taxes on a monopolist's behavior.

➤ How to use the theory of monopoly to explain the possible unintended consequences of an import quota imposed on a domestic monopolist.

➤ How to use the welfare implications of the theories of perfect competition and monopoly to explain the welfare effects of mergers.

➤ How monopolists price durable goods such as fine art reproductions and land.

➤ How to use the Cournot-Nash model of oligopoly pricing to explain the possible welfare effects of subsidizing a domestic oligopolist.

➤ How the Prisoner's Dilemma model can be used to explain why the nation's best colleges and universities colluded to fix the aid packages offered to individual students.

➤ How the theory of predatory pricing can explain pricing behavior in the airline industry during the 1990s.

▼▼▼ 16.1 Taxing Monopolists

corporate income tax

A tax on the profits earned by corporations.

value-added tax

A tax on the value added at each stage of production for every good and service produced in a country.

The United States taxes the profits earned by corporations by using a **corporate income tax**, which is actually a corporate profit tax. Many other countries, including the United Kingdom and Germany, rely heavily on taxes on consumption, such as a national sales tax or **value-added tax (VAT)**, to collect taxes from their corporations. A VAT taxes the value added at each stage of production for every good and service produced in a country. "Value added" is the difference between the value of output at the end of a stage of production and the value of output at the beginning of that stage. If the value added at each stage of production for every good or service is taxed, a VAT is equivalent to a tax on the entire gross domestic product of a country. This section analyzes the different impacts of a tax on a monopolist's income and a consumption tax on a good or service produced by a monopolist.

A Consumption Tax on a Good Produced by a Monopolist

Suppose that most corporations have some monopoly power and face downward-sloping demand curves such as those depicted in Figure 16.1. Initially, the monopolist's marginal and average costs are represented by the horizontal line $LRMC_0 = LRAC_0$, and therefore, the monopolist produces under conditions of constant returns to scale with constant long-run marginal and average costs. The monopolist maximizes profit by producing q_0, where $LRMC_0 = MR$, and charging price p_0. Consumer surplus equals the triangle that contains the sum of the shaded purple, green, and orange areas $A + B + F$. The monopolist's economic profits equal the rectangle that contains the shaded blue, red, and yellow areas, $C + D + E$.

Consider a per-unit, or excise, tax t on the consumption of a monopolist's good. Such a tax shifts both the $LRMC$ and $LRAC$ curves up vertically by the amount of the

Figure 16.1 A Consumption Tax on a Monopolist

A consumption tax—here, a per-unit tax—placed on a monopolist results in a decrease in output from q_0 to q_t and an increase in price from p_0 to p_t. The tax decreases consumer surplus by the sum of the green rectangle B and orange triangle F. Profit decreases by the sum of the red and yellow areas $D + E$, but increase by the smaller green area B. The red area D represents tax revenue. There is a deadweight loss due to the tax t, equal to the sum of the orange and yellow areas $E + F$.

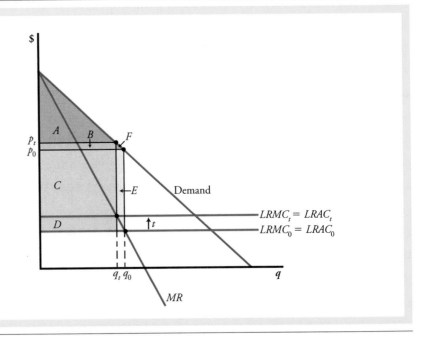

tax, so the post-tax marginal and average cost curves would be $LRMC_t = LRAC_t$. The tax results in a decrease in output to q_t and an increase in price to p_t.

Consider the welfare implications of the tax. After the tax is imposed, consumer surplus equals the purple triangle A, and has decreased by the green rectangle B and orange triangle F. Profit now equals the sum of the green and blue rectangles B and C. Profit has decreased by the amount represented in the red and yellow areas $D + E$, but increased by the green area B. The green rectangle B represents a transfer from consumer surplus to monopoly profit. Such a transfer does not change total welfare. The red rectangle D equals tq_t, or the total amount of taxes collected by the government. This represents a transfer from monopoly profit to government tax revenue. Assuming the government spends the tax revenue wisely, the transfer of the red area D from the monopolist to the government does not affect total social welfare. The sum of the orange and yellow areas $E + F$, however, represents an additional deadweight loss due to the per-unit tax. The per-unit tax, therefore, results in an increase in the deadweight loss to society.

A Tax on a Monopolist's Profit

Now consider a corporate income, or profit, tax imposed on the monopolist as a percentage of profit. Figure 16.2 depicts the effect of the profit tax. Before imposing the tax, consumer surplus equals the area of the purple triangle A and the monopolist earns positive economic profit equal to the sum of the green and blue rectangles $B + C$. In the United States, the federal corporate income tax is approximately one-third of a large corporation's profit; therefore, in Figure 16.2, the blue rectangle C was drawn to equal approximately one-third of the monopolist's before-tax profit. If the monopolist continues to produce q_0 units of output after the government imposes the tax, the firm will pay a tax equal to the blue area C and keep the green area B as after-tax profit.

The monopolist wants to maximize its after-tax profit; therefore, the critical question is whether the monopolist can take any action to increase the size of that profit. Consider the impact on $LRMC$ of a corporate income tax. Regardless of the size of the tax, the tax has *no* impact on marginal costs. Because marginal cost is unaffected by the tax, the

Figure 16.2 A Profit Tax on a Monopolist
Before the profit tax, consumer surplus equals the purple triangle A and profit equals the sum of the green and blue rectangles $B + C$. The profit tax takes a percentage of total profit, here equal to the blue rectangle C. In this case, there is no change in the monopolist's output or price and no additional deadweight loss.

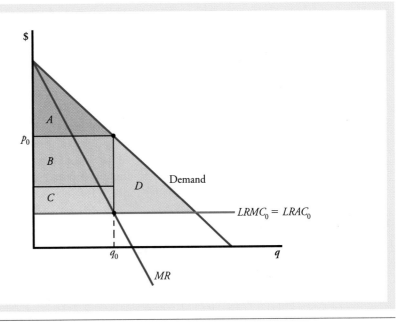

Table 16.1 Corporate Income Tax Rate Brackets

Profit is more than	But not more than	Then the tax is	Of the amount over
$0	$50,000	15%	$0
$50,000	$75,000	$7,500 + 25%	$50,000
$75,000	$100,000	$13,750 + 34%	$75,000
$100,000	$338,000	$22,250 + 39%	$100,000
$338,000	$10,000,000	$113,900 + 34%	$335,000
$10,000,000	———	$3,400,000 + 35%	$10,000,000

monopolist maximizes after-tax profit by continuing to produce q_0 units and charge price p_0. The corporate profit tax has no impact on consumer surplus. Furthermore, for every dollar of reduced profit for the monopolist, the government gains exactly one dollar of revenue, which ideally the government uses for productive purposes. Unlike the per-unit tax, there is no additional deadweight loss associated with the corporate profit tax.

If you are skeptical of the argument that a profit tax does not affect the monopolist's output and price, consider a slightly different explanation. The monopolist desires to keep the largest possible after-tax profit, which is represented by the largest possible green area B. However, the green area B is two-thirds of the green plus blue areas $B + C$, so the monopolist must maximize the total size of the green plus blue areas $B + C$. Profit is maximized where $LRMC = MR$, or at an output of q_0. If the monopolist were to attempt to pass the tax on to consumers by raising price above p_0, MR would be greater than MC and the total size of the green plus blue areas $B + C$ would be smaller. If the monopolist attempted to decrease price below p_0, MR would be less than MC and the total size of the green plus blue areas $B + C$ would also be smaller. With a tax based on a percentage of profit, the only way to maximize after-tax profit is to maximize pre-tax profit, so the tax has no impact on how the monopolist behaves.

The federal corporate income tax is complex, due to the set of marginal tax brackets shown in Table 16.1. This strange series of marginal tax brackets that first goes up, then down, then up again, might raise questions about the behavioral incentives of such a tax. In the case of the corporate profit tax on a monopolist, however, the behavior of the monopolist will not be affected by the tax. Therefore, if most corporations have some degree of market power and wish to maximize profit, these unusual-looking tax brackets will have no distortionary impact on corporate behavior.

The argument presented here implies only that a corporate profit tax on a monopolist has no impact on consumer or producer surplus. Remember, however, that the existence of monopoly power creates a deadweight loss for society equal to the orange area D in Figure 16.2. Although a corporate profit tax does not increase the size of this deadweight loss triangle, it also does not decrease or eliminate the deadweight loss.

16.2 The Impact of an Import Quota on a Domestic Monopoly

In some markets, the existence of foreign competitors who are willing to sell their goods at competitive prices on the world market greatly limits the market power of a domestic monopolist. In the American automobile and steel industries, for example, foreign competition has been a problem for domestic producers for over 40 years. This has resulted in periodic trade protection, such as tariffs and quotas, for these domestic industries. It may appear that protection from imports would always benefit the domestic monopoly at the expense of the foreign exporters; however, the restrictions may serve the interests of both domestic and foreign firms. This result may help to explain why foreign firms sometimes agree to "voluntary" trade restrictions.

The Theoretical Impact of a Quota

Consider the case of an import quota imposed on foreign firms. Figure 16.3 depicts the market situation before the quota is imposed. In Figure 16.3(a), the *LRMC* and *LRAC* curves represent the long-run marginal and average costs for a domestic monopolist. In Figure 16.3(b), the competitive world market is a constant-cost industry; therefore, as long as the foreign producers cover their minimum average cost of production p_f, they can produce an unlimited quantity of the good for export. The long-run supply curve for foreign firms, therefore, is the horizontal line LRS_f in Figure 16.3(b); foreign firms are willing to export an unlimited supply of the good to the United States at the world price p_f. Given this worldwide, constant-cost, perfectly competitive market, the American monopolist will be forced to take the price p_f as given and produce an output of q_d in panel (a).

Now suppose that the United States imposes an import quota of q_q units on the foreign firms. In Figure 16.3(b), the new foreign supply curve is the thick red supply curve LRS_q, which consists of a horizontal segment up to q_q units and a vertical segment at the quota quantity of q_q. Figure 16.4 depicts the impact of the quota. The total market demand in the United States is the entire blue demand curve D_{US}, including both the light- and dark-blue line segments. Before the quota is imposed, the monopolist takes the price p_f as given; therefore, the domestic monopolist supplies quantity q_d where $LRMC = p_f$. The foreign firms have an infinitely elastic long-run supply curve LRS_f from Figure 16.3(b), and supply the quantity $q_{us} - q_d$. The total quantity demanded is q_{us}. After the quota is imposed, for prices greater than or equal to p_f, we can derive the domestic monopolist's demand curve by subtracting the quota quantity q_q from the blue market

---

Figure 16.3 A Domestic Monopolist in a Competitive World Market

In a competitive world market, firms are able to produce with the perfectly elastic LRS_f supply curve in panel (b). This establishes the price as p_f in the domestic market. The domestic monopolist in panel (a) would then produce where p_f equals marginal cost. If a quota is imposed of q_q units, the new foreign supply curve is the heavy red LRS_q right angle supply curve in panel (b).

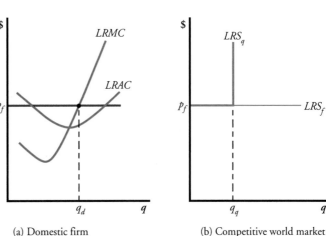

(a) Domestic firm   (b) Competitive world market

Figure 16.4 The Impact of an Import Quota
With a quota of q_q, the domestic monopolist faces the heavy light blue demand curve for prices above p_f and maximizes profit by producing where $LRMC = MR_M$, at quantity q_m and price p_m.

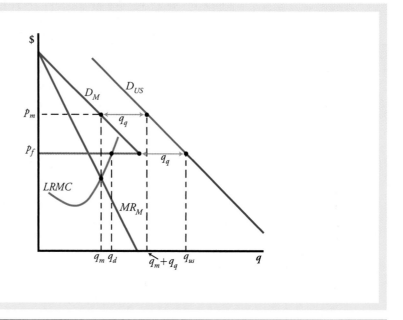

demand curve. This yields the residual demand curve D_M and the corresponding marginal revenue curve MR_M. For prices below p_f, the foreign firms would be unwilling to supply the U.S. market, because price would be below their costs. Therefore, the dark-blue segment of the demand curve D_{US} is also part of the monopolist's demand curve. Before the quota is imposed, the monopolist faced a horizontal demand curve and was a price taker at $p = p_f$. After the quota is imposed, the monopolist faces a downward-sloping demand curve and is a price setter.

The monopolist maximizes profit by setting $LRMC = MR_M$, producing an output q_m, and setting price equal to p_m. The foreign firms export q_q units to the United States and total output is $q_m + q_q$. The quota not only benefits the domestic monopolist, but the foreign firms as well, because it increases the price to p_m, which is above the foreign firms' minimum long-run average cost of p_f. Both the domestic monopolist and the foreign firms are now able to earn short-run positive economic profits.

Import Quotas in the American Automobile Industry

Our model can be used to explain the impact of American trade policy on the automobile industry in the early 1980s. Following the oil price shock of 1973–74, the American automobile producers, who were still highly dependent on large fuel-guzzling cars, began losing their market share to Japanese producers of small fuel-efficient cars. As a result, imports from Japan increased by more than 80 percent between 1973 and 1976.[1] By 1980, Japanese cars held a 28 percent share of the American market.[2] That year, General Motors lost $750 million and Ford lost $1.5 billion. Chrysler faced a far worse financial crisis, when it lost $1.7 billion and was saved from bankruptcy by a massive federal government bailout. In 1981, these problems led the American automobile industry to lobby

[1] John E. Kwoka, Jr. "Automobiles," in Larry L. Duetsch, ed., *Industry Studies, 2nd Edition.* Armonk, NY: M.E. Sharpe, 1998, p. 10.

[2] *Ibid.*

voluntary exports restraint (VER)

A voluntary agreement by one country to restrict exports of a good to another country.

Congress and President Reagan to impose trade restrictions on Japanese automobiles. As a result of this lobbying effort, the Japanese agreed to "voluntarily" restrict the number of Japanese automobiles exported to the United States. These restrictions were voluntary only because the alternative was a set of mandatory restrictions.

These **voluntary exports restraints**, or **VERs**, initially limited the sale of Japanese-manufactured cars in the United States to 1.68 million units in 1981 and 1982.[3] This number represented a significant reduction from the 1.9 million Japanese cars sold in the United States in 1980. In the context of Figure 16.4, the quota q_q equaled 1.68 million units, and $q_{US} - q_d$ equaled 1.9 million units. According to the analysis in Figure 16.4, the price of both American and Japanese cars would increase from p_f to p_m as a result of the VER. The figure also implies that the number of American cars sold would decrease from q_d to q_m. Several studies have shown that this is exactly what happened. For example, according to economist Robert Feenstra, the price of Japanese cars increased by 20 percent almost immediately, which represented a $1,000 increase per car, or a $1.7 billion increase in revenues for the Japanese producers.[4] American companies also increased their domestic prices by an average of 11 percent, matching the $1,000 price increase of the Japanese.[5]

By limiting the number of units that could be exported to the United States, the VER provided an incentive for the Japanese producers to reduce the number of small inexpensive cars, with small price-cost margins, such as Toyota Corollas and Honda Civics, exported to the United States. Larger, more expensive cars, with much higher price-cost margins replaced these small cars. The Japanese manufacturers also began to develop new luxury models specifically for the American market. In fact, the Toyota Lexus stands for "Luxury EXport for the United States." One of the major ironies of the VER was that in the long run, it resulted in much greater competition for the American producers of luxury cars such as GM's Cadillac and Ford's Lincoln Town Car.

To further compound the bad news for the American producers, the major Japanese car exporters, looking for ways around the export limitations, decided to produce automobiles in the United States. Honda began assembling Accords in the United States in 1982, and the following year, Nissan began manufacturing pickup trucks in the U.S. Toyota began producing Camrys in America in 1988. By 1992, there were 1.16 million automobiles produced by Japanese companies in the United States.[6] On the positive side for the United States, the entry of Japanese automobile firms into the American market increased the supply of domestically produced cars and created a large number of new jobs in the United States. Between 1982 and 1989, Japanese producers (either individually or jointly with American manufacturers) built enough new capacity in the United States to produce 2.38 million automobiles.[7] The expansion of Japanese producers into the United States had a negative impact on the market shares of the remaining American automobile manufacturers, General Motors, Ford, and at the time, Chrysler.

When the VER agreement between Japan and the United States expired in 1985, the Japanese Ministry of Trade and Industry (MITI) decided to continue to voluntarily restrict the export of cars to the United States. This decision strongly suggests that the VERs helped the Japanese companies in the long run. This action may have been at least

---

[3] *Ibid.*, p. 11.

[4] R. Feenstra, "Voluntary Export Restraints in U.S. Autos, 1980–81," in R. Baldwin and A. Kruger, eds., *The Structure and Evolution of Recent U.S. Trade Policy.* Chicago: University of Chicago Press, 1984.

[5] Kwoka, Jr., "Automobiles," *op cit.*, p. 12.

[6] F. M. Scherer. *Industry Structure, Strategy, and Public Policy.* New York: Harper Collins, 1996, p. 321.

[7] John E. Kwoka, Jr., *op cit.*, p. 20.

however, the huge profit being earned by Japanese manufacturers under the VER certainly played a role in MITI's decision.

In the short run, the biggest losers from the VER were undoubtedly American consumers who bought cars. They had to pay higher prices for fewer cars, and they lost the option of being able to purchase many small Japanese cars that virtually disappeared from the American market. In the long run, these restraints probably did more to help the Japanese economy than the American economy. However, American consumers also gained some benefits in the long run because the VERs led directly to the introduction of some popular new luxury car models, such as the Toyota Lexus LS 400 and ES 250 and the Nissan Maxima, into the United States. These new models have stood up quite well to the test of the American marketplace and continue to sell well. American automobile workers also have gained some benefits in the long run, as Japanese firms hired workers to produce cars in the United States.

▼▼▼ 16.3 The Attempted Merger of Office Depot and Staples

Recall from Chapter 12 that in addition to taxes and trade restrictions, firms with market power in the United States must abide by antitrust laws, including the Clayton Act, which forbids mergers that significantly lessen competition. On September 4, 1996, Office Depot and Staples announced plans to merge to form the world's largest chain of office superstores. The Federal Trade Commission (FTC), however, did not support this plan. Office Depot and Staples were the two largest office superstore chains with the third major chain being Office Max. According to Office Depot and Staples, the merger would result in economic efficiencies that would lower costs and result in lower prices for consumers. The FTC saw the proposed merger quite differently and moved to block it. They argued that the merger would reduce competition in the office superstore market and result in higher prices and reduced consumer surplus.

Office Depot and Staples contended that the entire concept of an office superstore was built on the idea of providing consumers with low prices by passing on the cost savings associated with purchasing goods in large volumes from suppliers. They argued that the combined purchases of Office Depot and Staples would enable the combined firm to obtain even larger volume discounts. Furthermore, the merger would reduce administrative, marketing, and distribution costs. Staples argued that the merger would result in sufficient efficiency gains to lower average prices by 3 percent.

The FTC countered Staples' argument by presenting evidence that in markets where Staples was the only office superstore, prices were 11.6 percent higher than in markets where Staples competed with Office Depot.[8] Similarly, in markets where Office Depot was the only office superstore, prices were 8.6 percent higher than in markets where Office Depot competed with Staples. The FTC also presented evidence that in markets where Staples and Office Max competed, but Office Depot did not, prices were 4.9 percent higher than in markets where all three chains competed with each other; and in markets where Office Depot and Office Max competed, but Staples did not, prices were 2.5 percent higher than in markets where all three competed.[9] Based on a statistical analysis,

---

[8] Serdar Dalkir and Frederick R. Warren-Boulton. "Prices, Market Definition, and the Effects of Merger: Staples–Office Depot (1997)," in John E. Kwoka, Jr., and Lawrence J. White, eds. *The Antitrust Revolution, 3rd Edition.* New York: Oxford University Press, 1999, p. 152.

[9] *Ibid.*

the FTC staff concluded that on average, the merger would increase prices by 7.3 percent in markets where the two firms currently competed against each other.[10]

The Economic Efficiency Effects of Mergers

The proposed Office Depot–Staples merger suggested that mergers may result in both an increase in market power and a reduction in costs due to increased efficiencies. The positive effects of increased efficiencies must thus be balanced against the negative effects of increased market power. Economist Oliver Williamson developed a model to explain this tradeoff.[11] Figure 16.5 presents his analysis, which is static and ignores the potential dynamic impacts of mergers on the rate of technological advance. As you learned in Chapter 11, these dynamic impacts may be more important than the static impacts analyzed here. Furthermore, to simplify the analysis, Williamson assumed that a merger in a competitive market would transform that market into a monopoly. This is a somewhat extreme assumption; however, as long as a merger increases the market power of the merged firms, it enables the new larger consolidated firm to increase its prices, and the implications of Williamson's model hold. Keeping these cautions in mind, we can use the model to better understand the theoretical issues involved in the proposed Office Depot–Staples merger.

MERGERS WITH NET NEGATIVE EFFICIENCY EFFECTS In Figure 16.5, we assume that prior to the merger, the industry performed competitively, with output equal to q_1 and price equal to p_1, which equals marginal cost MC_1. Suppose that the merger results in the creation of a monopoly. After the merger, because of efficiency gains, marginal costs are reduced to MC_2; but because of increased monopoly power, output declines to q_2, the level at which $MC_2 = MR$, and price increases to p_2. The merger

Figure 16.5 The Welfare Effects of a Horizontal Merger
A merger improves efficiency and reduces costs from $MC_1 = AC_1$ to $MC_2 = AC_2$. However, the merger reduces competition, therefore resulting in a monopoly. The merger reduces output from q_1 to q_2 and increases price from p_1 to p_2. The red triangle y represents the deadweight loss from the merger; the green rectangle z represents the cost saving.

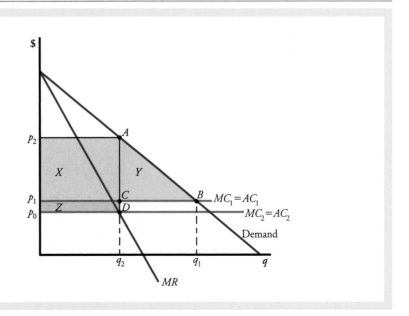

[10] *Ibid.*, p. 153.

[11] Oliver E. Williamson, "Economics as an Antitrust Defense: The Welfare Tradeoffs," *American Economic Review*, Vol. 58, March 1968, pp. 18–36.

reduces consumer surplus by the blue and red areas (X and Y) but it also reduces the costs of producing the q_2 units sold by the green area (Z). The blue rectangle X represents the transfer from consumer surplus to producer profit that results from the merger. The red triangle Y represents the deadweight loss resulting from the merger. If the red deadweight loss triangle Y is larger than the green rectangle Z, as it is in Figure 16.5, then the merger has a net negative effect. If the red deadweight loss triangle Y is smaller than the green rectangle Z, then the merger has a net positive effect.

MERGERS WITH NET POSITIVE EFFICIENCY EFFECTS Figure 16.6 depicts a numerical example in which a merger takes place in an industry with demand curve $p = 100 - 0.25Q$. Before the merger, the industry performed competitively, with output equal to 280 and price equal to marginal cost, $MC_1 = \$30$. After the merger, marginal costs fall to $MC_2 = \$10$, but output declines to 180, the level at which $MC_2 = MR$, and price increases to $p_2 = \$55$. The merger reduces consumer surplus by the sum of the blue and red areas (X and Y), $p_2ABp_1 = 180(25) + (1/2)(25 \times 100) = \$5,750$. However, it also reduces the costs of producing 180 units by the green rectangle (Z), $p_1CDp_0 = 180 \times 20 = \$3,600$. The blue rectangle ($X$), $p_2ACp_1 = 180 \times 25 = \$4,500$, represents a transfer from consumer surplus to producer profit. The red triangle $Y = (1/2)(25 \times 100) = \$1,250$, represents the deadweight loss resulting from the merger. Because the red deadweight loss Y \$1,250, is smaller than the green cost savings area Z \$3,600, this merger has a net positive effect.

To understand the implications of Figures 16.5 and 16.6, it is necessary to understand the trade-off of market power for cost reductions. If the effects of the cost reductions exceed the effects of the market power increase, the merger has, on balance, a positive efficiency effect; whereas if the effects of the market power increase exceed the effects of the cost reduction, the merger has, on balance, a negative efficiency effect. Given constant marginal cost, the elasticity of demand is the most important factor determining whether a merger has a net positive or negative effect in the Williamson model. We know from the Lerner Index that the monopolist's price-cost margin increases as demand becomes more inelastic. Furthermore, an increase in the monopolist's price-

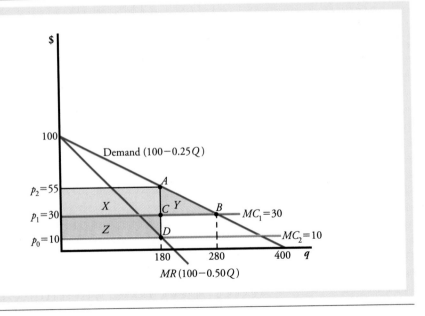

Figure 16.6 A Cost-Reducing Merger Resulting in a Welfare Gain
Here the merger reduces output from 280 to 180 units and increases price from $30 to $55. The deadweight loss is equal to the area of the red triangle Y, which equals $1,250. Production costs are reduced by the green rectangle Z, equal to $3,600.

cost margin causes an increase in the deadweight loss, due to monopoly. The more inelastic demand, therefore, the greater the deadweight loss resulting from the merger and the greater the likelihood that the merger has a net negative welfare effect. For example, demand is more inelastic in Figure 16.5 than in Figure 16.6, and this helps explain why there is a net welfare loss in Figure 16.5 and a net welfare gain in Figure 16.6.

Office Depot–Staples Merger Court Ruling

Returning to the Office Depot–Staples case: the FTC voted 4-1 to oppose the merger. The firms appealed the Commission's decision, but on June 30, 1997, District Court Judge Thomas F. Hogan found in favor of the FTC and granted a preliminary injunction against the merger.[12] The Judge concluded that in many geographic markets, the two firms would have a dominant market share of more than 45 percent of the office superstore market, and this dominance would result in higher prices for consumers. The government used an analysis consistent with Williamson's and concluded that the potential reductions in competition were greater than the potential cost savings, and as a result, the court prevented the merger.

16.4 Product Durability and Monopoly Power

In November 2002, the Metropolitan Museum of Art in New York was selling a limited edition etching by artist Helen Frankenthaler entitled "Midnight," for $8,500.[13] Only 71 copies of this limited edition were or will ever be produced. If $8,500 sounds a bit too steep for your budget, you could instead purchase a limited edition Waterford® Crystal Cogsworth Clock from the Disney Store for a mere $275. Only 1,000 copies of the Cogsworth Clock have been or will ever be produced.[14] Why do many artists and companies limit the reproduction of their artwork to a fixed number of pieces instead of setting a price for a reproduction and permitting consumers to buy as many as they wish at that price? Disney, for example, could set the price of the Cogsworth Clock at $275 without any restriction on the number it would sell.

durable goods

Goods that last for a long period of time, sometimes indefinitely; examples include land, artwork, and DVDs.

non-durable goods

Goods that have a short life-span, such as food, clothing, and toiletries.

Goods such as artwork, DVDs, and parcels of land last almost indefinitely and are called **durable goods**. Durability differentiates these goods from **non-durable goods** such as ready-to-eat cereals, computers, and clothing, all of which have finite lives and must be replaced at some point in the not too distant future. Nobel Prize–winning economist Ronald Coase wrote the seminal work on the impact of product durability on monopoly pricing.[15] The following analysis is based on Coase's work.

The Monopoly Price for a Durable Good

Suppose Aunt Annie has bequeathed her nephew Ben 100 majestic acres of undeveloped land on the southern coast of Mount Desert Island in Maine. Acadia National Park occupies a majority of Mount Desert Island, which also includes the popular tourist destination of Bar Harbor. Aunt Annie, who was an independently wealthy pretzel tycoon, had strenuously protected the land from developers. Ben, however, lives in Vermont and wants to sell the land. Ben's only objective is to maximize profit.

---

[12] *Federal Trade Commission v. Staples, Inc.*, No. 97–701 (1997).

[13] *http://www.metmuseum.org/store/*, November 11, 2002.

[14] *http://Disney.store.go.com*, November 11, 2002.

[15] Ronald H. Coase, "Durability and Monopoly," *Journal of Law & Economics*, Vol. 15, 1972, pp. 143–49.

The demand for these acres is given by:

$$Q = 106.6666 - 0.00026666P$$

or:

$$p = \$400,000 - \$3,750Q \qquad (16.1)$$

Figure 16.7 shows this demand curve. Suppose the entire marginal cost of selling an additional acre is \$1,000 in legal fees. The red *MC* curve in Figure 16.7 is therefore horizontal up to 100 acres and vertical at 100 acres. For the linear demand curve $p = 400,000 - 3,750Q$, the marginal revenue curve is:

$$MR = \$400,000 - \$7,500Q \qquad (16.2)$$

Profit maximization requires setting $MR = MC$, or:

$$MR = \$400,000 - \$7,500Q = \$1,000 = MC$$

$$Q = \frac{399,000}{7,500} = 53.2$$

$$p = \$400,000 - \$3,750(53.2) = \$200,500$$

Having done all the necessary calculations, Ben tells his real estate agent to set the price per acre at \$200,500. He then calculates his profit if the 53.2 acres were to sell at that price:

$$\text{profit} = TR - TC = 53.2(\$200,500) - 53.2(\$1,000)$$

$$= \$10,666,600 - \$53,200 = \$10,613,400$$

Figure 16.7 The Monopoly Market for a Durable Good
The monopoly owner of 100 acres of land on Mount Desert Island would prefer to set a monopoly price of \$200,500 per acre and sell 53.2 acres, thus yielding a monopoly profit of \$10,613,400. However, buyers would not buy any acres at the monopoly price, because they would realize that it would be rational for the monopolist to sell the remaining 46.8 acres later at a competitive price of \$25,000 per acre.

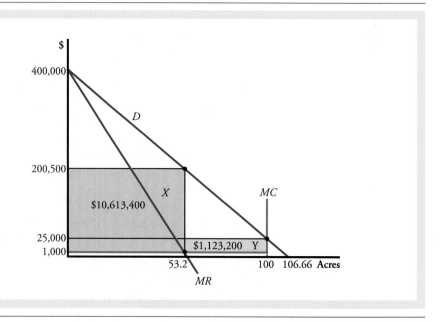

The profit of $10,613,400 equals the large green rectangle X in Figure 16.7. Thanks to Aunt Annie, Ben's about to become a multimillionaire.

The Instability of the Pure Monopoly Price

According to Coase, however, no-one will buy an acre at a price of $200,500. He argued that potential buyers know that the 100 acres are a completely durable good. Potential buyers also know that once Ben sells the 53.2 acres at $200,500 per acre, he would still own an additional 46.8 acres of land on Mount Desert Island. Furthermore, once Ben sells the first 53.2 acres for $200,500 per acre, he would be foolish not to sell the remaining acres. He could, for example, sell the remaining acres at a price of $25,000 per acre and earn an additional profit of 46.8 ($25,000 − $1,000) = $1,123,200, equal to the blue rectangle Y in Figure 16.7. That's more than one million dollars of additional profit waiting to be earned. Notice that the price of $25,000 per acre is the *competitive price* where the red *MC* curve intersects the demand curve. If Ben reduces the price to $25,000 per acre, he benefits, but the owners of the first 53.2 acres are going to be very upset. Because all potential buyers realize that it is rational for Ben to eventually reduce the price to $25,000, nobody will be willing to buy an acre at $200,500. In fact, no matter what price Ben attempts to charge above the competitive price of $25,000, the same result would ensue. According to Coase, Ben has to sell the acres at the competitive price of $25,000 per acre. If he can sell the land only at $25,000 per acre, he earns a profit of only 100($25,000) − 100($1,000) = $2,400,000. This is far below the potential monopoly profit of $10,613,400.

In order to avoid the implication of Coase's argument and be able to charge the profit-maximizing price of $200,500 per acre, Ben must figure out a way to protect buyers from the possibility of a future price decline. One solution would be to sell 53.2 acres at $200,500 per acre and donate the remaining 46.8 acres to the federal government with a guarantee that the government would never develop the land. Another solution would be a low-price guarantee clause (recall Application 13.3) written into every sales contract. Ben could guarantee all buyers that if the price were ever reduced below $200,500 per acre, then all prior buyers would receive a refund of the difference in the price per acre. For example, if Ben sold an acre to a buyer for $175,000, then he would have to refund $25,500 per acre to each and every buyer of the original 53.2 acres sold. Lowering the price then becomes an extremely costly action. An alternative to a low-price guarantee with a similar effect is a **leasing-only policy**, whereby Ben refuses to sell any acres, but will only rent the 53.2 acres at the monopoly rental rate. He would then have little incentive to lease more than 53.2 acres—that is, the profit-maximizing number of acres—because if he rented more than 53.2 acres at a lower rental rate, once the leases expired on the original 53.2 acres rented at the monopoly rent, future rents on those original 53.2 acres would have to be reduced to the new lower rental rate.

Coase's argument explains why artists produce limited editions of their artwork and Disney produces limited editions of its Cogsworth Clock. By insuring that there will be only 71 copies of Helen Frankenthaler's "Midnight" and 1,000 copies of Disney's Cogsworth Clock, the sellers ensure to buyers that the value of these collectibles will not decline significantly in the future. It also explains why on November 11, 1999, Disney announced that it would release 10 of its most popular animated movies, called its "Platinum Collection," beginning with *Snow White and the Seven Dwarfs* and including *Bambi*, *The Lion King*, and *Cinderella*, on DVD and video-cassette for a limited time only of one year for each film.[16]

leasing-only policy

A pricing policy under which a firm will lease a good, but refuse to sell it.

---

[16] "Disney Unleashes Videos," *CNN Money*, November 11, 1999, *http://money.cnn.com*.

Recall from the NAFTA application in Chapter 10 that in perfectly competitive markets, free trade *always* results in increased welfare for both the domestic and foreign countries. In recent years, however, economists have used the Cournot-Nash model to show that strategic trade policies such as tariffs and subsidies may improve domestic welfare in international oligopolies. One possible government intervention is to grant a subsidy to domestic firms. The same basic conclusions drawn from the subsidy case have also been drawn using other types of government intervention such as tariffs and import quotas.

The Cournot–Nash Equilibrium without Government Intervention

Using the Cournot-Nash framework, consider a model with one domestic American firm, Boeing; one foreign firm, Airbus; and no government intervention. To simplify the analysis, we assume that the product, commercial aircraft, is sold only in the domestic market. The foreign firm, therefore, produces only for export. The demand in the American market is $P = 120 - (1/20)Q$, where P is price in millions of dollars per plane and Q is quantity of planes. For both firms $MC = \$30$, or $30 million per plane, and fixed costs equal $10,000 million, so $TC = 10,000 + 30q$. The existence of fixed costs does not affect marginal cost, so MC remains equal to $30 million.

First, we derive Boeing's reaction function:

$$P = 120 - \frac{1}{20}(q_A + q_B) = \left(120 - \frac{1}{20}q_A\right) - \frac{1}{20}q_B$$

Setting $MR_B = MC$ yields:

$$MR_B = \left(120 - \frac{1}{20}q_A\right) - \frac{1}{10}q_B = 30 = MC$$

Solving for q_B, we obtain:

$$\frac{1}{10}q_B = 90 - \frac{1}{20}q_A$$

$$q_B = 900 - \frac{1}{2}q_A \qquad (16.3)$$

Because all conditions are symmetric for Airbus, Airbus's reaction function is:

$$q_A = 900 - \frac{1}{2}q_B \qquad (16.4)$$

Substituting Airbus's reaction function, Equation 16.4, into Boeing's reaction function, Equation 16.3, yields the following Cournot-Nash equilibrium price and quantity:

$$q_B = 900 - \frac{1}{2}\left(900 - \frac{1}{2}q_B\right) = 900 - 450 + \frac{1}{4}q_B$$

$$\frac{3}{4}q_B = 450$$

$$q_B = \frac{1800}{3} = 600$$

Again by symmetry, $q_A = 600$. To obtain price, substitute $q_B = q_A = 600$ back into the demand curve: $P = \$120 - (\$1/20)(q_A + q_B) = \$120 - (\$1/20)(1,200) = \$120 - \$60 = \$60$. Each firm produces 600 planes and sells them at a price of $60 million per plane.

Figure 16.8 shows the initial reaction functions for Boeing and Airbus in dark teal. The Cournot–Nash equilibrium is achieved at point C where the two dark-teal reaction functions intersect at $q_B = q_A = 600$. To obtain profit for each firm, calculate $TR - TC$:

$$\pi_B = \pi_A = Pq - FC - MCq = \$60(600) - \$10,000 - \$30(600) = \$8,000$$

where π_B represents profit for Boeing, and π_A represents profit for Airbus. Each firm earns an economic profit of $8 billion.

In Figure 16.9, the purple triangle X depicts consumer surplus in the American market, which is calculated as follows:

$$\text{consumer surplus} = (1/2)(\$60)(1,200) = \$36,000$$

Consumer surplus equals $36 billion, and Boeing earns a profit of $8 billion; consequently, domestic profit plus consumer surplus equals $44 billion.

The Cournot–Nash Equilibrium with a Government Subsidy

Suppose that the United States government decides to help Boeing compete by granting a subsidy, s, of $3.3 million per plane. Boeing's total costs become:

$$TC_B = FC + MCq_B - sq_B = \$10,000 + (\$30 - \$3.3)q_B = \$10,000 - \$26.7q_B$$

Figure 16.8 Cournot–Nash Equilibrium for Boeing and Airbus
In the absence of a subsidy, Boeing and Airbus have identical cost and demand conditions and the two reaction functions $q_B = 900 - (1/2)q_A$ and $q_A = 900 - (1/2)q_B$ are the two dark-teal line reaction functions, which intersect at the Cournot–Nash equilibrium $q_B = q_A = 600$. With a subsidy of $s = \$3.3$ million per plane, Boeing's reaction function becomes $q_B = 933 - (1/2)q_A$, which is the light-teal line in the figure. The new Cournot–Nash equilibrium is at $q_B = 644$ and $q_A = 578$.

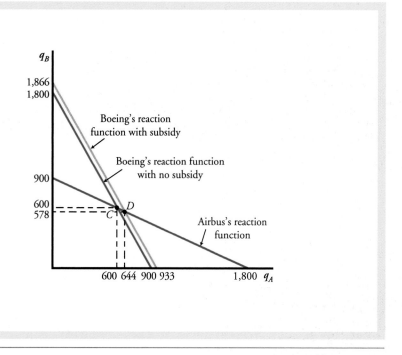

Figure 16.9 The Effect of a Subsidy in an Oligopoly World Market
Before the subsidy, the price of a plane was $60 million and American consumers purchased 600 planes from Boeing and 600 planes from Airbus, for a total of 1,200 planes. Consumer surplus equals the area of the purple triangle X. After the subsidy, the price declines to $58.9 million per plane and buyers purchase 1,222 planes at the lower price. The subsidy increases consumer surplus by the area of the green trapezoid Y.

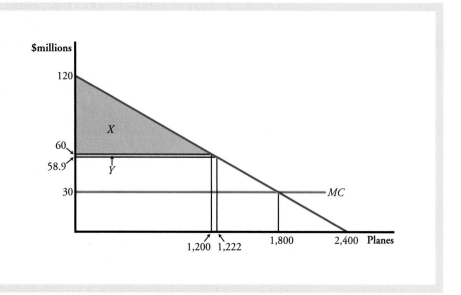

Boeing's effective marginal cost is now:

$$MC_B = MC - s = \$30 - \$3.3 = \$26.7$$

We can derive Boeing's new reaction function as follows:

$$MR_B = \$120 - \$\frac{1}{20} q_A - \$\frac{1}{10} q_B = \$26.7 = MC_B$$

or:

$$\$\frac{1}{10} q_B = \$93.3 - \$\frac{1}{20} q_A$$

$$q_B = 933 - \frac{1}{2} q_A \qquad (16.5)$$

With the subsidy, Boeing has a cost advantage over Airbus. To solve for the new Cournot-Nash equilibrium, substitute Airbus's reaction function from Equation 16.4, into Boeing's reaction function, Equation 16.5, and obtain Boeing's equilibrium output:

$$q_B = 933 - \frac{1}{2}\left(900 - \frac{1}{2} q_B \right)$$

or:

$$q_B = 933 - 450 + \frac{1}{4} q_B = 483 + \frac{1}{4} q_B$$

Therefore:

$$\frac{3}{4} q_B = 483$$

$$q_B = \frac{4(483)}{3} = \frac{1932}{3} = 644$$

From Equation 16.4, Airbus's output is therefore:

$$q_A = 900 - \frac{1}{2} q_B = 900 - 322 = 578$$

Total industry output is $Q = 644 + 578 = 1,222$ planes, and $P = \$120 - (\$1/20)(1,222) = \$58.9$ million.

In Figure 16.8, Boeing's new reaction function with the subsidy is the light-teal line, and the new Cournot-Nash equilibrium is at point D. The subsidy increases Boeing's output to 644 and decreases Airbus's ouput to 578. Profit is now substantially different for each firm. Boeing produces more planes than Airbus and, including the subsidy, earns:

$$\pi_B = Pq - FC - MCq + sq = (\$58.9)(644) - \$10,000 -$$
$$\$30(644) + \$3.3(644) = \$10,736.8$$

Airbus earns:

$$\pi_A = Pq - FC - MCq = (\$58.9)(578) - \$10,000 - \$30(578) = \$6,704.2$$

With the subsidy, consumer surplus increases by the area of the green trapezoid Y in Figure16.9 to:

$$\text{consumer surplus} = \frac{1}{2}(\$61.1)(1,222) = \$37,332.1$$

Now the sum of consumer surplus and Boeing's profit equals $\$10,736.8 + \$37,332.1 = \$48,068.9$. The cost of the subsidy to U.S. taxpayers, however, equals $(\$3.3)(644) = \$2,125.2$. Subtracting the cost of the subsidy from the sum of consumer surplus and Boeing's profit yields $\$48,068.9 - \$2,125.2 = \$45,943.7$ or \$45.944 billion.

In the absence of government intervention, total American consumer surplus plus Boeing's profit equaled \$44 billion. With the subsidy, total consumer surplus plus Boeing's profit minus the cost of the subsidy equals \$45.944 billion. The United States is better off, because its total welfare increases as a result of the subsidy. In a world of oligopoly and Cournot-Nash behavior, trade restrictions may improve domestic welfare and may be a rational public policy option. This analysis helps explain why governments often engage in strategic trade policies aimed at helping their domestic industries in oligopoly markets such as steel, automobiles, electronics, and aircraft.

It is important to note that if equal government subsidies were provided to both Boeing and Airbus, welfare would be reduced in both countries, because the subsidies would result in a larger decrease in price, a smaller market share for the doemstic producer, and some of the gains in producer surplus would go to the firm in the other country. As a result, the cost of the subsidies would be greater than the gains in domestic producer and consumer surplus. However, remember that in an oligopoly world market, it is possible for a country to increase domestic welfare if it alone provides a subsidy to its domestic industry.

▼▼▼ 16.6 Collusion in the Ivy League

The eight Ivy League universities (Brown, Columbia, Cornell, Dartmouth, Harvard, Princeton, University of Pennsylvania, and Yale) and the Massachusetts Institute of Technology (MIT) are among the most selective and expensive universities in the country.

These schools compete to attract top high school students from all over the world. The price for tuition and room and board to attend any of these schools is approximately $37,000 per year. Many students, however, receive sharp discounts off the "sticker price" in the form of financial aid packages that include both grants, which are not repaid, and loans, which are repaid. The typical financial aid packages offered in 2002 at these schools averaged over $23,000 per year.

Competition for Students and the Prisoner's Dilemma

One way to view the competition between these institutions is as an oligopoly game in which the objective is to obtain the best possible students for the lowest possible financial aid cost. Table 16.2 shows a possible game matrix. Here we assume that Harvard and Princeton consider themselves direct competitors for the top students. If one of the schools is more generous with financial aid than the other, it will be able to attract more of the best students. If both schools provide the same level of aid, they split the top students 50-50. If one school provides high aid packages and the other provides low aid packages, the school providing greater aid obtains 75 percent of the top students. As Table 16.2 shows, *High aid* is a dominant solution, and the Nash equilibrium is for both schools to provide generous aid packages. Although *High aid, High aid* is the Nash equilibrium; it is not the best possible outcome for the schools. The schools would be better off if they both offered *Low aid*, because they could obtain equally good students for a lower cost.

One solution to the problem facing Harvard and Princeton is for representatives of the schools to meet each year and discuss the aid packages offered to each and every student admitted to both schools. Suppose a student, Barbara, has been admitted to both Harvard and Princeton. Before the meeting, Harvard considered Barbara's financial need to be $24,500 and Princeton considered Barbara's need to be $22,000. At the meeting, the schools agree to split the difference and both offer Barbara $23,250. Barbara then selects a school based entirely on her educational preference and not the financial aid packages offered. In the absence of the meeting, if Barbara based her decision on her aid package, she would have selected Harvard and it would have cost Harvard $24,500 in aid. After the meeting, regardless of her choice, it costs whichever school she chooses $23,250 in aid. The schools have saved a collective $1,250.

The Ivy League and MIT Solve the Prisoner's Dilemma

As early as the 1950s and continuing until 1991, the Ivy League schools and MIT would send representatives to meet and set the aid packages offered to every student. At first,

Table 16.2 **Prisoner's Dilemma Game Played by Harvard and Princeton (Harvard's percentage of top students, Princeton's percentage of top students)**

		Princeton's Action	
		High Aid	Low Aid
Harvard's Action	High Aid	50 / 50	75 / 25
	Low Aid	25 / 75	50 / 50

the group set the packages only for student athletes, but the meetings quickly expanded to consider the aid packages offered to all students. In the 1970s, a second group of 14 selective colleges set up meetings for the same purpose. This group consisted of Amherst, Barnard, Bowdoin, Bryn Mawr, Colby, Middlebury, Mount Holyoke, Smith, Trinity, Tufts, Vassar, Wellesley, Wesleyan, and Williams.

In 1991, the United States Department of Justice (DOJ) filed an antitrust suit charging the Ivy League schools and MIT (but not the other group of 14 colleges) with violating the Sherman Act's prohibition against "restraints of trade."[17] The DOJ contended that the schools had conspired to restrain price competition for students receiving financial aid in order to reduce the schools' financial aid costs and increase their revenues. All eight of the Ivy League universities signed a consent decree agreeing to stop the meetings. MIT, however, decided to fight the case in court. In 1992, the District Court found that MIT had violated the Sherman Act.[18] In 1993, however, an Appeals Court overturned the District Court's ruling and ordered a new trial.[19] MIT and the Department of Justice then reached an out-of-court settlement that permitted the schools to share general guidelines on financial aid without actually meeting to discuss an individual student's aid package.[20]

Although the specifics of the case are interesting—particularly MIT's defense that argued, in part, that the elimination of the meetings would result in fewer needy students receiving aid—the economic aftermath of the agreement is more interesting for our purposes. Once the meetings were eliminated, the schools were once again faced with a Prisoner's Dilemma leading them toward a policy of increasing their aid packages. In 1998, Princeton was the first school to break with tradition when it replaced all low-income student loans with grants that did not have to be repaid. Princeton claimed that the new policies increased the percentage of students on scholarship from 38 percent to 42 percent for the class of 2003.[21] In addition, the percentage of admitted aid students who actually enrolled at Princeton increased from 60 percent before the new policy to 65 percent for the class of 2003. In response to Princeton's change, Yale then overhauled its financial aid policies.[22] Yale decided to exempt up to $150,000 of a family's savings, home equity, and other assets from consideration when it determined a student's financial need. In January 2001, when Princeton replaced all student loans with grants, the university guaranteed that if a student was accepted, Princeton would meet the student's entire financial need without requiring the student to borrow any money.[23] For students fortunate enough to be accepted at Princeton this was a remarkable opportunity; but it was also a very expensive policy. According to Princeton officials, funding for the new policy came from additional expenditures of $57 million out of the University's endowment.[24]

It will be surprising if the other Ivy League schools and MIT, not to mention Stanford and many other highly selective colleges and universities, are not forced to offer similar types of generous aid packages in order to compete for the best students. If this happens, the Prisoner's Dilemma, which the meetings helped to solve, will not have been solved in the end.

---

[17] *United States v. Brown University, et al.*, 805 F.Supp. 288 (1992).

[18] *Ibid.*

[19] *United States v. Brown University, et al.*, 5 F.3d 658 (1993).

[20] "MIT Press Release on the Overlap Group Settlement," December 22, 1993, *http://www-tech.mit.edu.*

[21] "Princeton University Further Increases its Support for Students on Financial Aid," Princeton University Office of Communications, January 31, 2000, *http://www.princeton.edu.*

[22] Kate Mason, "Financial Aid in a Changing Ivy World," *Yale Herald*, March 4, 1999, *http://www.yaleherald.com.*

[23] Bill Beaver, "Princeton Approves 'No-loan' Aid Program," *The Daily Princetonian*, February 5, 2001, *http://www.uwire.com.*

[24] *Ibid.*

16.7   Possible Predatory Pricing in the Airline Industry

Many oligopoly games deal with non-cooperative behavior where one firm is attempting to maintain its market power at the expense of other firms. The predatory pricing game in Chapter 15 is one such game. Recall that in the predatory pricing game, even a weak dominant firm responded aggressively to all entry early in the game in order to create a tough reputation. It was this aggressive response to all entry that allowed the dominant firm to deter future entry. The dominant firm's behavior increased the probability in the minds of potential entrants that the dominant firm was really a strong firm, even if it was actually weak. For several years, many economists and the U.S. Department of Justice (DOJ) were suspicious that American Airlines (American) was behaving in a manner consistent with the predatory pricing model.

The American Airlines Case

In 1999, the DOJ decided that based on the complaints of several small low-cost carriers (LCCs), there was sufficient evidence to file an antitrust complaint against American.[25] Several LCCs complained that immediately upon entry into any of American's markets, American slashed fares and dramatically increased the number of flights in that market. On May 13, 1999, the DOJ filed a monopolization case claiming that American had attempted to monopolize airline passenger service to and from the Dallas/Ft. Worth International Airport. In part, the suit charged that:

> American has been or will be able to recoup the costs of its predatory strategy by, among other things: reducing its capacity and increasing its fares to monopoly levels following the exit of an LCC from a DFW [Dallas/Ft. Worth] city pair; preventing expansion by LCCs into other DFW markets in which American has monopoly power; and establishing a reputation as a carrier that will employ predatory strategies to drive an LCC out of DFW city pairs, thereby deterring future entry by other LCCs into DFW markets.[26]

The government complained about many of American's actions, but it based its legal challenge primarily on charges of predatory behavior toward three LCCs, Vanguard Airlines, Western Pacific Airlines, and Sun Jet Airlines. In 1998, American was the second largest airline in the United States, and it earned more than $1.7 billion in profit on sales of over $15 billion. It operated a large fleet of over 850 airplanes. Dallas/Ft. Worth International Airport was American's largest and most profitable hub, and American's Dallas routes accounted for $2 billion of its $15 billion in revenues in 1998. American carried 70 percent of all passengers traveling nonstop from Dallas in 1998.

According to the DOJ's complaint, American had monopoly power on many of its Dallas routes because it was the only nonstop carrier. Due to a lack of competition, American was able to charge higher fares than it charged on other routes where it faced more competition. These high fares made Dallas a relatively attractive potential market for the LCCs, many of which were small start-up airlines. When an LCC entered a market, fares typically declined and traffic increased as new consumers were attracted to air travel. The government charged that beginning in 1993, American's management adopted a predatory strategy to deal with the entry of LCCs into Dallas. If any LCC

---

[25] *United States v. AMR Corporation*, Civil Action No. 99–1180-JTM, May 13, 1999, *http://www.usdoj.gov.*
[26] *Ibid.*

offered service to Dallas, American expanded capacity and lowered fares until that entrant was driven from the market. American recognized the significant short-run costs of such a strategy, but it believed that these losses were simply a good "investment" in the future. As chairmen and CEO of American Robert Crandall noted in 1996, "[I]f you are not going to get them [LCCs] out then no point to diminish profit."[27]

The following evidence of American's aggressive behavior was presented at trial. Vanguard Airlines began operating in 1994 with three daily round-trip, non-stop flights between Kansas City and Dallas. When Vanguard entered, American dominated the Dallas–Kansas City market with eight daily round-trip flights at an average one-way fare of $108. In 1995, American matched Vanguard's one-way fare of $80. American also added six additional daily round-trip flights. According to documents presented by the DOJ, American's strategy was "to drive [Vanguard] from the market."[28] If that was the intention, American was successful. In December 1995, Vanguard pulled out of the Dallas–Kansas City market. American immediately reduced its number of daily Dallas–Kansas City round-trips from 14 to 11 and increased fares. During the next six months, its average one-way fare ranged from $112 to $147, or as much as 80 percent higher than its $80 fare in the face of Vanguard's competition. American responded similarly to Vanguard's entry into the Dallas–Wichita, Dallas–Cincinnati, and Dallas–Phoenix markets. After Vanguard entered each of these markets, American greatly expanded its service and reduced fares.

In 1994, Sun Jet entered the Dallas market with very limited service to Newark, Long Beach, and Tampa. At first, because Sun Jet's Dallas service was so limited, American did not consider it to be a threat to its monopoly markets in Dallas; however, it was concerned about the possibility of Sun Jet creating a future hub in Dallas. In October 1996, when Sun Jet added a third daily Dallas–Long Beach round-trip, American decided to reenter the Dallas–Long Beach market, which it had abandoned as unprofitable in 1994. In January 1997, American began offering three daily round trips to Long Beach and matched Sun Jet's fares. In August, American added a fourth flight. In January 1998, Sun Jet left the Dallas–Long Beach market.

Western Pacific entered the Dallas–Colorado Springs (COS) market in April 1995 with two daily round-trips. Prior to Western Pacific's entry, American had charged an average $150 one-way fare on its Dallas–Colorado Springs route. In July 1995, American added two additional daily round-trip flights, and lowered its fares below $100. American's actions caused Western Pacific to reduce its daily flights between Dallas and Colorado Springs from two to one. In March 1997, Western Pacific attempted to add one daily round-trip, but American responded by adding another flight and replacing its standard jets with large jumbo jets on the route. On October 15, 1997, Western Pacific pulled out of the Dallas–Colorado Springs market. Shortly thereafter, Western Pacific filed for bankruptcy.

American's behavior appears to have been consistent with the implications of the predatory pricing game developed in Chapter 15; however, according to District Court Judge J. Thomas Marten, it did not violate the Sherman Act. On April 27, 2001, Judge Marten dismissed the case.[29] In predatory pricing antitrust cases, most federal courts currently rely on a price *below average variable cost* standard of liability. The judge ruled that American had never priced below its average variable costs. According to Judge Marten, the government had also failed to prove that American had the ability to recoup its lost revenues after the exit of the LCCs. Another key to the ruling was that American had

---

[27] *Ibid.*, p. 14.

[28] *United States v. AMR Corporation*, Civil Action No. 99–1180-JTM, May 13, 1999, *http://www.usdoj.gov*, p. 7.

[29] *United States v. AMR Corporation*, 2001–1 Trade Cas. ¶73,251 (D. Kan. Apr. 27, 2001).

only *matched* the fares of the LCCs, but had not *undercut* their fares. The judge failed to accept the DOJ's argument that American could drive the LCCs from the market by expanding capacity without undercutting fares. Judge Marten also rejected the reputation for predation arguments put forth by the Department of Justice. Even if the DOJ had proven that predatory pricing had taken place on some routes, legal liability could not be based solely on American's "reputation for predation," because there was no legal precedent for such an antitrust claim.

A Different Legal Standard: Canadian Airline Pricing Guidelines

In recent years, the Canadian Competition Bureau, which is responsible for administering and enforcing Canadian antitrust policy, complained about Air Canada's practice of increasing capacity and reducing fares in markets threatened by LCCs. As a result of these complaints, the Competition Bureau established Canadian guidelines for legal behavior entitled "The Abuse of Dominance in the Airline Industry."[30] The Bureau's general standard for predatory pricing is a price below **avoidable costs**, which are the portion of total fixed costs that are *not* sunk. However, the Canadian guidelines also note:

avoidable costs

The recoverable portion of total fixed costs; that is, the portion of fixed costs that are not sunk.

> The practice of operating capacity at fares that do not cover the avoidable cost of providing the service does not require that the fares charged by the dominant airline be lower than the fares set by the competitor in order to be considered anti-competitive. Airlines differ in many ways, such as in the quality of service they provide, the schedule they offer, and their frequent flyer programs. The Bureau does not consider that matching the dollar price of a competitor for travel on a specific flight is the same as charging the same real price for the same quality and quantity. An airline with a superior frequent flyer program or schedule could meet the dollar price of a competitor, and in fact force the rival to set substantially lower fares to attract customers.[31]

The Canadian Competition Bureau took a different approach to predatory pricing in the Canadian airline industry than Judge Marten took in his American Airlines ruling. The Canadian Competition Bureau's approach was more sympathetic to the theoretical justifications for predatory pricing.

In this chapter, we have seen how knowledge of microeconomic theory is critical to implementing wise public policies toward monopoly and oligopoly industries. For analyzing a wide variety of issues ranging from tax and trade policies to antitrust policies, governments must rely on policy makers with an understanding of the microeconomic models of monopoly and oligopoly developed in the previous five chapters.

Summary

1. Taxes on consumption reduce a monopolist's output and increase the size of the deadweight loss due to monopoly. Taxes on profit, however, have no effect on the monopolist's output or price, and therefore do not increase the deadweight loss due to monopoly.

---

[30] *Enforcement Guidelines on: The Abuse of Dominance in the Airline Industry.* Hull, Quebec: Information Centre Competition Bureau Industry Canada, February 2001.

[31] *Ibid.*, p. 8.

2. A quota placed on imports to protect a domestic monopolist results in an increase in the price of both the domestic and imported good, and therefore can increase the foreign firms' profits as well as the domestic monopolist's profit. The quota can also encourage the foreign firms to produce the good in the domestic market.

3. Mergers between direct competitors often reduce production costs and increase monopoly power. Such mergers may have either a net positive or negative effect on economic efficiency, depending on which of these two effects is greater: the efficiency effect or the monopoly power effect.

4. In order to charge a monopoly price for a durable good such as art reproductions, collectibles, or land, the monopolist must convince consumers that more of the durable good will not be made available in the future. Otherwise, consumers will refuse to pay the monopoly price for the durable good, because they realize that more of the good will be sold in the market. The monopolist can solve this durable good pricing problem by committing to never increasing the supply of the good.

5. In a world of perfect competition, free trade always maximizes domestic welfare. However, in a world of oligopoly, a subsidy to a domestic oligopolist can increase domestic welfare.

6. The Prisoner's Dilemma can force even non-profit institutions such as colleges and universities to collude to solve the dilemma. If collusion is legally prevented, the Prisoner's Dilemma is likely to result in numerous defections away from the collusive outcome.

7. The effective use of predatory pricing requires aggressive conduct toward all entrants in order to deter future entry. American Airlines' conduct toward entrants into the Dallas–Ft. Worth market in the 1990s while consistent with predatory behavior aimed at deterring entry, was not found to violate the antitrust laws.

Self-Test Problems

1. Consider a competitive market with demand given as $P = 300 - (1/3)Q$ and $MC_1 = AC_1 = 40$.

   a. Solve for the output, price, and consumer surplus in this competitive market.

   b. Consider a potential merger. After the merger, the market has monopolistic tendencies, but there is a cost savings as a result of the merger. $MC_2 = AC_2 = 20$. Solve for the output, price, consumer surplus, and producer surplus as a result of the merger.

   c. You have just been hired by the FTC to analyze this merger. Is the net effect negative or positive? Include a graph in your explanation.

2. Consider two firms (u for U.S. and f for foreign) in an oligopolistic market. The two firms act as Cournot duopolists. The total costs for each firm are identical: $TC = 5,000 + 20q$. MC for each firm is 20. The market demand is $P = 182 - (1/10)Q$, where Q represents market output $= q_u + q_f$.

   a. Solve for each firm's Cournot reaction functions.

   b. Solve for price, each firm's output, each firm's profit, and consumer surplus.

   c. Now suppose the U.S. government is considering subsidizing the U.S. market of $3 per unit. Solve for the new U.S. firm's reaction function.

   d. Solve for price, each firm's output, each firm's profit, and consumer surplus in this case.

   e. Is the U.S better off as a result of the subsidy? Explain.

Questions and Problems for Review

1. From Section 16.1, we learned that an excise tax, or per-unit tax, leads to a deadweight loss. Does the deadweight loss increase or decrease as demand becomes more elastic? Analyze using a graph.

2. Consider a competitive market with demand given as $P = 800 - 10Q$. $MC_1 = 180$.

   a. Solve for the output, price, and consumer surplus in this competitive market.

   b. Consider a potential merger. After the merger, the market has monopolistic tendencies, but there are cost savings as a result of the merger and $MC_2 = 60$. Solve for the output, price, consumer surplus, and producer surplus as a result of the merger.

   c. You have just been hired by the FTC to analyze this merger. Is the net effect negative or positive? Include a graph in your explanation.

3. Consider the market for small cars: The U.S. demand for such cars is $P = 12,000 - (1/2)Q$. The domestic supply of cars is $P = 1,000 + (1/2)Q_d$ and the foreign supply for small cars to the United States is $P = 1,000 + Q_f$.

   a. What is the equilibrium price and quantity of small cars in the U.S. with free trade? How much do foreign firms supply? What quantity would the domestic firms supply? (Recall that the market supply is constructed by horizontally summing the two individual supply curves.)

   b. Calculate consumer surplus and domestic producer surplus. What is the total welfare in this market?

   c. Suppose the government imposed a quota equal to 2400 units on small cars. What would be the new equilibrium price and quantity? How many small cars would domestic firms supply? How much would the foreign firms supply?

   d. Calculate consumer surplus and domestic producer surplus. What is total welfare in this market? Is the quota a good domestic policy? Explain.

   e. Why might the foreign producers of small cars voluntarily agree to the quota set by the U.S. government? Explain.

4. Your very wealthy grandmother has just died and left you 25 very famous paintings. The paintings are all by equally talented, famous, dead artists. The demand for paintings of this type is $P = 2.9 - 0.09 Q$, where prices are reflected in millions of dollars. You are considering selling the paintings. To do so, you must hire an art professional and a lawyer. The marginal cost to sell each painting $= 0.02$ (again, in millions of dollars).

   a. What would be your policy to sell these paintings if you are not familiar with Coase's work? Solve for the output sold, the price, and profit as a profit-maximizing monopolist.

   b. Why might you not be able to get rid of the paintings at the price set in question 4(a)?

   c. Explain what types of policies you could put into place to increase your chances of selling the paintings at the prices set in question 4(a).

5. Consider two firms (u for U.S. and f for foreign) in an oligopolistic market. The two firms act as Cournot duopolists. The total costs for each firm are identical: $TC = 5,000 + 20q$. MC for each firm is 20. The market demand is $P = 182 - (1/10)Q$, where Q represents market output $= q_u + q_f$. (Note that these are the same functions as Self-Test Problem 2.)

   a. Solve for each firm's Cournot reaction functions.

   b. Solve for price, each firm's output, each firm's profit, and consumer surplus.

   c. Now suppose the U.S. government is considering putting a tariff on foreign producers of $3 per unit. This is essentially a per-unit tax on foreign producers. Solve for the new foreign firm's reaction function.

   d. Solve for price, each firm's output, each firm's profit, consumer surplus, and government revenue in this case.

   e. Is the U.S better off as a result of the tariff? Explain.

6. Consider two firms (u for U.S. and f for foreign) in an oligopolistic market. The two firms act as Cournot duopolists. The total costs for each firm are identical: $TC = 20,000 + 20q$. MC for each firm is 20. The market demand is $P = 200 - (1/5)Q$, where Q represents market output $= q_u + q_f$.

   a. Solve for each firm's Cournot reaction functions.

b. Solve for price, each firm's output, each firm's profit, and consumer surplus.

c. Now suppose the U.S. government is considering subsidizing the U.S. producer by $5 per unit. Solve for the new U.S. firm's reaction function.

d. Solve for price, each firm's output, each firm's profit, and consumer surplus in this case.

e. Is the U.S better off as a result of the subsidy? Explain.

7. In Section 16.6, we learned of the financial aid game that many Ivy League colleges have played. Assume that Harvard manages to create some consumer loyalty among the top students with a huge advertising campaign. Now, if Harvard offers the low-aid package and MIT the high-aid package, Harvard will still get 45 percent of the top students. And if Harvard offers the high-aid package while MIT offers the low-aid package, Harvard will get 90 percent of the top students. If the aid packages are the same, Harvard will get 80 percent of the top students.

a. Reconstruct the payoff matrix associated with the financial aid game with these new payoffs.

b. What is the Nash equilibrium of this game? Is this game a Prisoner's Dilemma?

c. Does it make sense for Harvard to spend all this money on the advertising campaign to try to distinguish itself from the other Ivy League schools?

8. In Youngstown, Ohio, airline travelers have the choice of departing from three different airports, all within approximately a one-hour drive: Akron, Pittsburgh, and Cleveland. Pittsburgh is southeast of Youngstown, Cleveland is northwest of Youngstown, and Akron is west of Youngstown. In Pittsburgh, approximately 88 percent of the flights leaving on any given day are operated by USAirways. Although Cleveland is a hub for Continental Airlines, they do not dominate the market like USAirways does in Pittsburgh. There are five airlines to choose from in Akron, including the low-cost carrier, Air Tran. The Cleveland and Akron airports are close substitutes for each other, as travelers from Akron might consider departing out of either airport. Similarly, travelers from Cleveland view Akron as a possible airport for departure, given that they are only approximately 45 minutes from each other. Pittsburgh is too far for those from Cleveland or Akron to consider. Recently, Tom, who lives in Youngstown, decided to take his family to San Diego, California. After checking prices at each of the airports, he narrowed his decision down to the lowest fares from Cleveland and Pittsburgh: departing from Cleveland airport on American Airlines for $226 per ticket or departing from Pittsburgh airport on USAirways for $430. Does this outcome support the strategic behavior of airlines described in Section 16.7? Explain.

9. Recall the result of the possible predatory pricing in the airlines industry. How do most federal courts define predation? Does this definition make sense to you? Why do you think the court doesn't use average total cost?

Internet Exercises

Visit *http://www.myeconlab.com/waldman* for this chapter's Web exercises. Answer real-world economics problems by doing research on the Internet.

Part 5 Factor Markets, Investment, Time, and Risk

Chapter 17
Factor Markets

Over the past 20 years, professional sports leagues in North America have seen their seasons interrupted by numerous strikes as players and owners have fought aggressively during labor negotiations. Major league baseball experienced strikes in 1981, 1985, and 1994. In 1982 and 1987, the National Football League (NFL) experienced strikes. During the 1998–1999 season, the National Basketball Association lost almost half of its regular season games to a strike. Why have professional sports leagues been so susceptible to strikes during the past quarter-century? To answer this question, we must first understand how the conduct of monopoly buyers and monopoly suppliers of inputs differs from the conduct of competitive buyers and suppliers of inputs. In this chapter, we explore how competitive and monopolized factor markets operate, and how these differences in market structures affect economic performance.

You will also learn how the globalization of factor markets has changed how and where goods and services are produced. Forty years ago, many inexpensive products—from cars and electronics to clothing and toys—were produced in Japan and exported to the United States. In the 1960s, the label "Made in Japan" had a low-quality connotation for most American consumers. Today, the opposite is true; the "Made in Japan" label, especially on cars or electronics, has a high-quality reputation for most Americans. Furthermore, many of the low-quality items that used to be labeled "Made in Japan" are now labeled "Made in China" or "Made in Bangladesh." Likewise, the inexpensive cars and televisions that used to be made in Japan are now made in South Korea. What changed in the intervening years? Perhaps the most important change was the dramatic increase in labor productivity and wages in Japan. This chapter will show that

Learning Objectives

After reading Chapter 17, you will have learned:

➤ How to derive the demand and supply for an input in a competitive input market.

➤ How to identify the equilibrium in a competitive input market, both when the demand for the final product is produced in a competitive market and when the final product is produced in a monopolized market.

➤ How to identify the equilibrium in a monopsony input market where there is only one buyer of the input.

➤ How to identify the equilibrium in an input market where a monopolist supplies the input.

➤ How to identify the equilibrium in a bilateral monopoly input market where there is both a monopsonist buyer and a monopolist supplier of the input.

Featured Applications

➤ 17.1 Application Why Do Social Workers with MSW Degrees Earn So Much Less than Lawyers?

➤ 17.2 Application Marx's Labor Theory of Value

➤ 17.3 Application The NCAA's Control Over Student-Athlete Compensation

➤ 17.4 Application Are Union Wages Higher than Non-Union Wages?

➤ 17.5 Application Bilateral Monopoly Power in the Baseball Labor Market the simultaneous increase in labor productivity and wages that occurred in Japan is consistent with a smooth-working competitive labor market, as is the movement of production from countries with high wages to countries with lower wages. To understand why the production of some products is transferred from one country to another over time, it is necessary to understand the operation of competitive factor markets, including the labor market.

We begin this chapter by analyzing equilibrium in competitive factor markets and then proceed to examine how market imperfections affect the competitive equilibrium. We also examine the efficiency implications for factor markets of various market structures in the product market.

17.1 The Supply and Demand for Inputs in a Competitive Market

The market demand for an input in a perfectly competitive input market is derived in a manner analogous to the way the market demand for a product was derived in a perfectly competitive product market in Chapter 4. In the case of the demand for a product or service, the demand curve is derived by adding up the demand curves for each individual consumer. In the case of inputs, such as labor or raw materials, the market demand curve is derived by adding up the demand curves for each individual firm. To derive the market demand curve for labor, therefore, it is first necessary to derive the demand curve for labor for an individual firm. Next, we will derive the firm's demand in the short run and then in the long run.

The Demand for an Input in the Short Run with One Variable Input

To derive a firm's short-run demand curve for a variable input such as labor, in a perfectly competitive market for the input, we begin with the firm's short-run production function $Q = f(L,K^*)$, where K^* represents a fixed amount of capital. Recall from Equation 7.17 in Chapter 7 that for the production function $Q = f(L,K^*)$:

$$SRMC = \frac{w}{MP_L} \tag{17.1}$$

where $SRMC$ is the firm's short-run marginal cost, w is the wage, and MP_L is the marginal product of labor.

In Equation 17.1, there is an inverse relationship between MP_L and $SRMC$. Furthermore, we know from Chapter 8 that profit-maximizing firms shut down if price is less than average variable cost, and therefore profit-maximizing firms always produce an output where short-run marginal cost is greater than or equal to average variable cost. Because profit maximization requires that $SRMC > AVC$, profit maximization also requires that, in equilibrium, $SRMC$ must be increasing. Therefore, from Equation 17.1, MP_L must be decreasing and profit-maximizing firms must hire labor on the downward-sloping portion of the MP_L curve.

Consider, for example, the demand curve for labor for one bakery. In Figure 17.1, the green curve identifies the marginal product of labor curve, MP_L. To maximize profit, the bakery continues to hire additional workers, as long as the value of the bread pro-

Figure 17.1 The Short-Run Demand for Bakers
The green MP_L curve comes directly from the production function and shows the relationship between the number of bakers and the marginal product per baker. To derive the blue demand curve for bakers, MRP_L, multiply MP_L by the price of bread.

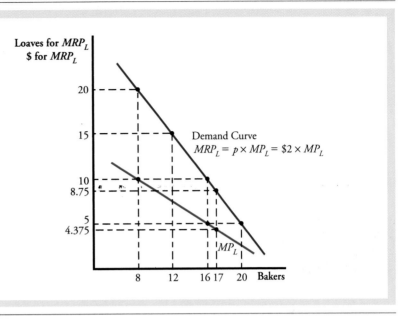

duced by an additional worker is greater than or equal to the wage paid to that worker. To determine the value of the extra bread produced by the marginal baker, it is necessary to know not only the MP_L, but also the marginal revenue generated from the sale of the marginal baker's output. The extra revenue generated by hiring one additional baker is called the **marginal revenue product of labor**, MRP_L, and is defined as:

marginal revenue product of labor, MRP_L

The extra revenue generated for a firm when it hires one additional unit of labor, or $MR \times MP_L$.

$$MRP_L = \frac{\Delta TR}{\Delta L} = \frac{\Delta TR}{\Delta q}\frac{\Delta q}{\Delta L} = MR \times MP_L \qquad (17.2)$$

Recall that in a perfectly competitive market, firms take the prices of all inputs and outputs as given, and marginal revenue equals price; that is, $MR = p$, so Equation 17.2 can be rewritten as:

$$MRP_L = p_b \times MP_L \qquad (17.3)$$

where p_b is the price of bread. For example, if the price of bread equals \$2 per loaf, the blue curve in Figure 17.1 depicts the MRP_L curve, where $MRP_L = p_b \times MP_L = \$2 \times MP_L$.

Suppose the competitive wage for a baker is \$8.75 per hour. The firm takes the wage as fixed and hires an additional baker, as long as the MRP_L is greater than or equal to \$8.75. In Figure 17.1, if the firm has already hired seven bakers, the MRP_L for the eighth baker is \$20, so with the wage $w = \$8.75$, the firm earns an *additional* \$11.25 (\$20 − \$8.75) in profit if it hires the additional eighth baker. Similarly, if the firm has already hired eleven bakers, the MRP_L for the twelfth baker is \$15, so the firm earns an *additional* \$6.25 (\$15 − \$8.75) in profit if it hires the additional twelfth baker. For profit maximization, the firm continues to hire additional bakers until seventeen bakers have been hired, because the $MRP_L = \$8.75 = w$ for the seventeenth baker. The MP_L for the seventeenth baker is 4.375 loaves. Notice that the MRP_L *equals* the wage for the last baker hired, but for every baker hired up to the seventeenth baker, the MRP_L is greater than the wage.

Using the knowledge from Equation 17.1 that $SRMC = w/MP_L$, we calculate $SRMC$ for this bakery's production function (shown in the last column of Table 17.1).

Table 17.1 Calculation of the Short-Run Marginal Cost from the Marginal Product of Labor Curve

Labor	MP_L	$MRP_L = p(MP_L) = 2MP_L$	$SRMC = w/MP_L$
8	10.0	$20.0	$8.75/10 = $0.875
12	7.5	$15.0	$8.75/7.5 = $1.167
16	5.0	$10.0	$8.75/5 = $1.75
17	4.375	$8.75	$8.75/4.375 = $2.00
20	2.5	$5.0	$8.75/2.5 = $3.50

Consistent with the theory of perfect competition, the price of bread must equal the marginal cost of producing bread, and the profit-maximizing firm hires workers up to the point where $p = SRMC = \$2$. In Table 17.1, for each additional baker hired up to the 17th baker, that is, for all $L < 17$, $p > SRMC$, and therefore the firm increases its profit by hiring more bakers and expanding output. With the hiring of the 17th worker, $p = \$2 = SRMC$, so profit is maximized. However, if more than 17 bakers were hired, profit would be reduced, because $p < SRMC$ for $L > 17$.

To summarize, for any wage w, the firm hires bakers up to the point where $MRP_L = w$. The firm's demand curve for labor, therefore, is the firm's blue MRP_L curve in Figure 17.1. If the wage were increased to $10, the firm would hire 16 bakers; if the wage were decreased to $5, the firm would hire 20 bakers.

COMMON ERROR 17.1 **Confusing an Individual's Productivity with Marginal Productivity**

Students often confuse the concept of an individual worker's productivity with the concept of that same worker's marginal productivity. An individual's productivity is based on their skill and work effort, but an individual's marginal productivity is a characteristic of the production process. To understand the difference, suppose you applied for a job making subs at your local Subway restaurant on weeknights between 6:00 and 8:00 PM. As part of the application, the manager asks you to come into the restaurant and make subs before the restaurant opens to show how productive you are at making subs. Working alone on the sub production line, you are able to make a sub every two minutes, or 30 subs an hour. Thirty subs an hour measures your productivity as a worker based on your skill and work effort.

When you arrive for your first evening shift at 6:00 that evening, you discover that the manager has hired you as the fifth worker on that busy shift. The other four workers have been working at the restaurant for several months. All five of you are making subs at a frantic pace during most of the busy dinner rush hour, but you find yourself making far fewer than 30 subs an hour. In fact, you are constantly waiting for access to the cheese, the fillings, or the vegetables, because one of your co-workers is in the way. At the end of your shift, the manager informs you that with four workers, the sub crew was able to make 100 subs in an hour, and that your addition to the workforce increased output to 110 subs an hour. Your marginal productivity was 10 subs an hour. Because you have to share access to the fixed input, the sub production line, with your four co-workers, your marginal productivity is far below your individual productivity of 30 subs per hour based on your skill and effort making subs. This difference can best be understood by realizing that a worker's productivity is a personal characteristic of the worker, whereas a worker's marginal productivity is a characteristic of the production process, not of the individual worker. Don't make the common mistake of confusing these two concepts.

The Demand for an Input in the Long Run

From Chapter 7, we know that if the amount of capital increases or decreases, the marginal product of labor also increases or decreases. Therefore, an increase in the amount of capital employed increases the marginal revenue product of labor. The MP_L and MRP_L curves in Figure 17.1 assume that capital is fixed at K^* units. Any change in the amount of capital shifts both the MP_L and MRP_L curves. The MP_L and MRP_L curves shift upward or downward, depending on whether there is an increase or decrease in the stock of capital. Similarly, if there is an increase or decrease in labor employed, there are more or fewer workers available to work with each unit of capital. Consequently, the marginal product of capital increases or decreases, and the marginal revenue product of capital also increases or decreases, depending on whether there is an increase or decrease in the number of workers.

THE FIRM'S DEMAND FOR AN INPUT WITH CONSTANT OUTPUT PRICES
In Figure 17.2, we consider the impact of a decrease in the wage from $8.75 to $5.00 per hour. In the short run, capital is fixed at K^*, and therefore the firm increases labor employed from 17 bakers at point A to 20 bakers at point B on the dark-green MRP_L curve. In the long run, however, the increase in the number of workers causes an increase in the marginal product of capital, MP_K, and the marginal revenue product of capital, MRP_K. At any given cost of capital r, the firm will now use more capital. Suppose at a wage $w = \$5.00$, the optimal amount of capital in the long run is K^{**}. With capital increased to K^{**}, the MRP_L curve shifts upward to the light-green MRP_L curve, and in the long run, the firm will hire 22 workers at point C.

The same exercise can be replicated for any wage above or below $w = \$8.75$. This replication yields the blue long-run demand curve for labor in Figure 17.2. The firm's demand for labor is therefore more elastic in the long run than the short run, because in the long run, as wages increase, the firm can substitute capital for labor.

THE INDUSTRY DEMAND CURVE FOR AN INPUT Having derived the firm's demand curve for bakers, we are ready to derive the bakery industry's demand curve for bakers. In deriving the firm's demand curve in Figure 17.2, we assumed that the price of bread remained constant at $2.00 per loaf. However, if the wage paid to bakers decreases,

Figure 17.2 The Long–Run Demand for Bakers with Constant Bread Prices
In the long run, a decline in the wage from $8.75 to $5.00 increases capital from K^* to K^{**}, and this increases the MRP_L from the dark-green curve to the light-green curve. The blue long-run demand for labor is derived by considering the impact of all possible changes in the wage on the use of capital and the impact of the change in capital on the MRP_L.

the marginal cost of producing bread decreases. As a result, the industry's supply curve increases, leading to an increase in the equilibrium quantity and a *decrease* in the equilibrium price of bread. Conversely, if the wage paid to bakers increases, the marginal cost of producing bread increases, the industry's supply curve decreases, and as a result, the equilibrium quantity decreases and the equilibrium price of bread increases.

Figure 17.3 analyzes the impact of a decrease in wages from $8.75 to $5.00 per hour on the industry demand for bakers with variable bread prices. An industry-wide decrease in bakers' wages results in an increase in the supply of bread, which decreases the equilibrium price of bread. Suppose as a result of a decrease in wages from $8.75 to $5.00 per hour, the equilibrium price of bread decreases from $2.00 to $1.75 per loaf. In Figure 17.3(a), the decrease in the price of bread decreases $MRP_L = p_b \times MP_L$ from $MRP_L = \$2.00 \times P_L$ to $MRP_L = \$1.75 \times MP_L$, and shifts the firm's demand curve for labor from the light-green demand curve to the dark-green demand curve. As a result of this decrease in the demand for labor, at $w = \$5.00$, the firm hires only 20 bakers instead of 22 bakers.

Figure 17.3(b) assumes that there are 100 competing bakeries. The industry's demand curve for bakers is derived by adding up the 100 individual firm demand curves. If the price of bread is $2.00, the industry demand curve is the light-green demand curve in panel (b). At a wage of $8.75, each firm would demand 17 bakers, and the industry would demand 1,700 bakers. When the wage declines to $5.00, the price of bread declines to $1.75, and the industry demand curve is the dark-green demand curve in panel (b). At a wage of $5.00, each firm demands 20 bakers, and the industry demands 2,000 bakers. Once again, the same exercise can be replicated for any wage above or below $w = \$8.75$; this replication yields the blue industry demand curve for bakers in panel (b).

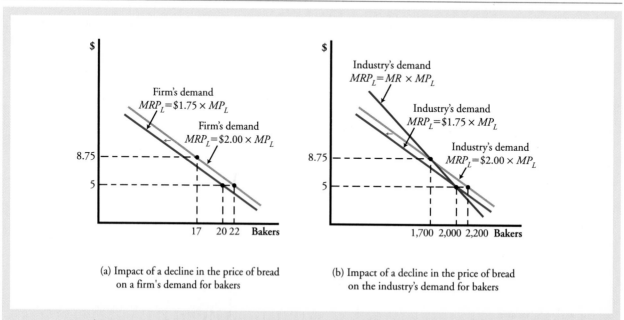

(a) Impact of a decline in the price of bread on a firm's demand for bakers

(b) Impact of a decline in the price of bread on the industry's demand for bakers

Figure 17.3 The Industry Demand for Bakers with Variable Bread Prices
When $w = \$8.75$, the price of bread is $2.00 and the firm and industry demand for bakers is represented by the light-green demand curves in panels (a) and (b). When the wage declines to $5.00, the price of bread declines to $1.75, and the firm and industry demand curves decline to the dark-green curves. The blue demand curve in panel (b) is derived by considering the impact of all possible changes in the wage on the price of bread, and the impact of these price changes on the MRP_L.

▲▲▲ 17.1 APPLICATION Why Do Social Workers with MSW Degrees Earn So Much Less than Lawyers?

Shortly after one of my nieces received her second graduate degree, a Masters of Social Work (MSW) from the University of Michigan, she expressed frustration over the fact that all of her job offers were paying between $26,000 and $35,000 a year. Compounding her feeling of injustice was the fact that another niece, who also spent seven years in college, but to get a law degree, was earning over $150,000 a year. I responded to my niece by explaining that workers generally get paid according to the supply and demand for their services. Furthermore, because there are large variations in the supply and demand for different types of workers, there are vast differences in wages for different jobs.

Consider, for example, the 2001 wage estimates by the United States Bureau of Labor Statistics in the table. The table shows the tremendous variation in the earnings of different types of workers. My niece with an MSW was apparently receiving offers that were in line with social workers'

typical earnings. My lawyer niece, on the other hand, was doing considerably better than the average lawyer.

Notice that economics professors earn more than professors of social work, but less than law professors. Not surprisingly, surgeons earn more than any other professionals, with dentists and other types of physicians close behind. Airline pilots and flight engineers earn, on average, more than lawyers. And while a handful of models make large fortunes, most are on the low end of the earnings ladder, well behind the average computer systems analyst and more in line with a typical travel agent. Finally, workers who provide the important service of taking care of our nation's young children are paid the lowest wages of all the professions listed.

Despite the apparent injustice of some of these wage differentials, they result from dramatically different supply and demand conditions in each of these various labor markets and are consistent with competitive market conditions.

Application Table 17.1 **2001 Wage Estimates for Various Jobs**

Occupational Title	2001 Mean Hourly Wage ($)	2001 Mean Annual Wage ($)
Social Workers, Medical and Public Health	18.29	38,050
Social Workers, Mental Health and Substance Abuse	16.34	33,980
Lawyers	44.19	91,920
Economists, including Market Research Analysts	34.78	72,350
Economics Teachers, College	N/A	65,620
Social Work Teachers, College	N/A	53,480
Law Teachers, College	N/A	79,130
Surgeons	65.85	137,050
Family and General Practice Physicians	52.89	110,020
Psychiatrists	54.60	113,570
Pediatricians	56.03	116,550
Psychologists, Clinical, Counseling, and School	25.77	53,500
Dentists	53.28	110,820

(continued)

Application Table 17.1 **Continued**

Occupational Title	2001 Mean Hourly Wage ($)	2001 Mean Annual Wage ($)
Computer Systems Analysts	30.63	63,710
Air Traffic Controllers	40.07	83,350
Sales and related occupations	13.91	28,920
Models	10.87	22,600
Fire Fighters	17.25	35,880
Police Patrol Officers	20.17	41,950
Flight Attendants	N/A	46,880
Child Care Workers	8.16	16,980
Automotive Mechanics	15.32	31,870
Aircraft Mechanics	20.41	42,460
Carpenters	17.36	36,110
Electricians	20.75	43,160
Truck Drivers, Heavy and Tractor-Trailer	16.20	33.690
Bus Drivers	14.15	29,420
Aircraft Pilots and Flight Engineers	N/A	99,400
Travel Agents	13.09	27,230

In the long run, a decrease in the wage sets off a chain reaction of events. First, the lower wage increases the number of bakers hired, which results in an increase in the marginal product of capital, which in turn increases the marginal revenue product of capital, and in the long run, the amount of capital employed. The increase in capital employed in turn increases the marginal product of labor and increases the firm's demand for labor. In addition, a decrease in wages decreases the marginal cost of production and increases industry supply, which in turn decreases the equilibrium product price, and this decrease in product price reduces the marginal revenue product of labor and decreases the firm's demand for labor, thus reducing the industry's demand for labor.

DERIVED DEMAND From the analysis thus far, there is a very strong connection between the market for a final product, such as bread, and the market for inputs, such as bakers. This connection is so strong that economists call the demand for inputs a **derived demand**, because the demand is ultimately derived from the consumer demand for the final product or service. In our example, the demand for bakers is a derived demand from the demand for bread. Any factor that affects the bread market therefore also affects the demand for bakers. If the demand for bread increases, the price of bread increases, the MRP_L for bakers increases, and the demand for bakers increases.

derived demand

The term used to describe an industry's demand for an input that depends on the industry's level of output, which in turn depends on the demand for the final product or service produced by the input.

COMMON ERROR 17.2 Believing that Jobs Requiring Greater Talents and Abilities are Always Rewarded with Higher Incomes

Michael Jordan, Nicole Kidman, Tom Cruise, Katie Couric, Donovan McNabb, Paul McCartney, Jennifer Lopez, John Grisham, J. K. Rowling, and Bill Gates have all used their varied talents to amass personal fortunes. There is no doubt that people of the highest abilities in their respective professions often earn very large incomes. As a result of this observed relationship between talent and income among the very best in their respective fields, students often incorrectly generalize the relationship between the most talented individuals and income to mean that jobs requiring great ability and skill always pay higher wages than jobs requiring less ability and skill; and in addition, that jobs requiring similar abilities and skills always pay similar wages. Such reasoning is incorrect.

Consider, for example, the fact that far fewer people have the talents and skills to be professional dancers (this category does not include dancing teachers) than professional airline flight attendants. Yet in 2001, the mean annual wage for professional dancers was $28,770 compared to a mean wage of $46,880 for flight attendants. What's more, jobs that appear to require the same talents and skills often pay vastly different wages. For example, professional dancers probably need to be at least as talented and skilled as professional musicians and singers, but musicians and singers earned a mean annual income of $46,690 in 2001, which was 62.3 percent higher than the mean income for dancers. Furthermore, the top 10 percent of musicians and singers earned over $93,960 in 2001, compared to only $56,660 for the top 10 percent of dancers. Something besides talent and skill must account for such a large gap in earnings between

flight attendants and dancers and between musicians and singers and dancers.

The concept of derived demand can explain these earning gaps. The demand for flight attendants is ultimately derived from the demand for airline passenger seats, while the demand for professional dancers is derived from the demand for theater seats to see performances, plays, and shows. There is a far greater demand for airline passenger seats than seats at professional dance performances, and therefore, the derived demand for flight attendants is much greater than the derived demand for professional dancers. Because of the much greater derived demand for the (some would say) less-talented and less-skilled flight attendants, they earn wages far higher than the more talented and more skilled professional dancers. Similarly, the demand for musicians and singers is derived not only from the demand for seats at public musical performances, but also from the demand for CDs and videos of their performances. The derived demand for musicians and singers, therefore, is also far greater than the derived demand for dancers, and as a result, despite the similarity in talents and skills required to become a professional musician and singer and a professional dancer, the musicians and singers earn far greater average incomes.

Never forget that the demand for labor is a derived demand, and wages are set by the interaction of the derived demand and the supply of labor within particular segments of the labor market. As a result, there is not necessarily a positive relationship between wages and the degree of talents and skills required for a job.

The Elasticity of Demand for an Input

Because the prices of inputs are affected by many public policies, such as an increase in the minimum wage or a decrease in taxes on a firm's plant and equipment, it is often important for economists and policy makers to understand the characteristics of input demand curves; particularly how responsive the quantity demanded for an input is to a change in its price. That is, it is important to understand the elasticity of demand for an input. The elasticity of demand for an input is defined exactly like any other elasticity as the percentage change in the quantity demanded of the input with respect to a 1 percent change in the input's price. There are five major factors that affect the elasticity of demand for an input:

1. *The elasticity of demand for the final product or service.* In Figure 17.3(b), suppose the demand curve for bread were perfectly elastic at p_b = $2.00 per loaf. The industry demand for bakers would then be the light-green demand curve labeled MRP_L = $2.00 × MP_L. If the wage decreased from $8.75 to $5.00 per hour, the quantity demanded of bakers would increase from 1,700 to 2,200. If the demand for bread is not perfectly elastic and if the price of bread decreases from $2.00 to $1.75 per loaf when the wage decreases from $8.75 to $5.00, then the industry demand for bread is the blue demand curve MRP_L = MR × MP_L in Figure 17.3(b). In this case, if the wage decreases from $8.75 to $5.00, the quantity demanded would increase only from 1,700 to 2,000 bakers. As the demand for the final product, bread, becomes more inelastic, so does the demand for the input, bakers. Similarly, if the demand for bread is inelastic, then the demand for flour will also be inelastic. In contrast, if the demand for hotels and motels is elastic, then the demand for hotel workers (housekeepers, bellhops, maintenance workers, etc.) will also be elastic.

2. *The ease or difficulty of substituting one input for another in the production function.* In the production function $q = f(x_1, x_2, x_3,..., x_n)$, the easier it is to substitute one input for another, the more elastic the demand for inputs. Automobile manufacturers, for example, can substitute plastic bumpers for aluminum bumpers. If the price of aluminum bumpers increases, automobile manufactures will substitute plastic bumpers for aluminum bumpers. The demand for aluminum bumpers as an input in the automobile industry will therefore be elastic. In contrast, automobile manufacturers cannot substitute plastic tires (or any other type of tires) for rubber tires; therefore, the demand for rubber tires will be inelastic.

3. *The elasticity of supply for substitute inputs.* If the price of input x_1 increases, but the supply curves for substitute inputs such as x_2 or x_3 are highly inelastic, then the demand curve for input x_1 will be highly inelastic, because firms will be unable to substitute inputs x_2 or x_3 for x_1 without dramatically driving up the prices of those substitute inputs. For example, during a major energy crisis in 1973–74, the price of oil quadrupled in a just few months. Firms attempted to turn to coal as an alternative source of energy. Because the short-run supply of coal was fairly inelastic, however, the price of coal also increased dramatically. The increase in the price of coal greatly limited the ability of firms to switch from oil to coal to meet their energy needs, and as a result, the short-run demand for oil was highly inelastic.

4. *The ratio of the input cost to total costs.* The larger the ratio of an input's costs to total costs, the greater is the elasticity of demand for the input. For example, consider the demand for labor in two industries: the custom tailoring industry, where clothing is made to order from measurements, and the electricity distribution industry. In the custom-tailoring industry, most of the firm's costs are the labor costs of making the clothing by hand, so labor makes up a large percentage of total costs. In the electricity distribution industry, most of the firm's costs are the large capital costs necessary to distribute electricity, so labor makes up a small percentage of total costs. If there is a 10 percent increase in wages in each industry, it will affect the total costs for custom-tailoring firms much more than it will affect the total costs of electricity distribution firms. As a result, the demand for labor will decrease more in custom tailoring than in electricity dis-

tribution: The demand for labor in custom tailoring therefore will be more elastic than the demand for labor in the electricity distribution.

5. *Time: The demand for inputs is more elastic in the long run than the short run.* In the short run, when input prices increase, it is often technologically difficult (if not impossible) to substitute for those inputs. Returning to the energy crisis of 1973–74: Prior to the crisis, the world's industrial economies had built their capital equipment on the assumption that there would be a continuous supply of relatively inexpensive oil as the primary energy source for running their capital equipment. In the short run, therefore, it was extremely difficult for the industrial economies to reduce their dependence on oil. However, in response to the energy crisis in the long run, the world's economies adjusted their capital stock to be much more energy-efficient and much less dependent on oil as their primary energy source. As a result, the long-run demand for oil proved to be much more elastic than the short-run demand.

The Market Demand Curve for an Input

Once we derive all of the industry demand curves for an input, it is a straightforward process to add the various industry demand curves together to obtain the market demand curve. Any one industry makes up a very small percentage of the total market demand for labor. To obtain the total market demand curve, it is necessary to add up all of the industry demand curves for labor.

The Supply of Inputs in a Competitive Industry

In a perfectly competitive input market, the individual firm has no control over the price of its inputs. Just as a perfectly competitive firm is a price taker in the product market, it is also a price taker in the input market.

THE SUPPLY CURVE FACED BY THE FIRM Figure 17.4 considers a farmer who uses fertilizer as an input to produce corn. In panel (a), the market supply and demand for fertilizer yields an equilibrium price of $200 per ton. The firm in panel (b) takes the price

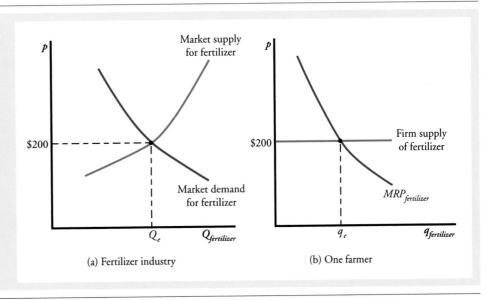

Figure 17.4 **The Supply of Fertilizer for a Competitive Firm**
In panel (a), the supply and demand curve for fertilizer determine the equilibrium price of fertilizer to be $200 per ton. In panel (b), the individual farmer takes the price of fertilizer as fixed, and therefore faces a perfectly elastic input supply curve at the equilibrium price.

(a) Fertilizer industry

(b) One farmer

of fertilizer as given at $200 per ton, equates $200 to the $MRP_{fertilizer}$, and purchases q_e tons of fertilizer. The supply curve of fertilizer as viewed by one farmer is perfectly elastic.

THE MARKET SUPPLY CURVE FOR AN INPUT In Figure 17.4(a), the market supply curve for fertilizer is drawn as a normal, upward-sloping supply curve. The supply curves for virtually every input, from fertilizer and pesticides to oil and coal, will be upward-sloping, for exactly the same reason that the supply curves for products and services are upward-sloping: they reflect the increasing opportunity cost of production as output increases. Because the short-run and long-run marginal costs of producing inputs typically increase with increased production, the supply curves for most inputs are upward-sloping.

There is, however, one important exception to this upward-sloping rule—an individual's supply of labor. In Chapter 5, we examined the impact of supply-side tax cuts on work effort and savings, and discovered that because income and substitution effects operate in opposite directions, tax cuts could either increase or decrease the supply of labor. We can use the same analysis to explore a typical worker's supply curve of labor. In Figure 17.5(a),

Figure 17.5 An Individual Worker's Choice Between Income and Leisure

In panel (a), given the utility function $U(L,I)$, the consumer can consume a maximum of 24 hours a day in leisure. At a wage of w_1, she chooses L_1 hours of leisure; at a wage of w_2, she chooses L_2 hours of leisure; and at a wage of w_3, she chooses L_3 hours of leisure. This results in the backward-bending supply curve for labor in panel (b). The points A, B, and C in panel (b) correspond to the points A, B, and C in panel (a).

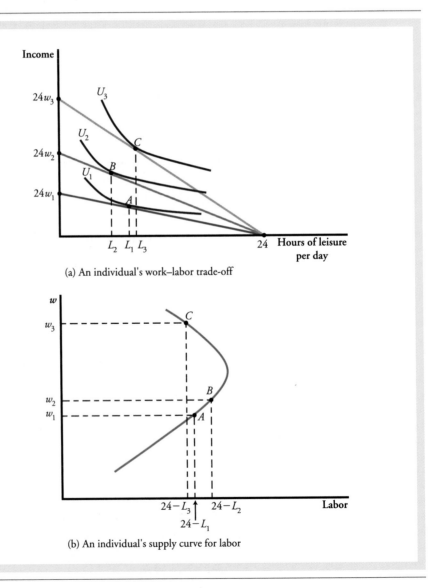

(a) An individual's work–labor trade-off

(b) An individual's supply curve for labor

the worker's utility function is $U(L, I)$, where L is leisure and I is income. Our worker can choose a maximum of 24 hours of leisure a day, so the leisure intercept is 24 hours. The income intercept is 24 hours times the wage. When the wage is w_1, the consumer takes L_1 hours of leisure per day, and supplies $24 - L_1$ hours of work per day. When the wage increases to w_2, the consumer decreases her leisure to L_2 hours and increases her quantity supplied of labor to $24 - L_2$ hours per day. Figure 17.5(b) shows this movement as the movement from point A to point B on her supply curve of labor. When the wage increases to w_3, however, the consumer increases her leisure to L_3 hours and decreases her quantity supplied of labor to $24 - L_3$ hours per day. Figure 17.5(b) shows this movement as the movement from point B to point C on her supply curve of labor, thereby resulting in a *backward-bending supply curve for labor*.

INCOME AND SUBSTITUTION EFFECTS ON AN INDIVIDUAL'S SUPPLY OF LABOR As the wage increases, the substitution effect causes our worker to consume *less* leisure and work more; however, the income effect causes her to consume *more* leisure and work less. When the wage increases from w_1 to w_2, the substitution effect dominates the income effect and she works *more*. However, when the wage increases from w_2 to w_3, the income effect dominates the substitution effect and she works *less*.

17.2 Equilibrium in a Competitive Factor Market

Competitive factor markets and competitive product markets are in equilibrium when supply equals demand. In a competitive labor market, this occurs where all workers earn the same wage, and this wage equals the MRP_L of the last worker hired. The efficiency implications of this equilibrium condition in the labor market are quite different, however, depending on whether the product market is competitive or monopolized. In this section, we consider these different efficiency implications.

Equilibrium with Competitive Factor and Product Markets

Recall from Chapter 9 that competitive product markets are efficient because price equals marginal cost. In competitive factor markets, there is an analogous efficiency condition—the marginal revenue product of the factor equals the price of the factor, which in the labor market translates into equality between the marginal revenue product of the last worker hired and the wage. When all factor and product markets are competitive, the marginal revenue product of labor measures the value to consumers of the products or services produced by the last worker hired (that is, what consumers are willing to pay for those products or services), and the wage measures the opportunity cost to the firm and to society of the last worker. It follows that in equilibrium, the marginal benefit to society of the last worker hired equals the extra cost to society of the last worker hired. As long as the $MRP_L > w$, firms hire additional labor, and this additional labor improves efficiency, because the value to society of their output (MRP_L) is greater than the cost to society (w) of hiring these additional workers.

ECONOMIC RENT In panel (a) of Figure 17.6, where the production function is $q = f(L,K)$, the total wage payment w_eL is represented by the sum of the blue area C and green area B. If firms could pay each additional worker a different wage that precisely equaled the minimum wage he or she would accept to enter the workforce, firms would be able to move slowly up the red supply curve as they hired each additional worker, and hire L_e workers for

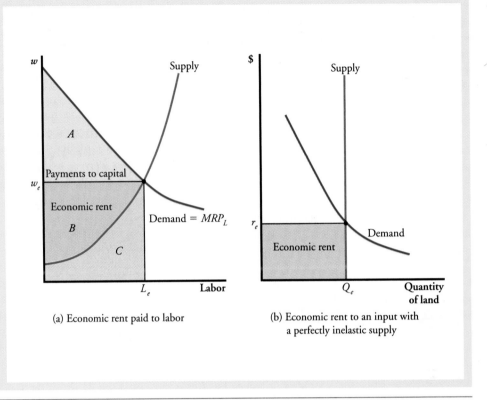

Figure 17.6 Economic Rent Earned by Labor and Land

For the production function $q = f(L,K)$, the blue area C represents the minimum payments to labor necessary to induce L_e units of labor into the workforce. At $w = w_e$, total labor payments include both the blue and green areas $B + C$. The green area B represents the economic rent paid to labor over and above the minimum payments necessary to induce these workers into the labor force. The yellow area A represents the payment to capital. In panel (b), for an input (such as land) with a perfectly inelastic supply curve, all of the payments to the input are economic rent, represented here by the green rectangle.

(a) Economic rent paid to labor

(b) Economic rent to an input with a perfectly inelastic supply

economic rent

The difference between the total payments to obtain a given quantity of an input and the minimum payments necessary to obtain the same quantity of that input.

a total cost equal to the blue area C. In competitive labor markets, however, all workers are paid the same wage, w_e. Therefore, the green area B represents the additional payments to labor over and above the minimum payments necessary to induce L_e workers into the labor force. This green area B is called labor's **economic rent**, which is the difference between the total payments to a given quantity of a factor and the minimum payments necessary to obtain that quantity of the factor.

As mentioned earlier, given the production function $q = f(L,K)$, the total payments to labor are represented by the rectangle equal to the sum of the green and blue areas, area $B + C$, but this rectangle does not represent the total value of the products produced by the firms hiring these L_e workers. We can calculate the total value of the products produced by adding up the MRP_L for each worker. Consequently, the first worker hired has the largest MRP_L and each additional worker has a lower MRP_L. In Figure 17.6(a), the total value of the products produced by all workers equals the entire area under the demand curve for labor, which consists of the blue, green, and yellow areas $A + B + C$. The sum of the blue and green areas $B + C$ equals the payment to labor. The yellow area A represents the payment to the only other factor of production in our production function—capital.

The extent to which a factor of production receives economic rent depends on the elasticity of supply for that factor. The more inelastic the supply, the greater the economic rent. One factor of production with a very inelastic supply curve is land. In fact, in the short run, the supply of land is perfectly inelastic. In Figure 17.6(b), the supply of land is perfectly inelastic and the entire payment to land is an economic rent. If the demand for land increases or decreases, the economic rent would increase or decrease accordingly.

▲▲▲ 17.2 APPLICATION Marx's Labor Theory of Value

Karl Marx railed against capitalists for their exploitation of the working class. He believed the profit represented by the yellow area A in Figure 17.6(a) showed how capitalists exploited workers. Marx questioned why capitalists should be permitted to keep the profits that resulted from the work of the lower classes, without which there would be no profits. We can use modern economic theory to analyze Marx's argument, keeping in mind that these theoretical tools were not available to Marx. Marx's argument goes like this: The workers sell their labor to the capitalist at a wage equal to the marginal revenue product of the last worker hired, and the capitalist uses these workers to produce products that have a higher total value than the total payments to labor. The source of Marx's *surplus value* is that labor is a source of more product value than the total wage payments made to labor. In other words, according to Marx, if labor input were zero, then the total output of society would also be zero.

In the light of modern theory, we might ask why the argument cannot be turned around by noting that Marx's argument could just as easily have shown that in the market for capital, capital receives a total payment that is less than the total value of the products produced using capital. For example, see the figure, with two inputs, capital and labor. In equilibrium, K_e units of capital are supplied at an equilibrium price r_e. Capital receives economic rent equal to the green area B, and labor receives a payment equal to the yellow area A. The capitalist is "forced" to rent all capital at the equilibrium rent of r_e, even though the MRP_K is greater than r_e for all units of capital employed except the last unit. Therefore, *capital* is exploited and the excess goes to labor represented by the yellow area A.

Marx contended, however, that capital equipment, like all products, was manufactured by exploiting workers. In other words, because you cannot produce capital equipment without workers, all value originates with labor. Capital goods are nothing more than the stored-up

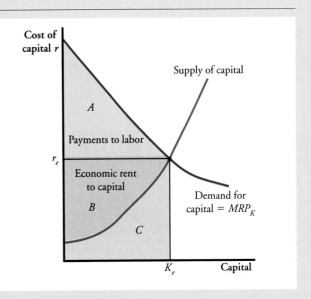

Application Figure 17.2
In equilibrium, K_e units of capital are supplied at an equilibrium price r_e. Capital receives economic rent equal to the green area B, and labor receives a payment equal to the yellow area A.

productive power of past exploited workers. Very few people still accept Marx's theory of surplus value. Rather, there is a growing recognition that value is generated by all inputs in the production process, including labor, capital, raw materials, and managerial talent. Furthermore, as capitalists supply more capital, the marginal revenue product of labor MRP_L increases, and as a result, so do wages. Marx underestimated this very important point: over time, capitalism generates more capital, thereby increasing the real wage of workers, and as a result, increasing the average worker's standard of living. To have a modern efficient economy, workers need capital as much as capital needs workers.

Equilibrium in a Competitive Factor Market with a Monopoly in the Product Market

In a world of competitive markets, if the input market for input x is perfectly competitive, firms take the prices of all inputs and outputs as given, and marginal revenue equals price, so $MRP_x = p \times MP_x$. In a monopolized product market, however, $MR < p$, so the $MRP_x = MR \times MP_x$ is less than $p \times MP_x$. If the input market for input x is competitive, but the product market is monopolized, $MRP_x \neq p \times MP_x$.

Recall that the marginal revenue product of labor is defined as:

$$MRP_L = \frac{\Delta TR}{\Delta L} = \frac{\Delta TR}{\Delta q}\frac{\Delta q}{\Delta L} = MR \times MP_L$$

In Figure 17.7, with a monopolized product market, the demand curve for labor is the green curve $MRP_L = MR \times MP_L$, which lies below the blue curve that identifies $p \times MP_L$. Because the labor market is competitive, the monopolist—like a competitive firm—faces a perfectly elastic supply curve for labor at the competitive equilibrium wage w_c. The monopolist hires additional workers as long as $MRP_L > w_c$. Equilibrium is at point A where $MRP_L = w_c = w_m$. From a social standpoint, the value of the prod-

value of the marginal product of labor, VMP_L

The value to society of the products produced by the last worker hired, which equals $p \times MP_L$.

ucts produced by the last worker hired equals the **value of the marginal product of labor, VMP_L**, which equals $p \times MP_L$, and represents what the monopolist can receive in revenue from the products produced by the last worker hired. If the monopolist hired additional workers beyond L_m, continuing up to the hiring of the L_c worker, the additional workers would produce products that are valued by society above the wage paid to these workers; however, the monopolist does *not* hire these workers. This creates an economic inefficiency. Just as the monopolist restricts output below the socially optimal level, because $p > MC$ in the product market, the monopolist restricts the amount of labor hired below the socially optimal level, because the value to society of hiring additional workers, $VMP_L = p \times MP_L$, is greater than the cost to society w of hiring those workers.

If the labor market operated efficiently in the monopolized product market, labor would be hired up to the point where $VMP_L = p \times MP_L = w_c$ at point C. The socially optimal number of workers, L_c, is therefore greater than L_m, and the monopolist hires too few workers. This results in a deadweight loss equal to the shaded orange triangle ABC, which measures the welfare loss to society because the monopolist hires too few workers.

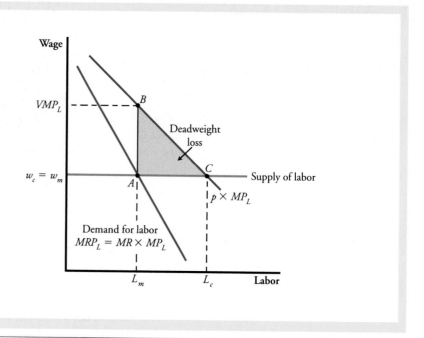

Figure 17.7 The Labor Market with Monopoly in the Product Market
If monopoly exists in the product market, $MRP_L < (p \times MP_L)$ because $MR < p$ for a monopolist. The green MRP_L demand curve for labor is below the blue curve that represents the value of the marginal product of labor. The monopolist equates the supply of labor to MRP_L and hires L_m units of labor at a wage w_m. The orange triangle ABC represents the deadweight loss due to monopoly.

▼▼▼ 17.3 Factor Markets with Monopoly Buyers: The Case of Monopsony Power

monopsony

A market with only one buyer.

monopsonist

The only buyer of a good or input.

marginal expenditures on labor, ME_L

The extra expenditures associated with hiring one additional unit of labor.

Monopsony is a market with only one buyer of a good or service. Economists call the only buyer in a monopsony market a **monopsonist**. The key difference between a monopsonist buyer of an input and a competitive buyer is that the monopsonist's purchases have a direct impact on the price of the input. A monopsonist is not a price taker in the market for inputs. Instead, the monopsonist is aware that if it increases its purchases of an input, it drives up the price of that input, and thereby drives up its own costs. The classic historical example of monopsony was the company mill or mining town in the United States and Europe in the mid-nineteenth century. In such towns, one company owned the only mill or mine in town, and because of a lack of labor mobility, was viewed as the only possible place to work. In the first half of the twentieth century, Alcoa was a monopolist in the primary aluminum industry, and as a result, was a monopsonist buyer of bauxite ore, which is a necessary input in the production of aluminum. Today, the United States government is a monopsonist buyer in many labor markets, including postal workers, air traffic controllers, airport security workers, and military personal, and the National Collegiate Athletic Association (NCAA) serves to facilitate American colleges' and universities' monopsony buying power over amateur athletes in football and basketball.

Table 17.2 Calculation of the Marginal Expenditure on Labor Curve

Labor (L)	Wage (w) (Average Expenditure)	Marginal Expenditure on Labor ($ME_L = w + L(\Delta w/\Delta L) = w + (1/2)L$)
0	10.0	—
5	12.5	15 = 12.5 + (1/2)5
10	15.0	20 = 15 + (1/2)10
15	17.5	25
20	20.0	30
25	22.5	35
30	25.0	40
35	27.5	45
40	30.0	50
45	32.5	55
50	35.0	60
55	37.5	65
60	40.0	70
65	42.5	75
70	45.0	80
75	47.5	85
80	50.0	90

Monopsony and the Marginal Expenditure on an Input

If a firm has monopsony power over an input with an upward-sloping supply curve, it must pay an increasingly higher price to hire additional units of the input. As a result, the extra cost of hiring additional units of the input includes not only the cost of hiring the last unit, but the higher price that must be paid to previously hired inputs. Table 17.2 and Figure 17.8 illustrate the effect of monopsony in the labor market where a monopsonist faces an upward-sloping supply curve for labor, $w = 10 + (1/2)L$. To simplify the analysis, assume the monopsonist is a price taker in the product market, so $MRP_L = p \times MP_L$. The **marginal expenditures on labor, ME_L**, are the extra expenditures associated with hiring one additional unit of labor. To calculate ME_L, we divide the change in total expenditures by the change in the number of workers hired:

$$ME_L = \frac{\Delta TE}{\Delta L}$$

We calculate ME_L at a given wage by considering what happens if there is a small increase or decrease in wages. In Figure 17.8, consider an increase in the wage from w_1 to w_2. When the

Figure 17.8 A Monopsony Labor Market
In a monopsony labor market, the marginal expenditure on labor, ME_L, is greater than the wage. The light-red ME_L curve is therefore above the dark-red supply curve of labor. The monopsonist hires labor up to the point where ME_L equals the demand for labor. In this case, $L = 35$ workers. To hire 35 workers, the monopsonist need pay a wage only equal to $27.50, which is well below $MRP_L = 45.

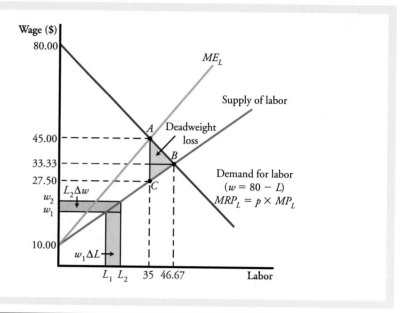

wage increases, the quantity supplied of labor also increases from L_1 to L_2, and total expenditures on labor increase from $w_1 L_1$ to $w_2 L_2$. The change in TE equals the sum of the green rectangle ($w_1 \Delta L$) and blue rectangle ($L_2 \Delta w$) and can be written as:

$$\Delta TE = w_1 \Delta L + L_2 \Delta w \tag{17.4}$$

For a very small change in the wage, we can drop the subscripts and rewrite Equation 17.4 as:

$$\Delta TE = w\Delta L + L\Delta w \tag{17.5}$$

Dividing Equation 17.5 by ΔL yields the ME_L:

$$ME_L = \frac{\Delta TE}{\Delta L} = w\frac{\Delta L}{\Delta L} + L\frac{\Delta w}{\Delta L} = w + L\frac{\Delta w}{\Delta L} \tag{17.6}$$

With an upward-sloping supply of labor curve, $\Delta w / \Delta L$ is always positive, and therefore the ME_L is always greater than the wage. To calculate ME_L from Equation 17.6 for the supply curve $w = 10 + (1/2)L$, we need only recognize that $\Delta w / \Delta L = 1/2$. Therefore, from Equation 17.6, $ME_L = w + L(\Delta w / \Delta L) = (10 + (1/2)L) + (1/2)L = 10 + L$. Table 17.2 calculates ME_L for the supply curve $w = 10 + (1/2)L$. Notice that $ME_L > w$ for all wages. The monopsonist's marginal expenditure on labor is therefore always greater than the wage.

Figure 17.8, in which the demand curve for labor is $w = 80 - L$, uses the calculations from Table 17.2 to draw the monopsonist's ME_L curve. The light-red ME_L curve, $ME_L = 10 + L$, has the same intercept as the red supply curve, but is twice as steep. To maximize profit, the monopsonist hires workers as long as the MRP_L—that is, the demand for labor—is greater than or equal to the marginal expenditure on labor. The firm hires 35 workers at point A, where $MRP_L = ME_L = 45. To obtain the wage, the monopsonist goes down to point C on the supply curve and pays $w = 27.50. The wage of $27.50 is much less than the marginal expenditure on labor of $45. The 35th worker is paid a wage of $27.50, but to hire the 35th worker, the monopsonist must raise wages

▲▲▲ 17.3 APPLICATION The NCAA's Control Over Student–Athlete Compensation

College athletics is a big business. In 1997, schools that belonged to the National Collegiate Athletic Association (NCAA) received over $3.5 billion in revenues.[*] The most important input for college sports programs are the coaches and players. There is no restriction placed on the salaries and benefits paid to schools' head coaches in major football and basketball programs, and competition among schools for the top head coaches is intense. As a result, salaries for top coaches are very high. When Rick Pitino became the head basketball coach at Louisville in 2001, his reported total compensation package was about $2 million a year. He joined Duke's Mike Krzyzewski ($1.6 million), Kentucky's Tubby Smith ($1.2 million), Florida's Billy Donovan ($1.2 million), and Michigan State's Tom Izzo ($1.2 million) as the highest-paid college basketball coaches. Among football coaches, Steve Spurrier of Florida earned over $2 million per year before he left Florida to become the coach of the Washington Redskins. While these coaches receive huge financial packages, their student-athlete players toil for tuition, room and board, and incidental expenses not to exceed "the cost of attendance at the school."

How much are college football players underpaid? According to one estimate, if 50 percent of Division I football revenues were distributed equally among all 11,000 players, each player would receive approximately $38,000 annually. Using marginal revenue product estimates for top college football and basketball players, economist Robert Brown estimated that in the early 1990s, the MRP_L for top football stars was about $600,000 and for top basketball stars the MRP_L was $1 million.[†] These stars were certainly not being paid anywhere near the value of their marginal revenue products. If the NCAA's monopsony control over payments and eligibility for student-athletes was eliminated, it is reasonable to assume that competition among colleges for top athletes would result in much higher student-athlete compensation packages, including direct payments to athletes over and above the cost of attending college. Whether such competition for athletes would be a good or bad thing for the competitive balance in college athletics, however, is debatable.

[*] John L. Fizel and Randall W. Bennett, "College Sports," in Walter Adams and James Brock, *The Structure of American Industry, 10th Edition.* Upper Saddle River, NJ: Prentice Hall, 2001, p. 323.

[†] Robert W. Brown, "An Estimate of the Rent Generated by a Premium College Football Player," *Economic Inquiry*, Vol. 31, 1993, pp. 671–684; and Robert W. Brown, "Measuring Cartel Rents in the College Basketball Recruitment Market," *Applied Economics*, Vol. 26, 1994, pp. 27–34.

for all of the previous 34 workers, and therefore the ME_L of the 35th worker is greater than the wage paid to the 35th worker.

Monopsony creates an economic inefficiency by restricting hiring below the socially optimal level. In Figure 17.8, the socially optimal quantity is 46.67 units of labor where the wage, $w = \$33.33$, equals the MRP_L. The monopsonist hires too few workers and pays them a wage that is too low. Society loses, because if hired, each of the additional 11.67 workers between the 35th worker and the 46.67th worker would contribute a value to society as measured by $MRP_L = p \times MP_L$ that would be greater than their wage. The deadweight loss due to monopsony equals the shaded orange triangle *ABC*.

▼▼▼ 17.4 Factor Markets with Monopoly Power

In this section, we examine how the owners of inputs can have market power and how that market power affects the input market. Three types of market power over inputs are particularly common: control of a necessary raw material; control of a necessary technology, often though ownership of a patent; and control of the supply of labor through a labor union. For over a century, De Beers' control over the supply of raw diamonds was an example of how one firm could control the supply of an important raw material. Until very recently, if a jeweler needed diamonds, he or she had to go through De Beers to obtain them. In the case of a patent, the owner of the patent can earn large monopoly profit. Microsoft's patent control over the operating system installed on most of the world's personal computers is an example of monopoly created through the control of technology. All of the major personal computer manufacturers install one of Microsoft's operating systems on most of their computers, so Microsoft has a great deal of market power over those manufacturers. The analysis of De Beers' control over raw diamonds or Microsoft's monopoly power over operating systems would look exactly like the analysis of monopoly power in Chapters 11 and 12. The case of labor unions, however, presents some new and interesting problems, and therefore, we confine the remainder of the analysis in this section to unions.

Unions and Monopoly Power in the Labor Market

In Figure 17.9, consider a labor market with the blue demand curve and the red supply curve. In a competitive market, the equilibrium wage is w_c and the equilibrium quantity is L_c. Suppose that the workers are able to form an effective union. The union could decide on any of a number of possible policy objectives. One possible objective would be to maximize the economic rent accruing to its members. An alternative objective would be to maximize the number of workers hired. Finally, the union might decide to maximize the total payments to its members.

If the union decides to maximize the number of workers hired, it will permit the competitive market to function normally, because the number of employed workers will be maximized at a wage of w_c. In this case, there will be no restriction of union membership, which probably serves as a social club as much as a traditional union.

Suppose the union decides to maximize the total payments to its members. Recall from Chapter 2 that total expenditures on a product or service are maximized where demand is unit-elastic and $MR = 0$. Furthermore, from Equation 11.4 in Chapter 11,

Figure 17.9 The Impact of a Labor Union
If the union elects to maximize the number of workers hired, it will result in a wage equal to w_c. If the union decides instead to maximize the total payments to its members, it will negotiate for a wage equal to w_R, where the demand for labor is unit-elastic. If the union wants to maximize the economic rent accruing to its members, it equates MR to MC and negotiates a wage of w_M, and labor receives an economic rent equal to the shaded blue area A. Maximization of economic rent results in a deadweight loss equal to the shaded orange area B.

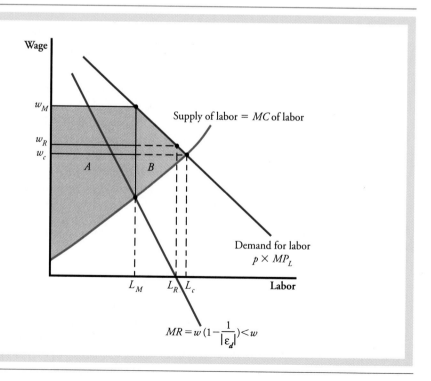

we know that $MR = p(1 - (1/|\varepsilon_p|)) < p$. In the labor market, because the price of labor is expressed as wage w, $MR = w(1 - (1/|\varepsilon_p|)) < w$. If the union decides to maximize the total payments to its members, $MR = 0$, and therefore it will negotiate a wage equal to w_R, and L_R workers will be hired, where demand is unit-elastic, that is, where $|\varepsilon_p| = 1$, and $MR = 0$. Given this objective, the union must restrict its membership below L_R.

Finally, if the union decides to maximize the economic rent of its members, it will negotiate a wage of w_M, and L_M workers will be hired, where $MR = MC$, because in the labor market, the marginal cost of labor is the supply curve of labor. Maximum rent equals the blue shaded area A in Figure 17.9. Although a wage of w_M maximizes labor's economic rent, it results in fewer employed workers, L_M, than either of the other two objectives. Furthermore, maximization of economic rent results in a deadweight loss equal to shaded orange area B.

Not all workers will benefit if the labor union decides to maximize economic rent, because fewer workers will be employed. In a competitive market, L_c workers are hired in Figure 17.9, so a rent-maximizing union eliminates $L_c - L_M$ jobs in the unionized industry. What happens to these workers? Suppose we divide the labor market into two sectors, a unionized sector and a non-unionized sector. In panels (a) and (b) in Figure 17.10, if the union decides to maximize the number of workers hired and allows the competitive market to operate, the wage will equal the competitive wage w_c in both sectors. If the union succeeds in bargaining for the rent-maximizing wage during the next round of contract negotiations, the wage in the unionized sector rises to w_M, but the number of unionized workers employed declines to U_M.

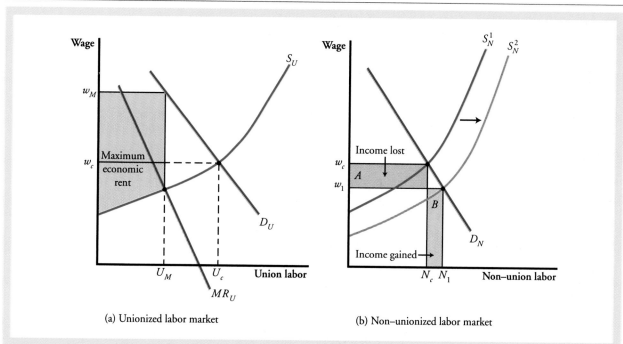

(a) Unionized labor market   (b) Non-unionized labor market

Figure 17.10 The Impact of a Union on the Non-Unionized Labor Market
If unions succeed in increasing wages in the unionized sector from w_c to w_M in panel (a), there will be an increase in the supply of labor in the non-unionized sector and the supply curve in panel (b) will increase from the dark-red supply curve S_N^1 to the light-red supply curve S_N^2. As a result, wages decline in the non-unionized sector, and if demand in the non-unionized sector is inelastic, the total payments to non-unionized labor also decline.

▲▲▲ **17.4 APPLICATION**   Are Union Wages Higher than Non–Union Wages?

Economists specializing in the study of labor markets have studied the impact of labor unions on wages in many countries and during many time periods and observed that union workers earn higher wages than non-union workers. In one study, economist David Card separated American workers into 10 "skill deciles" from the least skilled to the most skilled and analyzed the impact of labor unions on wages in 1973–74 and 1993. Card found that among men, from 1973–74 to 1993, there was a large decrease in the percentage of unionized workers in every skill category except the most skilled decile. Among women, between 1973–74 and 1993, there was a decrease in the percentage of unionized workers in the bottom five skill categories, but an increase in the percentage of unionized workers in the sixth, ninth, and tenth skill deciles. These shifting patterns of union membership resulted primarily from two forces: the reduction in the importance of manufacturing employment in the U.S. economy and the increased degree of unionization among public sector employees, many of whom were highly skilled—for example, educators.

Card found that unions appear to increase wages far more for less-skilled workers than for highly skilled workers. For example, among the least-skilled men, in 1993, non-union wages were generally 29 percent lower than for unionized workers. The figures were similar for the least-skilled women in 1993. Among the least-skilled women, union wages were between 23 and 26 percent higher than non-union wages.

One of Card's findings appears to contradict our theory that unions increase wages: In the highest two skill deciles among men, there was no evidence that wages were higher among union workers; in fact, wages were higher among non-union workers. Card's explanation for this finding is that within different skill categories, there are specific factors that determine whether a particular worker joins a union, and these factors would cause differences in the wages earned by union and non-union workers, even in the absence of unions. Card adjusted for these differences, which imply that among low-skill groups, in the absence of unions, higher wage earners tend to be union members, and among the highest skill groups, in the absence of unions, lower wage earners tend to be union members. After adjusting for these intragroup differences, a wage gap existed within all skill categories for all workers among both men and women.

Many of the $U_c - U_M$ workers who lose their jobs are likely to look for work in the non-unionized sector. As shown in Figure 17.10(b), these workers search for employment in the non-unionized sector. As a result, the supply curve in the non-unionized sector increases from the dark-red supply curve S_N^1 to the light red supply curve S_N^2. Employment in the non-unionized sector increases from N_c to N_1, but the wage declines from w_c to w_1. Increased wages in the unionized sector result in decreased wages in the non-unionized sector. Union workers gain, but non-union workers lose. Furthermore, if the demand in the non-unionized sector is *inelastic*, then when the wage declines from w_c to w_1, the orange shaded area A representing a *decrease* in labor income will be greater than the green shaded area B representing an *increase* in labor income, and the total payments to labor in the non-unionized sector will decline.

▼▼▼   **17.5   Factor Markets with Bilateral Monopoly Power**

bilateral monopoly

A market with monopoly power on both the supply and demand sides of the market; that is, a market with a monopsonist buyer and a monopolist seller.

In many industries with strong labor unions, the unions negotiate with strong monopsonist buyers of labor. The Major League Baseball Players Union, the United Automobile Workers, the National American Postal Workers Union, and the National Air Traffic Controllers Association all negotiate with strong monopsonist buyers. A market with monopoly power on both the supply and demand sides is called a **bilateral monopoly**. Bilateral monopoly also exists in many non-labor input markets. For example, when Intel sells computer microprocessors to Dell, Hewlett-Packard, Compaq, IBM, and Gateway, it is selling to buyers with significant market power.

Figure 17.11 depicts a bilateral monopoly labor market. The union wants to maximize economic rent by equating supply to *MR* and desires to negotiate a wage equal to w_2. The monopsonist wants to equate the marginal expenditure on labor to the demand for labor and wishes to negotiate a wage equal to w_1. There is a large gap between the two wages. In Figure 17.11, the monopsonist also wants to hire fewer workers than the union wants to supply. The negotiated wage is likely to lie somewhere between w_1 and w_2.

Exactly where the final wage agreement settles depends on the negotiating abilities of both sides. If the union threatens a long strike, the wage may settle close to w_2. On the other hand, if the monopsonist threatens to produce the good in a foreign country using low-wage labor, the wage may end up closer to w_1.

In this chapter, we have explored how firms choose their profit-maximizing levels of various inputs by examining the relationship between the marginal revenue product of an input and the cost of the input. This method works well for most inputs such as labor and raw materials. When dealing with investment decisions regarding capital, however, this method is typically incomplete because most capital goods are durable goods that last many years, and therefore, a consideration of time must be incorporated into capital goods investment decisions. Chapter 18 examines how firms consider time when making investments in capital goods.

Figure 17.11 Bilateral Monopoly in a Labor Market
In the case of bilateral monopoly, the monopsonist wishes to equate ME_L to demand and hire L_1 workers at a low wage of w_1. The union monopolist wishes to equate *MR* to supply and to hire L_2 workers at a high wage of w_2. The final wage will be a negotiated wage somewhere between w_1 and w_2.

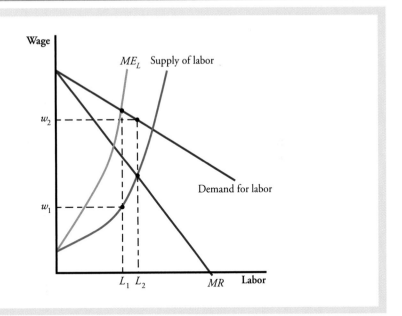

▲▲▲ 17.5 APPLICATION Bilateral Monopoly Power in the Baseball Labor Market

In monopsony input markets, there is only one buyer of the input. Perhaps the most famous example of monopsony power in this century was major league baseball's

monopsony power over its players, until a series of negotiated agreements eliminated the reserve clause in players' contracts. The reserve clause tied a player to one team for

(continued)

life, unless the player was traded or released.

In several cases in the late 1960s and early 1970s, the courts ruled that baseball—among all professional sports—was the only one exempt from the antitrust laws. A series of strikes and threatened strikes, however, resulted in a change in the reserve clause system in 1976. Beginning with the 1976 season, any player refusing to sign a contract became a free agent at the end of the season. In 1977, the contract was changed so that any player with six years of major league experience could become a free agent simply by notifying his current team that he intended to become a free agent. During this period of restricted free agency, free agents were subject to a free agent draft that limited the number of teams that could compete for their services. Following a 50-day strike during the 1981 season and another strike in 1985, another agreement was reached which called for salary arbitration for players with three years' major league experience, compensation in the form of an amateur draft pick for teams that lost free agents, and the elimination of the free agent draft. Following a series of court rulings in the late 1980s, another agreement was signed in 1990 that signaled the beginning of the modern period of unrestricted free agency for players with six years of major league experience.

Prior to 1976, the baseball teams were monopsonists. In the late 1970s, the teams were limited monopsonists, and since 1990, there has been bilateral monopoly in the market for baseball players' services. This table compares the salaries

Application Table 17.5 Salaries of Top Baseball Players Under the Reserve Clause (1969), Restricted Free Agency (1976), and Unrestricted Free Agency (1990)

Player	Actual Salary	Salary in 1991 Dollars
Reserve Clause Period, 1969		
Alou, Filepe	60,000	224,400
Chance, Dean	55,000	205,700
Davis, Tommy	69,000	258,060
Flood, Curt	90,000	336,600
Pinson, Vada	60,500	226,270
Restricted Free Agency, 1976		
Brock, Lou	185,000	445,850
Jackson, Reggie	185,000	445,850
Morgan, Joe	200,000	482,000
Palmer, Jim	177,500	427,775
Ryan, Nolan	170,000	409,700
Unrestricted Free Agency, 1990		
Gooden, Dwight	1,916,667	2,012,500
Puckett, Kirby	2,700,000	2,835,000
Scott, Mike	2,187,500	2,296,875
Valenzuela, Fernando	2,200,000	2,310,000
Yount, Robin	3,200,000	3,360,000

for a number of top players. The salaries in real 1991 dollars are much higher under free agency than in either of the other two periods. Salaries were also much lower during the 1969 season, when the reserve clause was fully in force. Before the era of free agency and under the reserve clause system, major league baseball was able to pay players a monopsony wage that was far below the equilibrium wage in a competitive market. Under the system, teams paid players a fraction of their value to the team, as indicated by the huge salary differentials in the table. An abrupt change in the salary structure was brought about by the series of strikes and threatened strikes in baseball. Organized labor therefore proved to be an offsetting monopoly power against the monopsony power of the teams.

Summary

1. The firm's demand curve for an input x in the short run is derived from the input's marginal revenue product (MRP_x), where $MRP_x = MR \times MP_x$. In the long run, all inputs are variable and the firm's demand curve for an input is more elastic than in the short run, because it is possible to substitute inputs in the production function. The long-run demand for an input is a derived demand that depends on the demand for the final product or service. The market supply curve for an input is typically upward-sloping, except that the supply of labor for an individual worker may be backward-bending. Firms take the price of inputs as fixed, and therefore face input supply curves that are perfectly elastic.

2. Equilibrium in a competitive input market for input x with a competitive product market occurs where $MRP_x = MR \times MP_x = p_{output} \times MP_x = p_x$, which results in economic efficiency in the input market. Equilibrium in a competitive input market for input x with a monopolized product market occurs where $MRP_x = p_x = MR \times MP_x < p_{output} \times MP_x = VMP_x$, which results in economic inefficiency in the input market and a deadweight loss for society.

3. In a monopsony input market for input x, there is only one buyer of the input and equilibrium occurs where the marginal expenditure on x equals the marginal revenue product but is greater than the price of the input; that is, $ME_x = MRP_x = p_{output} \times MP_x > p_x$. This results in a deadweight loss to society.

4. In a monopolized input market for input x with a competitive product market, the economic rent accruing to the input is maximized at an equilibrium where the marginal cost of supplying an additional unit of the input equals the marginal revenue associated with employing an additional unit of the input. At this equilibrium, the price of the input is above the marginal cost of the input, so there is a deadweight loss to society, because the value of the marginal product of the input is greater than the marginal cost of the input.

5. In a bilateral monopoly input market where there is both a monopsonist buyer and a monopolist supplier of the input, the monopsonist buyer wants to pay a low price for the input and the monopolist supplier wants to charge a high price for the input. The final price of the input will typically be a negotiated price somewhere between the monopsonist's preferred low price and the monopolist's preferred high price.

Self-Test Problems

1. Consider a firm with $MP_L = 10/\sqrt{L}$. The price of the product is equal to $3.
   a. Solve for the firm's MRP_L.
   b. If the firm takes the wage as given and $w = 10$, how much labor should the firm hire?

2. Consider a competitive labor market in which the demand for labor is $w = 17 - 0.05L$ and the supply for labor is $w = 3 + 0.05 L$.
   a. Solve for the equilibrium wage w_e and labor L_e. Calculate payments to capital, economic rent, total wage payments to labor, and total value of products. On a graph, label each of these areas.
   b. Calculate the elasticity of supply at the equilibrium point.
   c. Now assume the supply curve for labor is $w = 1.6 + 0.06 L$. Solve for the new equilibrium wage rate and labor hired in the market. Calculate elasticity of supply at the equilibrium point with the new supply curve. Calculate economic rent with the new supply curve.

d. What can you say about the relationship between the elasticity of the supply curve and the value of economic rent?

3. Consider a monopsonist that operates in a perfectly competitive output market. The monopsonist's demand for labor is $MRP_L = 240 - 2L$. The supply of labor is $w = 40 + L$.

a. Solve for the marginal expenditure of labor, ME_L, of the monopsonist.

b. Solve for the wage the monopsonist will set, w_m, and the amount of labor the monopsonist will hire, L_m.

c. Solve for the wage paid and the labor hired if this were a competitive labor market.

Questions and Problems for Review

1. Consider a perfectly competitive firm that produces baseball caps, which sell for $5 apiece. The following is a firm's short-run production function. The firm also operates in a competitive labor market, and the wage is $150 per day.

Quantity of Labor (L) Per Day	Total Number of Baseball Caps Produced
0	0
10	20
20	50
30	90
40	140
50	180
60	210
70	230

a. Calculate MRP_L.
b. Determine how much labor the firm should hire.
c. Calculate $SRMC$ for each of the values of output.
d. Discuss the relationship between $SRMC$ and MP_L.

2. Consider the table in question 1.
a. Graph the MRP_L curve and the labor hired if the wage is $150 per day.
b. Assume the wage increases to $200 per day. Describe what will happen in the short run. Show this change on the same graph.
c. What might be the likely long-term effects of this change in wages? Show these possible changes on the same graph.
d. Graph a hypothetical long-run demand for labor. Of course, you don't have numbers, but pay

attention to the relative shape of the long-run demand compared to the short-run demand for labor.

3. Analyze the effects of the following situations on a firm's derived demand for bakers. Assume that bread is a normal good and is produced in a competitive environment.
a. Consumer income increases.
b. Bakers participate in training that helps increase the productivity of workers.
c. A well-publicized health report says that carbohydrates are your worst enemy for weight gain and heart disease.
d. The number of firms producing bread increases.

4. Assume that there are 100 firms in the industry in the table in question 1. Assume that the wage is first $150 per day and then increases to $200 per day. Graphically analyze the effect of this increase in wages on the industry demand curve and explain in writing.
a. What would happen to the supply of baseball caps and the price of baseball caps as wages increase?
b. What would you expect to happen to the firm's demand for labor?
c. Roughly sketch the industry demand curve for labor if we allow the price of the product to change as a result of the wage increase. (You don't have numbers, but concentrate on the relative shape.)

5. In each of the following scenarios, comment on which market would be more elastic. Explain.
a. The demand for heart surgeons versus the demand for fast food workers.
b. The demand for heart surgeons this year versus the demand for heart surgeons for the next 20 years.

c. The demand for glass in beer bottling versus the demand for glass in automobile production.

6. Assume a local fast food restaurant operates in a competitive labor market. The demand for labor is $w = 15 - (1/2)L$ and the supply for labor is $w = -3 + (1/2)L$.

    a. Solve for the equilibrium wage, w_e, in the competitive market.

    b. The firm's $MP_L = 24/(5\sqrt{L})$. The price of the product is \$5. Solve for the firm's MRP_L and the total amount of labor the firm will hire.

    c. Draw a graph showing the profit-maximizing level of labor the firm hires.

7. Assume that George has convex indifference curves for leisure. He chooses to work 10 hours when the wage is \$8, 12 hours when the wage is \$10, and 8 hours when the wage is \$15.

    a. Draw a graph showing George's choice between income and leisure.

    b. From your graph in question 7(a), construct George's supply curve for labor.

    c. Using substitution and income effects, explain why George's supply curve defies the upward-sloping rule.

8. Consider a firm with the following market demand curve for labor: $w = 400 - (1/2)L$ and market supply for labor: $w = 80 + (1/2)L$.

    a. Solve for the equilibrium wage, w_e, and quantity of labor, L_e. Draw a graph of the demand and supply of labor. Label w_e and L_e.

    b. Calculate payments to capital, economic rent, total wage payments to labor, and total value of products. On your graph, label each of these areas.

    c. Calculate the elasticity of supply at the equilibrium point.

    d. Now assume the supply curve for labor changes to $w = 16 + 0.7L$. Solve for the new equilibrium wage rate and quantity of labor hired. Draw the new supply curve on your graph from question 8(a).

    e. Calculate elasticity of supply at the equilibrium point with the new labor supply curve.

    f. Calculate economic rent with the new supply curve.

    g. What can you say about the relationship between the elasticity of labor supply and the value of economic rent?

9. Consider a bookstore on a small college campus. Demand for its product is $P = 194.5 - (1/2)Q$. Its production function is $Q = KL$, and K is fixed at 4. Thus, its production function is $Q = 4L$, and $MP_L = 4$. The supply curve of labor is $w = 4 + 0.0625L$.

    a. First, let's assume the bookstore is operating in a competitive environment with demand $P = 194.5 - (1/2)Q$. Solve for the demand for labor in this case, VMP_L. Solve for the competitive equilibrium wage, w_c, and quantity of labor, L_c.

    b. Instead, the bookstore operates in a monopoly market with demand $P = 194.5 - (1/2)Q$. Calculate the monopolist's demand for labor, MRP_L. Solve for the quantity of labor the monopolist will hire, L_m, and the wage it will pay, w_m.

    c. For the same labor market, compare the wage paid and labor hired in a competitive output market versus the wage paid and labor hired in a monopoly output market.

10. Consider a product market with demand $P = 100 - Q$. The firm's production function is $Q = KL$, and K is fixed at 10. Thus, the firm's production function is $Q = 10L$, and the $MP_L = 10$. The supply curve of labor is $w = 10 + 10L$.

    a. First, let's assume the firm is operating in a competitive product market. Solve for the demand for labor in this case, VMP_L. Solve for the competitive equilibrium wage, w_c, and quantity of labor, L_c. Draw a graph of the demand and supply of labor. Label w_c and L_c.

    b. Instead, we know the product market is operated by a monopolist. Calculate the monopolist's demand for labor, MRP_L. Solve for the quantity of labor the monopolist will hire, L_m, and the wage it will pay, w_m. Label L_m and w_m on the graph in question 10(a).

    c. For the same labor market, compare the wage paid and labor hired in a competitive output market versus the wage paid and labor hired in a monopoly output market.

11. Consider a monopsonist operating in a perfectly competitive output market. The monopsonist's demand for labor is $MRP_L = 32 - (1/2)L$. The supply of labor is $w = 2 + L$.

    a. Solve for the marginal expenditure of labor, ME_L, of the monopsonist.

b. Solve for the wage the monopsonist will set, w_m, and the quantity of labor the monopsonist will hire, L_m.

c. Solve for the wage and the quantity of labor hired if this were a competitive labor market.

12. Consider a monopsonist operating in a perfectly competitive output market. The monopsonist's demand for labor is $MRP_L = 5{,}008 - 5L$. The supply of labor is $w = 10 + L$.

a. Solve for the marginal expenditure of labor, ME_L, of the monopsonist.

b. Solve for the wage the monopsonist will set, w_m, and the quantity of labor the monopsonist will hire, L_m. Graph this situation in question 12 and label L_m and w_m.

c. Solve for the wage paid and the quantity of labor hired if this were a competitive labor market. Show the values of w_c and L_c on the graph in question 12(b).

13. Explain the difference between MRP_L and VMP_L. When are the two equal? When are they different?

14. What do we mean when we say a firm has monopsony power? Is it possible for a firm to be both a monopolist and a monopsonist? Is it possible for a firm to be a monopolist but not a monopsonist?

15. Consider a competitive labor market with a demand curve for labor equal to $w = 60 - L$ and a supply curve of labor equal to $w = 6 + (1/2)L$.

a. Solve for the competitive equilibrium wage, w_c, and labor, L_c. Calculate economic rent and total wage payments.

b. Suppose the workers in this market form an effective union, $MR = 60 - 2L$. Solve for the amount of labor hired, the wage demanded, economic rent, and total wage payments if the union's goal is to *maximize total payments* to its members.

c. Suppose instead the union wishes to maximize economic rent to its members. Solve for the amount of labor hired, the wage demanded, economic rent, and total wage payments.

d. How do you know that the wage and labor hired in question 15(b) in fact do maximize total payments to its members and the wage and labor hired in question 15(c) in fact do maximize economic rent?

16. Consider George from question 7. He chooses to work ten hours when the wage is $8, twelve hours when the wage is $10, and eight hours when the wage is $15.

a. Redraw the graph showing George's choice between income and leisure.

b. Now consider Irma. She also works ten hours when the wage is $8, but she chooses to work eight hours when the wage increases to $10 and only work six hours when the wage increases to $15. On the same graph as in question 16(a), draw a set of indifference curves that would show Irma's choice between income and leisure. (Hint: You should use a different color pen for Irma's indifference curves.)

c. Compare the shape of George's and Irma's indifference curves. What can you say about George's preferences relative to Irma's? How do the relative shapes of the indifference curves show this?

d. Draw a supply curve of labor for Irma. With respect to substitution and income effects, what is true for Irma at all points on her supply curve?

17. Consider a labor market dominated by a union. The union and management just finished negotiations and came to an agreement. The union was able to demand a higher wage, but made concessions. Some of the jobs currently being advertised due to vacancy would not be filled. The total number of people employed will fall as a result of this concession. On a graph, show the effects that this negotiated contract might have in the non-unionized labor market.

18. Consider a competitive labor market with a demand curve for labor equal to $w = 80 - 2L$ and a supply curve of labor equal to $w = 8 + L$.

a. Solve for the competitive equilibrium wage, w_c, and labor, L_c. Calculate economic rent and total wage payments.

b. Suppose that the workers in this market form an effective union, $MR = 80 - 4L$. Solve for the quantity of labor hired, the wage demanded, economic rent, and total wage payments if the union's goal is to maximize total payments to its members.

c. Suppose instead that the union wishes to maximize economic rent to its members. Solve for the quantity of labor hired, the wage demanded, economic rent, and total wage payments if the union's goal is to maximize economic rent to its members.

d. Verify that the wage and quantity of labor hired in question 18(b) in fact do maximize total payments to the union's members and the wage and quantity of labor hired in question 18(c) in fact do maximize economic rent.

19. Consider the market described in question 15 in which the demand curve for labor equals $w = 60 - L$ and the supply curve of labor equals $w = 6 + (1/2)L$ and $MR = 60 - 2L$.

a. Suppose that this market is a bilateral monopoly. Solve for the quantity of labor the monopsonist hires and the wage the monopsonist pays.

b. Recall from question 15 the wage requested and labor hired if the union wants to maximize economic rent. What is the range of the final wage if this were a bilateral monopoly? Discuss how the final wage will be determined.

20. Consider the market described in question 18 in which the demand curve for labor equals $w = 80 - 2L$ and the supply curve of labor equals $w = 8 + L$ and $MR = 80 - 4L$.

a. Suppose that this market is a bilateral monopoly. Solve for the quantity of labor the monopsonist hires and the wage the monopsonist pays.

b. Solve for the wage requested and labor hired if the union wants to maximize economic rent. What is the range of the final wage if this were a bilateral monopoly? Discuss how the final wage will be determined.

 ## Internet Exercises

Visit *http://www.myeconlab.com/waldman* for this chapter's Web exercises. Answer real-world economics problems by doing research on the Internet.

Chapter 18

Investment, Time, and Risk

Few relationships in economics have received more attention than the relationship between risk and rate of return on an investment. Theory suggests that investors will invest in a risky investment only if it pays a higher rate of return than less-risky investments. For example, a comparison of the cumulative return on $1,000 invested in five investments of progressively increasing risk—U.S. Treasury bills, long-term U.S. government bonds, long-term corporate bonds, the Standard & Poor's stock fund, and small company stocks—between December 1925 and June 1995 shows us that the differences in accumulated wealth are very large. An investment of $1,000 in short-term U.S. Treasury bills in 1925 grew to only $12,520 in 1995, compared to $30,680 in long-term U.S. government bonds, $44,150 in long-term corporate bonds, $973,850 in the Standard & Poor's stock fund, and $3,425,250 in the small company stock fund. These figures show not only the relationship between risk and rate of return, but also the relationship between time and cumulative return. In this chapter, we explore the relationship between time, risk, and rate of return on investments.

Investing in stocks and bonds is one type of risk, but there are many other types of risk faced by companies and individuals, some of which cannot be predicted or measured. For example, prior to the tragedies of September 11, 2001, many airlines were planning to invest in new aircraft. Following the tragedies, however, these airlines cancelled their investment orders. Because of an ill-fated turn of events that ran counter to their expected growth, Boeing and Airbus laid off thousands of workers. The airline and aircraft manufacturing industries, however, were not the only companies affected by the attacks. The travel industry as a whole took an enormous hit. From there, the downward trend spiraled. Other industries cancelled their investment plans as well. These industries included everything from dry cleaners and shoe manufacturers to investment banks and retail chains. Why did all of these companies curtail their long-run investment plans? In this chapter, we explore how time and risk affect business investment.

Now let's consider a more personal investment decision. Given the uncertain times just described, consider the following: Suppose your grandparents gave you a $10,000 gift to invest in the stock market. How do you decide whether to invest the entire amount in one stock or spread your investments over many stocks? Should you use the services of a financial advisor, pick the stocks yourself off of the Internet, or pick the stocks by throwing darts at a newspaper page listing all available stocks? Should you ask your grandparents for permission to purchase other investments such as bonds instead of stocks? Or, should you invest in your own small business? These are the types of investment decisions millions of individuals face every day. In this chapter, we examine how rational, knowledgeable investors would answer each of these questions.

18.1 Intertemporal Investment Decisions: The Importance of Time and Discounting

Time is one of the most important factors affecting firms' investment decisions. A firm's decision to purchase a capital good, such as a new plant or a new piece of heavy machinery, differs from its decision to hire more labor or purchase additional raw materials, in large part because of very different time horizons for these decisions. Once a firm purchases a new capital good, the firm is stuck with that decision for years to come. Labor, on the other hand, can be laid off on short notice, and raw material orders can be quickly cancelled. Because capital equipment lasts for 5, 10, 15, 20, or more years, and because new equipment often cannot be easily shut down or discarded, investment decisions have impacts not only on current profit, but on future profit as well.

Present Value and Discounting

Chapter 4 introduced the concept of present value to incorporate time into consumers' consumption decisions. Recall from Chapter 4 that $X/(1 + r)$ is the present value of a promise to pay X dollars in one year at interest rate r. The value of $X/(1 + r)$ represents the amount a lender, such as a bank, would lend a borrower in year 1 if the borrower promised to repay X in year 2. To understand intertemporal investment decisions, it is first necessary to expand our understanding of the concept of present value beyond the intertemporal consumption model presented in Chapter 4.

Because X dollars invested today at an interest rate r would increase in value to $X(1 + r)$ dollars in one year, $X(1 + r)(1 + r) = X(1 + r)^2$ in two years, and $X(1 + r)^t$ in t years, the present value of $X(1 + r)^t$ dollars received t years from today equals $X(1 + r)^t/(1 + r)^t = X$ dollars. If $X = \$100$ and $r = 10$ percent, then the present value of $\$110$ received in one year is $\$100$, because it is necessary to invest $\$100$ today to receive $\$110$ in one year. Similarly, the present value of $\$121$ received in two years is $\$100$ today. By similar reasoning, the promise to pay X dollars t years from today has a present value of:

$$\text{present value} = \frac{X}{(1 + r)^t}$$

Therefore, at an interest rate of 10 percent, the promise to pay $\$100$ in one year has a present value of $\$90.91$, because the present value of $\$100$ received in one year $= \$100/(1.1) = \$90.909$.

THE PRESENT VALUE OF PROFIT For a typical firm, suppose π_t represents the firm's profit in time period t, and $(1 + r)$ represents the rate at which the firm is willing to trade future for present income just as it represented the rate at which an individual would trade future for present consumption in Chapter 4. The r in $(1 + r)$ is the firm's *discount rate*. The **discount rate** measures how consumers or firms value future income compared to current income; the higher the discount rate, the lower the value of future income compared to current income. In the following equation, π_{pv} represents the firm's present value of profit that it expects to earn over the next n years:

discount rate

The rate at which consumers or firms are willing to trade future income for present income.

$$\pi_{pv} = \frac{\pi_1}{(1 + r)} + \frac{\pi_2}{(1 + r)^2} + \frac{\pi_3}{(1 + r)^3} + \ldots + \frac{\pi_n}{(1 + r)^n} \qquad (18.1)$$

The maximization of long-run profit implies the maximization of π_{pv}. Equation 18.1 shows that the maximization of long-run profit depends not only on the annual flow of economic profit, π, but also critically depends on the discount rate r. Firms with short time horizons place a low value on future profits and are willing to trade current profit for future profit only at a high interest rate, and therefore have high discount rates. These firms want to earn high profits in early periods even if it means sacrificing large future profits. Firms with longer time horizons are willing to trade current profits for future profits at a low interest rate, and therefore have lower discount rates. These firms are willing to sacrifice current profits in order to earn higher profits in the future. For example, a firm owned by an individual nearing retirement with no heirs might have a very high discount rate, while a corporation with a very long-term time horizon would have a very low discount rate. Assuming n goes to infinity and π_t is constant and equal to π for all values of t, then Equation 18.1 can be written as:

$$\pi_{pv} = \frac{\pi}{(1 + r)} + \frac{\pi}{(1 + r)^2} + \frac{\pi}{(1 + r)^3} + \ldots \qquad (18.2)$$

Factoring out $1/(1 + r)$ from the right side of Equation 18.2 yields:

$$\pi_{pv} = \frac{1}{(1 + r)}\left(\pi + \frac{\pi}{(1 + r)} + \frac{\pi}{(1 + r)^2} + \ldots\right)$$

$$\pi_{pv} = \frac{1}{(1 + r)}(\pi + \pi_{pv})$$

$$\pi_{pv}(1 + r) = \pi + \pi_{pv}$$

$$\pi_{pv} + r\pi_{pv} = \pi + \pi_{pv}$$

$$\pi_{pv} = \frac{\pi}{r} \qquad (18.3)$$

GENERALIZING PRESENT VALUE CALCULATIONS Equation 18.2 can be generalized for any sum beginning at any time t, not just for $t = 1$. Consider the following sum:

$$\pi_{pv} = \sum_{t=c}^{\infty} \frac{\pi}{(1 + r)^t} = \frac{\pi}{(1 + r)^c} + \frac{\pi}{(1 + r)^{c+1}} + \frac{\pi}{(1 + r)^{c+2}} + \ldots \qquad (18.4)$$

where c is any number less than, equal to, or greater than zero. In Equation 18.4, c represents the time when the flow of profit begins. If the profit flow begins in the current time period, $c = 0$. If the profit flow begins in a future time period, $c > 0$. If the profit flow began in a past time period, $c < 0$. Factoring out $1/(1 + r)^{c-1}$ in Equation 18.4 yields:

$$\pi_{pv} = \frac{1}{(1 + r)^{c-1}}\left[\frac{\pi}{(1 + r)} + \frac{\pi}{(1 + r)^2} + \frac{\pi}{(1 + r)^3} + \cdots\right]$$

$$= \frac{1}{(1 + r)^{c-1}}\left[\frac{\pi}{r}\right] = \frac{\pi}{r(1 + r)^{c-1}} \tag{18.5}$$

For example, consider the following two infinite sums using Equation 18.5 and a discount rate $r = 0.10$; the first for $c = 4$, and the second for $c = -4$. The first sum begins at $t = 4$:

$$\pi_{pv} = \frac{\$100}{(1 + 0.1)^4} + \frac{\$100}{(1 + 0.1)^5} + \frac{\$100}{(1 + 0.1)^6} + \cdots$$

$$= \frac{\$100}{0.1(1 + 0.1)^3} = \frac{\$100}{0.1(1.1)^3} = \frac{\$100}{0.1(1.33)} = \$751.88$$

The second sum begins at $t = -4$:

$$\pi_{pv} = \frac{\$100}{(1 + 0.1)^{-4}} + \frac{\$100}{(1 + 0.1)^{-3}} + \frac{\$100}{(1 + 0.1)^{-2}} + \cdots$$

$$= \frac{\$100}{0.1(1 + 0.1)^{-5}} = \frac{\$100}{0.1(1.1)^{-5}} = \frac{\$100}{\dfrac{0.1}{(1.1)^5}} = \frac{\$100(1.1)^5}{0.1} = \$1,610$$

Knowing how to use Equation 18.5 to calculate the present value of future income streams will be extremely useful as we proceed through the remainder of this chapter.

Table 18.1 identifies the present value of $100 earned 1, 5, 10, 20, and 30 years in the future at discount rates of 1, 5, 10, 15, and 20 percent. At a 10 percent discount rate, $100 earned in ten years is worth only $100/(1.1)^{10} = \$38.55$ today. Notice that dollars received in the distant future are worth little today. For example, at a 10 percent discount rate, $100 earned in 30 years is worth only $100/(1.1)^{30} = \$5.73$ today.

The Value of a Bond or Perpetuity

One important use of discounting is to determine the value of *bonds* and *perpetuities*. When the government or a corporation wishes to borrow from the public, it typically sells a debt security called a **bond**. The purchaser of a bond gives the issuer of the bond

bond

A debt security issued by a government or a firm where the purchaser lends the issuer a lump sum of money today in return for a promise from the issuer to pay a finite stream of future payments.

Table 18.1 **Present Value of $100 Payable in Future Years at Various Discount Rates**

Discount Rate	1 Year	5 Years	10 Years	20 Years	30 Years
0.01	99.01	95.15	90.53	81.95	74.19
0.05	95.24	78.35	61.39	37.69	23.14
0.10	90.91	62.09	38.55	14.86	5.73
0.15	86.96	49.72	24.72	6.11	1.51
0.20	83.33	40.19	16.15	2.61	0.42

coupon

The annual interest payment on a bond.

perpetuity

A debt security where the purchaser lends the issuer a lump sum of money today in return for a promise from the issuer to pay a fixed amount of income to the purchaser forever.

a lump sum of money today in return for a promise from the issuer to pay a finite stream of future payments. The annual interest payment on a bond is called a **coupon**. For example, suppose a firm wants to borrow $10,000 for 10 years, so it issues a $10,000 bond that pays a coupon of $800 per year. The purchaser of the bond pays $10,000 today and receives a promise from the firm to pay an $800 coupon for each of the next 10 years, plus a promise to repay the principle of $10,000 in 10 years. The coupon payment identifies the annual interest rate on the bond. In this case, the interest rate is $800/$10,000 = 0.08, or 8 percent. A **perpetuity** differs from a bond because it pays a fixed amount to the lender *forever*.

To determine the value of a bond to its buyer, we calculate the present value of the payment stream. Suppose, for example, a bond is sold for $1,000 and pays a coupon of $100 per year for each of the next 10 years and a principal repayment in the tenth year of $1,000. Using Equation 18.1, the discounted present value of the bond, PV, is:

$$PV = \frac{\$100}{(1 + r)} + \frac{\$100}{(1 + r)^2} + \frac{\$100}{(1 + r)^3} + \cdots + \frac{\$100}{(1 + r)^{10}} + \frac{\$1,000}{(1 + r)^{10}}$$

At a discount rate of zero, the present value of the bond equals $PV = 10(\$100) + \$1,000 = \$2,000$. As the discount rate increases above zero, the present value will continuously decline. Using Equations 18.3 and 18.5, we can simplify the calculation of the present value of the bond as follows:

$$PV = \frac{\$100}{r} - \frac{\$100}{r(1 + r)^{10}} + \frac{\$1,000}{(1 + r)^{10}}$$

where from Equation 18.3, the first term on the right side, $\$100/r$, equals the present value of an annual payment of $100 forever with the first payment being made in one year. Using Equation 18.5, the second term on the right side, $-\$100/r(1 + r)^{10}$, subtracts out from the first term the present value of the payments that would be made from $t = 11$ to $t = \infty$ on a bond that pays a $100 coupon forever. Therefore, the first two terms on the right side, $\$100/r - \$100/r(1 + r)^{10}$, measure the present value of the 10 years of coupon payments on the bond. The third term on the right side is the present value of the principal repayment that is received in 10 years.

If the purchaser of the bond has a 5 percent discount rate, the present value of the bond is:

$$PV = \frac{\$100}{.05} - \frac{\$100}{(.05)(1.05)^{10}} + \frac{\$1000}{(1.05)^{10}}$$

$$= \$2,000 - \$1,227.83 + \$613.91 = \$1,386.08$$

At a 10 percent discount rate, the present value is $1,000; at a 15 percent discount rate, the present value is $749.06; and at a 20 percent discount rate, the present value of the bond is $580.75. Figure 18.1 shows the present value of this bond at discount rates between zero and 20 percent. The higher the discount rate, the lower the present value of the bond.

To find the present value of a perpetuity, which, beginning in year 1, pays $1,000 per year forever, use Equation 18.3 to calculate:

$$PV = \frac{\$1,000}{(1 + r)} + \frac{\$1,000}{(1 + r)^2} + \frac{\$1,000}{(1 + r)^3} + \cdots = \frac{\$1,000}{r}$$

At a 5 percent discount rate, the present value of the perpetuity is $20,000; at a 10 percent discount rate, the present value is $10,000; at 15 a percent discount rate, the present

Figure 18.1 The Present Value of a Bond
If a bond pays $100 for each of the next ten years and pays a $1,000 principal payment in ten years, its present value will decline as indicated in the graph as the interest rate increases.

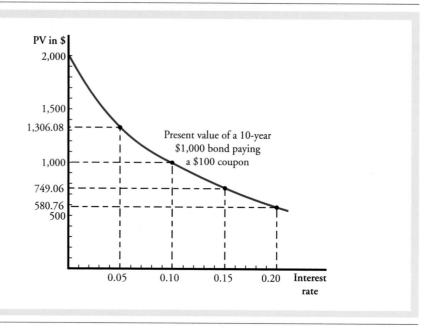

value is $6,666.67; and at a 20 percent discount rate, the present value of the perpetuity is $5,000.

Government and corporate bonds are sold in the bond market in the same way that shares of stock are sold in the stock market. Buyers and sellers agree to exchange a bond at an equilibrium price p. The **yield** on a bond is simply the rate of return on the market price (market value) of the bond. The **face value** of the bond equals the principal payment to the owner when the bond reaches maturity. To determine the yield or rate of return on a bond, rewrite Equation 18.1 in the following form:

yield

The rate of return on a bond.

face value

The principal payment to the owner of a bond when the bond reaches maturity.

$$p = \frac{x_1}{(1 + rr)} + \frac{x_2}{(1 + rr)^2} + \cdots + \frac{x_n}{(1 + rr)^n} + \frac{principal}{(1 + rr)^n} \qquad (18.6)$$

where p is the market price of the bond, rr is the rate of return or yield on the bond, x_i is the coupon payment to the bondholder in year i, and *principal* is the principal payment to the bondholder at maturity. The buyer knows the price of the bond (p), the coupon payments (the values of x_i for all i), and the principal payment (*principal*); therefore, the only unknown in Equation 18.6 is the yield or rate of return rr. Despite the fact that Equation 18.6 contains only one unknown variable, rr, there is no quick method for calculating rr without a computer.

▲▲▲ 18.1 APPLICATION Calculating the Yield on a Bond

There is a method for calculating the yield on a bond using a calculator, which takes a bit of time, but is fairly uncomplicated. Every business day, the *Wall Street Journal* publishes a list of bond sales from the previous business day. On October 10, 2001, for example, the fol-

lowing two bond sales were listed in the table on the next page. Bond listings have a standard format that includes: the name of the issuing company, the coupon on the bond per $100 of face value, the year of maturity, the coupon times 100 divided by the closing (current) price

(continued)

of the bond, the day's volume of sales in hundreds of shares, the day's closing price of the bond, and the change in the closing price from the previous day's closing price.

The bond's closing price or value is listed as a percentage, with 100 equaling the face value of the bond, which equals the principal payment when the bond reaches maturity. Most bonds have face values of $1,000, but using percentages instead of actual dollar values does not affect the calculation of the bond's yield.

The first bond is a Time Warner bond with a coupon of $7.75; therefore, the bond pays $7.75 interest annually per $100 of face value. The bond reaches maturity in 2005, and the current ratio of the coupon times 100 to the price is 7.1 ($775/$109). On October 9, 2001, the closing price was $109, and the price was up $1.00 from the previous day's closing price of $108. Because the bond reaches maturity in 2005, the bondholder receives a coupon payment of $7.75 per $100 of face value in each of the next four years, 2002–2005. In addition, the bondholder receives a principal payment of $100 (equal to the face value of the bond) when the bond matures in 2005. To calculate the yield on the bond, we set up the following equation:

$$\$109 = \frac{\$7.75}{(1 + rr)} + \frac{\$7.75}{(1 + rr)^2} +$$

$$\frac{\$7.75}{(1 + rr)^3} + \frac{\$7.75}{(1 + rr)^4} + \frac{\$100}{(1 + rr)^4}$$

Using Equations 18.3 and 18.5, this equation can be simplified to:

$$\$109 = \frac{\$7.75}{rr} - \frac{\$7.75}{rr(1 + rr)^4} + \frac{\$100}{(1 + rr)^4}$$

If the price of a bond equals $100, the yield always equals the coupon payment on the bond. If the price of a bond is greater than $100, as it is for this bond with a price of $109, the yield is less than the coupon payment on the bond. Finally, if the price of a bond is less than $100, the yield is greater than the coupon payment on the bond.

To solve for rr, we begin by noticing that the price of the bond, $109, is greater than the face value of the bond, which equals $100. Because there is an inverse relationship between the price of a bond and its yield, the yield on the bond will be less than the $7.75 coupon that the bond is paying on the $100 face value.

We next calculate the value of the right side of the equation for a value of rr less than 7.75 percent. Let's start by setting rr equal to 6.7 percent, or approximately 1 percent below 7.75 percent. If $rr = 0.067$, the right side of the equation equals $115.67 − $89.24 + $77.15 = $103.58, which is well below the $109 price of the bond. The yield must therefore be less than 6.7 percent. Using trial and error, and setting $rr = 0.052$, the right side value is $149.04 − $121.69 + $81.65 = $109! The yield or rate of return on the Time Warner bond is 5.2 percent. While this trial and error procedure is a bit time-consuming, the calculations are not difficult with a calculator. On October 9, 2001, the Time Warner bond had a yield of only 5.2 percent, which was well below the 7.1 percent listed in the newspaper as the ratio of the annual payment to the price of the bond, and even farther below the coupon payment on the bond of $7.75 per $100, or 7.75 percent.

The second bond, which matures in 2006, was issued by Lucent Technologies and sold for only $79.125. To determine the yield on this bond, we set up the following equation:

$$\$79.125 = \frac{\$7.25}{rr} - \frac{\$7.25}{rr(1 + rr)^5} + \frac{\$100}{(1 + rr)^5}$$

In this case, the price of the bond, $79.125, is well below the face value of the bond, which equals $100. The yield on the bond must therefore be greater than the $7.25 coupon that the bond was paying on its $100 face value. The equation is solved when $rr = 0.1321$. The yield on the bond is quite high at 13.21 percent.

Why would any investor be willing to purchase the Time Warner bond yielding 5.2 percent when they could

Issuing Company	Coupon Payment	Year of Maturity	Ratio of Coupon Payment to Price	Volume (100s)	Closing Price	Change in Price From Yesterday
Time Warner	7 3/4	05	7.1	23	109	+1
Lucent	7 1/4	06	9.2	1250	79 1/8	−3 3/4

(continued)

purchase the Lucent bond yielding 13.21 percent? There is a rational explanation: In October 2001 the risk of purchasing the Lucent bond was much greater than the risk of purchasing the Time Warner bond. Despite its higher yield, investors were selling the Lucent bond on October 8, 2001, in droves, driving the price of the bond down from $82.875 to $79.125 in just one day. In October 2001, Lucent was in deep financial trouble, and there were rumors that the firm might file for bankruptcy protection. If Lucent went bankrupt and defaulted on its bonds, its bonds yielding 13.21 percent would be worthless. Time Warner, on the other hand, was in excellent financial condition in October 2001, and therefore there was little risk of default on the Time Warner bond. Time Warner's strong financial condition did not last for long after October 2001. On January 11, 2001, AOL and Time Warner completed a merger; by early 2003, the merger had proven to be a financial disaster for AOL Time Warner. As a result, the price of AOL Time Warner bonds declined and the yields on the bonds increased.

▼▼▼ 18.2 The Firm's Investment Decision

Every day, firms make thousands of investment decisions concerning whether to build new plants and purchase new capital equipment. They make the decision to invest by comparing the present value of the expected cash flow generated by the investment with the present value of the cost of the investment. In this section, we analyze two common methods used to make such long-run investment decisions, the *net present value* and the *internal rate of return*.

The Net Present Value Criterion

net present value (NPV) criterion

An investment decision-making criterion where the present value of the expected cash flow minus the present value of the costs of an investment are calculated, and the investment is undertaken if the calculation results in a positive value.

The **net present value (NPV) criterion** states that if the present value of the expected cash flow generated by an investment is greater than the present value of the cost of the investment, then a firm should make the investment. Conversely, if the present value of the expected cash flow is less than or equal to the cost, then the firm should not proceed with the investment. Suppose, for example, that an investment costs C today and is expected to generate a cash flow beginning next year of X_1, X_2, X_3, ... X_n over the next n years. The net present value, NPV, of this investment is defined as:

$$NPV = -C + \frac{X_1}{(1 + r)} + \frac{X_2}{(1 + r)^2} + \frac{X_3}{(1 + r)^3} + \cdots + \frac{X_n}{(1 + r)^n} \quad (18.7)$$

where r is the firm's discount rate. If $NPV > 0$, the firm undertakes the investment. If $NPV < 0$, the firm does not undertake the investment. Knowing the firm's discount rate is critical to solving Equation 18.7 and determining the NPV of an investment; therefore, we next turn our attention to an examination of how a firm determines its discount rate r.

The Firm's Discount Rate

The discount rate on a particular project is the rate of return on the firm's *next best* alternative investment project with the same risk. In other words, the discount rate is the *opportunity cost* of capital invested in projects with the same risk. It is necessary for the firm to put projects in different risk categories, because investors insist on earning higher rates of return on riskier investments.

For "safe" or low-risk investments, a common measure of the opportunity cost of capital is the rate of return on a 10-year United States Treasury bond. Because there is essentially no risk of the United States government defaulting on its bonds, the return on a government bond is considered a risk-free return. Firms and individuals always have the opportunity to invest in risk-free U.S. government bonds.

Consider the following hypothetical example. Suppose that prior to September 11, 2001, Disney was considering building a Phantasmic theme restaurant at its MGM Studios theme park at Walt Disney World in Orlando. The restaurant would cost $6 million to build and Disney expected it to generate a cash flow of $1 million per year for each of the next 10 years. After 10 years, Disney planned to completely change the theme of the restaurant and expected to sell the salvageable equipment for $1.2 million. Based on these estimates, Disney needed to determine whether it should build the new restaurant. If the *NPV* of the investment is positive, Disney should build the restaurant. The answer depends on Disney's discount rate for this particular project. A Disney World theme park restaurant prior to September 11, 2001, would have been a very low-risk investment. If Disney believed the restaurant to be a risk-free investment, it would use a discount rate equal to the yield on a 10-year U.S. treasury bond. If a 10-year treasury bond yielded 5 percent interest, the *NPV* of the restaurant investment was:

$$NPV = -\$6 + \frac{\$1}{1.05} + \frac{\$1}{(1.05)^2} + \cdots + \frac{\$1}{(1.05)^{10}} + \frac{\$1.2}{(1.05)^{10}} \qquad (18.8)$$

We can simplify Equation 18.8 using Equations 18.3 and 18.5:

$$NPV = -\$6 + \frac{\$1}{.05} - \frac{\$1}{(.05)(1.05)^{10}} + \frac{\$1.2}{(1.05)^{10}}$$

$$NPV = -\$6 + \$20 - \$12.28 + \$0.74 = \$2.46$$

NPV = $2.46 million, and therefore, Disney should have built the new restaurant, because the *NPV* was greater than 0.

Disney's decision was dependent on the firm's discount rate. Suppose that Disney had to decide whether to build the new Phantasmic restaurant after September 11, 2001. Disney would now believe that building a theme park restaurant would be a much riskier investment than purchasing a government bond. As a result, suppose the company used a higher discount rate equal to the 10 percent rate of return on moderately risky corporate bonds. The *NPV* would then be:

$$NPV = -\$6 + \frac{\$1}{0.1} - \frac{\$1}{(0.1)(1.1)^{10}} + \frac{\$1.2}{(1.1)^{10}}$$

$$NPV = -\$6 + \$10 - \$3.86 + \$0.46 = \$0.6$$

At a 10 percent discount rate, *NPV* = $600,000. The *NPV* is much lower, but Disney should still build the restaurant because *NPV* > 0.

In addition to increasing Disney's discount rate, the events of September 11, 2001, would almost certainly reduce Disney's expected cash flow from the restaurant. Suppose the tragedy reduced expected park attendance and cash flow by 25 percent, so that expected cash flow is $750,000 per year. *NPV* would then be:

$$NPV = -\$6 + \frac{\$0.75}{0.1} - \frac{\$0.75}{(0.1)(1.1)^{10}} + \frac{\$1.2}{(1.1)^{10}}$$

$$NPV = -\$6 + \$7.5 - \$2.90 + \$0.46 = -\$0.94$$

NPV = −$940,000. Because *NPV* is now less than zero, Disney should not build the restaurant.

The Internal Rate of Return Criterion

internal rate of return (IRR)

The discount rate for which the net present value of an investment equals zero.

An alternative to the net present value criterion for evaluating investments is the **internal rate of return (IRR)** of an investment, which is the discount rate for which the net present value of the investment equals zero. The internal rate of return criterion for an investment states that if the *IRR* is greater than the firm's required rate of return on investments, the firm should undertake the investment; if the *IRR* is less than the firm's required rate of return, the firm should not undertake the investment. What is the firm's required rate of return? If the firm is borrowing to pay for the investment, the required rate of return will be the cost of borrowing. The firm then undertakes the investment if and only if the *IRR* is greater than the firm's cost of borrowing.

For any investment, there always exists at least one *IRR*. Consider our original Disney restaurant example prior to September 11, 2001, with a cash flow of $1 million per year for each of the next 10 years and salvageable equipment that Disney sells for $1.2 million in 10 years. The internal rate of return, *IRR*, is calculated by setting the *NPV* equal to zero as follows:

$$NPV = -\$6 + \frac{\$1}{1 + IRR} + \frac{\$1}{(1 + IRR)^2} + \cdots$$

$$+ \frac{\$1}{(1 + IRR)^{10}} + \frac{\$1.2}{(1 + IRR)^{10}} = 0 \qquad (18.9)$$

Using Equations 18.3 and 18.5 to simplify Equation 18.9, we have:

$$-\$6 + \frac{\$1}{IRR} - \frac{\$1}{(IRR)(1 + IRR)^{10}} + \frac{\$1.2}{(1 + IRR)^{10}} = 0$$

Solving by trial and error, *IRR* = 0.121:

$$-\$6 + \frac{\$1}{0.121} - \frac{\$1}{(0.121)(1.121)^{10}} + \frac{\$1.2}{(1.121)^{10}}$$

$$= -\$6 + 8.26 - 2.63 + 0.38 = 0.01 \cong 0$$

Prior to September 11, 2001, the restaurant's internal rate of return was 12.1 percent. If Disney's cost of borrowing were less than 12.1 percent, Disney would build the restaurant; if Disney's cost of borrowing were greater than 12.1 percent, Disney would not build the restaurant.

Real Versus Nominal Discount Rates and Cash Flows

In calculating the *NPV* of an investment, the firm must be careful to distinguish between *real* and *nominal* values for the cash flows and the discount rate. Real values adjust for inflation; nominal values do not. The real interest rate on a bond measures the increase in real purchasing power that the purchaser receives each year. The difference between the real and nominal interest rate can be closely approximated by:

$$\text{real interest rate} \cong \text{nominal interest rate} - \text{rate of inflation}$$

For example, if a government bond pays a nominal 7 percent interest rate each year and the inflation rate is 2 percent, then the real interest rate is approximately 5 percent.

The use of the nominal interest rate overstates the increase in purchasing power to the lender each year. Suppose an individual purchases a $10,000 one-year bond paying a nominal 7 percent interest rate. The bond holder receives a $700 interest payment plus

▲▲▲ **18.2 APPLICATION**   How Lotteries Misrepresent Jackpot Values

Powerball is one of the major national lotteries. On February 19, 2003, Powerball was played in 24 states plus the District of Columbia, and the jackpot was advertised as $34,000,000. When any of the major national lotteries, such as Powerball or Mega Millions, advertise a huge jackpot, the administrators of the lottery always advertise one very large potential payout. What the lotteries rarely mention in their advertising is that the large payout is based on a much smaller annual payout over decades. For example, a Powerball grand prize winner has the option of receiving an annual payment for 30 years or an alternative cash payment today. On February 19, 2003, the Powerball jackpot of $34,000,000 was based on 30 annual payments of $1,133,333, with the first payment made immediately, and the remaining 29 payments made on an annual basis. Alternatively, the jackpot winner could choose a cash payment of $18,700,000 today.

In order to determine which of these alternatives is better, the grand prize winner has to compare the present value of the stream of payments over 30 years with a single payment today. To simplify the analysis, we ignore the tax implications of the different payment methods. The present value of a payment of $1,133,333 for 30 years starting with an immediate first payment today is:

$$PV = \$1,133,333 + \frac{\$1,133,333}{(1 + r)} + \frac{\$1,133,333}{(1 + r)^2} + \cdots + \frac{\$1,133,333}{(1 + r)^{29}}$$

The winner of the lottery would have to select a discount rate and calculate the present value of the stream of payments in the preceding equation. If the present value of the stream is greater than $18,700,000, then the winner should select the stream of payments over time. However, if the present value of the stream is less than $18,700,000, then the winner should select the immediate payment.

One way to approach this issue is to calculate the discount rate at which the winner would be indifferent between the two choices. This requires setting the present value of the stream equal to the cash payment, or solving the following equation for the discount rate r:

$$\$18,700,000 = \$1,133,333 + \frac{\$1,133,333}{(1 + r)} + \frac{\$1,133,333}{(1 + r)^2} + \cdots + \frac{\$1,133,333}{(1 + r)^{29}}$$

Using Equation 18.5:

$$\$18,700,000 = \frac{\$1,133,333(1 + r)}{r} - \frac{\$1,133,333}{r(1 + r)^{29}}$$

Solving the equation for the discount rate r yields $r = 0.0479$, or $r = 4.79\%$. If a lottery winner had a discount rate greater than 4.79%, he would choose the cash payment. If the winner had a discount rate less than 4.79%, he would choose the stream of annual payments.

The Powerball lottery officials were using a rather low discount rate in February 2003 compared with the rate at which many individuals would discount future income. Because the lottery's discount rate is quite low, many winners would be expected to choose the cash payment today over the stream of payments for 30 years, and this is exactly what recent Powerball winners have done. In 2002, there were 10 jackpot winners in the Powerball game. Of those winners, nine elected the cash payment and only one elected the stream of payments. These cash payments varied from a low of $16,982,345 to a high of $170,505,876. In 2001, there were also 10 winners, and all of them elected the cash payment. By using a low discount rate, the lottery organizers are creating a strong incentive for winners to choose the cash payment.

a $10,000 principal repayment next year. In nominal terms, the bond holder sacrificed $10,000 of purchasing power this year in return for $10,700 of purchasing power next year. In real terms, however, if the price index is 1.00 today and inflation is 2 percent, then the price index next year is 1.02. In return for sacrificing $10,000 in purchasing power today, the lender receives $10,700/$1.02 = $10,490.20 in purchasing power next year, or slightly under a 5 percent real return.

> ## COMMON ERROR 18.1   Inconsistently Using Nominal and Real Values in Determining Net Present Value
>
> Students often make one common error in calculating the net present value of an investment: They fail to be consistent in their use of real and nominal values for the expected cash flows and the discount rate. This can lead to serious problems and poor investment decisions. In calculating *NPV*, it is critical to be consistent and use either all real values or all nominal values in the numerator and denominator. Failure to follow this procedure may result in an incorrect investment decision. Suppose the firm evaluated all of the cash flow figures in the numerator in nominal terms, but used the real discount rate in the denominator. *NPV* would then be overestimated, and the firm might invest in a project where the correct *NPV* is negative. On the other hand, if the firm evaluated all of the cash flow figures in real terms, but used the nominal discount rate, *NPV* would then be underestimated, and the firm might not invest in a project where the correct *NPV* is positive.
>
> In the Disney restaurant example, Disney correctly used all real values in Equation 18.8. Suppose the nominal discount rate were 13 percent, and the rate of inflation were 8 percent; therefore, the real discount rate was 5 percent. If Disney incorrectly used real cash flow values in the numerators, but the nominal discount rate of 13 percent in the denominators, then the calculated *NPV* would be:
>
> $$NPV = -\$6 + \frac{\$1}{0.13} - \frac{\$1}{(0.13)(1.13)^{10}} + \frac{\$1.2}{(1.13)^{10}}$$
>
> $$NPV = -\$6 + \$7.69 - \$2.27 + \$0.35 = -\$0.23$$
>
> With a negative *NPV*, Disney would now incorrectly decide not to invest in the restaurant. However, if Disney used nominal values for both the cash flow and the discount rate, then *NPV* equals:
>
> $$NPV = -6 + \frac{1(1.08)}{1.13} + \frac{1(1.08)^2}{(1.13)^2} + \cdots$$
> $$+ \frac{1(1.08)^{10}}{(1.13)^{10}} + \frac{1.2(1.08)^{10}}{(1.13)^{10}}$$
>
> Because $1.08/1.13 \cong 1/1.05 = 0.95$, the equation can be written as:
>
> $$NPV = -6 + \frac{1}{1.05} + \frac{1}{(1.05)^2} + \cdots$$
> $$+ \frac{1}{(1.05)^{10}} + \frac{1.2}{(1.05)^{10}}$$
>
> which yields the following *NPV* that is the same as the *NPV* using all real values:
>
> $$NPV = -\$6 + \frac{\$1}{0.05} - \frac{\$1}{(0.05)(1.05)^{10}} + \frac{\$1.2}{(1.05)^{10}}$$
>
> $$NPV = -\$6 + \$20 - \$12.28 + \$0.74 = \$2.46$$
>
> Using all nominal values, *NPV* is positive, and the investment would be undertaken. Do not make the common error of mixing real and nominal values when calculating the *NPV* of an investment.

18.3   The Impact of Risk on Investment Decisions

In Chapter 6, we explored how risk affects consumer and producer behavior. Recall that firms can use diversification to reduce risk. Diversification requires a firm to reduce its risk by choosing an appropriate collection of investments, some of which are high-risk gambles and some low-risk gambles. The classic example used in Chapter 6 was of a small factory in a tourist town where there is a 50-50 chance of either heavy rain or sun for the season, and no way to predict the weather in advance. The factory can manufacture either umbrellas or sunglasses. If the factory produces just sunglasses and the season turns out to be sunny, profit will be $50,000; if it is rainy, profit will be zero. The firm then has a 50 percent probability of earning $50,000 and a 50 percent probability of earning zero;

therefore, the expected value of profit is $25,000. If the factory produces just umbrellas and there is rain, profit will be $50,000; but if there is sun, profit will be zero. Once again, the firm then has a 50 percent probability of earning $50,000 and a 50 percent probability of earning zero, and the expected value of profit is $25,000.

What if we allow the owner to diversify and produce umbrellas for half the year and sunglasses for half the year? In Chapter 6, we assumed that in this case, whether the season turns out to be rainy or sunny, profit is guaranteed to be $25,000. Note that the expected value of profit from producing only umbrellas, only sunglasses, or half of each is the same: $25,000. However, if the firm is risk-averse—that is, has decreasing marginal utility of income—the expected utility of a guaranteed $25,000 is greater than the expected utility associated with a 50 percent chance of earning $50,000 and a 50 percent chance of earning zero. Through diversification, the firm can thus increase its expected utility.

As the example illustrates, diversification can reduce many risks. Using the same investment strategy, someone investing in the stock market might reduce their risk by holding a small number of shares of many stocks rather than a large number of shares of one stock. As long as the individual stocks that make up the diversified group of stocks move differently in response to economic shocks, diversification will reduce risk. Investing in an umbrella manufacturer and sunglasses manufacturer in light of uncertain weather conditions is therefore a good way to reduce risk; investing in a sunglasses manufacturer and a suntan lotion manufacturer would not be.

Returning to our chapter's opening example, what would you do if you received a $10,000 gift from your grandparents? You could reduce your risk by purchasing shares in many different companies, rather than investing in just one company. *Mutual funds* serve investors' desires to reduce risk in exactly this way, by enabling individual investors to hold stock in many different companies. A **mutual fund** collects investment funds from a large number of individual investors, places these funds into one large pool, and uses the pool of funds to purchase stock in many different companies. In this way, individual investors can diversify their holdings far more broadly than if they purchased stock on their own. If a mutual fund held shares in every company listed on the New York Stock Exchange, it would be very highly diversified.

Diversifiable and Nondiversifiable Risk

Diversification can eliminate many types of risk. Risk that can be eliminated through diversification is called **diversifiable risk**. Risk that cannot be eliminated through diversification is called **nondiversifiable risk** or **market risk**. It is sometimes useful to think of diversifiable risk as risk that affects only a small number of assets, whereas nondiversifiable risk affects a large number of assets. The risk of investing in just a few stocks is primarily diversifiable risk, because purchasing a broader base of stocks can reduce it. Similarly, the risk undertaken by life and automobile insurance companies is also diversifiable risk, because by selling insurance to many different individuals, the companies can reduce their risk.

Going back to our Disney example: There is diversifiable risk associated with Disney's restaurant investment decision. For example, Disney can reduce its risk by investing in many different capital projects besides its new Phantasmic theme restaurant in Walt Disney World. It can build new restaurants in all of its theme parks in Orlando, Anaheim, Tokyo, and Paris; it can also reduce its risk by investing in capital projects at its other companies, such as ABC and ESPN. If people travel, they will spend money at the theme park restaurants, but if they stay home, they will watch more television and the ratings will improve for ABC and ESPN. Furthermore, the owners of the Walt Disney

mutual fund

An investment fund that collects funds from a large number of individual investors, places these funds into one large pool, and uses the pool to purchase stock in many different companies.

diversifiable risk

Risk that can be eliminated through diversification.

nondiversifiable risk

Risk that cannot be eliminated through diversification.

market risk

An alternative name for nondiversifiable risk.

Company, its stockholders, can diversify their investments by holding shares in many companies beside Disney.

What then constitutes nondiversifiable risk? One example is risk associated with fluctuations in general economic conditions. The economic downturn that resulted from the terrorist attacks on the World Trade Center and the Pentagon on September 11, 2001, was nondiversifiable risk. These tragedies initially caused the stock market to decline dramatically across the board, increasing the risk associated with corporate investment throughout the world. No amount of diversification could have eliminated this risk. Economic shocks of various kinds, such as an unanticipated oil price shock, a financial crisis in Southeast Asia, or an unexpected increase in interest rates, are other examples of nondiversifiable risk.

Figure 18.2 shows that total risk can be divided into diversifiable and nondiversifiable risk. Diversifiable risk is a function of the number of stocks owned; nondiversifiable risk is independent of the number of stocks owned. According to professors of finance Stephen Ross, Randolph Westerfield, and Bradford Johnson, the purchase of 10 of the 30 stocks used to measure the Dow Jones Industrial Average (DJIA) eliminates a great deal of diversifiable risk associated with investing in the stock market and the purchase of all 30 DJIA stocks eliminates virtually all of the diversifiable risk.[1]

The Capital Asset Pricing Model (CAPM)

capital asset pricing model, or **CAPM**

A model used to measure the risk on a particular capital investment by comparing that risk with the risk of investing in the entire stock market.

We now examine how firms include risk in their net present value calculations. The most commonly used method is called the **capital asset pricing model**, or the **CAPM**. The CAPM measures the risk on a particular capital investment by comparing that risk with the risk of investing in the entire stock market. Suppose an individual invested in the entire stock market; that is, bought every single stock offered for sale. The investor would bear no diversifiable risk, because she would be completely diversified; she would, how-

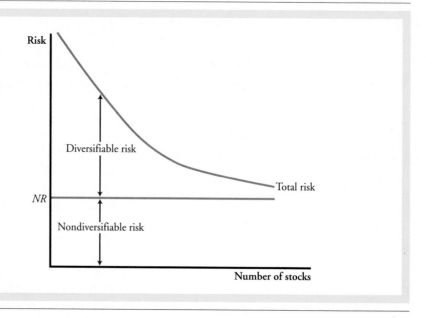

Figure 18.2 Diversifiable and Nondiversifiable Risk
Investing in a larger number of stocks decreases diversifiable risk, but does not reduce nondiversifiable risk. Nondiversifiable risk, *NR*, is independent of the number of stocks owned.

---

[1] Stephen A. Ross, Randolph W. Westerfield, and Bradford D. Johnson, *Fundamentals of Corporate Finance, 5th Edition.* Burr Ridge, IL: Irwin McGraw-Hill, 2000, pp. 394–395.

ever, bear some nondiversifiable risk. Because investment in the entire market includes some nondiversifiable risk, she would demand a risk premium for investing in the market instead of investing in risk-free government bonds. If the return on the entire market is r_m and the return on risk-free government bonds is r_f, then the risk premium is $(r_m - r_f)$.

AN INVESTMENT'S ASSET BETA If an investor is considering investing in the stock of just one company, he can use the capital asset pricing model to calculate the risk premium he would demand to invest in that stock. According to the CAPM, he would demand a risk premium on that stock that is proportional to the risk premium on the entire market, so that:

$$\text{risk premium} = r_i - r_f = \beta(r_m - r_f)$$

asset beta, β

A measure of the nondiversifiable risk associated with an investment; it measures the nondiversifiable risk associated with an investment compared to an investment in the entire stock market.

or:

$$r_i = r_f + \beta(r_m - r_f)$$

where r_i is the expected return on the stock, and β, called the **asset beta**, is a measure of the nondiversifiable risk associated with the investment. The asset beta β is related only to nondiversifiable risk. Because borrowers know that lenders can eliminate all of their diversifiable risk, they will not pay a risk premium to lenders to cover diversifiable risk. The asset beta measures the nondiversifiable risk associated with a particular investment compared to an investment in the entire market.[2] For an investment in the entire market, the risk premium is $r_m - r_f$, and therefore $\beta = 1$.

Investments that are riskier than investing in the entire market have asset betas greater than 1. Investments that are less risky than investing in the entire market have asset betas that are less than 1. Some investments are more highly correlated with movements in the stock market than others. If a 1 percent decrease in the value of the market, r_m, is associated with a 2 percent decrease in the return on a particular investment, then $\beta = 2$ for that investment. This investment has a very high positive correlation with the entire market and is quite risky. If another investment only decreases by 0.5 percent when r_m decreases by 1 percent, it has a $\beta = 0.5$. This investment is much less closely correlated with investments in the entire market and is much less risky.

Profits in the airline and steel industries are very sensitive to macroeconomic shocks, and therefore have relatively high asset betas. Profits in the ready-to-eat cereal, soaps and detergents, and food-processing industries are much less sensitive to macroeconomic shocks, and therefore have relatively low asset betas. Table 18.2 identifies estimated betas for the Walt Disney Company and some leading firms in the airline,

Table 18.2 **Some June 2003 Values of Beta**

Company	Beta
Walt Disney Company	0.99
US Airways	1.81
United Airlines	2.14
Northwest Airlines	1.74
U.S. Steel	1.51
AK Steel Holding Corp.	1.34
Procter & Gamble	0.01
Gillette	0.48
Clorox	0.41
Campbell Soup	0.43
H.J. Heinz	0.30
Kellogg	0.09
General Mills	0.04

---

[2] In statistics, β is technically defined as:

$$\beta = \frac{\text{cov}(r_i, r_m)}{\text{var}(r_m)},$$

where $\text{cov}(r_i, r_m)$ is the covariance of r_i and r_m, which is a measure of the linear association between r_i and r_m; and $\text{var}(r_m)$ is the variance of r_m, which measures the dispersion of r_m around its mean value. This ratio, and therefore β, measures the volatility of the investment i divided by the volatility of the entire market.

steel, personal care, and food-processing industries in June 2003. As expected, β is significantly greater than 1.00 for the airline and steel firms, but less than 0.50 for all the other firms except for the Walt Disney Company, which has a beta of 0.99.

If the β associated with a particular stock investment is known, it is possible to calculate the correct discount rate to use in calculating the *NPV* of that investment. The discount rate is:

$$\text{discount rate} = r_f + \beta(r_m - r_f) \qquad (18.10)$$

For a stock investment, calculating Equation 18.10 is straightforward. Over many years, the risk premium on the entire stock market, $r_m - r_f$, has averaged approximately 8 percent. If the current risk-free return on government bonds is 5 percent, then:

$$\text{discount rate} = 0.05 + \beta(0.08)$$

By following past trends in a stock's value, it is possible to calculate the stock's β. As Table 18.2 indicates, for U.S. Steel in June 2003, β = 1.51, and therefore the discount rate for an investment in U.S. Steel stock is:

$$\text{discount rate} = 0.05 + 1.51(0.08) = 0.1708$$

Investment in U.S. Steel's stock is quite risky and should be discounted at 17.08 percent. By comparison, Table 18.2 indicates that for General Mills, β = 0.04, and therefore the discount rate for an investment in General Mills stock is:

$$\text{discount rate} = 0.05 + 0.04(0.08) = 0.0532$$

Investment in General Mills' stock is nor very risky and should be discounted at only 5.32 percent.

DISCOUNTING A PARTICULAR CAPITAL PROJECT   Calculating β for a particular capital project is more complicated. For example, what β should Disney use to evaluate its restaurant project at the MGM Studios? It is virtually impossible for Disney to calculate β for investments in restaurants in theme parks. Economists have argued that the correct discount rate for a specific investment such as a theme park restaurant is the weighted average of the expected rate of return on the firm's stock and the interest rate paid on the firm's bonds. This measure provides an estimate of how risky investors believe it is to invest in Disney. If we know Disney's β, we can use the CAPM to calculate Disney's expected rate of return on its stock. According to *Marketguide.com*, in June 2003, Disney's β equaled 0.99. The expected return on Disney's stock was therefore:

$$r_{Disney} = 0.05 + 0.99(0.08) = 0.1292$$

If Disney paid an average interest rate of 7 percent on its bonds, and equity (stock) and debt (bond) financing were used equally by Disney to raise investment funds, then the correct discount rate for the restaurant investment would be:

$$\text{discount rate} = 0.5(0.1292) + 0.5(0.07) = 0.0996$$

If Disney raised only 25 percent of its funds through the sale of bonds, then:

$$\text{discount rate} = 0.75(0.1292) + 0.25(0.07) = 0.1144$$

Firms use the CAPM to determine the discount rate to use when calculating the net present value of an investment. According to the CAPM, the larger the firm's asset beta, the larger the firm's discount rate, and the less likely the firm is to undertake an investment.

The Stock Market and the Efficient Markets Hypothesis

Risk also affects individual investors' investment decisions, such as how much to invest in stocks compared to bonds. People who have never studied economics sometimes believe that economists know how to beat the stock market; that is, how to pick a select group of stocks that will on average earn a higher rate of return than the entire stock market. The truth is that economics can teach a great deal about the behavior of the stock market, but these lessons cannot make anyone a brilliant day trader (a person whose profession is to buy and sell their own stocks for personal profit). Quite to the contrary, the economists' lessons concerning the market should warn you of the perils of becoming a day trader. The overwhelming majority of economists believe that the stock market behaves as an **efficient market**, meaning that the stock market *immediately* and *instantaneously* incorporates all information into stock prices. According to the **efficient market hypothesis**, no financial analyst or guru can, on average, predict how a particular stock is going to perform relative to the market in a way that insures beating the market. Recall that at the beginning of this chapter you were asked if you should select stocks by using the services of a financial advisor, picking the stocks yourself, or picking stocks by throwing darts at a newspaper listing of stocks. As amazing as it may seem, the efficient market hypothesis suggests that, on average, throwing darts is as good as either of the other methods!

To understand why economists believe in the efficient market hypothesis, we begin by examining the underlying factors that determine the value of a share of stock. The stock value of a company should reflect the discounted value of the company's expected future flow of profit. In other words the value of a firm's stock should be:

$$\pi_{pv} = \frac{\pi_1}{(1 + r)} + \frac{\pi_2}{(1 + r)^2} + \frac{\pi_3}{(1 + r)^3} + \ldots + \frac{\pi_n}{(1 + r)^n} \qquad (18.11)$$

where π_t represents the firm's expected profit in time period t, r is the firm's discount rate, and π_{pv} represents the firm's present value of profit.

Many financial services firms contend that they can predict future stock prices by studying the fundamentals of the market. These firms use **fundamental analysis** to predict which stocks are good investments. Fundamental analysis firms examine every aspect of market conditions that might affect stock prices, from the overall macroeconomic environment to specific industry and firm conditions. A second method used to predict future stock prices is **technical analysis** of past stock behavior. Financial services firms that use technical analysis graph the past behavior of a stock's price and try to identify patterns to predict future behavior.

Both fundamental analysis and technical analysis seem like reasonable approaches to investing in the stock market, so why don't economists believe that these financial advisors can "beat the market"? The key to understanding the efficient markets hypothesis is that all information is *instantaneously* incorporated into a stock's price. Suppose, for example, that there is a rumor that Pfizer is developing a new and improved version of Viagra with fewer side effects and no risk of heart attack, at least not from the drug. All of Pfizer's expected future profit increases and as a result, the value of Pfizer's stock increases instantly as investors rush to purchase Pfizer shares. Fundamental analysis firms quickly send out a newsletter informing clients to buy Pfizer stock. Long before the clients receive the newsletter, however, the market will have instantaneously incorporated this news into the value of Pfizer's stock. By the time the clients buy the stock, the equilibrium price will have increased dramatically. None of the clients will be able to buy a share below the new higher equilibrium price. Who benefits from Pfizer's announcement?

---

efficient market

A market that incorporates all information immediately and instantaneously into the price of the good.

efficient market hypothesis

A theory predicting that no financial expert can, on average, predict how a particular stock or group of stocks is going to perform relative to the market in a way that ensures beating the rate of return on the entire stock market.

fundamental analysis

A method of predicting future stock prices by studying the fundamentals of the market; that is, studying all aspects of market conditions that might affect stock prices.

technical analysis

A method of predicting future stock prices by studying graphs and patterns of a stock's past price behavior to predict the stock's future price behavior.

Only those investors who were lucky enough to hold Pfizer stock before the rumor impacted the market.

Thus far we've debunked the fundamental analysts as market gurus, but what about the technical analysts? Can they beat the market? Once again, the instantaneous transmission of information defeats any attempt by the technical analysts to beat the market. Suppose technical analysts observe that investors are much more likely to buy stocks in the spring and summer and sell stocks in the fall and winter. These analysts inform their clients of this finding, and word quickly spreads throughout the entire financial services industry. Firms advise their clients to buy stocks in the fall and winter when prices are low, and sell stocks in the spring and summer when prices are high. As a result, increased demand drives stock prices up in the fall and winter, and decreased demand drives stock prices down in the spring and summer. Before long, the technical analysts would be unable to identify a spring–summer, fall–winter pattern to stock prices. Although this is a simple pattern, the efficient market hypothesis suggests that no matter how complicated the pattern, as soon as knowledge of the pattern is known, changes in demand cause the pattern to disappear.

The efficient market hypothesis implies that over an extended period of time, the present value of a company's future profit is the primary determinant of the value of a company's stock. Because short-term fluctuations in a company's stock price occur quite often, however, such fluctuations should be eliminated as the market incorporates accurate information into the present value of the firm's profit. As Application 18.3 shows,

---

COMMON ERROR 18.2 **Believing That Investors Can Regularly Beat the Market**

Many students taking their first economics course make the common error of assuming that by studying economics they will learn how to invest and become rich in the stock market. These students are greatly disappointed to learn that studying economics cannot make them any wiser when it comes to buying and selling stocks. Few theories have been more thoroughly tested than the efficient market hypothesis. The overwhelming majority of studies have confirmed the validity of the hypothesis. However, if the efficient market hypothesis is true, why are there so many talking heads on CNBC and CNN Financial telling us how to beat the market? The answer is surprisingly simple: luck. We generally don't hear from the unlucky financial advisors on CNBC, but they exist in numbers equal to the lucky ones. Consider how luck affects the market for financial services. If 100,000 people select a stock portfolio by throwing darts at the stock page of the newspaper, most of them will earn a normal rate of return, give or take a few percent. However, a few dart throwers will earn rates of return far higher than normal. Suppose one percent of our 100,000 dart throwers, or 1,000 people, earn very high rates of return. That creates 1,000 potential experts! These 1,000 "experts" sell their advice on tel-

evision or in market newsletters trying to convince others that they can beat the market.

If luck determines the markets winners, is the efficient market hypothesis a useless tool for investors? Not at all. There are some practical lessons to be learned from the efficient market hypothesis that can help prevent students from making some common errors. First, don't subscribe to investment newsletters. The information they contain is worthless by the time you receive the newsletter. This advice alone can save you hundreds or thousands of dollars. Second, because stocks are riskier than bonds, over the long term, stocks earn a higher rate of return than bonds. You should therefore consider investing in stocks as well as bonds. Third, because stock prices rise in the long run, and because it is virtually impossible to time the economic shocks that cause the market to rise or fall, many economists recommend a strategy of buying and holding stocks until you approach retirement age. The buy and hold strategy also limits the commissions you pay every time you buy or sell a share of stock. Fourth, if you can't beat the market, then invest in the market itself; that is, be highly diversified in a broad number of stocks. Finally, don't drop out of school or leave a good job to become a day trader.

▲▲▲ 18.3 APPLICATION   Booms and Busts in the Stock Market

If the stock market behaves as the efficient market hypothesis suggests, how could the NASDAQ rise to a value of 5,041, and then decline to 1,386 between March 2000 and September 2001? From time to time the stock market experiences speculative booms followed by downward corrections or busts. A speculative boom begins, rationally enough, when some economic shock results in optimism in the future of the economy, which leads investors to expect high future corporate profits. This happened in the 1920s, when the post-war economic expansion resulted in a market boom, and again in the mid-1990s when the Internet technological explosion resulted in another market boom. During every major speculative boom, investors expected stock prices to rise, so they rushed into the market to purchase stocks at "cheap" prices. The more people thought the market would rise, the more people wanted to buy stocks and the faster prices increased.

Historically, every time there has been a speculative boom, some event or series of events has occurred to destroy investors' optimism, and the market collapsed back to its normal, long-run growth path. In 1929, the collapse was precipitated by a decline in macroeconomic activity, combined with an unwise tightening of the credit market, which made it impossible for many investors to pay back loans they had taken out to purchase stocks. In March 2000, the decline was precipitated by the realization that many Internet companies had little or no hope of ever earning a profit. Investors began to sell high-tech stocks as fast as they possibly could, driving the NASDAQ down by *72.5 percent* in just 18 months. The Dow Jones Industrial Average (DJIA) fared a bit better, declining from 11,723 in January 2000 to 8,062 in September 2001. The decline in the NASDAQ, combined with a slowing economy that appeared headed toward recession, had led to a large decline in the DJIA even before the terrorist attacks of September 11, 2001. Those attacks worsened the downward spiral. Consistent with the efficient market hypothesis, when the market finally settled, the 10-year return on the DJIA was in line with the normal, long-run trend of the market.

short-term fluctuations in the stock market have moved the market dramatically off of its long-term trend, but historically, the market has always returned to that long-term trend.

▼▼▼ 18.4   Intertemporal Production Decisions: The Pricing of Exhaustible Natural Resources

In the first three sections of this chapter, we have seen that investment decisions must take time into consideration. In this section, we examine the importance of time in production decisions, such as the determination of a firm's optimal intertemporal pricing pattern. In Chapter 15, we simplified our analysis of limit pricing by ignoring time and discounting; however, a thorough understanding of the limit pricing model requires discounted future profit in order to compare the present value of future profit with current profit. In this section, we use the pricing of exhaustible natural resources such as oil, coal, natural gas, gold, silver, copper, and uranium to explain how time can have an important impact on firms' production decisions. Companies that own claims to natural resources must decide how to extract them over time. The firm's objective, of course, is to maximize the present value of profit. In this section, we analyze how to price exhaustible resources in both competitive and monopolized markets.

Competitive Markets for Exhaustible Resources

When analyzing a competitive market for an exhaustible natural resource, we maintain the basic assumptions of a perfectly competitive market: Buyers and sellers are price takers, the product is homogeneous, entry and exit is easy, and all economic agents have perfect information. Incorporating time into our analysis requires the discounting of future income and costs.

We consider a simple two-period model. Suppose that a gold mining company can sell its gold either today or next year. The marginal cost of mining a kilogram is c, and the price per kilogram in period t is p_t. If the current interest rate is r, then the mining company earns $(p_1 - c)$ on each kilogram sold this year and discounted income $(p_2 - c)/(1 + r)$ on each kilogram sold next year. There are three possible relationships between income earned this year and next year:

1. $(p_1 - c) > (p_2 - c)/(1 + r)$
2. $(p_1 - c) < (p_2 - c)/(1 + r)$
3. $(p_1 - c) = (p_2 - c)/(1 + r)$

Consider the company's incentives under each of these conditions. If $(p_1 - c) > (p_2 - c)/(1 + r)$, the gold is worth more if it is extracted and sold today than next year, and therefore, the company should sell all of its gold this year. If $(p_1 - c) < (p_2 - c)/(1 + r)$, the company should sell all of its gold next year. Finally, if $(p_1 - c) = (p_2 - c)/(1 + r)$, then the company should be indifferent between selling gold this year and next year.

If the market is competitive, consider what happens to the market price under each of the three possible relationships. If $(p_1 - c) > (p_2 - c)/(1 + r)$, then every company would attempt to sell all of their gold immediately, and p_1 would decrease as sellers attempted to unload their gold. If $(p_1 - c) < (p_2 - c)/(1 + r)$, no gold would be sold this year, and as a result p_1 would increase as buyers bid up the price. If $(p_1 - c) = (p_2 - c)/(1 + r)$, however, there is no reason for p_1 or p_2 to increase or decrease. Therefore, the equilibrium condition is $(p_1 - c) = (p_2 - c)/(1 + r)$, which can be written as:

$$(p_2 - c) = (1 + r)(p_1 - c) = (p_1 - c) + r(p_1 - c) \qquad (18.12)$$

From Equation 18.12, equilibrium requires that the net price, $(p - c)$, increases at the rate of interest r. This argument can be generalized for any time period t; therefore, $(p_{t+1} - c) = (p_t - c) + r(p_t - c)$. Figure 18.3 shows this equilibrium pattern for $p_0 = 200$, $c = 100$, and $r = 0.10$.

Figure 18.3 The Price of Exhaustible Resources
The net price of an exhaustible resource increases at the rate of interest. If the rate of interest is 10 percent, $c = 100$, and the current price = 200, then the net price rises by 10 percent per year.

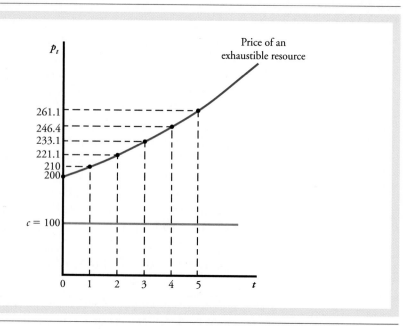

▲▲▲ **18.4 APPLICATION** The War in Iraq and the Price of Oil

In the months leading up to the 2003 war in Iraq, there was a great deal of fear that a war might seriously disrupt the world oil market. Many political and military experts believed that in the event of war, Saddam Hussein would blow up many of Iraq's oil wells as well as oil wells in Kuwait and Saudi Arabia. As a result, there was great concern that a war would cause future oil prices to increase dramatically.

Consider the impact of the pre-war expectations in the context of our model. Suppose that prior to the threat of war, the oil market was in equilibrium, so $(p_1 - c) = (p_2 - c)/(1 + r)$. The threat of war dramatically increased the expected future price of oil, which we identify as p_2^{war}. With a large increase in the expected future price of oil, $p_2^{war} > p_2$, and the market would no longer be in equilibrium, because $(p_1 - c) < (p_2^{war} - c)/(1 + r)$. According to our model, oil producers would want to sell all of their oil next year, and therefore would reduce their current supplies. Suppose the reduction in the current supply of oil increases the current price from p_1 to p_1^{war}. A new equilibrium would be established only when $(p_1^{war} - c) = (p_2^{war} - c)/(1 + r)$.

In spring 2003, the scenario played out exactly as predicted by the model. In the months leading up to the Iraq war, oil, gasoline, and heating oil prices increased dramatically. The average price per gallon of regular gasoline in the United States increased from less than $1.40 in December 2002 to over $1.70 in March 2003. It turned out that the war lasted only a few weeks, and there were no serious disruptions of oil supplies from the Middle East. After the war, expectations were that sanctions against Iraq would be lifted and Iraq would increase its oil production. As a result, there was a significant decrease in expected future oil prices and the scenario played out in reverse. With lower expected future oil prices, the current price of oil decreased dramatically.

But what about the "price equals marginal cost rule" for equilibrium in competitive markets; in this case, isn't that rule being violated by Equation 18.12? Although it's true that $p_t > c$, there is another important cost that must be considered: the opportunity cost of mining and selling gold *today*. Any gold sold this year cannot be sold in the future and can never be replenished. The opportunity cost of extracting an exhaustible natural resource is called the **user cost of production**. In our two-period model, the opportunity cost of selling one additional unit of gold this year is not selling it next year, so the mining company sacrifices $(p_2 - c)$ in net income next year by selling gold today. The present value of $(p_2 - c)$ received next year is $(p_2 - c)/(1 + r)$ today, which in equilibrium equals $(p_1 - c)$. The user cost of production at $t = 1$, therefore, is $(p_1 - c)$, and for any time t, the user cost of production is $(p_t - c)$. The sum of the marginal cost of production, c, and the marginal user cost of production, $(p_t - c)$, is $(c + (p_t - c))$, which equals p_t. Therefore, total marginal cost equals price.

user cost of production

The opportunity cost of extracting an exhaustible natural resource.

One common way of thinking about exhaustible resources is to compare resources in the ground to money in the bank. Because the resource price goes up at the rate of interest, firms can keep their exhaustible resources in the ground and earn an interest rate r on these resources exactly the way that firms and individuals can keep money in the bank and earn an interest rate r on the money. Essentially, gold in the ground is like money in a bank.

Monopoly Markets for Exhaustible Resources

If an exhaustible resource is monopolized or an effective cartel behaves like a monopolist, the equilibrium outcome changes, because price is greater than marginal revenue. When a monopolist considers whether to extract an additional unit this year or next, it compares $(MR_t - c)$ with $(MR_{t+1} - c)/(1 + r)$. Once again, there are three possibilities:

1. $(MR_t - c) > (MR_{t+1} - c)/(1 + r)$. In this case, the monopolist should extract more this year.

2. $(MR_t - c) < (MR_{t+1} - c)/(1 + r)$. In this case, the monopolist should extract less this year.
3. $(MR_t - c) = (MR_{t+1} - c)/(1 + r)$. In this case, the monopolist is extracting the correct amount this year, and therefore, this is the monopolist's equilibrium condition.

Equilibrium requires:

$$(MR_t - c) = \frac{(MR_{t+1} - c)}{(1 + r)}$$

$$(MR_{t+1} - c) = (MR_t - c) + r(MR_t - c) \tag{18.13}$$

With monopoly, net marginal revenue, $MR - c$, increases at the rate of interest.

How rapidly does the monopolist's net price increase over time if net marginal revenue increases at the rate of interest? The monopolist faces a downward-sloping demand curve. In Figure 18.4, we assume demand is $p_t = 500 - q_t$, $p_t = 300$, $q_t = 200$, and for simplicity, $c = 0$. It follows that $MR_t = 500 - 2q_t = 500 - 2(200) = 100$. If $r = 0.10$, net marginal revenue increases at 10 percent each year, and from Equation 18.12, with $c = 0$, $MR_{t+1} = MR_t + rMR_t = 100 + (0.10)(100) = 110$. If $MR_{t+1} = 110$, then $MR_{t+1} = 110 = 500 - 2q_{t+1}$, or $q_{t+1} = 250 - 55 = 195$, and $p_{t+1} = 500 - 195 = 305$. The percentage increase in the net price is $5/300 = 0.0167$, or only 1.67 percent. The percentage increase in the net price is less than the rate of interest.

Compared to a competitive industry, the monopolist charges a higher current price and increases its price much more slowly. Furthermore, by charging a high current price, the monopolist depletes the resource more slowly and serves the interest of conservation.

Figure 18.4 The Monopoly Price of an Exhaustible Resource
The monopolist originally produces $q_t = 200$, $MR_t = 100$, and $p_t = 300$. If $r = 0.10$, at $t = t + 1$, net marginal revenue increases by 10 percent to 110, but net price rises only by 1.67 percent to $p_{t+1} = 305$.

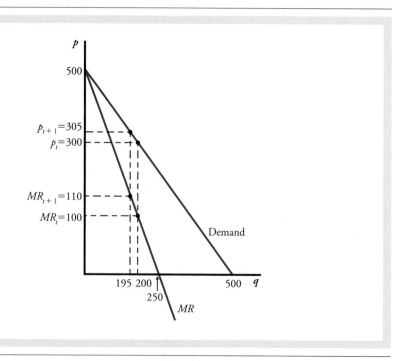

In the absence of changes in demand and supply conditions, net price increases at the rate of interest in competitive exhaustible resource industries.

In many real-world industries, however, net prices do not rise consistently at the rate of interest, because changes occur in demand and supply conditions. For example, if new reserves are found, supply increases and shifts the predicted price path downward. On the other hand, increases in demand shift the price path upward, while technological changes that reduce marginal extraction costs shift the price path downward. Of course, changes in the interest rate also shift the price path. Because changes in supply and demand conditions occur frequently, exhaustible resource prices typically do not follow the smooth paths predicted by our model.

We have seen in this chapter that optimal investment and production decisions require a consideration of time and risk. Time is incorporated into optimal decision-making by discounting future income and costs. Risk is incorporated through the value of the discount rate; the riskier the investment, the higher the discount rate. Failure to discount future income and costs often results in poor investment and production decisions.

Summary

1. To determine the present value of investments that yield profits into the distant future, it is necessary to discount future earnings and costs. The higher the discount rate, the lower the present value of the future profit stream. Discounting is also used to calculate the present value of a bond or perpetuity that promises to pay the holder a fixed annual payment for years into the future.

2. Firms often use either the net present value criterion (NPV) or the internal rate of return (IRR) criterion to calculate whether to undertake a specific investment. If the NPV of an investment is positive, then the discounted expected profit from the investment are greater than the discounted costs and the firm should undertake the investment. If the NPV is negative, the firm should not undertake the investment. The IRR for an investment is the discount rate for which the NPV equals zero. If the IRR is greater than the opportunity cost of capital for the investment, then the firm should undertake the investment; otherwise, it should not undertake the investment. In determining the NPV of an investment it is important to use either all real values or all nominal values for the flow of profit and the discount rate.

3. Risk can be classified as either diversifiable risk, which can be eliminated through diversification, or nondiversifiable risk, which cannot be eliminated through diversification. According to the capital asset pricing model (CAPM), investors demand a risk premium on a particular stock that is dependent on the risk of the particular stock and is proportional to the risk premium on the entire stock market. Specifically, investors demand a risk premium on that stock so that:

$$r_i = r_f + \beta(r_m - r_f)$$

where r_i is the expected return on the stock, and β, called the asset beta, is a measure of the nondiversifiable risk associated with the investment. Because the stock market behaves as an efficient market, the only way to beat the market, on average, is to be lucky.

4. In a competitive market for an exhaustible resource, the net price of the resource increases over time at a rate equal to the interest rate. In a monopolized market for

an exhaustible resource, the net price of the resource increases over time at a rate that is less than the interest rate. However, because many other factors affect the supply and demand for exhaustible resources over time, in the real world, prices do not behave with the smooth price patterns predicted by the model.

Self-Test Problems

1. Suppose that the city government of Youngstown, Ohio, is trying to decide whether to build a $15 million sports arena. The sports arena is expected to generate cash flow of $1.2 million per year for 20 years. After that point, the arena will most likely be outdated and torn down. However, members of the city council believe that they will be able to sell the land in 20 years for $2 million.

   a. Some city council members consider the investment to be low-risk and would like to use a discount rate of 0.04. What do these council members decide to do about the arena?

   b. Other city council members consider this investment quite risky and would like to use a discount rate of 0.08. What do these council members decide to do about the arena?

2. A company invests in a one-year bond that pays $900 for a $10,000 bond. At the end of the year, the company gets the $10,000 returned to them.

   a. What is the nominal interest rate?

   b. Assume the price index is 1 this year and inflation is 3.4 percent. What is the bond's real rate of return?

Questions and Problems for Review

1. Assume a firm's discount rate is 0.07.

   a. Calculate the present value of $100 payable in the following years: 1 year, 5 years, 10 years, 20 years, and 30 years.

   b. Compare your results to those in Table 18.1. For a given year, what happens to the present value as the discount rate increases? For a given discount rate, what happens to the present value as the number of years in the future that the payment is made increases?

2. Provide an explanation for the values in question 1. For example, what does it mean to say the present value of $100 five years from now is $71.30?

3. Your grandmother is a cautious person and chooses to invest in bonds only. She buys a bond that guarantees a payment of $80 for the next 10 years and a principal payment in the tenth year of $800.

   a. Calculate the discounted present value of the bond if the discount rate is 10 percent.

   b. Calculate the discounted present value of the bond if the discount rate is 15 percent.

   c. If your grandmother paid $800 for the bond initially, did she make a good investment? Explain how your answer might depend on the discount rate.

4. Assume that your grandmother invests in a perpetuity that pays $80 each year.

   a. Calculate the present value of the perpetuity if the discount rate is 10 percent.

   b. Calculate the present value of the perpetuity if the discount rate is 15 percent.

5. Consider the following bond listing from March 8, 2003.

Issuing Company	Annual Payment	Year of Maturity	Annual Payments/ Current Price	Volume of Sales	Closing Price	Change in Price
X	9.75	07	9.11	22	107	−1
Y	8.5	06	8.15	31	92	+1/2

a. Would the yield of the bond issued by company X be less than, greater than, or equal to 9.75 percent? Explain.

b. Would the yield of the bond issued by company Y be less than, greater than, or equal to 8.5 percent? Explain

6. Consider the information in question 5. Solve for the yield of the bond issued by company X. Solve for the yield of the bond issued by company Y.

7. Suppose that hypothetically Disney is deciding whether to build a theme park in Canada. The cost of the park would be $20 billion. The park is expected to generate $1.5 billion in revenue for 50 years. After 50 years, it is unclear what will happen. The shareholders of Disney consider this a pretty risky investment and want to be cautious. Thus, they will use a discount rate of 0.1. Determine whether Disney should build the theme park in Canada.

8. Consider question 7. Although the shareholders consider this investment to be risky, they are willing to compromise a bit on the discount rate used. What sort of discount rate compromise would have to be made in order to decide to invest in the project? (For example, does $r = 0.09$ work? What about $r = 0.08$?)

9. If Sally pays a nominal interest rate of 8 percent on her car loan and inflation is 3 percent, what is the real rate of Sally's car loan?

10. A company invests in a one-year bond that pays $8,000 for the year for a $100,000 bond. At the end of the year, it gets the $100,000 back.

a. What is the nominal interest rate?

b. Assume the price index is 1 this year and inflation is 2.8 percent. What is the bond's real rate of return?

11. Consider the Disney Canadian theme park example from question 7. Recall that Disney would choose not to invest given the discount rate of 10 percent. Suppose the Chair of Disney's Board realizes that Disney used real costs and revenues but the nominal rather than the real discount rate in calculating the NPV of the park.

a. How will this mistake affect the net present value of the investment?

b. Assume that the inflation rate is 3 percent. Calculate the net present value using the real discount rate. What should Disney do?

12. Give an example of diversifiable risk. Give an example of nondiversifiable risk.

13. Interpret what it means for US Airways to have a β value equal to 1.81. Interpret a β value equal to 0.09, such as the value for Kellogg's.

14. As of September 2002, the return on the entire stock market had fallen overall since September 11, 2001.

a. Calculate the discount rate an investor should use for US Airways stock if the return on the entire market is valued at -0.04 and the current risk-free return on government bonds is 5 percent.

b. Calculate the discount rate an investor should use for Kellogg's stock if the return on the market is valued at -0.04 and the current risk-free return on government bonds is 5 percent.

c. What does it mean to have a negative discount rate? Do you see problems with using only the information in the past year?

15. The return on the market used in question 14 is a short-term return. If an investor follows the chapter's advice of "buy and hold," then they can use the risk premium on the entire stock market, which is approximately 8 percent. Assume that the current risk-free return on government bonds is 5 percent.

a. Calculate the discount rate for Kellogg's and US Airways in this case.

b. Discuss the differences in the two discount rates calculated. Which investment is less risky? Is this verified by the β value?

16. Let's assume that the return on risk-free government bonds equals 0.04 and that the risk premium on the entire stock market is 8 percent. US Steel's β = 1.51 and it is trying to decide whether to build another plant. Assume that US Steel pays an average interest rate of 5 percent on its bonds. Assume that stocks and bonds are going to be used equally for financing the project. What value of the discount rate should US Steel use in order to evaluate this investment?

17. Consider the same example as in question 16, but this time consider that US Steel plans to use 60 percent stock financing and only 40 percent bond financing to finance the investment. What discount rate should the firm use to evaluate the investment? Given this discount rate, would you say the investment has some risk involved?

18. Explain what is meant by a speculative boom. Does the existence of periodic speculative booms negate

the accuracy of the efficient markets hypothesis? Explain.

19. Analyze the discovery of more gold on the user cost of production and the net price of gold over time.

20. A commonly used example of monopoly is De Beers diamonds. De Beers has primary control of diamonds as an input. How might it be good for society that diamonds are controlled by a monopolist?

 ## Internet Exercises

Visit *http://www.myeconlab.com/waldman* for this chapter's Web exercises. Answer real-world economics problems by doing research on the Internet.

Part 6 General Equilibrium, Information, Externalities, and Public Goods

Chapter 19
General Equilibrium and Efficiency

In just six months, from October 1973 to March 1974, the Organization of Petroleum Exporting Countries (OPEC) increased the official price of a barrel of oil by over 400 percent. Furthermore, in 1979, the price of oil again increased dramatically as a result of the Iranian revolution. On both occasions, these huge price increases set off a chain reaction of price changes in other markets. As the price of oil increased, the supply curves for gasoline and heating oil decreased significantly, resulting in an increase in the equilibrium price and a decrease in the equilibrium quantities of gasoline and heating oil. This large increase in the price of gasoline in turn resulted in a large decrease in the demand for large gas-guzzling automobiles and an increase in the demand for small, fuel-efficient automobiles. Meanwhile, the large increase in the price of heating oil resulted in an increase in the demand for wood stoves and wood. In addition, this increase in the price of oil resulted in an increase in the demand and price of coal, because coal is an excellent substitute for oil in the generation of electricity. As the price of electricity increased, the cost of production for most manufactured goods increased. This, in turn, resulted in a large general price increase for manufactured goods. These large oil price shocks ultimately resulted in many other price changes.

Up to this point in the text, we have been concerned primarily with how a change in demand, costs, or market structure affects a particular market. For example, how a decrease in the supply of oil affects the price of oil, or how the imposition of a minimum wage affects the labor market. In this chapter, we advance our analysis to consider how a change in demand, costs, or market structure in one industry can have an impact on many other industries. Furthermore, we will explore how a market economy adjusts to a change in one

Learning Objectives

After reading Chapter 19, you will have learned:

➤ The difference between a partial and general equilibrium analysis of an economic shock, and when it is appropriate to use each type of analysis.

➤ How to use an Edgeworth box diagram to analyze Pareto efficiency in exchange, and the first and second theorems of welfare economics.

➤ How to use an Edgeworth box diagram to analyze Pareto efficiency in production, and how Pareto efficiency in production is related to the production possibilities curve.

➤ The mathematical conditions for general equilibrium and Pareto efficiency in a perfectly competitive economy.

➤ How factors such as monopoly power, selective excise taxes, and externalities prevent an economy from achieving Pareto efficiency.

Featured Applications

➤ 19.1 Application Low-Carb Diets and General Equilibrium

➤ 19.2 Application Pareto Efficiency and Halloween Candy

➤ 19.3 Application Economic Inefficiency in the Former Soviet Union

➤ 19.4 Application How the Economy Adjusts to a Change in Tastes

➤ 19.5 Application The Gains from Trade Revisited

market and is able to move from one efficient equilibrium to a new efficient equilibrium. We will also see that in a general equilibrium framework, factors such as monopoly power, taxes, restrictions on free trade, and pollution can prevent an economy from achieving efficiency. We begin by examining the difference between partial equilibrium and general equilibrium analysis.

▼▼▼ 19.1 Moving from Partial Equilibrium to General Equilibrium

partial equilibrium analysis

The impact of a change in supply or demand in one market only—the market directly impacted.

general equilibrium analysis

The impact of a price change in one market on the equilibrium prices and quantities in all other markets.

With few exceptions, analysis in the previous chapters has been partial equilibrium analysis. **Partial equilibrium analysis** considers the impact of a change in supply or demand in one market only. The *ceteris paribus* assumption, by holding all other things constant, is the classic way that economists announce they are engaged in a partial equilibrium analysis. In comparison to partial equilibrium analysis, **general equilibrium analysis** considers the impact of a price change in one market on the equilibrium prices and quantities in all other markets.

The General Equilibrium Impact of an Economic Shock

To better understand the difference between partial equilibrium and general equilibrium analysis, consider this: suppose the U.S. Surgeon General announced that scientists are convinced that eating two ounces of soy protein a day greatly reduces the risk of virtually all types of cancer. Partial equilibrium analysis of the impact of this announcement on the soybean market would assume that all other things are held constant, and conclude that the demand for soybeans would increase, which would cause an increase in the equilibrium price and quantity of soybeans. Partial equilibrium analysis would end there. General equilibrium analysis would recognize the myriad other effects of this announcement, such as a decrease in the demand for beef, fish, pork, chicken, turkey, and peanut butter. General equilibrium analysis would also recognize that the demand for Asian food restaurants would also increase, as would the demand for Boca burgers and Morningstar Farms soy products. In this chapter, we consider how the conditions for general equilibrium differ from the conditions for partial equilibrium.

Beef, pork, chicken, and fish are excellent protein substitutes for each other. In Figure 19.1, these markets are initially in equilibrium where the dark-red supply curves intersect the dark-blue demand curves. The initial equilibrium prices are p_b = \$7.00, p_c = \$3.00, p_p = \$4.00, and p_f = \$10.00. Each of the four dark-blue demand curves is drawn *ceteris paribus*; that is, assuming that prices in the other three markets are constant. For example, the demand curve D_{b0} in the beef market assumes that p_c = \$3.00, p_p = \$4.00, and p_f = \$10.00, and D_{c0} in the chicken market assumes that p_b = \$7.00, p_p = \$4.00, and p_f = \$10.00, etc.

Various types of major economic shocks cause changes not only in those markets most directly affected by the shock, but in many other markets as well. Consider, for example, the general equilibrium impact of the hypothetical discovery of mad cow disease in cattle in the United States. Mad cow disease is an always-fatal cattle disease that causes large holes to develop in a steer's or cow's brain. If a human ate beef infected with mad cow disease, he or she might develop the same fatal disorder. Suppose mad cow disease is discovered in a steer in Iowa. As a result, many cattle ranchers are required to destroy their entire herds; in Figure 19.1(a) the supply curve for beef shifts dramatically

Figure 19.1 General Equilibrium
Initially, the four markets are in general equilibrium, with p_b = $7.00, p_c = $3.00, p_p = $4.00, and p_f = $10.00. With the discovery of mad cow disease in the U.S., the supply and demand for beef both decrease to S_{b1} and D_{b1} and p_b increases to $12.00. The increase in the price of beef results in an increase in the demand for chicken, pork, and fish, increasing prices to p_c = $4.00, p_p = $4.75, and p_f= $10.50. As the prices of chicken, pork, and fish increase, there is a *feedback effect* on the beef market, increasing demand for beef to D_{b2} and increasing the price of beef to $12.50. This effect itself causes a further increase in the demand for chicken, pork, and fish. Eventually, a new general equilibrium is attained with p_b = $12.80, p_c = $4.60, p_p = $5.00, and p_f= $10.75.

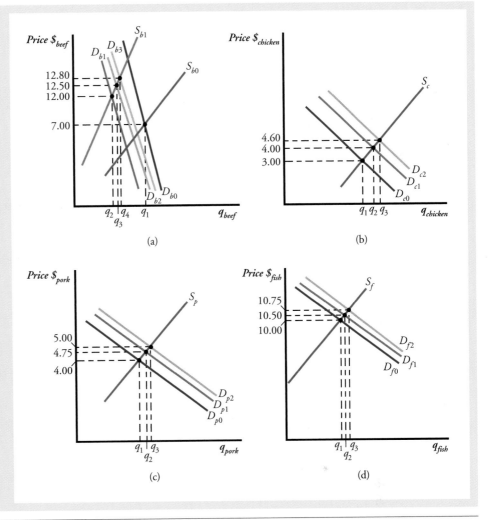

(a)

(b)

(c)

(d)

left to the light-red supply curve S_{b1}. This discovery also decreases demand to D_{b1} because of a change in tastes, as consumers' health concerns associated with eating beef increase. Partial equilibrium analysis would end there. The new equilibrium price of beef would be $12.00.

General equilibrium analysis considers the impact of the change in the price of beef and the change in tastes due to mad cow disease on the chicken, pork, and fish markets. As a result of the increased price of a substitute good and the lower health concerns associated with eating chicken, pork, or fish compared to beef, the demand curves for each of these substitute products would increase to the medium-blue curves D_{c1}, D_{p1}, and D_{f1} in panels (b), (c), and (d) respectively. These new demand curves assume that the price of beef is $12.00. The new equilibrium prices are p_c = $4.00, p_p = $4.75, and p_f = $10.50. The impact of the change in the beef market on each of these other markets is called a *spillover effect*. A **spillover effect** refers to a change in one market's equilibrium as a result of a change in another market's equilibrium.

Given these new prices for chicken, pork, and fish, the demand curve for beef would no longer be D_{b1} in panel (a), because that demand curve was drawn on the assumption that the prices of chicken, pork, and fish were $3.00, $4.00, and $10.00 respectively.

spillover effect

A change in one market's equilibrium as a result of a change in another market's equilibrium.

feedback effect

A change in market A's equilibrium, which results from a change in another market's equilibrium, which was caused initially by a change in market A.

Given the new higher prices for these substitute products, the demand curve for beef increases to the demand curve D_{b2} in panel (a) and the price of beef increases to $12.50. The shift in the demand for beef from D_{b1} to D_{b2} is called a *feedback effect*. A **feedback effect** refers to a change in market A's equilibrium—here the beef market equilibrium—that results from a change in another market's equilibrium—here the equilibriums in the chicken, pork, and fish markets—that was caused by an initial change in market A.

With the price of beef increasing to $12.50, the demand curves for chicken, pork, and fish in panels (b), (c), and (d) once again shift to the right to the light-blue demand curves, and the prices of chicken, pork, and fish all increase. These price changes in turn cause another shift to the right in the demand curve for beef to D_{b3} in panel (a). Eventually, the four markets reach a new general equilibrium where the demand curves are D_{b3}, D_{c2}, D_{p2}, and D_{f2}, respectively, and where the *ceteris paribus* assumption holds once again. In the new general equilibrium, the price of beef is $12.80 in panel (a) and the demand curve for beef, D_{b3}, is drawn on the assumption that $p_c = \$4.60$, $p_p = \$5.00$, and $p_f = \$10.75$, while the demand curve for chicken D_{c2} in panel (b) is drawn on the assumption that $p_b = \$12.80$, $p_p = \$5.00$, and $p_f = \$10.75$, etc.

▲▲▲ 19.1 APPLICATION   Low-Carb Diets and General Equilibrium

For almost 40 years the late Dr. Robert Atkins was the bane of America's nutritionists. Atkins advocated a diet very low in carbohydrates, such as bread, pasta, potatoes, and rice, and very high in proteins and fats, such as beef, chicken, fish, butter, mayonnaise, and bacon. Most doctors and dieticians still consider the Atkins Diet a prescription for heart disease and an early death. Instead of this diet, mainstream medicine advocates a diet low in fat and protein and high in carbohydrates. Beginning in 1999, with a *Time* article entitled, "The Low-Carb Diet Craze," however, several articles appeared questioning the conventional wisdom among doctors. The *New York Times Magazine* published an article, "What if Fat Doesn't Make You Fat?" on July 7, 2002, that provided some evidence of successful diet and health outcomes on low-carbohydrate diets. *Consumer Reports* reported (almost apologetically) in an issue devoted to diets that—much to the magazine's surprise—a survey of readers reported far more success on the Atkins Diet than on any low-fat diet. These articles were followed up by the results of a six-month study from Duke University and two articles in the *Journal of the American Medical Association* that reported better diet and health outcomes among a group of low-carbohydrate dieters than a control group of low-fat dieters.

We can analyze the direct economic impact of this new information on the low-carbohydrate diet book market using a partial equilibrium analysis. The demand for all of these books increased dramatically, and suddenly the top four non-fiction books on the *New York Times* bestseller list were *Dr. Atkins' New Diet Revolution*, *The Carbohydrate Addict's Diet Book*, *Protein Power*, and *Sugar Busters*. A partial equilibrium analysis might end there, by noting that there was a large increase in the demand for low-carbohydrate diet books. But a partial equilibrium analysis would explain little about the economic impact of the low-carbohydrate diet craze.

Using a general equilibrium analysis, we learn that the low-carbohydrate diet fad not only increased the demand for low-carb diet books, but also the demand for beef, pork, chicken, and fish, and decreased the demand for pasta, bread, and bagels. Upscale restaurants in New York City were being told to hold the bread, but add the bacon. The changing nature of demand caused new products and new companies to emerge. Since 2000 an estimated 800-plus new products making a no-carb or low-carb claim were introduced into the market. Companies introduced everything from low-carb candy and meal bars to low-carb bread, muffins, and pasta. The consumption of eggs, sausage, and bacon reached a 10-year high in 2003; and after many years of declining beef sales, the demand for beef increased by 1.6 percent in 1999, and the demand for pork increased by 2.3 percent. As this example shows, a general equilibrium analysis is necessary to have any true sense of the scope of the impact of this change in eating habits on the American economy.

When to Use General Equilibrium Analysis

Deciding whether to use partial or general equilibrium analysis depends on the particular change and market being analyzed. Partial equilibrium analysis is commonly used to investigate a change in a market in which the impact on other markets is either relatively unimportant or so widely dispersed that there is little impact on any particular market. For example, when the government increases the excise tax on cigarettes, it probably has little impact on any other markets. Because the demand for cigarettes is highly inelastic, the tax will result in a higher price and a slightly lower quantity demanded for cigarettes. Perhaps the tax will increase the demand for nicotine substitute products such as NicoDerm. However, the decision whether to quit smoking cigarettes is probably not based primarily on price for most consumers. Any other impact of the cigarette tax is likely to be minimal. In this case, partial equilibrium analysis is sufficient for analyzing the effects of the cigarette tax.

Taxes levied on other industries might have a greater general equilibrium impact. For example, if the government were to impose a 10 percent tax on airline tickets, it would significantly affect not only the airline industry, but also many other markets. Such a tax would decrease the demand and price for tourist destinations such as Las Vegas, Hawaii, and Disney World. Conversely, it might increase the demand and price for tourist destinations such as Vermont, Williamsburg, Virginia, San Francisco, and Disneyland, which are a short drive from the nation's major population centers. The tax would also reduce the demand and price for jet fuel, but increase the demand and price for gasoline. These impacts would be large enough that they should be considered when analyzing the impact of an airline ticket tax.

In this airline ticket tax example, the implications of a partial equilibrium analysis differ from the implications of a general equilibrium analysis. Partial equilibrium analysis suggests a large, permanent decline in airline traffic as a result of the tax—and that's as far as it goes. A general equilibrium analysis, however, recognizes the feedback effects of the tax on the airline as well as other related industries. For example, as a result of the tax, the price of gasoline increases relative to the price of jet fuel, because more people are opting to drive and fewer are opting to fly. This increases the relative cost of driving and decreases the relative cost of flying, and thereby offsets some of the direct impact of the tax. Furthermore, the increase in hotel rates in tourist destinations such as Vermont and Disneyland, combined with a decrease in hotel rates at more distant tourist destinations such as Las Vegas and Orlando, increases the demand for flying to more distant but now relatively cheaper tourist destinations such as Las Vegas and Disney World. Failure to consider these effects might considerably overestimate the negative impact of the tax on the airline industry.

19.2 Pareto Efficiency in Exchange

The concept of Pareto efficiency appeared in several previous chapters. Recall that a Pareto improvement is any change within society that makes at least one person better off without hurting anyone. Any potential Pareto improvement not undertaken represents a wasted opportunity to make someone better off. Anytime we can identify an unexploited Pareto improvement, we are therefore operating inefficiently from society's point of view. A Pareto-efficient situation is one in which all possible Pareto improvements have been exhausted.

The elimination of inefficiency within firms and households is necessary, but not sufficient, for Pareto efficiency. Every individual firm, household, and government

Parents of young children who go trick-or-treating might observe an excellent example of a movement from a Pareto-inefficient equilibrium to a Pareto-efficient equilibrium every Halloween. For many years, my two children returned home after hours of trick-or-treating and immediately dumped all their candy onto the floor in front of them. For the next ten minutes, they would exchange candy. My daughter would inevitably attempt to take advantage of her little brother, but he was quite savvy in the ways of candy, so she had no success attempting to sway him away from his favorite treats. First, a box of Junior Mints was exchanged for a Twizzler, then a 3 Musketeers bar was traded for a Kit-Kat bar, then a red lollipop for a green lollipop. Before too long, the piles in front of each child bore no resemblance to the piles they had started with.

My children had, in fact, behaved in an economically rational manner. They were busy exhausting each and every possible Pareto-improving trade. Any trade that made one of them better off without hurting the other was completed, and most of the trades made them both better off. In the end, they each looked contentedly at their piles of candy knowing that further trades would not improve their situation. Each ended up with more of the types of candy they liked most. They had achieved Pareto efficiency.

agency could eliminate all inefficiency under its direct control, yet there might still be Pareto inefficiency, because there might be a reallocation of resources between firms, or between one set of households and another, that would qualify as a Pareto improvement.

The Edgeworth Box Diagram

To better understand how trade can improve economic efficiency, we begin with a simple pure-exchange economy with two consumers, Monica and Rachel, and two goods, food (F) and clothing (C). Monica's and Rachel's utility functions are $U_M = U_M(F,C)$ and $U_R = U_R(F,C)$ respectively. At this point, we are not concerned with how or by whom the goods were produced, but simply how they are initially allocated. The entire exchange economy consists of 200 units of food and 100 units of clothing. Initially, Monica and Rachel divide the food and clothing equally, so each has 100 units of food and 50 units of clothing.

Edgeworth box diagram

A rectangular diagram that depicts either all of the possible allocations of two goods between two consumers, or all of the possible allocations of two inputs between two production goods.

Figure 19.2 identifies this initial equilibrium as point A in an *Edgeworth box diagram,* named after political economist F. Y. Edgeworth. An **Edgeworth box diagram** depicts either all of the possible allocations of two goods between two consumers, or all of the possible allocations of two inputs between two production goods. Using an Edgeworth box diagram, it is possible to draw the indifference curves for both Monica and Rachel on one graph. Monica's indifference curves are the red indifference curves using point G as the origin for her utility function and measuring Monica's food on the x-axis and her clothing on the y-axis. If Monica held all 200 units of food and 100 units of clothing, she would be consuming at point H. At point H, Rachel would have no food or clothing. *Now turn your textbook upside down.* At point H, Rachel has no goods, so this is the origin for her utility function. Rachel's indifference curves are the blue indifference curves using point H as the origin for her utility function and measuring Rachel's food on the x-axis and Rachel's clothing on the y-axis. As we move along Rachel's x-axis she consumes more food and simultaneously Monica consumes less food. Similarly, as we move along Rachel's y-axis, she consumes more clothing and Monica consumes less clothing. *Now turn your textbook right-side up.* At point A, Monica and Rachel each consume 100 units of food and 50 units of clothing.

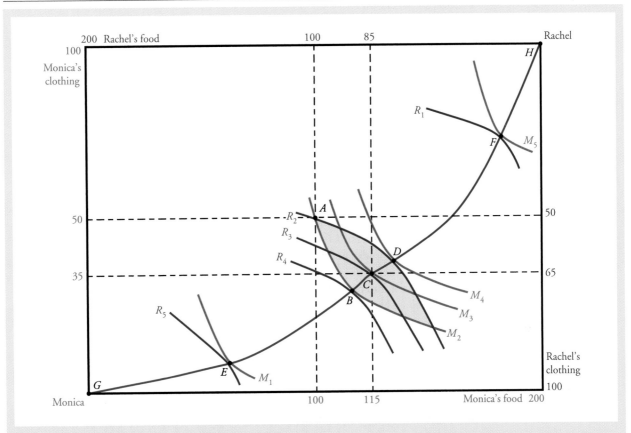

Figure 19.2 An Edgeworth Box and Efficiency in Exchange
If the goods were initially divided equally between Monica and Rachel, the women would consume at point *A*. By completing a Pareto-efficient trade that moves them into the orange shaded area, both Monica and Rachel increase their utility, and are better off. The only Pareto-efficient points are the points of tangency between Monica's and Rachel's indifference curves. These points make up the green contract curve.

Is point *A* a Pareto-efficient point? At point *A*, Monica's level of utility is M_2 and Rachel's level of utility is R_2. Suppose Monica agreed to give Rachel some clothing in exchange for some food. Because Monica and Rachel are such good friends, Monica trades by moving along her red indifference curve M_2. As Monica trades along indifference curve M_2, her utility remains unchanged, so Monica is equally well off as she was at point *A*. Rachel's utility increases continuously, however, as she moves along indifference curve M_2 from point *A* to point *B*. Each of the movements along M_2 from point *A* to point *B* results in a Pareto improvement, because Rachel is made better off while Monica is no worse off. Any movement along M_2 beyond point *B*, however, begins to reduce Rachel's utility, and therefore, would be Pareto-inefficient. At point *B*, any movement along M_2 in either direction reduces Rachel's utility without changing Monica's utility, and therefore, is Pareto-inefficient. The point *B* represents a Pareto-efficient point, because any movement away from point B in any direction makes either Monica or Rachel, or both of them, worse off. For example, moving from point *B* toward point *C* makes Monica better off but Rachel worse off.

Now suppose that beginning at point *A*, Rachel agrees to give Monica some food in exchange for some clothing by moving along her blue indifference curve R_2. As Rachel trades along indifference curve R_2, her utility remains unchanged. Monica's utility increases, however, as we move along indifference curve R_2 from point A to point D. Each of the movements along R_2 from point A to point D results in a Pareto improvement, because Monica is made better off while Rachel is no worse off. Any movement along R_2 beyond point D reduces Monica's utility, and therefore would be Pareto-inefficient. At point D, any movement along R_2 in either direction reduces Monica's utility without changing Rachel's utility, and therefore is Pareto-inefficient. The point D represents another Pareto-efficient point, because any movement away from point D in any direction makes either Monica or Rachel, or both of them, worse off. For example, moving from point D toward point C makes Rachel better off but Monica worse off.

So far we have identified two Pareto-efficient points, B and D. The major geometric characteristic of both points B and D is that Monica's indifference curve is tangent to Rachel's indifference curve. Beginning at point A, however, Monica and Rachel can make an *infinite* number of possible Pareto-improving trades. Any movement from point A to any of the infinite number of points in the orange shaded area results in an increase in utility for *both* Monica and Rachel. For example, if Monica trades 15 units of clothing to Rachel in exchange for 15 units of food, the new consumption point is C. At point C, Monica is on indifference curve M_3 and Rachel is on indifference curve R_3. Both Monica and Rachel are better off at point C than at point A. Is point C Pareto-efficient? The two indifference curves are tangent at point C, and therefore, point C is another Pareto-efficient point.

How many Pareto efficient points exist in the Edgeworth box in Figure 19.2? Any point of tangency between one of Monica's indifference curves and one of Rachel's indifference curves is a Pareto-efficient point. In Figure 19.2, the green curve represents the locus of all points of tangency between two indifference curves. There are an infinite number of tangencies in the Edgeworth box diagram. In fact, there are an infinite number of tangencies on the green curve segment connecting points B and D or points B and C. All of the points on the green curve are Pareto-efficient and together these points make up the **contract curve**, defined as the locus of Pareto-efficient points in an Edgeworth box diagram.

contract curve

The locus of all Pareto-efficient points in an Edgeworth box diagram.

In addition to the green contract curve, there are two other Pareto-efficient points in the Edgeworth box: points G and H. At point G, Rachel has all the food and clothing and Monica has nothing. Any movement away from point G makes Monica better off but makes Rachel worse off and is therefore Pareto-inefficient. Similarly, at point H, Monica has all the food and clothing and Rachel has nothing. Any movement away from point H makes Rachel better off but makes Monica worse off. We may all agree that points G and H seem unfair; however, they are Pareto-efficient points. Pareto efficiency, therefore, has nothing to do with society's sense of fairness and equity.

A Mathematical Approach to Pareto Efficiency

Figure 19.3 reproduces Figure 19.2 with one addition: Figure 19.3 identifies Monica's and Rachel's marginal rates of substitution (*MRS*) at point A. Recall that the *MRS* at a point on an indifference curve equals the absolute value of the slope of the indifference curve at that point. For Monica, at point A, $MRS_M = |-MU_F/MU_C| = 3$. For Rachel, you might want to turn your book upside down to see that at point A, $MRS_R = |-MU_F/MU_C| = 1/2$.

At point A, Monica is the food lover and is willing to trade 3 units of clothing for one unit of food. Rachel is the clothing lover and is willing to trade only 1/2 unit of clothing for 1 unit of food. Suppose Monica offers Rachel one unit of clothing in

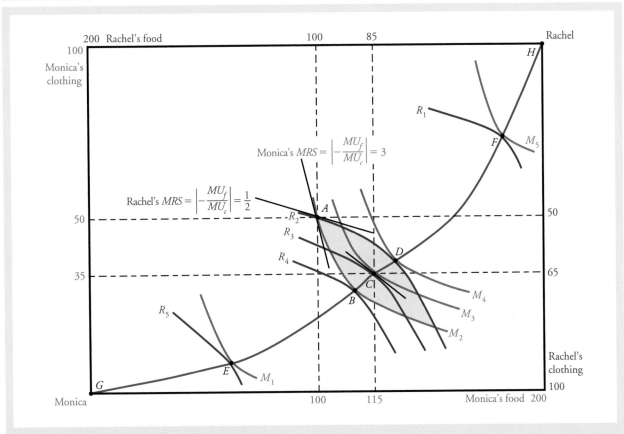

Figure 19.3 Disequilibrium in the Edgeworth Box
At point A, Monica's MRS is 3 and Rachel's MRS is 1/2. Because their marginal rates of substitution are not equal, point A is not Pareto-efficient. They both have the same MRS anywhere along the green contract curve where their indifference curves are tangent. This is the mathematical condition for Pareto efficiency.

exchange for one unit of food. This trade would make Monica better off, because she would be willing to trade up to 3 units of clothing to get a unit of food. Therefore, if Monica can get one unit of food for one unit of clothing she is better off. Should Rachel accept the offer? Rachel would be no worse off if she received 1/2 unit of clothing in exchange for a unit of her food, and therefore, if she receives one entire unit of clothing in exchange for a unit of food, she is better off. Rachel should accept the trade. Using the same reasoning, if Monica offers Rachel more than 1/2 unit of clothing in exchange for a unit of food, Rachel would be better off. Furthermore, as long as Monica sacrifices less than 3 units of clothing to obtain a unit of food, she will be better off. As long as the terms of trade are between 3 units of clothing for one unit of food and 1/2 unit of clothing for one unit of food, both Monica and Rachel will benefit from the trade. This reasoning can be generalized to any point in the Edgeworth box where $MRS_M \neq MRS_R$. As long as their marginal rates of substitution differ, it is possible to make both Monica and Rachel better off by trading.

Returning to point A; suppose Monica trades 15 units of clothing for 15 units of Rachel's food, so that the new consumption equilibrium point is at C on the contract curve. At point C, $MRS_M = MRS_R = \left| -MU_F/MU_C \right|$. This is the condition for Pareto efficiency. This reasoning holds no matter how many consumers are in our exchange economy. If we added a third consumer, Phoebe, to our economy, then Pareto efficiency in exchange would require that $MRS_M = MRS_R = MRS_P = |-MU_F/MU_C|$. For any pure exchange economy with n consumers:

$$MRS_1 = MRS_2 = MRS_3 = \ldots = MRS_n = \left| -\frac{MU_F}{MU_C} \right| \qquad (19.1)$$

Consumer Equilibrium: Adding Prices to the Model

In an exchange economy with many consumers, it would be awkward, if not impossible, to have each consumer running around attempting to trade with every other consumer. Market economies instead rely on prices to achieve Pareto efficiency. Each consumer and producer is free to buy or sell goods at their current prices. Figure 19.4, in which we again begin at point A, illustrates this situation. Even if there are many other consumers in this economy, Monica and Rachel will have to move from point A to a point on the contract curve if the economy is to achieve Pareto efficiency.

Assume that there are 2,000 consumers in our simple exchange economy and that 1,000 of them have tastes that are identical to Monica's and 1,000 have tastes that are

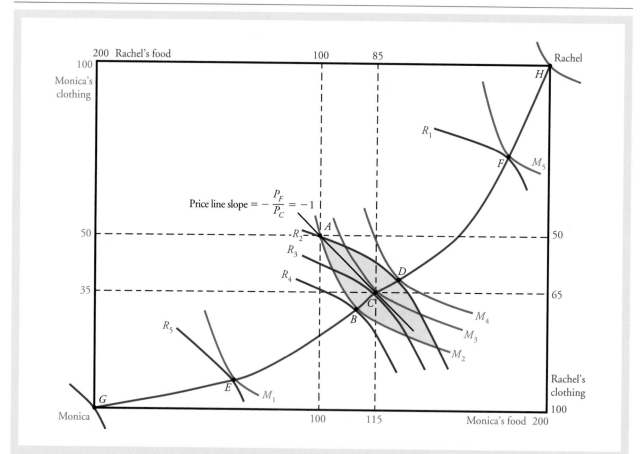

Figure 19.4 Prices and Efficiency in Exchange
If Monica and Rachel are initially at point A and the price ratio is $P_F/P_C = 1$, Monica can sell 15 units of clothing and use the income to buy 15 units of food, while Rachel can sell 15 units of food and use the income to buy 15 units of clothing. The new equilibrium would be Pareto-efficient at point C.

identical to Rachel's. Suppose the price ratio is $P_F/P_C = 1$. Starting at point A, Monica and Rachel can buy and sell food and clothing along the linear budget constraint connecting points A and C. To increase her utility, Monica can sell some of her clothing and buy food. Rachel, on the other hand, can sell some food and buy clothing. Suppose Monica sells 15 units of clothing for $15 and then uses the $15 to buy 15 units of food. Monica can then move from point A to point C. Notice that point C maximizes Monica's utility at M_3, given her budget constraint. Similarly, Rachel can sell 15 units of food for $15 and use the $15 to buy 15 units of clothing. Rachel will then move from point A to point C. At point C, Rachel's utility is maximized at R_3, given her budget constraint.

Did we rig this result by setting the price ratio equal to one, and thereby insuring that Monica and Rachel could trade and move from point A to point C? In one sense the result was rigged because the price ratio insured that both the food and clothing markets were in equilibrium—supply equals demand. With a price ratio equal to one, the food market is in equilibrium, because the quantity that each Rachel-type consumer wants to supply, 15 units, equals the quantity that each Monica-type consumer demands. With 1,000 Monica types and 1,000 Rachel types, the total quantity supplied equals 15,000 and the total quantity demanded equals 15,000 for both food and clothing.

In another sense, however, the result was not rigged. In Figure 19.5, suppose the price ratio equals 3, with $P_F = 3$ and $P_C = 1$. Starting at point A, we know that Monica's marginal rate of substitution at point A equals 3, and therefore, for Monica:

$$MRS_M = \left| -\frac{MU_F}{MU_C} \right| = 3 = \left| -\frac{P_F}{P_C} \right|$$

Monica is already in equilibrium at point A because the MRS_M equals the price ratio, and therefore Monica is not willing to buy or sell either good at a price ratio $P_F/P_C = 3$. At a price ratio of $P_F/P_C = 3$, Rachel would want to sell food and use the proceeds to buy clothing. Unfortunately for Rachel, however, Monica is not willing to buy food or sell clothing at that price ratio, and Rachel has nobody to sell to or buy from. At a price ratio of three, Rachel's demand for clothing would result in an excess demand for clothing, and her supply of food would result in an excess supply of food. Given the excess demand for clothing, the price of clothing would increase, and given the excess supply of food, the price of food would decrease. If the price of food decreases to two and the price of clothing increases to two, then the price ratio is once again equal to one and Monica and Rachel will achieve equilibrium by moving along the budget line with a slope of -1 from point A to point C.

Prices might not adjust immediately to their final equilibrium levels. For example, suppose the excess supply of food resulted in a price decrease for food from $3 to $2.50, and the excess demand for clothing resulted in a price increase from $1 to $1.25. The new price ratio would be two. At a price ratio equal to two, Monica would be willing to sell some clothing and buy some food, and Rachel would be willing to sell some food and buy some clothing. The markets, however, will only be in equilibrium if the quantity supplied equals the quantity demanded. Otherwise, prices will adjust further in order to move the markets closer to their final equilibriums. Only when both markets are in equilibrium will there be no further price changes.

The First Theorem of Welfare Economics

Our finding that prices will adjust to move consumers to the contract curve is one of the most important results of general equilibrium analysis. What we have found is that starting at point A in Figure 19.2, with only two consumers, Monica and Rachel, the final equilibrium will be somewhere on the green contract curve between point B and

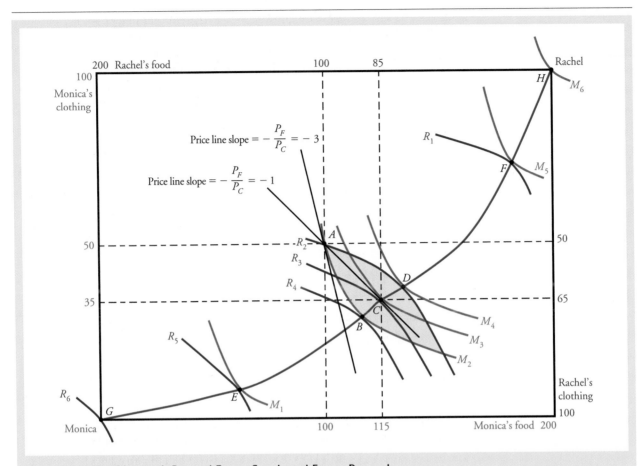

Figure 19.5 The Edgeworth Box and Excess Supply and Excess Demand
If Monica and Rachel are initially at point A and the price ratio is $P_F/P_C = 3$, Monica will be in equilibrium and will not be willing to trade. Rachel, however, would want to sell food and buy clothing at that price ratio. At a price ratio equal to 3, there would be an excess supply of food and an excess demand for clothing. As a result of the excess supply and excess demand, the price of food decreases and the price of clothing increases. If the price of food decreased and the price of clothing increased, so that the new price ratio is $P_F/P_C = 1$, then Monica and Rachel would reach Pareto efficiency at point C.

first theorem of welfare economics

A theorem stating that in a competitive exchange economy, all Pareto-improving moves will be made ensuring that the economy will be Pareto-efficient in its final equilibrium.

point D. The better Rachel is at bargaining, the closer the equilibrium will be to point B. The better Monica is at bargaining, the closer the equilibrium will be to point D. In the previous section, we saw that with 2,000 consumers, the ability of prices to adjust to changing supply and demand conditions insures that the economy reaches a Pareto-efficient point. This result is extremely important and extremely strong, because it guarantees that in a competitive exchange economy, all Pareto-improving moves will be made and the final equilibrium will be Pareto-efficient. We call this result the **first theorem of welfare economics**.

As a concept, the first theorem of welfare economics is closely related to Adam Smith's concept of the invisible hand. Of course, Smith was not using modern economic theory and Edgeworth box diagrams when he wrote in the late 18th century; however, Smith theorized that without any government intervention, the individual behavior of consumers and producers each working in their own self-interest would guarantee that society's resources would be allocated in an efficient manner. Formally, in the terminology of modern economics, the invisible hand implies that in an economy with n consumers:

$$MRS_1 = MRS_2 = MRS_3 = \cdots = MRS_n = \left| -\frac{MU_F}{MU_C} \right| = \left| -\frac{P_F}{P_C} \right| \qquad (19.2)$$

According to Equation 19.2, in equilibrium in a competitive economy, the marginal rates of substitution between any two goods for all consumers must be equal. This is another way of expressing the first theorem of welfare economics.

What About Equity?

In each of Figures 19.2 through 19.5, the green contract curve consists of an infinite number of possible Pareto-efficient allocations of food and clothing. Although every point on the contract curve is Pareto-efficient, the equity implications of the various points are radically different. Point G might be Pareto-efficient, but it sure won't seem equitable to poor Monica, who is left freezing and starving at point G. Meanwhile, Rachel certainly won't be happy at point H. Pareto efficiency implies nothing about equity.

In Figure 19.6, the green curve identifies all of the Pareto-efficient utility possibilities in our simple exchange economy. Monica's utility (U_M) is measured on the x-axis and Rachel's utility (U_R) is measured on the y-axis. The points G, E, B, C, D, F, and H in Figure 19.6 correspond to the same points on the contract curve in Figure 19.5. At point G, for example, Monica's utility is zero, because she has no food or clothing, while Rachel's utility is R_6. Moving up the contract curve to point E, Monica's utility is M_1 and Rachel's utility is R_5. Each of the points on the green contract curve in Figure 19.5 can

Figure 19.6 The Welfare Frontier
The utility possibilities curve, or welfare frontier, identifies all of the Pareto-efficient utility combinations for society. It is derived from the locus of points on the contract curve in Figures 19.2 through 19.5. Any points to the north, east, or northeast of a point on the welfare function, such as any point in the red shaded area in relation to point C, are impossible to reach because *both* Monica and Rachel would be better off in the red area compared to point C. If the social welfare function is $W = W(U_M, U_R)$ depicted by the purple indifference curves, society's welfare is maximized at point C.

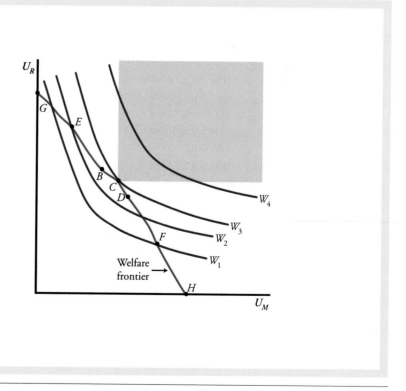

utility possibilities curve, or welfare frontier

A curve identifying all possible Pareto-efficient combinations of utility for consumers in an exchange economy; that is, the possible utility combinations for points on the contract curve in an Edgeworth box diagram.

be used to derive a unique point on the green *utility possibilities curve* in Figure 19.6. The **utility possibilities curve**, or **welfare frontier**, identifies all of the possible combinations of utility it is possible to achieve along the Pareto-efficient contract curve.

If society is on its welfare frontier, Pareto efficiency is achieved, and it is impossible to reallocate goods in a way that makes one person better off without hurting someone else. It is impossible, therefore, to reallocate goods in a way that moves society to a point either due north, due east, or northeast from any point on the welfare frontier. For example, suppose society is currently at point *C*. Because it is impossible to make one consumer better off without hurting the other, it is impossible to move to any of the points in the red shaded area in Figure 19.6. A similar exercise can be done beginning at any point on the welfare frontier, and in this way all of the points outside of the welfare frontier can be eliminated as possible utility combinations. As for the points inside the welfare frontier: These points represent possible utility combinations, but at any of these points, the goods can be reallocated to increase both Monica's and Rachel's utility. The points inside the welfare frontier, therefore, are Pareto-inefficient and represent all of the infinite number of points in the Edgeworth box that are not on the contract curve.

Is it possible to determine which point on the welfare frontier is best for society? Some economists have suggested addressing this question by using a **social welfare function** that is analogous to a consumer's utility function and which expresses society's well-being as a function of the utilities of its members. For our simple exchange economy, the social welfare function is:

$$W = W(U_M, U_R)$$

social welfare function

An expression of society's well-being as a function of the utilities of its individual members.

where W is society's welfare, U_M is Monica's utility, and U_R is Rachel's utility. Given normal convex preferences, the social welfare function yields a series of indifference curves depicting combinations of U_M and U_R that result in equal levels of social welfare, like the purple indifference curves in Figure 19.6. To maximize social welfare in this case, goods should be allocated to reach point *C* on the welfare frontier.

When considering equity and welfare, we enter squarely into the realm of normative economics, in which societies are forced to make value judgments concerning the distribution of income between consumers. The theoretical concept of a social welfare function seems quite reasonable, but actually identifying a real-world social welfare function is virtually impossible. Derivation of the welfare function requires society to make a series of interpersonal utility comparisons. Suppose, for example, the distribution of goods initially gave everything to Rachel and nothing to Monica at point *G* in Figure 19.6. Society might make a value judgment that from an equity standpoint, this is unacceptable. One possible solution to this equity problem would be to place a goods tax on Rachel and transfer these taxed goods to Monica. Such a tax and transfer policy would not improve economic efficiency, because point *G* is Pareto-efficient. Society, however, might make a normative judgment that it prefers many points on the welfare function to point *G*.

If we tax Rachel to give to Monica, can anyone say with certainty that the utility lost by Rachel is less than the utility gained by Monica? No matter how well intentioned the motivation to achieve equity, when society makes interpersonal utility comparisons, they almost invariably result in difficult and controversial political choices. Despite the political difficulties, such choices are made all the time by societies attempting to redistribute income from one group to another. The United States redistributes income to the poor through a variety of welfare programs, including direct welfare payments, food stamps, housing subsidies, and Medicaid. Not all redistribution programs are aimed at helping

egalitarians

A group of 19th-century philosophers who argued for an equal distribution of income.

Marxists

Followers of the 19th-century economist and sociologist Karl Marx, who believed that income should be distributed "to each according to their needs."

Utilitarians

A group of 19th-century philosophers who argued for the maximization of society's total utility.

Darwinism

Philosophy of the 19th-century followers of Charles Darwin's theory of natural selection and survival of the fittest; in economics, the Darwinist philosophy argues against any government interference with the market outcome.

Rawlsian theory

Theory of John Rawls, who believed that the preferred income allocation should maximize the utility of the individual with the lowest utility in society.

the poor, however. For example, farm subsidies redistribute income from taxpayers at large to farmers. College grants redistribute income from taxpayers to college students, and child-care tax credits redistribute income from taxpayers in general to taxpayers with young children. Some government programs even appear to redistribute income from the relatively poor to the relatively wealthy. For example, the tax deduction for interest paid on a home mortgage redistributes income to generally wealthier homeowners.

What is the proper way to redistribute income? This question has haunted economists and philosophers for centuries. **Egalitarians** wanted an equal distribution of income, like the distribution at point *A* in Figure 19.5. **Marxists** wanted to distribute "to each according to their needs." **Utilitarians** wanted to maximize society's total utility and hoped to reach a point like *C* on indifference curve W_3 in Figure 19.6. Supporters of **Darwinism** were staunch believers in survival of the fittest and argued against any government interference with the market outcome. During the peak of Darwinism in the late 19th century, many economists and philosophers supported a completely *laissez-faire* attitude toward redistribution. In contrast, John Rawls suggested that the preferred income allocation should maximize the utility of the individual with the lowest utility in society. **Rawlsian theory** recognized that the more egalitarian forms of redistribution are likely to reduce the work incentives of the most productive members of society. To maintain these incentives, Rawls was willing to permit the more productive members of society to receive higher incomes, as long as these higher incomes increased output and did not reduce the incomes of the poorest members of society.

Modern industrial economies have incorporated elements of all of these theories into their views of equity. Although these societies rely primarily on the market mechanism to distribute income in line with the marginal revenue product of each worker, they have not completely ignored the positions of the Marxists, Utilitarians, and Rawlsians. All industrial economies take care of their poorest citizens through a series of direct income transfers, the provision of education, and at least minimal levels of health care.

COMMON ERROR 19.1 **Failing to Understand That There is No Connection Between Pareto Efficiency and Equity**

When students first study Pareto efficiency in exchange using an Edgeworth box diagram, they often have a difficult time understanding that there is no connection between equity and efficiency. This can lead to problems if a student is asked: Where is the best place to be in the Edgeworth box diagram? A common response is "at the midpoint." The midpoint, of course, is the point of equal distribution. Is that point also Pareto-efficient? It can be, but as we discovered in Figure 19.2, there is no reason to believe that it will be. There are an infinite number of Pareto-efficient points along the contract curve, but there is no reason to believe that the midpoint is one of them.

The confusion between Pareto efficiency and equity sometimes causes students to make a second common error. In Figure 19.5 and Figure 19.6, many students make the error of thinking that point *C* is more efficient than point *H*, because at point *H*, Monica has all of the goods and Rachel has nothing. Such an argument requires a normative interpersonal utility comparison between Monica and Rachel. In terms of Pareto efficiency, it is impossible to make such comparisons. Both point *C* and point *H* are efficient points. There is nothing more to be said about efficiency with regard to these points. Of course, in terms of equity, almost everyone, including Monica, would probably concede that point *C* is more equitable than point *H*.

The Second Theorem of Welfare Economics

Is the Rawlsian view—that there is a trade-off of efficiency for equity—necessarily correct? In Figure 19.7, suppose resources are initially distributed at point W, where Monica has 62 units of food and 34 units of clothing, and Rachel has 138 units of food and 66 units of clothing. Monica's level of utility is M_1, and Rachel's is R_4. Left to the powers of the invisible hand, prices would adjust to move Monica and Rachel to point Y on the contract curve. Society might decide that point W is an unfair initial distribution, because Rachel has so many more goods than Monica. To solve this equity problem, suppose the government places a tax on Rachel of 16 units of clothing and 38 units of food and transfers these goods to Monica. The goods would then be distributed equally at point A, but Monica and Rachel will not remain at point A for long. The invisible hand would now move Monica and Rachel to point C on the contract curve.

Has the tax on Rachel and transfer to Monica reduced economic efficiency? The total amount of goods allocated between Rachel and Monica has not been reduced, and

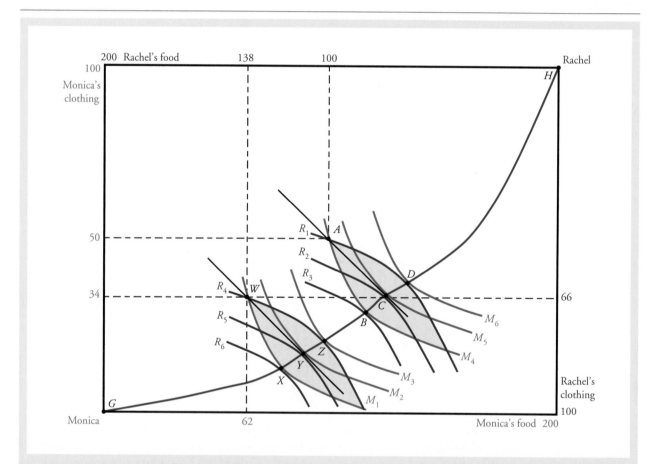

Figure 19.7 The Second Theorem of Welfare Economics

Suppose the economy is initially at point W, and the government decides that point W is unfair to Monica, so it decides to transfer goods from Rachel to Monica such that the goods are distributed equally at point A. According to the first theorem of welfare economics, in a free market economy, the invisible hand will move Rachel and Monica from point A to a point on the contract curve like point C. Increasing equity does not result in a reduction in efficiency. This is the primary lesson of the *second theorem of welfare economics.*

the final equilibrium point C is Pareto-efficient. There is apparently no theoretical reason why the redistribution of goods from Rachel to Monica has to reduce efficiency. This is the lesson of the **second theorem of welfare economics**, which states that every point on the contract curve is a competitive equilibrium for some initial allocation of goods. The implication of the second theorem of welfare economics is that no matter how resources are allocated in an Edgeworth box, the invisible hand will ensure that Pareto efficiency is obtained. There is no necessary trade-off of efficiency and equity in exchange.

This story seems to contradict much of what economists believe about the impact of taxes on economic incentives and efficiency. They believe that taxes do affect work incentives and can have an impact on the total output produced by society. Productive efficiency, therefore, is likely to be affected by a tax that transfers income from one group to another. We now turn to an analysis of efficiency in production.

second theorem of welfare economics

A theorem stating that given convex indifference curves, every point on the contract curve is a competitive equilibrium for some initial allocation of goods; implies that by selecting a suitable price ratio, any point on the contract curve can be reached from some initial distribution of income.

19.3   Efficiency in Production

Having examined Pareto efficiency in exchange, we turn our attention to Pareto efficiency in production. In many respects, the analysis of efficiency in production is completely analogous to the analysis of efficiency in exchange. The concepts introduced in the previous section—particularly the Edgeworth box—will be used extensively in this section.

The Edgeworth Box and Production Efficiency

Suppose in Figure 19.8 that two goods, food and clothing, are produced using two inputs, labor and capital. The production functions for food and clothing are $F = g(L,K)$ and $C = f(L,K)$, where F and C represent quantities of food and clothing, and L and K represent quantities of labor and capital. Assume that the economy has a fixed amount of labor, $\overline{L}$, and a fixed amount of capital, $\overline{K}$, available to produce either food or clothing. Using an Edgeworth box diagram, it is possible to graph the isoquants for food and clothing on one graph the way Monica's and Rachel's indifference curves were graphed on one graph. The isoquants for food are the red isoquants using point O_F as the origin for food production and measuring labor input on the x-axis and capital input on the y-axis. Now turn your textbook upside down. The isoquants for clothing are the blue isoquants, using point O_C as the origin for food production and measuring labor input on the x-axis and capital input on the y-axis. At point O_F, all labor and capital are employed in the production of clothing, and food output is zero; while at point O_C, all labor and capital are employed in the production of food, and clothing output is zero. On any isoquant F_i, the quantity of food equals F_i units; and on any isoquant C_i, the quantity of clothing equals C_i units.

In Figure 19.8, a point is Pareto-efficient if it is impossible to reallocate inputs so as to increase the output of one good without reducing the output of the other. As in any Edgeworth box diagram, the points of tangency between one of the red food isoquants and one of the blue clothing isoquants are Pareto-efficient. The green curve represents the locus of points of tangency between two isoquants, or all the Pareto-efficient points. These points make up the contract curve, which contains an infinite number of points.

Suppose production initially takes place at point A. L_2 units of labor go into food production and $\overline{L} - L_2$ units of labor go into clothing production. Capital is distributed with K_2 units going into food production and $\overline{K} - K_2$ units going into clothing production. At point A, F_2 units of food are produced and C_2 units of clothing are produced. Point A

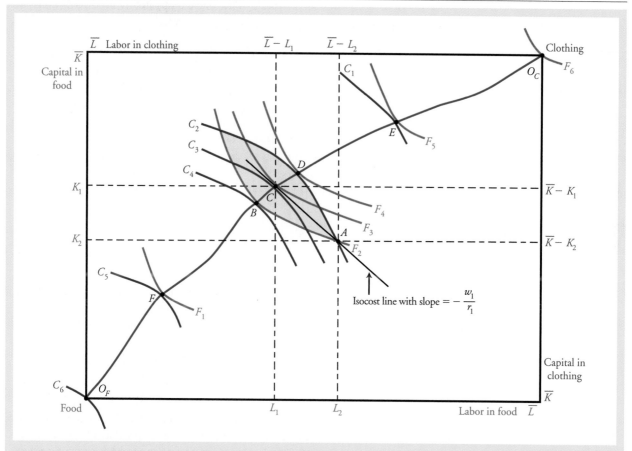

Figure 19.8 The Edgeworth Box and Efficiency in Production
The Edgeworth box depicts all of the possible allocations of labor and capital between food and clothing. Suppose inputs were initially divided between food and clothing at point A. By completing a Pareto-efficient trade that moves the producers into the orange shaded area, the output of both food and clothing can be increased, and therefore the economy is better off. The only Pareto-efficient points in the Edgeworth box are the points of tangency between the food and clothing isoquants. These points of tangency make up the green contract curve. Starting at point A, if the input price ratio is w_1/r_1, the food producer should fire workers and rent more capital, and the clothing manufacturer should hire more workers and rent fewer units of capital until production reaches point C on the contract curve.

is inefficient because it is possible to reallocate labor and capital and produce more of both food and clothing. If $L_2 - L_1$ units of labor are transferred from food production into clothing production, and $K_1 - K_2$ units of capital are transferred from clothing production into food production, the economy moves to point C. When inputs are reallocated in this manner, food output increases from F_2 units to F_3 units and clothing output increases from C_2 units to C_3 units. All of the points in the shaded orange area represent Pareto-improving moves from point A, because at each of these points, the output of both food and clothing is greater than at point A. To exhaust all Pareto-improving moves, it is necessary to move to a point on the contract curve where two isoquants are tangent.

Recall from Chapter 7 that the absolute value of the slope of an isoquant at a point measures the marginal rate of technical substitution, or the *MRTS*. The *MRTS* measures the rate at which labor can be substituted for capital while still producing the same level of output. In Chapter 7, we discovered that the *MRTS* measures the ratio of the marginal product of labor to the marginal product of capital:

$$MRTS = \frac{MP_L}{MP_K}$$

At every point on the contract curve, the slope of the isoquant for food equals the slope of the isoquant for clothing, and therefore the *MRTS* is equal for both production functions. On the contract curve, it follows that:

$$MRTS_{food} = MRTS_{clothing} = \frac{MP_L}{MP_K} \tag{19.3}$$

At points off the contract curve—for example *A*—the absolute value of the slope of the blue isoquant C_2 is greater than the absolute value of the slope of the red isoquant F_2, and therefore, at point *A*:

$$\left.\frac{MP_L}{MP_K}\right|_{clothing} > \left.\frac{MP_L}{MP_K}\right|_{food}$$

Suppose that the economy is at point *A*, and labor is transferred from food production to clothing, and capital is transferred from clothing production to food production. The transfer of labor from food production to clothing production causes the MP_L in clothing to decrease and the MP_L in food to increase; and the transfer of capital from clothing production to food production causes the MP_K in clothing to increase, and the MP_K in food to decrease. As a result, the $MP_L/MP_K|_{clothing}$ decreases and the $MP_L/MP_K|_{food}$ increases. The transfer of inputs should continue until a Pareto-efficient equilibrium is attained on the contract curve.

Adding Input Prices to the Model

Suppose that the price of labor is *w* and the rental price of capital is *r*. From Chapter 7, we also know that long-run cost minimization requires a tangency between the firm's isoquant and the firm's isocost line. The absolute value of the slope of the isocost lines equals the input price ratio, *w/r*, and therefore, cost minimization requires:

$$MRTS = \frac{MP_L}{MP_K} = \frac{w}{r} \tag{19.4}$$

Assume that there are 1,000 firms in our simple economy, with 500 identical firms producing food and 500 identical firms producing clothing. Staring at point *A* in Figure 19.8, suppose the input price ratio is w_1/r_1. Firms can hire inputs along the black isocost line connecting points *A* and *C*. To increase output at the same cost, a food producer can fire some workers and rent additional capital. A clothing manufacturer, on the other hand, can increase output at the same cost if it uses less capital and hires more workers. If our typical food producer fires $L_2 - L_1$ workers and rents $K_1 - K_2$ additional units of capital, its total cost remains constant, but output increases from F_2 to F_3. Similarly, if our clothing manufacturer hires $L_2 - L_1$ workers and rents $K_1 - K_2$ fewer units of capital, its total cost remains constant, but output increases from C_2 to C_3. The price mechanism enables the economy to achieve Pareto efficiency at point *C*.

The Production Possibilities Curve

The contract curve in Figure 19.8 represents the locus of all Pareto-efficient points. Along this curve, it is impossible to increase food output without decreasing clothing output and vice versa. In Figure 19.9, food production is measured along the x-axis and clothing production is measured along the y-axis. Each point on the contract curve in Figure 19.8 corresponds to a point on the green curve in Figure 19.9. The points O_F, F, B, C, D, E, and O_C in Figure 19.9 correspond to the same points in Figure 19.8. In Figure 19.8, for example, if all inputs are used to produce food, the maximum amount of food production is F_6 at point O_C. This corresponds to the food intercept in Figure 19.9 where F_6 units of food are produced and no clothing is produced. If all inputs are used to produce clothing, the maximum amount of clothing production is C_6 at point O_F, which corresponds to the clothing intercept in Figure 19.9, where C_6 units of clothing are produced and no food is produced. Beginning at the clothing intercept, more food can be produced only if some clothing is sacrificed. If the economy moves from point O_F to point F in Figure 19.8, food output increases to F_1 units and clothing output decreases to C_5. Continuing along the contract curve in Figure 19.8, if the economy moves from point F to point B, food output increases to F_2 and clothing output declines to C_4.

The green curve in Figure 19.9 should look familiar, because it was probably the first curve you saw in your introductory economics course. It is the **production possibilities curve**, which identifies all of the possible efficient combinations of food and clothing that the economy is capable of producing, given current resource constraints. If the economy is on its production possibilities curve, Pareto efficiency is achieved. All the points outside of the production possibilities curve lie outside the Edgeworth box, and are therefore impossible. Points inside the production possibilities curve are possible, but represent all of the inefficient points that are off the contract curve in the Edgeworth box.

As the economy moves from one point to another along the production possibilities curve, it is possible to identify the amount of one good that must be sacrificed to produce more of the other good. In other words, it is possible to identify the opportunity cost of producing more of one good in terms of the other good. If the economy moves from point B to point C, for example, one unit of clothing must be sacrificed to obtain

production possibilities curve

A curve identifying all of the possible efficient combinations of goods and services that the economy is capable of producing, given current resource constraints.

Figure 19.9 The Production Possibilities Curve

The production possibilities curve represents all of the Pareto-efficient points on the contract curve in Figure 19.8. Each point on the contract curve corresponds to exactly one point on the production possibilities curve. The absolute value of the slope of the production possibilities curve at a point measures the *marginal rate of transformation* or *MRT*, which measures the opportunity cost of food in terms of clothing. As more food is produced, the opportunity cost of producing food increases, and therefore the *MRT* increases as well.

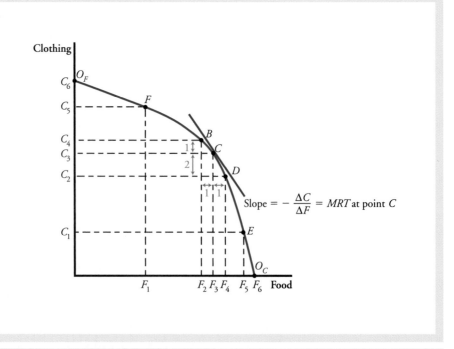

one additional unit of food, so the opportunity cost of an additional unit of food is one unit of clothing. If the economy moves from point C to point D, two units of clothing must be sacrificed to obtain one additional unit of food, so the opportunity cost of an additional unit of food is two units of clothing.

As we move continuously down the production possibilities curve from point O_F to O_C, the opportunity cost of an additional unit of food is $\Delta C/\Delta F$. If ΔF is very small, then $\Delta C/\Delta F$ equals the slope of the production possibilities curve at a point. In Figure 19.9, the slope of the line tangent to the production possibilities curve at point C measures precisely the opportunity cost of food at that point, and the absolute value of the slope measures the **marginal rate of transformation** or **MRT**. The *MRT* measures the opportunity cost of producing one more unit of one good in terms of the number of units of another good that must be sacrificed. In Figure 19.9, because the *MRT* continuously increases as food production increases, the production possibilities curve is concave, or bowed out from the origin. Production possibilities curves are almost always concave, because the opportunity cost of producing more of a good increases as more of the good is produced.

marginal rate of transformation, MRT

The opportunity cost of producing one more unit of one good in terms of the number of units of another good that must be sacrificed.

The *MRT* precisely at point C must be greater than 1 and less than 2. If the *MRT* equals 1.5 at point C, the opportunity cost of producing an additional unit of food is 1.5 units of clothing. The dollar cost of producing one more unit of food must therefore be 1.5 times the dollar cost of producing one more unit of clothing. For example, if at point C, one more unit of clothing can be produced for \$10.00 in extra input costs, then the cost of producing one more unit of food must be $(1.5)(\$10.00) = \$15.00$. The *MRT* therefore, equals the ratio of the marginal cost of producing food to the marginal cost of producing clothing:

$$MRT = \left| -\frac{\Delta C}{\Delta F} \right| = \left| -\frac{MC_F}{MC_C} \right| \tag{19.5}$$

▲▲▲ 19.3 APPLICATION   Economic Inefficiency in the Former Soviet Union

Prior to the 1980s, the Soviet Union's style of communism was an extreme form of a command economy in which central planners in Moscow made every resource allocation decision. The Soviet state owned virtually all the means of production, including land, factories, and capital equipment. The central planners set production quotas for firms, and—at least in theory—allocated inputs consistent with meeting those quotas. The central planners also set the prices for all consumer goods, raw materials, capital, and labor.

In the figure, we assume that the central planners allocated 75 percent of the available labor and 50 percent of the available capital to military goods and 25 percent of the available labor and 50 percent of the available capital to consumer goods. The planners therefore forced the economy to produce at point A with an output of M_1 units of military goods and C_1 units of consumer goods.

Point A is inefficient because it is far from the contract curve. The economy was capable of producing a great deal more of both goods. It was possible, for example, to reallocate inputs by transferring 40 units of labor from military goods to consumer goods and 20 units of capital from consumer goods to military goods, increasing the output of military goods to M_3 and the output of consumer goods to C_3. In the absence of omnipotent planners, it was almost impossible to achieve Pareto efficiency in the Soviet command economy. If the firms were meeting their quotas, there was no incentive to shift resources from one sector to another.

Under the Soviet style of communism, firms became adept at meeting their quotas, in part by making sure they had an excess supply of inputs. The worst thing that could happen for a firm was to be highly efficient and meet its quota using fewer inputs than the central planners

(continued)

allocated it. In this case, fewer inputs would be allotted to the firm the next year. This created some bizarre economic incentives. Hotels burned heating fuel on warm days to ensure that they used up their entire allotment. Automobile factories wasted steel to ensure that they used all the steel they received from the central planners.

The figure illustrates that the Soviet command economy was stuck at point *A*, far from the contract curve and therefore far from the production possibilities curve. Eventually the inefficiencies built into the system became so great that they contributed to the entire society coming apart at the seams. The dissolution of the Soviet Union in December 1991 has not been a cure-all for the economies of the new countries that emerged from the former Soviet Union. With little or no history of capitalism, Russia, for example, has struggled tremendously in the transition to a market economy. The old inefficient factories are now mostly controlled by private monopolists, who charge high monopoly prices for goods that are inferior in quality by Western European standards. While Russia has struggled mightily in its transition, states such as Poland and the Czech Republic, which had long histories of market economies prior to the end of World War II, have had far greater success.

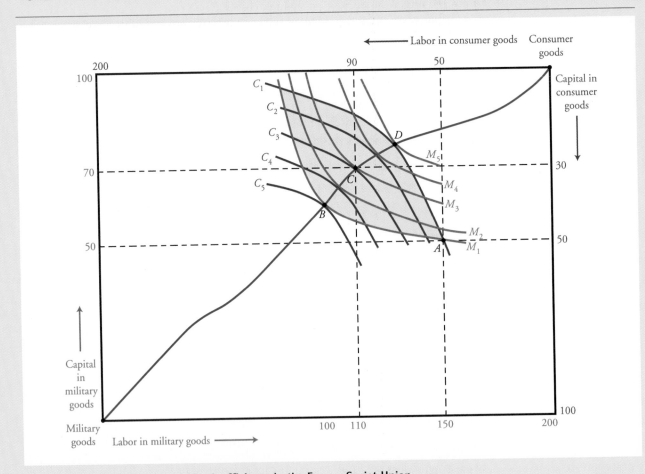

Application Figure 19.3 Production Inefficiency in the Former Soviet Union
In the former Soviet Union, central planners decided how many inputs each industry would receive. If resources were allocated by the planners at point *A*, with 75 percent of labor and 50 percent of capital going into military goods, the economy is producing inefficiently, because it is not producing on the contract curve, and therefore it is not producing on its production possibilities curve. With no free-market price mechanism to correct the inefficiency, there is no reason for the economy to move from point *A*, and it remains permanently mired in inefficiency.

19.4 General Equilibrium in a Perfectly Competitive Economy

Having established the conditions for Pareto efficiency in both exchange and production, we are ready to bring the two sides of the market together and establish the necessary conditions for a Pareto-efficient economy. A Pareto-efficient economy must operate simultaneously on the production possibilities curve *and* on the consumers' contract curve, where the marginal rates of substitution are equal for all consumers for all pairs of goods. In a perfectly competitive economy, the price mechanism enables the economy to achieve this outcome.

On the consumer side of the market, Equation 19.2 showed that in an efficient economy with n consumers, the following consumer equilibrium conditions must hold:

$$MRS_1 = MRS_2 = MRS_3 = \cdots = MRS_n = \left| -\frac{MU_F}{MU_C} \right| = \left| -\frac{P_F}{P_C} \right|$$

On the production side of the market, in equilibrium in a perfectly competitive market, price must equal marginal cost, so if the food and clothing markets are perfectly competitive, $P_F = MC_F$, $P_C = MC_C$, and:

$$\left| -\frac{MU_F}{MU_C} \right| = \left| -\frac{P_F}{P_C} \right|$$

Furthermore, from Equation 19.5, we know that the ratio of marginal costs equals the marginal rate of transformation, so:

$$MRT = \left| -\frac{MC_F}{MC_C} \right| = \left| -\frac{P_F}{P_C} \right|$$

Equations 19.2 and 19.5 tie the consumption and production sides of the market together through the price mechanism. In a Pareto-efficient economy, the *MRS* and *MRT* both equal the price ratio:

$$MRS = \left| -\frac{MU_F}{MU_C} \right| = \left| -\frac{P_F}{P_C} \right| = \left| -\frac{MC_F}{MC_C} \right| = MRT \qquad (19.6)$$

Figure 19.10 identifies an economy in general equilibrium. The point of production on the production possibilities curve determines the size of the Edgeworth box. The economy produces at point C, where the *MRT* equals the price ratio P_F/P_C. In general equilibrium, F_3 units of food and C_3 units of clothing are produced. Monica and Rachel reach equilibrium in exchange at point X, where Monica consumes F_1 units of food and C_1 units of clothing, and Rachel consumes $F_3 - F_1$ units of food and $C_3 - C_1$ units of clothing. At point X, the *MRS* also equals the price ratio P_F/P_C. All of the conditions in Equation 19.6 are fulfilled in Figure 19.10, and therefore the economy has achieved Pareto efficiency, where it is impossible to make anyone better off without hurting someone else.

Figure 19.10 General Equilibrium in a Perfectly Competitive Economy
In an economy in which all markets are perfectly competitive, the production point on the production possibilities curve, here point C, determines the size of the Edgeworth box for Monica and Rachel to allocate goods. In a Pareto-efficient general equilibrium, $MRS = MRT$, so the slope of the production possibilities curve at point C must equal the slopes of the indifference curves for Monica and Rachel at point X. If $MRS \neq MRT$, prices will adjust to cause a movement along the production possibilities curve, and eventually the equality between MRS and MRT will be reestablished.

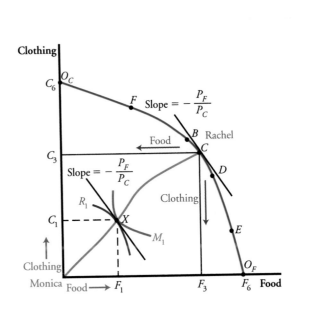

▲▲▲ 19.4 APPLICATION   How the Economy Adjusts to a Change in Tastes

Application 19.1 examined the impact of a significant change in consumer tastes, the widespread adoption of a low-carbohydrate diet by millions of Americans, and we saw that the impact could be analyzed only using a general equilibrium approach. Given the tools developed in the last three sections, it is now possible to explain exactly how the economy adapts to such a change in tastes. To simplify the analysis, consider an economy with two goods, beef and pasta. According to Equation 19.6, to achieve Pareto efficiency, the following economic conditions must hold:

$$MRS = \left| -\frac{MU_b}{MU_p} \right| = \left| -\frac{P_b}{P_p} \right| = \left| -\frac{MC_b}{MC_p} \right| = MRT$$

where MU_b represents the marginal utility of beef, MU_p represents the marginal utility of pasta, P_b represents the price of beef, P_p represents the price of pasta, MC_b repre-

sents the marginal cost of producing beef, and MC_p represents the marginal cost of producing pasta.

If consumers' tastes change in favor of beef compared to pasta, then the MU_b increases and the MU_p decreases, and as a result, $|-MU_b/MU_p|$ increases. Therefore, the economy would no longer be in equilibrium, because $|-MU_b/MU_p| > |-P_b/P_p|$. Prices would have to adjust to re-equate the ratio of the marginal utilities to the ratio of prices. The price of beef would have to increase relative to the price of pasta. As the price of beef increases, producers increase the quantity supplied of beef, and the marginal cost of producing beef increases.

The figure on the following page shows this adjustment process graphically. Initially, the economy is producing q_3^b units of beef and q_4^p units of pasta at point B on its production possibilities curve. The economy's two consumers, Will and Grace, are in equilibrium at point A,

(continued)

where Will consumes q_1^b units of beef and q_2^p units of pasta, and Grace consumes $q_3^b - q_1^b$ units of beef and $q_4^p - q_2^p$ units of pasta. Will is on his initial orange indifference curve, and Grace is on her initial teal indifference curve.

After Will and Grace switch to a low-carbohydrate diet, their indifference curves become steeper. At point A, Will's indifference curve is the dashed red curve, and Grace's indifference curve is the dashed blue curve. Because these two curves are no longer tangent, but intersect at point A, Will and Grace are no longer in equilibrium, and their marginal rates of substitution no longer equal the price ratio P_b/P_p. Both Will and Grace are now willing to trade away more pasta to get additional units of beef, so the demand for beef increases. As the demand for beef increases and the demand for pasta decreases, the price ratio P_b/P_p increases, and the economy moves along its production possibilities curve from point B to point D. The increase in the price ratio to P_b'/P_p' increases the economy's output of beef to q_4^b and decreases the output of pasta to q_3^p. The size of the Edgeworth box has changed dramatically, and Will and Grace move to point C, their new equilibrium point on the new contract curve. Will's consumption of beef has increased from q_1^b to q_2^b, and Grace's consumption of beef has increased from $q_3^b - q_1^b$ to $q_4^b - q_2^b$. Meanwhile, Will's consumption of pasta has decreased from q_2^p to q_1^p and Grace's consumption of pasta has changed from $q_4^p - q_2^p$ to $q_3^p - q_1^p$. It is not clear whether Grace's consumption of pasta has increased or decreased in this case. Will has responded to the low-carb diet craze by increasing his beef consumption *and* reducing his pasta consumption, while Grace has responded primarily by increasing her beef consumption, with little change in her pasta consumption. At the new equilibrium point C, the slopes of their indifference curves are equal to the slope of the production possibilities curve; therefore, the economy is once again Pareto-efficient and:

$$MRS = \left| -\frac{MU_b}{MU_p} \right| = \left| -\frac{P_b'}{P_p'} \right| = \left| -\frac{MC_b}{MC_p} \right| = MRT$$

Did the American economy respond to the low-carb diet craze in the manner depicted in the figure? In October

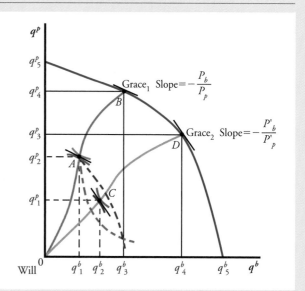

Application Figure 19.4
Before the low-carb diet craze, Will and Grace are in equilibrium at point A, where there is a tangency between Will's orange indifference curve and Grace's teal indifference curve. Because of the low-carb diet fad, their indifference curves become steeper, and there is no longer an equilibrium at point A. As the price ratio P_b/P_p increases, Will and Grace move to a new equilibrium at point C, where both consume more beef. The equilibrium on the production possibilities curve moves from point B to point D, so the economy produces more beef and less pasta.

1999, CNN reported that "[a]fter nearly three decades on the downswing, red meat is suddenly back in culinary fashion. The increased demand has sent wholesale prices soaring, up 20 percent or more during the past year for select beef cuts."[1] According to *http://beef.org*, the official Web site of the beef industry, demand in the fourth quarter of 2000 increased for the seventh consecutive quarter following 20 years of continuous declines.[2] In fact, 1999 was the first year the demand for beef had increased since 1980. The economy appears to have adjusted to the new change in tastes exactly as predicted by our general equilibrium model.

---

[1] Ceci Rodgers, "Beef Boosted by Protein Diets, Y2K," *http://www.cnn.com*.

[2] "The U.S. Beef Industry: Demand, Spending and Consumption," Factsheet March 2001, *http://www.beef.org*.

19.5 Failures to Achieve Pareto Efficiency

The economy achieves Pareto efficiency when all markets are perfectly competitive and the government permits the invisible hand to work without interference. Any movement away from perfect competition tends to move the economy away from its Pareto-efficient equilibrium. Among the most common types of market imperfections are monopoly, taxes, and externalities in production or consumption. In this section, we examine how these market imperfections prevent an economy from reaching Pareto efficiency.

Monopoly

Monopoly destroys the Pareto efficiency conditions as shown in Equation 19.6, because the monopoly price is greater than marginal cost. If the market for clothing were monopolized by a cartel, while the market for food remained competitive, the price of clothing would be greater than marginal cost. If the monopolist increases the price of clothing from P_C to P_{CM}, Equation 19.6 would be transformed into the following inequality:

$$MRS = \left| -\frac{MU_F}{MU_C} \right| = \left| -\frac{P_F}{P_{CM}} \right| < \left| -\frac{MC_F}{MC_C} \right| = MRT \qquad (19.7)$$

With monopoly, the price ratio no longer equals the marginal rate of transformation.

In Figure 19.11, the green curve is the production possibilities curve and the analysis is simplified by assuming that all consumers can be represented by one set of indifference curves, which can be thought of as representing society's preferences or the preferences of the only consumer in the economy. The Pareto-efficient general equilibrium in a perfectly competitive economy is at point A, where indifference curve U_2 is tangent to the production possibilities curve. Point A maximizes utility subject to the

Figure 19.11 Monopoly and Inefficiency
With perfect competition, the economy reaches an efficient equilibrium at point A. If the clothing industry is monopolized, the price of clothing increases from P_C to P_{CM} and point A is no longer efficient in exchange. Consumers will adjust their consumption patterns to the new price ratio by demanding more food and less clothing. Eventually, the economy moves to point C, where efficiency in exchange has been reestablished. Consumers, however, are worse off at point C than at point A, and the economy is no longer efficient.

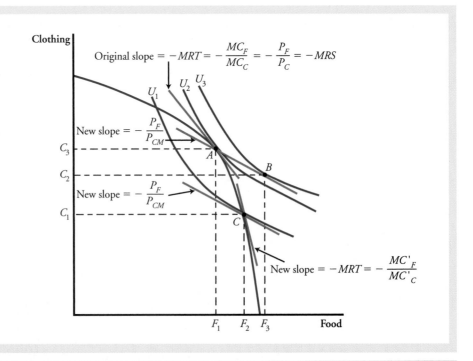

production possibilities curve output constraint. At point A, all of the Pareto-efficient conditions in Equation 19.6 hold.

If the clothing market is monopolized, the price ratio decreases to P_F/P_{CM}. Initially, the economy is at point A. But with the market monopolized, at point A, MRS (the absolute value of the slope of indifference curve U_2) is greater than the price ratio, so point A is no longer efficient in exchange. Given the new price ratio, consumers want to consume at point B on indifference curve U_3, but they can't, because point B is beyond the production possibilities curve. At the new price ratio, consumers demand F_3 units of food, but only F_1 units are supplied; therefore, an excess demand exists for food equal to $F_3 - F_1$ units. Similarly, at the new price ratio, consumers demand only C_2 units of clothing, but the monopolist supplies C_3 units; therefore, the monopolist supplies too much clothing equal to $C_3 - C_2$ units. The monopolist responds to its excess production of clothing by reducing output, and the food manufacturers respond to the excess demand for food by increasing output. In order to reestablish efficiency in exchange *and* efficiency in production, the economy must move to a point on the production possibilities curve where MRS equals the new price ratio. This new equilibrium occurs at point C. Monopolization of the clothing market has resulted in a decrease in clothing production, an increase in food production, and a decrease in utility. Consumers are clearly worse off at point C than at point A.

The economy is also worse off at point C despite the achievement of efficiency in both exchange and production. Efficiency in exchange is achieved because MRS equals the price ratio, and efficiency in production is achieved because the economy is producing on its production possibilities curve. The problem with monopoly is that it drives a wedge between the price ratio and MRT; this, in turn, prevents the economy from achieving Pareto efficiency. The shift from point A to point C results in an increase in the MRT, because the marginal cost of producing food increases to MC_F' as the economy produces more food, and the marginal cost of producing clothing decreases to MC_C' as the economy produces less clothing.

General equilibrium analysis adds considerable insight into the analysis of monopoly. Chapters 11 and 12 emphasized that monopoly resulted in a reduction in output to below the efficient level and created economic inefficiency. In Figure 19.11, monopoly reduces output in the monopolized market and increases output in competitive markets, as inputs are transferred from the monopolized market into the production of goods and services in competitive markets. The transferring of inputs into competitive markets reduces some of the negative impact of monopoly. The monopoly distortion results in an economy that produces too little clothing and too much food.

Excise Tax

A selective excise tax on clothing creates exactly the same distortion as the monopolization of the clothing market created in the previous section, because it drives a wedge between the price ratio and MRT. Just as monopolization of the clothing industry increases P_C and decreases the price ratio P_F/P_C, a per-unit excise tax equal to t increases the price of clothing from P_C to $P_C + t$, and decreases the price ratio from P_F/P_C to $P_F/(P_C + t)$. In Figure 19.11, suppose our efficient economy is initially at point A when the government places an excise tax on clothing. In exactly the same manner that monopoly caused the economy to move from point A to point C, the excise tax on clothing causes the economy to move to a new equilibrium with more food production and less clothing production. Therefore, the tax causes the economy to move down the production possibilities curve toward a point like C. The excise tax distortion also results in an economy that produces too little clothing and too much food.

> ### COMMON ERROR 19.2   Believing That Because Excise Taxes Prevent an Economy from Achieving Pareto Efficiency, All Excise Taxes Are Bad
>
> Students sometimes misinterpret Figure 19.11 to mean that all selective excise taxes have negative economic effects, because they cause economic distortions and prevent an economy from achieving Pareto efficiency. Their reasoning is this: If selective excise taxes always cause price distortions that eliminate Pareto efficiency, why do governments use such taxes at all? Wouldn't society be better off relying entirely on the invisible hand to solve all economic problems? These two questions solicit the more important question: What does the government do with its tax dollars? By ignoring government expenditures in our utility function, we have eliminated the possibility that a combination of taxation and government expenditures might increase society's utility.
>
> In Figure 19.11, consumer utility is a function of units of food and clothing alone. However, if consumer utility is a function of food, clothing, and public education, then an excise tax on clothing devoted to improving public education might increase utility, even though it causes a distortion in the choice between food and clothing. Don't make the common error of thinking that *all* taxes are bad merely because they distort consumer choices among different goods and prevent an economy from achieving Pareto efficiency.

Externalities

negative externalities

A social cost of production or consumption that is not considered to be a cost to the producer or consumer.

positive externalities

A social benefit of production or consumption that is not considered to be a benefit to the producer or consumer.

In addition to monopoly and taxes, any factor that distorts the equality between price and marginal cost will prevent the attainment of Pareto efficiency. In addition to monopoly power and taxes, some of the more common distortions result from the existence of *negative* and *positive externalities*. **Negative externalities** refer to a social cost of production or consumption that is not considered a cost to the producer or consumer. The most common example is pollution. **Positive externalities** refer to a social benefit of production or consumption that is not considered a benefit to the producer or consumer. A common example is immunizations that prevent the spread of diseases even to people who are not immunized. Chapter 21 considers externalities in more detail. This section explains why externalities distort the Pareto-efficient relationship between price and marginal cost.

Suppose food production results in negative externalities because fertilizers and pesticides pollute the environment. Because farmers do not pay directly for the cost of the pollution they create, farmers do not consider these externalities to be a cost of production, and therefore farmers underestimate the marginal cost of producing food. With competition, the price of food equals marginal cost, excluding pollution costs. This creates a distortion in Equation 19.6, because $P_F/P_C < MC_F/MC_C = MRT$.

The distortion caused by pollution is exactly the same as the distortion caused by monopoly or selective excise taxes. Because of pollution in agriculture, the economy would produce at a point like *C* in Figure 19.11, where $P_F/P_C < MC_F/MC_C = MRT$. The price of food is too low relative to the price of clothing, and therefore, once again, too much food is produced relative to clothing.

In this chapter, we have seen how in a world with perfect competition in all markets, allowing the market system to operate without government interference ensures Pareto efficiency. This is a powerful theoretical argument in favor of competition. We also have seen how market failures such as monopoly and externalities can prevent an economy from attaining Pareto efficiency. In the next chapter, we will discover how asymmetric information in many different types of market situations can also prevent Pareto efficiency.

▲▲▲ 19.5 APPLICATION   The Gains from Trade Revisited

In Chapter 10, we explored the gains from trade in a partial equilibrium framework. However, economists prefer to analyze the gains from trade using a general equilibrium framework. In the figure, the green curve is the production possibilities curve for a domestic economy that produces and consumes two goods, clothing and food. Once again, the set of purple indifference curves represent society's preferences or the preferences of the only consumer in the economy. In the absence of trade, the economy would be Pareto-efficient and produce and consume at point A, with a domestic price ratio equal to P_{cd}/P_{fd}.

Suppose that the domestic economy has a comparative advantage in producing food compared to the rest of the world, but the rest of the world has a comparative advantage in producing clothing compared to the domestic economy. The domestic price ratio P_{cd}/P_{fd} is therefore greater than the world price ratio P_{cw}/P_{fw}. If the domestic economy opens up its markets to free trade, it can trade with other countries at the lower price ratio P_{cw}/P_{fw}. Instead of producing at point A, the domestic economy should shift production to point B, where the production possibilities curve is tangent to the light-red line that has a slope equal to the slope of the world price ratio. With trade, the domestic economy increases its production of food from F_2 units to F_3 units and decreases its production of clothing from C_2 units to C_1 units. Point B is efficient in production, because it's on the production possibilities curve, but it is not efficient in exchange, because at point B, MRS—the slope of indifference curve U_1—is greater than the world price ratio, P_{cw}/P_{fw}. To maximize utility, the domestic economy exports $F_3 - F_1$ units of food, imports $C_3 - C_1$ units of clothing, and consumes at point C. Trade enables the economy to consume beyond its production possibilities curve. The

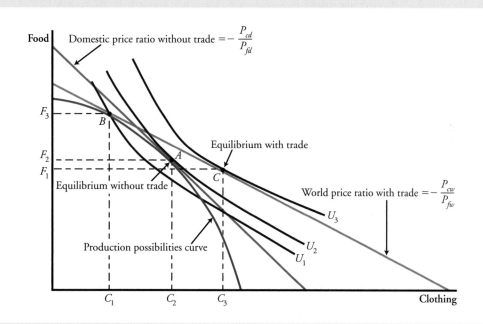

Application Figure 19.5 The Gains from Trade in General Equilibrium
In a closed economy without trade, the efficient point on the production possibilities curve is A, where $MRS = MRT$. If the price ratio with trade, P_{cw}/P_{fw} is less than the price ratio without trade, P_{cd}/P_{fd}, it is possible for trade to make the domestic economy better off. With free trade, the economy should produce at point B on the production possibilities curve, where the $MRT = P_{cw}/P_{fw}$, trade along the light-red world price ratio line, and consume at point C, where $MRS = P_{cw}/P_{fw}$. Trade permits the economy to consume beyond its production possibilities curve and thereby increases society's utility from U_2 to U_3.

(continued)

light-red world price ratio line is the consumption possibilities curve with trade. Production at point *B* is efficient in production, because point *B* is on the production possibilities curve, and consumption at point *C* is efficient in exchange, because *MRS* equals the world price ratio. Trade has increased society's utility from U_2 to U_3, so society is better off with trade.

The economy depicted in the figure could represent the American economy. The United States is the world's most efficient producer of food, but is a relatively high-cost producer of clothing. Compared to countries like India, China, or Poland, the United States has a comparative advantage in food production compared to clothing production. As a result, the United States produces more food than it consumes and exports a great deal of food to the rest of the world. In exchange for food, the United States imports most of the clothing consumed by Americans.

Summary

1. Partial equilibrium analysis considers the direct impact of an exogenous change in economic conditions on *one* market. General equilibrium analysis considers all of the impacts of an economic change on *all* markets in the economy. Partial equilibrium analysis is appropriate when an exogenous economic shock has no significant impact on any other markets except the market most directly affected by the shock. General equilibrium analysis is appropriate when an economic shock impacts many different markets, either directly or indirectly.

2. Using an Edgeworth box diagram, it is possible to show that in a perfectly competitive pure exchange economy, the first theorem of welfare economics ensures that prices will adjust to guarantee that all Pareto-improving moves will be made and the final equilibrium will be Pareto-efficient. The contract curve is the locus of all points of tangency between the two consumers' indifference curves in the Edgeworth box. Furthermore, the second theorem of welfare economics states that every point on the contract curve is a competitive equilibrium for some initial allocation of goods in the Edgeworth box. This theorem implies that no matter how resources are initially allocated in a perfectly competitive market, the invisible hand ensures that Pareto efficiency will eventually be obtained, and therefore, there is no necessary trade-off of efficiency and equity in exchange.

3. An Edgeworth box diagram can also be used to analyze Pareto efficiency in production, and to show how the Pareto-efficient points on the contract curve—which identifies all of the efficient input combinations in the Edgeworth box diagram—correspond to the points on the production possibilities curve.

4. In a Pareto-efficient perfectly competitive economy, the marginal rate of transformation, *MRT,* and the marginal rate of substitution, *MRS,* must both equal the price ratio. Mathematically, this implies: $MRS = \left| -MU_F/MU_C \right| = \left| -P_F/P_C \right| = \left| -MC_F/MC_C \right| = MRT$. These conditions for Pareto efficiency must hold in a perfectly competitive economy.

5. Monopoly power, selective excise taxes, and externalities all prevent an economy from achieving Pareto efficiency, because all of these economic conditions drive a wedge between the marginal rate of substitution and the marginal rate of transformation in equilibrium, and therefore, in equilibrium $MRS \neq MRT$.

1. Consider the following initial endowments for Fred and Ethel. Fred has 50 hot dogs and 20 gallons of juice. Ethel has 100 hot dogs and 30 gallons of juice.

   a. Draw an Edgeworth box depicting the situation described. (For consistency, put gallons of juice on the *x*-axis and hot dogs on the *y*-axis.) Label the initial point *A*.

   b. At the initial endowment point, Fred is willing to give up three hot dogs for one gallon of juice and Ethel is willing to give up five hot dogs for one gallon of juice. Draw in the Edgeworth box an indifference curve for Fred and an indifference curve for Ethel that might show this situation. (You do not need to show the numerical information exactly, but concentrate on the relationship between Fred and Ethel's *MRS*.) Is point *A* Pareto-efficient? Explain.

   c. Given the situation at the initial endowment point, shade in the area of possible gains from trade. Explain why Fred and Ethel would be willing to trade in this area.

   d. Although there are many possibilities, draw a Pareto-efficient point given the initial endowments. Label the point *B*. Draw an indifference curve for both Fred and Ethel at that point. What is true about the *MRS* for Fred and Ethel at the Pareto-efficient point?

2. Consider a world of trucks (good *x*) and cars (good *y*). The total amount of labor to produce both goods is 500 and the total amount of capital to produce both goods is 1,000. Initially, 200 units of labor and 400 units of capital are used to produce trucks. At this point, the production of both cars and trucks is Pareto-efficient.

   a. Depict the information in a production Edgeworth box. Label everything carefully.

   b. What condition is held at the point of Pareto efficiency in production?

   c. Draw a hypothetical contract curve. Show, with isoquants, that the points on the contract curve are Pareto-efficient.

1. Consider the market for low-carbohydrate diet books.

   a. Chapter 19 discusses the effect the Atkins Diet has had on the market for these books. Graphically show the partial equilibrium effects that the Atkins Diet has had on the market for these diet books.

   b. Graphically analyze the spillover effects on the markets for bagels and beef.

   c. What other goods might we analyze in order to have a more thorough general equilibrium analysis? Discuss what types of feedback effects might occur when we consider all the goods.

2. Chapter 19 discusses the results of the surgeon general announcing that two ounces of soy a day greatly reduced the risk of virtually all types of cancer.

   a. Graphically show the partial equilibrium effects that the announcement might have on the soybean market.

   b. Graphically analyze the spillover effects on the markets for Asian food restaurants, Boca burgers, peanut butter, and beef.

   c. Looking at your results to question 2(b), consider any feedback effects. Show the feedback effects on your graphs.

3. Consider an announcement from the surgeon general that red grapes help lower the risk of heart attacks.

   a. Analyze the result of this announcement using a partial equilibrium analysis.

   b. What markets might you include in a general equilibrium analysis? What markets are likely to be included in any spillover effects? Discuss the spillover effects of any relevant goods.

   c. What might be the feedback effect of this announcement?

   d. Why is the general equilibrium analysis more relevant in this situation?

4. Explain whether partial equilibrium or general equilibrium analysis is more appropriate for each of the following situations. Does the appropriate analysis change if we are more interested in the short run versus the long run?

   a. Excise tax on all alcohol (liquor, beer, and wine).

   b. Excise tax on wine only.

   c. Additional excise tax on gasoline.

5. Consider a world with the following initial endowments for George and Martha. George has forty pizzas and five six-packs of cola. Martha has ten pizzas and twenty six-packs of cola.

   a. Draw an Edgeworth box depicting the situation. (For consistency, put six-packs of cola on the *x*-axis and pizzas on the *y*-axis.) Label the initial point *A*.

   b. At the initial endowment point, George is willing to give up 5 pizzas for one six-pack of cola, and Martha is willing to give up one pizza for one six-pack of cola. Draw an indifference curve for George and an indifference curve for Martha that might show this situation in the Edgeworth box. (You do not need to use the exact numerical information, but concentrate on the relationship between George and Martha's *MRS*.) Is point *A* Pareto-efficient? Explain.

   c. Given the situation at the initial endowment point, shade in the area of gains from trade. Explain why George and Martha would be willing to trade in this area.

   d. Although there are many possibilities, draw a Pareto-efficient point given the initial endowments, and label it point *B*. Draw an indifference curve for both Martha and George at that point. What is true about the *MRS* for George and Martha at the Pareto-efficient point?

6. Consider a world with the following initial endowments for George and Martha. George has fifteen pizzas and twenty six-packs of cola. Martha has twenty-five pizzas and ten six-packs of cola.

   a. Draw an Edgeworth box depicting the situation. (For consistency, put six-packs of cola on the *x*-axis and pizzas on the *y*-axis.) Label the initial point *A*.

   b. At the initial endowment point, George is willing to give up one pizza for one six-pack of cola and Martha is willing to give up three pizzas for one six-pack of cola. Draw an indifference curve for

George and an indifference curve for Martha that might show this situation in the Edgeworth box. (You do not need to use the exact numerical information, but concentrate on the relationship between George and Martha's *MRS*.) Is point *A* Pareto-efficient? Explain.

   c. Given the situation at the initial endowment point, shade in the area of gains from trade. Explain why George and Martha would be willing to trade in this area.

   d. Although there are many possibilities, draw a Pareto-efficient point given the initial endowments. Label the Pareto-efficient point *B*. Draw an indifference curve for both Martha and George at that point. What is true about the *MRS* for George and Martha at the Pareto-efficient point?

7. Henry has forty boxes of cereal (*C*) and twenty pounds of bananas (*B*). At this point, Henry is willing to trade three boxes of cereal for one pound of bananas. Mary has forty boxes of cereal and fifty pounds of bananas. At this point, Mary is willing to trade one box of cereal for one pound of bananas.

   a. Draw an Edgeworth box showing the initial endowments. (Put *B* on the *x*-axis and *C* on the *y*-axis.) Label the initial endowment point *A*.

   b. Now Henry exchanges nine boxes of cereal for three pounds of Mary's bananas. Label this new point *B*. After the exchange, they are both willing to trade two boxes of cereal for one pound of bananas (their $MRS_{BC} = 2$). Are both Henry and Mary better off? Show this using the Edgeworth box diagram.

8. Jane has sixteen liters of cola and four sandwiches. Bob has four liters of cola and eight sandwiches. With these endowments, Jane's *MRS* of cola for sandwiches is two, and Bob's *MRS* of soft drinks for sandwiches is one. Draw an Edgeworth box diagram to show whether this allocation is Pareto-efficient. If it is, explain why. If it is not, explain why not.

9. Consider Rebecca (*R*) and Mary (*M*). Rebecca has twenty theatre tickets and ten bottles of wine. Mary has 0 theatre tickets and 0 bottles of wine.

   a. Draw an Edgeworth box depicting this situation. Label the initial endowment, point *A*.

   b. Is this initial point Pareto-efficient? Is there an area in the Edgeworth box that represents the possible gains from trade?

c. Consider Figure 19.6 in the text. Which point or points best reflects the initial endowment in this problem?

10. Gilligan and the Skipper are stranded on Gilligan's Island. Suppose that one day they go out gathering food. Gilligan returns with forty mangos and the Skipper with twenty coconuts.

a. In an Edgeworth box diagram, show their initial endowment point. Explain why it is unlikely (although not impossible) that this endowment is Pareto-efficient.

b. Suppose that Gilligan and the Skipper decide to split the mangos and coconuts equally. Each receives twenty mangos and ten coconuts. After this redistribution, Gilligan is willing to trade two mangos for onecoconut, while the Skipper is willing to trade two mangos for four coconuts. Is this new distribution efficient? If not, show in your graph how Gilligan and the Skipper might redistribute the mangos and coconuts in a Pareto-efficient manner.

11. Consider Figures 19.2 and 19.6 in the text. Comment on the following statement: Points *B*, *C*, and *D* are more efficient than points *G* and *H*. In your comment, explain the difference between these groups of points.

12. Describe the relationship between equity and Pareto efficiency. Carefully explain your answer.

13. Consider question 7 and the initial endowment. Let's assume the government decides to improve equity by taxing Mary fifteen pounds of bananas and redistributing it to Henry.

a. Label the new endowment point after the redistribution point *C*. Assume at this point that the *MRS* for Henry does not equal the *MRS* for Mary.

b. In what way will the first theorem of welfare economics and the second theorem of welfare economics be applied to this problem?

14. Henry has thirty boxes of cereal (*C*) and twenty pounds of bananas (*B*). At this point, Henry is willing to trade two boxes of cereal for one pound of bananas. Mary has ten boxes of cereal and fifty pounds of bananas. At this point, Mary is willing to trade 1/2 box of cereal for one pound of bananas.

a. Draw an Edgeworth box showing the initial endowments. (Put *B* on the *x*-axis and C on the *y*-axis.)

b. Discuss what would happen if the price ratio of bananas to cereal were equal to 2 ($P_b/P_c = 2$). What would we expect to happen to the price ratio? Explain. Give the range of values that the price ratio must equal in order to facilitate trade between Henry and Mary.

15. Consider a world that produces two goods: televisions and clothing. Television producers are currently allocated 400 units of labor and 400 units of capital. Clothing producers are currently allocated 800 units of labor and 200 units of capital. At this point, assume $MRTS_{tv} > MRTS_c$.

a. Draw an Edgeworth box for this situation. Label the initial allocation of labor and capital point *A*.

b. Discuss how labor and capital should be transferred and how this transfer changes the marginal products. Show a point of efficient production, given your initial endowment point and the shape of your isoquants.

16. Consider a world that produces food and clothing. The total amount of labor to produce both goods is 2,000 and the total amount of capital to produce both goods is 800. Initially, food production is using 1,200 units of labor and 300 units of capital. Clothing production is using 800 units of labor and 500 units of capital. At this point, the production of food and clothing is Pareto-efficient.

a. Draw a production Edgeworth box depicting the information. Label everything carefully.

b. What condition holds at the point of Pareto efficiency in production?

c. Draw a hypothetical contract curve. Show, with isoquants, that the points on the contract curve are Pareto-efficient.

17. Consider a world with two goods: food and clothing. There is a total of 1,000 units of labor and 500 units of capital to be allocated among the two goods. The points listed, in the table on the next page, are all on the contract curve:

a. Showing labor on the *x*-axis and capital on the *y*-axis, draw an Edgeworth box showing the Pareto efficient points from the table. (Use food's origin in the lower-left corner.) Draw in the contract curve.

b. From the Pareto-efficient points, draw a Production Possibilities Curve (PPC). Label each of the points from the table. Is there anything unusual about this PPC?

Labor Allocated to Food	Capital Allocated to Food	Food Produced	Clothing Produced	Point Labeled
0	0	0	2,832	A
250	125	354	2,124	B
500	250	708	1,416	C
750	375	1,062	708	D
1,000	500	1,416	0	E

c. Explain the relationship between the contract curve and the production possibilities curve.

18. One of the most important concepts to understand about general equilibrium is the concept of Pareto efficiency.

   a. What do economists mean by Pareto efficiency?

   b. What are the technical conditions required for Pareto efficiency?

   c. Suppose that currently the $MRS = MU_x/MU_y > MC_x/MC_y = MRT$ in an economy. Show this condition in a graph. How could the price mech-anism lead the economy to adjust to reach a Pareto-efficient equilibrium?

19. How might an excise tax prevent an economy from attaining Pareto efficiency?

20. Consider an economy with two goods: x and y. Good x is produced in a competitive market, and good y is produced with a monopolized market. Using the conditions of Pareto efficiency, explain why this economy would be Pareto-inefficient.

Internet Exercises

Visit *http://www.myeconlab.com/waldman* for this chapter's Web exercises. Answer real-world economics problems by doing research on the Internet.

Chapter 20
Asymmetric Information

One of the necessary assumptions of a perfectly competitive market is perfect information. All buyers and sellers must be fully informed about all relevant characteristics of the good or service, and about market conditions. No seller or buyer can enjoy the advantage of inside information not readily available to everyone else. Perfect information ensures that no buyer or seller can take advantage of another buyer or seller. All of us have had our economic well-being reduced by a lack of perfect information from time to time. In November 2001, for example, I purchased a copy of the movie *Shrek* on DVD from a local discount store for the advertised sale price of $19.95, $2.00 off the suggested retail price of $21.95. I took the DVD home and my son immediately opened it. A few hours later, while shopping in another store, I noticed that this store's price for the *Shrek* DVD was $17.95. My consumer surplus had been reduced by $2.00 by my lack of perfect information.

Many cases of imperfect information are much more costly to society than the preceding example. Consider, for instance, many of the dot-com companies that were started up in the late 1990s. Owners founded these companies with dreams of eventual fortunes, but knew that immediate profits were not in the cards. However, they did not share this information with their investors. As a result, investors had imperfect information that led them to invest in these companies. Many of these investors, who lost most or all of their money, also didn't know that these dot-com owners had jumped into the dot-com market with an idea, but no plan, which ended up leading to the companies' demise.

Other situations in which imperfect information results in economic problems include:

- *Labor markets.* When an employer hires an employee, the employer has less-than-perfect knowledge about how hard the employee will work. Ideally, employers would hire only hard-working employees, but by hiring from the pool of all available workers, that outcome is extremely unlikely. Many employees put in a half-hearted work effort and cost companies millions of dollars a year in lost productivity.

Learning Objectives

After reading Chapter 20, you will have learned:

➤ Why, if only sellers, but not buyers, know the quality of used cars offered for sale, only lemons are sold, in the lemons model.

➤ How the problem of adverse selection evolves in insurance markets and causes insurance companies to insure predominantly high-risk individuals, and how insurance companies attempt to solve the problems associated with adverse selection.

➤ How the problem of moral hazard arises in insurance situations whenever an insured individual's unobserved actions can affect the probability or magnitude of a payment to that insured individual, and why this problem results in insurance companies offering only partial insurance rather than full insurance.

➤ How employers use a college education as a signal of worker quality, even if the skills learned in college are not directly transferable to college graduates' jobs, and how companies use warranties to signal the quality of their products.

➤ How principal-agent problems are defined, why they arise when an agent in rational pursuit of his own goals behaves in a manner that reduces the principal's welfare, why principal-agent problems are common in large corporations, and how firms attempt to solve these problems.

Featured Applications

➤ 20.2 Application Adverse Selection and Medicare Costs

➤ 20.3 Application The IMF and Moral Hazard

➤ 20.4 Application Automobile Reliability and Warranties

➤ 20.5A Application Principal-Agent Problems and Waldman's Summer Job

➤ 20.5B Application Henry Ford and Efficiency Wages

➤ 20.5C Application The Principal-Agent Problem and Franchising

- *Insurance markets.* Insurance companies constantly face another problem associated with imperfect information—it is difficult to separate out good insurance risks from bad risks when they offer homeowners', life, automobile, or medical insurance. To guard against insuring too many bad risks, the companies charge higher rates to all their policyholders. These high rates only serve to drive the low-risk candidates out of the market for insurance and leave mostly the high-risk candidates as their customers.

- *Used car markets.* Many used car buyers are greatly disappointed with their cars, because they have major mechanical problems. This is another example of imperfect information, because sellers know a great deal more about the quality of used cars than buyers, and as a result, sellers mostly end up holding onto good used cars and selling bad used cars, which are called "lemons." This results in negative consequences not only for the unfortunate buyers of lemons, but also for the owners of good used cars, because those owners cannot sell their cars for a profit.

These examples are just the tip of the iceberg of imperfect information's destruction of economic efficiency. In fact, if you present most economists with an example of some strange type of economic behavior, it's more likely than not that the economist will try to explain the phenomenon by stating: "It must be some kind of imperfect information." In this chapter, we examine some of the major economic problems created by *asymmetric information.* (Recall from Chapter 13 that asymmetric information describes a situation in which some economic agents know different information than other agents.) We will also explore the potential solutions to the problems associated with asymmetric information.

20.1 The Lemons Model

The seminal economics article dealing with asymmetric information, entitled "The Market for Lemons: Quality Uncertainty and the Market Mechanism," was written by George Akerlof in 1970.[1] Akerlof's argument, for which he won a Nobel Prize, can be presented in the form of a simple game. The game has two players: a seller and a buyer of a used car. The seller offers a used car for sale and knows whether the car is a good car or a lemon. The buyer is unaware of the quality of the car; however, the buyer knows the probability distribution of good cars and lemons.

Figure 20.1 depicts the extensive form of the basic lemons game. Recall from Chapter 13 that Nature is a pseudo-player who takes a random action in a game. Furthermore, recall from Chapter 15 that a *node* is a point in an extensive form of a game at which a player or Nature takes an action or the game ends. In Figure 20.1, at the node Nature, Nature randomly selects either a good car or a lemon to sell. The dotted lines encircling nodes B_1 and B_2 indicate that the buyer's information remains the same after Nature selects the type of car for sale. This means that after Nature selects a car, the buyer doesn't know whether she is at node B_1 or B_2. The move at the node

---

[1] George Akerlof, "The Market for Lemons: Quality Uncertainty and the Market Mechanism," *Quarterly Journal of Economics*, Vol. 90, pp. 599–617 (November 1970).

Figure 20.1 The Extensive Form of the Lemons Game
At the node Nature, Nature randomly selects either a good car or a lemon. The buyer then makes an offer price that the seller accepts or rejects. The seller will accept an offer for a good car only at a price greater than or equal to $12,000, and the seller will accept an offer for a lemon only at a price greater than or equal to $6,000. The only price offer that both buyer and seller will accept is $P = \$6,000$ for a lemon.

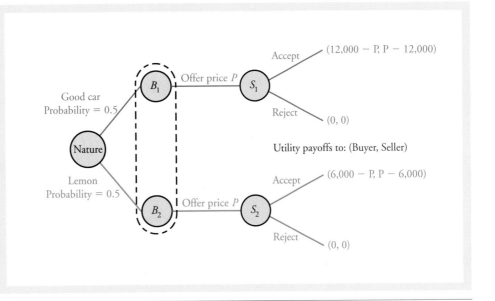

Nature and the move at either node B_1 or B_2 are made *simultaneously*. Nature selects a car and the buyer makes a price offer to the seller. If the distribution of good cars and lemons is 50 percent each, all the buyer knows is that there is a 50 percent chance of being at node B_1 and a 50 percent chance of being at node B_2. The buyer must make an offer to buy the car for a price P.

The payoffs are levels of utility after the offer is either accepted or rejected by the seller. For convenience, we assume a base value of utility equal to zero to both the buyer and the seller if no trade takes place. In the simplest version of the model, as presented in Figure 20.1, both the buyer and seller have identical tastes and there are only two types of cars. We depict the quality of a car by θ. Good cars have a quality value $\theta = \$12,000$ and lemons have a quality value $\theta = \$6,000$. If a trade takes place, the buyer's utility payoff is $\theta - P$ and the seller's utility payoff is $P - \theta$.

If the buyer knew the type of car, her decision would be easy: she would offer $12,000 for a good car or $6,000 for a lemon. However, the buyer doesn't know the quality of the car, but she does know the expected value of a car: its Expected Value is $0.5(\$12,000) + 0.5(\$6,000) = \$9,000$. Consequently, the buyer offers $9,000 for the car selected by Nature. The seller knows that the buyer knows the expected value of a car is $9,000. The seller, however, would offer only lemons for sale at $P = \$9,000$, because the seller's payoff from a good car sold at $P = \$9,000$ is $\$9,000 - \$12,000 = -\$3,000 < 0$, so the seller would reject $9,000 for a good car. The seller would accept $9,000 for a lemon, however, because $\$9,000 - \$6,000 > 0$. The act of accepting an offer of $9,000 for the car informs the buyer that the car is a lemon.

As soon as the seller accepts the offer of $9,000 for the car, the buyer knows she is at node B_2, and therefore, she will reject the car at $P = \$9,000$ because $\$6,000 - \$9,000 < 0$. In fact, the buyer will reject the car if $P > \$6,000$, because the seller will offer only lemons for prices above $6,000. In Figure 20.1, the seller knows that the maximum price the buyer will pay for a lemon is $6,000. Assuming sellers are indifferent between selling or keeping their lemons at $P = \$6,000$, sellers sell all their lemons for $P = \$6,000$. All the lemons get sold for $P = \$6,000$ and none of the good cars get sold. The existence of the bad cars drives the good cars out of the market.

Is this result an artifact of the assumption that there are only two types of cars: good cars worth $12,000 and lemons worth $6,000? Let's assume instead that there exists a continuum of different-quality cars. For example, suppose the quality of cars is uniformly distributed between lemons worth $6,000 and good cars worth $12,000. If 600,100 cars are available for sale, Nature can draw from 100 cars of each quality (100 cars valued at $6,000, 100 cars valued at $6,001, 100 cars valued at $6,002 ... 100 cars valued at $12,000). The average quality is still equal to $9,000, with 300,000 cars of quality less than $9,000 and 300,000 cars of quality greater than $9,000 available for Nature to draw from. Suppose that the buyer offers to pay the expected value $P = \$9,000$ for a car. The buyers know that the only cars sellers are willing to sell for $9,000 have values less than or equal to $9,000. The average quality of the cars offered for sale at $P = \$9,000$, therefore, is only $7,500, and the buyer knows this. The buyer therefore lowers her price offer to $7,500, which equals the expected value of the cars offered for sale. If the price offer is lowered to $7,500, the seller accepts the price offer only for a car worth between $6,000 and $7,500, so the average value of the cars sold declines to $6,750. However, if the price offer is lowered to $6,750, the sellers accept only offers for cars worth between $6,000 and $6,750, so the average value of the cars sold is $6,375. You should be able to see where this analysis is headed: the price offer keeps declining until it reaches $6,000 and the number of cars sold is a mere 100 vehicles. Asymmetric information has caused the entire market to collapse!

To this point, despite the absence of good cars being sold, there has been no efficiency loss as a result of the asymmetric information, because buyers and sellers have identical tastes and value the cars equally; therefore, from an efficiency standpoint, it doesn't matter whether a seller or buyer owns the car. We now expand the model to make it more realistic by assuming that buyers value any given car more highly than sellers. Assume, for example, that buyers place a 20 percent higher value on any car than do sellers, so the payoffs to a trade have changed. If a trade takes place, and the seller's quality is still measured by θ, then the buyer's utility payoff is $(1.2)\theta - P$, and the seller's utility payoff is $P - \theta$.

Table 20.1 shows how this inequality affects the game. The first column shows the quality range to the sellers for cars sold. Now look across the second row, where all cars priced between $6,000 and $6,500 are sold: in this case, the average value of a car to a seller is $\overline{\theta} = \$6,250$ and the expected value of a car to a buyer equals $1.2\,\overline{\theta} = \$7,500$. In the price range $6,000 - \$6,500$, the expected value of a car to a buyer, $7,500, is greater than the price $P = \$6,500$ sellers are willing to accept. At $P = \$6,500$, buyers would want to purchase more cars than sellers offer for sale and there would be an excess demand for cars. In Table 20.1, the market is in equilibrium only when all cars in the price range between $6,000 and $9,000 are sold at a price of $9,000. At a price $P = \$9,000$, all cars in the price range between $6,000 and $9,000 are sold and the expected value of a car sold to the seller equals $7,500. The expected value to a buyer equals $1.2\,\overline{\theta} = 1.2(\$7,500) = \$9,000$, so the expected value to the buyer equals the price, and equilibrium is achieved.

Figure 20.2 shows the equilibrium condition. The x-axis measures $\overline{\theta}$, the expected value of a car to sellers, and the y-axis measures the price that buyers and sellers are willing to pay or accept respectively for a car of quality $\overline{\theta}$. The red willingness-to-sell curve graphs price P as a function of $\overline{\theta}$ from Table 20.1, and the blue willingness-to-buy curve graphs the price buyers are willing to pay as a function of $\overline{\theta}$ from Table 20.1. The willingness-to-sell curve equals the willingness-to-buy curve only at equilibrium when $P = \$9,000$ and $\overline{\theta} = \$7,500$. For any value of $\overline{\theta} < \$7,500$, the willingness-to-buy curve is above the willingness-to-sell curve, so there is an excess demand; and for any value of $\overline{\theta} > \$7,500$, the willingness-to-sell curve is above the willingness-to-buy curve, so there is an excess supply.

Table 20.1 **Supply and Demand for Cars in the Lemons Model**

Quality Range to the Sellers for Cars Sold	Average Value of the Cars Sold to the Sellers ($\bar{\theta}$)	Price P	Expected Value to a Buyer $(1.2)(\bar{\theta})$	Excess Demand or Excess Supply
6,000	6,000	6,000	7,200	Excess demand
6,000–6,500	6,250	6,500	7,500	Excess demand
6,000–7,000	6,500	7,000	7,800	Excess demand
6,000–7,500	6,750	7,500	8,100	Excess demand
6,000–8,000	7,000	8,000	8,400	Excess demand
6,000–8,500	7,250	8,500	8,700	Excess demand
6,000–9,000	7,500	9,000	9,000	Equilibrium
6,000–9,500	7,750	9,500	9,300	Excess supply
6,000–10,000	8,000	10,000	9,600	Excess supply
6,000–10,500	8,250	10,500	9,900	Excess supply
6,000–11,000	8,500	11,000	10,200	Excess supply
6,000–11,500	8,750	11,500	10,500	Excess supply
6,000–12,000	9,000	12,000	10,800	Excess supply

Figure 20.2 **Equilibrium in the Lemons Model with Continuously Variable Quality**

The x-axis measures the expected value of a car to sellers, $\bar{\theta}$, and the y-axis measures the price P. The red willingness-to-sell curve graphs price P as a function of quality $\bar{\theta}$, and the blue willingness-to-buy curve graphs the price buyers would be willing to pay as a function of quality $\bar{\theta}$. For any value of $\bar{\theta} < \$7,500$, the willingness-to-buy curve is above the willingness-to-sell curve, so there is an excess demand. For any value of $\bar{\theta} > \$7,500$, the willingness-to-sell curve is above the willingness-to-buy curve, so there is an excess supply. The willingness-to-sell curve equals the willingness-to-buy curve only when $P = \$9,000$ and $\bar{\theta} = \$7,500$, so this is the equilibrium price.

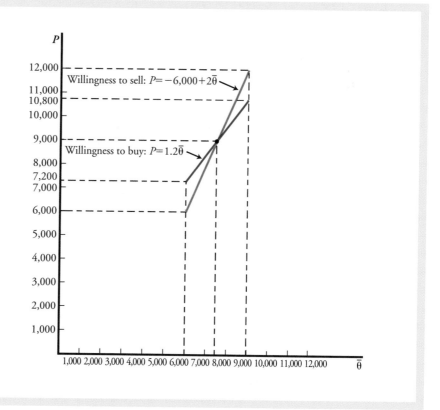

COMMON ERROR 10.1 **Believing That Pareto Efficiency Is Achieved in the Lemons Model Because the Quantity Demanded Equals the Quantity Supplied**

Students often believe that because in Figure 20.2 in equilibrium the quantity demanded equals the quantity supplied, the result is Pareto-efficient. This is incorrect. In fact, there is a serious efficiency problem in Figure 20.2. Buyers value all of the cars more highly than sellers, and in a market with perfect information, all of the cars should and would be sold, and every sale

is a Pareto-improving sale. In Figure 20.2, however, only half the cars are sold. Cars valued by sellers at more than $9,000 are not sold, even though each of these cars is valued more highly by some buyer than the current owner. Asymmetric information prevents the market from achieving Pareto efficiency.

▼▼▼ 20.2 Adverse Selection

adverse selection

A situation in which less desirable buyers or sellers are more likely to engage in a market exchange than more desirable buyers or sellers because buyers or sellers do not have sufficient information to determine the true quality of the product being exchanged.

The lemons model is an excellent example of one of the major problems associated with asymmetric information: *adverse selection*. **Adverse selection** refers to any situation where products of different qualities are sold at the same price because buyers or sellers do not have sufficient information to determine the true quality of the products. Based on the lemons model explored in Table 20.1 and Figure 20.2, buyers cannot determine the quality of a car before they purchase the car, and as a result, cars with qualities ranging between $6,000 and $9,000 to their sellers are all sold at a uniform price of $9,000. Some unlucky buyers pay $9,000 for lemons worth only $7,200 to these buyers. Meanwhile, no high-quality cars valued by sellers above $9,000 are sold at all. The adverse selection problem causes too few of the high-quality cars to be sold.

Insurance and the Adverse Selection Problem

The adverse selection problem is nowhere more apparent than in the insurance market. In Chapter 6, we analyzed the insurance market and discovered that insurance companies are in the business of insuring risk-averse individuals with income Y and utility functions $U = f(Y)$. By definition, these risk-averse individuals have diminishing marginal utility of income, and therefore have concave utility functions when income is graphed on the x-axis and total utility $U(Y)$ is graphed on the y-axis. Recall that these risk-averse individuals are willing to pay a risk premium for insurance.

Let's briefly review our insurance example from Chapter 6. There we assumed that an individual has a $200,000 home in an area where the average risk of fire in a given year is known to be 2 percent. In the event of a fire, the individual suffers $100,000 in damages to his home. Without insurance, the individual faces a gamble where he loses $100,000 with probability 0.02 each year, and loses nothing with probability 0.98. This gamble has an annual expected value of $0.02(-\$100,000) + 0.98 (\$0) = -\$2,000$. Suppose that the individual is permitted to buy insurance that covers all losses in the event of a fire. The yearly charge for the insurance is X. Buying insurance therefore implies a gamble that pays $(-X)$ with certainty. We then asked: What is the greatest amount of money X per year that an individual will pay for insurance? If the individual is risk-averse with utility function $U(Y) = \sqrt{100 + 0.001Y}$, we determined that he would be willing to pay a maximum of $3,960 per year to insure his house against an annual 2 percent chance of $100,000 in damages. The individual was willing to pay a risk premium of $1,960 above the expected loss of $2,000.

Realistically, however, the probability of having a fire will not be 2 percent for all homeowners. For high-risk homeowners, the risk will be greater than 2 percent, and for low-risk homeowners, the risk will be less than 2 percent. Recall from Chapter 6 that as the probability of having a fire increases above 2 percent, a premium based on a 2 percent risk of a fire looks like a good deal for the homeowner. On the other hand, as the probability of having a fire decreases below 2 percent, a premium based on a 2 percent risk of a fire looks like a bad deal. Unless the insurance company can calculate the exact probability of a particular house burning down, it cannot calculate the correct premium to charge for that specific house. Such precise risk calculations are impossible. If the insurance company bases its premium on the assumption that every house has a 2 percent probability of burning down, most homeowners with a probability greater than or equal to 2 percent will purchase insurance, while many homeowners with a probability less than 2 percent will not purchase insurance. This outcome is nothing more than the lemons model result in a somewhat different guise. Consequently, only high-risk homeowners purchase insurance. Adverse selection results in a pool of insured homeowners that comes disproportionately from the group of high-risk homeowners. The low-risk homeowners are driven out of the market and the insurance companies are left with a bunch of lemons, in the form of high-risk customers.

When an insurance company finds itself in the position of insuring a majority of high-risk policyholders, it will have to increase its rates to cover the increased probability of a fire. However, rate increases serve only to drive more of the low-risk homeowners away from the company, thus compounding the firm's problems. This analysis is valid for all types of insurance markets. In each market, the insurance company faces an adverse selection problem that tends to result in a disproportionately large share of high-risk individuals purchasing insurance.

Dealing with the Problem of Adverse Selection

One effective way to solve the adverse selection problem is to obtain more information. Insurance companies attempt to sort out high-risk from low-risk policyholders in a variety of ways. For example, before customers purchase homeowners' insurance, the company typically asks the following questions: Do you have smoke detectors on every floor? Does anyone living in the house smoke? How far is the house from a fire station? Is the local fire department professional or volunteer? How far is the nearest fire hydrant? Do you have a central alarm system? Do you have a sprinkler system? Is the house constructed of wood, brick, cement, or other materials? Is the house located in a wooded area with a high probability of a forest fire?

Similarly, to obtain life insurance, in addition to asking a long list of questions about an applicant's health history and living patterns, insurance companies usually demand a medical examination by a company-approved doctor. Automobile insurance companies look carefully at an applicant's history of accidents and automobile insurance claims, as well as the applicant's age. Young teenagers have the highest risk of serious automobile accidents, and young males in particular are in an extremely high-risk category. Once insurance companies gather all of this information, they place an applicant in a particular risk category and charge policy premiums based on these categories. For example, a 30-year-old non-smoking female professor will pay far less for health insurance than a 40-year-old male lumberjack smoker.

Another method used by insurance companies is to sell insurance to everyone in a large group. For example, many employers offer health insurance benefits through only

▲▲▲ 20.2 APPLICATION   Adverse Selection and Medicare Costs

Adverse selection problems arise in medical insurance programs if it is possible for healthy people to move to a medical insurance pool that sick people want to avoid. Such a flow of healthy individuals out of one insurance pool and into another results in a serious adverse selection problem in the pool that is left with mostly sick individuals. Many employers offer their employees multiple health insurance options. Typically, at least one of these plans is a health maintenance organization plan (HMO) and another is an indemnity plan such as Blue Cross/Blue Shield. An HMO plan usually requires patients to see only healthcare professionals employed by the HMO and to use only hospitals that are either owned by or approved by the HMO. An indemnity plan permits patients to choose any healthcare professional and any hospital anywhere in the country. The premium for an HMO insurance plan is typically lower than the premium for an indemnity plan. In addition to high premiums associated with indemnity plans, they also generally have large deductibles for doctors' bills, which the patient must pay before the plan will reimburse any expenses.

Healthy patients tend to prefer the low-cost HMO coverage; sicker individuals with serious life-threatening conditions tend to prefer high-cost indemnity plans, because they want to go to the best doctors and hospitals in the country to treat their serious illnesses. Furthermore, if a healthy person becomes sick, he or she can switch from an HMO to an indemnity plan, thereby exacerbating the adverse selection problem for the indemnity plans. Adverse selection tends to leave indemnity health plans with a pool of high-cost sick people and

forces these plans to charge extremely high rates, which in turn forces even more healthy people out of these indemnity plans.

Senior citizens make the same healthcare choices as younger individuals. Younger and healthier seniors tend to select lower-cost HMO coverage, while older and sicker seniors who can afford it select more flexible indemnity plans. Medicare, however, reimburses HMOs on a per-subscriber basis, based on the average healthcare costs of all retirees, with some minor adjustments for risk. Because HMOs have a subscriber base of younger and healthier seniors compared to the senior population at large, Medicare pays HMOs a per-subscriber fee that is significantly greater than the actual cost per subscriber. For example, one study done by the Health Care Financing Administration found that the ratio of HMO subscriber costs per patient to indemnity plan costs was only 0.85. In another study prepared for the U.S. Congress, the Physician Payment Review Commission found that spending per new HMO patient was, on average, 37 percent less than spending on indemnity plan patients in the six months prior to their enrollment in an HMO, and spending on patients who left HMOs to join indemnity plans was 60 percent higher in the six months after they switched plans; thus suggesting that healthier patients leave their indemnity plans to join HMOs, and sicker patients leave their HMOs to join indemnity plans. These studies suggest that adverse selection ends up costing the government—and ultimately taxpayers—a great deal of money under the current Medicare reimbursement system.

one company. Because everyone in the company must enroll in the plan, there is no adverse selection problem within that group of insured individuals; the healthy and the unhealthy are insured together. Similarly, many employers provide life insurance policies for all their employees, which enables the insurance company to overcome its adverse selection problem and offer the group life insurance at relatively low cost.

Consumers have insufficient information to make informed decisions in many other markets besides used cars and insurance. In these markets, the government sometimes attempts to reduce or solve adverse selection problems by mandating the disclosure of information to uniformed parties. For example, in the United States, food manufacturers must conform to food labeling that tells consumers a great deal about the nutritional content of packaged foods. Similarly, the U.S. government requires cigarette manufacturers to divulge the tar and nicotine content of their cigarettes, appliance manufacturers to disclose the energy efficiency of their products, and automobile manufacturers to reveal the fuel mileage of their cars. Furthermore, in the United States, the Federal Trade Commission is authorized to prevent firms from using false or deceptive forms of advertising. As a result, firms producing low-quality products are less likely to attempt to trick consumers, and as a result, firms producing high-quality products can advertise without being accused of hiding the truth. Finally, many states require homeowners to reveal in writing all of their homes' significant defects to potential buyers before selling a house.

20.3 Moral Hazard

Insurance companies face another serious asymmetric information problem in addition to adverse selection. If a person is fully insured against a loss, there is less incentive to behave carefully. For example, suppose the Woody family is building a house on a five-acre lot in a heavily forested area where there is a considerable risk of a fire. The house costs $300,000, and if the Woodys leave all the surrounding forest intact, there is a 2 percent chance the house will burn down completely in a given year. Therefore, the expected value of their loss from a fire is $E(V) = 0.98(0) + 0.02(-\$300,000) = -\$6,000$. Recall from Chapter 6 that ignoring administrative costs, the actuarially fair insurance premium if the Woodys leave the forest intact is $6,000. However, if every year the family cuts down all the forest and shrubbery on the acre immediately surrounding the house, the risk of the house burning down decreases to just 0.5 percent and the expected value of their loss from a fire is $E(V) = 0.995(0) + 0.005(-\$300,000) = -\$1,500$. The actuarially fair insurance premium if they clear the half-acre is $1,500. Similarly, if the Woodys cut down all the forest and shrubbery on the half-acre surrounding the house, the risk of the house burning down is 1.0 percent and the expected value of their loss from a fire is $E(V) = 0.99(0) + 0.01(-\$300,000) = -\$3,000$. Furthermore, if the family does not cut down the surrounding forest every year, the forest grows back quickly and the fire risk increases rapidly. The more acres the family cuts down annually, the lower the risk of a fire, but the less beautiful the house.

Suppose that an insurance company offers a policy to the Woodys for an annual premium of $X, and the company agrees to pay the family in the event of a fire. There are two possible types of insurance: *full insurance* and *partial insurance*. With **full insurance**, the company agrees to pay for the complete value of the house if it burns down; that is, because the house is worth $300,000, the company pays the Woodys $300,000 if the house burns down. With **partial insurance**, the company agrees to pay less than the complete value of the house.

In Figure 20.3, the Woody family's demand curve for acres of forest cleared with full insurance is D_{FI}, and without any insurance is D_{NI}. If the marginal cost of clearing an acre is $300, without insurance, the Woodys clear an acre in order to reduce the risk of fire to 0.5 percent. However, if the Woodys are fully insured, they are less concerned about a fire and more concerned about keeping the house looking beautiful, so they only clear a half-acre. The Woodys behave more carefully with regard to the risk of fire if they are not insured. This creates a *moral hazard* problem for the insurance company. **Moral hazard** arises in insurance situations whenever an insured individual's unobserved actions can increase the probability or magnitude of a payment to that insured individual. In other words, if you're insured against a particular type of loss, you behave less carefully than if you're not insured against that type of loss. In the case of the Woodys, if they are fully insured, they will clear only a half-acre annually.

full insurance

An insurance policy that pays for the complete value of the asset being insured.

partial insurance

An insurance policy that pays less than the complete value of the asset being insured.

moral hazard

A situation that arises in insurance markets whenever an insured individual's unobserved actions can affect the probability or magnitude of a payment to that insured individual.

Figure 20.3 Moral Hazard in the Insurance Market
With no insurance, the demand for acres of forest cleared is D_{NI} and the family clears an acre. With full insurance, the demand is D_{FI} and the family clears a half-acre. With partial insurance, the demand is D_{PI} and the family clears 0.75 acres. The family is more careful if it is not fully insured.

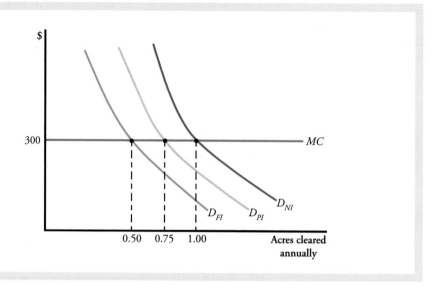

Insurance with Asymmetric Information

An economic problem arises because of asymmetric information in insurance markets. With perfect information, the insurance company and the Woody family would both be able to observe the family's behavior, in which case the optimal and actual outcome would be for the Woodys to clear an acre at a cost of $300 and pay $1,500 for an actuarially fair policy with full insurance. The total cost to the family would be $1,800 a year. Because the insurance company is able to monitor the family's behavior, it knows that the Woodys clear an acre every year, and therefore can charge the actuarially fair premium of $1,500.

Unfortunately, real-world insurance situations, like the Woody family's situation, are almost always situations of asymmetric information, where only the insured knows if he is behaving carefully or carelessly. Suppose the Woodys know how many acres they have cleared but the insurance company does not. If the insurance company offers the family full insurance for a $1,500 premium, how will the Woodys behave? In Figure 20.3, with full insurance, the Woodys always clear a half-acre. With asymmetric information and full insurance, the family has no incentive to behave carefully and clear an acre, because regardless of their behavior, they receive compensation for the full value of their house in the case of a fire. Of course, the insurance company knows that with asymmetric information and full insurance, the Woody family will never behave carefully, and therefore, the only full insurance policy the company will offer will be for a much higher premium than $1,500. But the problem is even more complicated. Only the Woodys know their demand curve is D_{FI} with full insurance, but the insurance company knows nothing about their demand curve. The insurance company might, for instance, assume that the Woodys would not clear any acres if they were fully insured, and the company would then offer a full insurance premium only at the very high premium of $6,000 per year. At such a high premium, the family would likely reject the policy offer. Full insurance is rare in insurance markets with asymmetric information, because it is too expensive.

There is, however, an alternative to full insurance: the insurance company can offer a partial insurance policy that pays less than the value of the house in case of a fire. With partial insurance, the Woodys bear some of the financial burden of a fire, and therefore they have a greater incentive to behave carefully and clear more acres. For example, sup-

▲▲▲ 20.3 APPLICATION The IMF and Moral Hazard

The International Monetary Fund (IMF) is a lender of last resort for countries faced with serious economic crises. Suppose that central banks in developing countries know that if their policies result in an economic crisis, the IMF will always bail them out. These banks would then take riskier actions than usual. Many economists believe this is exactly what has happened in Mexico and Southeast Asia over the past 25 years. Financial problems often begin simply enough, when banks in developing countries respond to an economic shock by borrowing money. Because interest rates in developed countries are relatively low compared to domestic interest rates in these developing countries, the banks borrow primarily from foreign lenders.

Asia's huge increase in debt in 1997 was an excellent example of such borrowing. Foreign banks were willing to extend more and more debt to these troubled economies, because in the end, the international banks knew that the IMF would bail these countries out in order to prevent a total currency collapse. For example, foreign bankers loaned enormous sums to insolvent banks in Korea not because the bankers were unaware of the Korean banks' looming insolvency, but because they knew that the Korean government and the IMF would ultimately protect the foreign banks from any losses.

As the price of a bailout, the IMF typically forces countries to raise taxes to pay back their IMF loans. Increased taxation is the IMF's required price that these countries must pay in order to avoid the bankruptcy of many of the domestic and foreign banks that hold these debts. Local politicians and the bankers favor higher taxes on the general population as an alternative to currency depreciation and bank bankruptcies. In the end, the IMF's payback conditions facilitate the next round of bad borrowing and the next crisis. If the IMF refused to bail out a country in crisis, the country's currency would depreciate dramatically, driving up the cost of imported goods and causing a lower standard of living. Furthermore, some banks would go bankrupt; however, there would be a much lower risk of future episodes of risky borrowing.

The IMF has not been the only financial institution facilitating risky banking decisions. In the early 1980s, U.S. savings and loan associations (S&Ls) began investing in highly speculative real estate deals. Because the Federal Savings and Loan Insurance Corporation (FSLIC) insured the S&L depositors, the managers of many S&Ls failed to seriously evaluate the risks of many of their investments. When the real estate market collapsed in some parts of the country—particularly in the South and Southwest—over 1,000 savings and loans went bankrupt. In 1989, the FSLIC ran out of funds to cover depositors' insured losses, and it essentially went bankrupt. As a result, the government was forced to abolish the FSLIC and transfer its activities to the Federal Deposit Insurance Corporation (FDIC), which had previously insured only deposits in non–savings and loan institutions. The cost to U.S. taxpayers was hundreds of billions of dollars.

---

deductible

The dollar amount of an insurance claim that the insured must pay before the policy begins to pay any benefits.

pose that the insurance company agrees to pay the cost of all fire damage except for a *deductible* of X for a premium between $1,500 and $6,000. An insurance **deductible** is the dollar amount of an insurance claim that the insured must pay before the policy begins to pay any benefits. The larger the deductible, the greater the incentive to behave carefully, and the lower the necessary insurance premium. For example, the insurance company and the Woody family might be willing to agree on a policy with a $5,000 deductible and a $2,500 premium, and as a result, the family's demand curve would be D_{PI} in Figure 20.3 and the Woodys would clear three-quarters of an acre annually. Suppose with 0.75 acres cleared, the probability of a fire is 0.75 percent. Then from the insurance company's perspective, the expected value of the Woodys' loss is $E(V) = 0.9925(0) + 0.0075(-\$295,000) = -\$2,212.50$, so a premium of $2,500 is greater than the actuarially fair premium. Notice that the Woodys would be much better off financially with perfect information, in which case they would clear an acre and pay a total cost of $1,800 for their insurance *and* the cost of clearing the acre. In equilibrium in insurance markets with asymmetric information, the insurance companies offer only partial insurance, and because of deductibles, the insured behaves more carefully than she would with full insurance.

Solutions to the Problem of Moral Hazard

In our model, partial insurance with a deductible makes it possible to have an insurance market at prices buyers can afford. Partial insurance is extremely common in the insurance industry. In fact, most insurance policies have some type of deductible. Automobile collision insurance policies typically include deductibles ranging from $100 up to thousands of dollars. Insurance companies greatly reduce premiums for collision insurance as the size of the deductible increases, because the larger the deductible, the more likely a driver is to be careful.

> **indemnity plans**
>
> A health insurance policy that pays for medical services when they are provided.

Health insurance policies also rely heavily on deductibles. **Indemnity plans**, like Blue Cross/Blue Shield, pay a fee for medical services provided. Such insurance plans typically have high deductibles that require the patient to pay hundreds of dollars for medical services before the plan begins to pay. Insurance companies also rely extensively on *co-insurance* to reduce the moral hazard problem. **Co-insurance** requires the insured to make a partial payment toward any medical expenses provided. For example, in addition to large deductibles, most medical indemnity plans pay only 80 percent of the bills for medical services up to some maximum amount. Under such a plan, if you receive a doctor's bill for $1,000, your co-insurance payment toward the bill is $200. Pre-paid **health maintenance organizations (HMOs)**, which provide most medical services for one fixed insurance payment, usually have much lower co-insurance payments than do indemnity plans. Many HMOs require a co-insurance payment of only $10 per visit for services rendered within the HMO's service network. Most medical insurance plans also require co-insurance payments for prescription drugs, which can range from $5 up to $50 or more per prescription, depending on the plan.

> **co-insurance**
>
> An insurance policy that requires the insured to make a partial payment toward any expenses beyond the policy's deductible.

> **health maintenance organizations (HMOs)**
>
> A pre-paid health insurance plan that provides most medical services for one fixed insurance payment.

▼▼▼ 20.4 Market Signaling

Why do you go to college? When asked this question, many students answer, "to get a better job." But why does a college degree get you a better job? Do students learn skills in college that are important to their employers? Some do, but many a sociology, philosophy, history, or English major goes to work for a large corporation where they use little if any of the course-specific knowledge gained in the classroom. Many economics majors go into sales-related jobs working for large corporations selling everything from pharmaceuticals and college textbooks to clothing and computer equipment. Do economics courses teach you how to sell products? Most probably don't. Although going to college may not train you in a specific skill for your first post-graduate job, or any future jobs, going to college certainly signals to potential employers that you are an intelligent person. Furthermore, the more prestigious the college and the higher your GPA, the stronger is the signal of your apparent intelligence and ability.

An Economic Model of Education as a Signal

> **market signaling**
>
> The use of an observable action as an indicator of a hidden characteristic.

Nobel Laureate A. Michael Spence was the first economist to view education primarily as a job market signal of quality to employers.[2] **Market signaling** is a way for sellers of a good or service to convey hidden information about quality to buyers. We begin with a

---

[2] A. Michael Spence, "Job Market Signalling," *Quarterly Journal of Economics*, Vol. 87 pp. 355–374 (August 1973).

simple model, where a worker's college educational background serves as a signal of the potential quality of his or her work. In this model, college education has no direct impact on the worker's productivity. High-quality workers are more productive because they are more efficient, not because they are well educated.

One way to illustrate educational signaling is to think of it as a game. The education game is played between a worker and two employers as follows:

1. Nature specifies a worker as either high quality or low quality with probability 0.5. The worker knows her quality, but employers do not. Low-quality workers produce output $q = 6.00$ and high-quality workers produce output $q = 16.50$.
2. The worker selects a level of college education s, where $s = 0$ if the worker does not attend college and $s = 1$ if the worker attends college.
3. The two employers each offer the worker a wage w that is a function of the amount of schooling, s, so the wage can be expressed as $w(s)$.
4. The worker accepts one of the two contracts or rejects both.
5. Output $q = 6.00$ if a low-quality worker accepts a wage offer, or output $q = 16.50$ if a high-quality worker accepts a wage offer.
6. College-educated workers receive a wage $w(1) = 16.50$, and workers without a college education receive a wage $w(0) = 6.00$.
7. The worker's payoff, π_{worker}, is her wage minus her cost of education $72s/q$, and the employer's payoff, $\pi_{employer}$, is the firm's profit, so:

$$\pi_{worker} = w - 72s/q \quad \text{if the worker accepts contract } w(s)$$
$$\pi_{worker} = 0 \quad \text{if the worker rejects both contract offers}$$
$$\pi_{employer} = q - w \quad \text{for the employer whose contract is accepted}$$
$$\pi_{employer} = 0 \quad \text{for the employer whose contract is rejected}$$

A crucial assumption of the Spence model is that the cost of education, $72s/q$, is greater for low-quality workers ($72/6.00 = 12$) than high-quality workers ($72/16.50 = 4.36$). The thinking behind this assumption is that high-quality workers complete school in less time than low-quality workers, and therefore have lower opportunity costs of education. Low-quality workers take more time to complete school, because they are capable of completing fewer courses each year and/or because they fail more courses along the way toward a degree.

Competition between employers ensures that firms hire workers as long as the wage equals the value of the worker's output. Therefore, given our assumptions and competition between employers, employers hire low-quality workers if $w(s) = w(0) = q_L = 6.00$, and employers hire high-quality workers if $w(s) = w(1) = q_H = 16.50$. Consider the choices for a low-quality and a high-quality worker. For a low-quality worker, comparing the profit if they don't go to school with profit if they do yields:

$$\pi_{worker}^{low} = w(0) - 0 = 6.00 - 0 = 6.00 > w(1) - \frac{72}{6.00} = 16.50 - 12 = 4.50$$

The low-quality worker is better off not going to college. Making the same comparisons for a high-quality worker:

$$\pi_{worker}^{high} = w(0) - 0 = 6.00 - 0 = 6.00 < w(1) - \frac{72}{16.50} = 16.50 - 4.36 = 12.14$$

The high-quality worker is better off going to college.

The equilibrium for the education game is:

$$s(low\text{-}quality\ worker) = 0; s(high\text{-}quality\ worker) = 1$$

and:

$$w(0) = 6.00; \; w(1) = 16.50$$

Only high-quality workers get an education, so employers identify the high-quality workers and pay them a wage equal to 16.50. Low-quality workers elect not to get an education, so employers identify the low-quality workers and pay them a wage equal to 6.00.

In this simple game, college education seems to be wasteful, because it imposes costs on society but does nothing to increase workers' productivity. Although this may be a disturbing conclusion, there are reasons to believe that even if a college education is only a signaling device, we are better off with a college education system. College enables employers to match workers with jobs more efficiently. In the absence of college, employers would be unable to differentiate between high-quality workers and low-quality workers. Suppose, for example, there were only two jobs in a corporation: clerks and technical analysts. The existence of colleges enables employers to hire low-quality workers to be clerks and high-quality workers to be analysts. Without a college education signal, many of the clerks would be high-quality and underutilized, and many of the analysts would be low-quality and under-productive.

Warranties as a Signal

Signaling is also used by manufacturers to signal the quality of their products. The true quality of many goods is impossible to determine before consumers purchase them. Consider the purchase of a new automobile: A consumer can purchase a new car that is the best-quality car ever built, or a lemon. It is only after the purchase that the consumer has any idea about the true quality of the car. One solution to this information problem is for the automobile manufacturer to signal the quality of the car by offering a warranty against mechanical defects for a certain number of months or miles. Warranties are offered on many different products, from cars and major appliances to electronic equipment and high-quality tools. The best warranty is a lifetime warranty that guarantees repair or replacement for the life of the product. Sears offers a lifetime warranty on all of its Craftsman tools, and Eddie Bauer and L.L. Bean offer lifetime warranties on many of their products, including clothing. With a lifetime warranty, a customer can't lose. If the product is in any way defective, it will be replaced. It is as if the customer were fully informed about the quality of the product, in which case she would purchase only high-quality products.

Why would a company ever guarantee a product for life? Suppose consumers cannot determine the quality of a product until after they have purchased it. Assume further that:

1. A low-quality product is less costly to produce, so that if a low-quality product is sold without a warranty at the same price as a high-quality product, the manufacturer earns more profit on the low-quality product.
2. If both low-quality and high-quality products are sold with lifetime warranties, it is less expensive to sell a high-quality product, because of the high replacement costs associated with low-quality products.

Given these assumptions, is it profitable for a high-quality producer to signal their products' quality to consumers by offering a lifetime warranty? Suppose we measure quality as q, where q is the probability that the product will not break in a given period and is constant in every time period. Therefore, if a product never breaks and never has to be replaced, it is of perfect quality $q = 1$, and if a product breaks and has to be replaced in every time period, it is of quality $q = 0$. If $TC(q)$ represents the total cost of producing and replacing a good of quality q, $c(q)$ represents the production cost of producing the good of quality q, r is the firm's discount rate, and $(1 - q)$ is the constant probability that the product will break and have to be replaced in any future period, then the total cost of a product of quality q with a lifetime warranty is the sum of the current production cost $c(q)$ plus the replacement costs in future periods, or:

$$TC(q) = c(q) + \frac{(1 - q)}{(1 + r)}c(q) + \frac{(1 - q)}{(1 + r)^2}c(q) + \cdots \tag{20.1}$$

With a lifetime warranty, the expected present value of replacing the good in any future period must be considered in calculating total costs. The first term on the right side of Equation 20.1 is the current cost of producing a good of quality q, the second term is the expected present value of replacing a good of quality q next year, and the third term is the expected present value of replacing a good of quality q in two years.

Using algebra, Equation 20.1 can be simplified to:

$$TC(q) = c(q) + c(q)\left[\frac{(1 - q)}{(1 + r)} + \frac{(1 - q)}{(1 + r)^2} + \cdots\right] = c(q)\left(1 + \frac{(1 - q)}{r}\right) \tag{20.2}$$

If the product is of perfect quality, it never breaks, $q = 1$, and total discounted cost, $TC(1)$, equals the initial cost of production $c(1)$. Recalling our assumption that if both low-quality and high-quality products are sold with lifetime warranties, it is less expensive to produce and sell a high-quality product, total cost $TC(q)$ must be a decreasing function with respect to increases in quality q, and therefore total cost $TC(q)$ must be minimized for a product that never breaks with $q = 1$.

Suppose a producer of a high-quality product sets price p equal to cost, so the firm makes a normal profit, that is:

$$p = TC(q) = c(q)\left(1 + \frac{(1 - q)}{r}\right) \tag{20.3}$$

A high-quality manufacturer earns a normal, or zero, economic profit; however, consider the possibilities for a low-quality manufacturer. A low-quality producer can offer the

---

COMMON ERROR 20.2 | **Thinking That Low-Quality Producers Are More Likely to Offer Good Warranties than High-Quality Producers**

Before examining the model of how warranties are used to signal quality, I usually ask my students if they think low-quality or high-quality producers are more likely to offer good warranties. Typically, roughly half the students make the common error of thinking that a company producing a low-quality product must compensate for that low quality by offering reluctant buyers a good warranty. The problem with this reasoning is that competitive producers of higher-quality products who offer the same warranty will have significantly lower costs because costs, $(c(q))(1 + [(1 - q)/r])$, are lower with a higher value of quality q. In

fact, with a product of perfect quality that never breaks, $q = 1$, and costs are minimized and equal $c(1)$. For any lower-quality product $q < 1$, and if the lower-quality product is offered with the same warranty, $TC(q) = (c(q))(1 + [(1 - q)/r]) > c(1)$. In a competitive market, price equals $TC(q)$, and the lower-quality producers, who have higher costs if they offer a warranty, will not be able to survive. Only the producers of high-quality products, therefore, offer excellent warranties. Don't make the common error of assuming that the producers of lower-quality products are more likely to offer good warranties.

▲▲▲ 20.4 APPLICATION   Automobile Reliability and Warranties

Between 1980 and 2000, the average quality of American-built automobiles improved dramatically compared to European- and Japanese-built cars. In April 2001, the magazine *Consumer Reports* compared the reliability of American-, European-, and Japanese-built cars and found that the reliability of American-built cars improved by over 70 percent since 1980, and the dependability gap between American-built and foreign-built cars was greatly reduced.

If the *Consumer Reports'* findings are accurate, then our model suggests that American automobile manufacturers should have signaled to consumers that reliability had improved by improving their warranties. This is exactly what happened. In the late 1970s and early 1980s, American manufacturers offered basic warranties of either 12 months or 12,000 miles on most of their models. In the 1980s, the basic warranty was improved to 36 months or 36,000 miles, and in 2001,

DaimlerChrysler offered a 7-year or 100,000-mile powertrain warranty on some Chrysler models. American manufacturers have indeed signaled their improved quality by offering much better warranties.

In 2001, several South Korean automobile manufacturers also used improved warranties to signal quality to consumers. These South Korean firms produce the Hyundai, Kia, and Daewoo brands. The South Korean models had some early quality problems and were in danger of failing to compete in the North American market when the companies began to offer 5-year bumper-to-bumper warranties and 10-year powertrain warranties. Consumers responded by purchasing significantly more of these models. According to Hyundai, its extended warranties were the top reason why consumers chose Hyundais. Hyundai claimed that the increased costs of the warranties were more than offset by increased sales volume and lower marketing expenditures.

product without a lifetime warranty; however, that would mean the low quality of the product is revealed to consumers. Alternatively, the low-quality manufacturer can offer a lifetime warranty; however, at a price p, the low-quality manufacturer would sustain an economic loss, because $TC(q)$ increases as quality q decreases and the high-quality producer is earning only a normal profit of zero at price $p = TC(q)$. Low-quality firms, therefore, cannot offer lifetime warranties and survive. They are forced to offer either weaker warranties or no warranty at all. In either case, the high-quality manufacturer succeeds in signaling its high quality to consumers by offering a lifetime warranty.

▼▼▼   20.5   The Principal–Agent Problem

principal

A person or group of people who hire another person or group of people to achieve an objective for the principal.

agent

The person or group hired to achieve the principal's objective.

principal-agent problem

A problem that arises when an agent in rational pursuit of his own goals behaves in a manner that reduces the principal's welfare.

In this chapter, we have explored several ways in which asymmetric information distorts economic choices. In the adverse selection, moral hazard, and signaling models, one player has more information than another. In each of these models, one economic agent's welfare is dependent on the actions of another economic agent. For example, in the adverse selection and moral hazard insurance games, the insurance company's welfare is dependent on the policyholder's action; and in the education game, the employer's welfare is dependent on the worker's action. In the insurance games, the policyholder has better information than the company; and in the education game, the worker has better information than the employer. In principal-agent games, the **principal** is a person or group of people who hire another person or group of people to achieve an objective for the principal. The **agent** is the person or group hired to achieve the principal's objective. A **principal-agent problem** arises when an agent in rational pursuit of his own goals behaves in a manner that reduces the principal's welfare. This is clearly not Pareto-efficient, as the agent makes himself better off while making the principal worse off.

The Separation of Ownership from Control in Large Corporations

One of the most significant principal-agent problems arises when the ownership of a corporation is separated from effective control over the daily operations of the firm. A corporation's owners are its stockholders, and a large corporation typically has many owners. While there are many owners in the modern corporation, the day-to-day corporate business decisions are made by a handful of professional managers. In theory, the stockholders elect a board of directors to oversee the managers, ensuring that the owners' interests are represented. In practice, however, the managers often select the candidates for the board of directors for most corporations. Few stockholders typically attend a corporation's annual meeting. Instead, they make the managers their proxies, or give them permission to vote on their behalf at meetings. Consequently, many corporate boards of directors are more of a rubber-stamp body, rather than an independent group that vigilantly examines the management's decisions and protects the stockholders' interests. In modern corporations, managers generally have a great deal more knowledge about their businesses' daily operations than stockholders, so the stockholders are the principals and the managers are their agents. The principal's (stockholder's) welfare is ultimately dependent on the agent's (manager's) performance.

Why does it matter whether owners or managers control the firm? Let's start by accepting a central assumption of microeconomic theory: Individuals act to maximize their own utility. This principle applies to managers, whether they are operating firms or behaving as consumers. The managers who run firms maximize profits as long as it's in their best interest. Profit maximization and utility maximization, however, may conflict with each other as managers pursue objectives other than maximizing profits.

Solving the Separation of Ownership and Control Principal–Agent Problem

To solve the principal-agent problem, the stockholders have a strong incentive to compensate the managers in a way that encourages them to act in the stockholders' best interests. The stockholders can work with either a carrot or a stick in their interactions with managers. For example, consider the following game played by a group of stockholders and a manager:

1. Both players are risk-neutral.
2. The stockholders offer a manager a contract that pays a wage greater than or equal to zero and is a function of revenues R generated by the firm, so that $w(R) \geq 0$.
3. The manager either accepts the contract offer, or rejects the offer, in which case he receives his *reservation utility*, $U_r = 210$, which equals the wage he could earn in his next best job offer. His **reservation utility** is the lowest utility the worker will accept and work for the company; if his utility is any lower, he will work somewhere else or not at all.
4. The manager's work effort, e, is either high, in which case $e = 100$, or low, in which case $e = 0$.
5. Nature selects revenues according to Table 20.2.
6. The stockholders' payoff is $R - w$. If he accepts the contract offer, the manager's utility payoff is the wage *minus* his work effort, $w - e$. If he rejects the contract, his utility payoff is his reservation utility $U_r = 210$.

reservation utility

The lowest utility a worker will accept to work for a company.

We begin by noting that under any fixed wage contract that is independent of the level of revenues—that is, where $w = w(200) = w(600)$—the manager will always provide

Table 20.2 Revenues in the Stockholder-Manager Game

Effect ↓	Probability of Revenues		
	$R = 200$	$R = 600$	Total
Low, $e = 0$	0.5	0.5	1.0
High, $e = 100$	0.1	0.9	1.0

a low work effort to avoid the cost ($e = 100$) of a high work effort. With any fixed wage contract, therefore, low effort is a dominant strategy. Furthermore, the lowest fixed wage contract that the manager will accept is $w(200) = w(600) = 210$, because such a contract yields a utility of $210 - e = 210 - 0 = 210$, which just covers the manager's reservation utility. However, if the stockholders offer a fixed wage contract below 210, the manager will work somewhere else or not at all. If the stockholders offer a fixed wage contract $w = 210$, the manager exerts a low work effort, and the payoffs to the manager and stockholders respectively are:

$$\text{Payoff to the manager} = 210 \tag{20.4}$$

$$\text{Expected payoff to the stockholders} = 0.5(200 - 210)$$
$$+ 0.5(600 - 210) = -5 + 195 = 190 \tag{20.5}$$

Next, we calculate the conditions under which the manager will exert a high work effort. To induce the manager to work hard, the wage contract must ensure that the expected utility payoff from working hard at least covers the manager's reservation utility of 210. From Table 20.2, if the manger's work effort is high, there is a 10 percent probability of generating revenues of 200 and a 90 percent probability of generating revenues of 600. Therefore, one necessary condition for providing a high work effort is that:

$$\text{Expected utility from high effort} \geq 210$$
$$E(U) = 0.1(w(200) - 100) + 0.9(w(600) - 100) \geq 210 \tag{20.6}$$

or:

$$E(U) = 0.1(w(200)) - 10 + 0.9(w(600)) - 90 \geq 210$$
$$E(U) = 0.1(w(200)) + 0.9(w(600)) \geq 310 \tag{20.7}$$

Equation 20.7 shows that in order to induce a high work effort, the expected utility from the contract offer must be greater than or equal to 310.

There is a second necessary condition to induce a high work effort: the manager's expected utility from a high work effort must be greater than or equal to the expected utility from a low work effort. Mathematically:

$$\text{Expected utility from high effort} = E(U)_{high} - 100 \geq E(U)_{low}$$
$$= \text{Expected utility from low effort}$$
$$0.1(w(200)) + 0.9(w(600)) - 100 \geq 0.5(w(200)) + 0.5(w(600))$$

or:

$$(0.1 - 0.5)(w(200)) + (0.9 - 0.5)(w(600)) = 0.4(w(600) - w(200)) \geq 100$$
$$w(600) - w(200) \geq 100/0.4 = 250 \tag{20.8}$$

Equation 20.8 states that the wage gap, or the difference between the wage if revenues equal 600 and the wage if revenues equal 200, must be greater than or equal to 250.

The manager will provide a high work effort only if Inequalities 20.7 and 20.8 both hold. Furthermore, the game assumes that it is impossible to pay a negative wage, because $w(R) \geq 0$. There are an infinite number of possible contracts that will induce a high work effort, but the stockholders will be willing to offer a contract only if it results in a stockholders' payoff that is greater than the payoff of 190 (from Equation 20.5) associated with a fixed wage contract $w = 210$. One contract that fulfills the necessary conditions is $w(200) = 100$ and $w(600) = 350$. The stockholders offer a contract that pays 100 if revenues are 200 and pays 350 if revenues are 600. The expected utility payoff to the manager is:

$$E(U) = 0.1(w(200)) + 0.9(w(600)) - 100 = 0.1(100) + 0.9(350) - 100$$
$$= 10 + 315 - 100 = 225 \qquad (20.9)$$

The manager's expected utility payoff of 225 with this variable wage contract is greater than the payoff of 210 with a fixed wage contract, so the manager prefers the variable wage contract. The stockholders' expected payoff is:

$$E(R - w) = 0.1(200 - 100) + 0.9(600 - 350) = 10 + 225 = 235 \quad (20.10)$$

The payoff of 235 to stockholders is greater than the payoff of 190 with a fixed wage contract $w = 210$ in Equation 20.5. A contract of $w(200) = 100$ and $w(600) = 350$ succeeds in inducing a high work effort from the manager. By tying the manager's wage to his performance, both the manager and the stockholders are better off.

The stockholders can do even better by offering the following contract: $w(200) = 0$ and $w(600) = 345$. This contract fulfills Inequalities 20.7 and 20.8 because:

$$E(U) = 0.1(w(200)) + 0.9(w(600)) = 0.1(0) + 0.9(345) = 310.5 \geq 310$$

and

$$w(600) - w(200) = 345 - 0 = 345 \geq 250$$

The expected utility payoff to the manager is:

$$E(U) = 0.1(w(200)) + 0.9(w(600)) - 100 = 0.1(0) + 0.9(345) - 100$$
$$= 0 + 310.5 - 100 = 210.5$$

The expected payoff to stockholders is:

$$E(R - w) = 0.1(200 - 0) + 0.9(600 - 345) = 20 + 229.5 = 249.5$$

The stockholders can structure many contracts that will induce the managers to put forth a high work effort. These contracts all have one thing in common: They base the managers' rewards on performance. This explains why so many corporations tie executive pay, bonuses, and stock options to corporate performance.

▲▲▲ **20.5A APPLICATION**   Principal–Agent Problems and Waldman's Summer Job

When I was in college, I learned firsthand about the principal-agent problem from two summer job experiences. You may recall from Chapter 13 that for two summers I drove a Good Humor ice cream truck. In this position, I was essentially my own boss. I worked six 16-hour days a week on straight commission; therefore, the more ice cream I sold, the more money I made. On most days, I did not even stop to eat lunch or dinner, but instead ate in the truck. The opportunity cost of stopping to eat a meal was too high! Working on straight commission, there was no principal-agent problem.

After driving the truck for two summers, I decided to look for an easier, 9-to-5 summer job with weekends off. I was hired by Philco-Ford, which was a major American manufacturer of color televisions and other appliances in the 1950s and 1960s. I worked in the accounting department as the timekeeper for a manufacturing plant in Philadelphia. I was the summer replacement for a 20-year veteran on the job, and I was paid a straight salary based on a 40-hour work week. My job was to collect all of the daily time cards ("punch cards" in those days), mark down the number of hours each employee worked on the card, and then run the cards through a card-reading machine that recorded the hours worked on the employees' payroll records.

The first week, the job took me about five hours a day; by the third week, the same tasks took me, at most, three hours a day. My supervisor cared only about my completing my work, which I did every day. By the end of the third week, I could not find anything to do after 11:00 in the morning, so I went to lunch a bit early before returning back to the plant at 1:00. By the fifth week on the job, I realized that nobody had any idea what I did after I completed my record-keeping chores around 10:30 in the morning. I began leaving for lunch at 10:30, and after lunch I'd go to a local park, where I'd play basketball or softball with a group of high school students before returning to the plant around 4:00 so that I could punch out.

Philco-Ford, as the principal, was a victim of the principal-agent problem. I spent most of my days shirking my job, and my shirking was completely unobserved by my supervisor. It was a case of asymmetric information: I knew I was not putting in any type of serious work effort, but my supervisor was completely oblivious to my behavior. I assume that if I had asked for more work I would have been supplied with other tasks, but it was in my interest to get paid by Philco-Ford for playing basketball or softball. You might say that for about eight weeks during the summer of 1970, I was a professional athlete!

Efficiency Wage Theory

Well, then say I, what's the use you learning to do right when it's troublesome to do right and ain't no trouble to do wrong, and the wages is just the same?
Mark Twain, *The Adventures of Huckleberry Finn*, 1884

In the stockholder-manager model developed in the previous section, the manager was willing to work for a fixed wage of 210, but the stockholders benefited from offering a contract with an expected wage that was considerably higher than 210. The first contract analyzed was $w(200) = 100$ and $w(600) = 350$, which has an expected wage payment of $0.1(100) + 0.9(350) = 325$. Even with a contract $w(200) = 0$ and $w(600) = 345$ that pays zero if revenues are 200, the expected wage payment is $0.1(0) + 0.9(345) = 310.5$. The stockholders are willing to pay wages well above the manager's reservation wage in order to induce the manager to work hard.

Suppose that only one firm offered its workers a contract based on performance and every other firm offered a contract with a fixed wage, $w = 210$. Potential managers working at other companies would be lining up to work at the company paying a higher expected wage based on performance. Of course, it is irrational for other companies to pay a fixed wage of 210, so we would expect that all other corporations would also offer a wage contract based on performance, to prevent managers from shirking. You might think that once all the firms pay a higher wage, the incentive to work hard would disappear, because the reservation wage would rise to the higher expected wage. However, there is a catch: If all firms pay a higher expected wage, the quantity demanded for labor must decline as the wage increases. This generates some involuntary unemployment at the higher wage level. Workers now have an incentive not to shirk: If they shirk and as a result get fired, there is an unemployed worker waiting in the wings to take the worker's place. This pool of unemployed workers keeps employed workers from underperforming and prevents shirking. This is the fundamental argument behind *efficiency wage theory* developed by Shapiro and Stiglitz, and Yellen.[3] **Efficiency wage theory** argues that firms pay higher wages in order to prevent workers from shirking.

efficiency wage theory

A theory that firms pay wages above the equilibrium wage in order to prevent workers from shirking.

Efficiency wage theory can be explained using Figure 20.4. Suppose the supply of labor is fixed at L^* and the equilibrium wage in a competitive labor market is w^* if workers work hard. If firms pay a wage w^*, however, all workers shirk, because even if a shirking worker is fired, she can find another job paying w^* at another company where all the workers are also shirking. To avoid shirking, firms must pay a wage above w^*. What wage is high enough to prevent shirking? According to Yellen and Stiglitz, the minimum wage necessary to avoid shirking is inversely related to the level of unemployment; that is, the higher the level of unemployment, the lower is the wage necessary to prevent shirking.[4] The logic is that if unemployment is high, workers know that if they shirk they could be

Figure 20.4 Efficiency Wage Theory

Suppose the supply of labor is fixed at L^* and the equilibrium wage in a competitive labor market is w^*. If the wage is w^*, all workers shirk, because even if a shirking worker is fired, she can find another job paying w^*. To avoid shirking, firms must pay a wage above w^*. The orange non-shirking constraint depicts the inverse relationship between the unemployment rate and the minimum wage necessary to prevent shirking. The non-shirking constraint intersects the demand curve at w_{eff} where unemployment equals $L^* - L_{eff}$, which is exactly the unemployment necessary to avoid shirking at a wage w_{eff}.

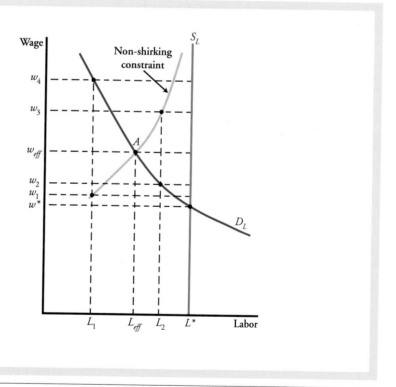

[3] Carl Shapiro and Joseph Stiglitz, "Equilibrium Unemployment as a Worker Discipline Device," *American Economic Review*, Vol. 74, pp. 433–44 (June 1984); Janet Yellen, "Efficiency Wage Models of Unemployment," *American Economic Review*, Vol. 74, pp. 200–205 (May 1984); and Joseph Stiglitz, "The Causes and Consequences of Dependence of Quality on Price," *Journal of Economic Literature*, Vol. 25, pp. 1–48 (March 1987).

[4] Yellen, *supra*, note 3; and Stiglitz, *supra*, note 3.

non-shirking constraint

An inverse functional relationship between the unemployment rate and the minimum wage necessary to prevent shirking.

fired and remain unemployed for a long time. Fear of unemployment therefore prevents workers from shirking. As the level of unemployment decreases, the fear of remaining unemployed for an extended period decreases, and it becomes necessary to pay workers a higher wage to avoid shirking.

In Figure 20.4, the orange upward-sloping **non-shirking constraint** depicts the inverse relationship between the unemployment rate and the minimum wage necessary to prevent shirking. Consider, for example, a wage w_2. At a wage w_2, unemployment equals the excess supply of labor $L^* - L_2$. This is a fairly low level of unemployment. At this low level of unemployment, there is little threat that if a worker is fired, she will be unemployed for an extended period of time. The firm would have to pay a high wage of w_3 on the non-shirking constraint to prevent shirking. On the other hand, at a wage w_4, unemployment equals the excess supply of labor, $L^* - L_1$. This is a high level of unemployment, and workers would be justified in feeling fear if they were fired, as they would be unemployed for an extended period of time. Given this high level of unemployment, the firm can prevent shirking by paying a low wage of w_1 on the non-shirking constraint. The non-shirking constraint intersects the demand curve at w_{eff} where unemployment equals $L^* - L_{eff}$, which is exactly the unemployment necessary to avoid shirking at a wage w_{eff}. At any wage below w_{eff}, shirking will occur, and the firm will increase wages to prevent shirking. At any wage above w_{eff}, the firm is paying a wage that is higher than the wage necessary to prevent shirking, and the firm will lower wages to increase profit. In equilibrium, firms pay the efficiency wage w_{eff}, hire L_{eff} workers, and the level of unemployment equals $L^* - L_{eff}$. The equilibrium efficiency wage is where the orange non-shirking constraint intersects the demand curve at point A.

Macroeconomists have used efficiency wage theory to help explain the inflexibility of wages and the existence of unemployment. Microeconomists find the model to be a fascinating example of how firms faced with principal-agent problems in the workforce can induce a greater work effort by paying wages above the equilibrium wages.

▲▲▲ 20.5B APPLICATION   Henry Ford and Efficiency Wages

Perhaps the best-known example of paying efficiency wages is Henry Ford's decision to pay his workers the then-astronomical sum of $5.00 a day in January 1914. Working on a production line, as many of Ford's workers did at the turn of the century, was monotonous and boring. Prior to January 1914, Ford had previously paid bonuses to some of his workers to help improve efficiency; by 1913, however, the company had a serious problem with employee turnover and low productivity. To solve these problems, Ford turned to one of his plant's general managers, John R. Lee, who was probably the first modern labor manager. After an extensive study, Lee determined that "...the chief causes of dissatisfaction and unrest among employees ... included: long hours, low wages, bad housing, wrong home influences, domestic troubles, unsanitary working conditions, and poor man-

agement by foremen and superintendents." On January 12, 1914, the company announced that it was reducing the workday from nine hours to eight hours and raising pay for most unskilled workers from $2.34 to $5.00 a day.

The Ford plan was actually a profit-sharing plan where workers received a daily wage plus the difference between the daily wage and $5.00 if the workers demonstrated "thrift, good habits, and good home conditions." For an unskilled worker, the daily wage remained $2.34, but he received an additional $2.66 if he was certified by the company as having good work habits. To monitor employees, Ford set up the Ford Sociological Department. After investigating an employee, the Sociological Department placed the employee in one of three groups: workers in the first group received the full additional wage; workers in the second group received

(continued)

the higher wage, but were warned that they had to show improvement in order to continue to receive the higher wage; and workers in the third group did not qualify for the higher wage unless they showed improvement. Ford's $5.00 wage was part of a broader social engineering policy as well as an efficiency wage; workers were also evaluated in areas that would today be considered off-limits, such as their home lives, living conditions, and how they spent their wages.

Did the $5.00 wage improve efficiency? Henry Ford stated in 1915 that:

> The increased efficiency of the men under the plan has been from 15 to 20 percent with reference to the work produced, which is further emphasized when you consider that the improvement was made in an eight-hour day versus the comparison in a nine-hour day.[*]

When asked why he had instituted the $5.00 wage, Ford replied that he "concluded that machinery was playing such a part in production that if men could be induced to speed up machinery, there would be more profit in the high wage than the low wage."[†] More specifically, the $5.00-day reduced the turnover rate from a huge 370 percent in 1913 to just 16 percent in 1915, and the rate of absenteeism declined from 10 percent in 1913 to 2.5 percent in 1914. The percentage of workers classified as "good" by the Sociological Department also increased over time.

During World War I, the unemployment rate declined substantially and wages throughout the American economy increased. As a result, Ford's turnover rate increased to 51 percent in 1918. In response, Ford increased the minimum daily wage to $6.00 in 1919. According to one analyst, however, Ford needed a $10.00 wage in 1919 to maintain the same efficiency wage incentives as the $5.00 wage had provided in 1914.

The evidence suggests that Ford's $5.00 wage worked perfectly as an efficiency wage. The higher wage succeeded in improving the quality of the workforce and labor productivity. Furthermore, consistent with efficiency wage theory, when the unemployment rate decreased, the efficiency wage had to increase to maintain workers' incentives. In an empirical study, economists Daniel Ruff and Lawrence Summers provided evidence that Ford's $5.00 wage was indeed an efficiency wage.

---

[*]Stephen Meyer III, *The Five Dollar Day: Labor Management and Social Control in the Ford Motor Company 1908–1921*. Albany, NY: State University of New York Press, 1981, p. 120.

[†]*Ibid.*, p. 120.

Franchising

franchising

An alternative to company ownership of outlets in which a company sells the right to open outlets under its trademark to independent entrepreneurs.

franchisor

In a franchising agreement, the company that sells the right to open outlets under its trademark to independent entrepreneurs.

franchisee

In a franchising agreement, the independent entrepreneur who purchases the right to open outlets under the franchisor's trademark.

When you enter a McDonald's or Subway restaurant, more likely than not, the restaurant is not owned and operated by McDonald's Corporation or Subway, but instead by an independent *franchisee*. An alternative to company ownership is **franchising**, in which a **franchisor**, such as McDonald's Corporation, sells the right to open outlets under its trademark to independent entrepreneurs called **franchisees**. Typically, the franchisee pays the franchisor a fixed franchise fee plus a royalty based on sales. One of the advantages of franchising over company ownership is that franchisees have a strong incentive to run their outlets as active owner-managers who attempt to prevent workers from shirking.

One of the primary theories advanced to explain the rapid worldwide growth of franchising is that principal-agent problems make it difficult for owners to monitor managers as chains expand rapidly. Franchise chains typically begin with one or a few company-owned outlets in one geographic area, so initially the owners are able to effectively monitor workers and deter shirking. As a chain expands beyond a few outlets in one region, however, it becomes increasingly difficult for the owners to monitor each outlet. One possible solution is to hire high-quality managers to prevent shirking, but rapid expansion makes it difficult to find enough high-quality managers. Furthermore, managers have an incentive to shirk themselves, so managerial oversight is likely to be moderately successful at best. Franchising has become a common method of trying to reduce the principal-agent problem associated with rapid chain expansion.

▲▲▲ 20.5C APPLICATION   The Principal–Agent Problem and Franchising

Franchising has become an important force in the global economy. Many of the 10 fastest growing franchises in 2002 are common household names, including 7-Eleven, Subway, Jackson Hewitt Tax Service, KFC, McDonald's, and Budget Rent-A-Car. Others are somewhat less well known, such as Kumon Math & Reading Centers, Curves, Coverall Cleaning Concepts, and Jani-King. Company-owned units represent a small percentage of total units for most of these rapidly growing franchisors, making up less than 1 percent of the units for five of the ten companies (Kumon, Curves, Coverall, Subway, and Jani-King), and never more than 27.3 percent (McDonald's).

Several studies have provided evidence suggesting that franchisors use franchising to solve principal-agent problems. For example, based on efficiency wage theory, economist Alan Krueger theorized that to avoid shirking, company-owned fast food restaurants would pay higher wages than franchised restaurants. Franchisees prevent shirking by closely monitoring their workers, whereas franchisor-owned outlets must rely on hired managers and therefore must pay efficiency wages to prevent shirking. Consistent with this theory, Krueger found that company-owned restaurants paid higher wages and were more likely to provide their employees with fringe benefits such as free meals, paid vacations, paid holidays, and insurance than franchised restaurants.

Economist Seth Norton approached the principal-agent-franchising relationship from a different perspective by theorizing that if franchising solves principal-agent problems, then franchising should be more common in firms in which effective monitoring is more difficult. For example, if a chain is growing rapidly or is geographically dispersed, it is difficult to effectively monitor workers from one centrally located corporate headquarters. Because of their relatively large number of workers, businesses with higher labor-to-sales ratios will also have difficulty monitoring workers. Using data from the restaurant and motel industries, Norton found that the percentage of franchised outlets in a company was significantly and positively related to the company's degree of geographic dispersion, rate of sales growth, and labor-to-sales ratio. These results support the theory that firms turn to franchising when it is more difficult to monitor workers.

If franchising is so effective in preventing principal-agent problems, why do many firms such as McDonald's, KFC, and 7-Eleven operate many company-owned outlets? Company-owned outlets might provide franchisors with any or all of the following advantages:

1. Experimentation with new products, like McDonald's yogurt parfait or Wendy's stuffed pita; or new techniques, like self-serve soft-drink stations or drive-through-only outlets.
2. A yardstick to measure the performance of franchisees.
3. Ability for franchisors to measure differences in demand conditions in different markets, which helps the franchisor to assess the performance of franchises located in different markets. For example, if McDonald's has at least some company-owned restaurants in midtown Manhattan and Portland, Maine, the firm can more easily understand differences in the demand and performance of its franchises in New York City and small New England cities.
4. The existence of company-owned outlets makes the threat of terminating weak franchises more credible, because franchises can be more easily converted into company-owned outlets.
5. Company-owned outlets increase the franchisor's financial stake in maintaining the overall quality of the system, because a real or perceived decline in quality has a greater negative impact on the franchisor. Company-owned outlets therefore serve to ensure franchisees that the value of their franchises will be maintained or increased.

Despite these reasons for maintaining or expanding the number of company-owned outlets, all of the ten fastest-growing franchisors in 2002 relied overwhelmingly on franchising to expand their businesses. As these firms expanded, the benefits of avoiding principal-agent problems appear to have dominated the benefits associated with expanding the percentage of company-owned outlets, so these companies increased their reliance on franchising.

Summary

1. In the lemons model, only sellers know the quality of used cars offered for sale, but only buyers know the distribution of the quality of cars. Therefore, buyers offer sellers the mean value of all cars sold, and sellers sell only cars worth the mean value or less. As a result, high-quality cars are eliminated from the market.

2. The lemons model is an example of adverse selection where products of different qualities are sold at the same price because buyers or sellers do not have sufficient information to determine the true quality of the products. Insurance companies are constantly faced with problems of adverse selection, because the companies cannot identify the true risks associated with insuring an individual client. As a result, high-risk individuals are more likely to purchase insurance than are low-risk individuals, and this drives up insurance rates, which further eliminates low-risk individuals from the insurance pool. The most common solution to the problem of adverse selection is to gather more information.

3. Moral hazard is another problem associated with asymmetric information in the insurance market: It exists whenever an insured individual's unobserved actions can affect the probability or magnitude of a payment to that insured individual. A fully insured individual has much less incentive to behave carefully than a partially insured individual. Because insurance companies cannot directly observe or monitor the insured's behavior, insurance companies attempt to find other ways to encourage their insured clients to behave carefully, and therefore companies agree to provide partial insurance only with a substantial deductible, which places a substantial portion of any financial losses directly on the insured.

4. In many markets with asymmetric information, sellers use signaling to convey information about the quality of their products to buyers. For example, employees use the attaining of a college education to signal employers of their ability to do high-quality work; and companies use warranties to signal the high quality of their products to buyers.

5. A principal-agent problem arises in any situation in which an agent in rational pursuit of his own goals behaves in a manner that reduces the principal's welfare. Principal-agent problems are common in large corporations, because stockholder ownership is separated from managerial control, and as a result, managers do not always act in the owners' best interests. Principal-agent problems also arise when employers hire employees, but wages are not directly tied to worker performance, so the workers have a strong incentive to shirk. To prevent shirking, employers may have to pay efficiency wages above the equilibrium wage. Franchising is used to overcome principal-agent problems in retailing and services because franchises are operated by owners who have a greater incentive to closely monitor their workers than managers hired by large corporations.

Self-Test Problems

1. Consider a perfectly competitive insurance market with perfect information. Assume that there are only two possibilities for Megan, an owner of a car worth $30,000: she can either crash, in which case she totals the car with $30,000 in damages, or she can avoid a crash. If Megan is a careful driver, then the

probability that she will crash and total her car is 0.10. If Megan is a careless driver, then the probability that she will crash and total her car is 0.80.

a. Solve for the actuarially fair insurance premium charged if Megan is careful and the insurance company fully insures the car.

b. Solve for the actuarially fair insurance premium charged if Megan is careless and the insurance company fully insures the car.

c. With perfect information, will Megan choose to be careful or careless? Explain your reasoning.

d. With asymmetric information, the insurance company does not know whether Megan is careful or careless. Does asymmetric information increase the likelihood that Megan is careful or careless? Explain your reasoning.

2. Consider Spence's general model of education as a signal. Assume that the output of low-quality workers is 4 and the output of high-quality workers is 15. Assume that the cost of education is equal to $48s/q$, where $s = 1$ if the worker attends college and $s = 0$ if the worker doesn't attend college. Show that the low-quality worker is better off not going to college and the high-quality worker is better off going to college.

3. Consider the following model with a manager and a group of stockholders. Both players are risk-neutral. Assume that the manager has two different levels of work effort, e, and his utility payoff is the wage, w, minus e, that is, $w - e$. Assume that the manager's reservation utility is 250. The stockholders' profit is $R - w$.

Revenues in the Stockholder-Manager Game

Effort	Probability of Revenues		
	$R = 300$	$R = 800$	Total
Low, $e = 0$	0.5	0.5	1.0
High, $e = 75$	0.1	0.9	1.0

a. If the stockholders offer a fixed wage contract equal to the reservation utility, solve for the payoffs to the manager and to the stockholders.

Now assume that the stockholders decide to provide an incentive to induce the manager to put forth high effort by offering a wage linked to the revenues generated by the manager.

b. Solve for the minimum expected utility from the contract offer that will induce a high work effort.

c. Solve for the wage gap that will ensure the manager's expected utility from a high work effort is greater than or equal to the expected utility from a low work effort.

d. Find one such wage offer that the stockholders would be willing to make and that satisfies both the conditions in questions 3(b) and (c). Prove that your specific example will give stockholders a higher payoff than the fixed wage contract.

Questions and Problems for Review

1. Which of these situations describe a market of perfect information?

a. Mary buys a used Toyota Camry with a limited warranty but no service record.

b. Joe buys a used Honda Accord without a warranty but some information about the car's service record.

c. Sally is an insurance agent and has just written an auto insurance policy for the 16-year-old daughter of a "good-driver" customer.

d. Henry owns a pizza shop and hires a young woman with a good driving record to deliver pizzas.

2. If the used car market is a lemons market, how would you expect the repair record of used cars that are sold to compare with the repair record of used cars that are not sold? Explain your reasoning.

3. Assume two players: a buyer and seller of a used car. The seller knows whether the car is a good car or a lemon and the buyer knows the probability distribution of good cars and lemons. Assume that the probability of a good car is 70 percent and the probability of a lemon is 30 percent. Assume that both buyers and sellers have identical tastes and there are only two types of cars. Good cars have a quality value of $20,000 and lemons have a quality value of $10,000.

a. What is the expected value of a car? Given this information, how will the buyer be informed whether the car is a lemon?

b. What would the Akerlof lemons model predict to be the final outcome of this game? In other words, which cars will be sold and for how much? Explain.

c. In general, what happens to the end result if we assume that buyers value any given car more highly than sellers? Explain.

4. Name three specific markets in which adverse selection is present. Explain why there is a problem.

5. Discuss the application of the lemons model in the insurance market. In what ways do insurance companies deal with adverse selection?

6. Suppose a bank issued credit cards over the Internet at a fixed interest rate to all approved applicants—for example, at 11.9 percent. Explain why this bank would face an adverse selection problem. How might the bank solve the problem? Would your solution make some customers unhappy? Explain your reasoning.

7. Suppose in the Woody family example in Section 20.3, the family loves the forest surrounding its home so much that it refuses to clear any of the forest after purchasing an insurance policy for $2,500 with a $5,000 deductible. What would the Woodys demand curve look like in Figure 20.3? Is the $2,500 cost of the policy still actuarially fair? If not, what would be the new actuarially fair insurance premium? If the company sent an inspector out to check whether the Woodys had cleared any forest and she discovered that none had been cleared, how might the company respond when the policy expired? Are there any possible responses other than raising the premium to the actuarially fair level? Explain your reasoning.

8. Explain why insurance companies rarely offer full insurance. How do partial insurance policies typically affect the policyholder's behavior? There is one exception to the partial insurance rule with regard to automobile insurance: Most policies offer partial collision insurance, but full insurance on broken glass windows. Why would most insurance companies be willing to fully insure a broken windshield but not a broken bumper?

9. Make a counter-argument as to why moral hazard might not be as huge a problem in automobile insurance as indicated in the text.

10. College students often drive cars that are owned by their parents, who also pay the insurance premiums and the cost of fixing up the cars if the student is in an accident. How might this arrangement result in a moral hazard problem for the parents? If parents pay for the students' parking tickets on campus, how might this make the parents' problems worse? What is a solution to the parents' moral hazard problem? Explain your reasoning.

11. Many economists argue that it is too easy for businesses and individuals to declare bankruptcy. How might easy bankruptcy laws create moral hazard problems?

12. Consider Spence's general model of education as a signal. Assume that the output of low-quality workers is 5 and the output of high-quality workers is 15. Assume the cost of education is $55s/q$, where $s = 1$ if the worker attends college and $s = 0$ if the worker doesn't attend college. Show that the low-quality worker is better off not going to college and the high-quality worker is better off going to college.

13. What is the key assumption that keeps a low-quality producer from offering a lifetime warranty?

14. What type of signal is Kia (a South Korean firm) sending with its 100,000-mile/10-year warranty? What impact might this have on the market for American cars? Explain.

15. What might be one solution Philco-Ford could have implemented to reduce the principal-agent problem associated with Waldman's summer job? Discuss the advantages and disadvantages of this solution.

16. Using the assumptions of the stockholders-manager model presented in the chapter, consider the following game. The stockholders and the manager are both risk-neutral. Assume that the manager has two different levels of work effort (e), and his utility payoff is the wage, w, minus e. Assume the manager's reservation utility is 300. The stockholders' profit is $R - w$.

Revenues in the Stockholder-Manager Game

| Effort | Probability of Revenues | | |
	$R = 400$	$R = 1,200$	Total
Low, $e = 0$	0.5	0.5	1.0
High, $e = 150$	0.1	0.9	1.0

a. If the stockholders offer a fixed wage contract equal to the reservation utility, solve for the payoffs to the manager and to the stockholders.

Now assume that the stockholders decide to provide an incentive to induce the manager to put forth high effort by offering a wage linked to the revenues generated by the manager.

b. Solve for the minimum expected utility from the contract offer that will induce a high work effort.

c. Solve for the wage gap that will ensure the manager's expected utility from a high work effort is greater than or equal to the expected utility from a low work effort.

d. Find one such wage offer that the stockholders would be willing to make and that satisfies both the conditions in questions 16(b) and (c). Prove that your specific example will give stockholders higher payoff than under the fixed wage contract.

17. Consider a vertical labor supply equal to 20, a demand for labor equal to $w = 480 - 10L$, and a non-shirking constraint equal to $w = 280 + L$.

a. Solve for the equilibrium wage and quantity of labor if firms do not pay an efficiency wage. What is the value of the non-shirking constraint at the equilibrium wage and labor?

b. Solve for the amount of labor demanded and the efficient wage w_{eff}, above which the firm is paying a wage that is higher than the wage necessary to prevent shirking and below which shirking will occur. What is unemployment at w_{eff}?

18. Discuss the differences between moral hazard and adverse selection.

19. In what way does the use of a large franchising system help to reduce the principal-agent problem? Does franchising completely eliminate all the potential principal-agent problems? Why might even a small franchise (with one location) still face a principal-agent problem?

20. Suppose one in every ten DVDs of computer games for children is defective. The defective DVDs, however, cannot be identified except by those who own them. Once a DVD is opened, the DVD is unable to be returned to the store for a full refund, but can be returned to a used DVD store to be reconditioned. Assume that the DVDs do not depreciate with use. Consumers are risk-neutral and value non-defective DVDs at $25 each. If defective DVDs can be returned for $10, how much would consumers be willing to pay for a new DVD? Explain. If manufacturers charged $25.00 for new DVDs, how many would they sell? If the manufacturers changed their policy to permit any defective DVD to be returned for a full refund, what would happen to the percentage of defective DVDs? Do the manufacturers face an adverse selection problem? Do they face a moral hazard problem? Explain your reasoning.

Internet Exercises

Visit *http://www.myeconlab.com/waldman* for this chapter's Web exercises. Answer real-world economics problems by doing research on the Internet.

Chapter 21
Externalities and Public Goods

Anyone who has ever walked outside in Los Angeles on a smog alert day or driven on the northern portion of the New Jersey Turnpike with the windows open on a warm summer afternoon knows about the cost of air pollution. Industrial plants spew pollution into the air in California and New Jersey causing pain and discomfort for many; not to mention serious health problems for people with asthma, emphysema, cystic fibrosis, or other lung diseases. As noted in Chapter 19, pollution is the most common example of a *negative externality*, a cost of production or consumption that negatively affects a third party but is not considered a cost by the producer or consumer. When negative externalities exist, the invisible hand fails to produce Pareto efficiency; consequently, some form of government intervention is necessary to obtain an efficient outcome.

I often ask my students, most of whom live in the Eastern part of the United States: "How many of you have ever visited Yellowstone National Park?" Usually, 10 to 20 percent say they have been to Yellowstone at least once. I then ask: "How many of you would be willing to pay taxes each year to maintain and improve the beauty of Yellowstone National Park?" Typically, 90 to 100 percent of my students say they would be willing to pay such a tax. Many students who have never been to Yellowstone have a demand for the park. These students obtain some utility from Yellowstone National Park without ever having stepped foot in it. If we measured the demand for Yellowstone National Park based only on how much actual visitors are willing to pay to maintain the park, we would underestimate the demand. As a result, too few resources would be devoted to Yellowstone. This raises a difficult question: How many of our resources should the nation be willing to devote to Yellowstone and other national parks?

In this chapter, we examine the different government options available to correct for externalities, including direct regulations and taxes. We will see that it is difficult to correct for the inefficiencies caused by externalities (defined in the following section). In this chapter, we will also examine why the demand for goods such as Yellowstone National Park differs from the demand for a sweater or a meal at a restaurant. We will see that because of certain characteristics of national parks, the invisible hand cannot find the true demand for national parks, and therefore fails to allocate the correct amount of resources to maintain national parks.

▼▼▼   21.1   Externalities

externality

Any cost or benefit from an action undertaken by a producer or a consumer that affects other producers or consumers but is not incorporated into the market price for any good or service.

An **externality** refers to any cost or benefit from an action undertaken by a producer or a consumer that affects other producers or consumers, but is not incorporated into the market price for any good or service. The most commonly used example of a *negative externality* is air or water pollution. For example, in the absence of government intervention, if a chemical manufacturer generates air pollution, it imposes a cost on consumers living downwind from the chemical plant; however, the cost of the pollution is not incorporated into the price of the chemicals produced at the plant. Many other examples exist as well. Smokers impose negative externalities on non-smokers when they light up in public places. College students who stay up all night playing loud music that rocks the resident hall impose negative externalities on other students who are trying to sleep or study. As noted in Chapter 19, in contrast to negative externalities, there are also positive externalities, or the benefits of production or consumption that accrue to other consumers or producers, but are not incorporated into the market price of any good or service. Common examples include immunizations that prevent the spread of diseases to people who are not immunized, an apiary that pollinates the surrounding neighborhood, and the benefits to society at large from educating children.

Negative Externalities

marginal external cost (MEC)

Negative externalities associated with producing one more unit of a good or service.

marginal social cost (MSC)

The extra cost to society of producing one more unit of a good or service; equals the sum of the marginal private cost and the marginal external cost.

When most people think of externalities, they think of negative effects imposed on them from the production or consumption of a good or service. Economists wishing to quantify these costs use the concept of **marginal external costs** (MEC) for a good or service to measure the negative externalities associated with producing one more unit of the good or service. Another important measure of costs including externalities is the **marginal social cost** (MSC) of a good or service, which is the sum of the marginal private cost and the marginal external cost of producing one more unit of a good or service.

Figure 21.1 depicts how pollution can distort efficiency. Lumber mills cause pollution by dumping dangerous chemicals, such as dioxin, into rivers and streams. Dioxin is a powerful carcinogen (that is, a cancer-causing agent), and is also known to cause damage to the human immune and reproductive systems and severe developmental disorders in children. Paper mills create dioxin by burning chlorinated waste products and by chlorine bleaching. The lumber mill owners, unless they live close to the rivers into which the companies dump the waste chemicals, have little reason to be personally concerned about the dumping of dioxin. Furthermore, the owners pay no direct cost for dumping dioxin into rivers.

In Figure 21.1, the $S_{private}$ curve is the private supply curve for lumber. It includes all of the costs of producing lumber except the external cost of pollution, which is represented by the curve $MEC_{pollution}$. The total marginal social cost of production (shown as S_{social} in figure 21.1) is the summation of the private cost, $S_{private}$, and the marginal external cost of pollution, $MEC_{pollution}$. In the absence of government intervention, the lumber mills ignore the pollution costs, $MEC_{pollution}$, and produce output q_e at price p_e where

Figure 21.1 Negative Externalities, Pollution
The private supply curve for lumber is $S_{private}$. The total social cost of production is the vertical summation of the private cost $S_{private}$ and the marginal external cost of pollution, $MEC_{pollution}$, which equals the curve S_{social}. The lumber industry ignores the pollution costs and produces output q_e at price p_e with a deadweight loss equal to the orange triangle ABC. The government can place either a tax based on output tax $t = t(q) = MEC_{pollution}$, or a constant tax per unit equal to t_1. The tax $t(q) = MEC_{pollution}$ shifts the supply curve to S_{social}, and the constant tax t_1 shifts the supply curve to S_{tax}. With either tax, the industry produces the socially optimal output q_{so}.

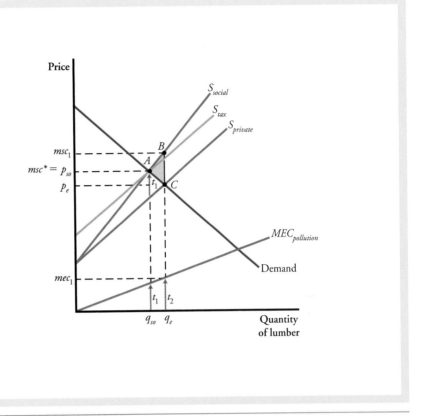

the demand curve intersects the $S_{private}$ curve at point C. At output q_e, the marginal social cost of production, msc_1 (at point B), which includes both private costs and marginal external costs, is greater than price p_e.

The socially efficient output must consider both the private and marginal external cost of production, and occurs at the socially optimal output q_{so}, where the demand curve intersects the S_{social} curve at point A. The socially optimal output is q_{so} and the socially optimal price is p_{so}. There is a deadweight loss associated with production at q_e, because for every unit produced between q_{so} and q_e the marginal social cost including the marginal external cost of pollution is greater than the price consumers are willing to pay for lumber. The deadweight loss equals the orange triangle ABC, which measures the difference between the total cost of producing the units between q_{so} and q_e (area $q_{so}ABq_e$) and the total value of those units to consumers (area $q_{so}ACq_e$).

To correct for the externality, the government intervenes in the lumber market. One possible intervention would be to place a tax on lumber producers. If it is possible to determine the precise $MEC_{pollution}$ curve, then a tax on lumber producers could be based on output. An optimal tax would be a function of output produced, such that the tax $t = t(q) = MEC_{pollution}$. For every additional unit produced, the tax would increase. For example, in Figure 21.1, the tax on the q_{so}th unit of output equals t_1 and the tax on the q_eth unit would equal t_2. Such a tax would be incorporated as an additional cost of production for lumber producers and would shift the industry supply curve from $S_{private}$ to S_{social}. The tax would *internalize* the externality for producers; that is, would force the producers to consider the cost of pollution as an explicit marginal cost of production. With a tax $t(q) = MEC_{pollution}$, the socially optimal output would be produced.

Because it is often difficult, if not impossible, to identify the $MEC_{pollution}$ curve, governments typically use a much simpler constant per-unit tax on output to try to reduce pollution. In Figure 21.1, the optimal per-unit tax equals t_1, which equals the marginal external cost of pollution associated with producing the q_{so}th unit. A per-unit tax t_1 would shift the supply curve to the light-red supply curve S_{tax}. The problem with a constant per-unit tax is that because the marginal external cost increases with output, any change in demand conditions requires a new per-unit tax to achieve the socially optimal output. If demand increases, the tax t_1 will be too small; and if demand decreases, the tax t_1 will be too large.

Positive Externalities

marginal external benefit (MEB)

Positive externalities associated with producing one more unit of a good or service.

marginal social benefit (MSB)

The extra benefit to society of producing one more unit of a good or service; equals the sum of the marginal private benefit and the marginal external benefit.

As noted earlier, some markets exhibit positive externalities. The **marginal external benefit (MEB)** for a good or service measures the positive externalities associated with producing one more unit of the good or service. The **marginal social benefit (MSB)** of a good or service is the sum of the marginal private benefit and the marginal external benefit of producing one more unit of a good or service.

The market for immunizations is an example of a market with positive externalities. The larger the percentage of the population that is immunized against a disease, the lower the probability that anyone—including those who are not immunized—will contract the disease. Society benefits from wide-reaching immunization programs because such programs prevent some individuals who cannot be immunized from contracting the disease. For example, pediatricians recommend that infants receive DPT (diphtheria, pertussis, and tetanus) shots when they are two months, four months, and six months old. Some infants, however, have violent life-threatening reactions to their first pertussis or whooping cough portion of the vaccine and cannot receive the remaining DPT shots. Instead, these infants are given DT shots at ages four months and six months old and are not immunized against whooping cough. Every year, there are cases of whooping cough throughout the world. For non-immunized children, it is extremely beneficial if all of the children who can safely receive the DPT shots are immunized. A larger percentage of protected children lowers the likelihood of a whooping cough epidemic among non-immunized children, because they are less likely to be exposed to the disease.

In Figure 21.2, in the case of DPT immunizations, the marginal social benefit curve MSB is the vertical summation of the private demand curve for DPT immunizations $D_{private}$ and the marginal external benefit curve MEB. The MEB curve measures the positive social benefits of immunizations that are not considered to be direct benefits to the recipients of the immunizations. The consumer of the q_eth immunization is willing to pay a price p_e for the immunization, and in addition, all of the other members of society receive benefits valued at meb_1 when the q_eth consumer is immunized. The rest of society is therefore willing to pay meb_1 to see that the q_eth consumer is immunized. In the absence of government intervention, the private market will result in q_e immunizations at a price p_e, where the private demand curve $D_{private}$ intersects the supply curve $S_{private}$ at point A. At q_e, the marginal external benefit of immunizations is meb_1, and the marginal social benefit equals $msb_1 = p_e + meb_1$, which is greater than price p_e. Because at output q_e, marginal social benefits are greater than price, the output q_e is socially inefficient.

The socially efficient output considers both the private benefits and the social benefits of immunizations and occurs at the socially optimal output, q_{so}, where the MSB curve intersects the supply curve, $S_{private}$ (at point C). The socially optimal output is q_{so} and the socially optimal price is p_{so}. There is a deadweight loss associated with production at q_e because for every immunization between q_e and q_{so}, the marginal social benefits, including the marginal external benefits, are greater than the opportunity costs of providing

Figure 21.2 Positive Externalities of Immunizations

The marginal social benefit curve *MSB* is the vertical summation of the private demand curve for DPT immunizations $D_{private}$ and the marginal external benefit curve *MEB*. The private market will result in q_e immunizations at a price p_e, where the private demand curve $D_{private}$ intersects the supply curve $S_{private}$. At output q_e, marginal social benefits, msb_1, are greater than price, p_e, and therefore the output q_e is socially inefficient with a deadweight loss equal to orange triangle *ABC*. The government can subsidize immunizations with either a subsidy based on output $s = s(q) = MEB$, or a constant subsidy per immunization equal to s_2. The subsidy $s(q) = MEB$ shifts the demand curve to *MSB*; and the constant subsidy s_2 shifts the demand curve to $D_{subsidy}$. With either subsidy, the industry produces the socially optimal output q_{so}.

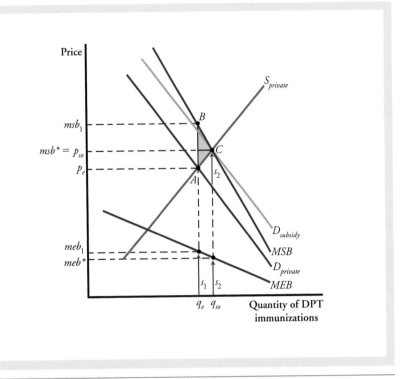

those immunizations. The deadweight loss equals the orange triangle *ABC*, which measures the difference between the total social benefits of the immunizations between q_e and q_{so} (area q_eBCq_{so}) and the total cost of those immunizations (area q_eACq_{so}).

To correct for the positive externality, the government must intervene in the market. One possible intervention would be to provide a subsidy directly to the individuals who receive immunizations. If it is possible to determine the precise *MEB* curve, then a subsidy could be based on the quantity of immunizations. An optimal subsidy would be a function of the quantity of immunizations q, such that the subsidy $s = s(q) = MEB$. For every additional person immunized, the subsidy would decrease, because the *MEB* of additional immunizations decreases. For example, in Figure 21.2, the subsidy on the q_eth immunization equals s_1 and the subsidy on the q_{so}th immunization equals s_2. Such a subsidy would increase the demand for immunizations by decreasing the out-of-pocket costs of obtaining an immunization for recipients, and would increase the demand curve from $D_{private}$ to *MSB*. The subsidy would internalize the positive externality for consumers; that is, it would reduce the out-of-pocket price of immunizations, and therefore increase the market demand for immunizations. With a subsidy $s(q) = MEB$, the socially optimal number of immunizations, q_{so}, would be provided.

Because it is almost impossible to identify the precise *MEB* curve, governments usually provide a simpler constant per-unit subsidy to recipients of immunizations. In Figure 21.2, the optimal per-unit subsidy equals s_2, which equals the marginal external benefit of providing the q_{so}th immunization, meb^*. A per-unit subsidy s_2 would shift the demand curve to the light-blue demand curve $D_{subsidy}$. The problem with a constant per-unit subsidy is that because the marginal external benefit decreases with output, any change in supply requires a new per-unit subsidy to achieve the socially optimal number of immunizations. If supply increases, the subsidy s_2 will be too large; and if supply decreases, the subsidy s_2 will be too small.

▲▲▲ **21.1 APPLICATION** The Positive Externalities from Education

Individuals invest in education to increase their value in the labor market. Investments in education pay substantial private dividends. According to the U.S. Bureau of the Census, the private returns to education are quite substantial, with non–high school graduates earning a mean income of $15,616 in 2000, compared to $24,030 for high schools graduates, $48,378 for college graduates, $82,915 for college graduates with a doctorate, and $99,856 for college graduates with a professional degree. Economists Orley Ashenfelter and Cecelia Rouse researched the private returns to education between 1979 and 1993 and estimated that the rate of return from one additional year of education increased from 6.2 percent in 1979 to 10 percent in 1993. Investments in education generally pay large dividends indeed.

In addition to the private returns to education, there are positive externalities associated with education at every level. In his famous book *Capitalism and Freedom,* Nobel Laureate Milton Friedman called these positive externalities "neighborhood effects." He wrote:

A stable and democratic society is impossible without a minimum degree of literacy and knowledge on the part of most citizens and without widespread acceptance of some common set of values. Education can contribute to both. In consequence, the gain from education of a child accrues not only to the child or his parents but also to other members of the society.[*]

In support of Friedman's belief that education makes for better citizens, several studies have shown that education influences voting more than any other socioeconomic variable. In fact, a 1996 United States Department of Education study found that 57 percent of Americans with four or more years of college voted in 1994, compared to just 30.6 percent of high school graduates.

Other studies have shown that increased levels of education significantly reduce the likelihood of committing a crime, and that increased education has a greater impact than increased income on reducing crime. Increased levels of education also reduce reliance on welfare programs. According to the United States Department of Education, "[i]n 1996, 25–34-year-olds who were high school graduates were 10 times as likely as college graduates to have received income from Aid to Families with Dependent Children or public assistance income."[†] Finally, evidence suggests that women with a college education are much less likely than women with only a high-school education to have an out-of-wedlock child.

Education also provides positive social benefits by increasing economic growth. Education enables a society to develop and diffuse new ideas and inventions more quickly. Studies have suggested that 10–25 percent of the growth in output in the United States is a direct result of increased levels of education. By increasing labor productivity, education increases the standard of living for all citizens in a society.

[*]Milton Friedman, *Capitalism and Freedom.* Chicago: University of Chicago Press, 1982, p. 86.
[†]U.S. Department of Education, National Center for Education Statistics, *The Condition of Education 1998*, NCES 98–013.

▼▼▼ 21.2 Alternative Methods of Government Intervention

In the previous section, we used taxes or subsidies to internalize the externality. We saw that it is difficult to identify the correct tax or subsidy if the cost or benefit of the externality varies with output. Three different methods of government intervention have been used in markets with negative externalities: direct regulation or standards, taxes or fees, and marketable externality permits. Each of these interventions has certain advantages and disadvantages, which this section considers.

Standards and Taxes

Administratively, the easiest method of eliminating a negative externality such as pollution is to establish standards for pollution reduction and then monitor adherence to ensure that the standards are met. Standards may not be as efficient as taxes are in reducing pollution. First, we consider the impact of standards and taxes in the simplest case where all firms have the same marginal costs of pollution abatement MC_A. Then we analyze the case of abatement costs differing across firms. Finally, we examine how uncertainty affects the choice of policies.

EQUAL ABATEMENT COSTS FOR ALL FIRMS
In Figure 21.3, the economic good of pollution reduction is measured in percent on the x-axis, and marginal social benefits and marginal costs of pollution abatement for a typical firm are measured on the y-axis. As increasing amounts of pollution are reduced, the marginal social benefits of further reductions decline dramatically. On the other hand, marginal abatement costs increase as additional pollution is reduced, because it becomes more difficult to reduce additional pollution as the environment becomes cleaner. In fact, the marginal cost of reducing the last few percentage points of pollution approaches infinity.

In Figure 21.3, the optimal level of pollution reduction is 65 percent, where the marginal cost of abatement curve, MC_A, intersects the marginal social benefits curve MSB. To require more than a 65 percent reduction in pollution would be inefficient, because the marginal costs of pollution reduction beyond 65 percent are greater than the marginal benefits. One way to eliminate 65 percent of pollution is for the government to mandate producers to reduce their emissions by 65 percent and then monitor compliance. The total cost of compliance with the mandated standards equals the area under the MC_A curve up to a 65 percent reduction, or the shaded orange area X.

effluent charge

A tax or fee imposed for pollution discharged into the air or water.

Alternatively, the government can require the firms to pay a fee or tax of f for every percent of pollution a firm emits into the environment. Such a tax or fee for pollution discharged into the air or water is called an **effluent charge**. Because the marginal cost of

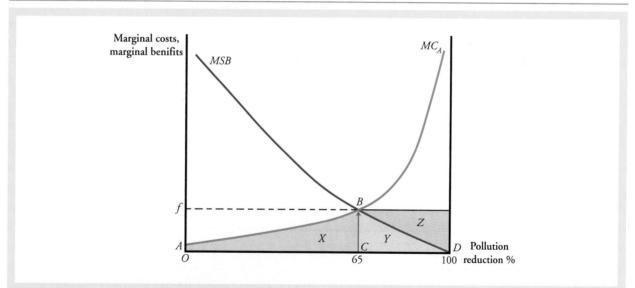

Figure 21.3 Optimal Level of Pollution Reduction
The optimal level of pollution reduction is where the marginal cost of abatement curve MC_A intersects the marginal social benefit curve MSB at 65 percent. The total cost of a government mandate to reduce pollution by 65 percent equals the area under the MC_A curve up to a 65 percent reduction, or the shaded orange area X. If the government requires firms to pay a fee or tax of f for every percent of pollution emitted into the environment, the firms also reduce pollution by 65 percent at a total cost equal to the orange area X and pay a fee equal to the sum of the blue and green areas $Y + Z$.

reducing pollution up to 65 percent is less than f, the firm would find it profitable to reduce pollution up to 65 percent. Further reductions, however, would not make economic sense, because the firms would be better off paying the fee f rather than paying the higher marginal cost of pollution reduction. In equilibrium, the firms reduce pollution by 65 percent at a cost equal to the orange area X and pay a fee equal to the sum of the blue area Y and green area Z, which equal 35f. The total social benefits of reducing the remaining 35 percent of pollution, which equal the blue area Y under the marginal social benefit curve between 65 and 100 percent, are considerably less than the marginal social cost of reducing the remaining 35 percent of pollution, which equals the entire area under the MC_A curve.

With equal abatement costs for all firms, firms prefer the 65 percent reduction standard in Figure 21.3, because the total cost of the standard equals the orange area X and is less than the total cost of the fee, which equals the orange area X plus the blue area Y plus green area Z. From a social standpoint, however, the fee may have an advantage. In Figure 21.4, if a 65 percent standard is in effect, firms have an incentive to find new technologies that reduce the cost of pollution abatement. Suppose a new technology can lower the marginal costs of pollution abatement from MC_A to MC_{A2}. The new total variable cost of reducing pollution by 65 percent equals the orange shaded area Y in Figure 21.4. The new technology reduces the firm's cost of meeting the 65 percent standard by the brown shaded area X, and therefore, if the fixed cost of developing the new technology is less than the brown area X, the development of the technology has a positive efficiency effect. However, as long as the 65 percent reduction standard is in effect, firms have no incentive to pay any additional costs to reduce pollution by more than 65 percent,

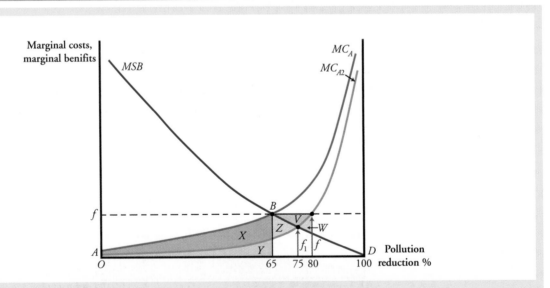

Figure 21.4 Comparing Standards and Fees
With a 65 percent standard, if new technology lowers the marginal cost of pollution abatement from MC_A to MC_{A2}, the total variable cost of reducing pollution equals the orange area Y. The new technology reduces the firm's cost of meeting the 65 percent standard by the brown shaded area X. As long as a 65 percent reduction standard is in effect, firms have no incentive to reduce pollution by more than 65 percent. With a fee f, if a new technology reduced the marginal abatement cost to MC_{A2}, the firm reduces pollution by 80 percent. In this case, the blue triangle Z is larger than the light-red triangle W, so the fee is more efficient. However, if the blue triangle Z is smaller than the light-red triangle W, the standard is more efficient; and if the blue triangle Z equals the light-red triangle W, the standard and the fee are equally inefficient.

even though the optimal level of pollution reduction with the lower abatement costs, MC_{A2}, is 75 percent. Unless the government changes the standard to 75 percent (which might take quite a long time—if it happens at all, given the slow pace at which government agencies sometimes work), the new technology results in an inefficiently high level of pollution and a deadweight loss equal to the blue triangle Z in Figure 21.4.

With a fee f, if a new technology with a fixed development cost less than the sum of the areas $X + Z + V$ reduced the marginal abatement cost to MC_{A2}, the firm would have an incentive to reduce pollution to below 65 percent. In fact, with a fee f, the firm would reduce pollution by 80 percent, which is more pollution reduction than the socially optimal 75 percent reduction. Unless the government lowers the fee to f_1, the new technology results in an inefficiently *low* level of pollution and a deadweight loss equal to the light-red triangle W.

Is a 65 percent standard or a fee f more efficient if the cost of pollution abatement decreases from MC_A to MC_{A2}? It depends on whether the blue triangle Z is larger than, smaller than, or equal to the light-red triangle W. If the blue triangle Z is larger than the light-red triangle W, as it is in Figure 21.4, the fee is more efficient. If the blue triangle Z is smaller than the light-red triangle W, the standard is more efficient. If the blue triangle Z equals the light-red triangle W, the standard and the fee are equally inefficient. The result depends on the shapes of the marginal social benefit and marginal abatement cost curves.

Differing Abatement Costs Across Firms Up to this point, we have assumed that the costs of pollution abatement are equal for all firms. It is more likely, however, that the costs of abatement vary across firms. In Figure 21.5, the marginal costs of sulfur dioxide abatement for Xcel Energy of Minneapolis, Minnesota, and OtterTail Power Company of Fergus Falls, Minnesota, which serves rural upstate Minnesota and North Dakota, are MC_X and MC_{OT}, respectively. Suppose the government mandates that both firms reduce their emissions of sulfur dioxide by 150 tons. The marginal abatement cost of the last ton reduced is MC_1 for OtterTail and MC_3 for Xcel. This is an inefficient outcome. The marginal cost of pollution reduction is much greater for Xcel than OtterTail. Society's total costs of pollution reduction can be reduced significantly if more of the burden is shifted from Xcel to OtterTail. In fact, as long as the marginal cost of pollution reduction is greater for Xcel than OtterTail, the burden should be shifted to OtterTail. To minimize the total social costs of pollution reduction, the marginal cost of pollution reduction must be equal for both firms.

COMMON ERROR 21.1 | **Believing That the Socially Optimal Level of Pollution Reduction Is 100 Percent**

In Figure 21.3, the socially optimal level of pollution reduction is 65 percent. Yet, if you ask a staunch environmentalist: "What is the optimal level of sulfur dioxide emissions from automobiles?" the response is likely to be that society should eliminate all sulfur dioxide emissions from cars. The thinking is that because all emissions cause some environmental damage, the sensible goal should be to eliminate all such emissions. Of course, given current technology, achieving such a goal would probably require eliminating automobiles.

To an economist, such reasoning is incorrect. Additional pollution should be eliminated only if the marginal benefits from abatement are greater than or equal to the marginal cost of abatement. Unless the marginal benefits exceed the marginal costs for all pollution, the socially optimal level of pollution reduction will be less than 100 percent.

Figure 21.5 Pollution Abatement with Differing Costs

The marginal costs of sulfur dioxide abatement for Xcel and OtterTail are MC_X and MC_{OT}, respectively. To minimize the total social costs of 300 tons of pollution reduction, Xcel should reduce pollution by 120 tons and OtterTail should reduce pollution by 180 tons, so the marginal cost of pollution reduction is equal for both firms.

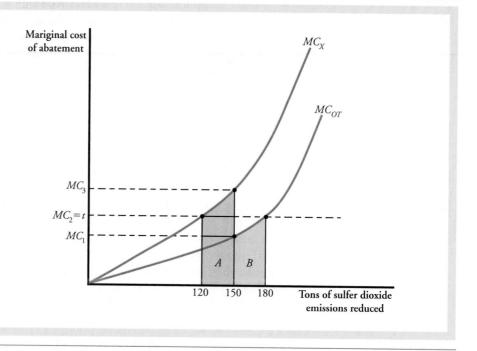

Alternatively, the government could place an effluent charge of $t = MC_2$ on every ton of sulfur dioxide emitted into the atmosphere. Xcel would reduce emissions by 120 tons and pay the fee for emissions greater than 120 tons, while OtterTail would reduce emissions by 180 tons. The shift from a standard to a fee system reduces pollution reduction costs for Xcel and society at large equal to the green area A. In exchange for these savings, OtterTail's pollution reduction costs increase by a smaller amount, equal to the red area B. The fee results in the same total reduction of 300 tons of sulfur dioxide emissions, but at a much lower social cost than the 150-ton standard. In fact, with a fee, the marginal abatement cost is equal for both firms, and therefore total social costs of pollution reduction are minimized.

UNCERTAINTY AND THE OPTIMAL POLLUTION ABATEMENT POLICY If the marginal social benefit curve and the marginal cost of abatement curves are known with certainty, a fee system can be imposed in order to reduce pollution for a lower total cost than a standard would. In Figure 21.6, suppose that the regulatory authorities do not know the MSB and MC_A curves with certainty. The government can therefore only estimate the optimal standard or fee. The marginal social benefit curve MSB, equals $10,000 - q_{SO_2}$, and the marginal cost of abatement curve is $MC_A = 650 + (1/4)q_{SO_2}$. The socially optimal level of sulfur dioxide reduction is where $MSB = MC_A$, or where:

$$MSB = 10,000 - q_{SO_2} = 650 + \frac{1}{4}q_{SO_2} = MC_A$$

$$\frac{5}{4} \; q_{SO_2} = 9,350$$

$$q_{SO_2} = \frac{4(9,350)}{5} = 7,480$$

The socially optimal fee is therefore $MC_A = 650 + (1/4)(7,480) = 2,520$.

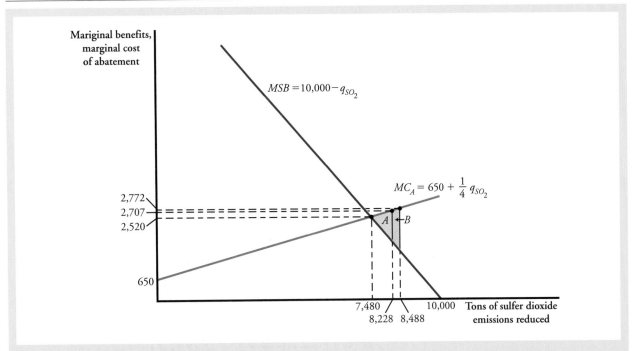

Figure 21.6 Uncertainty and the Optimal Pollution Abatement Policy

If the marginal social benefit curve is $MSB = 10,000 - q_{SO_2}$, and the marginal cost of abatement curve is $MC_A = 650 + (1/4)q_{SO_2}$, the optimal reduction in sulfur dioxide emissions is 7,480 tons and the optimal fee is $2,520 per ton. If the government sets a standard that is 10 percent too high, the deadweight loss equals the area of the red triangle A. If the government sets a fee that is 10 percent too high, the deadweight loss equals the area of the red triangle A plus the orange trapezoid B.

Suppose that due to uncertainty, the government sets the standard or fee 10 percent above the socially optimal standard or fee. If the standard is set 10 percent above the optimal level, the standard is $q_{SO_2} = 7,480 + 0.1(7,480) = 8,228$, and the marginal cost of abatement is $MC_A = 650 + (1/4)(8,228) = 2,707$. The resulting deadweight loss equals the red triangle A in Figure 21.6.

If the fee is set 10 percent above the socially optimal level, the fee is $f_2 = 2,520 + 0.1(2,520) = 2,772$, and therefore, $MC_A = 2,772 = 650 + (1/4)q_{SO_2}$ or $q_{SO_2} = 4(2,122) = 8,488$. The resulting deadweight loss equals the red triangle A plus the orange trapezoid B in Figure 21.6. In this case, the fee results in a larger deadweight loss than the standard. This is not the only possible result, though. The result in Figure 21.6 is driven by the highly elastic, or very flat, marginal cost of abatement curve. If instead, the marginal cost of abatement curve were highly elastic, or very steep, then a 10 percent error in the standard would result in a larger deadweight loss than a 10 percent error in the fee. With uncertainty, therefore, a fee can be more or less efficient than a standard.

Marketable Pollution Permits

pollution permit

A license issued by a government agency that gives the holder the legal right to emit a certain quantity of a pollutant into the environment.

A third method of government intervention is to issue marketable *pollution permits,* sometimes called "licenses to pollute." A **pollution permit**, issued by a government agency, gives the holder of the permit the legal right to emit a certain quantity of a pollutant into the environment. In Figure 21.7, the economic bad, tons of sulfur dioxide emissions, is measured on the *x*-axis, and the marginal cost of abatement, MC_A, is measured on the *y*-axis. The *x*-intercept represents the maximum amount of sulfur dioxide

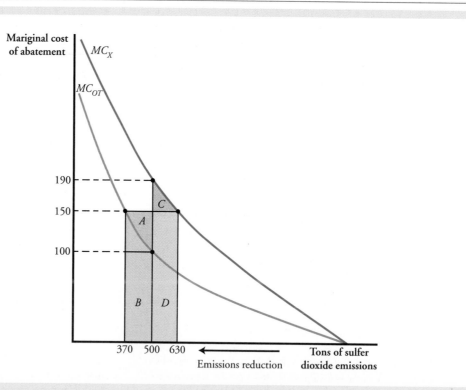

Figure 21.7 Marketable Pollution Permits

Initially, the government grants each firm 500 tons of sulfur dioxide permits. Xcel offers OtterTail $150 per permit for 130 permits or $19,500, which equals the red rectangle D. The $19,500 received by OtterTail equals the rectangle composed of the green and orange areas A + B. OtterTail reduces its emissions from 500 tons to 370 tons for a total cost equal to the orange shaded area B under the MC_{OT} curve. Xcel increases its emissions to 630 tons of sulfur dioxide. The trade benefits Xcel, because the price it pays for the permits equals the red rectangle D, which is less than the costs it would have to pay to clean up the additional 130 tons of sulfur dioxide, which equals the sum of the blue and red areas, C + D, under the MC_X curve.

emitted by the firms. As we move to the left along the x-axis, the amount of pollution decreases, and therefore the marginal cost of abatement increases.

Suppose that the government's objective is to permit a maximum of 1,000 tons of sulfur dioxide to be emitted by both firms. In Figure 21.7, the marginal abatement cost is once again higher for Xcel, MC_X, than for OtterTail, MC_{OT}. Initially, the government grants each firm 500 tons of sulfur dioxide permits. The penalty for emitting more than the firm's permitted allotment of sulfur dioxide is severe: The firm must pay a penalty of $2,000 per excess ton of emissions, and it loses a ton of its allotted permits for the following year.

If both firms use all of their allotted permits and emit 500 tons of pollution, the marginal cost of eliminating one less ton of pollution for (the 501st ton of emissions) Xcel is just a bit less than $190, and the marginal cost of eliminating one less ton of pollution for OtterTail is just a bit less than $100. Suppose that Xcel approaches OtterTail with an offer to purchase one ton of OtterTail's permits for $180. If accepted, the offer saves Xcel just under $190 in abatement costs for a price of $180. OtterTail should jump at this offer, because it can reduce its emissions to 499 tons for just a bit more than $100. OtterTail makes almost $80 by selling the permit to Xcel. This is a Pareto-improving exchange that makes both firms better off.

How many such Pareto-improving trades can the two firms complete? As long as the marginal abatement cost of an additional ton of sulfur dioxide is less for OtterTail than Xcel, the two firms can complete a Pareto-efficient trade. In Figure 21.7, suppose Xcel offered OtterTail $150 per permit for 130 permits or $19,500. The $19,500 cost to Xcel equals the red rectangle D in Figure 21.7, and the $19,500 received by OtterTail equals the rectangle composed of the green and orange areas $A + B$. OtterTail can reduce its emissions from 500 tons to 370 tons for a total cost equal to the orange-shaded area B under the MC_{OT} curve. The trade therefore benefits OtterTail, because the revenues it receives (the sum of the green and orange areas, $A + B$) are greater than the costs of its abatement (the orange area B). Xcel now has enough permits to increase its emissions to 630 tons of sulfur dioxide. The trade also benefits Xcel, because the price it pays for the permits, which equals the red rectangle D, is less than the costs it would have to pay to clean up the additional 130 tons of sulfur dioxide, which equals the sum of the blue and red areas, $C + D$, under the MC_X curve. Once the firms complete the exchange of 130 tons of permtis, no further Pareto-improving trades are possible, because the marginal cost of pollution abatement is equal to $150 per ton for both firms.

By using marketable permits, the government succeeds in reaching its goal of reducing sulfur dioxide emissions by 1,000 tons in the most cost-effective manner. The invisible hand is at work in this market, because all Pareto-improving trades will be completed. If the government makes millions of permits available in a free market, a competitive market evolves and firms having high marginal costs of abatement purchase permits from firms with lower marginal costs of abatement. Of course, there is no guarantee that the government will issue the socially optimal number of permits, and therefore there is no guarantee of a socially efficient outcome. However, the marketable permit system guarantees that the total cost of reducing pollution, given the number of permits, will be minimized.

▲▲▲ 21.2 APPLICATION   Bottle Bills and Recycling

Ten states and one county in Missouri have laws referred to as "bottle bills," which require a refundable deposit on all beer, malt, and soft drink container sales. Generally, these states, California, Connecticut, Delaware, Iowa, Maine, Massachusetts, Michigan, New York, Oregon, and Vermont—require a five-cent deposit on each container. The figure depicts the theoretical rationale behind bottle bills. The x-axis measures the number of bottles purchased and thrown away. These bottles enter the nation's solid waste system and must be disposed of in landfills. The vertical blue line on the right represents the total number of bottles purchased by consumers, which equals B_p. The marginal social cost of bottles that are thrown away, MSC; the marginal cost of recycling bottles to consumers, MCR; and the deposit per bottle are measured along the y-axis. The number of bottles recycled is measured by moving to the left along the x-axis, away from point B_p and toward the origin.

The red curve is the *marginal cost of recycling* (to consumers) curve, MCR. There are two ways to interpret the MCR curve. Moving left along the x-axis away from B_p, the marginal cost of recycling an additional bottle increases as more bottles are recycled. Alternatively, moving to the right along the x-axis, as the refundable deposit on a bottle decreases, the opportunity cost of throwing a bottle away decreases, and therefore consumers throw away more bottles. In this alternative interpretation, the MCR curve can be thought of as a "demand for throwing bottles away curve": The higher the price of throwing bottles away—that is, the higher the deposit—the lower the quantity demanded for throwing bottles away.

Moving to the right along the x-axis, the green marginal social cost curve, MSC, measures the marginal social cost of throwing away bottles. The most significant social costs are those of solid waste disposal and of litter, and the increased energy costs associated with having to

(continued)

replace the discarded bottles with bottles made out of new materials rather than bottles made out of recycled materials. Alternatively, moving from right to left, the green curve measures the marginal benefits of increased recycling, including the decreased costs of solid waste disposal, the decreased cost of litter, and the decreased cost of energy.

In 40 states and the District of Columbia, there are no mandated deposits, and consumers operate under a policy of "no deposit, no return." Consumers in these states can recycle bottles on a voluntary basis. If this figure represents a state without a bottle bill, consumers will throw away B_v bottles and voluntarily recycle $B_p - B_v$ bottles. This is inefficient, because the marginal benefits of increased recycling are greater than the marginal cost of recycling, MCR. There is a deadweight loss associated with a voluntary recycling policy equal to the orange area A.

Suppose instead that the figure represents a state with a bottle bill that requires a five-cent refundable deposit per bottle. With a five-cent deposit, consumers throw away B_{bb} bottles and recycle $B_p - B_{bb}$ bottles, which is the socially optimal outcome because $MSC = MCR = 0.05$.

Studies have shown that bottle bills result in dramatic reductions in litter and solid waste and save energy. These studies suggest that bottle bills reduce beverage container litter by between 70 and 85 percent and overall levels of litter by between 30 and 65 percent. According to the Container Recycling Institute, in 1995, the 10 states with bottle bills recycled 1.63 million beverage containers compared to only 1.33 million in all non-deposit states combined.[*]

There is little doubt that bottle bills reduce litter, decrease solid waste management costs, and save energy—but at what cost? A study in 2000 prepared for the Michigan Great Lakes Protection Fund suggested that the costs are quite substantial, because of the distributors' and retailers' costs of collecting and processing containers. Net benefits of $24.04 million occur to residents (consumers) and $9.27 million in benefits occur to the state government, while net costs of $34.91 million occur to distributors. Retailers bear a particularly large ($92.81 million) annual burden, because of the high costs of collecting and sorting containers. The bottom line is that the Michigan bottle bill imposed a net monetary cost of $94.46 million annually. Do these numbers

---

Application Figure 21.2
Impact of a Bottle Bill
In a state with a bottle bill that requires a five-cent refundable deposit per bottle, consumers throw away B_{bb} bottles and recycle $B_p - B_{bb}$ bottles, which is the socially optimal outcome, because $MSC = MCR = 0.05$. Without a bottle bill, consumers throw away B_v bottles and there is a deadweight loss equal to the orange area A.

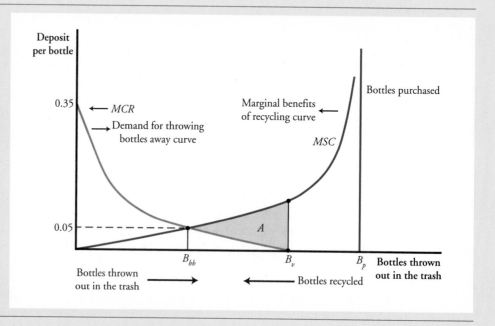

(continued)

[*] Bottle Bill Statistics, *http://www.fiu.edu.*

imply that Michigan would be better off without a bottle bill? The figures used in the Michigan study measured benefits in terms of market prices. Market prices, however, are likely to significantly underestimate the benefits from an environmental policy with positive externalities. The correct measure of benefits should be based on what consumers are willing to pay for the benefits accruing from the bottle bill. For example, would consumers worried about greenhouse gas emissions be willing to pay more or less than the market price of the energy saved through recycling containers? Most importantly, the study failed to measure what Michigan residents were willing to pay for a cleaner environment with far less litter strewn across the state's parks and highways.

▼▼▼   21.3   Externalities, Property Rights, and the Coase Theorem

In 1960, economist Ronald Coase published a paper entitled, "The Problem of Social Cost," in which he presented a theory that showed how problems created between two parties because of externalities can always be solved through negotiation, as long as the negotiations are costless, there are zero *transaction costs*, and the law assigns the responsibility for damages to one of the two parties.[1] **Transaction costs** are the costs of negotiating and enforcing an agreement between two parties. Because most agreements require some legal fees, transaction costs are rarely zero in the real-world; however, Coase's paper revolutionized the way scholars in the fields of economics, law, political science, and philosophy think about externalities.

transaction costs

The costs of negotiating and enforcing an agreement between two parties.

Property Rights

property rights

The legal rules regarding who owns a resource and what the owner can do with that resource.

To understand Coase's theorem, we must begin by defining the *property rights* to a piece of property. **Property rights** are the legal rules regarding what individuals and firms can do with their property. For example, if you own a piece of land, you have property rights over that land and the property rights might specify that you can build, drill for oil, erect a theme park, or sell the land. Similarly, if you have the appropriate property rights over a lake, you can fish, water ski, or swim in the lake; or, the property rights might specify that you can drain the lake, drill for oil in the lake, or dump chemicals in the lake and kill all the fish.

PROPERTY RIGHTS ASSIGNED TO A POLLUTER Coase suggested that by assigning property rights to one of the two parties in a dispute over externalities, all problems of externalities could be solved efficiently. In Figure 21.8, we assume that a lumber mill dumps a maximum of 150 tons of dioxin into a river. The marginal benefits of dioxin abatement for the nearby community of Shrek Valley are $MB_A = 600 - 4t$, and the marginal costs of abatement for the mill are $MC_A = 2t$, where t represents tons of dioxin. Therefore, the socially optimal level of dioxin abatement is obtained by equating MB_A to MC_A, or:

$$MB_A = 600 - 4t = 2t = MB_A$$

$$t = \frac{600}{6} = 100$$

The socially optimal level of dioxin abatement is 100 tons.

---

[1] Ronald Coase, "The Problem of Social Cost," *Journal of Law and Economics*, Vol. 3, No.1–44, 1960.

Figure 21.8 The Coase Theorem and Pollution Abatement
The marginal benefits of abatement for the community are $MB_A = 600 - 4t$. The marginal costs of abatement for the mill are $MC_A = 2t$, where t represents tons of dioxin. If property rights are assigned to the lumber mill, the community offers $200 per ton of dioxin abatement, and the mill eliminates 100 tons of dioxin at a total cost of $10,000, which equals area C. The community pays $20,000 to the mill owners, and its consumer surplus increases by area A. The result is socially efficient, because $MB_A = MC_A$. If the community is assigned the property rights, the mill owners offer to pay $10,000 (equal to areas $D + E$) to the community for the right to dump 50 tons of dioxin into the river, and the result is again socially efficient.

Suppose that the government assigns the property rights to the river to the lumber mill; that is, the mill owners, not the citizens of Shrek Valley, own the right to use the river. Assigning the property rights to the lumber mill is equivalent to the common real-world situation where an industry pollutes a river without any government intervention. In such real-world situations, the industry has been granted *de facto* property rights.

Although the community may feel helpless at this point because the mill can dump dioxin into the river with impunity, the community still has options. If negotiations between the community and mill owners are free of any transactions costs, the citizens of Shrek Valley can call a meeting with the lumber mill owners to negotiate a solution to the problem. Suppose that the community holds a public meeting and decides to offer the mill owners $200 per ton of dioxin abatement. At $200 per ton, the mill owners find it profitable to eliminate the first 100 tons of dioxin dumped into the river at a total cost of $10,000 (which equals the area C in Figure 21.8) in return for a payment of $200(100) = $20,000. The mill owners are $10,000 better off. The citizens of Shrek Valley make a payment of $20,000 to the mill owners, and in return receive an increase in consumer surplus equal to the triangle A (which equals $20,000), so the community is better off. At $200 per ton of dioxin abatement, the mill would not reduce more than 100 tons of dioxin, because the MC_A is greater than $200 per ton for any further reductions. The final result is socially efficient, because $MB_A = MC_A$ for the 100th ton of abatement.

Why would the community offer to pay $200 per ton to the mill owners rather than attempt to "low-ball" the owners with an offer below $200 per ton? For example, why not offer $100 per ton? In this case, the mill would find it profitable to reduce dioxin by only 50 tons for a payment of $100(50) = $5,000. Once the community leaders realized that the mill had reduced dioxin by only 50 tons, they would realize that the marginal benefits for additional tons of abatement are much greater than $100 per ton, and therefore would make an additional offer to the mill owners to reduce additional dioxin at a higher price. Only when the price reached $200 per ton would it no longer be in the community's interest to offer a higher price per ton of abatement.

PROPERTY RIGHTS ASSIGNED TO THE COMMUNITY Now suppose that the government assigns the property rights to the river to the community; that is, the citizens of Shrek Valley own the river. Does this mean that the mill owners are now in big trouble because the citizens of Shrek Valley can completely ban the dumping of dioxin in the river? Such a complete ban would cost the mill owners a total clean-up cost equal to the sum of the areas $C + D + E + F$, or $22,500. The mill owners can now call a meeting with the citizens to negotiate a solution to the dioxin problem.

Suppose that the mill owners offer to pay $200 per ton for any dioxin dumped into the river. At $200 per ton, the mill owners find it profitable to eliminate the first 100 tons of dioxin dumped into the river at a total cost of $10,000 (which equals the area C in Figure 21.8). The mill owners are $10,000 better off if they eliminate the first 100 tons of dioxin rather than pay the community $20,000 for the right to dump those first 100 tons into the river. The mill owners would offer to pay $10,000 (equal to the sum of areas $D + E$) to the community for the right to dump the remaining 50 tons into the river. The payment of $10,000 for the right to dump 50 tons into the river is less than the cost of $12,500 (equal to the sum of areas $D + E + F$) to clean up those last 50 tons of dioxin. The citizens of Shrek Valley would gladly accept the offer because the company's payment of $10,000 is greater than the total benefits to the citizens of the abatement of the final 50 tons of dioxin, which equals only $5,000 (the area D). The mill owners would not offer to reduce more than 100 tons of dioxin, because the MC_A is greater than $200 per ton for any further reductions. The final result is once again socially efficient, because $MB_A = MC_A$ for the 100th ton of abatement.

Why would the mill offer to pay $200 per ton for dioxin dumped into the river rather than attempt to low-ball the citizens of Shrek Valley with an offer below $200 per ton; for example, $100 per ton? Certainly the mill owners could offer $100 per ton for the right to dump dioxin into the river. However, the community would permit the company to dump only 25 tons of dioxin into the river for a payment of $100(25) = $2,500. The mill would then be forced to reduce its emissions by 125 tons and for each of the 75 tons of abatement beyond the first 50 tons, the marginal cost of abatement to the company would be greater than $100. Once the company realized that it would cost them more than $100 per ton to reduce emissions beyond 50 tons, the mill owners would realize that they would be better off making an additional offer to the community to pay a higher price for the right to dump dioxin into the river. Only when the offer price reached $200 per ton, would it no longer be in the company's interest to offer a higher price per ton for pollution permits. Summarizing the Coase theorem: *If transactions costs are zero and legal property rights are clearly defined, bargaining between two parties will always result in an efficient outcome.*

The Coase Theorem and Transactions Costs

The Coase theorem is dependent on the assumption of cost-free negotiations. In the real world, however, negotiations are rarely cost-free: in fact, legal fees usually present a substantial cost to individuals or firms engaged in any type of negotiations with another party. Suppose that in our previous example, the lumber mill has the property rights to the river. Because it is extremely difficult for the thousands of members of the community to negotiate with the owners of the lumber mill, the first thing the community does is to hire an attorney, Jay Cochrane. The community agrees to pay Mr. Cochrane a fee equal to $60 per ton of dioxin abatement he can obtain from the mill. Transaction costs are now substantial for the community.

Hiring Mr. Cochrane reduces the community's marginal benefit curve by $60 per ton of dioxin abatement; therefore, the new marginal benefit curve is $MB_A = 540 - 4t$. In Figure 21.9, the community will no longer be willing to offer $200 per ton of abatement to the mill owners. Because the community's marginal benefit curve is now $MB_A = 540 - 4t$, the community's optimal level of dioxin abatement is obtained by equating $MB_A = 540 - 4t$ to MC_A, or:

$$MB_A = 540 - 4t = 2t = MB_A$$

$$t = \frac{540}{6} = 90$$

The community's optimal level of dioxin abatement is 90 tons.

With the lower marginal benefits curve, the community is willing to offer just $180 per ton of abatement. At $180 per ton, the mill owners agree to reduce dioxin emissions by just 90 tons, which is 10 percent below the socially optimal level of abatement. As a result of these transaction costs, there is a deadweight loss equal to the orange shaded triangle X, which equals $(1/2)(\$60)(10) = \$300$. The higher the legal fee charged by Mr. Cochrane, the larger the deadweight loss.[2]

Figure 21.9 Coase Theorem with Non-Zero Transaction Costs
The lumber mill has the property rights and the community hires an attorney for a fee equal to $60 per ton of negotiated dioxin abatement. Hiring an attorney reduces the community's marginal benefit curve to $MB_A = 540 - 4t$, and the community is willing to offer only $180 per ton of abatement, and the mill owners agree to reduce dioxin emissions by 90 tons, which is 10 percent below the socially optimal level of abatement. There is a deadweight loss equal to the orange triangle.

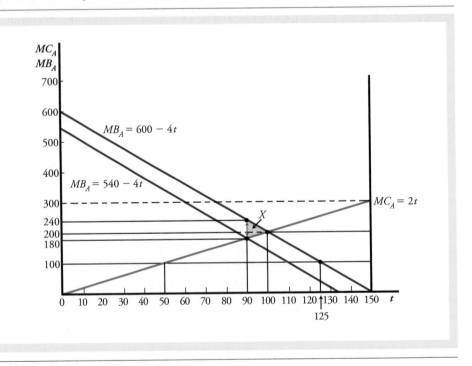

[2] Transaction costs are not the only reason why the Coase theorem may be invalid. Two other potential problems are the existence of asymmetric information between the community and the mill and the likelihood of the mill going bankrupt if the community owns the property rights. These problems can also prevent Coase-type negotiations from achieving economic efficiency.

▲▲▲ 21.3 APPLICATION   Applying the Coase Theorem: The EPA's Marketable Allowance Program

In March 1994, the United States Environmental Protection Agency (EPA) introduced a marketable pollution permit program to deal with the nation's acid rain problem, which is caused by sulfur dioxide emissions. The program gives clean-air property rights to the EPA, which sets limits on the number of permits issued. The program enables firms and individuals to engage in negotiations consistent with the Coase theorem.

Since its inception, the marketable pollution permit program has expanded dramatically; it is now the cornerstone of the EPA's acid rain reduction program. The EPA's permits are called "allowances," and each allowance permits a firm to emit a ton of sulfur dioxide. At the end of each year, each business unit that emits sulfur dioxide must hold allowances to cover its emissions. The allowances are fully marketable goods that can be bought, sold, traded, or banked for use in future years. Any individual, corporation, government, independent broker, environmental group, or private citizen is free to buy and sell allowances, including environmental groups such as the Sierra Club.

In 2000, the EPA placed a ceiling or "cap" of 8.95 million allowances each year. The EPA keeps track of who holds each allowance. Anyone holding allowances has an account with the EPA, and all allowance transfers must be recorded. At the end of the year, if a polluter's allowances are greater than the polluter's emissions of sulfur dioxide, the allowance can be carried forward into the next year. However, if a polluter's allowances are less than the polluter's emissions, the polluter must pay a penalty and surrender allowances for the following year. In 1998, the financial penalty for excess emissions was $2,581 per excess ton of sulfur dioxide.

The program has shown remarkable growth since its inception. The number of trades increased from 2 million in 1995 to over 14 million in 2000. Between August 1994 and August 2000, the average monthly price of an allowance fluctuated widely around the long-run average of approximately $150, falling as low as $69 in March 1996 and rising as high as $212 in May and June 1999. The market for sulfur dioxide allowances has behaved like a competitive commodity market, with prices rising and falling as market conditions have changed.

According to the EPA, the sulfur dioxide allowance program has reduced emissions by 6 million tons per year compared to 1980 levels, and remarkably, at a cost 75 percent below the EPA's original cost projections. When the program is fully implemented in 2010, the EPA predicts sulfur dioxide emissions will be half of their 1980 levels. The agency estimates that the sulfur dioxide reductions result in more than $50 billion per year in health benefits to Americans.

▼▼▼ 21.4   The Problem of a Common Resource

Perhaps the most important lesson to be learned from the Coase theorem is the importance of assigning property rights to one of the parties in a negotiation. Regardless of who holds the property rights, the efficient outcome will be reached through negotiations if transaction costs are zero.

But what happens in cases where property rights are not clearly identified? Consider a large body of water, such as a lake, or a sea to which commercial fishermen have access but no country or individual has clearly defined property rights. Examples include the Mediterranean Sea, ocean fishing waters beyond any nation's territorial waters, or the Caspian Sea in Central Asia, which is bordered by five countries. As additional fishing boats enter these waters, the marginal product per boat eventually declines because of the law of diminishing returns.

Suppose that a particular lake has the marginal product per boat shown in Table 21.1. The marginal product curve is $MP_B = 550 - 50B$; where MP_B represents the marginal product per boat, and B represents the number of boats on the lake. As more boats

Table 21.1 The Problem of the Commons

Boats	Fish Caught	MP_B	AP_B
0	0	—	—
1	500	500	500
2	950	450	475
3	1,350	400	450
4	1,700	350	425
5	2,000	300	400
6	2,250	250	375
7	2,450	200	350
8	2,600	150	325
9	2,700	100	300
10	2,750	50	275
11	2,750	0	250

go out fishing, the total number of fish caught increases, but at a decreasing rate. Furthermore, as the number of boats increases, the average product per boat also decreases, but at a slower rate than the marginal product per boat. In Table 21.1, the average product per boat curve is $AP_B = 525 - 25B$.

Figure 21.10 shows the marginal product and average product curves along with the marginal cost curve $MC = 300$ fish. The marginal cost of sending another boat onto the lake is 300 fish. This means that a boat must catch and sell 300 fish per day to cover the extra opportunity cost of one day's fishing. To determine the equilibrium number of boats fishing on the lake on a typical day, we must first ask this question: from the perspective of an individual boat crew waiting to go out on the lake, how many fish would the crew expect to catch? We know the following from Table 21.1:

- The first boat out expects to catch 500 fish.
- The second boat out on the lake knows that the total catch with two boats is 950 fish. Both boats are equally likely to pull any given fish out of the water, and therefore the second boat expects to catch half of the total catch, or $950/2 = 475$ fish. The second boat adds only 450 fish to the total catch, but expects to return to the dock with 475 fish.
- The third boat on the lake knows that the total catch with three boats will be 1,350 fish. All three boats are equally likely to pull any given fish out of the water, and therefore the third boat expects to catch one-third of the total catch, or $1,350/3 = 450$ fish. The third boat adds only 400 fish to the total catch, but expects to return to the dock with 450 fish.
- Each additional boat expects to return to the dock with a catch equal to the AP_B, and therefore boats continue to go out as long as AP_B is greater than or equal to MC per boat.

It follows that in Figure 21.10, nine boats will be fishing on the lake and $AP_B = MC = 300$ fish.

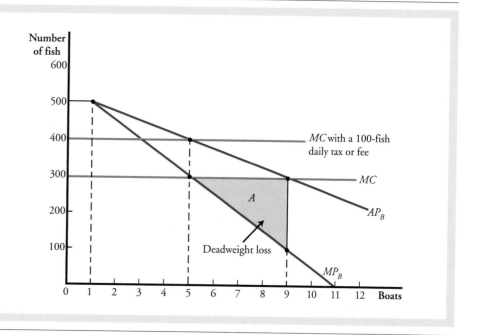

Figure 21.10 The Problem with a Common Fishing Resource

Boats go out fishing as long as AP_B is greater than or equal to $MC = 300$ fish per boat, so nine boats fish on the lake. The efficient number of boats is five, where $MP_B = MC = 300$. With nine boats, the deadweight loss equals the orange triangle.

There is a serious efficiency problem with nine boats on the lake. While the average product of the ninth boat is 300 fish, the marginal product is only 100 fish. This situation is inefficient, because the marginal cost of sending the ninth boat onto the lake is 300 fish, but the boat only adds 100 fish to the total catch. Consequently, it costs society far more in resources expended (300 fish) to send out the ninth boat than the contribution the boat makes (100 fish) to society's catch of fish. In Figure 21.10, the efficient number of boats is five, where the $MP_B = MC = 300$. The sixth, seventh, eighth, and ninth boats contribute less to society than their marginal costs. The deadweight loss equals the orange triangle A.

While the efficient number of boats is five, and the efficient number of total fish caught is 2,000, in the absence of well-defined property rights, 2,700 fish will be caught each day. Because 35 percent more than the socially optimal number of fish are caught each day, the lake will quickly become depleted as the number of reproducing fish rapidly declines. In Figure 21.11, as the number of fish in the lake declines, the MP_B and AP_B curves decline from the dark-blue curves AP_{B1} and MP_{B1} to the light-blue curves AP_{B2} and MP_{B2}, and the number of boats on the lake declines from 9 to 4. However, even as the number of boats and the total catch declines, the lake is still being over-fished! The new deadweight loss in Figure 21.11 equals the orange triangle A.

According to the Coase theorem, there are efficient solutions to the problem of the common fishing resource. Suppose that one individual or a government buys the lake. With clearly defined property rights, the lake owner would have an incentive to maximize the economic surplus value derived from the lake each day by limiting the number of fishing boats. In Figure 21.10, the government could either limit the number of boat permits to five per day or charge a 100-fish-per-day tax per boat, which would increase MC to 400 fish. Either policy would result in five boats per day fishing on the lake and eliminate the deadweight loss.

If the lake owner were a private monopolist, that would also solve the problem. The monopolist would want to maximize profit from those fishing on the lake. To do this, the monopolist could either own all the boats on the lake and limit the number going

Figure 21.11 Depletion of a Common Fishing Resource

As the number of fish in the lake declines, the MP_B and AP_B curves decline from the dark-blue curves AP_{B1} and MP_{B1} to the light blue curves AP_{B2} and MP_{B2}, and the number of boats declines from 9 to 4. With 4 boats, the lake is still being over-utilized and the deadweight loss equals the orange triangle A.

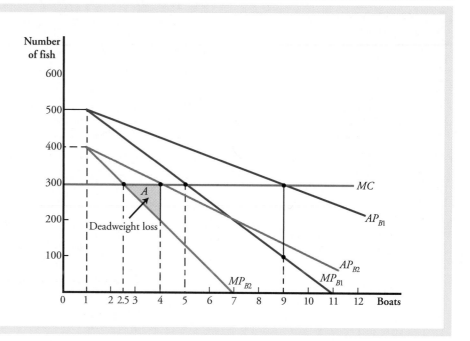

out to five per day, or could charge each boat a 100-fish daily fee. As shown in Figure 21.10, the fee would raise the marginal cost of fishing from 300 fish to 400 fish, and therefore only five boats would go out on the lake each day. At the end of each day, the monopolist would collect fees equal to 500 fish, and each of the boats would go home with 400 − 100 = 300 fish. The boat owners would earn a normal profit equal to zero, as they would without clearly defined property rights, and the monopolist lake owner would earn monopoly profit equal to 500 fish.

If the property rights to the lake are assigned to a fishing cooperative composed of the nine boat owners that were originally fishing on the lake, the result will also be efficient. The cooperative will want to maximize its joint profit. This can be done only if it limits the number of boats on the lake to five per day. It could then divide the 500 fish profit equally among all nine boat owners. The nine boat owners would each earn a profit of 55.55 (500/9) fish per day, which is better than the zero profit they would each earn with nine boats. As long as property rights to the lake are clearly defined, the efficient number of boats will end up on the lake.

▲▲▲ 21.4 APPLICATION   Caviar at $65 an Ounce!

Sturgeon fish in the Caspian Sea produce beluga caviar, which is widely regarded as the highest-quality caviar in the world. In 2001, the price of beluga caviar reached $65 per ounce! At the same time, you could purchase salmon caviar produced in the United States or Avruga caviar produced in Spain for approximately $6.00 per ounce. Why was beluga caviar 10 times more expensive than other caviars?

The Caspian sea is the world's largest inland sea, covering more than 149,000 square miles. Until the breakup of the Soviet Union in 1991, the Soviet Union and Iran were the only countries bordering the Caspian Sea. The

(continued)

two countries agreed to manage tightly and limit the catch of sturgeon each year. As a result, the annual catch in the 1980s was approximately 22,000 tons per year.

Since the breakup of the Soviet Union, five countries have bordered the Caspian Sea: Russia, Iran, Azerbaijan, Turkmenistan, and Kazakhstan. Only Iran has continued to effectively manage its section of the Caspian Sea. The United Nations Convention on International Trade in Endangered Species (CITES) has accused the other four countries of failing to protect the Caspian Sea from environmental damage, and more importantly, from illegal sturgeon poaching. According to CITES, the high price of Caspian Sea caviar has made the sea a "magnet for illegal fishing and even organized crime." In December 2001, the World Wildlife Fund reported that 80 percent of the sturgeon and caviar sold in Moscow was produced illegally. In addition, it was estimated that because of over-fishing, poaching, and environmental damage, the sturgeon catch was down to a mere 1,000 tons; an incredible 95 percent reduction from 1980s levels. Making matters worse, Russia, Azerbaijan, Turkmenistan, and Kazakhstan are all poor countries that cannot afford to put much of their resources into pollution control or anti-poaching enforcement.

In the 1990s, rapid worldwide economic growth and the stock market boom fueled the demand for beluga caviar. The combination of rapidly increasing demand and a 95 percent reduction in supply of beluga caviar resulted in a price of $65.00 per ounce. In December 2001, the crisis led Russia, Azerbaijan, and Kazakhstan to place a complete ban on both commercial fishing for sturgeon in the Caspian Sea and the export of black caviar. The key to successfully bringing back the sturgeon population, however, is finding a method of stopping poachers.

▼▼▼ 21.5 Public Goods

The following lyrics come from a 1988 song by the children's song writer Tom Chapin:[3]

> *Someone's gonna use it after you*
> *Someone needs that water when you're through*
> *'Cause the water, land and air*
> *These are things we've got to share*
> *Someone's gonna use it after you.*

In these lyrics, Mr. Chapin shows an understanding of an important economic concept. Some goods, like clean air and water, are consumed by all of us simultaneously. Furthermore, when I consume clean air, I can't prevent you from simultaneously consuming it. Clean air has two important economic characteristics: it is both *nonrival* and *nonexcludable* in consumption. A good is **nonrival** in consumption if my consumption of the good does not affect your ability to consume the good. If I am able to breathe clean air, it does not affect your ability to also breathe the same clean air. A good is **nonexcludable** if limiting its consumption to a select group of consumers is impossible or prohibitively expensive. Once again, clean air fits this definition. If I consume clean air, there is no possible way, short of locking you in a room with pumped-in dirty air, of excluding you from clean air.

Public goods are goods that are nonrival in consumption. Some public goods are also nonexcludable. Goods that are both nonrival and nonexcludable are called **pure public goods**. Examples include clean air and water, over-the-air (but not cable or satellite) television and radio broadcasting, and national defense. Some public goods are nonrival, but excludable: such goods are called **club goods** or **collective goods**. Examples include a college lecture, a rock concert, and cable or satellite television. By comparison, **private goods** are both rival and excludable. Do not be confused by the term "public goods": not all public goods are produced by the government. The term simply refers to the characteristics of

nonrival

Describes a good whose consumption by one person does not affect the consumption of the same good by another person or persons; for example, an uncrowded highway.

nonexcludable

Describes a good with the characteristic that it is impossible or prohibitively expensive to limit its consumption to a select group of consumers; for example, clean air.

public good

A good that is nonrival in consumption, such as an uncrowded park.

pure public good

A good that is both nonrival and nonexcludable; for example, national defense.

club good

A good that is nonrival but excludable; for example, a college class lecture.

---

[3] Tom Chapin and John Forster, *Family Tree*, ©1988 Sundance Music, Inc., A&M Records.

collective good

Another term for a club good.

private good

A good that is both rival and excludable.

a good, and not to the provision of the good. Public goods can be produced in the private sector, and the government can produce private goods that are both rival and excludable.

Table 21.2 illustrates some examples of goods that are both nonrival and nonexcludable, as well as other types of goods. Notice that some goods move from one category to another, depending on the specific conditions of consumption. Highways, for example, can fit into any one of the four categories, depending on whether the highway is crowded or a toll road. Crowded toll highways have the characteristic of private goods in that they are both rival and excludable. On the other hand, uncrowded non-toll highways have the characteristics of a pure public good. An uncrowded toll road, however, is nonrival but excludable, and a crowded non-toll highway is nonexcludable but rival.

Clean air and water present another interesting case of similar goods placed in different categories. Clean air is a pure public good, because it is nonrival and nonexcludable. Clean water, however, can be rival but nonexcludable. Consider the Sea of Galilee, which runs into the Jordan River and then into the Dead Sea. Israel and Jordan share the waters of the Sea of Galilee and the Jordan River; however, if the water enters the Dead Sea, it is extremely expensive to make it useful for humans. The waters of the Jordan River are therefore rival, in the sense that Jordan cannot use any water that Israel withdraws and Israel cannot use any water that Jordan withdraws. The water, however, is nonexcludable because each country borders the Sea of Galilee and the Jordan River and therefore cannot be prevented from withdrawing water from the Sea of Galilee or the Jordan River. Water rights were a very important part of the peace treaty between Israel and Jordan.

The Efficient Provision of Public Goods

One of the most common examples of a pure public good is an uncrowded public park. Uncrowded public parks are nonrival and nonexcludable. Central Park in New York or

Table 21.2 Different Types of Economic Goods

| | | Rival | |
		Yes	No
Excludable	**Yes**	**Private goods**	**Club goods or collective goods**
		Jeans	Cable and satellite television broadcasts
		Food	College class lecture broadcasts
		Deodorant	Pay-for-use Web sites
		Crowded toll highways	Uncrowded toll highways
			Rock concert broadcasts
	No	**Common resources**	**Pure public goods**
		Sturgeon in the Caspian Sea	National defense
		Oil reserves in the ocean	Over-the-air television and radio broadcasts
		Swimming in a small local lake	Clean air
		Clean water	Free Web sites
		Crowded national parks	Uncrowded national parks
		Crowded non-toll highways	Uncrowded non-toll highways

Hyde Park and Hempstead Heath in London are excellent examples of large public parks that are typically nonrival and nonexcludable, except when crowded. Even small towns like Hamilton, New York, often have beautiful public parks that are rarely crowded, and are therefore typically nonrival and nonexcludable.

Throughout most of this text, we have primarily analyzed the demand and supply for private goods. To determine the demand for rival and excludable private goods, we ask the following question: what is the quantity of the good that all buyers in a market would like to buy at each possible price over a given period of time? For example, suppose Bruce, Elton, Paul, and Art are the only four buyers in the market for jeans. If jeans are $30, and Bruce demands 7 pairs, Elton demands 2 pairs, Paul demands 5 pairs, and Art demands 3 pairs, the total demand for jeans at a price of $30 is 17 pairs of jeans. We obtain the demand curve for a private good by adding the quantities demanded at any given price or by adding the individual demand curves horizontally.

For a public good, it is incorrect to engage in a similar exercise of adding demand curves horizontally, because the goods are nonrival and nonexcludable. The same quantity of the good is shared by all, and all consumers consume the same quantity of the good. Now, however, consider the marginal benefit for acres of park land for two types of consumers: Type A and Type B. Assume that Type A's marginal benefit curve for park land is $MB_A = 100 - 25q$, and Type B's marginal benefit curve is $MB_B = 300 - 50q$; where q is the size of the park in acres, and MB_i is the marginal benefit obtained by the ith consumer from the last acre. The marginal benefit curve measures how much they would be willing to pay for the last acre of parkland.

In Figure 21.12 (a), the curves MB_A and MB_B identify the two marginal benefit curves. For a one-acre park, the Type A consumer would be willing to pay $75 and the

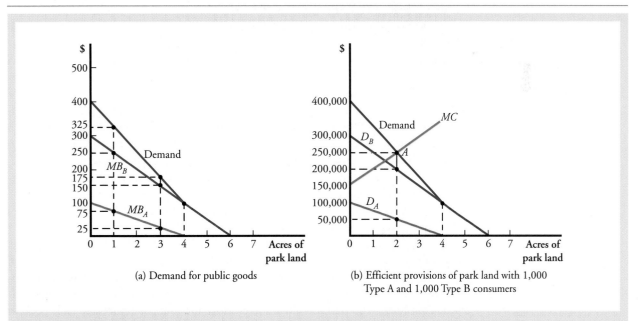

(a) Demand for public goods

(b) Efficient provisions of park land with 1,000 Type A and 1,000 Type B consumers

Figure 21.12 The Demand and Efficient Provision of Public Goods
In panel (a), the marginal benefit curves for Type A and Type B consumers are MB_A and MB_B, respectively. The demand for park land is obtained by adding the two green marginal benefit curves vertically to obtain the blue demand curve. In panel (b), with 1,000 Type A and 1,000 Type B consumers, the efficient number of acres is 2, where the marginal cost curve intersects the demand curve at point A. Efficiency can be achieved if each Type A consumer contributes $50 and each Type B consumer contributes $200, such that the total contributions are $250,000.

Type B consumer would be willing to pay $250. We can find the demand for park land by adding the two green marginal benefit curves vertically to obtain the blue demand curve for acres of park land. Together, Type A and Type B consumers would be willing to pay $325 for a one-acre park. For a three-acre park, the Type A consumer would be willing to pay $25 per acre and the Type B consumer would be willing to pay $150 per acre, so together they would be willing to pay $175 per acre. For any park bigger than four acres, the Type A consumer would not be willing to pay anything and the entire demand curve is Type B's marginal benefit curve.

If there were 1,000 Type A consumers and 1,000 Type B consumers in a community, the demand for park land would be the blue demand curve in panel (b) of Figure 21.12. In Figure 21.12(b), the marginal cost per acre is identified along with the demand curve. The efficient number of acres is 2, where the marginal cost curve intersects the demand curve at point A. One possible way to achieve efficiency is for each of the 1,000 Type A consumers to contribute $50 for a total of $50,000, and each Type B consumer to contribute $200 for a total of $200,000, such that the total contributions equal $250,000.

There are the following three potential serious problems associated with the optimal provision of public goods:

- It is difficult, if not impossible, to identify accurately the demand for public goods.
- Because it is difficult to identify demand, private markets generally do not supply the optimal quantity of a public good.
- Even if demand can be identified, it is difficult for the community to determine who should pay what for the public good.

Free-Rider Effects

Looking at Figure 21.12(b), suppose that a community wants to determine the demand for a park. You approach a Type B consumer and tell her that the community is considering building a two-acre park. You first must determine how much she and the other residents of the town would be willing to pay for the park, so you ask her: "How much can we count on you to pledge to the park fund?" The Type B consumer thinks to herself: if I tell the truth and pledge $200, it will cost me $200 to enjoy the park, but if I lie and tell them $100 or $50 or even nothing, and the park is built through the contributions of the other 1,999 residents, then I can receive all of the benefits of the park at a cost far below what I'm actually willing to pay. After reflecting on the question for a moment, the Type B consumer responds: "I'd be happy to pledge $100 to the park fund." When the Type A consumer is asked the same question, he answers, "$10." Together they have volunteered to contribute $110, even though the two of them would actually be willing to pay $250 for a two-acre park. The community will be in big trouble if it relies on voluntary contributions to the park.

Our Type A and Type B consumers were both being quite rational in their responses. They realized that if they could pass the bulk of the cost onto someone else and the park gets built, they will enjoy the same benefits as if they had contributed more. In the language of economics, our Type B and Type A consumers wanted to be *free riders*. **Free riders** are consumers who purposefully underestimate the value of a nonexcludable good in order to obtain the benefits at a reduced or zero cost.

free riders

Consumers who obtain the benefits of consuming a nonexcludable good without paying the full price because other consumers are paying for the good.

The larger the population consuming the public good, the greater the potential free-rider problem. With 1,000 Type A and 1,000 Type B consumers involved in building the park, each consumer might quickly realize it is seemingly in their interest not to reveal their true demand for the park. If all 2,000 consumers act like free riders, a two-acre park will never be built, because the community will falsely believe that there is no significant demand for the park.

Consider the free-rider problem on an even larger scale. Suppose that the nation wants to determine the answer to the question we asked at the beginning of this chapter: "How much of the nation's resources should we devote to Yellowstone and other national parks?" We need to determine 300 million Americans' demands for their national parks. If asked this question, many Americans would surely answer that they would contribute nothing. For some Americans that would be an honest response, but for many, it would be an attempt to free-ride on the generosity of their fellow citizens.

The Political Provision of Public Goods

Because of serious free-rider problems, governments through the budgetary process must provide public goods such as national defense, local fire and police protection, and environmental protection. Federal, state, and local legislatures decide how much to spend and then how to raise the money through taxes, fees, or borrowing. Modern democratic states use simple majority voting in legislatures to decide most fiscal policies. Using this voting method, each member of the legislature gets one vote, and if more than half of those voting support a bill, the bill passes. Does simple majority voting result in a clear-cut and optimal outcome? Suppose that the U.S. Congress is debating the defense budget and that there are three proposals: one is to spend $250 billion, the second is to spend $300 billion, and the third is to spend $350 billion. Three representatives have the preferences depicted in Figure 21.13(a). Representative A's preferences are, in order of preference: first, to spend $250 billion; second, to spend $300 billion; and third, to spend $350 billion. Representative B's preferences are: first, to spend $300 billion; second, to spend $350 billion; and third, to spend $250 billion. Representative C's preferences are: first,

---

▲▲▲ 21.5 APPLICATION   Stephen King and *The Plant*

In June 2000, horror novelist Stephen King announced that he was going to publish a book, *The Plant*, in installments over the Internet. At the time, King noted, "I think that the current technology is rapidly turning the whole idea of copyright into a risky proposition—not quite a joke, but something close to it."[*] King's idea was that readers would download an installment from his Web site and voluntarily send him $1.00 in the mail per installment. He warned that he would cease publication if too many people stole the story.

The Plant became a classic example of a public good. It was nonrival, because anyone could purchase a copy over the Internet, and it was nonexcludable, because King was not charging a fee to enter the Web site or even to download an installment. Did readers free-ride? They

certainly did. When only 46 percent of readers paid for the fourth installment, King decided to uproot *The Plant* after completing the sixth installment. Officially, King stated that he was only suspending publication because he had other important projects to complete. Economists, however, would be suspicious of that explanation. For one thing, Mr. King angered a lot of his best fans who had paid for the first four installments when he announced the suspension of publication. It is unlikely that he would have angered so many fans if he could have made a profit by continuing to write installments. It will probably be a long time before another Stephen King novel appears on the Internet with instructions to download and pay for the book on a voluntary basis.

[*] M. J. Rose, "Stephen King, the E-Publisher," *Wired News*, June 11, 2000, *http://www.wired.com*.

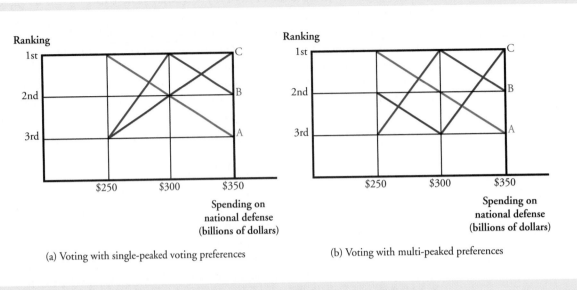

(a) Voting with single-peaked voting preferences

(b) Voting with multi-peaked preferences

Figure 21.13 Majority Voting with Single-Peaked and Multi-Peaked Voter Preferences
In panel (a), as long as all of the preferences of voters show a single-peaked pattern as they do here, the median voter wins regardless of the sequence of voting. In this case, the outcome is always $300 billion. In panel (b), with multi-peaked preferences, anything can happen with majority voting, depending on the order of voting. Beginning with $250 billion versus $300 billion, the final outcome is a defense budget of $350 billion. Beginning with $300 billion versus $350 billion, results in a $250 billion budget. Beginning with $250 billion versus $350 billion, $300 billion wins. The outcome is indeterminate.

COMMON ERROR 21.2 **Believing That Because of Free–Rider Effects, Public Goods Are Always Undersupplied**

Free-rider effects result in an underestimate of the demand for public goods such as parks and highways. As a result of free-rider effects, it is common for students to think that public goods are always undersupplied. There are, however, reasons why public goods might be oversupplied. One reason is that many public goods tend to benefit some subgroups of society more than others, while the tax costs of the public goods are borne by everyone. For example, highways are typically used by only some of the people living in a political jurisdiction. If it takes 51 percent of voters to approve the highway expenditure, that 51 percent of voters will have to pay only 51 percent of the cost of the highway, while 49 percent of the costs will be borne by other taxpayers. Part of the cost is borne by non-beneficiaries; and as a result, the 51 percent of taxpayers benefiting from the highway perceive the cost of the highway to be lower than it would be if the beneficiaries had to pay 100 percent of the cost. This makes it easier to put together political coalitions to support particular public goods expenditures, and it can lead to an oversupply of public goods.

Voters may also favor increased expenditures on public goods if the costs seem to be hidden. For example, some taxes are more visible to taxpayers than others: Income taxes tend to be more visible than sales taxes. If public goods are paid for out of less-visible taxes, they may incorrectly appear to be costless to taxpayers. This problem is compounded by the government's ability to borrow to pay for public goods. Public goods paid for by borrowing may give the impression of being costless to taxpayers receiving the benefits. As a result of these political factors, public goods may be oversupplied. Don't make the common error of assuming that because of free-rider effects, public goods are always undersupplied.

single-peaked preferences

The preferences of voters who prefer the median choice to at least one of the available extreme choices.

to spend $350 billion; second, to spend $300 billion; and third, to spend $250 billion. In this case, all three voters have **single-peaked preferences**, meaning that none of the voters prefer both of the extreme choices of $250 billion and $350 billion to the median choice of $300 billion; that is, the median choice of $300 billion is never the third choice of a voter.

Because there are more than two options, voting might be done by pitting two options against each other and then pitting the winning option against the remaining option. Here are the three possible voting patterns:

1. Begin with $250 billion versus $300 billion. Representatives B and C prefer $300 billion, so $300 billion wins. Now consider $300 billion versus $350 billion. Representatives A and B prefer $300 billion, so the final outcome is a defense budget of $300 billion.
2. Begin with $300 billion versus $350 billion. Representatives A and B prefer $300 billion, so $300 billion wins. Now consider $300 billion versus $250 billion. Representatives B and C prefer $300 billion, so $300 billion wins again.
3. Begin with $250 billion versus $350 billion. Representatives B and C prefer $350 billion, so $350 billion wins. Now consider $350 billion versus $300 billion, and once again $300 billion wins, because A and B prefer $300 billion.

No matter what order the voting takes place, $300 billion always wins.

In Figure 21.13(a), a budget of $300 billion is the median voter's preference, which represents the median alternative to the extremes. As long as all of the preferences of voters show a single-peaked pattern as they do in Figure 21.13, the median voter will win regardless of the sequence of voting.

What happens if some voters' preferences follow a pattern that is *multi-peaked* rather than single-peaked? Individuals with **multi-peaked preferences** prefer the extremes to the median choice. In Figure 21.13(b), Representative C prefers the extremes to the median, she prefers both a $350 billion and a $250 billion defense budget to a $300 billion budget, so her preferences show multiple peaks at $250 and $350. This type of preference is not that unusual. In many cases, for example, representatives want a program either carried out correctly or not at all. For example, a representative might believe that the Department of Defense should build a nuclear defense system correctly or spend just a small amount on an experimental prototype, rather than spend an intermediate amount on a mediocre system.

multi-peaked preferences

The preferences of voters who prefer all the available extreme choices to the median choice.

Consider voting using the preferences in Figure 21.13(b). Here are the three possible voting patterns:

1. Begin with $250 billion versus $300 billion. Representatives A and C prefer $250 billion, so $250 billion wins. Now consider $250 billion versus $350 billion. Representatives B and C prefer $350 billion, so the final outcome is a defense budget of $350 billion.
2. Begin with $300 billion against $350 billion. Representatives A and B prefer $300 billion, so $300 billion wins. Now consider $300 billion versus $250 billion. Representatives A and C prefer $250 billion, so $250 billion wins.
3. Begin with $250 billion versus $350 billion. Representatives B and C prefer $350 billion, so $350 billion wins. Now consider $350 billion versus $300 billion. Representatives A and B prefer $300 billion, so $300 billions wins.

voting paradox

Kenneth Arrow's statement that in order for majority voting to give non-arbitrary results, voters must have single-peaked preferences.

In the absence of single-peaked preferences, anything can happen depending on the order of voting. *The result is indeterminate!* The preceeding result is the **voting paradox** described by economist Kenneth Arrow, which states that in order for majority voting to give non-arbitrary results, voters must have single-peaked preferences.[4] The voting paradox does *not* imply that majority voting cannot work.

Even if voters have single-peaked preferences, however, there is still no guarantee that the efficient level of national defense will be provided. Majority voting fails to consider either the voter's strength of preferences or how much citizens are actually willing to contribute to national defense. In fact, it is difficult for any government to determine the optimal level of national defense, environmental protection, or any other public good. The reality is that in the area of public goods, where free-rider problems run rampant, not only is the private market likely to fail to provide the correct level of these goods, but so is the government.

Given the voting paradox, it usually makes for good public policy to rely on the private sector to supply private goods and services whenever possible. The government should intervene only in cases of serious market failures. And that is one of the important lessons to take from this book—free markets without government interference usually work pretty well at providing society with an optimal level of goods and services.

As this book comes to an end, it is also important to recognize, however, that there are many instances when free markets fail to provide an efficient solution to the problems of what to produce, how to produce it, and for whom to produce it. Problems arise in numerous instances of asymmetric information, imperfectly competitive product markets, externalities, public goods, and distributional concerns. Hopefully, you have learned how to identify when these problems exist. Furthermore, if you follow the most basic lessons of microeconomics—for example, that there is no free lunch and every action has opportunity costs associated with it—you will make better decisions throughout your personal and professional life, and that is the true value of an understanding of this important field.

Summary

1. An externality is any cost or benefit from an action undertaken by a producer or a consumer that affects other producers or consumers, but is not incorporated into the market price for any good or service. Both negative and positive externalities prevent society from achieving Pareto efficiency, unless the government intervenes and forces the externality to be internalized by producers or consumers.

2. Governments commonly use standards, taxes, or marketable permits to deal with the problems of externalities. In the case of negative externalities, these methods fail to achieve efficiency unless the method results in the marginal benefit of abatement of the externality being equal to the marginal cost of abatement. In the case of pollution, if abatement costs are identical for all firms, then all firms should reduce the pollution by the same amount to achieve efficiency; if abatement costs differ across firms, then all firms should reduce pollution by different amounts, but in equilibrium, the marginal cost of pollution abatement should be equal for all firms. Marketable pollution permits guarantee efficiency, because in equilibrium, the permits are held by those who value them most.

3. According to the Coase theorem, if property rights are legally assigned and there are zero transaction costs of negotiations in the market, it is always possible to negotiate an efficient solution to the problems of externalities. In the case of pollution, if the property rights are assigned to the polluter, the community will negoti-

[4] Kenneth J. Arrow, *Social Choice and Individual Values.* New York: John Wiley and Sons, Inc., 1951.

ate a "bribe" to the polluter to reduce pollution to an optimal level. If the property rights are assigned to the public, the polluter will negotiate to pay the community for the right to pollute.

4. The problem of a common resource is that without clearly defined property rights, all firms want to extract the natural resources from the common resource as long as the value of the average product is greater than marginal cost even though the value of the marginal product is less than marginal cost. As a result, producers attempt to extract common resources too quickly resulting in overuse of the common resource.

5. Public goods are nonrival in consumption. Goods that are both nonrival and nonexcludable are called pure public goods. The demand for public goods is obtained by adding the individual demand curves for a public good vertically, not horizontally. Achieving efficiency in the provision of public goods is complicated by the free-rider effect, in which consumers who are free riders assume that others will pay for the public good if they don't, and who therefore purposefully underestimate the value of a nonexcludable public good in order to obtain the benefits at a reduced or zero cost. The voting process is used to decide how many public goods should be produced relative to private goods, but the efficiency implications of the political voting process are difficult to determine: public goods may end up being undersupplied, oversupplied, or supplied efficiently.

 ## Self-Test Problems

1. Assume that the demand for paper is $P = 100 - q$, and that paper is produced in a perfectly competitive market where negative externalities exist. Firms perceive their supply as $S_{private} = 10 + q$. On the other hand, government agencies have found the $MC_{pollution} = (1/2)q$.

   a. Solve for the level of output produced and the price charged in the absence of government intervention.

   b. Solve for the socially optimal level of output and price. Calculate the deadweight loss.

   c. Draw a graph depicting the situation. Label q_e, p_e, q_{so}, p_{so}, and the deadweight loss on your graph.

   d. Solve for the per-unit tax that would efficiently internalize the externality.

   e. Discuss the general problems with the per-unit tax approach. For example, is the socially optimal level of output still attained if the demand for paper increases?

2. The local city government is deciding whether to tear down houses in a run-down neighborhood to build a park. The park would have no user fee, but the city does need to assess the demand for such a park. After a poll, twenty people indicated their $MB = 100 - 30Q$, thirty people indicated their $MB = 200 - 30Q$, and forty people indicated their $MB = 300 - 30Q$, where $Q = $ number of houses to be razed. The MC per torn-down house is estimated to be \$9,600.

   a. Calculate the demand for this public good.

   b. Solve for the optimal size of the park (how many houses to tear down).

 ## Questions and Problems for Review

1. Give two examples of negative externalities other than pollution, smoking, and loud music.

2. Give two examples of positive externalities other than immunizations, an apiary, and education.

3. Consider a good produced in a perfectly competitive market where negative externalities exist.

   a. Explain how negative externalities prevent the attainment of efficiency. Illustrate with a graph.

b. Explain and graphically show how a per-unit tax can be used to achieve the socially optimal level of output. How is the optimal amount of the tax determined? What effects will a tax have on prices, output, and the amount of the negative externality generated?

4. Assume the demand for automobiles is $P = 20,000 - 20q$. Assume that automobiles are produced in a perfectly competitive environment market where negative externalities exist. Firms perceive their supply to be $S_{private} = 112 + 2q$. On the other hand, government agencies have found $MC_{pollution} = q$.

   a. Solve for the level of output produced and price charged in the absence of government intervention.

   b. Solve for the socially optimal level of output (may not work out to a whole number) and price. Calculate the deadweight loss.

   c. Draw a graph depicting the equilibrium situation. Label q_e, P_e, q_{so}, P_{so}, and calculate the deadweight loss on your graph.

   d. Solve for the per-unit tax that will efficiently internalize the externality.

   e. Discuss the general problems with the per-unit tax approach. For example, is the socially optimal level of output still attained if the demand for paper increases?

5. Consider a good produced in a perfectly competitive market where positive externalities exist.

   a. Explain how positive externalities prevent the attainment of efficiency. Illustrate with a graph.

   b. Explain and show on a graph how a per-unit tax subsidy can be used to achieve the socially optimal level of output. How is the optimal amount of the tax subsidy determined? What effects will a subsidy have on prices, output, and the amount of the positive externality generated?

6. Describe what Milton Friedman means by "neighborhood effects." How would you suggest dealing with the problems associated with neighborhood effects? Be specific.

7. The State of Ohio recently threatened to balance the state budget by cutting public library funding, thus basically causing the elimination of 18 of the 19 public library branches in Mahoning County, Ohio. Rochelle, a local economist, immediately wrote to the governor, state representatives, and state senators asking them to reconsider the cuts. In her letter, she argued that the public library system has positive externalities. Explain what types of benefits might be felt by third parties through the funding of the public library system.

8. Suppose that a firm's marginal cost of pollution abatement is $2 + 8Q$ and the marginal benefit of pollution abatement is $1,478 - 10Q$, where Q is the pollution reduction in percent.

   a. Solve for the optimal level of pollution abatement.

   b. Calculate the cost to the firm to achieve the optimal level of pollution abatement.

   c. Solve for the fee that would ensure the optimal level of pollution abatement.

   d. In what ways is the functional form of $MC = 2 + 8Q$ given in this problem unrealistic?

9. Suppose that a firm's marginal cost of pollution abatement is $2 + 8Q$ and the marginal benefit of pollution abatement is $1,478 - 10Q$, where Q is the pollution reduction in percent as in Question 8. Now, suppose for a fixed development cost equal to 20, new technology lowers the MC of pollution abatement to $MC_2 = 7Q$.

   a. Solve for the efficient level of pollution abatement with the new technology.

   b. Solve for the level of abatement that would occur with the fee imposed in question 8. What is the deadweight loss associated with this excessive amount of abatement?

   c. Calculate the deadweight loss if the government continues with a mandated pollution abatement and monitoring program at the old optimal level of abatement.

   d. Solve for the optimal fee the government should impose to ensure optimal abatement with the new technology.

10. Consider question 8 again. Consider the marginal cost of pollution abatement equal to $2 + 8Q$ and the marginal benefit of pollution abatement equal to $1,478 - 10Q$, where Q is the pollution reduction in percent.

   a. Solve for the deadweight loss if the government were to set a pollution abatement standard that is 10 percent above the socially optimal standard.

   b. Solve for the deadweight loss if the government were to set a fee that is 10 percent above the socially optimal level.

   c. In this case, which error results in a smaller deadweight loss?

11. How does the outcome of the situation described in Figure 21.8 change with the assignment of property rights to different parties? How does this support the Coase theorem?

12. For each of the following situations, discuss whether the Coase theorem is applicable. Explain.

   a. Two cottages share a small pond. One cottager fishes, while the other prefers to hold games of water polo.

   b. The heat from a copper smelter interferes with the neighboring ice company, but aids an adjacent dry cleaner.

   c. The pollution from a copper smelter drifts out over a surrounding residential area.

13. Assume that the marginal benefit of abating pollution is $MB = 800 - 2t$ and the marginal cost of abatement is $MC = 2t$, where t is the number of tons of pollution abated.

   a. Solve for the optimal level of pollution abatement in tons. What is the additional cost of abating the last ton of pollution?

   b. If there are no transaction costs, what would be the level of abatement if property rights were assigned to consumers? What would be the level of abatement if property rights were assigned to producers?

   c. Calculate the impact of the existence of transaction costs equal to $40 per ton of abatement on the level of abatement t. What is the deadweight loss associated with the $40 per ton transaction costs?

14. You are an amateur astronomer. You have just purchased a house in the country where there is very little light pollution, so that you can use your telescopes. Three months after you purchase your home, a new house is built a mile away. The owner of this new house installs many powerful outside lights around his house and leaves them on all night. He claims that the lights make him feel more secure. Explain how the Coase theorem may be applicable to this situation.

15. Assume that there is a common lake where the residents fish in order to earn income; $AP_B = 300 - 20B$ and $MP_B = 300 - 40B$, where B is the number of boats on the lake and AP_B and MP_B are the average product and marginal product per boat. In addition, the marginal opportunity cost of sending another boat out on the lake is 100 fish.

   a. Solve for the optimal number of boats. If property rights are not assigned, solve for the number of boats that fish on the lake.

   b. If the government gains the property rights to the lake, what tax might it impose to ensure the socially optimal number of boats on the lake?

16. For each of the following goods, discuss whether the good is nonrival or rival and whether it is nonexcludable or excludable.

   a. Pizza.

   b. The Pennsylvania Turnpike on a low-travel weekday.

   c. A city park that charges no admission.

   d. An uncrowded state park that charges admission.

   e. A crowded state park that charges admission.

17. Consider the marginal benefit in dollars that three consumers receive from miles of paved bike paths (Q). Sarah's $MB = 75 - 25Q$. Jacqueline's $MB = 100 - 25Q$. Jonathan's $MB = 125 - 25Q$.

   a. Solve for the market demand curve for this public good.

   b. If the marginal cost of producing an additional mile of a paved bike path is constant at $150, how many miles should be provided? How much should Sarah, Jacqueline, and Jonathan each pay for the efficient number of miles of paved bike paths?

   c. How might free-riding cause an inefficient number of miles of bike paths to be provided?

18. Discuss the following statement: Public goods must be provided by local, state, or federal government.

19. Explain the meaning of Kenneth Arrow's voting paradox. Can you think of an issue where you have multi-peaked preferences? Explain why you have such preferences in this case.

20. Explain the difference between how the demand for private goods is calculated and the way in which the demand for public goods is calculated.

Internet Exercises

Visit *http://www.myeconlab.com/waldman* for this chapter's Web exercises. Answer real-world economics problems by doing research on the Internet.

Answer Key

Chapter One: Introduction

Answers to Self-Test Problems

1. The number in attendance at a national park on a Sunday depends on three things: the temperature, degree of cloudiness, and the amount of rainfall. For each additional degree of temperature, holding the cloudiness and amount of rainfall constant, the amount of people visiting the national park on a Sunday will increase by 10,000 people. Holding temperature and rainfall constant, for each percentage increase in the amount of sky covered by clouds, the amount of people visiting the national park on a Sunday will decrease by 15,000 people. Finally, holding temperature and cloudiness constant, for each additional inch of rain, the amount of people attending the national park on a Sunday will decrease by 20,000 people. Of course, all three of these factors affect Sunday attendance. For example, on a 70° partly-cloudy (30% cloudiness) Sunday with no rainfall, the model predicts that 250,000 people will visit the national park [10(70) − 15(30) − 20(0) = 250].

2. Remember that a Pareto improvement occurs whenever the outcome of a trade is such that at least one person is better off and no one is harmed.

   a. No. Although the mugger would be better off, I'll be worse off.

   b. Yes. Since the trade is voluntary, it must be the case that no one is worse off as a result of the trade and most likely both children are better off.

   c. No. This question involves normative issues. The removal of all tariffs and all quotas would most likely make some producers, consumers, or countries better off and harm at least some producers, consumers, or countries. For example, if the United States imports unlimited amounts of foreign steel with no tariffs, then most likely some domestic steel manufacturers will be harmed by this decision (possibly some domestic steel workers would lose their jobs). It is difficult to make such a huge decision without harming at least someone.

   d. No. While it will help some of those looking for apartments, rent control often causes long-term shortages in housing; thus, some people who want to rent at the lower price will be unable to find housing. In addition, the landlords might argue that a lower rent harms them. Sometimes rent controls cause apartment quality to fall as well, which hurts some tenants.

   e. No. In this case, while landlords would be getting more revenue, those paying the low rents will most likely be harmed by possibly having their new rents higher than they are willing or able to pay. However, some consumers would be better off (those who were previously unable to find apartments because of a shortage).

Answers to Odd-Numbered Questions and Problems for Review

1. Your answers will vary. One possible answer is provided here. *Microeconomist:* How will a decrease in interest rates by the Federal Reserve Bank affect the level of investment spending in the automobile industry? *(positive).* Should the autoworkers union negotiate a wage decrease in exchange for more union workers hired? *(normative). Macroeconomist:* What will be the effect of unemployment if the Federal Reserve lowers interest rates? *(positive).* Should the government's definition of unemployment include those who are not working but have given up looking for work (discouraged workers)? *(normative).*

3. The list is lengthy, but might include the following assumptions: Ecuador wages are lower than U.S. wages. Ecuador and U.S. workers produce the same products. The skill level of Ecuadorian workers is equal to that of U.S. workers. The quality of the product produced in Ecuador is the same as that produced in the United States. The United States does not trade with other countries. The U.S. workforce is not unionized.

5. a. Market equilibrium is ruled out because presumably the firm could decrease its use of electricity and lower its costs of producing, thus increasing profits. So the seller is not doing the best it can do and should want to change its behavior.

   b. Pareto efficiency is ruled out because there is room for Pareto improvement, in the sense that less use of electricity won't harm the firm and will use less resources, so that the saved electricity can be allocated to the production of a different good and other producers will be made better off. This answer assumes that electricity is a "scarce" resource.

c. Social optimality is ruled out because Pareto efficiency has not been achieved. The firm is no worse off by using less electricity and society is better off by conserving electricity. Presumably the electric company is not hurt, since the electricity could get allocated to the production of another good.

Chapter Two: Supply and Demand

Answers to Self-test Problems

1. a. See Figure 2A.1. Mining equipment is an input; thus supply for silver will shift right from S_1 to S_2 due to a decrease in the price of an input. Equilibrium price falls from p_1 to p_2 and equilibrium quantity increases from q_1 to q_2.

   b. See Figure 2A.1. Supply will shift right from S_1 to S_2 due to an improvement in technology. Equilibrium price falls from p_1 to p_2 and equilibrium quantity increases from q_1 to q_2.

   c. See Figure 2A.2. Mercury is a complement to silver. The demand for silver will shift left from D_1 to D_2 due to the rise in the price of a complement. Equilibrium price will fall from p_1 to p_2 and equilibrium quantity will fall from q_1 to q_2.

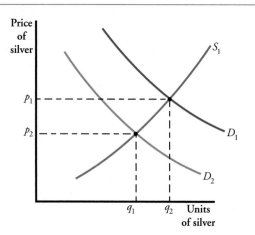

Figure 2A.2

d. See Figure 2A.2. Due to change in tastes, the demand for silver will shift left from D_1 to D_2. Equilibrium price will fall from p_1 to p_2 and equilibrium quantity will fall from q_1 to q_2.

e. See Figure 2A.3. Since expectations shift both supply and demand, this change in expectations will shift demand right from D_1 to D_2 and shift supply left from either S_1 to S_2 or from S_1 to S_3 or from S_1 to S_4. Since we don't know the size of the shifts, an increase in demand and decrease in supply will increase the equilibrium price of silver, but have an indeterminate effect on equilibrium quantity. Note that if the supply shift is bigger (S_1 to S_4) than the demand shift, then the equilibrium quantity will fall from q_1 to q_3. If

Figure 2A.1

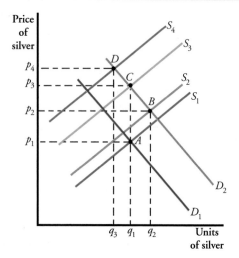

Figure 2A.3

the supply shift is smaller (S_1 to S_2) than the demand shift, then the equilibrium quantity will increase from q_1 to q_2. And finally, if the supply shift is equal (S_1 to S_3) to the demand shift, then the equilibrium quantity will stay the same at q_1. In all three cases, equilibrium price increases. If you draw only one shift in supply, you might have quantity increase (similar to point B) or quantity stay the same (similar to point C), or quantity decrease (similar to point D).

f. See Figure 2.4(a) on page 26 in the text. A change in taste toward silver fillings will cause an increase in demand. Equilibrium price and equilibrium quantity will increase. (It is possible that because the price of gold decreases, the supply of silver might increase as well. But the dominant effect here is the change in tastes, thus the demand for silver increases. Don't over-think this.)

g. See Figure 2.4(c) on page 26 in the text. The price of gold decreases. Since gold is a substitute for silver, the demand for silver will shift left (decrease) from D_1 to D_2. Since gold is an alternative good in production, the supply for silver will increase (shift right) from S_1 to S_2. The equilibrium price falls, but the effect on equilibrium quantity is indeterminate. In this case, however, because the increase in the supply of gold results from a technological advance, it is likely that the increase in the supply of silver will be relatively small.

h. This situation will shift the supply for gold to the right and dramatically drop the price of gold. The decrease in the price of gold will have

the same effects as in question 1(g). However, in this case the supply effect will likely be greater than in question 1(g).

2. Set $q_s = q_d$; $10 + (1/2)P = 100 - 2P$; $2.5P = 90$; $P = 36$; $q = 10 + (1/2)(36) = 28$ or $q = 100 - 2(36) = 28$.

b. Using Equation 2.2, $\varepsilon_p = -(\Delta q_s/\Delta p_s)(p_s/q_s) = -(-2) \times (36/28) = 2.57$.

c. For a one-dollar increase, at $P = 37$, $q_d = 100 - 2(37) = 26$, and using the arc elasticity formula, $\varepsilon_p = -(\Delta q/\Delta p)[(p_1 + p_2)/(q_1 + q_2)] = -(-2) \times [(36 + 37)/(28 + 26)] = 2 \times (73/54) = 2.70$.

For a one-dollar decrease, at $P = 35$, $q_d = 100 - 2(35) = 30$, and using the arc elasticity formula, $\varepsilon_p = -(\Delta q/\Delta p)[(p_1 + p_2)/(q_1 + q_2)] = -(-2) \times [(36 + 35)/(28 + 30)] = 2 \times (71/58) = 2.45$.

The answers will be different, since the arc formula takes the average of the point of origin (equilibrium price) and the new price. Since the new price is different for a one-dollar increase ($37) than a one-dollar decrease ($35), then the answers for arc elasticity will be different.

3. Using the formula $\varepsilon_p = \%\Delta q/\%\Delta p$, we know that $0.63 = \%\Delta q/30$. Solving this equation yields $\%\Delta q = 18.9$. Thus a 30% decrease in the price of milk causes quantity demanded to increase by 18.9%. Since demand for milk is inelastic, we know a decrease in price will cause total revenue to decrease.

Answers to Odd–Numbered Questions and Problems for Review

1. a. See Figure 2.4(b) on page 26 in the text. Supply will decrease (shift left), since the price of an input increases. Equilibrium price will rise and equilibrium quantity will fall.

b. See Figure 2.4(a) on page 26 in the text. Demand will increase (shift right), since the price of a complement falls. Equilibrium price will increase and equilibrium quantity will increase.

c. See Figure 2A.2 on page 26 in the text. The price of a substitute falls, so demand for raisin bran falls (shift left). Equilibrium price and equilibrium quantity both fall.

d. See Figure 2.4(b) on page 26 in the text. The drought will increase the price of bran, which is an input. Supply of raisin bran will decrease (shift left), since the price of an input increases.

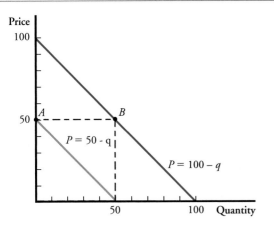

Figure 2A.4

Equilibrium price will rise and equilibrium quantity will fall.

e. See Figure 2.4(a) on page 26 in the text. Demand will increase (shift right), due to a change in tastes and preferences. Equilibrium price will increase and equilibrium quantity will increase.

f. See Figure 2.4(a) on page 26 in the text. Demand will increase (shift right), due to an increase in income, as long as raisin bran is a normal good. Equilibrium price will increase and equilibrium quantity will increase.

3. There is a shortage. The black market helps to allow trades between those willing to pay more than the price ceiling (the actual price of the ticket). Depending on how the black market works, this could also hurt consumers—for instance, if scalpers simply buy many of the tickets at the price ceiling and then sell them at a higher price.

5. No. The market is not in equilibrium. There is excess supply, so the price (salary) is too high to clear the market.

7. Although prices are high, consumers have the opportunity to consume goods that they were unable to consume in the past due to severe shortages. Consumers also save lots of time that they used to spend waiting in lines to purchase goods.

9. Exogenous variables: price of grapefruit juice and consumer's income; endogenous variables: quantity and price of orange juice.

11. See Figure 2A.4. At point A, demand is infinitely elastic (elasticity of demand is equal to infinity). At point B, demand is unit-elastic (elasticity of demand equals 1) because $P = 50$ is the midpoint of the demand curve $P = 100 - q$.

13. Studio apartments on the Upper West Side of Manhattan because there are more substitutes available.

15. Income elasticity of demand for Cliff Notes equals 1 also.

17. a. Supply would be a vertical line.

b. Supply would be a horizontal line.

19. a. Very strong substitutes (e.g., fresh salmon and frozen salmon).

b. Substitutes, but not very strong (e.g., electricity with the price of natural gas).

c. Very strong complements (e.g., salsa and tortilla chips).

d. Complements, but not very strong (e.g., salt and tequila).

Chapter Three: Theory of Consumer Behavior

Answers to Self-Test Problems

1. See Figure 3A.1 for graph of points.

a. A is preferred to E because A has the same amount of good X as E and more of good Y (non-satiation).

b. D is preferred to C, because D has more of both goods than C (non-satiation).

B is preferred to E, because we know that A and B are equally preferred (given) and A is better than E (question 1(a)), so by transitivity, B is better than E.

C is preferred to B. Convexity says that C cannot be on the same indifference curve as A and B, because the slope from A to C ($-2/5$) equals the slope from C to B, and therefore, C is on a line connecting points A and B. Because convex indifference curves are bowed in toward the origin, C must be on a higher indifference curve.

D is preferred to B. Under non-satiation, we know that D is preferred to A, and by transitivity, because A is equally preferred to B, then we know that D is preferred to B.

c. D is most preferred; then C; then B and A are equally preferred; then finally E is the least preferred.

2. a. Since she can freely buy or sell X at $2 and freely buy or sell Y at $4, then she has the equivalent of income worth (200 × $2) + (100 × $4) = $800. So the budget constraint is: $2X + $4Y = $800.

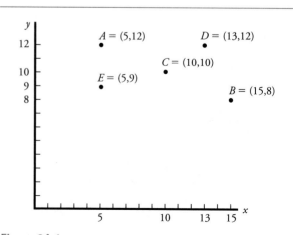

Figure 3A.1

b. See Figure 3A.2. Point E is the initial point of consumption.

3. a. See Figure 3A.3. Note that the indifference curves are straight, downward-sloping lines. For example, U_1 represents a utility level of 2. The equation for the utility function on U_1 is $2 = x + y$, or $y = 2 - x$. The slope of the indifference curve is always equal to -1. For every unit of y given up, a unit of x must be gained to maintain the same level of utility. U_4 is preferred to U_3, which is preferred to U_2, which is preferred to U_1. Given non-satiation, we see the point (2,2) is on U_2, where $U = 4$ must be better than the point (1,1), which is on U_1, where $U = 2$.

b. See Figure 3A.3. The budget constraint is represented by the green line. The slope is equal to

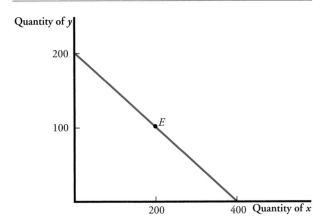

Quantity of y

200

100

E

200   400 Quantity of x

Figure 3A.2

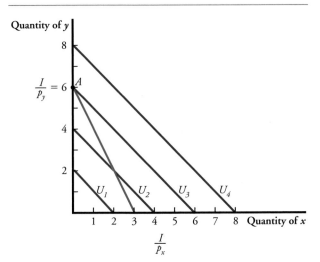

Quantity of y

8

$\frac{I}{P_y} = 6$ A

4

2

U_1 U_2 U_3 U_4

1 2 3 4 5 6 7 8 Quantity of x

$\frac{I}{P_x}$

Figure 3A.3

$-P_x/P_y = -\$4/\$2 = -2$. The budget constraint intercepts the y-axis at the point $I/P_y = \$12/\$2 = 6$. The budget constraint intercepts the x-axis at the point $I/P_x = \$12/\$4 = 3$.

c. The consumer will buy 6 units of y and no units of x at point A in Figure 3A.3. At this point, the consumer gets the maximum utility possible, given his budget constraints. If the consumer buys at any other point on the budget constraint, the utility will be less than at the point (0,6) and the consumer does not have enough income to afford to be on U_4.

Answers to Odd-Numbered Questions and Problems for Review

1. a. $A = (0,1)$ is indifferent to $B = (1,0)$.
   $A = (3,5)$ is preferred to $B = (4,2)$.
   $B = (4,8)$ is preferred to $A = (3,10)$.
   $B = (16,6)$ is preferred to $A = (8,3)$.

   b. Most preferred: (16,6) (4,8) (3,10) (8,3) (3,5) (4,2) and finally (0,1) and (1,0) are equally preferred.

   c. We know that $U(x_0, y_0) = x_0 y_0 = U(x_1,y_1) = x_1 y_1$. $U(2x_0, 2y_0) = (2x_0)(2y_0) = 4x_0 y_0$. $U(2x_1,2y_1) = (2x_1)(2y_1) = 4x_1 y_1$. Since $x_0 y_0 = x_1 y_1$, then it must be true that $4x_0 y_0 = 4x_1 y_1$.

   d. There are many, but $U = (xy)^2$ is a possible answer because it does not change the utility ranking of baskets.

3. If study time is measured as time spent studying for both economics and English, then the student could spend far fewer hours studying for a marginally lower grade in economics (because the technique works so well, they could give up many hours studying economics and lower their economics grade only a tiny bit), but devote those many hours to English, and increase his English score a great deal.

5. Note that values of x and y are both positive in all four quadrants. The reference of the origin continues to change.
   Quadrant I: MUx > 0 (as x increases, keeping y constant, U increases) and $MUy > 0$ (as y increases, keeping x constant, U increases); non-satiation is satisfied, because utility increases as quantities of both goods increase; convexity is satisfied because on a line connecting any two points on any indiffer-

ence curve, all the points on the line have higher utility than the points on the indifference curve.

Quadrant II: MUx > 0 and MUy < 0 (as y increases, keeping *x* constant, *U* decreases), non-satiation not satisfied in *Y* (more *Y* is worse than less—good *y* is a "bad"), but is satisfied in *x*; and convexity is satisfied.

Quadrant III: MUx < 0 and MUy < 0; non-satiation is not satisfied for both *x* and *y* (both *x* and *y* are "bads"); and convexity is satisfied because on a line connecting any two points on any indifference curve, all the points on the line have higher utility than the points on the curve.

Quadrant IV: MUx < 0 and MUy > 0, non-satiation is not satisfied in *X* (less *X* is better) but is satisfied in *y*; and convexity is satisfied.

7. See Figure 3A.4. Let $P_{x0} = 5$ and $P_{y0} = 20$ and $U_0 = 100$. The original budget constraint is the line *AB*.

   a. The budget constraint will rotate from *AB* to *DB*.

   b. The budget constraint will rotate from *AB* to *AC*.

   c. The budget constraint will shift out from *AB* to *EF*. *AB* is parallel to *EF*.

   d. The budget constraint will shift in from *AB* to *DC*. *AB* is parallel to *DC*.

   e. There will be no change in the budget constraint. It will remain *AB*.

9. See Figure 3A.5. Currently, the consumer is at a point like point *A*, where $MRS_{bp} = MU_p/MU_b > P_p/P_b$. The consumer can reach a higher indifference curve by increasing the consumption of pizza

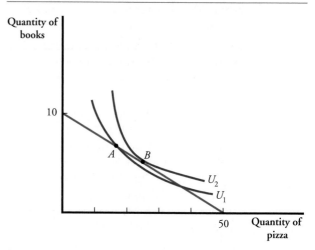

Figure 3A.5

(and thus lowering MU_p) and decreasing the consumption of books (and thus increasing MU_b) until the point where $MU_p/MU_b = P_p/P_b$, like at point *B*.

11. With $MU_p/MU_c = 5/2$, it follows that in equilibrium $p_p/p_c = 5/2$, or $p_p = (5/2)p_c$. Nikki's budget constraint is initially $100 = p_c(25) + (5/2)p_c(10)$ or $100 = 50p_c$. So $p_c = 2$ and $p_p = (5/2)p_c = 10/2 = 5$. Therefore, the initial budget constraint in Figure 3A.6 is the dark green line $q_c = (100/2) - (5/2)q_p$ and the initial equilibrium is point *A*. When income increases to \$150, the budget constraint shifts to the light green line and the new equilibrium point is *B*. The income consumption path,

Figure 3A.4

Figure 3A.6

ICP, is a horizontal line through points A and B. Cheese is neither a normal nor an inferior good because it has an income elasticity of zero. Pretzels are a normal good because Nikki consumes more pretzels as her income increases.

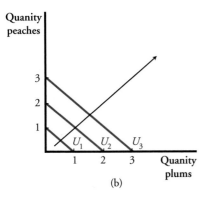

Figure 3A.7

13. a. See Figure 3A.7(a). Tortilla chips and salsa are perfect complements for Emma. The arrow indicates the direction of increasing preference through the map.

   b. See Figure 3A.7(b). Plums and peaches are perfect substitutes for Dan. The arrow indicates the direction of increasing preference through the map.

15. See Figure 3A.8. We would expect Alice to consume more green beans than Jessica, given the same prices and income, since Alice likes green beans better. Notice that Alice's indifference curves are much steeper than Jessica's. We'd expect Jessica to consume more peas than Alice, given the same prices and income, since Jessica likes peas better. However, in equilibrium, since $MRS_{bp} = P_b/P_p = 3/2$, then $MRS_{bp} = 3/2$ for both Jessica and for Alice. (The numbers are not important, just the fact that Alice consumes more green beans and Jessica consumes more peas.)

17. See Figure 3A.9. Note that U_4 is preferred to U_3, which is preferred to U_2, which is preferred to U_1. In panel (a), food is good and garbage is bad. The consumer must be compensated with more and more additional food to accept more garbage. In panel (b), both goods are bads, so the indifference curves are concave because less is better than more of both goods. In panel (b), all the points on a line connecting any two points on an indifference curve have higher utility than the points on the curve.

19. a. See Figure 3A.10. Note that the man will maximize utility by spending all his income on good x.

   b. 0   c. 0   d. 1   e. 1

Alice

Jessica

Figure 3A.8

Figure 3A.9

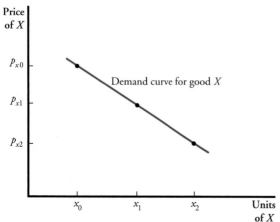

Figure 3A.10

Chapter Four: Further Topics in Consumer Theory

1. See Figure 4A.1. In each panel, the substitution effect (*SE*) is represented by the movement from point *A* to *C* and the income effect (*IE*) is represented by the movement from point *C* to *B*. The total effect (*TE*) is represented by the movement from point *A* to *B*. The substitution effect for good *X* is measured by the distance from x_1 to x_S, the income effect is measured by the distance from x_S to x_2, and the total effect is measured by the distance from x_1 to x_2. For good *Y*, the substitution effect is measured by the distance y_1 to y_S, the income effect by the distance y_S to y_2, and the total effect by the distance y_1 to y_2.

2. a. Before the tariff, Harry buys: $20 = 50 - 0.05q$; $0.05q = 30$; $q = 600$. After the tariff, Harry buys: $25 = 50 - 0.05q$; $0.05q = 25$; $q = 500$.

   b. The government will collect $\$5 \times 500 = \$2,500$ in tariff revenue.

   c. The change in consumer surplus will be $(1/2)(500 + 600) \times 5 = 2,750$. Or, at \$20, the consumer surplus $= (1/2)(50 - 20)(600) = 9000$. After the tariff, consumer surplus $= (1/2)(50 - 25)(500) = 6,250$. The change is 2,750.

   d. Presumably, Harry would be willing to pay as much as \$2,750 for the tariff to be stopped. So, Harry will hire the lobbyist, since after the

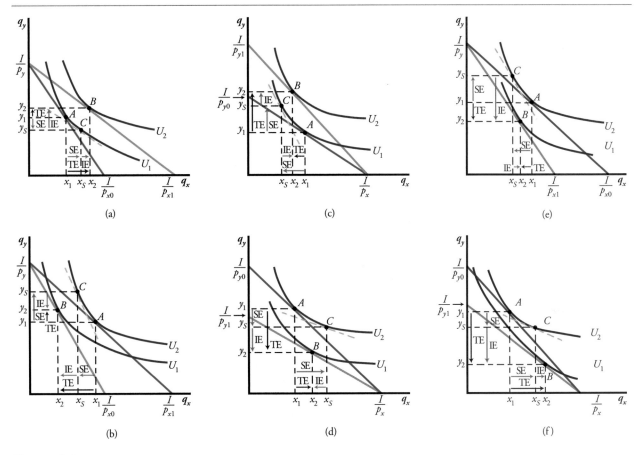

Figure 4A.1

$2,700 payment, he still has $50 more in consumer surplus than if the tariff were to be
imposed.

3. You would choose plan *B*. Under Plan *A*, you have
an endowment of $5,000 in each period, so with *r*
= 0.05 the most you could spend in period 2 is
$5,000 + (1.05)$5,000 = $10,250 if you saved
the entire $5,000 received in period 1. Plan *B* is
better because you can spend $10,500 in period 2.

Answers to Odd-Numbered Questions and Problems for Review

1. See Figure 4.2(b) on page 90 in the text. Potatoes
are an inferior good. If the price of potatoes
decreases, the substitution effect says to buy more
potatoes. In this case, the income effect must say to
buy fewer potatoes and be equal to the substitution
effect but in the opposite direction in order for the
consumption of potatoes to be the same. Thus,
since relative income increases with a price

decrease, the decrease in potato consumption
because of the income effect would indicate that
potatoes are an inferior good.

3. Yes, you are normal. For *Y*, the income effect is just
exactly equal (in the opposite direction) to the substitution effect. When the price of *X* falls, the
income effect says to consume more *X* and less *Y*
and the income effect (if *X* and *Y* are normal) says
to consume more *X* and more *Y*. Thus, the consumption of *X* will increase, and if your consumption of *Y* stays the same, the *SE* and *IE* on *Y* are
merely canceling each other out.

5. The graph is very similar to Figure 4.2(b) on page
90 in the text except for a price increase instead of
price decrease. The analysis is very similar to question 1. For an increase in the price of movie tickets,
then the *SE* would say to decrease the consumption
of movie tickets and increase the consumption of
other goods. Movie tickets must be inferior and
thus a decrease in relative income will cause the *IE*

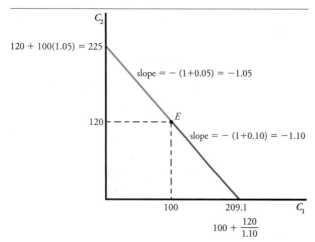

Figure 4A.2

to say buy more movie tickets. The *SE* and *IE* must be equal (but opposite) directions for movie tickets. If popcorn is normal, then the *IE* effect will indicate to buy less. In the case of popcorn, we have the *IE* outweighing the *SE* in order for Zach's consumption of popcorn to decrease.

7. Most likely a statistical estimation will be more accurate than "rules of thumb," but there are many factors to consider. How accurate has the "rule of thumb" been? Are we able to get the data that we need to do the careful econometric model estimation? How expensive will it be to perform the econometric study (entering the data, hiring someone to do the programming, analyzing the results, etc.)? Will the marginal benefit (perhaps in better estimation and cost savings in the long run on less excess inventory) of using the econometric estimation exceed the marginal cost of implementing the program?

9. Considering the demand shifters, the model has considered price of related goods and income. It does not appear to include factors that might affect tastes and preferences, number of buyers, or expectations. There are no leading economic indicators that might give an indication of how well the economy is doing overall. (For example, if much of the demand for wood stoves is for new homes or new cabins, then the model should include some indicator of the building activity of these new homes.) There is also no use of the price of alternative fuel sources such as electricity or natural gas. Given these exclusions, the model would be expected to do a fair job of estimating demand. Also, it is not clear what functional form is assumed for demand.

If the model assumes a linear demand, then the estimation may yield inaccurate results if demand is not linear.

11. Consumers certainly gain more total consumer surplus from their consumption of water. The amount consumers would be willing to pay for the first few gallons of water rather than go without water entirely is extremely high. The demand curve for water is highly inelastic for the first units consumed then levels off after we have consumed the amount of water necessary to live. (We all might also be willing to pay a lot for water to ensure we have enough to drink without being dehydrated, to cook with, and to clean ourselves with. After that point, the marginal value might drop dramatically.) The price of water, however, is relatively low because the supply is large. Thus, the consumer surplus is very large for water. The price of diamonds is very high relative to water (because of a small supply) and thus the total consumer surplus is probably relatively small for diamonds compared to water. The difference between what we are willing to pay and what we actually pay is much greater for water than diamonds.

13. Same. Consider the midpoint of demand, where we know the price elasticity is 1. The midpoint of an individual demand curve is $P = 25$. The midpoint of the market demand curve ($q = 500 - 10P$ or $P = 50 - (1/10)Q$) is also $P = 25$. So elasticity of demand equals 1 at $P = 25$ for both the individual and market demand curves. Similarly, at $P = 40$, the elasticity of demand is 4 for both demand curves. Try any P and the elasticity will be the same.

15. See Figure 4A.2. Note the line has a small kink in it at the income endowment point E. The slope above point E is -1.05 (on the light green segment) and the slope below point E is -1.1 (on the dark green segment). Given the small differences in the slope, it is difficult to see, but the line below point E is slightly steeper than the line above point E so there is a small kink in the budget constraint.

17. What your friend is doing is sometimes called "consumption smoothing." Your friend's future income has dramatically increased and thus he is borrowing today on the income he expects "tomorrow" (after his uncle dies). There is a very large income effect associated with the inheritance and because current consumption is a normal good for your friend, he is spending a great deal more on current consumption.

19. a. See Figure 4A.3. With the increase in the interest rate, the consumer consumes more in period 1 (saves less). The supply of savings is downward-sloping.

b. See Figure 4A.3.

c. For an increase in the interest rate:

- SE (point A to point C): C_1 decreases and C_2 increases.
- IE for a saver (point C to point B): if C_1 and C_2 are normal goods, then C_1 and C_2 both increase.
- TE (point A to point B): C_2 increases. C_1 increases in this case (and savings decreases), since $IE > SE$ for C_1. For an upward-sloping supply curve of savings, $SE > IE$ for C_1. For a downward-sloping supply curve of savings, $IE > SE$ for C_1.

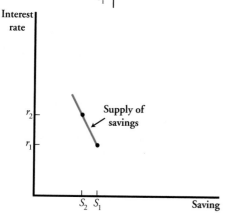

Figure 4A.3

Chapter Five: Applying Consumer Theory

Answers to Self-Test Problems

1. See Figure 5A.1. With the change in the market-clearing price of chicken, the budget constraint rotates inward, becoming steeper, from line *ch* to *cj*. The fixed price of chicken is still 2 rubles, so we would expect the price of a coupon to be 18 rubles. The typical consumer would now be more willing to sell coupons and less willing to buy them. The opportunity cost of using the coupons to buy chickens is much higher now. If the coupons are transferable, the budget constraint (line *fbg* in Figure 5.8(a) on page 132) will be higher along the *y*-axis. See line *fbg* in Figure 5A.1. If a consumer sold 10 coupons for 18 rubles each, he could now have 680 rubles to spend on other goods. On the other hand, given the large market-clearing price, point *g* rotates inward from 50 in Figure 5.8(a) to 34 in Figure 5A.1. The end result will depend on the tastes of the consumer and could differ depending on whether we have a consumer like in Figure 5.8(a) or a consumer like the one in Figure 5.8(b). With an increase in the market clearing equilibrium price, the excess demand would be greater and the lines would be longer; therefore, the social cost of a first-come first-served policy would typically be higher.

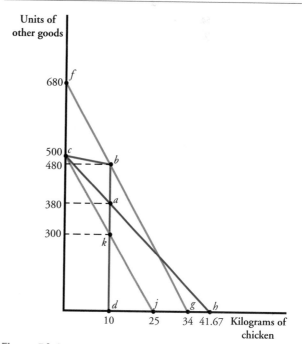

Figure 5A.1

2. See Figure 5A.2. With an increase in wages, the substitution effect says to take less leisure time and work more (since the opportunity cost of leisure has increased). If leisure is a normal good, as in Figure 5A.2(a), the income effect says to increase the consumption of leisure. In this case, the income effect outweighs the substitution effect, resulting in one hour more leisure (one hour less work) as the wage rate increases. In Figure 5A.2(b), this results in a backward bending supply curve for labor.

3. See Figure 5A.3. If the government eliminates the excise tax, Abby's budget constraint will rotate from *CF* to *CD*. We know as a result of a decrease in the price of movie tickets, the *SE* results in an increase in *MT* and a decrease in *OG*. Assume two normal goods, the *IE* results in an increase in *MT* and an increase in *OG*. Thus, the consumption of movie tickets will definitely increase and the consumption of *OG* will depend on the size of the effects. Now, basically by imposing a lump-sum tax, the government is taking away the income effect of the tax reduction. The budget constraint will shift to *GE* through point *A*. We know Abby will buy more *MT* as a result of

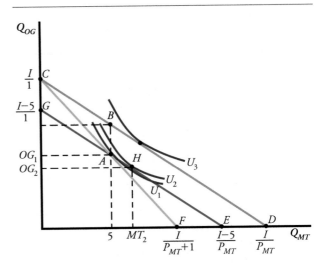

Figure 5A.3

the change in taxes and less *OG*. In our graph, Abby is better off as a result of the change in tax laws. She moves from point *A* on U_1 to point *H* on U_2.

Answers to Odd–Numbered Questions and Problems for Review

1. It is typically much easier politically to give grants-in-kind. For example, there is a fear recipients would spend cash foolishly. See "Political Issues" in Section 5.1 on page 124.

3. See Figure 5.5(a) on page 127 in the text. This student chooses to consume 4,000 units of public school if public schools exist. But with no public schools, the student would consume E_2, which is greater than 4,000. Finally, with a voucher system, the student would consume E_3. This student will consume more education with the voucher system.

5. See Figure 5A.4. The ticket plan shifts the budget constraint from the straight line *XYZ* to the light green kinked line *XYAW* in panels (a), (b), and (c). In panel (a), this consumer increases his purchase of tickets from 7 to 10 and we see why the Skychiefs sell the ticket books—to sell more tickets and increase attendance. In panel (b), tickets are an inferior good, and this consumer purchases fewer tickets (13) with the books than without (14). In panel (c), tickets are a normal good and we see that if tickets are normal it is impossible for the consumer to purchase fewer tickets with the ticket books. The team must believe that tickets are a normal good for the great majority of fans.

(a)

(b)

Figure 5A.2

(a) Impact of a ticket coupon book

(b) Tickets are an inferior good

(c) Tickets are a normal good

Figure 5A.4

7. Remember Abby, who was better off with the income tax than the excise tax in Self-Test Problem 3? Both taxes generated the same revenue. From a consumer standpoint, as long as we have convex indifference curves, the consumer prefers the income tax (see Figure 5.15 on page 140 in text as well).

9. See Figure 5A.5. George initially buys D_1 drugs at point A. With the subsidy, George buys even more drugs (D_3) at point B. George would be better off on U_3 with the equal cost cash payment. With the cash payment, George would purchase more drugs D_2 (provided they are a normal good) than with no subsidy, D_1, but less drugs than with the subsidy plan, D_3.

11. This example is similar to chicken rationing in the former Soviet Union. Gas rationing most likely made consumers worse off due to the opportunity cost of standing in lines, similar to a movement from point B to point A in Figure 5.7 on page 131 in the text. Yes, by issuing tradable vouchers, most consumers could be made better off (the buyers

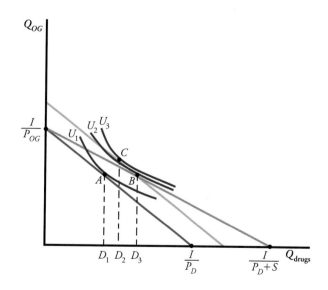

Figure 5A.5

and sellers of the vouchers) like in Figures 5.8(a) and 5.8(b) on page 132 in the text.

13. See Figure 5A.6. No, due to the relative price change in the price of heating oil, the substitution effect guarantees that the consumers will still consume less oil, $H_2 < H_3$.

15. Yes. See Figure 5.11 on page 135 and Self-Test Problem 5.2. If $IE > SE$, then an increase in wage can actually increase leisure and decrease work effort.

17. See Figure 5A.7. Assuming that the flat fee covers an unlimited number of bags, the budget constraint changes from XZ to XY and then horizontal to infinity. The consumer in panel (a) is better off with the fixed fee, but in (b) the consumer is better off with a per bag charge. Most consumers probably have a high MU_G (marginal utility of garbage

removal) for many bags removed each week, and therefore, their indifference curves will be steep until the number of bags removed is large. This means most consumers probably prefer a fixed fee.

19. Jack may be like the consumer in Figure 5.1 on page 122 and continue to buy the same as under the food stamp program. Either the food stamps or the cash would move Jack from point X to point Y in Figure 5.1. On the other hand, if Jack is like the consumer depicted in Figure 5.2 on page 123, then Jack would be better off with the cash. In this case, Jack would move from point X to Y, decreasing his consumption of food and increasing his consumption of other goods. This particular consumer, in Figure 5.2, is exactly who policy-makers are most worried about, in the sense that they have no con-

Figure 5A.6

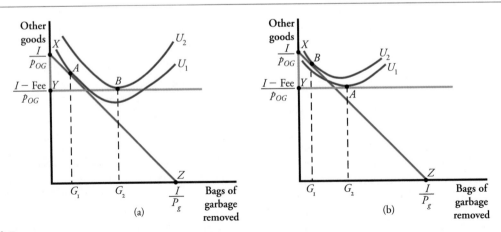

Figure 5A.7

trol over what types of other goods Jack will spend the $200 on. Of course, in Figure 5.1, Jack also spends more on other goods as a result of the program and may buy goods such as cigarettes and liquor that policy-makers object to.

Chapter Six: Uncertainty

Answers to Self-Test Problems

1. **a.** See Figure 6A.1.

   b. Gamble 1 is that you buy insurance and your house does not end up getting robbed. Gamble 2 is that you don't buy insurance and your house does end up getting robbed.

   c. $E(G_1) = 0.02\,(29.200) + 0.98\,(29,200) =$
   $584 + 28,616 = 29,200$

   $E(G_2) = 0.02\,(-30,000) + 0.98\,(30,000) =$
   $-600 + 29,400 = 28,800$

2. **a.** See Figure 6A.2.

   b. $E(A) = 0.3\,(40,000) + 0.7(60,000) =$
   $12,000 + 42,000 = 54,000$

   $E(B) = 0.3\,(30,000) + 0.3\,(50,000) +$
   $0.4\,(70,000) = 9,000 + 15,000 + 28,000 =$
   $52,000$

   c. $U(40,000) = 10 + 200 = 210$

   $U(60,000) = 10 + 244.95 = 254.95$

   $E\,(U(A)) = 0.3\,(210) + 0.7\,(254.95) = 63 +$
   $178.47 = 241.47$

   $U(30,000) = 10 + 173.21 = 183.21$

   $U(50,000) = 10 + 223.61 = 233.61$

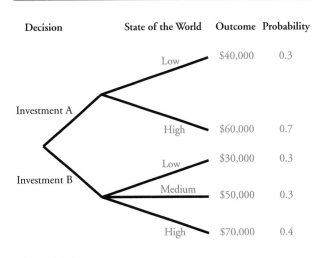

Decision	State of the World	Outcome	Probability
Investment A	Low	$40,000	0.3
	High	$60,000	0.7
Investment B	Low	$30,000	0.3
	Medium	$50,000	0.3
	High	$70,000	0.4

Figure 6A.2

$U(70,000) = 10 + 264.58 = 274.58$

$E(U(B)) = 0.3\,(183.21) + 0.3(233.61) +$
$0.4(274.58) = 54.96 + 70.08 + 109.83 =$
234.87

In this case, investment A will be chosen since it has the higher expected utility.

3. The gamble G_1 can be described as having an 80% probability that I can earn $2,000 and a 20% probability that I will lose $1,000.

   $E(U(G_1)) = 0.8\,U(4,000) + 0.2\,U(1,000) =$
   $0.8(63.24) + 0.2(31.62) = 50.59 + 6.32 = 56.91.$

   The amount of income, C, that would guarantee an expected utility of 56.91 can be found by solving:

   $(C + 2,000)^{1/2} = 56.91.$ So, $C + 2000 = (56.91)^2$ and $C = 3,238.75 - 2,000 = 1,238.75.$

   The gamble G_2 is whether I should pay the expert to appraise the jersey. In this case, I gain information and thus will know with certainty whether to buy the jersey. The new gamble will be that you get no income with probability 20% (if the expert reveals that the shirt is a fake) and gain $2,000 with 80% probability.

   $E\,U(G_2) = 0.8\,U(4,000) + 0.2\,U(2,000) =$
   $0.8(63.24) + 0.2(44.72) = 50.59 + 8.94 = 59.53.$

   The certainty equivalent, or the amount of income that I would value as highly as the gamble itself can be found by solving:

   $(C + 2,000)^{1/2} = 59.53.$ So, $C + 2,000 =$
   $(59.53)^2$ and $C = 3,543.82 - 2,000 = 1,543.82.$

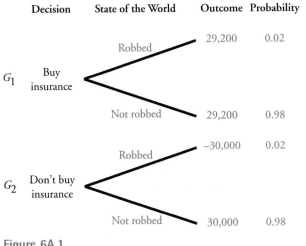

Decision	State of the World	Outcome	Probability
G_1 Buy insurance	Robbed	29,200	0.02
	Not robbed	29,200	0.98
G_2 Don't buy insurance	Robbed	−30,000	0.02
	Not robbed	30,000	0.98

Figure 6A.1

Hiring the expert turns a gamble worth $1,238.75 into a gamble worth $1,543.82. Thus, the value of the information from the expert is equal to $1,543.82 − $1,238.75 = $305.07. This is the maximum amount I would be willing to pay the expert.

Answers to Odd-Numbered Questions and Problems for Review

1. Becoming an actor might be considered a risky thing to do. Although there is the potential for big earnings, there is also a very high probability of not making it. Thus, perhaps those who are risk-averse are more likely to become lawyers and those who are risk-loving are more likely to become actors.

3. Some economists believe that consumers are risk-averse for large losses in income and risk-loving for large gains in income. So, it is possible for consumers to have *VNM* utility functions that are concave for low incomes but convex for high incomes. See Application 6.2 on page 159 for more information and an example.

5. **a.** Gathering information.

   b. Flexibility or diversification (there is some small gamble in keeping it at home).

   c. Flexibility.

   d. Information.

   e. Flexibility.

   f. Insurance.

7. They do many things, such as: buy a radar detector, follow others who are speeding or who have a radar detector, watch carefully in typical hiding places for police, slow down going downhill where police are more likely to expect speeding, drive a car that isn't as noticeable, or simply slow down!

9. Let G_1 be the gamble of buying the stock and G_2 be the gamble of using the stock broker. Let C_1 be the certainty equivalent of G_1 and C_2 be the certainty equivalent of G_2.

   a. $E(U(G_1)) = 0.6(100 \ln(4,000)) + 0.4(100 \ln(1,000)) = 773.95$

   $E(U(G_2)) = 0.6(100 \ln(4,000)) + 0.4(100 \ln(2,000)) = 801.68$

   $100 \ln(C_1) = 773.95$ or $\ln(C_1) = 773.95/100 = 7.7395$; so $C_1 = 2,297.32$

   $100 \ln(C_2) = 801.68$ or $\ln(C_2) = 801.68/100 = 8.0168$; so $C_2 = 3,031.46$

You would be willing to pay the broker $3,031.46 − $2,297.32 = $734.14.

   b. $E(U(G_1)) = 0.6(100(4,000)) + 0.4(100(1,000)) = 280,000$

   $E(U(G_2)) = 0.6(100(4,000)) + 0.4(100(2,000)) = 320,000$

   $100(C_1) = 280,000$; so $C_1 = 2,800$

   $100(C_2) = 320,000$; so $C_2 = 3,200$

   You would be willing to pay the broker $3,200 − $2,800 = $400.

   c. $E(U(G_1)) = 0.6((4,000)^3/1,000) + 0.4((1,000)^3/1,000) = 38,800,000$

   $E(U(G_2)) = 0.6((4,000)^3/1,000) + 0.4((2,000)^3/1,000) = 41,600,000$

   $(C_1)^3/1,000 = 38,800,000$; so $C_1 = 3,385.40$

   $(C_2)^3/1,000 = 41,600,000$; so $C_2 = 3,464.96$

   You would be willing to pay the broker $3,464.96 − $3,385.40 = $79.56.

11. For risk-averse or risk-loving individuals, the rank in expected value of income doesn't necessarily coincide with the rank in the expected utility of that income. In the case of risk-neutral consumers, it is valid to calculate the expected value of income to make decisions.

13. Consumer A will be most likely to buy lottery tickets because she is risk-loving. Consumer B is risk-averse. Consumer C is risk-neutral.

15. Yes. The homeowner is willing to pay $1,800 beyond the actuarially fair premium to insure against the gamble, so he will accept a premium only $750 above the actuarially fair premium. The insurance company is charging $750 above its expected loss, so they too are willing to provide the insurance. Both the homeowner and the insurance company win.

17. **a.** Greg is risk-averse and will have a utility function shaped like that in Figure 6.3 on page 155.

   b. Kristin is risk-loving and will have a utility function shaped like that in Figure 6.4 on page 157.

   c. Art is risk-averse up to $100 million in income. At that point, his utility function changes and becomes risk-loving. Thus, his utility function is a combination of Figure 6.3 up to $100 million in income, and Figure 6.4 after $100 million in income. Art's *VNM* utility function is shaped like the function in the Application Function 6.2 on page 159.

19. Jill's home will have higher actuarially fair insurance premium. Jill is more likely to buy insurance, because she has a higher likelihood of her house being damaged by forest fire or other scenarios. The problem is that only the consumers with higher risk will buy the insurance. This is why insurance companies do not charge the same premium and attempt to get as much information about the situation in order to determine the actuarially fair premium for each house.

21. They most likely do not have the same *VNM* utility functions. In the case of those who choose bonds, they are likely to be more risk-averse. Those who choose stocks are likely to be less risk-averse or risk-loving. Because most individuals are risk-averse, the expected earnings on stocks should be higher than on bonds. Otherwise, few people would buy the riskier stocks.

Chapter Seven: The Theory of Production, Costs, and Profits

Answers to Self-Test Problems

1. **a.** See Figure 7A.1. The firm is currently at point A. The slope of the isoquant $= -1$. The slope of the isocost curve is $-w/r = -2$. Note the absolute value of the slope of the isocost curve is larger than the absolute value of the slope of the isoquant.

   b. If the firm currently uses K_1 units of capital, it could be in a short-run equilibrium if in the short run the firm wants to produce Q_0 units because its only choice is to operate at point A with K_1 units of capital.

   c. It is not a long-run minimizing equilibrium, because $MRTS < w/r$ or $MP_L/MP_K < w/r$. The firm should decrease labor and increase capital until it is at point B. At point B, $MRTS = w/r$ and the isocost is tangent to the isoquant. In the long run, the firm is able to produce Q_0 units at a cost of C_0 rather than the higher short-run cost of C_1. For a cost of C_1, the firm can produce Q_1 units in the long run.

   d. The output expansion path would be flatter than (below) the one depicted in Figure 7A.1.

   e. Nothing will happen to *SRMC*, since *SRVC* has not changed. *SRAC* will increase (shift upward), since *SRTC* has increased. Since every point on the *SRAC* has increased, *LRAC* will also increase (shift up).

2. See Figure 7A.2. Currently the firm is operating at point A, where $MRTS > P_c/P_s$. The firm's costs are currently $20 (20) + 60 (40) = 2,800$. The firm could produce 50,000 square feet of shopping space in the mall at a lower cost by increasing the use of cement and decreasing the use of steel to a point like point B. Notice that C_0 is lower than the isocost curve $C = 2,800$. In the long run, at point B, $MRTS = P_c/P_s = 1/3$.

3. Let $Q(L,K) = 0.5KL$. Let's double all inputs: $Q(2L, 2K) = 0.5(2K)(2L) = 2KL = 4 \times Q(L,K) > 2 \times Q(L,K)$. This production function exhibits increasing returns to scale. In this case, a doubling of all inputs will more than double out-

Figure 7A.1

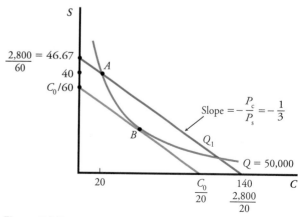

Figure 7A.2

put. If you increase all inputs by a factor $t > 0$, output increases by more than t times the original output.

Let $Q(L,K) = 2L + 3K$. Let's double all inputs: $Q(2L, 2K) = 2(2L) + 3(2K) = 4L + 6K = 2(2L + 3K) = 2 \times Q(L,K)$. This production function exhibits constant returns to scale. In this case, a doubling of all inputs will exactly double output. If you increase all inputs by a factor $t > 0$, output increases by exactly t times the original output. The $MRTS$ is constant for this production function because you can always substitute 1 unit of L for 2/3 unit of K; therefore, $MRTS = MP_L/MP_K = 2/3$.

Answers to Odd-Numbered Questions and Problems for Review

1. Answers will vary, but listed in the table below is a sample of the types of answers you might have given.

3. True; similar to the analysis in Figure 3.3 in Chapter 3 on page 52, where we learn indifference curves will never cross.

5. The isoquants will look like those in Figure 7.4(b) on page 182. In this case, capital and labor are complements. Assume $L = 3$ and $K = 3$ and $Q = 3$. If the firm tries to substitute K for L by decreasing K to 2 units and increasing L to 4 units, output will fall to $Q = 2$. The only way to increase output is to increase both L and K. Thus the inputs can be used only in fixed proportions and are perfect complements.

7. Let $Q_0 = f(L,K)$. Let $a > 1$, decreasing returns to scale implies that $f(aL, aK) = bQ_0 < aQ_0$.
$LRAC(Q_0) = (wL + rK)/Q_0$.
$LRAC(bQ_0) = (waL + raK)/bQ_0 = a(wL + rK)/bQ_0 = a/b \times LRAC(Q_0)$
Since $b < a$, $a/b > 1$, so $LRAC(bQ_0) > LRAC(Q_0)$ and thus, $LRAC$ is increasing.

9. a. See Figure 7A.3. At points A, B, C, and D, and any other point on the OEP, the $MRTS = w/r = 1$.

   b. OEP will shift to OEP_2. Given the wage rate decrease, a firm will increase labor and decrease

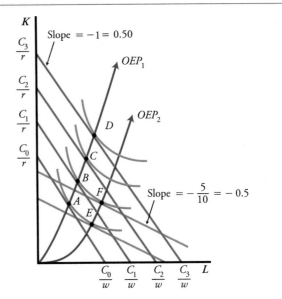

Figure 7A.3

capital to produce a particular level of output. Thus the new expansion path is flatter than before. At the new wage rate of 5, $MRTS = 1/2$ at any level of output.

   c. The decrease in wages does not change the fact that $MRTS = 1$ at points A, B, C, and D, but these points are no longer on the new long-run OEP.

11. The firm is not minimizing its long-run costs, since $MRTS > w/r$. The firm should decrease K and increase L until $MRTS = 2$. The firm might be minimizing its short-run costs. In the short run, the firm might be producing its optimal output utilizing a level of fixed capital K where $MRTS = 3$ but $w/r = 2$.

13. See Figure 7A.4. The firm is currently operating at a point, like point A, which is not on $LRAC$. In the case of constant returns to scale, because $LRAC$ is constant, the points of tangency between $SRAC$ and $LRAC$ occur at the minimum points on each $SRAC$ curve.

Type of Firm	Inputs	Outputs
Automobile manufacturer	Steel, machinery, labor, paint, tires	Automobiles
Bank	Tellers, managers, loan officers, computers	Provides checking and savings service, loans
Newspaper Publisher	Print press, reporters, editors, computers	Newspapers

Figure 7A.4

Figure 8A.1

15. a. Constant returns to scale. *LRAC* is horizontal.

b. Decreasing returns to scale. *LRAC* is upward-sloping.

c. Increasing returns to scale. *LRAC* is downward-sloping.

If $\alpha + \beta = 1$, constant returns to scale.

If $\alpha + \beta < 1$, decreasing returns to scale.

If $\alpha + \beta > 1$, increasing returns to scale.

17. *SRMC* will be minimized at the point of diminishing returns to labor, here the level of q corresponding with $q = (50, \overline{K})$. *AVC* will be minimized at a higher level of output. See Figure 7.7 on page 192 in the text.

19.

Q	TFC	TVC	TC	MC	AFC	AVC	ATC
1	50	12	62	12	50	12	62
2	50	22	72	10	25	11	36
3	50	30	80	8	16.67	10	26.67
4	50	40	90	10	12.5	10	22.5
5	50	55	105	15	10	11	21

Chapter Eight: Perfectly Competitive Product Markets

Answers to Self-Test Problems

1. a. See Figure 8A.1. The firm's short-run supply curve is equal to *SRMC* above minimum *AVC*. In this case, it is the entire *SRMC* curve. Note that at a price less than 2, the firm will not choose to produce in the short run. For each price, the firm would set $P = MC$; thus, if $P = 2$, $q = 1$; if $P = 4$, $q = 2$, etc.

b. $P = MR$. The firm will produce output as long as $MR > MC$ and will not produce a given level of output if $MR < MC$. If $P = 15$, the firm will produce $q = 7$. Notice that although $MR = 15 > MC = 14$ for $q = 7$, the firm would choose not to produce $q = 8$, because at that point, $MR < MC$. If $P = \$9$, $q = 4$. If $P = 1$, the firm would not produce, because for all levels of output, $MR < AVC$. The firm would produce $q = 0$ at $P = 1$.

Output	MC	AVC	ATC	Profit	Producer Surplus
1	2	2	18	−9	7
2	4	3	11	−4	12
3	6	4	9.333	−1	15
4	8	5	9	0	16
5	10	6	9.2	−1	15
6	12	7	9.667	−4	12
7	14	8	10.286	−9	7
8	16	9	11	−16	0
9	18	10	11.778	−25	−9
10	20	11	12.6	−36	−20

c. See the table above. For each level of output, profits are calculated as $(P - ATC) \times q$, so for example, at $q = 1$, $(9 - 18) \times 1 = -9$. Since the table implies discrete units of production, calculate producer surplus as the difference between price and marginal cost, for each level of q. For example, at $q = 1$, $PS = 9 - 2 = 7$. Now, for $q = 2$, producer surplus is calculated as the summation of PS at $q = 1$ and PS at $q = 2$. So, producer surplus $= 7 + (9 - 4) = 12$. This method continues for each level of output in the table. Notice, PS could also be calculated as $PS = TR - VC = q(P - AVC)$.

At a price of $9, to maximize profit, the firm should produce $q = 4$. This coincides with our analysis in Self-Test Problem 1(b).

At a price of $9, to maximize producer surplus, the consumer should produce $q = 4$ as well.

The difference between profits and producer surplus $= -16$. $FC = 16$ and this explains why $q = 4$ is the quantity that will maximize both profits and producer surplus, since the difference is a fixed value that does not vary with output.

2. a. We know the firm's short-run supply is determined by $P = SRMC$, so $P = 2q_i$, or $q_i = P/2$. Since there are n firms in the industry, the industry supply curve is $Q_s = nP/2$. We also know that profits $= 0$ in the long run for each firm.
   Profits $= TR - SRTC = (P \times q_i) - SRTC = (P \times q_i) - (q_i^2 + 1) = 0$.
   Substituting $q_i = P/2$ gives us: $P(P/2) - [(P/2)^2 + 1] = P^2/2 - P^2/4 - 1 = 0$. $P^2/4 = 1$. $P^2 = 4$. $P = 2$. If $P = 2$, then $Q_d = 52 - p = Q_s = 50$, so $Q_s = 50 = n(2)/2$ or $n = 50$. Each firm produces $q_i = P/2 = 2/2 = 1$. Each firm's profits $= (\$2 \times 1) - (1^2 + 1) = 2 - 2 = 0$.

b. In the short run, the increase in demand will cause equilibrium price to rise, but at that higher equilibrium price, firms will earn profits; therefore, there will be an incentive for entry. Firms will enter until profits equal zero again. Thus, the price at which profits equal zero will stay the same, at $P = 2$. There are now 51 firms in the industry and profits $= 0$ for each firm. Mathematically, the firm's short-run supply is not affected by the change in demand; therefore, the equation where we solved for $P = 2$ in Self-Test Problem 2(a) has not changed. If $P = 2$, it implies $Q_d = 53 - p = 51$, and thus, $n = 51$.

3. a. See Figure 8A.2. First, consider the case of a constant-cost industry. Then we will consider an increasing cost industry. The firm is initially at a long-run equilibrium at point E. An excise tax of $100 would affect both the average total cost and the marginal cost curves of the firm, causing each curve to shift vertically up by the amount of the tax (t). Since industry short-run supply is the horizontal summation of firm's marginal cost curves, then the short-run industry supply curve will shift up by the amount of the tax as well, from S_1 to S_2 in panel (a). The equilibrium price increases from p_1 to p_2 and firms adjust their output to q_2 and earn losses equal to the shaded box $ABDC$ in Figure 8A.2(b).

b. In the long run, firms will exit this industry, shifting industry supply in panel (a) to the left. Firms will continue to exit until economic profits $= 0$, which is at p_3. Note that at p_3 the full

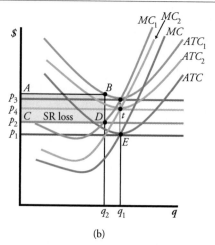

Figure 8A.2

burden of the tax has been passed onto consumers (price has risen by the exact amount of the tax). So economic profits equal zero and $p_3 - p_1 = 100$. Firms produce q_1 again, but industry output has fallen to Q_3.

c. Total tax revenue = $\$100 \times Q_3 = (p_3 - p_1) \times Q_3$ or the rectangle $p_3 GRp_1$ on the industry graph.

Now, let's do the same thing for an increasing-cost industry.

a. The easiest way to analyze this effect is to assume initially that the cost curves still shift up by the full amount of the tax to MC_1 and ATC_1 in Figure 8A.2(b). In the short run, price increases to p_2, firm output decreases to q_2, and firms earn economic losses. Thus the short-run analysis is exactly the same as with constant cost. (Technically, as supply shifts from S_1 to S_2, the firm's cost curves will decrease. But let's ignore that possibility for the very short run, since it would take a while for the input markets to adjust to this lower level of output demanded (and thus lower level of inputs demanded).

b. Now in the long run, firms will exit as a result of the losses. Industry supply will shift from S_2 to S_4. Simultaneously, ATC and MC will shift down (we do not know the exact sizes of the shift) to MC_2 and ATC_2, due to the decrease in industry output which decreases input prices. The price at which profits equal zero is p_4, which is lower than p_3. The industry output (Q_4) is greater than Q_3 in the long run constant cost case (not as many firms have to exit, because the price at which firms earn economic profit equal to zero is lower in the increasing cost case). Long-run equilibrium price increases, but not by the full amount of the tax. Firms increase output from q_2, and as drawn, the long-run equilibrium output returns to q_1.

c. Total tax revenue is $100 \times Q_4$ represented by the shaded blue area in panel (a).

d. In the increasing cost case, the producer is not able to pass the entire amount of the tax onto consumers, therefore, the industry quantity demanded does not fall by as much as a result of the tax, and thus tax revenues are higher under the scenario of an increasing-cost industry than with a constant-cost industry.

Answers to Odd-Numbered Questions and Problems for Review

1. Answers might slightly vary with different explanations, but here is the basic argument. Perfect information is difficult to assess and achieve. See table below.

Product	Many Buyers/ Many Sellers	Homogeneity	Free Entry and Free Exit	Perfect Information
Grade A winter wheat	Yes	Yes	Yes	Yes
Corn	Yes	Yes	Yes	Yes
Saudi light crude oil	No—a member of OPEC cartel (Organization of Petroleum Exporting Countries)	Yes	No — natural resource makes it difficult for just anyone to drill for oil	Yes — we see the announcements of the prices OPEC sets after they meet
Bananas	Yes	Yes	Yes	Yes
Automobiles	No—relatively few large sellers	No	No—very costly to enter, advertising	No—buyers not perfectly informed
Pork bellies	Yes	Yes	Yes	Yes

(continued)

Product	Many Buyers/ Many Sellers	Homogeneity	Free Entry and Free Exit	Perfect Information
Wine	Yes	No	Yes	No—buyers not perfectly informed
Computers	No—relatively few sellers (Apple, Dell, Compaq, Gateway, IBM)	No	No—costly advertising to enter	No—buyers not perfectly informed
Video games	No—very few sellers (X-box, Playstation, Nintendo, Sega)	No	No	No—buyers not perfectly informed

3. Assuming a long-run equilibrium, a firm that lowers its own price will actually sustain an economic loss with the lower price ($P < ATC$). There would be no incentive for this firm to do so. No other firm is going to follow such a decision given that this one firm's choice will have no impact on the market as a whole. Thus, in the long run, such a firm would have to raise price again to earn zero economic profits or leave the industry due to losses.

5. False. This would imply that the firm would choose to produce on the downward-sloping section of its MC curve. A firm would never choose to produce there. See Figure 8.4 on page 216.

7. a. Short-run industry supply equals 100 of the short-run firm supply curves, $SRMC = 4q \rightarrow q = (SRMC)/4 \rightarrow Q_{industry} = 100q = 100((SRMC)/4) \rightarrow Q = 25(SRMC)$ or because $SRMC = p$, $Q = 25p$. Setting supply equal to demand: $25p =$ $130 - p$, $26p = 130$, $p = 5$. Short-run equilibrium price is 5.

   b. Long-run equilibrium price is calculated by setting average cost equal to marginal cost. $AC = (SRTC)/q = (2q^2 + 8)/q = 2q + (8/q) = 4q = SMRC \rightarrow 2q = 8/q \rightarrow q^2 = 4 \rightarrow q = 2$. Therefore, $SMRC = p = 4q = 8$. Long-run equilibrium price is 8. Note: Because the long-run equilibrium price is above the short-run price, firms are sustaining economic losses in the short run.

   c. With long-run equilibrium price 8, long-run industry equilibrium quantity is $Q = 130 - p = 122$. Because each firm produces $q = 2$ units in the long-run equilibrium, there must be 61 firms in the industry in long-run equilibrium. Therefore, 39 firms must leave the industry.

9. a. See Figure 8A.3. Initially the firm is at point B, earning zero economic profit. Because the tax is

Industry

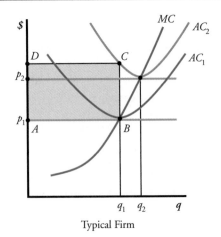
Typical Firm

Figure 8A.3

a fixed percentage of total profit (assuming that the tax is on accounting profit, not zero economic profit, for then the tax would be zero!), then the firm's AC curve increases to AC_2, but the MC curve does not. The short run price remains p_1 and at q_1, firms will earn economic losses equal to the area $ADCB$.

b. See Figure 8A.3. In the long run, firms will exit the industry, market price will increase, industry output will fall, and each firm's output will increase to q_2. Because the tax is accounted for in the new AC curve, the after-tax profit of the firm will return to zero.

11. Economic profit is different than accounting profit. Remember that economic costs include the value of the resources used to produce that good in their best alternative use. Similarly, economic profit is considered compared to the next best alternative for the firm. So, a firm earning zero economic profit is doing just as well (not better, not worse) than it could do in its next best alternative use of its resources. In long-run equilibrium, the firms are earning accounting profit, but after the opportunity costs of all inputs are taken into account, the firms are doing as well as they could in their next best alternative.

13. a. $P_e = 20$ and $Q_e = 60$.

b. We know the firm's minimum AVC occurs at $q = 2$. Thus, for every other level of output, AVC is greater than \$22. This firm should produce $q = 0$, because $P < AVC$ for any level of output.

15. a. The analysis is essentially identical to Self-Test Problem 8.3. See Figure 8A.2. The short-run impact is the following: MC and ATC shift vertically upward by the amount of the tax. Industry supply also shifts up vertically by the amount of the tax. Industry output falls, equilibrium price increases, firm output falls, and firms earn losses.

b. The price does not rise by the full amount of the tax in the short run, because price is determined where $S = D$, and because demand is downward sloping, S shifting up by the amount of the tax will not cause price to increase by the full amount of the tax.

c. In the long run, the price will not rise by the full amount, because as industry output falls, firms' costs also fall. The MC and ATC curves will shift down slightly (but not to their original levels). Thus, in Figure 8A.2(b), the price at which profits equal zero will be higher than the original price p_1, but not equal to $p_1 + \$1$.

17. a. See Figure 8A.4. In both panels, point E is initially the long-run equilibrium. In (b), firm's costs shift down by the amount of the subsidy, s, to ATC_1 and MC_1. In (a), industry supply also shifts by the amount of the subsidy to S_2. Short-run equilibrium price falls to p_2, firm output increases to q_2, in (b), and the firm is earning positive economic profits.

b. In the long run, firms will enter due to profits. In (a), supply will shift from S_2 to S_3. Long-run equilibrium price will fall to p_3. In (b), firm output

(a)

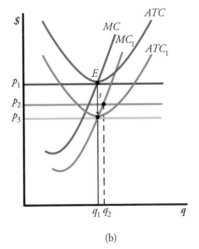

(b)

Figure 8A.4

will decrease to its original level q_1. Note that $p_3 = (p_1 - s)$. The price falls by the full amount of the subsidy.

c. In (a), the cost to the government is equal to $Q_3 \times s$, which is represented by the area p_1GRp_3.

d. Less. In Figure 8A.4(b), the ATC curves would shift up as a result of the increase in industry output. The price would therefore not fall by the full amount of the subsidy and the industry output would not be as high as Q_3 in (a). Thus the cost of the subsidy would be lower under an increasing-cost industry.

19. a. $q = 8$; profits $= TR - TC = 8(\$40) - \$260 = \$60$; producer surplus $= TR - TVC = \$320 - \$210 = 110$.

b. $q = 7$; profits $= TR - TC = 7(\$35) - \$222 = 23$; producer surplus $= 73$.

c. $q = 0$; Profits $= -50$ (smaller losses than if produced $q = 6$)

d. $q = 8$ like in question 19(a). Profits $= -40$ (100 less than in part a).

Chapter 9: The Invisible Hand at Work

Answers to Self-test problems

1. a. See Figure 9A.1. The supply curve shifts out by the amount of the quota to $S_{domestic\ and\ quota}$.

b. The equilibrium in the market will be p_1^*, which is equal to $p^*(1 + t)$ from Application Figure 9.2 on page 250. Thus, domestic producers sup-

ply q_2 and the government sells $(q_3 - q_2)$ import licenses for $(p_1^* - p^*)$. The government raises revenue equal to the orange area of the rectangle $bcef$.

c. The analysis here is the same as in Application 9.2 on page 250. Consumers lose the green, pink, orange, and red areas. Domestic producers gain the green area.

d. Graphically, the welfare loss is exactly the same under both policies. In addition, if the government sells the import licenses at $(p_1^* - p_1)$, the government raises the same amount of money with a license system as a tariff. If, alternately, the government issues the licenses for free, foreign producers will prefer a quota to a tariff.

2. a. See Figure 9A.2. Clearly, consumers would prefer plan 2 to plan 1. With plan 1, their consumer surplus is the triangle ABp_1, and with plan 2, their consumer surplus is the triangle ACp_2.

b. Clearly, producers would prefer plan 1. With plan 1, producer surplus is the area $FEBp_1$. With plan 2, their producer surplus is actually negative. It includes triangle FEp_2 − triangle ECG. Since ECG looks bigger than FEp_2, producer surplus is negative.

c. From society's standpoint, both plans appear to be equal. In the case of plan 1, there is deadweight loss because output Q_1 is produced where $p_1 > MC$. Deadweight loss is equal to the area BHE. Total surplus is the area $ABEF$. In the case of plan 2, there is deadweight loss, because output Q_2 is

Figure 9A.1

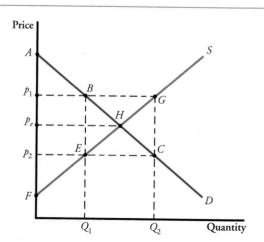

Figure 9A.2

produced where $MC > p_2$. In this case, total surplus is equal to the area $AHF - HGC$. Thus, deadweight loss equals HGC. Since HGC looks to be the same size as BHE, it doesn't appear as though (from society's standpoint) there is a preference as to which plan is better. Both plans result in an equal deadweight loss to society.

3. By setting supply = demand, we get $40 - q = 10 + q$; $30 = 2q$; $q = 15$; $P = 40 - 15 = 25$. See Figure 9A.3 for a graph. Equilibrium is at point E.

a. For the tenth unit, consumers will pay $P = 40 - 10 = \$30$.

b. Consumer surplus before the regulation was the area $AEG = (1/2)(40 - 25)(15) = 112.5$. After regulation, consumer surplus is $ABC = (1/2)(40 - 30)(10) = 50$. Consumers lose 62.5 in consumer surplus as a result of the regulation. The loss in consumer surplus is represented by the area $CBEG$.

Producer surplus before the regulation was the area $HEG = (1/2)(25 - 10)(15) = 112.5$. After regulation, producer surplus is equal to trapezoid $HFBC = (1/2)[(30 - 20) + (30-10)] \times 10 = (1/2)(10 + 20)(10) = (1/2)(30)(10) = 150$. Producers gain 37.5 as a result of the regulation. The gain in producer surplus is represented by the area $CBIG$ (equal to 50) and a loss of IEF (equal to 12.5), for a net gain of 37.5.

c. As a whole, society loses. Total surplus before regulation = $CS + PS = 225$. After regulation,

total surplus = $CS + PS = 200$, for a net loss of 25 in total surplus. This loss of 25 is deadweight loss, represented by area BEF. Of that area, IEF is a loss in producer surplus and BEI is the part of the loss in consumer surplus that was not transferred to producers.

Answers to Odd-Numbered Questions and Problems for Review

1. Remember that ultimately, the welfare of all individuals matters. We do believe that individuals themselves can best judge what is in their best interest, but we also know we want only trades to occur that involve Pareto improvement. Potentially, selfishness could involve behavior that distorts the market and causes us to move away from the Pareto-efficient level of output (we will talk more about this type of behavior and negative externalities in Chapter 21). Furthermore, most of us have utility functions that include the well being of others, including not only family and friends, but other members of society as well. Therefore, most of us are willing to trade some of our own income to increase the incomes of others.

3. No. Fairness is a normative concept, and its definition will be different for each person. It is difficult to say what should go into our criteria for fairness. Recall from the text that it is a common error to assume that consumer surplus is more socially desirable than producer surplus. But by the same notion, our measure of total surplus does not allow us to build any kind of favoritism for one group over another into the social assessment, yet society makes such normative judgments every day.

5. a. See Figure 9A.4(a). As supply shifts up by the amount of the tax, output decreases to Q_2. In the case of D and S, sloping downward and upward respectively, both consumers and producers bear some of the burden of the tax; thus there is a loss in consumer surplus due to the higher price paid and lower output consumed (Q_2), and there is a loss in producer surplus due to the lower price that producers receive net of the tax ($p_2 - t$) and the lower output (Q_2). Deadweight loss equals area ABC.

b. See Figure 9A.4(b). In the case of a perfectly inelastic demand, consumers bear the entire burden of the tax, paying a price of $p_2 = p_1 + t$.

Figure 9A.3

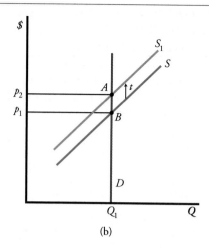

(a)   (b)

Figure 9A.4

There is no deadweight loss; only a transfer from consumers to government of p_2ABp_1.

c. In the case of perfectly inelastic supply, producers bear the entire burden of the tax. Since Q would not change, again, there is no deadweight loss; only a transfer from producers to government equal to the government revenue.

7. a. See Figure 9A.5(a). Market price increases by the full amount of the tax from P_1 to $P_1 + t$. In (a), market output decreases to Q_t. Firm output stays the same, but fewer firms are in the industry because firms sustained losses in the short run.

   b. In the long run, producers receive the same after-tax price they were receiving before the tax, but output has fallen from Q_1 to Q_t, so producers forced to leave are worse off. In addition,

producers are all worse off in the short run because they sustain economic losses. Consumers pay a higher price and output has fallen, so the loss in consumer surplus is represented by the orange and green areas $(p_1 + t)AEp_1$. But of that loss, the green area $(p_1 + t)ABp_1$, goes to the government in the form of tax revenue. Social welfare decreases by the orange triangle area AEB.

   c. The policy reduces TS, so it may not be justified. However, if there are large social benefits associated with what the government does with the tax revenues, there could be a net benefit to society of the tax policy.

9. No. A Pareto improvement occurs only if someone can be made better off without making anyone else worse off. It is difficult to determine whether the

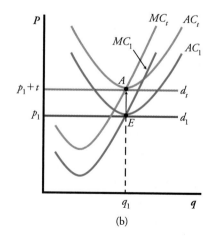

(a)   (b)

Figure 9A.5

government should proceed with the policy, but this determination will most likely involve normative economics. For example, if the 5% hurt are millionaires, many of us might agree to go along with the policy, but of course, that gets into normative economics, in the sense that we are assuming our welfare is better than theirs.

11. The figure is similar to Figure 9A.2. Assume that p_2 is the ceiling and p_e is the equilibrium price where supply equals demand. Consumer surplus would increase from AHp_e to ACp_2. Producer surplus would decrease from FHP_e to (p_2EF minus EGC). Total surplus has fallen by the area HGC. (HEC is a gain, to consumers, but a loss to producers, so it cancels out.) HGC is a loss to producers and since $MC > p$ at Q_2, it is part of deadweight loss. Obviously consumers will like this policy, because they gain, and producers will be opposed to this policy, because they lose producer surplus as a result. This policy is not a Pareto improvement, because one group is better off, but the other group is worse off and certainly society is worse off as a whole.

13. a, b, and e are all positive statements. The statements can be proven or refuted with a graph or specific statistics.

   c. With the words "better off" and "long run," it becomes likely that opinions as to what is "better off" and what is the "long run" will trigger a normative analysis. On the other hand, one may be able to use a graphical framework with standard measures of total surplus and long run to prove or refute this statement. Given the way the statement is worded, it will mostly likely be a normative analysis.

   d. This is a normative statement. What does "inefficiently" mean? The analysis is based on a value judgment of whether the government spends inefficiently. Thus normative analysis would follow.

15. Change in consumer surplus is 87.5. Change in producer surplus is 87.5. Cost of subsidy is $200, which is paid by taxpayers. Change in CS + change in PS − cost of subsidy = −25. It is negative. Given that the change in surplus has not covered the cost of the subsidy, the decision to subsidize was probably political in nature and probably involved normative issues other than simply how TS would increase.

Chapter 10: Using the Model of Perfect Competition

Answers to Self-Test Problems

1. a. Set U.S. demand equal to U.S. supply:

   $80 - Q_{US} = 20 + Q_{US}$

   $60 = 2Q_{US}$

   $Q_{US} = 30$

   $P_{US} = 20 + 30 = 50$

   In the rest of the world (row), set demand equal to supply:

   $-26 + 2 Q_{row} = 79 - Q_{row}$

   $3Q_{row} = 105$

   $Q_{row} = 35$

   $P_{row} = 79 - 35 = 44$

   In reference to Figure 10.4 on page 267, P_{US} is the same as p_4 in panel (a). P_{row} is the same as p_2 in panel (b).

   b. In order to solve for the equilibrium price, we must first calculate the total supply for U.S. and foreign, and to do that, we need to solve for exports. Horizontally, we must subtract: $Q^S_{row} - Q^D_{row}$. We get:

   $Q^S_{row} - Q^D_{row} = P/2 + 13 - (79 - P) = P/2 + 13 - 79 + P = (3/2)P - 66$

   Our export supply is therefore $Q_{ex} = (3/2)P - 66$. Next, we must calculate the sum of U.S. + foreign supply. We add $Q^S_{US} + Q_{ex}$, and get $P - 20 + (3/2)P - 66 = (5/2)P - 86 = Q^S_{US} + Q_{ex}$. Solving for P, we get $P = (2/5)Q_{USex} + 34.4$. Now we are ready to set the summed supply = U.S. demand:

   $(2/5)Q + 34.4 = 80 - Q$

   $(7/5)Q = 45.6$

   $Q = 32.57$

   $P = 80 - 32.57 = 47.43$

   Note that at $P = 47.43$, $Q_{ex} = (3/2)P - 66 = (3/2)(47.43) - 66 = 5.14$;

   $Q_{US} = P - 20 = 47.43 - 20 = 27.43$.

   The amount supplied by the U.S. (27.43) plus the amount exported by the rest of the world (5.14) = 32.57, the total amount demanded by the U.S. In terms of Figure 10.4, $p_3 = 47.43$, $Q_1 = 27.43$, $Q_2 = 30$, $Q_3 = 32.57$ in panel (a). In panel (b), $q_1 = 31.57$, $q_2 = 35$, $q_3 = 36.71$.

c. The gains from trade are area C in Figure 10.4(a) on page 267, for the United States and area F in Figure 10.4(b), for the rest of the world. For the United States, $1/2 \times (2.57)(5.14) = 6.6049$ and for the rest of the world, $1/2 \times (3.43)(5.14) = 8.8151$.

2. a. Set $S = D$, and $150 - Q = 30 + 1/2 \times Q$:

$120 = (3/2)Q$

$Q = 80$

$P = 150 - 80 = 70$

b. At a price support of $85, $Q_s = 110$ and the $Q_d = 65$, thus there is a surplus of 45. The cost to the government would be $\$85 \times 45 = 3,825$.

c. If the market clears, the market price is $70. The government must pay the difference between the target price, $80, and the market price, $70, $\times$ (the base acreage $\times$ the program yield $= 80$), thus it will cost the government ($\$80 - \$70)(80) = \$800$.

Answers to Odd-Numbered Questions and Problems for Review

1. The analysis in Figure 10.2 on page 263 shows that output or price might not increase with legalization. However, if money is not spent on education, then this is not the case. In addition, it is assumed that education will decrease the demand back to the original demand curve, which might or might not be the case.

3. As with any political or economic decision, there are winners and losers. The people who oppose NAFTA are the people with a great deal to lose, such as U.S. manufacturers and workers in industries affected by NAFTA. For example, the text discusses the plight of U.S. tomato farmers and workers. There are many groups such as tomato farmers that have a great deal to gain from opposition to the legislation. On the other hand, those who gain from free trade are often consumers who individually gain only a bit from the agreements, and therefore, are not inclined to spend much political effort in support of free trade legislation.

5. The problem is approached exactly like Self-Test Problem 1.

a. In the United States, $P = 90$ and $Q = 40$. In the rest of world, $P = 60$ and $Q = 60$.

b. $P = 75$, $Q = 55$; of this the United States will supply 32.5 and 22.5 will be exported by rest of world.

c. The U.S. gains from trade equal 168.75. The rest of world gains from trade equal 168.75.

7. It had to do with historical circumstances. Hoover acted during the beginning of the Great Depression that saw farmers' incomes destroyed. It also had to do with the importance and necessity of the goods. If all wheat farmers or dairy farmers had gone out of business in 1929, there would have been a huge crisis in the United States. Obviously, wheat and milk are still necessities. Justification cannot be given as easily, however, for providing government assistance to retail chain stores that go out of business. Most countries continue to behave as if it is vital to their well-being to maintain their agricultural production.

9. Figure 10.9(a) on page 279 depicts a situation in which demand is less elastic than supply and consumer surplus decreases with a ban on kidney sales. If demand is more elastic than supply (like in Figure 10.9(b)), a ban on kidney sales will increase consumer surplus. In general, the more *inelastic* demand and the more *elastic* supply, the more likely a ban on kidney sales is to decrease consumer surplus.

Chapter 11: Monopoly and Monopolistic Competition

Answers to Self-Test Problems

11. a. Using the twice-as-steep rule, we know $MR = 480 - 10Q$. Setting $MR = MC$, we get: $480 - 10Q = 20$; $10Q = 460$; $Q = 46$; $P = 480 - 5(46) = 250$.

b. Profits $= TR - TC = 250 \times 46 - (400 + 20 \times 46) = 11,500 - 1,320 = 10,180$.

c. See Figure 11A.1. Note: The hard part is drawing AC. It's best to calculate AC at $Q = 46$. $AC = 1,320/46 = 28.7$. Profits $= (P - AC) \times Q = (250 - 28.7) \times 46 = 10,179.8$ (due to rounding, we won't get exactly 10,180).

2. a. Step 1: Horizontally sum both firms' marginal cost curves:

$MC_a = 9 + 3q_a; q_a = (1/3)MC_a - 3$
$MC_b = 21 + 3q_b; q_b = (1/3)MC_b - 7$
$q_a + q_b = (2/3)MC - 10$

Figure 11A.1

Figure 11A.2

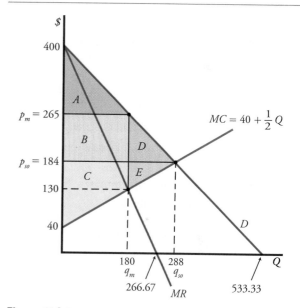

Figure 11A.3

$Q + 10 = (2/3)MC$

$MC = (3/2)Q + 15$

Now, set $MC = MR$. Using the twice-as-steep rule, $MR = 335 - (1/2)Q$

$335 - (1/2)Q = (3/2)Q + 15$

$320 = 2Q$

$Q = 160$; At $Q = 160$, $MC = (3/2)160 + 15 = 255$

The MC for each firm must be equal, so

$q_a = (1/3)MC_a - 3 = (255/3) - 3 = 82$

$q_b = (1/3)MC_b - 7 = (255/3) - 7 = 78$

Note that $q_a + q_b = 160$.

b. To get price, plug the total market output into the demand function. $P = 335 - (1/4)(160) = 295$.

c. See Figure 11A.2.

3. a. Using the twice-as-steep rule, $MR = 400 - (3/2)Q$. Setting $MR = MC$ gives us:

$400 - (3/2)Q = 40 + (1/2)Q$; $360 = 2Q$; $Q_m = 180$; $P_m = 400 - (3/4)(180) = 400 - 135 = 265$

So, $Q_m = 180$ and $P_m = 265$.

b. See Figure 11A.3. Triangle A is consumer surplus; areas C and B are producer surplus.

c. Consumer surplus $= (1/2)(400 - 265) \times 180 = 12,150$. Producer surplus is a trapezoid. The area of a trapezoid is $(1/2)(h_1 + h_2) \times b$, where h_1 and h_2 are the two different heights and b is

the base. At $Q = 180$, $MC = 40 + (1/2)(180) = 130$. Areas C and $B =$ producer surplus $= (1/2)[(265 - 130) + (265 - 40)] \times 180 = (1/2)(135 + 225) \times 180 = (1/2) \times 360 \times 180 = 32,400$.

d. $P = MC$; $400 - (3/4)Q = 40 + (1/2)Q$; $(5/4)Q = 360$; $Q_{so} = 288$; $P_{so} = MC = 40 + (1/2)(288) = 184$.

e. Consumer surplus $= (1/2)(400 - 184) \times 288 = 31,104$. Producer surplus $= (1/2)(184 - 40) \times 288 = 20,736$. Consumer surplus is equal to areas A, B, and D in Figure 11A.3. Producer surplus is equal to areas C and E.

f. Deadweight loss equals $(1/2)(265 - 130) \times (288 - 180) = 1/2 \times 135 \times 108 = 7,290$. Note that the difference between consumer surplus at the socially optimal level and consumer surplus at the monopoly output is equal to 18,954. Of this loss, the area B $((265 - 184) \times 180 = 14,580)$ gets transferred to producers in the form of producer surplus. The loss to consumers is the area D, which is equal to $[(1/2)(265 - 184) \times (288 - 180)] = (1/2) \times 81 \times 108 = 4,374$. The remainder of the triangle (area E) represents the portion of deadweight loss that is a loss in producer surplus $= (1/2)(184 - 130) \times (288 - 180) = (1/2) \times 54 \times 108 = 2,916$.

Answers to Odd-Numbered Questions and Problems for Review

1. This situation implies that demand intersects the upward-sloping section of *LRAC*. This situation might be like Figure 11A.4. In this case, entry would be likely to occur, but it need not if other barriers to entry exist.

3. a. Economies of scale–structural barriers.

  b. Structural barriers–absolute cost advantage.

  c. Structural barriers–absolute cost advantage–borrow funds at lower interest rates.

  d. Structural barriers–absolute cost advantage–advertising.

  e. Strategic barrier–predatory pricing.

  f. Government-imposed barrier.

5. a. $Q = 60$; $P = 370$; profits $= 14,380$.

  b. See Figure 11A.5. Profits are the green shaded rectangle $(P - ATC) \times Q$. Getting the actual shape of the *ATC* curve is difficult. The most important point is the point $(60, 130.33)$.

7. a. $Q = 12$; $P = 320$.

  b. $Q = 125$; $P = 270$.

  c. With $P = 320$, elasticity of demand equals 1.067 for the original demand curve. At $P = 320$, $Q = 100$ for the new demand curve, elasticity of demand equals 1.6. Thus, the new demand is more elastic than the old demand at $P = 320$. The explanation holds. This example is similar to the situation depicted in Figure 11.10 on page 303.

9. a. $Q = 25$; $P = 77$.

  b. See Figure 11A.6. Consumer surplus is area A and producer surplus is area B.

  c. Consumer surplus $= (1/2)(75)(25) = 937.5$; producer surplus $= (75)(25) = 1,875$; total welfare $= 937.5 + 1,875 = 2,812.5$.

  d. $P_{so} = 2$; $Q_{so} = 50$.

  e. $(1/2)(150)(50) = 3,750$.

  f. $DWL = (1/2)(75)(25) = 937.5$. The entire DWL is a loss in consumer surplus, because there was no producer surplus at the socially

Figure 11A.4

Figure 11A.5

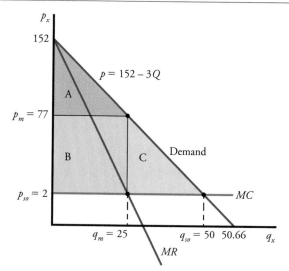

$p = 152 - 3Q$

p_x

152

$p_m = 77$

$p_{so} = 2$

A

B

C

Demand

MC

$q_m = 25$

$q_{so} = 50$ 50.66

q_x

MR

Figure 11A.6

optimal level. Deadweight loss equals area C in Figure 11A.6.

11. **a.** $Q = 38$; $P = 104$; profits $= 2,888$.

b. $Q = 40$; $P = 100$; profits $= 3,200$.

c. $DWL = (1/2)(38)(76) = 1,444$.

d. There are two ways to think about this. First, the deadweight loss triangle that equals $(1/2)(80 - 38)(104 - 20) = (1/2)(42)(84) = 1,764$. Second, each of the 38 units produced by the inefficient monopolist has cost that are 28 instead of 20, so there is an additional loss equal to 8 (38) $= 304$. Total $DWL = 1,764 + 304 = 2,068$.

13. Following Schumpeter's argument, in a dynamic world, Microsoft's investment in R&D can be used as an argument that they are helping to ensure that the economy will progress at an optimal rate of technological progress.

15. Similar to Figure 11.14 on page 314, DiGiorno's demand curve would shift in from panel (a) to panel (b). We would expect that as more substitutes became available for DiGiorno's pizza, demand would become more elastic.

17. **a.** There are now many firms, and product differentiation is the key to identifying the rising-crust pizza market as monopolistically competitive. In addition, advertising plays a key role in helping create product differentiation in the minds of consumers.

b. The point of this question is primarily to get you to think about how difficult it is to answer

such a question. Perhaps, however, most of the consumer surplus has been obtained in this market, in which case 11.17(a) would be more likely.

19. **a.** $MR = P(1 - 1/|\varepsilon_p|)$. From the demand $P = 160 - 4Q$, for $P = 120$, $Q = 40/4 = 10$. We know $MR = 160 - 8Q$; so for $Q = 10$, $MR = 80$. Therefore, $MR = 80 = 120(1 - 1/|\varepsilon_p|)$, and solving for ε_p, $120 - 80 = 120/|\varepsilon_p|$, or $|\varepsilon_p| = 120/40 = 3$. Price elasticity of demand $= 3$ at $P = 120$. Using similar reasoning, price elasticity of demand $= 1$ at $P = 80$, and price elasticity of demand $= 0.6$ at $P = 60$.

b. $MR = 160 - 8Q$.

c. Using $p(1 - 1/|\varepsilon_p|)$, at $P = 120$, we have $MR = 120(1 - 1/3) = 120 \times 2/3 = 80$ and using MR from question 19(b), we have $MR = 160 - 8(10) = 80$. It works!

Chapter 12: Additional Monopoly Topics: Pricing Strategies and Public Policy

Answers to Self-Test Problems

1. **a.** See Figure 12A.1. Set $MR = MC$ in each market. In adult market: $MR = 30 - (2/5)q_a$, using the twice-as-steep rule. Set $MR_a = MC$; $30 - (2/5)q_a = 2$; $(2/5)q_a = 28$; $q_a = 70$; $P_a = 30 - (1/5)(70) = 16$.

In children market, $MR = 10 - (1/5)q_c$. Set $MR_c = MC$; $10 - (1/5)q_c = 2$; $(1/5)q_c = 8$; $qc = 40$; $P_c = 10 - (1/10)(40) = 6$.

b. Adult: consumer surplus $= (1/2)(30 - 16) \times 70 = 490$ (area A) and producer surplus $= (16 - 2) \times 70 = 980$ (area B).

Children: consumer surplus $= (1/2)(10 - 6) \times 40 = 80$ (area C); producer surplus $= (6 - 2) \times 40 = 160$ (area D).

Because $MC = AC$, profits and producer surplus are equal.

Total: consumer surplus $= 570$ and producer surplus/profits $= 1,140$. Total surplus $= 570 + 1,140 = 1,710$.

c. See Figure 12A.2. We need to horizontally sum the two demand curves: $P_a = 30 - (1/5)q_a$; $(1/5)q_a = 30 - P_a$; $q_a = 150 - 5P_a$; $P_c = 10 - (1/10)q_c$; $(1/10)q_c = 10 - P_c$; $q_c = 100 - 10 P_c$; $Q = q_a + q_c = 150 - 5P + 100 - 10 P$; $Q = 250 - 15P$ for $P \leq 10$. The kink will occur at $P = 10$. Note that at $P = 10$, $q_a =$

(a)

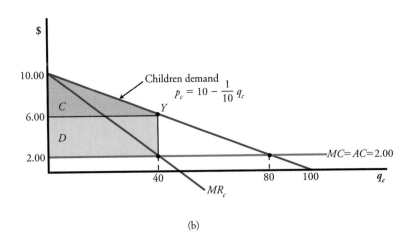

(b)

Figure 12A.1

$150 - 5(10) = 100$ and $Q = 250 - 15(10) = 100$. For prices less than 10, the market demand curve is $Q = 250 - 15P$ or:

$P = 16.67 - (1/15)Q$ or $P = 16.67 - 0.067Q$

$MR = 16.67 - (2/15)Q$ or $MR = 16.67 - 0.133Q$.

d. Now, set $MR = MC$ and get: $16.67 - (2/15)Q = 2$; $14.67 = (2/15)Q$; $Q = 110$ (note that depending on how you round 16 2/3, you might get a small decimal place after 110, but we know from our answer in question 1(a), that $Q = 110$, so we will round to 110).

$P = 16.67 - (1/15)(110) = 9.34$. (See Figure 12A.2.) Note that at $Q = 100$, MR in the adult market $= -10$. And MR from the market demand curve $= 3.34$. There is a big jump in the MR curve at $Q = 100$.

e. Producer surplus $=$ profits $= (9.34 - 2) \times 110 = 807.4$ (green area $YZVW$). Consumer surplus

$=$ the area of the trapezoid $XSTY +$ the area of the triangle SZT. Using the formula of $(1/2)(h_1 + h_2) \times$ b, where h_1 and h_2 represent the two different heights of the trapezoid, we get consumer surplus $= (1/2)(20.66 + .66) \times 100 + (1/2)(0.66) \times 10 = 1,066 + 3.3 = 1,069.3$. Total surplus $= 807.4 + 1,069.3 = 1,876.7$.

f. The monopolist prefers separating the two markets, as its profits are equal to 1,140 under that method and only 807.4 without price discrimination.

g. Total welfare $= 1,710$ under price discrimination. Total welfare $= 1,876.7$ under single-pricing policy. In this case, total welfare is reduced by 166.7 with price discrimination.

2. a. Using the twice-as-steep rule, $MR = 200 - 8Q$. Set $MR = MC$; $200 - 8Q = 8$; $192 = 8Q$; $Q = 24$; $P = 200 - 4(24) = 104$.

Profits $= (104 - 8) \times 24 = 2,304$ (area B in Figure 12A.3(a)).

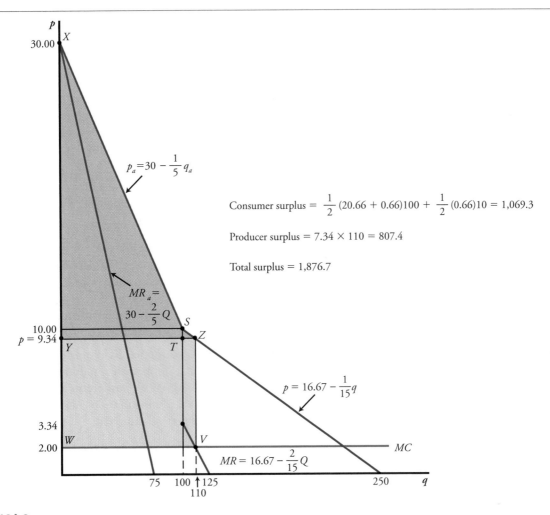

Consumer surplus $= \dfrac{1}{2}(20.66 + 0.66)100 + \dfrac{1}{2}(0.66)10 = 1{,}069.3$

Producer surplus $= 7.34 \times 110 = 807.4$

Total surplus $= 1{,}876.7$

Figure 12A.2

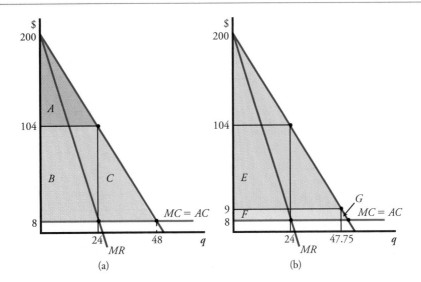

(a)   (b)

Figure 12A.3

b. See Figure 12A.3(a). If the monopolist charges $P = MC$, then $200 - 4Q = 8$; $192 = 4Q$; $Q = 48$; $P = 200 - 4(48) = 8 = MC$. The tariff would be equal to consumer surplus $= (1/2)(200 - 8) \times 48 = 4,608$ (areas $A + B + C$). Thus, profits would be 4,608, which is higher than 2,304 (area B) in question 2(a).

c. In Figure 12A.3(b), if price equals 9, then $9 = 200 - 4Q$; $191 = 4Q$; $Q = 47.75$. In this case, the optimal fixed fee would be $(1/2)(200 - 9) \times 47.75 = 4,560.125$ (green area E). In addition, the course earns a profit of $47.75 (9 - 8) = 47.75$ (blue area F) from a price of 9. So total profits equal the sum of areas E and F or 4,607.875, which is still less than 4,608 with $P = 8$. The difference is the small yellow triangle G in Figure 12A.3(b).

3. a. If the monopolist charges $P = MC = 8$, then: $8 = 200 - 4Q_1$; $4Q_1 = 192$; $Q_1 = 48$ and $8 = 122 - 6Q_2$; $6Q_2 = 114$; $Q_2 = 19$.

The fixed fee can only be equal to what the consumers of the lower demand will pay. Thus, it is equal to $(1/2)(114) \times 19 = 1,083$. Profits are equal to $2 \times 1,083 = 2,166$.

b. If the monopolist eliminates the low-volume consumer, it can charge a fee that the high-volume user will pay. Consumer surplus for the high demand is equal to $(1/2)(192)(48) = 4,608$. The low-volume user would never pay this fixed fee; thus they are eliminated. Profits to the firm will be 4,608. The monopolist earns more profit by eliminating the low-volume user than by charging a low fixed fee to keep them in.

Answers to Odd–Numbered Questions and Problems for Review

1. a. $Q = 58$; $P = 62$.

b. $Q = 116$; lowest price is at MC, so $P = 4$.

c. Non-discriminating monopolist: consumer surplus $= 1,682$; producer surplus $= 3,364$; total welfare $= 5,046$. First-degree price discrimination: producer extracts all consumer surplus for itself. Consumer surplus $= 0$; producer surplus $= 6,728$; total welfare $= 6,728$.

d. As you can see, although total welfare is higher under the first-degree price discrimination case, certainly consumer surplus isn't higher in that case (because it equals 0).

3. a. See Figure 12A.4.

b. Total revenue $= 100(20) + 60(15) + 30(10) + 10(5) = 3,250$.

c. Producer surplus is the sum of the three areas $X + Y + Z$ in Figure 12A.4. Producer surplus $= \$1,500 + \$600 + \$150 = \$2,250$. Consumer surplus is the light-red shaded areas, $(A + B + C + D)$ which we are unable to calculate.

5. a. See Figure 12A.5. The demand curve is $P = 133.33 - (1/3)Q$ for prices less than 100. The kink occurs at the point $(100,100)$.

b. $P = 76.67$ and $Q = 170$.

c. Consumer surplus is labeled as the purple area A and producer surplus is labeled as the green area B. Consumer surplus $= (1/2)(100)(100) + (1/2)(23.33)(100 + 170) = 5,000 + 3,149.55 = 8,149.55$ and producer surplus $=$ profits $= 9,633.9$. Total welfare $= 17,783.45$.

d. Profits with price discrimination (question 4) are 11,300. Profits with a uniform price (Problem 5) are 9,633.9. Thus, profits are higher with price discrimination. The monopolist would prefer to price discriminate.

e. With price discrimination, consumer surplus $= 4,050 + 1,600 = 5,650$, and producer surplus or profits $= 8,100 + 3,200 = 11,300$. Total surplus $= 16,950$. Total surplus without discrimination (question 5) is higher, at 17,783.45. Thus, price discrimination in this case reduces total welfare.

Figure 12A.4

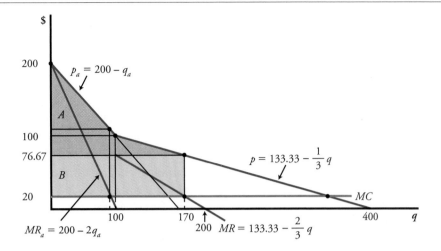

Figure 12A.5

7. a. $Q = 120$; $P = MC = 5$; fixed fee $= 36,000$. Profits $= 6,000$.

b. If $P = 6$, $Q = 119.8$, and fixed fee $= 35,880.1$; Profits $= 35,880.1 + (6 - 5) \times 119.8 - 30,000 = 5,999.90$. Profits are lower with a $1 increase in price.

9. a. First-degree

b. Second-degree

c. Third-degree

11. a. $P = MC = 4$; $Q_1 = 196$; $Q_2 = 175.79$. Fixed fee $= \$14,678.465$. Profits $= \$29,356.93$.

b. At $P = 5$, $Q_1 = 195$; $Q_2 = 174.74$; Fixed fee $= 14,503.42$. Profits $= 2(\text{Fixed Fee}) + (p - mc)(q_1 + q_2) = 2(14,503.42) + (5 - 4)(195 + 174.74) = 29,376.58$.

c. In this case, the firm is better off raising price by $1. Profits are higher under this scenario by $19.65. Our analysis is similar to Figure 12.7 on page 334. In this case, area E is bigger than area C.

13. a. Total revenue under separate prices is $560. Under pure bundling, total revenue is $600.

b. The team picks pure bundling.

c. The demand curves are negatively correlated. Jonathan is willing to pay a higher price than Nathaniel for the regular season but a lower price than Nathaniel for the playoffs. Pure bundling will yield greater profits only if the two demands are negatively correlated.

15. a. Negatively correlated because Anna will pay more for chicken nuggets than Alex and Alex will pay more for fries than Anna.

b. Profits are highest by charging $2.55 for chicken nuggets and $1.50 for fries. Profits are $2.55 in this case.

c. Pure bundling profits are $3.

d. Mixed bundling. Anna will buy only chicken nuggets. Alex will buy a bundle: Profits = $3.02, higher than in the pure bundling case.

17. a. $Q = 27.386$; $P = 226.14$; profits $= 4,107.92$.

b. $Q = 47.43$; $P = 25.66$; by nature of Ramsey price, profits $= 0$.

c. Consumer surplus in question 17(a) is 3,749.96. Consumer surplus in question 17(b) is 11,248.97. The increase in consumer surplus is equal to the difference or 7,499.01. (Note: Due to rounding, if you calculate the actual area of the trapezoid that represents the change in consumer surplus, you might get 7,499.56.)

19. Recall for Chapter 11 that X inefficiencies refer to a situation in which less than the maximum output is produced from a given set of inputs because managers have objectives other than profit maximization. X inefficiencies often exist in regulated firms because regulated firms often assume that the regulatory commission will guarantee the firm a profit, and therefore, the firm's managers have less incentive to minimize costs. In fact, under a rate of return method of regulation, managers may have an incentive to have higher costs than necessary so that the firm's profits and rate of return will decrease and the firm can then request a rate hike. Rate of return price regulation might also encourage firms to use too much capital relative to other inputs in an attempt to raise the regulated firm's rate base.

Chapter 13: An Introduction to Game Theory

Answers to Self-Test Problems

1. **a.** First pretend you are X. If X thinks Y will charge $9, then X will offer a "2 for 1" deal, because X will get 6,000 (instead of 4,000). If X thinks Y will offer a "2 for 1"deal, then X should also offer a "2 for 1" deal and get 3,000 (instead of 1,000). So, no matter what strategy Y chooses, X will always choose a "2 for 1" deal. So, X has a dominant strategy to offer a "2 for 1" deal. Similarly, now pretend you are Y. If Y thinks X will charge $9, then Y will choose to offer a "2 for 1" deal because it will get 6,000 (instead of 4,000). If Y thinks X will offer a "2 for 1" deal, then Y will choose to also offer a "2 for 1" deal because he will get 3,000 (instead of 1,000). So, no matter what strategy X plays, Y will always choose a "2 for 1" deal, so Y has a dominant strategy to offer a "2 for 1" deal. Thus, both players have a dominant strategy to offer a "2 for 1" deal, and the Nash equilibrium of the game is for both X and Y to offer a "2 for 1" deal.

   b. The game is a Prisoner's Dilemma, because both players are worse off at the Nash equilibrium than if they both charge a price of $9.00.

2. **a.** See Figure 13A.1. The Nash equilibrium is reached by working backwards. We can see that if the entrant stays out, then the incumbent will continue to profit-maximize (the only choice). Also, if the entrant enters, the incumbent is better off choosing to continue to profit-maximize. Thus, the incumbent has a dominant strategy to "continue to profit-maximize." With this knowl-edge, the entrant knows if it doesn't enter, it will earn 0, but if it does enter, it will get 30. Thus, the entrant chooses to enter, and the incumbent will continue to profit-maximize. The entrant will earn 30 and the incumbent will earn 50.

   b. Because the game is played once, the incumbent's threat to fight could not be credible. This possibility of forgoing current profits for future gain is not built into a game played one time.

3. **a.** This game is a game with no pure Nash equilibrium. If Pepsi thinks Coke will play *Low price*, then Pepsi will play *Low price*, but if Pepsi thinks Coke is going to choose *Heavy advertising*, then Pepsi will choose *Heavy advertising*. Thus, Pepsi chooses the same strategy as Coke. However, if Coke thinks Pepsi will choose *Low price*, then Coke will choose *Heavy advertising*, and if Coke thinks Pepsi will choose *Heavy advertising*, then Coke will choose *Low price*. Thus, Coke does the exact opposite of whatever Pepsi chooses. Neither firm has a dominant strategy, and there is no pure Nash equilibrium for this game.

   b. To solve the game, let's follow the same notation as in the text. Let θ = the probability that Coke chooses the strategy *Low price* and $(1 - \theta)$ = the probability that Coke chooses the strategy *Heavy advertising*. Let ρ = the probability that Pepsi chooses the strategy *Low price* and $(1 - \rho)$ = the probability that Pepsi chooses the strategy *heavy advertising*. We know that Coke's optimal strategy will result in equal profits for Pepsi, regardless of whether Pepsi plays *Low price* 100 percent of the time or plays *Heavy advertising* 100 percent of the time. The equation to solve is:

$$600\theta + 400(1 - \theta) = 400\theta + 500(1 - \theta)$$
$$600\theta + 400 - 400\theta = 400\theta + 500 - 500\theta$$

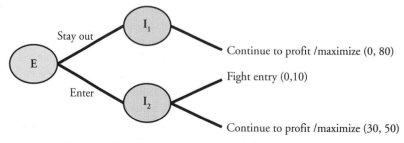

Figure 13A.1 ($millions entrant's profit, $millions incumbent's profit)

$300\theta = 100$

$\theta = 1/3$

$(1 - \theta) = 2/3$

Similarly, we know that Pepsi's optimal strategy will result in equal profits for Coke, regardless of whether Coke plays *Low price* 100 percent of the time or *Heavy advertising* 100 percent of the time. The equation to solve is:

$500\rho + 700 (1 - \rho) = 800\rho + 500 (1 - \rho)$

$500\rho + 700 - 700\rho = 800\rho + 500 - 500\rho$

$200 = 500\rho$

$2/5 = \rho$

$(1 - \rho) = 3/5$

Answers to Odd-Numbered Questions and Problems for Review

1. **a.** Your payoff matrix would mimic that of Table 13.1 on page 354.

   b. Both Joe and Jerry have a dominant strategy to locate their hot dog stands in the middle.

   c. The Nash equilibrium is for both Joe and Jerry to locate in the middle. They will each get 50% of the profits.

3. **a.** A has a dominant strategy to advertise big and B has a dominant strategy to give free stuff away.

   b. The Nash equilibrium is for A to advertise big and B to give free stuff away.

5. **a.** George has a dominant strategy to shout insults.

   b. Henry has a dominant strategy to shout insults.

   c. The Nash equilibrium is for both George and Henry to shout insults.

7. Betsy's husband needs to take a microeconomics class. He is going to be very disappointed when Betsy comes home with $100. As we know from Common Error 13.1 on page 357, the only way Stacey would have been willing to trade is if she had $100. Betsy had more than $100 before she traded and should not have been willing to trade, but if she followed her husband's advice, she will be very disappointed.

9. **a.** Both Venezuela and Saudi Arabia have a dominant strategy to defect: increase output.

   b. The Nash equilibrium is for both Venezuela and Saudi Arabia to defect.

   c. The game is a Prisoner's Dilemma, because both players end up getting lower profits at the Nash equilibrium than they could have by keeping the collusive agreement.

11. In the real world, the two countries are obviously not playing the game one time only. The game is considered infinitely repeated because neither country would know the end of the game (when they will stop competing with each other). The countries can learn over time about the likely actions of their competitors and then create punishment strategies for those countries who cheat.

13. **a.** See Figure 13A.2.

   b. No matter what Coke chooses, Pepsi will choose to develop the product. Given that Pepsi will always choose to develop the product, Coke will also develop the product. The Nash is for Coke and Pepsi to both develop the product. The payoffs will be 600 to Coke and 600 to Pepsi.

15. **a.** Martha does not have a dominant strategy.

   b. Harvey does not have a dominant strategy.

   c. There are two Nash equilibria for this game. Either they both go to the symphony or they both go to the basketball game.

17. **a.** Firm A does not have a dominant strategy.

   b. Firm B has a dominant strategy to develop a new product.

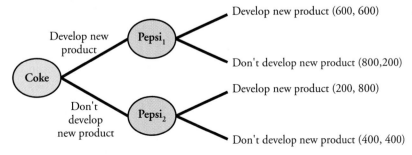

Figure 13A.2 (Coke's profit, Pepsi's profit)

c. The Nash equilibrium is for A to offer a sale and B to develop a new product.

d. This game is not a Prisoner's Dilemma.

19. a. Pepsi does not have a dominant strategy.

b. Coke does not have a dominant strategy.

c. There is no pure Nash equilibrium. The mixed strategy equilibrium is that the probability that Coke will play *Develop new product* is 1/2. The probability that Coke will play *Don't develop new product* is 1/2. The probability that Pepsi will play *Advertise heavy* is 1/2. The probability that Pepsi will play *Lower price* is 1/2.

Chapter 14: Oligopoly

Answers to Self-Test Problems

1. a. Let's consider Firm A first. $P = 100 - 4q_a - 4q_b$ because Firm A assumes q_b is constant; we can then use the twice-as-steep rule to get MR, using $(100 - 4q_b)$ as the constant. $MR_a = (100 - 4q_b) - 8q_a$. Firm A sets $MR_a = MC_a$, so $100 - 4q_b - 8q_a = 4$; $96 - 4q_b = 8q_a$; $q_a = 12 - (1/2)q_b$. Similarly, because the cost functions are identical, Firm B's reaction function is: $q_b = 12 - (1/2)q_a$.

b. Plugging Firm B's reaction function into Firm A's reaction function, we get:
$q_a = 12 - (1/2)(12 - (1/2)q_a)$; $q_a = 12 - 6 + (1/4)q_a$; $(3/4)q_a = 6$; $q_a = 8$
$q_b = 12 - (1/2)(8) = 12 - 4 = 8$
$Q = q_a + q_b = 8 + 8 = 16$
$P = 100 - 4(16) = 36$
Profits to Firm A $= 8(36 - 4) = 256$
Profits to Firm B $= 8(36 - 4) = 256$.
Total profits $= 512$.

c. If this were a collusive agreement, the firms would combine and act as a monopolist to maximize joint profits:
$MR = 100 - 8Q$
Setting $MR = MC$, we get $100 - 8Q = 4$; $8Q = 96$ and $Q = 12$.
With q_b on the y-axis and q_a on the x-axis, the collusion curve would be a downward-sloping line with a slope of -1 from the point (0,12) to the point (12,0). For every additional unit of output Firm A produces, Firm B must produce 1 less in order to keep the collusive agreement.

$P = 100 - 4(12) = 52$
Because the firms are identical, $q_a = q_b = 6$. Profits to Firm A $= (52 \times 6) - (4 \times 6) = 288$; Profits to Firm B $= (52 \times 6) - (4 \times 6) = 288$. Total profits $= 576$.

If Firm A increases output by 1 unit to 7 units, then total output would be 13 and $P = 100 - 4 \times 13 = 48$. Profits to Firm A $= (48 \times 7) - (4 \times 7) = 308$, which is higher than the old profit of 288. Firm B would have a similar incentive to cheat on the agreement. This collusive agreement is not stable.

d. If A is a Stackelberg leader, it takes the Cournot reaction curve for Firm B as constant. Thus, Firm A's demand curve becomes:
$P_a = 100 - 4q_a - 4q_b = 100 - 4q_a - 4(12 - (1/2)q_a) = 100 - 4q_a - 48 + 2q_a$
$P_a = 52 - 2q_a$
Using the twice-as-steep rule, $MR = 52 - 4q_a$. Setting $MR_a = MC_a$; $52 - 4q_a = 4$; $48 = 4q_a$; $q_a = 12$; $q_b = 12 - (1/2)(12) = 6$.
$Q = q_a + q_b = 12 + 6 = 18$. Price $= 100 - 4(18) = 28$. Profits to Firm A $= (28 \times 12) - (4 \times 12) = 288$. Profits to Firm B $= (28 \times 6) - (4 \times 6) = 144$. Total profits $= 432$.

e. Total output is higher and price is lower under the Stackelberg model, so it is more allocatively efficient. The distribution of output is such that Firm A has higher profits under Stackelberg, because it is the leader. In fact, it earns the same profits as it would in the collusive agreement. Firm B earns lower profits in Stackelberg than in the Cournot model.

2. a. If there is no product differentiation, then $P_h = P_k = MC = 1.5$.

b. Solve Harvey's demand for $p_h = f(p_k)$.
$q_h = 5 - (1/5)p_h + (1/10)p_k$; $(1/5)p_h = 5 - q_h + (1/10)p_k$; (1) $p_h = 25 + (1/2)p_k - 5q_h$
Using the twice-as-steep rule and recognizing that $25 + (1/2)p_k$ is a constant for Harvey, we have: $MR_h = 25 + (1/2)p_k - 10 q_h$. Set $MR_h = MC_h$; $25 + (1/2)p_k - 10 q_h = 1.5$; $23.5 + (1/2)p_k = 10 q_h$; (2) $q_h = 2.35 + (1/20)p_k$. Remember that our goal is to get $p_h = f(p_k)$. Thus, so far, we had $p_h = f(p_k, q_h)$ in Equation (1), but Equation (2) gives us $q_h = f(p_k)$, so if

we plug Equation (2) into Equation (1), we will get our reaction function. Doing that yields:

$p_h = 25 + (1/2)p_k - 5(2.35 + (1/20)p_k)$

$p_h = 25 + (1/2)p_k - 11.75 - (1/4)p_k$

$p_h = 13.25 + (1/4)p_k$

Similarly, because the demand functions and cost functions are identical, we have

$p_k = 13.25 + (1/4)p_h.$

c. To solve for price, we substitute Kim's reaction function into Harvey's reaction function:

$p_h = 13.25 + (1/4)(13.25 + (1/4)p_h)$

$p_h = 13.25 + 3.3125 + (1/16)p_h$

$(15/16)p_h = 16.5625$

$p_h = 17.67$

$p_k = 13.25 + (1/4)(17.67) = 17.67$

To get output, we can plug numbers into Equation (2) or the original demand. Either way, we get:

$q_h = 2.35 + (1/20)(17.67) = 3.23$ or $q_h = 5 - (1/5)(17.67) + (1/10)(17.67) = 3.23$

$q_k = 2.35 + (1/20)(17.67) = 3.23$ or $q_k = 5 - (1/5)(17.67) + (1/10)(17.67) = 3.23$

3. a. See Figure 14A.1. To solve for the residual demand, we must horizontally subtract the fringe supply from the market demand curve. Thus, we need to get both market demand and fringe supply as $q = f(P)$.

Market demand: $P = 208 - 4Q; 4Q = 208 - P; Q = 52 - (1/4)P$

Fringe supply: $P = 10 + 2q_f; P - 10 = 2q_f; q_f = P/2 - 5$

$q_d = Q - q_f = (52 - (1/4)P) - (P/2 - 5) = 52 - (1/4)P - P/2 + 5$

$q_d = 57 - (3/4)P$

Solving $P = f(q_d)$ so we can get MR by the twice-as-steep rule, we have:

$(3/4)P = 57 - q_d; P = 76 - (4/3)q_d$

$MR_d = 76 - (8/3)q_d$

b. The firm sets $MR_d = MC_d$ to determine the output and price:

$76 - (8/3)q_d = 4 + (1/3)q_d$

$72 = 3q_d; q_d = 24$

To get price, we plug q_d back into the dominant firm's demand curve:

$P = 76 - (4/3)(24) = 44$

c. The fringe takes the price of 44 as given and produces:

$q_f = (1/2)P - 5 = (1/2)(44) - 5 = 17$

Note: A way to verify your answer is to find price using market demand and market output. $Q = q_d + q_f = 24 + 17 = 41$. Using market demand, at $Q = 41$, $P = 208 - 4(41) = 44$.

d. See Figure 14A.1.

Answers to Odd-Numbered Questions and Problems for Review

1. a. $q_a = 6 - (1/2)q_b$ and $q_b = 6 - (1/2)q_a$.

   b. $q_a = q_b = 4$. $P = 10$. Profits to Firm A = Profits to Firm B = 32.

   Total output equals 8. Total profits = 64.

3. a. $Q = 6$; $q_a = q_b = 3$. With q_b on the y-axis and q_a on the x-axis, the collusion curve would be a downward-sloping line with a slope of -1 from (0,6) to (6,0). For every additional unit of output Firm A produces, B must produce 1 less in order to keep the collusive agreement. $P = 14$; profits to Firm A = Profits to Firm B = 36. Total profits = 72.

   b. Now, $Q = 7$; $q_a = 4$. $P = 12$; and profits to Firm A = $40 > 36$. Therefore, there is an incentive for Firm A to cheat. Of course, Firm B also has an incentive to cheat.

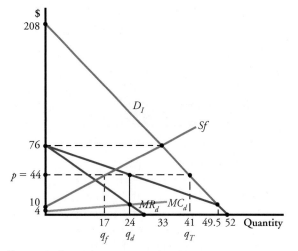

Figure 14A.1

5. $q_a = 6$; $q_b = 3$; $P = 8$; profits to Firm A = 36; profits to Firm B = 18; total output = 9; total profits = 54.

7. a. Firm A would be expected to be the Stackelberg leader because it has lower costs than Firm B.

   b. $q_b = 5.875 - (1/2)q_a$.

   c. $P_a = 14.25 - q_a$.

   d. $q_a = 6.125$; $q_b = 2.8125$; $Q = 8.9375$; $P = 8.125$; profits to Firm A = 37.516; profits to Firm B = 15.82; total profits = 53.336.

9. $q_a = q_b = 6$; $Q = 12$; $P = MC = 2$; profits to each firm = 0.

11. All numbers have been rounded to two decimal places. See table below.

   Note that Stackelberg has higher Q and lower P than Cournot. Collusion has highest P and lowest Q. The Bertrand outcome is best because price equals marginal cost, so the outcome is allocatively efficient.

13. a. $P = MC = 1$.

   b. $p_a = 4 + (1/3)p_b$; $p_b = 4 + (1/3)p_a$
   $p_a = p_b = 6$; $q_a = q_b = 15$.

   c. Price is much higher (6 instead of 1).

15. a. $P = 166 - (2/3)q_d$.

   b. $q_d = 81$; $P = 112$.

   c. $q_f = 106$.

   d. See Figure 14A.2.

17. Axelrod's three characteristics for the punishment are that: it is nice toward competitors; it punishes all defections; and it forgives defectors who return to the fold. The trigger strategy described may be nice in the sense that it doesn't punish until the firm actually cheats, but it doesn't allow for any forgiveness. It does punish, but forever. Tit-for-tat follows all three characteristics.

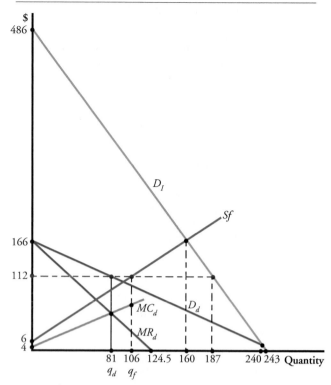

Figure 14A.2

19. The dominant firm allows for one firm to dictate price and the others to take the price as given. The fringe essentially acts as a competitive firm, setting the price equal to its supply (MC). However, the price leader model allows for firms to switch roles over time and for different firms to be the leader. It doesn't assume that there is one firm that dominates the market, although the leader may stay constant over time. The other firms in the industry are not so much price-takers as decision-makers based on the price leader's signal.

Model	Price	q_a	q_b	Q	Profits to A	Profits to B	Total Profits
Cournot (14.1)	10	4	4	8	32	32	64
Collusion (14.3)	14	3	3	6	36	36	72
Stackelberg (14.5)	8	6	3	9	36	18	54
Stackelberg with lower costs (14.7)	8.13	6.13	2.81	8.94	37.52	15.82	53.34
Bertrand (14.9)	2	6	6	12	0	0	0

Chapter 15: Strategic Behavior

Answers to Self-Test Problems

1. a. Using the twice-as-steep rule, $MR = 180 - 4Q$. Set $MR = MC$:

$180 - 4Q = 20$; $4Q = 160$; $Q = 40$

$P = 180 - 2(40) = 100$; profits $= 40(100 - 20) = 3,200$

b. If the monopolist keeps its output fixed at 40, then the residual demand for the potential entrant is: $P = 180 - (2 \times 40) - 2q_{pe}$; $P = 100 - 2q_{pe}$.

c. $MR_{pe} = 100 - 4q_{pe}$. Setting $MR = MC$, we get $100 - 4q_{pe} = 30$; $q_{pe} = 17.5$; $P = 100 - 35 = 65$.

The profits for the potential entrant $= (65 - 30) \times 17.5 = 612.5$.

The monopolist must lower its price to 65, and its profits $= (65 - 20) \times 40 = 1,800$.

d. If the monopolist charges $P = 30$, that will completely deter entry. Plugging $P = 30$ into demand $30 = 180 - 2Q$; $150 = 2Q$; $Q_m = 75$. Profits $= (30 - 20) \times 75 = 750$. The potential entrant would incur a loss if it entered.

e. Your extensive form would look exactly like Figure 15.3 on page 410. At node M_1, there are two choices: $q = 40$, $p = 100$ ($\$0$, $\$3,200$); and $q = 75$, $p = 30$ (0, 750). At node M_2, there are two choices: $q = 40$, $P = 65$ (612.5, $1,800$); and $q = 75$, $P = 30$ (loss, 750).

f. To find the Nash Equilibrium, we know that in each case, the monopolist would produce $q = 40$. Given that the entrant knows this, the entrant will enter and earn 612.5 in profits, rather than stay out and earn 0 in profits. The threat to limit price is not credible.

g. If the potential entrant trembled and stayed out, the monopolist would choose to produce 40 (not limit price) and earn $\$3,200$ in profits. A limit-pricing policy would not be reasonable, because it reduces the monopolist's profits.

2. a. Using the twice-as-steep rule, $MR = 200 - 4Q$; set $MR = MC$ to get

$200 - 4Q = 20$; $180 = 4Q$; $Q = 45$; $P = 200 - (2 \times 45) = 110$; profits $= (110 - 20) \times 45 = 4,050$.

b. If demand is $P = 240 - 2Q$, then $MR = 240 - 4Q$ and $MR = MC$ gets us:

$240 - 4Q = 20$; $220 = 4Q$; $Q = 55$; $P = 240 - 2(55) = 130$

Profits $= (130 - 20) \times 55 - A$; profits $= 6,050 - A$. Given that profits before the increase in advertising were 4,050, the monopolist would be willing to spend slightly less than $\$2,000$ on advertising.

c. The elasticity of demand $= |(-1/2)(130/55)| = |-1.18|$.

d. If the elasticity of demand is $|-1.18|$ then we have: $(A/7,150) = 0.2/1.18$; $A = \$1,211.86$. The monopolist maximizes profit by spending $\$1,211.86$ on advertising.

Answers to Odd-Numbered Questions and Problems for Review

1. a. $Q = 90$; $P = 210$; profits $= 16,200$.

b. $P = 210 - 2q_{pe}$.

c. $q_{pe} = 42.5$; $P = 125$; profits $= 3,612.5$; profits to monopolist $= 8,550$.

d. $P = 40$; $q = 175$; profits $= 1750$.

3. a. Your extensive form would look exactly like Figure 15.3 on page 410. At node M_1, there are two choices: $q = 90$, $p = 210$ ($\$0$, $\$16,200$); and $q = 175$, $p = 40$ (0, 1750). At node M_2, there are two choices: $q = 90$, $P = 125$ ($3,612.5$, $8,550$); and $q = 175$, $P = 40$ (loss, $1,750$).

b. The Nash equilibrium is that in each case, the monopolist would produce $q = 90$. Given that the entrant knows this, the entrant will enter and earn 3,612.5 in profits, rather than stay out and earn 0 in profits. The threat to limit price is not credible.

c. If the potential entrant trembled and stayed out, the monopolist would choose to produce 90 (not limit price) and earn $\$16,200$ in profits. A limit-pricing policy would not be reasonable, because it reduces the monopolist's profits.

5. Limit-pricing behavior occurs before entry and entails maintaining a low price to prevent entry. Predatory pricing is a strategy to drive a competitor out of the market after entry has occurred by lowering price such that the entrant sustains an economic loss. In one policy (limit pricing) there is no entry and in the other (predatory pricing) there is entry.

7. Recall that with symmetric information, even if the potential entrant trembles, it is best for the monopolist *not* to limit price. Thus, limit pricing is never a credible threat under symmetric information. However, with asymmetric information, the potential entrant does not know whether the monopolist is a high-cost or low-cost producer. If the probability of the monopolist being low-cost is high enough, but in actuality the monopolist is high-cost, then it is likely that a high-cost monopolist will charge a low price in order to prevent potential entrants from gaining information regarding the monopolist's true costs and at the same time, prevent entry. Thus, there are scenarios, with asymmetric information, in which limit pricing is possible.

9. The game is played with perfect, complete, certain, and symmetric information. Therefore, if the game is played any finite number of times, the end result is still the same because of the chain store paradox. By backward induction, at each time period, it is best for the entrant to enter and the incumbent to accommodate entry.

11. There are many possibilities: limit pricing, predatory pricing, could try to raise rival's costs through lobbying, advertising, or providing complementary goods and services. Certainly, proliferating the market with products is a way to deter entry. Finally, the firm could build excess capacity such that there is no room for the entrant as well.

13. a. $Q = 50$; $P = 210$; profits $= 7,500$.

   b. $Q = 60$; $P = 240$; profits $= 10,800 - A$. The monopolist would spend at most $3,300.

   c. elasticity $= |(-1/3)(240/60)| = |-1.33|$.

   d. $A/PQ = \varepsilon_A/|\varepsilon_p| \rightarrow A/(240)(60) = 0.25/1.33 \rightarrow A = 0.25(14,400)/1.33 = 2,706.77$

15. a. For Philip Morris, $e_A = .07$. For Nestlé, $e_A = 0.122$.

   b. For Philip Morris, quantity demanded will increase by 0.07% for every 1% increase in its advertising. For Nestlé, quantity demanded will increase by 0.122% for every 1% increase in its advertising expenditures.

   c. The Dorfman-Steiner model is one for monopoly. It does not consider that the firm may have competition from rivals. In oligopoly, advertising can cause a competitive response and cause competitors to also increase their advertising expenditures. The model does not take the competitive response into account.

17. This is an example of product proliferation. In addition, Coca-Cola has recently introduced Vanilla Coke and Diet Vanilla Coke. In addition, advertising and product differentiation are essential strategies. Note the attention given to the logo for the product, which indicates gearing up for a major advertising campaign.

19. a. $q_m = 90$; $p = 120$; profit $= 90(120 - 30) = 8,100$

   b. $q_m = 67.5$; $p = 97.5$; profit $= 67.5(97.5 - 30) = 4,556.25$

   $q_{pe} = 45$; $p = 97.5$; profit $= 45(97.5 - 30) - 3,000 = 37.5$

   c. $q_m = 70$; $p = 95$; profit $= 70(95 - 25) - 1,600 = 3,300$

   $q_{pe} = 45$; $p = 95$; profit $= 45(95 - 30) - 3,000 = -75$

   d. $q_m = 92.5$; $p = 117.5$; profit $= 92.5(117.5 - 25) - 1,600 = 6,956.25$

   e. See Figure 15A.1 on the following page. The Nash equilibrium is for the monopolist to choose capacity $q = 135$ and the potential entrant to stay out.

Chapter 16: Using the Models of Monopoly and Oligopoly

Answers to Self-Test Problems

1. a. See Figure 16A.1. If the market is competitive, then $P = MC$ and $300 - (1/3)Q = 40$; $(1/3)Q = 260$; $Q = 780$; $P = MC = 40$. Consumer surplus $= (1/2)(300 - 40)(780) = 101,400$.

   b. Using the twice-as-steep rule, $MR = 300 - (2/3)Q$. After the merger, the firm is a monopoly and thus sets $MR = MC$. $300 - (2/3)Q = 20$; $280 = (2/3)Q$; $Q = 420$; $P = 300 - (1/3)(420) = 160$. Consumer surplus $= (1/2)(300 - 160)(420) = 29,400$. Producer surplus $= 420(160 - 20) = 58,800$. Total welfare $= 88,200$.

   c. This merger has a net negative effect. The red and yellow areas ($A + B$) are the loss in consumer surplus as a result of the merger (72,000). Of this, the red area (A) gets transferred to producers $420(160 - 40) = 50,400$. The yellow area (B) $= (1/2)(780 - 420) \times (160 - 40) = 21,600$ is deadweight loss. The analysis doesn't end there, though, because there is a gain due to

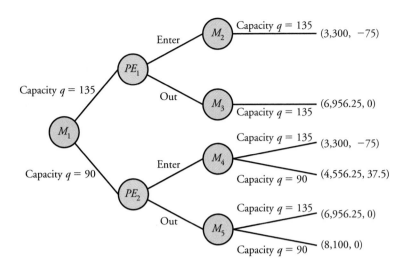

Figure 15A.1 (Monopolist's profits, Potential entrant's profits)

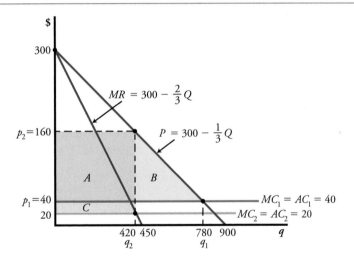

Figure 16A.1

the cost savings of the merger. This is represented by the blue rectangle (C): $20 \times 420 = 8,400$. Because the deadweight loss (21,600) is bigger than the cost savings gain (8,400), this merger has a net negative effect. The difference in these two areas gives us the total welfare loss of 13,200.

2. a. Because the firms are identical, we will do the work only for one firm.

$P = 182 - (1/10)q_f - (1/10)q_u$. From the U.S. perspective, q_f is constant. Thus, using the twice-as-steep rule, we have: $MR_u = 182 - (1/10)q_f - (2/10)q_u$. Setting $MR_u = MC$ gives

us: $182 - (1/10)q_f - (1/5)q_u = 20$; $162 - (1/10)q_f = (1/5)q_u$; $q_u = 810 - (1/2)q_f$. Similarly, $q_f = 810 - (1/2)q_u$.

b. Plugging the foreign firm's reaction function into the U.S. firm's reaction function gives us: $q_u = 810 - (1/2)(810 - (1/2)q_u)$; $q_u = 810 - 405 + (1/4)q_u$; $(3/4)q_u = 405$; $q_u = 540$; $q_f = 810 - (1/2)(540) = 540$. $Q = 1080$;

$P = 182 - (1/10)(1080) = 74$. Profits to each firm $= 74(540) - (5000 + (20 \times 540)) = 39,960 - 15,800 = 24,160$. Consumer surplus

= $(1/2)(182 - 74) \times 1,080 = 58,320$.
Consumer surplus + profits to U.S. = 82,480.

c. The TC function for the U.S. changes to 5,000 + $(20 - 3)q_u = 5000 + 17q_u$. Similarly, the MC of the U.S. firm has decreased to $17 as a result of the subsidy. The U.S. has a new reaction function, because its MC has changed. Set $MR_u = MC_u$ and get: $182 - (1/10)q_f - (1/5)q_u = 17$; $165 - (1/10)q_f = (1/5)q_u$; $q_u = 825 - (1/2)q_f$. The foreign firm's reaction function has not changed.

d. Plugging the foreign firm's reaction function into the U.S. firm's reaction function gives us: $q_u = 825 - (1/2)(810 - (1/2)q_u)$; $q_u = 825 - 405 + (1/4)q_u$; $(3/4)q_u = 420$; $q_u = 560$; $q_f = 810 - (1/2)(560) = 530$; $Q = 1,090$; $P = 182 - (1/10)(1,090) = 73$. Profits to the U.S. firm are = $(73 \times 560) - (5,000 + (17 \times 560)) = 40,880 - 14,520 = 26,360$; profits to the foreign firm are = $(73 \times 530) - (5,000 + (20 \times 530)) = 23,090$. Consumer surplus = $(1/2)(182 - 73) \times 1,090 = 59,405$.

e. As a result of the subsidy, consumer surplus increases by 1,085. In addition, profits to the U.S. firm increase by 2,200. The cost of the subsidization program is equal to $3 \times 560 = 1,680$. Thus, there is a net gain $(1,085 + 2,200 - 1,680 = 1,605)$ to the U.S. as a result of this policy. The U.S. is better off (consumers and producers are better off collectively by more than the cost of the subsidy program).

Answers to Odd-Numbered Questions and Problems for Review

1. Take Figure 16.1 on page 438 and draw a more elastic demand curve than the one drawn in that figure. You will see that deadweight loss is larger for a more elastic demand curve. For a given increase in price, the responsiveness to the price change will be larger; thus more output will be lost as a result of the tax.

3. a. Market supply: $P = 1,000 + (1/3)Q$; $Q = 13,200$; $P = 5,400$; $q_d = 8,800$; $q_f = 4,400$.

b. Consumer surplus = 43,560,000; domestic producer surplus = 19,360,000; total welfare = 62.92 million.

c. $Q = 12,200$; $P = 5,900$; $q_d = 9,800$; $q_f = 2,400$.

d. Consumer surplus = 37,210,000; domestic producer surplus = 24,010,000; total welfare = 61.22 million. Although the quota raised domestic producer surplus by 4.65 million, it is not a good domestic policy, because total welfare falls.

e. Similar to Section 16.2, the foreign producers may agree to this policy if they can earn a larger profit at a higher price-cost margin on more expensive products.

5. a. $q_u = 810 - (1/2)q_f$; and $q_f = 810 - (1/2)q_u$.

b. $q_f = q_u = 540$; $Q = 1,080$; $P = 74$; profits to U.S. = profits to foreign = 24,160; consumer surplus = 58,320.

c. $q_f = 795 - (1/2)q_u$.

d. $q_u = 550$; $q_f = 520$; $Q = 1,070$; $P = 75$; profits to foreign = 22,040; profits to U.S. = 25,250; consumer surplus = 57,245; government revenue = $3 \times 520 = 1,560$.

e. There is a net gain of 15 in total welfare, before considering government revenue. Consumer surplus falls by 1,075 as a result of the policy, but profits increase by 1,090. Thus, the net gain is 15. In addition, the government brings in 1,560 in revenue; thus the U.S. overall is better off by 1,575 as a result of the tariff, even though consumers are worse off.

7. a. Payoffs are (Harvard's percentage of top students, MIT's percentage of top students).

		MIT's action	
		High aid	Low aid
Harvard's action	High aid	(80,20)	(90,10)
	Low Aid	(45,55)	(80,20)

b. The Nash equilibrium is still for both firms to offer high aid. Notice that both Harvard and MIT could do just as well by offering a low aid package. This game is a Prisoner's Dilemma in the sense that it forces the universities to spend more than they have to in order to obtain students. They could do just as well as they do offering high aid, by each offering low aid.

c. Because the advertising campaign still creates a Prisoner's Dilemma, it might not be worth spending the money. On the other hand, Harvard is now able to attract 80% of the top students, rather than 50%, so it may be worth the investment. It all depends on the cost of the advertising campaign, which is not stated in the problem. Note: This example is hypothetical. Advertising would probably not create this kind of a diversion in the student choices. Usually, money talks!

9. The federal courts define predatory pricing as pricing below average variable cost. The definition makes sense from the standpoint that AVC is what determines, in the short run, whether a firm should still stay in business. Recall that a firm can still decide to operate even though it is earning losses, as long as $P > AVC$, so from that perspective, it would not make sense to consider average (total) cost. However, a $P < AVC$ standard permits firms to behave very aggressively toward competitors and requires a firm to price below its shut-down price to be guilty of predatory pricing. This standard may permit some truly predatory behavior, which can reduce the level of competition.

Chapter 17: Factor Markets

Answers to Self-Test Problems

1. **a.** $MRP_L = MP_L \times \text{price} = 30/\sqrt{L}$.

   b. The firm sets $MRP_L = $ wage. Thus, it sets $30/\sqrt{L} = 10; 3 = \sqrt{L}; L = 9$.

2. **a.** See Figure 17A.1. Setting demand = supply, we get $17 - 0.05 L = 3 + 0.05 L; 14 = 0.1 L; L = 140; w = 17 - 0.05(140) = 10$. Payments to capital equal (area C): $(1/2)(17 - 10) \times 140 = 490$. Economic rent (area A) $= (1/2)(10 - 3) \times 140 = 490$. Total wage payments $= w \times L = 10 \times 140 = 1,400$ (area $A + B + E$).

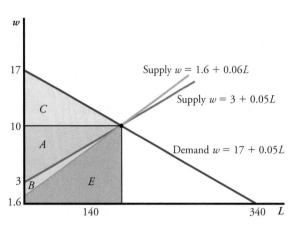

Figure 17A.1

Total value of the products (area $A + B + C + E$) = total wage payments + payments to capital = $1400 + 490 = 1,890$.

   b. The elasticity of supply = $(1/0.05) \times 10/140 = 1.429$.

   c. Setting demand equal to the new supply curve gives us: $1.6 + 0.06L = 17 - 0.05L$
   $0.11L = 15.4; L = 140; w = 1.6 + 0.06(140) = 10$; elasticity of supply = $(1/0.06) \times 10/140 = 1.19$. Economic rent equals $(1/2)(10 - 1.6) \times 140 = 588$ (area $A + B$).

   d. As supply becomes less elastic, economic rent increases.

3. **a.** The marginal expenditure of labor, $ME_L, = w + L(\Delta w/\Delta L) = (40 + L) + L(1) = 40 + 2L$.

Quantity of labor (L) per day	Total number of baseball caps produced	MP_L	$MRP_L = MP_L \times \text{price}$	$SRMC = w/MP_L$
0	0	—	—	—
10	20	20	100	7.5
20	50	30	150	5
30	90	40	200	3.75
40	140	50	250	3
50	180	40	200	3.75
60	210	30	150	5
70	230	20	100	7.5

b. The monopsonist sets $MRP_L = ME_L$, so $240 - 2L = 40 + 2L$; $200 = 4L$; $L_m = 50$. The monopsonist sets wage based on supply, thus $w_m = 40 + L = 40 + 50 = 90$.

c. In a competitive market, the demand for labor = supply for labor. $240 - 2L = 40 + L$; $3L = 200$; $L_c = 66.67$; $w_c = 40 + 66.67 = 106.67$.

Answers to Odd-Numbered Questions and Problems for Review

1. a. See table below.

b. $L = 60$. The firm always operates on the downward sloping section of the MP_L curve, so $L = 60$, not 20.

c. See table.

d. $SRMC = w/MP_L$. Thus, they are inversely related. When MP_L increases, $SRMC$ falls, and vice versa.

3. a. Demand for bread increases, and price of bread increases; thus demand for bread makers shifts right (increases).

b. MP_L increases; thus demand for bread makers shifts right (increases).

c. Demand for bread decreases, and price of bread decreases; thus demand for bread makers shifts left (decreases).

d. Supply for bread increases, and because this is a competitive market, firms must have been earning economic profit before entry, therefore, the production of bread will increase and so will the derived demand for bakers.

5. a. Demand for fast-food workers is more elastic. Heart surgery has less elastic demand than fast food.

b. The long run is more elastic.

c. Demand for glass in beer bottling is more elastic, because beer producers can choose aluminum cans instead. However, even though glass is a small part of the production process in automobiles, it is difficult to substitute with something other than glass in the production process.

7. a. Graph is similar, but not identical to Figure 17.5 on page 474, with $24w_1 = 192$; $24w_2 = 240$; $24w_3 = 360$. Points A in Figure 17.5(a) are (Leisure, Income), (14,80); $B = (12,120)$; and $C = (16,120)$. Unlike Figure 17.5, in your figure,

point C should be on a horizontal line going through point B.

b. There are three points on the supply curve, with labor on the x-axis and wage on the y-axis: (10,8), (12,10), (8,15). The graph is backwards-bending, similar to Figure 17.5.

c. In this case, from Point A to B, George's substitution effect on leisure is bigger than his income effect; from B to C, George's income effect on leisure is bigger than his substitution effect. In the case of individual labor supply, we often see a violation of the upward-sloping rule.

9. a. $VMP_L = p(MP_L) = (194.5 - (1/2)L) 4 = 778 - 2L$. $L_c = 375.27$; $w_c = 27.45$.

b. $MRP_L = MR(MP_L) = (194.5 - L)4 = 778 - 4L$; $L_m = 190.52$; $w_m = 15.908$.

c. The wage is higher in a competitive market and the amount of labor hired is higher in a competitive market. The wage is lower and the amount of labor hired is lower in a monopoly market.

11. a. $ME_L = w + L\Delta w/\Delta L = (2 + L) + L(1) = 2 + 2L$.

b. Set $ME_L = MRP_L$; so $2 + 2L = 32 - 1/2L$ and $L_m = 12$; $w_m = 14$.

c. Set $MRP_L = w$; so $32 - 1/2L = 2 + L$ and $L_c = 20$; $w_c = 22$.

13. They are both demand curves for labor. The term VMP_L implies a competitive output market and is calculated as price $\times MP_L$. MRP_L is the generic term for the demand for labor, but for comparison, if MRP_L is calculated as $MR \times MP_L$, then it is always lower than VMP_L for a monopolist but $MRP_L = VMP_L$ for a competitive firm.

15. a. $L_c = 36$; $w_c = 24$. Economic rent = 324; total payments = 864.

b. $L = 30$; $w = 30$; economic rent = 495; total payments = 900.

c. $L = 21.6$; $w = 38.4$; economic rent = 583.2; total payments = 829.44.

d. In question 15(b), total payments are the highest where the elasticity of demand equals 1 and $MR = 0$. In question 13(c), economic rent is the highest where $MR =$ supply of labor because the supple curve of labor measures the marginal cost to the union of hiring an extra worker.

17. Figure 17.10 on page 483 illustrates this situation. As a result of the concessions, the supply for non-unionized labor will increase, which will lower the wage in the non-unionized sector. This will cause an income loss for those already working in the non-unionized sector.

19. **a.** $L_m = 27$; $w_m = 19.5$.

b. $L = 21.6$ and $w = 38.4$ from question 15(c). The wage will be negotiated to be somewhere between 19.5 and 38.4. It will depend on the negotiating abilities of both sides.

Chapter 18: Investment, Time, and Risk

Answers to Self-Test Problems

1. **a.** $NPV = -15 + (1.2/1.04) + (1.2/1.04^2) + \cdots + (1.2/1.04^{20}) + (2/1.04^{20})$, which can be simplified to $NPV = -15 + (1.2/0.04) - (1.2/(0.04)(1.04^{20})) + (2/1.04^{20}) = -15 + 30 - 13.69 + 0.912 = 2.22$. City council members using 0.04 as the discount rate will agree to build the sports arena.

b. $NPV = -15 + (1.2/0.08) - (1.2/(0.08)(1.08^{20})) + (2/1.08^{20}) = -15 + 15 - 3.22 + .43 = -2.79$. City council members using 0.08 as the discount rate will not agree to build the sports arena.

2. **a.** The nominal interest rate is $900/10{,}000 = 9\%$.

b. The real interest rate must take into account the new price index of 1.034. Thus, the lender sacrifices $10,000 in purchasing power today to get $10,900/1.034 = $10,541.59 in purchasing power tomorrow. The real rate of return is: 541.59/100,000, or 5.42 %.

Answers to Odd-Numbered Questions and Problems for Review

1. **a.** 93.46, 71.30, 50.83, 25.84, 13.14.

b. As the discount rate increases, the present value decreases. As the number of years increases, present value decreases.

3. **a.** $PV_{10\%} = (80/0.10) - (80/(0.10)(1.10)^{10}) + (800/(1.10)^{10}) = 800 - 308.43 + 308.43 = 800$.

b. $PV_{15\%} = (80/0.15) - (80/(0.15)(1.15)^{10}) + (800/(1.15)^{10}) = 533.33 - 131.83 + 197.75 = 559.25$.

c. In neither case did she make a good investment. In the first case, the present value is exactly equal to what she paid for it. In the second case, the present value is less than what she paid for it.

5. For X, the yield will be less than 9.75 because the price is greater than 100. For Y, the yield will be greater than 8.5 because the price is less than 100.

7. Assuming the best possible salvage scenario for Disney, the company salvages $20 billion in 50 years, so $NPV = -20 + (1.5/0.10) - (1.5/(0.10)(1.10)^{50}) + (20/(1.10)^{50}) = -20 + 15 - 0.13 + 0.17 = -4.96$. The $NPV < 0$, and this assumes that Disney sells the park for $20 billion in 50 years. Disney should not build the park.

9. Approximately 5%.

11. **a.** The net present value was underestimated using a nominal discount rate of 10%.

b. Assuming Disney salvages nothing in 50 years (about the worst possible assumption for Disney), $NPV = -20 + (1.5/0.07) - (1.5/(0.07)(1.07)^{50}) = -20 + 21.43 - 0.73 = 0.70$. The $NPV > 0$, so Disney should invest.

13. **a.** For US Airways, a 1-percent decrease in the value of the stock market is associated with a 1.81% decrease in the rate of return on US Airways stock. For Kellogg's, a 1-percent decrease in the value of the stock market is associated with a 0.09% decrease in the rate of return on Kellogg's stock. Investing in US Airways is much riskier than investing in the market in general and investing in Kellogg's is much less risky.

15. **a.** Kellogg's: $r_K = 0.05 + 0.09(0.08) = 0.0572$. US Airways: $r_{US} = 0.05 + 1.81(0.08) = 0.1948$.

b. Investing in Kellogg's is much less risky, and therefore, has a much lower discount rate. This is verified by Kellogg's having a much lower value of beta, which is less than 1. Investing in US Airways is much riskier, and therefore, has a much higher discount rate. This is verified by US Airways having a value of beta which is greater than 1.

17. The stock discount rate $= 0.04 + 1.51(0.08) = 0.1608$. Given this method of financing, the discount rate used should equal $0.60(0.1608) + 0.40(0.05) = 0.0965 + 0.02 = 0.1165$. Because the discount rate is larger than 10% (in an economy in which government bonds are paying 4%), yes, it is risky. This is also reflected in the value of beta being greater than 1.

19. The supply of gold would increase, driving down the equilibrium price of gold $p_t - c$ in every period t.

Because $p_t - c$ is the user cost of production, the user production cost would decrease. The graph of the net price of gold would show a downward shift and then again continue on its upward trend at the rate of interest.

Chapter 19: General Equilibrium and Efficiency

Answers to Self-Test Problems

1. **a.** See Figure 19A.1. Remember that one point will show the initial endowment of both consumers.

   b. At point A, Ethel's MRS is greater than Fred's. Note that your graph will depend on which consumer is at what origin. We placed Ethel in the upper-right corner and Fred in the lower-left corner. Point A is not Pareto-efficient. There are ways to trade so that *both* Ethel and Fred will be better off. (The indif-

ference curves are not tangent, because the MRS for Fred and for Ethel is not equal.)

c. The orange shaded area is the area where gains from trade can be made. Because Ethel is willing to give up more hot dogs for juice than Fred, they can both become better off through trade. Thus, Ethel will be willing to give up hot dogs for additional juice, and the area of gains from trade must reflect that Ethel will be better off giving up hot dogs for more juice. Similarly, Fred will accept hot dogs and give up juice. For example, if Ethel gives up four hot dogs for one juice, then Ethel will be on a higher indifference curve, because she was willing to give up five hot dogs for one juice and Fred will be on a higher indifference curve because he was willing to accept less than four hot dogs for one juice.

d. At the Pareto-efficient point, B, the indifference curves are tangent and $MRS^{Ethel} = MRS^{Fred}$.

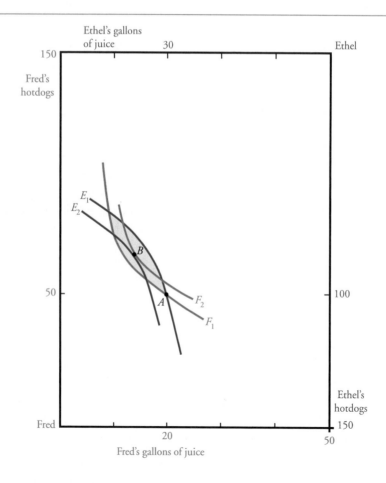

Figure 19A.1

The Pareto-efficient point will be somewhere in the yellow area (or if only one consumer gains through trade, point B could be along U_F or U_E).

2. **a.** See Figure 19A.2. The current Pareto-efficient point is E.

b. The isoquants are tangent and the $MRTS_{trucks} = MRTS_{cars}$.

c. We do not have enough information to know the actual shape of the contract curve, but the isoquants are tangent at any point on the green contract curve. See Figure 19A.2.

Answers to Odd–Numbered Questions and Problems for Review

1. **a.** See Figure 19A.3. The demand for low-carbohydrate diet books will increase to D_{L1}.

b. The demand for beef would increase to D_{b1}, but the demand for bagels would decrease to D_{b2}.

c. Although initially many on the Atkins diet might think "eat more beef," the increase in the price of beef might cause demand for substitute goods such as bacon, chicken, peanut butter, cheese, and pork to increase. In order to do a true general equilibrium analysis, we must consider the effect on steak-house restaurants, as well as other substitutes for beef. As the prices of these substitutes for beef increase, there is a feedback on the demand for beef—it increases.

3. **a.** A graph would be very similar to Figure 19A.3. The demand for red grapes would increase.

b. The demand for other goods, such as red grape juice (and maybe red wine) might increase. The demand for goods such as green grapes and other fruits might decrease, as well as the demand for other types of juices (such as white grape juice).

c. A feedback effect might be a decrease in the demand for red grapes because the price of white grapes has decreased.

d. General equilibrium analysis is more appropriate here because the Surgeon General's announcement would have significant impacts on many other markets in addition to the red grape market.

5. **a.** See Figure 19A.4.

Figure 19A.2

Figure 19A.3

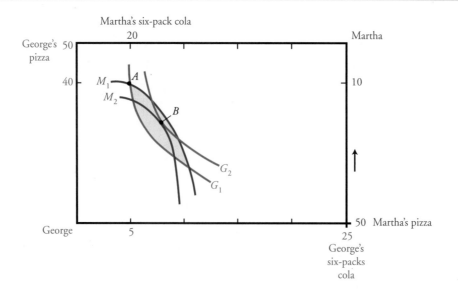

Figure 19A.4

b and c. Point A is not Pareto-efficient, because $MRS_{George} > MRS_{Martha}$. Both George and Martha will be willing to trade because both can be made better off by trading (George will give up pizza for more cola and Martha will give up cola for more pizza).

d. At point B, the indifference curves are tangent, and $MRS_{George} = MRS_{Martha}$.

7. a. See Figure 19A.5.

b. Mary and Henry are both better off (the trade occurred in the area where gains from trade can be made). After the trade, point B is Pareto-efficient. (Note: ignore points C and D for this problem.)

9. a. See Figure 19A.6.

b. The initial endowment is Pareto-efficient. There are no possible trades that will make Rebecca better off without making Mary worse off.

c. Assuming "R" is Rebecca and "M" is Mary, then point G (where Rebecca has the highest utility and Mary has none) is the relevant point in Figure 19.6 on page 531.

11. Although some of these points may seem more equitable than others, they are all equally efficient. Point G represents the situation in which Rachel is allocated all the goods and Monica nothing. Point H represents the situation in which where Monica is allocated all the goods and Rachel nothing. Points in between on the contract curve are all efficient (where $MRS_{Rachel} = MRS_{Monica}$).

Figure 19A.6

13. a. See Figure 19A.5. The initial allocation is point A. The new allocation, after the tax, is point C.

b. The first theorem says that *All Pareto-improving moves will be made and the final equilibrium will be Pareto-efficient.* Thus, given an allocation at point C, we would expect trade to occur until we reach a Pareto-efficient outcome (such as point D). The Second Theorem of Welfare Economics says that *Increasing equity does not result in a reduction in efficiency.* Therefore, by reallocating the bananas to improve equity, we still end up at a Pareto-efficient point (such as point D) after trade occurs between Henry and Mary.

15. a. See Figure 19A.7.

Figure 19A.5

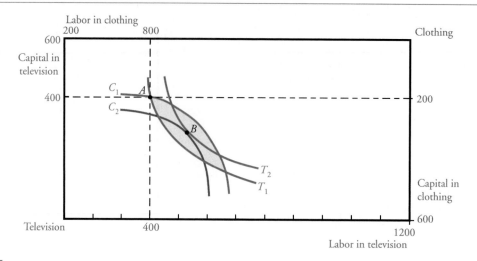

Figure 19A.7

b. Given $MRTS_{tv} > MRTS_c$, more labor and less capital should be allocated to television production. As labor in televisions increases, MP_L^{tv} will decrease and if capital in televisions decreases, MP_K^{tv} will increase. Thus $MRTS_{tv} = MP_L^{tv}/MP_K^{tv}$ will fall. At the same time, if less labor and more capital are allocated to clothing production, then we would expect $MRTS_c$ to increase, due to the increase in MP_L^c and the decrease in MP_K^c. Eventually, a Pareto-efficient point will be achieved, similar to point B in Figure 19A.7.

17. a. See Figure 19A.8(a). The green upward-sloping line is the contract curve. The isoquants for food and clothing are tangent to one another at points A, B, C, D, and E.

b. See Figure 19A.8(b). In this example, the *PPF* has a constant slope, which is unusual.

c. There is a one-to-one correspondence between the points on the contract curve and the points on the *PPF*. The only difference is that using the contract curve, efficient outputs are reflected in the level of output on the isoquants in the

Figure 19A.8(a)

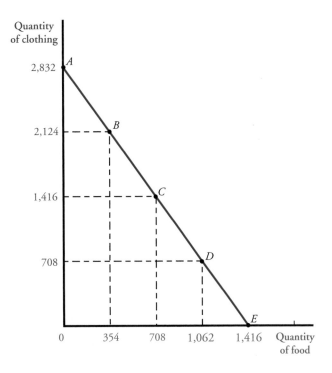

Figure 19A.8(b)

Edgeworth box, whereas because output is measured on the axes for the Production Possibilities Curve (*PPC*), efficient outputs are measured directly on the *PPC*. Labor and capital are only implicitly included in the *PPC* as assumptions that at each output combination, the amount of labor and capital is allocated in a Pareto-efficient manner. This efficient use of labor and capital is shown directly by the contract curve.

19. In a small, two-good world, the excise tax distorts the price ratio that enables us to achieve Pareto efficiency. If an economy is Pareto-efficient, we know that for any two goods *x* and *y*, MRS = $|-MU_x/MU_y| = |-P_x/P_y| = |-MC_x/MC_y| = MRT$. An excise tax, *t*, on good *x* raises the price of *x* above marginal opportunity costs of production such that $(P_x + t) > MC_x$. As a result, MRS = $|-MU_x/MU_y| = |-(P_x + t)/P_y| > |-MC_x/MC_y| = MRT$. With MRS > MRT, Pareto efficiency is not achieved. However, read Common Error 19.2 to understand that the existence of this distortion doesn't necessarily imply that all excise taxes are bad.

Chapter 20: Asymmetric Information

Answers to Self-Test Problems

1 a. If Megan is a careful driver, the probability that she will crash the car is 0.1 and the probability that she will not crash the car is 0.9. The expected value of her loss is $E(v) = 0.1(-30,000) + 0.9(0) = -3,000$. The premium to fully insure Megan and guarantee the insurance company zero profits is $3,000.

b. If Megan is a careless driver, the probability that she will crash the car is 0.8 and the probability that she will not crash the car is 0.2. The expected value of her loss is $E(v) = 0.8(-30,000) + 0.2(0) = -24,000$. The premium to fully insure Megan and guarantee the insurance company zero profits is $24,000.

c. With perfect information, the insurance company's premium is $3,000 if she is careful and $24,000 if she is not. Because the company always knows if she is careful or careless, she will always be careful.

d. Asymmetric information greatly increases the likelihood that she is careless. Once she is insured, her incentive to drive carefully is greatly reduced. This is why it is extremely unlikely that Megan will be able to purchase full insurance.

2. The low-quality worker would earn profits of $w(0) - 0 = 4$ if he doesn't go to college. He would earn profits of $w(1) - 48/q_L = 15 - 12 = 3$. In this case, the low-quality worker earns more by not going to college.

The high-quality worker would earn 4 if he didn't go to college. If he did go to college, he would earn $w(1) - 48/q_h = 15 - 48/15 = 15 - 3.2 = 11.8$. In this case, $11.8 > 4$ and the high-quality worker should go to college. Remember that this model has many assumptions, including that the cost of going to college is higher for the low-quality worker than the high-quality worker.

3. a. In this case, the manager will exert low effort. The manager's payoff will be the reservation utility of 250. The stockholder's payoff $= .5(300 - 250) + .5(800 - 250) = 25 + 275 = 300$.

b. The first condition needed in order to induce the manager to work hard is that the wage contract must insure that the expected utility payoff from working hard at least covers the manager's reservation utility of 250.

$0.1(w(300) - 75) + 0.9(w(800) - 75) \geq 250$

$0.1w(300) - 7.5 + 0.9w(800) - 67.5 \geq 250$

$0.1w(300) + 0.9w(800) \geq 325$

$E(U_{high\ effort}) \geq 325$. The minimum utility to guarantee a high effort from the manager is 325.

c. This condition states that we need the manager's expected utility from a high work effort to be greater than or equal to the expected utility from a low work effort:

$0.1w(300) + 0.9w(800) - 75 \geq 0.5w(300) + 0.5w(800)$

$(0.1 - 0.5)w(300) + (0.9 - 0.5)w(800) \geq 75$

$0.4[w(800) - w(300)] \geq 75$

$w(800) - w(300) \geq 75 / 0.4$

$w(800) - w(300) \geq 187.5$

d. One possible answer is to choose $w(300) = 100$ and $w(800) = 475$. Note that condition question 20(b) is satisfied: The expected utility payoff to the manager is equal to $0.1(100 - 75) + 0.9(475 - 75) = 2.5 + 360 = 362.5 > 325$.

Condition question 20(c) is satisfied since the differential is $475 - 100 = 375 > 187.5$. And finally, the payoff to stockholders would be: $R - w = 0.1(300 - 100) + 0.9(800 - 475) = 20 + 292.5 = 312.5$ which is greater than the payoff of 300 under a fixed wage.

Note that there are many possibilities that work but all three conditions must be met.

Answers to Odd-Numbered Questions and Problems for Review

1. None of them exhibit perfect information.

3. a. Expected value = $17,000. The seller will not be willing to sell a good car for $17,000, thus the buyer will be informed that the car is a lemon if the seller is willing to accept $17,000 or less for the car the buyer wants to buy.

b. The final outcome will be that only the lemons get sold for $10,000 a car.

c. With the new assumption (depending on the functions given), more than just the lemons will be sold. However, if all the cars are not sold (most likely outcome), then there is an efficiency problem, because buyers value all of the cars more highly than sellers.

5. Given a particular insurance premium, based on an assumed risk level, only those customers with risk levels at or greater than the assumed risk level will buy insurance. Thus, in the end, only the high-risk customers purchase insurance and those with lower risk are driven from the market. The insurance companies are left with the "lemons" (those with high-risk only). There are many ways in which insurance companies try to deal with this, mostly by collecting more information from the customer or by pooling individuals into large groups and selling insurance to everyone in the group.

7. The demand curve would be a vertical line, that is, perfectly inelastic at $q = 0$. The $2,500 cost of the policy would no longer be actuarially fair. The actuarially fair premium would be $0.98(\$0) + 0.02(-\$300,000) = -\$6,000$. The company might respond by raising the premium to at least $6,000 per year. It might also respond by canceling the policy or requiring that the Woodys permit the insurance company to have some land cleared at the Woody family's expense.

9. Although it is true that once a driver has insurance they might be more likely to drive less carefully, many people are carrying precious cargo (their children, pets, etc.) that would cause them to think twice about driving carelessly, insurance or not. Most people also want to prevent the opportunity costs of an accident, including personal injury, property damage, and aggravation.

11. Easy bankruptcy laws create a moral hazard problem because if consumer's debts are easily forgiven, then the opportunity cost of declaring bankruptcy is not very high and this encourages consumers or businesses to overspend without thinking of the full financial ramifications. The danger is that the creditors are left with bills that don't get paid, and these creditors then raise prices to those who do spend within their means.

13. In the model presented in Section 20.4, two assumptions are key: the cost of production, $c(q)$, increases as quality q decreases and the high-quality producer is earning a normal profit.

15. The company could have hired a manager to monitor Waldman's work. Because there is a principal-agent problem with every worker, it could get quite costly to continue to hire managers to monitor workers. In addition, there is the possibility that the manager could shirk his job and Philco-Ford would therefore just be paying one more person to shirk. Another possible solution would have been to pay him a high enough efficiency wage to prevent shirking, but this would also require finding him additional tasks to do.

17. a. The equilibrium is: $L_e = 20$; $w_e = 280$. The value of non-shirking constraint at $L = 20$ is 300.

   b. Setting demand equal to the non-shirking constraint, $480 - 10L = 280 + L$; so $L_{eff} = 18.18$, $w_{eff} = 298.18$; unemployment = 1.82.

19. Franchising reduces the scale of a franchiser's direct operations, and therefore, the franchiser does not need to keep a close watch over a large number of stores. Because of their smaller scale, it is easier to keep track of the efficiency of their workers. However, this does not mean that there are no potential principal-agent problems with franchising. Unless a franchise owner is at a store twenty-four hours a day, seven days a week, there is the potential for the workers to be less productive than the franchise owners expect them to be; that is, workers may still shirk.

Chapter 21: Externalities and Public Goods

Answers to Self-Test Problems

1. a. See Figure 21A.1. Setting $S_{private}$ = demand, we get: $10 + q = 100 - q$; $2q = 90$; $q_e = 45$; $p_e = 55$.

   b. $S_{social} = S_{private} + MC_{pollution} = 10 + q + (1/2)q = 10 + 1.5q$

   Setting S_{social} = demand yields: $10 + 1.5q = 100 - q$; $2.5q = 90$; $q_{so} = 36$; $p_{so} = 64$.

   The marginal cost to society (mc^*) of producing $q_e = 10 + 1.5(45) = 77.5$. The firm's perceived cost (p_e) is 55. Deadweight loss = $(1/2)(q_e - q_{so}) \times (mc - p_e) = (1/2)(45 - 36)(77.5 - 55) = 101.25$.

   c. Deadweight loss is labeled as the orange area ABC, similar to Figure 21.1 on page 583.

   d. You can figure the tax by computing $MC_{pollution}$ at $q_{so} = 36$. $MC_{pollution} = (1/2)(36) = 18$. (Note that $S_{tax} = 10 + q + 18 = 28 + q$; setting S_{tax} = demand gives us: $100 - q = 28 + q$; $2q = 72$; $q = 36 = q_{so}$).

   e. The problem with the per-unit tax approach, when $MC_{pollution}$ is not constant, is that the tax will change each time the market changes. For example, if demand changes and q_{so} changes,

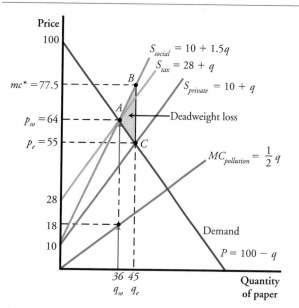

Figure 21A.1

then the optimal tax in order for the firm to internalize the externality will change.

2. a. See Figure 21A.2. Demand curves for public goods are determined by vertically summing all demand (*MB*) curves. In this case, the first 20 residents have a combined demand of: $MB = 2000 - 600Q$, and the next 30 residents have a combined demand of: $MB = 6,000 - 900Q$, and the last 40 residents have a combined demand of: $MB = 12,000 - 1,200Q$. Adding those together, we get the blue kinked demand curve *XABY* in Figure 21A.2.

b. If $MC = 9,600$, then by setting $MB = MC$, we get: $MB = 18,000 - 2,100Q = 9,600$; $Q = 4$. Four houses should be torn down to reach the socially optimal level, provided that no resident has underestimated their MB curve, due to free riding. Notice that only the second and third groups should pay for the park.

Answers to Odd-Numbered Questions and Problems for Review

1. There are many possible answers. Your neighbor paints his house bright pink and orange. A dump truck operator becomes your neighbor and parks his truck in front of your house. A movie patron whispers throughout a movie. There are many other possible answers.

3. a. The problem is that in equilibrium the marginal social cost is greater than the marginal social benefit. See Figure 21.1 on page 583, where $q_e > q_{so}$ illustrates the economic inefficiency.

b. Again referring to Figure 21.1, your graph should show a tax that either: (1) shifts the $S_{private}$ curve up by the optimal tax t_1; or (2) shifts the $S_{private}$ curve up by the actual cost of the pollution, that is, by the $MEC_{pollution}$ curve. The tax will increase price, decrease output, and reduce the amount of the negative externality generated.

5. a. The problem is that in equilibrium the marginal social benefit is greater than the marginal social cost. See Figure 21.2 on page 585, where $q_e < q_{so}$ illustrates the economic inefficiency.

b. Again referring to Figure 21.2, your graph should show a subsidy to the consumer that either: (1) shifts the $D_{private}$ curve up by the optimal subsidy s_2; or (2) shifts the $D_{private}$ curve up by the actual marginal external benefit, that is, by the *MEB* curve. The subsidy will increase price, increase output, and increase the amount of the positive externality generated.

7. A similar argument to that of education can be made that public libraries generate positive externalities. By having a place to learn to read, and continue to read, library users are educating themselves to become better and more productive citi-

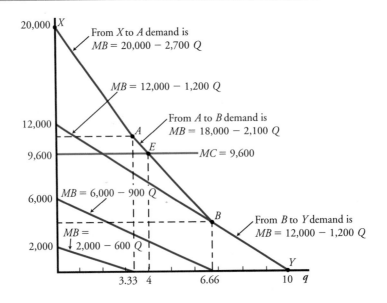

Figure 21A.2

zens. Application 21.1 outlines the specific benefits of education. In addition, at certain branches, the library serves as a place for many young students to go until their parents arrive home from work. All of society benefits by having the students in an educational setting rather than roaming the streets and getting into trouble.

9. a. 86.94 percent.

   b. The fee from question 8 was 658. Thus, the firm would now want to abate by 94 percent. Deadweight loss equals $(1/2)(94 - 86.94)(658 - 538) = 423.6$. In Figure 21.4 on page 588, this is area W.

   c. Deadweight loss of having the firm continue at an abatement of 82 percent from question 8 would be $(1/2)(86.94 - 82)(658 - 574) = 207.48$. In Figure 21.4, this is area Z.

   d. Given the new technology, the fee should be lowered to 608.58.

11. Whether the community or the mill owners are given the property rights, the end result is the same. The socially efficient level of dioxins dumped into the river will be attained. This supports Coase's theorem that as long as transactions costs are zero and property rights are clearly defined, bargaining between two parties will always result in an efficient outcome.

13. a. $t = 200$; $MC = 400$.

    b. If transactions costs are zero, then $t = 200$ regardless of whether the property rights are assigned to consumers or producers.

    c. $t = 190$ and deadweight loss $= 200$.

15. a. $B = 5$ is optimal. $B = 10$ is what will happen without property rights assigned.

    b. A tax of $100 will raise MC to 200 and ensure $B = 5$.

17. a. For prices greater than 75, we add all three demand curves, and $MB = 300 - 75Q$.

    b. $MC = 150 = 300 - 75Q$, so $Q = 2$; Sarah would pay $25, Jacqueline would pay $50, and Jonathan would pay $75, for a total of $150.

    c. All three riders have an incentive to free-ride and hope the others pay for the path. For example, suppose they each say they are willing to pay only $25, then the optimal miles of bike path would not get paved because demand would be underestimated.

19. When preferences are not single-peaked, anything can happen with voting depending on the order choices are presented. In the absence of single-peaked preferences, the result of the votes cannot be predicted. It will depend on the order in which items are voted upon. There are many possible choices where individuals have multi-peaked preferences. For example, suppose you can either purchase great stereo speakers for $2,000, medium quality speakers for $800, or cheap speakers for $150. You might prefer the $2,000 speakers but if you cannot currently afford them, you next prefer to purchase the $150 speakers now, and hope to save in order to purchase the $2,000 speakers in the future. The $800 speakers are a poor third choice.

Glossary

absolute cost advantage   A situation where some firm or firms can produce any given level of output at lower average cost than other firms. **288**

accounting costs   The costs reported by bookkeepers in a firm's official financial statement. **188**

actions   All of the possible moves a player can make in a game. **352**

actuarially fair insurance premium   The amount of money an insurance company must charge each insured to break even. **162**

adverse selection   A situation in which less desirable buyers or sellers are more likely to engage in a market exchange than more desirable buyers or sellers because buyers or sellers do not have sufficient information to determine the true quality of the product being exchanged. **558**

advertising elasticity of demand   The percentage change in quantity demanded associated with a 1 percent change in advertising expenditures. **423**

advertising-to-sales ratio   The ratio of the firm's advertising expenditures to sales; a common measure of the intensity of a firm's advertising. **290, 423**

agent   The person or group hired to achieve the principal's objective. **568**

Agricultural Adjustment Act   A 1933 U.S. law that established the nation's first price supports on major crops. **273**

Agricultural Market Transition Act   A 1996 U.S. law that ended direct price supports for wheat, corn, barley, cotton, rice, sorghum, and oats, but continued paying farmers who agreed to use their land exclusively for agricultural purposes subject to certain land-conservation requirements. **277**

Agricultural Marketing Act   A 1929 U.S. law that first established a fund to support farm prices. **273**

allocative efficiency   The socially optimal amount of a good to produce where the marginal benefit of producing another unit equals its marginal cost. **307**

arbitrageurs   Economic intermediaries who buy a good at a low price in hopes of reselling it at a higher price. **29**

arc elasticity of demand   A measure used to calculate the elasticity of demand between two points on a demand curve by dividing the change in quantity by the average of the two quantities and the change in price by the average of the two prices. **33**

asset beta, β   A measure of the nondiversifiable risk associated with an investment; it measures the nondiversifiable risk associated with an investment compared to an investment in the entire stock market. **507**

asset market   The coming together of economic agents to buy and sell valuable assets such as stocks and bonds among themselves. **9**

asymmetric information   Description of a game in which different players have different amounts of information when players take actions, with some players knowing more than other players. **358**

average fixed cost (*AFC*)   Fixed cost divided by output, or *FC/Q*. **192**

average product   For a given input, total output divided by the number of units of the input. **177**

average variable cost (*AVC*)   Variable cost divided by output, or *VC/Q*. **192**

avoidable costs   The recoverable portion of total fixed costs; that is, the portion of fixed costs that are not sunk. **458**

barrier to entry   Any market condition that enables established firms to increase their prices above perfectly competitive long-run levels for an extended period of time without attracting entry. **286**

Bertrand model   A model developed by Joseph Bertrand that criticized Cournot's model by arguing that if firms assume that all other firms hold their prices constant, Cournot's logic results in an entirely different outcome, with price equal to marginal cost. **388**

bilateral monopoly   A market with monopoly power on both the supply and demand sides of the market; that is, a market with a monopsonist buyer and a monopolist seller. **484**

black market   A market in which goods are sold illegally in violation of a price ceiling law. **29**

bond   A debt security issued by a government or a firm where the purchaser lends the issuer a lump sum of money today in return for a promise from the issuer to pay a finite stream of future payments. **496**

budget constraint   A locus of points depicting all of the market baskets it is possible for the consumer to purchase. **61**

bundling   A special case of a tie-in sale where the two goods are purchased in fixed proportions. **332**

capital asset pricing model, or CAPM   A model used to measure the risk on a particular capital investment by comparing that risk with the risk of investing in the entire stock market. 506

capital goods   Goods used to produce other goods, such as a firm's plant and equipment. 176

capital markets   All of the markets for obtaining investment funds, such as the stock market, the bond market, and banks and other lending institutions. 290

certain information   Description of a game in which nature never takes an action after any other player has taken an action. 358

certainty equivalent   The fixed income an individual would accept instead of taking a gamble, such that the individual would be indifferent between accepting this fixed income and taking the gamble; that is, the VNM utility of the fixed income equals the VNM utility of the gamble. 160

ceteris paribus   A Latin expression meaning "all else the same." Commonly assumed in economics when analyzing the impact of a change in one particular variable on another variable. 17

chain store paradox   A model developed by Richard Selton that argues that in any finite game, entry will always be accommodated in a game with perfect, certain, complete, and symmetric information, because fighting in early rounds cannot deter entry in later rounds. 415

Clayton Act   An antitrust law passed in 1914 that outlawed certain specific types of firm behavior. 340

club good   A good that is nonrival but excludable; for example, a college class lecture. 603

Cobb-Douglas production function   A commonly used production function of the general form $Q = AL^aK^b$ where Q is the quantity of output; L is the quantity of labor input; K is the quantity of capital input; and A, a, and b are positive constants. 193

Cobb-Douglas utility function   A commonly used utility function of the general form $U(x,y) = x^ay^{(1-a)}$ where x is the quantity of good X, y is the quantity of good Y, and a is a positive constant. 89

co-insurance   An insurance policy that requires the insured to make a partial payment toward any expenses beyond the policy's deductible. 564

collective good   Another term for a club good. 604

collusion curve   A curve identifying all the output combinations that firms can produce to maximize joint industry profits. 383

command system   An economic system that solves the problem of resource allocation by having the government tell households and firms what goods to produce, how to produce them, and for whom to produce them. 4

Commodity Credit Corporation (CCC)   A government agency established to make loans to farmers in return for the farmer's crops as collateral. 273

Common Agricultural Policy (CAP)   The price support system used by the European Union (E.U.). 277

common knowledge   Description of a game in which all players know all the information and they know that all the other players also know all the information. 356

comparative statics   The process of changing one exogenous variable and observing the effect on the equilibrium values of one or more endogenous variables. 24

complement goods   Two goods or services where an increase in the price of one good or service results in a decrease in the quantity demanded of the other good or service. 17

complete information   Description of a game in which either nature does not take the first action or nature takes the first action and all of the players observe that action. 357

constant elasticity demand curve   Refers to a demand curve where the elasticity of demand is the same at each and every point. 39

constant returns to scale   A production function where if when all inputs are increased (decreased) by a fixed proportion t, output increases (decreases) by the same proportion t. 183

constant-cost industry   An industry in which factor prices are independent of industry output, so input prices are unaffected as industry output expands or contracts. 232

consumer surplus   The difference between the maximum amount consumers are willing to pay for a given quantity of a good and what they actually have to pay to obtain that quantity of the good. 102

contract curve   The locus of all Pareto-efficient points in an Edgeworth box diagram. 526

corner solution   A consumer equilibrium where the consumer prefers to purchase a quantity equal to zero of some good or service. 71

corporate income tax   A tax on the profits earned by corporations. 438

coupon   The annual interest payment on a bond. 497

Cournot-Nash equilibrium   The equilibrium outcome in a simultaneous move game where all the firms assume that the outputs of all the other firms in the industry will remain constant. 382

cross-price effects The change in quantity demanded of one good in response to a price change of another good. **75**

cross-price elasticity of demand The percentage change in the quantity demanded of one good associated with a one percent change in the price of another good. **41**

Darwinism Philosophy of the 19th-century followers of Charles Darwin's theory of natural selection and survival of the fittest; in economics, the Darwinist philosophy argues against any government interference with the market outcome. **533**

deadweight loss Losses of consumer and producer surplus that are not transferred to other parties, and therefore, measure the misallocation of resources. **308**

decision tree A schematic diagram showing how alternative actions result in different results. **147**

decreasing returns to scale A production function where when all inputs are increased (decreased) by a fixed proportion t, output increases (decreases) by less than the proportion t. **183**

decreasing-cost industry An industry in which factor prices are inversely related to industry output, so input prices decrease as industry output expands and increase as industry output contracts. **233**

deductible The dollar amount of an insurance claim that the insured must pay before the policy begins to pay any benefits. **563**

derived demand The term used to describe an industry's demand for an input that depends on the industry's level of output, which in turn depends on the demand for the final product or service produced by the input. **470**

diminishing marginal returns In the short run, diminishing marginal returns exist when an additional unit of a variable input contributes less to total output than the addition of the previous unit of the input contributed, holding all other inputs fixed. **179**

discount rate The rate at which consumers or firms are willing to trade future income for present income. **495**

diseconomies of scale A term used to describe a long-run cost function where $LRAC$ are increasing so the $LRAC$ curve is upward-sloping. **205**

diversifiable risk Risk that can be eliminated through diversification. **505**

diversification The process of reducing risk by varying the collection of gambles. **165**

dominant strategy A strategy that is always the best strategy, no matter what strategy choices are made by opponents. **354**

duopolists The two firms in an oligopoly market with only two firms. **352**

durable goods Goods that last for a long period of time, sometimes indefinitely; examples include land, artwork, and DVDs. **447**

dynamic efficiency Efficiency over time; requiring an optimal rate of technological advance. **311**

dynamic model A model that deals with changes over time. **311**

econometrics The branch of economics specializing in the use of statistical techniques to test the validity of economic models. **7, 99**

economic agent A single decision-making unit, such as an individual consumer, a business firm, or a government. **8**

economic bad A good for which marginal utility is negative, so the consumer prefers less of the good rather than more of the good. Pollution is a common example. **55**

economic cost The value of an input in its best alternative employment; that is, the opportunity cost of using the input. **188**

economic rent The difference between the total payments to a given quantity of a factor of production and the minimum payments necessary to obtain that quantity of the factor. **310, 476**

economies of scale A term used to describe a long-run cost function where $LRAC$ are decreasing so the $LRAC$ curve is downward-sloping. **204**

Edgeworth box diagram A rectangular diagram that depicts either all of the possible allocations of two goods between two consumers, or all of the possible allocations of two inputs between two production goods. **524**

efficiency wage theory A theory that firms pay wages above the equilibrium wage in order to prevent workers from shirking. **573**

efficient A situation where it is impossible to reallocate resources to make at least one person better off without making someone else worse off. **11**

efficient market A market that incorporates all information immediately and instantaneously into the price of the good. **509**

efficient market hypothesis A theory predicting that no financial expert can, on average, predict how a particular stock or group of stocks is going to perform relative to the market in a way that ensures beating the rate of return on the entire stock market. **509**

effluent charge A tax or fee imposed for pollution discharged into the air or water. **587**

egalitarians A group of 19th-century philosophers who argued for an equal distribution of income. **533**

elastic Refers to goods whose quantities demanded are sensitive to price changes; specifically, any market demand where a one percent change in price results in more than a one percent change in quantity demanded. **31**

elasticity The percentage change in one variable associated with a one percent change in another variable. **31**

elasticity of supply The percentage change in the quantity supplied of a good associated with a one percent change in the good's own price. **43**

endogenous variable A variable in a model whose numerical value is determined by the model. **23**

envelope curve A curve that is derived entirely from a series of points taken from other curves. **202**

equilibrium A situation where every economic agent is doing the best it can, and therefore no economic agent wants to change its behavior. **10**

equilibrium A strategy combination consisting of the best strategy for each player in a game. **353**

excess burden A measure of how much more one tax reduces consumers' utility compared to another tax. **141**

excess capacity As an entry barrier, the decision to build large amounts of capacity so that incumbents can respond aggressively to entry by dramatically increasing output and lowering price. **292**

excess demand The amount by which the quantity demanded exceeds the quantity supplied because the price of a good is below the equilibrium price. **22**

excess supply The amount by which the quantity supplied exceeds the quantity demanded because the price of a good is above the equilibrium price. **22**

excise tax A tax placed on one particular good, such as the federal excise taxes on cigarettes, liquor, and gasoline. **139**

exogenous variable A variable in a model whose numerical value is determined outside the model and therefore is taken as given. **23**

expected utility Given a VNM utility function, the weighted average of a gamble's utility, where each utility is weighted by its probability. **153**

expected value The weighted average of a gamble's outcomes, where each outcome is weighted by its probability. **149**

extensive form An alternative term used to describe a game tree. Technically, the extensive form has a somewhat broader meaning, because it describes all the payoffs in a game, while a game tree describes only the outcomes. **362**

externality Any cost or benefit from an action undertaken by a producer or a consumer that affects other producers or consumers but is not incorporated into the market price for any good or service. **582**

face value The principal payment to the owner of a bond when the bond reaches maturity. **498**

factor market The coming together of households and other economic agents so that the households can sell their control over resources such as land, labor, and capital to the other economic agents. **9**

factor payments The income received by households in the form of wages, interest, rent, and profit for the factors supplied to other economic agents. **9**

Federal Trade Commission (FTC) Act A law, passed in 1914, establishing the Federal Trade Commission as an independent government agency to control business behavior. **340**

feedback effect A change in market A's equilibrium, which results from a change in another market's equilibrium, which was caused initially by a change in market A. **522**

financial sector In an economy, the banks, savings and loans, and other institutions that are in the business of borrowing funds from savers and lending those funds out to borrowers. **106**

first theorem of welfare economics A theorem stating that in a competitive exchange economy, all Pareto-improving moves will be made ensuring that the economy will be Pareto-efficient in its final equilibrium. **530**

first-degree price discrimination The practice of charging each consumer the maximum price they are willing to pay to purchase a good. **324**

flexibility A method of reducing risk by maintaining the ability to make a decision after the state of the world is known. **166**

franchisee In a franchising agreement, the independent entrepreneur who purchases the right to open outlets under the franchisor's trademark. **575**

franchising An alternative to company ownership of outlets in which a company sells the right to open outlets under its trademark to independent entrepreneurs. **575**

franchisor In a franchising agreement, the company that sells the right to open outlets under its trademark to independent entrepreneurs. **575**

free riders Consumers who obtain the benefits of consuming a nonexcludable good without paying the full price because other consumers are paying for the good. **606**

full insurance An insurance policy that pays for the complete value of the asset being insured. **561**

fundamental analysis A method of predicting future stock prices by studying the fundamentals of the market; that is, studying all aspects of market conditions that might affect stock prices. **509**

future value of the income stream Identifies the consumer's maximum future consumption if the consumer saves all current income. **110**

gains from trade The net increase in welfare that occurs to a country as a result of trade. **268**

gamble A set of possible outcomes combined with the probability of each outcome. **149**

game theory The study of how interdependent economic agents make decisions fully aware of the fact that their actions affect each other. **352**

game tree A method of describing a sequential game by showing the actions available to each player at every point in the game as a series of branches from that point. **362**

general equilibrium analysis The impact of a price change in one market on the equilibrium prices and quantities in all other markets. **520**

general sales taxes Taxes on all goods consumed, such as a state sales tax. **139**

Giffen good A good with a positively sloped demand curve, because the consumer purchases more of the good as the price increases. **74**

global market A market that is not restricted to a limited geographic area. **10**

government-imposed entry barriers Government regulations that prohibit or limit entry. **287**

grants-in-kind Government welfare programs that pay benefits in the form of goods or services instead of cash; for example, food stamp programs, housing subsidies, and Medicaid. **122**

health maintenance organizations (HMOs) A pre-paid health insurance plan that provides most medical services for one fixed insurance payment. **564**

imperfect information Description of a game in which at least one player is unaware of some action or actions taken by some other player or players before taking an action. **357**

income-consumption path A curve showing all of the possible consumer equilibrium points associated with every possible level of income, *ceteris paribus*. **76**

income effect The change in the consumption of a good associated with a change in the consumer's real income holding relative prices constant. **88**

income elasticity of demand The percentage change in the quantity demanded of a good associated with a one percent change in income. **41**

income endowment point Identifies the consumption point if the consumer neither borrows nor saves. **110**

incomplete information Description of a game in which some players have more information than other players at the beginning of the game, because nature moves first and nature's move is unobserved by at least one of the players. **357**

increasing returns to scale A production function where when all inputs are increased (decreased) by a fixed proportion t, output increases (decreases) by more than the proportion t. **183**

increasing-cost industry An industry in which factor prices are positively related to industry output, so input prices increase as industry output expands and decrease as industry output contracts. **233**

indemnity plans Health insurance policy that pays for medical services when they are provided. **564**

indifference curve A curve depicting all of the possible market baskets that provide the consumer with a given level of utility or satisfaction. **50**

inefficient A situation where there is a way of reallocating resources to make at least one person better off without making anyone else worse off. **11**

inelastic Refers to goods whose quantities demanded are insensitive to price changes; specifically, any market demand where a one percent change in price results in less than a one percent change in quantity demanded. **32**

inferior goods Goods or services that consumers purchase in smaller quantities as consumers' incomes increase. **17**

infinite game A static game that is repeated forever. **397**

information How much each player knows at each point in a game. **352**

information structure A description of how much information each player has at different points in a game. **356**

interior solution A consumer equilibrium where the consumer purchases positive amounts of all available goods. **69**

internal rate of return (IRR) The discount rate for which the net present value of an investment equals zero. **502**

intertemporal consumption plan The consumer's intended consumption pattern over time beginning in the present period and covering all future periods. **106**

inverse demand curve The price of a good as a function of the quantity demanded; i.e., $p = f(q)$. **102**

isocost curve   A curve identifying all the different combinations of inputs the firm can purchase at current input prices for a given amount of total cost.   197

isoquant   A level curve that identifies all of the input combinations that, when used as efficiently as possible, can produce a given level of output.   181

kinked demand curve model   An oligopoly model in which a firm's demand curve is based on the assumptions that if it independently raises price, its competitors maintain their prices, whereas a price decrease will be matched. As a consequence, the firm's demand curve is highly elastic for price increases but highly inelastic for price decreases.   399

Laffer curve   Shows how tax revenues are related to marginal tax rates.   133

laissez-faire   An economic philosophy that argues for an absence of government intervention in the marketplace.   251

the law of demand   The inverse relationship between price and quantity demanded.   17

law of diminishing returns   A relationship between inputs and outputs which states that as additional units of a variable input are added to a production process with at least one fixed input, eventually the increment in output associated with adding additional units of the variable input must decrease.   179

leading economic indicators   A group of data series and indices that provide advanced warning of short-run changes in the level of business activity.   98

leasing-only policy   A pricing policy under which a firm will lease a good, but refuse to sell it.   449

Lerner Index   A measure of market power as $(p - MC)/P = 1/|\varepsilon_p|$. The Lerner Index ranges from zero to one.   304

limit price   The highest possible price a monopolist can charge and still prevent entry.   408

limit pricing   A strategy of charging a price below the short-run profit-maximizing price in order to deter entry.   292

local market   A market that is restricted to a limited geographic area.   10

long run   The time horizon over which the firm can change all of its inputs, and therefore all inputs are variable.   175

long-run supply curve   All of the combinations of price and industry output that result in zero economic profit in the long run.   232

low-price guarantee   A promise made by a seller to match or beat a competitor's lower price.   361

macroeconomics   The study of the overall level of economic activity in an entire economy, such as the level of output, unemployment, inflation, and growth.   3

marginal expenditures on labor, ME_L   The extra expenditures associated with hiring one additional unit of labor.   479

marginal external benefit (MEB)   Positive externalities associated with producing one more unit of a good or service.   584

marginal external cost (MEC)   Negative externalities associated with producing one more unit of a good or service.   582

marginal product   For a given input, the additional output obtained from a one-unit increase in the amount of the input employed, holding the amounts of all other inputs fixed.   177

marginal profit   The rate of change of profit with respect to a change in output.   213

marginal rate of intertemporal substitution (MRIS) Measures the rate at which consumers are willing to trade future consumption for present consumption: It equals MU_p/MU_f, where MU_p is the marginal utility of present consumption and MU_f is the marginal utility of future consumption.   107

the marginal rate of substitution, MRS_{xy}   The rate at which a consumer is willing to sacrifice one good (y) in return for more of another good (x).   53

marginal rate of technical substitution   The rate at which one input can be substituted for another input while still producing the same level of output.   182

marginal rate of transformation, MRT   The opportunity cost of producing one more unit of one good in terms of the number of units of another good that must be sacrificed.   539

marginal revenue   The rate of change of revenue with respect to a change in output.   213

marginal revenue product of labor, MRP_L   The extra revenue generated for a firm when it hires one additional unit of labor, or $MR \times MP_L$.   465

marginal social benefit   The extra contribution that an additional unit of a good makes to total social welfare, typically represented for an additional unit of output as the vertical distance from the quantity axis up to the demand curve.   248

marginal social benefit (MSB)   The extra benefit to society of producing one more unit of a good or service; equals the sum of the marginal private benefit and the marginal external benefit.   584

marginal social cost (MSC)   The extra cost to society of producing one more unit of a good or service; equals the sum of the marginal private cost and the marginal external cost. **582**

marginal social cost curve   The extra social cost of producing an additional unit of output, typically represented for an additional unit of output as the vertical distance from the quantity axis up to the supply curve. **248**

marginal utility   The extra utility (satisfaction) associated with consuming an extra unit of a good. **58**

market   The coming together of buyers and sellers with the potential of exchanging goods or services. **3**

market demand   The relationship that specifies the quantity of a good that all buyers in a market would like to buy at each possible price over a given period of time, holding constant all other factors except the price. **16**

market demand curve   A graph showing the quantity of a good that buyers in the market would like to buy at different prices. **18**

market demand curve   The horizontal summation of all of the individual consumers' demand curves. **96**

market demand function   The quantity demanded of a good in terms of the prices of all goods and income, such that if $q_i(p_1,\ldots,p_n,I_i)$ is consumer i's demand for good q as a function of n different prices and consumer i's income, the market demand function is:

$$Q_m = \sum_{i=1}^{m} q_i(p_1, \ldots, p_n, I_i)$$

where m is the total number of consumers. **97**

market risk   An alternative name for nondiversifiable risk. **505**

market signaling   The use of an observable action as an indicator of a hidden characteristic. **564**

market structure   The number and size distribution of the economic agents in a market. **11**

market supply   The relationship that specifies the quantity of a good that all sellers in a market would like to sell at each possible price over a given period of time, holding constant all other factors except the price. **20**

market supply curve   A graph showing the quantity of a good that sellers in the market would like to sell at different prices. **21**

market system   An economic system that solves the problem of resource allocation by permitting households and firms to pursue their own self-interests and make individual decisions. **4**

Marxists   Followers of the 19th-century economist and sociologist Karl Marx, who believed that income should be distributed "to each according to their needs." **533**

microeconomics   The study of the behavior of individual economic decision-makers such as households, businesses, and governments. **3**

minimum efficient scale (MES)   The smallest level of output for which long-run average cost is at its minimum. **287**

mixed bundling   A pricing policy where firms give consumers a choice of paying for more than one good either separately or bundled. **337**

mixed strategy   A game in which the players' optimal strategies are to choose their actions randomly. **365**

mixed-strategy Nash equilibrium   An optimal set of random actions that maximize the players' expected outcomes in a game. **367**

model   A simplified and abstract representation of the real world. **5**

money illusion   A situation where consumers believe they are better off when their nominal income increases, even if prices increase by an equal or greater percent. **72**

monopolist   The only seller in a monopoly market. **286**

monopolistically competitive market   A market where there are no significant entry barriers, but firms face downward-sloping demand curves because of the existence of some product differentiation. **313**

monopoly   A market where there is only one seller and there are no close substitute products. **286**

monopsonist   The only buyer of a good or input. **479**

monopsony   A market with only one buyer. **479**

moral hazard   A situation that arises in insurance markets whenever an insured individual's unobserved actions can affect the probability or magnitude of a payment to that insured individual. **561**

multi-peaked preferences   The preferences of voters who prefer all the available extreme choices to the median choice. **609**

mutual fund   An investment fund that collects funds from a large number of individual investors, places these funds into one large pool, and uses the pool to purchase stock in many different companies. **505**

Nash equilibrium   An equilibrium in a game where all players are doing the best they can given the choices of their opponents. **354**

natural monopoly   A market where it is most efficient for one firm to supply the entire output in that market. **342**

nature A pseudo-player added by the game theorist to take random actions at some point or points in a game. 357

negative externalities A social cost of production or consumption that is not considered to be a cost to the producer or consumer. 546

negative income tax A program that would guarantee poor families a certain minimum level of income based on family size and certain other needs criteria. Instead of paying taxes, the government would send these families cash benefits. 122

net present value (NPV) criterion An investment decision-making criterion where the present value of the expected cash flow minus the present value of the costs of an investment are calculated, and the investment is undertaken if the calculation results in a positive value. 500

neuter good A good that the consumer is completely indifferent about, and therefore, more of the good does not increase or decreases the consumer's utility; as a result, the indifference curves are either horizontal (if good X is a neuter good) or vertical (if good Y is a neuter good). 55

node A point in an extensive form of a game at which a player or nature takes an action, or the game ends. 412

nominal income The monetary value (in dollars, euros, pesos, pounds, yen, etc.) of what the consumer has available to spend. 62

nondiversifiable risk Risk that cannot be eliminated through diversification. 505

non-durable goods Goods that have a short life-span, such as food, clothing, and toiletries. 447

nonexcludable Describes a good with the characteristic that it is impossible or prohibitively expensive to limit its consumption to a select group of consumers; for example, clean air. 603

nonrival Describes a good whose consumption by one person does not affect the consumption of the same good by another person or persons; for example, an uncrowded highway. 603

non-shirking constraint An inverse functional relationship between the unemployment rate and the minimum wage necessary to prevent shirking. 574

non-zero-sum game A game in which the combined payoffs in each cell of the payoff matrix vary, so one player's loss is not always equal to the other player's gain. 358

normal form The presentation of a game in the form of a matrix consisting of all the game's possible strategy combinations. 362

normal goods Goods or services that consumers purchase in larger quantities as consumers' incomes increase. 17

normal or zero economic profit Profit when total revenue equals total cost so the firm is exactly covering its opportunity cost of its investment; that is, it is doing as well as it could if it invested in the next best alternative investment. 216

normative economic analysis The study of what should be, requiring the use of value judgments to determine whether the predicted outcomes of economic actions are positive or negative. 12

opportunity cost The economic cost of undertaking any action; equal to the value of the best alternative action sacrificed. 3

outcome The combined result of a decision and a state of the world. 147

outcomes All of the possible results of the strategies that the players can select in a game; that is, the set of all possible game payoffs. 353

output expansion path (OEP) The locus of points of tangency between every possible isoquant and the corresponding lowest possible isocost curve. 201

Pareto efficiency An allocation of goods and services where it is impossible to reallocate the goods and services in a way that makes anyone better off without making someone else worse off. 11

Pareto improvement A reallocation of goods or services that makes at least one person better off without making anyone else worse off. 11

parity price A price support established with the objective of ensuring that farmers' real incomes remain comparable to the incomes earned by manufacturing workers. 273

partial equilibrium analysis The impact of a change in supply or demand in one market only—the market directly impacted. 520

partial insurance An insurance policy that pays less than the complete value of the asset being insured. 561

payoffs The profit or utility the players expect to receive after taking actions in a game. 352

perfect complements Two goods where the marginal rate of substitution of one for the other is either infinite or zero, and therefore the indifference curves are right angles. 54

perfect complements In production, two inputs are perfect complements if they can be used only in fixed proportions. 183

perfect discrimination Another term for first-degree price discrimination. 324

perfect information Description of a game in which each player knows all of the actions taken by all of the other players before taking an action. 356

perfect substitutes Two goods where the marginal rate of substitution of one for the other is always constant, and therefore the indifference curves are straight lines. **54**

perfect substitutes In production, two inputs are perfect substitutes if they can always be substituted for one another at a fixed rate. **183**

perfectly elastic Refers to a good with an elasticity of demand that is mathematically undefined (equal to infinity) and has a horizontal demand curve. **39**

perfectly inelastic Refers to a good with an elasticity of demand equal to zero that has a vertical demand curve. **39**

perpetuity A debt security where the purchaser lends the issuer a lump sum of money today in return for a promise from the issuer to pay a fixed amount of income to the purchaser forever. **497**

players The economic agents that make decisions in a game. **352**

pollution permit A license issued by a government agency that gives the holder the legal right to emit a certain quantity of a pollutant into the environment. **591**

positive economic analysis Uses economic models to predict the actual consequences of actions. **12**

positive externalities A social benefit of production or consumption that is not considered to be a benefit to the producer or consumer. **546**

predatory pricing A strategy of aggressively lowering price with the objective of driving entrants out of the market and preventing potential entrants from entering. **292**

predatory pricing A strategy of expanding output aggressively and cutting price so that competitors sustain economic losses, with the intention of driving competitors from the market. **414**

present value of the income stream Identifies the value today of all current and future income. **110**

price ceiling A maximum legal price for a good established by a government. **27**

price discrimination The practice of charging different consumers different prices for the same product. **324**

price elasticity of demand The percentage change in the quantity demanded of a good associated with a one percent change in the good's own price. **31**

price floor A minimum legal price for a good established by a government. **29**

price leader The firm in an oligopoly that is first to change price in response to a change in an industry's underlying demand or cost conditions. **400**

price leadership A model of oligopoly behavior in which the firms depend on one firm to signal price changes to the other firms, who then decide whether to follow the changes. **399**

price supports Laws that prevent prices from falling below legally set limits. **272**

price-consumption path A curve showing all of the possible consumer equilibrium points associated with every possible price for one good, *ceteris paribus*. **74**

price-takers Economic agents who take the market price as fixed and beyond their control. **210**

the principle of diminishing marginal rate of substitution A rule stating that for any convex indifference curve when moving down the curve from the top (northwest) to the bottom (southeast), the absolute value of that curve's slope must be continuously declining. **54**

principal A person or group of people who hire another person or group of people to achieve an objective for the principal. **568**

principal-agent problem A problem that arises when an agent in rational pursuit of his own goals behaves in a manner that reduces the principal's welfare. **568**

Prisoner's Dilemma A game in which all the players have a dominant strategy that results in a worse outcome than if they pursued some other strategy or strategies. **359**

private good A good that is both rival and excludable. **604**

producer surplus The excess earned by the firm's factors of production, including the owners of capital and labor, over and above what they would earn if the firm did not sell any output. **222**

product market The coming together of economic agents to buy and sell goods and services. **9**

product proliferation The strategic decision to preempt potential entrants by creating brands to fill every available product niche. **427**

production function The relationship between inputs and the maximum possible output that can be produced using those inputs over a given period of time and given the current state of technology. **176**

production possibilities curve A curve identifying all of the possible efficient combinations of goods and services that the economy is capable of producing, given current resource constraints. **538**

productive efficiency Producing any level of output at the lowest possible long-run average cost (lowest opportunity costs) for that output. **308**

profit maximization The fundamental economic assumption that firms always attempt to make the largest profit possible by maximizing the difference between their total revenues and total costs. **174**

property rights   The legal rules regarding who owns a resource and what the owner can do with that resource. **595**

public good   A good that is nonrival in consumption, such as an uncrowded park. **603**

pure bundling   A pricing policy where firms will sell two goods only if they are sold together; that is, consumers cannot buy either good by itself. **337**

pure public good   A good that is both nonrival and nonexcludable; for example, national defense. **603**

Ramsey price   A price that maximizes total social benefits in a market subject to the constraint that profits cannot be negative. **343**

rate base   The total value of invested capital in the regulated portion of a company. **343**

rate-of-return regulation   A regulatory pricing policy that attempts to set the price of a regulated good at a level that results in zero or normal economic profit. **343**

Rawlsian theory   Theory of John Rawls, who believed that the preferred income allocation should maximize the utility of the individual with the lowest utility in society. **533**

reaction function   A function identifying one firm's optimal output (price) response to every possible output (price) produced (charged) by competitors. **379**

real income   The maximum number of units of goods and services the consumer can buy. **62**

real wages   The real buying power of wages measured as the ratio of the wage, w, to the consumer price index, CPI, or w/CPI. **268**

relative price   The price of a good expressed as the number of units of another good that must be sacrificed to obtain one more unit of the good. **62**

relative valuation   The way that different consumers value different goods in relation to each other: for example, if Smith and Jones are both willing to pay more for good A than good B, but Smith is willing to pay more than Jones for A, while Jones is willing to pay more than Smith for B, then Smith has a higher relative valuation of good A and Jones has a higher relative valuation of good B. **337**

rental rate   The amount that another firm would pay to use a unit of capital for a specified period of time—typically an hour or a day. **188**

repeated game   The same game played over and over again by the same players. **360**

requirements tie-in sales   A special case of a tie-in sale where the two goods are purchased in variable proportions;

typically, the buyer agrees to purchase its entire requirements of one good in order to be permitted to purchase the other good. **332**

reservation price   The highest price a consumer is willing to pay for an additional unit of a good. **254, 324**

reservation utility   The lowest utility a worker will accept to work for a company. **569**

residual demand curve   A demand curve that is the leftover portion of an industry demand after a group of firms in the industry have chosen their outputs. **377**

resource allocation   How society decides to distribute its scarce resources, in terms of what goods and services to produce, how to produce them, and for whom to produce them. **3**

resources   The land, labor, raw materials, and machinery used to produce goods and services. **2**

returns to scale   A long-run production concept that refers to how output changes when all inputs are varied in equal proportions. **183**

returns to varying proportions   How output changes when inputs are varied in both their amounts and proportions. **186**

risk   A situation where an action has more than one possible result and the probability of each result is known. **146**

risk premium   The difference between the expected value of a gamble and the gamble's certainty equivalent. **161**

risk-averse   Term used to describe an individual always preferring a sure thing to a risky gamble with the same expected outcome as the sure thing. **155**

risk-loving   Term used to describe an individual always preferring a risky gamble to a sure thing if the expected outcome of the gamble equals the outcome of the sure thing. **155**

risk-neutral   Term used to describe an individual who is indifferent between a sure thing and a risky gamble with the same expected outcome as the sure thing. **155**

Rule of Reason   An important legal precedent establishing that only unreasonable attempts to monopolize violate the Sherman Act. **340**

scarcity   The fundamental economic problem that available resources are insufficient to satisfy human desires for goods and services. **2**

school vouchers   Government grants that families can use to purchase education in either the public or private sector. **124**

second theorem of welfare economics   A theorem stating that given convex indifference curves, every point on the contract curve is a competitive equilibrium for some initial allocation of goods; implies that by selecting a suitable price ratio, any point on the contract curve can be reached **535**

second-degree price discrimination   The practice of offering all consumers the same price schedule and permitting consumers to self-select into the different price categories of the schedule. **324**

sequential games   Games where players take turns moving. **362**

Sherman Act   The first federal antitrust law passed in 1890; it made price fixing and monopolization illegal. **340**

short run   The time horizon over which at least one of the firm's inputs is fixed. **174**

short-run average cost (*SRAC*)   Short-run total cost divided by output, or *SRTC/Q*. **192**

short-run firm supply curve   A curve identifying the quantity of output the firm would offer for sale in the short run at each and every market price. **214**

short-run fixed cost   The total cost of using all of the inputs whose levels are fixed in the short run. **190**

short-run marginal cost   The change in total cost (or total variable cost) associated with the production of one additional unit of output, holding at least one input fixed. **191**

short-run total cost   The minimum possible cost of producing a given output, given that some inputs are fixed. **190**

short-run total cost   The total cost of all inputs used to produce output in the short run. **191**

short-run total product curve   A curve identifying how much output is produced when the amount of a variable input is changed, holding all other inputs fixed. **187**

short-run variable cost   The total cost of using all of the inputs whose levels vary with output. **190**

shut down rule   A rule stating that a profit-maximizing firm should stop producing output whenever total variable cost exceeds total revenue, regardless of the output produced; or, stated differently, whenever price is less than average variable cost, regardless of the output produced. **217**

single-peaked preferences   The preferences of voters who prefer the median choice to at least one of the available extreme choices. **609**

social optimum   A normative state where society is as well off as possible. **12**

social welfare function   An expression of society's well-being as a function of the utilities of its individual members. **532**

specialization   The narrowing of tasks performed by an input such as labor or machinery. **184**

spillover effect   A change in one market's equilibrium as a result of a change in another market's equilibrium. **521**

Stackelberg follower   The firm that moves second in the Stackelberg game. **383**

Stackelberg leader   The firm that moves first in the Stackelberg game. **383**

static efficiency   Efficiency at a precise moment in time; requiring price to equal marginal cost among other conditions. **311**

static model   A model that deals with viewing the world at a precise moment in time. **311**

strategic entry barriers   Market conduct by established firms aimed specifically at reducing the probability of entry. **287**

strategies   A set of rules telling the players which actions to select at a given point in a game. **352**

strong monopolist   In a predatory pricing game, a monopolist that is always predatory. **416**

structural entry barriers   The basic elements of market structure that may act to deter entry: economies of scale, absolute cost advantages, high capital cost requirements, and product differentiation. **287**

substitute goods   Two goods or services where an increase in the price of one good or service results in an increase in the quantity demanded of the other good or service. **17**

substitution effect   The change in the consumption of a good associated with a change in its relative price holding the consumer's level of utility constant. **88**

sunk costs   Costs that have already been incurred and cannot be recovered. **189**

supply-side tax cuts   Income tax reductions aimed at increasing work effort and savings rates. **133**

symmetric information   Description of a game in which all the players have the same information when each player takes an action. **358**

target price   A price established by a government agency calculated to cover the full costs of production, including a normal profit. **274**

technical analysis   A method of predicting future stock prices by studying graphs and patterns of a stock's past price behavior to predict the stock's future price behavior. **509**

technological improvement   A change in production technique that enables the same quantity of a good to be produced with fewer inputs. **20**

third-degree price discrimination   The practice of separating consumers into different groups, each with a different elasticity of demand and charging a higher price to consumers in the group with a more inelastic demand. 324

tie-in sales   A pricing policy that requires consumers to purchase one good in order to be permitted to purchase another good. 332

tit-for-tat   A strategy in a Prisoner's Dilemma game in which a player starts off cooperating in the first round, and in every subsequent round adopts its opponent's strategy in the previous round. 397

total deficiency payment (TDP)   A lump sum payment to a farmer that guarantees a minimum price per bushel based on the farmer's historical number of planted acres and the yield per acre. 274

total effect   The change in the quantity demanded of a good associated with a price change. 87

total expenditures   Total expenditures on any good or service are calculated by taking the product of the price and the quantity purchased. 34

total fixed cost   The total cost of all of the inputs whose levels are fixed. 191

total surplus   The sum of consumer surplus and producer surplus; often used as a measure of economic welfare. 243

total variable cost   The total cost of all of the inputs whose levels vary with output. 191

traditional system   An economic system that solves the problem of resource allocation by having households and firms produce and distribute goods the way they have been produced and distributed in the past. 4

transaction costs   The costs of gathering information and using a market to make a transaction. Also, the costs of negotiating and enforcing an agreement between two parties. 290, 595

tremble   The small probability that a player will make a mistake and choose the wrong action in a game. 410

two-part tariff   A pricing policy consisting of a fixed or lump sum payment for a good or service combined with a per-unit user charge. 332

uncertain information   Description of a game in which nature takes an action after another player has taken an action. 358

uncertainty   A situation where an action has more than one possible result and the probability of each result is unknown. 146

unit elastic or **unitary elastic**   Refers to any market demand where a one percent change in price results in a one percent change in quantity demanded. 32

user cost of production   The opportunity cost of extracting an exhaustible natural resource. 513

utilitarians   A group of nineteenth century philosophers who believed the amount of satisfaction consumers received from consuming goods and services could be measured in terms of a number of pleasure units. They also argued for the maximization of society's total utility. 252, 533

utility function   A mathematical formula that assigns numerical utility to bundles of goods in a way that guarantees that if the consumer prefers one bundle to another bundle, the preferred bundle is assigned a higher number; and if the consumer is indifferent between two bundles, both bundles are assigned the same number. 56

utility maximization   The condition of consumer equilibrium where the consumer chooses from all of the possible market baskets on the budget constraint, the basket that yields the highest level of utility (satisfaction). 68

utility possibilities curve, or **welfare frontier**   A curve identifying all possible Pareto-efficient combinations of utility for consumers in an exchange economy; that is, the possible utility combinations for points on the contract curve in an Edgeworth box diagram. 532

value of the marginal product of labor, VMP_L The value to society of the products produced by the last worker hired, which equals $p \times MP_L$. 478

value-added tax   A tax on the value added at each stage of production for every good and service produced in a country. 438

voluntary exports restraint (VER)   A voluntary agreement by one country to restrict exports of a good to another country. 443

von Neumann–Morgenstern (VNM) utility function   A utility function expressed as the expected value of utility of an uncertain event such that, if $U(c_i)$ represents the utility associated with event c_i, p_i represents the probability of event c_i, and there are n possible events; then the von Neumann– Morgenstern utility is $p_1 U(c_1) + p_2 U(c_2) + \ldots + p_n U(c_n)$. 153

voting paradox   Kenneth Arrow's statement that in order for majority voting to give non-arbitrary results, voters must have single-peaked preferences. 609

weak monopolist   In a predatory pricing game, a monopolist that is only predatory if it believes it will increase its future profit in other markets to at least compensate for its lower current profit. 416

work–leisure trade-off   The rate at which consumers are willing to sacrifice additional income for leisure, typically represented by an indifference curve mapping. 134

X-inefficiency A situation in which less than the maximum output is produced from a given set of inputs because managers have objectives other than profit maximization. 310

yield The rate of return on a bond. 498

zero-sum game A game in which one player's gain is exactly matched by another player's loss. 353

Sources

Chapter 2

Application 2.1
Competition Commission of the United Kingdom, *Supermarkets: A Report on the Supply of Groceries from Multiple Stores in the United Kingdom*, October 2000; and "Tesco Cuts Spark Supermarket Price War", *The Guardian*, September 17, 2001.

Application 2.2
"Hot and Cold Real Estate Markets in the San Francisco Bay Area," *Federal Reserve Bank of San Francisco Economic Letter*, August 6, 1999; and Elizabeth Razzi, "Sanity Returns to the Housing Market," *Kiplinger's Personal Finance*, January 2001.

Application 2.4B
Mark Stephenson, "Milk Price Volatility, Federal Price Supports and Risk Management," National Program for Integrated Dairy Risk Management Education & Research, The United States Department of Agriculture, *http://www-agecon.ag.ohio-state.edu*; Gregory Conko, "Free Markets for Milk?" Competitive Enterprise Institute, June 29, 1999; and "Focus Price Squeeze," *Newshour with Jim Lehrer*, National Public Radio, March 31, 2000.

Application 2.5
Milton Friedman, "Stop Taxing Non-Addicts," *Reason Magazine*, October 1988; David W. Rasmussen and Bruce L. Benson, *The Economic Anatomy of a Drug War: Criminal Justice in the Commons*, Lantham, MD: Rowman & Littlefield, 1994.

Table 2.2
H.S. Houthakker and Lester D. Taylor, *Consumer Demand in the United States: Analysis and Projections, 2nd Ed.* (Cambridge, MA: Harvard University Press, 1970); D.J. DeVoretz and K.G. Salvanes, "Market Structure for Farmed Salmon," *American Journal of Agricultural Economics*, 75: 227–33 (1993); J. Wasserman, *Excise Taxes, Regulation, and the Demand for Cigarettes* (Santa Monica, CA: The Rand Corporation, 1988); J. Putnam and J. Allshouse, "Food Consumption, Prices and Expenditures, 1970–1990," SB-840, Economic Research Service, USDA (1992); C. Nichol, "Elasticities of Demand for Gasoline in Canada and the United States," Working Paper, University of Regina, (2000); Tae H. Oum, W. G. Waters II, and Jong Say Young, "A Survey of Recent Estimates of Price Elasticities of Demand for Transport," The World Bank, Working Papers, Transportation Division, WPS, 359 (January 1990).

Table 2.3
D.J. DeVoretz and K.G. Salvanes, "Market Structure for Farmed Salmon," *American Journal of Agricultural Economics*, Vol. 75 (1993), pp. 227–233; Gary W. Brester and Michael K. Wohlgenant, "Estimating Interrelated Demands for Meats Using New Measures for Ground and Table Beef," *American Journal of Agricultural Economics*, Vol. 73 (November 1991), pp. 1182–1194; Erik Brynjolfsson, "Some Estimates of the Contribution of Information Technology to Consumer Welfare," MIT Sloan School, Working Paper #161 (January 1994); Trisha Bezmen and Craig A. Depken II, "School Characteristics and the Demand for College," *Economics of Education Review*, Vol. 17, No. 2 (1998); J. Wasserman, *Excise Taxes, Regulation, and the Demand for Cigarettes* (Santa Monica, CA: The Rand Corporation, 1988); and Daniel B. Suits, "Agriculture," in Walter Adams and James W. Brock, eds., *The Structure of American Industry* (Upper Saddle River, NJ: Prentice Hall, 2001), p. 4.

Table 2.4
D.J. DeVoretz and K.G. Salvanes, "Market Structure for Farmed Salmon," *American Journal of Agricultural Economics*, Vol. 75 (1993), pp. 227–233; Gary W. Brester and Michael K. Wohlgenant, "Estimating Interrelated Demands for Meats Using New Measures for Ground and Table Beef," *American Journal of Agricultural Economics*, November (1991), pp. 1182–1194; F. Gasmi, J.J. Laffont,

and Q. Vuong, "Econometric Analysis of Collusive Behavior in the Soft-Drink Market," *Journal of Economics and Management Strategy* (Summer 1992), pp. 277–311; C. Hsiao and D. Mountain, "Estimating Short-Run Income Elasticities of Demand for Electricity by Using Cross-Sectional Categorized Data," *Journal of the American Statistical Association* (June 1985), pp. 259–65; and E.T. Fuji et al., "An Almost Ideal Demand System for Visitor Expenditures," *Journal of Transport Economics and Policy*, May 1985.

Application 2.6
Basic Petroleum Data Book, Vol. 13, September 1993; and Robert E. Hall and Marc Lieberman, *Economics: Principles and Applications*, Cincinnati, OH: South Western, 2001, pp. 75–76.

Chapter 3

Application 3.6
Theresa Agovino, "Largest Donations Smaller in 2001," *Los Angeles Times*, January 1, 2002.

Chapter 6

Application 6.1
New York Times, May 30, 1993.

Application 6.2
Melissa Schettini Kearney, "State Lotteries and Consumer Behavior," NBER Working Paper #9330, Cambridge, MA: National Bureau of Economic Research, 2002; and "Powerball: Someone could be $292 Million Richer," *http://CNN.com*, July 29, 1998.

Chapter 7

Application 7.2
Mimi Swartz and Sherron Watkins, *Power Failure: The Inside Story of the Collapse of Enron*. New York: Doubleday Publishing, 2003.

Application 7.3A
Marj Charlie "Few Small Miners Left Now Face the Prospect of a Hostile New Law," *The Wall Street Journal*, 1992; "Mining Reform: A Pickaxe Too Far," *The Economist*, 25 April 1992; and Marc Humphries and Carol Hardy Vincent, "Mining on Federal Lands," *CRS Issue Brief for Congress*, Washington: National Council for Science and the Environment, May 3, 2001.

Application 7.3B
Bridget Eklund, "Presence of Mind: Industrial Robots Are Smarter and Cheaper Than Ever," Red Herring, August 1, 2000; Imogen Foulkes, "Robot Investment on the Rise," *BBC News, news.bbc.co.uk*.

Application 7.5
Paul J. Gertler and Donald M. Waldman, "Quality-Adjusted Cost Functions and Policy Evaluation in the Nursing Home Industry," *Journal of Political Economy*, 100, 1992.

Chapter 8

Application 8.1
http://www.adage.com; M. Maremont, "Braun, Sonicare Brush Up on Their Legendary Feud," *The Wall Street Journal*, April 30, 1999, A1; Susan Greco, "Legal Distraction Kills IPO," *Inc.*, October 15, 1999; and Shona Crabtree, "Gillette in Toothbrush Battle," North Andover *Eagle-Tribune*, January 9, 1999, p. 2.

Application 8.5
John Shea, "Do Supply Curves Slope Up?" *Quarterly Journal of Economics*, 108(1), February 1993: 1–32.

Application Table 8.3
Gernot Klepper, "Industrial Policy in the Transport Aircraft Industry," in Paul Krugman and Alasdair Smith, eds. *Empirical Studies of Strategic Trade Policy* (Chicago: University of Chicago Press, 1994), p. 116.

Application Table 8.5
John Shea, "Do Supply Curves Slope Up?" *Quarterly Journal of Economics*, 108(1), February 1993: 1-32.

Chapter 10

Table 10.1
Paul J. Brounstein, et al., *Patterns of Substance Abuse and Delinquency Among Inner City Adolescents.* Washington, DC: The Urban Institute, 1989.

Table 10.2
United States Bureau of the Census. *Statistical Abstract of the United States:* 1993, Washington DC: United States Government Printing Office, p. 658.

Chapter 11

Application 11.1A
Rochelle Ruffer and Don E. Waldman, "Microsoft," in David I. Rosenbaum, ed. *Market Dominance: How Firms Gain, Hold, or Lose It and the Impact on Economic Performance.* Westport, CT: Praeger, 1998, pp. 153–193.

Application Table 11.1B
Advertising Age, September 25, 2002.

Application Table 11.2
Timothy F. Breshnahan, "Departures from Marginal-Cost Pricing in the American Automobile Industry," *Journal of Econometrics,* Vol. 17 (1981): p. 201–227; Elie Appelbaum, "The Estimation of the Degree of Oligopoly Power," *Journal of Econometrics,* Vol. 19 (1982): pp. 287–299; Robert H. Porter, "A Study of Cartel Stability: The Joint Committee, 1880–1896," *Bell Journal of Economics,* Vol. 14 (1983): pp. 301–314; Mark J. Roberts, "Testing Oligopoly Behavior," *International Journal of Industrial Organization,* Vol. 2 (1984): pp. 367–383; Pablo T. Spiller and Edward Favaro, "The Effects of Entry Regulation on Oligopolistic Interaction: The Uruguayan Banking Sector," *Rand Journal of Economics,* Vol. 15 (1984): pp. 244–254; Valerie Y. Suslow, "Estimating Monopoly Behavior with Competitive Recycling: An Application to Alcoa," *Rand Journal of Economics,* Vol. 17 (1986): pp. 389–403; Margaret E. Slade, "Interfirm Rivalry in a Repeated Game: An Empirical Test of Tacit Collusion," *The Journal of Industrial Economics,* Vol. 35 (1987): pp. 499–516; F. Gasmi, J.J. Laffont, and Q. Vuong, "Econometric Analysis of Collusive Behavior in a Soft Drink Market," *Journal of Economics and Management Strategy,* Vol. 1 (1992): pp. 277–311; G. Ellison, "Theories of Cartel Stability and the Joint Executive Committee," *Rand Journal of Economics,* Vol. 25 (1994): pp. 37–57; Satish Y. Deodhar and M. Sheldon, "Is Foreign Trade (Im)perfectly Competitive? An Analysis of the German Market for Banana Imports," *Journal of Agricultural Economics,* Vol. 46 (September 1995): pp. 336–348; and William Nebesky, B. Starr McMullen, and Man-Keung Lee, "Testing for Market Power in the U.S. Motor Carrier Industry," *Review of Industrial Organization,* Vol. 10 (1995): pp. 559–576.

Application 11.3
Charles R. Babcock, "Patent Fight Tests Drug Firms' Clout," *Washington Post*, October 30, 1999, A01; and Sidney Wolf, "Who's Pulling the Strings in Washington?" Washington, DC: *Public Citizen*, October 14, 2002, *http://www.citizen.org.*

Application Table 11.3
Public Citizen Analysis of Lobby Disclosure Reports filed with the Secretary of the U.S. Senate and Clerk of the U.S. House pursuant to the Lobby Disclosure Act of 1995.

Application 11.4

"DiGiorno Campaign Delivers Major Sales, *USA Today*, April 1, 2002; *http://www.freschetta.com*; Anne Schamberg, "Some Frozen Pizza Rises above the Rest," *Milwaukee Journal Sentinel*, March 31, 2002.

Chapter 14

Application 14.2

Wendy Bounds, "Fuji Will Buy Wal-Mart's Photo Business," *Wall Street Journal*, July 9, 1996, p. A3; Claudia C. Deutsch, "Fuji in Deal with Wal-Mart for Photofinishing Plants," *New York Times*, July 9, 1996, p. D4; "Japanese Companies in the U.S.: Photo Equipment and Copiers," *Japan-U.S. Business Reports*, No. 323, August 1996, *http://www.jei.org*; and "Can George Fisher Fix Kodak?" *Business Week*, October 20, 1997.

Application Table 14.3

http://www.usairways.com and *http://www.southwest.com*, August 28, 2002.

Application 14.4

United States v. United States Steel Corporation 251 US 417 (1920); Erwin A. Blackstone, "Limit Pricing and Entry in the Copying Machine Industry," *Quarterly Review of Economics and Business*, Winter 1972, pp. 57–65; Thomas Whiteside, "Where Are They Now?" *New Yorker*, February 17, 1951, pp. 39–58; and Richard T. Pascale, "Perspectives on Strategy: The Real Story Behind Honda's Success," *California Management Review*, Vol. 26, 1984, pp. 47–72.

Chapter 15

Application 15.1

Henry Grabowski and John Vernon, "Longer Patents for Lower Imitation Barriers: The 1984 Drug Act," *American Economic Review*, Vol. 76, p. 195, May 1986; Henry Grabowski and John Vernon, "Brand Loyalty, Entry, and Price Competition in Pharmaceuticals After the 1984 Act," *Journal of Law & Economics*, Vol. 35, p. 331, October 1992; and Robin Margolis, "Prescription Drug Manufacturers Get Warning on Prices," *Healthspan*, Vol. 10, p. 19, March 1993.

Application 15.2

American Drugs et al. v. Wal-Mart Stores, Faulkner County, AR, E-92-1158, October 1993; and *Wal-Mart Stores v. American Drugs, et al.*, 891 S.W. 2d 30 (1995).

Application 15.3

John Sutton, *Sunk Costs and Market Structure: Price Competition, Advertising, and the Evolution of Concentration* (Cambridge, MA: MIT Press, 1991); *http://www.money.cnn.com*, July 6, 2001; and *http://www.plada.com/jsp/about.jsp*, September 30, 2002.

Application Table 15.4

Advertising Age, *http://www.adage.com*.

Application 15.5

Federal Trade Commission v. Kellogg et al., FTC Docket 8883 (1981).

Application 15.6

D. West and B. Von Hohenbalken, "Empirical Tests for Predatory Reputation," *Canadian Journal of Economics* 19 (February 1986): p. 160.

Chapter 16

Table 16.1

Smith, Conley & Associates, pc, Certified Public Accountants, *http://www.cpatax.net*.

Chapter 17

Application Table 17.1
United States Bureau of Labor Statistics, *http://www.bls.gov.*

Common Error 17.2
United States Bureau of Labor Statistics, *http://www.bls.gov.*

Table 17.5
James Quirk and Rodney D. Fort, *Pay Dirt: The Business of Professional Sports.* (Princeton, NJ: Princeton University Press, 1997), p. 230.

Chapter 18

Table 18.2
http://www.marketguide.com.

Chapter 19

Application 19.1
Gary Taubes, "What If Fat Doesn't Make You Fat?" *New York Times Magazine*, July 7, 2002; Catherine Valenti, "Low-Carb Craze," *http://abcnews.com*; and Joel Stein, "The Low-Carb Diet Craze," *Time*, November 1, 1999.

Chapter 20

Application 20.2
Gerald Riley, Cynthia Tudor, Yen-pin Chiang, and Melvin Ingber, "Health Status of Medicare Enrollees in HMOs and Fee-for-Service in 1994." *Health Care Financing Review*, Vol. 17, No. 4, Summer 1996; and "Risk Selection and Risk Adjustment in Medicare," Chapter 15 in the Annual Report to Congress, Physician Payment Review Commission, Washington, DC, 1996.

Application 20.3
Charles W. Calomiris, *The Postmodern Bank Safety Net: Lessons from Developed and Developing Economies*, Washington, DC: American Enterprise Institute, 1997; and Charles W. Calomiris, "The IMF's Moral Hazard," *American Enterprise Institute, http://www.aei.org.*

Application 20.4
David Kiley, "Chrysler Expands Warranties to Attract More Buyers," *http://USAToday.com*, November 1, 2001.

Application 20.5B
Stephen Meyer III, *The Five Dollar Day: Labor Management and Social Control in the Ford Motor Company 1908–1921.* Albany, NY: State University of New York Press, 1981; and Ray Batchelor, *Henry Ford: Mass Production, Modernism and Design.* Manchester, UK: Manchester University Press, 1994; and Daniel Raff and Lawrence Summers, "Did Henry Ford Pay Efficiency Wages?" *Journal of Labor Economics*, January 1987.

Application 20.5C
Alan B. Krueger, "Ownership, Agency, and Wages: An Examination of Franchising in the Fast Food Industry," *Quarterly Journal of Economics*, Vol. 106, pp. 75–101, 1991; Seth W. Norton, "An Empirical Look at Franchising As an Organizational Form," *Journal of Business*, Vol. 64, No. 4, pp. 197–218, 1988; and *http://www.entrepreneur.com.*

Chapter 21

Application 21.1

Orley Ashenfelter and Cecelia Rouse, "Schooling, Intelligence, and Income in America: Cracks in the Bell Curve," National Bureau of Economic Research, Working Paper 6902, January 1999; Raymond E. Wolfinger and Steven J. Rosenstone, *Who Votes?* New Haven, CT: Yale University Press, 1980; and W. Russell Neuman, *The Paradox of Mass Politics: Knowledge and Opinion in the American Electorate.* Cambridge, MA: Harvard University Press, 1986; Joshua Hall, "Investment in Education: Private and Public Returns," Report to the Joint Economic Committee of the United States Congress, January 2000, *http://www.house.gov*; Ann Dryden White and Helen Tauchen, "Work and Crime: An Exploration Using Panel Data," National Bureau of Economic Research, Working Paper 4794, July 1994; A.J. Beck and B.E. Shipley, "Recidivism of Prisoners Released in 1983," Bureau of Justice Statistics Special Report NCJ-116261. Washington, DC: U.S. Department of Justice, 1989; and Amara Bachu, *Fertility of American Women: June 1995*, U.S. Bureau of the Census, Current Population Report Series P20-499.

Application 21.2

Final Report of the Temporary State Commission on Returnable Beverage Containers, March 27, 1985, p. 62; Projection from the Center for Management Analysis, School of Business and Public Administration for Long Island University; *New York State Returnable Container Act: A Preliminary Study*, 1984; Oregon Department of Environmental Quality, *Oregon's Bottle Bill: The 1982 Report*, p. 26; U.S. General Accounting Office, Report to Congress by the Comptroller General of the United States, *Potential Effects of a National Mandatory Deposit on Beverage Containers*, December 7, 1977, p. 54; U.S. General Accounting Office, Report to Congress by the Comptroller General of the United States, *States' Experience with Beverage Container Deposit Laws Shows Positive Benefits*, December 11, 1980, p. 9; Michigan Department of Transportation, Maintenance Division, *Michigan Roadside Litter Composition Survey, Final Report*, December 1979; Iowa Department of Transportation, Highway Division, *Litter Survey*, April 1980; John Stutz and Carrie Gilbert, *Michigan Bottle Bill: A Final Report to Michigan Great Lakes Protection Fund*, *http://www.deq.state.mi.us/ogl/michigan_bottle_bill.htm*, July 10, 2000, p. 12; and Bottle Bill Statistics, *http://www.fiu.edu*.

Application 21.3

U.S. Environmental Protection Agency, "$20 Billion Emission Trading Market Goes Online," *http://www.epa.gov*.

Application 21.4

James Arnold, "Crunch Time for Caspian Caviar," *BBC News*, June 19, 2001, *http://www.bbc.co.uk*.

Application 21.5

Tara McKelvey, "Stephen King Plows Under 'Plant' E-book," *USA Today*, November 29, 2000; and M.J. Rose, "Stephen King, the E-Publisher," *Wired News*, June 11, 2000, *http://www.wired.com*.

Index